Random House

LATIN-AMERICAN
SPANISH

Dictionary

Spanish-English
English-Spanish

David L. Gold
Doctor in Romance Philology
University of Barcelona

Random House

NEW YORK

Library of Congress Cataloging-in-Publication Data

Gold, David L.
    Random House Latin-American Spanish dictionary :
    Spanish-English
        English-Spanish / David L. Gold.
            p.   cm.
    ISBN   0-679-45294-X (HC)
            0-375-70084-6 (PB)
    1. Spanish language—Provincialisms—Latin American
    Dictionaries.
    2. Spanish language—Dictionaries—English. 3. English
    language—Dictionaries—Spanish. I. Title.
    PC4822.G65 1997
    463'.21—dc20   96-27274
                                        CIP

Contents

Preface

Selection of Vocabulary

The aim of this dictionary is to cover as much current vocabulary as possible, as well as certain items found in standard works of Modern Spanish and English literature.

This dictionary includes items often omitted in other bilingual dictionaries—road and street signs, for example—though few things could be as frustrating (and, sometimes, as dangerous) as seeing such signs but not knowing what they mean (in this dictionary, all kinds of public notices are enclosed by the symbols « » in Spanish and by double quotation marks in English). Also, many vocabulary items consisting of more than one word have been treated here (see for instance **do** in the English-Spanish section).

For lack of space, however, not every current or useful item could be included and a selection of material was thus necessary.

Spanish Spelling and Alphabetization

On January 1, 1959, the Spanish language academies changed certain spelling rules and on April 27, 1994, they eliminated **ch** and **ll** as separate letters of the alphabet. Thus, whereas words like **chico** and **chocolate** were formerly alphabetized under their own letter (**ch,** which came between c and d) and words like **llamar** and **llegar** were formerly alphabetized under their own letter (**ll,** which came between l and m), words containing **ch** or **ll,** in whatever part of the word they may appear, are now alphabetized as they would be in English (**chico** therefore now appears under c and **llegar** under l).

Field Labels

Only essential field labels are given in this dictionary. For example, the label *medicine* or *pathology* is unnecessary at **flebitis** 'phlebitis' (in the Spanish-English section) because both the Spanish and the English words refer only to the pathological condition so called in those languages.

In contrast to that entry, we do need a label at **foca** 'seal' (in the Spanish-English section) because English **seal** has several meanings and only the zoological one is intended here. Anglophones looking up **foca** thus need the label *zoology.*

Spatial Labels for Spanish

Spatial variation in Spanish ranges from nil to extreme. On one hand, the words for 'flower' and 'mother-in-law', for example, are everywhere **flor** and **suegra** respectively. On the other hand, the language has many words for 'bus' and 'ballpoint pen'.

In the absence of trustworthy sources, spatial labels are best dispensed with, though some are given in this dictionary when I have been able to ascertain at first hand that a less than universal usage is found in a certain area.

In general, this dictionary emphasizes Spanish of the Western Hemisphere. In particular, it tries to convey some of the spatial variation that may be found from country to country within that area. Therefore, certain usages are labeled *Latin American* (if they are used in at least many Western Hemispheric countries) and others are given more restricted labels, like *Argentina* and *Mexico* (if they appear to be limited to just certain countries).

Spatial characterizations in this dictionary should be interpreted in a minimal way. For instance, *Mexican* means that the usage so labeled is found in Mexico but it says nothing about whether that usage is present or absent elsewhere (something which only further research could determine).

Subentries

If a main entry head is repeated in a subentry in exactly the same form, it is abbreviated to its first letter (for instance, at **fin** in the Spanish-English section we find **a f. de,** which stands for **a fin de**). If the main entry head appears in any other form, the full form is given in the subentry (thus, at **fin,** the subentry head **a fines de** is spelled without abbreviation).

Irregular Spanish Verbs and the Direction "See . . ."

If a Spanish verb is irregular, it has been treated in one of two ways: either its principal parts are shown (see for example the end of the entry for **caber**) or you are referred to an analogous irregular verb for guidance (see for example the end of the entry for **comparecer,** where you are directed to **conocer**). Thus, since the irregular form **conozco,** is shown at **conocer** (it being irregular in the sense that it has a z), you may infer that **comparecer** has the irregular form **comparezco.**

One of the consequences of the changes in Spanish spelling of January 1, 1959, is that a new kind of orthographically irregular verb has come into existence (for example ahijar, ahincar, ahitar, ahuchar, ahumar, ahusar, cohibir, prohibir, prohijar, rehilar, rehusar, sahumar, sobrehilar, and trashumar).

If "See . . . " is all you find at an entry, you are being directed to a synonym. Thus, "descompasarse See descomedirse" means that the translations of descomedirse are those of descompasarse too.

Spanish Equivalents of 'you'

Today's Spanish, when taken as a whole, has at least six equivalents of 'you': tú, vos, usted (abbreviated to Vd.), su merced (all of which are used in addressing one person), ustedes (abbreviated to Vds.), vosotros, vosotras, and sus mercedes (all used in addressing more than one person).

When you occurs in this dictionary, usually only one of those words has been chosen to translate it, though three are never used here: su merced, sus mercedes, because they are now limited to only a small area of the Spanish-speaking world (the Cundinamarca Savanna, in Colombia) and even there they are now obsolescent, and vos, because the verb forms corresponding to this pronoun often vary from country to country.

Usually, the selection of one pronoun or another in this dictionary has been arbitrary, in which case any of the others could just as easily have been chosen. For example, for How are you? the translation '¿Cómo está Vd.?' is offered, yet any of the other pronouns could appear instead (with, in certain cases, a different verb form).

In certain cases, however, not all pronouns (whether actually used or just implicit) would be appropriate. For example, among the translations of please . . . are imperative forms of servirse . . . . Because servirse in this sense is a formal usage (found mostly in impersonal writing like application blanks), it is not found in any familiar form of the imperative. The dictionary therefore gives ¡sírvase . . . ! (where the understood subject is usted, a formal pronoun). It could also have given ¡sírvanse . . . ! (where the understood subject is ustedes, likewise a formal pronoun), but not any form in which the subject were an informal pronoun.

Masculine and Feminine, Male and Female

As women engage in more and more activities once the domain of men, a growing number of Spanish nouns formerly used only in the masculine gender are being used in the feminine too. This dictionary thus labels nauta, paracaidista, púgil, pugilista, recluta, reservista, and seminarista, for example, as both masculine and feminine (the gender to be chosen depending on the gender of the person in question). For the user's convenience, the gender of Spanish nouns is indicated not only in the Spanish-English section but also in the English-Spanish one.

Many sample Spanish phrases and sentences in this dictionary can refer to people of either gender. For example, under wish in the English-Spanish section the sample sentence I wished him a Merry Christmas is translated 'Le deseé unas Pascuas muy felices' and 'Le felicité las Pascuas'. Since they both also mean 'I wished her a Merry Christmas', the sentence could as easily have contained her rather than him. It should therefore not be inferred that every phrase or sentence referring to a male cannot refer to a female (or vice versa). In this dictionary, male and female references have been chosen randomly, hopefully in equal number.

In other cases, a slight change is needed to turn a male reference into a female one or vice versa. For instance, He was within an ace of being killed (under within, prep., in the English-Spanish section) is rendered by 'Por poco le matan'. Changing he to she and le to la will yield a correct equivalence referring to a female. Since it would have taken up too much space to indicate those alternate equivalences, they are not given here, but with just an elementary knowledge of both languages, users of this dictionary will be able to make the necessary changes and thus have at their disposal many more sample phrases and sentences than it supplies.

A dictionary of any living language can always be improved, all the more so a dictionary of two living languages. Additions, corrections, and other suggestions will be received with thanks. They should be addressed to:

Random House Reference &
Information Publishing
Random House, Inc.
201 East 50th St.
New York, NY 10022-7703
U.S.A.

To Sol Steinmetz, editorial director of Random House Reference & Information Publishing, and to his staff go my thanks for their help in seeing this dictionary into print.

D.L.G.
September
1996

The Basics of Spanish Pronunciation

Whereas the fit between English spelling and pronunciation has for centuries been less than ideal (think, for example, of the various pronunciations of **-ough,** as in **although, bough, cough,** and **slough**), the fit between today's Spanish spelling and pronunciation is quite good, thanks to the regulatory efforts of the Spanish academies.

Because of that good fit, Spanish-speakers learn to read and spell faster than English-speakers, there is no such thing as a Spanish spelling bee, and Spanish spelling is a good basis for teaching the rudiments of Spanish pronunciation. The following instructions thus take spelling as their starting point. Pronunciation is described in two ways: with phonetic symbols (enclosed in slashes or brackets) and by way of approximate comparisons with English. A wavy line separates variants (like **esnob ~ snob**). A stress mark (') means that the syllable following it is stressed (as in [re'lo]). An asterisk indicates a nonexistent form (like English *****llion**). A right-facing "arrow"(>), or "greater than" sign, means 'became in Spanish' (as in English **rum** and French **rhum > ron ~ romo**).

As may be expected of a language that has been used for many centuries, over a vast area, and by diverse people, Spanish is now pronounced in various ways. Of the many current pronunciations, two are offered as most suitable for speakers of Spanish as a second language. The two standards are identical to a large extent, differing chiefly with respect to the pronunciation of c before **e; c** before **i; z** in any position; and, optionally, **ll** in any position.

To the extent that the two standards differ, features belonging to just one of them are labeled either *Standard 1* or *Standard 2* below.

Features labeled *Standard 1* are accepted as standard in Spain but not in the Western Hemisphere. Features labeled *Standard 2* are accepted as standard in the Western Hemisphere but not in Spain. If you speak Spanish mostly with Spaniards or mostly with people in or from the Western Hemisphere, your choice of standard will thus be straightforward. If you speak with people from both areas, you can either try to master both standards or, if you want to follow just one of them no matter to whom you speak, pick Standard 2.

In the Western Hemisphere, features labeled *Standard 1* are often either erroneously admired as being "the correct pronunciation of the language" or, quite the opposite, disdained as highfalutin (which are precisely the same reactions to British English frequently heard in English-speaking areas outside Europe). Neither standard, however, is intrinsically better than the other.

If possible, review the material given here with a speaker of Standard Spanish and hear how the sample words, phrases, and sentences are pronounced.

a is pronounced /a/, which is similar to the second vowel of the English interjection **aha!** and the vowel of the English interjection **ah,** although much shorter in duration.

See also "Diphthongs and Triphthongs" below.

b has three pronunciations. At the beginning of an utterance, after [m] (whether represented by **m** or by **n**), or after [n] (whether represented by **n** or by **m**), the letter **b** is pronounced [b], which is similar to the pronunciation of the first consonant of English **beach, broth, pebble,** etc. For example, in the sentence **Bulgaria envió a ambos embajadores en un barco japonés,** each of the four instances of **b** (and the one instance of **v**) is so pronounced.

Before /č/, /f/, /t/, /k/, /s/, /x/, or /θ/ in the same word (see **ch** [under **c**], **f, t, c, g,** and **c** respectively for interpreting those symbols), **b** is pronounced [p] (see **p** for interpreting that symbol), as in **subtítulo, absceso, subjefe,** and, in Standard 1, **subcentral.** That rule also holds before [p] in the same word (with the further result that [p] + [p] is reduced to [p]; hence the first two syllables of **subproducto,** for example, are [supro]) and for [p] before /s/ in the same word (with the further result that [ps] may be reduced to [s.] In certain words, nonpronunciation of **b** became so widespread that the only spelling now used is without that letter, for instance **ofuscar** and its derivatives (contrast English **obfuscate, obfuscation,** etc.).

At the end of a word, more than one pronunciation of **b** may be heard. For example, **club** may be [klub], [kluβ], or [klu]. Its plural (**clubs**) may be [klups], [klus], and possibly [kluβs] (unless the plural **clubes** is used, whose universal pronunciation is [kluβɛs] (see the next paragraph for interpreting [β] and e for interpreting [ɛ])]. All of the foregoing holds for compounds of club, like aeroclub. In esnob ~ snob, the final b is pronounced [b].

In all other positions (for example, habas, hablar, and habré), b is pronounced [β] a sound absent in English, which is made by bringing the lips close together without letting them touch each other (as if you were blowing dust away or blowing out a match or candle), expelling air through the mouth, and vibrating the vocal cords. This sound is thus similar to /v/ (as in English very and vowel), except that the latter is made by making the lower lip touch the upper teeth. English-speakers should not mistake Spanish [β] for English /v/.

It follows from the foregoing that if the position of b in the utterance changes, its pronunciation may change. Contrast, for example, these three utterances: (1) **Bulgaria mandó embajadores a ambos países,** (2) **En Bulgaria viven unos cuantos rusos,** and (3) **Iremos a Bulgaria.** In (1), the b of **Bulgaria** is pronounced [b] because it comes at the beginning of an utterance; in (2) the same b is also pronounced [b] because it comes after [m] (see the instructions for n on its pronunciation as [m]); but in (3) the same b is pronounced [β] because none of the conditions for pronouncing it [b] is met.

Similarly, when the word baba is pronounced in isolation, the first b is rendered [b] and the second b as [β], but in the phrase **la baba,** the first b is no longer at the beginning of an utterance (nor is it preceded by the sounds [m] or [n]), hence the phrase is pronounced [laβaβa].

Or, if the b of club is pronounced, it will be [β] before a vowel. So too the final letter of esnob, which is always pronounced.

See also v and, on **tranvía,** "Miscellaneous" below.

c has several pronunciations. If it is followed by e or i, the letter c is pronounced /θ/ in Standard 1 and [s] in Standard 2. The pronunciation of /θ/ in Spanish is similar to that of th in English thatch, think, etc., but made with somewhat more protrusion of the tongue. The sound [s] is similar to the pronunciation of s in English say, simple, etc., though in northern Spain [s] is often produced with the tip of the tongue higher in the mouth than in other varieties of Spanish, the result being that this sound has a hushing quality there (similar to Modern Greek /s/), which English-speakers should not mistake for /š/, which is the pronunciation of sh in English shall, should, etc.

Although Standard 1 has /θ/ for c before e or i, people who use that pronunciation will not be put off if they hear you pronounce the c as [s], because the latter is widespread (though not standard) in Spain. In the Western Hemisphere, c before e or i is always pronounced [s] and never /θ/. Speakers of Western Hemispheric Spanish will react to /θ/ either as "the correct pronunciation" ("though we don't use it") or as a highfalutin pronunciation (unless it comes from people who are to the manner born, i.e., many Spaniards). Thus, whereas it is desirable though not obligatory that you use Standard 1 in Spain, you would be well advised to use only Standard 2 in the Western Hemisphere, where /θ/ is bound to elicit a sharp reaction of one kind or another (as sharp as British **drawing pin, lorry,** or **trunk call** instead of **thumbtack, truck, long-distance call** would probably elicit in the United States).

Most speakers pronounce the combination ch, wherever it is found, as /č/, which is similar to the pronunciation of ch in English child, church, etc. Speakers who know Catalan or, at least, are aware of the Catalan pronunciation of ch, may pronounce this letter combination as /k/ in Catalan-origin proper nouns used in Spanish, like the family names Escrich and Roch (see the next paragraph on Spanish /k/). The letter combination tch (as in catch) is pronounced /č/ (in general, that sound at the end of a word is extremely rare, being limited to Catalan-origin proper nouns ending in -ch but not pronounced in Catalan fashion and to recent borrowings from English like catch and punch).

If c ends a syllable that is not the last syllable in the word and the next syllable begins with any consonant except /t/ (for instance **accionista, facsímil,** and **técnico**), you have an alternative: c may be pronounced either /k/ or /g/. Spanish /k/ is similar to the pronunciation of c in English escape, scandal, etc., but different from that of c in English cape, coop, etc. To achieve a good rendition of Spanish /k/, hold your open palm in front of your mouth and pronounce first cape and coop, then escape and scandal. When pronouncing the first two words, you felt a noticeable puff of air on your palm, but in the last two words you felt almost no puff at all. A noticeable puff of air accompanying a speech sound is called *aspiration;* sounds pronounced with aspiration are *aspirated;* and those pronounced without it are *unaspirated.* Spanish /k/ (like Spanish /p/ and /t/) is always unaspirated, wherever it occurs. Thus, you should have no trouble with Spanish es-**capar** and **escándalo** because here /k/ occurs after [s] and as an English speaker you will automatically pronounce it as unaspirated (just as you would the c of the English cognates of those words: escape and scandal). It is in other positions that you have to be careful not to aspirate: **claro, crear, tocología**, etc. (contrast them with their English cognates, all of which have an aspirated /k/: **clear, create, tocology**). See **g** for interpreting [g]. Note that if **c** is followed by **c**, the next letter is always **e** or **i** (as in **accionista** and **confección**). In such cases, you have an alternative with respect to the first **c** (either /k/ or [g] is correct) and the second **c** is pronounced according to either of the instructions given above for **c** before **e** or **i**.

If **c** ends a syllable that is not the last syllable in the word and the next syllable begins with /t/, it is pronounced /k/ in most words (like **actor** and **actriz**) and in at least one you may pronounce it /k/ or not pronounce it at all (**coctel** and its plurals: **coctels ~ cocteles**). In the place name **Vitoria** the absence of /k/ has been universal for so long that that is now its only spelling (in contrast to the female given name **Victoria** and the common noun **victoria**).

If **c** or **k** ends the last syllable of the word, that letter is pronounced /k/ at least in **cinc ~ zinc, clac, copec, frac, Nueva York**, and **tic-tac**, whereas in **biftec, bistec**, and **coñac** many speakers do not pronounce it (likewise in the plural of the last word, **coñacs**).

In all other cases (as in **aclarar, acoplar, acreditar, capaz, chucruta, claro**, and **creer**), **c** is pronounced /k/.

See also **k, ll** (under **l**), **q, s**, and **z**.

d has several pronunciations. At the beginning of an utterance, after [n], or after /l/, this letter is pronounced [d], which is similar to the pronunciation of **d** in English **dear, dust**, etc., with this difference: in the production of Spanish [d], the tongue touches the lower edge of the upper front incisors.

When between two vowels, when preceded by a vowel and followed by **r**, or when at the end of a word and not preceded by **r** (as in **pedir, Pedro**, and **libertad**), the letter **d** is pronounced [ð], which is similar to the pronunciation of **th** in English **that, there**, etc., but less interdental than English [ð] (in the production of the Spanish sound, the tip of the tongue gently touches the lower edge of the upper incisors).

If **d** is at the end of a word and it is preceded by **r** (as in **lord, milord**), it is silent. In the plurals, no matter how they are spelled, **d** is never present, hence never pronounced: **lores, milores.**

It follows from the foregoing that if the position of **d** in the utterance changes, its pronunciation may change. Contrast, for example, these three utterances: (1) **Dinamarca mandó embajadores a doce países**, (2) **En Dinamarca viven unos cuantos americanos**, and (3) **Iremos a Dinamarca**. In (1), the **d** of **Dinamarca** is pronounced [d] because it comes at the beginning of an utterance; in (2) the same **d** is also pronounced [d] because it comes after [n]; but in (3) the same **d** is pronounced [ð] because none of the conditions for pronouncing it [d] is met. Similarly, when the word **dedo** is pronounced in isolation, the first **d** is rendered [d] (and the second one [ð]), but in the phrase **mi dedo**, the first **d** is no longer at the beginning of an utterance (nor is it preceded by [n] or /l/); hence the phrase is pronounced [miðeðo].

e has two pronunciations. The instruction given in some books that **e** is pronounced [e] when stressed and [ɛ] when unstressed does not hold true for today's Spanish and may never have been an accurate description of its pronunciation in any variety of the language.

Here are better guidelines for **e** (except when it is part of a diphthong or triphthong):

If **e** is found in a syllable ending in a consonant (see "Syllabification" below), it is pronounced [ɛ], which is similar to the pronunciation of **è** in French or to the vowel of **bet, let, met**, etc., as pronounced in Standard English, that is, with considerable lowering of the jaw. For example, **embaldosar, fresco, hablen**, and **mestizo**.

If **e** ends a syllable and the next one begins with **r, rr**, or **t**, it is pronounced [ɛ]. For instance, **pero, caballete** (the first **e**), **cerrar**, and **jinete**.

Otherwise, **e** is pronounced [e], which is similar to the pronunciation of **é** in French, that is, the jaw is lowered only minimally (the closest English comes to having a sound like [e] is probably the vowel of **ache, rake, stake**, etc.). For example, **caballete** (the second **e**), **hablé, mesa**, and **poeta**. **Caballete** thus has both renditions of **e**, though the plural of that word, **caballetes**, has only [ɛ], because here the last syllable ends in a consonant.

Many Spanish verbs show variation between -ar and -ear, like **bazucar ~ bazuquear, chapurrar ~ chapurrear** (**e** is optional in **Yugoeslavia ~ Yugoslavia** and in **yugoeslavo ~ yugoslavo**).

See also "Diphthongs and Triphthongs" below.

f is pronounced /f/, which is similar to the pronunciation of **f** in English **fate, feet**, etc. For example, **afectar, fecha, golf, golfo, ¡uf!**. See also **h**.

g has several pronunciations. At the beginning of an utterance and when followed by **a, o, u**, or a consonant letter except **n** (as in **gato, goma, gusto, glaciar**, or **grave**), **g** is pronounced [g], which is similar to the pronunciation of g in English get, go, gumption, etc.

At the beginning of a word and when followed by n, the letter g is silent (as in gnomo). That pronunciation is in fact so widespread and reputable that a g-less spelling is now acceptable and is in fact preferred in this dictionary (see "Miscellaneous" below).

When g is preceded by n and is followed in the next syllable of the same word by a, o, u, ü, or a consonant letter (as in angosto, ángulo, ungüento, englobar, and engrasar), it is pronounced [g].

When g occurs at the end of a syllable and is preceded by n, it is silent, as in bumerang. In older borrowings from other languages, that g was systematically or sometimes omitted, as in sterling > esterlina, pudding > pudín.

Before e or i (as in gemir and gigante), except if it comes at the end of a word, the letter g is pronounced /x/, which is absent in most varieties of current English. This sound is similar to the pronunciation of ch in German Bach, that of ch in Israeli Hebrew zecher, and that of ch in Scots English loch, Lochaber, etc. Press the back of the tongue against the soft palate, expel air (as if coughing), and do not vibrate the vocal chords.

If g ends a syllable that is not the last syllable of the word (as in dogma and the first syllable of zigzag), this letter is pronounced [g]. In such cases, the next syllable always begins with a consonant.

Otherwise, g is pronounced [ɣ], a sound absent in English, which is made by bringing the back of the tongue close to the soft palate (without letting them touch), expelling air through the mouth, and vibrating the vocal chords. Examples are hago and hígado.

It follows from the foregoing that if the position of g in the utterance changes, its pronunciation may change. Contrast, for example, these three utterances: (1) Grecia mandó embajadores, (2) En Grecia viven unos cuantos italianos, and (3) Iremos a Grecia. In (1), the g of Grecia is pronounced [g] because it comes at the beginning of an utterance; in (2) the same g is also pronounced [g] because it comes after [n]; but in (3) the same g is pronounced [ɣ] because none of the conditions for pronouncing it [g] is met.

h is silent. In older Spanish, this letter was pronounced /h/ (a sound similar to the first consonant of here, how, and huddle in Standard English), which has remained in a few words in the guise of /x/ (see g for interpreting that symbol). In such cases, h has been replaced by j (cante jondo and joder, from older cante hondo and hoder respectively).

In at least four words, both spellings remain standard: halar ~ jalar, halón ~ jalón, holgorio ~ jolgorio, ¡hopo! and ¡jopo! (in the first variant of each pair, the h is not now pronounced). To at least some Spanish ears, the variants with /x/ are more emphatic or affective than those without it.

Since h is now silent, its presence or absence does not affect pronunciation. Thus, Ghana and Lesotho, for example, are pronounced exactly as if spelled without that letter. In some words, h is optional and the tendency to omit it can only be encouraged: armonizar ~ harmonizar, baraúnda ~ barahúnda, Rodesia ~ Rhodesia.

Many words that in older Spanish had f now have h. In a few instances, variants with both f and h remain in today's Spanish. They may be either full synonyms of each other or less than full synonyms (like faz and haz, forma and horma).

See also g and w.

i has two pronunciations. When representing a full vowel, it is pronounced [i], which is similar to the vowel of English beet, feet, sheen, etc., but shorter (for instance, dicho, isla, and cursi). When bearing a dieresis, this letter is likewise pronounced [i], as in pïada (were the dieresis absent, ia here would represent a diphthong).

When i represents part of a diphthong or a triphthong (see "Diphthongs and Triphthongs" below), it is pronounced [y], which is similar to the pronunciation of y in English year, yes, or yolk. Thus, miel and tiesto are pronounced [myɛl] and [tyɛsto].

See also y.

j is almost always pronounced /x/ (see g for interpreting that symbol). A notable exception is reloj, which many speakers pronounce [re'lo]. That pronunciation of reloj is so widespread that reló is an alternate spelling of the singular form, but only in informal writing. In the plural, everyone pronounces /x/ and therefore writes the j: relojes.

See x.

k, which is now found only in recent borrowings from other languages, is pronounced /k/ (see c for interpreting that symbol). The letter combination ck (as in crack, flashback, shock, snack, stock) is pronounced /k/.

l when not doubled is pronounced /l/, which is formed by putting the tip of the tongue against the sockets of the upper incisors, the remainder of the tongue lying flat. Spanish /l/ thus does not have the hollow sound of English /l/, in whose formation the back of the tongue rises toward the palate.

The letter combination **ll** (which always begins a syllable) has two pronunciations in Standard Spanish: /λ/ (which is similar to the pronunciation of **lli** in English **million** or that of **li** in **vermilion**) and [y], which is similar to the pronunciation of **y** in English **year, yes,** or **yolk.** Since English words like **million** and **vermilion** actually have [ly] rather than /λ/, that is, [l] ends one syllable of those English words and [y] begins the next one (whereas Spanish **ll,** except at the end of a word, always begins a syllable), English-speakers should be careful not to misinterpret /λ/ as [ly]. To achieve a good rendition of Spanish /λ/, pronounce **million** as if it did not contain **mi-,** that is, as if it were * llion. Good practice words are those beginning with **ll** (like **llamar, llegar,** and **llorar**) since here you are forced to pronounce /λ/ at the beginning of a syllable. See also **ñ** and "Syllabification" below.

In Spain, although /λ/ is still prestigious, it has been going out of use for decades as more and more people switch to [y] (in the unvarnished pronunciation of Madrid, for example, /λ/ has disappeared entirely). Spaniards now using /λ/ natively are mostly from northern Spain or, if not from that part of the country, they first learned [y] and later intentionally replaced that sound by the more prestigious /λ/. You may thus use either pronunciation in speaking to Spaniards, but /λ/ has a cachet in Spain that [y] lacks. Standard 1 therefore has /λ/.

In the Western Hemisphere, **ll** is pronounced /λ/, [y], /ž/, or /š/, according to area or speaker (/ž/ is similar to the pronunciation of **z** in English **azure** and of **zs** in the name **Zsa Zsa;** /š/ is similar to the pronunciation of **sh** in English **shall, should,** etc.). You may want to pick the sound your interlocutors use or, if you want to choose a SINGLE pronunciation that most speakers of Western Hemispheric Spanish will find acceptable (whatever they themselves use), take /λ/ or [y] (though /λ/ might sound a tad highfalutin to certain Spanish-speakers in the Western Hemisphere who do not use it themselves).

If you want to pick a SINGLE pronunciation of **ll** acceptable both in Spain and in the Western Hemisphere, take /λ/. However, if you do, you should also choose Standard 1 for the pronunciation of **c** before **e** or **i** and of **z** when speaking to Spaniards, since it seems that no speakers of the language in Spain who pronounce **ll** as /λ/ follow Standard 2 for those other two letters. With regard to the Western Hemisphere, since Standard 2 for those other two letters co-occurs there with all of the pronunciations of **ll** (/λ/, [y], /ž/, /š/), you have four choices, the only selection not recommended for this part of the world being Standard 1 for **c** before **e** or **i** and for **z** in all positions (whatever pronunciation of **ll** you may choose).

l is optional in **belfo ~ befo.**

m: Traditionally, Spanish does not have [m] at the end of a word when it is pronounced in isolation. Consequently, in many words borrowed from other languages ending in that sound, it was replaced by [n] (see the next section for interpreting that symbol) and the word was respelled accordingly (for example, **harén, ínterin, Jerusalén, macadán, querubín, ron, serafín**). However, a few words (all learned borrowings from Latin and recent borrowings from other languages) end in **m** (for example, **álbum, factótum, ídem, médium, memorándum, ultimátum,** and **vademécum**) and that letter also appears in the Spanish names of many places outside Spanish-speaking areas, like **Bírmingham, Búckingham, Siam,** and **Vietnam.** Both [m] and [n] are heard in such words, depending on people's ability to pronounce [m] at the end of a word (as more and more Spanish-speakers study other languages, they find it easier to produce that sound in that position) and their interest in maintaining the supposedly "correct" (i.e., non-Spanish) pronunciation of that letter. The unaffected pronunciation is [n] (and **mm** in **súmmum** is always pronounced as if it were a single **m**), but if in another form of the word the **m** is followed by a vowel, it is pronounced according to rule, i.e., [m] (as in **siamés**).

In all other positions, **m** is pronounced [m], which is similar to the pronunciation of **m** in English **make, might,** etc. For example, **amar, almirante, ambos, mayor.**

n has several pronunciations. If immediately followed by a labial consonant (represented by **b, f, m, p,** or **v**) whether in the same word or in the next one, it is pronounced [m] (as in the words **anfitrión, inmediato, anverso** or the sentences **insiste en bucear, insiste en pelear,** and **en muchos casos hay más**). Since [m] + [m] is reduced to a single [m], **en muchos casos** actually has just one [m].

It follows from the foregoing that the word **tampoco** and the phrase **tan poco** are pronounced identically, as are the word **ciempiés** and the phrase **cien pies** (each of those words is in fact derived from the corresponding phrase); **Edimburgo** and **Nuremberg** also show the replacement of [n] by [m] before a labial.

However, [n] + [m] (as in **insomne**) is not reduced.

Before /k/ or [g] (as in **aunque** and **angosto**), **n** is pronounced [ŋ], which is similar to the final consonant of **long, sing,** and **song** as pronounced in Standard English.

In all other positions (as in **Anatolia, andan** and **nombrar**), n is pronounced [n], which is similar to the pronunciation of **n** in English **hand, near,** etc.

Instances of [n] + [n] are reduced to a single [n], as in the words **ennegrecer, ennoblecer, perenne, sinnúmero** or a phrase like **sin número** (the word **connoto** and the phrase **con Otto** are thus pronounced identically), though an effect of the double [n] remains: the preceding **e** is pronounced [ɛ], not [e], that is, as if the first syllable ended in the first [n].

Instances of [m] + [n], however, are not reduced (as in **amnesia** and **amnistiar**).

Spanish-speakers who know Catalan or, at least, are aware of the pronunciation of **ny** in that language at the end of a word, pronounce it [n] in Catalan-origin proper nouns used in Spanish (like the family names **Capmany, Castany,** and **Fortuny**). Others pronounce it [ni].

See also **m**, "Stress," and, on **tranvía**, "Miscellaneous" below.

ñ is pronounced /ɲ/ which is similar to the pronunciation of **ny** in English **canyon** or **ni** in English **onion**. Since English words like those two actually have [ny] rather than /ɲ/ (that is, [n] ends one syllable and [y] begins the next one), English-speakers should be careful not to misinterpret /ɲ/ as [ny]. To achieve a good rendition of Spanish /ɲ/ (which always begins a syllable), pronounce **canyon** as if it did not contain **ca-**, that is, as if it were *nyon, or **onion** as if it were *nion. Good practice words are those beginning with **ñ** (like **ñiquiñaque** and **ñoño**) since here you are forced to pronounce /ɲ/ at the beginning of a syllable.

See also **ll** (under **l**).

o has two pronunciations, neither of which can easily be described with reference to English. In a syllable ending in a consonant (see "Syllabification" below), this letter is pronounced somewhat like the **o** of English **port** or short (for instance **pondré** and **sondear**). Otherwise (that is, when o ends the syllable), it is pronounced somewhat like the **o** of English **coke** or **tote** (for instance, **codo** and **lodo**). The words **costo** and **zonzo** thus contain an example of each kind of o. The two kinds of /o/ are similar to the closed and open /o/ of Italian.

See also "Diphthongs and Triphthongs" below.

p, where it is pronounced, stands for [p], which is similar to the pronunciation of **p** in English **space, spear, spook,** etc., but different from that of **p** in English **pike, peak, poke,** etc. To achieve a good rendition of Spanish [p], hold your open palm in front of your mouth and pronounce first **pike, peak, poke,** then **space, spear, spook.** When pronouncing the first three words, you felt a noticeable puff of air on your palm, but in the last three words you felt almost no puff at all. A noticeable puff of air accompanying a speech sound is called *aspiration;* sounds pronounced with aspiration are *aspirated;* and those pronounced without it are *unaspirated.* Spanish [p] (like Spanish /k/ and /t/) is always unaspirated, wherever it occurs. Thus, you should have no trouble with Spanish **espacio, especial, especie,** etc. because here [p] occurs after [s] and as an English-speaker you will automatically pronounce it as unaspirated (just as you would the English cognates of those words: **space, special,** and **species**). It is in other positions that you have to be careful not to aspirate: **particular, poeta, puerta,** etc. (contrast them with their English cognates, all of which have an aspirated [p]: **particular, poet, port**).

Spanish **ps** at the beginning of a word is pronounced [s]. Some pretentious Spanish-speakers may tell you that the "correct" pronunciation is [ps], but that would be as artificial as pronouncing English **psyche, psychology,** etc., in that way. In fact, non-pronunciation of **p** in the combination **ps** at the beginning of a word is so entrenched in Spanish that the preferred spelling is now **s** (this dictionary thus gives only **sicología, sicólogo,** etc. and not the older spellings **psicología, psicólogo,** etc.). See "Miscellaneous" below.

Before /t/, some speakers pronounce **p** as [p] and some do not pronounce it at all. Thus, some write **excerpta, septiembre,** etc., and some **excerta, setiembre,** etc. Although both are correct, the spelling with **p** is preferred in this dictionary (except in the first word, for which both forms are given). Whether or not one pronounces the **p** of **óptimo,** it seems that standard spelling requires that the word always be spelled with that letter.

At the end of a word, you may have an alternative: in **galop,** for example, the **p** may be pronounced [p] or be silent.

The number of instances in which **p** is silent or may be silent is small.

q is always followed by **ue** or **ui.** The sequence **que** is pronounced either [kɛ] or [ke] and **qui** is pronounced [ki] (for example, **quince**) or [ky] (for instance, **quien**) (see "Diphthongs and Triphthongs" below).

To represent the sound sequences [kwe], [kwɛ], and [kwi], Spanish has **cue, cue,** and **cui** respectively (as in **cueva, cuestión,** and **cuidar**).

Because **q** is always followed by **u,** if Spanish-speakers borrow words containing just **q** from other languages, that letter is changed to **k.** Thus, the Spanish names of Iraq and Qatar, for example, are **Irak** and **Katar.**

r has two pronunciations. At the beginning of a word or when it comes after **l, n,** or **s** (for example, **reir, alrededor, enrojecer,** and **Israel**), this letter has the same pronunciation as **rr** (see below).

If **b** ends one syllable and **r** begins the next one in the same word (see "Syllabification" below), **r** is pronounced exactly like **rr** (for example **subrayar** if syllabified **sub-ra-yar**). If **b** + **r** belong to the same syllable (for instance **bramar** and **lubricar**), **r** is pronounced with one flip of the upper front part of the tongue against the sockets of the upper incisors (for instance **subrayar** if syllabified **su-bra-yar**). See "Syllabification" below on the alternative now permitted in words beginning with the prefix **sub-**.

In all other positions, **r** is likewise pronounced with one flip of the upper front part of the tongue against the sockets of the upper incisors (for instance, **leer, para, pera, pero, tercero,** and **treinta**).

rr is pronounced with a trill (several flips) of the upper front part of the tongue against the sockets of the upper incisors (for instance, **parra, perra, perro,** and **sierra**). Thus, **para** and **parra** are different words, with different pronunciations and different meanings. The same applies to **caro** and **carro, pera** and **perra, pero** and **perro, torero** and **torrero,** and other pairs of words.

s has several pronunciations. When it represents the plural ending of nouns recently borrowed from other languages, it is silent in certain words, like **cabarets, carnets, complots, conforts, superávits, tíckets, trusts, vermuts.**

Before the letters **b, v, d, g** (but only when this letter is not followed by **e** or **i**), **l, m, n,** or **r** (whether any of those eight letters appear in the same word as **s** or they appear in the next word), you have an alternative (in both standards) if **s** is not the last letter of the word: it may be pronounced [z] (a sound similar to the pronunciation of z in English **zebra, zoo,** etc.) or [s] (see **c** for interpreting that symbol): **esbelto, esdrújulo, esgrimir, isla, esmalte, Israel, los baúles, los varones, los dedos, los guantes, los lagos, los maestros, los nervios, los ratones,** etc. If **s** is the last letter, only [s] is found (for instance, in the family name **Pons**).

If **s** is followed by **r** (whether in the same word or in the next one), besides the two pronunciations suggested above [s] or [z]), a third possibility is not to pronounce the **s** at all and, as a compensation, trill the **r** more. The word **Israel** (and its derivatives) thus has three pronunciations: [isrraɛl], [izrraɛl], and [irrraɛl].

Otherwise, **s** is pronounced [s] (as in **ese, especial, hablas, hasta, insistir, seco**).

If **s** is followed by **h,** the foregoing paragraph applies, except in the case of Spanish words recently borrowed from other languages or words modeled on such recently borrowed words, in which **sh** constitutes a unit, to be pronounced /š/ (a sound similar to the pronunciation of sh in English **shall, sheet, should,** etc.). Thus, in **deshacer,** an old Spanish word not recently borrowed from another language, the instructions about **s** apply and the **h** is silent (hence the first two syllables of that word are [desa]), whereas in **riksha** and **yídish, sh** is pronounced /š/.

Spanish spelling does not distinguish the two kinds of **sh,** which you can, however, partly distinguish in this way: **sh** at the beginning or at the end of a word is of recent non-Spanish origin. If **sh** appears in the middle of a word, you have to know its origin to determine how that letter combination should be pronounced, though this rule of thumb will almost always hold: a word beginning **desh-** is likely not to be a recent borrowing from another language; rather, it probably consists of the centuries-old Spanish negating prefix **des-** and a word beginning with **h-**. Furthermore, the recent borrowings are often easily identified because of their unusual spelling (for example, it is clear that **riksha** is new).

Traditionally, no Spanish words began with **s** followed by a consonant, as a result of which Spanish-speakers either dropped **s** when borrowing non-Spanish words so beginning or, more frequently, added **e** to them: Dutch **sloeren** > **eslora,** Dutch **skiff,** English **skiff,** French **esquif,** French **skiff,** Italian **schifo,** and/or Portuguese **esquife** > **esquife,** English **sterling** > **esterlina,** Italian **strambotto** > **estrambote,** Latin **scientia** > **ciencia,** etc.

S is optional in **quizá ~ quizás.**

See also **b, c, t, z,** and "Syllabification" below.

t, except before **l** in the same word, is pronounced [t], which is similar to the pronunciation of t in English **stake, steer, stoop,** etc., but different from that of t in English **take, teak, took,** etc. To achieve a good rendition of Spanish /t/, hold your open palm in front of your mouth and pronounce first **take, teak, took,** then **stake, steer, stoop.** When pronouncing the first three words, you felt a noticeable puff of air on your palm, but in the last three words you felt almost no puff at all. A noticeable puff of air is called *aspiration;* sounds pronounced with aspiration are *aspirated;* and those pronounced without it are *unaspirated.* Spanish /t/ (like Spanish /k/ and /p/) is always unaspirated, wherever it occurs. Thus, you should have no trouble producing an unaspirated /t/ in Spanish estado, estimar, estúpido, etc. because here /t/ occurs after [s] and as an English-speaker you will automatically pronounce it as unaspirated (just as you would the English cognates of those words: state, esteem, and stupid). It is in other positions that you have to be careful not to aspirate: tocar, tabla, Túnez, etc. (contrast them with their English cognates, all of which have an aspirated /t/: touch, table, Tunisia). Furthermore, Spanish /t/ is made by touching the tip of the tongue against the upper incisors (in contrast to English /t/, in whose production the tongue touches the gums).

In three positions, t may not be pronounced as described above. First, before l or m in the same word (as in atleta, aritmético, and ritmo) you have an alternative: t may be pronounced as described or it may be pronounced [ð] (see d for interpreting that symbol).

Second, the t of the prefix post- is not pronounced if it is followed by any pronounced consonant letter except r, so much so that alternate spellings without t are also found and they are in fact the preferable ones, for instance, posguerra and posmeridiano. (but also postergar, etc.).

Third, t at the end of a word may be silent. Probably many, most, or all Spanish-speakers pronounce it in cenit, déficit, fagot, mamut, superávit, and el Tíbet ~ el Tibet, whereas in other words final t is silent, for instance cabaret, carnet, complot, tícket, trust, and vermut, which are pronounced as if written *cabaré, *carné, *compló, *tique, *trus, and *vermú (the plurals are pronounced identically to their singulars. In still other words you have an alternative: confort is pronounced either [kom'for] or [kom'fort] (the plural conforts has both variants too).

u has several pronunciations. In the combinations gue, gui, que, and qui, the letter u is silent. For example, guedeja [geðexa] ~ [ɣeðexa], quedar [keðar], and quien [kyɛn] (see q and e on the pronunciation of those letters).

When u represents part of a diphthong or a triphthong (see "Diphthongs and Triphthongs" below), it is pronounced [w], which is similar to the first sound of English win and won. Thus, puesto and seudónimo, for example, are pronounced [pwɛsto] and [sewðonimo].

If a u bears a dieresis, it is pronounced [w]. Thus, lingüista is pronounced [lingwista].

In all other cases, u is pronounced [u], which is similar to the vowel of English coot or toot, although in the production of the Spanish sound the lips are more rounded and the vowel is of shorter duration than in the production of the English one. For example, ducha, hubo, u, Unamuno, and uno.

v has two pronunciations. At the beginning of an utterance or after n (which in this position is pronounced [m]), the letter v is pronounced [b], which is similar to the first consonant of English beach, broth, pebble, etc. In all other positions, this letter is pronounced [β] (see b for interpreting that symbol). For example, in the sentence ¿Verdad que en el anverso de la medalla se ve un pavo real?, the first and fifth words have [b] and the tenth and twelfth have [β].

Therefore, the instructions for pronouncing b and those for pronouncing v are identical (depending on the position of those letters in the utterance), as a consequence of which pairs of words like baca and vaca or hube and uve are homophones in today's Spanish and, as a further consequence of which, if you hear [b] or [β], you cannot tell whether it is to be represented by b or by v unless you know how to spell the word.

If people try to tell you that b is pronounced in one way and v in another in today's Spanish, tell them that is a figment of their imagination. Spelling differences (like baca vs. vaca) are misleading them into thinking they hear a difference (or believing there should be a difference) when none in fact exists. The fact that native speakers of the language less skilled in spelling often write b when v is required or vice versa is proof enough that no difference in pronunciation is made.

w, which is found only in borrowings from Germanic languages and French, has several pronunciations. In several words, it is pronounced as if it were b or v and in such cases alternate spellings with v are found too: wagneriano ~ vagneriano, Westfalia ~ Vestfalia. The forms with v are preferable.

In at least a few words, w is pronounced [w] (a sound similar to the first sound of English win and won) and for one of them an alternate spelling with u exists: Malawi, Taiwán, Zimbabwe.

In whisky, the letter combination wh is pronounced [w] by those who want to show off their knowledge of English and [gw] or [ɣw] by those who speak normally (the choice of [gw] or [ɣw] depends on the position of the word in the utterance; see the instructions for g).

Whereas **Trans World Airlines** is shortened to the initialism **TWA** in English, in Spanish it is shortened to the acronym **la TWA**, which is pronounced /la'tua/.

x has several pronunciations. For a time, the recommended pronunciation was [ks]. Later, [gz] in certain positions was allowed as an alternate pronunciation. Today, those instructions, especially the one calling for [ks] wherever **x** occurs, would probably result in a pronunciation no native speaker uses and which would sound artificial. The following suggestions are more realistic for our times.

If **x** occurs before a consonant (as in **experiencia**, **extremidad** and **mixto**), pronounce it [s]. That pronunciation is probably most frequent in words beginning with the prefix **ex-** followed by a consonant, for example **excelente**, widely pronounced [ɛsθelɛnte] or [ɛselɛnte]. In the latter pronunciation, [s] + [s] becomes a single [s], though an effect of the double [s] remains: the preceding **e** is pronounced [ɛ], not [e], that is, as if the first syllable ended in a consonant, i.e., as if it ended in the first [s].

If **x** occurs between vowels, you have an alternative in certain words (**examen** and **exiguo**, for example, may be pronounced with [ks], [gz], or [s]) but not in others (for instance, all Spanish-speakers, it seems, now pronounce **sexo** with [ks]).

At the end of a word, the pronunciation of **x** is in flux. In **ántrax**, **Benelux**, **dux**, **fénix**, **látex**, and **tórax**, [ks] seems to be most frequent if not universal today, whereas in **clímax** and **flux**, [s] may now be more frequent.

At least some exceptions to those pronunciations are heard in words of Native American origin: for example, in **México** and **mexicano**, the **x** is now always pronounced [x] (those are the spellings official and universal in Mexico; elsewhere, **Méjico**, **mejicano** are used); in **Xochimilco** (a Mexican place name), the **x** is always pronounced [s].

Further exceptions are certain given and family names, which are found in two variants: one preserving a now archaic spelling with **x** (like **Xavier** and **Ximénez**) and the other spelled in modern fashion with **j** (**Javier** and **Jiménez**). Here, **x** is pronounced /x/, that is, just like **j**.

y has several pronunciations. In the word **y**, it is pronounced [i] (see **i** for interpreting that symbol).

When it represents the first or last segment of a diphthong or triphthong (see "Diphthongs and Triphthongs" below), as in **ya**, **yegua**, **yunque**, **ley**, **rey**, **soy**, and **Paraguay**, the letter **y** is pronounced [y] (see **ll** [under l] for interpreting that symbol).

In certain varieties of Spanish, [y] is pronounced with more occlusion, so that it has come to be close to [ž] if not actually that sound (see **ll** [under l] for interpreting the latter symbol); and in still other varieties it is pronounced with so much occlusion that it has come to be close to [ǰ] if not actually that (ǰ is similar to the first consonant of English **Jacob**, **Jerusalem**, **Jew**, etc.). Both Standard 1 and Standard 2 have [y] rather than [ž] or [ǰ], except in the emphatic pronunciation of **yo** (as in ¡yo, y yo sólo, soy el dueño aquí!), for which [ǰo] is a widespread rendition acceptable in both standards.

Certain family names have two spelling variants, an archaic one with **y** and one spelled in modern fashion with **i** (like **Yglesias ~ Iglesias**). Here, **y** is pronounced /i/, that is, just like **i**.

See also **n** with regard to **ny**.

z has several pronunciations. In Standard 1, you have an alternative:
(1) In all positions, pronounce it [θ] (see **c** for interpreting that symbol). Or,
(2) Before the letters **b**, **v**, **d**, **g**, **l**, **m**, **n**, or **r** (whether in the same word or in the next one), pronounce it [ð] (see **d** for interpreting that symbol) and in all other positions pronounce it [θ] (see **c** for interpreting that symbol).
In Standard 2, you have an alternative:
(3) In all positions, pronounce it [s] (see **s** for interpreting that symbol). Or,
(4) Before the letters **b**, **v**, **d**, **g**, **l**, **m**, **n**, or **r** (whether in the same word or in the next one), pronounce it [z] and in all other positions pronounce it [s] (see **s** for interpreting that symbol).

That is to say, if you pronounce **c** before **e** or **i** as [θ], you must follow instruction (1) or (2) above. If you pronounce **c** before **e** or **i** as [s], you must follow instruction (3) or (4) above.

Furthermore, if you choose to pronounce **s** as [s] before **b**, **v**, **d**, **g**, **l**, **m**, **n**, or **r**, you must pronounce **z** before any of those eight letters as [θ] (= Standard 1) or as [s] (= Standard 2); if you choose to pronounce **s** as [z], you must pronounce **z** before any of those eight letters as [ð] (= Standard 1) or [z] (= Standard 2).

Thus, in the sentence **César el hazmerreír de toda la isla**, for example, you have these choices for the **c** of the first word, the **z** of the third word, and the **s** of the seventh word:
c [θ] + z [θ] + s [s] (= Standard 1)
c [θ] + z [ð] + s [z] (= Standard 1)
c [s] + z [s] + s [s] (= Standard 2)
c [s] + z [z] + s [z] (= Standard 2)

The same restrictions apply to any individual word. Thus, **civilización**, for example, must be pronounced either [θiβiliθaθyon] (= Standard 1) or [siβilisasyon] (= Standard 2).

Diphthongs and Triphthongs

Spanish has fifteen diphthongs and six triphthongs.

Eight of the diphthongs begin with a semivowel:
ia [ya] is spelled **ya** at the beginning of a word, e.g., **desahuciar, yámbico.**
ua [wa] (e.g., **guardar**).
ie [ye] or [yɛ] is spelled **ye** at the beginning of a word, e.g., **agüero, bien, higiene, siete, yema.** The rules for choosing [e] or [ɛ] (see **e**) apply to [ye] and [yɛ] too.
ue [we] or [wɛ] is spelled **üe** after **g** that is not pronounced [x], e.g., **huelga, hueste, huevo, vergüenza.** The rules for choosing [e] or [ɛ] (see **e**) apply to [we] or [wɛ] too.
io and yo [yo], e.g., **soslayar, yo.** The spelling **io** at the beginning of a word is an imitation of Greek.
uo [wo] (e.g., **arduo**).
iu [yu] is spelled **yu** at the beginning of a word, e.g., **triunfo, yugo.**
ui [wi] (spelled **uy** in **muy**), e.g., **cuidar, muy.** For **uy** representing [uy], see **uy** in the next section.

Take care to pronounce diphthongs beginning with a semivowel as diphthongs and not as two syllables. Thus, whereas English **barrio** has three syllables, Spanish **barrio** has two (**ba-rrio**), pronounced [barryo].

Six of the diphthongs end in a semivowel:
ai [ay] is spelled **ay** at the end of most words; rarely, **ay** is found in the middle of a word (e.g., **aimará ~ aymará, hay, Raimundo, Seychelles**). If **ay** occurs before a vowel in the same word, it represents not a diphthong but /a/ + /y/ and each of those sounds belongs to a different syllable (thus, **aya** and **haya** for example are syllabified **a-ya** and **ha-ya**).
au [aw] (e.g., **caudillo**).
ei is almost always pronounced [ey] and is almost always spelled **ey** at the end of a word, e.g., **reina, rey.** A pronunciation exception is **reir**, which is pronounced as if spelled *reír. If **ey** occurs before a vowel in the same word, it represents not a diphthong but /e/ + /y/ and each of those sounds belongs to a different syllable (thus, **reyes** and **leyenda** for instance are syllabified **re-yes** and **le-yen-da**).
eu [ew] (e.g., **seudónimo**).
oi is almost always pronounced [oy] and is spelled **oy** at the end of a word (e.g., **hoy**)

and in certain family names in other positions too (like **Goytisolo**). A pronunciation exception is **oir**, which is pronounced as if spelled *oír. If **oy** occurs before a vowel in the same word, it represents not a diphthong but /o/ + /y/ and each of those sounds belongs to a different syllable (thus, **Goya** is syllabified **Go-ya**).
uy, which always occurs at the end of a word, is almost always pronounced [uy] (as in **¡huy!, Jujuy**). The exception is **muy**, whose pronunciation is given in the previous section. If **uy** occurs before a vowel in the same word, it represents not a diphthong but /u/ + /y/ and each of those sounds belongs to a different syllable (thus, **cuyo** and **tuyas** are syllabified **cu-yo** and **tu-yas**).

The triphthongs are:
iai [yay] (e.g., **despreciáis**).
iau [yaw] (e.g., **miau**).
iei [yey] (e.g., **despreciéis**).
uai [way] (spelled **uay** at the end of a word), e.g., **evaluáis, Uruguay.**
uau [waw] (e.g., **guau**).
uei [wey] (spelled **uey** at the end of a word), e.g., **evaluéis, buey.**

Syllabification

Spanish is a consonant-vowel language, that is, syllables preferably end in a vowel (though many exceptions are found). Therefore, a single consonant and the vowel following it usually form a syllable or, expressed otherwise, a single consonant between two vowels usually goes with the following vowel (thus, **ba-jo, a-dhe-sión**). Since **ch, ll, ñ**, and **rr** represent a single consonant, the syllabification is, for example, **mu-cha-cho, ha-llar, ni-ño, ba-rrio**, and **haz-me-rreír.**

The consonant clusters **bl, cl, dl, fl, gl, pl, tl, br, cr, dr, fr, gr, pr**, and **tr** form a syllable with the following vowel, for instance, **ha-blar, a-cla-rar, a-flo-jar, a-glo-me-rar, a-pla-zar, a-tle-ta, a-bra-zar, a-cre-di-tar, a-drede, a-fran-ce-sar, a-gre-gar**, and **a-pren-der.**

When representing /š/, **sh** is not divided, whereas if a consonant letter + **h** is found in the middle of a word and the **h** is silent, the **h** begins a new syllable: **al-ha-ra-ca, clor-hi-dra-to, des-hi-dra-tar, in-hu-ma-ción.**

All other clusters of two consonants between vowels (including diphthongs and triphthongs) are usually divided, so that the first consonant belongs to the preceding syllable and the second consonant to the following syllable, for example, **a-cos-tar-se, ac-tuar, cuer-do, en-car-gar, es-la-vo, fras-co, Is-ra-el, llan-ta, per-di-ción, sol-da-du-ra**, and **der-vi-che.** Subject to that rule are also instances of double **c** or **n**, as in **per-fec-ción** and **en-ne-gre-cer.**

If a cluster of three or more consonants stands between vowels, the last two consonants are usually **bl, cl, dl, fl, gl, pl, tl, br, cr, dr, fr, gr, pr,** or **tr** and they go with the following syllable, for instance, **tem-blar, ten-dré, ex-plo-tar, tem-prano.**

If a cluster of three or more consonants stands between vowels and if the second consonant is **s,** the **s** goes with the preceding syllable, for example **ins-tan-te** and **pers-pec-ti-va.**

If one vowel follows another and they do not constitute a diphthong (see above), they belong to separate syllables, for instance, **ma-es-tro, cre-o, le-er, to-a-lla.** Accordingly, if **i** or **u** (which represent respectively [y] or [w] in diphthongs and triphthongs) represents a vowel, it belongs in a separate syllable and that fact is indicated by a stress mark. Thus, **ahínco** (three syllables: **a-hín-co**), **búho** (two syllables: **bú-ho**), **traído** (three syllables: **tra-í-do**), **prohíbo** (three syllables: **pro-hí-bo**), **Raúl** (two syllables: **Ra-úl**), **haría** (three syllables: **ha-rí-a**), **haríais** (three syllables: **ha-rí-ais**), etc.

If **y** is preceded and followed by a vowel, it forms a diphthong with the following one and therefore belongs in the following syllable, for instance, **ca-yo, tu-yo, cre-yó.** In fact, all diphthongs and triphthongs (see the list above) form syllables of their own. In contrast, identical contiguous vowels (as in **creer**) and vowels that do not form diphthongs or triphthongs (as in **leal**), as well as diphthongs or triphthongs dissolved by the stress mark (see the examples from **ahínco** to **haríais** in the previous paragraph), form separate syllables (thus, **cre-er, le-al,** etc.).

It is permissible but not obligatory to set aside the foregoing rules in the case of prefixes, which one may consider as forming syllables of their own (whether or not such would be the case if the rules were followed) or which one may, rather, subject to the rules. For example, **ab-ro-ga-ción** or **a-bro** . . . , **des-a-bro-char** or **de-sa** . . . , **ex-a-cer-ba-ción** or **e-xa** . . . , **sub-li-mar** or **su-bli** . . . (in each pair, the first variant reflects treatment of the prefix as a syllable in its own right, no matter what the rules would require, and the second variant shows syllabification when the rules are suspended). The same applies to solid compounds: **nos-o-tros** or **no-so-tros, vos-o-tras** or **vo-so-tras,** etc.

The foregoing paragraph not withstanding, the rules must be followed with respect to a succession of three consonant letters, the second of which is **s,** in which case **s** belongs with the preceding, not the following letter (thus, as already noted, **ins-tante, pers-pect-ti-va,** not **in-st** . . . , **per-sp** . . .) and with

respect to prefixes if the first letter immediately following them is **h** (thus, **des-ha-cer** and **des-hi-dra-tar,** not **de-sha** . . . or **de-shi** . . .).

Stress

Most Spanish words have only one primary stress, which can be determined from the spelling according to these rules:

(1) If a word is spelled with a stress mark, stress the syllable in which it is found (like **águila, bíceps, fórceps, hablarán, Martínez**), the only exception being **ó,** which is not stressed (this is the form taken by the conjunction **o** when it appears between two Arabic numerals, the purpose of the mark being solely to prevent misinterpretation of the conjunction as the Arabic numeral for zero; thus, **6 ó 7,** for instance, means '6 or 7').

(2) If a word contains no stress mark:
  [2.A] Stress the last syllable if the word ends in:
    [2.A.i] a vowel letter + **y** (like **convoy, Uruguay, virrey**),
    [2.A.ii] a consonant letter other than **n** or **s** (like **consentir, David, lateral**),
    [2.A.iii] **n** not preceded by a vowel letter (like **Isern**),
    [2.A.iv] **s** not preceded by a vowel letter (like **Fontanals, Casals**).
  [2.B] Stress the next-to-last syllable if the word ends in:
    [2.B.i] a vowel letter other than **y** (like **casi, habla, hable, hablo, fatuo, patria, sitio**),
    [2.B.ii] a vowel letter + **n** (like **consienten, hablan**),
    [2.B.iii] a vowel letter + **s** (like **consientes, hablas**).

Catalan-origin names like **Capmany, Castany, Fortuny** are stressed on the vowel immediately preceding **-y** (thus, stress [man], [tan], [tun]).

The triplets **árbitro, arbitro, arbitró; público, publico, publicó; término, termino, terminó; tráfago, trafago, trafagó;** and **válido, valido, validó** illustrate several possibilities.

Miscellaneous

It is noted above that [m] + [m], [n] + [n], [p] + [p], and [s] + [s] are respectively reduced to one [m], [p], and [s]. Since the number of instances of [s] + [s] is not the same in all varieties of Spanish, the number of reductions to [s] varies accordingly. For example, **absceso** is pronounced [apseso] only where c before e (or i) is pronounced [s] (otherwise it is rendered [apθeso]); see also **excelente** in the remarks on **x**.

Reduction of identical contiguous sounds (whether vowels or consonants) is widespread in Spanish, whether within a word or between two words. Thus, [a] + [a] is reduced to [a] both in the word **portaaviones** and in a phrase like **a ambos**; or, [ε] + [e] is reduced to [e] in the word **sobreexcitar** and in a phrase like **este efecto** (in this regard, [e] and [ε] are considered "identical"; the same holds true for the two kinds of /o/; hence reduction is found in a sentence like **escojo ocho opciones**). The spellings **guardagujas, guardalmacén, remplazar, sobrentender**, etc., are in fact used too and they are preferable. In many cases, only spellings reflecting a reduction are now found, for example, **aprensión, prensil**, and **represible** (contrast those forms with their English cognates: **apprehension, prehensile**, and **reprehensible**).

In certain cases, however, two contiguous sounds are pronounced separately (by some speakers) or reduced to a single, slightly longer than usual one (by other speakers), for example in **creer** and its derivatives having **ee**. When to reduce to a single vowel and when not to reduce or to reduce to a single, slightly longer vowel must be learned individually for each word.

Other simplifications preferred in this dictionary are, at the beginning of a word, **g** instead of **gn, m** instead of **mn**, and **s** instead of **ps** (see, for example, **nomo, nemotecnia**, and **seudónimo**), as well as spellings like **oscuro** and **sustituir**.

Two sounds may influence each other. **Tranvía**, for example, is pronounced [trambia] because the sound represented by **v** causes the **n** to be pronounced [m] and the sound represented by **n** causes the **v** to be pronounced [b].

In both standards, vowels are relatively short, though in stressed syllables and when a vowel results from a reduction of two identical vowels, they are slightly longer than usual (thus, sentences **vi a ambos** and **vi ambos**, for instance, differ slightly in the length of /a/). You need not make an effort to lengthen a vowel in a stressed syllable because that will in most cases come naturally as a result of the stress on the vowel in that syllable. In Buenos Aires Spanish, as a consequence of Italian influence, stressed syllables are noticeably longer than unstressed ones. That feature is not recommended.

English, especially British English, is a stress-timed language (it has rhythm in which stressed syllables tend to occur at regular intervals of time, regardless of the number of intervening unstressed syllables) whereas Spanish is a syllable-timed language (with rhythm in which syllables are approximately equal in duration and thus tend to follow one another at regular intervals). Consequently, speakers of English, especially British English, tend to reduce unstressed syllables (as in the British pronunciation of **momentary, pattern**, and **secretary**), whereas Spanish-speakers tend to pronounce each syllable distinctly and do not often slur over any of them. Spanish-speakers thus often react to English-accented Spanish as one in which *se comen las vocales* 'the vowels are swallowed up' and speakers of English (especially of British English) tend to react to Spanish-accented English as "overly precise" (to get an idea of the difference between stress- and syllable-timed languages, contrast American and British pronunciations of **momentary** and **secretary:** Americans pronounce each syllable of those words with more or less the same degree of distinctiveness, whereas Britishers pronounce only the first syllable distinctly and slur over the others; thus, American English is more syllable-timed and British English more stress-timed). To pronounce Spanish correctly, English-speakers should therefore give each vowel its full value.

Formerly, in the Spanish-speaking world, the pronunciation and spelling of words borrowed from other languages were routinely changed so that they conformed to Spanish norms. Thus for example, **bowline > bolina, coolie > culí, goal > gol, kerosene > kerosén, ketch > queche, Quaker > cuáquero, shilling > chelín, sweater > suéter, trolley bus > trolebús, volt > voltio, yacht > yate**; English and/or French **bureau > buró**, English **jacket** and/or French **jaquette > chaqué** and **chaqueta**; English **packet boat** and/or French **paquebot > paquebote**; English **pudding** and/or French **pudding > pudín**; English and/or French **restaurant > restaurante ~ restorán**; English **role** and/or French **rôle > rol**; English **toupée** and/or French **toupet > tupé**; French **bivouac > vivac** (which was later completely hispanized to **vivaque**), **boudin > budín, boulevard > bulevar, bourgeois > burgués, corset > corsé, meeting > mitin, nécessaire > neceser, purée > puré, terreplain > terraplén, vaudou > vodú**; German **Schomberg > chambergo**; and, from various languages, **zar** 'tsar'. Or, non-Spanish /š/ usually became /č/ (not only in **chambergo** but also in **bolchevique, chal, champán ~ champaña, champú, coqueluche, derviche**, and **fetiche**) or /s/ (as in **Visnú**).

Now, however, the trend is to retain non-

Spanish spellings, though not necessarily non-Spanish pronunciations, with the result that the good fit between Spanish spelling and pronunciation is in certain words absent.

After the death of Francisco Franco (1975), the non-Spanish languages of Spain, long discouraged or suppressed in various ways up to that time, gained or regained their legitimate rights, although an unfortunate consequence thereof has been the use of non-Spanish spellings in certain Spanish words referring to elements of the cultures of which those languages are the vehicle. Thus, not uncommon in today's Spanish are Catalan spellings like "Catalunya" and "Convergencia i Unió" and Basque spellings like "batzoki," "txistu," and "txistulari." The Spanish language academies recognize only **Cataluña, Convergencia y Unión, bachoqui, chistu,** and **chistulari.**

All of which is to say that from the spelling of a recent Spanish borrowing from another language you may not be able to infer its pronunciation fully. But, on the whole, the number of Spanish words in which the fit between spelling and pronunciation is less than optimal or whose pronunciation is in some way unusual is still small.

D.L.G.

Los sonidos del inglés americano

Vocales y diptongos

a se pronuncia más cerrado que la *a* de *paro* (por ejemplo: **act, at, bat, hat, marry**); también se encuentra este sonido en palabras deletreadas con: -ah- (da*h*lia), -ai- (pl*ai*d), -al- (ha*l*f), -au- (l*au*gh), -ua- (g*ua*rantee).

a se pronuncia más cerrado que la *e* de *hablé* y como si fuera seguido de *i* (por ejemplo: **age, gate, rate**); también se encuentra este sonido en palabras deletreadas con: -ai- (r*ai*n, *ai*r), -aigh- (str*aigh*t), -au- (g*au*ge), -ay- (s*ay*), -ea- (st*ea*k), -ei- (v*ei*l, w*ei*gh), -ey- (ob*ey*).

a equivale aproximadamente a la *a* de *sentado* y *bajo* (por ejemplo: **ah, father, part**); también se encuentra este sonido en palabras deletreadas con: -al- (c*a*lm), -e(r)- (sergeant), -ea(r)- (h*ea*rt), -ua- (g*ua*rd).

a equivale aproximadamente a la *e* de las palabras francesas *de* y *le* (por ejemplo: *a*lone, *a*bout); también se encuentra este sonido en palabras deletreadas con: -e- (syst*e*m), -i- (eas*i*ly), -o- (gall*o*p), -u- (circ*u*s), -y- (martyr).

e equivale aproximadamente a la *e* de *templo* y *perro* (por ejemplo: **edge, set, merry**); también se encuentra este sonido en palabras deletreadas con: a-, -a- (*a*ny, m*a*ny), -ai- (s*ai*d), -ay- (s*ay*s), -ea- (l*ea*ther), -ei- (h*ei*fer), -eo- (j*eo*pardy), -ie- (fr*ie*nd).

e equivale aproximadamente a la *i* de *Chile* (por ejemplo: **be, equal, secret**); también se encuentra este sonido en palabras deletreadas con: ea- (*ea*ch, t*ea*), -ee- (f*ee*, k*ee*p), -ei- (rec*ei*ve), -eo- (p*eo*ple), -ey- (k*ey*), -ie- (f*ie*ld), -y- (cit*y*).

i se pronuncia menos cerrado que la *i* de *Chile* (por ejemplo: **if, big, fit, mirror**); también se encuentra este sonido en palabras deletreadas con: e- (*E*ngland), -ee- (b*ee*n), -ei- (counterf*ei*t), -ia- (carr*ia*ge), -ie- (s*ie*ve), -o- (w*o*men), (b)u(s)- (b*u*siness), -y- (sympathetic).

i equivale aproximadamente a la *ai* de *aire*, *baile* (por ejemplo: **bite, ice, pirate**); también se encuentra este sonido en palabras deletreadas con: ais- (*ai*sle), -ei- (h*ei*ght, st*ei*n), eye (*eye*), -ie- (p*ie*), -igh- (h*igh*), is- (*i*sland), -uy- (b*uy*), -y- (cycle, sky), -ye- (l*ye*).

o se pronuncia más cerrado que la *o* de *supo* (por ejemplo: **hope, go, oh, over**); también se encuentra este sonido en palabras deletreadas con: -au- (m*au*ve), -aux (f*au*x pas), -eau (b*eau*), -ew (s*ew*), -oa- (r*oa*d), -oe (t*oe*), -oo- (br*oo*ch), -ot (dep*ot*), -ou- (s*ou*l), -ow (fl*ow*), -owe- (*owe*).

o se pronuncia más cerrado que la *o* de *corre* (por ejemplo: **alcohol, order, raw**); también se encuentra este sonido en palabras deletreadas con: -a- (t*a*ll), -al- (w*a*lk),-au- (*au*thor, v*au*lt), -augh- (c*augh*t), -oa- (br*oa*d), -oo- (fl*oo*r), -ough- (s*ough*t).

oi equivale aproximadamente a la *oy* de *doy* (por ejemplo: **oil, joint, voice**); también se encuentra este sonido en palabras deletreadas con: -awy- (l*awy*er), -oy- (b*oy*).

oo se pronuncia menos cerrado que la *u* de *insulto* (por ejemplo: **book, foot**); también se encuentra el sonido en palabras deletreadas con: -o- (w*o*lf), -ou- (t*ou*r), -u- (p*u*ll).

oo se pronuncia más largo que la *u* de *susto* (por ejemplo: **too, ooze, fool**); también se encuentra este sonido en palabras deletreadas con: -eu- (man*eu*ver), -ew (gr*ew*), -o (wh*o*), -o . . . e (m*o*ve), -oe (can*oe*), -ou- (tr*ou*pe), -u . . . e (r*u*le), -ue (fl*ue*), -ui- (s*ui*t).

ou equivale aproximadamente a la *au* de *aurora* (por ejemplo: **loud, out**); también se encuentra este sonido en palabras deletreadas con -ow (br*ow*, c*ow*, pl*ow*).

u equivale aproximadamente a la *iu* de *ciudad* (por ejemplo: **cue, use, utility**); también se encuentra este sonido en palabras deletreadas con: -eau- (b*eau*ty), -eu- (f*eu*d), -ew (f*ew*), hu- (*hu*man), hu . . . e (*hu*ge), -iew (v*iew*), you (*you*), yu . . e (*yu*le).

u es sonido intermedio entre la *o* de *borro* y la *a* de *barro*, algo parecido a la proununciación de la *eu* francesa de *peur*; (por ejemplo: **up, sun, mud**); también se encuentra este sonido en palabras deletreadas con: o- (*o*ther), -o- (s*o*n), -oe- (d*oe*s), o . . . e (l*o*ve), -oo- (bl*oo*d), -ou (tr*ou*ble).

Consonantes

b equivale aproximadamente a la *b* de *burro* y *hombre* (por ejemplo: **bed, amber,**

rub); también se encuentra en palabras dele-treadas con -bb- (ho*bb*y) y -be (lo*be*).

ch equivale aproximadamente a la *ch* es-pañola (por ejemplo: **chief, beach**); también se encuentra en palabras deletreadas con: -tch- (ca*tch*, bu*tch*er), -te- (righ*te*ous), -ti-(ques*ti*on), -tu- (na*tu*ral).

d equivale aproximadamente a la *d* de *onda* (por ejemplo: **do, odor, red**); también se encuentra en palabras deletreadas con -dd- (la*dd*er) y -de (fa*de*).

f equivale aproximadamente a la *f* es-pañola (por ejemplo: **feed, safe**); también se encuentra en palabras deletreadas con -ff- (mu*ff*in) y -fe (li*fe*).

g equivale aproximadamente a la *g* de *globo* (por ejemplo: **give, fog**); también se encuen-tra en palabras deletreadas con -gg (e*gg*), gh- (*gh*ost), y -gue (pla*gue*).

h se pronuncia más aspirado pero menos áspero que la *j* española en *jabón* (por ejem-plo: **hit, hope**); también se encuentra en palabras deletreadas con wh- (*wh*ere, *wh*ich, *wh*o).

j equivale aproximadamente a la *y* de *yo* en su pronunciación enfática (p.ej. . . . *yo, y yo sólo soy el dueño aquí!*) o como la *y* de *cónyuge* en ciertas modalidades del español (por ejemplo: **just, joke**); también se encuentra en palabras deletreadas con: -dg- (ju*dg*e), -di-(sol*di*er), -ge (sa*ge*), -gg- (exa*gg*erate), gi-(*gi*n).

k (por ejemplo: **keep, make, token**); tras consonante equivale aproximadamente a la *k* española; en otras posiciones se pronuncia como los anglohablantes con fuerte acento inglés pronuncian la *k* española, o sea con as-piración; también se encuentra en palabras deletreadas con: -c- (*c*ar), -cc- (a*cc*ount), ch- (*ch*aracter), -ck (ba*ck*).

l se pronuncia aproximadamente como la *l* de *lago* (por ejemplo: **leap, sail**); también se encuentra en palabras deletreadas con -le (mi*le*) y -ll (ca*ll*), y puede formar sílaba (p.ej. **bottle** y **middle**).

m equivale aproximadamente a la *m* es-pañola (por ejemplo: **more, drum, him, summer**).

n equivale aproximadamente a la *n* de *bueno* (por ejemplo: **now, sunny**); también se encuentra en palabras deletreadas con gn- (*gn*at) y kn- (*kn*ife), y puede formar sílaba (p.ej. **button** y **mitten**).

ng (por ejemplo: **sing, Washington**) equi-vale aproximadamente a la *n* de *blanco*.

p (por ejemplo: **pool, spool, supper, stop**) tras consonante equivale aproximadamente a la *p* española; en otras posiciones se pro-nuncia como los anglohablantes con fuerte acento inglés pronuncian la *p* española, o sea con aspiración.

r se pronuncia como los anglohablantes con fuerte acento inglés pronuncian la *r* de *pero*, o sea que se eleva la punta de la len-gua hacia el paladar (sin tocarlo) y doblada para atrás (por ejemplo: **red, hurry, near**); también se encuentra en palabras dele-treadas con -re (pu*re*), rh- (*rh*ythm), y wr- (*wr*ong).

s equivale aproximadamente a la *s* de *salir*, pero algo más tensa y larga (por ejemplo: **see, kiss**); también se encuentra en palabras dele-treadas con: ce- (*ce*nter, ra*ce*r), ci- (*ci*ty, a*ci*d), -ce (mi*ce*), ps- (*ps*yche), sc- (*sc*ene).

sh equivale aproximadamente a la *ch* de las palabras francesas *changer* and *chapeau* (por ejemplo: **ship, wash**); también se en-cuentra en palabras deletreadas con: -ce- (o*ce*an), -ch- (ma*ch*ine), -ci- (spe*ci*al), s(u)- (*s*ugar), -sci- (con*sci*ence), -si- (man*si*on), -ss- (ti*ss*ue, mi*ss*ion), -ti- (cap*ti*on).

t (por ejemplo: **team, ten, steam, bit**); tras consonante equivale aproximadamente a la *t* española; en otras posiciones se pronuncia como los anglohablantes con fuerte acento inglés pronuncian la *t* de *también* o de *tomar*, o sea con aspiración; también se encuentra en palabras deletreadas con: -bt (dou*bt*), -cht (ya*cht*), -ed (talk*ed*), -ght (bou*ght*), -te (bi*te*), th- (*th*yme), -tt- (bo*tt*om), tw- (*tw*o).

th (por ejemplo: **thin, ether, path**) equi-vale aproximadamente a la *z* española en el norte de España.

th (por ejemplo: **that, the, either, smooth**) equivale aproximadamente a la *d* de *adoptar*.

v (por ejemplo: **voice, river, live**) equivale aproximadamente a la *b* de *haba* pero labio-dental en vez de bilabial.

w (por ejemplo: **west, witch, away**) equi-vale aproximadamente a la *u* de *puesto*.

y (por ejemplo: **yes, beyond**) equivale aproximadamente a la *i* de *bien*; también se encuentra en palabras deletreadas con -i- (on*i*on, un*i*on), -j- (halle*l*ujah), and -ll- (torti-*ll*a).

z (por ejemplo: **zoo, lazy, zone**) equivale aproximadamente a la *s* de *isla* y *mismo* en ciertas modalidades del español, pero con más sonoridad; también se encuentra en algunas palabras deletreadas con: -s (ha*s*), -se (ri*se*), x- (*x*ylophone), y -zz- (buzzard, fu*zz*); o con el sonido /zh/ en **azure, brazier,** que equivale aproximadamente a la *ll* del español de la gente mayor de la ciudad de Buenos Aires (o sea, como la *j* de la palabra francesa *bonjour*). El sonido /sh/ también se encuentra en ciertas palabras deletreadas con -ge (gara*ge,* mira*ge*), -si- (vi*si*on), y su- (plea*su*re).

Spanish Irregular Verbs

Infinitive	Present	Future	Preterit	Past Part.
andar	ando	andaré	anduve	andado
caber	quepo	cabré	cupe	cabido
caer	caigo	caeré	caí	caído
conducir	conduzco	conduciré	conduje	conducido
dar	doy	daré	di	dado
decir	digo	diré	dije	dicho
estar	estoy	estaré	estuve	estado
haber	he	habré	hube	habido
hacer	hago	haré	hice	hecho
ir	voy	iré	fui	ido
jugar	juego	jugaré	jugué	jugado
morir	muero	moriré	morí	muerto
oir	oigo	oiré	oí	oído
poder	puedo	podré	pude	podido
poner	pongo	pondré	puse	puesto
querer	quiero	querré	quise	querido
saber	sé	sabré	supe	sabido
salir	salgo	saldré	salí	salido
ser	soy	seré	fui	sido
tener	tengo	tendré	tuve	tenido
traer	traigo	traeré	traje	traído
valer	valgo	valdré	valí	valido
venir	vengo	vendré	vine	venido
ver	veo	veré	vi	visto

Las Formas del Verbo Inglés

1. Se forma la 3ª persona singular del tiempo presente exactamente al igual que el plural de los sustantivos, añadiendo **-es** o **-s** a la forma sencilla según las mismas reglas, así:

(1)	teach	pass	wish	fix	buzz		
	teaches	passes	wishes	fixes	buzzes		
(2)	place	change	judge	please	freeze		
	places	changes	judges	pleases	freezes		
(3a)	find	sell	clean	hear	love	buy	know
	finds	sells	cleans	hears	loves	buys	knows
(3b)	think	like	laugh	stop	hope	meet	want
	thinks	likes	laughs	stops	hopes	meets	wants
(4)	cry	try	dry	carry	deny		
	cries	tries	dries	carries	denies		

Cinco verbos muy comunes tienen 3ª persona singular irregular:

(5)
go	do	say	have	be
goes	does	says	has	is

2. Se forman el tiempo pasado y el participio de modo igual, añadiendo a la forma sencilla la terminación **-ed** o **-d** según las reglas que siguen:

(1) Si la forma sencilla termina en **-d** o **-t,** se le pone **-ed** como sílaba aparte:

end	fold	need	load	want	feast	wait	light
ended	folded	needed	loaded	wanted	feasted	waited	lighted

(2) Si la forma sencilla termina en cualquier otra consonante, se añade también **-ed** pero sin hacer sílaba aparte:

(2a)
bang	sail	seem	harm	earn	weigh
banged	sailed	seemed	harmed	earned	weighed

(2b)
lunch	work	look	laugh	help	pass
lunched	worked	looked	laughed	helped	passed

(3) Si la forma sencilla termina en **-e,** se le pone sólo **-d:**

(3a)
hate	taste	waste	guide	fade	trade
hated	tasted	wasted	guided	faded	traded

(3b)
free	judge	rule	name	dine	scare
freed	judged	ruled	named	dined	scared

(3c)
place	force	knife	like	hope	base
placed	forced	knifed	liked	hoped	based

(4) Una **-y** final que sigue a cualquier consonante se cambia en **-ie** al añadir la **-d** del pasado/participio:

cry	try	dry	carry	deny
cried	tried	dried	carried	denied

3. Varios verbos muy comunes forman el tiempo pasado y el participio de manera irregular. Pertenecen a tres grupos.

(1) Los que tienen una sola forma irregular para tiempo pasado y participio, como los siguientes:

bend	bleed	bring	build	buy	catch	creep	deal
bent	bled	brought	built	bought	caught	crept	dealt
dig	feed	feel	fight	find	flee	get	hang
dug	fed	felt	fought	found	fled	got	hung
have	hear	hold	keep	lead	leave	lend	lose
had	heard	held	kept	led	left	lent	lost
make	mean	meet	say	seek	sell	send	shine
made	meant	met	said	sought	sold	sent	shone
shoot	sit	sleep	spend	stand	strike	sweep	teach
shot	sat	slept	spent	stood	struck	swept	taught

(2) Los que tienen una forma irregular para el tiempo pasado y otra forma irregular para el participio, como los siguientes:

be	beat	become	begin	bite
was	beat	became	began	bit
been	beaten	become	begun	bitten
blow	break	choose	come	do
blew	broke	chose	came	did
blown	broken	chosen	come	done
draw	drink	drive	eat	fall
drew	drank	drove	ate	fell
drawn	drunk	driven	eaten	fallen
fly	forget	freeze	give	go
flew	forgot	froze	gave	went
flown	forgotten	frozen	given	gone
grow	hide	know	ride	ring
grew	hid	knew	rode	rang
grown	hidden	known	ridden	rung
rise	run	see	shake	shrink
rose	ran	saw	shook	shrank
risen	run	seen	shaken	shrunk
sing	sink	speak	steal	swear
sang	sank	spoke	stole	swore
sung	sunk	spoken	stolen	sworn
swim	tear	throw	wear	write
swam	tore	threw	wore	wrote
swum	torn	thrown	worn	written

(3) Los que no varían del todo, la forma sencilla funcionando también como pasado/participio; entre éstos son de mayor frecuencia:

bet	burst	cast	cost	cut
hit	hurt	let	put	quit
read	set	shed	shut	slit
spit	split	spread	thrust	wet

El Plural del Sustantivo Inglés

A la forma singular se añade la terminación **-es** o **-s** de acuerdo con las reglas siguientes.

(1) Si el singular termina en **-ch, -s, -sh, -x** o **-z**, se le pone **-es** como sílaba aparte:

match	glass	dish	box	buzz
matches	glasses	dishes	boxes	buzzes

(2) Si el singular termina en **-ce, -ge, -se** o **-ze,** se le pone una **-s** que con la vocal precedente forma sílaba aparte:

face	page	house	size
faces	pages	houses	sizes

(3) Una **-y** final que sigue a cualquier consonante se cambia en **-ie** a ponérsele la **-s** del plural:

sky	city	lady	ferry	penny
skies	cities	ladies	ferries	pennies

(4) Los siguientes sustantivos comunes tienen plural irregular:

Man	woman	child	foot	mouse	goose
men	women	children	feet	mice	geese

wife	knife	life	half	leaf	deer
wives	knives	lives	halves	leaves	deer

List of Abbreviations Used in This Dictionary

a adjective
abb abbreviation
acc accusative
adv adverb
aer aeronautics
agr agriculture
anat anatomy
ant antiquated
arch architecture
archeol archeology
art. article
art art
ast astronomy
astrol astrology
aut automobiles
aux auxiliary
biol biology
bot botany
cards card games
carp carpentry
chem chemistry
com commerce
comp comparative
condit conditional
conjunc conjunction
cul culinary
dance dancing
dat dative
dim diminutive
ecc ecclesiastical
elec electricity
eng engineering
ent entomology
euphem euphemism
f feminine
fig figurative
fig inf used figuratively in
   informal speech or writing
fut future
gen generally; genitive
geog geography

geol geology
geom geometry
gram grammar
gym gymnastics
her heraldry
hist history
icht ichthyology
imperf imperfect
impers impersonal
ind indicative
indef art. indefinite article
inf informal
infin infinitive
insep inseparable
interj interjection,
   exclamation
interr interrogative
iron ironical
irr irregular
Lat. Am. Latin America
law law
ling linguistics
lit literature
m masculine
mas masonry
math mathematics
mech mechanics
med medical
met metallurgy
mf masculine or feminine
mil military
min mineralogy
mus music
myth mythology
n noun
naut nautical
nav naval
neut neuter
opt optics
orn ornithology

part participle
pers personal; person
pharm pharmacy
phil philosophy
phon phonetics
phot photography
phys physics
physiol physiology
pl plural
poet poetic
pol political
pol econ political economy
poss possessive
prep preposition
pres present
print printing
pron pronoun
psy psychology
rad radio
rw railway
s substantive, noun
sew sewing
sing singular
spirit spiritualism
sport sports
subjunc subjunctive
sup superlative
surg surgery
surv surveying
tan tanning
theat theater
theol theology
univ university
v aux auxiliary verb
vi intransitive verb
vr reflexive verb
vt transitive verb
WH Western Hemispheric
   Spanish
zool zoology

SPANISH-ENGLISH
Dictionary

A

a *f*, name of the letter A

a *prep* to; at; on; by; in, into; up to; according to; if, etc. 1. Denotes the direct complement of verb before objects representing specified persons or animals, personified nouns, pronouns referring to specific persons (**alguien, entrambos, cualquiera,** etc.), demonstrative or relative pronouns, collective nouns representing persons (**el público, la muchedumbre,** etc.), names of countries, cities, rivers, etc., except where these invariably take the def. art., e.g. **Dejé a Varsovia,** I left Warsaw, *but* **Dejé el Perú,** I left Peru. 2. Introduces indirect obj. when this is a noun governed by a verb implying motion, or an emphatic pers. pron., e.g. **Nos conviene a ti y a mí,** It suits both you and me. It is also used before indirect obj. to avoid ambiguity when there is both an indirect and direct obj. 3. Denotes the complement of verb when this is an infin., e.g. **Enseñó a pintar a María,** He taught Mary to paint. 4. Indicates direction or destination, e.g. **Vamos a Edimburgo,** We are going to Edinburgh. 5. Signifies location, or point of time when action takes place, e.g. **Vinieron a las doce.** They came at twelve o'clock. 6. Describes position of persons or things, e.g. **Se sentaron a la puerta,** They sat down at the door. **La casa queda a la derecha,** The house is on the right. 7. Denotes interval of time or place between one thing and another, e.g. **de tres a cinco de la tarde,** from three to five in the afternoon, **de calle a calle,** from street to street. 8. Expresses manner of action, e.g. **a la francesa,** in the French way, **bordado a mano,** embroidered by hand. 9. Indicates rate or price, e.g. **a cuatro pesetas la libra,** at four pesetas the lb. 10. Indicates difference or comparison, e.g. **Va mucho de querer a hacer,** There's a difference between wishing and doing. 11. Sometimes is synonymous with **hasta, según, hacia** and governs almost all parts of speech. Has many idiomatic uses. 12. Before infin. sometimes has conditional sense, e.g. **A haber sabido las noticias no lo hubiéramos hecho,** If we had heard the news we would not have done it. 13. With certain nouns, adjectives, and infinitives forms adverbial phrases, e.g. **poco a poco,** little by little, **a veces,** sometimes, **a ciegas,** blindly, etc. **¡a ver!** let's see! *Colombia* hello! (on telephone). **A + el** becomes **al,** e.g. **al rey,** to the king. **Al +** infin. means when or on, e.g. **al marcharme yo,** when I left (on my leaving); *Lat. Am.* **al año** a year later; *Lat. Am.* **a la semana** a week later; *Lat. Am.* **al mes** a month later

abacería *f*, grocery shop

abacero (-ra) *n* grocer

ábaco *m, arch* abacus; counting frame

abad *m*, abbot

abajo *adv* under; underneath; below; down. Used immediately after noun in adverbial phrases, e.g. **cuesta a., escalera a.,** downhill, downstairs. *interj* Down with! e.g., **¡A. el rey!** Down with the king! **venirse a.,** to fall down; *fig* collapse

abalanzamiento *m*, balancing; rushing upon; dashing

abalanzar *vt* to balance; impel violently; *vr* throw oneself upon; attack, rush upon; (*with prep a*) rush into, risk. **Se abalanzó hacia ellos,** He rushed toward them

abalear *vt, Lat. Am.* to shoot at

abalorio *m*, glass bead; bead work

abanderado *m*, standardbearer; *Argentina* valedictorian

abanderizar *vt* to organize in groups; *vr* band together

abandonado *a* deserted; forlorn; helpless; indolent, careless; slovenly

abandonamiento *m*, desertion; forlornness; helplessness; carelessness; slovenliness

abandonar *vt* to forsake, desert; neglect; leave; give up; renounce; *vr* neglect oneself; grow discouraged; (*with prep a*) give oneself over to

abandono *m*, abandonment; defencelessness; forlornness; dilapidation; renunciation; neglect; slovenliness; debauchery

abanicar *vt* to fan

abanico *m*, fan; anything fan-shaped; *inf* sword; railway signal; *naut* derrick. **en a.,** fan-shaped

abaniqueo *m*, fanning; swinging; oscillation; gesticulation

abaratar *vt* to cheapen, make less expensive; *vr* fall in price

abarca *f*, leather sandal, worn chiefly in the Basque provinces

abarcador(-ra) *n* one who clasps or embraces; monopolist

abarcadura *f*, **abarcamiento** *m*, inclusion; scope

abarcar *vt* to clasp, encircle; include, comprise; undertake, attempt; monopolize

abarquillar *vt* to shape into a roll; roll; curl

abarracar(se) *vi* and *vr mil* to go into barracks

abarrancadero *m*, rough road; ravine, precipice; *fig* difficult situation

abarrancar *vt* to ditch; make a ravine; *vr* fall into a pit; stick (in the mud, etc.); get into difficulties; *naut* run aground

abarrotería *f, Mexico* grocery store, grocery, grocer's

abarrotero, -a *mf Lat. Am.* grocer

abarrotes *m pl, Lat. Am.* groceries

abastar *vt* see **abastecer**

abastecedor (-ra) *a* provisioning, supplying. *n* provider; purveyor, supplier; caterer

abastecer *vt irr* to supply, provide; purvey. See **conocer**

abastecimiento *m*, providing; supply, provision; catering; supplies

abasto *m*, provisions, food; *com* supply. *adv* plentifully, abundantly

abate *m*, abbé

abatido *a* dejected, depressed; spiritless; discouraged; crushed, humbled; *com* depreciated

abatimiento *m*, dejection, depression; humiliation; discouragement; falling; lowering; (*aer naut*) drift

abatir *vt* to knock down; overthrow; demolish; lower, take down; droop; humiliate; discourage; *naut* dismantle; *vi* (*aer naut*) drift; *vr* be despondent, despair; humble oneself; swoop down (of birds). **a. el vuelo,** to fly down

ABC *m*, ABCs (e.g. **el ABC de la física,** the ABCs of physics)

abdicación *f*, abdication

abdicar *vt* to abdicate; revoke, cancel; give up (rights, opinions)

abdomen *m*, abdomen

abdominal *a* abdominal

abecé *m*, ABCs

abecedario *m*, ABCs, alphabet; reading book, primer

abedul *m*, birch tree; birch wood

abeja *f*, bee. **a. maestra,** queen bee. **a. obrera,** worker

abejar *m*, beehive

abejero (-ra) *n* beekeeper

abejón *m*, drone; hornet

abejorro *m*, bumblebee

aberración *f*, deviation; error, lapse; (*ast phys biol*) aberration

abertura *f*, opening; aperture, gap, hole; fissure, cleft; mountain pass; naturalness, frankness

abeto *m*, yew-leaved fir

abierto *a* free, unobstructed; open, not enclosed; open, full-blown (flowers); frank, sincere. *adv* openly

abigarrado *a* variegated; varied; speckled

abigarrar *vt* to variegate; vary; speckle; fleck; spot; dapple

abigotado *a* having a thick moustache

abintestato *a law* intestate

abismal *a* abysmal

abismar *vt* to plunge into an abyss; depress, sadden; *vr* despair; be plunged in thought, be abstracted; be amazed

abismo *m*, chasm, abyss, gulf; hell

abjuración *f*, abjuration

abjurar *vt* to forswear, retract

ablactar *vt* to wean

ablandamiento *m*, softening; placating

ablandante *a* softening; placatory

ablandar *vt* to soften; appease, placate; loosen; relax; *vi* and *vr* be softened; be appeased; grow less stormy; (elements) decrease in force

ablandecer *vt irr* to soften. See **conocer**

ablución *f*, ablution

abnegación *f*, abnegation, self-sacrifice

abnegado *a* self-sacrificing

abnegarse *vr irr* to deprive oneself, sacrifice oneself. See **cegar**

abobado *a* bewildered; foolish-looking, silly

abobar *vt* to daze, bewilder; make stupid

abocado *a* full-flavoured, pleasant (of wine)

abocar *vt* to seize with the mouth; bring nearer; transfer (contents of one jug to another); *vr* meet, assemble; *vi naut* enter (a channel, port, etc.). **abocarse (con . . .),** to contact (. . .), get in touch (with . . .)

abocetado *a art* unfinished; sketchy

abochornado *a* flushed (of the face); ashamed; embarrassed

abochornar *vt* to overheat, make flushed; shame; embarrass; *vr* (plants) dry up

abofetear *vt* to slap, hit; buffet

abogacía *f*, legal profession; practice of law; advocacy

abogaderas, abogaderías *f pl Lat. Am.* hair-splitting, specious arguments, legalistics

abogado (-da) *n* lawyer

abogar *vi* to defend at law; intercede for; advocate, champion

abolengo *m*, lineage, descent, family; inheritance

abolición *f*, abolition

abolir *vt* to abolish; cancel; annul

abolladura *f*, bruise; dent; embossment

abollar *vt* to bruise; dent

abombado *a* convex; domed; *Mexico* tight (tipsy)

abombar *vt* to make convex; *inf* deafen, bewilder; *vr* begin to putrefy; get intoxicated; *Mexico* become tight, get tight (tipsy)

abominable *a* abominable

abominación *f*, abomination; loathing, detestation

abominar *vt* to abominate, loathe, detest

abonable *a* subscribable; payable

abonado (-da) *a* trustworthy, reliable; ready, prepared, inclined. *n* subscriber; season ticket holder (for concerts, etc.)

abonanzar *vi impers* to clear up, be fine (weather)

abonar *vt* to guarantee; go surety for; improve, better; manure; ratify, confirm; pay; *com* place to the credit of; *vr* subscribe, become a subscriber; take out (season tickets, etc.)

abonaré *m*, *com* due bill; promissory note, I.O.U.

abono *m*, subscription; voucher; guarantee; manure. **a. verde,** leaf mold. **en a. de,** in payment of; in support of

aboquillado *a* tipped (of cigarettes)

abordar *vt naut* to board a ship; *naut* collide, run into; accost, tackle; undertake; *vi naut* put into port

aborigen *a* aboriginal

aborígenes *m pl*, aborigines

aborrachado *a* bright red; highly colored; flushed

aborrascarse *vr* to grow stormy

aborrecedor (-ra) *a* hateful. *n* hater, loather

aborrecer *vt irr* to hate, loathe; desert offspring (animals, birds). See **conocer**

aborrecible *a* hateful, detestable

aborrecimiento *m*, hate, detestation; dislike

abortar *vt* to abort; foil (a plot); *vi med* miscarry; fail, go awry

abortivo *a* abortive

aborto *m*, abortion; miscarriage; monster; failure

abotagarse *vr* to swell up, become bloated

abotonador *m*, button-hook

abotonar *vt* to button; *vi* bud, sprout

abra *f*, cove, small bay; narrow gorge; fissure, cleft; *Argentina* clearing (in a forest)

abrasador *a* burning, flaming

abrasamiento *m*, burning; ardour, heat

abrasar *vt* to burn; dry up, parch (plants); squander, waste; shame; *vi* burn; *vr* be very hot, glow; burn with passion

abrasión *f*, abrasion

abrasivo *a* and *m*, abrasive

abrazadera *f*, clasp; clamp

abrazamiento *m*, embracing

abrazar *vt* to embrace, clasp in one's arms; follow, adopt; engage in; seize, take advantage of; comprise, include; surround; take in hand; clamp; clasp. **abrazarse a,** to clutch, hang on to

abrazo *m*, embrace

abrelatas *m*, can opener

abrevar *vt* to water cattle; irrigate, water

abreviación *f*, abbreviation, shortening; summary; hastening

abreviador *m*, abridger, condenser

abreviar *vt* to abbreviate, shorten; hasten, accelerate; condense, abridge. **a. tiempo,** to save time. **Y para a. . . . ,** And, to cut a long story short . . .

abreviatura *f*, abbreviation, contraction; shorthand

abridor *m*, opener; ear-ring (for keeping holes in ears open). **a. de guantes,** glove-stretcher. **a. de láminas,** engraving needle. **a. de latas,** can opener

abridura *f*, (act of) opening (e.g. of a trunk)

abrigada *f*, **abrigadero** *m*, sheltered place

abrigar *vt* to shelter, protect (against the cold, etc.); defend, help; hold (opinions); nurse (a hope, etc.); cover; *vr* take shelter; wrap oneself up

abrigo *m*, shelter; defence; protection; help; sheltered place; wrap, coat; *naut* haven

abril *m*, April; youth; *pl poet* years

abrillantar *vt* to cut in facets like a diamond; polish, burnish; cause to shine; *fig* improve, add lustre to

abrir *vt* to open; reveal; unlock; slide the bolt of; extend, spread out; cleave; engrave; clear (the way, etc.); begin; head; lead; separate; dig; inaugurate. *vi* unfold (flowers); expand; **en un abrir y cerrar de ojos,** in the twinkling of an eye, in the wink of an eye; *vr* open; expand; (*with con*) confide in. **a. el camino (a . . .),** to pave the way (for . . .). **abrirse camino,** to make one's way; **abrirse paso a codazos,** to elbow one's way out, (or through)

abrochador *m*, button-hook

abrochar *vt* to button; fasten, clasp; hook up (a dress, etc.); buckle; *Lat. Am.* **abrocharse (con . . .)** struggle (with . . .), wrestle (with . . .)

abrogación *f*, repeal, annulment

abrogar *vt* to repeal, annul

abrojo *m*, thistle; *bot* caltrops; thorn, prickle; *pl* submerged rocks in sea

abroncar *vt inf* to bore, annoy

abrumador *a* burdensome, crushing, oppressive; troublesome, tiresome; exhausting

abrumar *vt* to weigh down; overwhelm, oppress; weary, exhaust; *vr* grow misty

abrupto *a* steep; rough, broken (ground); rugged

absceso *m*, abscess

absentismo *m*, absenteeism

ábside *mf, arch* apse. *m, ast* apsis

absolución f, (ecc and law) absolution; remission, pardon

absoluta f, mil discharge

absolutista mf absolutist

absoluto a absolute; categorical; inf despotic. **en a.,** absolutely

absolver vt irr to absolve; acquit (of a charge). law **a. de la instancia,** to dismiss the case. See **mover**

absorbente a and m, absorbent

absorber vt to absorb; consume, use up; attract, hold (the attention, etc.); imbibe

absorción f, absorption

absortar vt to amaze, dumbfound

absorto a amazed, astounded; abstracted, lost in thought

abstemio a abstemious

abstención f, abstention

abstenerse vr irr to refrain; abstain. See **tener**

abstinencia f, abstinence; fasting

abstinente a abstemious; temperate

abstracción f, abstraction; preoccupation; absent-mindedness

abstracto a abstract. **en a.,** in the abstract

abstraer vt irr to abstract; consider separately; vi (with de) do without, exclude; vr be preoccupied; let one's thoughts wander. See **traer**

abstraído a retired, recluse; preoccupied; absent-minded

abstruso a abstruse

absurdidad f, absurdity; folly, nonsense

absurdo a ridiculous, absurd. m, piece of folly, nonsense

abuchear vt vi to boo, hoot, jeer

abuela f, grandmother; old woman, dame

abuelo m, grandfather; gen pl ancestor; old man; pl grandparents

abulia f, lack of will-power, abulia

abúlico a abulic, lacking will-power

abultado a bulky, large; voluminous; exaggerated

abultamiento m, bulkiness; enlargement, increase; mound; exaggeration

abultar vt to enlarge, increase; exaggerate; model in rough (sculpture); vi be bulky; be large

abundancia f, abundance, plenty

abundante a abundant, plentiful; abounding (in)

abundar vi to be plentiful, abound

aburrido a boring, tedious, dull; tired, weary

aburrimiento m, boredom, dullness; wearisomeness, tediousness

aburrir vt to bore; inf spend (time, money); (birds) desert the nest; vr grow bored; be weary

¡abusado! Mexico careful!, look out!, watch out!

abusar vi to abuse; exceed one's rights, go too far; (with de) take advantage of

abusivo a abusive

abuso m, abuse. **a. de confianza,** abuse of trust

abyección f, degradation, misery; abjectness, servility

abyecto a abject, wretched; servile

acá adv hither, here; at this time, now. **a. y acullá,** hither and thither. **desde ayer a.,** from yesterday until now

acabable a terminable, finishable; achievable

acabado a complete; perfect; expert, consummate; old, worn out; ill, infirm. m, finish

acabamiento m, finishing, completion; end; death, decease

acabar vt to end, terminate; finish; complete, perfect; kill; (with con) destroy, finish off; suppress; squander; vi end; die; be destroyed; (with de + infin) to have just (e.g. **Acaba de salir,** He has just gone out); vr end, be exhausted, run out of (e.g. **Se le acabó el dinero,** His money ran out); fade, grow weak; be destroyed. **Se les acabaron las dudas,** Their doubts were cleared up. **a. de desconcertar,** to nonplus completely; **a. de decidirse,** to come to a decision; **a. de saber,** to finally learn

acacia f, bot acacia

academia f, academy

académico (-ca) a academic. n academician. **a. de la lengua,** member of the Royal Spanish Academy

acaecer vi irr to happen, occur. See **conocer**

acaecimiento m, happening, occurrence, event

acalambrarse (muscle) to contract with cramps. **Estar acalambrado,** to have cramps

acalenturarse vr to grow feverish

acallar vt to quieten, hush; soothe, appease

acalorado a hot; fervent; fig heated

acaloramiento m, excitement, agitation, vehemence; ardour

acalorar vt to warm; aid, encourage; excite, stimulate; stir, move (to enthusiasm); inflame, rouse; tire (by exercise); vr grow hot; become agitated or excited; become heated (arguments)

acamar vt to lay flat (plants by the wind); vr be flattened (plants); lie down (animals); go rotten (fruit)

acampar vi and vt to encamp

acanalar vt to groove; striate, flute; corrugate; furrow, channel

acantilado a steep, precipitous; shelving (ocean-bed). m, cliff

acanto m, (arch bot) acanthus

acantonamiento m, billeting; cantonment

acantonar vt to billet or quarter troops

acaparador (-ra) n monopolist

acaparar vt com to monopolize, corner; seize, take possession of

acápite m, WH new paragraph

acaracolado a spiral, winding, twisting

acardenalar vt to bruise; vr be bruised; be covered with livid marks

acarear vt to face; face up to, meet with courage

acariciador (-ra) a caressing, loving. n fondler

acariciar vt to caress; brush, touch lightly; cherish, treat affectionately; toy with (a suggestion)

acarraladura f, Lat. Am. run (in a stocking)

acarreador (-ra) n carrier, carter

acarreamiento, acarreo m, cartage, carting; transport, carriage; occasioning

acarrear vt to cart, transport; occasion, bring (gen. evil). **La guerra acarreó la carestía,** The war brought scarcity

acartonado a shriveled; shrunken; of cardboard; fig forced (dialogue)

acaso m, chance. adv by chance; perhaps, perchance. **por si a.,** in case (e.g. **Por si a. venga,** In case he comes)

acatable a venerable, worthy

acatamiento m, respect; reverence; observance

acatar vt to treat with respect, honor, revere; observe

acatarrar vt, Lat. Am. to annoy, bother, pester

acatarrarse vr to catch a cold; Argentina booze up, tank up

acaudalado a wealthy, well-to-do

acaudalar vt to make money; hoard up wealth; acquire (learning, etc.)

acaudillar vt mil to command, lead; head (a party, etc.)

acceder vi (with prep a) to concede, grant; accede to, agree to

accesibilidad f, accessibility; approachableness

accesible a accessible; approachable

accesión f, agreement, acquiescence; accession; accessory; feverish attack

acceso m, access; paroxysm, outburst; med attack

accesorio a accessory

accesorios m pl, accessories; theat properties

accidentado a rough, uneven; stormy, troubled (life, etc.)

accidentar vt to cause (someone) an accident; vr be the victim of an accident; be seized by a fit

accidente m, chance; accident, mishap; illness, indisposition; med fit; gram accidence; mus accidental. **a. del**

trabajo, accident at work. **por a.,** by chance, accidentally

acción *f,* action; battle; skirmish; *mech* drive; *com* share; gesture; lawsuit; *lit* action (of play, etc.); *art* posture, pose. **a. de gracias,** thanksgiving; *com* **a. liberada,** paid-up share. **a. privilegiada,** preference share

accionar *vi* to gesture, gesticulate; *Lat. Am.* act, be active

accionista *mf com* shareholder

acechar *vt* to spy upon, watch; lie in ambush for

acecho *m,* spying upon, watch; waylaying, ambush. **al a.,** in ambush; on the watch

acechona *f,* waylaying; ambush

acecinar *vt* to salt and dry (meat); *vr* (persons) wither, dry up

acedar *vt* to make bitter, sour; embitter, displease; *vr* turn sour; wither (plants)

acefalía *f,* acephalia, headlessness

acéfalo *a* acephalous

aceitar *vt* to oil, lubricate; rub with oil

aceite *m,* olive oil; oil. **a. de hígado de bacalao,** cod-liver oil. **a. de linaza,** linseed oil. **a. de ricino,** castor-oil. **a. de trementina,** oil of turpentine

aceitera *f,* woman who sells oil; oil can; oil bottle; *pl* cruet

aceitero *m,* oil seller. *a* oil

aceitoso *a* oily

aceituna *f, bot* olive

aceitunado *a* olive-colored

aceitunero (-ra) *n* olive picker; olive seller. *m,* warehouse for storing olives

aceituno, olive tree; *a, Lat. Am.* olive-colored

aceleración *f,* speed, haste; acceleration

aceleradamente *adv* hastily, swiftly

acelerador *a* accelerating. *m,* hastener; *aut* accelerator

acelerar *vt* to hasten, speed up; accelerate

acémila *f,* beast of burden, mule

acendrado *a* pure, unblemished, spotless

acendrar *vt* to refine (metals); purify, make spotless

acento *m,* accent; tone, inflection; *poet* voice, words. **a. agudo,** acute accent. **a. circunflejo,** circumflex accent. **a. grave,** grave accent. **a. ortográfico,** graphic accent, written accent. **a. tónico,** tonic accent

acentuación *f,* accentuation, stress; emphasis

acentuar *vt* to accent; stress, emphasize; *vr* become evident, become marked, be noticeable

aceña *f,* water-mill; irrigation water-wheel; chain-well

acepción *f,* meaning, significance, acceptation. **a. de personas,** partiality, preference

acepilladura *f,* sweeping, brushing; planing; wood-shaving

acepillar *vt* to sweep, brush; plane; *inf* brush up, polish up

aceptabilidad *f,* acceptability

aceptable *a* acceptable

aceptación *f,* acceptance; popularity; approval

aceptador (-ra) *a* accepting. *n* acceptor

aceptar *vt* to accept; approve; accept a challenge; *com* honor

acequia *f,* ditch, trench; irrigation channel

acera *f,* sidewalk, pavement. **a. del sol,** sunny side of the street

acerado *a* steel; steel-like; strong, tough; mordant, incisive

acerar *vt* to steel; treat (liquids) with steel; harden, make obdurate

acerbidad *f,* bitterness, acerbity, sourness; harshness, cruelty

acerbo *a* sour, tart, bitter; cruel, harsh

acerca de *adv* about, concerning

acercamiento *m,* approach

acercar *vt* to bring nearer; *vr* be near at hand, draw near; (*with prep a*) approach

acerico *m,* small cushion; pincushion

acero *m,* steel; blade, sword; *pl* bravery, spirit; *inf* good appetite. **a. inoxidable,** stainless steel

acérrimo *a sup* extremely strong, mighty; most harsh; most resolute, unflinching; very strong (taste, smell)

acerrojar *vt* to lock, padlock; bolt

acertado *a* well-aimed; fitting, suitable; wise; successful

acertar *vt irr* to hit the mark; find, come across; succeed (in), achieve; guess, find out; **No acertaba a explicármelo,** I couldn't quite understand it. **a. por chambra,** to make a lucky guess. *vi* be successful; thrive (of plants); (*with prep a* + *infin*) happen, occur, come to pass. *Pres. Ind.* **acierto, aciertas, acierta, aciertan.** *Pres. Subjunc.* **acierte, aciertes, acierte, acierten**

acertijo *m,* riddle

acervo *m,* pile, heap; *fig* storehouse, wealth (e.g. of words)

acetato *m,* acetate

acético *a* acetic

acetileno *m,* acetylene

achacar *vt* to attribute, impute, assign. **achacable a,** imputable to

achacoso *a* ailing, ill, sickly

achantarse *vr inf* to hide from danger; put up with, bear

achaparrado *a* stocky

achaque *m,* ailment, illness (permanent); *inf* period, menstruation; pregnancy; matter, affair; pretext; failing, bad habit. **En a. de . . . ,** Re . . . , concerning . . .

achatamiento *m,* flattening

achatar *vt* to flatten, make flat

achicado *a* childish

achicar *vt* to make smaller, diminish; drain, bail out; depreciate, belittle

achicarse *vr* to get smaller

achicharrar *vt cul* to overcook; overheat; annoy, importune

achicoria *f,* chicory

achique *m,* bailing, draining

achispado *a inf* tipsy

achubascarse *vr* to become overcast, grow stormy

achuchar *vt inf* to squeeze, hug; jostle, push against

achuchón *m, inf* shove, push; hug, squeeze

achulado *a inf* brazen, tough

aciago *a* unhappy, ill-omened; fateful

acíbar *m,* aloe tree; bitter aloes; sorrow, bitterness

acibarar *vt* to add bitter aloes to; embitter, sadden

acicalado *a* polished; neat; well-groomed. *m,* polishing, burnishing (of weapons)

acicalador (-ra) *a* polishing. *n* polisher. *m,* burnisher (machine)

acicalar *vt* to burnish (weapons); adorn, deck; *vr* dress oneself with care

acicate *m,* Moorish spur; incitement, stimulus

acicatear *vt* to induce, spur on. **a. la curiosidad,** arouse curiosity

acidez *f,* acidity, bitterness

acidia *f,* indolence; sluggishness

ácido *a* acid; sour; harsh. *m,* acid. **a. fénico,** carbolic acid. **a. graso,** fatty acid

acidular *vt chem* to acidulate

acídulo *a chem* acidulous

acierto *m,* good hit, bull's-eye; success; achievement; cleverness; dexterity, skill; wisdom, sense; tact

acimut *m, ast* azimuth

aclamación *f,* acclamation; shout of acclamation. **por a.,** unanimously

aclamador (-ra) *a* acclaiming. *n* applauder, acclaimer

aclamar *vt* to acclaim; applaud

aclaración *f,* explanation; elucidation

aclarado *m,* rinse; rinsing

aclarador, aclaratorio *a* explanatory

aclarar *vt* to clarify, purify; clear; rinse (clothes); explain; thin; *vi* clear; (sky) clear up; dawn

aclimatación *f,* acclimatization; *Lat. Am.* air-conditioning

aclimatar *vt* to acclimatize

acné *m,* acne

acobardar *vt* to intimidate, frighten

acocear *vt* to kick; *inf* insult, humiliate

acocharse *vr* to squat, crouch

acocil *m, Mexico* freshwater shrimp

acodalar *vt* to prop

acodiciar *vt* to yearn for, covet, desire

acogedizo *a* gathered haphazardly

acogedor (-ra) *a* welcoming, friendly; inviting (e.g. a chair or room); *n* protector

acoger *vt* to receive, welcome, admit; protect, harbour; *vr* take refuge; (*with prep a*) make use of, resort to; **acogerse a sagrado,** seek sanctuary

acogida *f,* reception, welcome; protection, shelter; meeting place; confluence (of waters). **tener buena a.,** to be well received

acogollar *vt* to protect, cover (plants); *vi* sprout, shoot

acogotar *vt* to fell by a blow on the neck; *inf* knock out

acolada *f,* accolade

acolitar *vi* to serve as an altar boy, serve as an altar girl

acólito *m,* acolyte

acomedido, -a *Lat. Am.* helpful, obliging

acometedor (-ra) *a* capable, enterprising; aggressive. *n* aggressor, attacker

acometer *vt* to attack furiously; undertake; take in hand; overcome (of sleep, etc.)

acometida *f,* **acometimiento** *m,* assault, onrush; undertaking

acometividad *f,* aggressiveness; *Argentina* touchiness

acomodable *a* easily arranged

acomodación *f,* adjustment; adaptation; accommodation

acomodadizo *a* accommodating, easy-going

acomodado *a* suitable; convenient; wealthy, well-off; comfort-loving; moderate, low (of price)

acomodador (-ra) *n* theater attendant, usher

acomodamiento *m,* agreement, transaction; accommodation

acomodar *vt* to arrange, adjust, accommodate; adapt; appoint; place; reconcile; employ, take on; equip, provide; lodge; *vi* suit, be convenient; *vr* compromise, agree

acomodaticio *a* accommodating

acomodo *m,* post, employment; arrangement; settlement

acompañamiento *m,* accompaniment; following, retinue; *mus* accompaniment; *theat* crowd, chorus

acompañanta *f,* chaperon; maid, servant

acompañante *m, mus* accompanist

acompañar *vt* to accompany; follow, escort; enclose (a letter, etc.); *mus* accompany

acompasado *a* rhythmic; deliberate, slow

acondicionado *a* conditioned; (*with bien or mal*) in good or bad condition; of good or bad quality; good- or ill-natured. **reflejo acondicionado** *med* conditioned reflex

acondicionar *vt* to prepare; mend, repair; *vr* condition oneself

acongojar *vt* to sadden, grieve; oppress

aconsejable *a* advisable

aconsejar *vt* to advise; *vr* (*with con*) consult, ask advice of

acontecedero *a* possible

acontecer *vi irr impers* to happen. See **conocer**

acontecimiento *m,* event, occurrence

acopiar *vt* to collect, amass, gather

acopio *m,* collection, store; accumulation, gathering

acopladura *f,* **acoplamiento** *m,* (*carp. mech*) joint; coupling; yoking; mating (of animals)

acoplar *vt* to join, couple; yoke; mate (animals); reconcile (opinions); *vr inf* fall in love

acoquinar *vt inf* to intimidate, terrify

acorazado *a* (*nav mil*) armoured, iron-clad. *m,* iron-clad, battleship

acorcharse *vr* to dry up, shrivel; go numb (limbs)

acordadamente *adv* by common consent, unanimously; deliberately, after due thought

acordar *vt irr* to decide unanimously; resolve; remind; tune; harmonize (colors); *vi* agree; *vr* remember; come

to an agreement. **Si mal no me acuerdo,** If memory serves me right. *Pres. Ind.* **acuerdo, acuerdas, acuerda, acuerdan.** *Pres. Subjunc.* **acuerde, acuerdes, acuerde, acuerden**

acorde *a* agreed; in harmony; in agreement. *m, mus* chord; harmony

acordeón *m,* accordion; (slang) crib sheet

acordonar *vt* to lace; cordon off, surround; mill (coins)

acornear *vt* to butt, toss (bulls)

acorralamiento *m,* corralling, penning

acorralado *a* at bay, intimidated

acorralar *vt* to corral, pen; confine; corner, silence (in argument); frighten; harass

acorrer *vt* to aid, assist; *vi* run, hasten; *vr* take refuge

acortamiento *m,* shortening

acortar *vt* to shorten; *vr* be speechless, be shy. **a. las velas,** to take in sail

acosador (-ra) *a* persecuting. *n* persecutor

acosamiento *m,* persecution

acosar *vt* to persecute relentlessly; annoy, harass

acostado *a* in bed; stretched out; *her* couchant

acostar *vt irr* to lay down, stretch out; put to bed; *vi* lean, tilt; *vr* lie down; go to bed; *naut* come alongside. See **contar**

acostumbrado *a* accustomed, usual

acostumbrar *vt* to habituate, accustom; *vi* be in the habit of (e.g. **Acostumbramos ir a la playa en el verano,** We generally go to the seashore in summer); *vr* (*with prep a*) become used to

acotación *f,* noting; marginal note; stage direction; ordnance survey number

acotar *vt* to annotate; mark out boundaries; fix, establish; accept; *inf* choose; testify; fill in elevation figures (on a map); *vr* seek refuge

acotejar *vt, Lat. Am.* to arrange, put in order

acre *a* bitter, sour; harsh; biting, mordant. *m,* acre (land measure)

acrecencia *f,* **acrecentamiento** *m,* increase; addition

acrecentar *vt irr* to increase; augment; promote, prefer. See **acertar**

acrecer *vt irr* to increase; augment. See **conocer**

acreción *f,* accretion

acreditado *a* accredited, well-reputed; respected

acreditar *vt* to prove; verify; accredit; recommend; sanction, authorize; vouch for, guarantee; *com* credit

acreedor (-ra) *n* creditor; claimant. *a* deserving. **a. hipotecario,** mortgagee

acreencia *f,* debt; *com* claim

acribillar *vt* to riddle with holes; wound repeatedly; pelt; torment; *inf* pester, harass

acriminación *f,* accusation

acriminador (-ra) *a* incriminating. *n* accuser

acriminar *vt* to accuse, charge

acrimonia *f,* acrimony

acriollarse *vr, Lat. Am.* to adopt local customs, go native

acrisolar *vt* to refine, purify (metals); perfect; clarify, elucidate

acrobacia *f,* acrobatics

acróbata *mf* acrobat

acrobático *a* acrobatic

acromatópsico *a* color-blind

acróstico *a* and *m,* acrostic

acta *f,* minutes, record; certificate of election (as deputy to Cortes, etc.); *pl* deeds (of a martyr). **a. matrimonial,** marriage register

actitud *f,* attitude

activar *vt* to stimulate, make active; accelerate, hasten

actividad *f,* activity; movement, bustle. **en a.,** in action; at work

activo *a* active. *m, com* assets

acto *m,* act, deed, action; act, law; act (of a play); public ceremony; *pl* minutes (of a meeting), proceedings (of a conference). **a. continuo** *or* **a. seguido,** immediately afterwards. **a. vandálico,** act of vandalism. **los Actos de los Apóstoles,** Acts of the Apostles. **en a.,** in the act (of doing). **en el a.,** in the act; immediately

actor *m*, actor; *law* plaintiff

actriz *f*, actress

actuación *f*, operation, functioning; action; *pl* legal functions, judicial acts

actual *a* present; contemporary

actualidad *f*, present, present time; topic of interest. **actualidades**, current events. **en la a.**, at the present time

actuar *vt* to operate, set in motion; *vi* act; exercise legal functions

actuario (de seguros) *m*, actuary

acuarela *f*, water-color painting

acuarelista *mf* water-colorist

acuario *m*, aquarium; Aquarius

acuartelamiento *m*, billeting (of troops); billet, quarters

acuartelar *vt* to billet

acuático, acuátil *a* aquatic

acuatinta *f*, aquatint

acuatizar *vi*, *Lat. Am.* to land on water, touch down on water

acuchillado *a* taught by experience, schooled

acuchillar *vt* to hack, cut about; stab, put to the sword; slash (sleeves, etc.); *vr* fight with swords, daggers

acucia *f*, fervor, zeal; yearning, longing

acuciar *vt* to incite; goad; stimulate; encourage

acuciosidad *f*, eagerness, fervor, zeal

acucioso *a* eager, fervent, keen, zealous

acuclillarse *vr* to squat, crouch

acudir *vi* to go, repair (to); come; go or come to the aid of; attend, be present; **No me acude ningún ejemplo a la memoria,** No example comes to mind; resort (to), seek protection; reply, respond

acueducto *m*, aqueduct

acuerdo *m*, motion, resolution; decision; harmony, agreement; opinion, belief; remembrance; report; meeting (of members of a tribunal); *art* harmony (of colors). **de a.**, in agreement, in conformity; unanimously. **estar de a. (con),** to agree (with). **estar de acuerdo en** (+ inf.), to agree to (+ inf.) **ponerse de a.**, to come to an understanding

acuilmarse *vr Central America* to get depressed, get the blues

acuitar *vt* to distress, trouble; grieve

acumulación *f*, accumulation, collection

acumulador (-ra) *a* accumulative. *m*, accumulator, storage battery. *n* collector, accumulator

acumulamiento *m*, accumulation (act)

acumular *vt* to accumulate, amass, collect; accuse, charge with

acuñación *f*, minting, coining; wedging

acuñador (-ra) *n* coiner, stamper; wedge. *m*, coining machine

acuñar *vt* to mint, stamp, coin; wedge

acuoso *a* aqueous, watery

acurrucarse *vr* to huddle; curl up; crouch

acusación *f*, accusation; *law* charge; *law* prosecution

acusado (-da) *a* accused; prominent; well-defined; *n* accused; *law* defendant

acusador (-ra) *a* accusing. *n* accuser; *law* prosecutor

acusar *vt* to accuse; blame; denounce; *com* acknowledge receipt; *law* prosecute; *law* charge. **acusarle a uno las cuarenta,** *inf* to give someone a piece of one's mind

acusatorio *a* accusatory

acusón (-ona) *n inf* telltale, sneak, informer

acústica *f*, acoustics

acústico *a* acoustic

adagio *m*, adage; *mus* adagio

adalid *m*, chieftain; head, leader

adamado *a* effeminate; refined; genteel

adamantino *a* adamantine

adaptabilidad *f*, adaptability

adaptación *f*, adaptation

adaptar *vt* to adapt, make suitable; *vr* adapt oneself

adarme *m*, tittle, jot. **por adarmes,** in bits and pieces, in drabs and driblets

adecentar *vt* to make decent; tidy up; *vr* tidy oneself

adecuación *f*, adequacy; suitability

adecuado *a* adequate; suitable

adecuar *vt* to proportion, fit; *fig* tailor

adefesio *m*, *inf* folly, absurdity (gen. *pl*); extravagant attire; guy, sight

adelantado *a* precocious; forward, pert; fast (clocks); early (of fruit); excellent; capable, proficient. *m*, *ant* provincial governor *or* chief justice *or* captain-general (Spanish history). **por a.**, in advance

adelantamiento *m*, promotion, furtherance; progress, advancement; betterment; improvement; *ant* office of **adelantado**; anticipation

adelantar *vt* to advance, move on; hasten; forestall; overtake; move forward (the hands of clocks); improve, better; beat, excel; place in front; *vi* progress, advance; be fast (clocks); grow, develop; *vr* come forward

adelante *adv* on, forward; further on; straight ahead. **¡A.!** Onward!; Come in! **de hoy en a.,** henceforth, from today

adelanto *m*, anticipation; progress; *com* payment in advance. **el a. de la hora,** moving the clock forward

adelgazamiento *m*, loss of weight; slenderness; thinness

adelgazar *vt* to make slender or thin; *fig* split hairs; whittle, taper; *vi* grow slender or thin

ademán *m*, posture, attitude; gesture; *pl* behaviour, manners

además *adv* besides, in addition; moreover. **a. de,** as well as

adentro *adv* inside, within

adentros *m pl*, private thoughts (e.g. **Pensé para mis adentros,** I thought to myself). *Interj* **¡Adentro!** Come in!; Go in!

adepto *a* affiliated; adept, proficient

aderezamiento *m*, dressing; seasoning; embellishment

aderezar *vt* to deck, embellish; cook; *cul* season; *cul* dress; prepare; repair, mend; guide, direct; dress (cloth)

aderezo *m*, dressing, adornment; beautifying; finery, ornament; preparation; seasoning; set of jewels; horse's trappings; gum starch (for dressing cloth); equipment

adeudar *vt* to owe; be dutiable (goods); *com* debit; *vi* become related (by marriage); *vr* run into debt

adeudo *m*, debt; customs duty; *com* debit

adherencia *f*, adherence; adhesion

adherente *a* adhesive; connected, attached. *mf* adherent, follower; *m pl*. **adherentes,** accessories, requisites

adherirse *vr irr* to adhere, stick; follow; believe (in). See **herir**

adhesión *f*, adhesion; adherence

adhesivo *a* adhesive

adición *f*, addition; *Argentina* check (in a restaurant)

adicional *a* additional, extra

adicionar *vt* to add up; add to

adicto (-ta) *a* addicted, fond; joint. *n* addict; follower; disciple; *Lat. Am.* (drug) addict

adiestrador (-ra) *n* trainer, coach; guide, teacher

adiestrar *vt* to train, coach; guide, teach; lead; *vr* practise, perfect oneself

adietar *vt med* to put on a diet

adifés *adv*, *Central America* deliberately, on purpose

adinerado *a* wealthy, well-off, rich

adiós *interj* Good-bye!; Hello, God be with you! (used as greeting). *m*, farewell

aditamento *m*, addition

adive *m*, jackal

adivinación *f*, divination; guess

adivinanza *f*, divination; riddle; puzzle. **adivinanzas,** guessing games. **no estar para jugar a las a.,** to be in no mood for guessing games

adivinar *vt* to prophesy, foretell; divine; guess; solve, guess (riddles, etc.)

adivino (-na) *n* soothsayer, prophet

adjetivo *a* adjectival. *m*, adjective

adjudicación *f*, adjudication, award

adjudicador (-ra) *n* adjudicator

adjudicar *vt* to adjudge; award; *vr* appropriate

adjudicatario (-ia) *n* recipient (of a prize, etc.); grantee

adjuntar *vt* to enclose (with a letter, etc.)

adjunto *a* attached; enclosed, accompanying; assistant, deputy; adjectival. *m*, addition, supplement

administración *f*, administration; direction, control; administratorship

administrador (-ra) *a* administrative. *n* administrator. **a. de correos,** postmaster

administrar *vt* to control, manage; provide, supply; administer. **administrarse el tiempo,** to budget one's time

administrativo *a* administrative, executive

admirable *a* admirable

admirablemente *adv* admirably, excellently

admiración *f*, amazement; admiration; wonder; exclamation mark

admirador (-ra) *a* admiring. *n* admirer

admirar *vt* to admire; surprise, amaze (e.g. **Me admira su acción,** His action surprises me); to see (e.g. **Desde la colina se pueden admirar varios edificios de la ciudad,** From the hill several buildings in the city can be seen); *vr* (*with de*) be surprised at or by

admirativo *a* admiring; admirable, excellent

admisibilidad *f*, allowability, permissibility

admisible *a* admissible; permissible

admisión *f*, admission; acceptance; allowance

admitir *vt* to admit; receive, accept; tolerate, brook; allow, permit

admonición *f*, admonition, warning; reprimand

adobar *vt* to prepare; *cul* garnish; pickle (meat); cook; dress (hides)

adobo *m*, repairing; dressing (for cloth, leather); *cul* savory sauce; pickling sauce; make-up, cosmetic

adocenado *a* ordinary; narrow-minded

adoctrinar *vt* to instruct

adolecer *vi irr* to fall ill; (*with de*) suffer from (diseases, defects); *vr* be sorry for, regret. See **conocer**

adolescencia *f*, adolescence

adolescente *a* and *mf* adolescent

adonde *adv* (*interr* **a dónde**) where to, whither (e.g. **¿A dónde fuiste?** Where did you go to?)

adondequiera *adv* wherever

adopción *f*, adoption

adoptador (-ra) *a* adopting. *n* adopter

adoptar *vt* to adopt (children); make one's own; embrace (opinions); take (decisions)

adoptivo *a* adoptive

adoquín *m*, cobble-stone; *fig* blockhead

adoquinado *m*, cobbling, paving. *m*, cobbled pavement

adoquinar *vt* to pave with cobble-stones

adorable *a* adorable

adoración *f*, worship, adoration. **A. de los Reyes,** Adoration of the Magi; Epiphany

adorador (-ra) *a* adoring. *n* adorer

adorar *vt* to adore; worship; (*with en*) dote on; *vi* pray

adormecedor *a* soporific, drowsy

adormecer *vt irr* to make drowsy; soothe, lull; hush to sleep; *vr* go to sleep (limbs); fall asleep; (*with en*) persist in. See **conocer**

adormecimiento *m*, sleepiness; lulling asleep; numbness

adormitarse *vr* to doze, take a nap, snooze

adornamiento *m*, adornment, decoration

adornar *vt* to deck, beautify; decorate; trim, embellish; adorn (of virtues, etc.)

adorno *m*, decoration, adornment; ornament; trimming. **de a.,** ornamental; flowering (shrubs)

adquiridor (-ra) *a* acquiring. *n* acquirer

adquirir *vt irr* to acquire, get; achieve, obtain. *Pres. Ind.* **adquiero, adquieres, adquiere, adquieren.** *Pres. Subjunc.* **adquiera, adquieras, adquiera, adquieran**

adquisición *f*, acquirement; acquisition. **poder de a.,** purchasing power

adquisidor (-ra) *a* acquiring. *n* acquirer, obtainer

adquisitivo *a* acquisitive

adquisividad *f*, acquisitiveness

adrazo *m*, salt-water still

adrede *adv* on purpose, intentionally

adrenalina *f*, adrenaline

adscribir *vt* to ascribe, attribute; appoint (to a post, etc.)

adscripción *f*, ascription, attribution; appointment

aduana *f*, customs house, customs. **pasar por la a.,** to go through customs

aduanero *a* customs. *m*, customs officer

aducir *vt irr* to adduce, allege, cite; add. See **conducir**

adueñarse (de) *vr* to appropriate, take possession (of)

adulación *f*, adulation, flattery

adulador (-ra) *a* fawning. *n* flatterer

adular *vt* to flatter, fawn over, adulate

adulonería *f*, *Lat. Am.* flattery, fawning

adulteración *f*, adulteration; falsification

adulterador (-ra) *a* adulterant. *n* adulterator; falsifier; coiner

adulterar *vi* to commit adultery; *vt* adulterate; falsify

adulterino *a* adulterous; false

adulterio *m*, adultery

adúltero (-ra) *a* adulterous; corrupt. *n* adulterer

adulto (-ta) *a* and *n* adult

adunar *vt* to join, unite; unify, combine

adusto *a* extremely hot (of climate); grave, austere; standoffish, reserved

advenedizo *a* foreign, alien; strange, unknown; upstart; newly rich; *Lat. Am.* novice, tyro

advenimiento *m*, advent, arrival; ascension (to the throne)

advenir *vi irr* to come, arrive; happen, befall. See **venir**

adventicio *a* casual, accidental; *bot* adventitious

adverbio *m*, adverb

adversario (-ia) *n* adversary, rival; opponent

adversidad *f*, adversity, misfortune, sorrow

adverso *a* unfavorable, contrary, adverse; opposite

advertencia *f*, warning; introduction, preface; remark

advertido *a* capable, clever; experienced; expert

advertir *vt irr* to observe, notice; warn; advise; feel, be conscious of; point out, indicate; inform; discover. See **sentir**

adyacencia *f*, *Argentina* nearness, proximity

adyacente *a* adjacent, near-by, neighboring

aeración *f*, aeration

aéreo *a* aerial; airborne; airy; air; aeronautic; unsubstantial, fantastic. **correo a.,** airmail. **línea aérea** airline

aerobismo *m*, aerobics

aerodinámica *f*, aerodynamics

aeromozo, -a *mf*, *Lat. Am.* flight attendant

aeronauta *mf* aeronaut, balloonist

aeronáutica *f*, aeronautics

aeronáutico *a* aeronautic

aeropuerto *m*, airport

aeróstato *m*, dirigible

afabilidad *f*, affability, geniality, friendliness

afable *a* affable, genial, pleasant

afamado *a* famous, well-known

afamar *vt* to make famous

afán *m*, effort; manual labor; desire, anxiety **a. de mando,** thirst for power

afanar *vt* to press, urge on; filch; *vr* toil, labor; (*with por*) work hard to, try to

afanoso *a* hard, laborious; hard-working, painstaking; eager, anxious

afasia *f*, *med* aphasia

afear *vt* to make ugly; distort, deform; blame; criticize

afección *f*, fondness, affection; complaint, ailment, trouble

afectación *f*, affectation

afectado *a* affected

afectar *vt* to feign, assume; affect; move, touch; *law* encumber; *Lat. Am.* damage, hurt, injure

afectivo *a* affective

afecto *a* fond, affectionate; *law* encumbered; (*with prep a*) addicted to. *m*, emotion, sentiment; affection

afectuosidad *f*, affectionateness

afectuoso *a* affectionate, fond

afeitada *f*, shave, shaving

afeitar *vt* to shave; make up (one's face); adorn, beautify

afeite *m*, cosmetic; make-up (for the complexion)

afelpado *a* velvet-like, plushy

afeminación *f*, effeminacy; weakness, languor

afeminado *a* effeminate

afeminar *vt* to make effeminate; weaken; *vr* grow effeminate

aferradamente *adv* tenaciously, persistently, obstinately

aferramiento *m*, seizing, clutching; *naut* furling; *naut* grappling; mooring, anchoring; obstinacy

aferrar *vt* to seize, clutch; *naut* take in, furl; *naut* grapple; *vi naut* anchor; *vr* (*with con, en, a*) persist in, insist on

afestonado *a* festooned

Afganistán Afghanistan

afgano (-na) *a* and *n* Afghan

afianzamiento *m*, fastening, fixing; propping; grasping; guarantee, security

afianzar *vt* to fasten, fix; prop; consolidate (e.g. one's power); guarantee, be security for; grasp

afición *f*, propensity, inclination; fondness. **tomar a. (a),** to take a liking to

aficionado (-da) *a* amateur. *n* amateur, fan, enthusiast. **ser a a.,** to be fond of, have a liking for

aficionar *vt* to inspire liking or affection; *vr* (*with prep a*) take a liking to, grow fond of; become an enthusiast of

afijo *m*, *gram* affix

afiladera *f*, whetstone, grindstone

afilado *a* sharp, keen (of edges)

afilador *m*, grinder (of scissors, etc.); razor strop

afilalápices *m*, pencil sharpener

afilar *vt* to sharpen; grind, whet; taper; *Lat. Am.* flatter; *Lat. Am.* court, woo; *vr* grow thin; taper

afiliación *f*, affiliation

afiliar *vt* (*with prep a*) to affiliate with; *vr* (*with prep a*) become affiliated with; join, become a member of

afiligranado *a* filigree; delicate, fine; slender

afilón *m*, steel, knife sharpener; razor-strop

afín *a* nearby, contiguous; similar, related. *mf* relative by marriage

afinador *m*, tuning key; tuner (of pianos, etc.)

afinar *vt* to finish, perfect; *fig* polish, refine; tune (musical instruments); refine (metals); *vi* sing in tune; *vr* grow refined

afinidad *f*, affinity, analogy; relationship (by marriage); *chem* affinity

afirmación *f*, affirmation, statement

afirmadamente *adv* firmly

afirmar *vt* to make firm; fix, fasten; affirm; *vr* steady oneself; hold on to

afirmativa *f*, affirmative

afirmativo *a* affirmative

aflicción *f*, affliction, grief

aflictivo *a* sorrowful, grievous

afligir *vt* to sadden; afflict, trouble; *vr* lament, mourn

aflojamiento *m*, slackening; loosening; diminution

aflojar *vt* to slacken; loosen; *vi* relax, weaken; abate, diminish. **a. el paso,** to slow down

afluencia *f*, crowd, concourse; eloquence, fluency

afluente *a* fluent, eloquent. *m*, tributary (river)

afluir *vi irr* to crowd, swarm; flow (into). See **huir**

afonía *f*, *med* aphonia, loss of voice; hoarseness

afónico *a* hoarse

aforismo *m*, aphorism

aforrador (-ra) *n* one who lines jackets, etc.

aforrar *vt* to line (clothes, etc.); *vr* wrap oneself up; *inf* gormandize

afortunadamente *adv* luckily, fortunately

afortunado *a* lucky, fortunate; happy; stormy

afortunar *vt* to bring luck to, make happy

afrancesado (-da) *a* Francophile; Frenchified. *n* Francophile

afrancesamiento *m*, adoption of the French way of life; servile imitation of everything French

afrancesar *vt* to make French, gallicize; Frenchify; *vr* become a Francophile

afrenta *f*, insult, affront; disgrace

afrentar *vt* to insult; *vr* be ashamed

afrentoso *a* insulting, outrageous; disgraceful

África Africa

africanismo *m*, Africanism

africano -na *a* and *n* African

afrodisíaco *a* and *m*, aphrodisiac

afrontar *vt* to place opposite; confront; face (danger, etc.)

afuera *adv* outside, out

afueras *f pl*, suburbs, outskirts

afusilar *vt*, *Lat. Am.* to shoot

agachada *f*, crouch, duck; jerk

agachar *vt inf* bend, bow; *vr inf* crouch down; lie low, hide

agalla *f*, oak-apple; tonsil (gen. *pl*); *zool* gill; *inf* gall, cheek

agalludo, -a *a*, *Argentina* mean, stingy, tight; bold, daring

ágape *m*, agape; banquet, feast

Agar Hagar

agárico *m*, *bot* agaric

agarrada *f*, *inf* brawl, scuffle

agarradero *m*, handle; heft; *inf* influence, pull

agarrado *a inf* tight-fisted, mean

agarrar *vt* to grip, grasp; seize, take; *inf* nab (jobs); *vr* grip, hold on

agarro *m*, hold; grip, grasp

agarrotar *vt* to garrotte; tighten (ropes, etc.); press, squeeze; *vr* (limbs) go numb

agasajar *vt* to indulge, spoil, pet; receive kindly; entertain; caress

agasajo *m*, indulgence, kindness; affability, geniality; entertainment; gift, offering

agauchado *a* gaucho-like

agazapar *vt inf* to nab, catch; *vr inf* squat, crouch

agencia *f*, influence, agency

agenciar *vt* to negotiate, arrange; procure, manage

agenda *f*, notebook; agenda

agente *m*, agent. **a. de bolsa** or **a. de cambio,** bill broker. **a. de negocios,** business agent. **a. de policía,** police officer. **a. fiscal,** revenue officer

agerasia *f*, sickness-free old age

agestado *a* used generally with advs. **bien** or **mal,** well or ill-featured

agigantado *a* enormous, gigantic; outstanding, extraordinary

ágil *a* agile, nimble; easy to use (e.g. **un libro ágil,** a book easy to use)

agilidad *f*, agility, nimbleness

agilizar *vt* to make agile, limber; refresh one's knowledge of (e.g. **Quiero agilizar mi español,** I want to refresh my knowledge of Spanish); to enable; *vr* limber up

agitación *f*, shaking; agitation, excitement

agitador (-ra) *a* stirring; agitating. *n* agitator. *m*, stirrer, stirring rod

agitar *vt* to stir; shake; agitate, excite. **a. una cuestión,** raise a question; discuss a question

aglomeración *f*, agglomeration

aglomerar *vt* to agglomerate, amass

aglutinación *f*, agglutination

aglutinar(se) *vt* and *vr* to stick, agglutinate

agnóstico (-ca) *a* and *n* agnostic

agobiar *vt* to bow, bend down; *fig* weigh down, oppress; *vr* bend (beneath a weight)

agobio *m*, bowing, bending down; oppression, burden, weight

agolparse *vr* to rush, crowd, swarm

agonía *f*, agony, anguish

agonizante *a* dying

agonizar *vt* to attend a dying person; *inf* pester, annoy; *vi* be dying (gen. **estar agonizando**)

agorar *vt* to prophesy, foretell

agorero (-ra) *a* prophetic; ill-boding. *n* seer, augur

agostarse *vt* and *vr* to dry up, shrivel

agosto *m*, August; harvest. *inf* **hacer su a.,** to make hay while the sun shines

agotable *a* exhaustible

agotado *a* exhausted; out of print (of books)

agotador *a* exhausting; exhaustive

agotamiento *m*, exhaustion

agotar *vt* to drain off (water); empty (a glass); exhaust; run through (money); study thoroughly, examine closely (a subject)

agraciado *a* graceful; pretty

agraciar *vt* to lend grace to; make pretty; favor

agradable *a* agreeable, pleasant

agradar *vt* to be pleasing, like, please (e.g. **Me agrada su sinceridad,** I like his sincerity)

agradecer *vt irr* to be grateful for; thank for; *fig* repay, requite. See **conocer**

agradecido *a* grateful; thankful

agradecimiento *m*, gratitude; thankfulness

agrado *m*, pleasure; desire; liking; amiability, affability

agrandar *vt* to enlarge

agrario *a* agrarian

agrarismo *m*, *Mexico* farmers' movement, peasant movement

agravación *f*, **agravamiento** *m*, aggravation, worsening

agravador *a* aggravating; worsening; increasing

agravar *vt* to aggravate, increase; oppress (taxes, responsibilities); make worse; exaggerate; *vr* grow worse

agraviador -ra *a* offensive. *n* offender

agraviar *vt* to offend; wrong; *vr* take offence, be insulted

agravio *m*, offence, insult; wrong, injury

agraz *m*, unripened grape; verjuice; *fig* bitterness

agredir *vt* to attack

agregación *f*, association, aggregation; total, collection, aggregate

agregado *m*, aggregate; assistant; attaché; *Lat. Am.* sharecropper

agregar *vt* to add; collect, amass; appoint (to a post). **agregarse a . . . ,** to join . . . (e.g. an association)

agresión *f*, aggression

agresivo *a* aggressive

agresor (-ra) *a* and *n* aggressor

agreste *a* rural, rustic; wild; uncouth, rude

agriar *vt* to make bitter or sour; exasperate, provoke

agrícola *a* agricultural; *mf* agriculturalist, farmer

agricultura *f*, agriculture

agridulce *a* bitter-sweet

agrietarse *vr* to crack, split

agrimensor *m*, surveyor

agrimensura *f*, surveying

agrio *a* bitter, sour; rough, uneven (ground); brittle; sharp (of color contrast); unsociable; disagreeable

agronomía *f*, agronomy

agrónomo *a* agronomic. *m*, agronomist

agrupación *f*, congregation, assembly; group; crowd; crowding, grouping

agrupar *vt* to assemble, group; *vr* crowd, cluster

agrura *f*, bitterness; sourness; asperity

agua *f*, water; rain; slope of a roof; *pl* shot or watered effect on silks, etc.; medicinal waters; waves; water (of precious stones). **a. abajo,** down-stream. **a. arriba,** upstream. **a. bendita,** holy water. **a. cruda,** hard water. **a. de colonia,** eau de Cologne. **a. dulce,** fresh water. **a. fresca,** cold water. **a. nieve,** sleet. **a. oxigenada,** hydrogen peroxide. *fig inf* **estar con el a. al cuello,** to be in low water. *fig inf* **estar entre dos**

aguas, to be between two fires. *naut* **hacer a.,** to leak. **Todo eso es ya a. pasada,** That's all water under the bridge

aguacate *m*, avocado

aguacero *m*, heavy rainfall, shower

aguada *f*, water supply on board ship; flood (in mines); watering station; *art* water color

aguadero *m*, (animals') watering place

aguado *a* watery; abstemious; watered

aguador (-ra) *n* water carrier, water seller; drawer (of water)

aguafiestas *mf fig inf* wet blanket

aguafuerte *f*, etching

aguaje *m*, tide, waves; sea current; water supply (on board ship); wake (of a ship)

aguamanil *m*, washstand; pitcher, ewer

aguamanos *m*, water for washing hands; pitcher

aguamarina *f*, aquamarine

aguamiel *f*, honey and water, hydromel

aguantable *a* tolerable, bearable

aguantar *vt* to bear, tolerate, endure; restrain, resist, oppose; *vr* bear in silence, keep quiet

aguante *m*, patience, endurance; resistance

aguar *vt* to water down (wine, etc.); spoil (fun, etc.); *vr* be filled with water; be flooded; become watery or thin

aguardar *vt* to await; expect; allow time to (debtors)

aguardentería *f*, liquor shop

aguardentoso *a* spirituous, containing **aguardiente;** hoarse, husky (of the voice)

aguardiente *m*, liquor. **a. de caña,** rum

aguarrás *m*, oil of turpentine

aguatinta *f*, aquatint

aguatocha *f*, pump (for water, etc.)

aguaturma *f*, Jerusalem artichoke

agudeza *f*, sharpness; keenness; distinctness; alertness; cleverness; witty sally, repartee; wit; swiftness

agudo *a* sharp; alert, clever; (*geom med*) acute; fine, keen; rapid; high-pitched; strong (of scents, etc.)

agüero *m*, omen, sign; prophecy, prediction

aguerrido *a* veteran, war-hardened

aguerrir *vt defective* to harden to war; toughen

aguijada *f*, goad, spur

aguijar *vt* to prick (with a goad); urge on, encourage (animals); incite, instigate; spur on; *vi* walk swiftly

aguijón *m*, goad; sting; thorn, prickle; spur; incitement, stimulus. **tener aguijones,** to be on pins and needles

aguijonazo *m*, prick (with a goad)

águila *f*, eagle; master mind. **a. caudal** *or* **a. real,** royal eagle. **á. o sol,** *Mexico* heads or tails

aguileña *f*, *bot* columbine

aguileño *a* aquiline

aguilón *m*, *arch* gable; boom (of a crane)

aguinaldo *m*, Christmas present; New Year's gift

aguja *f*, needle; hand, pointer; hatpin; engraver's burin; switch; *rw* point; *rw* rail; obelisk; spire; bodkin; knitting needle; crochet hook; (compass) needle. *pl bot* plumelet. **a. capotera, a. de zurcir,** darning needle. **a. de marear** *naut*, binnacle; mariner's compass. **a. de media,** knitting needle. **a. espartera,** packing needle

agujerear *vt* to perforate, make holes in

agujero *m*, hole, aperture; needle maker or seller; needle case

agujeta *f*, lace (for shoes, etc.); *pl* muscular pains, aches; tip, gratuity

agusanarse *vr* to become worm-infested

aguzadura *f*, sharpening, grinding, whetting

aguzar *vt* to sharpen; grind, whet; stimulate, encourage; urge on, incite

ahechadura *f*, chaff (of grain)

ahembrado *a* effeminate

aherrojar *vt* to put (a prisoner) in irons; oppress

aherrumbrar *vt* to give the color or taste of iron to; *vr* taste or look like iron; go rusty

ahí *adv* there; over there. **de a.,** thus, so. **por a.,** somewhere about, near at hand.

ahidalgado *a* gentlemanly; noble, generous

ahijado (-da) n godchild; protégé

ahijar vt to adopt (children); mother (animals); attribute, impute; vi bring forth offspring; bot sprout. See **prohibir**

ahincado a earnest, eager

ahincar vt to urge, press; vr hurry, hasten. See **prohibir**

ahínco m, earnestness, eagerness

ahitar vt to stuff with food; bore, disgust. See **prohibir**

ahíto a full of food; fig fed up. m, indigestion

ahogado (-da) a drowned; suffocated; stuffy, unventilated; stifling. n drowned person; victim of suffocation

ahogamiento m, drowning; suffocation

ahogar vt to drown; suffocate; put out (the fire); stifle (yawns, etc.); suppress, extinguish; tire; overwater (plants); vr naut sink, founder; drown; suffocate

ahogo m, anxiety, grief; difficulty in breathing, oppression; asthma; embarrassment; suffocation; straitened circumstances

ahondamiento m, in-depth treatment (e.g. **el a. de un problema,** in-depth treatment of a problem)

ahondar vt to deepen; excavate, dig; go into thoroughly; go deep into, penetrate; vr (earth) subside

ahora adv now; very soon; just now, a short time ago. conjunc whether; now. **a. bien,** well now, given that. **a. mismo,** immediately, at once. **por a.,** for the present

ahorcado (-da) n hanged man

ahorcar vt to execute by hanging, hang. inf **a. los hábitos,** to leave the priesthood, cease to be an ecclesiastic

ahorita adv, Mexico right away, right now

ahormar vt to adjust, shape; break in (new shoes); make (a person) see reason

ahorquillar vt to prop up (trees) with forks; vr grow forked

ahorrar vt to free (slaves); save, economize; avoid, eschew; vr avoid; remove clothing

ahorro m, economy, thrift; pl savings

ahuchar vt to hoard; expel, drive away

ahuciar vt take possession of (a house)

ahuecar vt to hollow out; loosen; shake out; puff out, inflate; put on a solemn voice; hoe, dig; inf vr puff oneself out; put on airs

ahumada f, smoke signal

ahumado a smoked; smoky

ahumar vt to smoke (herrings, etc.); fill with smoke; vi smoke, burn; vr be full of smoke; taste smoked; inf get drunk. See **desahuciar**

ahusado a spindle-shaped

ahuyentar vt to frighten off; drive away; dismiss, banish (anxiety, etc.); vr flee

airadamente adv wrathfully, angrily

airado a angry

airar vt to annoy, anger; vr grow annoyed

aire m, air; atmosphere (sometimes pl); breeze, wind; bearing, appearance; vanity; (horse's) gait; futility, frivolity; grace, charm; gracefulness; mus air; mus tempo. **a. popular,** popular tune. **al a. libre,** in the open air, outdoors. inf **beber los aires (por),** to yearn (for)

aireación f, airing; ventilation

airear vt to air; ventilate; aerate; vr take the air; catch a chill

airecito m, Lat. Am. breeze, gentle wind

airosidad f, gracefulness; jauntiness

airoso a airy, open; windy, breezy, fresh; graceful; handsome; jaunty; victorious, successful

aislacionismo m, pol isolationism

aislacionista mf pol isolationist

aislado a isolated; remote; individual; single; elec insulated

aislador m, phys insulator

aislamiento m, isolation; phys insulation

aislante a isolating; insulating

aislar vt to isolate; elec insulate; vr become a recluse; become isolated

¡ajá! interj inf Aha! Good!

ajar vt to crease, crumple, spoil; humiliate; vr fade, wither (flowers)

ajedrecista mf chess player

ajedrez m, chess

ajenjo m, bot wormwood; absinthe

ajeno a alien; belonging to another; various, diverse; free, exempt; unsuitable; irrelevant

ajetrear vt to tire out, exhaust; vr be overtired

ajetreo m, exhaustion, fatigue

ají m, Lat. Am. chili, red pepper; chili sauce; **estar hecho un ají** to be hopping mad, be fuming

ajo m, garlic; inf make up, paint; disreputable affair, shady business; curse, oath. inf **revolver el a.,** to stir up trouble

ajorca f, bracelet; slave bangle

ajornalar vt to hire by the day

ajuar m, trousseau; household equipment

ajustado a exact; tight-fitting; trim

ajustador (-ra) a adjusting. n adjuster. m, tight-fitting jacket

ajustamiento m, adjustment; agreement

ajustar vt to adjust; fit; arrange; make an agreement about; reconcile; settle (accounts); engage, employ; retain (a barrister); regulate; tune up (a motor); vi fit; vr adapt oneself. inf **a. cuentas viejas,** to settle old accounts

ajuste m, fitting; adjustment; agreement; arrangement; print make-up; reconciliation; settlement; regulation; engagement, appointment

ajusticiado (-da) n executed person

ajusticiar vt to put to death

al (contraction of a + el). 1. prep a + m. def. art., to the, e.g. **Han ido al mar,** They have gone to the sea. 2. prep a + el used as dem. pron to that, to the one, e.g. **Mi sombrero se parece mucho al que tiene Vd.,** My hat is very similar to the one you have. al + infin. means when, as, at the same time as, e.g. **Al llamar a la puerta la vi en el jardín,** As I was knocking at the door, I saw her in the garden

ala f, zool wing; row, line; brim (of a hat); eaves; (arch aer mil bot) wing; blade (of propeller); fin (of fish); pl courage. **a. del corazón,** anat auricle. **arrastrar el a.,** to woo, flirt with. fig **cortar** (or **quebrar**) **las alas (a),** to clip a person's wings

alabador (-ra) n praiser, extoller

alabanza f, praise; eulogy

alabar vt to praise; vr brag, boast

alabastrino a alabastrine, alabaster

alabastro m, alabaster

alacena f, cupboard; recess; closet; safe (for food)

alacrán m, scorpion

alacre a, Mexico agile, nimble

alacridad f, alacrity, eagerness; Mexico agility, nimbleness

alado a winged; feathered; fig soaring

alambicado a sparing, frugal; subtle; euphuistic

alambicar vt to distil; examine carefully, scrutinise; make over-subtle or euphuistic (of style)

alambique m, still

alambrada f, mil wire-entanglement

alambrado m, wire-netting; mil wire-entanglement; wire cover

alambrar vt to wire (fence)

alambre m, wire; sheep bells. **a. espinoso,** barbed wire

alambrera f, wire fence; wire-netting; wire cover

alambrista mf tight-rope walker; (Mexico) wetback

alameda f, poplar wood or grove; avenue of poplars

álamo m, poplar. **a. temblón,** aspen tree

alano m, mastiff

alarde m, mil parade; display, ostentation. **hacer a. de,** to brag about

alargamiento m, lengthening; stretching

alargar vt to lengthen; prolong; pass, hand (things); pay out (ropes, etc.); increase; vr go away, depart; be wordy, spread oneself; lengthen

alarido *m,* yell, shout; shriek, scream; howl; yelp; cry (of a seagull)

alarma *f,* alarm. **a. aérea,** air-raid warning

alarmante *a* alarming

alarmar *vt* to give the alarm; frighten; *vr* be alarmed

alarmista *mf* alarmist

alazán *a* sorrel-colored. *m,* sorrel horse

alazo *m,* flap or stroke of the wings

alba *f,* dawn; *ecc* alb, vestment. **al a.,** at dawn

albacea *mf* executor, executrix; testator

albanés (-esa) *a* and *n* Albanian. *m,* Albanian language

albañil *m,* mason, bricklayer

albañilería *f,* masonry; bricklaying

albarda *f,* pack-saddle; *Lat. Am.* saddle

albardilla *f,* small saddle; pad; small pillow; *arch* coping

albaricoque *m,* apricot

albaricoquero *m,* apricot tree

albarrada *f,* stone wall; mud fence

albatros *m,* albatross

albear *vi* to become white, whiten

albedrío *m,* free will; fancy, caprice

albéitar *m,* veterinary surgeon; farrier

alberca *f,* reservoir, tank; vat; artificial lake; *Lat. Am.* (swimming) pool

albergar *vt* to shelter; nourish, harbor; *vi* and *vr* take refuge or shelter; lodge

albergue *m,* shelter, refuge; den, lair; hospitality; lodging; asylum

albo *a* pure white

albóndiga *f,* forced meat ball, rissole

albor *m,* whiteness; dawnlight, dawn. **a. de la vida,** life's dawning, childhood

alborada *f,* dawn; reveille; *mil* dawn attack; *mus* aubade

alborear *vi* to grow light, dawn

albornoz *m,* burnouse

alborotado *a* impulsive; turbulent; noisy; excitable

alborotar *vt* to disturb; *vi* make a noise; be gay; *vr* riot; grow rough (sea)

alboroto *m,* noise; confusion; tumult; riot; rejoicing, gaiety

alborotos *mpl, Argentina, Central America, Peru* popcorn

alborozar *vt* to overjoy, gladden; *vr* rejoice, be glad

alborozo *m,* gladness, rejoicing, joy

albricias *f pl,* reward for bringer of good tidings. *interj* **¡A.!** Joy! Congratulations!

álbum *m,* album

albúmina *f,* albumin

albur *m, icht* dace; chance, risk. **al a. de,** at the risk of

alcachofa *f,* artichoke

alcahuete *m,* procurer, go-between, pimp, pander; *fig inf* protector, screen; *inf* scandalmonger

alcahuetear *vt* to procure, act as a go-between for; *vi* be a pimp or a procuress

alcaide *m,* governor of a fortress *ant;* governor of a prison

alcalde *m,* mayor; magistrate. *inf* **tener el padre a.,** to have a friend at court

alcaldesa *f,* mayoress

alcaldía *f,* office or authority of an alcalde

álcali *m, chem* alkali

alcalino *a* alkaline

alcance *m,* reaching, attainment; range (of firearms, etc.); scope; arm's length or reach; pursuit; stop press *or* extra edition (newspapers); *com* deficit; importance; *pl* talent; capacity. **al a. de la voz,** within call. **hombre de cortos alcances,** a limited, dull man. **poner al a. de,** to make available to; make intelligible to

alcancía *f,* money-box; coin bank, piggy bank

alcanfor *m,* camphor

alcantarilla *f,* little bridge; sewer; culvert; bed for electric cable

alcantarillado *m,* sewage system; main sewer

alcanzable *a* obtainable; attainable

alcanzadizo *a* attainable, easily reached

alcanzar *vt* to overtake; reach; range (of guns, etc.); at-

tain; achieve; understand; *fig* equal (in attainments); live at the same time as, be contemporaneous with; be capable of, be able; *vi* reach; share, participate in; be enough

alcaparra *f, bot* caper; caper bush

alcaucil *m,* (in most places) wild artichoke; (in some places) cultivated artichoke

alcazaba *f,* fortress (within a walled town or city), casbah

alcázar *m,* fortress; royal residence, castle; *naut* quarterdeck

alción *m, orn* kingfisher

alcista *mf* speculator (on Stock Exchange)

alcoba *f,* bedroom; alcove, recess; Moorish flute

alcohol *m,* alcohol; galena; eye black (cosmetic); spirits of wine. **a. desnaturalizado,** industrial alcohol, methylated spirit. **a. metílico,** wood alcohol

alcohólico *a* alcoholic

alcoholismo *m,* alcoholism

alcor *m,* hill; slope

Alcorán *m,* Koran

alcornoque *m,* cork tree; dunderhead, dolt

alcorza *f, cul* icing, sugar-paste

alcorzar *vt cul* to ice, cover with sugar; decorate, adorn

alcurnia *f,* lineage, family, descent

alcuza *f,* oil-bottle; oil-can; cruet

aldaba *f,* door knocker; bolt, latch; *pl* protectors, influential helpers. *inf* **tener buenas aldabas,** to have plenty of pull

aldabada *f,* rap with the knocker; sudden shock

aldabeo *m,* knocking

aldea *f,* village

aldeano (-na) *a* village; country, ignorant. *n* villager; countryman, peasant

aldehído *m, chem* aldehyde

aleación *f,* alloy

alear *vi* to flutter, beat the wings; flap one's arms; recuperate, grow well; *vt* alloy

aleatorio *a* accidental, fortuitous

aleccionamiento *m,* teaching, training, coaching

aleccionar *vt* to teach, train, coach

aledaño *a* adjoining; border. *m,* boundary, border

alegación *f,* allegation, statement

alegar *vt* to allege, state; cite; *vi law* bring forward, adduce

alegato *m, law* speech (for the prosecution or defence)

alegoría *f,* allegory

alegórico *a* allegorical

alegorizar *vt* to interpret allegorically, treat as an allegory

alegrar *vt* to make happy, gladden, rejoice; adorn, beautify; stir (fires); *vr* be glad, rejoice; *inf* be merry (tipsy)

alegre *a* joyful, glad; cheerful, gay; bright (colors, etc.); pretty, attractive; *inf* risqué; *inf* flirtatious, light

alegría *f,* joy, gladness; cheerfulness, gaiety; *pl* public rejoicings

alegrón *m,* sudden unexpected joy; *inf* flash of light. *a inf* flirtatious

alejamiento *m,* placing at a distance, removal; withdrawal

Alejandría Alexandria

alejar *vt* to place at a distance, remove; withdraw; ward off (dangers, etc.); *vr* depart, go away; withdraw. **alejarse de,** to abandon (a belief, custom, superstition, etc.)

alelar *vt* to make silly or stupid

aleluya *mf,* alleluia. *m,* Eastertide. *f,* small Easter cake; *inf* daub, poor painting; *inf* doggerel; joy, rejoicing

alemán (-ana) *a* and *n* German. *m,* German language

Alemania Germany

alentada *f,* deep breath

alentado *a* valiant, spirited; proud; *Argentina* strong, vigorous

alentador *a* encouraging, inspiring, stimulating

alentar vi irr to breathe; vt encourage, inspire; vr be encouraged. See **sentar**

alerce m, larch tree and wood

alergia f, allergy

alergólogo m, allergist

alero m, projecting roof; splashboard (of carriages); eaves; gable end

alerón m, aer aileron

alerta adv watchfully. interj Take care! Look out! **estar ojo a.**, to be on the watch

alerto a watchful, alert

aleta f, dim small wing; fin

aletargado a lethargic; comatose

aletargamiento m, lethargy

aletargar vt to cause lethargy; vr become lethargic

aletazo m, flapping, beating (of wings); inf theft

aletear vi to flap the wings, flutter; move the arms up and down; become convalescent

aleteo m, fluttering, flapping of wings; beating, palpitation (of heart)

aleve a See **alevoso**

alevosía f, law malice; treachery

alevoso a law malicious; treacherous

alfabético a alphabetical

alfabetización f, literacy work

alfabetizador m, literacy worker

alfabeto m, alphabet. **a. manual,** sign language

alfalfa f, bot lucerne

alfandoque m, Lat. Am. cheesecake; maraca

alfanje m cutlass; Mexico machete

alfar m, potter's workshop; pottery; earthenware

alfarería f, pottery shop; potter's workshop; potter's craft

alfarero m, potter

alfeñique m, cul icing, sugarpaste; inf affectation

alférez m, mil ensign; second lieutenant; lieutenant. nav **a. de fragata,** sub-lieutenant. nav **a. de navío,** lieutenant

alfil m, bishop (in chess)

alfiler m, pin; brooch with a pin; tiepin; pl pin-money, dress-allowance; fig inf **no estar uno con sus alfileres,** to have a slate loose. inf **vestido de veinticinco alfileres,** dressed to the nines

alfiletero m, needle-case

alfombra f, carpet; rug

alfombrado m, carpeting

alfombrar vt to carpet

alfombrilla eléctrica f, electric pad or blanket

alfombrista m, carpet merchant; layer of carpets

alforja f, saddle-bag; mil knapsack

alforza f, sew tuck; inf scar

alforzar vt sew to tuck

alga f, alga, seaweed

algalia f, civet

algarabía f, Arabic; inf gibberish; din of voices, uproar

algarada f, troop of horse; uproar, hubbub; outcry

algarroba f, bot carob bean

algazara f, Moorish war cry; rejoicing, merriment; noise, clamor

álgebra f, algebra; art of bone setting

algebrista mf bonesetter; algebraist

álgido a icy cold

algo indef pron some, something (e.g. **Se ve que hay a. que le molesta,** You can see that something is irritating him). adv somewhat, a bit. **en a.,** in some way

algodón m, cotton plant; cotton flower; cotton fabric; candy floss (UK), cotton candy (USA). **a. en rama,** cotton-wool. **a. hidró-filo,** absorbent cotton wool. **a. pólvora,** nitrocellulose

algodonal m, cotton plantation

alguacil m, policeman, constable; ant city governor; short-legged spider

alguien indef pron someone, somebody, e.g. **Dime si viene a.,** Tell me if anyone comes

algún abb of **alguno** bef. m sing noun, e.g. **a. libro**

alguno a (abb **algún** bef. m, sing) some, any. indef pron someone, somebody; pl some, some people. **alguno que otro,** a few

alhaja f, jewel; ornament; treasure, precious object; inf gem, excellent person (also ironic, e.g. **Es una a.,** He's a fine fellow)

alhajar vt to adorn with jewels, bejewel; furnish, equip

alharaca f, vehemence, demonstration, fuss (gen. pl)

alheña f, bot privet; henna

alhóndiga f, corn exchange; public granary

aliado (-da) a allied. n ally

alianza f, alliance; pact, agreement; relationship (by marriage); sum total, whole (of factors, etc.); wedding-ring

aliarse vr to join together, become allies; be associated

alicaído a drooping; inf weak, exhausted; discouraged, downhearted; come down in the world

alicates m pl, pincers, pliers

aliciente m, attraction, inducement

alícuota f, a aliquot; proportional. **partes alícuotas,** aliquot parts

alienación f, alienation

alienado a insane, mad

alienar vt See **enajenar**

alienista mf med alienist

aliento m, breathing; breath; courage, spirit; encouragement. **el posterior a.,** one's last breath. **cobrar a.,** to regain one's breath; take heart. **de un a.,** in one breath; without stopping

alifafe m, inf ailment; tumor on horse's hock

aligación f, binding together, alligation

aligeramiento m, lightening, reduction in weight

aligerar vt to lighten, make less heavy; quicken, hasten; ease, alleviate; moderate; shorten, abbreviate

alimaña f, destructive animal

alimentación f, nourishment; feeding

alimentar vt to feed; nourish; encourage, foment; assist, aid; keep, support

alimenticio a nourishing; feeding

alimento m, food, nourishment; stimulus, encouragement; pl alimony; allowance

alindar vt to mark the boundary of; beautify, adorn; vi border, be contiguous

alineación f, alignment

alinear vt to align, range in line; dress (troops); vr fall into line

aliñar vt to decorate, adorn; cul season; prepare; set (bones)

aliño m, decoration, ornament; preparation; condiment, seasoning; setting (bones)

aliquebrado a broken-winged; inf down in the mouth

alisador (-ra) a smoothing; polishing. n polisher

alisar vt to smooth; polish; sleek; plane; comb lightly

alisios m pl, trade winds

aliso m, alder tree and wood

alistador m, enroller

alistamiento m, enlistment; conscription; enrolment

alistar vt to enrol, list; enlist; conscript; prepare, get ready; vr enrol; mil enlist; get ready

alitranca f, Chile, Peru brake

aliviar vt to lighten; alleviate, mitigate; relieve; ease; quicken (one's step); hasten, speed up; steal

alivio m, lightening; relief; alleviation; ease

aljaba f, quiver (for arrows); Lat. Am. fuchsia

aljibe m, tank, cistern; watership or tanker

aljófar m, small irregular shaped pearl; dew-drop, rain-drop, tear drop

aljofifa f, floorcloth

allá adv there; to that place. **más a.,** farther on, beyond. Used in conjunction with phrases of time, indicates remoteness, e.g. **a. en tiempos de los Reyes Católi-cos,** long ago in the time of the Catholic Monarchs. **a. por 1900,** way back in 1900

allanamiento m, leveling, flattening; condescension,

affability; (police) raid, (police) search acceptance of a judicial finding

allanar *vt* to level, flatten; overcome (difficulties); soothe; break into (a house, etc.); give entrance to the police; *vr* collapse (buildings, etc.); abide by, adapt oneself (to); condescend, be affable. **a. el camino (a . . .)**, to pave the way (for . . .)

allegado (-da) *a* near, allied; related. *n* follower, ally

allegar *vt* to gather, collect; draw nearer; *agr* reap; add; *vi* arrive

allende *adv* beyond; besides. **de a. el mar,** from beyond the sea

allí *adv* there; to that place, thereto; thereupon, then. **por a.,** through there; that way

alma *f,* soul; living person; essence, core; vivacity, animation; energy, vitality; spirit, ghost; core (of a rope). **a. de cántaro,** fool, ninny. **a. de Dios,** simple soul, kind person. **a. en pena,** soul in purgatory. **¡A. mía!** My darling! **con todo el a.,** with all my heart. **Lo siento en el a.,** I feel it deeply

almacén *m,* warehouse; store, shop

almacenaje *m,* cost of storage

almacenar *vt* to store; put in store; hoard

almacenero *m,* warehouseman, storekeeper

almacenista *mf* owner of a store; assistant, salesman (saleswoman)

almáciga *f,* mastic; tree plantation or nursery

almagre *m, min* red ocher; stain, mark

almanaque *m,* calendar, almanac

almeja *f, icht* clam

almenara *f,* beacon fire

almendra *f,* almond; kernel; crystal drop (of chandeliers, etc.); cocoon; bean (of cocoa tree, etc.). **a. garapiñada,** sugar almond

almendro *m,* almond tree

almendruco *m,* green almond

almete *m,* casque, helmet; helmeted soldier

almiar *m,* haystack, hayrick

almíbar *m,* sugar syrup; nectar

almibarado *a* syrupy; *inf* sugary

almibarar *vt* to coat with sugar; preserve (fruit) in syrup; flatter with sweet words

almidón *m,* starch

almidonado *a* starched; *fig inf* stiff, unbending; prim, starchy

almidonar *vt* to starch

alminar *m,* minaret (of mosque)

almirantazgo *m,* Admiralty; admiralship; Admiralty Court

almirante *m,* admiral

almizcle *m,* musk

almizcleño *a* musk (of scents)

almizclero *a* musky. *m, zool* musk-deer

almocafre *m, agr* hoe; trowel, dibble

almohada *f,* pillow; pillowcase; cushion. *inf* **aconsejarse** *or* **consultar con la a.,** to think over (a matter) carefully, sleep on it

almohadilla *f, dim* small cushion; lace or sewing cushion; pin cushion

almohadillado *a* cushioned; padded

almoneda *f,* auction; furniture sale

almonedear *vt* to auction; sell off (furniture)

almorranas *f pl,* hemorrhoids

almorzar *vi irr* to lunch; breakfast. See **forzar**

almuercería *f, Mexico* lunch counter, luncheonette

almuecín, almuédano *m,* muezzin

almuerzo *m,* luncheon; breakfast (not so usual)

alocado *a* feather-brained, reckless; crazy, wild

alocución *f,* allocution, address, harangue

áloe *m, bot* aloe

alojado (-da) *m,* billeted soldier. *n* lodger, guest

alojamiento *m,* lodging; dwelling; *mil* billeting; *naut* steerage; camp, encampment

alojar *vt* to lodge; billet, quarter (troops); insert, introduce; *vi* and *vr* lodge; live, dwell

alondra *f, orn* lark

alopatía *f, med* allopathy

alpaca *f,* alpaca (animal and fabric); nickel silver

alpargata *f,* sandal with hemp sole

alpargatero (-ra) *n* manufacturer or seller of alpargatas

Alpes, los the Alps

alpestre *a* Alpine; rock (of plants); mountainous, lofty

alpinismo *m,* mountaineering

alpinista *mf* mountaineer, climber

alpino *a* Alpine

alpiste *m,* bird seed

alpro *f,* (Alianza para el Progreso)

alquería *f,* farmstead

alquiladizo *a* rentable, hirable

alquilador (-ra) *n* hirer

alquilamiento *m,* See **alquiler**

alquilar *vt* to rent; hire out; hire; *vr* hire oneself out, serve on a wage basis

alquiler *m,* hiring out; renting; rental; hire; wages. **de a.,** for hire, on hire

alquimia *f,* alchemy

alquimista *mf* alchemist

alquitrán *m,* tar, pitch. **a. mineral,** coal tar

alquitranado *a* tarred. *m, naut* tarpaulin

alrededor *adv* around, round about. **a. de,** around; approximately, about (e.g. **a. de cinco dólares,** about $5)

alrededores *m pl,* environs, surrounding country

Alsacia Alsace

alsaciano (-na) *a* and *n* Alsatian

alta *f,* certificate of discharge from hospital

altanería *f,* hawking; haughtiness, disdain; superciliousness

altanero *a* soaring, high-flying (of birds); supercilious; haughty, disdainful

altar *m,* altar. **a. mayor,** high altar

altavoz *m,* loudspeaker; megaphone

altearse *vr* to rise, grow steep (of land)

alterabilidad *f,* alterability, changeability

alteración *f,* alteration, change; debasement (of coinage); agitation

alterar *vt* to change, alter; debase (coinage); disturb, agitate; *vr* grow angry; become excited

altercación, f. altercado *m,* altercation, quarrel

altercar(se) *vi* and *vr* to quarrel, dispute, altercate

alternación *f,* alternation

alternado *a* alternate

alternador *a* alternating. *m, elec* alternator

alternante *a* alternating

alternar *vt* to alternate; make one's debut as a **matador;** *vi* alternate; (*with con*) have dealings with, know

alternativa *f,* alternative, option; service performed by turns; alternation

alternativo *a* alternative

alterno *a* alternative; *bot* alternate

alteza *f,* altitude, height; sublimity, perfection; **(A.)** Highness (title)

altibajo *m,* embossed velvet; *pl inf* rough ground; *inf* vicissitudes of fortune

altillo *m,* hillock, eminence; garret, attic

altímetro *m, aer* altimeter

altiplano *m* plateau; **el A.** the High Andes, the high Andean plateau

altiplanicie *f,* plateau; highland

altisonante *a* sonorous; sublime; high-flown; pompous

altitud *f,* altitude, height

altivez *f,* arrogance, haughtiness

altivo *a* arrogant, haughty

alto *a* high; tall; difficult, arduous; sublime; deep; most serious (of crimes, etc.); dear (of price); small, early (hours). *m,* height; eminence, hill; story, floor; *mil* halt; red light (traffic light). *adv* up, above, on high; loudly. *interj* **¡A.!** *mil* Halt! *mil* **A. Mando,** High Command. **las altas horas de la noche,** the small (or early) hours. **en alta voz,** in a loud voice. **en alto,** on high; up above. **hacer alto,** to halt, stop

altozano *m,* mound, hillock; viewpoint, open space

altruismo *m*, altruism
altruista *a* altruistic. *mf* altruist
altura *f*, height; altitude; *geom* altitude or height; top, peak; sublimity; tallness
alucinación *f*, **alucinamiento**, *m*, hallucination
alucinado *m*, person suffering from hallucinations
alucinador *a* hallucinatory, deceptive
alucinar *vt* to dazzle, fascinate; deceive
alud *m*, avalanche
aludir *vi* to allude (to); refer (to), cite
alumbrado *m*, lighting; *pl* illuminati
alumbramiento *m*, lighting, supply of light; childbirth
alumbrar *vt* to light, illuminate; give sight to the blind; instruct, teach; inflict (blows); hoe vine roots; *vi* give birth to a child; *vr inf* grow tipsy
alumbre *m*, alum
aluminio *m*, aluminum
alumno (-na) *n* ward, adopted child; pupil. **a. externo,** day pupil. **a. interno,** boarder
alunizar *vi* to land on the moon
alunizaje *m*, landing on the moon, moon-landing
alusión *f*, allusion
alusivo *a* allusive, suggestive; hinting
aluvial *a* alluvial
aluvión *m*, alluvium. **de a.,** alluvial
alverjana *f*, *Lat. Am.* pea
alza *f*, rise (of temperature, etc.); increase (in price); front sight (of guns)
alzacuello *m*, high collar, clerical collar; neck stock
alzada *f*, horse's stature; mountain pasture; *law* appeal
alzado *a* fraudulent (of bankruptcy); fixed (of price); *Mexico* haughty, proud *m*, theft; *Lat. Am.* wild; insolent; rebellious; *arch* front elevation
alzamiento *m*, raising, lifting; higher bid (at auction); rising, rebellion; fraudulent bankruptcy
alzaprima *f*, lever; wedge; bridge (of string instruments)
alzar *vt* to raise; lift up; elevate (the Host); steal, remove; hide; gather in the harvest; build, construct; *naut* heave; *vr* rise (of temperature, mercury, price, etc.); make a fraudulent bankruptcy; *law* appeal; (*with con*) run off with, steal. *naut* **a. la vela,** to set sail
ama *f*, mistress of the house; owner; housekeeper; wet nurse. **a. de casa,** housemaker, housewife. **a. de leche,** foster-mother. **a. de llaves** *or* **a. de gobierno,** housekeeper. **a. seca,** children's nurse
amabilidad *f*, lovableness; kindness; niceness, goodness, helpfulness
amable *a* lovable; kind; nice, good, helpful
amador (-ra) *a* loving. *n* lover, admirer
amadrigar *vt* to welcome, receive well; *vr* go into a burrow or lair; go into seclusion
amaestrar *vt* to train, instruct; tame; break in (horses)
amagar *vt* and *vi* to threaten; *vt* show signs of (diseases, etc.); *vr inf* hide
amago (contra . . .), threat (to . . .), menace (to . . .)
amainar *vt naut* to take in the sails; *vi* drop (of the wind); *vt* and *vt* relax (efforts, etc.)
amaine *m*, dropping, abatement (of the wind)
amalgama *f*, *chem* amalgam
amalgamación *f*, amalgamation
amalgamar *vt* to amalgamate; *vr* be amalgamated
amamantamiento *m*, suckling, nursling
amamantar *vt* to suckle
amancillar *vt* to discredit, dishonor; tarnish; stain
amanecer *vi irr* to dawn; arrive or be somewhere *or* be doing, at dawn (e.g. **Amanecimos en el barco,** Dawn came while we were on the ship. **Amanecimos escribiendo la carta,** The day broke as we were writing the letter); appear at daybreak; begin to appear. *m*, dawn, daybreak. See **conocer**
amanerado *a* mannered; affected
amaneramiento *m*, manneredness; mannerism
amanerarse *vr* to acquire mannerisms or tricks of style; become affected
amansador (-ra) *a* soothing, calming. *n* appeaser

amansar *vt* to tame; appease, moderate; soothe, pacify; break in (horses)
amante *a* loving. *mf* lover
amanuense *mf* amanuensis, secretary, clerk
amanzanar to lay out the streets of
amañar *vt* to execute with skill; *vr* grow skilful
amaño *m*, skill, dexterity; *pl* schemes, intrigues; tools, equipment
amapola *f*, poppy
amar *vt* to love
amaranto *m*, *bot* amaranth
amarar *vi* to alight on the water (of hydroplanes)
amarchantarse con *vr*, *Lat. Am.* deal regularly with, do business with
amargar *vi* to taste or be bitter; *vt* make bitter; embitter
amargo *a* bitter; embittered; grievous, sad. *m*, bitterness; *pl* bitters
amargor *m*, **amargura**, *f*, bitter taste, bitterness; trouble, affliction, pain
amaricado *a inf* effeminate
amarillear *vi* to look yellow; turn yellow; tend to yellow
amarillento *a* yellowish, turning yellow
amarilleo *m*, yellowing
amarillez *f*, yellowness
amarillo *a* and *m*, yellow
amarilloso *a*, *Lat. Am.* yellowish, turning yellow
amarra *f*, *naut* cable, thick rope
amarradero *m*, *naut* mooring berth; mooring-post; hitchingpost or ring
amarraje *m*, *naut* mooring charge
amarrar *vt* to tie up, hitch; moor
amarre *m*, mooring; hitching
amartelar *vt* to make jealous; court, woo, make love to; *vr* be jealous; fall madly in love
amartillar *vt* to hammer, knock; cock (firearms)
amasadera *f*, kneading-trough
amasador (-ra) *a* kneading. *n* kneader
amasar *vt* to knead; massage; scheme, plot
amasia *f*, concubine
amasiato *m*, concubinage
amasijo *m*, *cul* dough; kneading; portion of plaster or mortar; *inf* hotchpotch, mixture; scheme, plot
amatista *f*, amethyst
amazacotado *a* heavy, dense; *fig* stodgy (of writings, etc.)
amazona *f*, Amazon; independent woman; woman rider; woman's riding habit
ambages *m pl*, maze, intricate paths; circumlocutions
ámbar *m*, amber. **a. gris,** ambergris
ambarino *a* amber
Amberes Antwerp
ambición *f*, ambition
ambicionar *vt* to long for; desire eagerly; be ambitious to
ambicioso *a* ambitious; eager, desirous
ambidextro *a* ambidextrous
ambiente *a* ambient, surrounding. *m*, air, atmosphere; environment
ambigú *m*, cold buffet; buffet (in theaters, etc.)
ambigüedad *f*, ambiguity
ambiguo *a* ambiguous
ámbito *m*, precincts; boundary, limit; compass, scope
amblar *vi* to pace (of a horse)
ambos, *a m pl*, **ambas** *a f pl*, both, e.g. **ambas casas,** both houses
ambulancia *f*, ambulance. **a. de correos,** railway post office. **a. fija,** field-hospital
ambulante *a* walking; traveling, wandering
amedrentar *vt* to frighten, scare; intimidate
ameliorar *vt* to better, improve
amelonado *a* melon-shaped; *inf* madly in love
amén *m*, amen, so be it. **a. de,** besides, in addition to. *inf* **en un decir a.,** in a trice
amenaza *f*, threat

amenazador, amenazante *a* menacing, threatening
amenazar *vt* to threaten; *vt* and *vi* presage, be pending
amenguamiento *m*, lessening, diminution; discredit; loss of prestige
amenguar *vt* to lessen, decrease; dishonor, discredit
amenidad *f*, amenity; agreeableness
amenizar *vt* to make pleasant or attractive
ameno *a* pleasant; entertaining; agreeable, delightful
América America
América del Norte North America
América del Sur South America
americana *f*, (man's) jacket
americanismo *m*, usage typical of Western-Hemisphere Spanish
americano (-na) *a* Western Hemispheric; *mf* native of the Western Hemisphere; resident of the Western Hemisphere
ameritar *vt WH* to deserve, merit
ametrallador *m*, machine-gunner
ametralladora *f*, machine-gun
amianto *m*, *min* amianthus, asbestos
amiba *f*, *zool* ameba
amicísimo *a sup.* **amigo,** most friendly
amiga *f*, woman friend; mistress, lover; dame, schoolmistress; dame school
amigabilidad *f*, friendliness, amicability
amigable *a* friendly, amicable; harmonious; suitable
amígdala *f*, tonsil
amigdalitis *f*, tonsillitis
amigo (-ga) *a* friendly; fond, addicted. *n* friend. *m*, lover. *inf* **ser muy a. de,** to be very friendly with; be very keen on or fond of
amilanado *a* cowed, spiritless
amilanar *vt* to terrify, intimidate; *vr* grow discouraged
aminorar *vt* to diminish, lessen
amistad *f*, friendship; liaison; favor; *pl* acquaintances, friends
amistar *vt* to introduce, make known to each other; bring about a reconciliation between or with
amistoso *a* friendly
amnesia *f*, amnesia
amnistía *f*, amnesty
amnistiar *vt* to concede an amnesty, pardon
amo *m*, head of the house; master; owner; overlord; overseer. **a. de huéspedes,** keeper of a boarding house. **Nuestro A.** Our Lord. *inf* **ser el a. del cotarro,** to rule the roost
amoblado *m*, *Central America, Mexico* furniture
amodorramiento *m*, stupor, deep sleep
amodorrarse *vr* to fall into a stupor; fall into a heavy sleep
amoladera *f*, whetstone
amolador *m*, scissors grinder; knife grinder; sharpener
amoladura *f*, grinding, whetting, sharpening
amolar *vt irr* to grind, sharpen; *inf* pester, annoy. See **colar**
amoldar *vt* to mold; adjust; *vr* adapt oneself
amonedar *vt* to coin, mint
amonestación *f*, warning; advice. **correr las amonestaciones,** to publish banns of marriage
amonestador (-ra) *a* warning, admonitory. *n* admonisher
amonestar *vt* to warn; advise; rebuke; *ecc* publish bans of marriage
amoníaco *m*, ammonia
amontillado *m*, kind of pale, dry sherry
amontonamiento *m*, accumulation; gathering, collection; piling up, heaping
amontonar *vt* to pile up, heap; gather; collect; accumulate; *vr inf* fly into a rage
amor *m*, love; beloved; willingness, pleasure; *pl* love affairs; caresses. **a. propio,** self-esteem; vanity. *inf* **con mil amores,** with great pleasure. **por a. de,** for love of; for the sake of
amoral *a* amoral
amoratado *a* livid, bluish

amorcillo *m*, *dim.* little love; unimportant love affair; Cupid
amordazar *vt* to muzzle; gag; prevent speaking
amorfo *a* amorphous
amorío *m*, *inf* wooing, love making; *pl* love affairs
amoroso *a* loving; gentle; mild, balmy
amorrar *vi inf* to hang one's head; sulk, be sullen
amortajar *vt* to wrap in a shroud; enshroud
amortiguador *m*, *mech* shock absorber. *aut* **a. de los muelles,** shock-absorber
amortiguamiento *m*, softening, deadening; mitigation, lessening
amortiguar *vt* to soften, deaden; absorb (shocks); moderate, mitigate; soften (colors)
amortización *f*, amortization
amortizar *vt* to amortize; recover, redeem; suppress, abolish (posts)
amoscarse *vr inf* to be piqued or annoyed; become agitated
amostazar *vt inf* to annoy; *vi* become peeved
amotinador (-ra) *a* mutinous, rebellious. *n* rebel, mutineer; rioter
amotinar *vt* to incite to rebellion; unbalance, unhinge (mind); *vr* rebel; riot; *fig* be unhinged
amovible *a* movable, removable; removable (of officials, etc.)
amovilidad *f*, movability, removability; liability to discharge or dismissal
amparador (-ra) *a* protective; sheltering. *n* protector, defender, helper; shelterer
amparar *vt* to protect, favor, help; shelter; *vr* take refuge, take shelter; defend oneself
amparo *m*, shelter, refuge; protection, favor, help; defense
amper *m*, *elec* ampere
amperímetro *m*, *elec* ammeter
amperio *m*, *elec* ampere
ampliable *a* amplifiable
ampliación *f*, enlargement, increase, extension; *phot* enlargement
ampliador (-ra) *a* enlarging. *n* enlarger
ampliadora *f*, *phot* enlarger
ampliar *vt* to extend, enlarge, increase; *phot* enlarge
amplificación *f*, extension, amplification; *phot* enlargement
amplificar *vt* to enlarge; extend; increase; amplify, expatiate upon
amplio *a* wide; extensive; roomy, ample; prolix
amplitud *f*, extension; width; spaciousness, amplitude
ampolla *f*, blister; ampoule; bubble; *elec* bulb
ampulosidad *f*, pomposity, redundancy (of style)
ampuloso *a* pompous, high-flown (style)
amputación *f*, amputation
amputar *vt* to amputate
amuchachado *a* boyish
amueblar *vt* to furnish; provide with furniture
amuinar *vt*, *Mexico* to anger, make angry
amuleto *m*, amulet, charm
amurallar *vt* to surround with a wall, wall
amurrarse *vr*, *Lat. Am.* get depressed, get the blues
amusgar *vt* and *vi* to flatten the ears (animals); *vt* screw up the eyes (to see better)
ana *f*, ell (measure)
anacardo *m*, cashew (nut)
anacoreta *mf* anchorite, hermit
anacreóntico *a* Anacreontic
anacrónico *a* anachronous
anacronismo *m*, anachronism
ánade *mf* duck
anadear *vi* to waddle (like a duck)
anadeo *m*, waddle
anadino (-na) *n* duckling
anadón *m*, drake
anáfora *f*, anaphora
anafrodisíaco *a* anaphrodisiac
anagrama *m*, anagram

analectas *f, pl* analects

anales *m, pl* annals

analfabetismo *m,* illiteracy

analfabeto (-ta) *a* and *n* illiterate

analgesia *f,* analgesia

analgésico *a* and *m, med* analgesic

análisis *m,* analysis; *gram* parsing

analista *mf* analyst

analizar *vt* to analyse

analogía *f,* analogy

analógico, análogo *a* analogous

ananás *m,* pineapple

anaquel *m,* shelf, ledge

anaranjado *a* and *m,* orange (color)

anarquía *f,* anarchy

anárquico *a* anarchical

anarquismo *m,* anarchism

anarquista *mf* anarchist

anatema *mf,* anathema

anatomía *f,* anatomy

anatómico *a* anatomical

anca *f,* croup, hindquarters of a horse

ancianidad *f,* old age; seniority; oldness

anciano (-na) *a* old; ancient. *n* old person

ancla *f,* anchor. **a. de la esperanza,** sheet anchor. **echar anclas,** to anchor

ancladero, anclaje *m,* anchorage

anclar *vi* to anchor

ancón *m,* cove, *Mexico* corner

áncora *f,* anchor; refuge, haven

ancho *a* wide, broad. *m,* width, breadth. *inf* **a mis (tus, sus,** etc.) **anchas** *or* **anchos,** at my (your, his, etc.) ease, with complete freedom

anchoa *f,* anchovy

anchura *f,* width, breadth; ease, freedom; extent

anchuroso *a* very wide; extensive; spacious

andada *f,* wandering, roving; hard bread roll; pasture; *pl* trail, tracks. *fig inf* **volver a las andadas,** to return to one's old tricks

andaderas *f pl,* go-cart (for learning to walk)

andador *a* walking; swift walking; wandering. *m,* walker; garden path; *pl* leading-strings, reins

andadura *f,* walk, gait; pace, step

Andalucía Andalusia

andaluz (-za) *a* and *n* Andalusian

andaluzada *f, inf* exaggeration, tall story

andamio *m,* scaffolding; stand, platform

andanada *f, naut* broadside; cheapest priced seat in a bullring; *inf* dressing-down, scolding

andante *a* walking, strolling; errant (of knights). *a* and *m, mus* andante

andanza *f,* happening, occurrence; *pl* doings, deeds. **buena a.,** good fortune

andar *vi irr* to walk; move; work, operate, run (machines, etc.); progress, get along (negotiations, etc.); be, feel; elapse (of time); be occupied; behave; (*with prep a*) administer (blows, etc.); (*with en*) upset, turn over (papers, etc.); ride in or on (cars, bicycles, etc.); be engaged in; (*with con*) use, handle; *vt* traverse. *m,* gait, walk. **a. por los cuarenta,** to be in one's forties. **a. con paños tibios,** not to be firm. **a. con pies de plomo,** to be extremely cautious. **a. tras,** to follow, go after; persecute; desire ardently (things). **andarse a la flor del berro,** to sow one's wild oats. *fig inf* **andarse por las ramas,** to beat about the bush. **¡Anda!** Get along with you!; Hurry up!; You don't say so! **¡Andando!** Let's go get going!, Let's get a move on it! *Preterite* **anduve,** etc. *Imperf subjunc* **anduviese,** etc.

andariego *a* swift walking; wandering, vagrant

andarín (-ina) *n* good walker; professional walker

andas *f pl,* kind of stretcher; bier

andén *m,* railway platform; *Lat. Am.* sidewalk

andero *m,* bearer (of a bier)

andinismo *m, Lat. Am.* mountain climbing **andinista** *mf Lat. Am.* mountain climber

andino *a* Andean

andorrano (-na) *a* and *n* Andorran

andrajo *m,* rag, wisp of cloth, tatter

andrajoso *a* ragged, tattered

andurriales *m pl,* byways, unfrequented paths; remote places

anécdota *f,* anecdote

anecdótico *a* anecdotal

anegación *f,* drowning; flooding, inundation

anegar *vt* to drown; inundate; shipwreck; *vr* drown; be flooded

anejo *a* attached, annexed. *m,* annexed borough

anemia *f,* anemia

anémico *a* anemic

anémona, anémone *f,* anemone. **anémona de mar,** sea-anemone

anestesia *f,* anesthesia

anestesiador (-ra) *n* anesthetist

anestesiar *vt* to anesthetize

anestésico *a* and *m,* anesthetic

aneurisma *mf med* aneurism

anexar *vt* to annex

anexión *f,* annexation

anexo *a* attached, joined. *m,* annex

anfibio *a* amphibious. *m,* amphibian

anfiteatro *m,* amphitheater; operating theater; dissecting room; morgue; *theat* dress-circle

anfitrión *m, inf* host, one who entertains guests

ánfora *f,* amphora; *Lat. Am.* ballot box

angarillas *f pl,* hand barrow; table cruet; yoke and panniers

ángel *m,* angel; *Lat. Am.* (hand) microphone **á. de la guarda,** guardian angel. **estar con los ángeles,** to be in Heaven (euphem. for 'to be dead')

angelical, angélico *a* angelic; divine, excellent

angina *f, med* angina, tonsillitis. **a. de pecho,** angina pectoris

anglicanismo *m,* Anglicanism

anglicano (-na) *a* and *n* Anglican

anglicismo *m,* anglicism

anglo (-la) *a* and *n* Angle. *a* Anglo-

anglófilo (-la) *n* Anglophile

anglosajón (-ona) *a* and *n* Anglo-Saxon. *m,* Anglo-Saxon language

angostar *vi* and *vt* to narrow; tighten

angosto *a* narrow; tight

angostura *f,* narrowness; tightness; narrow pass; strait; *fig* tight corner, fix

anguila *f, icht* eel; *pl naut* slipway, slips

angula *f, icht* elver (young eel)

ángulo *m,* angle. **á. inferior izquierdo,** lower lefthand corner. **á. inferior derecho,** lower righthand corner. **á. superior izquierdo,** upper lefthand corner. **á. superior derecho,** upper righthand corner. **á. recto,** right angle

anguloso *a* angulate; angular, gaunt; cornered

angustia *f,* anguish, grief

angustiante *a* distressing

angustiar *vt* to grieve; afflict; *vr* be full of anguish

anhelación *f,* panting, hard breathing; yearning, longing

anhelar *vi* to pant, breathe with difficulty; *vi* and *vt* long for, yearn for, desire

anhélito *m,* pant, hard breathing

anhelo (de) *m,* longing (for), desire (for), yearning (for)

anheloso *a* difficult, labored (of breathing); anxious, longing

anidar *vi* to nest (birds); swell; *vt* shelter, protect; *vr* nest; dwell; nestle

anilla *f,* curtain ring; *pl* gymnastic rings

anillo *m,* finger ring; small ring; coil (of serpents and ropes). **a. de compromiso** *Mexico* engagement ring. *inf* **venir como a. al dedo,** to fit like a glove; come just at the right moment

ánima *f,* soul, spirit; soul in purgatory; bore (of firearms); *pl* prayer bell for the souls of the departed

animación *f*, liveliness, gaiety; animation, vivacity; bustle, movement

animal *m*, animal; *inf* dolt, brute. *a* animal; *inf* brutish, doltish

animalada *f*, *inf* stupidity, foolishness

animalidad *f*, animalism

animar *vt* to animate; encourage, incite; invigorate, enliven; make gay, cheer up; make attractive, adorn; *vr* take heart; make up one's mind; cheer up; grow gay

animismo *m*, animism

ánimo *m*, soul, spirit; courage; endurance, fortitude; will, intention; mind. **con ánimo de + inf., **with the intention of + *ger*. **¡Á.! **Courage!

animosidad *f*, hatred, animosity, dislike

animoso *a* spirited, lively; valiant

aniñado *a* childlike, childish

aniquilable *a* destructible

aniquilación *f*, destruction, annihilation; suppression; decay

aniquilador (-ra) *a* destructive, annihilating. *n* destroyer

aniquilamiento *m*, See **aniquilación**

aniquilar *vt* to annihilate, destroy completely; *vr* waste away, decay

anís *m*, aniseed, anise; anisette (liqueur)

anisar *vt* to flavor with aniseed

anisete *m*, anisette

aniversario *a* annual. *m*, anniversary

Anjeo Anjou

ano *m*, anus

anoche *adv* last night; the previous night

anochecer *vi irr* to grow night; become dark; be in a place *or* be doing something at nightfall (e.g. **Anochecimos en Lérida, **We were in Lerida at nightfall). *vr poet* be obscured or darkened. *m*, nightfall, dusk. See **conocer**

anochecida *f*, dusk, late twilight

anodino *a med* anodyne; ineffective, useless; inoffensive. *m*, anodyne

anomalía *f*, anomaly, inconstancy, irregularity; *ast* anomaly

anómalo *a* anomalous, abnormal, unusual

anonadación, *f*, **anonadamiento** *m*, destruction, annihilation; despair, melancholy; suppression

anonadar *vt* to destroy, annihilate; suppress; *fig* overwhelm, depress; humble

anónimo *a* anonymous. *m*, anonymity; anonymous letter; unsigned literary work

anormal *a* abnormal; irregular, unusual. *mf* abnormal person

anormalidad *f*, abnormality; irregularity, inconsistency

anotación *f*, annotation; *Lat. Am.* score (in sports)

anotador (-ra) *n* annotator

anotar *vt* to annotate; note down

anquilostoma *m*, *med* hookworm

ánsar *m*, goose; drake

ansarino *a* goose. *m*, gosling

anseático *a* Hanseatic

ansia (de) *f*, anxiety, trouble; grief; longing (for), yearning (for); greed

ansiar *vt* to long for, yearn for; covet, desire

ansiedad *f*, anxiety, anguish, worry

ansión *f*, intense desire

ansioso *a* anxious; grievous, painful; eager, desirous; greedy

anta *f*, *zool* elk; obelisk

antagónico *a* antagonistic

antagonismo *m*, antagonism

antagonista *mf* antagonist, adversary

antaño *adv* last year, yesteryear; long ago

antártico *a* antarctic

ante *m*, *zool* elk; suede; buffalo

ante *prep* in the presence of, before; regarding, in the face of (e.g. **a. deber tan alto, **in the face of so noble a duty)

anteado *a* beige, buff-colored, fawn

anteanoche *adv* the night before last

anteayer *adv* the day before yesterday

antebrazo *m*, forearm

antecámara *f*, antechamber

antecedente *m*, antecedent. **antecedentes** *m pl* background (of a case, situation, etc.)

antecedentemente *adv* previously

anteceder *vt* to precede

antecesor (-ra) *a* previous. *n* predecessor. *m*, forebear, ancestor

antecoger *vt* to carry in front, lead before; pick too soon

antecomedor *m*, breakfast nook, breakfast room

antedata *f*, antedate

antedatar *vt* to antedate

antedicho *a* aforementioned, aforesaid

antediluviano *a* antediluvian

antelación *f*, advance, anticipation

antellevar *vt*, *Mexico* to knock down, run over

antemano, de *adv* in advance, beforehand

antemeridiano *a* antemeridian, forenoon

antena *f*, antenna; *rad* aerial

antenacido *a* born prematurely

antenombre *m*, title (placed before name)

anteojera *f*, horse's blinker; eyeglass case

anteojo *m*, spy-glass, small telescope; *pl* horse's blinkers; eyeglasses, glasses; spectacles; goggles

antepagar *vt* to pay in advance

antepalco *m*, vestibule of a box in a theater

antepasado *a* previous, past. *m*, ancestor (gen. *pl*)

antepecho *m*, parapet; windowsill; railing, balustrade; front (of a theater box, etc.); *naut* bulwark

antepenúltimo *a* antepenultimate, second from the last

anteponer *vt irr* to place before; prefer, favor. See **poner**

anteproyecto *m*, first sketch, preliminary work or plan

antepuerta *f*, door-curtain, portiere; *mil* anteport

anterior *a* previous, former; anterior; aforementioned, preceding

anteriormente *adv* beforehand, previously

antes *adv* before; rather, on the contrary; previously. **a. bien, **rather, sooner. **a. con a.** *or* **cuanto a., **as soon as possible

antesala *f*, antechamber

antevíspera *f*, two days previously

antiaéreo *a* antiaircraft. *m pl*. **(cañones) antiaéreos, **A.A. guns

anticiclón *m*, anticyclone

anticipación *f*, anticipation; advance

anticipada *f*, foul thrust (in fencing, etc.)

anticipadamente *adv* in advance; prematurely

anticipado *a* in advance; premature

anticipador *a* anticipatory

anticipar *vt* to anticipate; foresee; forestall; advance (money); lend; *vr* happen before time; (*with prep a*) act in advance of, anticipate; get ahead of oneself

anticipo *m*, anticipation, advance; advance payment; sum of money lent

anticlerical *a* anticlerical

anticlímax *m*, anticlimax

anticonstitucional *a* unconstitutional

anticuado *a* antiquated, ancient

anticuario *m*, antiquarian, antique dealer

antídoto *m*, antidote

antiesclavista *a* antislavery. *mf* antislavist

antiespasmódico *a* and *m*, *med* antispasmodic

antiestético *a* unesthetic

antietimológico *a* non-etymological, unetymological

antifaz *m*, mask; face-covering

antiflogístico *a* and *m*, *med* antiphlogistic

antigramatical *a* ungrammatical

antigualla *f*, antique; ancient custom; anything out-of-date

antiguamente *adv* in time past, formerly

antiguamiento *m*, seniority

antigüedad *f*, antiquity; ancients; length of service (in an employment); *pl* antiquities

antiguo *a* ancient, very old; antique; senior (in an employment); former. *m*, senior member (of a community, etc.). *m pl*, ancients. **A. Testamento,** Old Testament. **de a.,** from ancient times. **en lo antiguo,** in ancient times; in former times, in days of yore

antillano (-na) *a* and *n* of or from the Antilles

Antillas, las the Antilles

antílope *m*, antelope

antimacasar *m*, antimacassar

antimilitarismo *m*, antimilitarism

antimilitarista *a* antimilitaristic

antimonárquico *a* antimonarchical

antimonio *m*, *met* antimony

antipalúdico *a* antimalarial

antipara *f*, screen, shield

antiparras *f pl*, *inf* spectacles, eyeglasses, glasses

antipatía *f*, antipathy

antipático *a* disagreeable; unattractive

antipatriótico *a* unpatriotic

antípoda *a* and *m*, or *f*, antipode

antiquísimo *a sup*, *antiguo*, most ancient

antisemita *a* anti-Semitic. *mf* anti-Semite

antisemitismo *m*, anti-Semitism

antiséptico *a* and *m*, antiseptic

antisifilítico *a med* anti-syphilitic

antisocial *a* antisocial

antítesis *f*, antithesis

antitético *a* antithetic, contrasted

antófago *a* anthophagous, flower-eating

antojadizo *a* capricious, fanciful, whimsical

antojarse *vr* to have a fancy for, want (e.g. **Se me antoja marcharme al campo,** I have a yen to go to the country); suspect, imagine

antojito *m*, *Mexico* typical Mexican dish (of food)

antojo *m*, caprice, fancy, whim; desire, will; *pl* birthmark

antología *f*, anthology

antólogo *m*, anthologist

antonomasia *f*, antonomasia. **por a.,** by analogy, by transference

antorcha *f*, torch, flambeau

antracita *f*, anthracite

ántrax *m*, *med* anthrax

antro *m*, cave, cavern; *anat* antrum

antropofagia *f*, cannibalism, anthropophagy

antropófago (-ga) *a* cannibalistic. *n* cannibal

antropología *f*, anthropology

antropológico *a* anthropological

antropólogo *m*, anthropologist

antropometría *f*, anthropometry

antropomorfo *a* anthropomorphous

antroposofía *f*, anthroposophy

antruejo *m*, three days of carnival before Lent

anual *a* yearly, annual

anualidad *f*, annuity

anuario *m*, directory, yearbook, handbook

anubarrado *a* covered with clouds, cloudy

anublado *a* lowering, overcast; clouded

anublar *vt* to cloud; darken, obscure; blight (plants); *vr* cloud over; become blighted or mildewed

anudar *vt* to knot; tie, fasten; join; continue; **a. amistad de,** to strike up a friendship with. **a. la corbata, to** put on one's tie, tie one's tie; *vr* grow stunted

anulable *a* annulable, voidable

anulación *f*, annulment, abrogation

anular *a* annular, ring-shaped. *vt* to annul; *math* cancel out

anuloso *a* annulate, formed of rings

anunciación *f*, *ecc* Annunciation; announcement

anunciador (-ra), *n* **anunciante** *mf* announcer; advertiser

anunciar *vt* to announce; publish, proclaim; advertise; foretell, presage. **Anuncian lluvia,** The forecast calls for rain

anuncio *m*, announcement; publication, proclamation; advertisement; presage, omen. **a. luminoso,** sky-sign

anverso *m*, obverse, face

anzuelo *m*, fish-hook; *cul* fritter; *inf* attraction, inducement

añadido *m*, hair-switch; make-weight

añadidura *f*, addition; make-weight, extra

añadir *vt* to add; increase

añagaza *f*, decoy bird; enticement, lure

añejo *a* very old

añicos *m pl*, fragments, small pieces. **hacer a.,** to break into fragments

añil *m*, indigo; indigo blue

año *m*, year; *pl* birthday. **a. bisiesto,** leap-year. **a. económico,** fiscal year. **A. Nuevo,** New Year. **tener (siete) años,** to be (seven) years old. **los Años Bobos,** the period from 1874 to 1898 in Spain

añoranza *f*, homesickness, loneliness; nostalgia

añorar *vi* to be homesick or lonely

añoso *a* very old, full of years

añublo *m*, mildew

aojamiento *m*, evil eye, wicked spell

aojar *vt* to bewitch, place under a spell; spoil, frustrate

aojo *m*, evil eye; magic spell

aorta *f*, *anat* aorta

aovillarse *vr* to roll oneself into a ball; curl up

apabullante *a* crushing, flattening

apacentadero *m*, grazing land, pasture

apacentamiento *m*, pasturage; grazing

apacentar *vt irr* to put out to grass; teach, instruct; satisfy (one's desires); *vr* graze (cattle). See **acertar**

apachurrar *vt*, *Mexico* to press (button, etc.)

apacibilidad *f*, agreeableness; mildness; peaceableness

apacible *a* agreeable; mild; peaceable; calm, peaceful

apaciguamiento *m*, appeasement, soothing, pacification

apaciguar *vt* to appease, pacify; calm

apadrinar *vt* to act as godfather to; be best man to (at a wedding); act as a second for (in a duel); sponsor; favor

apagable *a* extinguishable

apagado *a* timid, nervous; pale (of colors); dull, lusterless

apagador (-ra) *a* quenching. *n* extinguisher. *m*, candle-snuffer; damper (of a piano)

apagaincendios *m*, ship's fire-extinguisher

apagamiento *m*, quenching, extinguishment

apagar *vt* to extinguish, put out; *fig* quench, moderate; slake (lime); *art* tone down (colors); shut off (engines)

apagarrisas *mf* crapehanger, killjoy, wet blanket

apagavelas *m*, candle-snuffer

apalabrar *vt* to make an appointment with; discuss, consider

apaleamiento *m*, beating, thrashing

apalear *vt* to beat, thrash; knock down with a stick

apandillarse *vr* to form a gang or group

apañar *vt* to take away, remove; seize; steal; dress, get ready; *inf* wrap up; patch, repair; *vr inf* grow skilful

apaño *m*, dexterity, skill; craft, guile

aparador *m*, sideboard; workshop; *ecc* credence (table); *Mexico* (shop) window

aparato *m*, apparatus; equipment, utensils; pomp, ostentation; symptoms; sign, circumstance, token. **a. digestivo,** digestive system; digestive tract. **a. fonador,** speech apparatus

aparatoso *a* showy, ostentatious. **incendio. a.,** conflagration, large fire

aparear *vt* to match, make equal; pair; mate (animals); *vr* love in pairs

aparecer(se) *vi* and *vr irr* to appear; seem; be. See **conocer**

aparecido *m*, apparition, specter

aparejador *m*, overseer, foreman; *naut* rigger

aparejar *vt* to prepare, make ready; saddle (horses); prime, size; rig (a ship)

aparejo *m*, preparation, arrangement; harness, trappings; *naut* rigging; *naut* gear; priming, sizing; *mech* tackle; *pl* equipment

aparentar *vt* to pretend, simulate

aparente *a* seeming, apparent; obvious, visible; suitable, proper

aparición *f*, appearance, arrival; apparition, phantom

apariencia *f*, appearance, looks, probability, likelihood; outward semblance; *pl theat* scenery

apartadamente *adv* apart, in private; secretly

apartadero *m*, passing place for cars; railway siding; grass verge. **a. ferroviario,** railway marshaling yard

apartado *a* distant, far off; secluded; different. *m*, post-office box; secluded room; smelting house; sorting of cattle; selection of bulls for a bullfight

apartamento *m Lat. Am.* (*except Argentina*) apartment

apartamiento *m*, separation; withdrawal, retiral; seclusion; apartment, flat; *law* withdrawal of an action

apartar *vt* to separate; remove (e.g. an obstacle), take away; *rw* shunt; dissuade; sort; *vr* obtain a divorce; *law* withdraw an action. **apartarse de la tradición,** to depart from tradition

aparte *adv* aside, on one side; separately; *theat* aside; besides; beyond. *m*, *theat* aside; paragraph; space between words. **¡Aparte!** Move to one side!

apartidario *a* non-partisan

apasionado (-da) *a* impassioned; fervent, devoted; passionate; enthusiastic. *n* admirer, lover; enthusiast

apasionamiento *m*, passion

apasionar *vt* to arouse to passion; pain; *vr* (*with por*) grow passionately fond of; become enthusiastic for

apatía *f*, apathy

apático *a* apathetic

apeadero *m*, mounting-block; halt, stopping place; wayside railway station; pied-à-terre, occasional dwelling

apear *vt* to dismount; hobble (horse); survey, map out; fell a tree; *fig* overcome (difficulties); *inf* dissuade; prop; remove, bring down; scotch (a wheel); *vr* dismount; alight, step off

apechugar *vi* to push with the breast; *inf* put up with reluctantly

apedazar *vt* to tear; break; mend, repair

apedrear *vt* to stone; stone to death; *vi impers* hail; *vr* be damaged by hail (crops)

apegarse *vr* to grow fond (of), become attached (to)

apego *m*, fondness, inclination; affection, attachment

apelación *f*, *law* appeal; *inf* doctor's consultation

apelante *a* and *mf law* appellant

apelar *vi law* to appeal; (*with prep a*) have recourse to; *vi* be of the same color (horses)

apellidar *vt* to name, call; acclaim; call to arms; *vr* be named

apellido *m*, surname; nickname; call to arms; clamor; name

apenar *vt* to grieve, afflict; cause sorrow

apenarse *vr Lat. Am.* to be ashamed

apenas *adv* scarcely; immediately, as soon as; with trouble or difficulty

apéndice *m*, appendix, supplement; *anat* appendix

apendicitis *f*, appendicitis

Apeninos, los the Apennines

apeo *m*, survey; scaffolding; prop, support

apercibimiento *m*, preparation; provision; warning; *law* summons

apercibir *vt* to prepare, furnish; warn; *law* summon

apergaminarse *vr inf* to shrivel, dry up (with old age, etc.)

aperitivo *a* aperitive. *m*, aperient; aperitive, appetiser

apertura *f*, opening; inauguration; reading (of a will)

apesadumbrar *vt* to sadden, afflict, grieve

apestar *vt* to infect with the plague; catch the plague; *fig* corrupt; *inf* pester, annoy; *vi* stink

apestoso *a* stinking, putrid

apetecer *vt irr* to want, desire; attract. See **conocer**

apetecible *a* attractive, desirable

apetencia *f*, appetite; desire

apetito *m*, appetite

apetitoso *a* appetising; tasty, savory; attractive

apiadarse *vr* (*with de*) to have compassion on, be sorry for

ápice *m*, apex; peak, summit, top; orthographic accent; iota, tittle; crux (of a problem)

apicultor (-ra) *n* apiarist, beekeeper

apicultura *f*, apiculture, beekeeping

apilar *vt* to pile, heap

apimplado, -a *a*, *Lat. Am.* boozed up, drunk

apiñado *a* crowded, serried

apiñamiento *m*, crowding; congestion

apiñar *vt* to group together, crowd; *vr* crowd

apio *m*, celery

apisonadora *f*, steam-roller; roller

apisonar *vt* to roll, stamp, flatten, ram down; tamp, pack down (e.g. tobacco in a pipe)

apizarrado *a* slate-colored

aplacable *a* appeasable, placable

aplacamiento *m*, appeasement

aplacar *vt* to appease, calm; moderate, mitigate

aplacible *a* agreeable, pleasant

aplanacalles *mf, Lat. Am.* idler, lay about, lazybones

aplanar *vt* to flatten, level; roll (pastry); *inf* dumbfound, overwhelm; *vr* collapse (buildings); lose heart

aplastar *vt* to flatten, squash, crush; *inf* squash flat, floor

aplaudir *vt* to applaud, clap; praise, commend, approve

aplauso *m*, applause; clapping, plaudit; approbation, commendation

aplazamiento *m*, postponement; appointment; summons

aplazar *vt* to summon, arrange a meeting; postpone; adjourn

aplicabilidad *f*, applicability

aplicable *a* applicable

aplicación *f*, application; diligence, assiduity; appliqué, ornamentation

aplicado *a* diligent, hardworking; appliqué

aplicar *vt* to apply; impute; intend, destine (for processions); *law* adjudge; *vr* engage in; apply oneself. **a. el oído,** to listen intently. **a. sanciones,** *pol* to impose sanctions

aplomado *a* self-possessed, dignified; leaden, lead-colored

aplomar *vt* and *vi* to plumb, test with a plumb-line; *vr* collapse, fall down

aplomo *m*, self-possession, dignity; sang-froid

apocado *a* spiritless, timid; base, mean

Apocalipsis *m*, Apocalypse

apocalíptico *a* apocalyptic

apocamiento *m*, timidity, pusillanimity; depression, discouragement; shyness; baseness, meanness

apocar *vt* to diminish, reduce; humiliate, scorn

apócrifo *a* fictitious, false; apocryphal. **Apócrifos,** Apocrypha

apodar *vt* to nickname

apoderado *a* authorized. *m*, attorney; deputy; proxy

apoderar *vt* to authorize; grant powers of attorney to; *vr* (*with de*) seize, take possession of

apodo *m*, nickname

apogeo *m*, *ast* apogee; *fig* zenith, peak (of fame, etc.)

apolillar *vt* to eat clothes (moths); *vr* be moth-eaten

apologista *mf* apologist

apólogo *m*, apologue, moral fable

apoltronarse *vr* to grow idle

apoplejía *f*, apoplexy

aporrear *vt* to beat, cudgel; *vr* work hard, slog away

aportación *f*, contribution; occasionment

aportar *vt* to cause, occasion; contribute; *vi naut* reach port; **El buque aportó a Nueva York,** The ship reached New York, The ship sailed into New York harbor; arrive at an unexpected place

aposentador *m*, usher; *mil* billeting officer

aposentar *vt* to lodge, give hospitality to; *vr* lodge, settle down

aposento *m*, room; suite, apartments; lodging, accommodation; *theat* box

aposición *f*, *gram* apposition

apósito *m*, poultice, external application; (medical) dressing

apostadero *m*, *naut* naval station; placing or stationing (of soldiers)

apostar *vt irr* to bet; station (soldiers); *vi* compete, rival. See **contar**

apostasía *f*, apostasy

apóstata *mf* apostate

apostilla *f*, marginal note, gloss

apóstol *m*, apostle

apostólico *a* apostolic

apóstrofe *m*, or *f*, apostrophe, hortatory exclamation

apóstrofo *m*, *gram* apostrophe

apostura *f*, neatness, spruceness

apotegma *m*, apothegm, maxim

apoteosis *f*, apotheosis

apoyar *vt* (*with en*) to lean against; rest upon; *vt* uphold, favor; confirm, bear out; droop the head (horses); second (a motion); *vi* (*with en*) rest on; lean against; *vr* (*with en*) rest on; lean against; **apoyarse de codos,** to lean on one's elbows; be upheld by; *fig* be founded on; *fig* depend on, lean on

apoyo *m*, support, prop; windowsill; sill; assistance; backing, support

apreciable *a* appreciable; estimable; important

apreciación *f*, appreciation; valuation, estimate

apreciador (-ra) *a* appreciatory. *n* appreciator

apreciar *vt* to estimate (values); appreciate; like, esteem, have a regard for

apreciativo *a* appreciative

aprecio *m*, valuation; appreciation, regard

aprehender *vt* to apprehend, catch; seize (contraband); understand, grasp

aprehensión *f*, seizure, apprehension

apremiador, apremiante *a* urgent, pressing

apremiar *vt* to hurry; urge, press; force, oblige; burden, oppress (with taxes)

apremio *m*, insistence, pressure; compulsion; demand note

aprendedor (-ra) *n* learner

aprender *vt* to learn. **a. de memoria,** to learn by heart

aprendiz (-za) *a* apprentice

aprendizaje *m*, apprenticeship. **hacer el a.,** to serve an apprenticeship

aprensión *f*, capture; fear, apprehension; suspicion, fancy; prejudice, scruple

aprensivo *a* apprehensive, nervous, fearful

apresar *vt* to nab, catch; capture (a ship); imprison; fetter

aprestar *vt* to prepare, arrange; dress (fabrics)

apresto *m*, preparation, arrangement; dressing (for cloth)

apresurar *vt* to quicken; *vr* hasten, be quick

apretado *a* difficult, dangerous; tight; crabbed (of handwriting); clustered (e.g. **casas apretadas alrededor de la sinagoga,** houses clustered around the synagogue). *inf* mean, close-fisted. *m*, small close handwriting

apretadura *f*, tightening, compression

apretar *vt irr* to tighten; compress; urge on, press; harass, vex; trouble, worry; speed up; squeeze; press (bells, gun triggers, etc.); *vi* increase, grow worse (storms, heat, etc.); pinch, hurt (shoes). **a. los pasos,** to quicken one's pace. *inf* **a. a correr,** to take to one's heels. **¡Aprieta!** *inf* Nonsense! It can't be! See **acertar**

apretón *m*, squeeze, grip, pressure; *inf* sprint, spurt; *inf* fix, pickle. **a. de manos,** handshake

apretujamiento *m*, squeezing together

apretujar *vt inf* to squeeze, hug

aprieto *m*, crowd, crush; urgency; *inf* jam, trouble, fix

aprisa *adv* quickly, in a hurry

aprisco *m*, cattle-shed; sheepfold

aprisionar *vt* to imprison; bind, fetter; tie

aprobación *f*, approbation, approval, commendation; ratification (of a bill); pass (in an examination)

aprobado *m*, pass certificate (in examinations)

aprobar *vt irr* to approve; pass (in an examination). See **contar**

aprontar *vt*, *Lat. Am.* to pay in advance, prepay

apropiación *f*, appropriation; application; adaptation

apropiado *a* appropriate, suitable, proper

apropiar *vt* to appropriate; adapt, fit; *vr* appropriate, take possession

aprovechable *a* usable, available

aprovechado *a* advantageous; assiduous, conscientious; capable; thrifty

aprovechador *a* self-seeking

aprovechamiento *m*, utilization, employment; exploitation; profitable use

aprovechar *vi* to be advantageous or useful; be beneficial; make progress (in studies, etc.); *vt* use; profit by; *vr* take advantage of, make use of. **¡Que aproveche!** May it do you good! (said to anyone eating)

aprovisionar *vt* to provision, supply

aproximación *f*, approximation; consolation prize (in a lottery)

aproximadamente *adv* approximately; nearly, almost

aproximar *vt* to bring or draw nearer; *vr* approach; be almost, be approximately; draw closer

aptitud *f*, aptitude, ability; fitness; propensity

apto *a* suitable, fitting; competent. **no apta para menores,** not suitable for children (of films, etc.)

apuesta *f*, bet, wager; competition

apuestas benéficas de fútbol football pools

apuesto *a* elegant; handsome, well set-up

apuntación *f*, noting down; note; *mus* notation

apuntador (-ra) *n* note-taker; observer. *m*, *theat* prompter; *theat* stage-manager

apuntalar *vt* to prop, prop up, underpin, bolster

apuntamiento *m*, summary; *law* indictment, minute

apuntar *vt* to aim (a gun, etc.); point to, indicate; note down; mark; sketch; sharpen; bet (at cards); fasten temporarily; *inf* mend; *theat* prompt; suggest, hint (e.g. **La fecha está apuntada en varios manuscritos,** The date is hinted at in various manuscripts); *vi* begin to appear. *inf* **a. y no dar,** to promise and do nothing

apunte *m*, abstract; note; annotation; sketch; *theat* prompt or prompter or prompt book or cue; stake in a card game

apuñalado *a* dagger-shaped

apuñalar *vt* to stab, attack with a dagger

apurado *a* poor, needy; dangerous; difficult; accurate, exact; hurried

apurar *vt* to purify; drain; exhaust; finish, conclude; examine closely, scrutinize (e.g. **apurar una materia,** to exhaust a subject, examine a subject thoroughly); irritate, make impatient; urge on, hasten; *vr* be anxious, fret; *Lat. Am.* hurry, hurry up

apuro *m*, difficulty, fix; poverty, want; anxiety, worry. **pasar apuros,** to have a hard time

aquejar *vt* to afflict; weary, beset, harass; *vr* complain, hurry

aquel, a m aquella, a f aquellos, a m pl aquellas a f pl, that, those; that or those over there (farther off than **ese**)

aquel *m*, charm, attraction, it

aquél, aquélla, aquéllos, aquéllas *dem pron m, f,* sing. and pl., that, the one, those, those ones; the former. e.g. **La casa que ve usted a lo lejos aquélla es la vivienda de mi tío,** The house that you see in the distance, that is my uncle's dwelling. **Éste no me gusta pero aquél sí,** I do not like the latter, but I like the former

aquelarre *m*, witches' sabbath

aquello *dem pron neut* that; the fact; the matter, the affair, the former (remark, idea, etc.). e.g. **Todo a. por fin acabó,** All that came to an end at last. **a. de,** the fact that

aquende *adv* on this side (rarely used)

aquí *adv* here. **de a.,** hence the fact that. **¡He a.!** Behold!

aquietar *vt* to calm, soothe

aquilatar *vt* to assay; scrutinize; examine, weigh up (persons)

aquistar *vt* to attain, acquire

ara *f,* altar; **en aras de,** in honor of; for the sake of

árabe *a* Arab, Arabic. *mf* Arab. *m,* Arabic (language)

arabesco *a* Arabic. *m, art* arabesque

Arabia Saudita Saudi Arabia

arábigo *a* Arabic. *m,* Arabic (language)

arácnido *m, zool* arachnid

arado *m,* plow

arador *a* plowing. *m,* plowman. **a. de la sarna,** *ent* scabies mite

aragonés (-esa) *a* and *n* Aragonese

araguato *m, Lat. Am.* howler monkey

arahuaco *a* and *n* Arawak, Arawakian

arancel *m,* tariff, duty, tax

arancelar to charge tuition for (e.g. **a. la universidad,** charge tuition for college studies)

arancelario *a* tariff, tax; customs

arándano *m, bot* bilberry

arandela *f,* candle-dripper; *mech* washer; wall candelabrum

araña *f,* spider; chandelier; *Lat. Am.* whore

arañacielos *m,* skyscraper

arañar *vt* to scratch; *inf* scrape together, hoard

arañazo *m,* scratch

arar *vt* to plough. **a. en el mar,** to labor in vain

arbitrador (-ra) *n* arbitrator

arbitraje *m,* arbitration; arbitrament, decision

arbitrar *vt* to judge freely; *law* arbitrate, mediate; devise; invent; marshal (money, resources, etc.); draft (a law) *vr* make shift, contrive

arbitrariedad *f,* arbitrariness

arbitrario *a* arbitral, mediatory; arbitrary, capricious

arbitrio *m,* free will; arbitration; means, way; discretion; arbitrament, judgment; *pl* rates, municipal taxes

árbitro (-ra) *a* arbitrary. *n* arbiter. *m, sport* umpire; referee

árbol *m,* tree; *mech* shaft; *naut* mast; axis of a winding stair. **a. de amor** *or* **a. de Judas,** Judas tree. **a. de la ciencia (del bien y del mal),** Tree of Knowledge (of good and evil). **a. de levas,** *mech* camshaft. **a. del pan,** breadfruit tree. *naut* **a. mayor,** mainmast. **a. motor** *mech,* drivingshaft

arbolado *a* tree-covered, wooded. *m,* copse, woodland

arboladura *f, naut* masts and spars

arbolar *vt* to hoist (flags); *naut* fit with masts; place upright; *vr* rear, prance (horses)

arboleda *f,* copse, grove, spinney

arbotante *m,* flying buttress

arbusto *m,* shrub, woody plant

arca *f,* chest; money-box, coffer; ark; *pl* (treasury) vaults. **a. caudal,** strong box. **a. de agua,** watertower. **a. de la alianza.** *or* **a. del testamento,** Ark of the Covenant (Bible). **a. de Noé,** Noah's Ark; lumber box

arcabucero *m,* arquebusier; maker of arquebuses

arcabuz *m,* arquebus

arcada *f,* arcade; series of arches; *pl* sickness, nausea

árcade *a* and *mf* Arcadian

arcaico *a* archaic

arcaísmo *m,* archaism

arcángel *m,* archangel

arcano *a* secret. *m,* mystery, arcanum

arce *m, bot* maple tree

archifeliz *a* extremely happy, in bliss

archimillonario (-ia) *a* and *n* multimillionaire

archipiélago *m,* archipelago

Archipiélago de Colón *m,* Galapagos Islands

archivar *vt* to place in an archive; file (papers)

archivero *m,* archivist, keeper of the archives; librarian; registrar; (Mexico) file cabinet, filing cabinet

archivista *mf* archivist; file clerk, filing clerk

archivo *m,* archives

arcilla *f,* clay

arcilloso *a* clayey, like or full of clay

arcipreste *m,* archpriest

arco *m, geom* arc; *mil* bow; bow (of a stringed instrument); hoop (of casks, etc.); *arch* arch; *Lat. Am.* goal (in sports). **a. del cielo** *or* **a. de San Martín** *or* **a. iris,** rainbow. **a. voltaico,** electric arc. *mus* **para a.,** for strings

arder *vi* to burn; shine, gleam; *fig* burn (with passion, etc.); *vt* to set alight, burn

ardid *a* crafty. *m,* trick, stratagem

ardiente *a* burning; ardent, passionate; vehement; enthusiastic; flame-colored; fiery-red

ardilla *f,* squirrel; *Lat. Am.* wheeler-dealer

ardite *m,* ancient Spanish coin of little value; *fig* farthing, fig, straw. **no valer un a.,** to be not worth a straw

ardor *m,* great heat; zeal, earnestness; passion, ardor; courage

ardoroso *a* ardorous

arduo *a* arduous

área *f,* area; small plot of ground; common threshing floor; arc (surface measure)

arena *f,* sand; arena; grit, gravel. **a. movediza,** quicksand

arenal *m,* quicksand; sand pit; sandy place

arenero (-ra) *n* sand merchant. *m,* sand-box (carried by railway engines)

arenga *f,* harangue, discourse *Argentina* argument, fight, quarrel

arenilla *f,* sand (for drying writing)

arenisca *f,* sandstone

arenisco *a* sandy

arenque *m,* herring

arete *m,* earring

argamasa *f,* mortar

argayo *m,* landslide; (Asturias) **a. de nieve,** avalanche

Árgel Algiers

Argelia Algeria

argelino (-na) *a* and *n* Algerian

argentado *a* silvered; silvery

argénteo *a* silver; silvery

argentífero *a* silver-yielding

argentino (-na) *a* silvery. *a* and *n* Argentinian. *m,* Argentinian gold coin

argento *m,* silver. **a. vivo,** mercury

argolla *f,* thick metal ring (for hitching, etc.); croquet (game); stocks, pillory; hoop, iron arch; *Lat. Am.* wedding ring

argonauta *m, myth* Argonaut; *zool* paper nautilus, argonaut

argucia *f,* sophism, quibble; subtlety

argüir *vt irr* to deduce, imply; prove; reveal, manifest; accuse; *vi* argue, debate; dispute, oppose. See **huir**

argumentación (-ra) *a* argumentative. *n* arguer

argumentar *vi* to argue; dispute; oppose

argumento *m,* contention, case; theme (of a book, etc.); argument, discussion

aridez *f,* aridity, dryness; drought; sterility, barrenness; dullness, lack of interest

árido *a* dry, arid; sterile, barren; uninteresting, dull

ariete *m, mil* battering ram

arisco *a* unsociable, surly; wild, shy (animals)

arista *f, bot* arista, awn, beard; pebble; edge, side

aristocracia *f,* aristocracy

aristócrata *mf* aristocrat

aristocrático *a* aristocratic

aristotélico *a* Aristotelian

aritmética *f,* arithmetic

aritmético (-ca) *a* arithmetical. *n* arithmetician

arlequín *m,* harlequin; *inf* fool, buffoon; Neapolitan ice-cream

arma *f,* weapon; *mil* arm, branch; bull's horn; *pl* troops, army; means, way; arms, coat of arms. **a. arrojadiza,** missile. **a. blanca,** steel weapon. **a. de fuego,** firearm. **¡Armas al hombro!** Shoulder Arms! **armas portátiles,** small arms. *inf* **de armas tomar,** belligerent; resolute. **pasar por las armas,** *mil* to shoot. **presentar las armas,** *mil* to present arms. **ser a. de dos filos,** *fig* to cut both ways

armada *f,* navy, armada; fleet, squadron; *Argentina* lasso

armadía *f,* raft, pontoon

armador (-ra) *n* supplier, outfitter. *m,* shipowner; pirate, privateer; jacket; assembler, fitter

armadura *f,* armature, armor; frame, framework; skeleton (of a building); skeleton (of vertebrates); *phys* armature; plate armor (of persons)

armamento *m, mil* armament; arms, military equipment

armar *vt* to arm; *mech* mount; man (guns); put together, assemble; roll (a cigaret); reinforce (concrete); *inf* arrange, prepare; *inf* occasion (quarrels); *inf* outfit; *naut* equip; commission (a ship); *vr* prepare oneself, arm oneself. **a. caballero,** to knight. **a. los remos,** to ship the oars. *inf* **armarla,** to cause a row or quarrel

armario *m,* cupboard; wardrobe. **a. de luna,** wardrobe with a mirror

armatoste *m,* unwieldy piece of furniture; *fig inf* dead weight, clumsy person; snare

armazón *f,* frame, framework; ship's hulk. *m, anat* skeleton

armenio (-ia) *a* and *n* Armenian. *m,* Armenian language

armería *f,* armory; heraldry; gunsmith's craft or shop

armero *m,* gunsmith, armorer; stand for weapons. **a. mayor,** Royal Armorer

armiño *m,* ermine

armisticio *m,* armistice

armón de artillería *m,* gun-carriage

armonía *f,* harmony; friendship, concord; *mus* harmony

armónica (de boca) *f,* mouth-organ

armónico *a* harmonious. *a* and *m, mus* harmonic

armonio *m,* harmonium

armonioso *a* harmonious

armonización *f, mus* harmonization

armonizar *vt* to bring into harmony; *mus* harmonize

arnero *m, Lat. Am.* sieve

arnés *m,* armor; harness; *pl* horse trappings; *inf* equipment, tools

aro *m,* hoop; rim (of wheel, etc.); napkin-ring; croquet hoop; *bot* wild arum; child's hoop; *Lat. Am.* earring **a. de empaquetadura,** *mech* gasket

aroma *m,* aroma, fragrance; balsam; sweet-smelling herb

aromático *a* aromatic

arpa *f,* harp. **a. eolia,** Eolian harp

arpar *vt* to scratch, claw; tear, rend

arpegio *m, mus* arpeggio

arpía *f,* harpy

arpicordio *m,* harpsichord

arpista *mf* harpist, harp player

arpón *m,* harpoon

arponear *vt* to harpoon

arponero *m,* harpooner; harpoon maker

arquear *vt* to arch; bend; beat (wool); gauge (ship's capacity); *vi* retch

arqueo *m,* arching; bending, curving; *naut* tonnage; gauging (of ship's capacity); *com* examination of deposits and contents of safe

arqueología *f,* archeology

arqueológico *a* archeological

arqueólogo *m,* archeologist

arquero *m, com* cashier, treasurer; *mil* archer

arquitecto *m,* architect. **a. de jardines,** landscape gardener

arquitectura *f,* architecture

arquitrabe *m,* architrave

arrabal *m,* suburb, district; *pl* outskirts

arracada *f,* pendant-earring

arracimarse *vr* to cluster; group

arraigadamente *adv* deeply, firmly

arraigado *a* deep-rooted; firm; convinced

arraigar *vi* to take root; *vi* and *vr fig* become established, take hold; *vr* settle; take up residence

arraigo *m,* rooting; settlement, establishment; landed property

arrancaclavos *m,* nail-puller

arrancadero *m, sport* starting-point

arrancar *vt* to uproot; pull out; wrench; tear off; extirpate; obtain by threats; clear one's throat; *vt* and *vi naut* put on speed; *vi* start (a race); *inf* leave, quit; derive, originate **¡Arrancan!** And they're off! (races)

arrancarse *vr, Lat. Am.* to kick the bucket, pop off

arranque *m,* uprooting; extirpation; wrenching, pulling, seizing; stimulus (of passion); sudden impulse; *mech* start; *mech* starter. **a. automático,** self-starter

arras *fpl,* dowry; coins given by bridegroom to his bride; earnest money, token

arrasamiento *m,* demolition, destruction; leveling

arrasar *vt* to demolish, destroy; level; fill to the brim; *vi* and *vr* clear up (sky). **ojos arrasados de lágrimas,** eyes brimming with tears

arrastrado *a inf* poverty-stricken, wretched; *inf* knavish; unhappy, unfortunate

arrastrar *vt* to drag; trail; convince; haul; *vi* trail along or touch the ground; trump (at cards); *vr* crawl, creep; shuffle along; humble oneself

arrastre *m,* dragging, trailing; haulage; trumping (at cards); *Central America, Mexico,* clout, pull

¡arre! *interj* Gee up! Get along!

arrear *vt* to spur on, whip up (horses, etc.). *interj inf* **¡Arrea!** Hurry up! Get on!

arrebañar *vt* to pick clean, clear; eat or drink up

arrebatado *a* precipitate, headlong; rash; flushed, red

arrebatador *a* overwhelming; violent; bewitching, captivating; delightful

arrebatamiento *m,* abduction; seizure; fury; ecstasy

arrebatar *vt* to abduct, carry off; seize, grab; attract, charm; grip (the attention); *vr* be overcome with rage

arrebatiña *f,* grab; scuffle, scrimmage

arrebato *m,* fit (gen. of anger); ecstasy, rapture

arrebozar *vt* to muffle; envelop

arrebujarse *vr* to huddle; wrap oneself up

arrechucho *m, inf* fit of rage; sudden slight ailment

arreciar *vi* to increase in intensity; *vr* grow strong

arrecife *m,* reef (in the sea); stone-paved road

arredrar *vt* to separate, remove; force back, repel; terrify

arregazar(se) *vt* and *vr* to tuck up one's skirts

arreglado *a* regular; regulated; ordered; methodical

arreglar *vt* to regulate; arrange; adjust, put right; tidy; make up (the face); *vr* (*with prep a*) conform to; (*with con*) reach an agreement with. **Me voy a a.,** I am going to make myself presentable. *inf* **arreglárselas,** to shift for oneself

arreglo *m,* arrangement; rule; regulation; method, order; agreement; adjustment; compromise

arrellanarse *vr* to settle comfortably in one's chair; be happy in one's work

arremangar *vt* to roll up (sleeves, trousers, etc.); *vr inf* make a decision

arremango *m,* rolling or tucking up (of sleeve, etc.)

arremetedor (-ra) *n* attacker, assailant

arremeter *vt* to attack, assail; *vi* launch oneself (at); *fig* spoil the view, shock the eye

arremetida *f,* attack, assault

arremolinarse *vr* to crowd, cluster, group

arrendador (-ra) *n* landlord; renter; hirer; tenant

arrendamiento *m,* letting, renting; hiring; rental; agreement, lease

arrendar *vt irr* to let, lease; hire; rent (as a tenant); train (horses); tie up (horses); restrain; mimic, imitate. See **recomendar**

arrendatario (-ia) *a* rent, lease. *n* tenant; lessee; hirer. **a. de contribuciones,** tax farmer

arreo *m*, ornament; apparel; *pl* horse trappings; appurtenances, equipment

¡Arrepa! But look!, Hold on!, Hold your horses!, Not so fast!

arrepentimiento *m*, repentance

arrepentirse *vr irr* to repent. See **sentir**

arrestado *a* courageous, audacious, bold

arrestar *vt* to arrest, detain; *vr* be bold, dare

arresto *m*, arrest; detention; imprisonment; audacity, boldness

arriada *f*, lowering (of a boat); taking in (of sail)

arriar *vt naut* to strike (colors); take in (sail); pay out (ropes, etc.); lower (boats); flood, inundate

arriate *m*, garden border; avenue, walk; trellis (for plants)

arriba *adv* up, above; overhead; upstairs; earlier, before; upwards (with prices). *interj* **¡A.!** Up with!; Long live! **de a. abajo,** from head to foot, from one end to the other; completely, wholly

arribada *f, naut* arrival. **de a.,** emergency (port)

arribar *vi naut* to arrive; put into an emergency port; reach, arrive at; *inf* convalesce; attain; *naut* drift

arribista *mf* social climber

arriero *m*, farrier; muleteer

arriesgado *a* dangerous, risky; rash, daring

arriesgar *vt* to risk; *vr* run into danger; dare, risk

arrimado *m, Mexico* parasite

arrimar *vt* to bring or draw near; abandon (professions, etc.); lay aside, discard; *inf* administer (blows); *naut* stow (cargo); *vr* (*with prep a*) lean against, rest on; join, go with; seek the protection of. **Cada cual se arrima a su cada cual,** Birds of a feather flock together

arrimo *m*, bringing or placing near; leaning or resting against; abandonment, giving up; protection; staff, support

arrinconado *a* remote, secluded; forgotten, neglected

arrinconar *vt* to discard, lay aside; corner, besiege; set aside, dismiss; forsake; *vr* go into retirement, withdraw

arriscado *a* craggy, rugged; bold, resolute; sprightly, handsome

arriscarse *vr Lat. Am.* to dress to kill, dress to the nines

arro, arro, arro purrrr (echoic of a cat's purr)

arrobamiento *m*, ecstasy, rapture; trance

arrobar *vt* to charm, entrance; *vr* be enraptured; be in ecstasy

arrodillar *vt* to cause to kneel down; *vi* and *vr* kneel down

arrogancia *f*, arrogance; courage; majesty, pride

arrogante *a* arrogant, haughty; courageous; proud, majestic

arrogar *vt* to adopt (as a son); *vr* usurp, appropriate

arrojadizo *a* easily cast or hurled; projectile

arrojado *a* bold, determined; rash

arrojar *vt* to throw, hurl, cast; shed (light, etc.; e.g. **La cuenta arroja un total de cien dólares,** The bill shows a total of a hundred dollars); *com* show (a balance, etc.); put out (sprouts); dismiss, send away; *vr* cast oneself; (*with prep a*) hurl oneself against or upon; undertake, venture upon. **a. de sí (a),** to get rid of, dismiss

arrojo *m*, daring, intrepidity; boldness

arrollar *vt* to roll; make into a roll, roll up; defeat (the enemy); silence, confound; rock to sleep; bear along, carry off

arromar *vt* to blunt; flatten

arropar *vt* to wrap up, cover

arrostrar *vt* to confront, defy, face up to; *vr* fight hand to hand. **a. las consecuencias,** *fig* to face the music

arroyada *f*, gorge, gully; course, channel; flood

arroyo *m*, stream, brook; street gutter; road, street; *fig* flood, plenty

arroz *m*, rice

arrozal *m*, rice field

arruga *f*, wrinkle; fold, pleat; crease

arrugamiento *m*, wrinkling; fold, pleating; crumpling, creasing; corrugation

arrugar *vt* to wrinkle; pleat; corrugate; crumple, crease. **a. el ceño,** to knit one's brow, scowl

arruinamiento *m*, ruin, decay, decline

arruinar *vt* to ruin; destroy, damage severely

arrullar *vt* to bill and coo (doves); lull to sleep; *inf* whisper sweet words to, make love to

arrullo *m*, cooing of doves; lullaby

arrumaco *m, inf* embrace, caress (gen. *pl*); ornament in bad taste

arrumaje *m, naut* stowage; clouds on the horizon

arrurruz *m*, arrowroot

arsenal *m*, dockyard; arsenal; *fig* store (of information, etc.)

arsénico *m*, arsenic

arte *mf*, art; skill; ability; talent; guile, craftiness. **las bellas artes,** fine arts. *inf* **no tener a. ni parte en,** to have nothing to do with, have no part in

artefacto *m*, machine, mechanism, apparatus; device, appliance. **a. atómico,** atomic bomb

arteria *f, med* artery; main line (of communication)

artería *f*, craftiness, guile

arterial *a* arterial

artesa *f*, wooden trough; kneading bowl

artesano (-na) *n* artisan; mechanic

artesiano *a* artesian

artesón *m*, bucket, pail; *arch* curved ceiling-panel; paneled ceiling

artesonado *a arch* paneled (ceiling). *m*, paneled ceiling

ártico *a* Arctic

articulación *f*, joint, articulation; jointing; enunciation, pronunciation

articular *vt* to joint, articulate; enunciate, pronounce clearly

articulista *mf* article writer

artículo *m*, finger knuckle; heading; article; *anat* joint; *gram* article; *pl* goods, things. **a. de fondo,** leading article (in a newspaper). **a. de primera necesidad,** prime necessity, essential

artífice *mf* craftsman, artificer; author, creator; forger

artificial *a* artificial

artificio *m*, skill, art; appliance, contraption, mechanism; trick, cunning device; guile, craftiness

artificioso *a* skilful; artificial; crafty, cunning

artillería *f*, artillery. **a. de costa,** coastal guns. **a. ligera, a. montada, a. rodada** or **a. volante,** field artillery

artillero *m*, gunner

artimaña *f*, trick, ruse, stratagem

artista *mf* artist; performer

artístico *a* artistic

artrítico *a med* arthritic

artritis *f, med* arthritis

arveja *f, bot* vetch; *Lat. Am.* pea

arzobispo *m*, archbishop

as *m*, Roman copper coin; ace (*aer* cards, etc.)

asa *f*, handle; pretext, excuse

asadero *m, Mexico* cottage cheese

asado *m, cul* roast

asador *m, cul* roasting-spit; roaster

asadura *f, cul* chitterlings; offal

asalariar *vt* to fix a salary for

asaltador (-ra) *a* attacking. *n* assailant, attacker

asaltar *vt* to storm, besiege; assault, attack; occur to (ideas); come on suddenly (illness)

asalto *m*, storming, besieging; assault, attack; bout (in fencing, boxing, wrestling); round (in a fight)

asamblea *f*, congregation, assembly; meeting; legislative assembly; *mil* assembly (bugle call)

asambleísta *mf* member of an assembly

asar *vt cul* to roast; grill; *vr* be burning-hot; *fig* burn (with enthusiasm)

asaz *adv* sufficiently, enough; very; in abundance. *a* sufficient; many

asbesto *m*, asbestos

ascalonia *f, bot* shallot

ascendencia *f*, lineage, ancestry, origin

ascendente *a* ascending

ascender *vi irr* to ascend, climb; be promoted; (*with prep a*) amount to (bills, etc.); *vt* promote. See **entender**

ascendiente *mf* ancestor, forbear. *m*, influence, ascendancy

ascensión *f*, ascension; promotion; *ast* exaltation

ascenso *m*, ascent; promotion, preferment

ascensor *m*, lift, elevator

ascensorista *mf* elevator operator

asceta *mf* ascetic

ascético *a* ascetic

ascetismo *m*, asceticism

asco *m*, nausea; repugnance, loathing; revolting thing. *inf* **Me da a.,** It sickens me

ascua *f*, live coal, ember. **estar como una a. de oro,** to be as bright as a new pin. **estar en ascuas,** *fig* to be on pins

aseado *a* clean, tidy

asear *vt* to tidy, make neat; clean up; decorate, adorn

asechanza *f*, ambush; trick, snare, stratagem

asechar *vt* to ambush, waylay; *fig* lay snares for

asediador (-ra) *n* besieger

asediar *vt* to besiege; pester, importune

asedio *m*, siege; importunity

asegurado (-da) *a* insured. *n* insured person

asegurador (-ra) *a* insuring. *n* insurer

asegurar *vt* to fasten, make secure; pinion, grip; reassure, soothe; assert, state; *com* insure; guarantee; ensure, secure; *vr com* insure oneself; (*with de*) make sure of

asemejar *vt* to imitate, copy; make similar to; *vr* (*with prep a*) be like, be similar to

asenderear *vt* to make a pathway through; persecute, harass

asenso *m*, assent. **dar a.,** to believe, give credence (to)

asentaderas *f pl, inf* buttocks, seat

asentado *a* prudent, circumspect; permanent, stable

asentamiento *m*, seating; settlement, residence; prudence, judgment

asentar *vt irr* to seat; place; fasten, fix; found; plant (flags); pitch (a tent); establish, make firm; smooth; hone (razors); estimate, budget, arrange, set forth; note down; affirm, believe; *com* enter (in an account); *vi* fit (clothes); *vr* seat oneself; alight (birds); settle (liquids); *arch* settle, subside; to be located (e.g. **El edificio se asienta en una esquina,** The building is located on a corner). **a. la mano en,** to strike hard. See **acertar**

asentimiento *m*, assent; consent, approval

asentir *vi irr* to assent, agree; (*with en*) consent to. See **sentir**

aseñorado *a* refined, gentlemanly; ladylike; presumptuous

aseo *m*, cleanliness, neatness

asepsia *f*, asepsis

asequible *a* attainable; obtainable

aserción *f*, assertion

aserradero *m*, sawmill; saw-pit

aserrador (-ra) *n* sawyer

aserrar *vt irr* to saw. See **acertar**

aserrín *m*, sawdust

aserruchar *vt, Lat. Am.* to saw

asertivo *a* assertive

aserto *m*, assertion

asesinar *vt* to assassinate, murder

asesinato *m*, assassination, murder

asesino *mf* assassin, murderer; murderess

asesor (-ra) *n* assessor

asesorar *vt* to give advice; *vr* take legal advice; seek advice

asestar *vt* to aim (firearms); fire; deal (a blow)

aseveración *f*, assertion, statement

aseveradamente *adv* affirmatively

aseverar *vt* to affirm, assert

asfaltado *m*, asphalting; asphalt pavement

asfaltar *vt* to asphalt

asfalto *m*, asphalt

asfixia *f, med* asphyxia

asfixiante *a* asphyxiating

asfixiar *vt* to asphyxiate

así *adv* thus, so, in this way; like this (e.g. **en días a.,** on days like this); even if; so that, therefore. **a. a.,** middling, so-so. **a. como a.,** as well as; as soon as. **a. las cosas,** that being the case, **a. que,** as soon as, immediately; consequently, thus

asiático (-ca) *a* and *n* Asiatic

asidero *m*, hold, grasp; handle, haft; pretext, excuse

asido a wedded to (e.g. a belief)

asiduo *a* assiduous

asiento *m*, seat; place, position; site; base (of a vase, etc.); lees, sediment; indigestion; *arch* subsidence, settling; treaty, pact; contract; note, reminder; *com* entry; permanence, stability; prudence; bit (of a bridle); *pl* buttocks, seat. **estar de a.,** to be established (in a place)

asignación *f*, assignation; appropriation (of money); salary; portion, share

asignar *vt* to assign; apportion; destine, intend; appoint

asignatario, -a *mf Lat. Am.* heir, heiress, legatee

asignatura *f*, subject (of study in schools, etc.)

asilar *vt* to give shelter to; receive; put into an institution

asilo *m*, shelter, refuge; sanctuary, asylum; *fig* protection, defence; home, institution

asimetría *f*, asymmetry

asimétrico *a* asymmetrical

asimiento *m*, hold, grasp; attachment, affection

asimilación *f*, assimilation

asimilar *vt* to compare, liken; (*bot zool gram*) assimilate; *vi* resemble, be like; *fig* assimilate, digest (ideas)

asimismo *adv* similarly, likewise

asir *vt irr* to grasp, take hold of; seize; *vi* take root (plants); *vr* (*with de*) lay hold of; take advantage of; make an excuse to. *Pres. Ind.* **asgo, ases,** etc. *Pres. Subjunc.* **asga,** etc.

asirio (-ia) *a* and *n* Assyrian. *m*, Assyrian language

asistencia *f*, presence, attendance; minimal attendance required (e.g. **Los alumnos tienen que completar una a.,** Pupils must attend a certain number of classes) assistance, help; service, attendance; medical treatment; remuneration; *pl* allowance. **a. pública,** Public Assistance. **a. social,** social work

asistenta *f*, daily maid; waiting-maid

asistente *m*, assistant; *mil* orderly

asistir *vt* to accompany; assist, help; attend, treat; (*with de*) act as; *vi* (*with prep a*) be present at, attend; follow suit (in cards)

asma *f*, asthma

asmático (-ca) *a* asthmatic. *n* asthma sufferer

asnal *a* asinine; brutish, stupid

asno *m*, ass

asociación *f*, association; company, partnership; society, fellowship

asociado (-da) *n* associate; member; partner

asociar *vt* to associate; *vr* associate oneself; join together; form a partnership

asolación, f. asolamiento *m*, destruction, ruin

asolar *vt irr* to destroy, devastate, lay flat; *vr* wither; settle (liquids). See **contar**

asoldar *vt irr* to employ, engage, hire. See **contar**

asolear *vt* to expose to the sun; *vr* sun oneself; become sunburnt

asomada *f*, brief appearance; vantage point

asomar *vt* to show, allow to appear, put forth; *vi* begin to show; *vr* show oneself, appear; *inf* be flushed (with wine); (*with prep a, por*) look out of. **asomarse a la ventana,** to show oneself at, or look out of, the window

asombrar *vt* to shade, shadow; darken (a color); terrify; amaze

asombro *m*, fright, terror; amazement; wonder, marvel

asombroso *a* amazing; marvellous, wonderful

asonancia *f*, assonance; congruity, harmony

asordar *vt* to deafen

asorocharse *vr, Peru* to come down with altitude sickness, get altitude sickness

aspa *f,* cross; sail of a windmill

aspaviento *m,* exaggerated display of emotion; gesture (of horror, etc.); **hacer aspavientos,** to make a fuss

aspecto *m,* look, appearance; aspect, outlook

aspereza *f,* roughness, harshness; ruggedness, rockiness; severity, asperity

áspero *a* rough, harsh; uneven, rocky; jarring, grating; hard, severe

aspersión *f, ecc* aspersion; sprinkling

áspid *m,* asp, viper

aspiración *f,* breath; breathing; aspiration, desire; *mus* pause

aspirador (de polvo) *m,* vacuum cleaner

aspirante *m,* aspirant, novice; office-seeker; applicant

aspirar *vt* to breathe in, inhale; *gram* aspirate; *(with prep a)* aspire to, desire

aspirina *f,* aspirin

asquear *vi* and *vt* to hate, loathe

asquerosidad *f,* filthiness, loathsomeness; vileness, hatefulness

asqueroso *a* nauseating; loathsome, revolting; vile, hateful

asta *f,* lance, spear, pike; horn (of bull); antler; flagstaff; shaft. **a media a.,** at half-mast

asterisco *m,* asterisk

astigmático *a* astigmatic

astigmatismo *m,* astigmatism

astil *m,* handle, pole, shaft; bar of a balance; beam feather

astilla *f,* splinter

astillar *vt* to splinter, chip

astillero *m,* shipyard; rack for lances and pikes

astilloso *a* splintery, fragile

astracán *m,* astrakhan

astringente *a* astringent

astringir *vt* to tighten up; compress; constrain

astro *m,* heavenly body

astrolatría *f,* astrolatry, star worship

astrología *f,* astrology

astrológico *a* astrological

astrólogo (-ga) *n* astrologist

astronauta *m,* astronaut

astronomía *f,* astronomy

astronómico *a* astronomical

astrónomo *m,* astronomer

astucia *f,* astuteness, guile, craftiness

asturiano (-na) *a* and *n* Asturian

astuto *a* guileful, crafty, astute

asueto *m,* day's holiday

asumir *vt* to assume; adopt, appropriate

asunción *f,* assumption

asunto *m,* matter, theme, subject; business, affair

asustadizo *a* timid, nervous, easily frightened

asustar *vt* to frighten; **que asusta,** terribly (e.g. **Es de una ñoñería que asusta,** It's a terribly timid thing to do) *vr* be frightened

atablar *vt* to roll, flatten (earth)

atacado *a inf* hesitant; mean, stingy

atacador (-ra) *a* attacking. *n* aggressor, attacker

atacar *vt* to attack; fasten, button; fit (clothes); ram (guns); *fig* press hard, corner (persons). **a. a los nervios,** to jar on the nerves

ataché *m. Central America* (paper) clip

atadero *m,* rope, tie, cord; hook, ring, etc. (for hitching); hindrance, impediment; hitching or fastening point

atado *m,* bundle, roll

atadura *f,* tying, stringing, fastening, tie; knot; connection

atajar *vi* to take a short cut; *vt* intercept, cut off; screen off, divide; impede, stop; interrupt (people); **atajarle la palabra a uno,** to cut somebody off, interrupt *vr* be overcome (by fear, shame, etc.)

atajo *m,* short cut, quick way; cutting, abbreviation; division. *inf* **echar por el a.,** to go to the root of (a matter)

atalaya *f,* look out, watch tower; observation point. *m,* lookout

atalayar *vt* to scan, watch; spy upon

atalón *m,* atoll, coral island

atañadero: en lo atañadero a with regard to, with respect to

atañer *vi impers* to concern, affect; belong, pertain

ataque *m, (mil med)* attack; quarrel, fight

atar *vt* to tie; fasten; lace; stop, paralyse; *vr* get in a fix; confine oneself. **a. cabos,** to put two and two together

atardecer *vi irr impers* to grow dusk. See **conocer**

atardecer *m,* dusk, evening

atarear *vt* to set to work, assign work to; *vr* work hard

atarugar *vt* to wedge; stop up; plug; block; *inf* silence, shut up; stuff, cram; *vr fig inf* lose one's head

atasajar *vt* to cut up, jerk (beef, etc.)

atascadero *m,* deep rut, boggy place; impediment, obstacle

atascar *vt* to plug; block up; stop (a leak); hinder, obstruct; *vr* stick in the mud; be held up or delayed; *inf* get stuck in a speech

atasco *m,* obstruction, block

ataúd *m,* coffin

ataviar *vt* to deck, apparel, adorn

atavío *m,* get-up, dress, apparel; *pl* ornaments

atavismo *m,* atavism

ate *m, Mexico* kind of Turkish delight

ateísmo *m,* atheism

atejonarse *vr Mexico* to hide

atelaje *m,* team, yoke (of horses); trappings, harness; *inf* trousseau

atemperación *f,* moderation, mitigation; tempering

atemperar *vt* to moderate, mitigate; adapt, adjust; temper, cool. **atemperarse a la realidad,** to adjust to reality

Atenas Athens

atenazar *vt* to grip, grasp; torture

atención *f,* attention; solicitude, kindness; courtesy, civility; *pl* business affairs. *interj* **¡A.!** Take care! Look out!; *mil* Attention! **en a. (a),** taking into consideration. **estar en a.,** (patient) to be under treatment

atender *vt irr* to await, expect; take care of, look after; *vi (with prep a)* attend to, listen to; *vi* remember. See **entender**

ateneo *m,* atheneum. *a* Athenian

atenerse *vr irr (with prep a)* to abide by; resort to, rely on. See **tener**

ateniense *a* and *mf* Athenian

atentado *a* prudent, sensible; secret, silent. *m,* infringement, violation; attempt (on a person's life); crime

atentar *vt irr* to do illegally; attempt a crime; *vr* proceed cautiously; restrain oneself. See **acertar**

atento *a* attentive; courteous, civil. *adv* taking into consideration. **su atenta (atta),** *com* your favor

atenuación *f,* attenuation, diminution

atenuante *a* attenuating; extenuating (of circumstances)

atenuar *vt* to attenuate, diminish; extenuate

ateo (-ea) *a* atheistic. *n* atheist

aterirse *vr defective* to grow stiff with cold

aterrador *a* terrifying; dreadful

aterraje *m, (aer, naut)* landing

aterramiento *m,* horror, terror; terrorization; *naut* landing; ruin, demolition

aterrar *vt irr* to demolish; discourage; cover with earth; *vi* land; *vr naut* draw near to land. See **acertar**

aterrizaje *m, aer* landing. **a. forzoso,** forced landing. **campo de a.,** landing field

aterrizar *vi aer* to land, touch down

aterrorizar *vt* to terrify; terrorize

atesar *vt Lat. Am.* to tighten (up)

atesorar *vt* to hoard, treasure up

atestación *f,* attestation, affidavit

atestar *vt irr* to stuff, cram; insert; *inf* stuff with food; crowd, fill with people. See **acertar**

atestar *vt* to attest, testify

atestiguación *f*, deposition, testimony

atestiguar *vt* to testify, attest

atetar *vt* to suckle; *vi* suck

atezado *a* bronzed, sunburnt; black

ático *a* Attic; *m*, penthouse

atiesar *vt* to stiffen

atildar *vt* to place a tilde over; blame, criticize; decorate, ornament

atimia *f*, loss of status

atinado *a* pertinent, relevant

atinar *vi* to find by touch; discover by chance; guess; hit the mark

atinente a . . . concerning . . .

atingencia *f*, *Lat. Am.* connection, relationship

atingir *vt*, *Lat. Am.* to concern, relate to

atisbadura *f*, watching, spying, prying

atisbar *vt* to spy upon, watch

atisbo *m*, prying, watching; suspicion, hint

atisbón *a* penetrating (mind, vision)

atizador *m*, poker (for the fire)

atizar *vt* to poke (the fire); dowse, snuff; trim (lamps); excite, rouse; *inf* slap, wallop

atlántico *a* Atlantic. *m*, Atlantic Ocean

atleta *m*, athlete

atlético *a* athletic

atletismo *m*, athletics

atmósfera *f*, atmosphere

atmosférico *a* atmospheric

atolladero *m*, rut; mud; bog

atolón *m*, atoll, coral island

atolondrado *a* scatter-brained, flighty

atolondramiento *m*, rashness, recklessness; bewilderment

atolondrar *vt* to bewilder, confuse

atómico *a* atomic

átomo *m*, atom; speck, particle

atónito *a* amazed, astounded

atontar *vt* to confuse, daze; make stupid; stun

atormentador (-ra) *a* torturing. *n* tormentor; torturer

atormentar *vt* to torment; torture; grieve, harass

atorrante *a* and *mf* (Argentina) good-for-nothing

atracadero *m*, jetty, landingstage

atracar *vt inf* to stuff with food; *naut* tie up, moor; hold up, rob; *vi naut* moor, stop; *vr inf* guzzle, gorge

atracción *f*, attraction

atraco (a) *m*, hold up (of), ambush (of)

atracón *m*, *inf* gorge, fill; surfeit. **darse atracones de,** to gorge oneself on

atractivo *a* attractive. *m*, attraction, charm

atractriz *a* attracting; *f*, force of attraction; (fig.) lure

atraer *vt irr* to attract; charm, enchant. See **traer**

atragantarse *vr* to choke; *inf* be at a loss, dry up (in conversation)

atraíble *a* attractable, able to be attracted

atrancar *vt* to bar the door; obstruct, block; hinder; *vi inf* stride; skip (in reading)

atrapar *vt inf* grab, seize, catch; net, obtain; deceive

atrás *adv* behind, back; past; previously. **¡A.!** Back! **años a.,** years ago

atrasado *a* slow (of clocks); backward; old-fashioned; hard-up, poor. **a. mental,** retarded person

atrasar *vt* to delay, retard; fix a later date than the true one; put back (clocks). *vi* be slow (clocks); *vr* be late; be left behind

atraso *m*, delay; backwardness, dullness; slowness (clocks); lateness; *pl* arrears. **El reloj lleva cinco minutos de a.,** The watch is five minutes slow

atravesado *a* slightly squint-eyed; mongrel, crossbreed; half-caste; ill-intentioned

atravesar *vt irr* to lay across, put athwart; cross, traverse; pierce; obstruct; *naut* lie to; *vr* be among, mingle (with); interrupt; interfere, take part in; quarrel; occur, arise. See **confesar**

atrayente *a* attractive

atreverse *vr* to dare, risk, venture; be overbold or insolvent

atrevido *a* bold, audacious; hazardous, dangerous; brazen, impudent

atribuible *a* attributable

atribución *f*, attribution; perquisite, attribute

atribuir *vt irr* to impute, attribute; assign, turn over to; *vr* take upon oneself, assume. See **huir**

atributo *m*, attribute, quality

atril *m*, lectern, reading desk; music stand

atrincherar *vt* to protect with entrenchments; *vr* entrench oneself

atrio *m*, atrium; hall, vestibule; *arch* parvis

atrocidad *f*, atrocity, cruelty; *inf* terrific amount; enormity, crime

atrofia *f*, atrophy

atrofiarse *vr* to atrophy

atrojarse *vr Mexico* to be stumped, be stuck (for an answer)

atronado *a* harebrained, foolish

atronar *vt irr* to deafen, stun with noise; confuse, daze. See **tronar**

atropelladamente *adv* in disorder, helter-skelter

atropellado *a* rash, foolhardy

atropellar *vt* to trample upon; thrust out of the way; knock down; disregard, violate (feelings); insult, abuse; transgress; do hastily; *vr* act rashly

atropello *m*, trampling; road accident; knocking over; upsetting; violation; outrage

atroz *a* atrocious, savage; monstrous, outrageous; *inf* terrific, enormous

atufar *vt* to irritate, vex; *vr* grow irritated; turn sour (wine, etc.)

atún *m*, tunny fish

aturdido *a* reckless, scatterbrained, silly; thoughtless; stunned

aturdimiento *m*, daze; confusion, bewilderment

aturdir *vt* to daze; confuse, bewilder; amaze; stun

atusar *vt* to trim (hair, beard); *agr* prune; smooth down (hair); *vr* dress over-carefully

audacia *f*, audacity

audaz *a* audacious, daring

audibilidad *f*, audibility

audición *f*, audition

audiencia *f*, audience, hearing; *law* audience; audience chamber

audífono *m*, hearing aid

audioteca *f*, audio library

auditor *m*, magistrate, judge

auditorio *a* auditory. *m*, audience

auge *m*, *fig* zenith, height; *ast* apogee

augusto *a* august, awesome

aula *f*, lecture or class room; *poet* palace

aullar *vi* to howl; bay

aullido *m*, howl; baying

aumentar(se) *vt vi vr* to increase, augment

aumentativo *a gram* augmentative

aumento *m*, increase; progress; enlargement; *Mexico* postscript **ir en a.,** to increase; advance, progress; prosper

aun *adv* even. **A. los que viven lejos han de oíros,** Even those who live far must hear you. **a. así** *or* **a. siendo así,** even so. **a. ayer,** only yesterday. **a. cuando,** even if. **más a.,** even more. **ni a. si,** not even if.

aún *adv* still, yet. **A. no te creen** *or* **No te creen a.,** They still don't believe you **¿A. se lo darás?** *or* **¿Se lo darás a.?** Will you still give it to her?

aunque *conjunc* although, even if, even though. It takes the Indicative referring to statement of fact and Subjunctive referring to a hypothesis, e.g. **A. vino, no lo hizo,** Although he came, he did not do it. **A. él cantase yo no iría allí,** Even though he sang (were to sing), I should not go there

aura *f*, zephyr, gentle breeze; popularity, approbation; aura. **a. epiléptica,** *med* epileptic aura

áureo *a* gold, gilt; golden

auricular *a* auricular. *m*, little finger; receiver, ear-piece (of a telephone); earphone (radio)

aurífero *a* gold-yielding, auriferous

auriga *m*, charioteer

aurora *f*, dawn; genesis, beginnings. **a. boreal,** aurora borealis, Northern Lights

auscultación *f*, *med* auscultation

auscultar *vt med* to auscultate

ausencia *f*, absence. **en ausencia de,** in the absence of

ausentar *vt* to send away; *vr* absent oneself

ausente *a* absent. *mf* absent person

auspicio *m*, augury, prediction; favor, patronage; *pl* auspices

austeridad *f*, austerity; mortification of the flesh

austero *a* austere, ascetic; severe, harsh; honest, upright

austral *a* southerly, austral

australiano (-na) *a* and *n* Australian

austríaco (-ca) *a* and *n* Austrian

austrófilo *a* and *n* Austrophile

autenticación *f*, authentication

autenticar *vt* to authenticate, attest; prove genuine

autenticidad *f*, authenticity

auténtico *a* authentic

autero, -a *mf*, *Lat. Am.* car thief

auto *m*, *law* sentence, decision; *theat* one-act allegory (gen. religious); *pl* proceedings. **a. de fe,** auto-da-fé. **a. de reconocimiento,** search-warrant. **a. sacramental,** one-act religious drama on theme of mystery of the Eucharist. **hacer a. de fe de,** to burn

autobiografía *f*, autobiography

autobús *m*, motor bus, bus

autocitarse *vr* to quote from one's own works

autoclave *m*, pressure cooker

autocracia *f*, autocracy

autócrata *mf* autocrat

autocrático *a* autocratic

autocrueldad *f*, self-inflicted pain

autodescubrimiento *m*, self-discovery

autodidacto *a* autodidactic; self-educated, self-taught

autódromo *m*, speedway

autógeno *a* autogenous, self-generating

autogiro *m*, *aer* autogyro

autografía *f*, autography

autográfico *a* autographic, in lithographic reproduction

autógrafo *a* autographical. *m*, autograph

autoinducción *f*, self-induction

autómata *m*, automaton

automático *a* automatic. *m*, *sew* press stud

automatismo *m*, automatism

automejoramiento *m*, self-improvement

automóvil *m*, automobile, motor car. *a* automatic

automovilismo *m*, motoring

automovilista *mf* motorist

autonombrarse *vr* to call oneself, go by the name of

autonomía *f*, autonomy

autónomo *a* autonomous

autopista *f*, motor road

autopsia *f*, *med* autopsy, post-mortem

autor (-ra) *n* agent, originator; author; inventor; *law* perpetrator

autoridad *f*, authority; pomp, show

autoritario *a* authoritarian; authoritative

autorización *f*, authorization

autorizado *a* approved, authorized, responsible

autorizar *vt* to authorize; *law* attest, testify; cite, prove by reference; approve; exalt

autorretratarse *vr* to have one's portrait painted, sit for one's portrait

autorretrato *m*, self-portrait

autostopista *mf* hitchhiker (Spain)

autosugestión *f*, autosuggestion

auxiliador (-ra) *a* assistant; helpful. *n* helper, assistant

auxiliar *vt* to help, aid; attend (the dying). *m*, *univ* lecturer. *a* assisting

auxiliaría *f*, *univ* lectureship

auxilio *m*, help, aid, assistance

aval *m*, *com* endorsement; voucher

avalar *vt* to enhance. **avalado por la tradición,** hallowed by tradition

avalentado *a* boastful, bragging

avalorar *vt* to value, estimate; put spirit into, encourage

avance *m*, advance; advance payment; balance sheet; attack

avanzada *f*, *mil* advance guard

avanzado *a* advanced, progressive

avanzar *vt* to advance; promote; *vi* advance; attack; grow late (time)

avanzo *m*, balance sheet; price estimate

avaricia *f*, greed, avarice

avaricioso, avariento *a* avaricious, greedy

avaro (-ra) *a* miserly; greedy. *n* miser

avasallador *a* dominating; *fig* overwhelming; enslaving

avasallar *vt* to subdue, dominate; *vr* become a vassal; surrender, yield

ave *f*, bird. **a. de paso,** migratory bird; *fig* bird of passage. **a. de rapiña,** bird of prey. **a. fría,** *orn* plover. **ave cantora,** songbird

avecinarse *vr* to be approaching (e.g. **el año que avecina,** the coming year)

avecindarse *vr* to take up residence (in a place)

avellana *f*, hazel nut

avellano *m*, *bot* hazel

avemaría *f*, Hail Mary (prayer); Angelus; rosary bead. *inf* **en un a.,** in a trice

avena *f*, oats; *poet* oaten pipe. **a. loca,** wild oats

avenal *m*, oatfield

avenar *vt* to drain (land); drain off (liquids)

avenencia *f*, agreement, arrangement; transaction; conformity, harmony

avenida *f*, flood, spate; avenue; abundance; way, approach (to a place)

avenido *a* (*with bien or mal*) well *or* ill-suited

avenidor (-ra) *n* arbitrator, mediator

avenir *vt irr* to reconcile; *vi* happen (used in infinitive and third singular and plural); *vr* be reconciled; agree; compromise, give way; harmonize (things); (*with con*) get on with, agree with. See **venir**

aventador *m*, *agr* winnower; pitchfork

aventajado *a* outstanding, talented; advantageous. *m*, *mil* private who enjoys extra pay

aventajar *vt* to improve, better; promote, prefer; excel; *vr* (*with prep a*) surpass, excel. **Te aventajo en diez años,** I'm ten years older than you

aventamiento *m*, winnowing

aventar *vt irr* to fan; air, ventilate; winnow; *inf* drive away, expel; *vr* be inflated; *inf* flee; smell (bad meat). See **sentar**

aventón *m*, *Mexico* hitch, lift, ride

aventura *f*, adventure; chance, luck; risk, danger

aventurar *vt* to risk, hazard

aventurero (-ra) *a* adventurous; unscrupulous; intriguing; undisciplined (of troops). *n* adventurer

avergonzar *vt irr* to shame; make shy, abash; *vr* be ashamed; be shy or sheepish. *Pres. Ind.* **avergüenzo, avergüenzas, avergüenza, avergüenzan.** *Pres. Subjunc.* **avergüence, avergüences, avergüence, avergüencen**

avería *f*, aviary; damage (to merchandise); loss, harm; *elec* fault; breakdown. **a. gruesa,** general average (marine insurance)

averiarse *vr* to be damaged; deteriorate; break down

averiguable *a* examinable, investigable; discoverable

averiguación *f*, inquiry, investigation; discovery

averiguar *vt* to investigate, inquire into; discover, ascertain. **¡averígüelo Vargas!** Beats me!, Search me!

averigüetas *mf*, *Lat. Am.* snoopers, nosy parker

averío *m*, flock of birds

aversión *f*, aversion, repugnance

avestruz *m*, ostrich
avetado *a* veined, mottled, streaked
avezar *vt* to accustom; *vr* grow accustomed (to)
aviación *f*, aviation
aviador *m*, aviator
aviar *vt* to outfit, equip; prepare, make ready; *inf* speed up; caulk (ship). *fig inf* **estar aviado,** to be in a mess
avidez *f*, avidity, greed; longing, desire
ávido *a* avid, greedy
avieso *a* twisted, crooked; ill-natured; sinister; *m Colombia* abortion
avillanado *a* countrified; gross, vulgar; boorish
avío *m*, preparation, provision; picnic lunch; money advanced (to miners or laborers); *pl inf* equipment, tools. **avíos de pesca,** fishing tackle
avión *m*, airplane; *orn* martin or swift. **a. de bombardeo,** bomber. **a. de caza,** fighter plane. **a. de combate nocturno,** night fighter. **a. de hostigamiento,** interceptor. **a. de reacción,** jet airplane. **a. de transporte,** *aer* transport. **a. en picado,** dive-bomber. **a. taxi,** air taxi. **por a.,** by airmail «**Avión**» "Airmail"
avioneta *f*, light airplane, small airplane
avisado *a* shrewd, sensible. **mal a.,** ill-advised, imprudent
avisar *vt* to inform, acquaint; warn; advise
aviso *m*, notice, announcement; warning; advice; care, caution; attention; shrewdness, prudence. **estar sobre a.,** to be on call; be on the alert
avispa *f*, wasp
avispado *a inf* smart, clever, quick; wide-awake
avispar *vt* to goad, prick; *inf* rouse, incite; *vr* be uneasy, fret
avispero *m*, wasp's nest; swarm of wasps; *fig inf* hornet's nest
avispón *m*, hornet
avistamiento *m*, sighting, spotting (e.g. of a ship)
avistar *vt* to descry, sight, spot; *vr* **avistarse con,** to interview
avituallar *vt* to victual, supply with food
avivar *vt* to enliven; stimulate, encourage; stir (fire); trim (wicks); brighten (colors); inflame; vivify, invigorate; *vi* revive, recover
avizor *m*, watcher, spy. *a* watchful, vigilant
avizorar *vt* to watch, spy upon
avutarda *f*, bustard
axila *f*, *bot* axil; *anat* axilla, armpit
axioma *m*, axiom
axiomático *a* axiomatic
¡ay! *interj* Alas! Woe is me! *m*, complaint, sigh
ayer *adv* yesterday; a short while ago; in the past. *m*, past
ayllu *m*, *Peru* Native American commune
ayo *m*, tutor
ayote *m*, *Mexico, Central America* pumpkin
ayuda *f*, help, assistance; enema; clyster; watch dog. *m*, **a. de cámara,** valet
ayudador (-ra) *a* helping, assisting. *n* helper
ayudante *m*, assistant; teaching assistant; *mil* adjutant. **a. a cátedra,** *univ* assistant lecturer. **a. de plaza,** post adjutant
ayudar *vt* to assist; help, aid; *vr* make an effort; avail oneself of another's help
ayunador (-ra) *a* fasting. *n* faster; abstainer
ayunar *vi* to fast
ayuno *m*, fast. *a* fasting; ignorant, unaware. **en a.** *or* **en**

ayunas, before breakfast, fasting; *inf* ignorant, unaware
ayuntamiento *m*, meeting, assembly; municipal government; town hall; sexual union
azabache *m*, *min* jet
azada *f*, *agr* spade; hoe
azadón *m*, *agr* hoe
azafata *f*, queen's waiting-maid *ant*; flight attendant
azafate *m*, flat basket; small tray
azafrán *m*, *bot* saffron; crocus
azafranado *a* saffron-colored
azahar *m*, flower of orange, lemon or sweet lime tree
azar *m*, chance, hazard; unexpected misfortune; losing card or throw of dice
azararse *vr* to go wrong, fail (negotiations, etc.); grow nervous; become confused; blush
azaroso *a* unlucky, ill-omened; hazardous
ázimo *a* unleavened (bread)
ázoe *m*, nitrogen
azogar *vt* to silver (mirrors, etc.); slake lime; *vr* suffer from mercury poisoning; *inf* grow uneasy, be agitated
azogue *m*, *min* mercury, quick-silver; market-place
azolve *m*, silt
azoramiento *m*, alarm, terror; confusion, stupefaction; incitement
azorar *vt* to alarm, terrify; confuse, stun, dumbfound; excite, stimulate; encourage
azotacalles *mf inf* idler, street loafer
azotaina *f*, *inf* whipping, spanking
azotamiento *m*, flogging, beating, whipping
azotar *vt* to whip, beat, flog; acourge, ravage; knock against or strike repeatedly
azotazo *m*, spank
azote *m*, whip; scourge; lash, blow with a whip; spank, slap; misfortune, disaster. *inf* **azotes y galeras,** monotonous diet
azotea *f*, flat terrace roof
azotera *f*, *Lat. Am.* beating, thrashing
azozador party whip, whip
azteca *a* and *mf* Aztec
azúcar *m*, sugar. **a. blanco** *or* **a. de flor,** white sugar. **a. de pilón,** loaf sugar. **a. moreno,** brown sugar. **a. quebrado,** brown sugar. **a. y canela,** sorrel gray (of horses)
azucarado *a* sugary; sugared, sugar-coated; *inf* honeyed, flattering
azucarar *vt* to coat with sugar; sweeten; *inf* soften, mitigate; *vr* crystallize; go sugary (jam)
azucarera *f*, sugar-basin
azucarero *a* sugar-producing (e.g. province)
azucarillo *m*, *cul* bar made of white of egg and sugar for sweetening water
azucena *f*, white lily. **a. de agua,** water-lily
azuela *f*, adze
azufre *m*, sulphur
azul *a* and *m*, blue. **a. celeste,** sky blue, azure. **a. de mar** *or* **a. marino,** navy blue. **a. de ultramar,** ultramarine. **a. turquí,** indigo
azulado *a* bluish, blue
azulear *vi* to look bluish, have a blue tint
azulejo *m*, ornamental glazed tile
azurumbado *m*, *Central America* dumb, silly, stupid; boozed up, drunk
azuzar *vt* to set on (dogs); irritate, provoke; incite, urge

B

baba *f*, saliva; secretion (of snails, etc.); viscous fluid (of plants). *inf* **caérsele (a uno) la b.,** to ooze satisfaction; be dumbfounded
babador, babero *m*, bib, feeder
babear *vi* to dribble, slaver; *fig inf* slobber over, be sloppy

babel *m*, babel
babélico *a* Babelian, Babel-like confused; unintelligible
Babia, estar en to be daydreaming
babieca *mf inf* stupid person. **Babieca** *f*, the Cid's horse
Babilonia Babylon
babilónico *a* Babylonian

bable *m*, Asturian (language)

babor *m*, *naut* larboard, port

babosa *f*, slug; young onion

baboso *a* slavering; *fig inf* "sloppy"; *inf* incompetent, useless; *Lat. Am.* dumb, stupid

babucha *f*, heelless slipper, babouche

babuino *m*, *zool* baboon

baca *f*, luggage carrier (on roof of bus, etc.)

bacalao *m*, codfish

bacanales *f pl*, Bacchanalia

bacante *f*, Bacchante

bacará *m*, baccarat (card game)

baceta *f*, pool (in card games)

bache *m*, rut (in road); pothole

bacheo *m*, repairing of streets

bachiller *mf* high-school graduate *m*, *inf* babbler. *f*. **bachillera,** *inf* blue-stocking; garrulous woman

bachillerarse *vr* to graduate as a bachelor

bachillerato *m*, baccalaureate, bachelor's degree

bacho *m*, *Peru* fib, tall tale

bacía *f*, bowl; barber's circular shaving-dish; barber's trade sign

bacilar *a* bacillary

bacilo *m*, bacillus

bacterial, bacteriano *a* bacterial

bactericida *m*, bactericide

bacteriología *f*, bacteriology

bacteriológico *a* bacteriological

bacteriólogo *m*, bacteriologist

báculo *m*, staff; walking-stick; *fig* support. **b. episcopal,** bishop's crozier

badajo *m*, clapper (of a bell); chatterbox, gossip

badana *f*, cured sheepskin, chamois leather, wash-leather; sweat band; *inf* **zurrar (a uno) la b.,** to take the hide off; insult

badén *m*, channel made by rain, furrow; conduit

badulaque *m*, *inf* good-for-nothing

bagaje *m*, *mil* baggage; beast of burden, transport animal; luggage

bagatela *f*, trifle, oddment, bagatelle

bagazo *m*, oilcake, bagasse

bagual *a* *WH* untamed, wild; doltish, dull. *m*, untamed horse, wild horse

bahía *f*, bay, harbor

bailable *a* dance (of music). *m*, *theat* dance number

bailador (-ra) *n* dancer

bailar *vi* to dance; spin round. **b. al son que le toca,** to adapt oneself to circumstances

bailarín *a* dancing. *m*, professional dancer. **b. de cuerda, bailarín de la cuerda floja,** tightrope dancer

bailarina *f*, ballerina

baile *m*, dance; ball; ballet. **b. de máscaras, b. de trajes,** fancy-dress ball. **b. de San Vito,** St. Vitus' dance. **b. ruso,** ballet

bailotear *vi* to jig about; dance

baja *f*, drop, diminution; fall (in price, etc.); *mil* casualty; discharge. *inf* **darse de b.,** to leave an employment

bajada *f*, descent, fall; slope, incline; hollow, depression. **b. de aguas,** roof gutter

bajalato *m*, pashalik

bajamar *f*, low tide

bajamente *adv* basely, abjectly

bajar *vi* to descend; go down; get off; drop; fall, decrease; *vt* lower, take down, bring down; let down; dismount, alight; bend, droop; drop; reduce (price); *fig* lower (voices); humiliate, humble; **b. a tierra,** to step ashore; **b. la cabeza ante,** to submit to (e.g. a judgment) *vr* alight, dismount; humble oneself

bajel *m*, *naut* galley, ship

bajeza *f*, base action; meanness; *fig* humble estate, lowliness. **b. de ánimo,** timorousness

bajío *m*, *naut* shallows, shoal; depression, hollow

bajista *mf* speculator, bear (Stock Exchange)

bajo *a* low; short, not tall; downcast; under; subordinate; pale (of colors); humble (origin); base; coarse; vulgar; cheap (price); low (sounds). *m*, depth; shoal, sand bank; *mus* bass; *pl* petticoats, skirts; horses' hoofs. *adv* beneath, below. *prep* under, beneath. **b. juramento,** upon oath. **bajo relieve,** bas relief. **en voz baja,** in a low voice. **planta baja,** ground floor. **por lo b.,** in a whisper; in secret, on the sly

bajolatino *a* Low Latin

bajón *m*, *mus* bassoon; bassoon player; *fig inf* downfall

bajonista *mf* bassoon player

bala *f*, bullet, ball; bale. **b. fría,** spent bullet. **b. luminosa,** tracer bullet. **b. perdida,** stray bullet. *inf* **como una b.,** like a shot

balacear *vt*, *Central America, Mexico* to shoot (at)

balada *f*, ballad, song

baladí *a* worthless, insignificant

baladro *m*, yell, outcry, shout

baladrón *a* braggart

baladronada *f*, bravado, bragging

balagar *m*, straw rick

balance *m*, balance; swinging, oscillation; rolling, rocking (of a ship, etc.); doubt, insecurity, *com* balance; *com* balance sheet **b. de situación** *Lat. Am.* balance sheet

balancear *vi* to swing; oscillate; vacillate, hesitate; *vt* balance; *vr* balance oneself; rock or swing oneself

balanceo *m*, balancing; rocking; swinging; rolling (of a ship, etc.)

balancín *m*, swing-bar; whipple-tree; balance beam; tight-rope dancer's pole; minting-mill; yoke (for carrying pails); *pl naut* lifts

balandra *f*, *naut* sloop, cutter

balanza *f*, balance; scale; judgment; comparison. **b. de comercio,** balance of trade. **en balanzas,** in doubt or danger, in the balance

balar *vi* to bleat (sheep)

balasto *m*, *rw* ballast

balaustrada *f*, balustrade

balaustre *m*, baluster

balazo *m*, shot; bullet wound

balbuceo *m*, stammering; babbling; lisping **balbuceos** *fig* beginnings, early stages (e.g. **los b. de la literatura yídica,** the beginnings of Yiddish literature)

balbuciente *a* stammering; babbling; lisping

balbucir *vi irr defective* to stammer; lisp; babble; read hesitantly. See **lucir**

Balcanes, los the Balkans

balcón *m*, balcony

baldaquín *m*, canopy, baldachin

baldar *vt* to cripple; impede, obstruct

balde *m*, bucket

balde (en) *adv* in vain. **de b.,** gratis, free of charge

baldear *vt naut* to wash the decks

baldío *a* untilled; fallow; useless, worthless; vagrant

baldón *m*, insult; dishonor

baldonar *vt* to insult

baldosa *f*, paving stone; tile

baldrufa *f*, top, spinning top

balduque *m*, red tape

Baleares, las Islas the Balearic Islands

baleárico *a* Balearic

balido *m*, bleat, bleating

balística *f*, ballistics

baliza *f*, *naut* buoy, beacon

balizamiento *m*, marking with beacons, marking with buoys; traffic signs and signals

ballena *f*, whale; whalebone

ballenero *a* whaling. *m*, whaler

ballesta *f*, crossbow; spring (of carriages)

ballestería *f*, archery; crossbowmen

ballestero *m*, archer; crossbowman; crossbow maker

balneario *a* pertaining to public baths; bathing; holiday; spa. *m*, watering place, spa

balompié *m*, football (game)

balón *m*, large ball; football; *chem* balloon; bundle; bale. **b. de ensayo,** *fig* feeler

baloncesto *m*, *sport* basket ball

balota *f*, ballot

balotaje *m*, balloting; run-off election

balotar *vi* to ballot
balsa *f*, pond; raft
balsadera *f*, ferry
bálsamo *m*, balm
balsero *m*, ferryman; rafter (person fleeing a country by raft, rowboat, etc.)
báltico *a* Baltic. **el Mar Báltico** the Baltic Sea
baluarte *m*, bulwark; bastion; protection, defence
bamboleante *a* swaying, swinging; *fig* tottering (e.g. empire)
bambolearse *vr* to sway; swing; totter; be shaky; stagger
bamboleo *m*, rocking; swinging; tottering; staggering; reeling
bambolla *f*, *inf* ostentation, swank
bambú *m*, bamboo
banal *a* banal, commonplace
banana *f*, banana
banasta *f*, big basket
banastero (-ra) *n* basket maker or dealer
banca *f*, bench; card game; stall; *com* banking
bancada *f*, rowing seat
bancal *m*, oblong garden plot; terrace
bancario *a* banking, bank
bancarrota *f*, bankruptcy. **hacer b.,** to go bankrupt
banco *m*, form, bench; rowing seat; settle; seat; *carp* bench; *com* bank; *naut* bar, shoal; school (of fish). **b. azul,** government benches in Spanish Parliament. **b. de arena,** sand-bank. **b. de descuento,** discount bank. **b. de emisión, banco emisor,** bank of issue. **b. de hielo,** iceberg. **b. de nivel,** benchmark
banda *f*, wide ribbon; sash; ribbon, insignia; strip; border; party, group; gang; flock (of birds); zone, belt; side (of ship); *mus* band; cushion (billiards); *her* bar, bend. **b. elástica,** rubber band. *naut* **dar a la b.,** to lie along
bandada *f*, flock (of birds)
bandeja *f*, tray, salver
bandera *f*, banner, flag; colors, standard. **b. de popa,** ensign. **jurar la b.,** (*mil nav*) to take the oath of allegiance
banderilla *f*, banderilla (bullfighting)
banderillear *vt* to put banderillas on bulls
banderillero *m*, man who puts banderillas on bulls
banderín *m*, *dim* small flag; recruiting post
banderizo *a* factious; vehement, excitable
banderola *f*, banderole, pennon; bannerole
bandido (-da) *a* and *n* outlaw, fugitive. *m*, bandit; highwayman; rogue, desperado
bando *m*, proclamation, order; faction, group, party
bandola *f*, *mus* pandora, pandore
bandolerismo *m*, brigandage
bandolero *m*, robber, footpad, brigand
bandolín *m*, mandolin
bandurria *f*, *mus* mandolin
banjo *m*, banjo
banquero *m*, banker
banqueta *f*, three-legged stool; seat; footstool; *Mexico* sidewalk
banquete *m*, banquet, feast
banquetear *vt* and *vi* to banquet
banqueteo *m*, banqueting, feasting
bañadera *f*, *Argentina* bathtub
bañado *m*, chamber pot; *WH* marshy land, marsh; **bañados** *pl* marsh
bañador (-ra) *a* bathing. *n* bather. *m*, bathing dress; bath, vat
bañar *vt* to bathe; coat, cover; dip; lave, wash; *fig* bathe (of sunlight, etc.). *vr* take a bath; bathe
bañera *f*, bath attendant; bathtub
bañista *mf* bather; one who takes spa waters
baño *m*, bathing; bath; bathroom; bathtub; bagnio; Turkish prison; covering, coat; *pl* mineral baths, spa. **b. de China** *Argentina* shower bath, shower **b. de mar,** sea bath. **b. de María,** double saucepan. **b. de sol,**

sunbath. **casa de baños,** public baths. **cuarto de b.,** bathroom
bao *m*, *naut* beam
baptisterio *m*, baptistery; *ecc* font
baquelita *f*, bakelite
baqueta *f*, ramrod; *pl* drumsticks; *mil* gauntlet
bar *m*, bar; café
barahúnda *f*, See **baraúnda**
baraja *f*, pack (of cards); game of cards
barajar *vt* to shuffle (cards); jumble, mix; *vi* quarrel
baranda *f*, handrail, banister; cushion (of billiard table)
barandilla *f*, *dim* railing
barata *f*, *Mexico* bargain sale, sale
baratija *f*, (gen. *pl*) trifle, oddment
baratillo *m*, second-hand article, frippery; second-hand shop or stall; bargain counter
barato *a* cheap; easy. *m*, bargain sale. *adv* cheaply
baratura *f*, cheapness
baraúnda *f*, uproar, confusion
barba *f*, chin; beard; whiskers; fin; barb (of a feather); *m*, actor who plays old men. *f pl*, fibers of plants. **b. bien poblada,** a thick beard. **barbas de ballena,** whalebone. *fig inf* **echar a las barbas,** to throw in a person's face. **en la barba, en las barbas,** to ones face (e.g. **Me lo dijeron en las barbas.** They told me so to my face). **hacer la b.,** to shave; *inf* annoy
barbacoa *f*, *WH* barbecue; trellis (for climbing plants)
barbado *a* bearded. *m*, shoot; sucker; transplanted plant
barbárico *a* barbarian; barbaric
barbaridad *f*, barbarity; blunder; atrocity; outrage; *inf* huge amount. **¡Qué b.!** How awful! You don't say so!
barbarie *f*, barbarism; barbarity, cruelty
barbarismo *m*, barbarism; cruelty; barbarians
bárbaro (-ra) *a* and *n* barbarian. *a* fierce; headstrong; uncivilized. **como un b.,** like crazy (e.g. **estudiar como un b.,** to study like crazy)
barbechar *vt* to plow; leave fallow
barbecho *m*, *agr* fallow; first plowing
barbería *f*, barber shop
barbero *m*, barber; *Guatemala, Mexico* flatterer
barbihecho *a* fresh-shaved
barbilampiño *a* smooth-faced, beardless, clean-shaven
barbilindo *a* dandified, dappy; *m*, dandy
barbilla *f*, point of the chin; chin. **acariciar la b. (de),** to chuck under the chin
barbiquejo *m*, *naut* bobstay; hat-guard
barbudo *a* heavily bearded
barbulla *f*, *inf* babble, chatter, murmur of voices
barca *f*, small boat, bark; barge. **b. de pasaje,** ferryboat. **b. plantaminas** minelayer
barcada *f*, boat-load; ferry crossing
barcaza *f*, *naut* lighter; barge. **b. de desembarco,** landingcraft
barcelonés (-esa) *a* and *n* of or from Barcelona
barcino *a* ruddy (of animals); fawn and white; *inf* turncoat (of politicians)
barco *m*, boat; ship; hollow, rut. **b. barredero,** trawler. **b. siembraminas,** minelayer
barda *f*, horse armor; thatch; *carp* shingle; (Mexico) cement fence, cement wall
bardal *m*, thatched wall; mud wall
bardar *vt* to thatch
bardo *m*, poet, bard
bario *m*, barium
barítono *m*, baritone
barloventear *vi naut* to tack; ply to windward; *inf* wander about
barlovento *m*, *naut* windward
barnacla *f*, barnacle
barniz *m*, varnish; glaze; smattering, veneer
barnizar *vt* to varnish; glaze
barométrico *a* barometric
barómetro *m*, barometer
barón *m*, baron
baronesa *f*, baroness
barquero *m*, boatman; bargee; *ent* water-boatman

barquillero *m,* seller of wafers; waffle-iron

barquillo *m,* wafer, cornet

barquín *m,* furnace bellows

barra *f,* bar; ingot; railing (in courtroom); sandbank; fault (in cloth); lever, crossbar; (in cricket) bail; *mus* bar. **b. de jabón de afeitar,** shaving-stick. **a barras derechas,** without deceit

barrabasada *f, inf* wilfulness, escapade

barraca *f,* cabin, hut; stall; sideshow; *Latin Am.* barracks **b. de tiro,** shooting gallery

barracón *m,* side-show; stall

barragana *f,* concubine, mistress

barranca, *f,* **barranco** *m,* furrow, channel, rut; gorge; difficulty, fix

barrancoso *a* rutty, uneven

barredor (-ra) *n* sweeper

barredura *f,* sweeping; *pl* sweepings; rubbish

barrena *f,* borer, gimlet, drill, auger. *aer* **b. de cola,** tailspin

barrenar *vt* to drill, bore; blast (in quarries)

barrendero (-ra) *n* sweeper, scavenger

barrenero *m,* driller; blaster

barreno *m,* blast hole; bore, drill; vanity; *Lat. Am.* mania, pet peeve

barreño *m,* earthenware bowl (for dish washing, etc.)

barrer *vt* to sweep; *fig* clear, make a clean sweep

barrera *f,* barrier; barricade; *fig* obstacle. **b. de golpe,** automatic gate (at level crossings, etc.). **b. de minas,** minefield

barriada *f,* district; quarter (of a city); *Peru* slum, shanty town

barrica *f,* cask; barrel

barricada *f,* barricade

barriga *f, inf* belly

barrigón, barrigudo *a* pot-bellied

barril *m,* barrel; cask; water-butt

barrilero *m,* cooper

barrio *m,* district, quarter; suburb. **barrios bajos,** slums, back streets. **el otro b.,** the other world, Eternity

barrizal *m,* muddy place; claypit

barro *m,* mud; clay; earthenware drinking vessel; *inf* money

barroco *a* baroque

barroso *a* muddy; pimpled; mud-colored

barrote *m,* thick iron bar; stave, bond

barruntar *vt* to conjecture; suspect

barrunto *m,* conjecture; indication, sign

bártulos *m pl,* household goods; *fig* means, wherewithal

barullo *m, inf* confusion, disorder; mob

basa *f,* base; *arch* pedestal; foundation, basis

basalto *m,* basalt

basar *vt* to base, place on a base; *fig* found, base; *vr (with en)* rely upon, base oneself on

basca *f,* (gen. *pl*) nausea; retching; wave of anger

báscula *f,* weighing-machine, platform-scale; weighbridge

base *f,* base; (*chem geom mil*) base; basis; *arch* pedestal; *mus* root. **sin b.,** baseless

básico *a* basic

Basilea Basel, Basle

basílica *f,* palace; church, basilica

basquear *vi* to retch; feel squeamish

bastante *a* sufficient, enough. *adv* sufficiently; enough; fairly; a good deal; somewhat. **Hace b. calor,** It is quite hot. **Tengo b.,** I have enough. **Tenemos b. tiempo,** We have sufficient time

bastar *vi* to suffice. **¡Basta!** Enough! No more! Stop! **¡Basta de . . . !** Enough of . . . ! **Basta decir que . . . ,** Suffice it to say that . . .

bastardía *f,* bastardy, illegitimacy; baseness, meanness

bastardilla *f, print* italics

bastardo (-da) *a* bastard; spurious. *n* bastard

bastear *vt sew* to baste

bastidor *m,* embroidery frame; *art* stretcher (for can-

vas); *theat* wing; *mech* underframe; chassis, carriage; frame (of a window). *fig* **entre bastidores,** behind the scenes

bastilla *f, sew* hem; bastille

bastimentar *vt* to provision; supply

bastimento *m,* supplies; provisioning

bastión *m,* bastion

basto *m,* pack-saddle; ace of clubs; clubs (cards). *a* rude; tough; *fig* unpolished, rough

bastón *m,* cane, walking-stick; rod (of office); truncheon. **b. de junquillo,** Malacca cane. **empuñar el b.,** to take control, take over. **meter el b.,** to mediate

bastonear *vt* to cane; stir with a stick

basura *f,* rubbish, refuse; dung; sweepings

basural *m, Lat. Am.* garbage dump

basurero *m,* dustman; dunghill, rubbish dump; kitchen middens; dust-bin

bata *f,* dressing-gown; smoking-jacket; old-fashioned dress; overall, smock

batacazo *m,* bump, noise of a fall; *pol* dark horse

batahola *f, inf* hurly-burly, hubbub

batalla *f,* battle; *fig* struggle, conflict; tournament; *art* battle-piece. **b. campal,** pitched battle

batallador *a* fighting, warlike

batallar *vi* to battle, fight; dispute, argue; hesitate

batallón *m,* battalion

batata *f,* sweet potato, yam

batayola *f, naut* rail

batea *f,* wooden tray; punt

bateador, -a *mf, Lat. Am.* batter

batear *vt, Lat. Am.* to bat

batería *f,* (*mil elec naut*) battery. **b. de cocina,** kitchen utensils. **b. de pilas secas,** dry battery. **b. de teatro,** stage lights. **b. eléctrica,** electric battery

baticola *f,* crupper

batida *f,* game drive; attack; *met* beating

batido *a* beaten (of metals); shot (of silk); trodden, worn (roads, etc.). *m, cul* batter; hunting party

batidor *m,* beater; scout; outrider; hair comb; *cul* whisk. **b. de oro** (or **de plata),** gold (or silver) beater

batiente *m,* jamb (of door, etc.); damper (piano); leaf (of door); place where sea beats against cliffs, etc.

batihoja *m,* gold beater; metal worker

batimiento *m,* beating

batín *m,* smoking-jacket; man's dressing-gown

batintín *m,* Chinese gong

batir *vt* to beat, slap; demolish; dismantle, take down (stall, etc.); hammer, flatten; batter; *fig* beat (of sun, etc.); stir; pound; churn; comb (hair); vanquish, defeat; coin; reconnoiter, beat; throw down or drop; *vr* fight; swoop (birds of prey). **b. palmas,** to clap, applaud

batista *f,* cambric, batiste

baturrillo *m,* hotchpotch (gen. food); *inf* farrago, medley

batuta *f,* baton, conductor's wand. **llevar la b.,** *inf* boss the show, call the music, be in charge, to rule the roost

baúl *m,* trunk; *inf* belly; *Lat. Am. also* trunk (of a car) **b. escaparate** or **b. mundo,** wardrobe trunk

bauprés *m, naut* bowsprit

bausán (-ana) *n* guy, strawman; puppet; fool, idiot; lazybones

bautismo *m,* baptism

bautista *m,* baptizer, baptist. **San Juan B.,** St. John the Baptist

bautisterio *m,* baptistery

bautizar *vt* to baptize, christen; *inf* nickname; *inf* water (wine); accidentally shower with water

bautizo *m,* baptism; christening party

baya *f,* berry

bayeta *f,* baize; flannel

bayo (-ya) *a* bay (of horses)

Bayona Bayonne

bayoneta *f,* bayonet. **b. calada,** fixed bayonet

bayonetazo *m,* bayonet thrust

baza *f*, tricks taken (playing cards). *fig inf* **meter b.**, to stick one's oar in

bazar *m*, bazaar; shop, store; department store

bazo *m*, *anat* spleen. *a* yellow-brown

bazucar, bazuquear *vt* to shake or stir (liquids)

bazuqueo *m*, shaking or stirring of liquids

be *f*, letter B. *m*, baa

beata *f*, devout woman; *inf* pious hypocrite, prude; Sister of Mercy; over-religious woman

beatería *f*, sanctimoniousness; bigotry

beatificación *f*, beatification

beatificar *vt* to make happy; sanctify; beatify

beatífico *a* beatific

beatitud *f*, blessedness, beatitude; happiness

beato (-ta) *a* happy; blessed, beatified; devout; prudish. *n* devout person; over-pious person

beba *f*, *Argentina* baby (girl)

bebé *m*, baby

bebedero *a* drinkable. *m*, drinking trough or place

bebedizo *a* drinkable. *m*, draught of medicine; love-potion; poisonous drink

bebedor (-ra) *a* drinkable. *n* drinker; toper

beber *vt* to drink; absorb; *vi* toast, drink to the health (of); tipple. *m*, drinking; drink

bebida *f*, drink; beverage; alcoholic liquor

beca *f*, academic scarf or sash; scholarship, exhibition

becado, becario *m*, exhibitioner, scholarship holder

becerra *f*, calf; *bot* snapdragon

becerro *m*, bullock; bull calf; calf-skin. **b. marino**, *zool* seal

Beda el Venerable the Venerable Bede

bedel *m*, beadle; servitor, university porter

beduino (-na) *a* and *n* Bedouin. *m*, savage, blood-thirsty man

befar *vt* to mock, ridicule

befo *a* thick-lipped; knock-kneed. *m*, animal's lip

begonia *f*, *bot* begonia

bejín *m*, *bot* puff-ball; spoilt child

bejuco *m*, rattan

beldad *f*, beauty; belle

beldar *vt* *agr* to winnow

Belén Bethlehem

belén *m*, nativity, manager; *inf* bedlam; *inf* gossip

belfo *a* thick-lipped

belga *a* and *mf* Belgian

Bélgica Belgium

bélgico *a* Belgian

Belgrado Belgrade

Belice Belize

belicista *adj* war, militaristic; *mf* warmonger

bélico *a* warlike, military

belicoso *a* bellicose, aggressive; warlike

beligerancia *f*, belligerency

beligerante *a* and *mf* belligerent

belitre *a* *inf* knavish, cunning

bellaco (-ca) *a* artful, cunning. *n* knave; *Lat. Am.* untamed horse

belladona *f*, belladonna

bellaquería *f*, roguery, knavery, cunning

bellasombra *f*, umbra tree

belleza *f*, beauty, loveliness, fairness

bello *a* beautiful

bellota *f*, acorn; carnation bud; ornamental button, knob

bemol *a* and *m*, *mus* flat. *inf* **tener bemoles**, to be thorny, be difficult

bencina *f*, benzine; petrol, gasoline, gas

bendecir *vt* *irr* to praise, extol; bless; dedicate, consecrate. See **decir**

bendición *f*, benediction; blessing; consecration; *pl* marriage ceremony. **b. de la mesa**, grace before meals

bendito (-ta) *a* holy, blessed; fortunate; simple. **ser un b.**, to be a simpleton; be a good soul. **¡Benditos los ojos que te ven!** It's so nice to see you!

benedictino (-na) *a* and *n* Benedictine. *m*, Benedictine liqueur

beneficencia *f*, beneficence; charitable institutions

beneficiación *f*, benefaction

beneficiado (-da) *n* beneficiary. *m*, incumbent of a benefice

beneficiador (-ra) *n* benefactor

beneficiar *vt* to benefit; improve; cultivate (land); exploit (mine); purchase (directorship, etc.); sell at a loss (bonds, etc.)

beneficiario (-ia) *n* beneficiary

beneficiencia *f*, beneficence, charity

beneficio *m*, benefit; profit; cultivation (land, etc.); working (mine); *ecc* benefice; *theat* benefit

beneficioso *a* beneficial; useful

benéfico *a* beneficent; kind, helpful; charitable

benemérito *a* benemeritus, worthy, meritorious

beneplácito *m*, approbation; consent

benevolencia *f*, benevolence, goodwill

benévolo *a* benevolent, kind

Bengala Bengal

bengalí *a* and *mf* Bengali

benignidad *f*, kindness; mildness (of the weather, etc.)

benigno *a* kind; benign; mild; balmy

beodo (-da) *a* drunk, intoxicated. *n* drunkard

berbén *m*, *Mexico* scurvy

Berbería Barbary

bereber *a* and *mf* Berber

berenjena *f*, eggplant

bergante *m*, rascal, rogue

berilo *m*, beryl

Berlín Berlin

berlinés (-esa) *a* and *n* of or from Berlin

bermejear *vi* to be or look reddish

bermejo *a* reddish; red; redgold; carroty (of hair)

bermellón *m*, vermilion

bernardina *f*, lie; boast; gibberish

bernardo (-da) *a* and *ecc* Bernardine (Order of St. Bernard)

berquelio *m*, berkelium

berrear *vi* to low, bellow; yell, squall; shriek; *vr* reveal, confess

berrido *m*, lowing, bellowing; *inf* yell

berrinche *m*, *inf* tantrum, fit, fit of sulks

berro *m*, watercress

berroqueña *f*, granite

berza *f*, cabbage

besamanos *m*, ceremony of kissing royal hand, levee; kissing fingers (in salute)

besar *vt* to kiss; *inf* brush against, touch (of things); *vr* kiss one another; *inf* bang into, knock against one another

beso *m*, kiss; knock, collision

bestia *f*, quadruped (especially horses or mules); beast. *mf inf* nasty piece of work. **b. de carga**, beast of burden. **como una b.**, like a dog (e.g. **Trabajo como una b.** I work like a dog)

bestial *a* bestial; brutal; beastly

bestialidad *f*, brutality; bestiality; beastliness

bestialismo *m*, bestiality (sexual orientation)

besuquear *vt inf* to cover with kisses; *vr inf* spoon, make love

besuqueo *m*, *inf* kissing and spooning

betabel *m*, *Mexico* beetroot

bético *a* Andalusian

betún *m*, bitumen; shoe blacking; kind of cement. **b. de Judea** *or* **b. judaico,** asphalt

bezo *m*, blubber lip; proud flesh (of a wound)

bezudo *a* thick-lipped

biberón *m*, feeding bottle

Biblia *f*, Bible

bíblico *a* biblical

bibliófilo *m*, bibliophile

bibliografía *f*, bibliography

bibliográfico *a* bibliographical

biblioteca *f*, library; book series. **b. por subscripción,** circulating library

bibliotecario (-ia) *n* librarian

bibliotecnia, bibliotecología, biblioteconomía *f*, library science
bicarbonato *m*, bicarbonate
bíceps *m*, biceps
bicherío *m*, *Lat. Am.* bugs, insects
bicho *m*, any small animal or reptile; quadruped; fighting bull; scarecrow, sight. **b. viviente,** *inf* living soul. **mal b.,** rogue
bicicleta *f*, bicycle, bike. **ir** (*or* **andar** *or* **montar**) **en b.,** to bicycle, bike, go by bicycle, go by bike
bicoca *f*, *inf* trifle, bagatelle
bicolor *a* bicolored
bidé *m*, bidet
biela *f*, axle-tree; connecting-rod; big-end
bielda *f*, pitchfork; *agr* winnowing
bien *m*, ideal goodness, perfection; benefit, advantage; welfare; *pl* property, wealth. *adv* well; willingly; happily; perfectly; easily; enough, sufficient; all right! very well! **b. que,** although. **b. de equipo,** capital good. **bienes muebles,** movables, goods and chattels. **bienes raíces,** real estate. **el B. y el Mal,** Good and Evil. **¡Está b.!** All right! **no b.,** scarcely, as soon as. **si b.,** although, even if. **¿Y b.?** And so what? Well, then; What next?
bienal *a* biennial
bienamado *a* dearly beloved
bienandante *a* prosperous; happy
bienandanza *f*, happiness, welfare; prosperity
bienaventurado *a* blessed, holy; happy; *inf* over-simple, innocent, foolish
bienaventuranza *f*, blessedness
bienestar *m*, wellbeing; ease; comfort
bienhablado *a* well-spoken; civil, polite
bienhadado *a* fortunate, happy
bienhechor (-ra) *a* kind, helpful. *n* benefactor
bienintencionado *a* well-meaning
bienio *m*, biennium, space of two years, period of two years
bienquisto *a* respected; generally esteemed
bienvenida *f*, safe or happy arrival; welcome. **dar la b.,** to welcome
bienvivir *vi* to live comfortably; live decently or uprightly
bies *m*, bias, cross; slant
bife *m* *Argentina* beefsteak, steak
biftec *m*, beefsteak, steak
bifurcación *f*, bifurcation; fork, branch, junction
bifurcarse *vr* to fork, branch
bigamia *f*, bigamy
bígamo (-ma) *a* bigamous. *n* bigamist
bigornia *f*, anvil
bigote *m*, moustache; *pl* whiskers
bigotudo *a* moustached, whiskered
bikini *m*, bikini
bilateral *a* bilateral
bilingüe *a* bilingual
bilioso *a* bilious
bilis *f*, bile
billar *m*, billiards; billiard table
billete *m*, note, short letter; ticket; banknote. **b. circular,** excursion ticket. **b. de abono,** season ticket. **b. de andén,** platform ticket. **b. de banco,** banknote. **b. de favor,** free ticket. **b. de ida y vuelta,** round trip ticket. **b. entero,** full fare. **b. kilométrico,** tourist ticket. **b. sencillo,** one-way. **medio b.,** half-fare
billón *m*, billion
bimestral *a* bimonthly
bimestre *a* bimonthly. *m*, two months' duration; money paid or received at two-monthly intervals
bimotor *a* two-motor. *m*, twin-engined aircraft
binario *a* binary
bincha *f*, *Lat. Am.* hairband
binóculo *m*, opera glasses
biofísica *f*, biophysics
biografía *f*, biography
biográfico *a* biographical

biógrafo (-fa) *n* biographer; (Chile) movie theater (e.g. **¡Vamos al biógrafo!** Let's go to the movies!)
biología *f*, biology
biológico *a* biological
biólogo *m*, biologist
biombo *m*, screen
bioquímica *f*, biochemistry
bioquímico *m*, biochemist
bipartido *a* bipartite
bípedo *a* and *m*, biped
biplano *m*, biplane
biplaza *a* two-seater
birla *f*, skittle
birlar *vt* to bowl from where the bowl stopped; *inf* knock down; snatch away; *inf* rob
birlocha *f*, child's kite
Birmania Burma
birmano (-na) *a* and *n* Burmese
birreta *f*, biretta
birrete *m*, biretta; university cap; cap
bis *adv* twice; repeat; encore. *a* duplicate; **B** (in addresses, e.g., **Calle de Alcalá 18bis,** 18b Alcalá St.)
bisabuela *f*, great-grandmother
bisabuelo *m*, great-grandfather
bisagra *f*, hinge; shoemaker's polisher
bisbís *m*, game of chance
bisbisar *vt inf* to mutter; whisper
bisbiseo *m*, *inf* muttering; murmuring; whispering
bisecar *vt* to bisect
bisección *f*, *geom* bisection
bisectriz *f*, bisector
bisel *m*, bevel, chamfer
bisiesto *a* leap and *m*, leap (year)
bisílabo *a* two-syllabled
bismuto *m*, bismuth
bisnieto (-ta) *n* great-grandchild
bisonte *m*, bison
bisoño (-ña) *a* inexperienced, raw. *n* recruit; *inf* greenhorn
bistec *m*, beef steak
bisturí *m*, surgical knife
bisunto *a* grubby, greasy
bisutería *f*, imitation jewelry
bituminoso *a* bituminous
bivalvo *a* bivalve
Bizancio Byzantium
bizantinismo *m*, Byzantinism
bizarría *f*, handsomeness; dash; verve; gallantry, courage; magnificence; liberality; whim, caprice
bizarro *a* handsome; dashing; gallant, courageous; liberal; splendid, magnificent
bizcaitarrismo *m*, doctrine of Basque autonomy; Basque autonomy movement
bizco *a* squint-eyed, cross-eyed
bizcocho *m*, biscuit; spongecake; bisque
bizma *f*, poultice. **poner bizmas,** to poultice
biznieto *n* See **bisnieto**
blanca *f*, old Spanish coin; *inf* penny; *mus* minim. **sin b.,** penniless
blanco *a* white; fair-skinned; blank, vacant; *inf* cowardly. *m*, target; blank left in writing; white person; interval. **b. de España,** whiting. **b. de la uña,** half-moon of the nail. **dar en el b.,** to hit the mark. **en b.,** blank, unused; *inf* in vain; uncomprehendingly; (of nights) sleepless
blancor, *m.* blancura *f*, whiteness; fairness (of skin)
blandear *vt* to moderate, soothe; brandish; *vi fig* give way, yield
blandir *vt* to brandish, wield, flourish
blando *a* soft; mild (weather); delicate; kind; peaceable; delicate, effeminate; *inf* cowardly
blandón *m*, wax taper
blandura *f*, softness; poultice; blandishment, compliment; mildness (of weather); gentleness, affability; luxury

blanquear vt to bleach; whitewash; whiten; vi appear white; show white

blanquecino a whitish

blanqueo m, whitening; whitewashing; bleaching

blanquillo m, *Central America, Mexico* egg; *Chile, Peru,* white peach

blanquizal m, pipe-clay

blasfemador (-ra) a blaspheming. n blasphemer

blasfemar vi to blaspheme; curse, swear

blasfemia f, blasphemy; insult

blasfemo (-ma) n blasphemer. a blasphemous

blasón m, heraldry; escutcheon; glory, honor. **una familia con antiguos blasones,** a family of ancient lineage

blasonar vt to blazon; vi boast, brag, blazon abroad

bledo m, blade, leaf. **no importar un b.,** not to matter a straw

blenda f, *min* blende

blindado a *nav* armored, ironclad

blindaje m, *nav* armor-plating; *mil* blindage

blindar vt to plate with armor, to case with steel

blofista mf, *Lat. Am.* bluffer

blonda f, blonde (of lace)

blondo a fair, blond, flaxen-haired

bloque m, block, slab

bloquear vt to blockade; besiege

bloqueo m, blockade; siege; blocking; freezing (of assets). **violar el b.,** to run the blockade

blusa f, blouse

boa f, boa, large snake. m, boa (fur)

boato m, outward show, ostentation

bobería f, foolishness, stupidity

bóbilis, bóbilis (de) adv inf free of charge; without effort

bobina f, bobbin, spool, reel; *elec* coil; spool (of fishing rod)

bobo (-ba) a stupid, idiotic; simple, innocent. n fool. m, clown, jester

boca f, mouth; pincers (of crustaceans); entrance or exit; mouth (of a river), gulf, inlet; orifice, opening; muzzle (of guns); cutting edge (of tools); taste (of wine, etc.). **b. abajo,** face down, prone. **b. arriba,** on one's back, face up, supine. **b. del estómago,** pit of the stomach. **b. rasgada,** large mouth. **a b.,** verbally. **a b. de jarro,** point-blank. **a pedir de b.,** just as one would wish. **de b.,** by word of mouth. *inf* **sin decir esta b. es mía,** without a word, in silence

bocacalle f, entrance (to a street); street junction

bocadillo m, narrow ribbon; sandwich

bocado m, mouthful. **b. de reyes,** delicacy, exquisite dish (of food); snack; bite; (horse's) bit; bridle; pl preserved fruit cut up

bocamanga f, wrist (of sleeve)

bocana f, *Lat. Am.* estuary

bocanada f, mouthful (of liquid); cloud (of smoke). **b. de aire,** gust of wind

boceto m, sketch; outline; rough-cast model

bocha f, *sport* bowl; pl bowls

bochorno m, sultry weather; heat, stuffiness; blush, hot flush; shame

bochornoso a sultry; shameful

bocina f, trumpet; megaphone; foghorn; hooter; *aut* horn; horn (of gramophone); *ast* Ursa Minor

bocio m, *med* goiter

bocoy m, hogshead; large cask

boda f, wedding, marriage. **bodas de oro,** fiftieth (golden) anniversary. **bodas de plata,** silver wedding anniversary

bodega f, wine-cellar; storeroom; stockroom; granary; *Puerto Rico* grocery store; *naut* hold (of ship)

bodegón m, eating-house; tavern; *art* still-life; genre picture

bofes m pl, lungs, lights. *inf* **echar los b.,** to work oneself to death

bofetada f, **bofetón** m, blow, slap; box on the ear

boga f, rowing; fashion, vogue; *mech* bogie. mf oarsman, rower. **estar en b.,** to be fashionable

bogador (-ra) n rower, oarsman

bogar vi to row

bogavante m, lobster

bogotano (-na) a and n of or from Bogotá

bohemio (-ia) a and n gipsy; bohemian; Bohemian. m, archer's short cloak

bohío m, *Lat. Am.* hut

boicotear vt to boycott

boicot, boicoteo m, boycott

boina f, Basque cap; beret

bola f, globe; ball; *sport* bowl; *arch* balloon; *inf* trick, lie; (Cuba) rumor; *Mexico* shoeshine, shine. **b. de nieves,** snowball. *inf* **dejar rodar la b.,** to let things slide

bolardo m, bollard

bolchevismo m, Bolshevism

bolea f, (tennis) volley; throw

bolera f, bowling alley

bolero m, bolero; dancer; *inf* top hat; *Mexico* bootblack

boleta f, admission ticket; billet ticket; warrant; voucher; summons, ticket, traffic ticket

boletería f. *Lat. Am.* ticket office, box office

boleto m. *Lat. Am.* ticket

boletín m, bulletin; admission ticket; pay warrant; *com* price list; learned periodical. **b. de noticias,** news bulletin. **b. meteorológico,** weather report

boliche m, jack (in bowls); cup-and-ball toy; small oven (for charcoal); dragnet; *Mexico* bowling **juego de b.,** bowls

bólido m, *ast* bolide, meteor

bolillo m, bobbin (lace making); *Mexico* roll (food)

bolina f, *naut* bowline; *naut* sounder; *inf* uproar, tumult

bolita f, pellet

boliviano(-na) a and n Bolivian. m, silver coin

bollo m, bread roll; bun; bulge, bruise (in metal); *med* lump

bollón m, round-headed or brass-headed nail; *bot* bud (especially vines)

bolo m, skittle, ninepin; pillow (for lace making); Cuban coin; *med* large pill; *fig inf* blockhead; pl skittles (game of)

bolsa f, purse; bag; footmuff; fold, pucker; pouch; exchange, stock exchange, capital, money; prize money; *med* sac; *min* pocket. **b. de estudio,** scholarship grant. **b. de trabajo,** labor exchange. **b. de valores,** stock exchange. **bajar** (or **subir**) **la b.,** to fall (or rise) (of stock exchange quotations). **jugar a la b.,** to speculate on the stock exchange

bolsillo m, pocket; purse; money

bolsista mf stock-broker; speculator (on the stock exchange)

bomba f, *mech* pump; pumping engine; bomb; *mil* shell; lamp globe; *inf* improvised verses; *inf* drinking bout. **¡B.!** Listen! Here goes! **b. de incendios,** fire-engine. **b. marina,** waterspout. **b. de mecha atrasada,** time bomb. **b. volante,** flying-bomb. **a prueba de b.,** bombproof. **arrojar bombas,** to bomb. *inf* **caer como una b.,** to be a bombshell

bombachos m pl, baggy, loose-fitting; m pl, plus fours

bombardear vt to bombard; bomb; shell

bombardeo m, bombardment, bombing; shelling

bombardero m, gunner, bombardier; *aer* bomber. **b. pesado,** *aer* heavy bomber. **Servicio de b.,** Bomber Command

bombástico a bombastic, high sounding

bombazo m, bombshell; bomb crater; noise of an exploding bomb

bombear vt to pump; bombard, shell; praise

bombero m, worker of a pressure pump; fireman; mortar, howitzer

bombilla f, *naut* lantern; (*elec phys*) bulb; small pump; straw for drinking maté *WH*

bombillo m, w.c. siphon; handpump

bombo m, big drum or player of it; *naut* barge, ferry; ballot box; exaggerated praise

bombón m, bonbon, sweet

bombonera f, box for toffee, etc.

bonachón *a inf* genial, good-natured

bonaerense *a* and *mf* of or from the Province of Buenos Aires

Bonaira Bonaire

bonancible *a* calm (of weather, sea)

bonanza *f*, fair weather; prosperity

bondad *f*, goodness; kindness, helpfulness. **Tenga la b. de . . . ,** Be good enough to . . . , Please . . .

bondadoso *a* good, kind

bonete *m*, academic cap; *zool* reticulum (ruminants); *ecc* biretta. **gran b.,** important person. *inf* **a tente b.,** insistently

bonetero (-ra) *n* seller or maker of caps and birettas

boniato *m, Lat. Am.* sweet potato, yam

bonificación *f*, bonus; allowance, discount

bonísimo, *a sup* **bueno** extremely good

bonito *a* pretty; graceful; (ironical) fine. *m, icht* striped tunny

bono *m*, voucher; *com* bond, certificate. **b. postal,** postal money order. **bono del gobierno,** government bond

boñiga *f*, cow-dung, animal manure

boqueada *f*, gasp, opening of the mouth. **dar las boqueadas, estar en las últimas boqueadas,** to be at the last gasp

boquear *vi* to gasp; be dying; *inf* be at last gasp (of things); *vt* say, utter

boquera *f*, sluice (in irrigation canal)

boquerón *m*, large opening; *icht* anchovy (fish); whitebait

boquete *m*, narrow entrance, aperture; gap, breach; hole

boquiabierto *a* open-mouthed; amazed

boquiancho *a* wide-mouthed

boquiasombrado *a* gaping

boquilla *f, dim* small mouth; mouthpiece (of wind instruments, etc.); cigar- or cigarette-holder; gas-burner; nozzle; tip (of cigarettes)

boquirroto *a inf* loquacious, indiscreet

borbollar *vi* to bubble, foam, froth

borbollón, borbotón *m*, gushing, bubbling, welling up. **a borbollones,** in a torrent; hastily, impetuously

borbotar *vi* to gush out, well up

borda *f*, hut, cabin; *naut* gunwale

bordado *m*, embroidery

bordador (-ra) *n* embroiderer

bordar *vt* to embroider; *fig* perform perfectly

borde *m*, edge; fringe; verge; rim; mount (of a picture); brim (of a hat); side (of ship). *a* wild (of plants); illegitimate. **estar lleno hasta los bordes,** to be full to the brim

bordear *vt* to border, trim with a bordear; line (a street, e.g. **Diez mil personas bordearon las calles durante el desfile,** Ten thousand people lined the streets during the parade)

bordillo *m*, curbstone, curb.

bordo *m*, side (of ships); border, edge. **a b.,** on board

bordón *m*, pilgrim's staff; monotonous repetition; refrain; *mus* bass string; *fig* guide, stay

borgoña *m*, Burgundy wine

borgoñón (-ona) *a* and *n* Burgundian

bórico *a* boric

boricua *a*, **borinqueño, -a** *a, mf* Puerto Rican

borla *f*, tassel; puff (for powder). *fig* **tomar la b.,** to take one's doctorate, graduate

bornear *vt* to bend, twist; *arch* hoist into position; *vr* warp (wood)

borra *f*, yearling ewe; thickest wool; wad-stuffing; lees, sediment; fluff, dust; *inf* trash. **b. de algodón,** cotton-waste

borrachera *f*, drunkenness; orgy, carousal; *inf* blunder

borrachín (-ina) *n* tippler, toper

borrachito *a* high (on liquor), tipsy

borracho (de) *a* drunk (on), intoxicated (with); *inf* blind (with rage, etc.). *n* tippler, drunkard

borrador *m*, rough draft. **en borrador,** in the works (e.g. **Tiene dos ensayos en borrador,** She has two essays in the works). **estar en borrador,** to be in the works

borradura *f*, erasure

borrajear *vt* to scribble

borrar *vt* to erase; cross out; blot out; *fig* obliterate

borrasca *f*, storm, tempest; peril, danger; *inf* orgy

borrascosidad *f*, storminess

borrascoso *a* stormy; disordered, turbulent

borrego (-ga) *n* lamb; *inf* nincompoop, simpleton; *m pl*, fleecy clouds; white horses (waves)

borrico (-ca) *n* donkey; fool. *m, carp* sawing-horse

borrón *m*, blot; rough draft; defect; *fig* stigma

borroso *a* blurred, indistinct; full of dregs, muddy

boscaje *m*, grove, group of trees, thicket

Bósforo, el the Bosporus

bosque *m*, wood, forest

bosquejar *vt art* to sketch; sketch out, draft; model in rough (sculpture); outline

bosquejo *m*, outline, sketch; rough plan or idea; unfinished work. **en bosquejo,** grosso modo

bostar *m*, ox barn

bostezar *vi* to yawn

bostezo *m*, yawning; yawn

bota *f*, small wineskin; barrel, butt; boot. **b. de montar,** riding boot. **botas de campaña,** top-boots. **botas de vadear,** waders

botada, botadura *f*, launching (of a ship)

botador *m*, thrower; boating-pole; *carp* nail-puller

botafuego *m, mil* linstock; *inf* quick-tempered, irascible person

botalón *m, naut* boom. **b. de foque,** jib-boom

botana *f, Lat. Am.* bite (to eat), snack

botánica *f*, botany

botánico (-ca) *a* botanical. *n* botanist

botar *vt* to fling; launch (boat); *Lat. Am.* to discard, throw away, throw out *naut* shift the helm; *vi* jump; bounce, rebound; rear, prance (horses)

botarate *m, inf* madcap, devil-may-care

botarel, botarete *m, arch* abutment, buttress, flying buttress

botarga *f*, motley; harlequin

bote *m*, thrust (with lance, etc.); rearing (of horse); rebound; *aer* bump; open boat; small bottle, jar. **b. salvavidas,** lifeboat. *inf* **de b. en b.,** chockfull

botella *f*, bottle; bottleful; flask

botica *f*, chemist's shop; medicines, remedies; physic; store, shop; medicine chest

boticario *m*, apothecary, chemist

botija *f*, earthen jug; *slang* chunky person

botijo *m*, earthenware jar with spout and handle

botillería *f*, ice-cream bar

botín *m*, gaiter; buskin; booty

botiquín *m*, first-aid kit; medicine chest

botón *m*, bud; button; knob, handle; switch (electric); press button (bell); *bot* center; button (on a foil); *mech* stud

botonero (-ra) *n* button maker or seller

bóveda *f, arch* vault, arch; crypt; cavern. **b. celeste,** sky

boxeador *m*, boxer

boxear *vi sport* to box

boxeo *m, sport* boxing

boya *f, naut* buoy; float

boyante *a* floating; light, buoyant; prosperous

boyar *vi naut* to float

boyero *m*, cowherd

boza *f*, painter (of a boat)

bozal *m*, muzzle; nosebag; harness bells. *mf inf* greenhorn; *a* wild, untamed (horses)

bozo *m*, down which precedes beard; muzzle; headstall; lips, snout

bracero *m*, one who offers his arm (to a lady); day laborer; strong man. **de b.,** arm-in-arm

bracete *m*, small arm. **de b.,** arm-in-arm

bracmán *m*, Brahmin

braga *f*, (gen. *pl*) breeches; knickerbockers; hoist or pulley rope

bragazas *m, inf* weak-willed, fellow, soft specimen
braguero *m, med* truss
bragueta *f,* fly (of breeches)
brahmanismo *m,* Brahmanism
bramante *a* roaring. *m,* twine, pack-thread
bramar *vi* to roar; rage; *fig* howl (of the wind, etc.)
bramido *m,* bellowing; roaring; yell of rage; *fig* howling (wind, sea, etc.)
brancada *f,* drag net
branquia *f,* (gen. *pl*) *icht* gill
branquial *a* branchiate
braquicefalia *f,* brachycephaly
braquiotomía *f, surg* brachiotomy, amputation of the arms
brasa *f,* live coal. **estar como en brasas,** to be like a cat on hot bricks
brasero *m,* brazier; *Mexico* fireplace
Brasil Brazil
brasileño (-ña) *a* and *n* Brazilian
bravata *f,* bravado; threat
braveza *f,* ferocity, savageness; valor; violence, fury (of elements)
bravío *a* savage, untamed; wild (plants); uncultured
bravo *a* valiant; surly, rude; independent, strong-minded, good, excellent; savage (animals); stormy (sea); rough, rugged; violent, angry; *inf* sumptuous, magnificent.
bravura *f,* ferocity (animals); courage (persons); boastful threat
braza *f, naut* fathom; stroke (in swimming)
brazado *m,* armful
brazal *m,* armlet, brassard
brazalete *m,* bracelet; brassard
brazo *m,* arm; upper arm; front paw; *mech* arm; branch (of chandelier, etc.); bough; arm (of chair); power, courage; *pl* protectors; workmen, hands. **b. de mar,** firth, arm of the sea. **a b. partido,** in unarmed fight, man to man. **con los brazos abiertos,** welcomingly; willingly, gladly. **dar los brazos (a),** to embrace. *inf* **hecho un b. de mar,** dressed up to the nines
brea *f,* pitch, tar; sacking, canvas
brebaje *m,* beverage; unpleasant drink; *naut* draught (of beer, grog, etc.)
brecha *f, mil* breach; opening; *fig* impression (on mind). **morir en la b.,** to fight to the last ditch; die in harness
brécol *m, bot* broccoli
brega *f,* fight; quarrel; disappointment, trick. **andar a la b.,** to work hard. **dar b.,** to play a trick
bregar *vi* to fight; work hard; *fig* struggle; **bregarse con,** to tackle (a problem)
Brema Bremen
breña *f,* rough ground, bramble patch
breñal *m,* scrub, brushwood
breñoso *a* rugged, rocky
Bretaña Brittany
brete *m,* fetters, shackles; *fig* fix, squeeze, tight spot, tight squeeze (e.g. **Estoy en un brete.** I'm in a tight spot)
bretón (-ona) *a* and *n* Breton. *m,* Breton (language)
breva *f,* early fig; early acorn; *fig* advantage, "plum"; *inf* peach (girl); *inf* windfall, piece of luck; Havana cigar
breve *a* brief; concise. *m,* papal brief. *f, mus* breve. **en b.,** shortly, concisely; in a short while, soon
brevedad *f,* brevity **a la mayor brevedad** *Lat. Am.* as soon as possible
breviario *m,* breviary
brezal *m,* heath, moor
brezo *m, bot* heath
bribón (-ona) *n* rogue, ruffian. *a* knavish, dishonest; lazy
bribonada *f,* knavery, mischievous trick
bribonear *vi* to idle; play tricks, be a rogue
bribonería *f,* rascality, vagrant life
brida *f,* bridle
brigada *f, mil* brigade; *naut* division of fleet; beasts of burden. **brigada millonaria,** (Castroist Cuba) team of

thirty sugarcane cutters who cut a million or more arrobas in one harvest
brillante *a* sparkling, brilliant; *fig* outstanding. *m,* diamond
brillantez *f,* brightness, luster; fame; *fig* brilliance
brillantina *f,* brilliantine
brillar *vi* to shine, sparkle, gleam, glisten; *fig* be brilliant or outstanding
brillo *m,* brilliancy, brightness, shine; fame, glory; distinction, brilliance, splendour
brincar *vi* to spring, leap, skip, frisk; *fig inf* skip, omit; *inf* grow angry; *vt* jump a child up and down
brinco *m,* leap, spring; skip, frolicking
brindar *vi* to invite, provoke (of things); (*with prep a or por*) drink the health of, toast; *vt* and *vi* give, present; offer; *vr* offer one's services
brindis *m,* toast (drink)
brío *m,* vigor; spirit, courage; gusto, verve
brioso *a* vigorous, enterprising; spirited, courageous; dashing, lively
briqueta *f,* briquette
brisa *f,* breeze; grape pressings
británico *a* British
brizna *f,* shred, paring; blade (grass); filament, fiber; string (of bean-pod, etc.); splinter, chip
briznar *vi, Lat. Am.* to drizzle
broca *f,* reel; tack (shoemaker's); *mech* drill, bit
brocado *m,* brocade. *a* brocade or embroidered like brocade
brocal *m,* puteal (of a well); mouthpiece (of wineskin); metal ring (of sword-sheath)
brocamantón *m,* large jeweled brooch
brocatel *m,* imitation brocade
brocha *f,* brush. **b. de afeitar,** shaving brush. **de b. gorda,** crudely painted. **pintor de b. gorda,** decorator
brochada *f,* stroke (of the brush)
brochado *a* brocaded, embossed
brochadura *f,* fastening, set of hooks and eyes
broche *m,* clasp, fastening; brooch; hooks and eyes; *Lat. Am.* (paper) clip
brochón *m,* whitewash brush
broma *f,* merriment; joke, jest; ship-worm. **b. literaria,** literary hoax
bromear(se) *vi* and *vr* to joke, make fun
bromista *a* joking, jesting; mischievous. *mf* genial person; prankster, tease
bromo *m,* bromine
bronca *f, inf* shindy
bronce *m,* bronze; brass; *poet* gun, bell, trumpet; bronze statue; sunburn
bronceado *a* bronzed; sunburnt. *m,* sunburn
broncear *vt* to bronze; sunburn
bronco *a* rough, coarse; brittle; (of metals); harsh (voice, musical instruments); rigid, stiff; surly
bronconeumonía *f,* bronchopneumonia
bronquial *a* bronchial
bronquio *m,* (gen. *pl*) bronchi
bronquitis *f,* bronchitis
broquel *m,* shield; *fig* protection
broquelero *m,* shield maker; quarrelsome man
broqueta *f,* skewer
brotadura *f,* budding
brotar *vi* to germinate, sprout; gush forth (water); issue forth, burst out; *fig* appear (of rash); *fig* begin to appear; *vt* to bring forth; produce (of earth)
brote *m,* bud, sprout; *fig* germ, genesis; iota, jot, atom
broza *f,* garden rubbish; debris; thicket
bruces (a or de) *adv* face downwards. **caer de b.,** to fall flat. Also with other verbs: *dar, echarse,* etc.
bruja *f,* witch; owl; *inf* hag
brujear *vi* to practise witchcraft
brujería *f,* witchcraft
brujo *m,* magician, wizard
brújula *f,* magnetic needle; compass; mariner's com-

pass. **b. de bolsillo,** pocket compass. **b. giroscópica,** gyrocompass

bruma *f,* haze; sea-mist

brumoso *a* misty, hazy

bruno *a* dark brown

bruñido *m,* polishing; burnish

bruñidor (-ra) *a* polishing. *n* burnisher. *m,* polisher (instrument)

bruñir *vt* to polish, burnish; *inf* apply make up

brusco *a* brusque, rude; blunt; sudden, unexpected; sharp (of bends)

Bruselas Brussels

bruselense *a* and *mf* of or from Brussels

brusquedad *f,* brusquerie, rudeness; bluntness; suddenness, unexpectedness; sharpness (of a bend)

brutal *a* brutal

brutalidad *f,* brutality; *fig* brutishness; viciousness

bruto *a* stupid, unreasonable; vicious; unpolished, rough. *m,* animal (gen. quadruped). **en b.,** in the rough; *com* in bulk. **diamante en b.,** an uncut diamond

bruza *f,* strong brush; scrubbing brush

Bs. As. abbrev. of Buenos Aires

bu *m, inf* bogey man

buba *f,* pustule; *pl* buboes

bubónico *a* bubonic

bucal *a* buccal

bucanero *m,* buccaneer

búcaro *m,* arsenical clay; jar made of arsenical clay

buceador *m,* diver

bucear *vi* to work as a diver; swim under water; *fig* investigate

bucéfalo *m,* bucephalus; *inf* fool, blockhead

buceo *m,* diving; dive; *fig* investigation

buchaca *f, Lat. Am.* saddlebag; billiard pocket

buche *m,* craw or crop; mouthful; wrinkle, pleat; *inf* stomach, belly. *fig inf* inmost heart

bucle *m,* ringlet, curl

bucólico *a* bucolic

budismo *m,* Buddhism

budista *a* and *mf* Buddhist

budín *m,* pudding

buen *a abb* of **bueno,** good. Used before *m,* singular nouns and infinitives used as nouns, e.g. **un b. libro,** a good book. **el b. cantar,** good singing

buenamente *adv* easily; comfortably, conveniently; willingly

buenaventura *f,* good luck; fortune told from hand

bueno (see buen) *a* good; kind; useful; convenient; pleasant; healthy; large (drink, etc.); simple, innocent; suitable; sufficient; opportune. **¡B.!** Good!; Enough!; *Mexico* Hello! (on telephone); All right! **a buenas,** willingly. **de buenas a primeras,** at first sight, from the beginning. **hacer bueno,** to prove, justify (a claim)

buey *m,* ox. **b. suelto,** *inf* freelance; bachelor

búfalo (-la) *n* buffalo

bufanda *f,* scarf

bufar *vi* to bellow; snort; *inf* snort with rage

bufete *m,* desk, writing table; lawyer's office or practice; sideboard

bufido *m,* snort; bellow

bufo *a* comic. *m,* clown, buffoon

bufón *m,* buffoon, clown; jester. *a* comical, clownish

bufonada *f,* buffoonery, clowning; raillery, taunt

bufonear(se) *vr* and *vi* to joke, jest, parody

bufonería. See **bufonada**

buhardilla *f,* garret; skylight

búho *m,* owl; *inf* hermit, unsociable person

buhonería *f,* pedling, hawking; pedler's wares

buhonero *m,* pedler

buido *a* sharp-pointed; sharp

buitre *m,* vulture

bujía *f,* candle; candlestick; *elec* candle-power; *aut* sparking plug

bula *f,* (Papal) bull

bulbo *m, bot* bulb. **b. dentario,** pulp (of teeth)

bulboso *a* bulbous

bulevar *m,* boulevard, promenade

bulla *f,* noise; bustle; confusion; fuss. *inf* **meter a b.,** to throw into great confusion

bullente *adj* boiling, bubbling; frothey (beer); swarming, teeming. **b. de sol,** drenched in sunlight, sundrenched

bullebulle *mf* busybody; madcap

bullicio *m,* noise, bustle; rioting; uproar

bullicioso *a* noisy, merry, boisterous; rebellious; lively, restless

bullir *vi* to boil; foam, bubble; *fig* seethe; *fig* swarm (insects); bustle; *vt* move, stir; *vr* stir, give signs of life

bulto *m,* bulk, mass, size; form of person, etc., seen indistinctly; swelling; bust, statue; bundle, package, piece of luggage; pillowcase. *fig inf* **poner de b.,** to put clearly, emphasize. **ser de b.,** to be obvious

bumerang *m,* boomerang

buñolería *f,* bun or waffle shop

buñuelo *m,* bun; waffle, fritter; *fig* botch

buque *m,* ship, vessel; capacity of ship; ship's hull. **b. barreminas,** minesweeper. **b. de guerra,** battleship, man-of-war. **b. de vapor,** steamer. **b. de vela,** sailing ship. **b. escuela,** trainingship. **b. mercante,** merchant vessel. **b. submarino,** submarine. **b. transbordador,** train-ferry

burbuja *f,* bubble

burbujear *vi* to bubble

burdel *m,* brothel; *inf* untidy, noisy place. *a* lascivious

burdo *a* coarse, tough

burgalés (-esa) *a* and *n* of or from Burgos

burgo *m,* borough, burgh

burgomaestre *m,* burgomaster

burgués (-esa) *a* and *n* bourgeois

burguesía *f,* bourgeoisie

buriel *a* dark red

buril *m,* burin, engraver's tool

burla *f,* mockery; joke, jest; trick. **b. burlando,** without effort; negligently. **de burlas,** in fun. **entre burlas y veras,** half-jokingly

burlador *a* mocking. *m,* libertine, rake; deceiver

burlar *vt* to play a trick on; deceive; disappoint; *vr* and *vi* (*with de*) make fun of, laugh at, ridicule

burlesco *a* jocular, comic, burlesque

burlón (-ona) *a* joking; mocking, scoffing. *n* joker; scoffer

buró *m,* bureau, writing-desk; *Mexico* night table

burocracia *f,* bureaucracy

burócrata *mf* bureaucrat

burocrático *a* bureaucratic

burocratismo *m,* bureaucracy, red tape

burra *f,* she-ass; foolish, unteachable woman; painstaking, patient woman

burrajo *m,* dry stable dung used as fuel

burro *m,* ass, donkey; sawing-horse; card game

bursátil *a com* relating to the stock exchange; financial

busca *f,* search; hunting party; research; pursuit

buscado *adj* deliberate, intentional (negligence, etc.)

buscador (-ra) *n* searcher; investigator. *m,* finder (of a camera, etc.)

buscapié *m,* hint or suggestion; *fig* feeler

buscapiés *m,* squib, cracker, firecracker

buscapleitos *mf Lat. Am.* troublemaker

buscar *vt* to search, look for; pursue. **ir a b.,** to go to look for, go and get; bring, fetch

buscarruidos *mf inf* quarrel maker

buscavidas *mf inf* busybody; *inf* go-getter

buscón (-ona) *n* searcher; pickpocket, thief, swindler, rogue

buscona *f,* prostitute

busilis *m, inf* knotty problem, snag; **ahí está el b.,** there's the rub; core, main point

búsqueda (de) *f,* search (for)

busto *m,* art bust, head and shoulders

butaca *f,* armchair; *theat* orchestra stall; seat (in movies, etc.)

butifarra *f*, sausage made principally in Catalonia and the Balearic Islands; *inf* badly fitting stocking

buzo *m*, diver

buzón *m*, mailbox; letter-box; canal, channel; sluice

C

C. abbrev. of ciudadano

¡ca! *interj* Fancy! Oh no!

cabal *a* just, exact; perfect; complete; faultless. *interj* Exactly! **por sus cabales,** according to plan; perfectly

cábala *f*, cabala; divination; *inf* intrigue. **hacer cábalas,** to venture a guess

cabalgada *f*, cavalcade; foray, raid

cabalgador (-ra) *n* rider, horseman

cabalgadura *f*, riding horse; beast of burden

cabalgar *vi* to ride a horse; ride in procession

cabalístico *a* cabalistic; mysterious

caballa *f*, mackerel

caballada *f*, pack of horses; stud (of horses)

caballeresco *a* gentlemanly; knightly; chivalrous

caballería *f*, riding animal; cavalry; knightly deed or quest; any of Spanish Military Orders; knight-errantry; knighthood; chivalry; share of the spoils of war; horsemanship. **c. andante,** knight-errantry. **c. ligera,** *mil* light horse. **c. mayor,** horses, mares, mules. **c. menor,** asses, donkeys

caballeriza *f*, stable; stud of horses; staff of a stable

caballerizo *m*, head stable-groom. **c. mayor del rey,** Master of the King's Horse

caballero *m*, gentleman; cavalier; knight. **c. andante,** knight-errant. *inf* **c. de industria,** adventurer, sharper. **el C. de la Mancha,** the Knight of La Mancha. **el C. Sin Miedo y Sin Tacha,** the Seigneur de Bayart. **c. del hábito,** knight of one of the Spanish Military Orders. **c. novel,** untried knight. **armar c.,** to dub a knight

caballerosidad *f*, gentlemanliness; nobility; generosity; chivalry

caballeroso *a* gentlemanly; noble; generous; chivalrous

caballete *m*, ridge (of a roof); *mil* wooden horse; brake (for flax and hemp); *agr* furrow; easel; sawing-frame; trestle; bridge (of the nose)

caballito *m*, *dim* little horse; *pl* merry-go-round; automatic horse gambling game; circus equestrian act. **c. del diablo,** dragonfly

caballo *m*, horse; (chess) knight; (Spanish cards) queen; sawing-frame; *pl* cavalry. **c. balancín,** rocking horse. **c. de batalla,** war-horse; *fig* hobby-horse; forte; crux. **c. de cartón,** hobby-horse; rocking horse. **c. de carrera,** racehorse. **c. de tiro,** draft-horse. **c. de vapor,** horsepower. **c. marino,** sea-horse. **a c.,** on horseback. **A c. regalado no le mires el diente,** Never look a gift horse in the mouth. **caer bien a c.,** to have a good seat (on a horse). **ser un c. loco en una cacharrería,** to be like a bull in a china shop

cabaña *f*, hut, cabin, cottage; flock (of sheep); drove (of mules); *Argentina* cattle ranch; *art* pastoral scene; balk (billiards)

cabaret *m*, cabaret, nightclub

cabaretero *m*, nightclub owner

cabeceada *f*, *Lat. Am.* nod (of the head)

cabecear *vi* to nod; shake the head in disapproval; move the head from side to side; toss the head (horses); (*aer naut*) pitch; sway (of a carriage); lean; *vt* refoot (socks); head (wine)

cabeceo *m*, nod, shake (of head); (*naut aer*) pitching; lurching (of a carriage, etc.); bight (of river)

cabecera *f*, top, upper portion, head; seat of honor; bedhead; river source; capital (country or county); illustrated chapter heading; pillow; inscription, heading

cabecilla *dim f*, small head. *mf inf* hothead. *m*, rebel leader

cabellera *f*, head of long hair; hair-switch; tail (of comet)

cabello *m*, hair; head of hair; silk (of maize). *fig inf* **asirse de un c.,** to clutch at a straw

cabelludo *a* hairy; *bot* fibrous

caber *vi irr* to be room for, contain; fit into, go into (e.g. **No cabemos todos en este coche,** There isn't room for all of us in this car); happen, befall, have (e.g. **No les cupo tal suerte,** They did not have such luck— Such luck did not befall them); be possible (e.g. **Todo cabe en Dios,** All things are possible with God). **No cabe más,** There's no room for anything else; *fig* That's the limit. *fig* **no c. en sí,** to be beyond oneself (with joy, pride, etc.). **No cabe duda de que,** There's no doubt that. *Pres. Ind.* **quepo, cabes,** etc. *Fut.* **cabré,** etc. *Conditional* **cabría,** etc. *Preterite* **cupe, cupiste,** etc. *Pres. Subjunc.* **quepa, quepas,** etc. *Imperf. Subjunc.* **cupiese,** etc.

cabestrar *vt* to halter

cabestrillo *m*, sling; thin chain (for ornament). **en c.,** in a sling (e.g. **Tenía el brazo en c.,** His arm was in a sling)

cabestro *m*, halter; sling; leading ox

cabeza *f*, head; top, upper end; nail-head; brain; mind; judgment; self-control; edge (of book); peak, summit; source, origin; individual, person; head of cattle; capital city. *m*, leader, chief, head. *mech* **c. de biela,** big-end. *inf* **c. de chorlito,** scatterbrain (person). **c. de hierro,** blockhead. *mil* **c. de puente,** bridgehead. **c. de partido,** principal town of a region. **c. de turco,** scapegoat. **irse la c. (a alguien),** to feel giddy. *fig inf* **meter a uno en la c.,** to put into someone's head. *inf* **quebrarse la c.,** to rack one's brains. *inf* **quitar a uno de la c. (una cosa),** to dissuade; get an idea out of someone's head

cabezada *f*, blow with or on the head; nod; headshake; headstall; *naut* pitching. **dar cabezadas,** to nod, go to sleep

cabezal *m*, small head pillow; *surg* pad; bolster; narrow mattress; *mech* head

cabezo *m*, summit (of mountain); hill; *naut* reef

cabezón *m*, tax-register; collar-band; head-opening (of a garment)

cabezudo *a* large-headed; *inf* obstinate; *inf* heady (of wine). *m*, carnival grotesque

cabida *f*, space, capacity; extent, area

cabildear *vi* to canvass votes, lobby

cabildo *m*, *ecc* chapter; municipal council; meeting; meeting place of council. **c. abierto,** town meeting

cabina *f*, cabin. **c. telefónica** phone booth

cabinero, -a *mf*, *Lat. Am.* flight attendant

cabizbajo *a* crestfallen; pensive, melancholy

cable *m*, end; string (of bridge); cable's length; **c. aéreo,** overhead cable. **c. alimentador,** feed line. **c. eléctrico,** electric cable

cabo *m*, end, extremity; stump, stub; handle, shaft, haft; leader; *geog* cape; end, conclusion; *naut* rope; ply (of wool, etc.); *mil* corporal; *pl* accessories (clothes); horse's tail and mane. **c. de maestranza,** foreman. **c. de mar,** naval quartermaster. **c. furriel,** *mil* quartermaster. **al c.,** in the end. **llevar a c.,** to finish

Cabo de Hornos Cape Horn

cabotaje *m*, *naut* coasting trade

cabra *f*, nanny-goat; goat. **c. montesa,** wild goat

cabrerizo (-za) *a* goatish. *m*, goatherd

cabrero (-ra) *m*, goatherd; *a Argentina* bad-tempered, cantankerous

cabria *f*, winch, hoist

cabrilla *f*, *carp* saw-horse; *pl ast* Pleiades; burn marks on legs from sitting too near fire; white crests (of waves)

cabrillear *vi* to foam, froth (the sea)

cabrío *a* goatish. *m*, herd of goats. **macho c.**, male goat, he-goat

cabriola *f*, fouetté (in dancing); spin in the air (acrobats); curvet (horses); caper

cabriolar *vi* to curvet; caper, skip

cabriolé *m*, cabriolet; short cape with or without sleeves

cabritilla *f*, dressed kid; lambskin, etc.

cabrito *m*, *zool* kid; *pl* toasted maize, popcorn

cabrón *m*, billy goat, buck, he-goat; *inf* complaisant husband, cuckhold; *Chile* owner or operator of a brothel

cabrona *f*, *Chile* bawd, madam

cabruno *a* goatish

cabujón *m*, *min* uncut gem; unpolished ruby; *pl* vignettes

cacahual *m*, cacao plantation

cacahuete *m*, *bot* peanut, monkey nut

cacao *m*, *bot* cacao tree; cacaonut

cacarear *vi* to crow, cackle; *vt* *inf* boast

cacareo *m*, crowing, cackling; *inf* boast

cacatúa *f*, cockatoo

cacera *f*, irrigation channel

cacería *f*, hunting party; hunting bag, booty; *art* hunting scene

cacerola *f*, stew-pot, casserole

cachalote *m*, sperm whale

cachano *m*, Old Nick

cachar *vt* to break in fragments; split (wood)

cacharrería *f*, crockery store

cacharro *m*, coarse earthenware vessel; *inf* decrepit, worthless object

cachazudo *a* phlegmatic, slow

cachear *vt* to search (a person) for weapons

Cachemira Kashmir

cachemira *f*, cashmere

cacheo *m*, search (of persons) for weapons

cachetada *f*, *Lat. Am.* slap (in the face)

cachete *m*, blow on the head or face with one's fist; cheek (especially fat one)

cachetero *m*, dagger

cachetina *f*, hand-to-hand fight

cachimba *f*, *Lat. Am.* pipe (for smoking)

cachiporra *f*, club, bludgeon

cachivache *m*, *inf* (gen. *pl*) trash; pots, pans, utensils

cacho *m*, small slice (gen. of bread or fruit)

cachón *m*, breaker, wave; small waterfall

cachorro (-rra) *n* puppy; cub. *m*, small pistol

cacillo *m*, ladle; basting spoon

cacique *m*, Indian chief, cacique; *inf* political "boss"

caciquismo *m*, political "bossism"

caco *m*, pickpocket, thief; *inf* poltroon

cacofonía *f*, cacophony

cacografía *f*, cacography

cacto *m*, cactus

cacumen *m*, *inf* brains, acumen

cada *a* every, each. **c. cual,** each. **c. que,** whenever; every time that. **c. y cuando que,** whenever

cadalso *m*, scaffold; platform, stand

cadáver *m*, corpse

cadavérico *a* cadaverous, ghastly

cadena *f*, chain; link, tie; *fig* bond; *fig* sequence (of events); *law* imprisonment; *arch* buttress; grand chain (dancing); **c. de montañas,** range of mountains. **c. perpetua,** life imprisonment

cadencia *f*, cadence; rhythm; *mus* measure, time; *mus* cadenza

cadencioso *a* rhythmic

cadente *a* falling, declining; decaying, dying; rhythmic

cadera *f*, hip; flank

cadete *m*, *mil* cadet

cadi *mf* caddy

Cádiz Cadiz

caducar *vi* to become senile; become invalid, be annulled; expire, lapse; *fig* be worn out

caduceo *m*, Mercury's wand

caducidad *f*, decrepitude; lapse, expiry

caduco *a* senile; decrepit; perishable; lapsed; obsolete

caduquez *f*, senility

caedizo *a* ready to fall; timid, cowardly, weak

caer *vi irr* to fall, drop; drop out or off; suit, fit, become; fail; fade (colors); *fig* drop (voice); (*with sobre*) attack, fall upon; (*with en*) fall in or on to; decay, collapse; understand; (*with preps. a, hacia*) *fig* look on to, face; (*with por, en*) *fig* fall on, occur on; *vr aer* crash; fly off (buttons, etc.). **c. de cabeza,** to fall head foremost. **c. en conflicto (con),** to come into conflict (with) **c. en las manos de uno,** to come into somebody's possession (come to be owned by somebody). **c. en gracia,** to make a good impression, arouse affection. **caerse de suyo,** to be self-evident. **c. por tierra,** (plan, etc.) to fall through. **Cayó enfermo,** He was taken ill. **cayendo y levantando,** dying *Pres. Ind.* **caigo, caes,** etc. *Pres. Part.* **cayendo.** *Preterite* **cayó cayeron.** *Pres. Subjunc.* **caiga,** etc.

café *m*, coffee (tree, berry, drink); café, coffeehouse. **c. con leche,** café au lait. **c. negro** *Lat. Am. (except Columbia)* black coffee. **c. solo** *Spain* black coffee. **c. tinto** *Colombia* black coffee

cafeína *f*, caffeine

cafetal *m*, coffee plantation

cafetera *f*, coffeepot; *Peru* cab, taxi

cafeto *m*, coffee tree

cafiche *m*, *Argentina, Chile* pimp

caficultor *m*, coffee-grower

caficultura *f*, coffee-growing

cafúa *f*, *Argentina* clink, slammer

cagadas *f pl*, droppings, dung

cagar(se) *vi vt vr* to evacuate (bowels); *vt inf* spoil, make a botch of

cagarruta *f*, dung of sheep, deer, rabbits, etc.

caída *f*, falling; fall; ruin; failure; close (of day); *fig* falling off; hanging (curtains, etc.); diminution; incline; *pl* coarse wool; *inf* repartee. **a la c. de la tarde,** at the end of the afternoon. **a la c. del sol,** at sunset

caído (-da) *a* debilitated, languid; lapsed; (of a shoulder) sloping. **los caídos,** the fallen, the dead (in war, etc.)

caimán *m*, alligator; *inf* shark, astute person

caite *m*, *Central America* sandal

caja *f*, box; safe, cash box; coffin; (of a vehicle) body; *mus* drum; case (of piano, watch, etc.); cavity; well (of a stair); *com* cash; cash-desk; cashier's office; *bot* sheath. **c. de ahorros,** savings bank. **c. de caudales,** strong-box. *print* **c. de imprenta,** type case. **c. de música,** musical box. **c. de reclutamiento,** recruiting office. **c. de velocidades,** gearbox. **c. registradora,** cash register. **c. torácica,** rib cage, thoracic cage

cajero (-ra) *m*, boxmaker; *n com* cashier; pedler **c. automático,** automatic teller, automatic teller machine, bank machine, money machine

cajetilla *f*, packet (cigarettes, etc.)

cajón *m*, chest, locker, case; drawer. **c. de municiones,** ammunition-box

cajonera *f*, *ecc* chest of drawers in sacristy; *agr* frame

cal *f*, lime. **c. muerta,** slaked lime. **c. viva,** quicklime. *fig inf* **de c. y canto,** tough, strong

cala *f*, sample slice (of fruit); *naut* hold; *surg* probe; cove, small bay; *bot* iris

calabacera *f*, *bot* pumpkin or gourd plant

calabacín *m*, kind of vegetable marrow; *inf* dolt

calabaza *f*, *bot* pumpkin (plant and fruit); gourd; *inf* dolt. **dar calabazas,** to refuse (suitor); flunk (an examinee). *inf* **llevar calabazas,** to get the sack; be jilted

calabobos *m*, *inf* drizzle

calabocero *m*, jailer

calabozo *m*, dungeon; prison cell; pruning knife

41

calada f, soaking, wetting through; flight of bird of prey; swoop. **dar una c.,** fig inf to dress down

calado a soaked, wet through. m, sew open-work; fretwork; naut draught of a ship; water level; pl lace. **c. hasta los huesos,** soaked to the skin; madly in love

calador m, one who does open or fretwork; caulking iron; borer; surg probe

calafate m, caulker

calafatear vt naut to caulk

calamaco m, Mexico kidney bean

calamar m, zool squid, calamary

calambre m, cramp. **c. del escribiente,** writer's cramp

calamidad f, misfortune, calamity

calamina f, min calamine

calamitoso a calamitous; unfortunate, unhappy

cálamo m, ancient flute; stalk (of grass); poet pen

calamocano a maudlin, tipsy

calandria f, orn calender, lark; mech calender; treadmill. mf inf malingerer

calaña f, sample; model; pattern; kind, quality; temperament; cheap fan

calar vt to permeate, soak through; pierce; do openwork (in cloth, paper, metal); cut a sample slice from fruit; pull (hat, etc.) well down on head; put down (an eyeshade or visor); fix (bayonets, etc.); inf understand (persons); inf guess, realize; naut let down; vi naut draw (water); vr be drenched, wet through; swoop (birds of prey); inf sneak in. a calcareous

calar m, limestone deposit or region

calatear vt, Peru to undress

calato, -a a, Peru naked, nude; broke, penniless

calavera f, skull. m, dare-devil, madcap; roué; Mexico taillight

calaverada f, inf dare-devilment, foolishness; escapade

calcañar m, heel (of foot)

calcar vt to trace (drawing); press with foot; copy servilely, imitate

calcáreo a calcareous

calce m, rim of a wheel; wedge; tyre

calcés m, naut masthead

calceta f, stocking; fetter. inf **hacer c.,** to knit

calcetería f, hosiery shop; hosiery trade

calcetero (-ra) n hosier; hose maker or darner

calcetín m, sock

calcificación f, med calcification

calcinación f, calcination

calcinar vt to calcine

calcio m, calcium

calco m, tracing (drawing)

calcografía f, chalcography

calcografiar vt to transfer; make chalcographies of

calcomanía f, transfer

calculación f, calculation

calculado a calculated

calculador a calculating. m, calculating machine, comptometer

calcular vt to calculate

cálculo m, calculation; math estimate; investigation; conjecture; (math med) calculus. **c. hepático,** med gallstone

calda f, heating; pl hot mineral baths

caldear vt to heat

caldeo m, heating

caldera f, cauldron; cauldron full; WH teapot; eng boiler. **c. de vapor,** steam-boiler

calderería f, coppersmith's trade and shop

calderero m, boiler maker; coppersmith; tinker

calderilla f, holy water stoup; any copper coin

caldero m, small cauldron; casserole; kettle

calderón m, large cauldron; mus rest; mus trill; pause

caldo m, broth; salad dressing; pl agr oil, wine, vegetable juices

calefacción f, heating. **c. central,** central heating

calendario m, calendar. **c. deportivo,** fixture card. **c. gregoriano,** Gregorian calendar

calendas f pl, calends. **en las c. griegas,** at the Greek calends

caléndula f, marigold

calentador a heating, warming. m, heater; warming-pan

calentamiento m, heating, warming

calentar vt irr to heat, warm; rev-up (an engine); hasten; inf spank; vr warm oneself; be in heat (animals); grow excited. See **acertar**

calentura f, fever

calenturiento a feverish

calera f, lime-pit; lime-kiln; fishing smack

calesa f, calash, calèche, chaise (two-wheeled carriage)

calesita f, Lat. Am. merry-go-round

caleta f, cove, creek

caletre m, inf discernment, head, sense

calibrar vt to calibrate; gauge

calibre m, mech gauge; bore, caliber; diameter (tubes, pipes, etc.)

calidad f, quality; role; character, temperament; condition, requisite; importance, gravity; personal particulars; nobility; pl qualities of the mind. **c. originaria,** rank and birth. **c. de oficio,** justification for action. **en c. de,** in the capacity of

cálido a warm, hot; warming, heating; vehement, ardent; art warm

calidoscopio m, kaleidoscope

calientalibros mf, bookworm (person)

calientapiés m, footwarmer

calientaplatos m, hot plate, plate-warmer

caliente a warm, hot; excited; art warm

calientito a piping hot

califa m, caliph

calificable a classifiable; qualifiable

calificación f, classification; qualification; judgment; mark, place (examinations)

calificar vt to class; authorize; judge (qualities); fig ennoble; vr prove noble descent

calificativo a gram qualifying. m, epithet

californio (-ia) a and n Californian

caliginoso a murky, dark

caligrafía f, calligraphy

calígrafo m, calligraphist

caliqueño m, cheroot

calistenia f, callisthenics

cáliz m, chalice; poet cup; bot calyx

caliza f, limestone

calizo a calcareous

callado a silent; reserved; secret

callar(se) vi and vr to say nothing, keep silent; stop speaking; stop making any sound (persons, animals, things); vt conceal, keep secret; omit, leave out; inf interj ¡**Calle!** You don't say so! **Quien calla otorga,** Silence gives consent

calle f, street. **c. de un sentido, c. de una corrida** Mexico one-way street. **c. de una sola mano** Argentina one-way street inf **abrir c.,** to clear the way. inf **dejar en la c.,** to leave destitute. inf **echar a la c.,** put out of the house, to throw out of the house; make known, publish. **ponerse en la c.,** to go out

calleja, callejuela f, small street, alley, side street

callejear vi to walk the streets, wander about the streets, loaf around the streets

callejero a fond of gadding. m, street directory

callejón m, alley, lane. **c. sin salida,** cul-de-sac; fig impasse

callicida m, corn cure

callista mf chiropodist

callo m, corn, callosity; med callus; pl tripe

calloso a callous, horny

calma f, calm, airlessness; serenity; composure; quiet, tranquillity, peace. **c. chicha,** dead calm. **en c.,** at peace; tranquil; calm (of the sea)

calmante a calming, soothing. med a and m, sedative, tranquilizer

calmar *vt* to soothe, calm; moderate, mitigate; pacify; quench (thirst); *vi* grow calm; moderate; be becalmed

calmoso *a* calm, tranquil; *inf* sluggish, lazy; imperturbable

calor *m*, heat; ardor, vehemence; cordiality; *fig* heat (of battle); excitement

caloría *f*, *phys* calorie

calórico *a phys* caloric, thermic

calorífero *a* heat-giving. *m*, heater, radiator

calumnia *f*, calumny; *law* slander

calumniador (-ra) *a* slandering. *n* calumniator, slanderer

calumniar *vt* to calumniate; *law* slander

calumnioso *a* calumnious, slanderous

caluroso *a* hot, warm; cordial, friendly; enthusiastic; ardent, impassioned; excited

calva *f*, bald patch on head; worn place (cloth, etc.); bare spot, clearing (trees, etc.)

Calvario *m*, Calvary; *inf* series of disasters; *inf* debts

calvero *m*, clearing (in a wood); chalk or marl pit

calvicie *f*, baldness

calvo *a* bald; bare, barren (land); worn (cloth, etc.)

calza *f*, breeches (gen. *pl*); wedge; *inf* stocking. *inf* **tomar calzas,** to beat it

calzada *f*, roadway. **c. romana,** Roman road

calzado *m*, footwear, shoes

calzador *m*, shoehorn

calzadura *f*, wedging (of a wheel); act of putting on shoes; felloe of a wheel

calzar *vt* to put on shoes; wear (spurs, gloves, etc.); wedge, block (wheel); scotch (a wheel). *fig inf* **c. el coturno,** don the buskin; write in the sublime style; write a tragedy, write tragedies. **calzarse a una persona,** to have a person in one's pocket

calzón *m*, breeches (gen. *pl*). *fig inf* **ponerse los calzones,** to wear the breeches (of a woman)

calzonazos *m*, *inf* weak-willed, easily led fellow

calzoncillos *m pl*, drawers, pants

calzoneras *fpl*, *Mexico* pants buttoned down the sides

cama *f*, bed; bedstead; bedhanging; lair, form; floor (of a cart); check (of bridle) (gen. *pl*). **c. de campaña,** camp bed. **c. de matrimonio,** double bed. **c. de monja,** single bed. **c. de operaciones,** operating table. **c. turca,** settee-bed. **guardar c.,** to stay in bed

camada *f*, brood, litter; *inf* gang

camafeo *m*, cameo

camaleón *m*, chameleon; *inf* changeable person

cámara *f*, chamber; hall; house (of deputies); granary; *naut* state room; chamber (firearms, mines); *phys* camera; human excrement; *aut* inner tube. **c. acorazada,** strong-room. **c. alta,** Upper House. **c. baja** *or* **c. de los comunes,** lower house, house of commons. **c. de comercio,** chamber of commerce. **c. oscura,** (optics) dark room

camarada *mf* pal, companion, comrade

camaradería *f*, comradeship, companionship

camarera *f*, waiting-maid; waitress; chambermaid; stewardess

camarero *m*, waiter; papal chamberlain; chamberlain; steward; valet. **c. mayor,** lord chamberlain

camarilla *f*, palace or other clique, coterie; *inf* backscratch

camarín *m*, *theat* dressing-room; closet; boudoir; cage (of a lift); niche

camarón *m*, prawn, shrimp; tip, reward

camarote *m*, cabin; berth

cambalachear *vt inf* to barter

cambalache *m*, *Lat. Am.* secondhand shop; exchange

cámbaro *m*, sea-crab

cambiable *a* exchangeable; changeable

cambiante *a* exchanging; changing. *m*, sheen, luster (gen. *pl*); money changer

cambiar *vt* to exchange; convert. *vt* and *vi* change, alter; *vi* and *vr* to veer (wind). **c. de aire,** get a change of scenery. **c. de frente,** to face about; *fig* change front

cambio *m*, exchange; change; *com* rate of exchange; money change; *com* premium on bills of exchange. **a c. de, en c. de,** in exchange for; instead of. **en c.,** instead, on the other hand. **c. de velocidad,** *aut* gear-changing. **letra de c.,** bill of exchange. **libre c.,** free trade

cambista *mf* money changer. *m*, banker

cambullón *m*, *Lat. Am.* swindle

cambur *m*, *Venezuela* banana

camelar *vt inf* to woo; seduce

camelia *f*, camelia. **c. japonesa,** japonica

camelo *m*, *inf* eyewash

camellero *m*, camel keeper or driver

camello *m*, camel. **c. pardal,** giraffe

camellón *m*, furrow; drinking trough; *Mexico* island, traffic island, median strip

camilla *f*, couch; small round skirted table with brazier underneath; stretcher, litter

camillero *m*, *mil* stretcher-bearer

caminador *a* in the habit of walking a great deal

caminante *mf* walker, traveler

caminar *vi* to travel; walk; *fig* move on, go (inanimate things). *fig inf* **c. derecho,** to walk uprightly

caminata *f*, long, tiring walk; excursion

caminejo *m*, worn path

camino *m*, road; route; journey; way, means; **c. de hierro,** railway. **c. de mesa,** table-runner. **c. de sirga,** towpath. **c. real,** highway, main road. **de c.,** on the way, in passing. **ponerse en c.,** to set out

camión *m*, truck. **c. de volteo, c. volquete** dump truck; *Mexico* bus; truck

camionera *f*, *Mexico* bus station

camioneta *f*, light truck, pick-up truck; *WH* station wagon

camisa *f*, shirt, stiff shirt; thin skin (of fruit); sloughed skin of snakes; coat (of whitewash, etc.); *mech* jacket; mantle (gas). **c. de fuerza,** straitjacket. **dejar sin c.,** *inf* to leave penniless

camisería *f*, shirt shop or factory

camisero (-ra) *n* shirt maker or seller

camiseta *f*, undershirt, T-shirt. **c. de fútbol,** soccer player's jersey

camisola *f*, stiff shirt; ruffled shirt

camisón *m*, large wide shirt; night shirt

camomila *f*, chamomile

camorra *f*, *inf* brawl, shindy. **armar c.,** to start a row

camote *m*, *Lat. Am.* sweet potato

campal *a* field, country

campamento *m*, camping; *mil* encampment; camp; jamboree

campana *f*, bell; anything bell-shaped; church, parish. **c. de chimenea,** mantelpiece. **c. de hogar,** hood, shutter (of a fireplace)

campanada *f*, peal of a bell; scandal

campanario *m*, belfry, bell tower

campanear *vi* to ring bells frequently

campaneo *m*, bell-ringing; chime

campanero *m*, bell-founder; bell ringer

campanil *m*, small belfry, campanile

campanilla *f*, hand-bell; bubble; any bell-shaped flower

campante *a* outstanding; *inf* proud, satisfied

campanudo *a* bell-shaped; sonorous (of words); pompous (of speech)

campaña *f*, level country; campaign. *naut* voyage, cruise. **correr la c.,** to reconnoiter. **la C. del Desierto,** the War against the Gauchos (in Argentina)

campar *vi* to camp. *inf* **c. por sus respetos,** to stand on one's own feet

campeador *a* mighty in battle

campear *vi* to go out to graze; grow green (crops); excel; *mil* be engaged in a campaign, reconnoiter

campechano *a inf* hearty; frank; cheerful; generous

campeche *m*, *bot* logwood

campeón *m*, champion; advocate, defender

campeonato *m*, championship

campesinado *m*, peasantry

campesino (-na) *a* rural, rustic. *n* country dweller
campestre *a* rural
campiña *f*, expanse of cultivated land; countryside, landscape
campo *m*, country (as opposed to urban areas); field; *fig* sphere, province; (*phys her mil*) field; *art* ground; *mil* camp, army; plain ground (of silks, etc.). «**C. Abierto**», "Miscellaneous" (e.g. as the title of a section in a book catalog). **c. de aterrizaje,** *aer* landing-field. **c. de batalla,** battlefield. **c. de concentración,** concentration camp. **c. de experimentación,** testing ground. **c. de golf,** golf course. **c. de prisioneros** *mil* prison camp. **c. de tiro,** rifle-range. **c. santo,** graveyard. **c. visual,** field of vision. **a c. abierto,** in the open air. **a c. travieso,** cross-country
camuflaje *m*, camouflage
camuflar *vt* to camouflage
can *m*, dog; trigger; *arch* modillion; *ast* Dog Star
cana *f*, gray hair
Canadá Canada
canadiense *a* and *mf* Canadian
canal *m*, canal. *mf*, *geol* subterranean waterway; channel; *anat* canal, duct; defile, narrow valley; gutter; drinking trough; animal carcass. **abrir en c.,** to open up, split open
canalera *f*, roof gutter
canaleta *f*, (wooden) trough; gutter (on roof)
canalete *m*, paddle
canalización *f*, canalization; *elec* main, mains; piping, tubing
canalizar *vt* to make canals or channels; regulate waters of rivers, etc.; canalize
canalón *m*, gutter, spout; shovel hat; pantile
canalla *f*, *inf* mob, rabble. *m*, *inf* scoundrel
canallesco *a* scoundrely, knavish; despicable
canana *f*, cartridge belt
canapé *m*, sofa
canario (-ia) *m*, canary. *a* and *n* pertaining to or native of the Canary Islands.
canasta *f*, hamper, basket; card game
canastilla *f*, small basket; layette
canastillo *m*, basket-work tray
cáncamo *m*, ring-bolt
cancamusa *f*, *inf* trick, deception
cancel *m*, draftscreen; *ecc* screen
cancela *f*, wrought-iron door
cancelación *f*, cancellation; expunging
cancelar *vt* to cancel; expunge, annul; abolish, blot out; pay off, clear (a mortgage)
cancelaría *f*, papal chancery
cancelario *m*, chancellor (universities)
cáncer *m*, cancer
cancerar *vt* to consume; weaken; mortify; *vr* suffer from cancer; become cancerous
cancerbero *m*, *myth* Cerberus; *fig* unbribable guard
canceroso *a* cancerous
cancha *f*, *sport* fronton; (tennis) court; cockpit; yard; hippodrome; widest part of a river; road; toasted maize. **estar en su cancha** *Argentina, Chile* to be in one's element. **tener cancha** *Argentina* to be experienced; *Venezuela* have charisma, charm, allure
canciller *m*, chancellor; foreign minister; assistant vice-consul
cancillería *f*, chancellorship; chancellery; foreign ministry
canción *f*, song; lyric poem; musical accompaniment; old name for any poetical composition. **volver a la misma c.,** *fig* to be always harping on the same theme
cancionero *m*, collection of songs and verses; songbook
cancionista *mf* singer; song writer
candado *m*, padlock; earring
candeal *a* white (of bread)
candela *f*, candle; horse-chestnut flower; candlestick; *inf* fire. **en c.,** *naut* vertical (of masts, etc.)
candelabro *m*, candelabrum

candelero *m*, candlestick; lamp; candle maker or seller; *naut* stanchion
candente *a* candescent, red-hot
candidatear *vi* to run (for office)
candidato (-ta) *n* candidate
candidatura *f*, candidature
candidez *f*, simplicity, ingenuousness; candidness
cándido *a* white; simple, ingenuous; candid, frank
candil *m*, oil lamp; Greek lamp; tips of stag's horns; *inf* cock of a hat
candileja *f*, oil reservoir of lamp; *pl* footlights, floats
candor *m*, extreme whiteness; sincerity, candor; simplicity, innocence
candoroso *a* candid, open; simple, honest
canela *f*, *bot* cinnamon; *fig* anything exquisitely perfect
canelo *m*, cinnamon tree. *a* cinnamon-colored
cangilón *m*, pitcher, jar; bucket (for water); dredging bucket
cangreja *f*, *naut* gaffsail. **c. de mesana,** *naut* jigger
cangrejo *m*, crab. **c. de mar,** sea-crab. **c. ermitaño,** hermit crab
canguro *m*, kangaroo
caníbal *a* and *mf* cannibal
canibalismo *m*, cannibalism
canica *f*, marble (for playing with)
canícula *f*, dog days; *ast* Dog star
caniculares *m pl* dog days
canijo *a* *inf* delicate, sickly; anemic, stunted
canilla *f*, long bone of leg or arm; any principal bones in bird's wing; tap, faucet; spool, reel; fault (in cloth)
canillera *f*, *Lat. Am.* cowardice; fear
canillito, -a *mf*, *Lat. Am.* newsboy, newsgirl
canino *a* canine
canje *m*, (diplomacy, *mil., com.*) exchange, substitution. **c. de prisioneros,** exchange of prisoners
canjear *vt* to exchange
cano *a* white-haired, hoary; ancient; *poet* white
canoa *f*, canoe; launch. **c. automóvil,** motor launch
canoero (-ra) *n* canoeist
canódromo *m*, dog-race track
canon *m*, rule; (*ecc print*) canon; catalog; part of the Mass; *mus* canon, catch; tax. *pl* canon law
canónico *a* canonic, canonical
canónigo *m*, canon; prebendary
canonización *f*, canonization
canonizar *vt* to canonize; extol, exalt; approve, acclaim
canonjía *f*, canonry, canonship; *inf* sinecure
canoso *a* white-haired, hoary
cansado (-da) *a* tired; weary; exhausted; decadent; tiresome; *inf* fed up. *n* bore, tedious person
cansancio *m*, fatigue, weariness
cansar *vt* to tire, weary; *agr* exhaust soil; bore; badger, annoy; *vr* be tired; grow weary
cansino *a* worn-out (of horses, etc.)
cantable *a* singable; *mus* cantabile
cantábrico (-ca) *a* and *n* Cantabrian
cantante *a* singing. *mf* professional singer
cantar *vi* to sing; twitter, chirp; extol; *inf* squeak, creak; *fig* call (cards); *inf* squeal, confess. *m*, song. **C. de los Cantares,** Song of Songs. **cantarlas claras,** to call a spade a spade
cántara *f*, pitcher, jug
cantárida *f*, Spanish fly
cántaro *m*, pitcher, jug; jugful; varying wine measure; ballot box; tax on spirits and oil
cantata *f*, cantata
cantatriz *f*, singer, prima donna
cante *m*, song; singing
cantera *f*, *min* quarry; capacity, talent
cantería *f*, stone-cutting; quarrying; building made of hewn stone
cantero *m*, stone-cutter; quarryman
cántico *m*, *ecc* canticle; *poet* poem
cantidad *f*, quantity; large part; portion; sum of money; quantity (prosody). **c. llovida,** rainfall

cantiga *or* **cántiga** *f,* old poetic form designed to be sung

cantil *m,* cliff; steep rock

cantimplora *f,* water cooler; canteen (of water); siphon

cantina *f,* wine cellar; canteen; refreshment room

cantinero *m,* sutler; owner of a canteen

canto *m,* singing; song; canto; epic or other poem; end, rim, edge; non-cutting edge (knives, swords); pebble, stone; angle (of a building). *mus* **c. llano,** plain-song. **al c. del gallo,** at cockcrow. **de c.,** on edge

cantón *m,* province, region; corner (of a street); cantonment; *her* canton, quartering

cantonera *f,* corner-piece (books, furniture, etc., as ornament); angle-iron; bracket, small shelf

cantor (-ra) *a* singing. *n* singer; song-bird

Cantórbery Canterbury

cantuja *f, Peru* underworld slang

canturía *f,* singing exercise; vocal music; monotonous song; droning; *mus* execution, technique

canturreo, *m,* **canturria** *f,* humming; droning

canturriar *vi inf* to hum, sing under one's breath

caña *f,* stalk; reed; bone of arm or leg; leg (of a trouser, stocking, boot, etc.); marrow; *bot* cane; tumbler, glass; wine measure; gallery (of mine); *pl* mock joust on horseback using **cañas** as spears. **c. de azúcar,** sugar-cane. **c. de pescar,** fishing rod. **c. del timón,** tiller *naut*

cañada *f,* glen, gulch, gully, hollow, ravine, vale, cattle path; *WH* brook, cattle track

cañal *m,* cane-break; weir (for fish)

cañamazo *m,* hempen canvas; embroidery canvas; embroidered canvas

cañamelar *m,* sugar-cane plantation

cáñamo *m,* hemp; *Lat. Am.* marijuana

cañar *m,* canebrake; growth of reeds; fishgarth made of reeds

cañavalera *f,* canefield

cañaveral *m,* cane-brake; *WH* bamboo field

cañazo *m,* blow with a cane

cañería *f,* conduit; pipe; piping

cañero *m,* pipe layer

caño *m,* pipe, tube, sewer; organ pipe; jet (of water); mine gallery

cañón *m,* pipe, cylindrical tube; flue; quill (of birds); cannon; soft down; *arch* shaft (of column); stack (of a chimney). **c. antiaéreo,** A.A. gun. **c. antitanque,** anti-tank gun. **c. de escalera,** well of a staircase; *slang* terrific-looking, absolutely gorgeous (e.g. mujer cañón)

cañonazo *m,* cannon shot; roar of a cannon

cañoneo *m,* cannonade; bombardment

cañonería *f, mil* group of cannon; *mus* set of organ pipes

cañonero *m,* gunboat

cañuto *m, bot* internode; small pipe or tube; *inf* talebearer

caoba *f, bot* mahogany

caos *m,* chaos; confusion

caótico *a* chaotic

capa *f,* cloak; cape; *ecc* cope; coating; layer; cover; coat (animals); *fig* cloak, disguise; *geol* stratum. **la c. del cielo,** the canopy of heaven. *fig inf* **echar la c. al toro,** to throw one's cap over the windmill. *naut* **estarse** (*or* **ponerse**) **a la c.,** to lie to

capacete *m,* helmet

capacha *f* basket; *Argentina, Chile* clink, jug (jail)

capacidad *f,* capacity; extension, space; mental capacity, talent; opportunity; means; *law* capacity. **c. de compra,** buying power, purchasing power. **c. de producción,** output

capacitación *f,* qualification, (act of) qualifying; (act of) training

capacitar *vt* to capacitate, qualify, enable

capadura *f,* castration

capar *vt* to castrate, geld; *inf* diminish, reduce

caparazón *m,* caparison, horse blanket; waterproof cover; hood (of carriages); nosebag; shell (insects, crustaceans)

capataz *m,* foreman; steward; overseer

capaz *a* capacious; large, spacious; capable, competent; *law* able

capcioso *a* deceitful, artful; captious, carping

capear *vt* to steal a cape; play the bull with a cape (bullfighting); *inf* put off with excuses, deceive; *naut* lie to

capelo *m,* cardinal's hat; cardinalate

capellán *m,* chaplain; any ecclesiastic

capeo *m,* playing the bull with a cape (bullfighting)

caperuza *f,* hood, pointed cap; *arch* coping-stone

capigorrón *a inf* loafing. *m,* loafer, idler

capilar *a* capillary

capilaridad *f,* capillarity

capilla *f,* cowl, hood; chapel; *ecc* chapter; *ecc* choir. **c. ardiente,** chapelle ardente. **estar en c.,** to await execution (criminals); *inf* be in suspense, await anxiously

capillero *m,* sexton; churchwarden

capillo *m,* baby's bonnet; cocoon of silkworm; flowerbud

capirotazo *m,* box on the ear; fillip

capirote *m,* academic hood and cap; hood (falconry); tall pointed cap. **ser tonto de c.,** *inf* to be a complete fool

capitación *f,* poll-tax, capitation

capital *a* relating to the head; capital (sins, etc.); main, principal. *m,* capital, patrimony; *com* capital stock. *f,* capital (city). **c. pagado,** paid-in capital stock

capitalino, -a *Lat. Am.* of the capital; *n* native of the capital; resident of the capital

capitalismo *m,* capitalism

capitalista *a* capitalistic. *mf* capitalist

capitalización *f,* capitalization

capitalizar *vt* to capitalize

capitán *m,* captain, skipper; chief, leader; ringleader. *aer* **c. de aviación,** group captain. **c. de fragata,** *nav* commander. **c. de puerto,** harbor master. **c. general de ejército,** field-marshal

capitana *f,* admiral's ship; *inf* captain's wife

capitanear *vt* to captain, command; *fig* guide, lead

capitanía *f,* captaincy; captainship

capitolio *m,* dignified building; *arch* acropolis; Capitol

capitulación *f,* agreement, pact; capitulation; *pl* marriage articles

capitular *a* capitulary, belonging to a Chapter. *m,* capitular, member of a Chapter. *vi* to make an agreement; capitulate; sing prayers; arrange order

capítulo *m, ecc* Chapter; meeting of town council, etc.; chapter (of book); item (in a budget); determination, decision

capó *m, aut* hood

capón *a* castrated; gelded. *m,* capon; bundle of firewood or vines

caponera *f,* coop for fattening capons; *inf* gaol; *inf* place where one lives well free of charge

capota *f, bot* head of teasel; bonnet; hood (of vehicles)

capote *m,* short, brightly colored cape (used by bullfighters); cape coat; (cards) slam; *inf* scowl

capricho *m,* caprice, fancy; strong desire

caprichoso *a* capricious; whimsical

caprichudo *a* headstrong; capricious

cápsula *f,* cartridge-case; bottlecap; (*bot med chem zool*) capsule

captar *vt* gain, attract (goodwill, attention, etc.); *mech* collect; monitor (foreign broadcasts)

captor *m,* capturer

captura *f, law* capture; seizing, arrest

capturar *vt* to capture; arrest, apprehend

capucha *f,* hood; cowl; *print* circumflex accent

capuchina *f,* Capuchin nun; *bot* nasturtium; table-lamp with an extinguisher

capucho *m,* cowl

capullo *m,* cocoon; flower bud; acorn cup; *anat* prepuce

caqui *m,* khaki; khaki color

cara *f,* face; likeness, aspect; façade, front; surface; side (of metal, etc.); mien. **c. a c.,** face to face; frankly; openly. *inf* **c. de juez,** severe face. *inf* **c. de pascua,** smiling face. *inf* **c. de vinagre,** sour face. **c. o cruz,** heads or tails. **c. o sello** *Argentina, Chile,* heads or tails **de c.,** opposite. **hacer a dos caras,** to be deceitful, be two-faced. **hacer c. (a),** to stand up to

caraba *f, slang* 25-centimo coin

cárabe *m,* amber

carabina *f,* carbine; rifle

carabinazo *m,* report of a carbine

carabinero *m,* carabineer; customs' guard, revenue guard; customs officer, customs official

caracol *m,* snail; snail's shell; cure; *zool* cochlea; winding stair. **c. marino,** periwinkle. **¡Caracoles!** Fancy!

caracola *f,* conch shell used as a horn

caracolear *vi* to prance from side to side (horses)

carácter *m,* sign, mark; character, writing (gen. *pl*); style of writing; brand (animals); nature, temperament; character, individuality, strong-mindedness, energy, firmness; condition, state, capacity. **comedia de c.,** psychological play. **en su c. de,** as in one's capacity as. **caracteres de imprenta,** printing types

característica *f,* quality, characteristic; *math* characteristic; actress who plays the part of an old woman

característico *a* characteristic, distinctive. *m,* actor who plays roles of old men

caracterización *f,* characterization; *theat* make-up

caracterizar *vt* to characterize; confer an office, honor, dignity, on; *theat* create a character; *vr theat* to make up, dress as, a character

caraíta *a* and *mf* Karaite

¡caramba! *interj* gosh!; blast!

carámbano *m,* icicle

carambola *f,* cannon (billiards); *inf* double effect; *inf* trick, deception

caramelo *m,* caramel; toffee

caramillo *m,* flageolet; small flute, pipe; gossip, intrigue

carancho *m, Argentina* vulture; *Peru* owl

carantamaula *f, inf* hideous mask; ugly person

carapacho *m,* carapace, shell

carátula *f,* mask; *fig* dramatic art, the theater

caravana *f,* caravan, group of traders, pilgrims, etc. (especially in East); *inf* crowd of excursionists, picnickers, etc.

¡caray! *interj* blast!; gosh!

carbólico *a* carbolic

carbón *m,* coal; charcoal; black chalk, crayon. **c. bituminoso,** soft coal. **c. de coque,** coke. **c. de leña,** charcoal. **c. mineral,** anthracite. **mina de c.,** coal-mine

carbonada *f, Lat. Am.* meat stew

carboncillo *m,* charcoal crayon

carbonear *vt* to turn into charcoal; *naut* coal

carboneo *m,* coaling

carbonera *f,* coal-cellar, coal-house, etc.; coal-scuttle; woman who sells charcoal or coal; charcoal burner

carbonería *f,* coal or charcoal merchant's office

carbonero *a* relating to coal or charcoal. *m,* collier; charcoal maker; coal merchant; *naut* coal-ship

carbónico *a chem* carbonic

carbonífero *a* carboniferous

carbonizar *vt* to carbonize

carbono *m, chem* carbon

carbunco *m, med* carbuncle

carbúnculo *m,* carbuncle, ruby

carburador *m,* carburetor

carcaj *m,* quiver (for arrows); *Mexico* rifle case

carcajada *f,* burst of laughter, guffaw. **reírse a carcajadas,** to roar with laughter

carcajearse *vi* to guffaw

carcamal *m, inf* dotard

cárcel *f,* prison, jail

carcelario *a* prison, jail

carcelero (-ra) *a* jail. *n* jailer

cárcola *f,* treadle (of a loom)

carcoma *f,* wood-worm; dry rot; *fig* gnawing care; spendthrift

carcomer *vt* to gnaw wood (worms); *fig* undermine (health, etc.); *vr* be worm-eaten

carda *f,* card, carding; teasel head; card brush; *inf* reprimand

cardador (-ra) *n* carder, comber

cardadura *f,* carding; carding frame

cardar *vt* to card, tease; brush up (felt, etc.)

cardenal *m,* cardinal; cardinal bird; bruise

cardenalato *m,* cardinalate, cardinalship

cardenillo *m,* verdigris; *art* verditer

cárdeno *a* livid

cardíaco *a med* cardiac

cardinal *a* principal; cardinal (point); *gram* cardinal (number)

cardiógrafo *m, med* cardiograph

cardiograma *m, med* cardiogram

cardo *m, bot* thistle

carear *vt* to confront; compare; *vi* turn towards, face; *vr* meet; come together

carecer *vi irr* to be short; lack, need (e.g. **Carece de las condiciones necesarias,** It lacks the necessary conditions). See **conocer**

carencia *f,* shortage, lack

carestía *f,* shortage, scarcity; famine; dearness, high price

careta *f,* mask; beekeeper's veil; fencing mask. *fig* **quitar la c. (a),** to unmask

carey *m, zool* shell turtle; tortoise-shell

carga *f,* loading; *elec* charging, charge; load; burden, weight; cargo; explosive charge; *fig* imposition; tax; duty, obligation. *naut* **c. de profundidad,** depth charge

cargadero *m,* place where goods are loaded or unloaded

cargado *a* loaded; heavy, sultry; strong (tea, coffee). **c. de cadenas,** (prisoner, etc.) in chains. **c. de espaldas,** round-shouldered

cargador *m,* loader; porter; dockhand; pitchfork; rammer; *mech* stoker; *elec* charger

cargamento *m, naut* cargo, freight, shipload

cargar *vt* to load; charge (guns, etc.); stoke; overburden; tax, impose; blame for, charge with; *inf* annoy, bore; *Argentina inf* to kid, tease; *com* charge, book; *mil* attack; (football) tackle; *vi* tip, slope; (*with con*) carry away; be loaded with (fruit); assume responsibility; (*with sobre*) importune, urge; lean against; *vr* turn (head, etc.); lower, grow darker (sky); (*with de*) be abundant (in or with); load oneself with

cargazón *f,* cargo; loading; heaviness; darkness (of the sky)

cargo *m,* loading; load, weight; post, office; duty, obligation; management, charge; care; *com* debit; accusation. *com* **el c. y la data,** debit and credit. **hacerse c. de,** to take charge of; understand; consider carefully. **ser en c. (a),** to be debtor (to)

cargosear *vt, Lat. Am.* to annoy, pester

cargoso, -a *a, Lat. Am.* annoying, pestering

cariancho *a inf* broadfaced

cariacontecido *a* crestfallen, disappointed; glum

cariarse *vr* to become carious

caribe *a* Caribbean. *mf* cannibal, savage

caricatura *f,* caricature

caricaturista *mf* caricaturist

caricaturizar *vt* to caricature

caricia *f,* caress

caridad *f,* charity; charitableness; alms

caries *f,* caries

carilargo *a inf* long-faced

carilla *f, dim* small face; mask; page (of a book)

carilleno *a inf* plump-faced, round-faced

carillón *m,* peal (of bells)

cariño *m,* affection; love; caress affectionately (gen. *pl*); fondness, inclination. **con c.,** affectionately

cariñoso *a* affectionate; loving; kind

carioca *a* of Rio de Janeiro; *n* native of Rio de Janeiro; resident of Rio de Janeiro
carirredondo *a inf* roundfaced
carismático *a* charismatic
caritativo *a* charitable
cariz *m,* appearance of the sky; look, face; aspect; *inf* outlook (for a business deal, etc.)
carlista *a* and *mf* Carlist
carmelita *a* and *mf* Carmelite
carmen *m,* country house and garden (Granada); song; poem
carmesí *a* crimson. *m,* crimson color; cramoisy
carmín *m,* red, carmine color; red wild rose-tree and flower
carnada *f,* bait
carnaje *m,* salted meat
carnal *a* carnal; lascivious; materialistic, worldly; related by blood
carnalidad *f,* carnality
carnaval *m,* carnival. **martes de c.,** Shrove Tuesday
carnavalesco *a* carnival
carne *f,* flesh; meat; pulpy part of fruit; carnality, **c. concentrada,** meat extract. **c. congelada,** frozen meat. **c. de gallina** *fig* gooseflesh. **c. de membrillo,** quince cheese or conserve. **c. y hueso,** *fig* flesh and blood. *inf* **cobrar carnes,** to put on weight. **poner toda la c. en el asador,** *inf* to put all one's eggs in one basket
carné de conductor *Argentina* driver's license
carnerada *f,* flock of sheep
carnerero (-ra) *n* shepherd
carnero *m,* sheep; mutton; mortuary; charnel-house; family burial vault. **c. marino,** *zool* seal
carnestolendas *f pl* three days of carnival before Ash Wednesday
carnet *m,* notebook, diary; identity card; membership card, pass. **c. de chófer,** driver's license
carnicería *f,* butcher's shop; carnage, slaughter
carnicero *a* carnivorous; inhuman, cruel. *m,* butcher
carnívoro *a* carnivorous. *m,* carnivore
carnosidad *f,* proud flesh; local fat; fatness
carnoso *a* meaty; fleshy; full of marrow; *bot* pulpy, juicy
caro *a* beloved; expensive; dear. *adv* expensively; dear
carolingio (-ia) *a* and *n* Carolingian
carótida *f,* carotid artery
carpa *f,* *icht* carp. **c. dorada,** goldfish; *Lat. Am.* tent; awning
carpanta *f,* *inf* violent hunger; *Mexico* gang
Cárpatos, los Montes the Carpathian Mountains
carpeta *f,* table or chest cover, doily; writing case; portfolio; docket, letter file
carpetazo, dar *vt* to shelve (a project, etc.)
carpintear *vi* to carpenter
carpintería *f,* carpenter's shop; carpentry
carpinteril *a* carpentering
carpintero *m,* carpenter, joiner; *theat* scene-shifter. **c. de carretas,** wheelwright. **c. de ribera,** shipwright
carraca *f,* rattle; ratchet-drill
Carrapempe *m,* Old Nick
carrascal *m,* field of pinoaks
carraspear *vi* to clear one's throat, cough
carraspera *f,* *inf* hoarseness
carrera *f,* run; race; racing; racecourse; *ast* course; high road; route; *mas* layer, course; line, row; *fig* ladder (in stockings, etc.); course; duration (of life); career, profession; conduct; girder. **c. de fondo,** long-distance race. **c. de relevos, c. de equipos,** relay race. **a c. abierta, a c. tendida,** at full speed
carrerista *mf* racing enthuriast; professional racer
carreta *f,* long, narrow two-wheeled cart; wagon; tumbril
carretada *f,* cart-load; *inf* great deal, mass
carretaje *m,* cartage; carriage, transport
carrete *m,* spool, reel, bobbin; fishing reel; *elec* coil; *phot* film spool
carretear *vt* to cart; drive a cart

carretera *f,* high road; highway
carretería *f,* number of carts; carting trade; cartwright's yard
carretero *m,* cartwright; carter, driver
carretilla *f,* wheelbarrow; hand cart; railway truck; squib. **de c.,** *inf* mechanically, without thought; *(with saber, repetir,* etc.) by rote
carretón *m,* truck, trolley; hand cart
carril *m,* wheel mark; furrow, rut; cart road, narrow road; rail (railways, etc.)
carrillera *f,* jaw (of some animals); chin strap; *pl* bonnet strings, etc.
carrillo *m,* cheek; jowl
carriola *f,* truckle bed; curricle
carro *m,* cart; cartload; car, chariot; carriage (of a typewriter, etc.); chassis; *ast* Plow, Great Bear; *Lat. Am.* automobile, auto, car; *mil* **c. blindado,** armored car. *mil* **c. de asalto,** tank. **c. de mudanzas,** moving van. **c. de regar,** watercart
carrocería *f,* place where carriages are made, sold, repaired; *aut* coachwork, body shop
carrocha *f,* eggs (of insects)
carrochar *vi* to lay eggs (insects)
carromato *m,* road wagon; covered wagon
carroña *f,* putrid flesh, carrion
carroza *f,* elegant coach; state coach; carriage; float (for tableaux, etc.); *naut* awning
carruaje *m,* carriage; any vehicle
carta *f,* letter; charter; royal order; playing card; chart, map. **c. certificada,** registered letter. **c. de amparo,** safe-conduct. **c. de crédito,** *com* letter of credit. **c. de marear,** sea chart. **c. de naturaleza,** naturalization papers. **c. de pésame,** letter of condolence. **c. de venta,** *com* bill of sale. **c. ejecutoria de hidalguía,** letters patent of nobility. **carta-poder,** letter of proxy, proxy. **cartas rusas,** (game of) consequences. **poner las cartas boca arriba,** *fig* to lay one's cards on the table
cartabón *m,* set-square; shoemaker's slide; quadrant
cartaginés (-esa) *a* and *n* Carthaginian
Cartago Carthage
cartapacio *m,* note-book; schoolbag, satchel; file, batch of papers
cartear *vi* cards to play low; *vr* to correspond by letter
cartel *m,* placard, poster; cartel; pasquinade, lampoon. **fijar carteles,** to placard
cartela *f,* tablet (for writing); slip (of paper, etc.); *arch* console, bracket
cartelera *f,* billboard
cartelero *m,* billpaster, billsticker
carteo *m,* correspondence (by letter)
cartera *f,* pocketbook; wallet; dispatch-case; portfolio; notebook; pocket flap; office of a cabinet minister; *com* shares
cartería *f,* sorting room (in a post-office)
carterista *mf* pickpocket
cartero *m,* mail carrier, postman
cartesiano (-na) *a* and *n* Cartesian
Cartesio Descartes
carteta *f,* lansquenet (card game)
cartilaginoso *a* cartilaginous
cartílago *m,* cartilage
cartilla *f,* first reading book; primer; certificate of ordination; note-book; liturgical calendar. **c. de racionamiento,** ration book
cartografía *f,* cartography
cartógrafo *m,* map maker
cartón *m,* pasteboard, cardboard; *arch* bracket; *art* cartoon, design
cartucho *m,* cartridge; paper cone
cartuja *f,* Carthusian Order or monastery
cartujano *a* Carthusian
cartujo *m,* Carthusian monk; *inf* taciturn, reserved man
cartulina *f,* Bristol board, oaktag, pasteboard, card
carúncula *f,* caruncle, comb of cock, etc.
casa *f,* house; home; household; residence, dwelling;

family house; *com* firm. **c. consistorial,** town hall. **c. cuna,** crèche. **c. de campo,** country-house. **c. de empeño,** pawnshop. **c. de huéspedes,** boarding house, lodging-house. **c. de los sustos,** haunted house (at amusement park). **c. de moneda,** mint. **c. de socorro,** First Aid Post. **c. de vecindad,** tenement. **c. mala,** house of ill repute. **c. solar** *or* **c. solariega,** family seat. **en c.,** at home (also sport usage). **poner c.,** to set up house

casaca *f,* dress coat. **volver la c.,** to become a turncoat, change one's allegiance

casación *f, law* cassation

casadero *a* marriageable

casadoro *m, Costa Rica* bus

casamiento *m,* marriage; wedding

casar *vt* to marry (of a priest); *law* repeal; *inf* marry off; join; match, harmonize; *vi* and *vr* (*with con*) to get married

casar *m,* group of houses

casca *f,* grape skin; tan (bark); shell, peel, rind

cascabel *m,* small bell (for harness, etc.). **serpiente de c.,** rattlesnake. *inf* **ser un c.,** to be feather-brained

cascabeleo *m,* jingling of bells

cascabillo *m,* husk (of cereals)

cascada *f,* cascade; waterfall

cascadura *f,* cracking, crack

cascajo *m,* gravel, shingle; *inf* broken, old things, junk; nuts

cascanueces *m,* nutcrackers

cascar *vt* to crack, split, break; *inf* beat; *fig inf* break down (of health); *vi inf* talk, chatter

cáscara *f,* shell; peel, rind; bark. *med* **c. sagrada,** cascara

cascarón *m,* eggshell; *arch* vault

cascarrabias *mf inf* spitfire

cascarriento, -a *Argentina* filthy; greasy

casco *m,* cranium; broken fragment of china, glass, etc.; crown of hat; helmet; tree of saddle; bottle; tank, pipe; barrel; *naut* hull; hoof; quarter (of fruit); *pl inf* head. **c. colonial,** sun-helmet. **c. respiratorio,** smoke-helmet

cascote *m,* rubble, ruins

caseoso *a* cheesy

caserío *m,* group of houses; country house

casero *a* home made; home bred; familiar; informa; *inf* domesticated, home-loving; domestic. *m,* landlord; caretaker; tenant

caserón *m,* large tumbledown house, mansion, hall

caseta *f,* hut; cottage; booth, stall. **c. de baños,** bathing van

casi *adv* almost, nearly. **c. c.,** very nearly

casilla *f,* hut; cabin; lodge; ticket office; pigeon-hole; *Argentina, Chile* post-office box *aer* **c. del piloto,** cockpit

casillero *m,* file cabinet, filing cabinet; locker (as in a locker room); set of pigeonholes; *sports* scoreboard; *rw* crossing guard

casino *m,* casino; club

caso *m,* happening, event; chance, hazard; occasion, opportunity; case, matter; (*med gram*) case. **en el c. de,** in a position to (e.g. **No estamos en el c. de pagar tanto dinero.** We are in no position to pay so much money). **en tal c.,** in such a case. **en todo c.,** in any case. **no hacer c. de,** to take no notice of. **venir al c.,** to be opportune

caspa *f,* dandruff; scab

¡cáspita! *interj* Amazing! Wonderful!

casquete *m,* helmet; skullcap; half wig

casquijo *m,* gravel

casquillo *m,* tip, cap, ferrule; socket; arrow-head; metal cartridge-case

casquivano *a inf* giddy, feather-brained

casta *f,* race; caste; breed (animals); kind, species, quality. **de buena c.,** pedigree (e.g. **perros de buena c.,** pedigree dogs)

castaña *f, bot* chestnut; knot, bun (of hair)

castañar *m,* chestnut plantation or grove

castañetear *vi* to play the castanets; snap one's fingers; chatter (of teeth); knock together (of knees)

castaño *a* chestnut-colored. *m,* chestnut tree; chestnut wood. **c. de Indias,** horse-chestnut tree

castañuela *f,* castanet. **tocar las castañuelas,** to play the castanets

castellán *m,* castellan

castellano (-na) *n* Castilian; Spaniard. *m,* Spanish (language); castellan. *a* Castilian; Spanish

casticismo *m,* purity (of language); Spanish spirit; traditionalism

castidad *f,* chastity

castigador *a* punishing. *m,* punisher; *inf* lady-killer

castigadora *f, inf* man-hunter

castigar *vt* to punish; chastise; chasten, advise; pain, grieve; correct, edit; decrease (expenses); *com* allow a discount

castigo *m,* punishment; emendation, correction

Castilla Castile

castillo *m,* castle; howdah. **c. de naipes,** house of cards. **c. de proa,** *naut* forecastle. **c. fuerte,** fortified castle. *inf* **hacer castillos en el aire,** to build castles in the air or in Spain

castizo *a* pure-blooded; prolific; pure (of language); typically Spanish; traditional

casto *a* chaste; pure, unsullied

castor *m, zool* beaver (animal and fur); soft, woollen cloth

castración *f,* castration, gelding

castrado *a* castrated. *m, inf* eunuch

castrador *m,* castrator; gelder

castrapo *m,* mixed Spanish and Galician spoken in Galicia, Spain

castrar *vt* to castrate, geld; prune; remove honeycomb from hives; weaken

castrense *a* military

castrista *v* and *mf* Castroite

casual *a* accidental, casual

casualidad *f,* chance, coincidence. **por c.,** by chance. **ser mucha c. que . . . ,** to be too much of a coincidence that . . .

casucha *f, inf* tumbledown hut

casuista *a* casuistic. *mf* casuist

casuística *f,* casuistry

casulla *f,* chasuble

cata *f,* tasting; taste, sample; *Lat. Am.* parrot

catabolismo *m,* catabolism

cataclismo *m,* cataclysm

catacumbas *f pl,* catacombs

catador *m,* taster, sampler

catadura *f,* tasting; look, countenance (gen. qualified)

catafalco *m,* catafalque

catalán (-ana) *a* and *n* Catalan, Catalonian. *m,* Catalan (language)

catalejo *m,* telescope

cataléptico *a* cataleptic

catálisis *f, chem* catalysis

catalítico *a* catalytic

catalogar *vt* to catalogue, list

catálogo *m,* catalogue, list

Cataluña Catalonia

cataplasma *f,* cataplasm

catapulta *f,* catapult

catar *vt* to taste, sample; see, examine; inspect; regard

catarata *f,* cataract, waterfall; *med* cataract (of the eyes)

catarral *a* catarrhal

catarro *m,* catarrh; common cold

catástrofe *f, lit* tragic climax; catastrophe

catastrófico *a* catastrophic

catavino *m,* taster (cup)

catavinos *mf,* professional wine taster; *inf* tippler, tavern haunter

cate *m, slang* flunk (failure in a course at school)

catecismo *m,* catechism

catecúmeno (-na) *n* catechumen

cátedra *f,* university chair; chair in a Spanish **instituto;**

professorship; university lecture room; subject taught by professor; reading desk, lectern; *ecc* throne; *ecc* see. **c. del espíritu santo,** pulpit. **c. de San Pedro,** Holy See

catedral *f,* and *a* cathedral

catedrático (-ca) *n* professor

categoría *f, phil* category; class, rank

categórico *a* categorical, downright

cateo *m, WH* sampling; prospecting; house search (by the police)

catequismo *m,* catechism; question and answer method of teaching

catequista *mf* catechist

catequizar *vt* to catechize; persuade, induce

caterva *f,* crowd, throng; jumble, collection

catéter *m, surg* probe; catheter

catoche *m, Lat. Am.* bad temper

catódico *a elec* cathodic

cátodo *m,* cathode

catolicidad *f,* catholicity; catholic world

catolicismo *m,* Catholicism

católico (-ca) *a* universal, catholic; infallible. *a* and *n* Catholic (by religion)

catorce *a* fourteen; fourteenth. *m,* number fourteen; fourteenth (of days of month)

catorzavo *a* fourteenth

catre *m,* camp-bed; truckle-bed; cot

Cáucaso, el the Caucasus

cauce *m,* river or stream bed; ditch, irrigation canal

cauchal *m,* rubber plantation

cauchera *f,* rubber tree

cauchero *m,* rubber planter; rubber-plantation worker

caucho *m,* caoutchouc, rubber; *Lat. Am.* tire

caución *f,* caution, precaution; surety; security

caucional *a* See **libertad**

caudal *m,* wealth, capital; flow, volume (of water); plenty, abundance (e.g. **un c. de conocimientos,** a wealth of knowledge)

caudaloso *a* carrying much water; wealthy; abundant

caudillo *m,* head, leader; chief tain. **el C.,** (title of Francisco Franco)

causa *f,* cause; reason, motive; lawsuit; *law* trial. **c. final,** *phil* final cause. **c. pública,** public welfare. **ser c. bastante para . . . ,** to be reason enough to . . .

causador (-ra) *a* motivating. *n* occasioner, originator

causalidad *f,* causality

causante *a* causative, causing. *m, law* principal; *Mexico* taxpayer

causar *vt* to cause; occasion

causticidad *f,* causticity; mordacity

cáustico *a* burning, caustic; scathing; mordant; *surg* caustic

cautela *f,* caution; astuteness, cunning

cauteloso *a* cautious; cunning

cauterio *m,* cautery

cauterización *f,* cauterization

cauterizar *vt* to cauterize

cautivar *vt* to capture; captivate, charm; attract; *vi* become a prisoner

cautiverio *m,* captivity

cautivo (-va) *a* and *n* captive

cauto *a* cautious; prudent; sly

cava *f,* digging (especially vines); wine cellar in royal palaces

cavador (-ra) *n* digger, hoer

cavadura *f,* digging, hoeing; sinking (wells)

cavar *vt* to dig, hoe; sink (wells); *vi* hollow; *fig* go deeply into a thing

caverna *f,* cavern, cave; *med* cavity (generally in the lung)

cavernícola *a* cave. **hombre c.,** cave-man

cavernoso *a* cavernous; caverned; *fig* hollow (cough, etc.); deaf

cavidad *f,* cavity; sinus; cell

cavilación *f,* caviling

cavilar *vt* to cavil; criticize

caviloso *a* captious

caz *m,* channel, canal; head-race, flume

caza *f,* hunting; hunt, chase; game. *m, aer* fighter. *aer* **c. lanzacohetes,** rocket-launching aircraft. **c. nocturno,** night fighter. *naut* **dar c.,** to pursue

cazaautógrafos *mf,* autograph hunter

cazabombardero *m, aer* fighter bomber

cazadero *m,* hunting ground

cazador *a* hunting. *m, mil* chasseur; huntsman

cazadora *f,* huntress; jacket; forage cap

cazadotes *m,* dowry hunter

cazafortunas *mf* fortune hunter

cazar *vt* to hunt, chase; *fig inf* run to earth; *fig inf* catch out; *inf* overcome by flattery

cazasubmarino *m,* submarine chaser

cazatorpedero *m, naut* torpedo-boat destroyer

cazo *m,* ladle; dipper

cazolada *f,* panful

cazoleta *f,* small pan; bowl (of pipe, etc.); sword guard; boss of a shield; pan (of a firelock)

cazuela *f,* earthenware cooking dish; stew-pot; part of theater formerly reserved for women; *theat* gallery

cazumbrón *m,* cooper

cazurro *a inf* unsociable; surly, boorish

c.c.p. abbrev. of **con copia para**

ce *f,* name of the letter C. *interj* Look! Chist! **ce por be,** in detail

cebada *f,* barley (plant and grain). **c. perlada,** pearl barley

cebadal *m,* barley field

cebadera *f,* nose-bag; barley bin

cebadero *m,* barley dealer

cebado *a* on the prowl; having tasted human flesh (animal)

cebar *vt* to feed or fatten (animals); fuel, feed (furnace, etc.); prime, charge (fire-arms, etc.); start up (machines); bait (fish hook); stimulate (passion, etc.); *vi* stick in, penetrate (nails, screws, etc.); *vr* put one's mind to; grow angry. **cebarse en vanas esperanzas,** to nurture vain hopes

cebo *m,* fodder; detonator; encouragement, food; bait

cebolla *f,* onion; onion bulb; any bulbous stem; oil bulb (of lamp). **c. escalonia,** shallot

cebollana *f,* chive

cebollero (-ra) *n* onion seller

cebolleta *f,* leek; young onion

cebollino *m,* onion seed; onion bed; chive

cebra *f,* zebra

ceca *f,* mint (for coining money); name of mosque in Cordova. **de C. en Meca,** from pillar to post, hither and thither

cecear *vi* to lisp

ceceo *m,* lisping

ceceoso *a* lisping

cecial *m,* dried fish

cecina *f,* dried salt meat

cedazo *m,* sieve, strainer

ceder *vt* to cede, give up; transfer; *vi* give in, yield; diminish, decrease (fever, storm, etc.); fail, end; happen, turn out; sag, give, stretch. **No c. la fama a,** to be no less famous than

cedro *m,* cedar tree; cedar wood. **c. dulce,** red cedar

cédula *f,* document, certificate, card; *ecc* **c. de comunión,** Communion card. **c. personal,** identity card. **c. real,** royal letters patent

céfiro *m,* west wind; *poet* zephyr

cegajoso *a* blear-eyed

cegar *vi irr* to become blind; *vt* to put out the eyes; *fig* blind; wall up, close up, stop up; infatuate. *Pres. Ind.* **ciego, ciegas, ciega, ciegan.** *Pres. Subjunc.* **ciegue, ciegues, ciegue, cieguen**

cegato *a inf* short-sighted

ceguedad, ceguera *f,* blindness; delusion; ignorance

Ceilán Ceylon

ceja *f,* eyebrow; cloud cap; mountain peak; *mus* bridge (of stringed instruments). *fig* **quemarse las cejas,** to burn the midnight oil

cejar *vi* to go backwards; give way, hesitate

cejijunto *a* having eyebrows that almost meet, beetle-browed

cejo *m,* river mist

cejudo *a* having long thick eyebrows

celada *f,* helmet; ambush; fraud, trick

celador (-ra) *a* watchful, zealous. *n* supervisor; caretaker; guard (at a museum, etc.)

celaje *m,* sky with scudding clouds (gen. *pl*); skylight, window; promising sign, presage

celar *vt* to be zealous in discharge of duties; spy upon; watch; oversee, superintend; conceal; engrave

celda *f,* cell

celdilla *f,* cell (bees, wasps, etc.); (*zool bot*) cell; *bot* capsule

celebérrimo, *a sup* **célebre** most celebrated

celebración *f,* celebration; applause

celebrador (-ra) *n* celebrator; applauder

celebrante *a* celebrating. *m, ecc* celebrant

celebrar *vt* to celebrate; applaud; praise; venerate; hold, conduct; **c. que** + *subj.* to be happy that, be glad that. *vt* and *vi ecc* officiate; *vr* take place

célebre *a* famous

celebridad *f,* fame, celebrity; magnificence, show, pomp

celeridad *f,* celerity

celeste *a* celestial, heavenly

celestial *a* celestial, heavenly; perfect, delightful; *inf* foolish (ironical)

celestina *f,* procuress (allusion to *Tragicomedia de Calixto y Melibea*)

celibato *m,* celibacy; *inf* bachelor

célibe *a* celibate, unmarried. *mf* unmarried person

celo *m,* enthusiasm, ardor; religious zeal; devotion; jealousy; heat, rut; *pl* jealousy, suspicion. **dar celos (a),** to make jealous

celosía *f,* lattice; Venetian blind

celoso *a* zealous; jealous; suspicious

célula *f,* cell

celular *a* cellular

celuloide *f,* celluloid

celulosa *f,* cellulose

celuloso *a* cellular

cementación *f,* cementation

cementar *vt* to cement

cementerio *m,* cemetery

cemento *m,* cement

cena *f,* evening meal; supper; Last Supper

cenacho *m,* marketing bag

cenáculo *m,* cenacle

cenador *m,* diner out; arbor, pergola

cenagal *m,* quagmire; *fig* impasse

cenagoso *a* miry, muddy

cenar *vi* to dine, sup; *vt* eat for evening meal, sup off

cenceño *a* slim, thin

cencerrada *f,* noisy mock serenade given to widows or widowers on the first night of their new marriage

cencerrear *vi* to jingle; *inf* play out of tune; bang in the wind, rattle; squeak

cencerreo *m,* jingling; jangle; rattling; squeaking

cencerro *m,* cow-bell

cendal *m,* gauze; *ecc* stole; barbs of a feather

cenefa *f,* border; valance, flounce; edging

cenicero *m,* ash-pan; ash-pit; ash-tray

ceniciento *a* ash colored, ashen. **la Cenicienta,** Cinderella

cenit *m, ast* zenith; *fig* peak, summit

ceniza *f,* ash, cinders

cenotafio *m,* cenotaph

cenote *m, Central America, Mexico* cenote (deep natural well or sinkhole)

censo *m,* census; agreement for settlement of an annuity; annual ground rent; leasehold

censor *m,* censor; censorious person; *univ* proctor

censual *a* pertaining to census, annuity, rents

censualista *mf* annuitant

censura *f,* censorship; criticism; blame, reproach; scandal, gossip; *psy* censorship

censurable *a* reprehensible; censorable

censurar *vt* to judge; censure; criticize

centauro *m, myth* centaur

centavo *m,* hundredth part; cent; *Lat. Am.* centavo

centella *f,* lightning; spark; flash; *fig* spark (of anger, affection, etc.)

centellador *a* flashing

centellear *vi* to flash; twinkle; sparkle

centelleo *m,* scintillation; sparkle; flash

centén *m,* Spanish gold coin once worth 100 reals and later 25 pesetas

centena *f,* hundred

centenal, centenar *m,* hundred; centenary; rye field. **a centenares,** by the hundred, in crowds

centenario (-ia) *a* centenary. *n* centenarian. *m,* centenary

centeno *m, bot* rye

centésimo *a* and *m,* hundredth

centígrado *a* centigrade

centigramo *m,* centigram

centilitro *m,* centiliter

centímetro *m,* centimeter. **c. cúbico,** cubic centimeter, milliliter

céntimo *a* hundredth. *m,* centime (coin)

centinela *mf mil* sentry, sentinel; person on watch. **estar de c.,** to be on sentry duty; be on guard

centolla *f,* marine crab

centón *m,* patchwork quilt

central *a* central; centric. *f,* head office; central depot; mother house. **c. de fuerza,** power-house. **c. telefónica,** telephone exchange

centralilla, centralita *f,* local exchange, private exchange

centralismo *m,* centralism

centralización *f,* centralization

centralizador *a* centralizing

centralizar *vt* to centralize

centrar *vt* to center

céntrico *a* central, centric; centrally located; downtown

centrífugo *a* centrifugal

centrípeto *a* centripetal

centro *m,* center; headquarters, meeting place, club; center, hub; middle; core (of a rope); *fig* focus. *phys* **c. de gravedad,** center of gravity. **c. de mesa,** table center-piece. *anat* **centro nervioso,** nerve center

Centroamérica *f.* Central America

centroamericano (-na) *a* and *n* Central American

céntuplo *a* centuple

centuria *f,* century

ceñidamente tightly (e.g. **un argumento c. organizado,** a tightly organized plot)

ceñido *a* thrifty; wasp-waisted; slender waisted; fitting (of garments)

ceñidor *m,* girdle, belt

ceñir *vt irr* to girdle; surround; shorten, abbreviate; *vr* be moderate (speech, expenditure, etc.); conform, confine oneself (to). **ceñirse a las reglas,** to abide by the rules. *Pres. Ind.* **ciño, ciñes, ciñen.** *Pres. Part.* **ciñendo.** *Preterite* **ciñó, ciñeron.** *Pres. Subjunc.* **ciña,** etc. *Imperf. Subjunc.* **ciñese,** etc.

ceño *m,* band, hoop; frown; *fig* dark outlook

ceñudo *a* frowning

cepa *f,* stump; vine-stock; root (tails, antlers, etc.); *fig* origin, trunk (of a family); *biol* strain. **de la más pura c.,** of the best quality

cepillar *vt* to brush; plane; smooth

cepillo *m,* brush; *carp* plane; poor-box, offertory-box. **c. para los dientes,** toothbrush. **c. para ropa,** clothes-brush. **c. para el suelo,** scrubbing-brush. **c. para las uñas,** nail-brush

cepo *m,* bough; wooden stocks; snare; trap; poor-box; collecting-box

cera *f,* beeswax; wax; wax candles, etc., used at a function. *inf* **ser como una c.,** to be like wax (in the hands of)

cerador *m,* floor waxer (person)

ceradora *f,* floor waxer (machine)

cerámica *f,* ceramics; ceramic art, pottery

cerámico *a* ceramic

cerbatana *f,* blow-pipe, popgun; pea-shooter; ear-trumpet

cerca *f,* fence, wall

cerca *adv* near. **c. de,** near to; almost, nearly (e.g. **c. de las once,** nearly eleven o'clock)

cercado *m,* enclosure, fenced in place; fence

cercanía *f,* nearness, proximity; (gen. *pl*) outskirts, surroundings

cercano *a* near, neighboring; impending, early

cercar *vt* to enclose; build a wall or fence round; to lay siege to; crowd round; *mil* surround

cercenamiento (a) *m,* curtailment (of)

cercenar *vt* to lop off the ends, clip; curtail, diminish; abridge; whittle

cerciorar *vt* to assure, confirm; *vr* make sure

cerco *m,* ring, hoop; fence; siege; small conversational circle; spin, circling; halo (sun, moon); frame; sash (of a window). **poner c. (a),** to lay siege to, blockade

cerda *f,* sow; bristle

Cerdeña Sardinia

cerdo *m,* pig, hog

cerdoso *a* bristly

cereal *a* and *m,* cereal

cerebelo *m, anat* cerebellum

cerebral *a* cerebral

cerebro *m,* cerebrum; brain; intelligence

cerebro-espinal *a* cerebrospinal

ceremonia *f,* ceremony; function, display; formality. **de c.,** ceremonial; formally. **por c.,** for politeness' sake

ceremonial *a* ceremonial. *m,* ceremony; rite; protocol (rules of behavior)

ceremonioso *a* ceremonious; formal, over-courteous

cerero *m,* wax-chandler

cereza *f,* cherry

cerezal *m,* cherry orchard

cerezo *m,* cherry tree; cherry wood

cerilla *f,* wax taper; match; ear wax

cerillo *m, Mexico* match

cerner *vt irr* to sieve; watch, observe; *fig* sift, clarify; *vi* bolt (of plants); drizzle; *vr* waddle; hover; threaten (of evil, etc.). *Pres. Ind.* **cierno, ciernes, cierne, ciernen.** *Pres. Subjunc.* **cierna, ciernas, cierna, ciernan**

cernícalo *m, orn* kestrel; *inf* lout

cernidillo *m,* drizzle; teetering walk

cernido *m,* sifting, sieving; sifted flour

cerniduras *f pl,* siftings

cero *m, math* zero; naught; (tennis) love. *fig inf* **ser un c.,** to be a mere cipher

cerote *m,* cobbler's wax. *inf* fear

cerquillo *m,* tonsure; welt (of a shoe); *Lat. Am.* fringe

cerquita *adv* very near, hard by

cerradero, *m,* cerradera *f,* bolt staple; catch of a lock; clasp or strings of a purse

cerradizo *a* closable, lockable

cerrado *a* closed; compact; incomprehensible, obscure; overcast, cloudy; *inf* taciturn; secretive. *m,* enclosure

cerradura *f,* fastening, lock; closing, locking

cerraja *f,* lock (of a door); bolt

cerrajería *f,* locksmith's craft; locksmith's workshop or shop

cerrajero *m,* locksmith

cerramiento *m,* closing, locking up; fence; enclosure, shooting preserve; partition wall

cerrar *vt irr* to close; lock, fasten, bolt; shut up; *mech* shut off, turn off; fold up; block or stop up; seal (letters, etc.); close down; terminate; obstruct; (*with con*) attack; *vi* close; close in (of night, etc.); *vr* heal up (wounds); close (flowers); *rad* close down; crowd together; *fig* stand firm. *inf* **cerrarse la espuela,** to take a nightcap,

have a last drink. **c. la marcha,** to bring up the rear. **al c. la edición,** stop press. See **acertar**

cerrazón *f,* dark, overcast sky heralding a storm

cerril *a* rough, rocky; wild, untamed (cattle, horses); *inf* boorish

cerro *m,* neck of an animal; spine, backbone; hill. *fig* **irse por los cerros de Úbeda,** to go off the track, indulge in irrelevancies

cerrojo *m,* bolt (of a door, etc.); lock (of a door, gun, etc.)

certamen *m,* contest; competition; match

certero *a* well-aimed; sure, well-timed; knowledgeable, sure

certeza, certidumbre *f,* certitude, assurance

certificación *f,* certification; certificate; affidavit

certificado *a* certified; registered. *m,* registered letter; certificate

certificar *vt* to certify; register (letter, etc.)

certificatorio *a* certifying or serving to certify

certísimo *a* a learned form of the superlative of **cierto** (see **certísimo**)

certitud *f,* certitude

cervantino *a* Cervantine

cervecería *f,* brewery; ale-house

cervecero (-ra) *n* brewer; beer seller

cerveza *f,* beer, ale. **c. negra,** stout

cerviz *f,* cervix, nape (of neck). **doblar** (*or* **bajar**) **la c.,** to humble oneself

cesación *f,* cessation, stopping

cesante *a* dismissed; pensioned off. **declarar c. (a),** to dismiss (a person from a post). **estar c.,** to be out of a job

cesantía *f,* status of dismissed or retired official; retirement pension

cesar *vi* to cease, stop, end; leave an employment; desist; retire

cesáreo *a* Cesarean; imperial

cese *m,* stopping of payment for an employment

cesión *f,* cession; transfer; resignation; *law* release

cesionario (-ia) *n* cessionary, transferee

césped *m,* grass, sward; sod, lawn

cesta *f,* basket, hamper; *sport* racket; cradle (for a wine bottle)

cestada *f,* basketful

cestería *f,* basketmaking, basketweaving; basket factory; basket shop; basketwork

cestero (-ra) *n* basket maker or seller

cesto *m,* basket, hamper, skip

cesura *f,* cesura

cetorrino *m,* basking shark

cetrería *f,* falconry

cetrino *a* greenish-yellow; sallow; citrine; melancholy; reserved, aloof

cetro *m,* scepter; verge; reign

chabacanería *f,* bad taste; vulgarity

chabacano *a* vulgar, common; rude, uncouth

chacal *m, zool* jackal

cháchara *f, inf* empty chatter; verbiage

chacharear *vi* to chatter; gabble, cackle

chacharero *a inf* chattering; talkative

chacolotear *vi* to clatter, clink (loose horseshoe)

chacota *f,* merriment, mirth

chacotear *vi inf* to be merry, have fun

chacotón *a* of a boisterous humor

chacra *f, Lat. Am.* small farm, small holding

chafado *a* taken aback; disappointed

chafallar *vt inf* to mend carelessly, botch

chafandín *m,* vain fool

chafar *vt* to flatten; crumple, crease (clothes); *inf* heckle

chafarrinar *vt* to stain, mark, blot

chaflán *m,* bevel edge, chamfer

chagrén *m,* shagreen leather

chagüe *m, Central America* bog, marsh, swamp

chal *m,* shawl

chalán *m,* horse-dealer

chalana *f, naut* wherry, lighter

chalanear vt to bargain; indulge in sharp practice

chalar vt to drive mad; enamour

chaleco m, waistcoat; cardigan

chalequear vt, Mexico to pilfer, swipe

chalina f, flowing scarf, artist's bow

Chalo pet form of the male given name Carlos 'Charles', hence = English Chuck; Bud, Mac (in direct address to a male whose name one does not know)

chalote m, shallot

chalupa f, shallop; launch; canoe; long boat, ship's boat

chamar vt inf to palm off, barter

chamarasca f, brushwood, tinder

chamarilero (-ra) n secondhand dealer

chamarreta f, sheepskin jacket; Mexico jacket

chambergo a pertaining to the Chambergo regiment. m, broad-brimmed hat

chambón a inf awkward, clumsy; lucky

chambonada f, inf blunder; fluke, chance

chambra f, dressing-jacket, peignoir, negligee

chamicera f, piece of scorched earth (woodland, etc.)

chamorro a close-cropped, shorn (hair)

champán m, champagne. **c. obrero,** humorous cider

champaña m, champagne

champar vt inf to cast in a person's face, remind

champú m, shampoo

chamuscar vt to scorch; singe

chamusquina f, scorching; singeing; inf brawl

chanada f, inf trick, mischievous act

chancaca f, Lat. Am. syrup cake

chancada f, Lat. Am. dirty trick

chancearse vr to joke

chancero a joking, facetious

chancho, -a mf, Lat. Am. pig

chanchollada f, dirty trick, foul play, trick

chanchullo m, inf fraud

chanciller m, chancellor

chancillería f, chancery

chancla f, down at heel shoe; heelless slipper

chancleta f, heelless slipper, babouche. mf inf ninny

chanclo m, overshoe; Wellington

chanfaina f, cul savory fricassee

chanflón a tough, coarse; ungainly

changador m. Argentina porter

chantaje m, blackmail

chantajista mf blackmailer

chantar vt to put on, clothe; inf tell plainly. inf **c. sus verdades,** to tell hometruths

chanza f, joke, jest

chanzoneta f, canzonetta; inf joke

¡chao! Argentina, Chile bye!

chapa f, plate, sheet; veneer; clasp; inf prudence, common sense; rouge. **c. de hierro,** sheet-iron. **c. de identidad,** number plate

chapado a la antigua a old-fashioned

chapalear vi to dabble in water; splash; clatter (of a horseshoe)

chapaleo m, dabbling, paddling; splash; clattering, clink (of a horseshoe)

chapaleteo m, lapping of water; splashing (of rain)

chaparrear vi to pour with rain

chaparrón m, heavy shower of rain, downpour

chapear vt to veneer; vi clatter (loose horseshoe)

chaperón m, hood

chapeta f, dim clasp; red flush or spot on cheek

chapetón (-ona) n WH recently arrived European, especially Spaniard

chapín m, cork-soled leather overshoe (for women) ant

chapino a and m, Mexico contemptuous Guatemalan

chapodar vt to prune, lop off branches; cut down, reduce

chapotear vt to sponge, moisten, damp; vi paddle, splash; dabble or trail the hands (in water)

chapoteo m, moistening, sponging; paddling, splashing; dabbling

chapucear vt to botch, do badly; bungle

chapuceramente adv awkwardly. **hablar el japonés c.,** to speak broken Japanese

chapucería f, roughness, poor workmanship; botch

chapucero a rough, badly finished; bungling, clumsy, awkward

chapurrado a broken (e.g. **hablar un italiano c.,** to speak broken Italian)

chapurrar, chapurrear vt to speak badly (a language); jabber; inf mix (drinks)

chapuz m, ducking, submerging; plunge; unimportant job; clumsiness

chapuzar vt to duck, submerge; plunge

chaqué m, morning coat; morning suit

chaqueta f, jacket; mech casing

chaquete m, backgammon

chaquetilla f, short jacket; coatee; blazer

chaquetón m, short coat. **c. de piloto,** aer pea-jacket

charabán m, charabanc

charada f, charade

charamusca f, Lat. Am. firewood, kindling

charanguero a rough, badly finished; clumsy. m, Andalusian boat

charca f, pond, pool; reservoir

charco m, puddle; inf sea

charla f, inf chatter; conversation; talk, informal lecture

charlar vi inf to prattle, chatter; chat, converse; give a talk (on)

charlatán (-ana) a loquacious, garrulous; indiscreet; fraudulent, false. n charlatan; chatterer

charlatanería f, loquacity, garrulity; quackery

charlatanismo m, charlatanism, quackery

charnela f, hinge; hinged joint

charol m, japan, varnish; patent leather

charolar vt to japan, varnish

charolista mf, varnisher

charpa f, pistol-belt; sling

charrán (-ana) n rogue, trickster

charranada f, roguery, knavery

charrería f, tawdriness; gaudiness

charretera f, mil epaulet; garter

charro a churlish, coarse; flashy, tawdry

chasca f, brushwood, firewood

chascar vi to creak, crack; clack (the tongue); swallow

chascarrillo m, inf amusing anecdote, good story

chasco m, trick, practical joke; disappointment. **llevarse un c.,** to meet with a disappointment

chasis m, aut chassis; phot plate-holder; mech underframe

chasquear vt to play a trick on; wag (one's tongue); crack (a whip, one's knuckles); break a promise, disappoint; vi creak, crack; meet with a disappointment

chasquido m, crack (of whip); creaking (of wood); click (of the tongue)

chatarra f, scrap iron; junk

chato a flat-nosed; flat

chauvinismo m, chauvinism

chaval a inf young. m, lad

chaveta f, mech bolt, pin, peg, cotter, key

checo (-ca) a and n Czech. Czech (language)

Chejov Chekov

chelín m, shilling

Chengis-Jan Genghis Khan

chepa f, inf hunch (back); hump

cheque m, check. **c. cruzado,** crossed check

chica f, girl; inf dear

chicana f, chicanery

chicano (-na) a and n Chicano, American of Mexican ancestry

chicha f, Lat. Am. corn liquor

chícharo m, pea

chicharrón m, cul crackling; burnt meat; inf sunburnt person

chichón m, bruise, bump

chichonera f, child's protective hat (something like a straw crash-helmet)

chicle m, chewing gum

chiclero *m,* chicle-gatherer
chico *a* little, small; young. *m,* little boy; youth; *inf* old boy, dear. **Es un buen c.,** He's a good fellow
chicoleo *m, inf* compliment
chicote *mf* sturdy child. *m, inf* cigar; *Lat. Am.* whip
chifla *f,* whistling, whistle; tanner's paring knife
chiflado *a inf* cracked, daft; crack-brained
chifladura *f,* whistling; *inf* whim, mania, hobby
chiflar *vi* to whistle; *vt* to make fun of, hiss; pare or scrape leather; *inf* swill, tipple; *vr inf* have a slate loose; be slightly mad; *inf* lose one's head over, adore
chifle *m,* whistle, whistling; decoy call (birds)
chiflón *m, Lat. Am.* draft (of air)
chile *m, bot* red pepper, chilli
chileno (-na) *a* and *n* Chilean
chilla *f, Argentina* fox
chillador *a* screaming, shrieking
chillar *vi* to scream, shriek; creak; squeak; jabber (monkeys, etc.); *art* be strident (of colors)
chillería *f,* shrieking, screaming
chillido *m,* scream, shriek; squeak (of mice, etc.); jabber (of monkeys, etc.)
chillón *a inf* screaming, yelling; strident, piercing; crude, loud (colors)
chimenea *f,* chimney; funnel; fireplace; kitchen range
chimpancé *m,* chimpanzee
china *f,* pebble; porcelain, china; Chinese silk
chinche *f,* bedbug; thumbtack, drawing-pin. *mf inf* bore
chinchona *f,* quinine
chinchorrería *f, inf* impertinence, tediousness; gossip
chinela *f,* mule, slipper; overshoe, patten *ant*
chinero *m,* china cupboard
chinesco *a* Chinese. **a la chinesca,** in Chinese fashion
chingana *f, Lat. Am.* bar
chino (-na) *a* and *n* Chinese. *m,* Chinese (language)
Chipre Cyprus
chiquero *m,* pigsty; stable for bulls
chiquillada *f,* childishness, puerility
chiquillería *f, inf* crowd of children
chiquillo (-lla) *n* small boy
chiquito (-ta) *a dim* **chico,** tiny, very small. *n* little one, small boy
chiripa *f,* (billiards) fluke; *inf* happy coincidence, stroke of luck; lucky guess
chirivía *f, bot* parsnip; *orn* wagtail
chirlar *vi inf* to gabble, talk loudly
chirlo *m,* knife wound, sabre cut; knife scar
chirona *f, inf* jail
chirriador *a* sizzling, crackling; creaking, squeaking
chirriar *vi* to sizzle, crackle; creak, squeak; squawk; *inf* croak, sing out of tune
chirrido *m,* squawk; croaking; noise of grasshoppers; squeaking; creaking, creak
¡chis! *interj* Shh! Silence!
chisme *m,* gossip, tale; *inf* small household utensil, trifle
chismear *vt* to tell tales, gossip
chismero (-ra), chismoso (-sa) *a* gossiping, talebearing. *n* gossip, tale bearer
chispa *f,* spark; ember; *elec* spark; tiny diamond; small particle; wit; quickwittedness; *inf* drunkenness. **c. del encendido,** ignition spark
chispazo *m,* flying out of a spark, sparking; damage done by spark; *inf* gossip, rumor
chispeante *a* sparking; sparkling; *fig* scintillating (with wit etc.)
chispear *vi* to throw out sparks, spark; sparkle, gleam; *fig* scintillate; drizzle gently
chisporrotear *vi inf* to sputter; fizz
chisposo *a* sputtering, throwing out sparks
chistar *vi* to speak, break silence (gen. used negatively)
chiste *m,* witticism, bon mot; amusing incident; joke
chistera *f,* creel (for fish); *inf* top-hat, tile
chistoso *a* joking; amusing, funny
chiticallando *adv* quietly, stealthily; *inf* on the quiet, in secret
¡chito! ¡chitón! *interj* Hush! Sh!

chiva *f, Colombia, Panama* bus; *Venezuela* beard, goatee; **chivas** *f, Venezuela* hand-me-downs
chivo *n zool* kid. **c. expiatorio,** scapegoat
chocante *a* colliding; provoking; shocking; surprising
chocar *vi* to collide; strike (against); run into; fight, clash; *vt* clink (glasses); provoke, annoy; surprise, shock. **¡Choca cinco!** Clasp five!, Gimme five!, Put it there!, Give some skin! (invitation to shake hands)
chocarrería *f,* coarse joke
chochear *vi* to be senile; *fig inf* dote (on)
chocho *a* senile; *fig inf* doting
choco *m,* small hump, hunchback
chocolate *m,* chocolate; drinking chocolate. **c. a la española,** thick chocolate. **c. a la francesa,** French drinking chocolate
chocolatería *f,* chocolate factory or shop
chocolatero (-ra) *a* fond of chocolate. *n* chocolate maker or seller
chófer *m,* chauffeur; driver
chompa *f, Lat. Am.* jumper, pullover
chonta *f, Lat. Am.* palm tree
chopera *f,* grove or plantation of black poplar trees
chopo *m, bot* black poplar; *inf* gun
choque *m,* collision; shock; jar; *med* concussion; fight; clink (of glasses); clash; *mil* skirmish
choricera *f,* sausage-making machine
choricero (-ra) *n* sausage maker
chorizo *m,* kind of pork sausage; counterweight
chorrear *vi* to spout, jet; drip; *fig inf* trickle, arrive slowly
chorreo *m,* drip, dripping; spouting, gushing
chorrera *f,* spout; drip; jabot, lace front
chorro *m,* jet; stream (of water, etc.); *fig* shower. **a chorros,** in a stream; in abundance, plentifully
chova *f,* rook; carrion crow; jackdaw
choza *f,* hut, cabin; cottage
chubasco *m,* squall, downpour; storm; transitory misfortune
chuchería *f,* gewgaw, trinket; savory titbit; snaring, trapping
chucruta *f,* sauerkraut
chueca *f,* round head of a bone; small ball; game like shinty; *inf* practical joke
chueco *a Mexico* bent, crooked, twisted
chufa *f, bot* chufa; *inf* joke, trick
chufería *f,* place where drink made of **chufas** is sold
chufla *f,* flippant remark
chufleta *f, inf* joke; taunt
chulada *f,* mean trick, base action; drollery
chulería *f,* drollness; attractive personality
chuleta *f, cul* cutlet, chop; mutton-chop; *inf* slap
chulo *a* droll, amusing; attractive. *m,* slaughterhouse worker; bullfighter's assistant; pimp; rogue
chumbera *f,* prickly pear; Indian fig
chupada *f,* sucking; suck; suction
chupado de cara, c. de mofletes *a* lantern-jawed
chupador *a* sucking. *m,* baby's comforter or dummy
chupar *vt* to suck; absorb (of plants); *fig inf* drain, rob; *vr* grow thin. **chuparse los dedos,** *inf* to lick one's lips; be delighted
chupatintas *mf, inf* scrivener, clerk (scornful)
churdón *m,* raspberry cane; raspberry; raspberry vinegar
churrería *f,* place where **churros** are made or sold
churrero (-ra) *n* maker or seller of **churros**
churrigueresco *a* Churrigueresque
churro *a* coarse (of wool). *m, cul* a kind of fritter eaten with chocolate, coffee, etc.
churumbela *f, mus* pipe; reed for drinking mate WH
chusco *a* droll, witty, amusing
chusma *f,* galley hands, crew; rabble, mob
chutar *vt sport* to shoot (a goal)
chuzo *m, mil* pike
chuzón *a* wily, suspicious, cunning
cianuro *m,* cyanide

ciar *vi* to go backwards; *naut* row backwards; *fig* make no headway (negotiations)

ciática *f*, sciatica

ciático *a* sciatic

cicatería *f*, niggardliness, avarice

cicatero *a* avaricious, niggardly, mean

cicatriz *f*, cicatrice; *fig* scar, mark, impression

cicatrizar *vt* to cicatrize, heal; *vr* scar over

cíclico *a* cyclic, cyclical

ciclismo *m*, bicycling

ciclista *mf* cyclist

ciclo *m*, cycle (of time). **c. artúrico, c. de Artús,** Arthurian Cycle. **c. de conferencias,** series of lectures

ciclón *m*, cyclone

ciclópeo *a* cyclopean

cicuta *f*, hemlock

cid *m*, great warrior, chief. **el Cid,** national hero of Spanish wars against the Moors

cidra *f*, citron

cidro *m*, citron tree

ciego *a* blind; dazed, blinded; choked up. *m*, blind man; *anat* cæcum. **a ciegas,** blindly; heedlessly

cielo *m*, sky, firmament; atmosphere; climate; paradise; Providence; bliss, glory; roof, canopy; *inf* darling. **a c. abierto,** in the open air. **parecer un c.,** to be heavenly

ciempiés *m*, centipede

cien *a* abb. **ciento,** hundred. Used always before substantives (e.g. **c. hombres,** 100 men)

ciénaga *f*, swamp; morass

ciencia *f*, science; knowledge; erudition, ability. **ciencias naturales,** natural science. **a c. cierta,** for certain, without doubt (gen. with *saber*)

cienmilésimo *a* hundred-thousandth

cieno *m*, slime, mud; silt

científico *a* scientific. *m*, scientist

ciento (cf. **cien**) *a* hundred; hundredth. *m*, hundred. **por c.,** per cent.

cierne, en in flower; *fig* in the early stages, in embryo

cierre *m*, closing, shutting; closing time of shops, etc.; fastening; fastener; clasp (of a necklace, handbag, etc.). **c. cremallera,** zip fastener. **c. metálico,** doorshutter

ciertamente *adv* certainly; undoubtedly; indeed

ciertísimo *a* everyday form of the superlative of **cierto** (see **certísimo**)

cierto *a* certain, sure; true; particular (e.g. **c. hombre,** a certain man (note no *def. art.*)). **un c. sabor,** a special flavor. **una cosa cierta,** something certain. **no, por c.,** no, certainly not. **por c.,** truly, indeed

cierva *f*, hind

ciervo *m*, stag. **c. volante,** stagbeetle

cierzo *m*, northerly wind

cifra *f*, number; figure; sum total; cipher, code; monogram; abbreviation

cifrar *vt* to write in cipher; summarize, abridge; (*with en*) be dependent on; depend on

cigarra *f*, *ent* cicada, harvest fly

cigarral *m*, (Toledo) countryhouse and garden or orchard

cigarrera *f*, woman who makes or sells cigars; cigarcabinet; cigar-case

cigarrería *f*, *Lat. Am.* tobacco shop

cigarrillo *m*, cigarette

cigarro *m*, cigar; *Lat. Am.* cigarette

cigüeña *f*, *orn* stork; *mech* crank

ciliar *a* ciliary

cilicio *m*, hairshirt

cilindrar *vt* to roll; calendar; bore

cilindrero *m*, organ grinder

cilíndrico *a* cylindrical

cilindro *m*, cylinder; roller

cima *f*, summit; top of trees; apex; *arch* coping; head (thistle, etc.); *fig* aim, goal, end

cimbalero (-ra) *n* cymbalist

címbalo *m*, cymbal

cimborrio *m*, *arch* cupola; cimborium

cimbrar, cimbrear *vt* to bend; brandish; *vr* sway (in walking)

cimbreño *a* graceful, lithe, willowy

cimbreo *m*, swaying, bending

cimbrón *m*, *Lat. Am.* vibration

cimentar *vt irr* to lay foundations; refine (gold, metals, etc.); found; *fig* ground (in virtue, etc.). See **acertar**

cimera *f*, crest of helmet

cimiento *m*, foundation (of a building); bottom; groundwork; origin, base. **abrir los cimientos,** to lay the foundations

cimitarra *f*, scimitar

cinabrio *m*, cinnabar; vermilion

cinc *m*, zinc

cincel *m*, chisel; burin, engraver

cincelador (-ra) *n* engraver; chiseler

cincelar *vt* to chisel; carve; engrave

cincha *f*, girth of a saddle

cinchar *vt* to tighten the saddle girths

cincho *m*, belt, girdle; iron hoop

cinco *a* and *m*, five; fifth. **a las c.,** at five o'clock

cincuenta *a* and *m*, fifty; fiftieth

cincuentavo *a* fiftieth

cincuentenario *m*, fiftieth anniversary

cincuentón (-ona) *a* and *n* fifty years old (person)

cine, cinema *m*, cinema, movies. **c. sonoro,** sound film

cinemática *f*, *phys* kinematics

cinematografía *f*, cinematography

cinematografiar *vt* to film

cinematográfico *a* cinematographic

cinematógrafo *m*, cinematograph; cinema

cínico *a* cynical; impudent; untidy. *m*, cynic

cinismo *m*, cynicism

cinta *f*, ribbon; tape; strip; film (cinematograph). **c. métrica,** tape-measure

cintillo *m*, hatband; small ring set with gems

cinto *m*, belt, girdle. **c. de pistolas,** pistol-belt

cintoteca *f*, tape library

cintura *f*, waist; belt; girdle

cinturón *m*, large waist; belt girdle; sword-belt; that which encircles or surrounds. **c. de seguridad,** seat belt

ciprés *m*, *bot* cypress tree or wood

cipresal *m*, cypress grove

cipresino *a* cypress; cypresslike

circasiano (-na) *a* and *n* Circassian

circo *m*, circus; amphitheater

circón *m*, zircon

circuir *vt. irr* to surround, encircle. See **huir**

circuito *m*, periphery; contour; (*elec phys*) circuit. **corto c.,** short circuit

circulación *f*, circulation; traffic. **c. de la sangre,** circulation of the blood. **calle de gran c.,** busy street

circular *a* circular. *f*, circular. *vt* to pass round; *vi* circle; circulate; move in a circle; move about; run, travel (traffic)

circulatorio *a* circulatory

círculo *m*, circle; circumference; circuit; casino, social club

circuncidar *vt* to circumcise; modify, reduce

circuncisión *f*, circumcision

circunciso *a* circumcised

circundar *vt* to surround

circunferencia *f*, circumference

circunflejo *a* circumflex. **acento c.,** circumflex accent

circunlocución *f*, circumlocution

circunnavegación *f*, circumnavigation

circunnavegar *vt* to circumnavigate

circunscribir *vt* to circumscribe. *Past Part.* **circunscrito**

circunscripción *f*, circumscription

circunspección *f*, circumspection; seriousness, dignity

circunspecto *a* circumspect; serious, dignified

circunstancia *f*, circumstance; incident, detail; condition. **c. agravante,** aggravating circumstance. **c. atenuante,** extenuating circumstance. **bajo las circunstancias,** in the circumstances. **de circunstancias,** occasional (e.g. **poesías de circunstancias,**

occasional verse). **estar al nivel de las circunstancias,** to rise to the occasion

circunstanciado *a* circumstantiated, detailed

circunstancial *a* circumstantial; occasional (e.g. **poesías circunstanciales,** occasional verse)

circunstante *a* surrounding; present. *mf* person present, bystander

circunvecino *a* adjacent, neighboring

circunvolución *f,* circumvolution

cirial *m,* processional candlestick

cirio *m,* wax candle

cirro *m, med* scirrhus; *bot* tendril; *zool* cirrus

cirrosis *f,* cirrhosis

cirroso *a med* scirrhous; (*zool bot*) cirrose

ciruela *f,* plum; prune. **c. claudia, c. veidal,** greengage. **c. damascena,** damson

ciruelo *m,* plum tree

cirugía *f,* surgery

cirujano *m,* surgeon

cisco *m,* coal dust, slack coal; *inf* hubbub, quarrel

cisma *m,* or *f,* schism; disagreement, discord. **el C. de Occidente,** the Western Schism

cismático *a* schismatic; discordant, inharmonious

cisne *m,* swan

cisterciense *a* Cistercian

cisterna *f,* water-tank, cistern

cístico *a* cystic

cistitis *f,* cystitis

cita *f,* appointment; quotation, citation

citable *a* quotable

citación *f,* quotation; *law* summons

citar *vt* to make an appointment; cite, quote; *law* summon. **c. en comparecencia,** to summon to appear in court

cítara *f, mus* zither

citatorio *m,* summons

citerior *a* hither, nearer

citrato *m, chem* citrate

cítrico *a* citric

ciudad *f,* city; municipal body. **la c. señorial,** the Aristocratic City (Ponce, Puerto Rico)

ciudadanía *f,* citizenship

ciudadano (-na) *a* city; civic, born in or belonging to a city. *n* citizen; burgess; bourgeois. **c. de honor,** freeman (of a city)

ciudadela *f,* citadel

cívico *a* civic; patriotic; *Lat. Am.* police officer

civicultura *f,* raising of civets

civil *a* civil; civilian; polite

civilidad *f,* politeness, civility

civilización *f,* civilization

civilizador *a* civilizing

civilizar *vt* to civilize; educate; *vr* grow civilized; be educated

civismo *m,* civism; patriotism; civics

cizalla *f,* shears, shearing machine; metal filings

cizaña *f, bot* darnel, tare; vice, evil; dissension, discord (gen. with *meter* and *sembrar*)

clac *m,* opera-hat; tricorne

clamar *vi* to cry out; *fig* demand (of inanimate things); vociferate; speak solemnly

clamor *m,* outcry, shouting; shriek, complaint; knell, tolling of bells

clamorear *vt* to implore, clamor (for); *vi* toll (of bells)

clamoroso *a* noisy, clamorous

clandestino *a* clandestine, secret

clangor *m, poet* blare, bray (of trumpet)

claqué *m,* tap-dance

clara *f,* white of egg; bald patch (in fur); *inf* fair interval on a rainy day

claraboya *f,* skylight; *arch* clerestory

claramente *adv* clearly, evidently

clarear *vt* to clear; give light to; *vi* to dawn; grow light; *vr* be transparent; *inf* reveal secrets unwittingly

clarete *m,* claret (wine); claret color. *a* claret; claretcolored

claridad *f,* clearness; transparency; lightness, brightness; distinctness; clarity; good reputation, renown; plain truth, home truth (gen. *pl*)

clarificación *f,* clarification; purifying, refining

clarificar *vt* to illuminate; clarify, purify; refine (sugar, etc.)

clarín *m,* bugle; clarion; organ stop; bugler

clarinete *m,* clarinet; clarinet player

clarión *m,* white chalk, crayon

clarividencia *f,* perspicuity, clear-sightedness

clarividente *a* perspicacious, clear-sighted

claro *a* clear; light, bright; distinct; pure, clean; transparent, translucent; light (of colors); easily understood; evident, obvious; frank; cloudless; shrewd, quick-thinking; famous. *m,* skylight; space between words; break in a speech; space in procession, etc.; *art* (gen. *pl*) high lights. *interj* **¡C.!** or **¡C. está!** Of course! **a las claras,** openly, frankly

claroscuro *m,* chiaroscuro; monochrome

clase *f,* class, group; kind, sort, quality; class (school, university); lecture room; lecture, lesson; order, family. **c. dirigente,** ruling class. **c. media,** middle class. **c. social,** social class

clasicismo *m,* classicism

clasicista *a* and *mf* classicist

clásico *a* classic; notable; classical. *m,* classic

clasificación *f,* classification

clasificador (-ra) *n* classifier. **c. de billetes,** ticketpunch

clasificar *vt* to classify, arrange. **c. correspondencia,** to file letters

claudicación *f,* limping; negligence; hesitancy, weakness; backing down

claudicar *vi* to limp; be negligent; hesitate, give way

claustral *a* cloistral

claustro *m,* cloister; council, faculty, senate (of university); monastic rule

claustrofobia *f,* claustrophobia

cláusula *f,* clause. **c. de negación implícita,** contraryto-fact clause. **c. principal,** main clause. **c. subordinada,** dependent clause, subordinate clause. **c. sustantiva,** noun clause

clausura *f,* sanctum of convent; claustration; solemn ending ceremony of tribunal, etc. **la vida de c.,** monastic or conventual life

clava *f,* club, truncheon; *naut* scupper

clavadizo *a* nail-studded (doors, etc.)

clavar *vt* to nail; fasten with nails; pierce, prick; set gems (jeweler); spike (cannon, gum); *fig* fix (eyes, attention, etc.); *inf* cheat

clave *m,* clavichord. *f,* code, key; *mus* clef; *arch* keystone; plug (telephones). **c. (de),** key to. *mus* **c. de sol,** treble clef

clavel *m, bot* carnation plant and flower

clavelito *m, bot* pink plant and flower

clavero (-ra) *n* keeper of the keys. *m,* clove tree

clavetear *vt* to stud with nails; *fig* round off (business affairs)

clavicordio *m,* clavichord

clavícula *f,* clavicle

clavija *f,* peg, pin; plug; peg of stringed instrument; axle-pin

clavo *m,* nail, spike, peg; corn (on foot); anguish. **c. de especia,** clove. **c. de herradura,** hob-nail

claymore *f,* claymore

clemátide *f, bot* clematis

clemencia *f,* mildness; clemency; mercy

clemente *a* mild; clement; merciful

cleptomanía *f,* kleptomania

cleptómano (-na) *a* and *n* kleptomaniac

clerecía *f,* clergy

clerical *a* belonging to the clergy; clerical

clericalismo *m,* clericalism

clerigalla *f,* (*contemptuous*) dog-collar men

clérigo *m,* cleric, clergyman; clerk (in Middle Ages)

clero *m,* clergy

cliente *mf* client, customer; protégé, ward
clientela *f,* patronage, protection; clientele
clima *m,* climate, clime
climatérico *a* climacteric
climático *a* climatic
climatología *f,* climatology
clímax *m,* climax
clínica *f,* clinic, nursing home; department of medicine or surgery
clínico *a* clinical
clíper *m, (aer* and *naut)* clipper
clisar *vt print* to cast from a mold, stereotype
clisé *m, print* stereotype plate
cloaca *f,* sewer, drain; *zool* cloaca
cloquear *vi* to go broody (hen); cluck
cloqueo *m,* cluck, clucking
cloquera *f,* broodiness (hens)
clorato *m,* chlorate
clorhídrico *a* hydrochloric
cloro *m,* chlorine
clorofila *f,* chlorophyll
cloroformizar *vt* to chloroform
cloroformo *m,* chloroform
clorosis *f,* chlorosis
cloruro *m,* chloride
club *m,* club
clueca *f,* broody hen
clueco *a* broody (hens); *inf* doddering
C.N.T. initialism of Confederación Nacional de Trabajo
coacción *f,* coercion
coactivo *a* coercive
coadjutor *m,* co-worker, assistant
coadunar *vt* to join or mingle together
coadyuvar *vt* to assist
coagulación *f,* coagulation
coagular *vt* to coagulate; clot; curdle
coágulo *m,* clot; coagulation; congealed blood
coalición *f,* coalition
coartada *f,* alibi. **probar la c.,** to prove an alibi
coartar *vt* to limit, restrict
coautor (-ra) *n* co-author
cobalto *m,* cobalt
cobarde *a* cowardly; irresolute. *m,* coward
cobardía *f,* cowardice
cobayo *m,* guinea-pig
cobertera *f,* lid, cover
cobertizo *m,* overhanging roof; shack, shed, hut. **c. de aeroplanos,** *aer* hangar
cobertura *f,* covering; coverlet; wrapping
cobija *f,* imbrex tile; cover; *Lat. Am.* blanket
cobijar *vt* to cover; shelter
cobra *f, zool* cobra; rope or thong for yoking oxen; retrieval (of game)
cobradero *a* that which can be collected, recoverable
cobrador *m,* collector, receiver. *a* collecting. **c. de tranvía,** tram conductor
cobranza *f,* receiving, collecting; collection of fruit or money
cobrar *vt* to collect (what is owed); charge; earn; regain, recover; feel, experience (emotions); wind, pull in (ropes, etc.); gain, acquire; retrieve (game); *vr* recuperate. **c. ánimo,** to take courage. **c. cariño (a),** to grow fond of. **c. fuerzas,** to gather strength. **c. importancia,** to gain importance. **¿Cuánto cobra Vd.?** How much do you charge?; How much do you earn?
cobre *m, min* copper; copper kitchen utensils; *pl mus* brass; *Lat. Am.* (copper) cent, centavo
cobrizo *a* containing copper; copper-colored
cocacolonizar *vt* (United States) to gain economic control of . . . and introduce into its pop culture
cocacolonización *f,* economic domination by the United States and introduction of its pop culture
cocaína *f,* cocaine
cocción *f,* coction
coceador *a* inclined to kick; kicking (animals)
coceadura *f,* kicking

cocear *vi* to kick; *inf* kick against, oppose
cocedero *a* easily cooked
cocer *vt. irr* to boil; cook; bake (bricks, etc.); digest; *surg* suppurate; *vi* boil (of a liquid); ferment; *vr* suffer pain or inconvenience over a long period. *Pres. Ind.* **cuezo, cueces, cuece, cuecen.** *Pres. Subjunc.* **cueza, cuezas, cueza, cuezan**
cochayuyo *m, Lat. Am.* edible seaweed
coche *m,* carriage, car. **c. camas,** sleeping car. **c. -camioneta,** station wagon. **c. cerrado,** *aut* sedan. **c. de muchos caballos,** high-powered car. **c. de plaza,** hackney-carriage. **c. fúnebre,** hearse. **c. -línea,** inter-city bus. *f, Ecuador* puddle
cochera *f,* coach house; tramway depot
cochero *m,* coachman; driver. *a* easily cooked
¡cochi! (call to pigs)
cochina *f,* sow
cochinería *f, inf* filthiness; mean trick
cochinilla *f,* wood louse; cochineal insect; cochineal
cochinillo *m,* sucking-pig. **c. de Indias,** guinea-pig
cochino *m,* pig; *inf* filthy person. *a* filthy
cocido *a* boiled, cooked, baked. *m,* dish of stewed meat, pork, chicken, with peas, etc.
cociente *m,* quotient
cocimiento *m,* cooking; decoction
cocina *f,* kitchen; pottage; broth; cookery. **c. de campaña,** field-kitchen. **c. económica,** cooking range
cocinar *vt* to cook; *vi inf* meddle, interfere
cocinería *f, naut* galley
cocinero (-ra) *n* cook, chef
cocinilla *f,* spirit-stove
coco *m, bot* coconut tree and fruit; coconut shell; grub, maggot; bogeyman; hobgoblin; *inf* grimace. *inf* **ser un c.,** to be hideously ugly
cocacolismo *n inf* economic dependence on the United States and adoption of its pop culture
cocodrilo *m,* crocodile
cócora *mf inf* bore, nosy Parker
cocotal *m,* grove of coconut palms
cocotero *m,* coconut palm
coctel *m,* cocktail
cocuyo *m,* firefly
codal *a* cubital. *m,* shoot of a vine; prop, strut; frame of a hand-saw
codazo *m,* blow or nudge of the elbow. **dar codazos,** to elbow, shoulder out of the way
codear *vi* to jostle; elbow, nudge; *vr* be on terms of equality with
codeína *f,* codeine
codelincuente *mf* partner in crime, accomplice
codera *f,* elbow rash; elbow-piece or patch
codeso *m,* laburnum
códice *m,* codex
codicia *f,* covetousness; greed
codiciar *vt* to covet
codicilo *m,* codicil
codicioso (-sa) *a* covetous; *inf* hardworking. *n* covetous person
codificación *f,* codification
codificar *vt* to codify, compile
código *m,* code of laws. **c. civil,** civil laws. **c. de la circulación, c. de la vía pública,** highway code, traffic code. *naut* **c. de señales,** signal code. **c. penal,** criminal laws. **c. postal,** zip code
codillo *m,* knee (of quadrupeds); shaft (of branch); bend (pipe, tube); stirrup
codo *m,* elbow; angle, bend (pipe, tube); cubit. *inf* **hablar por los codos,** to chatter
codorniz *f, orn* quail
coeducación *f,* co-education
coeficiente *m,* coefficient
coercer *vt* to restrain, coerce
coerción *f, law* coercion
coercitivo *a* coercive
coetáneo (-ea) *a* contemporaneous. *n* contemporary
coevo *a* coeval

coexistencia f, co-existence
coexistir vi to co-exist
cofia f, hairnet; coif
cofín m, basket
cofradía f, confraternity, brotherhood or sisterhood **c. de gastronomía,** eating club (US), dining society (UK)
cofre m, trunk, chest (for clothes); coffer
cogedor m, collector, gatherer; dustpan; coal-shovel
coger vt to seize, hold; catch; take, collect, gather; have room for; take up or occupy space; find; catch in the act; attack, surprise; reach; **c. un berrinche,** have a fit, have a tantrum. vi have room, fit
cogida f, gathering, picking; inf fruit harvest; toss (bull-fighting)
cogido m, pleat, fold; crease. **estar c. de tiempo** to be pressed for time.
cogitabundo a very pensive
cognación f, cognation; kinship
cognoscitivo a cognitive
cogollo m, heart (of lettuce, etc.); shoot; topmost branches of pine tree
cogote m, nape (of neck)
cogulla f, monk's habit
cohabitación f, cohabitation
cohabitar vt to cohabit
cohechador (-ra) a bribing. n briber
cohechar vt to bribe, corrupt, suborn
cohecho m, bribing; bribe
coherencia f, coherence, connection
coherente a coherent
cohesión f, cohesion
cohesivo a cohesive
cohete m, rocket
cohetero m, firework manufacturer
cohibir vt to restrain; repress. See **Prohibir.**
cohombrillo m, dim gherkin
cohombro m, cucumber
cohonestar vt fig to gloss over, cover up; make appear decent (actions, etc.)
cohorte f, cohort
coima f, Lat. Am. bribe
coincidencia f, coincidence
coincidir vt to coincide; (two or more people) be in the same place at the same time. **c. con que . . .** to agree that . . .
coito m, coitus
cojear vi to limp; wobble, be unsteady (of furniture); fig inf go wrong or astray; inf suffer from (vice, bad habit)
cojera f, lameness, limp
cojijoso a peevish
cojín m, cushion; pad; pillow (for lace-making)
cojinete m, small cushion; mech bearing. **c. de bolas,** ball-bearing
cojo a lame; unsteady, wobbly (of furniture, etc.)
col f, cabbage. **c. de Bruselas,** Brussels sprouts
cola f, tail; train (of gown); shank (of a button); queue; tailpiece (of a violin, etc.); appendage; glue. **c. de milano,** carp dovetail. **c. de pescado,** isinglass. **formar c.,** to line up, queue up
colaboración f, collaboration. **en c.,** joint (e.g. **obra en colaboración,** joint work)
colaboracionista mf collaborationist
colaborador (-ra) n collaborator
colaborar vt to collaborate
colación f, conferment of a degree; collation (of texts); light repast; cold supper; area of a parish
colada f, wash; bleaching; mountain path; met casting; inf trusty sword (allusion to name of one of the Cid's swords)
coladero m, colander, sieve, strainer; narrow path
colador m, colander
coladura f, straining, filtration; inf untruth; inf howler, mistake
colapso m, med prostration, collapse
colar vt irr to filter, strain; bleach; met cast; vi go through a narrow place; inf drink wine; vr thread one's way; inf

enter by stealth, steal in; inf tell untruths. Pres. Ind. **cuelo, cuelas, cuela, cuelan.** Pres. Subjunc. **cuele, cueles, cuele, cuelen**
colateral a collateral
colcha f, bedspread, counterpane, quilt
colchadura f, quilting
colchero m, quilt maker
colchón m, mattress. **c. de muelles,** spring-mattress. **c. de viento,** air-bed
colchoneta f, pad, thin mattress
coleada f, wag of the tail
colear vi to wag the tail
colección f, collection
coleccionador (-ra) n collector
coleccionar vt to collect
coleccionista mf collector
colecta f, assessment; collection (of donations); ecc collect; voluntary offering
colectivero m, bus driver
colectividad f, collectivity; body of people
colectivismo m, collectivism
colectivista a collectivist
colectivo a collective; Argentina (local) bus
colector m, gatherer; collector; tax-collector; water-pipe; water-conduit; elec commutator, collector
colega m, colleague
colegiado a collegiate
colegial (-la) a college, collegiate. n student; pupil; fig inf novice
colegiarse vr to meet as an association (professional, etc.)
colegiata f, college church
colegiatura f, scholarship, fellowship (money granted a student); tuition (fee paid by a student), tuition fee, tuition fees
colegio m, college; school; academy; association (professional); council, convocation; college or school buildings. **c. de abogados,** bar association. **c. de cardenales,** College of Cardinals. **c. electoral,** polling-booth. **c. militar,** military academy
colegir vt irr to collect, gather; deduce, infer. See **elegir**
cólera f, bile, anger. m, cholera. **montar en c.,** to fly into a rage
colérico a angry; choleric; suffering from cholera
colesterina f, chem cholesterol
coleta f, pigtail; queue; inf postscript
coletazo m, blow with one's tail, lash with one's tail; lash of a dying fish; fig last hurrah
coleto m, leather jerkin; inf body of a man
colgadero a able to be hung up. m, coat-hanger, hook
colgadizo a overhanging. m, overhanging roof
colgadura f, hangings, drapery, tapestries. **c. de cama,** bedhangings
colgajo m, tatter; bunch (of grapes, etc.); surg skin lap
colgar vt irr to hang up; decorate with hangings; inf hang, kill; vi hang, be suspended; fig be dependent. See **contar**
colibrí m, hummingbird
cólico m, colic
colicuar vt to dissolve
coliflor f, cauliflower
coligarse vr to confederate, unite
colilla f, stub (of a cigar or cigarette)
colina f, hill; cabbage seed; chem choline
colindante a adjacent, contiguous
coliseo m, coliseum; theater
colisión f, collision; abrasion, bruise; fig clash (of ideas)
colitis f, colitis
collado m, hill, hillock
collar m, necklace; chain of office or honor; collar (dogs, etc.)
collera f, horse collar; Chile cuff link
collerón m, horse collar
colmado a abundant. m, provision shop
colmar vt to fill to overflowing; bestow generously, heap upon

colmena *f,* beehive
colmenero (-ra) *n* beekeeper
colmillo *m,* canine tooth; tusk; fang
colmilludo *a* having large canine teeth; tusked; fanged; sagacious
colmo *m,* overflow; highest point; completion, limit, end. **ser el c.,** *inf* to be the last straw. **el c. de los colmos,** the absolute limit
colocación *f,* placing, putting; situation, place; employment; *sport* placing; order, arrangement; *ling* collocation
colocar *vt* to place, put, arrange; place in employment. **c. bajo banderas,** to draft (into the armed forces). *vr* place oneself
colocho *m, Guatemala* (naturally) curly hair
colofón *m, print* colophon
colofonia *f,* solid resin (for bows of stringed instruments, etc.)
colombiano (-na) *a* and *n* Colombian
colombina *f,* columbine
colombofilia *f,* pigeon fancying
colonia *f,* colony; plantation
coloniaje *m, Lat. Am.* colonial period; colonial government
colonial *a* colonial
colonización *f,* colonization
colonizador (-ra) *a* colonizing. *n* colonizer
colonizar *vt* to colonize; settle
colono *m,* settler, colonist; farmer
coloquio *m,* colloquy, conversation, talk; colloquium
color *m,* color; dye; paint; rouge; coloring; pretext, excuse; character, individuality; *pl* natural colors. **c. estable, c. sólido,** fast color. **mudar de c.,** to change color. **de c.,** colored. **so c.,** under the pretext. **ver las cosas c. de rosa,** to see things through rose-colored glasses
colorado *a* colored. *WH* red, reddish; *inf* blue, obscene; specious
colorante *a* coloring. *m,* dyestuff; coloring (substance)
colorar *vt* to color; dye
colorear *vt* to color; pretext; *fig* whitewash, excuse; *vi* show color; be reddish; grow red, ripe (tomatoes, cherries, etc.)
colorero *m,* dyer
colorete *m,* rouge
colorido *m,* coloring, color
colorín *m,* goldfinch; bright color
colosal *a* colossal, enormous; extraordinary, excellent
coloso *m,* colossus; *fig* outstanding person or thing, giant; **el C. del Norte, el Gran C. del Norte,** (contemptuous epithet for the United States of America)
columbino *a* pertaining to a dove; dovelike; candid, innocent; purply-red
columbrar *vt* to discern in the distance, glimpse; conjecture, guess
columna *f, mil arch print* column; *fig* protection, shelter; *naut* stanchion. **c. cerrada,** *mil* etc. mass formation. **c. de los suspiros,** agony column (in a newspaper)
columnata *f,* colonnade
columpiar *vt* to swing; dangle (one's feet); *vr inf* sway in walking; swing
columpio *m,* swing
colusión *f,* collusion
colusorio *a* collusive
coma *f, gram* comma. *m, med* coma
comadre *f,* midwife; *inf* procuress, go-between; *inf* pal, gossip
comadrear *vi inf* to gossip
comadreja *f, zool* weasel
comadrón *m,* accoucheur
comadrona *f,* midwife
comandancia *f, mil* command; commandant's H.Q.
comandante *m,* commandant; commander; major; squadron-leader. *a mil* commanding. **c. en jefe,** commanding officer
comandar *vt mil* to command

comandita *f, com* sleeping partnership; private company
comando *m, mil* commando
comarca *f,* district, region
comatoso *a* comatose
comba *f,* bend, warping; jump rope, skipping-rope; camber (of road)
combadura *f,* curvature; warping; camber (of a road)
combar *vt* to bend; twist; warp; camber
combate *m,* fight, combat; mental strife; contradiction, opposition. **c. judicial,** trial by combat. **dejar fuera de c.,** (a) (boxing) to knock out
combatiente *m,* combatant, soldier
combatir *vi* to fight; *vt* attack; struggle against (winds, water, etc.); contradict, oppose; *fig* disturb, trouble (emotions)
combi *m, Mexico* minibus
combinación *f,* combination; list of words beginning with same letter; project; concurrence; underskirt, petticoat. **estar en c. (con),** to be in cahoots (with), connive (with)
combinar *vt* to combine; (*mil nav*) join forces; arrange, plan; *chem* combine; **combinar para + inf.** (two or more people) to make arrangements to + inf.
combustible *a* combustible. *m,* fuel
combustión *f,* combustion. **c. activa,** rapid combustion. **c. espontánea,** spontaneous combustion
comedero *a* edible. *m,* feeding-trough; dining-room
comedia *f,* comedy; play; theater; comic incident; *fig* play-acting, theatricalism. **c. alta,** art theater. **c. de costumbres,** comedy of manners. **c. de enredo,** play with very involved plot. *inf* **hacer la c.,** to play-act, pretend
comediante *m,* actor; *inf* dissembler.
comedianta *f,* actress
comedido *a* courteous; prudent; moderate
comedimiento *m,* courtesy; moderation; prudence
comedir *vt irr* to prepare, premeditate; *vr* restrain oneself, be moderate; offer one's services. See **pedir**
comedor *a* voracious. *m,* dining-room
comendador *m,* knight commander
comendatorio *a* commendatory (of letters)
comensal *mf* table companion
comentador (-ra) *n* commentator
comentar *vt* explain (document); *inf* comment
comentario (a) *m,* commentary (on)
comentarista *mf* commentator
comento *m,* comment; commentary
comenzante *mf* beginner, novice. *a* initial
comenzar *vt vi irr* to begin, commence. See **empezar**
comer *m,* eating; food. *vi* to eat; feed; dine. *vt* eat; *inf* enjoy an income; waste (patrimony); consume, exhaust; fade (of colors); *vr* be troubled, uneasy, remorseful. **ser de buen c.,** to have a good appetite; taste good. **tener que c.,** to be obliged to eat; have to eat; have enough to eat
comerciable *a* marketable; sociable, pleasant (of persons)
comercial *a* commercial
comerciante *a* trading. *mf* merchant, trader
comerciar *vt* to trade; have dealings (with)
comercio *m,* trade, commerce; intercourse, traffic; illicit sexual intercourse; shop, store; tradesmen; commercial quarter of town
comestible *a* edible, eatable. *m,* (gen. *pl*) provisions
cometa *m, ast* comet. *f,* kite (toy). **c. celular,** box-kite
cometedor (-ra) *n* perpetrator
cometer *vt* to entrust, hand over to; commit (crime, sins, etc.); *com* order
cometido *m,* charge, commission; moral obligation; function
comezón *f,* itching, irritation; hankering, longing
cómico *a* comic; funny, comical. *m,* actor; comedian. **c. de la legua,** strolling player
comida *f,* food; meal; dinner; eating. **c. corrida** *Mexico*

table d'hôte **c. de gala,** state banquet. **c. de prueba,** *med* test meal

comienzo *m,* beginning, origin

comilón (-ona) *a inf* gluttonous. *n* glutton

comillas *f pl, gram* inverted commas

comino *m, bot* cumin. **no valer un c.,** to be not worth a jot

comisar *vt* to confiscate, sequestrate

comisaría *f,* commissaryship; commissariat. **c. de policía,** police station

comisario *m,* deputy, agent; commissary, head of police; commissioner; *Argentina,* purser. **alto c.,** high commissioner. **c. propietario,** stockholders' representative

comisión *f,* perpetration, committal; commission; committee; *com* commission

comisionado (-da) *a* commissioned. *m,* commissary

comisionar *vt* to commission

comisionista *mf com* commission agent

comiso *m, law* confiscation, sequestration; contraband

comité *m,* committee

comitiva *f,* retinue, following

como *adv* like, as; in the same way; thus, accordingly; in the capacity of; so that; since. *conjunc* if *(followed by subjunc.)*; because. **c. no,** unless. **¿Cómo?** How? In what way? Why? Pardon? What did you say? *interj* **¡Cómo!** What! You don't say! **¡Cómo no!** Why not! Of course! Surely! **¿Cómo que . . . ?** What do you mean that . . . ?

cómo *m,* the wherefore. **no saber el porqué ni el c.,** not to know the why or wherefore

cómoda *f,* chest of drawers

comodidad *f,* comfort; convenience; advantage; utility, interest

comodín *m,* (in cards) joker

cómodo *a* comfortable; convenient; opportune

comodón *a inf* comfort-loving; easy-going; egoistical

comodoro *m, naut* commodore

comoquiera que *adv* by any means that, anyway; whereas, given that

compacto *a* compact, dense; close (type)

compadecer *vt irr* to pity; *vr (with* de*)* sympathize with; pity; harmonize, agree with. See **conocer**

compadre *m, inf* pal; *Argentina* bully

compaginación *f,* joining, fixing; *print* making-up

compaginar *vt* to fit together; join, put in order; harmonize, square (e.g. **compaginé una cuenta con la otra,** I squared one account with the other); *print* make up

compañero (-ra) *n* companion, comrade; fellow-member; partner (games); *fig* pair, fellow, mate (things). **c. de armas,** brother-in-arms, companion-at-arms. **c. de cabina,** boothmate. **c. de exilio,** companion in exile, fellow exile. **c. de generación,** contemporary, person of the same generation. **c. de viaje,** traveling companion; *pol* fellow traveler (communist sympathizer)

compañía *f,* company; *(com mil)* society, association; theatrical company; *(com mil)* company. **C. de Jesús,** Order of Jesus. **c. de la zarza,** guild of guards and woodcutters for autos de fe. **c. de navegación,** shipping company. **c. por acciones,** joint stock company

comparable *a* comparable

comparación *f,* comparison

comparar *vt* to compare; collate

comparativo *a* comparative

comparecencia *f,* (gen. *law)* appearance

comparecer *vi irr law* to appear (before tribunal, etc.); present oneself. See **conocer**

comparendo *m, law* summons

comparsa *f,* retinue; *theat* chorus; troop of carnival revelers dressed alike. *mf theat* supernumerary actor

comparte *mf law* partner; accomplice

compartimiento *m,* share, division; railway carriage. *naut* **c. estanco,** compartment

compartir *vt* to share out, divide; participate

compás *m,* compasses; callipers; size; compass, time;

range of voice; *(naut min)* compass; *mus* time, rhythm, bar, marking time. **c. de mar,** mariner's compass. **c. de puntas,** dividers, callipers. **fuera de c.,** *mus* out of time; out of joint (of the times). *mus* **llevar el c.,** to beat time

compasar *vt* to measure with compasses; arrange or apportion accurately; *mus* put into bars

compasillo *m, mus* $\frac{4}{4}$ measure

compasivo *a* compassionate; tender-hearted

compatibilidad *f,* compatibility

compatible *a* compatible

compatriota *mf* compatriot

compeler *vt* to compel, force

compendiar *vt* to abridge, summarize

compendio *m,* compendium. **en c.,** briefly

compendioso *a* summary, condensed; compendious

compenetración *f,* co-penetration; intermingling

compenetrado (de) *a* thoroughly convinced (of)

compenetrarse *vr* to co-penetrate; intermingle

compensación *f,* compensating; compensation

compensar *vt* to equalize, counterbalance; compensate

compensatorio *a* compensatory; equalizing

competencia *f,* competition, contest; rivalry; competence; aptitude; *law* jurisdiction

competente *a* adequate, opportune; rightful, correct; apt, suitable; learned, competent

competer *vi irr* to belong to; devolve on; concern. See **pedir**

competición *f,* competition

competidor (-ra) *n* competitor

competir *vi irr* to compete, contest; be equal (to), vie (with). See **pedir**

compilación *f,* compilation

compilador (-ra) *n* compiler. *a* compiling

compilar *vt* to compile

compinche *mf inf* pal, chum

complacencia *f,* satisfaction, pleasure

complacer *vt irr* to oblige, humor; *vr (with en)* be pleased or satisfied with; delight in, like to. See **nacer**

complaciente *a* pleasing; obliging, helpful

complejidad *f,* complexity

complejo *a* complex; intricate. *m,* complex. **c. de inferioridad,** inferiority complex

complementario *a* complementary

complemento *m,* complement (all meanings)

completar *vt* to complete; perfect

completo *a* full; finished; perfect

complexión *f,* physical constitution

complexo *a* complex; intricate

complicación *f,* complication

complicar *vt* to complicate; muddle, confuse; *vr* be complicated; be muddled or confused

cómplice *mf* accomplice

complicidad *f,* complicity

complot *m, inf* conspiracy, plot, intrigue

complutense *a* native of, or belonging to, Alcalá de Henares

componedor (-ra) *n* repairer; arbitrator; bone-setter; *mus* composer; writer, author, compiler; *print* compositor

componenda *f,* mending, repair; *inf* settlement; compromise, arbitration; *inf* shady business

componente *a* and *m,* component

componer *vt irr* to construct, form; *mech* resolve; compose, create; *print* compose; prepare, concoct, mend, repair; settle (differences); remedy; trim; correct, adjust; *lit mus* compose; add up to, amount to; *vi* write (verses); *mus* compose; *vr* dress oneself up. **c. el semblante,** to compose one's features; *inf* **componérselas,** to fix matters, use one's wits. See **poner**

componible *a* reparable, mendable; able to be arranged or adjusted

comportamiento *m,* conduct; deportment

comportar *vt* to tolerate; *vr* behave, comport oneself

composición *f,* composition; repair; arrangement,

compromise; *print* composition; *gram* compound; *chem* constitution; *mech* resolution

compositor (-ra) *n mus* composer; *print* compositor

Compostela Compostella

compostura *f*, composition, structure; repair; neatness (of person); adulteration; arrangement, agreement; discretion, modesty

compota *f*, fruit preserve, compote; thick sauce

compotera *f*, jam or preserve dish

compra *f*, buying; marketing, shopping; purchase. **estar de compras,** *euphem* to be in the family way. **ir de compras,** to go shopping

comprable *a* purchasable

comprador (-ra) *a* purchasing. *n* purchaser; buyer; shopper

comprar *vt* to buy; bribe

comprender *vt* to encircle, surround; include, comprise, contain; understand

comprensible *a* comprehensible

comprensión *f*, comprehension, understanding

comprensivo *a* understanding; comprehensive

compresa *f*, *med* compress, swab; pack (for the face, etc.)

compresión *f*, compression; squeeze

compresivo *a* compressive

compresor *m*, compressor; *aut aer* supercharger

comprimido *m*, tablet, pill

comprimir *vt* to compress; squeeze; restrain; *vr* restrain oneself

comprobación *f*, verification; checking; proof

comprobante *a* verifying; confirmatory

comprobar *vt irr* to verify, check; confirm, prove. See **probar**

comprobatorio *a* confirmatory; verifying; testing

comprometedor *a inf* compromising; jeopardizing

comprometer *vt* to submit to arbitration; compromise; imperil, jeopardize; *vr* pledge oneself; *inf* compromise oneself

comprometido *a* awkward, embarrassing; (e.g. literature of a writer) committed, engagé

compromiso *m*, compromise, agreement, arbitration, commitment, obligation; appointment, engagement; jeopardy; difficulty

compuerta *f*, half-door, wicket, hatch; floodgate, sluice. **c. flotante,** floating dam

compuesto *a* and *past part* made-up, built-up; composite; circumspect; *bot gram* compound. *m*, composite; preparation, compound

compulsar *vt* to collate; *law* make a transcript of

compulsivo *a* compelling

compunción *f*, compunction

compungir *vt* to cause remorse or pity; *vr* repent; sympathize with, pity

computable *a* computable

computación *f*, **cómputo** *m*, calculation, computation

computador (-ra) *n* computer

computar *vt* to compute

cómputo *m*, computation; estimate

comulgar *vt* to administer Holy Communion; *vi* receive Holy Communion

comulgatorio *m*, communion rail, altar rail

común *a* general, customary, ordinary; public, communal; universal, common; vulgar, low. *m*, community, population; water-closet. **en c.,** in common; generally. **por lo c.,** generally. **sentido c.,** common sense

comuna *f*, *Lat. Am.* district

comunal *a* communal; common. *m*, commonalty

comunero *a* popular, affable, democratic. *m*, joint owner; commoner; *hist* commune

comunicable *a* communicable; communicative, sociable

comunicación *f*, communication; (telephone) call, message; letter (to the press); *mil* communiqué; *pl* lines of communication, transport

comunicado *m*, official communication, communiqué; letter (to the press)

comunicante *a* communicating

comunicar *vt* to communicate; transmit; impart, share; *vr* **comunicarse con,** (door) to open onto (e.g. **Esta puerta se comunica con el jardín.** This door opens onto the garden); communicate, converse, correspond with each other

comunicativo *a* communicative; talkative, not reserved

comunidad *f*, the common people; community; generality, majority; *pl hist* Commune

comunión *f*, communion; intercourse, fellowship; *ecc* Communion

comunismo *m*, communism

comunista *a* and *mf* communist

comunistófilo, comunistoide *a* fellow-traveling; *n* fellow traveler

comúnmente *adv* commonly, generally; frequently

con *prep* with; by means of; in the company of; towards, to; although (followed by *infin.*, but generally translated by an inflected verb, e.g. **C. ser almirante, no le gusta el mar,** Although he is an admiral, he doesn't like the sea); by (followed by *infin.* and generally translated by a gerund, e.g. **c. hacer todo esto,** by doing all this). **c. bien,** safe and sound, safely (e.g. **Llegamos con bien.** We arrived safely.) **c. cuentagotas,** sparingly; stingily. **c. que,** so, then. **c. tal que,** provided that, on condition that. **c. todo,** nevertheless. **¿Con . . . ?** Is this . . . ? (on the telephone, e.g. **¿Con el Sr. Piñangos?** Is this Mr. Piñangos?)

conato *m*, effort, endeavor; tendency; *law* attempted crime

concatenación *f*, concatenation

concavidad *f*, concavity; hollow

cóncavo *a* concave. *m*, concavity; hollow

concebible *a* conceivable

concebimiento *m*. See **concepción**

concebir *vi irr* to become pregnant; conceive, imagine; understand; *vt* conceive, acquire (affection, etc.). See **pedir**

concedente *a* conceding

conceder *vt* to confer, grant; concede; agree to

concejal *m*, councillor; alderman

concejil *a* pertaining to a municipal council; public

concejo *m*, town council; town hall; council meeting

concentración *f*, concentration

concentrado *a* concentrated; (of persons) reserved

concentrar *vt* to concentrate

concéntrico *a* concentric

concepción *f*, conception; idea, concept; *ecc* Immaculate Conception

conceptismo *m*, *lit* Concetism (cf. *Euphuism*)

conceptista *a* and *mf* concettist

concepto *m*, idea, concept; epigram; opinion. **en mi c.,** in my opinion; judgment. **por c. de,** in payment of

conceptuar *vt* to judge, take to be; believe; imagine

conceptuoso *a* witty, ingenious

concernencia *f*, respect, relation

concerniente *a* concerning

concernir *vi irr defective* to concern. See **discernir**

concertadamente *adv* methodically, orderly; by arrangement, or agreement

concertar *vt irr* to arrange, settle, adjust; bargain; conclude (business deal); harmonize; compare, correlate; tune instruments; *vi* reach an agreement. See **acertar**

concertina *f*, concertina

concertista *mf mus* performer, soloist; *mus* manager. **c. de piano,** concert pianist

concesión *f*, conceding, grant; concession; lease

concesionario *m*, *law* concessionaire, leaseholder

concho *m*, *Lat. Am.* dregs, sediment

conciencia *f*, consciousness; conscience; conscientiousness. **c. doble,** dual personality. **ancho de c.,** broad-minded. **a c.,** conscientiously

concienzudo *a* of a delicate conscience, scrupulous; conscientious

concierto *m*, methodical arrangement; agreement; *mus* concert; *mus* concerto. **de c.**, by common consent

conciliable *a* reconcilable compatible

conciliábulo *m*, conclave, private meeting; secret meeting

conciliación *f*, conciliation; similarity, affinity; protection, favor

conciliador *a* conciliatory

conciliar *m*, councilor. *vt* to conciliate; *fig* reconcile (opposing theories, etc.). **c. el sueño,** to induce sleep, woo sleep. *vr* win liking (or sometimes dislike)

concilio *m*, council; *ecc* assembly; conciliary decree; findings of council

concinidad *f*, concinnity

concino *a* concinnous

concisión *f*, conciseness, brevity

conciso *a* concise

concitar *vt* to stir up, foment

conciudadano (**-na**) *n* fellow citizen; fellow countryman

cónclave *m*, conclave; meeting

concluir *vt irr* to conclude, finish; come to a conclusion, decide; infer, deduce; convince by reasoning; *law* close legal proceedings; *vr* expire, terminate. **c. con,** to put an end to. See **huir**

conclusión *f*, finish, end; decision; close, denouement; theory, proposition (gen. *pl*); deduction, inference; *law* close. **en c.,** in conclusion

conclusivo *a* final; conclusive

concluyente *a* concluding; convincing; conclusive

concomer *vi inf* to give a shrug, shrug one's shoulders; fidget with an itch. **c. de placer,** to itch with pleasure

concomitancia *f*, concomitance

concomitante *a* and *m*, concomitant

concordable *a* conformable

concordador (**-ra**) *a* peacemaking. *n* peacemaker

concordancia *f*, harmony, agreement; (*mus gram*) concord; *pl* concordance

concordar *vt irr* to bring to agreement; *vi* agree. See **acordar**

concordato *m*, concordat

concorde *a* agreeing; harmonious

concordia *f*, concord, agreement, harmony; written agreement

concreción *f*, concretion

concretar *vt* to combine, bring together; make concise; resume; *vr fig* confine oneself (to a subject) to hammer out, work out (an agreement)

concreto *a* concrete, real, not abstract. **en c.,** in definite terms; finally, to sum up

concubina *f*, concubine, mistress

concubinato *m*, concubinage

conculcación *f*, trampling, treading; violation

conculcador *m*, violator

conculcar *vt* to trample under foot, tread on; break, violate

concupiscencia *f*, concupiscence, lust; greed

concupiscente *a* concupiscent, lustful; greedy

concurrencia *f*, assembly; coincidence; attendance; help, influence

concurrido *a* crowded; busy; frequented

concurrir *vi* to coincide; contribute; meet together; agree, be of same opinion; compete (in an examination, etc.)

concurso *m*, crowd, concourse; conjunction, coincidence; help; competition; (tennis) tournament; competitive examination; invitation to offer tenders. **c. de acreedores,** creditors' meeting. **c. interno,** competitive examination for a position open to staff members only

concusión *f*, concussion; shock; extortion

concha *f*, shell; turtle-shell; prompter's box; cove, creek; anything shell-shaped. *fig* **meterse en su c.,** to

retire into one's shell. *inf* **tener más conchas que un galápago,** to be very cunning

conchado *a* scaly, having a shell

condado *m*, earldom; county

condal *a* of an earl, earl's; of a count, count's; of Barcelona

conde *m*, earl; king of the gypsies

condecir (**con**) *vi* to agree (with)

condecoración *f*, conferment of an honor, decoration; medal

condecorar *vt* to confer a decoration or medal

condena *f*, *law* sentence; punishment; penalty

condenable *a* culpable, guilty; worthy of damnation

condenado (**-da**) *a* damned; wicked, harmful. *n law* convicted criminal

condenador *a* condemning; incriminating; blaming

condenar *vt law* to pronounce sentence (on), convict; condemn; disapprove; wall or block or close up. **c. a galeras,** to condemn to the gallies. *vr* blame oneself; be eternally damned

condenatorio *a* condemnatory; incriminating

condensación *f*, condensation

condensador *a* condensing. *m*, (*elec mech chem*) condenser

condensante *a* condensing

condensar *vt* to condense; thicken; abridge

condesa *f*, countess

condescendencia *f*, affability, graciousness

condescender *vi irr* to be obliging, helpful, agreeable. See **entender**

condescendiente *a* affable, gracious

condestable *m*, *hist* constable, commander-in-chief

condición *f*, condition; quality; temperament, character; (social) position; rank, family; nobility, circumstance; stipulation, condition, requirement. **estar en condiciones de,** to be in a position to. **no estar en condiciones de,** to be in no condition to

condicional *a* conditional

condicionar *vi* to come to an agreement, arrange; *vt* impose conditions

condigno *a* condign

condimentación *f*, *cul* seasoning

condimentar *vt* to flavor, season (food)

condimento *m*, condiment, flavoring

condiscípulo *m*, schoolfellow

condolencia *f*, compassion; condolence

condolerse *vr* (*with de*) to sympathize with, be sorry for. See **doler**

condonar *vt* to condone

conducción *f*. **conducencia,** *f*, transport, conveyance, carriage; guiding; direction, management; *phys* conduction; *mech* control-gear. *aut* **c. a izquierda,** left-hand drive

conducente *a* conducting, conducive

conducir *vt irr* to transport, convey, carry; *phys* conduct; guide, lead; manage, direct; *aut* drive; conduce; *vi* be suitable; *vr* behave, conduct oneself. *Pres. Ind.* **conduzco, conduces,** etc. *Preterite* **conduje, condujiste,** etc. *Pres. Subjunc.* **conduzca, conduzcas,** etc. *Imperf. Subjunc.* **condujese,** etc.

conducta *f*, transport, conveyance; management, conduct, direction; behavior

conductibilidad *f*, *phys* conductivity

conductivo *a* conductive

conducto *m*, pipe, conduit, drain, duct; *fig* channel, means; *anat* tube

conductor (**-ra**) *n* guide; leader; driver (vehicles); *m*, *phys* conductor. **c. de caballos,** teamster. **c. de entrada,** *rad* lead-in. **c. del calor,** heat-conductor. **c. eléctrico,** electric wire or cable

conectar *vt elec* to connect, switch on; couple; attach, join

conectivo *a* connective; (*elec mech*) connecting

conejera *f*, rabbit-warren; *inf* low dive or haunt

conejillo de Indias *m*, guineapig

conejo *m*, rabbit

conejuno *a* rabbit, rabbit-like

conejuna *f,* rabbit fur, coney

conexión *f,* connection; *elec* switching on, connection; joint; joining; *pl* friends, connections; *elec* wiring

conexo *a* connected

confabulación *f,* confabulation, conspiracy

confabular *vi* to confer; *vr* scheme, plot

confalón *m,* standard, banner

confección *f,* making; confection; making-up; concoction, remedy; ready-made garment

confeccionador (-ra) *n* maker (of clothes, etc.)

confeccionar *vt* to make; prepare; make up (pharmaceuticals)

confederación *f,* alliance, pact; confederacy, federation

confederarse *vr* to confederate, be allied

conferencia *f,* conference, meeting; lecture; (telephone) long-distance call (US), trunk call (UK)

conferenciante *mf* lecturer

conferencista *mf, Lat. Am.* lecturer

conferenciar *vi* to confer

conferir *vt irr* to grant, concede; consider, discuss; compare, correlate. See **herir**

confesable *a* acknowledgeable, avowable

confesar *vt irr* to avow, declare; acknowledge, admit; *ecc* hear confession; *vr ecc* confess. *Pres. Ind.* **confieso, confiesas, confiesa, confiesan.** *Pres. Subjunc.* **confiese, confieses, confiese, confiesen**

confesión *f,* confession

confesional *a* confessional

confesionario, confesonario, confesorio *m, ecc* confessional

confeso *a* confessed; converted (of Jews). *m, ecc* lay brother

confesor *m,* confessor

confeti *m,* confetti

confianza *f,* confidence, trust; assurance, courage; over-confidence, conceit; intimacy; familiarity. **de c.,** reliable (e.g. **persona de c.,** reliable person); informal (e.g. **reunión de c.,** informal meeting). **en c.,** in confidence, confidentially

confianzudo *a inf* overconfident

confiar *vi (with en)* to trust in, hope; *vt (with prep a or en)* entrust, commit to the care of; confide in

confidencia *f,* trust; confidence; confidential information

confidencial *a* confidential

confidente (-ta) *a* trustworthy, true. *m,* seat for two. *n* confidant(e); spy

configuración *f,* configuration, form, lie

configurar *vt* to shape

confín *m,* boundary, frontier; limit. *a* boundary

confinado *a* banished. *m, law* prisoner

confinar *vi (with con)* to be bounded by, contiguous to; *vt* banish; place in confinement

confirmación *f,* corroboration; *ecc* confirmation

confirmar *vt* to corroborate; uphold; *ecc* confirm

confiscación *f,* confiscation

confiscar *vt* to confiscate

confitar *vt* to candy, crystallize or preserve (fruit, etc.); *fig* sweeten

confite *m,* bonbon, sugared almond, etc.

confitería *f,* confectionery

confitero (-ra) *n* confectioner

confitura *f,* preserve, jam

conflagración *f,* conflagration, blaze; uprising, rebellion

conflicto *m,* strife, struggle; spiritual conflict; *fig* difficult situation

confluencia *f,* confluence; crowd

confluir *vi irr* to meet, flow together (rivers); run together (roads); crowd. See **huir**

conformación *f,* conformation; make-up, structure (e.g. of an organization)

conformar *vt* to fit, adjust; *vr* agree, be of the same opinion; submit, comply; to make up (e.g. **los grupos**

sociales que conforman este país, the social groups who make up this country)

conforme *a* similar, alike; consistent; in agreement; long-suffering, resigned. *adv* according (to), in proportion (to)

conformidad *f,* conformity; similarity; resignation; agreement, harmony; proportion, symmetry. **de c.,** by common consent. **en c.,** according to

confort *m,* comfort

confortante *a* comforting; consoling; strengthening (of beverages)

confortar *vt* to comfort, reassure; encourage; console

confortativo *a* comforting; comfortable; strengthening, warming (of beverages); encouraging, cheering

confrontación *f,* confrontment; comparison (of texts, etc.)

confrontar *vt* to bring face to face; compare, correlate; *vi* face; *(with con)* be contiguous to, border on

confucianismo *m,* Confucianism

confundible *a* mistakable, liable to be confused

confundimiento *m,* confounding; mistaking; confusion

confundir *vt* to mix, confuse; jumble together; mistake; *fig* confound (in argument); humble; bewilder, perplex; *vr* be mixed together; mistake, confuse; be ashamed; be bewildered

confusión *f,* confusion; perplexity; shame; jumble

confuso *a* mixed, upset; jumbled; obscure; indistinct; blurred; bewildered

confutación *f,* confutation

confutar *vt* to confute

conga *f,* conga (dance; drum)

congelación *f,* freezing; congealment. **punto de c.,** freezing point

congelar *vt* to congeal; freeze

congeniar *vi* to be congenial

congénito *a* congenital

congestión *f, med* congestion

congestionar *vt* to congest; *vr med* be overcharged (with blood)

conglomeración *f,* conglomeration

conglomerar *vt* to conglomerate

congoja *f,* anguish, anxiety, grief

congraciarse *(con), vr* to ingratiate oneself (with), get into the good graces (of)

congratulación *f,* congratulation

congratular *vt* to congratulate; *vr* congratulate oneself

congratulatorio *a* congratulatory

congregación *f,* gathering, meeting, congregation; brotherhood, guild

congregar(se) *vt* and *vr* to meet, assemble

congresista *mf* member of a congress

congreso *m,* congress; conference, meeting; sexual intercourse

congrio *m,* conger eel

congruencia *f,* suitability, convenience; *math* congruence

congruente *a* convenient, opportune; *math* congruent

cónico *a* conical, tapering *math* conic

conífera *f,* conifer

conífero *a* coniferous

conjetura *f,* conjecture

conjetural *a* conjectural

conjeturar *vt* to conjecture surmise

conjugación *f,* conjugation

conjugar *vt* to conjugate

conjunción *f,* connection, union association; *(ast gram)* conjunction

conjuntivitis *f,* conjunctivitis

conjunto *a* united, associated adjoining; mingled; mixed (with) bound, affiliated. *m,* whole; combo, ensemble (of musicians). **c. habitacional,** housing complex, housing project

conjura, conjuración *f,* conspiracy, plot

conjurador (-ra) *n* conspirator, plotter; exorcist

conjurar *vi* to conspire, plot *vt* swear, take an oath; exorcise; implore, beg; ward off (danger)

conjuro *m,* plot, conspiracy, spell, incantation; entreaty

conllevar *vt* to share (troubles) bear, put up with; endure

conmemoración *f,* commemoration

conmemorar *vt* to commemorate

conmemorativo *a* commemorative

conmensurable *a* commensurable

conmigo *pers. pron* 1st pers. sing. *mf* with myself, with me

conminar *vt* to threaten

conminatorio *a* threatening

conmiseración *f,* commiseration, compassion, pity

conmoción *f,* disturbance (mind or body); upheaval, commotion. **c. eléctrica,** electric shock

conmovedor *a* moving, pitiful; stirring, thrilling

conmover *vt irr* to perturb, stir; move to pity. **c. los cimientos de,** to shake the foundations of; *vr* be emotionally moved. See **mover**

conmutable *a* commutable

conmutación *f,* commutation

conmutador *m, elec* commutator; change-over switch

conmutar *vt* to commute; *elec* switch, convert

conmutatriz *f, elec* converter

connato *a* contemporary

connatural *a* innate, inborn

connaturalizar *vt* to connaturalize

connaturalizarse (con) *vr* to become accustomed (to), become acclimated (to)

connivencia *f,* connivance

connotación *f,* connotation

connotado, -a *a, Lat. Am.* well-known

connotar *vt* to connote

cono *m,* (*geom bot*) cone. **el C. Sur,** the Southern Cone

conocedor (-ra) *n* one who knows; connoisseur; expert

conocer *vt irr* to know; understand; observe, perceive; be acquainted (with); conjecture; confess, acknowledge; know carnally; *vr* know oneself; know one another. **conocerle a uno la voz,** to recognize somebody's voice (e.g. **Le conozco la voz. I recognize her by her voice.**) **conocerle a uno en su manera de andar,** to recognize somebody by his gait, recognize somebody by his walk. *Pres. Ind.* **conozco, conoces,** etc. *Pres. Subjunc.* **conozca,** etc.

conocido (-da) *a* illustrious, distinguished. *n* acquaintance

conocimiento *m,* knowledge; understanding; intelligence; acquaintance (*not* friend); consciousness; *com* bill of lading; *pl* knowledge, learning

conque *conjunc* so, so that (e.g. **¿C. Juan se va?** So John's going away?)

conquista *f,* conquest

conquistador (-ra) *a* conquering. *n* conqueror

conquistar *vt* to conquer; *fig* captivate, win

consabido *a* aforesaid, beforementioned

consagración *f,* consecration; dedication

consagrar *vt* to consecrate; dedicate, devote; deify; *vr* (*with prep a*) dedicate oneself to, engage in

consanguíneo *a* consanguineous

consciente *a* conscious; aware; sane. *m, psy* conscious

conscripción *f,* conscription

conscripto *m,* conscript

consecución *f,* obtainment; attainment

consecuencia *f,* consequence, outcome; logical consequence, conclusion; importance; consistence (of people)

consecuente *a* consequent, resultant; consistent. **c. consigo mismo,** self-consistent *m,* consequence; *math* consequent

consecutivo *a* consecutive, successive

conseguir *vt irr* to obtain, achieve. See **seguir**

conseja *f,* story, fairy-tale; old wives' tale

consejero (-ra) *n* adviser; member of council. *m.* **c. de estado,** counselor of state

consejo *m,* advice; council, commission, board; council chamber or building. **c. de administración,** board of directors. **c. de guerra,** council of war. **c. del reino,** council of the realm. **c. privado,** privy council

consenso *m,* consensus of opinion, unanimity

consentido *a* complaisant (of husband); spoilt, over-indulged

consentimiento *m,* consent; assent

consentir *vt irr* to permit, allow; believe; tolerate, put up with; over-indulge, spoil; *vr* crack, give way (furniture, etc.). **c. en,** to consent to; to agree to. See **sentir**

conserje *m,* concierge, porter; warden or keeper (of castle, etc.)

conserjería *f,* conciergerie, porter's lodge; warden's dwelling (in castles, etc.)

conserva *f,* jam; preserve; pickles; *naut* convoy. **en c.,** preserved, tinned

conservación *f,* upkeep; preservation, maintenance; *cul* preserving; conservation. **c. refrigerada,** cold-storage

conservador (-ra) *a* keeping, preserving. *a* and *n* preserver; *pol* conservative; traditionalist. *m,* curator

conservadurismo *m,* conservatism

conservar *vt* to keep, maintain, preserve; keep up (custom, etc.); guard; *cul* preserve. **c. en buen estado,** to keep in repair

conservatorio *m,* conservatoire; academy; *Lat. Am.* greenhouse. **c. de música,** academy of music, conservatoire

considerable *a* considerable; worthy of consideration, powerful; numerous; large; important

consideración *f,* consideration, attention; reflection, thought; civility; importance. **en c. de,** considering

considerado *a* considerate; prudent; distinguished; important

considerar *vt* to consider, reflect upon; treat with consideration (persons); judge, estimate, feel (e.g. **Considero que . . .** I feel that . . .)

consigna *f, mil* watchword; left luggage office

consignador (-ra) *n com* consigner, sender

consignar *vt* to assign, lay aside; deposit; *com* consign; entrust, commit; put in writing; *law* deposit in trust; book (a suspect)

consignatario *m, law* trustee; mortgagee; *com* consignee. **c. de buques,** shipping agent

consigo *pers. pron* 3rd sing. and pl. *mf* with himself, herself, oneself, yourself, yourselves, themselves

consiguiente *a* consequent, resulting. *m,* consequence. **por c.,** in consequence

consistencia *f,* solidity; consistence, density; consistency, congruity, relevance

consistente *a* of a certain consistency; solid

consistir *vi* (*with en*) to consist in; be comprised of; be the result of

consistorio *m,* consistory; municipal council (in some Spanish towns); town hall

consola *f,* console table; piertable; *mech* bracket

cónsola *f,* radio cabinet

consolación *f,* consolation

consolador (-ra) *n* comforter, consoler

consolar *vt irr* to comfort, console. **consolarse de + inf.,** to console oneself for + *pp.* See **contar**

consolidación *f,* consolidation; stiffening

consolidar *vt* to consolidate; strengthen; combine, unite; *vr law* unite

consomé *m,* consommé

consonancia *f,* harmony; agreement

consonante *a* consonant, consistent. *m,* rhyme. *f, gram* consonant

consonantismo *m,* consonantism, consonant system

consorcio *m,* partnership; trust; intimacy, common life

consorte *mf* consort; companion, associate, partner; spouse

conspicuo *a* outstanding, distinguished; conspicuous

conspiración *f,* conspiracy

conspirador (-ra) *n* conspirator

conspirar *vi* to conspire; plot, scheme; tend, combine

constancia *f*, constancy, steadfastness; stability, steadiness; transcript (of grades); *Lat. Am. law* deposition. **c. de estudios,** transcript (of grades)

constante *a* constant; durable; *mech* steady, non-oscillating. *m*, constant

Constantinopla Constantinople

Constanza Constance (female given name and lake)

constar *vi* to be evident, be clear; *(with de)* be composed of, consist of, comprise

constelación *f, ast* constellation; climate

consternación *f*, dismay, alarm

consternarse *vr* to be dismayed or alarmed

constipado *m, med* cold; chill

constiparse *vr* to catch a cold or chill

constitución *f*, constitution; composition, make-up (e.g. **la c. del suelo,** the make-up of the soil)

constitucional *a* constitutional

constituir *vt irr* to constitute, form; found, establish; *(with en)* appoint, nominate; *fig* place in (a difficult situation, etc.); *vr (with en* or *por)* be appointed or authorized; be under (an obligation). See **huir**

constituyente, constitutivo *a* and *m*, constituent

constreñir *vt irr* to constrain, oblige; constrict; constipate. See **ceñir**

constricción *f*, constriction; contraction, shrinkage

construcción *f*, construction; art or process of construction; fabric, structure; *gram* construction; building, erection. **c. de caminos,** road making. **c. naval,** shipbuilding

constructor (-ra) *a* building, constructive. *n* builder; constructor

construir *vt irr* to construct; build, make; *gram* construct. See **huir**

consuelo *m*, consolation; comfort, solace; joy, delight

cónsul *m*, consul

consulado *m*, consulate. **c. general,** consulate general

consulta *f*, deliberation, consideration; advice; reference; conference, consultation

consultar *vt* to discuss, consider; seek advice, consult. **consultarlo con la almohada,** *fig* to sleep on it, think it over, mull it over

consultor (-ra) *a* consultative, advisory; consulting. *n* consultant; adviser. **c. externo,** outside consultant

consultorio *m, med* consulting rooms; surgery; technical information bureau

consumación *f*, consummation; completion, attainment; extinction, end

consumado *a* consummate; *inf* thorough, perfect

consumar *vt* to consummate; complete, accomplish, perfect

consumido *a inf* emaciated, wasted away; timid, spiritless

consumidor (-ra) *a* consuming. *n* consumer, user

consumir *vt* to destroy; consume, use; waste away, wear away; *ecc* take communion; *inf* grieve; *vr* be destroyed; *inf* be consumed with grief

consumo *m*, consumption; demand. **c. de combustible,** fuel consumption

contabilidad *f*, bookkeeping; accounts; accounting

contable *m*, bookkeeper

contacto *m*, contact (also *elec mil*). **en c.,** in common (e.g. **Los dos libros tienen mucho en c.** The two books have much in common.)

contado *a* few; infrequent; rare. **al c.,** *com* cash down. **por de c.,** presumably; of course, naturally

contador *a* counting. *m*, accountant; *law* auditor; counter (in banks); *elec* meter, counter; *naut* purser. **c. oficial,** *Argentina* certified public accountant. **c. público titulado,** certified public accountant

contaduría *f*, counting house; accountant's office; auditorship; *theat* box-office; *naut* purser's office

contagiar *vt* to infect; corrupt, pervert; *vr (with con, de* or *por)* be infected by or through

contagio *m*, infection; contagious disease; *fig* contagion, perversion, corruption

contagioso *a* infectious; *fig* catching, contagious

contaminación *f*, contamination, pollution

contaminar *vt* to pollute, contaminate; infect; *fig* corrupt

contante *a* ready (of money)

contar *vt irr* to count; recount, tell; place to account; include, count among; *vi* calculate, compute. **contarle a uno las cuarenta,** *inf* to give someone a piece of one's mind. **c. con,** to rely upon; reckon upon. *Pres. Ind.* **cuento, cuentas, cuenta, cuentan.** *Pres. Subjunc.* **cuente, cuentes, cuente, cuenten**

contemplación *f*, meditation, contemplation; consideration

contemplar *vt* to consider, reflect upon; look at, contemplate; indulge, please

contemplativo *a ecc* contemplative; reflective, thoughtful; kind, indulgent

contemporáneo (de) *a* contemporaneous (to *or* with) *n* contemporary

contemporizar *vi* to temporize, gain time

contencioso *a* contentious, argumentative; *law* litigious

contender *vi irr* to contain; restrain, hold back; comprise; *vr* control oneself. See **entender**

contendiente *mf* contestant

contener *vt irr* to contain; include; comprise; hold back; restrain; check, repress; hold down, subdue; suppress, put down; *vr* contain oneself; keep one's temper; keep quiet; refrain. See **tener**

contenido *m*, contents. *a* contained; *fig* restrained; reserved (of persons)

contentamiento *m*, contentment

contentar *vt* to satisfy, please; *com* endorse; *vr* be pleased or satisfied

contento *a* happy; content; satisfied; pleased. *m*, pleasure; contentment. **no caber de c.,** to be overjoyed

contestación *f*, reply, answer; discussion, argument, dispute

contestar *vt* to reply, answer; confirm, attest; *vi* accord, harmonize

contexto *m*, context

contextura *f*, structure; context; physique, frame

contienda *f*, struggle, fight; quarrel, dispute; discussion

contigo *pers. pron* 2nd sing. *mf* with thee, with you

contigüidad *f*, proximity, nearness

contiguo *a* adjacent, near

continencia *f*, moderation, self-restraint; continence; chastity; containing

continental *a* continental. *m*, express messenger service; *Puerto Rico* person from the mainland United States

continente *a* continent. *m*, container; demeanor, bearing; *geog* continent; mainland

contingencia *f*, contingency; risk, danger

contingente *a* incidental; fortuitous; dependent; *m, mil* taskforce, contingent

continuación *f*, continuation; prolongation; sequel (of a story, etc.)

continuador (-ra) *n* continuer

continuar *vt* to continue; *vi* continue; last, remain, go on; *vr* be prolonged

continuidad *f*, continuity

continuo *a* continuous, steady, uninterrupted; persevering, tenacious; persistent; lasting, unremitting. *m*, a united whole. **de c.,** continuously

contonearse *vr* to swing the hips (in walking); strut

contorno *m*, contour, outline; (gen. *pl*) environs, surrounding district

contorsión *f*, contortion

contorsionista *mf* contortionist

contra *prep* against, counter, athwart; opposed to, hostile to; in front of, opposite; towards. *m*, opposite view or opinion. *f, inf* difficulty, trouble. **c. la corriente,** upstream. **el pro y el c.,** the pros and cons. **en c.,** in opposition, against

contraalmirante m, rear admiral

contraataque m, counterattack

contraaviso m, countermand

contrabajo m, doublebass; player of this instrument; deep bass voice

contrabalancear vt to counterbalance; fig compensate

contrabandista a smuggling. mf smuggler

contrabando m, contraband; smuggling

contracción f, contraction; shrinkage; abridgment; abbreviation

contracubierta f, book jacket, jacket

contradanza f, square dance

contradecir vt irr to contradict; vr contradict oneself. See **decir**

contradicción f, contradiction

contradictorio a contradictory

contraer vt irr to shrink, reduce in size, shorten; abridge; contract (matrimony, obligations); fig acquire (diseases, habits); vr shorten, contract, shrink. See **traer**

contrafuerte m, buttress, counterfort, abutment; geog spur

contrahacer vt irr to forge, counterfeit; mimic; imitate. See **hacer**

contrahecho a deformed

contralor m, comptroller

contraloría f, comptrollership, office of comptroller (position); comptroller's office (place)

contralto m, contralto (voice)

contraluz f, counterlight

contramaestre m, naut boatswain; overseer, superintendent, foreman

contramarcha f, retrogression; mil countermarch

contramedida f, counter-measure

contraorden f, countermand

contrapedalear vi to backpedal

contrapelo a adv the wrong way of the hair, against the grain; inf reluctantly, distastefully

contrapeso m, counterpoise, counterweight; balancing-pole (acrobats); fig counterbalance; makeweight

contraponer vt irr to compare; place opposite; oppose. See **poner**

contraproducente a counteractive, counterproductive, unproductive, self-deceiving; self-defeating

contrapuesto a opposing, divergent

contrapunto m, counterpoint

contrariar vt to counter, oppose; impede; vex, annoy

contrariedad f, contrariety, opposition; obstacle; vexation, trouble

contrario (-ia) a opposite; hostile, opposed; harmful; adverse, contrary. n adversary; opponent. m, obstacle. f. **contraria,** contrary, opposite. **al contrario,** on the contrary. **llevar la contraria (a),** to oppose; contradict

contrarreforma f, counter-Reformation

contrasentido m, wrong sense, opposite sense (of words); contradiction of initial premise; self-contradiction; nonsense

contraseña f, countersign; mil password

contrastar vt to contrast; oppose, resist; check (weights and measures); assay; mech calibrate, gauge; vi contrast

contraste m, contrast; opposition, difference; weights and measures inspector; dispute, clash. **en c. a,** in contrast to

contrata f, **contrato,** m, contract. **contrato de arrendamiento,** lease

contratación f, hiring; com transaction; commerce, trade

contratapa f, back cover (of a periodical, etc.)

contratar vt to contract, enter into an agreement; make a bargain (with), deal (with); hire, contract

contratiempo m, mishap, accident

contratista mf contractor

contratorpedero m, torpedoboat destroyer

contravención f, contravention; violation. **en c. a,** in violation of

contraveneno m, med antidote; remedy, precaution

contravenir vt irr to infringe, contravene. See **venir**

contraventana f, shutter (for windows)

contravidriera f, storm window

contrayente a contracting. mf contracting party (used of matrimony)

contribución f, contribution; tax. **c. sobre la propiedad,** property tax

contribuir vt irr to pay (taxes); contribute. See **huir**

contribuyente a contributing; contributory. mf contributor; taxpayer

contrición f, contrition

contrincante m, competitor, candidate (public examinations); rival, opponent

contrito a contrite

control m, control; checking. **c. de precios,** price control

controlar vt to control

controversia f, controversy

controvertir vi and vt irr to dispute, argue against, deny. See **sentir**

contumacia f, obstinacy; law contumacy

contumaz a stubborn; impenitent; law contumacious; med obstinate, resistant (to cure)

contumelia f, contumely

conturbar vt to perturb, make anxious, disturb; vr be perturbed

contuso a contused, bruised

convalecencia f, convalescence; convalescent home

convalecer vi irr to convalesce, get better; fig recover, regain (influence, etc.). See **conocer**

convaleciente a and mf convalescent

convalidar vt to ratify, confirm

convecino a nearby; neighboring

convencedor a convincing

convencer vt to convince; prove beyond doubt, demonstrate to (persons); be convincing (e.g. **No convence,** It's not convincing; He's not convincing). vr be convinced

convencimiento m, conviction, belief, assurance

convención f, pact, formal agreement; harmony, conformity; convention

convencional a conventional (all meanings)

convencionalismo m, conventionality

convenido a agreed

conveniencia f, conformity, harmony, adjustment; experience, suitability, convenience; advantage; agreement, pact; post as domestic; ease, comfort; pl income; social conventions

conveniente a convenient, opportune; suitable, fitting; profitable; useful; decorous. **tener por c. + inf,** to think it fitting to + inf, find it appropriate to + inf

convenio m, pact, treaty; com agreement, contract

convenir vi irr to agree; assemble, congregate; belong; be suitable; vr agree; suit oneself. **No me conviene salir esta tarde,** It does not suit me to go out this afternoon. **Me convendría pasar un mes allí,** It would be a good idea (or a wise thing) for me to spend a month there. See **venir**

conventillo m, Lat. Am. tenement

convento m, convent; monastery; religious community

conventual a conventual; monastic. m, ecc conventual

convergencia f, convergence

convergir vi to converge; fig coincide (views, etc.)

conversación f, conversation; intercourse, company; law criminal conversation

conversar vi to converse; chat; live with others; know socially

conversión f, conversion; change, transformation; com conversion; mil wheel; wheeling

converso (-sa) n convert

convertible a convertible

convertir vt irr to change, transform; convert; reform;

vr be transformed; be converted; be reformed. See **sentir**

convexo *a* convex

convicción *f,* conviction; certitude; *law* conviction

convicto (-ta) *a* and *n law* convict

convidado (-da) *n* guest

convidar *vt* to invite (persons); encourage, provoke; entice, attract; *vr* invite oneself; offer one's services

convincente *a* convincing

convite *m,* invitation; banquet; party

convivencia *f,* coexistence, common life, life together. **c. pacífica,** peaceful coexistence

convivial *a* convivial

convivir *vi* to live together, live under the same roof

convocación *f,* convocation

convocar *vt* to convene, convoke

convoy *m,* convoy; escort; following; cruet-stand

convoyar *vt* to convoy, escort

convulsión *f,* convulsion

convulsivo *a* convulsive

conyugal *a* conjugal

cónyuge *mf* husband or (and) wife (used gen. in *pl*)

coñac *m,* brandy

coñete *a, Chile, Peru* mean, stingy

cooperación *f,* cooperation

cooperador (-ra) *a* cooperative. *n* cooperator, collaborator

cooperar *vt* to cooperate

cooperativa *f,* cooperative society

cooperativo *a* cooperative

coordenada *f,* coordinate

coordinación *f,* coordination

coordinar *vt* to coordinate, classify

copa *f,* wineglass, goblet; glassful; top branches (of trees); crown (of hat); *cards* heart; gill (liquid measure); *inf* drink, glass; *pl cards* hearts (in Spanish pack, goblets)

copal *m, Central America, Mexico* resin

copartícipe *mf* co-partner, partaker, participant

copec *m,* kopeck

Copenhague Copenhagen

copernicano *a* Copernican

copero *m,* cupbearer; sideboard; cocktail cabinet

copete *m,* lock, tress (hair); tuft, crest; forelock (horses); head, top (ice-cream, drinks); *inf* **de alto c.,** aristocratic; socially prominent

copetudo, -a *a, Lat. Am.* tufted, crested; haughty, stuck-up

copia *f,* abundance, plenty; copy, reproduction; transcript; imitation

copiador (-ra) *a* copying. *n* copier; transcriber. *m,* copybook

copiar *vt* to copy

copioso *a* abundant, plentiful

copla *f,* couplet; popular four-line poem; couple, pair; *pl inf* verses

coplero (-ra) *n* balladmonger; poetaster

copo *m,* cop (of a spindle); snowflake

copón *m,* large goblet; *ecc* ciborium, chalice

coprófago *a* coprophagous

copropietario (-ia) *n* coproprietor, coowner

copto (-ta) *n* Copt

cópula *f,* connection; coupling; joining; copulation

copularse *vr* to copulate

coque *m,* coke

coqueluche *f,* whooping cough

coqueta *f,* coquette, flirt

coquetear *vi* to flirt

coqueteo *m,* coquetry; flirtation

coquetería *f,* coquetry

coquetón *a* coquettish

coraje *m,* courage, valor; anger

coral *m,* coral. *f,* coral snake. *m, bot* coral tree; *pl* coral beads

coral *a* choral

coralina *f,* coral (polyp).

coraza *f,* cuirass; shell (of tortoise); armor-plate, armor (ships, etc.)

corazón *m,* heart; courage, spirit; love, tenderness; goodwill, benevolence; core (of a fruit); *fig* pith. **de c.,** sincerely. **tener el c. en la mano,** to wear one's heart on one's sleeve

corazonada *f,* feeling, instinct; presentiment, apprehension

corbata *f,* necktie; scarf; ribbon (insignia)

corbatería *f,* necktie shop

corbatero *m,* necktie maker; necktie dealer; tie rack

Córcega Corsica

corchea *f, mus* quaver

corchete *m, sew* hook and eye; hook

corcho *m, bot* cork, cork bark; stopper, cork; cork mat; bee hive

corcova *f,* hump, abnormal protuberance

corcovado (-da) *a* hunchbacked, crooked. *n* hunchback

corcovear *vi* to curvet, caper

cordaje *m, naut* cordage, tackling, rope

cordel *m,* cord; *naut* line. **a c.,** in a straight line

cordelería *f,* rope making; ropeyard; cordage

cordelero (-ra) *n* rope maker

cordera *f,* ewe lamb; sweet, gentle woman

corderillano, -a *a, Argentina, Chile* Andean

cordero *m,* lamb; dressed lambskin; peaceable, mild man; Jesus (gen. **Divino C.**)

cordial *a* warming, invigorating; affectionate, loving, friendly. *m, med* cordial

cordialidad *f,* cordiality, friendliness

cordillera *f,* mountain range

Córdoba Cordova

cordobán *m,* cured goatskin; Cordovan leather, Spanish leather

cordobés (-esa) *a* and *n* Cordovan

cordón *m,* cord; cordon; *ecc* rope girdle; *arch* stringcourse

cordoncillo *m,* rib (in cloth); ridge, milling (of coins); *sew* piping

cordura *f,* good sense, prudence

Corea Korea

coreografía *f,* choreography; art of dancing

coreográfico *a* choreographic

coreógrafo *m,* choreographer

corintio (-ia) *a* and *n* Corinthian

Corinto Corinth

corista *m, ecc* chorister. *mf theat* member of the chorus

cornada *f,* horn thrust or wound (bulls, etc.)

cornamenta *f,* horns (bulls, deer, etc.)

córnea *f,* cornea

corneja *f,* carrion or black crow

córneo *a* horny, corneous

corneta *f, mus* bugle; *mus* cornet; swineherd's horn; *mil* pennon. *m,* bugler; *mil* cornet. **c. de monte,** hunting horn

cornetín *m, dim* **corneta,** *mus* cornet; cornet player

cornezuelo *m, dim* little horn; *med* ergot; *bot* variety of olive

cornisa *f,* cornice

cornucopia *f,* cornucopia, horn of plenty; sconce; mirror

cornudo *a* horned. *m,* cuckold. **el C.,** the Devil

coro *m,* choir; chorus; *arch* choir. **hacer c. (a),** to listen to, support. **saber de c.,** to know by heart

corolario *m,* corollary

corona *f,* garland, wreath; halo; (*ast arch*) corona; crown (of tooth); crown (of head); tonsure; crown (coin); royal power; kingdom; triumph; reward; summit, height, peak; circlet (for candles)

coronación *f,* coronation; coping stone

coronamiento *m,* coronation; coping stone; *fig* crowning touch; *naut* taffrail

coronar *vt* to crown; crown (in draughts); complete, round off; *vr* be crowned; crown oneself; be tipped or capped

coronel *m,* colonel

coronela *f, inf* colonel's wife

coronelía *f,* colonelcy

coronilla *f, dim* small crown; crown of head; *fig inf* **estar hasta la c.,** to be fed up

coroza *f,* dunce's cap

corpiño *m,* bodice

corporación *f,* corporation, body, association

corporal *a* and *m, ecc* corporal

corporativo *a* corporate, corporative

corpóreo *a* corporeal

corporizar *vt* to embody

corpulento *a* corpulent, stout

Corpus *m,* Corpus Christi

corpúsculo *m,* corpuscle

corral *m,* yard; pen, enclosure, corral; old-time theater. **c. de madera,** timber yard. *inf* **hacer corrales,** to play truant

correa *f,* leather strap or thong; flexibility; *mech* belt, band

corrección *f,* correction; correctness; punishment; emendation. **c. de pruebas,** proofreading, proofing, reading proof

correccional *a* correctional. *m,* reformatory

correcto *a* correct; well-bred; unexceptionable, irreproachable; regular (of features)

corredera *f,* link (engines); *mech* slide; *naut* log; racecourse; *inf* procuress

corredizo *a* easy to untie; running (of knots); sliding

corredor (-ra) *n* runner. *m, com* broker; corridor; *inf* meddler; *inf* procurer, pimp. *a* running. **c. de bolsa,** stockbroker

corregible *a* corrigible

corregidor *m,* Spanish magistrate; *ant* mayor

corregidora *f,* wife of corregidor; mayoress

corregir *vt irr* to correct; scold, punish; moderate, counteract; *mech* adjust; *vr* mend one's ways. **c. pruebas,** to read proof. *Pres. Ind.* **corrijo, corriges, corrige, corrigen.** *Pres. Part.* **corrigiendo.** *Pres. Subjunc.* **corrija, corrijas,** etc. *Imperf. Subjunc.* **corrigiese,** etc.

correligionario (-ia) *n* coreligionist; fellow-supporter or believer

correlón, -ona *a Mexico, Venezuela* cowardly

correntada *f, Argentina* rapids

correo *m,* courier; mail; post-office; letters. **c. aéreo,** air-mail. **c. certificado,** registered mail. **a vuelta de c.,** by return of mail. **tren c.,** mail train

correr *vi* to run; race; sail, steam; flow; blow; flood; extend, stretch; pass (of time); fall due (salary, etc.); be current or general; (*with con*) be in charge of or responsible for; *vt* run (a horse); fasten, slide (bolts, etc.); draw (curtains); undergo, suffer; sell, auction; *inf* steal; *fig* embarrass; spread (a rumor, etc.); catch, make (bus, train, etc.); *vr* slide, glide, slip; run (of colors); *inf* spread oneself, talk too much. **c. cañas,** to participate in a mock joust using reeds as spears

correría *f,* raid, foray; excursion, trip

correspondencia *f,* relationship, connection; intercourse, communication; correspondence, letters; equivalence, exact translation

corresponder *vi* to requite, repay; be grateful; belong to, concern; devolve upon, fall to; suit, harmonize (with); fit; *vr* correspond by letters; like or love each other

correspondiente *a* suitable; proportionate; corresponding. *mf* correspondent

corresponsal *mf* correspondent (especially professional); *com* agent

corretear *vi* to wander about the streets; gad

correveidile *mf inf* tale-bearer, gossip

corrida *f,* race, run; *aer* taxiing; bull fight (abb. for **c. de toros**)

corrido *a* extra, over (of weight); embarrassed; experienced

corriente *a* current, present; well-known; usual, customary; fluent (style); ordinary, average; easy. *f,* flow, stream; *fig* course (of events, etc.); *elec* current. *adv* quite, exactly. *elec* **c. alterna,** alternating current. **c. continua,** direct current. **c. de aire,** draught. **estar al c.,** to be informed (of something)

Corriente del Golfo Gulf Stream

corrillo *m,* knot, group, huddle (of people)

corro *m,* circle, group; ring (for children's games)

corroboración *f,* corroboration, confirmation

corroborar *vt* to fortify; corroborate, support

corroer *vt irr* to corrode, waste away; *fig* gnaw. See **roer**

corromper *vt* to rot; mar; spoil, ruin; seduce; corrupt (texts); bribe; *fig* contaminate, corrupt; *vi* stink; *vr* putrefy, not; be spoilt; *fig* be corrupted

corrosión *f,* corrosion

corrosivo *a* corrosive

corrugación *f,* corrugation, wrinkling

corrupción *f,* rot, putrefaction; corruption, depravity; decay; stink; bribery; falsification (of texts); corruption (of language, etc.)

corrupto *a* corrupt

corruptor (-ra) *n* corrupter

corsario *m,* pirate; privateer

corsé *m,* corset

corsetería *f,* corset shop or manufactory

corso (-sa) *a* and *n* Corsican

corta *f,* felling, cutting

cortacircuitos *m, elec* circuit breaker, cut-out; disconnecting switch

cortado *a* fitting, proportioned; disjointed (style); confused, shamefaced

cortador *m,* cutter; cutter-out (dresses, etc.); butcher

cortadura *f,* cut, wound; cutting (from periodicals); defile; *pl* clippings, cuttings

cortafrío *m,* cold chisel; *carp* hammer-head chisel

cortalápices *m,* pencil sharpener

cortante *a* cutting; sharp; piercing (of wind, etc.); trenchant; *m, Argentina* scissors *pl.*

cortapapel *m,* paper-knife

cortapisa *f,* condition, stipulation

cortaplumas *m,* penknife

cortapuros *m,* cigar cutter

cortar *vt* to cut; cut out (dresses, etc.); switch off, shut off (water, electricity, etc.); cleave, divide; cut (cards); pierce (wind, etc.); interrupt, impede; omit, cut; *fig* interrupt (conversation); decide, determine; *vr* be confused or shamefaced; curdle, turn sour (e.g. **Se cortó la leche,** The milk turned sour); split, fray; chap

cortavidrios *m,* diamond, glasscutter

cortaviento *m,* windscreen

corte *f,* court (royal); retinue; yard; *pl* Spanish parliament. *m,* cutting, cut; blade, cutting edge; cutting out, dressmaking; length, material required for garment, shoes, etc.; cut, fit; style; book edge; *arch* section; means, expedient; counting of money (in a till). **c. de caja,** counting of money (in a till). **c. trasversal,** side view

cortedad *f,* shortness, brevity; smallness; stupidity, dullness; timidity, shyness. **c. de fuerzas,** lack of strength

cortejar *vt* to accompany, escort; woo, court

cortejo *m,* courtship, wooing; suite, accompaniment; gift, present; homage, attention; *inf* lover, beau

cortés *a* polite, attentive, courteous, civil

cortesana *f,* courtesan

cortesano *a* court; courtly. *m,* courtier

cortesía *f,* politeness, courtesy; attentiveness; civility; gift, present; favor. **c. internacional,** courtesy of nations. **c. de boca mucho vale y poco cuesta.** Courtesy is worth much and costs little

corteza *f, bot* bark; *anat* cortex; skin, peel, crust; aspect, appearance; roughness. **c. terrestre,** Earth's crust, crust of the Earth. **de c.,** superficial (e.g. explanation)

cortijo *m,* farmhouse and land

cortina *f,* curtain; *fig* veil; *inf* heel taps; *mil* curtain, screen. **c. de fuego de artillería,** anti-aircraft barrage. **c. de globos de intercepción,** balloon barrage. **c. de humo,** smoke screen. **c. metálica,** metal shutter

cortinaje *m*, curtains, hangings

corto *a* short, brief; timid, bashful; concise; defective; stupid, dull; tongue-tied, inarticulate. **c. circuito,** *elec* short-circuit. **c. de alcances,** dull-witted. **c. de vista,** short-sighted

coruscar *vi* to glitter, shine

corvadura *f*, bend; curvature

corveta *f*, curvet, prancing; *a, Central America* bow-legged

corvetear *vi* to curvet

corzo *m*, roe-deer, fallow-deer

cosa *f*, thing. **c. rara,** strange to relate; an extraordinary thing. **como si tal c.,** as though nothing had happened. *inf* **poquita c.,** a person of no account

cosaco (-ca) *a* and *n* Cossack

coscorrón *m*, blow on the head, cuff

cosecha *f*, harvest; harvest time; reaping, gathering, lifting; yield, produce; crop, shower (of honors, etc.). **c. de vino,** vintage

cosechar *vi* and *vt* to harvest, reap

coseno *m*, cosine

coser *vt* to sew, stitch; join, unite; press together (lips, etc.). **c. a puñaladas,** to stab repeatedly

Cosme Cosmo

cosmético *a* and *m*, cosmetic

cósmico *a* cosmic

cosmografía *f*, cosmography

cosmógrafo *m*, cosmographer

cosmonave *f*, spaceship

cosmopolita *a* and *mf* cosmopolitan

cosmopolitismo *m*, cosmopolitanism

cosmos *m*, cosmos

cospel *m*, blank (from which to stamp coins); to ken; subway to ken

cosquillas *f pl*, tickling. **hacer c. (a),** to tickle

cosquillear *vt* to tickle

cosquilleo *m*, tickle, tickling

cosquilloso *a* ticklish; hypersensitive, touchy

costa *f*, cost; expense; coast; *pl law* costs. **a c. de,** by dint of; at the cost of. **a toda c.,** at all costs

Costa del Oro, la the Gold Coast

Costa de Marfil Ivory Coast

costado *m*, *anat* side; *mil* flank; side; *pl* line of descent, genealogy. *naut* **dar el c.,** to be broadside on

costal *m*, sack, bag

costanero *a* sloping; coast, coastal

costar *vi irr* to cost; cause. See **contar**

costarriqueño (-ña) *a* and *n* Costa Rican

coste *m*, cost, price

costear *vt* to pay for, defray the expense of; *naut* coast; *Argentina* pasture; *vr* pay (for itself)

costilla *f*, (*anat aer naut arch*) rib; *fig inf* better half, wife; *pl inf* back, behind

costillaje, costillar *m*, *anat* ribs; *naut* ship's frame

costoso *a* expensive, costly; valuable; dear, costly, difficult

costra *f*, crust; scab; rind (of cheese)

costumbre *f*, habit; custom

costumbrista *mf* writer on everyday life and customs. *a* (of literary work) dealing with life and customs

costura *f*, sewing; seam; needlework; *carp* joint; riveting

costurar, costurear *vi*, *Lat. Am.* to sew

costurera *f*, seamstress

costurero *m*, work-box, sewing bag

cota *f*, *surv* elevation, height; coat (of mail); quota. **c. de malla,** chain-mail

cotangente *f*, cotangent

cotejar *vt* to compare; collate

cotejo *m*, comparison; collation

cótel *m*, cocktail, drink

cotelera *f*, cocktail shaker

cotí *m*, ticking (cloth)

cotidiano *a* daily

cotizable *a* valued at; (of prices, shares) quoted

cotización *f*, *com* quotation; *com* rate. **boletín de c.,** price list (of shares, etc.)

cotizar *vt com* to quote (prices, rates)

coto *m*, enclosed ground; boundary stone; preserve, covert; hand's breadth; end, stop, limit. **c. de caza,** game preserve

cotorra *f*, small green parrot; magpie; *inf* chatterbox

cotufa *f*, earthnut; titbit; *inf* **pedir cotufas en el golfo,** to ask for the moon; **cotufas** *f pl Venezuela* popcorn

coyote *m*, coyote, prairie wolf; *Mexico* fixer (anyone who can pull strings to cut red tape or achieve something illegally); smuggler (of goods or people)

coyuntura *f*, *anat* joint; juncture, occasion

coz *f*, kick, recoil (of gun); butt (of a rifle); *inf* slap in the face, unprovoked rudeness. **dar coces,** to kick

craneal *a* cranial

cranearse *vr*, *Chile* to burn the midnight oil

cráneo *m*, cranium, skull

crápula *f*, drunkenness; depravity, immorality, debauchery

craquear *vt* to crack (petroleum)

crasitud *f*, greasiness; fatness; crassness

craso *a* fat, greasy; thick; unpardonable, crass (often with *ignorancia*). *m*, fatness; ignorance

creación *f*, creation; universe, world; foundation, establishment; appointment (dignitaries)

creador (-ra) *n* creator, originator. *m*, God. *a* creative

crear *vt* to create; found, institute, establish; make, appoint

crecer *vi irr* to grow; grow up; increase in size; grow longer; wax (moon); come in (of the tide); increase in value (money); *vr* become more sure of oneself; swell with pride; grow in authority. See **nacer**

creces *f pl*, increase, interest. **con c.,** fully, amply. **pagar con c.,** *fig* to pay with interest

crecida *f*, swollen river or stream; food; rising (of the tide)

crecido *a* grown up; considerable; abundant, plentiful; large; full; serious, important

crecidos *m pl*, widening stitches (knitting)

creciente *a* growing; rising (of the tide); crescent (moon). *m*, *her* crescent. *f*, rising of the tide; crescent moon

crecimiento *m*, growing; growth, development; increase (in value, money); waxing (of moon)

credenciales *f pl*, credentials

credibilidad *f*, credibility

crédito *m*, belief, credence; assent, acquiescence; reputation, name; favor, popularity, acceptance; *com* credit; *com* letter of credit. **créditos activos,** assets. **créditos pasivos,** liabilities. **a c.,** on credit

credo *m*, creed. *inf* **en un c.,** in a jiffy

credulidad *f*, credulity

crédulo *a* credulous

creencia *f*, belief; religion, sect, faith

creer *vt irr* to believe; think, consider, opine; think likely or probable. **¡Ya lo creo!** I should just think so! Rather! **creerse la divina garza,** *Mexico* to think one is God's gift to the world. **creerse descender del sobaco de Jesucristo,** to think one is God's gift to the world. *Pres. Part.* **creyendo.** *Preterite* **creyó, creyeron.** *Imperf. Subjunc.* **creyese,** etc.

creíble *a* credible

creído, -a *a*, *Lat. Am.* credulous, trusting

crema *f*, cream (of milk); custard mold, cream, shape; face cream; cold cream; elect, flower (of society, etc.)

cremación *f*, cremation; burning, incineration

cremallera *f*, *mech* rack; ratch; zip fastener. **colgar la c.,** to give a house-warming

crematístico *a* economic, financial

crematorio *m*, crematorium. *a* burning; cremating

cremor *m*, *chem* cream of tartar

cremoso *a* creamy

crencha *f*, parting (of the hair); each side of parting

crepitación *f*, crackling, sputtering; hissing; roar (of a fire); *med* crepitation

crepitar *vi* to crackle; sputter; hiss; roar (of a fire); *med* crepitate

crepuscular *a* twilight

crepúsculo *m,* twilight, half light

cresa *f,* maggot; cheese-mite; fly's egg

Creso Croesus

crespo *a* curly, frizzy (hair); rough (of animal's fur); curled (leaves); artificial, involved (style)

crespón *m,* crape

cresta *f,* comb (of cock, etc.); tuft, topknot (birds); plume; summit, top (of mountains); crest (of a wave); *her* crest

Creta Crete

creta *f,* chalk

cretense *a* Cretan

cretinismo *m,* cretinism

cretino (-na) *a* and *n* cretin

creyente *a* believing; religious. *mf* believer

cría *f,* rearing; bringing up; nursing; suckling; breeding; brood; litter

criada *f,* servant, maid

criadero *m, min* vein, deposit; tree nursery, plantation; breeding farm or place. *a* prolific

criado *m,* servant. *a* bred, brought up (used with *bien* or *mal,* well or badly brought up)

criador (-ra) *n* breeder, keeper, raiser. *a* creating; rearing; creative; fertile, rich

criandera *f. Lat. Am.* nursemaid, wet nurse

crianza *f,* feeding, suckling; lactation; manners. **buena** (or **mala**) **c., good (or bad) breeding or upbringing**

criar *vt* to create; procreate; rear, educate, bring up; feed, nurse, suckle; raise (birds, animals); inspire, give rise to. **Me crié raquítico,** I grew up delicate

criatura *f,* being, creature; man, human being; infant; small child; fetus; *fig* puppet, tool

criba *f,* sieve, cribble

cribar *vt* to sieve; riddle (earth, etc.)

crimen *m,* crime. **c. pasional,** crime of passion

criminal *a* and *m,* criminal

criminalidad *f,* guilt; crime ratio; delinquency

criminalista *mf* criminal lawyer; criminologist

criminología *f,* criminology

crin *f,* horsehair; (gen. *pl*) mane

crinolina *f,* crinoline

crío *m, inf* kid, brat

criollo (-lla) *a* and *n* creole. *a* indigenous, native

cripta *f,* crypt

criptografía *f,* cryptography

criquet *m, sport* cricket

crisantemo *m,* chrysanthemum

crisis *f,* crisis. **c. de desarrollo,** growing pains. **c. de vivienda,** housing shortage

crisma *m,* or *f,* chrism

crisol *m,* crucible; melting pot

crispado *a* stiffened

crispar *vt* to cause to contract or twitch; *vr* twitch. *inf* **Se me crispan los nervios,** My nerves are all on edge

cristal *m,* crystal; glass; windowpane; mirror; water. **c. tallado,** cut glass

cristalería *f,* glassware; glass manufacture; glass panes; glass and china shop

cristalino *a* crystalline. *m,* lens (of the eye)

cristalización *f,* crystallization

cristalizar *vi* to crystallize; *fig* take shape; *vt* cause to crystallize

cristalografía *f,* crystallography

cristiandad *f,* Christendom

cristianismo *m,* Christianity; Christendom

cristianizar *vt* to convert to Christianity, christianize

cristiano (-na) *a* and *n* Christian. *a inf* watered (of wine). *m, inf* Spanish (contrasted with other languages); *inf* soul, person

cristino (-na) *a* and *n* supporting, or follower of, Queen Regent Maria Cristina during Carlist wars

cristo *m,* Christ; crucifix. *inf* **donde C. dio las tres voces,** in the middle of nowhere

cristus *m,* Christ-cross; alphabet. **no saber el c.,** to be extremely ignorant

criterio *m,* criterion, standard; judgment, discernment; opinion. **a c. de,** in the opinion of. **según mi c.,** in my opinion

crítica (a) *f,* criticism (of)

criticar *vt* to criticize; censure, find fault with, blame

crítico *a* critical; censorious; dangerous, difficult; *med* critical. *m,* critic; fault-finder

criticón (-ona) *a* censorious, hyper-critical. *n* fault-finder

Croacia Croatia

croar *vi* (frog) to croak

croata *a* and *mf* Croatian

croché *m,* crochet work

crol *m,* crawl (swimming)

cromado *a* chromium-plated

cromático *a* chromatic

crómico *a* chromic

cromo *m,* chrome; chromium; chromolithograph

crónica *f,* chronicle; diary of events

crónico *a* chronic; inveterate

cronista *mf* chronicler

cronología *f,* chronology

cronológico *a* chronological

cronómetro *m,* stop-watch

croqueta *f,* croquette

croquis *m,* sketch, outline, drawing. **c. de nivel,** (optical) foresight

crótalo *m,* rattlesnake; snapper (kind of castanet)

cruce *m,* crossing; point of intersection; crossroads

crucero *m, ecc* cross-bearer; crossroads; *arch* transept; *ast* Cross; *naut* cruiser

crucificar *vt* to crucify; *fig inf* torment, torture

crucifijo *m,* crucifix

crucifixión *f,* crucifixion

crucigrama *m,* crossword puzzle

cruda *f, Mexico* hangover

crudelísimo *a sup* **cruel,** most cruel, exceedingly cruel

crudeza *f,* rawness, uncookedness; unripeness; rawness (silk, etc.); crudeness; harshness; *inf* boasting

crudo *a* uncooked, raw; green, unripe; indigestible; raw, natural, unbleached; harsh, cruel; cold, raw; *inf* boastful. **crudos de petróleo,** *m pl* crude oil

crueldad *f,* cruelty; harshness

cruento *a* bloody

crujía *f,* passage, corridor; *naut* midship gangway

crujidero *a* crackling; creaking; crispy; clattering; rustling; chattering

crujido *m,* creak, crack, crackling, rustle

crujir *vi* to creak, crackle, rustle

crup *m,* croup

crupié *m,* croupier

crustáceo *a* and *m,* crustacean

cruz *f,* cross; tails (of coin); withers (of animals); insignia, decoration; affliction, trouble; *ast* Southern Cross; *print* dagger, obelisk, obelus. **c. doble,** diesis, double dagger. **c. de mayo,** May cross. **c. gamada,** swastika. *inf* **¡C. y raya!** An end to this! **en c.,** in the shape of a cross. *inf* **hacerse cruces,** to be left speechless, be dumbfounded

cruza *f, Lat. Am.* intersection

cruzada *f,* crusade; crossroads; campaign

cruzado *a* cross; double-breasted (of coats). *m,* crusader; member of military order

cruzamiento *m,* crossing; intersection

cruzar *vt* to cross; intersect; interbreed; bestow a cross upon; *naut* cruise; *Chile, Peru* quarrel with; *vr* take part in a crusade; cross one another; coincide; *geom* intersect

cu *f,* name of the letter Q

cuaco *m, Lat. Am.* horse

cuacuac *m,* quack (of a duck)

cuaderna *f, naut* ship's frame, timber; double fours (backgammon)

cuaderno *m,* notebook, jotter, account book; *inf* card pack. *naut* **c. de bitácora,** logbook

cuadra f, stable; ward, dormitory; hall, large room; quarter of a mile; *Lat. Am.* block (of houses)

cuadrado a square; perfect, exact. m, square; (*carp mil math*) square; window-frame; clock (of a stocking)

cuadragésima f, Quadragesima

cuadragésimo a fortieth

cuadrángulo m, quadrangle

cuadrante m, quadrant; dial, face

cuadrar vt (*math carp*) to square; make square; vi correspond, tally; fit, be appropriate. vr *mil* stand at attention; *fig inf* dig one's heels in

cuadrática f, quadratic equation

cuadrático a quadratic

cuadratura f, squareness; (*math ast*) quadrature

cuadrienio m, space of four years

cuadriga f, quadriga

cuadrilátero m, quadrilateral; boxing ring. a quadrilateral

cuadrilongo a and m, oblong

cuadrilla f, gang; company, band, group; police patrol; quadrille (dance); matadors and their assistants (at a bull fight). **c. carrillana,** track gang

cuadrimotor a *aer* four-engined

cuadrivio m, quadrivium

cuadro m, square; picture-frame; frame (of bicycle); flowerbed; *theat* tableau, scene; spectacle, sight; board (of instruments); description (in novel, etc.); *mil* command, officers; square (of troops). **c. de distribución,** *elec* main switchboard. **c. enrejado,** play pen. **cuadro de costumbres,** word-picture of everyday life and customs. **cuadro vivo,** tableau vivant. **a cuadros,** checked, in squares

cuadrúpedo (-da) a and n quadruped

cuadruple a quadruple

cuadruplicar vt to quadruple

cuajada f, curd (of milk)

cuajar m, maw (of a ruminant)

cuajar vt to coagulate; curdle; vi *inf* achieve, get away with; vr be coagulated or curdled; *inf* be packed or chock full; get stuck (e.g. a piece of food in one's throat)

cuajarón m, clot (of blood, etc.)

cuajo m, rennet; coagulation; curdling; *anat* abomasum

cual *rel. pron* sing. *mf* and *neut. pl* **cuales,** which; who; such as (e.g. **Le detuvieron sucesos cuales suelen ocurrir,** He was detained by events such as usually happen). **a c. mas,** vying (with) (e.g. **Los dos canónigos a c. más grueso,** The two canons each fatter (vying in fatness) than the other). **c.** is used with *def. art* **el (la, lo, los, las) cual(es),** which, when the antecedent is a noun (e.g. **Juan saltó en el barco, el c. zarpó en seguida,** John jumped into the boat which sailed at once). **por lo c.,** for which reason. *adv* like (gen. literary or poet.). **¿cuál?** *interr. pron* (no article) which? what? e.g. **Aquí tienes dos cuadros, ¿cuál de ellos te gusta?** Here are two pictures, which one do you like? Also expresses an implicit question, e.g. **No sé cuál te guste,** I don't know which you will like. **¡cuál!** *adv interj* how! **c. . . . . c.** *indef pron* some . . . some

cualesquier a *pl* of **cualquier**

cualesquiera a *pl* of **cualquiera**

cualidad f, quality; characteristic; talent

cualitativo a qualitative

cualquier *abb* of **cualquiera,** any; *pl* **cualesquier.** Only used as abb. *before* noun

cualquiera a *mf* any, e.g. **una canción c.,** any song. *pron* anybody, each, anyone whatsoever, whoever (e.g. **¡C. diría que no te gusta!** Anyone would say you don't like it!) *inf* **un c.,** a nobody

cuán *adv* how (e.g. **¡C. bello es!** How beautiful it is). Used only before a or *adv.* Abb. of cuanto

cuando *adv* when; if. *interr* **¿cuándo?** *conjunc* although; since; sometimes; *prep* during (e.g. **c. la guerra,** during the war) **c. más,** at most, at best. **c. menos,** at the least. **c. no,** if not (e.g. **Es agnóstica**

cuando no atea, She's an agnostic, if not an atheist) **de c. en c.,** from time to time

cuandoquiera *adv* whenever

cuanta, teoría de la f, quantum theory

cuantía f, quantity, amount; importance, rank, distinction

cuantiar vt to value, estimate; tax

cuantidad f, quantity

cuantioso a large, considerable; numerous; plentiful, abundant

cuantitativo a quantitative

cuanto a as much as, all the; *pl* as many as, all the (e.g. **Te daré cuantas muñecas veas allí,** I'll give you all the dolls you see there). a. correlative the . . . the, as . . . as (e.g. **C. más tanto, mejor,** The more the better). **cuánto,** a and *pron interr* and *interj* how much; *pl* how many (e.g. **¡Cuánto tiempo sin verla!** How long without seeing her!) *pron neut* **cuanto,** as much as, all that (e.g. **Te daré c. quieras,** I shall give you all that you wish). *adv* **cuanto,** as soon as. **c. antes,** as soon as possible. **c. a** or **en c. a,** concerning. *adv* and *conjunc* **c. más,** all the more (e.g. **Se lo diré c. más que tenía esa intención,** I shall tell him all the more because I meant to do so). *adv* **en c.,** as soon as, immediately (e.g. **Lo haré en c. venga,** I shall do it immediately he comes). **en c. a,** with regard to. **por c.,** inasmuch, for this reason. *adv interr* **¿Cuánto?** How much? How long? *adv interj* How! How much! (e.g. **¡Cuánto me gustaría ir!** How much I should like to go!)

cuaquerismo m, Quakerism

cuáquero (-ra) n Quaker

cuarenta a and m, forty; fortieth. **esas son otras cuarenta** *Argentina, Peru* that's a different story, that's a horse of another color

cuarentena f, fortieth; period of forty days, months or years; Lent; quarantine

cuarentón (-ona) n person forty years old

cuaresma f, Lent

cuaresmal a Lenten

cuarta f, quarter, fourth; hand's breadth; *mus* fourth; *ast* quadrant

cuarteadura f, crack

cuartear vt to quarter, divide into quarters; cut or divide into pieces

cuartel m, barracks; *naut* hatch; quarter, fourth; *her* quarter; district, ward; flowerbed; *inf* house, accommodation; *mil* quarter, mercy; *mil* billet, station. *mil* **c. general,** general headquarters

cuartelada f, *naut* quarter; military rebellion, military uprising, mutiny

cuartelazo m, military rebellion, military uprising, mutiny

cuarteta f, quatrain

cuarteto m, *mus* quartet; *poet* quatrain

cuartilla f, sheet of paper; liquid measure; quarter of an arroba; pastern (horses)

cuarto m, room; quarter, fourth; point (of compass); watch (on battleships); *ast* quarter, phase; portion, quarter; joint (of meat); *pl* quarters (of animals); *inf* penny, farthing. a quarter, fourth. **c. creciente,** first phase (of moon). **c. de hora,** quarter of an hour. **c. doble** *Mexico* double room. **c. sencillo** *Mexico* single room. **en c.,** *print* in quarto. *inf* **no tener un c.,** to be broke

cuarzo m, quartz

cuasidelito m, *law* technical offence

cuasimodo m, *ecc* Low Sunday, Quasimodo

cuatrillón m, quadrillion

cuatrimestre a of four months' duration. m, space of four months

cuatrimotor m, *aer* four-engine airplane

cuatrisílabo a quadrisyllabic

cuatro a four; fourth. m, figure four; fourth (of days of months); playing-card with four spots; *mus* quartet. **el c. de mayo,** the fourth of May. **Son las c.,** It is four o'clock

cuatrocientos *a* four hundred; four hundredth.

cuba *f,* barrel, cask; tub, vat; *inf* pot-bellied person; *inf* drunkard, toper

cubano (-na) *a* and *n* Cuban

cubería *f,* cooperage

cubeta *f, dim* keg, small cask; bucket, pail; *phot* developing dish

cubicar *vt math* to cube; *geom* measure the volume of

cúbico *a* cubic

cubículo *m,* cubicle

cubierta *f,* cover; envelope; casing; deck (of ship); tire cover; book-jacket; pretext, excuse. **c. de escotilla,** *naut* companion-hatch. **c. de paseo,** promenade deck

cubierto *m,* cover, place at table; course (of a meal); table d'hôte, complete meal; roof. **un c. de doscientas pesetas,** a two hundred peseta meal

cubil *m,* lair, den (of animals)

cubilete *m, cul* mold; dice box; conjurer's cup

cubismo *m,* cubism

cubista *mf* cubist. *a* cubistic

cubo *m,* bucket, pail; *mech* socket; *math* cube; hub (of a wheel); mill-pond

cubrecama *m,* bedspread

cubrimiento *m,* covering

cubrir *vt* to cover; *mil* defend; spread over, extend over; conceal, hide; *com* cover; dissemble; *arch* roof; *vr* cover one's head; pay, meet (debts, etc.); cover or protect oneself (by insurance, etc.). *Past Part.* **cubierto**

cucaña *f,* greasy pole; *inf* snip, cinch, bargain

cucaracha *f,* cockroach

cuchara *f,* spoon; ladle; *naut* boat scoop; scoop, dipper. *fig* **meter c.,** to stick one's oar in

cucharada *f,* spoonful; ladleful

cuchí *m, Peru* hog

cúchi *a inf Venezuela* cute, sweet

cuchicheador (-ra) *n* whisperer

cuchichear *vi* to whisper

cuchicheo *m,* whisper; whispering; murmur

cuchillada *f,* knife thrust or wound; *pl* (in sleeves, etc.) slashes; fight, blows

cuchillería *f,* cutler

cuchillo *m,* knife; *sew* gore, gusset (gen. *pl*); authority, power; anything triangular in shape. **pasar a c.,** to put to the sword

cuclillas, en *adv* in a squatting position

cuclillo *m, orn* cuckoo; *inf* cuckold

cuco *a inf* pretty, cute; crafty, smart

Cucufo *m,* the Devil

cuculla *f,* cowl, hood

cucurucho *m,* paper cornet

cueca *f, chile* cueca (Chilean dance)

cuello *m, anat* neck; neck (of bottle, etc.); *sew* neck; collar; necklet (of fur, etc.)

cuenca *f,* socket (of eye); *geog* catchment-basin; gorge, deep valley. **c. de un río,** river-basin

cuenta *f,* count, counting; calculation; account; bead; charge, responsibility; reckoning; explanation, reason; *com* bill. **c. a cero, c. a la inversa, c. atrás,** countdown. **c. corriente,** current account. **cuentas alegres, cuentas galanas,** *inf* idle dreams, illusions. **c. pendiente,** outstanding account. *inf* **caer en la c.,** to tumble to, realize. **llevar la c.,** to reckon, keep account. **tener en c.,** countless. **tener en c.,** to bear in mind

cuentacorrentista *mf* one who has a bank account

cuentagotas *m,* dropper, dropping tube

cuentakilómetros *m,* speedometer

cuentapasos *m,* pedometer

cuentista *mf* storyteller; *inf* gossip

cuento *m,* story, tale; narrative; calculation; *inf* gossip, fairytale; *math* million. **c. de viejas,** old wives' tale. *fig inf* **dejarse de cuentos,** to go straight to the point. *inf* **Va de c.,** It is told, they say

cuerda *f,* rope; cord; string; *geom* chord; *mus* string; catgut; chain (of clock); *mus* chord; vocal range. **dar c. (a),** to wind up (a watch); lead on, make talk. **de cuerdas cruzadas,** overstrung (of a piano)

cuerdo *a* sane; prudent; levelheaded

cuerno *m, anat* horn; feeler, antenna; *mus* horn; horn (of the moon). **c. de abundancia,** horn of plenty. *inf* **poner en los cuernos de la luna,** to praise to the skies

cuero *m,* hide, pelt; leather. **c. charolado,** patent leather. **en cueros,** stark naked

cuerpo *m, anat* body or trunk; flesh (as opposed to spirit); bodice; volume, book; main portion; collection; size, volume; physical appearance; corpse; group, assembly; corporation, association; *geom* solid; *chem* element; thickness, density; *mil* corps. **c. de bomberos,** fire brigade. **c. de guardia,** guardhouse. **c. de la vida,** staff of life; *inf* **dar con el c. en tierra,** to fall flat. **de c. entero,** *art* full-length (portrait). **en c.,** without a coat, lightly clad. **un c. a c.,** a clinch (in wrestling)

cuervo *m,* raven; crow

cuesco *m,* stone, seed, pip

cuesta *f,* slope, incline, gradient. **c. abajo (arriba),** down (up) hill. **a cuestas,** on one's back; having the responsibility of

cuestión *f,* problem, question; quarrel, disagreement; affair, matter; torture

cuestionable *a* doubtful, questionable

cuestionar *vt* to discuss, debate

cuestionario *m,* questionnaire

cueva *f,* cave, cavern; basement, cellar. *fig* **c. de ladrones,** den of thieves

cuévano *m,* hamper, basket

cui *m, Lat. Am.* guinea pig

cuico, -a *mf, Argentina, Chile* foreigner, outsider; *Mexico, informal* cop (police officer)

cuidado *m,* carefulness, pains; attention; charge, care, responsibility; anxiety, fear. *interj* **¡C.!** Careful! Look out! **Me tiene sin c. su opinión,** I am not interested in his (your) opinion. *inf* **estar al c. de,** to be under the direction of. **estar de c.,** to be dangerously ill

cuidadoso (de) *a* careful (about *or* with); anxious (about); concerned (with); watchful; conscientious

cuidar *vt* to care for; tend; take care of, look after; mind, be careful of; *vr* look after oneself

cuita *f,* misfortune, anxiety, trouble

cuitado *a* unfortunate, worried; timid, bashful, humble

cuitla *f, Mexico* poultry manure

culata *f, anat* haunch; butt (of fire-arms); back, rear; *aut* sump

culebra *f,* snake; *inf* trick, joke; *inf* sudden uproar. **hacer c.,** to stagger along

culebrear *vi* to wriggle; grovel; meander, wind

culí *m,* coolie

culinario *a* culinary

culminación *f,* culmination, peak; *ast* zenith

culminante *a* culminating; *fig* outstanding

culminar *vi* to culminate (in)

culo *m,* buttocks, seat; rump; anus; base, bottom. **c. de lámpara,** *arch* pendant; *print* tail-piece

culpa *f,* fault; blame. **echar la c. (a),** to blame. **por c. de,** through the fault of. **tener la c.,** to be to blame

culpabilidad *f,* guilt

culpable *a* culpable

culpado (-da) *n* culprit

culpar *vt* to blame, accuse; criticize, censure

cultígeno *m,* cultigen

cultismo *m,* cultism (Gongorism); learned form, learnedism, learned word

cultivación *f,* cultivation; culture

cultivador (-ra) *n* cultivator; planter

cultivar *vt* to cultivate; develop; exercise, practise (professions); culture (bacteriology)

cultivo *m,* cultivation; farming; culture (bacteriological)

culto *a* cultivated; educated; cultured; elegant, artificial (style). *m,* worship; cult; religion, creed; homage

cultura *f,* cultivation; culture. **de c. universitaria,** college-educated

cultural *a* cultural

cumbre *f,* peak, crest, summit; *fig* zenith, acme

cumpleaños *m,* birthday

cumplidamente *adv* fully, completely

cumplido *a* complete; thorough; long; plentiful; courteous, punctilious; fulfilled. *m,* courtesy, attention; formality. **gastar cumplidos,** to stand on ceremony; be formal

cumplimentar *vt* to congratulate; perform, carry out

cumplimentero *a* over-complimentary; *inf* gushing

cumplimiento *m,* fulfilment, performance; courtesy, formality; completion; complement

cumplir *vt* to perform, carry into effect; reach (of age); keep (promises). **c. su palabra,** to keep one's word; *vi* perform a duty; expire, fall due; serve the required term of military service; be necessary, behove; *vr* be fulfilled, come true. **por c.,** as a matter of form

cumulativo *a* cumulative

cúmulo *m,* heap, pile; great many, host, mass, myriad; (cloud) cumulus, thunderhead

cuna *f,* cradle; foundling hospital; birthplace; origin, genesis; *pl* cat's cradle (game)

cundir *vi* to extend, spread (gen. liquids); be diffused (news); expand, grow

cuneco, -a *mf Venezuela* baby of the family

cuneiforme *a* wedge-shaped, cuneiform

cunero **(-ra)** *n* foundling, orphan

cuña *f,* wedge; *mech* quoin. *mil* **practicar una c.,** to make a wedge

cuñada *f,* sister-in-law

cuñado *m,* brother-in-law

cuño *m,* die, stamp; *fig* impression; mark on silver, hallmark. **de viejo c.,** old-guard (e.g. socialites)

cuota *f,* quota; share; subscription; fee

cupé *m,* coupé

Cupido *m,* Cupid; philanderer

cuplé *m,* couplet; song

cupo *m,* quota; share; tax rate; *mil* contingent

cupón *m,* coupon

cúpula *f, arch* dome, cupola; *bot* cup

cuquería *f,* craftiness, smartness; cuteness, prettiness

cura *m,* parish priest; *inf* Roman Catholic priest. *f,* cure (e.g. **La enfermedad tiene c.,** The illness can be cured); healing; remedy. **c. de almas,** cure of souls. **primera c.,** first aid. *inf* **c. de misa y olla,** ignorant priest

curación *f,* cure, remedy; healing

curador **(-ra)** *n* curer, salter. *m, (Scots law)* curator. *a* curing; healing

curaduría *f, law* guardianship

curanderismo *m,* quackery, charlatanism; quack medicine

curandero **(-ra)** *n* quack doctor; charlatan

curar *vi* to heal, cure; *(with de)* take care of; care about, mind; *vt* cure, salt; treat medically (bandage, give medicines, etc.); cure (leather); bleach (cloth); season (timber); *fig* remedy (an evil)

curasao *m,* curaçao (drink)

curativo *a* curative

curato *m, ecc* parish, cure

Curazao Curaçao

cúrcuma *f,* turmeric

cureña *f,* gun-carriage

curia *f, law* bar; tribunal; *ecc* curia; care, attention

curiana *f,* cockroach

curiche *m,* swamp

curiosear *vi* to pry; be curious (about); meddle, be a busybody

curiosidad *f,* curiosity; inquisitiveness, meddlesomeness; neatness; carefulness, conscientiousness; curio

curioso *a* curious; inquisitive; interesting, odd; neat, clean; conscientious, careful

Curita *f, trademark* Band-Aid

cursado *a* experienced, versed

cursante *m,* student

cursar *vt* to frequent, visit; do repeatedly; study, attend classes, take courses (e.g. **¿En qué escuela cursan?** At what school are you studying?); expedite (public admin.)

cursi *a inf* vulgar, in bad taste; loud, crude

cursilería *f, inf* vulgarity, bad taste

cursillo *m,* minicourse, short course; short series of lectures

cursiva *f,* italics. **en c.,** in italics, italicized

cursivo *a* cursive

curso *m,* course, direction; duration, passage (time); progress; route; course of study; academic year; succession, series; *com* tender

curtido *m,* tanning; leather; tanned leather (gen. *pl*)

curtidor *m,* tanner

curtiduría *f,* tannery

curtimiento *m,* tanning; effect of weather on the complexion; toughening-up; hardening

curtir *vt* to tan; *fig* bronze (complexions); make hardy, harden up; *vr* be weatherbeaten; be hardy. *inf* **estar curtido en,** to be experienced in; be expert at

curul *a* **curule** *m,* seat (in parliament)

curva *f,* curve; bend. *surv* **c. de nivel,** contour line

curvatura, curvidad *f,* curvature

curvo *a* curved; bent. *m,* curve

cusma *f, Lat. Am.* sleeveless shirt, tunic

cúspide *f,* peak, summit; *(geom arch)* cusp

custodia *f,* custody; guardianship, care; *ecc* monstrance; custodian, keeper; guardian; guard

custodiar *vt* to watch, guard; look after, care for; *naut* convoy

custodio *a* guardian; guarding; custodial. *m,* custodian; guard. **angel c.,** guardian angel

cutama *f, Argentina* blanket; *Chile* bag, sack

cutáneo *a* cutaneous, skin

cúter *m, naut* cutter

cutícula *f,* cuticle

cutis *m,* complexion; skin (sometimes *f*)

cuyo (cuya, cuyos, cuyas) *rel pron poss* whose, of which (e.g. **el viejo cuya barba era más blanca que la nieve,** the old man whose beard was whiter than snow). *interr* **¿Cúyo?** Whose? (e.g. **¿Cúyos son estos lápices?** Whose pencils are these?) (gen. **de quién** or **de quiénes** is used rather than **cúyo**). *m,* beau, lover

D

dable *a* practicable, possible

daca Give me!

dactilografía *f,* typewriting

dactilógrafo (-fa) *n* typist

dactilología *f,* dactylology

dadista *mf, Mexico* gambler

dádiva *f,* gift, present

dadivoso *a* generous, liberal

dado *m,* die; *arch* dado. *conjunc* **d. que,** given that, supposing that. **cargar los dados,** to load the dice

dador (-ra) *n* giver, donor. *m, com* bearer; *com* drawer (of a bill of exchange)

daga *f,* dagger

daguerrotipo *m,* daguerreotype

daifa *f,* concubine

¡dale! *interj* Stop! No more about . . . !

dalia *f, bot* dahlia

dallar *vt* to scythe (grass)

dalle *m,* scythe

dálmata *a* and *mf* Dalmatian

dalmática *f,* dalmatic, loose tunic or vestment

dalmático (-ca) *a* and *n* Dalmatian

daltoniano *a* color-blind

daltonismo *m,* color-blindness

dama *f,* lady; noblewoman; lady-in-waiting; lady-love; mistress, concubine; queen (chess); king (checkers); *theat* **d. primera,** leading lady

damajuana *f,* demijohn

damas *f pl,* checkers (game)

damasceno (-na) *a* and *n* Damascene

Damasco Damascus

damasco *m,* damask

damasquino *a* damascened (swords, etc.)

damería *f,* prudery, affectation

damisela *f,* damsel; *inf* woman of the town

damnificar *vt* to injure

dandi *m,* dandy

dandismo *m,* dandyism

danés (-esa) *a* Danish. *n* Dane. *m,* Danish (language)

danta *f, zool* tapir

dantesco *a* Dantesque

danubiano *a* Danubian

Danubio, el the Danube

danza *f,* dance; set (of dancers); *fig inf* dirty business. **d. de arcos,** dance of the arches. **d. de cintas,** maypole dance. **d. de monos,** amusing spectacle

danzador (-ra) *n* dancer; *a* dancing

danzante (-ta) *n* dancer; *fig inf* live wire; *inf* busybody

danzar *vt* and *vi* to dance; *vi* jump up and down, rattle; *inf* interfere, meddle

danzarín (-ina) *n* good dancer; *inf* meddler; *inf* playboy

danzón *m,* Cuban dance

dañable *a* harmful; worthy of condemnation

dañado *a* evil, perverse; damned; spoiled, damaged

dañador (-ra) *a* harmful. *n* injurer, offender

dañar *vt* to hurt, harm; damage, spoil; *vr* spoil, deteriorate

dañino *a* destructive (often of animals); hurtful, harmful. **animales dañinos,** vermin, pests

daño *m,* hurt; damage; loss. *law* **daños y perjuicios,** damages. **hacerse d.,** to hurt oneself

dañoso *a* hurtful, harmful

dar *vt irr* to give; wish, express (congratulations, etc.); hand over; concede, grant; inspire; produce, yield; cause, create; sacrifice; propose, put forward; take (a walk); believe, consider; deliver (blows, etc.); administer (medicine); provide with; apply, coat with; occasion; perform (plays); propose (a toast); give forth, emit; set (norms), render (thanks, etc.); hold (banquets, etc.); proffer, hold out; *vi* to strike (clocks); (*with prep a*) overlook, look on to (e.g. **Su ventana da a la calle,** His window looks on to the street); (*with con*) find, meet (things, persons); (*with de*) fall on, fall down (e.g. **Dio de cabeza,** He fell head first. **Dio de espaldas,** He fell on his back); (*with en*) fall into, incur; insist on or persist in (doing something); acquire the habit of (e.g. **Dieron en no venir a vernos,** They took to not coming to see us); solve, guess (riddles, etc.); strike, wound, hurt (e.g. **La bala le dio en el brazo,** The bullet struck him in the arm); (*with por*) decide on (e.g. **Di por no hacerlo,** I decided not to do it). *vr* to yield, give in; (*with prep a*) engage in, devote oneself to; (*with por*) think or consider oneself (e.g. **Me di por muerto,** I gave myself up for dead). **d. alas a,** to propagate, spread (a belief). **darse a la vela,** to set sail. **darse la mano,** to shake hands. **darse por buenos,** to make up a quarrel, be friends. **darse prisa,** to hurry up, make haste. **darse uno a conocer,** to make oneself known. **darse uno por entendido,** to show that one understands; be grateful. **No se me da un bledo,** I don't care a straw. **d. abajo,** to fall down. **d. bien por mal,** to return good for evil. **d. a conocer,** to make known. **d. a entender,** to suggest, hint. **d. a luz,** to give birth; publish, issue. **d. cuenta de,** to give an account of. **d. de baja,** *mil* to muster out, discharge. **d. de comer,** to feed. **d. de sí,** to stretch, expand; pro-

duce, yield; give of itself (oneself, himself, themselves) (either in good or bad sense). **d. diente con diente,** to chatter (of teeth), shiver. **d. el pésame,** to tender condolences. **d. en cara,** *fig inf* to throw in one's face. **d. en el clavo,** *fig* to hit the mark. **d. en qué pensar,** to make suspicious, cause to think. **d. fe,** to certify, attest. **d. fiado,** to give on credit. **d. fianza,** to give security. **d. fin a,** to finish. **d. licencia,** to permit, allow. **d. los buenos días,** to wish good day or good morning. **d. mal,** to have bad luck at cards. **d. parte de,** to announce; issue a communiqué about (e.g. **Dieron parte de la pérdida del buque,** They announced the loss of the ship). **d. prestado,** to lend. **d. qué decir,** to cause a scandal. **d. qué hacer,** to cause trouble. **d. razón de,** to give an account of. **d. sobre uno,** to assault a person. **d. un abrazo,** to embrace. **d. voces,** to shriek; call out. *inf* **Donde las dan las toman,** It's only tit-for-tat. *inf* **No me da la real gana,** I darn well don't want to. *Pres. Ind.* **doy, das,** etc. *Preterite* **di, diste,** etc. *Pres. Subjunc.* **dé,** etc. *Imperf. Subjunc.* **diese,** etc.

Dardanelos, los the Dardanelles

dardo *m,* (*mil sport*) dart; *icht* dace; lampoon

dares y tomares *m, pl* give and take; *inf* back-chat. Generally used with *andar, haber* or *tener*

dársena *f, naut* dock

darviniano *a* Darwinian

darvinismo *m,* Darwinism

darvinista *mf* Darwinian

data *f,* date (calendar); *com* credit

datar *vt* to date; *vi* (*with de*) date from; *vr com* credit

dátil *m, bot* date

datilado *a* date-like or date-colored

datilera *f, bot* date-palm

dativo *m, gram* dative

dato *m,* datum; basis, fact

davídico *a* Davidic

de *f,* name of letter D. *prep* of (possessive) (e.g. **Este cuadro es de Vd.,** This picture is yours); from (place and time) (e.g. **Vengo de Madrid,** I come from Madrid. **de vez en cuando,** from time to time); with, of, from, as the result of (e.g. **Lloraban de miedo,** They were crying with fright. **Murió de un ataque del corazón,** He died from a heart attack); for, to (e.g. **Es hora de marchar,** It is time to leave); with (of characteristics) (e.g. **el señor de los lentes,** the gentleman with the eyeglasses. **el cuarto de la alfombra azul,** the room with the blue carpet); when, as (e.g. **De niños nos gustaban los juguetes,** When we were children we liked toys); by (e.g. **Es un ensayo del mismo autor,** It is an essay by the same author. **Fue amado de todos,** He was loved by all. **Es hidalgo de nacimiento,** He is a gentleman by birth). Indicates the material of which a thing is made (e.g. **La mesa es de mármol,** The table is marble). Indicates contents of a thing (e.g. **un vaso de leche,** a glass of milk). Shows manner in which an action is performed (e.g. **Lo hizo de prisa,** He did it hurriedly). Shows the use to which an article is put (e.g. **una mesa de escribir,** a writing-table. **una máquina de coser,** a sewing-machine. **un caballo de batalla,** a war-horse). Sometimes used for emphasis (e.g. **El tonto de tu secretario,** That fool of a secretary of yours). Used by Spanish married women before husband's family name (e.g. **Señora Martínez de Cabra,** Mrs. Cabra (née Martínez)). Used after many adverbs (generally of time or place) to form prepositional phrases (e.g. **detrás de,** behind. **enfrente de,** opposite to; in front of. **de acá para allá,** here and there. **de allí a poco,** shortly afterward. **de allí a pocos días,** a few days later. **de bamba,** by chance. **de cabo a rabo,** from cover to cover. **además de,** besides, etc.). Used at beginning of various adverbial phrases (e.g. **de noche,** at night. **de día,** by day. **de antemano,** previously, **la persona de mi derecha,** the person at my right, etc.). Used partitively before nouns, pronouns, adjectives (e.g. **Estas historias ti-**

enen algo de verdad, These stories have some truth in them. **¿Qué hay de nuevo?** What's the news?) Forms many compound words (e.g. **deponer, denegar,** etc.). With **"uno"** means "at" (e.g. **Lo cogió de un salto,** He caught it at one bound). **de a** is used before expressions of price, weight, etc. (e.g. **un libro de a cinco pesetas,** a five-peseta book)

dea *f, poet* goddess

deán *m,* dean

debajo *adv* underneath; below

debate *m,* discussion, debate; dispute

debatible *a* debatable

debatir *vt* to discuss, debate, argue

debe *m, com* debtor

debelación *f,* conquest

debelador (-ra) *a* conquering. *n* conqueror

debelar *vt* to conquer, overthrow

deber *vt* to owe (e.g. **Le debo mil pesetas,** I owe him one thousand pesetas). Used as auxiliary verb followed by infinitive, to be obliged to (e.g. **Debía haberlo hecho,** I ought to have done it. **Deberá hacerlo,** He will have to do it); be destined to (e.g. **La princesa que más tarde debió ser reina,** The princess who later was destined to be queen); be essential, must (e.g. **La cuestión debe ser resuelta,** The question must be settled); (*with de + infin.*) indicates supposition) (e.g. **Debe de tener cincuenta años,** He is probably about fifty. **Debía de sufrir del corazón,** He probably suffered from heart trouble); (preceded by a negative *with de + infin.*) be impossible (e.g. **No debe de ser verdad,** It can't be true)

deber *m,* duty, obligation; debt. **hacer su d.,** to do one's duty

debidamente *adv* justly, rightly; duly

debido *a* correct, due. **d. a,** owing to, because of

débil *a* weak; *fig* spineless; frail

debilidad *f,* weakness; feebleness

debilitación *f,* debilitation

debilitante *a* weakening

debilitar *vt* to weaken; *vr* become weak

débito *m,* debit, debt; duty

debutar *vi* to appear for the first time, make one's début

década *f,* decade

decadencia *f,* decadence, decline

decadente *a* decadent, decaying

decaer *vi irr* to fail (persons); decay, decline. See **caer**

decagramo *m,* decagram

decaimiento *m,* decadence; *med* prostration

decalaje *m, aer* stagger

decalitro *m,* decaliter

decálogo *m,* decalogue, the Ten Commandments

decámetro *m,* decameter

decampar *vi mil* to decamp

decanato *m,* deanery; *univ* dean's rooms

decano *m,* senior member; *univ* dean

decantación *f,* decantation

decantar *vt* to decant (wines); praise

decapitación *f,* decapitation

decapitar *vt* to decapitate, behead

decena *f,* ten; *mus* tenth

decenal *a* decennial

decenario *m,* decade

decencia *f,* propriety, decency; decorum, modesty

decenio *m,* decade

deceno *a* tenth

decentar *vt irr* to begin, cut (loaves, etc.); *fig* undermine (health, etc.); *vr* suffer from bedsores. See **acertar**

decente *a* decent, honest; respectable; suitable; tidy

decepción *f,* disillusionment, disappointment

dechado *m,* model, ideal; *sew* sampler; exemplar, ideal

decible *a* expressible

decidero *a* that which can be safely said

decidido *a* decided; resolute, determined

decidir *vt* to resolve, decide; *vr* make up one's mind

decidor (-ra) *a* talkative, fluent, eloquent. *n* good talker

decigramo *m,* decigram

décima *f,* tenth; tithe; ten-line stanza of eight-syllable verse

decimal *a* decimal; pertaining to tithes. **sistema d.,** metric system

decímetro *m,* decimeter

décimo *a* tenth. *m,* tenth part; tenth of a lottery ticket

decimoctavo *a* eighteenth

decimocuarto *a* fourteenth

decimonono *a* nineteenth

decimoquinto *a* fifteenth

decimoséptimo *a* and *m,* seventeenth

decimosexto *a* sixteenth

decimotercio *a* thirteenth

decir *vt irr* to say; name; indicate, show; tell. **d. bien,** to go with, suit; speak the truth; be eloquent. **d. entre** (*or* **para**) **sí,** to say to oneself. *inf* **d. nones,** to refuse. **¡Diga!** Hello! (telephone). *inf* **el que dirán,** public opinion (what will people say!). **Es d.,** That is to say. **Se dice,** It is said, people say. *Pres. Ind.* **digo, dices,** etc. *Pres. Part.* **diciendo.** *Past Part.* **dicho.** *Fut.* **diré,** etc. *Condit.* **diría,** etc. *Preterite* **dije,** etc. *Pres. Subjunc.* **diga,** etc. *Imperf. Subjunc.* **dijese,** etc.

decir *m,* saying, saw; maxim, witticism (often *pl.*)

decisión *f,* decision, resolution; *law* judgment; firmness, strength (of character)

decisivo *a* decisive

declamación *f,* declamation, oration; *theat* delivery; recitation

declamador (-ra) *a* declamatory. *n* reciter; orator

declamar *vi* to make a speech, declaim; recite

declamatorio *a* declamatory, rhetorical

declaración *f,* declaration; exposition, explanation; confession; statement; *law* deposition. **d. jurada,** affidavit, sworn statement

declaradamente *adv* avowedly

declarante *a* declaring. *mf law* deponent

declarar *vt* to declare; make clear, explain; *law* find; *vi law* give evidence; *vr* avow, confess (one's sentiments, etc.); show, reveal itself

declarativo, declaratorio *a* explanatory, declaratory

declinación *f,* fall, descent; decadence, decay; *ast* declination; *gram* declension. *inf* **no saber las declinaciones,** not to know one's ABC, be very ignorant

declinante *a* declining; sloping

declinar *vi* to slope; diminish, fall; decline, deteriorate; *fig* near the end; *vt gram* decline

declive, m. declividad *f,* slope, incline; gradient

decocción *f,* decoction

decoloración *f,* decoloration; decolorization

decomisar *vt* to confiscate, seize

decoración *f,* decoration; ornament; embellishment; *theat* scenery

decorado *m, theat* scenery, décor

decorador *m,* decorator

decorar *vt* to adorn, ornament; *poet* decorate, honor

decorativo *a* decorative

decoro *m,* respect, reverence; prudence, circumspection; decorum, propriety; integrity, decency; *arch* decoration

decoroso *a* decorous, honorable, decent

decrecer *vi irr* to decrease, grow less. See **conocer**

decreciente *a* decreasing

decrepitación *f, chem* decrepitation, crackling

decrepitar *vi chem* to decrepitate, crackle

decrépito *a* decrepit

decrepitud *f,* decrepitude

decretar *vt* to decree, decide; *law* give a judgment (in a suit)

decreto *m,* decree, order; judicial decree

decuplar, decuplicar *vt* to multiply by ten

décuplo *a* tenfold

decurso *m,* course, lapse (of time)

dedada *f,* thimbleful, finger; pinch

dedal *m,* thimble; finger-stall

dédalo *m,* labyrinth

dedeo *m, mus* touch

dedicación f, dedication (all meanings)

dedicar vt to dedicate; devote; consecrate; vr (with prep a) dedicate oneself to, engage in

dedicatoria f, dedication (of a book, etc.)

dedicatorio a dedicatory

dedil m, finger-stall

dedillo, saber al fig to have at one's fingertips, know perfectly

dedo m, finger; toe; finger's breadth. **d. anular,** third (ring) finger. **d. de en medio** or **del corazón,** middle finger. **d. índice,** forefinger. **d. meñique,** little finger. **d. pulgar,** thumb or big toe. fig inf **a dos dedos de,** within an inch of. fig inf **chuparse los dedos,** to smack one's lips over. inf **estar unidos como los dedos de la mano,** to be as thick as thieves

deducción f, inference, deduction; derivation; (mus math) progression

deduciente a deductive

deducir vt irr to deduce, infer; deduct, subtract; law plead, allege in pleading. See **conducir**

deductivo a deductive

defecación f, purification; defecation

defecar vt to clarify, purify; defecate

defección f, defection

defectible a deficient; imperfect

defecto m, defect, fault; imperfection

defectuoso a imperfect, defective

defender vt irr to defend, protect; maintain, uphold; forbid; hinder; vr defend oneself. See **entender**

defendible a defensible

defensa f, defence; protection; (hockey) pad; law defense; sport back; pl mil defenses; naut fenders. **d. química,** chemical warfare. mil **defensas costeras,** coastal defenses

defensiva f, defensive

defensivo a defensive. m, safeguard

defensor (-ra) n defender. m, law counsel for the defense

deferencia f, deference

deferente a deferential

deferir vi irr to defer, yield; vt delegate. Pres. Ind. **defiero, defieres, defiere, defieren.** Pres. Part. **defiriendo.** Preterite **defirió, defirieron.** Pres. Subjunc. **defiera,** etc. Imperf. Subjunc. **defiriese,** etc.

deficiencia f, defect, deficiency

deficiente a faulty, deficient

déficit m, deficit

definible a definable

definición f, definition; decision

definido a definite

definir vt to define; decide

definitivo a definitive. **en definitiva,** definitely; in short

deflagración f, sudden blaze, deflagration

deflagrador m, elec deflagrator

deflagrar vi to go up in flames

deformación f, deformation; rad distortion

deformado a deformed; misshapen

deformador (-ra) a disfiguring, deforming. n disfigurer

deformar vt to deform; vr become deformed or misshapen

deformidad f, deformity; gross error; vice, lapse

defraudación f, defrauding; deceit

defraudador (-ra) n defrauder

defraudar vt to defraud; usurp; frustrate, disappoint; impede

defuera adv outwardly, externally

defunción f, decease, death

degeneración f, degeneration. **d. grasienta,** fatty degeneration

degenerado (-da) a and n degenerate

degenerar vi to degenerate

deglución f, swallowing, deglutition

deglutir vi and vt to swallow

degollación f, decollation, throat slitting

degolladero m, slaughterhouse; execution block

degollador m, executioner

degolladura f, slitting of the throat

degollar vt irr to behead; slit the throat; fig destroy; (fig theat) murder; inf annoy, bore. Pres. Ind. **degüello, degüellas, degüella, degüellan.** Pres. Subjunc. **degüelle, degüelles, degüelle, degüellen**

degollina f, inf massacre

degradación f, degradation; humiliation, debasement; art gradation, shading (colors, light)

degradante a degrading, humiliating

degradar vt to degrade; humiliate; art grade, blend; vr degrade oneself

degüello m, decollation; havoc, destruction; haft (of swords, etc.)

degustación f, act of tasting or sampling

dehesa f, pasture, meadow

deicida mf deicide (person)

deicidio m, deicide (act)

deidad f, divinity; deity, idol

deificación f, deification

deificar vt to deify; overpraise

deífico a deific, divine

deísmo m, Deism

deísta mf deist. a deistic

dejación f, relinquishment, abandonment

dejadez f, slovenliness; neglect; laziness; carelessness

dejado a lazy; neglectful; slovenly; discouraged, depressed

dejamiento m, relinquishment; negligence; lowness of spirits; indifference

dejar vt to leave; omit, forget, allow, permit (e.g. **Déjame salir,** Let me go out); yield, produce, entrust, leave in charge; believe, consider; intend, appoint; cease, stop; forsake, desert; renounce, relinquish; bequeath; give away; vr neglect oneself; engage (in); lay oneself open to, allow oneself; abandon oneself (to), fling oneself (into); fig be depressed or languid; (with de + infin.) cease to (e.g. **Se dejó de hacerlo,** He stopped doing it); vi (with de + adjective) be none the less, be rather (e.g. **No deja de ser sorprendente,** It isn't any the less surprising). **d. aparte,** to omit, leave out. **d. atrás,** to overtake; fig leave behind, beat. **d. caer,** to let fall. **dejarse caer,** to let oneself fall; fig inf to let fall, utter; appear suddenly. **dejarse vencer,** to give way, allow oneself to be persuaded

dejo m, relinquishment; end; accent (of persons); savor, after-taste; negligence; fig touch, flavor

del contraction of **de + el,** (def. art. m.) of the (e.g. **del perro,** of the dog)

delación f, accusation, denunciation

delantal m, apron

delante adv before, in front, in the presence (of)

delantera f, front, front portion; theat orchestra stall, front seat; front (of garment). **tomar la d.,** to take the lead; inf steal a march on

delantero a fore, front. m, postilion; sport forward. **d. centro,** sport centerforward

delatable a impeachable; blameworthy

delatar vt to inform against, accuse; impeach

delator (-ra) a denunciatory, accusing. n denouncer, informer

delectación f, delectation, pleasure

delegación f, delegation; proxy

delegado (-da) n delegate; proxy

delegar vt to delegate

deleitable a delightful

deleitar vt to delight, charm, please; vr delight (in)

deleite m, delight; pleasure

deleitoso a delightful, pleasant

deletéreo a deleterious; poisonous

deletrear vi to spell; fig decipher

deletreo m, spelling; fig decipherment

deleznable a fragile, brittle; slippery; brief, fugitive, transitory

délfico a Delphic

delfín m, (icht ast) dolphin; dauphin

delfina f, dauphiness
Delfos Delphi
delgadez f, thinness; slenderness, leanness
delgado a slim; thin; scanty; poor (of land); sharp, perspicacious
delgaducho a slenderish, somewhat thin
deliberación f, deliberation; consideration; discussion
deliberadamente adv deliberately
deliberante a deliberative, considering
deliberar vi to deliberate, consider; vt decide after reflection; discuss
delicadez f, weakness; delicacy; hypersensitiveness; amiability
delicadeza f, delicacy; fastidiousness; refinement, subtlety; sensitiveness; consideration, tact; scrupulosity
delicado a courteous; tactful; fastidious; weak, delicate; fragile, perishable; delicious, tasty; exquisite; difficult; embarrassing; refined, discriminating, sensitive; scrupulous; subtle; hypersensitive, suspicious. **d. de salud,** in poor health
delicia f, pleasure, delight; sensual pleasure
delicioso a delightful, agreeable, pleasant
delimitar vt to delimit
delincuencia f, delinquency
delincuente a and mf delinquent
delineación f, delineation; diagram, design, plan
delineador (-ra), n delineante m, draftsman, designer
delineamiento m, delineation
delinear vt to delineate; sketch; describe
delinquimiento m, delinquency; crime
delinquir vi irr to commit a crime. Pres. Ind. **delinco.** Pres. Subjunc. **delinca**
deliquio m, faint, swoon
delirante a delirious
delirar vi to be delirious; act or speak foolishly
delirio m, delirium; frenzy; foolishness, nonsense. **d. de grandezas,** illusions of grandeur
delito m, delict, offense against the law, crime
delta f, fourth letter of Greek alphabet. m, delta (of a river)
delusorio a deceptive
demacración f, emaciation
demacrado a emaciated
demacrarse vr to become emaciated
demagogia f, demagogy
demagógico a demagogic
demagogo (-ga) n demagogue
demanda f, petition, request; collecting (for charity); collecting box; want ad; question; search; undertaking; com order or demand; law claim
demandadero (-ra) n convent or prison messenger; errandboy
demandado (-da) n law defendant; law respondent
demandante mf law plaintiff
demandar vt to ask, request; desire, yearn for; question; law claim
demarcación f, demarcation, limit
demarcar vt to fix boundaries, demarcate
demás a other. adv besides. **lo d.,** the rest. **los (las) d.,** the others. **por d.,** useless; superfluous. **por lo d.,** otherwise; for the rest
demasía f, excess; daring; insolence; guilt, crime. **en d.,** excessively
demasiado a too; too many; too much. adv excessively
demencia f, madness, insanity
demencial a insane
dementar vt to render insane; vr become insane
demente a insane, mad. mf lunatic
demérito m, demerit, fault
demeritorio a undeserving, without merit
demisión f, submission, acquiescence
democracia f, democracy
demócrata mf democrat
democrático a democratic
democratizar vt to make democratic

demoledor (-ra) a demolition. n demolisher
demoler vt irr to demolish, destroy, dismantle. See **moler**
demolición f, demolition, destruction, dismantling
demoníaco a devilish; possessed by a demon
demonio m, devil; evil spirit. interj **¡Demonios!** Deuce take it! inf **tener el d. en el cuerpo,** to be always on the move, be very energetic
demontre m, inf devil
demora f, delay; naut bearing; com demurrage
demorar vt to delay; vi stay, remain, tarry; naut bear
demorón, -ona a, Lat. Am. slow
demostrable a demonstrable
demostración f, demonstration; proof
demostrador (-ra) a demonstrating. n demonstrator
demostrar vt irr to demonstrate, explain; prove; teach. See **mostrar**
demostrativo a demonstrative. gram **pronombre d.,** demonstrative pronoun
demudación f, change; alteration
demudar vt to change, vary; alter, transform; vr change suddenly (color, facial expression, etc.); grow angry
denario a denary. m, denarius
denegación f, denial; refusal
denegar vt irr to deny, refuse. See **acertar**
dengoso a fastidious, finicky
dengue m, affectation, faddiness, fastidiousness
denigrable a odious
denigración f, slander, defamation (of character)
denigrante a slanderous
denigrar vt to slander; insult
denodado a valiant, daring
denominación f, denomination
denominador a denominating m, math denominator
denominar vt to name, designate
denostada f, insult
denostar vt irr to revile, insult. See **acordar**
denotar vt to denote, indicate
densidad f, density; closeness, denseness; phys specific gravity; obscurity
denso a compact, close; thick, dense; crowded; dark, confused
dentado a toothed; pronged; dentate
dentadura f, set of teeth (real or false). **d. de rumiante,** teeth like an ox. **d. postiza,** false teeth
dental a dental
dentar vt irr to provide with teeth, prongs, etc.; vi cut teeth. See **sentar**
dentellada f, gnashing or chattering of teeth; bite; toothmark
dentellar vt to chatter, grind, gnash (teeth)
dentellear vt to bite, sink the teeth into
dentera f, (dar) to set one's teeth on edge; fig inf make one's mouth water
dentición f, teething, dentition
dentífrico m, toothpaste
dentista mf dentist
dentro adv within, inside. **d. de poco,** soon, shortly. **por d.,** from the inside; on the inside
dentudo a having large teeth
denudación f, denudation; geol erosion
denudar vt to denude
denuedo m, courage, daring
denuesto m, insult
denuncia f, denunciation, accusation
denunciante a accusing. mf law denouncer
denunciar vt to give notice, inform; herald, presage; declare, proclaim; denounce; law accuse
denunciatorio a denunciatory
deparar vt to furnish, offer, present
departamental a departmental
departamento m, department; compartment (railway); branch, section; Argentina apartment. **d. de lactantes,** nursery (in a hospital)
departir vi to converse
depauperación f, impoverishment; med emaciation

depauperar *vt* to impoverish; *vr med* grow weak, become emaciated

dependencia *f,* dependence; subordination; dependency; *com* branch; firm, agency; business affair; kinship or affinity; *pl arch* offices; *com* staff; accessories

depender *vi (with de)* to be subordinate to; depend on; be dependent on, need

dependiente (-ta) *a* and *n* dependent, subordinate. *m,* employee; shop assistant

depilar *vt* to depilate

depilatorio *m,* depilatory

deplorar *vt* to deplore, lament

deponente *a* deposing; affirming. *mf* deponent. *gram* **verbo d.,** deponent verb

deponer *vt irr* to lay aside; depose, oust; affirm, testify; remove, take from its place; *law* depose; *Central America, Mexico* throw up, vomit. See **poner**

deportación *f,* deportation

deportar *vt* to exile; deport

deporte *m,* sport; *pl* games. **d. de vela,** sailing; boating

deportismo *m,* sport

deportista *a* sporting. *mf* sportsman (sportswoman)

deportivo *a* sporting

deposición *f,* affirmation, statement; *law* deposition; degradation, removal (from office, etc.)

depositador (-ra) *a* depositing. *n* depositor

depositar *vt* to deposit; place in safety; entrust; lay aside, put away; *vr chem* settle

depositaría *f,* depository; trusteeship; accounts office

depositario (-ia) *a* pertaining to a depository. *n* depositary, trustee

depósito *m,* deposit; depository; *com* depot, warehouse; *chem* deposit, sediment; tank, reservoir; *mil* depot. **d. de bencina, d. de gasolina,** gas tank; service station. **d. de municiones,** munitions dump. *com* **en d.,** in bond. **Queda hecho el d. que marca la ley,** Copyright reserved

depravación *f,* depravity

depravar *vt* to deprave, corrupt; *vr* become depraved

deprecación *f,* supplication, petition; deprecation

deprecar *vt* to supplicate, petition; deprecate

depreciación *f,* depreciation, fall in value

depreciar *vt* to depreciate, reduce the value (of)

depredación *f,* depredation, robbery

depredar *vt* to pillage

depresión *f,* depression. **d. nerviosa,** nervous breakdown

depresivo *a* depressive; humiliating

deprimir *vt* to depress, compress, press down; depreciate, belittle; *vr* be compressed

depuración *f,* cleansing, purification; *pol* purge

depurar *vt* to cleanse, purify; *pol* purge

derecha *f,* right hand; *pol* (gen. *pl*) Right. *mil* **¡D.!** Right Turn! **a la d.,** on the right

derechamente *adv* straight, directly; prudently, justly; openly, frankly

derechera *f,* direct road

derechista *mf pol* rightist

derecho *a* straight; upright; right (not left); just, reasonable; *sport* forehand. *adv* straightaway. *m,* right; law; just claim; privilege; justice, reason; exemption; right side (cloth, etc.); *pl* dues, taxes; fees. **d. a la vía,** right of way. **d. de apelación,** right to appeal. **d. de visita,** (international law) right of search. **derechos de aduana,** customhouse duties. **derechos de entrada,** import duties. **según d.,** according to law. **usar de su d.,** to exercise one's right

derechura *f,* directness, straightness; uprightness; *Lat. Am.* good luck

deriva *f,* (*naut aer*) drift, leeway

derivación *f,* origin, derivation; inference, consequence; *gram* derivation

derivar *vi* to originate; *naut* drift; *vt* conduct, lead; *gram* derive; *elec* tap

dermatología *f,* dermatology

dermatólogo *m,* dermatologist

derogación *f,* repeal, annulment; deterioration

derogar *vt* to annul, repeal; destroy, suppress

derogatorio *a law* repealing

derrama *f,* apportionment of tax

derramado *a* extravagant, wasteful

derramamiento *m,* pouring out; spilling; scattering

derramar *vt* to pour out; spill; scatter; apportion (taxes); publish abroad, spread; *vr* be scattered; overflow

derrame *m,* spilling; leakage; overflow; scattering; slope

derredor *m,* circumference. **al** (*or* **en**) **d.,** round about

derrelicto *a* abandoned; derelict. *m, naut* derelict

derrengado *a* crooked; crippled

derretimiento *m,* melting; thaw; liquefaction; *inf* burning passion

derretir *vt irr* to melt, liquefy; waste, dissipate; *vr* be very much in love; *inf* be susceptible (to love); *inf* long, be impatient. See **pedir**

derribar *vt* to demolish; knock down; fell; throw down; *aer* shoot down; throw (in wrestling); *fig* overthrow; demolish, explode (a myth); control (emotions); *vr* fall down; prostrate oneself; throw oneself down. **d. el chapeo,** *humorous* to doff one's hat

derribo *m,* demolition; debris, rubble; throw (in wrestling)

derrocadero *m,* rocky precipice

derrocar *vt* to throw down from a rock; demolish (buildings); overthrow, oust

derrochador (-ra) *a* wasteful, extravagant. *n* spendthrift

derrochar *vt* to waste, squander

derroche *m,* squandering

derrota *f,* road; route, path; *naut* course; *mil* defeat

derrotar *vt* to squander; destroy, harm; *mil* defeat; *vr naut* drift, lose course

derrotero *m, naut* course; *naut* ship's itinerary; number of sea charts; means to an end, course of action

derrotismo *m,* defeatism

derrotista *mf* defeatist

derruir *vt irr* to demolish (a building). See **huir**

derrumbadero *m,* precipice; risk, danger

derrumbamiento *m,* landslide; collapse, downfall

derrumbar *vt* to precipitate; *vr* throw oneself down, collapse, tumble down (buildings, etc.)

derrumbe *m,* collapse; subsidence

derviche *m,* dervish

desabarrancar *vt* to pull out of a ditch or rut; extricate (from a difficulty)

desabillé *m,* deshabille

desabor *m,* insipidity

desabotonar *vt* to unbutton; *vi* open (flowers)

desabrido *a* insipid, poor-tasting; inclement (weather); disagreeable; unsociable; homely, plain (woman)

desabrigar *vt* to uncover; leave without shelter

desabrigo *m,* want of clothing or shelter; poverty, destitution

desabrimiento *m,* insipidity; harshness, disagreeableness; melancholy, depression

desabrir *vt* to give a bad taste (to food); annoy, trouble

desabrochar *vt* to unbutton, untie; open; *vr inf* confide, open up

desacatar *vt* to behave disrespectfully (towards); lack reverence

desacato *m,* irreverence; disrespect

desacertado *a* wrong, erroneous; imprudent

desacertar *vi irr* to be wrong; act imprudently. See **acertar**

desacierto *m,* mistake, miscalculation, blunder

desacomodado *a* lacking means of subsistence; poor; unemployed (servants); troublesome

desacomodar *vt* to incommode, make uncomfortable; inconvenience; dismiss, discharge

desaconsejado *a* ill-advised

desaconsejar *vt* to advise against, dissuade

desacoplar *vt* to disconnect

desacordar *vt irr mus* to put out of tune; *vr* (*with de*) forget. See **acordar**

desacorde *a* discordant, inharmonious; *mus* out of tune

desacostumbrado *a* unaccustomed; unusual

desacostumbrar *vt* to break of a habit

desacotar *vt* to remove (fences); refuse, deny; *vi* withdraw (from agreement, etc.)

desacreditar *vt* to discredit

desacuerdo *m*, disagreement, discord; mistake; forgetfulness; swoon, loss of consciousness

desadeudar *vt* to free from debt

desadornar *vt* to denude of ornaments

desadorno *m*, lack of ornaments; bareness

desafecto *a* disaffected; hostile. *m*, disaffection

desaferrar *vt irr* to untie, unfasten; *fig* wean from; *naut* weigh anchor. See **acertar**

desafiador (**-ra**) *a* challenging. *n* challenger. *m*, duelist

desafiar *vt* to challenge; compete with; oppose; *Mexico* fight

desafinar *vi mus* to go out of tune; *fig inf* speak out of turn

desafío *m*, challenge; competition; duel

desaforado *a* lawless; outrageous; enormous

desaforar *vt* to infringe (laws, etc.); *vr* be disorderly

desaforrar *vt* to remove the lining of or from

desafortunado *a* unfortunate

desafuero *m*, act of injustice; outrage, excess

desagarrar *vt inf* to release, loosen; unhook

desagraciado *a* ugly, unsightly

desagraciar *vt* to disfigure, make ugly

desagradable *a* disagreeable; unpleasant

desagradar *vi* to be disagreeable, displease (e.g. **Me desagrada su voz,** I find his voice unpleasant)

desagradecer *vt irr* to be ungrateful (for). See **conocer**

desagradecido *a* ungrateful

desagradecimiento *m*, ingratitude

desagrado *m*, displeasure, dislike, dissatisfaction

desagraviar *vt* to make amends, apologize; indemnify

desagravio *m*, satisfaction, reparation; compensation

desagregar(se) *vt and vr* to separate

desaguadero *m*, drain, waste pipe

desaguar *vt* to drain off; dissipate; *vi* flow (into sea, etc.)

desagüe *m*, drainage; outlet, drain; catchment

desaguisado *a* outrageous, lawless. *m*, offense, insult

desahogado *a* brazen, insolent; clear, unencumbered; in comfortable circumstances

desahogar *vt* to ease, relieve; *vr* unburden oneself; recover (from illness, heat, etc.); get out of debt; speak one's mind

desahogo *m*, relief, alleviation; ease; comfort, convenience; freedom, frankness; unburdening (of one's mind). *inf* **vivir con d.,** to be comfortably off

desahuciar *vt* to banish all hope; give up, despair of the life of; put out (tenants); *Chile* dismiss

desahúcio *m*, ejection, dispossession (of tenants); *Chile* dismissal

desahumar *vt* to clear of smoke

desairado *a* unattractive, graceless, ugly; unsuccessful, crestfallen; slighted

desairar *vt* to disdain, slight, disregard; underrate (things)

desaire *m*, gracelessness, ugliness; insult, slight

desalabanza *f*, disparagement; criticism

desalabar *vt* to censure, disparage

desalación *f*, desalinization

desalado *a* anxious, precipitate, hasty

desalar *vt* to remove the salt from; take off wings; *vr* walk or run at great speed; long for, yearn

desalentar *vt irr* to make breathing difficult (work, fatigue); discourage; *vr* be depressed or sad. See **sentar**

desaliento *m*, depression, discouragement, dismay

desalinear *vt* to throw out of the straight

desaliñado *a* slovenly; slipshod

desaliñar *vt* to disarrange, make untidy, crumple

desaliño *m*, untidiness, slovenliness; negligence, carelessness

desalmado *a* soulless, conscienceless; cruel

desalmamiento *m*, inhumanity, conscienceless-ness; cruelty

desalmidonar *vt* to remove starch from

desalojamiento *m*, dislodgement, ejection

desalojar *vt* to dislodge, remove, eject; *vi* move out, remove

desalquilado *a* untenanted, vacant

desalquilar *vt* to leave, or cause to leave, rented premises

desalterar *vt* to soothe, calm

desamar *vt* to cease to love; hate

desamarrar *vt* to untie; separate; *naut* unmoor

desamor *m*, indifference; lack of sentiment or affection; hatred

desamotinarse *vr* to cease from rebellion; submit

desamparar *vt* to abandon, forsake; leave (a place)

desamparo *m*, desertion; need

desamueblado *a* unfurnished

desamueblar *vt* to empty of furniture

desandar lo andado *vt irr* to retrace one's steps. See **andar**

desangrar *vt med* to bleed; drain (lake, etc.); impoverish, bleed; *vr* lose much blood

desangre *m*, *Lat. Am.* bleeding, loss of blood

desanidar *vi* to leave the nest; *vt* eject, expel

desanimado *a* downhearted; (of places) dull, quiet

desanimar *vt* to discourage, depress

desanublar, *vt* **desanublarse** *vr* to clear up (weather)

desanudar *vt* to untie; disentangle

desaojar *vt* to cure of the evil eye

desapacibilidad *f*, disagreeableness, unpleasantness

desapacible *a* disagreeable; unpleasant; unsociable

desaparecer *vt irr* to cause to disappear; *vi and vr* disappear. See **conocer**

desaparecido *a* late (deceased); *mil* missing

desaparejar *vt* to unharness

desaparición *f*, disappearance

desapegar *vt* to unstick, undo; *vr* be indifferent, cast off a love or affection

desapego *m*, lack of affection or interest, coolness

desapercibido *a* unnoticed; unprovided, unprepared

desapestar *vt* to disinfect

desapiadado *a* merciless

desaplicación *f*, laziness, lack of application; carelessness, negligence

desaplicado *a* lazy; careless

desapoderado *a* precipitate, uncontrolled; furious, violent

desapoderar *vt* to dispossess, rob; remove from office

desapolillar *vt* to free from moths; *vr inf* take an airing

desaposentar *vt* to evict; drive away

desapreciar *vt* to scorn

desaprensivo *a* unscrupulous

desapretar(se) *vt and vr irr* to slacken. See **acertar**

desaprisionar *vt* to release from prison

desaprobación *f*, disapproval

desaprobar *vt irr* to disapprove; disagree with. See **probar**

desapropiamiento *m*, renunciation or transfer of property

desapropiarse *vr* to renounce or transfer (property)

desaprovechado *a* unprofitable; backward; unintelligent

desaprovechar *vt* to take no advantage of, waste; *vi fig* lose ground, lose what one has gained

desapuntar *vt* to unstitch; lose one's aim

desarbolar *vt naut* to unmast

desarenar *vt* to clear of sand

desarmador *m*, *Mexico* screwdriver

desarmar *vt* to disarm; dismantle, dismount; appease

desarme *m*, disarming; disarmament

desarraigar *vt* to pull up by root (plants); extirpate; suppress; eradicate (opinion, etc.); exile

desarraigo *m*, uprooting; extirpation; eradication; exile

desarrebujar *vt* to disentangle, uncover; explain

desarreglado *a* disarranged; untidy; intemperate, immoderate

desarreglar *vt* to disarrange

desarreglo *m*, disorder; disarrangement; irregularity

desarrendar *vt irr* to unbridle a horse; end a tenancy or lease. See **recomendar**

desarrollar *vt* to unroll; increase, develop, grow, unfold; explain (theory); *vr* develop, grow

desarrollo *m*, unrolling; development; growth; explanation

desarropar *vt* to uncover, remove the covers, etc. from

desarrugar *vt* to take out wrinkles or creases

desarticulación *f*, disarticulation

desarticular *vt* to disarticulate; *mech* disconnect

desaseado *a* dirty; unkempt, slovenly

desaseo *m*, dirtiness; slovenliness

desasimiento *m*, loosening; liberality; disinterestedness; indifference, coldness

desasir *vt irr* to loosen, undo. *vr* disengage oneself. See **asir**

desasnar *vt inf* to instruct, educate, polish

desasosegar *vt irr* to disturb, make anxious. See **cegar**

desasosiego *m*, uneasiness, disquiet

desastre *m*, disaster, calamity

desastroso *a* unfortunate, calamitous

desatacar *vt* to unfasten, undo, unbutton

desatadura *f*, untying

desatar *vt* to untie; melt, dissolve; elucidate, explain; *vr* loosen the tongue; lose self control; lose all reserve; unbosom oneself

desatascar *vt* to pull out of the mud; free from obstruction; extricate from difficulties

desataviar *vt* to strip of ornaments

desatavío *m*, carelessness in dress, slovenliness

desatención *f*, inattention, abstraction; incivility

desatender *vt irr* to pay no attention to; disregard, ignore. See **entender**

desatentado *a* imprudent, ill-advised; excessive, immoderate

desatento *a* inattentive, abstracted; discourteous

desatinado *a* foolish, imprudent, wild

desatinar *vt* to bewilder; *vi* behave foolishly; lose one's bearings

desatino *m*, folly, foolishness, imprudence, rashness; blunder, faux pas, mistake

desatracar *vi naut* to push off

desatrancar *vt* to unbar the door; remove obstacles

desaturdir *vt* to rouse (from torpor, etc.)

desautorizar *vt* to remove from authority; discredit

desavenencia *f*, disharmony, disagreement

desavenido *a* disagreeing, discordant

desavenir *vt irr* to upset. See **venir**

desaventajado *a* disadvantageous; unfavorable, inferior

desaviar *vt* to lead astray; deprive of a necessity; *vr* lose one's way

desayunador *m*, breakfast nook

desavisado *a* unaware, unprepared

desavisar *vt* to take back one's previous advice

desayunarse *vr* to have breakfast, eat breakfast

desayuno *m*, breakfast

desazón *f*, insipidity, lack of flavor; poorness (soil); anxiety, trouble; vexation

desazonar *vt* to make insipid; make anxious, worry; vex; *vr* feel out of sorts

desbancar *vt* to break the bank (gambling); supplant

desbandada *f*, dispersal, rout. **a la d.,** in confusion or disorder

desbandarse *vr* to disband, retreat in disorder; *mil* desert

desbaratado *a inf* corrupt, vicious

desbaratar *vt* to spoil, destroy; dissipate, waste; foil, thwart (a plot); *mil* rout; *vi* talk foolishly; *vr* go too far, behave badly

desbarbado *a* beardless

desbastar *vt carp* to plane, dress; polish, refine, civilize

desbocado *a* (of tools) blunt; runaway (of a horse); *inf* foul-tongued; *Lat. Am.* overflowing (its banks)

desbocar *vt* to break the spout or neck (of jars, etc.); *vi* run (into) (of streets, etc.); *vr* bolt (horses); curse, swear

desboquillar *vt* to remove or break a stem or mouthpiece

desbordamiento *m*, overflowing, flood

desbordarse *vr* to overflow; lose self-control. **d. en alabanzas para,** to heap praise on

desbravar *vt* to break in (horses, etc.); *vi* grow less savage; lose force, decrease

desbrozar *vt* to free of rubbish, clear up

descabalgadura *f*, alighting (from horses, etc.)

descabalgar *vi* to alight (from horse); *vt* dismantle (gun)

descabellado *a* disheveled; ridiculous, foolish

descabellar *vt* to disarrange, ruffle (hair)

descabezado *a* headless; rash, impetuous

descabezar *vt* to behead; cut the top off (trees, etc.); *fig inf* break the back of (work); *vi* abut, join; *vr* (*with con* or *en*) rack one's brains about

descacharrado, -a *a, Central America* dirty, filthy, slovenly

descalabazarse *vr inf* to rack one's brains

descalabradura *f*, head wound or scar

descalabrar *vt* to wound in the head; wound; harm

descalabro *m*, misfortune, mishap

descalzar *vt* to remove the shoes and stockings; undermine; *vr* remove one's shoes and stockings; lose a shoe (horses)

descalzo *a* barefoot

descaminar *vt* to lead astray; pervert, corrupt

descamisado (-da) *a inf* shirtless; ragged, poor. *n inf* down and out, outcast; vagabond

descansadero *m*, resting place

descansado *a* rested, refreshed; tranquil

descansar *vi* to rest, repose oneself; have relief (from anxiety, etc.); sleep; *agr* lie fallow; sleep in death; (*with en*) trust, have confidence in; (*with sobre*) lean on or upon; *vt* (*with sobre*) rest (a thing) on another. **¡Que en paz descanse!** May he rest in peace!

descanso *m*, rest, repose; relief (from care); landing of stairs; *mech* bench, support; *mil* stand easy

descarado *a* impudent, brazen

descararse *vr* to behave impudently

descarbonizar *vt* to decarbonize

descarga *f*, unloading; *naut* discharge of cargo; *elec* discharge; *mil* volley. **d. cerrada,** dense volley, fusillade

descargadero *m*, wharf

descargador *m*, unloader, docker; *elec* discharger

descargar *vt* to unload; *mil* fire; unload (fire-arms); *elec* discharge; rain (blows) upon; *fig* free, exonerate; *vi* disembogue (of rivers); burst (clouds); *vr* relinquish (employment); shirk responsibility; *law* clear oneself

descargo *m*, unloading; *com* acquittance; *law* answer to an impeachment

descargue *m*, unloading

descarnado *a* fleshless; scraggy; spare, lean

descarnador *m*, dental scraper; tanner's scraper

descarnar *vt* to scrape off flesh; corrode; inspire indifference to earthly things

descaro *m*, impudence

descarriar *vt* to lead astray; *vr* be lost, be separated (from others); *fig* go astray

descarrilamiento *m*, derailment

descarrilar *vi* to run off the track, be derailed

descarrío *m*, losing one's way

descartar *vt* to put aside; *vr* discard (cards); shirk, make excuses

descarte *m*, discard (cards); excuse, pretext

descascarar *vt* to peel; shell; *vr* peel off

descendencia *f*, descendants, offspring; lineage, descent

descender *vi irr* to descend; flow (liquids); (*with de*) descend from, derive from; *vt* lower, let down. See **entender**

descendiente *mf* descendant, offspring. *a* descending

descendimiento *m*, descent

descenso *m*, descent; lowering, letting down; degradation

descentralizar *vt* to decentralize

desceñir(se) *vt* and *vr irr* to ungird, remove a girdle, etc. See **ceñir**

descepar *vt* to tear up by the roots; *fig* extirpate

descercado *a* unfenced, open

descercar *vt* to pull down a wall or fence; *mil* raise a siege

descerrajar *vt* to remove the locks (of doors, etc.)

descifrable *a* decipherable

descifrador *m*, decipherer, decoder

descifrar *vt* to decipher; decode

descinchar *vt* to loosen or remove girths (of horse)

desclavar *vt* to remove nails; unnail, unfasten

descoagular *vt* to liquefy, dissolve, melt

descobijar *vt* to uncover; undress

descocado *a inf* brazen, saucy

descoco *m, inf* impudence

descogollar *vt* to prune a tree of shoots; remove hearts (of lettuces, etc.)

descolar *vt irr* to cut off or dock an animal's tail; *Mexico* slight, snub. See **colar**

descolgar *vt irr* to unhang; lower; *vr* lower oneself (by rope, etc.); come down, descend; *inf* come out (with), utter. See **volcar**

descoloramiento *m*, discoloration

descolorar *vt* to discolor; *vr* be discolored

descolorido *a* discolored; pale-colored; pallid

descollar *vi irr* to excel, be outstanding. See **degollar**

descomedido *a* excessive, disproportionate; rude

descomedimiento *m*, disrespect, lack of moderation, rudeness

descomedirse *vr irr* to be disrespectful or rude. See **pedir**

descompasarse *vr* See **descomedirse**

descomponer *vt irr* to disorder, disarrange; *chem* decompose; unsettle; *vr* go out of order; rot, putrefy; be ailing; lose one's temper. See **poner**

descomposición *f*, disorder, confusion; discomposure; *chem* decomposition; putrefaction

descompostura *f*, decomposition; slovenliness, dirtiness, untidiness; impudence, rudeness

descompuesto *a* rude, impudent; *Lat. Am.* tipsy; *Venezuela* ill, sick

descomunal *a* enormous, extraordinary

desconcertar *vt irr* to disorder, disarrange; dislocate (bones); disconcert, embarrass; *vr* disagree; be impudent. See **acertar**

desconcharse *vr* to flake off, peel

desconcierto *m*, disorder, disarrangement; dislocation; embarrassment; disagreement; impudence

desconectar *vt* to disconnect; switch off

desconfianza *f*, lack of confidence

desconfiar *vi* to lack confidence

desconformidad *f*, See **disconformidad**

desconformismo *m*, non-conformism

desconocer *vt irr* to forget; be unaware of; deny, disown; pretend ignorance; not to understand (persons, etc.). See **conocer**

desconocido (-da) *a* unknown; ungrateful. *n* stranger; ingrate

desconocimiento *m*, unawareness; ignorance; ingratitude

desconsiderado *a* inconsiderate; discourteous; rash

desconsolación *f*, affliction, trouble

desconsolar *vt irr* to afflict, make disconsolate; *vr* grieve, despair. See **colar**

desconsuelo *m*, anguish, affliction, despair

descontar *vt irr com* to make a discount; ignore, discount; take for granted, leave aside. See **contar**

descontentadizo *a* discontented, difficult to please; fastidious, finicky

descontentar *vt* to displease; *vr* be dissatisfied

descontento *m*, discontent, dissatisfaction

descontextualizar *vt* to take out of context

descontrolarse *vr* to lose control, lose control of oneself.

desconveniencia *f*, inconvenience, unsuitability, disagreement

desconvenir *vi irr* to disagree; be unsuitable, unsightly or odd (things). See **venir**

descorazonamiento *m*, depression, despair

descorazonar *vt* to tear out the heart; depress, discourage

descorchar *vt* to take the cork from cork tree; draw a cork (bottles); force, break into (safes)

descorrer *vt* to re-run (race, etc.); draw back (curtains, etc.); *vi* run, flow (liquids)

descorrimiento *m*, overflow (liquids)

descortés *a* impolite

descortesía *f*, impoliteness, discourtesy

descortezadura *f*, peeling (of bark)

descortezar *vt* to decorticate; remove crust (bread, etc.); polish, civilize

descoser *vt sew* to unpick; *vr* be unpicked; be indiscreet or tactless

descosido *a* tactless, talkative; *fig* disjointed; desultory; unsewn. *m*, *sew* rent, hole

descoyuntamiento *m*, dislocation (bones); irritation, bore; ache, pain

descoyuntar *vt* to dislocate (bones); bore, annoy; *vr* be dislocated

descrédito *m*, fall in value (things); discredit (persons)

descreer *vt irr* to disbelieve; depreciate, disparage (persons). See **creer**

descreído (-da) *a* unbelieving. *n* unbeliever; infidel

descremar *vt*, *Lat. Am.* to skim (milk)

describir *vt* to describe; outline, sketch. *Past Part.* **descrito**

descripción *f*, description; *law* inventory

descriptible *a* describable

descriptivo *a* descriptive

descuajar *vt* to liquefy; *inf* discourage; *agr* pull up by the root

descuartizar *vt* to quarter; joint (meat); *inf* carve, cut into pieces, break up

descubierto *a* bareheaded; exposed. *m*, deficit. **al d.**, openly, in the open, without shelter. **girar en d.**, to overdraw (a bank account)

descubridero *m*, viewpoint, lookout

descubridor (-ra) *n* discoverer; inventor; explorer. *m*, *mil* scout

descubrimiento *m*, find; discovery; revelation; newly discovered territory

descubrir *vt* to reveal; show; discover; learn; unveil (memorials, etc.); *vr* remove one's hat; show oneself, reveal one's whereabouts. *Past Part.* **descubierto**

descuello *m*, extra height; *fig* pre-eminence; arrogance

descuento *m*, reduction; *com* rebate, discount

descuidado *a* negligent; careless; untidy; unprepared

descuidar *vt* to relieve (of responsibility, etc.); distract, occupy (attention, etc.); *vi* and *vr* be careless; *vr* (*with de* or *en*) neglect

descuido *m*, carelessness, negligence; oversight, mistake; incivility; forgetfulness; shameful act

desde *prep* since, from (time or space); after (e.g. **d. hoy,** from today). **d. la ventana,** from the window. **d. allá,** from the other world. **d. aquella época,** since that time

desdecir *vi irr* (*with de*) to degenerate, be less good than; be discordant, clash; be unworthy of; *vr* unsay one's words, retract. See **decir**

desdén *m*, indifference, coldness; disdain, scorn

desdentado *a* toothless; *zool* edentate

desdentar *vt* to remove teeth

desdeñar *vt* to scorn; *vr* (*with de*) dislike, be reluctant

desdeñoso *a* disdainful, scornful

desdibujado *a* badly drawn; blurred, confused

desdicha *f*, misfortune; extreme poverty, misery. **por d.**, unfortunately

desdichado *a* unfortunate; *inf* timid, weak-kneed

desdicharse *vr* to bewail one's fate

desdinerarse una fortuna *vr* to spend a fortune

desdoblar *vt* to unfold

desdorar *vt* to remove the gilt; *fig* tarnish, sully

desdoro *m*, discredit, dishonor

deseable *a* desirable

desear *vt* to desire; yearn or long for

desecar *vt* to dry; *vr* be desiccated

desechar *vt* to reject, refuse; scorn; cast out, expel; put away (thoughts, etc.); cast off (old clothes); turn (key); give up

desecho *m*, residue, rest, remains; cast-off; scorn; *Lat. Am.* shortcut

desembalar *vt* to unpack

desembanastar *vt* to take out of a basket; *inf* unsheath (sword); *vr* break loose (animals); *inf* get out, alight

desembarazar *vt* to clear of obstruction; disembarrass, free; vacate; *vr fig* rid oneself of obstacles

desembarazo *m*, freedom, insouciance, naturalness

desembarcadero *m*, landing-stage

desembarcar *vt* to unload; *vi* disembark; alight from vehicle

desembarco *m*, disembarkation, landing; staircase landing

desembargar *vt* to free of obstacles or impediments; *law* remove an embargo

desembargo *m*, *law* removal of an embargo

desembarque *m*, disembarkation, landing

desembarrancar *vt* and *vi naut* to refloat

desembaular *vt* to unpack from a trunk; disinter, empty; *inf* unbosom oneself

desembocadero *m*, exit, way out; mouth (rivers, etc.)

desembocadura *f*, mouth (rivers, etc.); street opening

desembocar *vi* (*with en*) to lead to, end in; flow into (rivers)

desembolsar *vt* to take out of a purse; pay, spend

desembolso *m*, disbursement; expenditure

desemboscarse *vr* to get out of the wood; extricate oneself from an ambush

desembozar *vt* to unmuffle

desembozo *m*, uncovering of the face

desembragar *vt mech* to disengage (the clutch, etc.)

desembravecer *vt irr* to tame, domesticate. See **conocer**

desembriagar(se) *vt* and *vr* to sober up (after a drinking bout)

desembrollar *vt inf* to disentangle, unravel

desemejanza *f*, unlikeness

desemejar *vi* to be unlike; *vt* disfigure, deform

desempacar *vt* to unpack

desempapelar *vt* to unwrap, remove the paper from; remove wallpaper

desempaquetar *vt* to unpack

desemparejar *vt* to split (a pair); make unequal

desemparentado *a* without relatives

desempedrar *vt irr* to take up the flags (of a pavement). See **acertar**

desempeñar *vt* to redeem (pledges); free from debt; fulfil (obligations, etc.); take out of pawn; hold, fill (an office); extricate (from difficulties, etc.); perform, carry out; *theat* act

desempeño *m*, redemption of a pledge; fulfilment (of an obligation, etc.); performance, accomplishment; *theat* acting of a part

desempolvar *vt* to free from dust, dust

desenamorar *vt* to kill the affection of; *vr* fall out of love

desencadenar *vt* to unchain, unfetter; *fig* unleash, let loose; *vr fig* break loose

desencajamiento *m*, disjointedness, dislocation; ricketiness, broken-down appearance

desencajar *vt* to disconnect, disjoint; dislocate; *vr* be out of joint; be contorted (of the face); be tired looking

desencaje *m*, See **desencajamiento**

desencantar *vt* to disenchant

desencanto *m*, disenchantment; disillusionment

desencerrar *vt irr* to set at liberty; unlock; disclose, reveal. See **acertar**

desenchufar *vt* to disconnect, unplug (electric plugs, etc.)

desenclavijar *vt* to remove the pegs or pins; disconnect, disjoint

desencoger *vt* to unfold, spread out; *vr* grow bold

desencolerizar *vt* to placate; *vr* lose one's anger, grow calm

desenconar *vt* to reduce (inflammation); appease (anger, etc.); *vr* become calm

desencono *m*, reduction of inflammation; appeasement (of anger, etc.)

desencordelar *vt* to untie the ropes (of), unstring

desencorvar *vt* to straighten (curves, etc.)

desenfadado *a* expeditious; natural, at ease; gay; forward, bold; wide, spacious

desenfadar *vt* to appease, make anger disappear

desenfado *m*, freedom; ease; unconcern, frankness

desenfrailar *vi* to leave the cloister, become secularized; *inf* emancipate oneself

desenfrenar *vt* to unbridle (horses); *vr* give rein to one's passions, etc.; break loose (storms, etc.)

desenfreno *m*, license, lasciviousness; complete freedom from restraint

desengalanar *vt* to strip of ornaments

desenganchar *vt* to unhook; uncouple; unfasten; unharness

desengañador *a* undeceiving

desengañar *vt* to undeceive, disillusion

desengaño *m*, undeceiving, disabuse; disillusionment

desengarzar *vt* to loosen from its setting; unlink, unhook, unclasp

desengastar *vt* to remove from its setting (jewelry, etc.)

desengrasar *vt* to remove the grease from, clean; *vi inf* grow thin

desenlace *m*, loosening, untying; *lit* denouement, climax (of play, etc.)

desenlatar *vt*, *Lat. Am.* to open (canned food)

desenlazar *vt* to untie, unloose; *lit* unravel (a plot)

desenlosar *vt* to remove flagstones

desenmarañar *vt* to disentangle; *fig* straighten out

desenmascarar *vt* to remove the mask from; *fig* unmask

desenmudecer *vi irr* to be freed of a speech impediment; break silence, speak. See **conocer**

desenojar *vt* to soothe, appease; *vr* distract oneself, amuse oneself

desenojo *m*, relenting, abatement of anger

desenredar *vt* to disentangle; *fig* set right; straighten out; *vr* extricate oneself, get out of a difficulty

desenredo *m*, disentanglement; *lit* climax

desenroscar *vt Lat. Am.* to unscrew

desentablar *vt* to tear up planks or boards; disorder, disrupt

desentenderse *vr irr* (*with de*) to pretend to be ignorant of; take no part in. See **entender**

desenterrador *m*, disinterrer, unearther

desenterramiento *m*, disinterment; *fig* unearthing, recollection

desenterrar *vt irr* to unbury, disinter; rummage out; *fig* unearth, bring up, recall. See **acertar**

desentoldar *vt* to take away an awning; *fig* strip of ornament

desentonar *vt* to humiliate; *vi mus* be out of tune;

speak rudely; *vr* be inharmonious; raise the voice (anger, etc.), behave badly

desentono *m*, bad behavior, rudeness; *mus* discord; grating quality or harshness (of voice)

desentorpecer *vt irr* to restore feeling to (numbed limbs); free from torpor; *vr* become bright and intelligent. See **conocer**

desentramparse *vr inf* free oneself from debt

desentrañar *vt* to disembowel; *fig* unravel, penetrate; *vr* give away one's all

desentumecer *vt irr* to free from numbness (limbs); *vr* be restored to feeling (numb limbs). See **conocer**

desenvainar *vt* to unsheath; *inf* reveal, bring into the open

desenvoltura *f*, naturalness, ease, freedom; eloquence, facility (of speech); effrontery, audacity, shamelessness (especially in women)

desenvolver *vt irr* to unroll; unfold; *fig* unravel, explain; *fig* develop, work out (theories, etc.); *vr* unroll; unfold; lose one's timidity, blossom out; be over-bold; extricate oneself (from a difficulty). See **resolver**

desenvuelto *a* natural, easy; impudent, bold

deseo *m*, desire, will, wish

deseoso *a* desirous, wishful

desequilibrar(se) *vt* and *vr* to unbalance

desequilibrio *m*, lack of balance; confusion, disorder; mental instability

deserción *f*, *mil* desertion. **d. estudiantil,** school dropout

desertar *vt mil* to desert; *inf* quit

desertor *m*, *mil* deserter; *inf* quitter

deservicio *m*, disservice

desesperación *f*, desperation, despair; frenzy, violence

desesperado *a* desperate, hopeless; frenzied

desesperanza *f*, despair; hopelessness

desesperanzar *vt* to render hopeless; *vr* despair, lose hope

desesperar *vt* to make hopeless; *inf* annoy, make furious; *vr* lose hope, despair; be frenzied

desestañar *vt* to unsolder

desestimación *f*, disrespect, lack of esteem; rejection

desestimar *vt* to scorn; reject

desfachatado *a inf* impudent, brazen

desfachatez *f*, *inf* effrontery, cheek

desfalcador (-ra) *a* embezzling. *n* embezzler

desfalcar *vt* to remove a part of; embezzle

desfalco *m*, diminution, reduction; embezzlement

desfallecer *vt irr* to weaken; *vi* grow weak; faint, swoon. See **conocer**

desfallecimiento *m*, weakness, languor; depression, discouragement; faint, swoon

desfavorable *a* unfavorable; hostile, contrary

desfavorecer *vt irr* to withdraw one's favor, scorn; disfavor; oppose. See **conocer**

desfiguración *f*, deformation; disfigurement

desfigurar *vt* to deform, misshape; disfigure; *fig* disguise, mask; obscure, darken; distort, misrepresent; *vr* be disfigured (by rage, etc.)

desfijar *vt* to unfix, pull off, remove

desfiladero *m*, defile, gully

desfilar *vi* to walk in file; *inf* file out; *mil* file or march past

desfile *m*, *mil* march past; parade; walk past; procession

desflecarse (en) *vr* to disintegrate (into)

desfloración *f*, defloration

desflorar *vt* to tarnish, stain; deflower, violate; *fig* touch upon, deal lightly with

desfortalecer *vt irr mil* to dismantle a fortress. See **conocer**

desfruncir *vt* to unfold, shake out

desgaire *m*, untidiness, slovenliness; affectation of carelessness (in dress); scornful gesture. **al d.,** with an affectation of carelessness, negligently

desgajar *vt* to tear off a tree branch; break; *vr* break off; dissociate oneself (from)

desgalgar *vt* to throw headlong

desgana *f*, lack of appetite; lack of interest, indifference; reluctance

desganar *vt* to dissuade; *vr* lose one's appetite; become bored or indifferent, lose interest

desgarbado *a* slovenly, slatternly; gawky, graceless

desgarrado *a* dissolute, vicious; impudent, brazen

desgarrador *a* tearing; heart-rending

desgarrar *vt* to tear; *vr* leave, tear oneself away

desgarro *m*, tearing; rent, breach; boastfulness, impudence, effrontery; *Lat. Am.* phlegm

desgastar *vt* to corrode, wear away; spoil, corrupt; *vr* lose one's vigor, grow weak; wear away

desgaste *m*, attrition; wearing down or away; corrosion; wear and tear

desgobernado *a* uncontrolled (of persons)

desgobernar *vt irr* to upset or rise against the government; dislocate (bones); *naut* neglect the tiller; *vr* affect exaggerated movements in dancing. See **recomendar**

desgobierno *m*, misgovernment; mismanagement; maladministration; disorder, tumult

desgomar *vt* to ungum (fabrics)

desgorrarse *vr* to doff one's cap, doff one's hat

desgoznar *vt* to unhinge; *vr fig* lose one's self-control

desgracia *f*, misfortune, adversity; mishap, piece of bad luck; disgrace, disfavor; disagreeableness, brusqueness; ungraciousness. **por d.,** unhappily, unfortunately

desgraciado *a* unfortunate, unhappy; unlucky; dull, boring; disagreeable

desgraciar *vt* to displease; spoil the development (of), destroy; maim; *vr* fall out of friendship; be out of favor; turn out badly, fail; be destroyed or spoiled; be maimed

desgranar *vt agr* to thresh, flail; *vr* break (string of beads, etc.)

desgrasante *m*, grease remover

desgreñar *vt* to dishevel the hair; *vr inf* pull each other's hair, come to blows

desguarnecer *vt irr* to strip of trimming; *mil* demilitarize; *mil* disarm; dismantle; unharness. See **conocer**

desguazar *vt* to break up (ships)

deshabitado *a* uninhabited, empty

deshabitar *vt* to desert, quit, leave (a place)

deshabituar *vt* to disaccustom; *vr* lose the habit, become unaccustomed

deshacer *vt irr* to undo; destroy; *mil* rout, defeat; take to pieces; melt; pulp (paper); untie (knots, etc.); open (parcels); diminish, decrease; break in pieces, smash; *fig* obstruct, spoil; *vr* be wasted or spoiled; be full of anxiety; vanish; try or work very hard; injure oneself; be emaciated, grow extremely thin; (*with de*) part with. **d. agravios,** to right wrongs. See **hacer**

desharrapado *a* tattered, shabby

deshebillar *vt* to unbuckle

deshebrar *vt* to unravel; shred

deshecha *f*, pretense, evasion; courteous farewell; obligatory departure

deshechizar *vt* to disenchant

deshelar *vt irr* to thaw, melt. See **acertar**

desherbar *vt irr* to pull up weeds. See **acertar**

desheredar *vt fig* lower oneself

desherrar *vt irr* to unfetter, unchain; strike off horseshoes; *vr* lose a shoe (horses). See **acertar**

desherrumbrar *vt* to remove the rust from; clean off rust from

deshidratación *f*, dehydration

deshidratar *vt* to dehydrate

deshielo *m*, thaw

deshilado *a* in single file. *m*, *sew* drawn-thread work (gen. *pl*). **a la deshilada,** *mil* in file formation; secretly

deshiladura *f*, unraveling

deshilar *vt* to unravel; *sew* draw threads; *cul* shred, grate

deshilvanado *a fig* disjointed, disconnected

deshilvanar *vt sew* to remove the tacking threads

deshincar *vt* to pull out, remove, draw out

deshinchar *vt* to remove a swelling; deflate; lessen the anger of; *vr* decrease, subside (swellings); deflate; *inf* grow humble

deshojar *vt* to strip the leaves from, strip the petals from; *Lat. Am.* husk (corn); peel (fruit)

deshollejar *vt* to skin, peel (fruit); shell (peas, etc.)

deshollinador *m*, chimney-sweep; wall-brush; chemical chimney cleaner

deshollinar *vt* to sweep chimneys; clean down walls; *inf* examine closely

deshonestidad *f*, immodesty, shamelessness; indecency

deshonesto *a* shameless, immodest; dissolute, vicious; indecent

deshonor *m*, dishonor; disgrace, insult

deshonra *f*, dishonor

deshonrabuenos *mf inf* slanderer; degenerate

deshonrador (-ra) *a* dishonorable. *n* dishonorer

deshonrar *vt* to dishonor; insult; seduce (women)

deshonroso *a* dishonorable, insulting, indecent

deshora *f*, inconvenient time. **a d.,** *or* **a deshoras,** at an inconvenient time, unseasonably; extempore

deshuesar *vt* to bone, remove the bone (from meat); stone (fruit)

deshumedecer *vt irr* to dry; *vr* become dry. See **conocer**

desidia *f*, negligence; laziness

desidioso *a* negligent; lazy

desierto *a* deserted, uninhabited, solitary. *m*, desert; wilderness

designación *f*, designation; appointment

designar *vt* to plan, intend; designate; appoint

designio *m*, intention, idea

desigual *a* unequal; uneven (ground); rough; arduous, difficult; changeable

desigualar *vt* to make unequal; *vr* prosper

desigualdad *f*, inequality; unevenness, rockiness; *fig* changeability; variability

desilusión *f*, disillusionment; disappointment

desilusionar *vt* to disillusion; *vr* become disillusioned; be undeceived

desinclinar *vt* to dissuade

desinfectante *a* and *m*, disinfectant

desinfectar *vt* to disinfect

desinflar *vt* to deflate

desinterés *m*, disinterestedness

desinteresado *a* disinterested; generous

desinteresarse *vr* to lose interest, grow indifferent

desistencia, *f*, **desistimiento** *m*, desistance, ceasing

desistir *vi* to desist; cease; *law* renounce

desjuntamiento *m*, separation; division

desjuntar(se) *vt* and *vr* to separate; divide

deslavado *a* brazen, impudent

deslavar *vt* to wash superficially; spoil by washing, take away the body of (cloth, etc.)

desleal *a* disloyal, treacherous

deslealtad *f*, disloyalty

desleír *vt irr* to dissolve; dilute. See **reír**

deslenguado *a* shameless, foulmouthed

deslenguar *vt* to remove the tongue; *vr inf* be insolent

desliar *vt* to untie, undo, unloose

desligadura *f*, untying, loosening

desligar *vt* to unfasten, unbind; *fig* solve, unravel; relieve of an obligation; *mus* play staccato; *vr* come unfastened, grow loose. **desligarse de,** to weasel out of, wiggle out of (a promise)

deslindador *m*, one who fixes boundaries or limits

deslindar *vt* to fix the boundaries (of); limit, circumscribe

deslinde *m*, demarcation, boundary

desliz *m*, slipping, slip, slide; skid; indiscretion, slip; peccadillo, trifling fault

deslizadero *m*, slippery place; chute

deslizadizo *a* slippery

deslizar *vt* to slip, slide; skid; *vr* commit an indiscretion; speak or act unwisely; escape, slip away; slip; skid

deslucido *a* fruitless, vain; stupid, clumsy, awkward; discolored; tarnished, dull; unsuccessful

deslucimiento *m*, clumsiness, gracelessness; failure, lack of success

deslucir *vt irr* to fade; discolor, stain; tarnish; spoil; sully the reputation of; *vr* do a thing badly, fail at. See **lucir**

deslumbrador *a* dazzling

deslumbramiento *m*, brilliant light, glare, dazzle; bewilderment, confusion

deslumbrar *vt* to dazzle; confuse, bewilder; *fig* daze (with magnificence)

deslustrar *vt* to dull, dim, tarnish; frost (glass); discredit, sully (reputation)

deslustre *m*, dullness, tarnish; frosting (of glass); disgrace, stigma

deslustroso *a* ugly, unsuitable, unbecoming

desmadejar *vt* to debilitate, enervate

desmalezar *vt, Lat. Am.* to clear the underbrush from; weed

desmán *m*, outrageous behavior; disaster, misfortune

desmandado *a* disobedient

desmandar *vt* to cancel, revoke (orders); withdraw (an offer). *vr* behave badly; stray

desmantelado *a* dismantled, dilapidated

desmantelamiento *m*, dismantling; dilapidation

desmantelar *vt* to dismantle; abandon, forsake

desmaña *f*, lack of dexterity, clumsiness, awkwardness

desmañado *a* clumsy, awkward, unhandy

desmayado *a* pale, faint (of colors); weak (of a voice)

desmayar *vt* to cause to faint; *vi* grow discouraged, lose heart; *vr* swoon, faint

desmayo *m*, depression, discouragement; faint, swoon

desmedido *a* disproportionate; excessive

desmedirse *vr* to misbehave, go too far

desmedrado *a* thin, emaciated; deteriorated, spoiled

desmedrar *vt* to spoil, ruin; *vi* deteriorate; decline

desmedro *m*, impairment; decline, deterioration. **en d. de,** to the detriment of

desmejora *f*, deterioration

desmejorar *vt* to spoil, impair, cause to deteriorate; *vr* deteriorate; *vi* and *vr* decline in health; lose one's beauty

desmelenar *vt* to ruffle or dishevel the hair

desmembración *f*, dismemberment

desmembrar *vt* to dismember; separate, divide

desmemoriarse *vr* to forget, lose one's memory

desmenguar *vt* to reduce, decrease; *fig* diminish

desmentida *f*, action of giving the lie to

desmentir *vt irr* to give the lie to; contradict, deny; lower oneself; behave unworthily; *vi* deviate (from right direction, etc.). See **sentir**

desmenuzar *vt* to crumble, break into small pieces; *fig* examine in detail; *vr* be broken up

desmeollar *vt* to remove the marrow of

desmerecedor *a* unworthy

desmerecer *vt irr* to become undeserving of; *vi* deteriorate; be inferior to. See **conocer**

desmesura *f*, insolence; disproportion; excess

desmesurado *a* disproportionate; excessive, enormous; insolent, uncivil

desmesurar *vt* to disarrange, disorder; *vr* be insolent

desmigajar(se) *vt* and *vr* to crumble

desmigar *vt cul* to make breadcrumbs

desmilitarizar *vt* to demilitarize

desmochar *vt* to lop off the top; pollard (trees)

desmonetización *f*, demonetization; conversion of coin into bullion

desmonetizar *vt* to convert money into bullion; demonetize; *vr* depreciate (shares, etc.)

desmontable *a* movable; sectional

desmontadura *f*, clearing; deforestation; leveling; demounting, dismounting

desmontar *vt* to clear wholly or partly of trees or shrubs; clear up (rubbish); level (ground); dismantle; dismount; uncock (firearms); *vi* and *vr* dismount (from horse, etc.)

desmonte *m*, clearing of trees and shrubs; clearing, cleared ground; timber remaining

desmoralización *f*, demoralization, corruption

desmoralizador *a* demoralizing

desmoralizar *vt* to demoralize, corrupt

desmoronamiento *m*, crumbling; decay, ruin

desmoronar *vt* to destroy, decay; crumble; *vr* crumble away, fall into ruin; decline, decay; wane, fade (power, etc.)

desmovilización *f*, demobilization

desmovilizar *vt* to demobilize

desnacificación *f*, denazification

desnatar *vt* to skim; *fig* take the cream or best

desnaturalización *f*, denaturalization

desnaturalizar *vt* to denaturalize; exile; deform, disfigure, pervert; *vr* give up one's country

desnivel *m*, unevenness; slope, drop

desnivelar(se) *vi* and *vr* to become uneven

desnudar *vt* to undress; *fig* despoil, strip, denude; *vr* undress oneself; deprive oneself

desnudez *f*, nudity; nakedness; bareness; plainness

desnudo *a* nude; ill-clad; bare, naked; clear, patent; *fig* destitute (of grace, etc.). *m*, *art* nude

desnutrición *f*, malnutrition

desobedecer *vt irr* to disobey. See **conocer**

desobediencia *f*, disobedience

desobediente *a* disobedient

desobligar *vt* to free from obligation; offend, hurt

desocupación *f*, lack of occupation; leisure

desocupado *a* idle; vacant, unoccupied

desocupar *vt* to empty; vacate; *vr* give up an employment or occupation

desodorante *a* and *m*, deodorant

desoir *vt irr* to pay no attention, pretend not to hear. See **oir**

desojar *vt* to break the eye of (needles, etc.); *vr* gaze intently

desolación *f*, destruction, desolation; affliction

desolador *a* desolate; grievous

desolar *vt irr* to lay waste, destroy; *vr* grieve, be disconsolate. See **contar**

desoldar *vt* to unsolder; *vr* become unsoldered

desolladero *m*, slaughterhouse

desollado *a inf* impertinent, barefaced. *m*, carcass

desolladura *f*, flaying, skinning; *inf* slander

desollar *vt* to flay, skin; harm, discredit. **d. vivo,** *inf* to extort an exorbitant price; slander. See **contar**

desopinado *a* discredited

desopinar *vt* to discredit, defame

desorden *m*, disorder, disarray; confusion; excess

desordenado *a* disordered; vicious; licentious

desordenar *vt* to disorder; confuse; *vr* go beyond the just limits; behave badly; be impertinent

desorganización *f*, disorganization

desorganizador *a* disorganizing

desorganizar *vt* to disorganize; disband

desorientación *f*, disorientation, loss of bearings; lack of method, confusion

desorientar *vt* to disorient; perplex, confuse; *vr* lose one's way; be disoriented

desovar *vi* to spawn

desove *m*, spawning; spawning season

desovillar *vt* to unwind; uncoil; uncurl; explain, clarify

despabiladeras *f pl*, snuffers

despabilado *a* alert, wide-awake; watchful, vigilant

despabiladura *f*, snuff of a candle, lamp, etc.

despabilar *vt* to snuff (a candle); trim (lamps); hasten; expedite; finish quickly; steal, rob; *fig* quicken (intelligence, etc.); *inf* kill; *vr* rouse oneself, wake up

despachador **(-ra)** *n* dispatcher, sender

despachar *vt* to expedite; dispatch, conclude; forward, send; attend to correspondence; sell; dismiss; *inf* serve in a shop; *inf* kill; *vi* hasten; carry letters to be signed (in offices, etc.); *vr* get rid of

despachero, -a *mf Chile* shopkeeper, storekeeper

despacho *m*, transaction, execution; study; office, room; department; booking-office; dispatch, shipment; expedient; commission, warrant; dispatch (diplomatic); telegram; telephone message. **d. particular,** private office

despachurrar *vt inf* to crush, squash; recount in a muddled fashion; *fig* squash flat, confound

despacio *adv* slowly, little by little; deliberately, leisurely. *interj* Careful! Gently now!

despacito *adv inf* very slowly

despalmador *m*, dockyard

despampanar *vt agr* to prune vines; *inf* amaze, stun, astound; *vi inf* relieve one's feelings; *vr inf* receive a serious injury (through falling)

desparpajar *vt* to spoil; *vi inf* chatter

desparpajo *m*, *inf* loquaciousness, pertness; disorder, muddle

desparramar *vt* to disperse, scatter; squander, waste (money, etc.); *vr* amuse oneself; be dissipated

despavorido *a* terrified, panicstricken

despechar *vt* to anger; make despair; *inf* wean; *vr* be angry; be in despair

despecho *m*, rancor, malice; despair. **a d. de,** in spite of

despechugar *vt* to cut off the breast (fowls); *vr inf* show the bosom

despectivo *a* contemptuous, depreciatory

despedazar *vt* to cut or break into pieces; *fig* break (heart, etc.)

despedida *f*, dismissal, discharge; seeing off (a visitor, etc.); farewell, good-by

despedir *vt irr* to throw out, emit, cast up; dismiss, discharge; see off (on a journey or after a visit); banish (from the mind); get rid of; *vr* say good-by; leave (employment). See **pedir**

despedregar *vt* to clear of stones

despegadamente *adv* uninterestedly, unconcernedly, indifferently

despegado *a inf* indifferent, unconcerned, cold

despegar *vt* to unstick; unglue; separate, detach; *vr* become estranged; come apart or unstuck; *vi aer* take off. **sin d. los labios,** without saying a word

despegue *m*, *aer* take-off

despeinar *vt* to disarrange the hair; undo the coiffure

despejado *a* lively, sprightly; logical, clear-cut; cloudless; spacious, unobstructed, clear

despejar *vt* to clear, free of obstacles; **d. el camino de,** to clear the way for; *fig* elucidate, solve; *math* find the value of; *vr* smarten up, grow gay; amuse oneself; clear up (weather, sky, etc.); improve (a patient)

despejo *m*, freeing of obstacles; smartness, gaiety; grace, elegance; perkiness; clear-sightedness, intelligence

despeluzar *vt* to disorder the hair; cause the hair to stand on end; horrify; *vr* stand on end (hair); be horrified or terrified

despeluznante *a* hair-raising, terrifying

despellejar *vt* to flay, skin; slander

despendedor **(-ra)** *n* spendthrift, waster

despender *vt* to spend; waste

despensa *f*, larder, pantry; store (of food); *naut* steward's room; stewardship

despensero **(-ra)** *n* steward; caterer; victualler; *naut* steward

despeñadero *m*, precipice, crag; dangerous undertaking, risk. *a* steep, precipitous

despeñar *vt* to precipitate, fling down from a height,

hurl down; *vr* fling oneself headlong; throw oneself into (vices, etc.)

despeño *m*, precipitation; headlong fall; *fig* collapse, ruin

despepitar *vt* to remove seeds or pips; *vr* vociferate; act wildly; *inf* desire, long (for)

desperdiciador (-ra) *a* squandering, wasting. *n* squanderer

desperdiciar *vt* to squander; *fig* misspend, waste

desperdicio *m*, waste; remains, leftovers (gen. *pl*)

desperdigar *vt* to separate, sever; scatter

desperecerse *vr irr* to crave, yearn (for). See **conocer**

desperezarse *vr* to stretch oneself

desperfecto *m*, imperfection, flaw; slight deterioration

despernado *a* weary, footsore

despertador (-ra) *a* awakening. *n* awakener. *m*, alarm clock; incentive, stimulus

despertar *vt irr* to awaken; bring to mind, recall; incite, stimulate; *vi* waken; *fig* wake up, become more intelligent. See **acertar**

despiadado *a* cruel, merciless

despicar *vt* to satisfy, content; *vr* revenge oneself

despierto *a* wide-awake, clever

despilfarrado *a* ragged, shabby; wasteful; spendthrift

despilfarrar *vt* to squander, waste

despilfarro *m*, slovenliness; waste, extravagance; mismanagement, maladministration

despintar *vt* to paint out; wash off the paint; efface, blot out; disfigure, deform; *vi* be unlike or unworthy (of); *vr* fade (colors); forget

despiojar *vt* to remove lice, delouse; *inf* rescue from misery

despique *m*, vengeance, revenge

despistar *vt* to throw off the scent; mislead

desplacer *vt irr* to displease. *m*, disgust, displeasure, sorrow. See **placer**

desplantar(se) *vt* and *vr* to deviate from the vertical

desplazamiento *m*, *naut* displacement

desplegadura *f*, unfolding

desplegar *vt irr* to unfold; spread open; *fig* reveal, disclose, explain; evince, display; *mil* deploy troops; *vr* unfold, open (flowers, etc.); *mil* deploy. See **cegar**

despliegue *m*, unfolding; spreading out; evincing, demonstration; *mil* deployment

desplomar *vt* to put out of the straight, cause to lean (walls, buildings); *vi* lean, tilt (buildings); topple, fall down (walls, etc.); collapse (people); be ruined

desplome *m*, collapse

desplomo *m*, tilt, cant, deviation from vertical

desplumar *vt* to remove feathers, pluck; rob, despoil

despoblación *f*, depopulation. **d. forestal,** deforestation

despoblado *m*, wilderness; deserted place

despoblar *vt* to depopulate; despoil, rob; *vr* become depopulated

despojador (-ra) *a* robbing, despoiling. *n* despoiler

despojar *vt* to plunder, despoil; dispossess; *vr* (*with de*) remove (garments, etc.); relinquish, give up

despojo *m*, pillaging, spoliation; booty, plunder; butcher's offal; *pl* remains, leavings; debris, rubble; corpse

despolvorear *vt* to remove dust; *fig* shake off

desposado *a* recently married; fettered, handcuffed. **los desposados,** the newlyweds

desposar *vt* to perform the marriage ceremony; *vr* become betrothed; marry

desposeer *vt* to dispossess; *vr* renounce one's possessions. See **creer**

desposeimiento *m*, dispossession

desposorio *m*, betrothal, promise of marriage; (gen. *pl*) wedding, marriage

déspota *m*, despot, tyrant

despótico *a* tyrannical

despotismo *m*, despotism

despotricarse *vr* to rave (against), rail (against)

despreciable *a* worthless, contemptible

despreciar *vt* to scorn, despise; *vr* despise oneself

despreciativo *a* contemptuous, scornful

desprecio *m*, contempt, scorn

desprender *vt* to loosen, remove, unfix; give off (gases, etc.); *vr* work loose, give way; deduce, infer; give away, deprive oneself (of)

desprendido *a* disinterested; generous

desprendimiento *m*, loosening; removal, separation; emission; indifference, lack of interest; generosity; impartiality

despreocupación *f*, fair mindedness, impartiality; lack of interest

despreocupado *a* unprejudiced, broadminded; indifferent, uninterested

despreocuparse *vr* to shake off prejudice; (*with de*) pay no attention to; set aside

desprestigiar *vt* to discredit; *vr* lose prestige; lose caste

desprestigio *m*, loss of prestige, discredit

desprevenido *a* unprepared, improvident

desproporción *f*, disproportion

desproporcionado *a* disproportionate; out of proportion

despropósito *m*, nonsense, absurdity

desproveer *vt irr* to deprive of necessities. See **creer**

despueble *m*, depopulation

después *adv* afterwards, after, next (of time and place) (e.g. **Vendrá d. de Pascua,** He will come after Easter. **Zaragoza viene d. de Madrid,** Saragossa comes after Madrid)

despuntar *vt* to blunt the point; *naut* double, sail round; *vi* show green, sprout; appear (the dawn); grow clever; *fig* stand out, excel

desquiciamiento *m*, unhinging; disconnecting; *fig* upsetting, throwing out of gear; downfall, fall from favor

desquiciar *vt* to unhinge; disconnect; *fig* throw out of gear, upset; banish from favor; *vr* become unhinged; *fig* be disordered; upset

desquitar(se) *vt* and *vr* to retrieve a loss; take revenge, retaliate

desquite *m*, compensation; revenge

desrielar *vt*, *Lat. Am.* to derail

destacamento *m*, *mil* detachment

destacar *vt mil* to detach; *vr* excel; be prominent; be conspicuous; *art* stand out

destajador *m*, smith's hammer

destajar *vt* to cut (cards); set forth conditions, stipulate, contract; *Lat. Am.* cut up

destajista *mf* pieceworker; jobber (worker)

destajo *m*, piecework; job. **a d.,** quickly and diligently. *inf* **hablar a d.,** to chatter, talk too much

destapar *vt* to remove the cover or lid; reveal, uncover; *vr* be uncovered; reveal oneself. **no destaparse,** to keep quiet, be mum

destartalado *a* tumble-down, rickety; poverty-stricken

destechado *a* roofless

destejar *vt* to remove tiles or slates; leave unprotected

destejer *vt* to unweave, unravel; *fig* undo, spoil

destello *m*, gleam, sparkle, brilliance; flash, beam, ray; *fig* gleam (of talent)

destemplado *a* out of tune; inharmonious; intemperate; *art* inharmonious; *inf* out of sorts, indisposed

destemplanza *f*, inclemency, rigor (weather); intemperance, excess, abuse; *inf* indisposition; lack of moderation (actions, speech)

destemplar *vt* to disturb, upset, alter; *mus* put out of tune; put to confusion; *vr* be unwell; *fig* go too far, behave badly; lose temper (metals)

destemple *m*, *mus* being out of tune; *med* indisposition; uncertainty (weather); lack of temper (metals); disturbance, disorder; intemperance, excess, confusion

desternillarse de risa to shake with laughter

desterrado (-da) *a* exiled. *n* exile

desterrar *vt irr* to exile; shake off the soil; *fig* discard, lay aside; extirpate (an error). See **recomendar**

destetar *vt* to wean

destete *m*, weaning

destiempo, a *adv* untimely, inopportunely

destierro *m*, banishment, exile; place of exile; remote place

destilación *f*, distillation

destilador (-ra) *n* distiller. *m*, still

destilar *vt* to distil; filter; *vi* to drip

destilatorio *a* distilling. *m*, distillery; still

destilería *f*, distillery

destinar *vt* to destine; appoint; assign

destino *m*, fate, destiny; post, appointment; destination. **con d. a,** going to, bound for

destitución *f*, destitution; discharge, dismissal

destituir *vt irr* (*with de*) to dismiss or discharge from (employment); deprive of. See **huir**

destorcer *vt irr* to untwist; straighten out; *vr naut* drift. See **torcer**

destornillado *a* reckless; *fig inf* with a screw loose

destornillador *m*, screwdriver

destornillamiento *m*, unscrewing

destornillar *vt* to unscrew; *vr* act rashly

destrenzar *vt* to unplait. **destrenzarse las cintas,** to unlace one's shoes

destreza *f*, dexterity; agility

destrón *m*, blind person's guide

destronamiento *m*, dethronement

destronar *vt* to dethrone, depose; oust

destroncamiento *m*, detruncation

destroncar *vt* to lop, detruncate (trees); dislocate, disjoint; mutilate; *fig* ruin, seriously harm; tire out; *Lat. Am.* uproot *vr* be exhausted or tired

destrozar *vt* to destroy; break in pieces, shatter; *mil* wipe out, annihilate; squander, dissipate

destrozo *m*, destruction, ruin; shattering; *mil* rout; dissipation, waste

destrozón *a* hard on wearing apparel, shoes, etc.

destrucción *f*, destruction; ruin, irreparable loss

destructible *a* destructible

destructivo *a* destructive

destructor (-ra) *a* destructive. *n* destroyer. *m, nav* destroyer

destruible *a* destructible

destruir *vt irr* to destroy, ruin, annihilate; frustrate, blast, disappoint; deprive of means of subsistence; squander, waste; *vr math* cancel. See **huir**

desuello *m*, flaying, skinning; forwardness, impertinence; extortion, fleecing. *fig inf* **¡Es un d.!** It's highway robbery!

desunión *f*, disunion, separation; *fig* discord, disharmony

desunir *vt* to disunite, separate; *fig* cause discord or disharmony

desusarse *vr* to fall into disuse, become obsolete

desuso *m*, disuse

desvaído *a* gaunt, lanky; pale, faded, dull (of colors)

desvainar *vt* to shell (peas, beans)

desvalido *a* unprotected, helpless

desvalijar *vt* to rifle (a suitcase, etc.); swindle

desvalimiento *m*, defenselessness, lack of protection; lack of favor; desertion, abandonment

desvalorización *f*, devaluation

desván *m*, garret

desvanecer *vt irr* to cause to disappear; disintegrate; make vain; remove; *vr* evaporate; faint, swoon; grow vain or conceited. See **conocer**

desvanecimiento *m*, faintness, loss of consciousness; vanity, conceit

desvarar *vt* to slip, slide; *naut* refloat

desvariar *vi* to be delirious; rave, talk wildly

desvarío *m*, foolish action, absurdity; delirium; monstrosity; whim, caprice

desvedar *vt* to raise a ban or prohibition

desvelar *vt* to keep awake; *vr* be sleepless; (*with por*) take great care over

desvelo *m*, sleeplessness, vigil; care, attention, vigilance; anxiety. **con d.,** watchfully

desvencijar *vt* to loosen, disconnect, disjoint; *vr* work loose, become disjointed

desventaja *f*, disadvantage. **estar en d.,** to be at a disadvantage

desventajoso *a* disadvantageous

desventura *f*, misfortune

desventurado *a* unfortunate; timid, faint-hearted; miserly

desvergonzado *a* shameless, brazen, impudent

desvergonzarse *vr irr* to be brazen, be impudent. See **avergonzar**

desvergüenza *f*, insolence; shamelessness

desvestir(se) *vt* and *vr irr* to undress. See **pedir**

desviación *f*, deviation, deflection

desviadero *m*, diversion; *rw* siding

desviar *vt* to divert, deflect; dissuade

desvío *m*, deviation; indifference, coldness; repugnance

desvirgar *vt* to deflower

desvirtuar *vt* to decrease in strength or merit

desvivirse *vr* (*with por*) to adore, love dearly; yearn for, be dying to; do one's best to please, (e.g. **Juan se desvive por servirme,** John does his best to help me)

detallar *vt* to tell in detail; relate

detalle *m*, detailed account; detail, particular

detallismo *m*, meticulous attention to details

detective *mf* detective

detector *m*, detector; *rad* catwhisker

detención *f*, stop, halt; delay; prolixity; arrest, detention. **con d.,** carefully, meticulously

detener *vt irr* to detain, stop; arrest; retain, keep; *vr* go slowly; tarry; halt, stop; (*with en*) pause over, stop at. See **tener**

detenido *a* timid, irresolute; miserable, mean

deterioración *f*, deterioration

deteriorar(se) *vt* and *vr* to deteriorate

determinación *f*, determination; daring; decision

determinado *a* resolute, determined

determinar *vt* to determine, limit; discern, distinguish; specify, appoint; decide, resolve; *law* define, judge; *vr* make up one's mind

determinativo *a* determining

determinismo *m*, determinism

determinista *mf* determinist. *a* deterministic

detersorio *a* and *m*, detergent

detestable *a* detestable

detestación *f*, detestation

detestar *vt* to abominate, detest

detonación *f*, detonation

detonador *m*, detonator

detonar *vi* to detonate

detractor (-ra) *a* slandering *n* detractor, slanderer

detraer *vt irr* to detract, take away; separate; slander. See **traer**

detrás *adv* behind, after (place). **por d.,** in the rear; *fig* behind one's back

detrimento *m*, detriment; moral harm. **en d. de,** to the detriment of

deuda *f*, debt; fault, offence; sin. **d. exterior,** foreign debt. **estar en d. con,** to be indebted to. **Perdónanos nuestras deudas,** Forgive us our trespasses

deudo *m*, relative, kinsman; kinship, relationship

deudor (-ra) *a* indebted. *n* debtor. **d. hipotecario,** mortgagor

devanadera *f*, bobbin, reel, spool; winder (machine)

devanador (-ra) *n* winder (person). *m*, spool, bobbin

devanar *vt* to reel, wind. *inf* **devanarse los sesos,** to rack one's brains

devanear *vi* to rave, talk nonsense

devaneo *m*, delirium; foolishness, nonsense; dissipation; love affair

devastación *f*, devastation

devastar *vt* to devastate, lay waste; *fig* destroy, ruin

develador *m*, betrayer

devengar *vt* to have a right to, earn (salary, interest, etc.)

devoción *f*, piety; affection, love; pious custom; prayer

devocionario *m*, prayer book

devolución *f*, restitution, return; its devolution

devolutivo *a law* returnable

devolver *vt irr* to restore to original state; return, give back; repay; **devolverse** *vr Lat. Am.* to come back, go back, return. See **resolver**

devorador (-ra) *a* devouring. *n* devourer

devorar *vt* to devour; destroy, consume

devoto (-ta) *a* devout, pious; devoted, fond. *n* devotee. *m*, object of devotion

día *m*, day; daylight; *pl* name or saint's day; birthday (e.g. **Hoy son los días de María,** This is Mary's saint's day (or birthday)). **d. de Año Nuevo,** New Year's Day. **d. de asueto,** day off. **d. de ayuno** or **de vigilia,** fast day. **d. del cura,** *humorous* wedding day. **d. del juicio,** Day of Judgment. **d. de los difuntos,** All Souls' Day. **d. de recibo,** at home day. **d. de Reyes,** Epiphany (when Spanish children receive their Christmas presents). **d. de trabajo** or **d. laborable,** working day. **d. por medio,** every other day. **días caniculares,** dog days. **d. por d.,** day by day. **al d.,** up to date; per day. **al otro d.,** next day. **¡Buenos días!** Good morning! Good day! **de d.,** by day. **de d. en d.,** from day to day. **de un d. a otro,** any time now, very soon. **el d. de mañana,** tomorrow, the near future. **un d. sí y otro no,** every other day. **vivir al d.,** to live up to one's income

diabético *a* diabetic

diablillo *m*, *dim* devilkin, imp; *inf* madcap

diablo *m*, devil; Satan; *fig* fiend. *inf* **d. cojuelo,** mischievous devil; *fig inf* imp. *inf* **Anda el d. suelto,** The Devil's abroad, there's trouble. *inf* **tener el d. en el cuerpo,** to be as clever as the Devil; be mischievous

diablura *f*, mischief, prank; devilry

diabólico *a* diabolical, devilish; *inf* fiendish, iniquitous

diaconisa *f*, deaconess

diácono *m*, deacon

diadema *f*, diadem; crown; tiara

diafanidad *f*, transparency

diáfano *a* transparent, diaphanous

diafragma *m*, *anat mech* diaphragm; sound-box (of a phonograph)

diagnosticar *vt med* to diagnose

diagnóstico *a* diagnostic. *m*, diagnosis. **d. precoz,** early diagnosis

diagonal *a* diagonal; oblique

diagrama *m*, diagram

diagramación *f*, layout (of a publication)

dialectal *a* dialect

dialéctica *f*, dialectic

dialéctico *a* dialectic. *m*, logician

dialecto *m*, dialect

dialogar *vi* to hold dialogue, converse; *vt* write dialogue

diálogo *m*, dialogue

diamante *m*, diamond; miner's lamp; glass-cutting diamond. **d. bruto,** rough diamond

diamantífero *a* diamond-bearing

diamantino *a* diamantine; *poet* adamant

diamantista *mf* diamond-cutter; diamond merchant

diámetro *m*, diameter

diana *f*, *mil* reveille; bull's-eye (of a target); the moon

¡diantre! *interj inf* the deuce!

diapasón *m*, *mus* tuning fork; diapason; neck (of violins, etc.). **d. normal,** tuning fork. **d. vocal,** pitch-pipe

diapositiva *f*, *phot* diapositive; (lantern) slide

diario *a* daily. *m*, diary; daily paper; daily expenses. **d. de navegación,** ship's log. **d. de viaje,** travel diary, trip journal

diarismo *m*, *Lat. Am.* journalism

diarista *mf* journalist, diarist

diarrea *f*, diarrhea

diatónico *a mus* diatonic

diatriba *f*, diatribe

diávolo *m*, diabolo (game)

dibujante *m*, sketcher; draftsman; designer

dibujar *vt art* to draw; describe, depict; *vr* appear, be revealed; be outlined, stand out

dibujo *m*, drawing; sketch, design, pattern; depiction, description. **d. a la pluma,** pen-and-ink drawing. **d. a pulso,** freehand drawing. **d. del natural,** drawing from life

dicción *f*, word; diction, language, style

diccionario *m*, dictionary

díceres *m pl WH* news

diciembre *m*, December

dictado *m*, title of honor; dictation; *pl* promptings (of heart, etc.). **escribir al d.,** to write to dictation

dictador *m*, dictator

dictadura *f*, dictatorship

dictamen *m*, judgment, opinion

dictaminar *vi* to give judgment or opinion

dictar *vt* to dictate; suggest, inspire; *Lat. Am.* give (a lecture). **dictar fallo,** to hand down a decision, render judgment

dictatorial, dictatorio *a* dictatorial

dicterio *m*, taunt, insult

dicha *f*, happiness; good fortune. **por d.,** by chance; fortunately

dicharacho *m*, *inf* vulgar expression, slangy expression

dicho *m*, saying, phrase, expression; witty remark; *law* declaration; *inf* insult. *a* said, aforementioned. *past part* **decir,** "said." **D. y hecho,** No sooner said than done. **Del d. al hecho hay muy gran trecho,** There's many a slip 'twixt the cup and the lip. **Lo d. d.,** The agreement stands

dichoso *a* happy; lucky; *inf* blessed, wretched, darn

didáctica *f*, didactics

didáctico *a* didactic

diecinueve *a* and *m*, nineteen

diecinuevavo *a* and *m*, nineteenth

dieciochavo *a* and *m*, eighteenth

dieciocheno *a* See **décimoctavo**

dieciocho *a* and *m*, eighteen

dieciséis *a* and *m*, sixteen

dieciseisavo *a* and *m*, sixteenth

dieciseiseno *a* See **décimosexto**

diecisiete *a* and *m*, seventeen

diecisieteavo *a* and *m*, seventeenth

diente *m*, tooth; tooth (of saw, etc.); tusk; cog (of wheel); prong (of fork); tongue (of a buckle). **d. de leche,** milk-tooth. *bot* **d. de león,** dandelion. **d. de perro,** *sew* feather-stitch. *inf* **dar d. con d.,** to chatter (teeth). *fig inf* **enseñar** (or **mostrar**) **los dientes,** to show one's teeth; threaten. *inf* **estar a d.,** to be famished. **hablar entre dientes,** to mutter; fume, grumble. *inf* **tener buen d.,** to have a good appetite. **traer a uno entre dientes,** to loathe someone; speak scandal of

Diepa Dieppe

diestra *f*, right hand; protection

diestro *a* right (hand); skilful, dextrous; shrewd; astute, cunning; favorable, happy. *m*, expert fencer; bullfighter; halter; bridle

dieta *f*, *med* diet; *inf* fast, abstinence; legislative assembly; travel allowance (gen. *pl*); day's journey of ten leagues; daily fee (gen. *pl*)

dietario *m*, household accounts' book

dietética *f*, dietetics

dietético *a* dietetic

dietista *mf* dietician

diez *a* ten; tenth. *m*, ten; decade of rosary

diezmar *vt* to tithe; decimate; punish every tenth person

diezmero (-ra) *n* tax-gatherer

diezmesino *a* ten months old

diezmillo *m, Mexico* sirloin

diezmo *m,* ten per cent tax; tithe

difamación *f,* defamation, libel

difamador (-ra) *a* libeling. *n* libeler

difamar *vt* to libel; denigrate

difamatorio *a* libelous, defamatory

diferencia *f,* unlikeness, dissimilarity; *math* difference; dissension, disagreement. **a d. de,** unlike; in contrast to

diferenciación *f,* differentiation. **d. del trabajo,** division of labor

diferencial *a* differential

diferenciar *vt* to differentiate; change the function (of); *vi* dissent, disagree; *vr* be different, differ; distinguish oneself

diferente *a* different, various

diferir *vt irr* to delay, retard; postpone; suspend, interrupt; *vi* be different. See **discernir**

difícil *a* difficult

dificultad *f,* difficulty; impediment, obstacle; objection

dificultar *vt* to raise difficulties; put obstacles in the way; *vi* think difficult (of achievements)

dificultoso *a* difficult; *inf* ugly (face, figure, etc.)

difidencia *f,* mistrust; lack of faith, doubt

difidente *a* mistrustful

difracción *f,* diffraction

difractar *vt* to diffract

difteria *f,* diphtheria

difundir *vt* to diffuse (fluids); spread, publish, divulge; *rad* broadcast

difunto (-ta) *a* and *n* deceased. *m,* corpse

difusión *f,* diffusion; prolixity; *rad* broadcasting

difusivo *a* diffusive

difuso *a* widespread, diffuse; prolix, wordy

digerible *a* digestible

digerir *vt irr* to digest; bear patiently; consider carefully; *chem* digest. See **sentir**

digestible *a* easily digested

digestivo *a* digestive

digesto *m, law* digest

digitación *f, mus* fingering

digital *a* digital. *f, bot* foxglove, digitalis

dígito *a* digital. *m, (ast math)* digit

dignación *f,* condescension

dignarse *vr* to deign, condescend

dignatario *m,* dignitary

dignidad *f,* dignity, stateliness; serenity, loftiness; high office or rank; high repute, honor; *ecc* dignitary

dignificar *vt* to dignify

digno *a* worthy, deserving; upright, honorable; fitting, suitable, appropriate

digresión *f,* digression

dije *m,* charm; trinket, any small piece of jewelry; *inf* person of excellent qualities, jewel

dilacerar *vt* to lacerate, tear flesh; *fig* discredit

dilación *f,* delay

dilapidación *f,* waste, dissipation, squandering

dilapidar *vt* to waste, squander

dilatación *f,* expansion; enlargement, widening; prolongation; *surg* dilatation; respite (in trouble)

dilatador *a* dilating. *m, surg* dilater

dilatar *vt* to dilate, enlarge; expand; delay, postpone; spread, publish abroad; prolong; *vr* expand; be prolix, spread oneself; *Lat. Am.* to be slow, take a long time

dilatorio *a* procrastinating, dilatory

dilección *f,* affection, love

dilema *m,* dilemma

diletantismo *m,* dilettantism

diligencia *f,* care, conscientiousness, industry; haste, briskness; diligence (coach); *inf* business, occupation. **hacer sus diligencias,** to try one's best

diligenciar *vt* to set on foot, put into motion

diligente *a* diligent, conscientious, industrious; speedy, prompt

dilucidación *f,* elucidation, clarification

dilucidar *vt* to elucidate, clarify

dilución *f,* dilution

diluir *vt irr* to dilute. See **huir**

diluviar *vi* to teem with rain

diluvio *m,* flood, inundation; *inf* very heavy rain, deluge; overabundance

dimanación *f,* emanation, source

dimanar *vi (with de)* to rise in (rivers); proceed from, originate in

dimensión *f,* dimension; size, extent

dimes y diretes *m pl, inf* back-chat

diminutivo *a* diminutive; diminishing; *gram* diminutive

diminuto *a* defective, incomplete; minute, very small

dimisión *f,* resignation (of office, etc.)

dimisorias *f pl, ecc* letter dimissory. *inf* **dar d. a uno,** to give a person his marching orders, dismiss

dimitente *a* resigning; retiring. *mf* resigner (of a post)

dimitir *vt* to resign (office, post, etc.)

Dinamarca Denmark

dinamarqués (-esa) *a* Danish. *n* Dane

dinámica *f,* dynamics

dinámico *a* dynamic

dinamita *f,* dynamite

dinamo *f,* dynamo

dinasta *mf* dynast

dinastía *f,* dynasty

dinástico *a* dynastic

dineral *m,* large amount of money, fortune

dinero *m,* money; Peruvian coin; wealth, fortune; currency. **d. contante, d. junto,** ready cash, **Poderoso caballero es Don D.,** Money talks

dinosauro *m,* dinosaur

dintel *m,* lintel; *Lat. Am.* threshold

diocesano *a* diocesan

diócesis *f,* diocese

Dios *m,* God; deity. **¡D. le guarde!** God keep you! **¡D. lo quiera!** God grant it! **D. mediante,** God willing (D.V.). **¡D. mío!** Good gracious! **De menos nos hizo D.,** Nothing is impossible, Never say die. *inf* **haber (or armarse) la de D. es Cristo,** to be the deuce of a row. **¡No lo quiera D.!** God forbid! **¡Plegue a D.!** Please God! **¡Por D.!** For goodness sake! Heavens! **¡Válgame D.!** Bless me! **¡Vaya Vd. con D.!** Goodbye! Off with you! **¡Vive D.!** By God!

diosa *f,* goddess

diploma *m,* license, bull; diploma. **d. de suficiencia,** general diploma

diplomacia *f,* diplomacy; tactfulness; *inf* astuteness

diplomarse *vr, Lat. Am.* to get one's degree, receive one's degree

diplomático *a* diplomatic; tactful; *inf* astute. *m,* diplomat. **cuerpo d.,** diplomatic corps

dipsomanía *f,* dipsomania

diptongo *m,* diphthong

diputación *f,* deputation; mission

diputado (-da) *n* deputy, delegate. **d. a Cortes,** member of the Spanish Parliament, congressman

diputar *vt* to appoint, depute; delegate; empower

dique *m,* dike; dam; dry dock; *fig* bulwark, check; **d. flotante,** floating dock

dirección *f,* direction; management, control, guidance; directorate; instruction; information; order, wish, command; editorial board; directorship, managership; (postal) address; managerial office. **d. cablegráfica,** cable address. **d. particular,** home address

directiva *f,* board, governing body

directivo *a* directive, control, ling, guiding, managing

directo *a* direct; straight

director (-ra) *a* directing, controlling. *n* director; manager; principal, head (schools, etc.); editor. **d. del ceremonial,** chief of protocol. **d. de escena,**

stagemanager. **d. espiritual,** *ecc* father confessor. **d. gerente,** managing director

directorio *a* directory, advising. *m,* directory; directorate, board of directors

dirigible *m,* airship

dirigir *vt* to direct; regulate; govern; supervise; guide; *mus* conduct; address (an envelope, etc.); keep (a shop, etc.); edit; put (a question); point (a gun); cast (a glance); *vr* go; wend one's way. **d. la palabra (a),** to speak to, address. **d. la vista a,** to look towards, look in the direction of, turn towards, turn in the direction of. **dirigirse a,** to go towards; make one's way to

dirimir *vt* to annul, make void; break, dissolve; settle (disputes, etc.)

discernimiento *m,* discernment; judgment; discrimination

discernir *vt irr* to discern, distinguish. *Pres. Ind.* **discierno, disciernes, discierne, disciernen.** *Pres. Subjunc.* **discierna, disciernas, discierna, disciernan**

disciplina *f,* discipline; system, philosophy, education; submission, obedience; subject (arts or science); *pl* scourge

disciplinante *a* disciplinary. *m,* scourge

disciplinar *vt* to train; educate; scourge, beat; discipline; *vr* scourge oneself

disciplinario *a* disciplinary

discipulado *m,* pupilship, studentship; education, teaching; discipleship; body of pupils (of a school, etc.)

discípulo (-la) *n* pupil, student; disciple, follower

disco *m,* discus; disk; phonograph record; *ast* disk. **d. de señales,** railway signal. **d. giratorio,** turntable (of a phonograph)

discóbolo *m,* discus thrower

díscolo *a* willful, unmanageable

disconformidad *f,* disagreement; disconformity

discontinuo *a* intermittent, discontinuous

discordancia *f,* discord, disagreement

discordar *vi* to be discordant; disagree; *mus* be out of tune

discorde *a* discordant; *mus* dissonant

discordia *f,* discord, disagreement

discreción *f,* discretion; circumspection; prudence, good sense; shrewdness; pithy or clever saying. **a d.,** at discretion; at will; voluntarily. *mil* **darse** (*or* **entregarse**) **a d.,** to surrender unconditionally

discrecional *a* optional, voluntary

discrepancia *f,* discrepancy; disagreement

discrepar *vi* to be discrepant; differ; disagree

discreto *a* discreet; ingenious, witty

disculpa *f,* excuse

disculpabilidad *f,* pardonableness

disculpable *a* excusable

disculpar *vt* to excuse; forgive, pardon; *vr* apologize; excuse oneself

discurrir *vi* to wander, roam; flow, run (rivers, etc.); (*with en*) consider, think about; (*with sobre*) discourse on; *vt* invent; conjecture

discursivo *a* discursive; thoughtful, reflective

discurso *m,* reasoning power; oration, discourse; consideration, reflection; speech, conversation; dissertation. **d. aceptatorio,** acceptance speech

discusión *f,* discussion

discutible *a* debatable; disputable

discutir *vt* to discuss, debate, consider

disecar *vt anat* to dissect; stuff animals; mount plants

disección *f,* dissection

disector *m,* dissector, anatomist

diseminación *f,* dissemination

diseminar *vt* to disseminate; spread

disensión *f,* dissension

disentería *f,* dysentery

disentimiento *m,* dissent

disentir *vi irr* to dissent; disagree. See **sentir**

diseñador *m,* delineator, drawer

diseñar *vt* to outline, sketch

diseño *m,* outline, sketch; plan; description

disertación *f,* dissertation

disertar *vi* (*with sobre*) to discourse on, discuss, treat of

diserto *a* eloquent

disfavor *m,* disfavor, discourtesy, slight

disforme *a* deformed; ugly; enormous

disfraz *m,* disguise; mask; fancy dress; pretence

disfrazar *vt* to disguise; dissemble, misrepresent; *vr* disguise oneself; wear fancy dress

disfrutar *vt* to enjoy (health, comfort, friendship, etc.); reap the benefit of; *vi* take pleasure in, enjoy

disfrute *m,* enjoyment, use, benefit

disgregación *f,* separation, disjunction

disgregar *vt* to separate, disjoin

disgustado *a* annoyed; discontented, dissatisfied; melancholy, depressed

disgustar *vt* to displease, dissatisfy; annoy; *fig* depress; *vr* quarrel, fall out. **Me disgusta la idea de marcharme,** I don't like the idea of going away

disgusto *m,* displeasure, dissatisfaction; discontent; annoyance; affliction, sorrow, trouble; quarrel; boredom; repugnance

disidente *a* dissenting. *mf* dissenter, nonconformist

disidir *vi* to dissent

disímil *a* dissimilar, different, unlike

disimulación *f,* dissimulation, pretence

disimulado *a* feigned, pretended

disimular *vt* to dissemble; pretend, feign; put up with, tolerate; misrepresent, misinterpret

disimulo *m,* pretence, dissimulation; tolerance, patience

disipación *f,* dispersion; dissipation, frivolity; immorality

disipado *a* spendthrift; dissipated, frivolous

disipar *vt* to disperse; squander; *vr* evaporate; vanish, fade, disappear

dislate *m,* absurdity, nonsense

dislocación *f,* dislocation

dislocar *vt* to dislocate; *vr* dislocate; sprain

disminución *f,* diminution. **ir (una cosa) en d.,** to diminish, decrease; taper, grow to a point

disminuido físico *m,* physically impaired person, physically handicapped person

disminuir *vt and vi irr* to diminish, decrease. See **huir**

disociación *f,* dissociation. **d. nuclear,** nuclear fission

disociar *vt* to dissociate, separate; *chem* dissociate

disoluble *a* dissoluble

disolución *f,* dissolution; immorality, laxity; disintegration; loosening, relaxation

disolutivo *a* dissolvent, solvent

disoluto *a* dissolute, vicious

disolvente *m,* dissolvent, solvent

disolver *vt irr* to loosen, undo; *chem* dissolve; separate, disintegrate; annul. See **resolver**

disonancia *f,* dissonance; disagreement; *mus* dissonant

disonante *a* dissonant; discordant, inharmonious

disonar *vi irr* to be inharmonious; disagree. See **sonar**

dísono *a* dissonant

dispar *a* unequal; unlike, different

disparadero *m,* trigger of a firearm

disparador *m,* shooter, firer; trigger (of firearms); ratchet (of watch); *a, Mexico* lavish

disparar *vt* to shoot, fire; throw or discharge with violence; *vr* run precipitately; rush (towards); bolt (horses); race (of a machine); explode, go off; *inf* go too far, misbehave; *Mexico* spend lavishly

disparatado *a* foolish; absurd, unreasonable

disparatar *vi* to act or speak foolishly

disparate *m,* foolishness, nonsense

disparidad *f,* disparity, dissimilarity

disparo *m,* shooting; explosion; racing (of an engine); discharge; foolishness

dispendio *m,* squandering, extravagance

dispendioso *a* costly, expensive

dispensa *f,* dispensation; privilege

dispensable *a* dispensable; excusable

dispensación *f,* dispensation; exemption

dispensar *vt* to grant, concede, distribute; exempt; excuse, forgive
dispensario *m*, dispensary
dispepsia *f*, dyspepsia
dispéptico (-ca) *a* and *n* dyspeptic
dispersar *vt* to disperse, scatter, separate; *mil* rout
dispersión *f*, dispersion
disperso *a* dispersed, scattered; *mil* separated from regiment
displicencia *f*, disagreeableness, coldness; hesitation, lack of enthusiasm
displicente *a* unpleasant, disagreeable; difficult, peevish
disponer *vt irr* to arrange, dispose; direct, order; decide; prepare, get ready; *vi* (*with de*) dispose of, make free with; possess; have at one's disposal; *vr* prepare oneself to die; make one's will; get ready. See **poner**
disponible *a* disposable; available
disposición *f*, arrangement; order, instruction; decision; preparation; aptitude, talent; disposal; condition of health; temperament; grace of bearing; promptitude, competence; measure, step, preliminary; *arch* plan; proviso, stipulation; symmetry. **A la d. de Vd,** I (we, he, it, etc.) am at your disposal. **hallarse en d. de hacer una cosa,** to be ready to do something. **última d.,** last will and testament
dispositivo *a* directory, advisory
dispuesto *a* ready, prepared; handsome, gallant; clever, wide-awake. **bien d.,** well-disposed; well, healthy. **mal d.,** ill-disposed; disinclined; out of sorts, indisposed
disputa *f*, dispute. **sin d.,** undoubtedly
disputar *vt* to argue, debate; dispute, question; *fig* fight for
disquisición *f*, disquisition
distancia *f*, distance; interval of time; difference, dissimilarity; unfriendliness, coolness
distanciar *vt* to separate, place farther apart
distante *a* separated; distant; far off
distar *vi* to be distant (time and place); be different, unlike
distender(se) *vt* and *vr med* to distend, swell
distinción *f*, distinction, differentiation; difference, individuality; privilege, honor; clarity, order; distinction (of bearing or mind). **a d. de,** unlike, different from
distinguible *a* distinguishable
distinguido *a* distinguished, illustrious
distinguir *vt* to distinguish, discern; differentiate; characterize; esteem, honor, respect; discriminate; see with difficulty; make out; *vr* be different; excel, distinguish oneself
distintivo *a* distinguishing; distinctive. *m*, distinguishing mark
distinto *a* different; distinct; clear
distracción *f*, distraction; abstraction, heedlessness, absentmindedness; pleasure, amusement; licentiousness
distraer *vt irr* to lead astray; distract (attention); influence for bad; amuse. *vr* be absentminded; amuse oneself. See **traer**
distraído *a* abstracted, absentminded; inattentive; licentious *Lat. Am.* slovenly
distribución *f*, distribution; (gen. *pl*) share
distribuidor (-ra) *a* distributing. *n* distributor
distribuir *vt irr* to distribute; share out, divide. See **huir**
distributivo *a* distributive
distrito *m*, district
disturbio *m*, disturbance
disuadir *vt* to dissuade
disuasión *f*, dissuasion
disuasivo *a* dissuasive
disyunción *f*, disjunction
dita *f*, *Lat. Am.* debt
ditirambo *m*, dithyramb; excessive praise
diurético *a* diuretic
diurno *a* diurnal
diva *f*, prima donna; woman singer

divagación *f*, wandering, roaming; digression
divagar *vi* to wander, roam; digress
diván *m*, divan (Turkish supreme council); divan, sofa; collection of Arabic, Persian or Turkish poems
divergencia *f*, divergence; disagreement
divergente *a* divergent; conflicting, dissentient
divergir *vi* to diverge; dissent
diversidad *f*, diversity, unlikeness, difference; variety
diversificar *vt* to differentiate; vary
diversión *f*, pastime, amusement; *mil* diversion
diverso *a* diverse, unlike; *pl* various, many
divertido *a* amusing, funny, entertaining
divertir *vt irr* to lead astray, turn aside; entertain; *mil* create a diversion. *vr* amuse oneself. See **sentir**
dividendo *m*, dividend. **com d. activo,** dividend
dividir *vt* to divide; distribute; stir up discord; *vr* (*with de*) part company with, leave
divieso *m*, *med* boil
divinamente *adv* divinely; excellently, admirably, perfectly
divinidad *f*, divinity, Godhead; person or thing of great beauty
divino *a* divine; excellent, admirable, superb
divisa *f*, badge, emblem; *her* motto
divisar *vt* to glimpse, descry
divisibilidad *f*, divisibility
divisible *a* divisible
división *f*, division, partition; discord; (*math mil*) division; hyphen; apportionment; district, ward
divisor (-ra) *a* dividing, separating. *m*, math divisor. *n* divider, separator
divisoria *f*, dividing line
divisorio *a* dividing
divorciar *vt* to divorce; separate; *vr* be divorced, be separated
divorcio *m*, divorce
divulgación *f*, spreading, publication, propagation
divulgar(se) *vt* and *vr* to spread abroad, publish
do *m*, *mus* doh, C. *poet* where
dobladillo *m*, *sew* hem; turn-up (of a trouser)
doblado *a* stocky, thickset, sturdy; rocky, rough, uneven; dissembling. *m*, garret
dobladura *f*, fold, crease; crease mark
doblamiento *m*, doubling; folding
doblar *vt* to double, multiply by two; fold, double; bend; persuade, induce; *naut* double, sail round; turn, walk round; *vi ecc* ring the passing bell; *theat* double a role; *vr* fold, double; bend; bow; stoop; allow oneself to be persuaded
doble *a* double, twofold; duplicate; insincere, false; thick (cloth); *bot* double (flowers); hardy, robust. *m*, fold, crease; *ecc* passing-bell; Spanish dance step. *adv* double, twice. ecc **rito d.,** full rites
doblegar *vt* to fold; bend; brandish; dissuade in favor of another proposition; *vr* submit, give way, acquiesce
doblete *a* of medium thickness. *m*, imitation jewel
doblez *m*, fold, crease; fold mark. *mf*, double dealing, treachery
doblilla *f*, twenty-real coin
doblón *m*, doubloon
doce *a* twelve. *m*, twelve; twelfth (of the month). **las d.,** twelve o'clock
docena *f*, dozen. **la d. del fraile,** baker's dozen
docente *a* teaching
dócil *a* docile; obedient; flexible, easily worked (metals, etc.)
docilidad *f*, docility; obedience; flexibility
docto *a* learned, erudite
doctor (-ra) *n* doctor; physician; teacher. *f*, *inf* bluestocking
doctorado *m*, doctorate
doctorarse *vr* to get one's doctorate
doctrina *f*, doctrine; instruction, teaching; theory, conception; *ecc* sermon
doctrinar *vt* to teach, instruct

documentación f, documentation; collection of documents, papers

documental a documental. m, documentary film

documentar vt to document

Dodecaneso, el the Dodecanese

dogal m, halter; noose; slipknot. fig **estar con el d. a la garganta,** to be in a fix

dogma m, dogma

dogmático a dogmatic

dogmatizar vt to teach heretical doctrines; dogmatize

dólar m, dollar

dolencia f, ailment; pain; ache

doler vi irr to be in pain; be reluctant; vr be sorry, regretful; grieve; sympathize, be compassionate; complain. Pres. Ind. **duelo, dueles, duele, duelen.** Pres. Subjunc. **duela, duelas, duela, duelan**

doliente a suffering; ill; afflicted, sad. mf sufferer, ill person. m, chief mourner

dolo m, fraud; deception; deceit; law premeditation

dolor m, pain, ache; mental suffering. **d. sordo,** dull pain

dolorido a painful; afflicted, sad

doloroso a sad, regrettable; mournful, sorrowful; pitiful; painful

doloso a deceitful, fraudulent

domable a tamable; controllable

domador (-ra) n subduer, controller; wild animal tamer; horsebreaker

domadura f, taming, breaking in; controlling (emotions)

domar vt to tame, break in; control, repress (emotions)

domesticable a tamable; domesticable

domesticar vt to tame; domesticate; vr grow tame; become domesticated

domesticidad f, domesticity

doméstico (-ca) a domestic, domesticated; tame. n domestic worker

domiciliar vt to domicile; vr become domiciled, settle down; Mexico address (a piece of mail)

domiciliario a domiciliary

domicilio m, domicile; house

dominación f, domination; power, authority; command (of a military position, etc.); mil high ground; pl dominions, angels

dominador a dominating; overbearing

dominante a dominating; overbearing, domineering; dominant. f, mus dominant

dominar vt to dominate; repress, subdue; fig master (branch of knowledge); vi stand out; vr control oneself

dómine m, inf teacher; pedant, know-all

domingo m, Sunday. **d. de Cuasimodo,** Low Sunday. **d. de Pentecostés,** Whitsuntide Sunday. **d. de Ramos,** Palm Sunday. **d. de Resurrección,** Easter Sunday

dominguero a inf Sunday; special, excursion (trains)

dominicano (-na) a and n Dominican; native of Santo Domingo

dominio m, authority, power; rule, sovereignty; dominion (country); domain

dominó m, domino; game of dominoes

don m, gift; quality, characteristic; talent. **d. de gentes,** the human touch; charm

don m, title of respect equivalent to English Mr. or Esquire. Used only before given name and not before a family name, e.g. **don Juan Martínez,** or **don Juan**

donación f, donation, gift, grant

donador (-ra) a donating. n donor

donaire m, discretion, wit; witticism; gracefulness, elegance

donar vt to bestow, give; transfer; grant

donatario m, recipient, grantee

doncel m, squire, youth not yet armed; knight; male virgin; king's page

doncella f, virgin, maid; maidservant; lady's maid

donde adv where, wherein. Sometimes used as relative pronoun "in which" (e.g. **La casa d. estaba,** The house in which I was); Lat. Am. at the house of, at . . .'s; to the house of, to . . .'s (e.g. **Mi tía está donde mis abuelos** My aunt is at my grandparents' **Mi tío no fue donde mis primos** My uncle did not go to my cousins') interrog **¿dónde? ¿A dónde va Vd.?** Where are you going to? **¿De dónde viene Vd.?** Where do you come from? **¿Por dónde se va a Madrid?** Which is the way to Madrid?

dondequiera adv wherever, anywhere, everywhere

donoso a witty; graceful

donostiarra a and mf of or from San Sebastian (N. Spain)

donosura f, wit; grace; dash, verve

doña f, feminine equivalent of **don** (e.g. **D. Catalina Palacios**)

dorado a golden, gilded; fortunate, happy. m, gilding

dorador m, gilder

doradura f, gilding

dorar vt to gild; make golden; fig gild the pill; cul toast lightly; vr become golden

dormidero a soporiferous, narcotic; m, Lat. Am. roost (of chickens)

dormilón (-ona) a inf sleepy. n sleepyhead

dormir vi irr to sleep; spend the night; fig grow calm; sleep (tops); (with sobre) sleep on, consider; vt put to sleep; vr go to sleep; go slow over, neglect; be dormant; go numb (limbs). **d. como un lirón,** to sleep like a top. inf **d. la mona,** to sleep oneself sober. **entre duerme y vela,** half-awake. Pres. Ind. **duermo, duermes, duerme, duermen.** Pres. Part. **durmiendo.** Preterite **durmió, durmieron.** Pres. Subjunc. **duerma, duermas, duerma, duerman**

dormitar vi to doze

dormitivo a and m, sedative

dormitorio m, dormitory; bedroom

dorso m, back; dorsum

dos a two. m, two; second (of the month). **las d.,** two o'clock. **d. a d.,** two against two. **de d. en d.,** two by two. inf **en un d. por tres,** in a twinkling

doscientos a and m, two hundred; two hundredth

dosel m, canopy; dais

dosis f, dose; quantity

dotación f, endowment; naut crew; staff, workers; equipment

dotar vt to give as dowry; endow, found; fig endow (with talents, etc.); equip; apportion (salary)

dote mf, dowry. f, (gen. pl) gifts, talents. **dotes de mando,** capacity for leadership

dracma f, drachma; dram

draga f, dredger

dragado m, dredging

dragaminas m, nav minesweeper

dragar vt to dredge

dragón m, dragon; bot snapdragon; mil dragoon; zool dragon, giant lizard; ast Draco

dragona f, female dragon; mil shoulder-strap

dragonear vi, Lat. Am. to boast, brag

drama m, play; drama. **d. lírico,** opera

dramática f, dramatic art

dramático a dramatic; vivid, unexpected, moving

dramaturgo m, dramatist, playwright

drenaje m, drainage (of land and wounds)

Dresde Dresden

dril m, drill, cotton cloth

droga f, drug; falsehood, deception; nuisance

droguería f, chemist's shop; drug trade

droguero (-ra) n chemist, druggist

dromedario m, zool dromedary

druida m, Druid

dualidad f, duality

ducado m, dukedom; duchy; ducat

ducentésimo a two hundredth

ducha f, shower-bath; douche; stripe in cloth; furrow

ducho a experienced, skilful

dúctil *a* ductile (metals); adaptable, docile, flexible
ductilidad *f,* ductility; adaptability
duda *f,* doubt, hesitation; problem. **sin d.,** doubtless
dudable *a* doubtful
dudar *vi* to be in doubt; *vt* doubt, disbelieve
dudoso *a* doubtful; uncertain, not probable
duela *f,* hoop, stave
duelista *mf* dueler; duelist
duelo *m,* sorrow, grief; mourning; mourners; duel; (gen. *pl*) troubles, trials. **duelos y quebrantos,** *cul* fried offal. **sin d.,** in abundance
duende *m,* imp, elf, sprite, ghost
dueña *f,* owner, proprietress, mistress; duenna; married lady *ant*
dueño *m,* owner, proprietor; master (of servants). **d. de sí mismo,** self-controlled
Duero, el the Douro
duetista *mf* duetist
dula *f,* common pasture ground or herds
dulce *a* sweet; fresh, pure; fresh, not salty; fragrant; melodious; pleasant, agreeable; tender, gentle; soft (metals). *m,* sweetmeat, bonbon. **d. de almíbar,** preserved fruit.
dulcedumbre *f,* sweetness; softness
dulcémele *m,* dulcimer
dulcera *f,* preserve dish, fruit dish
dulcería *f,* See **confitería**
dulcificar *vt* to make sweet; alleviate, sweeten
dulcinea *f, inf* sweetheart; ideal

dulzaina *f, mus* flageolet
dulzura *f,* sweetness; gentleness; pleasure; meekness; agreeableness
duna *f,* (gen. *pl*) sand dune
Dunquerque Dunkirk
dúo *m, mus* duet
duodécimo *a* twelfth
duodeno *a* twelfth. *m, anat* duodenum
duplicación *f,* duplication
duplicado *m,* duplicate
duplicar *vt* to duplicate; double
duplicidad *f,* duplicity, falseness
duplo *a* double
duque *m,* duke
duquesa *f,* duchess
duración *f,* duration; durability
duradero *a* lasting; durable
durante *adv* during
durar *vi* to continue; endure, last
dureza *f,* hardness; *med* callosity; severity, harshness
durmiente *a* sleeping. *mf* sleeper; *m, arch* dormant
duro *a* hard; firm, unyielding; vigorous, robust; severe, inclement; exacting, cruel; *mus* metallic, harsh; *art* crude, too sharply defined; miserly, avaricious; obstinate; self-opinionated; unbearable, intolerable; merciless, hard; harsh (style). *m,* Spanish coin worth five pesetas
dux *m,* doge

E

e *f,* letter E. *conjunc* used instead of *y* (and) before words beginning with *i* or *hi,* provided this last is not followed by a diphthong (e.g. **e invierno, e hijos,** *but* **y hierro**)
¡ea! *interj* Well!; Come on!; Let's see! (often used with **pues**)
ebanista *mf* cabinetmaker
ebanistería *f,* cabinetmaker's shop; cabinetmaking or work
ébano *m,* ebony
ebonita *f,* ebonite, vulcanite
ebrio *a* intoxicated, inebriated
ebullición *f,* boiling, ebullition
ebúrneo *a* eburnine, ivory-like
echada *f,* throw, cast; pitch; fling; length of a man
echador (-ra) *n* thrower. *m, inf* chucker-out
echadura *f,* sitting on eggs to hatch them; (gen. *pl*) gleanings
echamiento *m,* throw, fling; throwing, casting; expulsion; rejection
echar *vt* to throw, fling; eject, drive away; cast out, expel; put forth, sprout; emit, give forth; cut (teeth); dismiss, discharge; couple (animals); pour (liquids); place, apply; put into, fill; turn (keys, locks); impute; attribute; impose (penalty, taxes, etc.); play (game); try one's luck; distribute; publish, make known; perform (plays); (*with por*) go in direction of; (*with prep a +* *infin.*) begin to (**e. a andar,** to begin to walk); *vr* throw oneself down, lie down; sit on eggs (birds); abate, calm (wind); apply oneself, concentrate on; rush (towards), fling oneself (upon). **e. abajo,** to overthrow; demolish. **e. aceite al fuego,** to add fuel to the flames. **e. a perder,** to spoil, deteriorate. *naut* **e. a pique,** to sink. **e. a vuelo,** to ring (bells). **e. carnes,** to put on weight, grow fat. **e. cuentas,** to reckon up. **e. de menos,** to miss; mourn absence of. **e. de ver,** to notice. *fig* **e. en cara,** to throw in one's face, reproach. **echarla de majo,** to play the gallant. **e. las cartas al correo,** to post the letters. **e. las cartas,** to tell fortunes. **e. el pie atrás,** *fig* to climb down; *fig* back out. **e. raíces,** to take root; **e. las bases de, e. los cimientos de,** to lay the foundation of, lay the foundation for. *fig* then become established. **e. rayos por la boca,** *fig* to fly into a rage. **e. suertes,** to draw lots. **echarlo todo a rodar,** to spoil

everything. **e. una mano,** to lend a hand. **echar un volado** *Mexico* to toss a coin
echazón *f,* throw, cast; jetsam
eclecticismo *m,* eclecticism
ecléctico (-ca) *a* and *n* eclectic
eclesiástico *a* ecclesiastical. *m,* ecclesiastic, clergyman; Ecclesiasticus
eclipsar *vt ast* to eclipse; surpass, outvie; *vr ast* be in eclipse; disappear
eclipse *m, ast* eclipse; retirement, withdrawal
eco *m,* echo; verse-echo; muffled sound; slavish imitation or imitator
economato *m,* trusteeship; cooperative store
econometría *f,* econometrics
economía *f,* economy, thrift; structure, organization; poverty, shortage; saving (of time, labor, etc.); *pl* savings. **e. dirigida,** planned economy. **e. doméstica,** domestic economy. **e. política,** political economy
económico *a* economic; thrifty; avaricious; cheap
economista *mf* economist
economizar *vt* to economize; save
ecónomo *m,* trustee, guardian
ecuación *f,* (*math* and *ast*) equation. **e. personal,** personal equation
ecuador *m,* equator
ecuánime *a* calm, unruffled; impartial
ecuanimidad *f,* calmness, serenity; impartiality
ecuatorial *a* equatorial
ecuatoriano (-na) *a* and *n* Ecuadorian
ecuestre *a* equestrian
ecuménico *a* ecumenical
eczema *m,* eczema
edad *f,* age; epoch; period. **e. de piedra,** Stone Age. **e. media,** Middle Ages. **de cierta e.,** middle-aged. **ser mayor de e.,** to have attained one's majority. **ser menor de e.,** to be a minor
edecán *m,* aide-de-camp
edema *m,* edema
Edén *m,* Eden; *fig* paradise
edición *f,* edition. **e. diamante,** miniature edition. **e. príncipe,** first edition
edicto *m,* edict, decree; public notice
edificación *f,* building, construction; edification

edificador (-ra) *a* uplifting, edifying; building. *n* builder

edificante *a* building, constructing; edifying

edificar *vt* to build, construct; edify

edificio *m*, building, structure, fabric

Edimburgo Edinburgh

editar *vt* (of a publisher) to publish; edit

editor (-ra) *n* publisher; editor

editorial *a* publishing; editorial. *m*, editorial, leading article

edredón *m*, down of an eiderduck; eiderdown, quilt

eduardiano (-na) *a* and *n* Edwardian

educable *a* educable

educación *f*, upbringing; education; good breeding, good manners

educado *a* educated. **ser mal e.,** to be badly brought up; be ill-mannered

educador (-ra) *a* educating. *n* educator

educando (-da) *n* pupil

educar *vt* to educate; bring up, train, teach, develop

educativo *a* educational, educative

educción *f*, eduction; inference, deduction

educir *vt irr* to educe; infer, deduce. See **conducir**

efe *f*, name of letter F

efectismo *m*, sensationalism; striving after effect

efectista *a* (*art lit*) striking, sensational

efectivo *a* effective; real. *m*, cash. **hacer e.,** to put into effect

efecto *m*, effect, result; purpose, intent; impression; *pl* assets; goods, chattels. **efectos de escritorio,** stationery. **efectos públicos,** public securities. **en e.,** in fact, actually. **llevar a e.,** to put into effect; make effective

efectuación *f*, accomplishment, execution

efectuar *vt* to accomplish, effect; make (a payment); *vr* be effected; happen, take place

eferente *a* efferent

efervescencia *f*, effervescence; excitement, enthusiasm

efervescente *a* effervescent

Éfeso Ephesus

eficacia *f*, efficacy; effectiveness

eficaz *a* efficacious; effective

eficiencia *f*, efficiency

eficiente *a* efficient, effective

efigie *f*, effigy; image, representation, symbol

efímero *a* ephemeral; brief

eflorescencia *f*, *chem* efflorescence

efluvio *m*, effluvium; exhalation

efugio *m*, subterfuge, evasion

efusión *f*, effusion; *fig* spate (of words, etc.)

efusivo *a* effusive, expansive

Egeo, Mar Aegean Sea

égida *f*, shield; egis, protection

egipcíaco (-ca), egipcio (-ia) *a* and *n* Egyptian

Egipto Egypt

egiptólogo (-ga) *n* Egyptologist

egoísmo *m*, egoism

egoísta *a* egoistic. *mf* egoist

egolatría *f*, self-love

egotismo *m*, egotism

egotista *a* egotistical. *mf* egotist

egregio *a* distinguished, celebrated

egresado *m*, graduate (of a certain school)

egresar (de . . .) *vi*, *Lat. Am.* to go out (of . . .), leave (. . .); be graduated (from . . .)

egreso *m*, *Lat. Am.* departure, leaving; graduation

eje *m*, axis; axle-tree; shaft; pivot, fundamental idea. **e. trasero,** rear-axle

ejecución *f*, accomplishment, performance; execution, technique; death penalty

ejecutable *a* feasible, practicable

ejecutante *mf mus* executant, performer

ejecutar *vt* to discharge, perform; put to death; (*art mus*) execute; serve (a warrant, etc.); *law* seize (property)

ejecutivo *a* executive; urgent

ejecutor *m*, executor

ejecutoria *f*, letters patent of nobility; *law* judgment, sentence

ejemplar *a* exemplary. *m*, copy, specimen; precedent; example; warning

ejemplificar *vi* to exemplify

ejemplo *m*, example, precedent; illustration, instance; specimen. **dar e.,** to set an example. **por e.,** for example

ejercer *vt* to practise (a profession); perform, fulfil; exercise, use

ejercicio *m*, exercise; practice; performance; exertion, effort; *mil* exercises (gen. *pl*). **ejercicios espirituales,** spiritual exercises. **ejercicios físicos,** physical training

ejercitar *vt* to exercise; train, teach; *vr* exercise; practice

ejército *m*, army

ejote *m*, *Central America, Mexico* string bean

el *def art. m*, *sing* the

él *pers pron sing m*, he; it (*f*. **ella.** *neut* **ello**) (e.g. **Lo hizo él,** He did it). Also used with prep. (e.g. **Lo hicimos por él,** We did it for him)

elaboración *f*, elaboration, working out

elaborado *a* elaborate

elaborar *vt* to elaborate; produce, work out

elasticidad *f*, elasticity; adaptability

elástico *a* elastic; adaptable. *m*, elastic tape; elastic material

ele *f*, name of letter L

elección *f*, choice; election; selection; discrimination

electivo *a* elective

elector (-ra) *n* elector, voter. *m*, German prince *ant*

electorado *m*, electorate

electoral *a* electoral

electricidad *f*, electricity

electricista *mf* electrician

eléctrico *a* electric; electrical

electrificación *f*, electrification

electrificar *vt* to electrify

electrizar *vt* to electrify; startle; *vr* be electrified

electrocución *f*, electrocution

electrocutar *vt* to electrocute

electrodo *m*, electrode

electroimán *m*, electromagnet

electrólisis *f*, electrolysis

electrolizar *vt* to electrolyze

electromagnético *a* electromagnetic

electromotriz *a* electromotive. **fuerza e.,** electromotive force

electrón *m*, electron

electroquímica *f*, electrochemistry

electroscopio *m*, electroscope

electrotecnia *f*, electrical engineering

electroterapia *f*, *med* electrotherapy

elefante (-ta) *n* elephant

elefantíasis *f*, elephantiasis

elefantino *a* elephantine

elegancia *f*, elegance, grace; fashionableness; *lit* beauty of style

elegante *a* elegant; graceful, lovely; fashionable, stylish

elegantoso, -a *a*, *Lat. Am.* = **elegante**

elegía *f*, elegy

elegíaco *a* elegiac

elegibilidad *f*, eligibility

elegible *a* eligible

elegir *vt irr* to select, prefer; elect. *Pres. Ind.* **elijo, eliges, elige, eligen.** *Pres. Part.* **eligiendo.** *Preterite* **eligió, eligieron.** *Pres. Subj.* **elija,** etc.

elemental *a* elemental; fundamental; elementary

elemento *m*, element; component, constituent; *elec* element; *pl* rudiments. *mil* **elementos de choque,** shock troops

elenco *m*, *Lat. Am.* cast (of characters)

elevación *f*, lifting, raising; height, high ground; elevation; altitude; *fig* eminence; elevation, advancement; ecstasy; raising (of the voice)

elevado *a* sublime, lofty

elevar *vt* to raise, lift; *fig* exalt; *vr* be in ecstasy, be transported. **elevarse de categoría,** to rise in status

elfo *m*, elf

elidir *vt* (phonetics) to elide

eliminación *f*, elimination

eliminador *a* eliminatory. *m*, eliminator

eliminar *vt* to eliminate

elíptico *a* elliptic

elíseo *m*, Elysium. *a* Elysian. **campos elíseos,** Elysian fields

elocución *f*, elocution; style of speech

elocuencia *f*, eloquence

elocuente *a* eloquent

elogiador (-ra) *a* eulogistic. *n* eulogist

elogiar *vt* to eulogize, praise

elogio *m*, eulogy, praise. «**Elogio de la Locura**», ''In Praise of Folly''

elote *m*, *Central America, Mexico* corn

elucidación *f*, elucidation, explanation

elucidar *vt* to elucidate, clarify

eludible *a* escapable, avoidable

eludir *vt* to elude, avoid

elusivo, -a *a*, *Lat. Am.* evasive, tricky

ella *pers. pron 3rd sing. f* she; it. See **él**

elle *f*, name of letter LL

ello *pers. pron 3rd sing. neut* that, the fact, it. **Ello es que . . . ,** The fact is that . . . **No tengo tiempo para ello,** I have no time for that

ellos, ellas *pers. pron 3rd pl. m* and *f*, they. See **él**

emaciación *f*, emaciation

emanación *f*, emanation; effluvium

emanar *vi* to emanate (from), originate (in)

emancipación *f*, emancipation; enfranchisement

emancipador (-ra) *a* emancipatory. *n* emancipator

emancipar *vt* to emancipate, free; enfranchise; *vr* emancipate oneself; become independent; free oneself

emascular *vt* to emasculate

embadurnar *vt* to smear, smudge, daub

embajada *f*, embassy; ambassadorship; embassy building; *inf* message

embajador *m*, ambassador; emissary

embajadora *f*, wife of ambassador; woman ambassador

embalador *m*, packer

embalaje *m*, packing; bale; wrapper; packing charge

embalar *vt* to pack

embaldosado *m*, tiled pavement or floor

embaldosar *vt* to tile, pave with tiles

embalsamador *a* embalming. *m*, embalmer

embalsamar *vt* to embalm; perfume

embalse *m*, dam; damming, impounding (of water)

embanastar *vt* to place in a basket; crowd, squeeze

embarazada *a f*, pregnant

embarazar *vt* to impede, hinder, embarrass; *vr* be hindered or embarrassed; be pregnant

embarazo *m*, difficulty, impediment; pregnancy; timidity, embarrassment

embarazoso *a* embarrassing; inconvenient; difficult, troublesome

embarcación *f*, ship, vessel; embarkation

embarcadero *m*, wharf, dock; quay; pier; jetty

embarcador *m*, shipper

embarcar *vt* to embark, ship; board (boat, train, etc.); *vr* embark; board

embarco *m*, embarking, embarkation

embargar *vt* to obstruct, impede; *law* seize; suspend, paralyse

embargo *m*, *law* seizure; embargo. **sin e.,** nevertheless, however

embarque *m*, loading, embarkation (goods)

embarrancar *vi naut* to run aground; *vr naut* be stuck on a reef or in the mud

embarrilar *vt* to barrel

embarullar *vt inf* to mix up, muddle; do hastily and badly

embastar *vt sew* to baste; tack

embaste *m*, *sew* basting; tacking stitch

embate *m*, beating of the waves; sudden attack; unexpected misfortune

embaucamiento *m*, trick, deception

embaucar *vt* to deceive, hoodwink

embaular *vt* to pack in a trunk; *inf* stuff with food

embazar *vt* to dye brown; hinder; amaze; *vr* be amazed; be tired or bored; be satiated

embebecer *vt irr* to entertain, amuse; engross, fascinate; *vr* be dumbfounded. See **conocer**

embebecimiento *m*, astonishment; absorption, engrossment

embeber *vt* to absorb; contain; shrink, contract; saturate; insert, introduce; incorporate; *vi* shrink; *vr* be amazed; master or absorb (a subject). **embedido en sus pensamientos,** absorbed in thought

embelecar *vt* to dupe, deceive, trick

embeleco *m*, deception, fraud

embelesar *vt* to astonish; fascinate, enchant; *vr* be astonished or fascinated

embeleso *m*, astonishment; fascination; charm

embellecer *vt irr* to embellish; *vr* beautify oneself. See **conocer**

embellecimiento *m*, beautifying, embellishment

emberizo *m*, *orn* yellow-hammer

embermejecer *vt irr* to dye red; shame, make blush; *vi* turn red or reddish; *vr* blush. See **conocer**

embestida *f*, assault, attack, onrush; *inf* importunity

embestir *vt irr* to rush upon, assault; *inf* importune, be a nuisance to; *vi fig inf* clash, be inharmonious. See **pedir**

emblema *m*, emblem; symbol; badge

emblemático *a* emblematic; symbolical

embobamiento *m*, stupefaction, amazement

embobar *vt* to entertain, fascinate; *vr* be dumbfounded

embobecer *vt irr* to make stupid. See **conocer**

embobecimiento *m*, stupefaction

embocadero *m*, narrow entrance, bottleneck; mouth of a channel

embocadura *f*, entrance by a narrow passage; *mus* mouthpiece; flavor (of wine); estuary, mouth of a river; *theat* proscenium

embocar *vt* to put in the mouth; go through a narrow passage; deceive; *inf* devour, wolf; initiate a business deal

embolador, -a *mf*, *Lat. Am.* bootblack

embolia *f*, embolism

émbolo *m*, *mech* piston, plunger

embolsar *vt* to place money in a purse; collect (a debt, etc.)

emborrachar *vt* to intoxicate; daze, stupefy; *vr* become intoxicated; run (of dyes)

emborrascarse *vr* to be furious; become stormy (weather); *fig* go downhill (business concern)

emborronar *vt* to blot; scribble, write hastily

emboscada *f*, ambuscade, ambush; intrigue, spying

emboscar *vt mil* to set an ambush; *vr* lie in ambush

embosquecer *vi irr* to become wooded. See **conocer**

embotar *vt* to blunt (cutting edge); *vi fig* weaken; *vr* become blunt

embotellado *m*, bottling; *fig* bottleneck

embotellador (-ra) *n* bottler. *f*. **embotelladora,** bottling outfit

embotellar *vt* to bottle; bottle up, prevent from escaping

embotijar *vt* to put into jars; *vr inf* be enraged

embozar *vt fig* to cloak, dissemble; muffle; *vr* muffle oneself up

embozo *m*, anything used to cover or muffle the face; pretense, pretext; facings (gen. *pl*); yashmak

embullo *m*, *Central America* noise; excitement; revelry

embragar *vt* to sling, lift; *mech* let in the clutch

embrague *m*, hoisting, slinging; *mech* clutch

embravecer *vt irr* to infuriate; *vr* be enraged; be boisterous (sea). See **conocer**

embravecimiento *m*, fury, rage

embrazadura *f*, grasping, clasping; handle, clasp

embreadura *f,* tarring

embrear *vt* to tar, paint with pitch

embriagador *a* intoxicating

embriagar *vt* to intoxicate; enrapture; *vr* become inebriated

embriaguez *f,* intoxication, inebriation; rapture

embriología *f,* embryology

embrión *m,* embryo; germ, rough idea

embrionario *a* embryonic

embrollar *vt* to entangle; embroil

embrollo *m,* tangle; falsehood; difficult situation

embromar *vt* to tease, chaff; trick, deceive; waste the time of; annoy; harm

embrujar *vt* to bewitch

embrutecer *vt irr* to make brutish or stupid; *vr* become brutish. See **conocer**

embudo *m, chem* funnel

embuste *m,* lie, fraud; *pl* trinkets

embustero (-ra) *a* deceitful, knavish. *n* liar, cheat, trickster

embutido *m,* inlaid work; *cul* sausage

embutir *vt* to inlay; stuff full, cram; *vt* and *vr inf* stuff with food

eme *f,* name of letter M

emergencia *f,* emergence; accident, emergency

emergente *a* emergent

emerger *vi* to emerge; have its source (rivers, etc.)

emérito *a* emeritus

emético *a* and *m,* emetic

emigración *f,* emigration; migration; number of emigrants

emigrado *m,* emigrant, emigré

emigrante *a* and *mf* emigrant

emigrar *vi* to emigrate; migrate

emigratorio *a* emigration

eminencia *f,* highland; importance, prominence; outstanding personality, genius; title given to cardinals

eminente *a* high, elevated; prominent, illustrious

emirato *m,* emirate

emisario (-ia) *n* emissary

emisión *f,* emission; *rad* broadcast; *com* issue (bonds, etc.); floating (of a loan)

emisor *m, elec* transmitter.

emisora *f, rad* broadcasting station

emitir *vt* to emit; *rad* broadcast; *com* issue (bonds, paper money, etc.); utter, give voice to

emoción *f,* emotion

emocional *a* emotional; emotive

emocionante *a* moving, causing emotion; thrilling

emocionar *vt* to cause emotion, move; *vr* be stirred by emotion; be thrilled

emoliente *a* and *m,* emollient

emolumento *m,* emolument (gen. *pl*)

empachado *a* awkward, clumsy

empachar *vt* to hinder, impede; disguise, dissemble; *vr* overeat, stuff; be bashful

empacho *m,* bashfulness, timidity; embarrassment, impediment; indigestion, satiety

empadronamiento *m,* census

empadronar *vt* to take the census

empalagar *vt* to cloy (of food); tire, annoy

empalagoso *a* sickly, oversweet; cloying; *fig* sugary, honeyed

empalar *vt* to impale

empalizada *f,* stockade, fencing

empalmar *vt* to dovetail; splice (ropes); clamp; *fig* combine (plans, actions, etc.); *vi* join (railroad lines); couple (railroad trains); *vr* palm (as in conjuring)

empalme *m,* connection; splicing; *fig* combination (of plans, etc.); railroad junction; continuation; palming, secreting

empanada *f,* savory turnover or pie; secret negotiations, intrigue

empanar *vt* to bread; *cul* cover with breadcrumbs; *agr* sow grain

empantanar *vt* to turn into marsh; embog; delay, embarrass

empañar *vt* to swaddle; tarnish, dim; blur; *fig* sully (fame, etc.)

empapar *vt* to saturate; absorb; impregnate; *vr* be saturated; absorb; *fig* be imbued

empapelado *m,* paperhanging; wallpaper

empapelador *m,* paperhanger

empapelar *vt* to wrap in paper; paper (a room, etc.)

empaque *m,* packing; paneling; *inf* mien, air; pomposity

empaquetador (-ra) *n* packer

empaquetar *vt* to pack; make up parcels or packages; overcrowd

emparedado (-da) *a* cloistered, reclusive. *n* recluse. *m, cul* sandwich

emparedar *vt* to shut up, immure; *vr* become a recluse

emparejar *vt* to pair, match; equalize, make level; *vi* come abreast (of); be equal

emparentar *vi irr* to become related by marriage. See **acertar**

emparrado *m,* vine arbor; vine prop; pergola

empastadura *f,* filling (of teeth)

empastar *vt* to cover with glue or paste; bind in boards (books); fill (teeth). **empastado en tela,** clothbound

empaste *m,* pasting, gluing; filling (teeth)

empatar *vt* to equal, tie with

empate *m,* tie, draw; dead heat

empavonarse *vr, Central America* to dress to the nines

empecatado *a* willful; evil-minded, wicked; incorrigible, impenitent; extremely unlucky

empecer *vt irr* to harm, damage; *vi* hinder. See **conocer**

empecinado, -a *a, Lat. Am.* pigheaded, stubborn

empedernido *a* stony-hearted, cruel

empedrado *a* dappled (horses); *fig* flecked (with clouds). *m,* paving; pavement

empedrar *vt irr* to pave with stones. See **acertar**

empegar *vt* to coat with pitch; mark with pitch (sheep)

empeine *m,* groin; instep

empellar *vt* to push, jostle

empellón *m,* hard push. *inf* **a empellones,** by pushing and shoving

empeñado *a* violent, heated (of disputes)

empeñar *vt* to pledge, leave as surety; pawn; oblige, compel; appoint as mediator; *vr* bind oneself, be under an obligation; *(with en)* insist on; persist in; *vr* intercede; mediate; *mil* begin (a battle). **empeñado en,** determined to, intent on

empeño *m,* pledge, surety; obligation, engagement; fervent desire; purpose, intention; determination, resolve; guarantor; *inf* influence, favor

empeoramiento *m,* worsening; deterioration

empeorar *vt* to make worse; *vi* and *vr* deteriorate, grow worse

empequeñecer *vt irr* to diminish, lessen; make smaller; belittle. See **conocer**

emperador *m,* emperor

emperatriz *f,* empress

emperezar *vt* to obstruct, hinder; *vr* be lazy

empernar *vt* to peg, bolt

empero *conjunc* but; nevertheless

empezar *vt irr* to begin, commence; initiate; *vi* begin. *Pres. Ind.* **empiezo, empiezas, empieza, empiezan.** *Preterite* **empecé, empezaste,** etc. *Pres. Subjunc.* **empiece, empieces, empiece, empecemos, empecéis, empiecen**

empicotar *vt* to pillory

empiezo *m, Lat. Am.* beginning

empilonar *vt, Lat. Am.* to pile up

empinado *a* steep; lofty; arrogant; exalted

empinar *vt* to raise; tip, tilt (drinking vessels); *vr* stand on tiptoe; rear, prance; tower, rise; *aer* zoom, climb steeply. *inf* **e. el codo,** to lift the elbow, tipple

empingorotado *a* important, prominent; *inf* stuck-up

empírico (-ca) *a* empiric. *n* quack, charlatan

empizarrado *m,* slate roof

empizarrar *vt* to roof with slate

emplastar *vt med* to apply plasters; make up; paint; *inf* hinder, obstruct; *vr* be smeared

emplasto *m, med* plaster; poultice; *inf* put-up job, fraud

emplazamiento *m,* placing, location; site; *law* summons; *naut* berth

emplazar *vt* to convene, arrange a meeting; *law* summon

empleado (-da) *n* employee; clerk. **e. público,** civil servant

emplear *vt* to employ; lay out, invest (money); use; *vr* be employed or occupied

empleo *m,* employment; investment, laying out (of money); occupation; post, office

emplomar *vt* to lead, solder or cover with lead; affix lead seals on or to; weight (a stick, etc.); *Argentina* fill (a tooth)

emplumar *vt* to feather; decorate with feathers; tar and feather

emplumecer *vi irr* to fledge, grow feathers. See **conocer**

empobrecer *vt irr* to impoverish; *vi* and *vr* become poor; decay. See **conocer**

empobrecimiento *m,* impoverishment

empollar *vt* to hatch; *vi* produce a brood (of bees); *inf* brood on, consider; *inf* grind, cram, swot (of students)

empollón (-ona) *n inf* plodder, grind, swot

empolvar *vt* to cover with dust; powder

emponzoñar *vt* to poison; pervert, corrupt

emporio *m,* emporium

empotrar *vt* to embed, implant; fix down

emprendedor *a* capable, efficient, enterprising

emprender *vt* to undertake; (*with prep a or con*) *inf* accost, tackle, buttonhole

empresa *f,* undertaking, task; motto, device; intention, design; management, firm; enterprise, deal

empresarial *a* entrepreneurial

empresario *m,* contractor; theatrical manager

empréstito *m,* loan

empujar *vt* to push; *fig* exert pressure, influence

empuje *m,* push; *arch* pressure; energy; power, influence

empujón *m,* violent thrust or push. *inf* **a empujones,** by pushing and shoving; intermittently

empuñar *vt* to grasp; grip; clutch

empurrarse *vr, Central America* to get angry

emu *m,* emu

emulación *f,* emulation, competition, rivalry

emulador *a* emulative

emular *vt* to emulate, rival, compete with

émulo (-la) *a* emulative, rival. *n* competitor, rival

emulsión *f,* emulsion

en *prep* in; into; on, upon; at; by. **en Madrid,** in Madrid. **en junio,** in June. **Se echó en un sillón,** He threw himself into an armchair. **Se transformó en mariposa,** It turned into a butterfly. **Hay un libro en la mesa,** There is a book on the table. **María está en casa,** Mary is at home. **en un precio muy alto,** at a very high price. **El número de candidatos ha disminuido en un treinta por ciento,** The number of candidates has decreased by thirty percent. **En** appears in a number of adverbial phrases, e.g. **en particular,** in particular, **en secreto,** in secret, **en seguida,** immediately. When it is used with a gerund, it means after, as soon as, when, e.g. **En llegando a la puerta llamó,** When he arrived at the door, he knocked. **En todas partes se cuecen habas,** That happens everywhere; It happens in the best of families

enaceitar *vt, Argentina* to oil

enagua *f,* slip, crinoline, petticoat

enajenación *f,* transference, alienation (property); abstraction, absent-mindedness. **e. mental,** lunacy

enajenar *vt* to transfer (property)

enaltecer *vt irr* to elevate, raise; exalt. See **conocer**

enamoradizo *a* susceptible, easily enamoured; fickle

enamorado *a* in love, lovesick; easily enamoured

enamorar *vt* to arouse love in; court, make love to; *vr* fall in love; (with *de*) become fond of (things)

enano (-na) *a* small, dwarf. *n* dwarf

enarbolar *vt* to hoist (flags); *vr* prance (horses); become angry

enardecer *vt irr* to kindle, stimulate (passion, quarrel, etc.); *vr* be afire (with passion); *med* be inflamed. See **conocer**

encabestrar *vt* to halter; lead, dominate

encabestrarse *vr, Lat. Am.* to dig one's heels in

encabezamiento *m,* census taking; tax register; tax assessment; heading, inscription, running head

encabezar *vt* to take the census of; put on the tax register; open a subscription list; put a heading or title to; lead, head; *vr* compound, settle by agreement (taxes, etc.)

encadenamiento *m,* fettering, chaining; connection, link, relation

encadenar *vt* to chain, fetter; *fig* link up, connect; *fig* paralyze. **encadenar el interés de,** to capture the interest of

encajar *vt* to insert, fit one thing inside another; force in; fit tightly; *inf* be opportune, fit in (often with *bien*); *vr* squeeze or crowd in; *inf* butt in, interfere

encaje *m,* fitting, insertion; socket, groove; joining; lace; inlay, mosaic

encajero, -a *mf,* lace maker; lace seller

encaladura *f,* whitewashing

encalar *vt* to whitewash

encalmado *a* calm; *com* dull

encalmarse *vr* to become calm (wind, weather)

encalvecer *vt irr* to grow bald. See **conocer**

encalladero *m, naut* sandbank, reef, shoal

encallar *vi naut* to run aground; *fig* be held up (negotiations, etc.)

encamado *a* bedridden, confined to one's bed; *m,* person confined to his bed

encamarse *vr* to go to bed (gen. illness); be laid flat (grain, etc.); crouch

encaminadura *f,* **encaminamiento** *m,* directing, forwarding, routing

encaminar *vt* to guide; direct; regulate; manage; promote, advance; *vr* (*with prep a*) make for, go in the direction of

encandecer *vt irr* to make incandescent. See **conocer**

encandilar *vt* to dazzle; mislead; *inf* poke (the fire); *vr* be bloodshot (eyes)

encanecer *vi irr* to grow gray- or white-haired; grow mold; grow old. See **conocer**

encanijar *vt* to make weak, sickly (gen. of babies); *vr* be delicate or ailing

encantado *a inf* daydreaming, abstracted; haunted; rambling (of houses)

encantador *a* captivating, bewitching, delightful. *m,* sorcerer, magician. **e. de serpientes,** snake charmer

encantamiento *m,* enchantment, spell, charm

encantar *vt* to enchant, weave a spell; delight, captivate, charm

encañada *f,* gorge, ravine

encañado *m,* trellis; pipeline

encañar *vt* to run water through a pipe; stake plants; wind thread on a spool

encañonar *vt* to run into pipes; pleat, fold

encapotarse *vr* to muffle oneself in a cloak; scowl; be overcast; lower (sky)

encapricharse *vr* to take a fancy (to); insist on having one's own way, be stubborn

encaramar *vt* to raise, lift; climb; praise, extol. **e. al poder,** to put in power (e.g. a dictator). **encaramarse por,** to climb up

encarar *vt* to place face to face; aim (at); *vt* and *vr* face; come face to face

encarcelación *f,* incarceration

encarcelar *vt* to imprison, jail; *carp* clamp

encarecer *vt irr* to raise the price; overpraise, exaggerate; recommend strongly; *vi* and *vr* increase in price. See **conocer**

encarecimiento *m*, increase (in price); enhancement; exaggeration. **con e.,** insistently, earnestly

encargado *m*, person in charge; manager; agent, representative. **e. de negocios,** chargé d'affaires

encargar *vt* to enjoin; commission; recommend; advise; *com* order

encargo *m*, charge, commission; order; office, employ; responsibility

encariñarse (*con*), *vi* to become fond (of)

encarnación *f*, incarnation

encarnadino *a* incarnadine

encarnado *a* incarnate; flesh-colored; red

encarnar *vi* to incarnate; pierce the flesh; *fig* leave a strong impression; *vt* symbolize, personify; *vr* mingle, blend

encarnizado *a* bloodshot (eyes); flesh-colored; bloody, cruel (gen. of battles)

encarnizamiento *m*, cruelty, fury

encarnizar *vt* to infuriate; *vr* devour flesh (animals); persecute, ill-treat

encaro *m*, stare, gaze; aim

encarrilar *vt* to set on the track or rails (vehicles); *fig* put right, set on the right track

encartamiento *m*, proscription; charter

encartar *vt* to proscribe, outlaw; place on the tax register; *law* summon, cite

encartonar *vt* to cover with cardboard; bind in boards (books)

encasar *vt surg* to set (a bone)

encasillado *m*, set of pigeonholes

encasillar *vt* to pigeonhole; file, classify

encasquetar(se) *vt* and *vr* to pull a hat well down on the head; *vr* get a fixed idea

encasquillador, -a *mf*, *Lat. Am.* blacksmith

encastillar *vt* to fortify with castles; *vr* retire to a castle; be headstrong, obstinate

encauzamiento *m*, channeling; *fig* direction

encauzar *vt* to channel; *fig* direct, guide

encefalitis *f*, encephalitis. **e. letárgica,** encephalitis lethargica, sleeping sickness. **enceguedor** *a* blinding, dazzling

encéfalo *m*, *anat* brain

encenagarse *vr* to wallow in mire; muddy oneself; take to vice

encendedor *a* lighting. *m*, lighter. **e. de bolsillo,** pocket lighter

encender *vt irr* to light; switch on; set fire to, kindle; arouse (emotions); inflame, incite; *vr* blush. See **entender**

encendido *a* high-colored; inflamed; ardent. *m*, *aut* ignition

encerado *a* wax-colored. *m*, oilskin; sticking plaster; blackboard; tarpaulin

enceramiento *m*, waxing

encerar *vt* to wax, varnish with wax; stain with wax; inspissate (lime)

encercar *vt*, *Lat. Am.* to encircle

encerotar *vt* to wax (thread)

encerrar *vt irr* to shut up, imprison; include, contain; *vr* go into seclusion. See **acertar**

encerrona *f*, *inf* voluntary retreat; *fig inf* tight corner

encespedar *vt* to cover with sod

enchilada *f*, *Mexico* rolled-up tortilla filled with meat or cheese and covered with sauce or cream

enchufar *vt* to connect tubes; *fig* combine (jobs, etc.); *elec* plug, connect

enchufe *m*, joint, fitting together (of tubes); *elec* wall socket, plug; part-time post; *inf* cushy job. **e. de reducción,** *elec* adapter

encía *f*, gum (of the mouth)

encíclica *f*, encyclical

enciclopedia *f*, encyclopedia

enciclopédico *a* encyclopedic

encierro *m*, act of closing or shutting up; prison; retreat, confinement

encima *adv* over; above; at the top; besides; (*with de*) on, on top of. **por e. de esto,** over and above this, besides this

encinta *a f*, pregnant

encintar *vt* to decorate with ribbons

enclavar *vt* to nail; pierce; embed; *inf* deceive

enclenque *a* ailing, weak; puny, anemic

enclocar *vi irr* to begin to brood (hens). See **contar**

encobar *vi* to hatch eggs

encoger *vt* to shrink, contract, recoil; discourage; *vi* shrink (wood, cloth, etc.); *vr* shrink from, recoil; be discouraged; be timid or bashful

encogimiento *m*, shrinkage; contraction; depression, discouragement; timidity; bashfulness

encoladura *f*. **encolamiento** *m*, gluing; sizing

encolerizar *vt* to anger; *vr* be angry

encomendar *vt irr* to charge with, entrust; recommend, commend; *vr* (*with prep a*) put one's trust in; send greetings to. See **acertar**

encomiar *vt* to eulogize, praise

encomienda *f*, commission, charge; knight commandership; insignia of knight commander; land formerly granted in America to *conquistadores*; recommendation, commendation; protection, defense; *pl* greetings, compliments, messages

encomio *m*, eulogy; strong recommendation

enconar *vt* to irritate, exasperate; *vr med* be inflamed; be exasperated; (*with en*) burden one's conscience with

encono *m*, rancor, resentment, ill will

encontrado *a* facing, opposite, in front; hostile, inimical, opposed (to)

encontrar *vt irr* to meet; find; *vi* meet; encounter unexpectedly; (*with con*) run into, collide with; *vr* be antagonistic; find; feel, be; differ, disagree (opinions); (*with con*) meet, come across. **e. eco,** to strike a responsive chord. **encontrarse con el cura de su pueblo,** to find someone who knows all about, meet someone who knows all about. **¿Cómo se encuentra Vd?** How are you? *Pres. Ind.* **encuentro,** etc. *Pres. Subjunc.* **encuentre,** etc.

encontrón *m*, collision, violent impact

encopetado *a* conceited, proud; of noble descent; prominent, important

encorajar *vt* to encourage, inspire, hearten; *vr* be angry

encordelar *vt* to cord, rope

encorsetar *vt* to correct

encorvadura *f*, bending, curving

encorvar *vt* to bend, curve; *vr* have a leaning toward, favor

encostrar *vt* to cover with a crust; *vr* form a crust

encrespador *m*, curling irons

encrespar *vt* to curl (hair); enrage; *vr* be curly (hair); stand on end (hair, feathers, from fright); be angry; grow rough (sea); become complicated, entangled

encrestado *a* crested; haughty, arrogant

encrestarse *vr* to stiffen the comb or crest (birds)

encrucijada *f*, crossroad, intersection; ambush

encrudecer *vt irr* to make raw-looking; annoy; *vr* be annoyed. See **conocer**

encuadernación *f*, bookbinding; binding (of a book); bookbinder's workshop. **e. en tela,** cloth binding

encuadernador (-ra) *n* bookbinder

encuadernar *vt* to bind (a book)

encuadrar *vt* to frame; fit one thing into another, insert; limit; *mil* enlist

encubar *vt* to put into casks (wine, etc.)

encubiertamente *adv* secretly; deceitfully

encubierto *a* concealed; secret

encubridor (-ra) *a* concealing, hiding. *n* hider; harborer; accomplice; receiver (of stolen goods); *law* accessory after the fact

encubrimiento *m*, hiding, concealment; *law* accessory before (after) the fact; receiving (of stolen goods)

encubrir *vt* to conceal; receive (stolen goods); *law* prosecute as an accessory. *Past. Part.* **encubierto**

encuentro *m*, collision; meeting, encounter; opposition, hostility; *mil* fight, skirmish; *arch* angle. **ir al e. de,** to go in search of. **salir al e. (de),** to go to meet; resist

encuerado, -a *a, Lat. Am.* naked, nude, in the buff

encuesta *f*, investigation, examination

encumbrado *a* elevated, high

encumbramiento *m*, act of elevating; height; aggrandizement, advancement

encumbrar *vt* to raise, elevate; exalt, promote; ascend, climb to the top; *vr* be proud; be lofty, tower

encurtido *m*, pickle

encurtir *vt* to pickle

ende *adv ant* there. **por e.,** therefore

endeble *a* weak, frail

endeblez *f*, weakness

endémico *a med* endemic

endemoniado *a* devil-possessed; *inf* fiendish, malevolent

endemoniar *vt* to possess with a devil; *inf* enrage

endentar *vt irr mech* to cut the cogs (of a wheel); engage, interlock (gears, wheels, etc.). See **regimentar**

endentecer *vi irr* to cut teeth. See **conocer**

enderezamiento *m*, straightening; directing, guiding; putting right, correction

enderezar *vt* to straighten; direct, guide; put right, correct; *vi* take the right road; *vr* straighten oneself; prepare to

endeudarse *vr* to contract debts; be under an obligation

endiablado *a* ugly, monstrous; *inf* fiendish

endiosar *vt* to deify; *vr* be puffed up with pride; be abstracted or lost in ecstasy

enditarse *vr, Lat. Am.* to go into debt

endocrino *a* endocrine

endocrinología *f*, endocrinology

endomingarse *vr* to put on one's Sunday best

endosante *m*, endorser

endosar *vt com* to endorse; transfer, pass on

endoso *m*, *com* endorsement

endrogarse *vr, Mexico* = **enditarse**

endulzar *vt* to sweeten; soften, mitigate

endurecer *vt irr* to harden; toughen, inure; make severe or cruel; *vr* grow hard; become hardened or robust; be harsh or cruel. **endurecerse al trabajo,** to become hardened to work. See **conocer**

endurecimiento *m*, hardness; obstinacy, tenacity

ene *f*, name of letter N

enemiga *f*, hostility, enmity

enemigo (-ga) *a* hostile. *n* enemy; antagonist. *m*, devil

enemistad *f*, enmity, hostility

enemistar *vt* to make enemies of; *vr* (*with con*) become an enemy of; cease to be friendly with

energético, -a *a, Lat. Am.* = **enérgico**

energía *f*, energy, vigor

enérgico *a* energetic, vigorous

energúmeno (-na) *n* energumen

enero *m*, January

enervación *f*, enervation

enervar *vt* to enervate, weaken; *fig* take the force out of (reasons, etc.)

enfadar *vt* to make angry; *vr* become angry; *Lat. Am.* to get bored

enfado *m*, anger; annoyance; trouble, toil

enfadoso *a* vexatious; troublesome, wearisome

enfaldada *f*, skirtful

enfaldar *vt* to tuck up the skirts; lop off lower branches (of trees)

enfangarse *vr* to cover oneself with mud; *inf* dirty one's hands, sully one's reputation; wallow in vice

énfasis *m*, or *f*, emphasis

enfático *a* emphatic

enfermar *vi* to fall ill; *vt* cause illness; *fig* weaken. **Enfermó del corazón,** He fell ill with heart trouble.

enfermedad *f*, illness; *fig* malady, distemper. **e. del sueño,** sleeping sickness

enfermería *f*, infirmary; hospital; first-aid station

enfermero, -a *mf* nurse

enfermizo *a* ailing, delicate; unhealthy, unwholesome

enfermo (-ma) *a* ill; *fig* corrupt, diseased; delicate, sickly. *n* patient. **e. venéreo,** person with a venereal disease

enfilar *vt* to place in line; string; *mil* enfilade

enflaquecer *vt irr* to make thin; weaken, enervate; *vi* grow thin; lose heart. See **conocer**

enflaquecimiento *m*, loss of flesh; discouragement

enfocar *vt* to focus; envisage

enfoque *m*, focus

enfoscado *a* ill-humored; immersed in business matters

enfrascar *vt* to bottle; *vr* (*with en*) plunge into, entangle oneself in (undergrowth, etc.); become engrossed or absorbed in

enfrenar *vt* to bridle; curb (a horse); restrain, repress; check

enfrente *adv* in front, opposite, facing; in opposition

enfriadero *m*, cooling place, cold cellar, root cellar

enfriamiento *m*, cooling

enfriar *vt* to cool; *fig* chill, make indifferent; *vr* grow cold; *fig* grow stormy (weather)

enfurecer *vt irr* to enrage. See **conocer**

enfurecimiento *m*, fury

enfurruñarse *vr inf* to fume, be angry; be disgruntled

engalanar *vt* to decorate, embellish. **engalanado como nunca,** dressed to the nines, dressed to kill

enganchar *vt* to hook; couple, connect; hitch, harness, yoke; *inf* seduce, hook; *mil* bribe into army; *vr* be hooked or caught on a hook; *mil* enlist

enganche *m*, hooking; coupling (of railroad trains, etc.); connection; yoke, harness; hook; *inf* enticement; *mil* enlistment; *Mexico* down payment

engañadizo *a* easily deceived, simple

engañador (-ra) *a* deceiving; deceptive. *n* deceiver, impostor

engañar *vt* to deceive; defraud, cheat; beguile, while away; hoax, humbug; *vr* be mistaken; deceive oneself. **e. como a un chino,** *inf* to pull the wool over a person's eyes. **Las apariencias engañan,** Appearances are deceptive

engañifa *f*, *inf* swindle, fraud

engaño *m*, deceit; deception, illusion; fraud; falsehood

engañoso *a* deceitful, false; fraudulent; deceptive, misleading

engarabatar *vt inf* to hook; *vr* become hooked, curved, crooked

engaratusar *vt, inf, Lat. Am.* = **engatusar**

engarce *m*, hooking; coupling; setting (of jewels)

engarzar *vt* to link, couple, enchain; hook; curl; set (jewels)

engastar *vt* to set (jewels)

engaste *m*, setting of (jewels)

engatusar *vt inf* to wheedle, coax, flatter

engendrador (-ra) *a* engendering; original. *n* begetter

engendrar *vt* to procreate; engender, produce, cause

engendro *m*, fetus; abnormal embryo; literary monstrosity

engestarse *vr, Mexico* to make a wry face

englobar *vt* to include, comprise, embrace

engolfarse *vr* to sail out to sea; (*with en*) *fig* be absorbed in

engomar *vt* to gum

engordar *vt* to fatten; *vi* grow fat; *inf* prosper, grow rich

engorde *m*, fattening (of stock)

engorrar *vt, Lat. Am.* to annoy, needle

engorro *m*, impediment, obstacle, difficulty

engorroso *a* difficult, troublesome

engranaje *m*, *mech* gearing, gear; *fig* connection, link

engrandecer *vt irr* to enlarge; augment; eulogize; promote, exalt. See **conocer**

engrandecimiento *m*, enlargement; increase; exaggeration, eulogization; advancement, promotion

engrasador *m*, greaser, lubricator; oiler

engrasar *vt* to grease; lubricate, oil; manure; stain with grease

engreimiento *m*, conceit, vanity

engreír *vt irr* to make conceited; *vr* become vain or conceited. See **reír**

engrescar(se) *vt* and *vr* to start a quarrel

engrosar *vt irr* to fatten, thicken; *fig* increase, swell; manure; *vi* put on weight, grow fat. See **contar**

engrudar *vt* to paste, glue

engrudo *m*, paste, glue

enguijarrado *a* pebbled. *m*, pebbled path

engullir *vt* to gobble, swallow

enhebrar *vt* to thread (needles); string

enhestar *vt irr* to erect; set upright; *vr* rise; rear up; straighten oneself up. See **acertar**

enhiesto *a* upright, erect

enhorabuena *f*, congratulation. *adv* well and good. **dar la e.,** to congratulate

enhoramala *adv* in an evil hour. *inf* **¡Vete e.!** Go to the devil!

enhorquetado *a* in the saddle

enigma *m*, enigma

enigmático *a* enigmatical

enjabonar *vt* to soap; *inf* soap down, flatter

enjaezar *vt* to harness (a horse)

enjalbegar *vt* to whitewash

enjambrar *vt* to hive bees; *vi* multiply, increase

enjambre *m*, swarm (of bees); crowd

enjaretado *m*, latticework

enjaular *vt* to cage; *inf* jail

enjoyar *vt* to adorn with jewels; beautify; set with precious stones

enjuagadura *f*, rinsing (the mouth); rinse water; mouthwash

enjuagar *vt* to rinse; *vr* rinse the mouth

enjuague *m*, rinse; rinsing; mouthwash; tooth mug; scheme, plan

enjugar *vt* to dry; cancel, write off; wipe, mop (perspiration, tears, etc.); *vr* grow lean

enjuiciar *vt* to submit a matter to arbitration; *law* prosecute; *law* render judgment; *law* adjudicate (a case)

enjundia *f*, animal fat or grease; *fig* substance; meat; strength, vigor; constitution, temperament

enjuto *a* dry; lean. *m pl*, brushwood; *cul* canapés, savories

enlace *m*, connection; link; tie; *chem* bond; alliance, relationship; marriage

enladrillado *m*, brick floor or pavement

enlardar *vt cul* to baste

enlazar *vt* to tie, bind; join, link; lasso; *vr* marry; be allied, related. **e. con,** to connect with (of trains); link up with

enlentecerse *vr* to decelerate, go slow, slow down

enlodar *vt* to muddy; *fig* smirch, sully

enloquecer *vt irr* to drive insane; *vi* go mad. See **conocer**

enlosado *m*, tile floor

enlosar *vt* to pave with flags

enlozar *vt*, *Lat. Am.* to enamel, glaze

enlucir *vt irr* to plaster (walls); polish (metals). See **lucir**

enlutar *vt* to put in mourning, drape with crepe; darken, obscure; sadden; *vr* go into mourning; become dark

enmaderar *vt* to panel in wood, board up

enmarañar *vt* to tangle, disorder (hair, etc.); complicate, confuse; *vr* be tangled; be sprinkled with clouds

enmaridar *vi* to take a wife

enmarillecerse *vr irr* to grow yellow. See **conocer**

enmascarar *vt* to mask; disguise, dissemble; *vr* be masked

enmasillar *vt* to putty

enmendar *vt irr* to correct, improve; reform; compensate, indemnify; *law* repeal; *vr* be improved or corrected; mend one's ways. See **acertar**

enmienda *f*, correction; reform; indemnity; compensation; amendment; *pl agr* fertilizers

enmohecer *vt irr* to rust; *vr* become moldy. See **conocer**

enmudecer *vt irr* to silence; *vi* become dumb; be silent. See **conocer**

enmugrecer *vt irr* to cover with grime; *vr* be grimy, dirty. See **conocer**

enmugrentar *vt*, *Chile* = **enmugrecer**

ennegrecer *vt irr* to dye black; make black; *vr* become black; become dark or cloudy. See **conocer**

ennoblecer *vt irr* to ennoble; enrich, embellish; adorn, befit. See **conocer**

ennoblecimiento *m*, ennoblement; enrichment

enojadizo *a* irritable, peevish

enojar *vt* to anger; annoy, irritate; *vr* be angry; rage, be rough (wind, sea)

enojo *m*, anger; resentment; vexations, troubles, trials (gen. *pl*). **con gran e. de,** much to the annoyance of

enojoso *a* annoying; troublesome, tiresome

enorgullecer *vt irr* to make proud; *vr* be proud. See **conocer**

enorme *a* enormous, huge; monstrous, heinous

enormidad *f*, hugeness; enormity; wickedness

enramar *vt* to intertwine branches; embower; *vi* branch (trees)

enrarecer *vt irr* to rarefy; *vr* become rarefied; grow rare. See **conocer**

enrarecimiento *m*, rarefaction

enredadera *f*, convolvulus. *a f*, climbing, twining (plant)

enredador (-ra) *a* mischievous, willful; intriguing, scheming; *inf* gossiping, meddlesome. *n* intriguer; *inf* meddler

enredar *vt* to catch in a net; put down nets or snares; entangle; sow discord; compromise, involve (in difficulties); *vi* be mischievous; *vr* be entangled; be involved (in difficulties)

enredo *m*, tangle; mischief, prank; intrigue, malicious falsehood; difficult situation; plot

enredoso *a* tangled; fraught with difficulties

enrejado *m*, railing, paling; trellis or latticework; *sew* openwork

enrejar *vt* to fence with a railing; cover with grating

enriquecer *vt irr* to enrich; exalt, aggrandize; *vi* grow rich; prosper, flourish. See **conocer**

enriscado *a* craggy, rocky

enristrar *vt* to couch (a lance); string (onions, etc.); *fig* surmount (difficulties); go straight to (a place)

enrojecer *vt irr* to redden; make blush; *vr* grow red; blush. See **conocer**

enroscar *vt* to twist, twine; *vr* turn (screw); twist; coil

ensaimada *f*, Spanish pastry cake

ensalada *f*, salad; hodgepodge

ensaladera *f*, salad bowl

ensalmar *vt surg* to set (bones); cure by spells

ensalmo *m*, spell, charm. **por e.,** as if by magic, rapidly

ensalzar *vt* to exalt, promote; praise

ensamblador *m*, joiner, assembler

ensambladura *f*, assemblage, joinery; joining; dovetailing

ensamblar *vt* to assemble; join, dovetail, mortise

ensanchador, -a *mf*, glove stretcher

ensanchar *vt* to widen, enlarge, extend; *sew* let out, stretch; *vr* put on airs

ensanche *m*, dilatation, widening; stretch; extension; *sew* turnings, letting out; (city) extension

ensangrentar *vt irr* to stain with blood; *vr* be bloodstained; be overhasty. See **regimentar**

ensañar *vt* to irritate, infuriate; *vr* be merciless (with vanquished)

ensartar *vt* to string (beads); thread (needles); spit, pierce; tell a string (of falsehoods)

ensayar *vt* to try out; *chem* test; *theat* rehearse; assay

ensayista *mf* essayist

ensayo *m*, test, trial; *lit* essay; assay; experiment; rehearsal. **e. general,** dress rehearsal

ensenada *f*, cove, inlet

enseñanza *f*, teaching; education; example, experience. **e. primaria,** elementary education. **e. secundaria,** secondary education. **e. superior,** higher education

enseñar *vt* to teach, instruct; train; point out; exhibit, show; *vr* become accustomed. **e. la oreja,** *fig* to show the cloven hoof

enseñorearse *vr* to take possession (of)

enseres *m pl,* household goods; utensils; equipment

ensilladero *m*, paddock

ensillar *vt* to saddle

ensimismarse *vr* to be lost in thought; *Lat. Am.* to become conceited

ensoberbecer *vt irr* to make haughty; *vr* become arrogant; grow rough (sea). See **conocer**

ensordecedor *a* deafening

ensordecer *vt irr* to deafen; *vi* become deaf; keep silent, refuse to reply. See **conocer**

ensuciar *vt* to soil, dirty; *fig* sully; *vr* be dirty; *inf* accept bribes

ensueño *m*, dream; illusion, fancy

entabicar *vt, Lat. Am.* to partition off

entablado *m*, stage, dais; wooden floor; planking

entablar *vt* to plank, floor with boards; board up; *surg* splint; undertake, initiate (negotiations, etc.); begin (conversations, etc.); *vr* settle (winds). **e. acción judicial,** to take legal action

entalegar *vt* to put into sacks or bags; hoard (money)

entalladura *f*, carving; sculpture; *carp* mortise, notch

entallar *vt* to carve; sculpture; engrave; notch, groove; tap (trees); fit (well or ill) at the waist

entallecer *vi irr* to sprout (plants). See **conocer**

entapizar *vt* to hang with tapestry; upholster; *fig* cover, carpet

entarimado *m*, wooden floor; dais

ente *m*, entity, being; *inf* object, individual

entechar *vt, Lat. Am.* to roof, to put a roof on

enteco *a* sickly, ailing, delicate

entendederas *f pl, inf* understanding

entendedor (-ra) *a* understanding, comprehending. *n* one who understands. **A buen e. pocas palabras,** A word to the wise is sufficient

entender *vt irr* to comprehend, understand; know; deduce, infer; intend; believe; *(with de)* be familiar with or knowledgeable about; *(with en)* have as a profession or trade; be engaged in; have authority in; *vr* understand oneself; have a reason (for behavior); understand each other; have an amatory understanding; be meant, signify; *(with con)* have an understanding with. **a mi e.,** in my opinion, as I see it. *Pres. Ind.* **entiendo, entiendes, entiende, entienden.** *Pres. Subjunc.* **entienda, entiendas, entienda, entiendan**

entendido *a* learned, knowledgeable

entendimiento *m*, understanding; mind, reason, intelligence

enteramente *adv* completely, entirely, wholly

enterar *vt* to inform, advise

entereza *f*, entirety; completeness; impartiality, integrity; fortitude, constancy; strictness, rigour

enternecer *vt irr* to make lukewarm, make tender; move to pity; *vr* be touched by compassion. See **conocer**

enternecimiento *m*, compassion, pity; tenderness

entero *a* entire; whole; robust, healthy; upright, just; constant, loyal; virgin; pure; *inf* strong, tough (cloth); *math* integral; *Lat. Am.* payment

enterrador *m*, gravedigger

enterrar *vt irr* to inter; outlive; bury, forget. See **acertar**

entibiar *vt* to make lukewarm; *fig* cool, temper

entidad *f*, entity; value, importance

entierro *m*, interment, burial; grave; funeral; buried treasure

entoldar *vt* to cover with an awning; hang with tapestry, etc., drape; cover (sky, clouds)

entomología *f*, entomology

entomológico *a* entomological

entomólogo *m*, entomologist

entonación *f*, intonation; modulation (voice); conceit

entonado *m*, haughty, conceited

entonar *vt* to modulate (voice); intone; blow (organ bellows); lead (song); *med* tone up; *art* harmonize; *vr* become conceited; *com* improve, harden (stock, etc.)

entonces *adv* then, at that time; in that case, that being so

entonelar *vt* to put in barrels or casks

entontecer *vt irr* to make stupid or foolish; *vr* become stupid. See **conocer**

entornar *vt* to leave ajar; half-close; upset, turn upside down

entorpecer *vt irr* to numb, make torpid; confuse, daze; obstruct, delay; *vr* go numb; be confused. See **conocer**

entorpecimiento *m*, numbness, torpidity; stupidity, dullness; delay, obstruction

entrada *f*, entrance; door, gate; admission; *cul* entree; admission ticket; *theat* house; takings, gate; *mil* entry; beginnings (of month, etc.); intimacy; right of entry. **entradas y salidas,** comings and goings; collusion; *com* ingoing and outgoing

entrampar *vt* to trap (animals); swindle; *fig inf* entangle (business affairs); *inf* load with debts; *vr* be bogged down; *inf* be in debt

entrante *a* incoming, entrant; next, coming (month)

entraña *f*, entrail; *pl* heart; *fig* center, core; humaneness; temperament. *inf* **no tener entrañas,** to be heartless, be without feeling

entrañable *a* intimate; dearly loved

entrar *vi (with en)* to enter, go into, come in; flow into; *fig* have access to; join, become a member; *fig* be taken by (fever, panic, etc.); *mil* enter; be an ingredient of; *(with por, en)* penetrate, pierce; *(with de)* embrace (professions, etc.); *(with prep a + infin)* begin to; *(with en + noun)* begin to be (e.g. **e. en calor,** begin to be hot) or begin to take part in (e.g. **e. en lucha,** begin to fight); *vt* introduce, make enter; *mil (with en)* occupy; *vr (with en)* squeeze in. **e. en apetito,** to work up an appetite, get an appetite. *inf* **no e. ni salir en,** to take no part in. *inf* **No me entra,** I don't understand it

entre *prep* between; among; to. **e. joyas,** among jewels. **E. las dos se escribió la carta,** Between them, they wrote the letter. **Dije e. mí,** I said to myself. **los días de e. semana,** weekdays. **e. tanto,** in the meanwhile.

entreabrir *vt* to leave ajar; half-open. *Past Part.* **entreabierto**

entreacto *m*, interval, entr'acte; small cigar

entrecano *a* going gray, grayish (hair)

entrecejo *m*, space between the eyebrows; frown

entrecerrar *vt, Lat. Am* to close halfway, half-close; leave ajar

entrecoger *vt* to intercept, catch; constrain, compel

entrecortado *a* intermittent (sounds); faltering, broken (voice)

entrecubiertas *f pl, naut* between decks

entredicho *m*, prohibition; *ecc* interdiction

entredós *m, sew* insertion

entrefino *a* middling, fairly fine

entrega *f*, handing over; delivery; *lit* part, serial; installment. **por entregas,** as a serial, serial (of stories)

entregar *vt* to hand over; deliver; surrender; *vr* give oneself up; surrender; submit; *(with prep a)* engage in, be absorbed in; *(with prep a or en)* give oneself over to (vice, etc.)

entreguista *mf* defeatist

entrelazar *vt* to interlace, intertwine; interweave

entrelistado *a* striped

entrelucir *vi irr* to show through, be glimpsed. See **lucir**

entremedias *adv* in between, halfway; in the meantime

entremés *m*, hors d'oeuvres (gen. *pl*); interlude, one-act farce

entremeter *vt* to place between or among; *vr* intrude; meddle, pry

entremetido (-da) *a* meddlesome. *n* busybody, meddler

entremetimiento *m*, meddlesomeness

entremezclar *vt* to intermingle

entrenador (-ra) *n* trainer; *sport* coach

entrenamiento *m*, training, exercise

entrenar(se) *vt* and *vr* to train; exercise; *sport* coach

entreoír *vt* to overhear; hear imperfectly

entrepaño *m*, *arch* panel; pier (between windows, etc.)

entrepiernas *f pl*, crotch

entresacar *vt* to choose or pick out; thin out (plants); thin (hair)

entresuelo *m*, mezzanine, entresol; ground floor

entresueño *m*, daydream

entretallar *vt* to carve in bas-relief; engrave; *sew* do openwork; intercept; *vr* connect, dovetail

entretejer *vt* to interweave; interlace; *lit* insert

entretela *f*, *sew* interlining

entretener *vt irr* to keep waiting; make more bearable; amuse, entertain; delay, postpone; maintain, upkeep; *vr* amuse oneself. See **tener**

entretenido *a* amusing, entertaining

entretenimiento *m*, amusement; pastime, diversion; upkeep, maintenance

entretiempo *m*, between seasons, spring or autumn

entreventana *f*, space between windows

entreverado *a* variegated; streaky (of bacon)

entreverar *vt* to intermingle

entrevista *f*, meeting, interview

entristecer *vt irr* to sadden; *vr* grieve. See **conocer**

entristecimiento *m*, sadness

entrometer *vt* See **entremeter**

entromparse *vt*, *Lat. Am.* to get angry

entronar *vt* See **entronizar**

entroncar *vt* to prove descent; *vi* be related, or become related (by marriage)

entronerar *vt* to pocket (in billiards)

entronizar *vt* to enthrone; exalt

entronque *m*, blood relationship, cognation; junction

entrucharse *vr*, *Mexico* to meddle into other people's business

entumecer *vt irr* to numb; *vr* go numb; swell, rise (sea, etc.). See **conocer**

enturbiar *vt* to make turbid or cloudy; confuse, disorder; *vr* become turbid; be in disorder

entusiasmar *vt* to inspire enthusiasm; *vr* be enthusiastic

entusiasmo *m*, enthusiasm

entusiasta *a* enthusiastic. *mf* enthusiast

enumeración *f*, enumeration

enumerar *vt* to enumerate

enunciación *f*, statement, declaration, enunciation

enunciar *vt* to state clearly, enunciate

envainar *vt* to sheathe

envalentonamiento *m*, boldness; braggadocio, bravado

envalentonar *vt* to make bold (gen. in a bad sense); *vr* strut, brag; take courage

envanecer *vt irr* to make vain or conceited; *vr* be vain; be conceited

envanecimiento *m*, conceit, vanity

envasador (-ra) *n* packer. *m*, funnel

envasar *vt* to bottle; barrel; sack (grain, etc.); pack in any container; pierce (with sword)

envase *m*, bottling; filling; container; packing

envejecer *vt irr* to make old, wear out; *vi* grow old. See **conocer**

envenenador (-ra) *n* poisoner

envenenamiento *m*, poisoning

envenenar *vt* to poison; corrupt, pervert; put a malicious interpretation on; embitter; *vr* take poison

envergadura *f*, wingspan

envés *m*, wrong side of anything; *inf* back. **al e.,** wrong side out

enviado *m*, messenger; envoy. **e. extraordinario,** special envoy

enviar *vt* to send, dispatch

enviciar *vt* to corrupt, make vicious; *vr* (*with con, en*) take to (drink, etc.)

envidia *f*, envy; emulation; desire (to possess)

envidiable *a* enviable

envidiar *vt* to envy, grudge; emulate

envidioso *a* envious

envilecer *vt irr* to debase; *vr* degrade oneself. See **conocer**

envinarse *vr*, *Mexico* to get drunk (on wine)

envío *m*, *com* remittance; consignment

envite *m*, stake (at cards); offer; push, shove

enviudar *vi* to become a widow or widower

envoltorio *m*, bundle

envoltura *f*, swaddling clothes; covering; wrapping

envolver *vt irr* to enfold; envelop; wrap up, parcel; *fig* contain, enshrine; swaddle, swathe; roll into a ball; confound (in argument); *mil* outflank; implicate (person). See **mover**

enyesado *m*, plastering; stucco

enyesar *vt* to plaster; *surg* apply a plaster bandage

enzarzar *vt* to fill or cover with brambles; *vr* be caught on brambles; set one person against another; get in difficulties; quarrel

eñe *f*, name of the letter Ñ

eón *m*, eon

eperlano *m*, smelt

épica *f*, epic

épico *a* epic

epicúreo (-ea) *a* epicurean; sensual, voluptuous. *n* epicure

epidemia *f*, epidemic

epidémico *a* epidemic

epifanía *f*, Epiphany, Twelfth Night

epiglotis *f*, epiglottis

epígrafe *m*, epigraph, inscription; title, motto

epigrafía *f*, epigraphy

epigrama *m*, inscription; epigram

epigramático (-ca) *a* epigrammatic. *n* epigrammatist

epilepsia *f*, epilepsy

epiléptico (-ca) *a* and *n* epileptic

epilogar *vt* to summarize, recapitulate

epílogo *m*, recapitulation; summary, digest; epilogue

episcopado *m*, episcopate; bishopric

episodio *m*, episode; digression

epistolar *a* epistolary

epitafio *m*, epitaph

epíteto *m*, epithet

epítome *m*, epitome; summary, abstract

época *f*, epoch, period; space of time. **é. de celo,** mating season. **é. de lluvias,** rainy season. **é. de secas,** dry season. **en aquella é.,** at that time

épodo *m*, *poet* epode

epopeya *f*, epic poem; *fig* epic

equidad *f*, fairness; reasonableness; equity

equidistancia *f*, equidistance

equidistante *a* equidistant

equilibrar *vt* to balance; *fig* maintain in equilibrium, counterbalance

equilibrio *m*, equilibrium; equanimity; *fig* balance

equilibrista *mf* equilibrist, tightrope walker

equino *a* equine. *m*, *arch* echinus; sea urchin

equinoccio *m*, equinox

equipaje *m*, luggage, baggage; *naut* crew

equipar *vt* to equip, furnish

equipo *m*, outfitting, furnishing; equipment; team; trousseau

equis *f*, name of the letter X

equitación *f*, horsemanship, riding

equitativo *a* equitable, just, fair

equivalencia *f*, equivalence, equality

equivalente *a* equivalent

equivaler *vi irr* to be equivalent; *geom* be equal. See **valer**

equivocación *f*, error, mistake

equivocadamente *adv* mistakenly, by mistake

equivocar *vt* to mistake; *vr* be mistaken or make a mistake. **equivocarse de medio a medio,** to be off by a long shot

equívoco *a* equivocal, ambiguous. *m*, equivocation

era *f*, era; threshing floor; vegetable or flower bed

erario *m*, public treasury, exchequer

erección *f*, raising; erection, elevation; foundation, institution

eremita *mf* hermit

erguir *vt irr* to raise; straighten; lift up; *vr* straighten up; tower; grow proud. *Pres. Ind.* **irgo** (or **yergo**), **irgues, irguen.** *Pres. Part.* **irguiendo.** *Preterite* **irguió, irguieron.** *Pres. Subjunc.* **irga** or **yerga,** etc.

erial *m*, uncultivated land

erigir *vt* to found, establish; promote, exalt. **erigirse contra,** to rise up against

erisipela *f*, erysipelas

erizado *a* standing on end (of hair); prickly, covered with bristles or quills. **e. de espinas,** bristling with thorns; covered with bristles or quills

erizar *vt* to set on end (hair); beset with difficulties; *vr* stand on end, bristle (hair, quills, etc.)

erizo *m*, hedgehog; husk (of some fruits); *inf* touch-me-not, unsociable person; *mech* sprocket wheel. **e. de mar,** sea urchin

ermita *f*, hermitage

ermitaño *m*, hermit

erogación *f*, *Lat. Am.* expenditure

erosión *f*, erosion

erótico *a* erotic

errabundo *a* wandering, errant, vagrant

erradamente *adv* erroneously

erradicable *a* eradicable

erradicación *f*, eradication

erradicar *vt* to eradicate

errante *a* wandering; erring; errant

errar *vi irr* to err, fail; rove, roam; wander (attention, etc.); *vr* be mistaken. *aut* **e. el encendido,** to misfire. *Pres. Ind.* **yerro, yerras, yerra, yerran.** *Pres. Subjunc.* **yerre, yerres, yerre, yerren**

errata *f*, misprint

errático *a* wandering, vagrant; *med* erratic

erre *f*, name of the letter R

erróneo *a* erroneous, mistaken

error *m*, error. **error de más,** an overestimate. **error de menos,** an underestimate

eructar *vi* to eructate, belch

eructo *m*, eructation, belching

erudición *f*, erudition

erudito *a* learned, erudite. *m*, scholar. **e. a la violeta,** pseudo-learned

erupción *f*, *med* rash; eruption

eruptivo *a* eruptive

es *vi 3rd pers. sing Pres. Ind.* of ser, is

esa *f*, *dem* a that. **ésa,** *f*, *dem. pron* that one; the former; the town in which you are (e.g. **Iré a é. mañana,** I shall come to your town tomorrow). Used generally in letters. See **ése**

esbeltez *f*, slenderness

esbelto *a* tall and slim and graceful, willowy

esbozar *vt* to sketch, outline

esbozo *m*, sketch; outline, rough plan, first draft

escabechar *vt* to pickle; dye (the hair, etc.); *inf* kill in anger; *inf* fail (an examination)

escabeche *m*, *cul* pickle; hair dye

escabechina *f*, *inf* heavy failure (in an examination)

escabel *m*, footstool; small backless chair; *fig* stepping-stone

escabioso *a* scabby, scabious

escabro *m*, scab, mange

escabroso *a* rough; rocky; uneven; rude, unpolished, uncivil; risqué, improper

escabullirse *vr irr* to escape; run away; slip out unnoticed. See **mullir**

escafandra *f*, diving suit, diving outfit

escala *f*, ladder; (*mus math*) scale; dial (of machines); proportion, ratio; stage, stopping place; measuring rule; *naut* port of call. **e. de toldilla,** companion ladder. *mus* **e. mayor,** major scale. **e. menor,** minor scale. *naut* **hacer e. en un puerto,** to call at a port

escalada *f*, escalade

escalafón *m*, salary scale; roll, list

escalamiento *m*, scaling, climbing; storming

escalar *vt* to scale; climb, ascend; storm, assail, enter or leave violently

escaldadura *f*, scalding; scald

escaldar *vt* to scald; make red-hot; *vr* scald or burn oneself. **Gato escaldado del agua fría huye,** Once bitten, twice shy

escalera *f*, staircase; stair. **e. abajo,** below stairs. **e. de caracol,** spiral staircase. **e. de mano,** ladder. **e. de tijera,** stepladder. **e. móvil,** escalator

escalfar *vt* to poach (eggs); burn (bread)

escalinata *f*, outside staircase or flight of steps, perron

escalofrío *m*, (gen. *pl*) shiver, shudder

escalón *m*, step, stair; rung (of a ladder); *fig* stepping-stone; grade, rank. **en escalones,** in steps

escalpar *vt* to scalp

escalpelo *m*, scalpel

escama *f*, *zool* scale; anything scale-shaped; flake; suspicion, resentment

escamar *vt* to scale (fish); make suspicious. *vr inf* be suspicious or disillusioned

escamondar *vt agr* to prune

escamoso *a* scaly

escamotear *vt* to make disappear; palm (in conjuring); steal

escamoteo *m*, disappearance; stealing

escampada *f*, *inf* clear interval on a rainy day

escampar *vi* to cease raining; clear up (of the weather, sky); stop (work, etc.)

escamujar *vt agr* to cut out superfluous wood (of trees, etc.)

escanciar *vt* to pour out wine; *vi* drink wine

escandalizar *vt* to shock, scandalize; disturb with noise; *vr* be vexed or irritated

escándalo *m*, scandal; commotion, uproar; bad example; viciousness; astonishment

escandaloso *a* disgraceful, scandalous; turbulent

escandallo *m*, *naut* deep-sea lead; random test

Escandinavia Scandinavia

escandinavo (-va) *a* and *n* Scandinavian

escansión *f*, scansion

escantillón *m*, template, pattern; rule

escaño *m*, bench with a back

escapada *f*, escape; escapade

escapar *vt* to spur on (a horse); *vi* escape; flee; avoid, evade; *vr* escape; leak (gas, etc.). **Se me escapó su nombre,** His name escaped me. **e. por un pelo,** to have a narrow escape

escaparate *m*, showcase, cabinet; shop window

escapatoria *f*, escape, flight; *inf* way out, loophole

escape *m*, flight; evasion; escape (gas, etc.); *aut* exhaust. **a e.,** at full speed

escápula *f*, scapula

escaque *m*, square (chessboard or checkerboard); *pl* chess

escaqueado *a* checked, worked in squares

escara *f*, scar

escarabajo *m*, beetle, scarab; *fig inf* dwarf; *pl inf* scrawl

escaramuza *f*, skirmish

escaramuzar *vi* to skirmish

escarapela *f*, cockade, rosette; brawl

escarbadientes *m*, toothpick

escarbar *vt* to scratch, scrabble (fowls); rootle, dig; rake out (the fire); inquire into

escarcha *f*, hoarfrost

escarchar vt cul to frost, ice; spread with frosting; vi freeze lightly

escarda f, weeding; fig weeding out

escardador (-ra) n weeder

escardar vt to weed; fig separate good from bad

escarificación f, scarification

escarlata f, scarlet; scarlet cloth

escarlatina f, scarlet fever

escarmentar vt irr to reprehend or punish severely; vi learn from experience, be warned. See **acertar**

escarmiento m, disillusionment, experience; warning; punishment, fine

escarnecedor (-ra) a mocking. n mocker

escarnecer vt irr to mock. See **conocer**

escarnio m, gibe, jeer

escarola f, endive; frilled ruff

escarpa f, steep slope, declivity; escarpment; Mexico pavement

escarpado a steep, precipitous

escarpín m, pump, slipper

escasear vt to dole out, give grudgingly; save, husband; vi be scarce or short; grow less

escasez f, meanness, frugality; want; shortage, scarcity

escaso a scarce; short; bare; parsimonious

escatimar vt to cut down, curtail

escatimoso a malicious, guileful

escayola f, plaster of Paris

escena f, theat stage; scene; scenery; theater, drama; spectacle, sight; episode, incident. **director de e.,** producer. **poner en e.,** theat to produce

escenario m, theat stage; scenario

escénico a scenic

escenografía f, scenography

escenógrafo (-fa) n scenographer, scene painter

escepticismo m, scepticism

escéptico (-ca) a sceptical. n sceptic

escindir vt to split

escisión f, cleavage, split; splitting; schism; disagreement

esclarecer vt irr to illuminate; ennoble, make illustrious; fig enlighten; elucidate; vi dawn. See **conocer**

esclarecido a distinguished, illustrious

esclavina f, short cape

esclavitud f, slavery; fraternity

esclavizar vt to enslave

esclavo (-va) n slave; member of a brotherhood. a enslaved. f, slave bracelet; ID bracelet

esclerosis f, sclerosis

esclerótica f, sclerotic

esclusa f, lock; sluice gate; weir

esclusero, -a mf, lock keeper

escoba f, broom, brush; bot yellow broom

escobada f, sweep, stroke (of a broom)

escobar vt to sweep with a broom

escobazo m, brush with a broom

escobero, -a brush maker; brush seller

escobilla f, brush

escocer vi irr to smart; fig sear; vr hurt, smart; be chafed. See **mover**

escocés (-esa) a Scots, Scottish. n Scot

Escocia Scotland

escoda f, claw hammer

escofina f, rasp, file

escoger vt to choose, select

escogido a choice, select

escolar a school; pupil. m, pupil

escolasticismo m, scholasticism

escolástico a scholastic

escoleta f, Mexico amateur band

escollera f, breakwater, sea wall, jetty

escollo m, reef; danger, risk; difficulty, obstacle

escolopendra f, centipede; hart's-tongue fern

escolta f, escort, guard

escoltar vt to escort; guard, conduct

escombrar vt to remove obstacles, free of rubbish; fig clean up

escombro m, debris, rubble, rubbish; mackerel

esconder vt to hide, conceal; fig contain, embrace; vr hide

escondidas, a adv secretly

escondite, escondrijo m, hiding place. **jugar al escondite,** to play hide-and-seek

escopeta f, shotgun. **e. de aire comprimido,** air gun, popgun. **e. de pistón,** repercussion gun. **e. de viento,** air gun

escopetazo m, gunshot; gunshot wound; fig bombshell

escopetear vt to shoot repeatedly

escopetero m, musketeer; gunsmith; man with a gun

escoplear vt carp to notch; chisel; gouge

escoplo m, chisel

escorbuto m, scurvy

escoria f, dross, slag; scoria, volcanic ash; fig dregs

escorial m, slag heap

escorpión m, scorpion; Scorpio

escorzo m, art foreshortening

escotado a low-cut (of dresses)

escotadura a low neck (of a dress); piece cut out of something; theat large trapdoor; recess

escotar vt to cut low in the neck (of dresses); pay one's share (of expenses)

escote m, low neck (of a dress); shortness (of sleeves); share (of expenses); lace yoke

escotilla f, naut hatch

escozor m, smart, pricking pain; irritation, prickle; heartache

escriba m, (Jewish hist.) scribe

escribanía f, secretaryship; notaryship; bureau, office; writing case; inkstand

escribano m, notary public; secretary

escribiente mf clerk

escribir vt to write; vr enlist; enroll; correspond by writing. Past Part. **escrito**

escrito m, writing, manuscript; literary or scientific work; law writ. **por e.,** in writing

escritor (-ra) n writer, author

escritorio m, escritoire; office

escritura f, writing; handwriting; law deed; literary work. **Sagrada E.,** Holy Scripture

escrófula f, scrofula

escrofuloso a scrofulous

escroto m, scrotum

escrúpulo m, scruple, qualm; conscientiousness; scruple (pharmacy)

escrupulosidad f, conscientiousness, scrupulousness

escrupuloso a scrupulous; exact, accurate

escrutador (-ra) n scrutinizer. a examining, inspecting

escrutar vt to scrutinize, examine; count (votes)

escrutinio m, scrutiny, examination; count (votes)

escuadra f, carpenter's square; architect's square; nav fleet; aer squadron; mil squad. **e. de agrimensor,** surv cross-staff

escuadrar vt (carp and mas) to square

escuadrilla f, squadron (airplanes, small ships)

escuadrón m, squadron

escualidez f, squalor, sordidness

escuálido a filthy, squalid; sordid; thin

escucha f, listening; peephole; mil sentinel

escuchar vt to listen; attend to, heed; vr like the sound of one's own voice

escudar vt to shield, protect

escudero m, squire, page; gentleman; shield maker

escudete m, escutcheon; shield; gusset; white water lily

escudilla f, bowl

escudo m, shield; escudo; escutcheon; protection, defense; ward (of a keyhole)

escudriñador (-ra) a searching; curious, prying. n scrutinizer; pryer

escudriñar vt to scrutinize; scan; investigate; pry into

escuela f, school; school building; style; (lit and art) school. **e. de artes y oficios,** industrial school. **e. industrial,** technical school. **e. normal,** normal school

escuelante m, Mexico schoolmaster

escueto *a* dry, bare, unadorned; simple, exact; unencumbered

escuincle *mf, Mexico* child

esculpir *vt* to sculpture; engrave

escultor (-ra) *n* sculptor

escultórico *a* sculptural

escultura *f*, sculpture; carving; modeling

escupidera *f*, spittoon

escupir *vi* to expectorate; *vt fig* spit out; cast away, throw out

escurreplatos *m*, dishrack, draining rack

escurrido *a* narrow-hipped; skintight (of skirts)

escurridor *m*, colander, sieve; dishrack; drainingboard

escurriduras *f pl*, lees, dregs

escurrir *vt* to drain to the dregs; wring, press out, drain; *vi* trickle, drip; slip, slide; *vr* slip away, edge away; escape, slip out; skid

esdrújulo *a gram* of words where the stress falls on the antepenultimate syllable

ese *f*, name of letter S; S-shaped link (in a chain). *inf* **andar haciendo eses,** to reel about drunkenly

ese *m, dem a* (*f*, **esa.** *pl* **esos, esas**) that; those. **ése,** *m, dem pron* (*f*, **ésa.** *neut* **eso.** *pl* **ésos, ésas**) that one; the former (e.g. **Me gusta éste, pero ése no me gusta,** I like this one, but I do not like that one

esencia *f*, essence, nature, character; extract; *chem* essence

esencial *a* essential

esfera *f, geom* sphere, globe, ball; sky; rank; face, dial; province, scope

esférico *a* spherical

esfinge *f*, sphinx

esforzado *a* valiant, courageous; spirited

esforzador *a* encouraging

esforzar *vt irr* to encourage; invigorate; *vr* make an effort. See **contar**

esfuerzo *m*, effort; courage; spirit; vigor; exertion; strain; *mech* stress. **sin e.,** effortless

esfumar *vt art* shade; *art* stump; dim; *vr* disappear

esfumino *m, art* stump

esgrima *f*, (art of) fencing

esgrimidor *m*, fencer, swordsman

esgrimir *vt* to fence; fend off

esguince *m*, dodging, twist; expression or gesture of repugnance; *med* sprain

eslabón *m*, link (in a chain); steel for producing fire. **e. perdido,** *fig* missing link

eslabonar *vt* to link; connect, unite

eslavo (-va) *a* Slavic. *n* Slav

eslora *f, naut* length (of a ship)

eslovaco (-ca) *a* Slovakian. *n* Slovak

esmaltador (-ra) *n* enameler

esmaltar *vt* to enamel; decorate, adorn

esmalte *m*, enamel; enamelwork; smalt; brilliance

esmerado *a* careful, painstaking

esmeralda *f*, emerald

esmerar *vt* to polish; *vr* (*with en*) take great pains with (or to)

esmeril *m*, emery

esmerilar *vt* to polish with emery

esmero *m*, great care, conscientiousness

esmoladera *f*, grindstone

esnob *a* snobbish. *mf* snob

eso *neut dem pron* that; the fact that; that idea, affair, etc.; about (of time) (e.g. **Vendrá a e. de las nueve,** He will come about nine o'clock). **Eso** refers to an abstraction, never to one definite object. **No me gusta e.,** I don't like that kind of thing. **e. es,** that's it. **por e.,** therefore, for that reason

esófago *m*, esophagus

esotérico *a* esoteric

espaciar *vt* to space; *print* lead; *vr* spread oneself, enlarge (upon)

espacio *m*, space; capacity; interval, duration; slowness; *print* lead

espaciosidad *f*, spaciousness; capacity

espada *f*, sword; matador; swordsman; (cards) spade. **entre la e. y la pared,** *fig* between a rock and a hard place; between undesirable alternatives.

espadachín *m*, good swordsman; bully, quarrelsome fellow

espadaña *f*, open belfry; gladiolus

espadería *f*, sword cutler's workshop or shop

espadero *m*, sword cutler

espadín *m*, small dress sword

espahí *m*, spahi

espalda *f, anat* back (often *pl*); *pl* rear, back portion; *mil* rear guard. **de espaldas,** with one's (its, his, etc.) back turned; on one's (its, etc.) back

espaldar *m*, backpiece of a cuirass; back (of chair); garden trellis, espalier

espaldarazo *m*, accolade

espaldera *f*, espalier, trellis

espantadizo *a* easily frightened

espantapájaros *m*, scarecrow

espantar *vt* to frighten, terrify; chase off; *vr* be amazed; be scared

espanto *m*, terror, panic; dismay; amazement; threat

espantoso *a* horrible, terrifying, awesome; amazing

España Spain

español (-la) *a* Spanish. *n* Spaniard. *m*, Spanish (language). **a la española,** in Spanish fashion

españolía *f*, Spanish colony, Spanish community (outside Spain)

españolismo *m*, love of things Spanish; Hispanism

españolizar *vt* to hispanize; *vr* adopt Spanish customs

esparadrapo *m*, court plaster

esparavel *m*, casting net

esparcimiento *m*, scattering; naturalness, frankness; geniality

esparcir *vt* to scatter, sprinkle, disperse; spread, publish abroad; entertain; *vr* be scattered; amuse oneself

espárrago *m*, asparagus

esparraguera *f*, asparagus plant; asparagus bed; asparagus dish

Esparta Sparta

espartano (-na) *a* and *n* Spartan

espartería *f*, esparto industry, esparto shop

esparto *m*, esparto grass

espasmo *m*, spasm

espasmódico *a* spasmodic

espátula *f*, spatula; palette knife

especia *f*, spice. **nuez de e.,** nutmeg

especial *a* special; particular

especialidad *f*, speciality; branch (of learning)

especialista *mf* specialist

especialización *f*, specialization

especializarse *vr* to specialize

especie *f*, class, kind; species; affair, matter, case; idea, image; news; pretext, appearance

especiería *f*, spice trade; spice shop

especiero (-ra) *n* spice merchant; spice rack

especificación *f*, specification. **e. normalizada,** standard specification

especificar *vt* to specify, particularize

específico *a* and *m*, specific patent medicine

espécimen *m*, specimen, sample

especioso *a* lovely, perfect; specious

espectacular *a* spectacular

espectáculo *m*, spectacle, sight; show, display

espectador (-ra) *n* spectator

espectral *a* spectral; faint, dim

espectro *m*, phantom, specter; *phys* spectrum

especulación *f*, conjecture; *com* speculation

especulador (-ra) *n* speculator

especular *vt* to examine, look at; (*with en*) reflect on, consider; *vi com* speculate

especulativo *a* speculative; thoughtful, meditative

espejería *f*, mirror shop or factory

espejero *m*, mirror manufacturer or seller

espejismo *m*, mirage; illusion

espejo *m*, mirror; *fig* model. **e. de cuerpo entero,** full-length mirror. **e. retrovisor,** rearview mirror

espejuelo *m*, small mirror; *min* selenite; *min* sheet of talc; *pl* lenses, eyeglasses

espeluznante *a* hair-raising

espeluznar *vt* to dishevel; untidy (hair, etc.); *vr* stand on end (hair)

espera *f*, waiting; expectation; *law* adjournment; caution, restraint; *law* respite

esperantista *mf* Esperantist

esperanto *m*, Esperanto

esperanza *f*, hope

esperanzar *vt* to inspire hope in

esperar *vt* to hope; expect; await; *(with en)* have faith in. **e. sentado,** *fig inf* to whistle for

esperma *f*, sperm, semen. **e. de ballena,** spermaceti

esperpento *m*, *inf* scarecrow, grotesque; folly, madness; fantastic dramatic composition

espesar *vt* to thicken; make closer; tighten (fabrics); *vr* thicken; grow denser or thicker

espeso *a* thick; dense; greasy, dirty

espesor *m*, thickness; density

espesura *f*, thickness; density; thicket; filth

espetar *vt cul* to spit, skewer; pierce; *inf* utter, give; *vr* be stiff or affected; *inf* push oneself in, intrude

espetera *f*, kitchen or pot rack

espetón *m*, *cul* spit; poker; large pin

espía *mf* spy. *f*, *naut* warp

espiar *vt* to spy upon, watch; *vi naut* warp

espiche *m*, sharp-pointed weapon or instrument; spit, spike

espiga *f*, *bot* spike, ear; sprig; *carp* peg; tang, shank (of sword); *carp* tenon, dowel; *naut* masthead; *her* garb

espigador (-ra) *n* gleaner

espigar *vt* to glean; *carp* tenon; *vi bot* begin to show the ear or spike; *vr bot* bolt; shoot up, grow (persons)

espigón *m*, sting; sharp point; breakwater; bearded spike (corn, etc.)

espigueo *m*, gleaning

espiguero *m*, *Mexico* granary

espín *m*, porcupine

espina *f*, thorn; prickle; splinter; fish bone; *anat* spine; suspicion, doubt

espinaca *f*, spinach

espinal *a* spinal

espinar *m*, thorn brake; *fig* awkward position. *vt* to prick, wound, hurt

espinazo *m*, backbone

espinilla *f*, shinbone; blackhead

espinoso *a* thorny; difficult, intricate

espión *m*, See **espía**

espionaje *m*, espionage; spying

espira *f*, *(geom arch)* helix; turn, twist (of winding stairs); whorl (of a shell)

espiración *f*, expiration; respiration

espiral *a* spiral. *f*, *geom* spiral; spiral watchspring

espirar *vt* to exhale, breathe out; inspire; encourage; *vi* breathe; breathe out; *poet* blow (wind)

espiritismo *m*, spiritualism

espiritista *a* spiritualist. *mf* spiritualist

espiritoso *a* lively, active, spirited; spirituous

espíritu *m*, spirit; apparition, specter; soul; intelligence, mind; mood, temper, outlook; underlying principle, spirit; devil (gen. *pl*) vigor, ardor, vivacity; *chem* essence; *chem* spirits; turn of mind. **E. Santo,** Holy Ghost

espiritual *a* spiritual

espiritualidad *f*, spirituality

espiritualismo *m*, *phil* spiritualism

espita *f*, spigot, tap; *inf* tippler

esplender *vi poet* to shine

esplendidez *f*, liberality, abundance; splendor, pomp

espléndido *a* magnificent; liberal; resplendent (gen. *pl*)

esplendor *m*, splendor, brilliance; distinction, nobility

esplendoroso *a* splendid, brilliant, radiant

espliego *m*, lavender

esplín *m*, spleen, melancholy

espolada *f*, prick with the spur

espolear *vt* to prick with the spur; encourage, stimulate

espoleta *f*, fuse (of explosives); breastbone (of fowls); wishbone. **e. de tiempo, e. graduada,** time fuse. **e. de seguridad,** safety fuse

espolón *m*, spur (of a bird or mountain range); *naut* ram; breakwater; buttress; *naut* fender

espolvorear *vt* to sprinkle with powder

esponja *f*, sponge

esponjadura *f*, sponging

esponjar *vt* to make spongy; sponge; *vr* swell with pride; *inf* bloom with health

esponjera *f*, sponge holder

esponjosidad *f*, sponginess

esponjoso *a* spongy, porous

esponsales *m pl*, betrothal; marriage contract

espontaneidad *f*, spontaneity

espontáneo *a* spontaneous

espora *f*, spore

esporádico *a* sporadic

esportillo *m*, bass, frail

esposa *f*, wife; *pl* handcuffs

esposo *m*, husband; *pl* husband and wife

espuela *f*, spur; stimulus; *(orn bot)* spur. **e. de caballero,** larkspur

espuelar *vt*, *Lat. Am.* to spur, spur on

espulgar *vt* to delouse; examine carefully

espuma *f*, froth, foam; *cul* scum; *fig* the best of anything, flower; *fig inf* **crecer como la e.,** to flourish like weeds

espumadera *f*, skimming ladle

espumajear *vi* to foam at the mouth

espumajoso *a* frothy, foaming

espumar *vt* to skim (soup, etc.); *vi* foam; increase rapidly

espumilla *f*, *Lat. Am.* meringue

espumoso *a* frothy, foaming

espurio *a* bastard; spurious

esputo *m*, sputum

esqueje *m*, *agr* cutting

esquela *f*, note; (printed) card

esqueleto *m*, skeleton; *Mexico*, blank, form (to be filled out) *inf* skinny person; framework

esquema *m*, diagram, layout sketch; scheme, plan. **e. de una máquina,** drawing of a machine

esquemático *a* schematic; diagrammatic

esquematizar *vt* to plan, outline

esquí *m*, ski, snowshoe

esquiador, -a *mf*, skier

esquiar *vi* to ski

esquila *f*, cattle bell; small bell, hand bell; sheep shearing; *(icht bot)* squill

esquilador *a* shearing. *m*, sheep shearer

esquiladora *f*, shearing machine

esquilar *vt* to shear, clip (sheep, etc.)

esquileo *m*, shearing; shearing time or place

esquilmar *vt* to harvest; impoverish

esquilmo *m*, harvest

esquimal *a* and *mf* Eskimo

esquina *f*, corner; *Lat. Am.* corner shop; village shop

esquinado *a* having corners; *fig* difficult to approach (people)

esquirol *m*, *inf* strikebreaker, blackleg

esquisto *m*, *min* slate; shale

esquivada *f*, *Lat. Am.* evasion

esquivar *vt* to avoid; *vr* slip away, disappear; excuse oneself

esquivez *f*, unsociableness; unfriendliness, aloofness

esquivo *a* unsociable, elusive, aloof

estabilidad *f*, stability; fastness (of colors)

estabilizar *vt* to stabilize

estable *a* stable; fast (of colors)

establecer *vt irr* to establish, found, institute; decree; *vr* take up residence; open (a business firm). See **conocer**

establecimiento *m*, law, statute; foundation, institution; establishment

establero *m*, stablegroom
establo *m*, stable
estaca *f*, stake, pole; *agr* cutting; cudgel
estacada *f*, fence; *mil* palisade; place fixed for a duel
estacar *vt* to stake; fence; tie to a stake; *vr fig* be as still as a post
estación *f*, position, situation; season; station (railroad, etc.); depot; time, period; stop, halt; building, headquarters; *bot* habitat; (*surv geom ecc*) station
estacional *a* seasonal; *ast* stationary
estacionamiento *m*, stationing; *aut* parking
estacionar *vt* to station, place; *aut* park (a car); *vr* remain stationary; place oneself
estacionario *a* motionless; *ast* stationary. *m*, stationer
estacionómetro *m*, *Mexico* parking meter
estada *f*, sojourn
estadía *f*, stay, sojourn; *art* sitting (of a model)
estadio *m*, racetrack; stadium; furlong
estadista *mf*, statistician; statesman, stateswoman
estadística *f*, statistics
estadístico *a* statistical
estadizo *a* stagnant
estado *m*, state; condition; rank, position; *pol* state; profession; status; *com* statement. **e. de guerra,** state of war; martial law. **e. mayor central,** (*nav mil*) general staff. **e. tapón,** *pol* buffer state. **tomar e.,** to marry; *ecc* profess; be ordained a priest
Estados Unidos de América United States of America
estadounidense *a* United States
estafa *f*, swindle
estafador (-ra) *n* swindler
estafar *vt* to swindle
estafeta *f*, courier, messenger; branch post office; diplomatic pouch
estagnación *f*, stagnation
estalactita *f*, stalactite
estalagmita *f*, stalagmite
estallar *vi* to explode; burst; *fig* break out
estallido *m*, explosion, report; crash, crack; *fig* outbreak; *aut* **e. de un neumático,** blowout (of a tire)
estambre *m*, woolen yarn, worsted; stamen
estameña *f*, serge
estampa *f*, illustration, picture; print; aspect; printing press; track, step; *met* boss, stud
estampación *f*, stamping; printing; imprinting. **e. en seco,** tooling (of a book)
estampado *a* printed (of textiles). *m*, textile printing; printed fabric
estampar *vt* to print, stamp; leave the print (of); bestow, imprint. **e. en relieve,** to emboss. **e. en seco,** to tool (a book)
estampería *f*, print or picture shop; trade in prints
estampero *m*, print dealer, picture dealer
estampido *m*, report, bang, detonation; crash
estampilla *f*, rubber stamp; seal; *Lat. Am (except Mexico)*, (postage) stamp
estampillar *vt* to stamp, imprint
estancación *f*, stagnation
estancado *a* stagnant; blocked, held up
estancar *vt* to check, stem; set up a monopoly; *fig* hold up (negotiations, etc.); *vr* be stagnant
estancia *f*, stay, residence; dwelling; lounge, living-room; stanza; *WH* farm; ranch
estanciero *m*, *WH* farmer; rancher
estanco *a naut* watertight. *m*, monopoly; shop selling government monopoly goods; archive
estandarte *m*, standard, flag. **e. real,** royal standard
estanque *m*, tank; pool; reservoir
estanquero (-ra) *n* seller of government monopoly goods (tobacco, matches, etc.)
estante *a* present; extant; permanent. *m*, shelf; bookcase; bin (for wine)
estantería *f*, shelving; shelves, bookcase
estantigua *f*, hobgoblin, specter; *fig inf* scarecrow
estañador *m*, tinsmith
estañar *vt* to tin; solder

estaño *m*, tin
estaquilla *f*, peg, cleat
estar *vi irr* to be. Indicates: 1. Position or place (e.g. **Está a la puerta,** He is at the door). 2. State (e.g. **Las flores están marchitas,** The flowers are faded). 3. Used to form the continuous or progressive tense (e.g. **Siempre está (estaba) escribiendo,** He is (was) always writing). 4. In contrast to verb *ser,* indicates impermanency (e.g. **Está enfermo,** He is ill). 5. **Estar** forms an apparent passive where no action is implied (e.g. **El cuadro está pintado al óleo,** The picture is painted in oils). 6. Used in some impersonal expressions (e.g. **¡Bien está!** All right! **¡Claro está!** Of course! etc.). **e. de,** to be in, or on, or acting as (e.g. **e. de prisa,** to be in a hurry. **e. de capitán,** to be acting as a captain). **e. para,** to be on the point of; to be nearly; to be in the mood for. **e. para llover,** to be on the point of raining. **e. por,** to remain to be done; have a mind to (e.g. **La historia está por escribir,** The story remains to be written). **e. a mano (con . . .)** *Lat. Am.* to be even (with . . .), be quits (with . . .) **e. bien,** to be well (healthy). *mech* **e. bajo presión,** to have the steam up. *pol* **e. en el poder,** to be in office. **e. en una cuenca,** *Dominican Republic* to be broke. **¿A cómo** (*or* **A cuántos) estamos?** What is the date? *Pres. Ind.* **estoy, estás, está, estamos, estáis, están.** *Preterite* **estuve,** etc. *Pres. Subjunc.* **esté, estés, esté, estén.** *Imperf. Subjunc.* **estuviese,** etc.
estarcir *vt* to stencil
estatal *a* state
estática *f*, *mech* statics
estático *a* static
estatizar *vt*, *Lat. Am.* to nationalize
estatua *f*, statue
estatuaria *f*, statuary
estatuir *vt irr* to establish, order. See **huir**
estatura *f*, stature, height (of persons)
estatuto *m*, statute, law
estay *m*, *naut* stay. **e. mayor,** *naut* mainstay
este *m*, east
este *m*, *dem a* this (*f*, **esta,** *pl* **estos, estas,** these). **éste,** *m*, *dem pron* this one; the latter. (*f*, **ésta,** *neut* **esto,** *pl* **éstos, éstas,** these ones; the latter) (e.g. **Aquel cuadro no es tan hermoso como éste,** That picture is not as beautiful as this one)
estela *f*, wake, track (of a ship)
estenografía *f*, shorthand
estenordeste *m*, east-northeast
estentóreo *a* stentorian
estepa *f*, steppe, arid plain
estera *f*, matting
esterar *vt* to cover with matting; *vi inf* muffle oneself up
estercoladura *f*, manuring
estercolar *vt* to manure
estercolero *m*, manure pile; driver of a dung cart
estereoscopio *m*, stereoscope
esterería *f*, matting factory, matting shop
esterero (-ra) *n* matting maker, matting seller
estéril *a* sterile, barren; unfruitful, unproductive
esterilidad *f*, sterility; barrenness, unfruitfulness
esterilización *f*, sterilization
esterilizador *a* sterilizing. *m*, sterilizer
esterilizar *vt* to make barren; *med* sterilize
esterilla *f*, mat, matting
esterlina *a f*, sterling. **libra e.,** pound sterling
esternón *m*, sternum
estero *m*, salt marsh
estertor *m*, stertorous breathing, rattle
estesudeste *m*, east-southeast
estética *f*, aesthetics. *a* aesthete
estético *a* aesthetic *m*, aesthete
estetoscopio *m*, stethoscope
esteva *f*, plow handle
estevado *a* bandy-legged
estiaje *m*, low water level (of rivers)
estibador *m*, stevedore, dock worker

estibar *vt naut* to stow

estiércol *m,* dung; manure

estigio *a* Stygian; (*fig poet*) infernal

estigma *m,* stigma

estigmatizar *vt* to brand; stigmatize; insult

estilar *vi* to be accustomed; *vt* draw up (document)

estilete *m,* stiletto, dagger; needle, hand, pointer; *med* stylet

estilista *mf* stylist

estilística *f,* stylism, stylistics

estilizar *vt* to stylize

estilo *m,* (*art arch lit*) style, writing instrument; gnomon, pointer; manner, way; *bot* style. **por el e.,** in some such way, like that

estilográfico *a* stylographic. **pluma estilográfica,** fountain pen

estima *f,* appreciation, esteem, consideration

estimable *a* estimable

estimación *f,* valuation, estimate; regard, esteem. **e. prudente,** conservative estimate

estimar *vt* to value, estimate; esteem, judge

estimulante *m, med* stimulant. *a* stimulating

estimular *vt* to stimulate, excite; goad on, encourage, incite

estímulo *m,* stimulus; incitement, encouragement

estío *m,* summer

estipendiar *vt* to pay a stipend to

estipendiario *m,* stipendiary

estipendio *m,* stipend, pay, remuneration

estipulación *f,* stipulation; *law* clause, condition

estipular *vt* to stipulate; arrange terms; *law* covenant

estirado *a* stretched out; tight, stiff; wire-drawn (metals); stiff, pompous; parsimonious

estirador *m,* wire drawer

estirar *vt* to stretch; iron roughly (clothes); *met* wiredraw; dole out (money); *fig* stretch, go beyond the permissible; *vr* stretch oneself

estirpe *f,* race, stock, lineage

estival *a* summer

esto *dem pron neut* this, this matter, this idea, etc. Always refers to abstractions, never to a definite object. **e. de,** the matter of. **e. es,** that's it; namely. **por e.,** for this reason. **a todo e.,** meanwhile

estocada *f,* sword thrust

Estocolmo Stockholm

estofa *f, sew* quilting; kind, quality

estofado *m,* stew. *a sew* quilted; stewed

estofar *vt sew* to quilt; make a stew

estoicismo *m,* stoicism

estoico (-ca) *n* stoic. *a* stoical

estolidez *f,* idiocy

estólido (-da) *a* idiotic. *a* idiot

estomacal *a* stomach

estómago *m,* stomach

estomático *a* pertaining to the mouth, oral

estomatitis *f,* stomatitis

estonio (-ia) *a* and *n* Estonian. *m,* Estonian (language)

estopa *f,* tow; oakum

estopilla *f,* batiste, lawn; calico, cotton cloth

estopín *m, mil* quick march

estoque *m,* rapier; narrow sword

estoquear *vt* to wound or kill with a rapier

estoqueo *m,* swordplay

estorbador (-ra) *a* obstructive. *n* obstructer

estorbar *vt* to obstruct, impede; hinder

estorbo *m,* obstruction; hindrance, nuisance

estornino *m,* starling

estornudar *vi* to sneeze

estornudo *m,* sneezing; sneeze

estrabismo *m, med* strabismus, squint, cast

estrada *f,* road, highway

estrado *m,* dais

estrafalario *a inf* slovenly, untidy; *inf* eccentric, odd

estragar *vt* to corrupt, spoil, vitiate; ruin, destroy

estrago *m,* devastation, destruction, ruin, havoc

estrambólico, -a *Lat. Am.* = **estrambótico**

estrambote *m,* refrain

estrambótico *a inf* eccentric, odd, outlandish

estrangul *m, mus* mouthpiece

estrangulación *f,* strangulation; *aut* throttling

estrangulador (-ra) *a* strangling. *n* strangler. *m, aut* throttle

estrangular *vt* to strangle

estraperlista *mf* black marketeer

estraperlo *m,* black market

estratagema *f,* stratagem, trick

estrategia *f,* strategy

estratégico *a* strategic

estratego *m,* strategist

estratificación *f,* stratification

estrato *m, geol* stratum

estratosfera *f,* stratosphere

estraza *f,* rag. **papel de e.,** brown paper

estrechar *vt* to make narrower, tighten; hold tightly, clasp; compel, oblige; *vr* tighten oneself up; reduce one's expenses; *fig* tighten the bonds (of friendship, etc.). **e. la mano,** to shake hands

estrechez *f,* narrowness; tightness; scantiness; poverty, want. **e. de miras,** narrowmindedness

estrecho *a* narrow; tight; intimate, close; austere, rigid; meanspirited. *m, geog* strait

estregadera *f,* shoe scraper; scourer

estregar *vt irr* to rub, scour, scrub, scrape, scratch. See **cegar**

estrella *f,* star; fortune, fate; anything star-shaped; *fig* star. **e. de la pantalla,** movie star. **e. de mar,** starfish. **e. de rabo,** comet. **e. fugaz,** shooting star. **tener e.,** to be born under a lucky star

estrellado *a* star-shaped; full of stars, starry; shattered, broken; fried (eggs)

estrellamar *f,* starfish

estrellar *vt inf* to shatter, break into fragments; fry (eggs); *vr* be starry or sprinkled with stars; be dashed against; fail in, come up against

estrellón *m,* large, artificial star (painted or otherwise); star-like firework; *Lat. Am.* crash

estremecer *vt irr* to cause to tremble; perturb; *vr* shudder, tremble. See **conocer**

estremecimiento *m,* shudder, trembling; agitation

estrenar *vt* to use or do for the first time; inaugurate; give the first performance of (plays, etc.); *vr* do for the first time; *com* make the first sale of the day

estreno *m,* commencement, inauguration; first appearance; *theat* first performance, opening night, premiere

estrenque *m,* strong esparto rope

estrenuo *a* strong, energetic, agile

estreñimiento *m,* constipation

estreñir *vt* to constipate

estrépito *m,* clamor, din, great noise; fuss, show

estrepitoso *a* noisy, clamorous

estreptomicina *f,* streptomycin

estría *f, arch* fluting, stria

estribadero *m,* prop, support, strut

estribar *vi* (*with en*) to lean on, rest on, be supported by; *fig* be based on

estribillo *m,* refrain

estribo *m,* stirrup; footboard, step, running board (of vehicles); *arch* buttress or pier; *fig* stay, support; *anat* stapes; *mech carp* stirrup piece. **perder los estribos,** to lose patience, forget oneself

estribor *m,* starboard

estricnina *f,* strychnine

estricto *a* strict, exact; unbending, severe

estridente *a* strident, shrill

estridor *m,* strident or harsh sound; screech; creak

estro *m,* inspiration

estrofa *f,* strophe; verse, stanza

estropajo *m,* scourer, dishcloth; worthless person or thing

estropajoso *a inf* indistinct, stammering; dirty and ragged; tough (meat, etc.)

estropear *vt* to spoil, damage; ruin, undo, spoil (plans, effects, etc.); ill-treat, maim; *vr* hurt oneself, be maimed; spoil, deteriorate

estropicio *m, inf* crash (of china, etc.)

estructura *f*, fabric, structure; *fig* construction

estructural *a* structural

estruendo *m*, din, clatter; clamor, noise; ostentation

estruendoso *a* noisy

estrujar *vt* to squeeze, crush (fruit); hold tightly, press, squeeze, bruise; *fig inf* squeeze dry

estrujón *m*, squeeze, pressure; final pressing (grapes)

estuario *m*, estuary

estucado *m*, stucco

estucar *vt* to stucco

estuco *m*, stucco; plaster

estuche *m*, case; casket, box; cover; sheath

estudiantado *m, Lat. Am.* student body, students

estudiante *mf* student

estudiantil *a inf* student

estudiantina *f*, strolling band of students playing and singing, generally in aid of charity

estudiantino *a inf* student

estudiantón *m, inf* grind

estudiar *vt* to study. **e. de,** study to be a (e.g. **e. de rabino,** study to be a rabbi); learn; *art* copy

estudio *m*, study; sketch; disquisition, dissertation; studio; diligence; *art* study; reading room, den

estudiosidad *f*, studiousness

estudioso *a* studious

estufa *f*, heating stove; hothouse; hot room (in bathhouses); drying chamber; *elec* heater

estufador *m*, stewpot or casserole

estufista *mf* stove maker or repairer, stove seller

estulto *a* foolish

estupefacción *f*, stupefaction

estupefacto *a* stupefied, stunned, amazed

estupendo *a* wonderful, marvelous

estupidez *f*, stupidity

estúpido *a* stupid

estupor *m, med* stupor; astonishment

estupro *m, law* rape

estuque *m*, stucco

estuquería *f*, stuccowork

esturión *m*, sturgeon

esvástica *f*, swastika

etapa *f, mil* field ration; *mil* halt, camp; stage, juncture. **a pequeñas etapas,** by easy stages (of a journey)

etcétera etcetera

éter *m*, ethèr; *poet* sky

etéreo *a* etheric; ethereal

eterizar *vt* to etherize

eternidad *f*, eternity

eternizar *vt* to drag out, prolong; eternize, perpetuate

eterno *a* eternal, everlasting; lasting, enduring

ética *f*, ethics

ético *a* ethical. *m*, moralist

etimología *f*, etymology

etimológico *a* etymological

etimologista *mf* etymologist

etimólogo *m*, etymologist

etiología *f*, etiology

etíope *a* and *mf* Ethiopian

Etiopía Ethiopia

etiqueta *f*, etiquette; label

etiquetero *a* ceremonious, stiff; prim

étnico *a* ethnic; heathen

etnografía *f*, ethnography

etnográfico *a* ethnographic

etnología *f*, ethnology

etnólogo *m*, ethnologist

etrusco (-ca) *a* and *n* Etruscan

eubolia *f*, discretion in speech

eucalipto *m*, eucalyptus

Eucaristía *f*, Eucharist

euclídeo *a* Euclidean

eufemismo *m*, euphemism

eufonía *f*, euphony

eufónico *a* euphonious

euforia *f*, resistance to disease; buoyancy, well-being

eufuismo *m*, euphuism

eugenesia *f*, eugenics

eugenésico *a* eugenic

eunuco *m*, eunuch

euritmia *f*, eurythmics

eurítmico *a* eurythmic

euro *m, poet* east wind

Europa Europe

europeizar *vt* to Europeanize

europeo (-ea) *a* and *n* European

éuscaro *a* Basque. *m*, Basque (language)

eutanasia *f*, euthanasia

evacuación *f*, evacuation

evacuar *vt* to vacate; evacuate, empty; finish, conclude (a business deal, etc.)

evadir *vt* to avoid, elude; *vr* escape; elope

evaluación *f*, valuation; estimation

evaluar *vt* to evaluate, estimate; gauge; value

evangélico *a* evangelical

evangelio *m*, Gospel; Christianity; *inf* indisputable truth

evangelista *m*, evangelist

evangelizar *vt* to evangelize

evaporación *f*, evaporation

evaporar(se) *vt* and *vr* to evaporate; disappear, vanish

evasión, evasiva *f*, subterfuge, evasion; flight, escape

evasivo *a* evasive

evento *m*, happening, event; contingency

eventual *a* possible, fortuitous; accidental (expenses); extra (emoluments)

eventualidad *f*, eventuality

evicción *f, law* eviction

evidencia *f*, proof, evidence. **ponerse en e.,** to put oneself forward

evidenciar *vt* to show, make obvious

evidente *a* obvious, evident

evitable *a* avoidable

evitación *f*, avoidance

evitar *vt* to avoid; shun, eschew

evocación *f*, evocation

evocador *a* evocative

evocar *vt* to evoke

evolución *f*, evolution; development; (*mil nav*) maneuver; change; *geom* involution

evolucionar *vi* to evolve; (*nav mil*) maneuver; change, alter

evolucionismo *m*, evolutionism

evolutivo *a* evolutional

ex *prefix* out of; from; formerly

exacción *f*, exaction; tax

exacerbación *f*, exacerbation

exacerbar *vt* to exasperate; exacerbate

exactitud *f*, exactitude; correctness; punctuality

exacto *a* exact; correct; punctual

exactor *m*, tax collector; tyrant, oppressor

exageración *f*, exaggeration

exagerador (-ra) *a* given to exaggerating. *n* exaggerater

exagerar *vt* to exaggerate

exaltación *f*, exaltation

exaltar *vt* to exalt, elevate; extol; *vr* grow excited or agitated

exalumna *f, Lat. Am.* alumna, graduate

exalumno *m, Lat. Am.* alumnus, graduate

examen *m*, inquiry; investigation, research; examination; *geol* survey. **e. parcial,** quiz (at school)

examinador (-ra) *n* examiner

examinando (-da) *n* candidate, examinee

examinar *vt* to inquire into; investigate; inspect; examine; *vr* take an examination

exangüe *a* bloodless, pale; exhausted, weak; dead

exánime *a* lifeless; spiritless, weak

exasperación *f*, exasperation

exasperador, exasperante *a* exasperating

exasperar *vt* to exasperate; irritate, annoy

excarcelar *vt* to release from jail
excavación *f,* excavation
excavador (-ra) *n* excavator. *f, mech* excavator
excavar *vt* to hollow; excavate; *agr* hoe (roots of plants)
excedente *a* exceeding; excessive; surplus
exceder *vt* to exceed; *vr* forget oneself, go too far
excelencia *f,* excellence, superiority; Excellency (title)
excelente *a* excellent; *inf* first-rate
excelso *a* lofty, high; eminent, mighty; sublime
excentricidad *f,* eccentricity
excéntrico *a* unconventional; erratic; *geom* eccentric
excepción *f,* exception
excepcional *a* exceptional
exceptuar *vt* to except
excerpta, excerta *f,* excerpt, extract
excesivo *a* excessive
exceso *m,* excess; *com* surplus; *pl* crimes, excesses. **e. de peso** *or* **e. de equipaje,** excess baggage
excisión *f,* excision
excitabilidad *f,* excitability
excitable *a* excitable, high-strung
excitación *f,* excitation; excitement
excitador *a* exciting, stimulating. *m, phys* exciter
excitar *vt* to excite, stimulate, provoke; *elec* energize; *vr* become agitated or excited
exclamación *f,* exclamation, interjection
exclamar *vi* to exclaim
excluir *vt irr* to exclude, keep out; reject, bar. See **huir**
exclusiva *f,* exclusion; special privilege, sole right
exclusive *adv* exclusively; excluded
exclusivismo *m,* exclusivism
exclusivista *a* exclusive. *mf* exclusivist
exclusivo *a* exclusive
excomulgado (-da) *a* and *n ecc* excommunicate; *inf* wicked (person)
excomulgar *vt* to excommunicate
excomunión *f,* excommunication
excoriar *vt* to flay, excoriate; *vr* graze oneself
excrecencia *f,* excrescence
excreción *f,* excretion
excremento *m,* excrement
excretar *vi* to excrete
excretorio *a* excretory
exculpación *f,* exoneration
exculpar(se) *vt* and *vr* to exonerate
excursión *f,* excursion, outing, trip; *mil* incursion
excursionarse *vr, Lat. Am.* to go on a trip, go on an outing, go on an excursion
excursionismo *m,* sightseeing; hiking
excursionista *mf* excursionist; hiker
excusa *f,* excuse
excusado *a* excused; exempt; unnecessary, superfluous; reserved, private. *m,* lavatory, toilet
excusar *vt* to excuse; avoid, ward off, prevent; exempt; *vr* excuse oneself
execración *f,* execration
execrar *vt* to execrate; denounce; loathe
exención *f,* exemption
exentar *vt* to exempt
exento *a* exempt; free, liberated; open (of buildings, etc.)
exequias *f pl,* obsequies
exfoliar *vt* to strip off; *vr* flake off
exhalación *f,* exhalation; shooting star; lightning; emanation, effluvium
exhalar *vt* to exhale, give off; *fig* give vent to
exhibición *f,* exhibition
exhibicionismo *m,* exhibitionism
exhibicionista *mf* exhibitionist
exhibir *vt* to exhibit, show
exhortación *f,* exhortation
exhortar *vt* to exhort
exhumación *f,* exhumation
exhumar *vt* to exhume, disinter
exigencia *f,* exigency; demand
exigente *a* exigent

exigir *vt* to exact, collect; need, require; demand
exigüidad *f,* exiguousness
exiguo *a* exiguous, meager
exliado, -a *Lat. Am. a* exiled, in exile; *mf* exile
eximio *a* most excellent; illustrious
eximir *vt* to exempt
existencia *f,* existence; *pl com* stock on hand
existir *vi* to exist, be; live
éxito *m,* success; result, conclusion
exitoso, -a *a, Lat. Am.* successful
éxodo *m,* Exodus; exodus, emigration. **é. rural,** rural depopulation
exoneración *f,* exoneration
exonerar *vt* to exonerate; discharge (from employment)
exorbitancia *f,* exorbitance
exorbitante *a* exorbitant, excessive
exorcismo *m,* exorcism
exorcista *m,* exorcist
exorcizar *vt* to exorcize
exordio *m,* exordium, introduction
exornar *vt* to adorn; embellish (*lit* style)
exótico *a* exotic, rare
expandir *vt* to expand
expansión *f,* expansion; recreation, hobby
expansivo *a* expansive; communicative, frank
expatriación *f,* expatriation
expatriarse *vr* to emigrate, leave one's country
expectante *a* expectant
expectativa *f,* expectancy; expectation
expectoración *f,* expectoration
expectorar *vt* to expectorate
expedición *f,* expedition; speed, promptness; *ecc* bull, dispensation; excursion; forwarding, dispatch
expediente *m, law* proceedings; file of documents; expedient, device, means; expedition, promptness; motive, reason; provision
expedir *vt irr* to expedite; forward, send, ship; issue, make out (checks, receipts, etc.); draw up (documents); dispatch, deal with. See **pedir**
expedito *a* expeditious, speedy
expeler *vt* to expel, discharge, emit
expendedor (-ra) *a* spending. *n* spender; agent; retailer; seller; *law* **e. de moneda falsa,** distributor of counterfeit money
expendeduría *f,* shop where government monopoly goods are sold (tobacco, stamps, etc.)
expender *vt* to spend (money); *com* retail; *com* sell on commission; *law* distribute counterfeit money
expendio *m, Lat. Am.* tobacco shop
expensas *f pl,* costs, charges
experiencia *f,* experience; practice, experiment
experimentación *f,* experiencing
experimentar *vt* to test, try; experience; feel
experimento *m,* experiment
experto (-ta) *a* practiced, expert. *n* expert
expiación *f,* expiation
expiar *vt* to expiate, atone for; pay the penalty of; *fig* purify
expiatorio *a* expiatory
expiración *f,* expiration
expirar *vi* to die; *fig* expire; die down; exhale, expire
explanación *f,* leveling; explanation, elucidation
explanada *f,* esplanade; *mil* glacis
explanar *vt* to level; explain
explayar *vt* to extend, enlarge; *vr* spread oneself, enlarge (upon); enjoy an outing; confide (in)
explicación *f,* explanation; elucidation
explicar *vt* to explain; expound; interpret, elucidate; *vr* explain oneself
explicativo *a* explanatory
explícito *a* explicit, clear
exploración *f,* exploration
explorador *a* exploring. *m,* explorer; prospector; boy scout; *mil* scout

explorar *vt* to explore; investigate; *med* probe
exploratorio *a* exploratory
explosión *f,* explosion; outburst, outbreak. **hacer falsas explosiones,** *mech* to misfire
explosivo *a* and *m,* explosive. **e. violento,** high explosive
explotación *f,* development, exploitation
explotar *vt* to work (mines); *fig* exploit
expoliación *f,* spoliation
expoliar *vt* to despoil
exponente *a* and *mf* exponent. *m, math* index
exponer *vt irr* to show, expose; expound, interpret; risk, jeopardize; abandon (child). See **poner**
exportación *f,* exportation; export
exportador (-ra) *a* export. *n* exporter
exportar *vt* to export
exposición *f,* exposition, demonstration; petition; exhibition; *lit* exposition; *phot* exposure; orientation, position
expósito (-ra) *a* and *n* foundling
expositor (-ra) *a* and *n* exponent. *n* exhibitor
expremijo *m,* cheese vat
exprés *a* express. *m,* messenger or delivery service; express train; transport office
expresar *vt* to express (all meanings)
expresión *f,* statement, utterance; phrase, wording; expression; presentation; manifestation; gift, present; squeezing; pressing (of fruits, etc.)
expresivo *a* expressive; affectionate
expreso *a* express; clear, obvious. *m,* courier, messenger
exprimelimones *m,* **exprimidera,** *f,* lemon squeezer
exprimidor de la ropa *m,* wringer, mangle
exprimir *vt* to squeeze, press (fruit); press, hold tightly; express, utter
expropiación *f,* expropriation
expropiar *vt* to expropriate; commandeer
expugnar *vt mil* to take by storm
expulsar *vt* to expel, eject, dismiss
expulsión *f,* expulsion
expurgar *vt* to cleanse, purify; expurgate
expurgatorio *a* expurgatory. *m, ecc* index
exquisitez *f,* exquisiteness
exquisito *a* exquisite, choice; delicate, delicious
extasiarse *vr* to fall into ecstasy; marvel (at), delight (in)
éxtasis *m,* ecstasy; rapture
extático *a* ecstatic
extemporáneo *a* untimely; inopportune, inconvenient
extender *vt irr* to spread; reach, extend; elongate; enlarge, amplify; unfold, open out, stretch; draw up (documents); make out (checks, etc.); *vr* stretch out; lie down; spread, be generalized; extend; last (of time); record; stretch, open out. **extenderse en,** to expatiate on. See **entender**
extensión *f,* extension; expanse; length; extent; duration; extension (logic)
extensivo *a* extensive, spacious; extensible
extenso *a* extensive, vast
extensor *a* extensor. *m,* chest expander
extenuación *f,* emaciation, weakness; extenuation
extenuar *vt* to exhaust, weaken; *vr* become weak
exterior *a* external; foreign (trade, etc.). *m,* outside, exterior; outward appearance
exterioridad *f,* outward appearance; outside, externality; *pl* ceremonies, forms; ostentation

exteriorizar *vt* to exteriorize, reveal
exterminador (-ra) *a* exterminating. *n* exterminator
exterminar *vt* to exterminate; devastate
exterminio *m,* extermination; devastation
externado *m,* day school
externarse *vr* to stand out
externo (-na) *a* external. *n* day
extinción *f,* extinction; extinguishment; abolition, cancellation
extinguir *vt* to extinguish; destroy
extintor *m,* fire extinguisher
extirpación *f,* extirpation
extirpador (-ra) *a* extirpating. *n* extirpator
extirpar *vt* to extirpate; *fig* eradicate
extorsión *f,* extortion
extorsionar *vt* to extort
extra *prefix* outside, without, beyond. *prep* besides. *a* extremely, most. *m, inf* extra
extracción *f,* extraction; drawing (lottery); origin, lineage; exportation
extractar *vt* to abstract, summarize
extracto *m,* abstract, summary; *chem* extract
extractor *a* extracting. *m,* extractor
extradición *f,* extradition
extraer *vt irr* to extract; draw out; export; *chem* extract. See **traer**
extranjero (-ra) *a* alien, foreign. *n* foreigner. *m,* abroad, foreign country
extrañar *vt* to exile; alienate, estrange; wonder at; miss, feel the loss of; *vr* be exiled; be estranged; be amazed (by); refuse (to do a thing)
extrañeza *f,* strangeness; estrangement; surprise
extraño *a* strange, unusual; foreign, extraneous
extraoficial *a* unofficial
extraordinario *a* extraordinary; special. *m, cul* extra course
extraterrenal, extraterreno *a, Lat. Am.* extraterrestrial, unearthly
extraterritorialidad *f,* exterritoriality
extravagancia *f,* eccentricity; queerness; folly
extravagante *a* eccentric; queer, strange; absurd
extravertido *m,* extrovert
extraviar *vt* to mislead; mislay; *vr* lose one's way; be lost (of things); *fig* go astray
extravío *m,* deviation, divergence; error; aberration, lapse
extremado *a* extreme
extremar *vt* to take to extremes; *vr* do one's best
extremaunción *f,* extreme unction
extremidad *f,* end; extremity; remotest part; edge; limit; *pl* extremities
extremista *a* and *mf* extremist
extremo *a* last, ultimate; extreme; furthest; great, exceptional; utmost. *m,* end, extreme; highest degree; extreme care; *pl* excessive emotional display
extremoso *a* immoderate, exaggerated; very affectionate
extrínseco *a* extrinsic
exuberancia *f,* abundance; exuberance
exuberante *a* abundant, copious; exuberant
exudar *vi* and *vt* to exude
exultación *f,* exultation; rejoicing
exultante *a* exultant
exultar *vi* to exult
eyaculación *f, med* ejaculation
eyacular *vt med* to ejaculate

F

fa *m, mus* fa, F
fabada *f,* dish of broad beans with pork, sausage or bacon

fábrica *f,* manufacture; making; factory, works; fabric, structure, building; creation; invention. **f. de papel,** paper mill. **marca de f.,** trademark

fabricación *f*, make; making; construction. **f. en serie,** mass production

fabricador (-ra) *a* creative, inventive. *n* fabricator; maker

fabricante *a* manufacturing. *m*, manufacturer; maker

fabricar *vt* to manufacture; make; construct, build; devise; invent, create

fabril *a* manufacturing

fabriquero *m*, manufacturer; churchwarden; charcoal burner

fábula *f*, rumor, gossip; fiction; fable; story, plot; mythology; myth; laughingstock; falsehood.

fabulista *mf* fabulist; mythologist

fabulosidad *f*, fabulousness

fabuloso *a* fabulous; fictitious; incredible, amazing

faca *f*, jackknife

facción *f*, rebellion; faction, party, band; feature (of the face) (gen. *pl*); military exploit; any routine military duty

faccionario *a* factional

faccioso (-sa) *a* factional; factious, seditious. *n* rebel

faceta *f*, facet (gems); aspect, view

facha *f*, *inf* countenance, look, face; guy, scarecrow. *naut* **ponerse en f.,** to lie to

fachada *f*, facade, front (of a building, ship, etc.); *inf* build, presence (of a person); frontispiece (of a book)

fachenda *f*, *inf* boastfulness, vanity

fachinal *m*, *Argentina* swamp

fachoso, -a *a*, *Lat. Am.* elegant, smart

facial *a* facial; intuitive

fácil *a* easy; probable; easily led; docile; of easy virtue (women). *adv* easy

facilidad *f*, easiness; facility, aptitude; ready compliance; opportunity

facilitar *vt* to facilitate, expedite; provide, deliver

facineroso *a* criminal, delinquent. *m*, criminal; villain

facistol *m*, *ecc* lectern; chorister's stand

facsímile *m*, facsimile

factibilidad *f*, feasibility, practicability

factible *a* feasible, practicable

facticio *a* factitious, artificial

factor *m*, *com* factor, agent; *math* factor; element; consideration

factoría *f*, agency; factorage; factory; merchants' trading post, especially in a foreign country

factótum *m*, *inf* factotum, handyman; *inf* busybody; confidential agent or deputy

factura *f*, *com* invoice, bill, account; *art* execution; workmanship; making

facturar *vt com* to invoice; register (luggage on a railroad)

facultad *f*, faculty; mental or physical aptitude, capability; authority, right; science, art; *univ* faculty; license

facultar *vt* to authorize, permit

facultativo *a* belonging to a faculty; optional, permissive. *m*, physician

facundia *f*, eloquence

facundo *a* eloquent

faena *f*, manual labor; mental work; business affairs (gen. *pl*)

faetón *m*, phaeton

fagocito *m*, phagocyte

fagot *m*, bassoon

fagotista *mf* bassoon player

faisán (-ana) *orn* cock (hen) pheasant

faisanera *f*, pheasantry

faja *f*, belt; sash, scarf; corset, girdle; *geog* zone; newspaper wrapper; *arch* fascia; swathing band

fajar *vt* to swathe; swaddle (a child)

fajero *m*, swaddling band

fajín *m*, ceremonial ribbon or sash worn by generals, etc.

fajina *f*, stack; brushwood; (*fort.*) fascine; *Mexico* lunch

fajo *m*, bundle, sheaf; *pl* swaddling clothes

falacia *f*, fraud, deceit; deceitfulness; fallacy

falange *f*, *mil* phalanx; *anat* phalange; (*Spanish pol.*) Falange

falangista *a* and *mf* Falangist

falaz *a* deceitful; fallacious

falda *f*, skirt; lap, flap, panel (of a dress); slope (of a hill); the lap; loin (of beef, etc.); brim of a hat; *pl inf* petticoats, women. **f. escocesa,** kilt. **f.-pantalón,** divided skirt, culottes.

faldellín *m*, skirt; underskirt

faldero *a* lap (dog); fond of the company of women

faldillas *f pl*, coattails

faldistorio *m*, faldstool

faldón *m*, long, flowing skirt; shirttail; coattail

falibilidad *f*, fallibility

falible *a* fallible

falla *f*, deficiency, defect; failure; *geol* displacement; bonfire (Valencia); *min* slide

fallar *vt law* to pass sentence; *vi* be deficient

fallecer *vi irr* to die; fail. See **conocer**

fallecimiento *m*, death, decease

fallido *a* frustrated; bankrupt

fallo *m*, *law* verdict; judgment

falsario *a* falsifying, forging, counterfeiting; deceiving, lying. *m*, falsifier, forger; counterfeiter

falseamiento *m*, falsifying; forging

falsear *vt* to falsify; forge; counterfeit; penetrate; *vi* weaken; *mus* be out of tune (strings)

falsedad *f*, falseness; falsehood

falsete *m*, spigot; *mus* falsetto voice

falsificación *f*, falsification; forgery

falsificador *a* falsifying; forging. *m*, falsifier; forger

falsificar *vt* to forge, counterfeit; falsify

falso *a* false; forged, counterfeit; treacherous, untrue, deceitful; incorrect; sham; vicious (horses). **de f.,** falsely; deceitfully

falta *f*, lack, shortage; defect; mistake; *sport* fault; shortcoming; nonappearance, absence; deficiency in legal weight of coin; *law* offense. **f. de éxito,** failure. **hacer f.,** to be necessary. **sin f.,** without fail

faltar *vi* to be lacking; fail, die; fall short; be absent from an appointment; not to fulfill one's obligations. **f. a,** to be unfaithful to, break (e.g. **Faltó a su palabra,** He broke his promise). *inf* **¡No faltaba más!** I should think not!; That's the limit!

falto *a* lacking, wanting; defective; wretched, mean, timid. **f. de personal,** short-handed

faltriquera *f*, pocket; hip pocket

falúa *f*, *naut* tender; longboat

falucho *m*, felucca

fama *f*, rumor, report; reputation; fame

famélico *a* ravenous

familia *f*, family; household; kindred. **ser de f.,** to run in the family

familiar *a* family; familiar; well known; unceremonious; plain, simple; colloquial (language). *m*, *ecc* familiar; servant; intimate friend; familiar spirit

familiaridad *f*, familiarity

familiarizar *vt* to familiarize; *vr* become familiar; accustom oneself

familiarmente *adv* familiarly

famoso *a* famous; notorious; *inf* excellent, perfect; *inf* conspicuous

fámula *f*, *inf* female servant

fámulo *m*, servant of a college; *inf* servant

fanal *m*, lantern (of a lighthouse); *naut* poop lantern; lantern; lamp glass

fanático (-ca) *a* fanatical. *n* fanatic; *inf* fan, enthusiast

fanatismo *m*, fanaticism

fanatizar *vt* to make fanatical; turn into a fanatic

fandango *m*, lively Andalusian dance; *Lat. Am.* rowdy party

fanega *f*, grain measure about the weight of 1.60 bushel; land measure (about $1\frac{1}{2}$ acres)

fanfarrón (-ona) *a inf* boastful, swaggering. *n* swashbuckler; boaster

fanfarronear *vi* to swagger; brag

fanfarronería *f,* bragging
fango *m,* mud, mire; degradation
fangoso *a* muddy, miry
fantasear *vi* to let one's fancy roam; boast
fantasía *f,* fancy, imagination; fantasy; caprice; fiction; *inf* presumption; *mus* fantasia
fantasma *m,* ghost, phantom; vision; image, impression; presumptuous person. *f, inf* scarecrow; apparition
fantasmagoría *f,* phantasmagoria
fantasmagórico *a* phantasmagoric
fantástico *a* fanciful, imaginary; fantastic, imaginative; presumptuous, conceited
fantoche *m,* puppet; *inf* yes-man, mediocrity
faquín *m,* porter, carrier
faquir *m,* fakir
farabute *mf, Argentina* rogue
faradio *m,* farad
faralá *m,* flounce, frill
faramallear *vi, Lat. Am.* to boast, brag
farándula *f,* profession of low comedian; troupe of strolling players; cunning trick
farandulero *m,* actor, strolling player. *a inf* plausible
faraón *m,* pharaoh; faro (card game)
fardel *m,* bag, knapsack; bundle
fardo *m,* bundle, bale, package
farfulla *f, inf* mumbling; gibbering. *mf inf* mumbler
farfullar *vt inf* to mumble; gibber; *inf* act in haste
faringe *f,* pharynx
faríngeo *a* pharyngeal
faringitis *f,* pharyngitis
farmacéutico *a* pharmaceutical. *m,* pharmacist
farmacia *f,* pharmacy
farmacología *f,* pharmacology
farmacólogo *m,* pharmacologist
faro *m,* lighthouse; beacon, guide; *aut* headlight
farol *m,* lantern, lamp; streetlamp; cresset
farola *f,* lamppost (generally with several branches); lantern
farolero *m,* lantern maker; lamplighter; lamp tender. *a inf* swaggering, braggart
fárrago *m,* hodgepodge
farruto, -a *a, Lat. Am.* sickly, weak
farsa *f,* old name for a play; farce; theatrical company; poor, badly constructed play; sham, trick, deception
farsante *m,* comedian; *ant* actor; *fig inf* humbug
fascinación *f,* evil eye; enchantment, fascination
fascinador (-ra) *a* bewitching; fascinating. *n* charmer
fascinante *a* fascinating
fascinar *vt* to bewitch, place under a spell; deceive, impose upon; attract, fascinate
fascismo *m,* fascism
fascista *a* and *mf* fascist
fase *f,* phase; aspect
fastidiar *vt* to disgust, bore; annoy; *vr* be bored
fastidio *m,* sickness, squeamishness; annoyance, boredom, dislike, repugnance
fastidioso *a* disgusting, sickening; annoying; boring, tiresome
fastuoso *a* ostentatious; pompous
fatal *a* fatal, mortal; predetermined, inevitable; ill-fated, unhappy, disastrous; evil
fatalidad *f,* fatality; inevitability; disaster, ill-fatedness
fatalismo *m,* fatalism
fatalista *a* fatalistic. *mf* fatalist
fatalmente *adv* inevitably, unavoidably; unhappily, unfortunately; extremely badly
fatídico *a* prophetic (gen. of evil)
fatiga *f,* fatigue; toil; difficult breathing; hardship, troubles (gen. *pl.*)
fatigar *vt* to tire; annoy; *vr* be tired
fatigoso *a* tired; tiring; tiresome, annoying
fatuidad *f,* fatuousness, inanity, foolishness; conceit; priggishness
fatuo *a* fatuous, foolish; conceited; priggish. *m,* self-satisfied fool. **fuego f.,** will-o'-the-wisp

fauces *f pl,* gullet
faul *m, Lat. Am.* foul
faulear *vt, Lat. Am.* to foul
fauna *f,* fauna
fauno *m,* faun
fausto *m,* pomp, magnificence, ostentation. *a* fortunate, happy
fautor *m,* protector, helper; accomplice. **f. de guerra,** warmonger
favonio *m, poet* zephyr, westerly wind
favor *m,* aid, protection, support; favor, honor, service; love favor, sign of favor. **a f. de,** in favor of; on behalf of
favorable *a* kind, helpful; favorable
favorecedor (-ra) *a* favoring, helping. *n* helper; protector
favorecer *vt irr* to aid, protect, support; favor; do a service, grant a favor. See **conocer**
favoritismo *m,* favoritism
favorito (-ta) *a* and *n* favorite
fayenza *f,* faience
faz *f,* face; external surface of a thing, side; frontage
fe *f,* faith; confidence, trust, good opinion; belief; solemn promise; assertion; certificate, attestation; faithfulness. **f. de erratas,** *print* errata. **dar f.,** *law* to testify. **de buena f.,** in good faith. **en f.,** in proof
fealdad *f,* ugliness; base action
febo *m,* Phoebus; *poet* sun
febrero *m,* February
febril *a* feverish; ardent, violent; passionate
feculento *a* starchy; dreggy
fecundación *f,* fecundation
fecundar *vt* to fertilize; fecundate
fecundidad *f,* fecundity; fertility, fruitfulness
fecundizar *vt* to fertilize; make fruitful
fecundo *a* fertile, fecund, prolific; abundant
fecha *f,* date. **a la f.,** at present, now. **hasta la f.,** up to the present (day)
fechar *vt* to date, write the date
federación *f,* federation, league
federal *a* federal. *mf* federalist
federalismo *m,* federalism
federalista *a* federal, federalist. *mf* federalist
federativo *a* federative
fehaciente *a law* authentic, attested
felicidad *f,* happiness; contentment, satisfaction; good fortune
felicitación *f,* congratulation
felicitar *vt* to congratulate; wish well; *vr* congratulate oneself
feligrés (-esa) *n* parishioner
feligresía *f,* parish
felino *a* and *m,* feline
feliz *a* happy; fortunate; skillful, felicitous (of phrases, etc.)
felón (-ona) *n* felon
felonía *f,* felony
felpa *f,* plush; *inf* drubbing, beating
felpilla *f,* chenille
felpudo *a* plush
femenino *a* feminine; female; *fig* weak
fementido *a* sly, false, treacherous, unfaithful
feminismo *m,* feminism
feminista *a* feminist. *mf* feminist
fémur *m,* femur, thigh bone
fenecer *vt irr* to conclude, finish; *vi* die; be ended. See **conocer**
fenecimiento *m,* end; death
fenicio (-ia) *a* and *n* Phoenician
fénico *a* phenic, carbolic
fénix *f,* phoenix
fenomenal *a* phenomenal; *inf* terrific
fenómeno *m,* phenomenon; *inf* something of great size
feo *a* ugly; alarming, horrid; evil. *m, inf* slight, insult
feraz *a* fruitful, fertile
féretro *m,* coffin; bier

feria *f*, fair, market; workday; holiday; rest
feriar *vt* to buy at a fair; bargain. *vi* cease work, take a holiday
fermentación *f*, fermentation
fermentar *vi* to ferment; be agitated; *vt* cause to ferment
fermento *m*, ferment; leaven; *chem* enzyme
ferocidad *f*, ferocity, cruelty
feroz *a* ferocious, cruel; *Lat. Am.* ugly
férreo *a* ferrous; hard, tenacious. **línea férrea,** railroad
ferrería *f*, ironworks
ferretería *f*, ironworks; ironmonger's shop; ironware, hardware
férrico *a* ferric
ferrífero *a* iron-bearing
ferrocarril *m*, railroad, railway; railroad train. **f. de cremallera,** rack railroad. **f. funicular,** funicular railway
ferroso *a* ferrous
ferroviario *a* railroad, railway. *m*, railroad employee
fértil *a* fertile; fruitful, productive
fertilidad *f*, fertility
fertilización *f*, fertilization
fertilizar *vt* to fertilize, make fruitful
férula *f*, ferule; *surg* splint; *fig* yoke, rule
fervor *m*, intense heat; fervor, devotion; zeal
fervoroso *a* fervent, zealous, devoted
festejar *vt* to feast, entertain; woo; celebrate; *vr* amuse oneself; *Mexico* to thrash
festejo *m*, feast, entertainment; courtship, wooing; *pl* public celebrations
festín *m*, private dinner or party; sumptuous banquet
festival *m*, musical festival; festival
festividad *f*, festivity; *ecc* celebration, solemnity; witticism
festivo *a* joking, witty; happy, gay; solemn, worthy of celebration. **día f.,** holiday
festón *m*, garland, wreath; festoon; border; scalloped edging
festonear *vt* to garland, festoon; border
fetal *a* fetal
fetiche *m*, fetish
fetichismo *m*, fetishism
fetidez *f*, fetidness, fetor, stink
fétido *a* stinking, fetid
feto *m*, fetus
feudal *a* feudal; despotic
feudalismo *m*, feudalism
fez *m*, fez
fiado, al *adv* on credit. **en f.,** on bail
fiador (-ra) *n* guarantor; bail. *m*, fastener, loop (of a coat, clock, etc.); safety catch, bolt. **salir f.,** to be surety (for); post bail
fiambre *m*, cold meat, cold dish; *inf* stale, out-of-date news, etc.; *inf* corpse
fiambrera *f*, lunchbox, lunchpail
fiambrería *f* delicatessen
fianza *f*, guarantee, bail; surety; security. *law* **dar f.,** to guarantee; post bail
fiar *vt* to go surety for, post bail; sell on credit; trust; confide; *vr* (*with de*) confide in; trust
fibra *f*, fiber; filament; energy, strength; *min* vein; grain (of wood)
fibroso *a* fibrous; fibroid
ficción *f*, falsehood; invention; fiction, imaginative creation; pretense
ficha *f*, chip, counter; domino; index card, filing card. **f. antropométrica,** personal particulars card
fichar *vt* to record personal particulars on a filing card; file, index
fichero *m*, filing cabinet; card catalog
fichú *m*, fichu, scarf
ficticio *a* fictitious
fidedigno *a* trustworthy, bona fide
fidelidad *f*, fidelity, honesty; loyalty; punctiliousness
fideos *m pl*, vermicelli. *m, inf* scraggy person

fiduciario *a law* fiduciary. *m, law* trustee
fiebre *f*, fever; great agitation, excitement. **f. de oro,** gold fever. **f. palúdica,** malarial fever. **f. puerperal,** puerperal fever. **f. tifoidea,** typhoid fever
fiel *a* faithful, loyal; true, exact. *m*, axis; pointer (of a scale or balance)
fieltro *m*, felt
fiera *f*, wild beast; cruel person
fiereza *f*, savageness, wildness; cruelty, fierceness; deformity
fiero *a* wild, savage; ugly, huge, enormous; horrible, alarming; haughty
fiesta *f*, merriment, gaiety; entertainment, feast; *inf* joke; festivity, celebration; public holiday; caress, cajolery (gen. *pl*); *pl* holidays. **f. fija** *ecc* immovable feast. *inf* **estar de f.,** to be making merry. **hacer f.,** to take a holiday. *inf* **Se acabó la f.,** It's all over and done with
fifiriche *a, Central America, Mexico* sickly, weak
figón *m*, eating house, diner
figulino *a* a fictile, made of terra cotta
figura *f*, shape, form; face; *art* image, figure; *law* form; court card; *mus* note; *theat* character, role; (*geom gram dancing*) figure. **f. de nieve,** snowman. *naut* **f. de proa,** figurehead. *fig* **f. decorativa,** figurehead. *fig* **hacer f.,** to cut a figure
figurado *a* figurative; rhetorical
figurar *vt* to shape, mold; simulate, pretend; represent; *vi* be numbered among; cut a figure; *vr* imagine
figurilla *mf inf* ridiculous, dwarfish figure. *f, art* statuette
figurín *m*, fashion plate or model
figuroso, -a *a, Lat. Am.* flashy, loud, showy
fijación *f*, fixing; nailing; sticking, posting; attention, fixity; *chem* fixation; firmness, stability
fijador *m*, (*med phot*) fixative; setting lotion; *art* varnish. *a* fixing
fijamente *adv* firmly; attentively
fijar *vt* to fix; glue, stick; nail; make firm; settle, appoint (a date); fix, concentrate (attention, gaze); (*phot med*) fix; *vr* decide; notice (e.g. **No me había fijado,** I hadn't noticed). **f. anuncios,** to post bills
fijeza *f*, fixedness; firmness, stability; constancy, steadfastness
fijo *a* firm; fixed; stable, steadfast; permanent; exact. **de f.,** certainly, without doubt
fila *f*, line, row; *mil* rank; antipathy, hatred. **en f.,** in a line
filacteria *f*, phylactery
filamento *m*, filament
filantropía *f*, philanthropy
filantrópico *a* philanthropic
filántropo *m*, philanthropist
filarmónico *a* philharmonic
filatelia *f*, philately, stamp collecting
filatélico *a* philatelic
filatelista *mf* philatelist, stamp collector
filete *m*, *arch* fillet; *cul* small spit; filet (of meat or fish); thread of a screw; *sew* hem
filiación *f*, filiation; affiliation, relationship; *mil* regimental register
filial *a* filial; affiliated
filibustero *m*, filibuster
filiforme *a* filamentous
filigrana *f*, filigree; watermark (of paper); *fig* delicate creation
filípica *f*, philippic
Filipinas, las the Philippines
filipino (-na) *a* and *n* Philippine
filisteo (-ea) *a* and *n* philistine
filmar *vt* to film
filo *m*, cutting edge; dividing line
filología *f*, philology
filológico *a* philological
filólogo *m*, philologist
filomela *f, poet* nightingale
filón *m*, *min* vein, lode; *fig* gold mine

filoso, -a *a, Lat. Am.* sharp
filosofar *vi* to philosophize
filosofía *f,* philosophy. **f. moral,** moral philosophy. **f. natural,** natural philosophy
filosófico *a* philosophic
filósofo *m,* philosopher. *a* philosophic
filoxera *f,* phylloxera
filtración *f,* filtration
filtrar *vt* to filter; *vi* filter through, percolate; *vr fig* disappear (of money, etc.)
filtro *m,* filter, strainer; love potion, philter
filudo, -a *a, Lat. Am.* = **filoso**
fin *m,* finish, end, conclusion; purpose, goal, aim; limit, extent. **a f. de,** in order to, so that. **a fines de,** toward the end of (with months, years, etc.) (e.g. **a fines de octubre,** toward the end of October). **en f.,** at last; in fine; well then! **por f.,** finally
finado (-da) *n* deceased, dead person
final *a* final. *m,* end, finish; *sport* final (gen. *pl*)
finalidad *f,* finality; purpose
finalista *mf sport* finalist
finalizar *vt* to conclude, finish; *vi* be finished; close (stock exchange)
finalmente *adv* finally
financiar *vt* to finance
financiero *a* financial. *m,* financier
finanzas *f pl,* finance
finar *vi* to die; *vr* desire, long for a thing
finca *f,* land, real estate; house property, country house, ranch
fineza *f,* fineness; excellence, goodness; kindness, expression of affection; good turn, friendly act; gift; beauty, delicacy
fingido *a* pretended; assumed; feigned; sham
fingimiento *m,* pretense; affectation, assumption
fingir *vt* to pretend, feign; imagine
finiquitar *vt* to close and pay up an account; *inf* end
finiquito *m,* closing of an account; final receipt, quittance; quietus
finito *a* finite
finlandés (-esa) *a* Finnish. *n* Finn. *m,* Finnish (language)
fino *a* fine; excellent, good; slim, slender, thin; delicate, subtle; dainty (of people); cultured, polished; constant, loving; sagacious, shrewd; *min* refined
finta *f,* feint (in fencing); menace, threat
finura *f,* fineness; excellence; delicacy; courtesy
fiordo *m,* fjord
firma *f,* signature; act of signing; *com* firm name, firm
firmamento *m,* firmament
firmante *a* signing. *mf* signatory
firmar *vt* to sign
firme *a* firm; hard; steady, solid; constant, resolute, loyal. *m,* foundation, base. *mil* **¡Firmes!** Attention! **batir de f.,** to strike hard
firmeza *f,* stability, firmness; constancy, resoluteness, loyalty
fiscal *a* fiscal. *m,* attorney general; public prosecutor; meddler. **f. de quiebras,** official receiver
fiscalizar *vt* to prosecute; pry into; meddle with; censure, criticize
fisco *m,* national treasury, exchequer, revenue
fisgar *vt* to harpoon; pry; *vi* mock, make fun of
fisgón (-ona) *a* prying; mocking. *n* pryer; mocker; eavesdropper
fisgoneo *m,* prying; eavesdropping
física *f,* physics
físico *a* physical. *m,* physicist; physician; physique
fisiología *f,* physiology
fisiológico *a* physiological
fisiólogo *m,* physiologist
fisioterapia *f,* physiotherapy
fisonomía *f,* physiognomy
fistol *m, Mexico* tie pin; crafty person, sly person
fístula *f,* pipe, conduit; *mus* pipe; *surg* fistula

fisura *f,* fissure
flaccidez *f,* flabbiness
fláccido *a* flaccid, soft, flabby
flaco *a* thin; weak, feeble; *fig* weak-minded; dispirited. *m,* failing, weakness. *inf* **hacer un f. servicio,** to do an ill turn. **estar f. de memoria,** to have a weak memory
flagelación *f,* flagellation
flagelante *m,* flagellant
flagelar *vt* to scourge; *fig* lash
flagelo *m,* whip, scourge
flagrante *a poet* refulgent; present; actual. **en f.,** in the very act, flagrante delicto
flagrar *vi poet* to blaze, be refulgent
flamante *a* resplendent; brand-new; fresh, spick-and-span
flamenco (-ca) *m, orn* flamingo. *a* and *n* Flemish. *a* Andalusian; gypsy; buxom, fresh
flan *m,* baked custard, creme caramel. **estar como un f.,** to shake like a leaf, be nervous
flanco *m,* side; *mil* flank
flanquear *vt mil* to flank
flanqueo *m, mil* outflanking
flaquear *vi* to grow weak; weaken; totter (buildings, etc.); be disheartened, flag
flaqueza *f,* weakness; thinness; faintness, feebleness; frailty, fault; loss of zeal
flato *m,* flatulence, gas
flatulento *a* flatulent, gassy
flauta *f,* flute
flautín *m,* piccolo
flautista *mf* flutist
flebitis *f,* phlebitis
flecha *f,* arrow, dart
flechar *vt* to shoot an arrow or dart; wound or kill with arrows; *inf* inspire love; *vi* bend a bow to shoot
flechazo *m,* wound with an arrow; *inf* love at first sight
flechero *m,* archer; arrow maker
fleco *m,* fringe; fringe (of hair)
fleje *m,* iron hoop (for barrels, etc.)
flema *f,* phlegm; sluggishness
flemático *a* phlegmatic; sluggish
flemón *m,* gumboil; abscess
flequero, -a *a, Lat. Am.* dishonest, tricky
flequillo *m,* fringe (of hair)
fletamento *m,* chartering (a ship)
fletar *vt* to charter a ship; embark merchandise or people
flete *m,* freightage; cargo, freight
flexibilidad *f,* flexibility; suppleness, adaptability
flexible *a* pliant, supple; flexible, adaptable. *m, elec* flex
flirtear *vi* to flirt
flirteo *m,* flirtation
flojedad *f,* flabbiness; weakness, feebleness; laziness, negligence
flojo *a* flabby; slack, loose; weak, feeble; lazy, slothful; poor (of a literary work, etc.)
floqueado *a* fringed
flor *f,* flower; best (of anything); bloom (on fruit); virginity; grain (of leather); compliment (gen. *pl*); menstruation (gen. *pl*). **f. de especia,** mace. **f. de la edad,** prime, youth. **f. del cuclillo,** mayflower. **f. del estudiante,** French marigold. **flores de mano,** artificial flowers. **flores de oblón,** hops. **a f. de,** on the surface of, level with. **andarse en flores,** *fig* to beat about the bush. **echar flores,** to pay compliments. **en f.,** in bloom
flora *f,* flora
floral *a* floral. **juegos florales,** poetry contest
florear *vt* to adorn with flowers; *vi* execute a flourish on the guitar
florecer *vi irr* to flower, bloom; flourish, prosper; *vr* grow mold (of cheese, etc.). See **conocer**
floreciente *a* flowering; prosperous
florecimiento *m,* flowering; prosperity
floreo *m,* witty conversation; flourish (on the guitar or in fencing)
florero *m,* vase; flower pot; *art* flower piece

florescencia *f,* flowering; flowering season, florescence

floresta *f,* grove, wooded park, woodland; *fig* collector of beautiful things; anthology

florete *m,* fencing foil

floricultor (-ra) *n* floriculturist

floricultura *f,* floriculture

floridamente *adv* elegantly, with a flourish

florido *a* flowery; best, most select; florid, ornate

florilegio *m,* anthology, collection

florín *m,* florin

florista *mf* artificial-flower maker; florist; flower seller

florón *m,* large flower; *arch* fleuron; honorable deed

flota *f,* fleet of merchant ships. **f. aérea,** air force

flotación *f,* floating. *naut* **línea de f.,** water line

flotador *a* floating. *m,* float

flotamiento *m,* floating

flotante *a* floating

flotar *vi* to float on water or in air

flote *m,* floating. **a f.,** afloat; independent, solvent

flotilla *f,* flotilla; fleet of small ships. **f. aérea,** air fleet

fluctuación *f,* fluctuation; hesitation, vacillation

fluctuante *a* fluctuating

fluctuar *vi* to fluctuate; be in danger (things); vacillate, hesitate; undulate; oscillate

fluidez *f,* fluidity

flúido *a* fluid; fluent. *m,* fluid; *elec* current

fluir *vi irr* to flow. See **huir**

flujo *m,* flow, flux; rising tide. **f. de sangre,** hemorrhage

fluminense *formal a* of Rio de Janeiro; *mf* native of Rio de Janeiro; resident of Rio de Janeiro

fluorescencia *f,* fluorescence

fluorescente *a* fluorescent

flus *m, Colombia, Venezuela* suit (of clothes)

fluvial *a* fluvial

flux *m,* flush (in cards)

foca *f, zool* seal

focal *a* focal

foco *m,* focus; center; origin; source; *theat* spotlight; core (of an abscess)

fofo *a* spongy, soft; flabby

fogata *f,* bonfire

fogón *m,* fire, cooking area, kitchen range, kitchen stove; furnace of a steamboiler; vent of a firearm

fogonazo *m,* powder flash

fogonero *m,* stoker

fogosidad *f,* enthusiasm; vehemence; ardor

fogoso *a* ardent; vehement; enthusiastic

folclórico *a* pertaining to folklore

folclorista *mf* folklorist

folículo *m,* follicle

folio *m,* leaf of a book or manuscript, folio. **en f.,** in folio

follaje *m,* foliage; leafy ornamentation; crude, unnecessary decoration; verbosity

folletín *m,* feuilleton, literary article; serial story; *inf* dime novel, potboiler

folletinista *mf* pamphleteer

folleto *m,* pamphlet, leaflet

follisca *f, Lat. Am.* brawl

follón *a* lazy; caddish; craven

fomentación *f, med* fomentation, poultice

fomentador *a* fomenting. *m,* fomenter

fomentar *vt* to warm, foment; incite, instigate; *med* apply poultices

fomento *m,* heat, shelter; fuel; protection, encouragement; *med* fomentation

fonda *f,* inn; restaurant

fondeadero *m,* anchorage, anchoring ground

fondear *vt naut* to sound; search a ship; examine carefully; *vi naut* anchor; *vr, Lat. Am.* get rich

fondillos *m pl,* seat (of the trousers)

fondista *mf* owner of an inn or restaurant

fondo *m,* bottom (of a well, etc.); bed (of the sea, etc.); depth; rear, portion at the back; ground (of fabrics);

background; *com* capital; *com* stock; *fig* fund (of humor, etc.); character, nature; temperament; *fig* substance, core, essence; *naut* bottom; *pl com* resources, funds. **f. de amortización,** sinking fund. **f. doble** *or* **f. secreto,** false bottom. **f. muerto, f. perdido** *or* **f. vitalicio,** life annuity. *com* **fondos inactivos,** idle capital. **a fondo,** completely, thoroughly. **artículo de f.,** editorial, lead article. *sport* **carrera de f.,** long-distance race. *naut* **irse a f.,** to sink, founder

fonética *f,* phonetics

fonético *a* phonetic

fonetista *mf* phonetician

fonógrafo *m,* phonograph

fonología *f,* phonology

fonológico *a* phonological

fontanar *m,* spring, stream

fontanería *f,* pipe laying, plumbing

fontanero *m,* pipe layer; plumber

forajido (-da) *a* fugitive, outlawed. *n* robber, fugitive

foramen *m, Lat. Am.* hole

forastero (-ra) *a* strange, foreign; alien, exotic. *n* stranger

forcejear *vi* to struggle; try, strive; oppose, contradict

forcejo *m,* struggle; endeavor; opposition, hostility

fórceps *m pl,* forceps

forense *a* forensic

forillo *m, theat* backdrop

forja *f,* forge

forjador *m,* smith, ironworker

forjar *vt* to forge; fabricate; create; counterfeit

forma *f,* shape, form; arrangement; method; style; manifestation, expression; formula, formulary; ceremonial; *print* form; manner; means, way; mold, matrix; style of handwriting. *law* **en debida f.,** in due form

formación *f,* formation; form, contour, shape; (*mil geol*) formation. **f. del censo,** census taking

formador *a* forming, shaping

formal *a* apparent, formal; serious, punctilious, steady; truthful, reliable; sedate; orderly, regular, methodical

formaldehído *m,* formaldehyde

formalidad *f,* orderliness, propriety; formality; requirement, requisite; ceremony; seriousness, sedateness; punctiliousness

formalismo *m,* formalism; bureaucracy, red tape

formalizar *vt* to put into final form; legalize; formulate, enunciate; *vr* take seriously (a joke)

formar *vt* to shape; form; educate, mold; *mil* form. **formarle causa a uno,** to bring charges against someone. *vr* develop, grow; *Mexico* get in line

formativo *a* formative

formato *m, print* format; *chem* formate

formidable *a* formidable, awe-inspiring; huge, enormous

fórmula *f,* formula; prescription; mode of expression. (*math chem*) **f. clásica,** standard formula

formular *vt* to formulate; prescribe

formulario *m, law* formulary; handbook

formulismo *m,* formulism; bureaucracy, red tape

fornicación *f,* fornication

fornicador (-ra) *a* and *n* fornicator

fornicar *vi* to fornicate

fornido *a* stalwart, muscular, strong

foro *m,* forum; law courts; law, bar, legal profession; *theat* back scenery; leasehold

forraje *m,* forage, fodder; foraging

forrajeador *m,* forager

forrajear *vt* to gather forage, go foraging

forrar *vt sew* to line; cover, encase, make a cover for

forro *m,* lining, inner covering; cover (of a book); *Argentina* condom; *Lat. Am.* fraud, swindle

fortalecedor *a* fortifying

fortalecer *vt irr* to fortify. See **conocer**

fortaleza *f,* vigor; fortitude; fortress; natural defense; *Lat. Am.* stench, stink. *aer* **f. volante,** flying fortress

fortificable *a* fortifiable

fortificación *f*, fortification
fortificador *a* fortifying
fortificar *vt* to fortify
fortísimo *a sup* **fuerte** extremely strong
fortuito *a* fortuitous, chance
fortuna *f*, fate, destiny; fortune, capital, estate; tempest. **por f.,** fortunately. **probar f.,** to try one's luck
forzado *a* forced, obliged. *m*, convict condemned to the galleys
forzador *m*, violator, seducer
forzar *vt irr* to force, break open; take by force; rape, ravish; oblige, compel. *Pres. Ind.* **fuerzo, fuerzas, fuerza, fuerzan.** *Preterite* **forcé, forzaste,** etc. *Pres. Subjunc.* **fuerce, fuerces, fuerce, forcemos, forcéis, fuercen**
forzoso *a* obligatory, unavoidable, necessary
forzudo *a* brawny, stalwart
fosa *f*, grave; socket (of a joint). **f. común,** potter's field.
fosar *vt* to undermine; dig a trench around
fosfato *m*, phosphate
fosforecer *vi irr* to phosphoresce. See **conocer**
fosforera *f*, matchbox
fosforero (-ra) *n* match seller
fosforescente *a* phosphorescent
fósforo *m*, phosphorus; match; morning star
fósil *a* and *m*, fossil; *inf* antique
foso *m*, hole, hollow, pit; trench; pit (in garages); *theat* room under the stage.
foto *f*, snapshot, photo
fotocopia *f*, photocopy
fotogénico *a* photogenic
fotograbado *m*, photogravure
fotografía *f*, photography; photograph
fotografiar *vt* to photograph
fotográfico *a* photographic
fotógrafo *m*, photographer
fotograma *m*, (cinema) shot
fotoquímica *f*, photochemistry
fotostato *m*, photostat
frac *m*, tail coat
fracasar *vi* to break, crumble, be shattered; collapse (of plans, etc.); fail; be disappointed
fracaso *m*, shattering; collapse (of plans, etc.); disaster; failure, disappointment, downfall
fracción *f*, division into parts; fraction. **f. impropia,** *math* improper fraction
fractura *f*, fracture. **f. conminuta,** compound fracture
fracturar *vt* to fracture
fragancia *f*, fragrance, perfume; renown, good name
fragante *a* fragrant; perfumed; flagrant
fragata *f*, frigate
frágil *a* fragile, brittle; perishable, frail; weak, sinful
fragilidad *f*, fragility; frailty, sinfulness
fragmentario *a* fragmentary
fragmento *m*, fragment
fragor *m*, noise, crash
fragosidad *f*, roughness, rockiness, unevenness
fragoso *a* craggy, rocky; rough; noisy, clamorous
fragua *f*, forge
fraguar *vt* to forge, work; plot, scheme; *vi* set (concrete, etc.)
fraile *m*, friar, monk. *inf* **f. de misa y olla,** ignorant friar
frailesco *a inf* pertaining to friars, friar-like
frambuesa *f*, raspberry
francachela *f*, *inf* binge
francés (-esa) *a* French. *n* Frenchman (-woman). *m*, French (language). **a la francesa,** in French fashion
francesilla *f*, *cul* French roll
Francia France
francmasón (-ona) *n* Freemason
francmasonería *f*, freemasonry
franco *a* generous, liberal; exempt; sincere, genuine, frank; duty-free; Frank; Franco (in compound words). *m*, franc (coin). **f. de porte,** post-free; prepaid
francotirador *m*, sharpshooter, franc tireur

franela *f*, flannel; *Lat. Am.* undershirt; T-shirt
frangir *vt* to divide, quarter
frangollar *vt* to scamp, skimp (work); botch, bungle
franja *f*, fringe; border, trimming; stripe. *rad* **f. undosa,** wave band
franjar *vt sew* to fringe, trim
franqueadora *f*, postage meter
franquear *vt* to exempt; make free, make a gift of; clear the way; stamp, prepay; free (slaves); *vr* fall in easily with others' plans; make confidences
franqueo *m*, exemption; bestowal, making free; postage, stamping; enfranchisement (of slaves)
franqueza *f*, exemption, freedom; generosity, liberality; sincerity, frankness
franquicia *f*, exemption from excise duties
franquista *mf* Franquist, supporter of Franco
frasco *m*, bottle, flask; powder flask or horn. **f. cuentagotas,** drop bottle
frase *f*, sentence; phrase; epigram; idiom, style. **f. hecha,** cliché
frasear *vt* to phrase
fraseología *f*, phraseology; wording
fratás *m*, plastering trowel
fraternal *a* brotherly
fraternidad *f*, fraternity, brotherhood
fraternizar *vi* to fraternize
fraterno *a* fraternal
fratricida *a* fratricidal. *mf* fratricide
fratricidio *m*, fratricide (act)
fraude *m*, fraud, deception
fraudulento *a* fraudulent
fray *m*, *abb* **fraile.** Always followed by a proper name (e.g. **F. Bartolomé,** Friar Bartholomew)
frazada *f*, blanket
frecuencia *f*, frequency. **f. radioeléctrica,** radiofrequency
frecuentación *f*, frequenting, visiting
frecuentador (-ra) *n* frequenter
frecuentar *vt* to frequent
frecuente *a* frequent
fregada *f*, *Lat. Am.* bother, hassle, nuisance
fregadero *m*, kitchen sink
fregado *m*, scrubbing; rubbing; scouring; washing; *inf* murky business
fregador *m*, kitchen sink; scrub brush; dishcloth. **f. mecánico de platos,** dishwasher
fregandera *f*, *Mexico* charwoman, cleaning woman
fregar *vt irr* to rub; scour; wash (dishes). See **cegar**
fregona *f*, kitchen maid
fregotear *vt inf* to clean or scour inefficiently
freiduría *f*, fried-fish shop
freír *vt irr cul* to fry. See **reír**
fréjol *m*, kidney bean
frenar *vt* to restrain, hold back; bridle, check; *mech* brake
frenesí *m*, madness, frenzy; vehemence, exaltation
frenético *a* mad, frenzied; vehement, exalted
freno *m*, bridle; *mech* brake; restraint, check. **f. de pedal,** foot brake. **f. neumático,** vacuum brake, pneumatic brake
frente *f*, brow, forehead; front portion; countenance; head; heading; beginning (of a letter, etc.). *m*, *mil* front. *mf* facade; front; obverse (of coins). *adv* in front, opposite. **f. a f.,** face to face. **con la f. levantada,** with head held high; proudly; insolently. **de f.,** abreast
freo *m*, strait, narrow channel
fresa *f*, strawberry plant and fruit (especially small or wild varieties); *mech* milling cutter, miller
fresadora *f*, milling machine
fresal *m*, strawberry bed
fresca *f*, cool air; fresh air; *inf* home truth
fresco *a* cool; fresh, new; recent; buxom, fresh-colored; calm, serene; *inf* impudent, cheeky, bold; thin (cloths). *m*, coolness; fresh air; *art* fresco. **al f.,** in the open air. **hacer f.,** to be cool or fresh
frescote *a inf* ruddy and corpulent

frescura f, coolness; freshness; pleasant verdure and fertility; inf cheek, nerve; piece of insolence; unconcern, indifference; calmness, serenity

fresero (-ra) n strawberry seller

fresno m, bot ash

fresón m, strawberry (large, cultivated varieties)

fresquera f, meat locker; cool place

fresquería f, Mexico refreshment stand

fresquista mf fresco painter

friable a brittle; friable, powdery

frialdad f, coldness, chilliness; med frigidity; indifference, lack of interest; foolishness; negligence

fríamente adv coldly; coolly, with indifference; dully, flatly

fricción f, friction

friccionar vt to rub; give a massage

friega f, friction, massage

frigidez f, See **frialdad**

frígido a frigid

frigio a and n Phrygian

frigorífico a refrigerative. m, refrigerator, cold-storage locker

frijol m, bean; bot kidney bean

frijoles refritos con queso mpl, Mexico twice fried Mexican beans with cheese

frío a cold; med frigid; indifferent, uninterested; dull, uninteresting; inefficient. m, coldness, chill; cold

friolera f, bagatelle, trifle, mere nothing

friolero a sensitive to cold

frisa f, frieze cloth

frisar vt to frizz, curl (cloth); scrub, rub; vi approach, be nearly (e.g. **Frisa en los setenta años,** He's nearly seventy)

friso m, frieze; dado, border

fritada f, cul fry, fried food

frito a fried

fritura f, frying; fried food

frivolidad f, frivolity

frivolité m, sew tatting

frívolo a frivolous, superficial; futile, unconvincing

fronda f, bot leaf; frond (of ferns); pl foliage

frondoso a leafy

frontera f, frontier; facade

fronterizo a frontier; facing, opposite

frontero a facing, opposite. m, (ant mil) frontier commander

frontispicio m, frontispiece; facade; fig inf face, dial

frontón m, pelota court; jai alai court; arch pediment; Mexico jai alai

frotamiento, frote m, rubbing, friction

frotar vt to rub

frotis m, med smear

fructífero a fruitful, fructiferous

fructuoso a fruitful, fertile; useful

frufrú m, rustle (of silk, etc.)

frugal a frugal; saving, economical

frugalidad f, frugality, abstemiousness, moderation

fruición f, enjoyment; fruition; satisfaction

fruir vi irr to enjoy what one has long desired. See **huir**

frunce m, sew shirring; gather; ruffling; tuck; pucker; wrinkle

fruncimiento m, wrinkling; puckering; sew shirring

fruncir vt to frown; purse (the lips); pucker; sew shirr, pleat, gather; reduce in size; conceal the truth; vr pretend to be prudish. **f. el ceño,** to knit one's brow, scowl

fruslería f, trifle, nothing

frustración f, frustration

frustrar vt to disappoint; frustrate, thwart

fruta f, fruit; inf consequence, result. **f. bomba** Cuba papaya **f. de hueso,** stone fruit. cul **f. de sartén,** fritter

frutal a fruit-bearing. m, fruit tree

frutar vi to bear fruit

frutería f, fruit

frutero (-ra) a fruit. n fruit seller. m, fruit dish; art painting of fruit; basket of imitation fruit

frútice m, bush, shrub

fruticultura f, fruit farming

fruto m, fruit; product, result; profit, proceeds; agr grain

fu spitting (of cats). interj expression of scorn. inf **ni f. ni fa,** neither one thing nor the other

fucsia f, fuchsia

fuego m, fire; conflagration; firing (of firearms); beacon; hearth, home; rash; ardor; heat (of an argument, etc.); interj **¡F.!** mil Fire! **fuegos artificiales,** fireworks. **a sangre y f.,** by fire and sword. mil **hacer f.,** to fire (a weapon). **pegar f.,** to set on fire

fuelle m, bellows; bag (of a bagpipe); sew pucker, wrinkle; hood (of a carriage, etc.); wind cloud; inf talebearer. **f. de pie,** foot pump

fuente f, stream, spring; fountain; meat dish; genesis, origin; source, headwaters; tap

fuera adv outside, out. interj get out! **f. de,** besides, in addition to. **f. de alcance,** out of reach. **f. de sí,** beside oneself (with rage, etc.). **de f.,** from the outside. **por f.,** on the outside, externally

fuereño, -a mf, Mexico foreigner

fuero m, municipal charter; jurisdiction; compilation of laws; legal right or privilege; pl inf arrogance. **los fueros de León,** the laws of León

fuerte a strong, resistant; robust; spirited, vigorous; hard (of diamonds, etc.); rough, uneven; impregnable; terrible, tremendous; overweight (of coins); active; efficacious, effective; expert, knowledgeable; gram strong; intense; loud; tough. m, fort; talent, strong point; mus forte. adv strongly; excessively. **tener genio f.,** to be quick-tempered

fuerza f, strength; power, might; force; efficacy; fortress; sew stiffening; mech power; violence; toughness, durability, solidity; potency; authority; courage; vigor; pl fig inf livewires, influential people. **a f. de,** by means of, by dint of. **a la f.,** forcibly. **en f. de,** because of, on account of. **por f. mayor,** by main force. **ser f.,** to be necessary

fuga f, flight, escape, running away; leak (gas, etc.); elopement; mus fugue; ardor, strength. **f. de cerebros,** brain drain

fugarse vr to run away; elope; escape

fugaz a fugitive; fleeting, brief

fugitivo (-va) a fugitive; runaway, escaping; transient. n fugitive

fulano (-na) n so-and-so, such a person **f., zutano, y mengano,** inf Tom, Dick, and Harry

fulcro m, fulcrum

fulgente, fúlgido a brilliant, shining

fulgor m, brilliance, brightness

fulgurar vi to shine, be resplendent, scintillate; flare

fulguroso a shining, sparkling

fulminante a med fulminant; fulminating; thundering. m, percussion cap

fulminar vt to fulminate (all meanings)

fulminato m, chem fulminate

fulmíneo, fulminoso a fulminous, pertaining to lightning

fullería f, cheating at play; craftiness, low guile

fullero (-ra) a cheating; crafty, astute. n cheat, cardsharper

fumadero m, smoking room

fumador (-ra) a smoking. n smoker. «**No fumadores**», "Nonsmoking" (area)

fumar vi to smoke; vr inf dissipate, waste

fumarola f, fumarole

fumigación f, fumigation

fumigador (-ra) n fumigator

fumigar vt to fumigate

fumigatorio a fumigatory. m, perfume burner

fumista mf stove maker; stove dealer; Argentina joker, tease

fumistería f, stove factory or store

funámbulo n tightrope walker, acrobat

función f, function; working, operation; *theat* performance; activity, duty; ceremony; celebration; *math* function; *mil* battle

funcional a functional

funcionamiento m, functioning

funcionar vi to function, work. «**No funciona**», "Out of order"

funcionario m, functionary, official; civil servant

funda f, case, cover, sheath; hold-all. **f. de almohada,** pillowcase

fundación f, foundation

fundadamente adv with reason, on good evidence

fundador (-ra) n founder, creator; originator

fundamental a fundamental

fundamento m, mas foundation; basis; basic principle, reason; origin, root

fundar vt to build, erect; base; found, institute; create, establish; vr (*with en*) found, base upon. **f. una compañía,** *com* to float a company

fundición f, foundry; smelting, founding, casting; cast iron; *print* font

fundido fotográfico m, composite photograph

fundidor m, founder, smelter.

fundir vt to melt; found, smelt; cast (metals); vr join together, unite; *elec* blow (fuses)

fúnebre a funeral; dismal, lugubrious, mournful

funerales m pl, funeral; *ecc* memorial masses

funerala, (a la) adv mil with reversed arms

funeraria f, funeral home, undertaker

funéreo a funereal, mournful

funestidad f, Mexico calamity, catastrophe

funesto a unlucky, unfortunate; mournful, melancholy, sad

fungoso a spongy, fungous

funicular a funicular

furgón m, wagon; van; guard's van, baggage car, luggage cart. **f. postal,** mail truck

furia f, myth fury; rage, wrath; fit of madness; raging, violence (of the elements); speed, haste

furibundo a frantic, furious; raging

fúrico a stark raving mad

furioso a furious, enraged; mad, insane; violent, terrible; enormous, excessive

furor m, fury, rage; poetic frenzy; violence; furor

furtivo a furtive; covert, clandestine; pirate (editions)

fusa f, demisemiquaver

fusco a dark

fuselado a streamlined

fuselaje m, fuselage

fusible a fusible. m, elec fuse; fuse wire

fusil m, rifle

fusilamiento m, execution by shooting

fusilar vt to execute by shooting; inf plagiarize

fusilazo m, rifle shot

fusión f, melting, liquefying; fusion, blending; mixture, union; com merger, amalgamation

fusionar vt to blend, fuse, merge; vr com combine, form a merger

fusta f, brushwood; whip

fustán m Lat. Am. skirt

fuste m, wood, timber; poet saddle; fig core, essence; importance, substance; shaft of a lance; arch shaft. **hombre de buen f.,** a man with a good (physical) constitution

fustigar vt to whip, lash; rebuke harshly

fútbol m, football; soccer

futbolista mf football player; soccer player

fútil a futile, ineffectual, worthless

futilidad f, futility, worthlessness

futura f, law reversion (of offices); inf fiancée

futurismo m, futurism

futurista mf futurist

futurístico a futuristic

futuro (-ra) a future. m, future. n inf betrothed

G

gabacho (-cha) a and n (inf scornful) Frenchman

gabán m, overcoat; cloak

gabardina f, gabardine; weatherproof coat

gabarra f, naut lighter, gabbard, barge

gabarro m, flaw (in cloth); knot (in stone); snag, drawback; slip, error (in accounts)

gabela f, duty, tax; imposition, burden

gabinete m, study, library; sitting room; den; pol cabinet; collection, museum, gallery; laboratory; boudoir; studio; display cabinet. **g. de lectura,** reading room

gablete m, arch gable

gacel, m. gacela f, gazelle

gaceta f, bulletin, review, record; newspaper; gazette (official Spanish government organ); inf newshound

gacetero (-ra) n newsdealer. m, news reporter

gacetilla f, news in brief, miscellany column, society news; gossip column; inf newshound

gacetillero m, paragrapher, penny-a-liner; reporter

gacha f, unglazed crock; pl pap; porridge

gaché m, (among the Romany) Andalusian; inf fellow

gacho a drooping, bent downward; slouch (hat); (of ears) lop; Mexico unpleasant

gachón a inf attractive, charming

gaélico a and m, Gaelic

gafar vt to claw; seize with a hook, hook; mend with a bracket (pottery)

gafas f pl, spectacles; goggles; spectacle earhooks; grapplehooks

gafete m, hook and eye; clasp

gaita f, bagpipe; hand organ; kind of clarinet; inf neck. **g. gallega,** bagpipe

gaitería f, crude, gaudy garment or ornament

gaitero a inf overmerry; loud, crude. m, piper

gajes m pl, salary; emoluments; perquisites

gajo m, branch, bough (gen. cut); little cluster (of grapes); bunch (of fruit); quarter (of oranges, etc.); prong (of forks, etc.)

gala f, evening or full dress; grace, wit; flower, cream, best; gala; pl finery; trappings; wedding presents. **de g.,** full dress. **hacer g. de,** to glory in, boast of

galactita f, fuller's earth

galaico a See **gallego**

galán m, handsome, well-made man; lover, wooer, gallant; theat leading man or one of leading male roles

galancete m, handsome little man; theat male juvenile lead

galano a smart, well-dressed; agreeable, pleasing; beautiful; ornamented; fig elegant (speech, style, etc.)

galante a gallant, courtly, attentive; flirtatious (of women); licentious

galanteador a flirtatious. m, philanderer; wooer

galantear vt to court; flirt with; make love to; fig procure assiduously

galanteo m, courtship; flirtation; love-making; wooing

galantería f, courtesy; attention, compliment; elegance, grace; gallantry; generosity, liberality

galanura f, showiness, gorgeousness; elegance, grace; prettiness

galápago m, freshwater tortoise; cleat

galardón m, reward, recompense, prize

galardonar vt to reward, recompense

gálata a and mf Galatian

galbana f, inf laziness, inertia

galbanoso a inf slothful

galdrufa f, top, spinning top

galeote m, galley slave

galera *f*, van, wagon, cart; *naut* galley; prison for women; *print* galley; *Central America, Mexico* shed. **echar a galeras,** to condemn to the galleys

galerada *f*, galley proof

galería *f*, gallery; corridor, passage; collection of paintings; *min* gallery, drift; *theat* gallery

galerna *f*, tempestuous northwest wind (gen. on Spanish north coast)

Gales Wales

galés (-esa) *a* Welsh. *n* Welshman. *m*, Welsh (language)

galga *f*, boulder, rolling stone; greyhound bitch

galgo *m*, greyhound. **g. ruso,** borzoi

Galia Gaul

gálibo *m*, *naut* mold; elegance

galicado *a* gallicized

galicismo *m*, gallicism

gálico *m*, syphilis. *a* gallic

Galilea Galilee

galileo (-ea) *a* and *n* Galilean

galimatías *m*, *inf* gibberish, nonsense

gallardear *vi* to behave with ease and grace

gallardete *m*, pennant; bunting

gallardía *f*, grace, dignity; spirit, dash; courage; liveliness

gallardo *a* handsome, upstanding; gallant; spirited; fine, noble; lively

gallear *vi inf* to put on airs; be a bully; shout, bawl (with anger, etc.); *fig inf* stand out

gallego (-ga) *a* and *n* Galician. *m*, Galician (language)

galleta *f*, biscuit; *inf* slap; anthracite, lump coal; small jar or vessel

gallina *f*, hen. *mf inf* coward. **g. ciega,** blindman's buff. *inf* **acostarse con las gallinas,** to go to bed early

gallinaza *f*, hen dung

gallinero (-ra) *n* poultry dealer. *m*, henhouse; brood of hens; *theat* gallery; babel, noisy place

gallito *m*, small cock; cock of the walk; bully

gallo *m*, *orn* cock; *inf* false note (in singing); *inf* boss, chief. **g. de viento,** weathercock. *inf* **alzar el g.,** to put on airs, boast. **Cada g. canta en su muladar,** Every man is boss in his own house. *inf* **Otro g. nos cantara,** Our lot (or fate) would have been very different

gallofero (-ra) *a* mendicant, vagabond. *n* beggar

galocha *f*, patten, clog; cap with earflaps

galón *m*, galloon, braid; *mil* stripe; gallon (measure)

galoneadura *f*, braiding, trimming

galonear *vt* to trim with braid

galop *m*, galop; gallopade

galopante *a* galloping (of consumption, etc.)

galopar *vi* to gallop; *mech* wobble

galope *m*, gallop. **a** or **de g.,** at the gallop; on the run, quickly. **andar a g. corto,** to canter

galopillo *m*, scullion

galopín *m*, ragamuffin, urchin; rogue, knave; *inf* clever rogue; *naut* cabin boy

galvanización *f*, galvanization

galvanizar *vt elec* to galvanize; electroplate; *fig* shock into life

gama *f*, *mus* scale; gamut, range; doe

gambado *a Lat. Am.* knock-kneed

gambito *m*, gambit (in chess)

gamella *f*, trough (for washing, feeding animals, etc.)

gamo *m*, buck (of the fallow deer)

gamuza *f*, chamois; chamois leather

gana *f*, appetite; wish, desire. **de buena g.,** willingly. **de mala g.,** reluctantly. **tener g. (de),** to wish, desire, want. **no tener g.,** to have no appetite, not be hungry. **No me da la g.,** I don't want (to), I won't

ganable *a* attainable; earnable

ganadería *f*, livestock; strain (of cattle); cattle raising; stock farm; cattle dealing

ganadero *m*, cattle raiser or dealer; herdsman

ganado *m*, livestock, herd; flock; hive (of bees); *inf* mob. **g. mayor,** cattle, mules, horses. **g. menor,** sheep, goats, etc. **g. moreno,** hogs, swine. **g. vacuno,** cattle

ganador (-ra) *a* winning. *n* winner

ganancia *f*, winning; gain, profit

ganancial, ganancioso *a* gainful, profitable; lucrative

ganapán *m*, laborer; porter; *inf* boor

ganar *vt* to gain; win; conquer; arrive at; earn; surpass; beat; achieve; acquire; *vi* prosper

ganchero *m*, lumberjack

ganchillo *m*, crochet hook; crochet. **hacer g.,** to crochet

gancho *m*, hook; stump (of a branch); shepherd's crook; crochet hook; *inf* trickster, pimp; *inf* scribble

ganchoso *a* hooked; bent; curved

gandujar *vt sew* to pleat, tuck, shirr

gandul (-la) *a inf* lazy. *n* lazybones, loafer

gandulería *f*, loafing, idleness

ganga *f*, *min* gangue, matrix; bargain, cinch

ganglio *m*, ganglion

gangoso *a* nasal; with a twang (of speech)

gangrena *f*, gangrene

gangrenarse *vr* to become gangrenous, mortify

gangrenoso *a* gangrenous

ganguear *vi* to speak nasally, or with a twang

ganoso *a* wishful, desirous, anxious

gansada *f*, *inf* impertinence, foolishness

ganso (-sa) *n* goose, gander; slow-moving person; yokel, bumpkin

ganzúa *f*, skeleton key; *inf* picklock, burglar; *inf* pumper, inquisitive person

gañán *m*, farm worker; day laborer; brawny fellow

gañido *m*, yowl, yelp, howl

gañir *vi irr* to yowl, yelp, howl (of dogs, etc.); crow, croak; *inf* talk hoarsely. See **mullir**

garabatear *vi* to hook, catch with hooks; scribble; *fig inf* beat around the bush

garabateo *m*, hooking; scribbling

garabato *m*, hook; *agr* weed clearer; scrawl, scribble; *inf* charm, sex appeal; pothook; boat hook; *pl* gestures, movements (with the hands)

garaje *m*, garage

garambaina *f*, tawdry finery gaudiness; *pl inf* grimaces of affectation; *inf* scribble, scrawl

garante *mf* guarantor; reference (person). *a* responsible, guaranteeing

garantía *f*, guarantee; security, pledge; *law* warranty

garantir *vt* to guarantee; warrant, vouch for

garañón *m Lat. Am.* stallion

garapiñar *vt* to ice, freeze (drinks, syrups, etc.); *cul* candy, coat with sugar

garbanzo *m*, chickpea. **g. negro,** *fig* black sheep

garbillar *vt agr* to sift; *min* riddle

garbo *m*, jaunty air; grace, elegance; frankness; generosity, liberality

garboso *a* attractive; handsome, sprightly, gay; graceful; munificent

garduña *f*, weasel; marten

garduño (-ña) *n inf* sneak thief

garete (ir or **irse al)** *naut* to be adrift

garfa *f*, claw (of a bird or animal)

garfear *vi* to catch with a hook, hook

garfio *m*, grappling iron, hook, drag hook, cramp; gaff

gargajear *vi* to expectorate

gargajo *m*, phlegm

garganta *f*, throat; gullet; instep; defile; neck, shaft, narrowest part

gargantear *vi* to warble, trill

gárgara *f*, gargling (gen. *pl*). **hacer gárgaras,** to gargle

gargarismo *m*, gargling; gargle

gárgol *a* rotten (eggs). *m*, groove, mortise

gárgola *f*, *arch* gargoyle; linseed

garguero *m*, windpipe; esophagus

garita *f*, sentry box; porter's lodge; hut; cabin. **g. de señales,** (railroad) signal box

garitero *m*, gambling house keeper; gambler

garito *m*, gambling house; profits of a gambling house

garra *f*, paw with claws; talon; hand; *mech* clamp, claw. *fig* **caer en las garras de,** to fall into the clutches (of)

garrafa *f*, decanter, carafe; carboy

garrapata *f, ent* tick
garrapatear *vi* to scribble
garrapaticida *m, Lat. Am.* insecticide
garrapato *m,* scribble, scrawl
garrido *a* handsome; gallant; elegant; graceful
garroba *f,* carob bean
garrocha *f,* goad. **salto a la g.,** pole jumping
garrotazo *m,* blow with a truncheon or cudgel. **dar garrotazos de ciego,** to lay about one
garrote *m,* truncheon, club; *med* tourniquet; garrote. **dar g. (a),** to strangle
garrotillo *m,* croup
garrucha *f,* pulley; *mech* gin block
garrulidad *f,* garrulity, loquaciousness
gárrulo *a* twittering, chirping (birds); garrulous; murmuring, babbling (wind, water, etc.)
ganuar *vi Lat. Am.* to drizzle
garza *f,* heron
garzo *a* blue (gen. of eyes)
gas *m,* gas; fumes. **g. asfixiante,** poison gas. **cámara de g.,** gasbag, gas chamber
gasa *f,* gauze. **tira de g.,** black mourning band
gasconada *f,* bravado, gasconade
gaseosa *f,* aerated water
gaseoso *a* gaseous
gasista *mf* gas fitter; gasman
gasolina *f,* gasoline, petrol
gasómetro *m,* gas meter; gasometer
gastado *a* worn; worn-out; exhausted
gastador (-ra) *a* extravagant, wasteful. *n* spendthrift. *m, mil* sapper; convict condemned to hard labor
gastar *vt* to spend (money); wear out; exhaust; ruin, destroy; display or have habitually; possess, use, wear; *vr* wear out; run down (of a battery)
gasto *m,* spending; expenditure; consumption (of gas, etc.); expense, cost, charge; wear (and tear). **g. suplementario,** extra charge
gástrico *a* gastric
gastritis *f,* gastritis
gastronomía *f,* gastronomy
gastronómico *a* gastronomic
gastrónomo (-ma) *n* gastronome
gata *f,* she-cat; wreath of mist; *inf* Madrilenian woman. **a gatas,** on all fours
gatada *f, inf* sly trick
gatear *vi* to climb like a cat; *inf* crawl on all fours; *vt inf* scratch (of a cat); steal, pinch
gatillo *m, dim* small cat; dental forceps; trigger (of gun); *inf* juvenile petty thief
gato *m,* cat; tomcat; moneybag or its contents; *mech* jack; mousetrap; *inf* cat burglar, sneak thief; *inf* Madrilenian; *carp* clamp. **g. atigrado,** tiger cat. **g. de algalia,** civet cat. **g. de Angora,** Persian cat. **g. montés,** wildcat. **g. romano,** tabby cat. **dar g. por liebre,** to serve cat for hare, to deceive; misrepresent. *inf* **Hay g. encerrado,** There's more to this than meets the eye
gatuno *a* feline
gaucho (-cha) *n* gaucho; cowboy, rider
gaveta *f,* drawer (of a desk)
gavia *f,* main topsail; *pl* topsails; crow's-nest
gavilán *m,* sparrow hawk; thistle flower; *Lat. Am.* ingrown toenail
gavilla *f,* sheaf (of corn, etc.); gang, rabble
gaviota *f,* seagull
gavota *f,* gavotte
gayo *a* gay, happy; showy, attractive. **gaya ciencia,** minstrelsy, art of poetry
gazapera *f,* rabbit warren; *inf* thieves' den; *inf* brawl
gazapo *m,* young rabbit; *inf* cunning fellow; fib, lie; slip, blunder
gazmoñería *f,* prudery, priggish affectation
gazmoño *a* hypocritical, prudish, priggish
gaznápiro (-ra) *n* ninny, simpleton
gaznate *m,* windpipe
gazpacho *m,* cold soup containing bread, onions, vinegar, olive oil, garlic, etc.

ge *f,* name of the letter G
gehena *m,* gehenna, hell
géiser *m,* geyser
gelatina *f,* gelatin. **g. incendiaria,** napalm. **g. seca,** cooking gelatin
gelatinoso *a* gelatinous
gélido *a poet* icy; very cold
gema *f,* gem; *bot* bud
gemelo (-la) *a* and *n* twin. *m pl,* field or opera glasses, binoculars; cuff links; *ast* Gemini
gemido *m,* groan, lament, moan
gemidor *a* groaning, moaning; wailing (of the wind, etc.)
gemir *vi irr* to moan, groan, lament; *fig* wail, howl. See **pedir**
gene *m,* gene
genealogía *f,* genealogy
genealógico *a* genealogical
genealogista *mf* genealogist
generación *f,* generation, reproduction; species; generation
generador *a* generative. *m, mech* generator
general *a* general; universal; widespread; common, usual. *m, (mil ecc)* general. **g. de división,** *mil* major general. **en** *or* **por lo g.,** generally
generalato *m,* generalship
generalidad *f,* majority, bulk; generality
generalísimo *m,* generalissimo, commander in chief
generalización *f,* generalization
generalizar *vt* to generalize; *vr* become widespread or general
generar *vt* to generate
genérico *a* generic
género *m,* kind; class; way, mode; *com* goods; species; genus; *gram* gender; cloth, material. **g. chico,** short theatrical pieces (gen. one act). **g. humano,** humankind
generosidad *f,* hereditary nobility; generosity, magnanimity; liberality, munificence; courage
generoso *a* noble (by birth); magnanimous; generous (of wine); munificent; courageous; excellent
genésico *a* genetic
génesis *m,* Genesis. *f,* beginning, origin
genial *a* of genius; highly talented; brilliant; characteristic, individual; pleasant; cheerful
genialidad *f,* genius; talent; brilliance; eccentricity, oddity
genio *m,* nature, individuality, temperament; temper; character; talent; genius; genie, spirit. **corto de g.,** unintelligent. **mal g.,** bad temper
genital *a* genital. *m,* testicle (gen. *pl*)
genitivo *a* reproductive, generative. *m, gram* genitive
Génova Genoa
gente *f,* people, a crowd; nation; army; *inf* family; followers, adherents. **g. baja,** rabble. **g. de bien,** honest folk; respectable people. **g. de paz,** friends (reply to sentinel's challenge). **g. fina,** nice, cultured people. **g. menuda,** children, small fry
gentecilla *f, dim inf* rabble; contemptible people
gentil *a* pagan, idolatrous; spirited, dashing, handsome; notable, extraordinary; graceful, charming
gentileza *f,* grace; elegance; beauty; verve, sprightliness; courtesy; show, ostentation
gentilhombre *m,* gentleman; handsome man; kind sir! **gentileshombres de cámara,** gentlemen-in-waiting
gentilicio *a* national; family
gentílico *a* pagan, idolatrous
gentilidad *f,* idolatry, paganism; heathendom
gentío *m,* crowd, throng
gentualla, gentuza *f,* canaille, rabble
genuflexión *f,* genuflection
genuino *a* pure; authentic, genuine; *Colombia* great, wonderful
geodesia *f,* geodesy
geodésico *a* geodesic
geografía *f,* geography

geográfico *a* geographical
geógrafo *m*, geographer
geología *f*, geology
geológico *a* geological
geólogo *m*, geologist
geometría *f*, geometry. **g. del espacio,** solid geometry
geométrico *a* geometrical
geranio *m*, geranium
gerencia *f*, *com* managership; manager's office; management
gerente *m*, *com* manager
germanía *f*, thieves' slang; association of thieves; sixteenth-century political brotherhood
germánico *a* germanic
germanófilo (-la) *a* and *n* germanophile
germen *m*, germ, sprout; *bot* embryo; genesis, origin
germinación *f*, germination
germinar *vi* to germinate, sprout; develop, grow
germinativo *a* germinative
gerundio *m*, *gram* gerund; *inf* pompous ass; *inf* tubthumper
gesta *f*, heroic deed. **cantar de g.,** epic or heroic poem
gestación *f*, gestation
gestear *vi* to gesture, grimace
gesticulación *f*, gesticulation; grimace
gesticular *vi* to grimace, gesticulate. *a* gesticulatory
gestión *f*, negotiation; management, conduct; effort, exertion; measure
gestionar *vt* to negotiate; conduct; undertake; take steps to attain
gesto *m*, gesture; facial expression; grimace; face, visage
gestor (-ra) *n* manager; partner; promoter. *a* managing
Getsemaní Gethsemane
giba *f*, hump, hunchback; *inf* nuisance, inconvenience
gibón *m*, gibbon
giboso *a* hunchbacked
gibraltareño *a* Gibraltarian
gigante *a* gigantic. *m*, giant.
giganta *f*, giantess
gigantesco *a* giant, gigantic; *fig* outstanding
gigantez *f*, gigantic size
gigantón (-ona) *n* enormous giant; carnival grotesque
gimnasia *f*, gymnastics
gimnasio *m*, gymnasium; school, academy
gimnasta *mf* gymnast
gimnástico *a* gymnastic
gimotear *vi inf* to whine (often used scornfully)
gimoteo *m*, *inf* whining, whimpering
ginebra *f*, gin (drink); confusion; babble, din
ginebrés (-esa), ginebrino (-na) *a* and *n* Genevan
gineceo *m*, (*bot* and in ancient Greece) gynaecium
ginecología *f*, gynecology
ginecológico *a* gynecological
ginecólogo (-ga) *n* gynecologist
girado *m*, *com* drawee
girador *m*, *com* drawer
giralda *f*, weathercock in the shape of a person or animal; tower at Seville
girar *vi* to revolve; deal (with), concern; turn, branch (streets, etc.); *com* trade; *mech* turn on, revolve; *vt* and *vi com* draw, cash. **g. en descubierto,** *com* to overdraw
girasol *m*, sunflower
giratorio *a* revolving, gyrating; swiveling
giro *m*, revolution, turn; revolving; trend; course (of affairs); style, turn (of phrase); threat; knife gash; *com* draft, drawing; *com* line of business, speciality. **g. postal,** postal order
giroscopio *m*, gyroscope
gis *m Lat. Am.* chalk; *Mexico also* pulque
gitanería *f*, cajolery, wheedling; gypsies; gypsy saying or action
gitanesco *a* gypsy, gypsy-like
gitano (-na) *a* gypsy; gypsy-like; seductive, attractive; sly. *n* gypsy
glaciar *m*, glacier
gladiador *m*, gladiator

glándula *f*, gland
glanco *a Lat. Am.* light green
glicerina *f*, glycerin, glycerol
globo *m*, *geom* sphere; globe, world; globe (*elec gas*); balloon. **g. aerostático,** air balloon. **g. terrestre,** world; geographical globe
globular *a* globular
glóbulo *m*, globule.
globuloso *a* globulous
gloria *f*, heavenly bliss; fame, glory; delight, pleasure; magnificence, splendor; *art* apotheosis, glory. *m*, *ecc* doxology
gloriar *vt* to praise; *vr* (*with de or en*) boast about; be proud of, rejoice in
glorieta *f*, bower, arbor; open space in a garden; street square
glorificación *f*, glorification
glorificador *a* glorifying
glorificar *vt* to exalt, raise up; glorify, extol; *vr* (*with de or en*) be proud of; glory in; boast of
glorioso *a* glorious; *ecc* blessed; boastful, bragging
glosa *f*, gloss; explanation, note
glosador (-ra) *n* glossator; commentator. *a* explanatory
glosar *vt lit* to gloss
glosario *m*, glossary
glosopeda *f*, foot-and-mouth disease
glotón (-ona) *a* greedy, gluttonous. *n* glutton
glotonería *f*, gluttony, greed
glucosa *f*, glucose
glúteo *a* gluteal
glutinoso *a* glutinous
gn- For words so beginning, see spellings without **g.**
gobernación *f*, government; governor's office or building; ministry of the interior, home office (abb. for **ministerio de G.)**
gobernador (-ra) *a* governing, *n* governor
gobernalle *m*, helm
gobernante *a* governing. *m*, *inf* self-appointed director or manager
gobernar *vt irr* to govern, rule; lead, conduct; manage; steer; control; *vi* govern; *naut* obey the tiller. See **recomendar**
gobierno *m*, government (all meanings); *naut* helm; control (of machines, business, etc.)
goce *m*, enjoyment; possession
godo (da) *a* Gothic; aristocratic, noble. *n* Goth; aristocrat
gol *m*, *sport* goal
gola *f*, throat; gullet; gorget; tucker, bib
goleta *f*, schooner
golf *m*, golf. **palo de g.,** golf club
golfear *vi* to loaf
golfería *f*, loafing; vagabondage; loafers
golfo (-fa) *m*, *geog* gulf; sea, ocean. *n* ragamuffin, urchin. *m*, *inf* loafer; lounge lizard, wastrel
golilla *f*, ruff; *Lat. Am.* scarf; *inf* magistrate
gollería *f*, dainty, tidbit; *inf* affectation, persnicketiness
gollete *m*, gullet; neck (of a bottle, etc.); *mech* nozzle
golondrina *f*, *orn* swallow; *Chile* moving van. **g. de mar,** tern
golosina *f*, tidbit, delicacy; desire, caprice; pleasant useless thing
goloso *a* fond of sweet things; greedy, desirous; appetizing
golpe *m*, blow, knock; pull (at the oars); ring (of a bell); *mech* stroke; crowd; fall (of rain, etc.); mass, torrent; misfortune; shock, collision; spring lock; beating (of the heart); flap (of a pocket); *sew* passementerie; surprise; point, wit; bet. **g. de estado,** coup d'état. **g. de fortuna,** stroke of fortune. **g. de mano,** rising, insurrection. **g. en vago,** blow in the air; disappointment. **g. franco,** *sport* free kick. **de g.,** suddenly; quickly
golpeadura *f*. **golpeo** *m*, knocking, striking; beating, throbbing
golpear *vt* and *vi* to knock, strike; beat, throb
goma *f*, gum, rubber; India rubber; rubber band

gomería *f*, tire store

gomero *a* gum; rubber. *m*, *WH* rubber planter

gomoso *a* gummy; gum

gónada *f*, gonad

góndola *f*, gondola

gondolero *m*, gondolier

gongorino *a* gongoristic, euphuistic

gonorrea *f*, gonorrhea

gordo *a* fat, stout; greasy, oily; thick (thread, etc.). *m*, animal fat, suet. *inf* **ganar el g.,** to win first prize (in a lottery, etc.)

gordura *f*, grease, fat; stoutness, corpulence

gorgojo *m*, weevil; *fig* dwarf

gorgoritear *vi inf* to trill, quaver

gorgorito *m*, *inf* quaver, tremolo, trill (gen. *pl*)

gorgoteo *m*, gurgle

gorjear *vi* to trill, warble; twitter; *vr* crow (of a baby)

gorjeo *m*, trill, shake; warbling, twitter; crowing, lisping (of a child)

gorra *f*, cap; bonnet; *mil* busby; hunting cap. **vivir de g.,** *inf* to sponge

gorrión *m*, sparrow

gorrista *mf inf* parasite; sponger

gorro *m*, cap; bonnet

gorrón *m*, smooth, round pebble; *mech* pivot, gudgeon; sponger, waster. *a* parasitical

gota *f*, drop (of liquid); gout

gotear *vi* to drop, trickle, drip; leak; drizzle; give or receive in driblets

goteo *m*, trickling, dripping

gotera *f*, dripping; trickle; leak; leakage; valance

gotero *m Lat. Am.* (medicine) dropper

gótico *a* Gothic; noble, illustrious

gotoso (-sa) *a* gouty. *n* sufferer from gout

gozar *vt* to enjoy, have; take pleasure (in), delight (in); know carnally; *vi* (*with de*) enjoy; have, possess

gozne *m*, hinge

gozo *m*, enjoyment, possession; gladness, joy; *pl* couplets in honor of the Virgin Mary or a saint. *inf* **¡Mi g. en el pozo!** I'm sunk! All is lost!

gozoso *a* glad, happy. *adv* gladly; with pleasure

grabado *m*, engraver's art; engraving; illustration, picture. **g. al agua fuerte,** etching. **g. al agua tinta,** aquatint

grabador (-ra) *n* engraver

grabadura *f*, act of engraving

grabar *vt* to engrave; *fig* leave a deep impression

gracejo *m*, humor, wit; cheerfulness

gracia *f*, grace; attraction, grace; favor; kindness, jest, witticism; pardon, mercy; pleasant manner; obligingness, willingness; *pl* thanks, thank you. **gracias a,** thanks to. **¡Gracias a Dios!** Thank God! Thank goodness! **las Gracias,** the Three Graces

grácil *a* slender; small

graciosidad *f*, beauty, perfection, grace

gracioso (-sa) *a* attractive, graceful, elegant; witty, humorous; free, gratis. *n theat* comic role; *m*, *theat* fool

grada *f*, step, stair; gradin, seat; stand, gallery; *agr* harrow; *naut* runway; *pl* perron, flight of stairs

gradación *f*, gradation; climax

gradería *f*, flight of steps

grado *m*, step, stair; degree (of relationship); university degree; grade, class (in schools); (*fig geom phys*) degree; will, desire. **de buen g.,** willingly. **en sumo g.,** in the highest degree

graduación *f*, graduation; *mil* rank; rating (of a ship's company). **g. de oficial,** *mil* commission

graduado *a* graded; *mil* brevet. *m*, graduate

gradual *a* gradual

graduar *vt* to classify; *mil* grade; confer a degree on; measure; test; *com* standardize; *mech* calibrate; *vr* graduate, receive a degree. **g. la vista,** to test the eyes. **graduarse de oficial,** *mil* to get one's commission

gráfica *f*, graph

gráfico *a* graphic; vivid

grafito *m*, graphite

grafología *f*, graphology

grajear *vi* to caw; gurgle, burble (of infants)

grajo *m*, *orn* rook

grama *f Dominican Republic, Venezuela* grass, lawn

gramática *f*, grammar. *inf* **g. parda,** horse sense

gramático *a* grammatical. *m*, grammarian

gramo *m*, gram

gran *a abb* See **grande.** Used before a singular noun. big; great; grand

grana *f*, grain, seed; seed time; cochineal; kermes; red

granada *f*, *mil* grenade, shell; pomegranate

granadero *m*, grenadier; *inf* very tall person; *Lat. Am.* riot policeman

granadilla *f*, passionflower

granadina *f*, grenadine

granar *vi agr* to seed; run to seed

granate *m*, garnet; dark red

Gran Bretaña Great Britain

grande *a* big, large; great, illustrious; grand. *m*, great man; grandee. **en g.,** in a large size; as a whole; in style, lavishly

grandeza *f*, largeness; greatness, magnificence; grandeeship; vastness, magnitude

grandilocuencia *f*, grandiloquence

grandílocuo *a* grandiloquent

grandiosidad *f*, grandeur, greatness

grandioso *a* grandiose, magnificent

grandor *m*, size

granear *vt agr* to sow; grain (of leather)

granero *m*, granary; grain-producing country

granito *m*, *dim* small grain; granite; small pimple

granizar *vi* to hail, sleet; *vi* and *vt fig* shower down, deluge

granizo *m*, hail, sleet; hailstorm; *fig* shower, deluge

granja *f*, grain; farmhouse; dairy farm, dairy

granjear *vt* to trade, profit, earn; obtain, acquire; *vr* gain, win

granjería *f*, farming; agricultural profits; earnings, profits

granjero (-ra) *n* farmer

Gran Lago Salado, el the Great Salt Lake

grano *m*, *agr* grain; (seed; bean (coffee, etc.); particle; markings, grain (of wood, etc.); pimple; grain (measure). *fig inf* **ir al g.,** to go to the root of the matter; come to the point

granuja *f*, grape pit. *m*, *inf* urchin, scamp; knave, rogue

granujiento *a* pimply

gránulo *m*, granule

granuloso *a* granulous

grapa *f*, cramp, dowel, clamp; block hook; *elec* cleat; staple

grasa *f*, fat; grease; oil; dripping, suet

grasiento *a* greasy; grubby, dirty

gratificación *f*, monetary reward; fee, remuneration; gratuity

gratificar *vt* to recompense; please, gratify

gratis *a* and *adv* gratis

gratitud *f*, gratitude

grato *a* pleasing, agreeable; free, gratuitous; *Lat. Am.* appreciative, grateful

gratuito *a* gratuitous, free; baseless, unfounded

grava *f*, gravel; stone chip, pebble; metal (of a road)

gravamen *m*, obligation; burden; tax

gravar *vt* to burden, weigh upon; tax

grave *a* heavy; important, momentous; grave; dignified, serious; sedate; tiresome; low-pitched, low; *gram* grave accent

gravedad *f*, *phys* gravity

gravitación *f*, *phys* gravitation; seriousness; sedateness; importance; enormity, gravity

gravitar *vi* to gravitate; lean or rest (upon)

gravoso *a* grievous, oppressive; onerous; costly

graznar *vi* to caw; cackle; quack; croak; sing stridently, screech

graznido *m*, caw; cackle; croaking; quack; screech

Grecia Greece

greco (-ca) *a* and *n* Greek

gregario *a* gregarious

gregoriano *a* Gregorian

gregüescos *m pl*, wide breeches (sixteenth and seventeenth centuries)

gremial *a* pertaining to a guild, union, or association. *m*, member of a guild, union, or association

gremio *m*, guild, corporation, union; society, association; (univ.) general council

greña *f*, tangled lock (of hair) (gen. *pl*); tangle, confused mass

gresca *f*, uproar, tumult; fight, row

grey *f*, flock, drove, herd; *ecc* flock, company; people, nation

griego (-ga) *a* and *n* Greek. *m*, Greek (language); *inf* gibberish

grieta *f*, fissure; crevice; chink; split; flaw; vein (in stone, etc.); *mech* leak

grietado *a* fissured; cracked

grifo *m*, griffin; tap; cock

grillo *m*, cricket; *bot* shoot; *pl* fetters, irons, chains; *fig* shackles

grima *f*, revulsion, horror

gringo (-ga) *n inf* foreigner (scornful)

gripe *f*, influenza; grippe

gris *a* and *m*, gray

grisú *m*, firedamp

gritador (-ra) *a* shouting. *n* shouter

gritar *vi* to shout, yell, scream; howl down; hoot

gritería *f*, shouting, yelling, clamor

grito *m*, shout, yell, shriek, scream. *inf* **poner el g. en el cielo,** to cry to high heaven, complain. **el Grito de Dolores** the Proclamation of Mexican Independence (1810)

groenlandés (-esa) *a* Greenland. *n* Greenlander

Groenlandia Greenland

grosella *f*, currant. **g. blanca,** gooseberry

grosería *f*, rudeness; roughness (of workmanship); ignorance; rusticity

grosero *a* coarse; rough; thick; unpolished, rude

grotesco *a* grotesque, absurd

grúa *f*, *mech* crane, hoist, derrick. **g. de pescante,** jib crane. **g. móvil,** traveling crane

gruesa *f*, twelve dozen, gross

grueso *a* stout, corpulent; large. *m*, bulk, body; major portion, majority; thick stroke (of a letter); thickness, density. **en g.,** in bulk

grulla *f*, *orn* crane

grumete *m*, ship's boy, cabin boy

grumo *m*, clot; heart (of vegetables); bunch, cluster; bud

gruñido *m*, grunt; growl

gruñidor *a* grunting; growling

gruñir *vi* to grunt; growl; grumble; squeak, creak (doors, etc.). *Pres. Part.* **gruñendo.** *Pres. Ind.* **gruño, gruñes,** etc.

grupa *f*, croup (of a horse); pillion (of a motorcycle)

grupera *f*, pillion (of a horse, etc.)

grupo *m*, knot, cluster; band, group; *art* group; *mech* set

gruta *f*, cavern, grotto

guacamayo *m*, macaw

guadamecí *m*, embossed decorated leather

guadaña *f*, scythe

guagua, *f Caribbean* bus

gualdo *a* yellow, golden

gualdrapa *f*, saddlecloth, trappings; *inf* tatter, rag

guante *m*, glove. **g. con puño,** gauntlet glove. **g. de boxeo,** boxing glove. **g. de cabritilla,** kid glove. **arrojar el g.,** to throw down the gauntlet; challenge, defy

guantelete *m*, gauntlet

guantería *f*, glove trade, shop, or factory

guantero (-ra) *n* glove maker or seller, glover

guapear *vi inf* to make the best of a bad job; *inf* pride oneself on being well dressed

guapeza *f*, prettiness; *inf* resolution, courage; *inf* smartness or showiness of dress; boastful act or behavior

guapo *a* pretty; handsome; *inf* daring, enterprising; *inf* smart, well-dressed, foppish; *inf* handsome. *m*, braggart, brawler; beau, lover; *inf* fine fellow, son of a gun

guaracha *f*, *Cuba, Puerto Rico* guaracha (vigorous dance in triple meter; music for this dance)

guarda *mf* keeper, guard. *f*, guarding, keeping, custodianship, preservation; guardianship; observance, fulfilment; flyleaf, end page (books); warder (of locks or keys); *mech* guard; guard (of a fan)

guardabarrera *mf* gatekeeper at a level crossing (railroad)

guardabarro *m*, mudguard

guardabosque *mf* gamekeeper

guardabrisa *m*, *aut* windshield; glass candle shield

guardacostas *m*, coast guard; *naut* revenue cutter

guardafrenos *m*, brakeman (railroad)

guardalmacén *mf* storekeeper

guardameta *mf* goalkeeper

guardamuebles *m*, furniture warehouse

guardapelo *m*, locket

guardapolvo *m*, dustcover; light overcoat; inner case of a pocket watch

guardar *vt* to keep; preserve, retain; maintain, observe; save, put aside, lay away; defend, protect; guard; *vr* (*with de*) avoid, guard against. **g. compás con,** to be in tune with. **guardarse mucho,** to think twice before. **g. silencio,** to keep silent. **¡Guarda!** Take care! **¡Guárdate del agua mansa!** Still waters run deep!

guardarropa *m*, cloakroom. *mf* cloakroom attendant; keeper of the wardrobe. *m*, wardrobe, clothes closet

guardarropía *f*, theatrical wardrobe

guardavía *m*, signalman (railroad)

guardería *f*, day nursery, day-care center

guardia *f*, guard, escort; protection; (*mil naut*) watch; regiment, body (of troops); guard (fencing). *m*, guardsman; policeman. **g. de asalto,** armed police. **g. de corps,** royal bodyguard. **g. civil,** civil guard. **g. marina,** midshipman. **g. municipal,** city police. *mil* **montar la g.,** to mount guard

guardián (-ana) *n* keeper; custodian; warden. *m*, watchman; jailer

guardilla *f*, attic, garret

guarecer *vt irr* to shelter, protect, aid; preserve, keep; cure; *vr* take shelter. See **conocer**

guarida *f*, lair, den; refuge, shelter; haunt, resort

guarismo *m*, *math* figure; number, numeral

guarnecer *vt irr* to decorate, adorn; *sew* trim, face, border; *mil* garrison; mas plaster. See **conocer**

guarnecido *m*, mas plastering

guarnición *f*, *sew* trimming, ornament, border, fringe; *mech* packing; *mil* garrison; setting (of jewels); guard (of a sword, etc.); *pl* harness; fittings

guarnir *vt naut* to reeve

guasa *f*, *inf* dullness, boringness; joke. **de g.,** jokingly

guasón *a inf* dull, tedious; humorous, jocose

guatemalteco (-ca) *a* and *n* Guatemalan

guau *m*, bowwow, bark of a dog

guayaba *f*, guava; guava jelly; *Lat. Am. also* hoax

Guayana Guiana

gubernamental *a* governmental

gubernativo *a* governmental; administrative

gubia *f*, *carp* chisel; gouge

guedeja *f*, long tress or lock of hair; forelock; lion's mane

Guernesey Guernsey

guerra *f*, war; struggle, fight; *fig* hostility. *inf* **dar g.,** to give trouble, annoy. **en g. con,** at war with. **la g. de Cuba,** the Spanish-American War

guerrear *vi* to make war, fight; oppose

guerrero (-ra) *a* war, martial; warrior; *inf* troublesome, annoying. *n* fighter. *m*, warrior, soldier

guerrillear *vi* to wage guerrilla warfare; fight as a guerrilla

guerrillero *m*, guerrilla fighter

guía *mf* guide, conductor; adviser, director. *f*, guide, aid;

guidebook; *mech* guide, slide; directory; signpost. **g. de ferrocarriles,** train schedule, railroad timetable. **g. de teléfonos,** telephone directory

guiar *vt* to guide; lead, conduct; *mech* work, control; *aut* drive; pilot; teach, direct, govern

guija *f,* pebble

guijarro *m,* smooth, round pebble; boulder; cobblestone

guijarroso *a* pebbly, cobbled

guijo *m,* gravel; granite chips; pebble

guillotina *f,* guillotine; paper-cutting machine

guillotinar *vt* to guillotine, decapitate

guinda *f,* mazard cherry; *naut* height of masts

guinea *f,* guinea

guinga *f,* gingham

guiñada *f,* wink; blink; *naut* yaw

guiñapo *m,* rag, tatter; sloven, ragamuffin

guiñar *vt* to wink; blink; *naut* yaw; *vr* wink at each other

guiño *m,* wink

guión *m,* royal standard; banner; summary; leader of a dance; *gram* hyphen; subtitle (in films). **g. mayor,** *gram* dash

guipuzcoano (-na) *a* and *n* Guipuzcoan

guirigay *m, inf* gibberish; uproar, babble

guirnalda *f,* garland, wreath

guisa *f,* way, manner; will, desire. **a g. de,** in the manner or fashion of

guisado *m, cul* stew; cooked dish

guisante *m, agr* pea; pea plant. **g. de olor,** sweetpea

guisar *vt* to cook; stew; *cul* prepare, dress; adjust, arrange

guiso *m,* cooked dish

güisquisoda *f Spain* highball

guitarra *f,* guitar

guitarrista *mf* guitar player

guito *a* vicious (horses, mules)

gula *f,* greed, gluttony

gusaniento *a* worm-eaten; maggoty

gusano *m,* worm; caterpillar; maggot; meek, downtrodden person. **g. de seda,** silkworm

gusanoso *a* wormy

gustar *vt* to taste, savor; try; *vi* be pleasing, give pleasure; like. **Me gusta el libro,** I like the book. **La película no me gustó,** I didn't like the film. **g. de,** to like, is used only when a person is the subject

gusto *m,* taste; flavor, savor; pleasure, delight; will, desire; discrimination, taste, style, fashion, manner; whim, caprice. **a g.,** to taste; according to taste. **con mucho g.,** with great pleasure. **dar g.,** to please. **de buen g.,** in good taste

gustoso *a* savory, palatable; willingly, with pleasure; pleasant, agreeable

gutapercha *f,* guttapercha

gutural *a* guttural

H

haba *f,* broad bean; bean (coffee, cocoa, etc.). **h. de las Indias,** sweetpea. **Esas son habas contadas,** That's a certainty

Habana, la Havana

habanero (-ra), habano (-na) *a* and *n* Havanese, from Havana. *m.* **habano,** Havana cigar

haber *m,* estate, property (gen. *pl*); income; *com* credit balance. **h. monedado,** specie

haber *vt irr* to have; catch, lay hands on (e.g. **El reo fue habido,** The criminal was caught). *v aux* (e.g. **Hemos escrito la carta,** We have written the letter). *v impers* to happen, take place; be. *3rd pers. sing Pres. Ind.* **ha** is replaced by **hay,** meaning there is or there are (e.g. **No hay naranjas en las tiendas,** There are no oranges in the shops). In certain weather expressions, **hay** means it is (e.g. **Hay luna,** It is moonlight). Used of expressions of time, **haber** means to elapse and **ha** (*3rd pers. sing Pres. Ind.*) has adverbial force of 'ago' (e.g. **muchos días ha,** many days ago). **h. de,** to be necessary (less strong than **h. que**) (e.g. **Hemos de verle mañana,** We must see him tomorrow. **He de hacer el papel de Manolo,** I am to play the part of Manolo). **h. que,** to be unavoidable, be essential. With this construction the form **hay** is used (e.g. **Hay que darse prisa,** We (or one) must hurry. **No hay que enojarse,** There's no need to get annoyed). **no h., más que pedir,** to leave nothing to be desired. **no h. tal,** to be no such thing. *inf* **habérselas con,** to quarrel or fall out with. **Hubo una vez . . . ,** Once upon a time . . . **¡No hay de qué!,** Don't mention it!; Not at all!; You're welcome! **No hay para que . . . ,** There's no point in. . . . **poco tiempo ha,** a little while ago. **¿Qué hay?** What's the matter?; What's new? **¿Qué hay de nuevo?** What's new? *Pres. Ind.* **he, has, ha, hemos, habéis, han.** *Fut.* **habré,** etc. *Condit.* **habría,** etc. *Preterite* **hube, hubiste, hubo, hubimos, hubisteis, hubieron.** *Pres. Subjunc.* **haya,** etc. *Imperf. Subjunc.* **hubiese,** etc.

habichuela *f,* kidney bean

hábil *a* clever; skillful; able; lawful

habilidad *f,* ability; skill; accomplishment; craftsmanship, workmanship

habilidoso *a* accomplished; able; skillful

habilitación *f,* habilitation; paymastership; equipment; furnishing

habilitado *m,* paymaster

habilitar *vt* to qualify; equip; furnish; habilitate; enable; *com* capitalize

habilitidad *f,* habitability

habitable *a* habitable

habitación *f,* habitation, dwelling; room in a house; residence; (*bot zool*) habitat; caretaking

habitante *m,* inhabitant

habitar *vt* to inhabit, reside in

hábito *m,* attire; *ecc* habit; use, custom; skill, facility; *pl* vestments; gown, robe. **tomar el h.,** to become a monk or nun

habitual *a* habitual, usual

habituar *vt* to accustom; *vr* accustom oneself; grow used (to)

habitud *f,* habit, custom; connection, relationship

habla *f,* speech; language; dialect; discourse. **al h.,** within speaking distance

hablado *a* spoken. **bien h.,** well-spoken; courteous. **mal h.,** ill-spoken; rude

hablador (-ra) *a* talkative; gossipy; *Mexico also* boastful. *n* chatterbox; gossip

habladuría *f,* gossip; impertinent chatter

hablanchín *a inf* chattering, gossiping

hablar *vi* to speak; converse; express oneself; arrange; (*with de*) speak about, discuss; gossip about, criticize; (*with por*) intercede on behalf of; *vt* speak (a language); say, speak; *vr* speak to one another. **no hablarse,** to not be on speaking terms. **h. a gritos,** to shout. **h. alto,** to speak loudly or in strong terms. **h. bien** (*or* **mal**), to be well- (or ill-) spoken; be polite (or rude). **h. claro,** to speak frankly. **h. consigo** *or* **h. entre sí,** to talk to oneself. *inf* **h. cristiano, h. en cristiano,** to speak clearly or intelligibly; speak frankly. **hablarlo todo,** to talk too much. **h. por h.,** to talk for talking's sake. *inf* **h. por los codos,** to chatter. **h. sin ton ni son,** to speak foolishly

hablilla *f,* rumor, tittletattle, gossip

hacecillo *m,* small sheaf; small bundle; *bot* fascicle; beam (of light)

hacedero *a* feasible, practicable

hacedor *m,* maker; steward, manager; Creator

hacendado (-da) *a* landed. *n* landowner; *WH* cattle rancher

hacendista *mf* political economist

hacendoso *a* diligent, hard-working

hacer *vt* to make; fashion, form, construct; do, perform; cause, effect; arrange, put right; contain; accustom, harden; pack (luggage); imagine, invent, create; improve, perfect; compel, oblige; deliver (speeches); compose; earn; *math* add up to; suppose, imagine (e.g. **Sus padres hacían a María en casa,** Her parents imagined that Mary was at home); put into practice, execute; play the part of or act like (e.g. **h. el gracioso,** to play the buffoon); shed, cast (e.g. **El roble hace sombra,** The oak casts a shadow); assemble, convoke (meetings, gatherings); give off, produce (e.g. **La chimenea hace humo,** The chimney is smoking); perform (plays); (*with el, la, lo, and some nouns*) pretend to be (e.g. **Se hizo el desconocido,** He pretended to be ignorant). (**h.** followed by infin. is sometimes translated by a past participle in English (e.g. **Lo hice h.,** I had it done).) *vi* to matter, be important, signify (e.g. **Su llegada no hace nada al caso,** His arrival makes no difference to the case. **Se me hace muy poco ...,** It matters to me very little . . .); be fitting or suitable; concern, be pertinent; match, go with; agree, be in harmony; (*with de*) act as, discharge duties of temporarily (e.g. **h. de camarero,** to be a temporary waiter); (*with por*) try to, attempt to (e.g. **Haremos por decírselo,** We shall try to tell him). *vi impers* Used in expressions concerning: 1. the weather. 2. lapse of time. English uses the verb 'to be' in both cases, e.g.:

1. **hace buen** (*or* **mal**) **tiempo,** it is fine (or bad) weather. **hace mucho frío,** it is very cold. **hace sol,** it is sunny. **hace viento,** it is windy. **¿Qué tiempo hace?** What is the weather like?

2. **hace** + an expression of time is followed by **que** introducing a clause (e.g. **Hace dos horas que llegamos,** It is two hours since we arrived) or **hace** + an expression of time may be followed by **desde** + a noun (e.g. **Hace dos años desde aquel día,** It is two years since that day)

When an action or state that has begun in the past is still continuing in the present, the Spanish verb is in the Pres. Ind., whereas the English verb is in the Perfect (e.g. **Hace un mes que la veo todos los días,** I have been seeing her every day for a month). This rule holds good with other tenses. English Pluperfect, Future Perfect, Conditional Perfect become in Spanish Imperfect, Future, Conditional, respectively. *naut* **h. agua,** to leak. **h. aguas,** to pass water, urinate. **h. alarde de,** to boast of. **h. América,** to strike it rich. **h. el amor a,** to make love to, court, woo. **h. autoridad,** to be authoritative. **h. a todo,** to have many uses; be adaptable. **h. bancarrota,** to go bankrupt. **h. un berrinche, hacerse un berrinche,** to have a fit, have a tantrum. *fig inf* **h. buena,** to justify. **h. calceta,** to knit. **h. cara** or **frente a,** to face; resist. **h. caso,** to take notice, mind (e.g. **¡No hagas caso!** Never mind!). **h. causas,** to bring charges, institute proceedings. **h. cuentas,** to reckon up. **h. daño,** to harm. *inf* **h. de las suyas,** to behave in his usual manner or play one of his usual tricks. **h. diligencias por,** to endeavor to. **h. fiesta,** to take a holiday. **h. fuerza,** to struggle. **h. fuerza a,** *fig* to do violence to (e.g. **Hizo fuerza a sus creencias,** He did violence to his beliefs). **h. h.,** to cause to be made (e.g. **He hecho hacer un vestido,** I have had a dress made). **h. juego,** to make a set, match (e.g. **El sombrero hace juego con el traje,** The hat goes with the dress). **h. la corte (a),** to court, woo. *fig inf* **h. la vista gorda,** to turn a blind eye. **h. la vida del claustro,** to lead a cloistered existence. **h. mal,** to do wrong; be harmful (food, etc.). **h. pedazos,** to break. **h. pinos** (or **pinitos**) to totter; toddle; stagger. *aer* **h. rizos,** to loop the loop. **h. saber,** to make known; notify. **h. seguir,** to forward (letters). **h. señas,** to make signs

(wave, beckon, etc.). *inf* **h. una que sea sonada,** to cause a big scandal. **¡Hágame el favor!** Please! *Pres. Ind.* **hago, haces,** etc. *Fut.* **haré,** etc. *Condit.* **haría,** etc. *Imperat.* **haz, haga, hagamos, haced, hagan.** *Preterite* **hice, hiciste, hizo, hicimos, hicisteis, hicieron.** *Pres. Subjunc.* **haga,** etc. *Imperf. Subjunc.* **hiciese,** etc.

hacerse *vr irr* to become (e.g. **Se ha hecho muy importante,** It (or he) has become very important); grow up (e.g. **Miguel se ha hecho hombre,** Michael has grown up (become a man)); develop, mature; pass oneself off as, pretend to be; (*with prep a*) become accustomed to or used to (e.g. **Me haré a este clima,** I shall grow used to this climate); withdraw or retire to (of places); (*with de or con*) provide oneself with. **h. a la vela,** to set sail. **h. a (uno),** to seem (e.g. **Eso que me cuentas se me hace increíble,** What you tell me seems incredible). *inf* **h. chiquito,** to be modest. **h. tarde,** to grow late; *fig* be too late. *See* **hacer**

hacia *prep* toward, near, about. **h. adelante,** forward, onward

hacienda *f,* country estate, land; property; *pl* domestic tasks; cattle. **h. pública,** public funds. **ministerio de h.,** national treasury, exchequer

hacina *f, agr* stack; heap, pile

hacinamiento *m,* stacking, piling; accumulation

hacinar *vt agr* to stack sheaves; accumulate, amass; pile up, heap

hacha *f,* large candle; torch; ax. **h. pequeña,** hatchet

hachazo *m,* stroke of an ax

hache *f,* name of the letter H

hachero *m,* candlestick; woodcutter, axman

hacho *m,* torch; beacon

hada *f,* fairy

hado *m,* fate; destiny

hagiografía *f,* hagiography

hagiógrafo *m,* hagiographer

Haití Haiti

haitiano (-na) *a* and *n* Haitian

halagar *vt* to caress; flatter; coax; please, delight

halago *m,* flattery; coaxing; caress; source of pleasure, delight

halagüeño *a* flattering; pleasing; caressing; hopeful, promising

halar *vt naut* to haul, tow

halcón *m,* falcon

halconero *m,* hawker, hunter

hálito *m,* breath; vapor; *poet* breeze

hallado *a* and *Past Part.* found, met. **bien h.,** welcome; happy, contented. **mal h.,** unwelcome; uneasy, discontented

hallador (-ra) *n* finder

hallar *vt* to find; meet; observe; discover; find out; *vr* be present; be, find oneself

hallazgo *m,* finding; thing found; finder's reward

halo *m,* halo

halterofilia *f,* weightlifting

hamaca *f,* hammock

hambre *f,* hunger; famine; desire, yearning. **tener h.,** to be hungry

hambriento *a* hungry; famished; *fig* starved (of affection, etc.)

Hamburgo Hamburg

hamo *m,* fishhook

hampa *f,* rogue's life; gang of rogues; underworld; slum

hangar *m,* hangar

haragán (-ana) *a* lazy, idle. *n* idler, lazybones

harapiento *a* ragged

harapo *m,* tatter, rag

haraposo *a* ragged

harén *m,* harem

harina *f,* flour; powder; farina. *inf* **ser h. de otro costal,** to be a horse of another color

harinero *a* relating to flour. *m,* flour merchant; flour bin

harinoso *a* floury, mealy; farinaceous

harmónica *f,* (*phys math*) harmonic

harmonizar vt to arrange (music)

harnear vt Lat. Am. to sieve, sift

harnero m, sieve

harón a slothful, slow; lazy, idle

harpillera f, sackcloth, sacking

hartar vt to satiate; tire, annoy; satisfy the appetite; shower (with blows, etc.)

hartazgo m, satiety

harto a satiated; tired (of), adv enough

hartón a Central America, Mexico gluttonous

hartura f, satiety; abundance

hasta prep until; as far as; down or up to. conjunc also, even. **h. la vista,** See you! Ciao! Au revoir! **h. mañana,** until tomorrow

hastial m, gable, end wall; boor, lout

hastío m, loathing; distaste; nausea

hato m, personal clothing; herd of cattle; gang (of suspicious characters); crowd, mob; inf group, party. inf **liar el h.,** to pack up

Hawai Hawaii

hay there is; there are. See **haber**

haya f, beech tree; beechwood

hayal m, wood of beech trees, beech plantation

hayuco m, beech mast

haz m, bundle, sheaf; mil file; pl fasces. f, visage; surface, face. **h. de la tierra,** face of the earth. **h. de luz,** beam of light. fig **ser de dos haces,** to be two-faced

haz 2nd pers Imperat **hacer**

hazaña f, exploit, prowess

hazañoso a heroic, dauntless, courageous

hazmerreír m, inf laughingstock

he interj and adv Hallo! Hist!; Behold! **¡Heme aquí!** Here I am. **he aquí,** here is . . .

hebilla f, buckle

hebra f, thread; fiber; flesh; min vein, streak; filament (textiles); grain (of wood); pl poet hair. inf **pegar la h.,** to start a conversation

hebraísmo m, Hebraism

hebraísta m, Hebraist

hebreo (-ea) a Hebraic, Jewish. n Jew. m, Hebrew (language)

hecatombe f, hecatomb; slaughter, massacre

hechicería f, sorcery; spell, enchantment

hechicero a bewitching, magic; charming, attractive

hechizar vt to bewitch; charm, attract, delight

hechizo m, magic spell; fascination, charm; delight, pleasure; a Lat. Am. homemade, produced locally, locally produced

hecho a developed, mature; accustomed, used; perfected, finished; ready-made. **h. una furia,** like a fury, very angry. **bien h.,** well-made, well-proportioned; well or rightly done

hecho m, deed, action; fact; happening; event. **los Hechos de los Apóstoles,** the Acts of the Apostles

hechura f, making, make; creation; form; figure, statue; lit composition; build (of body); fig puppet, creature; pl price paid for work done. **de h. sastre,** a tailor-made

hectárea f, hectare

hectógrafo m, hectograph

hectogramo m, hectogram

hectolitro m, hectoliter

hectovatio m, hectowatt

heder vi irr to stink; be intolerable. See **entender**

hediondez f, stink, stench

hediondo a stinking; intolerable, pestilential; obscene

hedonismo m, hedonism

hedonista mf hedonist

hegeliano a Hegelian

hegemonía f, hegemony

helada f, frost. **h. blanca,** hoarfrost

heladera f, refrigerator

helado a frozen; ice-cold; astounded, disdainful. m, iced drink; sherbet, ice cream

helamiento m, icing; freezing

helar vt irr to freeze; ice, chill; astound; discourage; vr

become iced; freeze; become ice-cold. v impers to freeze. See **acertar**

helecho m, fern

helénico a Hellenic

helenismo m, Hellenism

helenista mf Hellenist

helenizar vt to Hellenize

hélice f, spiral, helical line; screw, propeller; geom helix; ast Ursa Major

helicóptero m, aer helicopter

helio m, helium

heliógrafo m, heliograph

helioscopio m, helioscope

helióstato m, heliostat

helioterapia f, heliotherapy

heliotropismo m, heliotropism

heliotropo m, heliotrope; agate

helvecio (-ia) a and n Helvetian

hembra f, female; inf woman; nut of a screw; eye of a hook. inf **una real h.,** a fine figure of a woman

hemiciclo m, hemicycle; floor (of a legislative building)

hemisférico a hemispherical

hemisferio m, hemisphere

hemofilia f, hemophilia.

hemoglobina f, hemoglobin

hemorragia f, hemorrhage

hemorroides f, hemorrhoids

henchido a swollen

henchimiento m, swelling; inflation; filling

henchir vt irr to fill; stuff; swell. Pres. Ind. **hincho, hinches, hinche, henchid.** Pres. Part. **hinchiendo.** Pres. Subjunc. **hincha,** etc. Imperf. Subjunc. **hinchiese,** etc. Imperat. **hinche, hincha, hinchamos, henchid, hinchan**

hendedura f, fissure; rift

hender vt irr to split, crack; fig cleave (air, water, etc.); make one's way through. See **entender**

hendidura f, split, fissure, crack, chink

hendija f, Lat. Am. crack, crevice

henil m, hayloft

heno m, hay

hepático a hepatic

heráldica f, heraldry

heráldico a heraldic

heraldo m, herald; harbinger

herbaje m, herbage; pasture, grass; thick woolen cloth

herbario m, herbalist, botanist; herbarium. a herbal

herbívoro a herbivorous

herbolaria f, herbal

hercúleo a herculean

heredad f, landed property; country estate

heredar vt to inherit; make a deed of gift to; inherit characteristics, etc.; take as heir

heredera f, heiress

heredero m, heir; inheritor. **h. aparente,** heir apparent. **presunto h.,** heir presumptive

hereditario a hereditary

hereje mf heretic

herejía f, heresy

herencia f, inheritance; heredity; heritage

heresiarca mf heresiarch

herético a heretical

herida f, wound; insult; anguish. **h. contusa,** contusion. **h. penetrante,** deep wound

herir vt irr to wound; strike, harm; fig pierce (of sun's rays); fig pluck (strings of a musical instrument); impress (the senses); affect (the emotions); offend (gen. of words). Pres. Part. **hiriendo.** Pres. Ind. **hiero, hieres, hiere, hieren.** Preterite **hirió, hirieron.** Pres. Subjunc. **hiera, hieras, hiera, hiramos, hiráis, hieran.** Imperf. Subjunc. **hiriese,** etc.

hermafrodita a and mf hermaphrodite

hermafroditismo m, hermaphroditism

hermana f, sister; twin, pair (of things). **h. de leche,** foster sister. **h. política,** sister-in-law

hermanar vt to join; mate; harmonize; Chile to pair (like socks); *vt* and *vr* be the spiritual brother of, be compatible

hermanastra *f*, stepsister

hermanastro *m*, stepbrother

hermandad *f*, brotherhood; friendship, intimacy; relationship (of one thing to another); confraternity. **Santa H.,** Spanish rural police force instituted in the fifteenth century

hermano *m*, brother; pair, twin (of things); *ecc* brother. **h. de raza,** member of the same race. **h. político,** brother-in-law

hermético *a* hermetic

hermosear *vt* to embellish, beautify, adorn

hermoso *a* beautiful; shapely; handsome; fine, wonderful (weather, view, etc.)

hermosura *f*, beauty; pleasantness, attractiveness, perfection of form; belle

hernia *f*, hernia

héroe *m*, hero

heroicidad *f*, heroism

heroico *a* heroic

heroína *f*, heroine

heroismo *m*, heroism

herpes *m pl*, or *f pl*, herpes

herrada *f*, pail

herradero *m*, branding of livestock

herrador *m*, blacksmith

herradura *f*, horseshoe

herraje *m*, ironwork; *Lat. Am.* horseshoe

herramienta *f*, tool; set of tools

herrar *vt irr* to shoe horses; brand (cattle); decorate with iron. See **acertar**

herrería *f*, forge; ironworks; blacksmith's shop; clamor, tumult, confusion

herrero *m*, smith

herrete *m*, ferrule, tag

herrumbre *f*, rust; taste of iron

herrumbroso *a* rusty

hervidero *m*, boiling, bubbling; *fig* ebullition; swarm, crowd

hervir *vi irr* to boil; foam and froth (sea); seethe (emotions); surge (crowds); (*with en*) abound in, swarm with. See **sentir**

hervor *m*, boiling; ebullition, vigor, zest; seething, agitation

hesitación *f*, hesitation, doubt, uncertainty

hesitar *vi* to hesitate, vacillate

heterodina *a f*, *rad* heterodyne

heterodoxia *f*, heterodoxy

heterodoxo *a* heterodox

heterogeneidad *f*, heterogeneity

heterogéneo *a* heterogeneous

hético *a* hectic, consumptive

hexagonal *a* hexagonal

hexágono *m*, hexagon

hexámetro *m*, hexameter

hez *f*, (gen. *pl* **heces**) lees, dregs

hiato *m*, hiatus

hibernal *a* wintry

hibernés *a* Hibernian

hibisco *m*, hibiscus

hibridación *f*, hybridization

hibridismo *m*, hybridism

híbrido *a* and *m*, hybrid

hidalgo (-ga) *n* noble, aristocrat. *a* noble; illustrious; generous

hidalguía *f*, nobility; generosity, nobility of spirit

hidra *f*, *zool* hydra; poisonous snake; *ast* Hydra

hidratar *vt chem* to hydrate

hidrato *m*, hydrate. **h. de carbono,** carbohydrate

hidráulica *f*, hydraulics

hidráulico *a* hydraulic

hidroavión *m*, flying boat

hidrocarburo *m*, hydrocarbon

hidrocéfalo *a* hydrocephalic

hidrodinámica *f*, hydrodynamics

hidroeléctrico *a* hydroelectric

hidrofobia *f*, hydrophobia; rabies

hidrógeno *m*, hydrogen

hidrografía *f*, hydrography

hidrología *f*, hydrology

hidropesía *f*, dropsy

hidrópico *a* dropsical

hidroplano *m*, seaplane

hidroquinona *f*, hydroquinone

hidroscopio *m*, hydroscope

hidrostática *f*, hydrostatics

hidroterapia *f*, hydrotherapy

hiedra *f*, ivy

hiel *f*, gall, bile, bitterness, affliction; *pl* troubles

hielo *m*, ice, frost; freezing, icing; stupefaction; indifference, coldness. *inf* **estar hecho un h.,** to be as cold as ice

hiena *f*, hyena

hierático *a* hieratical

hierba *f*, grass; small plant; herb. **h. cana,** groundsel. **mala h.,** weed

hierbabuena *f*, *bot* mint

hierra *f*, branding time

hierro *m*, iron; brand with hot iron; iron or steel head of a lance, etc.; instrument or shape made of iron; weapon of war. **h. colado,** cast iron. **h. dulce,** wrought iron. **h. en planchas,** sheet iron. **h. viejo,** scrap iron

hígado *m*, liver; courage; *Central America, Mexico also* nuisance

higiene *f*, hygiene; cleanliness, neatness. **h. privada,** personal hygiene. **h. pública,** public health

higiénico *a* hygienic

higo *m*, fig. **h. chumbo,** prickly pear

higrómetro *m*, hygrometer

higuera *f*, fig tree

hija *f*, daughter; native of a place; offspring

hijastro (-ra) *n* stepchild

hijo *m*, son; child; native of a place; offspring; shoot, sprout; *pl* descendants. **h. de la cuna,** foundling. **h. de leche,** foster child. **h. natural,** natural child. **h. político,** son-in-law

hijuela *f*, little daughter; small mattress; small drain; side road; accessory, subordinate thing; piece of material for widening a garment; *law* part of an inheritance; *Lat. Am.* rural property

hila *f*, row, line; gut; *surg* lint (gen. *pl*)

hilacha *f*, thread raveled from cloth; fiber, filament. **h. de vidrio,** spun glass

hilado *m*, spinning; thread, yarn

hilandería *f*, spinning; spinning mill; mill. **h. de algodón,** cotton mill

hilandero (-ra) *n* spinner

hilar *vt* to spin; reason, infer, discourse

hilaridad *f*, hilarity; quiet happiness

hilaza *f*, yarn

hilera *f*, line, file, row; fine yarn; *mil* file, rank; *met* wire drawer; *mas* course (of bricks)

hilo *m*, thread; linen; wire; mesh (spiders, silkworm's web, etc.); edge (of a blade); thin stream (of liquid); thread (of discourse)

hilván *m*, *sew* basting; tack

hilvanar *vt sew* to baste

himen *m*, hymen

himeneo *m*, marriage, wedding

himnario *m*, hymnal

himno *m*, hymn

hin *m*, whinny, neigh

hincapié *m*, foothold. **hacer h.,** to insist, make a stand

hincar *vt* to thrust in; drive in, sink; *vr* kneel. **h. el diente,** to bite. **h. la uña,** to scratch. **hincarse de rodillas,** to kneel down

hinchado *a* puffed up, vain; pompous, high-flown, redundant (style)

hinchar *vt* to inflate; puff out (the chest); swell (of a river, etc.); exaggerate (events); *vr* swell; grow vain, be puffed up

hinchazón *f*, swelling; vanity, presumption; pomposity, euphuism (style)

hiniesta *f*, Spanish broom

hinojo *m*, *bot* fennel; knee. **de hinojos,** on bended knee

hipar *vi* to hiccup; pant (of dogs); be overanxious; be overtired; sob, cry

hipérbole *f*, hyperbole

hiperbólico *a* hyperbolical

hipercrítico *m*, hypercritic. *a* hypercritical

hipertrofiarse *vr* to hypertrophy

hípico *a* equine

hipnosis *f*, hypnosis

hipnótico *a* hypnotic. *m*, hypnotic drug

hipnotismo *m*, hypnotism

hipnotización *f*, hypnotization

hipnotizar *vt* to hypnotize

hipo *m*, hiccup; sob; longing, desire; dislike, disgust

hipocondría *f*, hypochondria

hipocondríaco (-ca) *a* hypochondriacal. *n* hypochondriac

hipocrático *a* Hippocratic

hipocresía *f*, hypocrisy

hipócrita *a* hypocritical. *mf* hypocrite

hipodérmico *a* hypodermic

hipódromo *m*, hippodrome, racetrack

hipopótamo *m*, hippopotamus

hipostático *a* hypostatic

hipoteca *f*, mortgage

hipotecable *a* mortgageable

hipotecar *vt* to mortgage

hipotecario *a* belonging to a mortgage

hipotenusa *f*, hypotenuse

hipótesis *f*, hypothesis

hipotético *a* hypothetical

hirsuto *a* hirsute, hairy

hirviente *a* boiling

hisca *f*, birdlime

hisopear *vt ecc* to sprinkle, asperse

hisopo *m*, *bot* hyssop; *ecc* hyssop, sprinkler; *Lat. Am.* also (paint)brush

hispánico *a* Spanish

hispanismo *m*, Hispanism

hispanista *mf* Hispanist

hispanoamericano (-na) *a* and *n* Spanish-American, Hispano-American

histeria *f*, hysteria

histérico *a* hysterical; hysteric

histerismo *m*, *med* hysteria

histología *f*, histology

histólogo *m*, histologist

historia *f*, history; narrative, story; tale; *inf* gossip (gen. *pl*); *art* historical piece. **h. natural,** natural history. **h. sagrada,** biblical history. *fig inf* **dejarse de historias,** to stop beating around the bush

historiador (-ra) *n* historian

historiar *vt* to narrate, relate; record, chronicle

histórico *a* historical; historic

historieta *f*, short story; anecdote

historiografía *f*, historiography

historiógrafo *m*, historiographer

histriónico *a* histrionic

hitlerismo *m*, Hitlerism

hito *m*, milestone; boundary mark; *fig* mark, target. **de h. en h.,** from head to foot

hocico *m*, snout; *inf* face, mug; *inf* angry gesture; *naut* prow. **meter el h.,** to stick one's nose into other people's business

hogaño *adv inf* during this year; at the present time

hogar *m*, hearth, fireplace; home, house; family life; firebox (of a locomotive)

hoguera *f*, bonfire

hoja *f*, *bot* leaf; petal; sheet (metal, paper, etc.); page (of book); blade (sharp instruments); leaf (door, window); sword. **h. de servicios,** service or professional record.

h. de tocino, side of bacon. **h. extraordinaria,** extra, special edition (of a newspaper). **h. volante,** handbill, supplement. **volver la h.,** to turn over (pages); change one's opinion; turn the conversation

hojalata *f*, tin plate

hojalatería *f*, tinware; tin shop

hojalatero *m*, tinsmith

hojalda, hojalde *m* = **hojaldre**

hojaldre *m*, or *f*, puff pastry

hojarasca *f*, withered leaves; excessive foliage; rubbish, trash

hojear *vt* to turn the leaves of a book; skip, skim, read quickly; *vi* exfoliate

hojuela *f*, *dim* little leaf; *bot* leaflet; pancake

¡hola! *interj* Hallo! Goodness!

Holanda Holland

holandés (-esa) *a* and *n* Dutchman (-woman) *m*, Dutch (language)

holgado *a* leisured, free; loose, wide; comfortable; well-off, rich

holganza *f*, repose, leisure, ease; idleness; pleasure

holgar *vi irr* to rest; be idle; be glad; be unused or unnecessary (things). *vr* enjoy oneself, amuse oneself; be glad. See **contar**

holgazán (-ana) *a* idle. *n* idler

holgazanear *vi* to idle

holgazanería *f*, idleness, sloth

holgorio *m*, rejoicing, festivity, merriment

holgura *f*, enjoyment, merrymaking; width; comfort, ease; *mech* free play

hollar *vt irr* to trample under foot; humiliate. See **degollar**

hollejo *m*, peel, thin skin (of fruit); *agr* chaff

hollín *m*, soot

holocausto *m*, holocaust. **el H.** the Holocaust

hológrafo *m*, holograph

hombradía *f*, manliness; courage

hombre *m*, man; adult; omber (cards). *interj* **¡h.!** *inf* Old fellow! You don't say so! **¡h. al agua!** Man overboard! **h. de bien,** honest, honorable man. **h. de estado,** statesman. **h. de muchos oficios,** jack-of-all-trades. **h. de negocios,** businessman; man of affairs. **h. de pro,** worthy man; famous man. **ser muy h.,** to be a real man, be very manly

hombrera *f*, epaulette; shoulderpad

hombro *m*, shoulder. **echar al h.,** to shoulder; undertake, take the responsibility of. **encogerse de hombros,** to shrug one's shoulders; be indifferent or uninterested

hombruno *a inf* mannish (of a woman)

homenaje *m*, allegiance; homage; veneration; respect

homeópata *a* homeopathic. *mf* homeopath

homeopatía *f*, homeopathy

homérico *a* Homeric

homicida *a* murderous, homicidal. *mf* murderer (-ess)

homicidio *m*, homicide (act)

homilía *f*, homily

homogeneidad *f*, homogeneity

homogéneo *a* homogeneous

homónimo *a* homonymous. *m*, homonym

homosexual *a* and *mf* homosexual

honda *f*, sling, catapult, slingshot

hondear *vt naut* to sound, plumb; *naut* unload; *Lat. Am.* to hit with a slingshot

hondo *a* deep; low; *fig* profound; deep, intense (emotion). *m*, depth

hondón *m*, depth, recess

hondonada *f*, hollow; glen; valley

hondura *f*, depth

hondureño (-ña) *a* and *n* Honduran

honestidad *f*, honorableness; virtue; respectability; modesty; courtesy

honesto *a* honorable, virtuous, modest; honest, just

hongo *m*, fungus; toadstool; bowler hat

honor *m*, honor; fame; reputation (women); modesty (women); praise; *pl* rank, position; honors

honorable *a* honorable
honorario *a* honorary. *m*, honorarium, fee
honorífico *a* honorary; honorable
honra *f*, self-respect, honor, personal dignity; reputation; chastity and modesty (women); *pl* obsequies
honradez *f*, honesty; honorableness, integrity; respectability
honrado *a* honest; honorable
honrar *vt* to respect; honor; *vr* to be honored
honroso *a* honor-giving, honorable
¡hopa! *interj Argentina* cut it out!, stop it!
hora *f*, hour; opportune moment; *pl* book of hours. **horas hábiles**, working hours. **horas muertas**, wee hours; wasted time. **a última h.**, at the last minute. **dar la h.**, to strike the hour. **¿Qué h. es?** What time is it?
horadar *vt* to bore, pierce
horario *a* hourly. *m*, timetable; hour hand of a clock; watch
horca *f*, gibbet, gallows; *agr* pitchfork; fork; prop for trees
horcajadas (a) *adv* astride
horcajadura *f*, crotch
horchata *f*, drink made of chufas or crushed almonds
horda *f*, horde
horizontal *a* horizontal
horizonte *m*, horizon. **nuevos horizontes,** new opportunities
horma *f*, mold; cobbler's last; stone wall. *fig inf* **hallar la h. de su zapato,** to find what suits one; meet one's match
hormiga *f*, ant
hormigón *m*, concrete. **h. armado,** ferro-concrete
hormiguear *vi* to itch; crowd, swarm
hormiguero *m*, anthill; crowd, swarm
hormona *f*, hormone
hornero (-ra) *n* baker
horno *m*, oven; furnace; kiln; bakery. **h. alfarero,** firing oven (for pottery). **h. de cocina,** kitchen stove. **h. de cuba,** blast furnace. **h. de ladrillo,** brick kiln. **alto h.,** iron-smelting furnace
horóscopo *m*, horoscope
horquilla *f*, forked stick; hairpin; hatpin; *agr* fork; hook. **viraje en h.,** hairpin turn
horrendo *a* horrible, frightful
hórreo *m*, granary, barn
horribilidad *f*, horribleness
horribilísimo *a sup* most horrible, exceedingly horrible
horrible *a* horrible
horrífico *a* horrific
horripilante *a* hair-raising, horrifying
horrísono *a poet* horrid-sounding, terrifying
horror *m*, horror; horribleness; atrocity, enormity
horrorizar *vt* to horrify; *vr* be horrified, be terrified
horroroso *a* dreadful, horrible; horrid; *inf* hideous, most ugly
hortaliza *f*, green vegetable, garden produce
hortelano *m*, market gardener
hortensia *f*, hydrangea
horticultura *f*, horticulture
horticultural *a* horticultural
hosanna *m*, hosanna
hosco *a* dark brown; unsociable, sullen; crabbed
hospedaje *m*, lodging; board, payment
hospedar *vt* to lodge, receive as a guest; *vr* and *vi* lodge, stay
hospedería *f*, hostelry, inn; lodging
hospedero (-ra) *n* innkeeper
hospicio *m*, hospice; almshouse, workhouse; lodging; orphanage
hospital *m*, hospital; hospice. **h. de sangre,** field hospital
hospitalario *a* hospitable
hospitalidad *f*, hospitality; hospitableness; hospital
hostelero (-ra) *n* innkeeper
hostería *f*, hostelry; inn

hostia *f*, *ecc* wafer, Host; sacrificial victim
hostigamiento *m*, harassment. **h. sexual,** sexual harassment
hostigar *vt* to chastise; harass; tease, annoy
hostil *a* hostile
hostilidad *f*, hostility
hostilizar *vt* to commit hostile acts against; antagonize
hotel *m*, hotel; villa
hotelero (-ra) *n* hotelkeeper
hoy *adv* today; at present. **h. día** *or* **h. en día,** today. **h. por h.,** day by day; at the present time. **de h. en adelante,** from today forward
hoya *f*, hole; grave; valley, glen; bed (of a river)
hoyo *m*, hole; pockmark; grave; hollow
hoyuelo *m*, *dim* little hole; dimple
hoz *f*, sickle; defile
hozar *vt* to root (pigs, etc.)
hucha *f*, large chest; strongbox; savings
hueco *a* empty; hollow; vain; hollow (sound); pompous (style); spongy, soft; inflated. *m*, hollow; interval of time or place; *inf* vacancy; gap in a wall, etc.
huelga *f*, strike; leisure; lying fallow; merrymaking. **h. de brazos caídos,** sit-down strike. **h. patronal,** lock-out strike
huelguista *mf* striker
huella *f*, footprint, track; footstep; tread (of stairs); *print* impression; vestige, trace. **h. digital,** fingerprint
huérfano (-na) *n* orphan. *a* unprotected, uncared for
huero *a* addled; empty, hollow
huerta *f*, kitchen garden; orchard; irrigation land
huerto *m*, orchard; kitchen garden
hueso *m*, bone; stone (of fruit); kernel, core; drudgery; cheap, useless thing of poor quality. *inf* **no dejar un h. sano,** to tear (a person) to pieces. **tener los huesos molidos,** to be tired out; be bruised
huésped (-da) *n* guest; host; innkeeper
hueste *f*, (gen. *pl*) army on the march; host; party, supporters
huesudo *a* bony
hueva *f*, fish roe
huevera *f*, egg seller; eggcup
huevo *m*, egg. **h. duro,** hard-boiled egg. **h. estrellado,** fried egg. **h. pasado por agua,** soft-boiled egg. **huevos revueltos,** scrambled eggs
hugonote (-ta) *a* and *n* Huguenot
huida *f*, flight, escape; bolting (of a horse); outlet
huir *vi irr* to flee; fly (of time); elope; run away, bolt; (*with de*) avoid. *Pres. Part.* **huyendo.** *Pres. Ind.* **huyo, huyes, huyen.** *Preterite* **huyó, huyeron.** *Pres. Subjunc.* **huya,** etc. *Imperf. Subjunc.* **huyese,** etc.
hule *m*, oilcloth; rubber; *Central America, Mexico* rubber tree
hulla *f*, coal mine, coal, soft coal
hullera *f*, colliery, coal mine
humanidad *f*, humanity; human nature; human weakness; compassion; affability; *inf* stoutness; *pl* study of humanities
humanismo *m*, humanism
humanista *mf* humanist. *a* humanistic
humanitario *a* humanitarian
humanizar *vt* to humanize
humano *a* human; understanding, sympathetic. *m*, human being
humareda *f*, cloud of smoke
humeante *a* smoking; smoky
humear *vi* to give forth smoke; give oneself airs; *Lat. Am.* fumigate; beat, thrash
humedad *f*, humidity; dampness; moisture
humedecer *vt irr* to moisten, wet, damp; *vr* grow moist. See **conocer**
húmedo *a* humid; damp; wet
humildad *f*, humility; lowliness; humbleness
humilde *a* meek; lowly; humble
humillación *f*, humiliation
humillante *a* humiliating; debasing; mortifying

humillar *vt* to humble; humiliate; *vr* humble one-self

humo *m*, smoke; vapor, fume; vanity, airs

humor *m*, *med* humor; temperament, disposition; mood. **de buen h.,** good-tempered. **de mal h.,** ill-tempered

humorada *f*, humorous saying, extravagance, witticism

humorismo *m*, humor, comic sense; humorousness

humorista *mf* humorist

humorístico *a* humorous

humoso *a* smoky, reeky

hundible *a* sinkable

hundido *a* sunken (of cheeks, etc.); hollow, deep-set (of eyes)

hundimiento *m*, sinking; collapse; subsidence (of earth)

hundir *vt* to sink; oppress; confound; destroy, ruin; *vr* collapse (building); sink; *fig inf* disappear

húngaro (-ra) *a* and *n* Hungarian. *m*, Hungarian (language)

Hungría Hungary

huracán *m*, hurricane

huraña *f*, shyness, unsociableness; diffidence; wildness (of animals, etc.)

huraño *a* shy, unsociable; diffident; wild (of animals, etc.)

hurgar *vt* to stir; poke, rake; touch; rouse, incite. *vr* pick one's nose

hurgón *m*, fire rake, poker; *inf* sword

hurgonada *f*, raking (of the fire, etc.)

hurguete *mf*, *Argentina* busybody, nosy parker

hurón (-ona) *n* ferret. *a* shy, unsociable

¡hurra! *interj* Hurrah!

hurtadillas (a) *adv* by stealth, secretly

hurtar *vt* to steal; encroach (sea, river); plagiarize; *vr* hide oneself

hurto *m*, theft. **coger con el h. en las manos,** *fig* to catch red-handed

husmear *vt* to sniff out; *inf* pry; *vi* smell bad (of meat)

huso *m*, spindle; bobbin

¡huy! *interj* (denoting pain or surprise) Oh!

I

ibérico *a* Iberian

ibero (-ra) *a* and *n* Iberian

íbice *m*, ibex

icnografía *f*, ichnography

icnográfico *a* ichnographical

icono *m*, icon

iconoclasta *a* iconoclastic. *mf* iconoclast

iconografía *f*, iconography

ictericia *f*, jaundice

ida *f*, setting out, departure, going; impetuous action; precipitancy; track, trail (of animals). **de i. y vuelta,** round trip (of tickets)

idea *f*, idea. *inf* **¡Qué ideas tienes!** What (odd) ideas you have!

ideal *a* ideal; perfect. *m*, model; ideal

idealidad *f*, ideality

idealismo *m*, idealism

idealista *a* idealistic. *mf* idealist

idealización *f*, idealization

idealizar *vt* to idealize

idear *vt* to imagine; devise; plan; design; draft, draw up

ideático, -a *a*, *Lat. Am.* eccentric

ídem *adv* idem

idéntico *a* identical

identidad *f*, identity

identificable *a* identifiable

identificación *f*, identification

identificar *vt* to identify; recognize; *vr* (*with con*) identify oneself with

ideografía *f*, ideography

ideograma *m*, ideogram, ideograph

ideología *f*, ideology. **i. racista,** racial ideology

ideológico *a* ideological

ideólogo (-ga) *n* ideologist; dreamer, planner

idílico *a* idyllic

idilio *m*, idyll

idioma *m*, language, tongue

idiomático *a* idiomatic

idiosincrasia *f*, idiosyncrasy

idiosincrásico *a* idiosyncratic

idiota *a* idiot; idiotic. *mf* idiot

idiotez *f*, idiocy

idiotismo *m*, *gram* idiom; ignorance

idiotizar *vt*, *Lat. Am.* to drive crazy, drive insane.

idólatra *a* idolatrous; adoring. *mf* idolater, heathen

idolatrar *vt* to idolize; worship, love excessively

idolatría *f*, idolatry; adoration, idolization

ídolo *m*, idol

idoneidad *f*, fitness, suitability; competence; capacity

idóneo *a* suitable; competent, fit

idus *m pl*, ides

iglesia *f*, church. **i. colegial,** collegiate church. **cumplir con la i.,** to discharge one's religious duties. **llevar a una mujer a la i.,** to lead a woman to the altar

ígneo *a* igneous

ignición *f*, ignition

ignominia *f*, ignominy, disgrace

ignominioso *a* ignominious

ignorancia *f*, ignorance. **pretender i.,** to plead ignorance

ignorante *a* ignorant; unaware, uninformed. *mf* ignoramus

ignorar *vt* to be unaware of, not to know

ignoto *a* unknown, undiscovered

igual *a* equal; level; even, smooth; very similar; alike; uniform; proportionate; unchanging; constant; indifferent; same. *mf* equal. *m*, *math* equal sign. **al i.,** equally. **sin i.,** peerless, without equal. **Me es completamente i.,** It's all the same to me

iguala *f*, equalizing; leveling; agreement, arrangement; cash adjustment

igualación *f*, equalization; leveling; arrangement, agreement; matching; *math* equation

igualador *a* equalizing; leveling

igualar *vt* to equalize, make equal; match; pair; level, flatten; smooth; adjust; arrange, agree upon; weigh, consider; *math* equate; *vi* be equal

igualdad *f*, equality; uniformity, harmony; evenness; smoothness; identity, sameness. **i. de ánimo,** equability, equanimity

igualitario *a* equalizing; egalitarian

igualmente *adv* equally; the same, likewise

ijada *f*, side, flank; pain in the side

ijadear *vt* to pant

ijar *m*, See **ijada**

ilación *f*, connection, reference

ilegal *a* illegal

ilegalidad *f*, illegality

ilegible *a* illegible, unreadable

ilegitimidad *f*, illegitimacy

ilegítimo *a* illegitimate; false

ileso *a* unharmed, unhurt

iletrado *a* unlettered, uncultured

Ilíada *f*, Iliad

iliberal *a* illiberal; narrow-minded

iliberalidad *f*, illiberality; narrow-mindedness

ilícito *a* illicit

ilicitud *f*, illicitness

ilimitado *a* unlimited, boundless

iliterato *a* illiterate, uncultured

ilógico a illogical
iluminación f, illumination; lighting. **i. intensiva,** floodlighting
iluminador (-ra) a lighting; illuminating. n art illuminator
iluminar vt to illuminate; light; art illuminate; enlighten; vr. Lat. Am. get drunk
iluminativo a illuminating
ilusión f, illusion; illusoriness; hope; dream
ilusionarse vr to harbor illusions
ilusivo a deceptive, illusive
iluso a deceived, deluded; dreamy; visionary
ilusorio a illusory; deceptive; null
ilustración f, illustration, picture; enlightenment; explanation; illustrated newspaper or magazine; erudition, knowledge; example, illustration
ilustrado a erudite, learned; knowledgeable, well-informed
ilustrador (-ra) a illustrative. n illustrator
ilustrar vt to explain, illustrate; enlighten, instruct; illustrate (books); make illustrious; inspire with divine light
ilustrativo a illustrative
ilustre a illustrious, distinguished
ilustrísimo a sup most illustrious (title of bishops, etc.)
imagen f, image; effigy, statue; idea; metaphor, simile. **i. nítida,** sharp image
imaginable a imaginable
imaginación f, imagination
imaginar vi to imagine; vt suppose, conjecture; discover, invent; imagine. **¡Imagínese!** Just imagine!
imaginario a imaginary
imaginativa f, imagination; common sense
imaginativo a imaginative
imaginería f, imagery
imán m, magnet; attraction, charm; imam
imanación f, magnetization
imanar vt to magnetize
imbécil a imbecile; stupid, idiotic. mf imbecile
imbecilidad f, imbecility; folly, stupidity
imberbe a beardless. inf **joven i.,** stripling
imbibición f, imbibing, absorption
imborrable a ineffaceable
imbuir vt irr to imbue. See **huir**
imitable a imitable
imitación f, imitation; reproduction, copy
imitado a imitation; imitated
imitador (-ra) a imitation; imitative. n imitator
imitar vt to imitate; counterfeit
imitativo a imitative
impacción f, impact
impaciencia f, impatience
impacientar vt to make impatient, annoy; vr grow impatient
impaciente a impatient
impacto m, impact. **i. de lleno,** direct hit
impago, -a Lat. Am. remaining to be paid, still to be paid, unpaid; m non-payment
impalpabilidad f, impalpability
impalpable a impalpable
impar a odd; unpaired; single, uneven. **número impar,** odd number
imparcial a impartial
imparcialidad f, impartiality
imparisilábico a imparisyllabic
impartible a indivisible
impasibilidad f, impassivity, indifference
impasible a impassive
impavidez f dauntlessness; serenity in the face of danger; Lat. Am. cheek, cheekiness, effrontery
impávido a dauntless; calm, composed, imperturbable; Lat. Am. cheeky, fresh
impecabilidad f, impeccability, perfection
impecable a impeccable, perfect
impedido a disabled
impedimento m, obstacle; hindrance; law impediment

impedir vt irr to impede; obstruct; prevent; thwart; disable; delay; poet amaze. See **pedir**
impeler vt to push; incite; drive; urge
impender vt to spend money
impenetrabilidad f, impenetrability; imperviousness; obscurity, difficulty
impenetrable a impenetrable, dense; impervious; fig unfathomable; obscure
impenitencia f, impenitence
impenitente a impenitent
impensado a unexpected, unforeseen
imperante a ruling, dominant
imperar vi to rule; command
imperativo a commanding. a and m, gram imperative
imperatorio a imperial, imperatorial
imperceptible a imperceptible
imperdible m, safety pin
imperdonable a unpardonable, inexcusable
imperecedero a undying, eternal, everlasting
imperfección f, imperfection, inadequacy; fault, blemish; weakness
imperfecto a imperfect; inadequate; faulty. a and m, gram imperfect
imperial a imperial. f, upper deck of a bus or streetcar
imperialismo m, imperialism
imperialista a imperialistic. mf imperialist
impericia f, inexpertness; unskillfulness, unhandiness
imperio m, empire; rule, reign; command, sway; imperial dignity; arrogance, haughtiness. fig inf **valer un i.,** to be priceless
imperioso a imperious
imperito a inexpert; clumsy, unskilled
impermeabilidad f, watertightness; imperviousness; impermeability
impermeabilizar vt to waterproof
impermeable a watertight, impermeable; impervious. m, raincoat, mackintosh
impertérrito a unafraid, dauntless
impertinencia f, impertinence, insolence; peevishness; fancy, whim; overexactness, meticulousness; interference, intrusion
impertinente a impertinent; irrelevant; inopportune; officious, interfering
imperturbabilidad f, imperturbability
imperturbable a calm, imperturbable
impetrar vt to obtain by entreaty; implore
ímpetu m, impetus, momentum; speed, swiftness; violence
impetuosidad f, impetuosity
impetuoso a impetuous; precipitate
impiedad f, cruelty, harshness; irreligion
impío a impious, wicked; irreverent, irreligious
implacabilidad f, implacability, relentless
implacable a implacable
implantación f, inculcation, implantation
implantar vt to inculcate, implant (ideas, etc.)
implicación f, implication; contradiction (in terms); complicity
implicar vt to implicate; imply, infer; involve, entangle; vi imply contradiction (gen. with negatives)
implicatorio a contradictory; implicated (in crime)
implícito a implicit; implied
implorante a imploring
implorar vt to implore, entreat
implume a without feathers, unfeathered
impolítico a impolitic; unwise, inexpedient; tactless
imponderabilidad f, imponderability
imponderable a imponderable, immeasurable; most excellent
imponencia f. Lat. Am. impressiveness
imponente a imposing, impressive; awe-inspiring
imponer vt irr to exact, impressive; impose; malign, accuse falsely; instruct, acquaint; fig impress (with respect, etc.); invest or deposit (money); print impose; give, bestow (a name). vr assert oneself. See **poner**
imponible a taxable; ratable

impopular *a* unpopular
impopularidad *f*, unpopularity
importable *a* importable
importación *f*, *com* importation; import
importador (-ra) *a* import, importing. *n* importer
importancia *f*, importance; magnitude
importante *a* important
importar *vi* to matter; be important; concern, interest; *vt* amount to; import; include, comprise. **¡No importa!** It doesn't matter! Never mind!
importe *m*, amount; value, cost. **i. bruto,** gross or total amount. **i. líquido** *or* **neto,** net amount
importunación *f*, importuning; importunity
importunadamente *adv* importunately
importunar *vt* to importune, pester
importunidad (*also* importunación) *f*, importunity
importuno *a* importunate, inopportune, ill-timed; persistent; tedious
imposibilidad *f*, impossibility
imposibilitado *a* disabled, crippled; incapable, unable
imposibilitar *vt* to disable; render unable; make impossible
imposible *a* impossible
imposición *f*, imposition; exaction; tax, duty, tribute; *print* makeup **i. de manos,** *ecc* laying on of hands
impostor (-ra) *n* impostor
impostura *f*, swindle, imposture; aspersion, slur, imputation
impotable *a* undrinkable
impotencia *f*, impotence
impotente *a* impotent; powerless
impracticabilidad *f*, impracticability; impassability (of roads, etc.)
impracticable *a* impracticable; impossible; impassable (roads, etc.)
imprecación *f*, imprecation; curse, malediction
imprecar *vt* to imprecate, curse
impregnación *f*, impregnation, permeation, saturation
impregnar *vt* impregnate; to permeate; *vr* become impregnated
impremeditado *a* unpremeditated
imprenta *f*, printing; printing house or office; print; letterpress
impreparación *f*, unpreparedness
imprescindible *a* indispensable, essential
impresión *f*, printing; impression; effect; influence; imprint, stamp; *print* impression; print. **impresión digital,** fingerprint
impresionable *a* impressionable, susceptible
impresionante *a* imposing; moving, affecting
impresionar *vt* to impress; affect; fix in the mind; *fig* move deeply, stir; (*rad* cinema) record
impresionismo *m*, impressionism
impresionista *mf* impressionist. *a* impressionistic
impreso *m*, (gen. *pl*) printed matter
impresor *m*, printer
imprevisión *f*, lack of foresight; improvidence
imprevisto *a* unforeseen, unexpected, sudden
imprevistos *m pl*, incidental expenses
imprimación *f*, priming (of paint, etc.)
imprimar *vt* to prime (of paint)
imprimir *vt* to print; stamp; impress upon (the mind)
improbabilidad *f*, improbability
improbable *a* improbable
improbo *a* vicious, corrupt, dishonest; hard, arduous
improductivo *a* unproductive; unprofitable, fruitless
impronta *f*, *art* cast, mold
impronunciable *a* unpronounceable; ineffable
improperio *m*, insult, affront
impropiedad *f*, inappropriateness; unsuitableness; impropriety
impropio *a* unsuitable; inappropriate; inadequate; improper
improporcionado *a* disproportionate, out of proportion
impróvido *a* improvident, heedless

improvisación *f*, improvisation
improvisador (-ra) *n* improviser
improvisamente *adv* unexpectedly, suddenly
improvisar *vt* to improvise
improviso, improvisto *a* unexpected, unforeseen. **al** (*or* **de**) **improviso,** unexpectedly
imprudencia *f*, imprudence, rashness, indiscretion
imprudente *a* imprudent, unwise, rash
impúbero *a* below the age of puberty
impudencia *f*, impudence, impertinence
impudente *a* brazen, impudent
impudicia *f*, immodesty, brazenness
impúdico *a* immodest, brazen
impuesto *m*, tax; duty. **i. de utilidades,** income tax. **i. sucesorio,** inheritance tax
impugnable *a* impugnable, refutable
impugnación *f*, refutation; contradiction
impugnar *vt* to refute, contradict; oppose; criticize
impulsar *vt* to impel; prompt, cause; drive, operate, propel
impulsión *f*, impulse; impetus; *mech* operation, driving; propulsion
impulsivo *a* impulsive; irreflexive, precipitate
impulso *m*, stimulus, incitement; impulse, desire; *mech* drive, impulse
impulsor (-ra) *a* driving, impelling. *n* driver, operator
impune *a* unpunished
impunemente *adv* with impunity
impunidad *f*, impunity
impureza *f*, impurity; lack of chastity; obscenity, indecency
impurificar *vt* to defile; make impure; adulterate
impuro *a* impure; adulterated; polluted; immoral, unchaste
imputable *a* imputable
imputación *f*, imputation
imputador (-ra) *n* imputer, attributer
imputar *vt* to impute; attribute
inacabable *a* endless, interminable, ceaseless; wearisome
inaccesibilidad *f*, inaccessibility
inaccesible *a* inaccessible; incomprehensible
inacción *f*, inaction
inaceptable *a* unacceptable
inactividad *f*, inactivity; quiescence; idleness
inactivo *a* inactive; idle; unemployed; *naut* laid-up
inadaptable *a* inadaptable
inadecuado *a* inadequate, insufficient
inadmisible *a* inadmissible
inadvertencia *f*, inadvertence; oversight, mistake, slip
inadvertido *a* unnoticed; inattentive; inadvertent, unintentional; negligent
inafectado *a* unaffected, natural
inagotable *a* inexhaustible, unfailing; abundant
inaguantable *a* unbearable, intolerable
inajenable *a* inalienable
inalámbrica *f*, radio station
inalienable *a* inalienable
inalterable *a* unalterable
inamovibilidad *f*, immovability
inamovible *a* immovable
inanición *f*, inanition
inanimado *a* inanimate
inapagable *a* inextinguishable
inapelable *a* unappealable; irremediable, inevitable
inapetencia *f*, lack of appetite
inaplazable *a* undeferrable, unable to be postponed
inaplicable *a* inapplicable
inaplicación *f*, laziness, inattention, negligence
inaplicado *a* lazy; inattentive; careless
inapreciable *a* inappreciable; invaluable
inarmónico *a* unharmonious, discordant
inarticulado *a* inarticulate
inasequible *a* unattainable; out of reach
inaudible *a* inaudible

inaudito *a* unheard of, unprecedented; extraordinary, strange

inauguración *f,* inauguration; induction; inception, commencement

inaugural *a* inaugural

inaugurar *vt* to inaugurate; induct

inaveriguable *a* unascertainable

inca *mf* Inca

incaico *a* Incan

incalculable *a* incalculable; innumerable

incalificable *a* indescribable, unclassable; vile

incandescencia *f,* incandescence, white heat

incandescente *a* incandescent

incansable *a* indefatigable; unflagging; unwearying

incapacidad *f,* incapacity; incompetence

incapacitar *vt* to incapacitate; disable

incapaz *a* incapable, incompetent; inefficient

incasable *a* unmarriageable; antimarriage

incásico, -a *a, Lat. Am.* Inca

incautarse *vr* to seize, take possession (of)

incauto *a* incautious; unwary

incendiar *vt* to set on fire, set alight

incendiario (-ia) *a* and *n* incendiary

incendiarismo *m,* incendiarism

incendio *m,* conflagration, fire; consuming passion

incensar *vt irr ecc* to cense, incense; flatter. See **acertar**

incensario *m,* incense burner, incensory

incentivo *m,* incentive; encouragement

incertidumbre *f,* uncertainty; incertitude

incesable, incesante *a* incessant, continuous

incesto *m,* incest

incestuoso *a* incestuous

incidencia *f,* incidence

incidente *a* incidental. *m,* incident, event, occurrence

incidir *vi* (*with en*) to incur, fall into (e.g. **Incidió en el pecado,** He fell into sin)

incienso *m,* incense; flattery

incierto *a* untrue, false; uncertain; unknown

incineración *f,* incineration

incinerador *m,* incinerator

incinerar *vt* incinerate, reduce to ashes

incipiente *a* incipient

incircunciso *a* uncircumcised

incisión *f,* incision

incisivo *a* sharp, keen; incisive, sarcastic, caustic

inciso *m,* clause; comma

incitación *f,* incitement; *fig* spur, stimulus

incitar *vt* to incite; stimulate, encourage

incivil *a* rude, discourteous, uncivil

incivilidad *f,* rudeness, incivility

inclasificable *a* unclassifiable

inclemencia *f,* harshness, severity; inclemency (of the weather). **a la i.,** at the mercy of the elements

inclemente *a* inclement

inclinación *f,* inclination; slope; slant; tendency, propensity; predilection, fondness; bow (in greeting); *geom* inclination

inclinar *vt* to incline, tilt, slant; bow; bend; influence; persuade; *vi* resemble; *vr* lean; stoop; tilt; tend, incline (to), view favorably (e.g. **Me inclino a creerlo,** I am inclined to believe it)

ínclito *a* famous, celebrated

incluir *vt irr* to comprise, embrace, contain; include, take into account. See **huir**

inclusa *f,* foundling home

inclusión *f,* inclusion; relationship, intercourse, friendship

inclusive *adv* including

inclusivo *a* inclusive

incluso *adv* including, inclusive. *prep* even

incoar *vt* to begin (especially lawsuits)

incobrable *a* irrecoverable; irredeemable

incógnita *f, math* X; unknown quantity; secret motive; unknown lady

incógnito *a* unknown. *m,* incognito, assumed name, disguise

incoherencia *f,* incoherence

incoherente *a* incoherent, disconnected, illogical

íncola *mf* resident, dweller, inhabitant

incoloro *a* colorless, uncolored

incólume *a* unharmed, unscathed; untouched, undamaged

incombustibilidad *f,* incombustibility

incomodar *vt* to disturb, incommode, inconvenience; annoy; *vr* disturb oneself, put oneself out; grow angry. **¡No se incomode!** Please don't move!; Please don't be angry!

incomodidad *f,* discomfort; inconvenience; trouble, upset; annoyance

incómodo *a* uncomfortable; inconvenient; troublesome, tiresome; *Argentina, Chile* fed up *m,* discomfort; inconvenience

incomparable *a* incomparable

incompartible *a* indivisible

incompasivo *a* unsympathetic, hard

incompatibilidad *f,* incompatibility

incompetencia *f,* incompetence

incompetente *a* incompetent

incomplejo, incomplexo *a* noncomplex, simple

incompleto *a* incomplete

incomponible *a* unrepairable, unmendable

incomprensibilidad *f,* incomprehensibility

incomprensible *a* incomprehensible

incomprensión *f,* incomprehension

incomunicado *a* in solitary confinement (of a prisoner)

incomunicar *vt* to sentence to solitary confinement; isolate, deprive of means of communication; *vr* become a recluse

inconcebible *a* inconceivable

inconciliable *a* irreconcilable

incondicional *a* unconditional; *Lat. Am.* fawning, servile

inconexión *f,* disconnectedness

inconexo *a* inconnected; incoherent

inconfeso *a* unconfessed

incongruencia *f,* incongruity

incongruente *a* incongruous, inappropriate

inconmensurabilidad *f,* incommensurability

inconmovible *a* immovable; unflinching, unshakable

inconmutable *a* unalterable, immutable, unchangeable

inconquistable *a* unconquerable; *fig* resolute, inflexible

inconsciencia *f,* unconsciousness; subconscious

inconsciente *a* unconscious, involuntary; subconscious

inconsecuencia *f,* inconsequence; inconsistency

inconsecuente *a* inconsequential; inconsistent

inconsideración *f,* thoughtlessness

inconsiderado *a* thoughtless; heedless, selfish

inconsiguiente *a* illogical, inconsistent

inconsistencia *f,* inconsistency

inconsistente *a* inconsistent

inconsolable *a* inconsolable

inconstancia *f,* inconstancy, infidelity

inconstante *a* inconstant, fickle

inconstitucional *a* unconstitutional

incontaminado *a* uncontaminated

incontestable *a* undeniable, unquestionable

incontinencia *f,* incontinence

incontinente *a* incontinent

incontrastable *a* insuperable, invincible; undeniable, unanswerable; *fig* unshakable, inconvincible

incontrovertible *a* undeniable, incontrovertible

inconvencible *a* inconvincible

inconveniencia *f,* discomfort; inconvenience; unsuitability

inconveniente *a* awkward, inconvenient; uncomfortable; inappropriate. *m,* inconvenience; obstacle, impediment; disadvantage

inconvertible *a* inconvertible

incorporación *f*, incorporation
incorporar *vt* to incorporate; cause to sit up, lift up; *vr* sit up, raise oneself; become a member, join (associations); be incorporated; blend, mix
incorporeidad *f*, incorporeity
incorpóreo *a* incorporeal; immaterial
incorrección *f*, incorrectness; indecorum, impropriety
incorrecto *a* incorrect; indecorous, unbecoming, improper
incorregible *a* incorrigible
incorrupción *f*, incorruption; purity; integrity; wholesomeness
incorrupto *a* incorrupt; pure; chaste
incredibilidad *f*, incredibility
incredulidad *f*, incredulity, scepticism
incrédulo (-la) *a* incredulous; atheistic. *n* atheist; unbeliever, sceptic
increíble *a* incredible; marvelous, extraordinary
incremento *m*, increment, increase
increpación *f*, scolding, harsh rebuke
increpar *vt* to scold, rebuke harshly
incriminante *a* incriminating
incriminar *vt* to incriminate, accuse; exaggerate (a charge, etc.)
incruento *a* bloodless, unstained with blood
incrustación *f*, incrustation; *art* inlay
incubación *f*, hatching; *med* incubation
incubadora *f*, incubator (for chickens)
incubar *vi* to sit on eggs (of hens); *vt* hatch; *med* incubate
inculcación *f*, inculcation, instillment
inculcar *vt* to press one thing against another; instill, inculcate; *vr* grow more fixed in one's views
inculpable *a* blameless, innocent
inculpar *vt* to blame; accuse
incultivable *a* uncultivatable; untillable
inculto *a* uncultivated, untilled; uncultured; uncivilized
incultura *f*, lack of cultivation; lack of culture
incumbencia *f*, obligation, moral responsibility, duty
incumbir *vi* to be incumbent on; concern
incumplimiento *m*, nonfulfilment
incurable *a* incurable; inveterate, hopeless
incuria *f*, negligence, carelessness
incurioso *a* incurious
incurrir *vi* (*with en*) to fall into (error, etc.); incur (dislike, etc.)
incursión *f*, incursion; inroad
indagación *f*, investigation, inquiry
indagador (-ra) *a* investigating, inquiring. *n* investigator
indagar *vt* to investigate, examine; inquire. **i. precios,** to inquire about prices
indebido *a* undue, immoderate improper; illegal, illicit
indecencia *f*, indecency; obscenity; impropriety
indecente *a* indecent; obscene; improper
indecible *a* unutterable, ineffable, unspeakable
indeciso *a* undecided; hesitant, irresolute; vague; noncommittal
indeclinable *a* obligatory; unavoidable; *gram* indeclinable, uninflected
indecoro *m*, impropriety, indecorum
indecoroso *a* indecorous, unbecoming; base, mean
indefectible *a* unfailing; perfect
indefectiblemente *adv* invariably
indefendible *a* indefensible
indefenso *a* unprotected, defenseless
indefinible *a* indefinable, vague; indescribable
indefinido *a* indefinite, vague; undefined; *gram* indefinite
indeleble *a* indelible
indeliberado *a* unpremeditated; unconsidered
indemme *a* unharmed, undamaged
indemnidad *f*, indemnity
indemnización *f*, compensation, indemnification; indemnity

indemnizar *vt* to indemnify, compensate
indemostrable *a* indemonstrable, incapable of demonstration
independencia *f*, independence
independiente *a* independent; self-contained
indescifrable *a* undecipherable; illegible
indestructible *a* indestructible
indeterminado *a* indeterminate; vague, doubtful, uncertain; hesitant, irresolute; *math* indeterminate
indiano (-na) *a* and *n* Indian; East Indian; West Indian. *m*, nouveau riche, one who returns rich from the Western Hemisphere
indicación *f*, indication; sign, evidence; intimation, hint
indicador *a* indicative. *m*, indicator. **i. del nivel de gasolina,** gas gauge
indicar *vt* to indicate; show; point out; simply, suggest; intimate
indicativo *a* indicative. *a* and *m*, *gram* indicative
índice *m*, index; indication, sign; library catalogue; catalogue room; hand (of a clock); pointer, needle (of instruments); gnomon (of a sundial); *math* index; forefinger. **I. expurgatorio,** the Index
indicio *m*, indication; sign; evidence. **indicios vehementes,** circumstantial evidence
índico *a* Indian
indiferencia *f*, indifference
indiferente *a* indifferent
indígena *a* native, indigenous. *mf* native
indigencia *f*, destitution, indigence; impecuniosity
indigenismo *m*, *Lat. Am.* Native American movement
indigente *a* destitute, indigent; impecunious
indigestión *f*, indigestion
indigesto *a* indigestible; *lit* muddled, confused; unsociable, brusque
indignación *f*, indignation, anger
indignado *a* indignant
indignar *vt* to anger, make indignant; *vr* grow angry
indignidad *f*, unworthiness; indignity; personal affront
indigno *a* unworthy; base, despicable
índigo *m*, indigo
indio (-ia) *a* Indian; blue. *n* Indian. *m*, indium
indirecta *f*, hint, covert suggestion, innuendo. *inf* **i. del padre Cobos,** strong hint
indirecto *a* indirect
indisciplina *f*, indiscipline
indisciplinado *a* undisciplined
indiscreción *f*, indiscretion
indiscreto *a* indiscreet
indiscutible *a* unquestionable, undeniable
indisoluble *a* indissoluble
indispensable *a* indispensable
indisponer *vt irr* to make unfit or incapable; indispose; make ill; (*with con or contra*) set against, make trouble with; *vr* be indisposed; (*with con or contra*) quarrel with. See **poner**
indisposición *f*, reluctance, disinclination; indisposition, brief illness
indistinguible *a* undistinguishable
indistinto *a* indistinct; indeterminate; vague
individual *a* individual; peculiar, characteristic. *m*, (tennis) single
individualidad *f*, individuality
individualismo *m*, individualism
individualista *a* individualistic. *mf* individualist
individuo (-ua) *a* individual; indivisible. *m*, individual; member, associate; *inf* self. *n inf* person
indivisibilidad *f*, indivisibility
indivisible *a* indivisible
indiviso *a* undivided
indócil *a* unmanageable; disobedient; brittle, unpliable (of metals)
indocilidad *f*, indocility; disobedience; brittleness (of metals)
indochino (-na) *a* and *n* Indochinese
indoeuropeo *a* Indo-European

indoísmo *m*, Hinduism

índole *f*, temperament, nature; kind, sort

indolencia *f*, idleness, indolence

indolente *a* nonpainful; indifferent, insensible; idle, indolent

indoloro *a* painless

indomable *a* untamable; invincible; indomitable; ungovernable, unmanageable

indomado *a* untamed

indómito *a* untamed; untamable; unmanageable, unruly; indomitable

indonesio (-ia) *a* and *n* Indonesian

indostanés *a* Hindustani

indostani *m*, Hindustani (language)

indubitable *a* unquestionable

inducción *f*, persuasion; *phys* induction

inducir *vt irr* to persuade, prevail upon; induce; infer, conclude. See **conducir**

inductivo, inductor *a* inductive

indudable *a* indubitable

indulgencia *f*, overkindness, tenderness; *ecc* indulgence

indulgente *a* indulgent, tender; tolerant

indultar *vt* to pardon; exempt

indulto *m*, amnesty; exemption; forgiveness; *ecc* indult

indumentaria *f*, clothing; outfit (of clothes)

industria *f*, assiduity, industriousness; pains, effort, ingenuity; industry. **i. pesada,** heavy industry. **i. cárnica,** meat industry. **i. extractivos,** mining industry

industrial *a* industrial. *m*, industrialist

industrialismo *m*, industrialism

industrialización *f*, industrialization

industriar *vt* to teach, train; *vr* find a way, manage, succeed in

industrioso *a* industrious; diligent, assiduous

inédito *a* unpublished; unedited

inefable *a* ineffable

ineficacia *f*, inefficiency; ineffectiveness

ineficaz *a* ineffective; inefficient

ineludible *a* unavoidable

ineptitud *f*, ineptitude

inepto *a* inept, incompetent; unfit, unsuitable

inequívoco *a* unequivocal

inercia *f*, inertia

inerme *a* defenseless, unprotected; (*bot zool*) unarmed

inerte *a* inert

inescrutable *a* inscrutable, unfathomable

inesperado *a* unexpected, sudden

inestabilidad *f*, instability

inestable *a* unstable

inestimable *a* inestimable

inevitable *a* inevitable

inexactitud *f*, inexactitude, inaccuracy; error, mistake

inexacto *a* inexact, inaccurate; erroneous

inexcusable *a* inexcusable, unforgivable; indispensable

inexhausto *a* inexhaustible

inexistente *a* nonexistent

inexorable *a* inexorable

inexperiencia *f*, inexperience

inexperto *a* inexperienced; inexpert

inexplicable *a* inexplicable

inexplorado *a* unexplored

inexplosible *a* inexplosive

inexpresivo *a* inexpressive; reticent

inexpugnable *a* impregnable; *fig* unshakable, firm; obstinate

inextinguible *a* inextinguishable; everlasting, perpetual

infalibilidad *f*, infallibility

infalible *a* infallible

infamación *f*, defamation

infamador (-ra) *a* slandering. *n* slanderer

infamar *vt* to defame, slander

infame *a* infamous, vile

infamia *f*, infamy; baseness, vileness

infancia *f*, infancy, babyhood; childhood

infanta *f*, female child under seven years; infanta, any Spanish royal princess; wife of a Spanish royal prince

infantado *m*, land belonging to an *infante* or *infanta*

infante *m*, male child under seven years; infante, any Spanish royal prince except an heir-apparent; infantryman. **i. de coro,** choir boy

infantería *f*, infantry

infanticida *a* infanticidal. *mf* infanticide (person)

infanticidio *m*, infanticide (act)

infantil *a* infantile, babyish; innocent, candid

infatigable *a* unwearying, indefatigable

infatuación *f*, infatuation

infatuar *vt* to infatuate; *vr* become infatuated

infausto *a* unlucky, unfortunate

infección *f*, infection

infeccioso *a* infectious

infectar *vt* to infect; corrupt, pervert; *vr* become infected; be corrupted

infecto *a* infected; corrupt, perverted; tainted

infecundidad *f*, sterility

infecundo *a* sterile, barren

infelice *a poet* unhappy, unfortunate

infelicidad *f*, unhappiness

infeliz *a* unhappy; unfortunate; *inf* simple, goodhearted

inferencia *f*, inference, connection

inferior *a* inferior; lower; second-rate; subordinate. *mf* inferior, subordinate

inferioridad *f*, inferiority

inferir *vt irr* to infer, deduce; involve, imply; occasion; inflict. See **sentir**

infernáculo *m*, hopscotch

infernal *a* infernal; devilish, fiendish; wicked, inhuman; *inf* confounded

inferno *a poet* infernal

infértil *a* infertile

infestación *f*, infestation

infestar *vt* to infest, swarm in; infect; injure, damage

infesto *a poet* harmful, dangerous

inficionar *vt* to infect; pervert, corrupt

infidelidad *f*, faithlessness, infidelity; disbelief in Christian religion; unbelievers, infidels

infidelísimo, *a sup* **infiel** most disloyal; most incorrect; most incredulous, faithless

infidencia *f*, disloyalty, faithlessness

infiel *a* unfaithful, disloyal; inaccurate, incorrect; infidel, unbelieving. *mf* infidel, nonbeliever

infierno *m*, hell; hades (gen. *pl*); *fig inf* inferno. **en el quinto i.,** very far off, at the end of the world. **en los quintos infiernos,** at the end of nowhere

infiltración *f*, infiltration; inculcation, implantation

infiltrar *vt* to infiltrate; imbue, inculcate

ínfimo *a* lowest; meanest, vilest, most base; cheapest, poorest (in quality)

infinidad *f*, infinity; infinitude; great number

infinitivo *a* and *m*, *gram* infinitive

infinito *a* infinite; endless; boundless; countless. *m*, math infinite. *adv* excessively, immensely

infinitud *f*, See **infinidad**

inflación *f*, inflation; distension; pride, vanity

inflacionismo *m*, inflationism

inflacionista *mf* inflationist

inflador *m*. Lat. Am. bicycle pump

inflamabilidad *f*, inflammability

inflamable *a* inflammable

inflamación *f*, inflammation; *eng* ignition

inflamador *a* inflammatory

inflamar *vt* to set on fire; *fig* inflame, excite; *vr* take fire; *med* become inflamed; grow hot or excited

inflamatorio *a med* inflammatory

inflar *vt* to inflate; blow up, distend; throw out (one's chest); exaggerate; make haughty or vain; *vr* be swollen or inflated; be puffed up with pride

inflexibilidad *f*, inflexibility; rigidity; immovability, constancy

inflexible *a* inflexible

inflexión *f*, bending, flexion; diffraction (optics); inflection

infligir *vt* to impose, inflict (penalties)

influencia *f*, influence; power, authority; *elec* charge

influir *vt irr* to influence; affect; (*with en*) cooperate in, assist with. See **huir**

influjo *m*, influence; flux, inflow of the tide

influyente *a* influential

información *f*, information; legal inquiry; report; research, investigation

informador (-ra) *a* informing, acquainting. *n* informant

informal *a* informal, irregular; unreliable (of persons); unconventional

informalidad *f*, irregularity; unconventionality; unreliability

informante *mf* informant

informar *vt* to inform, acquaint with; *vi law* plead; *vr* (*with de, en, or sobre*) find out about, investigate

informática *f*, information sciences

informativo *a* informative

informe *a* formless, shapeless. *m*, report, statement; information; *law* plea; *pl* data, particulars; references

infortificable *a* unfortifiable

infortuna *f*, *astrol* evil influence

infortunado *a* unfortunate

infortunio *m*, misfortune; unhappiness, adversity; mischance, ill luck

infracción *f*, transgression, infringement

infracto *a* imperturbable

infractor(-ra) *a* infringing. *n* transgressor, infringer

infrangible *a* unbreakable

infranqueable *a* insuperable, unsurmountable

infrarrojo *a* infrared

infrascrito *a* undersigned; undermentioned

infrecuente *a* infrequent

infringir *vt* to infringe, transgress, break

infructífero *a* unfruitful; worthless, useless

infructuosidad *f*, unfruitfulness; worthlessness, uselessness

infructuoso *a* fruitless; useless, worthless

infumable *a* unsmokable (of tobacco)

infundado *a* unfounded, groundless

infundio *m*, *inf* nonsense, untruth

infundir *vt* to infuse, imbue with

infusión *f*, infusion

ingeniar *vt* to devise, concoct, plan; *vr* contrive, find a way, manage

ingeniería *f*, engineering

ingeniero *m*, engineer. **i. agrónomo,** agricultural engineer. **i. de caminos, canales y puertos,** civil engineer. **i. radiotelegrafista,** radio engineer. **cuerpo de ingenieros,** royal engineers

ingenio *m*, mind; inventive capacity; imaginative talent; man of genius; talent, cleverness; ingeniousness; machine; guillotine (bookbinding)

ingeniosidad *f*, ingeniousness; witticism, clever remark

ingenioso *a* talented, clever; ingenious

ingénito *a* unengendered, unconceived; innate, inborn

ingente *a* huge, enormous

ingenuidad *f*, ingenuousness, naiveté

ingenuo *a* ingenuous, naive, artless, unaffected

Inglaterra England

ingle *f*, groin

inglés (-esa) *a* English; British. *n* Englishman; Briton. *m*, English (language); *inf* creditor. **a la inglesa,** in English fashion. **marcharse a la inglesa,** *inf* to take French leave

inglesismo *m*, Anglicism

ingobernable *a* ungovernable, unruly

ingratitud *f*, ingratitude

ingrato *a* ungrateful; irksome, thankless; disagreeable

ingrávido *a* light weight

ingrediente *m*, ingredient; *Argentina* appetizer

ingresar *vi* to return, come in (money); (*with en*) join, become a member of, enter

ingreso *m*, joining, entering, admission; *com* money received; opening, commencement; *pl* earnings, takings, revenue

ingurgitación *f*, *med* ingurgitation

ingurgitar *vt* to ingurgitate, swallow

inhábil *a* unskillful; unpracticed; incompetent, unfit; unsuitable, ill-chosen

inhabilidad *f*, unskillfulness; incompetence; unsuitability; inability

inhabilitación *f*, incapacitation; disqualification; disablement

inhabilitar *vt* to make ineligible; disqualify; incapacitate, make unfit; *vr* become ineligible; be incapacitated

inhabitable *a* uninhabitable

inhabitado *a* uninhabited, deserted

inhalación *f*, inhalation

inhalador *m*, *med* inhaler

inhalar *vt* to inhale

inhallable *a* nowhere to be found, unfindable

inhereditable *a* uninheritable

inherencia *f*, inherency

inherente *a* inherent, innate

inhestar *vt irr* to raise, lift up; erect. See **acertar**

inhibición *f*, inhibition

inhibir *vt law* to inhibit; *vr* inhibit or restrain oneself. See **prohibir**

inhibitorio *a law* inhibitory

inhonesto *a* indecent, obscene; immodest

inhospedable, inhospitalario *a* inhospitable; bleak, uninviting; exposed

inhospitalidad *f*, inhospitality

inhumación *f*, inhumation, burial

inhumadora *f*, crematory

inhumanidad *f*, inhumanity; brutality

inhumano *a* inhuman; brutal, barbarous

inhumar *vt* to bury, inter

iniciación *f*, initiation

iniciador (-ra) *a* initiating; *n* initiator

inicial *a* and *f*, initial

iniciar *vt* to initiate; admit, introduce; originate; *vr* be initiated; *ecc* take minor or first orders

iniciativa *f*, initiative

inicuo *a* iniquitous, most unjust, wicked

inimaginable *a* inconceivable

inimicísimo *a sup* **enemigo** most hostile

inimitable *a* inimitable

ininteligible *a* unintelligible

iniquidad *f*, iniquity, wickedness

injerir *vt irr* to insert, put within, introduce; interpolate; *vr* meddle. See **sentir**

injertar *vt agr* to graft

injerto *m*, *agr* graft; grafting; grafted plant, briar, or tree

injuria *f*, insult; slander; outrage; wrong, injustice; harm, damage

injuriador (-ra) *a* insulting. *n* offender, persecutor

injuriar *vt* to insult; slander; outrage; wrong, persecute; harm, damage

injurioso *a* insulting; slanderous; offensive, abusive; harmful

injusticia *f*, injustice; lack of justice; unjust action

injustificable *a* unjustifiable

injustificado *a* unjustified

injusto *a* unjust; unrighteous

inllevable *a* unbearable, intolerable

inmaculado *a* immaculate, pure

inmanejable *a* unmanageable; uncontrollable

inmanencia *f*, immanence

inmanente *a* immanent

inmarcesible, inmarchitable *a* unfading, imperishable

inmaterial *a* incorporeal; immaterial

inmaterialidad *f*, incorporeity; immateriality

inmaturo *a* immature; unripe

inmediación *f*, nearness, proximity; contact; *pl* outskirts, neighborhood, environs
inmediatamente *adv* near; immediately, at once
inmediato *a* adjoining, close, nearby; immediate, prompt
inmejorable *a* unsurpassable, unbeatable
inmemorable, inmemorial *a* immemorial
inmensidad *f*, vastness, huge extent; infinity; infinite space; immensity; huge number
inmenso *a* vast; infinite; immense; innumerable
inmensurable *a* immeasurable, incalculable
inmerecido *a* undeserved, unmerited
inmérito *a* wrongful, unjust
inmeritorio *a* unmeritorious, unpraiseworthy
inmersión *f*, immersion; dip
inmigración *f*, immigration
inmigrante *a* and *mf* immigrant
inmigrar *vi* to immigrate
inminencia *f*, imminence
inminente *a* imminent
inmiscuir *vt* to mix; *vr* meddle. May be conjugated regularly or like **huir**
inmisión *f*, inspiration
inmobiliario *a* concerning real estate
inmoble *a* immovable; motionless, immobile, stationary; *fig* unshakable, unflinching
inmoderación *f*, immoderateness, excess
inmoderado *a* immoderate; unrestrained, excessive
inmodestia *f*, immodesty
inmodesto *a* immodest
inmolación *f*, immolation
inmolador (-ra) *a* sacrificing. *n* immolator
inmolar *vt* to immolate; *fig* sacrifice, give up; *vr fig* sacrifice oneself
inmoral *a* immoral
inmoralidad *f*, immorality
inmortal *a* immortal
inmortalidad *f*, immortality
inmortalizar *vt* to immortalize
inmotivado *a* unfounded, without reason
inmoto *a* motionless, stationary
inmóvil *a* immovable, fixed; motionless; steadfast, constant
inmovilidad *f*, immovability; immobility; constancy, steadfastness
inmovilizar *vt* to immobilize
inmueble *m*, *law* immovable estate
inmundicia *f*, filth, nastiness; dirt; rubbish, refuse; obscenity, indecency
inmundo *a* dirty, filthy; obscene, indecent; unclean
inmune *a* exempt; *med* immune
inmunidad *f*, exemption; immunity
inmunizar *vt* to immunize
inmutabilidad *f*, immutability, changelessness; imperturbability
inmutable *a* immutable, unchangeable; imperturbable
inmutación *f*, change, alteration, difference
inmutar *vt* to change, alter, vary; *vr* change one's expression (through fear, etc.)
innato *a* innate; inherent; instinctive, inborn
innatural *a* unnatural
innavegable *a* unnavigable; unseaworthy (of ships)
innecesario *a* unnecessary
innegable *a* undeniable; indisputable, irrefutable
innoble *a* plebeian; ignoble
innocuo *a* harmless, innocuous
innovación *f*, innovation
innovador (-ra) *a* innovatory. *n* innovator
innovar *vt* to introduce innovations
innumerabilidad *f*, countless number, multitude
innumerable *a* innumerable, countless
innúmero *a* countless, innumerable
inobediencia *f*, disobedience
inobediente *a* disobedient
inobjetable *a*, *Lat. Am.* unobjectionable
inobservable *a* unobservable

inobservancia *f*, inobservance
inobservante *a* unobservant
inocencia *f*, innocence; simplicity, candor; harmlessness
inocentada *f*, *inf* naïve remark or action; fool's trap; practical joke
inocente *a* innocent; candid, simple; harmless; easily deceived
inocentón *a inf* extremely credulous and easily taken in
inocuidad *f*, innocuousness
inoculación *f*, inoculation
inoculador *m*, inoculator
inocular *vt* to inoculate; pervert, corrupt; contaminate
inodoro *a* odorless. *m*, toilet, lavatory
inofensivo *a* inoffensive, harmless
inolvidable *a* unforgettable
inoperable *a* inoperable
inopia *f*, poverty; scarcity
inopinable *a* indisputable, unquestionable
inopinado *a* unexpected, sudden
inoportunidad *f*, inopportuneness, unseasonableness; unsuitability
inoportuno *a* inopportune, untimely
inordenado *a* inordinate, immoderate, excessive
inorgánico *a* inorganic
inoxidable *a* rustless
inquebrantable *a* unbreakable; final, irrevocable
inquietador (-ra) *a* disturbing. *n* disturber
inquietar *vt* to disturb; trouble, make anxious, worry; *vr* be disquieted, worry
inquieto *a* restless; unquiet; fidgety; disturbed, anxious, worried, uneasy
inquietud *f*, restlessness; uneasiness; worry; trouble, care, anxiety
inquilinato *m*, tenancy; rent; *law* lease; (rental) rates
inquilino (-na) *n* tenant; lessee; *Chile* tenant farmer
inquina *f*, dislike, grudge
inquinar *vt* to contaminate, corrupt, infect
inquiridor (-ra) *a* inquiring, examining. *n* investigator
inquirir *vt irr* to inquire; examine, look into. See **adquirir**
inquisición *f*, inquiry, investigation; *ecc* Inquisition
inquisidor (-ra) *a* inquiring, investigating. *n* investigator. *m*, *ecc* inquisitor; judge
inquisitorial *a* inquisitorial
insaciabilidad *f*, insatiability
insaciable *a* insatiable
insalubre *a* unhealthy
insanable *a* incurable
insania *f*, insanity
insano *a* insane, mad
inscribir *vt* to inscribe; record; enter (a name on a list, etc.), register, enroll; engrave; *geom* inscribe. *Past Part.* **inscrito**
inscripción *f*, inscription; record, enrollment; registration; government bond
insecable *a* undryable, undrying
insecticida *a* insecticide
insecto *m*, insect
inseguridad *f*, insecurity
inseguro *a* insecure; unsafe; uncertain
insensatez *f*, folly, foolishness
insensato *a* foolish, stupid, mad
insensibilidad *f*, insensibility; imperception; callousness, hard-heartedness
insensibilizar *vt* to make insensible (to sensations)
insensible *a* insensible; imperceptive, insensitive; unconscious, senseless; imperceptible, inappreciable; callous
inseparabilidad *f*, inseparability
inseparable *a* inseparable
insepulto *a* unburied (of the dead)
inserción *f*, insertion; interpolation; grafting
insertar *vt* to insert; introduce; interpolate; *vr* (*bot zool*) become attached
inservible *a* useless; unfit; unsuitable

insidia f, insidiousness; snare, ambush
insidiador (-ra) a ensnaring. n schemer, ambusher
insidiar vt to waylay, ambush; set a trap for; scheme against
insidioso a insidious; treacherous; scheming, guileful
insigne a illustrious, famous; distinguished
insignia f, symbol; badge; token; banner, standard; naut pennant; pl insignia
insignificancia f, meaninglessness; unimportance, triviality; insignificance, insufficiency
insignificante a meaningless; unimportant; insignificant, small
insinuación f, insinuation; hint; implication; suggestion
insinuador a insinuating; suggestive, implicative
insinuar vt to insinuate; suggest, hint; vr ingratiate oneself; creep in
insinuativo a insinuative
insipidez f, tastelessness, insipidity; fig dullness
insípido a tasteless, insipid; dull, uninteresting, boring
insistencia f, insistence
insistente a insistent
insistir vi (with en or sobre) to lay stress upon, insist on; persist in
ínsito a inherent, innate
insociabilidad f, unsociability
insociable a unsociable
insolación f, insolation, exposure to the sun; sunstroke
insolar vt to expose to the sun's rays; vr contract sunstroke
insoldable a unsolderable, unable to be soldered
insolencia f, insolence; impudence, impertinence
insolentarse vr to grow insolent; be impudent
insolente a insolent; impudent, impertinent
insólito a unaccustomed; infrequent; unusual; unexpected
insolubilidad f, insolubility
insoluble a insoluble
insoluto a unpaid, outstanding
insolvencia f, insolvency
insolvente a insolvent
insomne a sleepless
insomnio m, insomnia
insondable a unfathomable, bottomless; inscrutable, secret
insoportable a intolerable, unbearable
insostenible a indefensible; arbitrary, baseless
inspección f, inspection; supervision; examination; inspectorship; inspector's office
inspeccionar vt to inspect; survey, examine. **i. una casa,** to view a house
inspector (-ra) a inspecting, examining. n supervisor. m, inspector; surveyor
inspiración f, inspiration; inhalation
inspirador (-ra) a inspiring. n inspirer
inspirar vt to breathe in, inhale; blow (of the wind); inspire; vr be inspired; (with en) find inspiration in, imitate
instabilidad f, instability; unsteadiness; shakiness; unreliability, inconstancy
instable a unstable
instalación f, plant, apparatus; erection, fitting; induction; installment, settling in
instalador (-ra) n fitter; one who installs (electricity, etc.)
instalar vt to appoint, induct; erect (a plant, etc.); install, put in; lay on; elec wire; vr install oneself, settle down
instancia f, instance; argument; suggestion; supplication; request; formal petition. **de primera i.,** in the first instance, firstly
instantánea f, phot snapshot
instantáneo a instantaneous
instante a urgent. m, second; instant, moment. **a cada i.,** every minute; frequently. **al i.,** at once, immediately. **por instantes,** continually; immediately

instar vt to press; persuade; insist upon; vi be urgent, press
instauración f, restoration; renewal; renovation; Lat. Am. establishment
instaurador (-ra) a renovating, renewing. n restorer, renovator
instaurar vt to restore; repair; renovate, renew; Lat. Am. establish, set up
instaurativo a restorative
instigación f, instigation, incitement
instigador (-ra) n instigator
instigar vt to instigate, incite; induce
instilación f, instillment, pouring drop by drop; inculcation, implantation
instilar vt chem instill; implant, inculcate
instintivo a instinctive
instinto m, instinct. **por i.,** by instinct, naturally
institución f, setting up, establishment; institution; teaching, instruction; pl institutes, digest
institucional a institutional
instituir vt irr to found, establish; institute; instruct, teach. See **huir**
instituto m, institute; secondary school. **i. de belleza,** beauty parlor, beauty salon
institutor m, founder, instituter; tutor
institutriz f, governess
instrucción f, teaching, instruction; knowledge, learning; education; pl orders; rules; instruction. **i. primaria,** primary education. **i. pública,** public education
instructivo a instructive
instructor (-ra) a instructive. n instructor
instruido a cultured, well-educated; knowledgeable
instruir vt irr to teach, instruct; train; inform, acquaint with; law formulate. See **huir**
instrumentación f, mus instrumentation
instrumentista mf mus instrumentalist; instrument maker
instrumento m, tool, implement; machine, apparatus; mus instrument; means, medium; legal document. **i. de cuerda,** string instrument. **i. de percusión,** percussion instrument. **i. de viento,** wind instrument
insuave a unpleasant (to the senses); rough
insubordinación f, insubordination, rebellion
insubordinado a insubordinate, unruly
insubordinar vt to rouse to rebellion; vr become insubordinate, rebel
insubsistencia f, instability
insubsistente a unstable; groundless, unfounded
insubstancial a insubstantial, unreal, illusory; pointless, worthless, superficial
insubstancialidad f, superficiality, worthlessness
insuficiencia f, insufficiency, shortage; incompetence, inefficiency
insuficiente a insufficient, scarce, inadequate
insufrible a insufferable, unbearable, intolerable
insular a insular
insulina f, insulin
insulsez f, insipidity, tastelessness; dullness; tediousness
insulso a insipid, tasteless; tedious; dull
insultador (-ra) a insulting. n insulter
insultante a insulting
insultar vt to insult; call names; vr take offense
insulto m, insult; sudden attack; sudden illness, fit; Argentina fit of fainting; Mexico indigestion
insumable a incalculable; excessive, exorbitant
insumergible a unsinkable
insumiso a rebellious
insuperable a insuperable
insurgente a insurgent, rebellious. m, rebel
insurrección f, insurrection
insurreccionar vt to incite to rebellion; vr rise in rebellion
insurrecto (-ta) n rebel
insustancial a See **insubstancial**

insustituible *a* indispensable

intacto *a* untouched; intact, uninjured; whole, entire; complete; pure

intachable *a* irreproachable; impeccable, perfect

intangibilidad *f,* intangibility

intangible *a* intangible

integración *f,* integration

integrar *vt* to integrate; *com* repay

integridad *f,* wholeness; completeness; integrity, probity, honesty; virginity

íntegro *a* integral, whole; upright, honest

integumento *m,* integument; pretense, simulation

intelectiva *f,* understanding

intelecto *m,* intellect

intelectual *a* intellectual

intelectualidad *f,* understanding, intellectuality; intelligentsia

inteligencia *f,* intelligence; intellect; mental alertness; mind; meaning, sense; experience, skill; understanding, secret agreement; information, knowledge; Intelligence, Secret Service

inteligente *a* intelligent; clever; skillful; capable, competent

inteligible *a* intelligible; understandable; able to be heard

intemperancia *f,* intemperance, lack of moderation

intemperante *a* intemperate

intemperie *f,* stormy weather. **a la i.,** at the mercy of the elements; in the open air

intempestivo *a* inopportune, ill-timed

intención *f,* intention; determination; purpose; viciousness (of animals); caution. *inf* **con segunda i.,** with a double meaning, slyly

intencionado *a* intentioned, disposed

intencional *a* intentional, designed, premeditated

intendencia *f,* management; supervision; administration; *pol* intendancy; *Argentina* mayoralty. *mil* **cuerpo de i.,** quartermaster corps, army supply corps

intendente *m,* director; manager; *pol* intendant; *Argentina* mayor. **i. de ejército,** quartermaster general

intensar *vt* to intensify

intensidad *f,* intensity; ardor; vehemence

intensificar *vt* to intensify

intensivo *a* intensive

intenso *a* intense; ardent; fervent, vehement

intentar *vt* to intend, mean; propose; try, endeavor; initiate. **i. fortuna,** to try one's luck

intento *m,* intention, determination; purpose. **de i.,** on purpose; knowingly

intentona *f, inf* foolhardy attempt

interacción *f,* interaction; reciprocal effect; *chem* reaction

intercalación *f,* interpolation; insertion

intercalar *vt* to intercalate; interpolate, include, insert

intercambiable *a* interchangeable

intercambio *m,* interchange

interceder *vi* to intercede, plead for

interceptación *f,* interception

interceptar *vt* to intercept; interrupt; hinder

intercesión *f,* intercession

intercesor (-ra) *a* interceding. *n* intercessor

intercutáneo *a* intercutaneous

interdecir *vt irr* to forbid, prohibit. See **decir**

interdicción *f,* interdiction, prohibition

interdicto *m,* interdict

interés *m,* interest; yield, profit; advantage; *com* interest; inclination, fondness; attraction, fascination; *pl* money matters. **i. compuesto,** compound interest. **intereses creados,** bonds of interest; vested interests

interesado *a* involved, concerned; biased; selfish

interesante *a* interesting

interesar(se) *vi* and *vr* to be interested; *vt com* invest; interest

interfecto (-ta) *n law* victim (of murder)

interferencia *f, phys* interference

interfoliar *vt* to interleave (of books)

ínterin *m,* interim. *adv* meanwhile, in the meantime

interinamente *adv* in the interim; provisionally

interinar *vt* to discharge (duties) provisionally, act temporarily as

interino *a* acting, provisional, temporary

interior *a* interior; inner; inside; indoor; inland; internal, domestic (policies, etc.); inward, spiritual. *m,* interior, inside; mind, soul; *pl* entrails

interiorizar *vt, Lat. Am.* to investigate closely, look into, scrutinize

interjección *f, gram* interjection, exclamation

interlinear *vt* to write between the lines; *print* lead

interlocución *f,* dialogue, conversation

interlocutorio *a law* interlocutory

intérlope *a* interloping. *mf* interloper

interludio *m,* interlude

intermediario (-ia) *a* and *n* intermediary. *m, com* middleman

intermedio *a* intermediate. *m,* interim; *theat* interval. **por i. de,** through, by the mediation of

intermisión *f,* intermission, interval

intermitencia *f,* intermittence

intermitente *a* intermittent

intermitir *vt* to interrupt, suspend, discontinue

internación *f,* going inside; penetration; taking into

internacional *a* international

internacionalismo *m,* internationalism

internacionalista *mf* internationalist

internacionalización *f,* internationalization

internado *m,* boarding school

internamiento *m,* internment

internar *vt* to take or send inland; *vi* penetrate; *vr (with en)* go into the interior of (a country); get into the confidence of; study deeply (a subject)

interno (-na) *a* interior; internal; inner; inside; boarding (student). *n* boarding school student; *med* intern

internuncio *m, ecc* internuncio; interlocutor; representative

interoceánico *a* interoceanic

interpaginar *vt* to interleave (of books)

interpelación *f, law* interpellation; appeal

interpelar *vt law* to interpellate; appeal to, ask protection from

interpolación *f,* interpolation, insertion; interruption

interpolador (-ra) *n* interpolator; interrupter

interpolar *vt* to interpolate; interject

interponer *vt* to interpose, insert, intervene; designate as an arbitrator; *vr* intervene. See **poner**

interposición *f,* interposition; intervention; mediation, arbitration

interpresa *f, mil* surprise attack

interpretación *f,* interpretation; translation

interpretador (-ra) *a* interpretative. *n* interpreter

interpretar *vt* to interpret; translate; attribute; expound, explain. **i. mal,** to misconstrue; translate wrongly

intérprete *mf* interpreter

interregno *m,* interregnum; *Lat. Am.* interim. **i. parlamentario,** parliamentary recess

interrogación *f,* interrogation, question; *gram* question mark

interrogador (-ra) *n* questioner

interrogante *a* interrogating. *m, print* question mark

interrogar *vt* to interrogate, question

interrogativo *a* interrogative

interrogatorio *m,* interrogatory

interrumpir *vt* to interrupt; hinder, obstruct; *elec* break contact

interrupción *f,* interruption; stoppage (of work); *elec* break

interruptor (-ra) *a* interrupting. *n* interrupter. *m, elec* switch, interruptor. **i. de dos direcciones,** *elec* two-way switch

intersticio *m,* interstice, crack, crevice; interval, intervening space

intervalo *m,* interval

intervención f, intervention; mediation, intercession; auditing (of accounts)

intervenir vi irr to take part (in); intervene, interfere; arbitrate, mediate; happen, occur; vt com audit. See **venir**

interventor (-ra) a intervening. n one who intervenes. m, auditor; inspector

intervocálico a intervocalic

intestado (-da) a and n law intestate

intestino a intestinal. m, intestine

íntima, intimación f, intimation, notification

intimar vt to intimate; inform, notify; vr penetrate; vr and vi become intimate or friendly

intimidación f, intimidation, terrorization

intimidad f, intimacy

intimidar vt to intimidate, terrorize, cow

íntimo a intimate; deep-seated, inward; private, personal

intitular vt to give a title to, entitle, call; vr call oneself

intolerable a intolerable; unbearable

intolerancia f, narrow-mindedness, intolerance, bigotry

intolerante a narrow-minded, illiberal; med intolerant

intonso a long-haired, unshorn; boorish, ignorant

intoxicación f, poisoning

intoxicar vt to poison

intraducible a untranslatable

intramuros adv within the town walls, within the city

intranquilidad f, disquiet, restlessness; anxiety

intranquilizador a disquieting, perturbing

intranquilizar vt to disquiet, make uneasy, worry

intranquilo a uneasy, anxious

intransferible a untransferable, not transferable

intransigencia f, intolerance, intransigence

intransigente a intolerant, intransigent

intransitable a impassable; unsurmountable

intransitivo a intransitive

intrascendente a, Lat. Am. unimportant

intratable a intractable; impassable; rough; unsociable, difficult

intrauterino a intrauterine

intravenoso a intravenous

intrepidez f, intrepidity, dauntlessness, gallantry

intrépido a intrepid, dauntless, gallant

intriga f, scheme, intrigue; entanglement; lit plot

intrigante mf intriguer, schemer

intrigar vi to intrigue, scheme, plot; **intrigarse** Lat. Am. to be intrigued, be puzzled

intrincación f, intricacy

intrincado a intricate

intrincar vt to complicate; obscure, confuse

intríngulis m, inf ulterior motive

intrínseco a intrinsic, inherent; essential

introducción f, introduction

introducir vt irr to introduce; insert; fit in; drive in; present, introduce; bring into use; cause, occasion; show in, bring in; vr interfere, meddle; enter. See **conducir**

introductor (-ra) n introducer

introito m, preamble, introduction; ecc introit; (theat ant) prologue

intromisión f, intromission; interference; geol intrusion

introspección f, introspection

introverso a introvert

intruso (-sa) a intruding, intrusive. n intruder

intuición f, intuition

intuir vt irr to know by intuition. See **huir**

intuitivo a intuitive

intuito m, glance, look, view

inulto a poet unavenged, unpunished

inundación f, flood; flooding; excess, superabundance

inundar vt to flood; swamp; fig inundate, overwhelm

inurbanidad f, discourtesy, impoliteness

inurbano a discourteous, uncivil, impolite

inusitado a unusual, unaccustomed; rare

inútil a useless

inutilidad f, uselessness

inutilizar vt to render useless; disable, incapacitate; spoil, damage

invadeable a impassable, unfordable

invadir vt to invade

invaginación f, invagination

invalidación f, invalidation

invalidar vt to invalidate

invalidez f, invalidity; disablement; infirmity

inválido (-da) a weak, infirm; invalid, null; disabled. n invalid; disabled soldier

invariable a invariable

invariación f, invariableness

invariante m, invariant

invasión f, invasion, encroachment, incursion

invasor (-ra) a invading; med attacking. n invader

invectiva f, invective

invencibilidad f, invincibility

invencible a invincible

invención f, invention, discovery; deception, fabrication, lie; creative imagination; finding (e.g. **i. de la Santa Cruz,** Invention of the Holy Cross)

invencionero (-ra) n inventor; schemer, deceiver

invendible a unsalable

inventar vt to invent; create; imagine; concoct, fabricate (lies, etc.)

inventariar vt to make an inventory of; com take stock of

inventario m, inventory; com stock taking

inventiva f, inventiveness, ingenuity; creativeness

inventivo a inventive

invento m, See **invención**

inventor (-ra) n inventor, discoverer; liar, storyteller

inverecundia f, impertinence, impudence

inverecundo a shameless, brazen

inverisímil a See **inverosímil**

invernáculo m, greenhouse; conservatory

invernada f, winter season; hibernation; Lat. Am. winter pasture

invernadero m, winter quarters; greenhouse

invernal a wintry; winter

invernar vi irr to winter; hibernate; be wintertime. See **acertar**

invernizo a wintry, winter

inverosímil a unlikely, improbable

inverosimilitud f, improbability

inversamente adv inversely

inverso a inverse; inverted

inversor, -a mf, Lat. Am. invester

invertebrado a and m, invertebrate

invertir vt irr to invert, transpose; reverse; com invest; spend (time). See **sentir**

investidura f, investiture

investigación f, investigation, examination; research; inquiry

investigador (-ra) a investigating. n investigator; researcher

investigar vt to investigate, examine; research on

investir vt irr to confer upon, decorate with; invest, appoint. See **pedir**

inveterado a inveterate

inviable a unfeasible

invicto a invincible; unconquered

invierno m, winter; rainy season

inviolabilidad f, inviolability. **i. parlamentaria,** parliamentary immunity

inviolable a inviolable; infallible

inviolado a inviolate

invisibilidad f, invisibility

invisible a invisible; m, Argentina hairpin; Mexico hairnet

invitación f, invitation

invitado (-da) n guest

invitar vt to invite; urge, request; allure, attract

invocación f, invocation

invocador (-ra) n invoker

invocar vt to invoke

involuntariedad f, involuntariness

involuntario *a* involuntary

invulnerabilidad *f*, invulnerability

invulnerable *a* invulnerable

inyección *f*, injection

inyectado *a* bloodshot (of eyes)

inyectar *vt* to inject

ipecacuana *f*, ipecac

iperita *f*, mustard gas

ir *vi irr* to go; bet (e.g. **Van cinco pesetas que no lo hace,** I bet five pesetas he doesn't do it); be different, be changed (e.g. **¡Qué diferencia va entre esto y aquello!** What a difference there is between this and that!); suit, be becoming, fit (e.g. **El vestido no te va bien,** The dress doesn't suit you); extend; lead, go in the direction of (e.g. **Este camino va a Lérida,** This road leads to Lerida); get along, do, proceed, be (e.g. **¿Cómo te va estos días?** How are you getting along these days?); come (e.g. **Ahora voy,** I'm coming now); *math* carry (e.g. **siete y van cuatro,** seven, and four to carry); *math* leave (e.g. **De quince a seis van nueve,** Six from fifteen leaves nine). With a gerund, **ir** indicates the continuation of the action, or may mean to become or to grow (e.g. **Iremos andando hacia el mar,** We shall go on walking toward the sea, or **Entre tanto iba amaneciendo,** In the meanwhile it was growing light). With a past participle, **ir** means 'to be' (e.g. **Voy encantado de lo que he visto,** I am delighted with what I have seen). With *prep a* + *infin*, **ir** means to prepare (to do) or to intend (to do) or to be on the point of doing (e.g. **Van a cantar la canción que te gusta,** They are going (or preparing) to sing the song you like). With *prep a* + *noun*, **ir** indicates destination (e.g. **Voy al cine,** I'm going to the cinema. **¿A dónde vamos?** Where are we going to?). **ir** + *con* means to go in the company of, or to do a thing in a certain manner (e.g. **Hemos de ir con cuidado,** We must go carefully). **ir** + *en* means to concern, interest (e.g. **¿Qué le va a él en este asunto?** What has this affair to do with him?). **ir** + *por* means to follow the career of, become (e.g. **Juan va por abogado,** John is going to be a lawyer). It also means to go and bring, or to go for (e.g. **Iré por agua,** I shall go and bring (or for) water). *vr* to go away, leave, depart; die; leak (of liquids); evaporate; overbalance, slip (e.g. **Se le fueron los pies,** He slipped (and lost his balance)); be worn out, grow old, deteriorate; be incontinent; *fig inf* **írsele a uno una cosa,** not to notice or not to understand a thing. *naut* **irse a pique,** to founder, sink. **Se le fueron los ojos tras María,** He couldn't keep his eyes off Mary. **i. a caballo,** to ride, go on horseback. **i. adelante,** to go on ahead, head; *fig inf* forge ahead, go ahead. **i. al cuartel,** to go into the army. **i. a una,** to cooperate in. **i. bien** *fig inf* to go on well; be well. **i. de brazo,** to walk arm in arm. **i. de compras,** to go shopping. **i. de juerga** *inf* to go on a binge. **i. de bicicleta** *or* **en coche,** to go by bicycle or to ride (in a car or carriage). **i. por,** to do things in order, take one thing at a time. *fig inf* **i. tirando,** to carry on, manage. **¿Cómo le va?** How are things with you? How are you getting along? *inf* **no irle ni venirle a uno nada en un asunto,** to be not in the least concerned in (an affair). **¡Qué va!** Rubbish! Nothing of the sort! **¿Quién va?** *mil* Who goes there? **Vamos,** Let's go (also used as an exclamation: Good gracious! You don't say so! Well!) **Vamos a ver . . . ,** Let's see. . . . **¡Vaya!** What a . . . !; Come now! Never mind! **¡Vaya a paseo!** *or* **¡Vaya con su música a otra parte!** Take yourself off! Get out! **¡Vaya con Dios!** God keep you! Good-bye! *Pres. Ind.* **voy, vas, va, vamos, váis, van.** *Pres. Part.* **yendo.** *Preterite* **fui, fuiste, fue, fuimos, fuisteis, fueron.** *Imperf.* **iba,** etc. *Pres. Subjunc.* **vaya,** etc. *Imperf. Subjunc.* **fuese,** etc. *Imperat.* **vé**

ira *f*, wrath, anger; vengeance; raging, fury (of elements); *pl* cruelties, acts of vengeance

iracundia *f*, irascibility, irritability; anger

iracundo *a* irascible, irritable, choleric; angry; raging, tempestuous

iranio (-ia) *a* and *n* Iranian

irascibilidad *f*, irascibility; petulance

iridiscencia *f*, iridescence

iridiscente *a* iridescent

iris *m*, rainbow; *anat* iris (of the eye)

irisación *f*, irisation

irisar *vi* to be iridescent

irlandés (-esa) *a* and *n* Irishman (woman)

Irlanda Ireland

ironía *f*, irony

irónico *a* ironical

iroqués (-esa) *a* and *n* Iroquois

irracional *a* irrational; illogical, unreasonable; *math* irrational, absurd

irracionalidad *f*, irrationality, unreasonableness

irradiación *f*, radiation, irradiation

irradiar *vt* to radiate, irradiate

irrazonable *a* unreasonable

irreal *a* unreal

irrealidad *f*, unreality

irrealizable *a* unachievable, unattainable

irrebatible *a* irrefutable, evident

irreconciliable *a* irreconcilable, intransigent

irrecuperable *a* irretrievable

irredimible *a* irredeemable

irreemplazable *a* irreplaceable

irreflexión *f*, thoughtlessness; impetuosity

irreflexivo *a* thoughtless; rash, impetuous

irreformable *a* unreformable

irrefragable *a* indisputable, unquestionable

irrefrenable *a* unmanageable, uncontrollable

irrefutable *a* irrefutable

irregular *a* irregular; infrequent, rare

irregularidad *f*, irregularity; abnormality; *inf* moral lapse

irreligión *f*, irreligion

irreligiosidad *f*, impiety, godlessness

irreligioso *a* irreligious, impious

irremediable *a* irremediable

irremediablemente *adv* unavoidably; hopelessly

irremisible *a* unpardonable, inexcusable

irremunerado *a* unremunerated, gratuitous

irreparable *a* irreparable

irreprensible *a* blameless, unexceptionable

irreprochable *a* irreproachable

irresistible *a* irresistible; ravishing

irresolución *f*, vacillation, indecision

irresoluto *a* hesitant, irresolute

irrespetuoso *a* disrespectful

irresponsabilidad *f*, irresponsibility

irresponsable *a* irresponsible

irreverencia *f*, irreverence

irreverente *a* irreverent

irrevocabilidad *f*, irrevocability, finality

irrevocable *a* irrevocable

irrigación *f*, irrigation

irrigador *m*, spray, sprinkler; *med* syringe, spray

irrigar *vt* (*med agr*) to irrigate

irrisible *a* ridiculous, laughable, absurd

irrisión *f*, derision; laughingstock

irrisorio *a* ridiculous; derisive

irritabilidad *f*, irritability, petulance, irascibility

irritable *a* irritable

irritación *f*, *med* irritation; petulance, exasperation

irritador *a* irritating; exasperating. *m*, irritant

irritante *a* irritating; exasperating

irritar *vt* to exasperate, annoy; provoke, inflame; (*med law*) irritate

írrito *a law* null, void

irrogar *vt* to occasion (damage, harm)

irrompible *a* unbreakable

irrumpir *vi* to enter violently, break in

irrupción *f*, irruption, incursion, invasion

irruptor *a* invading, attacking
isabelino *a* Isabelline (pertaining to Spanish Queen Isabella II (reigned 1830–68)); bay (of horses)
isla *f*, island; block (of houses)
islámico *a* Islamic
islamismo *m*, Islam
islamita *a* and *mf* Muslim
islandés (-esa), islándico (-ca) *a* Icelandic. *n* Icelander. *m*, Icelandic (language)
Islandia Iceland
isleño (-ña) *a* island. *n* islander; native of the Canary Islands
isleta *f*, islet
islote *m*, barren islet
isoca *f*, *Argentina* caterpillar
isométrico *a* isometric
isomorfo *a* isomorphic
isotermo *a* isothermal
isótope, isótopo *m*, isotope
israelita *mf* Israelite. *a* Israeli

istmeño (-ña) *n* native of an isthmus
ístmico *a* isthmian
istmo *m*, isthmus
Istmo de Suez, el the Suez Canal
Ítaca Ithaca
Italia Italy
italianismo *m*, Italianism
italianizar *vt* to italianize
italiano (-na) *a* and *n* Italian. *m*, Italian (language)
itálico *a* italic
iteración *f*, iteration, repetition
iterar *vt* to repeat, reiterate
iterativo *a* iterative, repetitive
itinerario *a* and *m*, itinerary
izar *vt naut* to hoist
izote *m*, yucca
izquierda *f*, left, left-hand side; *pol* left. ¡I.! *mil* Left face! **a la i.,** on the left
izquierdo *a* left, left-hand; left-handed; bent, twisted, crooked

J

jaba *f*, *Lat. Am.* basket; *Mexico* crate
jabalí *m*, wild boar
jabalina *f*, sow of wild boar; javelin
jabato *m*, young wild boar
jabón *m*, soap. **j. blando,** soft soap. **j. de olor** *or* **j. de tocador,** toilet soap. **j. de sastre,** French chalk, steatite
jabonadura *f*, soaping; *pl* soapsuds, lather
jabonar *vt* to soap; wash; *inf* dress down, scold
jaboncillo *m*, toilet soap; steatite
jabonera *f*, soapdish or box; soapwort
jabonería *f*, soap factory or shop
jabonoso *a* soapy
jaca *f*, pony; filly
jacal *m*, *Mexico* hut, shack
jácara *f*, gay, roguish ballad; song and dance
jácena *f*, *arch* beam, girder
jacinto *m*, hyacinth; jacinth. **j. de ceilán,** zircon. **j. occidental,** topaz. **j. oriental,** ruby
jaco *m*, short coat of mail; hack, jade
jactancia *f*, bragging, boasting
jactancioso (-sa) *a* boastful. *n* braggart
jactarse *vr* to brag, boast
jaculatoria *f*, ejaculatory prayer
jade *m*, *min* jade
jadeante *a* panting
jadear *vi* to pant
jadeo *m*, pant; panting; hard breathing
jaez *m*, harness (gen. *pl*); kind, sort; *pl* trappings
jaguar *m*, jaguar
jaiba *f*, *Lat. Am.* crab
jáibol *m*, *Lat. Am.* highball
jáilaif *m*, *Lat. Am.* high life
¡ja, ja, ja! *interj* Ha! ha! ha!
jalbegar *vt* to whitewash; make up the face
jalbegue *m*, whitewash
jalde *a* bright yellow
jalea *f*, jelly. **j. de membrillo,** quince jelly
jalear *vt* to encourage, urge on (by shouts, etc.)
jaleo *m*, act of encouraging dancers by clapping, shouting, etc.; Andalusian song and dance, *inf* uproar
jalón *m*, surveying rod
jamaicano (-na) *a* and *n* Jamaican
jamás *adv* never. **nunca j.,** never. **por siempre j.,** for always, forever
jamba *f*, jamb (of a door or window)
jambarse *vr*, *Lat. Am.* to overeat
jamelgo *m*, sorry nag, miserable hack
jamón *m*, ham
jamona *f*, *inf* plumpish middle-aged woman
jansenista *mf* and *a* Jansenist
Japón Japan

japonés (-esa) *a* and *n* Japanese. *m*, Japanese (language)
jaque *m*, check (in chess); braggart. **j. mate,** checkmate. **en j.,** at bay
jaquear *vt* to check (in chess); *mil* harass the enemy
jaqueca *f*, migraine, sick headache. *inf* **dar una j.,** to annoy
jarabe *m*, syrup. **j. tapatío,** Mexican hat dance
jarana *f*, roundhouse; *inf* revelry; fight, roughhouse; trick, deception
jarcia *f*, equipment; *naut* tackle, rigging (gen. *pl*); fishing tackle; *inf* heap, mixture, medley
jardín *m*, garden
jardinar *vt* to landscape
jardinera *f*, plant stand, jardiniere; open streetcar
jardinería *f*, gardening
jardinero (-ra) *n* gardener
jareta *f*, *sew* running hem; *naut* netting
jarra *f*, jar, jug. **en jarras,** arms akimbo
jarrero *m*, jug seller or manufacturer
jarrete *m*, calf (of the leg)
jarretera *f*, garter. **Orden de la J.,** Order of the Garter
jarro *m*, pitcher; jug; jar; vase
jarrón *m*, garden urn; vase
jaspe *m*, jasper
jaspeado *a* marbled, mottled; dappled; frosted (of glass)
jauja *f*, *fig* paradise, land of milk and honey
jaula *f*, cage; crate; miner's cage
jauría *f*, pack of hounds
jazmín *m*, jasmine. **j. amarillo,** yellow jasmine. **j. de la India,** gardenia
jefa *f*, forewoman; manager; leader, head
jefatura *f*, chieftainship; managership; leadership. **j. de policía,** police station or headquarters
jefe *m*, chief; head, leader; manager; *mil* commanding officer. *mil* **j. de estado mayor,** chief of staff. **j. del tren,** railroad guard
jengibre *m*, ginger
jeque *m*, sheik
jerarca *m*, hierarch
jerarquía *f*, hierarchy
jerárquico *a* hierarchical
jerez *m*, sherry
jerga *f*, thick frieze cloth; jargon
jergón *m*, straw or hay mattress, pallet; misfit (garments); *inf* fat, lazy person
Jericó Jericho
jerigonza *f*, jargon; gibberish
jeringa *f*, syringe
jeringar *vt* to inject; syringe; *inf* annoy

jeringuilla *f*, small syringe; mock orange
jeroglífico *a* hieroglyphic. *m*, hieroglyph
jersey *m*, jersey, sweater
Jerusalén Jerusalem
jesuita *m*, Jesuit
Jesús *m*, Jesus. *interj* Goodness!; Bless you! (said to someone after sneezing). **¡ay J.! ¡Alas!** *inf* **en un decir J.,** in a trice
jeta *f*, hog's snout; blubber lip; *inf* face, mug
jibia *f*, cuttlefish
jícama *f*, *Central America* sweet turnip
jícara *f*, small cup
jicote *m*, *Lat. Am.* wasp
jifa *f*, meat offal
jifia *f*, swordfish
jinete *m*, horseman, rider; horse soldier, cavalryman
jip *m*, jeep
jipijapa *f*, very fine straw. **sombrero de j.,** panama hat
jira *f*, strip of cloth; picnic; tour
jirafa *f*, giraffe
jirón *m*, rag; piece of a dress, etc.; portion of a whole
jitomate, *m*, *Mexico* tomato. See **tomate**
jiujitsu *m*, jujitsu
jocosidad *f*, pleasantry, jocularity; joke
jocoso *a* waggish; jocose, joyous
jocundidad *f*, jocundity
jocundo *a* jocund
jofaina *f*, washbowl
jónico (-ca) *a* Ionic. *n* Ionian. *m*, (metrics) Ionic foot
Jordán Jordan (river)
jornada *f*, day's journey; journey, trip; *mil* expedition; duration of a working day; opportunity; span of life; act of a drama. **a grandes jornadas,** by forced marches, rapidly
jornal *m*, day's wages or labor
jornalear *vi* to work by the day
jornalero (-ra) *n* day laborer; wage earner
joroba *f*, hump; *inf* impertinence, nuisance
jorobado (-da) *a* humpbacked. *n* hunchback
jota *f*, name of letter J; popular Spanish dance; jot, tittle (always used negatively). **no saber j.,** to be completely ignorant
joven *a* young. *mf* young man or woman
jovenzuelo (-la) *n* youngster, boy
jovialidad *f*, joviality, cheerfulness
joya *f*, jewel; present; *arch* astragal; *fig* a jewel of a person
joyería *f*, jeweler's shop or workshop
joyero *m*, jeweler; jewel box
juanete *m*, bunion; prominent cheekbone; *naut* topgallant sail
juanetudo *a* having bunions; with prominent cheekbones
jubilación *f*, retirement; pensioning off; pension
jubilado *a* retired
jubilar *vt* to pension off; excuse from certain duties; *inf* put aside as useless (things); *vr* rejoice; retire or be pensioned off
jubileo *m*, jubilee
júbilo *m*, rejoicing, merriment. **j. de vivir,** joie de vivre
jubiloso *a* jubilant, happy
jubón *m*, doublet; bodice
judaico *a* Judaic
judaísmo *m*, Judaism
judas *m*, Judas; traitor
judería *f*, Jewry
judesmo *m*, Judezmo (Romance language of Jews)
judía *f*, Jew (female); Jewish quarter, Jewish neighborhood; haricot bean. **judías verdes,** string beans
judicatura *f*, judicature; judgeship; judiciary
judío (-ía) *a* Jewish. *n* Jew. **j. errante,** wandering Jew
juego *m*, play, sport; gambling; hand (of cards); set; suite; *mech* play, working. **j. de café,** coffee set. **j. de los cientos,** piquet. **j. de manos,** sleight of hand, conjuring. **j. de naipes,** game of cards. **j. limpio,** fair play. **j. sencillo,** single (at tennis). **j. sucio,** foul play.

juegos florales, floral games, poetry contest. **juegos malabares,** juggling. **en j.,** in operation; at stake. **entrar en j.,** to come into play. **hacer j.,** to match. **hacer juegos malabares,** to juggle
juerga *f*, *inf* spree, binge. **ir de j.,** *inf* to go on a binge
jueves *m*, Thursday. **¡No es cosa del otro j.!** *inf* It's no great shakes! It's nothing to write home about!
juez *m*, judge. **j. arbitrador,** arbitrator; referee. **j. municipal,** magistrate
jugada *f*, play; playing; move, throw; *fig* bad turn
jugador (-ra) *a* gambling; playing. *n* gambler; player. **j. de manos,** conjurer
jugar *vi irr* to play; frolic; take part in a game; gamble; make a move (in a game); *mech* work; handle (a weapon); *com* intervene; *vt* play (a match); bet; handle (a weapon); risk. **j. el lance,** *fig* to play one's cards well. **j. limpio,** to play fair; *fig inf* be straightforward. **j. sucio,** to play foul. **jugarse el todo por el todo,** to stake everything. *Pres. Ind.* **juego, juegas, juega, juegan.** *Pres. Subjunc.* **juegue, juegues, juegue, jueguen**
jugarreta *f*, *inf* bad play; dirty trick
juglar *m*, entertainer; buffoon, juggler; minstrel
juglaresco *a* pertaining to minstrels
jugo *m*, sap; juice; *fig* essence. **j. de muñeca,** elbow grease
jugosidad *f*, juiciness, succulence; *fig* pithiness
jugoso *a* juicy, succulent; *fig* pithy
juguete *m*, toy; plaything; *fig* puppet
juguetear *vi* to frolic, gambol
jugueteo *m*, gamboling; play, dalliance
juguetería *f*, toy trade; toy shop
juguetón *a* playful
juicio *m*, judgment; wisdom, prudence; sanity, right mind; opinion; horoscope. **j. final,** Last Judgment. **j. sano,** right mind. **asentar el j.,** to settle down, become sensible. **estar fuera de j.,** to be insane. **pedir en j.,** to sue at law
juicioso *a* judicious; prudent
julepear *vt*, *Lat. Am.* to get scared, be terrified
julio *m*, July; *elec* joule
jumento *m*, ass; beast of burden
juncal *a* reedy; rushy; *inf* slim, lissome
juncar *m*, reedy ground
junco *m*, *bot* rush, reed; *naut* junk
junio *m*, June
junquillo *m*, jonquil; *arch* reed molding
junta *f*, joint; assembly, council; committee; union, association; session, sitting; entirety, whole; board, management. **j. de comercio,** board of trade. **j. directiva,** managerial board
juntamente *adv* jointly; simultaneously
juntar *vt* to join, unite (*with prep a or con*); couple; assemble; amass; leave ajar (door); *vr* (*with con*) frequent company of; meet; join; copulate
junto *a* united, together. *adv* (*with prep a*) near; *adv* together, simultaneously. **en j.,** altogether, in all
juntura *f*, joining; joint; seam; juncture
jura *f*, solemn oath; swearing
jurado *m*, jury; jury
juramentar *vt* to swear in; *vr* take an oath
juramento *m*, oath; curse, imprecation. **j. falso,** perjury, **prestar j.,** to take an oath
jurar *vt* to swear an oath; swear allegiance; *vi* curse, be profane
jurídico *a* juridical, legal
jurisconsulto *m*, jurisconsult
jurisdicción *f*, *law* jurisdiction; boundary; authority
jurisprudencia *f*, jurisprudence
jurista *mf* jurist
justa *f*, joust; tournament; contest
justar *vi* to joust
justicia *f*, justice; equity, right; penalty, punishment; righteousness; court of justice; *inf* death penalty, execution. **administrar j.,** to dispense justice

justiciero *a* just
justificable *a* justifiable
justificación *f*, justification, impartiality, fairness; convincing proof
justificar *vt* to justify, vindicate; adjust, regulate; prove innocent; *vr* justify oneself; prove one's innocence
justipreciar *vt* to appraise, value
justiprecio *m*, appraisement, valuation

justo *a* just; righteous, virtuous; exact, accurate; tight-fitting, close. *adv* justly; exactly; tightly
juvenil *a* young
juventud *f*, youthfulness, youth; younger generation
juzgado *m*, court of law; jurisdiction; judgeship
juzgar *vt* to judge, pass sentence on; decide, consider

K

ka *f*, name of the letter K
káiser *m*, kaiser
kan *m*, khan
kantiano *a* Kantian
Kenia Kenya
kermese *f*, kermis, festival
kerosén *m*, kerosene
kilo *prefix* meaning a thousand. *m*, *abb* kilogram
kilociclo *m*, *elec* kilocycle

kilogramo *m*, kilogram (2.17 lb.)
kilolitro *m*, kiloliter
kilometraje *m*, number of kilometers; mileage
kilométrico *a* kilometric. **billete k.,** tourist ticket
kilómetro *m*, kilometer (about $\frac{5}{8}$ mile)
kilovatio *m*, *elec* kilowatt
kiosco *m*, kiosk
klaxon *m*, *Mexico* horn

L

la *def art. f, sing* the (e.g. **la mesa,** the table). **la** is replaced by el *m, sing* before feminine nouns beginning with stressed *a* or *ha* (e.g. **el hambre,** hunger). **la** is sometimes used before names of famous women (e.g. **la Juana de Arco, la Melba** (Joan of Arc, Melba)) and is generally not translated. *pers pron acc f sing* her; it (e.g. **La veo venir,** I see her coming). *dem. pron* followed by *de*, or by *que* introducing relative clause, that of, that which, the one that, she who (e.g. **La casa está lejos de la en que escribo,** The house is far from the one in which I write). **la de** is used familiarly for Mrs. (e.g. **la de Jiménez,** Mrs. Jimenez). **la** means some, any, one, as substitution for noun already given (e.g. **Su hija lo haría si la tuviera,** Her daughter would do it if she had one)
lábaro *m*, labarum, standard
laberíntico *a* labyrinthine
laberinto *m*, labyrinth; *fig* tangle, complication; *anat* labyrinth of the ear
labia *f*, *inf* blarney, gab
labial *a* labial
labihendido *a* harelipped
labio *m*, lip; rim, edge. **l. leporino,** harelip. **cerrar los labios,** to close one's lips; keep silent
labor *f*, work, toil; sewing; needlework; husbandry, farming; silkworm egg; *min* working; trimming; plowing, harrowing; *Central America* small farm
laborable *a* workable; cultivable, tillable. **día l.,** workday
laborar *vt* to work; till; plow; construct; *vi* scheme, plot, plan; *Central America* work
laboratorio *m*, laboratory
laborear *vt* to work; till, cultivate; *naut* reeve
laboreo *m*, tilling, cultivation; working, development (of mines, etc.)
laboriosidad *f*, laboriousness, diligence
laborioso *a* industrious, diligent; laborious, tedious, hard
laborista *a* and *mf* belonging to the Labor Party
labra *f*, stonecutting; carving or working (metal, stone, or wood)
labrada *f*, fallow land ready for sowing
labradero *a* workable; cultivable, tillable
labrado *a* and *past part* worked; fashioned; carved; embroidered; figured, patterned. *m*, (gen. *pl*) cultivated ground
labrador *m*, laborer, worker; farmer; peasant
labradora *f*, peasant girl; farm girl
labradoresco, labradoril *a* rustic, peasant, farming

labrandera *f*, seamstress
labrantío *a* tillable, cultivable. *m*, farming
labranza *f*, tillage, cultivation; farm; farmland; farming; employment, work
labrar *vt* to work, do; carve; fashion, construct, make; *agr* cultivate, till; plow; embroider; sew; bring about, cause; *vi fig* impress deeply, leave a strong impression
labriego (-ga) *n* agricultural laborer; peasant
laca *f*, lac; lacquer, varnish; *art* lake (pigment)
lacayo *m*, groom; lackey; footman
lacear *vt sew* to trim with bows; tie, lace; snare, trap; *Lat. Am.* lasso
laceración *f*, laceration
lacerado *a* unhappy, unfortunate; leprous
lacerar *vt* to lacerate, mangle, tear; distress, wound the feelings of
lacería *f*, poverty, misery; toil, drudgery; trouble, affliction
lacero *m*, cowboy, one who uses a lasso; poacher
lacio *a* drooping, limp; withered, faded; straight (hair)
lacónico *a* laconic; concise; Laconian
lacra *f*, aftereffect, trace (of illness); vice; fault; *Lat. Am.* sore, ulcer
lacrar *vt* to impair the health; infect with an illness; injure, prejudice (the interests, etc.); seal with sealing wax
lacre *m*, sealing wax. *a* red
lacrimoso *a* tearful, lachrymose
lactancia *f*, lactation
lactar *vt* to suckle; feed with milk; *vi* take or drink milk
lácteo *a* lacteal; milky
ladear *vt* to incline; tilt; turn aside, twist; skirt, pass close to; reach by a roundabout way, go indirectly to; *vr* tilt; be in favor of, incline to; be equal to
ladeo *m*, tilt; sloping; turning aside
ladera *f*, slope, incline; hillside
ladería *f*, terrace on a hillside
ladero *a* lateral; *Argentina* helper
ladilla *f*, crab louse
ladino *a* eloquent; versatile linguistically; wily, crafty; *m*, Ladino (variety of Judezmo)
lado *m*, side; edge, margin; slope, declivity; faction, party; side, flank; face (of a coin); *fig* aspect, view; line of descent; means, way; favor, protection; *pl* helpers, protectors; advisers. **al l.,** near at hand. *inf* **dar de l. (a),** to cool off, fall out with. **dejar a un l. (una cosa),** to omit, pass over (a thing). **mirar de l.** or **de medio l.,** to look upon with disapproval; steal a look at

ladrar *vi* to bark; *inf* threaten without hurting
ladrido *m*, bark, barking; slander, gossip
ladrillado *m*, brick floor or pavement
ladrillar *vt* to floor or pave with bricks. *m*, brickyard; brickkiln
ladrillo *m*, brick; tile
ladrón (-ona) *a* robbing, thieving. *n* thief, robber; burglar. *m.* **l. de corazones,** ladykiller
ladronera *f*, thieves' den; thieving, pilfering; strongbox
lagar *m*, wine or olive press
lagarta *f*, female lizard; *inf* she-serpent, cunning female
lagartera *f*, lizard hole
lagartija *f*, wall lizard, small lizard
lagarto *m*, lizard; *inf* sly, artful person, fox; *inf* insignia of Spanish Military Order of Santiago
lago *m*, lake
lagotear *vi* *inf* to wheedle, play up to
lagotería *f*, wheedling, coaxing, flattery
lágrima *f*, tear; drop (of liquid); exudation, ozzing (from trees)
lagrimal *a* lachrymal
lagrimear *vi* to shed tears
lagrimeo *m*, weeping, crying; watering of the eyes
lagrimoso *a* tearful; watery (of eyes); sad, tragic
laguna *f*, small lake, lagoon; lacuna; gap, hiatus
lagunoso *a* boggy, marshy
laicismo *m*, secularism
laico *a* lay, secular
laja *f*, *Lat. Am.* flagstone, slab
lama *f*, ooze, slime. *m*, lama, Buddhist priest
lamaísmo *m*, lamaism
lambioche *a*, *Mexico* cringing, fawning
lameculos *mf* *inf* toady
lamedura *f*, licking; lapping
lamentable *a* lamentable
lamentación *f*, lamentation; lament
lamentador (-ra) *a* lamenting, wailing. *n* wailer, mourner
lamentar *vt* to mourn, lament, bewail; *vr* bemoan, bewail
lamento *m*, lament
lamentoso *a* lamenting, afflicted; lamentable
lamer *vt* to lick; pass the tongue over; touch lightly; lap
lámina *f*, sheet (of metal); lamina; engraving; illustration, picture; engraving plate
laminación *f*, lamination, rolling (of metals)
laminado *a* laminate; rolled (metals). *m*, rolling (of metals)
laminador *m*, rolling mill (for metals)
laminar *a* laminate; laminated. *vt* to roll (metals); laminate; lick
lampa *f*, *Chile, Peru* hoe
lámpara *f*, lamp; radiance, light, luminous body; grease spot. **l. de los mineros** *or* **l. de seguridad,** safety lamp. **l. de soldar,** blowpipe. **l. termiónica,** *rad* thermionic valve. **atizar la l.,** to trim the lamp; *inf* refill drinking glasses
lamparería *f*, lamp factory; lamp shop
lamparero (-ra), *n* lamparista *mf* lamplighter; lamp maker or seller
lamparilla *f*, night-light; *bot* aspen; small lamp
lamparón *m*, scrofula, king's evil; tumor (disease of horses)
lampazo *m*, *Lat. Am.* (floor) mop
lampiño *a* beardless, clean-shaven; smooth-faced; *bot* nonhirsute
lampista *mf* See **lamparero**
lamprea *f*, lamprey
lana *f*, wool; fleece; woolen garments or cloth; woolen trade (gen. *pl*)
lanar *a* wool; wool-bearing. **ganado l.,** sheep
lance *m*, throw, cast; casting a fishing line; catch of fish; crisis, difficult moment; *lit* episode; quarrel; move (in a game). *fig* **l. apretado,** difficult position, tight corner. **l. de fortuna,** chance, fate. **l. de honor,** affair of honor; duel

lancear *vt* to wound with a lance; lance
lancero *m*, *mil* lancer; *pl* lancers (dance and music)
lanceta *f*, lancet; *Lat. Am.* goad
lancha *f*, *naut* launch; lighter; ship's boat; small boat; flagstone. **l. bombardera** *or* **l. cañonera,** gunboat. **l. de salvamento,** ship's lifeboat. **l. escampavía,** patrol boat
lancinar *vt* *med* to lance
landa *f*, lande
landó *m*, landau
lanero *a* woolen. *m*, wool merchant; wool warehouse
langosta *f*, locust; lobster. **l. migratoria,** locust
langostín *m*, crayfish
languidecer *vi* *ir* to languish, pine. See **conocer**
languidez *f*, lassitude, inertia; languor
lánguido *a* listless, weak, languid; halfhearted; languishing, languorous
lanolina *f*, lanolin
lanosidad *f*, woolliness; down (on leaves, etc.)
lanoso, lanudo *a* woolly
lanza *f*, lance, spear; lancer; nozzle (of a hosepipe). **correr lanzas,** to joust (in a tournament). **estar con la l. en ristre,** to have the lance in rest; be prepared or ready. *inf* **ser una l.,** to be very clever
lanzabombas *m*, (*aer nav*) bomb release
lanzada *f*, lance or spear thrust
lanzadera *f*, weaver's shuttle; sewing machine shuttle. *inf* **parecer una l.,** to be constantly on the go
lanzador (-ra) *m*, batsman. *n* thrower, caster, tosser
lanzallamas *m*, flamethrower
lanzamiento *m*, throwing; cast, throw; *law* dispossession; *naut* launching
lanzaminas *m*, minelayer
lanzar *vt* to throw, cast, hurl; *naut* launch; vomit; *law* dispossess; *agr* take root; *vr* hurl oneself, rush; take (to), embark (upon)
lanzatorpedos (tubo) *m*, torpedo tube
lañar *vt* to clamp; clean fish (for salting)
lapa *f*, barnacle, limpet; *Mexico* scrounger
lapicera *f*, *Argentina* ballpoint (pen)
lapicero *m*, pencil holder, pencil case; mechanical pencil
lápida *f*, memorial tablet; gravestone
lapidar *vt* to stone, lapidate; throw stones at
lapidario *a* lapidary
lapislázuli *m*, lapis lazuli
lápiz *m*, graphite; pencil; crayon. **l. para los labios,** lipstick
lapizar *m*, graphite mine. *vt* to pencil
lapón (-ona) *a* Lappish. *n* Laplander. *m*, Sami (language)
lapso *m*, lapse, period, passage; slip, error, failure
laquear *vt* to lacquer, paint
lardear *vt* *cul* to baste
lardo *m*, lard; animal fat
lardoso *a* greasy; fat; oily
larga *f*, longest billiard cue; delay (gen. *pl*). **a la l.,** in the long run
largamente *adv* fully, at length; generously; widely, extensively; comfortably
largar *vt* to slacken, loosen; *naut* unfurl; set at liberty; *fig* *inf* let fly (oaths, etc.); administer (blows, etc.); *vr* *inf* quit, leave (in a hurry or secretly); *naut* set sail
largo *a* long; generous, liberal; abundant, plentiful; protracted; prolonged; expeditious; *pl* many long (e.g. **por largos años,** for many long years). *m*, *mus* largo; length. *inf* **¡L. de aquí!** Get out! **a la larga,** in length; eventually, finally; slowly; with many digressions. **a lo l.,** lengthwise; along the length (of); in the distance, far off; along, the length (of). *fig* **ponerse de l.,** to make one's debut in society; come of age
largor *m*, **largura** *f*, length
largucho, -a *a*, *Lat. Am.* lanky
largueza *f*, length; generosity, munificence
largura *f*, length
laringe *f*, larynx
laríngeo *a* laryngeal

laringitis *f,* laryngitis

larva *f,* larva; worm, grub; specter, phantom

las *def art. f pl,* of **la**. *the. pers pron acc f pl,* of **la,** them

lascivia *f,* lasciviousness

lascivo *a* lascivious, lewd; wanton

lasitud *f,* lassitude, weariness, exhaustion

laso *a* weary, exhausted; weak; untwisted (of silk, etc.)

lástima *f,* compassion, pity; pitiful sight; complaint, lamentation. **dar l.,** to cause pity. **Es l.,** It's a pity. **tener l. (a** *or* **de) to be sorry for (persons)**

lastimador *a* harmful, injurious; painful

lastimadura *f, Lat. Am.* injury, wound

lastimar *vt* to hurt, harm, injure; pity; *fig* wound, distress; *vr (with de)* be sorry for or about; complain, lament

lastimero *a* pitiful; mournful; injurious, harmful

lastimoso *a* pitiful, heartbreaking; mournful

lastrar *vt* to ballast

lastre *m,* ballast; good sense, prudence

lata *f,* can, tin; tin plate; can of food. **en l.,** canned, tinned (of food). *inf* **Es una l.,** It's a bore, It's an awful nuisance

latamente *adv* extensively, at length; broadly

latente *a* latent

lateral *a* lateral

látex *m,* latex

latido *m,* yelp, bark; beat; throb; palpitation

latifundios *m pl,* latifundia (large agricultural estates)

latigazo *m,* lash; crack of a whip; sudden blow of fate; *inf* draft (of wine, etc.); harsh scolding; *naut* jerk or flapping (of sails)

látigo *m,* whip, lash; cinch, girth of a saddle

latín *m,* Latin. **bajo l.,** low Latin. *inf* **saber l.,** to know the score; be smart

latinajo *m, inf* bad Latin

latinismo *m,* Latinism

latinista *mf* Latinist

latinizar *vt* to latinize; *vi inf* use Latin phrases

latino *a* Latin; lateen sail

latinoamericano (-na) *a* and *n* Latin-American

latir *vi* to yelp, howl; bark; throb, palpitate, beat **me late que . . .** *Mexico,* I have a hunch that . . .

latitud *f,* latitude; area, extent; breadth

latitudinario *a* latitudinarian

lato *a* extensive; large; broad (of word meanings)

latón *m,* brass

latonería *f,* brassworks; brass shop

latoso *a* boring, troublesome, annoying

latrocinio *m,* larceny

latvio (-ia) *a* and *n* Latvian

laúd *m,* lute

laudable *a* praiseworthy, laudable

laudatorio *a* laudatory

laurear *vt* to crown with laurel; honor, reward

laurel *m,* bay tree. **l. cerezo,** laurel. **l. rosa,** rosebay, oleander

láureo *a* laurel

lauréola *f,* laurel wreath

lauro *m,* bay tree; glory, triumph

Lausana Lausanne

lava *f,* lava

lavable *a* washable

lavabo *m,* washstand; cloakroom, lavatory

lavada *f,* load of wash, load

lavadedos *m,* fingerbowl

lavadero *m,* washing place; laundry

lavado *m,* washing; cleaning; wash. **l. al seco,** dry cleaning

lavadura *f,* washing

lavamanos *m,* washstand; lavatory

lavamiento *m,* washing, cleansing, ablution

lavanda *f,* lavender

lavandera *f,* laundress; washerwoman

lavandería *f,* laundry

lavandero *m,* laundry; laundryman

lavaplatos *m,* dishwasher; *Chile, Mexico* (kitchen) sink

lavar *vt* to wash; *fig* wipe out, purify; paint in watercolors. **l. al seco,** to dry-clean

lavativa *f,* enema; syringe, clyster; *inf* nuisance, bore

lavatorio *m,* washing, lavation; *ecc* lavabo; lavatory, washing place; *ecc* maundy

lavazas *f pl,* dirty soapy water

laxante *a* and *m,* laxative

laxar *vt* to loosen, relax; soften

laxitud *f,* laxity

laxo *a* lax; slack

laya *f, agr* spade; kind, sort, class

layar *vt agr* to fork

lazar *vt* to lasso

lazareto *m,* leper hospital; quarantine hospital

lazarillo *m,* boy who guides a blind person

lázaro *m,* lazar, beggar

lazo *m,* bow; knot of ribbons; tie; ornamental tree; figure (in dancing); lasso; rope, bond; lace (of a shoe); *fig* trap, snare; bond, obligation; slipknot. **l. corredizo,** running knot. *fig inf* **armar l.,** to set a trap. *inf* **caer en el l.,** to fall into the trap, be deceived

le *pers pron dat m,* or *f, 3rd pers sing* to him, to her, to it, to you (e.g. **María le dio el perro,** Mary gave him (her, you) the dog). Clarity may require the addition of **a él, a ella, a usted** (e.g. **Le dio el perro a ella,** etc.). *pers pron acc m, 3rd pers sing* him (e.g. **Le mandé a casa,** I sent him home)

leal *a* loyal; faithful (animals)

lealtad *f, agr* loyalty; faithfulness; sincerity, truth

lebrel *m,* greyhound

lección *f,* reading; lesson; oral test; warning, example. **l. práctica,** object lesson. **dar l.,** to give a lesson. **tomar la l.,** to hear a lesson

leccionista *mf* private teacher, coach, tutor

lechas *f pl,* soft roe; milt

leche *f,* milk; milky fluid of some plants and seeds; *Lat. Am.* good luck. *inf* **estar con la l. en los labios,** to be young and inexperienced

lechera *f,* milkmaid; milk can or jug; *Lat. Am.* cow

lechería *f,* dairy; dairy shop; *Lat. Am.* meanness

lechero (-ra) *a* dairy; milk; milky; milch, milk-giving. *n* milk seller. **industria lechera,** dairy farming

lecho *m,* bed; couch; animal's bed, litter; riverbed; bottom of the sea; layer; *geol* stratum

lechón *m,* suckling pig; hog; *inf* slovenly man

lechosa *f, Dominican Republic, Venezuela,* papaya

lechoso *a* milky

lechudo, -a *a, Lat. Am.* lucky

lechuga *f,* lettuce; frill, flounce. *inf* **como una l.,** as fresh as a daisy

lechuguero (-ra) *n* lettuce seller

lechuguilla *f,* ruff; ruche

lechuguina *f, inf* affected, overdressed young woman

lechuguino *m,* lettuce plant; *inf* young blood, gallant; *inf* foppish young man

lechuza *f,* barn owl

lector (-ra) *n* reader; lecturer

lectura *f,* reading; lecture; culture, knowledge

ledo *a* happy, content

leer *vt irr* to read; explain, interpret; teach; take part in an oral test. See **creer**

lega *f, ecc* lay sister

legación *f, ecc* legateship; legation

legado *m,* legacy; legate

legajo *m,* bundle, docket; file

legal *a* legal; legitimate; upright, trustworthy

legalidad *f,* legality

legalización *f,* legalization

legalizar *vt* to legalize

legamente *adv* ignorantly, stupidly

légamo *m,* mud, slime

legamoso *a* slimy

legañoso *a* bleary-eyed

legar *vt* to bequeath; send as a legate

legatario (-ia) *n* legatee, one to whom a legacy is bequeathed

legendario *a* legendary
legibilidad *f*, legibility
legible *a* legible
legión *f*, legion
legionario *a* and *m*, legionary
legislación *f*, legislation
legislador (-ra) *a* legislative. *n* legislator
legislar *vi* to legislate
legislativo *a* legislative
legislatura *f*, legislature
legista *mf* jurist; student of law
legítima *f*, portion of a married man's estate that cannot be willed away from his wife and children
legitimación *f*, legitimation
legitimar *vt* to legitimize
legitimidad *f*, legitimacy
legítimo *a* legitimate; real, true
lego *a* lay, secular. *m*, layman
legua *f*, league (approximately 5.573 meters). **a la l., de cien leguas, desde media l.,** from afar
legumbre *f*, pulse; vegetable
leída *f*, *Lat. Am.* reading. **de una leída** in one reading, at one go
leído *a* well-read
leila *f*, nocturnal Moorish merrymaking or dance
lejanía *f*, distance
lejano *a* distant, remote, far off
lejía *f*, lye; bleaching solution; *inf* dressing-down, scolding
lejos *adv* far off, far, distant. *m*, perspective, view from afar; *art* background. **a lo l.,** far off, in the distance. **de** *or* **desde l.,** from afar, from a distance
lelo *a* stupid; fatuous, inane
lema *m*, chapter heading; argument, summary; motto; theme, subject
lémur *m*, lemur
lencería *f*, linen goods; linen merchant's shop; linen closet
lencero *m*, linen merchant
lene *a* smooth, soft; kind, sweet, gentle; lightweight
lengua *f*, *anat* tongue; mother tongue, language; clapper of a bell; information. *mf* spokes. **l. de escorpión** *or* **mala l.,** scandalmonger, backbiter. **l. de fuego,** *ecc* tongue of fire, flame. **l. del agua,** waterline, tidemark. **l. de oc,** langue d'oc. **l. de oil,** langue d'oïl. **l. de tierra,** neck of land, promontory. **l. viva,** modern language. *inf* **andar en lenguas,** to be on every lip, be famous. *inf* **hacerse lenguas de,** to praise to the skies. *inf* **irse (a uno) la l.,** to be indiscreet, talk too much. **poner l.** *or* **lenguas en,** to gossip about. *inf* **tener mucha l.,** to be very talkative. **tomar l.** *or* **lenguas,** to find out about, inform oneself on
lenguado *m*, *icht* sole
lenguaje *m*, language; style; speech, idiom. **l. vulgar,** common speech
lengüeta *f*, *dim* little tongue; *mus* tongue (of wind instruments); barb (of an arrow); needle (of a balance)
lengüeterías *Lat. Am.* gossip
lenidad *f*, lenience, indulgence, mercy
lenitivo *a* lenitive; soothing. *m*, *med* lenitive; *fig* balm (of sorrow, etc.)
lente *m*, lens; *pl* eyeglasses. **l. de aumento,** magnifying glass
lenteja *f*, lentil; lentil plant
lentejuela *f*, sequin
lentitud *f*, lentitude; slowness, deliberation
lento *a* slow, deliberate; sluggish, heavy; *med* glutinous, adhesive
leña *f*, firewood; *inf* beating, birching. *fig* **echar l. al fuego,** to add fuel to the flame. *fig* **llevar l. al monte,** to carry coals to Newcastle
leñador (-ra) *n* woodcutter; firewood dealer
leñera *f*, woodpile; woodshed
leño *m*, wooden log; wood, timber; *poet* ship; *inf* blockhead
leñoso *a* woody, ligneous

león *m*, lion. *ast* Leo; valiant man; *Lat. Am.* puma. **l. marino,** sea lion
leona *f*, lioness; *Chile* confusion, mixup
leonera *f*, lion cage; lion's den; *inf* gambling den; *inf* lumber room; *Mexico* whore house
leonero (-ra) *n* lionkeeper; *inf* keeper of a gambling house
leonés (-esa) *a* and *n* Leonese
leopardo *m*, leopard
leperada *f*, *Central America, Mexico* coarse remark
lepra *f*, leprosy
leproso *a* leprous
lerdo *a* slow, lumbering (gen. horses); stupid, slow-witted, dull
les *pers pron dat 3rd pers pl mf*, to them (e.g. **Les dimos las flores,** We gave them flowers. **Les hablé del asunto,** I spoke to them about the matter)
lesbio (-ia) *a* and *n* lesbian
lesión *f*, lesion, wound; *fig* injury
lesionar *vt* to wound; *fig* injure
lesna *f*, awl
leso *a* wounded, hurt; offensive, injurious; *fig* unbalanced, perturbed (of the mind); *Lat. Am.* dumb, stupid. **crimen de lesa majestad,** crime of lèse-majesté
letal *a* lethal; deadly
letanía *f*, *ecc* litany
letargia *f*, *med* lethargy
letárgico *a* lethargic
letargo *m*, lethargy; indifference, apathy
letra *f*, letter (of alphabet); *print* type; penmanship, hand; *fig* letter, literal meaning; words (of a song); inscription; *com* bill, draft; cunning, shrewdness; *pl* learning, knowledge. **l. abierta,** *com* open credit. **l. de cambio,** *com* bill of exchange. **l. gótica,** Gothic characters. **l. itálica,** italics. **l. mayúscula,** capital letter. **l. paladial,** palatal. **facultad de letras,** faculty of arts. **La l. con sangre entra,** Learning is acquired with pain. **primeras letras,** early education, first letters
letrado *a* learned, educated; *inf* presumptuous; pedantic. *m*, lawyer
letrero *m*, label; inscription; poster, bill; sign, indicator. **l. luminoso,** illuminated sign
letrilla *f*, short poem, often set to music
letrina *f*, latrine
leva *f*, *naut* weighing anchor; *mil* levy, forced enrolment; tappet; *mech* lever; *mech* cam; *inf* **irse a l. y a monte,** to flee, beat it, quit
levadizo *a* able to be raised or lowered (bridges). **puente l.,** drawbridge
levadura *f*, leaven, yeast; rising (of bread)
levantada *f*, act of rising from bed
levantamiento *m*, raising, lifting; rebellion, revolt; ennoblement, elevation; settlement of accounts
levantar *vt* to raise (lift); pick up; build, construct; cancel, remove; encourage, rouse; recruit, enlist; cut (cards); leave, abandon; survey; disturb (game); produce, raise (a swelling); found, institute; increase (prices); raise (the voice); *fig* ennoble, elevate; cause, occasion; libel, accuse falsely; *vr* rise; get up; stand up; stand out, be prominent; rebel; leave one's bed after an illness. **l. bandera,** to rebel. **l. el campo,** to break camp. **levantarse del izquierdo,** *inf* to get out of bed on the wrong side
levante *m*, east; Levant; east wind
levantino (-na) *a* and *n* Levantine
levar *vt* *naut* to weigh anchor; *vr* set sail
leve *a* light (in weight); unimportant, trifling
levedad *f*, lightness (in weight); unimportance, levity, flippancy
leviatán *m*, leviathan
levita *m*, Levite; deacon. *f*, frock coat
levitación *f*, levitation
levítico *a* Levitical. *m*, Leviticus
levitón *m*, frock coat
léxico *m*, lexicon

lexicografía *f,* lexicography

lexicógrafo *m,* lexicographer

lexicólogo *m,* lexicologist

ley *f,* law; precept; regulation, rule; doctrine; loyalty, faithfulness; affection, love; legal standard (weights, measures, quality); ratio of gold or silver in coins, jewelry; statute, ordinance; *pl* the Law. **l. de préstamo y arriendo,** Lend-Lease Act. **ley suntuaria,** sumptuary law. *inf* **a la l.,** with care and decorum. **a l. de caballero,** on the word of a gentleman. **de buena l.,** *a* excellent; *adv* genuinely; in good faith. **de mala l.,** *a* disreputable, base; *adv* in bad faith

leyenda *f,* legend; inscription; story, tale

leyente *a* reading. *mf* reader

lezna *f,* awl

lía *f,* plaited esparto rope; *pl* lees, dregs

liar *vt* to fasten or tie up; wrap up, parcel; roll (a cigarette); *inf* entangle, embroil; *vr* take a lover, enter on a liaison. *inf* **liarlas,** to quit, sneak off; *inf* kick the bucket, die

libación *f,* libation

Líbano, el Lebanon

libar *vt* to suck; perform a libation; sip, taste; sacrifice

libelista *mf* libeler

libelo *m,* libel; *law* petition

libélula *f,* dragonfly

liberación *f,* liberation, freeing; receipt, quittance; *law* reconveyance (of mortgages)

liberador (-ra) *a* liberating, freeing. *n* liberator

liberal *a* generous, openhanded; liberal, tolerant; learned (of professions). *a* and *mf pol* liberal

liberalidad *f,* generosity, magnanimity

liberalismo *m,* liberalism

liberalizar *vt* to liberalize, make liberal

liberar *vt* to liberate

libérrimo *a sup* extremely free, most free

libertad *f,* liberty, freedom; independence; privilege, right (gen. *pl*); exemption; licentiousness; forwardness, familiarity; naturalness, ease of manner; facility, capacity; immunity. **l. caucional,** freedom on bail, release on bail. **l. de cultos,** freedom of worship; religious toleration. **l. vigilada,** *law* probation. **poner en l.,** to set at liberty; (*with de*) *fig* free from

libertador (-ra) *a* liberating, freeing. *n* liberator, deliverer

libertar *vt* to liberate, free; save, deliver; exempt

libertario (-ia) *a* anarchistic. *n* anarchist

libertinaje *m,* libertinage, licentiousness

libertino (-na) *a* debauched, licentious. *m,* libertine. *n* child of a freed slave

liberto (-ta) *n* freed slave, freedman

Libia Libya

libídine *f,* lust

libidinoso *a* libidinous, lustful

libio (-ia) *a* and *n* Libyan

libra *f,* pound (measure, coinage); *ast* Libra. **l. esterlina,** pound sterling. **l. medicinal,** pound troy

libración *f,* oscillation; *ast* libration

librador (-ra) *a* freeing, liberating. *n* deliverer, liberator. *m,* com drawer (of bill of exchange, etc.)

libramiento *m,* liberation, deliverance; *com* delivery; order of payment

libranza *f, com* draft. **l. de correos, l. postal** *Lat. Am.* (postal) money order

librar *vt* to liberate, free; protect (from misfortune); *com* draw (a draft); *com* deliver; place confidence in; issue, enact; *vi* bring forth children; *vr* (*with de*) escape from; get rid of

libre *a* free; at liberty, disengaged; unhampered, untrammeled; independent; bold, brazen; dissolute, vicious; exempt; vacant, unoccupied; unmarried; clear, free; mutinous, rebellious; isolated, remote; innocent; unharmed; *Mexico, Venezuela* taxi. **l. cambio,** free trade

librea *f,* livery

librecambio *m,* free trade

librecambista *a* free trade. *mf* free trader

librepensador (-ra) *a* freethinking. *n* freethinker

librepensamiento *m,* free thought

librera *f, Lat. Am.* bookcase

librería *f,* bookshop; book trade, bookselling; bookcase

librero *m,* bookseller; *Lat. Am.* bookcase. **l. anticuario,** antiquarian bookseller; rare-book dealer

libreta *f, cul* 1-lb. loaf; notebook; passbook, bankbook

libretista *mf* librettist

libreto *m,* libretto

librillo *m, dim* small book; book of cigarette papers; tub, pail; *zool* omasum

libro *m,* book; *mus* libretto; *zool* omasum. **l. copiador,** *com* letter book. **l. de actas,** minute book. **l. de caja,** *com* cash book. **l. de cheques,** checkbook. **l. de facturas,** *com* invoice book. **l. de reclamaciones,** complaint book. **l. de texto,** textbook. **l. diario,** *com* daybook. **l. mayor,** ledger. **l. talonario,** receipt book. *fig inf* **hacer l. nuevo,** to turn over a new leaf; introduce innovations

licencia *f,* permission, license; licentiousness; boldness, insolence; *univ* bachelor's degree, licentiate. **l. absoluta,** *mil* discharge. **l. de manejar** *Lat. Am.* driver's license

licenciado (-da) *a* pedantic; free, exempt; licensed. *n univ* bachelor; licentiate. *m,* discharged soldier

licenciar *vt* to allow, permit; license; dismiss, discharge; confer degree of bachelor or licentiate; *mil* discharge; *vr* become licentious; receive bachelor's degree or licentiate

licenciatura *f,* degree of licentiate or bachelor; graduation as such; licentiate course of study

licencioso *a* licentious, dissolute

liceo *m,* lyceum; *Lat. Am.* secondary school, high school

licitación *f,* bidding (at auction)

licitador *m,* bidder (at auction); *Lat. Am.* auctioneer

licitar *vt* to bid for (at auction)

lícito *a* permissible, lawful

licor *m,* liquor, alcoholic drink; liquid

licorera *f,* liqueur set; decanter

licuadora *f,* blender

licuar *vt* to liquefy

lid *f,* combat, fight; dispute, controversy. **en buena l.,** in fair fight; by fair means

líder *m,* leader; chief

lidia *f,* fighting; bullfight

lidiador (-ra) *n* combatant, fighter

lidiar *vi* to fight; *fig* struggle; (*with contra or con*) oppose, fight against; *vt* fight (a bull). **¡Cuánto tienen que l. con . . . !** *fig* What a struggle they have with . . . !

liebre *f,* hare

liendre *f,* nit

lienza *f,* narrow strip (of cloth)

lienzo *m,* linen; cotton; cambric; hemp cloth; *art* canvas

liga *f,* garter; bandage; birdlime; mixture, blend; *met* alloy; alliance, coalition; league (football, etc.)

ligación *f,* tying; binding; union

ligado *m, mus* legato; *mus* tie

ligadura *f,* bond, tie; binding, fastening; *fig* shackle, link; (*surg mus*) ligature; *naut* lashing

ligamento *m,* tie, bond; mixture; *anat* ligament

ligar *vt* to tie, bind; *met* alloy; join, connect; render impotent by sorcery; *mus* slur (notes); *vr* ally, join together; *fig* bind oneself. **l. cabos,** to put two and two together

ligazón *f,* fastening; union; bond

ligereza *f,* lightness (of weight); swiftness, nimbleness; fickleness; tactless remark, indiscretion

ligero *a* light (in weight); swift, nimble; light (sleep); unimportant, insignificant; easily digested (food); thin (fabrics, etc.); fickle, changeable. **l. de cascos,** frivolous, gay. **a la ligera,** lightly; quickly; without fuss. **de l.,** impetuously, thoughtlessly; easily, with ease

lignito *m,* lignite

lija *f,* dogfish; sandpaper

lijar *vt* to sandpaper

lila *f,* lilac bush and flower; lilac color. *a inf* foolish, vain

liliputiense *a* and *mf* Lilliputian

lima *f,* sweet lime, citron fruit; lime tree; file (tool); filing, polishing

limadura *f,* filing; polishing; *pl* filings

limar *vt* to file, smooth with a file; *fig* touch up, polish

limazo *m,* slime, viscosity (especially of snails, etc.)

limbo *m,* limbo; edge, hem; (*ast bot*) limb; limb (of a quadrant, etc.). *inf* **estar en el l.,** to be bewildered or abstracted

limen *m, poet* threshold; *psy* limen

limeño (-ña) *a* and *n* native of or belonging to Lima (Peru)

limero (-ra) *n* seller of sweet limes. *m,* sweet lime tree (citron)

limitación *f,* limitation; limit, extent, bound; district, area

limitado *a* dull-witted, limited

limitar *vt* to limit; curb, restrict; bound

límite *m,* limit, extent; boundary, border; end, confine

limítrofe *a* bordering, contiguous

limo *m,* mud, mire, slime; *Lat. Am.* lime tree

limón *m,* lemon; lemon tree

limonada *f,* lemonade. **l. seca,** lemonade powder

limonar *m,* lemon grove

limonero (-ra) *n* lemon seller. *m,* lemon tree

limosna *f,* alms

limosnear *vi* to beg, ask alms

limosnero, -a *a* charitable, generous. *a* charitable, generous. *mf* almoner; *Lat. Am.* beggar

limoso *a* slimy, muddy

limpiabarros *m,* shoe scraper

limpiabotas *m,* bootblack (person)

limpiachimeneas *m,* chimney-sweep

limpiador (-ra) *a* cleaning. *n* cleaner

limpiadura *f,* cleaning; *pl* rubbish

limpiamanos *m, Central America, Mexico* towel

limpiamente *adv* cleanly; dexterously, neatly; sincerely, candidly; generously, charitably

limpiametales *m,* metal polish

limpiaparabrisas *m,* windshield wiper

limpiapipas *m,* pipe cleaner

limpiar *vt* to clean; *fig* cleanse, clear; empty, free (from); *agr* thin out; *inf* steal, pinch; *inf* win (gambling); *vr* clean oneself

limpiauñas *m,* orange stick (for fingernails)

limpidez *f, poet* limpidity

límpido *a poet* limpid

limpieza *f,* cleanliness; cleaning; chastity; purity; altruism; uprightness, integrity; neatness, tidiness; dexterity, skill, precision; fair play

limpio *a* clean; pure, unalloyed, unmixed; neat, tidy; pure-blooded; unharmed, free. **en l.,** in substance; as a fair copy; clearly; *com* net

linaje *m,* lineage, family; offspring; kind; sort, quality

linajudo (-da) *a* highborn. *n* noble, aristocrat; one who alleges his noble descent

linaza *f,* linseed

lince *m,* lynx; *Mexico* wild cat; *fig.* fox, crafty person

linchamiento *m,* lynching

linchar *vt* to lynch

lindar *vi* to run together, be contiguous

linde *mf* limit, extent; boundary

lindero *a* bordering, contiguous. *m,* boundary. *inf* **con linderos y arrabales,** with many digressions

lindeza *f,* beauty, loveliness; witticism; *pl* (*inf ironical*) insults

lindo *a* lovely, beautiful; perfect, exquisite. *m, inf* fop (gen. **lindo don Diego**)

línea *f,* line; kind, class; ancestry, lineage; limit, extent; *mil* file; equator. **l. aérea,** airline. *naut* **l. de flotación,** waterline. **l. de toque,** touchline (in soccer). **l. recta,** direct line (of descent)

lineal *a* lineal; *computers* on-line

lineamento *m,* lineament

linear *a* linear. *vt* to line, mark with lines; *art* sketch

linfa *f, med* lymph; vaccine; *poet* water

linfático *a* lymphatic

lingote *m,* ingot; bar (of iron). **l. de fundición,** pig iron

lingüista *mf* linguist

lingüística *f,* linguistics

lingüístico *a* linguistic

linimento *m,* liniment

lino *m, bot* flax; linen; *poet* ship's sail, canvas

linóleo *m,* linoleum

linotipia *f,* linotype

linterna *f,* lantern; lighthouse; lamp. **l. sorda,** dark lantern

lío *m,* bundle; *inf* muddle, imbroglio; *inf* liaison, amour. *inf* **armar un l.,** to make a muddle, cause trouble. *inf* **hacerse un l.,** to get in a fix; get in a muddle

liquen *m,* lichen

liquidable *a* liquefiable

liquidación *f,* liquefaction; *com* clearance, sale; *com* settlement

liquidar *vt* to liquefy; *com* settle; *com* liquidate; finish; *vr* liquefy

liquidez *f,* liquidness

líquido *a* liquid; *com* net. *m,* liquid; *com* net profit

lira *f, mus* lyre; *ast* Lyra; lira (coin)

lírica *f,* lyrical verse, lyric

lírico *a* lyrical

lirio *m,* lily. **l. cárdeno,** yellow flag (iris). **l. de los valles,** lily of the valley

lirismo *m,* lyricism

lirón *m, zool* dormouse; *inf* sleepyhead

Lisboa Lisbon

lisiado *a* lame, crippled

lisiar *vt* to cripple, lame; *vr* be disabled; be lame

liso *a* smooth; sleek; unadorned, plain; unicolored

lisonja *f,* flattery, adulation

lisonjear *vt* to flatter; fawn upon; *fig* delight (the ear). **lisonjearse de . . . ,** to flatter oneself on . . .

lisonjero (-ra) *a* flattering; sweet, pleasant (sounds). *n* flatterer

lista *f,* strip of cloth; streak; rib; stripe; catalog, list. **l. de correos,** general delivery, poste restante. **l. de platos,** bill of fare; *Mexico* **l. de raya,** payroll. **pasar l.,** to call the roll; check the list

listado *a* streaked; striped; ribbed

listo *a* clever; expeditious, diligent; ready, prepared

listón *m,* ribbon; strip (of wood)

lisura *f,* smoothness; sleekness; flatness; sincerity

lisurero, -a *a, Peru* cheeky, impudent

litera *f,* litter; *naut* berth

literal *a* literal

literario *a* literary

literatear *vi* to write on literary subjects

literato (-ta) *a* literary. *n* writer, litterateur

literatura *f,* literature

litigación *f,* litigation

litigante *mf* litigant

litigar *vt* to litigate; *vi* dispute, argue

litigio *m,* lawsuit; dispute, argument

litigioso *a* litigious; quarrelsome, disputatious

litisexpensas *f pl, law* costs of a suit; legal expenses

litografía *f,* lithography

litografiar *vt* to lithograph

litoral *a* and *m,* littoral

litro *m,* liter; *Chile* coarse woolen cloth

Lituania Lithuania

liturgia *f,* liturgy

litúrgico *a* liturgical

liviandad *f,* lightness (of weight); fickleness; unimportance; frivolity; lewdness; act of folly, indiscretion

liviano *a* light weight; fickle; unimportant, trifling, frivolous; lascivious

lividez *f,* lividness

lívido *a* livid; *Lat. Am.* pale, pallid

liza *f,* list (at a tournament); arena

llaga *f,* ulcer; sore; grief, affliction; *fig* thorn in the flesh

llagar *vt* to ulcerate; make or produce sores; *fig* wound; *vr* be covered with sores

llama f, flame; ardor, vehemence; marsh; *zool* llama
llamada f, call; *mil* call-to-arms, call. **l. molestosa,** annoyance call, nuisance call
llamado a called; so-called
llamador (-ra) n caller. m, door knocker; doorbell
llamamiento m, calling; call; divine summons, inspiration; invocation, appeal; summons, convocation
llamar vt to call; invoke, call upon; summon, convoke; name; attract; vi knock (at a door); ring (a bell); vr be named, be called; *naut* veer (wind). **Se llama Pedro,** His name is Peter
llamarada f, flame, flash; blaze, flare (of anger, etc.)
llamativo a striking, showy; provocative
llamear vi to throw out flames, blaze
llampo m, *Lat. Am.* ore
llana f, mason's trowel; plain; surface of a page
llanada f, plain
llanamente adv frankly, plainly; naturally, simply; candidly, sincerely
llanero (-ra) n plain dweller
llaneza f, naturalness; candor; familiarity; simplicity (of style)
llano a flat, level; smooth, even; shallow (of receptacles); unaffected, homely, natural; plain (of dresses); manifest, evident; easy; straightforward, candid; informal; simple (of style). m, plain; level stretch of ground
llanta f, *aut* tire; rim, felloe. **l. de refacción** *Mexico* spare tire **l. de rueda,** wheel, rim
llanto m, weeping, flood of tears
llanura f, smoothness, evenness, levelness; plain
llave (de) f, key (to); spigot (of), faucet (of), tap (of); spanner, wrench; *elec* switch; clock winder; *mus* key; clef; *arch* keystone; *print* brace; *mech* wrench; lock (of a gun); tuning key; piston (of musical instruments); lock (in wrestling); *fig* key (of a problem or a study). **l. de transmisión,** sender (telegraphy). **l. inglesa,** monkey-wrench, spanner. **l. maestra,** master key, skeleton key. **echar la l.,** to lock. **torcer la l.,** to turn the key
llavero (-ra) n keeper of the keys. m, key ring. **l. de cárcel,** turnkey
llavín m, yale key, latchkey
llegada f, arrival, advent
llegar vi to arrive; last, endure; reach; achieve a purpose; be sufficient, suffice; amount (to), make; vt bring near, draw near; gather; vr come near, approach; all here. **l. a ser,** to become. **l. a un punto muerto,** to reach a deadlock. **l. hasta . . . ,** to stretch as far as . . .
llena f, spate, overflow
llenar vt to fill; occupy (a post); satisfy, please; fulfill; satiate; pervade; fill up (a form); vi be full (of the moon); vr inf stuff, overeat; *fig inf* be fed-up
lleno a full; replete; abundant; complete. m, full moon; *theat* full house; *inf* glut, abundance; perfection. **de l., de l. en l.,** entirely, completely
llenura f, abundance, plenty
lleva, llevada f, carrying, bearing
llevadero a tolerable, bearable
llevar vt to carry, transport; charge (a price); yield, produce; carry off, take away; endure, bear; persuade; guide, take; direct; wear (clothes); carry (a handbag, etc.); introduce, present; gain, achieve; manage (a horse); pass, spend (of time); (*with past part*) have (e.g. **Llevo escrita la carta,** I have written the letter); *math* carry; (*with prep. a*) surpass, excel. **l. a cabo,** to accomplish. **l. a cuestas,** to carry on one's back; support. **l. la correspondencia,** to look after the correspondence. **l. la delantera,** to take the lead. **l. luto,** to be in mourning. **l. por delante** *Argentina, Chile* to run over (e.g., a pedestrian) **llevarse bien,** to get on well, agree
llorar vi to weep, cry; drip; water (eyes); vt lament, mourn; bewail one's troubles
lloriquear vi to whine, snivel
lloriqueo m, whining, sniveling
lloro m, weeping, crying; flood of tears

llorón a weeping; sniveling, whining. m, long plume. **niño llorón,** crybaby
lloroso a tearful; grievous, sad; sorrowful
llovedizo a leaky; rainy
llover vi impers irr to rain; come in abundance (of troubles, etc.); vr leak (roofs, etc.). **l. a cántaros,** to rain in torrents, rain cats and dogs. **l. sobre mojado,** to add insult to injury. **como llovido,** unexpectedly. See **mover**
llovida f, *Lat. Am.* rain, shower
llovido m, stowaway
llovizna f, drizzle, fine rain
lloviznar vi to drizzle
lluvia f, rain; rainwater; *fig* shower; rose (of watering can) *Chile, Nicaragua* shower bath, shower
lluvioso a rainy, showery
lo def art. neut the thing, part, fact, what, that which. Used before adjectives, past participles, sometimes before nouns and adverbs (e.g. **Lo barato es caro,** Cheap things are dear (in the long run).) **Lo mío es mío, pero lo tuyo es de ambos,** What's mine is mine, but what is yours belongs to both of us. **Juan siente mucho lo ocurrido,** John is very sorry for what has happened. **a lo lejos,** in the distance). **lo . . . que,** how (e.g. **No sabes lo bueno que es,** You don't know how good he is). *pers pron acc m,* or *neut* him, it; that, it (e.g. **Lo harán mañana,** They will do it tomorrow). Means some, any, one, as substitute for noun already mentioned (e.g. **Carecemos de azúcar; no lo hay,** We are short of sugar; there isn't any). **Lo cortés no quita lo valiente,** One can be courteous and still insistent
loa f, praise, eulogy; *theat* prologue; short dramatic piece; *ant* dramatic eulogy
loable a praiseworthy
loar vt to praise; commend
lobero a wolf; wolfish
lobo (-ba) n wolf. m, (*bot anat*) lobe; *inf* drinking fit. **l. marino,** *zool* seal. *inf* **pillar un l.,** to get drunk
lóbrego a murky, dark; dismal; mournful, lugubrious
lobreguez f, obscurity, gloom, darkness
lóbulo m, lobe
locación f, *law* lease; agreement, contract
local a local. m, premises; place, spot, scene
localidad f, location; locality; place, spot; seat (in theaters, etc.)
localización f, localization, placing; place
localizar vt to localize
locamente adv insanely, madly; extraordinarily, extremely
loción f, lotion
loco (-ca) a insane, mad; rash, foolish, crazy; excessive, enormous; amazing; extraordinary; infatuated. n lunatic; rash person. *fig inf* **Es un l. de atar,** He's completely crazy!
locomoción f, locomotion
locomotor a locomotive
locomotora f, locomotive
locomóvil a and f, locomotive
locro m, *Lat. Am.* meat-and-vegetable stew
locuacidad f, loquacity
locuaz a loquacious
locución f, style of speech; phrase, idiom; *gram* locution
locuelo (-la) n madcap
locura f, insanity, lunacy; madness, fury; folly, foolishness
locutor (-ra) n (radio) announcer; commentator
locutorio m, locutory; phone booth
lodazal, lodazar m, muddy place; quagmire
lodo m, mud
lodoso a muddy
logarítmico a logarithmic
logaritmo m, logarithm
logia f, (Freemason's) lodge
lógica f, logic. *inf* **l. parda,** common sense
lógico (-ca) a logical. n logician

logística *f,* logistics

lograr *vt* to achieve, attain, obtain; enjoy; (*with infin*) succeed in; *vr* succeed in, achieve; reach perfection

logrear *vi* to borrow or lend at interest

logrero (-ra) *n* moneylender; monopolist, profiteer

logro *m,* achievement, attainment; profit, gain; usury, money-lending

loma *f,* knoll, hill

lombarda *f,* red cabbage

Lombardía Lombardy

lombardo (-da) *a* of or from Lombardy. *n* native of Lombardy (Italy). *m,* mortgage bank

lombriciento, -a *a, Lat. Am.* having worms, suffering from worms

lombriz *f,* earthworm, common worm. **l. intestinal,** intestinal worm. **l. solitaria,** tapeworm

lomo *m,* loin, back of a book; ridge between furrows; *pl* ribs; loins

lona *f,* canvas, sailcloth

lonchería *f, Lat. Am.* luncheonette, lunch counter, snack bar

Londres London

longanimidad *f,* longanimity, fortitude

longaniza *f, cul* pork sausage

longevidad *f,* longevity

longevo *a* long-lived

longísimo *a sup* **luengo** exceedingly long

longitud *f,* length; longitude. **l. de onda,** *rad* wavelength

lonja *f,* slice, rasher; *com* exchange; market; grocery store; woolen warehouse

lonjista *mf* provision merchant, grocer

lontananza *f,* distance (also *art*). **en l.,** in the distance, far off

loor *m,* praise

loquear *vi* to play the fool; romp

loro *m, orn* parrot

los *def art. m pl,* the, (e.g. **l. sombreros,** the hats). *pers. pron acc 3rd pers m pl,* them. **Tus cigarrillos no están sobre la mesa; los tengo en mi bolsillo,** Your cigarettes are not on the table; I have them in my pocket. Means some, any, ones, as substitution for noun already stated (e.g. **Los cigarros están en la caja si los hay,** The cigars are in the box, if there are any). Used demonstratively followed by *de* or *que* introducing relative clause, those of; those which, those who; the ones that (who) (e.g. **Estaba leyendo algunos libros de los que tienes en tu cuarto,** I was reading some books from among those which you have in your room)

losa *f,* flagstone; slab; tombstone

lote *m,* lot, portion, share

lotería *f,* lottery; lotto (game); lottery office

lotero (-ra) *n* seller of lottery tickets

loto *m,* lotus; lotus flower or fruit

loza *f,* porcelain, china

lozanía *f,* luxuriance (of vegetation); vigor, lustiness; arrogance

lozano *a* luxuriant, exuberant; vigorous, lusty; arrogant

lubricación *f,* lubrication

lubricante *a* lubricant

lubricar *vt* to lubricate

lúbrico *a* slippery, smooth; lascivious, lustful

lucera *f,* skylight

lucerna *f,* large chandelier; skylight

lucero *m,* evening star; any bright star; white star (on a horse's head); brilliance, radiance; *pl poet* eyes, orbs. **l. del alba,** morning star

lucha *f,* fight; struggle; wrestling match; argument, disagreement. **l. grecorromana,** wrestling. **l. igualada,** close fight. **l. libre,** catch-as-catch-can

luchador (-ra) *n* fighter; struggler

luchar *vi* to fight hand to hand; wrestle; fight; struggle; argue

lucidez *f,* brilliance, shine; lucidity, clarity

lucido *a* splendid, brilliant; sumptuous; fine, elegant

lúcido *a poet* brilliant; lucid; clear

luciente *a* bright, shining

luciérnaga *f,* glowworm

lucimiento *m,* brilliance, luster; success, triumph; elegance; display, ostentation

lucir *vi irr* to shine, scintillate; excel, outshine; be successful; *vt* illuminate; display, show off; show; *vr* dress elegantly; be successful; excel, be brilliant. *Pres. Ind.* **luzco, luces,** etc. *Pres. Subjunc.* **luzca,** etc.

lucrativo *a* lucrative

lucro *m,* gain, profit

lucroso *a* profitable

luctuoso *a* lugubrious, mournful

lucubración *f,* lucubration

ludibrio *m,* mockery, ridicule

luego *adv* immediately; afterward, later; then; soon, presently. *conjunc* therefore. **l. que,** as soon as. **desde l.,** immediately, at once; of course, naturally; in the first place. **hasta l.,** au revoir, good-by for the present

lueguito *adv Lat. Am.* at once, right away, right now; *Central America, Chile, Mexico* near, nearby

luengo *a* long

lugar *m,* place; spot; village, town, city; region, locality; office, post; passage, text; opportunity, occasion; cause, motive; place on a list; room, space; seat. **l. común,** commonplace. **en l. de,** instead of. **en primer l.,** firstly, in the first place. **hacer l.,** to make room, make way. *law* **No ha l.,** The petition is refused. **tener l.,** to take place; have the time or opportunity (to)

lugarejo *m,* hamlet

lugareño (-ña) *a* peasant, regional. *n* villager, peasant

lugarteniente *m,* lieutenant; substitute, deputy

lúgubre *a* lugubrious, dismal, mournful

luis *m,* louis (French coin)

lujo *m,* luxury; abundance, profusion. **artículos de l.,** luxury goods

lujoso *a* luxurious; abundant, profuse

lujuria *f,* lasciviousness; excess, intemperance

lujuriante *a* luxuriant, abundant, profuse

lujurioso *a* lascivious, voluptuous

lumbago *m,* lumbago

lumbre *f,* fire; light; splendor, lustre; transom window, opening, skylight; *pl* tinderbox

lumbrera *f,* luminary; skylight; dormer window; eminent authorit; *Mexico* box (in a theater or bullring)

luminar *m,* luminary (also *fig*)

luminaria *f,* illumination; fairy lamp, small light; lamp burning before the Sacrament in Catholic churches

luminosidad *f,* luminosity

luminoso *a* luminous; bright

luna *f,* moon; mirror; satellite; sheet of plate glass. **l. creciente,** new or rising moon. **l. de miel,** honeymoon. **l. llena,** full moon. **l. menguante,** waning moon. **media l.,** crescent moon

lunado *a* half-moon, crescent

lunar *m,* beauty spot; *fig* stain, blot (on reputation, etc.); blemish, slight imperfection. *a* lunar

lunático (-ca) *a* and *n* lunatic

lunes *m,* Monday

luneta *f,* lens (of eyeglasses), *theat* orchestra stall; (*arch mil*) lunette

lupa *f,* magnifying glass

lupanar *m,* brothel

lúpulo *m, bot* hop

lusitano (-na) *a* and *n* Lusitanian

lustrador *m,* polisher; *Lat. Am.* bootblack. **l. de piso,** floor polisher

lustrar *vt* to lustrate; purify; polish, burnish; roam, journey

lustre *m,* polish, sheen, gloss; glory, luster

lustro *m,* lustrum, period of five years; chandelier

lustroso *a* shining, glossy; brilliant; glorious, noble

luterano (-na) *a* and *n* Lutheran

luto *m,* mourning; grief, affliction; *pl* mourning draperies. **estar de l.,** to be in mourning

luxación *f, surg* luxation, dislocation
luz *f,* light; glow; brightness, brilliance; information, news; *fig* luminary; day, daylight; *pl* culture, learning; windows. **luces de estacionamiento,** parking lights. **a buena l.,** in a good light; in a favorable light; after due consideration. **a primera l.,** at dawn. **dar a l.,** to publish (a book); bring forth (children); reveal. **entre dos luces,** in the dawn light; in the twilight; *inf* tipsy. **media l.,** half-light, twilight

M

maca *f,* bruise or blemish on fruit; defect, flaw; *inf* fraud, swindle
macabro *a* macabre
macadán *m,* macadam
macagua *f, orn* macaw
macanudo *a* (*inf WH*) extraordinary; enormous; robust; fine, excellent
macarrones *m pl,* macaroni; *naut* stanchions
macarrrónico *a* macaronic, recondite, stylized
macarse *vr* to go bad, rot (fruit)
maceración *f,* maceration; steeping, soaking; mortification of the flesh
macerar *vt* to macerate; steep, soak; mortify
macero *m,* mace bearer
maceta *f, dim* small mace; handle, haft (of tools); stonecutter's hammer; flowerpot; *Lat. Am.* bouquet, bunch (of flowers)
macetero *m,* flowerpot stand; *Lat. Am.* flowerpot
machaca *f,* pestle; pulverizer. *mf inf* bore, tedious person
machacador (-ra) *a* crushing, pounding. *n* beater, crusher, pounder
machacar *vt* to crush, pound; *vi* importune; harp on a subject
machacón *a* tiresome, prolix
machado *m,* hatchet, ax
machete *m* machete
machetero *m,* one who cuts sugarcane with a machete
machihembrar *vt carp* to dovetail
machina *f,* derrick, crane; pile driver
macho *m,* male; male animal (he-goat, stallion, etc.); male plant; hook (of hook and eye); screw; *met* core; tap (tool); *inf* dunderhead, fool; *arch* buttress. *a* male; stupid, ignorant; vigorous, strong. **m. cabrío,** he-goat
machucadura *f,* **machucamiento** *m,* pounding, crushing; bruising
machucar *vt* to crush, pound; bruise
machucho *a* prudent, sensible; adult, mature
macicez *f,* solidity; massiveness; thickness
macilento *a* thin, lean, emaciated
macillo *m, dim* small mace; hammer (of a piano)
macis *f, cul* mace
macizar *vt* to block up, fill up
macizo *a* massive; compact, solid; *fig* well-founded, unassailable; thick; strong. *m,* solidity, compactness; bulk, volume; flowerbed; solid tire
macrocosmo *m,* macrocosm
macuco, -a *a, Lat. Am.* crafty, cunning, sly
mácula *f,* stain, spot; *fig* blot, blemish; *inf* trick, deception; *ast* macula
macuquero *m,* unauthorized worker of abandoned mines
madeja *f,* skein, hank; lock of hair; *inf* dummy, useless person
madera *f,* wood; timber; *inf* kind, sort; *mus* wind instruments. **m. contrachapada,** plywood. **m. de construcción,** timber. **maderas de sierra,** lumber wood. *inf* **ser de mala m.,** to be a ne'er-do-well
maderada *f,* lumber wood
maderaje *m,* woodwork, timber work
maderero *m,* timber merchant; lumberjack; carpenter
madería *f,* timber yard
madero *m,* wooden beam; log, piece of lumber; ship, vessel; *inf* blockhead or insensible person
madrastra *f,* stepmother; anything unpleasant
madraza *f, inf* overindulgent mother

madre *f,* mother; matron; cause, genesis; *inf* dame, mother; riverbed; dam; womb; main sewer; chief irrigation channel. **m. de familia,** mother; housewife. **m. de leche,** wet nurse. **m. política,** mother-in-law; stepmother. *inf* **sacar de m. (a),** to provoke, irritate (a person)
madreperla *f,* mother-of-pearl
madreselva *f,* honeysuckle
madrigado *a* twice-married (women); *inf* experienced, wide-awake
madrigal *m,* madrigal
madriguera *f,* rabbit warren; burrow, den, hole, lair; haunt of thieves, etc.
madrina *f,* godmother; matron of honor or bridesmaid; sponsor; patroness; prop; stanchion
madroncillo *m,* strawberry
madroño *m,* strawberry tree; tuft, spot; tassel
madrugada *f,* dawn, daybreak; early rising. **de m.,** at dawn
madrugador (-ra) *a* early rising. *n* early riser
madrugar *vi* to get up early; gain time; anticipate, be beforehand
maduración *f,* ripening; mellowing; preparation; ripeness; maturity
madurador *a* ripening; maturing
maduramente *adv* maturely; sensibly
madurar *vt* to ripen; mature; think out; *vi* ripen; grow mature, learn wisdom
madurez *f,* ripeness; maturity; mellowness; wisdom
maduro *a* ripe; mature; mellow; adult; wise
maestra *f,* schoolmistress; teacher, instructor; queen bee; guide, model
maestral *a* referring to the grand master of one of the Spanish military orders; teaching, pedagogic. *m,* mistral (wind); cell of a queen bee
maestranza *f, Lat. Am.* machine shop
maestrear *vt* to direct, control, manage; prune vines; *vi inf* bully, domineer
maestría *f,* mastery, skill; *univ* master's degree
maestril *m,* queen cell (of bees)
maestro *a* masterly; excellent; chief, main; midship. *m,* master, expert; teacher; instructor; master craftsman; *univ* master; *mus* composer; *naut* mainmast. **m. de armas,** fencing master. **m. de capilla,** *ecc* choirmaster. **m. de obras,** building contractor; master builder. **El ejercicio hace m.,** Practice makes perfect
Magallanes, Estrecho de Straits of Magellan
magdalena *f,* madeleine (cake); magdalen, penitent. *inf* **estar hecha una M.,** to be inconsolable
magia *f,* magic
mágica *f,* magic; enchantress, sorceress
mágico *a* magic; marvelous, wonderful. *m,* magician; enchanter, wizard
magín *m, inf* imagination; head, mind
magisterio *m,* teaching profession; teaching diploma; teaching post; pedantry, pompousness. **ejercer su m. en,** to be employed as a teacher in
magistrado *m,* magistrate; magistracy
magistral *a* magistral; authoritative, magisterial; pedantic, pompous
magistratura *f,* magistracy
magnanimidad *f,* magnanimity; generosity, liberality
magnánimo *a* magnanimous, generous, noble
magnate *m,* magnate
magnavoz *m, Mexico* loudspeaker
magnesia *f,* magnesia

magnesio *m*, magnesium
magnético *a* magnetic
magnetizar *vt* to magnetize; mesmerize
magneto *m*, magneto
magnificar *vt* to magnify, enlarge; praise, extol
magnificencia *f*, magnificence, pomp, splendor
magnífico *a* magnificent; splendid, wonderful, fine; excellent
magnitud *f*, magnitude; quantity; importance
magno *a* great; famous. **Alejandro M.,** Alexander the Great
magnolia *f*, magnolia
mago *m*, magician; *pl* magi
magra *f*, rasher (of bacon, ham)
magrez, magrura *f*, leanness; scragginess
magro *a* lean; scraggy. *m*, *inf* lean pork
magulladura *f*, **magullamiento** *m*, bruising; bruise, contusion
magullar *vt* to bruise
magullón *m*, *Lat. Am.* bruise
mahometano (-na) *a* and *n* Muslim
mahonesa *f*, mayonnaise
maíz *m*, corn
maizal *m*, cornfield
maja *f*, belle
majada *f*, sheepfold; dung
majaderear *vt*, *Lat. Am.* to nag, pester
majadería *f*, impertinence, insolence
majadero *a* persistent, tedious. *m*, bobbin (for lace making); pestle. *n* fool, bore
majador *m*, pestle
majar *vt* to pound, crush; *inf* importune, annoy
majestad *f*, majesty (title); dignity; stateliness
majestuosidad *f*, majesty; dignity
majestuoso *a* majestic; stately; dignified
majo *a* arrogant, aggressive; gaudily attired, smart; dashing, handsome; attractive, pretty; elegant, well-dressed. *m*, beau, gallant, man about town
majuelo *m*, new vine; species of white hawthorn
mal *a abb* **malo.** Used only before *m sing* nouns (e.g. **un m. cuarto de hora,** a bad quarter of an hour). *m*, evil; damage; harm; misfortune; illness, disease; trouble (e.g. **El m. es,** The trouble is). **m. de altura,** air sickness. **m. de ojo,** evil eye. **m. de piedra,** lithiasis, stone. **m. francés,** syphilis. **el m. menor,** the lesser of two evils. *interj* **¡M. haya!** A curse upon! **echar a m.,** to scorn (things); waste, squander. **llevar a m. (una cosa),** to take (a thing) badly, complain. **No hay m. que por bien no venga,** It's an ill wind that blows no one any good, Every cloud has a silver lining. **parar en m.,** to come to a bad end
mal *adv* badly; unfavorably; wrongly; wickedly; with difficulty; scarcely, barely. **m. que bien,** willingly or unwillingly; rightly or wrongly. **de m. en peor,** from bad to worse
mala *f*, mail, post. **m. real,** royal mail
malabarista *mf* juggler
malaconsejado *a* ill-advised; imprudent
malacostumbrado *a* badly trained, spoiled; having bad habits
malandante *a* evildoing; unfortunate, miserable; poor
malandanza *f*, evildoing; misfortune, misery; poverty
malandrín *a* wicked, ill-disposed. *m*, scoundrel, miscreant
malanga *f*, *Central America* kind of tuber resembling a sweet potato
malaquita *f*, malachite
malaria *f*, malaria
malaventura *f*, misfortune, adversity, bad luck
malaventurado *a* unfortunate, unlucky
malayo (-ya) *a* Malay. *n* Malayan
malbaratador (-ra) *a* wasteful, spendthrift. *n* squanderer, spendthrift
malbaratar *vt* to squander, waste; sell at a loss
malcasado *a* adulterous, unfaithful
malcasar(se) *vt* and *vr* to marry badly

malcomido *a* underfed
malcontento (-ta) *a* dissatisfied, discontented; rebellious. *n* malcontent, rebel
malcriado *a* badly brought up; ill-bred; spoiled, peevish
maldad *f*, badness; depravity, wickedness
maldecidor (-ra) *a* slanderous. *n* scandalmonger, slanderer
maldecir *vt irr* to curse; *vt* and *vi* slander, backbite. See **decir**
maldiciente *a* defamatory, slanderous; cursing, reviling. *m*, slanderer; curser
maldición *f*, malediction; curse, imprecation
maldispuesto *a* indisposed, ill; reluctant
maldita *f*, *inf* tongue. *inf* **soltar la m.,** to say too much, go too far
maldito *a* accursed; wicked; damned; poor (of quality); *inf* not a . . .
maleabilidad *f*, malleability, flexibility
maleable *a* malleable, flexible
maleante *a* rascally, villainous. *mf* evildoer
malecón *m*, breakwater
maledicencia *f*, slander, abuse, backbiting; cursing
maleficencia *f*, wrongdoing
maleficio *m*, (magic) curse; spell; charm
maléfico *a* malefic, harmful. *m*, sorcerer
malestar *m*, indisposition, slight illness; discomfort
maleta *f*, suitcase, valise, grip; *m*, *inf* clumsy matador; duffer (at games, etc.). **hacer la m.,** to pack a suitcase; *inf* prepare for a journey, get ready to leave
maletero *m*, seller or maker of traveling bags; porter
maletín *m*, small suitcase or valise
malevolencia *f*, malevolence, hatred, malice
malévolo *a* malevolent, malicious
maleza *f*, weeds; undergrowth; thicket
malgastador (-ra) *a* thriftless, wasteful. *n* squanderer
malgastar *vt* to waste (time); squander, throw away (money)
malhablado *a* foul-tongued, indecent
malhadado *a* ill-fated, unhappy
malhecho *a* deformed, twisted (persons). *m*, evil deed; wrongdoing
malhechor (-ra) *n* malefactor; evildoer
malhumorado *a* ill-humored, bad-tempered
malicia *f*, wickedness, evil; malice, maliciousness; acuteness, subtlety, shrewdness; craftiness, guile; *inf* suspicion
maliciar *vt* to suspect; spoil, damage; hurt, harm
malicioso *a* malicious; vindictive; wicked; shrewd, clever; *inf* suspicious; artful
malignidad *f*, malignancy, spite, ill will
maligno *a* malignant, spiteful; wicked; *med* malignant
malintencionado *a* ill-intentioned, badly disposed
malla *f*, mesh (of a net); coat of mail; *pl theat* tights. **m. de alambre,** wire netting. **cota de m.,** coat of mail
Mallorca Majorca
malmandado *a* disobedient; reluctant, unwilling
malmaridada *f*, adultress, faithless wife
malo *a* bad; wicked; evil; injurious; harmful; illicit; licentious; ill; difficult; troublesome, annoying; *inf* mischievous; knavish; rotten, decaying. *interj* **¡M.!** That's bad! You shouldn't have done that! That's a bad sign! **de malas,** unluckily, unhappily. **el M.,** the Evil One, the Devil. **estar m.,** to be ill. **Lo m. es,** The trouble is, The worst of it is. **por malas o por buenas,** willy-nilly, willingly or unwillingly. **ser m.,** to be wicked; be evil; behave badly (children)
malograr *vt* to lose (time); waste, throw away (opportunities); *vr* fall through, fail; wither, fade; die early, come to an untimely end
malogro *m*, loss, waste (time, opportunity); frustration; decline, fading; untimely death
malparar *vt* to ill-treat; damage. **quedar malparado,** to get the worst of
malparir *vt med* to miscarry
malparto *m*, miscarriage; abortion
malquerencia *f*, ill will, aversion, dislike

malquistar *vt* to stir up trouble; make unpopular; estrange; *vr* make oneself disliked
malquisto *a* unpopular, disliked
malsano *a* unhealthy
malta *m*, malt
maltés (-esa) *a* and *n* Maltese
maltraer *vt irr* to ill-treat; insult. See **traer**
maltraído, -a *a*, *Lat. Am.* shabby
maltratamiento *m*, abuse, ill usage; damage, deterioration
maltratar *vt* to ill-treat; abuse, insult; misuse, spoil, damage
maltrato *m*, maltreatment; misuse
maltrecho *a* ill-treated, bruised; abused, insulted; damaged
maltusiano *a* Malthusian
Malucas, las the Moluccas
malucho *a inf* off-color, below par, not well
malva *f*, mallow. **m. real, m. rosa,** *or* **m. loca,** hollyhock. **ser como una m.,** *fig inf* to be a clinging vine
malvado *a* evil, malevolent, fiendish. *n* villain, fiend
malvasía *f*, *bot* malvasia; malmsey (wine)
malvavisco *m*, *bot* marshmallow
malvender *vt* to sell at a loss
malversación *f*, malversation, maladministration; misappropriation (of funds)
malversador (-ra) *n* bad or corrupt administrator
malversar *vt* to misappropriate (funds)
Malvinas, las *fpl* the Falkland Islands
mama *f*, *inf* mamma, mommy; breast; udder
mamá *f*, mamma
mamado, -a *a*, *Lat. Am.* drunk, tipsy
mamar *vt* to suck (the breast); *inf* wolf, swallow; learn from an early age; enjoy, obtain unfairly; *vr* get drunk
mamario *a* mammary
mamarracho *m*, *inf* scarecrow, dummy; anything grotesque looking
mameluco *m*, mameluke; *inf* ninny, fool
mamífero *a* mammalian. *m*, mammal
mamotreto *m*, notebook, memorandum; *inf* large book or bulky file of papers
mampara *f*, folding screen; screen; partition
mamparo *m*, bulkhead
mampostería *f*, masonry, stonemasonry
mampostero *m*, stonemason
maná *m*, manna
manada *f*, handful; herd, flock; group, drove, crowd
manadero *m*, herdsman, drover; spring, stream
manantial *m*, fountain, source, spring; head (of a river)
manar *vi* to flow, stream; be plentiful
manatí *m*, sea cow, manatee
mancar *vt* to injure, maim; *vi* grow calm (elements)
manceba *f*, concubine; girl
mancebía *f*, brothel; youth, young days
mancebo *m*, youth, stripling; bachelor; shop assistant
mancha *f*, spot, smear, stain; blotch; plot of ground; patch of vegetation; stigma, disgrace
manchar *vt* to stain; smear; spot; speckle; disgrace; tarnish
manchuriano (-na) *a* and *n* Manchurian
mancilla *f*, stain; slur
mancillar *vt* to stain; *fig* smirch
manco (-ca) *a* maimed, disabled; one-handed; one-armed; armless; handless; incomplete, faulty. *n* disabled person
mancomunidad *f*, association, society; community, union; commonwealth; regional legislative assembly
mancorna, *f*, *Colombia* cuff link **mancuerna, mancuernilla** *f*, *Central America* cuff link
manda *f*, offer, suggestion, proposition; legacy
mandadero (-ra) *n* convent or prison messenger; errand boy (girl)
mandado *m*, order, command; errand
mandamiento *m*, order, command; *ecc* commandment; *law* writ; *pl inf* one's five fingers
mandar *vt* to order, command; bequeath, will; send;

control, drive; promise, offer; order (e.g. **Mandó hacerse un traje,** He ordered a suit to be made); *vr* walk unaided (convalescents, etc.); lead into one another (rooms, etc.); **¿Quién manda aquí?** Who is in charge here?
mandarín *m*, mandarin; *inf* bureaucrat; *Lat. Am.* bossy person, domineering person
mandarina *f*, mandarin (classical Chinese); mandarin orange
mandato *m*, mandate; command; *ecc* maundy. *pol* mandate. **cuarto m.,** fourth term (of President, Governor, etc.)
mandíbula *f*, jaw; jawbone, mandible
mandil *m*, long leather apron; apron; Freemason's apron; close-meshed fishing net; *Lat. Am.* (horse) blanket
mandilón *m*, *inf* coward, nincompoop
mandioca *f*, manioc, cassava; tapioca
mando *m*, authority, power; (*mil nav*) command; *eng* regulation; controls (of a machine, etc.). **m. a distancia,** remote control. *aer* **m. de dos pilotos,** dual-controlled. **mandos gemelos,** dual control. **al m. de,** under the command of; under the direction of
mandolín *m*. **mandolina** *f*, mandolin
mandón *a* domineering, bossy
mandril *m*, *mech* mandrel, chuck; *zool* mandrill
manear *vt* to hobble (a horse); manage, control
manecilla *f*, *dim* little hand; hand of a clock; *print* fist
manejable *a* manageable, controllable
manejar *vt* to handle; use, wield; control; manage, direct; ride (horses); *vr* manage to move around (after an accident, illness)
manejo *m*, handling; use, wielding; control; management, direction; horsemanship; intrigue
maneota *f*, hobble, shackle
manera *f*, manner, way, means; behavior, style (gen. *pl*); class (of people); *art* style, manner. **a la m. de,** like, in the style of. **de esa m.,** in that way; according to that, in that case. **de m. que,** so that. **en gran m.,** to a great extent. **sobre m.,** exceedingly
manga *f*, sleeve; bag; grip; handle; pipe (of a hose); strainer; waterspout; body of troops; beam, breadth of a ship; *pl* profits. **m. de viento,** whirlwind. **echar de m. a,** to make use of a person. *inf* **estar de m.,** to be in league. **tener m. ancha,** to be broad-minded. *fig inf* **traer (una cosa) en la m.,** to have (something) up one's sleeve
mangana *f*, lasso
manganilla *f*, sleight of hand; hoax, trick
mangle *m*, mangrove tree
mango *m*, handle, haft, stock; mango. **m. de cuchillo,** knife handle
mangonear *vi inf* to loaf, roam about; interfere, meddle
mangonero *a inf* meddlesome
mangosta *f*, mongoose
mangote *m*, *inf* long, wide sleeve; black oversleeve
manguera *f*, hose; sleeve, tube; airshaft; waterspout
manguero *m*, fireman; hoseman
manguito *m*, muff; black oversleeve; wristlet, cuff; *mech* bush, sleeve
manía *f*, mania, obsession; whim, fancy
maniabierto, -a *a*, *Lat. Am.* generous, giving, open-handed
maníaco (-ca) *a* maniacal; capricious, extravagant. *n* maniac
maniatar *vt* to handcuff; hobble (a cow, etc.)
maniático (-ca) *a* maniacal; capricious; faddy, fussy. *n* crank
manicomio *m*, insane asylum, mental hospital
manicura *f*, manicure
manicuro (-ra) *n* manicurist
manida *f*, lair, den; dwelling, habitation
manifestación *f*, declaration, statement; exhibition; demonstration; *ecc* exposition (of the Blessed Sacrament)
manifestante *mf* demonstrator

manifestar *vt irr* to declare, make known, state; exhibit, show; *ecc* to expose (the Blessed Sacrament). See **acertar**

manifiesto *a* obvious, evident. *m*, manifesto; *naut* manifest; *ecc* exposition of the Blessed Sacrament. **poner de m.,** to show; make public; reveal

manigua *f*, thicket, jungle (in Cuba)

manija *f*, handle, stock, haft; hand lever; clamp; tether (for horses, etc.)

manileño (ña) *a* and *n* Manilan

manilla *f*, bracelet; handcuff, manacle

maniobra *f*, operation, process; *mil* maneuver; intrigue; tackle, gear; handling, management; *naut* working of a ship; *pl* shunting (trains)

maniobrar *vi mil* to maneuver; *naut* handle, work (ships)

manipulación *f*, handling; manipulation; control, management

manipulador *a* manipulative. *m*, sending key (telegraphy)

manipular *vt* to handle; manipulate; manage, direct

manípulo *m*, maniple

maniquete *m*, black lace mitten

maniquí *m*, mannequin; dummy; *inf* puppet, weak person

manirroto (-ta) *a* wasteful, extravagant. *n* spendthrift

manivela *f, mech* crank, lever; *Lat. Am.* handle

manjar *m*, dish, food; pastime, recreation, pleasure. **m. blanco,** blancmange; *Lat. Am.* fudge

mano *f*, hand; coat, coating; quire (of paper); front paw (animals); elephant's trunk; side, hand; hand (of a clock); game (of cards, etc.); lead (at cards); way, means; ability; power; protection, favor; compassion; aid, help; scolding; *mus* scale; pestle; workers. *inf* editing, correction of a literary work (gen. by a person more skilled than the author). **m. de mortero,** pestle. **m. de obra,** (manual) labor. **manos muertas,** *law* mortmain. **m. sobre m.,** with folded hands; lazily, indolently. **a la m.,** at hand, nearby; within one's grasp. **a manos llenas,** in abundance, abundantly. **bajo m.,** in an underhand manner, secretly. **buenas manos,** cleverness, ability; dexterity. **de primera m.,** firsthand, new. **estar dejado de la m. de Dios,** to be very unlucky; be very foolish. **poner la m. en,** to ill-treat; slap, buffet. **Si a m. viene . . . ,** If by chance . . . **tender la m.,** to put out one's hand, shake hands. **traer entre manos,** to have on hand, be engaged in

manojo *m*, bunch, handful. **a manojos,** in handfuls; plentifully, in abundance

manolo (-la) *n* inhabitant of low quarters of Madrid noted for pride, gaiety, quarrelsomeness, and wit

manoseado *a* hackneyed

manosear *vt* to handle; paw, touch repeatedly; finger

manoseo *m*, handling; fingering; *inf* pawing, feeling

manotada *f*, slap, cuff

manotear *vt* to slap, cuff; *vi* gesticulate, gesture with the hands

manoteo *m*, gesticulation with the hands

manquedad *f*, disablement of hand or arm; lack of one of these; defect; incompleteness

mansalva (a) *adv* without danger

mansedumbre *f*, meekness; kindness; gentleness

mansión *f*, stay, visit; dwelling, abode; mansion

manso *a* soft, gentle; meek, mild; tame; peaceable, amiable; calm

manta *f*, blanket; horse blanket; traveling rug; *inf* hiding, thrashing. **m. de viaje,** traveling rug. *inf* **a m. de Dios,** in abundance. **dar una m.,** to toss in a blanket. *fig inf* **tirar de la m.,** to let the cat out of the bag

manteamiento *m*, tossing in a blanket

mantear *vt* to toss in a blanket

manteca *f*, lard; cooking fat; grease; *Argentina* butter. **como m.,** as mild as milk, as soft as butter

mantecada *f*, buttered toast

mantecado *m*, French ice cream

mantecoso *a* greasy

mantel *m*, tablecloth; altar cloth

mantelería *f*, table linen

mantelete *m*, (*ecc mil*) mantlet

mantener *vt irr* to maintain; keep, feed; support; continue, persevere with; uphold, affirm; keep up; *vr* support oneself; remain in a place; (*with en*) continue to uphold (views, etc.), persevere in. **mantenerse firme,** *fig* to stand one's ground. See **tener**

mantenimiento *m*, maintenance; support; sustenance, nourishment; affirmation; upkeep; livelihood

manteo *m*, tossing in a blanket; long cloak

mantequera *f*, churn; dairymaid; butter dish

mantequero *m*, dairyman; butter dish

mantequilla *f*, butter

mantero *m*, blanket seller or maker

mantilla *f*, mantilla; saddlecloth. *pl* baby's long clothes. **estar en mantillas,** to be in swaddling clothes; *fig* be in early infancy

manto *m*, cloak; cover, disguise; *zool* mantle; *min* layer

mantón *m*, shawl. **m. de Manila,** Manila shawl

mantuano (-na) *a* and *n* Mantuan

manuable *a* easy to handle or use, handy

manual *a* manual; handy, easy to use; docile, peaceable. *m*, manual, textbook; *ecc* book of ritual; notebook

manubrio *m*, handle, crank; *Lat. Am.* handlebars

manuela *f*, open carriage (Madrid)

manufactura *f*, manufacture; manufactured article; factory

manufacturar *vt* to manufacture

manufacturero *a* manufacturing

manumisión *f*, freeing (of a slave), manumission

manumitir *vt law* to free, enfranchise (slaves)

manuscrito *a* and *m*, manuscript

manutención *f*, maintenance; upkeep; protection

manzana *f*, apple; block (of houses); city square; Adam's apple; *Argentina* 2.5 acres; *Central America* 1.75 acres

manzanal *m*, apple orchard; apple tree

manzanar *m*, apple orchard

manzanilla *f*, white sherry wine; *bot* chamomile; chamomile tea; knob, ball (on furniture); pad (on an animal's foot)

manzano *m*, apple tree

maña *f*, skill, dexterity; craftiness, guile; vice, bad habit (gen. *pl*). **darse m. para,** to contrive to

mañana *f*, morning; tomorrow. *m*, future, tomorrow. *adv* tomorrow; in time to come; soon. **¡M.!** Tomorrow! Another day! Not now! (generally to beggars). **de m.,** early in the morning. **muy de m.,** very early in the morning. **pasado m.,** the day after tomorrow

mañanica *f*, early morning

mañear *vt* to arrange cleverly; *vi* behave shrewdly

mañero *a* shrewd, clever; easily worked; handy

mañoso *a* clever, skillful; crafty; vicious, with bad habits

mañuela *f*, low guile

mapa *m*, map; card. **m. en relieve,** relief map. **m. del estado mayor,** ordnance map. *inf* **no estar en el m.,** to be off the map; be most unusual (of things)

mapache *m*, raccoon

maqueta *f*, (*art arch*) model

maquiavélico *a* Machiavellian

maquiladora *f*, maquiladora (factory run by a U.S. company in Mexico to take advantage of cheap labor and lax regulation)

maquillaje *m*, makeup, cosmetics; making up (of the face)

maquillar (se) *vt* and *vr* to make up (the face, etc.)

máquina *f*, machine, mechanism; engine; apparatus; plan, scheme; machine, puppet; *inf* mansion; palace; plenty; locomotive; fantasy, product of the imagination. **m. de vapor,** steam engine. **m. de arrastre,** traction engine; tractor. **m. de coser,** sewing machine. **m. de escribir,** typewriter. **m. fotográfica,** camera. **m. de impresionar,** movie camera. **m. de imprimir,**

printing machine. **m. herramienta,** machine tool. **m. neumática,** air pump

maquinación f, intrigue, machination

maquinador (-ra) n intriguer, schemer

maquinal a mechanical

maquinar vt to intrigue, scheme, plot

maquinaria f, machinery; applied mechanics; mechanism

maquinista mf driver, enginer; mechanic; machinist; locomotive driver

mar mf sea; great many, abundance. **m. bonanza** or **m. en calma,** calm sea. **m. de fondo** or **m. de leva,** swell. **alta m.,** high seas. **a mares,** plentifully. **arar en el m.,** to labor in vain. naut **hacerse a la m.,** to put out to sea. **la m. de historias,** a great number of stories

maraña f, undergrowth; tangle; fig difficult position; intrigue; silk waste

marasmo m, med marasmus, atrophy; inactivity, paralysis

maravilla f, marvel, wonder; admiration; amazement; marigold. **a m.,** wonderfully. **a las mil maravillas,** to perfection, excellently. **por m.,** by chance; occasionally

maravillar vt to amaze, cause admiration; vr (with de) marvel at, admire; be amazed by

maravilloso a marvelous, wonderful

marbete m, label, tag; edge, border

marca f, mark, sign; brand; frontier zone, border country; standard, norm (of size); make, brand; measuring rule; sport record. **m. de fábrica,** brand, trademark. **m. de ley,** hallmark. **m. registrada,** registered name. **de m.,** excellent, of excellent quality

marcado a marked; pronounced; strong (of accents)

marcador a marking. m, marker; scoreboard; bookmark

marcar vt to mark; brand; embroider initials on linen; tell the time (watches); show the amount (cash register, etc.); dial (telephone); sport score (a goal); notice, observe; set aside, earmark; vr naut check the course. **m. el compás** to beat time

marcha f, departure; running, working; mil march; speed (of trains, ships, etc.); mus march; progress, course (of events). **m. atrás,** backing, reversing. **m. de ensayo,** trial run. **m. forzada,** mil forced march. **a largas marchas,** with all speed. **a toda m.,** at top speed; full speed ahead; by forced marches; mil **batir la m.,** to strike up a march. **en m.,** underway; working; in operation

marchamero m, customs official who checks and marks goods

marchamo m, customs mark on checked goods

marchante, -a mf Lat. Am. client, customer; dealer; merchant; pedlar

marchar vi to run; work; function; go; leave, depart; progress, proceed; mil march; go (clocks); vr leave, go away

marchitable a perishable, fragile

marchitar vt to wither, fade; blight, spoil; weaken; vr wither; be blighted

marchito a withered; faded; blighted, frustrated

marcial a martial; courageous, militant

marcialidad f, war-like spirit, militancy

marciano a Martian

marco m, mark (German coin); boundary mark; frame (of a picture, etc.). **m. de ventana,** window frame

Mar de las Indias Indian Ocean

Mar del Norte North Sea

marea f, tide; strand, water's edge; light breeze; drizzle; dew; street dirt. **m. creciente,** flood tide. **m. menguante,** ebb tide. **m. muerta,** neap tide

mareaje m, seamanship; ship's course

marear vt to navigate; sell; sell publicly; inf annoy; vr be seasick; feel faint; feel giddy; be damaged at sea (goods)

marejada f, surge, swell; high sea; tidal wave; commotion, uproar

mareo m, seasickness; nausea, dizziness; inf irritation, tediousness

mareta f, movement of the waves; sound, noise (of a crowd)

marfil m, ivory

marfileño a ivory; ivory-like

marfuz a spurned, rejected; deceitful

marga f, loam, marl

margarina f, margarine

margarita f, pearl; marguerite, oxeye daisy; daisy; periwinkle

margen mf edge, fringe, border, verge; margin (of a book); opportunity; marginal note. **dar m. para,** to provide an opportunity for; give rise to

marginal a marginal

margoso a loamy, marly

marica f, magpie. m, (offensive) homosexual; milksop

maricón m, (offensive) homosexual

maridable a marital, matrimonial

maridaje m, conjugal union and harmony; intimate relationship (between things)

maridar vi to get married; mate, live as husband and wife; vt unite, link, join together

marido m, husband

marihuana f, marijuana

marimacho m, inf mannish woman

marina f, coast, seashore; art seascape; seamanship; navy, fleet. **m. de guerra,** navy. **m. mercante,** merchant navy

marinera f, sailor's blouse

marinería f, profession of a sailor; seamanship; crew of a ship; sailors (as a class)

marinero m, sailor, seaman. **m. de agua dulce,** freshwater sailor (a novice). **m. práctico,** able seaman. **a la marinera,** in a seaman-like fashion

marinesco a seamanly

marino a marine, sea; seafaring; shipping. m, sailor, mariner

marioneta f, marionette, puppet

mariposa f, butterfly; night-light

mariposear vi to flutter, flit, fly about; flirt, be fickle; follow about, dance attendance on

mariquita f, ent ladybird; parakeet.

marisabidilla f, inf blue-stocking, know-it-all

mariscal m, mil marshal; field marshal; blacksmith

marisco m, shellfish

marisma f, bog, morass, swamp

marital a marital

marítimo a maritime, sea

marjal m, marshland, fen

marmita f, stewpot; copper, boiler; Mexico kettle

marmitón m, kitchen boy, scullion

mármol m, marble; work executed in marble

marmolería f, marble works; work executed in marble

marmolista mf marble cutter; dealer in marble

marmóreo a marble; poet marmoreal

marmota f, zool marmot; sleepyhead, dormouse

Mar Muerto Dead Sea

maroma f, rope, hawser; Lat. Am. tightrope

maromero, -a mf, Lat. Am. acrobat, tightrope walker; opportunist

marquesina f, marquee

marquetería f, marquetry

marrana f, sow; inf slattern, slut

marrano m, pig, hog; Marrano

marras (de) adv long ago, in the dim past

marrasquino m, maraschino liqueur

marro m, tick, tag (game)

marrón a maroon; brown. m, brown color; maroon color; quoit

marroquí a and mf Moroccan. m, Morocco leather

marroquín (-ina), marrueco (-ca) a and n Moroccan

Marruecos Morocco

marrullería f, flattery, cajolery

marrullero (-ra) a wheedling, flattering. n wheedler, cajoler

marsopa *f*, porpoise

marta *f*, sable; marten

martajar *vt*, *Lat. Am.* to grind, pound

Marte *m*, Mars

martes *m*, Tuesday. **m. de carnaval,** mardi gras

martillar *vt* to hammer; oppress

martillazo *m*, hammer blow

martilleo *m*, hammering; noise of the hammer; clink, clatter

martillero, -a *mf*, *Lat. Am.* auctioneer

martillo *m*, hammer; oppressor, tyrant; auction rooms. **a m.,** by hammering. **de m.,** wrought (of metals)

martín pescador *m*, kingfisher

martinete *m*, hammer (of a pianoforte); pile driver; drop hammer. **m. de báscula,** tilt hammer

Martinica Martinique

mártir *mf* martyr

martirio *m*, martyrdom

martirizar *vt* to martyr; torture, torment, martyrize; tease, annoy

marxismo *m*, Marxism

marzo *m*, March

mas *conjunc* but; yet

más *adv comp* more; in addition, besides; rather, preferably. *math* plus. **el (la,** etc.) **más,** *adv sup* the most, etc. **m. bien,** more; rather; preferably. **m. que,** only; but; more than; although, even if. **a lo m.,** at the most; at the worst. **a m.,** besides, in addition. **de m.,** superfluous, unnecessary, unwanted. **no . . . m. que,** only. **por m. que,** however; even if. **sin m. ni m.,** without further ado. **M. vale un mal arreglo que un buen pleito,** A bad peace is better than a good war

masa *f*, mass; dough; whole, aggregate; majority (of people); mortar. **en la m. de la sangre,** *fig* in the blood, in a person's nature

masada *f*, farmhouse and stock

masadero *m*, farmer; farm laborer

masaje *m*, massage

masajista *mf* masseur; masseuse

masato *m*, *Lat. Am.* drink made from bananas, fermented corn, yucca, etc.

mascadura *f*, chewing

mascar *vt* to chew; masticate; *inf* mumble, mutter

máscara *f*, mask; fancy dress; pretext, excuse. *mf* masquerader, reveler; *pl* masquerade. **m. para gases,** gas mask

mascarada *f*, masquerade; company of revelers

mascarero (-ra) *n* theatrical costumer, fancy-dress dealer

mascarilla *f*, death mask

mascarón *m*, large mask; *arch* gargoyle. **m. de proa,** *naut* figurehead

mascota *f*, mascot

masculinidad *f*, masculinity

masculino *a* masculine; male; manly, vigorous

mascullar *vt inf* to chew; mutter, mumble

masera *f*, kneading bowl; cloth for covering dough

masilla *f*, mastic, putty

masón (-ona) *n* Freemason

masonería *f*, freemasonry

masónico *a* masonic

masoquismo *m*, masochism

mastelero *a*, *naut* topmast

masticación *f*, mastication

masticar *vt* to masticate, eat; *inf* chew upon, consider

masticatorio *a* masticatory

mástil *m*, *naut* mast; upright, stanchion; pole (of a tent); stem, trunk; neck (of a guitar, etc.)

mastín *m*, mastiff

mastodonte *m*, mastodon

mastoides *a* mastoid

mastuerzo *m*, watercress; fool, blockhead

masturbación *f*, masturbation

masturbarse *vr* to masturbate

mata *f*, plant, shrub; stalk, sprig; grove, copse. **m. de pelo,** mat of hair

matacandelas *m*, candle snuffer

matachín *m*, mummer; butcher; *inf* swashbuckler

matadero *m*, slaughterhouse, abattoir; *Lat. Am.* brothel

matadura *f*, sore (on animals)

matafuego *m*, fire extinguisher; fireman

matalotaje *m*, ship's supplies, stores; *inf* hodgepodge

matamoros *a* swashbuckling, swaggering

matamoscas *m*, fly swatter

matanza *f*, killing, massacre, slaughter; butchery (animals); *inf* persistence, determination

matar *vt* to kill; quench (thirst); put out (fire, light); slake (lime); tarnish (metal); bevel (corners, etc.); pester, importune; suppress; compel; *art* tone down; *vr* kill oneself; be disappointed, grieve; overwork. **estar a m.,** to be at daggers drawn. **matarse por,** to try hard to; work hard for

matasanos *m*, *inf* quack (doctor); bad doctor

matasellos *m*, cancellation, postmark

mate *a* matte, unpolished, dull. *m*, checkmate (chess); maté, Paraguayan tea; gourd; vessel made from gourd, coconut, etc.

maté *m*, maté, Paraguayan tea

matemáticas *f pl*, mathematics. **m. prácticas,** applied mathematics. **m. teóricas,** pure mathematics

matemático *a* mathematical; exact. *m*, mathematician

materia *f*, matter; theme, subject matter; subject (of study); matter, stuff, substance; pus, matter; question, subject; reason, occasion. **m. colorante,** dye. **materias plásticas,** plastics. **materias primas,** raw materials. **en m. de,** concerning; in the matter of

material *a* material; dull, stupid, limited. *m*, material; ingredient; plant, factory; equipment. **m. móvil ferroviario,** rolling stock (railroads)

materialidad *f*, materiality; external appearance (of things)

materialismo *m*, materialism

materialista *a* materialistic. *mf* materialist; *Mexico* truckdriver

materializar *vt* to materialize; *vr* materialize; grow materialistic, grow less spiritual

maternidad *f*, maternity, motherhood

materno *a* maternal

matiz *m*, combination of colors; tone, hue; shade (of meaning, etc.)

matizar *vt* to combine, harmonize (colors); tint, shade; tinge (words, etc.)

matojo *m*, shrub, bush

matorral *m*, thicket, bush, undergrowth

matraca *f*, rattle; *inf* scolding, dressing-down; insistence, importunity

matraquear *vi* to make a noise with a rattle; *inf* scold

matriarcado *m*, matriarchy

matrícula *f*, list, register; matriculation; registration number (of a car, etc.). **m. de buques,** maritime register. **m. de mar,** mariner's register; maritime register

matriculación *f*, matriculation; registration

matricular *vt* to matriculate; enrol; *naut* register; *vr* matriculate; enroll, register

matrimonial *a* matrimonial

matrimonio *m*, marriage, matrimony; married couple. **m. a yuras,** secret marriage. **m. de la mano izquierda** *or* **m. morganático,** morganatic marriage. **contraer m.,** to get married

matritense *a* and *mf* Madrilenian

matriz *f*, uterus, womb; matrix, mold; *min* matrix; nut, female screw

matrona *f*, married woman; matron; midwife; female customs officer

matusalén *m*, Methuselah, very old man

matute *m*, smuggling; contraband; gambling den

matutero (-ra) *n* smuggler, contrabandist

matutino *a* matutinal, morning

maula *f*, trash; remnant; deception, fraud, trick. *mf inf* good-for-nothing; lazybones. *inf* **ser buena m.,** to be a trickster or a fraud

mauleria *f*, remnant stall; trickery

maullar *vi* to meow, mew (cats)

maullido *m*, meow, cry of the cat

Mauricio, Isla de Mauritius

mauritano (-na) *a* and *n* Mauritian

mausoleo *m*, mausoleum

maxilar *a* maxillary. *m*, jaw

máxima *f*, maxim, rule, precept, principle

máxime *adv* principally, chiefly

máximo *a sup* **grande** greatest, maximum, top. *m*, maximum

maya *f*, common daisy; May queen

mayal *m*, flail

mayo *m*, May; maypole; bouquet, wreath of flowers; *pl* festivities on eve of May Day

mayólica *f*, majolica

mayonesa *f*, mayonnaise

mayor *a comp* **grande** bigger; greater; elder; main, principal; older; high (mass, etc.); *mus* major. *mf* major (of full age). *a sup* **grande. el, la, lo mayor, los (las) mayores,** the biggest, greatest; eldest; chief, principal. **por m.,** in short, briefly; *com* wholesale

mayor *m*, head, director; chief clerk; *mil* major; *pl* ancestors

mayoral *m*, head shepherd; coachman, driver; foreman, overseer, supervisor, steward

mayorazgo *m*, *law* entail; entailed estate; heir (to an entail); eldest son; right of primogeniture

mayordoma *f*, steward's wife; housekeeper; stewardess

mayordomo *m*, steward, superintendent; butler; major-domo, royal chief steward

mayoreo *m*, *Lat. Am.* wholesale

mayoría *f*, majority

mayormente *adv* chiefly; especially

mayúscula *f*, capital letter, upper-case letter

mayúsculo *a* large; capital (letters). **letra mayúscula,** capital letter, upper-case letter

maza *f*, mallet; club, bludgeon; mace; bass drum stick; pile driver; bone, stick, etc., tied to dog's tail in carnival; *inf* pedant, bore; important person, authority; *Lat. Am.* hub (of a wheel). **m. de polo,** polo mallet

mazacote *m*, concrete; roughhewn work of art; *inf* stodgy overcooked dish; bore, tedious person

mazamorra *f*, dish made of cornmeal; biscuit crumbs; broken fragments, remains

mazapán *m*, marzipan

mazmorra *f*, dungeon

mazo *m*, mallet; bundle, bunch; importunate person; clapper (of a bell); *Argentina*, deck (of cards)

mazonería *f*, stonemasonry

mazonero *m*, stonemason

mazorca *f*, spindleful; spike, ear (of corn); cocoa berry; camarilla, group

mazurca *f*, mazurka

me *pers pron acc* or *dat 1st sing mf* me; to me

meandro *m*, meandering, twisting, winding; wandering

meato *m*, meatus

mecánica *f*, mechanics; mechanism, machinery; *inf* worthless thing; mean action

mecánico *a* mechanical; power-operated; base, illbred. *m*, engineer; mechanic

mecanismo *m*, mechanism; works, machinery

mecanizar *vt* to mechanize

mecanografía *f*, typewriting

mecanografiar *vt* to typewrite, type

mecanográfico *a* typewriting; typing; typewritten, typed

mecanografista *mf* **mecanógrafo (-fa)** *n* typist

mecate *m*, *Lat. Am.* twine; coarse person

mecedor *a* rocking, swaying. *m*, swing; *Lat. Am.* rocking chair

mecedora *f*, rocking chair

mecenas *m*, Maecenas, patron

mecer *vt* to stir, mix; shake; rock; swing

mecha *f*, wick; bit, drill; fuse (of explosives); match (for cannon, etc.); fat bacon (for basting); lock of hair; skein, twist; *Lat. Am.* fright, scare

mechar *vt cul* to baste, lard

mechero *m*, gas burner; pocket lighter; socket of a candlestick

mechón *m*, tuft, skein, bundle; lock of hair; wisp

medalla *f*, medal; medallion; plaque, round panel; *inf* piece of eight (coin)

medallón *m*, large medal; medallion; locket

media *f*, stocking

mediación *f*, mediation, arbitration; intercession

mediado *a* half-full. **a mediados (del mes,** etc.**),** toward the middle (of the month, etc.)

mediador (-ra) *n* mediator, arbitrator; intercessor

medianamente *adv* moderately; passably, fairly well

medianero (-ra) *a* middle; intervening, intermediate; mediatory. *n* mediator. *m*, owner of a semidetached house or of one in a row

medianía *f*, average; medium, mediocrity; moderate wealth or means

mediano *a* medium, average; moderate; *inf* middling, passable, fair

medianoche *f*, midnight

mediante *a* mediatory. *adv* by means of, by, through

mediar *vi* to reach the middle; get halfway; elapse half a given time; intercede, mediate; arbitrate; be in between or in the middle; intervene, take part

medicación *f*, medication

medicamento *m*, medicament, medicine, remedy

medicar *vt* to medicate

medicastro *m*, unskilled physician; quack, charlatan

medicina *f*, medicine; medicament

medicinar *vt* to attend; treat (patients)

medición *f*, measuring; measurements; survey (land); scansion

médico (-ca) *a* medical. *n* doctor of medicine. **m. de cabecera,** family doctor. **m. general,** general practitioner

medida *f*, measurement; measuring stick; measure, precaution (gen. with *tomar, adoptar,* etc.); gauge; judgment, wisdom; meter; standard. **a m. que,** while, at the same time as. **tomar las medidas (a),** *fig* to take a person's measure, sum him up. **tomar sus medidas,** to take his (their) measurements; take the necessary measures. **un traje hecho a m.,** a suit made to measure

medidor *m* *Lat. Am.* gauge, meter. **m. de aqua** water meter. **m. de gas** gas meter

medio *a* half; middle; intermediate; halfway. *m*, half; middle; *art* medium; spiritualist medium; proceeding, measure, precaution; environment, medium; middle way, mean; *sport* halfback. **m. galope,** canter. **m. tiempo,** *sport* halftime. **a medias,** by halves; half, partly. **de por m.,** by halves; in between; in the way. **estar de por m.,** to be in the way; take part in. *inf* **quitar de en m.,** to get rid of. *inf* **quitarse de en m.,** to go away, remove oneself

mediocre *a* mediocre

mediodía *m*, noon, meridian; south

medioeval *a* medieval

mediopelo *m*, lower middle class

mediquillo *m*, *inf* quack; medicine man (in the Philippines)

medir *vt irr* to measure; (metrics) scan; survey (land); compare; *vr* measure one's words; act with restraint. See **pedir**

meditabundo *a* pensive, meditative, thoughtful

meditación *f*, meditation; consideration, reflection

meditador *a* meditative, thoughtful

meditar *vt* to meditate, consider, muse

meditativo *a* meditative

mediterráneo *a* mediterranean; inland, landlocked

médium *m*, *spirit* medium

medra *f*, progress; improvement, betterment; growth; prosperity

medrar vi to flourish, grow; become prosperous or improve one's position

medro m, improvement, progress. See **medra**

medroso a timid, frightened; frightful, horrible

médula f, marrow; bot pith; fig essence, core

medusa f, jellyfish

mefistofélico a Mephistophelian

mefítico a noxious, mephitic, poisonous

megáfono m, megaphone

megalómano (-na) n megalomaniac

mejicano (-na) a and n Mexican

Méjico Mexico

mejilla f, anat cheek

mejillón m, sea mussel

mejor a comp **bueno** better. adv better; rather; sooner; preferably. a sup **bueno. el, la, lo mejor; los, las mejores,** the best; most preferable. **m. que m.,** better and better. inf **a lo m.,** probably, in all probability. **tanto m.,** so much the better

mejora f, improvement; bettering; progress; higher bid (at auctions)

mejorable a improvable

mejoramiento m, betterment, improvement

mejorar vt to improve; better; outbid; vi grow better (in health); improve (weather); make progress; rally (of markets). **Mejorando lo presente,** Present company excepted

mejoría f, improvement, progress; betterment; superiority; advantage, profit

mejunje m, inf brew, potion, cure-all, stuff; Lat. Am. mess

melado a honey-colored. m, cane syrup

melancolía f, melancholia; sadness, depression, melancholy

melancólico a melancholy, sad; depressing

melaza f, molasses

melena f, long side whiskers; loose, flowing hair (in women); overlong hair (in men); lion's mane. inf **andar a la m.,** to start a fight or quarrel. inf **traer a la m.,** to drag by the hair, force

melifluo a mellifluous, sweet-voiced; honeyed

melindre m, honey fritter; affectation, scruple, fastidiousness; narrow ribbon

melindroso a overfastidious, affected, prudish

mella f, nick, notch; dent; gap; harm, damage (to reputation, etc.). **hacer m.,** fig to make an impression (on the mind); mil breach, drive a wedge

mellar vt to nick, notch; dent; damage

mellizo (-za) a and n twin

melocotón m, peach; peach tree

melocotonero m, peach tree

melodía f, melody, tune; melodiousness

melódico a melodic, melodious

melodioso a melodious, tuneful, sweet-sounding

melodrama m, melodrama

melodramático a melodramatic

melón m, melon

melosidad f, sweetness

meloso a honeyed; sweet; gentle; mellifluous

membrana f, membrane

membrete m, note, memorandum; note or card of invitation; superscription; heading; address (of person)

membrillo m, quince tree; quince; quince jelly

membrudo a brawny, strong, muscular

memo a silly, stupid

memorable a memorable

memorándum m, notebook, jotter; memorandum

memorar(se) vt and vr to remember, recall

memoria f, memory; remembrance, recollection; monument; memorial; report; essay, article; codicil; memorandum; record, chronicle; pl regards, compliments, greetings; memoirs; memoranda. inf **m. de grillo,** poor memory. **de m.,** by heart. **flaco de m.,** forgetful. **hacer m.,** to remember

memorial m, notebook; memorial, petition

memorialista mf secretary, amanuensis

memorioso a mindful, unforgetful

mena f, min ore

menaje m, household or school equipment or furniture

mención f, mention. **m. honorífica,** honorable mention. **hacer m. de,** to mention

mencionar vt to mention

mendacidad f, mendacity, untruthfulness

mendaz a mendacious, untruthful

mendelismo m, Mendelism

mendicante a begging; ecc mendicant. mf beggar

mendicidad f, mendicancy, begging

mendigar vt to beg for alms; entreat, supplicate

mendigo (-ga) n beggar

mendoso a mendacious, untruthful; mistaken

mendrugo m, crust of bread

menear vt to sway, move; wag; shake; manage, control, direct; vr inf get a move on; sway, move; wriggle

meneo m, swaying movement; wagging; shaking; wriggling; management, direction; aer bump; inf spanking

menester m, lack, shortage; necessity; occupation, employment; pl physical necessities; inf tools, implements, equipment. **haber m.,** to need, require. **ser m.,** to be necessary or requisite

menesteroso a indigent, poverty-stricken, needy

menestra f, vegetable soup; dried vegetable (gen. pl)

mengano (-na) n so-and-so (used instead of the name of the person)

mengua f, decrease; lack, shortage; waning (of the moon, etc.); dishonor, disgrace; poverty

menguado (-da) a timid, cowardly; silly, stupid; mean, avaricious. n coward; fool; skinflint. m, narrowing stitch when knitting socks

menguante a ebb; waning; decreasing. f, ebb tide; decadence, decline. **m. de la luna,** waning of the moon

menguar vi to decrease; decline, decay; wane; ebb; narrow (socks); vt diminish; disgrace, discredit

menina f, child attendant (on Spanish royalty)

menino m, Spanish royal page; little dandy

menjurje m, See **mejunje**

menopausia f, menopause

menor a comp less, smaller; younger, minor; mus minor. m, minor. f, (logic) minor. a sup **el, la, lo m.; los, las menores,** the least; smallest; youngest. **m. de edad,** minor (in age). **por m.,** at retail; in detail

menoría f, subordination, dependence; inferiority; minority (underage); childhood, youth

menorista Lat. Am., a retail; mf retailer

menos adv less; minus; least; except. **m. de** or **m. que,** less than. **al m., por lo m.,** at least. **a m. que,** unless. **De m. nos hizo Dios,** Never say die, Nothing is impossible. **poco más o m.,** more or less, about

menoscabar vt to lessen, diminish, decrease; deteriorate, damage; disgrace, discredit

menoscabo m, decrease, diminishment; harm, damage, loss

menospreciable a despicable, contemptible

menospreciador (-ra) a scornful. n scorner, despiser

menospreciar vt to despise, scorn; underestimate, have a poor opinion of

menospreciativo a scornful, slighting, derisive

menosprecio m, scorn, derision; underestimation

mensaje m, message; official communication

mensajería f, carrier service; steamship line

mensajero (-ra) n messenger; errand boy

menso, -a a, Mexico dumb, silly, stupid

menstruación f, menstruation

menstruar vi to menstruate

mensual a monthly

mensualidad f, monthly salary, monthly payment

mensurable a measurable

mensurar vt to measure

menta f, menthe, mint; peppermint

mentado a celebrated, distinguished, famous

mental a mental

mentalidad f, mentality

mentalmente adv mentally

mentar *vt irr* to mention. See **sentar**

mentas *fpl, Argentina* reputation, gossip

mente *f,* mind; intelligence, understanding; will, intention

mentecatería *f,* folly, stupidity

mentecato (-ta) *a* foolish, silly; feeble-minded, simple. *n* fool, idiot

mentir *vi irr* to lie, be untruthful; deceive, mislead; falsify; *poet* belie; disagree, be incompatible; *vt* break a promise, disappoint. **m. como un bellaco,** to lie like a trooper See **sentir**

mentira *f,* lie, falsehood; error (in writing); *inf* white spot (on a fingernail); cracking (of fingerjoints). **m. oficiosa,** white lie. **Parece m.,** It seems incredible

mentiroso *a* lying, false; full of errors (literary works); deceptive

mentís *m,* giving the lie (literally, you lie); proof, demonstration (of error)

mentol *m,* menthol

mentón *m,* chin

menú *m,* menu

menudamente *adv* minutely; in detail, circumstantially

menudear *vt* to do frequently; do repeatedly; *vi* happen frequently; describe in detail; *com* sell by retail

menudencia *f,* minuteness, smallness; exactness, care, accuracy; trifle, worthless object; small matter; *pl* offal; pork sausages

menudeo *m,* repetition; description in detail; *com* retail. **al m.,** at retail

menudillos *m pl,* giblets; offal

menudo *a* minute, tiny; despicable; thin; small; vulgar; meticulous, exact; small (money). *m,* small coal; *m pl,* offal, entrails; small change (money). **a m.,** often, frequently. **por m.,** in detail, carefully; *com* in small lots

meñique *a inf* very small. *m,* little finger (in full, **dedo m.)**

meollo *m,* brain; *anat* marrow; *fig* essence, core, substance; understanding; *inf* **no tener m. (una cosa),** to be worthless, unsubstantial (things)

mequetrefe *m, inf* coxcomb, whippersnapper

meramente *adv* solely, simply, merely

mercachifle *m,* peddler; small merchant

mercadear *vi* to trade, traffic

mercadeo *m,* marketing (study of markets)

mercader *m,* dealer, merchant, trader. **m. de grueso,** wholesaler

mercadería *f,* See **mercancía**

mercado *m,* market; marketplace

mercancía *f,* goods, merchandise; commerce, trade, traffic

mercante *a* trading; commercial. *m,* merchant, dealer, trader

mercantil *a* mercantile, commercial

merced *f,* salary, remuneration; favor, benefit, kindness; will, desire, pleasure; mercy, grace; courtesy title given to untitled person (e.g. **vuestra m.,** your honor. Has now become **usted** and is universally used). **m. a,** thanks to. **estar uno a m. de,** to live at someone else's expense, be dependent on

mercenario (-ia) *n ecc* member of the Order of la Merced. *m, mil* mercenary; day laborer. *a* mercenary

mercería *f,* haberdashery, mercery

mercerizar *vt* to mercerize

mercero *m,* haberdasher, mercer

mercurio *m,* mercury, quicksilver; *ast* Mercury

merecedor *a* deserving, worthy

merecer *vt irr* to deserve, be worthy of; attain, achieve; be worth; *vi* deserve, be deserving. **m. bien de,** to deserve well of; have a claim on the gratitude of. See **conocer**

merecido *m,* due reward

merecimiento *m,* desert; merit

merendar *vi irr* to have lunch; pry into another's affairs; *vt* have (a certain food) for lunch. *inf* **meren-**

darse (una cosa), to obtain (a thing), have it in one's pocket. See **recomendar**

merendero *m,* lunchroom; tearoom

merengue *m, cul* meringue

meridiana *f,* daybed, chaise longue; siesta

meridiano *a* meridian. *m,* meridian. **a la meridiana,** at noon

meridional *a* meridional, southern

merienda *f,* tea, snack; lunch; *inf* hunchback. *inf* **juntar meriendas,** to join forces, combine interests

merino *a* merino. *m,* merino wool; shepherd of merino sheep

mérito *m,* merit; desert; worth, excellence. **de m.,** excellent, notable. **hacer m. de,** to mention

meritorio *a* meritorious. *m,* unpaid worker, learner

merluza *f,* hake; *inf* drinking bout. *inf* **pescar una m.,** to get drunk

merma *f,* decrease, drop; loss, waste, reduction; leakage

mermar *vi* to diminish, waste away, decrease; evaporate; leak; *vt* filch, pilfer; reduce, decrease

mermelada *f,* conserve, preserve; jam; marmalade

mero *a* mere; simple; plain

merodeador *a* marauding. *m,* marauder, raider

merodear *vi* to maraud, raid; *Mexico* make money illegally

merodeo *m,* raiding, marauding

mes *m,* month; menses, menstruation

mesa *f,* table; board, directorate; meseta, tableland; staircase landing; flat (of a sword, etc.); game of billiards. **m. de batalla,** post office sorting table. **m. de caballete,** trestle table. **m. de noche,** bedside table. **m. de tenis,** *Mexico* tennis court. **m. de tijeras,** folding table. **m. giratoria,** turntable. **alzar** (*or* **levantar) la m.,** to clear the table. **cubrir** (*or* **poner) la m.,** to set the table

mesada *f,* monthly wages, monthly payment

mesadura *f,* tearing of the hair or beard

mesarse *vr* to tear one's own hair or beard

mesenterio *m,* mesentery

mesera *f Mexico* waitress

mesero *m Mexico* waiter

meseta *f,* staircase landing; plateau, tableland

mesiánico *a* Messianic

Mesías *m,* Messiah

mesilla *f,* small table; laughing admonition; landing (of a stair)

mesnada *f,* association, company, society

mesocracia *f,* mesocracy; middle class, bourgeoisie

mesón *m,* inn, tavern

mesonero (-ra) *n* innkeeper; *Venezuela* waiter, waitress

mesta *f,* ancient order of sheep farmers; *pl* confluence, meeting (of rivers)

mester *m,* craft, occupation. **m. de clerecía,** learned poetic meter of the Spanish Middle Ages. **m. de juglaría,** popular poetry and troubadour songs

mestizo *a* half-breed; hybrid; cross-breed

mesura *f,* sedateness; dignity; courtesy; moderation

mesurado *a* sedate; dignified; moderate, restrained, temperate

meta *f,* goalpost *fig* aim, end; goal; goalkeeper

metabolismo *m,* metabolism

metáfora *f,* metaphor

metafórico *a* metaphorical

metal *m,* metal; brass; timbre of the voice; state, condition; quality, substance; *her* gold or silver; *mus* brass (instruments)

metalario *m,* metalworker

metálico *a* metallic. *m,* metalworker; coin, specie; bullion

metalistería *f,* metalwork

metalizar *vt* to metallize, make metallic; *vr* become metallized; grow greedy for money

metalurgia *f,* metallurgy

metalúrgico *a* metallurgical. *m,* metallurgist

metamorfosis *f,* metamorphosis

metano *m,* methane

metatarso *m*, metatarsus

metate *m*, *Central America, Mexico* flat stone for grinding and pounding

metátesis *f*, metathesis

metedor (-ra) *n* placer, inserter; smuggler, contrabandist

metellón, -ona *a*, *Mexico* meddling, meddlesome

metempsicosis *f*, metempsychosis

metemuertos *inf* meddler, Nosy Parker

meteórico *a* meteoric

meteorito *m*, meteorite

meteoro *m*, meteor

meteorología *f*, meteorology

meteorológico *a* meteorological

meteorologista *mf* meteorologist; weather forecaster

meter *vt* to place; put; introduce, insert; stake (gambling); smuggle; cause, occasion; place close together; persuade to take part in; *sew* take in fullness; deceive, humbug; cram in, pack tightly; *naut* take in sail; *vr* interfere, butt in; meddle (with); take up, follow (occupations); be overfamiliar; disembogue, empty itself (rivers, etc.); attack with the sword; (*with prep a*) follow (occupations); become, turn (e.g. **meterse a predicar,** to turn preacher); (*with con*) pick a quarrel with. **meterse en precisiones,** to go into details. *inf* **meterse en todo,** to be very meddlesome

metesillas y sacamuertos *m*, scene shifter, stagehand

metiche *a*, *Mexico* = **metellón**

meticulosidad *f*, meticulosity; timorousness

meticuloso *a* meticulous, fussy; timid, nervous

metido *a* tight; crowded; crabbed (of handwriting). *m*, *sew* material for letting out (seams). **m. en años,** quite old (person)

metílico *a* methylic

metimiento *m*, insertion, introduction; influence, sway

metódico *a* methodical

método *m*, method

metodología *f*, methodology

metralla *f*, *mil* grapeshot, shrapnel

métrica *f*, metrics

métrico *a* metric; metrical

metro *m*, (verse) meter; meter (measurement); subway, underground railway

metrónomo *m*, metronome

metrópoli *f*, metropolis, capital; see of a metropolitan bishop; mother country

metropolitano *a* metropolitan. *m*, metropolitan bishop

mexicano *Lat. Am.* = **mejicano**

México *Lat. Am.* = **Méjico**

mezcla *f*, mixture; blend, combination; mixed cloth, tweed; mortar

mezclar *vt* to mix, blend, combine; *vr* mix, mingle; take part; interfere, meddle; intermarry

mezcolanza *f*, *inf* hodgepodge

mezquindad *f*, poverty; indigence; miserliness; paltriness; meanness, poorness

mezquino *a* needy, impoverished; miserly, stingy; small, diminutive; unhappy; mean, paltry

mezquita *f*, mosque

mi *poss pron* my. *m*, *mus* mi, E

mí *pers pron acc gen dat 1st pers sing* me. Used only after prepositions (e.g. **Lo hicieron por mí,** They did it for me)

miaja *f*, See **migaja**

miasma *m*, miasma

miasmático *a* miasmatic, malarious

miau *m*, meow

mica *f*, *min* mica; coquette, flirt

micho (-cha) *n inf* puss, pussycat

micología *f*, mycology

micra *f*, micron, thousandth part of a millimeter

micro *m*, *Chile, Peru* (large, express) bus; *elsewhere in Lat. Am.* minibus

microbiano *a* microbial, microbic

microbio *m*, microbe

microbiología *f*, microbiology

microbrigada *f*, team of volunteer workers (in Castroist Cuba)

microcosmo *m*, microcosm

micrófono *m*, microphone

microonda *f*, microwave

microscópico *a* microscopic

microscopio *m*, microscope

miedo *m*, fear, apprehension, terror. **m. al público,** stagefright. **tener m.,** to be afraid

miedoso *a inf* fearful, nervous

miel *f*, honey. **m. de caña,** sugarcane syrup. *inf* **quedarse a media m.,** to see one's pleasure snatched away. *inf* **ser de mieles,** to be most pleasant or agreeable

mielitis *f*, myelitis

miembro *m*, *anat* limb; penis; member, associate; part, portion, section; *math* member

miente *f*, thought, imagination, mind. **parar** *or* **poner mientes en,** to consider, think about. **venírsele a las mientes,** to occur to one's mind

mientras *adv* while. **m. más . . .,** the more . . . . **m. que,** while (e.g. **m. que esperaba en el jardín,** while he was waiting in the garden). **m. tanto,** in the meanwhile

miércoles *m*, Wednesday. **m. de ceniza,** Ash Wednesday

mierda *f*, (*vulgar*) shit; *inf* filth

mies *f*, cereal plant, grain; harvest time; *pl* grain fields

miga *f*, breadcrumb; crumb; *inf* essence, core; substance; bit, scrap; *pl* fried breadcrumbs. *inf* **hacer buenas** (*or* **malas**) **migas,** to get on well (*or* badly) together

migaja *f*, breadcrumb; bit, scrap; trifle, mere nothing; *pl* crumbs (from the table); remains, remnants

migajón *m*, crumb (of a loaf): *fig inf* essence, substance, core

migración *f*, migration; emigration

migraña *f*, migraine

migratorio *a* migratory

mijo *m*, millet; maize

mil *a* thousand; thousandth; many, large number. *m*, thousand; thousandth. *inf* **Son las m. y quinientas,** It's extremely late (of the hour)

miladi *f*, my lady

milagrero *a inf* miraculous

milagro *m*, miracle; marvel, wonder. **¡M.!** Amazing! Just fancy!

milagroso *a* miraculous; marvelous, wonderful

milanés (-esa) *a* and *n* Milanese

mildeu *m*, mildew

milenario *a* millenary; millennial. *m*, millenary; millennium

milésimo *a* thousandth

milicia *f*, militia; military; art of war; military profession

miliciano *a* military. *m*, militiaman

milico *m*, *Lat. Am., derogatory* soldier

miligramo *m*, milligram

mililitro *m*, milliliter

milímetro *m*, millimeter

militante *a* militant

militar *a* military. *m*, soldier. *vi* to fight in the army; struggle (for a cause); *fig* militate (e.g. **Las circunstancias militan en favor de** (*or* **contra**) **sus ideas,** Circumstances militate against his ideas)

militarismo *m*, militarism

militarista *a* militaristic. *mf* militarist

militarizar *vt* to militarize; make war-like

milla *f*, mile

millar *m*, thousand; vast number (gen. *pl*)

millón *m*, million

millonario (-ia) *a* and *n* millionaire

millonésimo *a* millionth

milmillonésimo *a* billionth

milpa *f*, *Central America, Mexico* corn field

milpero, -a *mf*, *Lat. Am.* corn grower

mimar vt to spoil, overindulge; caress, fondle
mimbre mf osier; willow tree. m, wicker
mimbrear vi to sway, bend
mimbrera f, osier; osier bed; willow
mímica f, mimicry; mime
mímico a mimic
mimo m, mimic, buffoon; mime; caress, expression of affection, tenderness; overindulgence
mimoso a affectionate, demonstrative
mina f, mine; excavation, mining; underground passage; lead (in a pencil); (mil nav) mine; fig gold mine. mil **m. terrestre,** landmine
·minador m, excavator; nav minelayer; mil sapper
minar vt to excavate, mine; fig undermine; (mil nav) mine; work hard for
minarete m, minaret
mineraje m, exploitation of a mine, mining; mineral products
mineral a and m, mineral
mineralogía f, mineralogy
mineralógico a mineralogical
mineralogista mf mineralogist
minería f, mining, mineworking; mineworkers
minero a mining. m, miner, mineworker; source, origin
minga f, Lat. Am. voluntary communal labor
miniar vt art to illuminate
miniatura f, miniature
miniaturista mf miniaturist
mínima f, mus minim; very small thing or portion
mínimo a sup **pequeño** smallest; minimum; meticulous, precise. m, minimum; (meteorological) trough
ministerial a ministerial
ministerio m, office, post; pol cabinet; ministry; government office; government department.
ministrar vt and vi to fill; administer (an office); vt minister to; give, provide
ministro m, instrument, agency; minister of state, cabinet minister; clergyman, minister; minister plenipotentiary; policeman. **m. de estado,** secretary of state. **m. de gobernación,** secretary of the interior. **m. de hacienda,** treasurer. **m. de relaciones extranjeras,** foreign secretary. **primer m.** prime minister
minoración f, reduction, decrease
minorar vt to diminish, decrease
minoría f, minority, smaller number; minority (of age)
minoridad f, minority (of age)
minorista mf, Lat. Am. retailer
minucia f, smallness; morsel, mite; pl details, trifles, minutiae
minucioso a meticulous, precise, minute
minúsculo a minute, very small
minuta f, memorandum, minute; note; list, catalogue
minutero m, minute hand (of a clock)
minuto a minute, very small. m, minute
mío m. **mía,** f, (m pl. **míos,** f pl. **mías**) poss pron mine (e.g. **Las flores son mías,** The flowers are mine). **Mi** is used before nouns, not **mío.** Also used with article (e.g. **Este sombrero no es el mío,** This hat is not mine (my one)). **de mío,** by myself, without help. inf **¡Esta es la mía!** This is my chance!
miope a myopic. mf myopic person
miopía f, shortsightedness
miosota f, myosotis, forget-me-not
mira f, sight (optical instruments, guns); intention, design; mil watchtower; care, precaution. **andar, estar** or **quedar a la m.,** to be vigilant, be on the lookout
mirada f, look; gaze. **lanzar miradas de carnero degollado (a),** to cast sheep's eyes at
miradero m, object of attention, cynosure; observation post, lookout
mirador (-ra) n spectator. m, arch oriel; enclosed balcony; observatory
miramiento m, observation, gazing; scruple, consideration; precaution, care; thoughtfulness
mirar vt to look at, gaze at; observe, behold; watch; consider, look after; value, appreciate; concern; believe,

think; (with prep a) overlook, look on to; face; (with por) care for, protect; look after, consider. **m. contra el gobierno,** inf to be squint-eyed. **m. de hito en hito,** to look over, stare at. **mirarse en (una cosa),** to consider (a matter) carefully
miríada f, myriad, huge number
mirilla f, peephole
miriñaque m, trinket, ornament; crinoline
mirlarse vr inf to give oneself airs
mirlo m, blackbird; inf pompous air
mirón a inquisitive, curious
mirra f, myrrh
mirto m, myrtle
misa f, (ecc mus) mass. **m. de difuntos,** requiem mass. **m. del gallo,** midnight mass. **m. mayor,** high mass. **m. rezada,** low mass. **como en m.,** in profound silence. **oír m.,** to attend mass
misal m, missal
misantropía f, misanthropy
misantrópico a misanthropic
misántropo m, misanthrope
miscelánea f, medley, assortment, miscellany
misceláneo a assorted, miscellaneous, mixed
miscible a mixable
miserable a miserable, unhappy; timid, pusillanimous; miserly, mean; despicable
miseria f, misery; poverty, destitution; avarice, miserliness; inf poor thing, trifle
misericordia f, mercy, compassion
misericordioso a merciful, compassionate
mísero a inf fond of churchgoing
misérrimo a sup most miserable
misión f, mission; vocation; commission, duty, errand
misionar vi to missionize, act as a missionary; ecc conduct a mission
misionero m, missioner; missionary
Misisipí, el the Mississippi
misiva f, missive
mismo a same; similar; self (e.g. **ellos mismos,** they themselves); very, same (e.g. **Ahora m. voy,** I'm going this very minute). **Me da lo m.,** It makes no difference to me. **por lo m.,** for that selfsame reason
misógamo (-ma) n misogamist
misógino m, misogynist
misterio m, mystery
misterioso a mysterious
mística f, **misticismo** m, mysticism
místico a mystic
mistificación f, mystification; mystery; deception
mistificar vt to mystify; deceive
Misuri, el the Missouri
mitad f, half; middle, center. fig inf **cara m.,** better half. inf **mentir por la m. de la barba,** to lie barefacedly
mítico a mythical
mitigación f, mitigation
mitigador (-ra) a mitigatory. n mitigator
mitigar vt to mitigate, moderate, alleviate; appease
mitin m, mass meeting
mito m, myth
mitología f, mythology
mitológico a mythological
mitologista, mitólogo m, mythologist
mitón m, mitten
mitra f, miter; bishopric; archbishopric
mitrado a mitred
mixto a mixed, blended; hybrid; composite; mongrel. m, mixed train (carrying freight and passengers); sulphur match
mixtura f, mixture, blend; compound; mixture (medicine)
¡miz, miz! puss, puss!
moabita mf Moabite
mobiliario a movable (goods). m, furniture
moblaje m, household goods and furniture
mocasín m, moccasin

mocedad *f*, youth, adolescence; mischief, prank. *fig inf* **correr sus mocedades**, to sow one's wild oats

mochila *f*, knapsack; nosebag; military rations for a march

mocho *a* blunted, topless, lopped; *inf* shorn, cropped. *m*, butt, butt end

mochuelo *m*, owl; *inf* difficult job

moción *f*, motion, movement; impulse, tendency; divine inspiration; motion (of a debate)

moco *m*, mucus; candle drips; snuff of a candle. *inf* **caérsele el m.**, to be very simple, be easily deceived

mocoso (-sa) *a* running of the nose, sniffling; unimportant, insignificant. *n* coxcomb, stripling; *Lat. Am.* child

moda *f*, fashion. **estar** *or* **ser de m.**, to be fashionable, be in fashion. **la última m.**, the latest fashion

modales *m pl*, manners, behavior

modalidad *f*, form, nature; *mus* modality

modelado *m*, *art* modeling

modelar *vt art* to model; *vr* model oneself (on), copy

modelo *m*, example, pattern; model. *mf art* life model

moderación *f*, moderation; restraint, temperance, equability

moderado *a* moderate; restrained, temperate

moderador (-ra) *a* moderating. *n* moderator

moderantismo *m*, moderate opinion; moderate political party

moderar *vt* to moderate; temper, restrain; *vr* regain one's self-control; behave with moderation

modernidad *f*, modernity

modernismo *m*, modernism

modernista *a* modernistic; modern. *mf* modernist

modernización *f*, modernization

modernizar *vt* to modernize

moderno *a* modern. *m*, modern. **a la moderna**, in modern fashion

modestia *f*, modesty

modesto *a* modest

módico *a* moderate (of prices, etc.)

modificable *a* modifiable

modificación *f*, modification

modificador, modificante *a* modifying, moderating

modificar *vt* to modify; moderate

modismo *m*, idiom, idiomatic expression

modista *mf* dressmaker; couturier; milliner

modo *m*, mode, method, style; manner, way; moderation, restraint; civility, politeness (often *pl*); *mus* mode; *gram* mood. **m. de ser**, nature, temperament. **de m. que**, so that. **de ningún m.**, not at all, by no means. **de todos modos**, in any case

modorra *f*, deep sleep, stupor

modorro *a* drowsy, heavy

modoso *a* demure; well-behaved

modulación *f*, modulation

modulador (-ra) *a* modulative. *n* modulator, *m*, *mus* modulator

modular *vt* and *vi* to modulate

mofa *f*, mockery, ridicule, jeering

mofador (-ra) *a* jeering. *n* scoffer, mocker

mofarse *vr* (*with de*) to make fun of, jeer at

mofeta *f*, noxious gas; damp (gas); *zool* skunk

moflete *m*, *inf* plump cheek

mofletudo *a* plump-cheeked

mogol (-la) *a* and *a* Mongolian.

mogote *m*, hill; pyre, stack

mohín *m*, grimace

mohína *f*, grudge, rancor; sullenness; sulkiness

mohíno *a* depressed, gloomy; sulky; black or black-nosed (of animals)

moho *m*, mold, fungoid growth; moldiness; moss. *inf* **no criar m.**, to be always on the move

mohoso *a* mossy; moldy

mojada *f*, wetting; *inf* stab; sop of bread

mojador (-ra) *n* wetter. *m*, stamp moistener

mojar *vt* to wet; moisten; *inf* stab, wound with a dagger; *vi* take part in; meddle, interfere; *vr* get wet

mojicón *m*, kind of spongecake; *inf* slap in the face

mojiganga *f*, masquerade, mummer's show; farce; funny sight, figure of fun

mojigatería *f*, hypocrisy; sanctimoniousness; prudery

mojigato (-ta) *a* hypocritical; sanctimonious; prudish. *n* hypocrite; bigot; prude

mojón *m*, boundary marker; milestone; heap. **m. kilométrico**, milestone

molar *a* molar

molde *m*, mold, matrix; *fig* model, pattern. **de m.**, printed; suitably, conveniently; perfectly. **letra de m.**, printed letters, print

moldeador (-ra) *n* molder

moldear *vt* to mold, cast

moldura *f*, molding

moldurar *vt carp* to mold

molécula *f*, molecule

molecular *a* molecular

mole *f* mass, bulk

mole de guajolote *m*, *Mexico* turkey served with a heavy dark sauce made of different kinds of chiles, spices, etc.

moler *vt irr* to grind, crush; tire, exhaust; ill-treat; pester, annoy. **m. a palos**, to beat black and blue. *Pres. Ind.* **muelo, mueles, muele, muelen.** *Pres. Subjunc.* **muela, muelas, muela, muelan**

molestia *f*, inconvenience, trouble; annoyance; discomfort, pain; bore, nuisance. **Es una m.**, It's a nuisance

molesto *a* inconvenient, troublesome; annoying; painful; uncomfortable; boring, tedious

molestoso, -a *a*, *Lat. Am.* annoying, bothersome

moletón *m*, flannelet

molicie *f*, softness, smoothness; effeminacy, weakness

molienda *f*, milling; grinding; mill; portion ground at one time; *inf* exhaustion, fatigue; *inf* nuisance

molificar *vt* to mollify, appease

molimiento *m*, milling; grinding; exhaustion, fatigue

molinera *f*, (woman) miller; miller's wife

molinero *a* mill. *m*, miller

molinillo *m*, hand mill, small grinder; mincing machine; beater. **m. de café**, coffee mill

molino *m*, mill; harum-scarum, rowdy; bore, tedious person; *inf* mouth. **m. de rueda de escalones**, treadmill. **m. de viento**, windmill

molleja *f*, gizzard

mollera *f*, crown of the head; brains, sense. *inf* **ser duro de m.**, to be obstinate; be stupid

molusco *m*, mollusk

momentáneo *a* momentary, brief; instantaneous, immediate

momento *m*, moment, minute; importance; *mech* moment. **al m.**, immediately. **a cada m.**, all the time; frequently. **por momentos**, continually; intermittently

momería *f*, mummery

momero (-ra) *n* mummer

momia *f*, mummy

momificación *f*, mummification

momificar *vt* to mummify; *vr* become mummified

mona *f*, female monkey; *inf* imitator; drinking bout; drunk. *inf* **Aunque la m. se vista de seda, m. se queda**, Breeding will tell. *inf* **ser la última m.**, to be of no account, be unimportant

monacillo *m*, *ecc* acolyte

monada *f*, mischievous prank; affected gesture or grimace; small, pretty thing; childish cleverness; flattery; rash act; *pl* monkey shines

monaguillo *m*, *ecc* acolyte

monarca *mf* monarch

monarquía *f*, monarchy

monárquico (-ca) *a* monarchic. *n* monarchist

monarquismo *m*, monarchism

monasterio *m*, monastery; convent

monástico *a* monastic

monda *f*, skinning, peeling; *agr* pruning; cleansing; *Lat. Am.* beating, thrashing

mondadientes *m*, toothpick

mondar *vt* to skin, peel; *agr* prune; cut the hair; cleanse; free of rubbish; *inf* deprive of possessions; *Lat. Am.* to beat, beat up, thrash *vr* pick one's teeth

mondo *a* simple, plain; bare; unadulterated, pure

mondongo *m*, *Lat. Am.* tripe

moneda *f*, coin, piece of money; coinage; *inf* wealth; cash. **m. corriente**, currency. **m. metálica**, specie. **pagar en buena m.**, to give entire satisfaction. **pagar en la misma m.**, to pay back in the same coin, return like for like. *inf* **ser m. corriente**, to be usual or very frequent

monedero *m*, coiner, minter; handbag; purse

monería *f*, mischievous trick; unimportant trifle; pretty thing; childish cleverness, pretty ways

monetario *a* monetary. *m*, collection of coins and medals

monetización *f*, monetization

monigote *m*, *inf* boor; grotesque, puppet

monitor *m*, monitor

monitorio *a* monitory

monja *f*, nun; *pl* sparks

monje *m*, monk

monjil *a* nun-like. *m*, nun's habit

mono *a inf* pretty, attractive; amusing, funny. *m*, monkey; person given to grimacing; rash youth; coverall. *inf* **estar de monos**, to be on bad terms

monocromo *a* monochrome; monochromatic

monóculo *m*, monocle

monogamia *f*, monogamy

monógamo *a* monogamous. *n* monogamist

monografía *f*, monograph

monograma *m*, monogram

monolítico *a* monolithic

monolito *m*, monolith

monólogo *m*, monologue

monomanía *f*, monomania

monomaníaco (-ca) *n* monomaniac

monopatín *m*, scooter

monoplano *m*, monoplane

monopolio *m*, monopoly

monopolista *mf* monopolist

monopolizar *vt* to monopolize

monoteísmo *m*, monotheism

monoteísta *mf* monotheist

monotipia *f*, monotype

monotonía *f*, monotony; monotone

monótono *a* monotonous

monroísmo *m*, Monroe doctrine

monseñor *m*, monsignor

monserga *f*, *inf* rigmarole; jargon

monstruo *m*, monster; freak, monstrosity; cruel person; hideous person or thing

monstruosidad *f*, monstrousness, monstrosity

monstruoso *a* monstrous, abnormal; enormous; extraordinary; atrocious, outrageous

monta *f*, mounting a horse; total; *mil* mounting signal; breeding station (horses)

montacargas *m*, hoist, lift; freight elevator

montador *m*, mounter; mounting block

montadura *f*, mounting; mount, setting (of jewels)

montaje *m*, assembling, setting up (machines); presentation (of a book); (cinema) montage

montano *a* hilly, mountainous

montante *m*, upright, stanchion; tent pole

montaña *f*, mountain; mountainous country. **montañas rusas**, roller coaster (at an amusement park)

montañés (-esa) *a* mountain. *n* mountain dweller; native of Santander

montañoso *a* mountainous; hilly

montar *vi* to ascend, climb up, get on top; mount (a horse); ride (a horse); be important; *vt* get on top of; ride (a horse); total, amount to; set up (apparatus, machinery); *naut* sail around, double; set, mount (gems); cock (firearms); fine for trespassing; wind (a clock); command (a ship); *naut* carry, be fitted with (guns,

etc.). **m. a horcajadas en**, to mount astride; straddle. **montarse en cólera**, to fly into a rage

montaraz *a* mountain-dwelling; wild, savage; rude, uncivilized, uncouth. *m*, gamekeeper, forester

monte *m*, mount, hill; woodland; obstacle, impediment. **m. de piedad**, pawnshop. **m. pío**, savings fund

montenegrino (-na) *a* and *n* Montenegrin

montepío *m*, *Lat. Am.* pawnshop

montera *f*, cap; glass roof

montería *f*, hunt, chase; art of hunting

montero (-ra) *n* hunter, huntsman

montés *a* wild, savage, untamed

montevideano (-na) *a* and *n* Montevidean

montículo *m*, mound, hill

montón *m*, heap, pile; *inf* abundance, lot. *inf* **a, de** or **en m.**, all jumbled up together. **a montones**, in abundance

montonero, -a *mf* domineering, overbearing

montuoso *a* mountainous

montura *f*, riding animal, mount; horse trappings; setting up, mounting (artillery, etc.)

monumento *m*, monument; document, record; tomb

monzón *mf*, monsoon

moña *f*, doll; dressmaker's model; bow for the hair; bullfighter's black bow; baby's bonnet; *inf* drinking bout

moño *m*, bun, chignon; topknot (birds); bunch of ribbons; *pl* tawdry trimmings

moquete *m*, slap in the face

moquillo *m*, distemper (of animals)

mora *f*, blackberry; mulberry; bramble; Moorish girl, Moorish woman

morada *f*, dwelling, abode; sojourn, stay

morado *a* purple

morador (-ra) *n* dweller; sojourner

moral *a* moral, ethical. *f*, morality, ethics; morale. *m*, blackberry bush

moraleja *f*, moral, lesson

moralidad *f*, morality

moralista *mf* moralist

moralización *f*, moralization

moralizador (-ra) *a* moralizing. *n* moralizer

moralizar *vt* to reform, correct; *vi* moralize

moratoria *f*, moratorium

morbidez *f*, *art* morbidezza; softness

mórbido *a* morbid, diseased; *art* delicate (of flesh tones); soft

morbo *m*, illness. **m. gálico**, syphilis

morboso *a* ill; morbid, unhealthy

morcilla *f*, *cul* black pudding; (*inf theat*) gag

morcillero (-ra) *n* seller of black puddings; (*inf theat*) actor who gags

mordacidad *f*, corrosiveness; mordacity, sarcasm; *cul* piquancy

mordaz *a* corrosive; sarcastic, caustic, mordant; *cul* piquant

mordaza *f*, gag

mordedor *a* biting; scandalmongering

mordedura *f*, bite, biting

mordelón, -ona *mf*, *Central America, Mexico* given to taking bribes

morder *vt irr* to bite; nibble, nip; seize, grasp; corrode, eat away; slander; etch. *Pres. Ind.* **muerdo, muerdes, muerde, muerden.** *Pres. Subjunc.* **muerda, muerdas, muerda, muerdan**

mordida *f*, *Lat. Am.* bite; *Central America, Mexico* also bribe

mordiente *m*, fixative (for dyeing); mordant. *a* mordant (of acid)

mordiscar *vt* to nibble, bite gently; bite

mordisco *m*, nibble; nibbling; bite; biting; piece bitten off

morena *f*, moraine

moreno (-na) *a* dark brown; swarthy complexioned; dark (of people). *n inf* negro, mulatto

morera *f*, mulberry bush

morería *f*, Moorish quarter

morfina *f*, morphine

morfinómano (-na) *n* morphine addict

morfológico *a* morphological

morganático *a* morganatic

moribundo (-da) *a* moribund, dying. *n* dying person

morillo *m*, andiron, fire-dog

morir *vi irr* to die; fade, wither; decline, decay; disappear; yearn (for); long (to); go out (lights, fire); *vr* die; go numb (limbs); (*with por*) adore, be mad about. *inf* **m. vestido,** to die a violent death. **¡Muera!** Down with! *Past Part.* **muerto.** For other tenses see **dormir**

morisco (-ca) *a* Moorish. *n* Morisco, Moor converted to Christianity

mormón (-ona) *n* Mormon

mormonismo *m*, Mormonism

moro (-ra) *a* Moorish. *n* Moor; Mohammedan. *inf* **haber moros y cristianos,** to be the deuce of a row. *inf* **Hay moros en la costa,** The coast is not clear; There's trouble in the offing

moronga *f, Central America, Mexico* blood sausage

morosidad *f*, slowness, delay; sluggishness, sloth

moroso *a* slow, dilatory; sluggish, lazy

morra *f*, crown of the head

morral *m*, nose-bag; knapsack; game-bag; *inf* lout

morriña *f*, cattle plague, murrain; *inf* depression, blues; homesickness

morro *m*, anything round; hummock, hillock; round pebble; headland, cliff

morrón *m, Lat. Am.* hot red pepper

morsa *f*, walrus

mortaja *f*, shroud, winding sheet

mortal *a* mortal; fatal, deadly; on the point of death; great, tremendous; certain, sure. *mf* mortal

mortalidad *f*, humanity, human race; mortality, death-rate

mortandad *f*, mortality, number of deaths

mortecino *a* dead from natural causes (animals); weak; fading; dull, dead (of eyes); flickering; on the point of death or extinction

mortero *m*, mortar (for building); *mil* mortar; pounding mortar

mortífero *a* deadly, mortal

mortificación *f, med* gangrene; humiliation, wounding; mortification (of the flesh)

mortificar *vt med* to mortify; humiliate, wound, hurt; mortify (the flesh); *vr* become gangrenous

mortuorio *a* mortuary. *m*, funeral, obsequies

mosaico *a* and *m*, mosaic

mosca *f*, fly; *inf* nuisance; bore, pest; cash; *pl* sparks. *inf* **m. muerta,** underhanded person. *inf* **papar moscas,** to gape, be dumbfounded. *inf* **soltar la m.,** to give or spend money unwillingly

moscardón *m*, gadfly

moscatel *a* muscatel. *m*, muscatel (grapes and wine); *inf* pest, tedious person

Moscú Moscow

mosquear *vt* to drive off flies; reply crossly; whip; *vr* be exasperated; brush aside obstacles

mosquero *m*, flypaper

mosquete *m*, musket

mosquetería *f*, musketry; (*ant theat*) male members of the audience who stood at the back of the pit

mosquetero *m*, musketeer; (Spanish theater of the sixteenth and seventeenth centuries) male member of the audience who stood at the back of the pit

mosquitero *m*, mosquito net

mosquito *m*, mosquito; midge, gnat; *inf* tippler, drunkard

mostacera *f*, mustard pot

mostacho *m*, mustache, whiskers; *inf* smudge on the face

mostaza *f*, mustard plant or seed; *cul* mustard

mostela *f*, sheaf (of corn, etc.)

mosto *m*, must, unfermented wine

mostrador (-ra) *n* one who shows, exhibitor. *m*, shop counter; face of a watch

mostrar *vt irr* to show; indicate, point out; demonstrate, prove; manifest, reveal; *vr* show oneself, be (e.g. **Se mostró bondadoso,** He showed himself to be kind). *Pres. Ind.* **muestro, muestras, muestra, muestran.** *Pres. Subjunc.* **muestre, muestres, muestre, muestren**

mostrenco *a inf* stray, vagrant, homeless; *inf* dull, ignorant; *inf* fat, heavy

mota *f*, fault in cloth; mote, defect, fault; mound, hill; thread of cotton, speck of dust, etc.; fleck (of the sun, etc.); spot

mote *m*, maxim, saying; motto, device; catchword, slogan; nickname; *Lat. Am.* boiled corn

motear *vt* to speckle, dot, variegate, spot

motejar *vt* to nickname, call names, dub

motete *m*, motet

motín *m*, mutiny; riot

motivar *vt* to motivate, cause; explain one's reasons

motivo *a* motive. *m*, cause, motive; *mus* motif. **con m. de,** on account of, because of. **de m. propio,** of one's own free will

motocicleta *f*, motorcycle

motociclista *mf* motorcyclist

motor (-ra) *a* motive, driving. *m*, motor, engine. *n* (person) mover, motive force. **m. de combustión interna,** internal combustion engine. **m. de retroacción,** jet engine

motorista *mf* motorist, driver

movedizo *a* movable; insecure, unsteady; shaky; changeable, vacillating

mover *vt irr* to move; operate, drive; sway; wag; persuade, induce; excite; move (to pity, etc.); (*with prep a*) cause; *vi* sprout (plants); *vr* move. *Pres. Ind.* **muevo, mueves, mueve, mueven.** *Pres. Subjunc.* **mueva, muevas, mueva, muevan**

movible *a* movable; insecure, shaky. *m*, motive, cause, incentive

movilidad *f*, mobility; changeableness, inconstancy

movilización *f*, mobilization

movilizar *vt* to mobilize

movimiento *m*, movement; perturbation, excitement; *mus* movement; *lit* fire, spirit; *mech* motion, movement. *mil* **m. envolvente,** encircling movement

moza *f*, maid; girl; waitress. **m. de partido,** party girl, prostitute. **buena m.,** fine, upstanding young woman

mozalbete *m*, lad, stripling, boy

mozo *a* young, unmarried. *m*, boy, youth; bachelor; waiter; porter. **m. de cordel** *or* **m. de esquina,** street porter, message boy. **m. de estación,** railroad porter. **buen m.,** fine, upstanding young man

muaré *m*, moiré silk

mucama *f, Argentina* chambermaid

muceta *f, univ* hood, short cape (of a graduate's gown)

muchacha *f*, girl, lass; female servant

muchachada *f*, childish prank

muchachez *f*, boyhood; girlhood

muchachil *a* boyish; girlish

muchacho *m*, boy, youth; male servant

muchedumbre *f*, abundance, plenty; crowd, multitude; mass, mob

muchísimo *a sup* very much. *adv* very great deal, very much

mucho *a* much; plenty of; very; long (time); *pl* many, numerous. *adv* a great deal; much; very much; yes, certainly; frequently, often; very (e.g. **Me alegro m.,** I am very glad); to a great extent; long (time). **con m.,** by far, easily. **ni con m.,** nor anything like it, very far from it. **ni m. menos,** and much less. **por m. que,** however much

mucílago *m*, mucilage, gum

mucosa *f*, mucous membrane

mucoso *a* mucous

muda *f*, change, transformation; change of clothes; molting season; molt, sloughing of skin (snakes, etc.); change of voice (in boys)

mudable *a* changeable, inconstant

mudanza *f*, change; furniture removal; step, figure (in dancing); changeability, inconstancy

mudar *vt* to change; alter, transform; exchange; remove; dismiss (from employment); molt; slough the skin (snakes, etc.); change the voice (boys); *vr* alter one's behavior; change one's clothes; change one's residence, move; change one's expression; *inf* go away, depart

mudéjar *m*, *arch* style containing Moorish and Christian elements. *mf* Moor who remained in Spain under Christian rule

mudez *f*, dumbness; silence, muteness

mudo *a* dumb; silent, mute, quiet

mueblaje *m*, household goods and furniture

mueble *m*, piece of furniture; furnishing

mueblería *f*, furniture store or factory

mueblista *mf* furniture maker; furniture dealer

mueca *f*, grimace

muela *f*, grindstone; molar (tooth); millstone; flat-topped hill. **m. del juicio,** wisdom tooth. **dolor de muelas,** toothache

muellaje *m*, wharfage, dock dues

muelle *a* soft, smooth; voluptuous, sensuous; luxurious. *m*, spring (of a watch, etc.); wharf, quay; freight platform (railroad). **m. real,** mainspring (of a watch). **m. del volante,** hairspring.

muérdago *m*, mistletoe

muermo *m*, glanders

muerte *f*, death; destruction, annihilation; end, decline. *inf* **una m. chiquita,** a nervous shudder. **a m.,** to the death, with no quarter. **de m.,** implacably, inexorably (of hatred); very seriously (of being ill). **dar m. (a),** to kill. **estar a la m.,** to be on the point of death. **a cada m. de un obispo,** once in a blue moon

muerto (-ta) *a* dead; slaked (lime); *mech* neutral; faded, dull (colors); languid, indifferent. **m.** is used in familiar speech as *past part* **matar** (e.g. **Le ha muerto,** He has killed him). *n* corpse. *inf* **desenterrar los muertos,** to speak ill of the dead. *inf* **echarle a uno el m.,** to pass the buck. *inf* **estar m. por,** to be dying, yearning for. **ser el m.,** to be dummy (at cards)

muesca *f*, notch, mortise, groove

muestra *f*, shop sign; sample, specimen; pattern, model; demeanor; watch or clock face; sign, indication; poster, placard; *mil* muster roll. **hacer m.,** to show

muestrario *m*, sample book, collection of samples

mufla *f*, muffler (of a furnace)

mugido *m*, mooing or lowing (of cattle)

mugir *vi* to low or moo (cattle); bellow, shout; rage (elements)

mugre *f*, grease, grime, dirt

mugriento *a* grimy, greasy

muguete *m*, lily of the valley

mujer *f*, woman; wife. **m. de la vida airada** *or* **m. del partido** *or* **m. pública,** prostitute. **m. de la luna,** man in the moon. **m. de su casa,** good housewife. **tomar m.,** to take a wife

mujerero, -a *a*, *Lat. Am.* fond of women

mujeriego *a* womanly, feminine; (of men) dissolute, given to philandering. **cabalgar a mujeriegas,** to ride sidesaddle

mujeril *a* womanly, feminine

mula *f*, female mule; mule (heelless slipper); *Colombia* dope smuggler; *Mexico* junk, trash. *inf* **Se me fue la m.,** My tongue ran away with me

muladar *m*, refuse heap, junkpile, dunghill

mular *a* mule; mulish

mulatero *m*, mule hirer; muleteer

mulato (-ta) *a* and *n* mulatto

muleta *f*, crutch; bullfighter's red flag; support, prop

mullir *vt irr* to make soft, shake out (wool, down, etc.); *fig* prepare the way; *agr* hoe the roots (of vines, etc.). *Pres. Part.* **mullendo.** *Preterite* **mulló, mulleron.** *Imperf. Subjunc.* **mullese,** etc.

mulo *m*, mule

multa *f*, fine

multar *vt* to impose a fine on

multicolor *a* multicolored

multiforme *a* multiform

multilátero *a* multilateral

multimillonario (-ia) *a* and *n* multimillionaire

multiplicación *f*, multiplication

multiplicador (-ra) *n* multiplier. *m*, *math* multiplier

multiplicando *m*, multiplicand

multiplicar((se) *vt* and *vr* to multiply; reproduce

multiplicidad *f*, multiplicity

múltiplo *a* and *m*, multiple

multisecular *a* age-old, many centuries old

multitud *f*, multitude, great number; crowd; rabble, masses, mob

mundanal, mundano *a* worldly, mundane

mundial *a* world, worldwide

mundo *m*, world, universe; human race; earth; human society; world (of letters, science, etc.); secular life; *ecc* vanities of the flesh; geographical globe. **echar al m.,** to give birth to; produce, bring forth. **el Nuevo M.,** the New World, America. *inf* **medio m.,** half the earth, a great crowd. *inf* **ponerse el m. por montera,** to treat the world as one's oyster. **ser hombre del m.,** to be a man of the world. *inf* **tener m.** *or* **mucho m.,** to be very experienced, know the world. **todo el m.,** everyone. **venir al m.,** to be born. **ver m.,** to travel, see the world

mundología *f*, worldliness, experience of the world

munición *f*, *mil* munition; small shot. **mil m. de boca,** fodder and food supplies

municionero (-ra) *n* purveyor, supplier

municipal *a* municipal. *m*, policeman

municipalidad *f*, municipality

municipio *m*, municipality, town council

munificencia *f*, munificence, generosity

munífico *a* munificent, generous

muñeca *f*, *anat* wrist; doll; puppet; dressmaker's dummy; polishing pad; mannequin; boundary marker; *inf* flighty young woman

muñeco *m*, boy doll; puppet; *inf* playboy

muñir *vt irr* to summon, convoke; arrange, dispose. See **mullir**

muñón *m*, *surg* stump of an amputated limb; *mech* gudgeon

mural *a* mural

muralla *f*, town wall; rampart, fortification

murar *vt* to surround with a wall, wall in

murciélago *m*, *zool* bat

murga *f*, band of street musicians

murmullo *m*, whisper; whispering; rustling; purling; lapping, splashing; mumbling, muttering

murmuración *f*, slander, backbiting, gossip

murmurador (-ra) *a* gossiping, slanderous. *n* gossip, backbiter

murmurar *vi* to rustle (leaves, etc.); purl, lap, splash (water); whisper; mumble, mutter; *vi* and *vt inf* slander, backbite

murmurio *m*, rustling; lapping (of water); whispering; murmur; *inf* slander

muro *m*, wall; defensive wall, rampart

musaraña *f*, *zool* shrew; any small animal; *inf* ridiculous effigy, guy. *inf* **mirar a las musarañas,** to be absent-minded

muscular *a* muscular

musculatura *f*, musculature

músculo *m*, muscle; strength, brawn

musculoso *a* muscular; strong, brawny

muselina *f*, muslin

museo *m*, museum. **m. de pintura,** art gallery, picture gallery

musgo *m*, moss

musgoso *a* mossy, moss-grown

música *f*, music; melody, harmony; musical performance; musical composition; group of musicians; sheet music. *inf* **m. celestial,** vain words, moonshine. *inf* **m.**

ratonera, badly played music. *inf* **¡Vaya con su m. a otra parte!** Get out! Go to hell!

musical *a* musical

músico (-ca) *a* music. *n* musician. **m. ambulante,** strolling musician. **m. mayor,** bandleader

musitar *vi* to mutter, mumble

muslo *m,* thigh

mustango *m, Lat. Am.* mustang

mustio *a* sad, disheartened, depressed; faded, withered; *Mexico* hypocritical

musulmán (-ana) *a* and *n* Muslim

mutabilidad *f,* mutability, changeability

mutación *f,* change, mutation; sudden change in the weather; *theat* change of scene

mutilación *f,* mutilation; damage; defacement

mutilar *vt* to mutilate; spoil, deface, damage; cut short; reduce

mutis *m, theat* exit. **hacer m.** *theat* to exit; keep quiet, say nothing

mutismo *m,* mutism, dumbness; silence, speechlessness

mutualidad *f,* reciprocity, mutuality, interdependence; principle of mutual aid; mutual aid society

mutualismo *m,* mutualism, organized mutual aid

mutualista *mf* member of a mutual aid society

mutuante *mf com* lender

mutuo *a* reciprocal, mutual, interdependent

muy *adv* very; very much; much. Used to form absolute superlative (e.g. **m. rápidamente,** very quickly). Can modify adjectives, nouns used adjectivally, adverbs, participles (e.g. **María es m. mujer,** Mary is very much a woman (very womanly)). **m. temprano,** very early. **M. señor mío,** Dear Sir (in letters)

N

naba *f,* swede, turnip

nabar *m,* turnip field

nabo *m,* turnip; turnip root; any root stem; *naut* mast; stock (of a horse's tail)

nácar *m,* mother-of-pearl

nacarado, nacáreo *a* nacreous, mother-of-pearl

nacer *vi irr* to be born; rise (rivers, etc.); sprout; grow (plumage, fur, leaves, etc.); descend (lineage); appear (stars, etc.); originate; *fig* issue forth; appear suddenly; (*with prep a* or *para*) be destined for, have a natural leaning toward. **n. con pajitas de oro en la cuna,** to be born with a silver spoon in one's mouth. *vr* grow; sprout; *sew* split at the seams. *Pres. Ind.* **nazco, naces,** etc. *Pres. Subjunc.* **nazca,** etc.

nacido *a* and *past part* born; suitable, fit. *m,* (gen. *pl*) the living and the dead. **bien n.,** noble, well-born; well-bred. **mal n.,** base-born; ill-bred

naciente *a* growing; nascent. *m,* east

nacimiento *m,* birth; source (of rivers, etc.); birthplace; origin; lineage; *ast* rising; nativity crib, manger. **de n.,** from birth; by birth; born

nación *f,* nation; country; *inf* birth

nacional *a* national; native. *mf* citizen, national

nacionalidad *f,* nationality

nacionalismo *m,* nationalism

nacionalista *a* and *mf* nationalist

nacionalización *f,* naturalization; nationalization; acclimatization

nacionalizar *vt* to naturalize; nationalize

nacionalsindicalismo *m,* national syndicalism

nacionalsocialismo *m,* national socialism, nazism

nada *f,* void, nothingness. *pron indef* nothing. *adv* by no means. **casi n.,** very little, practically nothing. **¡De n.!** Not at all! Don't mention it! You're welcome! **No vale para n.,** He (it, she) is of no use

nadaderas *f pl,* water wings (for swimming)

nadador (-ra) *n* swimmer. *a* swimming

nadar *vi* to swim; float; have an abundance (of); *inf* be too large (of garments, etc.). **n. y guardar la ropa,** *fig* to sit on the fence

nadería *f,* trifle

nadie *pron indef* no one. *m, fig* a nobody

nadir *m,* nadir

nado *a* by swimming; afloat

nafta *f,* naphtha; *Argentina* gas, gasoline

naftalina *f,* naphthalene

naipe *m,* playing card; pack of cards

naire *m,* elephant keeper or trainer

nalga *f,* (gen. *pl*) buttock(s)

nana *f, inf* grandma; lullaby; *Mexico* wet nurse; nursery-maid

nao *f,* ship

napoleónico *a* Napoleonic

Nápoles Naples

napolitano (-na) *a* and *n* Neapolitan

naranja *f,* orange. **n. dulce,** blood orange. **n. mandarina,** tangerine. *inf* **media n.,** better half

naranjada *f,* orangeade

naranjal *m,* orange grove

naranjero (-ra) *n* orange seller

naranjo *m,* orange tree; *inf* lout, blockhead

narciso *m,* narcissus; dandy, fop. **n. trompón,** daffodil

narcótico *a* and *m,* narcotic

narcotizar *vt* to narcotize

narcotraficante *mf* drug dealer

nardo *m,* tuberose, spikenard, nard

narigudo *a* large-nosed; nose-shaped

nariz *f,* nose; nostril; snout; nozzle; sense of smell; bouquet (of wine). **n. perfilada,** well-shaped nose. **n. respingona,** snub nose. *inf* **meter las narices,** to meddle, interfere

narración *f,* narration, account

narrador (-ra) *a* narrative. *n* narrator

narrar *vt* to narrate, tell, relate

narrativa *f,* narrative; account; narrative skill

narrativo, narratorio *a* narrative

nata *f,* cream; *fig* the flower, elite; *pl* whipped cream with sugar

natación *f,* swimming. **n. a la marinera,** trudgen stroke

natal *a* natal; native. *m,* birth; birthday

natalicio *a* natal. *a* and *m,* birthday

natalidad *f,* birth rate

natatorio *a* swimming. *m,* swimming pool

natillas *f pl,* custard

natividad *f,* nativity; birth; Christmas

nativo *a* indigenous; native; innate

nato *a* born; inherent; ex officio

natura *f,* nature; *mus* major scale

natural *a* natural; native; indigenous; spontaneous; sincere, candid; physical; usual, ordinary; *mus* natural; unadulterated, pure; *her* proper. *mf* native, citizen. *m,* temperament; disposition; instinct (of animals); natural inclination. **al n.,** naturally, without art. **del n.,** art from life

naturaleza *f,* nature; character; disposition; instinct; temperament; nationality, origin; naturalization; kind, class; constitution, physique. **n. humana,** humankind. **n. muerta,** *art* still life

naturalidad *f,* naturalness; nationality

naturalista *mf* naturalist

naturalización *f,* naturalization; acclimatization

naturalizar *vt* to naturalize; acclimatize; *vr* become naturalized; become acclimatized

naturalmente *adv* naturally; of course

naturismo *m,* nature cure

naufragar *vi* to be shipwrecked; fail, be unsuccessful

naufragio *m*, shipwreck; disaster, loss
náufrago (-ga) *n* shipwrecked person. *m*, shark
náusea *f*, nausea (*pl* more usual); repugnance
nauseabundo, nauseoso *a* nauseous; nauseating, repugnant
nauta *mf* mariner
náutica *f*, navigation; yachting; seamanship
náutico *a* nautical
navaja *f*, razor; clasp knife; boar tusk; sting; *inf* slanderous tongue. **n. de afeitar,** (shaving) razor
navajada *f*, slash with a razor
navajero *m*, razor case
naval *a* naval
Navarra Navarre
navarro (-ra) *a* and *n* Navarrese
nave *f*, ship; *arch* nave. **n. aérea,** airship. *arch* **n. lateral,** aisle. **n. principal,** *arch* nave
navegable *a* navigable
navegación *f*, navigation; sea voyage
navegante *a* voyaging; navigating. *m*, navigator
navegar *vi* to navigate; sail; fly
navidad *f*, nativity; Christmas; *pl* Christmastime
naviero *a* shipping. *m*, ship owner
navío *m*, warship; ship. **n. de transporte,** transport. **n. de tres puentes,** three-decker
náyade *f*, naiad, water nymph
nazareno (-na) *a* and *n* Nazarene; Christian
Nazaret Nazareth
nazismo *m*, nazism
neblina *f*, fog; mist
nebulosidad *f*, nebulousness; cloudiness
nebuloso *a* foggy; misty; cloudy; somber, melancholy; confused, nebulous
necedad *f*, silliness
necesario *a* necessary; unavoidable
neceser *m*, dressing case. *sew* **n. de costura,** workbox
necesidad *f*, necessity; poverty, want; shortage, need; emergency. **de n.,** necessarily
necesitado (-da) *a* needy, poor. *n* poor person
necesitar *vt* to necessitate; compel, oblige; *vi* be necessary, need
necio *a* stupid; senseless; unreasonable
necrología *f*, necrology, obituary
necromancía *f*, necromancy
neerlandés *a* Dutch
nefando *a* iniquitous
nefario *a* nefarious
nefasto *a* disastrous, ill-omened
nefrítico *a* nephritic
nefritis *f*, nephritis
negable *a* deniable
negación *f*, negation; privation; negative; nay; *gram* negative particle; *law* traverse
negado *a* inept, unfitted; stupid
negar *vt irr* to deny; refuse; prohibit; disclaim; dissemble; disown; *law* traverse; *vr* refuse, avoid; decline (to receive visitors). See **acertar**
negativa *f*, denial; refusal; *phot* negative
negativo *a* negative
negligencia *f*, negligence; omission; carelessness; forgetfulness
negligente *a* negligent; careless; neglectful
negociable *a* negotiable
negociación *f*, negotiation; business affair, deal
negociado *m*, department, section (of a ministry, etc.); business; *Chile* shop, store; *elsewhere in Lat. Am.* shady deal
negociante *m*, businessman. *a* negotiating; trading
negociar *vi* to trade, traffic; negotiate
negocio *m*, occupation; trade; business; employment; transaction; *Argentina* shop, store; *pl* business affairs. **hombre de negocios,** businessman
negra *f*, black girl, black woman; *inf* honey, *WH* sweetheart
negrecer *vi irr* to become black. See **conocer**
negrero (-ra) *n* slave trader

negro *a* black; dark; melancholy; disastrous; *her* sable. *m*, black; black (color). **n. de humo,** lampblack
negrura *f*, blackness
negruzco *a* blackish
neme *m*, *Colombia* asphalt
nemotécnica *f*, mnemonics
nene (-na) *n inf* baby; darling
nenúfar *m*, white water lily
neo *m*, neon
neófito (-ta) *n* neophyte
neologismo *m*, neologism
neoyorquino (-na) *a* New York. *n* New Yorker
nepotismo *m*, nepotism
Neptuno *m*, *ast* Neptune; *poet* sea
nervio *m*, nerve; sinew; *bot* vein; vigor; *mus* string. **n. ciático,** sciatic nerve
nervioso *a* nervous; overwrought, agitated; vigorous; neural; sinewy; jerky (of style, etc.)
nervosidad *f*, nervousness; nervosity; flexibility (metals); jerkiness (of style, etc.); force, efficacy
nervudo *a* strong-nerved, vigorous
nesga *f*, *sew* gore
neto *a* neat; clean; pure; *com* net. *m*, *arch* dado
neumático *a* pneumatic. *m*, rubber tire
neumococo *m*, pneumococcus
neurálgico *a* neuralgic
neurastenia *f*, neurasthenia
neurasténico (-ca) *a* and *n* neurasthenic
neurología *f*, neurology
neurólogo *m*, neurologist
neurosis *f*, neurosis. **n. de guerra,** war neurosis; shell shock
neurótico (-ca) *a* and *n* neurotic
neutral *a* neutral; indifferent
neutralidad *f*, neutrality; impartiality, indifference
neutralizar *vt* to neutralize; counteract, mitigate
neutro *a* neuter; *chem* neutral; *mech* neuter; sexless
nevada *f*, snowfall
nevado *m*, *Lat. Am.* snow-capped mountain
nevar *vi irr impers* to snow. *Pres. Ind.* **nieva.** *Pres. Subjunc.* **nieve**
nevazón *f*, *Lat. Am.* blizzard, snowstorm
nevera *f*, refrigerator; icehouse
nevero *m*, ice-cream man; iceman
nevisca *f*, light snowfall
nevoso *a* snowy
nexo *m*, nexus; connection, union
ni *conjunc* neither, nor. **ni bien ni mal,** neither good nor bad. **ni siquiera,** not even. **¡Ni crea!, ¡Ni creas!** Nonsense!
niara *f*, haystack, rick
nicaragüeño (-ña) *a* and *n* Nicaraguan
nicho *m*, niche; recess (in a wall)
nicotina *f*, nicotine
nidada *f*, nest full of eggs; brood, clutch
nidal *m*, nest; nest egg; haunt; cause, foundation
nido *m*, nest; den; hole; dwelling; haunt. **n. de ametralladoras,** *mil* pillbox
niebla *f*, fog; mist; cloud; mildew; haze
nieto (-ta) *n* grandchild; descendant
nieve *f*, snow; whiteness. **deportes de n.,** winter sports
nigromancia *f*, necromancy
nigromante *m*, necromancer
nihilismo *m*, nihilism
nihilista *mf* nihilist
Nilo, el the Nile
nimbo *m*, halo, nimbus
nimiedad *f*, prolixity; *inf* fussiness; fastidiousness, delicacy
nimio *a* prolix; *inf* fussy; fastidious; *inf* parsimonious
ninfa *f*, nymph; *ent* chrysalis
ningún *a abb* of **ninguno.** Used before *m*, *sing* nouns only. **De n. modo,** In no way! Certainly not!
niña *f*, girl. **n. del ojo,** pupil (of the eye). **n. de los ojos,** apple of one's eye, darling
niñada *f*, childishness, foolish act

niñera *f,* nursemaid

niñería *f,* childish act; trifle; childishness, folly

niñez *f,* childhood; beginning, early days; *fig* cradle

niño (-ña) *a* childish; young; inexperienced; imprudent. *n* child; young or inexperienced person. **n. de la doctrina,** charity child. **n. terrible,** enfant terrible. **desde n.,** from childhood

nipón (-ona) *a* and *n* Japanese

níquel *m, chem* nickel

niquelar *vt* to chrome-plate

niquelera *f, Colombia* purse, change purse

nirvana *m,* nirvana

níspero *m,* medlar tree; medlar

níspola *f,* medlar

nitidez *f,* brightness, neatness, cleanliness

nítido *a* bright, neat, clean (often *poet.*)

nitrato *m,* nitrate

nítrico *a* nitric

nitrógeno *m,* nitrogen

nivel *m,* level; levelness. **n. de albañil,** plummet. **n. de burbuja,** spirit level. **a n.,** on the level. **estar al n. de las circunstancias,** to rise to the occasion; save the day

nivelación *f,* leveling

nivelador (-ra) *a* leveling. *n* leveler

nivelar *vt* to level; *fig* make equal

níveo *a* snowy; snow-white

no *adv* no; not. **no bien,** no sooner. **no sea que,** unless. **no tal,** no such thing

noble *a* noble, illustrious; generous; outstanding, excellent; aristocratic. *mf* nobleman (-woman)

nobleza *f,* nobility

noche *f,* night; darkness; confusion, obscurity. *inf* **n. toledana,** restless night. **¡Buenas noches!** Good night! **de n.,** by night. **esta n.,** tonight

nochebuena *f,* Christmas Eve

nochebueno *m,* yule log; Christmas cake

nocherniego *a* night, nocturnal

nochote *m, Mexico* cactus beer

noción *f,* notion, idea; *pl* elementary knowledge

nocividad *f,* noxiousness

nocivo *a* noxious

nocturno *a* nocturnal; melancholy. *m, mus* nocturne

nodriza *f,* wet nurse

nogal *m,* walnut tree; walnut wood

nómada *a* nomadic

nomadismo *m,* nomadism

nombradía *f,* renown

nombramiento *m,* naming; appointment; nomination

nombrar *vt* to name; nominate; appoint; mention (in dispatches, etc.)

nombre *m,* name; title; reputation; proxy; *gram* noun; *mil* password. **n. de pila,** Christian name. **por n.,** called; by name. **Su n. anda puesto en el cuerno de la Luna,** He (she) is praised to the skies

nomenclatura *f,* nomenclature

nómina *f,* list, register; payroll; amulet

nominación *f,* nomination, appointment

nominador (-ra) *a* nominating. *n* nominator

nominal *a* nominal

nominalismo *m,* nominalism

nominalista *a* nominalistic. *mf* nominalist

nomo *m,* gnome

nóstico (-ca) *a* and *n* gnostic

non *a* odd (of numbers)

nonada *f,* nothing, practically nothing

nonagenario (-ia) *a* and *n* nonagenarian

nonagésimo *a* ninetieth

nones *m, pl* certainly not, definitely not, nope

nopal *m,* nopal, prickly pear tree

noque *m,* tanner's vat

noquear *vt (boxing)* to knock out, K.O.

norabuena *f,* congratulation

nordeste *m,* northeast

nórdico (-ca) *a* and *n* Nordic

noria *f,* water well; chain pump; *inf* hard, monotonous work

norma *f,* square (used by builders, etc.); *fig* norm, standard, model

normal *a* normal, usual; standard, average. *f,* normal school, teacher's college (also **escuela n.**)

normalidad *f,* normality

normalista *mf* student at a teacher's college

normalización *f,* normalization; standardization

normalizar *vt* to make normal; standardize

Normandía Normandy

normando (-da) *a* Norman. *n* Northman; Norman

nornordeste *m,* northnortheast

nornorueste *m,* northnorthwest

noroeste *m,* northwest

norte *m,* north pole; north; north wind; polestar; *fig* guide

norteamericano (-na) *a* and *n* North American; (*U.S.A.*) American

norteño *a* northerly, northern

Noruega Norway

noruego (-ga) *a* and *n* Norwegian. *m,* Norwegian (language)

nos *pers pron pl mf acc* and *dat* (direct and indirect object) of **nosotros,** us; to us (e.g. **Nos lo dio,** He gave it to us)

nosotros, nosotras *pers pron pl mf* we; us. Also used with preposition (e.g. **Lo hicieron por nosotros,** They did it for us)

nostalgia *f,* nostalgia

nostálgico *a* nostalgic; melancholy; homesick

nota *f,* mark, sign; annotation, comment; *mus* note; memorandum; *com* bill, account; criticism, imputation; mark (in exams); repute, renown; note (diplomatic)

notabilidad *f,* notability

notable *a* notable, remarkable; outstanding, prominent; with distinction (examination mark). *m pl,* notabilities

notación *f, (mus math)* notation; annotation

notar *vt* to mark, indicate; observe, notice; note down; annotate; dictate, read out; criticize, reproach; discredit

notaría *f,* profession of a notary; notary's office

notarial *a* notarial

notario *m,* notary public

noticia *f,* rudiment, elementary knowledge; information; news (gen. *pl*); *pl* knowledge. **atrasado de noticias,** *fig* behind the times

noticiar *vt* to inform, give notice

noticiario *m,* news bulletin, newsreel.

noticiero *m,* newspaper

noticioso *a* informed; learned; newsy

notificación *f, law* notification. **n. de reclutamiento,** draft notice

notificar *vt* to notify officially; inform; warn

noto *a* known. *m,* south wind

notoriedad *f,* notoriety, publicity; flagrancy; fame, renown

notorio *a* well-known; notorious, obvious; flagrant

novatada *f, inf* ragging (of a freshman); blunder

novato (-ta) *a* new, inexperienced. *n* novice, beginner

novecientos *a* and *m,* nine hundred

novedad *f,* newness, novelty; change, alteration; latest news; surprise; *pl* novelties. **sin n.,** no change; all well (or as usual); safely, without incident

novel *a* new; inexperienced

novela *f,* novel; tale; falsehood. **n. caballista,** western, cowboy story. **n. por entregas,** serial (story)

novelero (-ra) *a* fond of novelty and change; fond of novels; fickle. *n* newshound, gossip

novelesco *a* novelistic; imaginary

novelista *mf* novelist

novelística *f,* art of novel writing

novena *f, ecc* novena, religious services spread over nine days

noveno *a* and *m,* ninth

noventa *a* and *m*, ninety; ninetieth

novia *f*, bride; fiancée

noviar con *vi*, *Argentina* to court, woo

noviazgo *m*, engagement, betrothal

noviciado *m*, novitiate; training, apprenticeship

novicio (-ia) *n ecc* novice; beginner, apprentice; unassuming person

noviembre *m*, November

novillada *f*, herd of young bulls; bullock baiting

novillo *m*, bullock. **hacer novillos,** to play truant

novilunio *m*, new moon

novio *m*, bridegroom; fiancé; novice, beginner

novísimo *a sup* **nuevo** newest; latest; most recent

nubada *f*, cloudburst, rainstorm; abundance, plenty

nubarrón *m*, dense, lowering cloud, storm cloud

nube *f*, cloud; *fig* screen, impediment. **n. de verano,** summer cloud; passing annoyance

nublado *a* cloudy; overcast. *m*, storm cloud; menace, threat; multitude, crowd

nublarse *vr* to cloud over

nubloso *a* cloudy; unfortunate, unhappy

nuca *f*, nape

núcleo *m*, kernel; stone, pip (of fruit); nucleus; *fig* core, essence

nudillo *m*, knuckle; *mas* plug

nudo *m*, knot; (*bot med*) node; joint; *naut* knot; *fig* bond, tie; *fig* crux, knotty point. **n. al revés,** granny knot. **n. de comunicaciones,** communication center. **n. de marino,** reef knot. **n. de tejedor,** sheet bend (knot). **n. en la garganta,** *fig* lump in the throat (from emotion)

nudoso *a* knotted, knotty; gnarled

nuera *f*, daughter-in-law

nuestro, nuestra *poss pron 1st pers pl mf* our; ours. **los nuestros,** our friends, supporters, party, profession, etc.

nueva *f*, news

Nueva Caledonia New Caledonia

Nueva Escocia Nova Scotia

Nueva Gales del Sur New South Wales

nuevamente *adv* again

Nueva Orleans New Orleans

Nueva York New York

Nueva Zelanda, Nueva Zelandia New Zealand

nueve *a* nine; ninth. *m*, number nine; ninth (of the month) (e.g. **el nueve de marzo,** March 9th). **a las nueve,** at nine o'clock

nuevo *a* new; fresh; newly arrived; inexperienced; unused, scarcely worn. **de n.,** again. **¿Qué hay de n.?** What's the news? What's new?

Nuevo México *m* New Mexico

nuez *f*, walnut; *anat* Adam's apple. **n. moscada,** nutmeg

nulidad *f*, nullity; incompetence, ineptitude; worthlessness

nulo *a* null, void; incapable; worthless

numen *m*, divinity; inspiration

numeración *f*, calculation; numbering

numerador *m*, numerator

numerar *vt* to number; enumerate; calculate

numerario *a* numerary. *m*, cash

numérico *a* numerical

número *m*, number; figure; numeral; size (of gloves, etc.); quantity; issue, copy; rhythm; *gram* number; item (of a program); *pl ecc* Numbers. **n. del distrito postal,** ZIP code. **n. quebrado,** *math* fraction. **sin n.,** numberless

numeroso *a* numerous; harmonious

numismática *f*, numismatics

nunca *adv* never. **n. jamás,** nevermore. **N. digas «De esta agua no beberé!»** Never say "Never!"

nuncio *m*, messenger; papal nuncio; *fig* harbinger

nupcial *a* nuptial

nupcialidad *f*, marriage rate

nupcias *f pl*, nuptials, marriage

nutria *f*, otter, nutria

nutrición *f*, nourishment; nutrition

nutrido *a* abundant; numerous

nutrimento *m*, nutriment; nourishment; nutrition; *fig* food, encouragement

nutrir *vt* to nourish; encourage; *fig* fill

nutritivo *a* nourishing, nutritive

Ñ

ñácara *f*, *Central America* sore, ulcer

ñaña *f*, *Lat. Am.* wet nurse; nursemaid; elder sister

ñaques *m pl*, odds and ends, rubbish

ñiquiñaque *m*, *inf* good-for-nothing, wastrel; *inf* trash

ñoco, -a *a*, *Lat. Am.* one-handed; missing a finger

ñoñería *f*, *inf* drivel; folly, stupidity

ñoño (-ña) *a inf* sentimental; foolish, idiotic. *n* fool.

O

o *f*, letter O. *conjunc* or, either. **o** becomes **u** before words beginning with **o** or **ho** (e.g. **gloria u honor**)

oasis *m*, oasis; *fig* refuge, haven

obcecación *f*, blindness; obstinacy; obsession

obcecar *vt* to blind; obsess; *fig* dazzle; darken

obduración *f*, obstinacy, stubbornness, obduracy

obedecer *vt irr* to obey; *fig* respond; bend, yield (metals, etc.); *vi* result (from), arise (from). See **conocer**

obedecimiento *m*, **obediencia** *f*, obedience

obediente *a* obedient; docile

obelisco *m*, obelisk

obertura *f*, *mus* overture

obesidad *f*, obesity

obeso *a* obese

óbice *m*, obstacle, impediment

obispado *m*, bishopric

obispo *m*, bishop. **o. sufragáneo,** suffragan bishop

óbito *m*, death, demise

obituario *m*, obituary; obituary column

objeción *f*, objection

objetar *vt* to object to, oppose

objetivar *vt* to view objectively

objetividad *f*, objectivity

objetivo *a* objective. *m*, *opt* eyepiece; object finder; aim, goal

objeto *m*, object; subject, theme; purpose; aim, goal. **sin o.,** without object; aimlessly

oblicuidad *f*, obliqueness

oblicuo *a* slanting, oblique

obligación *f*, obligation; *com* bond; *com* debenture; *pl* responsibilities; *com* liabilities

obligacionista *mf com* bond holder, debenture holder

obligado *m*, contractor (to a borough, etc.); *mus* obbligato

obligar *vt* to compel, oblige, constrain; lay under an obligation; *law* mortgage; *vr* bind oneself, promise

obligatorio *a* obligatory

oblongo *a* oblong

oboe *m*, oboe; oboe player, oboist

óbolo *m*, obol, ancient Greek coin

obra *f*, work; anything made; literary, artistic, scientific production; structure, construction; repair, alteration (to buildings, etc.); means, influence, power; labor, or time spent; action, behavior. **o. de caridad,** charitable act. **o. maestra,** masterpiece. **obras públicas,** public works. **poner por o.,** to put into effect; to set to work on. **o. de,** about, approximately

obrar *vt* to work; make, do; execute, perform; affect; construct, build; *vi* be, exist (things); act, behave. **o. mal,** to behave badly, do wrong

obrero (-ra) *a* working. *n* worker; *pl* workers

obscenidad *f,* obscenity

obsceno *a* obscene

obsequiar *vt* to entertain, be attentive (to); give presents (to); court, make love to. **Me obsequia con un reloj,** He is presenting me with a watch

obsequio *m,* attention; gift; deference. **en o. de,** as a tribute to

obsequioso *a* obliging, courteous, attentive

observable *a* observable

observación *f,* observation; remark

observador (-ra) *a* observing. *n* observer

observancia *f,* observance; respect, reverence

observar *vt* to notice; inspect, examine; fulfill; remark; watch, spy upon; *ast* observe

observatorio *m,* observatory

obsesión *f,* obsession

obsesionar *vt* to obsess

obseso *a* obsessed

obsidiana *f,* obsidian

obsolecer *vi* to obsolesce, become obsolete

obsoleto *a* obsolete

obstáculo *m,* impediment; obstacle

obstante, no *adv* in spite of; nevertheless

obstar *vi* to impede, hinder

obstetra *mf* obstetrician

obstetricia *f,* obstetrics

obstinación *f,* obstinacy

obstinado *a* obstinate, stubborn

obstinarse *vr* (*with en*) to persist in, insist on, be stubborn about

obstinaz *a* obstinate

obstrucción *f,* obstruction

obstruccionar *vt, Lat. Am.* to obstruct, stonewall

obstruccionismo *m,* obstructionism, stonewalling

obstruccionista *mf* obstructionist

obstruir *vt irr* to obstruct; block; hinder; *vr* become choked or stopped up (pipes, etc.). See **huir**

obtención *f,* obtainment; attainment, realization

obtener *vt irr* to obtain; attain; maintain, preserve. See **tener**

obturador *m,* stopper; shutter (of a camera)

obturar *vt* to stopper, plug; block, obstruct

obtuso *a* blunt, dull; (*geom* and *fig*) obtuse

obús *m,* howitzer; *mil* shell

obviar *vt* to obviate

obvio *a* obvious, evident, apparent

oca *f,* goose

ocasión *f,* occasion; opportunity; motive, cause; danger; risk; *inf* **asir la o. por la melena,** to take time by the forelock. **de o.,** second-hand

ocasional *a* chance, fortuitous; occasional

ocasionar *vt* to cause, occasion; excite, provoke; risk, endanger

ocaso *m,* sunset; west; dusk; decadence, decline

occidental *a* Western

occidente *m,* West, Occident

occiso *a* murdered; killed

oceánico *a* oceanic

océano *m,* ocean; immensity, abundance

oceanografía *f,* oceanography

ocelote *m,* ocelot

ochava *f,* eighth; *ecc* octave

ochavo *m, ant* small Spanish copper coin

ochenta *a* and *m,* eighty; eightieth

ochentón (-ona) *n* octogenarian

ocho *a* eight; eighth. *m,* figure eight; playing card with eight pips; eight; eighth day (of the month). **las o.,** eight o'clock

ochocientos *a* and *m,* eight hundred; eight-hundredth

ocio *m,* leisure, idleness; *pl* pastimes; leisure time

ociosidad *f,* idleness, laziness; leisure

ocioso (-sa) *a* idle; useless, worthless; unprofitable, fruitless. *n* idle fellow

ocozoal *m, Mexico* rattlesnake

ocre *m,* ocher

octágono *m,* octagon

octava *f,* octave

octaviano *a* Octavian

octavo *a* eighth. *m,* eighth. **en o.,** in octavo

octeto *m,* octet

octogenario (-ia) *a* and *n* octogenarian

octogésimo *a* eightieth

octubre *m,* October

óctuple *a* octuple, eightfold

ocular *a* ocular. *m,* eyepiece

oculista *mf* oculist

ocultación *f,* hiding, concealment

ocultamente *adv* secretly

ocultar *vt* to hide, conceal; disguise; keep secret

ocultismo *m,* occultism

oculto *a* hidden; secret; occult. **en o.,** secretly, quietly

ocupación *f,* occupancy; occupation, pursuit; employment, office, trade

ocupado *a* occupied; busy

ocupante *m,* occupant

ocupar *vt* to take possession of; obtain or hold (job); occupy, fill; inhabit; employ; hinder, embarrass; hold the attention (of); *vr* (*with en*) be engaged in, be occupied with; (*with con*) concentrate on (a business affair, etc.)

ocurrencia *f,* occurrence, incident; bright idea; witty remark

ocurrir *vi* to anticipate; happen, take place; occur, strike (ideas)

oda *f,* ode

odalisca *f,* odalisk

odiar *vt* to hate; *Chile* annoy, irk

odio *m,* hatred; malevolence

odioso *a* hateful, odious; *Argentina, Chile, Peru* annoying, irksome

odisea *f,* odyssey

odontología *f,* odontology

odontólogo *m,* odontologist

odorífero *a* odoriferous, fragrant

odre *m,* goatskin, wineskin; *inf* wine bibber

oesnorueste *m,* westnorthwest

oessudueste *m,* westsouthwest

oeste *m,* west

ofender *vt* to ill-treat, hurt; offend, insult; anger, annoy; *vr* be offended

ofendido *a* offended; resentful

ofensa *f,* injury, harm; offense, crime

ofensiva *f, mil* offensive. **tomar la o.,** to take the offensive

ofensivo *a* offensive

ofensor (-ra) *n* offender

oferta *f,* offer; gift; proposal; *com* tender. **o. y demanda,** supply and demand

oficial *a* official. *m,* official; officer; clerk; executioner; worker

oficiala *f,* trained female worker

oficialidad *f,* officialdom; officers

oficiar *vt ecc* to celebrate or serve (mass); communicate officially, inform; *inf* (*with de*) act as

oficina *f,* workshop; office; pharmaceutical laboratory; *pl* cellars, basement (of a house)

oficinesco *a* bureaucratic, red-tape

oficinista *mf* clerk, office employee, office worker

oficio *m,* occupation, employment; office, function, capacity; craft; operation; trade, business; official communication; office, bureau; *ecc* office. **Santo O.,** Holy Office. *fig* **buenos oficios,** good offices

oficiosidad *f*, diligence, conscientiousness; helpfulness; friendliness; officiousness

oficioso *a* conscientious; helpful, useful; officious; meddlesome; unofficial, informal

ofrecer *vt irr* to offer; present; exhibit; consecrate, dedicate; *vr* occur, suggest itself; volunteer. **¿Qué se le ofrece?** What do you require? What would you like? See **conocer**

ofrecimiento *m*, offer, offering

ofrenda *f*, *ecc* offering; gift, present

oftalmología *f*, ophthalmology

oftalmólogo *m*, oculist, ophthalmologist

ofuscación *f*. **ofuscamiento** *m*, obfuscation, dazzle; dimness of sight; mental confusion, bewilderment

ofuscar *vt* to dazzle, daze; dim, obfuscate; confuse, bewilder

ogro *m*, ogre

ohmio *m*, ohm

oídas, de *adv* by hearsay

oído *m*, sense of hearing; ear. **de o.**, by ear. **decir al o.**, to whisper in a person's ear. *mus* **duro de o.**, hard of hearing; having a bad ear (for music). **estar sordo de un o.**, to be deaf in one ear

oidor *m*, hearer; judge, *ant* magistrate

oir *vt irr* to hear; give ear to, listen; understand. *Pres. Part.* **oyendo.** *Pres. Ind.* **oigo, oyes, oye, oyen.** *Preterite* **oyó, oyeron.** *Pres. Subjunc.* **oiga,** etc. *Imperf. Subjunc.* **oyese,** etc.

oíslo *mf inf* better half

ojal *m*, buttonhole; slit, hole

¡ojalá! *interj* If only that were so! God grant!

ojeada *f*, glance

ojear *vt* to look at, stare at; bewitch; scare, startle

ojera *f*, dark shadow (under the eye); eye bath

ojeriza *f*, ill-will, spite

ojeroso *a* having dark shadows under the eyes, wan, haggard

ojete *m*, eyelet

ojinegro *a* black-eyed

ojiva *f*, ogive

ojo *m*, eye; hole; slit; socket; keyhole; eye (of a needle); span (of a bridge); core (of a corn); attention, care; mesh; spring, stream; well (of a staircase); *pl* darling. **¡Ojo!** Take care! **o. avizor,** sharp watch; lynx eye. **Ojos que no ven, corazón que no siente,** Out of sight, out of mind. **o. saltón,** prominent, bulging eye. **o. vivo,** bright eye. **a o. de buen cubero,** at a guess. **a ojos vistas,** visibly; patently

ojota *f*, *Chile*, sandal

ola *f*, billow; wave (atmospheric)

ole *m*, Andalusian dance

¡olé! *interj* Bravo!

oleada *f*, big wave, breaker; swell (of the sea); *fig* surge (of a crowd)

oleaginoso *a* oleaginous

oleaje *m*, swell, surge, billowing

olear *vt* to administer extreme unction

óleo *m*, oil; *ecc* holy oil (gen. *pl*). **al ó.,** in oils

oleoducto *m*, oil pipeline

oler *vt irr* to smell; guess, discover; pry, smell out; *vi* smell; *(with prep a)* smell of; smack of, be reminiscent of. *Pres. Ind.* **huelo, hueles, huele, huelen.** *Pres. Subjunc.* **huela, huelas, huela, huelan**

olfatear *vt* to sniff, snuff, smell; *inf* pry into

olfativo, olfatorio *a* olfactory

olfato *m*, sense of smell; shrewdness

olfatorio *a* olfactory

oliente (mal) *a* evil-smelling

oligárquico *a* oligarchic

olímpico *a* Olympic; Olympian

olisco, -a *a, Lat. Am.* spoiled, tainted (meat)

oliva *f*, olive tree; olive; barn owl; peace

olivar *m*, olive grove

olivo *m*, olive tree

olmeda *f*, **olmedo** *m*, elm grove

olmo *m*, elm tree

olor *m*, odor, scent, smell; hope, promise; suspicion; hint; reputation. **o. de santidad,** odor of sanctity

oloroso *a* fragrant, perfumed

olvidadizo *a* forgetful

olvidar(se) *vt* and *vr* to forget; neglect, desert. **Se me olvidó el libro,** I forgot the book. **Me olvidé de lo pasado,** I forgot the past

olvido *m*, forgetfulness; indifference, neglect; oblivion

olla *f*, stew pot; Spanish stew; whirlpool. **o. podrida,** rich Spanish stew containing bacon, fowl, meat, vegetables, ham, etc. **las ollas de Egipto,** the fleshpots of Egypt

ombligo *m*, navel; *fig* core, center

ominoso *a* ominous

omisión *f*, omission; carelessness, negligence; neglect

omiso *a* omitted; remiss; careless. **hacer caso o. de,** to set aside, ignore

omitir *vt* to omit

ómnibus *m*, bus

omnímodo *a* all-embracing

omnipotencia *f*, omnipotence

omnipotente *a* omnipotent, all-powerful

omnisciencia *f*, omniscience

omniscio *a* omniscient

omnívoro *a* omnivorous

omoplato *m*, scapula, shoulder blade

once *a* eleven; eleventh. *m*, eleven; eleventh (of the month). **las o.,** eleven o'clock

onceno *a* eleventh

onda *f*, wave; *fig* flicker (of flames); *sew* scallop; *phys* wave; ripple; *pl* waves (in hair). *rad* **o. corta,** short wave. **o. etérea,** ether wave. **o. sonora,** sound wave

ondeado *a* undulating; wavy; scalloped

ondeante *a* waving; flowing

ondear *vi* to wave; ripple; undulate; roll (of the sea); float, flutter, stream; *sew* scallop; *vr* swing, sway

ondeo *m*, waving; undulation

ondulación *f*, undulation; wave; wriggling; twisting. **o. permanente,** permanent wave, perm

ondulado *a* wavy; undulating; scalloped

ondular *vi* to writhe, squirm, wriggle; twist; coil; *vt* wave (in hair)

oneroso *a* onerous, heavy; troublesome

ónice *m*, onyx

onomástico *a* onomastic. **día o.,** saint's day

onomatopeya *f*, onomatopoeia

onza *f*, ounce. **por onzas,** by ounces; sparingly

onzavo *a* and *m*, eleventh

opacidad *f*, opacity; obscurity; gloom

opaco *a* opaque; dark; gloomy, sad

opalino *a* opaline

ópalo *m*, opal

opción *f*, option; choice, selection; *law* option

ópera *f*, opera

operación *f*, *surg* operation; execution, performance; *com* transaction

operar *vt surg* to operate; *vi* act, have an effect; operate, control; *com* transact

operario (-ia) *n* worker, hand; operator; mechanic

opereta *f*, operetta, light opera

opinar *vi* to have or form an opinion, think; judge, consider

opinión *f*, opinion, view; reputation

opio *m*, opium. **fumadero de o.,** opium den

opíparo *a* magnificent, sumptuous (banquets, etc.)

oponer *vt irr* to oppose; resist, withstand; protest against; *vr* oppose; be contrary or hostile (to); face, be opposite; object (to), set oneself against; compete (in public exams.). See **poner**

oporto *m*, port (wine)

oportunidad *f*, opportunity, occasion

oportunismo *m*, opportunism

oportunista *a* and *mf* opportunist

oportuno *a* opportune, timely

oposición *f*, opposition; resistance; antagonism; public competitive exam for a post; *(ast pol)* opposition

opositor (-ra) *n* opponent; competitor
opresión *f*, oppression; hardship; pressure. **o. de pecho,** difficulty in breathing
opresor (-ra) *a* oppressive. *n* oppressor
oprimir *vt* to oppress; treat harshly; press, crush; choke
oprobio *m*, opprobrium
optar *vt* to take possession of; (*with por*) choose
óptica *f*, *phys* optics; peepshow
óptico *a* optic, optical. *m*, optician
optimismo *m*, optimism
optimista *mf* optimist. *a* optimistic
óptimo *a sup* **bueno** best, optimal, optimum
opugnar *vt* to resist violently; *mil* assault, attack; impugn, challenge
opulencia *f*, opulence, riches; excess, superabundance
opulento *a* opulent, rich
opúsculo *m*, monograph, opuscule
oquedad *f*, hollow, cavity; superficiality, banality
ora *adv* now
oración *f*, oration, speech; prayer; *gram* sentence
oráculo *m*, oracle
orador (-ra) *n* orator; speech maker. *m*, preacher
oral *a* oral; verbal; buccal
orangután *m*, orangutan
orar *vi* to harangue, make an oration; pray; *vt* request, beg
orate *mf* lunatic
oratoria *f*, oratory, eloquence
oratorio *a* oratorical. *m*, oratory, chapel; *mus* oratorio
orbe *m*, sphere; orb; world
órbita *f*, *ast* orbit; *fig* sphere; *anat* orbit, eye socket
Órcades, las the Orkneys
ordalía *f*, (medieval hist.) ordeal
orden *mf* order, mode of arrangement; succession, sequence; group; system; orderliness, neatness; coherence, plan; *ecc* order, brotherhood; (*zool bot*) group, class; *arch* order; *math* degree. *f*, precept, command; *com* order; *pl ecc* ordination. (*mil naut*) **o. de batalla,** battle array. **o. de caballería,** order of knighthood. **o. del día,** order of the day. *ecc* **dar órdenes,** to ordain. **en o.,** in order; with regard (to). **por su o.,** in its turn; successively
ordenación *f*, order, orderly arrangement, disposition; ordinance, precept; *ecc* ordination
ordenador *m Spain* computer
ordenamiento *m*, ordaining; ordinance; edict
ordenancista *mf mil* martinet; disciplinarian
ordenanza *f*, order, method; command, instruction; ordinance, regulation (gen. *pl*). *m*, *mil* orderly
ordenar *vt* to put in order, arrange; command, give instructions to; decree; direct, regulate; *ecc* ordain; *vr* (*with de*) *ecc* be ordained as
ordeñadero *m*, milk pail
ordeñar *vt* to milk
ordinal *a* ordinal. *m*, ordinal number
ordinariez *f*, rudeness, uncouthness; vulgarity
ordinario *a* ordinary, usual; vulgar, coarse, uncultured; rude; commonplace, average, mediocre. *m*, *ecc* ordinary; carrier; courier. **de o.,** usually, ordinarily
orear *vt* to ventilate; *vr* dry; air; take the air
orégano *m*, wild marjoram
oreja *f*, external ear; lug; tab, flap; tongue (of a shoe). *inf* **con las orejas caídas,** down in the mouth, depressed
orejera *f*, earflap; mold board (of a plow)
orejudo *a* large- or long-eared
oreo *m*, zephyr; ventilation; airing
orfanato *m*, orphanage, orphan asylum
orfandad *f*, orphanhood; defenselessness, lack of protection
orfebre *mf* gold- or silversmith
orfebrería *f*, gold- or silverwork
orfeón *m*, choral society
organdí *m*, organdy
orgánico *a* organic; harmonious; *fig* organized
organillero(-ra) *n* organ grinder
organillo *m*, barrel organ

organismo *m*, organism; organization, association
organista *mf* organist
organización *f*, organization; order, arrangement
organizador (-ra) *a* organizing. *n* organizer
organizar *vt* to organize; regulate; constitute
órgano *m*, *mus* organ; (*anat bot*) organ; means, agency. **o. de manubrio,** barrel organ
orgasmo *m*, orgasm
orgía *f*, orgy
orgullo *m*, pride; arrogance
orgulloso *a* proud; haughty
orientación *f*, orientation; exposure, prospect; bearings
oriental *a* Oriental, Eastern. *mf* Oriental; *Argentina* Uruguayan
orientalismo *m*, Orientalism
orientalista *mf* Orientalist
orientar *vt* to orientate; *vr* find one's bearings; familiarize oneself (with)
oriente *m*, Orient, the East; luster (of pearls); youth, childhood; origin, source
orificio *m*, orifice; hole
oriflama *f*, oriflamme; standard, flag
origen *m*, origin, source, root; stock, extraction; reason, genesis. **dar o. a,** to give rise to. **país de o.,** native land
original *a* original; earliest, primitive; new, first-hand; novel, fresh; inventive, creative; eccentric; quaint. *m*, original manuscript; original; sitter (for portraits); eccentric
originalidad *f*, originality
originar *vt* to cause, originate; invent; *vr* spring from, originate (in)
originario *a* original, primary; primitive; native (of)
orilla *f*, limit, edge; hem, border; selvage; shore, margin; bank (of a river, etc.); sidewalk; brink, edge. **a la o.,** on the brink; nearly
orillar *vt* to settle, arrange, conclude; *vi* reach the shore or bank; *sew* leave a hem; *sew* border; leave a selvage on cloth
orillo *m*, selvage (of cloth)
orín *m*, rust; *pl* urine
orinal *m*, chamber pot, urinal
orinar *vi* to urinate
oriundo *a* native (of); derived (from)
orla *f*, border, fringe; selvage (of cloth, garments); ornamental border (on diplomas, etc.)
orlar *vt* to border; edge, trim
ornamentación *f*, ornamentation
ornamental *a* ornamental
ornamentar *vt* to ornament; embellish
ornamento *m*, ornament; decoration; gift, virtue, talent; *pl ecc* vestments
ornar *vt* to ornament, adorn, embellish
ornato *m*, decoration, ornament
ornitología *f*, ornithology
ornitológico *a* ornithological
ornitólogo *m*, ornithologist
oro *m*, gold; gold coins or jewelery; *fig* riches; *pl* diamonds (cards). **o. batido,** gold leaf. **o. en polvo,** gold dust. *fig* **como un o.,** shining with cleanliness. **el as de oros,** the ace of diamonds
orondo *a* hollow; *inf* pompous; *inf* swollen, spongy
oropel *m*, brass foil; showy, cheap thing; trinket; tinsel
orquesta *f*, orchestra
orquestación *f*, orchestration
orquestal *a* orchestral
orquestar *vt* to orchestrate
orquídea *f*, orchid
ortega *f*, *orn* grouse
ortiga *f*, *bot* nettle
orto *m*, rising (of sun, stars)
ortodoxia *f*, orthodoxy
ortodoxo *a* orthodox
ortografía *f*, orthography
ortográfico *a* orthographical
ortopedia *f*, orthopedics

ortopédico (-ca) *a* orthopedic. *n* orthopedist
ortopedista *mf* orthopedist
oruga *f,* caterpillar
orzuelo *m, med* sty; trap (for wild animals)
os *pers pron 2nd pl mf dat and acc of* **vos** and **vosotros** you, to you
osa *f,* she-bear; *ast* **O. mayor,** Big Bear; **O. menor,** Little Bear
osadía *f,* boldness, audacity
osado *a* daring, bold
osamenta *f,* skeleton; bones (of a skeleton)
osar *vi* to dare; risk, venture
osario *m,* charnel house, ossuary
oscilación *f,* oscillation
oscilante *a* oscillating
oscilar *vi* to oscillate, sway; hesitate, vacillate
ósculo *m,* kiss, osculation
oscurantismo *m,* obscurantism
oscurantista *a* and *mf* obscurantist
oscurear *Mexico* = **oscurecer**
oscurecer *vt irr* to darken; *fig* tarnish, dim, sully; confuse, bewilder; express obscurely; *art* shade; *vn* grow dark; *vr* cloud over (sky); *inf* disappear (things, gen. by theft). See **conocer**
oscuridad *f,* darkness; gloom, blackness; humbleness; obscurity, abstruseness
oscuro *a* dark; humble, unknown; abstruse, involved; obscure; uncertain, dangerous. **a oscuras,** in the dark; ignorant
óseo *a* osseous
osera *f,* bear's den
osezno *m,* bear cub
osificación *f,* ossification
osificarse *vr* to ossify
ósmosis *f,* osmosis
oso *m,* bear. **o. blanco,** polar bear
ostensible *a* ostensible; obvious
ostensión *f,* show, display, manifestation
ostensivo *a* ostensive
ostentación *f,* manifestation; ostentation
ostentar *vt* to exhibit, show; boast, show off

ostentoso *a* magnificent, showy, ostentatious
osteópata *mf* osteopath
osteopatía *f,* osteopathy
ostión, *m, Mexico* oyster
ostra *f,* oyster. **vivero de ostras,** oyster bed
ostracismo *m,* ostracism
otear *vt* to observe; look on at
otero *m,* hill, height, eminence
otología *f,* otology
otólogo *m,* otologist
otomana *f,* ottoman, couch
otomano *a* Ottoman
otoñal *a* autumnal, autumn, fall
otoño *m,* autumn, fall
otorgamiento *m,* granting; consent, approval; license; award
otorgar *vt* to grant; concede, approve; *law* grant, stipulate, execute
otro (-ra) *a* other, another. *n* another one
otrosí *adv* besides, moreover
ovación *f,* ovation, triumph; applause
ovacionar *vt* to applaud
oval *a* oval
óvalo *m,* oval
ovario *m,* ovary
oveja *f,* ewe
overol *m Lat. Am.* overalls
ovillar *vi* to wind thread into a ball; *vr* curl up; huddle
ovillo *m,* ball, bobbin (of thread); tangled heap (of things)
ovíparo *a* oviparous
OVNI *m,* UFO
ovulación *f,* ovulation
óvulo *m,* ovule
oxidación *f,* oxidation
oxidar *vt* oxidize; *vr* become oxidized
óxido *m,* oxide. **ó. de carbono,** carbon monoxide. **ó. de cinc,** zinc oxide
oxígeno *m,* oxygen
oyente *mf* hearer; *pl* audience
ozono *m,* ozone

P

pabellón *m,* pavilion; colors, flag; bell tent. **p. británico,** Union Jack. **p. de reposo,** rest home. **en p.,** stacked (of arms)
pábulo *m,* food; *fig* pabulum
pacedero *a agr* grazing, meadow
pacer *vi irr agr* to graze; *vt* nibble away; eat away. See **nacer**
paciencia *f,* patience
paciente *a* patient; long-suffering; complacent. *mf med* patient
pacienzudo *a* extremely patient or long-suffering
pacificación *f,* pacification; serenity, peace of mind
pacificador (-ra) *a* peace making; pacifying. *n* peace maker
pacificar *vt* to pacify; *vi* make peace; *vr* grow quiet, become calm (sea, etc.)
pacífico *a* pacific, meek, mild; peace-loving, peaceful. **el Océano P.,** the Pacific Ocean
pacifismo *m,* pacifism
pacifista *a* and *mf* pacifist
pacotilla *f,* goods. *inf* **hacer su p.,** to make one's packet or fortune. **ser de p.,** to be poor stuff; be jerry-built (of houses)
pactar *vt* to stipulate, arrange; contract
pacto *m,* agreement, contract; pact
padecer *vt irr* to suffer; feel keenly; experience, undergo; tolerate. **p. desnudez,** to go unclothed. **p. hambre,** to go hungry. See **conocer**
padecimiento *m,* suffering

padrastro *m,* stepfather; cruel father; *fig* impediment, obstacle; hangnail
padrazo *m, inf* indulgent father
padre *m,* father; stallion; head (of the family, etc.); *ecc* father; genesis, source; author, creator; *pl* parents; ancestors. **p. adoptivo,** foster father. **p. de familia,** paterfamilias. **P. Eterno,** Eternal Father. **p. nuestro,** Lord's Prayer. **P. Santo,** Holy Father, the Pope
padrear *vi* to take after one's father; *zool* reproduce, breed
padrejón *m, Argentina* stallion
padrino *m,* godfather; sponsor; second (in duels, etc.); patron; best man
padrón *m,* census; pattern, model; memorial stone
paella *f, cul* savory rice dish of shellfish, chicken, and meat
paga *f,* payment; amends, restitution; pay; payment of fine; reciprocity (in love, etc.)
pagadero *a* payable. *m,* date and place when payment is due
pagador (-ra) *n* payer. *m,* teller; wages clerk; paymaster
pagaduría *f,* pay office
paganismo *m,* paganism; heathenism
pagano (-na) *a* and *n* pagan; heathen
pagar *vt* to pay; make restitution, expiate; return, requite (love, etc.); *vr* (*with de*) become fond of; be proud of. **p. adelantado,** to prepay. *com* **p. al contado,** to pay cash. **p. la casa,** to pay the rent (for one's residence)
pagaré *m, com* promissory note, I.O.U.

página *f*, page (of a book); episode, occurrence
paginación *f*, pagination
paginar *vt* to paginate
pago *m*, payment; recompense, reward; region of vineyards, olive groves, etc.; *Argentina* area, region
paguro *m*, hermit crab
pailebote *m*, schooner
país *m*, country, nation; region; *art* landscape. **del p.,** typical of the country of origin (gen. of food)
paisaje *m*, countryside; landscape, scenery
paisajista, paisista *mf* landscape painter
paisano (-na) *n* compatriot; peasant; civilian
Países Bajos, los the Low Countries, the Netherlands
paja *f*, straw; chaff; trash; *fig* padding. **ver la p. en el ojo del vecino y no la viga en el nuestro,** to see the mote in our neighbor's eye and not the beam in our own
pajar *m*, barn
pájara *f*, hen (bird); kite (toy); *inf* jay; prostitute. **p. pinta,** game of forfeits
pajarear *vt* to snare birds; loaf, idle about
pajarera *f*, aviary
pajarero *m*, bird catcher or seller. *a inf* frivolous, giddy; *inf* gaudy (colors); *Lat. Am.* skittish (horse)
pajarita *f*, bow tie
pájaro *m*, bird. **p. bobo,** penguin. **p. carpintero,** woodpecker. *fig inf* **p. gordo,** big gun. **p. mosca,** hummingbird
pajarota *f*, *inf* canard, false report
paje *m*, page; *naut* cabin boy
pajera *f*, hayloft
pajizo *a* made of straw; covered or thatched with straw; strawcolored
pala *f*, paddle; blade (of an oar); shovel; spade; baker's peel (long-handled shovel); cutting edge of a spade, hoe, etc.; *sport* racket; vamp, upper (of a shoe); pelota or jai alai racket; tanner's knife; *inf* guile, cunning; cleverness, dexterity. **p. de hélice,** propeller blade. **p. para pescado,** fish server. *inf* **corta p.,** ignoramus; blockhead
palabra *f*, word; power of speech; eloquence; offer, promise; *pl* magic formula, spell. **p. de clave,** code word. **p. de matrimonio,** promise of marriage. **p. de rey,** inviolable promise. **palabras cruzadas,** crossword puzzle. **bajo p. de,** under promise of. **cuatro palabras,** a few words; short conversation. **de p.,** verbally, by word of mouth. **dirigir la p. a,** to address, speak to. **faltar a su p.,** to break one's promise. **llevar la p.,** to be spokesperson. **medias palabras,** halfwords; hint, insinuation. **su p. empeñada,** one's solemn word. **tener la p.,** to have the right to speak (in meetings, etc.) (e.g. **El señor Martínez tiene la p.,** Mr. Martinez has the floor)
palabrería *f*, verbosity, wordiness
palabrota *f*, *inf* coarse language; long word
palaciego (-ga) *a* pertaining to palaces; *fig* courtesan. *n* courtier
palacio *m*, palace; mansion
palada *f*, shovelful, spadeful; oar stroke
paladar *m*, *anat* palate; taste; discernment, sensibility
paladear *vt* to taste with pleasure, savor; enjoy, relish
paladín *m*, paladin
paladino *a* public, clear, open
palafrén *m*, palfrey
palafrenero *m*, groom; stablehand
palanca *f*, *mech* lever; handle; bar; (high) diving board. **p. de arranque,** starting gear. **p. de cambio de velocidad,** gear-changing lever. **p. de mando,** control stick
palangana *f*, washbasin
palanganear *vi*, *Lat. Am.* to show off
palanganero *m*, washstand
palanqueta *f*, *dim* small lever; jimmy
palastro *m*, sheet iron or steel
palatinado *m*, Palatinate
palatino *a* palatine

palatizar *vt* to palatilize
palazón *f*, woodwork
palco *m*, *theat* box; stand, raised platform, enclosure. **p. de platea,** orchestra
palenque *m*, enclosure; stand; platform; palisade
paleografía *f*, paleography
paleógrafo *m*, paleographer
paleolítico *a* paleolithic
paleología *f*, paleology
paleontología *f*, paleontology
palestra *f*, tilt yard
paleta *f*, *dim* little shovel; trowel; *art* palette; fireplace shovel; mason's trowel; *anat* shoulder blade; blade (of a propeller, ventilator, etc.); *chem* spatula
paliacate *m*, *Mexico* kerchief
paliación *f*, palliation; excuse
paliar *vt* to dissemble, excuse; palliate, mitigate
paliativo *a* palliative; extenuating
palidecer *vi irr* to turn pale. See **conocer**
palidez *f*, pallor, paleness
pálido *a* pale, pallid
paliducho *a* somewhat pale, palish; sallow
palillo *m*, *dim* small stick; toothpick; bobbin (for lacemaking); drumstick; *fig* chatter; *pl* castanets
palimpsesto *m*, palimpsest
palinodia *f*, *lit* palinode. **cantar la p.,** to eat one's words, recant
palio *m*, Greek mantle; cape; *ecc* pallium; canopy, awning
palique *m*, *inf* chat. **estar de p.,** to be having a chat
paliquear *vi* to chat
paliza *f*, caning, beating
palizada *f*, paling, fence; palisade, stockade. **p. de tablas,** hoarding
palma *f*, palm tree; palm leaf; date palm; palm (of the hand); hand; triumph. **llevarse la p.,** to bear away the palm; take the cake
palmada *f*, slap; *pl* hand-clapping
palmado *a* a web (of feet); palmy
palmar *a* palmaceous; palmar; clear, obvious. *m*, palm grove
palmatoria *f*, ferule, ruler; candlestick
palmear *vi* to clap hands
palmera *f*, palm tree
palmeta *f*, ferrule, ruler
palmetazo *m*, slap on the hand with a ruler; *fig* slap in the face
palmo *m*, span; hand's breadth. **p. a p.,** inch by inch, piecemeal
palmotear *vt* to applaud; clap
palo *m*, stick; rod; pole; timber, wood; wooden log; *naut* mast; blow with a stick; execution by hanging; suit (of playing cards); fruit stalk; *her* pale. **p. de Campeche,** logwood. **p. de hule,** rubber tree. **p. de rosa,** tulipwood. *naut* **p. mayor,** mainmast. *naut* **a p. seco,** under bare poles. **de tal p., tal astilla,** a chip off the old block; like father like son. **estar del mismo p.,** to be of the same mind, agree
paloma *f*, dove; pigeon; gentle person; *pl naut* white horses. **p. buchona,** pouter pigeon. **p. mensajera,** carrier pigeon. **p. torcaz,** wood pigeon
palomar *m*, dovecote; pigeon loft
palomero (-ra) *n* pigeon fancier; pigeon dealer
palomino *m*, young pigeon
palomo *m*, male pigeon; wood pigeon
palotes *m pl*, drumsticks; pothooks (in writing)
palpabilidad *f*, palpability
palpable *a* palpable, tangible
palpación *f*, *med* palpation
palpar *vt* to palpate, examine by touch; grope, walk by touch; *fig* see clearly
palpitación *f*, beating (of a heart); *med* palpitation; convulsive movement
palpitante *a* palpitating; quivering; beating; (of a question) burning

palpitar *vi* to beat (heart); throb, palpitate; shudder, move convulsively; *fig* manifest itself (passions, etc.)

me palpita que . . . *Argentina,* I have a hunch that . . .

palpo *m,* palp, feeler

palta *f, Lat. Am.* avocado (pear)

palúdico *a* marshy, swampy; malarial

paludismo *m,* malaria; paludism

palurdo (-da) *a inf* gross, rude, boorish. *n* boor

palustre *m,* mason's trowel. *a* marshy, swampy

pamela *f,* wide-brimmed straw sailor (woman's hat)

pamema *f, inf* unimportant trifle; *inf* caress

pampa *f,* pampa, treeless plain

pamplina *f, inf* nonsense, rubbish

pan *m,* bread; loaf; *cul* piecrust; *fig* food; wheat; gold leaf; *pl* cereals. **p. ázimo,** unleavened bread. **p. de oro,** gold leaf. **llamar al p. p. y al vino vino,** to call a spade a spade. **venderse como p. bendito,** to sell like hot cakes

pana *f,* velveteen, velours

panacea *f,* panacea; cure-all

panadería *f,* bakery trade or shop; bakery

panadero (-ra) *n* baker. *m pl,* Spanish dance

panadizo *m, med* whitlow; *inf* ailing person, crock

panal *m,* honeycomb; wasp's nest

Panamá Panama

panamá *m, Lat. Am.* Panama hat

panameño (-ña) *a* and *n* Panamanian

panamericanismo *m,* pan-Americanism

panarra *m, inf* simpleton

páncreas *m,* pancreas

pancreático *a* pancreatic

panda *f,* gallery of a cloister. *mf zool* panda

pandémico *a* pandemic

pandemonio *m,* pandemonium

pandereta *f,* tambourine

pandero *m,* tambourine; *inf* windbag

pandilla *f,* league, group; gang (of burglars, etc.); party, crowd, band

pane *f,* breakdown

panecillo *m, dim* roll (of bread)

panegírico *a* and *m,* panegyric

panel *m,* panel

panetela *f,* panada

pánfilo (-la) *a* sluggish, phlegmatic, slow-moving. *n* sluggard

panfleto *m,* pamphlet

paniaguado *m,* servant; favorite, protégé

pánico *a* and *m,* panic

panoja *f, bot* panicle; *bot* ear, beard, awn

panoli *a inf* doltish, stupid

panorama *m,* panorama; view

panorámico *a* panoramic

pantalón *m,* pant, trouser (gen. *pl*); knickers. **p. de corte,** striped trousers. **pantalones bombachos,** plus fours

pantalla *f,* lampshade; face screen; movie screen; shade, reflector

pantano *m,* marsh, swamp; impediment; artificial pool

pantanoso *a* marshy, swampy; *fig* awkward, full of pitfalls

panteísmo *m,* pantheism

panteón *m,* pantheon; *Mexico* cemetery

pantera *f,* panther; *Venezuela* jaguar, ocelot

pantomima *f,* pantomime; mime

pantorrilla *f,* calf (of the leg)

pantuflo *m,* house slipper

panza *f,* paunch, stomach; belly (of jugs, etc.). *inf* **un cielo de p. de burra,** a dark gray sky. **p. mojada** *Mexico* wetback

panzudo *a* paunchy

pañal *m,* diaper; shirttail; *pl* long clothes, swaddling clothes; infancy

pañería *f,* drapery stores; drapery

pañero (-ra) *n* draper

paño *m,* woolen material; cloth, fabric; drapery, hanging; tapestry; linen, bandage; tarnish or other mark;

naut canvas; *sew* breadth, width (of cloth); panel (in a dress); floor cloth, duster; livid mark on the face; *pl* garments. **p. de lágrimas,** consoler, sympathizer. **p. mortuorio,** pall (on a coffin). **paños menores,** underwear. **p. verde,** gambling table. **al p.,** *theat* from the wings, from without. *inf* **poner el p. al púlpito,** to hold forth, spread oneself

pañoleta *f,* kerchief, triangular scarf; fichu

pañuelo *m,* kerchief; handkerchief

papa *m,* pope; *inf* papa, daddy. *f, inf* potato; stupid rumor; nonsense; *pl* pap; *cul* sop; food

papá *m, inf* papa, daddy

papada *f,* double chin; dewlap

papado *m,* papacy

papagayo *m,* parrot

papal *m, Lat. Am.* potato field

papamoscas *m, orn* flycatcher; *inf* simpleton

papanatas *m, inf* simpleton

papar *vt* to sip, take soft food; *inf* eat; neglect, be careless about

paparrucha *f, inf* stupid rumor; nonsense

papel *m,* paper; document; manuscript; *theat* role, part; pamphlet; sheet of paper; paper, monograph, essay; guise, role; *theat* character. **p. carbón, p. carbónico,** carbon paper. **p. celofán,** cellophane. **p. cuadriculado,** graph paper, cartridge paper. **p. de calcar,** carbon paper; tracing paper. **p. de escribir,** writing paper. **p. de estaño,** tinfoil. **p. de estraza,** brown paper. **p. de fumar,** cigarette paper. **p. de lija,** emery- or sandpaper. **p. de paja de arroz,** rice paper. **p. de seda,** tissue paper. **p. de tornasol,** litmus paper. **p. del estado,** government bonds. **p. higiénico,** toilet paper. **p. moneda,** paper money. **p. pintado,** wallpaper. **p. secante,** blotting paper. **p. sellado,** official stamped paper. **hacer buen (mal) p.,** to do well (badly). **hacer el p. (de),** *theat* to act the part (of); feign, pretend

papelear *vi* to turn over papers, search among them; *inf* cut a dash

papeleo *m,* bureaucracy, red tape

papelera *f,* mass of papers; desk (for keeping papers)

papelería *f,* heap of papers; stationer's shop; stationery

papelero (-ra) *a* paper, stationery. *n* paper maker; stationer

papeleta *f,* slip or scrap of paper

papelista *mf* paper maker; stationer; paperhanger

papelucho *m,* old or dirty piece of paper; trash, worthless writing; *inf* rag (newspaper)

papera *f,* mumps

papilla *f,* pap; guile, wiliness

papillote *m,* curl-paper

papiro *m,* papyrus

papo *m,* dewlap; gizzard (of a bird); goiter. **p. de cardo,** thistledown

paquebote *m, naut* packet; mail boat; liner

paquete *m,* packet; parcel, package

paquidermo *m,* pachyderm

par *a* equal; alike; corresponding. *m,* pair, couple; team (of oxen, mules); peer (title); rafter (of a roof); *mech* torque, couple; *elec* cell. *f, par.* **a la p.,** jointly; simultaneously; *com* at par. **a pares,** two by two. **de p. en p.,** wide-open (doors, etc.). **sin p.,** peerless, excellent

para *prep* in order to; for; to; for the sake of (e.g. **Lo hice p. ella,** I did it for her sake); enough to (gen. with *bastante,* etc.); in relation to; toward; about to, on the point of (e.g. **Está p. salir,** He is on the point of going out). Expresses:

1. *Purpose* (e.g. **La educan p. bailarina,** They are bringing her up to be a dancer. **Lo dije p. ver lo que harías,** I said it to (in order to) see what you would do)

2. *Destination* (e.g. **Salió p. Londres,** He left for London)

3. *Use* (e.g. **seda p. medias,** silk for stockings; **un vaso p. flores,** a vase for flowers)

4. *An appointed time* (e.g. **Lo pagaré p. Navidad,** I will pay it at Christmas)

p. con, toward (a person) (e.g. **Ha obrado muy bien p. con mi hermano,** He has behaved very well toward my brother)

p. coneretar, to be exact, to wit

p. que, in order to, so that (e.g. **Lo puse en la mesa p. que lo vieses,** I put it on the table so that you would see it)

¿P. qué? Why? For what reason?

p. siempre, forever. **decir p. sí,** to say to oneself. **sin qué ni p. qué,** without rhyme or reason

parábola *f*, parable; *geom* parabola

parabrisas *m*, windshield

paracaídas *m*, parachute

paracaidista *mf* parachutist

parachoques *m, aut* bumper; buffer (railroad)

parada *f*, stopping, halting; stop; stoppage, suspension; halt; *mil* review; interval, pause; cattle stall; dam; gambling stakes; parry (in fencing); relay (of horses). **p. de coches,** taxi rank. **p. de tranvía,** streetcar stop. **p. discrecional,** request stop (buses, etc.)

paradear (con . . .) *vi, Argentina* to brag (about . . .)

paradero *m*, railroad station; stopping place; end, conclusion; whereabouts

paradisíaco *a* paradisaical

parado *a* still; indolent, lazy; unoccupied, leisured; silent, reserved; timid; unemployed

paradoja *f*, paradox

paradójico *a* paradoxical

parador *m*, inn, tavern, hostelry

parafina *f*, paraffin

parafrasear *vt* to paraphrase

paráfrasis *f*, paraphrase

paraguas *m*, umbrella

paraguayo (-ya) *a* and *n* Paraguayan

paragüería *f*, umbrella shop

paragüero (-ra) *n* umbrella maker, umbrella seller. *m*, umbrella stand

paraíso *m*, paradise; garden of Eden; heaven; (*inf theat*) gallery, gods

paraje *m*, place, locality, spot; state, condition

paralela *f, mil* parallel; *pl* parallel bars (for gymnastic exercises)

paralelismo *m*, parallelism

paralelo *a* parallel; analogous; similar. *m*, parallel, similarity; *geog* parallel

parálisis *f*, paralysis

paralítico (-ca) *a* and *n* paralytic

paralización *f*, paralysis; cessation; *com* dullness, quietness

paralizar *vt* to paralyze; stop

paramento *m*, ornament; trappings (of a horse); face (of a wall); facing (of a building). **paramentos sacerdotales,** liturgical vestments or ornaments

páramo *m*, paramo, treeless plain; desert, wilderness

parangón *m*, comparison; similarity

parangonar *vt* to compare

paraninfo *m, arch* paranymph, university hall; best man (weddings); messenger of good

paranoico *m*, paranoiac

parapetarse *vr* to shelter behind a parapet; take refuge behind

parapeto *m*, parapet

parapoco *mf inf* ninny, numskull

parar *vi* to stop, halt; end, finish; lodge; come into the hands of; *vt* stop; detain; prepare; bet, stake; point (hunting dogs); parry (fencing); *vr* halt; be interrupted; *Lat. Am.* to get up, stand up. **p. mientes en,** to notice; consider. **sin p.,** immediately, at once; without stopping

pararrayos *m*, lightning conductor

parasitario, parasítico *a* parasitic

parásito *m*, parasite; *fig* sponger; *pl rad* interference. *a* parasitic

parasitología *f*, parasitology

parasol *m*, sunshade; *bot* umbel

paratifoidea *f*, paratyphoid

parca *f*, Fate; *poet* death. **las Parcas,** the Three Fates

parcela *f*, plot, parcel (of land); atom, particle

parchar *vt, Lat. Am.* to mend, patch, patch up

parche *m, med* plaster; *aut* patch; drum; drumhead; parchment of drum; patch, mend

parcial *a* partial, incomplete; biased, prejudiced; factional, party; participatory

parcialidad *f*, partiality, bias, prejudice; party, faction, group; intimacy, friendship

parco *a* scarce, scanty; temperate, moderate; frugal

parcómetro *m Lat. Am. (except Argentina and Mexico)* parking meter

pardo *a* brown; gray, drab, dun-colored; cloudy, dark; husky (voices). *m*, leopard

pardusco *a* grayish; fawn-colored

parear *vt* to pair, match; put in pairs; compare

parecer *vi irr* to appear; look, seem; turn up (be found). *impers* believe, think (e.g. **me parece,** it seems to me, I think, my opinion is); *vr* look alike, resemble one another. See **conocer**

parecer *m*, opinion, belief; appearance, looks

parecido *a* (*with bien or mal*) good- or bad-looking. *m*, resemblance

pared *f*, wall; partition wall; side, face. **p. maestra,** main wall. **p. medianera,** party wall. **Las paredes oyen,** The walls have ears. *inf* **pegado a la p.,** confused, taken aback

pareja *f*, pair; dance partner; couple. **p. desparejada,** mismatched pair. **parejas mixtas,** mixed doubles (in tennis). **correr parejas** *or* **correr a las parejas,** to be equal; go together, happen simultaneously; be on a par

parejo *a* equal; similar; smooth, flat; even, regular

parentela *f*, relatives, kindred; parentage

parentesco *m*, kinship; relationship; affinity; *inf* connection, link

paréntesis *m*, parenthesis; digression. **entre p.,** incidentally

paresa *f*, peeress

paria *mf* pariah; outcast

parida *a f*, newly delivered of a child

paridad *f*, parity; analogy, similarity

pariente (-ta) *n* relative, relation; *inf* husband (wife)

parihuela *f*, wheelbarrow; stretcher

parir *vt* to give birth to; *fig* bring forth; reveal, publish; *vi* lay eggs

París Paris

parisiense *a* and *mf* Parisian

parla *f*, speech; loquaciousness, eloquence; verbiage

parlamentar *vi* to converse; discuss (contracts, etc.); *mil* parley

parlamentario *a* parliamentarian. *m*, member of parliament

parlamentarismo *m*, parliamentarianism

parlamento *m*, legislative assembly; parliament; discourse, speech; *theat* long speech; *mil* parley

parlanchín *a inf* talkative, chattering, loquacious

parlar *vt* and *vi* to speak freely or easily; chatter; reveal, speak indiscreetly; babble (of streams, etc.)

parlero *a* talkative; gossiping, indiscreet; talking (birds); *fig* expressive (eyes, etc.); prattling, babbling (brook, etc.)

parlotear *vi inf* to chatter, gossip

parloteo *m*, chattering, gossip

parnaso *m*, Parnassus; anthology of verse

paro *m, inf* work stoppage; lockout; *orn* tit. **p. forzoso,** unemployment

parodia *f*, parody

parodiar *vt* to parody

parodista *mf* parodist

parótida *f*, parotid gland; parotitis; mumps

parotiditis *f*, parotitis, mumps

paroxismo *m, med* paroxysm; frenzy, ecstasy, fit

parpadear *vi* to blink

parpadeo *m*, blinking

párpado *m*, eyelid

parque *m*, park; depot, park; paddock, pen. **p. de atracciones,** pleasure ground. **p. de** (*or* **para**) **automóviles,** car park, parking lot

parquear *vt, vi, Lat. Am.* to park

parquedad *f*, scarcity; moderation, temperance; parsimony, frugality

parquímetro *m Spain, Venezuela* parking meter

parra *f*, vine. **hoja de p.,** *fig* fig leaf

párrafo *m*, paragraph; *gram* paragraph sign. **p. aparte,** new paragraph. **echar un p.,** to chat, gossip

parranda *f, inf* binge; strolling band of musicians. **ir de p.,** to go on a binge

parricida *mf* parricide (person)

parricidio *m*, parricide (act)

parrilla *f, cul* griller, broiler; grill, gridiron; *eng* grate. *cul* **a la p.,** grilled

párroco *m*, parish priest; parson

parroquia *f*, parish church; parish; clergy of a parish; clientele, customers

parroquial *a* parochial

parroquiano (-na) *a* parochial. *n* parishioner; client, customer

parsimonia *f*, frugality, thrift; prudence, moderation

parsimonioso *a* parsimonious

parte *f*, part; share; place; portion; side, faction; *law* party; *theat* part, role. *m*, communication, message; telegraph or telephone message; (*mil nav*) communiqué. *f pl*, parts, talents. **p. actora,** *law* prosecution. **p. de la oración,** part of speech. **partes litigantes,** *law* contending parties. **dar p.,** to notify; (*mil naut*) report; give a share (in a transaction). **de algún tiempo a esta p.,** for some time past. **de p. de,** in the name of, from. **en p.,** partly. **por todas partes,** on all sides, everywhere. **ser p. a** *or* **ser p. para que,** to contribute to. **tener de su p.** (a), to count on the favor of. **la quinta p.,** one-fifth, etc.

partear *vt* to assist in childbirth

partera *f*, midwife

partero *m*, accoucheur

partición *f*, partition, distribution; (*aer naut*) accommodation

participación *f*, participation; notice, warning; announcement (of an engagement, etc.); *com* share

participante *a* and *mf* participant

participar *vi* to participate, take part (in); share; *vt* inform; announce (an engagement, etc.)

partícipe *a* sharing. *mf* participant

participio *m*, participle

partícula *f*, particle, grain; *gram* particle

particular *a* private; peculiar; special, particular; unusual; individual. *mf* private individual. *m*, matter, subject. **en p.,** especially; privately

particularidad *f*, individuality; speciality; rareness, unusualness; detail, circumstance; intimacy, friendship

particularizar *vt* to detail, particularize; single out, choose; *vr* (*with en*) be characterized by

partida *f*, departure; entry, record (of birth, etc.); certificate (of marriage, etc.); *com* item; *com* lot, allowance; *mil* guerrilla; armed band; expedition, excursion; game (of cards, etc.); rubber (at bridge, etc.); *inf* conduct, behavior; place, locality; death. *com* **p. doble,** double entry. **Las siete Partidas,** code of Spanish laws compiled by Alfonso X (1252–84)

partidarismo *m*, partisanship

partidario (-ia) *a* partisan. *n* adherent, disciple. *m*, partisan, guerrilla

partido *m*, party, group, faction; profit; *sport* match; team; agreement, pact. **p. conservador,** *pol* conservative party. **p. obrero** *or* **p. laborista,** *pol* labor party. **buen p.,** *fig* good match, catch. **sacar p. de,** to take advantage of, make the most of. **tomar p.,** to enlist; join, become a supporter (of)

partidor *m*, divider, apportioner; cleaver, chopper; hewer

partir *vt* to divide; split; crack, break; separate; *math* divide; *vi* go, depart; start (from). **p. como el rayo,** be off like a flash. *vr* disagree, become divided; leave, depart

partitura *f, mus* score

parto *m*, parturition, birth; newborn child; *fig* creation, offspring; important event

parturienta *a f*, parturient

parvedad *f*, smallness; scarcity; light breakfast (taken on fast days)

parvo *a* little, small

párvulo (-la) *n* child. *a* small; innocent, simple; lowly, humble

pasa *f*, raisin; *naut* channel; passage, flight (of birds). **p. de Corinto,** currant

pasacalle *m*, *mus* lively march

pasada *f*, passing, passage; money sufficient to live on; passage, corridor. **dar p.,** to let pass, put up with. *inf* **mala p.,** bad turn, dirty trick

pasadera *f*, steppingstone

pasadero *a* passable, traversable; fair (health); tolerable, passable. *m*, steppingstone

pasadizo *m*, narrow corridor or passage; alley, narrow street; *naut* alleyway

pasado *m*, past; *pl* ancestors. **Lo p., p.,** What's past is past. **p. de moda,** out of fashion, unfashionable

pasador *m*, bolt, fastener; *mech* pin, coupler; pin (of brooches, etc.); colander; *naut* marlin spike; shirt stud

pasajaretas *m*, bodkin

pasaje *m*, passing; passage; fare; passage money; *naut* complement of passengers; channel, strait; (*mus lit*) passage; *mus* modulation, transition (of voice); voyage; passage; covered way; road; *Lat. Am.* dead-end street

pasajero (-ra) *a* crowded public (thoroughfare); transitory, fugitive; passing; temporary. *n* passenger

pasamanería *f*, passementerie work, industry or shop

pasamano *m*, passementerie; banister, handrail; *naut* gangway

pasante *a* her passant. *m*, student teacher; articled clerk; apprentice; student. **p. de pluma,** law clerk

pasaporte *m*, passport; license, permission. **dar el p.** (a), *inf* to give the sack (to)

pasar *vt* to pass; carry, transport; cross over; send; go beyond, overstep; run through, pierce; upset; overtake; transfer; suffer, undergo; sieve; study; dry (grapes, etc.); smuggle; surpass; omit; swallow (food); approve; dissemble; transform; spend (time); *vi* pass; be transferred; be infectious; have enough to live on; cease; last; die; pass away; pass (at cards); be transformed; be current (money); be salable (goods); (*with prep a* + *infin*) begin to; (*with por*) pass as; have a reputation as; visit; (*with sin*) do without. *impers* happen, occur. *vr* end; go over to another party; forget; go stale or bad; *fig* go too far, overstep the mark; permeate. **p. contrato,** to draw up a contract; sign a contract. **p. la voz,** to pass the word along. **p. por alto (de),** to omit, overlook. **p. de largo,** to go by without stopping. **pasarse de listo,** to be too clever. **¡No pases cuidado! Don't worry!**

pasarela *f*, gangplank

pasatiempo *m*, pastime, hobby, amusement

pasavante *m*, *naut* safe conduct; navicert

pascua *f*, Passover; Easter; Christmas; Twelfth Night; Pentecost; *pl* twelve days of Christmas. **P. florida,** Easter Sunday. **dar las pascuas,** to wish a merry Christmas. **¡Felices pascuas!** Merry Christmas!

pascual *a* paschal

pase *m*, pass (with the hands and in football, etc.); safe conduct; free pass; thrust (in fencing)

paseante *mf* stroller, promenader, passerby

pasear *vt* to take a walk; parade up and down, display; *vi* take a walk; go for a drive; go for a ride (on horseback, etc.); stroll up and down; *vr* touch upon lightly, pass over; loaf, be idle; drift; float

paseo *m*, walk, stroll; drive; outing, expedition; promenade; boulevard. **p. a caballo,** ride on horseback

pasiega *f*, wet nurse

pasillo *m*, gallery; corridor; lobby; railway corridor; *sew* basting stitch

pasión *f*, suffering; passivity; passion; desire; *ecc* passion. **con p.,** passionately

pasionaria *f*, passionflower

pasividad *f*, passivity

pasivo *a* passive; inactive; *com* sleeping (partner); *gram* passive. *m*, *com* liabilities

pasmar *vt* to freeze to death (plants); dumbfound, amaze, stun; chill; *vr* be stunned or amazed

pasmo *m*, amazement, astonishment; wonder, marvel; *med* tetanus, lockjaw

pasmoso *a* astounding, amazing; wonderful

paso *a* dried (of fruit)

paso *m*, step; pace; passage, passing; way; footstep; progress, advancement; passage (in a book); *sew* tacking stitch; occurrence, event; *theat* short play; gait, walk; strait, channel; migratory flight (birds); *mech* pitch; event or scene from the Passion; armed combat; death; *Lat. Am.* ford. *pl* measures, steps. *adv* softly, in a low voice; gently. **p. a nivel,** level crossing. **p. a p.,** step by step. **p. doble,** quick march; Spanish dance. **p. volante,** (gymnastics) giant stride. **a cada p.,** at every step; often. **al p.,** without stopping; on the way, in passing. **ceder el p.,** to allow to pass. **de p.,** in passing; incidentally. **llevar el p.,** to keep in step. **marcar el p.,** to mark time. **salir al p. (a),** to waylay, confront; oppose. **seguir los pasos (a),** to follow; spy upon

paspa *f*, *Peru* chapped skin

paspadura *f*, *Argentina* = **paspa**

pasparse *vr*, *Lat. Am.* to chap, crack

pasquín *m*, **pasquinada** *f*, pasquinade, lampoon

pasta *f*, *cul* dough; paste; pastry; piecrust; batter; *cul* noodle paste; paper pulp; board (bookbinding). **ser de buena p.,** to be good-natured

pastar *vt* to take to pasture; *vi* graze, pasture

pastel *m*, cake; *art* pastel; pie; *inf* plot, secret understanding; cheating (at cards); *print* pie; *inf* fat, stocky person

pastelear *vi inf* to indulge in shady business (especially in politics)

pastelería *f*, cake bakery; cake shop; confectioner's art; confectionery

pastelero (-ra) *n* confectioner, pastry cook; *fig inf* spineless person, jellyfish

pastelillo *m*, *cul* turnover

pastelón *m*, meat or game pie

pasteurización *f*, pasteurization

pasteurizar *vt* to pasteurize

pastilla *f*, tablet, cake; lozenge; pastille, drop; tread (of a tire)

pasto *m*, grazing land, pasture; fodder; *fig* fuel, food; spiritual food. **a p.,** in plenty, abundantly. **de p.,** of daily use

pastor (-ra) *n* shepherd. *m*, *ecc* pastor

pastoral *a* rustic, country; *ecc* pastoral, *f*, pastoral poem; *ecc* pastoral letter

pastorear *vt* to graze, put to grass; *ecc* have charge of souls

pastorela *f*, pastoral

pastoreo *m*, pasturage, grazing

pastoril *a* shepherd, pastoral

pastoso *a* doughy; mealy; pasty; mellow

pata *f*, paw and leg (animals); foot (of table, etc.); duck; *inf* leg. **p. de gallo,** blunder; crow's-foot, wrinkle. **meter la p.,** to interfere, put one's foot in it. *inf* **tener mala p.,** to be unlucky

patada *f*, kick, stamp; *inf* step, pace

patagón (-ona) *a* and *n* Patagonian

patalear *vi* to stamp (with the feet)

pataleo *m*, kicking; stamping

pataleta *f*, *inf* convulsion; feigned hysterics

patán *m*, *inf* yokel; boor, churl

patanería *f*, *inf* boorishness, churlishness

patarata *f*, trash, useless thing; extravagant courtesy

patata *f*, potato

patatal, patatar *m*, potato patch

patatús *m*, *inf* petty worry; mishap; *med* stroke, fit

patear *vt inf* to stamp; *fig* walk on, treat badly; *vi inf* stamp the feet; be furiously angry; (*golf*) putt

patena *f*, engraved medal worn by country women; *ecc* paten

patentar *vt* to issue a patent; take out a patent, patent

patente *a* obvious, patent; *f*, patent; warrant, commission; letters patent. **p. de invención,** patent. **p. de sanidad,** clean bill of health

patentizar *vt* to make evident

paternidad *f*, paternity

paterno *a* paternal

patético *a* pitiable; pathetic, moving

patiabierto *a inf* knock-kneed

patibulario *a* heartrending, harrowing

patíbulo *m*, scaffold

paticojo *a inf* lame; wobbly; unsteady

patilla *f*, side whisker (gen. *pl*); *pl* old Nick, the Devil

patín *m*, skate; runner (of a sled); (*aer* and of vehicles) skid; *mech* shoe. **p. del diablo,** scooter. **p. de ruedas,** roller skate

patinador (-ra) *n* skater

patinaje *m*, skating; skidding (of planes and vehicles)

patinar *vi* to skate; slip, lose one's footing; skid (vehicles and planes)

patinazo *m*, skid (of a vehicle)

patinete *m*, child's scooter

patio *m*, courtyard; *theat* pit; *Mexico* shunting yard

patitieso *a inf* paralyzed in the hands or feet; openmouthed, amazed; stiff, unbending, proud

patituerto *a* crooked-legged; pigeon-toed; *inf* lopsided

patizambo *a* knock-kneed

pato *m*, duck; *inf* **pagar el p.,** to be a scapegoat

patógeno *a* pathogenic

patojo *a* waddling

patología *f*, pathology

patológico *a* pathological

patólogo *m*, pathologist

patoso *a fig* heavy, pedestrian, tedious

patraña *f*, nonsense, rubbish, fairy tale

patria *f*, motherland, native country; native place. **p. chica,** native region

patriarca *m*, patriarch

patriarcado *m*, patriarchy

patriarcal *a* patriarchal

patricio (-ia) *a* and *n* patrician

patrimonio *m*, patrimony

patriota *mf* patriot

patriótico *a* patriotic

patriotismo *m*, patriotism

patrocinar *vt* to protect, defend; favor, sponsor; patronize

patrocinio *m*, protection, defense; sponsorship; patronage

patrón (-ona) *n* patron, sponsor; patron saint; landlord; employer. *m*, coxswain; *naut* master, skipper; pattern, model; standard. **p. de oro,** gold standard

patronato *m*, patronage, protection; employers' association; charitable foundation. **p. de turismo,** tourist bureau

patronímico *a* and *m*, patronymic

patrono (-na) *n* protector; sponsor; patron; patron saint; employer

patrulla *f*, *mil* patrol; group, band

patrullar *vi* *mil* patrol; march about

patudo *a inf* large-footed

paulatinamente *adv* slowly, by degrees

pauperismo *m*, destitution, pauperism

pausa *f*, pause, interruption; delay; *mus* rest; *mus* pause. **a pausas,** intermittently

pausado *a* deliberate, slow. *adv* slowly, deliberately

pausar *vi* to pause

pauta *f*, standard, norm, design; *fig* guide, model

pava *f*, *Argentina* kettle; *Venezuela* broad-brimmed straw hat, *inf* bad luck

pavada *f*, flock of turkeys

pavana *f*, pavane, stately dance

pavero (-ra) *a* vain; strutting. *n* turkey keeper or vendor. *m*, broad-brimmed Andalusian hat; *mf*, *Chile*, *Peru* practical joker

pavimentación *f*, paving, flagging

pavimento *m*, pavement

pavo (-va) *n orn* turkey. **p. real,** peacock. *inf* **pelar la pava,** to serenade, court

pavón *m*, *orn* peacock; peacock butterfly; preservative paint (for steel, etc.); gunmetal

pavonear *vi* to strut, peacock (also *vr*); *inf* hoodwink, dazzle

pavor *m*, terror, panic

pavoroso *a* fearful, awesome, dreadful

payador *m*, *Argentina*, *Chile* gaucho minstrel

payasada *f*, clowning, practical joke; clown's patter

payasear *vi*, *Lat. Am.* to clown around

payaso *m*, clown

paz *f*, peace; harmony, concord; peaceableness. **¡P. sea en esta casa!** Peace be upon this house! (salutation). **estar en p.,** to be at peace; be quits, be even. **poner** (*or* **meter**) **p.,** to make peace (between dissentients). **venir de p.,** to come with peaceful intentions

pazguato (-ta) *n* simpleton, booby

pe *f*, name of the letter P. *inf* **de pe a pa,** from A to Z, from beginning to end

peaje *m*, toll (on bridges, roads, etc.)

peatón *m*, pedestrian; walker; country postman

pebete *m*, joss stick; fuse; *inf* stench

peca *f*, mole, freckle

pecado *m*, sin; fault; excess; defect; *inf* the Devil. **p. capital,** mortal sin

pecador *a* sinful. *m*, sinner. **¡P. de mí!** Poor me!

pecadora *f*, sinner; *inf* prostitute

pecaminoso *a* sinful

pecar *vi* to sin; trespass, transgress; (*with de*) be too . . . (e.g. **El libro peca de largo,** The book is too long)

peceño *a* pitch-black (horses, etc.); tasting of pitch

pecera *f*, goldfish bowl; aquarium

pechera *f*, shirt front; chest protector; bib, tucker; shirt frill; *inf* bosom

pecho *m*, *anat* chest; breast; bosom; mind, conscience; courage, endurance; *mus* quality (of voice); incline, slope. **p. arriba,** uphill. **abrir su p. a** (*or* **con**), to unbosom oneself to. **dar el p.** (**a**), to suckle. **de pechos,** leaning on. **echar el p. al agua,** *fig* to embark courageously upon. **tomar a pechos** (**una cosa**), to take (a thing) very seriously; take to heart

pechuga *f*, breast (of a bird); *inf* breast, bosom; slope, incline

pécora *f*, sheep, head of sheep; wily woman, serpent

pecoso *a* freckled; spotted (with warts)

pecuario *a agr* stock; cattle

peculiar *a* peculiar, individual

peculiaridad *f*, peculiarity

peculio *m*, private money or property

pecunia *f*, *inf* cash

pedagogía *f*, education, pedagogy

pedagogo *m*, schoolmaster; educationalist; *fig* mentor

pedal *m*, *mech* treadle, lever, *mus* pedal; *mus* sustained harmony. *aut* **p. de embrague,** clutch pedal

pedalear *vi* to pedal

pedante *a* pedantic. *mf* pedant

pedantería *f*, pedantry

pedazo *m*, bit, piece; lump; fragment, portion. *inf* **p. del alma, p. del corazón, p. de las entrañas,** loved one, dear one. **a pedazos** *or* **en pedazos,** in pieces, in bits. **hacer pedazos,** to break into fragments

pedernal *m*, flint; anything very hard

pedestal *m*, pedestal; base; stand; *fig* foundation

pedestre *a* pedestrian; dull, uninspired

pediatra *mf* pediatrician

pedicuro *m*, chiropodist

pedido *m*, *com* order; request, petition

pedigüeño *a* importunate, insistent

pedimento *m*, petition, demand; *law* claim; *law* motion

pedir *vt irr* to ask, request; *com* order; demand; necessitate; desire; ask in marriage. **p. aventón** *Mexico* to hitch a ride **p. en juicio,** *law* to bring an action against. *inf* **pedírselo** (**a uno**) **el cuerpo,** to desire (something) ardently. **a p. de boca,** according to one's wish. *Pres. Part.* **pidiendo.** *Pres. Ind.* **pido, pides, pide, piden.** *Preterite* **pidió, pidieron.** *Pres. Subjunc.* **pida,** etc. *Imperf. Subjunc.* **pidiese,** etc.

pedo *m*, fart

pedómetro *m*, pedometer

pedrada *f*, casting a stone; blow with a stone; innuendo

pedrea *f*, stone throwing; fight with stones; shower of hailstones

pedregal *m*, stony ground, rocky ground

pedregoso *a* stony

pedrera *f*, stone quarry

pedrería *f*, precious stones

pedrisco *m*, hailstone; shower of stones; pile of stones

pedrusco *m*, *inf* rough, unpolished stone

pega *f*, sticking; cementing; joining; pitch; varnish; *inf* joke; beating; *orn* magpie

pegadizo *a* sticky, gummy, adhesive; detachable, removable; *fig* clinging, importunate (of people)

pegado *m*, sticking plaster; patch

pegajoso *a* sticky, gluey; viscid; contagious, catching; *inf* oily, unctuous; *fig inf* cadging, sponging

pegar *vt* to stick; cement; join, fasten; press (against); infect with (diseases); hit, strike; give (a shout, jump, etc.); patch; *vi* spread, catch (fire, etc.); *fig* make an impression, have influence; be opportune; *vr cul* stick, burn; meddle; become enthusiastic about; take root in the mind. **p. un tiro** (**a**), to shoot

pegote *m*, sticking plaster; *fig inf* sponger; *inf* patch

peinado *m*, hairdressing or style; headdress. *a inf* effeminate, overelegant (men); overcareful (style). **un p. al agua,** a finger wave

peinador (-ra) *m*, peignoir, dressing gown; *Lat. Am.* dressing table. *n* hairdresser

peinadura *f*, brushing or combing of hair; *pl* hair combings

peinar *vt* to comb, dress the hair; card (wool); cut away (rock)

peine *m*, comb; *mech* hackle, reed; instep; *inf* crafty person

peinería *f*, comb factory or shop

peinero *m*, comb manufacturer or seller

peineta *f*, high comb (for mantillas, etc.)

peladilla *f*, sugared almond; smooth, small pebble

pelado *a* plucked; bare, unadorned; needy, poor; hairless; skinned; peeled; without shell; treeless

peladura *f*, peeling; shelling; skinning; plucking (feathers)

pelafustán *m*, *inf* good-for-nothing, scamp

pelagatos *m*, *inf* miserable wretch

pelágico *a* a pelagian, oceanic

pelagra *f*, pellagra

pelaje *m*, fur, wool

pelamesa *f*, brawl, fight; lock, tuft (of hair)

pelapatatas *m*, potato peeler

pelar *vt* to tear out or cut the hair; pluck; skin; peel; shell; rob, fleece; *vr* lose one's hair

peldaño *m*, step, stair, tread, rung

pelea *f*, battle; quarrel, dispute; fight (among animals); effort, exertion; *fig* struggle

peleador *a* fighting; quarrelsome, aggressive

pelear *vi* to fight; quarrel; struggle, strive. **p. como perro y gato,** to fight like cat and mouse. *vr* come to blows; fall out, become enemies

pelechar *vi* to get a new coat (of animals); grow new feathers (of birds); *inf* prosper, flourish; grow well

pelele *m*, effigy; *inf* nincompoop

peletería *f,* furrier; fur shop
peletero *m,* furrier; skinner
peliagudo *a* long-haired (animals); *inf* complicated, difficult; wily, downy
pelícano *m,* pelican
pelicorto *a* short-haired
película *f,* film. **p. fotográfica,** roll of film. **p. sonora,** sound film
peligrar *vi* to be in danger
peligro *m,* danger, peril. **correr p.** *or* **estar en p.,** to be in danger
peligroso *a* dangerous, perilous, risky
pelilargo *a* long-haired
pelirrojo *a* red-haired
pelleja *f,* hide, skin (of animals); sheepskin
pellejo *m,* hide; pelt; skin; wineskin; *inf* drunkard; peel, skin (of fruit)
pelliza *f,* fur or fur-trimmed coat
pellizcar *vt* to pinch, tweak, nip; pilfer
pellizco *m,* pinch, nip, tweak; pilfering, pinching; bit, pinch
pelmazo *m,* squashed mass; *inf* idler, sluggard; *inf* bore
pelo *m,* hair; down (on birds and fruit); fiber, filament; hair trigger (firearms); hairspring (watches); kiss (in billiards); nap (of cloth), grain (of wood); flaw (in gems); raw silk. **p. chino,** *Mexico* (naturally) curly hair **p. de camello,** camel's hair. **a p.,** in the nude; without a hat; opportunely. **en p.,** bareback (of horses). **hacerse el p.,** to do one's hair; have one's hair cut. *inf* **no tener p. de tonto,** to be smart, clever. *inf* **no tener pelos en la lengua,** to be outspoken. *inf* **tomar el p. (a),** to pull a person's leg. **venir a p.,** to be apposite; come opportunely
pelón *a* hairless; *fig inf* broke, fleeced
pelonería *f, inf* poverty, misery
pelota *f,* ball; ball game. **p. base,** baseball. **p. vasca,** pelota. **en p.,** stark naked
pelotari *m,* professional pelota player
pelotazo *m,* knock or blow with a ball
pelotear *vt* to audit accounts; *vi* play ball; throw, cast; quarrel; argue
pelotera *f, inf* brawl
pelotón *m,* big ball; lump of hair; crowd, multitude; *mil* platoon. **p. de ejecución,** firing squad
peltre *m,* pewter
peluca *f,* wig; periwig; *inf* scolding
peludo *a* hairy. *m,* long-haired rug
peluquería *f,* hairdressing establishment; hairdressing trade
peluquero (-ra) *n* hairdresser; barber
peluquín *m,* small wig
pelusa *f,* down, soft hair; fluff, nap
pena *f,* punishment, penalty; grief; pain, suffering; difficulty, trouble; mourning veil; hardship; anxiety; embarrassment; tail feather. **p. capital** *or* **p. de la vida,** capital punishment. **a duras penas,** with great difficulty. **so p. de,** under penalty of. **valer** (*or* **merecer**) **la p.,** to be worth while
penable *a* punishable
penacho *m,* topknot, crest (of birds); plume, panache; *inf* pride, arrogance
penado (-da) *a* difficult, laborious; painful, troubled, afflicted. *n* convict
penal *a* penal; punitive
penalidad *f,* trouble, labor, difficulty; *law* penalty
penar *vt* to penalize; punish; *vi* suffer; undergo purgatorial pains; *vr* suffer anguish. **p. por,** to long for
penca *f, bot* fleshy leaf; lash, strap, cat-o'-nine-tails
penco *m, inf* wretched nag
pendejo *m,* pubic hair; *inf* coward; jerk
pendencia *f,* fight; quarrel
pendenciar *vi* to fight; quarrel
pendenciero *a* quarrelsome, aggressive
pender *vi* to hang; depend; be pending
pendiente *a* pending; hanging; *com* outstanding. *m,* earring; pendant. *f,* slope, incline; gradient

péndola *f,* feather, plume; quill pen; pendulum (of a clock)
pendolista *mf* calligrapher
pendón *m,* pennon, banner; *bot* shoot; *inf* lanky, slatternly woman; *pl* reins
péndulo *a* pendulous, hanging. *m,* pendulum
pene *m,* penis
peneque, *m, Mexico* roll of maize dough filled with cheese
penetrabilidad *f,* penetrability
penetración *f,* penetration; understanding, perspicuity; sagacity, shrewdness
penetrador *a* penetrating, perspicacious; sagacious, acute
penetrante *a* penetrating; deep; piercing (of sounds); acute, shrewd
penetrar *vt* to penetrate; permeate; master, comprehend; (*with en*) enter
penetrativo *a* piercing
penicilina *f,* penicillin
península *f,* peninsula. **la P.** the Iberian Peninsula
Península Ibérica, la the Iberian Peninsula
penique *m,* penny
penitencia *f,* penitence, repentance; penance
penitencial *a* penitential
penitenciaría *f,* penitentiary
penitente *a* penitent, repentant. *mf* penitent
penoso *a* laborious, difficult; grievous; painful; troublesome; *inf* foppish; *Lat. Am.* shy, timid
pensado *a* premeditated, deliberate. **de p.,** intentionally. **mal p.,** malicious, evil-minded
pensador *a* thinking; pensive. *m,* thinker
pensamiento *m,* mind; thought; idea; suspicion, doubt; heartsease pansy; maxim; intention, project
pensar *vt irr* to think; purpose, intend; (*with en, sobre*) reflect upon; think about; *vt* feed (animals). **p. entre sí, p. para consigo** *or* **p. para sí,** to think to oneself. See **acertar**
pensativo *a* reflective, pensive
pensil *a* hanging. *m,* hanging garden; delightful garden
pensión *f,* pension, allowance; boarding house; private hotel; scholarship grant; cost of board; trouble, drudgery
pensionado (-da) *a* pensioned; retired. *n* scholarship holder. *m,* boarding school
pensionar *vt* to pension, grant a pension to; charge a pension on
pensionista *mf* pensioner; boarder
pentágono *m,* pentagon. *a* pentagonal
pentámetro *m,* pentameter
Pentateuco *m,* Pentateuch
Pentecostés *m,* Pentecost, Whitsuntide
penúltimo *a* next to the last, penultimate
penuria *f,* scarcity; want, penury
peña *f,* crag, rock; boulder; group of friends; club. **ser una p.,** to be stony-hearted
peñasco *m,* craggy peak
peñascoso *a* craggy, rocky
peñón *m,* rock; cliff; peak
peón *m,* pedestrian; laborer; *South America* farmhand; top (toy); piece (chess, checkers); *mech* axle; infantryman. **p. caminero,** road mender. **p. de ajedrez,** pawn (in chess)
peonada *f,* day's manual labor; gang of laborers
peonar *vi, Argentina* to do manual labor
peonía *f,* peony
peonza *f,* top; teetotum
peor *a comp* **malo** worse. *adv comp* **mal,** worse. *a sup* **el (la, lo) peor; los (las) peores,** the worst. **p. que p.,** worse and worse. **tanto p.,** so much the worse
pepino *m,* cucumber plant; cucumber; *fig* pin, straw
pepita *f, min* nugget; pip, seed (of fruit)
péptico *a* peptic
pequeñez *f,* littleness, smallness; pettiness; childhood; infancy; trifle, insignificant thing; meanness, baseness

pequeño *a* little, small; petty; very young; short, brief; humble, lowly

pequero, -a *mf, Argentina* cardsharp

pera *f*, pear; goatee; *fig* plum, sinecure

peral *m*, pear tree; pearwood

perca *f, icht* perch

percal *m*, percale, calico

percalina *f*, percaline, binding cloth

percance *m*, perquisite, attribute (gen. *pl*); disaster, mischance

percebe *m*, (gen. *pl*) goose barnacle

percentaje *m*, percentage

percepción *f*, perception; idea, conception

perceptible *a* perceptible

perceptivo *a* perceptive

perceptor (-ra) *a* perceptive. *n* observer

percha *f*, stake, pole; coat hanger; perch (for birds); rack (for hay); hall stand, coat and hat stand, coatrack

perchero *m*, hall stand; clothes rack; row of perches (for fowl, etc.)

percibir *vt* to collect, draw, receive; perceive; understand, grasp

percibo *m*, perceiving; collecting, drawing, receiving

percolador *m*, percolator (coffee)

percusión *f*, percussion; shock, vibration

percusor *m*, hammer (of a firearm)

percutir *vt* to percuss, strike

perdedor (-ra) *a* losing. *n* loser

perder *vt* to lose; throw away, squander; spoil, destroy; *vi* fade (of colors); *vr* lose one's way, be lost; be confused or perplexed; be shipwrecked; take to vice, become dissolute; be spoiled or destroyed; disappear; love madly. **p. la chaveta (por),** to go out of one's head (for), be wild (about). **p. la ocasión,** to let the chance slip. **p. los estribos,** to lose patience. **p. terreno,** to lose ground. **perderse de vista,** to be lost to sight. **echarse a p.,** to spoil, be damaged. See **entender**

perdición *f*, loss; perdition, ruin; damnation; depravity, viciousness

pérdida *f*, loss; waste. **p. cuantiosa,** heavy losses

perdidamente *adv* ardently, desperately; uselessly

perdigón *m*, young partridge; decoy partridge; hailstone, pellet, shot

perdigonada *f*, volley of hailstone; hailstone wound

perdiguero (-ra) *n* game dealer; setter, retriever

perdiz *f*, partridge. **p. blanca,** ptarmigan

perdón *m*, pardon, forgiveness; remission. **con p.,** with your permission; excuse me

perdonable *a* pardonable, excusable

perdonar *vt* to pardon, forgive; remit, excuse; exempt; waste, lose; give up (a privilege)

perdonavidas *m, inf* bully, braggart

perdulario *a* careless, negligent; slovenly; vicious, depraved

perdurable *a* perpetual, everlasting; enduring, lasting

perdurar *vi* to last, endure

perecedero *a* brief, fugitive, transient; perishable. *m, inf* poverty, want

perecer *vi irr* to end, finish; perish, die; suffer (damage, grief, etc.); be destitute; *vr (with por)* long for, crave; desire ardently. See **conocer**

peregrinación *f*, journey, peregrination; pilgrimage

peregrinamente *adv* rarely, not often; beautifully, perfectly

peregrinar *vi* to journey, travel; make a pilgrimage

peregrino (-na) *a* and *n* pilgrim. *a* migratory (birds); rare, unusual; extraordinary, strange; beautiful, perfect

perejil *m*, parsley; *inf* ornament or apparel (gen. *pl*); *pl* honors, titles

perengano (-na) *n* so-and-so, such a one

perenne *a* incessant, constant; *bot* perennial

perennidad *f*, perpetuity

perentoriedad *f*, peremptoriness; urgency

perentorio *a* peremptory; conclusive, decisive; urgent, pressing

pereza *f*, laziness; languor, inertia; slowness, deliberateness

perezoso *a* lazy; languid; slothful; slow, deliberate. *m, zool* sloth

perfección *f*, perfection; perfecting, perfect thing, virtue, grace

perfeccionamiento *m*, perfecting; progress, improvement

perfeccionar *vt* to perfect; complete

perfectamente *adv* perfectly; quite, entirely

perfecto *a* perfect; excellent, very good; complete; whole; *gram* perfect

perfidia *f*, perfidy, treachery

pérfido *a* perfidious, treacherous

perfil *m*, ornament, decoration; outline, contour; profile; section (of metal); fine stroke (of letters); *pl* finishing touches; politeness, attention, courtesy. **de p.,** in profile; sideways

perfilado *a* long, elongated (of faces, etc.)

perfilar *vt* to draw in profile; outline; *vr* place oneself sideways, show one's profile; *inf* dress up, titivate

perforación *f*, perforation, boring; hole

perforador *a* perforating, boring. *m, mech* drill

perforar *vt* to perforate, pierce; bore, drill, make a hole in

perfumador (-ra) *a* perfuming. *n* perfumer. *m*, perfume burner

perfumar *vt* to perfume; *vi* give off perfume

perfume *m*, perfume; scent, fragrance

perfumería *f*, scent factory; perfumery; perfume shop

perfumista *mf* perfumer

perfunctorio *a* perfunctory

pergamino *m*, parchment, vellum; document; diploma; *pl* aristocratic descent

pericardio *m*, pericardium

pericia *f*, expertness; skilled workmanship

pericial *a* expert, skillful

perico *m*, parakeet; giant asparagus

periferia *f*, periphery

periférico *a* peripheral

perifollos *m pl, inf* frills, flounces, finery

perifrástico *a* periphrastic

perilla *f*, pear-shaped ornament; goatee; imperial. **p. de la oreja,** lobe of the ear. **venir de p.,** to be most opportune

perillán *m, inf* rascal, rogue

perímetro *m*, perimeter; precincts

perínclito *a* distinguished, illustrious; heroic

perineo *m*, perineum

perinola *f*, top, teetotum

periodicidad *f*, periodicity

periódico *a* periodic. *m*, newspaper; periodical publication

periodicucho *m*, rag (bad newspaper)

periodismo *m*, journalism

periodista *mf* journalist

periodístico *a* journalistic

período *m*, period; *phys* cycle; menstruation period; *gram* clause; age, era

periostio *m*, periosteum

peripatético *a* peripatetic

peripecia *f*, sudden change of fortune, vicissitude

peripuesto *a inf* overelegant, spruce, too well-dressed; smart

periquete *m, inf* jiffy, trice

periquito *m*, parakeet; budgerigar

periscopio *m*, periscope

perito (-ta) *a* expert; skillful, experienced. *n* expert

peritoneo *m*, peritoneum

perjudicador (-ra) *a* injurious, prejudicial. *n* injurer

perjudicar *vt* to harm, damage, injure; prejudice

perjudicial *a* injurious, noxious, harmful; prejudicial

perjuicio *m*, injury, damage; harm; *law* prejudice

perjurador (-ra) *n* perjurer

perjurar *vi* to perjure oneself, commit perjury; swear, curse

perjurio *m*, perjury

perjuro (-ra) *a* perjured, forsworn. *n* perjurer

perla *f*, pearl; *arch* bead; *fig* treasure, jewel, dear. **de perlas,** excellent; exactly right

perlero *a* pearl

perlesía *f*, paralysis; palsy

perlino *a* pearly, pearl-colored

permanecer *vi irr* to stay, remain. **p. en posición de firme,** to stand at attention. See **conocer**

permanencia *f*, stay, sojourn; permanence

permanente *a* permanent; lasting, enduring

permeabilidad *f*, permeability

permisible *a* permissible, allowable

permisivo *a* permissive

permiso *m*, permission, leave; permit; (*mil* etc.) pass. **¡Con p.!** Excuse me!; Allow me!

permitir *vt* to permit, allow

permuta *f*, exchange

permutación *f*, permutation, interchange

permutar *vt* to exchange

pernear *vi* to kick; *inf* bustle; fret, be impatient

pernetas, en *adv* barelegged

perniciosidad *f*, perniciousness

pernicioso *a* pernicious

pernil *m*, *anat* hock; ham; leg of pork; leg (of trousers)

pernio *m*, hinge (of doors, windows)

perniquebrar *vt irr* to break the legs of. See **quebrar**

perno *m*, bolt, pin, spike

pernoctar *vi* to spend the night (away from home)

pero *conjunc* but. *m*, *inf* defect; difficulty, snag

perogrullada *f*, *inf* truism

perol *m*, *cul* pan

peroné *m*, fibula

peronista *a*, *mf* Peronist

peroración *f*, peroration

perorar *vi* to make a speech; *inf* speak pompously; ask insistently

peróxido *m*, peroxide

perpendicular *a* perpendicular. *f*, perpendicular

perpetración *f*, perpetration

perpetrar *vt* to perpetrate

perpetua *f*, *bot* immortelle, everlasting

perpetuación *f*, perpetuation

perpetuar *vt* to perpetuate; *vr* last, endure

perpetuidad *f*, perpetuity

perpetuo *a* everlasting; lifelong

perplejidad *f*, perplexity, bewilderment, doubt

perplejo *a* perplexed, bewildered, doubtful

perquirir *vt irr* to search carefully. See **adquirir**

perra *f*, bitch; *inf* sot, drunkard; tantrums. **p. chica,** five-cent coin. **p. gorda,** ten-cent coin

perrada *f*, pack of dogs; *inf* dirty trick

perramus *m*, *Argentina* raincoat

perrengue *m*, *inf* short-tempered person

perrera *f*, dog kennel; useless toil; *inf* tantrums

perrería *f*, pack of dogs; *inf* dirty trick; fit of anger

perrero *m*, dog fancier; kennel worker

perro *m*, dog. **p. caliente,** hot dog. **p. danés,** Great Dane. **p. de aguas,** poodle; spaniel. **p. de casta,** thoroughbred dog. **p. de lanas,** poodle. **p. de muestra,** pointer. **p. de presa,** bulldog. **p. de San Bernardo,** St. Bernard (dog). **p. de Terranova,** Newfoundland (dog). **p. del hortelano,** dog in the manger. **p. dogo,** bulldog. **p. esquimal** husky. **p. faldero,** lap dog. **p. lobo,** wolfhound. **p. pachón,** dachshund. **p. pastor alemán** *or* **p. policía,** German shepherd. **p. pequinés,** Pekingese. **p. perdiguero,** retriever. **p. pomerano,** spitz, Pomeranian (dog). **p. sabueso español,** spaniel. **p. zorrero,** foxhound. *inf* **A p. viejo no hay tus tus,** You can't fool an old dog. **vivir como perros y gatos,** *inf* to live like cat and dog

persa *a* and *mf* Persian. *m*, Persian (language)

persecución *f*, pursuit; persecution; annoyance, importuning

perseguidor (-ra) *a* pursuing; tormenting. *n* pursuer; tormentor, persecutor

perseguimiento *m*, pursuit

perseguir *vi irr* to pursue; persecute, torment; importune. See **seguir**

perseverancia *f*, perseverance

perseverante *a* persevering; constant

perseverar *vi* to persevere; last, endure

persiana *f*, Venetian blind; flowered silk material

pérsico *a* Persian. *m*, peach tree; peach

persignar *vt* to sign; make the sign of the cross over; *vr* cross oneself

persistencia *f*, persistence

persistente *a* persistent

persistir *vi* to persist

persona *f*, person; personage; character (in a play, etc.); (*gram ecc*) person. **de p. a p.,** in private, face to face

personaje *m*, important person, personage; character (in a play, etc.)

personal *a* personal. *m*, staff, personnel

personalidad *f*, personality

personalismo *m*, personality; personal question

personalizar *vt* to become personal, be offensive

personalmente *adv* personally

personarse *vr* to present oneself, call, appear

personificación *f*, personification

personificar *vt* to personify

perspectiva *f*, perspective; view; outlook; aspect, appearance. **p. aérea,** bird's-eye view

perspicacia *f*, perspicacity, shrewdness

perspicaz *a* perspicacious, clear-sighted

perspicuidad *f*, perspicuity

perspicuo *a* lucid, clear

persuadir *vt* to persuade

persuasible *a* persuadable

persuasión *f*, persuasion; belief, conviction, opinion

persuasiva *f*, persuasiveness

persuasivo *a* persuasive

pertenecer *vi irr* to belong; relate, concern. See **conocer**

perteneciente *a* belonging (to), pertaining (to)

pertenencia *f*, ownership, proprietorship; property, accessory

pértiga *f*, long rod; pole. **salto de p.,** pole vaulting

pertinacia *f*, pertinacity, doggedness

pertinaz *a* pertinacious, stubborn, dogged

pertinencia *f*, relevance, appropriateness

pertinente *a* relevant, apposite; appropriate

pertrechar *vt* to supply, equip; prepare, make ready

pertrechos *m pl*, *mil* armaments, stores; equipment, appliances

perturbación *f*, disturbance; agitation

perturbador (-ra) *a* disturbing. *n* disturber; heckler

perturbar *vt* to disturb; agitate

Perú *m* Peru

peruano (-na) *a* and *n* Peruvian

perversidad *f*, wickedness, depravity

perversión *f*, perversion; wickedness, evil

perversivo *a* perversive

perverso *a* wicked, iniquitous, depraved

pervertir *vt irr* to pervert, corrupt; distort. See **sentir**

pesa *f*, weight; clock weight; gymnast's weight. **pesas y medidas,** weights and measures

pesacartas *m*, letter scale, letter balance

pesada *f*, weighing

pesadez *f*, heaviness; obesity; tediousness, tiresomeness; slowness; fatigue

pesadilla *f*, nightmare

pesado *a* heavy; obese; deep (of sleep); oppressive (of weather); slow; unwieldy; tedious; impertinent; dull, boring; offensive

pesadumbre *f*, heaviness; grief, sorrow; trouble, anxiety

pésame *m*, expression of condolence. **dar el p.,** to present one's condolences

pesantez *f*, weight, heaviness; seriousness, gravity
pesar *m*, grief, sorrow; remorse. **a p. de,** in spite of
pesar *vi* to weigh; be heavy; be important; grieve, cause regret (e.g. **Me pesa mucho,** I am very sorry); influence, affect; *vt* weigh; consider. **Mal que me (te,** etc.) **pese . . . ,** Much as I regret . . .
pesaroso *a* regretful, remorseful; sorrowful
pesca *f*, fishery; angling, fishing; catch of fish. **p. a la rastra,** trawling. **p. deportiva** sport fishing. **p. mayor,** deep-sea fishing
pescadería *f*, fishery; fish store; fish market
pescadilla *f*, *icht* whiting
pescado *m*, fish (out of the water); salt cod
pescador (-ra) *n* fisherman; angler
pescante *m*, driving seat; coach box; jib (of a crane)
pescar *vt* to fish; *inf* catch in the act; acquire. **p. a la rastra,** to trawl
pescozón *m*, slap on the neck or head
pescuezo *m*, neck; throat; haughtiness, arrogance. **torcer el p.,** to wring the neck (of chickens, etc.)
pesebre *m*, manger, stable; feeding trough
pesero *m*, *Mexico* jitney, jitney taxi
pésimamente *adv* extremely badly
pesimismo *m*, pessimism
pesimista *a* pessimistic. *mf* pessimist
pésimo *a sup* **malo** extremely bad
peso *m*, weighing; weight; heaviness; gravity; importance; influence; load; peso (money); scale, balance. **p. bruto,** gross weight. **p. de joyería,** troy weight. **p. específico,** *phys* specific gravity. **p. pluma,** (*boxing*) featherweight
pespunte *m*, backstitch
pesquera *f*, fishing ground, fishery
pesquería *f*, fishing, angling; fisherman's trade; fishing ground, fishery
pesquero *a* fishing (of boats, etc.)
pesquisa *f*, investigation, examination; search
pesquisar *vt* to investigate, look into; search
pestaña *f*, eyelash; *sew* edging, fringe; ear, lug; *naut* fluke
pestañear *vi* to wink; blink; flutter one's eyelashes
pestañeo *m*, winking; blinking
peste *f*, plague, pestilence; nauseous smell; epidemic; pest; vice; *Chile* smallpox; *pl* oaths, curses. **p. bubónica,** bubonic plague. **p. roja** syphilis. **p. de las abejas,** foul brood. **echar pestes,** to swear; fume
pestífero *a* noxious
pestilencia *f*, plague, pestilence
pestilente *a* pestilential
pestillo *m*, latch; lock bolt. **p. de golpe,** safety latch
petaca *f*, cigarette or cigar case; tobacco pouch; *Mexico* suitcase.
pétalo *m*, petal
petardista *mf* swindler, impostor
petardo *m*, detonator; torpedo; firecracker; fraud
petición *f*, petition, request
peticionar *vt*, *Lat. Am.* to petition
peticionario (-ia) *n* petitioner. *a* petitionary
petimetra *f*, stylish and affected young woman
petimetre *m*, fop
petirrojo *m*, robin
petitorio *a* petitionary. *m*, *inf* importunity
peto *m*, breastplate; front (of a shirt); bib
pétreo *a* petrous
petrificación *f*, petrifaction
petrificar *vt* to petrify; *vr* become petrified
petrografía *f*, petrology
petróleo *m*, petroleum; oil, mineral oil. **p. bruto,** crude oil. **p. de lámpara,** kerosene
petrolero (-ra) *a* oil, petroleum. *n* petroleum seller; incendiarist. *m*, oil tanker
petrolífero *a* oil-bearing
petulancia *f*, insolence; vanity
petulante *a* insolent; vain
pez *m*, fish; *pl* Pisces. *f*, *chem* pitch. **p. sierra,** swordfish

pezón *m*, *bot* stalk; nipple; axle pivot; point (of land, etc.)
pezuña *f*, cloven hoof (of cows, pigs, etc.)
piada *f*, chirping, twittering
piadoso *a* compassionate; kind, pitiful; pious, religious
piafar *vi* to stamp, paw the ground (horses)
pianista *mf* piano maker; piano dealer; pianist
piano *m*, pianoforte. **p. de cola,** grand piano. **p. de media cola,** baby grand. **p. vertical,** upright piano
piante *a* chirping, twittering
piar *vi* to chirp, twitter
piara *f*, herd of swine; pack (of horses, etc.)
pibe, -a *mf*, *Argentina* kid, child
pica *f*, *mil* pike; bullfighter's goad; pike soldier; stonecutter's hammer. **a p. seca,** in vain. **pasar por las picas,** to suffer hardship. **poner una p. en Flandes,** to triumph over great difficulties
picacho *m*, peak, summit
picada *f*, prick; bite; peck; *aer* dive
picadero *m*, riding school; paddock (of a racetrack)
picado *a sew* pinked. *m*, *cul* hash
picador *m*, horse trainer; meat chopper; horseman armed with a goad (bullfights)
picadura *f*, puncture; prick; sting; *sew* pinking; peck (of birds); cut tobacco; black tobacco; beginning of caries in teeth
picajoso *a* hypersensitive, touchy, peevish
picamaderos *m*, woodpecker
picanear *vt*, *Lat. Am.* to goad on, spur on
picante *a* piquant; mordant; hot, highly seasoned. *m*, mordancy; pungency
picantería *f*, *Lat. Am.* restaurant specializing in spicy foods
picapleitos *m*, *inf* shady lawyer, pettifogger
picaporte *m*, latch, door catch; door knocker
picar *vt* to prick; sting; peck; bite; chop fine; mince; nibble (of fishing); irritate (the skin); *sew* pink; burn (the tongue); eat (grapes); goad; spur; stipple (walls); stimulate, encourage; split, cleave; *mil* harass; vex; *mus* play staccato; *vi* burn (of the sun); smart (of cuts, etc.); eat sparingly; *aut* knock; (*with en*) knock at (doors, etc.); *vr* be moth-eaten; go rotten (fruit, etc.); grow choppy (of the sea); be piqued; boast
picardear *vi* to play the rogue; behave mischievously
picardía *f*, knavery, roguery; mischievousness; practical joke; wantonness
picaresco *a* roguish, picaresque, knavish
pícaro (-ra) *a* knavish; base, vile; astute; mischievous. *n* rogue
picatoste *m*, kind of fritter
picaza *f*, magpie
picazo *m*, blow with a pike or anything pointed; peck, tap with a beak (of birds); sting
picazón *f*, itch, irritation; annoyance
pícea *f*, *bot* spruce
píceo *a* piscine, fish-like
pichincha *f*, *Argentina* bargain
pichón (-ona) *m*, male pigeon. *n inf* darling
pico *m*, beak (of birds); peak; woodpecker; odd amount (e.g. **treinta y p.,** thirty-odd); sharp point; spout (of a jug, etc.); *inf* mouth; blarney, gab. **p. de cigüeña,** crane's-bill. **p. de oro,** silver-tongued orator
picor *m*, burning sensation in the mouth; smarting; itching, irritation
picoso *a* pitted, marked by smallpox; *Mexico* hot, spicy (food)
picota *f*, pillory; peak; spire
picotazo *m*, peck; dab; sting, bite
picotear *vt* to peck (of a bird); *vi* toss the head (of horses); *inf* chatter senselessly; *vr inf* slang each other
picotero *a inf* chattering, talkative; indiscreet
pictórico *a* pictorial
picudo *a* pointed, peaked; having a spout; *inf* chattering; *Mexico* clever, crafty, sly
pie *m*, foot; stand, support; stem (of a glass, etc.); stan-

dard (of a lamp); *bot* trunk, stem; sapling; lees, sediment; *theat* cue; foot (measure); custom; (metrics) foot; motive, cause; pretext; (metrics) meter. **p. de cabra,** crowbar. **p. de imprenta,** printer's mark, printer's imprint. **p. de piña,** clubfoot. **p. de rey,** caliper. **p. palmado,** webfoot. **al p. de la letra,** punctiliously. *inf* **andar con pies de plomo,** to walk warily. **a p.,** on foot. **a p. firme,** without budging; steadfastly. *inf* **buscar tres pies al gato,** to look for something that isn't there; twist a person's words. **de a p.,** on foot. **en p. de guerra,** on a wartime footing. *inf* **poner pies en polvorosa,** to quit

piedad *f,* piety; pity, compassion; *art* pietà

piedra *f,* stone; tablet; *med* gravel. **p. de amolar,** whetstone, grindstone. **p. angular,** cornerstone (also *fig*). **p. caliza,** limestone. **p. clave,** keystone. **p. de construcción,** building stone; child's block. **p. de toque,** touchstone, test. **p. filosofal,** philosopher's stone. **p. fundamental,** foundation stone. **p. miliaria,** milestone. **p. mortuoria,** tombstone. *fig inf* **no dejar p. sin remover,** to leave no stone unturned. **no dejar p. sobre p.,** to demolish, destroy completely

piel *f,* skin; fur; hide; leather; peel (of some fruits); rind (of bacon). **p. de gallina,** *fig* goose flesh. **p. de rata,** horse blanket. **p. de Rusia,** Russian leather.

piélago *m,* high seas; sea, ocean; glut, superabundance

pienso *m, agr* fodder

pierna *f, anat* leg; *mech* shank; leg of a compass. *inf* **a p. suelta,** at one's ease. **en piernas,** barelegged

pietista *a* pietistic. *mf* pietist

pieza *f,* portion; piece; component part; room; *theat* play; roll (of cloth); piece (in chess, etc.); coin; piece (of music). **p. de recambio** *or* **de repuesto,** spare part. **p. de recibo,** reception room. *inf* **quedarse en una p.,** to be struck dumb

pífano *m,* fife; fife player, fifer

pigmentación *f,* pigmentation

pigmento *m,* pigment

pignoración *f,* hypothecation; pawning; mortgage

pignorar *vt* to hypothecate; pawn; mortgage

pigre *a* lazy; negligent, careless

pigricia *f,* laziness; negligence *Chile, Peru* trifle

pijama *m,* pajamas

pila *f,* trough, basin; heap, pile; *elec* battery; *ecc* parish; pier, pile; *phys* cell. **p. atómica,** atomic pile. **p. bautismal,** *ecc* font

pilar *m,* fountain basin; milestone; pillar

pilastra *f,* pier, pile; pilaster

pilche *m, Lat. Am.* calabash, gourd

píldora *f, med* pill; *inf* disagreeable news

pileta (de natación) *f, Argentina,* (swimming) pool

pillador (-ra) *n* pillaging, plundering. *n* plunderer

pillaje *m,* pillaging; looting; robbery, theft

pillar *vt* to pillage; steal, rob; seize, snatch; *inf* surprise, find out (in a lie, etc.). **pillarse el dedo,** to get one's finger caught (in a door, etc.)

pillastre *m, inf* rogue, ragamuffin

pillería *f, inf* gang of rogues; *inf* rogue's trick

pillo *m,* rogue, knave

pilón *m,* fountain basin; pestle; loaf sugar; pylon; *Mexico, Venezuela* gratuity, tip

pilongo *a* thin, lean

píloro *m,* pylorus

pilotaje *m,* pilotage; piling, pilework. **examen de p.,** flying test

pilotar *vt* to pilot

pilote *m, eng* pile

pilotear *vt* to pilot

piloto *m,* pilot; mate (in merchant ships). **p. de pruebas,** test pilo

pilsen *m, Chile* beer

pimentero *m,* pepper plant; pepper shaker

pimentón *m,* red pepper, cayenne

pimienta *f,* pepper. **p. húngara,** paprika. *inf* **ser como una p.,** to be sharp as a needle

pimiento *m,* pimento; capsicum; red pepper; pepper plant. **p. de cornetilla,** chili pepper

pimpollo *m,* sapling; sprout, shoot; rosebud

pina *f,* conical stone; felloe (of a wheel)

pinacoteca *f,* art gallery, picture gallery

pináculo *m,* pinnacle, summit; climax, culmination; *arch* finial

pinar *m,* pinewood

pincel *m,* paintbrush; artist, painter; painting technique. **p. para las cejas,** eyebrow pencil

pincelada *f,* brushstroke. **dar la última p.,** to add the finishing touch

pincelero (-ra) *n* seller or maker of paintbrushes; brush box

pinchadura *f,* prick, puncture, piercing; sting; nipping, biting

pinchar *vt* to prick; puncture; pierce; sting; nip, bite. **no p. ni cortar,** to be ineffective (of persons)

pinchazo *m,* prick; puncture; sting; incitement

pinche *m,* scullion, kitchen boy; *Argentina* minor office clerk; *a, Mexico* damn

pineda *f,* pinewood

pingajo *m, inf* tatter, rag

pingajoso *a inf* tattered, ragged

pingo *m, inf* tatter, rag; *pl inf* cheap clothes

pingüe *a* fat, greasy; fertile, rich

pingüino *m,* penguin

pino *a* steep. *m, bot* pine, deal; *poet* ship. **p. de tea,** pitch pine. **p. silvestre,** red fir

pinta *f,* spot; marking; mark; fleck; look, appearance; pint (measure); drop, drip; spot ball (in billiards)

pintamonas *mf inf* dauber

pintar *vt* to paint; describe, picture; exaggerate; *vi* show, manifest itself; *vr* make up (one's face). *inf* **pintarse solo para,** to be very good at, excel at

pintiparado *a* most similar, very alike; fitting, apposite

pintiparar *vt inf* to compare

pintor (-ra) *n* painter, artist. **p. callejero,** sidewalk artist, pavement artist. **p. de brocha gorda,** house painter

pintoresco *a* picturesque, quaint, pretty

pintorrear *vt inf* to daub, paint badly

pintura *f,* painting; paint, pigment; picture, painting; description. **p. a la aguada,** watercolor painting. **p. al fresco,** fresco. **p. al látex,** latex paint. **p. al óleo,** oil painting. **p. al pastel,** pastel drawing

pinturería *f,* paint store

pinturero *a inf* affected, conceited; dandified, overdressed

pinza *f,* clamp. **p. de la ropa,** clothes peg

pinzas *f pl,* pincers; pliers; tweezers; forceps. **p. hemostáticas,** arterial forceps

piña *f,* pineapple; cluster, knot (of people, etc.); pinecone

piñón *m,* pine nut; *mech* pinion, chain wheel

pío *a* pious; compassionate; good; piebald. *m,* chirping, cheep; *inf* longing

piocha *f, Lat. Am.* pickax

piojo *m,* louse

piojoso *a* lousy; avaricious, stingy

piola *f, Lat. Am.* cord, string; rope; tether

pionero *m,* pioneer

piorrea *f,* pyorrhea

pipa *f,* barrel, cask; tobacco pipe; pip (of fruits)

pipar *vi* to smoke a pipe

pipeta *f,* pipette

pipiar *vi* to chirp, twitter

pique *m,* pique, resentment. **a p. de,** on the verge of, about to. **echar a p.,** *naut* to sink; destroy. **irse a p.,** to sink, founder

piqueta *f,* pick, mattock; mason's hammer

piquete *m,* puncture, small wound; *mil* picket; pole, stake; small hole (in garments); picket (in strikes)

pira *f,* funeral pyre; bonfire

piragua *f,* piragua, canoe

pirámide *f,* pyramid

piraña *f* piranha
pirarse *vr inf* to slip away
pirata *a* piratical *mf* pirate; savage, cruel person
piratear *vi* to play the pirate
piratería *f*, piracy; plunder, robbery
pirático *a* piratical
pirca *f*, *Lat. Am.* dry-stone wall
pirenaico, pirineo *a* Pyrenean
pirético *a* pyretic
piriforme *a* pear-shaped
Pirineos, los the Pyrenees
piropear *vt inf* to pay compliments to
piropo *m*, carbuncle; *inf* compliment. **echar piropos,** to pay compliments
pirotécnico *a* pyrotechnical. *m*, pyrotechnist
pirrarse *vr inf* to desire ardently
pírrico *a* Pyrrhic
pirueta *f*, pirouette, twirl
pisada *f*, treading, stepping; footprint, footstep; stepping on a person's foot. **seguir las pisadas de alguien,** *fig* to follow in someone's footsteps, imitate someone
pisano (-na) *a* and *n* Pisan
pisapapeles *m*, paperweight
pisar *vt* to tread upon; trample upon; crush; *mus* press (strings); trespass upon; *vr, Argentina* to be mistaken
pisaverde *m, inf* fop, dandy
piscicultura *f*, pisciculture, fish farming
piscina *f*, fishpond; swimming pool; *ecc* piscina
piscolabis *m, inf* snack, light meal
piso *m*, treading, trampling; story, floor; flooring; apartment. **p. bajo,** ground floor
pisón *m*, rammer, ram
pisotear *vt* to trample; crush under foot; tread on; step on; humiliate, treat inconsiderately
pisoteo *m*, trampling under foot; treading
pista *f*, track, trail (of animals); circus ring; racetrack, racecourse. **p. de patinar,** skating rink. **p. de vuelo,** *aer* landing field. *inf* **seguir la p. a,** to spy upon
pistacho *m*, pistachio
pistar *va* to pestle, pound
pistero *m*, feeding cup
pistilo *m*, pistil
pisto, *m*, *Central America, slang* dough (money)
pistola *f*, pistol. **p. ametralladora,** machine gun.
pistolera *f*, holster; pistol case
pistolero *m*, gangster
pistoletazo *m*, pistol shot; pistol wound
pistón *m*, *mus* piston; *mil* percussion cap; *mech* piston
pitada *f*, blast on a whistle, whistling; impertinence
pitagórico (-ca) *a* and *n* Pythagorean
pitanza *f*, alms, charity; *inf* daily food; pittance, scanty remuneration
pitar *vi* to play the whistle; *vt* pay (debts); smoke; give alms to
pitido *m*, blast on a whistle; whistling (of birds)
pitillera *f*, cigarette case; female cigarette maker
pito *m*, whistle; *mus* fife. *inf* **Cuando pitos flautas, cuando flautas pitos,** It's always the unexpected that happens. *inf* **no valer un p.,** to be not worth a straw
pitoflero (-ra) *n* mediocre performer (gen. on a wind instrument); *inf* talebearer, gossip
pitón *m*, *zool* python; nascent horn (of goats, etc.); spout; protuberance; *bot* sprout
pitonisa *f*, *myth* pythoness; witch, enchantress
pitorrearse *vr* to ridicule, mock
pituitario *a* pituitary
pituso *a* small and amusing (of children)
pivote *m*, pivot, swivel, gudgeon
piyama *m*, pajamas
pizarra *f*, slate; blackboard
pizarral *m*. **pizarrería** *f*, slate quarry
pizarrín *m*, slate pencil
pizca *f*, *inf* atom, speck, crumb; jot, whit. **¡Ni p.!** Not a scrap!

pizpireta *a f, inf* coquettish; smart; dressed up
placa *f*, plate, disk; *art* plaque; *phot* plate; star (insignia). **p. recordatorio,** commemorative plaque
placabilidad *f*, placability, appeasability
pláceme *m*, congratulation
placentero *a* agreeable, pleasant
placer *vt irr* to please, give pleasure to, gratify. *m, naut* reef, sandbank; pleasure; wish, desire; permission, consent; entertainment, diversion. **a p.,** at one's convenience; at leisure. *Pres. Ind.* **plazco, places,** etc. *Preterite* **plugo, pluguieron.** *Pres. Subjunc.* **plazca,** etc. *Imperf. Subjunc.* **pluguiese,** etc.
placibilidad *f*, agreeableness, pleasantness
placible *a* agreeable, pleasant
placidez *f*, placidity, calmness, serenity
plácido *a* placid, calm, serene
placiente *a* pleasing, attractive
plácito *m*, decision, judgment, opinion
plafón *m*, ceiling light; *arch* panel
plaga *f*, plague; disaster, calamity; epidemic; glut; pest; grief
plagar *vt* (*with de*) to infect with; *vr* (*with de*) be covered with; be overrun by; be infested with
plagiar *vt* to plagiarize, copy; kidnap, hold for ransom
plagiario (-ia) *n* plagiarist; *Lat. Am.* kidnapper
plagio *m*, plagiary; kidnapping
plan *m*, plan; scheme; plane. **p. quinquenal,** five-year plan
plana *f*, sheet, page; mason's trowel; plain. **p. mayor,** (*mil nav*) staff
planadora *f*, steamroller
plancha *f*, sheet, slab, plate; flatiron; horizontal suspension (in gymnastics); *naut* gangway, gangplank; *inf* howler
planchado *m*, ironing; ironing to be done or already finished
planchador (-ra) *n* ironer
planchar *vt* to iron, press with an iron
planchear *vt* to plate (with metal)
planeador *m*, *aer* glider
planear *vt* to plan out; make plans for; *vi aer* glide
planeo *m*, *aer* glide
planeta *m*, planet
planetario *a* planetary. *m*, planetarium
planicie *f*, levelness, evenness; plain
planilla *f*, *Lat. Am.* application, application form, blank; payroll; list; ballot
plano *a* flat, level; plane. *m*, *geom* plane; plan, map; *aer* aileron, wing
planta *f*, *bot* plant; sole (of the foot); plantation; layout, plan; position of the feet (in dancing, fencing); scheme, project. **p. baja,** ground floor. **p. vivaz,** perennial plant. *inf* **buena p.,** good appearance
plantación *f*, planting; plantation, nursery
plantador (-ra) *n* planter. *m, agr* dibble. *f*, **plantadora,** mechanical planter
plantar *vt* to plant; erect; place; found, set up; pose (a problem); raise (a question, etc.); *inf* leave in the lurch; *vr* take up one's position; jib (of horses); oppose
planteamiento *m*, execution; putting into practice; planning; statement (of problems)
plantel *m*, nursery garden; training school, nursery
plantilla *f*, young plant; insole (of shoes); *mech* template, jig
plantío *m*, plantation, afforestation; planting. *a* planted or ready for planting (ground)
plantón *m*, plant or sapling ready for transplanting; *bot* cutting; doorkeeper, porter. **dar un p. (a),** to keep (a person) waiting a long time
plañidero (-ra) *a* mournful, piteous, anguished
plañido *m*, lament, weeping, wailing
plañir *vi* and *vt irr* to lament, wail, weep. See **tañer**
plasma *m*, plasma
plasmar *vt* to mold, throw (pottery)
plástica *f*, art of clay modeling; plastic
plástico *a* plastic; flexible, malleable, soft

plata *f*, silver; silver (coins); *Lat. Am.*, money; white. **p. labrada,** silverware

plataforma *f*, platform; running board (of a train); *rw* turntable

platal *m*, *Lat. Am.* wealth

plátano *m*, banana tree, banana; plantain; plane tree

platea *f*, *theat* pit. **butaca de p.,** pit stall

plateado *a* silvered; silver-plated; silvery

plateador *m*, plater

platear *vt* to electroplate, silver

platería *f*, silversmith's art or trade; silversmith's shop or workshop

platero *m*, silversmith; jeweler

plática *f*, conversation; exhortation, sermon; address, discourse

platicar *vt* and *vi* to converse (about)

platija *f*, plaice

platillo *m*, saucer; kitty (in card games); pan (of a scale); *pl* cymbals

platinado *m*, plating

platino *m*, platinum

platívolo *m*, flying saucer

plato *m*, plate; dish; *cul* course, dish; pan (of a scale). **p. sopero,** soup plate. **p. trinchero,** meat dish. *inf* **comer en un mismo p.,** to be on intimate terms. **nada entre dos platos,** much ado about nothing

platónico *a* Platonic

platonismo *m*, Platonism

platudo, -a *mf*, rich, wealthy, well-heeled

plausible *a* plausible, reasonable; commendable

playa *f*, beach, seashore, strand

plaza *f*, square (in a town, etc.); marketplace; fortified town; space; duration; employment, post.; *com* market. **p. de armas,** garrison town; military camp. **p. de toros,** bullring. **p. fuerte,** strong place, fortress. **sentar p.,** to enlist in the army

plazo *m*, term, duration; expiration of term, date of payment; installment. **a plazos,** *com* by installments, on the installment system

plazoleta *f*, small square (in gardens, etc.)

pleamar *f*, *naut* high water

plebe *f*, common people; rabble, mob

plebeyo (-ya) *a* plebeian. *n* commoner, plebeian

plebiscito *m*, plebiscite

plectro *m*, plectrum

plegable *a* foldable

plegadera *f*, folder; folding knife; paper folder

plegadizo *a* folding; collapsible; jointed

plegado *m*, pleating; folding

plegador *a* folding. *m*, folding machine

plegadura *f*, folding, doubling; fold, pleat

plegar *vt irr* to fold; pleat; *sew* gather; *vr* submit, give in. See **acertar**

plegaria *f*, fervent prayer

pleitear *vt* to go to court about; indulge in litigation

pleitista *a* quarrelsome, litigious

pleito *m*, action, lawsuit; dispute, quarrel; litigation. **p. de familia,** family squabble. **ver el p.,** *law* to try a case

plenamente *adv* fully, entirely

plenario *a* full, complete; *law* plenary

plenilunio *m*, full moon

plenipotencia *f*, full powers (diplomatic, etc.)

plenipotenciario *a* and *m*, plenipotentiary

plenitud *f*, fullness, completeness; plenitude, abundance

pleno *a* full. *m*, general meeting

pleonasmo *m*, *gram* pleonasm

pleonástico *a* pleonastic

pleuresía *f*, pleurisy

plexo *m*, plexus

pliego *m*, sheet (of paper); letter, packet of papers

pliegue *m*, fold, pleat; *sew* gather

plinto *m*, *arch* plinth (of a column); baseboard

plisar *vt* to pleat; fold

plomada *f*, plummet; sounding lead; plumb, lead

plomería *f*, plumbing; plumbing business; lead roofing

plomero *m*, plumber

plomizo *a* lead-like; lead-colored, gray

plomo *m*, lead (metal); plummet; bullet; *inf* bore, tedious person

pluma *f*, feather; pen; plumage; quill; penmanship; writer; writing profession. **p. estilográfica,** fountain pen. **a vuela p.,** as the pen writes, written in a hurry

plumado *a* feathered

pluma fuente *f*, *Lat. Am.* fountain pen

plumaje *m*, plumage, feathers; plume

plúmbeo *a* plumbeous, leaden

plúmeo *a* feathered, plumed

plumero *m*, feather duster; plume, feather; plumage

plumón *m*, down; feather bed *Lat. Am.* felt-tipped pen

plumoso *a* feathered

plural *a* and *m*, plural

pluralidad *f*, plurality; multitude, number

pluralizar *vt* to pluralize

plurilingüe *a* multilingual

pluscuamperfecto *m*, pluperfect

plusmarquista *mf sport* recordholder

plutocracia *f*, plutocracy

plutócrata *mf* plutocrat

plutocrático *a* plutocratic

pluviómetro *m*, rain gauge

poblacho *m*, miserable town or village

población *f*, peopling; population; town

poblado *m*, inhabited place; town; village

poblador (-ra) *a* populating. *n* colonist, settler

poblar *vt irr* to colonize; people, populate; breed fast; stock, supply; *vr* put forth leaves (of trees). See **contar**

pobre *a* poor; indigent, needy; mediocre; unfortunate; humble, meek. *mf* beggar, pauper, needy person. *inf* **ser p. de solemnidad,** to be down and out

pobrero *m*, *ecc* distributor of alms

pobretería *f*, poverty; needy people

pobretón *a* extremely needy

pobreza *f*, poverty, need; shortage; timidity; *min* baseness; poorness (of soil, etc.)

pocero *m*, well digger

pocilga *f*, pigsty; *inf* filthy place

poción *f*, potion, drink; mixture, dose

poco *a* little, scanty; *pl* few. *m*, small amount, a little. *adv* little; shortly, in a little while. **p. a p.,** by degrees, little by little; slowly. **p. más o menos,** more or less, approximately. **por p.,** almost, nearly (always used with the present tense, e.g. **Por p. me caigo,** I almost fell). **tener en p. (a),** to have a poor opinion of; undervalue

poda *f*, *agr* pruning; pruning season

podadera *f*, pruning knife

podar *vt agr* to prune, trim

poder *m*, power; authority; jurisdiction; *law* power of attorney; strength; ability; proxy; efficacy; possession; *pl* authority; power of attorney. **los poderes constituidos,** the established authorities; the powers that be. **p. de adquisición,** purchasing power. **casarse por poderes,** to be married by proxy

poder *vt irr* to be able to (e.g. **Podemos comprar estas naranjas,** We can (are able to) buy these oranges). **Dice que la calamidad podía haberse evitado,** He says that the disaster could have been averted). **p.** also expresses possibility (e.g. **Pueden haber ido a la ciudad,** They may have gone to the city. **¡Qué distinta pudo haber sido su vida!** How different his life might have been!). *impers* be possible. **a más no p.,** of necessity, without being able to help it; to the utmost. **no p. con,** to be unable to control or manage. **no p. hacer más,** to have no alternative, have to; be unable to do more. **no p. menos de,** to be obliged to, have no alternative but. **no p. contener su emoción,** to be overcome with emotion. **no p. ver a,** to hate (persons). *impers* **Puede que venga esta tarde,** He may come (perhaps he will come) this afternoon. *Pres. Part.* **pudiendo.** *Pres. Ind.* **puedo, puedes, puede, pueden.** *Fut.* **podré,** etc. *Condit.* **podría,** etc. *Preterite*

pude, pudiste, etc. *Pres. Subjunc.* **pueda, puedas, pueda, puedan.** *Imperf. Subjunc.* **pudiese,** etc.

poderío *m,* power, authority; sway, rule; dominion; wealth

poderoso *a* powerful; opulent; effective, efficacious; mighty, magnificent

podredumbre *f,* decay; pus; *fig* canker, anguish

podredura, podrición *f,* putrefaction; decay

podrido *a* rotten; putrid; corrupt; decayed

podrir *vt* See **pudrir**

poema *m,* poem. **p. sinfónico,** tone poem

poesía *f,* poetry, verse; lyric, poem

poeta *m,* poet

poetastro *m,* poetaster

poética *f,* poetics

poético *a* poetical

poetisa *f,* poetess

poetizar *vi* to write verses; *vt* poeticize

polaco (-ca) *a* Polish. *n* Pole. *m,* Polish (language)

polainas *f pl,* leggings, puttees, gaiters

polar *a* polar

polaridad *f,* polarity; polarization

polarización *f,* polarization

polarizar *vt* to polarize

polca *f,* polka

polea *f,* pulley; *naut* block

polémica *f,* polemic, controversy, dispute

polémico *a* polemical

polemista *mf* disputant, controversialist

polen *m,* pollen

polichinela *m,* Punchinello

policía *f,* police; government, polity, administration; civility, courtesy; cleanliness, tidiness. *m,* policeman. **p. urbana,** city police

policíaco *a* police; detective

policial *a* police; *m, Lat. Am.* police officer

policromo *a* polychrome

poliedro *m,* polyhedron

polifacético *a* many-sided

polifonía *f,* polyphony

polifónico *a* polyphonic

poligamia *f,* polygamy

polígamo (-ma) *a* polygamous. *n* polygamist

poligloto (-ta) *n* polyglot. *f,* polyglot Bible

polígono *a* polygonal. *m,* polygon

polilla *f,* moth; moth grub; destroyer, ravager

polimorfismo *m, chem* polymorphism

polimorfo *a* polymorphous

Polinesia Polynesia

polinesio (-ia) *a* and *n* Polynesian

polinización *f,* pollination

poliomielitis *f,* poliomyelitis, polio

pólipo *m, zool* polyp; octopus; *med* polyp

polisílabo *a* polysyllabic. *m,* polysyllable

polista *mf* polo player

politécnico *a* polytechnic

politeísmo *m,* polytheism

politeísta *a* polytheistic. *mf* polytheist

política *f,* politics; civility, courtesy; diplomacy; tact; policy

politicastro *m,* corrupt politician

político *a* political; civil, courteous; in-law, by marriage (relationships). *m,* politician

politiquear *vi inf* to dabble in politics, talk politics

politizarse *vr* to enter the political arena

póliza *f, com* policy; *com* draft; share certificate; revenue stamp; admission ticket; lampoon. **p. a prima fija,** fixed-premium policy. **p. de seguros,** insurance policy. **p. dotal,** endowment policy

polizón *m,* loafer, tramp; stowaway; bustle (of a dress)

polla *f,* pullet; *inf* flapper, young woman

pollada *f,* brood, hatch (especially of chickens)

pollastro (-ra) *n* pullet

pollera *f,* female poultry breeder or seller; chicken coop; go-cart; *Argentina, Chile* skirt

pollería *f,* poultry market or shop

pollero *n* poultry breeder; poulterer. *m,* hen coop; *Lat. Am.* gambler

pollino (-na) *n* young ass; donkey

pollo *m,* chicken; *inf* youth, stripling; *fig inf* downy bird. *inf* **p. pera,** young blood, lad. **sacar pollos,** to hatch chickens

polo *m,* pole (all meanings); *fig* support; popular Andalusian song; *sport* polo. **de p. a p.,** from pole to pole

polonés (-esa) *a* Polish. *n* Pole

Polonia Poland

poltrón *a* lazy, idle

poltronear *vi* to loaf about

poltronería *f,* idleness, laziness

polución *f, med* ejaculation

polvareda *f,* dust cloud; storm, agitation

polvera *f,* powder bowl; powder puff; powder compact

polvillo *m, Lat. Am.* blight

polvo *m,* dust; powder; pinch (of snuff, etc.); *pl* face or dusting powder. **Se hizo como por polvos de la madre celestina,** It was done as if by magic. *inf* **limpio de p. y paja,** gratis, for nothing; net (of profit)

pólvora *f,* gunpowder; bad temper. **p. de algodón,** guncotton.

polvorear *vt* to powder, dust with powder

polvoriento *a* dusty; powdery, covered with powder

polvorín *m,* very fine powder; powder magazine; powder flask

polvoroso *a* dusty; covered with powder

pomada *f,* pomade; salve, ointment

pomar *m,* orchard (especially an apple orchard)

pómez *f,* pumice stone (**piedra p.**)

pomo *m, bot* pome; pomander; nosegay; pommel, hilt (of a sword); handle; rose (of watering can)

pomología *f,* pomology, art of fruit growing

pompa *f,* pomp, splendor; ceremonial procession; air bubble; peacock's outspread tail; *naut* pump; billowing of clothes in the wind

Pompeya Pompeii

pomposidad *f,* pomposity

pomposo *a* stately, ostentatious, magnificent; inflated, pompous; florid, bombastic

pómulo *m,* cheekbone

ponchada *f Lat. Am.* great deal, large amount

ponche *m,* punch, toddy

ponchera *f,* punch bowl

poncho *a* lazy, negligent. *m,* military cloak; poncho, cape

ponderación *f,* weighing; reflection, consideration; exaggeration

ponderador *a* reflective, deliberate; exaggerated

ponderar *vt* to weigh; consider, ponder; exaggerate; overpraise

ponderosidad *f,* heaviness; ponderousness, dullness

ponderoso *a* heavy; ponderous; circumspect

ponedero *a* egg-laying (of hens). *m,* nest

ponencia *f,* clause, section; office of referee or arbitrator; report, referendum

poner *vt irr* to place, put; arrange; set (the table); bet, stake; appoint (to an office); call, name; lay (eggs); set down (in writing); calculate, count; suppose; leave to a person's judgment; risk; contribute; prepare; need, take; cause, inspire (emotions); make, cause; adapt; add; cause to become (angry, etc.); insult; praise; (*with prep a + infin*) begin to. **p. a contribución,** to lay under contribution, turn to account, utilize. **ponerle el cascabel al gato** or **el collar al gato,** to bell the cat. **p. los cuernos (a),** to cuckold. **p. al corriente,** to bring up to date, inform. **p. a prueba,** to test. **p. casa,** to set up house. *inf* **p. colorado a,** to make blush. **p. coto a,** to put a stop to, check. **p. en comparación,** to compare. **p. conato en,** to put a great deal of effort into. **p. en cotejo,** to collate. **p. en limpio,** to make a fair copy (of). **p. en marcha,** to start, set in motion. **p. en práctica,** to put into effect. **p. por caso,** to take as an example (e.g. **Pongamos por caso . . .** For example, . . .). **p. por encima (de),** to prefer. *vr* to place oneself; become; put on (garments, etc.); dirty or stain oneself; set (of the sun, stars); oppose; deck oneself, dress oneself up; arrive; (*with prep a + infin*) begin to. **ponerse al corriente,** to bring oneself up to date. **ponerse bien,** to improve; get better (in health). **ponerse colorado,** to blush, flush. **p. una base racional a la fe,** to give faith a rational foundation. **p. los cimientos de,** lay the foundation of, lay the foundations for. **p. una conferencia,** to make a long-distance call. *Pres. Ind.* **pongo, pones,** etc. *Fut.* **pondré,** etc. *Condit.* **pondría,** etc. *Imperat.* **pon.** *Past Part.* **puesto.** *Preterite* **puse, pusiste,** etc. *Pres. Subjunc.* **ponga,** etc. *Imperf. Subjunc.* **pusiese,** etc.

pongo *m Bolivia, Peru* Native American serf

pongueaje *m* **Bolivia, Peru** Native American serfdom

ponientada *f,* steady west wind

poniente *m,* west; west wind

pontazgo *m,* bridge toll

pontear *vt* to bridge; make bridges

pontificado *m,* pontificate, papacy

pontífice *m,* pontifex; pope, pontiff; archbishop; bishop

pontón *m, mil* pontoon; hulk used as a prison, hospital, store, etc.; wooden bridge

pontonero *m,* pontoneer, military engineer

ponzoña *f,* poison, venom

ponzoñoso *a* poisonous, venomous; noxious; harmful

popa *f, naut* stern, poop. **en p.,** abaft, astern, aft

popelina *f,* poplin

popote *m, Mexico* (drinking) straw

populachería *f,* cheap popularity with the rabble

populachero *a* mob, vulgar

populacho *m,* mob, rabble

popular *a* popular

popularidad *f,* popularity

popularizar *vt* to popularize; *vr* grow popular

populoso *a* populous, crowded

popurrí *m, cul* stew; potpourri; miscellany

poquedad *f,* paucity, scarcity; timidity, cowardice; trifle, mere nothing

poquísimo *a sup* **poco** very little

poquito *m,* very little

por *prep* for; by; through, along; during; because, as (e.g. **Lo desecharon p. viejo,** They threw it away because it was old); however (e.g. **p. bonito que sea,** however pretty it is); during; in order to (e.g. **Lo hice p. no ofenderla,** I did it in order not to offend her); toward, in favor of, for; for the sake of; on account of, by reason of (e.g. **No pudo venir p. estar enfermo,** He could not come on account of his illness); via, by (e.g. **p. correo aéreo,** by airmail); as for (e.g. **P. mí, lo rechazo,** As for me, I refuse it. **p. mi cuenta,** to my way of thinking; on my own); in exchange for (e.g. **Me vendió dos libros p. seis dólares,** He sold me two books for six dollars); in the name of; as a substitute for, instead of (e.g. **Hace mi trabajo p. mí,** He is doing my work for me); per. **Por** has several uses: 1. Introduces the agent after a passive (e.g. **La novela fue escrita p. él,** The novel was written by him). 2. Expresses movement through, along or about (e.g. **Andaban p. la calle,** They were walking along (or down) the street). 3. Denotes time at or during which an action occurs (e.g. **Ocurrió p. entonces un acontecimiento de importancia,** About that time an important event occurred). 4. Expresses rate or proportion (e.g. **seis por ciento,** six percent). 5. With certain verbs, means 'to be' and expresses vague futurity (e.g. **El libro queda p. escribir,** The book remains to be written). **p. cortesía,** by courtesy, out of politeness. **p. cortesía de,** by courtesy of. **p. escrito,** in writing. **p. fas o p. nefas,** by fair means or foul; at any cost. **p. mucho que,** however great, however much; in spite of, notwithstanding. **¿P. qué?** Why? **p. si acaso,** in case, if by chance. **estar p.,** to be about to; be inclined to. **P. un clavo se pierde la herradura,** For want of a nail, the shoe was lost.

porcelana *f,* porcelain, china; chinaware

porcentaje *m,* percentage

porche *m,* porch, portico

porcino *a* porcine. *m,* young pig; bruise

porción *f,* portion; *com* share; *inf* crowd; allowance, pittance

porcionista *mf* shareholder; sharer; boarding school student

pordiosear *vi* to ask alms, beg

pordioseo *m,* asking alms, begging

pordiosero (-ra) *a* begging. *n* beggar

porfía *f,* obstinacy; importunity; tenacity. **a p.,** in competition

porfiadamente *adv* obstinately

porfiado *a* obstinate, obdurate, persistent

porfiar *vi* to be obstinate, insist; persist

pórfido *m,* porphyry

pormenor *m,* particular, detail (gen. *pl*); secondary matter

pormenorizar *vt* to describe in detail

pornografía *f,* pornography

pornográfico *a* pornographic, obscene

poro *m,* pore; *Lat. Am. also* leek

porongo *m, Lat. Am.* calabash, gourd

porosidad *f,* porosity, permeability

poroso *a* porous, leaky

poroto *m, Lat. Am.* bean; *Chile* child, kid

porque *conjunc* because, for; in order that

porqué *m,* reason, wherefore, why; *inf* money. **el cómo y el p.,** the why and the wherefore

porquería *f, inf* filth, nastiness; dirty trick; rudeness, gross act; trifle, thing of no account

porquerizo, porquero *m,* swineherd

porra *f,* club, bludgeon; last player (in children's games); *inf* vanity, boastfulness; bore, tedious person

porrada *f,* blow with a club; buffet, knock, fall; *inf* folly; glut, abundance

porrazo *m,* blow with a club; buffet, knock, fall

porrear *vi inf* to insist, harp on

porrería *f, inf* folly; obduracy, persistence

porreta *f,* green leaves of leeks, onions, and cereals. *inf* **en p.,** stark-naked

porrino *m,* seed of a leek; young leek plant

porrón *m,* winebottle with a spout; earthenware jug

porsiacaso *m, Argentina, Venezuela* knapsack

portaaviones *m,* aircraft carrier

portachuelo *m,* defile, narrow mountain pass

portada *f,* front, facade; frontispiece; title page; portal, doorway

portado (bien *or* **mal)** *a* well- or ill-dressed or behaved

portador (-ra) *n* carrier. *m, com* bearer; *mech* carrier

portaestandarte *m,* standard-bearer

portafolio *m,* portfolio; *Lat. Am. also* briefcase

portafusil *m,* rifle sling

portal *m,* entrance, porch; portico; city gate

portalámpara *f,* lamp holder; *elec* socket

portalibros *m,* bookstrap

portalón *m,* gangway

portamanteo *m,* traveling bag

portamonedas *m,* pocketbook; handbag, purse

portanuevas *mf* bringer of news, newsmonger

portaobjetos *m,* stage (of a microscope)

portaplumas *m,* pen holder

portar *vt* to retrieve (of dogs); carry (arms); *vr* behave (well or badly); bear oneself, act; be well, or ill (in health)

portátil *a* portable

portavoz *m,* megaphone; spokesman, mouthpiece

portazgo *m,* toll; tollbooth

portazguero *m,* toll collector

portazo *m,* bang of the door; slamming the door in a person's face

porte *m,* transport; *com* carriage; postage; freight, transport cost; porterage; behavior, conduct; bearing, looks; capacity; volume; size, dimension; nobility (of descent); *naut* tonnage. **p. pagado,** charges prepaid

porteador *m,* carrier; porter; carter

portear *vt* to carry, transport; *vr* migrate (of birds)

portento *m*, marvel, prodigy, portent

portentoso *a* marvelous, portentous

porteño, -a *a* of Buenos Aires; native of Buenos Aires; resident of Buenos Aires

porteo *m*, porterage, cartage

portería *f*, porter's lodge; porter's employment; *sport* goal

portero (-ra) *n* doorman, doorkeeper; porter; concierge; janitor; *sport* goalkeeper. **p. eléctrico,** door buzzer

portezuela *f*, *dim* small door; carriage door; pocket flap

pórtico *m*, portico, piazza; porch; vestibule, hall

portillo *m*, breach, opening; defile, narrow pass; *fig* loophole

portón *m*, hall door, inner door; *Chile* back door

portorriqueño (-ña) *a* and *n* Puerto Rican

portuario *a* dock, port

portugués (-esa) *a* and *n* Portuguese. *m*, Portuguese (language)

portuguesada *f*, exaggeration

porvenir *m*, future time

¡porvida! *interj* By the saints! By the Almighty!

pos *prefix* after; behind. Also *adv* **en p.,** with the same meanings

posa *f*, tolling bell; *pl* buttocks

posada *f*, dwelling; inn, tavern; lodging; hospitality

posaderas *f pl*, buttocks

posadero (-ra) *n* innkeeper; boardinghouse keeper

posar *vi* to lodge, live; rest; alight, perch; *vt* set down (a burden); *vr* settle (liquids); (*with en or sobre*) perch upon

posdata *f*, P.S., postscript

pose *f*, *phot* time exposure; *inf* pose

poseedor (-ra) *n* possessor, holder

poseer *vt irr* to own, possess; know (a language, etc.); *vr* restrain oneself. **estar poseído por,** to be possessed by (passion, etc.); be thoroughly convinced of. See **creer**

posesión *f*, ownership, occupancy; possession; property, territory (often *pl*)

posesionarse *vr* to take possession; lay hold (of)

poseso *a* possessed of an evil spirit

posesor (-ra) *n* owner, possessor

posfecha *f*, postdate

posguerra *f*, postwar period

posibilidad *f*, possibility; probability; opportunity; means, chance; *pl* property, wealth

posibilitar *vt* to make possible, facilitate

posible *a* possible. *m pl*, property, personal wealth. **hacer lo p.** *or* **hacer todo lo p.,** to do everything possible; do one's best

posición *f*, placing; position; situation; status

positivamente *adv* positively, definitely

positivismo *m*, positivism

positivista *a* positivistic. *mf* positivist

positivo *a* positive; certain, definite; (*math elec*) plus; true, real

pósito *m*, public granary; cooperative association

posma *f*, *inf* sluggishness, sloth

poso *m*, sediment; lees, dregs; repose, quietness

posponer *vt irr* (*with prep a*) to place after; make subordinate to; value less than. See **poner**

posta *f*, post horse; stage, post; stake (cards)

postal *a* postal. *f*, postcard, postal card

poste *m*, post, stake

postema *f*, tumor, abscess; bore, tedious person

postergación *f*, delay; delaying; relegation; disregard of seniority (in promotion)

postergar *vt* to delay; disregard a senior claim to promotion

posteridad *f*, descendants; posterity

posterior *a* back, rear; hind; subsequent

posteriormente *adv* later, subsequently

postigo *m*, secret door; grating, hatch; postern; shutter (of a window)

postillón *m*, postilion

postizo *a* false, artificial, not natural. *m*, switch of false hair

postor *m*, bidder (at an auction)

postración *f*, prostration; exhaustion; depression, distress

postrar *vt* to cast down, demolish; prostrate, exhaust; *vr* kneel down; be prostrated or exhausted

postre *a* last (in order). *m*, *cul* dessert. **a la p.,** at last, finally

postrero *a* last (in order); rearmost, hindmost

postrimeramente *adv* lastly, finally

postrimería *f*, *ecc* last period of life

postulación *f*, entreaty, request

postulado *m*, assumption; supposition; working hypothesis; *geom* postulate

postulante (-ta) *n ecc* postulant, applicant, candidate

postular *vt* to postulate; *Lat. Am.* nominate

póstumo *a* posthumous

postura *f*, posture, bearing; laying (of an egg); bid (at an auction); position; agreement, pact; bet, stake; planting; transplanted tree. **p. de vida,** way of life

potable *a* drinkable. **agua p.,** drinking water

potación *f*, potation, drink

potaje *m*, stew, potage; dried vegetables; mixed drink; hotchpotch

potasa *f*, potash

potasio *m*, potassium

pote *m*, pot; jar; flowerpot; *cul* cauldron; *cul* stew

potencia *f*, power; potency; *mech* performance, capacity; strength, force; *math* power; rule, dominion

potencial *a* potential

potentado *m*, potentate

potente *a* potent; powerful; *inf* enormous

potestad *f*, authority, power; podesta, Italian magistrate; potentate; *math* power; *pl* angelic powers

potestativo *a law* facultative

potingue *m*, *inf* brew; mixture; lotion; medicine; filthy place, pigsty

poto *m*, *Lat. Am.* calabash, gourd; backside

potra *f*, filly

potrear *vt inf* to tease, annoy

potro *m*, colt, foal; rack (for torture); vaulting horse. **p. mesteño,** mustang

poyo *m*, stone seat

pozal *m*, pail, bucket

pozo *m*, well; shaft (in a mine). *aut* **p. colector,** crankcase

pozole, *m*, *Mexico* stew of pork, corn, chile, etc.

práctica *f*, practice; custom, habit; method; exercise

practicabilidad *f*, feasibility

practicable *a* feasible, practicable

prácticamente *adv* practically, in practice

practicante *m*, medical practitioner; medical student; *med* intern; first-aid practitioner

practicar *vt* to execute, perform; practice; make

práctico *a* practical; experienced, expert; workable. *m*, *naut* pilot

pradeño *a* meadow, prairie

pradera *f*, meadow, field; lawn

pradería *f*, meadowland, prairie

prado *m*, meadow; grassland; field; lawn; walk (in cities)

Praga Prague

pragmatista *a* pragmatic. *mf* pragmatist

pravedad *f*, wickedness, immorality, depravity

pravo *a* wicked, immoral, depraved

pre *m*, *mil* daily pay. *prep insep* pre-

preámbulo *m*, preamble, preface; importunate digression

prebenda *f*, *ecc* prebend, benefice; *inf* sinecure

preboste *m*, provost

precario *a* precarious, uncertain, insecure

precaución *f*, precaution, safeguard

precaucionarse *vr* to take precautions, safeguard oneself

precautelar *vt* to forewarn; take precautions

precaver *vt* to prevent, avoid; *vr* (*with de or contra*) guard against

precavido *a* cautious, forewarned

precedencia *f*, priority, precedence; superiority; preference, precedence

precedente *a* preceding. *m*, antecedent; precedent

preceder *vt* to precede; have precedence over, be superior to

preceptivo *a* preceptive; didactic

precepto *m*, precept; order, injunction; rule, commandment. **de p.,** obligatory

preceptor (-ra) *n* teacher, instructor, tutor, preceptor

preces *f pl*, *ecc* prayers; entreaties

preciado *a* excellent, esteemed, precious; boastful

preciar *vt* to esteem, value; valuate, price; *vr* boast

precintar *vt* to seal; rope, string, tie up

precinto *m*, sealing; roping, tying up; strap

precio *m*, price, cost; recompense, reward; premium; rate; reputation, importance; esteem. **p. de tasa,** controlled price

preciosidad *f*, preciousness; exquisiteness, fineness; richness; wittiness; *inf* loveliness, beauty; thing of beauty

precioso *a* precious; exquisite, fine, rare; rich; witty; *inf* lovely, delicious, attractive

preciosuna *f*, Lat. Am. thing of beauty

precipicio *m*, precipice; heavy fall; ruin, disaster

precipitación *f*, precipitancy, haste; rashness; *chem* precipitation

precipitadamente *adv* precipitately, in haste; rashly, foolishly

precipitado *a* precipitate; rash, thoughtless. *m*, *chem* precipitate

precipitar *vt* to precipitate, hurl headlong; hasten; *chem* precipitate; *vr* hurl oneself headlong; hasten, rush

precipitoso *a* precipitous; rash, heedless

precisamente *adv* exactly, precisely, just; necessarily. **Y p. en aquel instante llegó,** And just at that moment he arrived

precisar *vt* to fix, arrange; set forth, draw up, state; compel, force, oblige

precisión *f*, accuracy, precision; necessity, conciseness, clarity; compulsion, obligation

preciso *a* necessary, unavoidable; concise, clear; precise, exact

precitado *a* aforementioned

preclaro *a* illustrious, distinguished, celebrated

precocidad *f*, precocity

precognición *f*, foreknowledge

precolombino, -a *a* pre-Columbian

preconcebido *a* preconceived

preconcepto *m*, preconceived idea, preconceived notion

preconizar *vt* to eulogize, praise publicly

preconocer *vt irr* to know beforehand; foresee. See **conocer**

precoz *a* precocious

precursor (-ra) *a* precursory; preceding, previous. *n* precursor

predecesor (-ra) *n* predecessor

predecir *vt irr* to foretell, prophesy. See **decir**

predestinación *f*, predestination

predestinado (-da) *a* predestined; foreordained. *n* one of the predestined

predestinar *vt* to predestine, foreordain

predeterminar *vt* to predetermine

prédica *f*, *inf* (contemptuous) sermon

predicación *f*, preaching; homily, sermon

predicadera *f*, pulpit; *pl inf* talent for preaching

predicador (-ra) *a* preaching. *n* preacher

predicamento *m*, predicament; reputation

predicar *vt* to publish; manifest; preach; *vi* overpraise; *inf* lecture, scold. **p. en el desierto,** to preach to the wind

predicción *f*, prediction, prophecy

predilección *f*, predilection, preference, partiality

predilecto *a* favorite, preferred

predisponer *vt irr* to predispose. See **poner**

predisposición *f*, predisposition; tendency, prejudice

predominación *f*, predominance

predominante *a* predominant; prevailing

predominar *vi* and *vt* to predominate; prevail; tower above; overlook

predominio *m*, predominance, ascendancy, preponderance

preeminencia *f*, preeminence

preeminente *a* preeminent

preexistencia *f*, preexistence

preexistente *a* preexistent

preexistir *vi* to preexist, exist before

prefacio *m*, introduction, preface, prologue; *ecc* preface

prefecto *m*, prefect

prefectura *f*, prefecture

preferencia *f*, preference; superiority. **de p.,** preferred, favorite; preferably

preferente *a* preferable; preferential; preferred (of stock)

preferible *a* preferable

preferir *vt irr* to prefer; excel, exceed. *Pres. Part.* **prefiriendo.** *Pres. Ind.* **prefiero, prefieres, prefiere, prefieren.** *Preterite* **prefirió, prefirieron.** *Pres. Subjunc.* **prefiera, prefieras, prefiera, prefieran.** *Imperf. Subjunc.* **prefiriese,** etc.

prefijar *vt* to prefix

prefijo *m*, prefix

prefinir *vt* to fix a time limit for

prefulgente *a* brilliant, shining, resplendent

pregón *m*, public proclamation; marriage banns

pregonar *vt* to proclaim publicly; cry one's wares; publish abroad; eulogize, praise; proscribe, outlaw. **p. a los cuatro vientos,** *inf* to shout from the rooftops

pregonería *f*, office of the town crier

pregonero *m*, town crier

preguerra *f*, prewar period

pregunta *f*, question; *com* inquiry; questionnaire, interrogation. *inf* **andar** (*or* **estar**) **a la cuarta p.,** to be very hard up, be on the rocks. **hacer una p.,** to ask a question

preguntador (-ra) *a* questioning; inquisitive. *n* questioner; inquisitive person

preguntar *vt* to question, ask; (*with por*) inquire for; *vr* ask oneself, wonder

prehistoria *f*, prehistory

prehistórico *a* prehistoric

prejuicio *m*, prejudice

prejuzgar *vt* to prejudge, judge hastily

prelacía *f*, prelacy

prelación *f*, preference

prelado *m*, prelate

preliminar *a* preliminary, prefatory. *m*, preliminary

preludiar *vi* and *vt mus* to play a prelude (to); *vt* prepare, initiate

preludio *m*, introduction, prologue; *mus* prelude; *mus* overture

prematuro *a* premature, untimely; unseasonable; immature, unripe

premeditación *f*, premeditation

premeditar *vt* to premeditate, plan in advance

premiador (-ra) *a* rewarding. *n* rewarder

premiar *vt* to reward, requite

premio *m*, prize; reward; premium; *com* interest. **p. en metálico,** cash prize. *inf* **p. gordo,** first prize (in a lottery)

premioso *a* tight; troublesome, annoying; stern, strict; slow-moving; burdensome, hard; labored (of speech or style)

premisa *f*, premise; sign, indication

premonitorio *a* a premonitory

premura *f*, urgency, haste

prenda *f*, pledge; token, sign; jewel; article of clothing; talent, gift; loved one; *pl* game of forfeits

prendador (-ra) *n* pledger

prendamiento *m*, pawning

prendar *vt* to pawn; charm, delight; *vr* (*with de*) take a liking to

prender *vt* to seize; arrest; capture, catch. *vi* take root (plants); catch fire; be infectious

prendería *f*, second-hand shop

prendero (-ra) *n* second-hand dealer

prendimiento *m*, seizure, capture; arrest

prenombre *m*, given name, praenomen

prensa *f*, press; printing press; newspapers, the press. **dar a la p.,** to publish

prensado *m*, **prensadura** *f*, pressing; flattening; squeezing

prensar *vt* to press; squeeze

prensil *a* prehensile

preñado *a* pregnant; bulging, sagging (walls, etc.); swollen. *m*, pregnancy

preñez *f*, pregnancy; suspense

preocupación *f*, anxiety, preoccupation; prejudice

preocupadamente *adv* preoccupiedly, absentmindedly; with prejudice

preocupar *vt* to preoccupy; make anxious; bias, prejudice; *vr* be anxious; be prejudiced

preordinar *vt ecc* to predestine

preparación *f*, preparation; treatment; compound, specific

preparado *a* ready, prepared. *m*, preparation, patent food, etc.

preparar *vt* to prepare; *vr* prepare oneself; qualify

preparativo *a* preparatory. *m*, preparation

preparatorio *a* preparatory

preponderancia *f*, preponderance

preponderante *a* preponderant; dominant

preponderar *vi* to preponderate; dominate; outweigh

preponer *vt irr* to put before. See **poner**

preposición *f*, preposition

prepósito *m*, chairman, head, president; *ecc* provost

prepucio *m*, prepuce, foreskin

prerrogativa *f*, prerogative

presa *f*, hold, grasp; seizure, capture; booty; dam; lock (on rivers, canals); weir; ditch, trench; embankment; slice, bit. **hacer p.,** to seize; take advantage of (circumstances)

presagiar *vt* to prophesy, presage, bode

presagio *m*, presage, sign; presentiment, foreboding

présbita *a* long-sighted, farsighted

presbiterado *m*, priesthood; holy orders

presbiteriano (-na) *a* and *n* Presbyterian

presbítero *m*, priest

presciencia *f*, prescience, foresight

presciente *a* prescient, farsighted

prescindible *a* nonessential, able to be dispensed with

prescindir *vi* (*with de*) to pass over, omit; do without. **Prescindiendo de esto . . . ,** Leaving this aside. . . .

prescribir *vt* to prescribe, order

prescripción *f*, prescription

presea *f*, jewel, object of value

presencia *f*, presence, attendance; appearance; looks; ostentation. **p. de ánimo,** presence of mind

presenciar *vt* to be present at; witness, behold

presentación *f*, presentation; introduction; *Lat. Am. also* petition

presentar *vt* to show; present, make a gift of; introduce (persons); *vr* occur; present oneself; offer one's services

presente *a* present. *m*, gift; present time. *law* **Por estas presentes . . . ,** By these presents . . . . **tener p.,** to remember

presentimiento *m*, presentiment, apprehension

presentir *vt irr* to have a presentiment of. See **sentir**

preservación *f*, preservation, protection, saving

preservar *vt* to preserve, protect, save

preservativo *a* preservative. *m*, preservative, safeguard, protection

presidencia *f*, presidency; chairmanship; presidential seat or residence

presidencial *a* presidential

presidenta *f*, female president; president's wife; chairwoman

presidente *m*, president; chairman; head, director; presiding judge

presidiar *vt* to garrison

presidiario *m*, convict

presidio *m*, garrison; garrison town; fortress; penitentiary; imprisonment; *law* hard labor; assistance, protection

presidir *vt* to preside over; act as chairperson for; influence, determine

presilla *f*, loop, shank, noose; press stud; *Mexico* epaulet

presión *f*, pressure

preso (-sa) *n* prisoner, captive; convict

prestación *f*, lending, loan. **p. vecinal,** corvée

prestador (-ra) *a* lending, loan. *n* lender

prestamente *adv* expeditiously, promptly

prestamista *mf* moneylender; pawnbroker

préstamo *m*, loan; lending. **casa de préstamos,** pawnshop

prestar *vt* to lend; assist; pay (attention); give; *Lat. Am.* to borrow; *vi* be useful; give, expand; *vr* be suitable; lend itself; offer oneself. **tomar prestado,** to borrow

prestatario (-ia) *n* money borrower, debtor

preste *m*, celebrant of high mass. **el p. Juan,** title of Prester John

presteza *f*, speed; promptness, dispatch

prestidigitación *f*, prestidigitation

prestidigitador (-ra) *n* juggler, conjurer

prestigio *m*, magic spell, sorcery; trick, illusion (of conjurers, etc.); influence, prestige

prestigioso *a* illusory; influential

presto *a* quick, speedy; prompt, ready. *m*, pressure cooker. *adv* immediately; soon; quickly. **de p.,** speedily

presumido *a* conceited, vain; presumptuous

presumir *vt* to suppose, presume; *vi* be conceited

presunción *f*, supposition, presumption; vanity, presumptuousness

presuntivo *a* presumptive

presuntuosidad *f*, presumptuousness

presuntuoso *a* presumptuous, vain

presuponer *vt irr* to presuppose, assume; budget, estimate. See **poner**

presuposición *f*, presupposition

presupuesto *m*, motive, reason; supposition, assumption; estimate; *com* tender; national budget

presuroso *a* swift, speedy

pretencioso *a* pretentious, vain

pretender *vt* to seek, solicit; claim; apply for; attempt, try; woo, court

pretendiente (-ta) *n* pretender; candidate; petitioner; suitor

pretensión *f*, pretension; claim; *pl* ambitions

pretérito *a* past. *m*, preterite

pretextar *vt* to allege as a pretext or excuse

pretexto *m*, pretext, excuse

prevalecer *vi irr* to prevail; be dominant; take root (plants). See **conocer**

prevaleciente *a* prevailing; prevalent

prevaricador (-ra) *n* prevaricator

prevaricar *vi* to prevaricate

prevención *f*, prevention; precaution; prejudice; police station; *mil* guard room; foresight, prevision; preparation. **de p.,** as a precaution

prevenido *a* prepared; cautious, forewarned

prevenir *vt irr* to prepare; prevent, avoid; warn; prejudice; occur, happen; *fig* overcome (obstacles); *vr* be ready; be forewarned. See **venir**

preventivo *a* preventive

prever *vt irr* to foresee, forecast, anticipate. See **ver**

previamente *adv* previously, in advance

previo *a* previous, advance

previsión *f*, forecast; foresight, prevision, prescience. **p. social,** social insurance

previsor *a* farsighted, provident

prieto *a* almost black, blackish; tight; mean, avaricious; *Lat. Am.* dark-skinned, swarthy

prima *f, ecc* prime; *com* premium; female cousin

primacía *f,* supremacy, preeminence; primacy; primateship

primada *f, inf* act of sponging on, taking advantage of

primado *m,* primate; primateship

primario *a* primary. *m,* professor who gives the first lecture of the day

primavera *f,* springtime; primrose; figured silk material; beautifully colored thing; youth; prime

primaveral *a* spring, spring-like

primeramente *adv* first; in the first place

primerizo (-za) *n* novice; beginner; apprentice; first-born

primero *a* first; former; excellent, first-rate. *adv* first; in the first place. **primera enseñanza,** primary education. **primera materia,** raw material. **primer plano,** *art* foreground. **primera cura,** first aid. **de buenas a primeras,** all at once, suddenly

primicia *f,* first fruits; offering of first fruits; *pl* first effects

primitivo *a* original, early; primitive

primo (-ma) *a* first; excellent, fine. *n* cousin; *inf* simpleton; *inf* pigeon, dupe. **p. carnal,** first cousin. *inf* **hacer el p.,** to be a dupe. *inf* **ser prima hermana de,** to be the twin of (of things)

primogénito (-ta) *a* and *n* firstborn

primogenitura *f,* primogeniture

primor *m,* exquisite care; beauty, loveliness; thing of beauty

primoroso *a* beautiful; exquisitely done; dexterous, skillful

princesa *f,* princess

principado *m,* principality; princedom; superiority, preeminence

principal *a* chief, principal; illustrious; fundamental, first. *m,* head, principal (of a firm) *com* capital, principal; first floor

principalmente *adv* principally, chiefly

príncipe *m,* leader; prince. **p. de Asturias,** prince of Asturias. **p. de la sangre,** prince of the blood royal

principesco *a* princely

principiante (-ta) *n* beginner, novice; apprentice

principiar *vt* to begin, commence

principio *m,* beginning; principle; genesis, origin; rudiment; axiom; constituent. **al p.,** at first. **a principios,** at the beginning (of the month, year, etc.). **en p.,** in principle

pringar *vt cul* to soak in fat; stain with grease; *inf* wound; take part in a business deal; slander; *vr inf* appropriate, misuse (funds, etc.)

pringo *m, Lat. Am.* drop (of a liquid)

pringoso *a* greasy

pringue *mf,* animal fat, lard; grease spot

priora *f,* prioress

prioridad *f,* priority

prisa *f,* haste, speed; skirmish, foray. **a toda p.,** with all speed. **correr p.,** to be urgent. **dar p.,** to hasten, speed up. **darse** (*or* **estar de) p.,** to hurry

prisión *f,* prison, jail; seizure; captivity, imprisonment; *fig* bond; obstacle, shackle; *pl* fetters

prisionero (-ra) *n* prisoner; *fig* victim (of passion, etc.)

prisma *m,* prism

prismáticos *m pl,* field glasses

pristino *a* pristine

privación *f,* privation; lack, shortage; deprivation; degradation

privada *f,* toilet, privy, water closet

privadamente *adv* privately; individually, separately

privado *a* private; individual, personal. *m,* favorite; confidant

privar *vt* to deprive; dismiss (from office); interdict, forbid; *vi* prevail, be in favor; *vr* swoon; deprive oneself

privilegiar *vt* to privilege; bestow a favor on

privilegio *m,* privilege; prerogative; concession; copyright; patent

pro *mf* advantage, benefit. **el p. y el contra,** the pros and cons. **en p.,** in favor

proa *f,* prow, bow

probabilidad *f,* probability

probable *a* probable; likely; provable

probación *f,* proof, test; novitiate, probation

probado *a* tried, tested, proved

probar *vt irr* to prove; test; taste; try on (clothes); *vi* suit; (*with prep a* + *infin*) try to. **p. fortuna,** to try one's luck. *Pres. Ind.* **pruebo, pruebas, prueba, prueban.** *Pres. Subjunc.* **pruebe, pruebes, prueben**

probatorio *a* probationary

probidad *f,* probity, trustworthiness, honesty

problema *m,* problem

problemático *a* problematical, uncertain

probo *a* honest, trustworthy

procacidad *f,* insolence, pertness

procaz *a* insolent, pert, brazen

procedencia *f,* origin, source; parentage, descent; port of sailing or call

procedente *a* arriving or coming from

proceder *vi* to proceed; behave; originate, arise; continue, go on; act. *law* **p. contra,** to proceed against (a person)

procedimiento *m,* proceeding, advancement; procedure; legal practice; process

proceloso *a* tempestuous

prócer *a* exalted, eminent; lofty. *m,* exalted personage

procesado (-da) *n* defendant

procesamiento *m,* suing, suit; indictment

procesar *vt law* to proceed against, sue

procesión *f,* proceeding, emanating; procession; *inf* train, string. **andar** (*or* **ir) por dentro la p.,** to feel keenly without betraying one's emotion

proceso *m,* process; progress, advancement; lapse of time; lawsuit

proclama *f,* proclamation; announcement; publication of marriage banns

proclamación *f,* proclamation; acclaim, applause

proclamar *vt* to proclaim; acclaim; publish abroad; reveal, show

proclividad *f,* proclivity, tendency

procomún *m,* social or public welfare

procreación *f,* procreation

procreador (-ra) *a* procreative. *n* procreator

procrear *vt* to procreate, beget, engender

procuración *f,* procurement; assiduity, care; *law* power of attorney; *law* attorneyship

procurador (-ra) *m,* proxy; *law* attorney; proctor. *n* procurer

procurar *vt* to try, attempt; procure, get; exercise the profession of a lawyer

prodigalidad *f,* prodigality, lavishness; waste, extravagance

prodigar *vt* to waste, squander; lavish, bestow freely; *vr* make oneself cheap

prodigio *m,* marvel, wonder, prodigy; monster; miracle

prodigiosidad *f,* prodigiousness

prodigioso *a* wonderful; prodigious; monstrous; miraculous

pródigo (-ga) *a* wasteful, extravagant; lavish, generous. *n* spendthrift, wastrel, prodigal

producción *f,* production; output, yield; generation (of heat, etc.); crop

producir *vt irr* to produce; generate; yield, give; cause, occasion; publish; *vr* explain oneself; arise, appear, be produced. **p. efecto,** to have effect; take effect. See **conducir**

productividad *f,* productivity

productivo *a* productive; fertile; profitable

producto *m,* produce; product; profit; yield, gain; *math* product. *chem* **p. derivado,** by-product

productor (-ra) *a* productive. *n* producer

proemio *m,* prologue, preface, introduction

proeza *f*, prowess, gallantry; skill; *Lat. Am.* boast
profanación *f*, profanation
profanador (-ra) *n* profaner, transgressor
profanar *vt* to profane
profanidad *f*, profanity
profano *a* profane; dissolute; pleasure-loving, worldly; immodest; lay, ignorant
profecía *f*, prophecy; *ecc* Book of the Prophets; opinion, view
proferir *vt irr* to utter, pronounce. See **herir**
profesar *vt* to exercise, practice (professions); *ecc* profess; believe in; teach
profesión *f*, profession; trade, occupation; avowal, admission
profesional *a* professional
profesionalismo *m*, professionalism
profeso (-sa) *a ecc* professed. *n* professed monk
profesor (-ra) *n* teacher; professor
profesorado *m*, teaching staff; teaching profession; professorship; professorate
profeta *m*, prophet; seer
profético *a* prophetic
profetisa *f*, prophetess
profetizar *vt* to prophesy; imagine, suppose
proficiente *a* proficient
profiláctico *a* and *m*, prophylactic
prófugo (-ga) *a* and *n* fugitive from justice. *m*, *mil* one who evades military service
profundamente *adv* profoundly; acutely, deeply
profundidad *f*, depth; profundity, obscurity; *geom* depth; concavity; intensity (of feeling); vastness (of knowledge, etc.)
profundizar *vt* to deepen; hollow out; *fig* go into deeply, fathom
profundo *a* deep; low; *fig* intense, acute; abstruse, profound; *fig* vast, extensive; high. *m*, depth, profundity; *poet* ocean, the deep; *poet* hell
profuso *a* profuse, abundant; extravagant, wasteful
progenie *f*, descendants
prognosis *f*, prognosis; forecast
programa *m*, program; edict, public notice; plan, scheme; *univ* calendar; syllabus; timetable
progresar *vt* and *vi* to make progress; progress, advance
progresión *f*, progression; advancement, progress
progresista *a pol* progressive. *mf* progressive
progresivo *a* progressive; advancing
progreso *m*, progress, advancement; growth; improvement, development
prohibente *a* prohibitory, prohibitive
prohibición *f*, forbidding, prohibition
prohibicionista *mf* prohibitionist. *a* prohibitionist
prohibir *vt* to forbid, prohibit. «**Prohibido el paso,**» "No thoroughfare"
prohibitivo, prohibitorio *a* prohibitive
prohijador (-ra) *n* adopter (of a child)
prohijamiento *m*, child adoption; fathering (of a bill, etc.)
prohijar *vt* to adopt (children, ideas); *fig* father
prohombre *m*, master of a guild; respected, well-liked man
prójimo *m*, fellow man, brother, neighbor.
prole *f*, progeny, young offspring
proletariado *m*, proletariat
proletario *a* poor; common, vulgar. *m*, plebeian; pauper; proletarian
prolífico *a* prolific; abundant, fertile
prolijidad *f*, verbosity, prolixity; nicety, scruple; importunity, tediousness
prolijo *a* verbose, prolix; fussy, fastidious; tedious, importunate; *Argentina* indefatigable, untiring
prologar *vt* to prologue; provide with a preface
prólogo *m*, preface; prologue; introduction
prolongación *f*, lengthening; prolongation, protraction; extension
prolongado *a* prolonged; oblong, long

prolongar *vt* to lengthen; *geom* produce; prolong, spin out
promediar *vt* to distribute or divide into two equal portions; average; *vi* arbitrate; place oneself between two people; reach half-time
promedio *m*, average; middle, center
promesa *f*, promise; augury, favorable sign
prometedor (-ra) *a* promising. *n* promiser
prometer *vt* to promise; attest, certify; *vi* promise well, look hopeful; *vr* devote oneself to service of God; anticipate confidently, expect; become engaged (marriage). *inf* **prometérselas muy felices,** to have high hopes
prometido (-da) *n* betrothed. *m*, promise
prometimiento *m*, promise; promising
prominencia *f*, prominence, protuberance; eminence, hill
prominente *a* prominent, protuberant; eminent, elevated
promiscuar *vi* to eat meat and fish on fast days
promiscuidad *f*, promiscuity; ambiguity
promiscuo *a* indiscriminate, haphazard, promiscuous; ambiguous
promisión *f*, promise
promisorio *a* promissory
promoción *f*, promotion; batch, class, year (of recruits, students, etc.)
promontorio *m*, headland; promontory; cumbersome object
promotor (-ra) *a* promotive. *n* promoter; supporter
promover *vt irr* to promote, further, advance; promote (a person). **p. un proceso (a),** to bring a suit (against). See **mover**
promulgación *f*, promulgation
promulgar *vt* to publish officially, proclaim; promulgate. *law* **p. sentencia,** to pass judgment
pronombre *m*, pronoun
pronosticación *f*, prognostication; presage
pronosticar *vt* to prognosticate, forecast; presage
pronóstico *m*, omen, prediction; almanac; prognosis; sign, indication. **p. del tiempo,** weather forecast
prontitud *f*, quickness, promptness; quick-wittedness; *fig* sharpness, liveliness; celerity, dispatch
pronto *a* quick, speedy; prompt; ready, prepared. *m*, *inf* sudden decision. *adv* immediately; with all speed; soon. **de p.,** suddenly; without thinking. **por lo p.,** temporarily, provisionally
prontuario *m*, compendium, handbook; summary
pronunciación *f*, pronunciation
pronunciamiento *m*, military uprising; political manifesto; *law* pronouncement of sentence
pronunciar *vt* to pronounce, articulate; decide, determine; *law* pronounce judgment; give or make (a speech)
propagación *f*, propagation; dissemination; transmission
propagador *a* propagative. *m*, propagator
propaganda *f*, propaganda organization; propaganda
propagandista *mf* propagandist
propagar *vt* to reproduce; propagate, disseminate; *vr* reproduce, multiply; propagate, spread
propalar *vt* to disseminate, spread abroad
propasarse *vr* to go too far, forget oneself; overstep one's authority
propender *vi* to be inclined, have a leaning toward
propensión *f*, propensity, inclination; tendency
propenso *a* inclined, disposed; liable
propiamente *adv* properly, suitably
propiciación *f*, propitiation
propiciador (-ra) *a* propitiatory. *n* propitiator
propiciar *vt* to propitiate, appease
propiciatorio *a* propitiatory
propicio *a* propitious, auspicious; kind, favorable
propiedad *f*, estate, property; ownership; landed property; attribute, quality, property; *art* resemblance, naturalness
propietario (-ia) *a* proprietary. *n* proprietor, owner

propina f, gratuity, tip. *inf* **de p.,** in addition, extra

propinar vt to treat to a drink; administer (medicine); *inf* give (slaps, etc.)

propincuidad f, propinquity, proximity

propincuo a near, contiguous, adjacent

propio a own, one's own; typical, characteristic; individual, peculiar; suitable, apt; natural, real; same. *m,* messenger; *pl* public lands

proponente a proposing. *m,* proposer; *com* tenderer

proponer vt irr to propose, suggest; make a proposition; propose (for a post, office, etc.); *math* state; vr intend, purpose. **proponerse para un empleo,** to apply for a post. See **poner**

proporción f, proportion; chance, opportunity; size; *math* proportion

proporcionado a fit, suitable; proportionate; symmetrical

proporcional a proportional

proporcionar vt to allot, proportion; supply, provide, give; adapt

proposición f, proposition; motion (in a debate)

propósito m, proposal; intention, aim; subject, question, matter. **a p.,** suitable, apropos; by the way, incidentally. **de p.,** with the intention, proposing. **fuera de p.,** irrelevant

propuesta f, proposal, tender

propugnar vt to defend, protect

propulsar vt to repulse, throw back; propel, drive

propulsión f, repulse; propulsion

propulsor a driving, propelling. *m,* propeller

prorrata f, quota, share, apportionment. **a p.,** in proportion

prorratear vt to apportion, distribute proportionately, prorate

prorrogación f, prorogation, adjournment; extension (of time); renewal (of a lease, etc.)

prorrogar vt to extend, prolong; defer, suspend, prorogue; renew (leases, etc.)

prorrumpir vt (*with en*) to burst out; utter, give vent to, burst into

prosa f, prose; prosaism, prosaic style; *inf* dull verbosity; monotony, tediousness; *Lat. Am.* pomposity

prosaico a prosaic; prosy; monotonous, tedious; matter-of-fact

prosapia f, family, lineage, descent

proscenio m, proscenium

proscribir vt to proscribe, outlaw; forbid, prohibit. *Past Part.* **proscrito**

proscripción f, proscription

proscrito (-ta) n outlaw, exile

prosecución f, prosecution, performance; pursuit

proseguir vt to continue, proceed with. See **pedir**

proselitismo m, proselytism

prosélito m, convert, proselyte

prosificar vt to turn verse into prose

prosista mf prose writer

prosodia f, prosody

prospecto m, prospectus

prosperar vt to prosper; protect; vi flourish, prosper

prosperidad f, prosperity; wealth; success

próspero a favorable, propitious, fortunate; prosperous

próstata f, prostate

prostitución f, prostitution

prostituir vt irr to prostitute; vr become a prostitute; sell oneself, debase oneself. See **huir**

prostituta f, prostitute

protagonista mf hero or heroine, principal character; leading figure, protagonist

protección f, protection, defense; favor, aid

proteccionismo m, protectionism

proteccionista mf protectionist

protector a protective. *m,* protector; guard

protectorado m, protectorate

protectriz f, protectress

proteger vt to protect, defend; favor, assist

protegido (-da) n protégé

proteico a protean

proteína f, protein

protervia f, depravity, perversity

protervo a depraved, perverse

protesta, protestación f, protest; protestation, declaration

protestante a and *mf* Protestant

protestantismo m, Protestantism

protestar vt to declare, attest; (*with contra*) protest against; (*with de*) affirm vigorously

protesto m, *com* protest; objection

protocolizar vt to protocol, draw up

protocolo m, protocol

prototipo m, model, prototype

protuberancia f, protuberance, projection, swelling

provecto a ancient, venerable; mature, experienced

provecho m, gain, benefit; profit; advantage; progress, proficiency. **¡Buen p.!** Enjoy your food! Enjoy your meal! **ser de p.,** to be advantageous or useful

provechoso a beneficial; profitable; advantageous; useful

proveedor (-ra) n provider; purveyor, supplier

proveer vt irr to provide; furnish; supply; confer (an honor or office); transact, arrange. **p. de,** to furnish or supply with; fit with. See **creer**

provenir vi irr (*with de*) to originate in, proceed from. See **venir**

provenzal a and *mf* Provençal. *m,* Provençal (language)

proverbio m, proverb; omen; *pl* Book of Proverbs

providencia f, precaution, foresight; provision, furnishing; measure, preparation. **la Divina P.,** Providence

providencial a providential

próvido a provident, thrifty, careful; kind, favorable

provincia f, province; *fig* sphere

provincial a provincial. *m, ecc* provincial

provincialismo m, provincialism

provinciano (-na) a provincial. n provincial, rustic, countryman; native of Biscay

provisión f, stock, store; provision; supply; food supply (gen. *pl*); catering; means, way

provisional a temporary, provisional

provisor m, purveyor, supplier; *ecc* vicar general

provisorio, -a a, *Lat. Am.* = **provisional**

provocación f, provocation

provocador (-ra) a provocative. n provoker; instigator

provocar vt to provoke; incite; irritate; help, assist; *inf* vomit; *Lat. Am.* **¿te provoca ir al cine?** Would you like to go to the movies?

provocativo a provocative

próximamente adv proximately; soon; approximately

proximidad f, nearness, proximity (in time or space)

próximo a near, neighboring; next; not distant (of time)

proyección f, projection (all meanings)

proyectante a projecting, jutting

proyectar vt to throw, cast; plan, contrive; design; project; vr jut out; be cast (a shadow, etc.)

proyectil m, projectile

proyectista mf planner

proyecto a placed in perspective. *m,* project, plan, scheme; planning; intention, idea

proyector (-ra) n designer, planner. *m,* searchlight; spotlight; projector

prudencia f, prudence, sagacity, caution; moderation

prudencial a prudent, discreet; safe

prudente a prudent, cautious; provident

prueba f, proof; test; testing; trial; fitting (of garments); sample; taste; *law* evidence; (*phot print*) proof. *law* **p. de indicios** or **p. indiciaria,** circumstantial evidence. *phot* **p. negativa,** negative. *com* **a p.,** on approval; on trial; up to standard, perfect. **a p. de,** proof against (water, etc.). **poner a p.,** to put to the test, try out

prurito m, pruritus; desire, longing

ps- For words so beginning (e.g. *psicología, psiquiatría*), see spellings without **p**

púa *f,* prong; tooth (of a comb); quill (of a porcupine); *agr* graft; plectrum (for playing the mandolin, etc.); anxiety, grief; pine needle; *inf* crafty person

púber *a* pubescent

pubertad *f,* puberty

púbico *a* pubic

publicación *f,* publication; announcement, proclamation; revelation; publishing of marriage banns

publicador (-ra) *a* publishing. *n* publisher; announcer

publicar *vt* to publish; reveal; announce, proclaim; publish (marriage banns)

publicidad *f,* publicity; advertising, propaganda

publicista *mf* publicist; publicity agent

público *a* well-known, universal; common, general; public. *m,* public; audience; gathering, attendance. **dar al p.** *or* **sacar al p.,** to publish

pucherazo *m, inf* electoral fraud, vote-fixing

puchero *m, cul* kind of stew; stew pot; *inf* daily food; puckering of the face preceding tears

pudicia *f,* modesty; bashfulness; chastity

púdico *a* modest; bashful; chaste

pudiente *a* rich, wealthy; powerful

pudín *m,* pudding

pudor *m,* modesty; bashfulness, shyness

pudoroso *a* modest; shy

pudrir *vt* to rot, putrefy; irritate, worry, provoke; *vi* rot in the grave; *vr* rot; be consumed with anxiety

puebla *f,* town; population; gardener's seed setting

pueblada *f, Lat. Am.* riot; rebellion, revolt, uprising

pueblo *m,* town; village, hamlet; people, population, inhabitants; common people; working classes; nation

puente *mf* bridge; *mus* bridge (of stringed instruments); *naut* bridge; *carp* crossbeam, transom. **p. colgante,** suspension bridge. **p. levadizo,** drawbridge. **hacer p. de plata (a),** to remove obstacles for, make plain sailing

puerco *m,* pig; wild boar. *a* filthy; rough, rude; low, mean. **p. espín** *or* **p. espino,** porcupine. **p. marino,** dolphin. **p. montés** *or* **p. salvaje,** wild boar

puericultura *f,* child care

pueril *a* childish, puerile; foolish, silly; trivial

puerilidad *f,* puerility; foolishness; triviality

puerro *m,* leek

puerta *f,* door; gate; goal (football, soccer, hockey); means, way. **p. batiente,** swinging door. **p. caediza,** trapdoor. **p. corrediza,** sliding door. **p. de servicio,** tradesman's entrance. **p. falsa** *or* **p. secreta,** secret door; side door. **p. trasera,** back door. **a p. cerrada,** in camera; in secret. *inf* **dar con la p. en las narices (de),** to slam the door in a person's face; offend, insult. **llamar a la p.,** to knock at the door; be on the verge of happening. **tomar la p.,** to depart, go away

puerto *m,* harbor; port; defile, narrow pass; refuge, haven. **p. fluvial,** river port. **p. franco,** free port. **tomar p.,** to put into port; take refuge

Puerto Rico *m* Puerto Rico

puertorriqueño, -a *a* and *mf* Puerto Rican

pues *conjunc* then; since, as; for, because; well. *adv* yes, certainly. *conjunc* **p. que,** since, as

puesta *f, ast* setting, sinking; stake (in gambling). **p. al día,** aggiornamento, updating; modernization. **p. de largo,** coming of age; coming-out party. **p. del sol,** sunset

puesto *m,* post, job; booth, stall; beat, pitch; place, position; state, condition; *mil* encampment, barracks; office, position. **p. de los testigos,** witness box. **p. de mando,** command, position of authority.

puesto *a* (*with bien* or *mal*) well-or badly dressed. *conjunc* **p. que,** since, as; although

púgil *mf* pugilist, boxer

pugilato *m,* boxing; boxing match

pugilista *mf* boxer

pugna *f,* fight, struggle; rivalry, conflict

pugnante *a* hostile, conflicting, rival

pugnar *vi* to fight; quarrel; (*with con, contra*) struggle against, oppose; (*with por, para*) strive to

pugnaz *a* pugnacious

puja *f,* outbidding (at an auction); higher bid; push, thrust

pujador (-ra) *n* bidder or outbidder (at an auction)

pujante *a* strong, powerful, vigorous

pujanza *f,* strength, vigor

pujar *vt* to push on; bid or outbid (at an auction); *vi* stutter; hesitate, falter; *inf* show signs of weeping

pujo *m,* irresistible impulse; desire; will; purpose, intention

pulcritud *f,* beauty, loveliness, delicacy; fastidiousness, subtlety

pulcro *a* beautiful, lovely; delicate, fine; fastidious, subtle

pulga *f,* flea; small top (toy). **el juego de la p.,** tiddlywinks. *inf* **tener malas pulgas,** to be irritable

pulgada *f,* inch

pulgar *m,* thumb

pulgón *m,* aphid, greenfly

pulgoso *a* full of fleas

pulguiento *a, Lat. Am.* = **pulgoso**

pulidez *f,* elegance, fineness; polish, smoothness; neatness

pulido *a* elegant, fine; polished, smooth; neat

pulidor *m,* polisher (machine)

pulimentar *vt* to polish, burnish

pulir *vt* to polish, burnish; give the finishing touch to; beautify, decorate; *fig* polish up, civilize; *vr* beautify oneself; become polished and polite

pulmón *m,* lung

pulmonar *a* pulmonary

pulmonía *f,* pneumonia

pulpa *f,* fleshy part of fruit; *anat* pulp; wood pulp

pulpejo *m, anat* fleshy part, fat portion (of thumbs, etc.)

pulpería *f, WH* grocery, grocery store, general store; bar, tavern

púlpito *m,* pulpit

pulpo *m,* octopus. *inf* **poner como un p.,** to beat to a pulp

pulposo *a* pulpy, pulpous

pulquérrimo *a sup* **pulcro** most lovely, most exquisite

pulsación *f,* pulsation; throb, beat

pulsar *vt* to touch, feel; take the pulse of; *fig* explore (a possibility); *vi* beat (the heart, etc.)

pulsera *f,* bracelet; wrist bandage. **p. de pedida,** betrothal bracelet

pulso *m,* pulse; steadiness of hand; tact, diplomacy, circumspection. **a p.,** freehand (drawing). **tomar a p. (una cosa),** to try a thing's weight. **tomar el p. (a),** to take a person's pulse

pulular *vi* to pullulate, sprout; abound, be plentiful; swarm, teem; multiply (of insects)

pulverización *f,* pulverization; atomization

pulverizador *m,* atomizer, sprayer; scent spray

pulverizar *vt* to pulverize, grind, make into powder; atomize; spray

pulla *f,* lewd remark; strong hint; witty comment

¡pum! *interj* Bang! Thump!

pundonor *m,* (**punto de honor**) point of honor, sense of honor

pundonoroso *a* careful of one's honor; honorable, punctilious

pungir *vt* to prick, pierce; revive an old sorrow; *fig* wound, sting (passions)

punible *a* punishable

punitivo *a* punitive, punitory

punta *f,* sharp end, point; butt (of a cigarette); end, point, tip; cape, headland; trace, touch, suspicion; nib (of a pen); pointing (pointer dogs); *her* point; *pl* point lace. **p. de París,** wire nail. **p. seca,** drypoint, engraving needle. **sacar p.,** to sharpen; *inf* twist (a remark)

puntación *f,* dotting, placing dots over (letters)

puntada *f, sew* stitch; innuendo, hint

puntal *m, naut* draft, depth; stanchion, prop, brace, pile; *fig* basis, foundation; *Lat. Am.* bite (to eat), snack

puntapié *m,* kick

punteado *m,* plucking the strings of a guitar, etc.; sewing

puntear *vt* to make dots; *mus* pluck the strings of; play the guitar; sew; *art* stipple; *vi naut* tack

puntera *f,* mend in the toe of a stocking; toe cap; new piece on the toe of shoe; *inf* kick

puntería *f,* aiming (of a firearm); aim, sight (of a firearm); marksmanship

puntero *a* of a good aim, having a straight eye. *m,* pointer, wand; stonecutter's chisel

puntiagudo *a* pointed, sharp-pointed

puntilla *f,* narrow lace edging; headless nail, wire nail; brad, tack. **de puntillas,** on tiptoe

puntilloso *a* punctilious; overfastidious, fussy

punto *m.;* dot; point; pen nib; gun sight; *sew* stitch; dropped stitch, hole; weaving stitch, mesh; *gram* full stop, period; hole (in belts for adjustment); place, spot; point, mark; subject matter; *mech* cog; degree, extent; taxi stand; instant; infinitesimal amount; opportunity, chance; vacation, recess; aim, goal; point of honor. **p. de congelación,** freezing point. **p. de ebullición,** boiling point. **p. de fuga,** vanishing point. **p. de fusión,** melting point. **p. de partida,** starting point. **p. de vista,** point of view. **p. final,** *gram* period, full stop. **p. interrogante,** question mark. **p. menos,** a little less. **p. y coma,** semicolon. **p. cardinal,** cardinal point. **p. suspensivo,** *gram* ellipsis point, suspension point, leader, dot. **a p.,** in readiness; immediately. **en p.,** sharp, prompt (e.g. **a las seis en p.,** at six o'clock sharp)

puntoso *a* many-pointed

puntuación *f,* punctuation; *sport* score

puntual *a* punctual; punctilious; certain, indubitable; suitable, convenient

puntualidad *f,* punctuality; punctiliousness; certainty; exactitude, accuracy

puntualizar *vt* to describe in detail; give the finishing touch to, perfect; impress on the mind

puntualmente *adv* punctually; carefully, diligently; exactly

puntuar *vt* to punctuate

puntudo *a, Lat. Am.* = **puntiagudo**

punzada *f,* prick, sting; puncture, piercing; sudden pain, twinge, stitch; *fig* anguish, pain

punzar *vt* to pierce, puncture; prick; punch, perforate; *vi* revive, make itself felt (pain or sorrow)

punzón *m,* awl; punch; die; engraver's burin

puñado *m,* handful; a few, some, a small quantity. **a puñados,** in handfuls; liberally, lavishly

puñal *m,* dagger

puñalada *f,* dagger thrust; stab, wound; *fig* unexpected blow (of fate). **p. por la espalda,** stab in the back

puñetazo *m,* blow with the fist

puño *m,* fist; handful; cuff (of a sleeve); wristband; handle, head, haft; hilt (of a sword); *pl inf* guts, courage. **p. de amura,** *naut* tack. **p. de un manillar,** handlebar grip. *inf* **meter en un p.,** to overawe. *inf* **ser como un p.,** to be tightfisted; be small (in stature)

pupila *f,* female child ward; *anat* pupil; *inf* cleverness, talent

pupilaje *m,* pupilage, minority; boarding house, guesthouse; boarding school; price of board residence; dependence, bondage

pupilo (-la) *n* ward, minor; boarder; boarding school student; *Lat. Am.* prostitute, whore

pupitre *m,* desk, school desk

puquío *m Lat. Am.* spring (of water)

puramente *adv* purely; simply, solely; *law* unconditionally, without reservation

puré *m,* purée, thick soup

pureza *f,* purity; perfection, excellence; chastity; disinterestedness, genuineness; clearness

purga *f,* laxative, purge; waste product

purgación *f,* purging; menstruation; gonorrhea

purgante *a* purgative. *m,* purge, cathartic

purgar *vt* to cleanse, purify; expiate, atone for; (*med law*) purge; suffer purgatorial pains; clarify, refine; *vr* rid oneself, purge oneself

purgativo *a* purgative

purgatorio *m,* purgatory. *a* purgatorial

puridad *f,* purity; secrecy, privacy. **en p.,** openly, without dissembling; secretly, in private

purificación *f,* purification; cleansing

purificador (-ra) *a* purifying; cleansing. *n* purifier; cleanser

purificar *vt* to purify; cleanse; *vr* be purified

purificatorio *a* purificatory

Purísima (la) *f,* the Most Blessed Virgin

purista *mf* purist

puritano (-na) *a* puritanical. *n* Puritan

puro *a* pure; undiluted; unalloyed; unmixed; disinterested, honest; virgin; absolute, sheer; mere, simple. *m,* cigar. **de p.,** by sheer . . . , by dint of

púrpura *f,* purple; *poet* blood; purpura; *her* purpure; purple (cloth); dignity of an emperor, cardinal, consul

purpurear *vi* to look like purple; be tinged with purple

purpurina *f Lat. Am.* metallic paint

purulencia *f,* purulence

purulento *a* purulent

pus *m,* pus, matter

pusilánime *a* pusillanimous, timid, cowardly

pústula *f,* pustule

putativo *a* putative

putrefacción *f,* putrefaction; rottenness, putrescence

puto, -a *mf* prostitute

putrefacto *a* rotten, decayed

pútrido *a* putrid, rotten

puya *f,* goad

puyar *vt Lat. Am.* to jab, prick, stick; *fig* needle

puyazo *m,* prick with a goad

Q

que *pron. rel* all genders sing. and pl. who; which; that; whom; when (e.g. **Un poema en que habla de su juventud,** A poem in which he speaks of his youth. **El libro que tengo aquí,** The book (that) I have here. **No es oro todo lo que reluce,** All that glitters is not gold. **Un día que nos vimos,** One day when we met. *interr* **¿qué?** what? *interj* what a ———! what! how! (e.g. **¿Qué hay?** What's the matter? **¡Qué día más hermoso!** What a lovely day! **¿qué de . . . ?** how many? **¿qué tal?** how? *inf* **¿Qué tal estás hoy?** How are you today? **¿qué tanto?** how much? **¿a qué?** why? for what reason? (e.g. **¿A qué negarlo?** Why deny it?). *conjunc* that (e.g. **Me dijo que vendría,** He said (that) he would come). Means 'so that,' 'that,' 'for,' in commands (e.g. **Mandó que le trajesen el libro,** He ordered that they bring him the book (He ordered them to bring him the book)). Note that the translation of **que** is often omitted in English.

In compound tenses where the participle is placed first, **que** means 'when' (e.g. **llegado que hube,** when I had arrived). In comparisons, **que** means 'than' (e.g. **más joven que yo,** younger than I).

With subjunctives and expressing commands or wishes, **que** means 'let' (e.g. **¡Que venga!** Let him come!) Preceding a subjunctive, **que** is generally translated by 'to' (e.g. **Quiero, que venga** or **que llueva,** I want him to come *or* I want it to rain). Also means 'may' (e.g. **¡Que lo pase bien!** May you enjoy yourself! (I hope you . . .)). **es (era) que,** the fact is (was) that . . . **que . . . que,** whether . . . or . . .

quebrada *f,* mountain gorge, ravine; *com* bankruptcy; *Lat. Am.* brook, stream

quebradizo *a* brittle, fragile; ailing, infirm; delicate, frail

quebrado (-da) *m, math* fraction; *n com* bankrupt. *a* rough, uneven (ground); *med* ruptured; bankrupt; ailing, broken-down

quebradura *f,* snap, breaking; gap, crevice; hernia

quebraja *f,* split, crack; flaw (in wood, metal, etc.)

quebrantahuesos *m,* sea eagle, osprey; *inf* bore, tedious person

quebrantamiento *m,* crushing; splitting, cleaving; fracture, rupture; profanation, desecration; burglary; violation, breaking, infringement; fatigue; *law* annulment; exhaustion

quebrantanueces *m,* nutcrackers

quebrantaolas *m,* breakwater

quebrantar *vt* to break, shatter; crush, pound; transgress, infringe; break out, force; tone down, soften; moderate, lessen; bore, exhaust; move to pity; *inf* break in (horses); profane; overcome (difficulties); assuage, placate; *law* revoke (wills); *vr* be shaken or bruised, suffer from aftereffects

quebranto *m,* breaking, shattering; crushing, pounding; infringement; breaking out (from prison); weakness, exhaustion; compassion, pity; loss, damage; pain, suffering

quebrar *vt irr* to break, shatter; crush; impede, hinder; make pale (color, gen. of complexion); mitigate, moderate; bend, twist; overcome (difficulties); *vi* break off (a friendship); weaken, give way; go bankrupt; *vr med* suffer from hernia; be interrupted (of mountain ranges). **quebrarse los ojos,** to strain one's eyes. *Pres. Ind.* **quiebro, quiebras, quiebra, quiebran.** *Pres. Subjunc.* **quiebre, quiebres, quiebre, quiebren**

queda *f,* curfew; curfew bell

quedada *f,* stay, sojourn

quedar *vi* to stay, sojourn; remain; be left over; (*with por* + *infin.*) remain to be (e.g. **Queda por escribir,** It remains to be written); (*with por*) be won by or be knocked down to; be, remain in a place; end, cease; (*with en*) reach an agreement (e.g. **Quedamos en no ir,** We have decided not to go). **q. en esta alternativa . . . ,** to face this alternative: . . . . *vr* remain; abate (wind); grow calm (sea); (*with con*) keep, retain possession of. **q. bien o mal,** to behave well or badly, come off well or badly (in business affairs, etc.). **quedarse muerto,** to be astounded

quedo *a* still, motionless; quiet, tranquil. *adv* in a low voice; noiselessly. **de q.,** slowly, gradually. *interj* **¡Q.!** Quiet!

quehacer *m,* odd job; task; business (gen. *pl*)

queja *f,* lamentation, grief; complaint, grudge; quarrel

quejarse *vr* to lament; complain, grumble; *law* lodge an accusation (against)

quejido *m,* complaint, moan

quejoso *a* querulous, complaining

quejumbre *f,* complaint, whine; querulousness

quejumbroso *a* complaining, grumbling

quelite *m, Central America, Mexico* vegetables

quema *f,* burn; burning; fire, conflagration

quemadero *a* burnable. *m,* stake (for burning people)

quemado *m,* burned patch of forest; *inf* anything burned or burning

quemador (-ra) *m,* jet, burner. *n* incendiary

quemadura *f,* burn; scald; burning

quemajoso *a* smarting, burning, pricking

quemar *vt* to burn; dry up, parch; scorch; tan; bronze; scald; throw away, sell at a loss; *vi* burn, be excessively hot; *vr* be very hot; be dried up with the heat; burn with (passions); *inf* be near the attainment of a desired

end. **quemarse las cejas,** to burn the midnight oil, study too hard

quemazón *f,* burning; conflagration; intense heat; *inf* smarting; *inf* hurtful remark; *inf* vexation, soreness

quena *f* kind of Native American flute

querella *f,* complaint; quarrel, fight

querellarse *vr* to complain; lament, bemoan; *law* lodge an accusation; *law* contest a will

querelloso *a* complaining, grumbling, querulous

querencia *f,* love, affection; homing instinct; lair; natural inclination or desire

querer *vt irr* to desire, wish; want, will; attempt, endeavor; (*with a*) love. *impers* be on the point of. **q. decir,** to mean. **¿Qué quiere decir esto?** What does this mean? **sin q.,** unintentionally. See **entender**

querer *m,* affection, love

querido (-da) *m* lover; beloved; darling. *a* dear

querub, querube *poet* **querubín** *m,* cherub

querúbico *a* cherubic

quesadillas, *fpl, Mexico* maize dough with beans or cheese fried like a turnover

quesera *f,* dairymaid; dairy; cheese vat; cheese board; cheese dish

quesería *f,* dairy; cheese shop; season for making cheese

queso *m,* cheese. **q. de bola,** Dutch cheese. **q. rallado,** grated cheese

quetzal *m,* quetzal (monetary unit of Guatemala)

quevedos *m pl,* glasses, eyeglasses; pince-nez

¡quia! *interj inf* You don't say so!

quianti *m,* chianti

quicial *m,* doorjamb

quicio *m,* threshold; hinge; *mech* bushing. **fuera de q.,** out of order; unhinged. **sacar de q.,** to displace (things); annoy, irritate; drive crazy

quiebra *f,* breach, crack; rut, fissure; loss; bankruptcy

quiebro *m,* twisting of the body, dodging; *mus* trill

quien *rel pron mf pl* **quienes.** *interr* **quién, quiénes** who; whom; he (she, etc.) who, anyone who, whoever; which; whichever (e.g. **mis padres a quienes respeto,** my parents whom I respect. **Quien te quiere te hará llorar,** Whoever (he, those, who) love(s) you will make you weep. **¿Quién está a la puerta?** Who is at the door? **¿De quién es?** Whose is it? To whom does it belong?). *indef pron* one (*pl* some)

quienquiera *indef pron mf pl* **quienesquiera,** whosoever, whichever, whomsoever

quietador (-ra) *a* tranquilizing, soothing. *n* soother

quieto *a* quiet, still; peaceful, tranquil; virtuous, respectable

quietud *f,* stillness, repose; peacefulness; rest, quietness

quif *m,* hashish, marijuana

quijada *f,* jawbone, jaw; *mech* jaw

quijo *m,* ore (gold or silver)

quijotada *f,* quixotic action, quixotism

quijote *m,* cuisse; thigh guard; quixotic person

quijotesco *a* quixotic

quilate *m,* carat; degree of excellence (gen. *pl*). *inf* **por quilates,** in small bits, parsimoniously

quilla *f, naut* keel; breastbone (of birds)

quillotrar *vt inf* to encourage, incite; woo, make love to; consider; *vr inf* fall in love; dress up; whine, complain

quillotro *m, inf* incentive; indication, sign; love affair; puzzle, knotty point; compliment; dressing up

quimera *f,* chimera; fancy, vision; quarrel, dispute

quimérico *a* chimerical, fanciful

quimerista *mf* dreamer, visionary; quarreler, disputant

química *f,* chemistry

químico *a* chemical. *m,* chemist. **productos químicos,** chemicals

quimono *m,* kimono

quina *f,* cinchona; quinine; *pl* Arms of Portugal. *inf* **tragar q.,** to suffer in patience, put up with

quinario *m, Argentina* mud hut

quincalla *f*, cheap jewelery; fancy goods
quincallería *f*, cheap jewelery shop; hardware factory or industry; cheap jewelry; fancy goods
quince *a* and *m*, fifteen; fifteenth
quinceañero *f*, sweet sixteen party, sweet sixteen (in Spanish-speaking areas, held at age fifteen)
quincena *f*, fortnight, two weeks; bimonthly pay; *mus* fifteenth
quincenal *a* fortnightly; lasting a fortnight, lasting two weeks
quinceno *a* fifteenth
quincuagenario *a* quinquagenarian
quincuagésimo *a* fiftieth
quindécimo *a* fifteenth
quinientos *a* five hundred; five-hundredth. *m*, five hundred
quinina *f*, quinine
quinqué *m*, oil lamp, student's lamp, table lamp; perspicuity, talent
quinquenio *m*, period of five years, lustrum
quinta *f*, country house; *mus* fifth; conscripting men into army by drawing lots; *mil* draft
quintaesencia *f*, quintessence
quintal *m*, hundredweight
quintar *vt* to draw one out of every five; draw lots for conscription into the army; *vi* reach the fifth (day, etc., gen. of the moon)
quintería *f*, farm
quintero *m*, farmer; farmworker
quinteto *m*, quintet
Quintín, San. armarse (*or* **haber**) **la de San Q.** to quarrel, make trouble; be a row
quinto *a* fifth. *m*, one-fifth; *mil* conscript; duty of twenty percent; *law* fifth part of an estate. **quinta columna,** fifth column. **quinta esencia,** quintessence
quintuplicar *vt* to quintuplicate
quíntuplo *a* fivefold, quintuple

quiñón *m*, share of land owned jointly, share of the profits
quiosco *m*, kiosk, stand; pavilion, pagoda. **q. de música,** bandstand
quipo *m* quipu (Native American rope writing in Peru)
quiquiriquí *m*, cock-a-doodle-doo; *fig inf* cock of the walk
quiromancia *f*, chiromancy, palmistry
quiromántico (-ca) *n* chiromancer, palmist
quirúrgico *a* surgical
quirurgo *m*, surgeon
quisicosa *f*, *inf* riddle, puzzle, enigma
quisquilla *f*, trifle, quibble, scruple; prawn, shrimp
quisquilloso *a* quibbling, overscrupulous, fastidious; hypersensitive; irascible, touchy
quistarse *vr* to make oneself well-liked or loved
quiste *m*, *med* cyst
quita *f*, *law* discharge (of part of a debt)
quitaesmalte *m*, nail polish remover (for fingernails)
quitamanchas *mf*, dry cleaner, clothes cleaner
quitamotas *mf inf* flatterer, adulator
quitanieve *m*, snowplow
quitanza *f*, quittance; quietus
quitapesares *m*, *inf* consolation, solace, comfort
quitar *vt* to remove; take off or away; clear (the table); rob, steal; prevent, impede; parry (in fencing); separate; redeem (pledges); forbid; annul, repeal (laws, etc.); free from (obligations); *vr* shed, take off, remove; get rid of; leave, quit. **quitarse de encima (a),** to get rid of someone or something. **q. el polvo,** to dust. **de quita y pon,** detachable, removable; adjustable
quitasol *m*, parasol, sunshade
quitasueño *m*, *inf* sleep banisher, anxiety
quite *m*, hindering, impeding; obstruction; parry (in fencing). **estar al q.,** to be ready to protect someone
quizá, quizás *adv* perhaps. **q. y sin q.,** without doubt, certainly

R

rabadán *m*, head shepherd or herdsman
rabadilla *f*, rump, croup
rábano *m*, radish. **r. picante,** horseradish
rabel *m*, *mus* rebec; *inf* backside, seat
rabera *f*, tail-end; chaff, siftings
rabí *m*, rabbi
rabia *f*, rabies, hydrophobia; anger, fury. *inf* **tener r. (a),** to hate
rabiar *vi* to suffer from hydrophobia; groan with pain; be furious; (*with por*) yearn for, desire. **a r.,** excessively
rabieta *f*, *inf* tantrum
rabínico *a* rabbinical
rabinismo *m*, rabbinism
rabino *m*, rabbi. **gran r.,** chief rabbi
rabioso *a* rabid; furious, angry; vehement. **perro r.,** mad dog
rabo *m*, tail; *bot* stalk; *inf* train (of a dress); shank (of a button). **r. del ojo,** corner of the eye. *fig inf* **ir r. entre piernas,** to have one's tail between one's legs
rabón *a* tailless, docked; bobtailed
rabonear *vi*, *Lat. Am.* to play hookey
rabudo *a* big-tailed
racimo *m*, bunch (of grapes or other fruits); cluster; raceme
raciocinar *vi* to reason
raciocinio *m*, reasoning; ratiocination; discourse, speech
ración *f*, ration; portion (in a restaurant); meal allowance; *ecc* prebendary. *inf* **r. de hambre,** starvation diet; pittance, starvation wages
racional *a* reasonable, logical; rational
racionalidad *f*, reasonableness; rationality
racionalismo *m*, rationalism
racionalista *a* and *mf* rationalist. *a* rationalistic

racionalización *f*, rationalization
racionamiento *m*, rationing. *f*. **cartilla de r.,** ration book
racionar *vt* to ration
rada *f*, bay, cove; *naut* road, roadstead
radar *m*, radar
radiación *f*, radiation; *rad* broadcasting
radiactividad *f*, radioactivity
radiactivo *a* radioactive
radiador *m*, radiator (for heating); *aut* radiator
radial *a* radial
radiante *a phys* radiating; brilliant, shining; *fig* beaming (with satisfaction)
radiar *vi phys* to radiate; *vt* broadcast (by radio); *Lat. Am.* to cross off, delete, erase
radical *a* radical; fundamental; *pol* radical. *m*, *gram* root; (*math chem*) radical. *mf pol* radical
radicalismo *m*, radicalism
radicar(se) *vi* and *vr* to take root. **r. una solicitud,** file an application, submit an application. *vi* be (in a place)
radio *m*, (*geom anat*) radius; radium. *f*, radio
radioaficionado (-da) *n* radio amateur; *inf* ham, wireless fan or enthusiast
radioaudición *f*, radio broadcast
radiocomunicación *f*, radio transmission
radiodifundir *vt rad* to broadcast
radiodifusión, radioemisión *f*, *rad* broadcast; broadcasting
radiodifusora *f*, *Lat. Am.* = **radioemisora**
radioemisora *f*, radio station; (radio) transmitter
radioescucha *mf* radio listener
radiofotografía *f*, radiophotography; x-ray photograph. **tomar una r. de,** to x-ray
radiofrecuencia *f*, radiofrequency

radiografía *f*, radiography
radiografiar *vt* to x-ray, radiograph
radiografista *mf* radiographer
radiograma *m*, radiogram, cable
radiolocación *f*, radiolocation
radiología *f*, radiology
radiólogo *mf* radiologist
radiometría *f*, radiometry
radiómetro *m*, radiometer
radiorreceptor *m*, receiver, wireless set
radioscopia *f*, radioscopy
radioyente *mf* radio listener
radiotelefonía *f*, radiotelephony
radiotelegrafía *f*, radiotelegraphy
radiotelegráfico *a* radiotelegraphic, wireless
radiotelegrafista *mf* wireless operator
radiotelegrama *m*, radiogram, radiotelegram
radioterapia *f*, radiotherapy, radiotherapeutics
radiotransmisor *m*, (radio) transmitter
raedera *f*, scraper
raedor *a* scraping; abrasive
raedura *f*, scraping; rubbing; fraying
raer *vt irr* to scrape; abrade; fray; *fig* extirpate. See **caer**
ráfaga *f*, gust or blast of wind; light cloud; flash (of light)
rafe *m*, eaves
rafia *f*, raffia
raicear *vi*, *Lat. Am.* to take root
raído *a* frayed, threadbare; brazen, barefaced
raíz *f*, root. **r. amarga,** horseradish. **r. cuadrada (cúbica),** square (cubed) root. **r. pivotante,** tap root. **r. fuerte,** *Mexico* horseradish **a r.,** close to the root, closely. **a r. de,** as a result of; after. **de r.,** from the root, entirely. **echar raíces,** to take root
raja *f*, split, crack; chip, splinter (of wood); slice (of fruit, etc.)
rajadura *f*, splitting; crack, split, crevice; *geol* break
rajar *vt* to crack, split; slice; *vi inf* boast; chatter; *vr* crack, split; *inf* take back one's words
ralea *f*, kind, quality; (*inf* scornful) race, lineage
ralear *vi* to grow thin (cloth, etc.); behave true to type (gen. in a bad sense)
rallador *m*, *cul* grater
rallar *vt cul* to grate; *inf* bother, annoy
rallo *m*, *cul* grater; rasp
ralo *a* sparse, thin
rama *f*, bough, branch; *fig* branch (of family). *fig inf* **andarse por las ramas,** to beat around the bush. **en r.,** *com* raw; unbound (of books)
ramaje *m*, thickness of branches, denseness of foliage
ramal *m*, strand (of rope); halter; branch line (of a railroad); fork (of a road, etc.); ramification, division
ramalazo *m*, blow with a rope; mark left by this; bruise
rambla *f*, bed, channel, course; avenue, boulevard (in Catalonia)
ramera *f*, whore
ramificación *f*, ramification; *anat* bifurcation
ramificarse *vr* to branch, fork; *fig* spread
ramillete *m*, bouquet; table centerpiece; *bot* cluster
ramo *m*, *bot* branch; twig, spray; bouquet, bunch; wreath; *fig* branch (of learning, etc.); *com* line (of business); *fig* touch, slight attack. **Domingo de Ramos,** Palm Sunday
ramoso *a* branchy, thick with branches
rampa *f*, gradient, incline; *mil* ramp; launching site
ramplón *a* stout, heavy (of shoes); coarse; vulgar; bombastic
rana *f*, frog. **r. de San Antonio,** tree frog
ranchero *m*, *mil* cook; small farmer; *WH* rancher
rancho *m*, mess, rations; settlement, camp; hut, cabin; *inf* group, huddle; *WH* ranch; *naut* gang. **hacer r.,** *inf* to make room
rancidez *f*, rancidness; staleness; rankness; antiquity
ranciedad *f*, rancidness; antiquity, oldness; mustiness
rancio *a* rancid, rank; mellow (of wine); ancient; traditional; musty
rancotán *adv*, *Lat. Am.* in cash

rango *m*, grade, class; range; (*mil nav* and social) rank; file, line
ranura *f*, groove; rabbet; slot, notch
rapacidad *f*, rapacity, avidity, greed
rapador *a* scraping. *m*, *inf* barber
rapapolvo *m*, *inf* severe scolding, dressing-down
rapar(se) *vt* and *vr* to shave; *vt* crop, cut close (hair); *inf* steal, pinch
rapaz *a* rapacious. *m*, young boy. **ave r.,** bird of prey
rapaza *f*, young girl
rape *m*, *inf* hasty shave or haircut. **al r.,** close-cropped
rapidez *f*, speed, swiftness, rapidity
rápido *a* quick, swift; express (trains). *m*, torrent, rapid; express train
rapiña *f*, robbery, plundering, sacking
rapiñar *vt inf* to steal, pinch
raposa *f*, vixen, fox; *inf* wily person
raposo *m*, (male) fox
raposear *vi* to behave like a fox
rapsodia *f*, rhapsody
raptar *vt* to abduct; rob
rapto *m*, abduction, rape; snatching, seizing; ecstasy, trance; *med* loss of consciousness
raptor *m*, kidnapper, abductor
raquero *a* pirate. *m*, wrecker; pickpocket, dock rat
raqueta *f*, racket (tennis, badminton, squash rackets); croupier's rake. **r. de nieve,** snowshoe
raquianestesia *f*, spinal anesthesia
raquítico *a med* rachitic; small, minute; weak, feeble; rickety
raquitismo *m*, rickets
rarefacer(se) *vt* and *vr irr* to rarefy. See **satisfacer**
rareza *f*, rareness, unusualness; eccentricity; whim; oddity, curio
raridad *f*, rarity; thinness; scarcity
raro *a* rare, unusual, uncommon; notable, outstanding; odd, eccentric, queer; rarefied (gases, etc.). **rara vez,** seldom. **lo r. de,** the strange thing about (e.g. **Lo r. del caso es . . . ,** the strange thing about the case is . . .)
ras *m*, level. **a r.,** flush (with), nearly touching
rasa *f*, worn place in cloth; clearing, glade
rasar *vt* to level with a strickle; graze, brush, touch lightly; *vr* grow clear (of the sky, etc.)
rascacielos *m*, skyscraper
rascador *m*, scraper; ornamental hairpin
rascadura *f*, scraping; scratching
rascar *vt* to scratch; claw; scrape; twang (a guitar, etc.). *inf* **¡Que se rasque!** Let him put up with it! Let him lump it!
rascatripas *m*, *inf* caterwauler, squeaker (of violinists, etc.)
rascón *a* sour, tart
rasgado, -a *a*, *Lat. Am.* outspoken
rasgadura *f*, tearing; tear, rip, rent
rasgar(se) *vt* and *vr* to tear, rip; *vt* strum the guitar
rasgo *m*, flourish (of the pen); felicitous expression; characteristic, quality; *Lat. Am.* irrigation channel; *pl* features (of the face)
rasgón *m*, rip, tear
rasguear *vt* to strum, twang (the guitar); *vi* write with a flourish
rasgueo *m*, flourish (on a guitar); scratch (of a pen)
rasguñar *vt* to scratch, scrape; claw; *art* sketch
rasguño *m*, scratch; *art* sketch, outline
raso *a* flat; free of obstacles; glossy; clear (sky, etc.); plain; undistinguished; backless (chairs). *m*, satin. **al r.,** in the open air
raspa *f*, *bot* beard (of cereals); fishbone; bunch of grapes; *bot* husk; *carp* scraper
raspador *m*, eraser; scraper, rasp
raspadura *f*, scraping; erasing; shavings, filings; *Lat. Am.* brown sugar
raspar *vt* to scrape; erase; rob, steal; burn, bite (wine, etc.); *Lat. Am.* scold; *inf* to fail (student), fire (employee)
rastra *f*, trace, sign; sled; string of onions, etc.; anything

dragging; *agr* harrow; *agr* rake. **a la r.,** dragging; reluctantly. **pescar a la r.,** to trawl

rastreador *m, naut* minesweeper. *a* dragging

rastrear *vt* to trace, trail; drag, trawl; surmise, conjecture, investigate; *vi agr* rake; fly low

rastreo *m,* dragging (of lakes, etc.)

rastrero *a* dragging, trailing; low-flying; servile, abject; *bot* creeping. *m,* slaughterhouse employee

rastrillador (-ra) *n* raker; hackler

rastrilladora *f,* mechanical harrow

rastrillaje *m,* raking

rastrillar *vt* to rake; dress, comb (flax)

rastrillo *m, agr* rake; hackle; portcullis; *agr* rack

rastro *m, agr* rake; track, trail; wholesale meat market; slaughterhouse; trace, vestige; second-hand market (in Madrid)

rastrojo *m,* stubble; stubble field

rasura *f,* shaving

rasurar(se) *vt* and *vr* to shave

rata *f,* rat. *m, inf* pickpocket. **r. almizclera,** muskrat. *inf* **más pobre que las ratas,** poorer than a church mouse

rataplán *m,* rub-a-dub-dub, beating of a drum

ratear *vt* to rebate pro rata; apportion; thieve on a small scale, filch; *vi* crawl, creep

ratería *f,* filching, petty theft, picking pockets; meanness, parsimony

ratero (-ra) *n* pilferer, petty thief, pickpocket

ratificación *f,* ratification

ratificador (-ra) *n* ratifier

ratificar *vt* to ratify

ratificatorio *a* ratifying, confirmatory

rato *m,* short interval of time, while. **buen (mal) r.,** pleasant (unpleasant) time. **r. perdido,** leisure moment. **a ratos,** sometimes, occasionally. **de r. en r.,** from time to time. **pasar el r.,** *inf* to while away the time

ratón (-ona) *n* mouse

ratonera *f,* mousetrap; mousehole; mouse nest; *Lat. Am.* hovel. *fig* **caer en la r.,** to fall into a trap

ratonero, ratonesco, ratonil *a* mousy

rauco *a poet* hoarse

raudal *m,* torrent, cascade; *fig* flood, abundance

raudo *a* swift, rapid

ravioles *m pl,* ravioli

raya *f,* stripe, streak; limit, end; part (of the hair); boundary; *gram* dash; score (some games). *m, icht* ray. **pasar de r.,** to go too far; misbehave

rayadillo *m,* striped cotton

rayano *a* neighboring; border; almost identical, very similar

rayar *vt* to draw lines; streak; stripe; cross out; underline; rifle (a gun); *vi* verge (on), border (on); appear (of dawn, daylight); excel; be similar. **Raya en los catorce años,** He is about fourteen

rayo *m, phys* beam, ray; thunderbolt; flash of lightning; spoke; quick-witted person; capable, energetic person; sudden pain; disaster, catastrophe. **r. de sol,** sunbeam. **r. catódico,** cathode ray. **r. x,** x-ray. *fig* **echar rayos,** to breathe forth fury

rayón *m,* rayon

raza *f,* race; breed; lineage, family; kind, class; crack, crevice. **de r.,** purebred

razón *f,* reason; reasoning; word, expression; speech, argument; motive, cause; order, method; justice, equity; right, authority; proportion; *math* ratio, proportion. **r. de estado,** raison d'état, reasons of state. *com* **r. social,** firm, trade name. **a r. de,** at a rate of. **dar la r. (a),** to agree with. **estar puesto en r.,** to stand to reason. **tener r.,** to be in the right

razonable *a* reasonable; moderate

razonador (-ra) *n* reasoner

razonamiento *m,* reasoning

razonar *vi* to reason; speak; *vt* attest, confirm

razzia *f,* foray; pillaging, sacking; police raid

re *m, mus* re, D

reabsorción *f,* reabsorption

reacción *f,* reaction. **r. de Bayardo,** quick reaction of someone always ready to help those in distress

reaccionar *vi* to react

reaccionario (-ia) *a* and *n* reactionary

reaccionarismo *m,* reactionism

reacio *a* recalcitrant

reactivo *m,* reagent. *a* reactive; reacting

readmisión *f,* readmission

readmitir *vt* to readmit

reajustar *vt* to readjust

real *a* actual, real; kingly; royal; royalist; *fig* regal; *inf* fine, handsome. *m,* silver coin, real; *m pl,* encampment, camp. **alzar el r.,** *mil* to strike camp. **asentar el r.,** *mil* to encamp. **r. decreto,** royal decree. **sitio r.,** royal residence. **un r., sobre otro,** *inf* cash in full

realce *m,* raised or embossed work; renown, glory; *art* high light

realeza *f,* royalty, royal majesty

realidad *f,* reality; sincerity, truth. **en r.,** in fact, actually

realismo *m,* realism; regalism; royalism

realista *a* realistic; royalist. *mf* realist; royalist; regalist

realizable *a* realizable; practicable

realización *f,* realization; performance, execution

realizar *vt* to perform, execute, carry out; *com* realize. **r. beneficio,** to make a profit

realmente *adv* really, truly; actually

realzar *vt* to heighten, raise; emboss; exalt; enhance; *art* intensify (colors, etc.)

reanimar *vt* to reanimate; revive, restore, resuscitate; encourage

reanudación *f,* resumption, renewal

reanudar *vt* to resume, continue

reaparecer *vi irr* to reappear. See **conocer**

reaparición *f,* reappearance

rearmamento *m,* rearmament

rearmar *vi* to rearm

reasegurador *m,* underwriter

reasegurar *vt* to reinsure, underwrite

reaseguro *m,* reinsurance, underwriting

reasunción *f,* reassumption; resumption

reata *f,* string of horses or mules. **de r.,** in single file; *inf* blindly, unquestioningly; *inf* at once

rebaja *f,* diminution; *com* discount, rebate; remission

rebajar *vt* to lower; curtail, lessen; remit; *com* reduce in price; *mech* file; *elec* step down; humble, humiliate; *vr* cringe, humble oneself

rebajo *m,* reduction (in price, etc.); rabbet

rebanada *f,* slice, piece (of bread, etc.)

rebanar *vt* to cut into slices; split

rebaño *m,* flock, drove, herd; *ecc* flock

rebasar *vt* to exceed, go beyond; *mil* bypass

rebate *m,* altercation, dispute, quarrel

rebatiña *f,* grab; scrimmage. **andar a la r.,** to scuffle

rebatir *vt* to repulse, repel; fight again; fight hard; oppose, resist; *com* deduct; refuse, reject

rebato *m,* alarm, tocsin; *mil* surprise attack; panic, dismay

rebeca *f,* cardigan, jersey

rebeco *m, zool* chamois

rebelarse *vr* to mutiny, rebel; oppose, resist

rebelde *a* mutinous, rebellious; wilful, disobedient; stubborn. *mf* rebel

rebeldía *f,* rebelliousness; willfulness; stubbornness; *law* nonappearance

rebelión *f,* insurrection, revolt

rebenque *m, Lat. Am.* whip

rebién *adv* very well, extremely well

rebisabuelo (-la) *n.* See **tatarabuelo**

reblandecer *vt irr* to soften; *vr* become soft. See **conocer**

reblandecimiento *m,* softening; *med* flabbiness

reborde *m,* rim, edge; *mech* flange. **r. de acera,** curb

rebordear *vt* to flange

rebosar vi to overflow, run over; fig abound in; express one's feelings

rebotar vi to rebound; clinch (nails, etc.); refuse; vr change color; inf be vexed

rebote m, rebounding; rebound

rebotica f, back room of a pharmacy; back of a shop

rebozar vt to muffle up; coat with batter

rebozo m, muffling up, hiding the face; head shawl; pretense, excuse. fig **sin r.,** openly

rebueno a inf extremely good, fine

rebullicio m, uproar, clamor

rebullir vi to stir, show signs of movement; fig swarm, seethe

rebusca f, close search; gleaning; remains

rebuscado a affected, unnatural (of style)

rebuscar vt to search for; glean

rebuznar vi to bray

recadero (-ra) n messenger, errand boy

recado m, message; greeting, note; gift, present; daily marketing; outfit, implements; precaution, safeguard

recaer vi irr to fall again; med relapse; lapse, backslide; devolve, fall upon. See **caer**

recaída f, falling again; med relapse; lapse

recalar vt to impregnate; naut call at (a port), come within sight of land

recalcada f, pressing down, squeezing; emphasis; naut list

recalcar vt to press down; squeeze; pack tight; stress, emphasize; vi naut list; vr inf say over and over, savor one's words

recalcitrante a obdurate, recalcitrant

recalentador m, mech superheater

recalentar vt irr to overheat; superheat; reheat. See **sentar**

recamado m, raised embroidery

recámara f, dressing room; explosives chamber; breech of a gun; inf caution

recamarera f, Mexico chambermaid

recambio m, spare, spare part; com re-exchange

recantación f, retraction, recantation

recapacitar vi to search one's memory; think over

recapitulación f, summary, résumé

recapitular vt to recapitulate, summarize

recargar vt to recharge; load again; reaccuse; overcharge; overdress or overdecorate; vr med become more feverish. **r. acumuladores,** to recharge batteries

recargo m, charge; new load; law new accusation; overcharge, extra cost; med temperature increase

recatado a prudent, discreet, circumspect; modest, shy

recatar vt to hide, conceal; vr be prudent or cautious

recato m, caution, prudence; modesty, shyness, reserve

recauchutar vt to retread (tires)

recaudación f, collecting; collection (of taxes, etc.); tax collector's office

recaudador m, tax collector

recaudar vt to collect, recover (taxes, debts, etc.); deposit, place in custody

recaudo m, collecting; collection (of taxes, etc.); precaution, safeguard; law surety; Lat. Am. daily supply of vegetables

recelar vt to suspect, fear, mistrust; vr (with de) be afraid or suspicious of

recelo m, suspicion, mistrust, doubt, fear

receloso a suspicious, distrustful, doubtful

recepción f, receiving, reception; admission, acceptance; reception, party; law cross-examination

receptáculo m, receptacle, container; fig refuge; bot receptacle

receptador (-ra) n receiver (of stolen goods); accomplice

receptivo a receptive

receptor (-ra) a receiving. n recipient. m, elec receiver; wireless set. **r. de galena,** crystal set. **r. telefónico,** telephone receiver

receta f, med prescription; cul recipe

recetar vt med to prescribe; inf demand

rechapear vt to replate

rechazar vt to repulse; resist; refuse; oppose, deny (the truth of); contradict

rechazo m, recoil; rebound; refusal

rechinamiento, rechino m, squeaking, creaking; gnashing of teeth

rechinar vi to squeak, creak; gnash (teeth); chatter (teeth); do with a bad grace

rechoncho a squat, stocky, thickset

reciamente adv hard; strongly, firmly, vigorously

recibí m, com receipt

recibidor (-ra) a receiving. n recipient. m, reception room

recibimiento m, reception; welcome, greeting; reception room, waiting room; hall, vestibule

recibir vt to obtain, receive; support, bear; suffer, experience (attack, injury); approve; accept, receive; entertain; stand up to (attack); vr (with de) graduate as, take office as

recibo m, reception; com receipt; reception room, waiting room; hall, vestibule. com **acusar r.,** to acknowledge receipt

recidiva f, med relapse

recién adv recently, newly. Shortened form of **reciente** before a past participle (e.g. **r. llegado,** newly arrived)

reciente a recent; new; fresh

recinto m, precincts; neighborhood; premises, place

recio a strong; robust; bulky, thick; rough, uncouth; grievous, hard; severe (weather); impetuous, precipitate

recipiente a receiving. m, receptacle, container, vessel

reciprocar vt to reciprocate

reciprocidad f, reciprocity; reciprocation

recíproco a reciprocal

recitación f, recitation

recitado m, recitative

recitador (-ra) n elocutionist, reciter

recitar vt to recite, declaim

reclamación f, reclamation; objection, opposition; com claim

reclamar vi to oppose, object to; poet resound; vt call repeatedly; com claim; decoy (birds)

reclamo m, decoy bird; enticement, allurement; law reclamation; advertisement. **objeto de r.,** advertising sample. **venta de r.,** bargain sale

reclinación f, reclining; leaning

reclinatorio m, couch; prie-dieu

recluir vt irr to immure, shut up; detain, arrest. See **huir**

reclusión f, confinement, seclusion; prison

recluso (-sa) n recluse

recluta f, recruiting. mf mil recruit

reclutador m, recruiting office

reclutamiento m, recruiting

reclutar vt to enlist recruits, recruit; Argentina round up

recobrar vt to recover, regain; vr recuperate; regain consciousness

recobro m, recovery; mech pick-up

recocer vt irr to reboil; recook; overboil; overcook; anneal (metals); vr fig be tormented (by emotion), be all burned up. See **cocer**

recodo m, bend, turn, loop

recogedor a sheltering. m, agr gleaner

recoger vt to gather, pick; pick up; retake; collect (letters from a mailbox, etc.); amass; shrink, narrow; keep; hoard; shelter; reap, pick; vr withdraw, retire; go home; go to bed; retrench, economize; give oneself to meditation

recogida f, collection (of letters from a mailbox); withdrawal; retirement; harvest

recogido a recluse; cloistered, confined

recogimiento m, gathering, picking; collection, accumulation; seclusion; shelter; women's reformatory

recolección f, summary, résumé; harvest; collection (of taxes, etc.); ecc convent of a reformed order; mystic ecstasy

recoleto *a ecc* reformed (of religious orders); recluse

recomendable *a* commendable, recommendable

recomendación *f*, recommendation (all meanings)

recomendar *vt irr* to recommend (all meanings); entrust, commend. *Pres. Ind.* **recomiendo, recomiendas, recomienda, recomiendan.** *Pres. Subjunc.* **recomiende, recomiendes, recomiende, recomienden**

recompensa *f*, compensation; recompense, reward

recompensar *vt* to compensate; requite; reward, recompense

recomposición *f*, recomposition

recomprar *vt* to repurchase

reconcentrar *vt* to concentrate; dissemble; *vr* withdraw into oneself, meditate

reconciliable *a* reconcilable

reconciliación *f*, reconciliation

reconciliador (-ra) *a* reconciliatory. *n* reconciler

reconciliar *vt* to reconcile; *ecc* reconsecrate; *ecc* hear a short confession; *vr* become reconciled; *ecc* make an additional confession

recondicionar *vt* to rebuild, overhaul, recondition

recóndito *a* recondite

reconocer *vt irr* to examine, inspect; recognize; admit, acknowledge; own, confess; search; *pol* recognize; *mil* reconnoiter; (*with por*) adopt as (a son, etc.); recognize as; *vr* be seen, show; acknowledge, confess; know oneself. **Bien se reconoce que no está aquí,** It's easy to see he's not here. See **conocer**

reconocido *a* grateful

reconocimiento *m*, examination, inspection; recognition; acknowledgement, admission; search; *mil* reconnoitering; adoption; gratitude

reconquista *f*, reconquest

reconquistar *vt* to reconquer; *fig* recover, win back

reconstitución *f*, reconstitution

reconstituir *vt irr* to reconstitute. See **huir**

reconstituyente *m, med* tonic

reconstrucción *f*, reconstruction

reconstruir *vt irr* to reconstruct, rebuild; recreate. See **huir**

reconvención *f*, rebuke, reproof; recrimination; *law* countercharge

reconversión *f*, reconversion

recopilación *f*, summary, compendium; collection (of writings); digest (of laws)

recopilador *m*, compiler

recopilar *vt* to compile, collect

recordar *vt irr* to cause to remember, remind; remember; *vi* remember; awake. See **acordar**

recordatorio *m*, reminder. *a* commemorative (e.g. a plaque)

recorrer *vt* to travel over; pass through; wander around; examine, inspect; read hastily; overhaul, renovate

recorrido *m*, journey, run; *mech* stroke; overhaul. **r. de despegue,** *aer* take-off run

recortado *a bot* jagged, incised. *m*, paper cutout

recortar *vt* to clip, trim, pare; cut out; *art* outline; *vr* stand out (against), be outlined (against)

recorte *m*, clipping, paring; cutting; cutout; *art* outline; *pl* snippets, clippings. **r. de periódico,** newspaper cutting, newspaper clipping

recostar *vt irr* (*with en or contra*) to lean, rest against; *vr* (*with en or contra*) lean against, rest on; lean back; recline. See **contar**

recreación *f*, recreation, hobby

recrear *vt* to entertain, amuse; *vr* amuse oneself; delight (in), enjoy

recreo *m*, recreation, hobby; playtime, recess (in schools); place of amusement. **salón de r.,** recreation room

recriminación *f*, recrimination

recriminador *a* recriminatory

recriminar *vt* to recriminate

recrudecer(se) *vi* and *vr irr* to recur, return. See **conocer**

recrudescencia *f*, recrudescence, recurrence

rectángulo *m*, rectangle. *a* rectangular

rectificable *a* rectifiable

rectificación *f*, rectification; *mech* grinding

rectificador *m*, rectifier

rectificar *vt* to rectify; *mech* grind; *vr* mend one's ways; *mil* **r. el frente,** to straighten the line

rectilíneo *a* rectilinear

rectitud *f*, straightness; rectitude, integrity; exactness; righteousness

recto *a* straight; upright; erect; literal (meaning); just, fair; single-breasted (of coats); *m*, right angle; rectum

rector (-ra) *n* director; principal, headmaster. *m, ecc* rector

rectorado *m*, principalship, headmaster- (mistress-) ship, directorship; *ecc* rectorship

rectoría *f*, rectorate, rectorship

recua *f*, drove of beasts of burden; *inf* string or line (of things)

recubrir *vt* to re-cover; coat; plate. *Past Part.* **recubierto**

recuento *m*, calculation; recount; inventory

recuerdo *m*, memory, remembrance; memento; *pl* greetings, regards

reculada *f*, drawing back; recoil

recular *vi* to recoil, draw back; *inf* go back on, give up

recuperable *a* recoverable, recuperable

recuperación *f*, recovery, recuperation; *chem* recovery

recurrente *a* recurrent

recurrir *vi* to recur; (*with prep a*) have recourse to; appeal to

recurso *m*, recourse, resort; choice, option; reversion; petition; *law* appeal; *pl* means of livelihood; *fig* way out, last hope

recusar *vt* to refuse; challenge the authority (of)

red *f*, net; network; hairnet; railing, grating; *fig* snare; system (of communications, etc.); *fig* combination (of events, etc.); *elec* mains. **r. de arrastre,** trawl net. *fig inf* **caer en la r.,** to fall into the trap

redacción *f*, phrasing; editorial office; editing; editorial board

redactar *vt* to write, phrase; draw up; edit

redactor (-ra) *a* editorial. *n* editor

redada *f*, cast (of a fishing net); haul, catch

redecilla *f, dim* small net; netting; hairnet

redención *f*, redemption; ransom; deliverance, salvation; redeeming, paying off (a mortgage, etc.)

redentor (-ra) *a* redeeming, redemptive. *n* redeemer

redificar *vt* to rebuild

redifusión *f, rad* relay

redil *m*, sheepfold

redimible *a* redeemable

redimir *vt* to ransom; redeem, buy back; pay off (a mortgage, etc.); deliver, free; *ecc* redeem

reditar *vt* to reprint, reissue

rédito *m, com* income, revenue, interest, profit

redoblamiento *m*, redoubling; bending back (of nails, etc.); rolling (of a drum)

redoblar *vt* to redouble; repeat; bend back (nails, etc.); *vi* roll (a drum)

redoble *m*, doubling; redoubling; repetition; roll (of a drum)

redoma *f*, flask, vial

redomado *a* astute, crafty, sly; complete, perfect

redonda *f*, district; pasture ground; *naut* square sail; *mus* semibreve. **a la r.,** around

redondear *vt* to make round; round; free (from debt, etc.); *vr* acquire a fortune; clear oneself (of debts, etc.)

redondel *m*, traffic circle, rotary, roundabout

redondez *f*, roundness

redondo *a* round; circular; unequivocal, plain. *m*, round, circle; *inf* cash

reducción *f*, reduction; *mil* defeat, conquest; decrease; *com* rebate; (*math chem*) reduction

reducir *vt irr* to reduce; decrease, cut down; break up;

art scale down; *elec* step down; subdue; (*chem math surg*) reduce; exchange; divide into small fragments; persuade; *vr* be obliged to, have to; live moderately. See **conducir**

redundancia *f*, redundance

redundante *a* redundant

redundar *vi* to overflow; be excessive or superfluous; (*with en*) redound to

reduplicación *f*, reduplication

reduplicar *vt* to reduplicate

ree For words so beginning (e.g. *reeditar, reexportar*), see spellings with one **e**

refacción *f*, refection, light meal; compensation, reparation

refaccionar *vt*, *Lat. Am.* to fix, repair

refajo *m*, skirt, underskirt; *Colombia* mild drink consisting of champagne, soda and beer

refección *f*, refection, light meal

refectorio *m*, refectory

referencia *f*, report, account; allusion; regard, relation; *com* reference (gen. *pl*); consideration

referente *a* concerning, related (to)

referir *vt irr* to narrate; describe; direct, guide; relate, refer, concern; *vr* allude (to); refer (to); concern. See **sentir**

refinación *f*, refining

refinado *a* refined; polished, cultured; crafty

refinador *m*, refiner

refinamiento *m*, refinement, subtlety, care

refinar *vt* to refine, purify; polish, perfect

refinería *f*, refinery

reflector *a* reflecting. *m*, reflector; searchlight; shade (for lamps, etc.)

reflejar *vi phys* to reflect; *vt* consider; show, mirror; *vr fig* be reflected, be seen

reflejo *m*, reflection; image; glare. *a* reflex; considered, judicious

reflexión *f*, *phys* reflection; consideration, thought

reflexionar *vt* (*with en or sobre*) to consider, reflect upon

reflexivo *a phys* reflective; thoughtful

reflorecer *vi irr* to flower again; return to favor (ideas, etc.). See **conocer**

reflujo *m*, reflux, refluence; ebb tide

refocilar *vt* to warm up, brace up; give pleasure to; *vr* enjoy oneself

reforma *f*, reform; improvement; reformation; *hist* Reformation

reformación *f*, reform, improvement

reformador (-ra) *a* reformatory, reforming. *n* reformer

reformar *vt* to remake; reshape; repair, mend, restore; improve, correct; *ecc* reform; reorganize; *vr* mend one's ways, improve; control oneself

reformatorio *m*, reformatory. *a* reforming, reformatory

reformista *mf* reformist, reformer. *a* reformatory

reforzador *m*, *phot* reinforcing bath; *elec* booster

reforzamiento *m*, stiffening, reinforcing

reforzar *vt irr* to reinforce, strengthen, stiffen; encourage, inspirit. See **forzar**

refractar *vt* to refract

refractario *a* stubborn; (*phys chem*) refractory; unmanageable, unruly; fireproof

refrán *m*, proverb

refranero *m*, collection of proverbs

refregamiento *m*, rubbing; scrubbing, scouring

refregar *vt irr* to rub; scrub, scour; *fig inf* rub in, insist on. See **cegar**

refrenamiento *m*, curbing; control, restraint

refrenar *vt* to curb, check (horses); control, restrain

refrendar *vt* to countersign, endorse, legalize

refrescante *a* refreshing, cooling

refrescar *vt* to cool, chill; repeat; *fig* brush up, revise; *vi* be rested or refreshed; grow cooler; take the air; freshen (wind); take a cool drink; *vr* grow cooler; take the air; take a cool drink

refresco *m*, refreshment; cool drink; *Lat. Am.* soft drink, soda, pop

refresquería *f*, *Lat. Am.* refreshment stand

refriega *f*, affray, scuffle, rough-and-tumble

refrigeración *f*, refrigeration

refrigerador *m*, refrigerator

refrigerante *a* refrigerative; chilling; cooling. *m*, cooling chamber, cooler

refrigerar *vt* to chill; cool; freeze, refrigerate; refresh

refrigerio *m*, coolness; consolation; refreshment, food

refringente *a phys* refringent

refuerzo *m*, reinforcement, strengthening; aid, help

refugiado (-da) *a* and *n* refugee

refugiar *vt* to protect, shelter; *vr* take refuge

refugio *m*, refuge, shelter, protection; traffic island. **r. antiaéreo,** air raid shelter. **r. para peatones,** traffic island

refulgencia *f*, resplendence, splendor, brilliance

refulgente *a* resplendent, refulgent, dazzling

refulgir *vi* to shine, be dazzling

refundición *f*, recasting (of metals); adaptation; rehash, refurbishing

refundir *vt* to recast (metals); include, comprise; adapt; rehash, refurbish; *vi fig* promote, contribute to

refunfuñador *a* grumbling, fuming

refunfuñar *vi* to grumble, growl, fume

refunfuño *m*, grumble, fuming; snort

refutable *a* refutable

refutación *f*, refutation

refutar *vt* to refute

regadera *f*, watering can; irrigation canal; sprinkler; *Lat. Am.* shower bath, shower

regadío *m*, irrigated land; irrigation, watering. *a* irrigated

regajal, regajo *m*, pool, puddle; stream, brook

regalado *a* delicate, highly bred; luxurious, delightful

regalar *vt* to make a gift of, give; caress, fondle; indulge; cherish; entertain, regale; *vr* live in luxury

regalía *f*, royal privilege; right, exemption; perquisite, emolument

regaliz *m*, **regaliza** *f*, licorice

regalo *m*, gift, present; satisfaction, pleasure; entertainment, regalement; luxury, comfort

regalón *a inf* pampered

regalonear *vt*, *Lat. Am.* to pamper, spoil

regañadientes, a *adv* unwillingly, grumblingly

regañar *vi* to snarl (dogs); crack (skin of fruits); grumble, mutter; *inf* quarrel; *vt inf* scold

regaño *m*, angry look or gesture; *inf* scolding

regañón (-ona) *a inf* grumbling, complaining; scolding. *n inf* grumbler

regar *vt irr* to water, sprinkle with water; flow through, irrigate; spray; *fig* shower (with), strew. See **cegar**

regata *f*, regatta; small irrigation channel (for gardens, etc.)

regate *m*, twist of the body, sidestep; dribbling; (in soccer); *inf* dodging, evasion

regatear *vt* to haggle over, beat down (prices); resell, retail; dribble (a ball); *fig inf* dodge, avoid; *vi* bargain, haggle; *naut* take part in a regatta, race

regateo *m*, haggling, bargaining

regatero (-ra) *a* retail. *n* retailer

regatón (-ona) *m*, ferrule, tip. *a* haggling, bargaining. *n* haggler; retailer

regatonear *vt* to resell at retail

regazo *m*, lap, knees; *fig* heart, bosom

regeneración *f*, regeneration

regenerador (-ra) *n* regenerator. *a* regenerative, reforming

regenerar *vt* to regenerate, reform

regenta *f*, wife of the president of a court of session

regentar *vt* to fill temporarily (offices); rule, govern; manage, run (businesses)

regente *a* ruling. *mf* regent. *m*, president of a court of session; manager

regicidio *m*, regicide (act)

regidor *a* ruling, governing. *m*, magistrate, alderman

régimen *m*, administration, management; regime; (*med gram*) regimen; *mech* rating

regimentación *f*, regimentation

regimentar *vt irr* to form into regiments; regiment. *Pres. Ind.* **regimiento, regimientas, regimienta, regimientan.** *Pres. Subjunc.* **regimiente, regimientes, regimiente, regimienten**

regimiento *m*, *mil* regiment; administration, rule; *Lat. Am.* crowd (of people)

regio *a* royal; magnificent, regal. ¡**regio!** great!, wonderful!

región *f*, region, country; area, tract, space. **r. industrial,** industrial area

regionalismo *m*, regionalism

regionalista *mf* regionalist. *a* regional

regir *vt irr* to govern, rule; administer, conduct; *gram* govern; *vi* be in force (laws, etc.); work, function; *naut* obey the helm. See **pedir**

registrador *a* recording. *m*, registrar, keeper of records; recorder. **caja (registradora),** (cash) register

registrar *vt* to examine, inspect; search; copy, record; mark the place (in a book); observe, note; (of thermometers, etc.) record, show; look on to (houses, etc.); *vr* register (hotels, etc.)

registro *m*, search; registration, entry; record; recording; reading (of a thermometer, etc.); *mech* damper; registry; register (book); *mus* range, compass (voice); *mus* register (organ); (*mech print*) register; bookmark. **r. civil,** register of births, marriages, and deaths

regla *f*, ruler, measuring stick; rule, principle, guide; precept; system, policy; *med* period; moderation; method, order. **r. de cálculo,** slide rule. **r. T,** T-square. **en r.,** in due form. **por r.,** general, generally, as a rule

reglamentación *f*, regulation; rules and regulations

reglamentar *vt* to regulate

reglamento *m*, bylaw; regulation, ordinance

reglar *vt* to rule (lines); regulate; govern; control; *vr* restrain oneself, mend one's ways

regocijar *vt* to cheer, delight; *vr* enjoy oneself, rejoice

regocijo *m*, happiness, joy; cheer, merriment

regordete *a inf* chubby

regresar *vi* to return

regresión *f*, return; retrogression; regression

regreso *m*, return

reguera *f*, irrigation channel, ditch

regulación *f*, regulation; *mech* control, timing

regulador *m*, *mech* governor, regulator. *a* regulating, controlling

regular *vt* to adjust, regulate; *mech* govern. *a* methodical, ordered; moderate; average, medium; (*ecc mil geom gram*) regular; so-so, not bad; probable. **por lo r.,** generally

regularidad *f*, regularity

regularización *f*, regularization; regulation

regularizar *vt* to regularize; regulate

regurgitar *vi* to regurgitate

rehabilitación *f*, rehabilitation

rehabilitar *vt* to rehabilitate; *vr* rehabilitate oneself

rehacer *vt irr* to remake; repair, mend; *vr* recover one's strength; control one's emotions; *mil* rally. See **hacer**

rehén *m*, hostage (gen. *pl*); *mil* pledge, security

rehenchir *vt irr* to restuff; refill, recharge. See **henchir**

reherir *vt irr* to repulse

rehilar *vt* to spin too much or twist the yarn; *vi* totter, stagger; whizz (arrows, etc.). See **prohibir**

rehuir *vt irr* to withdraw; avoid; reject. See **huir**

rehusar *vt* to refuse, reject. See **desahuciar**

reimponer *vt irr* to reimpose. See **poner**

reimportación *f*, reimportation

reimpresión *f*, reprint

reimprimir *vt* to reprint

reina *f*, queen; queen (in chess); queen bee; peerless beauty, belle

reinado *m*, reign; heyday, fashion

reinante *a* reigning; prevalent

reinar *vi* to reign; influence; endure, prevail

reincidencia *f*, relapse (into crime, etc.), recidivism

reincidente *mf* backslider

reincidir *vi* to relapse (into crime, etc.)

reincorporar *vt* to reincorporate; *vr* join again, become a member again

reingresar *vi* to reenter

reingreso *m*, reentry

reino *m*, kingdom

reinstalación *f*, reinstatement

reinstalar *vt* to reinstate; *vr* be reinstalled

reintegración *f*, reintegration

reintegrar *vt* to reintegrate; *vr* be reinstated, recuperate, recover

reir *vi irr* to laugh; sneer, jeer; *fig* smile (nature); *vt* laugh at; *vr inf (with de)* scorn. **reírse a carcajadas,** to shout with laughter. *Pres. Part.* **riendo.** *Pres. Ind.* **río, ríes, ríe, ríen.** *Preterite* **rió, rieron.** *Pres. Subjunc.* **ría,** etc. *Imperf. Subjunc.* **riese,** etc.

reiteración *f*, reiteration, repetition

reiteradamente *adv* repeatedly, reiteratively

reiterar *vt* to reiterate, repeat

reivindicación *f*, *law* recovery

reivindicar *vt law* to recover

reja *f*, colter, plowshare; plowing, tilling; grating, grille; *Lat. Am.* jail, prison

rejado *m*, railing, grating

rejilla *f*, grating; grille, lattice; luggage rack (in a train); cane (for chairs, seats, etc.); wire mesh; small brazier; *elec* grid; *mech* grate

rejo *m*, *Lat. Am.* whip

rejuntar *vt* to point (a wall)

rejuvenecer *vt irr* to rejuvenate; *fig* revive; bring up to date; *vi* and *vr* be rejuvenated, grow young again, rejuvenesce. See **conocer**

rejuvenecimiento *m*, rejuvenation

relación *f*, relation; connection (of ideas); report, statement; narrative, account; *math* ratio; *law* brief; intercourse, association, dealings (gen. *pl*); list; analogy, relation. **tener relaciones con,** to have dealings with; be engaged or betrothed to; woo, court

relacionar *vt* to recount, narrate, report; connect, relate; *vr* be connected

relajación *f*, relaxation; recreation; laxity, dissoluteness

relajar *vt* to relax; recreate, amuse; make less rigorous; *law* remit; *vr* become relaxed; be dissolute, lax, or vicious

relamer *vt* to lick again; *vr* lick one's lips; *fig* overpaint, make up too much; ooze satisfaction, brag

relamido *a* overdressed; affected

relámpago *m*, lightning; flash, gleam; streak of lightning (of quick persons or things); flash of wit, witticism

relampaguear *vi* to lighten (of lightning); flash, gleam

relapso *a* relapsed, lapsed (into error, vice)

relatar *vt* to relate, narrate, report

relatividad *f*, relativeness; *phys* relativity

relativo *a* relevant, pertinent; relative, comparative; *gram* relative

relato *m*, narration, account, report

relator (-ra) *a* narrating. *n* narrator. *m*, *law* reporter

relavar *vt* to rewash, wash again

relección *f*, reelection

releer *vt irr* to reread; revise. See **creer**

relegación *f*, relegation

relegar *vt* to banish; relegate, set aside

relegir *vt irr* to reelect. See **elegir**

relente *m*, night dew, dampness; *inf* cheek, impudence

relevación *f*, *art* relief; release; remission, exemption

relevar *vt art* to work in relief; emboss; relieve, free; dismiss; excuse, pardon; aid, succor; *fig* aggrandize; *mil* relieve; *vi* carve in relief

relevo *m*, relay; *mil* relief

relieve *m*, *art* relief; *pl* leftovers, remains (of food). **alto r.,** high relief. **bajo r.,** low relief

religar *vt* to retie, fasten again; fasten more securely; solder

religión *f*, religion; creed, faith, philosophy; devotion, religious practice. **r. reformada,** Protestantism. **entrar en r.,** *ecc* to profess

religiosidad *f*, religiosity; religiousness; conscientiousness, punctiliousness

religioso (-sa) *a* religious; punctilious, conscientious; moderate. *n* religious

relinchar *vi* to whinny, neigh

reliquia *f*, residue (gen. *pl*); *ecc* relic; vestige, remnant, memento; permanent disability or ailment

rellanar *vt* to make level again; *vr* stretch oneself at full length

rellano *m*, landing (of a staircase); level stretch (of ground)

rellenar *vt* to refill, replenish; fill up; *mas* plug, point; *cul* stuff; *inf* cram with food (gen. *vr*)

relleno *m*, *cul* stuffing; replenishing; filling; *fig* padding (of speeches, etc.)

reloj *m*, clock; watch. **r. de arena,** hourglass. **r. de bolsillo,** watch. **r. de la muerte,** deathwatch beetle. **r. de péndulo,** grandfather clock. **r. de pulsera,** wristwatch. **r. de repetición,** repeater. **r. de sol** *or* **r. solar,** sundial

relojera *f*, clock stand; watch case

relojería *f*, watch or clock making; jeweler, watch maker's shop

relojero (-ra) *n* watch maker, watch repairer

reluciente a shining, sparkling; shiny

relucir *vi irr* to glitter, sparkle, gleam; *fig* shine, excel. See **lucir**

reluctante *a* unruly, refractory, disobedient

relumbrante *a* resplendent, dazzling

relumbrar *vi* to be resplendent, shine, glitter

remachar *vt* to rivet; *fig* clinch

remache *m*, riveting; rivet

remaduro, -a *a, Lat. Am.* overripe

remanente *m*, remains, residue

remanso *m*, backwater; stagnant water; sloth, dilatoriness

remar *vi* to row, paddle; scull; toil, strive

rematadamente *adv* completely, entirely, absolutely

rematado *a* beyond hope, extremely ill; utterly lost; *law* convicted

rematar *vt* to end, finish; finish off, kill; knock down at auction; *sew* finish; *vi* end; *vr* be ruined or spoiled

remate *m*, end, conclusion; extremity; *arch* coping; *arch* terminal; highest bid; auction. **de r.,** utterly hopeless

rematista *mf, Lat. Am.* auctioneer

rembarcar *vt* to reembark, reship

rembolsable *a* repayable

rembolsar *vt* to recover (money); refund, return (money)

rembolso *m*, repayment. **contra r.,** cash on delivery, C.O.D.

remedar *vt* to copy, imitate; mimic

remediador (-ra) *a* remedying. *n* benefactor, helper

remediar *vt* to remedy; aid, help; save from danger; prevent (trouble)

remedio *m*, remedy; emendation, correction; help; refuge, protection; *med* remedy. **No hay más r.,** There's nothing else to do, It's the only way open. **no tener más r.,** to be unable to help (doing something), be obliged to

remedo *m*, imitation; poor copy

remembranza *f*, remembrance, memory

rememorar *vt* to remember, recall to mind

remendar *vt irr* to mend, patch; darn; repair; correct. See **recomendar**

remendón (-ona) *n* cobbler; mender of old clothes

remero (-ra) *n* oarsman, rower; sculler

remesa *f*, remittance; consignment, shipment

remesar(se) *vt* and *vr* to pluck out (hair); *vt com* remit; consign

remezón *m*, *Lat. Am.* (earth) tremor

remiendo *m*, *sew* patch; mend, darn; emendation; *inf*

insignia of one of the Spanish military orders. **a remiendos,** *inf* piecemeal

remilgarse *vr* to preen oneself, be overdressed

remilgo *m*, affectation; mannerism; prudery, squeamishness

reminiscencia *f*, reminiscence; memory, recollection

remirado *a* wary, cautious, prudent, circumspect

remirar *vt* to revise, go over again; *vr* take great care over; behold with pleasure

remisión *f*, sending; remission; pardon, forgiveness; foregoing, relinquishment; abatement, diminution; *lit* reference, allusion

remise *m*, *Argentina* limousine, hired taxi

remiso *a* timid, spiritless; languid, slow

remitente *mf* sender. *a* sending

remitir *vt* to remit, send; pardon, forgive; defer, postpone; abate, diminish; relinquish, forgo; *lit* refer; *vr* remit, submit, consult; refer (to), cite

remo *m*, oar, scull, paddle; arm or leg (of men or animals, gen. *pl*); wing (gen. *pl*); hard, continuous toil; galleys. **al r.,** by dint of rowing; *inf* struggling with hardships

remojar *vt* to soak, steep; celebrate by drinking

remojo *m*, soaking, steeping

remolacha *f*, beet

remolcador *m*, *naut* tow, tug. *a naut* towing

remolcar *vt* (*naut aut*) to tow; *fig* press into service, use

remoler *vi, Lat. Am.* to live it up, live the life of Riley

remolinar *vi* to spin, whirl, eddy; *vr* throng, swarm

remolino *m*, whirlwind; eddy, swirl; whirlpool; crowd, throng, swarm; disturbance, riot

remolonear *vi inf* to loiter, lag; avoid work; be lax or dilatory

remolque *m*, towage, towing; towline; barge; *aut* trailer. **a r.,** on tow

remonta *f*, resoling (of shoes); leather gusset (of riding breeches); *mil* remount

remontar *vt* to scare off (game); *mil* supply with fresh horses; resole (shoes); *fig* rise to great heights (of oratory, etc.); *vr* soar (of birds); (*with prep a*) date from, go back to; originate in

remoquete *m*, blow with the fist; witticism; *inf* flirtation, courtship

rémora *f*, *icht* remora; delay, hindrance

remorder *vt irr* to bite again or repeatedly; *fig* gnaw, nag, cause uneasiness or remorse; *vr* show one's feelings. See **morder**

remordimiento *m*, remorse

remoto *a* distant, remote; unlikely, improbable

remover *vt irr* to remove, move; stir; turn over; dismiss, discharge. See **mover**

remozar *vt* to cause to appear young; freshen up, bring up to date; *vr* look young

remplazar *vt* to replace; exchange, substitute; succeed, take the place of

remplazo *m*, replacement; exchange, substitute; successor; *mil* replacement

remuda *f*, replacement, exchange

remudar *vt* to replace

remuneración *f*, remuneration; reward

remunerador (-ra) *a* remunerative, recompensing. *n* remunerator

remunerar *vt* to recompense, reward

remusgar *vi* to suspect, imagine

renacentista *a* renaissance

renacer *vi irr* to be reborn. See **nacer**

renacimiento *m*, rebirth; Renaissance

renacuajo *m*, tadpole; *mech* frog; *inf* twerp

rencarcelar *vt* to reimprison

rencarnación *f*, reincarnation

rencarnar(se) *vi* and *vr* to be reincarnated

rencilla *f*, quarrel, grievance, resentment

rencilloso *a* peevish, easily offended, touchy

rencor *m*, rancor, spite, old grudge. **guardar r.,** to bear malice

rencoroso *a* rancorous, malicious, spiteful

rencuadernar *vt* to rebind (books)
rencuentro *m*, collision; *mil* encounter, clash
rendición *f*, surrender; yield, profit
rendido *a* submissive, obsequious
rendija *f*, crevice, cleft, crack, fissure
rendimiento *m*, weariness, fatigue; submissiveness, obsequiousness; yield, profit; *mech* efficiency
rendir *vt irr mil* to cause to surrender; defeat; overcome, conquer; give back, return; yield, provide; tire, exhaust; vomit; pay, render; *vr* be exhausted, be worn out; surrender. *mil* **r. el puesto,** to retire from or give up a post. See **pedir**
renegado (-da) *n* renegade, apostate; turncoat; *inf* malignant person. *a* renegade
renegador (-ra) *n* blasphemer; foul-mouthed person
renegar *vt irr* to deny, disown; loathe, hate; *vi (with de)* apostatize; blaspheme; *inf* curse. See **cegar**
renganchar(se) *vt and vr mil* to reenlist
renganche *m*, *mil* reenlistment
renglón *m*, *print* line; *pl* writing, composition
renguear *vi*, *Lat. Am.* to limp
renguera *f*, *Lat. Am.* limp
reniego *m*, blasphemy; *inf* foul language, cursing
renitencia *f*, repugnance
renombrado *a* illustrious, famous
renombre *m*, surname; renown, reputation, fame
renovable *a* renewable, replaceable
renovación *f*, replacement; renewal; renovation; transformation, reform
renovador (-ra) *n* reformer; renovator. *a* renovating; reforming
renovar *vt irr* to renew; renovate; replace; exchange; reiterate, repeat. See **contar**
renta *f*, yield, profit; income; revenue; government securities; rent; tax
rentar *vt* to yield, produce an income
rentero (-ra) *n* tenant farmer. *m*, one who farms out land
rentista *mf* financier; bondholder; person who lives on a private income, rentier
rentístico *a* revenue, financial
renuente *a* refractory, willful
renuevo *m*, *bot* shoot; renewal
renuncia, renunciación *f*, renunciation; resignation; abandonment, relinquishment
renunciar *vt* to renounce; refuse; scorn; abandon, relinquish; resign; revoke (at cards). **r. a,** to give up
renuncio *m*, revoke (cards); *inf* falsehood
reñidamente *adv* strongly, stubbornly, fiercely
reñir *vi irr* to quarrel, dispute; fight; be on bad terms, fall out; *vt* scold; fight (battles, etc.). See **ceñir**
reo *mf* criminal; offender, guilty party; *law* defendant
reojo *m*, **(mirar de)** to look out of the corner of the eye; *fig* look askance
reorganizador (-ra) *a* reorganizing. *n* reorganizer
reóstato *m*, rheostat
repantigarse *vr* to stretch out one's legs, make oneself comfortable
reparable *a* remediable, reparable; worthy of note
reparación *f*, repair, mending; reparation, satisfaction; indemnity, compensation
reparada *f*, shying (of horses)
reparador *a* repairing, mending; faultfinding; restoring; satisfying, compensating
reparar *vt* to repair; restore; consider; correct, remedy; atone for, expiate; indemnify; hold up, detain; protect, guard; *(with en)* notice; *Lat. Am.* to ape, imitate, mimic; *vi* halt, be detained; *vr* control oneself
reparo *m*, repair; restoration; remedy; note, reflection; warning; doubt, scruple; guard, protection; parry (at fencing)
repartición *f*, distribution
repartidero *a* distributable
repartidor (-ra) *a* distributing. *n* distributor; tax assessor
repartimiento *m*, distribution, allotment; assessment

repartir *vt* to distribute; share out; allot; deal (cards); assess; *com* deliver
reparto *m*, distribution; assessment; delivery (of letters, etc.); *theat* cast; deal (at cards); *Lat. Am.* building site, construction site
repasador *m*, *Lat. Am.* dish cloth, dishrag
repasar *vt* to pass by again; peruse, reexamine; brush up, revise; skim, glance over; mend, repair (garments); edit, revise; hone
repaso *m*, second passage through; reexamination, perusal; revision, editing; brushing up, revision; repair, mending; *inf* dressing-down, scolding
repatriación *f*, repatriation
repatriado (-da) *n* repatriate
repatriar *vt* to repatriate; *vi and vr* return to one's own country
repecho *m*, steep slope. **a r.,** uphill
repelar *vt* to pull by the hair; put through its paces (of a horse); clip, cut; remove, diminish
repeler *vt* to repel, throw back; reject, refute
repelo *m*, anything against the grain; *inf* skirmish; reluctance, repugnance
repente *m*, *inf* sudden or unexpected movement. **de r.,** suddenly
repentino *a* sudden, unexpected
repentizar *vi mus* to sight-read
repercusión *f*, repercussion; vibration
repercutir *vi* to recoil, rebound; *vr* reverberate; reecho; *fig* have repercussions; *vt med* repel
repertorio *m*, repertory
repesar *vt* to reweigh, weigh again
repetición *f*, repetition; *art* replica, copy; repeater (in clocks); recital
repetidamente *adv* repeatedly
repetir *vt irr* to repeat, do over again; reiterate; *art* copy, make a replica of; recite. See **pedir**
repicar *vt* to chop, mince; peal (of bells); prick again; *vr* pride oneself (on), boast
repique *m*, chopping, mincing; peal, pealing (of bells); disagreement, grievance
repisa *f*, *arch* bracket; ledge; shelf. **r. de chimenea,** mantelpiece
replantar *vt* to replant; transplant
repleción *f*, repletion, satiety
replegar *vt irr* to refold, fold many times; *vr mil* retreat in good order. See **cegar**
repleto *a* replete
réplica *f*, reply, answer; replica
replicar *vi* to contradict, dispute; answer, reply. **¡No me repliques!** *inf* Don't answer back!
repliegue *m*, double fold, crease; doubling, folding; *mil* withdrawal
repoblación *f*, repeopling, repopulation
repoblar *vt* to repeople, repopulate
repollo *m*, white cabbage; heart (of lettuce, etc.)
reponer *vt irr* to replace; reinstate, restore; reply; *vr* recover, regain (possessions); grow well again; grow calm. See **poner**
reportación *f*, serenity, moderation
reportaje *m*, journalistic report
reportar *vt* to restrain, moderate; achieve, obtain; carry; bring; *vr* control oneself
reporte *m*, report, news; rumor
reporterismo *m*, newspaper reporting
reportero (-ra) *a* news, report. *n* reporter
reposado *a* quiet, peaceful, tranquil
reposar *vi* to rest, repose oneself; sleep, doze; lie in the grave; settle (liquids); rest (on)
reposición *f*, replacement; restoration; renewal; recovery (of health); *theat* revival
repositorio *m*, repository
reposo *m*, rest, repose; peace, tranquility; sleep
repostada *f*, *Lat. Am.* cheeky reply, saucy retort
repostería *f*, confectioner's shop; pantry; butler's pantry
repostero *m*, confectioner, pastry cook

repreguntar *vt* to cross-examine

reprender *vt* to scold, reprimand, rebuke

reprensible *a* reprehensible, censurable

reprensión *f*, scolding, reprimand, rebuke

represa *f*, damming, holding back (water); dam, lock; restraining, controlling

represalia *f*, reprisal (gen. *pl*); retaliation

represar *vt* to dam, harness (water); *naut* retake, recapture; *fig* restrain, control

representación *f*, representation; *theat* performance; authority; dignity; *com* agency; portrait, image; depiction, expression; petition

representador *a* representative

representante *a* representative. *mf* representative; actor; performer

representar *vt* to represent; *theat* perform; depict, express; describe, portray; *vr* imagine, picture to oneself

representativo *a* representative

represión *f*, repression; recapture

represivo *a* repressive

reprimenda *f*, rebuke, reprimand

reprimir *vt* to repress, restrain, control; *vr* restrain oneself

reprobación *f*, censure; reprobation

reprobar *vt irr* to reprove; censure; fail (in an exam). See **probar**

réprobo (-ba) *n* reprobate

reprochar *vt* to reproach

reproche *m*, reproaching; rebuke, reproach

reproducción *f*, reproduction. **r. a gran escala,** large-scale model

reproducir *vt irr* to reproduce. See **conducir**

reproductor (-ra) *a* reproductive. *n* breeding animal

reps *m*, rep (fabric)

reptil *a* reptilian; crawling. *m*, reptile

república *f*, republic; state, commonwealth. **la r. de las letras,** the republic of letters

República Dominicana Dominican Republic

República Malgache Republic of Madagascar

republicanismo *m*, republicanism

republicano (-na) *a* and *n* republican

repudiación *f*, repudiation

repudiar *vt* to cast off (a wife); repudiate, renounce

repuesto *a* retired, hidden. *m*, stock, provision; serving table; pantry; stake (at cards, etc.). **de r.,** spare, extra

repugnancia *f*, inconsistency, contradiction; aversion, dislike; reluctance; repugnance

repugnante *a* repugnant, loathsome

repugnar *vt* to contradict, be inconsistent with; hate, be averse to (e.g. **La idea me repugna,** I hate the idea)

repujado *m*, repoussé work

repujar *vt* to work in repoussé

repulir *vt* to repolish, reburnish; *vt* and *vr* make up too much, overdress

repulsa *f*, snub, rebuff; rejection; repulse

repulsar *vt* to decline, reject; repulse; deny, refuse; rebuff

repulsión *f*, repulsion; rebuff; aversion, dislike

repulsivo *a* repellent

repunta *f*, headland, cape; *fig* first sign; *inf* disgust; caprice; fight

reputación *f*, reputation

reputar *vt* to believe, consider (e.g. **Le reputo por honrado,** I believe him to be an honorable man); appreciate, esteem

requebrar *vt irr* to break into smaller pieces; make love to, woo; compliment, flatter. See **quebrar**

requemado *a* sunburned; brown

requemar *vt* to burn again; overcook; dry up, parch (of plants, etc.); burn (the mouth) (of spicy foods, etc.); *vr fig* suffer inwardly

requerimiento *m*, requirement, demand; *law* summons

requerir *vt irr* to inform, notify; examine; need, necessitate; require; summon; woo; persuade. See **sentir**

requesón *m*, cream cheese; curd

requetebién *adv inf* exceedingly well

requiebro *m*, compliment, expression of love; wooing, flirtation

requintar *vt, Lat. Am.* to tighten

requisa *f*, inspection, visitation; *mil* requisitionin; *Lat. Am.* confiscation

requisar *vt mil* to requisition

requisito *m*, requisite

res *f*, animal, beast; head of cattle; *Lat. Am.* steak

resabiar *vt* to make vicious, cause bad habits; *vr* contract bad habits or vices; be discontented; relish

resabio *m*, disagreeable aftertaste; bad habit, vice

resaca *f*, surf, undertow, surge; *com* redraft

resacar *vt* to distil

resalado *a inf* very witty; most attractive

resaltar *vi* to rebound; project, jut out; grow loose, fall out; *fig* stand out, be prominent

resalto *m*, rebound; projection

resarcir *vt* to compensate, indemnify

resbaladizo *a* slippery; difficult, delicate (of a situation)

resbalar *vi* to slip; slide; skid; err, fall into sin

resbalón *m*, slip; slide; skid; temptation, error

rescatador (-ra) *n* ransomer; rescuer

rescatar *vt* to ransom; redeem, buy back; barter; free, rescue; *fig* redeem (time, etc.)

rescate *m*, ransom; redemption; barter; amount of ransom

rescindir *vt* to annul, repeal, rescind

rescoldo *m*, ember, cinder; scruple, qualm, doubt

resentimiento *m*, deterioration, impairment; animosity, resentment

resentirse *vr irr* to deteriorate, be impaired; be hurt or offended. See **sentir**

reseña *f*, *mil* review; short description; review (of a book)

reseñar *vt mil* to review; describe briefly, outline

reserva *f*, store, stock; exception, qualification; reticence; restraint, moderation; (*ecc law*) reservation; (*mil naut*) reserve. **sin r.,** frankly, without reserve

reservación *f*, reservation; scruple

reservado *a* reserved, reticent; prudent, moderate; kept, reserved. *m*, reserved compartment; private apartment, private garden, etc.

reservar *vt* to keep, hold; postpone; reserve (rooms, etc.); exempt; keep secret; withhold (information); *ecc* reserve; *vr* await a better opportunity; be cautious

reservista *a* (*mil nav*) reserved. *mf* reservist

resfriado *m*, *med* cold, chill

resfriar *vt* to chill; *fig* cool, moderate; *vi* grow cold; *vr* catch a cold; *fig* cool off (of love, etc.)

resguardar *vt* to protect; shelter; *vr* take refuge; (*with de*) guard against; (*with con*) shelter by

resguardo *m*, protection, guard; *com* guarantee, security; *com* voucher; preservation; vigilance (to prevent smuggling, etc.); contraband guards

residencia *f*, stay, residence; home, domicile; *ecc* residence

residencial *a* residential; resident, residentiary

residente *a* resident. *mf* inhabitant. *m*, resident, minister resident (diplomatic)

residir *vi* to live, inhabit; reside officially; be found, be, exist

residuo *m*, residuum, remainder; *math* remainder; *chem* residue

resignación *f*, resignation; fortitude, submission

resignar *vt* to resign, relinquish; *vr* submit, resign oneself

resina *f*, resin

resistencia *f*, resistance, opposition; endurance; (*phys mech psy*) resistance

resistente *a* resistant; tough; hardy (of plants)

resistir *vi* to resist, oppose; reject; *vt* endure, bear; resist; *vr* fight, resist

resolución *f*, decision; boldness, daring; determination, resolution; decree

resoluto *a* resolute, bold; brief, concise; able, expert

resolver *vt irr* to determine, decide; summarize; solve; dissolve; analyze; (*phys med*) resolve; *vr* decide, determine; be reduced to, become; *med* resolve. *Pres. Ind.* **resuelvo, resuelves, resuelve, resuelven.** *Past Part.* **resuelto.** *Pres. Subjunc.* **resuelva, resuelvas, resuelva, resuelvan**

resollar *vi irr* to breathe; pant. See **degollar**

resonancia *f*, resonance, sonority, ring; fame, reputation

resonante *a* resonant; resounding

resonar *vi irr* to resound, echo. See **tronar**

resoplido, resoplo *m*, heavy breathing, pant, snort

resorber *vt* to reabsorb

resorción *f*, reabsorption

resorte *m*, *mech* spring; elasticity; *fig* means, instrument; *Lat. Am.* rubber band

respaldo *m*, back (of chairs, etc.); reverse side (of a piece of paper)

respectivo *a* respective

respecto *m*, relation, regard, reference. **con r. a,** *or* **r. a,** with regard to, with respect to, concerning

respetabilidad *f*, respectability; worthiness

respetable *a* worthy of respect; respectable; *fig* considerable, large

respetar *vt* to respect, revere

respeto *m*, respect, honor; consideration, reason. **de r.,** spare, extra; special, ceremonial

respetuoso *a* venerable, worthy of honor; respectful, courteous

respingar *vi* to flinch, wince, kick; *inf* be uneven, rise (hem of garments); *inf* do (a thing) grumblingly

respingo *m*, wincing; jerk, shake; *inf* gesture of reluctance or dislike

respiración *f*, breathing, respiration; ventilation

respiradero *m*, ventilator; air hole, vent; rest, breathing space

respirador *a* breathing; respiratory. *m*, respirator

respirar *vi* to breathe; exhale, give off; take courage; have a breathing space, rest; *inf* speak. **sin r.,** continuously, without stopping for breath

respiratorio *a* respiratory

respiro *m*, breathing; breathing space, respite

resplandecer *vi irr* to glitter, gleam; shine, excel. See **conocer**

resplandeciente *a* glittering, resplendent, shining

resplandor *m*, radiance, brilliance; glitter, gleam; majesty, splendor

responder *vt* to reply; satisfy, answer; *vi* reecho; requite, return; produce, provide; *fig* answer, have the desired effect; *com* (*with de*) answer for, guarantee; *com* correspond

respondón *a inf* pert, impudent, cheeky, given to answering back

responsabilidad *f*, responsibility

responsable *a* responsible

responso *m*, *ecc* response, responsory

respuesta *f*, answer, reply; response; refutation; repartee

resquebradura *f*, fissure, crevice, crack

resquebrajarse *vr* to crack, split

resquemar *vt* to bite, sting (of hot dishes)

resquicio *m*, crack, chink, slit; opportunity; *Lat. Am.* sign, trace, vestige

resta *f*, *math* subtraction; *math* remainder

restablecer *vt irr* to reestablish; restore; *vr* recover one's health; reestablish oneself. See **conocer**

restablecimiento *m*, reestablishment; restoration

restañar *vt* to re-tin; staunch

restar *vt math* to subtract; deduct; return (a ball); *vi* remain. **No me resta más que decir adiós,** It only remains for me to say good-by

restauración *f*, restoration; renovation

restaurante *m*, restaurant

restaurantero *m*, restaurant operator; restaurant owner; restaurateur

restaurar *vt* to recover, recuperate; renovate, repair; restore

restaurativo *a* and *m*, restorative

restinga *f*, sandbank, bar

restitución *f*, restitution

restituible *a* returnable, replaceable

restituir *vt irr* to return, give back; restore; reestablish; *vr* return to one's place of departure. See **huir**

resto *m*, rest, balance; *math* remainder; *pl* remains

restorán *m*, restaurant

restricción *f*, limitation, restriction

restrictivo *a* restrictive; restraining

restringir *vt* to limit, restrict; contract

resucitar *vt* to raise from the dead; *fig inf* revive; *vi* resuscitate

resuelto *a* audacious, daring; resolute, capable

resuello *m*, breathing; panting, hard breathing

resulta *f*, consequence, result; decision, resolution; vacant post. **de resultas de,** as the result of; in consequence of

resultado *m*, result, consequence, outcome

resultar *vi* to result, follow; turn out, happen; result (in); *inf* turn out well. **El vestido no me resulta,** The dress isn't a success on me

resumen *m*, summary. **en r.,** in short

resumir *vt* to summarize, abridge; sum up, recapitulate; *vr* be contained, be included

resurgimiento *m*, resurgence, revival

resurgir *vi* to reappear, rise again, revive; resuscitate

resurrección *f*, resurrection

retablo *m*, *arch* altarpiece, retable; frieze; series of pictures

retador, -a *mf*, *Lat. Am.* challenger

retaguardia *f*, rear guard. **a r.,** in the rear. **picar la r.,** to harass the rear guard

retajar *vt* to cut in the round; circumcise

retal *m*, clipping, filing, shaving; remnant

retama *f*, *bot* broom. **r. común** *or* **r. de olor,** Spanish broom. **r. de escobas,** common broom

retar *vt* to challenge; *inf* reproach, accuse

retardación *f*, retardment

retardar *vt* to retard, delay

retardo *m*, delay, retardment

retazo *m*, remnant, cutting; excerpt, fragment

retemblar *vi* to quiver, tremble constantly

retemplar *vt*, *Lat. Am.* to cheer up

retén *m*, stock, reserve, provision; *mil* reserve

retención *f*, retention

retener *vt irr* to keep, retain; recollect, remember; keep back; *law* detain; deduct. See **tener**

retenidamente *adv* retentively

retentiva *f*, retentiveness, memory

retentivo *a* retentive

reticencia *f*, reticence

reticente *a* reticent

retículo *m*, reticulum, network; *phys* reticle

retina *f*, retina

retintín *m*, ringing; tinkling; *inf* sarcastic tone

retiñir *vt* to tinkle, clink; jingle

retirada *f*, withdrawal; retirement; seclusion, refuge; *mil* retreat

retirado *a* remote, secluded; *mil* retired

retirar *vt* to withdraw; remove; repel, throw back; hide, put aside; *vr* withdraw; retire; *mil* retreat

retiro *m*, withdrawal; removal; seclusion, privacy; *mil* retreat; retirement; *ecc* retreat. **dar el r. (a),** to place on the retired list

reto *m*, challenge; threat

retocar *vt* to touch again or repeatedly; *phot* retouch; restore (pictures); *fig* put the finishing touch to

retoñar *vi* to sprout, shoot; *fig* revive, resuscitate

retoño *m*, sprout, shoot

retoque *m*, frequent touching; finishing touch; touch, slight attack

retorcer *vt irr* to twist; contort; confound with one's own argument; misconstrue, distort; *vr* contort; writhe. See **torcer**

retórica *f*, rhetoric; *pl inf* quibbling

retórico (-ca) *a* rhetorical. *n* rhetorician

retornar *vt* to return, give back; turn, twist; turn back; *vi* and *vr* return, go back

retorno *m*, return, going back; recompense, repayment; exchange; return journey

retorsión *f*, twisting, writhing; *fig* misconstruction

retortijón *m*, twisting, curling. **r. de tripas,** stomachache

retozar *vi* to skip, frisk, frolic, gambol; romp; *fig* be aroused (passions)

retozón *a* frolicsome

retracción *f*, drawing back, retraction

retractación *f*, retractation, recantation

retractar *vt* to retract, recant, withdraw

retráctil *a* retractile

retraer *vt irr* to bring back again; dissuade; buy back, redeem; *vr* take refuge; retire; withdraw; go into seclusion. See **traer**

retraído *a* fugitive, refugee; retired, solitary; timid, nervous, unsociable

retraimiento *m*, withdrawal; seclusion, privacy; refuge, asylum, sanctuary; timidity, unsociability

retranca *f, Lat. Am.* brake

retrancar *vt, Lat. Am.* to brake

retrasar *vt* to postpone, delay; turn back (the clock); *vi* be slow (of clocks); *vr* be behind time, be late; be backward (persons)

retraso *m*, lateness; delay, dilatoriness; loss of time (clocks); setting back (of the clock) (e.g. **El reloj lleva cinco minutos de r.,** The clock is five minutes slow)

retratar *vt* to paint or draw the portrait of; portray, describe; photograph; copy, imitate

retratería *f, Lat. Am.* photographer's studio

retratista *mf* portrait painter; photographer; portrayer

retrato *m*, portrait; portrayal; *fig* image, likeness

retrechería *f, inf* craftiness, evasiveness

retrete *m*, toilet, water closet

retribución *f*, recompense, reward

retribuir *vt irr* to recompense, reward. See **huir**

retroactivo *a* retroactive

retroceder *vi* to withdraw, move back, draw back; recede

retroceso *m*, retrocedence, withdrawal; *med* retrogression

retrogradación *f*, retrogression

retrógrado *a* retrogressive, retrograde; *pol* reactionary

retronar *vi irr* to bang, thunder, resound with noise. See **tronar**

retrospectivo *a* retrospective

retrotraer *vt irr* to antedate. See **traer**

retruécano *m*, antithesis; play on words, pun

retumbante *a* resounding; pompous, high-flown

retumbar *vi* to resound, echo, reverberate; roll (of thunder); roar (of a cannon)

retumbo *m*, reverberation, echo; rumble; roll (of thunder); roar (of a cannon, etc.)

reuma *m*, rheumatism

reumático *a* rheumatic

reumatismo *m*, rheumatism

reunión *f*, reunion, union; meeting; assembly, gathering

reunir *vt* to reunite; unite; join; gather, assemble; *vr* meet, assemble; unite

revacunación *f*, revaccination

revacunar *vt* to revaccinate

revalidación *f*, ratification, confirmation

revalidar *vt* to ratify, confirm; *vr* pass a final examination

revejido *a* prematurely old

revelación *f*, revelation; *phot* developing

revelador *a* revealing. *m, phot* developer

revelar *vt* to reveal; *phot* develop

revendedor (-ra) *a* reselling, retail. *n* retailer

revender *vt* to resell; retail (goods)

reventa *f*, resale; retail

reventar *vi irr* to burst, explode; break in foam (waves);

burst forth; *fig* burst (with impatience, etc.); *inf* explode (with anger, etc.); *vt* break, crush; *fig* wear out, exhaust; *inf* irritate, vex; *vr* burst; *fig* be exhausted. See **sentar**

reventón *a* bursting. *m*, explosion, bursting; steep hill; hole, fix, difficulty; uphill work, heavy toil

rever *vt irr* to look at again, revise; *law* retry. See **ver**

reverberación *f*, reflection (of light); reverberation, resounding

reverberar *vi* to reflect; resound, reverberate

reverbero *m*, reverberation; reflector; *Lat. Am.* small stove

reverdecer *vi irr* to grow green again; revive, acquire new vigor. See **conocer**

reverencia *f*, respect, veneration; bow; curtsy; *ecc* reverence (title)

reverencial *a* reverential, respectful

reverenciar *vt* to revere; honor; respect

reverendo *a* reverend; venerable; *inf* overprudent

reversión *f*, reversion

reverso *m*, wrong side, back; reverse side (of coins)

reverter *vi irr* to overflow. See **entender**

revertir *vi law* to revert

revés *m*, wrong side, back, reverse; cuff, slap; backhand (in ballgames); check, setback, reverse; disaster, misfortune. **al r.,** on the contrary; wrong side out. **de r.,** from left to right, counterclockwise

revesado *a* complicated, difficult; willful

revestimiento *m*, *mas* lining, coating

revestir *vt irr* to dress; *mas* coat, line; *fig* cover, clothe; *vr* be dressed or dress oneself; *fig* be captivated (by an idea); become haughty or full of oneself; rise to the occasion, develop qualities necessary. See **pedir**

reviejo *a* very old. *m*, dead branch (of trees)

revisar *vt* to revise; examine

revisión *f*, revision; reexamination; *law* retrial

revisor *a* revising, examining. *m*, reviser; ticket inspector

revista *f*, reexamination, revision; review, periodical; *theat* revue; reinspection; review (of a book, etc.); *law* new trial; *mil* review. **pasar r.,** to inspect; review

revivificación *f*, revivification

revivificar *vt* to revivify, revive

revivir *vi* to resuscitate; revive

revocación *f*, revocation, cancellation, annulment

revocar *vt* to revoke, annul; dissuade; repel; throw back; wash (walls); *law* discharge

revolcadero *m*, bathing place (of animals)

revolcar *vt irr* to knock down, trample underfoot; lay flat (in an argument); *vr* wallow; dig one's heels in, be obstinate. See **volcar**

revolotear *vi* to flutter, fly around; twirl; *vt* hurl, toss

revoltillo *m*, jumble, hodgepodge; confusion, tangle; *Venezuela* scrambled eggs

revoltoso *a* rebellious; mischievous, willful; intricate

revoltura *f, Mexico* dish of eggs and vegetables

revolución *f*, turn, revolution; rebellion, uprising; revolution

revolucionar *vt* to revolutionize

revolucionario (-ia) *a* and *n* revolutionary

revolver *vt irr* to turn over; turn upside down; wrap up; revolve; stir; reflect upon, consider; upset, cause disharmony; search through, disorder (papers, etc.); *vr* move from side to side; change (in the weather). See **resolver**

revólver *m*, revolver

revoque *m*, *mas* washing, whitewash; plastering

revuelco *m*, wallowing

revuelo *m*, second flight (of birds); irregular course of flight; disturbance, upset

revuelta *f*, second turn or revolution; revolt, rebellion; quarrel, fight; turning point; change of direction, turn; change (of opinions, posts, etc.)

revueltamente *adv* in confusion, higgledy-piggledy

revulsión *f*, revulsion

rexaminación *f*, reexamination

rexaminar *vt* to reexamine

rexpedir *vt* to forward, send on

rexportación *f,* reexport

rexportar *vt com* to reexport

rey *m,* king (in cards, chess); queen bee; *inf* swineherd; *fig* king, chief. *her* **r. de armas,** king-of-arms. **reyes magos,** magi. **día de Reyes,** Twelfth Night. **servir al r.,** to fight for the king

reyerta *f,* quarrel, row, rumpus

reyezuelo *m,* kinglet, petty king; golden-crested wren

rezagar *vt* to leave behind; postpone, delay; *vr* lag behind, straggle

rezar *vt* to pray, say prayers; say mass; *inf* state, say; *vi* pray; *inf* fume, grumble. **El edicto reza así,** The edict runs like this, The edict reads like this

rezo *m,* prayer; devotions

rezongar *vi* to grouse, grumble

rezumar(se) *vr* and *vi* to percolate, ooze through; *inf* leak out, be known

ría *f,* estuary, river mouth, firth

riachuelo *m,* rivulet, stream

riada *f,* flood. *aer* **r. de acero,** rain of flak

ribaldería *f,* ribaldry

ribaldo *a* ribald. *m,* knave

ribazo *m,* slope, incline

ribera *f,* bank, margin, shore, strand; *Lat. Am.* slum

ribereño (-ña) *a* and *n* riparian

ribero *m,* embankment, wall

ribete *m,* binding, border, trimming; stripe; increase, addition; dramatic touch, exaggeration; *pl* indications, signs

ribetear *vt sew* to bind, trim, edge

ricacho (-cha) *n inf* newly rich person, nouveau riche

ricahembra *f,* lady; daughter or wife of a Spanish noble *ant*

ricamente *adv* richly, opulently; beautifully, splendidly; luxuriously

ricino *m,* castor oil plant

rico *a* wealthy, rich; abundant; magnificent, splendid; delicious. **r. como Creso,** rich as Croesus

ricohombre *m,* nobleman *ant*

ricura *f, inf* richness, wealth

ridiculez *f,* absurd action or remark; ridiculousness; affectation; folly

ridiculizar *vt* to ridicule, poke fun at

ridículo *a* ridiculous, absurd; grotesque; preposterous, outrageous. *m,* reticule

riego *m,* watering, spraying; irrigation

riel *m,* ingot; rail (of a train or streetcar)

rielar *vi* to glimmer, glisten; glitter; shimmer

rienda *f,* rein (gen. *pl*); restraint; *pl* administration, government. **a r. suelta,** swiftly; without restraint

riesgo *m,* risk, danger

riesgoso, -a *a, Lat. Am.* dangerous, risky

rifa *f,* raffle; quarrel, disagreement

rifar *vt* to raffle; *vi* quarrel, fall out

rifle *m,* rifle

rigidez *f,* stiffness; rigidity; harshness

rígido *a* stiff; rigid; inflexible; severe, harsh

rigor *m,* severity, sternness; rigor; hardness; inflexibility; *med* rigor. **en r.,** strictly speaking. **ser de r.,** to be essential, be indispensable

rigorista *mf* martinet

riguroso *a* rigorous; harsh, cruel; austere, rigid; strict, exact, scrupulous

rijoso *a* quarrelsome; lascivious

rima *f,* rhyme, rime; heap; *pl* lyrics

rimador (-ra) *a* rhyming, rimer. *n* rhymer, rimer

rimar *vi* to compose verses; *vi* and *vt* rhyme, rime

rimbombo *m,* reverberation (of a sound)

rimero *m,* heap, pile

Rin, el the Rhine

rincón *m,* corner, angle; retreat, hiding place; *inf* home, nest, nook

rinconada *f,* corner, angle

rinconera *f,* corner cupboard; corner table

ringlera *f,* file, line, row

ringlero *m,* guiding line for writing

ringorrangos *m pl, inf* exaggerated flourishes in writing; *inf* unnecessary frills or ornaments

ringueletear *vi, Lat. Am.* to wander through the streets

rinoceronte *m,* rhinoceros

riñón *m,* kidney; *fig* center, heart; *pl anat* back

río *m,* river; *fig* stream, flood

rioja *m,* red wine from Rioja

rioplatense *a* of the River Plate area; *mf* native of the River Plate area; resident of the River Plate area

ripio *m,* remains, rest; debris, rubbish; *lit* padding; verbiage, prolixity. **no perder r.,** to lose no occasion or opportunity

riqueza *f,* riches, wealth; abundance; richness, magnificence

risa *f,* laugh; laughter; cause of amusement, joke

risco *m,* crag

riscoso *a* craggy

risible *a* laughable

risoles *m pl,* rissoles

risotada *f,* loud laugh

ristra *f,* string (of onions, etc.); file, line, row

risueño *a* smiling; cheerful; pleasant, agreeable; favorable, hopeful

rítmico *a* rhythmic

ritmo *m,* rhythm

rito *m,* rite

ritualismo *m,* ritualism

ritualista *mf* ritualist

rivalidad *f,* rivalry, competition; hostility

rivalizar *vi* to compete, rival

rizado *a,* curling; pleating, crimping; rippling, ruffling

rizar *vt* to curl (hair); ripple, ruffle (of water); pleat, crimp; *vr* be naturally wavy (of hair)

rizo *m,* curl, ringlet; cut velvet. *aer* **hacer el r.,** to loop the loop; *naut* to take in reefs

rizoso *a* naturally curly or wavy (hair)

robador (-ra) *a* robbing. *n* robber, thief. *m,* abductor

robar *vt* to rob; abduct; wash away, eat away (rivers, sea); remove honey from the hive; draw (in cards, dominoes); *fig* capture (love, etc.)

roblar *vt* to reinforce, strengthen; clinch

roble *m,* oak tree; oak; *fig* bulwark, tower of strength

robledo *m,* oak grove

roblón *m,* rivet

robo *m,* theft, robbery; booty

robustecer *vt irr* to strengthen. See **conocer**

robustez *f,* strength, robustness

robusto *a* vigorous, robust, hearty, strong

roca *f,* rock; *fig* tower of strength

roce *m,* rubbing, brushing, touching, friction; social intercourse

rociada *f,* dewing; sprinkling; dew-wet grass given as medicine to horses and mules; *fig* shower; general slander; harsh rebuke

rociar *vi* to fall as dew; drizzle; *vt* sprinkle, spray; *fig* shower (with)

rocín *m,* sorry nag; hack; *inf* ignoramus, boor

rocinante *m,* poor nag (alluding to Don Quixote's horse)

rocío *m,* dew; dewdrop; drizzle, light shower; *fig* sprinkling, spray

rocoso *a* rocky

rodaballo *m,* turbot; *inf* crafty man

rodada *f,* wheel mark or track

rodado *a* dappled (of horses)

rodaje *m,* wheeling; shooting (of a film)

rodante *a* rolling

rodar *vi* to roll; revolve, turn; run on wheels; wander, roam; be moved about; be plentiful, abound; happen successively; (*with por*) fall down, roll down

rodear *vi* to walk around; go by a roundabout way; *fig* beat around the bush; *vt* encircle, surround; besiege; *WH* round up (cattle)

rodela *f,* round shield; buckler

rodeno *a* red (of rocks, earth, etc.)

rodeo *m*, encirclement; indirect and longer way; trick to evade pursuit; *WH* rodeo, roundup; stockyard, cattle enclosure; *fig* beating around the bush; evasive reply

rodera *f*, rail, track, line; cart rut or track

rodilla *f*, knee; floor cloth. **de rodillas**, on one's knees. **ponerse de rodillas**, *or* **hincar las rodillas**, to kneel down

rodillazo *m*, push with the knee

rodillera *f*, kneecap, kneepad; mend at the knee of garments; bagginess of trouser knees

rodillo *m*, roller; traction engine; *print* inking roller; garden roller. **r. de pastas**, *cul* rolling pin

rododendro *m*, rhododendron

rodrigón *m*, stake, prop (for plants); *inf* old retainer who serves as a ladies' escort

roedor *a* gnawing; *fig* nagging; biting. *a* and *m*, rodent

roedura *f*, biting, gnawing; corrosion

roer *vt irr* to gnaw, nibble, eat; corrode, wear away; trouble, afflict. *Pres. Ind.* **roigo, roes**, etc. *Preterite* **royó, royeron.** *Imperf. Subjunc.* **royese**, etc.

rogación *f*, request, supplication, entreaty; *ecc* rogation

rogador (-ra) *a* requesting; beseeching. *n* suppliant

rogar *vt irr* to request; beseech, beg. See **contar**

rogativo *a* supplicatory, petitioning

roído *a* gnawed, eaten; *inf* miserable, stingy

rojal *a* red (of soil, etc.). *m*, red earth

rojear *vi* to appear red; be reddish

rojete *m*, rouge

rojez *f*, redness

rojizo *a* reddish

rojo *a* red; fair; red-gold (of hair); *pol* radical, red

rol *m*, roll, list

roldana *f*, pulley wheel

rollizo *a* round; plump, sturdy. *m*, log

rollo *m*, roll; *cul* rolling pin; log; town cross or pillar; anything rolled (paper, etc.); twist (of tobacco)

Roma Rome

romance *a* and *m*, romance (language). *m*, Spanish; ballad; romance of chivalry; *pl fig* fairy tales, excuses. **en buen r.,** *fig* in plain words

romancear *vt* to translate from Latin into the spoken language; translate into Spanish; paraphrase the Spanish to assist translation; *Lat. Am.* to flirt

romancero (-ra) *n* balladeer. *m*, collection of ballads

romancista *mf* romancist

románico *a* arch Romanesque

romanista *mf* expert in Roman law or Romance languages and literature

romanizar *vt* to romanize; *vr* become romanized

romano (-na) *a* and *n* Roman. **a la romana**, in the Roman way. **cabello a la romana**, *inf* bobbed hair

romanticismo *m*, romanticism

romántico (-ca) *a* romantic; emotional; fanciful. *n* romantic; romanticist

rombo *m*, rhombus

romería *f*, pilgrimage; excursion, picnic (made on a saint's day)

romero (-ra) *m*, rosemary. *n* pilgrim

romo *a* blunt, dull, unsharpened; flat (of noses); *m. Lat. Am.* rum

rompecabezas *m*, bludgeon; knuckleduster; *inf* teaser, puzzle, riddle; jigsaw puzzle

rompeimágenes *mf* iconoclast

rompeolas *m*, jetty, breakwater

romper *vt* to break; shatter, break into fragments; spoil, ruin; break up, plow; *fig* cut, divide (of water, etc.); *fig* end, break; interrupt; infringe, break; *vi* break; break (of waves); sprout, flower; (*with prep a*) begin to. **Rompió a hablar,** He broke into speech. *Past Part.* **roto**

rompiente *a* breaking. *m*, reef, shoal

rompimiento *m*, break, rupture; crack, split; breakage; infringement; plowing up; *fig* dividing (water, etc.); spoiling, ruining; opening (of buds, etc.)

ron *m*, rum

roncar *vi* to snore; *fig* roar, howl (of the sea, wind, etc.); *inf* brag

roncear *vi* to be dilatory or unwilling; *inf* flatter, cajole; *naut* lag behind, sail slowly

roncero *a* dilatory, slow; grumbling, complaining; cajoling, flattering; *Lat. Am.* sly

roncha *f*, wheal; bruise, bump; *inf* money lost through trickery; thin, round slice

ronco *a* hoarse, husky

ronda *f*, round, beat, patrol; serenading party; *inf* round (of drinks)

rondador *m*, watchman; roundsman; serenader; night wanderer

rondalla *f*, tale, fairy tale

rondar *vi* to patrol, police; walk the streets by night; serenade; *vt* haunt; hover about; *inf* overcome (of sleep, etc.)

ronquear *vi* to be hoarse

ronquera *f*, hoarseness

ronquido *m*, snore; hoarse sound

ronronear *vi* to purr (of cats)

ronzal *m*, halter

ronzar *vt* to munch, crack with the teeth

roña *f*, mange (in sheep); grime, filth; mold; moral corruption; *inf* stinginess; *inf* trick, deception

roñería *f*, *inf* meanness, stinginess

roñoso *a* scabby; filthy; rusty; *inf* mean, stingy

ropa *f*, fabric, material, stuff; clothes, wearing apparel; garment, outfit; robe (of office). **r. blanca**, underclothes; (domestic) linen. **r. hecha**, ready-made clothing. **r. talar**, long gown; cassock

ropaje *m*, clothes, garments; vestments; drapery; *fig* form, outline

ropavejería *f*, old-clothes shop

ropavejero (-ra) *n* old-clothes dealer

ropería *f*, clothier's shop or trade; wardrobe; cloakroom

ropero (-ra) *n* clothier; keeper of the wardrobe. *m*, wardrobe; charitable organization

ropilla *f*, doublet

ropón *m*, a loose-fitting gown generally worn over clothes

roque *m*, rook (in chess)

roqueño *a* rocky; hard as rock

roquete *m*, *ecc* rochet; barb of a lance

rorro *m*, *inf* infant, baby

rosa *f*, rose; anything rose-shaped; artificial rose; red spot on the body; *arch* rose window; *pl* rosettes. *m*, rose color. **r. de los vientos**, mariner's compass. **r. laurel**, oleander

rosado *a* rose-colored; rose; rosé (wines)

rosal *m*, rose tree. **r. de tallo**, standard rose tree

rosaleda, rosalera *f*, rose garden

rosario *m*, rosary; *fig* string; chain pump; *inf* backbone

rosbif *m*, roast beef

rosca *f*, screw and nut; *cul* twist (of bread or cake); spiral

roscado *a* twisted, spiral

rosear *vi* to turn to rose, become rose-colored

róseo *a* rose-colored

roseta *f*, *dim* small rose; rosette; rose of a watering can; rosette copper; *pl* toasted maize. **r. de fiebre,** rush of fever

rosetón *m*, large rosette; *arch* rose window

rosicler *m*, rose-pink (first flush of dawn)

rosillo *a* light red; roan (of horses)

rosmaro *m*, manatee, sea cow

roso *a* bald, worn; red

rosquete *m*, *Lat. Am.* bun

rosquilla *f*, ring-shaped cake

rosquillero (-ra) *n* seller of rosquillas

rostrituerto *a inf* wry-faced (from sadness or anger)

rostro *m*, bird's beak; face, visage. **conocer de r.,** to know by sight. **dar en r.,** *fig* to throw in one's face

rota *f*, *mil* defeat; *ecc* Rota; *bot* rattan

rotación *f*, rotation. **r. de cultivos,** rotation of crops

rotativa *f*, rotary printing press

rotativo *a* rotary

rotatorio *a* rotatory

rotisería *f, Lat. Am.* steakhouse; grillroom

roto *a* shabby, ragged; vicious, debauched

rotograbado *m,* rotogravure

rotonda *f,* rotunda

rótula *f,* rotula, patella

rotular *vt* to label; give a title or heading to

rótulo *m,* title; poster, placard; label

rotundamente *adv* tersely, roundly, plainly

rotundidad *f,* rotundity; roundness; finality (of words, etc.)

rotundo *a* round; rotund; sonorous; final, plain (of words, etc.)

rotura *f,* breaking, shattering; plowing up; breakage; rupture

roturar *vt agr* to break up, plow up

roya *f,* rust, mildew; tobacco

roza *f, agr* clearing (of weeds, etc.); ground ready for sowing. **de r. abierta,** open cast (of mining)

rozador *m, Lat. Am.* machete

rozadura *f,* rubbing, friction; abrasion, chafing

rozagante *a* long and elaborate (dresses); upstanding; handsome; strapping, fine

rozamiento *m,* grazing, brushing, rubbing; discord, disharmony, disagreement; *mech* friction

rozar *vt agr* to clear of weeds; crop, nibble; scrape; brush against, touch; *vi* brush, rub, touch; *vr* have dealings with, know; stammer; be like, resemble

rúa *f,* village street; highway

ruar *vi* to walk or ride through the streets; parade through the streets flirting with the ladies

rubeola *f,* rubella

rubí *m,* ruby; jewel (of a watch)

rubia *f, bot* madder; blonde (girl, woman)

rubicundez *f,* rubicundity, ruddiness, redness

rubicundo *a* red-gold; ruddy-complexioned; reddish

rubio *a* red-gold, gold; fair, blond

rubor *m,* blush, flush; bashfulness

ruborizarse *vr* to blush; be shamefaced

ruboroso *a* shamefaced; blushing

rúbrica *f,* rubric; personal mark, flourish added to one's signature

rubricar *vt* to sign and seal; sign with an X or other symbol; sign with a flourish

rubro *a* red

rucio *a* fawn, light-gray (of animals); *inf* going gray, gray-haired

rudamente *adv* rudely, abruptly, churlishly; roughly

rudeza *f,* roughness; rudeness, uncouthness; stupidity

rudimentario *a* rudimentary

rudimento *m,* embryo; *pl* rudiments

rudo *a* rough; unfinished; uncouth, boorish, rude; stupid

rueca *f,* distaff (in spinning); spinning wheel; curve, twist

rueda *f,* wheel; group, circle; spread of a peacock's tail; roller, castor; round piece or slice; turn, chance; succession (of events); wheel (used for torture). **r. libre,** freewheeling. *inf* **hacer la r. (a),** to flatter, make a fuss of

ruedero *m,* wheelwright

ruedo *m,* turning, rotation; circumference; lined hem of a cassock; circuit

ruego *m,* request, entreaty

rufián *m,* ruffian; pimp

rufo *a* fair; red-haired; curly-haired

rugido *m,* roaring, roar; creaking; gnashing; rumbling

rugir *vi* to roar; squeak, creak; gnash (the teeth)

ruibarbo *m,* rhubarb

ruido *m,* noise, din; disturbance; rumor. **hacer** (*or* **meter**) **r.,** to cause a sensation. *inf* **ser más el r. que las nueces,** to be much ado about nothing

ruidoso *a* noisy; notable

ruin *a* base, vile; despicable; mean; puny

ruina *f,* ruin, downfall; financial ruin; fall, decline; *pl* ruins

ruinar *vt* to ruin

ruindad *f,* baseness; meanness; pettiness, unworthiness; mean trick, despicable action

ruinoso *a* half-ruined; ruinous; useless, worthless

ruiseñor *m,* nightingale

ruleta *f,* roulette

rumano (-na) *a* and *n* Romanian. *m,* Romanian (language)

rumba *f* rumba; *Lat. Am.* party (celebration)

rumbo *m, naut* course, way, route; direction; *inf* swank; *Lat. Am.* party (celebration) **con r. a,** headed for, in the direction of. **hacer r. a,** to sail for; make for

rumboso *a inf* pompous, dignified; open-handed, generous

rumia *f,* rumination; cud

rumiante *a* and *mf zool* ruminant. *a inf* reflective, meditative

rumiar *vt zool* to ruminate; *inf* reflect upon, chew on; *inf* fume, rage

rumor *m,* noise; rumor; murmur, babble; dull sound

rúnico *a* runic

runrunearse *v impers* to be rumored

rupia *f,* rupee

ruptura *f, fig* rupture; *surg* hernia

rural *a* rustic, rural

ruralmente *adv* rurally

Rusia Russia

rusificar *vt* to russianize

ruso (-sa) *a* and *n* Russian. *m,* Russian (language)

rusticación *f,* rustication

rusticar *vi* to rusticate

rusticidad *f,* rusticity; boorishness, coarseness

rústico *a* rustic, country; boorish, uncouth. *m,* countryman; yokel; peasant. **en rústica,** in paper covers (of books)

ruta *f,* route; *fig* way. **r. de evitación,** bypass, detour

ruteno (-na) *a* and *n* Ruthenian. *m,* Ruthenian (language)

rutilante *a poet* sparkling, glowing

rutilar *vi poet* to gleam, sparkle

rutina *f,* routine

rutinario *a* routine

rutinero (-ra) *a* routinistic. *n* routinist

S

sábado *m,* Saturday; Jewish sabbath. **s. de gloria,** Easter Saturday

sábalo *m, icht* shad

sabana *f,* savannah

sábana *f,* bed sheet; altar cloth. *inf* **pegársele (a uno) las sábanas,** to be tied to the bed, get up late

sabandija *f,* any unpleasant insect or reptile; *fig* vermin

sabanero (-ra) *n* savannah dweller. *a* savannah

sabanilla *f,* small piece of linen (kerchief, towel, etc.); altar cloth

sabañón *m,* chilblain

sabatario *a* sabbatarian

sabático *a* sabbatical

sabatino *a* Saturday, Sabbath

sabedor *a* aware; knowledgeable, knowing

sabelotodo *mf inf* know-it-all

saber *m,* learning; wisdom

saber *vt irr* to know; be able to, know how; *vi* know; be shrewd, be well aware of; (*with prep a*) taste of; be like or similar to. **s. al dedillo,** *fig* to have at one's fingertips. **a s.,** viz., namely. *inf* **no s. cuántas son cinco,** not to know how many beans make five. **no s. dónde meterse,** to be overcome by shame; have the jitters. **No sé cuántos,** I don't know how many. **No sé quién,** I don't know who (which person). **No sé qué,** I don't know what. **un no sé qué,** a certain something; a touch (of). **¡Quién sabe!** Who knows!; Time will tell. *Pres. Ind.* **sé, sabes,** etc. *Fut.* **sabré,** etc. *Condit.* **sabría,** etc. *Preterite* **supe,** etc. *Pres. Subjunc.* **sepa,** etc. *Imperf. Subjunc.* **supiese,** etc.

sabiamente *adv* wisely, prudently

sabidillo (-lla) *a* and *n inf* know-it-all

sabiduría *f*, prudence; wisdom; erudition, learning; knowledge, awareness. **Libro de la S. de Salomón,** Book of Wisdom

sabiendas, a *adv* knowingly, consciously

sabihondo (-da) *n inf* know-it-all

sabio (-ia) *a* wise; learned, erudite; prudent, sagacious; knowing (of animals); performing (of animals). *n* wise person; scholar, erudite person

sablazo *m*, saber thrust or wound; *inf* sponging, taking advantage of. **dar un s. (a),** *inf* to sponge on; touch for money

sable *m*, saber; *her* sable; *inf* talent for sponging on people. *a her* sable

sablear *vi inf* to touch for invitations, loans, etc.; cadge

sablista *mf inf* sponger, cadger

saboneta *f*, hunting case watch, hunter

sabor *m*, taste, flavor; impression, effect. **a s.,** to taste; at pleasure

saboreamiento *m*, savoring; relishing, enjoyment

saborear *vt* to flavor, season; relish, savor; appreciate, enjoy; *vr* relish, savor; enjoy

saboreo *m*, tasting; savoring; relishing

sabotaje *m*, sabotage

saboteador *m*, saboteur

Saboya Savoy

saboyano (-na) *a* and *n* Savoyard

sabroso *a* tasty, savory, well-seasoned; delightful, delicious; *inf* piquant, racy; *Lat. Am.* garrulous, talkative

sabueso *m*, cocker spaniel. **s. de artois,** hound

sabuloso *a* sandy

saburra *f*, fur (on the tongue)

saca *f*, drawing out, removing; export, transport, shipping; removal, extraction; legal copy (of a document). **estar de s.,** to be on sale; *inf* be marriageable (of women)

sacabocados *m*, punch (tool); *inf* cinch, easy matter

sacabotas *m*, bootjack

sacabrocas *m*, tack puller

sacabuche *m*, *mus* sackbut; sackbut player; *inf* insignificant little man; *naut* hand pump

sacacorchos *m*, corkscrew

sacacuartos *m*, *inf* catchpenny

sacada *f*, territory cut off from a province

sacadineros *m*, *inf* catchpenny

sacamanchas *mf.* See **quitamanchas**

sacamantas *m*, *inf* tax collector

sacamiento *m*, removing, taking out

sacamuelas *mf* dentist; charlatan, quack; *inf* windbag

sacapotras *m*, *inf* unskilled surgeon

sacar *vt* to draw out; extract; pull out; take out; remove; dispossess, turn out; free from, relieve; examine, investigate; extort (the truth); extract (sugar, etc.); win (prizes, games); copy; discover, find out; elect by ballot; obtain, achieve; exclude; show, exhibit; quote, mention; produce, invent; manufacture; note down; put forth; unsheath (swords); bowl (in cricket); serve (in tennis). **s. a bailar,** to invite to dance. **s. a luz,** to publish, print; reveal, bring out. **s. a paseo,** to take for a walk. **s. de pila,** to be a godfather or godmother to. **s. en claro** *or* **s. en limpio,** to copy; conclude, infer, gather. **sacarse en conclusión que . . . ,** the conclusion is that . . .

sacarificar *vt* to saccharify

sacarina *f*, saccharine

sacasillas *mf*, *inf theat* stagehand

sacerdocio *m*, priesthood

sacerdotal *a* priestly

sacerdote *m*, priest

sacerdotisa *f*, priestess. **sumo s.,** high priestess

saciable *a* satiable

sachar *vt* to weed

sacho *m*, weeder

saciar *vt* to satisfy; satiate; *vr* be satiated

saciedad *f*, satiety, surfeit

saco *m*, handbag; sack, bag; sackful; sack coat; *biol* sac; *mil* sack, plundering. **s. de noche,** dressing case, weekend case. *inf* **no echar en s. roto,** not to forget, to remember

sacramentalmente *adv* sacramentally; in confession

sacramentar *vt* to consecrate; administer the Blessed Sacrament; hide, conceal

sacramentario (-ia) *n* sacramentalist; sacramentarian

sacramento *m*, sacrament; *ecc* Host; *ecc* mystery. **s. del altar,** Eucharist. **con todos los sacramentos,** with all the sacraments; done in order, complete with all formalities. **recibir los sacramentos,** to receive the last sacraments

sacratísimo *a* most sacred

sacrificadero *m*, place of sacrifice

sacrificador (-ra) *a* sacrificing. *n* sacrificer

sacrificar *vt* to sacrifice; slaughter; *vr* consecrate oneself to God; sacrifice oneself; devote or dedicate oneself (to)

sacrificio *m*, sacrifice; offering, dedication; surrendering, forgoing; compliance, submission. **s. del altar,** sacrifice of the mass

sacrilegio *m*, sacrilege

sacrílego *a* sacrilegious

sacristán *m*, sacristan; sexton; hoop (for dresses). *inf* **s. de amén,** yes-man. *inf* **ser gran s.,** to be very crafty

sacristana *f*, wife of a sacristan or sexton; nun in charge of a convent sacristy

sacristanía *f*, office of a sacristan or sexton

sacristía *f*, sacristy; vestry; office of a sacristan or sexton

sacro *a* sacred; *anat* sacral

sacrosanto *a* sacrosanct

sacudida *f*, shake, shaking; jerk, jar, jolt; twitch, pull; *aer* bump

sacudido *a* unsociable; difficult, wayward; determined, bold

sacudidor (-ra) *a* shaking; jerking. *n* shaker. *m*, carpet beater; duster

sacudidura *f*, shaking (especially to remove dust); jerking

sacudimiento *m*, shake, shaking; jerk; twitch, pull; jolt

sacudir *vt* to shake; flap, wave; jerk, twitch; beat, bang; shake off; *vr* shake off, avoid

sadismo *m*, sadism

sadista *mf* sadist

sadístico *a* sadistic

saduceo (-ea) *a* Sadducean. *n* Sadducee

saeta *f*, arrow, dart; clock hand, watch hand; magnetic needle; short sung expression of religious ecstasy; *ast* Sagitta

saetada *f*, **saetazo** *m*, arrow wound

saetera *f*, loophole; small window

saetero *a* arrow, arrow-like. *m*, archer, bowman

safado, -a *a*, *Lat. Am.* cheeky, impudent, saucy

saga *f*, saga

sagacidad *f*, sagacity

sagaz *a* sagacious, shrewd; farseeing; quick on the scent (dogs)

sagital *a* arrow-shaped

sagitario *m*, archer; *ast* Sagittarius

sagrado *a* sacred; holy; sacrosanct, venerable; accursed, detestable. *m*, sanctuary, refuge; haven

sagrario *m*, sanctuary; sacrarium

sagú *m*, sago

Sáhara, el the Sahara

sahornarse *vr* to chafe, grow sore

sahorno *m*, chafing, abrasion

sahumado *a* improved, rendered more excellent; perfumed; fumigated

sahumador *m*, perfumer; fumigating vessel

sahumar *vt* to perfume; fumigate. See **desahuciar**

sahumerio *m*, perfuming; fumigation; fume, smoke

saín *m*, fat, grease; sardine oil (for lamps); grease spot (on clothes)

sainar *vt* to fatten up (animals)

sainete *m*, *cul* sauce; *theat* one-act parody or burlesque; farce; delicacy, tidbit; delicate taste (of food)

sainetero *m*, writer of sainetes

sainetesco *a* pertaining to sainetes; burlesque, satirical

sajar *vt surg* to scarify

Sajonia Saxony

sajón (-ona) *a* and *n* Saxon

sal *f*, salt; wit; grace, gracefulness. **s. de cocina,** common kitchen salt. **s. de la Higuera,** Epsom salts. **s. gema,** rock salt. **s. marina,** sea salt. **sales inglesas,** smelling salts. *inf* **estar hecho de s.,** to be full of wit. *inf* **hacerse s. y agua,** to melt away, disappear (of riches, etc.)

sala *f*, drawing room; large room, hall; *law* courtroom; *law* bench; **s. de apelación,** court of appeal. **s. de hospital,** hospital ward. **s. de justicia,** court of justice. **s. de lectura,** reading room. *law* **guardar s.,** to respect the court

salacidad *f*, lewdness, salaciousness

saladero *m*, salting or curing place; *WH* meat packing factory

saladillo *m*, salt pork

salado *a* salty, briny; brackish; witty; attractive, amusing

salador (-ra) *a* salting, curing. *n* salter, curer. *m*, curing place

saladura *f*, salting, curing

salamandra *f*, salamander; fire sprite

salar *vt* to salt; season with salt; oversalt; cure, pickle (meat, etc.); *m*, *Lat. Am.* salt marsh

salario *m*, salary

salaz *a* lewd, lecherous

salazón *f*, salting, curing; salt meat or fish trade

salazonero *a* salting, curing

salchicha *f*, sausage

salchichería *f*, sausage shop

salchichero (-ra) *n* sausage maker, sausage seller

salchichón *m*, *cul* salami, kind of sausage

saldar *vt com* to settle, pay in full; sell out cheap; balance

saldista *mf* remnant buyer

saldo *m*, *com* balance; closing of an account; bargain sale. **s. acreedor,** credit balance. **s. deudor,** debit balance. **s. líquido,** net balance

salero *m*, saltshaker, saltcellar; salt storage warehouse; *inf* wit

saleta *f*, *dim* small hall; royal antechamber; court of appeal

salida *f*, going out; leaving; departure; sailing; exit, way out; projection, protrusion; *fig* escape, way out; outcome, result; witty remark; *mil* sally; *com* outlay, expense; *com* opening, sale, salability; environs, outskirts; *Argentina* bathrobe **s. de dólares,** dollar drain. **s. de tono,** *inf* an impertinent remark. **dar s.,** *com* to enter on the credit side

salidero *a* fond of going out; *m*, exit, way out

salidizo *m*, *arch* projection. *a* projecting

saliente *a* outgoing; salient, projecting. *m*, east; projection; salient. **s. continental,** continental shelf

salina *f*, salt mine; saltworks

salinero *m*, salt merchant; salter; salt worker

salino *a* saline. *m*, *med* saline

salir *vi irr* to go out; depart, leave; succeed in getting out; escape; appear (of the sun, etc.); sprout, show green; fade, come out (of stains); project, stand out; grow, develop; turn out, result; happen, take place; cost; sail; end (of seasons, time); lead off, start (some games); be published (books); do (well or badly), succeed or fail; appear, show oneself; be drawn, win (lot-

tery tickets); balance, come out right (accounts); be elected; become; give up (posts); lead to (of streets, etc.); *naut* overtake; (*with prep a*) guarantee, be surety for; resemble, be like; (*with con*) utter, come out with; commit, do inopportunely; succeed in, achieve (e.g. **Salió con la suya,** He got his own way); (*with de*) originate in; break away from (traditions, conventions); get rid of; (*with por*) stand up for, protect; go surety for, guarantee. *vr* leak; boil over; overflow; (*with con*) achieve, get; (*with de*) *fig* break away from. *theat* **s. a la escena,** to enter, come on to the stage. **s. de,** to recover (from an illness). **no acabar de s. de,** to not be completely recovered from. **s. del apuro,** to get out of trouble. **s. de estampía,** to stampede (of animals). **s. pitando,** *inf* to get out in a hurry. **Esta idea no salió de Juan,** This wasn't John's idea. **salga lo que saliere,** *inf* come what may. . . . *Pres. Ind.* **salgo, sales,** etc. *Fut.* **saldré,** etc. *Condit.* **saldría,** etc. *Pres. Subjunc.* **salga,** etc.

salitral *a* nitrous. *m*, saltpeter bed

salitre *m*, saltpeter

salitrería *f*, saltpeter works

salitrero *n* saltpeter worker or dealer

saliva *f*, saliva. *inf* **tragar s.,** to put up with; be unable to speak through emotion

salivación *f*, salivation

salival *a* salivary

salivar *vi* to salivate; spit

salmantino (-na) *a* and *n* Salamanca

salmear *vi* to intone psalms

salmista *mf* psalmist; psalmodist, psalm chanter

salmo *m*, psalm

salmodia *f*, psalmody; *inf* drone; psalter

salmodiar *vi* to chant psalms; *vt* drone

salmón *m*, salmon

salmonado *a* salmon-like

salmonera *f*, salmon net

salmonete *m*, red mullet

salmuera *f*, brine

salobre *a* salt, salty; brackish

salobridad *f*, saltiness

salomar *vi naut* to sing chanteys

salón *m*, drawing room; large room or hall; reception room; salon, reception, social gathering. **s. de muestras,** showroom

saloncillo *m*, *dim* small room; *theat* greenroom; rest room

salpicadura *f*, sprinkling, spattering, splashing

salpicar *vt* to sprinkle, scatter; bespatter, splash

salpicón *m*, *cul* kind of salmagundi; *inf* hodgepodge; spattering

salpimentar *vt irr* to season with pepper and salt; sprinkle; *fig* leaven, enliven (a speech, etc.). See **regimentar**

salpresar *vt* to preserve in salt, salt

salpullido *m*, rash, skin eruption

salsa *f*, sauce; gravy. **s. mahonesa** or **s. mayonesa,** mayonnaise sauce. **s. mayordoma,** sauce maître d'hôtel

salsera *f*, sauce boat, gravy boat

saltabanco *m*, mountebank; street entertainer, juggler

saltabarrancos *mf inf* madcap, harum-scarum

saltable *a* jumpable

saltadero *m*, jumping ground; fountain, jet

saltador (-ra) *a* jumping. *n* jumper; acrobat. *m*, jump rope, skip rope

saltamontes *m*, grasshopper

saltaojos *m*, peony

saltaparedes *mf inf* madcap, romp

saltar *vi* to jump, leap, spring; prance; frisk, gambol; rebound; blow up; burst, break asunder; pop (of corks); fly off, come off (buttons, etc.); gush out, shoot up (liquids); break apart, be shattered; be obvious, stand out; come to mind, suggest itself; show anger; *fig* let slip, come out with (remarks); *vt* leap or jump over; poke out (eyes); cover (the female); omit, pass over; blow up, explode. **s. a la cuerda,** to jump rope, play with a skip rope. **s. a la vista,** to be obvious, leap to the eye. **s. diciendo,** *inf* to come out with, say

saltarín (-ina) *a* dancing. *n* dancer

saltatriz *f,* ballet dancer, female acrobat

saltatumbas *m,* (*inf* contemptuous) cleric who makes his living off funerals

salteador *m,* highwayman

salteamiento *m,* highway robbery, holdup; assault, attack

saltear *vt* to hold up and rob; assault, attack; jump from one thing to another, do intermittently; forestall; surprise, amaze

salterio *m,* psaltery

saltimbanco, saltimbanqui *m, inf.* See **saltabanco**

salto *m,* jump, leap, bound; leapfrog (game); precipice, ravine; waterfall; assault; important promotion; omission (of words). **s. de agua,** waterfall. **s. de cama,** peignoir, bathrobe. **s. de campana,** overturning. *inf* **s. de mal año,** sudden improvement in circumstances. **s. de mata,** flight, escape. **s. mortal,** leap of death; somersault. **s. de pie,** spillway. **dar un s.,** to leap. **en un s.,** at one jump; swiftly

saltón *a* jumping, leaping; prominent (teeth, eyes). *m,* grasshopper

salubérrimo *a sup* **salubre** most healthy

salubre *a* salubrious, healthful

salubridad *f,* healthfulness

salud *f,* health; salvation; welfare, well-being; *ecc* state of grace; *pl* civilities, greetings. **¡S. y pesetas!** Here's to your good health and prosperity! (on drinking). **gastar s.,** to enjoy good health. *inf* **vender** (*or* **verter**) **s.,** to look full of health

saludable *a* healthy, wholesome

saludador (-ra) *a* greeting, saluting. *n* greeter. *m,* charlatan, quack

saludar *vt* to greet, salute; hail (as king, etc.); send greetings to; bow; *mil* fire a salute

saludo *m,* greeting, salutation; bow; (*mil nav*) salute

salutación *f,* greeting, salutation; Ave Maria

salutífero *a* salubrious

salva *f,* salutation, greeting; (*mil nav*) salvo, volley; salute (of guns); salver; ordeal (to establish innocence); solemn assurance, oath; sampling, tasting (of food, drink). **s. de veintiún cañonazos,** twenty-one–gun salute

salvación *f,* liberation, deliverance; salvation

salvado *m,* bran

salvador (-ra) *a* saving, redeeming. *n* deliverer. *m,* redeemer

salvadoreño (-ña) *a* and *n* Salvadorean

salvaguardia *m,* guard, watch. *f,* safeguard; protection, defense; safe conduct, passport

salvajada *f,* savagery, brutal action

salvaje *a* wild (plants, animals); rough, uncultivated; uncultured, uncivilized. *mf* savage

salvajismo *m,* savagery

salvamano, a *adv* safely

salvamente *adv* safely, securely

salvamento *m,* salvation; deliverance, security, safety; place of safety; salvage

salvante *adv inf* except, save

salvar *vt* to save; *ecc* redeem; avoid (difficulty, danger); exclude, except; leap, jump; pass over, clear; *law* prove innocent; *naut* save. **s. la diferencia,** to bridge the gap. *vi* taste, sample (food, drink); *vr* be saved from danger; *ecc* be redeemed

salvavidas *m,* life belt; safety belt; life preserver; traffic island

¡salve! *interj poet* hail!; Hail Mary, Salve Regina

salvedad *f,* qualification, reservation

salvia *f, bot* sage

salvilla *f,* salver

salvo *a* safe, unharmed; excepting, omitting. *adv* except. **a s.,** safely, without harm. **a su s.,** to his (her,

their) satisfaction; at his (her, etc.) pleasure. **dejar a s.,** to exclude, leave aside. **en s.,** in safety

salvoconducto *m,* safe conduct, pass

sallar *vt* to weed

samarita *a* and *mf* **samaritano (-na)** *a* and *n* Samaritan

samba *f* samba

sambenito *m,* penitent's gown (Inquisition); disgrace, dishonor

sambubia *f, Mexico* pineapple drink

Samotracia Samothrace

samotracio (-ia) *a* and *n* Samothracian

samoyedo (-da) *n* Samoyed

san *a abb* of **santo.** Used before masculine singular names of saints except **Santos Tomás** (*or* **Tomé**), **Domingo, Toribio**

sanable *a* curable

sanador (-ra) *a* healing, curing. *n* healer

sanalotodo *m, inf* cure-all, universal remedy

sanar *vt* to cure, heal; *vi* recover, get well; heal

sanatorio *m,* sanatorium; convalescent home

sanción *f,* authorization, consent; sanction; penalty

sancionable *a* sanctionable

sancionar *vt* to authorize, approve; sanction

sancochar *vt cul* to parboil, half-cook

sancocho *m,* parboiled meat

sandalia *f,* sandal

sándalo *m,* sandalwood

sandez *f,* foolishness, stupidity; folly

sandía *f,* watermelon

sandio *a* foolish, inane

sandunga *f, inf* attractiveness, winsomeness, grace; *Lat. Am.* carousing

sandunguero *a inf* attractive, appealing, winsome

saneado *a* unencumbered, nontaxable, free

saneamiento *m,* guarantee, security; indemnity; stabilization (of currency); drainage

sanear *vt com* to guarantee, secure; indemnify; stabilize (currency); drain (land, etc.)

Sanedrín *m,* Sanhedrin

sangradera *f,* lancet; channel, sluice, drain

sangrador *m,* phlebotomist; outlet, drainage

sangradura *f,* inner bend of the arm; *surg* bleeding; draining off

sangrar *vt surg* to bleed; drain off; *inf* extort money, bleed; *print* indent; draw off resin (from pines, etc.); *vi* bleed; *vr* bleed; have oneself bled; run (of colors)

sangre *f,* blood; lineage, family. **s. fría,** sang-froid. **a s. fría,** in cold blood, premeditated. **a s. y fuego,** by fire and sword, without quarter. *inf* **bullir la s.,** to have youthful blood in one's veins. **llevar en la s.,** *fig* to be in the blood. **subírsele la s. a la cabeza,** to grow excited. *fig inf* **tener s. de horchata,** to have milk and water in one's veins

sangría *f, surg* bloodletting; resin cut (on pines, etc.)

sangriento *a* bloody, bloodstained; bloodthirsty, cruel; mortal (insults, etc.); *poet* blood-colored

sangüesa *f,* raspberry

sanguijuela *f,* leech; *fig inf* sponger

sanguinaria *f,* bloodstone

sanguinario *a* vengeful, bloody, cruel

sanguíneo *a* blood; sanguineous; sanguine, fresh-complexioned; blood-colored

sanguinolento *a.* See **sangriento**

sanidad *f,* safety, security; healthiness; health department. **s. interior,** Public Health. **S. militar,** army medical corps

sanitario *a* sanitary, hygienic. *m, mil* medical officer

sano *a* healthy; safe, secure; healthful, wholesome; unhurt, unharmed; upright, honest; sincere; *inf* entire, undamaged; sane. **s. y salvo,** safe and sound. *inf* **cortar por lo s.,** to cut one's losses

San Pablo São Paulo

sánscrito *a* and *m,* Sanscrit

santa *f,* female saint

santamente *adv* in a saintly manner; simply

santero (-ra) *a* given to image worship. *n* accomplice (of a burglar); caretaker (of a hermitage); beggar

¡Santiago! *interj* St. James! (Spanish war cry). *m*, attack, assault

santiamén *m, inf* trice, twinkling

santidad *f*, sanctity; saintliness; godliness. **Su S.**, His Holiness

santificación *f*, sanctification

santificador (-ra) *a* sanctifying. *n* sanctifier

santificar *vt* to sanctify, make holy; consecrate; dedicate; keep (feast days)

santiguada *f*, crossing oneself; rough treatment, harsh reproof

santiguar *vt* to make the sign of the cross over; *inf* beat, rain blows on; *vr* cross oneself; *inf* be dumbfounded

santísimo *a sup* most saintly, most holy

santo *a* holy; saintly; saint (see **san**); consecrated; inviolate, sacred; *inf* simple, sincere, ingenuous. *m*, saint; image of a saint; saint's day, name day (of a person); *mil* password. **Santa Hermandad,** Holy Brotherhood (former name of the Spanish rural police force). **S. Oficio,** Holy Office, Inquisition. **S. y bueno,** Well and good, All right! *inf* **alzarse con el s. y la limosna,** to take the lot, make off with everything. **llegar y besar el s.,** to do in a trice. *inf* **No es s. de mi devoción,** I'm not very keen on him. *inf* **todo el s. día,** the whole blessed day

santón *m*, dervish, santon. *inf* hypocrite, sham saint

santoral *m*, book of saints; calendar of saints; choir book

santuario *m*, sanctuary

santurrón (-ona) *a* sanctimonious; hypocritical; prudish. *n* hypocrite

santurronería *f*, sanctimoniousness

saña *f*, fury, blind rage; lust for revenge, cruelty

sañoso, sañudo *a* furious, blind with rage; cruel

sapidez *f*, flavor, sapidity

sápido *a* tasty, savory

sapiencia *f*, wisdom; knowledge; erudition

sapino *m*, fir (tree)

sapo *m*, toad

saque *m, sport* serve, service; service or bowling line; *sport* server; *sport* bowler; bowling (in cricket)

saqueador (-ra) *a* looting, pillaging. *n* pillager, plunderer

saquear *vt* to pillage, plunder, sack

saqueo *m*, plundering, pillage, sacking

sarampión *m*, measles

sarao *m*, soirée, evening party

sarape, *m, Mexico* woolen shawl or blanket worn by males

sarasa *m*, (*inf* and contemptuous) pansy, faggot

sarcasmo *m*, sarcasm

sarcástico *a* sarcastic

sarcia *f*, load, cargo

sarcófago *m*, sarcophagus

sarda *f*, mackerel

sardana *f*, traditional Catalonian dance

sardina *f*, sardine. **s. arenque,** herring. **como sardinas en banasta,** *fig* packed like sardines

sardinal *m*, sardine net

sardinero (-ra) *a* sardine. *n* sardine seller or dealer. *m*, famous district of Santander

sardineta *f*, sprat; small sardine; *mil* chevron

sardónico *a* sardonic

sarga *f*, (silk) serge; willow

sargenta *f*, sergeant's wife; *inf* mannish, overbearing woman

sargentear *vt* to be in charge as a sergeant; command, captain; *inf* boss

sargento *m*, sergeant

sarita *f. Peru* straw hat

sarmentoso *a* vine-like; twining

sarmiento *m*, vine shoot

sarna *f*, scabies. **s. perruna,** mange. **más viejo que la s.,** *inf* older than the plague

sarnoso *a* itchy; mangy

sarraceno (-na) *a* Saracen. *n* Saracen; Moor

sarracina *f*, scuffle

sarrillo *m*, death rattle, rale; arum lily

sarro *m*, furry encrustation, scale; film; tartar (on teeth)

sarta *f*, string, link (of pearls, etc.); file, line

sartén *f*, frying pan. **tener la s. por el mango,** *inf* to be top dog

sastra *f*, female tailor; tailor's wife

sastre *m*, tailor. **ser buen s.,** *inf* to be an expert (in)

sastrería *f*, tailoring; tailor's shop

Satanás *m*, Satan; devil

satánico *a* satanic

satélite *m*, satellite; follower, admirer, sycophant

satén *m*, sateen

satinar *vt* to calender; glaze; satin (paper)

sátira *f*, satire

satírico *a* satiric

satirizar *vi* to write satires; *vt* satirize

sátiro *m*, satyr; *theat* indecent play

satisfacción *f*, settlement, payment; atonement, expiation; satisfaction; gratification; amends; complacency, conceit; contentment; apology. **tomar s.,** to avenge oneself

satisfacer *vt irr* to pay, settle; atone for, expiate; gratify; quench; fulfill, observe; compensate, indemnify; discharge, meet; convince, persuade; allay, relieve; reward; explain; answer, satisfy; *vr* avenge oneself; satisfy oneself. *Pres. Ind.* **satisfago, satisfaces,** etc. *Fut.* **satisfaré,** etc. *Condit.* **satisfaría,** etc. *Preterite* **satisfice,** etc. *Past Part.* **satisfecho.** *Pres. Subjunc.* **satisfaga,** etc. *Imperf. Subjunc.* **satisficiese,** etc.

satisfactorio *a* satisfactory

satisfecho *a* self-satisfied, complacent; happy, contented

sátrapa *m*, satrap; *inf* cunning fellow

saturación *f*, saturation

saturar *vt* to satiate, fill; saturate

saturnino *a* saturnine, melancholy, morose

saturnismo *m*, saturnism, lead poisoning

Saturno *m*, Saturn

sauce *m*, willow. **s. llorón,** weeping willow

saúco *m*, elder tree

saurio *a* and *m*, saurian

savia *f*, sap; energy, zest

sáxeo *a* stone, stony

saxófono *or* **saxofón** *m*, saxophone

saya *f*, skirt; long tunic

sayal *m*, thick woolen material

sayo *m*, loose smock; *inf* any garment. **cortar un s. (a),** *inf* to gossip behind a person's back

sayón *m*, executioner; *inf* hideous-looking man

sazón *f*, ripeness, maturity; season; perfection, excellence; opportunity; taste, flavor; seasoning. **a la s.,** at that time, then. **en s.,** in season; opportunely

sazonador (-ra) *a* seasoning. *n* seasoner

sazonar *vt cul* to season; mature; *vr* mature, ripen

se *object pron reflexive 3rd sing* and *pl mf* 1. Used as accusative (direct object) himself, herself, yourself, themselves, yourselves (e.g. **Juan se ha cortado,** John has cut himself). 2. Used as dative or indirect object to himself, at himself, herself, themselves, etc. (e.g. **María se mira al espejo,** Mary looks at herself in the mirror). Reciprocity is also expressed by reflexive (e.g. **No se hablan,** They do not speak to one another). When a direct object pron. (accusative) and an indirect object pron., both in the 3rd pers. (sing. or pl.), are used together, the indirect object pron. becomes **se** (instead of **le** or **les**) (e.g. **Se lo doy,** I give it to him). Many Spanish reflexive verbs have English equivalents that are not reflexive (e.g. **desayunarse,** to breakfast, **arrepentirse,** to repent, **quejarse,** to complain). Some intransitive (neuter) verbs have a modified meaning when used reflexively (e.g. **marcharse,** to go away, **dormirse,** to fall asleep). The passive may be formed by using **se** + 3rd pers. sing. of verb (e.g. **se dice,** it is said, people say). A number of impersonal phrases are also formed in this way (e.g. «**Se alquila,**» "To Let," «**Se vende,**» "For Sale"). The imperative is used in the same way (e.g. **Véase la página dos,** See page two)

sebáceo *a* sebaceous

sebo *m*, tallow; candle grease; fat, grease

seboso *a* tallowy; fat, greasy

seca *f*, drought; *naut* unsubmerged sandbank

secadero *m*, drying place, drying room

secadora *f*, dryer, drying machine, clothesdryer. **s. de cabello,** hairdryer

secafirmas *m*, blotting pad

secamente *adv* tersely, brusquely, curtly; dryly

secamiento *m*, drying

secano *m*, nonirrigated land; *naut* unsubmerged sandbank; anything very dry

secante *a* drying. *a* and *f*, *geom* secant. **papel s.,** blotting paper

secar *vt* to dry; desiccate; annoy, bore; *vr* dry; dry up (of streams, etc.); wilt, fade (of plants); become parched; grow thin, become emaciated; be very thirsty; become hard-hearted

sección *f*, act of cutting; section, part, portion; *geom mil* section. **s. cónica,** conic section. **s. de amenidades,** entertainment section (of a newspaper). **s. de reserva,** *mil* reserve list

seccionar *vt* to divide into sections, section

seccionario *a* sectional

secesión *f*, secession

secesionista *a* and *mf* secessionist

seco *a* dry; dried up, parched; faded, wilted; dead (plants); dried (fruits); thin, emaciated; unadorned; barren, arid; brusque, curt; severe, strict; indifferent, unenthusiastic; sharp (sounds); dry (wines). **a secas,** only; solely; simply, just. **en s.,** on dry land; curtly. *inf* **dejar s. (a),** to dumbfound, petrify

secreción *f*, segregation, separation; *med* secretion

secreta *f*, *law* secret trial or investigation; *ecc* secret(s); toilet, water closet

secretar *vt med* to secrete

secretaría *f*, secretaryship; secretary's office, secretariat

secretario (-ia) *n* secretary; amanuensis, clerk. *m*, actuary; registrar. **s. de asuntos exteriores** *or* **s. de asuntos extranjeros,** foreign secretary. **s. particular,** private secretary

secretear *vi inf* to whisper, have secrets

secreteo *m*, *inf* whispering, exchanging of secrets

secreto *m*, secret; secrecy, silence; confidential information; mystery; secret drawer. *a* secret; private, confidential. **en s.,** in secret, confidentially. **s. a voces,** open secret

secta *f*, sect

sectario (-ia) *a* and *n* sectarian. *n* fanatical believer

sectarismo *m*, sectarianism

sector *m*, sector

secuaz *mf* follower, disciple

secuela *f*, sequel, result

secuencia *f*, *ecc* sequence; (cinema) sequence

secuestrador (-ra) *a* sequestrating. *n* sequestrator

secuestrar *vt* to sequester; kidnap

secuestro *m*, sequestration; kidnapping; *surg* sequestrum

secular *a* secular, lay; centennial; age-old, ancient; *ecc* secular

secularización *f*, secularization

secularizar *vt* to secularize; *vr* become secularized

secundar *vt* to second, aid

secundario *a* secondary; accessory, subordinate; *geol* mesozoic

sed *f*, thirst; desire, yearning, appetite. **apagar** (*or* **matar**) **la s.,** to quench one's thirst. **tener s.,** to be thirsty

seda *f*, silk; bristle (boar, etc.). **s. cordelada,** twist silk. **s. ocal,** floss silk. **s. vegetal** *or* **s. artificial,** artificial silk. *inf* **como una s.,** as smooth as silk; sweet-tempered; achieved without any trouble

sedación *f*, calming, soothing

sedal *m*, fish line

sedar *vt* to soothe, calm

sedativo *a* and *m*, *med* sedative

sede *f*, *ecc* see; bishop's throne; *fig* seat (of government, etc.); Holy See (also **Santa S.**)

sedentario *a* sedentary

sedeño *a* silky; silken, made of silk

sedería *f*, silk goods; silks; silk shop

sedero (-ra) *a* silk. *n* silk weaver or worker; silk merchant

sedición *f*, sedition

sedicioso *a* seditious

sediento *a* thirsty; parched, dry (land); eager (for), desirous (of)

sedimentación *f*, sedimentation

sedimentar *vt* to leave a sediment; *vr* settle, form a sediment

sedimento *m*, sediment; dregs, lees; scale (on boilers)

sedoso *a* silky, silk-like

seducción *f*, seduction; temptation, blandishment, wile; charm, allurement

seducir *vt irr* to seduce; tempt, lead astray; charm, attract; corrupt, bribe. See **conducir**

seductivo *a* tempting; seductive, charming

seductor (-ra) *a* tempting; charming. *n* seducer; charming person

sefardí *mf* Iberian Jew or Jewess; *pl* Sephardim. *a* Sephardic

segadera *f*, sickle

segador *m*, reaper, harvester

segadora *f*, mowing machine, harvester; woman harvester

segar *vt irr* to scythe, cut down; reap, harvest; mow. See **cegar**

seglar *a* secular, lay. *mf* layman

segmento *m*, segment; *geom* segment. **s. de émbolo,** piston ring

segoviano (-na) *a* and *n* Segovian

segregación *f*, segregation

segregar *vt* to segregate, separate; *med* secrete

seguida *f*, continuation, prolongation. **de s.,** continuously; immediately. **en s.,** at once, immediately

seguidamente *adv* continuously; immediately

seguidilla *f*, popular Spanish tune and dance and verse sung to them; *inf* diarrhea

seguido *a* continuous, successive; direct, straight

seguidor (-ra) *a* following. *n* follower, disciple

seguimiento *m*, following, pursuit; continuation, resumption

seguir *vt irr* to follow; go after, pursue; prosecute, execute; continue, go on; accompany, go with; exercise (a profession); subscribe to, believe in; agree with; persecute; pester, annoy; imitate; *law* institute (a suit); handle, manage; *vr* result, follow as a consequence; follow in order, happen by turn; originate. *Pres. Part.* **siguiendo.** *Pres. Ind.* **sigo, sigues, sigue, siguen.** *Pres. Subjunc.* **siga,** etc. *Imperf. Subjunc.* **siguiese**

según *adv* according to; as. **s. parece,** as it seems. **s. y como,** as, according to

segunda *f*, *mus* second

segundar *vt* to repeat, do again; *vi* be second, follow the first

segundero *a agr* of the second flowering or fruiting. *m*, second hand (of a watch)

segundo *a* second. *m*, second in command, deputy head; *ast geom* second. **segunda intención,** double meaning. **segunda velocidad,** *aut* second gear. **de segunda mano,** second-hand. **sin s.,** without peer or equal

segundogénito (-ta) *a* and *n* secondborn

segundón *m*, second son; any son but the eldest

segurador *m*, surety, security (person)

seguramente *adv* securely, safely; surely, of course, naturally

seguridad *f*, security; safety; certainty; trustworthiness;

com surety; *Mexico* clasp, lock (of a suitcase, trunk, etc) **con toda s.,** with complete safety, surely, absolutely. **de s.,** *a* safety

seguro *a* secure; safe; certain, sure; firm, fixed; reliable, trustworthy; unfailing. *m,* certainty; haven, place of safety; *com* insurance; permit; *mech* ratchet. **s. contra incendio, accidentes, robo,** fire, accident, burglary insurance. **s. sobre la vida,** life insurance. **de s.,** surely, certainly. **en s.,** in safety. **s. social** *Lat. Am.* social security

seis *a* six; sixth. *m,* six; sixth (of the month); playing card or domino with six spots. **Son las s.,** It is six o'-clock

seiscientos *a* six hundred; six-hundredth. *m,* six hundred

selección *f,* selection, choice. **s. natural,** natural selection

seleccionar *vt* to select, choose

selectivo *a* selective

selecto *a* choice, select, excellent

sellado *m, Argentina* postage

sellador (-ra) *a* sealing, stamping. *n* sealer, stamper

selladura *f,* sealing, stamping

sellar *vt* to seal; stamp; end, conclude; close

sello *m,* seal; stamp. **s. fiscal,** stamp duty. **s. postal,** postage stamp. **s. y cruz** *Colombia,* heads or tails

selva *f,* forest, wood; jungle

Selva Negra, la the Black Forest

selvático *a* sylvan, wood, forest; wild

selvoso *a* wooded, sylvan

semafórico *a* semaphoric

semáforo *m,* semaphore, traffic light.

semana *f,* week; week's salary. **S. Mayor** *or* **S. Santa,** Holy Week. **entre s.,** during the week, on weekdays; weekdays

semanal *a* weekly; of a week's duration

semanario *a* weekly. *m,* weekly periodical

semanero, -a *a* employed by the week; paid by the week; person employed by the week; person paid by the week

semántica *f,* semantics

semántico *a* semantic

semblante *m,* facial expression, countenance; face; appearance, look, aspect. **componer el s.,** to pull oneself together, straighten one's face. **mudar de s.,** to change color, change one's expression; alter (of circumstances)

semblanza *f,* biographical sketch. **s. literaria,** short literary biography

sembradera *f,* sowing machine

sembradío *a agr* ready for sowing

sembrado *m,* sown land

sembrador (-ra) *a* sowing. *n* sower

sembradura *f, agr* sowing

sembrar *vt irr agr* to sow; scatter, sprinkle; spread, disseminate. See **sentar**

semeja *f,* resemblance, similarity; indication, sign (gen. *pl*)

semejante *a* like, similar; such a; *math* similar. *m,* similarity, imitation. *mf* fellow man

semejanza *f,* similarity, likeness. **a s. de,** in the likeness of; like

semejar(se) *vi* and *vr* to resemble

semen *m,* semen; *bot* seed

semental *a agr* seed; breeding (of male animals). *m,* stallion

sementar *vt agr* to sow

sementera *f, agr* sowing; sown land; seedbed; seedtime; *fig* hotbed, nursery, genesis

sementero *m,* seed bag; seed bed

semestral *a* biannual, half-yearly; lasting six months

semestre *a* biannual. *m,* half-year, period of six months; six months' salary; semester

semicírculo *m,* semicircle

semidifunto *a* half-dead

semidormido *a* half-asleep

semilla *f, bot* seed; *fig* germ, genesis

semillero *m,* seedbed; nursery; *fig* hotbed, origin

seminario *m,* seedbed; nursery; genesis, origin; seminary; tutorial. **s. conciliar,** theological seminary

seminarista *mf* seminarist

semiótica *f, med* symptomatology; semiotics

semita *mf* Semite. *a* Semitic

semítico *a* Semitic

semitismo *m,* Semitism

semitono *m, mus* semitone

semitransparente *a* semitransparent

semivivo *a* half-alive

sémola *f,* semolina

sempiterna *f,* everlasting flower; thick woolen material

sempiterno *a* eternal

sen *m,* senna

Sena, el the Seine

sena *f, bot* senna; six-spotted die

senado *m,* senate; senate house; any grave assembly

senador *m,* senator

senaduría *f,* senatorship

senario *a* senary

senatorio *a* senatorial

sencillez *f,* simplicity; naturalness; easiness; ingenuousness, candor

sencillo *a* simple; unmixed; natural; thin, light (fabric); easy; ingenuous, candid; unadorned, plain; single; sincere

senda *f,* path, footpath; way; means

senderear *vt* to conduct along a path; make a pathway; *vi* attain by tortuous means

sendero *m,* footpath, path

sendos, sendas *a m,* and *f pl,* one each (e.g. **Les dio sendos lápices,** He gave them each a pencil)

senectud *f,* old age

senescal *m,* seneschal

senil *a* senile

senilidad *f,* senility

seno *m,* hollow; hole; concavity; bosom, breast; chest; uterus, womb; any internal cavity of the body; bay, cove; lap (of a woman); interior (of anything), heart; gulf; *math* sine; *anat* sinus

sensación *f,* sensation

sensacional *a* sensational

sensacionalista *a* sensationalist

sensatez *f,* prudence, good sense

sensato *a* prudent, wise

sensibilidad *f,* sensibility

sensibilizar *vt phot* to sensitize

sensible *a* sensible, sensitive; tender, feeling; perceptible; noticeable, definite; sensitive; sad, regrettable

sensiblemente *adv* appreciably; perceptibly; painfully, sadly

sensiblería *f,* sentimentality, sentimentalism

sensiblero *a* oversentimental

sensitiva *f,* sensitive plant, mimosa

sensitivo *a* sensuous; sensitive, sensible

sensorio *a* sensory. *m,* sensorium

sensual *a* sensual; sensitive, sensible; carnal, voluptuous

sensualidad *f,* sensuality; sensualism

sensualismo *m,* sensualism; *phil* sensationalism

sensualista *mf phil* sensationalist; sensualist

sentadera *f, Lat. Am.* seat (of a chair)

sentadero *m,* resting place, improvised seat

sentado *a* prudent, circumspect

sentar *vt irr* to seat; *vi inf* suit, agree with (e.g. **No me sienta este clima (este plato),** This climate (dish) doesn't suit me); fit, become; *inf* please, satisfy, be agreeable to; *vr* sit down; *inf* leave a mark on the skin. *Pres. Ind.* **siento, sientas, sienta, sientan.** *Pres. Subjunc.* **siente, sientes, siente, sienten**

sentencia *f,* opinion, belief; maxim; *law* verdict, sentence; decision, judgment. *law* **fulminar** (*or* **pronunciar**) **la s.,** to pass sentence

sentenciador *a law* sentencing

sentenciar *vt law* to sentence; *inf* destine, intend
sentencioso *a* sententious
sentidamente *adv* feelingly; sadly, regretfully
sentido *m,* sense (hearing, seeing, touch, smell, taste); understanding, sense; meaning, interpretation, signification; perception, discrimination; judgment; direction, way. *a* and *past part* felt; expressive; hypersensitive, touchy. **s. común,** common sense. **costar un s.,** *fig inf* to cost a fortune. **perder el s.,** to lose consciousness
sentimental *a* emotional; sentimental; romantic
sentimentalismo *m,* emotional quality; sentimentalism
sentimiento *m,* feeling, sentiment; sensation, impression; grief, sorrow. **Le acompaño a usted en su s.,** I sympathize with you in your sorrow (bereavement)
sentina *f,* well (of a ship); *naut* bilge; cesspool; sink of iniquity
sentir *vt irr* to feel, experience; hear; appreciate; grieve, regret; believe, consider; envisage, foresee; *vr* complain; suffer; think or consider oneself; crack; feel, be; go rotten, decay (gen. with *estar* + *past part.*). *m,* view, opinion; feeling. **sin s.,** without feeling; without noticing. *Pres. Part.* **sintiendo.** *Pres. Ind.* **siento, sientes, siente, sienten.** *Preterite* **sintió, sintieron.** *Pres. Subjunc.* **sienta, sientas, sienta, sintamos, sintáis, sientan.** *Imperf. Subjunc.* **sintiese,** etc.
seña *f,* sign, mark; gesture; *mil* password; signal; *pl* address, domicile. **s. mortal,** definite or unmistakable sign. **dar señas,** to show signs, manifest. **hablar por señas,** to converse by signs
señal *f,* mark, sign; boundary stone; landmark; scar; signal; trace, vestige; indication, symptom, token; symbol, sign; image, representation; prodigy, marvel; deposit, advance payment. **s. de aterrizaje,** *aer* landing signal. **s. de niebla,** fog signal. **señales horarias,** *rad* time signal. **en s.,** as a sign, in proof of. **s. luminosa de la circulación,** traffic light, traffic robot
señaladamente *adv* especially, particularly, notably
señalado *a* famous, distinguished; important, notable
señalador *m, Argentina* bookmark
señalamiento *m,* marking; pointing out; appointment, designation
señalar *vt* to mark; indicate, point out; fix, arrange; wound; signal; stamp; appoint (to office); *vr* excel
señero *a* solitary, isolated
señor *a inf* gentlemanly. *m,* owner, master; mister, esquire; **(S.)** the Lord; lord, sire. **s. de horca y cuchillo,** feudal lord, lord of life and death
señora *f,* lady; owner, mistress; madam; wife. **s. de compañía,** chaperon; lady companion. **Nuestra S.,** Our Lady
señorear *vt* to control, run, manage; master; domineer; appropriate, seize; dominate, overlook; restrain (emotions); *vr* behave with dignity
señoría *f,* lordship (title and person); lordship, jurisdiction; area, territory; control, restraint
señoría *f,* dignity, sedateness; self-control
señorial *a* manorial; noble, dignified, lordly
señoril *a* lordly, noble, aristocratic
señorío *m,* lordship; jurisdiction; dominion
señorita *f,* young lady; miss; *inf* mistress of the house
señorito *m,* young gentleman; *inf* master of the house; master (address); *inf* young man about town
señuelo *m,* decoy; bait; allurement, attraction. **caer en el s.,** *fig inf* to fall into the trap
sepancuantos *m, inf* scolding, rebuke; spanking
separación *f,* separation
separado *a* separate
separador (-ra) *a* separating. *n* separator. *m,* filter. **s. de aceite,** oil filter
separar *vt* to separate; divide; dismiss (from a post); lay aside; *vr* retire, resign; separate
separatismo *m,* separatism
separatista *a* and *mf* separatist

septeno *a.* See **séptimo**
septentrión *m, ast* Great Bear; north
septentrional *a* north; northern
septeto *m,* septet
septicemia *f,* septicemia
séptico *a* septic
septiembre *m,* September
septillo *m, mus* septuplet
séptima *f, mus* seventh
séptimo *a* and *m,* seventh
septuagenario (-ia) *a* and *n* septuagenarian
septuagésimo *a* seventieth; septuagesimal. *m,* seventieth
séptuplo *a* sevenfold
sepulcral *a* sepulchral
sepulcro *m,* sepulcher
sepultador (-ra) *a* burying. *n* gravedigger; burier
sepultar *vt* to inter, bury; hide, cover up
sepultura *f,* interment; grave; tomb
sepulturero *m,* gravedigger
sequedad *f,* dryness, barrenness; acerbity, sharpness
sequía *f,* drought
séquito *m,* following, suite, retinue; general approval, popularity
ser *m,* essence, nature; being; existence, life. **El S. Supremo,** The Supreme Being, God
ser *vi irr* to be (e.g. **El sombrero es azul,** The hat is blue). **Ser** may agree with either subject or complement, though either when latter is *pl* the verb tends to be so too (e.g. **Son las once, (horas),** It is eleven o'clock. **Cien libras son poco dinero,** A hundred pounds is a small amount). If verbal complement is pers. pron., **ser** agrees with it both in number and person (e.g. **Son ellos,** It is they. **Soy yo,** It is I). In impers. phrases the pron. is not expressed (e.g. **Es difícil,** It is difficult. **Es sorprendente,** It is surprising). **ser** means to exist (e.g. **Pienso luego soy,** I think, therefore I am). **ser** (also **ser de** with nouns or obj. prons.) means to belong to, be the property of (e.g. **Este gato es mío,** This cat is mine. **El libro es de Juan,** The book belongs to John). Signifies to happen, occur (e.g. **¿Cómo fue eso?** How did that happen?). Means to be suitable or fitting (e.g. **Este vestido no es para una señora mayor,** This dress is not suitable for an elderly lady). Expresses price, to be worth (e.g. **¿A cuánto es la libra?** How much is it a pound?; How much is the pound (sterling) worth?). Means to be a member of, belong to (e.g. **Es de la Academia Española,** He is a member of the Spanish Academy). Means to be of use, be useful for (e.g. **Esta casa no es para una familia numerosa,** This house is no use for a large family). **Ser** expresses nationality (e.g. **Son francesas,** They are French. **Somos de Londres,** We are from London). *Auxiliary verb* used to form passive tense (e.g. **Esta historia ha sido leída por muchos,** This story has been read by many. **Fueron mandados al Japón,** They were sent to Japan. **s. de ver,** to be worth seeing. **s. para poco,** to be of little use, amount to little. **s. testigo de,** to witness. **¡Cómo es eso!** How can that be! Surely not! **¡Cómo ha de s.!** How should it be!; One must resign oneself. **Érase una vez** *or* **que érase,** Once upon a time. **es a saber,** viz., that is to say. **un sí es no es,** a touch of, a suspicion of). *Pres. Part.* **siendo.** *Pres. Ind.* **soy, eres, es, somos, sois, son.** *Fut.* **seré,** etc. *Condit.* **sería,** etc. *Preterite* **fui, fuiste, fue, fuimos, fuisteis, fueron.** *Imperf.* **era,** etc. *Past Part.* **sido.** *Pres. Subjunc.* **sea,** etc. *Imperf. Subjunc.* **fuese,** etc. *Imperat.* **sé**
sera *f,* large frail
seráfico *a* seraphic
serafín *m,* seraphim
serbal *m,* service tree
serena *f,* serenade; *inf* dew
serenar *vt* to calm; soothe; clear; *vr* grow calm; clear up (weather); clear (liquids); be soothed or pacified
serenata *f,* serenade

serenidad *f*, serenity, composure, tranquility; Serene Highness (title)

sereno *a* cloudless, fair; composed, serene. *m*, dew; night watchman

sericultor *m*, silk cultivator, sericulturist

sericultura *f*, silk culture

serie *f*, series, sequence, succession; *math* progression; (*biol elec*) series; break (in billiards)

seriedad *f*, seriousness, earnestness; gravity; austerity; sternness; importance; sincerity; solemnity

serigrafía *f*, silkscreen printing

serio *a* serious, earnest; grave; austere; stern; important; sincere, genuine; solemn. **en s.,** seriously

sermón *m*, sermon; scolding. **dar un s.,** to give a sermon; scold

sermonar *vi* to preach

sermonear *vi* to preach sermons; *vt* scold

sermoneo *m*, *inf* scolding

seroja *f*, withered leaves; brushwood

serpear *vi* to wind, twist; wriggle, squirm; coil

serpenteado *a* winding

serpentear *vi* to wind, twist, meander; stagger along; wriggle; coil; *aer* yaw

serpenteo *m*, winding, twisting; wriggling; coiling; *aer* yaw

serpentín *m*, *chem* worm; coil (in industry); *min* serpentine

serpentina *f*, *min* serpentine; paper streamer

serpentino *a* serpentine; *poet* winding, sinuous

serpiente *f*, snake, serpent; Satan, the Devil; *ast* Serpent. **s. de anteojos,** cobra. **s. de cascabel,** rattlesnake

serpollo *m*, *bot* shoot, new branch; sprout; sucker

serrado *a* serrate

serrallo *m*, harem, seraglio; brothel

serranía *f*, mountainous territory

serrano (-na) *a* mountain, highland. *n* highlander, mountain dweller

serruchar *vt*, *Lat. Am.* to saw, saw off

serrucho *m*, handsaw. **s. de calar,** fretsaw

Servia Serbia

servible *a* serviceable; useful

servicial *a* useful, serviceable; obliging, obsequious

servicio *m*, service; domestic service; cult, devotion; care, attendance; military service; set, service; department, section; present of money; cover (cutlery, etc., at table); domestic staff, servants. **s. informativo,** news service. **s. nocturno permanente,** all-night service. **hacer un flaco s. (a),** *inf* to do someone an ill turn. **prestar servicios,** to render service, serve

servidor (-ra) *n* servant, domestic; name by which one refers to oneself (e.g. **Un s. lo hará con mucho gusto,** I (your servant) will do it with much pleasure). *m*, wooer, lover; bowler (in cricket). **los servidores de una ametralladora,** the crew (of a gun). **Quedo de Vd. atento y seguro s.,** I remain your obedient servant (in letters), Yours faithfully

servidumbre *f*, serfdom; servitude; servants, domestic staff; obligation, duty; enslavement (by passions); right of way; use, service

servil *a* servile; humble

servilismo *m*, servility; abjectness; absolutism (Spanish history)

servilleta *f*, table napkin. **s. higiénica,** sanitary napkin

servilletero *m*, napkin ring

servio (-ia) *a* and *n* Serbian

servir *vi irr* to be employed (by), be in the service (of); serve (as), perform the duties (of); be of use; wait (on), be subject to. *mil* serve in the armed forces; wait at table; be suitable or favorable; *sport* serve; perform a service; follow the lead (cards); (*with de*) act as, be a deputy for; be a substitute for; *vt* serve; worship; do a favor to; woo, court; serve (food, drink); *vr* be pleased or willing, deign; help oneself to (food); (*with de*) make use of. **no s. para nada,** to be good for nothing, be useless. **No sirves para tales cosas,** You are no good

at this sort of thing. **Para s. a Vd,** At your service. **¡Sírvase de . . . !** (followed by infin.), Please! **s. de,** to serve as (e.g. **s. de base a,** to serve as a basis for). See **pedir**

sésamo *m*, sesame

sesenta *a* and *m*, sixty; sixtieth

sesentavo *a* and *m*, sixtieth

sesentón (-ona) *n inf* person of sixty

sesga *f*, *sew* gore

sesgadamente *adv* on the slant; askew; obliquely

sesgado *a* oblique, slanting

sesgar *vt sew* to cut on the bias; slant, slope; place askew, twist to one side

sesgo *a* slanting, oblique; serious-faced. *m*, slope, slant, obliquity; compromise, middle way. **al s.,** on the slant

sesión *f*, session, meeting; conference, consultation; *law* sitting; term. **abrir la s.,** to open the meeting. **levantar la s.,** to adjourn the meeting

seso *m*, brain; prudence; *pl* brains. **perder el s.,** to go mad; *fig* lose one's head

sestear *vi* to take an afternoon nap; rest; settle

sesteo *m*, *Lat. Am.* nap, siesta

sesudez *f*, prudence, shrewdness

sesudo *a* sensible, prudent

seta *f*, mushroom. **s. venenosa,** poisonous toadstool

setal *m*, mushroom bed, patch, or field

setecientos *a* and *m*, seven hundred; seven-hundredth

setenta *a* and *m*, seventy; seventieth

setentavo *a* and *m*, seventieth

setentón (-ona) *n* septuagenarian

seter *m*, setter (dog)

setiembre *m*. See **septiembre**

seto *m*, fence; hedge

seudo *a* pseudo

seudónimo *m*, pseudonym

severamente *adv* severely, harshly

severidad *f*, severity; harshness; strictness, rigor; austerity, seriousness

severo *a* severe; harsh; strict, rigid, scrupulous; exact; austere, serious

sevillanas *f pl*, Sevillian dance and its music

sevillano (-na) *a* and *n* of or from Seville, Sevillian

sexagenario (-ia) *n* sexagenarian

sexagésimo *a* sixtieth

sexo *m*, sex; (sexual) organ

sexología *f*, sexology

sexólogo (-ga) *n* sexologist

sexta *f*, *ecc* sext; *mus* sixth

sexteto *m*, sextet

sexto *a* sixth

sextuplicación *f*, multiplication by six

sextuplicar *vt* to multiply by six, sextuple

séxtuplo *a* sixfold

sexualidad *f*, sexuality

si *m*, *mus* B, seventh note of the scale. *conjunc* if; whether; even if, although. In conditional clause, **si**, meaning if, is followed by indicative tense unless statement be contrary to fact (e.g. **Si pierdes el tren, volverás a casa,** If you miss your train you will return home, *but* **Si hubieran venido habríamos ido al campo,** If they had come (but they didn't) we would have gone to the country). **Si** is used at the beginning of a clause to make expressions of doubt, desire, or affirmation more emphatic (e.g. **¡Si lo sabrá él, con toda su experiencia!** Of course he knows it, with all his experience. **¿Si será falsa la noticia?** Can the news be false?) **Si** also means whether (e.g. **Me preguntaron si era médico o militar,** They asked me whether I was a doctor or a soldier). Sometimes means even if, although (e.g. **Si viniesen no lo harían,** Even if they came they would not do it. **como si,** as if. **por si acaso,** in case, in the event of. **si bien,** although.

sí *pers pron reflexive 3rd pers m*, and *f*, *sing* and *pl* himself, herself, itself, themselves. Always used with prep. (e.g. **para sí,** for himself, herself, etc. **de por sí,** separately, on its own. **decir para sí,** to say to oneself)

sí adv yes. **sí** or **sí que** is frequently used to emphasize a verb generally in contrast to a previous negative (e.g. **Ellos no lo harán, pero yo sí,** They won't do it but I will). Often translated by 'did' (e.g. **No lo vi todo, pero lo que sí vi,** I didn't see it all, but what I did see . . .). m, assent; yes; consent. **dar el sí,** to say yes; agree; accept an offer of marriage

siamés (-esa) a and n Siamese. m, Thai (language)

sibarita a sybaritic. mf sybarite

sibarítico a sybaritic; sensual

sibaritismo m, sybaritism

siberiano (-na) a and n Siberian

sibila f, sibyl

sibilante a sibilant

sibilino a sibylline

sicario m, paid assassin

Sicilia Sicily

siciliano (-na) a and n Sicilian

sicoanálisis m, psychoanalysis

sicoanalista mf psychoanalyst

sicoanalizar vt to psychoanalyze

sicofanta, sicofante m, sycophant

sicología f, psychology

sicológico a psychological

sicólogo (-ga) n psychologist

sicomoro m, sycamore

sicopático a psychopathic

sicosis f, med psychosis

sicoterapia f, psychotherapy

SIDA m, AIDS

sideral, sidéreo a sidereal

sidra f, cider

siega f, reaping, harvesting; harvest time; harvest, crop

siembra f, agr sowing; seedtime; sown field

siempre adv always. **s. que,** provided that; whenever. **para s.,** forever. **por s. jamás,** for always, for ever and ever

siempreviva f, bot everlasting flower. **s. mayor,** houseleek

sien f, anat temple

sierpe f, serpent, snake; anything that wriggles; kite (toy); bot sucker; hideous person

sierra f, carp saw; ridge of mountains; sawfish; slope; hillside. **s. de cerrojero,** hacksaw. **s. de cinta,** handsaw

siervo (-va) n slave; servant; serf

siesta f, noonday heat; afternoon nap

siete a seven; seventh. m, seven; seventh (days of the month); playing card with seven spots; number seven. **las s.,** seven o'clock. inf **más que s.,** more than somewhat, extremely

sietemesino (-na) n seven-month-old child; fig inf young cock

sífilis f, syphilis

sifilítico (-ca) a and n syphilitic

sifón m, siphon; siphon bottle; soda water; mech trap

sigilar vt to seal; hide, conceal

sigilo m, seal; secrecy, concealment; silence, reserve

sigiloso a secret, silent

sigla f, acronym

siglo m, century; long time, age; social intercourse, society, world. **s. de oro,** golden age. **en** or **por los siglos de los siglos,** for ever and ever

signar vt to sign; make the sign of the cross over; vr cross oneself

signatario (-ia) a and n signatory

signatura f, print signature; mark, sign; mus signature

significación f, **significado** m, meaning; importance, significance

significante a significant

significar vt to signify, indicate; mean; publish, make known; vi represent, mean; be worth

significativo a significant

signo m, sign, indication, token; sign, character; math symbol; sign of the zodiac; mus sign; med symptom; ecc gesture of benediction; destiny, fate

siguemepollo m, inf streamer

siguiente a following; next, subsequent. **el día s.,** the next day

sílaba f, syllable

silabario m, speller, spelling book

silabear vi and vt to pronounce by syllables, syllabize

silabeo m, pronouncing syllable by syllable, syllabication

silábico a syllabic

sílabo m, syllabus, list

silba f, hissing (as a sign of disapproval)

silbador (-ra) a whistling; hissing. n whistler; one who hisses

silbar vi to whistle; whizz, rush through the air; vi and vt theat hiss

silbato m, whistle; air hole

silbido, silbo m, whistle, whistling; hiss, hissing

silenciador m, (aut firearms) silencer

silenciar vt to silence; keep secret

silenciario a vowed to perpetual silence

silencio m, silence; noiselessness, quietness; omission; disregard; mus rest. **en s.,** in silence; quietly; uncomplainingly. **pasar en s. (una cosa),** to pass over (something) in silence, omit. **s. de muerte,** deathly silence

silencioso a silent; noiseless; tranquil, quiet. m, (aut firearms) silencer

sílfide f, **silfo** m, sylph

silicato m, chem silicate

sílice f, chem silica

silla f, chair; riding saddle; mech rest, saddle; ecc see. **s. de manos,** sedan chair. **s. de montar,** riding saddle. **s. de posta,** post chaise. **s. de ruedas,** wheelchair. **s. de tijera,** deck chair; campstool. **s. giratoria,** swivel chair. **s. poltrona,** easy chair. inf **pegársele la s.,** to overstay one's welcome

sillar m, ashlar, quarry stone; horseback

sillería f, set of chairs; pew, choir stalls; chair factory; shop where chairs are sold; chair making; mas ashlar masonry

sillero (-ra) n chair maker or seller; saddler

silleta f, bedpan; fireman's lift

silletero m, runner, sedan chair carrier

sillín m, light riding saddle; seat, saddle (of bicycles, etc.)

sillón m, armchair; sidesaddle; Lat. Am. rocking chair. **s.-cama,** reclining chair. **s. de mimbres,** cane chair

silo m, agr silo; dark cavern, dark cave

silogismo m, syllogism

silogístico a syllogistic

silueta f, silhouette; figure

silúrico a silurian

siluro m, catfish; nav self-propelling torpedo

silva f, literary miscellany; metrical form

silvestre a bot wild; sylvan; uncultivated; savage

silvicultor m, forester

silvicultura f, forestry

sima f, abyss, chasm

simbiosis f, symbiosis

simbólico a symbolical

simbolismo m, symbolism

simbolista mf symbolist

simbolización f, symbolization

simbolizar vt to symbolize, represent

símbolo m, symbol. **s. de la fe,** ecc Creed

simetría f, symmetry

simétrico a symmetric; symmetrical

simetrizar vt to make symmetrical

símico a simian

simiente f, seed; semen; germ, genesis, origin

simiesco a apish, ape-like

símil a similar. m, comparison; simile

similar a similar

similitud f, similarity

simio (-ia) n ape

simón *m*, horse cab; cabdriver
simonía *f*, simony
simpatía *f*, liking, understanding, affection; fellow feeling; sympathy
simpático *a* friendly, nice, decent, congenial; sympathetic. **gran s.**, *anat* sympathetic
simpatizar *vi* to get on well, be congenial
simple *a* simple; single, not double; insipid; easy; plain, unadorned; stupid, silly; pure, unmixed; easily deceived, simple; naïve, ingenuous; mere; mild, meek. *mf* simpleton; fool
simpleza *f*, foolishness, stupidity; simplicity
simplicidad *f*, simplicity; candour, ingenuousness
simplicísimo *a sup* most simple, exceedingly simple
simplificable *a* simplifiable
simplificación *f*, simplification, simplifying
simplificador *a* simplifying
simplificar *vt* to simplify
simplista *mf* herbalist
simulación *f*, pretense, simulation
simulacro *m*, image, simulacrum; vision, fancy; *mil* mock battle
simuladamente *adv* pretendedly
simulador (-ra) *a* feigned. *n* dissembler
simular *vt* to feign, pretend
simultanear *vt* to perform simultaneously
simultaneidad *f*, simultaneousness
simultáneo *a* simultaneous
simún *m*, sandstorm
sin *prep* without (e.g. **Lo hizo s. hablar,** He did it without speaking). **s. embargo,** nevertheless. **s. fin,** endless. **s. hilos,** radio, wireless
sinagoga *f*, synagogue
sinapismo *m*, *med* mustard plaster; *inf* pest, bore
sincerarse *vr* to justify oneself; vindicate one's actions
sinceridad *f*, sincerity
sincero *a* sincere
síncopa *f*, *mus* syncopation; *gram* syncope
sincopar *vt* to syncopate; abbreviate
síncope *m*, syncope
sincrónico *a* synchronous
sincronismo *m*, synchronism
sincronizar *vt* to synchronize; *rad* tune in
sindéresis *f*, discretion, good sense
sindicación *f*, syndication
sindicado *m*, syndicate
sindical *a* syndical
sindicalismo *m*, syndicalism, trade unionism
sindicalista *mf* syndicalist, trade unionist. *a* syndicalistic, trade unionist
sindicar *vt* to accuse, charge; censure; syndicate
sindicato *m*, syndicate; trade union. **s. gremial,** trade union. **S. Internacional de Trabajadoras de la Aguja,** International Ladies' Garment Workers' Union
sindicatura *f*, (official) receivership
síndico *m*, *com* receiver, trustee
síndrome *m*, syndrome. **síndrome de inmunidad deficiente adquirida** acquired immunity deficiency syndrome
sinecura *f*, sinecure
sinergia *f*, synergy
sinfín *m*, countless number
sinfonía *f*, symphony
sinfónico *a* symphonic
sinfonista *mf* composer of symphonies, player in a symphony orchestra
sinfonola *f*, jukebox
singladura *f*, *naut* day's sailing; nautical twenty-four hours (beginning at midday)
singlar *vi* *naut* to sail a given course
singular *a* singular, single; individual; extraordinary, remarkable. *a* and *m*, *gram* singular
singularidad *f*, individuality, peculiarity; strangeness, remarkableness; oddness, eccentricity
singularizar *vt* to particularize, single out; *gram* make

singular, singularize; *vr* distinguish oneself, stand out; be distinguished (by)
sinhueso *f*, *inf* tongue (organ of speech)
siniestra *f*, left, lefthand
siniestro *a* left (side); vicious, perverse; sinister; unlucky. *m*, viciousness, depravity (gen. *pl*); shipwreck, sinking; disaster, catastrophe; *com* damage, loss
sinnúmero *m*, countless number
sino *m*, fate, destiny. *conjunc* but; except (e.g. **No lo hicieron ellos s. yo,** They didn't do it, I did. **no . . . s.,** not . . . , but); only (e.g. **No sólo lo dijo él s. ella,** Not only he said it, but she did too)
sínodo *m*, (*ecc ast*) synod; council
sinología *f*, sinology
sinólogo *m*, sinologist
sinonimia *f*, synonymy
sinónimo *a* synonymous. *m*, synonym
sinopsis *f*, synopsis
sinóptico *a* synoptic
sinrazón *f*, injustice, wrong
sinsabor *m*, unpleasantness, trouble; grief, anxiety
sintáctico *a* syntactic
sintaxis *f*, syntax
síntesis *f*, synthesis
sintético *a* synthetic
sintetizar *vt* to synthesize
síntoma *m*, symptom
sintomático *a* symptomatic
sintomatología *f*, symptomatology
sintonización *f*, *rad* tuning in
sintonizador *m*, *rad* tuner
sintonizar *vt* *rad* to tune in
sinuosidad *f*, sinuosity
sinuoso *a* sinuous, winding
sinvergüenza *mf* rascal, knave, rogue
sinvergüenzada *f*, *Lat. Am.* dirty thing (to do)
Sión Zion
sionismo *m*, Zionism
sionista *a* and *mf* Zionist
siquiatra *m*, psychiatrist
siquiatría *f*, psychiatry
síquico *a* psychic
siquiera *conjunc* although, even if. **s. . . . s.,** whether . . . or. *adv* at least; even (e.g. **Hay que pedir mucho para tener s. la mitad,** One must ask a great deal to get even half). **ni s.,** not even (e.g. **No había nadie, ni s. un perro,** There was no one, not even a dog)
Siracusa Syracuse
siracusano (-na) *a* and *n* Syracusan
sirena *f*, mermaid, siren; siren; foghorn
sirga *f*, towline
sirgar *vt* *naut* to track, tow
Siria Syria
sirio (-ia) *a* and *n* Syrian. *m*, Sirius
siroco *m*, sirocco
sirte *f*, sandbank, submerged rock
sirvienta *f*, female servant
sirviente *a* serving. *m*, servant
sisa *f*, pilfering; *sew* dart. **s. dorada,** gold lacquer
sisador (-ra) *n* filcher, pilferer
sisar *vt* to pilfer, filch, steal; *sew* take in, make darts in
sisear *vi* and *vt* to hiss (disapproval); sizzle
sísmico *a* seismic
sismógrafo *m*, seismograph
sismología *f*, seismology
sismológico *a* seismological
sismómetro *m*, seismometer
sistema *m*, system. **s. ferroviario,** railroad system. **s. métrico,** metric system
sistemático *a* systematic
sistematización *f*, systematization
sistematizar *vt* to systematize
sístole *f*, systole
sitiador *a* besieging. *m*, besieger
sitiar *vt* *mil* to lay siege to; surround, besiege
sitio *m*, place, spot; room, space; site; locality; *mil* siege,

blockade; *Lat. Am.* taxi stand **No hay s.,** There's no room

sito *past part* situated, located

situación *f,* situation; position; circumstances; condition, state; location

situado *past part* situated, placed. *m,* income, interest

situar *vt* to situate, locate, place; assign funds; *vr* place oneself

smoking *m,* tuxedo, tux, dinner jacket

snobismo *m,* snobbery

so *prep* under (used only with **color, pena, pretexto, capa**) (e.g. **so color de,** under the pretext of). *interj* **¡So!** Whoa! (to horses); *Lat. Am.* Hush!

soba *f,* rubbing; kneading; massaging; drubbing, beating; handling, touching

sobacal *a* underarm, axillary

sobaco *m,* armpit; *bot* axil

sobajar *vt* to squeeze, press

sobaquera *f, sew* armhole; dress shield

sobar *vt* to rub; knead; massage; beat, thrash; handle, touch, paw (persons); soften

soberanear *vi* to tyrannize, domineer

soberanía *f,* sovereignty; dominance, sway, rule; dignity, majesty

soberano (-na) *a* sovereign; superb; regal, majestic. *n* ruler, lord. *m,* sovereign (coin)

soberbia *f,* arrogance, haughtiness; conceit, presumption; ostentation, pomp; rage, anger

soberbio *a* haughty, arrogant; conceited; superb, magnificent; lofty, soaring; spirited (of horses)

sobón *a inf* overdemonstrative, mushy; *inf* lazy

sobordo *m, naut* manifest, freight list

sobornación *f,* bribing; bribery

sobornador (-ra) *a* bribing. *n* briber

sobornar *vt* to bribe

soborno *m,* bribing; bribe; inducement

sobra *f,* excess, surplus; insult, outrage; *pl* leftovers (from a meal); remains, residue; rubbish, trash. **de s.,** in abundance; in excess, surplus; unnecessary, superfluous; too well

sobradamente *adv* abundantly; in excess

sobrado *a* excessive; brazen, bold; wealthy, rich. *m,* garret

sobrante *a* surplus, leftover, remaining. *m,* remainder, surplus, excess

sobrar *vt* to exceed; have too much of (e.g. **Me sobran mantas,** I have too many blankets); *vi* be superfluous; remain, be left. *inf* **Aquí sobro yo,** I am in the way here, My presence is superfluous

sobrasada *f,* spicy sausage

sobre *prep* upon, on; above, over; concerning, about; apart from, besides; about (e.g. **s. las nueve,** at about nine o'clock) (indicates approximation); toward; after. *m,* envelope; address; superscription. **s. cero,** above freezing (Fahrenheit); above zero (Centigrade). **s. el nivel del mar,** above sea level. **s. manera,** excessively, extremely. **s. todo,** especially

sobreabundancia *f,* superabundance, excess

sobreabundante *a* superabundant

sobreabundar *vi* to be superabundant

sobreagudo *a* and *m, mus* treble (pitch)

sobrealiento *m,* heavy, painful breathing

sobrealimentación *f,* overfeeding; *aut* supercharge

sobrealimentar *vt aut* to supercharge

sobreasar *vt* to roast or cook again

sobrecama *f,* bedspread, quilt

sobrecarga *f,* overload; rope, etc., for securing bales and packs; additional trouble or anxiety

sobrecargar *vt* to overload; weigh down; *sew* oversew, fell

sobrecargo *m, naut* purser; flight attendant

sobrecarta *f,* envelope (for a letter)

sobreceja *f,* brow, lower forehead; frown

sobrecejo *m,* frown

sobrecielo *m,* canopy

sobrecoger *vt* to take by surprise; *vr* be frightened or apprehensive

sobrecogimiento *m,* fright, apprehension

sobrecomida *f,* dessert

sobrecoser *vt sew* to oversew, whip

sobrecrecer *vi irr* to grow too much. See **conocer**

sobrecubierta *f,* second lid or cover; dust jacket (of a book); *naut* upper deck

sobrecuello *m,* overcollar; loose collar

sobredicho *a* aforementioned, aforesaid

sobredorar *vt* to gild (metals); make excuses for

sobreedificar *vt* to build upon or above

sobreexcitar *vt* to overexcite

sobrefaz *f,* surface, exterior

sobreganar *vt* to make an excess profit

sobreguarda *m,* head guard; extra or second guard

sobreherido *a* lightly wounded

sobrehilar *vt* to oversew or overcast. See **prohibir**

sobrehumano *a* superhuman

sobrellenar *vt* to fill full

sobrellevar *vt* to help in the carrying of a burden; endure, bear; make excuses for, overlook; help

sobremesa *f,* tablecloth; after-dinner conversation. **de s.,** *fig* at the dinner table

sobrenadar *vi* to float

sobrenatural *a* supernatural; extraordinary, singular

sobrenombre *m,* additional surname; nickname

sobrentender *vt irr* to take for granted, understand as a matter of course; *vr* go without saying. See **entender**

sobrepaga *f,* overpayment; extra pay

sobreparto *m,* time after parturition; afterbirth

sobrepasar *vt* to exceed; outdo, excel

sobrepelliz *f,* surplice

sobreponer *vt irr* to place over; overlap; *vr* rise above (circumstances); dominate (persons). See **poner**

sobreprecio *m,* extra charge, rise in price

sobreproducción *f,* overproduction

sobrepuerta *f,* curtain pelmet; door curtain

sobrepujar *vt* to excel, surpass, outdo

sobrequilla *f,* keelson

sobrerrealista *a* and *mf* surrealist

sobrerrealismo *m,* surrealism

sobresaliente *a* overhanging; projecting; distinctive, outstanding; excellent, remarkable. *m,* "excellent" (mark in examinations). *mf theat* understudy

sobresalir *vi irr* to overhang, project; stand out; be conspicuous or noticeable; excel; distinguish oneself. See **salir**

sobresaltar *vt* to assail, rush upon; startle, frighten suddenly; *vi art* stand out, be striking; *vr* be startled or frightened

sobresalto *m,* sudden attack; unexpected shock; agitation; sudden fear. **de s.,** unexpectedly

sobresanar *vi* to heal superficially but not deeply; conceal, dissemble

sobrescribir *vt* to label; address, superscribe. *Past Part.* **sobrescrito**

sobrescrito *m,* address, superscription

sobresello *m,* second seal

sobrestante *m,* overseer; supervisor; foreman; inspector

sobresueldo *m,* additional salary, bonus

sobresuelo *m,* second flooring

sobretarde *f,* early evening, late afternoon

sobretodo *m,* overcoat

sobrevenida *f,* sudden arrival

sobrevenir *vi irr* occur, take place; supervene. See **venir**

sobrevidriera *f,* storm window; wire-mesh window guard

sobrevienta *f,* gust of wind; fury, violence; shock, surprise. **a s.,** suddenly

sobreviviente *a* surviving. *mf* survivor

sobrevivir *vi* to survive

sobriedad *f,* sobriety, moderation

sobrina *f,* niece

sobrino m, nephew
sobrio a sober, moderate, temperate
socaliña f, cunning, craft
socaliñero (-ra) a cunning. n trickster
socalzar vt mas to underpin
socapa f, blind, pretext. **a s.,** secretly; cautiously
socarra f, scorching, singeing; craftiness
socarrón a cunning, deceitful; malicious, sly (of humor, etc.)
socarronería f, cunning, craftiness; slyness (of humor, etc.); knavish action
socava f, undermining; agr hoeing round tree roots
socavar vt to undermine
sociabilidad f, sociability
sociable a sociable; social
social a social
socialdemócrata a and mf social democrat
socialismo m, socialism
socialista mf socialist. a socialistic
socialización f, socialization
socializar vt to socialize
sociedad f, society; association; com partnership; com company. com **s. anónima,** incorporated company, limited company. **S. de las Naciones,** League of Nations. **s. de socorros mutuos,** mutual aid society. **s. en comandita,** private company
socio (-ia) n associate, partner; member. **s. comanditario,** com silent partner
sociología f, sociology
sociológico a sociological
sociólogo (-ga) n sociologist
socolor m, pretext. adv (also **so c.**) under pretext
socollada f, naut flapping (of sails); pitching (of a ship)
socorredor (-ra) a aiding, succoring. n helper
socorrer vt to aid, succor, assist; pay on account
socorrido a helpful, generous, prompt to assist; well-equipped, well-furnished; well-supplied
socorro m, aid, help, assistance; payment on account; mil relief (provisions or arms)
socrático a socratic
sodio m, sodium
sodomía f, sodomy
sodomita mf sodomite. a sodomitic
soez a base, vile; vulgar
sofá m, sofa, couch
sofaldar vt to tuck up the skirts; disclose, reveal
sofisma m, sophism, fallacy
sofista a sophistic. mf sophist, quibbler
sofistería f, sophistry
sofístico a sophistic, fallacious
soflama f, thin flame; glow; flush, blush; specious promise, deception
soflamar vt to shame, make blush; promise with intent to deceive, swindle; vr cul burn
sofocación f, suffocation, smothering; shame; anger
sofocador, sofocante a suffocating; stifling
sofocar vt to suffocate, smother; extinguish; dominate, oppress; pester, importune; shame, make blush, make angry; agitate; vr be ashamed; be angry
sofocleo a Sophoclean
sofoco m, mortification, chagrin; shame; anger; suffocation, smothering; hot flush
sofreír vt irr to fry lightly. See **reír**
sofrenada f, sudden check, pulling up short (of horses); harsh scolding; moral restraint
sofrenar vt to pull up, check suddenly (horses); scold harshly; restrain, repress (emotions)
soga f, rope; land measure (varies in length). m, inf rogue, knave
soguería f, rope making; rope walk; rope shop; ropes
soguero m, rope maker or seller
soja f, soybean
sojuzgador (-ra) a conquering, oppressive. n conqueror, oppressor
sojuzgar vt to conquer, oppress, subdue
sol m, sun; sunlight; day; Peruvian coin; mus G, fifth

note of the scale, sol. **de s. a s.,** from sunrise to sunset. **hacer s.,** to be sunny. **morir uno sin s. sin luz y sin moscas,** inf to die abandoned by all. **no dejar a s. ni a sombra,** inf to follow everywhere; pester constantly. **tomar el s.,** to bask in the sun
solado m, paving; tile floor
solador m, tiler
solamente adv only; exclusively; merely, solely. **s. que,** only that; nothing but
solana f, sunny corner; Solarium
solanera f, sunburn; sunny spot
solapa f, lapel; excuse, pretext. **de s.,** inf secretly
solapado a cunning, sly
solapar vt sew to provide with lapels; sew cause to overlap; dissemble; vi sew overlap
solapo m, lapel; inf slap, buffet. **a s.,** inf secretly, slyly
solar vt irr to pave; sole (shoes). m, family seat, manor house; building site; lineage, family. a solar. See **colar**
solariego a memorial; of an old and noble family
solas, a adv alone, in private
solaz m, consolation; pleasure; relief, relaxation. **a s.,** enjoyably, pleasantly
solazar vt to solace, comfort; amuse; rest; vr be comforted; find pleasure (in)
soldada f, salary, wages, emoluments; (nav mil) pay
soldadesca f, soldiering, military profession; troops. **a la s.,** in a soldier-like way
soldadesco a military, soldier
soldado m, soldier; defender, partisan. **s. raso,** mil private
soldador m, solderer, welder; soldering iron
soldadura f, welding, soldering; correction, emendation
soldar vt irr to weld; mend by welding; correct, put right; mil wipe out, liquidate. See **contar**
solecismo m, solecism
soledad f, solitude; loneliness; homesickness; pl melancholy Andalusian song and dance (also f pl. **soleares**)
solemne a solemn; magnificent; formal; serious, grave, important; pompous; inf downright, complete
solemnidad f, solemnity; magnificence; formality; gravity, seriousness; solemn ceremony; religious ceremony; legal formality
solemnización f, solemnization
solemnizar vt to solemnize, celebrate; extol
soler vi irr defective to be in the habit, be used; happen frequently (e.g. **Solía hacerlo los lunes,** I generally did it on Mondays. **Suele llover mucho aquí,** It rains a great deal here). See **moler**
solercia f, shrewdness, ability, astuteness
solevantado a agitated; restless
solevantar vt to raise, push up; incite to rebellion. **s. con gatos,** mech to jack up
solfa f, mus sol-fa
solfear vt mus to sing in sol-fa; inf spank, buffet; inf scold
solfeo m, mus sol-fa; inf spanking, drubbing
solicitación f, request; application; solicitation; wooing; search (for a post); attraction, inducement
solicitador (-ra) a soliciting. n solicitor. m, agent; applicant
solicitante mf applicant, candidate
solicitar vt to solicit; request; apply for; make love to, court; seek (posts, etc.); try to, attempt to; manage (business affairs); phys attract; appeal to
solícito a solicitous; conscientious; careful
solicitud f, diligence; conscientiousness; solicitude; request; application; appeal, entreaty; petition; com demand. **a s.,** on request
solidaridad f, solidarity
solidario a law jointly responsible or liable
solideo m, ecc small skullcap
solidez f, solidity; fig force, weight (of arguments, etc.)
solidificación f, solidification
solidificar(se) vt and vr to solidify
sólido a compact, solid; thick; fast or lasting (of colors);

indisputable, convincing. *m*, (*geom phys*) solid; solidus (ancient coin)
soliloquiar *vi inf* to soliloquize, talk to oneself
soliloquio *m*, soliloquy
solio *m*, throne
solista *mf* soloist
solitario (-ia) *a* abandoned, deserted; solitary; secluded; solitude-loving. *n* recluse. *m*, solitaire diamond; hermit; solitaire (card game). **hacer solitarios,** to play solitaire (card game)
sólito *a* accustomed, wonted; customary, habitual
soliviantar *vt* to rouse, incite, excite
soliviar *vt* to help to lift up; *vr* half get up, raise oneself
sollastre *m*, scullion; brazen rogue
sollozante *a* sobbing
sollozar *vi* to sob
sollozo *m*, sob
solo *a* sole, only; alone; lonely; deserted, forsaken. *m*, solo performance; (cards) solo; solitaire (card game). **a solas,** alone; without help, unaided
sólo *or* **solo** *adv* only; merely, solely; exclusively
solomillo *m*, sirloin; filet (of meat)
solsticio *m*, solstice. **s. hiemal,** winter solstice. **s. vernal,** summer solstice
soltar *vt irr* to loosen; let go; disengage; untie; release; let drop; let out (a laugh, etc.); solve; *inf* utter; turn on (taps); set free; *vr* work loose; grow skillful; (*with prep. a + infin.*) begin to do (something). See **contar**
soltera *f*, spinster
soltería *f*, bachelorhood; spinsterhood
soltero *a* unmarried, single. *m*, bachelor
solterón *m*, confirmed bachelor
solterona *f*, confirmed old maid
soltura *f*, loosening; untying; freedom from restraint; ease, independence; impudence; immorality, viciousness; facility of speech; *law* release
solubilidad *f*, solubility
soluble *a* soluble, dissolvable; solvable
solución *f*, dissolution, loosening; (*math chem*) solution; answer, solution; payment, satisfaction; *lit* climax; conclusion, end (of negotiations)
solucionar *vt* to solve, find a solution for
solvencia *f*, *com* solvency
solventar *vt* to pay or settle accounts; solve (problems, difficulties)
solvente *a com* solvent
somático *a* somatic, corporeal
sombra *f*, shadow; shade; darkness, dimness; specter; phantom; defense, refuge, protection; resemblance, likeness; defect; *inf* luck; gaiety, charm; trace, vestige; *art* shading, shadow. **sombras chinescas,** shadow show. **a la s.,** in the shade; *inf* in jail. **hacer s.,** *fig* stand in the light, be an obstacle; protect. **ni por s.,** by no means; without warning. **no tener s. de,** to have not a trace of . . . . **tener buena s.,** *inf* to be witty or amusing and agreeable. **tener mala s.,** *inf* to bring bad luck, exert an evil influence upon; be dull and disagreeable
sombrear *vt* to shadow, shade; *art* shade; *vi* begin to show (of mustaches, beards)
sombrerera *f*, milliner; hatbox
sombrerería *f*, hat shop or trade; hat factory
sombrerero *m*, hatter; hat manufacturer
sombrerete *m*, *mech* bonnet, cap; cowl
sombrero *m*, hat; *mech* cap, cowl; sounding board; head (of mushrooms, toadstools). **s. calañés,** Andalusian hat. **s. chambergo,** broad-brimmed plumed hat. **s. de canal** *or* **teja,** shovel hat (worn by clergymen). **s. de copa,** top hat. **s. de jipijapa,** Panama hat. **s. de pelo** *Lat. Am.* top hat. **s. de tres picos,** three-cornered hat, cocked hat. **s. flexible,** soft felt hat. **s. hongo,** bowler (hat)
sombría *f*, shady spot
sombrilla *f*, sunshade
sombrío *a* dark; shadowy; overcast; *art* shaded; gloomy, melancholy

someramente *adv* superficially; briefly, summarily
somero *a* superficial, shallow; summary, rudimentary, brief
someter *vt* to put down, defeat; submit, place before; subject. **s. a votación,** to put to a vote. *vr* yield, surrender; (*with prep a*) undergo
sometimiento *m*, defeat; submission (to arbitration, etc.); subjection
somnambulismo *m*, somnambulism, sleepwalking
somnámbulo (-la) *a* somnambulistic. *n* somnambulist
somnífero *a* soporiferous
somnílocuo *a* somniloquous, sleeptalking
somnolencia *f*, somnolence
son *m*, sound; rumor; reason, motive; means, way; guise, manner. **al s. de,** to the sound of; to the music of. **en s. de,** in the manner of, as, like, under pretext of
sonadera *f*, nose blowing
sonado *a* famous; much admired or talked of. **hacer una que sea sonada,** *inf* to cause a great scandal; do something noteworthy
sonaja *f*, metal jingles on a tambourine; baby's rattle
sonajero *m*, baby's rattle
sonar *vi irr* to sound; be quoted, be mentioned; ring; *inf* be familiar, remember (e.g. **No me suena el nombre,** I don't remember the name); (*with prep a*) be reminiscent of; *vt* sound; ring; play on; clink; *vr* be rumored, be reported; blow one's nose. *Pres. Ind.* **sueno, suenas, suena, suenan.** *Pres. Subjunc.* **suene, suenes, suene, suenen**
sonata *f*, sonata
sonda *f*, *naut* taking of soundings, heaving the lead; sound, plummet, lead; dragrope; probe, sound
sondar *vt naut* to take soundings; probe; *inf* sound, try to find out; bore, drill
sondeable *a* fathomable
sondeo *m*, *naut* sounding; *min* drilling; probing
sonetear, sonetizar *vi* to write sonnets
sonetista *mf* sonneteer
soneto *m*, sonnet
sonido *m*, sound; literal meaning; rumor, report
sonochar *vi* to keep watch in the early hours of the night
sonoridad *f*, sonorousness
sonoro *a* sounding; resonant, loud; sonorous
sonreír, sonreírse *vi* and *vr irr* to smile; *vi* look pleasant (landscape, etc.); look favorable (of circumstances). **sonreír tras la barba,** to laugh to oneself. See **reír**
sonriente *a* smiling
sonrisa *f*, smile
sonrojar *vt* to cause to blush; *vr* blush
sonrosado *a* rosy, rose-colored, pink
sonrosar *vt* to make rose-colored; *vr* blush, flush
sonroseo *m*, blush, flush
sonsaca *f*, removal by stealth; pilfering; enticement; *fig* pumping (of a person for information)
sonsacar *vt* to remove by stealth; steal, pilfer; entice away; *fig* pump (a person for information), draw out
sonsonete *m*, rhythmic tapping or drumming; monotonous sound (gen. unpleasant); sarcastic tone of voice
soñador (-ra) *a* dreamy, sleepy. *n* dreamer
soñar *vt* to dream; imagine, conjure up; (*with con*) dream of; (*with prep a*) fear (of persons)
soñoliento *a* sleepy, drowsy; soothing; slow, leisurely
¡Soo! *interj* Whoa! (command to horses, etc.)
sopa *f*, sop, piece of bread; soup. **s. boba,** beggar's portion; life of ease at others' expense. **andar a la s.,** to beg one's way. **hecho una s.,** *inf* wet through
sopapo *m*, chuck under the chin; *inf* slap; valve
sopera *f*, soup tureen
sopero *m*, soup plate, soup bowl. *a* fond of soup
sopesar *vt* to try the weight of
sopetón *m*, blow, cuff. **de s.,** suddenly
soplado *f*, puff of wind
soplado *a inf* overelegant; haughty, stiff. *m*, fissure, chasm

soplador (-ra) *a* instigatory. *m*, blower, fan. *n* instigator; blower

soplar *vi* to blow; *vt* blow; blow away; inflate, blow up; filch, steal; instigate, inspire; accuse; fan; prompt, help out; *vr inf* eat and drink too much; *inf* be puffed up, grow haughty. *interj* ¡**Sopla!** *inf* You don't say so!

soplete *m*, blowpipe

soplo *m*, blow; blowing; instant, trice; *inf* hint, tip; *inf* accusation; *inf* tale-bearer; puff, breath (of wind)

soplón (-ona) *a inf* tale-bearing, backbiting. *n* talebearer. *m*, *aut* scavenger

soponcio *m*, *inf* fainting fit

sopor *m*, stupor; deep sleep

soporífero *a* soporiferous

soportable *a* bearable

soportador (-ra) *a* supporting. *n* supporter

soportal *m*, portico

soportar *vt* to bear; carry, support; put up with, tolerate

soporte *m*, rest, support; *mech* bearing; *mech* bracket, support; backup (of a computer file)

sorbedor (-ra) *a* supping, sipping. *n* sipper

sorber *vt* to suck; imbibe; swallow; *fig* absorb eagerly (ideas); sip

sorbete *m*, sherbet, iced drink; French ice cream

sorbo *m*, sucking; imbibition; swallow; sip; mouthful, gulp

sordamente *adv* secretly, quietly

sordera *f*, deafness

sórdido *a* dirty, squalid; mean, niggardly; sordid

sordina *f*, *mus* sordine, mute; *mus* damper. **a la s.,** on the quiet, in secret

sordo *a* deaf; silent, quiet; dull, muted (of sounds); insensible, inanimate; obdurate, uncompliant. **a la sorda** *or* **a lo s.** *or* **a sordas,** in silence, quietly

sordomudez *f*, deaf-muteness, deaf-mutism

sordomudo (-da) *a* and *n* deaf-mute

sorna *f*, slowness, sluggishness; craftiness, guile, knavery; malice

soroche *m*, *Peru* altitude sickness, mountain sickness

sorprendente *a* surprising, amazing

sorprender *vt* to surprise, amaze

sorpresa *f*, surprise; amazement; shock

sorpresivo, -a *a*, *Lat. Am.* sudden, unexpected; surprising

sortear *vt* to raffle; draw lots for; avoid artfully (difficulties, etc.); fight (bulls)

sorteo *m*, raffle; casting lots

sortero (-ra) *n* sorcerer; holder of a draw ticket

sortija *f*, ring (for a finger); ring (for a curtain, etc.); curl

sortilegio *m*, sorcery, magic

sortílego (-ga) *a* magic. *n* sorcerer, fortuneteller

sosa *f*, sodium carbonate, soda ash. **s. cáustica,** sodium-hydroxide, caustic soda, soda

sosegado *a* tranquil, peaceful, calm

sosegador (-ra) *a* soothing, calming. *n* appeaser, soother

sosegar *vt irr* to soothe, quiet; reassure; appease, moderate; *vi* grow still; rest, sleep; *vr* grow quiet; calm down, be appeased; grow still. See **cegar**

sosería *f*, insipidness; lack of wit, dullness; stupidity

sosia *f*, double, exact likeness (of persons)

sosiego *m*, calm; peace, tranquility

soslayar *vt* to slant, place in an oblique position; *fig* go around (a difficulty)

soslayo *a* slanting. **al s.,** obliquely, on the slant; askance

soso *a* saltless, insipid; dull, uninteresting; heavy (of people)

sospecha *f*, suspicion

sospechar *vt* and *vi* to suspect

sospechoso *a* suspicious. *m*, suspect

sostén *m*, support; *mech* stand, support; brassiere, bra, bustier; steadiness (of a ship)

sostenedor (-ra) *a* supporting. *n* supporter

sostener *vt irr* to support; defend, uphold; bear, tolerate; help, aid; maintain, support. **s. una conversación,** to carry on a conversation. See **tener**

sostenido *a mus* sostenuto, sustained. *a* and *m*, *mus* sharp

sostenimiento *m*, support; defense; toleration, endurance; maintenance, sustenance

sota *f*, jack, knave (in cards); *inf* baggage, hussy. *m*, foreman, supervisor. *prep* deputy, substitute (e.g. **sotamontero,** deputy huntsman)

sotabanco *m*, attic, garret

sotana *f*, gown, cassock, robe

sótano *m*, basement, cellar

sotavento *m*, leeward. **a s.,** on the lee

sotechado *m*, hut, shed

soterrar *vt irr* to bury in the ground; hide, conceal. See **acertar**

sotileza *f*, fine cord for fishing (in Santander province)

soto *m*, thicket, grove, copse

soviético *a* soviet

sovietismo *m*, sovietism

sovietizar *vt* to sovietize

sovoz, a *adv* in a low voice

su, sus *poss pron 3rd pers mf sing* and *pl* his, her, its, one's, your, their

suasorio *a* suasive, persuasive

suave *a* soft, smooth; sweet; pleasant, harmonious, quiet; slow, gentle; meek; delicate, subtle

suavidad *f*, softness, smoothness; sweetness; pleasantness; quietness; gentleness; meekness; delicacy

suavizador *a* softening, smoothing; soothing, quietening. *m*, razor strop

suavizar *vt* to soften; smooth; strop (a razor); moderate, temper; *mech* steady; quieten; ease

subalpino *a* subalpine

subalternar *vt* to put down, subdue

subalterno *a* subordinate. *m*, subordinate; *mil* subaltern

subarrendar *vt irr* to sublet. See **recomendar**

subarrendatario (-ia) *n* sublessee

subarriendo *m*, sublease, sublet

subasta *f*, auction sale. **sacar a pública s.,** to sell by auction

subastar *vt* to auction

subcentral *f*, substation

subclase *f*, subclass

subcolector *m*, assistant collector

subcomisión *f*, subcommittee

subconsciencia *f*, subconscious

subcutáneo *a* subcutaneous

subdelegar *vt* to subdelegate

subdirector (-ra) *n* deputy, assistant director

súbdito (-ta) *a* dependent, subject. *n* subject (of a state)

subdividir *vt* to subdivide

subdominante *f*, *mus* subdominant

subgénero *m*, subgenus

subgobernador *m*, deputy governor, lieutenant governor

subibaja *f*, seesaw, teetertotter

subida *f*, ascension, ascent; upgrade; rise; carrying up; raising (of a theater curtain)

subidero *m*, uphill road; mounting block; way up (to a higher level)

subido *a* strong (of scents); deep (of colors); expensive, high-priced; best, finest

subidor *m*, porter, carrier; elevator

subintendente *m*, deputy or assistant intendant

subir *vi* to ascend, climb, go up; mount; rise; *com* amount (to), reach; prosper, advance, be promoted; grow more acute (of illnesses); intensify; *mus* raise the pitch (of an instrument or voice); *vt* ascend, climb; pick up, take up; raise up; place higher; build up, make taller; straighten up, place in a vertical position; increase, raise (in price or value); *vr* ascend, climb. **s. a caballo,** to mount a horse. **subirse a la cabeza,** *inf* to go to one's head (of alcohol, etc.)

subitáneo *a* sudden

súbito *a* unexpected, unforeseen; sudden; precipitate, impulsive. *adv* suddenly (also **de s.**)

subjefe *m*, deputy chief, second in command
subjetividad *f*, subjectivity
subjetivismo *m*, subjectivism
subjetivo *a* subjective
subjuntivo *a* and *m*, subjunctive
sublevación *f*, **sublevamiento** *m*, rebellion, mutiny, uprising
sublevar *vt* to rouse to rebellion; excite (indignation, etc.); *vr* rebel
sublimación *f*, sublimation
sublimado *m*, *chem* sublimate
sublimar *vt* to exalt, raise up; *chem* sublimate
sublime *a* sublime
sublimidad *f*, sublimity, majesty, nobility
submarino *a* submarine. *m*, submarine. **s. de bolsillo** or **s. enano**, midget submarine
suboficial *m*, *mil* subaltern; *nav* petty officer
subordinación *f*, dependence, subordination
subordinado (-da) *a* and *n* subordinate
subordinar *vt* to subordinate
subprefecto *m*, subprefect
subproducto *m*, by-product
subrayar *vt* to underline; emphasize
subrepción *f*, underhand dealing; *law* subreption
subrepticio *a* surreptitious; clandestine
subrogación *f*, surrogation
subrogar *vt law* to surrogate, elect as a substitute
subs—For words so beginning not found here, see **sus-**
subsanar *vt* to make excuses for; remedy, put right; indemnify
subscriptor (-ra) *n* subscriber
subsección *f*, subsection
subsecretaría *f*, assistant secretaryship; assistant secretary's office
subsecretario (-ia) *n* assistant secretary
subsecuente *a* subsequent
subsidiario *a* subsidized; subsidiary
subsidio *m*, subsidy
subsiguiente *a* subsequent; next
subsistencia *f*, permanence; stability; subsistence, maintenance; livelihood
subsistir *vi* to last, endure; subsist, live; make a livelihood
subsuelo *m*, subsoil, substratum
subte *m*, *Argentina, informal* subway
subteniente *m*, *mil* second lieutenant
subterfugio *m*, subterfuge, trick
subterráneo *a* underground, subterranean. *m*, subterranean place
subtítulo *m*, subtitle; caption
subtropical *a* subtropical
suburbano (-na) *a* suburban. *n* suburbanite
suburbio *m*, suburb
subvención *f*, subsidy, subvention, grant
subvencionar *vt* to subsidize
subvenir *vt irr* to help, succor; subsidize. See **venir**
subversivo *a* subversive
subvertir *vt irr* to subvert, overturn, ruin. See **sentir**
subyugación *f*, subjugation
subyugador (-ra) *a* subjugating. *n* conqueror
subyugar *vt* to subjugate, overcome
succión *f*, suction
suceder *vi* to follow, come after; inherit, succeed. *impers* happen, occur
sucedido *m*, *inf* event, occurrence
sucesión *f*, succession; series; offspring, descendants; *law* estate
sucesivo *a* successive. **en lo s.,** in future
suceso *m*, happening, occurrence; course (of time); outcome, result
sucesor (-ra) *a* succeeding. *n* successor
suciedad *f*, dirt; filth, nastiness; obscenity
sucinto *a* succinct, brief, concise
sucio *a* dirty, unclean; stained; easily soiled; *fig* sullied, spotted; obscene; dirty (of colors); *fig* tainted, infected. **jugar s.,** *sport* to play in an unsporting manner

suco *m*, juice
sucoso *a* juicy
sucre *m* sucre (monetary unit of Ecuador)
suculencia *f*, succulence; juiciness
suculento *a* succulent; juicy
sucumbir *vi* to yield, give in; die, succumb; lose a lawsuit
sucursal *a* branch. *f*, *com* branch (of a firm)
sud *m*, south (gen. **sur**). Used in combinations like **sudamericano**
sudadero *m*, horse blanket; sudatorium, sweating bath
sudafricano (-na) *a* and *n* South African
Sudamérica *f* South America
sudamericano (-na) *a* and *n* South American
sudante *a* sweating, perspiring
sudar *vi* and *vt* to perspire, sweat; ooze; *vi inf* toil; *vt* bathe in sweat; *inf* give reluctantly. **s. frío,** to break out in a cold sweat. **s. la gota gorda,** *fig inf* to be in a stew
sudario *m*, shroud
sudeste *m*, southeast; southeast wind
sudexpreso *m*, southern express
sudoeste *m*, southwest; southwest wind
sudor *m*, sweat, perspiration; toil; juice, moisture, sap, gum
sudoroso *a* sweaty
sudsudeste *m*, southsoutheast
sudsudoeste *m*, southsouthwest
Suecia Sweden
sueco (-ca) *a* Swedish. *n* Swede. *m*, Swedish (language)
suegra *f*, mother-in-law
suegro *m*, father-in-law
suela *f*, sole (of a shoe); *icht* sole; tanned leather; base. **no llegarle a uno a la s. del zapato,** *inf* to be not fit to hold a candle to.
sueldo *m*, salary, wages; *ant* Spanish coin. **a s.,** for a salary, salaried
suelo *m*, ground, earth; soil; bottom, base; sediment, dregs; site, plot; floor; flooring; story; land, territory; hoof (of horses); earth, world; *pl* chaff of grain. **s. natal,** native land; besar el s., *inf* to fall flat. **dar consigo en el s.,** to fall down. **dar en el s. con,** to throw down; damage, spoil. *inf* **estar (una cosa) por los suelos,** to be dirt cheap
suelta *f*, loosening, unfastening; hobble (for horses); relay of oxen. **dar s. a,** to let loose, allow to go out for a time
sueltista *mf, Lat. Am.* freelance journalist, stringer
suelto *a* swift; competent, efficient; odd, separate; licentious; flowing, easy (style); loose, unbound. *m*, single copy (of a newspaper); loose change; newspaper paragraph
sueño *m*, dream; sleep; drowsiness, desire for sleep; vision, fancy. **s. pesado,** deep sleep. **conciliar el s.,** to court sleep. **echar un s.,** *inf* to take a nap. **en sueños,** in a dream; while asleep. **entre sueños,** between sleeping and waking. **¡Ni por sueño!** *inf* Certainly not! I wouldn't dream of it!
suero *m*, serum. **s. de la leche,** whey
suerte *f*, chance, luck; good luck; destiny, fate; condition, state; kind, species, sort; way, manner; bullfighter's maneuver; parcel of land. **de s. que,** so that; as a result. **echar suertes,** to draw lots. **tener buena s.,** to be lucky
sueste *m*, southeast; sou'wester (cap); *Lat. Am.* southeast wind
suéter *m*, sweater
suficiencia *f*, sufficiency; talent, aptitude; pedantry. **a s.,** enough
suficiente *a* sufficient, enough; suitable
sufijo *m*, suffix
sufragar *vt* to assist, aid; favor; pay, defray
sufragio *m*, aid, assistance; *ecc* suffragium, pious offering; vote; suffrage
sufragista *f*, suffragette
sufrible *a* bearable, endurable

sufrido *a* long-suffering, resigned; complaisant (of husbands); dirt-resistant (colors)

sufrimiento *m*, suffering, pain; affliction; tolerance

sufrir *vt* to suffer, undergo, experience; bear, endure; tolerate, put up with; allow, permit; resist, oppose; expiate; *vi* suffer

sugerir *vt irr* to suggest. See **sentir**

sugestión *f*, suggestion

sugestionable *a* easily influenced, open to suggestion

sugestionador *a* suggestive

sugestionar *vt* to suggest hypnotically; dominate, influence

sugestivo *a* suggestive, stimulating

suicida *a* suicidal, fatal. *mf* suicide (person)

suicidarse *vr* to commit suicide

suicidio *m*, suicide (act)

Suiza Switzerland

suiza *f*, row, rumpus, scrap

suizo (-za) *a* and *n* Swiss

sujeción *f*, subjection, domination; fastening, fixture; obedience, conformity

sujetador *m*, clamp; clip

sujetar *vt* to fasten, fix; hold down; grasp, clutch; subdue; *vr* (*with prep a*) conform to, obey. **s. con alfileres,** to pin up. **s. con tornillos,** to screw down

sujeto *a* liable, subject. *m*, topic, subject; person, individual; *gram phil* subject

sulfatar *vt* to sulphate

sulfato *m*, sulphate

sulfurar *vt* to sulphurate; *vr* grow irritated, become angry

sulfúrico *a* sulphuric

sulfuro *m*, sulphide

sulfuroso *a* sulphurous

sultán *m*, sultan

sultana *f*, sultana

suma *f*, total; amount, sum; *math* addition; summary, digest; computation. **en s.,** in brief, in short, finally

sumador (-ra) *n* summarizer; computator; adder

sumamente *adv* extremely, most

sumar *vt* to sum up, summarize; *math* add up

sumaria *f*, written indictment

sumariamente *adv* concisely, in brief; *law* summarily

sumario *a* brief, concise, abridged; *law* summary. *m*, summary, résumé, digest

sumergible *a* sinkable; submergible. *m*, submarine

sumergir *vt* to dip, immerse; sink, submerge; *fig* overwhelm (with grief, etc.); *vr* sink; dive; be submerged

sumersión *f*, immersion, dive, submersion

sumidero *m*, cesspool; drain; sink; pit, gully

suministración *f*. See **suministro**

suministrador (-ra) *n* purveyor

suministrar *vt* to purvey, supply, provide

suministro *m*, purveyance; provision; supply

sumir *vt* to sink; submerge; *ecc* consummate; *fig* overwhelm (with grief, etc.); *vr* fall in, become sunken (of cheeks, etc.); sink; be submerged; *Lat. Am.* cower, cringe

sumisión *f*, submission, obedience; *com* estimate, tender

sumiso *a* submissive, docile

sumista *mf* quick reckoner, computator. *m*, condenser, summarizer, abridger

sumo *a* supreme; high; tremendous, extraordinary. **a lo s.,** at the most; even if, although. **en s. grado,** in the highest degree

suntuosidad *f*, magnificence, luxury

suntuoso *a* magnificent, luxurious, sumptuous

supeditación *f*, subjection

supeditar *vt* to oppress; overcome, conquer; subordinate

superabundancia *f*, superabundance, excess; glut

superabundante *a* superabundant, excessive

superádito *a* superadded

superar *vt* to overcome, conquer; surpass; do better than

superávit *m*, *com* balance, surplus

superchería *f*, trickery, guile

superchero *a* guileful, wily

superconsciencia *f*, higher consciousness

supereminencia *f*, supereminence, greatest eminence

supereminente *a* supereminent

superentender *vt irr* to supervise, superintend. See **entender**

supererogación *f*, supererogation

superestructura *f*, superstructure

superficial *a* surface, shallow; superficial, rudimentary; futile

superficialidad *f*, superficiality; futility; shallowness

superficie *f*, area; surface; outside, exterior. **s. de rodadura,** tire tread

superfino *a* superfine

superfluidad *f*, superfluity

superfluo *a* superfluous, redundant

superfortaleza volante *f*, *aer* superfortress

superhombre *m*, superman

superintendencia *f*, supervision; superintendentship; higher administration

superintendente *mf* superintendent; supervisor

superior *a* higher, upper; excellent, fine; superior; higher (education, etc.). *m*, head, director; superior

superiora *f*, mother superior

superioridad *f*, superiority

superlativo *a* and *m*, superlative

superno *a* supreme

supernumerario (-ia) *a* and *n* supernumerary

superposición *f*, superposition

superproducción *f*, overproduction; superproduction

superrealismo *m*, surrealism

superrealista *a* surrealist

superstición *f*, superstition

supersticioso *a* superstitious

supervención *f*, *law* supervention

supervigilancia *f*, *Lat. Am.* supervision

supervivencia *f*, survival

superviviente *a* surviving. *mf* survivor

supino *a* supine; foolish, stupid. *m*, *gram* supine

suplantación *f*, supplanting

suplantador (-ra) *a* supplanting. *n* supplanter

suplantar *vt* to forge, alter (documents); supplant

suplefaltas *mf inf* scapegoat

suplementario *a* supplementary, additional

suplemento *m*, supplement; supply, supplying; newspaper supplement; *geom* supplement

suplente *m*, substitute, proxy; *fig* makeweight

súplica *f*, supplication, prayer; request

suplicación *f*, entreaty, supplication; *law* petition

suplicante *a* supplicatory; *law* petitioning. *mf* supplicator; *law* petitioner

suplicar *vt* to beg, supplicate; request; *law* appeal

suplicio *m*, torment, torture; execution; place of torture or execution; affliction, anguish. **último s.,** capital punishment

suplir *vt* to supply, furnish; substitute, take the place of; overlook, forgive

suponer *vt irr* to suppose, take for granted; simulate; comprise, include; *vi* carry weight, wield authority. See **poner**

suposición *f*, supposition; conjecture, assumption; distinction, talent, importance; falsity, falsehood

supositorio *m*, suppository

suprasensible *a* supersensible

supremacía *f*, supremacy

supremo *a* supreme; matchless, incomparable; last

supresión *f*, suppression; destruction, eradication; omission

suprimir *vt* to suppress; destroy, eradicate; omit, leave out. **s. una calle al tráfico,** to close a street to traffic, ban traffic from a street

supuesto *a* supposed; so-called; reputed. *m*, supposition, hypothesis. **por s.,** presumably; doubtless
supurar *vi* to suppurate
suputar *vt* to calculate, compute
sur *m*, south; south wind
surcador *m*, plowman
surcar *vt* to plow furrows; furrow, line; cut, cleave (water, etc.)
surco *m*, furrow; wrinkle, line; groove, channel; rut
surgidero *m, naut* road, roadstead
surgir *vi* to spout, gush, spurt; *naut* anchor; appear, show itself; come forth, turn up
surrealismo *m*, surrealism
surrealista *a* and *mf* surrealist
surtida *f*, hidden exit; false door; *naut* slipway
surtidero *m*, outlet, drain; jet, fountain
surtido *a* mixed, assorted. *m*, variety, assortment; stock, range. **de s.,** in everyday use
surtidor (-ra) *n* purveyor, supplier. *m*, fountain, jet. **s. de gasolina,** gasoline pump, gas pump
surtimiento *m*, assortment; stock
surtir *vt* to provide, supply, furnish; *vi* spurt, gush
surto *a* calm, reposeful; *naut* anchored
susceptibilidad *f*, susceptibility
susceptible *a* susceptible, open to; touchy, oversensitive
suscitar *vt* to cause, originate; provoke, incite; *vr* arise, take place
suscribir *vt* to sign; agree to; *vr* subscribe, contribute; take out a subscription (to a periodical, etc.). *Past Part.* **suscrito**
suscripción *f*, subscription; agreement, accession
susodicho *a* aforesaid
suspender *vt* to suspend, hang up; postpone, defer, stop; amaze, dumbfound; suspend (from employment); fail (an exam); adjourn (meetings); *vr* rear (of horses)
suspensión *f*, suspension; postponement, stoppage, deferment; amazement; failure (in an exam); adjournment (of a meeting); springs (of a car). *com* **s. de pagos,** suspension of payments. **con mala s.,** badly sprung (of a car)
suspensivo *a* suspensive
suspensivos *m, pl* suspension points, ellipsis points
suspenso *a* amazed, bewildered. *m*, failure slip (in an exam). **en s.,** in suspense
suspensor *m, Lat. Am.* suspender (for pants)
suspicacia *f*, suspiciousness; mistrust, uneasiness
suspicaz *a* suspicious, mistrustful
suspirado *a* eagerly desired, longed for
suspirar *vt* and *vi* to sigh. **s. por,** to long for
suspiro *m*, sigh; breath; glass whistle; *mus* brief pause, pause sign. **último s.,** *inf* last kick, end
suspirón *a* given to sighing

sustancia *f*, substance, juice, extract, essence; *fig* core, pith; *fig* meat; wealth, estate; worth, importance; nutritive part; *inf* common sense. *anat* **s. gris,** gray matter. **en s.,** in short
sustanciación *f*, substantiation
sustancial *a* substantial, real; important, essential; nutritive; solid
sustanciar *vt* to substantiate; summarize, extract, abridge
sustancioso *a* substantial; nutritive
sustantivo *a* and *m, gram* substantive, noun
sustentable *a* arguable, defensible
sustentación *f*, maintenance; defense
sustentar *vt* to sustain, keep; support, bear; nourish, feed; uphold, advocate. **s. un ciclo de conferencias,** to give a series of lectures
sustento *m*, maintenance, preservation; nourishment, sustenance; support
sustitución *f*, substitution
sustituible *a* substitutive, replaceable
sustituir *vt irr* to substitute. See **huir**
sustitutivo *a* substitutive
sustituto (-ta) *n* substitute
susto *m*, fright, shock; apprehension. **dar un s. (a),** to scare
sustracción *f*, subtraction
sustraer *vt irr* to remove, separate; rob, steal; *math* subtract; *vr* depart, remove oneself; avoid. See **traer**
sustrato *m*, substratum
susurrador (-ra) *a* whispering; murmuring; rustling. *n* whisperer
susurrante *a* whispering; murmuring; rustling
susurrar *vi* to whisper; murmur; rustle; babble, purl, prattle (of water); *vi* and *vr* be whispered abroad
susurro *m*, whispering, whisper; murmur; rustle; lapping
sutil *a* fine, thin; penetrating, subtle, keen
sutileza, sutilidad *f*, fineness, thinness; subtlety, penetration. **sutileza de manos,** dexterity; light-fingeredness; sleight of hand
sutilizaciones *f, pl* casuistry, hairsplitting, quibbling
sutilizar *vt* to make thin, refine; *fig* finish, perfect; *fig* split hairs, make subtle distinctions
sutura *f*, suture
suyo, suya *m*, and *f, pl* **suyos, suyas,** *poss pron* and *a 3rd pers* his; hers; its; yours; theirs; of his, of hers, etc. (e.g. **Este libro es suyo,** This book is his (hers, yours, theirs). **Este libro es uno de los suyos,** This book is one of his (hers, etc.). (**suyo** is often used with def. art. **el, la,** etc.) **los suyos,** his (hers, yours, etc.) family, following, adherents, etc. **de suyo,** of its very nature, of itself; spontaneously. **salirse con la suya,** to get one's own way. *inf* **ver la suyo,** to see one's opportunity

T

tabacal *m*, tobacco plantation
tabacalero (-ra) *a* tobacco. *n* tobacco merchant; tobacco planter
tabaco *m*, tobacco plant, tobacco leaf; tobacco; cigar. **t. de pipa,** pipe tobacco. **t. flojo,** mild tobacco. **t. rubio,** Virginia tobacco
tabalear(se) *vt* and *vr* to rock, sway, swing; *vi* drum with the fingers
tabaleo *m*, swaying, rocking; drumming with the fingers
tabanco *m*, market stall
tábano *m, ent* horsefly
tabanque *m*, potter's wheel
tabaque *m*, small osier basket (for fruit, sewing, etc.); large tack
tabaquera *f*, tobacco jar, tobacco tin; bowl of pipe tobacco; tobacco pouch; snuffbox

tabaquería *f*, tobacconist's shop
tabaquero (-ra) *a* tobacco. *n* tobacco grower; tobacco merchant; tobacco factory worker; tobacconist
tabaquismo *m*, nicotinism, nicotine poisoning
tabaquista *mf* tobacco expert; heavy smoker
tabardillo *m*, fever. **t. de tripas,** typhoid. **t. pintado,** typhus
tabardo *m*, tabard
taberna *f*, public house, tavern
tabernáculo *m*, tabernacle
tabernario *a* public house, tavern; low, vulgar
tabernera *f*, publican's wife; barmaid
tabernero *m*, publican; barman, drawer
tabicar *vt* to wall or board up; hide, cover up
tabique *m*, partition wall, inside wall; thin wall
tabla *f*, plank of wood, board; *met* plate; slab; flat side, face (of wood); *sew* box pleat; table (of contents, etc.);

art panel; vegetable garden; butcher's slab; butcher's stall; *pl* tablets (for writing); (*math* etc.) tables; stalemate (chess, checkers); draw (in an election); *theat* boards, stage. **t. de armonía,** sounding board (of musical instruments). **t. de lavar,** washboard. **t. de materias,** table of contents. **t. de multiplicación,** multiplication table. **t. rasa,** clean sheet (of paper, etc.); complete ignorance. **T. Redonda,** Round Table (of King Arthur). **escapar** *or* **salvarse en una t.,** to have a narrow escape, escape in the nick of time

tablacho *m,* sluice gate. **echar el t.,** *inf* to interrupt the flow of someone's remarks

tablado *m,* flooring; platform; *theat* stage; scaffold, gibbet. **sacar al t.,** to produce, put on the stage; to make known, publish

tablazón *f,* planks, boards; flooring; *naut* deck planks or sheathing

tablear *vt* to saw into planks; *sew* make box pleats in; hammer iron into sheets

tablero *m,* board (of wood); paneling, boarding; slab; shop counter; board (checkers, chess). **t. de instrumentos,** dashboard; instrument panel

tableta *f,* tablet; pastille, lozenge

tablilla *f,* small board; tablet; bulletin board, notice board

tablón *m,* thick plank; wooden beam; *inf* drinking bout

tabú *m,* taboo

tabuco *m,* miserable little room; hovel

taburete *m,* stool; tabouret

tacañería *f,* miserliness, niggardliness; craftiness

tacaño *a* miserly, niggardly; crafty

tacha *f,* imperfection, defect; spot, stain; fault; large tack. **poner t.,** to criticize, object to

tachable *a* censurable, blameworthy

tachar *vt* to criticize, blame; cross out, erase; charge, accuse

tacho de basura *m, Argentina* garbage can

tachón *m,* round-headed ornamental nail; *sew* gold or silver studs, trimming; crossing out, erasure

tachonar *vt* to stud with round-headed nails; *sew* trim with gold or silver studs or trimming

tachoso *a* imperfect, defective, faulty; spotted, stained

tachuela *f, carp* tack

tácito *a* silent, unexpressed; tacit, implied

taciturnidad *f,* taciturnity; reserve; melancholy

taciturno *a* taciturn; reserved; dismal, gloomy, melancholy

taco *m,* stopper, plug; billiard cue; rammer; wad, wadding (in a gun); pop gun; taco (filled tortilla); tear-off calendar; *Argentina,* heel (of a shoe) *inf* snack; obscenity, oath. **t. de papel,** writing tablet

tacón *m,* heel (of a shoe)

taconear *vi* to stamp with one's heels; walk heavily on one's heels; walk arrogantly

taconeo *m,* drumming or stamping of one's heels (gen. in dancing)

táctica *f,* method, technique; *mil* tactics; policy, way, means

táctico *a* tactical. *m, mil* tactician

táctil *a* tactile

tacto *m,* sense of touch; touch, feel; touching; skill; tact

tafetán *m,* taffeta; *pl* flags, standards. **t. de heridas** *or* **t. inglés,** court plaster

tafilete *m,* morocco leather

tahalí *m,* sword shoulder belt

tahona *f,* horse mill; bakery; baker's shop

tahonero (-ra) *n* miller; baker

tahúr *m,* gambler; cardsharper

tahurería *f,* gambling den; gambling; cheating at cards

Tailandia Thailand

taimado *a* knavish, crafty; obstinate, headstrong

taimería *f,* cunning, craftiness

taita *m,* daddy

taja *f,* cut, cutting; slice; washboard

tajada *f,* slice; strip, portion; steak, filet; *inf* cough; drinking bout; hoarseness

tajadera *f,* cheese knife; chisel; *pl* sluice gate

tajado *a* steep, sheer (of cliffs, etc.)

tajadura *f,* cutting, dividing, dissection

tajar *vt* to cut, chop; sharpen, trim (quill pens)

tajea *f,* culvert; aqueduct; drain; watercourse

tajear *vt, Lat. Am.* to cut up

Tajo, el the Tagus

tajo *m,* cut, incision; task; cutting (in a mountain, etc.); cut, thrust (of sword); executioner's block; chopping board; washboard; steep cliff, precipice

tajón *m,* butcher block; chopping board

tal *a pl* **tales,** such; said (e.g. **el t.** **Don Juan,** the said Don Juan). **tal** is always used before nouns and (except when meaning 'the said') without def. art. **un t.,** a certain (e.g. **un t. hombre,** a certain man). *pron* some, some people; someone; such a thing. *adv* so, thus. **t. para cual,** two of a kind, a well-matched pair; tit for tat. **con t. que,** *conjunc* on condition that, provided that. **No hay t.,** There is no such thing. *inf* **¿Qué t.?** How are you? What's the news? What's new?

tala *f,* felling or cutting down (of trees); cropping of grass (ruminants)

talabarte *m,* sword belt

talabartería *f,* saddlery

talador (-ra) *a* felling, cutting; destructive. *n* feller, cutter; destroyer

taladrar *vt* to drill, bore, gouge holes; pierce, perforate; punch (a ticket); assail or hurt the ear (sounds); *fig* go into deeply (a subject)

taladro *m,* drill, gimlet, gouge; drill hole, bore; puncher (for tickets, etc.)

tálamo *m,* marriage bed; (*bot anat*) thalamus

talán *m,* peal, tolling (of a bell)

talanquera *f,* barricade; parapet, fence, wall; refuge, asylum; safety, security

talante *m,* mode of execution, technique; personal appearance, mien; disposition, temperament; wish, desire; aspect, appearance. **de buen (mal) t.,** willingly (unwillingly)

talar *a* full-length, long (of gowns, robes, etc.)

talar *vt* to fell, chop down (trees); ravage, lay waste; prune (gen. olive trees)

talco *m, min* talc; sequin; tinsel

talcualillo *a inf* not too bad, fairly good; slightly better (of health)

taled *m,* prayer shawl, tales, tallit

talega *f,* sack, bag; sackful; money bag; *pl inf* cash wealth

talego *m,* narrow sack; *inf* dumpy person

talento *m,* talent (Greek coin); talent, gift, quality; intelligence, understanding; cleverness

talentoso *a* talented

talero *m, Argentina* whip

talión *m,* (**ley de**) law of retaliation

talismán *m,* talisman

talla *f,* carving (especially wood); cutting (of gems); reward for apprehension of a criminal; ransom; stature, height, size; height measuring rod

tallado *a* **bien** (or **mal**), well (or badly) carved; well (or badly) proportioned, of a good (or bad) figure

tallado *m,* carving

tallador *m,* metal engraver; die sinker

tallar *vt art* to carve; engrave; cut (gems); value, estimate; measure height (of persons)

tallarín *m,* (gen. *pl*) *cul* noodle

talle *m,* figure, physique; waist; fit (of clothes); appearance, aspect. *inf* **largo de t.,** long-waisted; long drawn out, overlong. **tener buen t.,** to have a good figure

tallecer *vi irr bot* to sprout, shoot. See **conocer**

taller *m,* workshop; factory; mill; workroom, atelier; industrial school; school of arts and crafts; studio

tallista *mf* engraver; wood carver; sculptor

tallo *m, bot* stalk; shoot; slice of preserved fruit; cabbage. **t. rastrero,** *bot* runner

talludo *a* long-stalked; lanky, overgrown; no longer young, aging (of women); habit-ridden

talmúdico *a* Talmudic

talón *m,* heel; heel (of a shoe); *com* counterfoil; luggage receipt; *com* sight draft; coupon; heel (of a violin bow). *inf* **apretar los talones,** to take to one's heels. *inf* **pisarle (a uno) los talones,** to follow on a person's heels; rival successfully

talonada *f,* dig in with the spurs

talonario *m,* stub book

tamaño *a comp* so big; so small (e.g. **La conocí tamaña,** I knew her when she was so high) (indicating her size with a gesture)); so great, so large (e.g. **tamaña empresa,** so great an undertaking). *m,* size

tamarindo *m,* tamarind

tambaleante *a* tottering, rickety; staggering

tambalear(se) *vi* and *vr* to totter, sway, shake; reel, stagger

tambaleo *m,* swaying; tottering; rocking; shaking; staggering, reeling

tambarillo *m,* chest with an arched lid

también *adv* also, too; in addition, as well

tambor *m, mus* drum; drummer; embroidery frame; *mech* drum, cylinder; roaster (for coffee, chestnuts, etc.). **t. mayor,** drum major. **a t.** (*or* **con t.**) **batiente,** with drums beating; triumphantly, with colors flying

tamborear *vi* to totter, sway; stagger, reel

tamboreo *m,* tottering, swaying; staggering, reeling

tamboril *m,* tabor

tamborilada *f, inf* slap on the back or face; *inf* fall on the bottom

tamborilear *vi* to play the tabor; *vt* eulogize, extol

tamborilero *m,* tabor player

tamborín *m,* tabor

Támesis, el the Thames

tamiz *m,* sieve

tamizar *vt* to sieve

tamo *m,* fluff; chaff

tampoco *adv* neither, not . . . either, nor . . . either; no more (e.g. **No lo ha hecho María t.,** Mary hasn't done it either)

tampón *m,* stamp moistener; *surg* tampon

tan *adv abb* **tanto** so, as. Used before adjectives and adverbs, excepting **más, mejor, menos, peor,** which need **tanto. t. . . . como,** as . . . as. **t. siquiera,** even (see **siquiera**). **t. sólo,** only, solely (e.g. **No vengo t. sólo para saludarte,** I do not come merely to greet you). **qué . . . t.,** what a . . . (e.g. **¡Qué día t. hermoso!** What a lovely day!)

tanda *f,* turn; opportunity; task; shift, relay; game (of billiards); bad habit; collection, batch, group; round (of a game); (*dance*) set

tándem *m,* tandem

tandeo *m,* allowance of irrigation water, turn for using water

Tangañica Tanganyika

tangente *a* and *f, geom* tangent

Tánger Tangier

tangerino (-na) *a* and *n* of or from Tangier, Tangerine

tanque *m, mil* tank; cistern, tank, reservoir; ladle, dipper

tanteador *m, sport* scorer, marker; scoreboard

tantear *vt* to measure, compare; consider fully; test, try out; *fig* probe, pump (persons); estimate roughly; *art* sketch, block in; *vt* and *vi sport* keep the score of

tanteo *m,* measurement, comparison; test; rough estimate; *sport* score

tanto *a* so much; as much; very great; as great; *pl* **tantos,** so many; as many (e.g. **Tienen tantas flores como nosotros,** They have as many flowers as we). In comparisons **tanto** is used before **más, mejor, menos, peor,** but generally **tan** is used before adjectives and adverbs (e.g. **¡Tanto peor!** So much the worse!). *pron dem* that (e.g. **por lo t.,** therefore, on that account). *m,* so much, a certain amount; copy of a document; man, piece (in games); point (score in games); *com* rate (e.g. **el t. por ciento,** the percentage, the rate); *pl* approximation, odd (e.g. **Llegaron cien hombres y tantos,** A hundred-odd men arrived). *adv*

so much; as much; so, in such a way. **t. . . . como,** the same as, as much as. **t. . . . cuanto,** as much as. **t. más,** the more. **t. menos,** the less (e.g. **Cuanto más (menos) dinero tiene t. más (menos) quiere,** The more (less) money he has, the more (less) he wants). **t. más (menos) . . . cuanto que,** all the more (less) . . . because. **algún t.,** a certain amount, somewhat. **al t. de (una cosa),** aware of, acquainted with (a thing). **en t.** *or* **entre t.,** meanwhile. **las tantas,** *inf* late hour, wee hours. **No es para t.,** *inf* It's not as bad as that, there's no need to make such a fuss; he (she, it) isn't equal to it. **otro t.,** the same, as much; as much more. **un t.,** a bit, somewhat

tañedor (-ra) *n mus* player

tañer *vt irr mus* to play; *vi* sway, swing. **t. la occisa,** to sound the death (in hunting). *Pres. Part.* **tañendo.** *Preterite* **tañó, tañeron.** *Imperf. Subjunc.* **tañese,** etc.

tañido *m,* tune, sound, note; toll, peal; ring

taoísmo *m,* Taoism

taoísta *mf* Taoist

tapa *f,* lid; cover; cover (of books)

tapaboca *m,* blow on the mouth; *f,* scarf, muffler; *inf* remark that silences someone

tapada *f,* veiled woman, one whose face is hidden

tapadera *f,* loose lid, top, cover

tapadero *m,* stopper

tapado *m, Argentina* coat, overcoat

tapador (-ra) *a* covering. *n* coverer. *m,* stopper; lid; cover

tapagujeros *m, inf* unskilled mason or bricklayer; *fig inf* stopgap (person)

tapar *vt* to cover; cover with a lid; muffle up, veil; hide, keep secret; close up, stop up

taparrabo *m,* loincloth; swimming trunks

tapete *m,* rug; tablecover. *inf* **t. verde,** gaming table. *fig* **estar sobre el t.,** to be on the carpet, be under consideration

tapia *f,* adobe; mud wall; fence. *inf* **más sordo que una t.,** as deaf as a post

tapiar *vt* to wall up; put a fence around, fence in

tapicería *f,* set of tapestries; tapestry work; art of tapestry making; upholstery; tapestry storehouse or shop

tapicero *m,* tapestry weaver or maker; upholsterer; carpet layer; furnisher

tapioca *f,* tapioca

tapisca *f Central America, Mexico* corn harvest

tapiz *m,* tapestry; carpet

tapizar *vt* to cover with tapestry; cover, clothe; upholster; carpet; hang with tapestry; furnish with hangings or drapes

tapón *m,* stopper; cork (of a bottle); plug; *surg* tampon

taponar *vt* to stopper, cork; plug; *surg* tampon; *mil* seal off

tapujarse *vr* to wrap oneself up, muffle oneself

tapujo *m,* scarf, muffler, face covering; disguise; *inf* pretense, subterfuge

taquera *f,* rack (for billiard cues)

taquería *f,* taco stand

taquigrafía *f,* shorthand

taquigrafiar *vt* to write in shorthand

taquigráfico *a* shorthand

taquígrafo (-fa) *n* shorthand writer, stenographer

taquilla *f,* booking office; box office; grille, window (in banks, etc.); rolltop desk, cupboard for papers; *theat* takings, cash

taquillero (-ra) *n* booking office clerk

tara *f,* tally stick; *com* tare

taracea *f,* inlaid work, marquetry

taracear *vt* to inlay

tarambana *mf inf* madcap

tarántula *f,* tarantula

tararear *vt* to hum a tune

tarareo *m,* humming, singing under one's breath

tarasca *f,* figure of a dragon (carried in Corpus Christi processions); *inf* hag, trollop

tarascada *f,* bite, nip; *inf* insolent reply

tarascar *vt* to bite; wound with the teeth

tardanza *f,* delay, tardiness; slowness

tardar *vi* to delay; be tardy, arrive late; take a long time. **a más t.,** at the latest

tarde *f,* afternoon. *adv* late. **¡Buenas tardes!** Good afternoon! **de t. en t.,** from time to time, sometimes. **hacerse t.,** to grow late. **Más vale t. que nunca,** Better late than never

tardecer *vi impers irr* to grow dusk. See **conocer**

tardecica, tardecita *f,* dusk, late afternoon

tardíamente *adv* late; too late

tardío *a* late; backward; behind; slow, deliberate

tardo *a* slow, slothful, tardy; late; dilatory; stupid, slowwitted; badly spoken, inarticulate

tarea *f,* task, work

tarifa *f,* price list; tariff

tarifar *vt* to put a tariff on

tarima *f,* stand, raised platform

tarín barín *adv inf* more or less, about

tarja *f,* large shield; ancient coin; tally stick. *inf* **beber sobre t.,** to drink on credit

tarjar *vt* to reckon by tally; *Lat. Am.* cross out, erase

tarjeta *f,* buckler, small shield; *arch* tablet bearing an inscription; title (of maps and charts); visiting card; invitation (card). **t. de visita,** visiting card. **t. postal,** postcard, postal card

tarquín *m,* mud, mire

tárraga *f,* old Spanish dance

tarro *m,* jar, pot; *Lat. Am.* top hat

tarso *m, anat* tarsus, ankle; *zool* hock; *orn* shank

tarta *f,* cake pan; cake; tart

tártago *m,* spurge; *inf* misfortune, disappointment

tartajear *vi* to stammer; stutter

tartajeo *m,* stammering; stutter

tartajoso (-sa) *a* stammering; stuttering. *n* stutterer

tartalear *vi inf* to stagger, totter; be speechless, be dumbfounded

tartamudear *vi* to stammer, stutter

tartamudeo *m.* **tartamudez** *f,* stammering; stuttering

tartamudo (-da) *n* stammerer

tartán *m,* tartan

tartana *f, naut* tartan; covered two-wheeled carriage

tartáreo *a poet* infernal, hellish

tártaro (-ra) *m,* cream of tartar; tartar (on teeth); *poet* hell, hades. *a* and *n* Tartar

tartufo *m,* hypocrite

tarugo *m,* thick wooden peg; stopper; wooden block; *a Lat. Am.* dumb, stupid

tasa *f,* assessment, valuation; valuation certificate; fixed price; standard rate; measure, rule

tasación *f,* valuation; assessment

tasador *m,* public assessor; valuer

tasajo *m,* salt meat; piece of meat

tasar *vt* to value; price; fix remuneration; tax; regulate; rate; dole out sparingly

tasca *f,* gambling den; tavern

tascar *vt* to dress (hemp, etc.); graze, crop the grass

tasquera *f, inf* quarrel, row, rumpus

tasquil *m,* wood splinter, chip

tata *m, inf WH* daddy

tatarabuela *f,* great-great-grandmother

tatarabuelo *m,* great-great-grandfather

tataradeudo (-da) *n* very old relative; ancestor

tataranieta *f,* great-great-granddaughter

tataranieto *m,* great-great-grandson

tatas, andar a *vt* to walk on all fours

¡tate! *interj* Stop!; Be careful!; Go slowly!; Now I understand!, Of course!

tatuaje *m,* tattooing

tatuar *vt* to tattoo

taumaturgia *f,* thaumaturgy, wonder-working

taumaturgo *m,* thaumaturge, magician

taurino *a* taurine; pertaining to bullfights

Tauro *m,* Taurus

tauromaquia *f,* bullfighting, tauromachy

tautología *f,* tautology

taxi *m,* taxi

taxidermia *f,* taxidermy

taxidermista *mf* taxidermist

taxista *m,* taxi driver

taxonomía *f,* taxonomy

taz a taz *adv* in exchange, without payment; even

taza *f,* cup; cupful; basin (of a fountain)

tazar(se) *vt* and *vr* to fray (of cloth)

tazón *m,* large cup; bowl

te *f,* name of the letter T. *mf* dat. and acc. of *pers pron 2nd pers sing* thee; you; to thee, to you. Never used with a preposition

té *m,* tea

tea *f,* torch; firebrand

teatral *a* theatrical

teatralidad *f,* theatricality

teatro *m,* theater; stage; dramatic works; dramatic art; drama, plays. **t. de variedades,** music hall. **t. por horas,** theater where short, one-act plays are staged hourly

teca *f,* teak

techado *m,* ceiling; roof

techador *m,* roofer

techar *vt* to roof

techo *m,* roof; ceiling; dwelling, habitation

techumbre *f,* ceiling; roof

tecla *f,* key (of keyed instruments); typewriter, linotype, or calculating machine key; *fig* difficult or delicate point. *inf* **dar en la t.,** to hit on the right way of doing a thing

teclado *m,* keyboard

tecleado *m, mus* fingering

teclear *vi* to finger the keyboard; run one's fingers over the keyboard; *inf* drum or tap with the fingers; *vt* tap (the keys, etc.); *inf* try out various schemes

tecleo *m,* fingering the keys; *inf* drumming with the fingers; scheme, means

técnica *f,* technique

tecnicismo *m,* technical jargon; technicality, technical term

técnico *a* technical. *m,* technician

tecnicolor *m,* technicolor

tecnología *f,* technology

tecnológico *a* technological

tecnólogo *m,* technologist

tecolote *m, Central America, Mexico* owl; *Mexico* cop (police officer)

tedero *m,* torch seller; torch holder

tedio *m,* tedium, boredom, ennui

tedioso *a* tedious, boring

teísmo *m,* theism

teísta *a* theistic. *mf* theist

teja *f,* tile, slate. *inf* **de tejas abajo,** in the normal way; in the world of men. **de tejas arriba,** in a supernatural way; in heaven

tejadillo *m,* roof (of a vehicle)

tejado *m,* roof

tejano, -a *a* and *ms* Texan. **tejanos** jeans

tejar *m,* tile works. *vt* to roof with tiles

Tejas *m* Texas

tejavana *f,* penthouse, open shed

tejedor (-ra) *a* weaving; *inf* scheming. *n* weaver; *inf* schemer

tejedura *f,* weaving; fabric; texture

tejeduría *f,* art of weaving; weaving shed or mill

tejemaneje *m, inf* cleverness, knack

tejer *vt* to weave; plait; spin a cocoon; arrange, regulate; concoct, hatch (schemes); wind in and out (in dancing)

tejero *m,* tile manufacturer

tejido *m,* texture, weaving; textile; *anat* tissue; fabric, material

tejo *m,* quoit, discus; metal disk; yew tree

tejón *m, zool* badger

tela *f,* fabric, material, cloth; membrane; film (on liquids); spiderweb, cobweb; inner skin (of fruit, vegetables); film over the eye; matter, subject; scheme, plot.

t. metálica, wire gauze. **en t. de juicio,** under consideration, in doubt. **llegarle a uno a las telas del corazón,** to hurt deeply, cut to the quick

telar *m,* loom, weaving machine; *theat* gridiron

telaraña *f,* cobweb; mere trifle, bagatelle. *inf* **mirar las telarañas,** to be absent-minded

telarañoso *a* cobwebby

telecomunicación *f,* telecommunication

telefonear *vt* to telephone, call

telefonía *f,* telephony. **t. sin hilos,** wireless telephony, broadcasting

telefónico *a* telephonic

telefonista *mf* telephone operator

teléfono *m,* telephone. **t. automático,** dial telephone. **llamar por t. (a),** to telephone, call, ring up

telefundir *vt* to telecast

telegrafía *f,* telegraphy. **t. sin hilos,** wireless telegraphy

telegrafiar *vt* to telegraph

telegráfico *a* telegraphic

telegrafista *mf* telegraph operator

telégrafo *m,* telegraph. **t. sin hilos,** wireless telegraph. *inf* **hacer telégrafos,** to talk by signs

telegrama *m,* telegram

telemetría *f,* telemetry

telémetro *m,* telemeter, rangefinder

teleología *f,* teleology

telepatía *f,* telepathy

telepático *a* telepathic

telescópico *a* telescopic

telescopio *m,* telescope

telespectador *m,* TV viewer, member of the television audience

teletipo *m,* teleprinter

televisión *f,* television

telilla *f,* film (on liquids); thin fabric

telón *m, theat* curtain; drop scene. **t. contra incendios, t. de seguridad,** *theat* safety curtain. **t. de boca,** drop curtain. **t. de foro,** drop scene

tema *m,* theme, subject; *mus* motif, theme; thesis, argument. *f,* obstinacy; obsession, mania; hostility, grudge, rancor

temático *a* thematic; pigheaded, obstinate

temblador (-ra) *a* trembling, shaking. *n* Quaker

temblante *a* shaking; quivering. *m,* bracelet

temblar *vi irr* to tremble, shake; wave, quiver; shiver with fear. See **acertar**

temblequear, tembletear *vi inf* tremble; shake with fear

temblón *a inf* trembling, shaking. *m, inf* aspen

temblor *m,* shake, trembling, shiver. **temblor (de tierra)** earthquake

tembloroso, tembloso *a* trembling, shaking, shivering, quivering

temedero *a* fearsome, dread

temedor (-ra) *a* fearful. *n* fearer, dreader

temer *vt* to fear, dread; suspect, imagine; *vi* be afraid

temerario *a* reckless, impetuous; thoughtless, hasty

temeridad *f,* recklessness, impetuosity, temerity; thoughtlessness; act of folly; rash judgment

temerón *a inf* swaggering, bombastic

temeroso *a* frightening, dread; fearful, timid; afraid, suspicious

temible *a* dread, awesome

temor *m,* fear

temoso *a* obstinate, headstrong

tímpano *m,* tabor; drumhead; block, flat piece; side of bacon. **t. de hielo,** iceberg, ice floe

temperación *f,* tempering

temperamento *m,* temperament, nature; compromise, agreement

temperar *vt* to temper; *Lat. Am.* spend the summer

temperatura *f,* temperature

temperie *f,* weather conditions

tempestad *f,* storm

tempestividad *f,* opportuneness, seasonableness

tempestivo *a* opportune, seasonable

tempestuoso *a* stormy

templa *f,* tempera; *pl anat* temples

templado *a* moderate; temperate (of regions); lukewarm; *mus* in tune; restrained (of style); *inf* brave, long-suffering. **estar bien (or mal) templado,** *inf* to be well (or badly) tuned (of musical instruments); be in a good (or bad) temper; be good- (or ill-) natured

templador (-ra) *n* tuner. *m,* tuning key

templadura *f,* tuning; tempering

templanza *f,* moderation; sobriety; mildness of climate

templar *vt* to tune; *met* temper; moderate; warm; allay, appease; anneal; *art* harmonize, blend; *naut* trim the sails; *vr* control oneself, be moderate; *vi* grow warm

temple *m,* weather conditions; temperature; temper (of metals, etc.); nature, disposition; bravery; mean, average; *mus* tuning. **al t.,** in tempera

templete *m, dim* shrine; niche (for statues); kiosk, pavilion

templo *m,* temple

temporada *f,* space of time, season, while. **de t.,** seasonal; temporary. **estar de t.,** to be out of town, on holiday

temporal *a* temporal; temporary; secular, lay; transient, fugitive. *m,* storm, tempest; rainy period; seasonal laborer

temporalidad *f,* secular character; temporality secular possession (gen. *pl*)

temporáneo, temporario *a* temporary, impermanent, fleeting

témporas *f pl,* Ember days

temporejar *vt naut* to lie to in a storm

temporero *a* temporary (of work)

temporizar *vi* to while away the time; temporize

tempranal *a* early fruiting

tempranear *vi, Lat. Am.* to get up early

tempranero *a* early

temprano *a* early. *adv* in the early hours; prematurely, too soon

temulento *a* intoxicated, drunken

ten con ten *m, inf* tact, diplomacy

tenacear *vi* to insist, be obstinate

tenacidad *f,* adhesiveness; resistance, toughness; obstinacy, tenacity

tenacillas *f pl, dim* small tongs; candle snuffers; sugar tongs; curling irons; tweezers

tenaz *a* adhesive; hard, resistant, unyielding; tenacious, obstinate

tenaza *f,* claw (of a lobster, etc.); *pl* tongs; pincers; pliers; dental forceps

tenazada *f,* seizing with tongs; strong bite, snap; rattle of tongs

tenazón (a or de) *adv* without taking aim, wildly; unexpectedly

tención *f,* retention, holding; grip

tendal *m,* awning; sheet for catching olives; *Lat. Am.* heap, lot, pile, large amount, large number

tendedero *m,* drying ground

tendedura *f,* laying out; stretching

tendencia *f,* tendency

tendencioso *a* tendentious, biased

tender *vt irr* to hang out; unfold, spread out; extend, hold out; *mas* plaster; *vi* tend, incline; *vr* lie down at full length; place one's cards on the table; gallop hard (of horses). See **entender**

tendero (-ra) *n* shopkeeper; retailer. *m,* tent maker

tendido *m,* row of seats in a bullfight arena; clothes hung out to dry; clear sky; *mas* plaster

tendón *m,* tendon

tenducha *f, inf* wretched little shop

tenebroso *a* dark, gloomy

tenedero *m, naut* anchoring ground, anchorage

tenedor *m,* table fork; possessor, retainer; *com* holder; payee. **t. de libros,** bookkeeper

teneduría *f,* employment of a bookkeeper. **t. de libros,** bookkeeping

tenencia *f*, possession; tenancy, occupation; lieutenancy

tener *vt irr* to have; hold; grasp; possess, own; uphold, maintain; contain; include; hold fast, grip; stop; keep (promises); lodge, accommodate; *(with en)* value, estimate (e.g. **Le tengo en poco,** I have a poor opinion of him); *(with para)* be of the opinion that (e.g. **tengo para mí,** my opinion is); *(with por)* believe, consider; *vi* be wealthy; *vr* steady oneself; hold on to; lean (on); rest (on); defend oneself; uphold; rely on; *(with por)* consider oneself as. **tener** is used to express: 1. *Age* (e.g. **¿Cuántos años tiene Vd?** How old are you?). 2. *Possession* (e.g. **Tenemos muchos sombreros,** We have a great many hats). 3. *Measurements* (e.g. **El cuarto tiene dieciocho metros de largo,** The room is eighteen meters long). Translated by 'be' when describing some physical and mental states (e.g. **Tenemos miedo,** We are afraid. **Tengo sueño,** I am sleepy. **Tienen frío (calor),** They are cold (hot)). Used as *auxiliary verb* replacing **haber** in compound tenses of transitive verbs (e.g. **Tengo escritas las cartas,** I have written the letters). **t. a bien,** to think fit, please, judge convenient. **t. algo en cuenta a uno,** to hold something against someone. **t. a menos de hacer (una cosa),** to scorn to do (a thing). **t. cruda,** to have a hangover. **t. curiosidad por,** to be curious about. **t. curiosidad por que** + *subj* to be interested that. **t. en aprecio,** to appreciate, esteem, value. **t. en cuenta,** to bear in mind. **t. en menos (a),** to despise (a person). **t. gana,** to want, wish; feel disposed; have an appetite. **t. lugar,** to take place, occur. **t. muchas partes cruzadas,** to be well-traveled. **t. mucho colegio** to be well-educated. **t. muy en cuenta,** to certainly bear in mind. **t. poco colegio,** to have had little education. **t. presente,** to remember. **t. que,** to have to (e.g. **tengo que hacerlo,** I must do it). **t. que ver (con),** to have something to do (with), be related to. **no tenerlas todas consigo,** *inf* to have the jitters. *Pres. Ind.* **tengo, tienes, tiene, tenemos, tenéis, tienen.** *Preterite* **tuve,** etc. *Fut.* **tendré,** etc. *Condit.* **tendría,** etc. *Pres. Subjunc.* **tenga,** etc. *Imperf. Subjunc.* **tuviese,** etc.

tenguerengue, en *adv* rickety, insecure

tenia *f*, tapeworm; *arch* fillet, narrow molding

teniente *a* owning; holding; unripe (of fruit); *inf* slightly deaf; stingy, mean. *m*, deputy, substitute; *mil* first lieutenant, lieutenant. **t. coronel,** lieutenant colonel. **t. de navío,** naval lieutenant. **t. general,** *mil* lieutenant general. **t. general de aviación,** air marshal

tenis *m*, tennis

tenor *m*, import, contents (of a letter, etc.); constitution, composition; *mus* tenor

tenorio *m*, rake, Don Juan, philanderer

tensar *vt* to tighten; tense

tensión *f*, tautness; tension; strain, stress; *elec* tension

tenso *a* taut; tight; tense

tentación *f*, temptation; attraction, inducement

tentáculo *m*, tentacle; feeler

tentadero *m*, yard for trying out young bulls for bull-fighting

tentador (-ra) *a* tempting; attractive. *n* tempter. *m*, the Devil

tentalear *vt* to examine by touch

tentar *vt irr* to touch, feel; examine by touch; incite, encourage; try, endeavor; test; tempt; *surg* probe. See **sentar**

tentativa *f*, endeavor, attempt; preliminary exam (at some univs.)

tentativo *a* tentative, experimental

tentemozo *m*, support, prop; tumbler (toy)

tentempié *m*, *inf* snack, bite

tenue *a* thin; slender, delicate; trivial, worthless, insignificant; pale; faint

tenuidad *f*, slenderness; delicacy; triviality, insignificance; paleness; faintness

teñidura *f*, dyeing, staining

teñir *vt irr* to dye; *art* darken; color, tinge; *vr* be dyed; be tinged or colored. See **ceñir**

teocracia *f*, theocracy

teocrático *a* theocratic

teodolito *m*, theodolite

teologal *a* theological

teología *f*, theology, divinity

teológico *a* theological

teologizar *vi* to theologize

teólogo *a* theological. *m*, theologian, divine; student of theology

teorema *m*, theorem

teoría *f*, theory

teórica *f*, theory

teórico *a* theoretical, speculative. *m*, theorist

teorizar *vt* to consider theoretically, theorize about

teoso *a* resinous, gummy

teosofía *f*, theosophy

teosófico *a* theosophical

teósofo *m*, theosophist

tepe *m*, sod, cut turf

tequila *f. Mexico* tequila, maguey brandy

terapeuta *mf* therapeutist

terapéutica *f*, therapeutics

terapéutico *a* therapeutic

terapia *f*, therapy

teratología *f*, teratology

tercena *f*, warehouse for storing government monopoly goods (tobacco, etc.)

tercenista *mf* person in charge of a tercena

tercer *a abb* of **tercero** third. Used before *m, sing* nouns

tercera *f*, procuress; *mus* third

tercería *f*, arbitration, mediation; temporary occupation of a fortress, etc.

tercero (-ra) *a* third; mediatory. *n* third; mediator. *m*, pimp; *ecc* tertiary; tithes collector; third person. **¡A la tercera va la vencida!** Third time lucky!

terceto *m*, tercet, triplet

tercia *f*, one-third; *ecc* tierce, third hour; storehouse for tithes. **tercias reales,** royal share of ecclesiastical tithes

terciana *f*, tertian fever

terciar *vt* to slant; sling sideways; divide into three; equalize weight (on beasts of burden); plow or dig for the third time; *agr* prune; *vr* be opportune, come at the right time. *vi* mediate, arbitrate; make up a number (for cards, etc.); reach the third day (of the moon); take part, participate

tercio *a* third. *m*, one-third; *mil* infantry regiment; *ant*, body of foreign volunteers; fishermen's association; *pl* brawny limbs of a man. **hacer t.,** to take part in; make up the number of. **hacer buen** (*or* **mal**) **t. a alguien,** to do someone a good (*or* bad) turn

terciopelo *m*, velvet; velveteen

terco *a* pigheaded, obstinate; hard, tough

tergiversación *f*, tergiversation, vacillation

tergiversar *vt* to tergiversate, shuffle, vacillate

termal *a* thermal

termas *f pl*, thermal springs, hot mineral baths; thermal

térmico *a* thermic

terminable *a* terminable

terminación *f*, conclusion, termination; end, finish; ending of a word; *gram* termination

terminador (-ra) *a* concluding. *n* finisher

terminal *a* terminal; final. *m*, *elec* terminal. **t. de carga,** cargo terminal

terminante *a* conclusive, definite; categorical

terminar *vt* to end, conclude; complete; *vr* and *vi* end

término *m*, limit, end; term; expression; boundary marker; district, suburb; space, period; state, condition; boundary; object, aim; appearance, demeanor, behavior (gen. *pl*); completion; *mus* tone; *(math law logic)* term. **t. medio,** *math* average; medium; compromise, middle way. **correr el t.,** to lapse (of time). **en primer t.,** *art* in the foreground. **medios términos,** evasions, excuses. **primer t.,** (cinema) closeup

terminología *f,* terminology
termita *f,* thermite. *m,* termite
termodinámica *f,* thermodynamics
termoeléctrico *a* thermoelectric
termómetro *m,* thermometer
Termópilas Thermopylae
termos *m,* thermos, vacuum bottle
termoscopio *m,* thermoscope
termóstato *m,* thermostat
termostático *a* thermostatic
terna *f,* triad, trio; set of dice
ternario *a* ternal, ternary
terne *a inf* bullying, braggartly; persistent, obstinate; robust. *mf* bully
ternera *f,* female calf; veal
ternero *m,* male calf
terneza *f,* tenderness, kindness; softness; softheartedness; endearment, caress, compliment (gen. *pl*)
ternilla *f,* cartilage, gristle
ternísimo *a sup* **tierno** most tender
terno *m,* triad; suit of clothes, three-piece suit; oath, curse
ternura *f,* softness; softheartedness; tenderness, kindness, sweetness
terquedad, terquería, terqueza *f,* obstinacy, obduracy
terracota *f,* terra cotta
terrado *m,* flat roof
Terranova Newfoundland
terraplén *m,* embankment; *mil* terreplein
terraplenar *vt* to fill up with earth; fill in (a hollow); make into an embankment; terrace
terrateniente *mf* landowner
terraza *f,* terrace; flat roof; flower border (of a garden)
terrazgo *m,* tillable land; rent for farming land
terregoso *a* lumpy, full of clods (of soil)
terremoto *m,* earthquake
terrenal *a* terrestrial
terreno *a* terrestrial. *m,* ground, land; *fig* sphere; region; soil; plot of land. **ganar t.,** *fig* to win ground, make progress. **medir el t.,** *fig* to feel one's way
térreo *a* earthy
terrero *a* earthly; low-flying, almost touching the ground; humble. *m,* flat roof; pile or mound of earth; deposit of earth, alluvium; target; mineral refuse
terrestre *a* terrestrial, earthly
terrezuela *f,* poor soil
terribilidad *f,* terribleness, horribleness; rudeness
terribilísimo *a sup* most terrible
terrible *a* terrible, horrible; rude, unsociable, ill-humored; enormous, huge
terrífico *a* terrible, frightful
territorial *a* territorial
territorialidad *f,* territoriality
territorio *m,* territory; jurisdiction. **t. bajo mandato,** mandated territory
terrizo *a* earthen
terrón *m,* clod (of earth); lump; *pl* lands, landed property. **t. de azúcar,** lump of sugar
terrorismo *m,* terrorism
terrorista *mf* terrorist
terrosidad *f,* earthiness
terroso *a* earthy; earthen
terruño *m,* plot of ground; native earth; country; soil
terso *a* smooth, shiny, glossy; *lit* elegant, polished (style)
tersura *f,* smoothness, glossiness; elegance (of style)
tertulia *f,* regular social meeting (gen. in cafés); conversational group; party; part of Spanish cafés set apart for players of chess, etc. **hacer t.,** to meet for conversation
tertuliano (-na) *n* **tertuliante,** *mf* **tertulio (-ia),** *n* member of a tertulia
terzuelo *m,* third, third part
Tesalia Thessaly
tesar *vt naut* to make taut; *vi* step backward, back (oxen)
tesela *f,* tessera, square used in mosaic work

teselado *a* tessellated
tesina *f,* master's essay, thesis
tesis *f,* thesis
teso *a* tight, taut, tense. *m,* hilltop; bulge, lump
tesón *m,* persistence, obstinacy, tenacity
tesonería *f,* stubbornness, obstinacy
tesorería *f,* treasury; treasuryship
tesorero (-ra) *n* treasurer
tesoro *m,* treasure; public treasury; hoard; *fig* gem, excellent person; thesaurus. **t. de duende,** fairy gold
tespíades *f pl,* the muses
testa *f,* head; face, front; *inf* sense, acumen. **t. coronada,** crowned head
testación *f,* erasure, crossing out
testado *a* testate
testador (-ra) *n* testator
testaferro *m, fig* figurehead, proxy
testamentar *vt* to bequeath
testamentaria *f,* execution of a will; *law* estate; executors' meeting
testamentario *a* testamental, testamentary
testamento *m, law* will; testament. **Antiguo T.,** Old Testament. **ordenar** (*or* **otorgar**) **su t.,** to make one's will
testar *vi* to make a will; *vt* erase, cross out
testarada *f,* a blow with the head; pigheadedness, stubbornness
testarrón *a inf* pigheaded
testarudez *f,* obstinacy, obduracy
testarudo *a* stubborn, obstinate
testera *f,* front, face; front seat (in a vehicle); upper half of an animal's face; tester, canopy
testículo *m,* testicle
testificación *f,* testification
testificar *vt* to testify; affirm, assert; attest, prove
testigo *mf* witness. *m,* proof, evidence. *law* **t. de cargo,** witness for the prosecution. *law* **t. de descargo,** witness for the defense. **t. de vista,** eyewitness. *law* **hacer testigos,** to bring forward witnesses
testimonial *a* confirmatory, proven
testimoniar *vt* to attest, confirm, bear witness to
testimoniero (-ra) *a* slanderous; hypocritical. *n* slanderer, hypocrite
testimonio *m,* testimony, proof; slander; affidavit
testuz *m,* front of the head (of some animals); nape (of animals)
teta *f,* mammary gland, breast; teat, dug, udder. **dar la t. (a),** to suckle
tétano, tétanos *m,* tetanus
tetera *f,* teapot; teakettle; *Lat. Am.* (feeding) bottle
tetilla *f, dim* rudimentary teat or nipple; nipple (of a nursing bottle)
tétrico *a* gloomy; somber
teután (-ona) *n* Teuton. *a* Teutonic
teutónico *a* Teutonic
textil *a* and *m,* textile
texto *m,* text; quotation, citation; textbook
textorio *a* textile
textual *a* textual
textualista *mf* textualist
textura *f,* texture; weaving; structure (of a novel, etc.); animal structure
tez *f,* complexion, skin
ti *pers pron 2nd sing mf dat acc abl* thee, you. Always used with prep. (e.g. **por ti,** by thee (you))
tía *f,* aunt; *inf* wife, mother, dame; *inf* coarse creature. **t. abuela,** grandaunt, great-aunt. *inf* **quedarse para t.,** to be left an old maid
tianguis *m, Central America, Mexico* open-air market
tiara *f,* ancient Persian headdress; papal tiara; coronet; dignity and power of the papacy
tiberino *a* Tiberine
tibetano (-na) *a* and *n* Tibetan. *m,* Tibetan (language)
tibia *f,* flute; tibia
tibieza *f,* tepidity; indifference, lack of enthusiasm
tibio *a* tepid, warm; indifferent, unenthusiastic

tiburón *m*, shark
ticket *m*, ticket; pass, membership card
tico, -a *mf inf* Costa Rican
tictac *m*, ticktock (of a clock)
tiempo *m*, time; season; epoch, period; chance, opportunity; leisure, free time; weather; *mus* tempo; *gram* tense; *naut* storm. **t. ha,** many years ago, long ago. **t. medio** *or* **medio t.,** *sport* halftime. **abrir el t.,** to clear up (of the weather). **ajustar los tiempos,** to fix the date (chronology). **a largo t.,** after a long time. **andando el t.,** in the course of time. **a su t.,** in due course, at the proper time. **a t.,** in time, at the right time. **a un t.,** simultaneously, at the same time. **cargarse el t.,** to cloud over (of the sky). **con t.,** in advance, with time; in time. **correr el t.,** to pass, move on (of time). **de t. en t.,** from time to time. **engañar** (*or* **entretener**) **el t.,** to kill time, while away the hours. *inf* **en t., de Maricastaña** *or* **del rey Perico,** long, long ago. **fuera de t.,** unseasonably, inopportunely; out of season. **ganar t.,** to gain time; *inf* hurry. **hacer t.,** to wait, cool one's heels; *fig* mark time. **perder el t.,** to waste time; misspend or lose time. **sentarse el t.,** to clear up (of the weather). **tomarse t.** (**para**), to postpone, take time for (or to)
tienda *f*, tent; *naut* awning, canopy; shop, store. **t. de abarrotes** *Lat. Am.* grocery store, grocery, grocer's **t. de antigüedades,** antique shop. **t. de campaña,** bell tent, pavilion. **t. oxígena,** oxygen tent
tienta *f*, astuteness; cleverness; *surg* probe; trying out young bulls for the bullring. **a tientas,** by touch, gropingly
tientaparedes *mf* one who gropes one's way
tiento *m*, touching, feeling; touch, feel; blind person's cane; tightrope walker's pole; manual control, steady hand; caution, care, tact; *mus* preliminary flourish; *inf* slap buffet; tentacle. **a t.,** by touch; unsurely, gropingly
tierno *a* soft; tender; kind; sweet; delicate; softhearted; fresh, recent; affectionate
tierra *f*, world, planet; earth; soil; ground; cultivated ground, land; homeland, native land; region; district, territory. **t. adentro,** inland. **t. de batán,** fuller's earth. **t. de Promisión,** Promised Land. **t. de Siena,** sienna. **besar la t.,** *inf* to fall down. **dar en t. con,** to throw down; demolish. **echar en t.,** *naut* to put ashore, land. **echar por t.,** *fig* to overthrow, destroy. **echar t. a,** *fig* to bury, forget. *inf* **la t. de María Santísima,** Andalusia. **por t.,** overland. **saltar en t.,** to land, disembark. **venir** (*or* **venirse**) **a t.,** to fall down, topple over
Tierra Santa Holy Land
tieso *a* hard, rigid, stiff; healthy, robust; taut; spirited, courageous; obstinate, stiff-necked; distant, formal. *adv* firmly, strongly
tiesto *m*, flowerpot; broken piece of earthenware
tiesura *f*, hardness, rigidity, stiffness; physical fitness; courageousness; obstinacy; formality, stiffness
tifoidea *f*, typhoid
tifón *m*, typhoon
tifus *m*, typhus. **t. exantemático,** trench fever
tigre *m*, tiger; ferocious person; *Lat. Am.* jaguar
tijera *f*, scissors (gen. *pl*); any scissor-shaped instrument; shears; drainage channel; carpenter's horse; scandalmonger, gossip
tijeretada *f*, cut or snip with scissors
tijeretear *vt* to cut with scissors; *inf* interfere arbitrarily
tijereteo *m*, scissor cut; click of the scissors
tila *f*, lime tree or flower; linden tree or flower; infusion made of lime flowers
tildar *vt* to cross out, erase; stigmatize; place a tilde over a letter
tilde *mf*, bad reputation; tilde; *f*, jot, iota
tilín *m*, tinkle, peal (of a bell)
tillar *vt* to lay wood floors
tilo *m*, lime tree
timador (-ra) *n inf* swindler, sharper, cheat

timar *vt* to swindle, cheat, deceive; *vr inf* exchange looks or winks
timba *f*, *inf* casino, gambling den; game of chance
timbal *m*, kettledrum
timbalero *m*, kettledrum player
timbrador *m*, stamper; stamping machine; rubber stamp
timbrar *vt* to stamp; place the crest over a coat of arms
timbre *m*, postage stamp; heraldic crest; excise stamp; bell, push-button; *mus* timbre; noble deed; personal merit; *Mexico* (postage) stamp; *Lat. Am.* description (of a person or goods)
timidez *f*, timidity, nervousness
tímido *a* timid, nervous
timo *m*, *inf* swindling, trick; thymus
timón *m*, *naut* helm; rudder; management, direction; stick of a rocket. **t. de dirección,** *aer* tailfin
timonear *vi naut* to steer
timonel, timonero *m*, helmsman, coxswain
timorato *a* godfearing; timid, vacillating
tímpano *m*, *anat* eardrum, tympanum; *mus* kettledrum; *arch* tympanum; *print* tympan
tina *f*, vat; flour bin; large earthenware jar; wooden tub; bath
tinaco *m*, *Mexico* (water) tank
tinada *f*, woodpile; cow shed
tinaja *f*, large earthenware jar; jarful
tinajero *m*, seller of earthenware jars
tinelo *m*, servants' hall
tinerfeño (-ña) *a* and *n* of or from Tenerife
tinglado *m*, overhanging roof; open shed; penthouse; intrigue
tiniebla *f*, gloom, darkness (gen. *pl*); *pl* profound ignorance; confusion of mind; *ecc* tenebrae
tino *m*, skilled sense of touch; good eye, accurate aim; judgment, shrewdness; vat. **sacar de t.** (**a**), to bewilder, confuse; irritate, exasperate. **sin t.,** without limit, excessively
tinta *f*, color, tint; ink; staining, dyeing; dye, stain; *pl* shades, colors; *art* mixed colors ready for painting. **t. china,** India ink. **t. simpática,** invisible ink. **recargar las tintas,** *fig* to overpaint, lay the colors on too thick. *inf* **saber de buena t.** (**una cosa**), to learn (a thing) from a reliable source
tintar *vt* to dye; color, tinge, stain
tinte *m*, dyeing, staining; color; dye; stain; dye house; pretext, disguise
tintero *m*, inkwell. *inf* **dejar** (*or* **quedársele a uno**) **en el t.,** to forget, omit (to say, write)
tintín *m*, ring, peal; clink; chink
tintinar *vi* to ring, tinkle; clink; jingle
tintineo *m*, ringing, tinkling; clinking; jingle
tinto *a* red (of wine). *m*, red wine; dark red
tintorera *f*, *Lat. Am.* shark
tintorería *f*, dyeing industry; dyeing and dry-cleaning shop
tintorero (-ra) *n* dyer; dry cleaner
tintura *f*, dyeing, staining; color, tint; dye; stain; tincture; smattering, slight knowledge
tinturar *vt* to dye; color, tinge, stain; give a superficial notion of
tiña *f*, ringworm; *inf* meanness, stinginess
tiñoso *a* mangy; afflicted with ringworm; *inf* mean, stingy
tiñuela *f*, shipworm
tío *m*, uncle; gaffer; fellow, chap; fool; stepfather; father-in-law. **t. abuelo,** granduncle, great-uncle
tiovivo *m*, merry-go-round
típico *a* typical
tiple *m*, soprano or treble voice. *mf* soprano
tipo *m*, model, pattern; type; print, type; species, group (of animals, etc.); *inf* guy, chap
tipografía *f*, typography
tipográfico *a* typographical
tipógrafo *m*, typographer
típula *f*, daddy-longlegs

tiquismiquis *m pl,* ridiculous scruples; affected courtesies. *a inf* faddy, fussy

tira *f,* strip, band, ribbon; stripe, rib. **t. cómica,** comic strip

tirabotas *m,* buttonhook

tirabuzón *m,* corkscrew; ringlet, curl; hair curler

tirada *f,* throwing; drawing; pulling; cast, throw; distance, space; *print* edition, issue; circulation (of a newspaper, etc.); stroke (in golf); lapse, interval (of time). **t. aparte,** reprint (of an article, etc.)

tiradero *m,* shooting butt

tirado *a inf* dirt-cheap. *m,* wire drawing

tirador (-ra) *n* thrower, caster; drawer, puller; marksman. *m,* handle, knob; *mech* trigger; bell rope, bell pull; *print* pressman. **t. de bota,** boot tag. **t. de gomas,** catapult. **t. de oro,** gold wire drawer

tiralíneas *m,* ruling pen

tiramiento *m,* pulling; stretching

tiramira *f,* long, narrow mountain range; long line of persons or things; distance

tiranía *f,* tyranny, despotism

tiranicida *mf* tyrannicide (person)

tiranicidio *m,* tyrannicide (act)

tiránico *a* tyrannical

tiranización *f,* tyranny, tyrannization

tiranizar *vt* to tyrannize over

tirano (-na) *a* tyrannous, tyrannical; *fig* overwhelming, dominating. *n* tyrant

tirante *a* taut; tense, strained. *m,* trace (of a harness); shoulderstrap; suspender (gen. *pl*); *arch* tie

tirantez *f,* tautness; tension, strain; straight distance between two points. **estado de t.,** *pol* strained relations

tiranuelo *m,* petty tyrant

tirar *vt* to throw, cast; fling, aim, toss; throw down, overthrow; pull; draw; discharge, shoot; stretch, pull out; rule, draw (lines); squander, waste; *print* print; *vi* attract; pull; (*with prep a*) turn to, turn in the direction of; incline, tend to; incline toward, have a tinge of (colors); try, aspire to; (*with de*) wield, unsheath, draw out (firearms, arms); *vr* cast oneself, precipitate oneself; throw oneself on. *inf* **ir tirando,** to carry on, get along somehow

tirilla *f, sew* shirt neckband

tiritaña *f,* thin silk material; *inf* mere nothing, trifle

tiritar *vi* to shiver with cold

tiritón *m,* shiver, shudder

Tiro Tyre

tiro *m,* throwing; throw, cast; toss, fling; try (in football); shooting; piece of artillery; report, shot (of a gun); discharge (firearms); shooting range or gallery; team (of horses); range (of firearms, etc.); hoisting cable; flight (of stairs); *min* shaft; *inf* trick; robbery, theft; innuendo, insinuation; grave harm or injury; *pl* sword belt. **t. de pichón,** pigeon shooting. **t. par,** four-in-hand. **a t.,** within firing range; within reach. **de tiros largos,** *inf* in full regalia

tirocinio *m,* apprenticeship

tiroideo *a* thyroid

tiroides *f,* thyroid gland

Tirol, el the Tyrol

tirón *m,* novice, beginner; pull, tug, heave. **de un t.,** with one tug; at one stroke, at one blow

tiroriro *m, inf* sound of a wind instrument; *pl inf* wind instruments

tirotearse *vr mil* to exchange fire; indulge in repartee

tiroteo *m,* shooting, exchange of shots; crackle (of rifle fire)

Tirreno, el Mar the Tyrrhenian Sea

tirria *f, inf* hostility, grudge, dislike

tirulato *a* dumbfounded, stupefied

tisana *f,* tisane

tísico (-ca) *a* tuberculous. *n* sufferer from tuberculosis, consumptive

tisis *f,* tuberculosis

tisú *m,* silver or gold tissue

titánico *a* titanesque; colossal, huge

títere *m,* puppet; *fig inf* dummy, grotesque; *inf* fool; obsession, fixed idea; *pl inf* circus; Punch and Judy show. *inf* **echar los títeres a rodar,** to upset the whole show; quarrel, fall out with. *inf* **no dejar t. con cabeza,** to destroy entirely, smash up completely; leave no one

titerero (-ra), titiritero (-ra), *n* **titerista** *mf* puppet showman; acrobat; juggler

tití *m,* marmoset

titilación *f,* quiver, tremor; twinkling, winking, gleam

titilador, titilante *a* quivering, trembling; twinkling

titilar *vi* to quiver, tremble; twinkle

titiritaina *f, inf* muffled strains of musical instruments; merrymaking, uproar

titiritar *vi* to tremble, shiver, shudder

titiritero (-ra) *n* puppet master; acrobat

titubear *vi* to totter, sway, rock; stutter, stammer; toddle; hesitate, vacillate

titubeo *m,* tottering, swaying; stuttering; hesitation

titulado *m,* titled person; one who holds an academic title

titular *a* titular. *vt* to entitle, call; *vi* obtain a title (of nobility); *vr* style oneself, call oneself

título *m,* title; heading; inscription; pretext, excuse; diploma, certificate; claim, right; noble title and its owner; section, clause; (univ.) degree; *com* stock certificate, bond; *com* title; caption; qualification, right, merit; basis of a claim or privilege; *pl com* securities, stocks. **t. de la columna,** *print* running title. **títulos de propiedad,** title deeds. **t. del reino,** title of nobility. **a t.,** under pretext

tiza *f,* chalk; whiting; calcined stag's antler

tiznar *vt* to make sooty; dirty, stain, begrime; *fig* sully, tarnish

tizne *m,* (sometimes *f*) soot; charcoal; stain (on one's honor, etc.); *agr* blight

tizón *m,* firebrand; *agr* blight; *fig* stain (on one's honor, etc.)

tizona *f, inf* sword (by allusion to name of that of the Cid)

tizonear *vi* to poke or rake the fire

toalla *f,* towel. **t. continua,** roller towel. **t. rusa,** Turkish towel

toallero *m,* towel rail

tobillera *f, inf* girl, flapper

tobillo *m,* ankle

tobogán *m,* toboggan; chute (in apartment buildings or amusement parks)

toca *f,* headdress; toque; wimple; coif

tocable *a* touchable

tocado *a fig* touched, half-crazy. *m,* headdress; coiffure, hairdressing

tocador (-ra) *n mus* player. *m,* dressing table; kerchief; boudoir; cloakroom; dressing room; dressing case

tocamiento *m,* touching, feeling; touch; *fig* inspiration

tocante *a* touching. **t. a,** concerning, with regard to

tocar *vt* to touch, feel; *mus* play; knock, rap; summon; ring, peal; brush against; discover by experience; persuade, inspire; mention, touch upon; *naut* touch bottom; *art* retouch, touch up. *vi* belong; stop (at), touch at; be one's turn; concern, interest; be one's lot; adjoin, be near to; be opportune; be allied or closely related to; find the scent (of dogs); *naut* to touch at a port. **Ahora me toca a mí,** Now it's my turn. **Es un problema que me toca de cerca,** It is a problem that touches me very nearly. **a toca teja,** *inf* in ready cash

tocayo (-ya) *n* namesake

tochedad *f,* boorishness, loutishness

tocho *a* boorish, loutish, countrified. *m,* iron bar

tocinería *f,* pork butcher's shop

tocinero *m,* pork butcher

tocino *m,* bacon; salt pork

tocología *f,* tokology, obstetrics

tocón *m,* stump (of a tree or an amputated limb)

todavía *adv* still; even; nevertheless; yet. **No han**

venido t., They have not come yet. **Queda mucho que hacer t.,** There is still much to be done.

todo *a* all; whole, entire; every, each. *m,* whole, entirety; whole word (in charades); all; *pl* all; everyone. *adv* wholly, entirely. **t. lo posible,** everything possible; all one can, one's best. **t. lo que,** all that which. **ante t.,** in the first place; especially, particularly. **así y t.,** nevertheless. **a t. esto,** in the meanwhile. **con t.** *or* **con t. esto** *or* **con t. y esto,** nevertheless, in spite of this. **del t.,** wholly, completely. **jugar el t. por el t.,** to risk everything on the outcome. **sobre t.,** especially. **y t.,** in addition, as well. **Todos somos hijos de Adán y Eva, sino que nos diferencia la lana y la seda,** We are all equal, but some of us are more equal than others

todopoderoso *a* all-powerful, almighty. *m,* the Almighty, God

toga *f,* toga; robe, gown

Tokio Tokyo

tolda *f* canvas; tent; shelter

toldadura *f,* awning; canopy; hanging, curtain

toldillo *m,* covered litter or sedan chair; *WH* mosquito net

toldo *m,* awning; canopy; pomp, show

tole *m,* outcry, uproar, tumult

toledano (-na) *a* and *n* Toledan

tolerable *a* bearable, tolerable

tolerancia *f,* tolerance, forbearance; permission

tolerante *a* tolerant, broad-minded

tolerantismo *m,* religious toleration

tolerar *vt* to put up with, bear, tolerate; overlook, allow, forgive

tolla *f,* marsh, bog

tollina *f, inf* spanking, whipping

tolmo *m,* tor

tolondro *a* stupid, heedless, reckless. *m,* bump, bruise

tolonés (-esa) *a* and *n* of or from Toulon

tolva *f,* chute (for grain, etc.)

toma *f,* taking; receiving; conquest, capture; dose (of medicine)

tomada *f,* taking; take; capture

tomadero *m,* handle, haft

tomadura *f,* taking; receiving; dose (of medicine). *inf* **t. de pelo,** leg-pull, joke

tomar *vt* to take; pick up; conquer; eat; drink; adopt; employ; contract (habits); engage (employees); rent; understand; steal; remove; buy; suffer; *fig* overcome (by laughter, sleep, etc.); choose; possess physically; *vi* (*with por*) go in the direction of; *vr* grow rusty; go moldy; (*with con*) quarrel with. **t. a chacota,** to take as a joke. **t. a pechos,** to take to heart. **t. el fresco,** to take the air. **tomarla con,** to contradict, oppose; bear a grudge. **t. la delantera,** to take the lead; excel, beat. **t. las de Villadiego,** *inf* to quit, show one's heels. **t. por su cuenta,** to undertake, take charge of; take upon oneself. **t. su desquite con,** to get even with. **Más vale un toma que dos te daré,** A little help is worth a lot of promises. **¡Toma!** *inf* Fancy! You don't say!; Of course! There's nothing new about that!

tomatal *m,* tomato bed, tomato patch; *Lat. Am.* tomato plant

tomate *m,* tomato; tomato plant; *Mexico* small green tomato; *inf* hole, potato (in stockings, etc.)

tomatera *f,* tomato plant

tomatero (-ra) *n* tomato seller

tómbola *f,* raffle (gen. for charity); jumble sale

tomillo *m,* thyme

tomo *m,* volume, book; importance, worth

ton *m, abb* **tono. sin t. ni son,** *inf* without rhyme or reason

tonada *f,* words of a song and its tune

tonadilla *f, dim* short song; comic song; *theat* musical interlude *ant*

tonadillero (-ra) *n* composer or singer of tonadillas

tonal *a* tonal

tonalidad *f,* tonality

tonar *vi poet* to thunder or lightning

tonel *m,* barrel; cask; butt

tonelada *f,* ton

tonelería *f,* cooperage; collection or stock of casks and barrels

tonelero *m,* cooper

tonga, tongada *f,* layer, stratum; *inf* task

tónica *f, mus* keynote

tónico *a* tonic. *m, med* tonic; pick-me-up

tonificador, tonificante *a* strengthening, invigorating tonic

tonillo *m, dim* monotonous singsong voice; regional accent

tonina *f,* tuna; dolphin

tono *m,* inflection, modulation; (*mus med art*) tone; pitch, resonance; energy, strength; style; manner, behavior; *mus* key; mode of speech. **bajar el t.,** *fig inf* to change one's tune. *inf* **darse t.,** to put on side, give oneself airs. **de buen (mal) t.,** in good (bad) taste

tonsila *f,* tonsil

tonsilitis *f,* tonsillitis

tonsura *f,* shearing; hair cutting; *ecc* tonsure

tonsurar *vt* to shear, clip; cut the hair off; *ecc* tonsure

tontaina *mf inf* ninny, fool

tontear *vi* to behave foolishly; play the fool

tontería *f,* foolishness, stupidity; piece of folly, trifle, bagatelle

tontiloco *a inf* crazy, daft

tontillo *m,* dress bustle; hoop (for dresses)

tontivano *a* vain, conceited

tonto (-ta) *a* silly, stupid, simple; foolish, absurd. *n* fool, idiot. '*m,* short coat, stroller. **t. de capirote,** *inf* an utter fool. **a tontas y a locas,** without rhyme or reason, topsy-turvy. **volver t. (a),** *fig inf* to drive crazy

topacio *m,* topaz

topar *vt* (*with con*) to run into, collide with, hit; meet unexpectedly; come across, find; *vi* butt (of horned animals); take a bet (in cards); consist in (of obstacles); meet with (difficulties); *inf* be successful

tope *m,* projection, part that juts out; obstacle, impediment; collision, bump; crux, difficult point; quarrel, fight; *mech* stop; *naut* masthead; *rw* buffer; *Mexico* speed bump. **hasta el t.,** completely full, full to the brim

topera *f,* molehill

topetada *f,* butt (of horned animals); *inf* knock, bang

topetar *vt* and *vi* to butt (of horned animals); *vt* meet, run into

topetón *m,* butt; collision, impact, bump; blow on the head

tópico *a* topical. *m,* topic, theme

topo *m, zool* mole; *inf* clumsy or shortsighted person; dolt, ninny

topografía *f,* topography

topográfico *a* topographical

topógrafo *m,* topographer

toque *m,* touch, touching; pealing, ringing (of bells); crux, essence; test, proof; touchstone; *met* assay; warning; *inf* tap (on the shoulder, etc.); *art* touch. **t. de luz,** *art* light (in a picture). **t. de obscuro,** *art* shade (in a picture). **t. de queda,** curfew. **t. de tambor,** beating of a drum. **dar un t. a,** *inf* to put to the test; pump (for information)

toquero (-ra) *n* manufacturer of headdresses

toquetear *vt* to keep touching, handle repeatedly

toquilla *f,* hatband, hat trimming; kerchief; small shawl

torácico *a* thoracic

toral *a* principal, chief, main

tórax *m,* thorax

torbellino *m,* whirlwind; spate of things; *inf* madcap

torcedero *a* twisted, crooked

torcedor *a* twisting. *m,* twister; cause of continual anxiety

torcedura *f,* twisting; sprain, wrench

torcer *vt irr* to twist; bend; turn, bear (of roads, etc.); slant, slope, incline; misconstrue, pervert; dissuade; wrench, sprain (muscles); corrupt (justice). **t. el gesto,** to make a wry face. *vr* turn sour (of wine, milk); *fig* go

astray; turn out badly (of negotiations). *Pres. Ind.*
tuerzo, tuerces, etc. *Pres. Subjunc.* **tuerza, tuerzas, tuerza, tuerzan**

torcida *f,* wick (of lamps, etc.)

torcido *a* bent, crooked, sloping, inclined; curved; dishonest, tortuous. *m,* silk twist

torcijón *m,* stomachache

torcimiento *m,* twisting; twist, turn; circumlocution; digression

tordo *a* piebald, black-and-white. *m, orn* thrush. **t. de campanario** *or* **t. de Castilla,** starling

toreador *m,* bullfighter

torear *vi* and *vt* to fight bulls; *vt* ridicule; exasperate, provoke; *inf* string along, deceive

toreo *m,* bullfighting

torera *f,* bullfighter's jacket

torero *a inf* bullfighting. *m,* bullfighter

torete *m, dim* small bull; *inf* problem, difficult question; engrossing topic of conversation

toril *m,* pen for fighting bulls

torio *m,* thorium

tormenta *f,* storm; misfortune, calamity; indignation, agitation

tormento *m,* torment; torture; pain; anxiety, anguish. **dar t. (a),** to torture; inflict pain (on)

tormentoso *a* stormy, tempestuous; *naut* pitching, rolling

torna *f,* return; restitution; backwater

tornaboda *f,* day after a wedding; rejoicings of this day

tornada *f,* return home; return visit, revisit; *poet* envoy

tornadizo (-za) *a inf* changeable. *n* turncoat

tornamiento *m,* return; change, transformation

tornar *vt* to return, give back; change, transform; *vi* return, go back; continue

tornasol *m,* sunflower; sheen, changing light; *chem* litmus

tornasolado *a* shot (of silk, etc.)

tornasolar *vt* to look iridescent; change the color of, cause to appear variegated

tornátil *a* turned (in a lathe); inconstant, changeable; *poet* spinning, revolving

tornatrás *mf* half-caste

tornaviaje *m,* return journey

tornavoz *m,* soundboard, sounding board

torneador *m,* turner; jouster, fighter in a tournament

tornear *vt sport* to put a spin on (balls); turn in a lathe; *vi* turn around, spin; fight in a tournament; turn over in the mind

torneo *m,* tournament

tornería *f,* turnery

tornero *m,* turner; lathe maker; convent messenger

tornillero *m, (inf mil)* deserter

tornillo *m,* screw; *(inf mil)* desertion

torniquete *m,* turnstile; tourniquet. **dar t. (a),** to pervert, misinterpret (meanings)

torniscón *m, inf* slap, buffet, blow; pinch

torno *m,* lathe; turntable (of a convent, etc.); turn, rotation; windlass; dumbwaiter; axletree; spinning wheel; bend, loop (in a river). **en t.,** round about, around; in exchange

toro *m,* bull; Taurus; *pl* bullfight. *inf* **t. corrido,** tough nut to crack, wise guy. *inf* **Ciertos son los toros,** So it's true (gen. of bad news)

toronja *f,* grapefruit

toroso *a* strong, vigorous, robust

torpe *a* heavy, slow, encumbered; torpid; clumsy, unskilled; stupid, dull-witted; obscene, indecent; base, infamous; ugly

torpedeamiento *m,* torpedoing, sinking

torpedear *vt* to torpedo

torpedeo *m,* torpedoing

torpedero *m,* torpedo boat

torpedo *m, icht* torpedo fish, electric ray; torpedo; sports car. **t. automóvil,** self-propelling torpedo

torpeza *f,* slowness, heaviness; torpidity; stupidity; lack of skill, clumsiness; indecency; ugliness; baseness, infamy

tórpido *a* torpid

torrar *vt* to toast, brown

torre *f,* tower; belfry, steeple; turret; rook (in chess); *naut* gun turret; stack, pile (of chairs, etc.); country house with a garden. **t. del tráfico,** traffic light. **t. de viento,** castle in the air, castle in Spain

torrefacción *f,* toasting (of coffee, etc.)

torrencial *a* torrential, rushing

torrente *m,* torrent; *fig* spate, rush; crowd

torrentoso, -a *a, Lat. Am.* = **torrencial**

torreón *m,* large fortified tower

torrero *m,* lighthouse keeper; gardener

torreznero (-ra) *n inf* lazybones, idler

torrezno *m,* rasher of bacon

tórrido *a* torrid

torsión *f,* twisting, torsion

torta *f,* cake; pastry, tart; *inf* slap. **t. de reyes,** traditional Twelfth Night cake

tortada *f,* meat pie, game pie

tortedad *f,* twistedness, crookedness

tortera *f,* cake pan; baking dish; whorl (of a spindle)

tortícolis *m,* crick (in the neck)

tortilla *f,* omelet; *Central America, Mexico* tortilla (corn pancake) **t. a la española,** potato omelet. **hacer t.,** to smash to atoms. **Se volvió la t.,** *inf* The tables are turned

tortillero, -a *mf Central America, Mexico* tortilla vendor

tórtola *f,* turtledove

tórtolo *m,* male turtledove; *inf* devoted lover

tortuga *f,* turtle; tortoise. **a paso de t.,** at a snail's pace

tortuosidad *f,* tortuousness; winding; indirectness; deceitfulness

tortuoso *a* tortuous; winding; disingenuous, deceitful

tortura *f,* twistedness; torture, torment; anguish, grief. **una t. china,** excruciating torture

torturador *a* torturing, tormenting

torturar *vt* to torture

torva *f,* squall of rain or snow

torzal *m,* sewing silk; twist, plait

tos *f,* cough. **t. ferina,** whooping cough

tosco *a* rough, unpolished; coarse; boorish, uncouth

toser *vi* to cough

tósigo *m,* poison, venom; anguish; affliction

tosigoso *a* poisoned, venomous

tosquedad *f,* roughness, lack of polish; coarseness; boorishness, uncouthness

tostada *f, cul* toast

tostadera *f,* toasting fork

tostado *a* golden brown, tanned. *m,* roasting (of coffee, etc.)

tostador (-ra) *n* toaster (of peanuts, etc.). *m,* toaster (utensil); coffee or peanut roaster

tostadura *f,* toasting; roasting (of coffee, etc.)

tostón *m,* buttered toast; anything overtoasted; roast pig; *inf* nuisance, bore

total *a* total, entire, whole; general. *m,* total. *adv* in short; so, therefore

totalidad *f,* whole; aggregate, entirety

totalitario *a* totalitarian

tótem *m,* totem

toxicidad *f,* toxicity

tóxico *a* toxic. *m,* toxic substance

toxicología *f,* toxicology

toxicológico *a* toxicological

tozo *a* dwarfish, small

tozudez *f,* obstinacy

tozudo *a* obstinate, obdurate

tozuelo *m,* scruff, fat nape (of animals)

traba *f,* setting (of a saw's teeth); tether (for horses); difficulty, obstacle; fastening; bond, tie; shackle; *law* distraint

trabacuenta *f,* mistake in accounts; argument, difference of opinion

trabajado *a* and *past part* wrought; fashioned; labored, exhausted, weary

trabajador (-ra) *a* working; conscientious. *n* worker

trabajar *vi* to work; function; stand the strain, resist (of machines, etc.); exert oneself, strive; toil, labor; operate, work; produce, yield (the earth fruits, etc.); *vt* work; till, cultivate; exercise (a horse); worry, annoy, weary; operate, drive; *vr* make every effort, work hard

trabajo *m*, work; toil, labor; operation, working; difficulty, obstacle; literary work; hardship, trouble; process; *pl* poverty; hardship. **t. a destajo,** piecework. **t. al ralenti,** go-slow tactics. **trabajos forzados** (*or* **forzosos**), *law* hard labor. **pasar trabajos,** to undergo hardships

trabajosamente *adv* painstakingly

trabajoso *a* difficult, hard; ailing, delicate; needy; afflicted

trabalenguas *m, inf* tongue twister, jawbreaker

trabamiento *m,* joining, fastening; uniting; initiation, commencement; shackling; hobbling (of horses)

trabar *vt* to join, unite, fasten; grasp, seize; set the teeth (of a saw); thicken; begin, initiate; hobble (of horses); reconcile, bring together, harmonize; shackle; *law* distrain; *vr* speak with an impediment; stutter, hesitate. **t. amistad,** to make friends. **t. conversación,** to get into conversation. **Se me trabó la lengua,** I began to stutter

trabazón *f,* join, union, fastening; connection; thickness, consistency

trabilla *f,* vest strap; dropped stitch (in knitting)

trabuca *f,* squib, Chinese firecracker, riprap

trabucar *vt* to turn upside down, upset; confuse, bewilder; mix up, confuse (news, etc.); pronounce or write incorrectly

trabucazo *m,* shot or report of a blunderbuss; *inf* calamity, unexpected misfortune

trabuco *m, mil* catapult; blunderbuss

trabuquete *m,* catapult

tracalada *f, Lat. Am.* crowd (of people); lot (large amount)

tracamundana *f, inf* barter, exchange of trash; hubbub, uproar

tracción *f,* pulling; traction

tracoma *f,* trachoma

tracto *m,* tract, area, expanse; lapse of time

tractor *m,* tractor. **t. de orugas,** caterpillar tractor

tractorista *mf* driver of a tractor, tractor driver

tradición *f,* tradition

tradicional *a* traditional

tradicionalismo *m,* traditionalism

tradicionalista *a* traditionalistic. *mf* traditionalist

traducción *f,* translation; interpretation, explanation

traducible *a* translatable

traducir *vt irr* to translate; interpret, explain; express. See **conducir**

traductor (-ra) *n* translator; interpreter

traedizo *a* portable, movable

traer *vt irr* to bring; attract; cause, occasion; wear, have on; quote, cite (as proof); compel, force; persuade; conduct, lead (persons); be engaged in; *vr* dress (well *or* badly). **t. consigo,** to bring with it; have or carry or bring with one. **t. entre manos,** to have on hand. *Pres. Ind.* **traigo, traes,** etc. *Pres. Part.* **trayendo.** *Preterite* **traje, trajiste,** etc. *Pres. Subjunc.* **traiga,** etc. *Imperf. Subjunc.* **trajese,** etc.

trafagador *m,* dealer, trafficker, merchant

tráfago *m,* traffic, trade; toil, drudgery

trafalmejas *a inf* rowdy, crazy, *mf inf* rowdy

traficante *mf* dealer, merchant, trader

traficar *vi* to trade; travel

tráfico *m,* traffic; trade, commerce

tragaderas *f pl,* throat, gullet. *inf* **tener buenas t.,** to be very credulous; be tolerant (of evil)

tragadero *m,* throat, gullet; sink, drain; hole, plug

tragador (-ra) *n* glutton, guzzler

tragahombres *mf inf* braggart, bully

trágala *m,* (**trágala tú, servilón**), title of Spanish Liberal song aimed at Absolutists; *inf* take that!

tragaleguas *mf inf* fast walker

tragaluz *m,* skylight; fan light

tragantón (-ona) *a inf* guzzling, greedy. *n* glutton

tragantona *f, inf* spread, large meal; swallowing with difficulty; *fig inf* hard pill to swallow

tragaperras *m, inf* vending machine, catchpenny

tragar *vt* to swallow; eat ravenously, devour; engulf, swallow up; believe, take in; tolerate, put up with; dissemble; consume, absorb

tragedia *f,* tragedy

trágico (-ca) *a* tragic. *n* tragedian; writer of tragedies

tragicomedia *f,* tragicomedy

tragicómico *a* tragicomic

trago *m,* swallow, gulp, draft; *fig inf* bitter pill. **a tragos,** *inf* little by little, slowly

tragón (-ona) *a inf* greedy, gluttonous. *n* glutton

tragonear *vt inf* to devour, eat avidly

traición *f,* treason, treachery. **a t.,** treacherously

traicionar *vt* to betray

traicionero (-ra) *a* treacherous. *n* traitor

traída *f,* conduction. **t. de aguas,** water supply

traidor (-ra) *a* treacherous. *n* traitor

traílla *f,* lead, leash (for animals)

traje *m,* dress, apparel; outfit, costume; suit. **t. de americana,** lounge suit. **t. de ceremonia** *or* **t. de etiqueta,** full-dress uniform; evening dress (men). **t. de luces,** bullfighter's gala outfit. **t. de montar,** riding habit. **t. de noche,** evening dress (women). **t. paisano,** civilian dress; lounge suit

trajín *m,* carriage, transport; busyness, moving around; bustle; clatter

trajinar *vt* to carry, transport; *Argentina* cheat, swindle; *vi* be busy, go about one's business

tralla *f,* rope, cord; lash (of a whip); whip

trama *f,* woof, texture (of cloth); twisted silk; intrigue, scheme; *lit* plot; olive flower

tramar *vt* to weave; prepare, hatch (plots); *fig* prepare the way for; *vi* flower (of trees, especially olive)

tramitación *f,* transaction, conduct; procedure, method

tramitar *vt* to transact, conduct, settle

trámite *m,* transit; negotiation, phase of a business deal; requirement, condition

tramo *m,* plot of ground; flight of stairs, staircase; stretch, expanse, reach, tract

tramontana *f,* north wind; arrogance, haughtiness

tramontano *a* ultramontane, from beyond the mountains

tramontar *vi* to cross the mountains; sink behind the mountains (of the sun); *vr* run away, escape

tramoya *f, theat* stage machinery; trick, deception, hoax

tramoyista *mf* stage carpenter; stagehand; sceneshifter; trickster, impostor, swindler

trampa *f,* trap, snare; trapdoor; flap of a shop counter; trouser fly; trick, swindle; overdue debt. *fig inf* **caer en la t.,** to fall into the trap. *inf* **coger en la t.,** to catch in a trap; catch in the act

trampal *m,* bog, marsh

trampantojo *m, inf* optical illusion, swindle

trampeador *a* swindling. *n* trickster, swindler

trampear *vi inf* to obtain money on false pretenses; struggle on (against illness, etc.); keep oneself alive, make shift; *vt* defraud, swindle

trampolín *m,* springboard; diving board; *fig* jumping-off place

tramposo (-sa) *n* debtor; cardsharper; swindler

tranca *f,* thick stick, cudgel; bar (of a window, etc.)

trancada *f,* stride

trancar *vt* to bar the door; *vi inf* oppose, resist; *vr, Lat. Am.* be constipated

trancazo *m,* blow with a stick; influenza, flu

trance *m,* crisis, difficult juncture; danger, peril. **t. de**

armas, armed combat. **a todo t.,** at all costs, without hesitation

tranco m, stride; threshold. *inf* **en dos trancos,** in a trice

tranquera f, stockade, palisade

tranquilar vt *com* to check off

tranquilidad f, tranquility, peace, quietness; composure, serenity

tranquilizador a tranquilizing, soothing

tranquilizar vt to calm, quiet; soothe

tranquilo a tranquil, quiet, peaceful; serene, composed

tranquiza f, *Mexico* beating, thrashing

transacción f, compromise, arrangement; transaction, negotiation, deal

transalpino a transalpine

transandino a transandean

transatlántico a transatlantic. m, (transatlantic) liner

transbordar vt to transship; transfer, remove goods from one vehicle to another

transbordo m, transshipment, transshipping; transfer, removal

transcendencia f See **trascendencia**

transcendental a. See **trascendental**

transcribir vt to transcribe; copy. *Past Part.* **transcrito**

transcripción f, transcription; copy, transcript

transcurrir vi to elapse, pass (time)

transcurso m, passage, lapse, course (of time)

transepto m, transept

transeúnte a transient, temporary. *mf* passerby; visitor, sojourner

transferencia f, transfer (from one place to another); *law* conveyance, transference. **t. bancaria,** bank draft

transferidor (-ra) a transferring. n transferrer; *law* transferor

transferir vt *irr* to transfer, move from one place to another; *law* convey (property, etc.); postpone. See **sentir**

transfiguración f, transfiguration

transfigurar vt to transfigure

transfijo a transfixed

transfixión f, transfixion

transformable a transformable

transformación f, transformation

transformador a transformative. m, *elec* transformer

transformar vt to transform; reform (persons); *vr* be transformed; reform, mend one's ways

transfregar vt *irr* to rub, scrub. See **cegar**

transfretar vt *naut* to cross the sea; vi spread

tránsfuga *mf* **tránsfugo** m, fugitive; political turncoat

transfundir vt to transfuse, pour from one vessel to another; imbue, transmit

transfusor a transfusive

transgredir vt to transgress, infringe

transgresión f, infringement, violation, transgression

transgresor (-ra) a infringing. n transgressor, violator

transición f, transition, change

transido a exhausted, worn-out, spent; niggardly, mean

transigencia f, tolerance, forbearance, indulgence

transigente a tolerant, forbearing

transigir vi to be tolerant; be broad-minded. vt put up with, tolerate

transitable a passable, traversable

transitar vi to cross, pass through; travel

transitivo a transitive

tránsito m, passage, crossing; transit; stopping place; transition, change; gallery of a cloister; *ecc* holy death. **de t.,** temporarily; in transit (of goods). **hacer tránsitos,** to break one's journey, stop

transitorio a transitory, fugitive, fleeting

translimitación f, trespass; bad behavior; armed intervention in a neighboring state

translimitar vt to overstep the boundaries (of a state, etc.); overstep the limits (of decency, etc.)

translucidez f, translucence, semitransparency

translúcido a translucent, semitransparent

transmarino a transmarine

transmigración f, transmigration

transmigrar vi to migrate; transmigrate (of the soul)

transmisión f, transmission. **t. del pensamiento,** thought transference

transmisor a transmitting. m, *elec* transmitter, sender

transmitir vt to transmit; *mech* drive

transmutable a transmutable

transmutación f, transmutation, transformation, change

transmutar vt to transmute, transform, change

transoceánico a transoceanic

transpacífico a transpacific

transparencia f, transparency; obviousness

transparentarse vr to be transparent; show through; *fig* reveal, give away (secrets)

transparente a transparent; translucent; evident, obvious. m, windowshade, blind

transpiración f, transpiration; perspiration

transpirar vi to perspire; transpire

transponer vt *irr* to move, transfer; transplant; transpose; vr hide behind; sink behind the horizon (of the sun, stars); be half-asleep. See **poner**

transportable a transportable

transportación f. See **transporte**

transportador (-ra) a transport. n transporter. m, *geom* protractor

transportamiento m. See **transporte**

transportar vt to transport; *mus* transpose; carry; vr *fig* be carried away by (anger, rapture)

transporte m, transport, carriage; cartage; *naut* transport; strong emotion, transport, ecstasy

transposición f, transposition

transpositivo a transpositive

transubstanciación f, transubstantiation

transubstanciar vt to transubstantiate, transmute

transversal, transverso a transverse

tranvía m, street railway; streetcar. **t. de sangre,** horse-drawn streetcar.

tranviario a streetcar. m, streetcar employee

trapacear vi to cheat, swindle

trapacete m, *com* daybook

trapacista *mf* trickster, swindler, knave

trapajoso a ragged, shabby, tattered

trápala f, noise, confusion, hubbub; noise of horse's hoofs, gallop; *inf* trick, swindle; prattling, babbling. *mf inf* babbler, prattler; trickster

trapalear vi to walk noisily, tramp; *inf* chatter, babble

trapatiesta f, *inf* brawl, row, quarrel

trapaza f, hoax, swindle

trapeador m, *Lat. Am.* (floor) mop

trapear vt, *Lat. Am.* to mop (the floor)

trapecio m, trapeze; *geom* trapezium, trapezoid

trapería f, old-clothes shop; old clothes, rags, trash, frippery

trapero (-ra) n old-clothes seller; rag merchant; ragpicker

trapezoide m, trapezium, trapezoid

trapichear vi *inf* to make shift, endeavor

trapiento a ragged, shabby

trapillo m, *inf* poverty-stricken lover; nest egg, savings. *inf* **de t.,** in a state of undress, in négligé

trapío m, *inf* spirit of a fighting bull; verve, dash, independent air (of women)

trapisonda f, *inf* uproar, brawl; hubbub, bustle; snare, fix

trapisondear vi *inf* to be given to brawling; scheme, intrigue

trapisondista *mf* brawler; schemer, trickster

trapo m, rag; *naut* canvas; bullfighter's cape; *pl* garments, bits and pieces. *inf* **poner como un t. (a),** to dress down, scold. *inf* **soltar el t.,** to burst out crying or laughing

trapujo m, *inf* trick; subterfuge

traque *m*, report, bang (of a rocket, etc.); fuse (of a firework)

tráquea *f*, trachea

traqueotomía *f*, tracheotomy

traquetear *vi* to crack, bang, go off with a report; rattle; jolt (of trains, etc.). *vt* shake, stir; *inf* paw, handle too much

traqueteo *m*, banging (of fireworks); creaking; rattling; jolting (of trains, etc.)

traquido *m*, report (of a gun); crack (of a whip); creak

tras *prep* after; behind; following, in pursuit of; trans- (in compounds). *m*, *inf* buttock; sound of a blow, bang, bump. **t. t.,** knocking (at a door); banging

trasalcoba *f*, dressing room

trasbarrás *m*, bang, bump, noise

trasbocar *vt*, *Lat. Am.* to vomit

trascendencia *f*, transcendence, excellence; consequence, result

trascendental *a* transcendental; important, far-reaching

trascender *vi irr* to spread to, influence; become known, leak out; exhale a scent; *vt* investigate, discover. See **entender**

trascocina *f*, back kitchen

trascolar *vt irr* to filter, strain; cross over, traverse. See **colar**

trascordarse *vr irr* to mix up, make a muddle of, forget. See **acordar**

trasechar *vt* to ambush, waylay

trasegar *vt irr* to upset, turn upside down; transfer, move from one place to another; empty, pour out, upset (liquids). See **cegar**

traseñalar *vt* to re-mark, mark again

trasera *f*, rear, back, rear portion

trasero *a* rear, back. *m*, hindquarters, rump; buttocks, seat; *pl inf* ancestors

trasgo *m*, imp, sprite, puck

trashumante *a* nomadic (of flocks)

trashumar *vi* to go from winter to summer pasture (or vice versa) (of flocks)

trasiego *m*, emptying, pouring out, upsetting (of liquids); decanting (of wines)

traslación *f*, removal, transfer; alteration (of the date for a meeting); metaphor

trasladable *a* removable, movable, transferable

trasladar *vt* to remove, transfer; move from one place to another; alter (the date of a meeting); translate; copy, transcribe; *vr* remove (from a place)

traslado *m*, removal; transfer; transcription

traslapar *vt* to cover, overlap

traslapo *m*, overlap, overlapping

traslucirse *vr irr* to be transparent or translucent; shine through; come out (of secrets); infer, gather. See **lucir**

traslumbramiento *m*, dazzle, glare, brilliance

traslumbrar *vt* to dazzle; *vr* flicker, glimmer; fade quickly, disappear

trasluz *m*, reflected light. **al t.,** against the light

trasminar *vt* to undermine, excavate; *vi* percolate, ooze; penetrate, spread

trasnochada *f*, previous night, last night; night's vigil; sleepless night; *mil* night attack

trasnochado *a* stale, old; weary; hackneyed; drawn, pinched

trasnochador (-ra) *n* one who watches by night or stays up all night; *inf* night owl, reveler

trasnochar *vi* to stay up all night; watch through the night; spend the night; *vt* sleep on, leave for the following day

trasnoche, trasnocho *m*, *inf* night out; night vigil

trasoir *vt irr* to hear incorrectly, misunderstand. See **oir**

trasojado *a* haggard, tired-eyed

trasoñar *vt irr* to imagine, mistake a dream for reality. See **contar**

traspalar *vt* to fork (grain); shovel; transfer, move

trasparencia *f*. See **transparencia**

traspasar *vt* to transfer, move; cross; *law* convey, make over to; pierce; transgress, flout; exceed one's authority; *fig* go too far; reexamine, go over again; give intolerable pain (of illness, grief). **se traspasa,** to be disposed of (houses, etc.)

traspaso *m*, transport, transfer; *law* conveyance; property transferred; price agreed upon

traspatio *m*, *Lat. Am.* backyard

traspié *m*, slip, catching of the foot, stumble; heel of the foot. **dar traspiés,** *inf* to blunder

trasplantación *f*, **trasplante** *m*, transplantation; emigration

trasplantar *vt agr* to transplant; *vr* emigrate

trasplante *m*, planting out

traspuesta *f*, transposition; back quarters; rear (of a house); back yard

traspunte *m*, *theat* prompter

traspuntín *m*, *aut* folding seat

trasquilar *vt* to cut the hair unevenly; shear (sheep); *inf* cut down, diminish

trasquilón *m*, cropping (of hair); shearing; *inf* money stolen by pilfering

trastada *f*, *inf* dirty trick, mean act

traste *m*, fret (of stringed instruments); tasting cup. **dar al t. con,** to spoil, upset, damage. *inf* **sin trastes,** topsy-turvy, without method

trastear *vt* to play well (on the mandolin, etc.); *inf* manage tactfully; *vi* move around, change (furniture, etc.); discuss excitedly

trastejar *vt* to repair the roof; renew slates; overhaul

trastienda *f*, back of a shop; room behind a shop; *inf* wariness, caution

trasto *m*, piece of furniture; (household) utensil; lumber, useless furniture; *theat* wing or set piece; *inf* useless person, ne'er-do-well; oddment, thing; *pl* implements, equipment

trastornable *a* easily overturned or upset; easily agitated

trastornar *vt* to turn upside down; perturb, disturb; *fig* overpower (of scents, etc.); disorder, upset; dissuade; make mad; derange the mind

trastorno *m*, upset; perturbation, anxiety; disorder; mental derangement; confusion (of the senses)

trastrabillar *vi* to stumble, slip; totter, sway; hesitate; stutter, be tongue-tied

trastrás *m*, *inf* last but one (in games)

trastrocamiento *m*, alteration, change; disarrangement

trastrocar *vt irr* to alter, change, disarrange; change the order of. See **contar**

trasudar *vt* to perspire

trasudor *m*, light perspiration

trasuntar *vt* to copy, transcribe; summarize

trasunto *m*, copy, transcript; imitation

trasver *vt irr* to see through or between, glimpse; see incorrectly. See **ver**

trasverter *vi irr* to overflow. See **entender**

trata *f*, slave trade. **t. de blancas,** white slave traffic

tratable *a* easily accessible, sociable, unpretentious

tratadista *mf* writer of a treatise; expert, writer on special subjects

tratado *m*, pact, agreement; treaty; treatise

tratador (-ra) *n* arbitrator

tratamiento *m*, treatment; courtesy title; address, style; *med* treatment; process

tratante *m*, merchant, dealer

tratar *vt* to handle, use; conduct, manage; have dealings with, meet, know (e.g. **Yo no le trato,** I don't know him); behave well or badly toward; care for, treat; discuss, deal with (e.g. **¿De qué trata el libro?** What is the book about?); propose, suggest; *chem* treat; (*with de*) address as, call; (*with de*) have amorous relations; (*with de*) try to, endeavor to; (*with en*) trade in; *vr* look after oneself, treat oneself; conduct oneself

trato *m*, use, handling; management; conduct, behavior; manner, demeanor; appellation, title; commerce, traffic; dealings, intercourse; treatment; agreement, arrangement. **t. colectivo,** collective bargaining

traumático *a* traumatic

traumatismo *m*, traumatism

• **través** *m*, slant, slope; mishap; (*mil arch*) traverse. **a t.** *or* **al t.,** across; through. **de t.,** athwart; through

travesaño *m*, crossbar; bolster; rung (of a ladder); *carp* traverse

travesear *vi* to run about, romp, be mischievous; lead a vicious life; speak wittily; move ceaselessly (of water, etc.)

travesía *f*, crossing; traverse; crossroad; side road or street; distance, space; sea crossing; crosswise position; stretch of road within a town

travestido *a* disguised, dressed up

travesura *f*, romping, frolic; mischief; prank; quick-wittedness

traviesa *f*, sleeping car, sleeper (railroad); *arch* rafter; distance between two points

travieso *a* transverse, crosswise; mischievous, willful; debauched; clever, subtle; ever-moving (of streams, etc.)

trayecto *m*, run, distance, journey; stretch, expanse, tract; fare stage

trayectoria *f*, trajectory; journey

traza *f*, plan, design, draft; scheme, project; idea, proposal; aspect, appearance; means, manner. **Hombre pobre todo es trazas,** A poor man is full of schemes (for bettering himself)

trazado *m*, designing, drawing; design, draft, model, plan; course, direction (of a canal, etc.)

trazador (-ra) *n* draftsman, designer; planner, schemer

trazar *vt* to plan, draft, design; make a drawing of; trace; describe; map out, arrange

trazo *m*, line, stroke; outline, contour, form, line; *art* fold in drapery; stroke of the pen

trebejar *vi* to frolic, skip, play

trebejo *m*, chessman, chess piece; utensil, article (gen. *pl*); plaything

trébol *m*, clover

trece *a* and *m*, thirteen, thirteenth. *m*, thirteenth (day of the month)

trecemesino *a* thirteen months old

trecho *m*, distance, space; interval (of time). **a trechos,** at intervals. **de t. en t.,** from time to time

trefe *a* pliable, flexible; light; spurious (of coins)

tregua *f*, truce, respite, rest. **dar treguas,** to afford relief, give a respite; give time

treinta *a* and *m*, thirty; thirtieth. *m*, thirtieth (day of the month)

treintavo *a* thirtieth

treintena *f*, thirtieth (part)

tremebundo *a* fearsome, dread

tremedal *m*, bog; quagmire

tremendo *a* fearful, formidable; awesome; *inf* tremendous, enormous

trementina *f*, turpentine

tremolar *vt* and *vi* to wave, fly (of banners); *fig* make a show of

tremolina *f*, noise of the wind; *inf* hubbub, confusion

trémulo *a* trembling, tremulous

tren *m*, supply, provision; outfit; equipment; pomp, show; railroad train; following, train; *Mexico also* streetcar, trolley car, trolley **t. ascendente,** up train (from coast to interior). *inf* **t. botijo,** excursion train. **t. con coches corridos,** corridor train. **t. correo,** mail train. **t. descendente,** down train (from interior to coast). **t. mixto,** train carrying passengers and freight. **t. ómnibus,** accommodation train, slow, stopping train. **t. rápido,** express

trencilla *f*, braid, trimming

trencillar *vt* to trim with braid, braid

trenza *f*, plait, braid; plait of hair; bread twist; *Lat. Am.* string (of onions). **en t.,** in plaits, plaited (of hair)

trenzadera *f*, linen tape

trenzar *vt* to plait, braid; *vi* curvet, prance *Lat. Am.* **tren-**

zarse (en . . .) get involved (in . . .), e.g. **trenzarse en una disputa** get involved in a dispute

trepa *f*, perforation, boring, piercing; climbing; creeping; *inf* half-somersault; grain, surface (of wood); craftiness, slyness; deception, fraud; beating, drubbing

trepador *a* climbing; crawling; *bot* creeping, climbing. *m*, climbing place

trepanación *f*, trepanning

trepanar *vt* to trepan

trepante *a* creeping; *bot* twining, climbing

trepar *vi* to climb, ascend; *bot* climb or creep; bore, perforate

trepatrepa *m*, jungle gym, monkey bars

trepidación *f*, trepidation, dread; vibration; jarring; shaking

trepidar *vi* to shiver, shudder; vibrate; shake; jar; *Lat. Am.* hesitate

trépido *a* shuddering, shivering; vibrating

tres *a* three; third. *m*, figure three; third (day of the month); three (of playing cards); trio. *inf* **como t. y dos son cinco,** as sure as two and two make four

trescientos *a* and *m*, three hundred; three-hundredth

tresillo *m*, omber (card game); *mus* triplet

tresnal *m*, *agr* stook, cock, sheaf

treta *f*, scheme; trick, hoax; feint (in fencing)

trezavo *a* thirteenth

tría *f*, selection, choice; worn place (in cloth)

triangulación *f*, triangulation

triángulo *a* triangular. *m*, (*geom mus*) triangle. **t. acutángulo,** acute triangle. **t. obtusángulo,** obtuse triangle. **t. rectángulo,** right-angled triangle

triar *vt* to select, pick out; *vi* fly in and out of the hive (of bees); *vr* grow threadbare, become worn

tribu *f*, tribe; species, family

tribulación *f*, tribulation, suffering

tribuna *f*, tribune; platform, rostrum, pulpit; spectators' gallery; stand. **t. de la prensa,** press gallery. **t. del jurado,** jury box. **t. del órgano,** organ loft

tribunado *m*, tribunate

tribunal *m*, law court; *law* bench; judgment seat; tribunal; board of examiners. **t. de menores,** children's court, juvenile court. *naut* **t. de presas,** prize court. **t. de primera instancia,** *law* petty sessions. **t. militar,** court-martial

tribuno *m*, tribune; political speaker

tributar *vt* to pay taxes; offer, render (thanks, homage, etc.)

tributario (-ia) *a* tributary; tax-paying, contributive. *n* taxpayer. *m*, tributary (of a river)

tributo *m*, contribution; tax; tribute, homage; census

tricenal *a* of thirty years' duration; occurring every thirty years

tricentésimo *a* three-hundredth

triciclo *m*, tricycle

tricolor *a* three-colored

tricorne *a* *poet* three-cornered, three-horned

tricornio *a* three-cornered. *m*, three-cornered hat

tricotomía *f*, trichotomy, division into three

tricromía *f*, three-color process

tridente *a* tridentate, three-pronged. *m*, trident

trienal *a* triennial

trienio *m*, space of three years

trifásico *a* three-phase

trifolio *m*, trefoil

trigal *m*, wheat field

trigésimo *a* thirtieth

trigo *m*, wheat plant; ear of wheat; wheat field (gen. *pl*); wealth, money. **t. sarraceno,** buckwheat. **t. tremés** *or* **t. trechel** *or* **t. tremesino** *or* **t. de marzo,** summer wheat

trigonometría *f*, trigonometry

trigueño *a* brunette, dark

triguero *a* wheat; wheat-growing. *m*, grain sieve; grain merchant

trilátero *a* three-sided, trilateral

trilingüe *a* trilingual

trilla *f*, red mullet; *agr* harrow; threshing; threshing season

trillado *a* frequented, trodden, worn (of paths); hackneyed

trilladora *f*, threshing machine

trillar *vt* to thresh; *inf* frequent; ill-treat

trillo *m*, threshing machine; harrow

trillón *m*, trillion

trilogía *f*, trilogy

trimestral *a* quarterly; terminal (in schools, etc.)

trimestre *a* quarterly; terminal. *m*, quarter, three months; term (in schools, etc.); quarterly payment; quarterly rent

trinado *m*, *mus* trill; twittering, shrilling (of birds)

trinar *vi mus* to trill; twitter, shrill; *inf* get in a temper, be furious

trincapiñones *m*, *inf* scatterbrained youth

trincar *vt* to fasten securely; tie tightly; pinion; *naut* lash, make fast; cut up, chop; *inf* tipple; *vi naut* sail close to the wind

trincha *f*, vest strap

trinchante *m*, table carver; carving fork; stonecutter's hammer

trinchar *vt* to carve (at table); *inf* decide, dispose

trinche *m Mexico* pitchfork; *elsewhere in Lat. Am.* fork

trinchera *f*, *mil* trench; cutting (for roads, etc.); trench coat

trinchero *m*, platter, trencher; serving table, side table

trineo *m*, sledge, sleigh

trinidad *f*, trinity

trinitaria *f*, *bot* heartsease

trinitario (-ia) *a* and *n ecc* Trinitarian

trino *a* triune; ternary. *m*, *mus* trill

trinomio *m*, trinomial

trinquete *m*, *naut* mainmast; mainsail; *sport* rackets; *mech* ratchet

trinquis *m*, *inf* draft, drink

trío *m*, trio

tripa *f*, entrail, gut; *inf* belly; inside (of some fruits). **hacer de tripas corazón,** *inf* to take heart, buck up. **revolver las tripas (a),** *fig inf* to make one sick

tripartición *f*, tripartition

tripartito *a* tripartite

tripicallos *m pl*, *cul* tripe

triple *a* triple; three-ply (of yarn)

triplicación *f*, trebling

triplicar *vt* to treble

trípode *m*, (sometimes *f*) three-legged stool or table; tripod; trivet

tríptico *m*, triptych

triptongo *m*, triphthong

tripulación *f*, crew (ships and aircraft)

tripulante *m*, crew member

tripular *vt* to provide with a crew, man; equip, furnish; serve in, work as the crew of

trique *m*, crack, creak. *inf* **a cada t.,** at every moment

triquiñuela *f*, *inf* evasion, subterfuge

triquitraque *m*, tap, rap; crack; firework

tris *m*, crack, noise of glass, etc., cracking; *inf* instant, trice. **estar en un t. (de),** to be on the verge (of), within an inch (of)

trisar *vt* to crack, break, splinter (of glass); *vi* chirp, twitter (especially of swallows)

trisca *f*, cracking, crushing, crackling (of nuts, etc.); noise, tumult

triscar *vi* to make a noise with the feet; gambol, frolic; creak, crack; *vt* blend, mingle; set the teeth of a saw

trisecar *vt* to trisect

trisemanal *a* three times weekly; every three weeks

trisílabo *a* trisyllabic

trismo *m*, lockjaw, trismus

triste *a* unhappy, sorrowful; melancholy, gloomy; sad; piteous, unfortunate; useless, worthless; *m*, *Lat. Am.* sad love song

tristeza, tristura *f*, unhappiness; melancholy, gloom; sadness; piteousness

tritón *m*, merman

triturar *vt* to crumble, crush; chew; masticate; ill-treat, bruise; refute, contradict

triunfada *f*, trumping (at cards)

triunfador (-ra) *a* triumphant. *n* victor

triunfal *a* triumphal

triunfante *a* triumphant

triunfar *vi* to triumph; be victorious, win; trump (at cards); spend ostentatiously

triunfo *m*, triumph; victory; trump card; success; booty, spoils of war; conquest

trivial *a* well-known, hackneyed; frequented, trodden; commonplace, mediocre; trivial, unimportant

trivialidad *f*, banality, triteness; mediocrity; triviality

trivio *m*, road junction

triza *f*, fragment, bit; *naut* rope. **hacer trizas,** to smash to bits

trizar *vt* to smash up, destroy

trocable *a* exchangeable

trocada, a la *adv* contrariwise; in exchange

trocador (-ra) *n* exchanger

trocar *vt irr* to exchange; vomit; distort, misconstrue; mistake; *vr* change, alter one's behavior; change places with another; be transferred. See **contar**

trocha *f*, short cut; trail, path, track

trochemoche, a *adv inf* without rhyme or reason, pell-mell

trocear *vt* to divide into pieces

trofeo *m*, trophy; victory; military booty

troglodita *a* and *mf* troglodyte. *m*, *fig* savage, barbarian. *mf* glutton

troj *f*, granary

trojero *m*, granary keeper

trola *f*, *inf* lie, nonsense, hoax

trole *m*, trolley

trolebús *m*, trolley car

trolero *a inf* deceiving, lying

tromba *f*, waterspout

trombón *m*, trombone; trombone player. **¡Trombones y platillos!** Great Scot!

trombosis *f*, thrombosis

trompa *f*, elephant's trunk; *mus* horn; proboscis (of insects); waterspout; humming top. **t. de Falopio,** fallopian tube

trompada *f*, *inf* bang, bump; blow, buffet, slap; collision

trompazo *m*, heavy blow, knock, bang

trompear *vi* to play with a top; *vt* knock about

trompero *m*, top maker. *a* deceiving, swindling

trompeta *f*, trumpet; bugle. *m*, trumpeter; bugler; *inf* ninny. **t. de amor,** sunflower

trompetada *f*, *inf* stupid remark, piece of nonsense

trompetazo *m*, bray of a trumpet; bugle blast; *inf* stupid remark

trompetear *vi inf* to play the trumpet or bugle

trompeteo *m*, trumpeting, trumpet call; sound of the bugle

trompetería *f*, collection of trumpets; metal organ pipes

trompetero *m*, trumpet or bugle maker or player

trompetilla *f*, *dim* little trumpet; ear trumpet

trompicar *vt* to make stumble, trip. *vi* stumble, trip up

trompicón *m*, stumble

trompo *m*, humming or spinning top; *inf* dolt, idiot

tronada *f*, thunderstorm

tronado *a* worn-out; threadbare, old; poor, poverty-stricken; down at the heels

tronar *v impers irr* to thunder; *vi* growl, roar (of guns); *inf* go bankrupt, be ruined; *inf* protest against, attack; *Central America, Mexico* execute, shoot; (*with con*) quarrel with. *Pres. Ind.* **trueno, truenas, truena, truenan.** *Pres. Subjunc.* **truene, truenes, truene, truenen**

troncal *a* trunk; main, principal

troncha *f*, *Lat. Am.* piece; slice

tronchar *vt* to break off, lop off (branches)

troncho *m*, *bot* stem, stalk, branch

tronco *m, anat bot* trunk; main body or line (of communications); trunk line; common origin, stock; *inf* blockhead, dolt; callous person. *fig* **estar hecho un t.,** to lie like a log; sleep like a log

tronera *f, naut* porthole; embrasure; slit window; pocket of a billiards table. *mf inf* madcap, harumscarum

tronido *m,* roll of thunder

trono *m,* throne; *ecc* tabernacle; shrine; kingly might; *pl* thrones, hierarchy of angels

tronzador *m,* two-handled saw

tronzar *vt* to smash, break into bits; *sew* pleat; exhaust, overtire

tropa *f,* crowd (of people); troops, military; *mil* call to arms; *pl* army. **t. de línea,** regiment of the line. **tropas de asalto,** storm troopers. **tropas de refresco,** fresh troops. **en t.,** in a crowd; in groups

tropel *m,* rush, surge (of crowds, etc.); bustle, confusion; crowd, multitude; heap, jumble (of things). **en t.,** in a rush; in a crowd

tropelía *f,* rush, dash; violence; outrage

tropezar *vi irr* to stumble, slip; (*with con*) meet unexpectedly or accidentally come up against, be faced with (difficulties); quarrel with or oppose; fall into (bad habits). See **empezar**

tropezón *m,* stumbling, slipping; stumbling block, obstacle. **a tropezones,** *inf* stumblingly; by fits and starts

tropical *a* tropical

trópicos *m pl,* tropics

tropiezo *m,* stumble; stumbling block, obstacle; hitch; impediment; slip, peccadillo, fault; difficulty, embarrassment; fight, skirmish; quarrel

tropo *m,* trope, figure of speech

troquel *m,* die, mold

trotaconventos *f, inf* go-between, procuress

trotamundos *mf, inf* globetrotter

trotar *vi* to trot; *inf* hurry, get a move on

trote *m,* trot; toil, drudgery. **t. corto,** jog-trot. **al t.,** with all speed

trotón (-ona) *a* trotting. *m,* horse. *f,* chaperone

trova *f,* verse; song, lay, ballad; love song

trovador (-ra) *m,* troubadour, minstrel. *n* poet

trovadoresco *a* pertaining to minstrels, troubadour

trovar *vi* to compose verses; write ballads; misconstrue, misinterpret

Troya Troy

troyano (-na) *a* and *n* Trojan

trozo *m,* part, fragment; piece, portion; *lit* selection. **t. de abordaje,** *nav* landing party

trucha *f,* trout. **t. asalmonada,** salmon trout

truchuela *f,* small trout; salt cod

truco *m,* trick, deception

truculencia *f,* harshness, cruelty, truculence

truculento *a* fierce, harsh, truculent

trueco *m,* exchange. **a t. de,** in exchange for; on condition that

trueno *m,* thunder; report, noise (of firearms); *inf* rake, scapegrace

trueque *m,* exchange. **a.** (*or* **en**) **t.,** in exchange

trufa *f, bot* truffle; nonsense, idle talk

trufar *vt cul* to stuff with truffles; *vi inf* lie, tell fibs

truhán (-ana) *a* knavish, roguish, comic. *n* knave, rogue; clown, buffoon

truhanear *vi* to be a trickster, behave like a knave; play the clown

truhanería *f,* knavery, act of a rogue; clowning, buffoonery; collection of rogues

truhanesco *a* knavish, scoundrelly; clownish

trujal *m,* oil or grape press; oil mill; vat for soap making

trujar *vt* to partition off

trulla *f,* uproar, tumult; crowd, throng

truncar *vt* to shorten, truncate; decapitate, mutilate; omit, cut out (words, etc.); curtail, abridge; mutilate, deform (texts, etc.)

truque *m,* card game; kind of hopscotch

trusa *f, Cuba,* bathing suit

trust *m, com* trust

tú *pers pron 2nd sing mf* thou, you. **tratar de t. (a),** to address familiarly; be on intimate terms with

tu *poss pron mf* thy, your. Used only before nouns

tuberculina *f,* tuberculin

tubérculo *m,* (*zool med*) tubercle; *bot* tubercle, tuber

tuberculoso *a* tubercular, tuberculous

tubería *f,* piping, tubing; pipe system; pipe factory

tuberosa *f,* tuberose

tuberoso *a* tuberous

tubo *m,* pipe, tube; lamp chimney; flue; *anat* duct, canal. **t. acústico,** speaking tube. **t. de ensayo,** test tube. **t. de escape,** exhaust pipe. **t. lanzatorpedos,** torpedo tube. **t. termiónico,** *rad* thermionic valve

tubular *a* tubular

tucán, tucano *m* toucan

tudesco *a* German

tueco *m,* stump (of a tree); wormhole (in wood)

tuerca *f,* nut (of a screw)

tuerto *a* one-eyed. *m, law* tort; *pl* afterpains. **a t.,** unjustly

tueste *m,* toasting

tuétano *m,* marrow. *inf* **hasta los tuétanos,** to the depths of one's being

tufillas *mf inf* easily irritated person

tufo *m,* strong smell, poisonous vapor; *inf* stink; side, airs, conceit (often *pl*); lock of hair over the ears

tugurio *m,* shepherd's hut; miserable little room; *inf* haunt, low dive

tul *m,* tulle

tulipa *f,* small tulip; lampshade

tulipán *m,* tulip

tullido *a* partially paralyzed; maimed, crippled

tullir *vt irr* to maim, cripple; paralyze; *vr* become paralyzed; be crippled. See **mullir**

tumba *f,* tomb; tumble, overbalancing; somersault; Catherine wheel

tumbar *vt* to knock down; kill, drop; *inf* overpower, overcome (of odors, wine). *vi* fall down; *naut* run aground; *vr inf* lie down, stretch oneself out

tumbo *m,* tumble, overbalancing; undulation (of ground); rise and fall of sea waves; imminent danger; book containing deeds and privileges of monasteries and churches

tumbón *a inf* crafty, sly; idle, lazy. *m,* trunk with an arched lid

tumefacción *f,* swelling

tumefacto, túmido *a* swollen

tumor *m,* tumor

túmulo *m,* tumulus; catafalque; mound of earth

tumulto *m,* riot, uprising; tumult, commotion, disturbance

tumultuario, tumultuoso *a* noisy, tumultuous, confused

tuna *f,* prickly pear tree or fruit; vagrant life; strolling student musicians (playing to raise money for charity)

tunante *a* rascally, roguish. *mf* rascal, scoundrel

tunantuelo (-la) *n inf* imp, little rascal

tunda *f,* shearing of cloth; *inf* sound beating, hiding

tundear *vt* to beat, drub, buffet

tundidora *f,* woman who shears cloth; cloth-shearing machine; lawn mower

tundir *vt* to shear (cloth); mow (grass); *inf* beat, wallop

tunecino (-na) *a* and *n* Tunisian

túnel *m,* tunnel

túnica *f,* tunic, chiton; tunicle; robe

tuno (-na) *a* knavish, rascally. *n* rascal, scoundrel

tupé *m,* forelock (of a horse); toupee; *inf* cheek, nerve

tupición *f, Lat. Am.* blockage, obstruction; cold (in the head)

tupido *a* thick, dense; obtuse, dull, stupid; *Lat. Am.* blocked up, obstructed

tupir *vt* to thicken, make dense; press tightly; *vr* stuff oneself with food or drink

turba *f,* crowd, multitude; peat

turbación *f*, disturbance; upset; perturbation; bewilderment, confusion; embarrassment

turbador (-ra) *a* disturbing, upsetting. *n* disturber, upsetter

turbamulta *f*, *inf* mob, rabble

turbante *a* upsetting, perturbing. *m*, turban

turbar *vt* to disturb, upset; make turbid, muddy; bewilder, confuse; embarrass

turbera *f*, peat bog

turbiedad *f*, muddiness (of liquids); obscurity

turbina *f*, turbine

turbio *a* turbid, muddy; troublous; turbulent, disturbed; obscure, confused (style); indistinct, blurred, *m pl*, lees, sediment (of oil)

turbión *m*, brief storm, squall; *fig* shower, rush

turbulencia *f*, turbidity, muddiness; turbulence, commotion; disturbance, confusion

turbulento *a* muddy, turbid; turbulent, disturbed; confused

turca *f*, *inf* drinking bout

turco (-ca) *a* Turkish. *n* Turk. *m*, Turkish (language)

turgencia *f*, swelling, turgidity

turgente *a med* turgescent; *poet* turgid, prominent, swollen

turismo *m*, touring, tourist industry. **coche de t.,** touring car

turista *mf* tourist

turno *m*, turn. **por t.,** in turn

turquesa *f*, turquoise

Turquía Turkey

turrón *m*, kind of nougat; almond paste; *inf* soft job, sinecure; civil service job

turulato *a inf* dumbfounded, speechless, inarticulate

¡tus! *interj* word for calling dogs. **sin decir t. ni mus,** *inf* without saying anything

tusa *f*, *Central America* corncob; whore; *Argentina* mane (of a horse)

tutear *vt* to address as tú (instead of the formal usted); treat familiarly

tutela *f*, guardianship; tutelage; protection, defense

tuteo *m*, the use in speaking to a person of the familiar tú instead of the formal used

tutor (-ra) *n* guardian. *m*, stake (for plants); protector, defender

tutoría *f*. See **tutela**

tuyo, tuya, tuyos, tuyas *poss pron 2nd sing* and *pl mf* thine, yours. Used sometimes with def. art. (e.g. **Este sombrero es el tuyo,** This hat is yours)

U

u *f*, letter U. *conjunc* Used instead of **o** or before words beginning with **o** or **ho** (e.g. **fragante u oloroso**)

ubérrimo *a sup* most fruitful; very abundant

ubicación *f*, situation, position, location

ubicar *vt* to place, situate; *vi* and *vr* be situated

ubicuidad *f*, ubiquity

ubicuo *a* omnipresent; ubiquitous

ubre *f*, udder

Ucrania Ukraine

ucranio (-ia) *a* and *n* Ukrainian

ucelele *m*, ukulele

¡uf! *interj* ugh!

ufanarse *vr* to pride oneself, put on airs

ufanía *f*, pride, conceit

ufano *a* conceited, vain; satisfied, pleased; expeditious, masterly

ujier *m*, usher

úlcera *f*, ulcer

ulcerar(se) *vt* and *vr* to ulcerate

ulceroso *a* ulcerous

ulpo *m*, *Chile, Peru* corn gruel

ulterior *a* farther, ulterior; subsequent

ulteriormente *adv* subsequently, later

ultimación *f*, ending, finishing

ultimar *vt* to end, conclude

ultimátum *m*, ultimatum

último *a* last; farthermost; ultimate; top; final, definitive; most valuable, best; latter; recent. «**Última Hora.**» "Stop Press." **a última hora,** *fig* at the eleventh hour. **en estos últimos años,** in recent years. **a últimos de mes,** towards the end of the month. **el ú. piso,** the top floor. **por ú.,** finally. *inf* **estar en las últimas,** to be at the end, be finishing

ultra, *adv* besides; (with words like *mar*) beyond; (as prefix) excessively

ultrajar *vt* to insult; scorn, despise

ultraje *m*, insult, outrage

ultrajoso *a* offensive, insulting, abusive

ultramar *m*, overseas, abroad

ultramarino *a* oversea; ultramarine. *m*, foreign produce (gen. *pl*)

ultramontano *a* ultramontane

ultrarrojo *a* infrared

ultratumba *adv* beyond the grave

ultravioleta *a* ultraviolet

úlula *f*, screech owl

ululación *f*, screech, howl; hoot of an owl

ulular *vi* to howl, shriek, screech; hoot (of an owl)

ululato *m*, ululation

umbilical *a* umbilical

umbral *m*, threshold; *fig* starting point; *arch* lintel. **atravesar** (*or* **pisar**) **los umbrales,** to cross the threshold

umbría *f*, shady place

umbrío *a* shady, dark

umbroso *a* shady

un *abb* of **uno, a,** one. Used before *m, sing f,* **una,** *indef art.* a, an; a; one

unánime *a* unanimous

unanimidad *f*, unanimity. **por u.,** unanimously

unción *f*, anointing; *ecc* Extreme Unction; unction, fervor

uncir *vt* to yoke

undécimo *a* eleventh

undísono *a poet* sounding, sonorous (waves, etc.)

undoso *a* wavy, rippling

undulación *f*, undulation; *phys* wave

undular *vi* to undulate; wriggle; float, wave (flags, etc.)

undulatorio *a* undulatory

ungimiento *m*, anointment

ungir *vt* to anoint

ungüento *m*, ointment; lotion; *fig* balm, unguent

unicelular *a* unicellular

único *a* unique; sole, solitary, only. **Lo ú. que se puede hacer es . . .,** The only thing one can do is . . .

unicolor *a* of one color

unicornio *m*, unicorn

unidad *f*, unity; unit; (*math mil*) unit. **u. de bagaje,** piece of baggage. (of drama) **u. de lugar,** unity of place. **u. de tiempo,** unity of time

unidamente *adv* jointly; harmoniously

unificación *f*, unification

unificar(se) *vt* and *vr* to unify, unite

uniformación *f*, standardization

uniformar *vt* to make uniform, standardize; put into uniform; *vr* become uniform

uniforme *a* uniform; same, similar. *m*, uniform

uniformidad *f*, uniformity

unigénito *a* only-begotten. *m*, Christ

unilateral *a* one-sided, unilateral

unión *f*, union; correspondence, conformity; agreement; marriage; alliance, federation; composition, mixture; combination; proximity, nearness; (mystic) union

unionista *mf pol* unionist

Unión Soviética Soviet Union

unir *vt* to unite, join; mix, combine; bind, fasten; connect, couple; bring together; marry; *fig* harmonize, conciliate; *vr* join together, unite; be combined; marry; (*with prep a* or *con*) be near to; associate with

unísono *a* unisonant. **al u.,** in unison; unanimously

unitario (-ia) *a* and *n* Unitarian

universal *a* universal; well-informed; widespread

universalidad *f,* universality

universalizar *vt* to make universal, generalize

universidad *f,* university; universality; universe

universitario *a* university

universo *a* universal. *m,* universe

uno (*f,* **una**) *a a,* one; single, only; same; *pl* some; about, nearly. *m,* one (number). **Tiene unos doce años,** He is about twelve. **unas pocas manzanas,** a few apples. *pron* someone; one thing, same thing; *pl* some people. **No sabe uno qué creer,** One doesn't know what to believe. **Unos dicen que no, otros que sí,** Some (people) say no, others yes. **Juan no tiene libros y le voy a dar uno,** John has no books and I am going to give him one. **Todo es uno,** It's all the same. **u. a u.,** one by one. **u. que otro,** a few. **u. y otro,** both. **unos cuantos,** a few, some. **Es la una,** It is one o'clock

untar *vt* to anoint; grease, oil; *inf* bribe; *vr* smear oneself with grease or similar thing; *fig inf* line one's pockets. **u. el carro,** *fig* to grease the wheels

unto *m,* grease; animal fat; *fig* balm; *Chile* shoe polish

untuoso *a* fat, greasy

uña *f,* nail (of fingers or toes); hoof, trotter, claw; stinging tail of scorpion; thorn; stump of tree branch; *naut* fluke; *fig inf* light fingers (gen. *pl*). **afilarse las uñas,** to sharpen one's claws, prepare for trouble. **comerse las uñas,** to bite one's nails. **caer en las uñas de,** to fall into the clutches of. **hincar la u. (en),** to stick the claws into; to defraud, overcharge. **ser u. y carne,** to be devoted friends

uñarada *f,* scratch with nails

uñero *m,* ingrowing nail, ingrown nail

¡upa! *interj* Up you get! Up you go! Upsy daisy! (gen. to children)

uranio *m,* uranium

urbanidad *f,* civility, good manners, urbanity

urbanismo *m,* town planning; housing scheme

urbanización *f,* urbanization

urbanizar *vt* to civilize, polish; urbanize

urbano *a* urban, city; urbane

urbe *f,* city, metropolis

urbícola *mf* city dweller

urdemalas *mf,* schemer, intriguer

urdidera *f,* warping-frame

urdimbre *f,* warp; scheming, plotting

urdir *vt* to warp; weave; scheme, intrigue

uréter *m,* ureter

uretra *f,* urethra

urgencia *f,* urgency; necessity; compulsion

urgente *a* urgent

urgir *vi* to be urgent; be valid, be in force (laws)

urinario *a* urinary. *m,* urinal

urna *f,* urn; ballot box; glass case

urraca *f,* magpie

Uruguay *m* Uruguay

uruguayo (-ya) *a* and *n* Uruguayan

usado *a* worn out; accustomed, efficient. *com* **al u.,** in the usual form. **ropa usada,** second-hand clothing, worn clothing

usanza *f,* custom, usage

usar *vt* to use; wear, make use of; follow (trade, occupation); *vi* be accustomed

usina *f, Argentina* power plant

uso *m,* use; custom; fashion; habit; wear and tear. **al u.,** according to custom. **al u. de,** in the manner of

usted *mf* you. *pl* **ustedes.** Often abbreviated to **Vd, V, Vds, VV** or **Ud, Uds**

usual *a* usual; general, customary; sociable

usufructo *m, law* usufruct; life-interest; profit

usura *f,* usury; profiteering. **pagar con u.,** to pay back a thousandfold

usurario *a* usurious

usurear *vi* to lend or borrow with usury; profiteer, make excess profits

usurero (-ra) *n* usurer; profiteer

usurpación *f,* usurpation

usurpador (-ra) *a* usurping. *n* usurper

usurpar *vt* to usurp

utensilio *m,* utensil; tool, implement (gen. *pl*)

uterino *a* uterine

útero *m,* uterus

útil *a* useful; profitable; *law* lawful (of days, etc.). *m,* usefulness, profit; *pl* **útiles,** utensils, tools

utilidad *f,* utility; usefulness; profit

utilitario *a* utilitarian

utilitarismo *m,* utilitarianism

utilizable *a* utilizable

utilización *f,* utilization

utilizar *vt* to utilize

utillaje *m,* machinery

utópico *a* Utopian

uva *f,* grape. **u. espina,** kind of gooseberry. **u. moscatel,** muscatel grape. *inf* **hecho una u.,** deaddrunk

uvero (-ra) *a* pertaining or relating to grapes, grape. *n* grape seller

uxoricidio *m,* uxoricide (act)

uxorio *a* uxorious

V

v *f,* letter V. **v doble** *or* **doble v,** letter W. **V** *or* **Vd, VV,** *abbs* **vuestra(s) merced(es),** *mf sing* and *pl* you

vaca *f,* cow. **v. de San Antón,** *ent* ladybug

vacación *f,* vacation, holiday (gen. *pl*); vacancy; act of vacating (employment). **vacaciones retribuídas,** paid vacation

vacada *f,* herd of cows

vacancia *f,* vacancy

vacante *a* vacant. *f,* vacancy

vacar *vi* to be vacant; take a holiday; retire temporarily; (*with prep a*) dedicate oneself to, engage in

vaciadero *m,* rubbish dump; sewer, drain

vaciado *m,* plaster cast; *arch* excavation

vaciamiento *m,* emptying; molding, casting; depletion

vaciar *vt* to empty; drain, drink; mold, cast; *arch* excavate; hone; copy; *vi* flow (into) (rivers); *vr inf* blurt out

vaciedad *f,* emptiness; foolishness, inanity

vacilación *f,* swaying; tottering; staggering; hesitation, perplexity

vacilada *Mexico, f* joke, trick (played on someone)

vacilante *a* swaying; tottering; staggering; hesitating, vacillating

vacilar *vi* to sway; totter; stagger; flicker; hesitate

vacío *a* empty, void; fruitless, vain; unoccupied, vacant, deserted; imperfect; hollow, empty; conceited, immature. *m,* hollow; *anat* flank; vacancy; shortage; *phys* vacuum. **v. de aire,** airpocket. **de v.,** unloaded (carts, etc.). **en v.,** in vacuo. *inf* **hacer el v. (a),** to send to Coventry

vacuidad *f,* emptiness; vacuity

vacuna *f,* cowpox; vaccine. **v. antivariolosa,** smallpox vaccine

vacunación *f,* vaccination

vacunar *vt* to vaccinate; inoculate

vacuno *a* bovine

vacuo *a* empty; vacant. *m*, void; vacuum

vadeable *a* fordable (rivers, etc.); *fig* surmountable

vadear *vt* to ford, wade; *fig* overcome (obstacles); *fig* sound, find out the opinion (of); *vr* behave

vademécum *m*, vade mecum; school satchel

vado *m*, ford; expedient, help

vagabundear *vi* to wander, roam, loiter

vagabundeo *m*, vagabondage

vagabundo (-da) *a* roving, wandering; vagrant. *n* tramp, vagabond

vagamundear *vi*. See **vagabundear**

vagancia *f*, vagrancy

vagar *m*, leisure; interval, pause. *vi* be idle or at leisure; wander, roam

vagido *m*, cry, wail (infants)

vago (-ga) *a* vagrant, idle; vague; *art* indefinite, blurred. *n* idler. *m*, tramp; loafer. **en v.,** unsuccessfully, vainly

vagón *m*, wagon; (railway) coach. **v. comedor,** dining car

vagoneta *f*, open truck (railways, mines, etc.)

vaguear *vi* to roam, wander; loaf

vaguedad *f*, vagueness; vague remark

vaharada *f*, whiff, exhalation

vahído *m*, vertigo, dizzy spell

vaho *m*, vapor, fume

vaina *f*, scabbard; *bot* sheath, pod; case (scissors, etc.); *Colombia* hassle. **¡Qué vaina!** What a hassle!

vainilla *f*, *bot* vanilla; *sew* drawn-thread work

vaivén *m*, swing, sway, seesaw; instability, fluctuation

vajilla *f*, china; dinner service

val *m*, *abb* valle

Valdepeñas *m*, red wine from Valdepeñas

vale *m*, *com* bond, I.O.U., promissory note; voucher; valediction; *Lat. Am.* buddy, pal

valedero *a* valid, binding

valedor (-ra) *n* protector, sponsor

valencia *f*, valency

valenciano (-na) *a* and *n* Valencian

valentía *f*, bravery; heroic deed; boast; (*art lit*) dash, imagination, fire; superhuman effort

valentón *a* boastful, blustering

valer *vt irr* to protect; defend; produce (income, etc.); cost; *vi* be worth; deserve; have power or authority; be of importance or worth; be a protection; be current (money); be valid; *vr* (*with de*) make use of. *m*, value, worth. **v. la pena,** to be worthwhile. **v. tanto como cualquiera,** to be as good as the next guy, be as good as the next fellow. **¡Válgame Dios!** Heavens! Bless me! **Más vale así,** It's better thus. **Vale más ser cola de león que cabeza de ratón.** Better a big frog in a small puddle than a small frog in a big puddle. *Pres. Ind.* **valgo, vales,** etc. *Fut.* **valdré,** etc. *Condit.* **valdría,** etc. *Pres. Subjunc.* **valga,** etc.

valeriana *f*, valerian

valeroso *a* active, energetic; courageous; powerful

valetudinario *a* valetudinarian

valía *f*, value, price; influence; worth; faction, party. **a las valías,** at the highest price

validación *f*, validation; force, soundness

validar *vt* to make strong; validate

validez *f*, validity

valido *a* favorite, esteemed. *m*, court favorite; prime minister

válido *a* firm, sound, valid; strong, robust

valiente *a* strong, robust; courageous; active; excellent; excessive, enormous (gen. *iron*); boastful

valija *f*, valise, suitcase, grip; mail bag; mail

valimiento *m*, value; favor; protection, influence

valioso *a* valuable; powerful; wealthy

valisoletano (-na) *a* and *n* of or from Valladolid

valla *f*, barricade, paling; stockade; *fig* obstacle. **v. publicitaria,** billboard

vallado *m*, stockade; enclosure; *Mexico* deep ditch

valle *m*, valley; vale; river-basin

valor *m*, worth, value; price; courage; validity; power; yield, income; insolence; *pl com* securities

valoración *f*, valuation; appraisement

valorar *vt* to value; appraise

valorización *f*, valuation

valquiria *f*, Valkyrie

vals *m*, waltz

valsar *vi* to waltz

valuación *f*. See **valoración**

valuar *vt* to value; appraise; assess

valva *f*, *zool* valve

válvula *f*, *mech* valve. *aut* **v. de cámara (del neumático),** tire-valve. **v. de seguridad,** safety-valve

vampiro *m*, vampire; *fig* bloodsucker

vanagloria *f*, vaingloriousness, conceit

vanagloriarse *vr* to be conceited

vanaglorioso (-sa) *a* conceited. *n* boaster

vanamente *adv* vainly; without foundation; superstitiously; arrogantly

vandálico *a* Vandal

vandalismo *m*, vandalism; destructiveness

vándalo (-la) *a* and *n* Vandal

vanguardia *f*, vanguard; *pl* outerworks. **a v.,** in the forefront

vanidad *f*, vanity; ostentation; empty words; illusion. *inf* **ajar la v. de,** to take (a person) down a peg

vanidoso (-sa) *a* vain; ostentatious. *n* conceited person

vano *a* vain; hollow, empty; useless, ineffectual; unsubstantial, illusory. *m*, span (bridge). **v. único,** single span. **en v.,** uselessly, in vain

vapor *m*, steam, vapor; fainting fit; steamboat; *pl* hysterics. **v. de ruedas, v. de paleta,** paddle steamer. **v. volandero,** tramp steamer. **al v.,** full steam ahead; *inf* with all speed

vaporable *a* vaporizable

vaporación *f*, evaporation

vaporización *f*, vaporization

vaporizador *m*, vaporizer; spray, sprayer

vaporizar *vt* to vaporize; spray

vaporoso *a* vaporous; ethereal; gauzy

vapulación *f*, **vapulamiento** *m*, whipping

vapular *vt* to whip

vapuleo *m*, whipping, spanking

vaquería *f*, herd of cattle; dairy; dairy farm

vaquero (-ra) *n* cowboy; **vaqueros,** *m*, *pl* jeans

vaquilla *f*, heifer

vara *f*, staff; rod; wand (of authority); vara (2.8 feet); shaft (of cart). **v. de aforar,** water gauge

varada *f*, *naut* running aground

varadero *m*, shipyard

varar *vi naut* to run aground; *fig* be held up (negotiations, etc.); *vt naut* put in dry dock

varear *vt* to knock down (fruit from tree); beat (with a rod); measure with a rod; sell by the rod; *vr* grow thin

variabilidad *f*, variableness

variable *a* variable; changeable, inconsistent

variación *f*, variation

variado *a* varied; variegated

variante *a* varying. *f*, variant; discrepancy

variar *vt* to vary; change; *vi* change; be different

varice *f*, varix

varicela *f*, chicken pox

varicoso *a* varicose

variedad *f*, variety; change; inconstancy, instability; alteration; variation; *biol* variety

varilla *f*, *dim* rod; rib (fan, umbrella). **v. de virtudes,** conjurer's wand. *mech* **v. percusora,** tappet rod

vario *a* different, diverse; inconstant, changeable; variegated; *pl* some, a few

variopinto *a* motley

varón *m*, male; man

varonil *a* male; manly

Varsovia Warsaw

varsoviano (-na) *a* and *n* of or from Warsaw

vasallaje *m*, vassalage; dependence; tribute money

vasallo (-lla) *n* vassal. *a* vassal; dependent

vasco (-ca), vascongado (-da) *a* and *n* Basque

vascuence *m*, Basque (language); *inf* gibberish

vaselina *f*, vaseline

vasija *f*, vessel, receptacle, jar

vaso *m*, receptacle; glass, tankard, mug; glassful; (*naut anat bot*) vessel; garden-urn; vase

vástago *m*, stem, shoot; offspring, descendant; piston rod

vastedad *f*, extensiveness, largeness, vastness

vasto *a* vast, extensive

vate *m*, bard; seer

vaticano *a* and *m*, Vatican

vaticinar *vt* to prophesy, foretell

vaticinio *m*, prediction

vatímetro *m*, water meter

vatio *m*, watt. **v. hora,** watt hour

ve *f*, name of the letter V. **v. doble** *or* **doble v.,** name of the letter W

vecinal *a* neighboring, adjacent

vecindad *f*, neighborhood; *Lat. Am.* slum. **buena v.,** good neighborliness. **hacer mala v.,** to be a nuisance to one's neighbors

vecindario *m*, neighborhood; population of a district

vecino (-na) *a* neighboring; near; similar. *n* neighbor; citizen; inhabitant

vector *m*, carrier (of disease)

veda *f*, close season; prohibition

vedamiento *m*, prohibition

vedar *vt* to forbid; prevent

vedija *f*, tangled lock of hair; piece of matted wool; curl (of smoke)

veedor (-ra) *a* prying. *n* busy-body. *m*, inspector; overseer

vega *f*, fertile lowland plain; meadow

vegada *f*. See **vez**

vegetable *a* and *m*, vegetable

vegetación *f*, vegetation

vegetal *a* vegetal; plant. *m*, vegetable, plant

vegetar *vi* to flourish, grow (plants); *fig* vegetate

vegetarianismo *m*, vegetarianism

vegetariano (-na) *a* and *n* vegetarian

vegetativo *a* vegetative

vehemencia *f*, vehemence

vehemente *a* vehement; vivid

vehículo *m*, vehicle; means, instrument

veinte *a* and *m*, twenty; twentieth

veintena *f*, a score

veinticinco *a* and *m*, twenty-five; twenty-fifth

veinticuatro *a* and *m*, twenty-four; twenty-fourth

veintidós *a* and *m*, twenty-two; twenty-second

veintinueve *a* and *m*, twenty-nine; twenty-ninth

veintiocho *a* and *m*, twenty-eight; twenty-eighth

veintiséis *a* and *m*, twenty-six; twenty-sixth

veintisiete *a* and *m*, twenty-seven; twenty-seventh

veintitrés *a* and *m*, twenty-three; twenty-third

veintiuno *a* and *m*, twenty-one; twenty-first. Abbreviates to **veintiún** before a noun (even if one or more adjectives intervene)

vejación *f*, ill-treatment, persecution

vejamen *m*, irritation, provocation; taunt; lampoon

vejar *vt* to ill-treat, persecute; plague

vejatorio *a* vexing, annoying

vejete *m*, *inf* silly old man

vejez *f*, oldness; old age; platitude. **vejeces,** *pl* ailments of old age. *inf* **a la v., viruelas,** the older the madder

vejiga *f*, bladder; blister. **v. natatoria,** float (of a fish)

vela *f*, vigil; watch; pilgrimage; sentinel, watchman; candle; *naut* sail; awning; night work, overtime. **v. de cangreja,** boom sail. **v. de mesana,** mizzen sail. **v. de trinquete,** foresail. **v. latina,** lateen sail. **a toda v.,** with all speed. **alzar velas,** to hoist sail. **en v.,** wakeful, without sleep. *inf* **estar entre dos velas,** to be tipsy

velación *f*, vigil; watch; marriage ceremony of veiling (gen. *pl*)

velada *f*, vigil; watch; evening party

velado *a* veiled; (of voice) thick, indistinct

velador (-ra) *a* watchful; vigilant. *m*, candlestick; small round table; *Mexico* lampshade. *n* watcher, guard

velar *vi* to watch, be wakeful; work overtime or at night; *ecc* watch; *fig* (*with por*) watch over, defend; *vt* veil; conceal; *phot* blur; (*with prep a*) wake (corpse); sit with (patient at night)

veleidad *f*, velleity; fickleness

veleidoso *a* inconstant, changeable

velero (-ra) *m*, sailing ship; sailmaker. *n* candlemaker

veleta *f*, weathercock; float, quill (fishing). *mf* changeable person

velís *m*, *Mexico* suitcase.

vello *m*, down, soft hair

vellocino *m*, wool; fleece

vellón *m*, fleece; copper and silver alloy formerly used in sense of 'sterling'; *ant* copper coin

vellosidad *f*, downiness, hairiness

velloso *a* downy, hairy

velludo *a* hairy, downy. *m*, plush, velvet

velo *m*, veil; curtain; *ecc* humeral veil; excuse, pretext; *zool* velum. **v. del paladar,** soft palate. **correr el v.,** to disclose a secret. **tomar el v.,** to take the veil, become a nun

velocidad *f*, speed; *mech* velocity. *aer* **v. ascensional,** rate of climb. *mech* **v. del choque,** speed of impact. **en gran v.,** by passenger train. **en pequeña v.,** by goods train

velocímetro *m*, *Mexico* speedometer

velódromo *m*, velodrome

velón *m*, oil lamp

velorio *m*, *Lat. Am.* (funeral) wake; dull party

veloz *a* swift; quick-thinking or acting

vena *f*, (*bot anat*) vein; streak, veining (in wood or stone); *min* seam; underground spring; inspiration. **estar de v.,** to be in the mood; be inspired

venablo *m*, javelin

venado *m*, venison; deer

venal *a* venous; saleable; venal

venalidad *f*, saleableness; venality

vencedor (-ra) *a* conquering. *n* conqueror

vencer *vt* to conquer; defeat; overcome, rise above; outdo, excel; restrain, control (emotions); convince, persuade; *vi* succeed, triumph; *com* fall due, mature; *com* expire; *vr* control oneself; twist, incline; *Argentina* wear out

vencible *a* conquerable; superable

vencimiento *m*, defeat; conquest, victory; bend, twist (of things); *com* expiration; *com* maturity (of a bill)

venda *f*, bandage; fillet. **tener una v. en los ojos,** to be blind (to the truth)

vendaje *m*, bandage

vendar *vt* to bandage; *fig* blind (generally passions)

vendaval *m*, strong wind

vendedor (-ra) *a* selling. *n* seller

vender *vt* to sell; betray; *vr* sell oneself; be sold; risk all (for someone); *fig* give away (secret); (*with por*) sell under false pretences. **v. al contado,** to sell for cash. **v. al por mayor,** to sell wholesale. **v. al por menor,** to sell retail. **venderse caro,** to be unsociable

vendí *m*, *com* certificate of sale

vendible *a* purchasable; saleable

vendimia *f*, vintage; profit, fruits

vendimiar *vt* to harvest the grapes; take advantage of; *inf* kill

veneno *m*, poison; venom; danger (to health or soul); evil passion

venenoso *a* poisonous, venomous

venera *f*, scallop-shell (pilgrim's badge); badge, decoration

veneración *f*, respect, veneration

venerador (-ra) *a* venerating. *n* venerator, respector

venerar *vt* to venerate; worship

venéreo *a* venereal

venero *m*, spring of water; horary line on sundial; origin, genesis; *min* bed

venezolano (-na) *a* and *n* Venezuelan

vengador (-ra) *a* avenging. *n* avenger

venganza *f*, revenge

vengar *vt* to avenge; *vr* avenge oneself

vengativo *a* vindictive

venia *f*, pardon, forgiveness; permission; inclination of head (in greeting); *law* license issued to minors to manage their own estate

venial *a* venial

venialidad *f*, veniality

venida *f*, arrival, coming; return; attack (fencing); precipitancy

venidero *a* future

venideros *m pl*, successors; posterity

venir *vi irr* to come; arrive; turn up (at cards); fit, suit; consent, agree; *agr* grow; follow, come after, succeed; result, originate; occur (to the mind); feel, experience; (*with prep a + infin.*) happen finally, come to pass; (*with en*) decide, resolve; *vr* ferment. **v. a menos**, to deteriorate, decline; come upon evil days. **v. a pelo**, to come opportunely, be just right. **v. a ser**, to become. **venirse abajo**, to fall, collapse. **¿A qué viene este viaje?** What is the purpose of this journey? **el mes que viene**, next month. **El vestido te viene muy ancho**, The dress is too wide for you. **Me vino la idea de marcharme**, It occurred to me to leave. **en lo por venir**, in the future. *Pres. Ind.* **vengo, vienes, viene, venimos, venís, vienen.** *Fut.* **viniendo.** *Fut.* **vendré**, etc. *Condit.* **vendría**, etc. *Preterite* **vine, viniste, vino, vinimos, vinisteis, vinieron.** *Pres. Subjunc.* **venga**, etc. *Imperf. Subjunc.* **viniese**, etc.

venta *f*, selling; sale; inn; *inf* wilderness; *pl com* turnover. **v. pública**, auction. **a la v.**, on sale. **la V. de la Mesilla**, the Gadsden Purchase

ventada *f*, gust of wind

ventaja *f*, advantage; profit

ventajoso *a* advantageous; *Lat. Am.* unscrupulous

ventana *f*, window. **v. de guillotina**, sash window. **v. sastrediza**, bay window. **echar algo por la v.**, to waste a thing

ventanal *m*, large window

ventanilla *f*, small window (as in railway compartments); grill (ticket office, bank, etc.); nostril

ventarrón *m*, high wind

ventear *v impers* to blow (of the wind); *vt* sniff air (animals); air, dry; investigate; *Lat. Am.* brand (an animal); *vr* be spoiled by air (tobacco, etc.)

ventero (-ra) *n* innkeeper

ventilación *f*, ventilation; ventilator; current of air

ventilador *m*, ventilating fan; ventilator

ventilar *vt* to ventilate; shake, winnow; air; discuss

ventisca *f*, snowstorm

ventiscar, ventisquear *v impers* to snow with a high wind

ventisquero *m*, glacier; snowfield, snowdrift; snowstorm

ventolera *f*, gust of wind; *inf* boastfulness; whim, caprice

ventolina *f*, *Lat. Am.* sudden gust (of wind)

ventor (-ra) *n* pointer (dog)

ventosa *f*, vent (pipes, etc.); *zool* sucker; *surg* cupping glass

ventoso *a* windy; flatulent

ventrículo *m*, ventricle

ventrílocuo (-ua) *a* ventriloquial. *n* ventriloquist

ventriloquia *f*, ventriloquism

ventrudo *a* big-bellied

ventura *f*, happiness; chance, hazard; risk, danger. **a la v.**, at a venture. **buena v.**, good luck. **por v.**, perhaps; by chance; fortunately

venturoso *a* fortunate

Venus *m*, Venus. *f*, beautiful woman, beauty

ver *vt irr* to see; witness, behold; visit, inspect, examine; consider; observe; know, understand; *Lat. Am.* look at,

watch (television, etc.) (*with de + infin.*) try to; *vr* be seen; show oneself, appear; experience, find oneself; exchange visits; meet. **v. mundo**, to travel. **V. y creer**, Seeing is believing. **A mi v.**, In my opinion. **¡A v.!** Let's see!; Wait and see! **no tener nada que v. con**, to have no connection with, nothing to do with. **Veremos**, Time will tell. **Verse en la casa**, to be a stay-at-home. **Ya se ve**, Of course, Naturally. *Pres. Ind.* **veo, ves**, etc. *Imperf.* **veía**, etc. *Past Part.* **visto.** *Pres. Subjunc.* **vea**, etc. *Imperf. Subjunc.* **viese**, etc.

vera *f*, edge; border; shore. **a la v.**, on the edge, on the verge

veracidad *f*, truthfulness, veracity

veranadero *m*, summer pasture

veraneante *mf* summer resident, summer vacationist, holiday-maker

veranear *vi* to spend the summer

veraneo *m*, summer vacation, summer holidays, summering

veraniego *a* summer; light, unimportant

verano *m*, summer; dry season *WH*

veras *f pl*, reality, truth; fervor, earnestness. **de v.**, really; in earnest

veraz *a* truthful, veracious

verbal *a* verbal; oral

verbena *f*, *bot* verbena, vervain; fair held on eve of a saint's day

verbigracia *adv* for instance. *m*, example

verbo *m*, word; vow; *gram* verb. **v. activo** *or* **v. transitivo**, active or transitive verb. **v. auxiliar**, auxiliary verb. **v. intransitivo** *or* **v. neutro**, intransitive or neuter verb. **v. reflexivo** *or* **v. recíproco**, reflexive verb

verbosidad *f*, verbosity

verboso *a* verbose, prolix

verdad *f*, truth, veracity; reality. **a la v.**, indeed; without doubt. **en v.**, in truth; indeed. **cantar cuatro verdades a alguien**, to tell someone a few home truths. **la pura v.**, the plain truth

verdadero *a* true; real; sincere; truthful

verdal *a* green. **ciruela v.**, greengage

verde *a* green; unripe; fresh (vegetables); youthful; immature, undeveloped; obscene, dissolute. *m*, green (color); verdure, foliage

verdear *vi* to look green; be greenish; grow green

verdecer *vi irr* to grow green, be verdant. See **conocer**

verdegay *a* and *m*, bright green

verdemar *a* and *m*, sea-green

verdín *m*, verdure; mold; verdigris

verdinegro *a* dark green

verdor *m*, verdure; greenness; strength; youth (also *pl*)

verdoso *a* greenish

verdugo *m*, hangman, executioner; wale, mark; shoot of tree; switch; whip; *fig* scourge; tyrant

verdulera *f*, greengrocer; market woman; *inf* harridan

verdulería *f*, greengrocer's shop

verdulero *m*, greengrocer

verdura *f*, verdure; green garden produce, vegetables (gen. *pl*); *art* foliage; obscenity

verecundo *a* bashful

vereda *f*, footpath; sheep track; *Argentina, Chile, Peru* sidewalk

veredicto *m*, *law* verdict; judgment, considered opinion

verga *f*, steel bow of crossbow; *naut* yard; *inf* penis

vergajo *m*, rod (for punishment)

vergel *m*, orchard

vergonzoso (-sa) *a* shameful; bashful, shamefaced. *n* shy person

vergüenza *f*, shame; self-respect; bashfulness, timidity; shameful act; public punishment

vericueto *m*, narrow, stony path

verídico *a* veracious; true, exact

verificación *f*, verification, checking; *law* **v. de un testamento**, probate

verificador (-ra) *a* verifying, checking. *n* inspector, checker

verificar vt to prove; verify; vr take place, happen; check; come true. elec **v. las conexiones,** to check the connections

verisímil a credible, probable

verisimilitud f, credibility

verismo m, realism; truthfulness

verja f, grating, grill; railing

vermífugo a and m, vermifuge

vermut m, vermouth

vernáculo a native, vernacular

vernal a vernal

veronés (-esa) a and n Veronese

verónica f, bot speedwell; veronica (bullfighting)

verosímil a credible, probable

verosimilitud f, verisimilitude, probability

verraco m, boar

verruga f, med wart; inf bore; defect

versar vi to revolve; (with sobre) concern, deal with (book, etc.); vr become versed (in)

versátil a zool versatile; changeable; fickle

versatilidad f, zool versatility; changeableness; fickleness

versículo m, versicle; verse (of the Bible)

versificación f, versification

versificador (-ra) n versifier

versificar vi to write verses; vt put into verse, versify

versión f, translation; version; account

verso m, poetry, verse; stanza; line (of a poem). **v. suelto,** blank verse

vertebrado a and m, zool vertebrate

vertedor m, drain, sewer; chute

verter vt irr to pour, spill; empty; translate; vi flow. See **entender**

vertical a and f, vertical

verticalidad f, verticality

vértice m, vertex

vertiente a emptying. mf, slope, incline; watershed; Lat. Am. also spring (of water)

vertiginoso a giddy; vertiginous

vértigo m, giddiness, faintness

vesícula f, blister; (anat bot) vesicle

vespertino a evening

vestíbulo m, hall, vestibule foyer

vestido m, dress; clothes; Panama, Peru suit

vestidura f, garment; pl vestments

vestigio m, footprint; trace, mark; remains; fig vestige

vestir vt irr to clothe, dress; adorn; embellish (ideas); fig disguise (truth); simulate, pretend; vi be dressed; vr dress oneself; fig be covered. See **pedir**

vestuario m, clothing, dress; theat wardrobe or dressing room; ecc vestry; mil uniform

Vesubio Vesuvius

veta f, vein; stripe, rib (fabric)

veterano (-na) a and n veteran

veterinaria f, veterinary science

veterinario a veterinary. m, veterinary surgeon

veto m, veto; prohibition

vetustez f, antiquity, oldness

vetusto a ancient, very old

vez f, time, occasion; turn; pl proxy, deputy, substitute. **a la v.,** simultaneously. **alguna v.,** sometime. **a su v.,** in its (her, his, their) turn. **a veces,** sometimes. **de una v.,** at the one time. **de v. en cuando,** from time to time. **en v. de,** instead of. **hacer las veces de,** to be a substitute for. **otra v.,** again. **Su cuarto es dos veces más grande que éste,** His room is twice as large as this one

vía f, way; road; railway track or gauge; anat tract; (mystic) way; route; conduct; pl procedure. **v. ancha,** broad gauge (railway). **v. angosta,** narrow gauge. **v. de agua,** naut leak. law **v. ejecutiva,** seizure, attachment. **v. férrea,** railway. **v. láctea,** Milky Way. **v. muerta,** railway siding. **v. principal,** main line. **v. pública,** public thoroughfare. **v. romana,** Roman road. **v. secundaria,** rw side line. **por v. aérea,** by air, by airplane

viabilidad f, viability

viable a viable; practicable; workable; passable

viaducto m, viaduct

viajante mf traveling salesman, commercial traveler

viajar vi to travel, journey, voyage

viaje m, journey; voyage; water-supply; travel journal; naut **v. de ensayo,** trial trip. **v. redondo,** circular tour. **¡Buen v.!** Have a good trip! Bon voyage!

viajero (-ra) a traveling. n traveler; passenger

vianda f, viand, victual (gen. pl); meal

viático m, ecc viaticum; provisions for a journey

víbora f, viper; Lat. Am. poisonous snake

viborezno m, young viper

vibración f, vibration; jar, jolt; thrill

vibrante a shaking; vibrant; thrilling

vibrar vt to shake, oscillate; vi vibrate; jar, jolt; quiver, thrill

vibratorio a vibratory, vibrative

vicaría f, vicarage; vestry

vicario a vicarious. m, vicar; curate; deputy

vicecónsul m, vice-consul

viceconsulado m, vice-consulate

vicepresidente (-ta) n vice president

vicesecretario (-ia) n assistant secretary

viciar vt to corrupt; adulterate; forge; annul; interpret maliciously, misconstrue; vr become vicious

vicio m, vice; defect; error, fraud; bad habit; excess, exaggerated desire; viciousness (animals); overgrowth (plants); peevishness (children). **tener el v. de,** to have the bad habit of. **el v. del juego,** fondness for gambling

vicioso a vicious; vigorous, overgrown; abundant; inf spoilt (children)

vicisitud f, vicissitude

víctima f, victim

victimar vt, Lat. Am. to murder

victimario, -a mf, Lat. Am. killer, murderer

¡víctor! interj Victor!; Long live!; Hurrah!

victoria f, victory, triumph; victoria

victoriano (-na) a and n Victorian

victorioso a victorious

vicuña f vicuna

vid f, vine

vida f, life; livelihood; human being; biography; vivacity. **v. airada,** dissolute life. **la v. allende la muerte,** life after death. **de por v.,** for life. **darse buena v.,** to live comfortably; enjoy one's life. **dar mala v.,** to ill-treat. **en la v.,** in life; never. **ganarse la v.,** to make one's living

vidente a, clairvoyant; seer

videograbación f, videotape

vidriar vt to glaze (earthenware)

vidriera f, glass window (gen. stained or colored)

vidriero m, glazier. a made of glass

vidrio m, glass; anything made of glass; fragile thing; touchy person. **v. inastillable,** safety-glass. **v. jaspeado,** frosted glass. **v. pintado** or **v. de color,** stainedglass. **v. plano,** plate glass. **v. soplado,** blown glass

vidrioso a brittle; slippery; fragile; hypersensitive; fig glazed (eyes)

vieja f, old woman

viejo a old; ancient; former; old-fashioned; worn out. m, old man

Viena Vienna

vienés (-esa) a and n Viennese

viento m, wind; scent (of game, etc.); guy (rope); upheaval; vanity. **v. en popa,** naut following wind; without a hitch, prosperously. **vientos alisios,** tradewinds. **v. terral,** land wind. **a los cuatro vientos,** in all directions. **contra v. y marea,** fig against all obstacles. **correr malos vientos,** to be unfavorable (of circumstances). **refrescar el v.,** to stiffen (of the breeze)

vientre m, stomach; belly; vitals; law venter

viernes m, Friday. **V. Santo,** Good Friday

viga f, beam, rafter; girder; joist; mill beam. **v. maestra,** main beam or girder

vigente *a* valid; in force (laws, customs)

vigésimo *a* twentieth

vigía *f*, watch tower; (gen. *m*) look-out, watch

vigilancia *f*, watchfulness, vigilance; watch patrol

vigilante *a* watchful. *m*, watcher; watchman. **v. escolar,** truant officer

vigilar *vi* to watch over; supervise

vigilia *f*, vigil; wakefulness; night study; *ecc* vigil, eve; wake; *mil* watch. **día de v.,** fast-day

vigor *m*, strength; activity; vigor, efficiency; validity

vigorizar *vt* to invigorate; exhilarate; encourage

vigoroso *a* strong, vigorous

vihuela *f*, lute

vil *a* vile, infamous; base; despicable; untrustworthy

vileza *f*, baseness; vileness, infamy

vilipendiar *vt* to revile

vilipendio *m*, vilification; contempt

villa *f*, villa; country house; town. **v. miseria** *Argentina* slum

villancico *m*, carol

villanesco *a* peasant; rustic, country

villanía *f*, humbleness of birth; vileness; villainy

villano (-na) *n* peasant. *a* rustic, country; boorish; base

vilo, en *adv* hanging in the air; *fig* in suspense

vilorta *f*, hoop; *mech* washer

vilote *mf*, *Lat. Am.* chicken, coward

vinagre *m*, vinegar

vinagrera *f*, vinegar bottle; table cruet; *Lat. Am.* heartburn

vinagreta *f*, vinegar sauce

vinagroso *a* vinegary; *inf* bad-tempered, acid

vinatero (-ra) *n* wine merchant. *a* wine

vincapervinca *f*, *bot* periwinkle

vinculación *f*, *law* entail

vincular *vt law* to entail; *fig* base; *vr* perpetuate. *a law* entail

vínculo *m*, tie, bond; *law* entail

vindicación *f*, vindication; justification; excuse

vindicador (-ra) *n* vindicator. *a* vindicative

vindicar *vt* to avenge; vindicate; justify; excuse

vindicativo *a* avenging; vindicatory

vinería *f*, *Lat. Am.* wineshop

vinícola *a* wine-growing; wine

vinicultor (-ra) *n* wine grower, viniculturalist

vinicultura *f*, wine-growing, viniculture

vinificación *f*, vinification

vinillo *m*, thin, weak wine

vino *m*, wine; fermented fruit juice. **v. de Oporto,** port wine. **v. generoso,** well-matured wine. **v. tinto,** red wine

vinoso *a* vinous; fond of wine

viña *f*, vineyard

viñador *m*, vineyard-keeper; vine-cultivator

viñedo *m*, vineyard

viñeta *f*, vignette

viola *f*, *mus* viola; *bot* viola, pansy. *mf* viola player

violación *f*, violation; infringement

violado *a* violet

violador (-ra) *n* violator. *m*, seducer

violar *vt* to violate; infringe; rape; spoil, harm

violencia *f*, violence; outrage; rape

violentar *vt* to force; falsify, misinterpret; force an entrance; *vr* force oneself

violento *a* violent; repugnant; impetuous, hasty-tempered; unnatural, false; unreasonable

violeta *f*, *bot* violet. *m*, violet color. **v. de febrero,** snowdrop

violín *m*, violin

violinista *mf* violinist

violón *m*, double-bass, bass viol; double-bass player

violoncelista *mf* cellist

violoncelo *m*, cello

viperino *a* viperine; venomous, evil

vira *f*, welt (of a shoe); dart

viraje *m*, *aut* change of direction; bend, turn

virar *vt naut* to put about; *phot* tone; *vi naut* tack; *aut* change direction. **v. de bordo,** *naut* to lay off

virgen *mf* virgin. *f*, *ast* Virgo

virginal *a* virginal; pure, unspotted

virginidad *f*, virginity

virgulilla *f*, comma; cedilla; accent; apostrophe; fine line

viril *a* manly, virile. *m*, clear glass screen

virilidad *f*, virility

virote *m*, arrow; shaft; *inf* young blood; *Mexico* roll (bread)

virreina *f*, vicereine

virreinato *m*, viceroyship

virrey *m*, viceroy

virtual *a* virtual; implicit

virtualidad *f*, virtuality

virtualmente *adv* virtually; tacitly

virtud *f*, virtue; power; strength, courage; efficacy. **en v. de,** in virtue of

virtuosidad *f*, virtuosity

virtuoso *a* virtuous; powerful, efficacious. *m*, virtuoso, artist

viruela *f*, smallpox (gen. *pl*)

virulencia *f*, virulence

virulento *a* virulent

virus *m*, virus

viruta *f*, wood-shaving

vis cómica *f*, the comic spirit

visa *f*, *Lat. Am.* visa

visado *m*, *Spain* visa

visaje *m*, grimace

visar *vt* to visa; endorse

viscosidad *f*, viscosity

viscoso *a* viscous, sticky

visera *f*, visor; eye-shade; peak (of a cap)

visibilidad *f*, visibility

visillo *m*, window-blind

visión *f*, seeing, sight; queer sight; vision; hallucination; *inf* scarecrow, sight

visionario (-ia) *a* and *n* visionary

visir *m*, vizier. **gran v.,** grand vizier

visita *f*, visit; visitor; inspection. **v. de cumplido,** formal call. **v. de sanidad,** health inspection. **hacer una v.,** to pay a call

visitación *f*, visitation; visit

visitador (-ra) *n* regular visitor. *m*, inspector. *a* visiting; inspecting

visitar *vt* to visit; inspect; *med* attend; *ecc* examine. **v. los monumentos,** to see the sights, go sightseeing

visiteo *m*, receiving or paying of visits

vislumbrar *vt* to glimpse; surmise, conjecture

vislumbre *f*, glimmer, glimpse; surmise, glimmering (gen. *pl*); semblance, appearance

viso *m*, view point, elevation; glare; shimmer, gleam; colored slip under transparent dress; semblance. **de v.,** prominent (persons)

visón *m*, mink

víspera *f*, eve; *ecc* day before festival; prelude, preliminary. *pl ecc* vespers. **en vísperas de,** on the eve of

vista *f*, vision, sight; view; eyes; eyesight; meeting, interview; *law* hearing (of a case); apparition; picture of a view; clear idea; connection (of things); proposition, intention; glance; *pl* window, door, skylight, opening for light. **v. corta,** short sight. **v. de lince,** sharp eyes. **a primera v.,** at first sight. **a v. de,** in sight of; in the presence of. **conocer de v.,** to know by sight. **dar una v.,** to take a look. **doble v.,** second sight; clairvoyance. **en v. de,** in view of, considering. **estar a la v.,** to be evident. *inf* **hacer la v. gorda,** to turn a blind eye. **¡Hasta la v.!** Good-bye! **perder de v. (a),** to lose sight of

vistazo *m*, glance. **echar un v.,** to cast a glance

visto *past part irr* **ver.** *law* whereas. **bien v.,** approved. **mal v.,** disapproved. **V. Bueno (V⁰ B⁰)** Approved, Passed. **v. que,** since, inasmuch as

vistoso *a* showy, gaudy; beautiful

visual *a* visual
vital *a* vital; essential
vitalicio *a* lifelong. *m*, life-insurance
vitalidad *f*, vitality
vitamina *f*, vitamin
vitando *a* odious; bad; vital
vitela *f*, vellum
vitícola *a* viticultural. *mf* viticulturist
viticultura *f*, viticulture
¡vítor! *interj* Victor!; Hurrah!; Long live!
vitorear *vt* to cheer; applaud, acclaim
vítreo *a* glassy, vitreous
vitrificar(se) *vt* and *vr* to vitrify
vitrina *f*, show-case; display cabinet; *Argentina, Chile, Venezuela* (shop) window
vitriólico *a* vitriolic
vitriolo *m*, vitriol
vitualla *f*, (gen. *pl*) victuals, provisions
vituperable *a* blameworthy, vituperable
vituperador (-ra) *a* vituperative. *n* vituperator
vituperar *vt* to censure, blame, vituperate
vituperio *m*, vituperation
viuda *f*, widow
viudedad *f*, widow's pension
viudez *f*, widowhood, widowerhood
viudita *f*, young widow
viudo *m*, widower
¡viva! *interj* Long live!; Hurrah!
vivacidad *f*, vivacity, gaiety; ardor, warmth; brightness
vivamente *adv* quickly, lively
vivandera *f*, vivandiere
vivandero *m*, sutler
vivaque *m*, bivouac
vivaquear *vi* to bivouac
vivar *m*, warren; aquarium; breeding ground; well (of a fishing boat); *vt, Lat. Am.* to cheer, shout hurrah (for ...)
vivaracho *a inf* sprightly, cheery, lively
vivaz *a* vigorous; quick-witted; sprightly; *bot* perennial; vivid, bright
víveres *m pl*, provisions; *mil* stores
vivero *m*, *bot* nursery; vivarium; small marsh
viveza *f*, quickness, briskness; vehemence; perspicuity; witticism; resemblance; brightness (eyes, colors); thoughtless word or act
vividero *a* habitable
vívido *a poet* vivid
vividor (-ra) *a* frugal, thrifty; dissolute. *n* liver; long-liver; libertine, rake
vivienda *f*, dwelling
viviente *a* living
vivificación *f*, vivification
vivificante *a* vivifying
vivificar *vt* to vivify; comfort
vivir *vi* to be alive, live; last, endure; (*with en*) inhabit. *m*, life. **¿Quién vive?** *mil* Who goes there? **v. a costillas ajenas,** to live at someone else's expense, live off someone else
vivisección *f*, vivisection
vivo *a* alive; intense, strong; bright; *mil* active; subtle, ingenious; precipitate; *fig* lasting, enduring; diligent; hasty; persuasive, expressive. *m*, edge. **al v., a lo v.,** to the life; vividly
vizcaíno (-na) *a* and *n* Biscayan
Vizcaya, el Golfo de the Bay of Biscay
vizconde *m*, viscount
vizcondesa *f*, viscountess
vocablo *m*, word
vocabulario *m*, vocabulary
vocación *f*, vocation; trade, profession
vocal *a* vocal; oral. *f*, *gram* vowel. *mf* voting member
vocalización *f*, vocalization
vocalizar *vi* to vocalize
voceador, -a *mf*, *Lat. Am.* newsvendor
vocear *vi* to cry out, shout; *vt* proclaim; call for; acclaim
vocerío *m*, shouting; clamor, outcry

vociferación *f*, vociferation, outcry
vociferar *vt* to boast (of); *vi* shout, vociferate
vocinglería *f*, clamor; babble, chatter
vocinglero *a* vociferous; prattling, babbling
vodca *m*, vodka
volada *f*, short flight; *Mexico* flat tire, flat. *mech* **v. de grúa,** jib
voladura *f*, explosion; blasting
volandas (en), volandillas (en) *adv* in the air, as though flying; *inf* in a trice
volante *a* flying; wandering, restless. *m*, frill, flounce; screen; fan (of a windmill); *mech* flywheel; *mech* balance wheel (watches); coiner's stamp mill; shuttlecock. *aut* **v. de dirección,** steering-wheel
volantón (-ona) *n* fledgeling
volar *vi irr* to fly (birds, insects, aviation); float in the air; hurry; disappear suddenly; burst, explode; jut out (buttresses, etc.); cleave (air) (arrows, etc.); *fig* spread (rumors); *vt* explode; blast; anger. See **contar**
volatería *f*, fowling; fowls; poultry; flock of birds; *fig* crowd (of ideas)
volátil *a* volatile; inconstant
volatilizar *vt* to volatilize
volatinero (-ra) *n* tight-rope walker, acrobat
volcán *m*, volcano; violent passion. **v. extinto,** extinct volcano
volcánico *a* volcanic
volcar *vt irr* to overturn, capsize; make dizzy; cause a change (of opinion); annoy; *vi* overturn. *Pres. Ind.* **vuelco, vuelcas, vuelca, vuelcan.** *Preterite* **volqué, volcaste,** etc. *Pres. Subjunc.* **vuelque, vuelques, vuelquen**
volear *vt* to strike in the air, volley; *agr* sow broadcast
voleo *m*, volley (tennis, etc.); high kick; straight punch
volframio *m*, wolfram, tungsten
volición *f*, volition
volquete *m*, tip-cart
voltaico *a* voltaic
voltaje *m*, voltage
voltario *a* versatile; capricious, headstrong
volteador (-ra) *n* acrobat
voltear *vt* to whirl, turn; overturn; change place (of); *arch* construct an arch or vault; *vi* revolve; tumble, twirl (acrobats)
volteo *m*, turning, revolution; whirl; overturning; twirling; *elec* voltage
voltereta *f*, somersault
volteriano *a* Voltairian
voltímetro *m*, voltmeter
voltio *m*, volt
volubilidad *f*, inconstancy, fickleness
voluble *a* easily turned; inconstant, changeable; *bot* twining
volumen *m*, bulk, size; volume, book
voluminoso *a* voluminous, bulky
voluntad *f*, will, volition; wish; decree; free will; intention; affection; free choice; consent. **a v.,** at will; by choice. **de buena v.,** of good will; willingly, with pleasure. **de su propia v.,** of one's own free will. **mala v.,** hostility, ill-will
voluntario (-ia) *a* voluntary; strong-willed. *n* volunteer
voluntarioso *a* self-willed
voluptuosidad *f*, voluptuousness
voluptuoso *a* voluptuous
volver *vt irr* to turn; turn over; return; pay back; direct, aim; translate; restore; change, alter; close (doors, etc.); vomit; reflect, reverberate; *vi* come back; continue (speech, etc.); bend, turn (roads); (*with prep a* + *infin.*) do something again (e.g. **v. a leer,** to read over again); (*with por* + *noun*) protect; *vr* become; go sour; turn. **v. a las filas,** *mil* to reduce to the ranks. **v. en sí,** to regain consciousness. **v. la cabeza,** to turn one's head. **volverse atrás,** *fig* to back out. **volverse loco,** to go mad. See **resolver**

vomitar *vt* to vomit; *fig* vomit forth; *fig* spit out (curses, etc.); *inf* burst into confidences

vomitivo *a* and *m*, emetic

vómito *m*, vomit

voracidad *f*, voracity

vorágine *f*, vortex, whirlpool

voraz *a* voracious; *Mexico* bold

vórtice *m*, whirlpool; *fig* vortex

vortiginoso *a* vortical

vos *pers pron 2nd pers sing* and *pl* you.

vosear *vt* to use the pronoun *vos*; address (someone) as *vos*

vosotros, vosotras *pers pron 2nd pers pl mf* you

votación *f*, voting

votador (-ra) *n* voter; swearer

votar *vi* and *vt* to vote; make a vow; curse, swear. **v. una proposición de confianza,** to pass a vote of confidence

votivo *a* votive

voto *m*, vote; vow; voter; prayer; curse; desire; opinion. **v. de calidad,** casting vote. **v. de confianza,** vote of confidence

voz *f*, voice; sound, noise; cry, shout (gen. *pl*); word; expression; *mus* singer or voice; *gram* mood; vote; rumor; instruction, order. **v. común,** general opinion. **a voces,** in a shout, loudly. **llevar la v. cantante,** *inf* to have the chief say

vuelco *m*, overturning

vuelo *m*, flight; wing; *sew* skirt-fullness; ruffle, frill; *arch* buttress. **v. a ciegas,** *aer* blind flying. **v. de distancia,** long-distance flight. **v. de patrulla,** patrol or reconnaissance flight. **v. de reconocimento,** reconnaissance flight. **v. nocturno,** *aer* night flying. **v. sin parar,** non-stop flight. **al v.,** on the wing; in passing; quickly. **alzar** (*or* **levantar**) **el v.,** to take flight

vuelta *f*, revolution, turn; bend, curve; return; restitution; recompense; repetition; wrong side; beating; *sew* facing, cuff; change (money); conning (lessons, etc.); stroll, walk; change; vault, ceiling; *sport* round; *mech* **vueltas por minuto,** revolutions per minute. **a v. de correo,** by return mail, by return of post. **a la v.,** on returning; overleaf. **dar la v.,** to turn round, make a détour. **dar una v.,** to take a stroll. **dar vueltas,** to revolve; search (for); consider. **media v.,** half turn

vuelto *m*, *Lat. Am.* change (money returned)

vuestro, vuestra, vuestros, vuestras *poss pron 2nd pl mf* your, yours

vulcanizar *vt* to vulcanize

vulgar *a* popular; general, common; vernacular; mediocre

vulgaridad *f*, vulgarity

vulgarismo *m*, vulgarism

vulgarización *f*, vulgarization; popularization

vulgarizar *vt* to vulgarize; popularize; translate into the vernacular; *vr* grow vulgar

vulgata *f*, Vulgate

vulgo *m*, mob

vulnerabilidad *f*, vulnerability

vulnerable *a* vulnerable

vulpeja *f*, vixen

vulpino *a* vulpine; crafty

W

wagneriano *a* Wagnerian

wáter *m*, toilet, water-closet

whisky *m*, whiskey

X

xenofobia *f*, xenophobia, hatred of foreigners

xilófago *a* xylophagous, wood-boring. *m*, wood-borer

xilófono *m*, xylophone

xilografía *f*, xylography

Y

y *conjunc* and. See **e**

ya *adv* already; formerly; soon; now; finally; immediately; well, yes, quite. Used of past, present and future time, and in various idiomatic ways. **Ha venido ya,** He has already come. **¡Ya caerá!** His time will come!, He will get his comeuppance! **Ya vendrá,** He will come soon. **¡Ya voy!** Coming! **¡Ya lo creo!** Of course!; I should think so! **¡Ya!** Quite!; I understand. **ya no,** no longer. **ya que,** since

yacaré *m*, *Lat. Am.* alligator

yacente *a* recumbent, reclining (statues, etc.)

yacer *vi irr* to be lying at full length; lie (in the grave); be situated, be; lie (with), sleep (with); graze by night. *Pres. Ind.* **yazgo** or **yazco, yaces,** etc. *Pres. Subjunc.* **yazga** or **yazca,** etc.

yacija *f*, bed; couch; tomb

yacimiento *m*, *geol* bed, deposit

yacio *m*, india-rubber tree

yaguré *m*, *Lat. Am.* skunk

yak *m*, yak

yanqui *a* and *mf contemptuous and offensive* North American (gen. U.S.A.)

yarda *f*, yard (English measure)

yate *m*, *naut* yacht

ye *f*, name of the letter Y

yegua *f*, mare

yelmo *m*, helmet

yema *f*, bud; yolk (of egg); sweetmeat; *fig* best of anything. **y. del dedo,** finger-tip

yerba mate *m* mate (drink)

yermo *a* uninhabited, deserted; uncultivated. *m*, wilderness, desert

yerno *m*, son-in-law

yerro *m*, error; mistake; fault

yerto *a* stiff, rigid

yesca *f*, tinder; fuel, stimulus

yeso *m*, gypsum, calcium sulphate; plaster; plaster cast

yesquero *m*, *Lat. Am.* (cigaret) lighter

yídish *n* and *a* Yiddish

yip *m* jeep

yo *pers pron 1st sing mf* I. **el yo,** the ego

yodo *m*, iodine

yuca *f*, yucca

yucateco (-ca) *a* and *n* Yucatecan

yugo *m*, yoke; nuptial tie; oppression; *naut* transom; *fig* **sacudir el y.,** to throw off the yoke

yugular *a anat* jugular. *m*, jugular vein

Yukón, el the Yukon

yunque *m*, anvil; patient, undaunted person; hard worker; *anat* incus

yunta *f*, yoke (of oxen, etc.)
yute *m*, jute fiber or fabric

yuxtaponer *vt irr* to juxtapose. See **poner**
yuxtaposición *f*, juxtaposition

Z

zabarcera *f*, vegetable seller
zaborda *f*, **zabordamiento** *m*, *naut* grounding, stranding
zabordar *vi naut* to run aground, strand
zacatín *m*, street or square where clothes are sold
zafadura *f*, *Lat. Am.* dislocation, sprain
zafar *vt* to embellish, garnish, adorn; *naut* lighten (a ship); *vr* escape, hide oneself; (*with de*) excuse oneself, avoid; get rid of
zafarrancho *m*, *naut* clearing the decks; *inf* damage; *inf* scuffle
zafiedad *f*, rudeness, ignorance, boorishness
zafio *a* rude, unlettered, boorish
zafiro *m*, sapphire
zafra *f*, olive oil container; sugar crop or factory; *min* waste
zaga *f*, rear. *m*, last player. **en z.**, behind. *inf* **no quedarse en z.**, not to be left behind; be not inferior
zagal *m*, youth; strong, handsome lad; young shepherd; full skirt
zagala *f*, maiden, girl; young shepherdess
zagual *m*, paddle
zaguán *m*, entrance hall; vestibule
zaguero *a* loitering, straggling. *m*, *sport* back
zahareño *a* untamable, wild (birds); unsociable, disdainful
zaherimiento *m*, upbraiding; nagging
zaherir *vt irr* to upbraid, reprehend; nag. See **herir**
zahína *f*, *bot* sorghum
zahón *m*, leather apron (worn by cowboys)
zahorí *m*, soothsayer; waterfinder; sagacious person
zahúrda *f*, pigsty
zaino *a* treacherous; vicious (horses); chestnut (horses); black (cows)
zalagarda *f*, ambush; skirmish; snare, trap; *inf* trick, ruse; *inf* mock battle
zalamería *f*, adulation, flattery
zalamero (-ra) *a* wheedling, flattering. *n* flatterer
zalea *f*, sheepskin
zalear *vt* to shake; frighten away (dogs)
zalema *f*, salaam
zamacuco *m*, *inf* oaf, dolt; *inf* drinking bout
zamarra *f*, sheepskin jacket
zamarrear *vt* to worry, shake (prey); *fig inf* beat up; *inf* floor, confound
zambo *a* knock-kneed
zambomba *f*, rustic drum
zambuco *m*, *inf* concealment (especially of cards)
zambullida *f*, plunge, submersion; thrust (in fencing)
zambullir *vt* to plunge in water, submerge; *vr* dive; hide oneself, cover oneself
zampar *vt* to conceal (one thing in another); eat greedily; (*with en*) arrive suddenly
zampatortas *mf inf* glutton
zampoña *f*, rustic flute; *inf* unimportant work
zanahoria *f*, carrot
zanca *f*, long leg (birds); *inf* long thin leg; *arch* stringboard (of stairs)
zancada *f*, swift stride
zancadilla *f*, trip (wrestling); *inf* trick, deceit. **echar la z. (a)**, to trip up
zancajear *vi* to stride about
zancajo *m*, heel-bone; torn heel (stocking, shoe); *inf* illshaped person. *inf* **no llegarle al z.**, to be immensely inferior to someone
zancajoso *a* flatfooted; slovenly
zanco *m*, stilt. *fig inf* **andar** (*or* **estar**) **en zancos**, to have gone up in the world

zancudo *a* long-legged
zangandungo (-ga) *n inf* loafer
zanganear *vi inf* to loaf
zángano *m*, *ent* drone; *inf* idler, parasite
zangolotear *vt inf* to shake violently; *vi* fuss about, bustle; *vr* rattle (windows, etc.)
zangoloteo *m*, shaking; rattling
zanguango *m*, *inf* lazybones
zanja *f*, trench, ditch; drain; furrow
zanjar *vt* to excavate; *fig* remove (obstacles)
Zanzíbar Zanzibar
zapa *f*, shovel, spade; *mil* sap; sandpaper
zapador *m*, *mil* sapper
zapapico *m*, pick-ax; mattock
zapaquilda *f*, *inf* she-cat
zapar *vi mil* to sap
zaparrastrar *vi inf* to trail along the floor (dresses)
zapata *f*, half-boot; piece of leather used to stop creaking of a hinge; *arch* lintel; (*naut mech*) shoe
zapatazo *m*, blow with a shoe; fall, thud; stamping (horses); flap (of sail)
zapateado *m*, dance in which rhythmic drumming of heels plays important part
zapatear *vt* to hit with a shoe; stamp feet; drum heels (in dancing); *inf* ill-treat; thump ground (rabbits); *vi* stamp (horses); *naut* flap (sails); *vr fig* stand one's ground
zapateo *m*, stamping; rhythmic drumming of heels
zapatera *f*, cobbler's wife; woman who makes or sells shoes
zapatería *f*, shoemaking; shoe shop
zapatero *m*, shoemaker; shoe seller. **z. remendón,** cobbler
zapateta *f*, caper, leap
zapatilla *f*, slipper; trotter, hoof
zapato *m*, shoe. **z. de hule** *Mexico*, galosh, rubber
zapatón *m*, *Lat. Am.* galosh, overshoe
¡zape! *interj inf* shoo! Used for frightening away cats; exclamation of surprise or warning
zapear *vt* to scare away cats; *inf* frighten off
zaque *m*, leather bottle, wineskin; *inf* drunkard, sot
zaquizamí *m*, garret; dirty little house or room
zar *m*, tsar
zarabanda *f*, saraband; *inf* racket, row
zaragata *f*, *inf* fight, brawl
Zaragoza Saragossa
zaragozano (-na) *a* and *n* Saragossan
zaragüelles *m*, *pl* wide pleated breeches
zaranda *f*, sieve, strainer, colander
zarandajas *f*, *pl inf* odds and ends
zarandar *vt* to sieve (grapes, grain); strain; *inf* pick out the best; *vr inf* move quickly
zarandillo *m*, small sieve, strainer; *inf* a live wire, energetic person; Spanish dance
zaraza *f*, chintz
zarcillo *m*, earring; *bot* tendril; *agr* trowel
zarco *a* light blue (generally eyes or water)
zarpa *f*, *naut* weighing anchor; paw
zarpada *f*, blow with a paw
zarpar *vt* and *vi naut* to weigh anchor, sail
zarza *f*, *bot* bramble, blackberry bush
zarzal *m*, bramble patch
zarzamora *f*, blackberry
zarzaparrilla *f*, sarsaparilla
zarzo *m*, hurdle; wattle
zarzoso *a* brambly
zarzuela *f*, comic opera; musical comedy
zarzuelista *mf* writer or composer of comic operas
¡zas! *m*, sound of a bang or blow

zascandil *m, inf* busybody
zatara *f,* raft
zeda *f,* name of the letter Z
zedilla *f,* cedilla
zenit *m.* See **cenit**
zepelín *m,* Zeppelin
zeta *f.* See **zeda**
zigzag *m,* zigzag
zigzaguear *vi* to zigzag
zinc *m,* zinc
zipizape *m, inf* row, quarrel
zoca *f,* square
zócalo *m, arch* socle; *Mexico* main square
Zócalo, el *m,* the Main Square (of Mexico City)
zoclo *m,* clog, sabot
zoco *m,* square; market; clog, sabot
zodiaco *m,* zodiac
zona *f,* girdle, band; strip (of land); zone; *med* shingles.
  z. de depresión, air pocket. **z. templada,** temperate
  zone. **z. tórrida,** torrid zone
zonal *a* zonal
zoncear *vi, Lat. Am.* to behave stupidly
zonzo, -a *a, Lat. Am.* silly, stupid
zoología *f,* zoology
zoológico *a* zoological
zoólogo *m,* zoologist
zopenco *a inf* oafish
zopo *a* maimed, deformed (hands, feet)
zoquete *m, carp* block; dowel; hunk of bread; *inf* short,
  ugly man; *inf* dunderhead
zorcico *m,* Basque song and dance
zorra *f,* vixen; fox; *inf* cunning person; *inf* prostitute; *inf*
  drinking bout; truck, dray
zorrera *f,* foxhole
zorrería *f,* foxiness; *inf* cunning
zorro *m,* fox; fox-skin; *inf* knave

zóster *f, med* shingles
zote *a* dull, ignorant
zozobra *f, naut* foundering, capsizing; anxiety
zozobrar *vi naut* to founder, sink; *naut* plunge, shiver;
  be anxious, vacillate
zueco *m,* sabot, clog
zulú *a* and *mf* Zulu
zumaque *m, bot* sumach tree; *inf* wine
zumba *f,* cow bell; jest
zumbar *vi* to buzz, hum; ring (of the ears); whizz;
  twang (of a guitar, etc.); *fig inf* be on the brink
zumbido *m,* buzzing, humming; ringing (in the ears);
  whizz; twanging (of a guitar, etc.); *inf* slap, blow
zumbón *a* waggish, jocose
zumo *m,* sap; juice; profit, advantage
zumoso *a* succulent, juicy
zupia *f,* wine lees; cloudy wine; *fig* dregs
zurcido *m, sew* darn; mend
zurcidor (-ra) *n* darner, mender. **z. de voluntades,**
  humorous pimp
zurcidura *f,* darning; mending; darn
zurcir *vt* to darn; mend, repair; join; *fig* concoct, weave
zurdo *a* left-handed
zurra *f, tan* currying; *inf* spanking; *inf* quarrel
zurrador *m, tan* currier, dresser
zurrapa *f,* (gen. *pl*) sediment, lees, dregs
zurrar *vt* to curry (leather); *inf* spank; *inf* dress down,
  scold
zurriagazo *m,* lash with a whip; *fig* blow of fate
zurriago *m,* whip
zurribanda *f, inf* whipping; fight, quarrel
zurriburri *m, inf* ragamuffin; mob; uproar
zurrido *m, inf* blow; dull noise
zurrir *vi* to have a confused sound, hum, rattle
zurrón *m,* shepherd's pouch; leather bag; *bot* husk
zutano (-na) *n inf* so-and-so, such a one

ENGLISH-SPANISH
Dictionary

A

a *n* (letter) a, *f*; *mus* la, *m*. **symphony in A major,** sinfonía en la mayor, *f*. **A1,** de primera clase; de primera calidad, excelente

a, an *indef art.* (one) un, *m*; una, *f*; (with weights, quantities) el, *m*; la, *f*; (with weeks, months, years, etc.) por, al, *m*; a la, *f*. The indef. art. is omitted in Spanish before nouns expressing nationality, profession, rank, and generally before a noun in apposition. It is omitted also before certain words such as **mil, ciento, otro, semejante, medio,** etc. Not translated in book titles, e.g., **A History of Spain,** Historia de España. *prep* a. In phrases such as **to go hunting,** ir a cazar. As prefix, see **abed, ashore,** etc. **Madrid, a Spanish city,** Madrid, ciudad de España. **three times a month,** tres veces al mes. **ten dollars an hour,** diez dólares por hora. **thirty miles an hour,** treinta millas por hora. **a certain Mrs. Brown,** una tal Sra. Brown. **a thousand soldiers,** mil soldados. **half an hour later,** media hora después

aback *adv naut* en facha; *fig* sorprendido, desconcertado. **to take a.,** desconcertar, coger desprevenido (a)

abacus *n* ábaco, *m*

abaft *adv naut* hacia la popa, en popa; atrás

abandon *vt* abandonar; dejar; desertar, desamparar; renunciar; entregar. *n* entusiasmo, fervor, *m*; naturalidad, *f*. **to a. oneself to,** (despair, vice, etc.) entregarse a

abandoned *a* entregado a los vicios, vicioso

abandonment *n* abandono, *m*; renunciación, *f*; deserción, *f*

abase *vt* humillar; degradar; abatir

abasement *n* humillación, degradación, *f*; abatimiento, *m*

abash *vt* avergonzar; confundir, desconcertar

abashed *a* avergonzado, confuso, consternado

abate *vt* disminuir, reducir; (a price) rebajar; (suppress) suprimir, abolir; (remit) condonar, remitir; (annul) anular; (moderate) moderar; (of pride, etc.) humillar; (of pain) aliviar. *vi* disminuir; moderarse; (of the wind and *fig*) amainar; cesar; apaciguarse, calmarse

abatement *n* disminución, *f*; reducción, *f*; mitigación, *f*; (of price) rebaja, *f*; supresión, *f*; remisión, *f*; (annulment) anulación, *f*; (of pride) humillación, *f*; (of the wind and of enthusiasm, etc.) amaine, *m*; (of pain, etc.) alivio, *m*

abattoir *n* matadero, *m*

abbey *n* abadía, *f*

abbreviate *vt* abreviar; condensar, resumir

abbreviation *n* abreviación, *f*; resumen, *m*, condensación, *f*; (of a word) abreviatura, *f*

abdicate *vt* renunciar; (a throne) abdicar

abdication *n* renuncia, *f*; abdicación, *f*

abdomen *n* abdomen, *m*

abdominal *a* abdominal

abduct *vt* raptar, secuestrar

abduction *n* rapto, *m*; (anat phil) abducción, *f*

abductor *n* anat abductor, *m*; raptor, *m*

aberration *n* aberración (also *ast phys biol*), *f*

abet *vt* ayudar, apoyar, favorecer; incitar, alentar; (in bad sense) ser cómplice de

abetment *n* ayuda, *f*, apoyo, *m*; instigación, *f*

abettor *n* instigador (-ra); cómplice, *mf*

abeyance *n* suspensión, *f*; expectativa, esperanza, *f*. **in a.,** en suspenso; vacante; latente

abhor *vt* detestar, odiar, aborrecer; repugnar

abhorrence *n* detestación, *f*, odio, aborrecimiento, *m*; repugnancia, *f*

abhorrent *a* detestable, odioso, aborrecible; repugnante

abide *vi* morar, quedar; *vt* aguardar; *inf* aguantar, sufrir. **to a. by,** atenerse a, cumplir; sostener

abiding *a* permanente, constante, perenne

ability *n* habilidad, facultad, *f*, poder, *m*; talento, *m*, capacidad, *f*. **to the best of my a.,** lo mejor que yo pueda

abject *a* abyecto, miserable; despreciable, vil; servil

abjure *vt* abjurar; renunciar; retractar

ablaze *a* en llamas, ardiendo. *a* brillante; (with, of anger, etc.) dominado por

able *a* capaz (de); (clever) hábil; competente; en estado (de); *law* apto legalmente, capaz; bueno, excelente. **to be a. to,** poder; ser capaz de; (know how) saber. **a.-bodied,** fuerte, fornido. **a.-bodied seaman,** marinero práctico, *m*

abloom *adv* en flor

ablution *n* ablución, *f*

ably *adv* hábilmente; competentemente

abnegation *n* abnegación, *f*

abnormal *a* anormal; irregular

abnormality *n* anormalidad, *f*; irregularidad, *f*

abnormally *adv* anormalmente; demasiado

aboard *adv* a bordo. *prep* a bordo de. **to go a.,** embarcarse, ir a bordo. **All a.!** ¡Viajeros a bordo!; (a train) ¡Viajeros al tren!

abode *n* morada, habitación, *f*; residencia, *f*; (stay) estancia, *f*

abolish *vt* abolir, suprimir, anular

abolition *n* abolición, supresión, *f*; anulación, *f*

abolitionist *n* abolicionista, *mf*

abominable *a* abominable, aborrecible; repugnante; execrable; *inf* horrible

abominably *adv* abominablemente

abominate *vt* abominar, aborrecer, detestar

abomination *n* abominación, *f*; aborrecimiento, *m*; horror, *m*

aboriginal *a* aborigen; primitivo

aborigines *n pl* aborígenes, *m pl*

abort *vi* abortar, malparir; *fig* malograrse

abortion *n* aborto, *Columbia* avieso *m*; *fig* fracaso, malogro, *m*

abortive *a* abortivo

abound *vi* abundar (en)

about *adv* (around) alrededor; (round about) a la redonda, en torno; (all over) por todas partes; (up and down) acá y acullá; por aquí, por ahí; en alguna parte; por aquí; (in circumference) en circunferencia; (almost) casi, aproximadamente; (by turns) por turnos, en rotación. *prep* alrededor de; en torno; por; (near to) cerca de; (on one's person) sobre; (on the subject of) sobre; (concerning) acerca de; (over) por, a causa de; en; (of) de; (with time by the clock) a eso de, sobre; (towards) hacia; (engaged in) ocupado en; (on the point of) a punto de. **a. here,** por aquí. **a. nothing,** por nada. **a. supper time,** hacia la hora de cenar. **a. three o'clock,** a eso de las tres. **A. turn!** ¡Media vuelta! (a la izquierda or a la derecha). **He wandered a. the streets,** Vagaba por las calles. **somewhere a.,** en alguna parte. **to be a. to,** estar para, estar a punto de. **to bring a.,** ocasionar, suceder. **to know a.,** saber de. **to set a.,** empezar, iniciar; (a person) acometer. **What are you thinking a.?** ¿En qué piensas?

above *adv* arriba; en lo alto; encima; (superior) superior; (earlier) antes; (higher up on a page, etc.) más arriba; (in heaven) en el cielo. *prep* encima de; por encima de; sobre; (beyond) fuera del alcance de; (superior to) superior a; (more than) más de; (too proud to) demasiado orgulloso para; (too good to) demasiado bueno para; (in addition to) además de, en adición a; (with degrees of temperature) sobre. *a* anterior; (with past participles) antes. **from a.,** desde arriba. **a. all,** sobre todo. **over and a. a.** **board,** *adv* abiertamente, con las cartas boca arriba. *a*

261

franco y abierto. **a. mentioned,** supradicho, susodicho, antes citado

abrasion *n* abrasión, *f*; rozadura, *f*; *geol* denudación, *f*

abrasive *a* abrasivo. *n* substancia abrasiva, *f*, abrasivo, *m*

abreast *adv* de frente, al lado uno de otro; *naut* por el través. **to keep a. of the times,** mantenerse al día. **to ride six a.,** cabalgar a seis de frente. **a. with,** al nivel de, a la altura de

abridge *vt* abreviar; resumir, condensar, compendiar; disminuir; reducir

abridgment *n* abreviación, *f*; resumen, *m*, sinopsis, *f*; disminución, *f*; reducción, *f*

abroad *adv* (out) fuera, afuera; (gone out) salido; ausente; (everywhere) en todas partes; (in foreign lands) en el extranjero. **to go a.,** salir de casa, echarse a la calle; ir al extranjero; (of rumors, etc.) propagarse, rumorearse

abrogation *n* abrogación, anulación, *f*

abrupt *a* (precipitous) escarpado, precipitado, abrupto; (unexpected) repentino, inesperado; (of persons) brusco, descortés; (of style) seco

abruptly *adv* bruscamente; repentinamente

abruptness *n* precipitación, *f*; brusquedad, *f*

abscess *n* absceso, *m*

abscond *vi* evadirse; huir, escaparse; (with money) desfalcar

absence *n* ausencia, *f*; alejamiento, *m*; (of mind) abstracción, *f*, ensimismamiento, *m*; (lack) falta, *f*. **leave of a.,** permiso para ausentarse, *m*; *mil* licencia, *f*, permiso, *m*

absent *a* ausente; alejado (de); (in mind) abstraído, ensimismado, distraído. *vt* ausentarse; alejarse. **the a.,** los ausentes. **a.-mindedness,** ensimismamiento, *m*, abstracción, *f*

absentee *n* ausente, *mf*

absenteeism *n* absentismo, *m*

absently *adv* distraídamente

absinthe *n* ajenjo, *m*

absolute *a* absoluto; perfecto; puro; (unconditional) incondicional; (downright) categórico; completo; (true) verdadero; (unlimited) ilimitado. **the a.,** lo absoluto

absolutely *adv* absolutamente; enteramente, completamente; realmente, categóricamente

absolution *n* (*ecc law*) absolución, *f*

absolutism *n* absolutismo, despotismo, *m*

absolutist *n* absolutista, *mf*

absolve *vt* absolver; (free) exentar, eximir; librar; exculpar

absorb *vt* absorber; (drink) beber; (use) gastar; (of shocks) amortiguar; (*fig* digest) asimilar; (engross) ocupar (el pensamiento, etc.). **to be absorbed in,** *fig* enfrascarse en, engolfarse en, estar entregado a

absorbent *a* and *n* absorbente, *m*. **a. cotton,** algodón hidrófilo, *m*

absorbing *a* absorbente; *fig* sumamente interesante

absorption *n* absorción, *f*; (*fig* digestion) asimilación, *f*; (engrossment) enfrascamiento, *m*, preocupación, abstracción, *f*

abstain *vi* abstenerse (de); evitar

abstemious *a* abstemio, abstinente; sobrio; moderado

abstention *n* abstención, *f*; abstinencia, *f*; privación, *f*

abstinence *n* abstinencia, *f*. **day of a.,** día de ayuno, *m*

abstinent *a* abstinente; sobrio

abstract *a* abstracto. *n* extracto, resumen, *m*; abstracción, *f*. *vt* abstraer; separar; extraer; (précis) resumir; (steal) substraer. **in the a.,** en abstracto

abstracted *a* distraído, desatento, absorto, ensimismado

abstraction *n* abstracción, *f*; (of mind) preocupación, desatención, *f*; (stealing) substracción, *f*

abstruse *a* abstruso, ininteligible; oscuro; recóndito

absurd *a* absurdo, grotesco; ridículo, disparatado; cómico

absurdity *n* absurdidad, ridiculez, *f*; disparate, *m*, tontería, *f*

abundance *n* abundancia, copia, *f*; muchedumbre (de), multitud (de), *f*; riqueza, *f*; prosperidad, *f*

abundant *a* abundante, copioso; rico. **to be a. in,** abundar en

abundantly *adv* en abundancia, abundantemente

abuse *n* abuso, *m*; (bad language) insulto, *m*, injuria, *f*. *vt* (ill-use) maltratar; (misuse) abusar (de); (revile) insultar, injuriar; (deceive) engañar

abuser *n* abusador (-ra); injuriador (-ra); (defamer) denigrante, *mf*

abusive *a* abusivo; (scurrilous) insultante, injurioso, ofensivo

abusively *adv* insolentemente, ofensivamente

abut (on) *vi* lindar con; terminar en; estar adosado a

abysmal *a* abismal

abyss *n* abismo, *m*, sima, *f*; (hell) infierno, *m*

acacia *n* acacia, *f*

academic *a* académico

academician *n* académico, miembro de la Academia, *m*

academy *n* academia, *f*; conservatorio, *m*; (school) colegio, *m*; (of riding, etc.) escuela, *f*. **A. of Music,** Conservatorio de Música, *m*

accede *vi* (to a throne) ascender (al trono); tomar posesión (de); (join) hacerse miembro (de); aceptar; (agree) acceder (a), consentir (en), convenir (en)

accelerate *vt* acelerar; apresurar; (shorten) abreviar

acceleration *n* aceleración, *f*

accelerator *n* (of a vehicle) acelerador, *m*

accent *n* acento (all meanings), *m*. *vt* acentuar

accentuate *vt* acentuar; dar énfasis a

accept *vt* aceptar; (believe) creer; recibir; admitir; (welcome) acoger

acceptability *n* aceptabilidad, *f*; mérito, *m*

acceptable *a* aceptable; admisible; agradable; (welcome) bien acogido

acceptably *adv* aceptablemente; agradablemente

acceptance *n* aceptación, *f*. **a. speech** discurso aceptatorio; (approval) aprobación, *f*; (welcome) buena acogida, *f*; *com* aceptación, *f*

access *n* acceso, *m*; entrada, *f*; (way) camino, *m*; *med* ataque, *m*; (fit) transporte, *m*; (advance) avance, *m*. **easy of a.,** accesible; fácil de encontrar

accessibility *n* accesibilidad, *f*

accessible *a* accesible; asequible

accession *n* (to the throne, etc.) advenimiento, *m*; aumento, *m*; (acquisition) adición, *f*; adquisición, *f*; *law* accesión, *f*

accessory *a* accesorio; secundario; suplementario, adicional. *n* accesorio, *m*; *law* cómplice, *mf*. **a. before the fact,** instigador (-ra). **a. after the fact,** encubridor (-ra)

accident *n* accidente, *m*; (chance) casualidad, *f*; (mishap) contratiempo, *m*. **by a.,** por casualidad, accidentalmente. **a. insurance,** seguro contra accidentes, *m*

accidental *a* accidental, casual, fortuito. *n* *mus* accidente, *m*

accidentally *adv* accidentalmente; por casualidad; sin querer

acclaim *vt* aclamar; proclamar; vitorear, aplaudir

acclamation *n* aclamación, *f*; aplauso, vítor, *m*

acclimatization *n* aclimatación, *f*

acclimatize *vt* aclimatar

accolade *n* acolada, *f*, espaldarazo, *m*

accommodate *vt* acomodar; ajustar; adaptar; (reconcile) reconciliar; (provide) proveer, proporcionar; (oblige) complacer; (fit) poner, instalar; (lodge) hospedar; (lend) prestar; (hold) tener espacio para, contener; (give a seat to) dar un sitio a. **to a. oneself to,** adaptarse a

accommodating *a* acomodadizo; (obliging) servicial

accommodation *n* acomodación, *f*; ajuste, *m*; adaptación, *f*; (arrangement) arreglo, *m*; (reconciliation) reconciliación, *f*; (lodging) alojamiento, *m*; (*aer naut*) partición, *f*; (space, room or seat) sitio, *m*; (loan) préstamo, *m*. **We found the accommodations good in**

this hotel, Estuvimos muy bien en este hotel. **a. ladder,** escalera real, *f*

accompaniment *n* acompañamiento, *m*

accompanist *n* acompañante (-ta)

accompany *vt* acompañar

accompanying *a* anexo *n* acompañamiento, *m*

accomplice *n* cómplice, comparte, *mf*

accomplish *vt* llevar a cabo, efectuar; terminar; (fulfil) cumplir; perfeccionar; (achieve) conseguir, lograr

accomplished *a* consumado; perfecto; culto; (talented) talentoso

accomplishment *n* efectuación, *f*; realización, *f*; logro, *m*; (fulfilment) cumplimiento, *m*; (gift) prenda, *f*, talento, *m*; *pl* **accomplishments,** partes, dotes, *f pl*; conocimientos, *m pl*

accord *n* acuerdo, *m*; unión, *f*; consentimiento, *m*; concierto, *m*, concordia, *f*; voluntad, *f*. *vt* otorgar, conceder. *vi* estar de acuerdo (con); armonizar (con). **of one's own a.,** espontáneamente. **with one a.,** unánimemente

accordance *n* acuerdo, *m*, conformidad, *f*; arreglo, *m*. **in a. with,** de acuerdo con, según, con arreglo a

according *adv* según, conforme. **a. as,** conforme a, a medida que. **a. to,** según

accordingly *adv* en consecuencia, por consiguiente; pues

accordion *n* acordeón, *m*. **to a.-pleat,** *vt* plisar

accost *vt* abordar, acercarse a; dirigirse a, hablar

account *vt* (judge) considerar, creer, juzgar, tener por. *vi* (for) explicar; (understand) comprender; (be responsible) responder de, dar razón de; justificar

account *n* (bill) cuenta, *f*; factura, *f*; (narrative) narración, relación, *f*; (description) descripción, *f*; historia, *f*; versión, *f*; (list) enumeración, *f*; (reason) motivo, *m*, causa, *f*; (importance) importancia, *f*; (weight) peso, *m*; (news) noticias, *f pl*; (advantage) provecho, *m*, ventaja, *f*. **by all accounts,** según lo que se oye, según voz pública. **current a.,** cuenta corriente, *f*. **outstanding a.,** cuenta pendiente, *f*. **on a.,** a cuenta. **on a. of,** a causa de, por motivo de. **on no a.,** de ninguna manera. **on that a.,** por lo tanto. **to be of no a.,** ser insignificante; ser de poca importancia; *inf* ser la última mona. **to give an a.,** contar, hacer una relación (de). **to give an a. of oneself,** explicarse. **to keep a.,** llevar la cuenta. **to settle accounts,** ajustar cuentas. **to take into a.,** considerar. **to turn to a.,** sacar provecho de. **a. book,** libro de cuentas, *m*

accountability *n* responsabilidad, *f*

accountable *a* responsable

accountancy *n* contabilidad, *f*

accountant *n* contador, *m*. **chartered a.,** contador autorizado, *m*. **accountant's office,** contaduría, *f*

accoutrement *n* atavío, *m*; equipo, *m*

accredit *vt* acreditar

accretion *n* acrecentamiento, aumento, *m*; *law* accesión, *f*

accrue *vi* resultar (de), proceder (de); originarse (en); aumentar

accumulate *vt* acumular; amontonar, atesorar. *vi* acumularse; aumentarse, crecer

accumulation *n* acumulación, *f*; amontonamiento, *m*

accumulative *a* acumulador; adquisitivo, ahorrador

accumulator *n elec* acumulador, *m*

accuracy *n* exactitud, corrección

accurate *a* exacto, correcto, fiel; (of persons) exacto, minucioso; (of apparatus) de precisión

accurately *adv* con exactitud, correctamente; con precisión

accursed *a* maldito

accusation *n* acusación, *f*. **to lodge an a.,** querellarse ante el juez

accusatory *a* acusatorio

accuse *vt* acusar

accused *n law* acusado (-da)

accuser *n* acusador (-ra)

accustom *vt* acostumbrar (a), habituar (a)

accustomed *a* acostumbrado, usual; general; característico

ace *n* as, *m*; *fig* pelo, *m*. **to be within an ace of,** estar a dos dedos de

acerbity *n* acerbidad, *f*; *fig* aspereza, *f*; severidad, *f*; sequedad, *f*

acetate *n* acetato, *m*

acetic *a* acético

acetylene *n* acetileno, *m*. **a. lamp,** lámpara de acetileno, *f*

ache *n* dolor, *m*; pena, *f*. *vi* doler. **My head aches,** Me duele la cabeza, Tengo dolor de cabeza

achievable *a* alcanzable, asequible; factible

achieve *vt* conseguir, lograr; (reach) alcanzar; (obtain) obtener, ganar

achievement *n* logro, *m*, realización, *f*; obtención, *f*; (deed) hazaña, *f*; (work) obra, *f*; (success) éxito, *m*; (discovery) descubrimiento, *m*; (victory) victoria, *f*

aching *n* dolor, *m*; pena, angustia, *f*. *a* doliente; afligido

achromatic *a* acromático

achromic *a* acrómico

acid *a* and *n* ácido, *m*. **fatty a.,** ácido graso, *m*

acidify *vt* acidificar

acidity *n* acidez, *f*

acidosis *n med* acidismo, *m*

acknowledge *vt* reconocer; confesar; (reply to) contestar a; (appreciate) agradecer. **to a. receipt,** *com* acusar recibo

acknowledgment *n* reconocimiento, *m*; confesión, *f*; (appreciation) agradecimiento, *m*; (reward) recompensa, *f*; (of a letter) acuse de recibo, *m*

acme *n* cumbre, *f*; *fig* auge, apogeo, *m*

acne *n* acné, *m*

acolyte *n* acólito, monacillo (male) *m*, acólita, monacilla *f*, (female)

acorn *n* bellota, *f*. **a. cup,** capullo de bellota, *m*. **a.-shaped,** en forma de bellota, abellotado

acoustic *a* acústico

acoustics *n pl* acústica, *f*

acquaint *vt* dar a conocer, comunicar, informar (de); dar parte (de); familiarizar (con). **to be acquainted with,** conocer; saber. **to make oneself acquainted with,** familiarizarse con; entablar amistad con

acquaintance *n* conocimiento, *m*; (person) conocido (-da), *pl* **acquaintances,** amistades, *f pl*. **to make their a.,** conocer (a), llegar a conocer (a)

acquiesce *vi* asentir (en), consentir (a)

acquiescence *n* acquiescencia, *f*, consentimiento, *m*

acquiescent *a* conforme; resignado

acquire *vt* adquirir, obtener; (diseases, habits) contraer; ganar; (learn) aprender

Acquired Immune Deficiency Syndrome *n* el síndrome de Inmunodeficiencia Adquirida, *m*

acquirement *n* adquisición, *f*; (learning) conocimiento, *m*; (talent) talento, *m*

acquirer *n* adquisidor (-ra)

acquisition *n* adquisición, *f*

acquisitive *a* adquisitivo

acquit *vt* (a debt) pagar; exonerar; *law* absolver; (a duty) cumplir. **to a. oneself well (badly),** portarse bien (mal); salir bien (mal)

acquittal *n* (of a debt) pago, *m*; *law* absolución, *f*; (of a duty) cumplimiento, *m*

acquittance *n* descargo, *m*; quitanza, *f*

acre *n* (measure) acre, *m*; *pl* **acres,** terrenos, campos, *m pl*. **1.75 acres** *Central America* manzana *f*. **2.5 acres** *Argentina* manzana *f*

acreage *n* acres, *m pl*

acrid *a* acre

acrimonious *a* acrimonioso, áspero; mordaz, sarcástico

acrimony *n* acrimonia, acritud, *f*; sarcasmo, *m*

acrobat *n* acróbata. Lat. Am. also maromero (-ra) *mf*

acrobatic *a* acrobático

acrobatics *n pl* acrobacia, *f*

acronym *n* sigla, *f*

acropolis *n* acrópolis, *f*

across *adv* a través, de través, transversalmente; (on the other side) al otro lado; de una parte a otra; (of the arms, etc.) cruzados, *m pl. prep* a través de; al otro lado de; (upon) sobre; por. **He went a. the road,** Cruzó la calle. **to run a.,** correr por; tropezar con; dar con. **a. country,** a campo travieso. **a. the way,** en frente

acrostic *n* (poema) acróstico, *m, a* acróstico

act *n* acción, obra, *f,* hecho, *m;* acto, *m; law* ley, *f; theat* acto, *m.* **in the act,** en el acto. **in the act (of doing),** en acto de (hacer algo). **in the very act,** en flagrante. **the Acts of the Apostles,** los Actos de los Apóstoles. **act of God,** fuerza mayor, *f.* **act of indemnity,** bill of indemnity

act *vt* (a play) representar, hacer; (a part) desempeñar, hacer (un papel); (pretend) simular, fingir. *vi* obrar, actuar, *Lat. Am.* accionar; (behave) portarse, conducirse; (function) funcionar; producir su efecto; (feign) fingir; (as a profession) ser actor. **to act as,** hacer de; cumplir las funciones de. **to act as a second,** (in a duel) apadrinar. **to act for,** representar; ser el representante de. **to act upon,** obrar sobre; afectar; influir en

acting *n* (of a play) representación (de una comedia), *f;* (of an actor) interpretación (de un papel), *f;* (as a hobby) el hacer comedia; (dramatic art) arte dramática, *f. a* interino, suplente; comanditario. **He is a. captain,** Está de capitán. **a. partner,** socio (-ia) comanditario (-ia)

action *n* acción, *f;* función, *f;* operación, *f;* (movement) movimiento, *m;* (effect) efecto, *m;* influencia, *f; law* proceso, *m; mil* batalla, acción, *f; lit* acción, *f.* **in a.,** en actividad; en operación; *mil* en el campo de batalla. **man of a.,** hombre de acción, *m.* **to be killed in a.,** morir en el campo de batalla. **to bring an a. against,** pedir en juicio, entablar un pleito contra. **to put into a.,** hacer funcionar; introducir. **to take a.,** tomar medidas (para). **to take a. against,** prevenirse contra; *law* proceder contra

actionable *a* procesable, punible

active *a* activo; ágil; diligente; *mil* vivo; enérgico; *gram* activo. **be a.** *Lat. Am.* accionar. **to make a.,** activar, estimular

activity *n* actividad, *f*

actor *n* actor, *m;* (in comedy) comediante, *m*

actress *n* actriz, *f;* (in comedy) comedianta, *f*

actual *a* actual, existente; real, verdadero

actuality *n* realidad, *f*

actually *adv* en efecto, realmente, en realidad

actuary *n* actuario de seguros, *m*

actuate *vt* mover, animar, excitar

acumen *n* cacumen, *m,* agudeza, sagacidad, *f*

acute *a* agudo; (shrewd) perspicaz; (of a situation) crítico. **a. accent,** acento agudo, *m.* **a.-angled,** acutángulo

acutely *adv* agudamente; (deeply) profundamente

acuteness *n* agudeza, *f;* (shrewdness) perspicacia, penetración, *f*

ad *n* anuncio, *m.* See **advertisement**

adage *n* refrán, proverbio, decir, *m*

Adam *n* Adán, *m.* **Adam's apple,** nuez de la garganta, *f*

adamant *a* firme, duro, inexorable

adamantine *a* adamantino

adapt *vt* adaptar; ajustar, acomodar; aplicar; (a play, etc.) refundir, arreglar; *mus* arreglar

adaptability *n* adaptabilidad, *f*

adaptable *a* adaptable

adaptation *n* adaptación, *f;* (of a play, etc.) refundición, *f;* (mus etc.) arreglo, *m*

adapter *n* (of a play, etc.) refundidor (-ra); *elec* enchufe de reducción, *f*

add *vt* añadir; juntar; (up) sumar. **add insult to injury,** al mojado echarle agua, añadir a una ofensa otra mayor. **to add to,** añadir a; (increase) aumentar, acrecentar. **to add up,** sumar. **to add up to,** subir a; (mean) querer decir.

adder *n* víbora, serpiente, *f*

addict *n* adicto (-ta). **to a. oneself to,** dedicarse a, entregarse a

addicted *a* aficionado (a), amigo (de), dado (a); adicto (a)

addiction *n* afición, propensión, *f;* adicción, *f*

addition *n* añadidura, *f; math* adición, suma, *f.* **in a. (to),** además de, también

additional *a* adicional

addled *a* huero, podrido; *fig* confuso

address *n* (on a letter) sobrescrito, *m;* (of a person) dirección, *f,* señas, *f pl;* (speech) discurso, *m;* (petition) memorial, *m,* petición, *f;* (dedication) dedicatoria, *f;* (invocation) invocación, *f;* (deportment) presencia, *f;* (tact) diplomacia, habilidad, *f; pl* **addresses,** corte, *f. vt* (a ball) golpear; (a letter) dirigir, poner el sobrescrito a, *Mexico* domiciliar; (words, prayers) dirigir (a); hablar, hacer un discurso. **to a. oneself to a task,** dedicarse a (or entregarse a or emprender) una tarea. **to deliver an a.,** pronunciar un discurso. **to pay one's addresses to,** cortejar, hacer la corte (a), galantear

addressee *n* destinatario (-ia)

adduce *vt* aducir, alegar; aportar

Aden Adén *m*

adenoids *n pl* amígdalas, *f pl*

adept *a* adepto, versado, consumado. *n* adepto, *m*

adequacy *n* adecuación, *f;* suficiencia, *f;* competencia, *f*

adequate *a* adecuado; proporcionado; suficiente; competente; a la altura (de)

adequately *adv* adecuadamente

adhere *vi* adherirse; pegarse; ser fiel (a); persistir (en)

adherence *n fig* adhesión, *f*

adherent *n* partidario (-ia)

adhesion *n* adherencia, *f;* (to a party, etc.) adhesión, *f*

adhesive *a* adhesivo; (sticky) pegajoso. **a. tape,** esparadrapo, *m; elec* cinta aisladora adherente, *f*

adipose *a* adiposo

adjacent *a* próximo, contiguo, adyacente, vecino

adjective *n* adjetivo, *m*

adjoin *vt* estar contiguo a, lindar con; juntar. *vi* colindar

adjoining *a* vecino, de al lado, adyacente; cercano

adjourn *vt* aplazar, diferir; (a meeting, etc.) suspender; levantar. *vi* retirarse. **The debate was adjourned,** Se suspendió el debate. **to a. a meeting,** levantar la sesión

adjournment *n* aplazamiento, *m;* (of a meeting) suspensión (de la sesión), *f*

adjudicate *vt* adjudicar; *law* declarar; juzgar. *vi* ejercer las funciones del juez; fallar, dictar sentencia

adjudication *n* adjudicación, *f; law* fallo, *m,* sentencia, *f;* (of bankruptcy) declaración (de quiebra), *f;* concesión, *f,* otorgamiento, *m*

adjudicator *n* adjudicador (-ra)

adjunct *n* atributo, *m;* accesorio, *m;* adjunto, *m; gram* adjunto, *m*

adjure *vt* conjurar; rogar encarecidamente

adjust *vt* ajustar; regular; arreglar; (correct) corregir; adaptar

adjustable *a* ajustable; regulable; desmontable; de quita y pon

adjustment *n* ajuste, *m;* regulación, *f;* arreglo, *m;* (correction) corrección, *f;* adaptación, *f; com* prorrateo, *m*

adjutant *n mil* ayudante, *m*

administer *vt* administrar; (laws) aplicar; (blows, etc.) dar; (an office) ejercer; (govern) regir, gobernar; (provide) suministrar; (an oath) tomar; (justice) hacer; (the sacraments) administrar; (with to) contribuir a. **to a. an oath,** tomar juramento (a)

administration *n* administración, *f;* (government) gobierno, *m;* dirección, *f;* (of laws) aplicación, *f;* distribución, *f*

administrative *a* administrativo; gubernativo

administrator *n* administrador, *m*

administratrix *n* administradora, *f*

admirable *a* admirable

admirably *adv* admirablemente

admiral *n* almirante, *m.* **A. of the Fleet,** almirante supremo, *m.* **admiral's ship,** capitana, *f*

admiration *n* admiración, *f*

admire *vt* sentir admiración por; (love) amar; (like) gustar; (respect) respetar

admirer *n* admirador (-ra); (amateur) aficionado (-da); apasionado (-da); (partisan) satélite, *m*; (lover) enamorado, amante, *m*

admiring *a* admirativo, de admiración

admissible *a* admisible; aceptable; lícito, permitido

admission *n* admisión, *f*; recepción, *f*; entrada, *f*; confesión, *f*, reconocimiento, *m*. **No a.!** Entrada prohibida. **right of a.,** derecho de entrada, *m*. **A. free,** Entrada libre. **a. ticket,** entrada, *f*

admit *vt* admitir; recibir; dejar entrar; hacer entrar, introducir; (hold) contener; (concede) conceder; (acknowledge) reconocer, confesar. **to a. of,** permitir; sufrir

admittance *n* admisión, *f*; entrada, *f*. **No a.!** Prohibida la entrada. **to gain a.,** lograr entrar

admittedly *adv* según opinión general; sin duda

admonish *vt* (advise) aconsejar; amonestar, advertir; (reprimand) reprender

admonition *n* amonestación, *f*; advertencia, *f*; admonición, *f*

admonitory *a* amonestador

ad nauseam *adv* hasta la saciedad

ado *n* (noise) ruido, *m*; (trouble) trabajo, *m*, dificultad, *f*; (fuss) barahúnda, *f*. **much ado about nothing,** mucho ruido y pocas nueces, nada entre dos platos. **without more ado,** sin más ni más

adolescence *n* adolescencia, *f*

adolescent *a* and *n* adolescente, *mf*

adopt *vt* adoptar. **a. local customs** *Lat. Am.* acriollarse

adopted *a* adoptivo

adoption *n* adopción, *f*; (choice) elección, *f*

adoptive *a* adoptivo

adorable *a* adorable

adoration *n* adoración, *f*. **A. of the Magi,** Adoración de los Reyes, *f*

adore *vt* adorar

adorer *n* adorador (-ra); amante, *m*

adoringly *adv* con adoración

adorn *vt* adornar, embellecer; (*fig* of persons) adornar con su presencia

adornment *n* adorno, *m*; ornamento, *m*; embellecimiento, *m*

adrenalin *n* adrenalina, *f*

Adriatic, the el (Mar) Adriático, *m*

adrift *a* and *adv* a merced de las olas; a la ventura. **to turn a.,** *inf* poner de patitas en la calle

adroit *a* hábil

adulate *vt* adular

adulation *n* adulación, *f*

adulatory *a* adulador

adult *a* and *n* adulto (-ta)

adult education *n* educación de los adultos, *f*

adulterate *vt* adulterar; falsificar; contaminar. *a* adulterado; falsificado; impuro

adulteration *n* adulteración, *f*; falsificación, *f*; impureza, *f*; contaminación, *f*

adulterer *n* adúltero, *m*

adulteress *n* adúltera, *f*

adulterous *a* adúltero

adultery *n* adulterio, *m*. **to commit a.,** cometer adulterio, adulterar

advance *n* avance, *m*; (progress) progreso, adelantamiento, *m*; (improvement) mejora, *f*; (of shares) alza, *f*; (of price) subida, *f*; (loan) préstamo, *m*; (in rank) ascenso, *m*; *pl* **advances,** (overtures) avances, *m pl*; (proposals) propuestas, *f pl*; (of love) requerimientos amorosos, *m pl*. **in a.,** de antemano, con anticipación, con tiempo, previamente; (of money) por adelantado. **a. guard,** *mil* avanzada, *f*. **a. payment,** anticipo, *m*, paga por adelantado, *f*

advance *vt* avanzar; (suggest) sugerir, proponer; (encourage) fomentar; (a person) ascender; (improve) mejorar; (of events, dates) adelantar; (of prices, stocks)

hacer subir; (money) anticipar; (of steps) tomar. *vi* avanzar; (progress) progresar; (in rank, studies, etc.) adelantar; (of prices) subir

advanced *a* avanzado; (developed) desarrollado; (mentally, of children) precoz; (course) superior. **a. research,** investigaciones superiores. **a. standing,** equivalencias, *f pl*. **a. views,** ideas avanzadas, *f pl*

advancement *n* adelantamiento, *m*; progreso, *m*; (encouragement) fomento, *m*; (in employment) promoción, *f*; prosperidad, *f*

advancing *a* que avanza; (of years) que pasan

advantage *n* ventaja, *f*; superioridad, *f*; (benefit) provecho, beneficio, *m*; interés, *m*; ocasión favorable, oportunidad, *f*; (tennis) ventaja, *f*. **to have the a. of,** tener la ventaja de. **to show to a.,** embellecer, realzar; aumentar la belleza (etc.) de. **to take a. of,** sacar ventaja de, aprovecharse de; (deceive) engañar. **to take a. of the slightest pretext,** asirse de un cabello

advantageous *a* ventajoso, provechoso. **to be a.,** ser de provecho

advent *n* advenimiento, *m*, llegada, *f*; *ecc* Adviento, *m*

adventitious *a* adventicio (all uses)

adventure *n* aventura, *f*; riesgo, *m*; (chance) casualidad, *f*; *com* especulación, *f*, *vt* aventurar, arriesgar. *vi* arriesgarse, osar

adventurer *n* aventurero, *m*; (one living by his wits) caballero de industria, *m*; (in commerce) especulador, *m*

adventuresome *a* de aventura

adventuress *n* aventurera, *f*

adventurous *a* aventurero; osado, audaz; (dangerous) peligroso, arriesgado

adverb *n* adverbio, *m*

adversary *n* adversario (-ia)

adverse *a* adverso; hostil (a); malo; desfavorable; (opposite) opuesto

adversity *n* adversidad, *f*

advertise *vt* anunciar. *vi* poner un anuncio; (oneself) llamar la atención

advertisement *n* anuncio, *m*; (poster) cartel, *m*; (to attract attention) reclamo, *m*. **to put an a. in the paper,** poner un anuncio en el periódico. **a. hoarding,** cartelera, *f*

advertiser *n* anunciante, *mf*

advertising *n* anuncios, *m pl*; publicidad, propaganda, *f*; medios publicitarios, *m pl*

advice *n* consejo, *m*; (warning) advertencia, amonestación, *f*; (news) noticia, *f*, aviso, *m*; *com* comunicación, *f*; (belief) parecer, *m*, opinión, *f*. **piece of a.,** consejo, *m*. **to follow the a. of,** seguir los consejos de. **to give a.,** dar consejos

advisability *n* conveniencia, *f*; prudencia, *f*

advisable *a* conveniente, aconsejable; prudente

advise *vt* aconsejar; (inform) avisar, informar

advised *a* avisado; premeditado. **ill-a.,** mal aconsejado; imprudente. **well-a.,** bien aconsejado; prudente

adviser *n* consejero (-ra)

advisory *a* asesor, consultivo, consultativo

advocacy *n* defensa, *f*; apología, *f*; abogacía, intercesión, *f*

advocate *n* *law* abogado (-da); defensor (-ra); (champion) campeón, *m*. *vt* abogar, defender; sostener, apoyar; recomendar

adze *n* azuela, *f*

Aegean, the el (Mar) Egeo, *m*

aegis *n* égida, *f*; protección, *f*

aerated *a* aerado; (of lemonade, etc.) gaseoso. **a. waters,** aguas gaseosas, *f pl*

aeration *n* aeración, *f*

aerial *a* aéreo, de aire; etéreo; fantástico. *n* (radio) antena, *f*. **indoor a.,** antena interior, *f*

aerobics *n* aerobismo *m*

aerodynamics *n* aerodinámica, *f*

aeronaut *n* aeronauta, *mf*

aeronautical *a* aeronáutico

aeronautics *n* aeronáutica, *f*

afar *adv* a lo lejos, en la distancia. **from a.,** desde lejos

affability *n* afabilidad, condescendencia, urbanidad, *f*

affable *a* afable, condescendiente

affably *adv* afablemente

affair *n* asunto, *m*, cosa, *f*; cuestión, *f*; (business) negocio, *m*; (*fam* applied to a machine, carriage, etc.) artefacto, *m*; (of the heart) amorío, *m*. **a. of honour,** lance de honor, *m*

affect *vt* afectar; influir; *med* atacar; (move) impresionar, conmover; enternecer; (harm) perjudicar; (frequent) frecuentar; (like) gustar de; (love) amar; (wear) vestir; (use) gastar, usar; (feign) aparentar; (boast) hacer alarde de

affectation *n* afectación, *f*

affected *a* afectado; influido; *med* atacado; (moved) conmovido, impresionado; enternecido; (inclined) dispuesto, inclinado; (artificial) artificioso; amanerado, afectado; (of style) rebuscado, artificial

affecting *a* conmovedor, emocionante

affection *n* afecto, cariño, *m*; amor, *m*; apego, *m*; simpatía, *f*; (emotion) emoción, *f*, sentimiento, *m*; *med* afección, enfermedad, *f*

affectionate *a* afectuoso, cariñoso; mimoso; (tender) tierno; expresivo

affectionately *adv* afectuosamente. **Yours a.,** tu cariñoso . . . , tu . . . , que te quiere

affective *a* afectivo

affidavit *n* declaración jurada, declaración jurídica *f*, atestiguación, *f*

affiliate *vt* afiliar; adoptar; *law* imputar; *law* legitimar

affiliation *n* afiliación, *f*; adopción, *f*; legitimación de un hijo, *f*

affinity *n* afinidad, *f*

affirm *vt* afirmar, aseverar, declarar; confirmar. *vi law* declarar ante un juez

affirmation *n* afirmación, aserción, *f*; confirmación, *f*; *law* declaración, deposición, *f*

affirmative *a* afirmativo. *n* afirmativa, *f*

affix *vt* fijar; pegar; añadir; (seal, one's signature) poner. *n gram* afijo, *m*

afflict *vt* afligir, atormentar, aquejar

affliction *n* aflicción, *f*; tribulación, pesadumbre, *f*; calamidad, *f*; miseria, *f*; (ailment) achaque, *m*

affluence *n* afluencia, *f*; abundancia, *f*; riqueza, *f*; opulencia, *f*

affluent *a* abundante; rico; opulento

afflux *n* afluencia, *f*; *med* aflujo, *m*

afford *vt* dar, proporcionar; producir; ofrecer; (bear) soportar; poder con; (financially) tener medios para; permitirse el lujo de; (be able) poder. **I could not a. to pay so much,** No puedo (podía) pagar tanto

afforest *vt* convertir en bosque

afforestation *n* conversión en bosque, *f*; plantación de un bosque, *f*

affray *n* riña, refriega, *f*

affront *n* afrenta, *f*, insulto, agravio, *m*. *vt* insultar, ultrajar, afrentar; (offend) ofender

Afghan *a* and *n* afgano (-na)

Afghanistan Afganistán, *m*

afield *adv* en el campo; lejos. **to go far a.,** ir muy lejos

afire *adv* en fuego, en llamas; *fig* ardiendo

aflame *adv* en llamas; *fig* encendido

afloat *adv* a flote; *naut* a bordo; (solvent) solvente; en circulación; (floating) flotante; (swamped) inundado; (in full swing) en marcha, en movimiento

afoot *adv* a pie; en marcha, en movimiento; en preparación. **to set a.,** iniciar, poner en marcha

aforementioned *a* antedicho, ya mencionado

aforesaid *a* consabido, dicho, susodicho

afraid *a* espantado; temeroso, miedoso. **I'm a. that . . . ,** Me temo que. . . . **to be a.,** tener miedo. **to make a.,** dar miedo (a)

afresh *adv* de nuevo, otra vez

African *a* and *n* africano (-na)

aft *adv* en popa; a popa. **fore and aft,** de proa a popa

after *prep* (of place) detrás de; (of time) después de; (behind) en pos de; (following) tras; (in spite of) a pesar de; (in consequence of) después de, a consecuencia de; (in accordance with) según; (in the style of) al estilo de, en imitación de. *adv* (later) después, más tarde; (subsequently) después (que); (when) cuando, a futuro, venidero. **day a. day,** día tras día. **on the day a.,** al día siguiente. **soon a.,** poco después. **to look a.,** cuidar de. **to go a.,** ir a buscar; seguir. **the day a. tomorrow,** pasado mañana. **What are you a.?** ¿Qué buscas? **a. all,** después de todo. **a. the manner of,** a la moda de, según la moda; al estilo de. **a.-dinner conversation,** conversación de sobremesa, *f*. **a. glow,** resplandor crepuscular, reflejo del sol poniente en el cielo, *m*. **a. life,** vida futura, *f*. **a. pains,** dolores de sobreparto, *m pl*. **a. taste,** dejo, resabio, *m*

afterbirth *n* placenta, *f*

aftermath *n* consecuencias, *f pl*, resultado, *m*

afternoon *n* tarde, *f*. **Good a.!** ¡Buenas tardes! **a. nap,** siesta, *f*. **a. tea,** el té de las cinco

afterthought *n* reflexión tardía, *f*; segunda intención, *f*. **to have an a.,** pensar en segundo lugar

afterwards *adv* después; más tarde

again *adv* (once more) otra vez, de neuvo; por segunda vez, dos veces; (on the other hand) por otra parte; (moreover) además; (likewise) también; (returned) de vuelta. Sometimes translated by prefix **re** in verbs. **as much a.,** otro tanto. **never a.,** nunca más. **not a.,** no más. **now and a.,** de vez en cuando. **to do a.,** volver a hacer, hacer de nuevo. **a. and a.,** repetidas veces

against *prep* (facing) enfrente de; contra; (in preparation for) para; (contrary to) contrario a; (opposed to) opuesto a; (near) cerca de. **a.,** oponer; estar enfrente de. **a. the grain,** a contrapelo

agate *n* ágata, *f*; heliotropo, *m*

age *n* edad, *f*; (generation) generación, *f*; (epoch) siglo, período, *m*; época, *f*; (old age) vejez, *f*; (majority) mayoría de edad, *f*, *vi* envejecer. **at any age,** a cualquier edad. **the golden age,** la edad de oro; (in literature, etc.) el siglo de oro. **from age to age,** por los siglos de los siglos. **to be of age,** ser mayor de edad. **to be under age,** ser menor de edad. **to come of age,** llegar a la mayoría de edad. **She is six years of age,** Ella tiene seis años. **age-old,** secular

aged *a* de la edad de; (old) anciano, viejo. **a girl a. four,** una niña de cuatro años

ageless *a* siempre joven; eterno

agency *n* órgano, *m*, fuerza, *f*; acción, *f*; influencia, *f*; intervención, *f*; mediación, *f*; *com* agencia, *f*. **through the a. of,** por la mediación (or influencia) de

agenda *n* agenda, *f*

agent *n* agente, *m*; *com* representante, *mf*; *law* apoderado (-da). **business a.,** agente de negocios, *m*

agglomerate *vt* and *vi* aglomerar(se)

agglomeration *n* aglomeración, *f*

agglutinate *vt* and *vi* aglutinar(se)

aggrandize *vt* engrandecer

aggrandizement *n* engrandecimiento, *m*

aggravate *vt* agravar, hacer peor; intensificar; (annoy) irritar, exasperar

aggravating *a* agravante, agravador; (tiresome) molesto; (annoying) irritante. **a. circumstance,** circunstancia agravante, *f*

aggravation *n* agravación, *f*, intensificación, *f*; (annoyance) irritación, *f*

aggregate *a* total. *n* agregado, conjunto, *m*. **in the a.,** en conjunto

aggression *n* agresión, *f*

aggressive *a* agresivo

aggressiveness *n* carácter agresivo, *m*, belicosidad, *f*

aggressor *n* and *n* agresor (-ra)

aggrieved *a* afligido; ofendido; lastimero

aghast *a* horrorizado, espantado; (amazed) estupefacto

agile *a* ágil; ligero, *Mexico* alacre; vivo

agility *n* agilidad, *f*; ligereza, *f*, *Mexico* alacridad *f*

agitate *vt* agitar; excitar; inquietar, perturbar; discutir. **to a. for,** luchar por; excitar la opinión pública en favor de

agitating *a* agitador

agitation *n* agitación, *f*; perturbación, *f*; discusión, *f*

agitator *n* agitador (-ra); (apparatus) agitador, *m*

aglow *a* and *adv* brillante, fulgente; encendido

agnostic *a* and *n* agnóstico (-ca)

agnosticism *n* agnosticismo, *m*

ago *adv* hace. **a short while ago,** hace poco. **How long ago?** ¿Cuánto tiempo hace? **long ago,** hace mucho. **many years ago,** hace muchos años. **I last saw him ten years ago,** La última vez que le vi fue hace diez años

agog *a* agitado; ansioso; excitado; impaciente; curioso. *adv* con agitación; con ansia; con curiosidad

agonize *vt* atormentar. *vi* sufrir intensamente; retorcerse de dolor

agonizing *a* (of pain) intenso, atormentador

agonizingly *adv* dolorosamente

agony *n* agonía, *f*; angustia, *f*; paroxismo, *m*. **a. column,** columna de los suspiros, *f*

agrarian *a* agrario

agree *vi* estar de acuerdo. **Do you a. or disagree?** ¿Coincides o discrepas?; convenir (en); acordar; ponerse de acuerdo, entenderse; (suit) sentar bien, probar; (consent) consentir (en); *gram* concordar, (get on well) llevarse bien; (correspond) estar conforme (con). **to a. to,** convenir en, consentir en. **to a. with,** estar de acuerdo con, apoyar; dar la razón a; (suit) sentar bien; *gram* concordar

agreeable *a* agradable; afable, amable; (pleasant) ameno, grato; conforme; dispuesto a (hacer algo); conveniente

agreeableness *n* (of persons) afabilidad, amabilidad, *f*; amenidad, *f*; deleite, *m*; conformidad, *f*

agreeably *adv* agradablemente; de acuerdo (con), conforme (a)

agreed *a* convenido, acordado; (approved) aprobado. *interj* ¡convenido! ¡de acuerdo!

agreement *n* acuerdo, *m*; pacto, *m*; acomodamiento, concierto, *m*; contrato, *m*; *com* convenio, *m*; conformidad, *f*; consentimiento, *m*; *gram* concordancia, *f*. **in a.,** conforme. **in a. with,** de acuerdo con; según. **to reach an a.,** ponerse de acuerdo

agricultural *a* agrícola. **a. engineer,** ingeniero agrónomo, *m*. **a. laborer,** labriego, *m*. **a. show,** exposición agrícola, *f*

agriculturalist *n* agrícola, *mf*

agriculture *n* agricultura, *f*

agronomist *n* agrónomo, *m*

agronomy *n* agronomía, *f*

aground *adv naut* varado, encallado. **running a.,** varada, *f*. **to run a.,** varar

ague *n* fiebre intermitente, *f*; *fig* escalofrío, *m*

ah! *interj* ¡ah! ¡ay!

aha! *interj* ¡ajá!

ahead *adv* delante; enfrente; al frente (de); a la cabeza (de); adelante; hacia delante; *naut* por la proa. **Go a.!** ¡Adelante! **It is straight a.,** Está directamente enfrente. **to go straight a.,** ir hacia delante; seguir (haciendo algo)

ahoy! *interj* ¡ah del barco!

aid *n* ayuda, *f*; socorro, auxilio, *m*; subsidio, *m*, *vt* ayudar; socorrer, auxiliar. **in aid of,** pro, en beneficio de. **first aid,** primera cura, *f*. **first aid post,** puesto de socorro, *m*. **to come or go to the aid of,** acudir en defensa de

aide-de-camp *n* edecán, *m*

AIDS *n* el SIDA, *m*

ail *vt* afligir, doler; pasar. *vi* estar indispuesto (or enfermo). **What ails me?** *inf* ¿Qué me pasa?

ailing *a* enfermizo, enclenque, achacoso

ailment *n* enfermedad, *f*, dolencia, *f*

aim *n* (of firearms) puntería, *f*; (mark) blanco, *m*; *fig* objeto, fin, *m*; *fig* intención, *f*, propósito, *m*, *vt* (a gun) apuntar; dirigir; (throw) lanzar; (a blow) asestar. *vi* apuntar (a); (a remark at) decir por; aspirar (a); intentar, proponerse. **Is your remark aimed at me?** ¿Lo

dices por mí? **to aim high,** apuntar alto; *inf* picar alto.

to miss one's aim, errar el tiro. **to take aim,** apuntar.

with the aim of, con objeto de, a fin de

aimless *a* aimlessly, *adv* sin objeto, a la ventura

air *n* aire, *m*, (all meanings). **by air,** en avión; (of mail) por avión; (of goods) por vía aérea. **in the air,** al aire; al aire libre; (as though flying) en volandas. **in the open air,** al aire libre, al fresco, a la intemperie. **to be on the air,** *rad* hablar por radio. **to give oneself airs,** darse tono, tener humos. **to take the air,** tomar el fresco; despegar. **air balloon,** globo aerostático, *m*; (toy) globo, *m*. **air-base,** base aérea, *f*. **air-bed,** colchón de viento, *m*. **air-borne (to become),** levantar el vuelo, despegar. **air-brake,** *mech* freno neumático, *m*. **air-chamber,** cámara de aire, *f*. **air chief marshal,** general del ejército del aire, *m*. **air-cock,** válvula de escape de aire, *f*. **air commodore,** general de brigada de aviación, *m*. **air conditioning,** purificación de aire, *f*. *Lat. Am.* aclimación, **air-cooled,** enfriado por aire. **air crash,** accidente de aviación, *m*. **air current,** corriente de aire, *m*. **air-cushion,** almohadilla neumática, *f*. **air-field,** campo de aviación, *m*. **air fleet,** flotilla aérea, *f*. **air force,** fuerza aérea, flota aérea, *f*. **air-gun,** escopeta de viento, *f*. **air-hole,** respiradero, *m*. **air-hostess,** azafata, *f*. **air-lift,** puente aéreo, *m*. **air-liner,** avión de pasajeros, *m*. **airline** línea aérea, aerolínea, *f*. **airmail,** correo aéreo, *m*. **by airmail,** por avión. **air marshal,** teniente general de aviación, *m*. **air-pocket,** bolsa (or vacío, *m*) de aire, *f*. **air pollution** contaminación atmosférica, *f*. **air pump,** bomba neumática, *f*. **air raid,** bombardeo aéreo, *m*. **air-raid shelter,** refugio antiaéreo, *m*. **air-raid warning,** alarma aérea, *f*. **air-route,** vía aérea, *f*. **air-screw,** hélice de avión, *f*. **air-shaft,** respiradero de mina, *m*. **air shuttle,** puente aéreo, *m*. **air squadron,** escuadrilla aérea, *f*. **air stream,** chorro de aire, *m*. **air taxi,** avión taxi, *m*. **air-tight,** herméticamente cerrado. **air valve,** válvula de aire, *f*. **air vice-marshal,** general de división de aviación, *m*

air *vt* airear, orear; secar al aire; ventilar; *fig* sacar a lucir; emitir; *fig* ostentar

aircraft *n* aparato, avión, *m*. **a. barrage,** cortina de fuego de artillería, *f*. **a.-carrier,** porta-aviones, *m*. **a. factory,** fábrica de aeroplanos, *f*

airily *adv* ligeramente, sin preocuparse; alegremente

airiness *n* airosidad, *f*; ventilación, *f*; situación airosa, *f*; (lightness) ligereza, *f*; alegría, *f*; frivolidad, *f*

airing *n* aireación, *f*; ventilación, *f*; secamiento, *m*; (walk) vuelta, *f*, paseo, *m*. **to take an a.,** dar una vuelta

airless *a* sin aire; falto de ventilación; sofocante

airman *n* aviador, *m*

airplane *n* aeroplano, avión, *m*. **jet-propelled a.,** aeroplano de reacción, *m*. **model a.,** aeroplano en miniatura, *m*

airport *n* aeropuerto, *m*

airsick *a* mareado en el aire, mareado

airway *n* vía aérea, *f*

airwoman *n* aviadora, *f*

airy *a* aéreo; (breezy) airoso; ligero; vaporoso; alegre; (vain) vano; (flippant) frívolo

aisle *n* nave lateral, ala, *f*

ajar *a* entreabierto, entornado. **to leave a.,** dejar entreabierto, entornar

akimbo *adv* en jarras. **with arms a.,** con los brazos en jarras

akin *a* consanguíneo, emparentado; análogo, relacionado; semejante

alabaster *n* alabastro, *m*, *a* alabastrino

alacrity *n* alacridad, *f*

alarm *n* alarma, *f*; toque de alarma, *m*; (tocsin) rebato, *m*; sobresalto, *m*, alarma, *f*. *vt* alarmar; *mil* dar la alarma (a); asustar. **to give the a.,** dar la alarma. **a. bell,** timbre de alarma, *m*. **a. clock,** despertador, *m*. **a. signal,** señal de alarma, *f*

alarming *a* alarmante

alarmingly *adv* de un modo alarmante; espantosamente
alarmist *n* alarmista, *mf*
alas! *interj* ¡ay!
alb *n* alba, *f*
Albanian *a* and *n* albanés (-esa); (language) albanés, *m*
albatross *n* albatros, *m*
albeit *conjunc* aunque, si bien; sin embargo
albinism *n* albinismo, *m*
albino *a* albino
album *n* álbum, *m*
albumin *n* albúmina, *f*
alchemist *n* alquimista, *m*
alchemy *n* alquimia, *f*
alcohol *n* alcohol, *m*. **industrial a.,** alcohol desnaturalizado, *m*. **wood a.,** alcohol metílico, alcohol de madera, *m*
alcoholic *a* alcohólico
alcoholism *n* alcoholismo, *m*
alcoholize *vt* alcoholizar
alcove *n* alcoba, *f*; nicho, *m*
alder *n* (tree and wood) aliso, *m*
alderman *n* concejal, *m*
ale *n* cerveza, *f*. **ale-house,** cervecería, *f*
alert *a* alerto; vigilante; despierto; vivo. *n* sirena, *f*. **to be on the a.,** estar sobre aviso; estar vigilante
alertly *adv* alertamente
alertness *n* vigilancia, *f*; viveza, *f*; prontitud, *f*
Alexandria Alejandría, *f*
alga *n* alga, *f*
algebra *n* álgebra, *f*
algebraic *a* algebraico
Algeria Argelia, *f*
Algerian *a* and *n* argelino (-na)
Algiers Argel, *m*
alias *adv* alias, por otro nombre. *n* nombre falso, seudónimo, *m*
alibi *n law* coartada, *f*. **to prove an a.,** probar la coartada
alien *a* ajeno; (foreign) extranjero; extraño; contrario. *n* extranjero (-ra). **a. to,** ajeno a; repugnante a. **Aliens Department,** Sección de Extranjeros, *f*
alienable *a* enajenable
alienate *vt* alejar, hacer indiferente; (property) enajenar, traspasar
alienation *n* desvío, *m*; enajenación, *f*; traspaso, *m*; enajenación mental, *f*
alight *vi* apearse (de), bajar (de); desmontar (de); (of birds, etc.) posarse (sobre)
alight *a* encendido, iluminado; en llamas
align *vt* alinear
alignment *n* alineación, *f*
alike *a* semejante; igual. *adv* del mismo modo; igualmente
alimentary *a* nutritivo; alimenticio. **a. canal,** tubo digestivo, *m*
alimentation *n* alimentación, *f*
alimony *n law* alimentos, *m pl*, pensión alimenticia, *f*
alive *a* viviente; vivo; del mundo; (busy) animado, concurrido; (aware) sensible; (alert) lleno de vida, enérgico, despierto. **He is still a.,** Aún vive. **He is the best man a.,** Es el mejor hombre que existe, Es el mejor hombre del mundo. **half-a.,** semivivo. **while a.,** en vida. **a. to,** consciente de, sensible de. **a. with,** plagado de, lleno de
alkali *n* álcali, *m*
alkaline *a* alcalino
alkaloid *n* alcaloide, *m*
all *a* todo; toda, *f*; todos, *m pl*; todas, *f pl*; (in games) iguales. *adv* enteramente, completamente; del todo; absolutamente. **after all,** después de todo; sin embargo. **at all,** nada; de ninguna manera; en absoluto. **fifteen all,** (tennis) quince iguales. **for good and all,** para siempre. **if that's all,** si no es más que eso. **in all,** en conjunto. **It is all one to me,** Me da igual. **not at all,** de ningún modo, nada de eso; nada; (never) jamás;

(as a polite formula) No hay de qué. **once for all,** una vez por todas; por última vez. **That is all,** Eso es todo. **all along,** (of time) siempre, todo el tiempo; (of place) a lo largo de, de un extremo a otro de. **all but,** (almost) casi, por poco; (except) todo menos. **all joking aside,** fuera de burla. **all of them,** todos ellos, *m pl*; todas ellas, *f pl*. **All right!** ¡Bien! ¡Está bien! ¡Entendido! **all that,** todo eso; (as much as) cuanto. **all that which,** todo lo que. **all those who,** todos los que, *m pl*; todas las que, *f pl*. **all the more,** cuanto más. **all the same,** sin embargo, a pesar de todo. **all the worse,** tanto peor
all *n* todo, *m*; todos, *m pl*; todas, *f pl*; (everyone, all men) todo el mundo. **to lose one's all,** perder todo lo que se tiene. **All is lost,** Todo se ha perdido. **all told,** en conjunto
all (*in compounds*) **all-absorbing,** que todo lo absorbe; sumamente interesante. **all-bountiful,** de suma bondad. **all-conquering,** invicto. **all-consuming,** que todo lo consume; irresistible; ardiente. **all-enduring,** resignado a todo. **All Fools' Day,** Día de los Inocentes, *m*, (December 28). **all-fours,** a cuatro patas; a gatas. **to go on all fours,** andar a gatas. **All hail!** ¡Salud! ¡Bienvenido! **all-important,** sumamente importante. **all-in insurance,** seguro contra todo riesgo, *m*. **all-in wrestling,** lucha libre, *f*. **all-loving,** de un amor infinito. **all-merciful,** de una compasión infinita, sumamente misericordioso. **all-powerful,** omnipotente, todo poderoso. **all-round,** completo, cabal; universal. **an all-round athlete,** un atleta completo. **All Souls' Day,** Día de las Ánimas, Día de los difuntos, *m*. **all-wise,** omniscio
allay *vt* calmar; (relieve) aliviar; apaciguar
allaying *n* alivio, *m*; apaciguamiento, *m*
allegation *n* alegación, *f*
allege *vt* afirmar, declarar; alegar
allegiance *n* lealtad, *f*; fidelidad, *f*; obediencia, *f*
allegorical *a* alegórico
allegory *n* alegoría, *f*
alleluia *n* aleluya, *m*
allergic *a* alérgico
allergist *n* alergólogo, *m*
allergy *n* alergia, *f*
alleviate *vt* aliviar
alleviation *n* alivio, *m*; mitigación, *f*
alley *n* callejuela, *f*, callejón, *m*; avenida, *f*; (skittle a.) pista de bolos, *f*. **a.-way,** *naut* pasadizo, *m*
alliance *n* alianza, *f*; parentesco, *m*
allied *a* aliado; allegado
alligator *n* caimán, *m*. **a. pear,** avocado, *Mexico* aquacate *m*
alliteration *n* aliteración, *f*
allocate *vt* asignar, destinar; distribuir, repartir
allocation *n* asignación, *f*; distribución, *f*, repartimiento, *m*
allotment *n* repartimiento, *m*, distribución, *f*; porción, *f*; lote, *m*; parcela de tierra, huerta, *f*
allow *vt* permitir; autorizar; dejar; tolerar, sufrir; (provide) dar; conceder, otorgar; (acknowledge) admitir; confesar; (discount) descontar; (a pension) hacer; deducir. **to a. for,** tener en cuenta; ser indulgente con; deducir; dejar (espacio, etc.) para
allowable *a* admisible, permisible; lícito, legítimo
allowance *n* ración, *f*; (discount) descuento, *m*; pensión, *f*; concesión, *f*; excusa, *f*; (subsidy) subsidio, *m*; (bonus) abono, *m*; (monthly) mesada, *f*. **to make a. for,** tener presente; hacer excusas para, ser indulgente con
alloy *n* aleación, *f*; liga, *f*; mezcla, *f*. *vt* alear, ligar; mezclar
allspice *n* guindilla de Indias, *f*
all-star game *n* juego de estrellas, *m*
allude *vi* aludir (a), referirse (a)
allure *vt* convidar, provocar; atraer; seducir, fascinar
allurement *n* (snare) añagaza, *f*; atracción, *f*; tentación, seducción, *f*

alluring *a* atractivo, seductor, tentador; (promising) halagüeño

allusion *n* alusión, referencia, *f;* insinuación, *f*

allusive *a* alusivo

ally *n* aliado (-da), allegado (-da); asociado (-da); (state) aliado, *m. vt* unir. **to become allies,** aliarse

almanac *n* almanaque, *m*

almighty *a* omnipotente

almond *n* almendra, *f;* (tree) almendro, *m.* **bitter a.,** almendra amarga, *f.* **green a.,** almendruco, *m.* **milk of almonds,** horchata de almendras, *f;* (for the hands) loción de almendras, *f.* **sugar a.,** almendra garapiñada, *f.* **a.-eyed,** con, or de, ojos rasgados. **a. paste,** pasta de almendras, *f.* **a.-shaped,** en forma de almendra, almendrado

almoner *n* limosnero (-ra) *mf*

almost *adv* casi; por poco

alms *n* limosna, *f.* **to ask a.,** pedir limosna, mendigar. **to give a.,** dar limosna. **a.-box,** cepillo de limosna, *m*

almsgiving *n* caridad, *f*

aloe *n* áloe, *m; pl* **aloes,** *med* acíbar, *m*

aloft *adv* arriba, en alto

alone *a* solo; solitario. *adv* a solas, sin compañía; solamente; únicamente. **to leave a.,** dejar solo; dejar en paz

along *adv* adelante; a lo largo; todo el tiempo. *prep* a lo largo de; por; al lado (de); en compañía (de). **Come a.!** ¡Ven! **all a.,** todo el tiempo, desde el principio; a lo largo de. **a. with,** junto con; en compañía de

alongside *adv* al lado; *naut* al costado. *prep* junto a, al lado de; *naut* al costado de. **to bring a.,** *naut* abarloar. **to come a.,** *naut* acostarse

aloof *adv* a distancia; lejos. *a* altanero, esquivo; reservado. **to keep a.,** mantenerse alejado

aloofness *n* alejamiento, *m;* esquivez, *f;* reserva, *f*

aloud *adv* en alta voz, alto

alpaca *n* alpaca, *f*

alphabet *n* alfabeto, *m;* abecedario, *m*

alphabetical *a* alfabético

Alpine *a* alpestre, alpino

Alps, the los Alpes, *m*

already *adv* ya; previamente

Alsatian *a* and *n* alsaciano (-na†). **A. dog,** perro policía, perro pastor alemán, perro lobo, *m*

also *adv* también, igualmente, además

altar *n* altar, *m.* **high a.,** altar mayor, *m.* **to lead a woman to the a.,** llevar a una mujer a la iglesia. **a.-cloth,** mantel del altar, *m.* **a.-piece,** retablo, *m.* **a.-rail,** mesa del altar, *f*

altar boy *n* acólito, monaguillo, *m*

altar girl *n* acólita, monaguilla, *f*

altar server *n* acólito, monaguillo, *m* (male), acólita, monaguilla, *f* (female)

alter *vt* cambiar; alterar; modificar; corregir; transformar; (clothes) arreglar. *vi* cambiar

alterable *a* alterable

alteration *n* cambio, *m,* alteración, *f;* modificación, *f;* corrección, *f;* innovación, *f;* (to buildings, etc.) reforma, *f;* renovación, *f;* arreglo, *m*

altercation *n* altercación, *f*

alternate *a* alternativo; (*bot* and of rhymes) alterno. *vt* and *vi* alternar

alternately *adv* alternativamente; por turno

alternating *a* alternador. **a. current,** *elec* corriente alterna, *f*

alternation *n* alternación, *f;* (of time) transcurso, *m;* turno, *m*

alternative *n* alternativa, *f, a* alternativo, alterno. **to have no a. but,** no poder menos de

alternatively *adv* alternativamente

alternator *n elec* alternador, *m*

although *conjunc* aunque, bien que; si bien; no obstante, a pesar de

altimeter *n aer* altímetro, *m*

altitude *n* altitud, elevación, *f;* altura, *f*

alto *n* (voice) contralto, *m;* (singer) contralto, *mf;* viola, *f*

altogether *adv* completamente; del todo; en conjunto

alto-relievo *n* alto relieve, *m*

altruism *n* altruísmo, *m*

altruist *n* altruista, *mf*

aluminum *n* aluminio, *m*

aluminum foil *n* hoja de aluminio, *f*

alumnus *n Lat. Am.* exalumno *m.*

alumna *n Lat. Am.* exalumna *f*

always *adv* siempre

amalgam *n* amalgama, *f;* mezcla, *f*

amalgamate *vt* amalgamar; combinar, unir. *vi* amalgamarse; combinarse, unirse

amalgamation *n* amalgamación, *f;* combinación, *f;* mezcla, *f*

amanuensis *n* amanuense, *mf;* secretario (-ia)

amass *vt* acumular, amontonar

amateur *a* and *n* aficionado (-da), (sports) no profesional. **a. theatricals,** función de aficionados, *f* **a. band** *Mexico* escoleta *f*

amateurish *a* no profesional; de aficionado; superficial; (clumsy) torpe

amatory *a* amatorio

amaze *vt* asombrar, sorprender; pasmar; confundir

amazed *a* asombrado; sorprendido; admirado; asustado

amazement *n* asombro, pasmo, *m;* sorpresa, *f;* (wonderment) admiración, *f;* estupor, *m*

amazing *a* asombroso, pasmoso; sorprendente

amazingly *adv* asombrosamente

Amazon *n* amazona, *f*

Amazon River, the el (Río de las) Amazonas, *m*

ambassador *n* embajador, *m*

ambassadress *n* embajadora, *f*

amber *n* ámbar, *m, a* ambarino

ambidextrous *a* ambidextro

ambiguity *n* ambigüedad, *f*

ambiguous *a* ambiguo, equivoco

ambition *n* ambición, *f*

ambitious *a* ambicioso. **to be a. to,** ambicionar

amble *n* (of a horse) paso de andadura, *m;* paso lento, *m. vi* (of a horse) andar a paso de andadura; andar lentamente

ambulance *n* ambulancia, *f.* **a. corps,** cuerpo de sanidad, *m.* **a. man,** sanitario, *m*

ambulatory *n* paseo, *m;* claustro, *m, a* ambulante

ambush *n* acecho, *m,* asechanza, *f; mil* emboscada, *f. vt* acechar, asechar; *mil* emboscar; sorprender. **to be in a.,** emboscarse, estar en acecho

amelioration *n* mejora, *f*

amen *n* amén, *m*

amenable *n* sujeto (a); responsable; dócil; fácil de convencer, dispuesto a ser razonable; dispuesto a escuchar. **to make a. to reason,** hacer razonable

amend *vt* enmendar; modificar. *vi* reformarse

amendment *n* enmienda, *f;* modificación, *f*

amends *n pl* reparación, *f;* satisfacción, *f;* compensación, *f.* **to make a.,** dar satisfacción

amenity *n* amenidad, *f*

America América, *f*

American *n* americano (-na); (U.S.A.) norteamericano (-na). *a* americano, de América; norteamericano, de los Estados Unidos. **Central A.,** *a* and *n* centroamericano (-na). **A. bar,** bar americano, *m*

Americanism *n* americanismo, *m*

Americanize *vt* americanizar

amethyst *n* amatista, *f*

amiability *n* amabilidad, afabilidad, cordialidad, *f*

amiable *a* amable, afable, cordial

amiably *adv* amablemente, con afabilidad

amianthus *n* amianto, *m*

amicable *a* amigable, amistoso

amice *n* amito, *m*

amid, amidst *prep* en medio de; entre; rodeado por

amidships *adv* en el centro del buque, en medio del navío

amiss *adv* mal; de más; (ill) indispuesto, enfermo;

(inopportunely) inoportunamente. *a* malo. **It would not come a.,** No vendría mal. **to take a.,** llevar a mal

ammeter *n elec* amperímetro, *m*

ammonia *n* amoníaco, *m*

ammoniacal *a* amoniacal

ammunition *n* munición, *f.* **a. box,** cajón de municiones, *m*

amnesia *n* amnesia, *f*

amnesty *n* amnistía, *f.* **to concede an a. to,** amnistiar

amok (to run a.) atacar a ciegas

among *prep* en medio de; entre; con

amoral *a* amoral

amorality *n* amoralidad, *f*

amorous *a* amoroso; (tender) tierno

amorousness *n* erotismo, *m*; galantería, *f*

amorphous *a* amorfo

amortization *n* amorcización, *f*

amortize *vt* amortizar

amount *n* importe, *m*, suma, *f*; cantidad, *f, vi* (to) subir a, ascender a, llegar a; valer; reducirse a. **gross a.**, importe bruto, *m*. **net a.**, importe líquido, importe neto, *m*. **It amounts to the same thing, then,** Es igual entonces, Viene a ser lo mismo pues. **What he says amounts to this,** Lo que dice se reduce a esto

amperage *n* amperaje, *m*

ampere *n* amper, amperio, *m*

amphibian *n* anfibio, *m*

amphibious *a* anfibio

amphitheater *n* anfiteatro, *m*

amphora *n* ánfora, *f*

ample *a* amplio; abundante; extenso, vasto; (sufficient) bastante, suficiente

amplification *n* amplificación, *f*

amplifier *n* amplificador, *m*

amplify *vt* amplificar; aumentar, ampliar

amplitude *n* amplitud, *f*; abundancia, *f*; extensión, *f*

amply *adv* ampliamente; abundantemente; suficientemente

amputate *vt* amputar

amputation *n* amputación, *f*

amulet *n* amuleto, *m*

amuse *vt* divertir, entretener, distraer. **to a. oneself,** divertirse; pasarlo bien

amusement *n* diversión, *f*, entretenimiento, *m*; (hobby) pasatiempo, *m*. **a. park,** parque de atracciones, *m*

amusing *a* divertido, entretenido; (of people) salado

amusingly *adv* de un modo divertido, entretenidamente

an. See **a**

Anabaptism *n* anabaptismo, *m*

Anabaptist *n* anabaptista, *mf*

anachronism *n* anacronismo, *m*

anachronistic *a* anacrónico

anagram *n* anagrama, *m*

analects *n pl* analectas, *f pl*

analgesia *n* analgesia, *f*

analgesic *a* and *n* analgésico, *m.*

analogous *a* análogo

analogy *n* analogía, *f*

analyse *vt* analizar

analysis *n* análisis, *m*

analyst *n* analista, *mf*

analytical *a* analítico

anaphora *n* anáfora, *f*

anaphrodisiac *a* anafrodisíaco

anarchic *a* anárquico

anarchism *n* anarquismo, *m*

anarchist *n* anarquista, *mf*

anarchy *n* anarquía, *f*

anastigmatic *a* anastigmático

anathema *n* anatema, *mf*

anathematize *vt* anatematizar

anatomic *a* anatómico

anatomically *adv* anatómicamente; físicamente

anatomist *n* anatomista, *mf*

anatomy *n* anatomía, *f*

ancestor *n* antepasado, abuelo, *m*

ancestral *a* de sus antepasados; de familia; hereditario. **a. home,** casa solariega, *f*

ancestry *n* antepasados, *m pl*; linaje, abolengo, *m*; estirpe, *f*; nacimiento, *m*; origen, *m*

anchor *n* ancla, *f. fig* áncora, *f. vt* sujetar con el ancla. *vi* anclar, echar anclas, fondear. **at a.,** al ancla. **drag a.,** ancla flotante, ancla de arrastre, *f.* **sheet a.,** ancla de la esperanza, *f; fig* ancla de salvación, *f.* **to drop a.,** anclar. **to ride at a.,** estar al ancla. **to weigh a.,** levar el ancla

anchorage *n* anclaje, *m*; ancladero, fondeadero, *m*; derechos de anclaje, *m pl*

anchovy *n* anchoa, *f,* boquerón, *m*

ancient *a* anciano; antiguo. *n pl* **ancients,** los antiguos. **from a. times,** de antiguo. **most a.,** antiquísimo

and *conjunc* y; (before stressed i or hi) e; (after some verbs and before infin.) de, a; que; (with) con; (often not translated before infins.). **Better and better,** Mejor que mejor. **I shall try and do it,** Trataré de hacerlo. **to come and see,** venir a ver. **We shall try and speak to him,** Procuraremos hablar con él

Andalusia Andalucía, *f*

Andalusian *a* andaluz. *n* andaluz (-za). **A. hat,** sombrero calañés, *m*

Andean *a* andino (-na), *Argentina, Chile also* corderillano (-na)

Andes, the los Andes, *f*

andiron *n* morillo, *m*

Andorran *a* and *n* andorrano (-na)

androgynous *a* andrógino

anecdotal *a* anecdótico

anecdote *n* anécdota, *f*

anemia *n* anemia, *f*

anemic *a* anémico

anemometer *n* anemómetro, *m*

anemone *n* anémona, anémone, *f*

aneroid *a* aneroide. *n* barómetro aneroide, *m*

anesthesia *n* anestesia, *f*

anesthetic *a* and *n* anestésico, *m.*

anesthetist *n* anestesiador (-ra)

anesthetize *vt* anestesiar

aneurism *n* aneurisma, *mf*

angel *n* ángel, *m*

angelic *a* angélico

angelica *n* angélica, *f*

anger *n* cólera, ira, *f,* enojo, *m, vt* enojar, encolerizar; hacer rabiar, *Mexico* amuinar

angina *n* angina, *f.* **a. pectoris,** angina de pecho, *f*

angle *n* ángulo, *m*; rincón, *m*; esquina, *f*; (of a roof) caballette, *m; fig* punto de vista, *m, vi* pescar con caña. **at an a.,** a un lado. **a.-iron,** hierro angular, *m.* **to a. for,** pescar; *fig* procurar obtener

Angle *a* and *n* anglo (-la)

angler *n* pescador (-ra) de caña

Anglican *a* and *n* anglicano (-na)

Anglicanism *n* anglicanismo, *m*

Anglicism *n* anglicismo, inglesismo, *m*

Anglicize *vt* inglesar

angling *n* pesca con caña, *f*

Anglo- (in compounds) anglo-. **A.-American,** *a* and *n* angloamericano (-na). **A.-Indian,** *a* and *n* angloindio (-ia). **A.-Saxon,** *a* and *n* anglosajón (-ona); (language) anglosajón, *m*

anglomania *n* anglomanía, *f*

anglophile *n* anglófilo (-la)

anglophobia *n* anglofobia, *f*

angora *n* angora, *f.* **a. cat,** gato de angora, *m.* **a. rabbit,** conejo de angora, *m*

angrily *adv* airadamente

angry *a* (of persons) enfadado, enojado, airado; (of waves, etc.) furioso; *med* inflamado; (red) rojo; (scowling) cenudo; (dark) obscuro. **to be a.,** estar enojado. **to get angry, to grow a.,** enojarse, enfadarse, *Lat. Am.*

entromparse; (of waves) encresparse; (of the sky) obscurecerse. **to make a.,** enojar

anguish *n* agonía, *f*, dolor, *m*; angustia, *f*. *vt* angustiar

angular *a* angular; (of features, etc.) anguloso

angularity *n* angulosidad, *f*

anhydrous *a* anhidro

aniline *n* anilina, *f*

animal *n* and *n* animal *m*. **a. fat,** grasa animal, *f*. **a. kingdom,** reino animal, *m*. **a. spirits,** *phil* espíritus animales, *m pl*; brío, *m*, energía, *f*

animalism *n* animalidad, *f*; sensualidad, *f*

animate *vt* animar; inspirar. *a* animado; viviente

animated *a* animado; vivo, lleno de vida

animation *n* animación, *f*; vivacidad, *f*; calor, fuego, *m*

animism *n* animismo, *m*

animosity *n* animosidad, hostilidad, *f*

aniseed *n* anís, *m*

anisette *n* (liqueur) anisete, *m*

ankle *n* tobillo, *m*. **a. bone,** hueso del tobillo, *m*. **a. sock,** calcetín corto, *m*

anklet *n* brazalete para el tobillo, *m*; (support) tobillera, *f*

annals *n pl* anales, *m pl*

anneal *vt* (metals) recocer; (glass) templar; (with oil) atemperar

annex *vt* unir, juntar; anexar. *n* anexo, *m*

annexation *n* anexión, *f*

annihilate *vt* aniquilar

annihilation *n* aniquilación,

anniversary *a* and *n* aniversario, *m*.

annotate *vt* anotar, acotar, comentar, hacer anotaciones a

annotation *n* anotación, *f*; nota, *f*

annotator *n* anotador (-ra), comentador (-ra)

announce *vt* proclamar; declarar; publicar; anunciar

announcement *n* proclama, *f*; declaración, *f*; publicación, *f*; anuncio, *m*; (of a betrothal) participación, *f*

announcer *n* anunciador (-ra); (radio or TV) locutor (-ra)

annoy *vt* exasperar, irritar, disgustar; molestar, incomodar, *Lat. Am.* acatarrar, cargosear, engorrar

annoyance *n* disgusto, *m*, exasperación, *f*; molestia, *f*, fastidio, *m*

annoying *a* enojoso, molesto, fastidioso, *Lat. Am.* cargoso

annual *a* anual. *n* anuario, *m*; calendario, *m*; planta anual, *f*

annually *adv* anualmente, cada año

annuitant *n* censualista, *mf*

annuity *n* anualidad, pensión vitalicia, *f*

annul *vt* anular

annulment *n* anulación, *f*

annunciation *n* anunciación, *f*. **the A.,** la Anunciación

anodyne *a* and *n* anodino, *m*

anoint *vt* untar; (before death) olear; (a king, etc.) ungir

anointing *n* unción, *f*

anomalous *a* anómalo

anomaly *n* anomalía, *f*

anonymity *n* anónimo, *m*

anonymous *a* anónimo. **a. letter,** anónimo, *m*

another *a* otro; (different) distinto. *n* otro, *m*; otra, *f*. **For one thing . . . and for a.,** En primer lugar . . . y además (y por otra cosa). **one after a.,** uno después de otro. **They love one a.,** Ellos se aman. **They sent it from one to a.,** Lo mandaron de uno a otro

answer *n* contestación, respuesta, *f*; (refutation) refutación, *f*; (pert reply) réplica, *f*; (solution) solución, *f*; *math* resultado, *m*; *law* contestación a la demanda, *f*

answer *vt* responder, contestar; (a letter, etc.) contestar a; (refute) refutar; (reply pertly) replicar; (write) escribir; (return) devolver; (suit) servir; (a bell, etc.) acudir a; (the door) abrir. *vi* contestar; (succeed) tener éxito; dar resultado. **to a. by return,** contestar a vuelta de correo, **to a. back,** replicar. **to a. for,** ser responsable por; ser responsable de; (speak for) hablar por; (guarantee) garantizar, responder de

answerable *a* responsable; refutable; (adequate) adecuado. **to make a. for,** hacer responsable de

answering machine *n* contestador telefónico, contestador, *m*

ant *n* hormiga, *f*. **ant-eater,** oso hormiguero, *m*. **ant-hill,** hormiguero, *m*

antagonism *n* antagonismo, *m*, hostilidad, oposición, *f*

antagonist *n* antagonista, *mf*

antagonistic *a* antagónico, hostil

antagonize *vt* contender; hacer hostil (a)

antarctic *a* antártico. *n* polo antártico, *m*

antecedent *a* and *n* antecedente, *m*.

antechamber *n* antecámara, antesala, *f*

antedate *vt* antedatar; anticipar

antediluvian *a* antediluviano

antelope *n* antílope, *m*

antenna *n* antena, *f*

anterior *a* anterior

anthem *n* antífona, *f*

anthologist *n* antólogo, *m*

anthology *n* antología, floresta, *f*

anthracite *n* antracita, *f*, carbón mineral, *m*

anthrax *n* ántrax, *m*

anthropological *a* antropológico

anthropologist *n* antropólogo, *m*

anthropology *n* antropología, *f*

anti-aircraft *a* antiaéreo. **A.A. gun,** cañón antiaéreo, *m*

antibody *n* anticuerpo, *m*

antic *n* travesura, *f*

Antichrist *n* Anticristo, *m*

anticipate *vt* (foresee) prever; anticipar; adelantarse a; (hope) esperar; (frustrate) frustrar; (enjoy) disfrutar con anticipación de

anticipation *n* anticipación, *f*; adelantamiento, *m*; esperanza, expectación, *f*. **in a. of,** en espera de

anticipatory *a* anticipador

anticlerical *a* anticlerical

anticlericalism *n* anticlericalismo, *m*

anticlimax *n* anticlímax, *m*

antidote *n* antídoto, contraveneno, *m*

antifreeze *n* anticongelante, *m*

Antilles, the las Antillas, *f*

antimony *n* antimonio, *m*

antipathetic *a* antipático

antipathy *n* antipatía, *f*

antipode *n pl* antípodas, *mf pl*

antiquarian *a* anticuario

antiquary *n* anticuario, *m*

antiquated *a* anticuado

antique *a* antiguo. *n* antigüedad, antigualla, *f*. **a. dealer,** anticuario, *m*. **a. shop,** tienda de antigüedades, *f*

antiquity *n* antigüedad, *f*; ancianidad, *f*

antireligious *a* antirreligioso

antirepublican *a* antirrepublicano

anti-Semitic *a* antisemita

anti-Semitism *n* antisemitismo, *m*

antiseptic *a* and *n* antiséptico, *m*

antisocial *a* antisocial

antithesis *n* antítesis, *f*

antithetic *a* antitético

antitoxin *n* antitoxina, *f*

antler *n* asta, *f*

antonym *n* contrario, *m*

antrum *n* antro, *m*

Antwerp Amberes, *m*

anus *n* ano, *m*

anvil *n* yunque, *m*, bigornia, *f*

anxiety *n* inquietud, intranquilidad, *f*; preocupación, *f*; ansiedad, *f*; curiosidad, *f*; impaciencia, *f*; (wish) deseo, afán, *m*

anxious *a* inquieto, intranquilo; preocupado; ansioso; impaciente; deseoso. **to be a.,** estar inquieto; apurarse. **to be a. to,** ansiar, tener deseos de. **to make a.,** preocupar, inquietar, intranquilizar

anxiously *adv* con inquietud; ansiosamente; impacientemente

any *a* cualquiera; (before the noun only) cualquier; (some) algún, *m*; alguna, *f*; (every) todo; (expressing condition or with interrogatives or negatives, following the noun) alguno, *m*; alguna, *f*, (is often not translated in a partitive sense, e.g. **Have you any butter?** ¿Tienes mantequilla?) *pron* algo; (with the relevant noun) algún, etc.; lo, *m*, and *neut*; la, *f*; los, *m pl*; las, *f pl*. **He hasn't any pity,** No tiene piedad alguna. **at any rate,** de todos modos; por lo menos. **If there is any,** Si lo (la, etc.) hay. **in any case,** venga lo que venga. **not any,** ninguno, *m*; ninguna, *f*. **Whether any of them . . . ,** Si alguno de ellos . . . **any further,** más lejos. **any longer,** más largo; (of time) más tiempo. **any more,** nada más; nunca más

anybody *n* and *pron* (someone) alguien; cualquiera, *mf*; (everyone) todo el mundo; (with a negative) nadie; (of importance) persona de importancia, *f*. **hardly a.,** casi nadie

anyhow *adv* de cualquier modo; (with a negative) de ningún modo; de cualquier manera; (at least) por lo menos, en todo caso; (carelessly) sin cuidado

anyone *n*. See **anybody**

anything *n* algo, *m*, alguna cosa, *f*; (negative) nada; cualquier cosa, *f*; todo (lo que). **a. but,** todo menos

anyway *adv* de todos modos, con todo; venga lo que venga; (anyhow) de cualquier modo

anywhere *adv* en todas partes, dondequiera; en cualquier parte; (after a negative) en (or a) ninguna parte

A.O.B. (any other business) asuntos varios (on an agenda)

aorta *n* aorta, *f*

apart *adv* aparte; a un lado; separadamente; separado (de); apartado (de). **a. from,** aparte de, dejando a un lado. **to keep a.,** mantener aislado; distinguir (entre). **to take a.,** desarmar. **wide a.,** muy distante

apartment *n* cuarto, *m*, habitación, *f*; (flat) piso, *Argentina* departamento, *elsewhere in Lat. Am.* apartamento *m*

apathetic *a* apático; indiferente

apathy *n* apatía, *f*; indiferencia, *f*

ape *n* simio, *m*

Apennines, the los Apeninos, *m*

aperitive *a* and *n* aperitivo, *m*.

aperture *n* abertura, *f*; agujero, *m*; orificio, *m*

apex *n* ápice, *m*

aphasia *n* afasia, *f*

aphorism *n* aforismo, *m*

aphrodisiac *a* and *n* afrodisíaco, *m*

apiary *n* colmenar, *m*

apiece *adv* cada uno; por persona

apish *a* simiesco, de simio; (affected) afectado; (foolish) tonto

aplomb *n* confianza en sí, *f*, aplomo, *m*

apocalypse *n* Apocalipsis, *m*

apocalyptic *a* apocalíptico

apocopate *vt* apocopar

Apocrypha *n* libros apócrifos, *m pl*

apocryphal *a* apócrifo

apogee *n* apogeo, *m*

apologetic *a* apologético

apologist *n* apologista, *mf*

apologize *vi* presentar sus excusas; disculparse, excusarse; (regret) sentir

apology *n* excusa, disculpa, *f*; defensa, apología, *f*; (makeshift) substituto, *m*

apoplectic *a* and *n* apoplético (-ca)

apoplexy *n* apoplegía, *f*

apostasy *n* apostasía, *f*

apostate *n* apóstata, *mf*, renegado (-da)

apostatize *vi* apostatar, renegar

apostle *n* apóstol, *m*. **Apostles' Creed,** el Credo de los Apóstoles

apostolic *a* apostólico

apostrophe *n* apóstrofe, *mf*; (punctuation mark) apóstrofo, *m*

Apothecaries' weight peso de boticario, *m*

apothegm *n* apotegma, *m*

apotheosis *n* apoteosis, *f*

appal *vt* horrorizar, espantar, aterrar

appalling *a* espantoso, horrible

apparatus *n* aparato, *m*; máquina, *f*; instrumentos, *m pl*

apparel *n* ropa, *f*; vestiduras, *f pl*; ornamento, *m*. *vt* vestir

apparent *a* aparente; visible; evidente, manifiesto; (of heirs) presunto. **to become a.,** manifestarse

apparently *adv* al parecer, aparentemente

apparition *n* aparición, *f*, fantasma, espectro, *m*

appeal *n* súplica, *f*; llamamiento, *m*; (charm) atracción, *f*, encanto, *m*; *law* apelación, alzada, *f*. *vi* (to) suplicar (a); hacer llamamiento (a); poner por testigo (a); recurrir a; llamar la atención de; interesar (a); (attract) atraer, encantar; *law* apelar. **It doesn't a. to him,** No le atrae, No le gusta. **to allow an a.,** revocar una sentencia apelada. **without a.,** inapelable

appealing *a* suplicante; atrayente

appealingly *adv* de un modo suplicante

appear *vi* (of persons and things) aparecer; (seem) parecer; (before a judge) comparecer, presentarse (ante el juez); (of books) publicarse; (of lawyers) representar; (of the dawn) rayar; (of the sun, etc.) salir; (show itself) manifestarse. **to cause to a.,** hacer presentarse; (show) hacer ver; (prove) demostrar, probar

appearance *n* aparición, *f*; (show, semblance or look, aspect) apariencia, *f*; presencia, *f*; aspecto, *m*; (in court of law) comparecencia, *f*; (of a book) publicación, *f*; (arrival) llegada, *f*; (view) perspectiva, *f*; (ghost) aparición, *f*, fantasma, *m*. **first a.,** (of an actor, etc.) debut, *m*; (of a play) estreno, *m*. **to all appearances,** según las apariencias. **to make one's first a.,** aparecer por primera vez; *theat* debutar. **Appearances are deceptive,** Las apariencias engañan

appease *vt* apaciguar, aplacar, pacificar; satisfacer

appeasement *n* apaciguamiento, aplacamiento, *m*, pacificación, *f*; satisfacción, *f*

appellant *a* and *n law* apelante, *mf*

appellation *n* nombre, *m*; título, *m*

append *vt* añadir; (a seal) poner; (enclose) incluir, anexar

appendage *n* accesorio, *m*; (*bot zool*) apéndice, *m*

appendicitis *n* apendicitis, *f*

appendix *n* apéndice, *m*

appertain *vi* pertenecer (a)

appetite *n* apetito, *m*; *fig* hambre, *f*; deseo, *m*. **to have a bad a.,** no tener apetito, estar desganado. **to have a good a.,** tener buen apetito. **to whet the a.,** abrir el apetito

appetizer *n* aperitivo, *Argentina* ingrediente *m*

appetizing *a* apetitoso

applaud *vt* and *vi* aplaudir; aclamar, ovacionar; celebrar

applause *n* aplauso, *m*; ovación, *f*; aprobación, alabanza, *f*

apple *n* manzana, *f*. **the a. of one's eye,** la niña de los ojos. **a. orchard,** manzanar, *m*. **a. sauce,** compota de manzanas, *f*. **a. tart,** pastel de manzanas, *m*. **a. tree,** manzano, *m*

appliance *n* aparato, *m*; instrumento, *m*; utensilio, *m*; máquina, *f*

applicability *n* aplicabilidad, *f*

applicable *a* aplicable

applicant *n* candidato, *m*; aspirante, *m*; solicitante, *mf*

application *n* aplicación, *f*; solicitud, *f*; petición, *f*; empleo, *m*. **on a.,** a solicitar

appliqué *a* aplicado. *n* aplicación, *f*

apply *vt* aplicar; (use) emplear; (place) poner; (give) dar; (the brakes) frenar; *vi* ser aplicable; ser a propósito; dirigirse (a); acudir (a); (for a post) proponerse para. **a. for,** solicitar, pedir; (a post) proponerse para. **a. for admission (to . . .),** solicitar el ingreso (en . . .). **a. oneself to,** ponerse a; dedicarse a, consagrarse a

appoint *vt* (prescribe) prescribir, ordenar; señalar; asignar; (furnish) amueblar; equipar; (create) crear, establecer; (to a post) nombrar, designar; (manage) gobernar; organizar. **at the appointed hour,** a la hora señalada. **well-appointed,** bien amueblado; bien equipado

appointive *a* por nombramiento

appointment *n* (assignation) cita, *f*; (to a post) nombramiento, *m*; (post, office) cargo, *m*; creación, *f*. **By Royal A.,** Proveedor de la Real Casa. **to make an a. with,** citar

apportion *vt* dividir; distribuir; prorratear; (taxes) derramar

apportionment *n* repartimiento, *m*, distribución, *f*; división, *f*; prorrateo, *m*

apposite *a* a propósito, pertinente, oportuno; justo

appositeness *n* pertinencia, oportunidad, *f*

appraisal *n* valoración, valuación, *f*; estimación, *f*

appraise *vt* valorar, tasar; estimar

appreciable *a* apreciable, perceptible

appreciably *adv* sensiblemente

appreciate *vt* (understand) darse cuenta de, comprender; estimar; apreciar; (distinguish) distinguir. *vi* encarecer, aumentar en valor; (of shares) subir, estar en alza

appreciation *n* (understanding) comprensión, *f*; apreciación, *f*; (recognition, etc.) aprecio, reconocimiento, *m*; (in value) aumento (en valor), *m*; subida de precio, *f*

appreciative *a* apreciativo

appreciatively *adv* con aprecio

appreciator *n* apreciador (-ra)

apprehend *vt* aprehender, prender; comprender, aprehender; (fear) temer

apprehension *n* aprehensión, comprensión, *f*; (fear) aprensión, *f*; (seizure) aprehensión, presa, *f*

apprehensive *a* aprehensivo; (fearful) aprensivo

apprehensiveness *n* aprehensión, *f*; (fear) aprensión, *f*, temor, *m*

apprentice *n* aprendiz (-za). **to bind a.,** poner de aprendiz

apprenticeship *n* aprendizaje, *m*. **to serve an a.,** hacer el aprendizaje

apprise *vt* dar parte (de), informar (de)

approach *vt* acercarse a; aproximarse a; (pull, etc. nearer) acercar, aproximar; (resemble) parecerse a, ser semejante a; (speak to) hablar con; entablar negociaciones con. *vi* acercarse, aproximarse. *n* acercamiento, *m*; (arrival) llegada, *f*; aproximación, *f*; (of night, etc.) avance, *m*; (entrance) entrada, *f*; avenida, *f*; vía, *f*; (step) paso, *m*; (to a subject) punto de vista (sobre), concepto (de), *m*; (introduction) introducción, *f*; *pl* **approaches,** (environs) alrededores, *m pl*, inmediaciones, *f pl*; (seas) mares, *m pl*; (overtures) avances, *m pl*

approachable *a* accesible

approaching *a* venidero, próximo, cercano

approbation *n* asentimiento, *m*; aprobación, *f*

appropriate *a* apropiado; conveniente; *vt* adueñarse de, tomar posesión de, apropiar

appropriately *adv* propiamente; convenientemente; justamente

appropriateness *n* conveniencia, *f*; justicia, *f*

appropriation *n* apropiación, *f*; aplicación, *f*; empleo, *m*

approval *n* aprobación, *f*; consentimiento, *m*. **on a.,** a prueba

approve *vt* aprobar; confirmar; (sanction) autorizar, sancionar; ratificar; estar contento (de); (oneself) demostrarse. *vi* aprobar

approved *a* aprobado; bien visto; (on documents) Visto Bueno (V° B°)

approximate *a* aproximado. *vt* acercar. *vi* aproximarse a (a)

approximately *adv* aproximadamente, poco más o menos

approximation *n* aproximación, *f*

appurtenance *n* accesorio, *m*, pertenencia, *f*

apricot *n* albaricoque, *m*. **a. tree,** albaricoquero, *m*

April *n* abril, *m*, *a* abrileño. **A. Fool's Day,** el 1° de abril; (in Spain) el Día de los Inocentes (December 28)

apron *n* delantal, *m*; (of artisans and freemasons) mandil, *m*. **to be tied to a mother's a.-strings,** estar cosido a las faldas de su madre. **a.-stage,** proscenio, *m*. **a.-string,** cinta del delantal, *f*

apse *n* ábside, *mf*

apt *a* apto, listo; propenso (a), inclinado (a); expuesto (a); (suitable) apropiado, oportuno

aptitude *n* aptitud, disposición, facilidad, *f*

aptly *adv* apropiadamente; justamente, bien

aquamarine *n* aguamarina, *f*

aquarelle *n* acuarela, *f*

aquarellist *n* acuarelista, *mf*

aquarium *n* acuario, *m*

Aquarius *n* Acuario, *m*

aquatic *a* acuático

aquatint *n* acuatinta, *f*

aqueduct *n* acueducto, *m*

aqueous *a* ácueo, acuoso

aquiline *a* aguileño

Arab *n* árabe. *n* árabe, *mf*

arabesque *n* arabesco, *m*

Arabian *a* árabe, arábigo. **The A. Nights,** Las Mil y Una Noches

Arabic *a* arábigo. *n* (language) arábigo, árabe, *m*

Arabist *n* arabista, *mf*

arable *a* cultivable, labrantío

Aragonese *a* and *n* aragonés (-esa)

arbiter *n* árbitro (-ra), arbitrador (-ra)

arbitrariness *n* arbitrariedad, *f*

arbitrary *a* arbitrario

arbitrate *vi* arbitrar, juzgar como árbitro; someter al arbitraje

arbitration *n* arbitraje, *m*

arbitrator. See **arbiter**

arbour *n* glorieta, *f*, emparrado, *m*

arc *n* arco, *m*. **arc-light,** lámpara de arco, *f*

arcade *n* arcada, *f*; galería, *f*; pasaje, *m*

arch *n* arco, *m*; (vault) bóveda, *f*. *vt* abovedar; arquear; encorvar

arch *a* (roguish) socarrón; (coy) coquetón

arch- *prefix* archi-

archaic *a* arcaico

archaism *n* arcaísmo, *m*

archangel *n* arcángel, *m*

archbishop *n* arzobispo, *m*

archenemy *n* mayor enemigo (-ga); Demonio, *m*

archeological *a* arqueológico

archeologist *n* arqueólogo, *m*

archeology *n* arqueología, *f*

archer *n* flechero, saltero, *m*; *mil* arquero, *m*

archery *n* ballestería, *f*

archery range *n* campo de tiro con arco, *m*

archfiend *n* demonio, *m*

arching *n* arqueo, *m*

archipelago *n* archipiélago, *m*

architect *n* arquitecto, *m*

architectural *n* arquitectónico

architecturally *adv* arquitectónicamente; desde el punto de vista arquitectónico

architecture *n* arquitectura, *f*

archive *n* archivo, *m*

archivist *n* archivero, *m*

archness *n* coquetería, *f*; malicia, *f*

archway *n* arcada, *f*, pasaje abovedado, *m*; arco, *m*

arctic *a* ártico; muy frío. **A. Circle,** Círculo ártico, *m*

ardent *a* ardiente; apasionado, vehemente; fogoso

ardently *adv* ardientemente; con vehemencia, apasionadamente

ardor *n* ardor, *m*,

arduous *a* arduo, difícil

arduousness *n* dificultad, arduidad, *f*

are *pl* of present indicative of **be.** See **be. There are,** Hay

area *n* área, *f*; superficie, *f*; (extent) extensión, *f*; espacio, *m*; región, *f*; (of a house) patio, *m*; (of a concert hall, etc.) sala, *f*

area code *n* característica, *f*, (Chile), código territorial (Spain), prefijo (Spain), código interurbano, código (Argentina), *m*

arena *n* arena, *f*

argent *n poet* blancura, *f*; *her* argén, *m*

Argentinian *a* and *n* argentino (-na)

argonaut *n* (*zool* and *myth*) argonauta, *m*

argot *n* jerga, *f*; (thieves') germanía, *f*

arguable *a* discutible

argue *vt* discutir; persuadir; (prove) demostrar. *vi* argüir, discutir; sostener. **to a. against,** hablar en contra de, oponer

arguing *n* razonamiento, *m*; argumentación, *f*; discusión, *f*

argument *n* argumento, *m*, *Argentina* arenga *f*

argumentative *a* argumentador; contencioso

arid *a* árido, seco

aridity *n* aridez, *f*

Aries *n* Aries, *m*

arise *vi* levantarse; (appear) surgir, aparecer; ofrecerse, presentarse; (of sound) hacerse oír; provenir (de); proceder (de); (result) hacerse sentir; (rebel) sublevarse

aristocracy *n* aristocracia, *f*

aristocrat *n* aristócrata, *mf*

aristocratic *a* aristocrático

Aristotelian *a* aristotélico

arithmetic *n* aritmética, *f*

arithmetical *a* aritmético

ark *n* arca, *f*. **Noah's ark,** arca de Noé, *f*. **Ark of the Covenant,** arca de la alianza, *f*

arm *n* (*anat geog mech* of a chair, a cross, and *fig*) brazo, *m*; (lever) palanca, *f*; (of a tree) rama, *f*, brazo, *m*; (sleeve) manga, *f*; *naut* cabo de una verga, *m*; (weapon) arma, *f*; (of army, navy, etc.) ramo, *m pl.* **arms,** *her* armas, *f pl*, escudo, *m*. **in arms,** en brazos; armado; en oposición. **To arms!** ¡A las armas! **to keep at arm's length,** guardar las distancias; tratar fríamente. **to lay down arms,** rendir las armas. **to present arms,** presentar las armas. **to receive with open arms,** recibir con los brazos abiertos. **to take up arms,** alzarse en armas, empuñar las armas. **under arms,** sobre las armas. **with folded arms,** con los brazos cruzados. **arm in arm,** del bracete, de bracero. **arm of the sea,** brazo de mar, *m*. **arm-rest,** brazo, *m*

arm *vt* armar; proveer (de); (*fig* fortify) fortificar. *vi* armarse

armada *n* armada, *f*

armament *n* armamento, *m*

armchair *n* sillón, *m*, silla poltrona, *f*

armed *a* armado

Armenian *a* and *n* armenio (-ia); (language) armenio, *m*

armful *n* brazado, *m*

armhole *n* sobaquera, *f*

arming *n* armamento, *m*

armistice *n* armisticio, *m*

armless *a* sin brazos

armor *n* armadura, *f*; (for ships, etc.) blindaje, *m*. *vt* blindar, acorazar. **(to) a.-plate,** *vt* blindar. *n* coraza, plancha blindada, *f*

armored *a* blindado, acorazado. **a. car,** carro blindado, *m*. **a. cruiser,** crucero acorazado, *m*

armory *n* armería, *f*

army *n* ejército, *m*; multitud, muchedumbre, *f*. **to be in the a.,** ser del ejército. **to go into the a.,** alistarse. **a. corps,** cuerpo del ejército, *m*. **a. estimates,** presupuesto del ejército, *m*. **a. list,** escalafón del ejército, *m*. **A. Medical Corps,** Sanidad Militar, *f*. **A. Supply Corps,** Cuerpo de Intendencia, *m*

aroma *n* aroma, *m*

aromatic *a* aromático

around *prep* alrededor de; por todas partes de; cerca de; (with words like corner) a la vuelta de. *adv* alrededor; a la redonda, en torno; por todas partes; de un lado para otro

arouse *vt* despertar; excitar. **a. (someone's) suspicions,** despertar las sospechas (de fulano)

arpeggio *n* arpegio, *m*

arraign *vt* acusar; *law* procesar

arraignment *n* acusación, *f*; *law* procesamiento, *m*

arrange *vt* arreglar; acomodar; poner en orden, clasificar, *Lat. Am.* acotejar; (place) colocar; (order) ordenar, disponer; (contrive) agenciar; organizar; preparar; *mus* adaptar; (of differences) concertar, ajustar. *vi* convenir, concertarse; arreglar; hacer preparativos

arrangement *n* arreglo, *m*; clasificación, *f*; disposición, *f*; (agreement) acuerdo, *m*; *mus* adaptación, *f*; *pl* **arrangements,** preparativos, *m pl*

array *n* (of troops) orden de batalla, *mf*; formación, *f*; colección, *f*; (dress) atavío, *m*, *vt* poner en orden de batalla; formar (las tropas, etc.); ataviar, adornar

arrears *n pl* atrasos, *m pl.* **in a.,** atrasado

arrest *vt* detener, impedir; (the attention) atraer; (capture) arrestar, prender; (judgment) suspender. *n* (stop) interrupción, parada, *f*; (hindrance) estorbo, *m*; (detention) arresto, *m*, detención, *f*; (of a judgment) suspensión, *f*. **under a.,** bajo arresto

arresting *a* que llama la atención, notable, muy interesante; asombroso, chocador

arrival *n* llegada, venida, *f*, advenimiento, *m*; *naut* arribada, *f*; entrada, *f*; el, *m*, (la, *f*), que llega. **on a.,** al llegar, a la llegada. **the new arrivals,** los recién llegados

arrive *vi* llegar; aparecer; (happen) suceder; *naut* arribar; entrar. **to a. at,** (a place or conclusion) llegar a

arrogance *n* arrogancia altivez, soberbia, *f*

arrogant *a* altivo, arrogante, soberbio

arrogate *vt* arrogar

arrow *n* saeta, flecha, *f*. **a.-head,** punta de flecha, *f*. **a.-shaped,** en forma de flecha, sagital. **a. wound,** flechazo, saetazo, *m*

arsenal *n* arsenal, *m*

arsenic *n* arsénico, *m*

arson *n* incendio premeditado, *m*

art *n* arte, *mf*; (cleverness) habilidad, *f*; (cunning) artificio, *m*. **Faculty of Arts,** Facultad de Letras, *f*. **fine arts,** bellas artes, *f pl*. **art exhibition,** exposición de pinturas, *f*. **art gallery,** museo de pinturas, *m*. **art school,** colegio de arte, *m*

arterial *a* arterial; (of roads) de primera clase. **a. forceps,** pinzas hemostáticas, *f pl*

artery *n* arteria, *f*

artesian *a* artesiano

artful *a* hábil, ingenioso; (crafty) astuto

artfully *adv* ingeniosamente; con astucia

artfulness *n* habilidad, ingeniosidad, *f*; astucia, maña, *f*

arthritic *a* artrítico

arthritis *n* artritis, *f*

artichoke *n* alcachofa, *f*. **Jerusalem a.,** aguaturma, *f*

article *n* artículo, *m*; (object) objeto, *m*, cosa, *f*; *pl* **articles,** escritura, *f*; contrato, *m*; estatutos, *m pl. vt* escriturar; contratar. **leading a.,** artículo de fondo, *m*. **articles of apprenticeship,** contrato de aprendizaje, *m*. **articles of association,** estatutos de asociación, *m pl.* **articles of war,** código militar, *m*

articulate *vt* articular; pronunciar, articular. *vi* estar unido por articulación; articular. *a* articulado; claro; expresivo

articulation *n* articulación, *f*, (all meanings)

artifice *n* artificio, *m*; arte, *m*, or *f*, habilidad, *f*

artificial *a* artificial; falso, fingido; afectado. **a. flowers,** flores de mano, *f pl.* **a. silk,** seda artificial, seda vegetal, *f*

artificiality *n* artificialidad, *f*; falsedad, *f*; afectación, *f*

artificially *adv* artificialmente; con afectación

artillery *n* artillería, *f*. **field a.,** artillería volante (or ligera or montada), *f*. **a. practice,** ejercicio de cañón, *m*

artilleryman *n* artillero, *m*

artisan *n* artesano (-na)

artist *n* artista, *mf;* (painter) pintor (-ra)
artiste *n* artista, *mf*
artistic *a* artístico
artistically *adv* artísticamente
artistry *n* habilidad artística, *f,* arte, *mf*
artless *a* natural; sencillo, cándido, inocente
artlessly *adv* con naturalidad; con inocencia
artlessness *n* naturalidad, *f;* sencillez, candidez, inocencia, *f*
art museum *n* museo de arte, *m*
Aryan *a* ario
as *adv conjunc rel pron* como; así como; (followed by infin.) de; (in comparisons) tan . . . como; (while) mientras; a medida que; (when) cuando, al (followed by infin.); (since) puesto que, visto que; (because) porque; (although) aunque; por; (according to) según; en; (in order that) para (que). **as a rule,** por regla general. **Once as he was walking,** Una vez mientras andaba. **as . . . as,** tan . . . como. **as far as,** hasta; en cuanto a. **as from,** desde. **as good as,** tan bueno como. **as if,** como si. **as it were,** por decirlo así, en cierto modo. **as many,** otros tantos (e.g. **six embassies in as many countries,** seis embajadas en otros tantos países). **as many as,** tanto . . . como; todos los que. **as soon as,** en cuanto, luego que, así que. **as soon as possible,** cuanto antes, *Lat. Am.* a la mayor brevedad posible. **as sure as can be,** sin duda alguna. **as to,** en cuanto a. **as usual,** como de costumbre. **as well,** también. **as well as,** (besides) además de; tan bien como. **as yet,** todavía.
asbestos *n* asbesto, amianto, *m*
ascend *vt* and *vi* subir; (on, in) subir a; ascender; (rise) elevarse; (a river) remontar. **to a. the stairs,** subir las escaleras. **to a. the pulpit,** subir al púlpito. **to a. the throne,** subir al trono
ascendancy *n* ascendiente, influjo, *m*
ascendant *n* elevación, *f. a* ascendente; predominante. **to be in the a.,** *fig* ir en aumento; predominar
ascending *a* ascendente
ascension *n* subida, ascensión, *f;* (of the throne) advenimiento (al trono), *m.* **The A.,** La Ascensión
ascent *n* subida, *f,* ascenso, *m;* elevación, *f;* (slope) cuesta, pendiente, *f*
ascertain *vt* averiguar, descubrir
ascertainable *a* averiguable, descubrible
ascertainment *n* averiguación, *f*
ascetic *a* ascético. *n* asceta, *mf*
asceticism *n* ascetismo, *m*
ascribable *a* imputable, atribuible
ascribe *vt* atribuir, adscribir, imputar
ascription *n* atribución, adscripción, *f*
asepsis *n* asepsia, *f*
aseptic *a* aséptico
asexual *a* asexual
ash *n* ceniza, *f;* cenizas, *f pl;* (tree and wood) fresno, *m; pl* **ashes,** cenizas, *f pl;* restos mortales, *m pl.* **mountain ash,** serbal, *m.* **ash-bin,** basurero, *m.* **ash-coloured,** ceniciento. **ash grove,** fresneda, *f.* **ashtray,** cenicero, *m.* **Ash Wednesday,** miércoles de ceniza, *m*
ashamed *a* avergonzado. **to be a. (of),** avergonzarse (de), *Mexico* apenarse (de). **to be a. of oneself,** avergonzarse, tener vergüenza de sí mismo
ashen *a* ceniciento; (of ash wood) de fresno; pálido como un muerto
ashlar *n* sillar, *m*
ashore *adv* a tierra; en tierra. **to go** or **put a.,** desembarcar
Asiatic *a* and *n* asiático (-ca)
aside *adv* a un lado; aparte. *n theat* aparte, *m.* **to set a.,** poner a un lado; (omit) dejar aparte; descontar; abandonar; (a judgment) anular. **to take a.,** llevar aparte
asinine *a* asnal
ask *vt* (a question; enquire) preguntar; (request; demand) pedir; (beg) rogar; (invite) invitar. **to ask a question,** hacer una pregunta. **to ask about,** preguntar acerca de. **to ask after,** preguntar por. **to ask**

down, invitar a bajar; invitar a visitar (a alguíen). **to ask for,** pedir; preguntar por. **ask for the moon,** pedir cotofas en el golfo. **to ask in,** invitar (a alguien) a entrar
askance *adv* al (or de) soslayo, de reojo; con recelo
askew *adv* oblicuamente; al lado; a un lado; sesgadamente
aslant *prep* a través de
asleep *a* and *adv* dormido. **to be a.,** estar dormido. **to fall a.,** dormirse
asparagus *n* espárrago, *m.* **a. bed,** esparraguera, *f*
aspect *n* aspecto, *m;* vista, *f;* apariencia, *f,* semblante, *m.* **to have a southern a.,** dar (mirar) al sur
asperity *n* aspereza, *f*
aspersion *n ecc* aspersión, *f;* calumnia, *f;* insinuación, *f*
asphalt *n* asfalto, *m, vt* asfaltar
asphyxia *n* asfixia, *f*
asphyxiate *vt* asfixiar
asphyxiating *a* asfixiante
aspirant *n* aspirante, candidato, *m*
aspirate *vt* aspirar. *n* letra aspirada, *f*
aspiration *n* aspiración, ambición, *f;* deseo, anhelo, *m; gram* aspiración, *f*
aspire *vi* aspirar (a), pretender, ambicionar; alzarse
aspirin *n* aspirina, *f*
ass *n* asno, *m*
assail *vt* atacar, acometer, arremeter
assailable *a* atacable
assailant *n* asaltador (-ra)
assassin *n* asesino, *mf*
assassinate *vt* asesinar
assassination *n* asesinato, *m*
assault *n* asalto, *m;* acometida, embestida, *f; fig* ataque, *m. vt* asaltar; acometer, embestir; atacar. **to take by a.,** tomar por asalto
assay *n* ensayo, *m, vt* ensayar, aquilatar
assayer *n* ensayador, *m*
assaying *n* ensaye, *m*
assemblage *n* reunión, *f;* (of a machine) montaje, *m;* (of people) muchedumbre, *f,* concurso, *m;* (of things) colección, *f,* grupo, *m*
assemble *vt* (persons) reunir, convocar; (things and persons) juntar; (a machine, etc.) armar, ensamblar. *vi* reunirse, congregarse; acudir
assembly *n* asamblea, *f;* reunión, *f; ecc* concilio, *m.* **a. line,** cadena de montaje, línea de montaje, *f.* **a. room,** sala de reuniones, *f;* sala de baile, *f*
assent *n* asentimiento, consentimiento, *m;* aprobación, *f;* (parliamentary, *law*) sanción, *f. vi* asentir (a), consentir (en); aprobar
assert *vt* mantener, defender; declarar, afirmar; hacer valer, reclamar. **to a. oneself,** imponerse, hacerse sentir; hacer valer sus derechos
assertion *n* aserción, afirmación, *f;* defensa, *f;* reclamación, *f*
assertive *a* afirmativo; dogmático
assess *vt* tasar, valorar; fijar, señalar; repartir (contribuciones, etc.)
assessment *n* tasación, *f;* fijación, *f;* repartimiento, *m*
assessor *n law* asesor (-ra); (of taxes) repartidor (-ra); (valuer) tasador, *m.* **public a.,** tasador, *m*
asset *n* ventaja, *f;* adquisición, *f;* cualidad, *f; pl* **assets,** fondos, *m pl; com* activo, *m,* créditos activos, *m pl*
assiduity *n* asiduidad, *f*
assiduous *a* asiduo
assiduously *adv* asiduamente, con asiduidad
assign *vt law* ceder; señalar, asignar; (appoint) destinar; fijar; atribuir, imputar. *n* cesionario (-ia)
assignation *n* asignación, *f;* cita, *f; law* cesión, *f*
assignment *n law* cesión, *f;* escritura de cesión, *f;* atribución, *f;* parte, porción, *f*
assimilable *a* asimilable
assimilate *vt* asimilar; incorporarse. *vi* mezclarse
assimilation *n* asimilación, *f;* incorporación, *f*
assimilative *a* asimilativo

assist *vt* ayudar; auxiliar, socorrer; (uphold) apoyar; (further) promover, fomentar. *vi* (be present) asistir (a)

assistance *n* ayuda, *f;* auxilio, socorro, *m;* apoyo, *m;* (furtherance) fomento, *m.* **public a.,** asistencia pública, *f*

assistant *n* ayudante, *m; ecc* asistente, *m;* (in a shop) dependiente (-ta); colaborador (-ra); (university) auxiliar, *m;* sub-. **a. secretary,** subsecretario (-ia). **a. secretaryship,** subsecretaría, *f*

associate *n* asociado (-da); miembro, *m;* socio (-ia); compañero (-ra), amigo (-ga); colega, *m;* colaborador (-ra); (confederate) cómplice, *mf a* asociado; auxiliar. *vt* asociar; unir, juntar. **to a. oneself with,** asociarse con; asociarse a. **to a. with,** frecuentar la compañía de, ir con

association *n* asociación, *f;* unión, *f;* sociedad, *f;* compañía, corporación, *f;* (connection) relación, *f.* **a. football,** fútbol, *m*

assonance *n* asonancia, *f*

assort *vt* clasificar; mezclar

assorted *a* surtido, mezclado. **They are a well-a. pair,** Son una pareja bien avenida

assortment *n* clasificación, *f,* arreglo, *m;* surtido, *m,* mezcla, *f*

assuage *vt* mitigar; suavizar; calmar; aliviar

assume *vt* asumir; tomar; apropiarse; (wear) revestir; (suppose) suponer; poner por caso

assumed *a* fingido, falso; supuesto

assumption *n* asunción, *f;* apropiación, arrogación, *f;* suposición, *f.* **Feast of the A.,** Fiesta de la Asunción, *f*

assurance *n* garantía, *f;* promesa, *f;* confianza, seguridad, *f;* (in a good sense) aplomo, *m,* naturalidad, *f;* (in a bad sense) presunción frescura, *f,* descaro, *m; com* seguro, *m*

assure *vt* asegurar

assured *a* aseguardo; seguro

assuredly *adv* seguramente

asterisk *n* asterisco, *m*

astern *adv* a popa; de popa; en popa; atrás

asthma *n* asma, *f*

asthmatic *a* asmático

astigmatic *a* astigmático

astigmatism *n* astigmatismo, *m*

astir *adv* en movimiento; (out of bed) levantado; excitado

astonish *vt* sorprender, asombrar

astonished *a* atónito, estupefacto

astonishing *a* sorprendente, asombroso

astonishment *n* asombro, *m,* sorpresa, estupefacción, *f*

astound *vt* aturdir, pasmar. **to be astounded,** *inf* quedarse muerto

astounding *a* asombroso

astray *adv* desviado, extraviado; por el mal camino. **to go a.,** errar el camino, perderse; *fig* descarriarse

astride *adv* a horcajadas. *prep* a horcajadas sobre; a ambos lados de

astringent *a* astringente

astrologer *n* astrólogo (-ga)

astrological *a* astrológico

astrology *n* astrología, *f*

astronaut *n* astronauta, *mf*

astronomer *n* astrónomo, *m*

astronomical *a* astronómico

astronomy *n* astronomía, *f*

astrophysics *n* astrofísica, *f*

astute *a* astuto, sagaz; (with knave, etc.) redomado, pícaro

astuteness *n* astucia, sagacidad, *f*

asunder *adv* en dos; separadamente; lejos uno de otro

asylum *n* asilo, *m;* (for the insane) manicomio, *m*

asymmetrical *a* asimétrico

asymmetry *n* asimetría, *f*

at *prep* a; en casa de; en; de; con; por; (before) delante de. Sometimes forms part of verb, e.g. **to aim at,** apuntar. **to look at,** mirar. May be translated by using pres. part., e.g. **They were at play,** Estaban jugando.

at a bound, de un salto. **at peace,** en paz. **at the doctor's,** en casa del médico. **at the crack of dawn,** al rayar el alba, al romper el alba. **at the head,** a la cabeza. **John is at Brighton,** Juan está en Brighton. **at the house of . . . , at . . .'s** en casa de, *Lat. Am. also* donde (e.g., **My cousin is at my grandmother's** Mi primo está en casa de mi abuela, Mi primo está donde mi abuela) **at first,** al principio. **at last,** por fin. **at no time,** jamás. **at once,** en seguida. **at most,** a lo más. **at one go** *Lat. Am.* de una leída. **at all events,** en todo caso. **What is he getting at?** ¿Qué quiere saber? **at home,** en casa. **at-home day,** día de recibo, *m*

atavism *n* atavismo, *m*

atavistic *a* atávico

atheism *n* ateísmo, *m*

atheist *n* ateo (-ea)

atheistic *a* ateo

Athens Atenas, *f*

athlete *n* atleta, *m*

athletic *a* atlético

athletics *n* atletismo, *m*

athwart *adv* de través. *prep* al través de; contra

Atlantic *a* and *n* atlántico *m.* **A. Charter,** Carta del Atlántico, *f.* **A. liner,** transatlántico, *m*

Atlantis Atlántida, *f*

atlas *n* atlas, *m*

atmosphere *n* aire, *m;* atmósfera, *f; fig* ambiente, *m*

atmospheric *a* atmosférico

atmospherics *n pl* perturbaciones eléctricas atmosféricas, *f pl*

atoll *n* atolón, *m*

atom *n* átomo, *m.* **splitting of the a.,** escisión del átomo, *f*

atomic *a* atómico. **a. bomb,** bomba atómica, *f.* **a. pile,** pila atómica, *f.* **a. theory,** teoría atómica, *f*

atomize *vt* pulverizar

atomizer *n* pulverizador, *m*

atone *vi* (for) expiar

atonement *n* expiación, *f*

atonic *a* átono, atónico

atrocious *a* atroz; horrible

atrocity *n* atrocidad, *f*

atrophy *n* atrofia, *f,* vi atrofiarse

attach *vt* (*law* of goods) embargar; (*law* of persons) arrestar; (fix) fijar; (tie) atar; (join) juntar; (stick) pegar; (connect) conectar; (hook) enganchar; (with a brooch, etc.) prender; (blame, etc.) imputar; (importance, etc.) dar, conceder; (assign) asignar; (attract) atraer; (enclose) adjuntar, incluir. *vi* pertenecer (a), ser indivisible (de). **to a. oneself to,** pegarse a; adherirse a, asociarse con; acompañar; hacerse inseparable de

attaché *n* agregado, *m.* **a. case,** maletín, *m*

attachment *n* (*law* of goods) embargo, *m,* vía ejecutiva, *f;* (*law* of persons) arresto, *m;* unión, *f;* conexión, *f;* (hooking) enganche, *m;* (with a brooch, etc.) prendimiento, *m;* (tying) atadura, *f;* (fixing) fijación, *f;* (affection) apego, cariño, *m;* (friendship) amistad, *f*

attack *n* ataque, *m; mil* ofensiva, *f;* (access) acceso, *m. vt* atacar

attacker *n* atacador (-ra), asaltador (-ra)

attain *vt* alcanzar, conseguir, lograr. *vi* llegar a; alcanzar

attainable *a* asequible, realizable; accesible

attainment *n* consecución, obtención, *f;* logro, *m; pl* **attainments,** prendas, dotes, *f pl*

attempt *vt* (try) procurar, tratar de, intentar; ensayar; querer; *law* hacer una tentativa (de), atentar. *n* tentativa, prueba, *f;* esfuerzo, ensayo, *m;* (criminal) atentado, *m,* tentativa, *f*

attend *vi* prestar atención (a); escuchar; (look after) cuidar (de); (serve) servir; (accompany) acompañar; (await) esperar. *vt* (be present) asistir (a); (of a doctor) visitar; (accompany) acompañar; (bring) acarrear, traer; (follow) seguir. **to be attended with,** traer consigo, acarrear

attendance *n* asistencia, presencia, *f;* (those present) público, *m,* concurrencia, *f;* servicio, *m;* (train) acompañamiento, *m; med* asistencia, *f,* tratamiento médico, *m.* **to be in a.,** acompañar (a)

attendant *a* que acompaña; que sigue; concomitante. *n* criado (-da); (keeper) guardián (-ana); (nurse) enfermero (-ra); (in a cloakroom) guardarropa, *f;* (in a theater) acomodador (-ra); (on a train) mozo, *m;* (waiter) camarero, *m;* (at baths) bañero (-ra)

attention *n* atención, *f;* cuidado, *m.* **A.!** ¡Atención!; *mil* ¡Firmes! **to pay a.,** prestar atención. **to stand to a.,** cuadrarse, permanecer en posición de firmes

attentive *a* atento; solícito; cortés, obsequioso

attentively *adv* con atención, atentamente; solícitamente

attentiveness *n* cuidado, *m;* cortesía, *f*

attenuate *vt* atenuar

attenuating *a* atenuante. **a. circumstance,** circunstancia atenuante, *f*

attenuation *n* atenuación, *f*

attest *vt* atestar. *vi* atestiguar, deponer, dar fe

attestation *n* atestación, deposición, *f;* (certificate) certificado, *m,* fe, *f*

attic *n* buhardilla, guardilla, *f,* desván, sotabanco, *m*

Attic *a* ático

attire *n* atavío, *m;* (dress) traje, *m;* (finery) galas, *f pl, vt* ataviar, vestir; engalanar

attitude *n* actitud, *f;* postura, *f;* posición, *f*

attorney *n* (solicitor) abogado (-da); (agent) apoderado (-da); (public) procurador, *m.* **power of a.,** poderes, *m pl* procuración, *f.* **A.-general,** fiscal, *m*

attract *vt* atraer; (charm) seducir, cautivar, apetecer; (invite) convidar; (goodwill, etc.) captar

attraction *n* atracción, *f;* atractivo, aliciente, encanto, *m*

attractive *a* atrayente; atractivo, seductivo; apetecible; encantador

attractively *adv* atractivamente

attributable *a* imputable, atribuible

attribute *vt* atribuir (a), achacar (a), imputar (a). *n* atributo, *m*

attribution *n* atribución, imputación, *f;* atributo, *m*

attrition *n* atrición, *f*

auburn *a* castaño, rojizo

auction *n* subasta, almoneda, *f;* venta pública, pública subasta, *f, vt* subastar. **to put up to a.,** sacar a pública subasta

auctioneer *n* subastador (-ra), *Lat. Am. also* licitador (-ra)

audacious *a* atrevido, audaz, osado, temerario; (shameless) descarado, impudente

audaciously *adv* osadamente; descaradamente

audacity *n* audacia, osadía, temeridad, *f,* atrevimiento, *m;* (shamelessness) descaro, *m,* desvergüenza, *f*

audibility *n* audibilidad, perceptibilidad, *f*

audible *a* audible, oíble

audibly *adv* en forma audible, perceptiblemente, en alta voz

audience *n* (interview and *law*) audiencia, *f;* oyentes, *m pl,* auditorio, público, *m.* **to give a.,** dar audiencia. **a. chamber,** sala de recepción, *f*

audiofrequency *n* audiofrecuencia, *f*

audit *vt* intervenir, examinar (cuentas). *n* intervención, *f,* ajuste (de cuentas), *m*

audition *n* audición, *f*

auditor *n* (hearer) oyente, *mf;* interventor, contador, *m*

auditorium *n* sala de espectáculos, *f*

auditory *a* auditivo, auditorio

Augean *a* de Augeas; muy sucio

auger *n* taladro, *m*

aught *n* algo. **For a. I know,** Por lo que yo sepa

augment *vt* aumentar, acrecentar. *vi* aumentarse, acrecentarse

augmentation *n* aumento, acrecentamiento, *m;* añadidura, *f*

augmentative *a* aumentativo

augur *n* agorero (-ra). *vt* and *vi* presagiar, anunciar; pronosticar, agorar

augury *n* predicción, *f;* agüero, presagio, pronóstico, *m*

August *n* agosto, *m*

august *a* augusto

Augustan *a* (of Roman emperor) augustal. **A. Age,** siglo de Augusto, *m*

Augustinian *a* and *n ecc* agustino (-na)

aunt *n* tía, *f.* **great-a.,** tía abuela, *f.* **A. Sally,** el pim, pam, pum

aura *n* exhalación, *f;* influencia psíquica, *f; med* aura, *f*

aural *a* auricular. **a. surgeon,** otólogo, *m*

auricle *n* (of the heart) aurícula, ala del corazón, *f;* oreja, *f,* pabellón de la oreja, *m*

aurora *n* aurora, *f.* **a. borealis,** aurora boreal, *f*

auspice *n* auspicio, *m*

auspicious *a* propicio, favorable, feliz

auspiciously *adv* próspero, felizmente

auspiciousness *n* buenos auspicios, *m pl;* felicidad, *f*

austere *a* severo, austero, adusto; ascético; (of style) desnudo

austerity *n* austeridad, severidad, *f;* ascetismo, *m;* (of style) desnudez, *f*

Australian *a* and *n* australiano (-na)

Austrian *a* and *n* austríaco (-ca)

authentic *a* auténtico

authenticate *vt* autenticar

authentication *n* autenticación, *f*

authenticity *n* autenticidad, *f*

author *n* autor, *m*

authoress *n* autora, *f*

author index *n* índice de autores, *m*

authoritarian *a* autoritario

authoritative *a* autoritario

authority *n* autoridad, *f;* poder, *m.* **to have on the best a.,** tener de muy buena fuente

authorization *n* autorización, *f*

authorize *vt* autorizar

authorship *n* profesión de autor, *f;* paternidad (literaria), *f;* origen, *m*

auto *n* = **automobile**

autobiographical *a* autobiográfico

autobiography *n* autobiografía, *f*

autocracy *n* autocracia, *f*

autocrat *n* autócrata, *mf*

autocratic *a* autocrático

autograph *n* autógrafo, *m*

autography *n* autografía, *f*

automatic *a* automático. **a. gate,** (at level crossings, etc.) barrera de golpe, *f.* **a. machine,** máquina automática, *f; inf* tragaperras, *m.* **a. pencil,** lapicero, *m*

automatically *adv* automáticamente

automatism *n* automatismo, *m*

automaton *n* autómata, *m*

automobile *n* automóvil, coche, *Lat. Am.* carro *m*

autonomous *a* autónomo

autonomy *n* autonomía, *f*

autopsy *n* autopsia, *f*

autosuggestion *n* autosugestión, *f*

autumn *n* otoño, *m*

autumnal *a* otoñal, de otoño

auxiliary *a* auxiliar. *n* auxiliador, *m*

avail *vi* servir; valer; importar. *vt* aprovechar. **to a. oneself of,** valerse de, aprovecharse de. **to no a.,** en balde

availability *n* utilidad, *f;* disponibilidad, *f;* provecho, *m;* (validity) validez, *f*

available *a* útil; disponible; aprovechable; válido

avalanche *n* alud, lurte, *m*

avarice *n* avaricia, *f*

avaricious *a* avaro, avaricioso

ave *interj* ¡ave! *n* avemaría, *f;* despedida, *f*

avenge *vt* vengar; vindicar. **to a. oneself for,** vengarse de

avenger *n* vengador (-ra)

avenging *a* vengador

avenue *n* avenida, *f*

aver *vt* afirmar, asegurar

average *n* promedio, término medio, *m;* (marine insurance) avería, *f, a* de promedio; típico; corriente; normal. *vt* hallar el término medio (de); prorratear, proporcionar; ser por término medio. **general a.,** (marine insurance) avería gruesa, *f.* **on the a.,** por término medio

averse *a* opuesto (a); desinclinado (a); enemigo (de); repugnante. **to be a. to,** no gustar de; oponerse a; estar desinclinado a; ser enemigo de; repugnar

aversion *n* aversión, *f*; repugnancia, *f*

avert *vt* apartar; (avoid) evitar

aviary *n* avería, pajarera, *f*

aviation *n* aviación, *f*

aviator *n* aviador (-ra)

avid *a* ávido

avidity *n* avidez, *f*

avidly *adv* ávidamente, con avidez

avocado *n* aguacate

avocation *n* pasatiempo, *m*, distracción, *f*; ocupación, *f*; profesión, *f*

avoid *vt* evitar; (pursuit) evadir, eludir; guardarse (de), rehuir; *law* anular

avoidable *a* evitable, eludible

avoidance *n* evitación, *f*

avow *vt* confesar; declarar

avowal *n* confesión, admisión, *f*

avowedly *adv* por confesión propia

avuncular *a* avuncular

await *vt* aguardar, esperar

awake *vt* despertar. *vi* despertarse. *a* despierto; vigilante; consciente (de); atento (a)

awakening *n* despertamiento, *m*

award *n* sentencia, decisión, *f*; adjudicación, *f*; (prize) premio, *m. vt* adjudicar; otorgar, conceder. **She was awarded a professorship in Greek,** Ganó unas oposiciones para una cátedra de griego

aware *a* consciente, sabedor. **to be well a. of,** saber muy bien. **to make a. of,** hacer saber

awash *adv* a flor de agua

away *adv* a distancia, a lo lejos; lejos; (absent) ausente; (out) fuera; (unceasingly) sin parar, continuamente; (wholly) completamente; (visibly) a ojos vistas. In verbs of motion **a.** is rendered by the reflexive, e.g. **to**

go a., marcharse. Sometimes not translated, e.g. **to take a.,** quitar. *interj* ¡fuera de aquí! ¡márchese Vd.!; ¡vámonos! ¡adelante! **nine miles a.,** a nueve millas de distancia. **a. in the distance,** allá a lo lejos. **She sang a.,** Ella seguía cantando

awe *n* temor reverente, *m*; horror, *m*; respeto, *m*; reverencia, *f, vt* intimidar, aterrar; infundir respeto (a). **to stand in awe of,** tener respeto (a), reverenciar

awesome *a* pavoroso, temible; aterrador; terrible; (august) augusto; (imposing) imponente

awestruck *a* espantado, aterrado

awful *a* terrible, pavoroso; horrible; temible; atroz; *inf* enorme. **How a.!** *inf* ¡Qué barbaridad!

awfully *adv* terriblemente; horriblemente; *inf* muy

awfulness *n* lo terrible; lo horrible; atrocidad, *f*; (of a crime, etc.) enormidad, *f*

awkward *a* difícil; peligroso; delicado; embarazoso; (of time, etc.) inconveniente, inoportuno; (of things) incómodo; (clumsy) torpe, desmañado; desagradable; (ungraceful) sin gracia. **the a. age,** la edad difícil

awkwardly *adv* torpemente; incómodamente; mal; con dificultad; sin gracia. **He is a. placed,** Se encuentra en una situación difícil

awkwardness *n* dificultad, *f*; peligro, *m*; delicadeza, *f*; inconveniencia, inoportunidad, *f*; (clumsiness) torpeza, desmaña, *f*; (ungracefulness) falta de gracia, *f*

awl *n* lezna, *f*, punzón, *m*

awning *n* toldo, palio, *m, Lat. Am.* carpa *f*; *naut* toldilla, *f*

awry *adv* a un lado; oblicuamente; *fig* mal. *a* torcido; *fig* descarriado

ax *n* hacha, *f*

axiom *n* axioma, *m*

axiomatic *a* axiomático

axis *n* eje, *m*; *zool* axis, *m.* **A. power,** nación del Eje

axle *n* eje, *m*; peón, árbol (de una rueda), *m.* **back a.,** eje trasero, *m.* **differential a.,** eje diferencial, *m.* **front a.,** eje delantero, *m*

ay *interj* sí. *n* voto afirmativo, *m*

azalea *n* azalea, *f*

Aztec *a* and *n* azteca, *mf*

azure *n* azul celeste, *m*

B

b *n* (letter) be, *f*; *mus* si, *m*

baa *n* balido, be, *m*, *vi* balar, dar balidos

babble *n* (chatter) charla, *f*; (of a child) gorjeo, *m*; (confused sound) vocinglería, barbulla, *f*, rumor, *m*; (of water) murmullo, susurro, *m. vi* charlar; (of children) gorjearse; (incoherently) balbucir; (water) murmurar, susurrar; (a secret) descubrir

babbler *n* charlatán (-ana)

babbling *n* garrulería, locuacidad, *f*; (incoherent speech) balbuceo, *m.* (of water) murmullo, *m. a* gárrulo, locuaz; balbuciente; murmurante

babel *n* babel, *m*

baboon *n* babuino, *m*

baby *n* bebé, crío, *m*; niño (-ña) de pecho; *fig* gran bebé, *m*; niño mimado, *m, a* infantil. **b. blue,** azul claro, *m.* **b. doll,** muñeca bebé, *f.* **b. girl** *Argentina* beba *f* **b. grand piano,** piano de media cola, *m.* **b. of the family** *Venezuela* cuneco (-ca) *mf*

baby carriage *n* coche de niños, *m*

baby-faced *a* con mejillas mofletudas

babyhood *n* infancia, niñez, *f*

babyish *a* infantil, aniñado, pueril

babysitter *n* cuidaniños, *mf*

baccalaureate *n* bachillerato, *m*

baccarat *n* bacará, *m*

bachelor *n* soltero, célibe, *m*; (of a university) licenciado, bachiller, *m*; (as a title) caballero, *m.* **confirmed b.,** solterón, *m.* **degree of b.,** licenciatura, *f.* **to receive the degree of b.,** licenciarse, bachillerarse

bachelorhood *n* soltería, *f*, celibato, *m*

bacillus *n* bacilo, *m*

back *n anat* espalda, *f*; (of an animal) lomo, espinazo, *m*; (reins, loins) riñones, *m pl*; (of chairs, sofas) respaldo, *m*; (of a book) lomo, *m*; (back, bottom) fondo, *m*; parte posterior, parte de atrás, *f*; (of a hand, brush and many other things) dorso, *m*; (of a coin) reverso, *m*; el otro lado de alguna cosa; (in football, hockey) defensa, *m*; *theat* foro, *m*; (of fire-arms) culata, *f*; (of a knife) canto, *m*; (upper portion) parte superior, *f. a* posterior, trasero; de atrás; (remote) alejado, apartado; inferior; (overdue; past; out of date) atrasado; (earlier) anterior; *anat* dorsal. **at the b.,** detrás; en el fondo; en la última fila. **at the b. of one's mind,** por sus adentros, en el fondo del pensamiento. **behind one's b.,** a espaldas de uno, en ausencia de uno. **half-b.,** medio, *m.* **on one's b.,** boca arriba; a cuestas. **to see the b. of,** *inf* ver por última vez, desembarazarse de. **to turn one's b. on,** volver la espalda (a). **with one's b. to the engine,** de espaldas a la máquina. **b. to b.,** espalda con espalda

back *vt* empujar hacia atrás; (a vehicle) dar marcha atrás; hacer retroceder; (line) reforzar; (support) apoyar; (sign) endosar; (bind) forrar; (bet on) apostar a; (a sail) fachear. *vi* retroceder; dar marchar atrás; (of the wind) girar; (with on to) dar sobre, dominar; (with down) abandonar (una pretensión, etc.). **to b. out,** salir, marcharse; volverse atrás; (retract) desdecirse

back *adv* detrás; atrás; otra vez, de nuevo; (returned) de vuelta; a alguna distancia; (at home) en casa. *interj*

¡atrás! **A few weeks b.,** Hace unas semanas, Unas semanas atrás. **It stands b. from the road,** Está a alguna distancia del camino. **to go b. to,** (of families, etc.) remontar a. **to come b.,** regresar. **to come b. again,** regresar de nuevo, regresar por segunda vez

back axle *n* eje trasero, *m*

backbite *vt* cortar (a uno) un sayo, desollarle (a uno) vivo, murmurar de

backbiter *n* mala lengua, *f,* murmurador (-ra)

backbiting *n* murmuración, detracción, maledicencia, *f, a* murmurador, detractor

backbone *n* espinazo, *m,* columna vertebral, *f.* **to the b.,** hasta la médula

backchat *n* dimes y diretes, *m pl;* insolencia, *f.* **to indulge in b.-c.,** andar en dimes y diretes

back door *n* puerta trasera, puerta de servicio, *f*

backed *a* (lined) forrado; (in compounds; of persons) de espalda; (of chairs) de respaldo

backer *n* (better) apostador, *m;* protector (-ra, -triz)

backfire *n* contrafuego *m,* falsa explosión, *f*

backgammon *n* chaquete, *m*

back garden *n* jardín de atrás, *m*

background *n* fondo, *m; art* último término, *m.* **in the b.,** en el fondo; *art* en último término; *fig* en las sombras; alejado, a distancia

backhand *n sport* revés, *m*

backhanded *a* de revés, dado con el revés de la mano; *fig* ambiguo, equívoco

backing *n* forro, *m;* (lining) refuerzo, *m;* (of a vehicle) marcha atrás, *f;* retroceso, *m;* (betting) el apostar (a); (wagers) apuestas, *f pl;* (*fig* support) apoyo, *m,* ayuda, *f;* garantía, *f*

backlog *n com* rezago de pedidos, *m*

back number *n* (of a periodical) número atrasado, *m*

back pedal *vi* contrapedalear.

back premises *n* parte trasera (de una casa, etc.), *f*

backroom *n* cuarto interior, *m,* habitación trasera, *f.* **b. boy,** investigador ocupado en trabajos secretos para el gobierno, *m*

back seat *n* asiento trasero, *m;* fondo, *m.* **to take a b.-s.,** permanecer en el fondo, ceder el paso

back shop *n* trastienda, *f*

backside *n* trasero, *m,* posaderas, nalgas, *f pl*

backslide *vi* recaer, reincidir

backslider *n* (in religion or politics) apóstata, *mf;* reincidente, *mf*

backsliding *n* apostasía, *f;* reincidencia, *f*

backstage *a* foro, fondo del escenario, *m, adv* hacia el foro; detrás de bastidores

backstaircase *n* escalera de servicio, *f;* escalera secreta, *f*

backstairs *n* escalera de servicio, *f; fig* vías secretas, *f pl, a* de cocina; *fig* secreto

backstitch *n sew* pespunte, *m, vt* and *vi* pespuntar

back street *n* calle secundaria, callejuela, *f; pl* **back streets,** barrios bajos, *m pl*

backstroke *n* reculada, *f; sport* revés, *m*

back tooth *n* muela, *f*

back view *n* vista de detrás, *f*

backward *a* hacia atrás; vuelto hacia atrás; (in development) atrasado, poco avanzado; lento; negligente; (shy) modesto; (late) tardío; atrasado; retrógrado; (dull) torpe; retrospectivo. *adv* hacia atrás; atrás; al revés; (of falling) de espaldas; (of time) al pasado. **to go b. and forward,** ir y venir. **b. and forward,** de acá para allá

backwardness *n* atraso, *m;* lentitud, *f;* negligencia, *f;* modestia, *f;* (lateness) tardanza, *f;* atraso, *m;* (dullness) torpeza, *f;* falta de progreso, *f*

backwards *adv.* See **backward**

backwash *n* agua de rechazo, *f*

backwater *n* remanso, *f*

back wheel *n* rueda trasera, *f, vi* contrapedalear

backwoods *n* monte, *m,* selva, *f*

back yard *n* corral, *m*

bacon *n* tocino, *m*

bacteria *n* bacteria, *f*

bacterial *a* bacterial, bacteriano

bactericide *n* bactericida, *m*

bacteriological *a* bacteriológico

bacteriologist *n* bacteriólogo, *m*

bacteriology *n* bacteriología, *f*

bad *a* malo; (wicked) perverso; (ill) enfermo, malo (with estar); (naughty; undutiful) malo (with ser); (of coins) falso; (of debts) incobrable; (rotten) podrido; (harmful) nocivo; (dangerous) peligroso; (of pains, a cold) fuerte; intenso; (of a shot) errado; (mistaken) equivocado; (unfortunate) desgraciado. *n* el mal, lo malo; (persons) los malos. **extremely bad,** pésimo. **from bad to worse,** de mal en peor. **It's too bad!** ¡Esto es demasiado! **to go bad,** (fruit) macarse; (food) estropearse. **bad habit,** mala costumbre, *f,* vicio, *m.* **to have the bad habit of,** tener el vicio de. **bad temper,** malhumor, mal genio, *Lat. Am.* catoche *m.* **bad-tempered,** malhumorado, *Argentina* cabrero. **bad turn,** flaco servicio, *m,* mala pasada, *f*

badge *n* insignia, *f;* (decoration) condecoración, *f;* símbolo, emblema, *m;* (mark) marca, *f*

badger *n* tejón, *m, vt* cansar, molestar

Bad Lands (of Nebraska and South Dakota) Tierras malas *f pl;* (of Argentina) la Travesía, *f*

badly *adv* mal. **extremely b.,** pésimamente. **to want something b.,** necesitar algo con urgencia. **b. done,** mal hecho. **b. disposed,** malintencionado

badminton *n* el juego del volante, *m*

badness *n* maldad, *f;* mala calidad, *f;* lo malo

bad-smelling *a* maloliente

baffle *vt* desconcertar; (bewilder) tener perplejo (a); contrariar, frustrar; (obstruct) impedir; (avoid) evitar. **to b. description,** no haber palabras para describir

baffling *a* desconcertante; difícil; confuso; perturbador; (of people) enigmático

bag *n* saco, *m;* talega, *f;* (hand) bolsa, *f,* saco (de mano), *m;* (for tools) capacho, *m;* (for sewing) costurero, *m;* (of bagpipes) fuelle, *m;* (saddle) alforja, *f;* (briefcase) cartera, *f;* (suitcase) maleta, *f;* (under the eye) ojera, *f;* (game shot) caza, *f. vt* entalegar; coger, cazar; matar; tomar. *vi* (of garments) arrugarse. **to clear out bag and baggage,** liar el petate. **a bag of bones,** (person) un manojo de huesos. **bag wig,** peluquín, *m*

bagatelle *n* bagatela, friolera, *f;* (game) billar romano, *m*

bagful *n* saco, *m;* bolsa, *f*

baggage *n* equipaje, *m; mil* bagaje, *m;* (madcap) pícara, *f;* (jade) mujerzuela, *f.* **b. master,** (railway) factor, *m.* **b. car,** furgón de equipajes, *m*

baggage rack *n* (of automobile) portaequipajes, *m*

baggy *a* (creased, of trousers) con rodilleras, arrugado; (wide) bombacho

bagpipe *n* gaita, *f*

bagpiper *n* gaitero, *m*

Bahamas, the las Islas Bahamas, las Islas Lucayas, *f*

bail *n law* fianza, caución, *f;* (person) fiador (-ra); (cricket) travesaño, *m,* barra, *f. vt law* poner en libertad bajo fianza; salir fiador (por); (a boat) achicar. **on b.,** en fiado. **to go b.,** dar fianza, fiar.

bailiff *n law* agente ejecutivo, *m;* alguacil, *m;* mayordomo, *m;* capataz, *m*

bait *n* cebo, *m;* anzuelo, *m;* (fodder) pienso, *m, vt* cebar; (feed) dar pienso (a); azuzar; atormentar; (attract) atraer

baiting *n* cebadura, *f;* combate, *m;* tormenta, *f*

bake *vt* cocer; hacer (pan, etc.). **I like to bake cakes,** Me gusta hacer pasteles; *fig* endurecer. *vi* cocerse

bakelite *n* bakelita, *f*

baker *n* panadero, hornero, *m.* **a baker's dozen,** la docena del fraile

bakery *n* panadería, *f*

baking *n* cocimiento, *m,* cocción, *f;* (batch) hornada, *f;* el hacer (pan, etc.) *a inf* abrasador. **b.-dish,** tortera, *f.* **b.-powder,** levadura química, *f*

balance *n* balanza, *f;* equilibrio, *m; com* balance, saldo, *m*; (in a bank) saldo (a favor del cuentacorrentista), *m*; *math* resto, *m*; *ast* Libra, *f*; (pendulum) péndola, *f*; (counterweight) contrapeso, *m*. **credit b.,** saldo acreedor, *m*. **debit b.,** saldo deudor, *m*. **net b.,** saldo líquido, *m*. **to lose one's b.,** perder el equilibrio. **to strike a b.,** hacer balance. **b. of power,** equilibrio político, *m*. **b. of trade,** balanza de comercio, *f*. **b.-sheet,** balance, avanzo, *Lat. Am.* balance de situación, *m*. **b. wheel,** (of watches) volante, *m*

balance *vt* balancear, abalanzar; contrapesar; (accounts) saldar; equilibrar; comparar; considerar, examinar. *vi* balancearse; ser de igual peso; equilibrarse; (accounts) saldarse

balance of trade *n* balanza comercial, *f*

balancing *n* balanceo, *m*; *com* balance, *m*. **b.-pole,** balancín, *m*

balconied *a* con balcones, que tiene balcones

balcony *n* balcón, *m*; galería, *f*; *theat* anfiteatro, *m*

bald *a* calvo; (of style) seco, pobre; *fig* desnudo, árido, pelado; sin adorno; (simple) sencillo. **to grow b.,** ponerse calvo, encalvecer

balderdash *n* galimatías, *m*, jerigonza, *f*; disparate, *m*

baldly *adv* secamente; sencillamente

baldness *n* calvicie, *f*; (of style) sequedad, pobreza, *f*; (bareness) desnudez, aridez, *f*

bale *n* (bundle) fardo, *m*; (of cotton, paper, etc.) bala, *f*

Balearic Islands, the las Islas Baleares, *f*

baleful *a* malicioso, siniestro, maligno

balk *n* obstáculo, *m*; (beam) viga, *f*; (billiards) cabaña, *f*. *vt* frustrar; impedir. *vi* resistirse, rehusar

Balkans, the los Balcanes, *m*

ball *n* globo, *m*, esfera, *f*; (plaything) pelota, *f*; (as in billiards, cricket, croquet) bola, *f*; (in football, basket-ball) balón, *m*; (shot) bala, *f*; (of wool, etc.) ovillo, *m*; (of the eye) globo (del ojo), *m*; (of the thumb) yema (del pulgar), *f*; (of the foot) planta (del pie), *f*; (dance) baile, *m*. *vi* apelotonarse. **red b.,** (in billiards) mingo, *m*. **to play b.,** jugar a la pelota. **to roll oneself into a b.,** aovillarse, hacerse un ovillo. **b.-and-socket joint,** articulación esférica, *f*. **b.-bearing,** cojinete de bolas, *m*

ballad *n* romance, *m*; (song) balada, *f*

ballast *n* (*naut* and *fig*) lastre, *m*; *rw* balasto, *m*. *vt* lastrar; llenar de balasto

ballerina *n* bailarina, *f*

ballet *n* baile ruso, ballet, *m*; baile, *m*. **b. master,** director de ballet, *m*

ballistics *n* balística, *f*

balloon *n* globo aerostático, *m*; *chem* balón, *m*; (toy) globo, *m*; *arch* bola, *f*. **captive b.,** globo cautivo, *m*. **b. barrage,** cortina de globos de intercepción, *f*. **b.-tyre,** neumático balón, *m*

balloonist *n* aeronauta, *mf*

ballot *n* votación, *f*; papeleta para votar, cédula de votación, *f*. *vi* votar, balotar. **b. box,** urna electoral, *f*

ballpoint, ballpoint pen *n* biro *m* (Argentina), birome *m* (Argentina, Uruguay), bolígrafo *m* (Spain), bolilápiz *m* (Mexico), esfero *m* (Colombia), esferográfica *f* (Colombia), estenógrafo *m* (Cuba), lapicera *f* (Argentina), lapicero *m* (Central America, Colombia), lápiz de pasta *m* (Chile), pluma esférica *f* (Spain), pluma esferográfica *f* (Spain), plumilla *f* (Venezuela), polígrafo *m* (Spain), punto bola, punto-bola, puntobola *f* (Bolivia), pluma de bola *f*, pluma atómica *f*

ballroom *n* salón de baile, *m*; salón de fiestas, *m*

ballroom dancing *n* baile de salón, *m*

balm *n* bálsamo, *m*; *fig* ungüento, *m*

balminess *n* fragancia, *f*; aroma, *m*; (gentleness) suavidad, *f*

balmy *a* balsámico; fragante; aromático; (soft) suave; (soothing) calmante

balsam *n* bálsamo, *m*

Baltic, the el (Mar) Báltico, *m*

balustrade *n* balaustrada, barandilla, *f*, antepecho, *m*

bamboo *n* bambú, *m*

bamboozle *vt* engatusar, embaucar

bamboozler *n* embaucador (-ra)

ban *n* interdicción, *f*; prohibición, *f*; bando, *m*. *vt* prohibir; proscribir

banal *a* banal, vulgar, trivial

banality *n* banalidad, vulgaridad, trivialidad, *f*

banana *n* (tree and fruit) plátano, *m*; (fruit) banana, *f*, *Venezuela* cambur *m* **b. plantation,** platanar, *m*

band *n* lista, tira, *f*; zona, *f*; (black mourning) tira de gasa, *f*; (sash) faja, *f*; (ribbon) banda; cinta, *f*; (bandage) venda, *f*; *mech* correa, *f*; *arch* listón, *m*; *mus* banda, *f*; (group) pandilla, *f*, grupo, *m*. *vt* congregar, reunir. *vi* reunirse, asociarse. **b.-saw,** sierra de cinta, *f*

bandage *n* venda, *f*, vendaje, *m*, *vt* vendar, poner un vendaje (in limbs, etc. or persons)

bandaging *n* vendaje, *m*

banderol *n* banderola, *f*

bandit *n* bandido, bandolero, *m*

bandmaster *n* músico mayor, *m*; director de orquesta, *m*

bandsman *n* músico, *m*

bandstand *n* quiosco de música, *m*

bandy *vt* cambiar, trocar; pasar de uno a otro

bandy-legged *a* estevado zanquituerto

bane *n* (poison) veneno, *m*; perdición, ruina, *f*; (nuisance) plaga, *f*

baneful *a* pernicioso, funesto; dañino; maligno

banefully *adv* funestamente; malignamente

bang *n* golpe, golpazo, *m*; (of an explosive, fire-arm) estallido, *m*, detonación, *f*; (of a firework) traque, *m*; (of a door) portazo, *m*; (with the fist) puñetazo, *m*; (noise) ruido, *m*; (fringe) flequillo, *m*. *vt* golpear; (beat) sacudir; (throw) lanzar, arrojar con violencia; (a door, etc.) cerrar de golpe, cerrar con violencia. *vi* golpear; estallar; (thunder) retronar; (in the wind) cencerrear. *interj* ¡pum! ¡zas!

banging *n* golpeadura, *f*; sacudidura, *f*; detonación, *f*; ruido, *m*

bangle *n* (slave b.) esclava, *f*; pulsera, *f*; brazalete, *m*; (for ankles) ajorca, *f*

banish *vt* desterrar; apartar; (from the mind) despedir, ahuyentar; (suppress) suprimir

banishment *n* destierro, *m*; expulsión, *f*; relegación, *f*; (suppression) supresión, *f*

banister *n* baranda, *f*, pasamano, *m*

banjo *n* banjo, *m*

banjoist *n* tocador (-ra) de banjo

bank *n* (of rivers, etc.) ribera, orilla, *f*, margen, *m*; (of clouds) banda, capa, *f*; (of sand, fog, snow) banco, *m*; (embankment) terraplén, *m*; *com* banco, *m*; (gaming) banca, *f*; (for foreign exchange) casa de cambio, *f*. **b. account,** cuenta corriente, *f*. **b. book,** libreta de banco, *f*. **b. clerk,** empleado del banco, *m*. **b. holiday,** fiesta oficial, *f*. **b.-note,** billete de banco, *m*. **b. stock,** acciones de un banco, *f pl*

bank *vi* estancar, represar; amontonar; poner (dinero) en un banco, depositar en un banco. *vi* tener cuenta corriente en un banco; (gaming) tener la banca; ser banquero; *aer* inclinarse al virar

banker *n* banquero, *m*, (also at cards); (money-changer) cambista, *mf*

banking *n com* banca, *f*; *aer* vuelo inclinado, *m*, *a com* bancario. **b. house,** casa de banca, *f*

bankrupt *a* insolvente, quebrado. *n* quebrado (-da). **to go b.,** declararse en quiebra, hacer bancarrota

bankruptcy *n* bancarrota, quiebra, *f*; *fig* pobreza, decadencia, *f*. **fraudulent b.,** quiebra fraudulenta, *f*. **b. court,** tribunal de quiebras, *m*

banner *n* bandera, *f*

banns *n pl* amonestaciones, *f pl*. **to forbid the b.,** impedir las amonestaciones. **to publish the b.,** decir las amonestaciones

banquet *n* banquete, *m*, *vt and vi* banquetear

banqueting *a* de banquetes. **b. hall,** sala de banquetes, *f*

bantam *n* gallina enana, *f*. **b. weight,** (*sport*) *a* de peso gallo. *n* peso gallo, *m*

banter *vt* and *vi* tomar el pelo (a). *n* chistes, *m pl*, burlas, *f pl*
baptism *n* bautismo, *m*; *fig* bautizo, *m*
baptist *n* bautista, *m*. **St. John the B.**, San Juan Bautista
baptistry *n* baptisterio, bautisterio, *m*
baptize *vt* bautizar
baptizing *n* bautizo, *m*
bar *n* barra, *f*; (of chocolate, soap) pastilla, *f*; *her* banda, *f*; (on a window) reja, *f*; (of a door) tranca, *f*, barrote, *m*; (bar lever) palanca, *f*; (of a balance) astil, *m*; *mus* barra, *f*; (in the sea, etc.) banco, alfaque, *m*; (barrier) barrera, *f*; (barrister's profession) foro, *m*, curia, *f*; *fig* tribunal, *m*; (in a court) barra, *f*; *fig* impedimento, *m*; (of light) rayo, *m*; (stripe) raya, *f*; (for refreshments) bar, *m*, *Lat. Am.* chingana *f* mostrador del bar, *m*. *vt* atrancar, abarrotar; impedir, obstruir; prohibir; exceptuar, excluir; (streak) rayar. **the b.**, el cuerpo de abogados. **to be called to the b.**, ser recibido como abogado en los tribunales. **b.-tender**, camarero del bar, *m*
bar association *n* colegio de abogados, *m*
barb *n* púa, *f*; (of an arrow, fish-hook, etc.) lengüeta, *f*; (of a lance) roquete, *m*; (of fish) barbilla, *f*; (of a feather) barba, *f*; (horse) caballo berberisco, *m*. *vt* proveer de púas; armar de lengüetas
Barbados Isla de Barbados, *f*
barbarian *a* bárbaro, barbárico. *n* bárbaro (-ra)
barbaric *a* barbárico, salvaje
barbarism *n* barbarismo, salvajismo, *m*; crueldad, *f*; (of style) barbarismo, *m*
barbarity *n* barbaridad, ferocidad, *f*
barbarous *a* feroz, cruel, salvaje; inculto
barbarously *adv* bárbaramente, cruelmente
barbarousness *n* barbaridad, *f*; crueldad, ferocidad, *f*
Barbary Berbería, *f*
barbecue *n* barbacoa, *f*
barbed wire *n* alambre de púas, alambre espinoso, *m*
barber *n* barbero, *m*. **barber shop,** barbería, *f*
Barcelona (of or from) *a* and *n* barcelonés (-esa)
bard *n* bardo, vate, *m*
bare *a* desnudo; descubierto; vacío; (mere) mero, solo; (worn) raído; pelado, raso; (unadorned) sencillo; (unsheathed) desnudo; (arid) árido; (curt) seco; (unprotected) desabrigado; pobre. *vt* desnudar; descubrir; revelar. **He bared his head,** Se descubrió. **to lay b.,** dejar al desnudo; revelar
bareback *a* que monta en pelo. *adv* en pelo
barefaced *a* descarado, desvergonzado, cínico
barefoot *a* descalzo
bareheaded *a* sin sombrero, descubierto
barelegged *a* en pernetas, en piernas
barely *adv* apenas; escasamente; meramente, solamente
bareness *n* desnudez, *f*; desadorno, *m*; (aridity) aridez, *f*; pobreza, *f*
bargain *n* contrato, *m*; pacto, acuerdo, *m*; (purchase) ganga, *f*. *vi* negociar; (haggle) regatear; (expect) esperar. **into the b.,** de añadidura, también. **It is a b.,** Es una ganga; Trato hecho. **to get the best of the b.,** salir ganando. **to strike a b.,** cerrar un trato. **b. counter,** sección de saldos, *f*. **b. sale,** venta de saldos, *Mexico* barata *f*
bargainer *n* negociador (-ra); regatón (-ona)
bargaining *n* negociación, gestión, *f*; (haggling) regateo, *m*
barge *n* (for freight) barcaza, gabarra, *f*; falúa, *f*; lancha, *f*. *vi* (into) tropezar con; dar empujones
baritone *n* barítono, *m*
barium *n chem* bario, *m*
bark *n* (of a tree) corteza, *f*; (quinine) quina, *f*; (boat, *poet*) barca, *f*; *naut* buque de tres palos, *m*; (of a dog) ladrido, *m*; (of a fox) aullido, *m*; (of a gun) ruido, *m*. *vi* (of a dog) ladrar; (of a fox) aullar; (of a gun) tronar
barking *n* ladridos, *m pl*; (of stags) rebramo, *m*; (of foxes) aullidos, *m pl*; (of guns) trueno, *m*
barley *n* cebada, *f*, *a* de cebada. **pearl b.,** cebada per-

lada, *f*. **b.-bin,** cebadera, *f*. **b. dealer,** cebadero, *m*. **b. field,** cebadal, *m*. **b.-water,** hordiate, *m*
barm *n* (froth on beer) giste, *m*; (leaven) levadura, *f*
barmaid *n* moza de bar, camarera, *f*
barn *n* pajar, granero, hórreo, *m*. **b.-owl,** lechuza, *f*
barnacle *n* lapa, *f*, barnacla, *m*
barometer *n* barómetro, *m*
barometric *a* barométrico
baron *n* barón, *m*
baroness *n* baronesa, *f*
Baron Munchausen el Barón de la Castaña
baroque *a* barroco. **the b.,** lo barroco
barracks *n mil* cuartel, *m*, caserna, *Lat. Am.* barraca *f*, *vt* acuartelar
barrage *n* presa de contención, *f*; *mil* cortina de fuego, *f*; (barrier) barrera, *f*; (of questions) lluvia, *f*. **b. balloon,** globo de intercepción, *m*
barrel *n* barril, *m*; tonel, *m*, cuba, *f*; (of a gun) cañón, *m*; *mech* cilindro, *m*; (of an animal) cuerpo, *m*. *vt* embarrilar, entonelar. **b.-organ,** organillo, órgano de manubrio, *m*
barrelled *a* embarrilado; (of guns, generally in compounds) de . . . cañones. **double-b. gun,** escopeta de dos cañones, *f*
barren *a* estéril; (of ground) árido; (fruitless) infructuoso
barrenness *n* esterilidad, *f*; aridez, sequedad, *f*; (fruitlessness) inutilidad, *f*
barrens *n* yermo, *m sing*, yerma, *f sing*
barricade *n* barricada, *f*; barrera, *f*, *vt* cerrar con barricadas; obstruir
barricading *n* el cerrar con barricadas; la defensa con barricadas (de)
barrier *n* barrera, *f*; impedimento, *m*; (for customs duties) portazgo, *m*
barring *prep* salvo, excepto, con la excepción de, menos
barrister *n* abogado (-da)
barrow *n* carretón, *m*; carretilla, *f*; (tumulus) túmulo, *m*
barter *n* cambio, trueque, *m*; tráfico, *m*, *vt* and *vi* cambiar, trocar; traficar
barterer *n* traficante, *mf*
basal *a* básico, fundamental
basalt *n* basalto, *m*
base *a* bajo, vil, ruin; soez; indigno; impuro; (of metals) de mala ley. *n* base, *f*; fundamento, *m*; pie, *m*; *arch* pedestal, *m*; (*mil chem geom*) base, *f*; (of a vase) asiento, *m*, *vt* basar; fundar. **b. action,** bajeza, *f*. **b. line,** *sport* línea de base, *f*. **b. metal,** metal común, *m*
baseball *n* pelota base, *f*
baseless *a* sin base; sin fundamento; insostenible
basely *adv* bajamente, vilmente
basement *n* sótano, *m*
baseness *n* bajeza, vileza, ruindad, *f*
bashful *a* vergonzoso, ruboroso; tímido, corto; (unsociable) huraño, esquivo
bashfully *adv* vergonzosamente; tímidamente
bashfulness *n* vergüenza, *f*, rubor, *m*; encogimiento, *m*, timidez, cortedad, *f*; (unsociableness) huraña, esquivez, *f*
basic *a* básico; fundamental
basic commodity *n* artículo básico, producto primario, *m*
basil (sweet) *n bot* albahaca, *f*
basilica *n* basílica, *f*
basilisk *n* basilisco, *m*
basin *n* vasija, *f*; (for washing) jofaina, *f*; (barber's) bacía, *f*; (of a fountain) taza, *f*; *anat* bacinete, *m*; (of a harbor) concha, *f*; (of a river) cuenca, *f*; (in the earth) hoya, *f*; (dock) dársena, *f*
basis *n* base, *f*; fundamento, *m*; elemento principal, *m*
bask *vi* calentarse; (in the sun) tomar el sol
basket *n* cesta, *f*; canasta, capacha, *Lat. Am.* jaba *f*; (frail) espuerta, *f*, **large b.,** banasta, *f*. **b. with a lid,** excusabaraja, *f*. **b. ball,** baloncesto, *m*. **b. maker** or **dealer,** banastero, cestero, *m*. **b. work** or

shop or **factory,** cestería, *f.* **b. work chair,** sillón de mimbres, *m*

basketful *n* cesta, cestada, *f*

Basque *a* and *n* vasco (-ca), vascongado (-da). *n* (language) vascuence, *m*

Basque Provinces, the las Provincias Vascongadas

bas-relief *n* bajo relieve, *m*

bass *n mus* bajo, *m;* (for tying) esparto, *m, a mus* bajo. **double b.,** contrabajo, *m.* **figured b.,** bajo cifrado, *m.* **b. clef,** clave de fa, *f.* **b. string,** bordón, *m.* **b. voice,** voz baja, *f*

bassinet *n* cochecito de niño, *m*

bassoon *n mus* bajón, fagot, *m*

bassoonist *n* bajonista, fagotista, *mf*

bastard *n* bastardo (-da), hijo (-ja) natural. *a* bastardo, ilegítimo; espurio

baste *vt sew* bastear, hilvanar, embastar; *cul* enlardar, lardear

basting *n sew* embaste, *m; cul* lardeamiento, *m.* **b. spoon,** cacillo, *m.* **b. stitch,** pasillo, *m*

bastion *n* bastión, baluarte, *m.* **to fortify with bastions,** abastionar

bastioned *a* abastionado, con bastiones

bat *n zool* murciélago, *m;* (in cricket) paleta, *f;* (in table tennis) pala, *f. vi* (cricket) golpear con la paleta. See **without**

batch *n* (of loaves, etc.) hornada, *f;* lote, *m;* (of recruits) promoción, *f*

bath *n* baño, *m;* (room) cuarto de baño, *m;* (vat) bañador, *m;* (for swimming) piscina cubierta, *f;* (in the open air) piscina al aire libre, *f; phot* baño, *m,* solución, *f. vt* bañar, lavar. **hot mineral baths,** termas, *f pl. Order of the B.,* Orden del Baño, *f.* **b. public baths,** casa de baños, *f.* **reinforcing b.,** *phot* reforzador, *m.* **to take a b.,** bañarse, tomar un baño. **b.-chair,** cochecillo de inválido, *m.* **b.-robe,** bata de baño, *f,* albornoz, *m.* **b. room,** cuarto de baño, *m.* **b. towel,** toalla del baño, *f.* **b. tub,** bañera, *f,* baño, *m, Argentina* bañadera *f*

bathe *vt* bañar, lavar; (of light, etc.) bañar, envolver. *vi* bañarse. *n* baño, *m.* **to go for a b.,** ir a bañarse

bather *n* bañista, *mf;* bañador (-ra)

bathing *a* de baño; balneario, *n* baño, *m.* **b. cap,** gorro de baño, *m.* **b. dress,** traje de baño, *m.* **b. gown,** albornoz, *m,* bata de baño, *f.* **b. machine,** caseta de baños, *f.* **b.-pool,** piscina, *f.* **b. resort,** estación balnearia, *f.* **b.-shoes,** calzado de baño, *m*

bathos *n* paso de lo sublime a lo ridículo, *m;* anticlímax, *m*

batiste *n* batista, *f*

baton *n* bastón de mando, *m; mus* batuta, *f;* (policeman's) porra, *f*

battalion *n* batallón, *m*

batten *vi* engordar (de); medrar, prosperar. **to b. down,** cerrar las escotillas

batter *n cul* batido, *m;* pasta, *f; sport* lanzador, *m. vt* apalear, golpear; (demolish) derribar, demoler; (with artillery) cañonear; batir. **to coat with b.,** rebozar. **to b. down,** derribar

battering ram *n* ariete, *m*

battery *n* (*mil nav*) batería, *f; elec* pila, batería, *f; law* agresión, *f.* **dry b.,** batería de pilas, *f.* **storage b.,** acumulador, *m.* **b. cell,** pila de batería eléctrica, *f*

battle *n* batalla, *f;* pelea, *f,* combate, *m;* (struggle) lucha, *f. vi* batallar, pelear; luchar. **b.-array,** orden de batalla, *f.* **b.-axe,** hacha de combate, *f.* **b.-cruiser,** acorazado, *m.* **b.-field,** campo de batalla, *m.* **b.-front,** frente de combate, *m.* **b.-piece,** *art* batalla, *f.* **b.-ship,** buque de guerra, *m*

battledore (and shuttlecock) *n* raqueta (y volante), *f*

battlement *n* almenaje, *m;* muralla almenada, *f*

bauble *n* (trifle) chuchería, fruslería, *f;* (fool's) cetro de bufón, *m*

bauxite *n* bauxita, *f*

Bavaria Baviera, *f*

Bavarian *a* and *n* bávaro (-ra)

bawdy *a* obsceno, indecente, escabroso

bawl *vi* chillar, vocear

bawling *n* vocerío, *m,* chillidos, *m pl*

bay *n geog* bahía, *f;* (small) abra, *f; bot* laurel, *m;* (horse) bayo, *m;* (howl) aullido, *m; arch* abertura, *f; rw* andén, *m. a* (of horses) bayo, isabelino. *vi* aullar. **at bay,** en jaque, acorralado. **sick-bay,** enfermería, *f.* **to keep at bay,** tener a distancia; tener alejado; entretener. **bay rum,** ron de malagueta, *m.* **bay window,** ventana saledíza, *f*

baying *n* aullido, *m*

bayonet *n* bayoneta, *f, vt* herir o matar con bayoneta. **fixed b.,** bayoneta calada, *f.* **b. charge,** carga de bayoneta, *f.* **b. thrust,** bayonetazo, *m*

Bayonne Bayona, *f*

bazaar *n* bazar, *m*

be *vi* ser; (of position, place, state, temporariness) estar; (exist) existir; (in impersonal expressions) haber; (of expressions concerning the weather and time) hacer; (remain) quedar; (leave alone) dejar; (do) hacer; (of one's health) estar; (of feeling cold, hot, afraid, etc. and of years of one's age) tener; (live) vivir; (belong) ser (de), pertenecer (a); (matter, concern) importar (a); (happen) ocurrir, suceder; (find oneself) hallarse, encontrarse, estar; (arrive) llegar (a); (cost) costar; (be worth) valer; (celebrate, hold) celebrarse, tener lugar; (forming continuous tense with present participle active or passive) estar; (with past participle forming passive) ser (this construction is often replaced by reflexive form when no ambiguity is entailed); (with infinitive expressing duty, intention) haber de; (must) tener que. **He is a soldier (doctor, etc.),** Es soldado (médico, etc.). **He is on guard,** Está de guardia. **They were at the door (in the house, etc.),** Estaban a la puerta (en la casa, etc.). **I am writing a letter,** Estoy escribiendo una carta (but this form is often replaced by a simple tense, e.g. escribo . . .). **It remains to be written,** Queda por escribir. **What is to be done?** ¿Qué hay que hacer? **Woe is me!** ¡Ay de mí! **to be hot (cold),** (of things) estar caliente (frío); (of weather) hacer calor (frío); (of persons) tener calor (frío). **How is John? He is well,** ¿Cómo está Juan? Está bien de salud. **It is daylight,** Es de día. **It is cloudy,** Está nublado. **She is 10,** Tiene diez años. **They are afraid,** Tienen miedo. **I am to go there tomorrow,** He de ir allí mañana. **What is to be will be,** Lo que tiene que ser será. **If John were to come we could go into the country,** Si viniera Juan podríamos ir al campo. **Be that as it may,** Sea como sea. **It is seven years since we saw him,** Hace siete años que no le vemos. **We have been here for three years,** Hace tres años que estamos aquí, Llevamos tres años aquí. **There is** or **there are,** Hay. **There will be many people,** Habrá mucha gente. **There were many people,** Había mucha gente. **There are many people,** Hay mucha gente. **It is three miles to the next village,** Estamos a tres millas del pueblo próximo. **So be it!** Así sea. **Your pen is not to be seen,** Tu pluma no se ve. **It is to be hoped that . . . ,** Se espera que . . . ; ¡Ojalá que . . . ! **The door is open,** La puerta está abierta. **The door was opened by Mary,** La puerta fue abierta por María. **He was accused of being a fascist,** Lo acusaron de fascista. **to be about to,** estar por; (of a more imminent action) estar para, estar a punto de. **to be in,** estar dentro; estar en casa. **to be off,** marcharse, irse. **Be off!** ¡Márchate! ¡Vete! ¡Fuera! **to be out,** estar fuera; haber salido; no estar en casa; (of a light, etc.) estar apagado. **to be up,** estar levantado. **to be up to,** proyectar, traer entre manos; urdir, maquinar

beach *n* playa, *f;* costa, *f. vt* (a boat) encallar en la costa. **b. shoes,** playeras, *f pl.* **b. suit,** vestido de playa, *m*

beach club *n* club de playa, *m*

beacon *n* (lighthouse) faro, *m;* (buoy) baliza, *f,* fanal, *m;* (watch-tower) atalaya, *f; fig* guía, *f. vt* iluminar. **b. fire,** almenara, *f*

bead *n* cuenta, *f;* (of glass) abalorio, *m;* (drop) gota, *f; arch* perla, *f;* (bubble) burbuja, *f;* (foam) espuma, *f; pl* **beads,** rosario, *m, vt* adornar con abalorios. **to tell one's beads,** rezar el rosario. **b. work,** abalorio, *m*

beading *n* abalorio, *m; arch* friso, listón, *m*

beadle *n* bedel, *m*

beadleship *n* bedelía, *f*

beagle *n* perro sabueso, *m*

beak *n* pico, *m;* punta, *f; naut* espolón, *m.* **to tap with the b.,** picotear

beaked *a* que tiene pico; (in compounds) de . . . pico

beaker *n* copa, *f; chem* vaso de precipitado, *m*

beam *n arch* madero, *m,* viga, *f;* (width of a ship) manga, *f;* (of a balance) palanca, *f;* (of a plough) cama, *f;* (of light) rayo, destello, *m; phys* rayo, *m;* (smile) sonrisa brillante, *f; pl* **beams,** (of a building) envigado, *m;* (of a ship) baos, *m pl.* **main b.,** *arch* viga maestra, *f.* **on her b.-ends,** de costado; *fig* arruinado; en la miseria. **b. feather,** astil, *m.* **b. of light,** rayo de luz, haz de luz, *m*

beam *vt* lanzar, emitir; difundir. *vi* brillar, fulgurar, destellar; estar radiante, estar rebosando de alegría

beaming *a* brillante; radiante

bean *n* haba, *f;* judía, alubia, *f;* (of coffee) grano, *m.* **broad b.,** haba, *f.* **French, haricot, kidney b.,** judía, *f.* **string b.,** judía verde, *f.* **b. field,** habar, *m*

bear *n zool* oso, *m;* (she-bear) osa, *f;* (Stock Exchange) bajista, *mf.* **Great B.,** *ast* Osa Mayor, *f,* Septentrión, *m.* **Little B.,** *ast* Osa Menor, *f.* **polar b.,** oso blanco, *m.* **b.-cub,** osezno, *m.* **bear's den,** osera, *f.* **b.-garden,** patio de osos, *m; inf* merienda de negros, *f.* **b.-hunting,** caza de osos, *f.* **b.-like,** osuno. **b.-pit,** recinto de los osos, *m*

bear *vt* and *vi* (carry) llevar; (show) ostentar; (company, etc.) hacer; (profess) profesar; (of spite, etc. and of relation) guardar; (have) tener; (fruit) dar; (give birth to) parir; (support) sostener; (endure) aguantar; (suffer) padecer, sufrir; (tolerate) tolerar, sufrir; (a strain, an operation, etc.) resistir; (lean on) apoyarse en; (experience) experimentar; (produce) producir, dar; (enjoy) disfrutar de; (use) usar; (impel) empujar; (occupy, hold) ocupar; (go) dirigirse. **It was suddenly borne in on them that . . . ,** De pronto vieron claro que . . . **I cannot b. any more,** No puedo más. **We cannot b. him,** No le aguantamos, No le sufrimos. **His language won't b. repeating,** Su lenguaje no puede repetirse. **to bring to b.,** ejercer (presión, etc.). **to b. a grudge,** guardar rencor (a), tener ojeriza (a). **to b. arms,** llevar armas; servir en el ejército o la milicia. **to b. company,** hacer compañía (a), acompañar (a). **to b. in mind,** tener en cuenta, tener presente; acordarse de. **to b. oneself,** conducirse, portarse. **to b. to the right,** ir hacia la derecha. **to b. witness,** atestiguar. **to b. false witness,** levantar falso testimonio. **to b. away,** llevarse; ganar. **to b. down,** hundir; derribar; bajar. **to b. down on,** avanzar rápidamente hacia; correr hacia; *naut* arribar sobre; (attack) caer sobre. **to b. in,** llevar adentro. **to b. off,** llevarse; ganar; *naut* apartarse de la costa. **to b. on, upon,** apoyarse en; (refer to) referirse a. **to b. out,** llevar fuera; confirmar; apoyar; justificar. **to b. up,** llevar arriba; llevar a la cumbre (de); sostener; (recover) cobrar ánimo; (against) resistir; hacer frente a. **to b. with,** soportar; sufrir; aguantar; llevar con paciencia; ser indulgente con

bearable *a* soportable; aguantable; tolerable

beard *n* barba, *f;* (of cereals) raspa, arista, *f, vt* desafiar. **thick b.,** barba bien poblada, *f*

bearded *a* con barba, barbudo

beardless *a* barbilampiño, desbarbado, imberbe, lampiño

bearer *n* llevador (-ra), portador (-ra); (of a bier) andero, *m; com* dador, portador, *m.* **good b.,** *agr* árbol fructífero, *m.* **to b.,** al portador

bearing *n* porte, *m;* postura, *f;* presencia, *f;* conducta, *f;* aspecto, *m;* relación, *f;* (meaning) significación, *f; naut* demora, orientación, *f; mech* cojinete, soporte, *m;* (endurance) tolerancia, *f; pl* **bearings,** (way) camino, *m;* her escudo de armas, *m.* **to get one's bearings,** orien-

tarse; encontrar el camino. **to lose one's bearings,** desorientarse; perderse. **to have a b. on,** tener relación con; tener que ver con; influir en

bearish *a* osuno; rudo, áspero

bearskin *n* piel de oso, *f;* birretina, *f*

beast *n* animal, bruto, *m;* cuadrúpedo, *m;* (cattle) res, *f;* bestia, *f.* **wild b.,** fiera, *f.* **b. of burden,** acémila, bestia de carga, *f.* **b. of prey,** animal de rapiña, *m*

beastliness *n* bestialidad, brutalidad, *f;* obscenidad, *f*

beastly *a* bestial, brutal; obsceno; *inf* horrible

beat *n* latido, *m,* pulsación, *f;* golpe, *m;* (of a drum) toque (de tambor), *m;* (of a clock) tictac, *m;* sonido repetido, *m;* vibración, *f*

beat *vt* and *vi* batir; golpear; (thrash) pegar, dar una paliza (a), *Lat. Am.* humear; (to remove dust, etc.) sacudir; (shake) agitar; (the wings) aletear; (hunting) batir; (excel) exceder, superar; ganar; (defeat) vencer; (of the rain, etc.) azotar; (a drum) tocar; (of the sun) batir, dar (en); (throb) latir, palpitar, pulsar. **to b. about the bush,** andarse por las ramas. **to stop beating about the bush,** dejarse de historias. **to b. a retreat,** *mil* emprender la retirada; huir. **to b. black and blue,** moler a palos. **to b. hollow,** vencer completamente; ganar fácilmente; aventajar con mucho. **to b. it,** *inf* escaparse corriendo. **to b. time,** *mus* llevar el compás; triunfar sobre la vejez. **to b. to it,** *inf* tomar la delantera. **to b. against,** golpear contra; chocar contra. **to b. back,** rechazar; (sobs, etc.) ahogar; reprimir. **to b. down,** (prices) regatear; (of the sun) caer de plomo, caer de plano; reducir; suprimir; destruir. **to b. off,** rechazar; echar a un lado. **to b. out,** hacer salir; (metals) batir; (a tune) llevar el compás (de). **to b. up,** *cul* batir; (a mattress) mullir; asaltar; maltratar

beaten *a* (of paths) trillado; (conquered) vencido; (of metals) batido; (dejected) deprimido; (trite) trivial, vulgar

beater *n* batidor, *m;* (for carpets) sacudidor (de alfombras), *m; cul* batidor, *m*

beatific *a* beatífico

beatification *n* beatificación, *f*

beatify *vt* beatificar

beating *n* batimiento, *m;* vencimiento, *m;* (thrashing) paliza, *f., Lat. Am. also* azotera, *f.;* (of the heart, etc.) palpitación, *f,* latido, *m;* (of metals) batida, *f;* (of a drum) rataplán, toque de tambor, *m;* (of waves) embate, *m;* (of wings) aleteo, aletazo, *m*

beatitude *n* beatitud, *f*

beau *n* galán, *m;* (fop) petimetre, *m*

beautiful *a* bello, lindo, hermoso; magnífico; excelente; exquisito; elegante; encantador, delicioso

beautifully *adv* bellamente; (richly) ricamente; admirablemente; magníficamente; elegantemente

beautify *vt* embellecer; hermosear; adornar. **to b. oneself,** arreglarse, ponerse elegante

beautifying *n* embellecimiento, *m;* adorno, *m*

beauty *n* belleza, hermosura, lindeza, *f;* magnificencia, *f;* excelencia, *f;* elegancia, *f;* encanto, *m;* (belle) beldad, Venus, *f.* **to lose one's b.,** desmejorarse, perder su hermosura. **b. contest,** concurso de belleza, *m.* **b. parlor,** salón de belleza, instituto de belleza, *m.* **b. sleep,** el primer sueño de la noche. **b. spot,** lunar, *m;* lunar postizo, *m;* (place) sitio hermoso, *m.* **b. treatment,** masaje facial, *m*

beaver *n* castor, *m;* (hat) sombrero de copa, *m;* (of helmet) babera, *f*

because *conjunc* porque. **b. of,** debido a, a causa de

beckon *vt* and *vi* hacer señas (a); llamar por señas, llamar con la mano

become *vi* volverse; llegar a ser, venir a ser; convertirse en; ponerse; hacerse; (befit) convenir; (suit) ir bien (a), favorecer. **He became red,** Se enrojeció. **The hat becomes you,** El sombrero te va bien. **He became king,** Llegó a ser rey. **What has b. of her?** ¿Qué es de ella?; (Where is she?) ¿Qué se ha hecho de ella? **b. binding,** adquirir carácter de compromiso

becoming *a* propio; correcto; decoroso; (suitable) conveniente; (of dress) que favorece, que va bien. **This dress is b. to you,** Este vestido te favorece

becomingly *adv* decorosamente

bed *n* cama, *f*, lecho, *m*; (of sea) fondo, *m*; (of river) cauce, *m*; *geol* yacimiento, *m*; (in a garden) cuadro, macizo (de jardín), *m*; (of a machine) asiento, *m*; (of a building) cimiento, *m*; *fig* fundamento, *m*, base, *f*, *vt* (plants) plantar; (fix) fijar, poner. **double bed,** cama de matrimonio, *f*. **single bed,** cama de monja, *f*. **in bed,** en cama. **to be gone to bed,** haber ido a la cama. **to be in bed,** estar acostado. **to get into bed,** meterse en cama. **to get out of bed,** levantarse de la cama. **to go to bed,** acostarse, ir a la cama. **to make the beds,** hacer las camas. **to put to bed,** acostar. **to stay in bed,** quedarse en cama, guardar cama. **bed-bug,** chinche, *f*. **bed-clothes,** ropa de cama, *f*. **bed-cover,** cubrecama, colcha, *f*. **bed-head,** cabecera, *f*. **bed-pan,** silleta, *f*. **bed-sore,** úlcera de decúbito, *f*

bedaub, bedazzle. See **daub, dazzle**

bedchamber *n* dormitorio, *m*, alcoba, *f*

bedded *a* con . . . cama(s). **a double-b. room,** un cuarto con dos camas; un cuarto con cama de matrimonio

bedding *n* ropa de cama, *f*; cama para el ganado, *f*

bedeck *vt* embellecer, adornar, engalanar

bedfellow *n* compañero de almohada, compañero de cama

bedlam *n* belén, manicomio, *m*; *fig* babel, *m*

bedraggled *a* mojado y sucio

bedridden *a* postrado en cama, inválido

bedrock *n* lecho de roca, *m*; *fig* principios fundamentales, fundamentos, *m pl*

bedroom *n* cuarto de dormir, dormitorio, *m*, habitación, *f*

bedside *n* lado de cama, *m*; cabecera, *f*. **b. manner,** mano izquierda, diplomacia, *f*. **b.-table,** mesa de noche, *f*

bedspread *n* colcha, cubrecama, sobrecama, *f*

bedstead *n* cama, *f*

bedtime *n* hora de acostarse, *f*

bee *n* abeja, *f*; (meeting) reunión, *f*, *a* abejuno. **queen bee,** rey, *m*, abeja maestra, *f*. **to have a bee in one's bonnet,** tener una manía (or idea fija). **to make a bee-line for,** ir directamente a. **bee-eater,** *orn* abejaruco, *m*. **bee hive,** colmena, *f*; abejar, *m*. **bee-keeper,** apicultor (-ra), colmenero (-ra), abejero (-ra), *f*. **bee's wax,** cera de abeja, *f*

beech *n* haya, *f*. **plantation of b. trees,** hayal, *m*. **b.-nut,** hayuco, *m*

beef *n* carne de vaca, *f*; (flesh) carne, *f*; (strength) fuerza, *f*. **roast b.,** rosbif, *m*. **b.-tea,** caldo, *m*

beefsteak *n* biftec, bistec, *Argentina* bife *m*

beer *n* cerveza, *f*. **b. barrel,** barril de cerveza, *m*. **b.-house,** cervecería, *f*. **b. mug,** jarro para la cerveza, *m*

beery *a* de cerveza; (tipsy) achispado

beet *n* remolacha, *f*. *Mexico* betabel *m* **b. sugar,** azúcar de remolacha, *Mexico* azúcar de betabel *m*

beetle *n* escarabajo, *m*. **b.-browed,** cejijunto

beetroot *n* remolacha, *f*, *Mexico* betabel *m*

befall *vi* acontecer, suceder, ocurrir. *vt* ocurrir (a), acontecer (a)

befit *vt* convenir (a), ser digno de

befitting *a* conveniente, apropiado; digno; oportuno

before *adv* delante; al frente; (of time), antes, anteriormente; (of order) antes; (already) ya. *prep* delante de; en frente de; (of time, order) ante; (in the presence of) ante, en presencia de; (rather than) antes de. **b. going,** antes de marcharse. **B. I did it,** Antes de que lo hiciera; Antes de hacerlo. **as never b.,** como nunca. **b. long,** en breve, dentro de poco. **b.-mentioned,** antes citado. **b. the mast,** al pie del mástil, e.g. **two years b. the mast,** dos años al pie del mástil

beforehand *adv* previamente, de antemano

befoul *vt* ensuciar; *fig* manchar, difamar

befriend *vt* proteger, ayudar, favorecer, amparar

beg *vt* pedir, implorar, suplicar. *vi* mendigar, pordiosear; vivir de limosna. **I beg to propose,** Me permito proponer; Tengo el gusto de proponer; (the health of) Brindo a la salud de. **I beg your pardon!** ¡Vd. dispense!; (when passing in front of anyone, etc.) Con permiso; (in conversation for repetition of a word) ¿Cómo? **to beg the question,** dar por sentado lo mismo que se trata de probar. **His conduct begs description,** No hay palabras para su comportamiento

beget *vt* procrear, engendrar; causar; suscitar

begetter *n* procreador (-ra); creador (-ra)

begetting *n* procreación, *f*; origen, *m*, causa, *f*

beggar *n* mendigo (-ga), pordiosero (-ra), *Lat. Am. also* llimosnero (-ra). **beggars can't be choosers,** a falta de pan, se conforma con tortillas (Mexico); *vt* empobrecer; arruinar. **to b. description,** no haber palabras para describir

beggarliness *n* mendicidad, *f*; pobreza, *f*

beggarly *a* miserable, pobre

beggary *n* miseria, pobreza, *f*

begging *a* mendicante, pordiosero. *n* mendicidad, *f*, pordioseo, *m*. **to go b.,** andar mendigando. **b. letter,** carta pidiendo dinero, *f*

begin *vt* and *vi* empezar; comenzar; iniciar; (a conversation) entablar; (open) abrir; inaugurar; tener su principio; nacer. **to b. to,** empezar a; (start on) ponerse a; (with laughing, etc.) romper a. **to b. with,** empezar por; para empezar, en primer lugar

beginner *n* principiante (-ta); (novice) novato (-ta); iniciador (-ra); autor (-ra)

beginning *n* principio, comienzo, *Lat. Am.* empiezo. *m*; origen, *m*. **at the b.,** al principio; (of the month) a principios (de). **from the b. to the end,** desde el principio hasta el fin, *inf* de pe a pa. **in the b.,** al principio. **to make a b.,** comenzar, empezar

begone *interj* ¡fuera! ¡márchate! ¡vete!

begonia *n* begonia, *f*

begrudge *vt* envidiar

beguile *vt* engañar; defraudar; (time) entretener; (charm) encantar, embelesar

beguilement *n* engaño, *m*; (of time) entretenimiento, *m*; (charm) encanto, *m*

beguilingly *adv* encantadoramente

behalf *n* (preceded by on or upon) por; (from) de parte (de); a favor (de); en defensa (de)

behave *vi* (oneself) conducirse, portarse; (act) obrar, proceder. **to b. badly,** portarse mal; obrar mal. **B.!** ¡Pórtate bien!

behavior *n* conducta, *f*; comportamiento, *m*; proceder, *m*; (manner) modales, *m pl*; *biol* reacción, *f*

behaviorism *n psy* behaviorismo, *m*

behead *vt* decapitar, descabezar

beheading *n* decapitación, *f*

behest *n* precepto, mandato, *m*

behind *adv* detrás; por detrás; atrás; hacia atrás; en pos; (of time and order) después; (late and in arrears) con retraso; (old-fashioned) atrasado. *prep* detrás de; por detrás de; inferior a; menos avanzado que. *n inf* trasero, *m*. **from b.,** por detrás. **to be b. time,** retrasarse; llegar tarde. **b. the back of,** a espaldas de. **b. the scenes,** entre bastidores. **b. the times,** *fig* atrasado de noticias; pasado de moda. **the ideology b. the French Revolution,** la ideología que informó la Revolución Francesa.

behindhand *a* (out of date) atrasado; (late) tardío; *adv* con retraso

behold *vt* ver, mirar, contemplar; presenciar. *interj* ¡he aquí! ¡mira!

beholden *a* obligado, agradecido

beholder *n* espectador (-ra). **the beholders,** los que lo presenciaban

beholding *n* contemplación, vista, *f*

behove *vt* incumbir, tocar, corresponder

beige *n* beige, color arena, *m*

being *n* existencia, *f*; operación, *f*; ser, *m*; (spirit) alma, *f*, espíritu, *m*; esencia, *f*. **human b.,** ser humano, *m*, alma viviente, *f.* **for the time b.,** por ahora, por el momento

bejewel *vt* enjoyar, adornar con joyas

belabor *vt* apalear, golpear

belated *a* tardío

belay *vt* amarrar

belch *n* eructo, *m;* detonación, *f;* (of a volcano) erupción, *f. vi* eructar. *vt* vomitar; (curses, etc.) escupir; despedir, arrojar

belching *n* eructación, *f;* (of smoke, etc.) vómito, *m,* emisión, *f*

beleaguer *vt* sitiar

belfry *n* campanario, *m*

Belgian *a* and *n* belga, *mf*

Belgium Bélgica, *f*

Belgrade Belgrado, *m*

belie *vt* desmentir, contradecir; defraudar

belief *n* creencia, *f;* fe, *f;* opinión, *f,* parecer, *m;* (trust) confianza, *f.* **in the b. that,** creyendo que, en la creencia de que

believable *a* creíble

believe *vt* and *vi* creer; opinar, ser de la opinión, parecer (a uno); confiar, tener confianza. **I b. not,** Creo que no, Me parece que no. **I b. so,** Creo que sí, Me parece que sí. **to make (a person) b.,** hacer (a uno) creer. **to b. in,** creer en; confiar en, tener confianza en

believer *n* persona que cree, *f;* creyente, *mf*

belittle *vt* achicar; conceder poca importancia a

bell *n* campana, *f;* (hand-bell) campanilla, *f;* (small, round) cascabel, *m;* (on cows, etc.) cencerro, *m,* esquila, *f;* (electric, push, or bicycle) timbre, *m;* (jester's) cascabeles, *m pl;* (cry of stag) bramido, *m. vt* poner el cascabel (a). *vi* (stags) bramar, roncar. **To bear away the b.,** *fig* llevarse la palma. **to ring the b.,** tocar el timbre; agitar la campanilla. **to ring the bells,** tocar las campanas. **to b. the cat,** ponerle el cascabel al gato, ponerle el collar al gato. **b.-boy,** botones, mozo de hotel, *m.* **b.-clapper,** badajo, *m.* **b.-flower,** campanilla, *f.* **b.-founder,** campanero, *m.* **b.-mouthed,** abocinado. **b.-pull,** tirador de campanilla, *m.* **b.-ringer,** campanero, *m.* **b.-shaped,** campanudo. **b.-tent,** pabellón, *m.* **b. tower,** campanario, *m*

belladonna *n* belladona, *f*

belle *n* beldad, *f*

belles-lettres *n pl* bellas letras, *f pl*

bellicose *a* belicoso, agresivo

bellicosity *n* belicosidad, *f*

belligerency *n* beligerancia, *f*

belligerent *a* beligerante; belicoso, guerrero. *n* beligerante, *mf*

bellow *n* (shout) grito, *m;* rugido, bramido, *m;* (of guns) trueno, *m. vi* gritar, vociferar; rugir, bramar; tronar

bellowing *n.* See **bellow**

bellows *n* fuelle, *m*

belly *n* vientre, *m,* barriga, *f;* (of a jug, etc.) panza, *f;* estómago, *m;* (womb) seno, *m. vt* hinchar. *vi* hincharse

belong *vi* pertenecer (a); tocar (a), incumbir (a); (to a place) ser de; residir en

belongings *n pl* efectos, *m pl;* posesiones, *f pl;* (luggage) equipaje, *m*

beloved *a* muy amado, muy querido. *n* querido (-da)

below *adv* abajo; (under) debajo; (further on) más abajo; (in hell) en el infierno; (in this world) en este mundo, aquí abajo. *prep* bajo; (underneath) debajo de; (after) después de; (unworthy of) indigno de; inferior a. **The valley lay b. us,** El valle se extendía a nuestros pies. **b. zero,** bajo cero

belt *n* cinturón, *m;* (of a horse) cincha, *f;* (corset) faja, *f; geog* zona, *f;* (of a machine) correa (de transmisión), *f*

beltway *n* anillo periférico, *m*

belvedere *n* mirador, *m*

bemoan *vt* deplorar, lamentar

bemoaning *n* lamentación, *f*

bemuse *vt* confundir, desconcertar

bench *n* banco, *m;* (with a back) escaño, *m;* mesa de

trabajo, *f;* (carpenter's, shoemaker's, in a boat, in parliament) banco, *m;* (judges) tribunal, *m*

bend *n* corvadura, curva, vuelta, *f;* (in a river, street) recodo, *m;* (on a road) codo viraje, *m;* (of the knee) corva, *f;* (in a pipe) codo, *m; naut* nudo, *m; her* banda, *f.* **sheet b.,** (knot) nudo de tejedor, *m*

bend *vt* encorvar; doblegar; torcer; (the head) bajar; (the body) inclinar; (steps) dirigir, encaminar; (the mind) aplicarse, dedicarse. *vi* encorvarse; doblegarse; torcerse; (arch) arquear; inclinarse. **to b. the knee,** arrodillarse. **on bended knee,** de rodillas. **to b. back,** *vt* redoblar; *vi* redoblarse; inclinarse hacia atrás. **to b. down,** agacharse; inclinarse. **to b. forward,** inclinarse hacia delante. **to b. over,** inclinarse encima de

bendable *a* que puede doblarse; plegadizo; flexible

bending *n* doblamiento, *m;* flexión, *f;* inclinación, *f. a* doblado; inclinado

beneath *adv* abajo; debajo; (at one's feet) a los pies de uno. *prep* bajo; debajo de; al pie de; (unworthy, inferior) indigno. **He married b. him,** Se casó fuera de su clase

Benedictine *a* benedictino. *n* benedictino, *m;* (liqueur) benedictino, *m*

benediction *n* bendición, *f;* gracia divina, merced, *f*

benefaction *n* beneficiación, *f;* buena obra, *f;* beneficio, favor, *m*

benefactor *n* bienhechor, *m;* protector, *m;* patrono, *m;* fundador, *m*

benefactress *n* bienhechora, *f;* protectora, *f;* patrona, *f;* fundadora, *f*

benefice *n* beneficio eclesiástico, *m,* prebenda, *f*

beneficence *n* beneficiencia, caridad, *f,* buenas obras, *f pl*

beneficent *a* benéfico, caritativo

beneficial *a* beneficioso; provechoso, útil

beneficiary *n* beneficiado (-da), beneficiario (-ia)

benefit *n* beneficio, bien, *m;* provecho, *m,* utilidad, *f;* (favor) favor, *m; theat* beneficio, *m;* (help) ayuda, *f,* servicio, *m. vt* beneficiar; aprovechar; (improve) mejorar. *vi* (with by) sacar provecho de; ganar. **for the b. of,** para; en pro de, a favor de. **b. society,** sociedad benéfica, *f*

benevolence *n* benevolencia, bondad, *f;* liberalidad, *f;* caridad, *f;* favor, *m*

benevolent *a* benévolo; bondadoso; caritativo. **b. society,** sociedad de beneficencia, *f*

benevolently *adv* benignamente, con benevolencia

Bengal Bengala, *f*

benighted *a* sorprendido por la noche; *fig* ignorante

benign, benignant *a* benigno

bent *n* talento, *m;* inclinación, afición, *f, a* torcido, *Mexico* chueco; encorvado; resuelto

benumb. See **numb**

benzine *n* bencina, *f*

bequeath *vt* legar, dejar (en el testamento); transmitir

bequest *n* legado, *m*

Berber *a* and *n* bereber, *mf*

bereave *vt* privar (de), quitar; arrebatar; afligir. **the bereaved parents,** los padres afligidos

bereavement *n* privación, *f;* (by death) pérdida, *f;* aflicción, *f*

bereft *a* privado (de); desamparado; indefenso. **utterly b.,** completamente solo

beret *n* boina, *f*

Berlin *a* and *n* (of or from) berlinés (-esa). *n* (carriage) berlina, *f*

Bermudas, the, *m* las Islas Bermudas

Bernard *n* Bernardo, *m.* **St. B. dog,** perro de San Bernardo, *m*

Berne Berna, *f*

berry *n* baya, *f;* (of coffee, etc.) fruto, *m, vi* dar bayas; coger bayas

berth *n* (bed) litera, *f;* (cabin) camarote, *m;* (anchorage) anclaje, fondeadero, *m;* (job) empleo, *m, vt* (a ship) fondear. **to give a wide b. to,** *naut* ponerse a resguardo de; apartarse mucho de; evitar

beseech vt suplicar, rogar, implorar; (ask for) pedir con ahinco

beseeching a suplicante, implorante. n súplica, f; ruego, m

beseechingly adv suplicantemente

beset vt atacar, acosar; aquejar, acosar, perseguir. **beset by personal misfortune,** acosado por las desgracias personales; (block) obstruir; (surround) rodear, cercar

besetting a usual, frecuente; obsesionante

beside, besides prep al lado de; cerca de; (compared with) en comparación de, comparado con; (in addition) además de; aparte de; excepto. adv además, también. **to be beside oneself,** estar fuera de sí

besiege vt sitiar; (assail) asaltar, asediar; (surround) rodear; importunar

besieged n sitiado (-da)

besieger n sitiador, m

besieging a sitiador. n sitio, asalto, m; asedio, m; importunación, f

besmear vt embadurnar, ensuciar

besotted a estúpido; embrutecido; atontado

bespangled a adornado con lentejuelas; brillante (con); (studded) salpicado (de)

bespatter vt manchar; derramar; salpicar

bespeak vt reservar; (goods) encargar; (signify) demostrar, indicar, significar; poet hablar

besprinkle vt rociar

best a sup of **good** and **well,** mejor; el (la) mejor, m, f., los (las) mejores, m pl, f pl. adv mejor; el mejor; (most) más. **as b. I can,** como mejor pueda. **at the b.,** cuando más, en el mejor caso. **He did it for the b.,** Lo hizo con la mejor intención. **the b.,** lo mejor. **to be at one's b.,** brillar; lucirse. **to do one's b.,** hacer todo lo posible. **to get the b. of,** llevar la mejor parte de; triunfar de (or sobre). **to make the b. of,** sacar el mayor provecho de. **The next b. thing to do is . . . ,** Lo mejor que queda ahora por hacer es . . . **b. man,** padrino de boda, m. **to be b. man to,** apadrinar, ser padrino de. **b. seller,** libro que se vende más, libro favorito, m

bestial a bestial

bestiality n bestialidad, f

bestir (oneself) vr menearse, moverse; preocuparse; (hurry) darse prisa

bestow vt (place) poner; (with upon) conferir, conceder, otorgar; (a present) regalar

bestowal n puesta, f; otorgamiento, m, concesión, f; (of a present) regalo, m, dádiva, f

bestride vt montar a horcajadas en; poner una pierna en cada lado de; cruzar de un tranco

bestseller n campeón de venta, éxito editorial, triunfo de librería, m

bet n apuesta, postura, f, vi apostar; (gamble) jugar. **What do you bet?** ¿Qué apuesta Vd.?

betake (oneself) vr acudir (a); darse (a); marcharse

bethink (oneself) vr pensar, reflexionar; (remember) recordar, hacer memoria; ocurrirse

Bethlehem Belén, m

betimes adv pronto; de buena hora, temprano; con tiempo

betoken vt presagiar, prometer; indicar

betray vt traicionar; revelar, descubrir; (a woman) seducir; (show) dejar ver

betrayal n traición, f; (of confidence) abuso (de confianza), m; (of a woman) seducción, f

betrayer n traidor (-ra)

betroth vt desposar(se) con, prometer(se). **to be betrothed to,** estar desposado con

betrothal n desposorio, m, esponsales, m pl; (duration) noviazgo, f

betrothed n desposado (-da), futuro (-ra)

better a comp of **good,** mejor; superior. adv mejor; más. vt mejorar; exceder. n apostador (-ra). **He has bettered himself,** Ha mejorado su situación. **It is b. to . . . ,** Es mejor . . . , Vale más . . . (followed by infin.). **little b.,** poco mejor; algo mejor; poco más. **much b.,** mucho mejor. **our betters,** nuestros superiores. **so**

much the b., tanto mejor. **the b. to,** para mejor. **to be b.,** ser mejor; (of health) estar mejor. **to get b.,** mejorar. **to get the b. of,** triunfar sobre, vencer. **b. half,** inf media naranja, f. **b. off,** mejor situado, más acomodado

betterment n mejora, f, mejoramiento, m; adelantamiento, avance, m

betting n apuesta, f

bettor n apostador (-ra)

between prep entre; en medio de; de. **the break b. Mr. X and Mrs. Y,** el rompimiento del Sr. X y la Sra. Y. adv en medio; entre los dos. **far b.,** a grandes intervalos. **b. now and then,** desde ahora hasta entonces. **b. one thing and another,** entre una cosa y otra. **b. ourselves,** entre nosotros

bevel n bisel, m, vt abiselar

beverage n brebaje, m, bebida, f

bevy n grupo, m; (of birds) bandada, f; (of roes) manada, f

bewail vt lamentar, llorar

bewailing n lamentación, f

beware vi guardarse (de); cuidar (de); desconfiar (de). interj ¡cuidado! ¡atención! **B. of imitations!** ¡Desconfiad de las imitaciones!

bewilder vt aturdir, abobar; dejar perplejo (a); confundir

bewildered a aturdido, abobado; perplejo; confuso

bewildering a incomprensible; complicado

bewilderment n aturdimiento, m; perplejidad, f; confusión, f

bewitch vt hechizar; fascinar, encantar

bewitching a encantador, hechicero, fascinante. n embrujamiento, encantamiento, m

bewitchingly adv de un modo encantador

bewitchment n. See **bewitching**

beyond prep más allá de; más lejos que; (behind) tras, detrás de; (of time) después de; fig fuera del alcance de; (without) fuera de; (above) encima de; (not including) aparte. adv más allá; más lejos; detrás. **b. doubt,** fuera de duda. **b. question,** indiscutible. **b. the sea,** allende el mar. **That is b. me,** Eso es demasiado para mí; Eso no está en mi mano; Eso está fuera de mi alcance. **the back of b.,** donde Cristo dio las tres voces, las quimbambas. **the B.,** la otra vida

Bhután Bután, m

bias n sesgo, bies, través, m; fig prejuicio, m; parcialidad, f, vt influir; predisponer. **to cut on the b.,** cortar al sesgo

biassed a parcial; tendencioso

bib n babero, m; pechera, f, vi beber mucho, empinar el codo

Bible n Biblia, f

biblical a bíblico. **b. history,** historia sagrada, f

bibliographer n bibliógrafo (-fa)

bibliographical a bibliográfico

bibliography n bibliografía, f

bibliophile n bibliófilo, m

bibulous a bebedor, borrachín

bicarbonate n bicarbonato, m

bicentenary n segundo centenario, m

biceps n bíceps, m

bicker vi disputar, altercar; (of stream, etc.) murmurar, susurrar; (of flame) bailar, centellear

bickering n altercado, argumento, m

bicycle n bicicleta, f, vi andar en bicicleta, ir de bicicleta

bicycle pump Lat. Am. inflador m

bicycling n ciclismo, m

bicyclist n biciclista, mf

bid n (at auction) postura, f; (bridge) puja, f; oferta, f, vt mandar, ordenar, invitar a; (at an auction) pujar, licitar. **to make a bid for,** (attempt) hacer un esfuerzo para; procurar. **to bid fair,** prometer; dar indicios de; dar esperanzas de. **to bid goodbye to,** decir adios (a), despedirse de. **to bid welcome,** dar la bienvenida (a)

biddable a obediente, dócil; manso

bidder *n* postor, *m*, pujador (-ra). **the highest b.**, el mejor postor

bidding *n* (order) orden, *f*; instrucción, *f*; invitación, *f*; (at an auction) postura, licitación, *f*. **to do a person's b.**, hacer lo que se le manda

bide *vt* aguardar, esperar. **to b. by,** (fulfil) cumplir con

bidet *n* bidé, *m*

biennial *a* bianual, bienal

bier *n* andas, *f pl*; féretro, ataúd, *m*

bifocal *a* bifocal

bifurcate *vt* and *vi* bifurcar(se)

bifurcation *n* bifurcación, *f*

big *a* grande; grueso; (grown up) mayor; (tall) alto; voluminoso; (vast) extenso, vasto; (full) lleno (de); (with young) preñada; importante. **to talk big,** echarla de importante. **big-boned,** huesudo. **big-end,** *aut* biela, *f*. **big game,** caza mayor, *f*. **big gun,** *inf* pájaro gordo, *m*

bigamist *n* bígamo (-ma)

bigamous *a* bígamo

bigamy *n* bigamia, *f*

bight *n* (in a rope) vuelta (de un cabo), *f*; (bay) ensenada, *f*

bigness *n* grandor, *m*; gran tamaño, *m*; altura, *f*; (tallness of a person) gran talle, *m*; (vastness) extensión, *f*; importancia, *f*

bigot *n* fanático (-ca)

bigoted *a* fanático, intolerante

bigotry *n* fanatismo, *m*, intolerancia, *f*

bikini *n* bikini, *m*

bilberry *n* arándano, *m*

bile *n* bilis, hiel, *f*; mal humor, *m*, cólera, *f*

bilge *n naut* pantoque, *m*, sentina, *f*. **b. water,** agua de pantoque, *f*

bilingual *a* bilingüe

bilious *a* bilioso

bill *n* (parliamentary) proyecto de ley, *m*; *law* escrito, *m*; *com* cuenta, *f*; (poster) cartel, *m*; (program) programa, *m*; (cast) repertorio, *m*; (bank note) billete de banco, *m*; (of a bird) pico, *m*; (for pruning) podadera, *f*. **due b.,** *com* abonaré, *m*. **Post no bills!** Se prohíbe fijar carteles. **b. of exchange,** letra de cambio, *f*. **b. of fare,** lista de platos, *f*; *fig* programa, *m*. **b. of health,** patente de sanidad, *f*. **b. of lading,** conocimiento de embarque, *m*. **b. of rights,** declaración de derechos, *f*. **b. of sale,** contrato de venta, *m*, carta de venta, *f*. **b.-broker,** agente de bolsa, agente de cambio, *m*. **b.-poster,** fijador de carteles, cartelero, *m*

bill *vt* anunciar; publicar; poner en el programa; fijar carteles en. **to b. and coo,** (doves) arrullar; *inf* besuquearse

billboard, *n* tablero publicitario, *m*

billed *a* (in compounds) de pico

billet *n* alojamiento, *m*; (of wood) pedazo (de leña), *m*; (job) empleo, destino, *m*, *vt* alojar (en or con)

billeting *n* alojamiento, *m*. **b. officer,** *mil* aposentador, *m*; oficial encargado de encontrar alojamiento, *m*

billiards *n pl* billar, *m*. **billiard ball,** bola de billar, *f*. **billiard cue,** taco, *m*. **billiard cushion,** baranda de la mesa de billar, *f*. **billiard marker,** marcador, *m*. **billiard match,** partida de billar, *f*. **billiard player,** jugador (-ra) de billar. **billiard pocket** *Lat. Am.* buchaca *f*. **billiard room,** sala de billar, *f*. **billiard table,** mesa de billar, *f*

billing *n* facturación, *f*

billion *n* billón, *m*; (U.S.A. and France) mil millones, *m pl*

billionth *a* billonésimo; (U.S.A. and France) milmillonésimo

bill of particulars *n* relación detallada, *f*

billow *n* oleada, *f*; *poet* ola, *f*; *fig* onda, *f*. *vi* hincharse, encresparse; ondular

billowy *a* ondulante, ondeante

bimonthly *a* bimestral

bin *n* hucha, *f*; arcón, *m*; recipiente, *m*; depósito, *m*; cajón, *m*; (for wine) estante, *m*

binary *a* binario

bind *vt* atar; unir, ligar; amarrar; (in sheaves) agavillar; (bandage) vendar; sujetar; fijar; aprisionar; (a book) encuadernar; *sew* ribetear; (oblige) obligar; comprometer; (constipate) estreñir; contratar (como aprendiz). **I feel bound to,** Me siento obligado a. **to b. over,** obligar a comparecer ante el juez

binder *n* encuadernador (-ra); *agr* agavilladora, *f*

binding *a* válido, valedero; obligatorio; **become b.,** adquirir carácter de compromiso; *med* constrictivo. *n* atadura, ligación, *f*; (of books) encuadernación, *f*; *sew* ribete, *m*

binge *n* parranda, juerga, *f*. **to go on the b.,** ir de parranda, ir de picos pardos, ir de juerga

binnacle *n naut* bitácora, *f*

binocular *a* binocular. *n pl* **binoculars,** binóculos, gemelos, *m pl*

binomial *a* and *n* binomio *m*.

biochemist *n* bioquímico, *m*

biochemistry *n* bioquímica, *f*

biographer *n* biógrafo (-fa)

biographical *a* biográfico

biography *n* biografía, vida, *f*

biological *a* biológico

biologist *n* biólogo, *m*

biology *n* biología, *f*

bipartite *a* bipartido

biped *n bot* abedul, *m*; (rod) vara, *f*, *a* de abedul. *vt* pegar con una vara, dar una paliza (a)

birch *n bot* abedul, *m*; (rod) vara, *f*, *a* de abedul. *vt* pegar con una vara, dar una paliza (a)

bird *n* pájaro, *m*; ave, *f*. **Birds of a feather flock together,** Cada cual se arrima a su cada cual. **hen b.,** pájara, *f*. **b.-call,** voz del pájaro, *f*, canto del ave, *m*. **b. catcher or vendor,** pajarero, *m*. **bird's-eye view,** vista de pájaro, perspectiva aérea, *f*. **b.-fancier,** aficionado (-da) a las aves; criador (-ra) de pájaros. **b.-like,** como un pájaro; de pájaro. **b.-lime,** liga, *f*. **to go b.-nesting,** ir a coger nidos de pájaros. **b. of paradise,** ave del paraíso, *f*. **b. of passage,** ave de paso, *f*. **b. of prey,** ave rapaz, *f*. **b.-seed,** alpiste, *m*

birth *n* nacimiento, *m*; (act of) parto, *m*; origen, *m*; (childhood) infancia, *f*; (family) linaje, *m*, familia, *f*; *fig* creación, *f*. **from b.,** de nacimiento. **to give b. to,** dar a luz, echar al mundo, parir. **b. certificate,** partida de nacimiento, certificación de nacimiento, *f*. **b. control,** anticoncepcionismo, *m*, regulación de la fecundidad, *f*. **b.-mark,** antojos, *m pl*. **b.-place,** lugar de nacimiento, *m*. **b.-rate,** natalidad, *f*

birthday *n* cumpleaños, *m*

birthright *n* derecho de nacimiento, *m*; herencia, *f*

Biscayan *a* and *n* vizcaíno (-na)

Biscay, the Bay of el Golfo de Vizcaya, *m*

biscuit *n* galleta, *f*; bizcocho, *m*. **b. box or maker,** galletero, *m*. **b.-like,** abizcochado

bisect *vt* dividir en dos partes iguales; *geom* bisecar

bisexual *a* bisexual

bishop *n* obispo, *m*; (in chess) alfil, *m*. **bishop's crozier,** báculo episcopal, cayado, *m*

bismuth *n* bismuto, *m*

bison *n* bisonte, *m*

bisque *n* porcelana blanca, *f*, bizcocho, *m*

bistoury *n* bisturí, *m*

bit *n* pedazo, *m*; (of grass, etc.) brizna, *f*; (moment) instante, *m*; (quantity) cantidad, *f*; (of a drill) mecha, *f*; (part) parte, *f*; (passage) trozo, *m*; (horse's) bocado, *m*; *inf* miga, *f*. **a bit,** un tanto, algo, un poco. **in bits,** en pedazos. **Not a bit!** ¡Nada!; ¡Ni pizca!; ¡Claro que no! **bit by bit,** poco a poco, gradualmente. **to give someone a bit of one's mind,** contarle cuatro verdades. **to take the bit between one's teeth,** desbocarse; *fig* rebelarse. **Wait a bit!** ¡Espera un momento!

bitch *n* (female dog) perra, *f*; (fox) zorra, *f*; (wolf) loba, *f*

bite *n* mordedura, *f*; mordisco, *m*; (mouthful, snack) bocado, *m*, *Lat. Am.* botana *f* (of fish and insects) picada, *f*; (hold) asimiento, *m*; (sting, pain) picadura, *f*; (pungency) resquemor, *m*; (offer) oferta, *f*; (*fig* mordancy) mordacidad, acritud, *f. vt* and *vi* morder; (gnaw) roer; (of fish, insects) picar; (of hot dishes) resquemar; (of acids) corroer; (deceive) engañar, defraudar; (of wheels, etc.) agarrar; (hurt, wound) herir. **to b. one's tongue,** morderse la lengua. **to b. the dust,** caer al suelo

biting *a* (stinging) picante; (mordant) mordaz, acre; (of winds, etc.) penetrante; satírico. *n* mordedura, *f;* rodura, *f*

bitter *a* amargo; (sour) agrio, ácido; (of winds) penetrante; (of cold) intenso; cruel. **to the b. end,** hasta la muerte; hasta el último extremo. **b.-sweet,** agridulce

bitterly *adv* amargamente; intensamente; cruelmente

bitterness *n* amargura, *f;* (sourness) acidez, *f;* (of cold) intensidad, *f;* crueldad, *f*

bitters *n pl* (drink) bíter, *m,* angostura, *f*

bitumen *n* betún, *m*

bivouac *n mil* vivaque, *m, vi* vivaquear

bizarre *a* raro, extravagante; grotesco

black *a* negro; obscuro; (sad) triste, melancólico; funesto; (wicked) malo, perverso; (sullen) malhumorado. *n* (color) negro, *m;* (mourning) luto, *m;* (negro) negro, *m;* (negress) negra, *f;* (stain) mancha, *f;* (dirt) tizne, *m. vt* ennegrecer; tiznar. **in b. and white,** por escrito. **to look on the b. side,** verlo todo negro. **b. art,** nigromancia, *f.* **b.-currant,** grosella negra, *f.* **b.-eyed,** ojinegro, con ojos negros. **b.-haired,** pelinegro, de pelo negro. **b.-lead,** plombagina, *f.* **b.-list,** lista negra, *f.* **b.-market,** estraperlo, mercado negro, *m.* **b.-marketeer,** estraperlista, *mf* **b.-out,** oscurecimiento, apagamiento, *m.* **b.-pudding,** morcilla, *f.* **b. sheep,** oveja negra, *f; fig* oveja descarriada, *f;* (of a family) garbanzo negro, *m.* **b.-water fever,** melanuria, *f*

blackberry *n* mora, zarzamora, *f;* (bush) zarza, *f,* moral, *m*

blackbird *n* mirlo, *m*

blackboard *n* encerado, *m,* pizarra, *f*

black coffee *Spain* café solo, *Colombia* café tinto, *elsewhere in Lat. Am.* café negro *m*

blacken *vt* ennegrecer; tiznar; *fig* manchar, desacreditar. *vi* ennegrecerse

black eye *n* ojo como un tomate, ojo morado, *m*

blackguard *n* tipo de cuidado, perdido, *m*

blackhead *n* espinilla, *f*

blacking *n* betún, *m*

blackish *a* negruzco

blackmail *n* chantaje, *m, vt* hacer víctima de un chantaje; arrancar dinero por chantaje (a)

blackmailer *n* chantajista, *mf*

blackness *n* negrura, *f;* obscuridad, *f;* (wickedness) maldad, perversidad, *f*

blacksmith *n* herrero (-ra) *mf, Lat. Am.* also encasquillador (-ra) *mf.* **blacksmith's forge,** herrería, *f*

bladder *n anat* vejiga, *f;* ampolla, *f;* (of sea-plants) vesícula, *f;* (of fish) vejiga natatoria, *f*

blade *n* (leaf) hoja, *f;* (of grass, etc.) brizna, *f;* (of sharp instruments) hoja, *f;* (of oar) pala, *f;* (of propeller) paleta, ala, *f*

bladed *a* de . . . hojas. **a two-b. knife,** un cuchillo de dos hojas

blame *n* culpa, *f;* responsabilidad, *f;* censura, *f. vt* culpar, echar la culpa (a); tachar, censurar, criticar; acusar. **You are to b. for this,** Vd. tiene la culpa de esto

blameless *a* inculpable; inocente; intachable; elegante

blamelessness *n* inculpabilidad, inocencia, *f;* elegancia, *f*

blameworthy *a* culpable, digno de censura, vituperable

blanch *vt cul* mondar; hacer palidecer. *vi* palidecer, perder el color

blanching *n* palidecimiento, *m; cul* mondadura, *f*

blancmange *n* manjar blanco, *m*

bland *a* afable, cortés; dulce, agradable

blandish *vt* adular, halagar, acariciar

blandishment *n* adulación, *f,* halago, *m,* caricia, *f*

blandness *n* afabilidad, urbanidad, *f;* dulzura, *f*

blank *a* en blanco; (empty) vacío; desocupado; pálido; (confused) confuso, desconcertado; (expressionless) sin expresión; (of verse) suelto; sin adorno. *n* blanco, hueco, *m;* papel en blanco, *m;* laguna, *f;* (form to be filled out) hoja *f, Mexico* esqueleto *m* **b. cartridge,** cartucho para salvas, cartucho de fogueo, *m.* **b. verse,** verso suelto, *m*

blanket *n* manta, frazada, *Lat. Am.* cobija *f;* (of a horse) sudadero, *Lat. Am.* mandil *m; fig* capa, *f. vt* cubrir con una manta. **to toss in a b.,** mantear. **wet b.,** aguafiestas, *mf.* **b. maker or seller,** mantero, *m.* **b. vote,** voto colectivo, *m*

blanketing *n* manteamiento, *m*

blankly *adv* con indiferencia; sin comprender; (flatly) categóricamente

blankness *n* confusión, *f,* desconcierto, *m;* (emptiness) vaciedad, *f;* indiferencia, *f;* incomprensión, *f*

blare *n* sonido de la trompeta o del clarín, *poet* clangor, *m;* (of a car horn) ruido, *m. vi* sonar

blarney *n* labia, *f. vt* lisonjear

blaspheme *vi* blasfemar. *vt* renegar de, maldecir

blasphemer *n* blasfemador (-ra), blasfemo (-ma)

blasphemous *a* blasfemo, blasfematorio

blasphemy *n* blasfemia, *f*

blast *n* (of wind) ráfaga (de viento), *f;* (of a trumpet, etc.) trompetazo, son, *m;* (of a whistle) pitido, *m;* (draft) soplo, *m;* explosión, *f; fig* influencia maligna, *f. vt* (rock) barrenar, hacer saltar; (wither) marchitar, secar; *fig* destruir; (curse) maldecir. **in full b.,** en plena marcha. **b.-furnace,** alto horno, horno de cuba, *m.* **b. hole,** barreno, *m*

blaster *n* barrenero, *m*

blasting *n* (of rock) voladura, *f;* (withering) marchitamiento, *m; fig* destrucción, ruina, *f;* (cursing) maldiciones, *f pl. a.* destructor; *fig* funesto. **b. charge,** carga explosiva, *f*

blatant *a* ruidoso; agresivo; llamativo; (boastful) fanfarrón

blaze *n* llama, *f;* fuego, *m;* conflagración, *f;* luz brillante, *f;* (of anger, etc.) acceso, *m. vi* llamear, encenderse en llamas; brillar, resplandecer. **a b. of colour,** una masa de color. **Go to blazes!** ¡Vete al infierno!

blazon *n her* blasón, *m; fig* proclamación, *f, vt* blasonar; adornar; proclamar

bleach *n* lejía, *f. vt* blanquear; descolorar. *vi* ponerse blanco; descolorarse

bleaching *n* blanqueo, *f.* **b. powder,** hipoclorito de cal, *m*

bleak *a* yermo, desierto; frío; expuesto; (sad) triste; severo

bleakness *n* situación expuesta, *f;* desnudez, *f;* frío, *m;* (sadness) tristeza, *f;* severidad, *f*

bleary-eyed *a* legañoso, cegajoso

bleat *n* balido, *m, vt* and *vi* balar, dar balidos

bleating *a* balador, que bala. *n* balido, *m*

bleed *vi* sangrar, echar sangre; sufrir. *vt* sangrar; arrancar dinero a

bleeding *n* hemorragia, *f;* sangría, *f, Lat. Am.* desangre *m*

blemish *n* imperfección, *f,* defecto, *m;* (on fruit) maca, *f;* (stain) mancha, *f;* deshonra, *f*

blend *n* mezcla, mixtura, *f;* combinación, *f;* fusión, *f. vt* mezclar; combinar. *vi* mezclarse; combinarse

blende *n min* blenda, *f*

blending *n* mezcla, *f;* fusión, *f*

bless *vt* bendecir; consagrar; (praise) alabar, glorificar; hacer feliz (a). **B. me!** ¡Válgame Dios!

blessed *a* bendito; *ecc* beato, bienaventurado; (dear) querido; feliz; *inf* maldito

blessedness *n* felicidad, *f;* bienaventuranza, *f*

blessing *n* bendición, *f;* (grace) bendición de la mesa, *f;* (mercy) merced, gracia, *f;* favor, *m;* (good) bien, *m.* **He gave them his b.,** Les echó su bendición

Bless you! (to someone who has sneezed) ¡Jesús!

blight *n agr* tizne, tizón, *m;* (of cereals) añublo, *m;*

(mould) roña, *f*; (greenfly) pulgón, *m*; *fig* influencia maligna, *f*; (frustration) desengaño, *m*; (spoil-sport) aguafiestas, *mf vt* atizonar; anublar; (wither) marchitar, secar; *fig* frustrar, destruir; malograr

blighter *n* bribón, *m*

blind *a* ciego; (secret) secreto; (of a door, etc.) falso; (closed) cerrado, sin salida; (unaware) ignorante; sin apreciación (de). **to be b.,** ser ciego; *fig* tener una venda en los ojos. **to be b. in one eye,** ser tuerto. **to turn a b. eye,** hacer la vista gorda. **b. alley,** callejón sin salida, *m*. **b. as a bat,** más ciego que un topo. **b. flying,** *aer* vuelo a ciegas, *m*. **b. man,** ciego, hombre ciego, *m*. **b. obedience,** obediencia ciega, *f*. **b. side,** (of persons) lado débil, *m*. **b. woman,** ciega, mujer ciega, *f*

blind *vt* cegar; poner una venda en los ojos (de); (dazzle) deslumbrar; hacer cerrar los ojos a; hacer ignorar

blind *n* persiana, *f*; (Venetian) celosía, *f*; (deception) pretexto, *m*; velo, *m*

blindfold *vt* vendar los ojos (a); *fig* poner una venda en los ojos (de). *a* and *adv* con los ojos vendados; a ciegas; con los ojos cerrados

blindly *adv* ciegamente; a ciegas; ignorantemente

blindman's buff *n* gallina ciega, *f*

blindness *n* ceguedad, *f*; ofuscación, *f*; ignorancia, *f*

blink *n* parpadeo, *m*, guiñada, *f*; (of light) destello, *m*; reflejo, *m*; *vi* parpadear, pestañear; (of lights) destellar

blinkers *n pl* anteojeras, *f pl*

bliss *n* felicidad, *f*; deleite, placer, *m*; *ecc* gloria, *f*

blissful *a* feliz

blissfulness *n*. See **bliss**

blister *n med* vesícula, *f*; ampolla, *f*; (bubble) burbuja, *f*. *vt* ampollar; *fig* herir

blithe *a* alegre

blithely *adv* alegremente

blitheness *n* alegría, *f*

blitzkrieg *n* blitzkrieg, *m*, guerra relámpago, *f*

blizzard *n* ventisca, nevasca, *f*

bloated *a* abotagado, hinchado; orgulloso; indecente

bloater *n* arenque ahumado, *m*

blob *n* masa, *f*; mancha, *f*; gota, *f*

block *n* bloque, *m*; (log) leño, *m*; *naut* polea, *f*; (for beheading and of a butcher) tajo, *m*; (for mounting) apeadero, *m*; (of shares, etc.) lote, *m*; (of houses) manzana, *Lat. Am.* cuadra *f*; (jam) atasco, *m*; (obstruction) obstrucción, *f*; (for hats) forma, *f*. **A chip off the old b.,** De tal palo tal astilla. **b. and tackle,** *naut* polea con aparejo. **b.-hook,** grapa, *f*. **b.-house,** *mil* blocao, *m*

block *vt* bloquear; cerrar (el paso); (stop up) atarugar, atascar; (a wheel) calzar; (a bill, etc.) obstruir; (hats) poner en forma. **to b. the way,** cerrar el paso.

blockade *n* bloqueo, *m*, *vt* bloquear. **to run the b.,** violar el bloqueo

blockhead *n* leño, zoquete, imbécil, *m*

blond(e) *a* (of hair) rubio; (of complexion) de tez blanca. *n* hombre rubio, *m*; (woman) rubia, mujer rubia, *f*. **peroxide b.,** rubia oxigenada, *f*. **b. lace,** blondina, *f*

blood *n* sangre, *f*; (relationship) parentesco, *m*; (family) linaje, *m*, prosapia, *f*; (life) vida, *f*; (sap) savia, *f*; jugo, *m*; (horse) caballo de pura raza, *m*; (dandy) galán, *m*. *vt* sangrar. **bad b.,** mala sangre, *f*; odio, *m*; mala leche, *f*. **blue b.,** sangre azul, *f*. **in cold b.,** a sangre fría, *f*. **My b. is up,** Se me enciende la sangre. **My b. runs cold,** Se me hiela la sangre. **to be in the b.,** llevar en la sangre. **b.-bank,** banco de sangre, *m*. **b.-bath,** matanza, *f*. **b.-colored,** de color de sangre, sanguíneo. **b.-feud,** venganza de sangre, *f*. **b.-guilt,** culpabilidad de homicidio, *m*. **b.-heat,** calor de sangre, *m*. **b.-letting,** sangría, *f*. **b. orange,** naranja dulce, *f*. **b.-plasma,** plasma sanguíneo, *m*. **b.-poisoning,** septicemia, *f*; infección, *f*. **b.-pressure,** presión sanguínea, *f*. **b. purity,** limpieza de sangre, *f*. **b.-red,** rojo como la sangre. **b.-relation,** pariente (-ta) consanguíneo(a). **b.-relationship,** consanguinidad, *f*. **b.-stain,** mancha de sangre, *f*. **b.-stained,** ensangrentado, manchado de

sangre. **b.-stone,** sanguinaria, *f*. **b.-sucker,** sanguijuela, *f*; *fig* vampiro, *m*; (usurer) avaro (-ra). **b.-vessel,** vaso sanguíneo, *m*

blooded *a* de sangre . . . ; de casta . . .

bloodhound *n* sabueso, *m*

bloodily *adv* sangrientamente; cruentamente; con ferocidad, cruelmente

bloodiness *n* estado sangriento, *m*; crueldad, ferocidad, *f*

bloodless *a* exangüe; pálido; incruento; anémico; indiferente

bloodshed *n* efusión de sangre, *f*; matanza, carnicería, *f*

bloodshot *a* (of the eye) inyectado

bloodthirstiness *n* sed de sangre, *f*

bloodthirsty *a* sanguinario, carnicero

bloody *a* sangriento; (of battles) encarnizado; (cruel) sanguinario, cruel

bloom *n* flor, *f*; florecimiento, *m*; (on fruit) flor, *f*; (prime) lozanía, *f*; (on the cheeks) color sano, *m*. *vi* florecer. **in b.,** en flor

blooming *a* florido; en flor; fresco; lozano; brillante

blossom *n* flor, *f*. *vi* florecer. **to b. out into,** hacerse, llegar a ser; (wear) lucir; (buy) comprarse

blossomed *a* con flores, de flores

blossoming *n* floración, *f*

blot *n* borrón, *m*; mancha, *f*. *vt* manchar; (erase) tachar; (dry) secar. **to b. out,** borrar; destruir; secar con papel secante

blotch *n* (on the skin, or stain) mancha, *f*

blotter *n com* libro borrador, *m*; teleta, *f*

blotting paper *n* papel secante, *m*

blouse *n* blusa, *f*

blow *n* golpe, *m*; bofetada, *f*; (with the fist) puñetazo, *m*; (with the elbow) codazo, *m*; (with a club) porrazo, *m*; (with a whip) latigazo, *m*; (blossoming) floración, *f*; (disaster) desastre, *m*, tragedia, *f*. **to come to blows,** venirse a las manos. **at a b.,** con un solo golpe; de una vez. **We are going for a b.,** Vamos a tomar el fresco. **b. below the belt,** golpe bajo, *m*. **b. in the air,** golpe en vago, *m*. **b. of fate,** latigazo de la fortuna, *m*

blow *vi* (of wind) soplar (el viento), hacer viento, correr aire; (pant) jadear, echar resoplidos; (of fuses) fundirse. *vt* (wind instruments) tocar; soplar; (inflate) inflar; (swell) hinchar. **to b. a kiss,** tirar un beso. **to b. one's nose,** sonarse las narices. **to b. away,** dispar; ahuyentar; llevar (el viento). **to b. down,** echar por tierra, derribar (el viento). **to b. in,** llevar adentro, hacer entrar (el viento); (windows, etc.) quebrar (el viento). **to b. off,** quitar (el viento). **to b. open,** abrir (el viento). **to b. out,** hacer salir (el viento); llevar afuera (el viento); (a light) matar de un soplo, apagar soplando. **to b. over,** pasar por (el viento); soplar por; disiparse; olvidarse. **to b. up,** (inflate) inflar; (the fire) avivar (el fuego); (explode) volar; (swell) hinchar

blowing *n* soplo, *m*; violencia, *f*; (blossoming) florecimiento, *m*. **b. up,** voleo, *m*; explosión, *f*

blow-up *n* (photograph) fotografía ampliada, *f*

blowzy *a* desaliñado

blubber *vi* gimotear; berrear. *n* (of the whale) grasa de ballena, *f*. **b.-lip,** bezo, *m*. **b.-lipped,** bezudo

bludgeon *n* cachiporra, porra, *f*; garrote, *m*; estaca, *f*. *vt* golpear con una porra, dar garrotazos (a)

blue *a* azul; (with bruises) amoratado; (sad) deprimido, melancólico; (obscene) verde; (dark) sombrío; (traditionalist) conservador. *n* azul, *m*; (sky) cielo, *m*; (for clothes) añil de lavandera, *m*; *pl* **blues,** melancolía, depresión, *f*; (homesickness) morriña, *f*. *vt* (laundry) añilar. **to look b.,** parecer deprimido; (of prospects, etc.) ser poco halagüeño. **b. black,** azul negro, *m*; (of hair) azabache, *m*. **b.-bottle,** *ent* moscón, *m*. **b.-eyed,** con ojos azules. **b. gum,** eucalipto, *m*. **B. Peter,** bandera de salida, *f*. **b. print,** fotocopia, *f*; plan, *m*

bluebell *n* campanilla, *f*

bluestocking *n* marisabidilla, doctora, *f*

bluff *a* (of cliffs, etc.) escarpado; (of persons) franco, campechano, brusco

bluffer *n Lat. Am.* blofista *mf*

bluffness *n* franqueza, brusquedad, *f*

bluish *a* azulado

bluishness *n* color azulado, *m*

blunder *n* desacierto, desatino, *m*; equivocación, *f*; (in a translation, etc.) falta, *f*. *vi* tropezar (con); desacertar; equivocarse; *inf* meter la pata. *vt* manejar mal; estropear

blunderer *n* desatinado (-da)

blundering *a* desacertado; equivocado; imprudente *n*. See **blunder**

blunt *a* romo, embotado; obtuso; (abrupt) brusco; franco; descortés; (plain) claro. *vt* enromar, embotar; (the point) despuntar; *fig* hacer indiferente; (pain) mitigar

bluntly *adv* sin filo; sin punta; bruscamente, francamente; claramente

bluntness *n* embotamiento, *m*; *fig* brusquedad, franqueza, *f*; claridad, *f*

blur *n* borrón, *m*; mancha, *f*; imagen indistinta, *f*. *vt* borrar; manchar; *phot* velar

blurred *a* borroso; indistinto; turbio

blurt (out) *vt* proferir bruscamente; revelar sin querer

blush *n* rubor, *m*; rojo, *m*. *vi* enrojecerse, ruborizarse, ponerse colorado; avergonzarse (por)

blushing *a* ruboroso; púdico

bluster *vi* (of the wind) soplar con furia; (of waves) encresparse, embravecerse; (of persons) bravear, fanfarronear. *n* furia, violencia, *f*; tumulto, *m*; fanfarronería, *f*

blustering *a* (of wind) violento, fuerte; (of waves) tumultuoso; (of people) fanfarrón, valentón

boar *n* verraco, *m*; (wild) jabalí, *m*

board *n* tabla, *f*; (for notices) tablón, *m*; (b. residence) pensión, *f*; (table) mesa, *f*; (food) comida, *f*; (for chess, checkers) tablero, *m*; (sign) letrero, *m*; (of instruments) cuadro, *m*; (bookbinding) cartón, *m*; *naut* bordo, *m*; (committee) junta, dirección, *f*; tribunal, *m*; *pl* boards *theat* tablas, *f pl*. **above b.,** abiertamente, sin disimulo. **free on b.,** (f.o.b.) franco a bordo. **in boards,** (of books) encartonado. **managerial b.,** junta directiva, *f*. **on b.,** a bordo. **on the boards,** *theat* en las tablas. **to go on b.,** ir a bordo. **b. and lodging,** pensión completa, casa y comida, *f*. **b. of directors,** consejo de administración, *m*. **b. of examiners,** tribunal de exámenes, *m*. **b. of trade,** junta de comercio, *f*; ministerio de comercio, *m*

board *vt carp* entablar, enmaderar; embarcar en; (*nav* a ship) abordar; (lodge) alojar, tomar a pensión

boarder *n* huésped (-da); (at school) pensionista, *mf* alumno (-na) interno (-na)

boarding *n* entablado, *m*; (planking) tablazón, *f*; (of a ship) abordaje, *m*; (of a train) subida (al tren), *f*. **b.-house,** casa de huéspedes, pensión, *f*. **b.-school,** pensionado, *m*

boarding gate *n* puerta de embarque, *f*

boast *n* jactancia, *f*; ostentación, *f*; (honor) gloria, *f*. *vi* jactarse, vanagloriarse, *Lat. Am.* dragonear, *Argentina* faramallear; alabarse; ostentar. **to b. about,** jactarse de; hacer gala de; gloriarse en

boaster *n* vanaglorioso (-sa), jactancioso (-sa)

boastful *a* vanaglorioso, jactancioso; ostentador

boastfulness *n* vanagloria, jactancia, *f*; fanfarronería, *f*; ostentación, *f*

boasting *n* alardeo, *m*; fanfarronería, *f*

boat *n* barco, *m*; bote, *m*; (in a fun fair) columpio, *m*, lancha, *f*; (for sauce or gravy) salsera, *f*. *vi* ir en barco; (row) remar; navegar. **to b. down,** bajar en barco. **b. up,** subir en barco. **b. building,** construcción de barcos, *f*. **b. club,** club náutico, *m*. **b. crew,** tripulación de un barco, *f*. **b.-hook,** bichero, garabato, *m*. **b.-house,** cobertizo de las lanchas, *m*. **b.-load,** barcada, *f*. **b.-race,** regata, *f*. **b.-scoop,** achicador, *m*. **b.-shaped,** en forma de barco. **b.-train,** tren que enlaza con un vapor, *m*

boating *n* pasear en bote, *m*; manejo de un bote, *m*; (rowing) remo, *m*. **b.-pole,** botador, *m*

boatman *n* barquero, *m*

boatswain *n* contramaestre, *m*. **boatswain's mate,** segundo contramaestre, *m*

bob *n* (curtsey) reverencia, *f*; (woman's hair) pelo a la romana, *m*; (of bells) toque (de campana), *m*. *vi* saltar; moverse. *vt* cortar corto. **long bob,** (hair) melena, *f*. **to bob up,** ponerse de pie; surgir. **to bob up and down,** subir y bajar; bailar. **bob-tail,** rabo corto, *m*. **bob-tailed,** rabón

Bob (pet form of *Robert*) Beto (Mexico)

bobbin *n* carrete, huso, *m*; (of wool, etc.) ovillo, *m*; (of looms, sewing machines) bobina, *f*; (in lace-making) bolillo, palillo, *m*

bobsleigh *n* trineo doble, *m*

bode *vt* presagiar, prometer. **to b. ill,** prometer mal. **to b. well,** prometer bien

bodice *n* corpiño, *m*

bodied *a* (in compounds) de cuerpo-

bodiless *a* incorpóreo

bodily *a* del cuerpo; físico; corpóreo; real; material; (of fear) de su persona. *adv* corporalmente; en persona, personalmente; en conjunto, enteramente; en una pieza

boding *a* ominoso, amenazador. *n* presagio, *m*; agüero, *m*

body *n anat* cuerpo, *m*; (trunk) tronco, *m*; (corpse) cadáver, *m*; (of a vehicle) caja, *f*; (of a motor-car) carrocería, *f*; (of a ship) casco, *m*; (of a church) nave, *f*; (centre) centro, *m*; (of a book, persons, consistency and *ast*) cuerpo, *m*; (person) persona, *f*; corporación, *f*; grupo, *m*; (of an army) grueso (de ejercito), *m*; organismo, *m*. **in a b.,** en masa, juntos (juntas); en corporación. **to have enough to keep b. and soul together,** tener de que vivir. **b.-snatcher,** junta cadáveres *mf* ladrón de cadáveres, *m*. **b.-snatching,** robo de cadáveres, *m*

bodyguard *n* guardia de corps, *f*; guardia, *f*; (escort) escolta, *f*

body language *n* el lenguaje del cuerpo, *m*

bog *n* pantano, marjal, *m*, marisma, *f*, *Central America* chagüe *m*

bogey *n* duende, *m*; (to frighten children) coco, *m*; (nightmare) pesadilla, *f*

boggy *a* pantanoso, fangoso

bogus *a* postizo, falso

Bohemian *a* and *n* bohemio (-ia)

boil *vi* bullir, hervir; (cook) cocer. *vt* hervir; cocer. *n* ebullición, *f*; *med* divieso, *m*. **to b. away,** consumirse hirviendo; *chem* evaporar a seco. **to b. over,** rebosar

boiler *n cul* marmita, olla, *f*; (of a furnace) caldera, *f*. **double-b.,** baño de María, *m*. **steam-b.,** caldera de vapor, *f*. **b.-maker,** calderero, *m*. **b. room,** cámara de la caldera, *f*. **b.-suit,** mono, *m*

boiling *n* ebullición, *f*, hervor, *m*; (cooking) cocción, *f*, *a* hirviente. **b. point,** punto de ebullición, *m*

boisterous *a* (of persons) exuberante, impetuoso; (stormy) tempestuoso, borrascoso; violento

boisterously *adv* impetuosamente, ruidosamente; tempestuosamente; con violencia

boisterousness *n* exuberancia, impetuosidad, *f*; violencia, *f*; tempestuosidad, borrascosidad, *f*

bold *a* intrépido, audaz, *Argentina* agulludo (determined) resuelto; (forward) atrevido; (showy) llamativo; (clear) claro. **b.-faced,** descarado, desvergonzado. **b.-faced type,** letra negra, *f*

boldly *adv* intrépidamente; descaradamente; resueltamente; claramente

boldness *n* intrepidez, valentía, *f*; resolución, *f*; (forwardness) osadía, *f*, descaro, atrevimiento, *m*; claridad, *f*

Bolivian *a* and *n* boliviano (-na)

Bolshevik *a* and *n* bolchevique, *mf*

Bolshevist *n* bolchevista, *mf*

bolster *n* travesaño, *m*. *vt* apuntalar; *fig* apoyar

bolt *n* pasador, cerrojo, *m*; (pin) perno, *m*; (knocker) aldaba, *f*; (roll) rollo, *m*; (flight) huida, *f*; (of a cross-bow) flecha, *f*; (from the blue) rayo, *m*. *adv* (upright) recto como una flecha; enhiesto; rígido. **b. and nut,** perno y tuerca, *m*

bolt *vt* echar el cerrojo (a); empernar; (*fam* eat) zampar. *vi* huir; (horses) desbocarse, dispararse; (plants) cerner. **to b. down,** cerrar con cerrojo. **to b. in,** entrar corriendo, entrar de repente. **to b. off,** marcharse corriendo. **to b. out,** *vi* salir de golpe. *vt* cerrar fuera

bolus *n* bolo, *m*

bomb *n* bomba, *f*, *vt* bombardear. **to be a b.-shell,** *fig* caer como una bomba. **b.-carrier,** portabombas, *m*. **b. crater,** bombazo, *m*. **b.-release,** (*aer nav*) lanzabombas, *m*. **b.-sight,** mira de avión de bombardeo, *f*

bombard *vt* bombardear, bombear; *fig* llover (preguntas, etc.) sobre

bombardier *n* bombardero, *m*

bombardment *n* bombardeo, *m*

bombast *n* ampulosidad, pomposidad, *f*

bombastic *a* bombástico, altisonante, pomposo

bomber *n* avión de bombardeo, bombardero, *m*. **dive b.,** bombardero en picado, *m*. **heavy b.,** bombardero pesado, *m*. **light b.,** bombardero ligero, *m*. **b. command,** servicio de bombardero, *m*

bombproof *a* a prueba de bomba

bonafide *a* fidedigno

bonbon *n* bombón, confite, dulce, *m*. **b. box,** bombonera, *f*

bond *n* lazo, vínculo, *m*; *chem* enlace, *m*; (financial) obligación, *f*; (security) fianza, *f*; (Customs) depósito, *m*; *pl* bonds, cadenas, *f pl*, a esclavo. **in b.,** en depósito. **bonds of interest,** intereses creados, *m pl*. **b.-holder,** obligacionista, *mf*

bondage *n* esclavitud, *f*; servidumbre, *f*; cautiverio, *m*; prisión, *f*

bone *n* hueso, *m*; (of fish) espina (de pez), *f*; (whale b.) ballena, *f*; *pl* bones, cuerpo, *m*, *vt* deshuesar; poner ballenas (a or en). **to be all skin and bones,** estar en los huesos. **to have a b. to pick with,** tener que arreglar las cuentas con. **b.-ash,** cendra, *f*

boned *a* (in compounds) de huesos; deshuesado, sin hueso

boner *n* gazapo, *m*, patochada, plancha, *f*

bonfire *n* fogata, hoguera, *f*

Bonn Bonn, *f*

bonnet *n* capota, *f*; (of babies) gorra, *f*; (of men) boina, *f*; (of chimney and of machines) sombrerete, *m*

bonny *a* sano; hermoso; (fat) gordo

bonus *n* paga extraordinaria, bonificación, *f*; sobresueldo, *m*; (of food, etc.) ración extraordinaria, *f*

bon vivant *n* alegre, vividor, *m*

bon voyage *interj* ¡buen viaje! ¡feliz viaje!

bony *a* huesudo; (of fish-bones) lleno de espinas; óseo

booby *n* pazguato, bobo, *m*. **b.-prize,** último premio, *m*. **b.-trap,** trampa, *f*; mil mina, *f*

book *n* libro, *m*; volumen, tomo, *m*; (of an opera) libreto, *m*, *vt* anotar en un libro; apuntar; (seats) tomar (localidades); (tickets) sacar (billetes); (of the issuing clerk) dar; (reserve) reservar; inscribir; consignar (a suspect); (engage) contratar; (invite) comprometer. **to turn the pages of a b.,** hojear un libro. **b.-ends,** sostén para libros, sujetalibros, *m*. **b.-keeper,** tenedor de libros, *m*. **b.-keeping,** teneduría de libros, *f*. **b.-maker,** apostador de profesión, *m*. **b. of reference,** libro de consulta, *m*. **b.-plate,** exlibris, *m*. **b.-post,** tarifa de impresos, *f*. **b.-shop,** librería, *f*. **b.-trade,** venta de libros, *f*; comercio de libros, *m*

bookbinder *n* encuadernador (-ra) de libros

bookbinding *n* encuadernación de libros, *f*

bookcase *n* armario de libros, *Lat. Am.* librero *m*

booking *n* (of rooms, etc.) reservación, *f*; (of tickets) toma, *f*; *com* asiento, *m*; (engagement) contratación, *f*. **b.-clerk,** vendedor (-ra) de billetes. **b.-office,** despacho de billetes, *m*; taquilla, *f*

bookish *a* aficionado a los libros; docto, erudito

bookishness *n* afición a los libros, *f*; erudición, *f*

bookmark *n* marcador, *m*

bookseller *n* librero, *m*

bookselling *n* venta de libros, *f*; comercio de libros, *m*

bookshelf *n* estante para libros, *m*

bookstall *n* puesto de libros, *m*

bookstrap *n* portalibros, *m*

bookworm *n* polilla que roe los libros, *f*; *fig* ratón de biblioteca, *m*

boom *n naut* botavara, *f*; (of a crane) aguilón, *m*; (noise) ruido, *m*; (of the sea) bramido, *m*; (thunder) trueno, *m*; (in a port) cadena de puerto, *f*; *com* actividad, *f*; (*fig* peak) auge, *m*, *vi* sonar; bramar; tronar; *com* subir; ser famoso. **b. sail,** vela de cangreja, *f*

boomerang *n* bumerang, *m*

boon *n* favor, *m*, merced, *f*; bien, *m*, ventaja, *f*; don, *m*; privilegio, *m*, *a* (of friends) íntimo

boor *n* monigote, patán, palurdo, *m*

boorish *a* rudo, zafio, rústico, cerril

boorishness *n* zafiedad, patanería, tosquedad, *f*

boost *vt elec* aumentar la fuerza de; *inf* empujar; subir; (advertise) dar bombo (a)

boot *n* bota, *f*; (of a car) compartimiento para equipaje, *m*. **button-boots,** botas de botones, *f pl*. **riding-boots,** botas de montar, *f pl*. **to b.,** además, de añadidura. **b.-maker,** zapatero, *m*. **b.-tag,** tirador de bota, *m*. **b.-tree,** horma de bota, *f*

bootblack *n* limpiabotas, *Mexico* bolero (-ra), *elsewhere in Lat. Am.* embolador (-ra), lustrador (-ra) *mf*

booted *a* con botas, calzado con botas; (in compounds) de botas . . .

bootee *n* botín, *m*

booth *n* puesto, *m*, barraca, *f*

bootlace *n* cordón para zapatos, *m*

bootlegger *n* contrabandista de alcohol, *m*

boots *n* mozo de hotel, botones, *m*

booze *vi* emborracharse. **b. up** *Argentina* acatarrarse *n* alcohol, *m*; borrachera, *f*

boozed up *Lat. Am.* apimplado (-da), *Argentina* acatarrado (-da), *Central America* azurumbado (-da)

boozer *n* borracho (-cha)

boracic *a* bórico. *n* ácido bórico, *m*

borax *n* bórax, *m*

Bordeaux *a* and *n* (of or from) bordelés (-esa). *n* (wine) vino de Burdeos, *m*

bordello *n* burdel, *m*

border *n* borde, *m*; (of a lake, etc.) orilla, *f*; (edge) margen, *m*; (of a diploma, etc.) orla, *f*; *sew* ribete, *m*, orla, *f*; (fringe) franja, *f*; (garden) arriate, *m*; (territory) frontera, *f*; límite, confín, *m*. *vt sew* orlar, ribetear; ornar (de); (of land) lindar con. **to b. on,** (of land) tocar, lindar con; (approach) rayar en. **b. country,** región fronteriza, *f*

borderer *n* habitante de una zona fronteriza, *m*; escocés (-esa) de la frontera con Inglaterra

borderland *n* zona fronteriza, *f*; lindes, *m pl*

borderline *n* frontera, *f*; límite, *m*; margen, *m*, *a* fronterizo; lindero; (uncertain) dudoso, incierto

bore *n* taladro, barreno, *m*; perforación, *f*; (hole) agujero, *m*; (of guns) calibre, *m*; (wave) oleada, *f*; (nuisance) fastidio, *m*; (dullness) aburrimiento, tedio, *m*; (person) pelmazo, *m*, machaca, *mf vt* taladrar, barrenar, horadar; perforar; hacer un agujero (en); (exhaust) aburrir; fastidiar. **It's a b.,** Es una lata. **to be bored,** aburrirse, fastidiarse

boredom *n* aburrimiento, *m*; tedio, hastío, *m*

boring *a* aburrido, pesado, tedioso; molesto, fastidioso. *n* taladro, *m*; horadación, *f*; sondeo, *m*; perforación, *f*

born *a* nacido; (by birth) de nacimiento; (b. to be) destinado a; natural (de). **He was b. in 1870.** Nació en 1870. **to be b.,** nacer, venir al mundo. **to be b. again,** renacer, volver a nacer. **well-b.,** bien nacido. **b. with a silver spoon in one's mouth,** Nacido de pie, Nacido un domingo

-borne trasmitido por . . . (e.g. **anthropod-b.,** trasmitido por los antrópodos)

borough *n* burgo, *m*; villa, *f*; ciudad, *f*. **b. surveyor,** arquitecto municipal, *m*

borrow *vt* pedir prestado; apropiarse, adoptar; copiar; (arithmetic) restar; (a book from a library) tomar prestado. **May I b. your pencil?** ¿Quieres prestarme tu lápiz?

borrower *n* el (la) que pide o toma prestado

borrowing *n* el pedir prestado, acto de pedir prestado, *m*

Bosnian *a* bosnio

bosom *n* pecho, *m*; (heart) corazón, *m*; (of the earth, etc.) seno, *m*. **b. friend,** amigo (-ga) del alma, amigo (-ga) íntimo (-ma)

Bosphorus, the el Bósforo, *m*

boss *n* (of a shield) corcova saliente, *f*; tachón, *m*; *arch* pinjante, *m. inf* amo, *m*; jefe, *m*. *vt* mandar; dominar. **political b.,** cacique, *m*

bossism *n* caudillaje, *m*

bossy *a* mandón, autoritario. **b. person** *Lat. Am.* mandarín *m*

botanical *a* botánico. **b. garden,** jardín botánico, *m*

botanist *n* botánico (-ca)

botany *n* botánica, *f*

botch *n* (clumsy work) chapucería, *f*; remiendo, *m. vt* chapucear, chafallar; (patch) remendar

both *a* and *pron* ambos, *m pl*; ambas, *f pl*; los dos, *m pl*; las dos, *f pl, adv* tan(to) . . . como; (and) y; a la vez, al mismo tiempo. **It appealed both to the young and the old,** Gustó tanto a los jóvenes como a los viejos. **b. of you,** ustedes dos, vosotros dos, vosotras dos. **b. pretty and useful,** bonito y útil a la vez

bother *n* molestia, *f*, fastidio, *m*; (worry) preocupación, *f*; dificultad, *f*; (fuss) alboroto, *m, Lat. Am.* fregada *f. vt* molestar, fastidiar, *Lat. Am.* acatarrar; preocupar. *vi* preocuparse

bottle *n* botella, *f*; (smaller) frasco, *m*; (babies) biberón, *m*; (for water) cantimplora, *f, vt* embotellar, envasar, enfrascar. **to b. up,** (liquids, capital, armies, navies) embotellar; (feelings) refrenar. **to bring up on the b.,** criar con biberón. **b.-green,** verde botella, *m*. **b.-neck,** (in an industry) embotellado, *m*; (in traffic) atascadero, *m*. **b.-washer,** fregaplatos, *mf*; (machine) máquina para limpiar botellas, *f*

bottle cap *n* corchalata, *f*

bottled *a* en botella; (of fruit, vegetables) conservado

bottleful *n* botella, *f*

bottler *n* embotellador (-ra)

bottling *n* embotellado, *m*; envase, *m*. **b. outfit,** embotelladora, *f*; (for fruit, etc.) aparato para conservar frutas o legumbres, *m*

bottom *n* base, *f*; (deepest part) fondo, *m*; (last place) último lugar, *m*; fundamento, *m*; (of a chair) asiento, *m*; (of a page, table, mountain, etc.) pie, *m*; (posterior) culo, *m*; (of a river) lecho, *m*; (of the sea) fondo, *m*; (of a ship) casco, *m*; (of a skirt) orilla, *f*; (truth) realidad, verdad, *f*; (basis) origen, *m*, causa, *f*. **at b.,** en realidad. **at the b.,** en el fondo. **false b.,** fondo doble, fondo secreto, *m*. **to be at the b. of,** ocupar el último lugar en; ser el causante de. **to get to the b. of,** descubrir la verdad de; profundizar en, analizar. **to sink to the b.,** (of ships) irse a pique

bottomed *a* (in compounds) de fondo . . .

bottomless *a* sin fondo; (of chairs, etc.) sin asiento; (unfathomable) insondable

boudoir *n* tocador, gabinete de señora, *m*

bough *n* rama, *f*, brazo (de un árbol) *m*

boulder *n* roca, peña, *f*; canto rodado, *m*; bloque de roca, *m*

boulevard *n* bulevar, *m*

bounce *n* bote, rebote, *m*; salto, *m*; (boasting) fanfarronería, *f, vi* rebotar; saltar, brincar. *vt* hacer botar o saltar

bouncing *a* (healthy) sano, robusto; vigoroso, fuerte

bound *n* límite, *m*; (jump) salto, brinco, *m, vt* limitar, confinar. *vi* saltar, brincar; (bounce) botar. **within**

bounds, dentro del límite. **b. for,** con destino a; (of ships) con rumbo a

boundary *n* límite, lindero, término, *m*; frontera, *f*; raya, *f*. **b. stone,** mojón, *m*

bounden *a* obligatorio, forzoso; indispensable

boundless *a* sin límites, infinito; inmenso

bounteous, bountiful *a* dadivoso, generoso; bondadoso

bountifulness *n* munificencia, dadivosidad, generosidad, *f*

bounty *n* generosidad, munificencia, *f*; don, *m*; (subsidy) subvención, *f*

bouquet *n* ramo, ramillete (de flores), *m, Lat. Am. also* maceta *f*; perfume, *m*; (of wine) nariz, *f*

Bourbon *a* borbónico. *n* Borbón (-ona)

bourgeois *a* and *n* burgués (-esa)

bourgeoisie *n* burguesía, mesocracia, *f*

bout *n* turno, *m*; (in fencing, boxing, wrestling) asalto, *m*; (of illness, coughing) ataque, *m*; (fight) lucha, *f*, combate, *m*; (of drinking) borrachera, *f*

bovine *a* bovino, vacuno

bow *n* (weapon) arco, *m*; (of a saddle) arzón (de silla), *m*; *mus* arco, *m*; (knot) lazo, *m*; (greeting) saludo, *m*; reverencia, inclinación, *f*; (of a boat) proa, *f*. **to tie a bow,** hacer un lazo. **bow and arrows,** arco y flechas, *m*. **bow-legged,** patizambo, *Central America* corveta, *f*. **bow window,** ventana saliente, *f*

bow *vi* inclinarse; hacer una reverencia, saludar; (remove the hat) descubrirse; *fig* inclinarse (ante); (submit) someterse (a), reconocer; agobiarse; *mus* manejar el arco. *vt* (usher in) introducir en, conducir a; doblar; inclinar. **to bow down (to),** humillarse ante; obedecer; (worship) reverenciar, adorar. **to bow out,** despedir con una inclinación del cuerpo

bowel *n* intestino, *m*; *pl* **bowels,** *fig* seno, *m*, entrañas, *f pl*

bower *n* (arbor) enramada, *f*; glorieta, *f*; (boudoir) tocador de señora, *m*

bowing *n mus* arqueada, *f*; saludo, *m*, *a* (of acquaintance) superficial

bowl *n* receptáculo, *m*; (of a fountain) taza, *f*; (of a pipe) cazoleta, *f*; (barber's) bacía, *f*; (for washing) jofaina, *f*; (for punch) ponchera, *f*; (goblet) copa, *f*; (for soup) escudilla, *f*; (for fruit) frutero, *m*; (for a spoon) paleta, *f*; (ball) boliche, *m. vt* tirar; (in cricket) sacar; (a hoop) jugar con; (in ninepins) tumbar con una bola. **to b. along,** recorrer; ir en coche o carruaje (por). **to b. over,** *fig* dejar consternado (a), desconcertar

bowler *n* (in cricket) servidor, *m*; (hat) sombrero hongo, *m*; (skittle player) jugador de bolos, *m*

bowling *n* (in cricket) saque, *m*; (skittles) (juego de) bolos, *m*; (juego de) boliche, *m*. **b. alley,** bolera, pista de bolos, *f*; salón de boliche, *m*. **b.-green,** bolera en cesped, *f*

bowls *n* juego de boliche, *m*

bowsprit *n* bauprés, *m*

bowstring *n* cuerda de arco, *f*

bow tie *n* pajarita, *f*

bow-wow *n* guau, *m*

box *n* caja, *f*; (case) estuche, *m*; (luggage) baúl, *m*, maleta, *f*; (for a hat) sombrerera, *f*; bot boj, *m*; *theat* palco, *m*, *Mexico* lumbrera, *f*; (for a sentry, signalman, etc.) garita, casilla, *f*; (on a carriage) pescante, *m*; (blow) cachete, *m*, bofetada, *f*; (for a horse) vagón, *m*. **post office box,** apartado de correos, *m*. **box-kite,** cometa celular, *f*. **box-maker,** cajero, *m*. **box office,** taquilla, *f, Lat. Am.* boletería *f*. **box-pleat,** *sew* tabla, *f*

box *vt* encajonar, meter en una caja. *vi* boxear. **to box the ears of,** calentar las orejas de. **to box up,** encerrar

boxer *n sport* boxeador, pugilista, *m*

boxing *n* encajonamiento, *m*; envase, *m*; *sport* boxeo, pugilato, *m*. **B. Day,** Día de San Esteban, *m*, (A Spanish child receives its Christmas presents on the Día de Reyes (Twelfth Night).) **b.-gloves,** guantes de boxeo, *m pl*. **b.-ring,** cuadrilátero de boxeo, *m*

box-office success *n* éxito de taquilla, *m*

boy *n* muchacho, niño, rapaz, *m*; (older) chico, joven, *m*. **new boy,** nuevo alumno, *m*. **old boy,** (of a school) antiguo alumno, *m*; (*fam* address) chico. **small boy,** chiquillo, pequeño, crío, *m*. **b. doll,** muñeco, *m*. **boy scout,** muchacho explorador, *m*

boycott *vt* boicotear. *n* boicot, *m*

boyhood *n* muchachez, mocedad, *f*; (childhood) niñez, *f*

boyish *a* muchachil; pueril; de niñez

brace *n* (prop) puntal, barrote, *m*; abrazadera, *f*; *carp* berbiquí, *m*; viento, tirante, *m*; freno (for the teeth), *m*, (pair) par, *m*; *pl* **braces,** tirantes, *m pl*. *vt* apuntalar; asegurar; *carp* ensamblar; *naut* bracear; (trousers) tirar; *fig* fortalecer, refrescar

bracelet *n* pulsera, *f*, brazalete, *m*, ajorca, *f*

bracing *a* (of air, etc.) fortificante, tónico; estimulador

bracken *n* helecho, *m*

bracket *n* consola, *f*; *arch* repisa, *f*; soporte, *m*; (on furniture, etc.) cantonera, *f*; *print* paréntesis angular, *m*; (for a light) brazo (de alumbrado), *m*. *vt print* poner entre paréntesis; juntar. **in brackets,** entre paréntesis. **They were bracketed equal,** Fueron juzgados iguales

brackish *a* salobre

brag *vi* jactarse, fanfarronear, *Lat. Am.* dragonear, *Argentina* faramallear *n* jactancia, *f*. **to b. about,** hacer alarde de

braggart *a* baladrón, jactancioso. *n* jactancioso, fanfarrón, *m*

bragging *n* jactancia, *f*

Brahmin *n* brahmán, *m*

Brahminism *n* brahmanismo, *m*

braid *n* trencilla, *f*, cordoncillo, *m*; (for trimming) galón, *m*; (plait) trenza, *f*. *vt* (hair) trenzar; (trim) galonear; acordonar, trencillar

brain *n* cerebro, *m*; entendimiento, *m*, inteligencia, *f*; talento, *m*; (common sense) sentido común, *m*; *pl* **brains,** sesos, *m pl*, (animal and human); cacumen, *m*. *vt* romper la crisma (a). **to blow one's brains out,** levantarse la tapa de los sesos. **to rack one's brains,** devanarse los sesos. **Brains Trust,** masa cefálica, *f*; consorcio de inteligencias, *m*. **b.-box,** cráneo, *m*. **b.-fever,** fiebre cerebral, *f*. **b.-storm,** crisis nerviosa, *f*. **b.-wave,** idea luminosa, *f*. **b.-work,** trabajo intelectual, *m*

brainchild *n* engendro, *m*

brain drain *n* fuga de cerebros, *f*

brained *a* de cabeza, de cerebro

brainless *a* sin seso; tonto

brainy *a* sesudo, inteligente, talentudo

braise *vt cul* asar

brake *n* (of vehicles and *fig*) freno, *m*, *Chile, Peru* alitranca *f* (flax and hemp) caballete, *m*; (carriage) break, *m*; (thicket) matorral, *m*. *vt* (vehicles) frenar; (hemp, etc.) rastrillar. **foot-b.,** freno de pedal, *m*. **hand-b.,** freno de mano, *m*. **b. hard,** frenar de repente. **to release the b.,** quitar el freno

bramble *n* zarza, *f*. **b. patch,** breña, *f*, zarzal, *m*

brambly *a* zarzoso

bran *n* salvado, *m*

branch *n* (of a tree, a family) rama, *f*; (of flowers, of learning) ramo, *m*; (of a river) tributario, afluente, *m*; (of roads, railways) ramal, *m*; (of a firm) sucursal, dependencia, *f*. *a* sucursal, dependiente; (of roads, railways) secundario. *vi* echar ramas; bifurcarse, dividirse; ramificarse. **to b. off,** bifurcarse, ramificarse. **to b. out,** extenderse; emprender cosas nuevas

branched *a* con ramas; *bot* ramoso; (of candlesticks) de . . . brazos

branchiness *n* ramaje, *m*, frondosidad, *f*

branching *n* ramificación, *f*; división, *f*. **b. off,** bifurcación, *f*

brand *n* tizón, *m*; (torch) tea, *f*; (on cattle, etc.) hierro, *m*; (trademark) marca de fábrica, *f*; marca, *f*; (stigma) estigma, *m*. *vt* marcar con el hierro, herrar; marcar; estigmatizar, tildar. **b.-new,** flamante

branding *n* (of livestock) herradero, *m*; (of slaves, crim-

inals) estigmatización, *f*; difamación, *f*. **b.-iron,** hierro de marcar, *m*

brandish *vt* blandir

brandy *n* coñac, *m*

brass *n* latón, *m*; *mus* metal, *m*; (tablet) placa conmemorativa, *f*; *inf* dinero, *m*. **the b.,** *mus* el metal. **b. band,** banda de instrumentos de viento, *f*. **b.-neck,** *inf* cara dura, *f*. **b. works** or **shop,** latonería, *f*

brassiere *n* sostén, *m*

brat *n* crío, *m*

bravado *n* bravata, *f*

brave *a* valiente, animoso, intrépido; espléndido, magnífico; bizarro. *n* valiente, *m*. *vt* desafiar, provocar; arrostrar

bravely *adv* valientemente; espléndidamente; bizarramente

bravery *n* valentía, *f*, valor, *m*, intrepidez, *f*, coraje, *m*; esplendidez, suntuosidad, *f*; bizarría, *f*

bravo *n* bandido, *m*; asesino pagado, *m*, *interj* ¡bravo! ¡ole!

bravura *n* bravura, *f*

brawl *n* camorra, reyerta, pelotera, *Lat. Am.* follisca *f. vi* alborotar; (of streams) murmurar. **to start a b.,** armar camorra

brawler *n* camorrista, *mf*

brawling *n* alboroto, *m*, vocinglería, *f*; (of streams) murmullo, *m*

brawn *n cul* embutido, *m*; músculo, *m*; (strength) fuerza, *f*

brawny *a* membrudo, musculoso, forzudo

bray *n* rebuzno, *m*; (of trumpets) clangor, *m*, *vi* rebuznar; sonar

brazen *a* de latón; (of voice) bronca; desvergonzado, descarado

brazier *n* (fire) brasero, *m*; latonero, *m*

Brazil el Brasil, *m*

Brazilian *a* and *n* brasileño (-ña)

Brazil nut *n* nuez del Brasil, *f*

breach *n* violación, contravención, *f*; (gap) abertura, *f*; (fissure) grieta, *f*; *geol* rajadura, *f*; *mil* brecha, *f*. *vt mil* hacer brecha (en); (in a line of defence) hacer mella (en). **b. of confidence,** abuso de confianza, *m*. **b. of promise,** incumplimiento de la palabra de casamiento, *m*. **b. of the peace,** alteración del orden público, *f*, quebrantamiento de la paz, *m*

bread *n* pan, *m*. **to earn one's b. and butter,** ganarse el pan. **brown b.,** pan moreno, *m*. **unleavened b.,** pan ázimo, *m*. **b. and butter,** pan con mantequilla, *m*; *fig* sustento diario, *m*. **b.-basket,** cesta de pan, *f*; *inf* estómago, *m*. **b.-bin,** caja del pan, *f*. **b.-crumb,** miga, *f*; migaja, *f*. **b.-knife,** cuchillo para cortar el pan, *m*. **b. poultice,** cataplasma de miga de pan, *f*. **b.-winner,** ganador (-ra) de pan, trabajador (-ra)

breadfruit tree *n* árbol del pan, *m*

breadth *n* anchura, *f*; latitud, *f*; liberalidad, *f*; *sew* ancho de una tela, *m*

breadthways *adv* a lo ancho

break *n* rotura, *f*; (opening) abertura, *f*; *geol* rajadura, *f*; (fissure) grieta, *f*; solución de continuidad, *f*; interrupción, *f*; (billiards) serie, *f*; (change) cambio, *m*; (in a boy's voice) muda (de la voz), *f*; (blank) vacío, *m*; (in the market) baja, *f*; intervalo, *m*; descanso, *m*; pausa, *f*; (truce) tregua, *f*; (clearing) clara, *f*; *mus* quiebra (de la voz), *f*; (carriage) break, *m*; (fam folly) disparate, *m*. **with a b. in one's voice,** con voz entrecortada. **b. of day,** aurora, alba, *f*. **at the b. of day,** al despuntar el alba

break *vt* romper; quebrar; quebrantar, fracturar; (breach) abrir brecha en; (in two) partir, dividir; (into pieces) hacer pedazos, despedazar; (into small pieces) desmenuzar; (into crumbs) desmigajar; (destroy) destrozar; (a blow) parar; (a law) infringir, violar; (the bank in gambling) quebrar; (a journey, etc.) interrumpir; (of a habit) desacostumbrar, hacer perder el vicio de; (a promise) no cumplir, faltar a; (a record) superar; (plow ground) roturar; (spoil) estropear; arruinar; *com* ir a la quiebra; (an official) degradar; (an animal) domar, amansar; (*fig* crush) subyugar; (betray) traicionar; (*fig* of silence, a spell, a lance, peace, the ranks) romper; (cushion) amortiguar; (lessen) mitigar; (disclose) revelar; *elec* interrumpir. **to b. one's promise,** faltar a su palabra. **to b. the ice,** *fig* romper el hielo. **to b. asunder,** romper en dos (partes); dividir. **to b. down,** derribar; echar abajo; destruir; (suppress) suprimir; subyugar; abolir; disolver. **to b. in,** (animals) domar, amaestrar; (persons) disciplinar; (new shoes) ahormar, romper. **to b. in two,** partir; dividir en dos; (split) hender. **to b. off,** separar, quitar; (a branch) desgajar; *fig* romper; interrumpir; cesar. **to b. open,** forzar, abrir a la fuerza. **to b. up,** hacer pedazos; (scatter) poner en fuga, dispersar; hacer levantar la sesión; (the ground) roturar; (parliament) disolver; (a ship) desguazar, deshacer (un buque)

break *vi* romperse; quebrarse; quebrantarse; (of beads) desgranarse; (burst) reventar, estallar; (of abscesses) abrirse; (of a boy's voice) mudar; (*fig* and of clouds, etc.) romperse; desaparecer; (of the dawn) despuntar (el alba), amanecer; (sprout) brotar; (of a ball) torcerse; (of fine weather) terminar; (change) cambiar; (of a storm) estallar. **to b. loose,** desasirse; *fig* desencadenarse. **to b. away,** escaparse, fugarse; (from a habit) romper con, independizarse de (another country); disiparse. **to b. down,** (of machinery, cars) averiarse; (fail) frustrarse, malograrse; (weep) deshacerse en lágrimas; (lose one's grip) perder la confianza en sí; (in health) sufrir una crisis de salud. **The car broke down,** El auto tuvo una avería. **to b. in,** (of burglars) forzar la entrada; irrumpir (en), penetrar (en); exclamar. **to b. in on,** sorprender; entrar de sopetón; invadir; interrumpir; caer sobre; molestar. **to b. into,** (force) forzar; (utter) romper a, prorrumpir en; empezar (a); pasar de repente a; (of time, etc.) ocupar; hacer perder. **to b. off,** (of speech) interrumpirse; cesar; (detach) desprenderse, separarse; (of branches) desgajarse. **to b. out,** huir, escaparse; *fig* estallar; aparecer; declararse; (of fire) tomar fuego; derramarse; (of an eruption) salir. **to b. over,** derramarse por; bañar. **to b. through,** abrirse paso (por); abrirse salida (por); atravesar; *fig* penetrar; (of the sun, etc.) romper (por). **to b. up,** (depart) separarse; (of meetings) levantarse la sesión; dispersarse; (smash) hacerse pedazos; disolverse; (of a school) cerrarse, empezar las vacaciones; (melt) fundir; desbandarse; (of a camp) levantar (el campo); (grow old) hacerse viejo; (be ill) estar agotado. **to b. with,** romper con; cesar; reñir con

breakable *a* quebradizo, frágil

breakage *n* rompimiento, quebrantamiento, *m*; cosa rota, *f*; fractura, *f*

breakdown *n* accidente, *m*; (of a machine) avería, *f*; *aut* pane, *f*; (failure) fracaso, *m*, falta de éxito, *f*; deterioración, *f*; (in health) crisis de salud, *f*. **b. gang,** pelotón de reparaciones, *m*

breaker *n* oleada, *f*

breakfast *n* desayuno, *m*. *vi* desayunar(se), tomar el desayuno. **to have a good b.,** desayunar bien. **b.-cup,** tazón, *m*. **b.-time,** hora del desayuno, *f*

breaking *n* rompimiento, *m*; quebrantamiento, *m*; fractura, *f*; ruptura, *f*; (in two) división, *f*; (into pieces) despedazamiento, *m*; (into small pieces) desmenuzamiento, *m*; (destruction) destrozo, *m*; (of a blow) parada, *f*; (of a law, etc.) violación, *f*; (of one's word) no cumplimiento, *m*; (of a journey, of sleep, etc.) interrupción, *f*; (escape) escape, *m*, huida, *f*; (of an animal) domadura, *f*; (of a boy's voice) muda (de la voz), *f*; (of news) revelación, *f*. **b. down,** demolición, *f*; (of negotiations) suspensión, *f*. **b. in,** irrupción, *f*; (of an animal) domadura, *f*; (training) entrenamiento, *m*. **b. open,** forzamiento, *m*; quebranto, *m*. **b. out,** huida, *f*, escape, *m*; *fig* estallido, *m*; aparición, *f*; declaración, *f*; (scattering) derramamiento, *m*; (of a rash) erupción, *f*. **b. up,** dispersión, *f*; disolución, *f*; fin, *m*; ruina, *f*; (of a school) cierre, *m*; (change in weather) cambio, *m*; (of a

meeting) levantamiento (de una sesión), *m*; (of the earth) roturación, *f*

breakneck *a* rápido, veloz, precipitado

breakwater *n* malecón, rompeolas, *m*

bream *n icht* sargo, *m*. **sea-b.,** besugo, *m*

breast *n* pecho, *m*; (of birds) pechuga, *f*; (of female animals) teta, mama, *f*; (heart) corazón, *m*, *vt* (the waves) cortar (las olas); luchar con; *fig* arrostrar, hacer frente a. **b.-bone,** esternón, *m*. **b. high,** alto hasta el pecho. **b.-pin,** alfiler de pecho, *m*. **b.-pocket,** bolsillo de pecho, *m*. **b.-stroke,** estilo pecho, *m*

breast cancer *n* el cáncer del seno, *m*

breasted *a* de pecho . . .; de pechuga . . .; de tetas . . . **a double-b. jacket,** una chaqueta cruzada. **a single-b. jacket,** una chaqueta

breastwork *n mil* parapeto, *m*

breath *n* aliento, *m*; suspiro, *m*; (phonetics) aspiración, *f*; (breeze) soplo (de aire), *m*; (of scandal, etc.) murmurio, *m*; (fragrance) perfume, *m*, fragancia, *f*; (life) vida, *f*. **in a b.,** de un instante. **in the same b.,** sin respirar. **out of b.,** sin aliento. **under one's b.,** por lo bajo, entre dientes. **to draw b.,** tomar aliento. **to get one's b. back,** cobrar aliento. **to hold one's b.,** contener el aliento. **to take one's b. away,** *fig* dejar consternado (a)

breathable *a* respirable

breathe *vi* respirar; vivir; (of air, etc.) soplar; (take the air) tomar el fresco; (rest) tomar aliento. *vt* respirar; exhalar; dar aire (a); (whisper) murmurar; (convey) expresar, revelar; (infuse) infundir. **to b. forth fury,** echar rayos. **to b. hard,** jadear. **to b. one's last,** exhalar el último suspiro. **to b. in,** inspirar

breathing *n* respiración, *f*; (of the air, etc.) soplo, *m*; (phonetics) aspiración, *f*. *a* que respira; viviente. **hard** or **heavy b.,** jadeo, resuello, resoplido, *m*. **b.-space,** *fig* respiro, *m*

breathless *a* jadeante, sin aliento; (dead) muerto; (sultry) sin un soplo de aire; intenso, profundo; (of haste) precipitado

breathlessly *adv* anhelosamente; con expectación

breathlessness *n* falta de aliento, *f*; respiración difícil, *f*; (death) muerte, *f*; (of weather) falta de aire, *f*

bred *a* criado. **ill (well) b.,** mal (bien) criado. **pure-b.,** de raza

breech *n anat* trasero, *m*; (of fire-arms) recámara, *f*

breeches *n* calzones, *m pl*; pantalones, *m pl*. **riding-b.,** pantalones de montar, *m pl*. **to wear the b.,** *fig* ponerse los calzones

breed *n* casta, raza, *f*; tipo, *m*; clase, *f*, *vt* procrear; engendrar, crear; (bring up) educar; criar. *vi* reproducirse; sacar cría; multiplicarse. **to b. in-and-in,** procrear sin mezclar razas

breeder *n* criador (-ra); animal reproductor, *m*

breeding *n* reproducción, *f*; cría, *f*; (upbringing) crianza, *f*; educación, *f*; instrucción, *f*; producción, *f*; creación, *f*, *a* de cría; (of male animals) semental; prolífico. **bad b.,** mala crianza, *f*. **good b.,** buena crianza, *f*. **cross b.,** cruzamiento de razas, *m*. **B. will out,** Aunque la mona se vista de seda, mona se queda. **b. farm,** criadero, *m*

breeze *n* brisa, *f*; vientecillo, *m*, soplo de aire, *m*, *Lat. Am.* airecito *m*; (argument) altercación, *f*, argumento, *m*; (of coke) cisco de coque, *m*. **fresh b.,** brisa fresca, *f*. **light b.,** brisa floja, *f*. **strong b.,** viento fuerte, viento muy fresco, *m*

breezy *a* con brisa, fresco; expuesto a la brisa; oreado; (of manner) animado, jovial

brethren *n pl* hermanos, *m pl*

Breton *a* and *n* bretón (-ona). *n* (language) bretón, *m*

brevet *n mil* graduación honoraria, *f*; nombramiento honorario, *m*. *vt mil* graduar

breviary *n* breviario, *m*

brevity *n* brevedad, *f*; concisión, *f*

brew *n* mezcla, *f*; brebaje, *m*. *vt* hacer (cerveza, té, etc.); preparar, mezclar; *fig* urdir, tramar. *vi* prepararse; urdirse; (storm) gestarse.

brewer *n* cervecero (-ra)
brewery *n* cervecería, fábrica de cerveza, *f*
brewing *n* elaboración de cerveza, *f*
briar *n* (wild rose) rosal silvestre, *m*; (heather) brezo, *m*. **b. pipe,** pipa de brezo, *f*
bribable *a* sobornable
bribe *n* soborno, cohecho, *m, Lat. Am.* coima *f vt* sobornar, cohechar. **to take bribes,** dejarse sobornar
briber *n* cohechador (-ra)
bribery *n* soborno, *m*
brick *n* ladrillo, *m*; (for children) piedra de construcción, *f*; bloque, *m*; *inf* buen chico, *m*, joya, *f, a de* ladrillo. *vt* enladrillar. **b.-floor,** ladrillado, *m*; **b.-kiln,** horno de ladrillo, *m*. **b.-maker,** ladrillero, *m*. **b.-yard,** ladrillar, *m*
bricklayer *n* albañil, *m*
bricklaying *n* albañilería, *f*
brickwork *n* masonería, *f*
bridal *a* nupcial; de la boda; de la novia. **b. bed,** tálamo, *m*. **b. cake,** torta de la boda, *f*. **b. shop,** tienda para novias, *f*. **b. shower,** despedida de soltera, despedida de soltería, *f*. **b. song,** epitalamio, *m*. **b. veil,** velo de la novia, velo nupcial, *m*. **b. wreath,** corona de azahar, *f*
bride *n* novia, desposada, *f*; (after marriage) recién casada, *f*
bridegroom *n* novio, *m*; (after marriage) recién casado, *m*
bridesmaid *n* madrina de boda, *f*; niña encargada de sostener la cola de la novia, *f*
bridge *n* (engineering, *mus naut*) puente, *m*; lomo (de la nariz), *m*; (game) bridge, *m*, *vt* construir un puente (sobre); pontear; (obstacles) salvar; evitar; (fill in) ocupar, llenar. **auction b.,** bridge por subasta, *m*. **contract b.,** bridge por contrato, *m*. **suspension-b.,** puente colgante, *m*. **b. toll,** pontazgo, *m*
bridgehead *n* cabeza de puente, *f*
bridle *n* brida, *f*; freno, *m*. *vt* embridar, enfrenar; *fig* reprimir. *vi* (of horses) levantar la cabeza; (of persons) erguirse; hacer un gesto despreciativo. **snaffle b.,** bridón, *m*. **b. path,** camino de herradura, *m*
brief *a* breve, corto; conciso; lacónico, seco; rápido; fugaz, pasajero. *n* (papal) breve, *m*; *law* relación, *f*; escrito, *m*. *vt* (a barrister) instruir. **to hold a b. for,** defender, abogar por. **b.-case,** portapapeles, *m*; cartera (grande), *f*
briefly *adv* brevemente; en pocas palabras; sucintamente; (tersely) secamente
brier *n* rosal silvestre, *m*; zarza, *f*
brigade *n* *mil* brigada, *f*; cuerpo, *m*; asociación, *f*
brigadier *n* brigadier, *m*
brigand *n* bandolero, bandido, *m*
brigandage *n* bandolerismo, *m*
bright *a* brillante, reluciente; vivo; cristalino; subido; claro; optimista; alegre; inteligente; (quick-witted) agudo; ilustre; (smiling) risueño; (of future, etc.) halagüeño. **to be as b. as a new pin,** estar como una ascua de oro. **b. blue,** azul subido, *m*. **b.-eyed,** con ojos vivos, con ojos chispeantes, ojialegre
Bright's disease *n* enfermedad de Bright, glomerulonefritis, *f*
brighten *vt* hacer brillar; (polish) pulir; (make happy) alegrar; (improve) mejorar. *vi* (of the weather) aclarar, despejarse (el cielo); sentirse más feliz; mejorar
brightly *adv* brillantemente; alegremente
brightness *n* brillo, *m*; claridad, *f*; esplendor, *m*; (of colors) brillantez, *f*; vivacidad, *f*; inteligencia, *f*; agudeza de ingenio, *f*
brilliance *n* fulgor, brillo, *m*, refulgencia, *f*; esplendor, *m*; lustre, *m*; talento, *m*; brillantez, gloria, *f*
brilliant *a* brillante. *n* (gem) brillante, *m*. **to be b.,** (in conversation, etc.) brillar; (be clever) ser brillante
brilliantine *n* brillantina, *f*
brim *n* (of a glass, etc.) borde, *m*; (of a hat) ala, *f*; margen, *m*, orilla, *f*. **to be full to the b.,** estar lleno hasta los bordes; *fig* rebosar. **eyes brimming with tears,** ojos arrasados de lágrimas

brimful *a* hasta el borde (or los bordes); *fig* rebosante
brimless *a* (of hats) sin ala
brimmed *a* (of hats) con ala
brimstone *n* azufre, *m*
brindled *a* atigrado, abigarrado
brine *n* salmuera, *f*; mar, *m*; *poet* lágrimas, *f pl*
bring *vt* traer; llevar; transportar; (take a person or drive a vehicle) conducir; *fig* acarrear, traer; causar, ocasionar; producir; crear; (induce) persuadir; hacer (ver, etc.); (be worth) valer; (sell for) vender por; *law* entablar (un pleito, etc.): (before a judge) hacer comparecer (ante); (present) presentar; (attract) atraer; (place) poner. **to b. home,** llevar a casa; *fig* hacer ver, hacer sentir; demostrar; (a crime) probar contra. **to b. near,** acercar. **to b. about,** efectuar, poner por obra; causar, ocasionar; (achieve) lograr, conseguir. **to b. again,** traer otra vez, llevar de nuevo. **to b. away,** llevarse. **to b. back,** devolver; traer; (of memories) recordar. **to b. down,** llevar abajo, bajar; (of persons) hacer bajar; (humble) humillar; hacer caer; (of prices) hacer bajar; arruinar; destruir. **to b. down the house,** *theat* hacer venirse el teatro abajo. **to b. forth,** (give birth to) dar a luz; producir; causar; sacar a luz. **to b. forward,** hacer adelantarse; empujar hacia adelante; *fig* avanzar; (allege) alegar; *com* llevar a nueva cuenta; presentar, producir. **brought forward,** *com* suma y sigue. **to b. in,** (things) llevar adentro; (persons) hacer entrar; introducir; aparecer con, presentarse con; (meals) servir; producir; declarar; (a verdict) dictar (sentencia de), fallar. **to b. into being,** poner en práctica; dar origen (a). **to b. off,** (a ship) poner a flote; (rescue) salvar, rescatar; (carry out) efectuar, poner en práctica; (achieve) conseguir, lograr. **B. me the glass off the table,** Tráeme el vaso que hay en la mesa. **to b. on,** causar, inducir; acarrear; iniciar. **He brought a book on to the stage,** Entró en escena llevando un libro (or con un libro). **to b. out,** sacar; poner afuera; (a person) hacer salir; publicar; (a play) poner en escena; sacar a luz; (an idea, jewels, etc.) sacar a relucir; revelar; demostrar; hacer aparecer; (a girl in society) poner de largo (a). **to b. over,** llevar al otro lado; hacer venir; traer; conducir; hacer cruzar; (convert) convertir. **to b. round,** traer; llevar; (from a swoon) sacar de un desmayo; curar; persuadir; conciliar. **to b. through,** hacer atravesar; llevar a través de; ayudar a salir (de un apuro); (an illness) curar de. **to b. to,** traer a; llevar a; (from a swoon) hacer volver en sí; *naut* ponerse a la capa. **He cannot b. himself to,** No puede persuadirse a. **to b. together,** reunir; (things) juntar, amontonar; reconciliar, poner en paz. **to b. under,** someter; sojuzgar; incluir. **to b. up,** llevar arriba, subir; (a person) hacer subir; hacer avanzar; (a price) hacer subir; ir (a); andar; (breed) criar; (educate) educar, criar; (in a discussion) hacer notar; vomitar. **to b. up the rear,** ir al fin (de); *mil* ir a la retaguardia. **well** (or **badly**) **brought up,** bien (o mal) educado. **to b. upon oneself,** buscarse, incurrir (en). **to b. up-to-date,** poner al día; refrescar; rejuvenecer
bringing *n* acción de llevar o traer, *f*; conducción, *f*; transporte, *m*. **b. forth,** producción, *f*. **b. in,** introducción, *f*. **b. out,** producción, *f*; publicación, *f*; (of a girl in society) puesta de largo, *f*. **b. under,** reducción, *f*; subyugación, *f*. **b. up,** educación, crianza, *f*
brink *n* borde, margen, *m*; (of water) orilla, *f*; *fig* margen, *m*. **on the b.,** al margen; a la orilla. **to be on the b. of,** (doing something) estar para, estar a punto de
briny *a* salado
briquette *n* briqueta, *f*, aglomerado de carbón, *m*
brisk *a* activo; vivo; animado; rápido, acelerado; enérgico
brisket *n* falda, *f*
briskly *adv* vivamente; enérgicamente; aprisa
briskness *n* actividad, *f*; viveza, *f*; animación, *f*; rapidez, *f*; energía, *f*
bristle *n* cerda, seda, *f*, *vi* erizarse
bristling *n* sardina noruega, .

bristly *a* erizado, cerdoso; espinoso; hirsuto
Bristol board *n* cartulina, *f*
British *a* británico. **the B.,** el pueblo británico; los ingleses
British Commonwealth, the la Mancomunidad Británica, *f*
Briton *n* inglés (-esa). **ancient B.,** britano (-na)
Brittany Bretaña, *f*
brittle *a* frágil, quebradizo, deleznable, friable
brittleness *n* fragilidad, friabilidad, *f*
broach *n cul* espetón, asador, *m*. *vt* espitar (un barril); abrir; *fig* introducir
broad *a* ancho; grande; (extensive) vasto, extenso; **a b. confession,** una confesión amplia; (full) pleno; (of accents) marcado; (of words) lato; (clear) claro; (of the mind) liberal, tolerante; (of humor, etc.) grosero; (general) general, comprensivo. **in b. daylight,** en pleno día. **b.-brimmed,** de ala ancha. **b.-faced,** cariancho. **b.-minded,** tolerante, liberal, ancho de conciencia, abierto al mundo. **b.-mindedness,** tolerancia, liberalidad, *f*. **to be b.-minded,** ser tolerante, tener manga ancha. **b.-shouldered,** ancho de espaldas
broadcast *n agr* siembra al vuelo, *f*; *rad* radiodifusión, radiotransmisión, emisión, *f*, *a* radiado. *adv* por todas partes; extensamente. *vt agr* sembrar a vuelo; *rad* radiodifundir, radiar, transmitir por radio; (news, etc.) diseminar
broadcaster *n* (lecturer) conferenciante, *mf*; radiodifusor (-ra); (announcer) locutor (-ra)
broadcasting *n* radiación, radiodifución, *f*; radio, *f*. **b.-station,** estación de radio, emisora, *f*. **b.-studio,** estudio de emisión, *m*
broaden *vt* ampliar, ensanchar. *vi* ampliarse, ensancharse
broad-leaved *a* frondoso
broadly *adv* anchamente; con marcado acento dialectal; de una manera general
broadness *n* anchura, *f*; extensión, vastedad, *f*; tolerancia, *f*; liberalidad, *f*; grosería, *f*; (of accent) acento marcado, *m*
broadside *n* (of a ship) costado, *m*; (of guns) andanada, *f*; *fig* batería, *f*; *print* cara de un pliego, *f*. **to be b. on,** dar el costado
brocade *a* and *n* brocado *m.. vt* decorar con brocado. **imitation b.,** brocatel, *m*
brocaded *a* decorado con brocado; de brocado
broccoli *n* bróculi, brécol, *m*
brochure *n* folleto, *m*
brogue *n* acento, *m*; acento irlandés, *m*; (shoe) zapato grueso, *m*
broil *vt* emparrillar, asar. *vi* asarse
broke *a* quebrado; (penniless) *Peru* calato
broken *a* roto; quebrado; (spiritless) abatido, desalentado; (infirm) agotado, debilitado; (ruined) arruinado; (of ground) desigual, escabroso; (of a language) chapucero; (spoilt) estropeado; imperfecto; incompleto; (loose) suelto; (of a horse, etc.) domado; (of the weather) variable; (of sleep) interrumpido; (of the heart, of shoes, etc.) roto; (of the voice, sobs, sighs) entrecortado; (of the voice through old age, etc.) cascada; (incoherent) incoherente. **b.-down,** (tired) rendido, agotado; arruinado; (not working) estropeado. **b.-hearted,** roto el corazón, angustiado. **b.-winged,** aliquebrado. **I speak broken Spanish,** Hablo el español chapuceramente
brokenly *adv* (of the voice) con voz entrecortada; a ratos; interrumpidamente
brokenness *n* interrupción, *f*; (of the ground) desigualdad, *f*; (of speech) imperfección, *f*
broker *n* corredor, *m*; (stock) corredor de bolsa, *m*
brokerage *n* corretaje, *m*
bromide *n* bromuro, *m*
bromine *n* bromo, *m*
bronchi *n pl* bronquios, *m pl*
bronchitis *n* bronquitis, *f*
broncopneumonia *n* bronconeumonía, *f*

Brontosaurus *n* brontosauro, *m*
bronze *n* bronce, *m*; objeto de bronce, *m*, *a* de bronce. *vt* broncear. **B. Age,** Edad de Bronce, *f*
brooch *n* broche, *m*; alfiler de pecho, *m*
brood *n* (of birds) nidada, *f*; (of chickens) pollada, *f*; (other animals) cría, *f*; prole, *f*, *vi* empollar. **to b. over,** meditar sobre, rumiar; (of mountains, etc.) dominar
broody *a* (of hens) clueca, *f*
brook *n* arroyo, riachuelo, *m*, *vt* tolerar, sufrir, permitir
broom *n* escoba, *f*; *bot* retama, *f*; hiniesta, *f*. **common b.,** retama de escobas, *f*. **Spanish b.,** retama común, retama de olor, hiniesta, *f*. **b.-handle,** palo de escoba, *m*
broomstick *n* palo de escoba, *m*
broth *n* caldo, *m*
brothel *n* burdel, lupanar, *m*, casa de trato, *f*
brother *n* hermano, *m*; (colleague) colega, *m*; *inf* compañero, *m*. **foster-b.,** hermano de leche, *m*. **half-b.,** medio hermano, *m*. **step-b.,** hermanastro, *m*. **b.-in-law,** hermano político, cuñado, *m*. **b.-officer,** compañero de promoción, *m*
brotherhood *n* fraternidad, *f*; *ecc* cofradía, *f*; hermandad, *f*
brotherliness *n* fraternidad, *f*
brotherly *a* fraterno
brow *n* frente, *f*; ceja, *f*; (of a hill) cresta, cumbre, *f*; (edge) borde, *m*. **to knit one's b.,** fruncir el ceño
browbeat *vt* intimidar, amenazar
browbeating *n* intimidación, *f*
brown *a* castaño; (gallicism often used of shoes, etc.) marrón; pardo; (of complexion, eyes, hair) moreno; (dark brown) bruno; (blackish) negruzco; (toasted) tostado; (burnt) quemado. *n* color moreno, *m*; color pardo, *m*; castaño, *m*; (from the sun) bronce, *m*. *vt* (toast) tostar; (a person) volver moreno, broncear; (meat) asar. *vi* tostarse; volverse moreno, broncearse; asarse. **b. bear,** oso pardo, *m*. **b. owl,** autillo, *m*. **b. paper,** papel de estraza, *m*. **b. study,** ensimismamiento, *m*, meditación, *f*. **b. sugar,** azúcar moreno (or quebrado), *m*
brownie *n* duende benévolo, *m*
brownish *a* morenucho; que tira a castaño o a bruno; parduzco; trigueño
brownness *n* color moreno, *m*
browse *vi* pacer; (through a publication) hojear (un libro)
browsing *n* apacentamiento, *m*; hojeo (de un libro), *m*; lectura, *f*, estudio, *m*
Bruges Brujas, *f*
bruise *n* cardenal, *m*. *Lat. Am.* magullón *m*; abolladura, *f*; (in metal) bollo, *m*; (on fruit) maca, *f*. *vt* acardenalar, magullar; abollar; (fruit) macar
bruising *n* magulladura, *m*; (of metal) abolladura, *f*; (crushing) machacadura, *f*; (boxing) boxeo, pugilato, *m*
brunette *n* trigueña, morena, *f*
brunt *n* peso, *m*; golpe, *m*; choque, *m*; esfuerzo, *m*. **to bear the b.,** soportar el peso; sufrir el choque; *inf* pagar el pato
brush *n* cepillo, *m*; (broom) escoba, *f*; (for whitewashing, etc.) brocha, *f*; (for painting) pincel, *m*; (of a fox) cola (de zorro), *f*; (undergrowth) breñal, matorral, *m*; (fight) escaramuza, *f*; (argument) altercación, *f*. **scrubbing-b.,** cepillo para fregar, *m*. **shoe-b.,** cepillo para limpiar los zapatos, *m*. **stroke of the b.,** brochada, *f*; pincelada, *f*. **whitewash-b.,** brochón, *m*. **b. maker** or **seller,** escobero (-ra); pincelero (-ra)
brush *vt* cepillar; (sweep) barrer; frotar; (touch) rozar; (touch lightly) acariciar. **to b. against,** rozar, tocar. **to b. aside,** echar a un lado; *fig* no hacer caso de; ignorar. **to b. off,** sacudir(se); quitar(se); (sweep) barrer. **to b. up,** (hair) (wool) cardar; (tidy) asear; (a subject) refrescar, repasar
brushing *n* acepilladura, *f*; (sweeping) barredura, *f*; (touching) roce, rozamiento, *m*; (of hair) peinadura, *f*
brushwood *n* enjutos, *m pl*, chamarasca, *f*; matorral, *m*

brusque *a* brusco, seco
brusquely *adv* secamente
brusqueness *n* brusquedad, *f*
Brussels *a* bruselense; de Bruselas. **B. lace,** encaje de Bruselas, *m*
Brussels sprouts *n pl* bretones, *m pl*
brutal *a* bestial, brutal; salvaje, inhumano
brutality *n* brutalidad, bestialidad, *f*; barbaridad, ferocidad, *f*
brutalize *vt* embrutecer
brutally *adv* brutalmente
brute *n* bruto, animal, *m*; salvaje, bárbaro, *m*. **b. force,** la fuerza bruta
brutish *a* bruto; sensual, bestial; grosero; salvaje; estúpido; ignorante. **to become b.,** embrutecerse
bubble *n* burbuja, *f*; borbollón, *m*, *vi* burbujear; borbollar, bullir, hervir
bubbling *n* burbujeo, *m*; hervidero, *m*; (of brooks) murmullo, *m*, *a* burbujeante; hirviente; (of brooks) parlero; (of wine) espumoso, efervescente
bubonic *a* bubónico. **b. plague,** peste bubónica, *f*
buccaneer *n* corsario, *m*; aventurero, *m*
Bucharest Bucarest, *m*
buck *n zool* gamo, *m*; (male) macho, *m*; (fop) galán, petimetre, *m*, *vi* (of a horse) caracolear; fanfarronear. **to pass the b.,** *inf* echarle a uno el muerto. **b.-rabbit,** conejo, *m*. **to b. up,** hacer de tripas corazón
bucket *n* cubo, balde, *m*, cubeta, *f*
buckle *n* hebilla, *f*. *vt* enhebillar, abrochar con hebilla. *vi* doblarse. **to b. to,** ponerse a hacer algo con ahinco
buckled *a* con hebillas
buckler *n* broquel, *m*, rodela, tarjeta, *f*
buckram *n* bocací, *m*
buckshot *n* perdigón, *m*
buckskin *n* ante, *m*
buckwheat *n* alforfón, trigo sarraceno, *m*
bucolic *a* bucólico, pastoril
bud *n* brote, *m*; botón, capullo, *m*; (of vines) bollón, *m*; (of vegetables) gema, *f*. *vi* brotar, germinar. *vt* injertar de escudete
Buddhism *n* budismo, *m*
Buddhist *n* budista, *mf*
budding *n* brotadura, *f*; (of roses, etc) injerto de escudete, *m*; *fig* germen, *m*
budge *vi* moverse, menearse. *vt* mover
budget *n* presupuesto, *m*; (of news, etc.) colección, *f*. *vi* presuponer
Buenos Aires (of or from the province of) *a* and *n* bonaerense, *mf*
buff *n* color de ante, *m*; piel de ante, *f*. **b.-colored,** anteado. **in the buff = naked, nude**
buffalo *n* búfalo, *f*
buffer *n* (railway) parachoques, *m*; (of cars) amortiguador, *m*. **b. state,** estado tapón, *m*
buffet *n* bofetón, *m*; bofetada, *f*; bar, *m*. *vt* abofetear; golpear; luchar con las olas
buffoon *n* bufón, *m*
buffoonery *n* bufonería, *f*
bug *n* chinche, *f*. **bugs** *Lat. Am.* bicherío *m*
bugbear *n* pesadilla, *f*
bugle *n* corneta, trompeta, *f*; (bead) abalorio, *m*. **b. blast,** trompetazo, *m*
bugler *n* trompetero, *m*
build *vt* edificar; (engines, ships, organs, etc.) construir; (a nest and *fig*) hacer; (have built) hacer, edificar; crear; formar; fundar. *n* estructura, *f*; (of the body) hechura, *f*; talle, *m*. **to b. castles in Spain,** hacer castillos en el aire. **built-up area,** zona urbana, *f*. **to b. up,** construir, levantar; (block) tapar; (business, reputation) establecer, crear. **to b. upon,** *fig* contar con, confiar en; esperar de
builder *n* constructor, *m*; maestro de obras, *m*; (laborer) albañil, *m*; creador (-ra), fundador (-ra); arquitecto, *m*
building *n* edificación, *f*; construcción, *f*; edificio, *m*; fundación, *f*; creación, *f*. **b. contractor,** maestro de obras, *m*. **b. material,** material de construcción, *m*. **b.**

site, solar, terreno, *m*. **b. timber,** madera de construcción, *f*
built-in *a* empotrado. **b. closet,** armario empotrado, *m*
bulb *n bot* bulbo, *m*; (*elec phys*) bombilla, *f*; (of an oil lamp) cebolla, *f*
bulbous *a* bulboso
Bulgarian *a* and *n* búlgaro (-ra)
bulge *n* bulto, *m*; hinchazón, *f*; protuberancia, *f*; *mil* bolsa (en el frente), *f*. *vi* hincharse; estar lleno (de)
bulging *a* lleno (de); con bultos; hinchado (de)
bulk *n* volumen, tamaño, *m*; bulto, *m*; (larger part) grueso, *m*; mayor parte, *f*; (of people) mayoría, *f*; (of a ship) capacidad, *f*. **in b.,** *com* en bruto, en grueso. **to b. large,** tener mucha importancia
bulkhead *n naut* mamparo, *m*
bulkiness *n* abultamiento, *m*; volumen, tamaño, *m*
bulky *a* voluminoso, grande, grueso
bull *n* toro, *m*; *ast* Tauro, *m*; (of some animals) macho, *m*; (Stock Exchange) alcista, *mf*; (of the Pope) bula (del Papa), *f*. **a b. in a china shop,** un caballo loco en una cacharrería. **to fight bulls,** torear. **b.-calf,** ternero, *m*. **bull's eye,** blanco, *m*; acierto, *m*. **b. fight,** corrida de toros, *f*. **b. fighter's gala uniform,** traje de luces, *m*. **b.-ring,** plaza de toros, *f*
bulldog *n* perro dogo, perro de presa, *m*
bulldozer *n* (excavator) tozodora, *f*
bullet *n* bala, *f*. **spent b.,** bala fría, *f*. **stray b.,** bala perdida, *f*. **b.-proof,** a prueba de bala, blindado
bulletin *n* boletín, *m*
bulletin board *n* tablero de anuncios, tablero de avisos, tablón, *m*
bulletproof vest *n* chaleco blindado, *m*
bullfighter *n* torero, *m* (on foot), toreador, *m* (on horseback)
bullfinch *n* pinzón real, *m*
bullion *n com* metálico, *m*; oro (or plata) en barras, *m*, *f*.
bullock *n* becerro, *m*; buey, *m*
bullpen *n* toril, *m* (bullfighting); calentador, *m* (baseball)
bully *n* valentón, perdonavidas, gallito, *m*; rufián, *Argentina* compadre *m*. *vt* intimidar; tratar mal. **b. beef,** vaca en lata, *f*
bulrush *n* anea, *f*
bulwark *n* baluarte, *m*; *naut* antepecho, *m*
bumblebee *n* abejorro, *m*
bump *n* golpe, *m*; ruido, *m*; choque, *m*; (bruise) chichón, *m*, roncha, *f*; *aer* sacudida, *f*, meneo, *m*. *vi* (against) tropezar con; (along) saltar en. *vt* chocar (contra)
bumper *n* copa llena hasta los bordes, *f*, vaso lleno, *m*; (of a car) parachoques, *m*. **a b. harvest,** una cosecha abundante
bumpkin *n* patán, villano, *m*
bumptious *a* fatuo, presuntuoso, presumido
bumpy *a* (of surface) desigual, escabroso; (of a vehicle) incómodo, con mala suspensión
bun *n* buñuelo, bollo, *m*; (hair) moño, *m*
bunch *n* (of fruit) racimo, *m*; manojo, *m*; (of flowers) ramo, *m*, *Lat. Am. also* maceta *f*; (tuft) penacho, *m*; (gang) pandilla, *f*, *vi* arracimarse, agruparse
bundle *n* atado, lío, *m*; (of papers) legajo, *m*; (of sticks) haz, *m*; (sheaf) fajo, *m*; (package) paquete, *m*; fardo, hatillo, *m*; (roll) rollo, *m*. *vt* atar, liar; envolver; empaquetar; (stuff) meter, introducir. **to b. in,** meter dentro (de). **to b. out,** despachar sin ceremonia, poner de patitas en la calle
bung *n* tapón, tarugo, *m*, *vt* atarugar
bungalow *n* casa de un solo piso, *f*
bungle *vt* estropear; hacer mal. *n* equivocación, *f*, yerro, *m*; cosa (o obra) mal hecha, *f*
bungling *a* chapucero, torpe
bunion *n* juanete (del pie), *m*
bunk *n* litera, *f*, *vi inf* poner pies en polvorosa, pirarse
bunker *n naut* pañol, *m*; (for coal) carbonera, *f*; (golf) hoya de arena, *f*
bunkum *n* patrañas, *f pl*

bunting *n* gallardete, *m*
buoy *n* boya, baliza, *f*, *vt* boyar; abalizar; *fig* sostener.
  light b., boya luminosa, *f*
buoyancy *n* flotación, *f*; *fig* optimismo, *m*, alegría, *f*
buoyant *a* boyante; ligero
burden *n* carga, *f*, peso, *m*; (of a ship) tonelaje, *m*, capacidad, *f*; (of a song) estribillo, *m*; (gist) esencia, *f*. *vt* cargar. **to be a b. on,** pesar sobre
burdensome *a* pesado, oneroso, gravoso; abrumador
burdensomeness *n* pesadez, *f*; agobio, *m*
bureau *n* buró, secreter, *m*; escritorio, *m*; (office) dirección, oficina, *f*; departamento, *m*
bureaucracy *n* burocracia, *f*
bureaucrat *n* burócrata, *mf*; *inf* mandarín, *m*
bureaucratic *a* burocrático
burgher *n* ciudadano (-na), vecino (-na)
burglar *n* ladrón de casas, escalador, *m*. **cat b.,** gato, *m*.
  b. alarm, alarma contra ladrones, *f*. **b. insurance,** seguro contra robo, *m*
burglary *n* robo nocturno de una casa, *m*
burgle *vi* robar una casa de noche. *vt* robar
burgundy *n* vino de Borgoña, borgoña, *m*
burial *n* entierro, *m*. **b.-ground,** campo santo, cementerio, *m*. **b. service,** misa de difuntos, *f*. **b. society,** sociedad de entierros, *f*
burlap *n* arpillera, *f*
burlesque *a* burlesco. *n* parodia. *f*. *vt* parodiar
burliness *n* corpulencia, *f*
burly *a* corpulento, fornido
burn *vt* quemar; calcinar; (bricks) cocer; cauterizar; (the tongue) picar; (dry up) secar; (the skin by sun or wind) tostar. *vi* quemar; arder; *fig* abrasarse (en). **b. at the stake,** *vt* quemar en la hoguera. **to b. to ashes,** reducir a cenizas. **to b. away,** consumir(se). **to b. oneself,** quemarse. **to b. the midnight oil** *Chile* cranearse **to b. up,** quemar del todo, consumir. **to b. with,** *fig* abrasarse en
burn *n* quemadura, *f*; (stream) arroyo, *m*
burnable *a* combustible
burner *n* quemador (-ra); mechero, *m*
burning *n* quema, *f*; incendio, *m*; fuego, *m*; (inflammation) inflamación, *f*; (pain) quemazón, *f*; abrasamiento, *m*. *a* en llamas; ardiente; intenso; (notorious) notorio, escandaloso; abrasador; palpitante. **b. question,** cuestión palpitante, *f*
burnish *vt* bruñido, *m*; lustre, brillo, *m*, *vt* bruñir; pulir, pulimentar, dar brillo a; (weapons) acicalar. *vi* tomar lustre
burnisher *n* bruñidor, acicalador, *m*
burnishing *n* bruñido, *m*; pulimento, *m*; (of weapons) acicalado, *m*
burr *n* *bot* cáliz de flor con espinas, *m*; *mech* rebaba, *f*; sonido fuerte de la erre, *m*
burrow *n* madriguera, *f*, vivar, *m*; (for rabbits) conejera, *f*. *vt* amadrigar; minar
bursar *n* tesorero, *m*; becario, *m*
bursary *n* tesorería, *f*; beca, *f*
burst *n* estallido, *m*, explosión, *f*; (in a pipe) avería, *f*, (fit) acceso, *m*; transporte, *m*; (effort) esfuerzo, *m*; (expanse) extensión, *f*, panorama, *m*. **b. of applause,** salva de aplausos, *f*
burst *vi* estallar; reventar; quebrarse; romperse; (overflow) desbordar; (of seams) nacerse; derramarse (por); (into laughter) romper a; (into tears) deshacerse en. *vt* quebrar; romper; hacer estallar. **to b. upon the view,** aparecer de pronto. **to b. into,** irrumpir en; (exclamations, etc.) prorrumpir en. **to b. into tears,** romper a llorar, deshacerse en lágrimas. **to b. open,** abrir con violencia; forzar
bursting *n* estallido, *m*; quebrantamiento, *m*; (overflowing) desbordamiento, *m*
bury *vt* enterrar, sepultar; sumergir; (hide) esconder, ocultar; (forget) echar tierra a
bus *n* (regular city bus) autobús *m* (Colombia, Spain, Venezuela), camión *m* (Mexico), camioneta *f* (Guate-

mala), casadoro *m* (Costa Rica), chiva *f* (Colombia, Panama, informal), colectivo *m* (Argentina, Bolivia), flota *f* (Colombia, informal), góndola *f* (Chile), guagua *f* (Canary Islands, Cuba), micro *m* (Chile), ómnibus *m* (Peru), omnibús *m* (Uruguay); (interurban bus), aerobús *m* (Venezuela), autobús (Argentina, Chile, Spain, Uruguay), camión, camión de primera clase *m* (Mexico), interprovincial *m* (Peru), pullmán *m* (Mexico); (interurban jitney bus) colectivo *m* (Colombia); (minibus) micro *m* (Colombia, Peru), liebre (Chile, informal) **double-decker bus,** ómnibus de dos pisos, *m*. **to travel by bus,** ir en autobús. **bus station,** estación de autobuses, *Mexico* camionera, *f*
busby *n* birretina, gorra de húsar, *f*
bush *n* arbusto, matojo, *m*; (undergrowth) maleza, *f*; tierra virgen, *f*; *mech* manguito, *m*
bushel *n* medida de áridos, *f*, (In England 8 gallons or 36.37 liters)
bushiness *n* espesura, *f*; densidad, *f*
bushy *a* lleno de arbustos; denso; espeso; grueso; (eyebrows, etc.) poblado
busily *adv* diligentemente, solícitamente; afanosamente, laboriosamente. **He was b. occupied in . . . ,** Estaba muy ocupado en . . .
business *n* ocupación, *f*; quehaceres, *m pl*; (matter) asunto, *m*, cosa, *f*; empleo, oficio, *m*; *com* negocio(s), *m*, *pl.*; casa comercial, *f*; (trade) comercio, *m*; (clients, connection) clientela, *f*; (right) derecho, *m*; *theat* juego escénico, *m*, pantomima, *f*. **He had no b. to do that,** No tenía derecho a hacer eso. **Mind your own b.!** ¡No te metas donde no te llaman! **on b.,** por negocios. **to be in b. for oneself,** tener negocios por su propia cuenta. **to mean b.,** hacer algo en serio; estar resuelto. **to send about his b.,** mandar a paseo (a). **to set up in b.,** establecer un negocio. **b. affairs,** negocios, *m pl*. **b. agent,** agente de negocios, *m*. **b. hours,** horas de trabajo, *f pl*. **b.-like,** formal, práctico, sistemático. **b. man,** hombre de negocios, negociante, *m*
business administration *n* administración de empresas, *f*
bust *n* *art* busto, bulto, *m*; pecho, *m*. **b. bodice,** sostén, *m*
bustard *n* avutarda, *f*
bustle *n* actividad, animación, *f*; confusión, *f*; (of a dress) polizón, tontillo, *m*. *vi* menearse, darse prisa. *vt* dar prisa (a)
bustling *a* activo; ocupado, atareado; animado; bullicioso, ruidoso
busy *a* ocupado; atareado; activo, diligente; (of places) animado, bullicioso; (of streets) de gran circulación; (officious) entrometido. **to b. oneself,** ocuparse (en, con); dedicarse (a), entregarse (a); (interfere) entremeterse (con). **to be b.,** estar ocupado; estar atareado, tener mucho que hacer. **b.-body,** bullebulle, *mf*, entremetido (-da), chismoso (-sa), *Argentina* hurguete *mf*
busyness *n* ocupación, *f*; laboriosidad, *f*; actividad, *f*
but *conjunc prep adv* pero; sino; (only) solamente; (except) menos; excepto; (almost) casi; que no; si no; (that) que; (nevertheless) sin embargo, empero, no obstante; (without) sin, sin que; (of time recently passed) no más que, tan recientemente. *n* pero, *m*. **He cannot choose but go,** No puede hacer otra cosa que marcharse. **to do nothing but . . . ,** (nosepor) únicamente . . . , no hacer más que . . . **but for,** a no ser por. **but yesterday,** solamente ayer. **but then (or but yet),** pero
butcher *n* carnicero, *m*. *vt* matar reses; hacer una carnicería en. **butcher's boy,** mozo del carnicero, *m*. **butcher's shop,** carnicería, *f*
butchery *n* carnicería, *f*; matanza, *f*
butler *n* mayordomo, *m*. **butler's pantry,** despensa, repostería, *f*
butt *n* (cask) tonel, *m*, pipa, *f*; (for water) barril, *m*; (of a cigarette, etc.) colilla, *f*; (of fire-arms) culata, *f*; (han-

dle) mango, cabo, *m*; (billiards) mocho, *m*; (earthwork) terrero, *m*; (*fig* object) objeto (de), *m*; (of bulls, etc.) topetada, *f*; *pl* **butts,** campo de tiro, *m*; (target) blanco, *m*. *vt* (toss) topar, acornear; (meet) tropezar (con). **to b. in,** *inf* entrometerse, meter baza; encajarse

butter *n* mantequilla, *f*, *vt* untar con mantequilla. **b.-dish,** mantequera, *f.* **b.-fingers,** torpe, *m.* **b.-knife,** cuchillo para mantequilla, *m.* **b.-milk,** suero de mantequilla, *m.* **b.-print,** molde para mantequilla, *m.* **b.-sauce,** mantequilla fundida, *f*

buttercup *n* ranúnculo, botón de oro, *m*

butterfly *n* mariposa, *f*

butterscotch *n* dulce de azúcar y mantequilla, *m*

buttocks *n pl* nalgas, posaderas, *f pl*

button *n* botón, *m*; *pl* **buttons,** botones, paje, *m*. *vt* abotonar, abrochar. *vi* abotonarse, abrocharse. **to press the b.,** apretar el botón. **b.-hook,** abotonador, *m*

buttonhole *n* ojal, *m*; flor que se lleva en el ojal, *f*. *vt sew* hacer ojales; (embroidery) hacer el festón; *inf* importunar

buttoning *n* abrochamiento, *m*

buttress *n* estribo, macho, contrafuerte, *m*; *fig* apoyo, sostén, *m*. *vt* afianzar, estribar; *fig* apoyar, sostener. **flying-b.,** arbotante, *m*

buxom *a* (of a woman) fresca, guapetona, frescachona

buxomness *n* frescura, *f*

buy *vt* comprar; obtener; (achieve) lograr; (bribe) sobornar. **to buy on credit,** comprar al fiado. **to buy back,** comprar de nuevo; redimir; (ransom) rescatar. **to buy for,** (a price) comprar por; (purpose or destination) comprar para. **to buy in,** (at an auction) comprar por cuenta del dueño. **to buy off,** librarse de uno con dinero. **to buy out,** (of a business) comprar la parte de un socio. **to buy up,** comprar todo, acaparar

buyable *a* comprable, que se puede comprar

buyer *n* comprador (-ra)

buying *n* compra, *f.* **b. back,** rescate, *m.* **b. up,** acaparamiento, *m*

buying power *n* capacidad de compra, *f*, valor adquisitivo, *m*

buzz *n* zumbido, *m*; (whisper) susurro, murmullo, *m*; (of a bell) sonido (del timbre), *m*, *vi* zumbar; susurrar

buzzer *n* zumbador, *m*; sirena, *f*; (bell) timbre, *m*

buzzing *a* zumbador, que zumba, *n*. See **buzz**

by *prep* por; de; en; a; con; (of place) cerca de, al lado de; (according to) según, de acuerdo con; (in front of, past) delante (de); (at the latest) antes de, al más tardar; (expressing agency) por; (by means of) mediante; (through, along) por; (upon) sobre; (for) para; (under)

bajo. **He will be here by Wednesday,** Estará aquí para el miércoles; (not later than) Estará aquí antes del miércoles (or el miércoles al más tardar). **How did he come by it?** ¿Cómo llegó a su poder? **He will come by train,** Vendrá en tren. **I know her by sight,** La conozco de vista. **There are three children by the first marriage,** Hay tres niños del primer matrimonio. **He goes by the name of Pérez,** Se le conoce por (or bajo) el nombre de Pérez. **six feet by eight,** seis pies por ocho. **They called her by her name,** La llamaron por su nombre. **two by two,** dos por dos. **The picture was painted by Cézanne,** El cuadro fue pintado por Cézanne. **drop by drop,** gota a gota. **by a great deal,** con mucho. **by all means,** naturalmente; de todos modos; cueste lo que cueste. **by chance,** por ventura. **by day (night),** de día (noche). **by daylight,** a la luz del día. **by doing it,** con hacerlo. **by myself,** solo; sin ayuda. **"By Appointment"** «Cita Previa». **by chance or by mischance,** por ventura o por desdicha. **an hour away by car,** a una hora de automóvil. **music by Brahms,** música de Brahms. **pull by the hair,** tirar por el pelo. **take by the hand,** llevar de la mano.

by *adv* (near) cerca; (before) delante; al lado; a un lado; aparte; (of time) pasado. **to put by,** (keep) guardar; (throw away) desechar; (accumulate) acumular; (put out of the way) arrinconar. **to pass by,** pasar; pasar delante (de). **by and by,** luego, pronto; más tarde. **by now,** ya, antes de ahora. **by the way,** entre paréntesis, a propósito; de paso; al lado del camino. **by-election,** elección parcial, *f.* **by-law,** reglamento, *m.* **by-pass,** ruta de evitación, *f*, desvío, *m*; (*mech elec*) derivación, *f. vi* desviarse de; *mil* rebasar. **by-product,** derivado, *m*; *chem* producto derivado, *m*; *fig* consecuencia, *f*; resultado, *m*

bye *n* (in cricket) meta, *f.* **by the bye,** a propósito, entre paréntesis

bye! *interj. Argentina, Chile* ¡chao!

bygone *a* pasado. **Let bygones be bygones,** Lo pasado pasado

byplay *n* pantomima, *f*, gestos, *m pl*; *theat* juego escénico, *m*, escena muda, *f*

bystander *n* espectador (-ra); *pl* **bystanders,** los circunstantes

bystreet *n* callejuela, *f*; calle pobre, *f*

byway *n* camino desviado, *m*; *fig* senda indirecta, *f*; *pl* **byways,** andurriales, *m pl*

byword *n* proverbio, *m*; objeto de burla o escándalo, *m*

Byzantine Empire, the el Imperio Bizantino, *m*

Byzantium Bizancio, *m*

C

c *n* (letter) c, *f*; *mus* do, *m*

cab *n* (horse-drawn) simón, *m*; (taxi) coche de alquiler, *m*; (of a locomotive) cabina del conductor, *f.* **cab-rank,** punto de coches, *m*

cabala *n* cábala, *f*

cabaret *n* cabaret, *m*; taberna, *f*

cabbage *n* col, berza, *f.* **red c.,** lombarda, *f.* **c. butterfly,** mariposa de col, *f*

cabin *n* cabaña, choza, *f*; *naut* camarote, *m*; (railway) garita, *f*; *aer* cabina, *f.* **c. boy,** grumete, galopín, mozo de cámara, *m.* **c. trunk,** baúl mundo, *m*

cabinet *n* (piece of furniture) vitrina, *f*; colección, exposición, *f*; *pol* gabinete, *m*; (of a radio) cónsola, *f.* **c.-maker,** ebanista, *m.* **c.-making,** ebanistería, *f.* **c. meeting,** consejo de ministros, *m.* **c. minister,** ministro, *m*

cable *n* amarra, maroma, *f*; cable, *m*; cable(grama), *m*, *vt* cablegrafiar. **electric c.,** cable eléctrico, *m.* **overhead c.,** cable aéreo, *m*

cabman *n* cochero de punto, simón, *m*

caboose *n naut* cocina, *f*

cache *n* escondite, escondrijo, *m*

cackle *vi* (of a hen) cacarear; (of a goose) graznar; (of humans) chacharear. *n* cacareo, *m*; graznido, *m*; cháchara, *f*

cacophony *n* cacofonía, *f*

cactus *n* cacto, *m*

cad *n* sinvergüenza, *m*; tipo de cuidado, *m*

cadaverous *a* cadavérico

caddish *a* mal educado, grosero

caddy *n* (for tea) cajita para té, *f*; (golf) cadi, *mf*

cadence *n* cadencia, *f*

cadet *n* hermano menor, *m*; *mil* cadete, *m*

cadge *vi* sablear. *vt* dar un sablazo (a)

cadger *n* sablista, *mf*; mendigo, *m*; (loafer) golfo, *m*

Cadiz Cádiz, *f*

cadmium *n* cadmio, *m*

café *n* café, *m*

cafeteria *n* bar automático, *m*

caffeine *n* cafeína, *f*

cage *n* (animal's, bird's) jaula, *f*; (of a lift) camarín, *m*; (for transporting miners) jaula, *f. vt* enjaular; encerrar

Cain, to raise armar lo de Dios es Cristo
cairn *n* montón de piedras, *m*
Cairo el Cairo, *m*
cajole *vt* lisonjear; engatusar, embromar; instar
cajolery *n* zalamerías, *f pl*; marrullería, *f*, engatusamiento, *m*
cake *n cul* pastel, *m*, torta, *f*; (of chocolate, etc.) pastilla, *f*. *vt* and *vi* cuajar; formar costra; (with mud) enlodar. **to sell like hot cakes,** venderse como pan bendito. **to take the c.,** llevarse la palma. **c. of soap,** pastilla de jabón, *f*. **c.-shop,** pastelería, *f*
calamine *n* calamina, *f*
calamitous *a* calamitoso, desastroso
calamity *n* calamidad, *f*; desastre, *m*, *Mexico also* funestidad *f*
calash *n* (carriage) calesa, carretela, *f*; (hood) capota, *f*
calcium *n* calcio, *m*
calculate *vt* calcular; adaptar. **to c. on,** contar con
calculated *a* premeditado. **to be c. to,** conducir a; ser a propósito para
calculatedly *adv* calculadamente
calculating *n* cálculo, *m*, *a* calculador; (of persons) interesado; (shrewd) perspicaz; atento. **c. machine,** máquina de calcular, *f*, calculador, *m*
calculation *n* cálculo, *m*; calculación, *f*
calculus *n* cálculo, *m*
calendar *n* calendario, *m*; almanaque, *m*; (university, etc.) programa, *m*
calender *n* calandria, *f*, *vt* calandrar, cilindrar
calf *n* becerro (-rra), ternero (-ra); (young of other animals) hijuelo, *m*; (of the leg) pantorrilla, *f*; (leather) cuero de becerro, *m*; piel, *f*. **calf's-foot,** pie de ternera, *m*. **c. love,** amor de muchachos, *m*
calibrate *vt* calibrar
calibre *n* calibre, *m*
calico *n* indiana, *f*; percal, *m*. **c.-printer,** fabricante de estampados, *m*
Californian *a* californio. *n* californio (-ia)
caliph *n* califa, *m*
calk. See **caulk**
call *n* llamada, *f*; (shout) grito, *m*; (of a bird) canto, *m*; (signal) señal, *f*; (visit) visita, *f*; (by a ship) escala, *f*; *mil* toque, *m*; (need) necesidad, *f*; (of religion, etc.) vocación, *f*; invitación, *f*; (demand) demanda, *f*; exigencia, *f*. **They came at my c.,** Acudieron a mi llamada. **c. to arms,** llamada, llamada a filas, *f*. **port of c.,** puerto de escala, *m*. **telephone c.,** llamada telefónica, *f*. **to pay a c.,** hacer una visita. **within c.,** al alcance de la voz. **c.-box,** cabina del teléfono, *f*. **c.-boy,** ayudante del traspunte, *m*
call *vi* llamar; gritar, dar voces; (visit) visitar, hacer una visita (a); venir; (stop) parar; (of a ship) hacer escala. *vt* llamar; (a meeting, etc.) convocar; (awaken) despertar, llamar; (say) decir; (appoint) nombrar; (at cards) declarar. **She is called Dorothy,** Se llama Dorotea. **Madrid calling!** ¡Aquí Radio Madrid! **Will you c. me at eight o'clock, please?** Haga el favor de despertarme (llamarme) a las ocho. **to c. at a port,** hacer escala en un puerto. **to c. a halt,** hacer alto. **to c. a strike,** declarar una huelga. **to c. names,** vituperar, injuriar. **to c. to account,** pedir cuentas (a). **to c. to arms,** tocar el arma; alarmar. **to c. to mind,** acordarse (de), recordar. **to c. to witness,** hacer testigo (de). **to c. back,** *vt* llamar; hacer volver; (unsay) desdecir. *vi* (return) volver; venir a buscar; ir a buscar. **I called back for the parcel,** Volví a buscar el paquete. **to c. for,** pedir a gritos; llamar; (demand) pedir; exigir; (collect a person) pasar a buscar; (parcels, etc.) ir (or venir) a recoger. **He called for help,** Pidió socorro a gritos. **to c. forth,** producir; provocar; inspirar; revelar; (bring together) reunir. **to c. in,** hacer entrar; invitar; (a specialist, etc.) llamar; (worn coin) retirar de la circulación; recoger. **to c. in question,** poner en duda. **to c. off,** (dogs, etc.) llamar; (a strike) cancelar; parar; terminar; (a person) disuadir (de); (postpone) aplazar; suspender; (refrain) desistir (de). **to c. on,** (visit) hacer

una visita (a), ir a ver, visitar; (of a doctor) visitar; (a person to do something) recurrir (a); (for a speech) invitar (a hablar); (invoke) invocar. **I shall now c. on Mr. Martínez,** Doy la palabra al señor Martínez. **to c. out,** *vt* hacer salir; provocar; inspirar; (challenge) desafiar, retar. *vi* gritar. **c. the roll,** pasar lista. **to c. over,** (names) pasar lista (de). **to c. up,** hacer subir; (to the army) llamar a filas (a); (telephone) llamar por teléfono (a); (memories) evocar. **to c. upon.** See **to c. on**
caller *n* visita, *f*
calligraphist *n* calígrafo, *m*
calligraphy *n* caligrafía, *f*
calling *n* llamamiento, *m*; (occupation) profesión, *f*; empleo, *m*; vocación, *f*; (of a meeting) convocación, *f*
callipers *n pl* compás de puntas, pie de rey, *m*
callisthenics *n pl* calistenia, *f*
callosity *n* callosidad, *f*
callous *a* (of skin) calloso; *fig* insensible, duro, inhumano
callously *adv* sin piedad
callousness *n* falta de piedad, inhumanidad, dureza, *f*
callow *a* (of birds) implume; (inexperienced) bisoño, inexperto, novato
callus *n* callo, *m*
calm *n* calma, *f*; paz, tranquilidad, *f*; sosiego, *m*; serenidad, *f*. *a* (of the sea) en calma; tranquilo; sereno; sosegado. *vt* calmar; tranquilizar; apaciguar. *vi* calmarse; tranquilizarse; sosegarse. **dead c.,** calma chicha, *f*
calming *a* calmante
calmly *adv* tranquilamente, sosegadamente; con calma
calmness *n* calma, tranquilidad, *f*; ecuanimidad, serenidad, *f*
caloric *a* calórico
calorie *n* caloría, *f*
calumniation *n* calumnia, *f*
calumniator *n* calumniador (-ra)
calumny *n* calumnia, *f*
calvary *n* calvario, *m*
calve *vi* (of a cow, etc.) parir
Calvinism *n* calvinismo, *m*
Calvinist *n* calvinista, *mf*
Calvinistic *a* calvinista
calyx *n* cáliz, *m*
cam *n mech* leva, *f*. **camshaft,** árbol de levas, *m*
camaraderie *n* compañerismo, *m*
camber *n* comba(dura), *f*
cambric *n* batista, *f*
camel *n* camello (-lla). **c.-driver,** camellero, *m*. **camel's hair,** pelo de camello, *m*
camellia *n* camelia, *f*
cameo *n* camafeo, *m*
camera *n phot* máquina fotográfica, *f*. **folding c.,** máquina fotográfica plegable, *f*. **in c.,** a puerta cerrada. **c. obscura,** cámara obscura, *f*
Cameroons, the el Camerón, los Camerones, *m*
camouflage *n* camuflaje, *m*, *vt* camuflar
camp *n* campamento, *m*; campo, *m*; *fig* vida de cuartel, *f*; (for school children, etc.) colonia, *f*; (party) partido, *m*. *vi* acampar; vivir en tiendas de campaña. **to break c.,** levantar el campo. **c.-bed,** cama de campaña, *f*. **c.-stool,** silla de campaña, *f*
campaign *n* campaña, *f*. *vi* hacer una campaña
campaigner *n* veterano, *m*; propagandista, *mf*
campaigning *n* campañas, *f pl*
camphor *n* alcanfor, *m*
camphorated *a* alcanforado
campus *n* recinto, *m* (Puerto Rico), ciudad universitaria, *f*
can *v auxil* poder; (know how to) saber. **You can go to the village when you like,** Puedes ir al pueblo cuando quieras. **I cannot allow that,** No puedo permitir eso. **What can they mean?** ¿Qué quieren decir? **If only things could have been different!** ¡Si solamente las cosas hubiesen sido distintas! **Can you**

come to dinner on Saturday? ¿Puede Vd. venir a cenar el sábado? **I can come later if you like,** Puedo (or Podría) venir más tarde si Vd. quiere. **Mary can** (knows how to) **play the piano,** María sabe tocar el piano **You can't eat your cake and have it too.** No hay rosa sin espinas

can *n* lata, *f*; (for carrying sandwiches, etc.) fiambrera, *f*. *vt* conservar en latas. **canopener,** abrelatas, *m*

Canada el Canadá, *m*

Canadian *a* canadiense. *n* canadiense, *mf*

canaille *n* gentualla, gentuza, *f*

canal *n* canal, *m*

canalization *n* canalización, *f*

canalize *vt* canalizar

canary *n* canario (-ia); color de canario, *m*; vino de Canarias, *m*. **roller c.,** canario de raza flauta, *m*. **c.-seed,** alpiste, *m*

Canary Islands, the las Islas Canarias, *m*

cancel *vt* cancelar; revocar; borrar; anular. **to c. out,** *math* anular

cancellation *n* cancelación, *f*; revocación, *f*; anulación, *f*

cancer *n med* cáncer, *m*; *ast* Cáncer, *m*

cancerous *a* canceroso. **to become c.,** cancerarse

candelabrum *n* candelabro, *m*

candescent *a* candente

candid *a* franco; sincero. **If I am to be c.,** Si he de decir la verdad, Si he de ser franco

candidate *n* candidato (-ta); aspirante, *m*

candidature *n* candidatura, *f*

candidly *adv* francamente; sinceramente

candidness *n* franqueza, *f*; sinceridad, *f*

candied *a* (of peel, etc.) almibarado, garapiñado

candle *n* vela, candela, *f*. **wax c.,** cirio, *m*. **You cannot hold a c. to him,** No llegas a la suela de su zapato, Ni llegas a sus pies, Ni le llegas a los pies. **The game is not worth the c.,** La cosa no vale la pena. **to burn the c. at both ends,** consumir la vida. **c.-grease,** sebo, *m*. **c.-light,** luz de las velas, *f*; luz artificial, *f*. **c.-maker,** candelero, *m*. **c.-power,** *elec* potencia luminosa, bujía, *f*. **c.-snuffer,** apagavelas, matacandelas, *m*

Candlemas *n* candelaria, *f*

candlestick *n* candelero, *m*, palmatoria, *f*; (processional) cirial, *m*

candor *n* franqueza, *f*; sinceridad, *f*; candor, *m*

candy *n* caramelo, bombón, *m*, *vt* garapiñar, almibarar

candytuft *n* carraspique, *m*

cane *n bot* caña, *f*; (for chair seats, etc.) rejilla, *f*; (walking stick) bastón, *m*; (for punishment) vara, *f*. *vt* apalear, pegar. **sugar-c.,** caña de azúcar, *f*. **c.-break,** cañaveral, *m*. **c. chair,** sillón de mimbres, *m*. **c.-sugar,** azúcar de caña, *m*. **c.-syrup,** miel de caña, *f*

canine *a* canino. *n* (tooth) diente canino, *m*

caning *n* paliza, *f*

canister *n* bote, *m*, cajita, *f*

canker *n* úlcera, *f*; (in trees) cancro, *m*; *fig* cáncer, *m*, *vt* roer; *fig* corromper

canned *a* en lata

cannibal *n* caníbal, *mf* antropófago (-ga). *a* caníbal, antropófago

cannibalism *n* canibalismo, *m*, antropofagía, *f*

canning *n* conservación en latas, *f*. **c. factory,** fábrica de conservas alimenticias, *f*

cannon *n* (fire-arm) cañón, *m*; (billiards) carambola, *f*, *vi* carambolear. **to c. into,** chocar con. **c.-ball,** bala de cañón, *f*. **c.-shot,** cañonazo, *m*

cannonade *n* cañoneo, *m*

canny *a* cuerdo, sagaz

canoe *n* canoa, *f*; piragua, *f*, *vi* ir en canoa

canoeist *n* canoero (-ra)

canon *n* (*ecc mus print*) canón, *m*; (dignitary) canónigo, *m*; (criterion) criterio, *m*. **c. law,** derecho canónico, *m*

canonical *a* canónico

canonization *n* canonización, *f*

canonize *vt* canonizar

canopy *n* dosel, toldo, *m*; palio, *m*; *fig* capa, bóveda, *f*. **the c. of heaven,** la capa (or bóveda) del cielo

cant *vt* inclinar; ladear. *vi* inclinarse; (be a hypocrite) camandulear. *n* (slope) inclinación, *f*, sesgo, desplomo, *m*; (hypocrisy) gazmoñería, *f*

Cantabrian *a* cantábrico

cantankerous *a* irritable, intratable, malhumorado, *Argentina* cabrero

cantankerousness *n* mal humor, *m*, irritabilidad, *f*

cantata *n* cantata, *f*

canteen *n* cantina, *f*; (water bottle) cantimplora, *f*. **c. of cutlery,** juego de cubiertos, *m*

canter *n* medio galope, *m*, *vi* andar a galope corto

canticle *n* cántico, *m*

canting *a* hipócrita

canto *n* canto, *m*

canton *n* (province and *her*) cantón, *m*, *vt* (of soldiers) acantonar

cantonment *n* acantonamiento, cantón, *m*

cantor *n ecc* chantre, *m*

canvas *n* lona, *f*; *art* lienzo, *m*; *naut* vela, *f*, paño, *m*. **under c.,** en tiendas de campaña; (of ships) a toda vela

canvass *vt* (votes, etc.) solicitar

canvasser *n* solicitador (-ra) (de votos, etc.)

canvassing *n* solicitación (de votos, etc.), *f*

canyon *n* cañón, *m*

canzonet *n* chanzoneta, *f*

cap *n* gorra, *f*; (with a peak) montera, *f*; (type of military headgear with brim at front) quépis, *m*; (cardinal's) birrete, *m*; *univ* bonete, *m*; (pointed) caperuza, *f*; (woman's old-fashioned) cofia, *f*; (jester's) gorro de bufón, *m*; (on a bottle) cápsula, tapa, *f*. *vt univ* conferir el grado (a). **cap and bells,** gorro de bufón, *m*. **cap and gown,** birrete y muceta, toga y birrete, toga y bonete. **to throw one's cap over the windmill,** echar la capa al toro. **to cap it all,** ser el colmo

capability *n* capacidad, *f*; aptitud, *f*

capable *a* capaz; competente; (of improvement) susceptible; (full of initiative) emprendedor

capably *adv* competentemente

capacious *a* espacioso; grande; extenso

capaciousness *n* capacidad, *f*; amplitud, *f*

capacitate *vt* capacitar

capacity *n* capacidad, *f*; calidad, *f*; aptitud, *f*. **in one's c. as,** en calidad de. **seating c.,** número de asientos, *m*; (in aircraft) número de plazas, *m*

caparison *n* caparazón, *f*

cape *n* (cloak) capa, *f*; (short) capotillo, *m*, capeta, *f*; (fur) cuello, *m*; *geog* cabo, promontorio, *m*. **c. coat,** capote, *m*

Cape Horn Cabo de Hornos, *m*

caper *vi* (gambol) brincar, saltar; cabriolar, corcovear; (play) juguetear. *n* travesura, *f*; zapateta, *f*; cabriola, *f*; (whim) capricho, *m*; *bot* alcaparra, *f*. **to c. about,** dar saltos, brincar; juguetear

capillarity *n* capilaridad, *f*

capillary *a* capilar. *n* vaso capilar, *m*

capital *a* capital; mortal; de muerte; de vida; principal; (of letters) mayúscula; (very good) excelente; (of the capital city) *Lat. Am.* capitalino *n* (city) capital, *f*; (letter) (letra) mayúscula, *f*; *com* capital, *m*; *arch* capitel, chapitel, *m*. **floating c.,** capital fluctuante, *m*. **idle c.,** fondos inactivos, *m pl*. **c. punishment,** pena de muerte, pena capital, pena de la vida, *f*. **C.!** ¡Estupendo! ¡Excelente! **to make c. out of,** aprovecharse de, sacar ventaja de

capitalism *n* capitalismo, *m*

capitalist *n* capitalista, *mf*

capitalistic *a* capitalista

capitalization *n* capitalización, *f*

capitalize *vt* capitalizar

capitally *adv* estupendamente

capitation *n* capitación, *f*

Capitol *n* Capitolio, *m*

capitulate *vi* capitular

capitulation *n* capitulación, *f*

capon *n* capón, *m*

caprice *n* capricho, *m*

capricious *a* caprichoso

capriciousness *n* carácter inconstante, *m*; lo caprichoso

Capricorn *n* Capricornio, *m*

capsize *vt naut* hacer zozobrar; volcar. *vi naut* zozobrar; volcarse

capsizing *n naut* zozobra, *f*; vuelco, *m*

capsule *n* (*bot med chem zool*) cápsula, *f*

captain *n* (*mil nav aer* and *sport*) capitán, *m*, *vt* capitanear. **to c. a team,** ser el capitán de un equipo. **group c.,** *aer* capitán de aviación, *m*

captaincy *n* capitanía, *f*

caption *n* (arrest) arresto, *m*; (heading) encabezamiento, título, pie, *m*; (cinema) subtítulo, *m*

captious *a* capcioso, caviloso

captivate *vt* cautivar, seducir

captivating *a* encantador, seductor

captive *a* cautivo, *n* cautivo (-va), prisionero (-ra), preso (-sa). **c. balloon,** globo cautivo, globo de observación, *m*

captivity *n* cautiverio, *m*

captor *n* el, *m*, (*f*, la) que hace prisionero (-ra)

capture *n* captura, *f*; presa, toma, *f*; *law* captura, *f*. *vt* prender, capturar; tomar

car *n* (chariot) carro, *m*; (tram) tranvía, *m*; (motor) automóvil, coche, *Lat. Am.* carro *m*; (on a train) coche vagón, *m*. **sleeping car,** coche camas, *m*. **car park,** parque de automóviles, *m*

carabineer *n* carabinero, *m*

carafe *n* garrafa, *f*

caramel *n* caramelo, *m*; azúcar quemado, *m*

carapace *n* carapacho, *m*

carat *n* quilate, *m*

caravan *n* caravana, *f*; coche de gitanos, *m*; coche habitación, *m*

caraway *n* alcaravea, *f*

carbarn *n* encierro, *m* (Mexico), cochera, cochera de tranvías, *f*, cobertizo, cobertizo para tranvías, *m*

carbide *n* carburo, *m*

carbine *n* carabina, *f*

carbohydrate *n* hidrato de carbono, *m*

carbolic *a* carbólico. **c. acid,** ácido fénico, *m*

carbon *n* carbono, *m*. **c. copy,** copia en papel carbón, *f*. **c. dioxide,** anhídrido carbónico, *m*. **c. monoxide,** óxido de carbono, *m*. **c. paper,** papel carbón, papel de calcar, *m*

carbonate *n* carbonato, *m*

carbonated *a* (beverage) carbónico (formal), con gas (informal)

carbonic *a* carbónico

carbonization *n* carbonización, *f*

carbonize *vt* carbonizar

carboy *n* damajuana, garrafa, *f*

carbuncle *n med* carbunco, *m*; (stone) carbúnculo, *m*

carburetor *n* carburador, *m*

carcass *n* (animal) res muerta, *f*; (corpse) cadáver, *m*; (body) cuerpo, *m*; (of a ship) casco, *m*

carcinoma *n* carcinoma, *m*

card *n* (playing) naipe, *m*; (pasteboard) cartulina, *f*; (visiting, postal, etc.) tarjeta, *f*; (index) ficha, *f*; (for wool, etc.) carda, *f*. *vt* (wool, etc.) cardar. **I still have a c. up my sleeve,** Me queda todavía un recurso. **to lay one's cards on the table,** poner las cartas boca arriba. **to play one's cards well,** *fig* jugar el lance. **admission c.,** billete de entrada, *m*. **post c.,** tarjeta postal, *f*. **visiting c.,** tarjeta de visita, *f*. **c.-case,** tarjetero, *m*. **c.-index,** fichero, *m*. *vt* poner en el fichero. **c.-sharper,** fullero, *m*. **c.-table,** mesa de juego, *f*. **c. trick,** juego de manos con cartas, *m*

cardboard *n* cartón, *m*, *a* de cartón

cardiac *a* cardíaco

cardigan *n* rebeca, chaqueta de punto, *f*

cardinal *a* cardinal. *n* cardenal, *m*. **c. number,** número cardinal, *m*. **c. points,** puntos cardinales, *m pl*

cardinalate *n* cardenalato, *m*

carding *n* (of wool, etc.) cardadura, *f*. **c. machine,** carda mecánica, *f*

cardiogram *n* cardiograma, *m*

care *n* cuidado, *m*; atención, *f*; inquietud, ansia, *f*; (charge) cargo, *m*. *vi* preocuparse; tener interés; (suffer) sufrir. **I don't c.,** Me es igual; No me importa. **I don't c. a straw,** No se me da un bledo. **They don't c. for eggs,** No les gustan los huevos. **We don't c. what his opinion is,** Su opinión nos tiene sin cuidado (or no nos importa). **to c. for,** cuidar, mirar por; (love) querer (a); (like) gustar. **Take c.!** ¡Cuidado! ¡Ojo! **Take c. not to spoil it!** ¡Ten cuidado que no lo estropees! **Would you c. to . . . ?** ¿Le gustaría . . . ? ¿Tendría inconveniente en . . . ? **c. of,** (on a letter, etc.) en casa de. **c.-free,** *a* libre de cuidados

careen *vt* carenar. *vi* dar a la banda

careening *n* carena, *f*

career *n* carrera, *f*; curso, *m*. *vi* correr a carrera tendida; galopar

careful *a* cuidadoso (de); atento (a); prudente. **Careful!, Be careful!** ¡Cuidado! ¡Cuidado! **to be c.,** tener cuidado

carefully *adv* con cuidado. **drive c.,** manejar con cuidado; cuidadosamente; prudentemente; atentamente

carefulness *n* cuidado, *m*; atención, *f*; prudencia, *f*

careless *a* sin cuidado; indiferente (a); insensible (a); negligente; (of mistakes, etc.) de (or por) negligencia

carelessly *adv* indiferentemente; negligentemente; descuidadamente

carelessness *n* indiferencia, *f*; negligencia, *f*; descuido, *m*; omisión, *f*

caress *n* caricia, *f*, *vt* acariciar

caressing *a* acariciador

caretaker *n* (of museums, etc.) guardián (-ana); (of flats, etc.) portero (-ra)

careworn *a* devorado de inquietud, ansioso

cargo *n* cargamento, *m*, carga, *f*. **c.-boat,** barco de carga, *m*

Caribbean *a* caribe

Caribbean Sea, the el Mar Caribe, *m*

caricature *n* caricatura, *f*, *vt* caricaturizar

caricaturist *n* caricaturista, *mf*

caries *n* caries, *f*

carious *a* cariado. **to become c.,** cariarse

Carmelite *a* carmelita. *n* carmelita, *mf*

carmine *n* carmín, *m*, *a* de carmín

carnage *n* carnicería, *f*

carnal *a* carnal; sensual

carnality *n* carnalidad, *f*

carnally *adv* carnalmente

carnation *n* clavel, *m*

carnival *n* carnaval, *m*, *a* de carnaval, carnavalesco

carnivore *n* carnívoro, *m*

carnivorous *a* carnívoro

carol *n* villancico, *m*; canto, *m*. *vi* cantar alegremente; (of birds) trinar, gorjear

Carolingian *a* carolingio

carotid *n* carótida, *f*

carousal *n* borrachera, *f*; holgorio, *m*, jarana, *f*

carouse *vi* emborracharse. *n* borrachera, orgía, *f*

carp *n* carpa, *f*, *vi* criticar, censurar

Carpathian Mountains, the los Montes Carpotes, *m*

carpel *n* carpelo, *m*

carpenter *n* carpintero, *m*, *vi* carpintear. **carpenter's bench,** banco de carpintero, *m*. **carpenter's shop,** carpintería, *f*

carpentry *n* carpintería, *f*

carpet *n* alfombra, *f*; *fig* tapete, *m*. *vt* cubrir de una alfombra, alfombrar; tapizar. **to be on the c.,** estar sobre el tapete. **c.-beater,** sacudidor de alfombras, *m*. **c. merchant,** alfombrista, *m*. **c. slippers,** zapatillas de fieltro, *f pl*. **c.-sweeper,** aspirador de polvo, *m*

carpeting *n* alfombrado, *m*

carping *a* capcioso, criticón

carriage *n* (carrying) transporte, porte, *m*; (deportment) porte, continente, *m*, presencia, *f*; (vehicle) carruaje, *m*; carroza, *f*; coche, *m*; (railway) departamento, *m*; (chassis) chasis, bastidor, *m*; (of a typewriter, etc.) carro, *m*. **hackney c.,** coche de plaza, *m*. **c. and pair,** carroza de dos caballos, *f*. **c. door,** portezuela, *f*. **c.-forward,** porte debido. **c.-free,** franco de porte. **c.-paid,** porte pagado

carrier *n* el, *m*, (*f*, la) que lleva; portador (-ra); *com* mensajero, *m*; (on a car, bicycle) portaequipajes, *m*; (of a disease) vector, *m*; (aircraft) porta-aviones, *m*. **c.-pigeon,** paloma mensajera, *f*

carrion *n* carroña, *f*. **c.-crow,** chova, *f*

carrot *n* zanahoria, *f*

carry *vt* llevar; transportar; traer; conducir; (*mil* of arms) portar; (have with one) tener consigo; (an enemy position) tomar, ganar; (a motion) aprobar; (oneself) portarse; (one's point, etc.) ganar; (in the mind) retener; (conviction) convencer; (involve) implicar; (influence) influir; (send) despachar, enviar; (contain) incluir, comprender. *vi* (of the voice, etc.) alcanzar, llegar. **The noise of the guns carried a long way,** El ruido de los cañones se oía desde muy lejos. **to fetch and c.,** traer y llevar. **to c. all before one,** vencer todos los obstáculos. **to c. into effect,** poner en efecto. **to c. one's audience with one,** captar (or cautivar) su auditorio. **to c. oneself well,** tener buena presencia. **to c. on one's back,** llevar a cuestas. **to c. the day,** quedar victorioso, quedar señor del campo. **to c. weight,** *fig* ser de peso. **to c. along,** llevar; (drag) arrastrar; conducir; acarrear. **to c. away,** llevar; llevarse, llevar consigo; (kidnap) robar, secuestrar; (of emotions) dominar; (by enthusiasm) entusiasmar; (inspire) inspirar. **to c. forward,** llevar a cabo; avanzar; fomentar; (bookkeeping) pasar a cuenta nueva. **to c. off,** (things) llevarse; (persons) llevar consigo (a); (abduct or steal) robar; (kill) matar; (a prize) ganar. **to c. (a thing) off well,** llevar la mejor parte, salir vencedor. **to c. on,** *vt* (a discussion, etc.) seguir, continuar. **c. on a conversation,** llevar una conversación; mantener; (a business, etc.) tener; dirigir. *vi* ir tirando; seguir trabajando. **to c. out,** realizar, llevar a cabo; hacer, ejecutar, efectuar; (a promise) cumplir. **to c. through,** llevar a cabo

carrying *n* transporte, *m*; (of a motion) adopción, *f*

cart *n* carro, *m*. *vt* acarrear; llevar. **c.-horse,** caballo de tiro, *m*. **c.-load,** carretada, *f*, carro, *m*. **c.-wheel,** rueda de carro, *f*; (somersault) voltereta, *f*

cartage *n* carretaje, transporte, porte, *m*

carte blanche *n* carta blanca, *f*

cartel *n* cartel, *m*

carter *n* carretero, *m*

Cartesian *a* cartesiano. *n* cartesiano (-na)

Carthage Cartago, *m*

Carthaginian *a* cartaginés. *n* cartaginés (-esa)

car thief *Lat. Am.* autero (-ra) *mf*

cartilage *n* cartílago, *m*

cartilaginous *a* cartilaginoso

cartographer *n* cartógrafo, *m*

cartography *n* cartografía, *f*

cartomancy *n* cartomancia, *f*

carton *n* caja de cartón, *f*

cartoon *n* (design for tapestry, etc.) cartón, *m*; caricatura, *f*

cartoonist *n* caricaturista, *mf*

cartridge *n* cartucho, *m*. **blank c.,** cartucho sin bala, *m*. **c.-belt,** cartuchera, canana, *f*. **c.-case,** cápsula de proyectil, *f*

carve *vt* tallar, labrar; grabar; cortar; (meat, etc.) trinchar; (a career, etc.) forjar, forjarse

carver *n* tallador, *m*; (at table) trinchador, *m*; (implement) trinchante, *m*

carving *n* talla, *f*; (design) tallado, *m*. **c.-knife,** trinchante, *m*

cascade *n* cascada, catarata, *f*, salto de agua, *m*; *fig* chorro, *m*. *vi* chorrear

case *n* caso, *m*; *law* proceso, *m*, causa, *f*; *gram* caso, *m*; *med* caso, *m*; enfermo (-ma); (box) caja, *f*; (for scissors,

etc.) vaina, *f*; (for a cushion, etc.) funda, *f*; (for jewels, manicure implements, etc.) estuche, *m*; (of a piano, watch and *print*) caja, *f*; (for documents) carpeta, *f*; (glass) vitrina, *f*; (for a book) sobrecubierta, *f*; (dressing) neceser, *m*. *vt* cubrir; forrar; resguardar. **packing-c.,** caja de embalaje, *f*. **c. of goods,** caja de mercancías, *f*; bulto, *m*. **in any c.,** en todo caso; venga lo que venga. **in c.,** por si acaso. **in c. of emergency,** en caso de urgencia. **in such a c.,** en tal caso. **in the c. of,** en el caso de; respecto a. **lower c.,** *print* caja baja, *f*. **upper c.,** *print* caja alta, *f*. **c.-hardened,** (of iron) templado; *fig* endurecido, indiferente

case closed! ¡asunto concluido!

casement window *n* ventana, *f*

cash *n* efectivo, metálico, *m*; dinero contante, *m*; *inf* dinero, *m*; *com* caja, *f*. *vt* cobrar; pagar, hacer efectivo. **hard or ready c.,** dinero contante, *m*. **to pay c.,** pagar al contado. **c. on delivery,** (C.O.D.) contra reembolso. **c. on hand,** efectivo en caja, *m*. **c.-book,** libro de caja, *m*. **c.-box,** caja, *f*. **c.-desk,** caja, *f*. **c. down,** pago al contado, *m*. **c. prize,** premio en metálico, *m*. **c.-register,** caja registradora, *f*

cashew *n* anacardo, *m*

cashier *n* cajero (-ra). *vt* degradar. **cashier's desk,** caja, *f*

cash machine *n* cajero automático, *m*

cashmere *n* cachemira, *f*

casino *n* casino, *m*

cask *n* pipa, barrica, *f*, tonel, *m*; cuba, *f*

casket *n* cajita, arquilla, *f*, cofrecito, *m*

Caspian Sea, the el (Mar) Caspio, *m*

casserole *n* cacerola, *f*

cassock *n* sotana, *f*

cast *vt* arrojar, tirar; (in fishing, the anchor, dice, darts, lots, a net, glances, blame, etc.) echar; (skin) mudar; (lose) perder; (a shadow, etc.) proyectar; (a vote) dar; (mold) vaciar; (accounts) echar, calcular; (a horoscope) hacer; (the parts in a play) repartir; (an actor for a part) dar el papel de; (metals) colar, fundir. **the shadow c. by the wall,** la sombra proyectada por el muro. **to c. anchor,** echar anclas, anclar. **to c. in one's lot with,** compartir la suerte de. **to c. something in a person's teeth,** echar en cara (a). **to c. lots,** echar suertes. **to c. about,** meditar, considerar; imaginar; (devise) inventar. **to c. aside,** desechar; poner a un lado; abandonar. **to c. away,** tirar lejos; desechar; (money) derrochar, malgastar. **to be c. away,** *naut* naufragar. **to c. down,** (overthrow) derribar, destruir; (eyes) bajar; (depress) desanimar, deprimir; (humiliate) humillar. **to be c. down,** estar deprimido. **c. iron,** *n* hierro colado, hierro fundido, *m*. **c.-iron,** *a* de hierro colado; *fig* inflexible. **to c. off,** quitarse; desechar; (a wife) repudiar; (desert) abandonar; (free oneself) librarse (de). **c.-off,** *n* desecho, *m*. **c.-off clothing,** ropa de desecho, *f*. **to c. out,** echar fuera; hacer salir; excluir. **to c. up,** echar; vomitar; (a sum) sumar; (something at a person) reprochar

cast *n* (of dice, fishing-line) echada, *f*; (of a net) redada, *f*; (worm) molde, *m*; (of a play) reparto, *m*, *Lat. Am.* elenco *m*; (of mind) inclinación, *f*; (in the eye) defecto en la mirada, *m*; (of colour) matiz, tinte, *m*. **c. of features,** facciones, *f pl*, fisonomía, *f*. **plaster c.,** vaciado, *m*

castanets *n pl* castañuelas, *f pl*

castaway *n* náufrago (-ga); *fig* perdido (-da)

caste *n* casta, *f*; clase social, *f*. **to lose c.,** desprestigiarse

castigate *vt* castigar

Castile Castilla, *f*

Castilian *a* castellano. *n* castellano (-na); (language) castellano, *m*

casting *n* lanzamiento, *m*; (of metals) fundición, colada, *f*; obra de fundición, *f*. **c.-net,** esparavel, *m*. **c.-vote,** voto de calidad, *m*

castle *n* castillo, *m*; (in chess) torre, *f*, roque, *m*. **to build castles in Spain,** hacer castillos en el aire

castor *n* *zool* castor, *m*; (for sugar) azucarero, *m*; (cruet)

convoy, *m*; (on chairs, etc.) ruedecilla, roldana, *f*.
c.-oil, aceite de ricino, *m*. **c.-sugar,** azúcar en polvo, *m*

castrate *vt* castrar, capar

castration *n* castración, capadura, *f*

casual *a* fortuito, accidental; ligero, superficial; *inf* despreocupado. **c. worker,** jornalero, *m*

casually *adv* por casualidad; de paso; negligentemente

casualness *n inf* negligencia, despreocupación, *f*

casualty *n* víctima, *f*; herido, *m*; *mil* baja, *f*; *pl* **casualties,** heridos, *m pl*; muertos, *m pl*. **c.-list,** lista de víctimas, *f*; *mil* lista de bajas, *f*

casuist *n* casuista, *mf*

casuistry *n* casuística, *f*

cat *n* gato (-ta). **She is an old cat,** Ella es una vieja chismosa. **to be like a cat on hot bricks,** estar como en brasas, **to let the cat out of the bag,** tirar de la manta. **to lead a cat-and-dog life,** vivir como perros y gatos. **cat's-cradle,** (game) cunas, *f pl*. **cat's paw,** (person) hombre de paja, *m*; *naut* bocanada de viento, *f*. **cat o' nine tails,** gato de siete colas, *m*, penca, *f*. **catwhisker,** *rad* detector, *m*

cataclysm *n* cataclismo, *m*

catacombs *n pl* catacumbas, *f pl*

catafalque *n* catafalco, *m*

Catalan *a* catalán (-ana). *n* catalán; (language) catalán, *m*

catalepsy *n* catalepsia, *f*

catalogue *n* catálogo, *m*, *vt* catalogar

catalysis *n* catálisis, *f*

cat-and-mouse *n* el juego de ratón, *m*

catapult *n mil* catapulta, *f*; *aer* catapulta (para lanzar aviones), *f*; (toy) tirador de gomas, *m*. *vt* tirar con una catapulta (or con un tirador de gomas); (throw) lanzar

cataract *n* catarata, cascada, *f*, salto de agua, *m*; (of the eye) catarata, *f*

catarrh *n* catarro, *m*; constipado, resfriado, *m*

catastrophe *n* catástrofe, *f*, desastre, *m*, *Mexico also* funestidad; (in drama) desenlace, *m*

catastrophic *a* catastrófico

catcall *n* silbido, *m*

catch *vt* coger; agarrar, asir; (capture) prender, haber; (a disease) contraer; (habit) tomar; (on a hook, etc.) enganchar; (surprise) sorprender; (understand) comprender; (hear) oír; (with blows, etc.) dar. *vi* (of a lock) encajarse; (become entangled) engancharse; (of a fire) encenderse. **to c. a glimpse of,** ver por un instante (a); alcanzar a ver, entrever. **to c. at,** asir; agarrarse (a); echar mano de; procurar asir; alargar la mano hacia; (an idea, etc.) adoptar con entusiasmo. **to c. on,** (be popular) tener éxito; (understand) comprender. **to c. out,** coger en el acto; coger en un error; *sport* coger. **to c. up,** coger; interrumpir. **to c. up with,** (a person) alcanzar; (news) ponerse al corriente de

catch *n* presa, *f*; (of fish) redada, pesca, *f*; (of a window, etc.) cerradura, *f*; (latch) pestillo, *m*; (trick) trampa, *f*; *mus* canon, *m*. **a good c.,** (matrimonial) un buen partido. **to have a c. in one's voice,** hablar con voz entrecortada. **c.-as-c.-can,** lucha libre, *f*

catching *a* contagioso

catchment *n* desagüe, *m*

catchword *n* reclamo, *m*; (theater cue) pie, apunte, *m*; (slogan) mote, *m*

catchy *a* atractivo. **It's a c. tune,** Es una canción que se pega

catechism *n* catequismo, *m*

categorical *a* categórico

category *n* categoría, *f*

cater *vi* proveer, abastecer. **to c. for all tastes,** atender a todos los gustos

caterer *n* despensero (-ra)

catering *n* provisión, *f*

caterpillar *n* oruga, *Argentina* isoca *f*. **c. tractor,** tractor de orugas, *m*

caterwaul *vi* (of a cat) maullar

caterwauler *n* (violinist, etc.) rascatripas, *m*

caterwauling *n* maullidos, *m pl*; música ratonera, *f*

catfish *n* siluro, *m*

catgut *n surg* catgut, *m*; *mus* cuerda, *f*

catharsis *n med* purga, *f*; *fig* catarsis, *f*

cathedral *n* catedral, *f*

Catherine wheel *n arch* rosa, *f*; (firework) rueda de Santa Catalina, *f*; (somersault) tumba, *f*

catheter *n* catéter, *m*

cathode *n* cátodo, *m*. **c. rays,** rayos catódicos, *m pl*. **c. ray tube,** tubo de rayos catódicos, *m*

cathodic *a* catódico

catholic *a* católico

Catholicism *n* catolicismo, *m*

catkin *n* amento, *m*. **male c.,** amento macho, *m*

catlike *a* de gato; gatuno

cattle *n* ganado vacuno, *m*; ganado, *m*; animales, *m pl*. **c.-dealer,** ganadero, *m*. **c.-lifter,** hurtador de ganado, *m*. **c.-pen,** corral, *m*. **c.-raiser,** criador de ganado, *m*. **c.-raising,** ganadería, *f*. **c.-ranch,** hacienda de ganado, estancia, *Argentina* cabaña *f*. **c.-show,** exposición de ganado, *f*. **c.-truck,** vagón de ferrocarril para ganado, *m*

cattle rustler *n* abigeo, cuatrero, ladrón de ganado, *m*

cattle rustling *n* abigeato, *m*

catty *a* gatuno; malicioso, chismoso

Caucasian *a* and *n* caucáseo (-ea)

cauldron *n* caldera, *f*

cauliflower *n* coliflor, *f*

caulk *vt* calafatear

caulker *n* calafate, *m*

caulking *n* calafateado, *m*. **c. iron,** calador, *m*

causality *n* causalidad, *f*

causative *a* causante

cause *n* causa, *f*; (reason) motivo, *m*, razón, *f*; (lawsuit) proceso, *m*. *vt* causar; ocasionar, suscitar; (oblige) hacer, obligar (a). **final c.,** *phil* causa final, *f*. **to have good c. for,** tener buen motivo para

causeway *n* dique, *m*; acera, *f*

caustic *a* cáustico; *fig* mordaz. **c. soda,** sosa cáustica, *f*

caustically *adv* mordazmente, con sarcasmo

causticity *n* causticidad, *f*

cauterization *n* cauterización, *f*

cauterize *vt* cauterizar

cautery *n* cauterio, *m*

caution *n* prudencia, cautela, *f*; (warning) amonestación, *f*; aviso, *m*. *vt* amonestar. **to proceed with c.,** ir con prudencia; ir despacio

"Caution" (road sign) «Precaución»

cautionary *a* (of tales) de escarmiento

cautious *a* cauteloso, cauto; prudente, circunspecto

cautiously *adv* cautamente; prudentemente. **to go c.,** *inf* ir con pies de plomo

cavalcade *n* cabalgata, *f*

cavalier *n* jinete, *m*; caballero, *m*; galán, *m*, *a* arrogante, altanero

cavalry *n* caballería, *f*. **c.-man,** jinete, soldado de a caballo, *m*

cave *n* cueva, caverna, *f*. **to c. in,** hundirse; desplomarse; *fig* rendirse. **c.-man,** hombre cavernícola, *m*

cavern *n* caverna, *f*

cavernous *a* cavernoso

caviar *n* caviar, *m*

cavil *vi* cavilar

cavity *n* cavidad, *f*; hoyo, *m*; hueco, *m*; (in a lung) caverna, *f*

cavy *n* cobayo (-ya), conejillo (-lla) de las Indias

caw *n* graznido, *m*, *vi* graznar, grajear

cawing *n* graznidos, *m*

cayenne *n* pimentón, *m*

cease *vi* cesar (de), dejar de; parar. *vt* cesar de; parar de; (payments, etc.) suspender; discontinuar. **C. fire!** ¡Cesar fuego!

ceaseless *a* incesante, continuo, sin cesar

ceaselessly *adv* sin cesar, incesantemente

ceasing *n* cesación, *f*. **without c.,** sin cesar

cedar *n* (tree and wood) cedro, *m*. **red c.,** cedro dulce, *m*

cede *vt* ceder, traspasar; (admit) conceder

cedilla *n* zedilla, *f*

ceiling *n* techo, *m*; *aer* altura máxima, *f*. **c. price,** máximo precio, *m*

celebrant *n ecc* celebrante, *m*

celebrate *vt* celebrar; solemnizar. **Their marriage was celebrated in the autumn,** Su casamiento se solemnizó en el otoño

celebrated *a* célebre, famoso

celebration *n* celebración, *f*; festividad, *f*

celebrity *n* celebridad, *f*

celerity *n* celeridad, *f*

celery *n* apio, *m*

celestial *a* celestial

celibacy *n* celibato, *m*

celibate *a* célibe. *n* célibe, *mf*

cell *n* celda, *f*; (*bot biol*) célula, *f*; (bees, wasps) celdilla, *f*; *elec* elemento, *m*

cellar *n* sótano, *m*; (wine) bodega, *f*

cellist *n* violoncelista, *mf*

cello *n* violoncelo, *m*

cellophane *n* (papel) celofán, *m*

cellular *a* celular, celuloso

cellule *a* célula, *f*

celluloid *n* celuloide, *f*

cellulose *n* celulosa, *f*

Celt *n* celta, *mf*

Celtic *a* celta

cement *n* cemento, *m*, *vt* cementar

cemetery *n* cementerio, *m*

cenotaph *n* cenotafio, *m*

cenote *n* cenote *m*

cense *vt* incensar

censer *n* incensario, *m*

censor *n* censor, *m*, *vt* censurar. **banned by the c.,** prohibido por la censura

censorious *a* severo; crítico

censoriousness *n* severidad, propensión a censurar, *f*

censorship *n* censura, *f*

censure *vt* censurar, culpar, criticar

census *n* censo, *m*. **to take the c.,** formar el censo, levantar el censo, tomar el censo, empadronar

census-taking *n* la formación del censo, la formación de los censos, *f*, el levantamiento del censo, el levantamientos de los censos, *m*

cent *n* (coin) centavo, *Lat. Am.* cobre (of copper) *m*. **per c.,** por ciento. **not to have a c., not to have a c. to one's name,** no tener donde caer muerto

centaur *n* centauro, *m*

centavo *n* centavo, *Lat. Am.* cobre (of copper) *m*

centenarian *a* and *n* centenario (-ia)

centenary *n* centenario, *m*, *a* centenario

center *n* centro, *m*; medio, *m*. *a* central; centro. *vt* centrar; concentrar (en). **nervous centers,** centros nerviosos, *m pl*. **c.-forward,** *sport* delantero centro, *m*. **c.-half,** *sport* medio centro, *m*. **c. of gravity,** centro de gravedad, *m*. **c.-piece,** centro, *m*

centerfold *n* páginas centrales, *f pl*

centigrade *a* centígrado

centigram *n* centigramo, *m*

centiliter *n* centilitro, *m*

centime *n* céntimo, *m*

centimeter *n* centímetro, *m*. **cubic c.,** centímetro cúbico, *m*

centipede *n* ciempiés, *m*

central *a* central; céntrico. **The house is very c.,** La casa es muy céntrica. **C. America** *n* Centroamérica *f* **C. American,** *a* and *n* centroamericano (-na). **c. depot,** central, *f*. **c. heating,** calefacción central, *f*

centralism *n* centralismo, *m*

centralist *n* centralista, *mf*

centralization *n* centralización, *f*

centralize *vt* centralizar

centrally *adv* centralmente; céntricamente

centric *a* céntrico; central

centrifugal *a* centrífugo

centripetal *a* centrípeto

centuple *a* céntuplo

centuplicate *vt* centuplicar

centurion *n* centurión, *m*

century *n* siglo, *m*, centuria, *f*

ceramic *a* cerámico

ceramics *n* cerámica, *f*

cereal *a* cereal. *n* cereal, *m*

cerebellum *n* cerebelo, *m*

cerebral *a* cerebral

cerebrospinal *a* cerebroespinal

cerebrum *n* cerebro, *m*

ceremonial *a* ceremonial; de ceremonia. *n* ceremonial, *m*

ceremonially *adv* ceremonialmente; con ceremonia

ceremonious *a* ceremonioso

ceremoniously *adv* ceremoniosamente

ceremoniousness *n* ceremonia, formalidad, *f*

ceremony *n* ceremonia, *f*. **to stand on c.,** gastar cumplidos. **without c.,** sin cumplidos

cerise *a* de color cereza

certain *a* (sure) seguro; cierto; (unerring) certero. **a c. man,** cierto hombre. **I am c. that . . . ,** Estoy seguro de que . . . **to know for c.,** saber con toda seguridad, saber a ciencia cierta. **to make c. of,** asegurarse de

certainly *adv* seguramente; ciertamente; (as a reply) sin duda; naturalmente. **c. not,** no, por cierto; claro que no

certainty *n* certidumbre, *f*; seguridad, *f*; convicción, *f*. **of a c.,** seguramente

certificate *n* certificado, *m*; fe, *f*; partida, *f*; *com* bono, título, *m*; diploma, *m*. *vt* certificar. **birth c.,** partida de nacimiento, *f*. **death c.,** partida de defunción, *f*. **marriage c.,** partida de casamiento, *f*

certificated *a* (of teachers, etc.) con título

certify *vt* certificar; atestiguar; declarar

certitude *n* certeza, certidumbre, *f*

Cerulean *a* cerúleo

Cervantine *a* cervantino

cervix *n anat* cerviz, *f*

Cesarean *a* cesáreo

cessation *n* cesación, *f*

cession *n* cesión, *f*

cessionary *n* cesionario (-ia)

cesspool *n* sumidero, *m*

cetacean *a* cetáceo. *n* cetáceo, *m*

Ceylon Ceilán, *m*

cf. cfr.

chafe *vt* (rub) frotar; (make sore) escocer, rozar. *vi* raerse, desgastarse; escocerse; *fig* impacientarse; *fig* irritarse, enojarse

chaff *n* (of grain) ahechadura, *f*; (in a general sense and *fig*) paja, *f*; tomadura de pelo, burla, *f*. *vt* (a person) tomar el pelo (a), burlarse de

chaffinch *n* pinzón, *m*

chafing *n* frotación, *f*; (soreness) excoriación, *f*; *fig* impaciencia, *f*. **c.-dish,** escalfador, *m*

chagrin *n* mortificación, decepción, *f*, disgusto, *m*, *vt* mortificar

chain *n* cadena, *f*, *vt* encadenar. **c. of mountains,** cadena de montañas, cordillera, *f*. **c.-gang,** cadena de presidiarios, *f*. **c.-mail,** cota de malla, *f*. **c.-stitch,** cadeneta, *f*. **c.-stores,** empresa con sucursales, *f*. **in chains,** cargado de cadenas (e.g., **prisoners in chains,** prisioneros cargados de cadenas)

chair *n* silla, *f*; *univ* cátedra, *f*; (of a meeting) presidencia, *f*. *vt* llevar en hombros (a). **C.!** ¡Orden! **easy-c.,** (silla) poltrona, *f*. **to be in the c.,** ocupar la presidencia; presidir. **to take a c.,** sentarse, tomar asiento. **to take the c.,** presidir. **swivel-c.,** silla giratoria, *f*. **wheel-c.,** silla de ruedas, *f*. **c.-back,** respaldo de una silla, *m*

chairman *n* presidente (-ta). **to act as c.,** presidir

chairmanship *n* presidencia, *f*

chaise longue *n* meridiana, tumbona, *f*

Chaldea Caldea, *f*

Chaldean *a* caldeo

chalet *n* chalet, *m*

chalice *n* cáliz, *m*

chalk *n* creta, *f*; (for writing, etc.) tiza, *f*, yeso, *m*. *vt* marcar con tiza; dibujar con tiza. **to c. up,** apuntar. **not by a long c.,** no con mucho

chalky *a* cretáceo; cubierto de yeso; (of the complexion) pálido

challenge *n* provocación, *f*; (of a sentry) quién vive, *m*; (to a duel, etc.) desafío, reto, *m*; *law* recusación, *f*; concurso, *m*. *vt* (of a sentry) dar el quién vive (a); desafiar; provocar; *law* recusar

challenger *n* desafiador (-ra)

challenging *a* desafiador, provocador

chamber *n* cuarto, *m*; sala, *f*; (bed-) dormitorio, *m*, alcoba, *f*; cámara, *f*; *mech* cilindro, *m*; (in a gun) cámara, *f*. **c. concert,** concierto de música de cámara, *m*. **c.-maid,** camarera, *f*. **c. music,** música de cámara, *f*. **c. of commerce,** cámara de comercio, *f*. **c.-pot,** orinal, *m*

chamberlain *n* camarero, *m*. **court c.,** chambelán, *m*. **Lord C.,** camarero mayor, *m*

chameleon *n* camaleón, *m*

chamfer *n* chaflán, bisel, *m*

chamois *n* gamuza, *f*, rebeco, *m*. **c. leather,** piel de gamuza, *f*

chamomile *n* camomila, manzanilla, *f*

champ *vt* mascar; morder. *vi fig* impacientarse

champagne *n* (vino de) champaña, *m*

champion *n* campeón, *m*; defensor (-ra)

championship *n* campeonato, *m*; (of a cause) defensa, *f*

chance *n* casualidad, *f*; suerte, fortuna, *f*; posibilidad, *f*; probabilidad, *f*; esperanza, *f*; (opportunity) ocasión, oportunidad, *f*. *a* fortuito; accidental. *vi impers* suceder, acontecer. *vt inf* arriesgar; probar. **by c.,** por casualidad; por ventura. **if by c.,** si acaso. **If it chances that . . . ,** Si sucede que; Si a mano viene que . . . **The chances are that . . . ,** Las probabilidades son que . . . **There is no c.,** No hay posibilidad; No hay esperanza. **to let the c. slip,** perder la ocasión. **to take a c.,** aventurarse, arriesgarse. **to c. to do,** hacer algo por casualidad. **to c. upon,** encontrar por casualidad.

chancel *n* antealtar, entrecoro, *m*

chancellery *n* cancillería, *f*

chancellor *n* canciller, *m*; *univ* cancelario, *m*. **C. of the Exchequer,** Ministro de Hacienda, *m*

chancellorship *n* cancillería, *f*

chancery *n* chancillería, *f*; (papal) cancelaría, *f*

chandelier *n* araña de luces, *f*

chandler *n* velero, *m*

change *vt* cambiar; transformar; modificar; (clothes) mudarse (de); (one thing for another) trocar; sustituir (por). *vi* cambiar; (clothes) mudarse. **All c.!** ¡Cambio de tren! **to c. a check,** cambiar un cheque. **to c. color,** cambiar de color; (of persons) mudar de color. **to c. countenance,** demudarse. **to c. front,** *fig* cambiar de frente. **to c. hands,** (of shops, etc.) cambiar de dueño. **to c. one's clothes,** cambiar de ropa, mudarse de ropa. **to c. one's mind,** cambiar de opinión. **to c. one's tune,** cambiar de tono. **to c. the subject,** cambiar de conversación. **to c. trains,** cambiar de trenes

change *n* cambio, *m*; transformación, *f*; modificación, *f*; variedad, *f*; (of clothes, feathers) muda, *f*; (theat of scene) mutación, *f*; (money) cambio, *m*; (small coins) suelto, *m*; (stock) bolsa, *f*; lonja, *f*; vicisitud, *f*; (of bells) toque (de campanas), *m*. **for a c.,** para cambiar, como un cambio; para variar. **small c.,** suelto, *m*, moneda suelta, *f*. **c. for the better,** cambio para mejor, *m*. **c. for the worse,** cambio para peor, *m*. **c. of clothes,** cambio de ropa, *m*; **c. of front,** *fig* cambio de frente, *m*. **c. of heart,** cambio de sentimientos, *m*; conversión, *f*. **c. of life,** menopausia, *f*. **c.-over,** cambio, *m*

changeability *n* mutabilidad, *f*; inconstancia, volubilidad, *f*

changeable *a* voluble; variable; cambiable

changeless *a* immutable; constante

changeling *n* niño (-ña) cambiado (-da) por otro

changing *a* cambiante. **c.-room,** vestuario, *m*

channel *n* (of a river, etc.) cauce, *m*; canal, *m*; (irrigation) acequia, *f*; (strait) estrecho, *m*; *fig* conducto, *m*; (furrow) surco, *m*, estría, *f*; (of information, etc.) medio, *m*. *vt* acanalar; (furrow) surcar; (conduct) encauzar

chant *n* canto llano, *m*; salmo, *m*. *vt* salmodiar; cantar; recitar

chantey *n* saloma, *f*

chaos *n* caos, *m*

chaotic *a* caótico, desordenado

chaotically *adv* en desorden

chap *vt* agrietar. *vi* agrietarse. *n inf* chico, *m*

chapbook *n* librito de cordel, *m*

chapel *n* capilla, *f*; templo disidente, *m*

chaperon *n* dama de compañía, señora de compañía, dueña, *f*, *vt* acompañar

chaplain *n* capellán, *m*

chaplaincy *n* capellanía, *f*

chaplet *n* guirnalda, *f*; rosario, *m*; (necklace) collar, *m*

chapter *n* (in a book) capítulo, *m*; *ecc* cabildo, capítulo, *m*. **a c. of accidents,** una serie de desgracias. **c. house,** sala capitular, *f*

char *vt* (a house, etc.) fregar, hacer la limpieza de; (of fire) carbonizar. *n inf* fregona, asistenta, *f*

character *n* carácter, *m*; (of a play) personaje, *m*; (role) papel, *m*; (eccentric) tipo, *m*. **Gothic characters,** caracteres góticos, *m pl*. **in c.,** característico; apropiado. **in the c. of,** en el papel de. **out of c.,** nada característico; no apropiado. **principal c.,** protagonista, *mf*. **c. actor,** actor de carácter, *m*. **c. actress,** actriz de carácter

characteristic *a* característico, típico. *n* característica, peculiaridad, *f*, rasgo, *m*

characterization *n* caracterización, *f*

characterize *vt* caracterizar

characterless *a* sin carácter; insípido, soso

charade *n* charada, *f*

charcoal *n* carbón de leña, *m*; (for blacking the face, etc.) tizne, *m*; *art* carboncillo, *m*. **c. burner,** carbonera, *f*. **c. crayon,** carboncillo, *m*. **c. drawing,** dibujo al carbón, *m*

charge *vt* cargar; (enjoin) encargar; (accuse) acusar (de); (with price) cobrar; (with a mission, etc.) encomendar, confiar; *mil* acometer, atacar. *vi mil* atacar; (a price) cobrar, pedir. **How much do you c.?** ¿Cuánto cobra Vd.? **to c. with a crime,** acusar de un crimen

charge *n* (load) carga, *f*; (price) precio, *m*; gasto, *m*; (on an estate, etc.) derechos, *m pl*; (task) encargo, *m*; (office or responsibility) cargo, *m*; (guardianship) tutela, *f*; (care) cuidado, *m*; exhortación, *f*; *law* acusación, *f*; *mil* ataque, *m*. **He is in c. of . . . ,** Está encargado de . . . ; Es responsable de . . . **The diamonds are in the c. of . . . ,** Los diamantes están a cargo de. **depth c.,** carga de profundidad, *f*. **extra c.,** gasto suplementario, *m*; (on a train) suplemento, *m*. **free of c.,** gratis. **c. for admittance,** entrada, *f*. **to bring a c. against,** acusar de. **to give (someone) in c.,** entregar (una persona) a la policía. **to take c. of,** encargarse de

chargé d'affaires *n* encargado de negocios, *m*

charger *n* caballo de guerra, corcel, *m*

chariness *n* cautela, *f*

chariot *n* carro, *m*

charioteer *n* auriga, *m*

charitable *a* caritativo, limosnero; benéfico

charitableness *n* caridad, *f*

charity *n* caridad, *f*; beneficencia, *f*; (alms) limosna, *f*. **c. child,** niño (-ña) de la doctrina

charlatan *n* charlatán (-ana); (quack) curandero, *m*

charlatanism *n* charlatanismo, *m*; curanderismo, *m*

charm *n* hechizo, *m*; ensalmo, *m*; (amulet) amuleto, *m*; (trinket) dije, *m*; (general sense) encanto, atractivo, *m*. *vt* encantar, hechizar, fascinar

charming *a* encantador; atractivo, seductor, fascinador

charm school *n* academia de buenos modales, *f*

chart *n naut* carta de marear, *f*; (graph) gráfica, *f*. *vt* poner en una carta

charter *n* carta, *f*; (of a city, etc.) fuero, *m*; cédula, *f*. *vt* (a ship) fletar; (hire) alquilar. **royal c.,** cédula real, *f*

Chartism *n* el cartismo, *m*

chartist *n* cartista, *mf*

charwoman *n* fregona, asistenta; mujer de hacer faenas, *Mexico* fregandera *f*

chary *a* cauteloso; desinclinado; frugal

chase *n* caza, *f*; seguimiento, *m*. *vt* cazar; dar caza (a); perseguir; (drive off) ahuyentar; *fig* disipar, hacer desaparecer; (engrave) cincelar. **to give c. to,** dar caza (a). **to go on a wild goose c.,** buscar pan de trastrigo

chasm *n* sima, *f*, precipicio, *m*; *fig* abismo, *m*

chassis *n* chasis, *m*

chaste *a* casto

chasten *vt* castigar; corregir; humillar, mortificar

chastened *a* sumiso, dócil

chastise *vt* castigar

chastisement *n* castigo, *m*

chastity *n* castidad, *f*

chat *vi* charlar, conversar. *n* conversación, charla, *f*. **They are having a c.,** Están charlando, Están de palique

chattels *n pl* bienes muebles, efectos, *m pl*

chatter *vi* charlar; hablar por los codos, chacharear; (of water) murmurar; (of birds) piar; (of monkeys, etc.) chillar; (of teeth) rechinar; (of a person's teeth) dar diente con diente. *n* charla, *f*; cháchara, parla, *f*; (of water) murmurio, *m*; (of birds) gorjeo, *m*; (of monkeys, etc.) chillidos, *m pl*

chatterbox *n* badajo, *m*, cotorra, *f*

chatterer *n* hablador (-ra)

chattering *n* charla, cháchara, *f*; (of teeth) rechinamiento, *m*, *a* gárrulo, chacharero, locuaz

chauffeur *n* chófer, *m*

cheap *a* barato; (of works of art) cursi. *adv* barato. **dirt c.,** baratísimo. **to be dirt c.,** estar por los suelos. **to hold** (something) **c.,** tener en poco, estimar en poco

cheapen *vt* disminuir el valor de; reducir el precio de

cheaply *adv* barato; a bajo precio

cheapness *n* baratura, *f*; precio módico, *m*; mal gusto, *m*, vulgaridad, *f*

cheat *n* engaño, fraude, *m*, estafa, *f*; (person) fullero (-ra), trampista, *mf* embustero (-ra). *vt* engañar; defraudar; (at cards) hacer trampas. **He cheated me out of my property,** Me defraudó de mi propiedad

cheating *n* engaño, *m*; fraude, *m*; (at cards) fullerías, *f pl*

check *n* (chess) jaque, *m*; revés, *m*; impedimento, *m*; contratiempo, *m*; (of a bridle) cama, *f*; (control) freno, *m*; control, *m*; (checking) verificación, *f*; (ticket) papeleta, *f*; (counterfoil) talón, *m*; (square) cuadro, *m*; (bill) cuenta, *f*, *Argentina* adición *f*; (bank) cheque, *m*. *vt* (chess) jaquear; (hamper) refrenar; detener; contrarrestar; (test) verificar. *vi* detenerse. **to c. off,** marcar. **to c. oneself,** detenerse; contenerse. **to c. up,** comprobar. **crossed c.,** cheque cruzado, *m*. **c. book,** libro de cheques, *m*

checked *a* (cloth) a cuadros

checker *vt* escaquear; (variegate) motear, salpicar; diversificar. **a checkered career,** una vida accidentada

checking *n* represión, *f*; control, *m*; verificación, *f*; comprobación, *f*

checkmate *n* mate, jaque, mate, *m*. *vt* dar mate (a); (plans, etc.) frustrar

checks and balances *n pl* frenos y contrapesos, *m pl*

cheek *n* mejilla, *f*; *inf* descaro, *m*; insolencia, *Lat. Am.* impavidez *f*. **They have plenty of c.,** Tienen mucha cara dura. **c. by jowl,** cara a cara; al lado de. **c.-bone,** pómulo, *m*

cheekiness *n* cara dura, insolencia, *Lat. Am.* impavidez *f*

cheeky *a* insolente, descarado, *Lat. Am.* impávido, *Peru* lisurero; (pert) respondón

cheer *n* alegría, *f*, regocijo, *m*; vítor, *m*; aplauso, *m*. *vt* animar; alegrar, regocijar; vitorear, aplaudir. **to be of good c.,** estar alegre; ser feliz. **C. up!** ¡Ánimo! **to c. up,** animarse, cobrar ánimo

cheerful *a* alegre; jovial; de buen humor. **It is a c. room,** Es un cuarto alegre

cheerfully *adv* alegremente; (willingly) con mucho gusto, de buena gana

cheerfulness *n* alegría, *f*; jovialidad, *f*; buen humor, *m*

cheering *n* vítores, *m pl*, aclamaciones, *f pl*, *a* animador

cheerleader *n* porro, *m*

cheerless *a* triste; sin alegría; (dank) obscuro, lóbrego

cheese *n* queso, *m*. **cream c.,** queso de nata, *m*. **grated c.,** queso rallado, *m*. **c.-dish,** quesera, *f*. **c.-mite,** cresa, *f*. **c.-paring,** *n* corteza de queso, *f*. *a inf* tacaño. **c.-vat,** quesera, *f*

cheesecake *m Lat. Am.* alfandoque *m*

cheesy *a* caseoso

chemical *a* químico. **c. warfare,** defensa química, *f*

chemicals *n pl* productos químicos, *m pl*

chemise *n* camisa (de mujer), *f*

chemist *n* químico, *m*. **chemist's shop,** farmacia, *f*; droguería, *f*

chemistry *n* química, *f*

cherish *vt* amar, querer; (a hope, etc.) abrigar, acariciar

cherry *n* (fruit) cereza, *f*; (tree and wood) cerezo, *m*. **c. brandy,** aguardiente de cerezas, *m*. **c. orchard,** cerezal, *m*

cherub *n* querub(e), querubín, *m*

cherubic *a* querúbico

chess *n* ajedrez, *m*. **c.-board,** tablero de ajedrez, *m*

chessman *n* pieza de ajedrez, *f*

chest *n* arca, *f*, cofre, *m*; cajón, *m*; *anat* pecho, *m*. **to throw out one's c.,** inflar el pecho. **c.-expander,** extensor, *m*. **c. of drawers,** cómoda, *f*

chested *a* (in compounds) de pecho . . .

chestnut *n* (tree) castaño, *m*; (fruit) castaña, *f*; (color) castaño, color castaño, *m*; (horse) caballo castaño, *m*; (joke) chiste del tiempo de Maricastaña, *m*, *a* castaño. **horse-c. tree,** castaño de Indias, *m*

chevron *n her* cabrio, *m*; (mil etc.) sardineta, *f*

chew *vt* mascar, masticar; (ponder) masticar

chewing *n* masticación, *f*. **c.-gum,** chicle, *m*

chianti *n* (wine) quianti, *m*

chiaroscuro *n* claroscuro, *m*

chic *n* chic, *m*, elegancia, *f*

chicanery *n* sofistería, *f*

chicken *n* pollo, *m*. **c.-hearted,** medroso, cobarde, timorato. **c.-pox,** varicela, *f*

chickenwire *n* alambrillo, *m*

chickpea *n* garbanzo, *m*

chickweed *n* pamplina, *f*

chicory *n* achicoria, *f*

chide *vt* reprender, reñir

chidingly *adv* en tono de reprensión

chief *n* jefe, *m*, *a* principal; primero; en jefe; mayor. **c.-of-staff,** jefe de estado mayor, *m*

chiefly *adv* principalmente; sobre todo

chieftain *n* caudillo, *m*; (of a clan) cabeza, jefe, *m*

chiffon *n* chifón, *m*, gasa, *f*

chiffonier *n* cómoda, *f*

chignon *n* moño, *m*

child *n* niño (-ña); hijo (-ja). *Mexico* escuincle *mf* **from a c.,** desde niño, desde la niñez. **with c.,** encinta, embarazada. **How many children have you?** ¿Cuántos hijos tiene Vd.? **child's play,** juegos infantiles, *m pl*; *fig* niñerías, *f pl*. **c. welfare,** puericultura, *f*

childbirth *n* parto, *m*

childhood *n* niñez, infancia, *f*. **from his c.,** desde su niñez, desde niño

childish *a* de niño; aniñado; pueril; fútil. **to grow c.,** chochear

childishly *adv* como un niño

childishness *n* puerilidad, *f*; futilidad, *f*

child labor *n* trabajo de menores, trabajo infantil, *m*

childless *a* sin hijos; sin niños

childlike *a* de niño, aniñado; pueril

children. See **child**

Chilean *a* and *n* chileno (-na)

chili *n* chile, pimento de cornetilla, *Lat. Am.* ají *m.* **c. sauce** *Lat. Am.* ají *m*

chill *n* frío, *m*; (of fear, etc.) estremecimiento, *m*; (illness) resfriado, *m*; (unfriendliness) frialdad, frigidez, *f, a* frío; (unfriendly) frígido. *vt* enfriar; helar; (with fear, etc.) dar escalofríos (de); (discourage) desalentar. *vi* tener frío; tener escalofríos. **to take the c. off,** templar, calentar un poco

chilliness *n* frío, *m*; (unfriendliness) frialdad, frigidez, *f*

chilly *a* frío; (sensitive to cold) friolero; (of politeness, etc.) glacial, frígido

chime *n* juego de campanas, *m*; repique, campaneo, *m*; armonía, *f. vi* (of bells) repicar; *fig* armonizar. **to c. the hour,** dar la hora

chimera *n* quimera, *f*

chimerical *a* quimérico

chimney *n* chimenea, *f*; (of a lamp) tubo (de lámpara), *m.* **c.-corner,** rincón de chimenea, *m.* **c.-pot,** sombrerete de chimenea, *m.* **c.-stack,** chimenea, *f.* **c.-sweep,** limpiador de chimeneas, deshollinador, *m*

chimpanzee *n* chimpancé, *m*

chin *n* barbilla, barba, *f*, mentón, *m.* **c.-rest,** mentonera, *f.* **c.-strap,** barboquejo, *m*; venda para la barbilla, *f*

china *n* china, porcelana, *f*; loza, *f. a* de porcelana; de loza. **c. cabinet,** chinero, *m*

chinchilla *n* (animal and fur) chinchilla, *f*

Chinese *a* and *n* chino (-na); (language) chino, *m.* **C. lantern,** farolillo de papel, *m.* **C. white,** óxido blanco de cinc, *m*

chink *n* resquicio, *m*, grieta, hendidura, *f*; (clink) retintín, tintineo, *m. vi* tintinar

chintz *n* zaraza, *f*

chip *n* astilla, *f*; (counter) ficha, *f. vt* picar; cincelar. **a c. off the old block,** de tal palo tal astilla. **c. potatoes,** patatas fritas, *f pl*

chiromancy *n* quiromancia, *f*

chiropodist *n* pedicuro, *m*, callista, *mf*

chiropody *n* pedicura, *f*

chiropractor *n* quiropráctico, *m*

chirp *vi* piar, gorjear. *n* pío, gorjeo, *m*

chirping *n* pïada, *f*, a gárrulo, piante

chisel *n* escoplo, cincel, *m, vt* cincelar. **cold c.,** cortafrío, *m*

chitchat *n* charla, *f*

chitterlings *n* asadura, *f*

chivalrous *a* caballeroso

chivalry *n* caballería, *f*; caballerosidad, *f. novel of c.,* novela de caballería, *f*

chive *n bot* cebollana, *f*, cebollino, *m*

chloral *n* cloral, *m*

chlorate *n* clorato, *m*

chloride *n* cloruro, *m*

chlorine *n* cloro, *m*

chloroform *n* cloroformo, *m, vt* cloroformizar

chlorophyll *n* clorófila, *f*

chock-full *a* lleno de bote en bote

chocolate *n* chocolate, *m, a* de chocolate. **thick drinking-c.,** chocolate a la española, *m.* **thin drinking-c.,** chocolate a la francesa, *m.* **c. shop,** chocolatería, *f*

choice *n* selección, *f*; preferencia, *f*; elección, *f*; opción, *f*; alternativa, *f*; lo más escogido. *a* escogido, selecto; excelente. **for c.,** con preferencia

choir *n* coro, *m.* **c.-boy,** niño del coro, *m.* **c.-master,** maestro de capilla, *m*

choke *vi* ahogarse; atragantarse; obstruirse. *vt* ahogar; estrangular. **to c. with laughter,** ahogarse de risa. **to c. back,** (words) tragar. **to c. off,** (a person) disuadir (de); quitarse de encima(a). **to c. up,** obstruir, cerrar, obturar; (hide) cubrir, tapar

choking *a* asfixiante, sofocante. *n* ahogamiento, *m*, sofocación, *f*

cholera *n* cólera, *m*

choleric *a* colérico

cholesterol *n* colesterina, *f*

choline *n* colina, *f*

choose *vt* escoger; elegir; optar por; (wish) querer, gustar. **They will do it when they c.,** Lo harán cuando les parezca bien. **If you c.,** Si Vd. quiere; Si Vd. gusta. **He was chosen as Mayor,** Fue elegido alcalde. **There is nothing to c. between them,** No hay diferencia entre ellos; Tanto vale el uno como el otro. **You cannot c. but love her,** No puedes menos de quererla

choosing *n* selección, *f*; (for an office, etc.) elección, *f*

chop *vt* cortar; (mince) picar; (split) hender, partir. *n* (meat) chuleta, *f*; (jaw) quijada, *f.* **to c. about, round,** (of the wind) girar, virar. **to c. down,** (trees) talar. **to c. off,** separar; cortar; tajar. **to c. up,** cortar en pedazos

chopper *n* hacha, *f*

choppy *a* picado, agitado

chopstick *n* palillo chino, *m*

choragus *n* corega, corego, *m*

choral *a* coral

chord *n* cuerda, *f*; *mus* acorde, *m*; **the right c.,** *fig* la cuerda sensible

choreographer *n* coreógrafo, *m*

choreographic *a* coreográfico

choreography *n* coreografía, *f*

chorister *n* corista, *m*

chorus *n* coro, *m*; (in revues) comparsa, *f*, acompañamiento, *m*; (of a song) refrán, *m.* **to sing in c.,** cantar a coro. **c. girl,** corista, *f*

chosen *a* escogido; elegido. **the c.,** los elegidos

chrestomathy *n* crestomatía, *f*

Christ *n* Cristo, Jesucristo, *m*

christen *vt* bautizar

Christendom *n* cristianismo, *m*, cristiandad, *f*

christening *n* bautizo, *m*, *a* bautismal, de bautizo

christian *a* cristiano. *n* cristiano (-na). **c. name,** nombre de pila, *m*

christianity *n* cristianismo, *m*

Christmas *n* Navidad, *f.* **A Merry C.!** ¡Felices Pascuas (de Navidad)! **Father C.,** Padre Noel, *m*; (Sp. equivalent) Los Reyes Magos. **C. box,** regalo de Navidad, *m.* **C. card,** felicitación de Navidad, *f.* **C. carol,** villancico de Navidad, *m.* **C. Day,** día de Navidad, *m.* **C. Eve,** Nochebuena, *f.* **C.-tide,** Navidades, *f pl.* **C. tree,** árbol de Navidad, *m*

Christopher Columbus Cristóbal Colón, *m*

chromate *n* cromato, *m*

chromatic *a* cromático

chrome *n* cromo, *m.* **c. yellow,** amarillo de cromo, *m*

chromic *a* crómico

chromium *n* cromo, *m.* **c.-plated,** cromado

chromosome *n* cromosoma, *m*

chronic *a* crónico; inveterado

chronicle *n* crónica, *f, vt* narrar

chronicler *n* cronista, *mf*

chronological *a* cronológico. **in c. order,** por orden cronológico

chronology *n* cronología, *f*

chronometer *n* cronómetro, *m*

chrysalis *n* crisálida, *f*

chrysanthemum *n* crisantemo, *m*

chubbiness *n* gordura, *f*

chubby *a* regordete, gordito. **c.-cheeked,** mofletudo

chuck *vt* (throw) lanzar, arrojar; (discontinue) abandonar, dejar. *n* (in a lathe) mandril, *m.* **to c. under the chin,** acariciar la barbilla (a). **to c. away,** derrochar; malgastar, perder. **to c. out,** echar, poner en la calle

chuckle *vi* reír entre dientes. *n* risa ahogada, *f*; risita, *f*

chum *n* compinche, camarada, *mf.* **to c. up with,** ser camarada (a)

chunk *n* pedazo, trozo, *m*

church *n* iglesia, *f*; (Protestant) templo, *m, vt* (a woman) purificar. **poor as a c. mouse,** más pobre que las ratas.

the C. of England, la iglesia anglicana. **to go to c.,** ir a misa; ir al templo. **c. music,** música sagrada, *f*
churchyard *n* cementerio, *m*
churl *n* patán, *m*
churlish *a* grosero, cazurro; (mean) tacaño, ruin
churn *n* mantequera, *f. vt* (cream) batir; *fig* azotar, agitar
chute *n* (for grain, etc.) manga de tolva, *f*; vertedor, *m*; (in flats and fun fairs) tobogán, deslizadero, *m*
ciborium *n* (chalice) copón, *m*; (tabernacle) sagrario, *m*; *arch* ciborio, *m*
cicada *n* cigarra, *f*
cicatrice *n* cicatriz, *f*
cicatrization *n* cicatrización, *f*
cicatrize *vt* cicatrizar. *vi* cicatrizarse
cider *n* sidra, *f*
cigar *n* cigarro, *m*. **c.-box,** cigarrera, *f.* **c.-case,** petaca, cigarrera, *f.* **c.-cutter,** corta-puros, *m*
cigarette *n* cigarrillo, pitillo, *Lat. Am.* cigarro *m*. **c.-butt,** colilla, *f.* **c.-case,** pitillera, *f.* **c.-holder,** boquilla, *f.* **c.-lighter,** encendedor de cigarrillos, *m.* **c.-paper,** papel de fumar, *m*
cinch *n* (of a saddle) cincha, *f; inf* ganga, *f; inf* seguridad, *f.* **c.-strap,** látigo, *m*
cinchona *n* quina, cinchona, *f*
cinder *n* ceniza, *f*; carbonilla, *f.* **red-hot c.,** rescoldo, *m.* **c.-track,** pista de ceniza, *f*
cinema, cinematograph *n* cine, cinematógrafo, *m*
cinematographic *a* cinematográfico
cinematography *n* cinematografía, *f*
cinemogul *n* magnate del cine, *mf*
cinnamon *n* (spice) canela, *f*; (tree) canelo, *m*; color de canela, *m*
cipher *n math* cero, *m; fig* nulidad, *f*; (code) cifra, *f*; monograma, *m.* **to be a mere c.,** ser un cero
Circassian *a* circasiano. *n* circasiano (-na)
circle *n* círculo, *m*; (revolution) vuelta, *f*; (group) grupo; *m*; (club, etc.) centro, *m*; (cycle) ciclo, *m. vt* dar vueltas alrededor de; rodear; ceñir; (on an application, examination, etc.) encerrar en un círculo. *vi* dar vueltas; (aircraft) volar en círculo; (of a hawk, etc.) cernerse. **dress-c.,** *theat* anfiteatro, *m.* **the family c.,** el círculo de la familia. **to come full c.,** dar la vuelta. **upper c.,** *theat* segundo piso, *m.* **vicious c.,** círculo vicioso, *m*
circlet *n* (of flowers, etc.) corona, *f*; (ring) anillo, *m*
circuit *n* circuito, *m*; (tour) gira, *f*; (revolution) vuelta, *f*; (radius) radio, *m.* **short c.,** corto circuito, *m.* **c.-breaker,** corta-circuitos, *m*
circuit court of appeals *n* tribunal colegial de circuito, *m*
circuitous *a* indirecto; tortuoso
circuitously *adv* indirectamente
circular *a* circular; redondo. *n* carta circular, *f*; circular, *f.* **c. tour,** viaje redondo, *m*
circularize *vt* enviar circulares (a)
circulate *vi* circular. *vt* hacer circular; poner en circulación; (news, etc.) divulgar, diseminar
circulating library *n* biblioteca por subscripción, *f*
circulation *n* circulación, *f*; (of a newspaper, etc.) tirada, circulación, *f.* **c. of the blood,** circulación de la sangre, *f*
circulatory *a* circulatorio
circumcise *vt* circuncidar
circumcised *a* circunciso
circumcision *n* circuncisión, *f*
circumference *n* circunferencia, *f*
circumflex *a* circunflejo. **c. accent,** acento circunflejo, *m*, (informal) capucha, *f*
circumlocution *n* circunlocución, *f*
circumnavigate *vt* circunnavegar
circumnavigation *n* circunnavegación, *f*
circumscribe *vt* circunscribir; *fig* limitar
circumscribed *a* circunscripto; *fig* limitado
circumscription *n* circunscripción, *f; fig* limitación, *f*, restricción, *f*

circumspect *a* circunspecto; discreto, correcto; prudente
circumspection *n* circunspección, *f*; prudencia, *f*
circumspectly *adv* con circunspección; prudentemente
circumstance *n* circunstancia, *f*; detalle, *m.* **aggravating c.,** circunstancia agravante, *f.* **attenuating c.,** circunstancia atenuante, *f.* **in the circumstances,** en las circunstancias. **in easy circumstances,** en buena posición, acomodado. **Do you know what his circumstances are?** ¿Sabes cuál es su situación económica? **under the circumstances,** bajo las circunstancias
circumstantial *a* circunstancial; detallado. **c. evidence,** prueba de indicios, *f*
circumvent *vt* frustrar; impedir
circumvention *n* frustración, *f*
circumvolution *n* circunvolución, *f*
circus *n* circo, *m*; plaza redonda, *f*; (traffic) redondel, *m*
cirrhosis *n* cirrosis, *f*
cirrus *n* (all meanings) cirro, *m*
cistern *n* tanque, *m*; cisterna, *f*, aljibe, *m*
citadel *n* ciudadela, *f*
citation *n law* citación, *f*; cita, *f*
citation dictionary *n* diccionario de autoridades, *m*
cite *vt* citar
citizen *n* ciudadano (-na); vecino (-na); natural, *mf.* **fellow c.,** conciudadano, *m*; compatriota, *mf*
citizenship *n* ciudadanía, *f*
citrate *n* citrato, *m*
citric *a* cítrico
citrine *a* cetrino
citron *n* (fruit) cidra, *f*; (tree) cidro, *m*
city *n* ciudad, *f, a* municipal
city-state *n* ciudad-estado, *f*, (plural: ciudades-estado)
civet *n* algalia, *f*
civic *a* cívico; municipal
civics *n* civismo, *m*
civil *a* civil; doméstico; (polite) cortés, atento; (obliging) servicial. **C. Aeronautics Board,** Dirección general de aeronáutica civil, *f.* **c. defense,** defensa pasiva, *f.* **c. engineer,** ingeniero de caminos, canales y puertos, *m.* **C. Service,** cuerpo de empleados del Estado, *m*
civilian *a* civil. *n* ciudadano (-na). **c. dress,** traje paisano, *m*
civility *n* civilidad, cortesía, *f*
civilization *n* civilización, *f*
civilize *vt* civilizar
civilized *a* civilizado
civilizing *a* civilizador
civilly *adv* civilmente, cortésmente
clack *n* golpeo, ruido sordo, *m*
clad *a* vestido
claim *vt* reclamar; pretender exigir; *law* demandar; (assert) afirmar. *vi law* pedir en juicio. *n* reclamación, *f*; pretensión, *f; law* demanda, *f*; (in a gold-field, etc.) concesión, *f*; (right) derecho, *m.* **to lay c. to,** pretender a; exigir. **to put in a c. for,** reclamar
claimant *n law* demandante, *mf*; pretendiente (-ta); *com* acreedor (-ra)
clairvoyance *n* doble vista, *f*
clairvoyant *n* vidente, *m*
clam *n* almeja, chirla, *f*
clamber *vi* trepar, encaramarse. *n* subida difícil, *f*
clamminess *n* viscosidad, humedad, *f*
clammy *a* viscoso; húmedo, mojado
clamor *n* clamor, estruendo, *m*; gritería, vocería, *f. vi* gritar, vociferar. **to c. against,** protestar contra. **to c. for,** pedir a voces
clamorous *a* clamoroso, ruidoso, estrepitoso
clamp *n* grapa, *f*; abrazadera, *f; carp* tornillo, *m*; (pile) montón, *m. vt* empalmar; sujetar, lañar
clan *n* clan, *m*; familia, *f*; partido, grupo, *m*
clandestine *a* clandestino, furtivo
clandestinely *adv* en secreto, clandestinamente
clang *vi* sonar; (of a gate, etc.) rechinar. *vt* hacer sonar. *n* sonido metálico, *m*; estruendo, *m*

clank *vi* dar un ruido metálico; crujir. *vt* hacer sonar; (glasses) hacer chocar. *n* ruido metálico, *m*; el crujir

clannish *a* exclusivista

clansman *n* miembro de un clan, *m*

clap *vt* (hands) batir; (spurs, etc.) poner rápidamente; (one's hat on) encasquetarse (el sombrero); (shut) cerrar apresuradamente. *vi* aplaudir. *n* (of the hands) palmada, *f*; (of thunder) trueno, *m*; (noise) ruido, *m*. **to c. eyes on,** echar la vista encima de. **to c. someone on the back,** dar una palmada en la espalda (a). **to c. the hands,** batir las palmas

clapper *n* (of a bell) badajo, *m*

clapping *n* aplausos, *m pl*

claque *n* claque, *f*

claret *n* clarete, *m*

clarification *n* clarificación, *f*; elucidación, *f*

clarify *vt* clarificar; elucidar, aclarar

clarinet *n* clarinete, *m*

clarinettist *n* clarinete, *m*

clarion *n* clarín, *m*

clarity *n* claridad, *f*; lucidez, *f*

clash *vi* chocar; encontrarse; (of events) coincidir; (of opinions, etc.) oponerse, estar en desacuerdo; (of colors) desentonar, chocar. *n* estruendo, fragor, *m*; choque, *m*; *mil* encuentro, *m*; (of opinions, etc.) desacuerdo, *m*; disputa, *f*

clasp *vt* (a brooch, etc.) abrochar, enganchar; (embrace) abrazar; (of plants, etc.) ceñir. *n* (brooch) broche, *m*; (of a belt) hebilla, *f*; (of a necklace, handbag, book) cierre, *m*; (for the hair) pasador, *m*. **to c. someone in one's arms,** tomar en los brazos (a), abrazar. **c.-knife,** navaja, *f*

class *n* clase, *f*; (kind) especie, *f*; (of exhibits, etc.) categoría, *f*. *vt* clasificar. **in a c. by itself,** único en su línea. **the lower classes,** las clases bajas. **the middle classes,** la clase media. **the upper classes,** la clase alta. **c.-mate,** condiscípulo (-la). **c.-room,** sala de clase, *f*, salón de clase, *f*. **c. war,** lucha de clases, *f*

classic *a* clásico. *n* clásico, *m*

classical *a* clásico

classicist *a* and *n* clasicista, *mf*

classifiable *a* clasificable

classification *n* clasificación, *f*

classified *a* (secreto) reservado, secreto; (advertisement) por palabras

classified advertisement *n* anuncio por palabras, *m*

classify *vt* clasificar

clatter *vi* hacer ruido; (knock) golpear; (of loose horseshoes) chacolotear. *vt* hacer ruido con; chocar (una cosa contra otra). *n* ruido, *m*; (hammering) martilleo, *m*; (of horseshoes) chacoloteo, *m*; (of a crowd) estruendo, *m*, bulla, *f*. **John clattered along the street,** Los pasos de Juan resonaban por la calle

clause *n gram* cláusula, *f*; *law* condición, estipulación, cláusula, *f*

claustrophobia *n* claustrofobia, *f*

clavichord *n* clavicordio, *m*

clavicle *n* clavícula, *f*

claw *n* garra, *f*; (of a lobster, etc.) tenaza, *f*; (hook) garfio, gancho, *m*. *vt* arañar, clavar las uñas en; (tear) desgarrar. **c.-hammer,** martillo de orejas, *m*

clay *n* arcilla, *f*; barro, *m*; (pipe) pipa de barro, *f*. **c.-pit,** barrizal, *m*

clayey *a* arcilloso

clean *a* limpio; puro, casto. *adv* limpio; completamente; exactamente. **to make a c. sweep (of),** no dejar títere con cabeza. **to make a c. breast of,** confesar sin tormento, no quedarse con nada en el pecho. **to show a c. pair of heels,** tomar las de Villadiego. **c. bill of health,** patente de sanidad, *m*. **c.-cut,** bien definido; claro. **c.-limbed,** bien proporcionado, gallardo. **c.-shaven,** lampiño; sin barba, bien afeitado

clean *vt* limpiar; (streets) barrer; (a floor) fregar; (dryclean) lavar al seco. **to c. one's hands (teeth),** limpiarse las manos (los dientes). **to c. up,** limpiar; (tidy) asear; poner en orden

cleaner *n* limpiador (-ra); (charwoman) fregona, *f*; (stain remover) sacamanchas, *m*; (drycleaner, person) tintorero (-ra)

cleaning *n* limpieza, *f*, *a* de limpiar. **dry-c.,** lavado al seco, *m*. **c. rag,** trapo de limpiar, *m*. **c. woman** *Mexico* fregandera

cleanliness *n* limpieza, *f*; aseo, *m*

cleanse *vt* limpiar; lavar; purgar; purificar

cleansing *n* limpieza, *f*; lavamiento, *m*; purgación, *f*; purificación, *f*

clear *a* claro; (of the sky) sereno, despejado; transparente; (free (from)) libre (de); (open) abierto; (of profit, etc.) neto; (of thoughts, etc.) lúcido; (apparent) evidente; explícito; (of images) distinto; absoluto; (whole) entero, completo. **c. majority,** mayoría absoluta, *f*. **c. profit,** beneficio neto, *m*. **c.-cut,** bien definido. **c.-headed,** perspicaz; inteligente. **c.-sighted,** clarividente

clear *vt* aclarar; despejar; limpiar; librar (de); quitar; (one's throat) carraspear; (*com* stock) liquidar; (of a charge) absolver; (one's character) vindicar; (avoid, miss) evitar; (jump) salvar, saltar; (a court, etc.) desocupar; (a debt) satisfacer; (an account) saldar; (a mortgage) cancelar; (win) ganar; hacer un beneficio de; (through customs) despachar en la aduana. *vi* (of sky, etc.) serenarse; escampar; (of wine, etc.) aclararse; despacharse en la aduana. **to c. the table,** levantar la mesa, levantar los manteles. **to c. the underbrush from** *Lat. Am.* desmalezar. **to c. the way,** abrir calle; *fig* abrir paso. **to c. away,** *vt* quitar; disipar. *vi* disiparse. **to c. off,** *vt* (finish) terminar; (debts) pagar; (discharge) despedir. *vi* (of rain) despejarse, escampar; marcharse. **to c. out,** *vt* limpiar; (a drain, etc.) desatascar; vaciar; echar. *vi* marcharse, escabullirse. **C. out!** ¡Fuera! **c. the decks,** hacer zafarrancho. **c. the decks for action,** hacer zafarrancho. **to c. up,** *vt* poner en orden; (a mystery, etc.) aclarar, resolver, *vi* (of weather) serenarse, escampar, despejarse

clearance *n* (of trees, etc.) desmonte, *m*; eliminación, *f*; expulsión, *f*; *mech* espacio muerto, *m*; despacho de aduana, *m*. **to make a c. of,** deshacerse de. **c. sale,** liquidación, venta de saldos, *f*

clearing *n* (in a wood) claro, *m*, *Argentina* abra *f*; desmonte, *m*; (*com* of goods) liquidación, *f*; (of one's character) vindicación, *f*. **c.-house,** casa de compensación, *f*

clearness *n* claridad, *f*

cleavage *n* hendimiento, *m*; (in views, etc.) escisión, *f*

cleave *vt* partir; abrir; (air, water, etc.) surcar, hender. *vi* partirse; (stick) pegarse, adherirse

cleaver *n* partidor, *m*; hacha, *f*

clef *n* clave, *f*. **treble c.,** clave de sol, *f*

cleft *n* hendedura, fisura, rendija, abertura, *f*. **c.-palate,** paladar hendido, *m*

clematis *n* clemátide, *f*

clemency *n* (of weather) benignidad, *f*; (of character, etc.) clemencia, *f*

clement *a* (of weather) benigno; (of character, etc.) clemente, benévolo

clench *vt* agarrar; (teeth, etc.) apretar; (a bargain) cerrar, concluir

clergy *n* clero, *m*, clérigos, *m pl*

clergyman *n* clérigo, *m*

cleric *n* eclesiástico, *m*

clerical *a* clerical; de oficina. **c. error,** error de oficina, *m*. **c. work,** trabajo de oficina, *m*

clericalism *n* clericalismo, *m*

clerk *n* (clergyman) clérigo, *m*; (in an office) oficinista, escribiente, *m*; oficial, *m*; secretario, *m*

clerkship *n* puesto de oficinista, *m*; escribanía, *f*; secretaría, *f*

clever *a* listo, inteligente; ingenioso; hábil; (dexterous) diestro

cleverly *adv* hábilmente; diestramente, con destreza

cleverness *n* talento, *m*; inteligencia, *f*; habilidad, *f*; (dexterity) destreza, *f*

cliché *n* frase hecha, frase de cajón, *f*
click *vi* (of the tongue) dar un chasquido; (of a bolt, etc.) cerrarse a golpe; hacer tictac. *vt* (one's tongue) chascar; (a bolt, etc.) cerrar a golpe. *n* golpe seco, *m*; tictac, *m*; (of the tongue) chasquido, *m*. **to c. one's heels together,** hacer chocar los talones
client *n* cliente, *mf*; (customer) parroquiano (-na), *Lat. Am. also* marchante (-ta) *mf*
clientele *n* clientela, *f*
cliff *n* acantilado, *m*, roca, escarpa, *f*
cliff dweller *n* hombre de la roca, hombre de las rocas, *m*, mujer de la roca, mujer de las rocas, *f*
climate *n* clima, *m*
climatic *a* climático
climatology *n* climatología, *f*
climax *n* culminación, *f*; (rhetoric) clímax, *m*; gradación, *f*; punto más alto, apogeo, cenit, *m*; (of a play, etc.) desenlace, *m*
climb *vt* and *vi* trepar; escalar; montar; subir; ascender. **rate of c.,** *aer* velocidad ascensional, *f*. **to c. down,** bajar; *fig* echar el pie atrás. **to c. over,** (obstacles) salvar. **to c. up,** encaramarse por; subir por; montar
climber *n* alpinista, *mf*; (plant) trepadera, enredadera, *f*; (social) arribista, *mf*
clinch *vt* (nails, etc.) remachar, rebotar; (a bargain, etc.) cerrar; (an argument, etc.) remachar. *n* (wrestling) cuerpo a cuerpo, *m*
cling *vi* pegarse (a); agarrarse (a); (of scents) pegarse; (follow) seguir. **They clung together for an instant,** Quedaron abrazados un instante
clinging *a* tenaz; (of plants, etc.) trepador; (of persons) manso, dócil. **to be a c. vine,** *inf* ser una malva
clinic *n* clínica, *f*
clinical *a* clínico
clink *vi* retiñir; (of glasses) chocarse. *vt* hacer sonar; (glasses) chocar. *n* retintín, *m*; (of a hammer) martilleo, *m*; sonido metálico, *m*; (of glasses) choque, *m*; (jail) *Argentina, Chile* capacha *f*
clip *vt* (grasp) agarrar; (sheep, etc.) esquilar; (trim) recortar, cercenar; (prune) podar; (a ticket) taladrar. *n* pinza, *f*; (paper-clip) sujetapapeles, *Central America* ataché, *elsewhere in Lat. Am.* broche *m*; *mech* grapa, escarpia, *f*; (for ornament) sujetador, *m*. **to c. a person's wings,** *fig* cortar (or quebrar) las alas (a)
clipper *n* (person) esquilador (-ra); (*naut* and *aer*) clíper, *m*; *pl* **clippers,** tenazas de cortar, *f pl*; (for pruning) podaderas, *f pl*; (punch) taladro, *m*
clipping *n* (of sheep, etc.) esquileo, *m*; (of a newspaper, etc.) recorte, *m*
clique *n* camarilla, *f*
cliquish *a* exclusivista
cloak *n* capa, *f*; manto, *m*; *fig* velo, *m*. *vt* encapotar; embozar; (conceal) ocultar, encubrir. **c. and sword play,** comedia de capa y espada, *f*. **c.-room,** guardarropa, *m*; (ladies') tocador, *m*; (on a station) consigna, *f*
clock *n* reloj, *m*; (of a stocking) cuadrado, *m*. **It is six o'clock,** Son las seis. **c.-face,** esfera de reloj, *f*. **c.-maker,** relojero, *m*. **c.-making,** relojería, *f*. **c.-work,** aparato de relojería, *m*. **to go like c.-work,** ir como un reloj. **c.-work train,** tren de cuerda, *m*
clockwise *a* and *adv* en el sentido de las agujas del reloj; de derecha a izquierda
clod *n* (of earth) terrón, *m*; (corpse) tierra, *f*; (person) zoquete, *m*. **c.-hopper,** patán, *m*
clog *n* (shoe) zueco, zoclo, *m*; (obstacle) estorbo, obstáculo, *m*. *vt* embarazar; estorbar, impedir; (block) obturar, cerrar; *fig* paralizar
cloister *n* claustro, *m*; convento, *m*. *vt* enclaustrar
cloistered *a* enclaustrado; retirado, aislado
close *a* estrecho; (of a prisoner) incomunicado; (reticent) reservado; (niggardly) tacaño, avaro; (scarce) escaso; (of friends) íntimo; (equal) igual; (lacking space) apretado; (dense) denso; (thick) tupido; compacto; (of a copy, etc.) fiel, exacto; (thorough) concienzudo; (careful) cuidadoso; (attentive) atento; (to the roots) a raíz; (of shaving) bueno; (of weather) pesado, sofo-

cante; (of rooms) mal ventilado. **at c. quarters,** de cerca. **It is c. to eight o'clock,** Son casi las ocho. **to press c.,** perseguir de cerca; fatigar. **c. at hand, c. by,** cerca; al lado; a mano. **c.-cropped,** (of hair) al rape. **c. fight,** lucha igualada, *f*. **c.-fisted,** tacaño, apretado. **c.-fitting,** ajustado, ceñido al cuerpo; pequeño. **c. season,** veda, *f*. **c.-up,** *n* (cinema) primer plano, *m*
close *n* (end) fin, *m*, conclusión, *f*; (of day) caída, *f*; *mus* cadencia, *f*; (enclosure) cercado, *m*; (square) plazoleta, *f*; (alley) callejón, *m*; (of a cathedral) patio, *m*. **at the c. of day,** a la caída de la tarde. **to bring to a c.,** terminar; llevar a cabo. **to draw to a c.,** tocar a su fin; estar terminando
close *vt* cerrar; (end) concluir, terminar; poner fin a. *vi* cerrar(se); (of a wound) cicatrizarse; cerrarse; (end) terminar(se), acabar, concluir. **to c. the ranks,** cerrar filas. **to c. about,** (surround) rodear, cercar; (envelop) envolver. **to c. down,** *vt* cerrar. *vi* cerrarse; *rad* cerrarse. **to c. halfway** entrecerrar **to c. in,** (surround) cercar; (of night) cerrar; caer; (envelop) envolver; (of length of days) acortarse. **to c. in on,** cercar. **to c. round,** envolver; (of water) tragar. **to c. up,** *vt* cerrar; cerrar completamente; obstruir. *vi* (of persons) acercarse; (of a wound) cicatrizarse; cerrarse
closed *a* cerrado. **"Road C.,"** Paso Cerrado. **to have a c. mind,** ser cerrado de mollera; sufrir de estrechez de miras
closely *adv* estrechamente; de cerca; (carefully) cuidadosamente; (exactly) exactamente; (attentively) con atención, atentamente
closeness *n* estrechez, *f*; densidad, *f*; (nearness) proximidad, *f*; (of a copy, etc.) fidelidad, exactitud, *f*; (stuffiness), falta de aire, *f*; (of friendship) intimidad, *f*; (stinginess) tacañería, *f*; (reserve) reserva, *f*
closet *n* camarín, *m*; (cupboard) alacena, *f*; (water) excusado, *m*
closing *n* cerramiento, *m*; (of an account) saldo, *m*. **c. time,** cierre, *m*, hora de cerrar, *f*
closure *n* conclusión, *f*; *pol* clausura, *f*
clot *n* coágulo, grumo, *m*. *vt* coagular. *vi* coagularse, cuajarse
cloth *n* tela, *f*; paño, *m*; (table) mantel, *m*; (clergy) clero, *m*. **She cleaned the books with a c.,** Ella limpió los libros con un paño. **in c.,** (of books) en tela
clothe *vt* vestir; cubrir; (with authority, etc.) revestir. **to c. oneself,** vestirse
clothes *n pl* vestidos, *m pl*, ropa, *f*. **a suit of c.,** un traje. **old c. shop,** ropavejería, *f*. **c.-basket,** cesta de la colada, *f*. **c.-brush,** cepillo para ropa, *m*. **c.-hanger,** percha, *f*. **c.-horse,** enjugador, *m*. **c.-line,** cuerda de la ropa, *f*. **c.-peg,** pinza de la ropa, *f*. **c.-prop,** palo para sostener la cuerda de la colada, *m*
clothier *n* ropero, *m*. **clothier's shop,** ropería, *f*
clothing *n* vestidos, *m pl*, ropa, *f*. **article of c.,** prenda de vestir, *f*
clotted *a* grumoso
cloud *n* nube, *f*. *vt* anublar, oscurecer; empañar; (blot out) borrar. *vi* anublarse. **to be under a c.,** estar bajo sospecha. **summer c.,** nube de verano, *f*. **storm-c.,** nubarrón, *m*. **c.-burst,** nubada, *f*, chaparrón, *m*. **c.-capped,** coronado de nubes
cloudiness *n* nebulosidad, *f*; obscuridad, *f*; (of liquids) turbiedad, *f*
cloudless *a* sin nubes, despejado; sereno, claro
cloudy *a* nublado, nubloso; obscuro; (of liquids) turbio
clout *n* *Central America, Mexico* arranque *m*
clove *n* clavo de especia, *m*; (of garlic) diente de ajo, *m*. **c.-tree,** clavero, *m*
cloven *a* hendido. **to show the c. hoof,** enseñar la oreja. **c. hoof,** pezuña, *f*
clover *n* trébol, *m*. **to be in c.,** nadar en la abundancia
clown *n* patán, *m*; bufón, tonto, *m*; (in a circus) payaso, *m*. *vi* hacer el tonto, hacer el payaso
clowning *n* payasada, *f*
clownish *a* grosero; palurdo, zafio; bufón
cloy *vt* empalagar

cloying *a* empalagoso

club *n* porra, cachiporra, clava, *f*; (gymnastic) maza, *f*; (hockey) bastón de hockey, *m*; (golf) palo de golf, *m*; (in cards) basto, *m*; (social) club, *m*. *vt* golpear. **to c. together,** asociarse, unirse. **We clubbed together to buy him a present,** Entre todos le compramos un regalo. **c.-house,** club, *m*

clubfoot *n* pie calcáneo, pie contrahecho, pie de piña, pie equino, pie talo, pie zambo, *m*

clubman *n* miembro de un club, *m*

cluck *vi* cloquear. *n* cloqueo, *m*

clucking *n* cloqueo, *m*

clue *n* indicio, *m*; (to a problem) clave, *f*; (of a cross-word) indicación, *f*; idea, *f*

clump *n* bloque, pedazo, *m*; (of trees) grupo, *m*; (of feet) ruido, *m*

clumsily *adv* torpemente; pesadamente

clumsiness *n* torpeza, *f*; falta de maña, *f*; pesadez, *f*

clumsy *a* torpe; desmañado; chapucero, sin arte; (lumbering) pesado; (in shape) disforme

cluster *n* (of currants, etc.) racimo, *m*; (of flowers) ramillete, *m*; grupo, *m*. *vi* arracimarse; agruparse. **They clustered round him,** Se agrupaban a su alrededor

clutch *vt* agarrar; sujetar, apretar. *n mech* embrague, *m*; (of eggs) nidada, *f*; *fig* garras, *f pl*. **to fall into the clutches of,** caer en las garras de. **to make a c. at,** procurar agarrar. **to throw in the c.,** *mech* embragar. **to throw out the c.,** *mech* desembragar. **c. pedal,** pedal de embrague, *m*

clutter *n* desorden, *m*, confusión, *f*, *vt* desordenar

coach *n* carroza, *f*; charabán, *m*; *rw* vagón, coche, *m*; (hackney) coche de alquiler, *m*; *sport* entrenador, *m*; (tutor) profesor particular, *m*. *vt sport* entrenar; (teach) preparar, dar lecciones particulares (a). **through c.,** coche directo, *m*. **c.-box,** pescante, *m*. **c.-house,** cochera, *f*

coaching *n sport* entrenamiento, *m*; lecciones particulares, *f pl*

coachman *n* cochero, *m*

coagulate *vi* coagularse. *vt* coagular, cuajar

coagulation *n* coagulación, *f*

coal *n* carbón, *m*; pedazo de carbón, *m*; (burning) brasa, *f*. *vi* carbonear, hacer carbón. *vt* proveer de carbón; carbonear. **to carry coals to Newcastle,** llevar leña al monte, elevar agua al mar. **to haul a person over the coals,** reprender a alguien. **c.-barge,** (barco) carbonero, *m*. **c.-black,** negro como el azabache. **c.-cellar, house,** carbonera, *f*. **c.-dust,** cisco, *m*. **c.-field,** yacimiento de carbón, *m*. **c.-gas,** gas de hulla, *m*. **c.-heaver,** cargador de carbón, *m*. **c.-merchant,** carbonero, *m*. **c.-mine,** mina de carbón, *f*. **c.-miner,** minero de carbón, *m*. **c.-scuttle,** carbonera, *f*. **c.-tar,** alquitrán mineral, *m*

coalesce *vi* fundirse; unirse; incorporarse

coalescence *n* fusión, *f*; unión, *f*; incorporación, *f*

coalition *n* coalición, *f*

coarse *a* (in texture) basto, burdo; tosco; (gross) grosero; vulgar. **c.-grained,** de fibra gruesa; (of persons) vulgar, poco fino. **c. woolen cloth** *Chile* litro *m*

coarsen *vt* (of persons) embrutecer. *vi* embrutecerse; (of the skin) curtirse

coarseness *n* basteza, *f*; tosquedad, *f*; (of persons) grosería, indelicadeza, *f*; vulgaridad, *f*

coast *n* costa, *f*; litoral, *m*. *vi* costear; deslizarse en un tobogán; dejar muerto el motor. **The c. is not clear,** Hay moros en la costa. **c.-guard,** guardacostas, *m*. **c.-line,** litoral, *m*

coastal *a* costanero, costero. **c. defences,** defensas costeras, *f pl*

coaster *n naut* barco costanero, barco de cabotaje, *m*

coasting *n naut* cabotaje, *m*

coat *n* abrigo, *m*; gabán, *m*; chaqueta, *f*; (animal's) capa, *f*; (of paint) mano, *f*. *vt* recubrir; (with paint, etc.) dar una mano de. **fur c.,** abrigo de pieles, *m*. **sports c.,**

Americana sport, *f*. **c. of arms,** escudo de armas, *m*. **c. of mail,** cota de malla, *f*. **c.-hanger,** percha, *f*

coating *n* (of paint, etc.) capa, mano, *f*

co-author *n* coautor, *m*

coax *vt* instar; halagar, engatusar, *Lat. Am. also* engaratusar; persuadir (a)

coaxing *n* ruegos, *m pl*; mimos, *m pl*, caricias, *f pl*; persuasión, *f*. *a* mimoso, zalamero; persuasivo

cob *n* (horse) jaca, *f*; (lump) pedazo, *m*; (swan) cisne macho, *m*

cobalt *n* cobalto, *m*. **c. blue,** azul cobalto, *m*

cobble *n* (stone) guijarro, *m*, *vt* (with stones) empedrar con guijarros; (shoes) remendar

cobbler *n* zapatero remendón, *m*. **cobbler's last,** horma, *f*. **cobbler's wax,** cerote, *m*

cobblestone *n* guijarro, *m*, piedra, *f*

cobelligerent *n* cobeligerante, *mf*

cobra *n* cobra, serpiente de anteojos, *f*

cobweb *n* telaraña, *f*

cobwebby *a* cubierto de telarañas; transparente; de gasa

cocaine *n* cocaína, *f*

coccyx *n* cóccix, *m*, *inf* rabadilla, *f*

cochlea *n* caracol (del oído), *m*

cock *n* gallo, *m*; (male) macho, *m*; (tap) grifo, *m*, espita, *f*; (of a gun) martillo, *m*; (weather-vane) veleta, *f*; (of hay) montón, *m*. *vt* (a gun) amartillar; (a hat) ladear; (raise) erguir, enderezar. **a cocked hat,** un sombrero de tres picos. **at half c.,** (of a gun) desamartillada *f..* **He cocked his head,** Erguió la cabeza. **The dog cocked its ears,** El perro aguzó las orejas. **to c. one's eye at,** lanzar una mirada (a). **c.-a-doodle-doo,** quiquiriquí, *m*. **c.-a-hoop,** triunfante, jubiloso; arrogante. **c.-crow,** canto del gallo, *m*. **c.-fight,** riña de gallos, *f*. **c.-of-the-walk,** gallito, *m*. **c.-sure,** pagado de sí mismo; completamente convencido

cockerel *n* gallo joven, gallito, *m*

cocker spaniel *n* cóquer, *m*

cockle *n* (bivalve) bucarda, *f*. *vi* arrugarse; (warp) torcerse; doblarse. **c.-shell,** (pilgrims') concha, *f*; (boat) cascarón de nuez, *m*

Cockney *a* londinense, de Londres. *n* londinense, *mf*

cockpit *n* gallería, *f*; *aer* casilla del piloto, *f*; *fig* arena, *f*

cockroach *n* cucaracha, *f*

cockscomb *n* cresta de gallo, *f*

cocktail *n* (drink) cótel, coctel, *m*. **to shake a c.,** mezclar un coctel. **c. party,** coctel *m*. **c. shaker,** cotelera, *f*

cocky *a* fatuo, presuntuoso

cocoa *n* cacao, *m*

coconut *n* coco, *m*; *inf* cabeza, *f*. **c. milk,** agua de coco, *f*. **c. shy,** pim, pam, pum, *m*. **c. tree,** cocotero, *m*

cocoon *n* capullo, *m*

cod *n* bacalao, *m*. **cod-liver oil,** aceite de hígado de bacalao, *m*

coddle *vt* criar con mimo, mimar, consentir

code *n* código, *m*; clave, *f*; (secret) cifra, *f*. *vt* poner en cifra. **signal c.,** *naut* código de señales, *m*. **c. word,** palabra de clave, *f*

codeine *n* codeína, *f*

codex *n* códice, *m*

codicil *n* codicilio, *m*

codification *n* codificación, *f*

codify *vt* codificar

coeducation *n* coeducación, *f*

coefficient *n* coeficiente, *m*

coequality *n* coigualdad, *f*

coerce *vt* forzar, obligar; constreñir

coercion *n* coerción, coacción, *f*

coercive *a* coercitivo, coactivo

coeval *a* coevo

coexist *vi* coexistir

coexistence *n* coexistencia, *f*

coffee *n* café, *m*. **black c.,** café solo, *m*. **white c.,** café con leche, *m*. **c.-bean,** grano de café, *m*. **c.-cup,** taza para café, *f*. **c.-house,** café, *m*. **c.-mill,** molinillo de

café, *m*. **c.-plantation,** cafetal, *m*. **c.-pot,** cafetera, *f*. **c.-set,** juego de café, *m*. **c.-tree,** cafeto, *m*
coffer *n* cofre, *m*; arca, caja, *f*
coffin *n* ataúd, féretro, *m*; caja, *f*
cog *n mech* diente (de rueda), *m*
cogency *n* fuerza, *f*
cogent *a* convincente, fuerte; urgente
cogitate *vi* pensar, considerar, meditar
cogitation *n* reflexión, meditación, consideración, *f*
cognac *n* coñac, *m*
cognate *a* (of stock) consanguíneo; afín; análogo; semejante
cognition *n* cognición, *f*
cognitive *a* cognoscitivo
cognizance *n* conocimiento, *m*; jurisdicción, *f*
cogwheel *n* rueda dentada, *f*
cohabit *vi* cohabitar
cohabitation *n* cohabitación, *f*
coheir *n* coheredero, *m*
coheiress *n* coheredera, *f*
cohere *vi* pegarse, adherirse; unirse
coherent *a* coherente; consecuente
cohesion *n* cohesión, *f*; coherencia, *f*
cohort *n* cohorte, *f*
coif *n* cofia, *f*; toca, *f*
coiffure *n* peinado, *m*; tocado, *m*
coil *vt* arrollar; (*naut* of ropes) adujar. *vi* arrollarse; enroscarse; serpentear. *n* rollo, *m*; (of a serpent and ropes) anillo, *m*; (of hair) trenza, *f*; *elec* carrete, *m*. **coil of smoke,** nube de humo, *f*. **to c. up,** hacerse un ovillo
coiling *n* arrollamiento, *m*; serpenteo, *m*
coin *n* moneda, *f*; *inf* dinero, *m*. *vt* acuñar; (a new word) inventar. **to pay back in the same c.,** pagar en la misma moneda
coinage *n* acuñación, *f*; moneda, *f*; sistema monetario, *m*; invención, *f*; (new word) neologismo, *m*
coincide *vi* coincidir (con); estar conforme, estar de acuerdo
coincidence *n* coincidencia, *f*; (chance) casualidad, *f*
coiner *n* acuñador de moneda, *m*; monedero falso, *m*; (of phrases, etc.) inventor, *m*
coitus *n* coito, *m*
coke *n* (carbón de) coque, *m*
colander *n* colador, *m*
cold *a* frío. *n* frío, *m*; *med* catarro, constipado, *m*. **I am c.,** Tengo frío. **It is c.,** Está frío; (weather) Hace frío. **to catch a c.,** acatarrarse, resfriarse. **to grow c.,** enfriarse; (of the weather) empezar a hacer frío. **in c. blood,** a sangre fría. **c.-blooded,** (fishes, etc.) de sangre fría; (chilly, of persons) friolero; (pitiless) insensible, sin piedad; (of actions) a sangre fría, premeditado. **c.-chisel,** cortafrío, *m*. **c. cream,** crema (para el cutis), *f*. **c.-hearted,** seco, insensible. **c.-shoulder,** *n* frialdad, *f*. *vt* tratar con frialdad (a). **c.-storage,** conservación refrigerada, *f*
coldly *adv* fríamente
coldness *n* frío, *m*; (of one's reception, etc.) frialdad, *f*; (of heart) inhumanidad, *f*
coleopterous *a* coleóptero
colic *n* cólico, *m*
coliseum *n* coliseo, *m*
colitis *n* colitis, *f*
collaborate *vi* colaborar (con)
collaboration *n* colaboración, *f*
collaborationist *n* colaboracionista, *mf*
collaborator *n* colaborador (-ra); (quisling) colaboracionista, *mf*
collapse *n* derrumbamiento, *m*; desplome, *m*; *med* colapso, *m*; (of buildings and *fig*) hundimiento, *m*; (of plans) frustración, *f*; (failure) fracaso, *m*. *vi* derrumbarse; (of buildings, etc.) hundirse, venirse abajo; (of persons, fall) desplomarse; *med* sufrir colapso; (of plans, etc.) frustrarse, venirse abajo. **George came to us after the c. of France,** Jorge vino a quedarse con nosotros después del hundimiento de Francia

collapsible *a* plegable
collar *n* (of a garment and of fur) cuello, *m*; (of a dog, etc., and necklace) collar, *m*. *vt* (seize) agarrar. **detachable c.,** cuello suelto, *m*. **high c.,** alzacuello, *m*. **c.-bone,** clavícula, *f*
collate *vt* cotejar; (to a benefice) colacionar
collateral *a* colateral
collation *n* colación, *f*
colleague *n* colega, *m*; compañero (-ra)
collect *vt* (assemble) reunir; (catch) coger; acumular; (call for) pasar a buscar, ir (or venir) a buscar; (pick up) recoger; (taxes, etc.) recaudar; coleccionar; (one's strength, etc. and debts, etc.) cobrar; (letters) recoger. *vi* reunirse, congregarse; acumularse. *n ecc* colecta, *f*. **to c. oneself,** reponerse
collected *a* (of persons) seguro de sí.
collection *n* reunión, *f*; (of data, etc.) acumulación, *f*; (of pictures, stamps, etc.) colección, *f*; (of a debt, etc.) cobranza, *f*; (of taxes, etc.) recaudación, *f*; (from a mail box) recogida, *f*; (of laws, etc.) compilación, *f*; *ecc* ofertorio, *m*; (of donations) colecta, *f*
collection agency *n* agencia de cobros de cuentas, *f*
collective *a* colectivo. **c. bargaining,** regateo colectivo, trato colectivo, *m*
collectivism *n* colectivismo, *m*
collector *n* (of pictures, etc.) coleccionador (-ra), coleccionista, *mf*; cobrador, *m*; *elec* colector, *m*
college *n* colegio, *m*; escuela, *f*; universidad, *f*. **C. of Cardinals,** Colegio de Cardenales, *m*
collegiate *a* colegial, colegiado. **c. church,** iglesia colegial, *f*
collide *vi* chocar (contra), topar (con); estar en conflicto (con). **c. head-on,** chocar frontalmente
collie *n* perro de pastor escocés, *m*
collier *n* minero de carbón, *m*; (barco) carbonero, *m*
collision *n* choque, *m*, colisión, *f*; (of interests, etc.) antagonismo, conflicto, *m*. **to come into c. with,** chocar con
Cologne Colonia, *f*
colloid *a* coloide. *n* coloide, *m*
colloquial *a* familiar
colloquialism *n* expresión familiar, *f*
colloquially *adv* en lenguaje familiar; familiarmente
colloquy *n* coloquio, *m*
collusion *n* colusión, *f*. **to be in c.,** *law* coludir; conspirar, estar de manga
Colombia Colombia, *f*
Colombian *a* colombiano. *n* colombiano (-na)
colon *n anat* colon, *m*; (punctuation) dos puntos, *m pl*
colonel *n* coronel, *m*
colonial *a* colonial. *n* habitante de las colonias, *m*. **c. government** *Lat. Am.* coloniaje *m* **C. Office,** Ministerio de Asuntos Coloniales, *m*. **c. period** *Lat. Am.* coloniaje *m*
colonist *n* colono, *m*; colonizador (-ra)
colonization *n* colonización, *f*
colonize *vt* colonizar. *vi* establecerse en una colonia
colonizer *n* colonizador (-ra)
colonizing *n* colonización, *f*, *a* colonizador
colonnade *n* columnata, *f*
colony *n* colonia, *f*
color *n* color, *m*; colorido, *m*; tinta, *f*; materia colorante, *f*; *pl* **colors,** insignia, *f*; bandera, *f*, estandarte, *m*; *naut* pabellón, *m*. *vt* colorar; pintar; iluminar; (influence) influir, afectar. *vi* colorarse; ruborizarse; encenderse. **fast c.,** color estable, color sólido, *m*. **regimental colors,** bandera del regimiento, *f*. **with colors flying,** con tambor batiente, a banderas desplegadas. **to be off c.,** estar malucho, estar indispuesto. **to change c.,** (of persons) mudar de color, mudar de color. **to give c. to,** (a story, etc.) hacer verosímil. **to lay the colors on too thick,** recargar las tintas. **to pass with flying colors,** salir triunfante. **under c. of,** so color de, a pretexto de. **c.-blind,** daltoniano. **c.-blindness,** daltonismo, *m*
Colorado beetle *n* escarabajo de la patata, *m*

colored *a* colorado; de color

coloring *n* (substance) colorante, *m*; (act of) coloración, *f*; *art* colorido, *m*; (of complexion) colores, *m pl*

colorist *n* colorista, *mf*

colorless *a* sin color, incoloro; *fig* insípido

colossal *a* colosal, gigantesco; enorme; *inf* estupendo

colossus *n* coloso, *m*

colt *n* potro, *m*; (boy) muchacho alegre, *m*

colter *n* reja, reja del arado, *f*

colt's-foot *n bot* fárfara, *f*

columbine *n bot* aguileña, *f*; (in pantomime) Colombina, *f*

column *n* columna, *f*. **Fifth c.,** quinta columna, *f*

columned *a* con columnas

columnist *n* periodista, *m*

coma *n* coma, *m*

comatose *a* comatoso

comb *n* peine, *m*; (for flax) carda, *f*; (curry) almohaza, *f*; (of cock) cresta, carúncula, *f*; (of a wave) cima, cresta, *f*; (honey) panal, *m*, *vt* (hair) peinar; (flax) rastrillar, cardar. **c. and brush,** cepillo y peine. **high c.,** peineta, *f*. **to c. one's hair,** peinarse

combat *vt* luchar contra, combatir, resistir. *vi* combatir, pelear. *n* combate, *m*; lucha, batalla, *f*. **in single c.,** cuerpo a cuerpo

combatant *n* combatiente, *m*, *a* combatiente

combative *a* belicoso, pugnaz

combination *n* combinación, *f*; mezcla, *f*; unión, *f*; asociación, *f*; *pl* **combinations,** camisa pantalón, *f*. **c. lock,** cerradura de combinación, *f*

combine *vt* combinar; reunir, juntar; *chem* combinar. *vi* combinarse; asociarse (con); *com* fusionarse. *n* asociación, *f*; *com* monopolio, *m*

combustible *a* combustible. *n* combustible, *m*

combustion *n* combustión, *f*. **rapid c.,** combustión rápida, *f*. **spontaneous c.,** combustión espontánea, *f*

come *vi* venir; llegar; avanzar; acercarse; (happen) suceder, acontecer; (result) resultar; (find oneself) encontrarse, hallarse; (become) llegar a ser; (begin to) ponerse (a), empezar (a). **Coming!** ¡Voy! ¡Allá voy! **C., c.!** ¡Vamos! ¡No es para tanto! ¡Ánimo! **I am ready whatever comes,** Estoy preparado venga lo que venga. **He comes of a good family,** Es (Viene) de buena familia. **I came to know him well,** Llegué a conocerle bien. **I don't know what came over me,** No sé lo que me pasó. **When I came to consider it,** Cuando me puse a considerarlo. **The bill comes to six thousand pesetas,** La cuenta sale a seis mil pesetas. **He comes up before the judge tomorrow,** Ha de comparecer ante el juez mañana. **What you say comes to this,** Lo que dice Vd. se reduce a esto. **What is the world coming to?** ¿A dónde va parar el mundo? **It does not c. within my scope,** No está dentro de mi alcance. **The party did not c. up to their expectations,** La reunión no fue tan divertida como esperaban. **to c. up with,** (a person) alcanzar (a). **to c. upon,** encontrar, hallar; tropezar con; encontrar por casualidad. **to c. upon evil days,** venir a menos

to c. home to, *fig* impresionar mucho, tocar en lo más íntimo; hacer comprender (a). **to c. into bloom,** empezar a tener flores, florecer. **to c. into one's head,** venir a las mientes. **to c. into the world,** venir al mundo. **to c. near,** acercarse; aproximarse, estar próximo. **to c. next,** venir después; suceder luego. **to c. to an end,** terminar, acabarse. **to c. to blows,** venir a las manos. **to c. to grief,** salir mal parado; (of schemes, etc.) malograrse. **to c. to hand,** venir a mano; (of letters) llegar a las manos (de). **to c. to life,** despertar; animarse; resucitarse. **to c. to nothing,** frustrarse; no quedar en nada. **to c. to pass,** suceder; realizarse. **to c. to terms,** ponerse de acuerdo. **to c. true,** cumplirse, verificarse. **to c. about,** suceder, acontecer, tener lugar; (of the wind) girar. **to c. across,** dar con, encontrar por casualidad; tropezar con. **to c. after,** (a situation) solicitar; (follow) seguir (a); venir más tarde (que); (succeed) suceder. **to c. again,** volver. **to c. along,** caminar (por); andar (por); (arrive) llegar. **C. along!** ¡Ven! ¡Vamos! ¡Andamos! **to c. at,** alcanzar; (attack) embestir, atacar; (gain) obtener, adquirir. **to c. away,** irse, marcharse; (break) des-

hacerse. **to c. back,** volver, regresar, *Lat. Am.* devolverse **c.-back,** *n inf* respuesta, *f*; contraataque, *m*. **to c. before,** llegar antes; preceder (a). **to c. between,** interponerse (entre), intervenir. **to c. by,** pasar por, pasar junto a; (acquire) obtener, adquirir; (achieve) conseguir. **to c. down,** bajar, descender; (in the world) venir a menos; (be demolished) demolerse; (collapse) derrumbarse, hundirse; (of prices) bajar; (of traditions, etc.) llegar e.g. **This work has c. down to us in two fifteenth-century manuscripts** Esta obra nos ha llegado en dos manuscritos del siglo quince; (fall) caer. **c.-down,** *n* caída, *f*; frustración, *f*; desengaño, *m*; desprestigio, *m*; pérdida de posición, *f*. **to c. down on a person,** cantar la cartilla (a). **to c. down with altitude sickness** *Peru* asorocharse **to c. forward,** avanzar, adelantarse; (offer) ofrecerse; presentarse. **to c. in,** entrar; (of money) ingresar; (of trains, etc.) llegar; (of the tide) crecer; (of the new year) empezar; (of fashion) ponerse de moda; (be useful) servir (para). **C. in!** ¡Adelante! ¡Pase Vd.! **to c. into,** (a scheme) asociarse con; (property) heredar; (the mind) presentarse a la imaginación, ocurrirse (a). **to c. off,** (happen) tener lugar; realizarse, efectuarse; (be successful) tener éxito; (break off) separarse (de); romperse. **to c. off well,** tener éxito; (of persons) salir bien. **c. off the press,** salir de prensas. **to c. on,** avanzar; (of actors) salir a la escena; (progress) hacer progresos; (develop) desarrollarse; (of pain, etc.) acometer (a); (arrive) llegar; (of a lawsuit) verse. **C. on!** ¡Vamos! ¡En marcha! **to c. out,** salir; (of stars) nacer; (of buds, etc.) brotar; (of the moon, etc.) asomarse; (of stains) borrarse, salir; (of a book) ver la luz, publicarse; (of secrets) divulgarse, saberse; (of a girl, in society) ponerse de largo; (on strike) declararse en huelga; (of fashions, etc.) aparecer. **to c. out with,** (a remark) soltar; (oaths, etc.) prorrumpir (en); (disclose) revelar, hacer público. **to c. round,** (to see someone) venir a ver (a); (coax) engatusar; (after a faint, etc.) volver en sí; (after illness) reponerse; (to another's point of view) aceptar, compartir. **to c. through,** pasar por; (trials, etc.) subir; salir de; (of liquids) salirse. **to c. to,** volver en sí. **to c. together,** reunirse, juntarse; venir juntos; unirse. **to c. under,** venir (or estar) bajo la jurisdicción de; (the influence of) estar dominado por; (figure among) figurar entre, estar comprendido en. **to c. up,** subir; (of sun, moon) salir; (of plants) brotar; (of problems, etc.) surgir; (in conversation) discutirse; (before a court) comparecer. **to c. up to,** (equal) igualar, ser igual (a); rivalizar con; (in height) llegar hasta. **He came up to them in the street,** Les abordó (or se les acercó) en la calle. **We have c. up against many difficulties,** Hemos tropezado con muchas dificultades. **This novel does not c. up to his last,** Esta última novela no es tan buena como la anterior.

comedian *n* actor cómico, comediante, *m*

comedy *n* comedia, *f*. **c. of manners,** comedia de costumbres, *f*

comeliness *n* hermosura, *f*

comely *a* hermoso

comer *n* el, *m*, (*f*, la) que viene. **all comers,** todo el mundo. **first c.,** primer (-ra) venido (-da)

comet *n* cometa, *m*

comfort *vt* consolar, confortar; (encourage) animar; (reassure) alegrar. *n* consuelo, *m*; satisfacción, *f*; comodidad, *f*; bienestar, *m*. **He lives in great c.,** Vive con mucha comodidad. **c.-loving,** comodón

comfortable *a* cómodo; (with income) suficiente; (consoling) consolador. **to make oneself c.,** ponerse cómodo

comfortably *adv* cómodamente; suficientemente; fácilmente; con facilidad; (well) bien. **He is c. off,** Está bien de dinero

comforter *n* consolador (-ra); (baby's) chupador, *m*; (scarf) bufanda, *f*

comforting *a* consolador

comfortless *a* incómodo, sin comodidad; desconsolador; (of persons) inconsolable, desconsolado

comic *a* cómico; bufo; satírico. *n* cómico, *m*; *pl* **comics,** (printed) historietas cómicas, *f pl.* **c. opera,** ópera cómicas, *f.* **c. paper,** periódico satírico, *m*

comical *a* cómico; divertido, gracioso

coming *a* (with year, etc.) próximo, que viene; (promising) de porvenir; (approaching) que se acerca. *n* venida, *f*; llegada, *f*; advenimiento, *m.* **c.-out party,** puesta de largo, *f.* **comings and goings,** entradas y salidas, *f pl*

comma *n* coma, *f.* **inverted commas,** comillas, *f pl*

command *vt* mandar, ordenar; (silence, respect, etc.) imponer; (an army, fleet, etc.) comandar; capitanear; (one's emotions) dominar; (have at one's disposal) disponer de; (a military position, view) dominar; (sympathy, etc.) despertar, merecer; (of price) venderse por. *vi* mandar. *n* orden, *f*; (*mil nav*) mando, *m*; (of an army, etc.) comandancia, *f*; (of one's emotions, etc.) dominio, *m*; (of a military position, etc.) dominación, *f*; disposición, *f.* **By Royal C.,** Por Real Orden; (of shops, etc.) Proveedor de la Real Casa. **The house commands lovely views of the mountains,** La casa tiene hermosas vistas de las montañas. **word of c.,** orden, *f.* **Yours to c.,** A la disposición de Vd.

commandant *n* comandante, *m*

commandeer *vt* (conscript) reclutar; *mil* requisar; expropiar

commander *n mil* comandante, *m*; *nav* capitán de fragata, *m*; (of order of Knighthood) comendador, *m.* **c.-in-chief,** generalísimo, *m.* **C. of the Faithful,** Comendador de los creyentes, *m*

commanding *a mil* comandante; imponente; (of manner) imperioso; dominante. **c. officer,** comandante en jefe, *m*

commandment *n* precepto, mandamiento, *m.* **the Ten Commandments,** los diez mandamientos

commando *n mil* comando, *m*

commemorate *vt* conmemorar

commemoration *n* conmemoración, *f*

commemorative *a* conmemorativo

commence *vt* comenzar, empezar, principiar. *vi* comenzar. **He commenced to eat,** Empezó a comer

commencement *n* principio, comienzo, *m*

commend *vt* (entrust) encomendar; recomendar; alabar

commendable *a* loable; recomendable

commendation *n* aprobación, alabanza, *f*, aplauso, *m*

commendatory *a* (of letters) comendatorio

commensurable *a* conmensurable

commensurate *a* proporcionado (a); conforme (a)

comment *n* observación, *f*; (on a work) comento, *m*; explicación, nota, *f. vi* hacer una observación (sobre); (a work) comentar, anotar. **to c. unfavorably on,** criticar

commentary *n* comentario, *m*; (on a person, etc.) comentos, *m pl*, observaciones, *f pl*

commentator *n* comentador (-ra); (of a work) comentarista, *mf*

commerce *n* comercio, *m*; negocios, *m pl*; (social) trato, *m*

commercial *a* comercial; mercantil. **c. traveler,** viajante, *mf*

commercialism *n* mercantilismo, *m*

commercialize *vt* hacer objeto de comercio

commercially *adv* comercialmente

commingle *vt* mezclar. *vi* mezclarse

commiserate *vi* compadecerse (de), apiadarse (de)

commiseration *n* conmiseración, compasión, *f*

commissariat *n* comisaría, *f*; *inf* despensa, *f*

commissary *n* comisario, *m*

commission *n* comisión, *f*; *mil* graduación de oficial, *f. vt* comisionar; (a ship) poner en servicio activo, armar; (appoint) nombrar. **in c.,** en servicio, activo. **out of c.,** (of ships) inutilizado; inservible. **c. agent,** comisionista, *mf* **to gain one's c.,** *mil* graduarse de oficial. **to put out of c.,** retirar del servicio; poner fuera de combate; estropear

commissionaire *n* portero, *m*

commissioned *a* comisionado. **c. officer,** oficial, *m*

commissioner *n* comisario, *m.* **High C.,** alto comisario, *m.* **c. for oaths,** notario, *m.* **c. of police,** jefe de policía, *m*

commit *vt* entregar (a); (a crime) cometer; (to prison) encarcelar; (for trial) remitir. **to c. oneself,** comprometerse. **to c. to memory,** aprender de memoria. **to c. to writing,** poner por escrito

commitment *n* (financial, etc.) obligación, responsabilidad, *f*; compromiso, *m*

committal *n* (of an offence) comisión, *f*; (placing, entrusting) entrega, *f*; (to prison) encarcelamiento, *m*; (legal procedure) auto de prisión, *m*

committee *n* comité, *m*; comisión, junta, *f*; consejo, *m.* **They decided in c.,** Tomaron la resolución en comité. **c. of management,** consejo de administración, *m*

commodious *a* espacioso, grande

commodiousness *n* espaciosidad, *f*

commodity *n* artículo, *m*, mercancía, *f*

commodore *n nav* jefe de escuadra, *m*; comodoro, *m*

common *a* común; general, corriente; universal; vulgar; (disparaging) cursi; (elementary) elemental. *n* pastos comunes, *m pl.* **He is not a c. man,** No es un hombre cualquiera; No es un hombre vulgar. **in c.,** en común. **the c. man,** el hombre medio. **the c. people,** el pueblo. **c. sense,** sentido común, *m.* **c. soldier,** soldado raso, *m.* **c. speech,** lenguaje vulgar, *m.* **c. usage,** uso corriente, *m*

commoner *n* plebeyo (-ya)

commonly *adv* comúnmente, por lo general

commonness *n* frecuencia, *f*; vulgaridad, *f*

commonplace *n* lugar común, *m*; trivialidad, *f. a* trivial

commons *n* el pueblo; (House of) Cámara de los Comunes, *f*; (food) provisiones, *f pl.* **to be on short c.,** comer mal, estar mal alimentado

Commonwealth *n* estado, *m*; república, *f*; comunidad (de naciones), *f*; mancomunidad, *f.* **the Commonwealth of Puerto Rico,** el Estado Libre Asociado de Puerto Rico, *m*

commotion *n* confusión, *f*; conmoción, perturbación, *f*; tumulto, *m*

communal *a* comunal

commune *n* comuna, *f*; comunión, *f. vi* conversar (con). **to c. with oneself,** hablar consigo

communicable *a* comunicable

communicant *n ecc* comulgante, *mf*; (of information) informante, *mf*

communicate *vt* comunicar; (diseases) transmitir. *vi* comunicarse (con); *ecc* comulgar

communication *n* comunicación, *f.* **lines of c.,** comunicaciones, *f pl.* **to get into c. with,** ponerse en comunicación con. **c.-cord,** (in a railway carriage) timbre de alarma, *m*

communicative *a* comunicativo; expansivo

communicativeness *n* carácter expansivo, *m*; locuacidad, *f*

communion *n* comunión, *f.* **Holy c.,** comunión, *f.* **to take c.,** comulgar. **c. card,** cédula de comunión, *f.* **c. cup,** cáliz, *f.* **c. table,** sagrada mesa, *f*; altar, *m*

communiqué *n* comunicación, parte, *f.* **to issue a c.,** dar parte

communism *n* comunismo, *m*

communist *n* comunista, *mf a* comunista

community *n* comunidad, *f.* **the c.,** la nación; el público. **c. center,** centro social, *m*

commutation *n* conmutación, *f*; reducción, *f*

commute *vt* conmutar; reducir

compact *n* (pact) acuerdo, pacto, *m*; (powder) polvorera, *f. a* compacto; firme; sólido; apretado, cerrado; (of persons) bien hecho; (of style) conciso, sucinto

compactness *n* compacidad, *f;* (of style) concisión, *f*

companion *n* compañero (-ra); camarada, *mf;* (of an Order) caballero, *m,* (or dama, *f). vt* acompañar. **lady c.,** señora de compañía, *f.* **c.-hatch,** cubierta de escotilla, *f.* **c.-ladder,** escala de toldilla, *f*

companionable *a* sociable, amistoso

companionably *adv* sociablemente, amistosamente

companionship *n* compañía, *f;* compañerismo, *m*

company *n* (*com mil* etc.) compañía, *f;* (ship's) tripulación, *f.* **I will keep you c.,** Te haré compañía. **to part c. with,** separarse de. **Present c. excepted!** ¡Mejorando lo presente! **They are not very good c.,** No son muy divertidos

company store *n* tienda de raya, *f* (Mexico)

comparable *a* comparable

comparably *adv* comparablemente

comparative *a* comparativo; relativo

comparatively *adv* comparativamente; relativamente

compare *vt* comparar. *vi* compararse; poder compararse. ser comparable. **beyond c.,** sin comparación; sin igual. **to c. favorably with,** no perder por comparación con. **to c. notes,** cambiar impresiones

comparison *n* comparación, *f.* **in c. with,** comparado con

compartment *n* compartimiento, *m; rw* departamento, *m*

compass *n* circuito, *m;* límites, *m pl;* alcance, *m;* (of a voice) gama, *f; naut* brújula, *f; pl* **compasses,** compás, *m. vt* (achieve) conseguir; (plan) idear, **mariner's c.,** compás de mar. *m,* rosa de los vientos, *f.* **pocket c.,** brújula de bolsillo, *f.* **to c. about,** cercar, rodear

compassion *n* compasión, *f.* **to have c. on,** apiadarse de, compadecerse de

compassionate *a* compasivo, piadoso. **c. leave,** permiso, *m*

compassionately *adv* compasivamente, con piedad

compatibility *n* compatibilidad, *f*

compatible *a* compatible, conciliable

compatriot *n* compatriota, *mf*

compel *vt* obligar (a), forzar (a); exigir; imponer. **His attitude compels respect,** Su actitud impone el respeto

compelling *a* compulsivo

compendious *a* compendioso, sucinto

compendium *n* compendio, *m;* resumen, *m*

compensate *vt* compensar; (reward) recompensar; (for loss, etc.) indemnizar. **to c. for,** compensar; indemnizar contra

compensation *n* compensación, *f;* (reward) recompensa, *f;* (for loss, etc.) indemnización, *f*

compensatory *a* compensatorio

compete *vi* competir (con); rivalizar; ser rivales; (in a competition) concurrir

competence *n* aptitud, *f;* capacidad, *f;* competencia, *f*

competent *a* competente; capaz

competently *adv* competentemente

competition *n* competencia, competición, rivalidad, *f;* emulación, *f;* (contest, etc.) concurso, *m.* **spirit of c.,** espíritu de competencia, *m*

competitive *a* competidor; de competición. **c. examination,** oposición, *f*

competitor *n* competidor (-ra)

compilation *n* compilación, *f*

compile *vt* compilar

compiler *n* compilador (-ra)

complacence *n* complacencia, satisfacción, *f;* contento de sí mismo, *m*

complacent *a* satisfecho; pagado de sí mismo

complacently *adv* con satisfacción

complain *vi* quejarse; lamentarse; *law* querellarse. **He complains about everything,** Se queja de todo

complainant *n law* demandante, *mf*

complaint *n* queja, *f;* lamento, *m; law* demanda, *f;* (ill-

ness) enfermedad, *f.* **to lodge a c. (against),** quejarse (de)

complaisance *n* afabilidad, cortesía, *f*

complaisant *a* complaciente, cortés, afable; (of husbands) consentido, sufrido

complement *n* complemento, *m;* total, número completo, *m. vt* completar

complementary *a* complementario

complete *a* entero; completo; perfecto; acabado. *vt* completar; acabar; (happiness, etc.) coronar, poner el último toque (a); (years) cumplir; (forms) llenar

completely *adv* completamente, enteramente

completeness *n* entereza, *f;* totalidad, *f*

completion *n* terminación, *f,* fin, *m*

complex *a* complejo. *n* complejo, *m.* **inferiority c.,** complejo de inferioridad, *m*

complexion *n* tez, *f,* cutis, *m; fig* carácter, *m*

complexity *n* complejidad, *f*

compliance *n* condescendencia, *f;* (subservience) sumisión, *f;* obediencia, *f.* **in c. with,** de acuerdo con, en conformidad con

compliant *a* condescendiente; sumiso, dócil; obediente

complicate *vt* complicar

complicated *a* complejo; complicado; enredado

complication *n* complicación, *f*

complicity *n* complicidad, *f.* **c. in a crime,** complicidad en un crimen

compliment *n* cumplido, *m,* cortesía, *f;* requiebro, *inf* piropo, *m;* favor, *m;* honor, *m;* (greeting) saludo, *m;* (congratulation) felicitación, *f. vt* cumplimentar; requebrar; (flatter) adular, lisonjear; (congratulate) felicitar. **They did him the c. of reading his book,** Le hicieron el honor de leer su libro. **to pay compliments,** hacer cumplidos; *inf* echar piropos

complimentary *a* lisonjero; galante. **c. ticket,** billete gratuito, *m*

comply *vi* (with) cumplir, obedecer; conformarse (con); consentir

component *a* componente. *n* componente, *m*

comport *vt* (oneself), comportarse

comportment *n* comportamiento, *m,* conducta, *f*

compose *vt* (all meanings) componer. **to c. oneself,** serenarse, calmarse. **to c. one's features,** componer el semblante

composed *a* sereno, tranquilo, sosegado

composer *n* compositor (-ra)

composite *a* compuesto; mixto. *n* compuesto, *m; bot* planta compuesta, *f*

composition *n* (all meanings) composición, *f*

compositor *n print* cajista, *mf*

composure *n* tranquilidad, serenidad, calma, *f;* sangre fría, *f,* aplomo, *m*

compote *n* compota, *f*

compound *vt* mezclar, componer; concertar. *a* compuesto. *n* compuesto, *m;* mixtura, *f.* **c. interest,** interés compuesto, *m*

comprehend *vt* comprender

comprehensible *a* comprensible

comprehensibly *adv* comprensiblemente

comprehension *n* comprensión, *f*

comprehensive *a* comprensivo

comprehensiveness *n* alcance, *m,* extensión, *f*

compress *vt* comprimir; condensar; reducir, abreviar. *n* compresa, *f*

compression *n* compresión, *f*

compressor *n* compresor, *m*

comprise *vt* comprender, abarcar, incluir

compromise *n* compromiso, *m,* transacción, *f;* componenda, *f. vt* (settle) componer, arreglar; (jeopardize) arriesgar; comprometer. *vi* transigir. **to c. oneself,** comprometerse

compromising *a* comprometedor

comptometer *n* calculador, *m*

compulsion *n* compulsión, fuerza, *f.* **under c.,** a la fuerza

compulsory *a* obligatorio. **c. measures,** medidas obligatorias, *f pl.* **c. powers,** poderes absolutos, *m pl*
compunction *n* compunción, *f,* remordimiento, *m;* escrúpulo, *m.* **without c.,** sin escrúpulo
computable *a* calculable
computation *n* computación, *f,* cómputo, *m*
compute *vt* computar, calcular.
computer *m* computador, *m* (Western Hemisphere), ordenador, *m* (Spain)
computer center *n* centro calculador, centro de computación, *m*
comrade *n* camarada, *mf* compañero (-ra)
comradeship *n* compañerismo, *m*
con *vt* estudiar; leer con atención; *naut* gobernar (el buque)
concatenation *n* concatenación, *f*
concave *a* cóncavo
conceal *vt* esconder, ocultar; (the truth, etc.) encubrir, callar; disimular
concealed *a* oculto; escondido; disimulado. **c. lighting,** iluminación indirecta, *f.* **c. turning,** (on a road) viraje oculto, *m*
concealment *n* ocultación, *f;* encubrimiento, *m;* (place of) escondite, *m;* secreto, *m*
concede *vt* conceder
conceit *n* presunción, vanidad, fatuidad, *f,* envanecimiento, *m.* **to have a good c. of oneself,** estar pagado de sí mismo
conceited *a* presumido, fatuo, vanidoso. **to become c.** *Lat. Am.* ensimismarse
conceivable *a* concebible, imaginable
conceivably *adv* posiblemente
conceive *vt* concebir; (affection, etc.) tomar; (an idea, etc.) formar; (plan) formular, idear. *vi* concebir; (understand) comprender; (suppose) imaginar, suponer
concentrate *vt* concentrar. *vi* concentrarse; (on, upon) dedicarse (a), entregarse (a); prestar atención (a), concentrar atención (en)
concentrated *a* concentrado
concentration *n* concentración, *f.* **c. camp,** campo de concentración, *m*
concentric *a* concéntrico
concept *n* concepto, *m*
conception *n* concepción, *f;* conocimiento, *m;* idea, *f,* concepto, *m.* **to have not the remotest c. of,** no tener la menor idea de
conceptualism *n* conceptualismo, *m*
concern *vt* tocar, tener que ver con, importar, concernir; interesar; referirse (a); tratar (de); (trouble) preocupar, inquietar; (take part in) ocuparse (de or con). *n* asunto, *m,* cosa, *f;* (share) interés, *m;* (anxiety) inquietud, *f;* solicitud, *f;* (business) casa comercial, firma, *f.* **as concerns . . . ,** en cuanto a . . . , respecto a . . . **It concerns the date of the next meeting,** Es cuestión de la fecha de la próxima reunión. **It is no c. of yours,** No tiene nada que ver contigo. **The book is concerned with the adventures of two boys,** El libro trata de las aventuras de dos muchachos
concerned *a* ocupado (en); afectado; (in a crime) implicado (en); (troubled) preocupado; inquieto, agitado
concerning *prep* tocante a, con respecto a, referente a, sobre
concert *n* acuerdo, concierto, *m,* armonía, *f; mus* concierto, *m, vt* concertar, acordar. **in c. with,** de acuerdo con. **c. hall,** sala de conciertos, *f*
concerted *a* concertado
concertina *n* concertina, *f*
concerto *n* concierto, *m*
concession *n* concesión, *f;* privilegio, *m*
concessionaire *n* concesionario, *m*
concierge *n* conserje, *m*
conciliate *vt* conciliar
conciliation *n* conciliación, *f*
conciliatory *a* conciliador
concise *a* conciso, breve, sucinto
concisely *adv* concisamente

concision *n* concisión, *f*
conclave *n* conciliábulo, *m;* (of cardinals) conclave, *m*
conclude *vt* concluir. *vi* concluirse
conclusion *n* conclusión, *f.* **in c.,** en conclusión, para terminar. **to come to the c. that . . . ,** concluir que . . .
conclusive *a* conclusivo, concluyente, decisivo
conclusively *adv* concluyentemente
conclusiveness *n* carácter decisivo, *m,* lo concluyente
concoct *vt* confeccionar; inventar
concoction *n* confección, *f;* mezcla, *f;* invención, *f;* (of a plot) maquinación, *f*
concomitant *a* concomitante. *n* concomitante, *m*
concord *n* concordia, buena inteligencia, armonía, *f;* (*mus gram*) concordancia, *f;* (of sounds) armonía, *f*
concordance *n* concordia, armonía, *f;* (book) concordancias, *f pl*
concordat *n* concordato, *m*
concourse *n* concurrencia, muchedumbre, *f*
concrete *a* concreto; de hormigón. *n* hormigón, *m. vt* concretar; cubrir de hormigón. **reinforced c.,** hormigón armado, *m*
concretion *n* concreción, *f*
concubine *n* concubina, manceba, *f*
concur *vi* coincidir, concurrir; estar de acuerdo, convenir (en)
concurrence *n* (agreement) acuerdo, consentimiento, *m,* aprobación, *f*
concurrent *a* concurrente; unánime; coincidente
concurrently *adv* concurrentemente
concussion *n* concusión, *f; med* concusión cerebral, *f*
condemn *vt* condenar; censurar, culpar; (forfeit) confiscar. **condemned cell,** celda de los condenados a muerte, *f*
condemnation *n* condenación, *f;* censura, *f*
condensation *n* condensación, *f*
condense *vt* condensar. *vi* condensarse
condenser *n* (*elec mech chem*) condensador, *m*
condescend *vi* dignarse; (in a bad sense) consentir (en); (with affability) condescender
condescending *a* condescendiente
condescendingly *adv* con condescendencia
condescension *n* condescendencia, *f;* afabilidad, *f*
condign *a* condigno
condiment *n* condimento, *m*
condition *n* condición, *f;* estado, *m; pl* **conditions,** condiciones, *f pl;* circunstancias, *f pl.* **on c. that,** con tal que; siempre que, dado que. **to be in no c. to,** no estar en condiciones de. **to change one's c.,** cambiar de estado. **to keep oneself in c.,** mantenerse en buena forma
conditional *a* condicional. **to be c. on,** depender de
conditionally *adv* condicionalmente
conditioned *a* acondicionado. **c. reflex,** reflejo acondicionado, *m*
condole *vi* condolerse (de); (on a bereavement) dar el pésame
condolence *n* condolencia, *f.* **to present one's condolences,** dar el pésame
condom *n* condón, *m, Argentina* forro, *m*
condone *vt* condonar, perdonar
conduce *vi* contribuir, conducir
conducive *a* que contribuye, conducente; favorable
conduct *n* conducta, *f. vt* conducir; guiar; *mus* dirigir; (oneself) portarse, conducirse; *phys* conducir. *vi mus* dirigir (una orquesta, etc.); *phys* ser conductor. **conducted tour,** excursión acompañada, *f;* viaje acompañado, *m*
conduction *n* conducción, *f*
conductive *a* conductivo
conductivity *n* conductibilidad, *f*
conductor *n* (guide) guía, *mf;* (of an orchestra) director, *m;* (on a tram, etc.) cobrador, *m; phys* conductor, *m*
conduit *n* conducto, *m;* cañería, *f;* canal, *m*
cone *n* (*bot geom* etc.) cono, *m*
confabulation *n* confabulación, *f*

confection *n* confección, *f*, *vt* confeccionar
confectioner *n* confitero (-ra); pastelero (-ra)
confectionery *n* confitería, pastelería, repostería, *f*
confederate *a* confederado; aliado. *n* confederado, *m*; (in crime) cómplice, *mf*. *vt* confederar. *vi* confederarse; aliarse
confederation *n* confederación, *f*
confer *vt* conceder, conferir; (an honor, etc.) otorgar, investir (con). *vi* consultar (con); deliberar, considerar
conference *n* conferencia, consulta, *f*; conversación, *f*
conferment *n* otorgamiento, *m*; concesión, *f*
confess *vt* confesar, reconocer; *inf* admitir; (of a priest) confesar; (of a penitent) confesarse. *vi* hacer una confesión; (one's sins) confesarse. **I c. that I was surprised,** No puedo negar que me sorprendió
confessed *a* confesado, declarado
confession *n* confesión, *f*; reconocimiento, *m*; declaración, *f*; religión, *f*; (creed) credo, *m*. **to go to c.,** confesarse. **to hear a c.,** confesar (a)
confessional *n* confesionario, *m*
confessor *n* confesor, *m*
confetti *n pl* confeti, papel picado *m*, serpentina, *f*
confidant *n* confidente, *m*
confidante *n* confidenta, *f*
confide *vi* confiar (a o en). *vt* confiar
confidence *n* confianza, *f*; seguridad, *f*; (revelation) confidencia, *f*. **in c.,** en confianza. **over-c.,** presunción, *f*. **to have c. in,** tener confianza en. **c. man,** caballero de industria, estafador, *m*. **c. trick,** timo, *m*
confident *a* confiado; seguro; (conceited) presumido
confidential *a* confidencial; de confianza. **c. clerk,** empleado (-da) de confianza. **c. letter,** carta confidencial, *f*
confidentially *adv* en confianza, confidencialmente
confidently *adv* confiadamente
confidingly *adv* con confianza
confiding *a* confiado
configuration *n* configuración, *f*
confine *vt* limitar; (imprison) encerrar. **confined space,** espacio limitado, *m*. **to be confined,** (of a woman) estar de parto, parir. **to be confined to one's room,** no poder dejar su cuarto. **to c. oneself to,** limitarse a
confinement *n* encierro, *m*, prisión, *f*; reclusión, *f*; (of a woman) parto, *m*. **to suffer solitary c.,** estar incomunicado
confines *n pl* límites, *m pl*; confines, *m pl*; fronteras, *f pl*
confirm *vt* confirmar; corroborar; *ecc* confirmar
confirmation *n* confirmación, *f*; (of a treaty) ratificación, *f*; *ecc* confirmación, *f*
confirmatory *a* confirmatorio
confirmed *a* inveterado
confiscate *vt* confiscar
confiscation *n* confiscación, *f*
conflagration *n* conflagración, *f*, incendio, *m*
conflict *n* conflicto, *m*; lucha, *f*. *vi* estar opuesto (a), estar en contradicción (con)
conflicting *a* opuesto; incompatible; (of evidence) contradictorio
confluence *n* confluencia, *f*
conform *vt* ajustar, conformar. *vi* ajustarse (a), amoldarse (a); conformarse (a); adaptarse (a)
conformation *n* conformación, *f*
conformity *n* conformidad, *f*. **in c. with,** en conformidad con, con arreglo a
confound *vt* confundir. **C. it!** ¡Demonio!
confounded *a* perplejo; *inf* maldito
confraternity *n* cofradía, hermandad, *f*
confront *vt* hacer frente (a), afrontar; salir al paso; confrontar
Confucianism *n* el confucianismo, *m*
confuse *vt* turbar, aturdir; confundir (con); (the issue) obscurecer; (disconcert) desconcertar, dejar confuso (a); dejar perplejo (a). **You have confused one thing with another,** Has confundido una cosa con otra. **My**

mind was confused, Mis ideas eran confusas; Tenía la cabeza trastornada
confused *a* confuso
confusing *a* turbador; desconcertante. **It is all very c.,** Todo ello es muy difícil de comprender
confusion *n* confusión, *f*. **covered with c.,** confuso, avergonzado. **to be in c.,** estar confuso; estar en desorden
confute *vt* (a person) confundir; (by evidence) refutar, confutar
congeal *vt* congelar; (blood) coagular. *vi* congelarse, helarse; coagularse
congealment *n* congelación, *f*; (of blood) coagulación, *f*
congenial *a* (of persons) simpático; propicio, favorable; agradable
congenital *a* congénito
congest *vt* atestar; amontonar; *med* congestionar
congested *a med* congestionado; (of places) atestado de gente; de mayor población; concurrido. **c. area,** área de mayor densidad de población, *f*
congestion *n med* congestión, *f*; densidad del tráfico, *f*; mayor densidad de población, *f*
conglomerate *a* conglomerado. *n* conglomerado, *m*
conglomeration *n* conglomeración, *f*
congratulate *vt* felicitar, dar la enhorabuena (a); congratular
congratulation *n* felicitación, enhorabuena, *f*; congratulación, *f*
congratulatory *a* de felicitación, congratulatorio
congregate *vi* congregarse, reunirse, juntarse
congregation *n* congregación, *f*; asamblea, reunión, *f*; (in a church) fieles, *m pl*; (parishioners) feligreses, *m pl*
congress *n* congreso, *m*. **C.-man,** miembro del Congreso, *m*
conical *a* cónico
conifer *n* conífera, *f*
coniferous *a* conífero
conjectural *a* conjetural
conjecture *n* conjetura, *f*, *vt* conjeturar
conjoint *a* asociado, conjunto
conjointly *adv* juntamente, en común
conjugal *a* conyugal
conjugate *vt* conjugar. *vi* conjugarse
conjugation *n* conjugación, *f*
conjunction *n* conjunción, *f*. **in c. with,** de acuerdo con
conjunctive *a* conjuntivo. *n* conjunción, *f*
conjunctivitis *n* conjuntivitis, *f*
conjure *vt* (implore) rogar, suplicar. *vi* (juggle) hacer juegos de manos. **a name to c. with,** un nombre todopoderoso. **to c. up,** (spirits) conjurar; *fig* evocar
conjurer, conjuror *n* (magician) nigromante, *m*; prestidigitador, *m*. **conjuror's wand,** varilla de virtudes, *f*
conjuring *n* prestidigitación, *f*, juegos de manos, *m pl*. **c. trick,** juego de manos, *m*. **c. up,** evocación, *f*
connect *vt* juntar, unir; (relate) relacionar; asociar; (*elec* and *mech*) conectar. *vi* juntarse, unirse; relacionarse; asociarse; (of events) encadenarse; (of trains) enlazar. **This train connects with the Madrid express,** Este tren enlaza con el expreso de Madrid. **They are connected with the Borgia family,** Están emparentados con los Borgia, Son parientes de los Borgia
connected *a* conexo; (coherent) coherente; relacionado; asociado; (in a crime) implicado; (by marriage, etc.) emparentado
connectedly *adv* coherentemente
connecting *a* que une; (*mech* and *elec*) conectivo; (of doors, etc.) comunicante. **c.-link,** *mech* varilla de conexión, *f*; *fig* lazo, *m*. **c.-rod,** biela, *f*
connection, connexion *n* conexión, *f*; unión, *f*; (of ideas) relación, *f*; (junction) empalme, *m*; (of trains, boats) enlace, *m*; (intimacy) intimidad, *f*; (relative) pariente, *m*; (of a firm, etc.) clientela, *f*; *elec* conexión, *f*. **in**

   c. with, con referencia a; en asociación con. **in this c.,** respecto a esto

conning tower *n* torre de mando, *f*

connivance *n* consentimiento, *m*; complicidad, *f*

connive (at) *vi* hacer la vista gorda, ser cómplice (en)

connotation *n* connotación, *f*

connote *vt* connotar

connubial *a* conyugal

conquer *vt* conquistar; vencer. *vi* triunfar

conquering *a* conquistador, vencedor; triunfante, victorioso

conqueror *n* conquistador, *m*; vencedor, *m*

conquest *n* conquista, *f*. **to make a c. of,** conquistar

consanguineous *a* consanguíneo

consanguinity *n* consanguinidad, *f*

conscience *n* conciencia, *f*. **in all c.,** en verdad. **with a clear c.,** con la conciencia limpia. **c.-stricken,** lleno de remordimientos

conscienceless *a* desalmado, falto de conciencia

conscientious *a* concienzudo; diligente. **c. objector,** objetor de conciencia, *m*

conscientiously *adv* concienzudamente

conscientiousness *n* conciencia, diligencia, *f*; rectitud, *f*

conscious *a* consciente. *n psy* consciente, *m*. **to become c.,** (after unconsciousness) volver en sí. **to become c. of,** darse cuenta de

consciously *adv* conscientemente, a sabiendas

consciousness *n* conciencia, *f*; conocimiento, sentido, *m*. **to lose c.,** perder el conocimiento, perder el sentido. **to recover c.,** recobrar el sentido, volver en sí

conscript *n* conscripto, *m*, *a* conscripto. *vt* reclutar

conscription *n* conscripción, *f*

consecrate *vt* consagrar; bendecir

consecration *n* consagración, *f*; dedicación, *f*

consecutive *a* consecutivo

consecutively *adv* consecutivamente

consensus *n* consenso, *m*, unanimidad, *f*. **c. of opinion,** opinión general, *f*

consent *vi* consentir. *n* consentimiento, *m*; permiso, *m*, aquiescencia, *f*. **by common c.,** de común acuerdo

consequence *n* consecuencia, *f*; resultado, *m*; importancia, *f*, **in c.,** por consiguiente. **in c. of,** de resultas de. **of no c.,** sin importancia

consequences *n* (game) cartas rusas, *f pl*

consequent *a* consecuente, consiguiente

consequential *a* consecuente; (of persons) fatuo, engreído

consequently *adv* por consiguiente, en consecuencia

conservation *n* conservación, *f*. **c. of energy,** conservación de energía, *f*

conservatism *n* conservadurismo, *m*

conservative *a* preservativo; conservador. *n* conservador (-ra), *m*. **c. party,** partido conservador, *m*

conservatoire *n* conservatorio de música, *m*

conservatory *n* invernáculo, invernadero, *m*

conserve *vt* conservar

consider *vt* considerar, pensar meditar; tomar en cuenta; examinar; (deem) juzgar; (believe) creer, estar convencido de (que); (of persons) considerar. **all things considered,** considerando todos los puntos, después de considerarlo todo

considerable *a* considerable

considerably *adv* considerablemente

considerate *a* considerado, solícito

considerately *adv* con consideración, solícitamente

consideration *n* consideración, *f*; reflexión, deliberación, *f*; remuneración, *f*. **out of c. for,** en consideración de; por consideración a. **to take into c.,** tomar en cuenta, tomar en consideración

considered *a* considerado

considering *prep* en consideración de, considerando, en vista de

consign *vt* consignar; *fig* enviar. **to c. to oblivion,** sepultar en el olvido

consignee *n* consignatorio, *m*

consignment *n* consignación, *f*; envío, *m*

consignor *n* consignador, *m*

consist *vi* consistir (en); ser compatible (con). **to c. of,** componerse de, consistir de

consistence, consistency *n* consistencia, *f*; compatibilidad, *f*; lógica, *f*; (of persons) consecuencia, *f*

consistent *a* compatible; lógico; (of persons) consecuente

consistently *adv* conformemente (a); consecuentemente

consolation *n* consuelo, *m*, consolación, *f*

console *vt* consolar; confortar. *n arch* cartela, *f*. **c. table,** consola, *f*

consolidate *vt* consolidar. *vi* consolidarse

consolidation *n* consolidación, *f*

consoling *a* consolador; confortador

consols *n pl* (títulos) consolidados, *m pl*

consonance *n* consonancia, *f*

consonant *a* consonante

consort *n* consorte, *mf*. **to c. with,** frecuentar la compañía de; ir con; acompañar (a). **prince c.,** príncipe consorte, *m*

conspicuous *a* conspicuo; prominente; notable. **to be c.,** destacarse; llamar la atención. **to make oneself c.,** ponerse en evidencia, llamar la atención

conspicuously *adv* visiblemente; muy en evidencia

conspiracy *n* conspiración, *f*; complot, *m*

conspirator *n* conspirador (-ra)

conspire *vi* conspirar

constable *n* agente de policía, *m*; (historical) condestable, *m*. **chief c.,** jefe de policía, *m*

constabulary *n* policía, *f*

constancy *n* constancia, *f*

constant *a* constante; incesante. *n* constante, *m*

Constantinople Constantinopla, *f*

constantly *adv* constantemente

constellation *n* constelación, *f*

consternation *n* consternación, *f*; espanto, terror, *m*

constipate *vt* estreñir

constipation *n* estreñimiento, *m*, constipación de vientre, *f*

constituency *n* distrito electoral, *m*

constituent *a* constituyente. *n* constituyente, *m*; componente, *m*; elector (-ra)

constitute *vt* constituir; nombrar; autorizar

constitution *n* constitución, *f*

constitutional *a* constitucional

constitutionally *adv* constitucionalmente

constrain *vt* obligar, forzar. **I felt constrained to help them,** Me sentí obligado a ayudarles

constrained *a* (of smiles, etc.) forzado; (of silences) violento; (of persons) avergonzado

constraint *n* fuerza, compulsión, *f*; (of atmosphere) tensión, *f*; (reserve) reserva, *f*; vergüenza, *f*

constrict *vt* apretar, estrechar

constriction *n* constricción, *f*

construct *vt* edificar; construir

construction *n* construcción, *f*; interpretación, *f*. **to put a wrong c. on,** interpretar mal

constructional *a* construccional

constructive *a* constructor

constructor *n* constructor, *m*

construe *vt* construir; (translate) traducir; *fig* interpretar

consul *n* cónsul, *m*

consular *a* consular

consular fees *n pl* derechos consulares, *m pl*

consulate *n* consulado, *m*. **c. general,** consulado general, *m*

consult *vt* consultar. *vi* consultar (con), aconsejarse (con)

consultant *n* (*med* and other uses) especialista, *m*

consultation *n* consulta, *f*

consultative *a* consultativo

consulting a consultor. **c. hours,** horas de consulta, f pl. **c. rooms,** consultorio, m

consume vt consumir; (eat) comerse, tragarse. vi consumirse. **to be consumed by envy,** estar consumido por la envidia. **to be consumed by thirst,** estar muerto de sed

consumer n consumidor (-ra)

consummate a consumido, perfecto. vt consumar

consummation n consumación, f

consumption n consumo, m; gasto, m; med tuberculosis, f. **fuel c.,** consumo de combustible, m

consumptive a destructivo; med tísico, hético. n tísico (-ca)

contact n contacto, m, vt ponerse en contacto con. **to be in c. with,** estar en contacto con

contagion n contagio, m

contagious a contagioso

contain vt contener; incluir; geom encerrar; (arithmetic) ser divisible por; (oneself) dominarse. **I could not c. myself,** No pude dominarme

container n recipiente, m; envase, m; (box) caja, f

contaminate vt contaminar; corromper

contamination n contaminación, f

contemplate vt contemplar; meditar, considerar; (plan) tener intención de, pensar, proponerse

contemplation n contemplación, f; meditación, f; expectación, esperanza, f; (plan) proyecto, m. **to have something in c.,** proyectar algo

contemplative a contemplativo

contemplatively adv contemplativamente; atentamente

contemporaneous a contemporáneo

contemporary a contemporáneo; (of persons) coetáneo; (of events, etc.) actual. n contemporáneo (-ea)

contempt n desprecio, menosprecio, m; desdén, m. **c. of court,** falta de respeto a la sala, f

contempt of court n rebeldía a la corte, f

contempt of law n rebeldía a la ley, f

contemptible a menospreciable, despreciable; vil

contemptibly adv vilmente

contemptuous a desdeñoso; despectivo; de desprecio. **to be c. of,** desdeñar; menospreciar, tener en poco (a)

contemptuously adv con desprecio, desdeñosamente

contend vi contender; (affirm) sostener, mantener. **He contended that . . . ,** Sostuvo que . . . ; **contending party,** law parte litigante, f

content n contenido, m; capacidad, f; (emotion) contento, m; satisfacción, f. a contento; satisfecho (de). vt contentar; satisfacer. **to one's heart's c.,** a pedir de boca; a gusto de uno; cuanto quisiera

contented a satisfecho, contento

contentedly adv con satisfacción, contentamente

contention n disputa, controversia, discusión, f; argumento, m, opinión, f

contentious a contencioso

contentment n contentamiento, m; contento, m

contest vt disputar; (a suit) defender; (a match, an election, etc.) disputar. n disputa, f; combate, m, lucha, f; (competition) concurso, m

contestant n contendiente, mf

context n contexto, m

contiguity n contigüidad, f

contiguous a contiguo, lindero, adyacente

continence n continencia, f

continent a continente. n continente, m

continental a continental

continental shelf n plataforma continental, f

contingency n contingencia, f

contingent a contingente. n mil contingente, m. **to be c. on,** (of events) depender de

continual a continuo

continually adv continuamente

continuance n continuación, f

continuation n continuación, f; prolongación, f

continue vi continuar; seguir; prolongarse; durar. vt

continuar; seguir; proseguir; perpetuar; (in an office) retener. **to be continued,** se continuará, continuará, seguirá

continuer n continuador (-ra)

continuity n continuidad, f

continuous a continuo. **c. performance,** sesión continua, f

continuously adv de continuo, continuamente

contort vt retorcer

contortion n contorsión, f

contortionist n contorsionista, m

contour n contorno, m; curva de nivel, f. **c. map,** mapa con curvas de nivel, m

contraband n contrabando, m

contrabandist n contrabandista, mf

contrabass n contrabajo, m

contraception n anticoncepción, f

contraceptive a anticonceptivo, m

contract n pacto, m; (com and law) contrato, m; (betrothal) esponsales, m pl; (marriage) capitulaciones, f pl; (cards) "Bridge," m. vt contraer; (acquire) adquirir, contraer; (a marriage, etc.) contraer; (be betrothed to) desposarse con; (by formal contract) contratar; pactar. vi (shrink) contraerse, encogerse; comprometerse por contrato. **breach of c.,** no cumplimiento de contrato, m. **c. party,** (of matrimony) contrayente, mf

contractile a contráctil

contraction n contracción, f (act or process); forma contracta, f (like isn't or can't)

contractor n contratista, mf

contradict vt contradecir; desmentir

contradiction n contradicción, f; negación, f

contradictory a contradictorio; opuesto (a), contrario (a)

contralto n (voice) contralto, m; (woman) contralto, f

contraption n inf artefacto, m

contrapuntal a mus de contrapunto

contrariness n inf testarudez, terquedad, f

contrariwise adv al contrario; al revés

contrary a contrario; opuesto (a); desfavorable, poco propicio; (of persons) difícil, terco. n contraria, f; (logic) contrario, m, adv en contra, contrariamente. **on the c.,** al contrario. **to be c.,** (of persons) llevar la contraria

contrast n contraste, m. vt contrastar (con). vi contrastar (con), hacer contraste (con)

contravene vt contravenir; atacar, oponerse (a)

contravention n contravención, f

contribute vt contribuir; (an article) escribir

contribution n contribución, f; (to a review, etc.) artículo, m

contributor n contribuyente, mf; (to a journal) colaborador (-ra)

contributory a contribuyente

contrite a penitente, arrepentido, contrito

contritely adv contritamente

contrition n contrición, penitencia, f, arrepentimiento, m

contrivance n invención, f; (scheme) treta, idea, estratagema, f; (machine) aparato, mecanismo, artefacto, m

contrive vt inventar; idear, proyectar. vi (succeed in) lograr, conseguir; (manage) arreglárselas

control n autoridad, f; dominio, m; gobierno, m; dirección, f; regulación, f; (restraint) freno, m; (biol and spirit) control, m; (of a vehicle) conducción, f; manejo, m, manipulación, f; pl **controls,** mech mando, m. vt dirigir, regir; regular; usar, manejar, manipular; controlar; (dominate) dominar; (curb) refrenar, reprimir; (command) mandar. **He lost c. of the car,** Perdió el mando (or control) del automóvil. **out of c.,** fuera de mando, fuera de control. **remote c.,** mando a distancia, m. **to c. oneself,** dominarse, contenerse. **to lose c. of oneself,** no lograr dominarse, perder el control. **c. stick,** aer palanca de mando, f. **c. tower,** aer torre de mando, f

controller *n* interventor, *m*; (device) regulador, *m*

controlling *n* See **control.** *a* regulador

controversial *a* debatible, discutible

controversy *n* controversia, *f*; argumento, *m*; altercación, disputa, *f*

contumacious *a* contumaz

contumacy *n* contumacia, *f*

contumely *n* contumelia, *f*

contusion *n* herida contusa, *f*

conundrum *n* acertijo, rompecabezas, *m*; problema, *m*

convalesce *vi* convalecer, estar convaleciente

convalescence *n* convalecencia, *f*

convalescent *a* convaleciente. *n* convaleciente, *mf*. **c. home,** casa de convalecencia, *f*

convene *vt* (a meeting) convocar; (person) citar. *vi* reunirse

convenience *n* conveniencia, *f*; (comfort) comodidad, *f*; utilidad, *f*; (advantage) ventaja, *f*; (public) retretes, *m pl.* **at one's c.,** cuando le sea conveniente a uno. **to make a c. of,** abusar de. **with all modern conveniences,** con todo el confort moderno

convenient *a* conveniente; apropiado; cómodo. **I shall make it c. to see him at 6 p.m.,** Arreglaré mis asuntos para verle a las seis

conveniently *adv* cómodamente; oportunamente; sin inconveniente

convent *n* convento, *m*

convention *n* convención, *f*

conventional *a* convencional

conventual *a* conventual. *n* conventual, *m*

converge *vi* convergir

convergence *n* convergencia, *f*

convergent *a* convergente

conversance *n* familiaridad, *f*, conocimiento, *m*

conversant *a* familiar, versado, conocedor. **c. with,** versado en

conversation *n* conversación, *f*. **to engage in c. with,** entablar conversación con

conversational *a* de conversación; (talkative) locuaz

conversationally *adv* en tono familiar; familiarmente; en conversación

converse *vi* conversar. **to c. by signs,** hablar por señas

conversely *adv* recíprocamente

conversion *n* conversión, *f*

convert *vt* convertir; transformar. *n* converso (-sa). **to become a c.,** convertirse

convertible *a* convertible; transformable

convex *a* convexo

convey *vt* transportar; conducir, llevar; (a meaning, etc.) comunicar, dar a entender; expresar; *law* traspasar

conveyance *n* transporte, *m*; conducción, *f*; medio de transporte, *m*; vehículo, *m*; carruaje, *m*; (of property) traspaso, *m*; (document) escritura de traspaso, *f*. **public c.,** coche de alquiler, *m*; ómnibus, *m*

convict *n* convicto, *m*; presidiario, *m*. *vt law* condenar; culpar. **c. settlement,** colonia penal, *f*

conviction *n* (of a prisoner) condenación, *f*; (belief) convencimiento, *m*, convicción, *f*

convince *vt* convencer

convincing *a* convincente

convivial *a* convivial

conviviality *n* jovialidad, *f*

convocation *n* convocación, *f*

convoke *vt* convocar

convolution *n* circunvolución, *f*; espira, *f*

convoy *vt* convoyar, escoltar. *n* convoy, *m*. **to sail in a c.,** navegar en convoy

convulse *vt* agitar; sacudir; estremecer. **to be convulsed with laughter,** desternillarse de risa, morirse de risa

convulsion *n* convulsión, *f*; conmoción, *f*

convulsive *a* convulsivo

coo *vi* arrullar; (of infants) gorjearse. *n* arrullo, *m*

cooing *n* arrullo, *m*

cook *n* cocinero (-ra). *vt* guisar, cocer, cocinar; (falsify) falsear

cooker *n* cocina, *f*. **gas c.,** cocina de gas, *f*

cookery *n* cocina, *f*. **c.-book,** libro de cocina, *m*

cooking *n* arte de guisar, *m*, or *f*; cocina, *f*; (of accounts, etc.) falsificación, *f*. **c. range,** cocina económica, *f*. **c.-stove,** cocina, *f*. **c. utensils,** batería de cocina, *f*

cool *a* fresco; bastante frío; (not ardent and of receptions, etc.) frío; (calm) sereno, imperturbable. *n* fresco, *m*. *vi* enfriarse; (of love, etc.) resfriarse; (of the weather) refrescar; (of persons) refrescarse. *vt* refrescar; enfriar. **to grow cooler,** (of weather) refrescarse; (of persons) tener menos calor. **It is c.,** Hace fresco. **to be as c. as a cucumber,** tener sangre fría. **c. drink,** bebida fría, *f*. **c.-headed,** sereno, imperturbable

coolie *n* culí, *m*

cooling *n* enfriamiento, *m*, a refrescante

coolly *adv* frescamente; fríamente, con frialdad; imperturbablemente; (impudently) descaradamente

coolness *n* frescura, *f*; (of a welcome, etc.) frialdad, *f*; (sangfroid) sangre fría, serenidad, *f*; aplomo, *m*

coop *n* gallinero, *m*; caponera, *f*, *vt* enjaular; encerrar. **to keep** (someone) **cooped up,** tener encerrado (a)

cooper *n* tonelero, barrilero, *m*, *vt* hacer barriles

cooperate *vi* cooperar; colaborar

cooperation *n* cooperación, *f*

cooperative *a* cooperativo. **c. society,** cooperativa, *f*

coopt *vt* elegir por votación

coordinate *vt* coordinar. *n math* coordenada, *f*. *a* coordenado

coordination *n* coordinación, *f*

coot *n* fúlica, *f*

cop *n* (police officer) polizonte, *mf, Ecuador,* chapa, *Mexico* cuico (-ca)

copartner *n* copartícipe, *mf*; socio (-ia)

cope *n ecc* capa, *f*; (of heaven) dosel, *m*, bóveda, *f*. **to c. with,** contender con; (a difficulty) hacer cara a, arrostrar

copeck *n* copec, *m*

Copenhagen Copenhague, *m*

copier *n* copiador (-ra)

coping *n arch* albardilla, *f*. **c.-stone,** teja cumbrera, *f*; *fig* coronamiento, *m*

copious *a* copioso, abundante

copiously *adv* en abundancia

copiousness *n* abundancia, *f*

copper *n* cobre, *m*; (coin) calderilla, *f*; (vessel) caldera, *f*. *a* de cobre. **c.-colored,** cobrizo. **c.-smith,** calderero, *m*. **c.-sulphate,** sulfato de cobre, *m*

copperplate *n* lámina de cobre, *f*; grabado en cobre, *m*

coppery *a* cobrizo

coppice *n* soto, bosquecillo, *m*. **c. with standards,** monte medio, *m*

coproprietor *n* copropietario, *m*

copse *n* arboleda, *f*, bosquecillo, *m*

copulate *vi* copularse

copulation *n* cópula, *f*

copy *n* copia, *f*; (of a book) ejemplar, *m*; (of a paper) número, *m*; manuscrito, *m*; (subject-matter) material, *m*. *vt* copiar; imitar; tomar como modelo (a). **rough c.,** borrador, *m*. **c.-book,** cuaderno de escritura, *m*

copy editor *n* redactor de textos, *m*

copying *n* imitación, *f*; transcripción, *f*. **c. ink,** tinta de copiar, *f*

copyist *n* copiador (-ra); (plagiarist) copiante, *mf*

copyright *n* derechos de autor, *m pl*; propiedad literaria, *f*. *a* protegido por los derechos de autor. *vt* registrar como propiedad literaria. **C. reserved,** Derechos reservados, Queda hecho el depósito que marca la ley

copywriter *n* escritor de anuncios, *m*

coquet *vi* coquetear; *fig* jugar (con)

coquetry *n* coquetería, *f*

coquette *n* coqueta, *f*

coquettish *a* coquetón; atractivo

coral *n* coral, *m*; (polyp) coralina, *f*. *a* de coral, coralino.

white **c.,** madrépora, *f.* **c. beads,** corales, *m pl.* **c.-island,** atalón, *m.* **c.-reef,** escollo de coral, *m.* **c. snake,** coral, *f*

corbel *n arch* ménsula, *f*

cord *n* cuerda, *f;* cordel, *m;* cordón, *m. vt* encordelar. **spinal c.,** médula espinal, *f.* **umbilical c.,** cordón umbilical, *m*

cordial *a* cordial; sincero, fervoroso. *n* cordial, *m*

cordiality *n* cordialidad, *f*

cordon *n* cordón, *m;* cinto, *m.* **to c. off,** acordonar

Cordova Córdoba, *f*

cordovan *a* cordobés. *n* (leather) cordobán, *m*

corduroy *n* pana de cordoncillo, *f*

core *n* (of a fruit) corazón, *m;* (of a rope) alma, *f,* centro, *m;* (of an abscess) foco, *m;* (of a corn) ojo, *m; fig* núcleo, *m;* esencia, *f;* lo esencial

coreligionist *n* correligionario (-ia)

corespondent *n* cómplice en un caso de divorcio, *mf*

Corinth Corinto, *m*

Corinthian *a* corintio. *n* corintio (-ia)

cork *n* corcho, *m;* (of a bottle) tapón, *m, a* de corcho. *vt* tapar con corcho, taponar; (wine) encorchar; (the face) tiznar con corcho quemado. **pop of a c.,** taponazo, *m.* **to draw a c.,** descorchar. **c.-jacket,** chaleco salvavidas, *m.* **c. tree,** alcornoque, *m*

corkscrew *n* sacacorchos, *m*

cormorant *n* cormorán, *m*

corn *n* grano, cereal, *m;* (wheat) trigo, *m;* (maize) maíz, *m;* (single seed) grano, *m;* (on the foot, etc.) callo, *m.* **Indian c.,** maíz, *m.* **c. cure,** callicida, *m.* **c.-exchange,** bolsa de granos, *f.* **c.-field,** campo de trigo, *m.* **c.-flower,** aciano, *m.* **c. liquor** *Lat. Am.* chicha *f*

cornea *n* córnea, *f*

corner *n* ángulo, *m;* (of a street or building) esquina, *f;* (of a room) rincón, *Mexico* ancón *m; aut* viraje, *m; com* monopolio, *m;* (of the eye) rabo, *m;* (Assoc. football) "corner," *m. vt* arrinconar; acorralar; *com* acaparar. **the four corners of the earth,** las cinco partes del mundo. **a tight c.,** un lance apretado, un apuro. **to drive into a c.,** *fig* poner entre la espada y la pared. **to look out of the c. of the eye,** mirar de reojo. **to turn the c.,** doblar la esquina; *fig* pasar la crisis. **c.-cupboard,** rinconera, *f.* **c. seat,** asiento del rincón, *m.* **c. shop** *Lat. Am.* esquina *f* **c.-stone,** piedra angular, *f.*

cornered *a* (of a person) acorralado, en aprieto; (of hats) de . . . picos. **three-c. hat,** sombrero de tres picos, *m*

cornet *n* (musical instrument) corneta, *f; mil* corneta, *m;* (paper) cucurucho, *m.* **c. player,** cornetín, *m*

cornflour *n* harina de maíz, *f*

cornice *n* cornisa, *f*

Cornish *a* de Cornualles

cornucopia *n* cornucopia, *f*

corollary *n* corolario, *m*

corona *n* (*ast arch*) corona, *f*

coronation *n* coronación, *f*

coroner *n* juez de guardia, *mf,* médico forense, *m*

coronet *n* (of a peer, etc.) corona, *f;* tiara, *f;* guirnalda, *f*

corporal *a* corporal, *n mil* cabo, *m;* (altar-cloth) corporal, *m.* **c. punishment,** castigo corporal, *m*

corporate *a* corporativo

corporation *n* corporación, *f;* concejo, cabildo municipal, *m;* (*com* U.S.A.) sociedad anónima, *f*

corporeal *a* corpóreo

corps *n* cuerpo, *m*

corpse *n* cadáver, *m*

corpulence *n* gordura, obesidad, *f*

corpulent *a* corpulento, grueso, gordo

corpus *n* cuerpo, *m.* **C. Christi,** Corpus, *m.* **c. delicti,** cuerpo del delito, *m*

corpuscle *n* corpúsculo, *m*

correct *a* correcto; exacto, justo. *vt* corregir; rectificar; amonestar, reprender

correction *n* corrección, *f;* rectificación, *f*

corrective *a* correctivo. *n* correctivo, *m*

correctness *n* corrección, *f;* exactitud, *f;* justicia, *f*

correlate *vt* poner en correlación. *vi* tener correlación

correlation *n* correlación, *f*

correspond *vi* corresponder (a); (by letter) escribirse, corresponderse

correspondence *n* correspondencia, *f; com* correo, *m.* **c. course,** curso por correspondencia, *m*

correspondent *n* correspondiente, *mf;* (*com* and journalist) corresponsal, *mf.* **special c.,** corresponsal extraordinario, *m*

corresponding *a* correspondiente. **c. member,** miembro correspondiente, *m*

corridor *n* corredor, pasillo, *m;* (railway) pasillo, *m; pol* corredor, *m.* **c. train,** tren con coches corridos, *m*

corroborate *vt* corroborar, confirmar

corroboration *n* corroboración, confirmación, *f*

corroborative *a* corroborativo, confirmatorio

corrode *vt* corroer, morder; *fig* roer

corrosion *n* corrosión, *f*

corrosive *a* corrosivo; mordaz

corrugate *vt* arrugar. *vi* arrugarse

corrugated *a* arrugado; ondulado. **c. iron,** chapa canaleta, *f*

corrugation *n* corrugación, *f,* arrugamiento, *m*

corrupt *a* corrompido; vicioso, desmoralizado. *vt* corromper. *vi* corromperse

corrupter *n* corruptor (-ra)

corruption *n* corrupción, *f*

corsage *n* corpiño, *m*

corset *n* corsé, *m, vt* encorsetar. **c. shop,** corsetería, *f*

Corsica Córcega, *f*

Corsican *a* corso. *n* corso (-sa)

cortege *n* séquito, acompañamiento, *m;* desfile, *m*

cortex *n bot anat* corteza, *f*

cortisone *n* (drug) cortisona, *f*

Corunna La Coruña, *f*

coruscation *n* brillo, *m*

corvette *n* corbeta, *f*

cosignatory *n* cosignatario (-ia)

cosine *n* coseno, *m*

cosiness *n* comodidad, *f*

cosmetic *a* cosmético. *n* afeite, cosmético, *m*

cosmic *a* cósmico

cosmographer *n* cosmógrafo, *m*

cosmography *n* cosmografía, *f*

cosmopolitan *a* cosmopolita. *n* cosmopolita, *mf*

cosmopolitanism *n* cosmopolitismo, *m*

cosmos *n* cosmos, universo, *m*

Cossack *a* cosaco. *n* cosaco (-ca)

cosset *vt* mimar, consentir

cost *vi* costar. *n* costa, *f,* coste, precio, *m; fig* costa, *f; pl* **costs,** *law* costas, *f pl.* **at all costs,** cueste lo que cueste, a toda costa. **to my c.,** a mi costa, *f.* **c. of living,** coste de la vida, *m.* **to c. a fortune,** costar un sentido

Costa-Rican *a* costarriqueño. *n* costarriqueño (-ña)

coster *n* vendedor (-ra) ambulante

costliness *n* alto precio, *m;* suntuosidad, *f*

costly *a* costoso; suntuoso, magnífico

costume *n* traje, *m;* (fancy-dress) disfraz, *m;* (tailored) traje sastre, *m;* "Costume," (among credits in films and plays) «Vestuario»

costumier *n* modista, *mf;* sastre, *m*

cot *n* (hut) choza, cabaña, *f;* (child's) camita, *f*

coterie *n* círculo, grupo, *m;* (clique) camarilla, *f*

cotillion *n* cotillón, *m*

cottage *n* cabaña, choza, *f;* casita, *f,* hotelito, *m;* torre, villa, *f* **c. cheese** *Mexico* asadero *m*

cotter *n* chaveta, llave, *f*

cotton *n* algodón, *m, a* de algodón. **I don't c. to the idea at all,** No me gusta nada la idea; La idea no me seduce. **sewing-c.,** hilo de coser, *m.* **c. goods,** géneros de algodón, *m pl.* **c. mill,** hilandería de algodón, algodonería, *f.* **c. plantation,** algodonal, *m.* **c.-seed oil,** aceite de semilla de algodón, *m.* **c.-spinner,** hilandero

(-ra) de algodón. **c.-wool,** algodón en rama, *m.*
c.-yarn, hilo de algodón, *m*

cottony *a* algodonoso

couch *n* sofá, canapé, *m;* (bed) lecho, *m;* (lair) cama, *f. vt* (lay down) acostar, echar; (a lance) enristrar; (express) expresar, redactar. *vi* acostarse; (crouch) agacharse; estar en acecho

cough *vi* toser. *n* tos, *f.* **to c. up,** escupir, expectorar. **c.-drop,** pastilla para la tos, *f*

coughing *n* tos, *f*

could. See **can**

council *n* consejo, *m;* junta, *f; ecc* concilio, *m.* **Privy C.,** consejo privado, *m.* **C. of the Realm,** Concejo del Reino, *m.* **to hold c.,** celebrar un consejo; aconsejarse (con); consultarse. **town c.,** ayuntamiento, *m.* **c. chamber,** sala consistorial, *f;* sala de actos, *f.* **c. houses,** casas baratas, *f pl.* **c. of war,** consejo de guerra, *m*

councilor *n* concejal, *m;* miembro de la junta, *m*

counsel *n* consultación, *f;* deliberación, *f;* consejo, *m; law* abogado, *m. vt* aconsejar. **a c. of perfection,** un ideal imposible. **to keep one's own c.,** no decir nada, callarse, guardar silencio. **to take c. with,** consultar (a), aconsejarse con

counselor *n* consejero, *m.* **c. of state,** consejero de estado, *m*

count *vt* contar; calcular; (consider) creer, considerar. *vi* contar. *n* cuenta, *f;* (of votes) escrutinio, *m; law* capítulo, *m.* **John simply doesn't c.,** Juan no cuenta para nada. **Erudition alone counts for very little,** La mera erudición sirve para muy poco. **to keep c. of,** tener cuenta de. **to lose c. of,** perder cuenta de. **to c. on,** contar con; (doing something) esperar. **to c. up,** contar

count *n* (title) conde, *m*

countenance *n* semblante, *m;* expresión de la cara, *f;* aspecto, *m;* (favor) apoyo, *m,* ayuda, *f. vt* autorizar, aprobar; apoyar, ayudar. **to put (a person) out of c.,** desconcertar (a)

counter *n* (in a bank) contador, *m;* (in a shop) mostrador, *m;* (in games) ficha, *f, adv* contra, al contrario; al revés. *a* opuesto (a), contrario (a). *vt* parar; contestar. **to run c. to my inclinations,** oponerse a mis deseos. **to c. with the left,** (boxing) contestar con la izquierda. **c.-attack,** contraataque, *m.* **c.-attraction,** atracción contraria, *f.* **c.-offensive,** contraofensiva, *f.* **c.-reformation,** contrarreforma, *f.* **c.-revolution,** contrarrevolución, *f*

counteract *vt* neutralizar; frustrar

counterbalance *n* contrapeso, *m, vt* contrabalancear; compensar, igualar

counterblast *n* denunciación, *f;* respuesta, *f*

countercharge *n* recriminación, *f. vt* recriminar; *law* reconvenir

counterfeit *a* falso, espurio; fingido. *n* falsificación, *f;* imitación, *f;* moneda falsa, *f;* (person) impostor (-ra). *vt* imitar; (pretend) fingir; (coins, handwriting, etc.) falsificar

counterfeiter *n* falsario (-ia)

counterfoil *n* talón, *m*

countermand *vt* contramandar; (an order) revocar, cancelar. *n* contraorden, *f;* revocación, *f*

countermarch *n* contramarcha, *f*

countermeasure *n* contramedida, *f*

counterpane *n* sobrecama, colcha, *f*

counterpart *n* contraparte, *f;* (of a document) duplicado, *m*

counterplot *n* contratreta, *f*

counterpoint *n mus* contrapunto, *m*

counterpoise *n* contrapeso, *m;* equilibrio, *m, vt* contrabalancear, contrapesar

countersign *n* contraseña, *f, vt* refrendar

countess *n* condesa, *f*

counting *n* cuenta, *f;* numeración, *f;* (of votes) escrutinio, *m.* **c.-house,** contaduría, *f*

countless *a* innumerable. **a c. number,** un sinfín, un sinnúmero

countrified *a* rústico, campesino

country *n* país, *m;* (fatherland) patria, *f;* región, campiña, tierra, *f;* (as opposed to town) campo, *m. a* del campo; campesino, campestre, rústico. **He lives in the c.,** Vive en el campo. **c. club,** club campestre, *m.* **c. cousin,** provinciano (-na). **c.-dance,** baile campestre, *m.* **c. gentleman,** hacendado, *m.* **c. girl,** campesina, *f;* aldeana, *f.* **c.-house,** finca, *f;* casa de campo, *f.* **c. life,** vida del campo, *f.* **c.-seat,** finca, *f*

countryman *n* campesino, *m;* hombre del campo, *m;* compatriota, *m*

countryside *n* campo, *m;* campiña, *f*

countrywoman *n* campesina, *f;* compatriota, *f*

county *n* condado, *m;* provincia, *f.* **c. council,** diputación provincial, *f.* **c. town,** cabeza de partido, *f;* ciudad provincial, *f*

county seat *n* cabecera municipal, cabeza de partido, *f*

coup *n* golpe, *m.* **c. d'état,** golpe de estado, *m*

coupe *n* cupé, *m*

couple *n* par, *m;* (in a dance, etc.) pareja, *f. vt* enganchar, acoplar; (in marriage) casar; (animals) aparear; (ideas) asociar; (names) juntar. **the young (married) c.,** el matrimonio joven

couplet *n* copla, *f*

coupling *n* enganche, acoplamiento, *m;* (of railway carriages) enganche, *m;* (of ideas) asociación, *f*

coupon *n* talón, *m;* cupón, *f*

courage *n* valor, *m.* **C.!** ¡Ánimo! **to muster up c.,** cobrar ánimo

courageous *a* valiente

courageously *adv* valientemente

courier *n* correo, *m,* estafeta, *f;* (guide) guía, *m;* (newspaper) estafeta, *f*

course *n* curso, *m;* (of time) transcurso, *m;* (of events) marcha, *f;* (of a river, etc.) cauce, *m;* (of stars) carrera, *f,* curso, *m;* (of a ship) derrota, *f,* rumbo, *m;* (way) camino, *m,* ruta, *f;* (of conduct) línea de conducta, *f;* actitud, *f;* (of study) curso, *m;* (of a meal) plato, *m;* (of an illness) desarrollo, *m; med* tratamiento, *m.* **He took it as a matter of c.,** Lo tomó sin darle importancia. **in due c.,** a su tiempo debido. **in the c. of time,** andando el tiempo, en el transcurso de los años. **of c.,** claro está; naturalmente. **Are you coming tomorrow? Of c.!** ¿Vienes mañana? ¡Ya lo creo! **the best c. to take,** lo mejor que se puede hacer, el mejor plantamiento, *m*

course *vt* cazar, perseguir; *poet* correr por, cruzar. *vi* (of blood, etc.) correr; cazar

court *n* (yard) patio, *m;* (tennis) campo de tenis, *m;* (fives, racquets) cancha, *f;* (royal) corte, *f;* (of justice) tribunal, *m;* (following) séquito, acompañamiento, *m. vt* hacer la corte (a); cortejar, pretender; solicitar; (sleep) conciliar. **to pay c. to,** (a woman) galantear, pretender; (a person) hacer la rueda (a), *Lat. Am.* afilar. **to respect the c.,** *law* guardar sala. **c. of appeal,** sala de apelación, *f.* **c. of justice,** sala de justicia, *f;* tribunal de justicia, *m.* **supreme c.,** tribunal supremo, *m.* **c.-card,** figura, *f.* **c.-dress,** traje de corte, *m.* **c. house,** palacio de justicia, *m.* **c. jester,** bufón, *m.* **c.-martial,** tribunal militar, *m.* **c.-plaster,** tafetán inglés, tafetán de heridas, *m.* **c.-room,** sala de justicia, *f*

courteous *a* cortés

courteousness *n* cortesía, *f*

courtesy *n* cortesía, *f;* favor, *m,* merced, *f;* permiso, *m*

courtier *n* cortesano, palaciego, *m*

courtliness *n* cortesía, urbanidad, *f;* dignidad, *f;* elegancia, *f*

courtly *a* cortés, galante; digno; elegante

courtship *n* noviazgo, *m;* galanteo, *m*

courtyard *n* patio, *m*

cousin *n* primo (-ma). **first c.,** primo (-ma) carnal. **second c.,** primo (-ma) segundo (-da)

cove *n* cala, abra, ensenada, *f,* ancón *m*

covenant *n* contrato, *m;* estipulación, *f;* pacto, *m;* alianza, *f. vt* prometer; estipular

Coventry, to send to, hacer el vacío (a)

cover *vt* cubrir; abrigar; (dissemble) disimular; (a distance) recorrer; (comprise) comprender, abarcar; (with confusion, etc.) llenar (de); (with a revolver, etc.) amenazar (con); (an overdraft, etc.) garantizar; (of stallions) cubrir; (of a hen and eggs) empollar; (a story, journalism) investigar. *n* cubierta, *f*; (for a chair, umbrella, etc.) funda, *f*; (of a saucepan, jar, etc.) tapa, *f*; (dish-cover) tapadera, *f*; (of a book) cubierta, tapa, *f*; (of a letter) sobre, *m*; (shelter) abrigo, *m*; protección, *f*; (undergrowth) maleza, *f*; *fig* velo, manto, *m*; (pretence) pretexto, *m*; *com* garantía, *f*. **outer c.,** cubierta de neumático, *f*. **to c. oneself with glory,** cubrirse de gloria. **to c. up,** cubrir completamente; (with clothes) arropar; (wrap up) envolver. **to c. with a revolver,** amenazar con un revólver. **to read a book from c. to c.,** leer un libro del principio al fin. **to take c.,** refugiarse, tomar abrigo. **under c.,** bajo tejado; al abrigo

cover charge *n* consumo mínimo, precio del cubierto, *m*

covering *n* cubrimiento, *m*; cubierta, *f*; envoltura, *f*; capa, *f*, abrigo, *m*. **c. letter,** carta adjunta, *f*

coverlet *n* colcha, sobrecama, *f*

covert *n* guarida, *f*. *a* oculto; furtivo

covertly *adv* secretamente, furtivamente

covet *vt* codiciar; ambicionar, suspirar por

covetous *a* codicioso; ávido; ambicioso

covetously *adv* codiciosamente; ávidamente

covetousness *n* codicia, avaricia, *f*; avidez, *f*; ambición, *f*

cow *vt* intimidar, acobardar

cow *n* vaca, *f*, *Lat. Am. also* lechera *f*; (of other animals) hembra, *f*. **c.-bell,** cencerro, *m*, zumba, *f*. **c.-catcher,** *aut* salvavidas, *m*. **c.-hide,** cuero, cuero de vaca, zurriago, *m*; penca, *f*. **c.-house,** establo, *m*, boyera, *f*. **c.-pox,** vacuna, *f*

coward *n* cobarde, *m*, *a* cobarde

cowardice *n* cobardía, *Argentina* canillera, *f*

cowardly *a* cobarde, *Mexico, Venezuela* correlón

cowboy *n* vaquero, *m*; gaucho, "cowboy," *m*

cower *vi* no saber dónde meterse; temblar, acobardarse

cowherd *n* vaquero, boyero, *m*

cowl *n* capucha, *f*; (of a chimney) sombrerete, *m*

coworker *n* colaborador (-ra)

cowshed *n* establo, *m*

cowslip *n* prímula, *f*

cox *n* timonel, *m*

coxcomb *n* (of a jester) gorra de bufón, *f*; mequetrefe, *m*

coxswain *n* patrón, *m*; (of a rowboat) timonel, *m*

coy *a* modoso, tímido; coquetón

coyly *adv* tímidamente; con coquetería

coyness *n* timidez, modestia, *f*; coquetería, *f*

cozy *a* cómodo; agradable; caliente. **You are very c. here,** Estás muy bien aquí

crab *n* (sea) cangrejo de mar, cámbaro, *m*, *Lat. Am. also* jaiba *m*; (river) cangrejo, *m*; *ast* Cáncer, *m*. *vt* (thwart) frustrar. **hermit c.,** cangrejo ermitaño, *m*. **c.-apple,** manzana silvestre, *f*. **c.-louse,** ladilla, *f*

crabbed *a* áspero, hosco, desabrido, arisco; (of handwriting) apretado, metido

crack *vt* hender; quebrantar, romper; (nuts) cascar; (a whip and fingers) chasquear; (a bottle of wine) abrir. *vi* (of earth, skin, etc.) agrietarse; romperse, quebrarse; (of the voice) romper; (of the male voice) mudar. *n* hendedura, rendija, *f*; quebraja, *f*; (of a whip) chasquido, *m*; (of a rifle) estallido, *m*; (blow) golpe, garrotazo, *m*, *a* excelente, de primera categoría; estupendo. **to c. a joke,** soltar un chiste. **to c. up,** *vt* dar bombo (a), alabar. *vi* (in health) quebrantarse; (airplane) cuartearse, estrellarse. **c.-brained,** chiflado; estúpido, loco

cracked *a* grietado; (of a bell, etc.) hendido; (of the voice) cascada; (of a person) chiflado

cracker *n* (firework) petardo, *m*; buscapiés, *m*

crackle *vi* (of burning wood, etc.) crepitar; (rustle) cru-

jir; (of rifle fire) tirotear. *n* crepitación, *f*; crujido, *m*; (of rifle fire) tiroteo, *m*

crackling *n*. See **crackle;** *cul* chicharrón, *m*

Cracow Cracovia, *f*

cradle *n* cuña, *f*; *fig* niñez, infancia, *f*; (for a limb) arco de protección, *m*; (for winebottle) cesta, *f*. *vt* mecer. **c.-song,** canción de cuna, *f*

craft *n* (guile) astucia, *f*; (skill) habilidad, *f*; arte, *mf*; (occupation) oficio manual, *m*; profesión, *f*; (guild) gremio, *m*; (boat) barco, *m*, embarcación, *f*

craftily *adv* astutamente

craftiness *n* astucia, *f*

craftsman *n* artífice, *m*; arte sano, *m*; artista, *m*

craftsmanship *n* arte, *m*, or *f*; habilidad, *f*; artificio, *m*

crafty *a* astuto, taimado, *Lat. Am.* macuco. **c. person** *Mexico* fistol *m*

crag *n* peña, *f*, risco, despeñadero, *m*

cragginess *n* escabrosidad, aspereza, fragosidad, *f*

craggy *a* escabroso, escarpado, peñascoso, riscoso

cram *vt* henchir; atestar; (one's mouth) llenar (de); (poultry) cebar; (a pupil) preparar para un examen; (a subject) empollar. *vi* (with food) atracarse. **The room was crammed with people,** La sala estaba atestada de gente

cramp *n med* calambre, *m*; (numbness) entumecimiento, *m*; (rivet) grapa, *f*. *vt* dar calambre (a); (numb) entumecer; (fasten) lañar; (*fig* hamper) estorbar. **to c. someone's style,** cortar los vuelos (a). **writer's c.,** calambre del escribiente, *m*

cramped *a* (of space) apretado, estrecho; (of writing) menuda

cranberry *n* arándano, *m*

crane *n orn* grulla, *f*; (machine) grúa, *f*. **jib c.,** grúa de pescante, *f*. **travelling c.,** grúa móvil, *f*. **to c. one's neck,** estirar el cuello. **crane's bill,** pico de cigüeña, *m*

cranium *n* cráneo, *m*

crank *n* (handle) manivela, *f*; (person) maniático (-ca). *vt* poner en marcha (un motor) con la manivela

crankiness *n* (crossness) irritabilidad, *f*, mal humor, *m*; (eccentricity) excentricidad, *f*

cranky *a* (cross) irritable, malhumorado; (eccentric) chiflado, maniático, excéntrico

cranny *n* hendedura, grieta, *f*

crape *n* crespón, *m*

crash *vi* caer estrepitosamente; romperse; estallarse; (of aircraft, cars) estrellarse; *fig* hundirse, arruinarse. *n* estrépito, estruendo, *m*; estallido, *m*; (of aircraft) accidente de aviación, *m*; (car) accidente, *m*, (or choque, *m*) de automóviles; (financial) ruina, *f*; *fig* hundimiento, *m*. **to c. into,** estrellarse contra, chocar con. **c. helmet,** casco, *m*. **c.-landing,** aterrizaje violento, *m*

crass *a* craso

crassness *n* estupidez, *f*

crate *n* (box) caja de embalaje, *f*; (basket) canasto, *m*, banasta, *Mexico* jaba *f*

crater *n* cráter, *m*

cravat *n* corbata, *f*

crave *vt* suplicar, implorar. **to c. for,** perecer por, suspirar por, anhelar

craven *a* cobarde, pusilánime. *n* poltrón, cobarde, *m*

craving *n* deseo vehemente, *m*, sed, *f*

crawfish *n* cangrejo de río, *m*; cigala, *f*

crawl *vi* arrastrarse; andar a gatas; andar a paso de tortuga; (abase oneself) humillarse; (be full of) abundar (en). *n* paso de tortuga, *m*; (swimming) arrastre *m*

crayfish *n* cangrejo de río, *m*; cigala, *f*

crayon *n* carbón, *m*; pastel, *m*; (pencil) lápiz de color, *m*. *vt* dibujar con pastel, etc. **c. drawing,** dibujo al carbón, *m*

craze *vt* enloquecer, volver loco (a). *n* manía, *f*, capricho, entusiasmo, *m*; (fashion) moda, *f*

crazily *adv* locamente

craziness *n* locura, *f*

crazy *a* loco; chiflado; (of structure) dilapidado. **He is c. about music,** Está loco por la música. **to be com-**

pletely c., (of persons) ser un loco de atar; ser completamente loco. **to drive c.,** volver loco (a)

creak vi (of shoes, chairs, etc.) crujir; (of gates, etc.) rechinar, chirriar. n crujido, m; chirrido, m

creaking n. See **creak**

creaky a crujiente, que cruje; chirriador

cream n crema, f; nata, f; fig flor, nata, f. a de nata. **whipped c.,** nata batida, f. **c. cake,** pastel de nata, m. **c.-cheese,** queso de nata, m. **c.-colored,** de color crema. **c.-jug,** jarro para crema, m. **c. of tartar,** cremor, tártaro, m

creamery n lechería, f

creamy a cremoso

crease n (wrinkle) arruga, f; (fold) pliegue, m; (in trousers) raya, f; (in cricket) línea de la meta, f. vt (wrinkle) arrugar; (fold) plegar; (trousers) poner la raya en. vi arrugarse

create vt crear; (appoint) nombrar; (produce) suscitar, producir

creation n creación, f; establecimiento, m; (appointment) nombramiento, m

creative a creador; de la creación

creativeness n facultad creativa, inventiva, f

creator n creador (-ra)

creature n criatura, f; animal, m. **c. comforts,** bienestar material, m

creche n casa cuna, f

credence n crédito, m, fe, creencia, f; ecc credencia, f. **to give c. to,** dar crédito (a), creer

credentials n pl credenciales, f pl

credibility n credibilidad, verosimilitud, f

credible a creíble, verosímil; (of persons) digno de confianza

credibly adv creíblemente

credit n crédito, m; reputación, f; honor, m; (com and banking) crédito, m; (in bookkeeping) data, f. vt dar fe (a), dar crédito (a); creer; atribuir; (bookkeeping) acreditar. **It does them,** Les hace honor. **on c.,** a crédito, al fiado. **open c.,** com letra abierta, f. **to give on c.,** dar fiado. **c. balance,** haber, m

creditable a loable, honroso, digno de alabanza

creditably adv honrosamente

creditor n acreedor (-ra); (bookkeeping) haber, m

credulity n credulidad, f

credulous a crédulo, Lat. Am. creído

credulously adv con credulidad, crédulamente

creed n credo, m

creek n caleta, abra, f

creel n (for fish) cesta de pescador, f

creep vi arrastrarse; (of plants and birds) trepar; (of infants) andar a gatas; (totter) hacer pinitos; (slip) deslizarse; (cringe) lisonjear, rebajarse; (of one's flesh) sentir hormigueo. **to c. about on tiptoe,** andar de puntillas. **to c. into a person's favor,** insinuarse en el favor de. **to c. in,** entrar sin ser notado (en); deslizarse en. **to c. on,** (of time) avanzar lentamente; (of old age, etc.) acercarse insensiblemente. **to c. out,** salir sin hacer ruido; escurrirse. **to c. up,** trepar por; subir a gatas

creeper n bot enredadera, f; orn trepador, m; zool reptil, m

creeping a bot trepante; zool trepador; (servile) rastrero

cremate vt incinerar

cremation n cremación, f

crematorium n crematorio, m; horno de incineración, m, inhumadora, f

creole a criollo. n criollo (-lla)

creolize vt acriollar

crescent n media luna, f; her creciente, m; calle en forma de semicírculo, f. a en forma de media luna; poet creciente

cress n bot berro, m

crest n (of a cock, etc.) cresta, f; (plume) penacho, m; (of a helmet) cimera, f; (of a hill) cumbre, cima, f; (of a wave) cresta, f. **family c.,** blasón, escudo, m

crested a Lat. Am. copetudo (-da)

crestfallen a cabizbajo, cariacontecido

cretan a cretense. n cretense, mf

cretin n cretino (-na)

crevasse n grieta en un ventisquero, f

crevice n intersticio, m, rendija, grieta, f

crew n (of ships, boats, aircraft) tripulación, f; (of a gun) servidores de una ametralladora, m pl; (gang) pandilla, cuadrilla, f

crib n pesebre, m; (child's) camita de niño, f; (plagiary) plagio, m. vt (plagiarize) plagiar; (steal) hurtar

crick n (in the neck) tortícolis, m

cricket n ent grillo, m; (game) cricquet, m. **c. ball,** pelota de cricquet, f. **c. bat,** paleta de cricquet, f. **c. ground,** campo de cricquet, m. **c. match,** partido de cricquet, m

cricketer n jugador de cricquet, m

crier n (town) pregonero, m

crime n crimen, m; ofensa, f, delito, m

Crimea, the la Crimea, f

Crimean War, the la guerra de Crimea, la guerra de Oriente, f

criminal a criminal. n criminal, m; reo, mf **C. Investigation Department,** (nearest equivalent) policía secreta, f. **c. laws,** código penal, m

criminally adv criminalmente

criminologist n criminalista, m

criminology n criminología, f

crimp vt (hair) rizar

crimson n carmesí, m. a de carmesí. vt teñir de carmesí. vi enrojecerse

cringe vi temblar; asustarse, acobardarse; inclinarse (ante)

cringing a servil, humilde; adulador, Mexico also lambioche

crinkle vi arrugarse; rizarse. vt arrugar. n arruga, f

crinoline a crinolina, f, miriñaque, guardainfante, m

cripple n tullido (-da); cojo (-ja). vt lisiar, tullir, estropear; fig paralizar

crisis n crisis, f

crisp a (of hair and of leaves) crespo; (fresh) fresco; (stiff) tieso; (of style) nervioso, vigoroso; (of manner) decidido; (of repartee) chispeante; (of tone) incisivo

crisscross vt (a body of water or land) surcar

criterion n criterio, m

critic n crítico, m; censor, m

critical a crítico

criticism n crítica, f

criticize vt criticar; censurar

critique n crítica, f

croak vi (of frogs) croar; (of ravens) graznar; (of persons) lamentarse, gruñir

croaking n canto de la rana, m; graznido, m

Croat a croata. n croata, mf

Croatia Crocia, f

crochet n ganchillo, m, vi hacer ganchillo. vt hacer (algo) de ganchillo. **c. hook,** aguja de gancho, f, ganchillo, m. **c. work,** croché, ganchillo, m

crockery n loza, f, cacharros, m pl. **c. store,** cacharrería, f

crocodile n cocodrilo, m. **c. tears,** lágrimas de cocodrilo, f pl

crocus n azafrán, m

croft n campillo, m; (farm) heredad, f

crofter n colono, m

crone n bruja, f

crony n compinche, mf

crook n curva, f; (staff) cayado, m; (swindler) caballero de industria, estafador, m, vt doblar, encorvar

crooked a curvo; encorvado; torcido, Mexico chueco; ladeado; (deformed) contrahecho; (of paths, etc.) tortuoso; (dishonest) torcido, tortuoso

crookedly adv torcidamente; de través

crookedness n encorvadura, f; tortuosidad, f; sinuosidad, f

croon vt and vi canturrear; cantar

crooner n cantante, mf

crop *n* (of birds) buche, *m*; (whip) látigo, *m*, fusta, *f*; (handle) mango, *m*; (harvest) cosecha, *f*; (of the hair) cortadura, *f. vt* cortar; (nibble) rozar; (hair) rapar. **Eton c.,** pelo a la garçonne, *m*. **to c. up,** aparecer, surgir

crop rotation *n* la rotación de cultivos, *f*

croquet *n* juego de la argolla, juego de croquet, *m*

croquette *n cul* croqueta, *f*

crosier *n* báculo, cayado del obispo, *m*

cross *n* cruz, *f*; *biol* cruzamiento, *m*; (sew bias) bies, *m*. **in the shape of a c.,** en cruz. **the Red C.,** la Cruz Roja. **c.-bearer,** *ecc* crucero, *m*

cross *vt* cruzar; atravesar; pasar por; (a check and animals) cruzar; (thwart) contrariar. **It did not c. my mind,** No se me ocurrió. **Our letters must have crossed,** Nuestras cartas deben haberse cruzado. **to c. oneself,** *ecc* persignarse. **to c. out,** tachar, rayar. **to c. over,** *vt* atravesar, cruzar. *vi* ir al otro lado

cross *a* transversal; cruzado; oblicuo; (contrary) opuesto (a); (bad-tempered) malhumorado. **c.-breed,** *a* mestizo, atravesado. **c.-country,** *a* a campo travieso. **c.-examination,** *law* repregunta, *f*, contrainterrogatorio, *m*. **c.-examine,** *vt law* repreguntar; interrogar. **c.-eyed,** bizco. **c.-fire,** *mil* fuego cruzado, *m sing* fuegos cruzados, *m pl*; *fig* tiroteo, *m*. **c.-grained,** (of wood) vetisesgado; (of persons) áspero, intratable, desabrido. **c.-legged,** con las piernas cruzadas. **c.-purpose,** despropósito, *m*. **at c.-purposes,** a despropósito. **c.-question,** *vt law* repreguntar; interrogar. **c. reference,** contrarreferencia, *f*. **c. section,** sección transversal, *f*. **c.-stitch,** punto cruzado, *m*. **c.-word puzzle,** crucigrama, *m*

crossbar *n* travesaño, *m*

crossbeam *n* viga transversal, *f*

crossbench *a* atravesada

crossbred *a* cruzado, mestizo; híbrido

crossbreed *n* mestizo (-za); híbrido, *m*

crossing *n* cruzamiento, *m*; (of the sea) travesía, *f*; (intersection) cruce, *m*; paso, *m*. **level c.,** paso a nivel, *m*. **pedestrian c.,** paso para peatones, *m*. **c.-sweeper,** barrendero, *m*

crossly *adv* con mal humor, con displicencia, irritablemente

crossness *n* irritabilidad, *f*, mal humor, *m*

crossroad *n* travesía, *f*; cruce, *m*; *pl* **crossroads,** cruce, cruce de caminos, *m sing* encrucijada, *f sing*

crosswise *adv* en cruz; a través

crotch *n* (of a tree) bifurcación, *f*; *anat* horcajadura, *f*; (of breeches) entrepiernas, *f pl*

crotchet *n mus* semínima, *f*; (fad) capricho, *m*; extravagancia, excentricidad, *f*

crotchety *a* caprichoso; raro, excéntrico; difícil

crouch *vi* acurrucarse, agacharse, acuclillarse

croup *n* (disease) crup, garrotillo, *m*; (of a horse) grupa, anca, *f*

croupier *n* coime, crupié, *m*

crow *n orn* cuervo, *m*; *orn* grajo, *m*; (of a cock) canto del gallo, cacareo, *m*; (of an infant) gorjeo, *m*. *vi* (of a cock) cantar, cacarear; (of an infant) gorjearse. **as the c. flies,** en línea recta. **to c. over,** gallear, cantar victoria. **crow's-foot,** pata de gallo, *f*. **crow's-nest,** *naut* gavias, *f pl*

crowbar *n* alzaprima, palanca, *f*

crowd *n* multitud, muchedumbre, *f*; concurso, *m*; vulgo, *m*; (majority) mayoría, *f*; *theat* acompañamiento, *m*. *vi* reunirse, congregarse; agolparse, remolinarse, apiñarse. *vt* (fill) llenar; atestar. **in a c.,** en tropel. **So many ideas crowded in on me,** Se me ocurrieron tantas ideas a la vez. **to follow the c.,** seguir la multitud; *fig* ir con la mayoría. **to c. in,** entrar en tropel. **to c. round,** cercar, agruparse alrededor de. **to c. together,** apiñarse. **to c. up,** subir en masa, subir en tropel

crowded *a* lleno; atestado, apiñado; (weighed down) agobiado; (of hours, etc.) lleno

crowing *n* cacareo, canto del gallo, *m*; (of an infant) gorjeos, *m pl*; (boasting) jactancia, *f*

crown *n* corona, *f*; (of the head) coronilla, corona, *f*; (of a hat) copa, *f*; *arch* coronamiento, *m*. *vt* coronar. **c. prince,** príncipe heredero, *m*

crowning *n* coronamiento, *m*; *arch* remate, *m*, *a* final; supremo

crozier *n*. See **crosier**

crucial *a* decisivo, crítico; difícil

crucible *n* crisol, *m*

crucifix *n* crucifijo, *m*

crucifixion *n* crucifixión, *f*

cruciform *a* cruciforme

crucify *vt* crucificar

crude *a* crudo; (of colors) chillón, llamativo; (uncivilized) cerril, inculto; (vulgar) cursi; (of truth, etc.) desnudo

crudity *n* crudeza, *f*

cruel *a* cruel

cruelty *n* crueldad, *f*

cruet *n* ánfora, vinagrera, *f*; (stand) angarillas, *f pl*, convoy, *m*

cruise *vi* cruzar, navegar; (of cars) correr. *n* viaje por mar, *m*

cruiser *n* crucero, *m*

crumb *n* miga, *f*; (spongy part of bread) migaja, *f. vt* (bread) desmigajar; desmenuzar. **c. brush,** recogemigas, *m*

crumble *vt* desmigajar, desmenuzar. *vi* desmoronarse, desmigajarse; *fig* hundirse, derrumbarse; *fig* desaparecer

crumbling *n* (of buildings, etc.) desmoronamiento, *m*; *fig* destrucción, *f*

crumple *vt* arrugar, ajar. *vi* arrugarse. **to c. up,** *vt* (crush) estrujar; (persons) dejar aplastado. *vi* (collapse) hundirse, derrumbarse; (of persons) desplomarse; (despair) desalentarse

crunch *vt* mascar; hacer crujir. *vi* crujir

crupper *n* baticola, *f*

crusade *n* cruzada, *f*

crusader *n* cruzado, *m*

crush *vt* aplastar; (to powder) moler, triturar; (grapes, etc.) exprimir; (crease) arrugar; (opposition, etc.) vencer; (annihilate) aniquilar, destruir; (abash) humillar, confundir; (hope, etc.) matar; (of sorrow, etc.) agobiar. **We all crushed into his diningroom,** Fuimos en tropel a su comedor. **to c. up,** machacar, moler; (paper, etc.) estrujar

crushing *a* (of defeats and replies) aplastante; (of sorrow, etc.) abrumador

crust *n* (of bread, pie) corteza, *f*; (scab) costra, *f*; (of the earth, snow) capa, *f. vt* encostrar. *vi* encostrarse. **c. of bread,** mendrugo de pan, *m*

crustacean *a* crustáceo. *n* crustáceo, *m*

crustily *adv* irritablemente, malhumoradamente

crustiness *n* mal humor, *m*, aspereza, *f*

crusty *a* costroso; (of persons) malhumorado, irritable; áspero

crutch *n* muleta, *f*; (fork) horquilla, *f*; (crotch) horcajadura, *f*

crux *n* problema, *m*; (knotty point) nudo, *m*

cry *vi* (weep) llorar; (shout) gritar; (exclaim) exclamar. *vt* (one's wares) pregonar. *n* grito, *m*. **to cry for help,** pedir socorro a voces. **to cry to high heaven,** poner el grito en el cielo. **to cry one's eyes out,** llorar a mares. **to cry down,** desacreditar. **to cry off,** desdecirse; volverse atrás. **to cry out,** *vt* gritar. *vi* dar gritos; gritar; *fig* clamar. **cry-baby,** niño (-ña) llorón (-ona)

crying *a* urgente; notorio. *n* gritos, *m pl*; (weeping) llanto, *m*, lamentaciones, *f pl*; (tears) lágrimas, *f pl*

crypt *n* cripta, *f*

cryptic *a* secreto, oculto

cryptography *n* criptografía, *f*

crystal *n* cristal, *m*. **c. set,** *rad* receptor de galena, *m*

crystal ball *n* bola de cristal, esfera de cristal, *f*

crystalline *a* cristalino

crystallization *n* cristalización, *f*

crystallize *vt* and *vi* cristalizar

crystallography *n* cristalografía, *f*
cub *n* cachorro (-rra)
Cuban *a* cubano. *n* cubano (-na)
cubbyhole *n* refugio, *m*; garita, *f*; cuarto pequeño, *m*; chiribitil, *m*
cube *n* cubo, *m*; (of sugar) terrón, *m*. *vt* cubicar. **c. root,** raíz cúbica, *f*
cubic *a* cúbico
cubicle *n* cubículo, *m*
cubism *n* cubismo, *m*
cuckold *n* cornudo, *m*
cuckoo *n* cuclillo, *m*; (cry) cucú, *m*. **c.-clock,** reloj de cuclillo, *m*
cucumber *n* cohombro *m*
cud *n* rumia, *f*. **to chew the cud,** rumiar
cuddle *vt* abrazar. *n* abrazo, *m*. **to c. up together,** estar abrazados
cudgel *n* porra, estaca, tranca, *f*, *vt* aporrear, apalear. **to c. one's brains,** devanarse los sesos. **to take up the cudgels for,** salir en defensa de
cue *n* *theat* pie, *m*; (lead) táctica, *f*; (hint) indicación, *f*; (of hair) coleta, *f*; (billiard) taco (de billar), *m*. **to take one's cue from,** tomar como modelo (a); seguir el ejemplo de
cueca *n* cueca *f*
cuff *vt* abofetear. *n* (blow) bofetón, *m*; (of sleeve) puño, *m*, bocamanga, valenciana, *f*.
cufflink *n* gemelo *m*, *Central America* mancuerna, mancuernilla *f*, *Chile* collera *f*, *Colombia* mancorna *f*
cuisine *n* cocina, *f*
cul-de-sac *n* callejón sin salida, *m*
culinary *a* culinario
cullender *n* colador, *m*
culminate *vi* culminar (en), terminar (en). **culminating point,** punto culminante, *m*
culmination *n* culminación, *f*; *fig* apogeo, punto culminante, *m*
culpability *n* culpabilidad, *f*
culpable *a* culpable
culpably *adv* culpablemente
culprit *n* culpado (-da)
cult *n* culto, *m*
cultivable *a* cultivable, labradero
cultivate *vt* cultivar
cultivated *a* cultivado; (of persons) culto, fino
cultivation *n* cultivación, *f*; (of the land) cultivo, *m*; (of persons, etc.) cultura, *f*
cultivator *n* cultivador (-ra); (machine) cultivador, *m*
cultural *a* cultural
culture *n* cultura, *f*; (bacteriology) cultivo, *m*, *vt* (bacteriology) cultivar
cultured *a* culto
culvert *n* alcantarilla, *f*
cumbersome *a* pesado; incómodo
cumulative *a* cumulativo
cumulus *n* cúmulo, *m*
cuneiform *a* cuneiforme
cunning *a* astuto, taimado, *Lat. Am.* macuco *n* (skill) habilidad, *f*; astucia, *f*
cup *n* taza, *f*; (*ecc* and *bot*) cáliz, *m*; *sport* copa, *f*; (hollow) hoyo, *m*, hondonada, *f*. **c.-final,** *sport* final de la copa, *m*. **c.-tie,** *sport* partido eliminatorio, *m*
cup-and-ball *n* boliche, *m*
cupboard *n* armario, *m*; (in the wall) alacena, *f*. **c. love,** amor interesado, *m*
cupful *n* taza, *f*
cupidity *n* avaricia, codicia, *f*
cup of sorrow *n* ramito de amargura, *m*
cupola *n* cúpula, *f*
cur *n* perro mestizo, *m*; canalla, *m*
curable *a* curable
curableness *n* curabilidad, *f*
curative *a* curativo, terapéutico
curator *n* (of a museum) director, *m*; (Scots law) curador, *m*
curb *n* (of a bridle) barbada, *f*; *fig* freno, *m*; (stone) bor-

dillo, *m*, guarnición, *f*. *vt* (a horse) enfrenar; *fig* refrenar, reprimir; (limit) limitar
curd *n* requesón, *m*; cuajada, *f*
curdle *vi* coagularse; (of blood) helarse. *vt* coagular; (blood) helar
cure *n* cura, *f*; *ecc* curato, *m*. *vt* curar; (salt) salar; *fig* remediar. **to take a c.,** tomar una cura. **c.-all,** panacea, *f*. **c. of souls,** cura de almas, *f*
curer *n* (of fish, etc.) salador, *m*; (of evils, etc.) remediador, *m*
curfew *n* toque de queda, *m*
curing *n* curación, *f*; (salting) saladura, *f*
curio *n* curiosidad, antigüedad, *f*
curiosity *n* curiosidad, *f*
curious *a* (all meanings) curioso
curiously *adv* curiosamente
curl *n* (of hair) rizo, bucle, *m*; (of smoke) penacho, *m*. *vt* rizar. *vi* rizarse; *sport* jugar al curling. **in c.,** rizado. **to c. one's lip,** hacer una mueca de desdén. **to c. up,** *vt* arrollar; *fig* dejar fuera de combate (a). *vi* hacerse un ovillo, enroscarse; (of leaves) abarquillarse; *fig* desplomarse; desanimarse. **c.-paper,** papillote, *m*
curlew *n* *orn* zarapito, *m*
curling *n* (game) curling, *m*, *a* rizado. **c.-tongs,** encrespador, *m*
curly *a* rizado, crespo
curmudgeon *n* erizo, misántropo, cara de viernes, *m*
currant *n* (dry) pasa de Corinto, *f*; (fresh) grosella, *f*. **black c.,** grosella negra, *f*; (bush) grosellero negro, *m*. **c.-bush,** grosellero, *m*
currency *n* uso corriente, *m*; moneda corriente, *f*, dinero, *m*; dinero en circulación, *m*; valor corriente, *m*; estimación, *f*
current *a* corriente; presente, de actualidad; (of money) en circulación. *n* (of water, etc., *fig* *elec*) corriente, *f*. **alternating c.,** *elec* corriente alterna, *f*. **direct c.,** *elec* corriente continua, *f*. **the c. number of a magazine,** el último número de una revista. **c. events,** actualidades, *f* *pl*
currently *adv* corrientemente, generalmente
curricle *n* carriola, *f*
curriculum *n* plan de estudios, *m*; curso, *m*
curriculum vitae *n* hoja de vida, *f*
curry *vt* (leather) zurrar; (a horse) almohazar; *cul* condimentar con cari. **to c. favor with,** insinuarse en el favor de. **c.-comb,** almohaza, *f*
curse *n* maldición, *f*; blasfemia, *f*; (ruin) azote, castigo, *m*. *vt* maldecir; (afflict) castigar. *vi* blasfemar, echar pestes
cursed *a* maldito; abominable, odioso
cursing *n* maldición, *f*; blasfemias, *f* *pl*
cursorily *adv* rápidamente; de prisa; superficialmente
cursory *a* rápido; apresurado; superficial
curt *a* seco, brusco; corto
curtail *vt* abreviar; reducir; disminuir
curtailment *n* abreviación, *f*; reducción, *f*; disminución, *f*
curtain *n* cortina, *f*; *theat* telón, *m*. *vt* poner cortinas (a) **drop c.,** telón de boca, *m*. **iron c.,** *pol* telón de acero, *m*. **to c. off,** separar por cortinas. **c.-lecture,** reprimenda conyugal, *f*. **c.-raiser,** entremés. *m*. **c.-ring,** anilla, *f*
curtly *adv* secamente, bruscamente
curtness *n* brusquedad, sequedad, *f*
curtsey *n* reverencia, cortesía, *f*, *vi* hacer una reverencia
curvature *n* curvatura, *f*
curve *n* curva, *f*; *mech* codo, *m*; (*aut* of a road) viraje, *m*. *vt* encorvar, torcer. *vi* encorvarse, torcerse; (of a road) hacer un viraje.
curved *a* curvo
curvet *n* corveta, cabriola, *f*, *vi* corvetear, corcovear, cabriolar
curvilinear *a* curvilíneo
cushion *n* almohada, *f*; cojín, *m*; (billiards) banda, *f*; (of fingers, etc.) pulpejo, *m*. *vt* proveer de almohadas; (a shock) amortiguar; suavizar
custard *n* flan, *m*, natillas, *f pl*

custodian *n* custodio, *m*; guardián, *m*; (of a museum, etc.) director, *m*

custody *n* custodia, *f*; guarda, *f*; prisión, *f*. **in safe c.,** en lugar seguro. **to take** (a person) **into c.,** arrestar

custom *n* costumbre, *f*; uso, *m*; *com* parroquia, clientela, *f*; (sales) ventas, *f pl*; *pl* **Customs,** aduana, *f*. **to go through the Customs,** pasar por la aduana. **Customs duty,** derechos de aduana, *m pl*. **Customs officer,** aduanero, *m*. **c.-house,** aduana, *f*

customarily *adv* habitualmente, por lo general

customary *a* acostumbrado, usual, habitual

customer *n* cliente, *mf* parroquiano (-na), *Lat. Am. also.* marchante (-ta). **He is a queer c.,** Es un tipo raro

customs barrier *n* barrera aduanera, barrera arancelaria, *f*

cut *vt* cortar; (diamonds) tallar; (hay, etc.) segar; (carve) labrar, tallar; (engrave) grabar; (a lecture, etc.) no asistir a; (cards) destajar, cortar; (*fig* wound) herir; (reduce) reducir; abreviar; (teeth) echar; (of lines) cruzar. *vi* cortar; cortar bien; (*fam* go) marcharse a prisa y corriendo. **I must get my hair cut,** He de hacerme cortar el pelo. **That cuts both ways,** Es una arma de dos filos. **His opinion cuts no ice,** Su opinión no cuenta. **Mary cut him dead,** María hizo como si no le reconociera. **to cut a caper,** dar saltos; hacer cabriolas. **to cut a person short,** echar el tablacho (a). **to cut and run,** poner los pies en polvorosa. **to cut for deal,** (cards) cortar para ver quién da las cartas. **to cut short,** (a career) terminar. **to cut to the quick,** herir en lo más vivo. **to cut across,** cortar al través; (fields, etc.) atravesar; tomar por un atajo. **to cut away,** *vt* quitar. *vi inf* poner pies en polvorosa. **to cut down,** derribar; (by the sword) acuchillar; (by death, etc.) segar, malograr; (expenses, etc.) reducir; (abbreviate) cortar, abreviar. **to cut off,** cortar, separar; amputar; (on a telephone) cortar la comunicación; (gas, water, etc.) cortar; (supply of food, etc.) interrumpir; (of death) llevarse. **to cut off with a shilling,** desheredar (a). **to cut out,** (dresses, etc.) cortar; (oust) suplantar. **He is not cut out for medicine,** No tiene la disposición para la medicina. **to cut up,** trinchar, cortar en pequeños trozos, *Lat. Am.* destajar; (afflict) entristecer, afligir. **to cut up rough,** *inf* ponerse furioso

cut *a* cortado. **well-cut features,** facciones regulares, *f pl*. **cut and dried opinion,** opinión hecha, idea fija, *f*; ideas cerradas, *f pl*. **cut glass,** cristal tallado, *m*

cut *n* corte, *m*; (with a whip) latigazo, *m*; (with a sword) cuchillada, *f*; (with a sharp instrument) tajo, *m*; cortadura, *f*; (in prices, etc.) reducción, *f*; (engraving) grabado, *m*; clisé, *m*; (of cards) corte, *m*. **short**

cut, atajo, *m*. **the cut of a coat,** el corte de un abrigo. **to give** (someone) **the cut direct,** pasar cerca de (una persona) sin saludarle. **cut-out,** *n* (paper) recortado, *m*; *elec* cortacircuitos, *m*. **cut-throat,** *n* asesino, *m*

cutaneous *a* cutáneo

cute *a* cuco, listo; mono

cuteness *n* cuquería, inteligencia, *f*; monería, *f*

cuticle *n* cutícula, *f*

cutlass *n* alfanje *m*

cutler *n* cuchillero, *m*

cutlery *n* cuchillería, *f*

cutlet *n* chuleta, *f*

cutter *n* cortador, *m*; *naut* cúter, *m*; escampavía, *f*

cutting *n* corte, *m*; (of diamonds) talla, *f*; (in a mountain, etc.) tajo, *m*; *agr* plantón, *m*; (of cloth) retazo, *m*; (newspaper) recorte, *m*. *a* cortante; *fig* mordaz. **newspaper c.,** recorte de periódico. **c. down,** (of trees) tala, *f*; reducción, *f*

cuttingly *adv* mordazmente, con malicia

cuttlefish *n* jibia, *f*

cyanide *n* cianuro, *m*

cycle *n* ciclo, *m*; período, *m*; (bicycle) bicicleta, *f*. *vi* ir en bicicleta

cyclic *a* cíclico

cycling *n* ciclismo, *m*

cyclist *n* ciclista, *mf*

cyclone *n* ciclón, *m*

Cyclopean *a* ciclópeo

Cyclopean task *n* obra ciclópea, *f*

cygnet *n* pollo del cisne, *m*

cylinder *n* cilindro, *m*; *mech* tambor, *m*. **c. head,** culata, *f*

cylindrical *a* cilíndrico

cymbal *n* címbalo, platillo, *m*

cymbalist *n* cimbalero (-ra)

cynic *n* cínico, *m*

cynical *a* cínico

cynicism *n* cinismo, *m*

cynosure *n* *ast* Osa Menor, *f*; blanco, *m*

cypress *n* (tree and wood) ciprés, *m*. **c. grove,** cipresal, *m*

Cypriot *a* chipriota. *n* chipriota, *mf*

Cyprus Isla de Chipre, *f*

cyst *n* quiste, *m*

cystic *a* cístico

Czech *a* checo. *n* checo (-ca); (language) checo, *m*

Czechoslovak *n* checoslovaco (-ca)

Czechoslovakia Checoslovaquia, *f*

Czechoslovakian *a* checoslovaco

D

d *n* (letter) de, *f*; *mus* re, *m*

dab *vt* golpear suavemente, tocar; (sponge) esponjar; (moisten) mojar. *n* golpecito, golpe blando, *m*; (small piece) pedazo pequeño, *m*; (blob) borrón, *m*; (peck) picotazo, *m*; *inf* experto (-ta). **to dab at one's eyes,** secarse los ojos

dabble *vt* mojar (en). *vi* chapotear; (engage in) entretenerse en; (meddle in) meterse en; (speculate in) especular en. **to d. in politics,** meterse en política

dabbler *n* aficionado (-da)

dace *n* dardo, albur, *m*

dachshund *n* perro pachón, *m*

daddy *n* papaíto, *m*. **d.-longlegs,** típula, *f*

daffodil *n* narciso trompón, *m*

daft *a* bobo, tonto, chiflado; loco

dagger *n* daga, *f*, puñal, *m*; *print* cruz, *f*. **to be at daggers drawn,** estar a matar. **to look daggers (at),** lanzar miradas de odio (hacia), mirar echando chispas. **d. thrust,** puñalada, *f*

daguerreotype *n* daguerrotipo, *m*

dahlia *n* dalia, *f*

daily *a* diario, de todos los días; cotidiano. *adv* diariamente, cada día, todos los días; cotidianamente. *n* (paper) diario, *m*. **d. bread,** pan cotidiano, pan de cada día, *m*. **d. help,** (person) asistenta, *f*. **d. pay,** jornal, *m*; mil pre, *m*

daintily *adv* delicadamente; elegantemente; con primor

daintiness *n* delicadeza, *f*; elegancia, *f*; (beauty) primor, *m*

dainty *a* delicado; elegante; primoroso, exquisito; (fastidious) melindroso, difícil. *n* bocado exquisito, *m*, golosina, *f*

dairy *n* lechería, *f*. **d. cattle,** vacas lecheras, *f pl*. **d.-farm,** granja, *f*. **d.-farmer,** granjero (-ra). **d.-farming,** industria lechera, *f*

dairymaid *n* lechera, *f*

dairyman *n* lechero, *m*

dais *n* estrado, *m*

daisy *n* margarita, *f*

dale *n* valle, *m*

dalliance *n* (delay) tardanza, *f*; (play) jugueteo, *m*; diversiones, *f pl*; (caresses) caricias, *f pl*, abrazos, *m pl*

dally *vi* tardar, perder el tiempo; entretenerse, divertirse; (make love) holgar (con); (with an idea) entretenerse con, jugar con

Dalmatian *a* dalmático, dálmata. *n* dálmata, *mf*. **D. dog,** perro dálmata, *m*

dalmatic *n* dalmática, *f*

daltonism *n* daltonismo, *m*

dam *n* (of animals) madre, *f*; (of a river, etc.) presa, *f*, embalse, *m*; (mole) dique, *m*; pared de retención, *f. vt* represar, embalsar; cerrar; (restrain) contener, reprimir

damage *n* daño, perjuicio, *m*; mal, *m*; avería, *f*; pérdida, *f*; (*fam* price) precio, *m*; *pl* **damages,** *law* daños y perjuicios, *m pl. vt* dañar, perjudicar, *Lat. Am.* afectar; estropear; deteriorar; (reputation, etc.) comprometer

damageable *a* que puede ser dañado; frágil

damaging *a* perjudicial; comprometedor

damascene *vt* damasquinar

Damascus Damasio, *m*

damask *n* (cloth) damasco, *m*; (steel) acero damasquino, *m*. *a* de damasco; damasquino. *vt* (metals) damasquinar; (cloth) adamascar. **d.-like,** adamascado. **d. rose,** rosa de Damasco, *f*

dame *n* dama, señora, *f*; *inf* madre, *f*; (schoolmistress) amiga, *f.* **to attend a d. school,** ir a la amiga

damming *n* embalse, *m*, represa, *f*; retención, *f*; represión, *f*

damn *vt* condenar al infierno; maldecir; vituperar. **D. it!** ¡Maldito sea!

damnable *a* detestable, infame; *inf* horrible

damnably *adv* abominablemente; *inf* horriblemente

damnation *n* condenación, perdición, *f*; maldición, *f*; vituperación, *f*

damned *a* condenado; maldito; detestable, odioso

damning *a* que condena; irresistible

damp *n* húmedo. *n* humedad, *f*; (mist) niebla, *f*; exhalación, *f*; (gas) mofeta, *f*; *fig* tristeza, depresión, *f. vt* humedecer, mojar; apagar, amortiguar; (depress) deprimir, entristecer; (stifle) ahogar; (lessen) moderar; (trouble) turbar. **d.-proof,** impermeable

damper *n* (of a chimney) registro de humos, *m*; (of a piano) batiente, *m*; (for stamps) mojador, *m*; (gloom) depresión, tristeza, *f*; (restraint) freno, *m*

dampish *a* algo húmedo

dampness *n* humedad, *f*

damsel *n* chica, muchacha, *f*; damisela, *f*

damson *n* ciruela damascena, *f.* **d. tree,** ciruelo damasceno, *m*

dance *n* danza, *f*; baile, *m. vi* bailar, danzar; saltar, brincar. *vt* bailar; hacer saltar. **to d. attendance on,** servir humildemente; hacer la rueda (a). **to lead someone a d.,** hacer bailar. **d. band,** orquestina, *f*; orquesta de jazz, *f.* **d. floor,** pista de baile, *f.* **d. hall,** salón de baile, *m.* **d. music,** música bailable, *f.* **d.-number,** (in a theater) bailable, *m.* **d. of death,** danza de la muerte, *f*

dancer *n* bailarín (-ina); danzador (-ra), bailador (-ra); *pl* **dancers,** (partners) parejas de baile, *f pl*

dancing *n* baile, *m*, danza, *f*. **d.-girl,** bailarina, *f*; (Indian) bayadera, *f.* **d.-master,** maestro de baile, *m.* **d. school,** academia de baile, *f.* **d. slipper,** zapatilla de baile, *f*

dandelion *n* diente de león, *m*

dandle *vt* mecer, hacer saltar sobre las rodillas, hacer bailar

dandruff *n* caspa, *f*

dandy *n* dandi, petimetre, barbilindo, *m*

Dane *n* danés (-esa). **Great D.,** perro danés, *m*

danger *n* peligro, *m*; riesgo, *m*. **out of d.,** fuera de peligro. **to be in d.,** correr peligro, peligrar, estar en peligro

dangerous *a* peligroso; arriesgado; nocivo

dangerously *adv* peligrosamente

dangerousness *n* peligro, *m*

dangle *vi* colgar, pender. *vt* dejar colgar; oscilar; (show) mostrar

Danish *a* danés, de Dinamarca. *n* (language) danés, *m*

dank *a* húmedo

dankness *n* humedad, *f*

Danube, the el (Río) Danubio, *m*

dapper *a* apuesto, aseado; activo, vivaz

dapple *vt* motear, salpicar, manchar. **d.-grey,** *a* rucio

dappled *a* (of horses) rodado, empedrado

Dardanelles, the los Dardanelos, *m*

dare *vi* atreverse, osar. *vt* arriesgar; desafiar, provocar; hacer frente a, arrostrar. *n* reto, *m*. **I d. say!** ¡Ya lo creo! ¡No lo dudo! **I d. say that . . . ,** No me sorprendería que . . . ; Supongo que . . . **d.-devil,** calavera, *m*; atrevido (-da), valeroso (-sa)

daring *a* intrépido, audaz; atrevido, *Argentina* agalludo (dangerous) arriesgado, peligroso. *n* audacia, osadia, *f*, atrevimiento, *m*; peligro, *m*

daringly *adv* atrevidamente

dark *a* oscuro; (of complexion, etc.) moreno; negro; lóbrego; (of colours) oscuro; misterioso, enigmático; secreto, escondido; (sad) funesto, triste; (evil) malo, malévolo; (ignorant) ignorante, supersticioso. *n* oscuridad, *f*; (shade) sombra, *f*; ignorancia, *f*. **after d.,** *a* nocturno. *adv* después del anochecer. **in the d.,** a oscuras; de noche; *fig* **be in the d.,** quedarse en la luna. **to become d.,** oscurecerse; (cloud over) anublarse; (become night) anochecer. **to keep d.,** *vt* tener secreto. *vi* esconderse. **d. ages,** los siglos de la ignorancia y de la superstición. **d.-eyed,** de ojos negros, ojinegro. **d. horse,** caballo desconocido, *m*; *pol* batacazo, *m*. **d. lantern,** linterna sorda, *f.* **d. room,** cuarto oscuro, *m*; *phot* laboratorio fotográfico, *m*; (optics) cámara oscura, *f*

darken *vt* obscurecer; sombrear; (of color) hacer más oscuro; (sadden) entristecer. *vi* obscurecerse; (of the sky) anublarse; (of the face with emotion) inmutarse

darkening *n* oscurecimiento, *m*

darkly *adv* oscuramente; misteriosamente; con malevolencia; secretamente; (archaic) indistintamente

darkness *n* oscuridad, *f*, tinieblas, *f pl*; oscuro, *f*; (of color) oscuro, *m*; (of the complexion) color moreno, *m*; (of eyes, hair) negrura, *f*; (night) noche, *f*; (ignorance) ignorancia, *f*; (privacy) secreto, *m*. **Prince of d.,** el príncipe de las tinieblas

darling *a* querido, amado; (greatest) mayor. *n* querido (-da); (favorite) el predilecto, la predilecta, el favorito, la favorita. **My d.!** ¡Amor mío! ¡Vida mía! ¡Pichoncito mío!

darn *vt* zurcir, remendar. *n* zurcido, remiendo, *m*

darner *n* zurcidor (-ra); (implement) huevo de zurcir, *m*

darning *n* zurcidura, *f*; zurcido, recosido, *m*. **d.-needle,** aguja de zurcir, *f.* **d. wool,** lana de zurcir, *f*

dart *n* dardo, *m*; movimiento rápido, *m*; avance rápido, *m*; *sew* sisa, *f. vi* lanzarse, abalanzarse (sobre); volar, correr, avanzar rápidamente. *vt* lanzar, arrojar; dirigir. **to make darts in,** *sew* sisar

Darwinian *a* darviniano. *n* darvinista, *mf*

Darwinism *n* darvinismo, *m*

dash *n* (spirit) fogosidad, *f*, brío, *m*; energía, *f*; (impact) choque, golpe, *m*; (mixture) mezcla, *f*; (of a liquid) gota, *f*; (of the pen) rasgo, *m*; (attack) ataque, *m*; avance rápido, *m*; (a little) algo, un poco (de); *gram* raya, *f*; (show) ostentación, *f*. **He made a d. for the door,** Se precipitó a la puerta, Corrió hacia la puerta. **to cut a d.,** hacer gran papel. **d.-board,** tablero de instrumentos, *m*

dash *vt* arrojar con violencia; (break) quebrar, estrellar; (sprinkle) rociar (con), salpicar (con); (mix) mezclar; (knock) golpear; (disappoint) frustrar, destruir; (confound) confundir; (depress) desanimar. *vi* (rush) precipitarse; quebrarse, estrellarse; chocar (contra); (of waves) romperse. **to d. to pieces,** hacer añicos, estrellar. **to d. along,** avanzar rápidamente; correr. **to d. away,** *vi* marcharse apresuradamente. *vt* apartar bruscamente. **to d. down,** *vi* bajar aprisa. *vt* derribar; (overturn) volcar; (throw) tirar. **to d. off,** *vi* marcharse rápidamente. *vt* hacer apresuradamente; (a letter, etc.) escribir de prisa; (sketch) bosquejar rápidamente. **to d. out,** *vi* salir precipitadamente; lanzarse a la calle. *vt* (erase) borrar; hacer saltar. **to d. through,** atravesar rápidamente; hacer de prisa. **to d. up,** llegar a prisa; (sprout) saltar

dashing *a* valiente; (spirited) fogoso, gallardo; majo, brillante. *n* choque, *m*; (breaking) quebrantamiento, *m*; (of the waves) embate, *m*

dastardly *a* cobarde

data *n pl* datos, *m pl*

data processing *n* elaboración electrónica de datos, *f*, recuento de datos, *m*

date *n* fecha, *f*; (period) época, *f*; (term) plazo, *m*; (duration) duración, *f*; (appointment) cita, *f*; *bot* dátil, *m*. *vt* fechar, datar; poner fecha a; asignar. *vi* datar (de), remontar (a). **out of d.,** anticuado; pasado de moda; (of persons) atrasado de noticias. **to be up to d.,** ser nuevo; ser de última moda; (of persons) estar al día. **to bring up to d.,** renovar; (of persons) poner al corriente. **to fix the d.,** señalar el día; (chronologically) ajustar los tiempos. **to d.,** hasta la fecha. **under d. (of),** con fecha (de). **up to d.,** hasta hoy, hasta ahora. **What is the d.?** ¿Qué fecha es? ¿A cómo estamos hoy? ¿A cuántos estamos hoy? **d. palm,** datilera, *f*

date of expiry *n* fecha de caducidad, *f*

daub *vt* barrar, embadurnar; manchar, ensuciar; untar; (paint) pintorrear. *n* embadurnamiento, *m*; (picture) aleluya, *f*

dauber *n* chafalmejas, pintamonas, *mf* pintor (-ra) de brocha gorda

daughter *n* hija, *f*. **adopted d.,** hija adoptiva, *f*. **little d.,** hijuela, *f*. **d.-in-law,** nuera, *f*

daughterly *a* de hija

daunt *vt* intimidar, acobardar; dar miedo (a), espantar; (dishearten) desanimar

dauntless *a* impávido, intrépido

dauphin *n* delfín, *m*

dawdle *vi* perder el tiempo; haraganear, gandulear

dawdler *n* gandul (-la)

dawdling *a* perezoso, lento

dawn *n* alba, madrugada, primera luz, *f*; *fig* aurora, *f*. *vi* amanecer, alborear, romper el día; (appear) mostrarse, asomar. **at d.,** a primera luz, al amanecer, de madrugada, al alba. **It had not dawned on me,** No me había ocurrido

day *n* día, *m*; luz del día, *f*; (day's work) jornada, *f*; (battle) batalla, *f*; (victory) victoria, *f*; *pl* **days,** (time) tiempos, *m pl*, época, *f*; (life) vida, *f*; (years) años, *m pl*, a diario. **all day long,** durante todo el día. **any day,** cualquier día. **by day,** de día. **by the day,** al día. **every day,** todos los días, cada día. **every other day,** un día sí y otro no, cada dos días. **from this day forward,** desde hoy en adelante. **from day to day,** de día en día. **Good day!** ¡Buenos días! **in these days,** en estos días. **in olden days,** en la antigüedad; *inf* en tiempos de Maricastaña. **in the days of,** en los tiempos; durante los años de; durante la vida de. **next day,** el día siguiente. **(on) the next day,** al día siguiente, al otro día. **one of these days,** un día de éstos. **some fine day,** el mejor día, de un día a otro. **the day after tomorrow,** pasado mañana. **the day before yesterday,** anteayer. **the day before,** la víspera. **to win the day,** ganar el día, salir victorioso. **day after day,** cada día, día tras día. **day by day,** día por día. **day in, day out,** sin cesar, día tras día. **day-book,** *com* libro diario, *m*. **day's holiday,** día de asueto, *m*; día libre, *m*. **day laborer,** jornalero, *m*. **day nursery,** guardería de niños, *f*. **day-pupil,** alumno (-na) externo (-na). **day-school,** externado, *m*. **day shift,** turno de día, *m*. **day-star,** lucero del alba, *m*. **day ticket,** billete de excursión, *m*

daybreak *n* alba, *f*, amanecer, *m*. **at d.,** al romper el día, al amanecer

daydream *n* ensueño, *m*; ilusión, *f*; fantasía, visión, *f*. *vi*

lit soñar despierto, dejar volar sus pensamientos; *fig* hacerse ilusiones

daydreamer *n* soñador (-ra); visionario (-ia)

daylight *n* luz del día, *f*, día, *m*; (contrasted with artificial light) luz natural, *f*. **in broad d.,** a plena calle, a plena luz, en plena luz del día. **It's d. robbery!** ¡Es un desuello! **d.-saving,** hora de verano, *f*

daytime *n* día, *m*. **in the d.,** durante el día

daze *vt* aturdir, confundir; (dazzle) deslumbrar. *n* aturdimiento, *m*, confusión, *f*; perplejidad, *f*

dazzle *vt* (camouflage) disfrazar; deslumbrar, ofuscar. *n* deslumbramiento, *m*; brillo, *m*, refulgencia, *f*

dazzling *a* deslumbrador; brillante

deacon *n* diácono, *m*

deaconess *n* diaconisa, *f*

dead *a* and *past part* muerto; inanimado; (withered) marchito; (deep) profundo; (unconscious) inerte; inmóvil; insensible; (numb) entumecido; (complete) absoluto, completo; (sure) certero, excelente; (useless) inútil; (of color and human character) apagado; sin espíritu; inactivo; (of eyes) mortecino; (of sound) sordo, opaco; (of villages, etc.) desierto, despoblado; (quiet) silencioso; (empty) vacío; (monotonous) monótono; (of fire) apagado; (with weight, language) muerto; *elec* interrumpido; *law* muerto civilmente. *adv* completamente, enteramente; del todo; directamente; exactamente; profundamente. **the d.,** los muertos. **in the d. of night,** en las altas horas de la noche. **to be d.,** estar muerto; haber muerto. **to be d. against,** estar completamente opuesto a. **to drop d.,** caer muerto; morir de repente. **to go d. slow,** ir muy lentamente. **to rise from the d.,** resucitar. **to sham d.,** hacer la mortecina, fingirse muerto. **to speak ill of the d.,** hablar mal de los muertos; *inf* desenterrar los muertos. **d. ball,** pelota fuera de juego, *f*. **d.-beat,** muerto de cansancio. **d. body,** cadáver, cuerpo muerto, *m*. **d. calm,** calma profunda, *f*; *naut* calma chicha, *f*. **d. certainty,** seguridad completa, *f*. **d.-drunk,** hecho una uva. **d. end,** callejón sin salida, *m*. **d. heat,** empate, *m*. **d. language,** lengua muerta, *f*. **d.-letter,** letra muerta, *f*; carta devuelta o no reclamada, *f*. **d.-lock,** punto muerto, *m*. **to reach a d.-lock,** llegar a un punto muerto. **d. march,** marcha fúnebre, *f*. **d. season,** temporada de calma, *f*. **d. set,** empeñado (en). **d. shot,** (person) tirador (-ra) certero (-ra) (shot) tiro certero, *m*. **d. silence,** silencio profundo, *m*. **d. stop,** parada en seco, *f*. **d. tired,** rendido. **d. weight,** peso muerto, *m*. **d. wood,** leña seca, *f*; material inútil, *m*

deaden *vt* amortiguar; (of pain) calmar; (remove) quitar; (of colours) apagar

deadening *n* amortiguamiento, *m*

deadliness *n* carácter mortal, *m*; implacabilidad, *f*

deadly *a* mortal; implacable; *inf* insoportable. *adv* mortalmente. **He was d. pale,** Estaba pálido como un muerto. **the seven d. sins,** los siete pecados mortales. **d. nightshade,** belladona, *f*

deadness *n* falta de vida, *f*; inercia, *f*; marchitez, *f*; (numbness) entumecimiento, *m*; desanimación, *f*; parálisis, *f*

Dead Sea, el mar Muerto, *m*

Dead Sea Scrolls, the los rollos del mar Muerto, *m pl*

deaf *a* sordo. **d. people,** los sordos. **to be d.,** ser sordo; padecer sordera. **to be as d. as a post,** ser más sordo que una tapia. **to become d.,** ensordecer, volverse sordo. **to fall on d. ears,** caer en saco roto. **to turn a d. ear,** hacerse el sordo. **d. aid,** audífono, *m*. **d.-and-dumb,** sordomudo. **d.-and-dumb alphabet,** alfabeto manual, abecedario manual, *m*. **d.-mute,** sordomudo (-da). **d.-mutism,** sordomudez, *f*

deafen *vt* asordar, ensordecer

deafening *a* ensordecedor

deafly *adv* sordamente

deafness *n* sordera, *f*

deal *n* (transaction) negocio, trato, *m*; (at cards) reparto, *m*; (wood) pino, *m*; (plank) tablón de pino, *m*. **a d., a**

great d., mucho. **a very great d.,** muchísimo. **to con-clude a d.,** cerrar un trato

deal vt repartir; (a blow) asestar, dar; (cards) dar; (justice) dispensar. **to d. a blow at,** asestar un golpe; fig herir (en); fig destruir de un golpe. **to d. in,** comerciar en, traficar en; ocuparse en; meterse en. **to d. out,** dispensar. **to d. with,** (buy from) comprar de; tener relaciones con, tratar; entenderse con; portarse con; (of affairs) ocuparse en, arreglar, dirigir; (contend) luchar con; (discuss) discutir, tratar de; (of books) versar sobre. **d. regularly with** Lat. Am. amarcharse con

dealer n traficante, mf mercader, m, Lat. Am. marchante (-ta); (at cards) el que da las cartas

dealing n conducta, f; proceder, m; trato, m; tráfico, m; pl **dealings,** relaciones, f pl; transacciones, f pl

dean n ecc deán, m; univ decano, m

dear a (beloved) querido, amado; (charming) encantador, simpático; (in letters) estimado, querido; (favorite) predilecto; (expensive) caro. n querido (-da) persona querida, f, bien amado (-da). adv caro. **Oh d.! ¡Dios mío! ¡Ay!**

dearly adv tiernamente, entrañablemente; caro

dearness n cariño, afecto, m, ternura, f; (of price) precio alto, m

dearth n carestía, f; (of news, etc.) escasez, f

death n muerte, f; (law and in announcements) fallecimiento, m, defunción, f. **to be at death's door,** estar a la muerte. **to put to d.,** ajusticiar. **to the d.,** a muerte. **untimely d.,** muerte repentina, f; malogro, m. **death's head,** calavera, f. **d. certificate,** partida de defunción, f. **d.-duties,** derechos de herencia, m pl. **d.-like,** cadavérico. **d.-mask,** mascarilla, f. **d. penalty,** pena de muerte, f. **d.-rate,** mortalidad, f. **d.-rattle,** sarrillo, m. **d.-trap,** lugar peligroso, m; fig trampa, f. **d.-warrant,** sentencia de muerte, f. **d.-watch bettle,** reloj de la muerte, m

deathbed n lecho mortuorio, lecho de muerte, m. **on one's d.,** en su lecho de muerte

deathblow n golpe mortal, m

deathly a mortal

death toll n (of a bell) doble, toque de difuntos, m; (casualties) número de muertos, saldo de muertos, m

debacle n fig ruina, f

debar vt excluir, privar

debase vt degradar, humillar, envilecer; (the coinage) alterar (la moneda)

debasement n degradación, humillación, f, envilecimiento, m; (of the coinage) alteración (de la moneda), f

debasing a degradante, humillante

debatable a discutible

debate n debate, m; discusión, f; disputa, f. vt and vi debatir; discutir; disputar; considerar

debater n discutidor (-ra); orador (-ra).

debating n discusión, f; argumentación, f

debauch vt corromper, pervertir; (a woman) seducir, violar. n libertinaje, m; borrachera, f

debauched a vicioso, licencioso

debauchee n libertino, vicioso, m

debauchery n libertinaje, mal vivir, m, viciosidad, licencia, f

debenture n obligación, f. **d. holder,** obligacionista, mf

debilitate vt debilitar

debilitating a debilitante

debilitation n debilitación, f

debility n debilidad, f

debit n débito, cargo, m; saldo deudor, m; "debe" de una cuenta, m. vt adeudar. **d. and credit,** el cargo y la data. **d. balance,** saldo deudor, m

debonair a gallardo, gentil, donairoso; alegre

debonairly adv gallardamente; alegremente

débris n escombros, desechos, m pl; ruinas, f pl; geol despojos, m pl

debt n deuda, Lat. Am. also dita f. **a bad d.,** una deuda incobrable. **to be in the d. of,** ser en cargo a; deber

dinero a; fig sentirse bajo una obligación. **to get into d.,** adeudarse, contraer deudas, Mexico endrogarse, elsewhere in Lat. Am. enditarse

debtor n deudor (-ra); com debe, m

debunk vt demoler

debut n (of a debutante) puesta de largo, f; (of a play, etc.) estreno, m. **to make one's d.,** ponerse de largo, presentarse en sociedad

debutante n debutante, f

decade n década, f, decenio, m; (of the rosary) decena, f

decadence n decadencia, f

decadent a decadente

decagramme n decagramo, m

decaliter n decalitro, m

decalogue n decálogo, m

decametre n decámetro, m

decamp vi mil decampar; escaparse, fugarse

decant vt decantar

decanter n garrafa, f

decapitate vt decapitar, descabezar

decapitation n decapitación, f

decarbonization n descarburación, f

decarbonize vt descarbonizar

decay vi (rot) pudrirse; degenerar; marchitarse; (of teeth) cariarse; (crumble) desmoronarse, caer en ruinas; decaer, declinar; (come down in the world) venir a menos, arruinarse. n pudrición, putrefacción, f; (of teeth) caries, f; (withering) marchitez, f; degeneración, f; desmoronamiento, m; ruina, f; (oldness) vejez, f; decadencia, declinación, f; (fall) caída, f

decease n fallecimiento, m, defunción, f, vi fallecer

deceased n finado (-da), difunto (-ta). a difunto

deceit n engaño, fraude, m; duplicidad, f

deceitful a engañoso, falso; embustero, mentiroso; ilusorio

deceitfully adv engañosamente

deceitfulness n falsedad, duplicidad, f

deceivable a fácil a engañar, engañadizo

deceive vt engañar; (disappoint) decepcionar, desilusionar; frustrar. **If my memory does not d. me,** Si la memoria no me engaña, Si mal no me acuerdo

deceiver n engañador (-ra); seductor, m

deceiving a engañador

December n diciembre, m

decency n decoro, m, decencia, f; pudor, m, modestia, f; conveniencias, f pl; inf bondad, f; (manners) cortesía, f, buenos modales, m pl

decennial a decenal

decent a decente; decoroso, honesto; púdico; (likable) simpático; (of things) bastante bueno; (honorable) honrado

decently adv decentemente

decentralization n descentralización, f

decentralize vt descentralizar

deception n engaño, m; ilusión, f

deceptive a engañoso, mentiroso, ilusorio

deceptively adv engañosamente

decide vt decidir; law determinar. vi decidir, resolver; acordar, quedar en; juzgar; law dictar sentencia, fallar

decided a decidido; (downright) categórico, inequívoco; resuelto; positivo; definitivo

decidedly adv decididamente; categóricamente; definitivamente

deciduous a bot caedizo

decigram n decigramo, m

decimal a decimal. **d. fraction,** fracción decimal, f. **d. point,** punto decimal, m. **d. system,** sistema métrico, m

decimate vt diezmar

decimation n gran mortandad, f; matanza, f

decimeter n decímetro, m

decipher vt descifrar; deletrear

decipherable a descifrable

decipherer *n* descifrador, *m*

decipherment *n* el descifrar; deletreo, *m*

decision *n* decisión, determinación, *f; law* sentencia, *f,* fallo, *m;* (agreement) acuerdo, *m;* (of character) firmeza, resolución, *f*

decisive *a* decísivo; terminante, conclusivo; crítico

decisively *adv* decisivamente

decisiveness *n* carácter decisivo, *m;* firmeza, resolución, *f;* decisión, *f*

deck *n* cubierta, *f;* (of cards) baraja (de naipes), *f. vt* adornar, ataviar; decorar. **between decks,** entrecubiertas, *f pl.* **lower d.,** cubierta, *f.* **promenade d.,** cubierta de paseo, *f.* **upper d.,** cubierta superior, *f.* **d.-cabin,** camarote de cubierta, *m.* **d.-chair,** silla de cubierta, silla de tijera, silla extensible, *f.* **d.-hand,** marinero, estibador, *m*

decked *a* ornado, ataviado; engalanado; *naut* de . . . puentes

declaim *vt* recitar. *vi* perorar, declamar

declamation *n* declamación, *f*

declamatory *a* declamatorio

declaration *n* declaración, *f;* manifiesto, *m;* proclamación, *f*

declaratory *a* declaratorio, declarativo

declare *vt* declarar; proclamar; afirmar; manifestar; confesar. *vi* declarar; *law* deponer, testificar. **to d. war (on)** declarar la guerra (a)

declaredly *adv* declaradamente, explícitamente, abiertamente

declension *n* declinación, *f*

declination *n* declinación, *f*

decline *n* declinación, decadencia, *f;* disminución, *f;* debilitación, *f;* (of the day) caída, *f;* (of stocks, shares) depresión, *f;* (illness) consunción, *f; (fig* setting) ocaso, *m, vi* declinar; inclinarse; decaer; disminuir; debilitarse; (refuse) negarse (a). *vt* (refuse) rechazar, rehusar; *gram* declinar; (avoid) evitar

declining *a* declinante. **in one's d. years,** en sus últimos años

declivity *n* cuesta, pendiente, *f,* declive, *m*

declutch *vi* desembragar

decoction *n* decocción, *f*

decode *vt* descifrar

decoder *n* descifrador, *m*

décolletee *a* escotado

decolouration *n* decoloración, *f*

decompose *vt* descomponer. *vi* descomponerse

decomposition *n* descomposición, *f*

decompressor *n* decompresor, *m*

decontaminate *vt* descontaminar

decontamination *n* descontaminación, *f*

decontrol *vt* suprimir las restricciones sobre

decorate *vt* adornar (con), embellecer; (by painting, etc.) decorar, pintar; (honor) investir (con), condecorar

decoration *n* decoración, *f; theat* decorado, *m;* (honor) condecoración, *f;* ornamento, *m*

decorative *a* decorativo

decorator *n* decorador, *m;* (interior) adornista, *m*

decorous *a* decoroso, decente; correcto

decorum *n* decoro, *m;* corrección, *f*

decoy *n* señuelo, *m;* añagaza, *f;* (trap) lazo, *m,* trampa, *f; fig* añagaza, *f. vt* (birds) reclamar, atraer con señuelo; *fig* tentar (con), seducir (con). **d. bird,** pájaro de reclamo, *m*

decrease *n* disminución, *f;* baja, *f;* reducción, *f;* (of the moon, waters) mengua, *f, vi* decrecer, disminuir; bajar; menguar. *vt* disminuir; reducir

decreasingly *adv* de menos en menos

decree *n* decreto, *m;* edicto, *m. vi and vt* decretar, mandar

decrepit *a* decrépito

decry *vt* desacreditar, rebajar

dedicate *vt* dedicar; consagrar; destinar; aplicar; (a book, etc.) dedicar. **to d. oneself to,** dedicarse a, consagrarse a, entregarse a

dedication *n* dedicación, *f;* consagración, *f;* (of a book, etc.) dedicatoria, *f*

dedicatory *a* dedicatorio

deduce *vt* derivar; deducir, inferir

deduct *vt* deducir; descontar

deduction *n* deducción, *f;* descuento, *m*

deductive *a* deductivo

deed *n* acción, *f;* hecho, acto, *m;* hazaña, *f;* (reality) realidad, *f; law* escritura, *f; law* contrato, *m.* **d. of gift,** escritura de donación, *f*

deem *vt* juzgar, creer, estimar

deep *a* profundo; (wide) ancho; (low) bajo; (thick) espeso; (of colours) subido; (of sounds) grave, profundo; (immersed (in)) absorto (en); (of the mind) penetrante; (secret) secreto; (intense) intenso, hondo; (cunning) astuto, artero; (dark) oscuro; (of mourning) riguroso. *n poet* piélago, mar, *m;* profundidad, *f;* abismo, *m, adv* profundamente; a una gran profundidad. **to be in d. waters,** *fig* estar con el agua al cuello. **to be three feet d.,** tener tres pies de profundidad. **to be d. in,** estar absorto en; (of debt) estar cargado de. **three d.,** tres de fondo. **d. into the night,** hasta las altas horas de la noche. **d.-felt,** hondamente sentido. **d. mourning,** luto riguroso, *m.* **d.-rooted,** arraigado. **d.-sea fishing,** pesca mayor, *f.* **d.-sea lead,** escandallo, *m.* **d.-seated,** íntimo, profundo; arraigado. **d.-set,** hundido

deepen *vt* profundizar, ahondar; (broaden) ensanchar; (intensify) intensificar; (increase) aumentar; (of colors) aumentar el tono de, intensificar. *vi* hacerse más profundo, hacerse más hondo; intensificarse; aumentarse; (of sound) hacerse más grave

deeply *adv* profundamente; intensamente; fuertemente

deepness *n* (cunning) astucia, *f;* see **depth**

deer *n* ciervo (-va), venado, *m, a* cervuno. **d.-hound,** galgo de cazar venados, *m.* **d.-skin,** piel de venado, *f.* **d.-stalking,** caza del ciervo, *f.*

deface *vt* desfigurar, mutilar; estropear; (erase) borrar

defacement *n* desfiguración, mutilación, *f;* afeamiento, *m;* borradura, *f*

defamation *n* difamación, denigración, *f*

defamatory *a* difamatorio, denigrante

defame *vt* difamar, denigrar, calumniar

default *n* omisión, *f,* descuido, *m;* falta, *f;* ausencia, *f; law* rebeldía, *f. vi* dejar de cumplir; faltar; no pagar. *vt law* condenar en rebeldía. **in d. of,** en la ausencia de

defaulter *n* el, *m,* (f, la) que no cumple sus obligaciones; delincuente, *mf;* desfalcador (-ra); *law* rebelde, *mf*

defeat *vt* vencer, derrotar; frustrar; (reject) rechazar; (elude) evitar; *fig* vencer, triunfar sobre. *n* derrota, *f;* vencimiento, *m;* frustración, *f;* rechazamiento, *m.* **to d. one's own ends,** defraudar sus intenciones

defeatism *n* derrotismo, *m*

defeatist *n* derrotista, *mf*

defecate *vt* defecar

defecation *n* defecación, *f*

defect *n* defecto, *m;* imperfección, *f;* falta, *f*

defection *n* defección, *f;* deserción, *f;* (from a religion) apostasía, *f*

defective *a* defectuoso; *gram* defectivo; falto; imperfecto; (mentally) anormal. *n* persona anormal, *f,* anormal, *m*

defectiveness *n* imperfección, *f;* deficiencia, *f;* defecto, *m*

defend *vt* defender; proteger; preservar; sostener; (a thesis) sustentar

defendant *n law* acusado (-da), procesado (-da), demandado (-da)

defender *n* defensor (-ra); (of a thesis) sustentante, *mf*

defense *n* defensa, *f;* justificación, *f; pl* **defenses,** defensas, *f pl;* obras de fortificación, *f pl.* **for the d.,** (of witnesses) de descargo; (of counsel) para la defensa. **in d. of,** en defensa de. **in one's own d.,** en su propia defensa. **d. in depth,** *mil* defensa en fondo, *f*

defenseless *a* indefenso, sin defensa
defenselessness *n* incapacidad de defenderse, *f*; debilidad, *f*, desvalimiento, *m*
defensible *a* defendible; justificable
defensive *a* defensivo. *n* defensiva, *f*. **to be on the d.,** estar a la defensiva
defensively *adv* defensivamente
defer *vt* (postpone) diferir, aplazar; suspender. *vi* (yield) deferir, ceder; (delay) tardar, aguardar. **deferred payment,** pago a plazos, *m*
deference *n* deferencia, *f*, respeto, *m*; consideración, *f*
deferential *a* deferente, respetuoso
deferment *n* aplazamiento, *m*; suspensión, *f*
defiance *n* desafío, *m*; provocación, *f*; oposición, *f*; insolencia, *f*. **in d. of,** en contra de
defiant *a* provocativo; insolente
defiantly *adv* de un aire provocativo; insolentemente
deficiency *n* falta, deficiencia, *f*; imperfección, *f*; defecto, *m*; omisión, *f*; (scarcity) carestía, *f*; (in accounts) déficit, *m*
deficient *a* deficiente; falto, incompleto; imperfecto; pobre; defectuoso; (not clever at) débil (en); (mentally) anormal. **to be d. in,** carecer de; ser pobre en
deficit *n* déficit, *m*; descubierto, *m*
defile *n* desfiladero, *m*. *vt* contaminar; profanar; manchar; deshonrar. *vi mil* desfilar
defilement *n* contaminación, *f*; corrupción, *f*; profanación, *f*
definable *a* definible
define *vt* definir; (throw into relief) destacar; fijar; *law* determinar
definite *a* definido; positivo; categórico; exacto; concreto. **d. article,** artículo definido, *m*
definitely *adv* positivamente; claramente. **definitely not!** ¡definitivamente no!
definiteness *n* carácter definido, *m*; exactitud, *f*; lo categórico
definition *n* definición, *f*
definitive *a* definitivo
deflate *vt* desinflar. *vi* desinflarse, deshincharse
deflation *n* desinflación, *f*
deflect *vt* desviar; apartar. *vi* desviarse; apartarse
deflection *n* desviación, *f*; apartamiento, *m*
defloration *n* desfloración, *f*
deflower *vt* desflorar
deforestation *n* desforestación, desmontadura, despoblación forestal, *f*
deform *vt* deformar, desfigurar; afear
deformation *n* deformación, *f*
deformed *a* deformado; contrahecho
deformity *n* deformidad, *f*
defraud *vt* defraudar
defrauder *n* defraudador (-ra)
defrauding *n* defraudación, *f*
defray *vt* sufragar, costear, pagar
defrayal *n* pago, *m*
defrost *vt* deshelar
deft *a* diestro; hábil
deftly *adv* con destreza; hábilmente
deftness *n* destreza, *f*; habilidad, *f*
defunct *a* and *n* difunto (-ta)
defy *vt* desafiar; (face) arrostrar; (violate) contravenir
degeneracy *n* degeneración, *f*; depravación, degradación, *f*
degenerate *a* and *n* degenerado (-da). *vi* degenerar
degeneration *n* degeneración, *f*
degradation *n* degradación, *f*; abyección, *f*
degrade *vt* degradar; envilecer, deshonrar
degrading *a* degradante
degree *n* grado, *m*; punto, *m*; clase social, *f*. **by degrees,** poco a poco, gradualmente, **five degrees below zero,** cinco grados bajo cero. **in the highest d.,** en sumo grado, en grado superlativo. **to a certain d.,** hasta cierto punto. **to receive a d.,** graduarse
degree-granting institution *n* plantel habilitado para expedir títulos, *m*

dehydrate *vt* deshidratar
dehydration *n* deshidratación, *f*
de-ice *vt* deshelar
deification *n* deificación, *f*
deify *vt* deificar, endiosar
deign *vi* dignarse. *vt* conceder
deism *n* deísmo, *m*
deist *n* deísta, *mf*
deity *n* deidad, divinidad, *f*; dios, *m*
dejected *a* abatido, desanimado, deprimido
dejectedly *adv* tristemente, abatidamente
dejection *n* abatimiento, desaliento, *m*, melancolía, *f*
delay *n* retraso, *m*, dilación, tardanza, demora, *f*. *vt* retrasar, demorar; (a person) entretener; (postpone) aplazar; (obstruct) impedir. *vi* tardar; entretenerse. **without more d.,** sin más tardar
delectable *a* deleitoso, delicioso
delectably *adv* deliciosamente
delectation *n* delectación, *f*, deleite, *m*
delegacy *n* delegación, *f*
delegate *n* delegado (-da). *vt* delegar, diputar
delegation *n* delegación, *f*
delete *vt* suprimir, borrar
deleterious *a* deletéreo
deletion *n* supresión, borradura, *f*
deliberate *a* premeditado, intencionado; (slow) pausado, lento. *vi* and *vt* deliberar, discurrir, considerar
deliberately *adv* (intentionally) con premeditación, a sabiendas, *Central America* adifés; (slowly) pausadamente, lentamente
deliberation *n* reflexión, deliberación, consideración, *f*; (slowness) lentitud, pausa, *f*
deliberative *a* deliberativo, de liberante
delicacy *n* delicadeza, *f*; fragilidad, *f*; suavidad, *f*; sensibilidad, *f*; escrupulosidad, *f*; (of health) debilidad, delicadez, *f*; (difficulty) dificultad, *f*; (food) manjar exquisito, *m*, golosina, *f*
delicate *a* delicado; fino; frágil; suave; exquisito; delicado (de salud); (of situations) difícil
delicatessen *n* (store) fiambrería, *f*
delicious *a* delicioso
deliciously *adv* deliciosamente
deliciousness *n* deleite, *m*, lo delicioso; excelencia, *f*, delicias, *f pl*
delict *n* delito, *m*
delictive *a* delictivo
delight *n* deleite, regocijo, *m*; encanto, *m*, delicia, *f*; placer, gozo, *m*. *vt* deleitar, encantar; halagar. *vi* deleitarse, complacerse. **to be delighted with,** estar encantado con. **to d. in,** deleitarse en, complacerse en; tomar placer en
delightful *a* delicioso, precioso, encantador
delightfully *adv* deliciosamente
delimit *vt* delimitar
delimitation *n* delimitación, *f*
delineate *vt* delinear, diseñar; *fig* pintar, describir
delineation *n* delineación, *f*; retrato, *m*; *fig* descripción, *f*
delineator *n* diseñador, *m*
delinquency *n* delincuencia, *f*; criminalidad, *f*; culpa, *f*; delito, *m*
delinquent *a* delincuente. *n* delincuente, *mf*
deliquescence *n* delicuescencia, *f*
deliquescent *a* delicuescente
delirious *a* delirante; desvariado; *inf* loco. **to be d.,** delirar, desvariar
delirium *n* delirio, desvarío, *m*. **d. tremens,** delírium tremens, *m*
deliver *vt* librar (de); salvar (de); (distribute) repartir; (hand over) entregar; (recite) recitar, decir; (a speech) pronunciar; comunicar; (send) despachar, expedir; (a blow) asestar; (give) dar; (bring) traer; (battle, a lecture) dar; (a woman, of a doctor) asistir en el parto a; (a child) traer al mundo; (a judgment) pronunciar. **to be delivered (of a child),** dar a luz. **to d. oneself up,** entregarse. **delivered free,** porte pagado.

deliverance *n* libramiento, rescate, *m*; redención, salvación, *f*; (of a judgment) pronuncia, *f*

deliverer *n* libertador (-ra); salvador (-ra); (distributor) repartidor (-ra); entregador (-ra)

delivery *n* (distribution) reparto, *m*, distribución, *f*; entrega, *f*; *law* cesión, *f*; (of a judgment) pronuncia, *f*; (of a speech) pronunciación, *f*; (manner of speaking) declamación, *f*; dicción, *f*; (of a child) parto, *m*. **on d.,** al entregarse. **The letter came by the first d.,** La carta llegó en el primer reparto. **d. man,** mozo de reparto, *m*. **d. note,** nota de entrega, *f*. **d. van,** camión de reparto, *m*

delivery truck *n* camioneta de reparto, furgoneta, *f*, sedán de reparto, *m*

dell *n* hondonada, *f*; pequeño valle, *m*

delouse *vt* despiojar, espulgar

Delphi Delfos, *m*

delta *n* (Greek letter) delta, *f*; (of a river) delta, *m*

delude *vt* engañar; ilusionar. **to d. oneself,** engañarse

deluded *a* iluso, engañado, ciego

deluge *n* diluvio, *m*. *vt* diluviar; inundar (con)

delusion *n* engaño, *m*, ceguedad, *f*; error, *m*; ilusión, *f*

delve *vt* and *vi* cavar; *fig* ahondar (en), penetrar (en), investigar

demagogic *a* demagógico

demagogue *n* demagogo (-ga)

demagogy *n* demagogia, *f*

demand *n* exigencia, *f*; *com* demanda, *f*; petición, *f*; *pol econ* consumo, *m*. *vt* exigir; requerir; pedir; (claim) reclamar. **in d.,** en demanda, *f*. **on d.,** al solicitarse. **to be in d.,** ser popular. **d. note,** apremio, *m*

demanding *a* exigente

demarcate *vt* demarcar

demarcation *n* demarcación, *f*

demean (oneself) *vr* degradarse, rebajarse

demeanor *n* conducta, *f*; continente, porte, aire, *m*; (manners) modales, *m pl*

demented *a* demente, loco

demerit *n* demérito, *m*

demi *prefix* semi; casi. **d.-tasse,** taza cafetera, jícara, *f*

demigod *n* semidios, *m*

demigoddess *n* semidiosa, *f*

demijohn *n* damajuana, *f*

demilitarize *vt* desmilitarizar

demise *n law* traslación de dominio, *f*; sucesión de la corona, *f*; (death) óbito, fallecimiento, *m*

demisemiquaver *n* fusa, *f*

demobilization *n* desmovilización, *f*

demobilize *vt* desmovilizar

democracy *n* democracia, *f*

democrat *n* demócrata, *mf*

democratic *a* democrático. **to make d.,** democratizar

demolish *vt* demoler, derribar; *fig* destruir; (eat) engullir, devorar

demolisher *n* demoledor, *m*; *fig* destructor (-ra)

demolition *n* demolición, *f*; derribo, *m*, *a* demoledor; de demolición. **d. squad,** pelotón de demolición, *m*

demon *n* demonio, diablo, *m*

demonetization *n* desmonetización, *f*

demonetize *vt* desmonetizar

demoniacal *a* demoníaco

demonology *n* demonología, *f*

demonstrable *a* demonstrable

demonstrably *adv* demostrablemente

demonstrate *vt* demostrar; mostrar, probar. *vi* hacer una demostración

demonstration *n* demostración, *f*; manifestación, *f*

demonstrative *a* demostrativo; (of persons) expresivo, mimoso. **d. pronoun,** pronombre demostrativo, *m*

demonstrator *n* demostrador (-ra)

demoralization *n* desmoralización, *f*

demoralize *vt* desmoralizar

demoralizing *a* desmoralizador

demur *vi* dudar, vacilar; objetar, protestar; poner dificultades. *n* objeción, protesta, *f*

demure *a* serio, modoso recatado; púdico; de una coquetería disimulada

demurely *adv* modestamente; con recato; con coquetería disimulada

demureness *n* seriedad, *f*, recato, *m*; modestia fingida, coquetería disimulada, *f*

demy *n* papel marquilla, *m*; becario de Magdalen College, Oxford, *m*

den *n* madriguera, guardia, *f*; (of thieves) cueva, *f*; (in a zoo) cercado, recinto, *m*; (study) gabinete, *m*; (squalid room) cuartucho, *m*

denaturalization *n* desnaturalización, *f*

denaturalize *vt* desnaturalizar

denial *n* negación, *f*; rechazo, *m*; contradicción, *f*; negativa, *f*

denizen *n* habitante, *m*; ciudadano (-na)

Denmark Dinamarca, *f*

denominate *vt* denominar, nombrar

denomination *n* denominación, *f*; secta, *f*; clase, *f*

denominational *a* sectario

denominator *n math* denominador, *m*

denote *vt* denotar, indicar; significar

dénouement *n* desenlace, desenredo, *m*; solución, *f*

denounce *vt* denunciar; delatar, acusar

denouncer *n* denunciante, *mf* delator (-ra)

dense *a* denso; espeso, compacto; tupido; impenetrable; *inf* estúpido

densely *adv* densamente; espesamente. **d. populated,** con gran densidad de población

density *n* densidad, *f*; espesor, *m*; consistencia, *f*; *inf* estupidez, *f*

dent *n* mella, *f*; (in metal) abolladura, *f*, *vt* mellar; abollar

dental *a* dental. *n* letra dental, *f*. **d. forceps,** gatillo, *m*. **d. mechanic,** mecánico dentista, *m*. **d. surgeon,** odontólogo, *m*

dental floss *n* seda dental, *f*

dentifrice *n* dentífrico, *m*

dentist *n* dentista, *mf*; odontólogo, *m*

dentistry *n* odontología, *f*

dentition *n* dentición, *f*

denture *n* dentadura, *f*

denudation *n* denudación, *f*

denude *vt* denudar, despojar, privar (de)

denunciation *n* denuncia, *f*; acusación, delación, *f*

denunciatory *a* denunciatorio

Denver boot *n* cepo, *m*

deny *vt* negar; desmentir; rehusar; rechazar; renegar (de); (give up) renunciar, sacrificar. **to d. oneself,** privarse (de); sacrificar; negarse

deodorant *a* and *n* desodorante *m*.

deodorize *vt* desinfectar, destruir el olor de

depart *vi* marcharse, irse, partir; (of trains, etc., and meaning go out) salir; (deviate) desviarse (de), apartarse (de); (go away) alejarse; (leave) dejar; (disappear) desaparecer; (alter) cambiar; (die) morir

departed *a* (past) pasado; desaparecido; (dead) difunto, muerto. *n* difunto (-ta)

department *n* departamento, *m*; sección, *f*; (of learning) ramo, *m*; (in France) distrito administrativo, *m*. **d. store,** grandes tiendas, *f pl*, (Argentina), grandes almacenes, *m pl*

departmental *a* departamental

departure *n* partida, ida, *f*. *Lat. Am.* egreso *m*; (going out, and of trains, etc.) salida, *f*; (deviation) desviación, el apartarse. **d. from the rules,** el apartarse de las reglas), *f*; (disappearance) desaparición, *f*; (change) cambio, *m*; (giving up) renuncia, *f*; (death) muerte, *f*. **to take one's d.,** marcharse

depend *vi* depender. **to d. on,** depender de; (rest on) apoyarse en; (count on) contar con; (trust) fiarse de; tener confianza en, estar seguro de. **That depends!** ¡Eso depende!

dependable *a* digno de confianza; seguro

dependence, dependency *n* dependencia, *f*; subordinación, *f*; (trust) confianza, *f*

dependent *a* dependiente; subordinado; condicional. *n* dependiente, *m*. **to be d. on,** depender de

depict *vt* representar; pintar; dibujar; *fig* describir, retratar

depiction *n* representación, *f*; pintura, *f*; dibujo, *m*; *fig* descripción, *f*

depilate *vt* depilar

depilatory *a* and *n* depilatorio *m*.

deplete *vt* agotar; disipar

depletion *n* agotamiento, *m*

deplorable *a* lamentable, deplorable

deplorably *adv* lamentablemente

deplore *vt* deplorar, lamentar

deploy *vt* desplegar. *vi* desplegarse. *n* despliegue, *m*

deployment *n* despliegue, *m*

deponent *n law* declarante, deponente, *mf a* deponente. **d. verb,** verbo deponente, *m*

depopulate *vt* despoblar

depopulation *n* despoblación, *f*

deport *vt* deportar

deportation *n* deportación, *f*

deportment *n* comportamiento, *m*; porte, aire, *m*; conducta, *f*

depose *vt* destronar; (give evidence) testificar, declarar

deposit *n* depósito, *m*; *geol* yacimiento, filón, *m*; sedimento, *m*. *vt* depositar. **to leave a d.,** dejar un depósito. **d. account,** cuenta corriente, *f*

deposition *n* deposición, *f*; *law* testimonio, *m*, declaración, *Lat. Am.* contancia *f*; (from the Cross) descendimiento, *m*, (de la Cruz)

depositor *n* depositador (-ra)

depository *n* depositaría, *f*, almacén, *m*; (of knowledge, etc.) pozo, *m*

depot *n* almacén, *m*; (military headquarters) depósito, *m*; (for army vehicles, etc.) parque, *m*; (for buses, etc.) estación, *f*

depravation *n* depravación, *f*

depraved *a* depravado, perverso, vicioso

depravity *n* corrupción, maldad, perversión, *f*

deprecate *vt* desaprobar, criticar; lamentar, deplorar

deprecatingly *adv* con desaprobación, críticamente

deprecation *n* deprecación, *f*; desaprobación, crítica, *f*

deprecatory *a* deprecativo; de desaprobación, de crítica

depreciate *vt* depreciar, rebajar; *fig* tener en poco, menospreciar. *vi* depreciarse, deteriorarse; bajar de precio

depreciatingly *adv* con desprecio

depreciation *n* (in value) amortización, depreciación, *f*; *fig* desprecio, *m*

depreciatory *a fig* despectivo, despreciativo

depredation *n* depredación, *f*

depress *vt* deprimir; (weaken) debilitar; (humble) humillar; (dispirit) abatir, entristecer; (trade) desanimar, paralizar

depressed *a* deprimido, desalentado, melancólico, triste; (of an area) necesitado

depressing *a* melancólico, triste; pesimista

depressingly *adv* con tristeza; con pesimismo

depression *n* depresión, *f*; (hollow) hoyo, *m*; (sadness) desaliento, abatimiento, *m*, melancolía, *f*; (in prices) baja, *f*; (in trade) desanimación, parálisis, *f*; *ast* depresión, *f*

deprivation *n* privación, *f*; pérdida, *f*

deprive *vt* privar (de), despojar (de); defraudar (de); *ecc* destituir (de)

depth *n* profundidad, *f*; (thickness) espesor, *m*; fondo, *m*; (of night, winter, the country) medio, *m*; (of sound) gravedad, *f*; (of colour, feeling) intensidad, *f*; (abstruseness) dificultad, *f*; (sagacity) sagacidad, *f*; *pl* **depths,** profundidades, *f pl*; abismo, *m*; lo más hondo; lo más íntimo. **to be 4 feet in d.,** tener cuatro pies de profundidad. **to the depths of one's being,** hasta lo más íntimo de su ser; hasta los tuétanos. **d. charge,** carga de profundidad, *f*

deputation *n* deputación, delegación, *f*

deputize (for) *vi* desempeñar las funciones de, substituir

deputy *n* (substitute) lugarteniente, *m*; (agent) representante, *m*; apoderado, *m*; (parliamentary) diputado, *m*; (in compounds) sub, vice. **d.-governor,** subgobernador, *m*. **d.-head,** subjefe, *m*; (of a school) subdirector (-ra)

derail *vt* (hacer) descarrilar, *Lat. Am.* desrielar

derailment *n* descarrilamiento, *m*

derange *vt* desordenar; desorganizar; turbar; (mentally) trastornar, hacer perder el juicio (a)

derangement *n* desorden, *m*; turbación, *f*; (mental) trastorno, *m*, locura, *f*

derby *n* carrera del Derby, *f*; (hat) sombrero hongo, *m*

deregulate *vt* desregular

deregulation *n* desregulación, *f*

derelict *a* abandonado, derrelicto. *n* derrelicto, *m*

dereliction *n* abandono, *m*; omisión, negligencia, *f*; descuido, *m*

deride *vt* burlarse de, mofarse de; ridiculizar

derision *n* irrisión, *f*, menosprecio, *m*

derisive *a* irrisorio; irónico

derisively *adv* irrisoriamente; con ironía, irónicamente

derivation *n* derivación, *f*

derivative *a* derivativo. *n* derivado, *m*

derive *vt* derivar; obtener; extraer; *fig* sacar, hallar. *vi* (from) derivar de; proceder de; remontar a

dermatitis *n* dermatitis, *f*

dermatologist *n* dermatólogo, *m*

dermatology *n* dermatología, *f*

derogatory *a* despectivo, despreciativo; deshonroso

derrick *n* grúa, machina, *f*; abanico, *m*

descant *n mus* discante, *m*. *vi mus* discantar; discurrir (sobre), disertar (sobre)

descend *vi* descender, bajar; (be inherited) pasar a; (fall) caer; (of the sun) ponerse. *vt* bajar. **to d. from,** descender de. **to d. to,** (lower oneself) rebajarse; (consider) venir a, considerar. **to d. upon,** caer sobre; (arrive unexpectedly) llegar inesperadamente, invadir

descendant *n* descendiente, *mf; pl* **descendants,** descendencia, *f*

descent *n* descenso, *m*; bajada, *f*; (slope) pendiente, cuesta, *f*; (attack) invasión, *f*, ataque, *m*; (lineage) descendencia, alcurnia, procedencia, *f*; (inheritance) herencia, *f*; transmisión, *f*. **D. from the Cross,** Descendimiento de la Cruz, *m*

describable *a* descriptible

describe *vt* describir; pintar

description *n* descripción, *f*

descriptive *a* descriptivo

descry *vt* divisar, descubrir; *poet* ver

Desdemona Desdémona, *f*

desecrate *vt* profanar

desecration *n* profanación, *f*

desert *vt* abandonar; dejar; (mil etc.) desertar. *vi* desertar. *a* solitario; inhabitado; desierto; *fig* árido. *n* desierto, *m*; soledad, *f*; (merit) mérito, *m*. **to receive one's deserts,** llevar su merecido

deserted *a* abandonado; desierto; solitario; inhabitado, despoblado

deserter *n* desertor, *m*

desertion *n* abandono, *m*, deserción, *f*; (mil etc.) deserción, *f*

deserve *vt* and *vi* merecer

deservedly *adv* merecidamente

deserving *a* merecedor; meritorio. **to be d. of,** merecer

desiccate *vt* desecar. *vi* desecarse

design *n* proyecto, *m*; plan, *m*; intención, *f*, propósito, *m*; objeto, *m*; modelo, *m*; (pattern) diseño, dibujo, *m*; arte del dibujo, *mf. vt* idear; proyectar; (destine) destinar, dedicar; diseñar, dibujar, delinear; planear. **by d.,** expresamente, intencionalmente

designate *vt* señalar; designar; (appoint) nombrar. *a* electo

designation *n* designación, *f*; nombramiento, *m*

designedly *adv* de propósito

designer *n* inventor (-ra), autor (-ra); delineador (-ra); dibujante, *mf*; (of public works, etc.) proyectista, *mf*

designing *a* intrigante, astuto

desirability *n* lo deseable; conveniencia, *f*; ventaja, *f*

desirable *a* deseable; conveniente; ventajoso; agradable; apetecible

desire *vt* desear; querer; ansiar, ambicionar; (request) rogar, pedir; (order) mandar. *n* deseo, *m*; ansia, aspiración, *f*; ambición, *f*; impulso, *m*; (will) voluntad, *f*. **to d. ardently,** perecerse por; suspirar por

desirous *a* deseoso (de); ambicioso (de); ansioso (de); impaciente (a); curioso (de)

desist *vi* desistir; dejar (de)

desk *n* pupitre, *m*; escritorio, buró, *m*; mesa de trabajo, *f*; (cashier's) caja, *f*; (teacher's, lecturer's; pulpit) cátedra, *f*

desolate *a* solitario; desierto; deshabitado; abandonado; arruinado; árido; (afflicted) desolado, angustiado. *vt* desolar; despoblar

desolation *n* desolación, *f*; aflicción, angustia, *f*, desconsuelo, *m*

despair *n* desesperación, *f*, *vi* perder toda esperanza. **His life is despaired of,** Se ha perdido la esperanza de salvarle (la vida). **to be in d.,** estar desesperado

despairing *a* desesperado

despairingly *adv* sin esperanza

desperate *a* desesperado; sin esperanza; irremediable; furioso; violento; (dangerous) arriesgado, peligroso; terrible

desperately *adv* desesperadamente; furiosamente; terriblemente

desperation *n* desesperación, *f*; furia, violencia, *f*

despicable *a* vil, despreciable; insignificante

despise *vt* despreciar; desdeñar

despiser *n* menospreciador (-ra)

despite *prep* a pesar de

despoil *vt* despojar, desnudar

despoiler *n* despojador (-ra)

despoliation *n* despojo, *m*

despondency *n* abatimiento, desaliento, *m*, desesperación, *f*

despondent *a* abatido, desanimado, deprimido

despondently *adv* con desaliento

despot *n* déspota, *m*

despotic *a* despótico

despotism *n* despotismo, *m*

dessert *n* postre, *m*, *a* de postre. **d. plate,** plato para postre, *m*. **d.-spoon,** cuchara de postre, *f*

destination *n* destinación, *f*

destine *vt* destinar; dedicar; predestinar

destiny *n* destino, *m*

destitute *a* indigente, menesteroso; desnudo (de); privado (de); desprovisto (de), falto (de); desamparado

destitution *n* destitución, indigencia, miseria, *f*; privación, falta, *f*; desamparo, *m*

destroy *vt* destruir; demoler; deshacer; (kill) matar; exterminar; (finish) acabar con

destroyer *n* destructor (-ra); *nav* destructor, cazatorpedero, *m*

destructible *a* destructible, destruible

destruction *n* destrucción, *f*; demolición, *f*; ruina, *f*; pérdida, *f*; muerte, *f*; exterminio, *m*; perdición, *f*

destructive *a* destructivo, destructor; (of animals) dañino. **d. animal,** animal dañino, *m*, alimaña, *f*

destructiveness *n* destructividad, *f*; instinto destructor, *m*

desultory *a* inconexo; sin método, descosido; irregular

detach *vt* separar, desprender; (unstick) despegar; *mil* destacar

detachable *a* separable, de quita y pon

detached *a* suelto, separado; (*fig* with outlook, etc.) imparcial; indiferente, despegado. **d. house,** hotelito, *m*

detachment *n* separación, *f*; *mil* destacamento, *m*; (*fig* of mind) imparcialidad, *f*; independencia (de espíritu, etc.), *f*; indiferencia, *f*

detail *n* detalle, *m*; pormenor, *m*, particularidad, *f*; circunstancia, *f*; *mil* destacamento, *m*. *vt* detallar; particularizar, referir con pormenores; *mil* destacar. **in d.,** detalladamente; al por menor; *inf* ce por be. **to go into details,** entrar en detalles

detain *vt* detener; (arrest) arrestar, prender; (withhold) retener; (prevent) impedir

detect *vt* descubrir; averiguar; (discern) discernir, percibir; *elec* detectar

detectable *a* perceptible

detection *n* descubrimiento, *m*; averiguación, *f*; percepción, *f*

detective *n* detective, *m*, *a* de detectives, policíaco. **d. novel,** novela policíaca, *f*

detector *n* descubridor, *m*; *elec* detector, *m*; *mech* indicador, *m*

detention *n* detención, *f*; (arrest) arresto, *m*; (confinement) encierro, *m*

deter *vt* desanimar, desalentar; acobardar; (dissuade) disuadir; (prevent) impedir

detergent *a* detersorio. *n* detersorio, *m*

deteriorate *vt* deteriorar. *vi* deteriorarse; empeorar

deterioration *n* deterioración, *f*; empeoramiento, *m*

determinable *a* determinable

determination *n* determinación, *f*; definición, *f*; resolución, decisión, *f*; *law* fallo, *m*; *med* congestión, *f*

determine *vt* determinar; definir; decidir, resolver; concluir; (fix) señalar; *law* sentenciar. *vi* resolverse, decidirse; (insist (on)) empeñarse en, insistir en

determined *a* determinado; resuelto, decidido; (of price) fijo

determining *a* determinante

determinism *n* determinismo, *m*

deterministic *a* determinista

deterrent *a* disuasivo. *n* freno, *m*. **to act as a d.,** servir como un freno

deterrent capability *n* poder de disuasión, *m*

detest *vt* detestar, abominar, aborrecer

detestable *a* detestable, aborrecible, abominable

detestation *n* detestación, abominación, *f*, aborrecimiento, *m*

dethrone *vt* destronar

detonate *vt* hacer detonar. *vi* detonar, estallar

detonation *n* detonación, *f*

detonator *n* detonador, *m*; señal detonante, *f*

detour *n* rodeo, *m*; desvío, *m*, desviación, *f*

detract *vt* quitar; (diminish) disminuir; (slander) detraer, denigrar

detraction *n* detracción, denigración, *f*

detractor *n* detractor (-ra); infamador (-ra)

detriment *n* detrimento, *m*; perjuicio, *m*; daño, *m*

detrimental *a* perjudicial

deuce *n* (dice, cards) dos, *m*; (tennis) "dos," *m*. **The d.!** ¡Diantre! **to be the d. of a row,** haber moros y cristianos. **D. take it!** ¡Demonios!

Deuteronomy *n* Deuteronomio, *m*

devaluation *n* desvalorización, *f*

devalue *vt* rebajar el valor de

devastate *vt* devastar, asolar

devastation *n* devastación, *f*

develop *vt* desarrollar; (make progress) avanzar, fomentar; perfeccionar; *phot* revelar. *vi* desarrollarse; crecer; avanzar, progresar; evolucionar

developer *n* *phot* revelador, *m*

development *n* desarrollo, *m*; evolución, *f*; progreso, avance, *m*; (encouragement) fomento, *m*; (event) acontecimiento, suceso, *m*; (product) producto, *m*; (working) explotación, *f*; *phot* revelación, *f*

deviate *vi* desviarse (de); (disagree) disentir (de)

deviation *n* desviación, *f*

device *n* (contrivance) aparato, artefacto, mecanismo, *m*; (invention) invento, *m*; (trick) expediente, artificio, *m*; (scheme) proyecto, *m*; (design) dibujo, emblema, *m*; (motto) divisa, leyenda, *f*; *pl* **devices,** placeres, caprichos, *m pl*

devil *n* diablo, Satanás, *m*; demonio, *m*; (printer's) aprendiz de impresor, *m*. **Go to the d.!** ¡Vete enhoramala! **He is a poor d.,** Es un pobre diablo. **little d.,** diablillo, *m*. **The devil's abroad,** Anda el diablo suelto. **The d. take it!** ¡Lléveselo el diablo! **to play the d. with,** arruinar por completo. **What the d.!** ¡Qué diablos! **d.-possessed,** endemoniado

devilish *a* diabólico, demoníaco; infernal

devilry *n* diablura, *f*; magia, *f*; demonología, *f*; (wickedness) maldad, *f*; crueldad, *f*

devious *a* desviado; tortuoso

deviousness *n* tortuosidad, *f*

devise *vt* idear, inventar; fabricar; *law* legar

deviser *n* inventor (-ra)

devitalize *vt* restar vitalidad, privar de vitalidad

devoid *a* desprovisto (de), privado (de); libre (de), exento (de)

devolve *vt* traspasar, transmitir. *vi* (on, upon) incumbir (a), corresponder (a), tocar (a)

devote *vt* dedicar; consagrar. **to d. oneself to,** darse a, dedicarse a; consagrarse a

devoted *a* fervoroso, apasionado; (faithful) fiel, leal

devotedly *adv* con devoción

devotee *n* devoto (-ta), admirador (-ra); aficionado (-da)

devotion *n* devoción, *f*; dedicación, *f*; (zeal) celo, *m*; afición, *f*; (loyalty) lealtad, *f*; *pl* **devotions,** rezos, *m pl*, oraciones, *f pl*

devotional *a* devoto, religioso, de devoción. **devotional literature,** literatura de devoción, *f*

devour *vt* devorar; consumir

devourer *n* devorador (-ra)

devouring *a* devorador; absorbente

devout *a* devoto, piadoso, practicante (e.g., **a d. Catholic,** un católico practicante)

devoutly *adv* piadosamente

devoutness *n* piedad, devoción, *f*

dew *n* rocío, sereno, relente, *m*; *fig* rocío, *m*, *vt* rociar; humedecer; (refresh) refrescar. **d.-drop,** aljófar, *m*, gota de rocío, *f*

dewlap *n* papada, *f*, papo, *m*

dewy *a* rociado, lleno de rocío; húmedo; (of eyes) lustroso

dexterity *n* destreza, *f*

dextrine *n* dextrina, *f*

dextrose *n* dextrosa, glucosa, *f*

dextrous *a* diestro; hábil, listo

diabetes *n* diabetes, *f*

diabetic *a* diabético

diabolical *a* diabólico

diadem *n* diadema, *f*

diagnose *vt* diagnosticar

diagnosis *n* diagnóstico, *m*, diagnosis, *f*

diagnostician *n* diagnóstico, *m*

diagonal *n* diagonal, *f*

diagram *n* diagrama, *m*; esquema, *f*; gráfico, *m*

diagrammatic *a* esquemático

dial *n* (sundial) reloj de sol, *m*; (of clocks, gas-meter) esfera, *f*; (of machines) indicador, *m*; (of a wireless set) cuadrante graduado, *m*; (of a telephone) marcador, disco, *m*. *vt* (a telephone number) marcar. **d. telephone,** teléfono automático, *m*

dialect *n* dialecto, *m*, habla, *f*, *a* dialectal

dialectic *a* dialéctico

dialectics *n* dialéctica, *f*

dialogue *n* diálogo, *m*. **to hold a d.,** dialogar

dialysis *n* diálisis, *f*

diameter *n* diámetro, *m*

diametrical *a* diametral

diamond *n* diamante, *m*; brillante, *m*; (tool) cortavidrios, *m*; (cards) oros (de baraja), *m pl*. **rough d.,** diamante bruto, *m*. **d.-bearing,** diamantífero. **d. cutter,** diamantista, *mf* **d. cutting,** talla de diamantes, *f*. **d. edition,** edición diamante, *f*. **d.-like,** adiamantado. **d. wedding,** bodas de diamante, *f pl*

diapason *n* diapasón, *m*

diaper *n* lienzo adamascado, *m*; (baby's) pañal, *m*; (woman's) servilleta higiénica, *f*

diaphanous *a* diáfano, transparente

diaphragm *n* diafragma, *m*

diarist *n* diarista, *mf*

diarrhea *n* diarrea, *f*

diary *n* diario, *m*

diastase *n* diastasa, *f*

diastole *n* diástole, *f*

diatribe *n* diatriba, denunciación violenta, *f*

dibble *n* plantador, *m*, *vt* and *vi* plantar con plantador

dice *n pl* dados, *m pl*. **to load the d.,** cargar los dados

dicky *n* (front) pechera postiza, *f*; (seat) trasera, *f*; (apron) delantal, *m*. **d. seat,** *inf* ahí te pudras, *m*

dictaphone *n* dictáfono, *m*

dictate *vt* dictar; mandar. *n* (order) dictamen, *m*; *fig* dictado, *m*

dictation *n* dictado, *m*. **to write from d.,** escribir al dictado

dictator *n* dictador, *m*

dictatorial *a* dictatorial, dictatorio, imperioso

dictatorship *n* dictadura, *f*

diction *n* dicción, *f*

dictionary *n* diccionario, *m*

dictum *n* dictamen, *m*; (saying) sentencia, *f*; *law* fallo, *m*

didactic *a* didáctico

die *vi* morir; fallecer, finar; (wither) marchitarse; (disappear) desvanecerse, desaparecer; (of light) palidecer; extinguirse; (end) cesar; (desire) ansiar, perecerse (por). **Never say die!** ¡Mientras hay vida, hay esperanza! **to die early,** morir temprano; malograrse. **to die a violent death,** tener una muerte violenta, *inf* morir vestido. **to die from natural causes,** morir por causas naturales; *inf* morir en la cama. **to die hard,** luchar contra la muerte; tardar en morir; tardar en desaparecer. **to die of a broken heart,** morir con el corazón destrozado, morir de pena. **to die away,** desaparecer gradualmente; extinguirse poco a poco; dejar de oírse poco a poco; cesar; pasar. **to die down,** extinguirse gradualmente; palidecer; dejar de oírse; desaparecer; (of the wind) amainar; perder su fuerza. **to die out,** desaparecer; olvidarse; dejar de existir; pasarse de moda

die *n* dado, *m*; *fig* suerte, *f*; (stamp) cuño, troquel, *m*; *arch* cubo, *m*. **The die is cast,** La suerte está echada. **die-sinker,** grabador en hueco, *m*

diehard *n* valiente, *m*; tradicionalista empedernido, *m*; partidario (-ia) entusiasta

Dieppe Diepa, *f*

dieresis *n* diéresis, crema, *f*

diesel *a* Diesel. **d. engine,** motor Diesel, *m*

diet *n* dieta, *f*, régimen dietario, *m*; (assembly) dieta, *f*. *vi* estar a dieta, hacer régimen

dietetic *a* dietético

dietetics *n* dietética, *f*

dietician *n* dietista, *mf*

differ *vi* diferenciarse; (contradict) contradecir; (disagree) no estar de acuerdo; disentir

difference *n* diferencia, *f*; disparidad, *f*; contraste, *m*; (of opinion) disensión, *f*; controversia, disputa, *f*. **to make no d.,** no hacer diferencia alguna; no afectar; dar lo mismo, no importar

different *a* distinto; diferente; vario, diverso

differential *a* diferencial. **d. calculus,** cálculo diferencial, *m*

differentiate *vt* diferenciar, distinguir. *vi* diferenciarse, distinguirse

differentiation *n* diferenciación, *f*

differently *adv* diferentemente

difficult *a* difícil. **to make d.,** dificultar

difficulty *n* dificultad, *f*. **d. in breathing,** opresión de pecho, *f*

diffidence *n* modestia, timidez, *f*; huraña, *f*; falta de confianza en sí mismo, *f*

diffident *a* modesto, tímido, huraño; sin confianza en sí mismo

diffidently *adv* tímidamente; vergonzosamente

diffract *vt* difractar

diffraction *n* difracción, *f*

diffractive *a* difrangente

diffuse *vt* difundir. *a* difuso; (long-winded) prolijo

diffuseness *n* difusión, *f*; prolijidad, *f*

diffusion *n* difusión, *f*; esparcimiento, *m*; diseminación, *f*

diffusive *a* difusivo

dig *vt* and *vi* cavar; excavar; (of animals) escarbar; (mine) zapar, minar; (into a subject) ahondar (en); (with the spurs) aguijonear, dar con las espuelas; (poke) clavar. **to dig one's heels in** *Lat. Am.* encabestrarse **to dig in**, enterrarse; *mil* abrir trincheras; *inf* arreglarse las cosas. **to dig out**, excavar; sacar cavando, sacar con azadón; extraer. **to dig up**, desenterrar; descubrir

digest *vt* clasificar; codificar; (food, also *chem.* and *fig.* tolerate and think over) digerir; (of knowledge and territory) asimilar. *vi* digerir. *n* compendio, resumen, *m*; *law* digesto, *m*; recopilación, *f*. **This food is easy to d.,** Este alimento es fácil de digerir; Este alimento es muy ligero

digestibility *n* digestibilidad, *f*

digestible *a* digerible, digestible

digestion *n* digestión, *f*; (of ideas) asimilación, *f*; *chem* digestión, *f*

digestive *a* digestivo

digger *n* cavador (-ra)

digging *n* cavadura, *f*; excavación, *f*; *pl* **diggings**, minas, *f pl*; excavaciones, *f pl*; *inf* alojamiento, *m*, posada, *f*

digit *n* dígito, *m*

digital *a* digital, dígito

digitalin *n* digitalina, *f*

digitalis *n* digital, *f*

dignified *a* serio, grave; majestuoso; (worthy) digno; solemne; altivo; noble

dignify *vt* dignificar, honrar; exaltar; dar dignidad (a); ennoblecer

dignitary *n* dignatario, *m*; dignidad, *f*

dignity *n* dignidad, *f*; (rank) rango, *m*; (post) cargo, puesto, *m*; (honor) honra, *f*; (stateliness) majestad, *f*; mesura, seriedad, *f*; (haughtiness) altivez, *f*; (nobility) nobleza, *f*. **to stand on one's d.,** darse importancia

digress *vi* divagar

digression *n* digresión, divagación, *f*

dike *n* dique, *m*; (ditch) acequia, *f*; canal, *m*; (embankment) zanja, *f*, *vt* represar

dilapidated *a* arruinado, destartalado; (of fortune) dilapidado; (of persons, families) venido a menos; (shabby) raído

dilapidation *n* deterioración, *f*; ruina, *f*, estado ruinoso, *m*

dilatation *n* dilatación, *f*; ensanche, *m*

dilate *vt* dilatar; ensanchar. *vi* dilatarse. **to d. upon,** extenderse sobre, dilatarse en

dilator *n* dilatador, *m*

dilatoriness *n* tardanza, *f*; (slowness) lentitud, *f*

dilatory *a* dilatorio, tardo; (slow) lento

dilemma *n* dilema, *m*

dilettante *n* diletante, *m*; aficionado (-da)

dilettantism *n* diletantismo, *m*

diligence *n* diligencia, *f*; asiduidad, *f*; (care) cuidado, *m*; (coach) diligencia, *f*

diligent *a* diligente, asiduo, aplicado, industrioso; (painstaking) concienzudo

dilute *vt* diluir; *fig* adulterar. *a* diluido

dilution *n* dilución, *f*; *fig* adulteración, *f*

diluvian *a* diluviano

dim *a* (of light) apagado, débil, tenue; (of sight) turbio; (dark) sombrío, oscuro; (blurred, etc.) empañado; indistinto, confuso. *vt* obscurecer; empañar; (dazzle) ofuscar; (eclipse) eclipsar; reducir la intensidad (de una luz); (of memories) borrar. **dim intelligence,** de brumoso seso

dimension *n* dimensión, *f*; (size) tamaño, *m*; (scope) extensión, *f*, alcance, *m*

dimensional *a* dimensional

diminish *vt* disminuir; reducir; debilitar, atenuar. *vi* disminuir; reducirse; debilitarse, atenuarse

diminishing *a* menguante

diminution *n* disminución, *f*; reducción, *f*; atenuación, *f*

diminutive *a* diminutivo. *n* diminutivo, *m*

diminutiveness *n* pequeñez, *f*

dimly *adv* obscuramente; vagamente; indistintamente. **dimly lit,** apenas alumbrado

dimness *n* oscuridad, *f*; deslustre, *m*; (of light) tenuidad (de la luz), *f*; confusión, *f*

dimple *n* hoyuelo, *m*

dimpled *a* con hoyuelos, que tiene hoyuelos

din *n* estrépito, estruendo, ruido, *m*; algarabía, barahúnda, *f*, *vt* ensordecer

dine *vi* (in the evening) cenar; (at midday) comer. *vt* convidar a cenar or a comer. **to d. out,** cenar or comer fuera

diner *n* (on a train) coche comedor, coche restaurante, *m*; cenador, *m*; comedor, *m*

ding-dong *n* tintín, *m*

dinghy *n* lancha, *f*; canoa, *f*, bote, *m*. **rubber d.,** canoa de goma, *f*

dinginess *n* deslustre, *m*; suciedad, *f*; oscuridad, *f*; (of a person) desaseo, *m*

dingy *a* deslucido, empañado; sucio; oscuro; (of persons) desaseado

dining car *n* coche comedor, vagón restaurante, *m*

dining room *n* comedor, *m*; refectorio, *m*

dining table *n* mesa del comedor, *f*

dinner *n* (in the evening) cena, *f*; (at midday) comida, *f*. **over the d. table,** de sobremesa. **d.-jacket,** smoking, *m*. **d. party,** cena, *f*. **d. plate,** plato, *m*. **d. roll,** panecillo, *m*. **d. service,** vajilla, *f*

dinosaur *n* dinosauro, *m*

dint (by d. of) a fuerza de, a costa de

diocesan *a* diocesano

diocese *n* diócesis, *f*

Dionysus Thrax Dionisio el Tracio, *m*

dioxide *n* dióxido, *m*

dip *n* inmersión, *f*; baño, *m*; (in the ground) declive, *m*; (in the road) columpio, *m*, depresión, *f*; (slope) pendiente, *f*; (candle) vela de sebo, *f*; (of the horizon) depresión (del horizonte), *f*; (of the needle) inclinación (de la aguja), *f*. *vt* sumergir; bañar; (put) poner. *vi* inclinarse hacia abajo. **to dip into a book,** hojear un libro. **to dip the colors,** saludar con la bandera. **to dip the headlights,** bajar los faros

diphtheria *n* difteria, *f*

diphthong *n* diptongo, *m*

diploma *n* diploma, *m*

diplomacy *n* diplomacia, *f*; tacto, *m*

diploma mill *n* fábrica de títulos académicos, *f*

diplomat *n* diplomático, *m*

diplomatic *a* diplomático. **d. bag,** valija diplomática, *f*. **d. corps,** cuerpo diplomático, *m*

diplomatically *adv* diplomáticamente

dipper *n* (ladle) cazo, *m*; *ast* Osa Mayor, *f*

dipsomania *n* dipsomanía, *f*

dipsomaniac *n* dipsómano (-na)

diptych *n* díptica, *f*

dire *a* espantoso, horrible; cruel; funesto

direct *a* directo; claro, inequívoco; (of descent) recto; (of electric current) continuo; exacto. *adv* directamente. *vt* dirigir; (command) ordenar, encargar; dar instrucciones. **d. action,** acción directa, *f*. **d. current,** corriente continua, *f*. **d. line,** línea directa, *f*; (of descent) línea recta, *f*. **d. object,** acusativo, *m*. **d. speech,** oración directa, *f*

direct dialing *n* discado directo, *m*

direction *n* dirección, *f*; rumbo, *m*; instrucción, *f*; (on a letter) sobrescrito, *m*; señas, *f pl*. **in the d. of,** en la dirección de; hacia; *naut* con rumbo a. **in all direc-**

tions, por todas partes; a los cuatro vientos. **to go in the d. of,** ir en la dirección de; tomar por. **Directions for use,** Direcciones para el uso. **d. indicator, d. signal,** (on car) indicador de dirección, *m*
directive *a* directivo, director
directly *adv* directamente; inmediatamente, en seguida
directness *n* derechura, *f*
director *n* director (-triz, -ora), **managing d.,** director gerente, *m*
directorate *n* directorio, *m*, junta directiva, *f*; cargo de director, *m*
directory *n* directorio, *m*, guía, *f*. **telephone d.,** guía de teléfonos, *f*
dirge *n* endecha, *f*, lamento, *m*; canto fúnebre, *m*
dirt *n* mugre, suciedad, *f*; (mud) lodo, *m*; (earth) tierra, *f*; (dust) polvo, *m*; *fig* inmundicia, *f*. **d.-cheap,** sumamente barato. **to be d. cheap,** (of goods) estar por los suelos. **d.-track,** pista de ceniza, *f*. **d.-track racing,** carreras en pista de ceniza, *f pl*
dirtiness *n* suciedad, *f*; (untidiness) desaseo, *m*; sordidez, *f*; (meanness) bajeza, *f*
dirty *a* sucio, *Central America* descacharrado; (untidy) desaseado; (muddy) enlodado; (dusty) polvoriento; (of weather) borrascoso; (sordid) sórdido; (base, mean) vil; (indecent) indecente, verde, obsceno. *vt* ensuciar. **d. trick,** mala pasada, *Lat. Am.* chancada *f*
disability *n* incapacidad, *f*; impotencia, *f*; desventaja, *f*
disable *vt* (cripple) estropear, tullir; hacer incapaz (de), incapacitar; imposibilitar; (destroy) destruir; *law* incapacitar legalmente
disabled *a* inválido; impedido, lisiado; (in the hand) manco; incapacitado; (of ships, etc.) fuera de servicio, estropeado. **d. soldier,** inválido, *m*
disablement *n* (physical) invalidez, *f*; inhabilitación, *f*; *law* impedimento, *m*
disabuse *vt* desengañar, sacar de un error
disadvantage *n* desventaja, *f*. **to be under the d. of,** sufrir la desventaja de
disadvantaged *a* (financially) de escasos recursos
disadvantageous *a* desventajoso
disaffected *a* desafecto
disaffection *n* desafecto, descontento, *m*
disagree *vi* no estar de acuerdo; diferir; (quarrel) reñir; (not share the opinion of) no estar de la opinión (de); (of food, etc.) sentar mal; no probar. **The meat disagreed with me,** La carne me sentó mal
disagreeable *a* desagradable; repugnante; (of persons) antipático, displicente
disagreeableness *n* lo desagradable; (of persons) displicencia, *f*
disagreeably *adv* desagradablemente; con displicencia
disagreement *n* desacuerdo, *m*; diferencia, *f*; desavenencia, *f*; discordia, *f*; (quarrel) riña, disputa, *f*; discrepancia, *f*
disallow *vt* negar; rechazar
disappear *vi* desaparecer. **to cause to d.,** hacer desaparecer
disappearance *n* desaparición, *f*
disappoint *vt* desilusionar; frustrar; (hopes) defraudar; (deprive) privar de; (annoy) contrariar; (break a promise) faltar (a la palabra)
disappointedly *adv* con desilusión, con desengaño
disappointing *a* desengañador; pobre; triste; poco halagüeño
disappointment *n* desengaño, *m*, decepción, *f*; frustración, *f*; desilusión, *f*; (vexation) contrariedad, *f*; contratiempo, *m*. **to suffer a d.,** sufrir un desengaño; *inf* llevarse un chasco
disapproval *n* desaprobación, *f*
disapprove *vt* desaprobar
disapproving *a* de desaprobación, severo
disapprovingly *adv* con desaprobación
disarm *vt* desarmar. *vi* desarmarse; deponer las armas
disarmament *n* desarme, *m*
disarrange *vt* desarreglar; descomponer, desajustar; (hair) despeinar

disarrangement *n* desarreglo, *m*; desajuste, *m*; desorden, *m*
disarray *n* desorden, desarreglo, *m*; confusión, *f*. *vt* desordenar, desarreglar
disarticulate *vt* desarticular
disarticulation *n* desarticulación, *f*
disaster *n* desastre, *m*; catástrofe, *m*; infortunio, *m*
disastrous *a* desastroso; funesto, trágico
disastrously *adv* desastrosamente
disastrousness *n* carácter desastroso, *m*
disavow *vt* repudiar; retractar
disavowal *n* repudiación, *f*
disband *vt* licenciar. *vi* desbandarse, dispersarse
disbelief *n* incredulidad, *f*; desconfianza, *f*
disbelieve *vt* and *vi* descreer, no creer; desconfiar (de)
disburse *vt* desembolsar, pagar
disbursement *n* desembolso, *m*
disc *n* disco, *m*
discard *vt* desechar, arrinconar, *Lat. Am.* botar; despedir; (at cards) descartar. *n* (at cards) descarte, *m*
discern *vt* discernir, distinguir, percibir
discerner *n* discernidor (-ra)
discernible *a* distinguible, perceptible
discerning *a* perspicaz, discernidor
discernment *n* discernimiento, *m*
discharge *vt* descargar; (a gun) disparar, tirar; (an arrow) lanzar; *elec* descargar; emitir; (dismiss) destituir, despedir; arrojar; *mil* licenciar; (exempt) dispensar (de); (exonerate) absolver, exonerar; (free) dar libertad (a); (from hospital) dar de baja (a); *law* revocar; (perform) cumplir, ejecutar; (pay) pagar, saldar; (of an abscess, etc.) supurar.
discharge *n* (of firearms) disparo, tiro, *m*; (of artillery) descarga, *f*; (of goods, cargo) descargue, *m*; *elec* descarga, *f*; (from a wound, etc.) pus, *m*, supuración, *f*; (from the intestine) flujo, *m*; (of a debt) pago, m.; *com* descargo, *m*; (receipt) carta de pago, quitanza, *f*; *mil* licencia absoluta, *f*; (dismissal) despedida, destitución, *f*; (exoneration) exoneración, *f*; (freeing) liberación, *f*; (from hospital) baja, *f*; (performance) cumplimiento, *m*; ejecución, *f*
disciple *n* discípulo (-la)
disciplinarian *n* disciplinario (-ia)
disciplinary *a* disciplinario
discipline *n* disciplina, *f*, *vt* disciplinar
disclaim *vt* renunciar (a); (repudiate) rechazar, repudiar
disclaimer *n* *law* renunciación, *f*; repudiación, *f*
disclose *vt* descubrir, revelar
disclosure *n* descubrimiento, *m*, revelación, *f*
discolor *vt* descolorar. *vi* descolorarse
discoloration *n* descoloramiento, *m*
discomfit *vt* desconcertar
discomfiture *n* desconcierto, *m*
discomfort *n* falta de comodidades, *f*; incomodidad, *f*; malestar, *m*; molestia, *f*; inquietud, *f*; dolor, *m*
discompose *vt* confusión, agitación, inquietud, *f*
disconcert *vt* desconcertar, turbar; (of plans, etc.) frustrar
disconnect *vt* separar; (of railway engines, etc.) desacoplar; desconectar; (of electric plugs) desenchufar
disconnected *a* inconexo; incoherente, deshilvanado
disconnectedness *n* inconexión, *f*; incoherencia, *f*
disconsolate *a* desconsolado, triste
disconsolately *adv* desconsoladamente, tristemente
disconsolateness *n* desconsuelo, *m*
discontent *n* descontento, disgusto, *m*, *vt* descontentar, desagradar
discontented *a* descontentadizo, descontento, disgustado
discontinuance *n* descontinuación, cesación, *f*; interrupción, *f*
discontinue *vt* descontinuar; cesar; interrumpir; (of payments, etc.) suspender. *vi* cesar
discontinuous *a* descontinuo; interrumpido; intermitente

discord n discordia, f; mus disonancia, f, desentono, m
discordant a discorde, poco armonioso; incongruo; mus disonante, desentonado. **to be d.,** discordar; ser incongruo; mus disonar
discount n descuento, m; rebaja, f. vt descontar; rebajar; balancear; (disconsider) desechar. **at a d.,** al descuento; bajo la par; fácil de obtener; superfluo; fig en disfavor, en descrédito. **rate of d.,** tipo de descuento, m. **d. for cash,** descuento por venta al contado, m
discourage vt desalentar, desanimar; oponerse a; disuadir; frustrar
discouragement n desaliento, m; desaprobación, oposición, f; disuasión, f; (obstacle) estorbo, m
discouraging a poco animador, que ofrece pocas esperanzas; (with prospect, etc.) nada halagüeño
discourse n discurso, m; plática, f; (treatise) disertación, f. vi (converse) platicar, conversar; (with on, upon) disertar sobre, discurrir sobre; tratar de
discourteous a descortés, desconsiderado
discourtesy n descortesía, f
discover vt descubrir; (see) ver; (realize) darse cuenta de; (show) manifestar; revelar
discoverable a que se puede descubrir; averiguable; distinguible, perceptible
discoverer n descubridor (-ra); revelador (-ra)
discovery n descubrimiento, m; revelación, f
discredit n descrédito, m; des honra, f; duda, f. vt dudar (de), no creer (en); desacreditar; deshonrar
discreditable a deshonroso, ignominioso, vergonzoso
discreet a discreto; prudente, circunspecto
discreetly adv discretamente; prudentemente
discrepancy n discrepancia, diferencia, f; contradicción, f
discrepant a discrepante; contradictorio, inconsistente
discretion n discreción, f; prudencia, circunspección, f; juicio, m; voluntad, f. **at d.,** a discreción. **at one's own d.,** a voluntad (de uno). **years of d.,** edad de discreción, f
discriminate vi distinguir (entre); hacer una distinción (en favor de or en perjuicio de). vt distinguir
discriminating a discerniente, que sabe distinguir, juicioso; culto; diferencial
discrimination n discernimiento, m; gusto, m; distinción, f; discriminación, f
discursive a discursivo; digresivo
discus n disco, m. **d. thrower,** discóbolo, m
discuss vt discutir; hablar de; debatir; (deal with) tratar; (fam a dish) probar; (a bottle of wine) vaciar
discussion n discusión, f; debate, m
disdain n desdén, m; altivez, f. vt desdeñar, desairar, despreciar. **to d. to,** desdeñarse de
disdainful a desdeñoso; altivo
disdainfully adv desdeñosamente
disease n enfermedad, f; fig mal, m. **infectious d.,** enfermedad contagiosa, f
diseased a enfermo; (of fruit, etc.) malo
disembark vt and vi desembarcar
disembarkation n desembarque, m; mil desembarco (de tropas), m
disembodied a incorpóreo
disembowel vt desentrañar, destripar
disenchant vt desencantar; deschechizar; desilusionar
disenchantment n desencanto, m; desilusión, f
disengage vt desasir; soltar; (gears) desembragar; (uncouple) desacoplar; (free) librar
disengaged a (free) libre
disentangle vt (undo) desatar, desanudar; separar; (of threads, etc., and fig) desenredar, desenmarañar. vi desenredarse
disentanglement n desatadura, f; separación, f; desenredo, m
disestablish vt separar (la Iglesia del Estado)
disestablishment n separación (de la Iglesia del Estado), f
disfavor n disfavor, m; (disapproval) desaprobación, f. vt desaprobar

disfigure vt desfigurar, afear; deformar; (mar) estropear
disfigurement n desfiguración, f; deformidad, f; defecto, m
disfranchise vt privar de los derechos civiles (a)
disfranchisement n privación de los derechos civiles, privación del derecho de votar, f
disgorge vt and vi vomitar; (of a river) desembocar (en); hacer restitución (de lo robado)
disgrace n vergüenza, ignominia, f; deshonra, f; (insult) afrenta, f; (scandal) escándalo, m; disfavor, m. vt deshonrar; despedir con ignominia. **in d.,** fuera de favor; desacreditado; (of children and animals) castigado
disgraceful a deshonroso; ignominioso; escandaloso
disgracefully adv escandalosamente
disgracefulness n ignominia, vergüenza, f; deshonra, f
disgruntled a refunfuñador, enfurruñado, malhumorado
disguise n disfraz, m; (mask) máscara, f. vt disfrazar; cubrir, tapar; (fig conceal) ocultar. **in d.,** disfrazado
disgust n repugnancia, aversión, f; aborrecimiento, m; asco, m. vt repugnar, inspirar aversión; disgustar; dar asco (a)
disgusted a asqueado; disgustado; furioso; (bored) aburrido
disgusting a repugnante; odioso, horrible; asqueroso
dish n (for meat, vegetables, fruit, etc.) fuente, f; (food) plato, m; pl **dishes,** platos, m pl, vajilla, f. vt servir; inf frustrar. **cooked d.,** guiso, m. **special d. for today,** plato del día, m. **to wash the dishes,** fregar los platos. **d.-cloth,** (for washing) fregador, m; (for drying) paño de los platos, m. **d.-cover,** cubre-platos, m. **d.-rack,** escurre-platos, m. **d.-washer,** lavaplatos, lavavajillas, m. **d.-water,** agua de lavar los platos, f
disharmony n falta de armonía, f; (disagreement) discordia, desavenencia, f; incongruencia, f; mus disonancia, f
dishearten vt desalentar, desanimar; desesperar; disuadir (de)
disheveled a despeinado, desgreñado; (untidy) desaseado
dishonest a falto de honradez, tramposo; fraudulento; falso, desleal, Lat. Am. also flequetero
dishonestly adv de mala fe, sin honradez; fraudulentamente; deslealmente
dishonesty n falta de honradez, falta de integridad, f; fraude, m; falsedad, deslealtad, f
dishonor n deshonra, f, vt deshonrar; com no pagar, o no aceptar, un giro
dishonorable a deshonroso
dishonorer n deshonrador (-ra); profanador (-ra)
disillusion vt desengañar, desilusionar
disillusionment n desilusión, f, desengaño, desencanto, m
disinclination n aversión, f
disincline vt desinclinar
disinfect vt desinfectar
disinfectant a and n desinfectante m.
disinfection n desinfección, f
disingenuous a tortuoso, doble, falso, insincero
disinherit vt desheredar
disinheritance n desheredación, f
disintegrate vt despedazar, disgregar. vi disgregarse; desmoronarse
disintegration n disgregación, f; disolución, f; desmoronamiento, m
disinter vt desenterrar
disinterested a desinteresado
disinterestedness n desinterés, m
disinterment n desenterramiento, m
disjointed a dislocado; desarticulado; incoherente, inconexo; (of a speech, etc.) descosido
disjointedness n descoyuntamiento, desencajamiento, m; incoherencia, f
disk n disco, m
dislike n aversión, f; antipatía, f; (hostility) animosidad,

f. vt desagradar, no gustar; repugnar. **I d. the house,** No me gusta la casa. **I d. them,** No me gustan

dislocate *vt* dislocar, descoyuntar; *fig* interrumpir

dislocation *n* dislocación, *f,* descoyuntamiento, *m*; *fig* interrupción, *f*

dislodge *vt* desalojar

dislodgement *n* desalojamiento, *m*

disloyal *a* desleal, infiel, falso

disloyalty *n* deslealtad, infidelidad, falsedad, *f*

dismal *a* lóbrego, sombrío; lúgubre; funesto; triste

dismantle *vt* (a ship or fort) desmantelar; (a machine) desmontar; (a house, etc.) desamueblar

dismantling *n* desmantelamiento, *m*

dismay *n* desmayo, desaliento, *m*; consternación, *f*; espanto, terror, *m*. *vt* desanimar; consternar; espantar, horrorizar

dismember *vt* desmembrar

dismemberment *n* desmembración, *f*

dismiss *vt* (from a job) despedir (de); (from an official position) destituir (de) *Chile* desahuciar (de); (bid good-bye to) despedirse de; (after military parade) dar la orden de romper filas; (thoughts) apartar de sí; ahuyentar; (discard) desechar, descartar; (omit) pasar por alto de; (disregard) rechazar; (a parliament, etc.) disolver; (a law case) absolver de la instancia. **to d. in a few words,** tratar someramente; hablar brevemente de

dismissal *n* despedida, *f*; (from an official post) destitución, *f, Chile* desahúcio *m*; apartamiento, *m*; (discard) descarte, *m*; (of a parliament, etc.) disolución, *f*

dismount *vi* apearse, desmontar, echar pie a tierra; bajar. *vt* desmontar; (dismantle) desarmar

disobedience *n* desobediencia, *f*

disobedient *a* desobediente

disobey *vt* and *vi* desobedecer

disobliging *a* poco servicial

disobligingly *adv* descortésmente

disorder *n* desorden, *m*; confusión, *f*; (unrest) perturbación del orden público, *f,* motín, *m*; (disease) enfermedad, *f*; (mental) enajenación mental, *f*; trastorno, *m*. *vt* desordenar, desarreglar; (of health) perjudicar; (the mind) trastornar. **in d.,** en desorden, desarreglado; (helter-skelter) atropelladamente

disordered *a* en desorden; irregular, desordenado; (of the mind and bodily organs) trastornado; (ill) enfermo; (confused) confuso

disorganization *n* desorganización, *f*

disorganize *vt* desorganizar

disorientate *vt* desorientar

disorientation *n* desorientación, *f*

disown *vt* repudiar; negar; renegar de

disparage *vt* menospreciar; desacreditar; denigrar; (spoil) perjudicar; (scorn) despreciar

disparagement *n* menosprecio, *m*; denigración, *f*; desprecio, *m*

disparagingly *adv* con desprecio

disparity *n* disparidad, *f*

dispassionate *a* desapasionado, sereno; imparcial; moderado

dispassionately *adv* con imparcialidad; serenamente; con moderación

dispatch *n* despacho, *m*; *com* envío, *m*; (message) mensaje, *m*; (communique) parte, *f*; (cable) telegrama, *m*; (promptness) prontitud, presteza, *f*; (execution) ejecución, muerte, *f*. *vt* despachar; enviar, remitir; (*fam* kill) despachar. **d.-case,** cartera, *f*. **d.-rider,** mensajero motociclista, *m*

dispel *vt* disipar

dispensable *a* dispensable

dispensary *n* dispensario, *m*

dispensation *n* distribución, *f*; (of the Pope, etc.) dispensa, *f*; (decree) ley, *f,* decreto, *m*; (of justice) administración, *f*

dispense *vt* dispensar; (of justice) administrar. **to d. with,** pasar sin, prescindir de

dispenser *n* dispensador (-ra); administrador (-ra)

dispersal *n* dispersión, *f*; disipación, *f*; esparcimiento, *m*

disperse *vt* dispersar; disipar; esparcir. *vi* dispersarse disiparse

dispirited *a* abatido, desanimado, deprimido; lánguido

dispiritedly *adv* desanimadamente, con desaliento; lánguidamente

displace *vt* desalojar; cambiar de situación; (of liquids) desplazar; (oust) quitar el puesto (a), destituir

displacement *n* desalojamiento, *m*; cambio de situación, *m*; (of liquid) desplazamiento, *m*; (from a post) destitución, *f*

display *n* exhibición, *f*; ostentación, *f*; presentación, *f*; (development) desarrollo, *m*; manifestación, *f*; (naval or military) maniobras, *f pl*; espectáculo, *m*; (pomp) pompa, *f*; fausto, *m*. *vt* exhibir; mostrar, manifestar; ostentar; (unfold) desplegar, extender; (develop) desarrollar. **d. cabinet,** vitrina, *f*

displease *vt* desagradar; ofender; enojar

displeasing *a* desagradable

displeasure *n* desagrado, *m*; disgusto, *m*; disfavor, *m*; indignación, *f*; enojo, *m*; (grief) angustia, *f*

disport *vi* (**oneself**), divertirse, entretenerse, recrearse; retozar, jugar

disposal *n* disposición, *f*; (transfer) cesión, enajenación, *f*; (sale) venta, *f*; (gift) donación, *f*. **I am at your d.,** Estoy a la disposición de Vd. **the d. of the troops,** la disposición de las tropas

dispose *vt* disponer; inclinar. *vi* disponer. **to d. of,** disponer de; (finish) terminar, concluir; (get rid of) deshacerse de; (give away) regalar; (sell) vender; (transfer) ceder; (of houses, etc.) traspasar; (kill) matar; (send) enviar; (use) servirse de; (refute) refutar. **"To be disposed of,"** (a business, etc.) «Se traspasa»

disposed *a* (in compounds) intencionado, dispuesto. **well-d.,** bien intencionado

disposition *n* disposición, *f*; (temperament) naturaleza, índole, *f,* temperamento, carácter, *m*; (humor) humor, *m*

dispossess *vt* desposeer (de); privar (de); desahuciar

dispossession *n* desposeimiento, *m*; desahúcio, *m*

disproportion *n* desproporción, *f*

disproportionate *a* desproporcionado

disproportionately *adv* desproporcionadamente

disprovable *a* refutable

disprove *vt* refutar

disputable *a* disputable; discutible

disputant *n* disputador (-ra)

dispute *n* disputa, controversia, *f*; altercación, *f*; discusión, *f*; debate, *m*. *vt* and *vi* disputar. **beyond d.,** *a* incontestable. *adv* incontestablemente; fuera de duda

disqualification *n* incapacidad, *f*; inhabilitación, *f*; impedimento, *m*; *sport* descalificación, *f*

disqualify *vt* incapacitar; inhabilitar; *sport* descalificar

disquiet *n* desasosiego, *m*; intranquilidad, inquietud, agitación, *f. vt* desasosegar, intranquilizar, perturbar, agitar

disquieting *a* intranquilizador, perturbador

disquisition *n* disquisición, *f*

disregard *n* indiferencia, *f*; omisión, *f*; descuido, *m*; (scorn) desdén, *m*. *vt* no hacer caso de, desatender; omitir; desconocer; descuidar; despreciar

disregardful *a* indiferente; negligente; desatento; desdeñoso

disrepair *n* deterioro, mal estado, *m*

disreputable *a* de mala fama; (shameful) vergonzoso, vil; (compromising) comprometedor; de mal aspecto, horrible; ruin

disreputably *adv* ruinmente; vergonzosamente

disrepute *n* disfavor, *m*; mala fama, *f*; deshonra, *f*; descrédito, *m*. **to come into d.,** caer en disfavor; perder su reputación

disrespect *n* falta de respeto, *f*; irreverencia, *f*

disrespectful *a* irrespetuoso, irreverente

disrobe *vt* desnudar. *vi* desnudarse

disrupt *vt* quebrar; desorganizar; interrumpir; separar

disruption *n* quebrantamiento, *m*; desorganización, *f*; interrupción, *f*; separación, *f*

dissatisfaction *n* descontento, desagrado, disgusto, *m*

dissatisfied *a* descontentado, malcontento, no satisfecho

dissect *vt* disecar; *fig* analizar

dissecting table *n* mesa de disección, *f*

dissection *n* disección, *f*; análisis, *m*

dissector *n* disector, *m*; *fig* analizador (-ra)

dissemble *vt* and *vi* disimular, fingir

dissembler *n* hipócrita, *mf*; disimulador (-ra)

disseminate *vt* diseminar; propagar, sembrar

dissemination *n* diseminación, *f*; propagación, *f*

dissension *n* disensión, *f*; disidencia, *f*

dissent *n* disentimiento, *m*, *vi* disentir, disidir

dissenter *n* disidente, *mf*

dissentient *a* disidente, divergente. **without one d. voice,** unánimemente

dissertation *n* disertación, *f*

disservice *n* deservicio, *m*

dissimilar *a* disímil, desemejante, diferente

dissimilarity *n* desemejanza, diferencia, disparidad, *f*

dissimulation *n* disimulación, *f*, disimulo, *m*

dissipate *vt* disipar; dispersar; (waste) derrochar, desperdiciar. *vi* disiparse; dispersarse; (vanish) desvanecerse; (of persons) ser disoluto

dissipated *a* (of persons) disipado, disoluto, vicioso

dissipation *n* disipación, *f*; (waste) derroche, *m*; libertinaje, *m*

dissociate *vt* disociar

dissociation *n* disociación, *f*

dissoluble *a* disoluble

dissolute *a* disoluto, vicioso, licencioso

dissoluteness *n* disolución, inmoralidad, *f*

dissolution *n* disolución, *f*; separación, *f*; muerte, *f*

dissolvable *a* soluble

dissolve *vt* disolver; derretir; (of parliament) prorrogar; (a marriage, etc.) anular; *fig* disipar. *vi* disolverse; derretirse; (vanish) desvanecerse, disiparse, evaporarse. **to d. into tears,** deshacerse en lágrimas

dissolvent *a* disolutivo. *n* disolvente, *m*

dissonance *n* disonancia, *f*; *fig* discordia, falta de armonía, *f*

dissonant *n* disonancia, *f*, *a* disonante

dissuade *vt* disuadir (de), apartar (de)

dissuasion *n* disuasión, *f*

distaff *n* rueca, *f*

distance *n* distancia, *f*; lontananza, *f*; lejanía, *f*; trecho, *m*; (of time) intervalo, *m*; (difference) diferencia, *f*. **at a d.,** a alguna distancia; lejos; (from afar) desde lejos. **from a d.,** desde (or de) lejos. **in the d.,** a lo lejos, en lontananza. **to keep at a d.,** mantener lejos; guardar las distancias (con). **to keep one's d.,** mantenerse a distancia; no intimarse, guardar las distancias. **What is the d. from London to Madrid?** ¿Qué distancia hay desde Londres a Madrid?

distant *a* distante; lejano; remoto; (of manner) frío, reservado; (slight) ligero; (of references, etc.) indirecto. **He is a d. relation,** Es un pariente lejano. **They are always rather d. with her,** La tratan siempre con bastante frialdad

distantly *adv* a distancia; a lo lejos; desde lejos; remotamente; (of manner) con frialdad; (slightly) ligeramente

distaste *n* aversión, repugnancia, *f*; disgusto, hastío, *m*

distasteful *a* desagradable

distemper *n* enfermedad, *f*; (in animals) moquillo, *m*; *fig* mal, *m*; (for walls) pintura al temple, *f*. *vt* desordenar, perturbar; (walls) pintar al temple

distend *vt* ensanchar; dilatar; inflar, henchir; *med* distender. *vi* ensancharse, etc.

distension *n* dilatación, *f*; inflación, *f*; henchimiento, *m*; *med* distensión, *f*

distil *vt* destilar; extraer. *vi* destilar; exudar

distillation *n* destilación, *f*; extracción, *f*; exudación, *f*

distiller *n* destilador (-ra)

distillery *n* destilería, *f*, destilatorio, *m*

distinct *a* distinto; diferente; claro; notable, evidente

distinction *n* distinción, *f*

distinctive *a* distintivo; característico

distinctive feature *n* *ling* rasgo pertinente, *m*

distinctly *adv* claramente; distintamente

distinctness *n* claridad, *f*; distinción, *f*; carácter distintivo, *m*

distinguish *vt* distinguir; discernir; caracterizar; (honor) honrar. *vi* distinguir, diferenciar

distinguishable *a* distinguible; perceptible, discernible

distinguished *a* distinguido; eminente; famoso, ilustre, egregio

distinguishing *a* distintivo

distort *vt* (twist) torcer; deformar; falsear; pervertir

distorting mirror *n* (at fairs) espejo de la risa, *m*; espejo deformador, *m*

distortion *n* deformación, *f*; torcimiento, *m*; contorsión, *f*; perversión, *f*; *rad* deformación, *f*

distract *vt* distraer; interrumpir; perturbar; (turn aside) desviar, apartar; (madden) enloquecer, volver loco (a)

distracted *a* aturdido; demente, loco

distractedly *adv* locamente; perdidamente

distraction *n* distracción, *f*; (amusement) diversion, *f*, pasatiempo, *m*; (bewilderment) confusión, *f*, aturdimiento, *m*; (madness) locura, *f*; frenesí, *m*. **to drive to d.,** trastornar, sacar de quicio.

distrain *vi* embargar

distraint *n* embargo, *m*

distraught *a* aturdido; desesperado; enloquecido

distress *n* dolor, *m*, aflicción, *f*; pena, *f*; miseria, penuria, *f*; (exhaustion) fatiga, *f*, cansancio, *m*; (pain) dolor, *m*; (misfortune) desdicha, *f*; apuro, *m*; (danger) peligro, *m*; *law* embargo, *m*. *vt* afligir, dar pena (a), llenar de angustia; cansar, fatigar; (pain) doler

distressed *a* afligido; necesitado, pobre

distressing *a* congojoso, doloroso, penoso

distributable *a* repartible

distribute *vt* (of justice, etc.) administrar; distribuir; repartir

distribution *n* (of justice) administración, *f*; distribución, *f*; reparto, *m*

distributive *a* distributivo

distributor *n* distribuidor (-ra); repartidor (-ra). **d. of false money,** expendedor (-ra) de moneda falsa

district *n* distrito, *m*; comarca, *f*; (of a town) barrio, *m*; (judicial) partido judicial, *m*, *Lat. Am.* comuna *f*; jurisdicción, *f*; región, zona, *f*

distrust *n* desconfianza, *f*; recelo, *m*, sospecha, *f*. *vt* desconfiar de, sospechar

distrustful *a* desconfiado, receloso, suspicaz

distrustfully *adv* desconfiadamente, con recelo

disturb *vt* perturbar; interrumpir; incomodar; (make anxious) inquietar; (alter) cambiar; (disarrange) desordenar, desarreglar. **to d. the peace,** perturbar el orden público

disturbance *n* perturbación, *f*; disturbio, *m*, conmoción, *f*; incomodidad, *f*; agitación, *f*; confusión, *f*; tumulto, *m*; desorden, *m*; *rad* parásitos, *m pl*

disturber *n* perturbador (-ra)

disturbing *a* perturbador; inquietador; conmovedor, impresionante, emocionante

disunion *n* desunión, *f*; discordia, *f*

disunite *vt* desunir; separar, dividir. *vi* separarse

disuse *n* desuso, *m*. *vt* desusar; desacostumbrar. **to fall into d.,** caer en desuso

ditch *n* zanja, *f*; (for defense, etc.) foso, *m*; (irrigation) acequia, *f*. *vt* zanjar; abarrancar. **to die in the last d.,** morir en la brecha

ditto *adv* ídem; también

ditty *n* canción, cantinela, *f*

diuretic *a* diurético

divan *n* diván, *m*

dive *n* buceo, *m*; *aer* picada, *f*, *vi* bucear; sumergirse (en); *aer* volar en picado; penetrar (en); (into a book) enfrascarse en. **to d. out,** salir precipitadamente. **to**

d.-bomb, bombardear en picado. **d.-bomber,** avión en picado, *m*. **d.-bombing,** bombardeo en picado, *m*
diver *n* buceador, *m*; buzo, *m*; (bird) somorgujo, *m*
diverge *vi* divergir
divergence *n* divergencia, *f*
divergent *a* divergente
diverse *a* diverso, vario
diversify *vt* diversificar
diversion *n* diversión, *f*; entretenimiento, *m*, recreación, *f*; pasatiempo, *m*; placer, *m*; *mil* diversión, *f*
diversity *n* diversidad, variedad, *f*
divert *vt* desviar; (amuse) divertir, entretener
diverting *a* divertido, entretenido
divide *vt* dividir; partir; separar; (cut) cortar; (share) repartir, distribuir; (hair) hacer la raya (del pelo); (of voting) provocar una votación. *vi* dividirse; separarse; (of roads, etc.) bifurcarse; (of voting) votar. **divided skirt,** *n* falda pantalón, *f*
dividend *n* dividendo, *m*. **d. warrant,** cupón de dividendo, *m*
dividers *n pl* compás de puntas, *m*
dividing *a* divisorio, divisor
divination *n* adivinación, *f*
divine *a* divino; sublime; *inf* estupendo. *n* teólogo, *m*. *vt* (foretell) vaticinar, pronosticar; presentir; (guess) adivinar
diving *n* buceo, *m*; *aer* picado, *m*. **d.-bell,** campana de bucear, *f*. **d.-board,** (low) trampolín, *m*; (high) palanca, *f*. **d.-suit,** escafandra, *f*
divining rod *n* vara divinatoria, *f*
divinity *n* divinidad, *f*; teología, *f*
divisibility *n* divisibilidad, *f*
divisible *a* divisible
division *n* división, *f*; separación, *f*; (distribution) repartimiento, *m*; (*mil math*) división, *f*; sección, *f*; grupo, *m*; (voting) votación, *f*; (discord) discordia, desunión, *f*. **without a d.,** por unanimidad, sin votar
divisor *n math* divisor, *m*
divorce *n* divorcio, *m*. *vt* divorciarse de; *fig* divorciar, separar. **to file a petition of d.,** poner una petición de divorcio
divorcee *n* (wife) divorciada, *f*; (husband) divorciado, *m*
divulge *vt* divulgar, revelar
dizzily *adv* vertiginosamente
dizziness *n* vértigo, *m*; mareo, *m*; (bewilderment) aturdimiento, *m*, confusión, *f*
dizzy *a* vertiginoso; mareado; confuso, perplejo, aturdido
do *vt* hacer; ejecutar; (one's duty, etc.) cumplir con; concluir; (cause) causar; (homage) rendir; (commit) cometer; (arrange) arreglar; (cook) cocer, guisar; (roast) asar; (*fam* cheat) engañar; (suffice) bastar; (act) hacer el papel (de); (*fam* treat) tratar (bien o mal); (learn) aprender; (exhaust) agotar; (walk) andar; (travel, journey) recorrer; (translate) traducir; (prepare) preparar. *vi* hacer; (behave) conducirse; (of health) estar (bien o mal); (act) obrar; (get on) ir; (be suitable, suit) convenir; (suffice) bastar; (of plants) florecer; (cook) cocerse; (last) durar. **Don't!** ¡No lo hagas! ¡Quieto! ¡Calla! **How do you do?** ¿Cómo está Vd.? ¡Buenos días! **Have done!** ¡Acaba de una vez! **It will do you good,** Te conviene; Te hará bien; Te sentará bien. **It will do you no harm,** No te perjudicará; No te hará daño. **I could do with one,** Me gustaría (tener) uno; (of drinks) Me bebería uno con mucho gusto. **That will do,** Eso basta; Se puede servirse de eso; Está bien así; (leave it alone) ¡Déjate de eso! (be quiet!) ¡No digas más! ¡Cállate! **That won't do,** Eso no es bastante; Eso no sirve; Eso no se hace así; Eso no se hace. **That will never do,** Eso no servirá; Eso no puede ser. **This will do,** (when buying an article) Me quedaré con éste; Me serviré de esto; Esto basta; Esto será suficiente; (is all right) Está bien así. **Thy will be done!** ¡Hágase tu voluntad! **to be doing,** estar haciendo; estar ocupado en (o con) hacer; (of

food) estar cocinando. **to be done for,** estar perdido; estar muerto. **to do better,** hacer mejor (que); (mend one's ways) enmendarse, corregirse; (improve) mejorar, hacer progresos; (in health) encontrarse mejor. **to do business with** *Lat. Am.* amarchantarse con. **to do nothing,** no hacer nada. **to do reverence,** rendir homenaje; inclinarse. **to do to death,** matar; asesinar; ejecutar. **to do violence to,** *fig* hacer fuerza a. **to do well,** hacer bien; obrar bien; (be successful) tener éxito; hacer buena impresión; (prosperous) tener una buena posición. **to do wonders,** hacer maravillas. **to have done with,** renunciar (a); dejar de usar; dejar de hacer, cesar; concluir, terminar; no tener más que ver con; (forsake) abandonar; (a person) romper con. **to have nothing to do,** no tener nada que hacer. **to have nothing to do with,** no tener nada que ver con; (of people) no tratar; (end a friendship) romper su amistad con, dejar de ver. **well done,** bien hecho; (of food) bien guisado; (of meat) bien asado. **What is to be done?** ¿Qué hay que hacer? ¿Qué se puede hacer? **What is to do?** ¿Qué pasa? ¿Qué hay? **When he had done speaking,** Cuando hubo terminado de hablar. **to do again,** hacer de nuevo, volver a hacer, rehacer; repetir. **He will not do it again,** No lo hará más. **to do away with,** quitar; eliminar; suprimir; hacer desaparecer; poner fin a; hacer cesar; destruir; matar. **to do by,** tratar (a), portarse con. **to do for,** arruinar; matar; (suffice) bastar para; ser a propósito para, servir para; (look after) cuidar; (as a housekeeper) dirigir la casa para. **to do out,** (a room) limpiar. **to do out of,** quitar; privar de; (steal) robar. **to do up,** (tie) atar; (fold) enrollar, plegar; envolver; (parcel) empaquetar; (arrange) arreglar; decorar; poner en orden; poner como nuevo; (iron) planchar; (launder) lavar y planchar; (tire) fatigar. **to do with,** (of people) tratar; (of things) tener que ver con; (put up with) poder con; poder sufrir. **to do without,** prescindir de; pasarse sin
do as an auxiliary verb is not translated in Spanish, e.g. **I do believe,** creo. **Do not do that,** no hagas eso. **I did not know,** no sabía
When it is used for emphasis, **do** is translated by **sí, ciertamente, claro** and similar words, e.g.:
She did not know, but he did, Ella no lo sabía pero él sí
You do paint well, Pintas muy bien por cierto
Do come this time, No dejes de venir esta vez
docile *a* dócil
dock *n* dique, *m*, dársena, *f*; (wharf) muelle, *m*; (in a law court) banquillo de los acusados, *m*; *bot* romaza, *f*. *vt* (a tail) descolar; cortar, cercenar; reducir; (money) descontar; (a ship) poner en dique. *vi* entrar en dársena, entrar en dique, entrar en muelle. **dry-d.,** dique seco, *m*. **floating-d.,** dique flotante, *m*. **d.-dues,** muellaje, *m*. **d. rat,** (thief) raquero, *m*
docker *n* estibador, descargador del muelle, *m*
docket *n* (bundle) legajo, *m*; extracto, *m*; minuta, *f*; (label) etiqueta, *f*, marbete, *m*
dockyard *n* arsenal, astillero, *m*
doctor *n* doctor (-ra); (medical practitioner) médico (-ca), asistir; (repair) reparar, componer; adulterar; mezclar drogas con; falsificar. *vi* ejercer la medicina. **family d.,** médico de cabecera, *m*. **to graduate as a d.,** doctorarse. **d. of divinity, laws, medicine,** doctor (-ra) en teología, en derecho, en medicina, *m*
doctoral *a* doctoral
doctorate *n* doctorado, *m*
doctrinaire *a* and *n* doctrinario (-ia)
doctrinal *a* doctrinal
doctrine *n* doctrina, *f*
document *n* documento, *m*. *vt* documentar; probar con documentos. **d.-case,** carpeta, *f*
documentary *a* documental; escrito, auténtico. **d. film,** película documental, *f*
documentation *n* documentación, *f*
Dodecanese, the el Dodecaneso, *m*
dodge *n* esguince, regate, *m*; evasiva, *f*; (trick) es-

tratagema, *m*, maniobra, *f*; artefacto, *m*. *vt* esquivar, evadir

doe *n* gama, *f*. **doe rabbit,** coneja, *f*

doer *n* hacedor (-ra); autor (-ra)

doeskin *n* ante, *m*, piel de gama, *f*

doff *vt* quitar; (of hats, etc.) quitarse; desnudarse de

dog *n* perro, *m*; (male) macho, *m*; (andiron) morillo, *m*; *ast* Can Mayor (or Menor), Sirio, *m*. *vt* perseguir; seguir los pasos de; espiar. **You can't deceive an old dog,** A perro viejo no hay tus tus. **to go to the dogs,** ir a las carreras de galgos; *fig* ir cuesta abajo. **mongrel dog,** perro mestizo, *m*. **thoroughbred dog,** perro de raza pura, *m*. **dog-collar,** collar de perro, *m*; *ecc* alzacuello, *m*. **dog-days,** días caniculares, *m pl*, canícula, *f*. **dog-eared** (of books) con las puntas de las hojas dobladas. **dog-fight,** lucha de perros, *f*; combate aéreo, *m*. **dog-fish,** lija, *f*, cazón, *m*. **dog in the manger,** el perro del hortelano. **dog-kennel,** perrera, *f*. **dog-latin,** bajo latín, *m*. **dog license,** matrícula de perros, *f*. **dog-racing,** carrera de galgos, *f*. **dog-rose,** escaramujo, *m*. **dog show,** exposición canina, *f*. **dog-tooth,** *arch* diente de perro, *m*. **dog-vane,** *naut* cataviento, *m*

doge *n* dux, *m*

dogged *a* persistente, tenaz, pertinaz, obstinado

doggedly *adv* tenazmente

doggedness *n* pertinacia, tenacidad, terquedad, persistencia, *f*

doggerel *n* malos versos, *m pl*; aleluyas, coplas de ciego, *f pl*, *a* malo, irregular

dogma *n* dogma, *m*

dogmatic *a* dogmático

dogmatize *vt* and *vi* dogmatizar; mostrarse dogmático

doh *n* *mus* do, *m*

doily *n* carpeta, *f*, pañito de adorno, *m*

doings *n pl* acciones, *f pl*; (deeds) hechos, *m pl*; (behavior) conducta, *f*; (happenings) acontecimientos, *m pl*; (works) obras, *f pl*; (things) cosas, *f pl*

doldrums *n pl* calmas ecuatoriales, *f pl*

dole *n* limosna, *f*; porción, *f*. **to d. out,** repartir; distribuir en porciones pequeñas; racionar; dar contra la voluntad de uno.

doleful *a* triste, lúgubre, melancólico; doloroso

dolefulness *n* tristeza, melancolía, *f*; dolor, *m*

doll *n* muñeca, *f*

dollar *n* dólar, *m*

dolly *n* muñeca, *f*; (for clothes) moza, *f*. **d.-tub,** cubo para la colada, *m*

dolman *n* dormán, *m*

dolphin *n* delfín, *m*

dolt *n* cabeza de alcornoque, *mf*, zamacuco, *m*

domain *n* territorio, *m*; heredad, posesión, propiedad, *f*; (empire) dominio, *m*

dome *n* cúpula, *f*; bóveda, *f*; (palace) palacio, *m*

domestic *a* doméstico; familiar; (home-loving) casero; (of animals) doméstico; (national) interior, nacional. *n* doméstico, sirviente, *m*; criada, *f*. **d. economy,** economía doméstica, *f*

domesticate *vt* domesticar

domesticated *a* (of animals) domesticado; (of persons) casero

domestication *n* domesticación, *f*

domesticity *n* domesticidad, *f*

domicile *n* domicilio, *m*, *vt* domiciliar

domiciliary *a* domiciliario

dominant *a* dominante; imperante. *n* *mus* dominante, *f*. **to be d.,** prevalecer

dominate *vt* and *vi* dominar

domination *n* dominación, *f*

domineer *vi* dominar, tiranizar. **to d. over,** mandar en

domineering *a* dominante, mandón, tiránico. **d. person** *Lat. Am.* mandarín *m*

Dominican *n* dominicano, *m*

Dominican Republic, the la República Dominicana, *f*

dominion *n* dominio, *m*; autoridad, soberanía, *f*; imperio, *m*; *pl* **dominions,** *ecc* dominaciones, *f pl*

Dominions, the los Dominios, *m*

domino *n* dominó, *m*. **to go d.,** nacer domino

don *n* (Spanish and Italian title) don, *m*; señor, *m*. *vt* ponerse, vestirse

donation *n* donación, dádiva, *f*; contribución, *f*

done *a* and *past part* hecho; (of food) cocido; (roasted) asado; (tired) rendido; (*fam* deceived) engañado. **Well d.!** ¡Bien hecho! **d. for,** arruinado; muerto; perdido; vencido; (spoilt) estropeado

donkey *n* borrico (-ca), burro (-rra). **d.-engine,** máquina auxiliar, *f*

donor *n* donador (-ra); dador (-ra)

doodle *v* borrajear, garabatear, hacer garabatos

doom *n* condena, *f*; (fate) suerte, *f*; (judgment) destino, *m*; ruina, *f*; juicio, *m*. *vt* sentenciar; condenar

doomsday *n* día del juicio final, *m*

door *n* puerta, *f*; entrada, *f*. **front d.,** puerta de entrada, *f*. **next d.,** la casa vecina; la puerta de al lado, la puerta vecina. **next d. neighbor,** vecino (-na) de al lado. **out of doors,** al aire libre; en la calle. **to knock at the d.,** llamar a la puerta. **to slam the d. in a person's face,** dar con la puerta en las narices de alguien. **d.-bell,** timbre (non-electric, campanilla, *f*) de llamada, *m*. **d.-jamb,** quicial, *m*. **d. keeper,** portero, *m*. **d.-knob,** tirador, *m*. **d.-knocker,** manija, *f*; picaporte, *m*, aldaba, *f*. **d.-plate,** placa, *f*. **d.-shutter,** cierre metálico, *m*. **d.-step,** peldaño de la puerta, *m*; umbral, *m*. **d.-way,** portal, *m*

dope *n* drogas, *f pl*, narcóticos, *m pl*; (news) información, *f*. **d. fiend,** morfinómano (-na)

dope-pusher *n* narcotraficante, *mf*

Doric *a* dórico

dormant *a* durmiente; latente; secreto; inactivo. **to go d.,** dormirse

dormer window *n* lumbrera, *f*

dormitory *n* dormitorio, *m*

dormouse *n* lirón, *m*

dorsal *a* dorsal

dory *n* (fish) dorado, *m*

dose, dosage *n*; dosis, *f*

dossier *n* documentación, *f*

dot *n* punto, *m*; *mus* puntillo, *m*; *pl* **dots,** *gram* puntos suspensivos, *m pl*. *vt* poner punto (a una letra); (scatter) salpicar. **on the dot,** (of time) en punto. **to dot one's i's,** poner los puntos sobre las íes

dotage *n* senectud, chochera, *f*

dotard *n* viejo chocho, *m*; vieja chocha, *f*; *inf* carcamal, *m*

dote *vi* chochear. **to d. on,** adorar en, idolatrar

doting *a* chocho

double *a* and *adv* doble; dos veces; (in a pair) en par; en dos; doblemente; (deceitful) doble, de dos caras, falso; ambiguo. *n* doble, *m*; duplicado, *m*; *theat* contrafigura, *f*; *pl* **doubles,** (tennis) dobles, *m pl*, juego doble, *m*. *vt* doblar; duplicar; (fold) doblegar; (the fist) cerrar (el puño); (*theat* and *naut*) doblar. *vi* doblarse; (dodge) volverse atrás, hacer un rodeo, dar (una vuelta); esquivarse. **to d. up,** *vt* envolver; arrollar; (a person) doblar. *vi* doblegarse; arrollarse; (collapse) desplomarse. **at the d.,** corriendo. **He was doubled up with pain,** El dolor se le hacía retorcerse. **mixed doubles,** parejas mixtas, *f pl*; dobles mixtos, *m pl*. **double two,** (telephone) dos dos. **with a d. meaning,** con segunda intención. **d.-barrelled,** de dos cañones. **d.-bass,** contrabajo, *m*. **d. bed,** cama de matrimonio, *f*. **d.-bedded,** con cama de matrimonio; con dos camas. **d.-breasted,** cruzado. **d.-chin,** papada, *f*. **d.-dealing,** duplicidad, *f*. **d.-edged,** de doble filo. **d.-entry,** *com* partida doble, *f*. **d.-faced,** de dos caras. **d.-jointed,** con articulaciones dobles

double room *Mexico* cuarto doble *m*

double-spaced *a* a doble espacio, a dos espacios

doublet *n* (garment) jubón, justillo, *m*; pareja, *f*, par, *m*

doubling *n* doblamiento, *m*; doblez, plegadura, *f*; duplicación, *f*; (dodging) evasiva, *f*, esguince, *m*

doubloon *n* doblón, *m*

doubly *adv* doblemente; con duplicidad

doubt *n* duda, *f*; incertidumbre, *f*; sospecha, *f*. *vt* and *vi* dudar; sospechar; titubear, hesitar; temer. **beyond all d.,** fuera de duda. **no d.,** sin duda. **There is no d. that,** No hay duda de que, No cabe duda de que. **When in d. . . . ,** En caso de duda . . .

doubter *n* incrédulo (-la)

doubtful *a* dudoso; incierto; perplejo; ambiguo; (of places) sospechoso

doubtfully *adv* dudosamente; inciertamente; irresolutamente; ambiguamente

doubtfulness *n* duda, incertidumbre, *f*; ambigüedad, *f*

doubtless *adv* sin duda, por supuesto; probablemente

douche *n* ducha, *f*, *vt* duchar

dough *n* pasta, masa, *f*; (money) lana, *f*

dour *a* huraño, adusto, austero

dourly *adv* severamente

douse *vt* zambullir; (a sail) recoger; *inf* apagar

dove *n* paloma, *f*. **d.-cote,** palomar, *m*

dovetail *n carp* cola de milano, *f*, *vt carp* machihembrar, empalmar; *fig* encajar

dowager *n* viuda, *f*; matrona, *f*. **d. countess,** condesa viuda, *f*

dowager empress *n* emperatriz viuda, *f*

dowdiness *n* desaliño, desaseo, *m*; falta de elegancia, *f*

dowdy *a* desaliñado, desaseado; poco elegante. *n* mujer poco elegante, *f*

dowel *n* espiga, clavija, *f*, zoquete, *m*, *vt* enclavijar

down *n* (of a bird) plumón, *m*; (on a peach, etc.) pelusilla, *f*; (hair) vello, *m*; (before the beard) bozo, *m*; (of a thistle, etc.) vilano, *m*. **ups and downs,** vicisitudes, *f pl*

down *a* pendiente; (of trains, etc.) descendente. *adv* abajo; hacia abajo; (lowered) bajado; (of the eyes) bajos; (on the ground) en tierra, por tierra; (stretched out) tendido a lo largo; (depressed) triste, abatido; (ill) enfermo; (fallen) caído; (of the wind) cesado; (closed) cerrado; (exhausted) agotado; *com* al contado; (of temperature) más bajo. *prep* abajo de; abajo; en la dirección de; (along) a lo largo de; por. **"Down"** (on elevators) «Para bajar». *interj* ¡Abajo!; ¡A tierra! **He went d. the hill,** Bajaba la colina. **He is d. now,** Ha bajado ahora; Está abajo ahora; Está derribado ahora. **The sun has gone d.,** Se ha puesto el sol. **His stock has gone d.,** *fig inf* Ha caído en disfavor. **Prices have come d.,** Los precios han bajado. **Their numbers have gone d.,** Sus números han disminuido. **to be d. and out,** estar completamente arruinado, ser pobre de solemnidad. **to boil d.,** reducir hirviendo. **to come d. in the world,** venir a menos. **while I was going d. the river,** mientras iba río abajo, mientras bajaba al río. **d. below,** allá abajo; abajo; en el piso de abajo. **D. on your knees!** ¡De rodillas! **d. to,** hasta. **d. spout,** tubo de bajada, *m*. **D. with!** ¡Abajo! ¡Muera! **d.-stream,** agua abajo. **d. train,** tren descendente, *m*

down *vt* derribar; vencer. **to d. tools,** declararse en huelga

downcast *a* bajo; cabizbajo, deprimido, abatido

downfall *n* caída, *f*; derrumbamiento, *m*; (failure) fracaso, *m*; (*fig* ruin) decadencia, ruina, *f*

downhearted *a* descorazonado, alicaído, desalentado

downhill *adv* cuesta abajo, hacia abajo. *a* en declive, inclinado. **to go d.,** ir cuesta abajo

downiness *n* vellosidad, *f*

downpayment *n Mexico* enganche *m*

downpour *n* chubasco (Mexico), aguacero, chaparrón, *m*

downright *a* franco, sincero; categórico, terminante; absoluto. *adv* muy; completamente

downstairs *adv* escalera abajo; al piso de abajo; en el piso bajo; abajo. *a* del piso de abajo. *n* planta baja, *f*; piso de abajo, *m*. **to go d.,** bajar la escalera; ir al piso de abajo

downtrodden *a* oprimido, esclavizado

downward *a* descendente; inclinado. *adv* hacia abajo

downy *a* velloso; (*fam* of persons) con más conchas que un galápago

dowry *n* dote, *mf*. **to give as a d.,** dotar

dowse *vt*. See **douse**

doze *vi* dormitar. *n* sueño ligero, *m*

dozen *n* docena, *f*

drab *a* pardo, parduzco, grisáceo; *fig* gris, monótono. *n* (slut) pazpuerca, *f*; (prostitute) ramera, *f*

drachma *n* dracma, *f*

draft *n* (detachment) destacamento, *m*; *com* giro, *m*, letra de cambio, *f*; (for the army, navy) conscripción, leva, *f*; (outline) bosquejo, *m*; proyecto, *m*; borrador, *m*. *vt* (detach) destacar; (recruit) reclutar; (outline) bosquejar, delinear; (draw up) redactar; proyectar

draft card *n* cartilla (Mexico), libreta de enrolamiento (Argentina), *m*

draft dodger *n* emboscado, prófugo, *m*

drafting *n* (*mil nav*) reclutamiento, *m*; (of a bill, etc.) redacción, *f*; (wording) términos, *m pl*

draftsman *n* dibujante, *m*; delineante, *m*; redactor, *f*

drag *n* (for dredging) draga, *f*; (harrow) rastrillo, *m*; (break) freno, *m*; (obstacle) estorbo, *m*; *aer* sonda, *f*. *vt* arrastrar; (fishing nets) rastrear; (harrow) rastrillar. *vi* (of the anchor) garrar; arrastrarse por el suelo; (of time) pasar lentamente; ir más despacio (que); (of interest) decaer, disminuir. **d.-hook,** garfio, *m*. **d.-net,** brancada, *f*

dragging *n* arrastre, *m*; (of lakes, etc.) rastreo, *m*, *a* rastrero; cansado

draggled *a* mojado y sucio

dragon *n* dragón, *m*. **d.-fly,** libélula, *f*, caballito del diablo, *m*

dragoon *n mil* dragón, *m*, *vt* someter a una disciplina rigurosa; obligar a la fuerza (a)

drain *n* desaguadero, *m*; (sewer) cloaca, alcantarilla, *f*; sumidero, *m*; *agr* acequia, *f*. *vt* desaguar; sanear; (lakes, etc.) desangrar; secar; (bail) achicar; (empty and drink) vaciar; (swallow) tragar; (*fig* of sorrow, etc.) apurar; (despoil) despojar; (deprive) privar (de); (impoverish) empobrecer; (exhaust) agotar. *vi* desaguarse; vaciarse; (with off) escurrirse. **to be well drained,** tener buen drenaje. **to d. the sump,** vaciar la culata. **to d. away,** vaciar. **d.-pipe,** tubo de desagüe, *m*

drainage *n* (of land) drenaje, *m*; desagüe, *m*; (of wounds) drenaje, *m*; (sewage) aguas del alcantarillado, *f pl*. **main d.,** drenaje municipal, *m*

draining *a* de desagüe; de drenaje. **d.-board,** escurridor, *m*

drake *n* ánade macho, *m*

dram *n* dracma, *f*; (of liquor) trago, *m*

drama *n* drama, *m*

dramatic *a* dramático

dramatically *adv* dramáticamente

dramatis personae *n pl* personajes, *m pl*

dramatist *n* dramaturgo, *m*

dramatization *n* versión escénica, *f*; descripción dramática, *f*; (of emotions) dramatización, *f*

dramatize *vt* dramatizar

drape *vt* colgar, cubrir; vestir

draper *n* pañero (-ra)

drapery *n* colgaduras, *f pl*; ropaje, *m*, ropas, *f pl*; pañería, *f*

drastic *a* drástico; enérgico, fuerte; **a drastic measure,** una medida avanzada, *f*

draught *n* (act of drawing) tiro, *m*; (of liquid) trago, *m*; (glass) vaso, *m*; (of a ship) calado, *m*; (of air) corriente de aire, *f*, Lat. Am. chiflón, *m*; (party) destacamento, *m*; *n pl* draughts, (game) damas, *f pl*. *vt* see **draft. on d.,** (of beer, etc.) por vaso. **d. horse,** caballo de tiro, *m*. **d. screen,** cancel, *m*

draughtboard *n* tablero de damas, *m*

draughtsman *n* dibujante, *m*; delineante, *m*; redactor, *m*; (piece in game) peón, *m*

draughtsmanship *n* arte del dibujo lineal, *m*; redacción (de un proyecto de ley), *f*

draughty *a* que tiene corriente de aire; expuesto a los vientos. **This room is d.,** Hay corriente de aire en esta habitación

draw *vt* tirar; arrastrar; traer; (pluck) arrancar; (attract) atraer; (extract) extraer; sacar; hacer salir; (unsheath) desenvainar; (a bow-string) tender; (cards, dominoes) tomar, robar; (threads) deshilar; (disembowel) destripar; (a check, etc.) girar, librar; (of a ship) calar; (of lines) hacer (rayas); (curtains) correr; (to draw curtains back) descorrer; (salary, money) cobrar, percibir; (obtain) obtener; (persuade) persuadir, inducir; (inhale) respirar; (a sigh) dar; (win) ganar; (a conclusion) deducir, inferir; (a distinction) hacer formular; *sport* empatar; (a number, etc.) sortear; (suck) chupar; (tighten) estirar; (lengthen) alargar; (comfort, etc.) tomar; (inspiration) inspirarse en; (obtain money) procurarse (recursos); (withdraw funds) retirar; (write) escribir; (draw) dibujar; (trace) trazar; (provoke) provocar. **to be drawn,** (of tickets in a lottery and cards) salir. **to d. lots,** echar suertes. **to d. water,** sacar agua. **to d. along,** arrastrar; conducir. **to d. aside,** tomar a un lado, tomar aparte; quitar de en medio, poner a un lado; (curtains) descorrer. **to d. away,** (remove) quitar; (a person) llevarse (a); apartar. **to d. back,** hacer recular; hacer retirarse; hacer volverse atrás; (curtains) descorrer. **to d. down,** hacer bajar; tirar a lo largo de (or por); bajar; (attract) atraer. **to d. forth,** hacer salir; hacer avanzar; tirar hacia adelante; conducir; (develop) desarrollar; sacar; hacer aparecer; (comment, etc.) suscitar. **to d. in,** tirar hacia adentro; sacar; acercar; atraer. **to d. off,** sacar; retirar; quitar; (water from pipes, etc.) vaciar; *print* tirar; (turn aside) desviar. **to d. on,** (of apparel) ponerse; (boots) calzarse; (occasion) ocasionar. **to d. out,** sacar fuera; hacer salir; tirar (de); (extract) extraer; (trace) trazar; (a person) hacer hablar. **to d. over,** poner encima de; arrastrar por; hacer acercarse (a), tirar hacia; atraer; persuadir. **d. prestige (from),** cobrar prestigio (de). **to d. round,** poner alrededor de. **to d. together,** reunir; acercar. **to d. up,** tirar hacia arriba; subir; sacar; extraer; (raise) levantar, alzar; (bring) traer; (bring near) acercar; (order) ordenar; *mil* formar; (a document) redactar; formular. **to d. oneself up,** erguirse

draw *vi* tirar; (shrink) encogerse; (wrinkle) arrugarse; (of chimneys, etc.) tirar; (a picture) dibujar; *sport* empatar; (move) moverse; avanzar, adelantarse; (of a ship) calar; (a sword) desnudar (la espada); (lots) echar suertes; (attract people) atraer gente; *com* girar. **to d. aside,** ponerse a un lado; retirarse. **to d. back,** retroceder, recular; retirarse; vacilar. **to d. in,** retirarse; (of days) hacerse corto; (of dusk) caer. **to d. off,** alejarse; apartarse, retirarse. **to d. on,** (approach) acercarse; avanzar; *com* girar contra; inspirarse en. **to d. out,** hacerse largo; (of a vehicle) ponerse en marcha, empezar a andar. **to d. round,** ponerse alrededor; reunirse alrededor. **to d. together,** reunirse. **to d. up,** parar.

draw *n* tirada, *f;* (of lotteries) sorteo, *m; sport* empate, *m;* atracción, *f; (fig* feeler) tanteo, *m.* **to be a big d.,** ser una gran atracción

drawback *n* desventaja, *f,* inconveniente, *m*

drawbridge *n* puente levadizo, *m*

drawee *n com* girado, *m*

drawer *n* tirador (-ra); (of water) aguador (-ra); extractor (-ra); (in a public-house) mozo de taberna, *m;* (designer) diseñador, *m;* (sketcher) dibujante, *mf; com* girador, *m;* (receptacle) cajón, *m; pl* **drawers,** (men's) calzoncillos, *m pl;* (women's) pantalones, *m pl*

drawing *n* (pulling) tiro, *m;* atracción, *f;* (extraction) extracción, *f;* saca, *f;* (in raffles, etc. and of lots) sorteo, *m;* (of money) percibo, *m; com* giro, *m;* (sketch) dibujo, *m;* (plan) esquema, *f.* **free-hand d.,** dibujo a pulso, *m.* **d. from life,** dibujo del natural, *m.* **d.-board,** tablero de dibujo, *m.* **d.-paper,** papel para dibujar, *m.* **d.-pin,** chinche, *f.* **d.-room,** salón, *m*

drawl *vi* hablar arrastrando las palabras

drawn *past part* See **draw.** *a* (tired) ojeroso, con ojeras, con un aspecto de cansancio; (with pain) desencajado.

long d. out, demasiado largo. **d. sword,** espada desnuda, *f.* **d.-thread work,** deshilados, *m pl*

dread *n* pavor, temor, terror, espanto, *m;* trepidación, *f,* miedo, *m. a* temible, espantoso, terrible; augusto. *vt* temer. *vi* tener miedo, temer. **in d. of,** con miedo de, con terror de

dreader *n* el, *m,* (*f,* la) que teme, temedor (-ra)

dreadful *a* terrible, pavoroso, espantoso, horroroso; formidable; augusto

dreadfully *adv* terriblemente, horriblemente

dreadfulness *n* horror, *m*

dream *n* sueño, *m;* ilusión, *f;* ensueño, *m;* fantasía, *f. vt* and *vi* soñar; imaginar. **He dreamed away the hours,** Pasaba las horas soñando. **I wouldn't d. of it!** ¡Ni por sueño! **in a d.,** en sueños; (waking) como en sueños; mecánicamente. **Sweet dreams!** ¡Duerme bien! **to d. of,** soñar con

dreamer *n* soñador (-ra); visionario (-ia)

dreamily *adv* como en sueños; soñolientamente; vagamente

dreaming *n* sueños, *m pl*

dreamland *n* reino de los sueños, *m*

dreamy *a* soñador; soñoliento; fantástico; (empty) vacío

dreariness *n* tristeza, *f;* melancolía, *f;* lobreguez, *f*

dreary *a* triste; melancólico; lóbrego

dredge *vt* dragar; (with sugar, etc.) espolvorear

dredger *n* draga, *f;* (for sugar) azucarera, *f;* (for flour) harinero, *m*

dredging *n* dragado, *m;* (sprinkling) salpicadura, *f.* **d. bucket,** cangilón, *m*

dregs *n pl* heces, *f pl,* posos, *m pl, Lat. Am.* concho *m* **to drain to the d.,** vaciar hasta las heces

drench *vt* mojar, calar. **He is drenched to the skin,** Está calado hasta los huesos

Dresden *n* Dresde, *f.* **D. china,** loza de Dresde, *f*

dress *vt* (with clothes) vestir; (arrange) arreglar; (the hair) peinar(se); (a wound) curar; (hides) adobar; (cloth) aprestar; (flax) rastrillar; (stone) labrar; (wood) desbastar; (prune) podar; (a garden) cultivar; (manure) abonar; *cul* aderezar; preparar; (season) condimentar; (a table) poner; (adorn) ataviar, adornar; revestir; (a dead body) amortajar. *vi* vestirse; ataviarse; (of troops) alinearse. **all dressed up and nowhere to go,** compuesta y sin novio. **dress to kill,** ataviarse a las mil maravillas; *Lat. Am.* arriscarse, *Central America* empavonarse **dressed up to the nines,** vestido de veinticinco alfileres. **Left (Right) d.!** ¡A la izquierda (A la derecha) alinearse! **to d. down,** (scold) poner como un trapo (a), dar una calada (a). **to d. up,** *vt* ataviar; (disguise) disfrazar. *vi* ponerse muy elegante; disfrazarse

dress *n* (in general) el vestir; (clothes) ropa, *f;* (frock) vestido, traje, *m;* (uniform) uniforme, *m; (fig* covering) hábitos, *m pl;* (appearance) aspecto, *m;* forma, *f.* **full d.,** (uniform) uniforme de gala, *m;* (civilian, man's) traje de etiqueta, *m;* (woman's) traje de gala, *m.* **morning d.,** (man's) traje de paisano, *m;* (woman's) vestido de todos los días, *m;* (man's formal dress) chaqué, *m.* **ready-made d.,** traje hecho, *m.* **d. allowance,** alfileres, *m pl.* **d.-circle,** anfiteatro, *m.* **d.-coat,** frac, *m.* **d. protector,** sobaquera, *f.* **d. rehearsal,** ensayo general, *m.* **d. shirt,** camisa de pechera dura, *f.* **d. suit,** (with white tie) traje de frac, *m;* (with black tie) smoking, *m.* **d. sword,** espada de gala, *f.* **d. tie,** corbata de smoking (or de frac), *f*

dresser *n* el que adereza; (of wounds) practicante (de hospital), *m;* (valet) ayuda de cámara, *m;* (maid) doncella, *f;* (of skins) adobador de pieles, *m;* (furniture) aparador, *m;* (in the kitchen) armario de la cocina, *m*

dressing *n* el vestir(se); aderezamiento, *m;* (for cloth) apresto, *m;* (of leather) adobo, *m;* (of wood) desbaste, *m;* (of stone) labrado, *m;* (manuring) estercoladura, *f;* (sauce) salsa, *f;* (seasoning) condimentación, *f;* (of a wound) cura, *f;* (bandage) apósito, *m,* vendaje, *m.* **d.-case,** neceser, *m,* saco de noche, *m.* **d.-down,** *inf* rapapolvo, *m.* **d.-gown,** (woman's) salto de cama, quimono, *m*; (man's) batín, *m*. **d.-jacket,** chambra, *f*; peinador, *m*. **d.-room,** *theat* camarín, *m*; (in a house) trasalcoba, recámara, *f*. **d.-station,** puesto de socorro, *m*. **d.-table,** tocador, *m*, mesa de tocador, *f*

dressmaker *n* modista, *mf*

dressmaking *n* confección de vestidos, *f*; arte de la modista, *mf*

dribble *vi* gotear; (slaver) babear. *vt* (in football) regatear. *n* (in football) regate, *m*

dried *a* seco; (of fruit) paso. **d. up,** (withered) marchito; (of people) enjuto. **d. fish,** cecial, *m*. **d. meat,** cecina, *f*

drift *n* (in a ship or airplane's course) deriva, *f*; (of a current) velocidad, *f*; (tendency) tendencia, *f*; (meaning) significación, *f*; (heap) montón, *m*; (aim) objeto, propósito, fin, *m*; *min* galería, *f*; (of dust, etc.) nube, *f*; (shower) lluvia, *f*; (impulsion) impulso, *m*; violencia, *f*. *vi* flotar, ir arrastrado por la corriente; amontonarse; *naut* derivar; *aer* abatir. *vt* llevar; amontonar. **drifts of sand,** arena movediza, *f*. **to d. into,** (war, etc.) entrar sin querer en; (habits) dar en la flor de; (a room, etc.) deslizarse en. **d.-wood,** madera de deriva, *f*

drill *n* (instrument) taladro, perforador, *m*, barrena, *f*; ejercicio, *m*, educación física, *f*; *mil* instrucción militar, *f*; (cloth) dril, *m*; *agr* sembradora mecánica, *f*; (for seeds) hilera, *f*; (discipline) disciplina, *f*; (teaching) instrucción, *f*. *vt* taladrar, barrenar; enseñar el ejercicio (a); enseñar la instrucción; disciplinar; (seed) sembrar en hileras. *vi* hacer el ejercicio; hacer la instrucción militar. **d. ground,** (in a barracks) patio de un cuartel, *m*; (in a school) patio de recreo, *m*. **d.-sergeant,** sargento instructor, *m*

drilling *n* (boring) perforación, *f*, barrenamiento, *m*; (of seeds) sembradura en hileras, *f*; ejercicios, *m pl*; (maneuvers) maniobras, *f pl*

drink *n* bebida, *f*; (glass of wine, etc.) copita, *f*; (of water, etc.) vaso, *m*. *vt* beber; tomar; (empty) vaciar. *vi* beber. **to d. the health of,** beber a la salud de, brindar por. **to give someone a d.,** dar a beber. **Would you like a d.?** ¿Quieres tomar algo? **to d. in,** absorber. **to d. off, up,** beber de un trago

drinkable *a* potable, bebedero

drinker *n* bebedor (-ra)

drinking *n* acción de beber, *f*; el beber, *m*; (alcoholism) bebida, *f*. *a* que bebe; aficionado a la bebida; (of things) para beber; (drinkable) potable; (tavern) de taberna. **d.-fountain,** fuente pública para beber agua, *f*. **d. place,** bebedero, *m*; bar, *m*. **d.-song,** canción de taberna, *f*. **d.-trough,** abrevadero, *m*; **d.-water,** agua potable, *f*

drip *vi* and *vt* chorrear, gotear; caer gota a gota; escurrir; destilar; chorrear. *n* goteo, *m*; gota, *f*; *arch* goterón, *m*

dripping *n* goteo, *m*; chorreo, *m*; (fat) grasa, *f*, a que gotea; mojado; que chorrea agua. **d.-pan,** grasera, *f*

drive *vt* empujar; arrojar; conducir; (grouse, etc.) batir; (a ball) golpear; (a nail, etc.) clavar; (oblige) compeler, forzar a; (a horse, plough, etc.) manejar; (*mech* work) mover; (cause to work, of machines) hacer funcionar; (a tunnel, etc.) abrir, construir; (a bargain, etc.) hacer; (cause) impulsar, hacer; (mad, etc.) volver. *vi* lanzarse; (of rain) azotar; (a vehicle) conducir; (in a vehicle) ir en (coche, etc.). **to let d. at,** (aim) asestar. **to d. a wedge,** hacer mella. **to d. home an argument,** convencer; hacer convincente. **What is he driving at?** ¿Qué se propone?; ¿Qué quiere?; ¿Qué quiere decir con sus indirectas? ¿A dónde quiere llegar con esto? **to d. along,** ir en coche o carruaje por; pasearse en coche o carruaje; conducir un auto, etc., por. **to d. away,** *vt* echar; (chase) cazar; (flies, etc.) sacudirse, espantar; (care, etc.) ahuyentar; (of persons) apartar, alejar. *vi* (depart) marcharse (en coche, etc.). **to d. back,** *vt* rechazar; (a ball) devolver. *vi* volver (en auto, etc.); (arrive) llegar. **to d. crazy, d. insane** enloquecer, *Lat. Am. also* idiotizar; **to d. down,** hacer bajar; arrojar hacia abajo; (in a vehicle) bajar (por). **to d. in, into,** *vt* hacer entrar; (of teeth, etc.) hincar; (nails) clavar; *fig* in-

troducir. *vt* entrar (en coche, carruaje); llegar (en coche, etc.). **to d. off,** See **away. to d. off the stage,** hacer dejar la escena, silbar. **to d. on,** *vt* empujar; hacer avanzar; (attack) atacar. *vi* seguir su marcha; seguir avanzando; emprender la marcha. **to d. out,** *vt* expulsar; hacer salir; (chase) cazar. *vi* salir (en coche, etc.). **to d. up,** *vi* llegar (en coche, etc.); parar. **to d. up to,** avanzar hasta, llegar hasta; conducir (el coche, etc.) hasta

drive *n* paseo (en coche, etc.), *m*; (avenue) avenida, *f*; (distance) trayecto, *m*; (journey) viaje, *m*; *mech* acción, *f*; conducción, *f*; *m*; mil ataque, *m*; (of a person) energía, *f*; campaña vigorosa, *f*; impulso, *m*. **left (right) hand d.,** conducción a la izquierda (derecha). **to take a d.,** dar un paseo en (auto, etc.). **to take for a d.,** llevar a paseo en (auto, etc.)

drive-in *n* automóvil, autocinema, *m*

drivel *n* vaciedades, patrañas, *f pl*, disparates, *m pl*, *vi* decir disparates, chochear

driver *n* conductor (-ra); chófer, *m*; (of an engine) maquinista, *m*; (of a cart) carretero, *m*; (of a coach, carriage) cochero, *m*; (of cattle, etc.) ganadero, *m*; (golf) conductor, *m*

driver's license *Spain* carné de chofer, *Argentina* carné de conductor, *m*, *elsewhere in Lat. Am.* licencia de manejar, *f*

"Driveway" «Vado Permante», «Paso de Carruajes»

driving *n* conducción, *f*; modo de conducir, *m*; paseo (en coche, etc.), *m*; impulsión, *f*. *a* de conducir; de chófer; para choferes; motor; propulsor; impulsor; de transmisión; *fig* impulsor; (violent) violento, impetuoso. **to go d.,** ir de paseo (en auto o carruaje). **d. mirror,** espejo retrovisor, *m*. **d. seat,** asiento del conductor, *m*; (of an old-fashioned coach, etc.) pescante, *m*. **d.-shaft,** *mech* árbol motor, *m*. **d. test,** examen para choferes, *m*. **d.-wheel,** volante, *m*; rueda motriz, *f*. **d.-whip,** látigo, *m*

drizzle *n* llovizna, *f*, *vi* lloviznar, *Lat. Am.* briznar

droll *a* chusco, gracioso. *n* bufón, *m*

drone *n* abejón, *m*; *fig* zángano, *m*; (hum) zumbido, *m*; (of a song, voice) salmodia, *f*, *vt* and *vi* (hum) zumbar; (of a song, voice) salmodiar; (idle) zanganear

droop *vi* inclinarse; colgar; caer; (wither) marchitarse; (fade) consumirse; (pine) desanimarse. *vt* bajar; dejar caer. *n* caída, *f*; inclinación, *f*

drooping *a* caído; debilitado; lánguido; (of ears) gacho; (depressed) alicaído, deprimido

drop *n* gota, *f*; (tear) lágrima, *f*; (for the ear) pendiente, *m*; (sweet) pastilla, *f*; (of a chandelier) almendra, *f*; (fall) caída, *f*; (in price, etc.) baja, *f*; (slope) pendiente, cuesta, *f*. **by drops,** a gotas. **d. bottle,** frasco cuentagotas, *m*. **d.-curtain,** telón de boca, *m*. **d.-hammer,** martinete, *m*. **d.-head coupé,** cupé descapotable, *m*. **d.-scene,** telón de foro, *m*

drop *vt* verter a gotas; destilar; (sprinkle) salpicar, rociar; dejar caer; soltar; (lower) bajar; (of clothes, etc.) desprenderse de, quitar; (lose) perder; (a letter in a mailbox) echar; (leave) dejar; (give up) renunciar (a); desistir (de); abandonar; (kill) tumbar; (a hint) soltar; (a curtsey) hacer. *vi* gotear, caer en gotas, destilar; (descend) bajar, descender; caer muerto; caer desmayado; (sleep) dormirse; (fall) caer; (of the wind) amainar; (of prices, temperature) bajar. **to let the matter d.,** poner fin a una cuestión. **to d. a line,** poner unas líneas. **to d. anchor,** anclar. **to d. behind,** quedarse atrás. **to d. in,** entrar al pasar. **d. in on somebody,** pasarse por casa de fulano, pasarse por el despacho de (etc.). **to d. off,** separarse (de); disminuir; (sleep) quedar dormido; (die) morir de repente. **to d. out,** separarse; (from a race, etc.) retirarse (de); quedarse atrás; desaparecer; ausentarse, apartarse; (decrease) disminuir; decaer. **He has dropped out of my life,** Le he perdido de vista. **to d. through,** (fail) fracasar; (of project) no dar resultado

dropping *n* gotera, *f*; gotas, *f pl*; (fall) caída, *f*; *pl* **droppings** (of a candle) moco, *m*; (dung) cagadas, *f pl*. **Con-**

stant d. wears away the stone, La gotera cava la piedra
dropsy *n* hidropesía, *f*
dross *n* escoria, *f*; (rubbish) basura, *f*
drought *n* aridez, *f*; (thirst) sed, *f*; (dry season) sequía, *f*
drove *n* manada, *f*, hato, *m*; (of sheep) rebaño, *m*; (crowd) muchedumbre, *f*
drown *vi* ahogarse. *vt* ahogar; sumergir; inundar; (*fig* of cries, sorrow, etc.) ahogar
drowning *n* ahogamiento, *m*; sumersión, *f*; inundación, *f*. **a que se ahoga**
drowse *vi* adormecerse
drowsily *adv* soñolientamente
drowsiness *n* somnolencia, *f*; sueño, *m*; (laziness) indolencia, pereza, *f*
drowsy *a* soñoliento; adormecedor, soporífero; (heavy) amodorrado. **to grow d.,** adormecerse. **to make d.,** adormecer
drubbing *n* tunda, zurra, felpa, *f*
drudgery *n* trabajo arduo, *m*, faena monótona, *f*
drug *n* droga, *f*; medicamento, *m*; narcótico, *m*. *vt* mezclar con drogas; administrar drogas (a); narcotizar. *vi* tomar drogas. **d. trade,** comercio de drogas, *m*. **d. traffic,** contrabando de drogas, narcotráfico *m*
drug addict *n* toxicómano, *Lat. Am.* adicto *m*
drug addiction *n* toxicomanía, *f*
druggist *n* droguero (-ra)
drum *n* tambor, *m*; (of the ear) tímpano (del oído), *m*; (cylinder) cilindro, *m*; (box) caja, *f*; *arch* cuerpo de columna, *m*. **bass d.,** bombo, *m*. **with drums beating,** con tambor batiente. **d.-head,** parche (del tambor), *m*. **d.-head service,** misa de campaña, *f*. **d.-major,** tambor mayor, *m*
drum *vt* and *vi* tocar el tambor; (with the fingers) tabalear, teclear; (with the heels) zapatear; (into a person's head) machacar. **to d. out,** *mil* expulsar a tambor batiente
drummer *n* tambor, *m*
drumming *n* ruido del tambor, *m*; (of the heels) taconeo, *m*; (of the fingers) tabaleo, tecleo, *m*
drumstick *n* palillo (de tambor), *m*
drunk *a* borracho, ebrio, *Lat. Am. also* iluminado, *Central America* azunumbaso *n* borracho, *m*. **to be d.,** estar borracho. **to get d.,** emborracharse, *Lat. Am. also* iluminarse; *inf* pillar un lobo, (on wine) *Mexico* envinarse. **to make d.,** emborrachar
drunkard *n* borracho (-cha)
drunken *a* borracho, ebrio
drunkenness *n* embriaguez, borrachera, ebriedad, *f*
dry *vi* secarse. *vt* secar; desaguar; (wipe) enjugar. **to dry one's tears,** enjugarse las lágrimas; *fig* secarse las lágrimas. **to dry up,** secarse; (of persons) acecinarse; (with old age) apergaminarse; (of ideas, etc.) agotarse; (be quiet) callarse
dry *a* seco; árido; estéril; (thirsty) sediento; (of wine) seco; (U.S.A.) prohibicionista; (squeezed) exprimido; (of toast) sin mantequilla; (*fig* chilly) aburrido; (sarcastic) sarcástico; (of humour) agudo. **on dry land,** en seco. **dry battery,** pila seca, *f*. **to dry-clean,** lavar al seco. **dry-cleaning,** tintorero (-ra). **dry-cleaning,** lavado al seco, *m*. **dry-cleaning shop,** tintorería, *f*. **dry goods,** lencería, *f*. **dry land,** tierra firme, *f*. **dry measure,** medida para áridos, *f*. **dry-nurse,** ama seca, *f*. **dry-point,** punta seca, *f*. **dry-rot,** carcoma, *f*. **dry-shod,** con los pies secos
drying *n* secamiento, *m*; desecación, *f*, *a* secante; seco; para secar. **d. ground,** tendedero, *m*. **d. machine,** secadora, *f*. (for the hair) secadora de cabello, *f*. **d. room,** secadero, *m*
dryly *adv* secamente
dryness *n* sequedad, *f*; aridez, *f*; (of humour) agudeza, *f*
dual *a* doble; *gram* dual. **d. control,** mandos gemelos, *m pl*. **d. personality,** conciencia doble, *f*
dualism *n* dualismo, *m*

duality *n* dualidad, *f*
dub *vt* (a knight) armar caballero; (call) apellidar; (nickname) motejar, apodar
dubbing *n* (of films) doblaje, *m*
dubious *a* dudoso, incierto; indeciso; problemático; ambiguo
dubiously *adv* dudosamente
dubiousness *n* carácter dudoso, *m*; incertidumbre, *f*; ambigüedad, *f*
Dublin Dublín, *f*
Dubliner *n* dublinés (-esa)
ducat *n* ducado, *m*
duchess *n* duquesa, *f*
duchy *n* ducado, *m*
duck *n* pato (-ta), ánade, *mf*; *sport* cero, *m*; (darling) vida mía, querida, *f*; (jerk) agachada, *f*; (under the water) chapuz, *m*; (material) dril, *m*; *mil* auto anfibio, *m*; *pl* **ducks,** pantalones de dril, *m pl. vi* agacharse; (under water) chapuzarse. *vt* zabullir, sumergir; bajar, inclinar
ducking *n* chapuz, *m*. **d.-stool,** silla de chapuzar, *f*
duckling *n* anadino (-na)
duct *n* conducto, canal, *m*; *bot* tubo, *m*
ductile *a* dúctil
ductility *n* ductilidad, *f*
ductless *a* sin tubos
due *a* debido; (payable) pagadero; (fallen due) vencido; (fitting) propio; (expected) esperado. *n* impuesto, *m*; derecho, *m*. **in due form,** en regla. **in its due time,** a su tiempo debido. **to fall due,** vencerse. **due bill,** *com* abonaré, *m*. **due west,** poniente derecho, *m*
duel *n* duelo, lance de honor, *m*; *fig* lucha, *f*. **to fight a d.,** batirse en duelo
dueling *n* el (batirse en) duelo
duelist *n* duelista, *m*
duenna *n* dueña, *f*
duet *n* dúo, *m*
duettist *n* duetista, *mf*
duffer *n* estúpido (-da); ganso, *m*; (at games, etc.) maleta, *m*
dug *n* teta, *f*
dugout *n* trinchera, *f*
duke *n* duque, *m*
dukedom *n* ducado, *m*
dulcet *a* dulce
dulcimer *n* dulcémele, *m*
dull *a* (stupid) lerdo, estúpido, obtuso; (boring, tedious) aburrido; (of pain, sounds) sordo; (of colors and eyes) apagado; (of light, beams, etc.) sombrío; (not polished) mate; (pale) pálido; (insipid) insípido, insulso; (of people) soso, poco interesante; (dreary, sad) triste; (gray) gris; (of mirrors, etc.) empañado; (of weather) anublado; (of hearing) duro; (slow) lento; lánguido; insensible; (blunt) romo; *com* encalmado, inactivo. **to find life d.,** encontrar la vida aburrida. **d. of hearing,** duro de oído, algo sordo. **d. pain,** dolor sordo, *m*. **d. season,** temporada de calma, *f*. **d.-eyed,** con ojos apagados. **d.-witted,** lerdo
dull *vt* (make stupid) entontecer; (lessen) mitigar; (weaken) debilitar; (pain) calmar, aliviar; (sadden) entristecer; (blunt) embotar; (spoil) estropear; (a mirror, etc.) empañar; (a polished surface) hacer mate, deslustrar; (of enthusiasm, etc.) enfriar; (tire) fatigar; (obstruct) impedir
dullness *n* (stupidity) estupidez, *f*; (boredom) aburrimiento, *m*; (heaviness) pesadez, *f*; (drowsiness) somnolencia, *f*; (insipidity) insipidez, insulsez, *f*; (of literary style) prosaísmo, *m*; (of persons) sosería, *f*; (of a surface) deslustre, *m*; (laziness) pereza, languidez, *f*; (slowness) lentitud, *f*; (tiredness) cansancio, *m*; (sadness) tristeza, *f*; (bluntness) embotamiento, *m*; (of hearing) dureza, *f*; *com* desanimación, *f*
dully *adv* (stupidly) estúpidamente; sin comprender; (insipidly) insípidamente; (not brightly) sin brillo; (slowly) lentamente; (sadly) tristemente; (tiredly) con cansancio; (of sound) sordamente

duly *adv* debidamente; puntualmente

dumb *a* mudo; callado; silencioso; *inf* tonto, estúpido, *Lat. Am. also* baboso, *Central America* azurumbado. **to become d.,** enmudecer. **to strike d.,** dejar sin habla. **d.-bell,** barra con pesas, *f.* **d. show,** pantomima, *f.* **d. waiter,** bufete, *m*

dumbfound *vt* dejar sin habla; confundir; pasmar

dumbness *n* mudez, *f,* mutismo, *m;* silencio, *m*

dummy *n* (tailor's, etc.) maniquí, *m;* (puppet) títere, *m;* cabeza para pelucas, *f;* (figurehead) hombre de paja, testaferro, *m;* (baby's) chupador, *m;* (at cards) el muerto. *a* fingido. **to be d.,** (at cards) ser el muerto

dump *n* depósito, *m;* vaciadero, *m. vt* depositar; (goods on a market) inundar (con)

dumping *n* depósito, *m;* vaciamiento, *m;* (of goods on a market) inundación, *f.* **"D. prohibited,"** «Se prohibe arrojar la basura»

dumps *n* murria, *f*

dun *vt* apremiar, importunar

dun-colored *a* pardo

dunce *n* asno, bobo, zoquete, *m.* **dunce's cap,** coroza, *f*

dunderhead *n* cabeza de alcornoque, zoquete, *m*

dune *n* duna, *f*

dung *n* estiércol, *m;* (of rabbits, mice, deer, sheep, goats) cagarruta, *f;* (of cows) boñiga, *f;* (of hens) gallinaza, *f.* **d.-cart,** carro de basura, *m*

dungarees *n* mono, *m,* pantalones-vaquero, *m pl*

dungeon *n* mazmorra, *f,* calabozo, *m*

dunghill *n* muladar, *m*

duodenum *n* duodeno, *m*

dupe *n* víctima, *f;* tonto (-ta). *vt* embelecar, engañar. **to be a d.,** *inf* hacer el primo

duplicate *a* duplicado, doble. *n* duplicado, *m;* copia, *f, vt* duplicar

duplication *n* duplicación, *f*

duplicator *n* copiador, *m*

duplicity *n* duplicidad, *f*

durability *n* duración, *f.* **This is a cloth of great d.,** Este es un paño que dura mucho, Este es un paño muy duradero

durable *a* duradero

duration *n* duración, *f*

duress *n* compulsión, *f;* (prison) prisión, *f*

during *prep* durante

dusk *n* atardecer, anochecer, *m;* (twilight) crepúsculo, *m;* (darkness) oscuridad, *f.* **at d.,** al atardecer, a la caída de la tarde

dusky *a* (swarthy) moreno; (black) negro; (dim, dark) oscuro; (of colors) sucio

dust *n* polvo, *m;* (cloud of dust) polvareda, *f;* (ashes) cenizas, *f pl;* (of coal) cisco, *m;* (sweepings) barreduras, *f pl;* (of grain) tamo, *m. vt* desempolvar, quitar (or sacudir) el polvo de; (cover with dust) polvorear; (scatter) salpicar; (sweep) barrer; (clean) limpiar. **d.-bin,** basurero, *m.* **d.-cart,** carro de la basura, *m.* **d. cloud,** polvareda, *f.* **d. jacket,** (books) sobrecubierta, *f.* **d.-pan,** recogedor de basura, *m.* **d.-sheet,** guardapolvo, *m.* **d. storm,** vendaval de polvo, *m*

duster *n* el, *m,* que quita el polvo; paño (para quitar el polvo), *m;* (of feathers) plumero, *m*

dustiness *n* empolvoramiento, *m;* estado polvoriento, *m*

dusting *n* limpieza, *f;* (sweeping) barredura, *f;* (powder) polvos antisépticos, *m pl*

dustman *n* basurero, *m*

dusty *a* polvoriento, polvoroso, empolvado; del color del polvo; (of colours) sucio. **It is very d.,** Hay mucho polvo. **to get d.,** llenarse (or cubrirse) de polvo

Dutch *a* holandés. **the D.,** los holandeses. **double D.,** griego, galimatías, *m.* **D. cheese,** queso de bola, *m.* **D. courage,** coraje falso, *m.* **D. woman,** holandesa, *f*

Dutchman *n* holandés, *m*

dutiable *a* sujeto a derechos de aduana

dutiful *a* que cumple con sus deberes; obediente, sumiso; respetuoso; excelente, muy bueno

dutifully *adv* obedientemente; respetuosamente

dutifulness *n* obediencia, docilidad, *f;* respeto, *m*

duty *n* deber, *m;* obligación, *f;* (greetings) respetos, *m pl;* (charge, burden) carga, *f;* (tax) derecho, impuesto, *m; mil* servicio, *m;* (guard) guardia, *f.* **off d.,** libre. **on d.,** de servicio. **to be on sentry d.,** estar de guardia. **to do d. as,** servir como. **to do one's d.,** hacer (or cumplir con) su deber. **to pay d. on,** pagar derechos de aduana sobre. **d.-free,** franco de derechos

dwarf *a* enano. *n* enano (-na). *vt* impedir el crecimiento de; empequeñecer

dwarfish *a* enano

dwell *vi* vivir, habitar; (with on, upon) (think about) meditar sobre, pensar en; (deal with) tratar de; hablar largamente de; (insist on) insister en; apoyarse en, hacer hincapié en; (pause over) detenerse en

dweller *n* habitante, *mf;* (more poetic) morador (-ra)

dwelling *n* vivienda, *f;* (abode) morada, habitación, *f;* residencia, *f;* casa, *f;* (domicile) domicilio, *m.* **d.-house,** casa, *f*

dwindle *vi* disminuirse; consumirse; (decay) decaer; (degenerate) degenerar. **to d. to,** reducirse a

dwindling *n* disminución, *f*

dye *vt* teñir, colorar. *n* tinte, *m;* (colour) color, *m.* **fast dye,** tinte estable, *m.* **dye-house,** tintorería, *f.* **dye-stuff,** materia colorante, *f.* **dye-works,** tintorería, *f*

dyed-in-the-wool *a* de pies a cabeza

dyeing *n* teñidura, tintura, *f;* (as a trade) tintorería, *f.* **d. and dry-cleaning shop,** tintorería, *f*

dyer *n* tintorero (-ra)

dyestuff *n* materia colorante, materia de tinte, materia tintórea, *f*

dying *a* moribundo, agonizante; de la muerte; (of light) mortecino; (last) último; supremo; (languishing) lánguido; (deathbed) hecho en su lecho mortuorio. **to be d.,** estar agonizando; (of light) fenecer. **to be d. for,** estar muerto por

dynamic *a* dinámico

dynamics *n* dinámica, *f*

dynamite *n* dinamita, *f*

dynamo *n* dinamo, *f*

dynastic *a* dinástico

dynasty *n* dinastía, *f*

dysentery *n* disentería, *f*

dyspepsia *n* dispepsia, *f*

dyspeptic *a* dispéptico. *n* dispéptico (-ca)

E

e *n* (letter) e, *f; mus* mi, *m*

each *a* cada (invariable), todo. *pron* cada uno, *m;* cada una, *f.* **e. of them,** cada uno de ellos. **They help e. other,** Se ayudan mutuamente, Se ayudan entre sí. **to love e. other,** amarse

eager *a* impaciente; ansioso, deseoso; ambicioso

eagerly *adv* con impaciencia; con ansia; ambiciosamente

eagerness *n* impaciencia, *f;* ansia, *f,* deseo, *m;* (promptness) alacridad, *f;* (zeal) fervor, *m*

eagle *n* águila, *f.* **royal e.,** águila caudal, águila real, *f.* **e.-eyed,** con ojos de lince, de ojo avizor. **have the eyes of an e.,** tener ojos de lince, tener vista de lince

ear *n* (outer ear) oreja, *f;* (inner ear and sense of hearing) oído, *m; bot* espiga, panoja, *f.* **to begin to show the ear,** (grain) espigar. **to be all ears,** ser todo oídos.

to give ear, dar oído. **to have a good ear,** tener buen oído. **to play by ear,** tocar de oído. **to turn a deaf ear,** hacerse el sordo. **ear-ache,** dolor de oídos, *m*. **ear-drum,** tímpano (del oído), *m*. **ear-flap,** orejera, *f*. **ear-phone, ear-piece,** auricular, *m*. **ear-piercing,** penetrante, agudo. **ear-shot,** alcance del oído, *m*. **to be within ear-shot,** estar al alcance del oído. **ear-trumpet,** trompetilla, *f*. **ear wax,** cerilla, *f*

eared *a* con orejas; de orejas; *bot* con espigas

earl *n* conde, *m*

earldom *n* condado, *m*

earlier, earliest *a comp* and *sup* más temprano; más primitivo; más antiguo; (first, of time) primero. *adv* más temprano; más pronto; antes

earliness *n* lo temprano; antigüedad, *f*, lo primitivo; (precocity) precocidad, *f*. **The e. of his arrival,** Su llegada de buena hora

early *a* temprano; primitivo; (of fruit, etc.) temprano, adelantado; (movement) primero (e.g. **early Romanticism,** el primer romanticismo); (person) de la primera época (e.g. **the early Cervantes,** Cervantes de la primera época); (work) un primer (e.g. **an early work of Unamuno's,** una primera obra de Unamuno); (advanced) avanzado; (precocious) precoz; (first, of time) primero; (in the morning) matutino; (near) próximo; cercano; (premature) prematuro; (of child's age) tierno; joven. **in the e. hours,** en las primeras horas; en las altas horas (de la noche). **e. age,** edad temprana, tierna edad, *f*. **e.-fruiting,** *agr* tempranal. **e. riser,** madrugador (-ra). **e.-rising,** *a* madrugador. **e. years,** primeros años, años de la niñez, *m pl*

early *adv* temprano; al principio (de); en los primeros días (de); desde los primeros días (de); (in the month, year) a principios (de); (in time) a tiempo; (in the day) de buena hora; (soon) pronto; (among the first) entre los primeros (de). **as e. as possible,** lo más temprano posible; lo más pronto posible. **to be e.,** llegar antes de tiempo; llegar de buena hora. **to get up e.,** madrugar. **to go to bed e.,** acostarse temprano. **too e.,** demasiado temprano. **e. in the morning,** de madrugada

earmark *vt* marcar; *fig* destinar, reservar

earn *vt* ganar; obtener, adquirir; (deserve) merecer

earnable *a* ganable

earnest *a* serio; fervoroso; diligente; sincero. **to be in e. about something,** tomarlo en serio; ser sincero (en). **e. money,** *f pl*

earnestly *adv* seriamente; fervorosamente; con diligencia; sinceramente, de buena fe

earnestness *n* seriedad, *f*; fervor, celo, *m*; diligencia, *f*; sinceridad, buena fe, *f*

earnings *n pl com* ingresos, *m pl*; (salary) salario, *m*; estipendio, *m*; (of a workman) jornal, *m*

earring *n* pendiente, arete, *Lat. Am. also* aro *m*

earth *n* tierra, *f*; (of a badger, etc.) madriguera, *f*; *rad* tierra, *f*. *vt* cubrir con tierra; *rad* conectar con tierra. **clod of e.,** terrón, *m*. **half the e.,** *inf* medio mundo, *m*. **on e.,** en este mundo, sobre la tierra

earthen *a* terrizo, terroso; (of mud) de barro

earthenware *n* alfar, *m*, a de loza, de barro

earthiness *n* terrosidad, *f*

earthly *a* terrestre, terrenal; de la tierra; (fleshly) carnal; (worldly) mundano; material. **There is not an e. chance,** No hay la más mínima posibilidad

earthquake *n* terremoto, temblor de tierra, *m*

earth tremor *n* movimiento sísmico, *m*

earthwork *n* terraplén, *m*

earthworm *n* gusano de tierra, *m*

earthy *a* térreo, terroso

earwig *n* tijereta, *f*

ease *n* bienestar, *m*; tranquilidad, *f*; descanso, *m*; (leisure) ocio, *m*; (comfortableness) comodidad, *f*; (freedom from embarrassment) naturalidad, *f*, desembarazo, desenfado, *m*; (from pain) alivio, *m*; (simplicity) facilidad, *f*. *vt* (widen) ensanchar; aflojar; (pain) aliviar; (lighten) aligerar; (moderate) moderar;

(soften) suavizar; (free) librar; (one's mind) tranquilizar. **in my moments of e.,** en mis ocios, en mis momentos de ocio. **Stand at e.!** *mil* ¡En su lugar descansen! **to be at e.,** estar a sus anchas; encontrarse bien; comportarse con toda naturalidad. **with e.,** fácilmente. **to e. off,** *vt* (naut cables, sails) arriar. *vi* sentirse menos, cesar

easel *n* caballete (de pintor) *m*

easily *adv* fácilmente. **The engine runs e.,** El motor marcha bien

easiness *n* facilidad, *f*; sencillez, *f*; (of manner) desembarazo, *m*, naturalidad, *f*

east *n* este, *m*; oriente, *m*, (of countries) Oriente, *m*; Levante, *m*. *a* del este; del oriente; (of countries) de Oriente, oriental; levantino. **e. North e.,** estenordeste, *m*. **e. South e.,** estesudeste, *m*. **e. wind,** viento del este, *m*

Easter *n* Pascua de Resurrección, *f*. **E. egg,** huevo de Pascua, *m*. **E. Saturday,** sábado de gloria, *m*. **E. Sunday,** domingo de Pascua, *m*

easterly *a* del este; al este. *adv* hacia el este

eastern *a* del este; de Oriente; oriental. *n* oriental, *mf*

easternmost *a* situado más al este

East Indies Indias Orientales, *f pl*

eastward *adv* hacia el este, hacia oriente

easy *a* fácil; sencillo; (comfortable) cómodo; (free from pain) aliviado; *com* flojo; (well-off) acomodado, holgado; (calm) tranquilo; tolerante; natural; afable, condescendiente; (of virtue, women) fácil. *adv* con calma; despacio. **I must make myself e. about,** he de tranquilizarme sobre. **Stand e.!** ¡En su lugar descansen! **to take it e.,** tomarlo con calma. **e.-chair,** (silla) poltrona, *f*. **easy come, easy go,** lo que por agua, agua (Mexico and Colombia), los dineros del sacristán cantando vienen y cantando se van (Spain). **e.-going,** acomodadizo; indolente; (morally) de manga ancha; (casual) descuidado

eat *vt* comer; (meals, soup, refreshments) tomar; (with a good, bad appetite) hacer; consumir; (corrode) corroer; desgastar. *vi* comer; (fam of food) ser de buen (or mal) comer. **to eat one's breakfast (lunch),** tomar el desayuno, desayunar (almorzar). **to eat one's words,** retractarse. **to eat away,** comer; consumir; corroer. **to eat into,** (of chemicals) morder; (a fortune) consumir; gastar. **eat out of s.b.'s hand,** comer de la mano de fulano, comer en la mano de fulano. **to eat up,** devorar (also *fig*)

eatable *a* comestible, comedero. *n pl* **eatables,** comestibles, *m pl*

eater *n* el, *m*, (f, la) que come

eating *n* el comer; comida, *f*. **e. and drinking,** el comer y beber. **e.-house,** casa de comidas, *f*

eau de cologne *n* agua de Colonia, *f*

eaves *n* rafe, alero, *m*. **under the e.,** debajo del alero

eavesdrop *vi* escuchar a las puertas; fisgonear, espiar

eavesdropper *n* fisgón (-ona)

eavesdropping *n* fisgoneo, *m*

ebb *n* (of the tide) reflujo, *m*; menguante, *f*; *fig* declinación, *f*; *fig* decadencia, *f*; (of life) vejez, *f*. *vi* (of tide) menguar; declinar; decaer. **to ebb and flow,** fluir y refluir. **to ebb away from,** dejar; dejar aislado. **ebb-tide,** marea menguante, *f*

ebonite *n* ebonita, *f*

ebony *n* ébano, *m*

ebullience *n* efervescencia, exuberancia, *f*

ebullient *a* efervescente, exuberante

ebullition *n* (boiling) ebullición, *f*, hervor, *m*; *fig* efervescencia, *f*, estallido, *m*

eccentric *a geom* excéntrico; raro, original; extravagante, excéntrico. *Lat. Am.* ideático. *n* persona excéntrica, *f*, original, *m*

eccentrically *adv* excéntricamente

eccentricity *n geom* excentricidad, *f*; rareza, extravagancia, excentricidad, *f*

Ecclesiastes *n* Eclesiastés, *m*

ecclesiastic *a* eclesiástico. *n* eclesiástico, clérigo, *m*

ecclesiastically *adv* eclesiásticamente
echo *n* eco, *m*; reverberación, resonancia, *f. vt* repercutir; *fig* repetir. *vi* resonar, retumbar, reverberar
echoing *a* retumbante. *n* eco, *m*
eclectic *a* and *n* ecléctico (-ca)
eclecticism *n* eclecticismo, *m*
eclipse *n ast* eclipse, *m, vt* eclipsar, hacer eclipse a. **to be in e.,** estar en eclipse
ecliptic *n ast* eclíptica, *f, a* eclíptico
eclog *n* égloga, *f*
economic *a* económico
economical *a* económico
economics *n* economía política, *f*
economist *n* economista, *mf*
economize *vt* economizar, ahorrar. *vi* hacer economías
economy *n* economía, *f.* **domestic e.,** economía doméstica, *f.* **political e.,** economía política, *f*
ecstasy *n* éxtasis, arrebato, *m*; transporte, *m.* **to be in e.,** estar en éxtasis
ecstatic *a* extático
Ecuador el Ecuador
Ecuadorian *a* and *n* ecuatoriano (-na)
ecumenical *a* ecuménico
eczema *n* eczema, *f*
eddy *n* remolino, *m, vi* remolinar; *fig* remolinear
edelweiss *n* inmortal de las nieves, *f*
edema *n med* edema, *m*
Eden *n* Edén, *m*
edge *n* (of sharp instruments) filo, *m*; (of a skate) cuchilla, *f*; margen, *mf*; (shore) orilla, *f*; (of two surfaces) arista, *f*; (of books) borde, *m*; (of a coin) canto, *m*; (of a chair, a precipice, a forest, a curb, etc.) borde, *m*; (extreme) extremidad, *f.* **on e.,** de canto; *fig* ansioso. **to be on e.,** *fig* tener los nervios en punta. **to set on e.,** poner de canto; (of teeth) dar dentera
edge *vt* (sharpen) afilar; *sew* ribetear; orlar; poner un borde (a); (cut) cortar. **to e. away,** escurrirse. **to e. into,** *vt* insinuarse. *vi* deslizarse en. **to e. out,** salir poco a poco
edged *a* afilado, cortante; (in compounds) de . . . filos; (bordered) bordeado; (of books) de bordes . . .
edgeways *adv* de lado; de canto. **He couldn't get a word in e.,** No pudo meter baza en la conversación
edging *n* borde, *m*; ribete, *m*
edibility *n* el ser comestible
edible *a* comestible
edict *n* edicto, *m*
edification *n* edificación, *f*
edifice *n* edificio, *m*
edify *vt* edificar
edifying *a* edificante, edificador, de edificación
Edinburgh Edinburgo, *m*
Edipus complex *n* complejo de Edipo, *m*
edit *vt* editar; (a newspaper, journal) ser director de; (prepare for press) redactar; (correct) corregir
editing *n* trabajo editorial, *m*; redacción, *f*; dirección, *f*; corrección, *f*
edition *n* edición, *f*; *print* tirada, *f.* **first e.,** edición príncipe, *f.* **miniature e.,** edición diamante, *f*
editor *n* (of a book) editor, *m*; (of a newspaper, journal) director, *m*
editorial *a* de redacción; editorial. *n* editorial, artículo de fondo, *m.* **e. staff,** redacción, *f*
editorial board consejo de redacción, *m*
editorship *n* dirección (de un periódico, de una revista), *f*
editress *n* (of a paper, journal) directora, *f*; editora, *f*
educability *n* educabilidad, *f*
educable *a* educable
educate *vt* educar; formar; (accustom) acostumbrar
educated *a* culto
education *n* educación, *f*; enseñanza, *f*; pedagogía, *f.* **chair of e.,** cátedra de pedagogía, *f.* **early e.,** primeras letras, *f pl.* **higher e.,** enseñanza superior, *f*
educational *a* educativo; pedagógico; instructivo
educationalist *n* pedagogo, *m*

educative *a* educativo
educator *n* educador (-ra)
educe *vt* educir; deducir; *chem* extraer
eduction *n* educción, *f*
Edwardian *a* and *n* eduardiano (-na)
eel *n* anguila, *f.* **electric eel,** gimnoto, *m.* **eel-basket,** nasa para anguilas, *f*
eerily *adv* fantásticamente; de modo sobrenatural
eeriness *n* ambiente de misterio, *m*; efecto misterioso, *m*
eerie *a* misterioso, fantástico; sobrenatural; lúgubre
efface *vt* borrar, destruir; quitar. **to e. oneself,** retirarse; permanecer en el fondo
effacement *n* borradura, *f*
effect *n* efecto, *m*; impresión, *f*; (result) resultado, *m*, consecuencia, *f*, (meaning) substancia, *f*, significado, *m*; *pl* **effects,** efectos, bienes, *m pl. vt* efectuar; producir. **in e.,** en efecto, efectivamente. **of no e.,** inútil. **striving after e.,** efectismo, *m.* **to feel the effects of,** sentir los efectos de; padecer las consecuencias de. **to put into e.,** poner en práctica; hacer efectivo. **to take e.,** producir efecto; ponerse en vigor
effective *a* eficaz; (striking) de mucho efecto, poderoso, vistoso. **to make e.,** llevar a efecto
effectively *adv* eficazmente; (strikingly) con gran efecto; efectivamente, en efecto
effectiveness *n* eficacia, *f*; efecto, *m*
effectuate *vt* efectuar
effeminacy *n* afeminación, *f*
effeminate *a* afeminado, adamado. **to make e.,** afeminar
efferent *a* eferente
effervesce *vi* estar efervescente, hervir
effervescence *n* efervescencia, *f*
effervescent *a* efervescente
effete *a* gastado; estéril; decadente
effeteness *n* decadencia, *f*; esterilidad, *f*
efficacious *a* eficaz
efficacy *n* eficacia, *f*
efficiency *n* eficiencia, *f*; buen estado, *m*; habilidad, *f*; *mech* rendimiento, *m*
efficient *a* (e.g. medicine) eficaz; eficiente; (person) competente, capaz
efficiently *adv* eficientemente; eficazmente; competentemente
effigy *n* efigie, imagen, *f*
efflorescence *n chem* eflorescencia, *f*; *bot* florescencia, *f*
effluvium *n* efluvio, *m*
effort *n* esfuerzo, *m.* **to make an e.,** hacer un esfuerzo. **make every effort to,** hacer lo posible por + *inf*; empeñar sus máximos esfuerzos en el sentido de + *inf*
effortless *a* sin esfuerzo
effrontery *n* descaro, *m*, insolencia, *f*
effulgence *n* esplendor, fulgor, *m*
effulgent *a* fulgente, resplandeciente
effusion *n* efusión, *f*
effusive *a* efusivo, expansivo
egg *n* huevo, *m.* **to egg on,** incitar (a). **boiled egg,** huevo cocido, *m.* **fried egg,** huevo frito, *m.* **hard egg,** huevo duro, *m.* **poached egg,** huevo escalfado, *m.* **scrambled egg,** huevos revueltos, *m pl.* **soft egg,** huevo pasado por agua, *m.* **to lay eggs,** poner huevos. **to put all one's eggs in one basket,** *fig* poner toda la carne en el asador. **egg-cup,** huevera, *f.* **egg dealer,** vendedor (-ra) de huevos. **egg flip,** huevo batido con ron, *m.* **eggplant,** berenjena, *f.* **egg-shaped,** aovado. **egg-shell,** cascarón, *m*; cáscara de huevo, *f.* **egg-shell china,** loza muy fina, *f.* **egg-spoon,** cucharita para comer huevos, *f.* **egg-whisk,** batidor de huevos, *m*
ego *n* yo
egoism *n* egoísmo, *m*
egoist *n* egoísta, *mf*
egoistic *a* egoísta
egoistically *adv* egoístamente
egotism *n* egotismo, *m*, egolatría, *f*
egotist *n* egotista, *mf*
egotistic *a* egotista

egregious *a* notorio

egress *n* salida, *f*

Egypt Egipto, *m*

Egyptian *a* egipcio. *n* egipcio (-ia); cigarrillo egipcio, *m*

Egyptologist *n* egiptólogo (-ga)

Egyptology *n* egiptología, *f*

eh? *interj* ¿eh? ¿qué?

eider *n* *orn* pato de flojel, *m*

eiderdown edredón, *m*

eight *a* and *n* ocho *m*. **He is e. years old,** Tiene ocho años. **It is e. o'clock,** Son las ocho. **e.-day clock,** reloj con cuerda para ocho días, *m*. **e. hundred,** *a* and *n* ochocientos *m*. **e.-syllabled,** octosilábico

eighteen *a* and *n* diez y ocho, *m*.

eighteenth *a* décimoctavo; (of the month) (el) diez y ocho, dieciocho; (of monarchs) diez y ocho. *n* décimoctava parte, *f*. **Louis the E.,** Luis diez y ocho

eightfold *a* óctuple

eighth *a* octavo, *m*; (of the month) (el) ocho; (of monarchs) octavo. *n* octavo, *m*

eighthly *adv* en octavo lugar

eightieth *a* octogésimo

eighty *a* and *n* ochenta, *m*.

either *a* and *pron* uno u otro, cualquiera de los dos; ambos (-as). *conjunc* o (becomes **u** before words beginning with **o** or **ho**). *adv* tampoco. **I do not like e.,** No me gusta ni el uno ni el otro (ni la una ni la otra). **e. ... or,** o . . . o

ejaculate *vt* exclamar, lanzar; *med* eyacular

ejaculation *n* exclamación, *f*; *med* eyaculación, *f*

ejaculatory *a* jaculatorio

eject *vt* echar, expulsar; *law* desahuciar; (emit) despedir, emitir

ejection *n* echamiento, *m*, expulsión, *f*; *law* desahúcio, *m*; (emission) emisión, *f*

eke (out) *vt* aumentar, añadir a

elaborate *a* elaborado; primoroso; elegante; complicado; (detailed) detallado; (of meals) de muchos platos; (of courtesy, etc.) estudiado. *vt* elaborar; amplificar

elaborately *adv* primorosamente; elegantemente; complicadamente; con muchos detalles

elaborateness *n* primor, *m*; elegancia, *f*; complicación, *f*; (care) cuidado, *m*; minuciosidad, *f*

elaboration *n* elaboración, *f*

elapse *vi* transcurrir, andar, pasar

elastic *a* elástico. *n* elástico, *m*. **e. band,** anillo de goma, *m*; cinta de goma, *f*. **e. girdle,** faja elástica, *f*

elasticity *n* elasticidad, *f*

elate *vt* alegrar; animar

elatedly *adv* alegremente; triunfalmente

elation *n* alegría, *f*, júbilo, *m*; triunfo, *m*

elbow *n* codo, *m*; ángulo, *m*; (of a chair) brazo, *m*. *vt* codear, dar codazos (a). **at one's e.,** a la mano. **nudge with the e.,** codazo, *m*. **to be out at e.,** enseñar los codos, tener los codos raídos; ser harapiento. **to e. one's way,** abrirse paso a codazos. **e.-chair,** silla de brazos, *f*. **e.-grease,** jugo de muñeca, *m*. **e.-piece** or **patch,** codera, *f*. **e. room,** libertad de movimiento, *f*

elder *a comp* mayor. *n* persona mayor, *f*; señor mayor, *m*; (among Jews and in early Christian Church) anciano, *m*; *bot* saúco, *m*

elderly *a* mayor

eldest *a sup* old (el, la, etc.) mayor. **e. daughter,** hija mayor, *f*. **e. son,** hijo mayor, *m*

elect *vt* elegir. *a* elegido; predestinado. *n* electo, *m*; elegido, *m*

election *n* *theol* predestinación, *f*; elección, *f*. **by-e.,** elección parcial, *f*

electioneer *vi* solicitar votos; distribuir propaganda electoral

electioneering *n* solicitación de votos, *f*; propaganda electoral, *f*

elective *a* electivo. *n* (subject at school) materia optativa, *f*

elector *n* elector (-ra); (prince) elector, *m*

electoral *a* electoral. **e. register,** lista electoral, *f*

electoral college colegio de compromisarios, *m*

electorate *n* electorado, *m*

electric, electrical *a* eléctrico; *fig* vivo, instantáneo. **e. arc,** arco voltaico, *m*. **e. engineer,** ingeniero electricista, *m*. **electric fan,** (Spain) ventilador, (Western Hemisphere) ventilador eléctrico, *m*. **e. fire,** estufa eléctrica, *f*. **e. immersion heater,** calentador de agua eléctrico, *m*. **e. light,** luz eléctrica, *f*. **e. pad,** alfombrilla eléctrica, *f*. **e. shock,** conmoción eléctrica, *f*. **e. washing-machine,** lavadora eléctrica, *f*. **e. wire** or **cable,** conductor eléctrico, *m*

electrically *adv* por electricidad

electrician *n* electricista, *mf*

electricity *n* electricidad, *f*

electrification *n* electrificación, *f*

electrify *vt* electrificar; *fig* electrizar

electro *prefix* (in compounds) electro. **e.-chemistry,** electroquímica, *f*. **e.-dynamics,** electrodinámica, *f*. **e.-magnet,** electroimán, *m*. **e.-magnetic,** electromagnético. **e.-plate,** *vt* galvanizar, platear. *n* artículo galvanizado, *m*. **e.-therapy,** electroterapia, *f*

electrocute *vt* electrocutar

electrocution *n* electrocución, *f*

electrode *n* electrodo, *m*

electrolysis *n* electrólisis, *f*

electrolyte *n* electrólito, *m*

electrolyze *vt* electrolizar

electrometer *n* electrómetro, *m*

electromotive *a* electromotriz. **e. force,** fuerza electromotriz, *f*

electron *n* electrón, *m*

electroscope *n* electroscopio, *m*

elegance *n* elegancia, *f*

elegant *a* elegante; bello

elegantly *adv* elegantemente, con elegancia

elegiac *a* elegíaco

elegy *n* elegía, *f*

element *n* elemento, *m*; factor, *m*; ingrediente, *m*; *elec* par, elemento, *m*; *chem, phys* cuerpo simple, *m*; *pl* **elements,** rudimentos, *m pl*, nociones, *f pl*; (weather) intemperie, *f*; (Eucharist) el pan y el vino. **to be in one's e.,** estar en su elemento

elemental *a* elemental; rudimentario, lo elemental

elementariness *n* el carácter, elemental

elementary *a* elemental; rudimentario; primario. **e. education,** enseñanza primaria, *f*

elephant *n* elefante (-ta). **e. keeper** or **trainer,** naire, *m*

elephantiasis *n* elefantíasis, *f*

elephantine *a* elefantino

elevate *vt* (the Host) alzar; elevar; (the eyes, the voice) levantar; (honor) enaltecer

elevated *a* noble, elevado, sublime; edificante; (drunk) achispado

elevation *n* elevación, *f*; enaltecimiento, *m*; (of style, thought) nobleza, sublimidad, *f*; (hill) eminencia, altura, *f*

elevator *n* (lift) ascensor, *m*; (for grain, etc.) montacargas, *m*

elevator shaft caja, *f*, hueco pozo, *m*

eleven *a* once. *n* once, *m*. **It is e. o'clock,** Son las once

eleventh *a* onceno, undécimo; (of month) (el) once; (of monarchs) once. *n* onzavo, *m*; undécima parte, *f*. **at the e. hour,** *fig* a última hora. **Louis the E.,** Luis once (XI)

elf *n* elfo, duende, *m*; (child) trasgo, *m*; (dwarf) enano, *m*

elfin *a* de duendes; de hada

elicit *vt* sacar; hacer contestar; hacer confesar; descubrir

elicitation *n* descubrimiento, *m*

elide *vt* elidir

eligibility *n* elegibilidad, *f*

eligible *a* elegible; deseable

eliminate *vt* eliminar; quitar

elimination *n* eliminación, *f*

eliminatory *a* eliminador
elision *n* elisión, *f*
elite *n* nata, flor, *f*
elixir *n* elixir, *m*
Elizabethan *a* de la época de la Reina Isabel I de Inglaterra
elk *n* ante, *m*
ell *n* (measure) ana, *f*
ellipse *n geom* elipse, *f*; óvalo, *m*
ellipsis *n gram* elipsis, *f*
elliptic *a geom, gram* elíptico
elm *n* olmo, *m*. **e. grove,** olmeda, *f*
elocution *n* elocución, *f*; (art of elocution) declamación, *f*
elocutionist *n* recitador (-ra), declamador (-ra)
elongate *vt* alargar; extender. *vi* alargarse; extenderse. *a* alargado; (of face) perfilado
elongation *n* alargamiento, *m*; prolongación, *f*; extensión, *f*
elope *vi* evadirse, huir; fugarse (con un amante)
elopement *n* fuga, *f*
eloquence *n* elocuencia, *f*
eloquent *a* elocuente
eloquently *adv* elocuentemente
else *adv* (besides) más; (instead) otra cosa, más; (otherwise) si no, de otro modo. **anyone e.,** (cualquier) otra persona; alguien más. **Anything e.?** ¿Algo más? **everyone e.,** todos los demás. **everything e.,** todo lo demás. **nobody e.,** ningún otro, nadie más. **nothing e.,** nada más. **or e.,** o bien, de otro modo; si no. **someone e.,** otra persona, otro. **somewhere e.,** en otra parte. **There's nothing e. to do,** No hay nada más que hacer; No hay más remedio
elsewhere *adv* a, or en, otra parte
elucidate *vt* elucidar, aclarar
elucidation *n* elucidación, aclaración, *f*
elucidatory *a* aclaratorio
elude *vt* eludir, evitar
elusive *a* (of persons) esquivo; fugaz; difícil de comprender
elusiveness *n* esquivez, *f*; fugacidad, *f*
Elysian *a* elíseo. **E. Fields,** campos elíseos, *m pl*
Elysium *n* elíseo, *m*
emaciate *vt* extenuar, demacrar, enflaquecer
emaciated *a* extenuado, demacrado. **to become e.,** demacrarse
emaciation *n* demacración, emaciación, *f*; *med* depauperación, *f*
emanate *vi* emanar (de), proceder (de)
emanation *n* emanación, *f*; exhalación, *f*
emancipate *vt* emancipar
emancipated *a* emancipado
emancipation *n* emancipación, *f*
emancipator *n* emancipador (-ra), libertador (-ra)
emancipatory *a* emancipador
emasculate *a* afeminado. *vt* emascular; *fig* afeminar; mutilar
emasculation *n* emasculación, *f*
embalm *vt* embalsamar; *fig* conservar el recuerdo de; perfumar
embalmer *n* embalsamador, *m*
embalmment *n* embalsamamiento, *m*
embankment *n* declive, *m*; ribera, *f*; terraplén, *m*; dique, *m*; (quay) muelle, *m*
embargo *n* embargo, *m*, *vt* embargar. **to put an e. on,** embargar. **to remove an e.,** sacar de embargo
embark *vi* embarcarse; lanzarse (a). *vt* embarcar
embarkation *n* (of persons) embarcación, *f*; (of goods) embarque, *m*
embarrass *vt* impedir; (financially) apurar; (perplex) tener perplejo; (worry) preocupar; (confuse) desconcertar, turbar; (annoy) molestar
embarrassed *a* turbado
embarrassing *a* embarazoso; desconcertante; molesto
embarrassingly *adv* de un modo desconcertante; demasiado

embarrassment *n* impedimento, *m*; (financial) apuro, *m*; (obligation) compromiso, *m*; (perplexity) perplejidad, *f*; (worry) preocupación, *f*; (confusion) turbación, *f*
embassy *n* embajada, *f*
embattled *a* en orden de batalla; *her* almenado
embed *vt* empotrar, enclavar; fijar
embellish *vt* embellecer; adornar
embellishment *n* embellecimiento, *m*; adorno, *m*
ember *n* rescoldo, *m*. **E. days,** témporas, *f pl*
embezzle *vt* desfalcar
embezzlement *n* desfalco, *m*
embezzler *n* desfalcador (-ra)
embitter *vt fig* amargar; envenenar
embittering *a* amargo
embitterment *n* amargura, *f*
emblazon *vt* blasonar; *fig* ensalzar
emblem *n* emblema, *m*
emblematic *a* emblemático
embodiment *n* incarnación, *f*; expresión, *f*; personificación, *f*; símbolo, *m*; síntesis, *f*
embody *vt* encarnar; expresar; personificar; incorporar; contener; formular; sintetizar. **to be embodied in,** quedar plasmado en
embolden *vt* animar, dar valor (a)
embolism *n med* embolia, *f*
emboss *vt* repujar, abollonar; estampar en relieve
embossment *n* abolladura, *f*; relieve, *m*
embrace *n* abrazo, *m*. *vt* abrazar, dar un abrazo (a); (*fig.* seize) aprovechar; (accept) aceptar; adoptar; (engage in) dedicarse a; (comprise) incluir, abarcar; (comprehend) comprender. **They embraced,** Se abrazaron
embroider *vt* bordar; embellecer; (a tale, etc.) exagerar; *vi* hacer bordado
embroiderer *n* bordador (-ra)
embroidery *n* bordado, *m*; labor, *f*. **e.-frame,** bastidor, *m*. **e. silk,** hilo de bordar, *m*
embroil *vt* enredar, embrollar; desordenar
embryo *n* embrión, *m*; *fig* germen, *m*. *a* embrionario
embryology *n* embriología, *f*
embryonic *a* embrionario
emend *vt* enmendar; corregir
emendation *n* enmienda, *f*; corrección, *f*
emerald *n* esmeralda, *f*, *a* de color de esmeralda. **e. green,** verde esmeralda, *m*
emerge *vt* emerger; surgir; *fig* salir; aparecer
emergence *n* emergencia, *f*; salida, *f*; aparición, *f*
emergency *n* urgencia, *f*; necesidad, *f*; emergencia, *f*; aprieto, *m*. **e. exit,** salida de urgencia, *f*. **e. port,** *naut* puerto de arribada, *m*
emergent *a* emergente; que sale; naciente
emery *n* esmeril, *m*. **to polish with e.,** esmerilar. **e.-paper,** papel de lija, *m*
emetic *a* and *n* emético, vomitivo, *m*.
emigrant *a* emigrante. *n* emigrante, *mf* emigrado, *m*
emigrate *vi* emigrar; *inf* trasladarse
emigration *n* emigración, *f*. **e. officer,** oficial de emigración, *m*
eminence *n* (hill) elevación, prominencia, *f*; eminencia (also as title), *f*; distinción, *f*
eminent *a* distinguido, eminente; famoso, ilustre; notable; conspicuo
eminently *adv* eminentemente
emir *n* amir, *m*
emissary *n* emisario (-ia); embajador (-ra); agente, *m*
emission *n* emisión, *f*
emit *vt* despedir; exhalar; emitir
emollient *a* emoliente, lenitivo. *n* emoliente, *m*
emolument *n* emolumento, *m*
emotion *n* emoción, *f*. **to cause e.,** emocionar
emotional *a* emocional, sentimental; emocionante
emotionalism *n* sentimentalismo, *m*
emotionalize *vt* considerar bajo un punto de vista sentimental
emotionally *adv* con emoción, sentimentalmente
emotionless *a* sin emoción

emotive *a* emotivo
emperor *n* emperador, *m*
emphasis (on) *n* énfasis (en), *mf*; insistencia especial (en), especial atención (a), *f*; accentuación, *f*
emphasize *vt* subrayar, dar énfasis a, poner de relieve, hacer resaltar, dar importancia a; acentuar; insistir en, hacer hincapié (en)
emphatic *a* enfático
emphatically *adv* con énfasis
empire *n* imperio, *m*
empiric *a* empírico
empiricism *n* empirismo, *m*
employ *n* empleo, *m*; servicio, *m*. *vt* emplear; ocupar; tomar; servirse de, usar. **How do you e. yourself?** ¿Cómo te ocupas? ¿Cómo pasas el tiempo?
employable *a* empleable; utilizable
employee *n* empleado (-da)
employer *n* el, *m*, (*f*, la) que emplea; dueño (-ña), amo (-a); patrón (-ona)
employment *n* empleo, *m*; uso, *m*; ocupación, *f*; aprovechamiento, *m*; (post) puesto, cargo, *m*; (situation) colocación, *f*. **e. exchange,** bolsa de trabajo, *f*
emporium *n* emporio, *m*; (store) almacén, *m*
empower *vt* autorizar; permitir; ayudar (a); dar el poder (para)
empress *n* emperatriz, *f*
emptiness *n* vaciedad, *f*; futilidad, *f*; vacuidad, *f*; (verbosity) palabrería, *f*
empty *a* vacío; (of a house, etc.) deshabitado, desocupado; (deserted) desierto; (vain) vano, inútil; frívolo; (hungry) hambriento. *n* envase vacío, *m*. *vt* vaciar; descargar. *vi* vaciarse; (river, etc.) desembocar, venir a morir en. **e.-handed,** con las manos vacías. **e.-headed,** casquivano
emptying *n* vaciamiento, *m*; abandono, *m*; *pl* **emptyings,** heces de la cerveza, *f pl*
emu *n* emu, *m*
emulate *vt* emular
emulation *n* emulación, *f*
emulative *a* emulador
emulsify *vt* emulsionar
emulsion *n* emulsión, *f*
emulsive *a* emulsivo
enable *vt* (to) hacer capaz (de); ayudar (a); autorizar (para); permitir (de)
enact *vt law* promulgar; decretar; (a part) hacer, desempeñar (un papel); (a play) representar; (happen) ocurrir, tener lugar
enaction *n law* promulgación, *f*
enamel *n* esmalte, *m*, *vt* esmaltar
enameler *n* esmaltador (-ra)
enameling *n* esmaltadura, *f*
enamor *vt* enamorar. **to be enamored of,** estar enamorado de; estar aficionado a
encamp *vt and vi* acampar
encampment *n* campamento, *m*
encase *vt* encajar; encerrar; (line) forrar
encasement *n* encaje, *m*; encierro, *m*
encephalitis *n* encefalitis, *f*. **e. lethargica,** encefalitis letárgica, *f*
enchant *vt* encantar, hechizar; fascinar, embelesar, deleitar
enchanter *n* encantador, *m*
enchanting *a* encantador, fascinador
enchantment *n* encantamiento, *m*; fascinación, *f*, encanto, deleite, *m*
enchantress *n* bruja, *f*; *fig* mujer seductora, *f*
encircle *vt* cercar; rodear; dar la vuelta (a)
enclose *vt* cercar; meter dentro de; encerrar; (with a letter, etc.) incluir, adjuntar
enclosed *a* (of letters) adjunto
enclosure *n* cercamiento, *m*; cercado, *m*; recinto, *m*; (wall) tapia, cerca, *f*; (with a letter) contenido adjunto, *m*
encomium *n* encomio, *m*
encompass *vt* cercar, rodear

encore *n* repetición, *f*, *interj* ¡bis!
encounter *n* encuentro, *m*; combate, *m*; conflicto, *m*; lucha, *f*. *vt* encontrar; atacar; tropezar con
encourage *vt* animar; alentar; estimular; incitar; ayudar; (approve) aprobar; (foster) fomentar
encouragement *n* ánimos, *m pl*; estímulo, incentivo, *m*; ayuda, *f*; (approval) aprobación, *f*; (promotion) fomento, *m*
encourager *n* instigador (-ra); ayudador (-ra); aprobador (-ra); fomentador (-ra)
encouraging *a* alentador; estimulante; fomentador; (favorable) halagüeño, favorable
encouragingly *adv* de un modo alentador; con aprobación
encroach *vi* usurpar; abusar (de); invadir; robar; (of sea, river) hurtar
encroaching *a* usurpador; invadiente
encroachment *n* usurpación, *f*; abuso, *m*; invasión, *f*
encrust *vt* encostrar; incrustar
encumber *vt* impedir, estorbar; llenar; (burden) cargar; (mortgage) hipotecar; (overwhelm) agobiar
encumbrance *n* impedimento, estorbo, *m*; gravamen, *m*; carga, *f*; (mortgage) hipoteca, *f*
encyclical *n* encíclica, *f*
encyclopedia *n* enciclopedia, *f*
encyclopedic *a* enciclopédico
encyclopedist *n* enciclopedista, *m*
end *n* fin, *m*; extremidad, *f*; extremo, *m*; conclusión, *f*; (point) punta, *f*; cabo, *m*; (district) barrio, *m*; cabeza, *f*; (death) muerte, *f*; (aim) objeto, intento, *m*; (purpose) propósito, *m*; (issue) resultado, *m*; (bit) fragmento, pedazo, *m*; (of a word) terminación, *f*. *vi* terminar; acabar; concluir; cesar; (in) terminar en; resultar en; (with) terminar con. *vt* terminar; acabar, dar fin a. **at an end,** terminado. **at the end,** al cabo (de); al extremo (de). **end of quotation,** fin de cita, final de la cita, *m*. **from end to end,** de un extremo a otro; de un cabo a otro. **in the end,** por fin, finalmente. **on end,** de pie, de cabeza, derecho; de punta; (of hair) erizado. **no end of,** un sinnúmero de. **to make both ends meet,** pasar con lo que se tiene. **to make an end of,** acabar con. **to put an end to,** poner fin a. **to the end that,** a fin de que, para que; con objeto de. **toward the end of,** (months, years, etc.) a fines de, a últimos de; hacia el fin de. **two hours on end,** dos horas seguidas. **end-paper,** guarda, *f*
endanger *vt* arriesgar, poner en peligro
endear *vt* hacer querer
endearing *a* que inspira cariño; atrayente; cariñoso
endearment *n* cariño, amor, *m*; caricia, terneza, *f*; palabra de cariño, *f*
endeavor *vi* procurar, intentar, hacer un esfuerzo. *n* esfuerzo, *m*, tentativa, *f*
endemic *a med* endémico
ending *n* fin, *m*; conclusión, *f*; *gram* terminación, *f*; cesación, *f*; (climax) desenlace, *m*
endive *n bot* escarola, *f*
endless *a* eterno; inacabable; infinito; sin fin; interminable; incesante
endlessly *adv* sin fin; incesantemente; sin parar
endlessness *n* eternidad, *f*; infinidad, *f*; continuidad, *f*
endocrine *a* endocrino. *n* secreción interna, *f*
endocrinology *n* endocrinología, *f*
end-of-season *a* por final de temporada (e.g., **end-of-season reductions,** rebajos por final de temporada, *m pl*. **end-of-season sale,** liquidación por final de temporada, *f*)
endogenous *a* endógeno
endorse *vt com* endosar; garantizar; (uphold) apoyar; confirmar
endorsee *n* endosatario (-ia)
endorsement *n com* endoso, *m*; aval, *m*, garantía, *f*; corroboración, confirmación, *f*
endorser *n com* endosante, *m*
endow *vt* dotar; fundar; crear
endowment *n* dotación, *f*; fundación, *f*; creación, *f*;

(mental) inteligencia, *f*; cualidad, *f*, don, *m*. **e. policy,** póliza dotal, *f*

endurable *a* sufrible, soportable; tolerable

endurance *n* aguante, *m*; resistencia, *f*; sufrimiento, *m*; tolerancia, *f*; paciencia, *f*; (lastingness) duración, continuación, *f*. **beyond e.,** intolerable, inaguantable. **e. test,** prueba de resistencia, *f*

endure *vt* soportar; tolerar; aguantar; sufrir; resistir. *vi* sufrir; (last) durar, continuar

enduring *a* permanente, perdurable; continuo; constante

enduringness *n* (lastingness) permanencia, *f*; paciencia, *f*; aguante, *m*

enema *n* lavativa, enema, *f*

enemy *n* enemigo (-ga); adversario (-ia); (in war) enemigo, *m*. *a* del enemigo, enemigo. **to be one's own e.,** ser enemigo de sí mismo. **to become an e. of,** enemistarse con; hacerse enemigo de, volverse hostil a

energetic *a* enérgico

energy *n* energía, fuerza, *f*, vigor, *m*

enervate *vt* enervar; debilitar. *a* enervado

enervation *n* enervación, *f*; debilitación, *f*

enfeeble *vt* debilitar

enfeeblement *n* debilitación, *f*, desfallecimiento, *m*

enfold *vt* envolver; abrazar

enforce *vt* (a law) poner en vigor; (impose) imponer a la fuerza; hacer cumplir; conseguir por fuerza; (demonstrate) demostrar

enforcement *n* (of a law) ejecución (de una ley), *f*; imposición a la fuerza, *f*; observación forzosa, *f*

enfranchise *vt* emancipar; conceder derechos civiles (a)

enfranchisement *n* emancipación, *f*; concesión de derechos civiles, *f*

engage *vt* empeñar; contratar; tomar en alquiler; tomar a su servicio; (seats, etc.) reservar; (occupy) ocupar; (attention) atraer; (in) aplicarse a, dedicarse a; *mil* combatir con, librar batalla con; atacar; (of wheels) endentar con. *vi* obligarse; dedicarse (a); tomar parte (en); (bet) apostar; *mil* librar batalla; (fight) venir a las manos. **to be engaged in,** traer entre manos, ocuparse en. **to become engaged,** prometerse. **Number engaged!** (telephone) ¡Están comunicando!

engaged *a* ocupado; (betrothed) prometido; reservado

engagement *n* obligación, *f*; compromiso, *m*; (date) cita, *f*; (betrothal) palabra de casamiento, *f*; (battle) combate, *m*, batalla, *f*. **I have an e. at two o'clock.** Tengo una cita a las dos

engagement gift regalo de esponsales, *m*

engaging *a* simpático, atractivo

engagingly *adv* de un modo encantador

engender *vt fig* engendrar; excitar

engine *n* máquina, *f*; motor, *m*; (locomotive) locomotora, *f*; (pump) bomba, *f*. **to sit with one's back to the e.,** estar sentado de espaldas a la máquina (or locomotora). **e. builder,** constructor de máquinas, *m*. **e. driver,** maquinista, *mf*. **e. room,** cuarto de máquinas, *m*. **e. works,** taller de maquinaria, *m*

engineer *n* ingeniero, *m*; mecánico, *m*, *vt fig* gestionar, arreglar. **civil e.,** ingeniero de caminos, canales y puertos, *m*. **Royal Engineers,** Cuerpo de Ingenieros, *m*

engineering *n* ingeniería, *f*; *fig* manejo, *m*. *a* de ingeniería

England Inglaterra, *f*

English *a* inglés. *n* (language) inglés, *m*. **in E. fashion,** a la inglesa. **to speak E.,** hablar inglés. **to speak plain E.,** hablar sin rodeos; hablar en cristiano. **E. Church,** iglesia anglicana, *f*. **E.-teacher,** maestro (-ra) de inglés. **English-translator,** traductor al inglés, *m*

English Channel, the el Canal de la Mancha

Englishman *n* inglés, *m*

Englishwoman *n* inglesa, *f*

engrain *vt* inculcar

engrave *vt* grabar; esculpir, cincelar; *fig* grabar

engraver *n* grabador (-ra); (tool) cincel, *m*

engraving *n* grabadura, *f*; (picture) grabado, *m*. **e. needle,** punta seca, *f*

engross *vt* (a document) poner en limpio; redactar; (absorb) absorber

engrossing *a* absorbente

engulf *vt* hundir, sumir, sumergir

enhance *vt* realzar; intensificar; aumentar; mejorar

enhancement *n* realce, *m*; intensificación, *f*; aumento, *m*; mejoría, *f*

enigma *n* enigma, *m*

enigmatic *a* enigmático

enjoin *vt* imponer; ordenar, mandar; encargar

enjoy *vt* disfrutar; gustar de; gozar de; poseer, tener. **to e. oneself,** recrearse, regocijarse; (amuse oneself) divertirse; entretenerse; pasarlo bien. **Did you e. yourself?** ¿Lo pasaste bien?

enjoyable *a* agradable; divertido, entretenido

enjoyableness *n* lo agradable; lo divertido

enjoyably *adv* de un modo muy agradable

enjoyer *n* el, *m*, (*f*, la) que disfruta; poseedor (-ra); (amateur) aficionado (-da)

enjoyment *n* posesión, *f*; goce, disfruto, *m*; (pleasure) placer, *m*; aprovechamiento, *m*; utilización, *f*; (satisfaction) satisfacción, *f*

enlarge *vt* agrandar; aumentar; ensanchar; extender; *phot* ampliar; dilatar; (the mind, etc.) ensanchar. *vi* agrandarse; ensancharse; aumentarse; extenderse. **an enlarged heart,** dilatación del corazón, *f*. **to e. upon,** tratar detalladamente, explayarse en

enlargement *n* engrandecimiento, *m*; ensanchamiento, *m*; *phot* ampliación, *f*; *med* dilatación, *f*; aumento, *m*; amplificación, *f*; (of a town, etc.) ensanche, *m*

enlarger *n phot* ampliadora, *f*

enlighten *vt* iluminar; aclarar; informar

enlightened *a* culto; ilustrado; inteligente

enlightening *a* instructivo

enlightenment *n* ilustración, *f*; cultura, civilización, *f*

enlist *vt mil* reclutar; alistar; obtener, conseguir. *vi mil* sentar plaza, sentar plaza de soldado; engancharse; alistarse

enlistment *n mil* enganche, *m*; reclutamiento, *m*; alistamiento, *m*

enliven *vt* animar; avivar; alegrar

enmity *n* enemistad, enemiga, hostilidad, *f*

ennoble *vt* ennoblecer; ilustrar

ennui *n* tedio, *m*; aburrimiento, *m*

enormity *n* enormidad, *f*; gravedad, *f*; atrocidad, *f*

enormous *a* enorme, colosal

enormously *adv* enormemente

enormousness *n* enormidad, *f*

enough *a* bastante, suficiente. *n* lo bastante, lo suficiente. *adv* bastante; suficientemente. *interj* ¡bastante! ¡basta! **to be e.,** ser suficiente; bastar. **two are enough,** con dos tenemos bastante, con dos tengo bastante

enquire. See **inquire**

enrage *vt* enfurecer, hacer furioso; *inf* hacer rabiar

enraged *a* furioso

enrapture *vt* entusiasmar, extasiar; (intoxicate) embriagar; (charm) encantar, deleitar

enrich *vt* enriquecer; (adorn) adornar, embellecer; (the land) fertilizar

enrichment *n* enriquecimiento, *m*; embellecimiento, *m*; (of the land) abono, *m*

enroll *vt* alistar; matricular; inscribir; (perpetuate) inmortalizar

enrollment *n* alistamiento, *m*; inscripción, *f*

ensconce *vt* acomodar, colocar; ocultar

ensemble *n* conjunto, *m*

enshrine *vt* poner en sagrario; guardar con cuidado; *fig* guardar como una reliquia

enshroud *vt* amortajar; envolver; esconder

ensign *n* (badge) insignia, *f*; (flag) enseña, bandera, *f*; pabellón, *m*; bandera de popa, *f*; *mil* alférez, *m*; (U.S.A. navy) subteniente, *m*

enslave *vt* esclavizar; *fig* dominar

enslavement *n* esclavitud, *f*

ensue *vt* conseguir. *vi* resultar; suceder, sobrevenir

ensuing *a* (next) próximo; (resulting) resultante

ensure *vt* asegurar; estar seguro de que; garantizar

entail *vt* traer consigo, acarrear; *law* vincular; *n law* vinculación, *f*; herencia, *f*

entangle *vt* enredar; coger; *fig* embrollar

entanglement *n* enredo, *m*; complicación, *f*; intriga, *f*; (*mil* of wire) alambrada, *f*

entangling *a* enmarañador (e.g., **entangling alliances,** alianzas enmarañadoras, *f pl*)

enter *vt* entrar en; penetrar; (of thoughts) ocurrirse; (join) ingresar en; entrar en; (become a member of) hacerse miembro de; (enroll) alistarse; (a university) matricularse; (inscribe) inscribir, poner en la lista; (note) anotar, apuntar; (a protest) hacer constar; (make) hacer; formular. *vi* entrar; *theat* salir (a la escena); penetrar; *com* anotarse. **to e. for,** *vt* inscribir. *vi* inscribirse, tomar parte en. **to e. into,** entrar en; formar parte de; (conversation) entablar (conversación); (negotiations) iniciar; considerar; (another's emotion) acompañar en; (an agreement, etc.) hacer; (sign) firmar; (bind oneself) obligarse a, comprometerse a; tomar parte en; (undertake) emprender; empezar; adoptar. **to e. up,** anotar, poner en la lista; registrar. **to e. upon,** comenzar, emprender; tomar posesión de; encargarse de, asumir; inaugurar, dar principio a

enteric *a* entérico

enteritis *n* enteritis, *f*

enterprise *n* empresa, *f*; aventura, *f*; (spirit) iniciativa, *f*, empuje, *m*

enterprising *a* emprendedor, acometedor; de mucha iniciativa

entertain *vt* (an idea, etc.) acariciar, abrigar; considerar; (as a guest) agasajar, obsequiar; recibir en casa; (amuse) divertir, entretener. *vi* ser hospitalario; tener invitados en casa; dar fiestas

entertaining *a* entretenido, divertido

entertainingly *adv* entretenidamente; (witty) graciosamente

entertainment *n* convite, *m*; fiesta, *f*; reunión, *f*; banquete, *m*; (hospitality) hospitalidad, *f*; (amusement) diversión, *f*, entretenimiento, *m*; espectáculo, *m*; función, *f*; concierto, *m*

enthrall *vt* seducir, atraer, encantar; absorber, captar la atención

enthralling *a* absorbente; atrayente, halagüeño

enthrallment *n* absorción, *f*; atracción, *f*

enthrone *vt* entronizar

enthronement *n* entronización, *f*

enthusiasm *n* entusiasmo, *m*

enthusiast *n* entusiasta, *mf*

enthusiastic *a* entusiasta. **to make e.,** entusiasmar. **to be e.,** entusiasmarse

enthusiastically *adv* con entusiasmo

entice *vt* tentar, inducir; atraer, seducir

enticement *n* tentación, *f*; atractivo, *m*

enticing *a* seduciente, atrayente; halagüeño

entire *a* entero; completo; intacto; absoluto; perfecto; íntegro; total

entirely *adv* enteramente; completamente; integralmente; totalmente

entirety *n* totalidad, *f*; integridad, *f*; todo, *m*

entitle *vt* (designate) intitular; dar derecho (a); autorizar. **to be entitled to,** tener derecho a

entity *n* entidad, *f*; ente, ser, *m*

entombment *n* sepultura, *f*, entierro, *m*

entomological *a* entomológico

entomologist *n* entomólogo, *m*

entomology *n* entomología, *f*

entourage *n* séquito, *m*; (environment) medio ambiente, *m*

entr'acte *n* entreacto, *m*

entrails *n* entrañas, tripas, *f pl*, intestinos, *m pl*

entrain *vi* tomar el tren, subir al tren

entrance *n* entrada, *f*; *theat* salida (a la escena), *f*; (into a profession, etc.) ingreso, *m*; alistamiento, *m*; (beginning) principio, *m*; (door) puerta, *f*; (porch) portal, *m*; (of a cave) boca, *f*. **e. fee,** cuota de entrada, *f*. **e. hall,** zaguán, *m*. **e. money,** entrada, *f*

entrance *vt fig* encantar, fascinar; ecstasiar

entrancing *a* encantador

entreat *vt* suplicar, implorar, rogar

entreating *a* suplicante, implorante

entreatingly *adv* de un modo suplicante; insistentemente

entreaty *n* súplica, instancia, *f*, ruego, *m*

entree *n* entrada, *f*

entrench *vt* atrincherar

entrenchment *n* atrincheramiento, *m*; *mil* parapeto, *m*; (encroachment) invasión, *f*

entresol *n* entresuelo, *m*

entrust *vt* confiar a (or en), encomendar a; encargar

entry *n* entrada, *f*; (passage) callejuela, *f*; (note) inscripción, apuntación, *f*; *com* partida, *f*; (registration) registro, *m*. **double e.,** *com* partida doble, *f*. **single e.,** *com* partida simple, *f*

entwine *vt* entrelazar, entretejer

enumerate *vt* enumerar

enumeration *n* enumeración, *f*

enumerative *a* enumerativo

enunciate *vt* enunciar; articular

enunciation *n* enunciación, *f*; articulación, *f*

envelop *vt* envolver, cubrir

envelope *n* sobre, *m*

envelopment *n* envolvimiento, *m*; cubierta, *f*

enviable *a* envidiable

envious *a* envidioso. **an e. look,** una mirada de envidia

enviously *adv* con envidia

environment *n* medio ambiente, *m*

environs *n* inmediaciones, *f pl*, alrededores, *m pl*

envisage *vt* hacer frente a; contemplar; imaginar

envoy *n* enviado, *m*; mensajero (-ra)

envy *n* envidia, *f*, *vt* envidiar

enzyme *n* fermento, *m*, enzima, *f*

eon *n* eón, *m*

epaulette *n* hombrera, *f*

ephemeral *a* efímero; *fig* fugaz, pasajero

Ephesus Efiso, *m*

Ephraim Efraín, *m*

Ephraimite *n* and *adj* efraíta, *mf*

epic *a* épico. *n* epopeya, *f*

epicenter *n* epicentro, *m*

epicure *n* epicúreo (-ea)

epicurean *a* epicúreo

Epicureanism *n* epicureísmo, *m*

epidemic *n* epidemia, *f*; plaga, *f*, *a* epidémico

epidermis *n* epidermis, *f*

epiglottis *n* epiglotis, *f*

epigram *n* epigrama, *m*

epigrammatic *a* epigramático

epigraph *n* epígrafe, *m*

epigraphy *n* epigrafía, *f*

epilepsy *n* epilepsia, alferecía, *f*

epileptic *a* and *n* epiléptico (-ca). **e. fit,** ataque epiléptico, *m*. **e. aura,** aura epiléptica, *f*

epilog *n* epílogo, *m*

epiphany *n* epifanía, *f*

Epirus Epiro, *m*

episcopacy *n* episcopado, *m*

episcopal *a* episcopal

episcopalianism *n* episcopalismo, *m*

episode *n* suceso, incidente, *m*; *lit* episodio, *m*

episodic *a* episódico

epistle *n* epístola, *f*

epistolary *a* epistolar

epitaph *n* epitafio, *m*

epithet *n* epíteto, *m*

epitome *n* epítome, *m*

epitomize *vt* resumir, abreviar

epoch *n* época, edad, *f*

epode *n* épodo, *m*

Epsom salts *n* sal de la Higuera, *f*

equability *n* igualdad (de ánimo), ecuanimidad, *f;* uniformidad, *f*

equable *a* igual, ecuánime; uniforme

equably *adv* con ecuanimidad; igualmente; uniformemente

equal *a* igual; uniforme; imparcial; equitativo, justo. *n* igual, *mf. vt* ser igual a; equivaler a; igualar; *sport* empatar. **to be e. to,** (of persons) ser capaz de; servir para; atreverse a; (circumstances) estar al nivel de; sentirse con fuerzas para. **without e.,** sin igual; (of beauty, etc.) sin par. **e. sign,** *math* igual, *m*

equality *n* igualdad, *f;* uniformidad, *f*

equalization *n* igualación, *f*

equalize *vt* igualar

equalizing *a* igualador; compensador

equally *adv* igualmente; imparcialmente

equanimity *n* ecuanimidad, *f*

equation *n* ecuación, *f*

equator *n* ecuador, *m*

equatorial *a* ecuatorial

equerry *n* caballerizo del rey, *m*

equestrian *a* ecuestre

equiangular *a* equiángulo

equidistance *n* equidistancia, *f*

equidistant *a* equidistante

equilateral *a* equilátero

equilibrist *n* equilibrista, *mf*

equilibrium *n* equilibrio, *m*

equine *a* equino; hípico; de caballo

equinoctial *a* equinoccial. **e. gale,** tempestad equinoccial, *f*

equinox *n* equinoccio, *m*

equip *vt* proveer; pertrechar; equipar

equipage *n* (train) séquito, tren, *m;* (carriage) carruaje, *m*

equipment *n* habilitación, *f;* equipo, *m;* pertrechos, *m pl;* material, *m;* aparatos, *m pl;* armamento, *m*

equitable *a* equitativo, justo

equitableness *n* equidad, justicia, *f*

equitably *adv* equitativamente, con justicia

equity *n* equidad, *f;* imparcialidad, justicia, *f*

equivalence *n* equivalencia, *f*

equivalent *a* and *n* equivalente, *m.* **to be e. to,** equivaler a

equivocal *a* equívoco, ambiguo

equivocally *adv* equivocadamente

equivocate *vi* usar frases equívocas, emplear equívocos, tergiversar

equivocation *n* equívoco, *m*

era *n* época, era, *f*

eradiation *n* irradiación, *f*

eradicable *a* erradicable

eradicate *vt* erradicar; destruir, extirpar; suprimir

eradication *n* erradicación, *f;* destrucción, *f;* supresión, *f*

erasable *a* borrable

erase *vt* borrar; tachar

eraser *n* goma de borrar, *f.* **ink e.,** goma para tinta, *f*

erasure *n* borradura, *f;* tachón, *m*

ere *conjunc* antes de (que), antes de. *prep* antes de

erect *a* (upright) derecho; erguido; vertical; (uplifted) levantado; (standing) de pie; (firm) firme, resuelto; (alert) vigilante. *vt* (build) edificar, construir; instalar; (raise) alzar; convertir

erectile *a* eréctil

erection *n* erección, *f;* construcción, edificación, *f;* (building) edificio, *m;* (structure) estructura, *f;* instalación, *f;* (assembling) montaje, *m*

erectly *adv* derecho

erectness *n* derechura, *f*

erg *n phys* ergio, *m*

ermine *n* armiño, *m, a* de armiño

erode *vt* corroer; comer; *geol* denudar

erosion *n* erosión, *f*

Erostrato Eróstrato

erotic *a* erótico

err *vi* desviarse; errar; desacertar; pecar

errand *n* mensaje, recado, *m;* encargo, *m;* misión, *f.* **e.-boy,** mandadero, mensajero, motril, mozo, recadero, *m*

errant *a* errante; (of knights) andante

erratic *a* (of conduct) excéntrico, irresponsable; (of thoughts, etc.) errante; *med* errático

erratum *n* errata, *f*

erring *a* extraviado; pecaminoso

erroneous *a* erróneo; falso; injusto

erroneously *adv* erróneamente; falsamente; injustamente

erroneousness *n* falsedad, *f*

error *n* error, *m;* equivocación, *f,* desacierto, *m;* (sin) pecado, *m.* **in e.,** por equivocación

erudite *a* erudito; sabio

erudition *n* erudición, *f*

erupt *vi* entrar en erupción, estar en erupción; *fig* salir con fuerza

eruption *n* erupción, *f*

erysipelas *n* erisipela, *f*

escalade *n* escalada, *f, vt* escalar

escalator *n* escalera automática, escalera eléctrica, escalera mecánica, escalera móvil, escalera rodante, *f*

escapable *a* evitable, eludible

escapade *n* escapada, *f;* aventura, *f*

escape *n* huida, fuga, *f;* evasión, evitación, *f;* (leak) escape, *m; fig* salida, *f. vt* eludir, evitar; (of cries, groans, etc.) dar, salir de. *vi* huir, fugarse, escapar; (slip away) escurrirse; librarse; salvarse; (leak) escaparse. **His name escapes me,** Se me escapa (or se me olvida) su nombre. **to e. notice,** pasar inadvertido. **to have a narrow e.,** salvarse en una tabla. **to e. from,** escaparse de; librarse de; huir de

escape clause *n* cláusula de salvaguardia, *f*

escaping *a* fugitivo

escarpment *n* escarpa, *f*

eschew *vt* evitar

eschewal *n* evitación, *f*

escort *n mil* escolta, *f;* (of ships) convoy, *m;* acompañamiento, *m;* acompañante, *m. vt mil* escoltar; (of ships) convoyar; acompañar

escritoire *n* escritorio, *m*

escudo *n* escudo, *m*

escutcheon *n* escudo, blasón, *m*

Eskimo *a* and *n* esquimal *mf*

esoteric *a* esotérico

esparto *n* esparto, *m*

especial *a* especial; particular

especially *adv* especialmente; ante todo; en particular

Esperantist *n* esperantista, *mf*

Esperanto *n* esperanto, *m*

espionage *n* espionaje, *m*

esplanade *n mil* explanada, *f;* bulevar, paseo, *m*

espousal *n* desposorio, *m; fig* adhesión (a una causa), *f*

espouse *vt* desposar; (a cause) abrazar; defender

espy *vt* divisar, ver, observar

esquire *n* escudero, *m;* (landowner) hacendado, *m;* (as a title) don (before given name)

essay *n* tentativa, *f; lit* ensayo, *m, vt* probar; procurar; (on an examination) tema, *m.* **essay question,** tema, *m*

essayist *n* ensayista, *mf*

essence *n* esencia, *f*

essential *a* esencial; indispensable, imprescindible; intrínseco. *n* artículo de primera necesidad, *m;* elemento necesario, *m*

essentially *adv* esencialmente

establish *vt* establecer; fundar; crear; erigir, *Lat. Am. also* instaurar; (constitute) constituir; (order) disponer; (prove) demostrar, probar; (take root, settle) arraigarse

established *a* establecido; arraigado; (proved) demostrado; bien conocido; (author) consagrado; (of churches) oficial

establishment *n* establecimiento, *m;* fundación, *f;* creación, *f, Lat. Am. also* instauración; institución, *f;*

(building) erección, *f*; arraigo, *m*; (house) casa, *f*; (church) iglesia oficial, *f*; demostración, *f*; reconocimiento, *m*

estate *n* estado, *m*; clase, *f*; condición, *f*; (land) propiedad, finca, *f*; fortuna, *f*; (inheritance) heredad, *f*, patrimonio, *m*; *law* bienes, *m pl*. **personal e.,** bienes muebles, *m pl*; fortuna personal, *f*. **third e.,** estado llano, *m*. **e. agent,** agente de fincas, *m*; agente de casas, *m*

esteem *n* estima, *f*, aprecio, *m*; consideración, *f*, *vt* estimar, apreciar; creer, juzgar

ester *n chem* éster, *m*

esthete *n* estético, *m*

esthetic *a* estético

esthetically *adv* estéticamente

esthetics *n* estética, *f*

estimable *a* apreciable, estimable

estimableness *n* estimabilidad, *f*

estimate *n* estimación, tasa, *f*; cálculos, *m pl*; apreciación, *f*; opinión, *f*; *pl* **estimates,** presupuesto, *m*. *vt* (value) avalorar, tasar; calcular, computar; considerar. *vi* hacer un presupuesto

estimation *n* opinión, *f*; cálculo, cómputo, *m*; (esteem) aprecio, *m*, estima, *f*

estrange *vt* enajenar; ofender

estrangement *n* enajenación, alienación, *f*

estuary *n* estuario, *m*, ría, *f*

etcetera etcétera. (Used as noun, *f*)

etch *vt* grabar al agua fuerte

etcher *n* grabador (-ra) al agua fuerte

etching *n* aguafuerte, *f*; grabado al agua fuerte, *m*. **e. needle,** punta seca, aguja de grabador, *f*

eternal *a* eterno; incesante. *n* (E.) el Eterno

eternally *adv* eternamente

eternity *n* eternidad, *f*

eternize *vt* eternizar

ether *n* éter, *m*

ethereal *a* etéreo; vaporoso, aéreo

etheric *a* etéreo

etherize *vt* eterizar

ethical *a* ético, moral; *n* droga de ordenanza, *f*

ethics *n* ética, *f*; (filosofía) moral, *f*

Ethiopia Etiopia, *f*

ethnic *a* étnico

ethnographic *a* etnográfico

ethnography *n* etnografía, *f*

ethnologist *n* etnólogo, *m*

ethnology *n* etnología, *f*

ethyl *n chem* etilo, *m*

ethylene *n chem* etileno, *m*

etiquette *n* etiqueta, *f*

Eton coat *n* chaquetilla, *f*

Eton collar *n* cuello de colegial, *m*

Etna, Mount el Etna

Etruscan *a* and *n* etrusco (-ca)

etymological *a* etimológico

etymologist *n* etimólogo, *m*, etimologista, *mf*

etymology *n* etimología, *f*

eucalyptus *n* eucalipto, *m*

Eucharist *n* Eucaristía, *f*

eucharistic *a* eucarístico

eugenic *a* eugenésico

eugenics *n* eugenesia, *f*

eulogist *n* elogiador (-ra), loador (-ra)

eulogistic *a* elogiador

eulogize *vt* elogiar, alabar, encomiar

eulogy *n* elogio, encomio, *m*; alabanza, *f*; panegírico, *m*

eunuch *n* eunuco, *m*

euphemism *n* eufemismo, *m*

euphonious *a* eufónico

euphony *n* eufonía, *f*

euphuistic *a* alambicado, gongorino

Eurasian *a* and *n* eurasio (-ia)

eurhythmic *a* eurítmico

eurhythmics *n* euritmia, *f*

European *a* and *n* europeo (-ea)

europeanize *vt* europeanizar

euthanasia *n* eutanasia, *f*

evacuate *vt* evacuar

evacuation *n* evacuación, *f*

evade *vt* evadir, eludir; evitar, esquivar; rehuir

evaluate *vt* evaluar, estimar; calcular

evaluation *n* evaluación, estimación, *f*

evanescent *a* transitorio, fugaz, pasajero

evangelical *a* evangélico

evangelicalism *n* evangelismo, *m*

evangelist *n* evangelista, *m*

evangelize *vt* evangelizar

evaporate *vi* evaporarse; desvanecerse. *vt* evaporar

evaporation *n* evaporación, *f*; desvanecimiento, *m*

evaporative *a* evaporatorio

evasion *n* (escape) fuga, *f*; evasión, *f*; evasiva, *f*, efugio, *m*, *Lat. Am.* esquivada, *f*

evasive *a* evasivo, ambiguo

evasively *adv* evasivamente

evasiveness *n* carácter evasivo, *m*

eve *n* víspera, *f*; *ecc* vigilia, *f*. **on the eve of,** la víspera de; *fig* en vísperas de

even *a* (flat) llano; (smooth) liso; igual; (level with) al mismo nivel (de); uniforme; (of numbers) par; (approximate, of sums) redondo; rítmico; invariable, constante; (of temper) apacible; (just) imparcial; (monotonous) monótono, igual; (paid) pagado; (*com* of date) mismo. **to get e. with,** pagar en la misma moneda, vengarse de. **to be e. (with . . .)** (be quits) *Lat. Am.* estar a mano (con . . .)

even *adv* siquiera; aun; hasta; (also) también. **not e.,** ni siquiera. **e. as,** así como, del mismo modo que. **e. if,** aun cuando, si bien. **e. now,** aun ahora; ahora mismo. **e. so,** aun así; (nevertheless) sin embargo. **e. though,** aunque; suponiendo que

even *vt* igualar; (level) allanar, nivelar; (accounts) desquitar; compensar; hacer uniforme

evening *n* tarde, *f*, atardecer, *m*; noche, *f*; *fig* fin, *m*, *a* vespertino, de tarde. **Good e.!** ¡Buenas tardes! ¡Buenas noches! **in the e.,** al atardecer. **tomorrow e.,** mañana por la tarde. **yesterday e.,** ayer por la tarde. **e. class,** clase nocturna, *f*. **e. dress,** (women) traje de noche, *m*; (men) traje de etiqueta, *m*. **e. meal,** cena, *f*. **e. paper,** periódico (or diario) de la noche, *m*. **evening primrose,** hierba del asno, onagra, *f*. **e. star,** estrella vespertina, estrella de la tarde, *f*; (Venus) lucero de la tarde, *m*

evenly *adv* igualmente; (on a level) a nivel; uniformemente; imparcialmente; (of speech) con suavidad

evenness *n* igualdad, *f*; (smoothness) lisura, *f*; uniformidad, *f*; imparcialidad, *f*; (of temper) ecuanimidad, serenidad, *f*

evensong *n* vísperas, *f pl*

event *n* incidente, suceso, acontecimiento, *m*; (result) consecuencia, *f*; resultado, *m*; caso, *m*; (athletics) prueba, *f*; (race) carrera, *f*. **at all events,** de todas maneras. **in such an e.,** en tal caso. **in the e. of,** en el caso de

eventful *a* lleno de acontecimientos; accidentado; memorable

eventual *a* eventual; final, último

eventuality *n* eventualidad, *f*

eventually *adv* a la larga, al fin

ever *adv* siempre; (at any time) jamás; alguna vez; nunca; (even) siquiera; (very) muy; (in any way) en modo alguno. **As fast as e. he can,** Lo más aprisa que pueda. **Be it e. so big,** Por grande que sea. **Did you e.!** ¡Habráse visto! ¡Qué cosa! **for e.,** para siempre. **for e. and e.,** para siempre jamás; (mostly ecclesiastical) por los siglos de los siglos; eternamente. **He is e. so nice,** Es muy simpático. **Hardly e.,** casi nunca. **I don't think I have e. been there,** No creo que haya estado nunca allí. **if e.,** si alguna vez; (rarely) raramente. **nor . . . e.,** ni nunca. **not . . . e.,** nunca. **e. after,** desde entonces; (afterward) después. **e. and anon,** de vez en cuando. **e. so little,** siquiera un poco; muy poco

evergreen *a* siempre verde. *n* planta vivaz, *f.* **e. oak,** encina, *f*

everlasting *a* eterno, perpetuo; (of colors) estable; incesante. **e. flower,** perpetua, *f*

evermore *adv* eternamente

every *a* todo; cada (invariable); todos los, *m pl;* todas las, *f pl.* **e. day,** todos los días, cada día. **e. now and then,** de cuando en cuando. **e. other day,** cada dos días

everybody *n* todo el mundo, *m;* todos, *m pl;* todas, *f pl;* cada uno, *m;* cada una, *f*

everyday *a* diario, cotidiano; corriente, de cada día, usual

everything *n* todo, *m;* (e. that, which) todo lo (que). **e. possible,** todo lo posible

everywhere *adv* por todas partes

evict *vt* desahuciar; expulsar

eviction *n* evicción, *f,* desahúcio, *m;* expulsión, *f*

evidence *n law* testimonio, *m,* deposición, *f;* indicios, *m pl;* evidencia, *f;* prueba, *f;* hecho, *m, vt* patentizar, probar. **to give e.,** dar testimonio, deponer

evident *a* evidente, patente, manifiesto; claro. **to be e.,** ser patente, estar a la vista

evidently *adv* evidentemente; claramente

evil *a* malo; malvado, perverso; de maldad; (unfortunate) aciago; de infortunio; (of spirits) diabólico, malo. *n* mal, *m;* maldad, perversidad, *f;* (misfortune) desgracia, *f.* **the E. one,** el Malo. **e.-doer,** malhechor (-ra). **e. eye,** mal de ojo, aojo, *m.* **e.-minded,** mal pensado; malintencionado. **e.-speaking,** maledicencia, calumnia, *f.* **e. spirit,** demonio, espíritu malo, *m*

evince *vt* evidenciar; mostrar

eviscerate *vt* destripar, desentrañar

evocation *n* evocación, *f*

evocative *a* evocador

evoke *vt* evocar

evolution *n* evolución, *f;* desarrollo, *m;* (nav, mil) maniobra, *f; math* extracción de una raíz, *f;* (revolution) revolución, vuelta, *f*

evolutionism *n* evolucionismo, *m*

evolutive *a* evolutivo

evolve *vi* evolucionar; desarrollarse. *vt* producir por evolución; desarrollar; pensar

ewe *n* oveja, *f.* **ewe lamb,** cordera, *f*

ewer *n* aguamanil, *m*

exacerbate *vt* exacerbar; agravar, empeorar

exacerbation *n* exacerbación, *f;* agravación, *f*

exact *a* exacto; fiel; metódico; estricto. *vt* exigir

exacting *a* exigente; severo, estricto; (hard) agotador, arduo

exaction *n* exigencia, *f;* extorsión, exacción, *f*

exactly *adv* exactamente; precisamente

exactness *n* exactitud, *f*

exaggerate *vt* exagerar; acentuar. *vi* exagerar

exaggerated *a* exagerado

exaggeration *n* exageración, *f*

exaggerator *n* exagerador (-ra)

exalt *vt* exaltar; enaltecer, elevar; (praise) glorificar, magnificar; (intensify) realzar; intensificar

exaltation *n* exaltación, elevación, *f;* alegría, *f,* júbilo, *m;* (ecstasy) éxtasis, arrobamiento, *m;* (of the Cross) exaltación, *f*

exalted *a* exaltado, eminente

exaltedness *n* exaltación, *f*

examination *n* examen, *m;* inspección, *f;* investigación, *f; law* interrogatorio, *m;* prueba, *f.* **to sit an e.,** examinarse. **written e.,** prueba escrita, *f*

examine *vt* examinar; inspeccionar; investigar; *law* interrogar; (search) reconocer; (by touch) tentar; observar; analizar. **to e. into,** examinar; considerar detenidamente; ahondar en

examinee *n* examinando (-da)

examiner *n* examinador (-ra); inspector (-ra)

examinership *n* cargo de examinador, *m*

examining *a* que examina; de examen; *law* interrogante

example *n* ejemplo, *m;* ilustración, *f;* (parallel) ejem-

plar, *m;* (warning) escarmiento, *m.* **for e.,** por ejemplo. **to set an e.,** dar ejemplo, dar el ejemplo.

exasperate *vt* exasperar, irritar; (increase) aumentar; (worsen) agravar

exasperating *a* exasperante, irritante, provocador

exasperation *n* exasperación, irritación, *f;* (worsening) agravación, *f;* enojo, *m*

excavate *vt* excavar; (hollow) vaciar

excavation *n* excavación, *f; arch* vaciado, *m*

excavator *n* excavador (-ra); (machine) excavadora, *f*

exceed *vt* exceder; (excel) superar, aventajar; (one's hopes, etc.) sobrepujar. *vi* excederse. **e. all expectations,** exceder a toda ponderación. **to e. one's rights,** abusar de sus derechos, ir demasiado lejos

exceedingly *adv* sumamente, extremadamente; sobre manera

excel *vt* aventajar, superar; vencer. *vi* sobresalir; distinguirse, señalarse; ser superior

excellence *n* excelencia, *f;* superioridad, *f;* perfección, *f;* mérito, *m;* buena calidad, *f*

excellency *n* (title) Excelencia, *f.* **Your E.,** Su Excelencia

excellent *a* excelente; superior; perfecto; magnífico; (in examinations) sobresaliente

excellently *adv* excelentemente; perfectamente; magníficamente

except *vt* exceptuar; omitir

except, excepting *prep* excepto, con excepción de; exceptuando; menos; salvo; fuera de. *conjunc* a menos que. **except for,** si no fuese por; con excepción de; fuera de

exception *n* excepción, *f;* objeción, protesta, *f.* **to make an e.,** hacer una excepción. **to take e. to,** protestar contra; tachar, criticar; desaprobar

exceptional *a* excepcional

excerpt *n* excerpta, *f,* extracto, *m, vt* extraer

excess *n* exceso, *m;* superabundancia, *f;* demasía, *f; com* superávit, *m.* **in e.,** en exceso, de sobra. **in e. of,** en exceso de; arriba de. **to e.,** excesivamente, demasiado. **e. fare,** suplemento, *m.* **e. luggage,** exceso de equipaje, *m;* (overweight) exceso de peso, *m*

excessive *a* excesivo; superabundante; inmoderado, desmesurado; exagerado

excessively *adv* excesivamente; exageradamente

excessiveness *n* exceso, *m;* superabundancia, *f;* exageración, *f*

exchange *n* cambio, trueque, *m;* (of prisoners) canje, *m;* (financial) cambio, *m;* (building) bolsa, lonja, *f;* (telephone) oficina central de teléfonos, *f. vt* cambiar (for, por); trocar; (replace) reemplazar; (prisoners) canjear; (of blows) darse; (pass from, into) pasar de . . . a. *vi* hacer un cambio. **in e. for,** en cambio de, a trueque de; por. **to e. greetings,** saludarse; cambiar saludos. **They exchanged looks,** Se miraron. **What is the rate of e.?** ¿Cuál es el tipo de cambio? **e. of prisoners,** canje de prisioneros, *m*

exchangeable *a* cambiable; trocable

exchequer *n* (public finance) Hacienda pública, *f;* tesorería, *f;* (funds) fondos, *m pl.* **Chancellor of the E.,** Ministro de Hacienda, *m*

excise *n* contribución indirecta, *f;* (customs and e.) Aduana, *f. vt* (cut) cortar, extirpar; imponer una contribución indirecta. **e. duty,** derecho de aduana, *m*

excise tax arbitrios, *m pl*

excision *n* excisión, *f;* extirpación, *f*

excitability *n* excitabilidad, *f*

excitable *a* excitable

excitation *n* excitación, *f*

excite *vt* emocionar; conmover; agitar; excitar; suscitar; provocar; incitar, instigar; (attention, interest) despertar; estimular. **to become excited,** emocionarse; exaltarse; (annoyed) acalorarse; (upset) agitarse

excitedly *adv* con emoción; acaloradamente; agitadamente

excitement *n* conmoción, *f;* agitación, *f, Central America* embullo *m;* (annoyance) acaloramiento, *m;* emoción, *f;*

estímulo, *m*; instigación, *f*, fomento, *m*; (amusement) placer, *m*

exciting *a* emocionante; conmovedor; agitador; muy interesante

exclaim *vt* and *vi* exclamar. **to e. against,** clamar contra

exclamation *n* exclamación, *f*. **e. mark,** punto de exclamación, *m*

exclamatory *a* exclamatorio

exclude *vt* excluir; exceptuar; evitar; (refuse) rechazar

exclusion *n* exclusión, *f*; exceptuación, *f*; eliminación, *f*

exclusive *a* exclusivo; (snobbish) exclusivista. **e. of,** no incluido; aparte de

exclusively *adv* exclusivamente; únicamente

exclusiveness *n* carácter exclusivo, *m*

exclusivism *n* exclusivismo, *m*

exclusivist *n* exclusivista, *mf*

excommunicate *vt* excomulgar. *a* excomulgado

excommunication *n* excomunión, *f*

excrement *n* excremento, *m*

excrescence *n* excrecencia, *f*

excrescent *a* que forma excrecencia; superfluo

excrete *vt* excretar

excretion *n* excreción, *f*

excretory *a* excretorio

excruciating *a* atormentador, angustioso; (of pain) agudísimo

excursion *n* excursión, *f*; expedición, *f*; (digression) digresión, *f*. **e. ticket,** billete de excursión, *m*. **e. train,** tren de excursionistas, *m*

excursionist *n* excursionista, *mf*; turista, *mf*

excusable *a* disculpable, excusable

excusably *adv* excusablemente

excuse *n* excusa, *f*; disculpa, *f*; pretexto, *m*; justificación, defensa, *f*. **to give as an e.,** pretextar

excuse *vt* disculpar, excusar; dispensar (de); librar (de); (forgive) perdonar; (defend) justificar, defender; (minimize) paiar; (oneself) disculparse. **E. me!** ¡Con permiso!; ¡Perdone Vd.!; ¡Dispense Vd.!

execrable *a* execrable, abominable

execrate *vt* execrar, abominar. *vi* maldecir

execration *n* execración, abominación, *f*; maldición, *f*

execute *vt* (perform) ejecutar, poner en efecto, realizar; (*art, mus*) ejecutar; (part in a play) hacer, desempeñar; (fulfil) cumplir; *law* otorgar (un documento); (kill) ajusticiar

execution *n* efectuación, realización, *f*; (*art, mus*) ejecución, *f*; (of part in a play) desempeño (de un papel), *m*; (fulfilment) cumplimiento, *m*; *law* otorgamiento (de un documento), *m*; (killing) suplicio, *m*, ejecución de la pena de muerte, *f*; (*law* seizure) ejecución, *f*

executioner *n* verdugo, *m*

executive *a* ejecutivo; administrativo. *n* poder ejecutivo, *m*

executor *n* administrador testamentario, *m*

executrix *n* administradora testamentaria, *f*

exegesis *n* exégesis, *f*

exegetical *a* exegético

exemplary *a* ejemplar

exemplification *n* ejemplificación, ilustración, demostración, *f*

exemplify *vt* ejemplificar; ilustrar, demostrar

exempt *vt* exentar, eximir; librar; dispensar, excusar. *a* exento; libre; excusado; inmune

exemption *n* exención, *f*; libertad, *f*; inmunidad, *f*

exercise *n* ejercicio, *m*; uso, *m*; (essay) ensayo, *m*; *pl* **exercises,** (on land or sea) maniobras, *f pl*. *vt* ejercer; usar, emplear; (train) ejercitar, entrenar; adiestrar; pasear, dar un paseo; (worry) preocupar. *vi* hacer ejercicio; ejercitarse; adiestrarse. **spiritual exercises,** ejercicios espirituales, *m pl*. **to take e. in the open air,** tomar ejercicio al aire libre. **to write an e.,** escribir un ejercicio. **e. book,** cuaderno de ejercicios, *m*

exert *vt* hacer uso de, emplear; ejercer, poner en juego; (deploy) desplegar. **to e. oneself,** hacer un esfuerzo

(para); esforzarse (de); trabajar mucho; tratar (de); apurarse, tomarse mucha molestia; preocuparse

exertion *n* esfuerzo, *m*; uso, *m*; (exercise) ejercicio, *m*; (good offices) diligencias, gestiones, *f pl*; buenos oficios, *m pl*

exhalation *n* exhalación, *f*; efluvio, *m*; vapor, *m*; humo, *m*

exhale *vt* exhalar; emitir, despedir. *vi* evaporarse; disiparse

exhaust *vt* agotar; (empty) vaciar; (end) acabar; apurar; consumir; (tire) rendir, cansar mucho; (weaken) debilitar; (a subject) tratar detalladamente. *n mech* escape, *m*; emisión de vapor, *f*; vapor de escape, *m*. **e. pipe,** tubo de escape, *m*

exhaustible *a* agotable

exhausting *a* cansado, agotador

exhaustion *n* agotamiento, *m*; rendimiento, cansancio, *m*; lasitud, *f*; postración, *f*

exhaustive *a* completo; minucioso

exhaustively *adv* detenidamente; detalladamente; minuciosamente

exhaustiveness *n* lo completo; minuciosidad, *f*

exhibit *vt* exhibir; manifestar, ostentar; revelar, descubrir; presentar. *vi* exhibir, ser expositor. *n* objeto exhibido, *m*; *law* prueba, *f*

exhibition *n* exposición, *f*; (performance) función, *f*; espectáculo, *m*; exhibición, *f*; (showing) manifestación, *f*; (grant) bolsa de estudio, beca, *f*

exhibitionism *n* exhibicionismo, *m*

exhibitionist *n* exhibicionista, *mf*

exhibitor *n* expositor (-ra)

exhilarate *vt* alegrar, alborozar

exhilarating *a* alegre; estimulador; vigorizador, tonificante

exhilaration *n* alegría, *f*, alborozo, regocijo, *m*

exhort *vt* and *vi* exhortar

exhortation *n* exhortación, *f*

exhumation *n* exhumación, *f*

exhume *vt* exhumar

exigence *n* exigencia, *f*; urgencia, *f*; (need) necesidad, *f*

exigent *a* exigente; urgente

exiguous *a* exiguo

exiguousness *n* exigüidad, *f*

exile *n* destierro, *m*; (person) desterrado (-da), *Lat. Am.* exiliado (-da) *mf* vt desterrar, *Lat. Am.* exiliar

exist *vi* existir

existence *n* existencia, *f*; (being) ser, *m*; (life) vida, *f*. **to bring into e.,** causar; producir

existentialism *n* existencialismo, *m*

existing *a* existente

exit *n* salida, *f*; partida, *f*; (death) muerte, *f*; *theat* mutis, *m*. *vi theat* hacer mutis. **to make one's e.,** salir; marcharse; irse; morir; *theat* hacer mutis

exodus *n* éxodo, *m*; salida, *f*; emigración, *f*; (Old Testament) Éxodo, *m*

exonerate *vt* exonerar

exoneration *n* exoneración, *f*

exorbitance *n* exorbitancia, *f*

exorbitant *a* exorbitante

exorcism *n* exorcismo, *m*

exorcist *n* exorcista, *m*

exorcize *vt* exorcizar, conjurar

exotic *a* exótico. *n* planta exótica, *f*; *fig* flor de estufa, *f*

expand *vt* extender; abrir; (wings, etc.) desplegar; (the chest, etc.) expandir; dilatar; (amplify) ampliar; (an edition) ampliar, aumentar; (develop) desarrollar; *fig* ensanchar; (increase) aumentar. *vi* dilatarse; hincharse; abrirse; extenderse; *fig* ensancharse; (increase) aumentarse

expanse *n* extensión, *f*

expansibility *n phys* expansibilidad, *f*; dilatabilidad, *f*

expansible *a phys* expansible; dilatable

expansion *n* expansión, *f*; extensión, *f*; dilatación, *f*; (amplification) ampliación, *f*; (development) desarrollo, *m*; *fig* ensanchamiento, *m*; (increase) aumento, *m*

expansionism *n* expansionismo, *m*

expansive *a* expansivo; (of persons) efusivo, expresivo, comunicativo, afable

expansiveness *n* expansibilidad, *f*; (of persons) afabilidad, *f*

expatiate (upon) *vi* extenderse en

expatiation *n* discurso, *m*; digresión, *f*

expatriation *n* expatriación, *f*

expect *vt* esperar; (await) aguardar; (suppose) suponer; (demand) exigir; (count on) contar con. *vi* creer

expectance *n* expectación, *f*; esperanza, *f*

expectant *a* expectante; (hopeful) esperanzado; (pregnant) embarazada

expectantly *adv* con expectación

expectation *n* expectación, *f*; (hope) esperanza, expectativa, *f*; probabilidad, *f*

expectorate *vt* expectorar. *vi* escupir

expectoration *n* expectoración, *f*

expedience *n* conveniencia, *f*; oportunidad, *f*; aptitud, *f*; (self-interest) egoísmo, *m*

expedient *a* conveniente; oportuno; apto; prudente; político. *n* expediente, recurso, medio, *m*

expedite *vt* acelerar; facilitar; (send off) despachar

expedition *n* expedición, *f*; (haste) celeridad, diligencia, *f*

expeditionary *a* expedicionario. **e. force,** fuerza expedicionaria, *f*

expeditious *a* expedito, pronto

expeditiously *adv* expeditamente, prontamente

expeditiousness *n* prontitud, *f*

expel *vt* expeler, expulsar; echar, arrojar; despedir

expend *vt* gastar, expender; (time) perder

expenditure *n* gasto, desembolso, *m, Lat. Am.* erogación *f*; (of time) pérdida, *f*

expense *n* gasto, *m*; pérdida, *f*; costa, *f*; *pl* **expenses,** expensas, *f pl*, gastos, *m pl*. **at the e. of,** a costa de. **to be put to great e.,** tener que gastar mucho. **to pay one's expenses,** pagar sus gastos

expensive *a* costoso; caro

expensively *adv* costosamente

expensiveness *n* lo costoso; costa, *f*

experience *n* experiencia, *f*. *vt* experimentar; sentir; sufrir. **by e.,** por experiencia

experienced *a* experimentado; experto; hábil; (lived) vivido

experiment *n* experimento, *m*; prueba, *f*; ensayo, *m*, tentativa, *f, vi* experimentar; hacer una prueba

experimental *a* experimental; tentativo

experimentally *adv* experimentalmente; por experiencia

expert *a* experto; perito; hábil; (finished) acabado. *n* experto, *m*, especialista, *mf*

expertly *adv* expertamente; hábilmente

expertness *n* pericia, *f*; maestría, *f*; habilidad, *f*; (knowledge) conocimiento, *m*

expiable *a* que se puede expiar

expiate *vt* expiar; reparar

expiation *n* expiación, *f*

expiatory *a* expiatorio

expiration *n* (breathing out) espiración, *f*; (ending) expiración, *f*; terminación, *f*; *com* vencimiento, *m*; (death) muerte, *f*

expiration date fecha de caducidad, *f*

expire *vi* (exhale) espirar; (die) morir, dar el último suspiro; (of fire, light) extinguirse; (end) expirar; terminar; *com* vencer

expiry *n* terminación, *f*; expiración, *f*; *com* vencimiento, *m*

explain *vt* explicar; aclarar; demostrar; exponer; (justify) justificar, defender. *vi* explicarse. **to e. away,** explicar; justificar

explainable *a* explicable

explanation *n* explicación, *f*; aclaración, *f*

explanatory *a* explicativo; aclaratorio

expletive *a* expletivo. *n* interjección, *f*

explicable *a* explicable

explicit *a* explícito

explode *vi* estallar; detonar; reventar. *vt* hacer estallar;

(a mine) hacer saltar; (a belief, etc.) hacer abandonar; desechar

exploit *n* hazaña, proeza, *f*; aventura, *f. vt* explotar

exploitation *n* explotación, *f*

exploiter *n* explotador (-ra)

exploration *n* exploración, *f*

exploratory *a* exploratorio

explore *vt* explorar; examinar; averiguar; investigar; (*med surg*) explorar

explorer *n* explorador (-ra)

explosion *n* explosión, *f*; estallido, *m*, detonación, *f*

explosive *a and n* explosivo, *m*. **high e.,** explosivo violento, *m*. **explosives chamber,** recámara, *f*

explosiveness *n* propiedad explosiva, *f*; lo explosivo; violencia, *f*

exponent *a and n* exponente, *mf*

export *n* exportación, *f, vt* exportar. **e. licence,** permiso de exportación, *m*. **e. trade,** comercio de exportación, *m*

exportation *n* exportación, *f*

exporter *n* exportador (-ra)

expose *vt* exponer; arriesgar; (exhibit) exhibir, (unmask) desenmascarar; descubrir; revelar; *phot* exponer; (ridicule) ridiculizar

exposed *a* descubierto; no abrigado; expuesto, peligroso

exposition *n* explicación, interpretación, *f*; declaración, *f*; (exhibition) exposición, *f*

expostulate *vi* protestar, **to e. with,** reprochar; reconvenir

expostulation *n* protesta, *f*; reconvención, *f*

exposure *n* exposición, *f*; (aspect) orientación, *f*; (scandal) revelación, *f*, escándalo, *m*; peligro, *m*; exposición al frío or al calor, *f*

expound *vt* exponer, explicar; comentar

expounder *n* intérprete, *mf*; comentador (-ra)

express *a* (clear) categórico, explícito, claro; expreso; (exact) exacto; (quick) rápido. *n* (messenger, post) expreso, *m*; (train) (tren) expreso, (tren) rápido, *m*; (goods) exprés, *m. vt* expresar; (a letter, etc.) mandar por expreso

expressible *a* decible

expression *n* expresión, *f*

expressionless *a* sin expresión

expressive *a* expresivo; que expresa

expropriate *vt* expropiar

expropriation *n* expropiación, *f*

expulsion *n* expulsión, *f*

expunge *vt* borrar; testar; omitir

expunging *n* borradura, *f*; testación, *f*; omisión, *f*

expurgate *vt* expurgar

expurgation *n* expurgación, *f*

expurgator *n* expurgador, *m*

expurgatory *a* expurgatorio

exquisite *a* exquisito, precioso, primoroso; excelente; (acute) agudo, intenso; (keen) vivo. *n* elegante, petimetre, *m*

exquisitely *adv* primorosamente, pulcramente; a la perfección

exquisiteness *n* primor. *m*; pulcritud, perfección, *f*; excelencia, *f*; (of pain) intensidad, *f*; (keenness) viveza, *f*

ex-serviceman *n* excombatiente, antiguo soldado, *m*

extant *a* estante; existente; viviente

extempore *a* improvisado

extemporize *vt and vi* improvisar

extend *vt* extender; (hold out) tender, alargar; (lengthen) prolongar; (a period of time) prorrogar, diferir; (make larger) ensanchar; (increase) aumentar; dilatar; ampliar; (offer) ofrecer; *vi* extenderse; dilatarse; continuar; (give) dar de sí, estirarse; (last) prolongarse, durar; (become known) propagarse

extensible *a* extensible

extension *n* extensión, *f*; expansión, *f*; (increase) aumento, *m*; prolongación, *f*; ampliación, *f*; *com* prórroga, *f*; (telephone number) extensión, *f*, interno, *m*

extension cord *n* cordón de extensión, *m*; ladrón *m*, (Mexico; slang)

extensive *a* extenso, ancho, vasto; grande, considerable; (comprehensive) comprensivo

extensively *adv* extensamente; generalmente

extensiveness *n* extensión, *f*; amplitud, *f*

extensor *n anat* extensor, *m*

extent *n* extensión, *f*; (degree) punto, *m*; (limit) límite, *m*. **to a great e.,** en gran parte; considerablemente. **to some e.,** hasta cierto punto. **to the full e.,** en toda su extensión; completamente. **to what e.?** ¿hasta qué punto?

extenuate *vt* atenuar, desminuir, mitigar, paliar

extenuating *a* atenuante

extenuation *n* atenuación, mitigación, *f*

exterior *a* exterior, externo; de fuera; (foreign) extranjero. *n* exterior, *m*; aspecto, *m*; forma, *f*

exterminate *vt* exterminar

extermination *n* exterminio, *m*

exterminator *n* exterminador (-ra)

exterminatory *a* exterminador

external *a* externo, exterior; (foreign) extranjero. *n pl* **externals,** apariencias, *f pl*; aspecto exterior, *m*; comportamiento, *m*

externally *adv* exteriormente

exterritorial *a* extraterritorial

exterritoriality *n* extraterritorialidad, *f*

extinct *a* extinto; (of light, fire) extinguido; suprimido

extinction *n* extinción, *f*

extinguish *vt* extinguir; apagar; *fig* eclipsar

extinguishable *a* apagable

extinguisher *n* apagador (-ra); (for fires) extintor, *m*; (snuffer) matacandelas, *m*

extinguishment *n* apagamiento, *m*; extinción, *f*; abolición, *f*; (destruction) aniquilamiento, *m*

extirpate *vt* extirpar

extirpation *n* extirpación, *f*

extol *vt* elogiar, encomiar, alabar; cantar

extoller *n* alabador (-ra)

extort *vt* arrancar, sacar por fuerza; exigir por amenazas

extortion *n* extorsión, *f*; exacción, *f*

extortionate *a* injusto; opresivo; (of price) exorbitante, excesivo

extra *a* and *adv* adicional; extraordinario; suplementario; (spare) de repuesto. *prefix* (in compounds) extra. *n* extra, *m*; suplemento, *m*; (of a paper) hoja extraordinaria, *f*; (actor) supernumerario (-ia). **e. charge,** gasto suplementario, *m*; (on the railway, etc.) suplemento, *m*. **e.-mural,** *a* de extramuros.

extract *vt* sacar; (chem math) extraer; extractar; (obtain) obtener. *n chem* extracto, *m*; (excerpt) cita, *f*

extraction *n* saca, *f*; extracción, *f*; obtención, *f*

extradite *vt* entregar por extradición

extradition *n* extradición, *f*

extraneous *a* extraño; (irrelevant) ajeno (a)

extraordinarily *adv* extraordinariamente, singularmente

extraordinariness *n* lo extraordinario; singularidad, *f*; (queerness) rareza, *f*

extraordinary *a* extraordinario; singular; (queer) raro, excéntrico; (incredible) increíble

extraterrestrial *a Lat. Am.* extraterrenal

extravagance *n* (in spending) prodigalidad, *f*, derroche, *m*; (of dress, speech) extravagancia, *f*; (foolishness) disparate, *m*; (luxury) lujo, *m*

extravagant *a* extravagante; (queer) extraño, raro; (wasteful) pródigo; (of persons) gastador, manirroto; (of price) exorbitante; excesivo

extravagantly *adv* extravagantemente; de un modo extraño; pródigamente; profusamente; excesivamente

extreme *a* extremo. *n* extremo, *m*. **in e.,** extremamente, en extremo, en sumo grado. **to carry to extremes,** llevar a extremos; **E. Unction,** Extremaunción, *f*

extremely *adv* sumamente; *inf* muy

extremism *n* extremismo, *m*

extremist *a* and *n* extremista, *mf*

extremity *n* extremidad, *f*; (point) punta, *f*; necesidad, *f*; *pl* anat extremidades, *f pl*; (measures) medidas extremas, *f pl*

extricate *vt* desenredar; librar; sacar

extrication *n* liberación, *f*

extrinsic *a* extrínseco

extrovert *n psy* extravertido, *m*

exuberance *n* exuberancia, *f*

exuberant *a* exuberante

exudation *n* exudación, *f*

exude *vt* exudar; rezumar; sudar. *vi* exudar; rezumarse

exult *vi* exultar; alegrarse

exultant *a* exultante, triunfante

exultantly *adv* con exultación; triunfalmente

exultation *n* exultación, *f*; triunfo, *m*

eye *n* ojo, *m*; (sight) vista, *f*; (look) mirada, *f*; atención, *f*; (opinion) opinión, *f*, juicio, *m*; (of a needle, of cheese) ojo, *m*; (of a hook) corcheta, *f*; *bot* yema, *f*; (of a potato) grillo, *m*. *vt* ojear; fijar los ojos en; examinar, mirar detenidamente. **bright eyes,** ojos vivos, *m pl*. **prominent eyes,** ojos saltones, *m pl*. **He couldn't keep his eyes off Mary,** Se le fueron los ojos tras María. **as far as the eye can reach,** hasta donde alcanza la vista. **before one's eyes,** a la vista de uno, ante los ojos de uno. **in my (etc.) eyes,** *fig* según creo yo, en mi opinión. **in the twinkling of an eye,** en un abrir y cerrar de ojos. **with an eye to,** pensando en. **with my own eyes,** con mis propios ojos. **with the naked eye,** con la simple vista. **to keep an eye on,** vigilar. **to make eyes at,** guiñar el ojo; mirar con ojos de enamorado. **to have one's eyes opened,** *fig* caérsele la venda. **eye-bath,** ojera, *f*. **eye-opener,** revelación, sorpresa, *f*. **eye-pencil,** pincel para las cejas, *m*. **eye-piece,** objetivo, ocular, *m*. **eye-shade,** visera, *f*. **eye-tooth,** colmillo, *m*. **eye-witness,** testigo ocular, testigo de vista, testigo presencial, *mf*

eyeball *n* globo ocular, *m*

eyebrow *n* ceja, *f*

eye care atención de la vista, *f*

eyed *a* que tiene ojos; (in compounds) de ojos . . ., con ojos . . .; con los ojos; (of a needle) con el ojo . . . **She is a blue-eyed child,** Es una niña de ojos azules

eyeglass *n* lente, *m*

eyelash *n* pestaña, *f*

eyeless *a* sin ojos

eyelet *n* ojete, *m*

eyelid *n* párpado, *m*

eyesight *n* vista, *f*

eyewash *n* colirio, *m*; *inf* camelo, *m*. **That's all e.!** ¡Eso es un camelo!

eyrie *n* nido (of any bird of prey), nido de águila (eagle's) *m*

F

f *n* (letter) efe, *f*; *mus* fa, *m*. **f sharp,** fa sostenido, *m*

fa *n mus* fa, *m*

fable *n* fábula, leyenda, historia, *f*, apólogo, cuento, *m*; (untruth) invención, mentira, *f*

fabled *a* celebrado, famoso

fabric *n* obra, fábrica, *f*; estructura, construcción, *f*; (making) manufactura, *f*; (cloth) tejido, paño, *m*; textura, *f*

fabricate *vt* fabricar, construir; (invent) fingir, inventar

fabrication *n* fabricación, manufactura, *f*; construcción, *f*; (lie) invención, ficción, *f*

fabulist *n* fabulista, *mf*

fabulous *a* fabuloso

façade *n* fachada, frente, *f*

face *n* superficie, *f;* (of persons) cara, *f,* rostro, *m;* (look) semblante, aire, *m;* (of coins) anverso, *m;* (grimace) mueca, *f,* gesto, *m;* (dial) esfera, *f;* (of gems) faceta, *f;* (of a wall) paramento, *m;* (front) fachada, frente, *f;* (effrontery) cara dura, *f,* descaro, *m.* **in the f. of,** ante; en presencia de. *mil* **Left f.!** ¡Izquierda! **on the f. of it,** juzgando por las apariencias. **to bring f. to f.,** confrontar (con). **to laugh in a person's f.,** reírse a la cara (de). **to make a f.,** hacer muecas. **to my f.,** en mi cara, en mis barbas. **to put a good f. on,** *fig* poner (or hacer) buena cara a. **to set one's f. against,** oponerse resueltamente a. **to straighten one's f.,** componer el semblante. **to throw in one's f.,** *fig* dar en rostro, dar en cara. **to wash one's f.,** lavarse la cara. **f. card,** figura (de la baraja), *f.* **f.-cloth,** paño para lavar la cara, *m.* **f. downward,** boca abajo. **f. lift,** operación estética facial, *f.* **f. of the waters,** faz de las aguas, *f.* **f. powder,** polvos de arroz, *m pl.* **f. to f.,** cara a cara, de persona a persona; frente a frente. **f. value,** significado literal, *m;* *com* valor nominal, *m*

face *vt* hacia; confrontar, hacer cara (a); (of buildings, etc.) mirar a, caer a (or hacia); *fig* arrostrar, enfrentarse con; *sew* guarnecer, aforrar. *vi* estar orientado. **to f. the facts,** enfrentarse con la realidad. **to f. the music,** *fig* arrostrar las consecuencias. **to f. about,** volver la espalda; *mil* dar una media vuelta, cambiar de frente. **to f. up to,** *fig* hacer cara a

faced *a* con cara . . . , de cara . . . ; *sew* forrado (de). **to be two-f.,** *fig* ser de dos haces

facer *n* puñetazo en la cara, *m; fig* dificultad insuperable, *f,* problema muy grande, *m*

facet *n* faceta, *f*

facetious *a* chancero, chistoso, jocoso

facetiousness *n* jocosidad, festividad, *f*

facial *a* facial. **f. expression,** expresión de la cara, *f,* semblante, *m*

facile *a* (frivolous) ligero (e.g., a deduction or inference)

facilitate *vt* facilitar

facilitation *n* facilitación, *f*

facility *n* facilidad, *f;* habilidad, destreza, *f*

facing *n sew* vuelta, *f;* (of a building) paramento, *m;* (of lumber) chapa *f;* encaramiento, *m*

facsimile *n* facsímile, *m*

fact *n* (event) hecho, suceso, *m;* (datum) dato, *m;* realidad, verdad, *f.* **as a matter of f.,** en realidad. **in f.,** en efecto, en realidad. **I know as a f.,** Tengo por cierto. **The f. is . . . ,** La verdad es (que) . . . **the f. that,** el hecho de que

fact-finding informador (e.g. **send s.b. on a fact-finding mission,** enviar a fulano en misión informadora)

faction *n* facción, *f,* partido, bando, *m;* (tumult) alboroto, *m*

factional *a* partidario

factious *a* faccioso, sedicioso

factiousness *n* espíritu de facción, *m;* rebeldía, *f*

factitious *a* falso; artificial

factor *n* (fact) factor, elemento, *m;* consideración, *f; math* factor, *m; com* agente, factor, *m*

factory *n* fábrica, manufactura, *f;* taller, *m.* **F. Act,** ley de trabajadores industriales, *f.* **f. hand,** operario (-ia)

factotum *n* factótum, *m*

factual *a* basado en hechos, objetivo

faculty *n* facultad, *f;* (talent) habilidad, *f,* talento, *m;* (university division) facultad, *f;* (teachers as a group) claustro de profesores, claustro de profesorado, *m;* (authorization) privilegio, *m,* autoridad, *f*

fad *n* capricho, *m,* chifladura, *f,* dengue, *m*

faddiness *n* manías, *f pl,* excentricidad, *f*

faddist *n* chiflado (-da)

faddy *a* caprichoso, dengoso, difícil, excéntrico

fade *vi* (of plants) marchitarse, secarse; (of color) palidecer, descolorarse; (vanish) disiparse, desaparecer; (of persons) desmejorarse; (of stains) salir. *vt* descolorar. **to f. away,** desvanecer; (of persons) consumirse. **f.-out,** *n* (cinema) desaparecimiento gradual, *m*

faded *a* (of plants) seco, marchito, mustio; (of colors) descolorado, pálido; (of people) desmejorado

fadeless *a* de colores resistentes; eterno, no olvidado; siempre joven

fading *a* que palidece; (of flowers) medio marchito; (of light) mortecino, pálido; decadente. *n* desaparecimiento, *m,* marchitez, *f;* decadencia, *f*

fag *n inf* pitillo, *m.* **f.-end,** fin, *m;* restos, *m pl,* sobras, *f pl;* (of a cigarette) colilla, *f;* (*offensive*) maricón. *vi* trabajar mucho. *vt* fatigar mucho; hacer trabajar.

faggot *n* haz (or gavilla) de leña, *f*

faience *n* fayenza, *f*

fail *vi* faltar; fracasar, malograrse; no tener éxito, salir mal; (of strength) decaer, acabarse; (be short of) carecer (de); *com* hacer bancarrota, suspender pagos. *vt* abandonar; (disappoint) decepcionar, engañar; (in exams) suspender. **Do not f. to see her,** No dejes de verla. **He failed to do his duty,** Faltó a su deber

fail *n* **without f.,** sin falta

failing *n* falta, *f;* (shortcoming) vicio, flaco, *m,* debilidad, *f;* malogro, fracaso, *m;* decadencia, *f*

failure *n* fracaso, *m;* falta de éxito, *f;* (in exams) suspensión, *f;* (of power) no funcionamiento, *m;* omisión, *f,* descuido, *m; com* quiebra, bancarrota, *f;* (decay) decadencia, *f.* **on f. of,** al fracasar; bajo pena de

fain *a* deseoso, muy contento. **He was f. to . . . ,** Se sintió obligado a . . . ; Quería

faint *a* débil; (dim) indistinto, vago, borroso; (of colors) pálido, desmayado; (weak) lánguido, desfallecido; (slight) superficial, rudimentario. *vi* perder el sentido, desmayarse. *n* desmayo, *m.* **to be f. with hunger,** estar muerto de hambre. **to cause to f.,** hacer desmayar. **f.-hearted,** pusilánime, medroso. **f.-heartedness,** pusilanimidad, *f*

faintly *adv* débilmente; en voz débil; indistintamente

faintness *n* languidez, debilidad, *f;* (swoon) desmayo, *m;* lo indistinto; lo borroso.

fair *n* feria, *f;* (sale) mercado, *m;* (exhibition) exposición, *f*

fair *a* (beautiful) hermoso, lindo, bello; (of hair) rubio; (of skin) blanco; (clear, fresh) limpio, claro; (good) bueno; (favorable) favorable, propicio, próspero; (of weather) despejado, sereno; (just) imparcial; (straightforward) honrado, recto, justo; (passable) regular, mediano; (of writing) legible; (proper) conveniente. *adv* honradamente; (politely) cortésmente; exactamente. **by f. means,** por medios honrados. **It's not f.!** ¡No hay derecho! **to become f.,** (of weather) serenarse. **to give a f. trial,** juzgar imparcialmente; dar una buena oportunidad; *law* juzgar imparcialmente. **to make a f. copy,** poner en limpio. **f.-haired,** de pelo rubio, rubio. **f. one,** una beldad, *f.* **f. play,** *sport* juego limpio, *m;* proceder leal, *m.* **f.-skinned,** de tez blanca, rubio. **f.-weather,** buen tiempo, *m,* bonanza, *f.* **f.-weather friends,** amigos de los días prósperos, *m pl*

fairing *n Brit* regalo de feria, *m.* **to give fairings,** feriar

fairly *adv* (justly) con imparcialidad; (moderately) bastante; totalmente, enteramente. **f. good,** bastante bueno; regular

fairness *n* belleza, hermosura, *f;* (of skin) blancura, *f;* (justness) imparcialidad, *f;* (reasonableness) justicia, equidad, *f;* (of hair) color rubio, oro, *m*

fairway *n naut* canalizo, paso, *m;* (golf) terreno sin obstáculos, *m*

fairy *n* hada, *f,* duende, *m, a* de hada, de duendes; *fig* delicado. **f.-gold,** tesoro de duendes, *m;* **f.-light,** lucecillo, *m;* luminaria, *f.* **f.-like,** aduendado, como una hada. **f.-ring,** círculo mágico, *m.* **f.-tale,** cuento de hadas, *m;* patraña, *f,* cuento de viejas, *m*

fairyland *n* país de las hadas, *m*

faith *n* fe, *f;* confianza, *f;* (doctrine) creencia, religión, filosofía, *f;* (honor) palabra, *f.* **in good f.,** de buena fe.

to break f., faltar a la palabra dada. **f.-healing,** curanderismo, *m*

faithful *a* fiel, leal; (accurate) exacto; (trustworthy) veraz. **the f.,** los creyentes

faithfully *adv* fielmente, lealmente; (accurately) con exactitud. **Yours f.,** Queda de Vd. su att. s.s.

faithfulness *n* fidelidad, lealtad, *f*; (accuracy) exactitud, *f*

faithless *a* infiel, desleal, pérfido.

faithlessness *n* infidelidad, deslealtad, traición, *f*

fake *vt* imitar, falsificar. *n* imitación, falsificación, *f*. **to f. up,** inventar

Falangist *a* and *n* falangista *mf*

falcon *n* halcón, *m*. **f. gentle,** *orn* neblí, *m*

falconry *n* cetrería, *f*

Falkland Islands, the *pl* las Malvinas, *fpl*

fall *n* caída, *f*; (of temperature, mercury) baja, *f*; (of water) salto de agua, *m*, catarata, cascada, *f*; (in value) depreciación, *f*; (in price and Stock Exchange) baja, *f*; (descent) bajada, *f*; (autumn) otoño, *m*; (declivity) declinación, *f*, declive, desnivel, *m*; (ruin) ruina, *f*; destrucción, *f*; (of night, etc.) caída (de la noche), *f*; (of snow) nevada, *f*; (of rain) golpe, *m*; (*theat* of curtain) caída, bajada, *f*; (surrender) capitulación, rendición, *f*; (of earth) desprendimiento de tierras, *m*; (of the tide) reflujo, *m*

fall *vi* caer; (of mercury, temperature) bajar; (collapse) desplomarse, hundirse, derrumbarse; (die) caer muerto; (descend) descender; (*theat* of the curtain) bajar, caer; (of a river into the sea, etc.) desembocar, desaguar; (of hair, draperies) caer; (decrease) disminuir; (of spirits) ponerse triste, sentirse deprimido; (sin) caer; (come upon) sobrevenir; (of dusk, etc.) caer, llegar; (strike, touch) tocar; (as a share) tocar en suerte; (as a duty, responsibility) tocar, corresponder; (of seasons) caer en; (of words from the lips) caer se (los labios); (say) decir, pronunciar palabras; (of exclamations) escaparse; (become) venir a ser; (happen) suceder; (be) ser. **fallen upon evil days,** venido a menos. **His face fell,** Puso una cara de desengaño. **Christmas falls on a Thursday this year,** Navidad cae en jueves este año. **to let f.,** dejar caer. **to f. a-**(followed by verb) empezar a. **He fell a-crying,** Empezó a llorar. **to f. again,** volver a caer, recaer. **to f. among,** caer entre. **to f. astern,** quedarse atrás. **to f. away,** (leave) abandonar, dejar; (grow thin) enflaquecer; marchitarse; (crumble) desmoronarse. **to f. back,** retroceder, volver hacia atrás. **to f. back upon,** recurrir a; *mil* replegarse hacia. **to f. backward,** caer de espaldas, caer hacia atrás. **to f. behind,** quedarse atrás. **to f. down,** venirse a tierra; venirse abajo, dar consigo en el suelo, caer. **to f. due,** vencer. **to f. flat,** caer de bruces; (be unsuccessful) no tener éxito. **to f. in,** caer en; (collapse) desplomarse; *mil* alinearse; (expire) vencer. **to f. into,** caer en. **to f. in with,** tropezar con; reunirse con, juntarse con; (agree) convenir en; **to f. off,** caer de; (of leaves, etc.) desprenderse de, separarse de; (abandon) abandonar; (diminish) disminuir. **to f. on,** caer de (e.g. **to f. on one's back,** caer de espaldas); (of seasons) caer en; (attack) echarse encima de, atacar. **to f. out,** (of a window, etc.) caer por; (happen) acontecer, suceder; (quarrel) pelearse, reñir; *mil* romper filas. **to f. out with,** reñir con. **to f. over,** volcar, caer; (stumble) tropezar con. **to f. short,** faltar; carecer, ser deficiente; (fail) malograrse, no llegar a sus expectaciones; (of shooting) errar el tiro. **to f. through,** caer por; (fail) malograrse, fracasar. **to f. to,** empezar a, ponerse a; (be incumbent on) tocar a, corresponder a; (attack) atacar. **to f. under,** caer debajo; caer bajo; sucumbir, perecer; (incur) incurrir en, merecer. **to f. upon,** (attack) caer sobre, acometer; acaecer, tener lugar; (be incumbent) tocar a

fallacious *a* falaz, engañoso, ilusorio

fallaciousness *n* falacia, *f*, engaño, *m*

fallacy *n* error, *m*, ilusión, *f*

fallen *a* caído; arruinado; degradado. **f. angel,** ángel caído, *m*. **f. woman,** perdida, mujer caída, *f*

fallibility *n* falibilidad, *f*

fallible *a* falible

falling *a* que cae, cayente. *n* caída, *f*; (of mercury, temperature) baja, *f*; (crumbling) desmoronamiento, *m*; (collapse) hundimiento, derrumbamiento, *m*; (of tide) reflujo, *m*; (of waterlevel) bajada, *f*; (in value) depreciación, *f*; (of prices and Stock Exchange) baja, *f*; (diminishment) disminución, *f*; (in level of earth) declinación, *f*; (*com* expiry) vencimiento, *m*; (*theat* of curtain) bajada, caída, *f*. **f. away,** (crumbling) desmoronamiento, *m*; desprendimiento de tierras, *m*; (desertion) deserción, *f*, abandono, *m*. **f. back,** retirada, *f*, retroceso, *m*. **f. down,** caída, *f*; derrumbamiento, *m*. **f. due,** vencimiento, *m*. **f. in,** hundimiento, *m*; (crumbling) desmoronamiento, *m*. **f. off,** caída de, *f*; (disappearance) desaparición, *f*; (diminution) disminución, *f*; (deterioration) deterioración, *f*. **f. out,** caída por, *f*; disensión, *f*. **f. short,** falta, *f*; carácter inferior, *m*; frustración, *f*. **f. star,** estrella fugaz, *f*

fallout caída radiactiva, llovizna radiactiva, precipitación radiactiva, *f*

fallow *a* (of color) leonado; *agr* barbechado; descuidado. *n* barbecho, *m*. *vt* barbechar. **to leave f.,** dejar en barbecho. **f. deer,** corzo (-za)

false *a* incorrecto, erróneo, equivocado; falso; (unfounded) infundado; (disloyal) infiel, traidor, desleal; (not real) postizo; artificial; de imitación; *mus* desafinado; (pretended) fingido; engañoso, mentiroso. **to play a person f.,** traicionar (a). **f. bottom,** fondo doble, *m*. **f. claim,** pretensión infundada, *f*. **f. door,** surtida, *f*. **f.-hearted,** pérfido, desleal. **f. teeth,** dientes postizos, *m pl*, dentadura postiza, *f*

falsehood *n* mentira, *f*

falseness *n* falsedad, *f*; (disloyalty) duplicidad, perfidia, traición, *f*

falsetto *n* falsete, *m*, voz de cabeza, *f*

falsification *n* falsificación, *f*; (of texts) corrupción, *f*

falsifier *n* falsificador (-ra)

falsify *vt* falsear, falsificar; (disappoint) defraudar, frustrar, contrariar

falter *vi* (physically) titubear; (of speech) balbucir, tartamudear; (of action) vacilar. **to f. out,** balbucir; hablar con voz entrecortada; decir con vacilación

faltering *a* titubeante; (of speech) entrecortado; vacilante. *n* temblor, *m*; vacilación, *f*

falteringly *adv* (of speech) balbuciente, en una voz temblorosa; con dificultad, vacilantemente

fame *n* fama, *f*; reputación, *f*; (renown) celebridad, *f*, renombre, *m*. **of ill f.,** de mala fama

famed *a* reputado; renombrado, célebre, famoso

familiar *a* íntimo, familiar; afable, amistoso; (ill-bred) insolente, demasiado familiar; (usual) corriente, usual, común; conocido. *n* amigo (-ga) íntimo (-ma); *ecc* familiar, *m*; demonio familiar, *m*. **to be f. with,** (a subject) estar versado en, conocer muy bien; (a person) tratar con familiaridad. **to become f. with,** acostumbrarse a; familiarizarse con; (a person) hacerse íntimo de

familiarity *n* intimidad, familiaridad, confianza, *f*; (friendliness) afabilidad, *f*; (over-familiarity) insolencia, demasiada familiaridad, *f*; (with a subject) conocimiento (de), *m*, experiencia (de), *f*

familiarize *vt* familiarizar, acostumbrar, habituar. *vr* familiarizarse

familiarly *adv* familiarmente; amistosamente

family *n* familia, *f*; (lineage) linaje, abolengo, *m*; (*bot zool*) familia, *f*; (of languages) grupo, *m*. *a* de familia; familiar; casero. **f. doctor,** médico de cabecera, *m*. **f. life,** vida de familia, *f*; hogar, *m*. **f. man,** padre de familia, *m*. **f. name,** apellido, *m*. **f. seat,** casa solar, *f*. **f. tree,** árbol genealógico, *m*

family quarrel disputa de familia, *f*

famine *n* hambre, *f*; carestía, escasez, *f*

famish *vt* matar de hambre. *vi* morirse de hambre

famished *a* hambriento

famous *a* famoso, célebre, renombrado; insigne, distinguido; *inf* excelente

famously *adv inf* muy bien, excelentemente

fan *n* abanico, *m*; *agr* aventador, *m*; *mech* ventilador, *m*; (on a windmill) volante, *m*; (amateur) aficionado (-da); (admirer) admirador (-ra); *arch* abanico, *m*. *vt* abanicar; *agr* aventar; ventilar. **fan oneself,** hacerse viento. **tap with a f.,** abanicazo, golpecito con el abanico, *m*. **f.-belt,** *mech* correa de transmisión del ventilador, *f*. **f.-light,** tragaluz, *m*. **f. maker** or **seller,** abaniquero (-ra). **f.-shaped,** en abanico, abanicado, en forma de abanico

fanatic *a* and *n* fanático (-ca)

fanaticism *n* fanatismo, *m*

fanaticize *vt* fanatizar

fancied *a* imaginario

fancier *n* aficionado (-da); (of animals) criador (-ra)

fanciful *a* romántico, caprichoso; fantástico

fancifulness *n* extravagancia, *f*; romanticismo, *m*

fancy *n* fantasía, imaginación, *f*; (idea) idea, *f*, ensueño, *m*; (caprice) capricho, antojo, *m*; (liking) afecto, cariño, *m*; gusto, *m*, afición, *f*; (wish) deseo, *m*; (fantasy) quimera, *f*, *a* imaginario; elegante, ornado; *com* de capricho, de fantasía; fantástico, extravagante. *vt* imaginar, figurarse; (like) gustar de; aficionarse a; antojarse. **I have a f. for . . . ,** Se me antoja. . . . **Just f.!** ¡Toma! ¡Quia! ¡Parece mentira! **to take a f. to,** (things) tomar afición a; (people) tomar cariño (a). **f.-dress,** disfraz, *m*. **f.-dress ball,** baile de trajes, *m*

fancy goods *n pl* artículos suntuarios *m pl*

fane *n* templo, *m*

fanfare *n* tocata de trompetas, *f*

fang *n* colmillo, *m*; raíz de un diente, *f*

fanged *a* que tiene colmillos; (of teeth) acolmillado

fangless *a* sin colmillos

fanner *n* abanicador (-ra); *agr* aventador, *m*

fanning *n* abaniqueo, *m*; *agr* avienta, *f*

fantastic *a* fantástico; extravagante

fantastically *adv* fantásticamente; extravagantemente

fantasy *n* imaginación, *f*; fantasía, quimera, visión, *f*; creación imaginativa, *f*

far *adv* lejos; a lo lejos; (much, greatly) mucho, en alto grado; (very) muy; (mostly) en gran parte. *a* lejano, distante; (farther) ulterior. **as far as,** tan lejos como; (up to, until) hasta; en cuanto, por lo que, según que. (e.g. **As far as we know,** Por lo que nosotros sepamos. **As far as we are concerned,** En cuanto a nosotros toca). **by far,** con mucho. **from far and near,** de todas partes. **from far off,** desde lejos. **He found far into the night,** Leyó hasta las altas horas de la noche. **how far?** ¿a qué distancia? ¿hasta qué punto? ¿hasta dónde? **How far is it to . . . ?** ¿Qué distancia hay a . . . ? **in so far as,** en tanto que. **on the far side,** al lado opuesto; al otro extremo. **so far,** tan lejos; (till now) hasta ahora. **to go far,** ir lejos. **far away,** *a* distante, remoto, lejano; *fig* abstraído. *adv* muy lejos. **far beyond,** mucho más allá. **far-fetched,** increíble, improbable. **far-off,** *a* distante. *adv* a lo lejos, en lontananza. **far-reaching,** de gran alcance. **far-sighted,** sagaz, presciente, previsor. **far-sightedness,** sagacidad, previsión, *f*

farce *n* farsa, *f*. *vt cul* embutir, rellenar

farcical *a* burlesco, cómico, sainetesco; absurdo, grotesco, ridículo

fare *n* (price) pasaje, precio del billete, *m*; (traveler) viajero (-ra), pasajero (-ra); (food) comida, *f*. *vi* pasarlo (e.g. **to f. well,** pasarlo bien). **bill of f.,** menú, *m*. **full f.,** billete entero, *m*. **f. stage,** trayecto, *m*

farewell *n* despedida, *f*, adiós, *m*. *a* de despedida. *interj* ¡adiós! ¡quede Vd. con Dios! **to bid f. to,** despedirse de

farewell address *n* discurso de despedida *m*

farflung de gran alcance, extenso, vasto; (empire) dilatado

farina *n* harina (de cereales), *f*; *chem* fécula, *f*, almidón, *m*; *bot* polen, *m*

farm *n* granja, hacienda, quintería, finca, chacra, *f*, cortijo, *m*. *vt* cultivar, labrar (la tierra); (taxes) arrendar. *vi* ser granjero. **to f. out,** (taxes) dar en arriendo. **f. girl,** labradora, *f*. **f. house,** alquería, casa de labranza, granja, *f*. **f. laborer,** labriego, peón, *m*. **f. yard,** corral de una granja, *m*

farmer *n* granjero, hacendado, quintero, *m*, agrícola, *mf*; (small) colono, labrador, *m*; (of taxes) arrendatario, *m*

farmers' movement *Mexico* agrarismo *m*

farmhand gañán, mozo, mozo de granja, peón *m*

farming *n* labranza, *f*, cultivo, *m*; agricultura, labor agrícola, *f*; (of taxes) arriendo, *m*. *a* de labranza, labradoril; agrícola

faro *n* (card game) faraón, *m*

farouche *a* huraño, esquivo

farrago *n* fárrago, *m*, mezcla, *f*

farrier *n* herrador, *m*

farther *adv* más lejos; (beyond) más adelante; (besides) además. *a* ulterior; más distante. **at the f. end,** al otro extremo; en el fondo. **f. on,** más adelante; más allá

farthest *adv* más lejos. *a* más lejano, más distante; extremo

farthing *n* cuarto, *m*; *fig* ardite, maravedí, *m*. **He hasn't a brass f.,** No tiene dos maravedís

fasces *n pl* fasces, *f pl*

fascinate *vt* fascinar; encantar, hechizar, seducir

fascinating *a* fascinador; encantador, seduciente

fascination *n* fascinación, *f*; encanto, hechizo, *m*

Fascism *n* fascismo, *m*

Fascist *a* and *n* fascista *mf*

fashion *n* (form) forma, hechura, *f*; (way) modo, *m*; (custom) costumbre, *f*, uso, *m*; (vogue) moda, *f*; (high life) alta sociedad, *f*; (tone) buen tono, *m*. *vt* hacer, labrar; inventar. **in Spanish f.,** a la española, al uso de España. **the latest f.,** la última moda. **to be in f.,** estar de moda. **to go out of f.,** dejar de ser de moda, perder la popularidad. **f. book,** revista de modas, *f*. **f. plate,** figurín, *m*

fashionable *a* de moda; elegante; de buen tono. **to be f.,** estar en boga, ser de moda. **f. world,** mundo elegante, mundo de sociedad, *m*

fashionableness *n* buen tono, *m*; elegancia, *f*

fashionably *adv* a la moda, elegantemente

fashion show desfile de modas, *m*, exhibición de modas, *f*

fast *a* (firm) firme; (secure) seguro; (strong) fuerte; (fixed) fijo; (closed) cerrado; (of boats) amarrado; (tight) apretado; (of colors) estable; (of trains) rápido; (of sleep) profundo; (of friends) leal, seguro; (quick) rápido, veloz; (of a watch) adelantado; (dissipated) disoluto. *adv* firmemente, seguramente; (quickly) rápidamente; (of sleep) profundamente; (tightly) estrechamente, apretadamente; (of rain) (llover) a cántaros; (ceaselessly) continuamente; (often) frecuentemente; (entirely) completamente. **to be f.,** (clocks) adelantar. **to make f.,** *naut* amarrar, trincar. **f. asleep,** profundamente dormido. **f. color,** color estable, color sólido, *m*

fast *n* ayuno, *m*, *vi* ayunar. **to break one's f.,** romper el ayuno. **f.-day,** día de ayuno, día de vigilia, *m*

fasten *vt* (tie) atar; (fix) fijar; sujetar; (stick) pegar; (a door) cerrar; (bolt) echar el cerrojo; *naut* trincar; (together) juntar, unir; (with buttons, hooks, etc.) abrochar; (on, upon) fijar en; *fig* imputar. *vi* fijarse; pegarse; (upon) agarrarse a, asir. **to f. one's eyes on,** fijar los ojos en. **to f. up,** cerrar; atar; (nail) clavar

fastener *n* (bolt) pasador, *m*; (for bags, clothes, etc.) cierre, *m*; (buckle) hebilla, *f*; (of a coat, etc.) tiador, *m*; (of a book, file) sujetador, *m*; (lock) cerrojo, *m*. **paper-f.,** sujetador de papeles, *m*. **patent-f.,** botón automático, *m*

fastening *n* atadura, *f*; sujeción, *f*, afianzamiento, *m*; (together) unión, *f*; (of a garment) brochadura, *f*; (of a handbag) cierre, *m*

fastidious *a* dengoso, melindroso, desdeñoso; (sensitive) sensitivo, delicado; (critical) discerniente, crítico

fastidiously *adv* melindrosamente

fastidiousness *n* dengues, melindres, *m pl*, nimiedad, *f*, desdén, *m*; sensibilidad, delicadeza, *f*; sentido crítico, *m*

fasting *n* ayuno, *m*. *a* and *part* de ayuno; en ayunas

fastness *n* firmeza, solidez, *f*; (stronghold) fortaleza, *f*; (retreat) refugio, *m*; (speed) velocidad, rapidez, *f*; (dissipation) disipación, *f*, libertinaje, *m*

fat *a* (stout) gordo, grueso; mantecoso, graso, seboso; (greasy) grasiento; (rich) fértil, pingüe; (productive) lucrativo. *n* (stoutness) gordura, *f*; (for cooking) manteca, *f*; (lard) lardo, *m*; (of animal or meat) grasa, *f*; sebo, saín, *m*; *fig* riqueza, *f*; *fig* fertilidad, *f*. **to grow fat,** engordarse, ponerse grueso

fatal *a* fatal, mortal; funesto

fatalism *n* fatalismo, *m*

fatalist *n* fatalista, *mf*

fatalistic *a* fatalista

fatality *n* fatalidad, *f*; infortunio, *m*, calamidad, *f*; muerte, *f*

fatally *adv* mortalmente, fatalmente; inevitablemente

fate *n* destino, sino, hado, *m*, providencia, *f*; fortuna, suerte, *f*; destrucción, ruina, *f*; muerte, *f*. **the Three Fates,** las Parcas

fated *a* fatal, destinado; predestinado

fateful *a* decisivo, fatal; aciago, ominoso

father *n* padre, *m*. *vt* prohijar, adoptar; (on or upon) atribuir (a), imputar (a). **Eternal F.,** Padre Eterno, *m*. **Holy F.,** Padre Santo, *m*. **indulgent f.,** padre indulgente, padrazo, *m*. **Like f. like son,** De tal palo tal astilla. **f. confessor,** *ecc* director espiritual, *m*. **f.-in-law,** suegro, *m*

fatherhood *n* paternidad, *f*

fatherland *n* patria, madre patria, *f*

fatherless *a* sin padre, huérfano de padre

fatherliness *n* amor paternal, *m*; sentimiento paternal, *m*

fatherly *a* paternal, de padre

fathom *n* *naut* braza, *f*. *vt* sondear; *fig* profundizar, tantear; (a mystery) desentrañar

fathomless *a* insondable; *fig* incomprensible, impenetrable

fatigue *n* fatiga, *f*, cansancio, *m*; *mil* faena, *f*; *mech* pérdida de resistencia, *f*. *vt* fatigar, cansar. **to be fatigued,** estar cansado, cansarse, fatigarse. **f. party,** *mil* pelotón de castigo, *m*

fatiguing *a* fatigoso

fatness *n* (stoutness) gordura, carnosidad, *f*; grasa, *f*, gordo, *m*; (richness) fertilidad, *f*; lo lucrativo

fatten *vt* engordar; (animals) cebar, sainar; (land) abonar, fertilizar. *vi* ponerse grueso, echar carnes

fatty *a* untoso, grasiento; *chem* graso. **f. acid,** ácido graso, *m*. **f. degeneration,** degeneración grasienta, *f*

fatuity *n* fatuidad, necedad, *f*

fatuous *a* fatuo, necio, lelo

faucet *n* canilla, llave, *f*, grifo, *m*

fault *n* defecto, *m*, imperfección, *f*; (blame) culpa, *f*; (mistake) falta, *f*, error, *m*; (in cloth) canilla, barra, *f*; *geol* falla, quiebra, *f*; *elec* avería, *f*; *sport* falta, *f*, *vi sport* cometer una falta. **to a f.,** excesivamente. **to be at f.,** (to blame) tener la culpa; (mistaken) estar equivocado; (puzzled) estar perplejo; (of dogs) perder el rastro. **to find f.,** tachar, culpar, criticar. **Whose f. is it?** ¿Quién tiene la culpa?

faultfinder *n* criticón (-ona)

faultiness *n* defectuosidad, imperfección, *f*

faultless *a* sin faltas; perfecto, sin tacha; impecable

faulty *a* defectuoso, imperfecto

fauna *n* fauna, *f*

favor *n* favor, *m*; (protection) amistad, protección, *f*, amparo, *m*; (permission) permiso, *m*, licencia, *f*; (kindness) merced, gracia, *f*; (gift) obsequio, *m*; (favoritism) favoritismo, *m*, preferencia, *f*; (benefit) beneficio, *m*; (badge) colores, *m pl*; *com* grata, atenta, *f*. *vt* favorecer, apoyar; mirar con favor, mostrar parcialidad (hacia);

(suit) favorecer; (be advantageous) ser propicio (a); (contribute to) contribuir a, ayudar; (resemble) parecerse (a). **Circumstances f. the idea,** Las circunstancias son propicias a la idea, Las circunstancias militan en pro de la idea. **I f. the teaching of modern languages,** Soy partidario de la enseñanza de lenguas vivas. **in f. of,** a favor de, en pro de. **in the f. of,** en el favor de. **out of f.,** fuera de favor; (not fashionable) fuera de moda. **to count on the f. of,** tener de su parte (a), contar con el apoyo de. **to do a f.,** hacer un favor. **to enjoy the f. of,** gozar del favor de. **to fall out of f.,** caer en desgracia; (go out of fashion) pasar de moda. **to grow in f.,** aumentar en favor

favorable *a* favorable; propicio, próspero

favorableness *n* lo favorable; lo propicio; benignidad, benevolencia, *f*

favored *a* favorecido; predilecto; (in compounds) parecido, encarado

favoring *a* favorecedor, propicio

favorite *a* favorito; predilecto, preferido. *n* favorito (-ta). **court f.,** valido, privado, *m*; (mistress) querida (de un rey), *f*; (lover) amante (de una reina), *m*. **to be a f.,** ser favorito

favoritism *n* favoritismo, *m*

fawn *n* *zool* cervato, *m*; (color) color de cervato, color de ante, *m*. *a* de color de cervato, anteado, pardo; (of animals) rucio, pardo. *vt* and *vi* parir la cierva. *vi* acariciar; (on, upon) adular, lisonjear

fawning *a* adulación, *Lat. Am.* adulonería *f*, a adulador, lisonjero, *Lat. Am. also* incondicional, *Mexico* lambioche

fear *n* miedo, temor, *m*, terror *m*, espanto *f*; (apprehension) ansiedad, aprensión, *f*, recelo, *m*; (respect) veneración, *f*. *vt* temer; recelar; (respect) reverenciar. *vi* tener miedo; estar receloso, estar con cuidado. **for f. of,** por miedo de. **for f. that,** por temor de que, por miedo de que. **from f.,** por miedo. **There is no f. of . . .,** No hay miedo de (que) . . .

fearer *n* temedor (-ra), el (la) que teme

fearful *a* miedoso, aprensivo, receloso; (cowardly) tímido, pusilánime; (terrible) horrible, espantoso, pavoroso; *inf* tremendo, enorme

fearfully *adv* con miedo; tímidamente; (terribly) horriblemente; *inf* enormemente

fearfulness *n* temor, miedo, *m*; (horribleness) lo horrible

fearless *a* sin miedo, intrépido, audaz

fearlessness *n* intrepidez, valentía, *f*

fearsome *a* temible, horrible, espantoso

feasibility *n* practicabilidad, posibilidad, *f*

feasible *a* factible, hacedero, practicable, ejecutable

feast *n* *ecc* fiesta, *f*; banquete, *m*; *fig* abundancia, *f*, *vi* regalarse. *vt* festejar, agasajar; (delight) recrear, deleitar. **immovable f.,** *ecc* fiesta fija, *f*. **movable f.,** fiesta movible, *f*. **f. day,** día de fiesta, *m*, festividad, *f*

feasting *n* banquetes, *m pl*; fiestas, *f pl*

feat *n* hazaña, proeza, *f*, hecho, *m*

feather *n* pluma, *f*; (of the tail) pena, *f*; *pl* **feathers,** plumaje, *m*; plumas, *f pl*. *vt* emplumar; adornar con plumas; (rowing) poner casi horizontal la pala del remo. **to f. one's nest,** *inf* hacer su agosto. **f.-bed,** plumón, colchón de plumas, *m*. **f.-brained,** casquivano, alocado, aturdido. **f.-duster,** plumero, *m*. **f.-stitch,** *sew* diente de perro, *m*. **f. weight,** (boxing) peso pluma, *m*

feathered *a* plumado, plumoso; adornado con plumas; (winged) alado

feathery *a* plumoso; como plumas

feature *n* rasgo, *m*, característica, *f*; (cinema) número de programa, *m*; *pl* **features** (of the face) facciones, *f pl*. *vt* dar importancia (a); (cinema) presentar. **f. film,** documentaria, *f*

febrile *a* febril

February *n* febrero, *m*

fecal *a* fecal

feces *n* heces, *f pl*; excremento, *m*

fecund *a* fecundo, fértil

fecundate *vt* fecundar

fecundity *n* fecundidad, fertilidad, *f*

federal *a* federal, federalista

federalism *n* federalismo, *m*

federalist *n* federalista, federal, *mf*

federate *vt* confederar. *vi* confederarse. *a* confederado

federation *n* confederación, federación, *f*; liga, unión, asociación, *f*

fed up *a Argentina, Chile* incomódo

fee *n* (feudal law) feudo, *m*; (homage) homenaje, *m*; (duty) derecho, *m*; (professional) honorario, estipendio, *m*; (to a servant) gratificación, *f*; (entrance, university, etc.) cuota, *f*; (payment) paga, *f*

feeble *a* débil; lánguido; enfermizo; (of light, etc.) tenue; *fig* flojo. **to grow f.,** debilitarse; disminuir. **f.-minded,** anormal

feebleness *n* debilidad, *f*; *fig* flojedad, *f*

feebly *adv* débilmente; lánguidamente

feed *n* alimento, *m*; (meal) comida, *f*; (of animals) pienso, forraje, *m*; *mech* alimentación, *f*. *vt* alimentar; dar de comer (a); (animals) cebar; *mech* alimentar; mantener; *fig* nutrir. *vi* comer, alimentarse; (graze) pastar. **to be fed up,** *inf* estar hasta la coronilla, estar harto. **to f. on,** alimentarse de; *fig* nutrirse de. **f. pipe,** tubo de alimentación, *m*

feedback retrocomunicación, *f*

feeder *n* el, *m*, (*f*, la) que da de comer a; (eater) comedor (-ra); (of a river) tributario, afluente, *m*; (bib) babero, *m*; *mech* alimentador, *m*; (cup for invalids) pistero, *m*

feeding *n* alimentación, *f*, *a* alimenticio, de alimentación. **f.-bottle,** biberón, *m*. **f.-cup,** pistero, *m*. **f.-trough,** pesebre, *m*

feel *n* (touch) tacto, *m*; (feeling) sensación, *f*; (instinct) instinto, *m*, percepción innata, *f*

feel *vt* (touch) tocar, tentar, palpar; (experience) sentir, experimentar; (understand) comprender; (believe) creer; (be conscious of) estar consciente de; (the pulse) tomar; examinar. *vi* sentir, ser sensible; sentirse, encontrarse; (to the touch) ser . . . al tacto, estar. **How do you f.?** ¿Cómo se siente Vd.? **I f. cold,** Tengo frío. **I f. for you,** Lo siento en el alma; Estoy muy consciente de ello. **I f. strongly that . . .,** Estoy convencido de que . . . **I f. that it is a difficult question,** Me parece una cuestión difícil. **It feels like rain,** Creo que va a llover. **to f. at home,** sentirse a sus anchas, sentirse como en su casa. **to f. hungry (thirsty),** tener hambre (sed). **to f. one's way,** andar a tientas; *fig* medir el terreno. **to f. soft,** ser blando al tacto. **to make itself felt,** hacerse sentir. **Your hands f. cold,** Tus manos están frías

feeler *n* (of insects) palpo, *m*, antena, *f*; tentáculo, *m*; *fig* tentativa, *f*, balón de ensayo, *m*

feeling *n* (touch) tacto, *m*; (sensation) sensación, *f*; (sentiment) sentimiento, *m*; emoción, *f*; (premonition) corazonada, intuición, premonición, *f*; (tenderness) ternura, *f*; (perception) sensibilidad, percepción, *f*; (passion) pasión, *f*; (belief) opinión, *f*, sentir, *m*. *a* sensible; tierno; (compassionate) compasivo; apasionado; (moving) conmovedor

feelingly *adv* con emoción; (strongly) enérgicamente, vivamente; (understandingly) comprensivamente

feign *vt* fingir; (invent) inventar, imaginar; simular; (allege) pretextar; (dissemble) disimular. *vi* disimular

feint *n* artificio, engaño, *m*; (in fencing) treta, finta, *f*. *vi* hacer finta

feldspar *n min* feldespato, *m*

felicitate *vt* felicitar, congratular, dar el parabién (a)

felicitation *n* felicitación, *f*, parabién, *m*

felicitous *a* feliz, dichoso, afortunado; (of phrases, etc.) feliz, acertado; oportuno

felicity *n* felicidad, dicha, *f*

feline *a* felino, gatuno, de gato. *n* felino, *m*

fell *n* (skin) piel, *f*; (upland) altura, cuesta de montaña, *f*. *a* cruel, feroz; (unhappy) aciago, funesto. *vt* talar, cortar; (knock down) derribar; *sew* sobrecoser

feller *n* talador, leñador, *m*

felling *n* corta, tala, *f*

fellow *n* compañero (-ra); (equal) igual, *mf*; (in crime) cómplice, *mf*; (man) hombre, *m*; (boy, youth) chico, *m*; (colleague) colega, *m*; (of a society) miembro, *m*; (of a pair of objects) pareja, *f*; *inf* tipo, chico, *m*. **He's a good f.,** Es un buen chico. **How are you, old f.?** ¡Hombre! ¿Cómo estás? **f.-citizen,** conciudadano (-na). **f.-countryman,** compatriota, *m*; paisano (-na). **f.-creature,** semejante, *mf* **f.-feeling,** simpatía, comprensión mutua, *f*. **f.-member,** compañero (-ra); colega, *m*. **f.-passenger,** compañero (-ra) de viaje. **f.-prisoner,** compañero (-ra) de prisión. **f.-student,** condiscípulo (-la). **f.-worker,** compañero (-ra) de trabajo; (collaborator) colaborador (-ra); (colleague) colega, *m*

fellowship *n* coparticipación, *f*; (companionship) compañerismo, *m*; (brotherhood) comunidad, confraternidad, *f*; (society) asociación, *f*; (grant) beca, *f*; (of a university) colegiatura, *f*

felon *n* reo, criminal, *mf*; felón (-ona); malvado (-da); (swelling) panadizo, *m*

felonious *a* criminal; pérfido, traidor

felony *n* felonía, *f*

felt *n* fieltro, *m*. **a f. hat,** un sombrero de fieltro

female *n* hembra, *f*, *a* femenino. (**f.** is often rendered in Sp. by the feminine ending of the noun, e.g. **a f. cat,** una gata; **a f. friend,** una amiga.) **This is a f. animal,** Este animal es una hembra. **f. screw,** hembra de tornillo, tuerca, *f*

feminine *a* femenino; mujeril, afeminado. **in the f. gender,** en el género femenino

feminism *n* feminismo, *m*

feminist *n* feminista, *mf*

feministic *a* feminista

femur *n anat* fémur, *m*

fen *n* marjal, pantano, *m*

fence *n* cerca, *f*; (of stakes) estacada, palizada, *f*; (hedge) seto, *m*; (fencing) esgrima, *f*; *mech* guía, *f*; *inf* comprador (-ra) de efectos robados. *vi* esgrimir; *fig* defenderse; *inf* recibir efectos robados. *vt* cercar; estacar; *fig* defender; proteger. **to sit on the f.,** *fig* estar a ver venir

fencer *n* esgrimidor, *m*

fencing *n* esgrima, *f*; palizada, empalizada, *f*. **f. mask,** careta, *f*. **f. master,** maestro de esgrima, maestro de armas, *m*. **f. match,** asalto de esgrima, *m*

fencesitter *n* bailarín de la cuerda flaja, *m*

fend (off) *vt* parar; defenderse de, guardarse de. *vi* (for) mantener, cuidar de. **to f. for oneself,** ganarse la vida; defenderse

fender *n* (round hearth) guardafuegos, *m*; *naut* espolón, *m*, defensas, *f pl*; *aut* parachoques, *m*

fennel *n bot* hinojo, *m*

ferment *n* fermento, *m*; fermentación, *f*; *fig* agitación, conmoción, efervescencia *f*. *vt* hacer fermentar; *fig* agitar, excitar. *vi* fermentar, estar en fermentación; *fig* hervirse, agitarse, excitarse

fermentation *n* fermentación, *f*

fern *n* helecho, *m*

ferny *a* cubierto de helechos

ferocious *a* feroz, bravo, salvaje

ferocity *n* ferocidad, braveza, fiereza, *f*

ferreous *a* férreo

ferret *n zool* hurón (-ona); **to f. out,** cazar con hurones; (discover) husmear, descubrir

Ferris wheel *n* estrella giratoria, gran rueda, novia, rueda de feria, *f*

ferroconcrete *n* hormigón armado, *m*

ferrous *a* ferroso

ferruginous *a* ferruginoso; aherrumbrado, rojizo

ferrule *n* herrete, regatón, *m*, contera, *f*; garrucha de tornillos, *f*

ferry *n* barca de transporte, *f*; barca de pasaje, *f*, transbordador, *m*. *vt* transportar de una a otra orilla, llevar en barca. *vi* cruzar un río en barca. **ferry across** *vt* transbordar. **F.-Command,** servicio de entrega y transporte de aeroplanos, *m*

ferryman n barquero, m
fertile a fértil, fecundo; (rich) pingüe; fig prolífico, abundante
Fertile Crescent, the el Creciente Fértil m
fertility n fertilidad, fecundidad, f
fertilization n biol fecundación, f; agr fertilización, f, abono, m
fertilize vt biol fecundar; agr fertilizar, abonar
fertilizer n abono, m
ferule n palmatoria, palmeta, férula, f
fervent a ardiente; fervoroso, intenso; (enthusiastic) entusiasta, apasionado
fervently adv con fervor, con vehemencia
fervor n ardor, fervor, m, pasión, f; (enthusiasm) entusiasmo, celo, m; vehemencia, f
festal a de fiesta; alegre, festivo, regocijado
fester vi ulcerarse, enconarse; fig inflamarse, amargarse. vt ulcerar
festival a de fiesta. n festividad, f; ecc fiesta, f; (musical, etc.) festival, m
festive a de fiesta; festivo, alegre
festivity n festividad, fiesta, f; (merriment) alegría, f, júbilo, m
festoon n festón, m, guirnalda, f. vt festonear
festschrift n libro de homenaje, libro jubilar, m
fetal a fetal
fetch vt traer; ir a buscar; ir por; llevar; (conduct) conducir; (of tears) hacer derramar lágrimas, hacer saltársele las lágrimas; (blood) hacer correr la sangre; (produce, draw) sacar; (a blow, a sigh) dar; (acquire) conseguir; (charm) fascinar; (of price) venderse por. **to go and f.,** ir a buscar. **to f. and carry,** vt (news) divulgar, publicar. vi estar ocupado en oficios humildes, trajinar. **to f. away,** llevarse; ir a buscar; venir a buscar. **to f. back,** devolver; (of persons) traer (a casa, etc.); traer otra vez. **to f. down,** bajar, llevar abajo; hacer bajar. **to f. in,** hacer entrar; (place inside) poner adentro; (persons and things) llevar adentro. **to f. out,** hacer salir; (bring out things) sacar; (put out) poner afuera; (an idea, etc.) sacar a relucir. **to f. up,** (a parcel, etc.) subir; (a person) hacer subir; llevar arriba
fete n fiesta, f
fetid a fétido, hediondo
fetidness n fetidez, f, hedor, m
fetish n fetiche, m
fetishism n fetichismo, m
fetter n grillete, m; pl **fetters,** grillos, m pl, cadenas, f pl; prisión, cárcel, f. vt encadenar, atar
fettle n condición, f, estado, m
fetus n feto, m
feud n enemistad, riña, f; (feudal law) feudo, m
feudal a feudal. **f. lord,** señor feudal, señor de horca y cuchillo, m
feudalism n feudalismo, m
feudatory a and n feudatario (-ia)
fever n fiebre, f; calentura, f; (enthusiasm) pasión, afición, f. **to be in a f.,** tener fiebre; (agitated) estar muy agitado. **to be in a f. to,** estar muy impaciente de. **puerperal f.,** fiebre puerperal, f. **tertian f.,** fiebre terciana, f. **yellow f.,** fiebre amarilla, f
feverish a febril; fig ardiente, febril, vehemente. **to grow f.,** empezar a tener fiebre, acalenturarse
feverishness n calentura, f; (impatience) impaciencia, f
few a and n pocos, m pl; pocas, f pl; algunos, m pl; algunas, f pl; (few in number) número pequeño (de), m. **a good f.,** bastantes, mf pl. **not a f.,** no pocos, m pl, (pocas, f pl). **the f.,** la minoría, f. **f. and far between,** raramente, en raras ocasiones; pocos y contados
fewer a comp menos. **The f. the better,** Cuantos menos mejor
fewest a sup (el) menos, m; el menor número (de), m; (el) menos posible de, m
fewness n corto número, m
fiancé(e) n novio (-ia); desposado (-da), prometido (-da)
fiasco n fiasco, mal éxito, fracaso, malogro, m

fiat n fiat, mandato, m, orden, f
fib n mentirilla, f, Peru bacho m vt, decir mentirillas, mentir
fibber n embustero (-ra), mentiroso (-sa)
fiber n fibra, f; filamento, m, hebra, f; (of grass, etc.) brizna, f; fig naturaleza, f
fibroid a fibroso. n fibroma, m
fibrous a fibroso
fibula n anat peroné, m
fichu n pañoleta, f, fichú, m
fickle a inconstante; mudable; (of persons) liviano, ligero, voluble
fickleness n inconstancia, f; mudanza, f; liviandad, f, ligereza, veleidad, volubilidad, f
fiction n ficción, f; invención, f; literatura narrativa, f; novelas, f pl. **legal f.,** ficción legal, ficción de derecho, f
fictitious a ficticio; imaginario; fingido
fictitiousness n carácter ficticio, m; falsedad, f
fiddle n violín, m. vt tocar . . . en el violín. vi tocar el violín; (fidget) jugar; perder el tiempo. **to play second f.,** tocar el segundo violín; fig ser plato de segunda mesa
fiddler n violinista, mf
fiddling a insignificante, trivial, frívolo
fidelity n fidelidad, f
fidget vi estar nervioso, estar inquieto; impacientarse; trajinar; (with) jugar con. vt molestar; impacientar
fidgetiness n inquietud, nerviosidad, f
fidgety a inquieto, nervioso. **to be f.,** tener hormiguillo
fiduciary a fiduciario. n fideicomisario (-ia)
fief n feudo, m
field n campo, m; (meadow) prado, m, pradera, f; (sown field) sembrado, m; (phys, her) campo, m; (of ice) banco, m; min yacimiento, m; (background) fondo, m; (campaign) campaña, f; (battle) batalla, lucha, f; (space) espacio, m; (of knowledge, etc.) especialidad, esfera, f; (hunting) caza, f; sport campo, m; (competitors) todos los competidores en una carrera, etc.; (horses in a race) el campo. a campal, pradeño; de campo; de los campos. vt sport parar y devolver la pelota. **in the f.,** mil en el campo de batalla, en campaña. **magnetic f.,** campo magnético, m. **to take the f.,** entrar en campaña. **f.-artillery,** artillería ligera, artillería montada, f. **f.-day,** (holiday) día de asueto, m; (day out) día en el campo, m; mil día de maniobras, m. **f.-glasses,** anteojos, gemelos, m pl. **f.-hospital,** hospital de sangre, m; ambulancia fija, f. **f.-kitchen,** cocina de campaña, f. **f.-marshal,** capitán general de ejército, m. **f.-mouse,** ratón silvestre, m. **f. of battle,** campo de batalla, m. **f. of vision,** campo visual, m. **f.-telegraph,** telégrafo de campaña, m
fielder n (baseball) jardinero (-ra)
field work prácticas de campo, f pl
fiend n diablo, demonio, m; malvado (-da); (addict) adicto (-ta). **morphia f.,** morfinómano (-ma)
fiendish a diabólico, infernal; malvado, cruel, malévolo
fiendishness n perversidad, crueldad, f
fierce a salvaje, feroz, cruel; (of the elements) violento, furioso; (intense) intenso, vehemente
fiercely adv ferozmente; violentamente, con furia; intensamente, con vehemencia
fierceness n ferocidad, fiereza, f; violencia, furia, f; intensidad, vehemencia, f
fieriness n ardor, m; (flames) las llamas, f pl; (redness) rojez, f; (irritability) ferocidad, irritabilidad, f; (vehemence) pasión, vehemencia, f; (of horses) fogosidad, f
fiery a ardiente; (red) rojo; (irritable) feroz, colérico, irritable; (vehement) apasionado, vehemente; (of horses) fogoso
fife n mus pífano, pito, m
fifteen a and n quince m.; (of age) quince años, m pl
fifteenth a and n décimoquinto m.; (part) quinzavo, m, décimaquinta parte, f; (of the month) (el) quince, m; (of monarchs) quince; mus quincena, f
fifth a quinto; (of monarchs) quinto; (of the month)

(el) cinco. *n* quinto, *m*; (part) quinto, *m*, quinta parte, *f*; *mus* quinta, *f*, **Charles V,** Carlos quinto. **f. column,** quinta columna, *f*

fifthly *adv* en quinto lugar

fiftieth *a* quincuagésimo; (part) quincuagésima parte, *f*, cincuentavo, *m*

fifty *a* and *n* cincuenta *m*.; (of age) cincuenta años, *m pl*

fiftyfold *a* and *adv* cincuenta veces

fig *n* higo, *m*; (tree) higuera, *f*; *fig* bledo, ardite, *m*. **green fig,** higo, *m*, breva, *f*. **I don't care a fig,** No se me da un higo. **to be not worth a fig,** no valer un ardite.

fig-leaf, hoja de higuera, *f*; *fig* hoja de parra, *f*

fight *n* lucha, pelea, *f*, combate, *m*; batalla, *f*; (struggle) lucha, *f*; (quarrel) riña, pelea, *Argentina* arenga *f*; (conflict) conflicto, *m*; (valor) coraje, brío, *m*. **hand-to-hand** *f*, cachetina, *f*. **in fair f.,** en buena lid. **to have a f.,** tener una pelea. **to show f.,** mostrarse agresivo

fight *vt* luchar contra, batirse con; (a battle) dar (batalla); (oppose) oponer, *Mexico* desafiar; (defend) defender, pelear por; hacer batirse. *vi* luchar, batirse, pelear; (with words) disputar; (struggle) luchar; (make war) hacer la guerra; (in a tournament) tornear. **to f. one's way,** abrirse paso con las armas. **to f. against,** luchar contra. **to f. off,** librarse de; sacudirse. **to f. with,** luchar con; pelear con; reñir con

fighter *n* luchador (-ra); combatiente, *m*; guerrero, *m*; duelista, *m*; (boxer) boxeador, *m*; *aer* (avión de) caza, *m*. **night f.,** *aer* (avión de) caza nocturno, *m*. **f.-bomber,** *aer* caza bombardero, *m*. **F. Command,** *aer* servicio de aviones de caza, *m*

fighting *n* lucha, *f*, combate, *m*; el pelear; (boxing) boxeo, *m*, *a* combatiente; (bellicose) agresivo, belicoso. **f.-man,** combatiente, guerrero, *m*

figment *n* ficción, invención, *f*

figurative *a* figurado, metafórico; figurativo; simbólico

figuratively *adv* en sentido figurativo; metafóricamente

figure *n* figura, *f*; forma, *f*; (statue) estatua, figura, *f*; (of a person) silueta, *f*; talle, *m*; (number) cifra, *f*, número, *m*; (quantity) cantidad, *f*; (price) precio, *m*; *geom, gram, dance* (skating) figura, *f*; (appearance) presencia, *f*, aire, *m*; (picture) imagen, *m*; (on fabric) diseño, *m*; *mus* cifra, *f*; *pl* **figures,** aritmética, *f*, matemáticas, *f pl*. *vt* figurar; (imagine) figurarse, imaginar; *mus* cifrar. *vi* figurar, hacer un papel; (calculate) calcular, hacer cuentas. **to f. out,** calcular; (a problem, etc.) resolver. **a fine f. of a woman,** *inf* una real hembra. **lay f.,** maniquí, *m*. **to be good at figures,** estar fuerte en matemáticas. **to cut a f.,** *fig* hacer figura. **to have a good f.,** tener buen talle. **f. of speech,** figura retórica, figura de dicción *f*; (manner of speaking) metáfora *f*. **f. dance,** baile de figuras, *m*, contradanza, *f*. **f.-head,** *naut* mascarón, *m*, (or figura, *f*) de proa; *fig* figura decorativa, *f*

figured *a* estampado, con diseños, labrado

figurine *n* figurilla, *f*

filament *n* filamento, *m*; hebra, *f*

filbert *n* avellana, *f*; (tree) avellano, *m*

filch *vt* sisar, ratear

filching *n* sisa, *f*

file *n* (line) fila, hilera, sarta, línea, *f*; *mil* fila, *f*; (tool) lima, *f*; (rasp) escofina, *f*; (list) lista, *f*, catálogo, *m*; (for documents) carpeta, *f*, cartapacio, *f*; (bundle of papers) legajo, *m*; (for bills, letters, etc.) clasificador, *m*; archivo, *m*; (in an archives) expediente *m*. **in a f.,** en fila; en cola

file *vt* hacer marchar en fila; (smooth) limar; (literary work) pulir; (classify) clasificar; (note particulars) fichar; (keep) guardar; (a petition, etc.) presentar, registrar. *vi* marchar en fila. **to f. in,** entrar en fila. **to f. off,** desfilar. **to file a brief,** presentar un escrito. **to f. letters,** clasificar correspondencia. **to f. past,** *mil* desfilar

filial *a* filial

filiation *n* filiación, *f*

filibuster *n* filibustero, pirata, *m*

filigree *n* filigrana, *f*, *a* afiligranado

filing *n* (with a tool) limadura, *f*; clasificación, *f*; (of a

petition, etc.) presentación, *f*, registro, *m*; *pl* **filings,** limaduras, *f pl*, retales, *m pl*. **f.-cabinet,** fichero, *m*. **f.-card,** ficha, *f*

fill *vt* llenar; (stuff) rellenar; (appoint to a post) proveer; (occupy a post) desempeñar; (imbue) henchir; (saturate) saturar; (occupy) ocupar; (a tooth) empastar, *Argentina* emplomar; (fulfil) cumplir; (charge, fuel) cargar; (with food) hartar. *vi* llenarse. **fill an order,** servir un pedido. **fill a prescription,** surtir una receta. **to f. the chair,** ocupar la presidencia; (university) ocupar la cátedra. **to f. the place of,** ocupar el lugar de; substituir; suplir. **It will be difficult to find someone to f. his place,** Será difícil de encontrar uno que haga lo que hizo él. **to f. to the brim,** llenar hasta los bordes. **to f. in, f. out,** (a form) llenar (or completar) (una hoja); (insert) insertar, añadir; (a hollow) terraplenar. **to f. out,** *vt* hinchar. *vi* hincharse; echar carnes; (of the face) redondearse. **to f. up,** colmar, llenar hasta los bordes; (an office) proveer; (block) macizar; (a form) completar, llenar

fillet *n* venda, cinta, *f*; (of meat or fish) filete, *m*; (of meat) solomillo, *m*; *arch* filete, *m*. *vt* atar con una venda o cinta; *cul* cortar en filetes

filling *n* envase, *m*; (swelling) henchimiento, *m*; (of a tooth) empastadura, *f*; (in or up, of forms, etc.) llenar, *m*. **f. station,** depósito de gasolina, *m*

fillip *n* capirotazo, *m*; (stimulus) estímulo, *m*; (trifle) bagatela, *f*. *vt* and *vi* dar un capirotazo (a); *vt* estimular, incitar

filly *n* jaca, potra, *f*

film *n* (on liquids) tela, *f*; membrana, *f*; (coating) capa ligera, *f*; (on eyes) tela, *f*; (cinema) película, cinta, *f*; *phot* película, *f*; *fig* velo, *m*; nube, *f*, *vi* cubrirse de un velo, etc. *vt* cubrir de un velo, etc.; filmar, fotografiar para el cine. **roll f.,** película fotográfica, *f*. **silent f.,** película muda, *f*. **talking f.,** película sonora, *f*. **to shoot a f.,** hacer una película. **to take part in a f.,** actuar, or tomar parte, en una película. **f. pack,** película en paquetes *f*. **f. star,** estrella de la pantalla (or del cine), *f*

film industry industria fílmica, *f*

filminess *n* transparencia, diafanidad, *f*

filmy *a* transparente, diáfano

filter *n* filtro, *m*. *vt* filtrar. *vi* infiltrarse; (*fig* of news) trascender, divulgarse. **f.-bed,** filtro, *m*. **f.-paper,** papel filtro, *m*

filth *n* inmundicia, suciedad, *f*; *fig* corrupción, *f*; *fig* obscenidad, *f*

filthiness *n* suciedad, *f*; escualidez, *f*; *fig* asquerosidad, *f*; *fig* obscenidad, *f*

filthy *a* inmundo, sucio; escuálido, *Argentina* cascarriento, *Central America* descacharrado; *fig* asqueroso; *fig* obsceno

filtrate *n* filtrado, *m*, *vt* filtrar

filtration *n* filtración, *f*

fin *n* (of fish) aleta, ala, *f*; (of whale) barba, *f*; *aer* aleta, *f*

final *a* último, final; (conclusive) conclusivo, decisivo, terminante. *n sport* finales, *m pl*; *univ* último examen, *m*. **f. blow,** *fig* golpe decisivo, *m*. **f. cause,** *phil* causa final, *f*

finale *n* final, *m*

finalist *n* finalista, *mf*

finality *n* finalidad, *f*; (decision) determinación, resolución, decisión, *f*

finally *adv* por fin, finalmente, por último, a la postre; (irrevocably) irrevocablemente

finance *n* hacienda pública, *f*, asuntos económicos, *m pl*; finanzas, *f pl*. *vt* financiar

financial *a* financiero, monetario. **f. year,** año económico, *m*

financially *adv* del punto de vista financiero

financier *n* financiero, *m*

find *vt* encontrar, hallar; (discover) descubrir, dar con; (invent) inventar, crear; (supply) facilitar, proporcionar; (provide) proveer; (instruct) instruir; *law* declarar. *vi law* fallar, dar sentencia. *n* hallazgo, *m*; descubrimiento, *m.* **I found him out a long time ago,** *fig* Hace tiempo que me di cuenta de cómo era él. **I found it possible to go out,** Me fue posible salir. **The judge found them guilty,** El juez les declaró culpables. **to f. a verdict,** *law* dar sentencia, fallar. **to f. one's way,** encontrar el camino. **to f. oneself,** hallarse, verse, encontrarse. **to f. out,** averiguar, descubrir. **to f. out about,** informarse sobre (or de)

finder *n* hallador (-ra); (inventor) inventor (-ra), descubridor (-ra); (telescope, camera) buscador, *m*

finding *n* hallazgo, *m*; (discovery) descubrimiento, *m*; *law* fallo, *m*, sentencia, *f*

fine *n* multa, *f*; (end) fin, *m*. **in f.,** en fin, en resumen

fine *vt* multar, cargar una multa a

fine *a* (thin) delgado; (sharp) agudo; (delicate) fino, delicado; (minute) menudo; (refined) refinado, puro; (healthy) saludable; (of weather) bueno; magnífico; (beautiful) hermoso, lindo; excelente; (perfect) perfecto; (good) bueno; elegante; (showy) ostentoso, vistoso; (handsome) guapo; (subtle) sutil; (acute) agudo; (noble) noble; (eminent, accomplished) distinguido, eminente; (polished) pulido; (affected) afectado; (clear) claro; (transparent) transparente, diáfano. *adv* muy bien. **a f. upstanding young man,** un buen mozo. **a f. upstanding young woman,** una real moza. **He's a f. fellow,** (ironically) Es una buena pieza. **That is all very f. but . . . ,** Todo eso está muy bien pero. . . . **to become f.,** (weather) mejorar

finely *adv* finamente; menudamente; elegantemente; (ironically) lindamente

fineness *n* (thinness) delgadez, *f*; (excellence) excelencia, *f*; delicadeza, *f*; (softness) suavidad, *f*; elegancia, *f*; (subtlety) sutileza, *f*; (acuteness) agudeza, *f*; (perfection) perfección, *f*; (nobility) nobleza, *f*; (beauty) hermosura, *f*

finery *n* galas, *f pl*, atavíos magníficos, *m pl*; adornos, *m pl*; primor, *m*, belleza, *f*

finesse *n* sutileza, diplomacia, *f*; estratagema, artificio, *m*; (cunning) astucia, *f*, *vi* valerse de estratagemas o artificios

finger *n* dedo, *m*; (of a clock, etc.) manecilla, *f*; (measurement) dedada, *f*; *fig* mano, *f*. *vt* manosear, tocar; (soil) ensuciar con los dedos; (steal) sisar; (*mus* a keyed instrument) teclear, (a stringed instrument) tocar. **first f.,** dedo índice, *m*. **fourth f.,** dedo anular, *m*. **little f.,** dedo meñique, *m*. **second f.,** dedo de en medio, dedo del corazón, *m*. **to burn one's fingers,** quemarse los dedos; *fig* cogerse los dedos. **to have at one's f.-tips,** *fig* saber al dedillo. **f.-board,** (of piano) teclado, *m*; (of stringed instruments) diapasón, *m*. **f.-bowl,** lavadedos, lavafrutas, *m*. **finger's breadth,** dedo, *m*. **f.-mark,** huella digital, *f*. **f.-nail,** uña del dedo, *f*. **f.-print,** impresión digital, *f*. **f.-stall,** dedil, *m*. **f.-tip,** punta del dedo, yema del dedo, *f*. **f.-wave,** peinado al agua, *m*

fingered *a* (in compounds) con dedos, que tiene los dedos . . .

fingering *n* (touching) manoseo, *m*; *mus* digitación, *f*; (*mus* the keys) tecleo, *m*; (wool) estambre, *m*

finial *n* pináculo, *m*

finicky *a* (of persons) dengoso, remilgado; (of things) nimio

finish *n* fin, *m*, conclusión, terminación, *f*; (final touch) última mano, *f*; perfección, *f*; (of an article) acabado, *m*; *sport* llegada, (*horse race*) meta, *f*. *vt* terminar, acabar, concluir; llevar a cabo, poner fin a; (perfect) perfeccionar; (put finishing touch to) dar la última mano a; (kill) matar; (exhaust) agotar, rendir; (overcome) vencer. *vi* acabar; concluirse. **to f. off,** acabar, terminar; (kill) matar, acabar con; (destroy) destruir. **to f. up,** acabar; (eat) comer; (drink) beber

finishable *a* acabable

finished *a* acabado, terminado, completo; perfecto; (careful) cuidadoso

finished goods *n pl* bienes terminados, *m pl*

finisher *n* terminador (-ra), acabador (-ra); pulidor (-ra); (final blow) golpe de gracia, *m*

finishing *a* concluyente. *n* terminación, *f*, fin, *m*; perfección, *f*; (last touch) última mano, *f*. **to put the f. touch,** dar la última pincelada

finite *a* finito

Finland Finlandia, *f*

Finn *n* finlandés (-esa)

Finnish *a* finlandés. *n* (language) finlandés, *m*

fir *n* abeto, sapino, pino, *m*. **red fir,** pino silvestre, *m*. **fir-cone,** piña de abeto, *f*. **fir grove,** abetal, *m*

fire *n* fuego, *m*; (conflagration) incendio, *m*; (on the hearth) lumbre, *f*, fuego, *m*; *fig* ardor, *m*, pasión, *f*; (shooting) fuego, tiro, *m*. **by f. and sword,** a sangre y fuego. **by the f.,** cerca del fuego; (in a house) al lado de la chimenea. **long-range f.,** *mil* fuego de largo alcance, *m*. **short-range f.,** *mil* fuego de corto alcance, *m*. **on f.,** en fuego, ardiendo, en llamas; *fig* impaciente; *fig* lleno de pasión. **to be between two fires,** *fig* estar entre dos aguas. **to make a f.,** encender un fuego. **to miss f.,** no dar en el blanco, errar el tiro. **to open f.,** *mil* hacer una descarga. **to set on f.,** prender fuego a, incendiar. **to take f.,** encenderse. **under f.,** bajo fuego. **f.-alarm,** alarma de incendios, *f*. **f.-arm,** arma de fuego, *f*. **f.-box,** hogar, *m*. **f.-brand,** tea, *f*. **f.-brigade,** cuerpo de bomberos, *m*. **f.-damp,** aire detonante, grisú, *m*, mofeta, *f*. **f.-dog,** morillo, *m*. **f.-drill,** (fire-fighters') instrucción de bomberos, *f*. (others') simulacro de incendio, *m*. **f.-engine,** autobomba, bomba de incendios, *f*. **f.-escape,** escalera de incendios, *f*. **f.-extinguisher,** apagador de incendio, extintor, matafuego, *m*. **f.-guard,** vigilante de incendios, *m*; alambrera, *f*. **f.-hose,** manguera de incendios, *f*. **f.-insurance,** seguro contra incendios, *m*. **f.-irons,** badil *m*. y tenazas *f pl*. **f.-lighter,** encendedor, *m*. **f.-screen,** pantalla, *f*. **f.-ship,** brulote, *m*. **f.-shovel,** badil, *m*, paleta, *f*. **f.-spotter,** vigilante de incendios, *m*. **f.-sprite,** salamandra, *f*. **f.-watching,** servicio de vigilancia de incendios, *m*

fire *vt* incendiar, prender (or pegar) fuego a; quemar; (bricks) cocer; (fire-arms) disparar; (cauterize) cauterizar; (*fig* stimulate) estimular, excitar; (inspire) inspirar; (*inf* of questions) disparar; (*inf* sack) despedir. *vi* encenderse; (shoot) hacer fuego, disparar (un tiro); (*inf* away) disparar; (up) enojarse. **to f. a salute,** disparar un saludo. *mil* **F.!** ¡Fuego!

firecracker *n* buscapiés *m*

fire department *n* parque de bomberos, servicis de bomberos, servicio de incendios, parque de bombas (Puerto Rico), *m*

firefly *n* cocuyo, *m*

fireman *n* bombero, *m*; (of an engine, etc.) fogonero, *m*. **fireman's lift,** silleta, *f*

fireplace *n* chimenea francesa, chimenea, *f*, *Mexico* brasero *m*; (hearth) hogar, *m*

fireproof *a* a prueba de incendios; incombustible

firer *n* disparador, *m*

firewood *n* leña, *Lat. Am.* charamusca *f*. **f. dealer,** leñador (-ra), vendedor (-ra) de leña

firework *n* fuego artificial, *m*

firing *n* (of fire-arms) disparo, *m*; (burning) incendio, *m*, quema, *f*; (of bricks, etc.) cocimiento, *m*; (of pottery) cocción, *f*; (cauterization) cauterización, *f*; (fuel) combustible, *m*; (*inf* sacking) despedida, *f*. **within f. range,** a tiro. **f.-line,** línea de fuego, *f*. **f.-oven,** (pottery) horno alfarero, *m*. **f.-squad,** pelotón de ejecución, *m*

firm *a* firme; (strong) fuerte; (secure) seguro; sólido; (resolute) inflexible, resoluto; severo; (steady) constante; (persistent) tenaz. *n com* casa (de comercio), empresa, *f*; razón social, *f*

firmament *n* firmamento, *m*

firmly *adv* firmemente; inflexiblemente; constantemente

firmness *n* firmeza, *f*; solidez, *f*; inflexibilidad, resolución, *f*; severidad, *f*; constancia, *f*; tenacidad, *f*

first *a* primero (primer before *m sing* nouns); (of monarchs) primero; (of dates) (el) primero. *n* primero, *m*; (beginning) principio, *m*. *adv* primero, en primer lugar; (before, of time) antes; (for the first time) por primera vez; (at the beginning) al principio; (ahead) adelante. **at f.,** al principio. **from the very f.,** desde el primer momento. **to appear for the f. time,** aparecer (or presentarse) por primera vez; *theat* debutar. **to go f.,** ir delante de todos, ir a la cabeza; ir adelante. **f. and foremost,** en primer lugar; ante todo. **f.-aid,** primera cura, *f.* **f.-aid post,** casa de socorro, *f.* **f.-aider,** practicante, *m.* **f.-born,** *a* and *n* primogénito (-ta). **f.-class,** *a* de primera clase; *fig* excelente. **f.-cousin,** primo (-ma) carnal, primo (-ma) hermano (-na). **f. edition,** edición príncipe, *f.* **f. floor,** primer piso, *m.* **f. fruits,** frutos primerizos, *m pl; fig* primicias, *f pl.* **f.-hand,** *a* original, de primera mano. **f. letters,** primeras letras, *f pl.* **f. night,** *theat* estreno, *m.* **f. of all,** primero, ante todo. **f.-rate,** *a* de primera clase

firstly *adv* en primer lugar, primero

firth *n* ría, *f*

fiscal *a* and *n* fiscal *m..* **f. year,** año económico, *m*

fish *n* pez, *m*; (out of the water) pescado, *m*; *inf* tipo, indivíduo, *m*. *vt* pescar; (out) sacar. *vi* pescar; *fig* buscar. **fried f.,** pescado frito, *m.* **He is a queer f.,** Es un tipo muy raro. **to be neither f. nor fowl,** no ser ni carne ni pescado. **to feel like a f. out of water,** sentirse fuera de su ambiente. **to f. in troubled waters,** A río revuelto ganancia de pescadores. **f.-eating,** *a* ictiófago. **f.-fork,** tenedor de pescado, *m.* **f.-glue,** cola de pescado, *f.* **f.-hook,** anzuelo, *m.* **f.-knife,** cuchillo de pescado, *m.* **f.-like,** de pez; como un pez, parecido a un pez. **f. roe,** hueva, *f.* **f.-server,** pala para pescado, *f*

fishbone *n* espina de pescado, raspa de pescado, *f*

fisherman *n* pescador, *m*

fishery *n* pesquería, *f*

fishing *n* pesca, *f, a* de pescar. **to go f.,** ir de pesca. **f.-boat,** bote de pesca, *m.* **f.-floats,** levas, *f pl.* **f.-line,** sedal, *m.* **f.-net,** red de pesca, *f.* **f.-reel,** carretel, carrete, *m.* **f.-rod,** caña de pescar, *f.* **f.-tackle,** aparejo de pesca, *m.* **f. village,** pueblo de pescadores, *m*

fishmeal harina de pescado, *f*

fishmonger *n* pescadero (-ra)

fishpond *n* vivero, *m*, piscina, *f*

fishwife *n* pescadora, *f*

fishy *a* de pescado; (of eyes, etc.) de pez, como un pez; (in smell) que huele a pescado; *inf* sospechoso; (of stories) inverosímil

fissure *n* grieta, hendidura, rendija, *f*; (*anat, geol*) fisura, *f*

fissured *a* hendido

fist *n* puño, *m*; *print* manecilla, *f*; (handwriting) letra, *f.* **with clenched fists,** a puño cerrado

fisticuff *n* puñetazo, *m*; *pl* **fisticuffs,** agarrada, riña, *f*

fit *n* espasmo, paroxismo, *m*; ataque, *m*; (impulse) acceso, arranque, *m*; (whim) capricho, *m*; (of a garment) corte, *m*; (adjustment) ajuste, encaje, *m*. **by fits and starts,** a tropezones, espasmódicamente. **fit of fainting** *Argentina, Venezuela* insulto *m*

fit *a* a propósito (para), bueno (para); (opportune) oportuno; (proper) conveniente, apto; (decent) decente; (worthy) digno; (ready) preparado, listo; (adequate) adecuado; (capable) capaz, en estado (de); (appropriate) apropiado; (just) justo. **It is not in a fit state to be used,** No está en condiciones para usarse. **to be not fit for,** no servir para; (through ill-health) no tener bastante salud para. **to think fit,** creer (or juzgar) conveniente. **fit for use,** usable. **fit to eat,** comestible

fit *vt* ajustar, acomodar, encajar; adaptar (a); (furnish) proveer (de), surtir (con); (of tailor, dressmaker) entallar, probar; (of shoemaker) calzar; (of garments, shoes) ir (bien o mal); (prepare) preparar; (go with) ser apropiado (a); (adapt itself to) adaptarse a. *vi* ajustarse, acomodarse, encajarse; adaptarse; (clothes) ir (bien o mal). **to fit in,** *vt* encajar; incluir. *vi* encajarse; caber; adaptarse. **to fit out,** equipar; proveer (de); preparar.

to fit up, montar, instalar; proveer (de). **to fit with,** proveer de

fitful *a* intermitente; espasmódico; caprichoso

fitfully *adv* por intervalos, a ratos; caprichosamente

fitly *adv* adecuadamente; justamente; apropiadamente

fitment *n* equipo, *m*; instalación, *f*; (of bookcase, etc.) sección, *f*; (furniture) pieza, *f*, mueble, *m*

fitness *n* conveniencia, *f*; aptitud, capacidad, *f*; oportunidad, *f*; salud, *f*; (good health) vigor, *m*

fitted *a* (of clothes) ajustado

fitter *n* ajustador, *m*; (mechanic) armador, mecánico, *m*; (tailoring) cortador, *m*; (dressmaking) probador (-ra)

fitting *n* encaje, ajuste, *m*; adaptación, *f*; (of a garment) prueba, *f*; (size) medida, *f*; (installation) instalación, *f*; **pl. fittings,** guarniciones, *f*; instalaciones, *f pl*; accesorios, *m pl. a* conveniente, justo; apropiado; adecuado; (worthy) digno; (of coats, etc.) ajustado. **f. room,** cuarto de pruebas, *m.* **f. in,** encaje, *m.* **f. out,** equipo, *m.* **f. up,** arreglo, *m*; (of machines) montaje, *m*; (of a house) mueblaje, *m*

five *a* and *n* cinco *m.*; (of the clock) las cinco, *f pl*; (of age) cinco años, *m pl.* **to be f.,** tener cinco años. **f. feet deep,** de cinco pies de profundidad. **f. feet high,** cinco pies de altura. **f.-finger exercises,** ejercicios de piano, *m pl.* **F.-Year Plan,** Plan Quinquenal, *m*

fivefold *a* quíntuplo

fix *n* aprieto, apuro, *m*; callejón sin salida, *m*. *vt* fijar; sujetar, afianzar; (bayonets) calar; (with nails) clavar; (*phot, chem, med*) fijar; (decide) establecer; (a date) señalar; (eyes, attention) clavar; (on the mind) grabar; estampar; (one's hopes) poner; (base) basar, fundar; (*inf* put right) arreglar, componer. *vi* fijarse; establecerse; determinarse. **to get in a fix,** hacerse un lío. **to fix a price,** fijar un precio. **to fix on, upon,** elegir, escoger; decidir, determinar. **to fix up,** arreglar; decidir; organizar; (differences) olvidar (sus disensiones)

fixation *n* obsesión, idea fija, *f*; (scientific) fijación, *f*

fixative *n* (*med, phot*) fijador, *m*; (dyeing) mordiente, *m*. *a* que fija

fixed *a* fijo; inmóvil; permanente; (of ideas) inflexible. **f. bayonet,** bayoneta calada, *f.* **f. price,** precio fijo, *m.* **f. star,** estrella fija, *f*

fixedly *adv* fijamente; resueltamente; firmemente

fixing *n* fijación, *f*; afianzamiento, *m*; arreglo, *m*; (of a date) señalamiento, *m.* **f. bath,** *phot* baño fijador, *m*

fixity *n* permanencia, *f*; inmovilidad, *f*; invariabilidad, *f*; firmeza, *f*

fixture *n* instalación, *f*; accesorio fijo, *m*; *sport* partido, *m*; *inf* permanencia, *f.* **f. card,** *sport* calendario deportivo, *m*

fizz *n* espuma, *f*; chisporroteo, *m. inf* champaña, *m. vi* (liquids) espumear; (sputter) chisporrotear

fizzle *n* (failure) fiasco, fracaso, *m. vi* chisporrotear; (out) apagarse; (fail) fracasar, no tener éxito

fjord *n* fiordo, *m*

flabbergast *vt* dejar con la boca abierta, dejar de una pieza

flabbiness, flaccidity *n* flaccidez, flojedad, *f*; *med* reblandecimiento, *m*; (of character) debilidad, flaqueza del ánimo, *f*

flabby, flaccid *a* fláccido, flojo; *fig* débil

flag *n* bandera, *f*; pabellón, estandarte, *m*; (small) banderola, *f*; (iris) (yellow) cala, *f*, (purple) lirio cárdeno, *m*; (stone) losa, *f.* **to dip the f.,** saludar con la bandera. **to hoist the f.,** izar la bandera. **to strike the f.,** bajar la bandera; (in defeat) rendir la bandera. **f. bearer,** portaestandarte, abanderado, *m.* **f.-day,** día de la banderita, *m*; (in U.S.A.) día de la bandera, *m.* **f.-officer,** almirante, *m*; vicealmirante, *m*; jefe de escuadra, *m.* **f. of truce,** bandera blanca, bandera de paz, *f*

flag *vi* flaquear, debilitarse; languidecer; (wither) marchitarse; decaer, disminuir. *vt* adornar con banderas; (signal) hacer señales con una bandera; (for a race, etc.) marcar con banderas; (with stones) enlosar, embaldosar.

flagellant *n* flagelante, *m*
flagellate *vt* flagelar
flagellation *n* flagelación, *f*
flageolet *n mus* caramillo, *m,* chirimía, *f.* **f. player,** chirimía, *m*
flagging *n* pavimentación, *f;* (floor) enlosado, *m. a* lánguido, flojo
flagon *n* frasco, *m;* botella, *f*
flagrancy *n* escándalo, *m,* notoriedad, *f*
flagrant *a* escandaloso, notorio
flagship *n* capitana, *f*
flagstaff *n* asta de bandera, *f*
flagstone *n* losa, lancha, *Lat. Am.* laja *f*
flail *n* mayal, *m*
flair *n* instinto natural, *m,* comprensión innata, *f;* habilidad natural, *f*
flak *n* cortina (or barrera) antiaérea, *f*
flake *n* escama, *f;* laminilla, hojuela, *f;* (of snow) copo, *m;* (of fire) chispa, *f. vt* cubrir con escamas, etc.; exfoliar; (crumble) hacer migas de, desmigajar. *vi* escamarse; (off) exfoliarse; caer en copos
flaky *a* escamoso; en laminillas; (of pastry) hojaldrado. **f. pastry,** hojaldre, *f*
flamboyance *n* extravagancia, *f, lit* ampulosidad, *f*
flamboyant *a arch* flamígero; extravagante, llamativo, rimbombante; (of style) ampuloso. **f. gothic,** gótico florido, *m*
flame *n* llama, *f; fig* fuego, *m. inf* amorío, *m, vi* flamear, llamear; arder, abrasarse; (shine) brillar; (up, *fig*) inflamarse; acalorarse. **f.-colored,** de color de llama, anaranjado. **f.-thrower,** lanzallamas, *m*
flaming *a* llameante; abrasador; (of colors) llamativo, chillón; (of feelings) ardiente, fervoroso, apasionado
flamingo *n orn* flamenco, *m*
Flanders flandes, *m*
flange *n mech* reborde, *m, vt* rebordear
flank *n* (of animal) ijada, *f;* (human) costado, *m;* (of hill, etc.) lado, *m,* falda, *f; mil* flanco, *m. a (mil nav)* por el flanco. *vt* lindar con, estar contiguo a; *(mil, nav)* flanquear. *vi* estar al lado de; tocar a, lindar con.
flannel *n* franela, *f, a* de franela
flannelette *n* moletón, *m*
flap *n* golpe, *m;* (of a sail) zapatazo, *m,* sacudida, *f;* (of a pocket) cartera, tapa, *f;* (of skin) colgajo, *m;* (of a shoe, etc.) oreja, *f;* (of a shirt, etc.) falda, *f;* (of a hat) ala, *f;* (of trousers) bragueta, *f;* (rever) solapa, *f;* (of a counter) trampa, *f;* (of a table) hoja plegadiza, *f;* (of the wings) aletazo, *m;* (of w.c.) tapa, *f. vt* sacudir, golpear, batir; agitar; (the tail) menear. *vi* agitarse; (of wings) aletear; (of sails) zapatear, sacudirse; colgar. **f.-eared,** de orejas grandes y gachas
flapjack *n cul* torta de sartén, *f;* (for powder) polvorera, *f*
flapper *n inf* polla, tobillera, chica "topolino," *f*
flapping *n* batimiento, *m;* (waving) ondulación, *f;* (of sails) zapatazo, *m;* (of wings) aleteo, *m*
flare *n* fulgor, *m,* llama, *f;* hacha, *f; aer* cohete de señales, *m; sew* vuelo, *m. vi* relampaguear, fulgurar; brillar; (of a lamp) llamear; (up) encolerizarse, salirse de tino; (of epidemic) declararse; (war, etc.) desencadenarse
flash *n* relámpago, centelleo, *m,* ráfaga de luz, *f;* brillo, *m;* (from a gun) fuego, fogonazo, *m;* (of wit, genius) rasgo, *m;* (of joy, etc.) acceso, *m. vi* relampaguear, fulgurar, centellear; brillar; cruzar rápidamente, pasar como un relámpago. *vt* hacer relampaguear; hacer brillar; (a look, etc.) dar; lanzar; (light) encender; (powder) quemar; transmitir señales por heliógrafo; *inf* sacar a relucir, enseñar. **shoulder-f.,** *mil* emblema, *m.* **to be gone like a f.,** desaparecer como un relámpago. **to f. out,** brillar, centellear. **f. of lightning,** relámpago, rayo, *m.* **f. of wit,** agudeza, *f,* rasgo de ingenio, *m*
flashback *n* episodio intercalado, *m,* retrospección, *f*
flashily *adv* llamativamente, con mal gusto
flashing *n* centelleo, *m,* llamarada, *f. a* centellador, relampagueante; brillante; chispeante

flashlight *n* luz de magnesio, *f;* (torch) lamparilla eléctrica, *f,* rayo, *m* (Mexico); **f. photograph,** magnesio, *m*
flashy *a* llamativo, de mal gusto, charro, *Lat. Am.* figuroso; frívolo, superficial
flask *n* frasco, *m,* redoma, botella, *f;* (for powder) frasco, *m;* (vacuum) termos, *m*
flat *a* llano; (smooth) liso; (lying) tendido, tumbado; (flattened) aplastado; (destroyed) arrasado; (stretched out) extendido; (of nose, face) chato, romo; (of tire) desinflado; (uniform) uniforme; (depressed) desanimado; (uninteresting) monótono; (boring) aburrido; *com* paralizado; (downright) categórico; absoluto; (net) neto; *mus* bemol; (of boats) de fondo plano. *adv* See **flatly.** *n* planicie, *f;* (of a sword) hoja, *f;* (of the hand) palma, *f;* (land) llanura, *f;* (apartment) piso, *m; mus* bemol, *m.* **to fall f.,** caer de bruces; *fig* no tener éxito. **to make f.,** allanar. **to sing f.,** desafinar. **f. boat,** barco de fondo plano, *m.* **f.-footed,** de pies achatados; *fig* pedestre. **f.-iron,** plancha, *f.* **f. roof,** azotea, *f*
flatly *adv* de plano; a nivel; (plainly) llanamente, netamente; (dully) indiferentemente; (categorically) categóricamente
flatness *n* planicie, *f;* llanura, *f;* (smoothness) lisura, *f;* (evenness) igualdad, *f;* (uninterestingness) insulsez, insipidez, *f;* aburrimiento, *m;* (depression) desaliento, abatimiento, *m*
flatten *vt* aplanar, allanar; aplastar; (smooth) alisar; (even) igualar; (destroy) derribar, arrasar, destruir; (dismay) desconcertar; (out) extender. *vi* aplanarse, allanarse; aplastarse
flattening *n* achatamiento, *m,* allanamiento, *m;* aplastamiento, *m;* igualación, *f*
flatter *vt* adular, lisonjear, halagar, engatusar, *Lat. Am.* also afilar, engaratusar; (of a dress, photograph, etc.) favorecer, (please the senses) regalar, deleitar; (oneself) felicitarse
flatterer *n* adulador (-ra), lisonjero (-ra), *Guatemala* barbero (-ra) *mf*
flattering *a* adulador; lisonjero; (promising) halagüeño; favoreciente; deleitoso
flattery *n* adulación, *Lat. Am.* adulonería *f*
flat tire llanta desinflada, *f*
flatulence *n* flatulencia, *f*
flatulent *a* flatulento
flaunt *vi* (flutter) ondear; pavonearse. *vt* desplegar; ostentar, sacar a relucir; enseñar
flaunting *n* ostentación, *f;* alarde, *m. a* ostentoso; magnífico; (fluttering) ondeante
flautist *n* flautista, *mf*
flavor *n* sabor, gusto, *m; cul* condimento, *m; fig* dejo, *m. vt cul* sazonar, condimentar; dar un gusto (de), hacer saborear (a); *fig* dar un dejo (de)
flavored *a* (in compounds) de sabor . . . ; sazonado; que tiene sabor de . . .
flavoring *n cul* condimento, *m; fig* sabor, dejo, *m*
flavorless *a* insípido, soso, sin sabor
flaw *n* desperfecto, *m,* imperfección, *f;* (crack) grieta, hendedura, *f;* (in wood, metals) quebraja, *f;* (in gems) pelo, *m;* (in fruit) maca, *f;* (in cloth) gabarro, *m; fig* defecto, error, *m;* (wind) ráfaga de viento, *f*
flawless *a* sin defecto; perfecto; impecable
flax *n* lino, *m.* **to dress f.,** rastrillar lino. **f.-comb,** rastrillo, *m.* **f. field,** linar, *m*
flaxen *a* de lino; (fair) rubio, blondo. **f.-haired,** de pelo rubio
flay *vt* desollar; (criticize) despellejar
flaying *n* desuello, *m,* desolladura, *f*
flea *n* pulga, *f.* **f. bite,** picada de pulga, *f*
fleck *n* pinta, mancha, *f,* lunar, *m;* (of sun) mota, *f;* (speck) partícula, *f;* (freckle) peca, *f. vt* abigarrar; manchar; (dapple) salpicar, motear
fledged *a* emplumecido, plumado; alado; *fig* maduro
fledgeling *n* volantón, *m; fig* niño (-ña); *fig* novato (-ta)

flee *vi* huir, fugarse, escapar; (vanish) desaparecer; (avoid) evitar, huir de. *vt* abandonar

fleece *n* vellón, *m*; lana, *f*; toisón, *m*. *vt* esquilar; *fig inf* pelar. **Order of the Golden F.,** Orden del Toisón de Oro, *f*

fleecy *a* lanudo, lanar; (white) blanquecino; (of clouds) borreguero. **f. clouds,** borregos, *m pl*

fleet *n* (navy) armada, *f*; escuadra, flota, *f*; *fig* serie, *f*, *a* alado, rápido, veloz. **F. Air Arm,** Aviación Naval, *f*. **f.-footed,** ligero de pies

fleeting *a* fugaz, momentáneo, efímero, pasajero

flesh *n* carne, *f*; (mankind) género humano, *m*, humanidad, *f*; (of fruit) pulpa, *f*. **a man of f. and blood,** un hombre de carne y hueso. **of one's own f. and blood,** de la misma sangre de uno. **to make one's f. creep,** dar carne de gallina (a). **f.-coloured,** encarnado, de color de carne. **f.-eating,** carnívoro. **f. wound,** herida superficial, *f*

fleshiness *n* carnosidad, gordura, *f*

fleshpot *n* marmita, *f*; *fig* olla, *f*. **the fleshpots of Egypt,** las ollas de Egipto

fleshy *a* carnoso, grueso; (of fruit) pulposo; suculento

fleur-de-lis *n* flor de lis, *f*

flex *n elec* flexible, *m*, *vt* doblar. *vi* doblarse

flexibility *n* flexibilidad, *f*; (of style) plasticidad, *f*; docilidad, *f*

flexible *a* flexible; dúctil, maleable; (of style) plástico; of) voice) quebradizo; adaptable; dócil

flexion *n* flexión, *f*; *gram* inflexión, *f*; *gram* flexión, *f*

flexor *n anat* músculo flexor, *m*

flick *n* golpecito, toque, *m*; (of the finger) capirotazo, *m*; *inf* cine, *m*, *vt* dar un golpecito a; dar ligeramente con un látigo; sacudir. **flick one's wrist** hacer girar la muñeca **to f. over the pages of,** hojear

flicker *n* estremecimiento, temblor, *m*; fluctuación, *f*; (of bird) aleteo, *m*; (of flame) onda (de una llama), *f*; (of eyelashes) pestañeo, *m*; (of a smile) indicio, *f*, *vi* agitarse; (of flags) ondear; vacilar

flickering *a* tenue; vacilante

flier *n* volador (-ra); aviador (-ra); piloto, *m*; fugitivo (-va)

flight *n* vuelo, *m*; (of bird of prey) colada, *f*; (flock of birds) bandada, *f*; (migration) migración, *f*; (of time) transcurso, *m*; (of imagination, etc.) arranque, *m*; (volley) lluvia, *f*; (of aeroplanes) escuadrilla (de aviones), *f*; (of stairs) tramo, tiro, *m*; (staircase) escalera, *f*; (of locks on canal, etc.) ramal, *m*; (escape) huida, fuga, *f*. **long-distance f.,** *aer* vuelo de distancia, *m*. **non-stop f.,** *aer* vuelo sin parar, *m*. **reconnaissance f.,** *aer* vuelo de reconocimiento, vuelo de patrulla, *m*. **test f.,** *aer* vuelo de pruebas, *m*. **to put to f.,** ahuyentar, poner en fuga. **to take f.,** alzar el vuelo. **f.-lieutenant,** teniente aviador, *m*. **f.-sergeant,** sargento aviador, *m*

flight attendant sobrecarbo, *Lat. Am.* aeromozo (-za), cabinero (-ra) *mf*

flightiness *n* frivolidad, veleidad, ligereza, *f*

flighty *a* frívolo, inconstante, veleidoso

flimsiness *n* falta de solidez, endeblez, *f*; fragilidad, *f*; (of arguments) futilidad, *f*

flimsy *a* endeble; frágil; fútil, insubstancial

flinch *vi* echarse atrás, retirarse (ante); vacilar, titubear. **without flinching,** sin vacilar; sin quejarse

fling *vt* arrojar, echar, tirar; lanzar; (scatter) derramar; (oneself) echarse; (oneself upon) echarse encima; *fig* confiar en. *vi* lanzarse; marcharse precipitadamente; saltar. *n* tiro, *m*; (of dice, etc.) echada, *f*; (gibe) sarcasmo, *m*, burla, chufleta, *f*; (of horse) respingo, brinco, *m*; baile escocés, *m*. **in full f.,** en plena operación; en progreso. **to have one's f.,** darse un verde, correrla. **to f. away,** *vt* desechar; (waste) desperdiciar, malgastar, perder. **to f. back,** (a ball) devolver; (the head) echar atrás. **to f. down,** tirar al suelo; arrojar; derribar. **to f. off,** *vt* rechazar; apartar; (a garment, etc.) quitar. *vi* marcharse sin más ni más. **to f. oneself down,** tumbarse; echarse; despeñarse (por). **to f. oneself head-**

long, despeñarse. **to f. open,** abrir violentamente, abrir de repente. **to f. out,** *vt* echar a la fuerza; (a hand) alargar, extender. *vi* salir apresuradamente. **to f. over,** (upset) volcar; arrojar por; abandonar. **to f. up,** lanzar al aire; levantar, erguir; renunciar (a), abandonar; dejar

flint *n* pedernal, *m*; (for producing fire) piedra de encendedor, *f*

flinty *a* pedernalino; *fig* endurecido

flippancy *n* levedad, ligereza, *f*; frivolidad, *f*; impertinencia, *f*

flippant *a* poco serio, ligero; frívolo; impertinente

flipper *n* aleta, *f*

flirt *n* (man) coquetón, castigador, *m*; (woman) coqueta, castigadora, *f*. *vt* (shake) sacudir; (move) agitar; (wave) menear. *vi* flirtear, coquetear; (toy with) jugar con; divertirse con

flirtation *n* flirteo, amorío, *m*

flirtatious *a* (of men) galanteador, castigador; (of women) coqueta

flit *vi* revolotear, mariposear; (move silently) deslizarse, pasar silenciosamente; (depart) irse, marcharse; mudarse por los aires. **to f. about,** ir y venir silenciosamente. **to f. past,** pasar como una sombra

flitch *n* (of bacon) hoja de tocino, *f*

float *n* masa flotante, *f*; (raft) balsa, *f*; *mech* flotador, *m*; (of fishing rod or net) corcho, *m*; (of fish) vejiga natatoria, *f*; (for swimming) nadadera, calabaza, *f*; (for tableaux) carroza, *f*; *pl* **floats,** *theat* candilejas, *f pl*. *vi* flotar; (flags, hair, etc.) ondear; (wander) vagar; *naut* boyar. *vt* poner a flote; hacer flotar; (a grounded ship) desencallar; (com a company) fundar; (a loan, etc.) emitir, poner en circulación; (launch a ship) botar; (flood) inundar

floating *n* flotación, *f*, flote, *m*; *com* fundación (de una compañía), *f*; (of a loan) emisión, *f*; (of a ship) botadura, *f. a* flotante; boyante; *com* en circulación, flotante; fluctuante, variable. **f. capital,** capital fluctuante, *m*. **f. debt,** deuda flotante, *f*. **f. dock,** dique flotante, *m*. **f. light,** buque faro, *m*. **f. population,** población flotante, *f*. **f. rib,** costilla flotante, *f*

flock *n* rebaño, *m*, manada, *f*; (of birds) bandada, *f*; *fig* grey, *f*; (crowd) multitud, muchedumbre, *f*; (parishioners) congregación, *f*; (of wool or cotton) vedija (de lana or de algodón), *f*; *pl* **flocks,** (for stuffing) borra, *f*. *vi* concurrir, reunirse, congregarse; ir en tropel; acudir; (birds) volar en bandada. **f.-bed,** colchón de borra, *m*

floe *n* banco de hielo, *m*

flog *vt* azotar; castigar

flogging *n* azotamiento, vapuleo, *m*

flood *n* inundación, *f*; (Bible) diluvio, *m*; (of the tide) flujo, *m*; *fig* torrente, *m*; (abundance) copia, abundancia, *f*; (fit) paroxismo, *m*. *vt* inundar; sumergir; (of tears) mojar. *vi* desbordar. **f. lighting,** iluminación intensiva, *f*

floodgate *n* compuerta (de esclusa), *f*

flooding *n* inundación, *f*; desbordamiento, *m*; *med* hemorragia uterina, *f*

floodtide *n* marea creciente, *f*

floor *n* suelo, piso, *m*; (wooden) entarimado, *m*; (story) piso, *m*; (of a cart) cama, *f*; *agr* era, *f*. *vt* entablar; echar al suelo, derribar; *fig* desconcertar, confundir. **on the f.,** en el suelo. **on the ground f.,** en el piso bajo. **to take the f.,** *fig* tener la palabra. **f. mop** *Lat. Am.* lampazo *m*. **f.-polisher,** lustrador de piso, *m*

flooring *n* tablado, *m*, tablazón, *f*; piso, *m*

flop *n* golpe, *m*; ruido sordo, *m*; (splash) chapoteo, *m*; *inf* fiasco, *m*. *vi* dejarse caer

flora *n* flora, *f*

floral *a* floral. **f. games,** juegos florales, *m pl*

Florence Florencia, *f*

Florentine *a* and *n* florentino (-na)

florescence *n* florescencia, *f*

florid *a* florido; demasiado ornado, cursi, llamativo; (of complexion) rubicundo

floridness n floridez, f, estilo florido, m; demasiada ornamentación, vulgaridad, f, mal gusto, m; (of complexion) rubicundez, f

florin n florín, m

florist n florista, mf

floss n seda floja, filoseda, f; (of maize) penacho, m; (of a cocoon) cadarzo, m. **f. silk,** seda floja, f

flotilla n flotilla, f

flotsam n pecio, m

flounce n volante, m, vi saltar de impaciencia. **to f. out,** salir airadamente

flounder n (nearest equivalent) icht platija, f; tumbo, m. vi tropezar; revolcarse; andar dificultosamente

flour n harina, f, vt enharinar. **f.-bin,** tina, f, harinero, m. **f. merchant,** harinero, m

flourish n movimiento, m; gesto, saludo, m; (of a pen) plumada, f; (on the guitar, in fencing) floreo, m; preludio, m; (fanfare) tocata (de trompetas), f; (of a signature) rúbrica, f; (in rhetoric) floreo, m. vi (of plants) vegetar; (prosper) prosperar, medrar; florecer; (of the guitar, in fencing) florear; mus preludiar; (with a pen) hacer plumadas (or rasgos de pluma); (of a signature) firmar con rúbrica; (sound a fanfare) hacer una tocata (de trompetas). vt agitar en el aire, blandir

flourishing a (of plants) lozano; floreciente; (prosperous) próspero; (happy) feliz

flourmill n molino de harina, m, fábrica de harina, f, molina harinero, m

floury a harinoso

flout vt burlarse de; despreciar, no hacer caso de

flow n flujo, m; corriente, f; chorro, m; (of water) caudal, m; (output) producción total, cantidad, f; (of the tide) flujo (de la marea), m; (of words) facilidad, f. vi fluir, manar; correr; (of the tide) crecer (la marea); (pass) pasar, correr; (result) resultar (de), provenir (de); (of hair, drapery) caer, ondular; (abound) abundar (en). **to f. away,** escaparse, salir. **to f. back,** refluir. **to f. down,** descender, fluir hacia abajo; (of tears) correr por. **to f. from,** dimanar de; manar de; fig provenir de. **to f. in,** llegar en abundancia. **to f. into,** (rivers) desaguar en, desembocar en. **to f. over,** derramarse por. **to f. through,** fluir por; atravesar; (water) regar. **to f. together,** (rivers) confluir

flower n flor, f; (best) flor y nata, crema, f. vi florecer. **in f.,** en flor. **No flowers by request,** (for a funeral) No flores por deseo del finado. **f.-bud,** capullo, m. **f.-garden,** jardín, m. **f. girl,** florista, vendedora de flores, f. **f. market,** mercado de flores, m. **f.-piece,** florero, m. **f. pot,** tiesto, m, maceta, f, Lat. Am. macetero m. **f. show,** exposición de flores, f. **f. vase,** florero, m

flowerbed n cuadro, macizo, m

flower car coche portacoronas, m

flowered a (in compounds) con flores; con dibujos de flores

floweriness n abundancia de flores, f; (of style) floridez, f, estilo florido, m

flowering n florecimiento, m. a floreciente; con flores; (of shrubs) de adorno. **f. season,** época de la floración, f

flowery a florido

flowing n flujo, m; derrame, m. a fluente, corriente; (of tide) creciente; (waving) ondeante; suelto; (of style) flúido

flow of capital corriente de capital, f

fluctuate vi fluctuar, vacilar; variar

fluctuating a fluctuante, vacilante; variable; (hesitating) irresoluto, dudoso

fluctuation n fluctuación, f; cambio, m, variación, f; (hesitancy) indecisión, vacilación, f

flue n (of a chimney) cañón, m; (of a boiler) tubo, m

fluency n fluidez, f

fluent a flúido; fácil

fluently adv corrientemente, con facilidad, de corrido

fluff n borra, pelusa, f, tamo, m

fluffy a velloso; (feathered) plumoso; (woolly) lanudo; (of hair) encrespado

fluid n flúido, líquido, m, a flúido

fluidity n fluidez, f

fluke n (in billiards) chiripa, f; naut uña, f; inf carambola, chiripa, chambonada, f. **by a f.,** de carambola, por suerte. **f.-worm,** duela del hígado, f

flunkey n lacayo, m; fig adulador, m

fluorescence n fluorescencia, f

fluorescent a fluorescente

fluorine n chem flúor, m

fluorite n fluorita, f

flurry n (of wind) ráfaga, f; (squall) chubasco, m; agitación, f; conmoción, f. vt agitar

flush n rubor, m; (in the sky) arrebol, rojo, color de rosa, m; emoción, f, acceso, m; sensación, f; (at cards) flux, m; vigor, m; (flowering) floración, f; abundancia, f; (of youth, etc.) frescura, f. a (level) igual, parejo; abundante; (generous) pródigo, liberal; (rich) adinerado. vi ruborizarse, enrojecerse, ponerse colorado; (flood) inundarse, llenarse (de agua, etc.); (of sky) arrebolarse. vt inundar, limpiar con un chorro de agua, etc., lavar; (of blood) circular por; (redden) enrojecer; (make blush) hacer ruborizarse; (exhilarate) excitar, animar; (inflame) inflamar, encender; (make level) igualar, nivelar. **f. with,** a ras de

flushing n rojez, f; (cleansing) limpieza, lavadura, f; (flooding) inundación, f

fluster n agitación, confusión, f, aturdimiento, m. vt agitar, poner nervioso (a); aturdir; (oneself) preocuparse. vi agitarse; estar nervioso, estar perplejo; (with drink) estar entre dos velas

flute n flauta, f; arch estría, f; (organ-stop) flautado, m. vi tocar la flauta, flautear; tener la voz flauteada. vt tocar (una pieza) en la flauta; (groove) encanutar, acanalar, estriar. **f. player,** flautista, mf

fluted a (grooved) acanalado

fluting n mus son de la flauta, m; (of birds) trinado, m; arch estría, f; sew rizado, m

flutter n (of wings) aleteo, m; (of leaves, etc.) murmurio, m; (of eyelashes) pestañeo, m; (of flags, etc.) ondeo, m, ondulación, f; (excitement) agitación, f; (stir) sensación, f; (gamble) jugada, f. vi (of birds) aletear; revolotear; (of butterflies) mariposear; (of flags) ondear; palpitar; (of persons) estar agitado. vt agitar; (the eyelashes) pestañear; (agitate) agitar, alarmar

fluttering n mariposeo, m; revoloteo, m; (of birds) aleteo, m; (of leaves, etc.) murmurio, m; (of flags, etc.) ondeo, m, ondulación, f; (of eyelashes) pestañeo, m

fluvial a fluvial

flux n flujo, m

fly n (insect) mosca, f; (on a fishhook) mosca artificial, f; (carriage) calesín, m; (of breeches) bragueta, f; theat bambalina, f; (of a tent) toldo, m; (flight) vuelo, m; (of a flag) vuelo, m. **fly-blown,** manchado por las moscas. **fly-by-night,** trasnochador (-ra). **fly-catcher,** orn papamoscas, m; matamoscas, m. **fly-fishing,** pesca con moscas artificiales, f. **fly-leaf,** guarda (de un libro), f. **fly-paper,** papel matamoscas, m. **fly-swatter,** matamoscas, m. **fly-wheel,** mech volante, m

fly vi volar; (flutter) ondear; (jump) saltar; (rush) lanzarse, precipitarse; (pass away) pasar volando, volar; (run off) marcharse a todo correr; (escape) huir, escapar; (seek refuge) refugiarse; (to the head, of intoxicants) subirse; (vanish) desaparecer. vt hacer volar; hacer ondear, enarbolar; (an airplane) pilotar, dirigir; (flee from) huir de; evitar. **to let fly (at),** descargar, tirar; fig saltar la sinhueso. **to fly about,** volar en torno de; revolotear. **to fly at,** lanzarse sobre; acometer, asaltar. **to fly away,** emprender el vuelo. **to fly back,** volar hacia el punto de partida; (of doors, etc.) abrir, or cerrar, de repente. **to fly down,** volar abajo. **to fly in,** volar dentro de; volar adentro; (of airplanes) llegar (el avión). **to fly in pieces,** hacerse pedazos. **to fly into a rage,** montarse en cólera. **to fly low,** rastrear; aer volar a poca altura. **to fly off,** emprender el vuelo; (hasten) marcharse volando; (of buttons, etc.) saltar (de), separarse (de). **to fly open,** abrirse de repente.

to fly over, volar por, volar por encima de. **to fly up-wards,** volar hacia arriba; subir

flying *n* vuelo, *m. a* volante, volador; que vuela; de volar; volátil; (hasty) rápido; (flowing) ondeante, ondulante. **to shoot f.,** tirar al vuelo. **with f. colors,** con banderas desplegadas, triunfante. **f.-boat,** hidroavión, *m.* **f.-buttress,** botarel, arbotante, *m.* **f.-column,** *mil* cuerpo volante, *m.* **f.-fish,** (pez) volador, *m.* **f.-fortress,** *aer* fortaleza volante, *f.* **f.-officer,** oficial de aviación, *m.* **f.-sickness,** mal de altura, *m.* **f.-squad,** escuadra ligera, *f.* **f.-test,** *aer* examen de pilotaje, *m*

foal *n* potro (-ra). *vi* and *vt* parir una yegua

foam *n* espuma, *f. vi* espumar; (of horses, etc.) echar espumarajos. **to f. and froth,** (of the sea) hervir. **f. at the mouth,** echar espuma por la boca.

foam rubber *n* caucho esponjoso, *m,* espuma de caucho, *f,* espuma sintética, *f*

foamy *a* espumoso

fob *n* bolsillo del reloj, *m*; faltriquera pequeña, *f. vt* (off) engañar con

focal *a* focal

focus *n* foco, *m*; centro, *m. vt* enfocar; concentrar. *vi* convergir. **in f.,** en foco

fodder *n* *agr* pienso, forraje, *m. vt* dar forraje (a)

foe *n* enemigo, *m*

fog *n* neblina, niebla, *f; fig* confusión, *f; fig* perplejidad, *f, vt* obscurecer; *phot* velar; *fig* ofuscar. *vi* hacerse nebuloso; *phot* velarse. **fog-signal,** señal de niebla, *f*

fogbound *a* rodeado de niebla; detenido por la niebla

fogey *n* obscurantista, *m.* **He is an old f.,** Es un señor chapado a la antigua

fogginess *n* oscuridad, neblina, *f*

foggy *a* nebuloso; *phot* velado. **It is f.,** Hay niebla

foghorn *n* sirena, *f*; bocina, *f*

foible *n* flaco, *m,* debilidad, *f*

foil *n* (sword) florete, *m*; (coat) hoja, *f*; (of a mirror) azogado, *m. vt* frustrar. **f. a plot,** desbaratar un complot. **She makes a good f. for her sister's beauty,** Hace resaltar la belleza de su hermana

foiling *n* frustración, *f*

foist *vt* imponer; insertar, incluir; engañar (con)

fold *n* doblez, *f,* pliegue, *m*; arruga, *f; sew* cogido, *m*; (for sheep) redil, aprisco, *m; fig* iglesia, congregación de los fieles, *f*; (in compounds) vez, *f. vt* doblar, plegar, doblegar; (the arms) cruzar (los brazos); (embrace) abrazar; (wrap) envolver; (clasp) entrelazar; (sheep) meter en redil, encerrar. *vi* doblarse, plegarse; cerrarse

folder *n* doblador (-ra); plegadera, *f*

folding *n* plegadura, *f,* doblamiento, *m*; (of sheep) encerramiento, *m, a* plegadizo. **f.-door,** puerta plegadiza, *f.* **f.-machine,** plegador, *m.* **f.-seat,** *aut* traspuntín, *f.* **f.-table,** mesa de tijeras, *f*; mesa plegadiza, *f*

foliage *n* follaje, *m,* frondas, *f pl.* **thick f.,** frondosidad, *f*

folio *n* folio, *m*; (a volume) infolio, *m. a* de infolio. *vt* foliar

folk *n* (nation) pueblo, *m,* nación, *f*; gente, *f; pl* **folks,** *inf* familia, *f*; parientes, *m pl.* **f.-dance,** danza popular, *f*

folklore *n* folclore, *m,* tradiciones folclóricas, *f pl*

folklorist *n* folclorista, *mf*

folksong *n* canción popular, *f*; romance, *m*; copla, *f*

folktale *n* conseja, *f,* cuento popular, *m*

follicle *n* (anat, bot) folículo, *m*

follow *vt* seguir; (pursue) perseguir; (hunt) cazar; (adopt) adoptar; (understand) comprender; (notice) observar. *vi* ir, or venir, detrás; (of time) venir después; (gen. impers.) seguir, resultar; seguirse. **as follows,** como sigue. **I shall f. your advice,** Seguiré tus consejos. **to f. on the heels of,** *fig* pisar los talones (a). **to f. suit,** (at cards) asistir, jugar el mismo palo; *fig* imitar. **to f. up,** proseguir; continuar; (pursue) perseguir; (enhance) reforzar. **f.-me-lads,** *inf* siguemepollo, *m*

follower *n* seguidor (-ra); adherente, secuaz, *mf*; (imitator) imitador (-ra); (lover) novio, *m*; *pl* **followers,** acompañamiento, séquito, *m*

following *n* séquito, acompañamiento, *m,* comitiva, *f*; partidarios, *m pl,* adherentes, *mf pl. a* siguiente; próximo. **f. wind,** viento en popa, *m*

folly *n* locura, extravagancia, absurdidad, tontería, *f,* disparate, *m*

foment *vt* (poultice) fomentar; provocar, incitar, instigar; (assist) fomentar, proteger, promover

fomentation *n* *med* fomentación, *f*; provocación, instigación, *f*; fomento, *m,* protección, *f*

fomenter *n* fomentador (-ra), instigador (-ra)

fond *a* (credulous) vano, crédulo, vacío; (doting) demasiado indulgente; (loving) cariñoso, tierno, afectuoso; (addicted to) aficionado a, adicto a, amigo de. **to be f. of,** (things) tener afición a, estar aficionado de; (people) tener cariño (a). **to grow f. of,** (things) aficionarse a; (people) tomar cariño (a)

fondle *vt* mimar, acariciar; jugar (con.)

fondly *adv* (vainly) vanamente, sin razón; cariñosamente, tiernamente

fondness *n* cariño, afecto, *m*; (for things) afición, inclinación, *f*; gusto, *m*

font *n* pila bautismal, *f; poet* fuente, *f; print* fundición, *f*

food *n* alimento, *m*; comida, *f,* el comer; (of animals) pasto, *m; fig* pábulo, *m*; materia, *f.* **She gave him f.** Le dio de comer. **You have given me f. for thought,** Me has dado en qué pensar. **f.-card,** cartilla de racionamiento, **food, clothing, and shelter** comida, abrigo y vivienda, *f.* **F. Ministry,** Ministerio de Alimentación, *m.* **f. value,** valor nutritivo, *m.* **food poisoning,** intoxicación alimenticia, *f*

foodstuffs *n pl* comestibles, víveres, *m pl*

fool *n* tonto (-ta), mentecato (-ta), majadero (ra) necio (-ia); (jester) bufón, *m*; (butt of jest) hazmerreír, *m*; víctima, *f; cul* compota de frutas con crema, *f, vi* tontear, hacer tonterías. *vt* poner en ridículo (a); (deceive) engañar, embaucar; (with) jugar con. **to make a f. of oneself,** ponerse en ridículo. **to f. about,** *vi* perder el tiempo, vagabundear. **to f. away,** malgastar, malbaratar. **fool's bauble,** cetro de bufón, *m.* **fool's cap,** gorro de bufón, *m*

foolhardiness *n* temeridad, *f*

foolhardy *a* temerario, atrevido

fooling *n* payasada, bufonada, *f*; (deceiving) engaño, *m,* burla, *f*

foolish *a* imprudente; estúpido, tonto; ridículo, absurdo; imbécil

foolishly *adv* imprudentemente; tontamente; imbécilmente

foolishness *n* imprudencia, *f*; estupidez, tontería, *f,* disparate, *m*; ridiculez, *f*; imbecilidad, *f*

foolproof *a* (of utensils, etc.) con garantía absoluta

foolscap *n* (nearest equivalent) papel de barba, *m*

fool's gold *n* pirita amarilla, *f,* sulfuro de hierro *m*

foot *n* pie, *m*; (of animals, furniture) pata, *f*; (of bed, sofa, grave, ladder, page, etc.) pie, *m*; (hoof) pezuña, *f*; (metric unit and measure) pie, *m; mil* infantería, *f*; (base) base, *f*; (step) paso, *m. a mil* de a pie; a pie. *vi* ir a pie; venir a pie; bailar. *vt* hollar; (account) pagar (una cuenta); (stockings) poner pie (a). **on f.,** a pie; (of soldiers) de a pie; (in progress) en marcha. **to go on f.,** ir a pie, andar. **to put one's best f. forward,** apretar el paso; *fig* hacer de su mejor. **to put one's f. down,** poner pies en pared, pararle firme el alto. **to put one's f. in it,** meter la pata. **to rise to one's feet,** ponerse de pie. **to set f. on,** pisar, hollar. **to set on f.,** poner en pie; *fig* poner en marcha. **to trample under f.,** pisotear. **f.-and-mouth disease,** glosopeda, *f.* **f.-brake,** freno de pedal, *m.* **f.-pump,** fuelle de pie, *m.* **f.-rule,** (nearest equivalent) doble decímetro, *m.* **f.-soldier,** soldado de a pie, infante, *m*

football *n* (game) fútbol, *m*; (ball) pelota de fútbol, *f.* **f. field,** campo de fútbol, *m.* **f. match,** partida de fútbol, *f.* **f. pools,** apuestas de fútbol, *f pl*; (in Spain) apuestas benéficas de fútbol, *f pl*

footballer *n* futbolista, *m*

footbath *n* baño de pies, *m*

footbridge *n* puente para peatones, *m*
footed *a* con pies; de pies . . . ; de patas . . .
footfall *n* pisada, *f*, paso, *m*
foothills *n pl* faldas de la montaña, *f pl*
foothold *n* hincapié, *m*; posición establecida, *f*
footing *n* hincapié, *m*; posición firme, *f*; condiciones, *f pl*; relaciones, *f pl*. **on a peacetime f.,** en pie de paz. **to be on an equal f.,** estar en pie de igualdad, estar en iguales condiciones. **to miss one's f.,** resbalar
footlights *n pl* canilejas, candilejas, *f pl*. **to get across the f.,** hacer contacto con el público
footman *n* lacayo, *m*
footnote *n* llamada a pie de página, nota a pie de página, *f*
footpath *n* senda, vereda, *f*, sendero, *m*
footprint *n* huella, pisada, *f*, vestigio, *m*
footsore *a* con los pies lastimados
footstep *n* paso, *m*; (trace) pisada, huella, *f*. **to follow in the footsteps of,** *fig* seguir las pisadas de
footstool *n* escabel, banquito, *m*
footwarmer *n* calientapiés, *m*
footwear *n* calzado, *m*
fop *n* petimetre, *m*
foppery *n* afectación en el vestir, *f*; vanidad, *f*
foppish *a* presumido, afectado; elegante
for *prep* (expressing exchange, price or penalty of, instead of, in support or favor of, on account of) por; (expressing destination, purpose, result) para; (during) durante, por; (for the sake of) para; (because of) a causa de; (in spite of) a pesar de; (as) como; (with) de; (in favor of) en favor de; (in election campaign) con (e.g., "Ecuadorians for Martínez!" ¡Ecuatorianos con Martínez!) (toward) hacia; (that) que, para que (with *subjunc*); a, (before) antes de; (searching for) en busca de; (bound for) con rumbo a; (regarding) en cuanto a; (until) hasta. What's for dinner? ¿Qué hay de comida? **center for** . . . centro de . . . (e.g., **Center for Applied Linguistics,** Centro de Lingüística Aplicada). **He is in business for himself,** Tiene negocios por su propia cuenta. **It is raining too hard for you to go there,** Llueve demasiado para que vayas allí. **It is not for him to decide,** No le toca a él decidirlo. **Were it not for . . . ,** Si no fuese por . . . **She has not been to see me for a week,** Hace una semana que no viene a verme. **It is impossible for them to go out,** Les es imposible salir. **but for all that,** pero con todo. **for ever,** por (or para) siempre. **for fear that,** por miedo de que. **for myself,** en cuanto a mí, personalmente. **for the present,** por ahora. **for what reason?** ¿para qué? ¿por cuál motivo? **for brevity's sake, for the sake of brevity,** por causa de la brevedad
for *conjunc* porque; visto que, pues, puesto que, en efecto, ya que
forage *n* forraje, *m*. *vt and vi* forrajear. **to f. for,** buscar. **f. cap,** gorra de cuartel, *f*
forager *n* forrajeador, *m*
foraging *n* forraje, *m*
forasmuch as *conjunc* puesto que, como que, ya que
foray *n* correría, cabalgada, *f*; saqueo, *m*
forbear *vt and vi* dejar (de), guardarse (de); abstenerse de; evitar; reprimirse (de); rehusarse (de); (cease) cesar (de); (be patient) ser paciente; ser tolerante
forbearance *n* abstención, *f*; tolerancia, transigencia, *f*; indulgencia, *f*; paciencia, *f*
forbearing *a* tolerance, transigente; generoso, magnánimo; paciente
forbid *vt* prohibir, defender (de); impedir. **I f. you to do it,** Te prohibo hacerlo. **The game is forbidden,** El juego está prohibido. **They have forbidden me to . . . ,** Me han defendido de . . . **Heaven f.!** ¡Dios no lo quiera!
forbidden *a* prohibido; ilícito. **f. fruit,** fruto prohibido, *m*
forbidding *a* repugnante, horrible; antipático, desagradable; (dismal) lúgubre; (threatening) amenazador. *n* prohibición, *f*

force *n* fuerza, *f*; violencia, *f*; vigor, *m*; (efficacy) eficacia, *f*; (validity) validez, *f*; (power) poder, *m*; (motive) motivo, *m*, razón, *f*; (weight) peso, *m*, importancia, *f*; (police) policía, *f*; *pl* **forces,** *mil* fuerzas, tropas, *f pl*. **by main f.,** por fuerza mayor. **in f.,** vigente, en vigor. **to be in f.,** estar vigente
force *vt* forzar; (compel) obligar, constreñir, precisar; (ravish) violar; *cul* rellenar; (impose) imponer; (plants) forzar; (the pace) apresurar; (cause) hacer; (a lock, etc.) forzar. **to f. oneself into,** entrar a la fuerza en; (a garment) ponerse con dificultad; imponerse a la fuerza. **to f. oneself to,** esforzarse a. **to f. the pace,** forzar el paso. **to f. away,** ahuyentar. **to f. back,** hacer retroceder; rechazar; (a sigh, etc.) ahogar. **to f. down,** hacer bajar, obligar a bajar; (make swallow) hacer tragar; (of airplanes) hacer tomar tierra. **to f. in,** introducir a la fuerza; obligar a entrar. **to f. into,** meter a la fuerza; obligar a entrar (en). **to f. on, upon,** imponer. **to f. open,** abrir a la fuerza; (a lock) romper, forzar. **to f. out,** hacer salir; empujar hacia fuera; (words) pronunciar con dificultad. **to f. up,** obligar a subir; hacer subir; hacer vomitar
forced *a* forzado; forzoso; afectado. **f. landing,** *aer* aterrizaje forzoso, *m*. **f. march,** *mil* marcha forzada, *f*
forceful *a* See **forcible**
forcemeat *n* picadillo, *m*; relleno, *m*. **f. ball,** albóndiga, *f*
forceps *n pl* fórceps, *m pl*; pinzas, *f pl*. **arterial f.,** pinzas hemostáticas, *f pl*
forcible *a* fuerte; a la fuerza; violento; enérgico, vigoroso; poderoso; *lit* vívido, gráfico, vehemente. **f. feeding,** alimentación forzosa, *f*
forcibleness *n* fuerza, *f*; vigor, *m*, energía, *f*; vehemencia, *f*
forcibly *adv* a la fuerza
forcing *n* forzamiento, *m*; compulsión, *f*. **f. frame,** semillero, *m*, especie de invernadero, *f*
ford *n* esguazo, vado, *m*. *vt* esguazar, vadear
fordable *a* esguazable, vadeable
fore *a* delantero; *naut* de proa. *adv* delante; *naut* de proa. **f.-and-aft,** *naut* de popa a proa.
forearm *n* antebrazo, *m*. *vt* armar de antemano; preparar
forebear *n* antecesor, *m*, ascendiente, *mf*
forebode *vt* presagiar, augurar, anunciar; presentir
foreboding *n* presagio, augurio, *m*; presentimiento, *m*, corazonada, *f*
forecast *n* pronóstico, *m*; proyecto, plan, *m*, *vt* pronosticar; proyectar. **weather f.,** pronóstico del tiempo, *m*
forecastle *n naut* castillo de proa, *m*
foreclose *vt* excluir; impedir; vender por orden judicial; anticipar el resultado de; decidir de antemano
foreclosure *n* venta por orden judicial, *f*; juicio hipotecario, *m*
foredoom *vt* predestinar
forefather *n* antepasado, antecesor, *m*
forefinger *n* índice, dedo índice, *m*
forefoot *n* pata delantera, *f*
forefront *n* delantera, primera línea, *f*; frente, *m*; vanguardia, *f*. **in the f.,** en la vanguardia; en el frente
foregoing *a* precedente, anterior
foregone *a* decidido de antemano; previsto
foreground *n* primer plano, primer término, frente, *m*. **in the f.,** *art* en primer término
forehand *a* derecho. **f. stroke,** golpe derecho, *m*
forehead *n* frente, *f*
foreign *a* extranjero; extraño; exótico; exterior; (alien) ajeno. **f. affairs,** asuntos extranjeros, *m pl*. **f. body,** cuerpo extraño, *m*. **f. debt,** deuda exterior, *f*. **F. Legion,** tercio extranjero, *m*. **F. Office,** Ministerio de Relaciones Extranjeras, *m*. **f. parts,** extranjero, *m*. **f. policy,** política internacional, *f*. **F. Secretary,** Secretario de Asuntos Extranjeros, Secretario de Asuntos Exteriores, Ministro de Relaciones Extranjeras, *m*. **f. trade,** comercio con el extranjero, *m*

foreigner *n* extranjero (-ra), *Argentina, Chile also* cuico (-ca), *Mexico also* fuereño (-ña) *mf*

foreignness *n* extranjerismo, *m*; (strangeness) extrañeza, *f*; lo exótico

foreknowledge *n* presciencia, precognición, *f*

foreland *n* promontorio, cabo, *m*

foreleg *n* pata delantera, *f*

forelock *n* guedeja, vedeja, *f*; (of a horse) copete, tupé, *m*. **to take time by the f.,** asir la ocasión por la melena

foreman *n* (of jury) presidente (del jurado), *m*; (of a farm) mayoral, *m*; (in a works) capataz, *m*

foremost *a* delantero; de primera fila; más importante. *adv* en primer lugar; en primera fila

forensic *a* forense, legal. **f. medicine,** medicina legal, *f*

foreordained *a* predestinado

forerunner *n* precursor (-ra), predecessor (-ra); (presage) anuncio, presagio, *m*

foresee *vt* prever, anticipar

foreseeing *a* presciente, sagaz

foreseer *n* previsor (-ra)

foreshadow *vt* anunciar, prefigurar; simbolizar; hacer sentir.

foreshorten *vt art* escorzar

foreshortening *n art* escorzo, *m*

foresight *n* presciencia, *f*; previsión, prudencia, *f*; (of gun) punto de mira, *m*; (optical) croquis de nivel, *m*

forest *n* bosque, *m*, selva, *f*. *vt* arbolar

forestall *vt* anticipar, saltear; prevenir; *com* acaparar

forestalling *n* anticipación, *f*

forestation *n* repoblación forestal, *f*

forester *n* silvicultor, guardamonte, ingeniero forestal, *m*; habitante de los bosques, *m*

forest fire incendio forestal, *m*

forestry *n* silvicultura, *f*

foresworn *a* perjuro

foretaste *n* muestra, *f*; presagio, *m*. *vt* gustar con anticipación

foretell *vt* predecir, profetizar; anunciar, presagiar

foreteller *n* profeta, *m*; presagio, *m*

foretelling *n* profecía, predicción, *f*

forethought *n* presciencia, previsión, *f*; prevención, *f*

forewarn *vt* prevenir

forewarning *n* presagio, *m*

forewoman *n* encargada, *f*; primera oficiala, *f*

foreword *n* prefacio, *m*, introducción, *f*

forfeit *n* pérdida, *f*; (fine) multa, *f*; (in games) prenda, *f*; (of rights, goods, etc.) confiscación, *f*. *a* confiscado. *vt* perder; perder el derecho o el título de

forfeiture *n* pérdida, *f*; confiscación, *f*; secuestro, *m*

forge *n* fragua, *f*; (smithy) herrería, *f*. *vt* and *vi* fraguar, forjar; (fabricate) inventar, fabricar; falsificar; (advance) avanzar lentamente. **to f. ahead,** abrirse camino; avanzar

forged *a* (of iron) forjado; (of checks, etc.) falso, falsificado

forger *n* falsificador (-ra), falsario (-ia); (creator) artífice, *mf*

forgery *n* falsificación, *f*

forget *vt* olvidar; descuidar. *vi* olvidarse. **to f. about,** olvidarse de, desacordarse de. **to f. oneself,** olvidarse de sí mismo; propasarse; (in anger) perder los estribos

forgetful *a* olvidadizo; descuidado, negligente

forgetfulness *n* olvido, *m*; descuido, *m*; falta de memoria, *f*

forging *n* fraguado, *m*; falsificación, *f*

forgivable *a* perdonable, excusable

forgive *vt* perdonar, disculpar, condonar; (debts) remitir

forgiveness *n* perdón, *m*; condonación, *f*; (remission) remisión, *f*

forgiving *a* misericordioso, clemente, dispuesto a perdonar

forgo *vt* renunciar, sacrificar, privarse de; abandonar, ceder

forgoing *n* renunciación, *f*, sacrificio, *m*; cesión, *f*

"For Immediate Occupancy" «De Ocupación Inmediata»

fork *n agr* horca, horquilla, *f*; (table fork) tenedor, *m*; bifurcación, *f*; (of rivers) confluencia, *f*; (of branches) horcadura, *f*; (of legs) horcajadura, *f*; (for supporting trees, etc.) horca, *f*; *mus* diapasón normal, *m*. *vt* hacinar con horca. *vi* bifurcarse; ramificarse

forked *a* bifurcado, hendido, ahorquillado. **f. lightning,** relámpago, *m*. **f. tail,** cola hendida, *f*

forlorn *a* abandonado, desamparado, desesperado. **f. hope,** aventura desesperada, *f*

forlornness *n* desamparo, *m*, miseria, *f*; desolación, *f*, desconsuelo, *m*

form *n* forma, *f*; figura, *f*; (shadowy) bulto, *m*; (formality) formalidad, *f*; ceremonia, *f*; *ecc* rito, *m*; método, *m*; regla, *f*; (in a school) clase, *f*; (lair) cama, *f*; (seat) banco, *m*; (system) sistema, *m*; (ghost) espectro, *m*; aparición, *f*; (to fill out) documento, *m*; hoja, *f*, *Mexico* esqueleto *m*; (state) condición, *f*; *lit* construcción, forma, *f*. **It is a matter of f.,** Es una pura formalidad. **in due f.,** en debida forma, en regla. **in the usual f.,** *com* al usado. **It is not good f.,** No es de buena educación

form *vt* formar; (a habit) contraer; (an idea) hacerse (una idea). *vi* formarse. **to f. fours,** *mil* formar a cuatro

formal *a* esencial; formal; ceremonioso, solemne; (of person) etiquetero, formalista. **f. call,** visita de cumplido, *f*

formaldehyde *n* formaldehído. *m*

formalism *n* formalismo, *m*

formality *n* formalidad, *f*; ceremonia, solemnidad, *f*

formally *adv* formalmente

format *n* formato, *m*

formation *n* formación, *f*; disposición, *f*, arreglo, *m*; organización, *f*; (mil, geol) formación, *f*

formative *a* formativo

forme *n print* forma, *f*, molde, *m*

former *a* primero; antiguo; anterior; pasado. **in f. times,** antes, antiguamente. **the f.,** ése, aquél, *m*; ésa, aquélla, *f*; aquéllos, *m pl*; aquéllas, *f pl*

former *n* formador (-ra); creador (-ra), autor (-ra)

formerly *adv* antiguamente, antes

formidable *a* formidable; terrible, espantoso

formless *a* informe

formlessness *n* falta de forma, *f*

formula *n* fórmula, *f*. **standard f.,** (*math, chem*) fórmula clásica, *f*

formulate *vt* formular

fornicate *vi* fornicar

fornication *n* fornicación, *f*

fornicator *n* fornicador (-ra)

forsake *vt* dejar, desertar; abandonar, desamparar; separarse de; (of birds, the nest) aborrecer; (one's faith) renegar de

forsaker *n* el, *m*, (la, *f*) que abandona; desertor, *m*; renegado (-da)

"For Sale" «Se Vende»

forsooth *adv* ciertamente, claro está

forswear *vt* abjurar; renunciar a. **to f. oneself,** perjurarse

forswearing *n* abjuración, *f*; renuncia, *f*; perjurio, *m*

fort *n* fortaleza, *f*, fuerte, *m*

forte *n* fuerte, *m*. *a mus* fuerte

forth *adv* (on) adelante, hacia adelante; (out) fuera; (in time) en adelante, en lo consecutivo; (show) a la vista. **and so f.,** y así en lo sucesivo; etcétera

forthcoming *a* próximo; futuro; en preparación

forthwith *adv* en seguida, sin tardanza

fortieth *a* cuadragésimo; cuarenta. *n* cuarentavo, *m*

fortifiable *a* fortificable

fortification *n* fortificación, *f*

fortify *vt* fortificar; fortalecer; confirmar; *fig* proveer (de)

fortitude *n* aguante, *m*, fortaleza, *f*, estoicismo, *m*

fortnight *n* quince días, *m pl*, dos semanas, *f pl*; quincena, *f*. **a f. ago,** hace quince días. **a f. tomorrow,**

mañana en quince. **in a f.,** dentro de quince días; al cabo de quince días. **once a f.,** cada quince días
fortnightly *a* quincenal. *adv* cada dos semanas, dos veces al mes. *n* revista quincenal, *f*
fortress *n* fortaleza, plaza fuerte, *f*
fortuitous *a* fortuito, accidental
fortuitously *adv* accidentalmente
fortuity *n* casualidad, *f*; accidente, *m*
fortunate *a* dichoso, feliz; afortunado; próspero. **to be f.,** (of persons) tener suerte
fortunately *adv* afortunadamente, por dicha, felizmente
fortune *n* suerte, fortuna, *f*, destino, *m*; (money) caudal, *m*, fortuna, *f*; bienes, *m pl*; buena ventura, *f*. **good f.,** buena fortuna, dicha, *f*. **ill f.,** mala suerte, *f*. **to cost a f.,** costar un sentido. **to make one's f.,** enriquecerse; *inf* hacer su pacotilla. to tell fortunes, echar las cartas. **f. hunter,** buscador de dotes, cazador de dotes, cazador de fortunas, aventurero, *m*. **f.-teller,** adivinadora, *f*; echadora de cartas, *f*. **f.-telling,** buenaventura, *f*
forty *a* and *n* cuarenta, *m*. **He is turned f.,** Ha cumplido los cuarenta. **person of f.,** cuarentón (-ona). **She is f.,** Tiene cuarenta años
forum *n* foro, tribuna *f*, (e.g., **to serve as a forum for discussion,** servir de tribuna de discusión)
forward *a* avanzado; adelantado; (of position) delantero; (ready) preparado; (eager) pronto, listo, impaciente; activo, emprendedor; (of persons, fruit, etc.) precoz; (pert) insolente, desenvuelto, atrevido. *adv* adelante; hacia adelante; (of time) en adelante; (farther on) más allá; hacia el frente; en primera línea. *vt* ayudar, promover; adelantar; (letters) hacer seguir; *com* expedir, remitir; (a parcel) despachar; (hasten) apresurar; (plants) hacer crecer. *n* sport delantero, *m*. **center-f.,** *sport* delantero centro, *m*. **from this time f.,** de hoy en adelante. **Please f.,** ¡Haga seguir! **putting f. of the clock,** el adelanto de la hora. **to carry f.,** *com* pasar a cuenta nueva. **to go f.,** adelantarse; estar en marcha, estar en preparación. **f. line,** *sport* delantera, *f*. **F.!** ¡Adelante!
forwarder *n* promotor (-ra); *com* remitente, *m*
forwarding *n* fomento, *m*, promoción, *f*; *com* expedición, *f*, envío, *m*
forwardness *n* progreso, adelantamiento, *m*; (haste) apresuramiento, *m*; (of persons, fruit, etc.) precocidad, *f*; (pertness) desenvoltura, insolencia, frescura, *f*, descaro, *m*; (eagerness) impaciencia, *f*
fossil *a* and *n* fósil, *m*.
fossilization *n* fosilización, *f*
fossilize *vt* fosilizar; petrificar. *vi* fosilizarse
foster *vt* provocar, promover, suscitar; (favor) favorecer, ser propicio a. **f.-brother,** hermano de leche, *m*. **f.-child,** hijo (-ja) de leche. **f.-father,** padre adoptivo, *m*. **f.-mother,** ama de leche, *f*. **f.-sister,** hermana de leche, *f*
foul *a* sucio, asqueroso, puerco; (evil-smelling) hediondo, fétido; (of air) viciado; impuro; (language) ofensivo; (coarse) indecente, obsceno; (harmful) nocivo, dañino; (wicked) malvado, infame; vil; (unfair) injusto; *sport* sucio; (ugly) feo; (entangled) enredado; (with corrections) lleno de erratas; (choked) atascado; (of weather) borrascoso, tempestuoso; malo, desagradable; (repulsive) repugnante. *n sport* juego sucio, *Lat. Am.* faul *m*. *vt* ensuciar; *naut* chocar, abordar; (block) atascar; (the anchor) enredar; *Lat. Am.* sports faulear; (dishonor) deshonrar. *vi* atascarse; (anchor) enredarse; *naut* chocar. **to fall f. of,** *naut* abordar (un buque); *fig* habérselas con. **by fair means or f.,** a las buenas o a las malas. **f. breath,** aliento fétido, aliento corrompido, *m*. **f. brood,** peste de las abejas, *f*. **f. language,** palabras ofensivas, *f pl*; lenguaje obsceno, *m*. **f. play,** juego sucio, *m*. **f. weather,** mal tiempo, tiempo borrascoso, *m*
found *vt* fundar; (metal, glass) fundir; (create, etc.) establecer
foundation *n* fundación, *f*; establecimiento, *m*; crea-

ción, *f*; *arch* cimiento, embasamiento, *m*; (basis) base, *f*; (cause) causa, *f*, origen, principio, *m*; (endowment) dotación, *f*; *sew* refuerzo, *m*. **to lay the f.,** poner las fundaciones. **f. stone,** piedra angular, *f*; *fig* primera piedra, *f*. **to lay the f. stone,** poner la piedra angular
founder *n* fundador (-ra); (of metals) fundidor, *m*. *vt* (a ship) hacer zozobrar. *vi* zozobrar, irse a pique; *fig* fracasar
foundering *n* naut zozobra, *f*
founding *n* fundación, *f*; establecimiento, *m*; (of metals) fundición, *f*
foundling *n* hijo (-ja) de la cuna, expósito (-ta). **f. hospital** or **home,** casa de cuna, casa de expósitos, inclusa, *f*
foundress *n* fundadora, *f*
foundry *n* fundición, *f*
fountain *n* fuente, *f*; (spring) manantial, *m*; (jet) chorro, *m*; (artificial) fuente, *f*, surtidero, *m*; (source) origen, principio, *m*. **f.-head,** fuente, *f*. **Fountain of Youth,** Fuente de la juventud, Fuente de Juvencio, *f*. **f. pen,** pluma estilográfica, *f*
four *a* and *n* cuatro, *m*. **It is f. o'clock,** Son las cuatro. **She is f.,** Tiene cuatro años. **on all fours,** a gatas. **f.-course,** (of meals) de cuatro platos. **f.-engined,** cuadrimotor. **f.-engined plane,** cuadrimotor, *m*. **f.-footed,** cuadrúpedo. **f.-horse,** de cuatro caballos. **f. hundred,** cuatrocientos. **f.-inhand,** tiro par, *m*. **f.-part,** (of a song) a cuatro voces. **f.-wheel brakes,** freno en las cuatro ruedas, *m*
fourfold *a* cuádruple
fourposter *n* cama de matrimonio, *f*
fourscore *a* and *n* ochenta, *m*.
foursome *n* partido de cuatro personas, *m*
fourteen *a* and *n* catorce, *m*. **He is f.,** Tiene catorce años
fourteenth *a* and *n* décimocuarto *m*.; (of the month) (el) catorce, *m*; (of monarchs) catorce. **April f.,** El 14 (catorce) de abril
fourth *a* cuarto; (of the month) el cuatro; (of monarchs) cuarto. *n* (fourth part) cuarta parte, *f*; *mus* cuarta, *f*. **f. dimension,** cuarta dimensión, *f*. **f. term,** (U.S.A. *pol*) cuarto mandato, *m*
fourthly *adv* en cuarto lugar
fowl *n* gallo. *m*; gallina, *f*; (chicken) pollo, *m*; (bird) ave, *f*; (barndoor f.) ave de corral, *f*. *vi* cazar aves. **f.-house** or **run,** gallinero, *m*
fox *n* zorro, *m*; (vixen) zorra, raposa, *Argentina* chilla *f*; *fig* zorro, taimado, *m*. *vi* disimular. *vt* (books) descolorar. **f.-brush,** cola de raposa, *f*. **f.-earth,** zorrera, *f*. **f.-hunting,** caza de zorras, *f*. **f. terrier,** fox-térrier, *m*
foxglove *n* digital, dedalera, *f*
foxhound *n* perro zorrero, *m*
foxiness *n* zorrería, astucia, *f*
foxtrot *n* foxtrot, *m*
foxy *a* de zorro; zorrero, astuto
foyer *n* foyer, salón de descanso, *m*
fraction *n* math fracción, *f*, número quebrado, *m*; pequeña parte, *f*; fragmento, *m*. **improper f.,** *math* fracción impropia, *f*. **proper f.,** *math* fracción propia, *f*
fractional *a* fraccionario
fractious *a* malhumorado, enojadizo
fractiousness *n* mal humor, *m*
fracture *n* surg fractura, *f*. *vt* fracturar. **compound f.,** fractura conminuta, *f*
fragile *a* frágil, quebradizo; (of persons) delicado
fragility *n* fragilidad, *f*
fragment *n* fragmento, *m*; trozo, pedazo, *m*. **to break into fragments,** hacer pedazos, hacer añicos
fragmentary *a* fragmentario
fragrance *n* fragancia, *f*, buen olor, perfume, aroma, *m*
fragrant *a* fragante, oloroso. **to make f.,** perfumar
frail *a* frágil, quebradizo; débil, endeble. *n* capacho, *m*, espuerta, *f*
frailty *n* fragilidad, *f*; debilidad, *f*
frame *n* constitución, *f*; sistema, *m*; organización, *f*; (of the body) figura, *f*, talle, *m*; (of window, picture) marco, *m*; (of machine, building) armadura, *f*; (of a bi-

cycle) cuadro (de bicicleta), *m*; *agr* cajonera, *f*; (embroidery) bastidor (para bordar), *m*; (skeleton) esqueleto, *m*; *lit* composición, construcción, *f*; (of spectacles) armadura, *f*; (of mind) disposición (de ánimo), *f*; humor, *m*. *vt* formar; construir; arreglar; ajustar; (a picture) enmarcar; componer, hacer; (draw up) redactar; (think up) idear, inventar; (words) articular, pronunciar. **f. a constitution,** elaborar una constitución

framer *n* fabricante de marcos, *m*; autor (-ra), creador (-ra), inventor (-ra)

framework *n* armadura, armazón, *f*, esqueleto, *m*; organización, *f*; (basis) base, *f*

franc *n* (coin) franco, *m*

franchise *n* (exemption) franquicia, *f*; privilegio, *m*; (vote) derecho de sufragio, *m*; (citizenship) derecho político, *m*

France Francia, *f*

Franche-Comté Franco-Condado, *m*

Franciscan *a* and *n* franciscano (-na)

Franco- (in compounds) franco- . . . *a* (Spanish *pol*— referring to General Franco) franquista

Francophile *a* and *n* afrancesado (-da)

Frank *n* franco (-ca), galo (-la)

frank *a* franco, cándido, sincero; abierto. *vt* franquear

frankincense *n* incienso, *m*

frankly *adv* francamente; sinceramente; cara a cara; sin rodeos, claramente; abiertamente. **to speak f.,** hablar claro, hablar sin rodeos

frankness *n* franqueza, *f*; sinceridad, *f*, candor, *m*

frantic *a* frenético, furioso, loco. **He drives me f.,** Me vuelve loco

fraternal *a* fraterno, fraternal

fraternity *n* fraternidad, hermandad, *f*

fraternization *n* fraternización, *f*

fraternize *vi* fraternizar

fratricidal *a* fratricida

fratricide *n* (person) fratricida, *mf*; (action) fratricidio, *m*

fraud *n* fraude, *m*; engaño, embuste, *Argentina also* forro *m*; (person) farsante, *m*, embustero (-ra)

fraudulence *n* fraudulencia, fraude, *f*

fraudulent *a* fraudulento

fraught *a* (with) cargado de; lleno de, preñado de

fray *n* refriega, riña, *f*; combate, *m*, batalla, *f*; (rubbing) raedura, *f*. *vt* raer, tazar. *vi* tazarse, deshilarse

frayed *a* raído

fraying *n* raedura, deshiladura, *f*

freak *n* monstruo, *m*; fenómeno, *m*; (whim) capricho, *m*

freakish *a* monstruoso; caprichoso; extravagante; raro, singular

freakishness *n* carácter caprichoso, *m*; extravagancia, *f*; rareza, extrañeza, *f*

freckle *n* peca, *f*. *vi* tener pecas; salir pecas (a la cara, etc.)

freckled *a* pecoso, con pecas

free *a* (in most senses) libre; independiente; emancipado; desembarazado; abierto; limpio (de); franco; (voluntary) voluntario; (self-governing) autónomo, independiente; accesible; (disengaged) desocupado; (vacant) vacío; (exempt) exento (de); (immune) immune (de); ajeno; gratuito; (loose) suelto; (generous) generoso, liberal; (vicious) disoluto, licencioso; (bold) atrevido; (impudent) insolente, demasiado familiar. *adv* gratis, gratuitamente. **There are two f. seats in the train,** Hay dos asientos libres en el tren. **to get f.,** libertarse. **to make f. with,** tomarse libertades con; usar como si fuera suyo. **to set f.,** poner en libertad. **f. agent,** libre albedrío, *m*. **f. and easy,** familiar, sin ceremonia. **f. gift,** *com* objeto de reclamo, *m*. **f.-hand drawing,** dibujo a pulso, *m*. **f. kick,** *sport* golpe franco, *m*. **f. love,** amor libre, *m*. **f. play,** rienda suelta, *f*; *mech* holgura, *f*. **f. port,** puerto franco, *m*. **f. speech,** libertad de palabra, *f*. **f. thought,** libre pensamiento, *m*. **f. ticket,** *theat* billete de favor, *m*. **f. trade,** *a* librecambista. *n* librecambio, *m*. **f. trader,** librecambista, *mf*. **f. verse,** verso libre, verso suelto, *m*. **f.-wheeling,**

desenfrenado, libre. **f. will,** propia voluntad, *f*; (theology) libre albedrío, *m*

free *vt* libertar; poner en libertad (a); librar (de); (slave) salvar; emancipar; exentar; (of obstacles, difficulties) desembarazar; **to f. from,** libertar de; librar de; (clean) limpiar de

freebooter *n* pirata, filibustero, *m*

freeborn *a* nacido libre, libre por herencia

freedman *n* liberto, *m*

freedom *n* libertad, *f*; independencia, *f*; exención, *f*; inmunidad, *f*; soltura, facilidad, *f*, franqueza, *f*; (over-familiarity) insolencia, *f*; (boldness) audacia, intrepidez, *f*; (of customs) licencia, *f*. **to receive the f. of a city,** ser recibido como ciudadano de honor. **f. of speech,** libertad de palabra, *f*. **f. of the press,** libertad de la prensa, *f*. **f. of worship,** libertad de cultos, *f*

freehold *n* feudo franco, *m*

freeing *n* liberación, *f*; emancipación, *f*; salvación, *f*; (from obstruction) desembarazo, *m*; limpieza, *f*

freelance *n* *mil* soldado libre, *m*; *pol* independiente, *m*; aventurero (-ra). **f. journalist,** periodista libre, *m*

freely *adv* libremente; francamente; generosamente; sin reserva

freeman *n* hombre libre, *m*; (of a city) ciudadano de honor, *m*

freemason *n* francmasón, *m*. **freemason's lodge,** logia masónica, *f*

freemasonry *n* francmasonería, masonería, *f*

freethinker *n* librepensador (-ra)

freeze *vt* helar; (meat, etc.) congelar; *fig* helar. *vi* helarse; congelarse; (*impers*, of the weather) helar. **to f. to death,** morir de frío

freezing *n* hielo, *m*; congelación, *f*. *a* glacial; congelante, frigorífico. **f. mixture,** mezcla frigorífica, *f*. **f. of assets,** bloqueo de los depósitos bancarios, *m*. **f.-point,** punto de congelación, *m*. **above f.-point,** sobre cero. **below f.-point,** bajo cero

freight *n* flete, *m*; porte, *m*. *vt* fletar

freighter *n* fletador, *m*; (ship) buque de carga, *m*

French *a* francés. *n* (language) francés, *m*; (people) los franceses, *m pl*. **in F. fashion,** a la francesa. **to take F. leave,** despedirse a la inglesa. **What is the F. for "hat"?** ¿Cómo se dice «sombrero» en francés? **F. spoken,** Se habla francés. **F. bean,** judía, *f*. **F. chalk,** jabón de sastre, *m*. **F. horn,** trompa, *f*. **F. lesson,** lección de francés, *f*. **F. marigold,** flor del estudiante, *f*. **F. polish,** barniz de muebles, *m*. **F. poodle,** perro (-rra) de aguas, *f*. **F. roll,** panecillo, *m*. **F. window,** puerta ventana, *f*

Frenchify *vt* afrancesar

Frenchman *n* francés, *m*. **a young F.,** un joven francés

Frenchwoman *n* francesa, mujer francesa, *f*. **a young F.,** una joven francesa, una muchacha francesa, *f*

frenzied *a* frenético

frenzy *n* frenesí, delirio, paroxismo, *m*

frequency *n* frecuencia, *f*. **high f.,** alta frecuencia, *f*. **low f.,** baja frecuencia, *f*

frequent *a* frecuente; (usual) común, corriente. *vt* frecuentar

frequentation *n* frecuentación, *f*

frequenter *n* frecuentador (-ra)

frequently *adv* frecuentemente, con frecuencia, muchas veces; comúnmente

fresco *n* *art* fresco, *m*, pintura al fresco, *f*. *vt* pintar al fresco

fresh *a* fresco; nuevo; reciente; (newly arrived) recién llegado; (inexperienced) inexperto, bisoño; (of water, not salt) dulce; puro; (healthy) sano; (brisk) vigoroso, enérgico; (vivid) vivo, vívido; (bright) brillante; (cheeky) fresco, *Lat. Am.* impávido. **f. complexioned,** recién (with past participle). **He came to us f. from school,** Vino a nosotros recién salido de su colegio. **We are going to take the f. air,** Vamos a tomar el fresco. **The milk is not f.,** La leche no está fresca. **f.-complexioned,** de buenos colores. **f. news,** noticias nuevas, *f pl*. **f. troops,** tropas nuevas, *f pl*, (reinforcements) tropas de refuerzo, *f pl.* **f. water,** agua fresca, *f;* (not salt) agua dulce, *f.* **f.-water shrimp** *Mexico* acocil *m.* **f. wind,** viento fresco, *m*

freshen *vt* refrescar; (remove salt) desalar. *vi* (wind) refrescar. **to f. up,** renovar; refrescar; (of dress, etc.) arreglar

freshly *adv* nuevamente; recientemente

freshness *n* frescura, *f;* (newness) novedad, *f;* (vividness, brightness) intensidad, *f;* pureza, *f;* (beauty) lozanía, hermosura, *f;* (cheek) frescura, *f,* descaro, *m*

freshwater *n* agua dulce, *f.* **f. sailor,** marinero de agua dulce, *m*

fret *n* agitación, *f;* ansiedad, preocupación, *f; arch* greca, *f;* (of stringed instrument) traste, *m. vt* roer; (of a horse) bocezar; (corrode) desgastar, corroer; (of the wind, etc.) rizar; (worry) tener preocupado (a); irritar, enojar; (lose) perder; (oneself) apurarse, consumirse; *arch* calar. *vi* torturarse, preocuparse, inquietarse; (complain) quejarse; (mourn) lamentarse, estar triste

fretful *a* mal humorado, mohíno, quejoso, irritable

fretfully *adv* irritablemente, con mal humor

fretwork *n* calado, *m*

Freudian *a* freudiano

friar *n* fraile, *m.* **Black f.,** dominicano, *m.* **Gray f.,** franciscano, *m.* **White f.,** carmelita, *m.* **f.-like,** frailesco

friction *n* frote, frotamiento, roce, *m; phys* rozamiento, *m;* fricción, *f.* **to give a f.,** friccionar, dar fricciones (a). **f. gearing,** engranaje de fricción, *m.* **f. glove,** guante de fricciones, *m*

Friday *n* viernes, *m.* **Good F.,** Viernes Santo, *m*

fried *a* frito. **f. egg,** huevo frito, *m*

friend *n* amigo (-ga); (acquaintance) conocido (-da); (Quaker) cuáquero (-ra); (follower) adherente, *m;* partidario (-ia); (ally) aliado (-da); *pl* **friends,** amistades, *f pl;* amigos, *m pl.* **a f. of yours,** un amigo tuyo, uno de tus amigos. **to make friends,** hacer amigos; (become friends) hacerse amigos; (after a quarrel) hacer las paces. **Friends!** (to sentinel) ¡Gente de paz!

friendless *a* sin amigos; desamparado

friendliness *n* amabilidad, afabilidad, cordialidad, amigabilidad, *f*

friendly *a* amistoso, amigable, amigo; afable, acogedor, simpático; propicio, favorable. **to be f. with,** ser amigo de. **f. society,** sociedad de socorros, *f*

friendship *n* amistad, intimidad, *f*

frieze *n* friso, *m;* (cloth) frisa, jerga, *f*

frigate *n nav* fragata, *f*

fright *n* terror, susto, *m;* (guy) espantajo, *m. vt* asustar. **to have a f.,** tener un susto. **to take f.,** asustarse

frighten *vt* espantar, dar un susto (a), alarmar, asustar; horrorizar; (overawe) acobardar. **to be frightened out of one's wits,** estar muerto de miedo. **to f. away,** ahuyentar, espantar

frightened *a* miedoso, tímido, medroso, nervioso

frightening *a* que da miedo; alarmante, amedrentador; horrible

frightful *a* horrible, espantoso, horroroso; *inf* tremendo, enorme

frightfully *adv* horrorosamente; *inf* enormemente

frigid *a* frío; helado; *med* impotente

frigidity *n* frialdad, frigidez, *f; med* impotencia, *f*

frigidly *adv* fríamente

frill *n sew* volante, *m;* (jabot) chorrera, *f;* (round a bird's neck) collarín de plumas, *m;* (of paper) frunce, *m. vt* alechugar; fruncir

fringe *n* fleco, *m,* franja, *f, Lat. Am.* cerquillo *f;* (of hair) flequillo, *m;* (edge) borde, *m,* margen, *mf.* **vt** guarnecer con fleco, franjar; adornar; (grow by) crecer al margen (de)

Frisian *a* and *n* frisón (-ona); (language) frisón, *m*

frisk *vi* retozar, brincar

friskiness *n* viveza, agilidad, *f*

frisky *a* retozón, juguetón

fritter *n cul* fruta de sartén, *f. vt* (away) malgastar, desperdiciar; perder

frivolity *n* frivolidad, ligereza, *f;* futilidad, *f*

frivolous *a* frívolo, ligero, liviano; (futile) trivial, fútil

frizz *vt* (cloth) frisar; (hair) rizar

frizzy *a* (of hair) crespo, rizado

fro *adv* hacia atrás. **movement to and fro,** vaivén, *m.* **to and fro,** de un lado a otro. **to go to and fro,** ir y venir

frock *n* vestido, *m;* (of a monk) hábito, *m;* (of priest) sotana, *f.* **f.-coat,** levita, *f*

frog *n* rana, *f.* **to have a f. in the throat,** padecer carraspera

frolic *n* (play) juego, *m;* (mischief) travesura, *f;* (folly) locura, extravagancia, *f;* (joke) chanza, *f;* (amusement) diversión, *f;* (wild party) holgorio, *m,* parranda, *f. vi* retozar, juguetear; divertirse

frolicsome *a* retozón, juguetón

from *prep* de; desde; (according to) según; (in the name of, on behalf of) de parte de; (through, by) por; (beginning on) a contar de; (with) con; **F.** (on envelope) Remite, Remitente. **He is coming here f. the dentist's,** Vendrá aquí desde casa del dentista. **Give him this message f. me,** Dale este recado de mi parte. **Judging f. his appearance,** Juzgando por su apariencia. **prices f. five hundred pesetas upward,** precios desde quinientos pesetas en adelante. **f. what I hear,** según mi información, según lo que oigo. **f. above,** desde arriba. **f. among,** de entre. **f. afar,** de lejos, desde lejos. **f. time to time,** de cuando en cuando, de vez en cuando

frond *n bot* fronda, *f*

front *n* frente, *f;* cara, *f; mil* frente, *m;* (battle line) línea de combate, *f;* (of a building) fachada, *f;* (of shirt) pechera, *f;* (at the seaside) playa, *f;* (promenade) paseo de la playa, *m;* (forefront) primera línea, *f;* (forepart) parte delantera, *f; theat* auditorio, *m;* (organization) organización de fachada, *f;* (impudence) descaro, *m, a* delantero; anterior; de frente; primero. *adv* hacia delante. *vi* mirar a, dar a; hacer frente a. **in f.,** en frente. **in f. of,** en frente de; (in the presence of) delante de, en la presencia de. **to face f.,** hacer frente. **to put on a bold f.,** hacer de tripas corazón. **f. door,** puerta de entrada, puerta principal, *f.* **f. line,** *mil* línea del frente, *f;* primera línea, *f.* **f. seat,** (at an entertainment, etc.) delantera, *f.* **f. organization** organización de fachada *f.* **f. tooth,** diente incisivo, *m.* **f. view,** vista de frente, *f;* vista de cerca, *f*

frontage *n* (of a building) fachada, *f;* (site) terreno de . . . metros de fachada, *m*

frontal *a mil* de frente; *anat* frontal

frontier *n* frontera, *f; fig* límite, *m. a* fronterizo

frontispiece *n* (of a building) frontispicio, *m,* fachada, *f;* (of a book) portada, *f*

frost *n* escarcha, *f;* helada, *f. vt* helar; *cul* escarchar; (glass) deslustrar; *fig* escarchar. *vi* helar. **f.-bitten,** helado

frostbite *n* efectos del frío, *m pl*

frosted *a* escarchado; helado; (of glass) deslustrado, opaco; *cul* escarchado

frostily *adv fig* glacialmente, con frialdad

frostiness *n;* frío glacial, *m*

frosting *n* escarcha, *f;* (of glass) deslustre, *m; cul* cobertura, escarcha, *f*

frosty *a* helado; de hielo; (of hair) canoso; *fig* glacial, frío. **It was f. last night,** Anoche heló

froth *n* espuma, *f; fig* frivolidad, vanidad, *f, vi* espumar, hacer espuma; echar espuma. *vt* hacer espumar; hacer echar espuma

frothiness *n* espumosidad, *f; fig* frivolidad, superficialidad, vaciedad, *f*

frothy *a* espumoso, espumajoso; *fig* frívolo, superficial

frown *n* ceño, *m;* cara de juez, expresión severa, *f;* desaprobación, *f;* (of fortune) revés, golpe, *m. vi* fruncir el ceño. **to f. at, on, upon,** mirar con desaprobación, ver con malos ojos; ser enemigo de; desaprobar

frowning *a* ceñudo; severo; amenazador

frowningly *adv* severamente

frowsiness *n* mal olor, *m;* (dirtiness) suciedad, *f;* (untidiness) desaliño, desaseo, *m*

frowsy *a* fétido, mal oliente; mal ventilado; (dirty) sucio; (untidy) desaliñado, desaseado

frozen *a* helado; cubierto de hielo; congelado; (*geog* and *fig*) glacial. **to be f. up,** estar helado. **f. meat,** carne congelada, *f*

frugal *a* económico; frugal; sobrio

frugality *n* economía, *f;* frugalidad, sobriedad, *f*

fruit *n* (in general sense) fruto, *m;* (off a tree or bush) fruta, *f; fig* fruto, *m;* resultado, *m,* consecuencia, *f. vi* frutar, dar fruto. **bottled f.,** fruta en almíbar, *f.* **candied f.,** fruta azucarada, *f.* **dried f.,** fruta seca, *f.* **first fruits,** primicias, *f pl.* **soft f.,** frutas blandas, *f pl.* **stone f.,** fruta de hueso, *f.* **f.-bearing,** frutal. **f.-cake,** pastel de fruta, *m.* **f.-dish,** frutero, *m.* **f. farming,** fruticultura, *f.* **f.-knife,** cuchillo de postres, *m.* **f. shop,** frutería, *f.* **f. tree,** frutal, *m*

fruiterer *n* frutero (-ra)

fruitful *a* fructuoso, fértil; prolífico, fecundo; provechoso

fruitfulness *n* fertilidad, *f;* fecundidad, *f;* provecho, *m*

fruition *n* fruición, *f*

fruitless *a* infructuoso, estéril; inútil

fruitlessness *n* infructuosidad, esterilidad, *f;* inutilidad, *f*

fruity *a* de fruta; (wines) vinoso; (of voice) melodioso

frump *n* estantigua, *f*

frumpish *a* estrafalario; fuera de moda

frustrate *vt* frustrar; defraudar; malograr; destruir; anular

frustration *n* frustración, *f;* defraudación, *f;* malogro, *m;* destrucción, *f;* desengaño, *m*

fry *n cul* fritada, *f, vt* freír. *vi* freírse. **small fry,** *inf* gente menuda, *f*

frying *n* fritura, *f,* el freír. **to fall out of the f.-pan into the fire,** ir de mal en peor, andar de zocos en colodros, ir de Guatemala en Guatapeor. **f.-pan,** sartén, *f*

fuchsia *n* fuscia, *Lat. Am.* aljaba, *f*

fuddle *vt* atontar, aturdir; embriagar, emborrachar

fudge *n* patraña, tontería, *f,* disparate, *m;* (food) *Lat. Am.* manjar *m. interj* ¡qué disparate! ¡qué va!

fuel *n* combustible, *m; fig* cebo, pábulo, *m. vt* cebar, echar combustible en. *vi* tomar combustible. **to add f. to the flame,** echar leña al fuego. **f. consumption,** consumo de combustible, *m.* **f.-oil,** aceite combustible, aceite de quemar, *m.* **f.-tank,** depósito de combustible, *m*

fueling *n* aprovisionamiento de combustible, *m*

fugitive *a* fugitivo; pasajero, perecedero; transitorio, efímero, fugaz. *n* fugitivo (-va); (from justice) prófugo (-ga); *mil* desertor, *m;* (refugee) refugiado (-da)

fugue *n mus* fuga, *f*

fulcrum *n mech* fulcro, *m*

fulfil *vt* cumplir; (satisfy) satisfacer; (observe) observar; guardar. **to be fulfilled,** cumplirse, realizarse

fulfilment *n* cumplimiento, *m;* desempeño, ejercicio, *m;* (satisfaction) satisfacción, realización, *f;* (observance) observancia, *f*

full *a* lleno; colmado; todo; pleno; (crowded) atestado; (replete) harto; abundante; (intent on) preocupado con, pensando en; (loose) amplio; (plentiful) copioso; (occupied) ocupado; completo; (resonant) sonoro; (mature) maduro; puro; perfecto; (satiated) saciado (de); (of the moon, sails) lleno; (weighed down) agobiado, abrumado; (detailed) detallado; (with uniform, etc.) de gala; (with years, etc.) cumplido. *n* colmo, *m;* totalidad, *f. adv* muy; completamente, totalmente. **f. many a flower,** muchas flores. **at f. gallop,** a galope tendido. **at f. speed,** a todo correr; a toda velocidad. **His hands are f.,** Sus manos están llenas. **The moon was at the f.,** La luna estaba llena. **in f.,** por completo; sin abreviaciones; integralmente. **in f. swing,** en plena actividad. **in f. vigor,** en pleno vigor. **to the f.,** completamente; hasta la última gota; a la perfección. **to be f. to the brim,** estar lleno hasta el

tope. **f.-blooded,** sanguíneo; de pura raza; *fig* viril, vigoroso; *fig* apasionado. **f.-blown,** en plena flor, abierto. **f. dress,** *a* de gala. *n* traje de etiqueta, traje de ceremonia, *m.* **f.-face,** de cara. **f.-flavored,** (wine) abocado. **f.-grown,** adulto; completamente desarrollado. **f.-length,** de cuerpo entero. **f. moon,** luna llena, *f;* plenilunio, *m.* **f. name,** nombre y apellidos, *m.* **f. powers,** plenos poderes, *m pl.* **f. scale,** tamaño natural, *m.* **f. scope,** carta blanca, *f;* toda clase de facilidades. **f. steam ahead,** a todo vapor. **f. stop,** *gram* punto final, *m*

full-color *a* a todo color. **full-color plates,** láminas a todo color

fuller *n* batanero, *m.* **fuller's earth,** tierra de batán, *f*

fulling *n* abatanadura, *f.* **f.-mill,** batán, *m*

fullness *n* abundancia, *f;* plenitud, *f;* (repletion) hartura, *f;* (of clothes) amplitud, *f;* (stoutness) gordura, *f;* (swelling) hinchazón, *f.* **She wrote with great f. of all that she had seen,** Describía muy detalladamente todo lo que había visto. **in the f. of time,** andando el tiempo

full-page *a* a toda plana. **full-page advertisement,** anuncio a toda plana.

full-time *a* de tiempo completo

fully *adv* plenamente; enteramente. **It is f. six years since . . . ,** Hace seis años bien cumplidos que . . . **It is f. 9 o'clock,** Son las nueve bien sonadas. **f. dressed,** completamente vestido

fulminant *a med* fulminante

fulminate *n chem* fulminato, *m. vi* estallar; fulminar. *vt* volar; fulminar

fulminous *a* fulmíneo, fulminoso

fulsome *a* servil; insincero, hipócrita; asqueroso, repugnante

fumble *vi* (grope) ir a tientas; procurar hacer algo; chapucear (con); (for a word) titubear

fumbling *n* hesitación, *f;* tacto incierto, *m. a* incierto; vacilante

fumblingly *adv* de manera incierta; a tientas

fume *n* vaho, humo, gas, *m;* emanación, *f;* mal olor, *m,* fetidez, *f; fig* vapor, *m;* (state of mind) agitación, *f;* frenesí, *m. vi* humear; refunfuñar, echar pestes, *Lat. Am.* estar hecho un ají

fumigate *vt* fumigar, *Lat. Am. also* humear; sahumar, perfumar; desinfectar

fumigation *n* fumigación, *f;* sahumerio, *m*

fumigator *n* fumigador (-ra); (apparatus) fumigador, *m*

fumigatory *a* fumigatorio

fuming *n* refunfuño, *m. a* refunfuñador

fumy *a* humoso

fun *n* diversión, *f,* entretenimiento, *m;* (joke) chanza, broma, *f,* burla, *f,* para divertirse; en chanza. **in fun,** de burlas. **to have fun,** divertirse. **to poke fun at,** burlarse de, mofarse de, ridiculizar

function *n* función, *f. vi* funcionar

functional *a* funcional

functionary *n* funcionario, *m. a* funcional

functioning *n* funcionamiento, *m*

fund *n* fondo, *m; pl* **funds,** fondos, *m pl; inf* dinero, *m.* **public funds,** fondos públicos, *m pl.* **sinking f.,** fondo de amortización, *m*

fundamental *a* fundamental, básico; esencial. *n* fundamento, *m*

fundamentally *adv* fundamentalmente, básicamente; esencialmente

funeral *a* funeral, fúnebre, funerario. *n* funerales, *m pl;* entierro, *m.* **to attend the f. (of),** asistir a los funerales (de). **f. feast,** banquetes fúnebres, *m pl.* **f. director,** director de pompas fúnebres, *m.* **f. procession,** cortejo fúnebre, *m.* **f. pyre,** pira funeraria, *f.* **f. service,** misa de difuntos, *f*

funereal *a* fúnebre, lúgubre

fungicide *n* anticriptógamo, *m*

fungous *a* fungoso

fungus *n* hongo, *m*

funicular *a* funicular. **f. railway,** ferrocarril funicular, *m*

funnel *n chem* embudo, *m; naut* chimenea, *f;* (of a chimney) cañón (de chimenea), *m.* **f.-shaped,** en forma de embudo

funnily *adv* de un modo raro

funniness *n* lo divertido; rareza, extrañeza, *f*

funny *a* cómico, gracioso; divertido; (strange) extraño, raro; (mysterious) misterioso. **It struck me as f.,** (amused me) Me hizo gracia; (seemed strange) Me pareció raro. **f.-bone,** hueso de la alegría, *m*

fur *n* piel, *f;* depósito, sarro, *m;* (on tongue) saburra, *f. a* hecho de pieles. *vt* forrar, or adornar, or cubrir, con pieles; depositar sarro sobre; (the tongue) ensuciarse la lengua. *vi* estar forrado, or adornado, or cubierto, con pieles; formarse incrustaciones; (of the tongue) tener la lengua sucia. **fur cap,** gorra de pieles, *f.* **fur cape,** cuello de piel, *m;* capa de pieles, *f.* **fur trade,** peletería, *f*

furbish *vt* pulir; renovar; limpiar

furious *a* furioso. **to become f.,** ponerse furioso, enfurecerse

furiously *adv* furiosamente, con furia

furiousness *n* furia, *f*

furl *vt* plegar; enrollar; *naut* aferrar

furlong *n* estadio, *m*

furlough *n mil* permiso, *m. vt* conceder un permiso (a). **on f.,** de permiso

furnace *n* horno, *m;* (of steam boiler) fogón, *m;* (for central heating) caldera de calefacción central, *f;* (for smelting) cubilote, *m*

furnish *vt* proveer (de), equipar (de), suplir (de); amueblar; (an opportunity) proporcionar; producir

furnished *a* amueblado, con muebles. **f. house,** casa amueblada, *f*

furnisher *n* decorador, *m;* proveedor (-ra)

furnishing *n* provisión, *f,* equipo, *m; pl* **furnishings,** accesorios, *m pl;* mobiliario, mueblaje, *m*

furniture *n* mobiliario, mueblaje, *Central America, Mexico* amoblado *m;* ajuar, equipo, *m;* avíos, *m pl; naut* aparejo, *m.* **a piece of f.,** un mueble. **to empty of f.,** desamueblar, quitar los muebles (de). **f. dealer** or **maker,** mueblista, *mf.* **f. factory,** mueblería, *f.* **f. polish,** crema para muebles, *f.* **f. mover,** transportador de muebles, *m;* (packer) embalador, *m.* **f. repository,** guardamuebles, *m.* **f. van,** carro de mudanzas, *m*

furor *n* furor, *m*

furred *a* forrado or cubierto or adornado de piel; (of the tongue) sucia

furrier *n* peletero, *m.* **furrier's shop,** peletería, *f*

furrow *n* surco, *m; carp* muesca, *f; arch* estría, *f;* (wrinkle) arruga, *f. vt* surcar

furry *a* cubierto de piel; parecido a una piel; hecho de pieles

further *a* ulterior, más distante; (other) otro; opuesto; adicional, más. *adv* más lejos; más allá; además; también; por añadidura. *vt* promover, fomentar; ayudar. **on the f. side,** al otro lado. **till f. orders,** hasta nueva orden. **f. on,** más adelante; más allá

furtherance *n* fomento, *m,* promoción, *f;* progreso, avance, *m*

furthermore *adv* además, por añadidura

furthest *a* (el, la, lo) más lejano or más distante; extremo. *adv* más lejos

furtive *a* furtivo

furtively *adv* furtivamente, a hurtadillas. **to look at f.,** mirar de reojo

fury *n* furor, enfurecimiento, *m,* rabia, *f;* violencia, *f;* frenesí, arrebato, *m;* furia, *f.* **like a f.,** hecho una furia. **to breathe forth f.,** echar rayos

fuse *n* (of explosives) espoleta, mecha, *f; elec* fusible, *m. vt* (metals) fundir; fusionar, mezclar. *vi* (metals) fundirse; mezclarse. **safety-f.,** espoleta de seguridad, *f.* **time-f.,** espoleta de tiempo, *f.* **to blow a f.,** fundir un fusible. **f. box,** caja de fusibles, *f.* **f. wire,** fusible, *m*

fuselage *n aer* fuselaje, *m*

fusible *a* fusible

fusillade *n* descarga cerrada, *f*

fusion *n* fusión, *f;* unión, *f;* (melting) fundición, *f*

fuss *n* agitación, *f;* (bustle) conmoción, bulla, *f;* bullicio, *m. vi* agitarse, preocuparse. *vt* poner nervioso. **There's no need to make such a f.,** No es para tanto. **to make a f. of,** (a person) hacer la rueda (a), ser muy atento (a); (spoil) mimar mucho (a). **to f. about,** andar de acá para allá

fussily *adv* nerviosamente; de un aire importante

fussy *a* meticuloso, nimio; nervioso; (of style) florido, hinchado; (of dress) demasiado adornado

fustigate *vt* fustigar

fusty *a* (moldy) mohoso; mal ventilado; mal oliente; (of views, etc.) pasado de moda

futile *a* fútil, superficial, frívolo; inútil

futility *n* futilidad, superficialidad, frivolidad, *f;* (action) tontería, estupidez, *f*

future *a* futuro, venidero. *n* futuro, porvenir, *m.* **in the f.,** en adelante, en lo venidero, en lo sucesivo. **for f. reference,** para información futura. **f. perfect tense,** *gram* futuro perfecto, *m.* **f. tense,** *gram* futuro, *m*

futurism *n* futurismo, *m*

futurist *n* futurista, *mf*

futuristic *a* futurístico

fuzz *n* tamo, *m,* pelusa, *f.* **f.-ball,** *bot* bejín, *m*

fuzzy *a* crespo rizado; velloso

G

g *n* (letter) ge, *f; mus* sol, *m.* **G clef,** clave de sol, *f*

gab *n inf* labia, *f.* **to have the gift of the gab,** tener mucha labia

gabardine *n* gabardina, *f*

gabble *vi* chacharear, garlar; hablar indistintamente; (of goose and some birds) graznar. *vt* decir indistintamente; decir rápidamente; (a language) chapurrear; mascullar. *n* cháchara, *f,* vocerío, *m;* (of goose and some birds) graznido, *m*

gabbler *n* charlatán (-ana), chacharero (-ra)

gabbling *n* See **gabble**

gable *n arch* gablete, hastial, *m.* **g.-end,** alero, *m*

gad *vi* corretear, callejear. **to gad about,** correr por todos lados; divertirse.

gadabout *n* azotacalles, *mf;* gandul (-la), vagabundo (-da)

gadding *a* callejero; vagabundo. *n* vagancia, *f;* vida errante, *f;* gandulería, *f*

gadfly *n ent* tábano, *m; inf* moscardón, *m*

gadget *n* accesorio, *m;* aparato, *m;* chuchería, *f*

Gadsden Purchase la Venta de la Meseta, *f*

Gael *n* escocés (-esa) del norte; celta, *mf*

Gaelic *a* gaélico. *n* gaélico, *m*

gaff *n* (hook) garfio, *m; naut* pico de cangrejo, *m; theat* teatrucho, *m*

gaffer *n* viejo, tío, abuelo, *m*

gag *n* mordaza, *f; theat* morcilla, *f. vt* amordazar; *fig* hacer callar. *vi theat* meter morcillas

gage *n* prenda, fianza, *f;* (symbol of challenge) guante, *m;* (challenge) desafío, *m.* See **gauge**

gagging *n* amordazamiento, *m*

gaggle *n* (cry) graznido, *m;* (of geese) manada (de ocas), *f. vi* graznar; cacarear

gaiety *n* alegría, *f;* animación, vivacidad, *f;* (entertainment) diversión, festividad, *f*

gaily *adv* alegremente

gain *n* ganancia, *f;* provecho, beneficio, *m;* (increase) aumento, *m;* (riches) riqueza, *f. vt* ganar; (acquire) conseguir; adquirir; obtener; conquistar; captar; (friends) hacerse; (reach) llegar a, alcanzar. *vi* ganar; (improve) mejorar; (of a watch) adelantarse. **What have they gained by going to Canada?** ¿Qué han logrado con marcharse al Canadá? **to g. ground,** *fig* ganar terreno. **to g. momentum** adquirir velocidad **to g. time,** ganar tiempo. **to g. on, upon,** acercarse a; (overtake) alcanzar; (outstrip) dejar atrás, pasar; (sea) invadir; (of habits) imponerse

gainful *a* ganancioso, lucrativo; ventajoso

gainfully *adv* ventajosamente; lucrativamente

gainsay *vt* contradecir; oponer; negar

gainsaying *n* contradicción, *f*; oposición, *f*; negación, *f*

gait *n* porte, andar, *m*; paso, *m*, andadura, *f*

gaiter *n* polaina, *f*; (spat) botín, *m*

gala *n* gala, fiesta, *f*. **g.-day.** día de fiesta, *m*. **g.-dress,** traje de gala, *m*

galaxy *n ast* vía láctea, *f*; *fig* constelación, *f*; grupo brillante, *m*

gale *n* vendaval, ventarrón, *m*; (storm) temporal, *m*; tempestad, *f*

Galician *a* and *n* gallego (-ga).

Galilean *a* and *n* galileo (-ea)

Galilee Galilea, *f*

gall *n* (on horses) matadura, *f*; (abrasion) rozadura, *f*; hiel, bilis, *f*; *fig* hiel, amargura, *f*; rencor, *m*; (American slang) descaro, *m*, impertinencia, *f*; *bot* agalla, *f*. *vt* rozar; *fig* mortificar, herir. **g.-apple,** agalla, *f*. **g.-bladder,** vejiga de la hiel, *f*. **g.-stone,** cálculo hepático, *m*

gallant *a* hermoso; (imposing) imponente, majestuoso; (brave) valiente, gallardo, valeroso, intrépido; (chivalrous) caballeroso; noble; (attentive to ladies, or amorous) galante. *n* galán, *m*. *vt* galantear, cortejar

gallantly *adv* (bravely) valientemente; caballerosamente; cortésmente; galantemente

gallantry *n* (bravery) valentía, *f*, valor, *m*; heroísmo, *m*, proeza, *f*; (chivalry) caballerosidad, *f*; (toward women, or amorousness) galantería, *f*

galleon *n* galeón, *m*

gallery *n* galería, *f*; pasillo, *m*; (of a cloister) tránsito, *m*; (cloister) claustro, *m*; (for spectators) tribuna, *f*; *theat* paraíso, gallinero, *m*; (theater audience) galería, *f*; (of portraits, etc.) galería, colección, *f*; (min, mil) galería, *f*; (building) museo, *m*. **art g.,** museo de pinturas, *m*

galley *n* (naut, print) galera, *f*; (kitchen) cocina, *f*; (rowboat) falúa de capitán, *f*. **to condemn to the galleys,** echar a galeras. **wooden g.,** *print* galerín, *m*. **g.-proof,** galerada, *f*. **g.-slave,** galeote, *m*

Gallic *a* gálico, galicano; francés

gallicism *n* galicismo, *m*

galling *a fig* irritante; mortificante

gallivant *vi* callejear, corretear; divertirse; ir de parranda

gallon *n* galón, *m*

galloon *n* galón, *m*, trencilla, *f*

gallop *n* galope, *m*. *vi* galopar; ir aprisa. *vt* hacer galopar, **at full g.,** a rienda suelta, a galope tendido. **to g. back,** volver a galope. **to g. down,** bajar a galope. **to g. off,** marcharse galopando; alejarse corriendo. **to g. past,** desfilar a galope ante. **to g. through,** cruzar a galope. **to g. up,** *vt* subir a galope. *vi* llegar a galope

gallopade *n* (dance) galop, *m*

galloping *n* galope, *m*; galopada, *f*. *a* que va a galope; *med* galopante. **g. consumption,** tisis galopante, *f*

gallows *n* patíbulo, *m*, horca, *f*; (framework) montante, *m*. **g.-bird,** criminal digno de la horca, *m*

galop *n* galop, *m*

galore *adv* a granel, en abundancia (e.g. **sunshine galore,** sol a granel)

galosh *n* chanclo, *m*

galvanic *a elec* galvánico; espasmódico

galvanize *vt* galvanizar

gambit *n* (chess) gambito, *m*; *fig* táctica, *f*

gamble *n* juego de azar, *m*; jugada, *f*; aventura, *f*; *com* especulación, *f*. *vi* jugar por dinero; especular; (with)

fig aventurar, arriesgar. **to g. on the Stock Exchange,** jugar en la bolsa. **to g. away,** perder al juego

gambler *n* jugador (-ra), *Mexico* dadista *mf*

gambling *n* juego, *m*. *a* jugador; de juego. **g.-den,** casa de juego, *f*, garito, *m*

gambol *n* salto, brinco, retozo, *m*; cabriola, *f*; juego, *m*. *vi* saltar, brincar, retozar; juguetear

game *n* juego, *m*; (match) partido, *m*; (jest) chanza, *f*; (trick) trampa, *f*; (birds, hares, etc.) caza menor, *f*; (tigers, lions, etc.) caza mayor, *f*; (flesh of game) caza, *f*; *pl* **games,** deportes, *m pl. a* de caza; (courageous) valiente, animoso, brioso; resuelto. *vi* jugar por dinero. **He is g. for anything,** Se atreve a todo. **big g. hunting,** caza mayor, *f*. **head of g.,** pieza de caza, *f*. **It is a g. at which two can play,** Donde las dan las toman. **The g. is not worth the candle,** La cosa no vale la pena. **The g. is up,** *fig* El proyecto se ha frustrado. **to make g. of,** (things) burlarse de; (persons) tomar el pelo a; mofarse de. **to play the g.,** *fig* jugar limpio. **to g. away,** perder al juego. **g. of cards,** juego de naipes, *m*. **g. of chance,** juego de azar, *m*. **g.-bag,** morral, *m*. **g. drive,** batida de caza, *f*. **g.-laws,** leyes de caza, *f pl*. **g.-licence,** licencia de caza, *f*. **g.-pie,** tortada, *f*. **g. preserve,** coto de caza, *m*

gamekeeper *n* guardabosque, *m*

gamely *adv* valientemente

gameness *n* valentía, resolución, fortaleza, *f*

gamete *n* gameto, *m*

gaming *n* juego, *m*, *a* de juego. **g.-house,** garito, *m*. **g.-table,** mesa de juego, *f*; *fig* juego, *m*

gammon *n* (of bacon) jamón, *m*. *vt* curar (jamón)

gamut *n* gama, *f*

gander *n* ganso, *m*

gang *n* cuadrilla, pandilla, *Mexico* carpanta *f*; (squad) pelotón, *m*; (of workers) brigada, cuadrilla, *f*; group, *m*. **g.-plank,** plancha, *f*

ganglion *n* ganglio, *m*; *fig* centro, *m*

gangrene *n* gangrena, *f*. *vt* gangrenar. *vi* gangrenarse

gangrenous *a* gangrenoso

gangster *n* pistolero, gángster, *m*

gangway *n* pasillo, *m*; *naut* plancha, *f*, pasamano, *m*; (opening in ship's side) portalón, *m*. **midship g.,** crujía, *f*

gap *n* brecha, *f*; abertura, *f*; (hole) boquete, *m*; (pass) desfiladero, paso, *m*; (ravine) hondonada, barranca, *f*; (blank) laguna, *f*, vacío, *m*; (crack) intersticio, *m*, hendedura, *f*, resquicio, *m*. **to fill a gap,** llenar un boquete; llenar un vacío

gape *vi* estar con la boca abierta, papar moscas. **to g. at,** mirar con la boca abierta

gaping *n* huelgo, *m*; abertura, *f*, *a* que bosteza; boquiabierto; abierto

garage *n* garaje, *m*. *vt* poner (un coche, etc.) en un garaje. **g. owner,** garajista, *mf*

garb *n* traje, vestido, *m*; uniforme, *m*; *her* espiga, *f*. *vt* vestir, ataviar

garbage *n* basura, inmundicia, *f*

garbage can basurero, tarro de la basura, *m*

garbage dump *Lat. Am.* basural *m*

garble *vt* falsear, mutilar, pervertir

garden *n* jardín, *m*; huerto, *m*; (fertile region) huerta, *f*. *a* de jardín. *vi* trabajar en el jardín, cultivar un huerto. **g. city,** ciudad jardín, *f*. **g.-frame,** semillero, *m*. **g. mold,** tierra vegetal, *f*. **g.-party,** fiesta de jardín, *f*. **g.-plot,** parterre, *m*. **g. produce,** hortalizas, legumbres, *f pl*. **g. roller,** rodillo, *m*. **g.-seat,** banco de jardín, *m*. **g. urn,** jarrón, *m*

gardener *n* jardinero, *m*

gardenia *n* gardenia, *f*; jazmín de la India, *m*

gardening *n* jardinería, *f*; horticultura, *f*. *a* de jardinería

gargantuan *a* gargantuesco; tremendo, enorme

gargle *n* (liquid) gargarismo, *m*; gárgaras, *f pl*. *vi* hacer gárgaras, gargarizar

gargling *n* gargarismo, *m*

gargoyle *n* gárgola, *f*

garish *a* cursi, llamativo, charro, chillón

garishness *n* cursería, ostentación, *f*, lo llamativo

garland *n* guirnalda, *f*; corona, *f*; (anthology) florilegio, *m*; *arch* festón, *m*. *vt* enguirnaldar

garlic *n* ajo, *m*

garment *n* prenda de vestir, *f*; traje, vestido, *m*; *fig* vestidura, *f*; (*fig* cloak) capa, *f*

garner *n* granero, *m*; tesoro, *m*; colección, *f*. *vt* atesorar, guardar

garnet *n* granate, *m*

garnish *n cul* aderezo, *m*; adorno, *m*. *vt cul* aderezar; embellecer, adornar

garnishing *n*. See **garnish**

garret *n* guardilla, buhardilla, *f*, desván, *m*

garrison *n* guarnición, *f*, presidio, *m*. *vt* guarnecer, presidiar. **g. town,** plaza de armas, *f*

garrotte *n* garrote, *m*. *vt* agarrotar, dar garrote (a)

garrulity *n* garrulidad, locuacidad, charlatanería, *f*

garrulous *a* gárrulo, locuaz, charlatán

garter *n* liga, *f*; (G.) Jarretera, *f*, *vt* atar con liga; investir con la Jarretera. **Order of the G.,** Orden de la Jarretera, *f*

gas *n* gas, *m*; *fig, inf* palabrería, *f*; (petrol) bencina, *f*, a de gas; con gas; para gases. *vt* asfixiar con gas; *mil* atacar con gas; saturar de gas. **gas attack,** ataque con gases asfixiantes, *m*. **gas-bag,** bolsa de gas, *f*; *inf* charlatán (-ana). **gas-burner,** mechero de gas, *m*. **gas-chamber,** cámara de gas, *f*. **gas detector,** detector de gases, *m*. **gas-fire,** estufa de gas, *f*. **gas-fitter,** gasista, *m*. **gas-fittings,** lámparas de gas, *f pl*. **gas-light,** luz de gas, *f*; mechero de gas, *m*. **gas-main,** cañería maestra de gas, *f*. **gas-man,** gasista, *m*. **gas-mantle,** camiseta incandescente, *f*. **gas-mask,** máscara para gases, *f*. **gas-meter,** contador de gas, *m*. **gas-pipes,** cañerías (or tuberías) de gas, *f pl*. **gas-ring,** fogón de gas, *m*. **gas-shell,** obús de gases asfixiantes, *m*. **gas-stove,** cocina de gas, *f*. **gas warfare,** guerra química, *f*. **gas-works,** fábrica de gas, *f*

Gascon *a* and *n* gascón (-ona)

Gascony Gascuña, *f*

gaseous *a* gaseoso

gash *n* cuchillada, *f*; herida extensa, *f*. *vt* acuchillar; herir extensamente

gasket *n* aro de empaquetadura, *m*

gasoline *n* gasolina, *f*; bencina, *f*

gasp *n* boqueada, *f*. *vi* boquear. **to be at the last g.,** estar agonizando. **to g. for breath,** luchar por respirar. **to g. out,** decir anhelante, decir con voz entrecortada

gastric *a* gástrico

gastritis *n* gastritis, *f*

gastronome *n* gastrónomo (-ma)

gastronomic *a* gastronómico

gastronomy *n* gastronomía, *f*

gate *n* puerta, *f*; cancela, verja, *f*; entrada, *f*; (of a lock, etc.) compuerta, *f*; (across a road, etc.) barrera, *f*; (money) entrada, *f*; *fig* puerta, *f*. **automatic g.,** (at level crossings, etc.) barrera de golpe, *f*. **to g.-crash,** asistir sin invitación. **g.-keeper,** portero, *m*; guardabarrera, *mf* **g.-money,** entrada, *f*. **g.-post,** soporte de la puerta, *m*

gateway *n* entrada, *f*; puerta, *f*; paso, *m*; vestíbulo, *m*; *fig* puerta, *f*

gather *vt* (assemble) reunir; (amass) acumular, amontonar; (acquire) obtener, adquirir; hacer una colección (de); cobrar; (harvest) cosechar, recolectar; (pick up) recoger; (pluck) coger; (infer) sacar en limpio, aprender; *sew* fruncir; (the brows) fruncir (el ceño). *vi* reunirse, congregarse; amontonarse; (threaten) amenazar; (sadden) amargar; (*fig* hover over) cernerse (sobre); (increase) aumentar, crecer; (be covered) cubrirse; (fester) supurar. *n sew* frunce, pliegue, *m*. **to g. breath,** tomar aliento. **to g. speed,** ganar velocidad. **to g. strength,** cobrar fuerzas. **I g. from Mary that they are going abroad,** Según lo que me ha dicho María, van al extranjero. **to g. in,** juntar; reunir; (harvest) cosechar; coger. **to g. together,** *vt* reunir. *vi* reu-

nirse. **to g. up,** recoger; coger; tomar; (one's limbs) encoger. **to g. up the threads,** *fig* recoger los hilos.

gatherer *n* cogedor, colector, *m*; (harvester) segador, *m*; (of grapes) vendimiador (-ra); (of taxes) recaudador, *m*

gathering *n* cogedura, *f*; (fruit, etc.) recolección, *f*; (of taxes) recaudación, *f*; amontonamiento, *m*; colección, *f*; *med* absceso, *m*; *sew* fruncimiento, *m*; (assembly) reunión, asamblea, *f*; (crowd) concurrencia, muchedumbre, *f*

gathers *n sew* fruncidos, pliegues, *m pl*

gauche *a* torpe, huraño

gaudily *adv* ostentosamente; brillantemente

gaudiness *n* ostentación, *f*; brillantez, *f*

gaudy *a* llamativo, vistoso, brillante, ostentoso

gauge *n* (of gun) calibre, *m*; (railway) entrevía, *f*; (for measuring) indicator, *m*; regla de medir, *f*; *naut* calado, *m*; *fig* medida, *f*; (test) indicación, *f*; (model) norma, *f*. *vt* calibrar; medir; estimar; (ship's capacity) arquear; (judge) juzgar; (size up) tomar la medida (de); *fig* interpretar; *sew* fruncir; (liquor) aforar. **broad (narrow) g. railway,** ferrocarril de vía ancha (estrecha), *m*. **pressure g.,** manómetro, *m*. **water g.,** indicador del nivel de agua, *m*

gauging *n* medida, *f*; (of ship's capacity) arqueo, *m*; (of liquor) aforamiento, *m*; *fig* apreciación, *f*; interpretación, *f*

Gaul Galia, *f*

gaunt *a* anguloso, huesudo, desvaído; (of houses, etc.) lúgubre

gauntlet *n* guante de manopla, *m*; (part of armor) manopla, *f*; guantelete, *m*. **to throw down the g.,** echar el guante, desafiar

gauntness *n* angulosidad, flaqueza, *f*

gauze *n* gasa, *f*; (mist) bruma, *f*. **wire-g.,** tela metálica, *f*

gauziness *n* diafanidad, *f*

gauzy *a* diáfano; de gasa

gavotte *n* gavota, *f*

gawkiness *n* torpeza, desmaña, *f*

gawky *a* anguloso, desgarbado, torpe

gay *a* alegre; festivo, animado; ligero de cascos, disipado; homosexual; (of colors) brillante, llamativo

Gaza Strip la franja de Gaza, *f*

gaze *n* mirada, *f*; mirada fija, *f*. *vi* mirar; mirar fijamente, contemplar

gazelle *n* gacel (-la)

gazer *n* espectador (-ra)

gazette *n* gaceta, *f*. *vt* publicar en la gaceta.

gazing *n* contemplación, *f*, *a* contemplador; que presencia, que asiste a

gear *n* (apparel) atavíos, *m pl*; (harness) guarniciones, *f pl*, arneses, *m pl*; (tackle) utensilios, *m pl*, herramientas, *f pl*; *naut* aparejo, *m*; *mech* engranaje, *m*; juego, *m*, marcha, *f*. *vt* aparejar, enjaezar; *mech* poner en marcha, hacer funcionar. *vi mech* engranar, endentar. **low g.,** pimera velocidad, *f*. **neutral g.,** punto muerto, *m*. **reverse g.,** marcha atrás, *f*. **second g.,** segunda velocidad, *f*. **three-speed g.,** cambio de marchas de tres velocidades, *m*. **top g.,** tercera (or cuarta—according to gear-box) velocidad, *f*. **to change g.,** cambiar de marcha, cambiar de velocidad. **to throw out of g.,** *fig* desquiciar. **g.-box,** caja de velocidades, *f*. **g.-changing,** cambio de velocidad, *m*. **g.-changing lever,** palanca de cambio de velocidad, palanca de cambio de marchas, *f*

gearing *n* engranaje, *m*

gee up *interj* ¡arre!

gehenna *n* gehena, *f*

geisha *n* geisha, *f*

gelatine *n* gelatina, *f*. **cooking g.,** gelatina seca, *f*

gelatinous *a* gelatinoso

geld *vt* capar, castrar

gelder *n* castrador, *m*

gelding *n* castración, capadura, *f*; caballo castrado, *m*; animal castrado, *m*

gelid *a* gélido, helado; *fig* frío, frígido

gem *n* piedra preciosa, *f;* joya, alhaja, *f; fig* joya, *f. vt* adornar con piedras preciosos; enjoyar

Gemini *n* (los) Gemelos

gender *n gram* género, *m;* sexo, *m*

gene *n biol* gene, *m*

genealogical *a* genealógico. **g. tree,** árbol genealógico, *m*

genealogist *n* genealogista, *mf*

genealogy *n* genealogía, *f*

general *a* general; universal; común; corriente; (usual) acostumbrado, usual; del público, público. *n* lo general; *(mil, ecc)* general, *m; inf* criada para todo, *f.* **in g.,** por lo general, en general, generalmente. **to become g.,** generalizarse. **to make g.,** generalizar, hacer general. **g. average,** (marine insurance) avería gruesa, *f.* **g. election,** elección general, *f.* **g. meeting,** pleno, mitin general, *m.* **g. opinion,** voz común, opinión general, *f.* **G. Post Office,** Oficina Central de Correos, *f.* **g. practitioner,** médico (-ca) general. **g. public,** público, *m.* **the general reader** el lector de tipo general *m*

generalissimo *n* generalísimo, *m*

generality *n* generalidad, *f*

generalization *n* generalización, *f*

generalize *vt* and *vi* generalizar

generally *adv* en general, por regla general, por lo general, generalmente; comúnmente, por lo común

generalship *n mil* generalato, *m;* (strategy) táctica, estrategia, *f;* dirección, jefatura, *f*

generate *vt* (beget) engendrar, procrear; *(phys, chem)* generar; *fig* producir, crear

generation *n* procreación, *f;* generación, *f; fig* producción, creación, *f.* **the younger g.,** los jóvenes

generative *a* generador

generator *n mech* generador, *m;* dínamo, *f*

generic *a* genérico

generosity *n* generosidad, *f;* liberalidad, *f*

generous *a* generoso; liberal, dadivoso, limosnero, *Lat. Am.* maniabierto; magnánimo; (plentiful) abundante; (of wines) generoso

generously *adv* generosamente; abundantemente

genesis *n* principio, origen, *m;* (G.) Génesis, *m*

genetic *a* genético

genetics *n* genética, *f*

Geneva Ginebra, *f*

genial *a* (of climate) agradable, bueno; (of persons) afable, bondadoso; de buen humor, bonachón

geniality *n* afabilidad, bondad, *f;* buen humor, *m*

genially *adv* afablemente

genie *n* genio, *m*

genital *a* genital, sexual. *n pl* **genitals,** genitales, *m pl*

genitive *a* and *n gram* genitivo *m.*

genius *n* genio, *m;* carácter, *m,* índole, *f;* ingenio, *m; inf* talento, *m*

Genoa Génova, *f*

Genoese *a* and *n* genovés (-esa)

genre *n* género, *m.* **g. painting,** cuadro de género, *m*

genteel *a* fino; (affected) remilgado, melindroso; de buen tono; de buena educación

gentile *a* and *n* gentil, *mf*

gentility *n* aristocracia, *f;* respetabilidad, *f*

gentle *a* noble, bien nacido, de buena familia; amable; suave; ligero; dulce; (docile) manso, dócil; (affectionate) cariñoso; bondadoso; sufrido, paciente, cortés; pacífico, tolerante. **He was a man of g. birth,** Era un hombre bien nacido. **"G. reader,"** «Querido lector». **g. wind** *Lat. Am.* airecito *m*

gentlefolk *n pl* gente de bien, gente fina, *f;* gente de buena familia, *f*

gentleman *n* caballero, señor, *m;* gentilhombre, *m.* **Ladies and gentlemen,** Señoras y caballeros, Señores. **young g.,** señorito, *m.* **to be a perfect g.,** ser un caballero perfecto. **g.-inwaiting,** gentilhombre de la cámara, *m*

gentlemanliness *n* caballerosidad, *f*

gentlemanly *a* caballeroso

gentleness *n* amabilidad, *f;* suavidad, *f;* dulzura, *f;* man-

sedumbre, docilidad, *f;* bondad, *f;* paciencia, *f;* cortesía, *f;* tolerancia, *f*

gentlewoman *n* dama, *f;* dama de servicio, *f*

gently *adv* suavemente; dulcemente; silenciosamente, sin ruido; (slowly) despacio, poco a poco. **g. born,** bien nacido

gentry *n* pequeña aristocracia, alta clase media, *f;* (disparaging) gentle, *f*

genuflect *vi* doblar la rodilla

genuflexion *n* genuflexión, *f*

genuine *a* puro; genuino; verdadero; real; sincero; auténtico

genuinely *adv* genuinamente; verdaderamente; realmente; sinceramente

genuineness *n* pureza, *f;* autenticidad, *f;* verdad, *f;* sinceridad, *f*

genus *n* género, *m*

geodesic *a* geodésico

geodesy *n* geodesia, *f*

geographer *n* geógrafo, *m*

geographical *a* geográfico

geographically *adv* geográficamente; desde el punto de vista geográfico

geography *n* geografía, *f*

geological *a* geológico

geologically *adv* geológicamente; desde el punto de vista geológico

geologist *n* geólogo, *m*

geologize *vi* estudiar la geología. *vt* estudiar desde un punto de vista geológico

geology *n* geología, *f*

geometric *a* geométrico

geometry *n* geometría, *f*

geophysics *n* geofísica, *f*

Georgian *a geog* georgiano; del principio del siglo diez y nueve

georgic *n* geórgica, *f*

geotropism *n* geotropismo, *m*

geranium *n* geranio, *m*

germ *n* embrión, germen, *m;* microbio, bacilo, *m; fig* germen, *m.* **g.-cell,** célula germinal, *f*

German *a* alemán; germánico. *n* alemán (-ana); (language) alemán, *m;* germano (-na), germánico (-ca). **Sudeten G.,** alemán (-ana) sudete. **G. measles,** rubeola, *f.* **G. silver** alpaca, *f,* melchor *m,* plata alemana *f*

germander *n bot* camedrio, *m*

germane *a* pertinente (a), a propósito (a)

Germanic *a* germánico. *n* (language) germánico, *m*

Germanization *n* germanización, *f*

Germanize *vt* germanizar. *vi* germanizarse

Germanophile *n* germanófilo (-la)

Germany Alemania, *f*

germicidal *a* bactericida

germicide *n* desinfectante, *m*

germinal *a* germinal. *n* (G.) germinal, *m*

germinate *vi* germinar, brotar. *vt* hacer germinar

germination *n* germinación, *f*

germinative *a* germinativo

gerund *n* gerundio, *m*

gerundive *n* gerundio adjetivado, *m*

Gestapo *n* Gestapo, *f*

gestation *n* gestación, *f*

gesticulate *vi* gesticular, hacer gestos; accionar. *vt* expresar por gestos

gesticulation *n* gesticulación, *f*

gesticulatory *a* gesticular

gesture *n* movimiento, *m;* gesticulación, *f;* (of the face) gesto, *m,* mueca, *f;* ademán, *m,* acción, *f. vi* gesticular. *vt* decir por gestos; acompañar con gestos

get *vt* (obtain) obtener; (acquire) adquirir; (buy) comprar; (take) tomar; (receive) recibir; (gain, win) ganar; (hit) acertar, dar; (place) poner; (achieve) alcanzar, lograr; (make) hacer; (call) llamar; (understand) comprender; (catch) coger; (procreate) procrear, engendrar; (induce) persuadir; (invite) convidar, invitar; (cause) hacer; (with have and past part.) tener;

giddy

(with have and past part. followed by infin.) tener que; (followed by noun and past part.) hacer; (fetch) buscar, ir a buscar; (order) mandar, disponer; (procure) procurar; (bring) traer; (money) hacer; (a reputation, etc.) hacerse; (a prize, an advantage) llevar; (learn) aprender; (be) ser. vi (become) hacerse; ponerse; venir a ser; (old) envejecerse; (angry) montar (en cólera), enojarse; (arrive) llegar a; (attain) alcanzar; (accomplish) conseguir, lograr; (drunk) emborracharse; (hurt) hacerse daño; (wet) mojarse; (cool) enfriarse; (money) hacer (dinero); (of health) ponerse; (find oneself) hallarse, encontrarse; (late) hacerse (tarde); (dark) empezar a caer (la noche), empezar a caer (la noche), empezar a oscurecer; (put oneself) meterse; (grow, be) estar; (on to or on top of) montar sobre, subir a. **He has got run over,** Ha sido atropellado. **It gets on my nerves,** Se me pone los nervios en punta. **Let's get it over!** ¡Vamos a concluir de una vez! **How do you get on with her?** ¿Cómo te va con ella? **She must be getting on for twenty,** Tendrá alrededor de veinte años. **to get a suit made,** mandar hacerse un traje. **to get altitude sickness** Peru asorocharse **to get better,** (in health) mejorar de salud; hacer progresos adelantar. **to get dark,** obscurecer. **to get depressed** Lat. Am. amurrarse **to get into conversation with,** trabar conversación con. **to get into bad company,** frecuentar malas compañías. **to get into the habit of,** acostumbrarse a. **to get married,** casarse. **to get near,** acercarse. **to get one's own way,** salir con la suya. **to get oneself up as,** disfrazarse de. **to get out in a hurry,** salir apresuradamente; marcharse rápidamente, inf salir pitando. **to get out of the way,** quitarse de en medio, apartarse. **to get rid of,** desembarazarse de, librarse de; salir de; perder. **to have got,** poseer; tener; padecer. **Get on!** ¡Adelante!; (to a horse) ¡Arre! (continue) ¡Sigue! **Get out!** ¡Fuera! ¡Largo de aquí! ¡Sal! **to get the blues = to get depressed. Get up!** ¡Levántate!; (to a horse) ¡Arre! **to get about,** moverse mucho; andar mucho; (attend to business affairs) ir a sus negocios; (travel) viajar; (get up from sick bed) levantarse; (go out) salir; (be known) saberse, divulgarse, hacerse público. **to get above,** subir a un nivel más alto (de). **to get across,** vi cruzar, atravesar. vt hacer cruzar. **to get along,** vi (depart) marcharse; (continue) seguir, vivir; (manage) ir, ir tirando. vt llevar; traer; hacer andar por. **How are you getting along?** ¿Cómo le va? **I am getting along all right, thank you,** Voy tirando, gracias. **to get along without,** pasarse sin. **to get angry** vi Central America empurrarse **to get at,** (remove) sacar; (find) encontrar; (reach) llegar a; alcanzar; (discover) descubrir; (allude to) aludir a; (understand) comprender. **to get away,** vi dejar (un lugar); marcharse, irse; (escape) escaparse. vt ayudar a marcharse; ayudar a escaparse. **to get away with,** llevarse, marcharse con; inf salir con la suya. **to get back,** vi regresar, volver; (get home) volver a casa; (be back) estar de vuelta. vt (recover) recobrar; (receive) recibir; (find again) hallar de nuevo. **to get depressed** Central America acuilmarse **to get down,** vi bajar, descender. vt bajar; (take off a hook) descolgar; (swallow) tragar; (note) anotar; escribir. **to get down on all fours,** ponerse en cuatro patas. **to get down to,** ponerse a (estudiar, trabajar, etc.). **to get in,** vi entrar en; lograr entrar en; (slip in) colarse en; (of political party) entrar en el poder; (of a club) hacerse socio de; (return) regresar; (home) volver a casa; (find oneself) hallarse, estar; (a habit) adquirir. vt hacer entrar en; (a club, etc.) hacer socio de; (a word) decir. **to get in line** Mexico formarse **to get into.** See **to get in. to get off,** vt apearse de; bajar de; (send) enviar; (from punishment) librar; (bid goodbye) despedirse de; (remove) quitar, sacar. vi apearse; bajar; (from punishment) librarse; (leave) ponerse en camino, marcharse. **to get on,** vi (wear) tener puesto; (progress) hacer progresos, adelantar; (prosper) medrar, prosperar; (suc-

ceed) tener éxito; avanzar; seguir el camino; (agree) avenirse. vt (push) empujar; (place) poner; (cause) hacer; (clothes) ponerse; (mount) subir a. **to get open,** abrir. **to get out,** vt hacer salir; sacar; (publish) publicar; divulgar. vi salir; escapar; **to get out of a jam,** salir de un paso; (descend) bajar (de). **to get over,** (cross) atravesar, cruzar; (an illness, grief, etc.) reponerse, reponerse de; (excuse) perdonar; (surmount) superar; (ground) recorrer. **to get round,** (a person) persuadir; (surround) rodear; (avoid) evitar; (difficulties) superar, vencer. **to g. one's degree** Lat. Am. diplomarse. **to get through,** pasar por; (time) pasar, entretener; (money) gastar; (finish) terminar; acabar; (pierce or enter) penetrar; (communicate) comunicar (con); (difficulties) vencer; (an exam) aprobar. **to get the blues** Central America acuilmarse **to get to,** llegar a; encontrar; (begin) empezar. **to get together,** vt reunir, juntar. vi reunirse, juntarse. **to get under,** ponerse debajo de; (control) dominar. **to get up,** vt (raise) alzar, levantar; (carry up things) subir; hacer subir; organizar; preparar; (learn) aprender; (linen) blanquear, colar; (ascend) subir; hacer; (dress) ataviar; (steam) generar; (a play) ensayar, poner en escena. vi levantarse; (on a horse) montar a caballo; (of the wind) refrescarse; (of the fire) avivarse; (of the sea) embravecerse. **to get up to,** llegar a; alcanzar

get-at-able a accesible

getting n adquisición, f; (of money) ganancia, f. **g. up,** preparación, f; organización, f; (of a play) representación (de una comedia), puesta en escena, f

get-up n atavío, m; (of a book, etc.) aspecto, m

gewgaw n chuchería, f

geyser n géiser, m; (for heating water) calentador (de agua), m

ghastliness n horror, m; palidez mortal, f; aspecto miserable, m; (boringness) tedio, aburrimiento, m; lo desagradable

ghastly a horrible; de una palidez mortal; cadavérico; (boring) aburrido; muy desagradable

ghetto n gueto m

ghost n fantasma, espectro, aparecido, m; (spirit) alma, f, espíritu, m; (shadow) sombra. f; (writer) mercenario, m. **Holy G.,** Espíritu Santo, m. **to give up the g.,** entregar el alma; perder la esperanza, desesperarse. **to look like a g.,** parecer un fantasma

ghostliness n espiritualidad, f; lo misterioso; palidez, f; tenuidad, f

ghostly a espiritual; espectral; misterioso; pálido; vaporoso, tenue; indistinto

ghost town n pueblo-fantasma, m

ghost word n palabra-fantasma, f

ghoul n vampiro, m

ghoulish a insano; cruel; sádico

giant n gigante, m; fig coloso, m, a gigantesco; de gigantes; de los gigantes. **g.-killer,** matador de gigantes, m. **g.-stride,** (gymnastics) paso volante, m

gibber vi hablar incoherentemente, hablar entre dientes; farfullar, hablar atropelladamente; decir disparates

gibberish n galimatías, m; jerigonza, f, griego, m

gibbet n horca, f, patíbulo, m. **to die on the g.,** morir ahorcado

gibbon n zool gibón, m

gibe n improperio, escarnio, m, burla, mofa, f. vi criticar. **to g. at,** burlarse de, ridiculizar, mofarse de

gibing a burlón, mofador. n mofas, burlas, f pl

gibingly adv burlonamente, con sorna

giblets n menudillos, m pl

giddily adv vertiginosamente; frívolamente; atolondradamente

giddiness n vértigo, m; atolondramiento, m; inconstancia, f; frivolidad, ligereza de cascos, f

giddy a vertiginoso; mareado; atolondrado, casquivano, frívolo; inconstante. **She felt very g.,** Se sintió muy mareada. **to make g.,** dar vértigo (a), marear

gift *n* regalo, *m*, dádiva, *f*; (quality) don, talento, *m*; prenda, *f*; poder, *m*; *law* donación, *f*; (offering) ofrenda, oblación, *f*. *vt* dotar. **deed of g.,** *law* escritura de donación, *f*. **in the g. of,** en el poder de, en las manos de. **I wouldn't have it as a g.,** No lo tomaría ni regalado. **Never look a g. horse in the mouth,** A caballo regalado no se le mira el diente. **g. of tongues,** don de las lenguas, genio de las lenguas, *m*

gifted *a* talentoso

gig *n* (carriage) carrocín, *m*; (boat) falúa, lancha, *f*; (for wool) máquina de cardar paño, *f*; (harpoon) arpón, *m*

gigantic *a* gigantesco; colosal, enorme

giggle *vi* reírse sin motivo; reírse disimuladamente. *n* risa disimulada, *f*

giggling *n* risa estúpida, *f*; risa nerviosa, *f*

gigolo *n* gigolo, mantenido, jinetero (Cuba), *m*

gild *vt* dorar; (metals) sobredorar; embellecer. **to g. the pill,** dorar la píldora

gilder *n* dorador, *m*

gilding *n* dorado, *m*, doradura, *f*; embellecimiento, *m*

Gileadite *n* and *a* galaadita, *mf*

gill *n* (of fish) agalla, branquia, *f*; (ravine) barranco, *m*; (measure) cierta medida de líquidos, *f*, ($\frac{1}{4}$ litro)

gilt *n* (of lady) dorado, *m*; pan de oro, *m*; relumbrón, *m*; *fig* encanto, *m*, a dorado, áureo. **g.-edged,** (of books) con los bordes dorados. **g.-edged security,** papel del Estado, *m*; valores de toda confianza, *m pl*

gimcrack *n* chuchería, *f. a* de baratillo, cursi; mal hecho

gimlet *n* barrena, *f*, taladro, *m*

gin *n* (drink) ginebra, *f*; (snare) trampa, *f. vt* (snare) coger con trampa. **g. block,** *mech* garrucha, *f*

ginger *n* jengibre, *m*; *inf* energía, *f*, brío, *m*, *a* rojo. *vt* sazonar con jengibre; *inf* animar, estimular. **g.-beer,** gaseosa, *f*

gingerly *adv* con gran cuidado; delicadamente

gingham *n* guinga, *f*

gingivitis *n* gingivitis, *f*

gipsy *n*. See **gypsy**

giraffe *n* jirafa, *f*

gird *vt* ceñir; (invest) investir; (surround) cercar, rodear; (put on) revestir. **to g. oneself for the fray,** prepararse para la lucha

girder *n* viga, jácena, *f*. **main g.,** viga maestra, *f*

girdle *n* (belt) cinturón, *m*; (corset) faja, *f*; circunferencia, *f*; zona, *f. vt* ceñir; *fig* cercar, rodear

girl *n* niña, *f*; chica, muchacha, *f*; (maidservant) criada, muchacha, *f*; (young lady) señorita, *f*. **a young g.,** una jovencita; (a little older) una joven. **old g.,** (of a school) antigua alumna, *f*; *inf* vieja, *f*; (*inf* affectionate) chica, *f*. **g. friend,** amiguita, *f*. **g. guide, girl scout,** exploradora, *f*. **girls' school,** colegio de niñas, colegio de señoritas, *m*

girlhood *n* niñez, *f*; juventud, *f*

girlish *a* de niña, de muchacha; (of boys) afeminado; joven

girth *n* (of horse, etc.) cincha, *f*; circunferencia, *f*; (of person) talle, *m*; (obesity) corpulencia, obesidad, *f*

gist *n* esencia, substancia, *f*, importe, *m*

give *vt* dar; (a present) regalar; (infect) contagiar; (impart) comunicar; (grant) otorgar; (allow, concede) conceder; (assign) asignar, señalar; (appoint) nombrar; (a toast) brindar (a la salud de); (a party, ball, etc.) dar; (a bill) presentar; (wish) desear; (punish) castigar; (pay) pagar; (hand over) entregar; (names at baptism) imponer; (produce) producir; dar; (cause) causar; (of judicial sentences) condenar a; (evoke) proporcionar; (provoke) provocar; (devote) dedicar, consagrar; (sacrifice) sacrificar; (evidence, an account, orders, a lesson, a performance, a concert) dar; (a cry, shout) lanzar, proferir; (a laugh) soltar; (describe) describir; (paint) pintar; (write) escribir; (offer) ofrecer; (show) mostrar; (transmit) transmitir; (heed, pain) hacer; (a speech) pronunciar, hacer; (award, adjudge) adjudicar; (ear) prestar (oído (a)). *vi* dar; ser dadivoso, mostrarse generoso; (give in) ceder; (be elastic) dar de sí; ablandarse; (collapse) hundirse. **G. them my best**

wishes! ¡Dales mis mejores recuerdos! **G. us a song!** ¡Cántanos algo! **I can g.** him a lift in my car, Puedo ofrecerle un asiento en mi auto. **I g. you my word,** Os doy mi palabra. **to g. a good account of oneself,** defenderse bien; hacer bien; salir bien. **to g. a person a piece of one's mind,** contarle cuatro verdades. **to g. chase,** dar caza (a). **to g. it to a person,** poner a uno como nuevo; reprender; (beat) pegar, dar de palos. **to g. of itself,** dar de sí. **to g. rise to,** dar lugar a, ocasionar, causar. **to g. way,** no poder resistir; (break) romperse; (yield) ceder; (collapse) hundirse; (retreat) retroceder. **to g. way to,** (retreat before) retirarse ante; (abandon oneself to) entregarse a, abandonarse a. **to g. away,** enajenar; dar; regalar; (sell cheaply) vender a un precio muy bajo; (get rid of) deshacerse de; (sacrifice) sacrificar; (a secret) revelar; (betray) traicionar; (expose) descubrir; (tell) contar; (a bride) conducir al altar. **He gave himself away,** Reveló su pensamiento sin querer. **to g. back,** *vt* devolver; restituir. *vi* retirarse, cejar. **to g. forth,** divulgar, publicar; (scatter) derramar; (emit) emitir, despedir; (smoke, rays) echar. **to g. in,** *vt* entregar; presentar. *vi* darse por vencido. **to g. in to,** (agree with) asentir en, consentir en; rendirse ante. **Mary always gives in to George,** María hace siempre lo que Jorge quiere. **to g. off,** (of odors, etc.) emitir, exhalar, despedir. **to g. out,** *vt* (tribute) distribuir, repartir; (allocate) asignar; (publish) publicar; (announce) anunciar; (reveal) divulgar; (allege) afirmar, hacer saber; (emit) emitir. *vi* (be exhausted) agotarse; (end) acabarse; (be lacking) faltar. **to g. over,** *vt* entregar; (transfer) traspasar; cesar de. *vi* cesar. **to g. up,** entregar; ceder; (renounce) renunciar (a); (sacrifice) sacrificar; (abandon) abandonar; (cease) dejar de; (as lost) dar por perdido; (of a patient) desahuciar; (a post) dimitir de; (return) devolver, restituir; (a problem) renunciar (a resolver un problema); (lose hope) perder la esperanza; (give in) darse por vencido. **I had given you up,** (didn't expect you), Creí que no ibas a venir. **to g. oneself up to,** entregarse a; dedicarse a; *mil* rendirse a. **to g. up one's seat,** ceder su sitio (or asiento). **to g. upon,** (overlook) dar sobre

give *n* elasticidad, *f*; el dar de sí; (concession) concesión, *f*. **g. and take,** concesiones mutuas, *f pl*. **g. away,** *inf* revelación indiscreta, *f*

given *a* dado; especificado; convenido; (with to) dado a, adicto a. **in a g. time,** en un tiempo dado. **g. that,** dado que

giver *n* dador (-ra); donador (-ra)

giving *a* = **generous**

gizzard *n* molleja, *f*. **It sticks in my g.,** *inf* No lo puedo tragar

glacial *a* glacial

glacier *n* glaciar, *m*

glad *a* feliz, alegre; contento, satisfecho; *inf* elegante. **to be g.,** alegrarse, estar contento, estar satisfecho. **to give the g. eye,** hacer ojos

gladden *vt* alegrar, regocijar

glade *n* claro, *m*; rasa, *f*

gladiator *n* gladiador, *m*

gladiolus *n bot* gladíolo, gladio, *m*; espadaña, *f*

gladly *adv* alegremente; con mucho gusto, gustoso, de buena gana

gladness *n* alegría, felicidad, *f*, contento, *m*; placer, *m*

glamorous *a* exótico; garboso

glamour *n* encanto, *m*, fascinación, *f*; garbo, *m*. **g. girl,** belleza exótica, *f*

glance *n* (of a projectile) desviación, *f*; (of light) vislumbre, *m*; relumbrón, centelleo, *m*; (look) vistazo, *m*, ojeada, *f*; mirada, *f*, *vi* desviarse; relumbrar, centellear, brillar; (with at) ojear, echar un vistazo a, lanzar miradas a; (a book) hojear; mirar; mirar de reojo; *fig* mirar brevemente. **at a g.,** con un vistazo; en seguida. **at the first g.,** a primera vista. **to g. off,** desviarse (al chocar). **to g. over,** repasar, echar un vistazo a; (a book) hojear

glancing *a* (of a blow) que roza

gland *n* (*anat*, *bot*) glándula, *f*; (in the neck) ganglio, *m*.
to have swollen glands, tener inflamación de los ganglios
glandular *a* glandular
glare *n* brillo, fulgor, *m*; luminosidad, *f*; reflejo, *m*; (look) mirada feroz, *f*. *vi* relumbrar, centellear; (stare) mirar con ferocidad, mirar fijamente
glaring *a* deslumbrante, brillante; (of colors) chillón, llamativo; (of looks) de mirada feroz; (flagrant) notorio, evidente
glaringly *adv* brillantemente; con mirada feroz; notoriamente
glass *n* vidrio, *m*; cristal, *m*; (glassware) artículos de vidrio, *m pl*; cristalería, *f*; (for drinking) vaso, *m*, copa, *f*; (pane) cristal, *m*; (mirror) espejo, *m*; (telescope) telescopio, *m*; catalejo, *m*; (barometer) barómetro, *m*; (hour-glass) reloj de arena, *m*; (of a watch) vidrio (de reloj), *m*; *pl* **glasses**, (binoculars) anteojos, *m pl*; (spectacles) gafas, lentes, *m pl*; (opera glasses) gemelos de teatro, *m pl*, *a* de vidrio; de cristal. *vt* vidriar. **John wears glasses,** Juan lleva gafas. **The g. is falling (rising),** El barómetro baja (sube). **to clink glasses,** trincar las copas. **to look in the g.,** mirarse en el espejo. **clear g.,** vidrio trasparente, *m*. **cut g.,** cristal tallado, *m*. **frosted g.,** vidrio jaspeado, *m*. **plate-g.,** vidrio plano, *m*; **safety g.,** vidrio inastillable, *m*. **stained g.,** vidrio de color, vidrio pintado, *m*. **under g.,** bajo vidrio; en invernáculo. **g. bead,** abalorio, *m*; cuenta de vidrio, *f*. **g.-blower,** soplador de vidrio, *m*. **g.-blowing,** el soplar de vidrio. **g. case,** escaparate, *m*. **g.-cloth,** paño para vasos, *m*. **g. eye,** ojo de cristal, *m*. **g. paper,** papel de vidrio, *m*. **g. roof,** techo de cristal, *m*. **g. window,** vidriera, *f*
glasscutter *n* cortador de vidrio, *m*
glassful *n* contenido de un vaso, *m*; vaso, vaso lleno, *m*, copa, *f*
glasshouse *n* fábrica de vidrio, *f*; vidriería, *f*; invernáculo, invernadero, *m*, estufa, *f*
glassware *n* cristalería, *f*
glassy *a* vitreo; (of eyes) vidrioso; *fig* cristalino; (smooth) liso, raso
glaucous *a* de color verdemar; *bot* glauco
glaze *n* barniz, *m*: lustre, brillo, *m*. *vt* poner vidrios (a); vidriar; barnizar; (paper, leather, etc.) satinar. *vi* (of eyes) vidriarse, ponerse vidrioso
glazier *n* vidriero, *m*
glazing *n* vidriado, *m*; barnizado, *m*; satinado, *m*; (material) barniz, *m*
gleam *n* rayo, destello, *m*; (of color) viso, *m*, mancha, *f*; *fig* rayo, *m*; (in the eye) chispa, *f*. *vi* relucir, centellear, resplandecer; brillar; reflejar la luz; *fig* brillar. **g. of hope,** rayo de esperanza, *m*
gleaming *a* reluciente, centelleante; brillante. *n* see **gleam**
glean *vt* espigar, rebuscar; recoger. *vi* espigar
gleaner *n* espigador, *m*; recogedor (-ra)
gleaning *n* espigueo, *m*; rebusca, recolección, *f*; *pl* **gleanings,** fragmentos, *m pl*
glee *n* alegría, *f*, júbilo, alborozo, *m*; *mus* canción para voces solas, *f*
gleeful *a* alegre, jubiloso, gozoso
gleefully *adv* alegremente, con júbilo
glen *n* cañada, *f*, cañón, *m*, hondonada, *f*
glib *a* locuaz, voluble; (easy) fácil
glibness *n* locuacidad, volubilidad, *f*; (easiness) facilidad, *f*
glide *n* deslizamiento, *m*; *aer* planeo, *m*. *vi* deslizarse; resbalar; *aer* planear. **to g. away,** escurrirse; desaparecer silenciosamente
glider *n* *aer* deslizador, planeador, *m*
gliding *n* *aer* vuelo sin motor, *m*
glimmer *n* luz trémula, luz débil, *f*, tenue resplandor, *m*; vislumbre, *m*. *vi* brillar con luz trémula, rielar *fig*; tener vislumbres (de)
glimpse *n* vistazo, *m*; vislumbre, *m*; indicio, *m*; impre-

sión, *f*; vista, *f*. *vt* entrever, divisar; tener una vista (de); ver por un instante; vislumbrar
glint *n* tenue resplandor, *m*; lustre, *m*; centelleo, *m*; reflejo, *m*; (in the eye) chispa, *f*. *vi* relucir, destellar, rutilar; reflejar
glisten *vi* brillar, relucir
glistening *a* coruscante; brillante, reluciente
glitter *n* brillo, resplandor, *m*, rutilación, *f*. *vi* brillar, resplandecer, relucir; rutilar. **All that glitters is not gold,** Todo lo que reluce no es oro
glittering *a* reluciente, resplandeciente; *fig* brillante
gloat (over) *vi* recrearse en, gozarse en, deleitarse en
globe *n* globo, *m*; esfera, *f*; (for fish) pecera, *f*; (for gas, electric light) globo, *m*. **geographical g.,** globo terrestre, *m*. **g.-trotter,** trotamundos, *mf*
globular *a* globular, esférico
globule *n* glóbulo, *m*
gloom *n* obscuridad, *f*; lobreguez, *f*, tinieblas, *f pl*; *fig* melancolía, tristeza, *f*; taciturnidad, *f*. *vi fig* ponerse melancólico; ser taciturno
gloomily *adv* obscuramente; *fig* tristemente; taciturnamente
gloomy *a* obscuro; sombrío, lóbrego; melancólico, triste; taciturno; (of prospects, etc.) poco halagüeño, nada atrayente
glorification *n* glorificación, *f*
glorify *vt* glorificar; exaltar; alabar
glorious *a* glorioso; espléndido, magnífico; insigne; *inf* estupendo
glory *n* gloria, *f*; esplendor, *m*, magnificencia, *f*; *art* gloria, *f*. *vi* recrearse, gozarse; glorificarse, jactarse. **to be in one's g.,** estar en la gloria. **to g. in,** hacer gala de, glorificarse en
gloss *n* (sheen) lustre, brillo, *m*; *fig* apariencia, *f*; (note) glose, *m*; (excuse) disculpa, *f*. *vt* pulir; glosar. **to g. over,** (faults) disculpar, excusar
glossary *n* glosario, *m*
glossiness *n* lustre, *m*, tersura, *f*; brillo, *m*
glossy *a* lustroso, terso; brillante; (of hair) liso
glottis *n* *anat* glotis, *f*
glottal stop *n* choque glótica, golpe de glotis, *m*
glove *n* guante, *m*; **evening gloves,** guantes largos, *m pl*. **to be hand in g. with,** juntar diestra con diestra. **to fit like a g.,** sentar como un guante. **to put on one's gloves,** ponerse los guantes. **g. shop,** guantería, *f*. **g.-stretcher,** ensanchador (-ra) de guantes, abridor (-ra) de guantes *mf*
glove compartment gaveta, guantera, *f*, guantero portaguantes *m*
glove-compartment light luz de portaguantes, *f*
glover *n* guantero (-ra)
glow *n* incandescencia, *f*; claridad, *f*; luz difusa, *f*; (heat) calor, *m*; (of color) intensidad, *f*; color vivo, *m*; (enthusiasm) ardor, entusiasmo, *m*; (redness) rojez, *f*; (in the sky) arrebol, *m*; (of pleasure, etc.) sentimiento de placer, *m*; sensación de bienestar, *f*. *vi* estar incandescente; arder; abrasarse; sentir entusiasmo; mostrarse rojo; experimentar un sentimiento de placer o una sensación de bienestar. **to g. with health,** estar rebosando de salud. **g.-worm,** luciérnaga, *f*
glower *n* ceño, *m*; mirada amenazadora, *f*. *vi* poner cara de pocos amigos, mirar airadamente; tener los ojos puestos (en)
glowing *a* candente, incandescente; ardiente; entusiasta; satisfecho; intenso; (bright) vivo; (red) encendido; (with health) rebosante de salud. *n* see **glow**
glowingly *adv* encendidamente; *fig* con entusiasmo
glucose *n* glucosa, *f*
glue *n* engrudo, *m*, cola, *f*. *vt* encolar, engrudar; pegar; *fig* fijar, poner. **He kept his eyes glued on them,** Tenía los ojos fijados (or pegados) en ellos. **g.-pot,** pote de cola, *m*
gluey *a* gomoso; pegajoso, viscoso
glueyness *n* viscosidad, *f*
gluing *n* encoladura, *f*
glum *a* deprimido, taciturno, sombrío

glumly *adv* taciturnamente

glut *n* superabundancia, *f*, exceso, *m*. *vt* (satiate) hartar; *fig* saciar; (the market) inundar

gluteal *a* glúteo

glutinous *a* glutinoso, pegajoso, viscoso

glutton *n* glotón (-ona); *fig* ávido (-da)

gluttonous *a* glotón, comilón

gluttony *n* glotonería, gula, *f*

glycerine *n* glicerina, *f*

gnarled *a* nudoso; (of human beings) curtido

gnash *vt* rechinar, crujir (los dientes)

gnashing *n* rechinamiento (de dientes), *m*

gnat *n* mosquito, *m*

gnaw *vt* roer; morder; (of wood by worms) carcomer; *fig* roer

gnawing *n* roedura, *f*; mordedura, *f*, *a* roedor; mordedor

gnome *n* nomo, *m*

gnostic *a* and *n* nóstico (-ca)

gnosticism *n* nosticismo, *m*

go *vi* ir; (depart) irse, marcharse; (go toward) dirigirse a, encaminarse a; (lead to of roads, etc.) conducir a, ir a; (vanish) desaparecer; (leave) dejar, salir de; (lose) perder; (pass) pasar; (of time) transcurrir, pasar; (be removed) quitarse; (be prohibited) prohibirse; (fall) caer; (collapse) hundirse; (be torn off) desprenderse; desgajarse; *mech* funcionar, trabajar, andar; (sound) sonar; (of the heart) palpitar, latir; (follow) seguir; (gesture) hacer un gesto; (be stated) decirse, afirmarse; (live) vivir; (wear) llevar; (turn out) salir, resultar; (improve) mejorar; (prosper) prosperar; (turn, become) ponerse; volverse; (to sleep) dormirse; (into a faint) desmayarse; (decay) echarse a perder, estropearse; (turn sour) agriarse; (become, adopt views, etc.) hacerse; (be sold) venderse; (be decided); decidirse, ser decidido; (have) tener; (by will) pasar; (belong) pertenecer; (receive) recibir; (have its place) estar; (put) ponerse; (going plus infin.) ir a; (die) morir, irse; (do a journey, a given distance) hacer; (a pace, step) dar; (take) tomar; (escape) escaparse, (contribute) contribuir (a); (harmonize) armonizar (con); (be current) ser válido; (be) ser; (of a document, etc., run) rezar, decir; (attend) asistir a; (be broken) estar roto; (be worn) estar raído; (be granted) darse, otorgarse. **It's gone five,** Ya dieron las cinco. **It's time to be going,** Es hora de marcharse. **Let's go!** ¡Vamos! **These two colours go well together,** Estos colores armonizan bien. **Well, how goes it?** Bueno, ¿qué tal? ¿Cómo te va? **Who goes there?** *mil* ¿Quién va? **to go and fetch,** ir a buscar. **to let go,** soltar; dejar ir. **to go one's way,** seguir su camino. **to go wrong,** salir mal, fracasar; (sin) descarriarse. **"Go!"** (traffic sign) «¡Siga!» **Go on!** ¡Adelante!; (continue) ¡Siga!; ¡Qué va! **to go about,** dar la vuelta a; rodear; recorrer; (undertake) emprender, hacer; intentar; (of news, etc.) circular; *naut* virar de bordo. **Go about your business!** ¡Métete en lo que te importa! **to go abroad,** ir al extranjero; salir a la calle; publicarse, divulgarse. **to go across,** cruzar, atravesar; pasar. **to go after,** andar tras; seguir; (seek) ir a buscar; (persecute) perseguir. **to go again,** ir de nuevo; (be present) asistir otra vez; volver. **to go against,** ir contra; militar contra; oponerse a; ser desfavorable a. **to go ahead,** adelantar, avanzar; progresar; prosperar; (lead) ir a la cabeza (de), conducir; *naut* marchar hacia adelante. **to go along,** andar por; recorrer; (depart) irse, marcharse. **go apartment-hunting,** ir en busca de piso. **to go along with,** acompañar (a). **to go aside,** quitarse de en medio; apartarse, retirarse. **to go astray,** perderse; extraviarse, descarriarse. **to go at,** atacar, acometer; (undertake) emprender; empezar a. **to go at it again,** *inf* volver a la carga. **to go away,** irse, marcharse; ausentarse; alejarse; desaparecer. **to go away with,** marcharse con; (an object) llevarse. **to go back,** volver, regresar, *Lat. Am.* devolverse; (retreat) retroceder, volverse atrás; (in history) remontarse a. **to go back on,** (a promise, etc.) faltar a; (retract) retractarse; (betray) traicionar. **to go backwards,** retroceder, cejar; desandar lo andado; *fig* deteriorar, empeorar. **to go backwards and forwards,** ir y venir; oscilar. **to go before,** (lead) ir a la cabeza de, conducir; anteceder; proceder; (a judge, etc.) comparecer ante. **to go behind,** ir detrás de; esconderse detrás de; seguir; (evidence, etc.) mirar más allá de. **to go between,** ponerse entre; interponerse; (as a mediator) mediar; (insert) intercalarse; (travel) ir entre; llevar cartas entre, ser mensajero de. **to go beyond,** ir más allá; exceder. **to go by,** pasar por; pasar cerca de, pasar junto a; ir por; (of time) transcurrir, pasar; (follow) seguir; guiarse por, atenerse a; (judge by) juzgar por; (a name) pasar por; tomar el nombre de. **to go down,** bajar, descender; (of the sun) ponerse; (sink) hundirse; sumergirse; (fall) caer; (be remembered) ser recordado; (believe) tragar; ser creído. **to go down again,** bajar de nuevo; volver a caer. **go Dutch,** ir a escote, ir a la gringa, ir a la par, ir a limón. **to go far,** ir lejos; influir mucho (en); impresionar mucho; (contribute) contribuir (a). **to go for,** (seek) ir en busca de; procurar tener; (attack) echarse encima de, atacar. **to go for a ride (by car, bicycle, on horseback),** dar un paseo (en coche, en bicicleta, a caballo). **to go forth,** salir; publicarse. **to go forward,** adelantar, avanzar; progresar; continuar; (happen) tener lugar. **to go from,** dejar, abandonar; separarse de, apartarse de; marcharse de. **to go in,** entrar en; (a railway carriage, etc.) subir a; (compete) concurrir. **to go in again,** volver a entrar en, entrar de nuevo en. **to go in and out,** entrar y salir; ir y venir. **to go in for,** entrar a buscar; dedicarse a, entregarse a; (buy) comprarse; tomar parte en; (an examination) tomar (un examen); (for a competition) entrar en (un concurso); (try) ensayar; arriesgar. **to go into,** entrar en; examinar; investigar; ocuparse con. **to go native** *Lat. Am.* acriollarse. **to go near,** acercarse a. **to go off,** marcharse; (explode) estallar; (of fire-arms) dispararse; (of the voice, etc.) perder (la voz, etc.); (run away) huir, fugarse. **to go off badly,** salir mal, fracasar, no tener éxito. **to go off well,** salir bien, tener éxito. **to go on,** subirse a; continuar; durar; avanzar; proseguir su marcha; progresar; prosperar; *theat* entrar en escena; (of clothes) ponerse; (rely on) apoyarse en. **to go on an excursion, go on an outing, go on a trip** *Lat. Am.* excursionarse. **Don't go on like that,** No seas así, No te pongas así. **This glove will not go on me,** No puedo ponerme este guante. **to be gone on a person,** *inf* estar loco por. **I went on to say . . . ,** Después dije; Continuando mi discurso dije . . . **It was going on for six o'clock when . . .** Serían alrededor de las seis cuando . . . **He is going on for fifty,** Raya en los cincuenta años. **to go on foot,** ir a pie. **to go on with,** continuar con; empezar. **to go out,** salir; (descend) bajar; (of fires, lights) extinguirse, apagarse; (of fashion, etc.) pasar (de); (the tide) menguar; (retire) retirarse; (in society) frecuentar la alta sociedad; (die) morir; (arouse) excitar. **to go out of** salir de, *Lat. Am. also* egresar de. **to go out of fashion,** pasar de moda. **to go out of one's way (to),** dejar su camino (para); (lose oneself) perder el camino, extraviarse; (take trouble) desvivirse (por), tomarse molestia (para). **to go over,** cruzar; pasar por encima; (to another party or to the other side) pasarse a; (read) repasar; examinar. **to go past,** pasar; pasar en frente de. **to go round,** dar la vuelta a; (revolve) girar; (surround) rodear; (of news, etc.) divulgarse; (be enough) ser suficiente para todos. **to go through,** ir por, pasar por; recorrer; (pierce) penetrar, atravesar; (examine) examinar; (suffer) padecer, sufrir; (experience) experimentar; (live) vivir; (of time) pasar; (of money) malgastar, derrochar; (die) morir. **to go through with,** llevar a cabo; terminar. **to go to,** ir a, encaminarse a; (a person) acercarse a, dirigirse a; (help, be useful) servir para; (be meant for) destinarse a; (rise of price) subir a; (find) encontrar; (of a bid) subir una apuesta hasta. **to go to**

war, declarar la guerra. **to go together,** ir juntos (juntas). **to go toward,** encaminarse hacia; ir hacia; (help) ayudar a. **to go under,** pasar por debajo de; (sink) hundirse; (fail) fracasar; (be bankrupt) arruinarse, declarare en quiebra; (the name of) hacerse pasar por. **to go up,** subir; ir arriba; (a tree) trepar; (a ladder, etc.) subir; (a river) ir río arriba; (to town) ir a; (explode) estallar. **to go up and down,** subir y bajar; oscilar; ir de una parte a otra. **to go upon,** subirse a; (rely on) apoyarse en; obrar según; emprender. **to go upstairs,** ir arriba; (to another story, as in a flat) subir al otro piso; subir la escalera. **to go up to,** acercarse a; (of a bid) subir una apuesta hasta. **to go with,** acompañar; (agree with) estar de acuerdo con; (of principles) seguir, ser fiel a; (harmonize) armonizar con; (be suitable to) ir bien con; convenir a; (*inf* get along) ir. **to go without,** marcharse sin; (lack) pasarse sin. **It goes without saying that . . .,** Huelga decir que **Where are you going with this?** (What do you mean?) ¿A dónde quieres llegar con esto?

go *n* (fashion) moda, boga, *f*; (happening) suceso, *m*; (fix) apuro, *m*; (energy) energía, *f*, empuje, brío, *m*; (turn) turno, *m*; (attempt) tentativa, *f*; (action) movimiento, *m*, acción, *f*; (bargain) acuerdo, *m*. **It's a go!** (agreed) ¡Trato hecho! ¡Acordado! ¡Entendidos! ¡Entendidas! **It is all the go,** Hace furor, Es la gran moda. **It is no go,** No puede ser, Es imposible. **Now it's my go,** Ahora me toca a mí, Ahora es mi turno. **on the go,** en movimiento; entre manos; ocupado. **to have a go,** probar suerte; procurar, tratar de; tener un turno

goad *n* garrocha, aguijada, *f,* aguijón, *m, Lat. Am.* lanceta *f; fig* acicate, estímulo, *m. vt* aguijar, picar; *fig* incitar, estimular, empujar. **prick with a g.,** aguijonazo, *m*

go-ahead *a* emprendedor: progresivo

goal *n* (posts in football, etc.) meta, portería, *f, Lat. Am.* arco, *m;* (score) gol, *m;* (in racing) meta, *f;* (destination) destinación, *f; fig* ambición, *f;* (purpose, objective) fin, objeto, *m.* **to score a g.,** marcar un gol. **g.-keeper,** guardameta, *m,* portero (-ra). **g.-post,** palo de la portería, *m*

goat *n* cabra, *f; ast* capricornio, *m.* **he-g.,** cabrón. *m.* **young g.,** cabrito, *m,* chivo (-va). **g.-herd,** cabrero, *m.* **g. skin,** piel de cabra, *f;* (wineskin) odre, *m*

goatee *n* pera, perilla, *f*

goatish *a* cabruno; de cabra; lascivo

gobble *vt* and *vi* engullir, tragar. *vi* (of turkey) gluglutear. *n* glugluteo, *m,* voz del pavo, *f*

go-between *n* trotaconventos, *f;* alcahuete, *m;* (mediator) medianero (-ra)

goblet *n* copa, *f*

goblin *n* trasgo, duende, *m*

go-by, to give the evitar; pasar por alto de; omitir

go-cart *n* andaderas, *f pl;* pollera, *f;* cochecito de niño, *m*

god *n* dios, *m; pl* **gods,** dioses, *m pl;* (in a theater) público del paraíso, *m;* paraíso, *m.* **By God!** ¡Vive Dios! **For God's sake,** ¡Por el amor de Dios!; ¡Por Dios! **Please God,** ¡Plegue a Dios! **Thank God!** ¡Gracias a Dios! **God Bless You!** (to someone who has sneezed) ¡Jesús! **God forbid!** ¡No lo quiera Dios! **God grant it!** ¡Dios lo quiera! **God keep you!** ¡Dios le guarde! ¡Vaya Vd. con Dios! **God willing,** Dios mediante. **My father, God rest his soul, was . . .,** Mi padre, que Dios perdone, era . . .

godchild *n* ahijado (-da)

goddess *n* diosa, *f; poet* dea, *f*

godfather *n* padrino, *m.* **to be a g. to,** ser padrino de, sacar de pila (a)

godfearing *a* timorato, temeroso de Dios; religioso

godforsaken *a* dejado de la mano de Dios; (of places) remoto, solitario

Godhead *n* divinidad, *f*

godkin *n* diosecillo, *m*

godless *a* impío, irreligioso; sin Dios

godlessness *n* impiedad, irreligiosidad, *f*

godlet *n* diosecilla, *m*

godlike *a* divino

godliness *n* piedad, *f;* santidad, *f*

godling *n* diosecillo, *m*

godly *a* devoto, piadoso, religioso

godmother *n* madrina, *f.* **fairy g.,** hada madrina, *f.* **to be a g. to,** ser madrina de

godparent *n* padrino, *m;* madrina, *f pl.* **godparents,** padrinos, *m pl*

godsend *n* bien, *m;* buena suerte, *f;* fortuna, *f*

go-getter *n* buscavidas, *mf*

goggle *n* mirada fija, *f; pl* **goggles,** anteojos, *m pl,* gafas, *f pl;* (of a horse) anteojeras, *f pl. vi* mirar fijamente; salirse a uno los ojos de la cabeza. **g.-eyed,** de ojos saltones. **g.-eyes,** ojos saltones, *m pl*

going *n* ida, *f;* (departure) partida, marcha, *f;* salida, *f;* (pace) paso, *m;* (speed) velocidad, *f.* **It was heavy g.,** El avance era lento; El progreso era lento; (of parties, etc.) Era aburrido. **The g. was difficult on those mountainous roads,** El conducir (or el ir o el andar) era difícil en aquellos caminos de montaña. **g. back,** vuelta, *f,* regreso, *m.* **g. down,** bajada, *f,* descenso, *m;* (of the sun, etc.) puesta, *f.* **g. forward,** avance, *m;* progreso, *m.* **g. in,** entrada, *f.* **g. in and out,** idas y venidas, *f pl.* **g. out,** salida, *f;* (of a fire, light) apagamiento, *m*

going *a* and *pres part* que va, yendo; que funciona. **G., g., gone** (at an auction) A la una, a las dos, a las tres. **goings-on,** (tricks) trapujos, *m pl;* (conduct) conducta, *f.* **g. concern,** empresa próspera, *f.* **g. to,** con destino a

going-away present *n* regalo de despedida, *m*

goiter *n* bocio, *m*

gold *n* oro, *m;* color de oro, *m. a* de oro; áureo. **All that glitters is not g.,** No es oro todo lo que reluce. **cloth of g.,** tela de oro, *f.* **dull g.,** oro mate, *m.* **light g.,** oro pálido, *m.* **old g.,** oro viejo, *m.* **g.-beater,** batidor de oro, *m.* **g.-digger,** minero de oro, *m;* (woman) aventurera, *f.* **g. dust,** oro en polvo, *m.* **g.-fever,** fiebre de oro, *f.* **g. lace,** galón de oro, *m.* **g. lacquer,** sisa dorada, *f.* **g. leaf,** pan de oro batido, *m.* **g.-mine,** mina de oro, *f.* **g. piece,** moneda de oro, *f.* **g. plate,** vajilla de oro, *f.* **g. standard,** patrón oro, *m.* **g.-thread,** hilo de oro, *m.* **g.-yielding,** *a* aurífero

golden *a* de oro; dorado; áureo; amarillo; *fig* feliz; excelente. **to become g.,** dorarse. **g. age,** edad de oro, *f.* **g.-crested wren,** abadejo, *m.* **g. hair,** cabellos dorados (or de oro), *m pl.* **G. Legend,** leyenda áurea, *f.* **g. mean,** justo medio, *m.* **g. rose,** rosa de oro, *f.* **g. rule,** regla áurea, *f.* **g. syrup,** jarabe de arce, *m.* **g. voice,** voz de oro, *f.* **g. wedding,** bodas de oro, *f pl*

goldfinch *n* jilguero, *m*

goldfish *n* carpa dorada, *f.* **g. bowl,** pecera, *f*

goldrush carrera de oro, *f*

goldsmith *n* orfebre, oribe, orífice, *m*

golf *n* golf, *m.* **g.-club,** (stick) palo de golf, *m;* (organization) club de golf, *m.* **g.-course,** campo de golf, *m*

golfer *n* jugador (-ra) de golf

gonad *n* gonada, *f*

gondola *n* góndola, *f*

gondolier *n* gondolero, *m*

gone *a* and *past part* ido; (lost) perdido; (ruined) arruinado; (dead) muerto; (past) pasado; (disappeared) desaparecido; (fainted) desmayado; (suppressed) suprimido; (pregnant) encinta; (drunk) borracho; (ended) terminado; (exhausted) agotado; (ill) enfermo. **far g.,** avanzado; (in years) de edad avanzada; (of illness) cerca de la muerte, muy enfermo; (in love) loco de amor; (drunk) muy borracho. **It is all g.,** No hay más. **It is g. seven o'clock,** Son las siete y pico, Son las siete ya

gong *n* gong, *m;* (Chinese) batintín, *m*

gonorrhea *n* gonorrea, *f*

good *a* bueno (before *m sing* nouns) buen; agradable; afortunado; (appropriate) apropiado, oportuno; (beneficial) provechoso, ventajoso; (wholesome) sano, saludable; (suitable) apto; (useful) útil; (kind) bondadoso; (much) mucho; (obliging) amable; (virtuous) virtuoso; (skilled) experto; (fresh) fresco; (genuine) genuino, legítimo; verdadero. *adv* bien. *interj* ¡bueno! ¡bien! **a g. deal,** mucho. **a g. many,** bastantes. **a g. turn,** un favor. **a g. way,** (distance) un buen trecho; mucho. **a g. while,** un buen rato. **as g. as,** tan bueno como. **Be so g. as to . . .** ! Haga el favor de, Tenga Vd. la bondad de (followed by infin.). **fairly g.,** *a* bastante bueno. *adv* bastante bien. **I'm g. for another five miles,** Tengo fuerzas para cinco millas más. **It was g. of you to do it,** Vd. fue muy amable de hacerlo, Vd. tuvo mucha bondad de hacerlo. **to be no g. at this sort of thing,** no servir para tales cosas. **to have a g. time,** pasarlo bien. **to make g.,** reparar; indemnizar; (accomplish) llevar a cabo, poner en práctica; justificar; (a promise) cumplir. **very g.,** *a* muy bueno. *adv* muy bien. **g.-feeling,** buena voluntad, *f.* **g.-fellowship,** compañerismo, *m;* buena compañía, *f.* **g.-for-nothing,** *n* papanatas, badulaque, *m.* **to be g.-for-nothing,** no servir para nada. **g. luck,** buena suerte, *Lat. Am. also* derechura, leche *f.* **g. manners,** buenos modales, *m pl;* buena crianza, educación, *f.* **g. nature,** buen natural, *m;* buen humor, *m.* **g.-natured,** de buen natural; de buen humor, bonachón. **g. offices,** buenos oficios, *m pl.* **g.-tempered,** de buen humor

good *n* bien, *m;* provecho, *m;* utilidad, *f; pl* **goods.** See separate entry. **I am saying this for your g.,** Lo digo para tu bien. **Much g. may it do you!** ¡Buen provecho te haga! **for g. and all,** para siempre jamás. **It is no g.,** Es inútil; No vale la pena. **the g.,** el bien; (people) los buenos. **They have gone for g.,** Se han marchado para no volver. **to do one g.,** hacer bien a uno; mejorar; ser provechoso (a uno); (suit) sentar bien (a uno). **What is the g. of . . . ?** ¿Para qué sirve . . . ?; ¿Qué vale . . . ? **g. and evil,** el bien y el mal

good-bye *interj* ¡adiós! *n* adiós, *m,* despedida, *f.* **to bid g.-b.,** decir adiós. **G.-b. for the present!** ¡Hasta la vista! ¡Hasta luego! **G.-b. until tomorrow, then,** Hasta mañana pues, adiós, Hasta mañana entonces

goodness *n* bondad, *f;* (of quality) buena calidad, *f;* (of persons) amabilidad, benevolencia, *f;* (essence) esencia, substancia, *f;* bien, *m;* excelencia, *f; interj* ¡Jesús! ¡Dios mío! **For g. sake!** ¡Por Dios! **I wish to g. that,** ¡Ojalá que . . . !

goods *n pl* bienes, efectos, *m pl;* artículos, *m pl; com* mercancías, *f pl,* géneros, *m pl.* **by g.-train,** en pequeña velocidad. **stolen g.,** objetos robados, *m pl.* **g. lift,** montacargas, *m.* **g. office,** depósito de mercancías, *m.* **g. station,** estación de carga, *f.* **g.-train,** tren de mercancías, *m.* **g. van,** furgón, *m.* **g. wagon,** vagon de mercancías, *m.*

good-smelling *a* oloroso

goodwill *n* benevolencia, *f;* buena voluntad, *f;* (of a business) clientela, *f*

goose *n* oca, *f,* ganso (-sa); plancha de sastre, *f. a* de oca. **g.-flesh,** *fig* carne de gallina, *f.* **g. girl,** ansarera, *f.* **g.-step,** paso de oca, *m*

gooseberry *n* uva espina, *f*

Gordian *a* gordiano. **G. knot,** nudo gordiano, *m*

gore *n* sangre, *f; sew* sesga, nesga, *f. vt* acornear; desgarrar; herir (con arma blanca)

gorge *n* (valley) cañón, barranco, *m;* (heavy meal) comilona, *f,* atracón, *m. vt* engullir, tragar. *vi* hartarse, atracarse

gorgeous *a* magnífico; espléndido, suntuoso; *inf* maravilloso, estupendo

gorgeously *adv* magníficamente

gorgeousness *n* magnificencia, *f;* suntuosidad, *f,* esplendor, *m*

gorilla *n* gorila, *m*

gormandize *vi* glotonear

gormandizer *n* glotón (-ona)

gorse *n* tojo, *m,* aulaga, *f*

gory *a* ensangrentado; sangriento

gosh *interj* ¡caray! ¡caramba!

goshawk *n orn* azor, *m*

gosling *n* ansarino, *m*

gospel *n* evangelio, *m;* doctrina, *f.* **The G. according to St. Mark,** El Evangelio según San Marcos. **to believe as g. truth,** creer como si fuese el evangelio. **to preach the G.,** predicar el evangelio

gossamer *n* hilo de araña, *m,* red de araña, telaraña, *f;* (filmy material) gasa, *f;* hilo finísimo, *m, a* de gasa; sutil, delgado, fino

gossip *n* murmurador (-ra), chismoso (-sa), hablador (-ra); (scandal) chisme, *m, Lat. Am. also* lengüeterías *fpl;* habladuría, murmuración, *f;* (obsolete, of a woman) comadre, *f;* (talk) charla, *f. vi* charlar, conversar; (in bad sense) murmurar, chismear; criticar. **to g. about,** charlar de; poner lenguas en, cortar un sayo (a); hablar mal de. **g. column,** gacetilla, *f*

gossiping *a* charlatán, hablador; chismoso, murmurador. *n* See **gossip**

Goth *n* godo (-da); bárbaro (-ra)

Gothic *a art* gótico; (of race) godo; bárbaro. *n* (language) gótico, *m;* arquitectura gótica, *f.* **G. characters,** letra gótica, *f*

gouge *n* gubia, *f. vt* escoplear. **to g. out,** vaciar; sacar

gourd *n* calabaza, *f*

gourmand *n* glotón, *m*

gourmet *n* gastrónomo, *m*

gout *n med* gota, *f*

gouty *a* gotoso

govern *vt* gobernar; regir; (guide) guiar; dominar; domar, refrenar; *gram* regir; (regulate) regular

governable *a* gobernable; manejable; dócil

governess *n* institutriz, *f;* (in a school) maestra, *f*

governing *a* gubernante; director; (with principle, etc.) directivo. *n* See **government**

government *n* gobierno, *m;* dirección, *f;* autoridad, *f.* **g. bond,** bono del estado, *m.* **g. house,** palacio del gobernador, *m.* **g. office,** oficina del gobierno, *f.* **g. stock,** papel del Estado, *m*

governmental *a* gubernamental, gubernativo.

Government Printing Office Talleres Gráficos de la Nación, *m pl*

governor *n* gobernador (-ra); vocal de la junta de gobierno, *mf;* (of a prison) director (-ra) (de una prisión); *mech* regulador, *m.* **g.-general,** gobernador general, *m*

governorship *n* gobierno, *m;* dirección, *f*

gown *n* toga, *f;* (cassock) sotana, *f;* (dressing-g.) bata, *f;* (for sleeping) camisa de noche, *f;* (bathing-wrap) albornoz, *m;* (dress) vestido, traje, *m*

Goyesque *a* goyesco

grab *n* asimiento, *m,* presa, *f; mech* gancho, *m. vt* arrebatar, asir, agarrar; *fig* alzarse con, tomar

grabber *n* cogedor (-ra); codicioso (-sa)

grace *n* elegancia, *f;* simetría, armonía, *f;* gracia, gentileza, *f,* donaire, *m;* encanto, *m;* (goodness) bondad, *f;* gracia, *f;* merced, *f,* favor, *m;* (period of time) plazo, *m;* (privilege) privilegio, *m; theol* gracia divina, *f;* (at table) bendición de la mesa, *f;* (as a title) excelentísimo, (to an archbishop) ilustrísimo. *vt* adornar; favorecer; honrar. **airs and graces,** humos, *m pl.* **the Three Graces,** las Gracias. **three days' g.,** plazo de tres días, *m.* **to get into a person's good graces,** congraciarse con; caer en gracia con. **to say g.,** bendecir la mesa. **with a bad g.,** a regañadientes. **with a good g.,** de buena gana. **g.-note,** *mus* nota de adorno, *f*

graceful *a* airoso, gentil, gracioso; elegante; bonito

gracefully *adv* airosamente; con gracia; elegantemente

gracefulness. See **grace**

graceless *a* réprobo; dejado de la mano de Dios; sin gracia

gracious *a* (merciful) piadoso, clemente; (urbane) afable, condescendiente, agradable. **Good g.!** ¡Vamos!, ¡Dios mío!

graciously *adv* afablemente; con benevolencia. **to be g. pleased,** tener a bien

graciousness *n* amabilidad, afabilidad, condescendencia, *f*

gradate *vt* graduar; *art* degradar

gradation *n* graduación, *f; mus* gradación, *f;* paso gradual, *m;* serie, *f*

grade *n* grado, *m;* (quality) calidad, clase, *f;* (in a school) clase, *f;* (gradient) pendiente, *f,* declive, *m. vt* graduar, clasificar; (cattle breeding) cruzar. **down g.,** cuesta abajo. **up g.,** cuesta arriba. **highest g.,** *n* primera clase, *f. a* de primera clase; de calidad excelente

gradient *n* declive, *m.* cuesta, pendiente, *f*

gradual *a* gradual. *n ecc* gradual, *m*

gradually *adv* gradualmente; poco a poco

graduate *n* licenciado (-da), *Lat. Am.* exalumno (na) *mf a* graduado. *vt* graduarse; (as a doctor) doctorarse. **to g. as,** recibirse de. **be graduated from** . . . *Lat. Am.* egresar de . . .

graduation *n* graduación, *f, Lat. Am.* egreso *m*

graft *n bot* injerto, *m; surg* injerto de piel, *m;* (swindle) estafa, *f;* (bribery) soborno, *m. vt bot* injertar; *surg* injertar un trozo de piel; *fig* injerir

grafting *n bot* injerto, *m; surg* injerto de piel, *m; fig* inserción, *f*

grain *n* (corn) grano, *m;* (cereal) cereal, *m,* or *f;* (seed, weight) grano, *m;* (trace) pizca, *f;* (of wood, etc.) hila, *m,* fibra, hebra, veta, *f;* (of leather) flor, *f;* (texture) textura, *f. vt* granear; granular; (wood, marble, etc.) vetear. **against the g.,** a contrapelo. **g. lands,** mieses, *f pl*

gram *n* gramo, *m*

grammar *n* gramática, *f.* **g. school,** instituto de segunda enseñanza, *m*

grammarian *n* gramático, *m*

grammatical *a* gramático

grammatically *adv* gramaticalmente, como la gramática lo quiere. (e.g., **She now speaks Catalan g.,** Ahora habla el catalán como la gramática lo quiere)

grammaticalness *n* corrección gramatical, *f*

gramophone *n* gramófono, *m.*

granary *n* granero, hórreo, *m,* troj, *f, Mexico* espiguero *m.* **g. keeper,** trojero, *m*

grand *a* magnífico, soberbio; imponente; (of dress) espléndido, vistoso; (of people) distinguido, importante; aristocrático; (proud) orgulloso; (of style) elevado, sublime; (morally) noble; augusto; (main) principal; (full) completo; *inf* estupendo, magnífico; (with duke, etc.) gran. *n* piano de cola, *m.* **g.-aunt,** tía abuela, *f.* **g. cross,** gran cruz, *f.* **g. duchess,** gran duquesa, *f.* **g. duke,** gran duque, *m.* **g. lodge,** (of freemasons) Gran Oriente, *m.* **g. master,** gran maestre, *m.* **g.-nephew,** resobrino, *m.* **g.-niece,** resobrina, *f.* **g. opera,** ópera, *f.* **g. piano,** piano de cola, *m.* **g.-stand,** tribuna, *f.* **g.-uncle,** tío abuelo, *m.* **g. vizier,** gran visir, *m.*

grandchild *n* nieto (-ta). **great-g.,** bisnieto (-ta). **great-great-g.,** tataranieto (-ta)

granddaughter *n* nieta, *f.* **great-g.,** bisnieta, *f.* **great-great-g.,** tataranieta, *f*

grandee *n* grande (de España, grande de Portugal), *m*

grandeur *n* magnificencia, *f;* grandiosidad, *f;* magnitud, grandeza, *f;* (pomp) pompa, *f,* fausto, *m*

grandfather *n* abuelo, *m.* **great-g.,** bisabuelo, *m.* **great-great-g.,** tatarabuelo, *m*

grandfather's clock reloj de péndulo, *m*

grandfatherly *a* de abuelo

grandiloquence *n* grandilocuencia, *f*

grandiloquent *a* grandílocuo

grandiose *a* grandioso, sublime; impresionante; imponente; (in a bad sense) extravagante: (of style) bombástico, hinchado

grand jury *n* jurado de acusación, jurado de jucio, *m*

grandmother *n* abuela, *f.* **great-g.,** bisabuela, *f.* **great-great-g.,** tatarabuela, *f*

grandness *n* magnificencia, *f;* aristocracia, *f;* (pride) orgullo, *m;* grandiosidad, *f;* (of style) sublimidad, *f;* (of character) nobleza, *f*

grandparent *n* abuelo, *m;* abuela, *f; pl* **grandparents,** abuelos, *m pl.* **great-grand-parents,** bisabuelos, *m pl.* **great-great-grandparents,** tatarabuelos, *m pl*

grandson *n* nieto, *m.* **great-g.,** bisnieto, *m.* **great-great-g.,** tataranieto, *m*

grange *n* granja, *f;* casa de campo, *f*

granite *n* granito, *m*

granny *n* abuelita, nana, *f;* abuela, *f.* **g. knot,** nudo al revés, *m*

grant *n* concesión, *f;* otorgamiento, *m;* donación, *f;* privilegio, *m;* (for study) beca, bolsa de estudio, *f;* (transfer) traspaso, *m,* cesión, *f. vt* conceder; (bestow) otorgar, dar; donar; (agree to) acceder a, asentir en; permitir; (transfer) traspasar; (assume) suponer. **to g. a degree,** expedir un título. **to g. a motion,** dar por entrada a una moción. **to take for granted,** descontar; dar por hecho, dar por sentado. **God g. it!** ¡Dios lo quiera! **granted that,** dado que

grantee *n* cesionario (-ia), adjudicatorio (-ia)

grantor *n* cesionista, *mf;* otorgador (-ra)

granulated *a* granulado

granule *n* gránulo, *m*

granulous *a* granuloso

grape *n* uva, *f.* **bunch of grapes,** racimo de uvas, *m.* **muscatel g.,** uva moscatel, *f.* **sour grapes,** uvas agrias, *f pl;* (phrase) ¡están verdes! **g.-fruit,** toronja, *f.* **g. gatherer,** vendimiador (-ra). **g. harvest,** vendimia, *f.* **g. juice,** mosto, *m.* **g.-shot,** metralla, *f.* **g. stone,** granuja, *f.* **g.-sugar,** glucosa, *f.* **g.-vine,** vid, parra, *f*

graph *n* gráfica, *f;* diagrama, *m*

graphic *a* gráfico

graphite *n* grafito, *m*

graphology *n* grafología, *f*

grapple *n naut* rezón, arpeo, *m;* lucha a brazo partido, *f. vt naut* aferrar; asir, agarrar. *vi naut* aferrarse. **to g. with,** luchar a brazo partido (con); *fig* luchar con

grappling *n naut* aferramiento, *m;* lucha cuerpo a cuerpo, *f;* (with a problem) lucha con, *f*

grasp *n* agarro, *m;* (reach) alcance, *m;* (of a hand) apretón, *m;* (power) garras, *f pl,* poder, *m;* (understanding) comprensión, *f;* inteligencia, capacidad intelectual, *f. vt* agarrar, asir; empuñar; abrazar; *fig* comprender, alcanzar; (a hand) estrechar. *vi* agarrarse. **within one's g.,** al alcance de uno. **to g. at,** asirse de

grasping *n* asimiento, *m;* (understanding) comprensión, *f,* a codicioso, tacaño, mezquino

graspingness *n* codicia, *f*

grass *n* hierba, *f;* (pasture) pasto, herbaje, *m;* (sward) césped, *m. vt* cubrir de hierba; sembrar de hierba; apacentar. **to hear the g. grow,** sentir crecer la hierba. **to let the g. grow,** *fig* dejar crecer la hierba. **to turn out to g.,** echar al pasto. **g.-blade,** brizna de hierba, *f.* **g.-green,** *a* and *n* verde como la hierba *m..* **g.-grown,** cubierto de hierba. **g.-land,** pradera, *f.* **g.-snake,** culebra *f.* **g. widow,** mujer cuyo marido está ausente

grasshopper *n* saltamontes, *m.* **grasshopper's chirp,** chirrido (del saltamontes), *m*

grassy *a* parecido a la hierba, como la hierba; cubierto de hierba; de hierba

grate *n* parrilla, *f;* (grating) reja, *f. vt* raspar, raer; *cul* rallar; (make a noise) hacer rechinar. *vi* rozar; (sounds) chirriar. **to g. on, upon,** (of sounds) irritar, molestar; chocar con. **to g. on the ear,** herir el oído

grateful *a* agradecido, reconocido; (pleasant) agradable, grato

gratefully *adv* agradecidamente; gratamente

gratefulness *n* agradecimiento, *m,* gratitud, *f;* (pleasantness) agrado, *m*

grater *n cul* rallador, *m*

gratification *n* satisfacción, *f;* (pleasure) placer, gusto, *m*

gratified *a* satisfecho, contento

gratify *vt* satisfacer; (please) gratificar, agradar

gratifying *a* satisfactorio, agradable

grating *n* reja, *f;* rejilla, *f; naut* jareta, *f;* (optics) retículo, *m;* (sound) rechinamiento, chirrido, *m. a* rechinante, chirriador; áspero

gratis *a* and *adv* gratis

gratitude *n* agradecimiento, *m,* gratitud, *f*

gratuitous *a* gratuito

gratuitousness *n* gratuidad, *f*

gratuity *n* gratificación, propina, *f*

grave *n* (hole) sepultura, fosa, *f;* (monument) tumba, *f,* sepulcro, *m; fig* muerte, *f.* **g.-digger,** enterrador, sepulturero, *m*

grave *a* grave; importante; serio; sobrio; (anxious) preocupado; (of accent) grave. *n* (grave accent) acento grave, *m*

gravel *n* grava, *f;* cascajo, casquijo, *m; med* arenillas, *f pl,* cálculo, *m*

gravely *adv* gravemente; seriamente

Graves' disease *n* bocio exoftálmico, *m*

gravestone *n* lápida mortuoria, *f*

graveyard *n* camposanto, cementerio, *m*

gravitate *vi* gravitar; tender

gravitation *n* gravitación, *f;* tendencia, *f*

gravitational *a* de gravitación, gravitacional, gravitatorio

gravitational pull *n* atracción gravitatoria, *f*

gravity *n phys* gravedad, *f;* seriedad, *f;* solemnidad, *f;* gravedad, *f;* (weight) peso, *m;* importancia, *f;* (enormity) enormidad, *f;* (danger) peligro, *m.* **center of g.,** centro de gravedad, *m.* **law of g.,** ley de la gravedad, *f.* **specific g.,** peso específico, *m*

gravy *n* salsa, *f;* jugo (de la carne), *m.* **g.-boat,** salsera, *f*

gray *a* gris; (of animals) rucio. *n* color gris, gris, *m;* caballo gris, *m.* **His hair is turning g.,** El pelo se le vuelve gris. **g.-haired,** de pelo gris. **g. matter,** materia gris, *f;* cacumen, *m.* **g. mullet,** *icht* mújol, *m.* **g. squirrel,** gris, *m.* **g. wolf,** lobo gris, *m*

grayish *a* grisáceo, agrisado; (of hair) entrecano

grayness *n* color gris, gris, *m; fig* monotonía, *f*

graze *n* abrasión, *f;* (brush) roce, *m, vi* pacer, apacentarse. *vt* pastorear, apacentar; (brush) rozar

grazing *n agr* apacentamiento, pastoreo, *m;* (brushing) rozadura, *f. a* que pace, herbívoro; (of land) pacedero. **g. land,** pasto, *m*

grease *n* grasa, *f;* (dirt) mugre, *f;* (of a candle) sebo, *m,* cera, *f. vt* engrasar; manchar con grasa; *fig inf* untar. **to g. the wheels,** *fig* untar el carro. **g.-box,** *mech* caja de sebo, *f.* **g.-gun,** engrasador de compresión, *m.* **g.-paint,** afeites de actor (or de actriz), *m pl.* **g.-proof paper,** papel impermeable, *m.* **g. spot,** lámpara, mancha de grasa, *f,* saín, *m*

greaser *n* engrasador, *m*

greasiness *n* graseza, *f;* lo aceitoso; untuosidad, *f*

greasing *n* engrasado, *m*

greasy *a* grasiento; (oily) aceitoso; (grubby) mugriento, bisunto, *Argentina* cascarriento; *fig* lisonjero. **g. pole,** cucaña, *f*

great *a* gran; grande; enorme; vasto; (much) mucho; (famous) famoso, ilustre; noble, sublime; (intimate) íntimo; importante; principal; poderoso; magnífico, impresionante; *inf* famoso, estupendo; (of time) largo; (clever) fuerte. **Alexander the G.,** Alejandro Magno. **the G. Mogul,** el Gran Mogul. **a g. deal,** mucho. **a g. man,** un grande hombre, un hombre famoso. **a g. many,** muchos (muchas). **He lived to a g. age,** Vivió hasta una edad avanzada. **so g.,** tan grande, tamaño. **the g.,** los grandes hombres. **g. on,** aficionado a. **g.-aunt,** tía abuela, *f.* **g.-grandchild,** etc. See **grandchild,** etc. **g.-hearted,** valeroso; magnánimo, generoso. **g. power,** gran poder, *m.* **G. War,** Gran Guerra, *f.* **the Great Schism,** el Gran Cisma, *m*

greater *a* comp. of **great,** mayor; más grande. **to make g.,** agrandar. **G. London,** el Gran Londres, *m*

greatest *a* sup. of **great,** más grande; mayor; máximo; más famoso; sumo

greatly *adv* mucho; con mucho; (very) muy; noblemente

greatness *n* grandeza, *f;* grandiosidad, *f;* extensión, vastedad, *f;* importancia, *f;* poder, *m;* majestad, *f;* esplendor, *m;* (intensity) intensidad, *f;* (enormity) enormidad, *f*

Greco- *prefix* (in compounds) greco-, greco

greed *n* (cupidity) codicia, rapacidad, avaricia, *f;* avidez, ansia, *f;* (of food) gula, glotonería, *f*

greedily *adv* codiciosamente; con avidez; (of eating) vorazmente

greedy *a* (for food) glotón; codicioso; ambicioso; ávido; deseoso

Greece Grecia, *f*

Greek *a* and *n* griego (-ga); (language) griego, *m.* **It's all G. to me,** Para mí es como si fuese en latín, Me es chino. **G. tunic,** peplo, *m*

green *a* verde; (inexpert) inexperto, bisoño; (recent) nuevo, reciente; (fresh) fresco; (of complexion) pálido, descolorido; (flowery) floreciente; (vigorous) lozano; (young) joven; (unripe) verde; (credulous) crédulo; (raw) crudo; (of wood, vegetables) verde. *n* verde, color verde, *m;* (vegetables) verdura, *f;* (meadow) prado, *m;* (turf) césped, *m;* (grass) hierba, *f;* (bowling) campo de juego, *m. vt* teñir (or pintar) de verde. **bright g.,** *n* verdegay, verde claro, *m.* **dark g.,** *n* verdinegro, *m.* **light g.,** *n* verde pálido, *m.* **to grow** or **look g.,** verdear. **g.-eyed,** de ojos verdes. **g. peas,** guisantes, *m pl.* **g. table,** tapete verde, *m*

greenery *n* follaje, *m;* verdura, *f*

greengrocery *n* verdulería, *f*

greenhorn *n* bisoño (-ña); papanatas, *m*

greenhouse *n* invernáculo, invernadero, *Lat. Am.* conservatorio *m*

greenish *a* verdoso. **g.-yellow,** cetrino

Greenland Groenlandia, *f*

Greenlander *n* groenlandés (-esa)

greenness *a* lo verde; verdor, *m,* verdura, *f;* (inexperience) falta de experiencia, *f;* (vigor) vigor, *m,* lozanía, *f;* (newness) novedad, *f;* (of wood, fruit) falta de madurez, *f*

greenroom *n theat* saloncillo, *m*

greenstuff *n* hortalizas, legumbres, *f pl*

greet *vt* saludar; recibir; (express pleasure) dar la bienvenida (a)

greeting *n* salutación, *f,* saludo, *m;* recepción, *f;* (welcome) bienvenida, *f; pl* **greetings,** recuerdos, *m pl*

gregarious *a* gregario

gregariousness *n* gregarismo, *m*

Gregorian *a* gregoriano

grenade *n* granada, bomba, *f.* **hand-g.,** bomba de mano, *f*

grey See **gray**

greyhound *n* galgo, lebrel, *m.* **g. bitch,** galga, *f;* **g. racing,** carreras de galgos, *f pl*

grid *n* (of electric power) red, *f;* rejilla, *f;* (for water, etc.) alcantarilla, *f*

gridiron *n cul* parrilla, *f;* (of electric power) red, *f; theat* telar, *m*

grief *n* angustia, pena, aflicción, *f;* dolor, suplicio, *m.* **to come to g.,** pasarlo mal, tener un desastre

grievance *n* injusticia, *f;* motivo de queja, *m*

grieve *vt* entristecer, afligir, angustiar; atormentar. *vi* entristecerse, afligirse, acongojarse. **to g. for,** lamentar: echar de menos

grievous *a* (heavy) oneroso, gravoso; opresivo; doloroso, penoso; lamentable; cruel. **g. error,** error lamentable

grievousness *n* (weight) peso, *m;* carácter opresivo, *m;* dolor, *m,* aflicción, *f;* enormidad, *f;* crueldad, *f*

griffin *n* grifo, *m;* (fig chaperon) carabina, *f;* (dog) grifón, *m*

grill *n cul* parrilla, *f;* (grating) rejilla, *f;* (before a window) reja, *f;* (food) asado a la parrilla, *m. vt cul* asar a la parrilla; (burn) quemar; (question) interrogar; (torture) torturar. *vi cul* asarse a la parrilla; (be burnt) quemarse. **g.-room,** parrilla, *f*

grille *n* reja, *f;* rejilla, *f;* (screen) verja, *f*

grilled *a cul* a la parrilla; con rejilla

griller *n cul* parrilla, *f*

grim *a* (fierce) feroz, salvaje; (severe) severo, ceñudo, adusto; inflexible; (frightful) horrible

grimace *n* mueca, *f,* gesto, mohín, visaje, *m, vi* hacer muecas

grime *n* mugre, *f;* suciedad, *f.* **to cover with g.,** enmugrecer

grimly *adv* severamente; sin sonreír; inflexiblemente; (without retreating) sin cejar; (frightfully) horriblemente; de un modo espantoso

grimness *n* (ferocity) ferocidad, *f;* (severity) severidad, *f;* inflexibilidad, *f;* (frightfulness) horror, *m,* lo espantoso

grimy *a* mugriento, sucio

grin *n* sonrisa grande, *f;* sonrisa burlona, *f;* (grimace) mueca, *f. vi* sonreír mostrando los dientes; sonreír bonachonamente; sonreír de un modo burlón

grind *vt* (to powder) pulverizar; moler; (break up) quebrantar; (oppress) agobiar, oprimir; (sharpen) afilar, amolar; (a barrel-organ) tocar (un manubrio); (the teeth) crujir, rechinar (los dientes); (into) reducir a; (*inf* teach) enseñar. *vi* moler; *fig inf* trabajar laboriosamente. *n fig inf* trabajo pesado, *m; n fig inf* estudiantón, *m*

grinder *n* (of scissors, etc.) afilador, *m;* (of an organ) organillero; (mill-stone) piedra de moler, *f;* (molar) muela, *f*

grinding *a* (tedious) cansado, aburrido; opresivo; (of pain) incesante. *n* pulverización, *f;* amoladura, *f;* (of grain) molienda, *f;* (polishing) pulimento, bruñido, *m;* (oppression) opresión, *f;* (of teeth) rechinamiento, *m*

grindstone *n* amoladera, afiladera, piedra de amolar, *f.* **to have one's nose to the g.,** batir el yunque

grinning *a* sonriente; riente; (mocking) burlón

grip *n* asimiento, agarro, *m;* (claws, clutches) garras, *f pl;* (hand) mano, *f;* (of shaking hands) apretón de manos, *m;* (of a weapon, etc.) empuñadura, *f;* (reach) alcance, *m;* (understanding) comprensión, *f;* (control) dominio, *m;* (bag) portamanteo, *m;* maleta, *f. vt* asir, agarrar; (of wheels) agarrarse; *mech* morder; (a sword, etc.) empuñar; (pinch) pellizcar; (surround) cercar; (understand) comprender; (press; to grip the hand and *fig* the heart) apretar; (fill) llenar; (the attention) atraer, llamar; (sway, hold) dominar

gripe *n* (*inf* pain) retortijón (de tripas), *m*

grisly *a* espantoso; repulsivo

grist *n* molienda, *f.* **Everything is g. to their mill,** Sacan partido de todo

gristle *n* cartílago, *m,* ternilla, *f*

gristly *a* cartilaginoso

grit *n* cascajo, *m;* polvo, *m; fig* firmeza (de carácter), *f;* (courage) valor, *m;* (endurance) aguante, *m*

gritty *a* arenoso, arenisco

grizzled *a* (of hair, etc.) gris; canoso; grisáceo

grizzly bear *n* oso (-sa) pardo (-da)

groan *n* gemido, *m. vi* gemir; (creak) crujir. **to g. out,** decir (o contar) entre gemidos. **to g. under,** sufrir bajo, gemir bajo; (of weight) crujir bajo

groaning *n* gemidos, *m pl. a* que gime, gemidor; (under a weight) crujiente

grocer *n* abacero (-ra) vendedor (-ra) de comestibles, *Lat. Am.* abarrotero (-ra). **grocer's shop,** tienda de comestibles, bodega, *f, Mexico* abarrotería, *f*

grocery *n* tienda de comestibles, tienda de ultramarinos, abarrotería, lonja, bodega, *f,* negocio de comestibles, *m; pl* **groceries,** provisiones, *f pl,* comestibles, *m pl, Lat. Am.* abarrotes *mpl*

groin *n anat* ingle, *f*

groom *n* (in a royal household) gentilhombre, *m;* lacayo, *m;* mozo de caballos, *m;* (of a bride) novio, *m. vt* (a horse) cuidar; (oneself) arreglarse. **She is always well groomed,** Está siempre muy bien arreglada

groomsman *n* padrino de boda, *m*

groove *n* ranura, muesca, *f;* estría, *f;* surco, *m; fig* rutina, *f. vt* entallar; estriar

grooved *a* con ranura; estriado

grope *vi* andar a tientas; (with for) buscar a tientas; procurar, encontrar, buscar. **to g. one's way toward,** avanzar a tientas hacia; *fig* avanzar poco a poco hacia

gropingly *adv* a tientas; irresolutamente

gross *n com* gruesa, *f;* totalidad, *f, a* grueso; denso, espeso; (unrefined) grosero; (great) grande; (crass) craso; total, *com* bruto; (tremendous) enorme. **in g.,** en

grueso. **g. amount,** total, *m; com* importe bruto, *m.* **g. weight,** peso bruto, *m*

grossly *adv* groseramente; (much) enormemente

grossness *n* gordura, *f;* (vulgarity) grosería, *f;* obscenidad, *f;* (enormity) enormidad, *f*

grotesque *a* grotesco; extravagante, estrambótico; ridículo. *n* grotesco, *m*

grotesqueness *n* lo grotesco; ridiculez, *f*

grotto *n* gruta, *f*

ground *n* suelo, *m;* (of water and *naut*) fondo, *m;* (earth) tierra, *f; fig* terreno, *m;* (strata) capa, *f; sport* campo, *m;* (parade) plaza (de armas), *f;* (background) fondo, *m;* (basis) base, *f,* fundamento, *m;* (reason) causa, *f;* motivo, *m;* (excuse) pretexto, *m; pl* **grounds,** jardines, *m pl,* parque, *m;* (sediment) sedimento, *m,* heces, *f pl;* (reason) causa, *f. vi naut* varar, encallar. *vt* poner en tierra; *naut* hacer varar; *elec* conectar con tierra; (base) fundar (en), basar (en); (teach) enseñar los rudimentos (de). *a* molido; en polvo; (of floors, stories) bajo; (of glass) deslustrado; *bot* terrestre. **common g.,** tierra comunal, *f; fig* tierra común, *f.* **He is on his own g.,** Está en terreno propio. **It fell to the g.,** Cayó al suelo; *fig* Fracasó. **It is on the g.,** Está en el suelo. **It suits me to the g.,** Me viene de perilla. **to break fresh g.,** *fig* tratar problemas nuevos. **to be well grounded in,** conocer bien los elementos (o rudimentos) de. **to cover g.,** cubrir terreno; recorrer; (in discussion) tocar muchos puntos. **to cut the g. from beneath one's feet,** hacer perder la iniciativa (a). **to give g.,** retroceder; perder terreno. **to raze to the g.,** echar por tierra, arrasar. **to stand one's g.,** resistir el ataque; no darse por vencido; *fig* mantenerse firme, mantenerse en sus trece. **to win g.,** ganar terreno. **g. coffee,** café molido, *m.* **g.-color,** (of paint) primera capa, *f;* (color de) fondo, *m.* **g.-floor,** piso bajo, *m.* **g. glass,** vidrio deslustrado, *m.* **g.-ivy,** hiedra terrestre, *f.* **g. nut,** cacahuete, *m.* **g.-plan,** *arch* planta, *f.* **g.-rent,** censo, *m.* **g.-sheet,** tela impermeable, *f;* **g. staff,** *aer* personal del aeropuerto, *m.* **g.-swell,** mar de fondo, *m*

grounded *a* fundado. **The airplanes are g.,** Los aviones están sin volar. **His suspicions are well g.,** Tiene motivos para sus sospechas

grounding *n naut* encalladura, *f;* (teaching) instrucción en los rudimentos, *f*

groundless *a* sin fundamento, inmotivado, sin causa, sin motivo

groundwork *n* fundamento, *m;* base, *f;* principio, *m*

group *n* grupo, *m. vt* agrupar. *vi* agruparse. **g. captain,** coronel de aviación, *m*

grouping *n* agrupación, *f*

grouse *n orn* ortega, *f. vi* rezongar, refunfuñar

grove *n* soto, boscaje, *m;* arboleda, *f*

grovel *vi* arrastrarse; *fig* humillarse

groveling *a fig* servil; ruin

grow *vi* crecer; (increase) aumentar; (become) hacerse; empezar a; llegar a; (turn) volverse, ponerse; (flourish) progresar, adelantar; (develop) desarrollarse; (extend) extenderse. *vt* cultivar; dejar crecer. **I grew to fear it,** Llegué a temerlo. **to g. cold,** ponerse frío; enfriarse; (of weather) empezar a hacer frío. **to g. fat,** engordar. **to g. hard,** ponerse duro; *fig* endurecerse. **to g. hot,** ponerse caliente; calentarse; (of weather) empezar a hacer calor. **to g. like Topsy,** crecer a la buena de Dios. **to g. old,** envejecer. **to g. tall,** crecer mucho; ser alto. **to g. again,** crecer de nuevo. **to g. into,** hacerse, llegar a ser; venir a ser. **to g. out of,** brotar de; originarse en; (a habit) desacostumbrarse poco a poco. **He is growing out of his clothes,** La ropa se le hace pequeña. **to g. up,** (of persons) hacerse hombre (mujer); desarrollarse; (of a custom, etc.) imponerse. **to g. on, upon,** crecer sobre; llegar a dominar; (make think) hacer creer, empezar a pensar; (of a habit) arraigar en

grower *n* cultivador (-ra)

growing *n* crecimiento, *m*; desarrollo, *m*; (increase) aumento, *m*; (of flowers, etc.) cultivación, *f*, *a* creciente

growing pains *n pl* crisis de desarrollo, *f*

growl *n* gruñido, *m*; reverberación, *f*; trueno, *m*. *vi* gruñir; (of guns) tronar; (of thunder) reverberar. **to g. out,** decir gruñendo

grown *a* crecido; maduro; adulto. **a g. up,** una persona mayor. **to be full-g.,** estar completamente desarrollado; haber llegado a la madurez. **g. over with,** cubierto de

growth *n* crecimiento, *m*; (development) desarrollo, *m*; (progress) progreso, adelanto, *m*; (increase) aumento, *m*; (cultivation) cultivo, *m*; (vegetation) vegetación, *f*; *med* tumor, *m*. **He has a week's g. on his chin,** Tiene una barba de una semana

grub *n* larva, *f*, gusano, *m*. *vt* (with up, out) desarraigar; cavar; desmalezar; *fig inf* buscar

grubbiness *n* suciedad, *f*; (untidiness) desaliño, *m*

grubby *a* lleno de gusanos; sucio; bisunto; desaliñado

grudge *n* motivo de rencor, *m*; rencor, resentimiento, *m*, ojeriza, *f*; mala voluntad, *f*; aversión, *f*. *vt* envidiar. **to bear a g.,** tener ojeriza

grudging *a* (niggardly) mezquino; envidioso; poco generoso; de mala gana; nada afable

grudgingly *adv* de mala gana, contra su voluntad; con rencor; a regañadientes

gruel *n* gachas, *f pl*

gruesome *a* pavoroso, horrible; macabro

gruff *a* (of the voice) bronco, grave, áspero; (of manner) brusco, malhumorado

gruffly *adv* en una voz bronca (or áspera); bruscamente, con impaciencia, malhumoradamente

gruffness *n* aspereza, bronquedad, *f*; brusquedad, sequedad, impaciencia, *f*, mal humor, *m*

grumble *n* ruido sordo, trueno, *m*; estruendo, *m*; (complaint) refunfuño, rezongo, *m*. *vi* tronar; refunfuñar, rezongar; hablar entre dientes; quejarse; protestar (contra). *vt* decir refunfuñando

grumbler *n* murmurador (-ra), refunfuñador (-ra)

grumbling *a* gruñón, refunfuñador; regañón; descontento. *n* See **grumble**

grumblingly *adv* a regañadientes, refunfuñando

grumpiness *n* mal humor, *m*, irritabilidad, *f*

grumpy *a* malhumorado, irritable

grunt *n* gruñido, *m*. *vi* gruñir

grunting *a* gruñidor

guarantee *n law* persona de quien otra sale fiadora, *f*; garantía, *f*; abono, *m*. *vt* garantizar; responder de; abonar; (assure) asegurar, acreditar

guarantor *n* garante, *mf*

guard *n* (watchfulness) vigilancia, *f*; (in fencing) guardia, *f*; (of a sword) guarnición, *f*; (sentry) centinela, *m*; (soldier) guardia, *m*; (body of soldiers) guardia, *f*; (escort) escolta, *f*; (keeper) guardián, *m*; (protection) protección, defensa, *f*; (of a train) jefe de tren, *m*. *vt* guardar; proteger, defender; vigilar; (escort) escoltar. **to g. against,** guardarse de. **the changing of the g.,** el relevo de la guardia. **to be on g.,** *mil* estar de guardia; (in fencing) estar en guardia. **to be on one's g.,** estar prevenido, estar alerta. **to be off one's g.,** estar desprevenido. **to mount g.,** *mil* montar la guardia; vigilar. **guard's van,** furgón de equipajes, *m*. **g.-house,** cuerpo de guardia, *m*; prisión militar, *f*

guarded *a* (reticent) reservado, circunspecto, prudente, discreto

guardedly *adv* prudentemente, con circunspección, discretamente

guardian *n* protector (-ra); guardián (-ana); *law* tutor, *m*. *a* que guarda; tutelar. **g. angel,** ángel de la guarda, ángel custodio, *m*; deidad tutelar, *f*

guardianship *n* protección, *f*; patronato, *m*; *law* curaduría, tutela, *f*

guardsman *n* guardia, *m*

Guatemalan *a* and *n* guatemalteco (-ca)

guava *n bot* guayaba, *f*

Guernsey Guernesy, *m*

guerrilla *n* guerrilla, *f*; (soldier) guerrillero, *m*. *a* de guerrilla. **g. warfare,** guerra de guerrillas, *f*

guess *n* adivinación, *f*; estimación, *f*; conjetura, *f*; sospecha, *f*. *vt* and *vi* adivinar; conjeturar; sospechar; imaginar; (suppose) suponer, creer; calcular. **to g. at,** formar una opinión sobre; imaginar. **a rough g.,** estimación aproximada, *f*. **at a g.,** a poco más o menos, a ojo de buen cubero. **g.-work,** conjeturas, suposiciones, *f pl*

guest *n* (at a meal) convidado (-da), invitado (-da); (at a hotel, etc.) cliente (-da); (houseguest) *Lat. Am.* alojado *biol* parásito, *m*. **g.-room,** alcoba de respeto, alcoba de honor, alcoba de huéspedes, *f*, cuarto de amigos, cuarto para invitados, *m*

guffaw *n* carcajada, *f*. *vi* reírse a carcajadas, soltar el trapo

Guiana Guayana, *f*

guidance *n* dirección, *f*; gobierno, *m*; (advice) consejos, *m pl*; inspiración, *f*

guide *n* (person) guía, *mf*; (girl g.) exploradora, *f*; (book and *fig*) guía, *f*; mentor, *m*; modelo, *m*; (inspiration) norte, *m*; *mech* guía, *f*. *vt* guiar; conducir; encaminar; dirigir; (govern) gobernar. **g.-book,** guía (de turistas), *f*. **g.-post,** poste indicador, *m*

guided tour *n* visita explicada, visita programada, *f*

guideline *lit* falsarregla, falsilla, *f*; *fig* pauta, *f*

guiding *a* que guía; directivo; decisivo. *n* See **guidance**

guild *n* gremio, *m*. *a* gremial. **g. member,** gremial, *m*

guilder *n* (coin) florín holandés, *m*

guile *n* astucia, superchería, maña, *f*

guileful *a* astuto

guileless *a* cándido, sin malicia, inocente

guilelessly *adv* inocentemente

guilelessness *n* inocencia, candidez, *f*

guillotine *n* guillotina, *f*. *vt* guillotinar

guilt *n* culpabilidad, *f*; crimen, *m*; (sin) pecado, *m*

guilt complex complejo de culpa, *m*

guiltily *adv* culpablemente; como si fuese culpable

guiltless *a* libre de culpa, inocente; puro; ignorante

guilty *a* culpable; delincuente; criminal. **to find g.,** encontrar culpable. **to plead g.,** confesarse culpable. **g. party,** culpable, *m*

Guinea Guinea, *f*

guinea *n* guinea, *f*. **g.-fowl,** gallina de Guinea, *f*. **g.-pig,** conejillo de Indias, cobayo, *m*

guise *n* manera, guisa, *f*; (garb) traje, *m*; máscara, *f*; *fig* pretexto, *m*. **under the g. of,** bajo el pretexto de; bajo la apariencia de

guitar *n* guitarra, *f*

guitarist *n* guitarrista, *mf*

gulf *n* golfo, *m*; abismo, *m*

Gulf Stream, the la Corriente del Golfo

gull *n orn* gaviota, *f*; (dupe) primo, *m*. *vt* engañar, timar, defraudar

gullet *n* esófago, *m*; garganta, *f*

gullibility *n* credulidad, *f*

gullible *a* crédulo

gully *n* hondonada, barranca, *f*; (gutter) arroyo, *m*

gulp *n* trago, sorbo, *m*. *vt* engullir, tragar; (repress) ahogar; (believe) tragar. **to g. up,** vomitar

gum *n* (of the mouth) encía, *f*; goma, *f*. *vt* engomar; pegar con goma. **gum arabic,** goma arábiga, *f*. **gum boots,** botas de goma, *f*. **gum-resin,** gomorresina, *f*. **gum starch,** aderezo, *m*. **gum tree,** eucalipto, *m*

gummy *a* gomoso

gumption *n* sentido común, seso, *m*

gun *n* arma de fuego, *f*; (handgun) fusil, *m*; (sporting g.) escopeta, *f*; (pistol) pistola, *f*, revólver, *m*; (cannon) cañón, *m*; (firing) cañonazo, *m*. **big gun,** *inf* pájaro gordo, *m*. **heavy gun,** cañón de grueso calibre, *m*. **gun-barrel,** cañón de escopeta, *m*. **gun-carriage,** cureña, *f*. **gun-cotton,** pólvora de algodón, *f*. **gun-fire,** cañonazos, *m pl*, fuego, *m*. **gun-metal,** bronce de cañón, *m*; pavón, *m*. **gun-room,** armería, *f*; (on a ship) polvorín, *m*. **gun-running,** contrabanda de armas, *f*. **gun-turret,** torre, *f*. **gun wound,** balazo, *m*

gunboat *n* cañonero, *m*, lancha bombardera, *f*
gunflint *n* piedra de escopeta, *f*
gunman *n* escopetero, armero, *m*; bandido armado, *m*; gángster, apache, *m*
gunner *n* artillero, *m*; escopetero, *m*
gun permit *n* licencia de armas, *f*, permiso de armas, *m*
gunpowder *n* pólvora, *f*
gunshot *n* escopetazo, *m*; tiro de fusil, *m*
gunsmith *n* escopetero, armero, *m*
gunwale *n naut* regala, borda, *f*
gurgle *n* murmullo, murmurio, gorgoteo, *m*; gluglú, *m*; (of a baby) gorjeo, *m*. *vi* murmurar; hacer gluglú; (of babies) gorjear
gurgling *a* murmurante; (of babies) gorjeador. *n* See **gurgle**
gush *n* chorro, *m*; (of words) torrente, *m*; (of emotion) efusión, *f*. *vi* chorrear, borbotar; surtir, surgir. **to g. out,** saltar, brotar a borbotones, salir a borbollones, salira borbotones. **to g. over,** *fig* hablar con efusión de
gushing *a* hirviente; (of people) efusivo, extremoso, empalagoso
gusset *n sew* escudete, *m*
gust *n* (of wind) ráfaga, bocanada (de aire), *f*; *fig* arrebato, acceso, *m*
gusto *n* brío, *m*; entusiasmo, *m*
gusty *a* borrascoso
gut *n* intestino, *m*, tripa, *f*; (catgut) cuerda de tripa, *f*; *naut* estrecho, *m*; *pl* **guts,** tripas, *f pl*; (content) meollo, *m*, substancia, *f*; (stamina) aguante, espíritu, *m*. *vt* (of

fish, etc.) destripar; (plunder) saquear; destruir por completo; quemar completamente
gutta-percha *n* gutapercha, *f*
gutter *n* canal, *m*; (of a street) arroyo (de la calle), *m*; (ditch) zanja, *f*; *fig* hampa, *f*. *vt* surcar. *vi* gotear; (of a candle) cerotear, gotear la cera. **g. spout,** canalón, *m*
guttersnipe *n* golfillo, *m*, niño (-ña) del hampa
guttural *a* gutural. *n* letra gutural, *f*
guy *n* (rope) viento, *m*; *naut* guía, *f*; (effigy) mamarracho, *m*; (scarecrow) espantajo, *m*, *vt* sujetar con vientos o guías; burlarse de
guzzle *vt* tragar, engullir. *vi* atracarse, engullir; emborracharse. *n* comilón, *m*; borrachera, *f*
guzzler *n* tragador (-ra); borracho (-cha)
gymnasium *n* gimnasio, *m*
gymnast *n* gimnasta, *mf*
gymnastic *a* gimnástico. **g. rings,** anillas, *f pl*
gymnastics *n* gimnasia, *f*
gynecological *a* ginecológico
gynecologist *n* ginecólogo (-ga)
gynecology *n* ginecología, *f*
gypsum *n* yeso, *m*
gypsy *n* gitano (-na). *a* gitano, gitanesco; (music) flamenco
gyrate *vi* girar, rodar
gyration *n* giro, *m*, vuelta, *f*
gyratory *a* giratorio
gyro-compass *n* brújula giroscópica, *f*
gyroscope *n phys* giroscopio, *m*

H

h *n* (letter) hache, *f*
ha *interj* ¡ah!
haberdasher *n* mercero, *m*
haberdashery *n* mercería, *f*
habiliment *n* vestidura, *f*; *pl* **habiliments,** indumentaria, *f*
habilitate *vt* habilitar
habilitation *n* habilitación, *f*
habit *n* costumbre, *f*, hábito, *m*; (temperament) temperamento, carácter, *m*; (use) uso, *m*; (of body) complexión, constitución, *f*; *ecc* hábito, *m*. **to be in the h. of,** soler, acostumbrar. **to have bad habits,** estar malacostumbrado. **to have the bad h. of,** tener el vicio (or la mala costumbre) de. **to contract the h. of,** contraer la costumbre de. **h. maker,** sastre de trajes de montar, *m*
habitable *a* habitable, vividero
habitat *n* (*bot*, *zool*) medio, *m*, habitación, *f*
habitation *n* habitación, *f*
habit-forming *a* enviciador, que crea vicio
habitual *a* habitual, acostumbrado, usual; constante, común
habitually *adv* habitualmente; constantemente; comúnmente
habituate *vt* habituar, acostumbrar
habituation *n* habituación, *f*
habitué *n* parroquiano (-na); veterano (-na)
hack *n* caballo de alquiler, *m*; rocín, jaco, *m*; (writer) escritor mercenario, *m*. *vt* acuchillar; tajar, cortar. *vi* cortar. **to h. to pieces,** cortar en pedazos; pasar a cuchillo
hacking *a* (of coughs) seco
hackle *n* (for flax, hemp) rastrillo, *m*
hackney carriage *n* coche de plaza, coche de alquiler, *m*
hackneyed *a* gastado, trillado, muy usado, repetido, resobado
hacksaw *n* sierra de cerrajero, sierra para metal, *f*
hackwork *n* trabajo de rutina, *m*
haddock *n* merlango, *m*, pescadilla, *f*
Hades *n* Hades, *m*; *inf* el infierno, *m*

haft *n* mango, tomadero, *m*, manija, *f*; puño, *m*
hag *n* bruja, *f*
haggard *a* ojeroso, trasnochado, trasojado
haggardly *adv* ansiosamente
haggardness *n* aspecto ojeroso, *m*
haggle *vi* regatear; vacilar
haggling *n* regateo, *m*, *a* regatón
hagiographer *n* hagiógrafo, *m*
hagiography *n* hagiografía, *f*
ha, ha! *interj* ¡ja, ja!
hail *n* (salutation) saludo, *m*; (shout) grito, *m*; aclamación, *f*; (frozen rain) granizo, *m*; (of blows) lluvia, *f*. *interj* ¡salve! *vt* saludar; llamar; aclamar; *fig* lanzar, echar. *vi* (hailstones) granizar; (blows, etc.) llover. **to h. from,** proceder de, ser natural de. **within h.,** al habla. **H. Mary,** Salve Regina, Avemaría, *f*
hailstone *n* granizo, pedrisco, *m*
hailstorm *n* granizada, *f*
hair *n* (single h.) cabello, *m*; (*zool*, *bot*) pelo, *m*; (of horse's mane) crin, *f*; (head of h.) cabellera, mata de pelo, *f*, pelo, *m*; (superfluous) vello, *m*; (fiber) fibra, *f*, filamento, *m*; (on the pen) raspa, *f*, pelo, *m*; *fig* pelo, *m*. **lock of h.,** bucle, rizo, *m*; mecha, *f*. **to dress one's h.,** peinarse. **to have one's h. cut,** hacerse cortar el pelo. **to part the h.,** hacer(se) la raya del pelo. **to put up one's h.,** hacerse el moño; (to "come out") ponerse de largo. **to tear one's h.,** mesarse los cabellos. **h. combings,** peinaduras, *f pl*. **h.-curler,** tirabuzón, *m*. **h. dryer,** secadora de pelo, *f*. **h. dye,** tinte para el pelo, *m*. **h.-net,** redecilla, *f*, *Mexico* invisible *m*. **h.-oil,** brillantina, *f*. **h.-raising,** horripilante, espeluznante. **h.-ribbon,** cinta para el pelo, *f*. **h.-shirt,** cilicio, *m*. **h. slide,** pasador, *m*. **h.-splitting,** sofistería, argucia, *f*; mez quinas argucias, quis quillas, *f pl*. **h.-spring,** muelle del volante, *m*. **h.-switch,** añadido, *m*. **h.-trigger,** pelo de una pistola, *m*
hairband *m Lat. Am.* bincha *f*
hairbreadth *n* pelo, *m*. **to have a h. escape,** escapar por un pelo.
hairbrush *n* cepillo para el cabello, *m*
hairdresser *n* peluquero (-ra), peinadora, *f*

hairdressing *n* peinado, *m*. **h. establishment** or **trade,** peluquería, *f*

haired *a* peludo, con pelo; (in compounds) de pelo . . .

hairless *a* sin pelo; calvo

hairlike *a* filiforme

hairpin *n* horquilla, *f*, *Argentina* invisible *m*. **h. bend,** viraje en horquilla, *m*

hairsplitting arguments *Lat. Am.* abogaderas, abogaderías *fpl*

hairy *a* peludo; velloso; *bot* hirsuto

Haiti Haití, *m*

Haitian *a* and *n* haitiano (-na)

hake *n* merluza, *f*

halcyon *n* alción, martín pescador, *m. a fig* feliz, sereno, tranquilo

hale *a* fuerte, sano, robusto. *vt* hacer comparecer

half *n* mitad, *f*; (school term) trimestre, *m. a* medio; *semi. adv* a medias; mitad; (almost) casi; insuficientemente; imperfectamente. **I don't h. like it,** No me gusta nada. **It is h.-past two,** Son las dos y media. **an hour and a h.,** una hora y media. **better h.,** *inf* media naranja, cara mitad, *f*. **by halves,** a medias. **in h.,** en dos mitades. **one h.,** la mitad. **to go halves,** ir a medias. **to h. close,** entornar. **to h. open,** entreabrir. **h. a bottle,** media botella, *f*. **h. a crown,** media corona, *f*. **h.-alive,** semivivo. **h. an hour,** media hora, *f*. **h.-and-h.,** mitad y mitad; en partes iguales. **h.-asleep,** semidormido, medio dormido. **h.-awake,** medio despierto, entre duerme y vela. **h.-back,** *sport* medio, *m*. **h.-baked,** medio cocido, crudo; *fig* poco maduro. **h.-binding,** encuadernación en media pasta, *f*. **h.-breed,** *a* mestizo. *n* cruce, *m*. **h.-brother,** hermanastro, hermano de padre, hermano de madre, *m*. **h.-caste,** mestizo, *m*. **h. circle,** semicírculo, *m*. **h.-closed,** entreabierto; medio cerrado. **h.-dead,** medio muerto; más muerto que vivo. **h.-done,** hecho a medias, sin acabar. **h.-dozen,** media docena, *f*. **h.-dressed,** medio desnudo. **h. fare,** medio billete, *m*. **h.-full,** medio lleno. **h.-hearted,** débil, poco eficaz, lánguido; indiferente, sin entusiasmo. **h.-heartedness,** debilidad, *f*; indiferencia, *f*. **h.-holiday,** media fiesta, *f*. **h.-hourly,** cada media hora. **h.-length,** (portrait) de medio cuerpo. **h.-length coat,** abrigo de tres cuartos, *m*. **h.-light,** media luz, *f*. **h.-mast,** a media asta. **h.-measure,** medida poco eficaz, *f*. **h.-moon,** *n* media luna, *f*; *ast* semilunio, *m*; (of a nail) blanco (de la uña), *m*. **h.-mourning,** medio luto, *m*. **h.-pay,** media paga, *f*. **h.-price,** a mitad de precio. **h.-seas-over,** *inf* entre dos velas. **h.-sister,** hermanastra, hermana de padre, hermana de madre, *f*. **h.-time,** *sport* media parte, *f*; medio tiempo, *m*. **h.-tone,** de medio tono. **h.-tone illustration,** fotograbado a media tinta, *m*. **h.-truth,** verdad a medias, *f*. **h.-turn,** media vuelta, *f*. **h.-way,** a medio camino; medio. **h.-witted,** medio loco, tonto, imbécil. **h.-year,** medio año, *m*. **h.-yearly,** semestral

half close *vt* entrecerrar

half title anteportada, falsa portada, portadilla, preportada, *f*

halibut *n* halibut, *m*; (genus) hipogloso, *m*

halitosis *n* halitosis, *f*

hall *n* (mansion) mansión, casa de campo, *f*, caserón, *m*; (public building) edificio, *m*, casa (de); (town h.) casa del ayuntamiento, *f*; (room) sala, *f*; (entrance) vestíbulo, *m*; (dining room) comedor, *m*; (of residence for students) residencia, *f*. **h. door,** portón, *m*, puerta del vestíbulo, *f*. **h. porter,** conserje, *m*. **h.-stand,** perchero, *m*

hallelujah *n* aleluya, *f*

hallmark *n* marca de ley, *f*; *fig* señal, *f*; indicio, *m*. *vt* poner la marca de ley sobre; *fig* sellar

halloo *vt* (hounds) azuzar; perseguir dando voces; (call) llamar

hallow *vt* santificar; reverenciar; (consecrate) consagrar

Halloween *n* la víspera de Todos los Santos, *f*

hallucination *n* alucinación, ilusión, *f*; visión, *f*; fantasma, *m*

hallucinatory *a* alucinador

halo *n* halo, nimbo, *m*

halogen *n chem* halógeno, *m*

halt *n* mil alto, *m*; cesación, *f*; interrupción, *f*; (on a railway) apeadero, *m*; (for trams, buses) parada, *f*. *vt* parar, detener. *vi* pararse, detenerse; *mil* hacer alto; cesar; interrumpirse; (in speech) titubear; (of verse) estar cojo; (doubt) dudar; (limp) cojear. **H.!** *mil* ¡Alto!

halter *n* ronzal, cabestro, *m*; (for hanging) dogal, *m*. *vt* encabestrar, cabestrar

halting *n* parada, *f*; interrupción, *f. a* (of gait) cojo; incierto; vacilante; (of speech) titubeante

halve *vt* partir (or dividir) en dos mitades

ham *n* jamón, *m*; *anat* pernil, *m*; (radio-operator) radioaficionado, *m*

Hamburg Hamburgo, *m*

hamlet *n* aldea, *f*, pueblecito, *m*

hammer *n* martillo, *m*; (stone cutter's) maceta, *f*; (mason's) piqueta, *f*; (of fire-arms) percusor, *m*; (of piano) macillo, *m*. *vt* amartillar, martillar, batir. **to throw the h.,** lanzar el martillo. **under the h.,** en subasta, al remate. **h. blow,** martillazo, *m*

hammering *n* martilleo, martillazo, *m*. **by h.,** a martillo

hammock *n* hamaca, *f*; *naut* coy, *m*

hamper *n* banasta, canasta, *f*, cesto grande, *m*. *vt* estorbar, dificultar, impedir; *fig* embarazar

hamster *n zool* hámster, *m*, marmota de Alemania, rata del trigo, *f*

hand *n* mano, *f*; (of animal) pata, mano, *f*; (worker) operario (-ia); obrero (-ra); (skill) habilidad, *f*; (side) mano, *f*, lado, *m*; (measure) palmo, *m*; (of a clock) manecilla, *f*; (of instruments) aguja, *f*; (applause) aplauso, *m*; (power) poder, *m*; las manos; (at cards) mano, *f*; (card player) jugador, *m*; (signature) firma, *f*; (handwriting) letra, escritura, *f*; (influence) influencia, parte, *f*. **old h.,** veterano; perro viejo. **at h.,** a mano, al lado, cerca. **have at h.,** tener a la mano. **at the hands of,** de manos de. **by h.,** a mano; (on the bottle) con biberón. **from h. to h.,** de mano a mano. **in h.,** entre manos; (of money) de contado. **in the hands of,** *fig* en el poder de. **"Hands wanted,"** «Se desean trabajadores.» **h. over h.,** mano sobre mano. **hand's breadth,** palmo, *m*. **Hands off!** ¡Fuera las manos! **Hands up!** ¡Manos arriba! **lost with all hands,** (of a ship) perdido con toda su tripulación. **off one's hands,** despachado; (of a daughter) casada. **on all hands,** por todas partes. **on h.,** entre manos; (of goods) existente; (present) presente. **on one's hands,** a cargo de uno. **on the one h.,** por un lado; a un lado. **on the other h.,** por otra parte; en cambio. **out of h.,** luego, inmediatamente; revoltoso. **to come to h.,** venir a mano; (of letters) llegar a las manos (de). **to get one's h. in,** ejercitarse. **to have a h. in,** intervenir en. **to have no h. in,** no tener arte ni parte en. **to have on h.,** traer entre manos. **to have the upper h.,** tener la sartén por el mango, llevar la ventaja. **to hold one's h.,** abstenerse; detenerse. **to hold hands,** cogerse de las manos. **to lay hands on,** tocar; poner mano en; echar mano a. **to set one's h. to,** emprender; (sign) firmar. **to shake hands,** estrechar la mano. **to stretch out one's hands,** tender las manos. **to take one's hands off,** no tocar. **with folded hands,** mano sobre mano. **with his hands behind his back,** con las manos en la espalda. **h.-in-h.,** cogidos (cogidas) de las manos. **h.-lever,** manija, *f*. **h.-loom,** telar de mano, *m*. **h. luggage,** equipaje de mano, *m*. **h.-made,** hecho a mano. **h.-mill,** molinillo, *m*. **h.-pump,** *n naut* sacabuche, *m*. **h. rail,** pasamano, *m*, baranda, balustrada, *f*. **h.-sewn,** cosido a mano. **h.-to-h.,** de mano en mano; (of a fight) a brazo partido, cuerpo a cuerpo. **h.-to-h. fight,** cachetina, *f*. **h.-to-mouth,** precario. **to live from h.-to-mouth,** vivir de día en día

hand *vt* dar; entregar; alargar. **to h. down,** bajar; (a person) ayudar a bajar; transmitir. **to h. in,** entregar; (a person) ayudar a entrar; (one's resignation) dimitir; (send) mandar, enviar. **to h. on,** transmitir. **to h. out,** vt distribuir; (a person) ayudar a salir; (from a vehicle) ayudar a bajar. vi inf pagar. **to h. over,** vt entregar. vi mil traspasar los poderes (a). **to h. round,** pasar de mano en mano; pasar; ofrecer. **to h. up,** subir; (a person) ayudar a subir

handbag n bolso, saco, monedero, m

handbill n anuncio, m

handbook n manual, compendio, tratado, m; anuario, m; (guide) guía, f

handbreadth n palmo, m

handcart n carretilla de mano, f, carretón, m

handcuff n esposa, f, grillo, m, (gen. pl). vt poner las esposas (a), maniatar

handed a (in compounds) que tiene manos; de manos . . . ; con las manos . . . **four-h.,** sport de cuatro personas. **one-h.,** manco

handful n puño, puñado, manojo, m. **to be a h.,** inf tener el diablo en el cuerpo. **in handfuls,** a manojos

handgrip n apretón de manos, m

handicap n desventaja, f; obstáculo, m; sport handicap, m; ventaja, f. vt fig perjudicar, impedir, dificultar. **the handicapped,** los lisiados, m pl

handicraft n mano de obra, f; (skill) destreza manual, f,

handiwork n mano de obra, f; trabajo manual, m; obra, f; (deed) acción, f, hecho, m

handkerchief n pañuelo, m

handle n mango, puño, m, Lat. Am. also manivela f; (lever) palanca, f; (of baskets, dishes, jugs) asa, f; (of doors, windows, drawers) pomo, m, (of a car door) picaporte m; (to one's name) designación, f; título, m; (excuse) pretexto, m. vt (touch) tocar; manejar; manipular; (treat) tratar; **h. with kid gloves,** tratar con guantes de seda; (deal in) comerciar en; tomar; (paw) manosear; (direct) dirigir; (control) gobernar; (pilot) pilotar; (a theme) explicar, tratar de. **h.-bar grip,** puño de un manillar, m

handlebars npl Spain guia fsg, manillar msg, Lat. Am. manubrio msg

handless a sin manos; manco; fig torpe

handling n manejo, m; manipulación, f; (treatment) trato, m, relaciones (con), f pl; (thumbing) manoseo, m; interpretación, f; art tratamiento, m, técnica, f

handmaid n sirvienta, criada, f; fig mayordomo, m

handsaw n sierra de mano, f, serrucho, m

handshake n apretón de manos, m

handsome a (generous) generoso; magnánimo; considerable; hermoso, bello; elegante; (of people) guapo; distinguido; excelente; (flattering) halagüeño. **He was a very h. man,** Era un hombre muy guapo

handsomely adv generosamente; con magnanimidad; elegantemente; bien

handsomeness n generosidad, f; magnanimidad, f; hermosura, f; elegancia, f; distinción, f

handspring n voltereta sobre las manos, f

handwork n obra hecha a mano, f, trabajo a mano, m; (needlework) labor de aguja, f

handworked a hecho a mano; (embroidered) bordado

handwriting n caligrafía, letra, escritura, f. **the h. on the wall,** la mano que escribía en la pared, f

handy a (of persons) diestro, mañoso, hábil; (of things) conveniente; útil; (near) cercano, a mano. adv cerca. **h.-man,** hombre de muchos oficios, m; factótum, m

hang vt colgar; suspender; (execute) ahorcar; (the head) bajar; dejar caer; (upholster) entapizar; (with wallpaper) empapelar; (drape) poner colgaduras en; (place) poner; (cover) cubrir. vi colgar, pender; estar suspendido; (be executed) ser ahorcado; (of garments) caer. n (of garments) caída, f; (of a machine) mecanismo, m; (meaning) sentido, m, significación, f. **to h. by a thread,** pender de un hilo. **h. in the balance,** estar en la balanza. **to h. fire,** estar (una cosa) en suspenso. **to h. loose,** caer suelto; (clothes) venir ancho. **to h.**

about, (surround) rodear, pegarse a; (frequent) frecuentar; (haunt) rondar; (be imminent) ser inminente, amenazar; (embrace) abrazar. **to h. back,** retroceder; quedarse atrás; fig vacilar, titubear. **to h. down,** colgar, pender; estar caído; caerse. **to h. on,** seguir agarrado (a); apoyarse en; fig persistir; (a person's words) estar pendiente de, beber; (remain) quedarse. **to h. out,** vt tender. vi (lean out) asomarse (por); (inf live) habitar. **to h. over,** colgar por encima; (brood) cernerse sobre; (lean over) inclinarse sobre; quedarse cerca de; (overhang) sobresalir; (overarch) abovedar; (threaten) amenazar. **to h. together,** (of persons) permanecer unidos; (of things) tener cohesión; (be consistent) ser lógico, ser consistente. **to h. up,** colgar; suspender; fig dejar pendiente, interrumpir. **to h. upon,** apoyarse en; (a person's words) beber las palabras de uno

hangar n cobertizo; aer hangar, m

hanger n colgadero, m; percha f. **h.-on,** parásito, m; dependiente, m

hanging n colgamiento, m; (killing) ahorcamiento, m; pl hangings, colgaduras, f pl, cortinajes, m pl. a pendiente colgante; péndulo; (of gardens) pensil. **It's not a h. matter,** No es una cuestión de vida y muerte. **h. bridge,** puente colgante, m. **h. committee,** junta (de una exposición,) f. **h. lamp,** lámpara de techo, f

hangman n verdugo, m

hangnail n padrastro, m

hangover n (after drinking) resaca, cruda (Mexico), f

hank n madeja, f

hanker vi (with after) ansiar, ambicionar; (with for) anhelar, suspirar por, desear con vehemencia

hankering n ambición, f; deseo vehemente, m

hanky-panky n superchería, f; engaño, m

hap n casualidad, suerte, f; suceso fortuito, m

haphazard n casualidad, f. a fortuito, casual

hapless a desgraciado, desdichado

haplessness n desgracia, desdicha, f

happen vi suceder, acontecer, ocurrir, pasar; (to be found, be) hallarse por casualidad; (take place) tener lugar, verificarse; (arise) sobrevenir. **Do you know what has happened to . . .?** ¿Sabes qué se ha hecho de . . .? **as if nothing had happened,** como si no hubiese pasado nada. **He turned up as if nothing had happened,** Se presentó como si tal cosa. **How did it h.?** ¿Cómo fue esto? **If they h. to see you,** Si acaso te vean. **I happened to be in London,** Me hallaba por casualidad en Londres. **It won't h. again,** No volverá a suceder. **whatever happens,** venga lo que venga

happening n suceso, acontecimiento, hecho, m, ocurrencia, f

happily adv felizmente; por suerte

happiness n felicidad, dicha, f; alegría, f, regocijo, m

happy a (lucky) afortunado; (felicitous) feliz, oportuno; feliz, dichoso; alegre, regocijado. **to be h.,** estar contento, ser feliz. **to be h. about,** alegrarse de. **to make h.,** hacer feliz, alegrar. **h.-go-lucky,** irresponsable, descuidado

harangue n arenga, f. vt arengar. vi pronunciar una arenga

harass vt hostigar, acosar; atormentar; preocupar; mil picar. **to h. the rear-guard,** picar la retaguardia

harbinger n fig precursor, heraldo, m; presagio, anuncio, m. vt anunciar, presagiar

harbor n puerto, m; (bay) bahía, f; (haven) asilo, refugio, m. vt dar refugio (a), albergar, acoger; (cherish) abrigar, acariciar; (conceal) esconder. **inner h.,** puerto, m. **outer h.,** puerto exterior, m. **to put into h.,** entrar en el puerto. **h. bar,** barra del puerto, f. **h.-dues,** derechos de puerto, m pl. **h.-master,** capitán de puerto, contramaestre de puerto, m

harborer n amparador (-ra), protector (-ra); (criminal) encubridor (-ra)

hard a duro; (firm) firme; difícil; laborioso, agotador; violento; poderoso; arduo; fuerte, recio; vigoroso, robusto; insensible, inflexible; cruel; (of weather) inclemente, severo; (unjust) injusto, opresivo; (stiff) tieso; (of water) cruda; (of wood) brava. *adv* duro; duramente; con ahínco; con fuerza; de firme; difícilmente; (of gazing) fijamente; severamente; (firmly) firmemente; vigorosamente; (of raining) a cántaros, mucho; (quickly) rápidamente; excesivamente; (much) mucho; (of bearing misfortune) a pechos; (attentively) atentamente; (heavily) pesadamente; (badly) mal; (closely) de cerca, inmediatamente. **It was a h. blow,** Fue un golpe recio. **to be h. put to,** encontrar difícil. **to go h.,** endurecerse. **to go h. with,** irle mal a uno. **to have a h. time,** pasar apuros, pasarlo mal. **to look h. at,** mirar atentamente, examinar detenidamente; mirar fijamente. **to be a h. drinker,** ser un bebedor empedernido. **h. and fast rule,** regla inalterable, *f.* **h.-bitten,** de carácter duro. **a h.-boiled egg,** un huevo duro. **h. breathing,** resuello, *m.* **h. by,** muy cerca. **h. cash,** efectivo, *m.* **h.-earned,** difícilmente conseguido; ganado con el sudor de la frente. **h.-featured,** de facciones duras. **h.-fisted,** tacaño. **h.-fought,** arduo, reñido. **h.-headed,** práctico, perspicaz. **h.-hearted,** duro de corazón, insensible. **h.-heartedness,** insensibilidad, *f.* **h. labor,** *law* trabajos forzados, *m pl,* presidio, *m.* **h.-mouthed,** (of horses) boquiduro. **h. of hearing,** duro de oído. **h.-up,** apurado. **to be very h.-up,** ser muy pobre; *inf* estar a la cuarta pregunta. **h.-wearing,** duradero; sufrido. **h.-won,** See **h.-earned. h.-working,** trabajador, laborioso, hacendoso, diligente

harden *vt* endurecer; (metal) templar; robustecer; (to war) aguerrir; (make callous) hacer insensible. *vi* endurecerse; hacerse duro; templarse; robustecerse (of shares) entonarse

hardening *n* endurecimiento, *m*; (of metal) temple, *m.* **h. of the arteries,** arteriosclerosis, *f*

hardiness *n* vigor, *m,* fuerza, robustez, *f*; audacia, *f*

hardly *adv* duramente; difícilmente; (badly) mal; severamente; (scarcely) apenas, casi. **h. ever,** casi nunca

hardness *n* dureza, *f*; severidad, *f*; inhumanidad, insensibilidad, *f*; (stiffness) tiesura, *f*; (difficulty) dificultad, *f*; (of water) crudeza, *f*; (of hearing) dureza de oído, *f*

hardship *n* penas, *f pl,* trabajos, *m pl*; infortunio, *m,* desdicha, *f*; (suffering) sufrimiento, *m*; (affliction) aflicción, *f*; (privation) privación, *f.* **to undergo h.,** pasar trabajos

hardware *n* ferretería, *f*

hardwood *n* madera brava, *f*

hardy *a* audaz, intrépido; (strong) fuerte, robusto; *bot* resistente

hare *n* liebre, *f.* **young h.,** lebrato, *m.* **h. and hounds,** rally paper, *m,* caza de papelitos, *f.* **h.-brained,** casquivano, atronado, con cabeza de chorlito. **hare's foot,** mano de gato, *f.* **h.-lip,** labio leporino, *m.* **h.-lipped,** labihendido

harebell *n* campanilla, campánula, *f*

harem *n* harén, serrallo, *m*

haricot *n* (green bean) judía, *f*; (dried bean) alubia, *f*

hark *vt* escuchar; oír. **to h. back,** volver al punto de partida; volver a la misma canción

harlequin *n* arlequín, *m*

harlequinade *n* arlequinada, *f*

harlot *n* ramera, prostituta, meretriz, *f*

harlotry *n* prostitución, *f*

harm *n* mal, *m*; daño, *m*; perjuicio, *m*; (danger) peligro, *m*; (detriment) menoscabo, *m*; (misfortune) desgracia, *f, vt* hacer mal (a); dañar, hacer daño (a); perjudicar. **And there's no h. in that,** Y en eso no hay mal. **to keep out of harm's way,** evitar el peligro; guardarse del mal

harmful *a* malo; dañino, perjudicial, nocivo; (dangerous) peligroso. **to be h.,** (of food, etc.) hacer mal (a); (of pests) ser dañino; (of behavior, etc.) perjudicar

harmfulness *n* lo malo; perniciosidad, *f*; daño, *m*; peligro, *m*

harmless *a* innocuo; inofensivo; inocente

harmlessness *n* innocuidad, *f*; inocencia, *f*

harmonic *n* (*phys math*) harmónica, *f*; *mus* armónico, *m, a mus* armónico

harmonica *n* armónica, *f*

harmonics *n* armonía, *f*; (tones) armónicos, *m pl*

harmonious *a* armonioso

harmoniously *adv* armoniosamente; *fig* en armonía

harmoniousness *n* armonía, *f*

harmonium *n* armonio, *m*

harmonization *n* armonización, *f*

harmonize *vt* armonizar. *vi* armonizarse, estar en armonía

harmony *n* armonía, *f*; *fig* paz, *f,* buenas relaciones, *f pl*; música, *f.* **to live in h.,** vivir en paz

harness *n* guarniciones, *f pl,* jaeces, *m pl*; (armor) arnés, *m. vt* enjaezar; (yoke) enganchar; (water) represar. **to die in h.,** *fig* morir en la brecha. **h. maker,** guarnicionero, *m.* **h. room,** guadarnés, *m*

harp *n* arpa, *f.* **t to h. on,** volver a la misma canción, volver a repetir

harpist *n* arpista, *mf*

harpoon *n* arpón, *m. vt* arponear

harpooner *n* arponero, *m*

harpsichord *n* arpicordio, *m*

harpy *n* arpía, *f*

harridan *n* bruja, *f*

harrow *n agr* rastra, *f,* escarificador, *m. vt agr* escarificar; *fig* lastimar, atormentar

harrowing *a* patibulario, conmovedor, atormentador, angustioso

harry *vt* devastar, asolar; (persons) robar; perseguir; (worry) atormentar; (annoy) molestar

harsh *a* áspero; (of voice) ronco; (of sound) discordante; (of colors) áspero; duro; chillón; severo, duro; (of features) duro; (of taste) ácido, acerbo

harshly *adv* severamente

harshness *n* (roughness) aspereza, *f*; (of voice) ronquedad, aspereza, *f*; (of sound) disonancia, *f*; (of colors) aspereza, *f*; severidad, *f*; dureza, *f*; (of taste) acidez, *f*

harum-scarum *n* tronera, saltabarrancos, *mf* molino, *m, a* irresponsable

harvest *n* cosecha, siega, *f*; recolección, *f*; *fig* producto, fruto, *m. vt* cosechar; recoger. **h. festival,** fiesta de la cosecha, *f*

harvester *n* segador, *m,* cosechero (-ra); (machine) segadora, *f*

hash *n* picado, *m. vt cul* picar

hashish *n* hachich, hachís, quif, *m*

hasp *n* pasador, *m*; sujetador, *m*

hassock *n* cojín, *m*

hassle *n Lat. Am.* fregada *f*

haste *n* prisa, rapidez, *f*; precipitación, *f*; urgencia, *f. vt* dar prisa (a); acelerar; precipitar. *vi* darse prisa; acelerarse; precipitarse. **in h.,** de prisa, aprisa. **to be in h.,** estar de prisa, llevar prisa. **in great h.,** muy aprisa, aprisa y corriendo, precipitadamente; con mucha prisa. **More h. less speed,** (Spanish equivalent. Words said by Charles III of Spain to his valet) ¡Vísteme despacio que voy de prisa!

hasten *vt* acelerar, apresurar; precipitar. *vi* darse prisa, apresurarse; moverse con rapidez; correr. **to h. one's steps,** apretar el paso. **to h. away,** marcharse rápidamente. **to h. back,** regresar apresuradamente. **to h. down,** bajar rápidamente. **to h. on,** seguir el camino sin descansar; seguir rápidamente. **to h. out,** salir rápidamente. **to h. towards,** ir rápidamente hacia; correr hacia. **to h. up,** subir aprisa, correr hacia arriba; darse prisa

hastily *adv* de prisa, rápidamente; con precipitación, precipitadamente; (angrily) impacientemente, airadamente; (thoughtlessly) sin reflexión

hastiness *n* rapidez, *f*; precipitación, *f*; (anger) impaciencia, irritación, *f*

hasty *a* rápido, apresurado; precipitado; (superficial)

superficial, ligero; (ill-considered) desconsiderado, imprudente; (angry) impaciente, irritable; violento, apasionado

hat *n* sombrero, *m*. **to pass round the h.,** pasar el platillo. **Andalusian h.,** sombrero calañés, *m*. **bowler h.,** sombrero hongo, *m*. **broad-brimmed h.,** sombrero chambergo, *m*. **Panama h.,** sombrero de jipijapa, *m*. **picture h.,** pamela, *f*. **shovel h.,** sombrero de teja, *m*. **soft felt h.,** sombrero flexible, *m*. **straw h.,** sombrero de paja, *m*. **three-cornered h.,** sombrero de tres picos, *m*. **top-h.,** sombrero de copa, *m*. **h. shop** or **trade,** sombrerería, *f*

hatband *n* cinta de sombrero, *f*, cintillo, *m*

hatbox *n* sombrerera, *f*

hatbrush *n* cepillo para sombreros, *m*

hatch *n* (wicket) compuerta, *f*; (trap-door) puerta caediza, *f*; *naut* escotilla, *f*; compuerta de esclusa, *f*; (of chickens) pollada, *f*; (of birds) nidada, *f*. *vt* (birds) empollar; incubar, encobar; *fig* tramar, urdir. *vi* empollarse, salir del cascarón; incubarse; *fig* madurarse. **to h. a plot,** urdir un complot, conspirar. **to h. chickens,** sacar pollos

hatchet *n* hacha pequeña, *f*, machado, *m*. **to bury the h.,** hacer la paz. **h.-faced,** de cara de cuchillo

hatching *n* incubación, *f*; (of a plot) maquinación, *f*

hatchway *n* *naut* escotilla, *f*

hate *n* odio, aborrecimiento, *m*, aversión, *f*; abominación, *f*. *vt* odiar, aborrecer, detestar; repugnar; saber mal, sentir. **I h. to trouble you,** Me sabe mal molestarle, Siento mucho molestarle. **to h. the sight of,** *inf* no poder ver (a)

hateful *a* odioso, aborrecible; repugnante

hatefulness *n* odiosidad, *f*, lo odioso; maldad, *f*

hater *n* aborrecedor (-ra). **to be a good h.,** saber odiar

hatful *n* un sombrero lleno (de)

hatless *a* sin sombrero, descubierto

hatpin *n* horquilla de sombrero, *f*

hatred *n* odio, aborrecimiento, *m*, detestación, *f*; aversión, enemistad, *f*

hatstand *n* perchera, *f*

hatter *n* sombrerero, *m*. **as mad as a h.,** loco como una cabra

haughtiness *n* altanería, arrogancia, altivez, soberbia, *f*, orgullo, *m*

haughty *a* altanero, arrogante, altivo, orgulloso *Lat. Am.* copetudo, *Mexico also* alzado

haul *n* (pull) tirón, *m*; (of fish) redada, *f*; (booty) botín, *m*. *vt* arrastrar, tirar de; *naut* halar. **to h. at, upon,** (ropes, etc.) aflojar, soltar, arriar. **to h. down,** (flags, sails) arriar

haulage *n* transporte, acarreo, *m*; coste de transporte, *m*. **h. contractor,** contratista de transporte, *m*

haunch *n* anca, culata, *f*; (of meat) pierna, *f*. **h.-bone,** hueso ilíaco, *m*

haunt *n* punto de reunión, lugar frecuentado (por), *m*; (lair) cubil, nido, *m*, guarida, *f*. *vt* frecuentar; rondar; (of ideas) perseguir; (of ghosts) aparecer, visitar. **It is a h. of thieves,** Es una cueva de ladrones

haunted *a* (by spirits) encantado

haunter *n* frecuentador (-ra); (ghost) fantasma, espectro, *m*

haunting *n* frecuentación, *f*; aparición de un espectro, *f*. *a* persistente

hautboy *n* oboe, *m*

hauteur *n* altivez, *f*

Havana la Habana, *f*. *n* (cigar) habano, *m*. (native) habanero (-ra), habano (-na)

have *vt* tener; poseer; (suffer) padecer; (spend) pasar; (eat or drink) tomar; (eat) comer; (a cigarette) fumar; (a bath, etc.) tomar; (a walk, a ride) dar; (cause to be done) mandar (hacer), hacer (hacer); (deceive) engañar; (defeat) vencer; (catch) coger; (say) decir; (allow) permitir; (tolerate) tolerar, sufrir; (obtain) lograr, conseguir; (wish) querer; (know) saber; (realize) realizar; (buy) comprar; (acquire) adquirir. As an auxiliary verb, haber (e.g. **I h. done it,** Lo he hecho, etc.). **As**

fate would h. it, Según quiso la suerte. **Do you h. to go?** ¿Tiene Vd. que marcharse? **H. him come here,** Hazle venir aquí. **I h. been had,** Me han engañado. **I h. a good mind to . . .,** Tengo ganas de . . . **I had all my books stolen,** Me robaron todos los libros. **You had better go,** Es mejor que te vayas. **I had rather,** Preferiría, Me gustaría más bien. **I h. had a suit made,** Mandé hacerme un traje, Hice hacerme un traje. **I would not h. had it otherwise,** No lo hubiese querido de otra manera. **I will not h. it,** No lo quiero; No quiero tomarlo; (object) No lo permitiré. **If we had known,** Si lo hubiésemos sabido. **It has to do with the sun,** Está relacionado con el sol, Tiene que ver con el sol. **Have a good trip!** ¡Buen viaje!, ¡Feliz viaje! **What are you going to h.?** ¿Qué quiere Vd. tomar? **Will you h. some jam?** ¿Quiere Vd. mermelada? **to h. breakfast,** desayunar. **to h. dinner, supper,** cenar. **to h. lunch,** almorzar. **to h. for tea,** invitar a tomar el té; (of food) merendar. **to h. tea,** tomar el té. **to h. it out with,** habérselas con. **to h. just,** acabar de. **I h. just done it,** Acabo de hacerlo. **to h. on hand,** traer entre manos. **to h. one's eye on,** no perder de vista (a), vigilar. **to h. one's tail between one's legs,** ir rabo entre piernas. **to h. to,** tener que; deber. **It has to be so,** Tiene que ser así. **to h. too much of,** sobrar, tener demasiado de. **He has too much time,** Le sobra tiempo. **to h. about one,** tener (or llevar) consigo. **to h. back,** aceptar; recibir. **to h. down,** hacer bajar. **She had her hair down,** El pelo le caía por las espaldas. **to h. in,** hacer entrar. **to h. on,** vestir, llevar puesto; (engagements) tener (compromisos). **to h. out,** hacer salir; llevar a paseo; llevar fuera; (have removed) hacerse sacar; quitar. **to h. up,** (persons) hacer subir; (things) subir; *law* llevar a (ante) los tribunales. **to h. with one,** tener consigo. **I h. her with me,** La tengo conmigo, Ella me acompaña

haven *n* puerto, *m*, abra, *f*; *fig* oasis, abrigo, refugio, *m*

haversack *n* mochila, *f*, morral, *m*

havoc *n* destrucción, ruina, *f*; *fig* estrago, *m*. **to wreak h. among,** destruir; *fig* hacer estragos entre (or en)

Hawaii Hawai, *m*

Hawaiian *a* and *n* hawaiano; *n* (language) hawaiano, *m*

hawk *n* halcón, *m*; gavilán, milano, *m*. *vi* cazar con halcón. *vt* vender mercancías por las calles; *fig* difundir. **h.-eyed,** de ojos de lince. **h.-nosed,** de nariz aguileña

hawker *n* halconero, *m*; (vendor) buhonero, *m*, vendedor (-ra) ambulante

hawking *n* caza con halcones, cetrería, *f*; (expectorating) gargajeo, *m*; (selling) buhonería, *f*

hawser *n* maroma, *f*, calabrote, *m*

hawthorn *n* espino, *m*. **white h.,** espino blanco, *m*

hay *n* heno, *m*. **to make hay while the sun shines,** hacer su agosto. **hay fever,** fiebre del heno, *f*. **hay-fork,** horca, *f*

hayloft *n* henil, *m*

haymaker *n* segador (-ra); (machine) segadora, *f*

haymaking *n* recolección del heno, *f*

haystack *n* almiar, *m*, niara, *f*

hazard *n* azar, *m*, suerte, *f*; riesgo, peligro, *m*; (game) juego de azar, *m*. *vt* arriesgar, aventurar. **at all hazards,** a todo riesgo

hazardous *a* azaroso, arriesgado, peligroso

haze *n* bruma, *f*; confusión, *f*

hazel *n* avellano, *m*. **h.-nut,** avellana, *f*

hazy *a* brumoso, calinoso; confuso

he *pers. pron* él. *m* (of humans) varón, *m*; (of animals) macho, *m*. **he who,** el que, quien. **he-goat,** macho cabrío, *m*. **he-man,** todo un hombre, hombre cabal, *m*

head *vt* golpear con la cabeza; encabezar; (lead) capitanear; (direct) dirigir, guiar; (wine) cabecear. *vi* estar a la cabeza de; dirigirse a. **headed for,** con rumbo a, en dirección a. **to h. off,** interceptar; desviar; *fig* distraer

head *n* *anat* cabeza, *f*; (upper portion) parte superior, *f*; (of a coin) cara, *f*; (hair) cabellera, *f*; (individual) persona, *f*; (of cattle) res, *f*; (of a mountain) cumbre, *f*; (of a ladder) último peldaño, *m*; (of toadstools) sombrero,

m; (of trees) copa, *f;* (of a stick) puño, *m;* (of a cylinder) culata, *f;* (of a river, etc.) manantial, origen, *m;* (of a bed) cabecera, *f;* (of nails, pins) cabeza, *f;* (froth) espuma, *f;* (flower) flor, *f;* (leaves) hojas, *f pl;* (first place) primer puesto, *m;* (of game, fish) pieza, *f;* (of a page, column) cabeza, *f;* (cape) cabo, *m;* (of an arrow, dart, lance) punta, *f;* (front) frente, *m;* (leader) jefe, cabeza, *m;* (chief) director (-ra), superior (-ra); presidente (-ta); (of a school) director (-ra); (of a cask) fondo, *m; mech* cabezal, *m;* (of an ax) filo, *m;* (of a bridge) cabeza, *f;* (of a jetty, pier) punta, *f;* (of a ship) proa, *f;* (of a flower) cabezuela, *f;* (of asparagus) punta, *f;* (of a table) cabeza, *f;* (of the family) jefe, cabeza, *m;* (seat of honor) cabecera, *f;* (title) título, *m;* (aspect) punto de vista, *m;* (division) capítulo, *m;* (management, direction) dirección, *f;* (talent) talento, *m,* cabeza, *f;* (intelligence) inteligencia, *f. a* principal; primero; en jefe. **at the h. of,** a la cabeza de. **crowned h.,** testa coronada, *f.* **from h. to foot,** de pies a cabeza; de hito en hito; de arriba abajo. **He took it into his h. to . . .,** Se le ocurrió de . . . **This story has neither h. nor tail,** Este cuento no tiene pies ni cabeza. **with h. held high,** con la frente levantada. **to come to a h.,** llegar a la crisis; llegar al punto decisivo. **to get an idea out of a person's h.,** quitar una idea a uno de la cabeza. **to keep one's h.,** *fig* conservar la sangre fría, no perder la cabeza. **to lose one's h.,** *fig* perder la cabeza. **to put into a person's h.,** *fig* meter (a uno) en la cabeza. **to run one's h. against,** golpear la cabeza contra. **h. first,** de cabeza. **h. of cattle,** res, *f.* **h. office,** central, *f.* **h. of hair,** cabellera, *f;* mata de pelo, *f.* **h.-on,** de cabeza. **h.-on collision,** choque de frente, *m.* **h. opening,** (of a garment) cabezón, *m.* **heads or tails,** cara o cruz (Spain), águila o sol (Mexico), cruz o sello (Argentina, Chile). **h. over heels,** de patas arriba. **h. over heels in love,** calado hasta los huesos. **h.-dress,** tocado, *m;* peinado, *m;* sombrero, *m.* **h. voice,** voz de cabeza, *f.* **h. waiter,** encargado de comedor, jefe de camareros, *m*
headache *n* dolor de cabeza, *m; fig* quebradero de cabeza, *m*
headboard *n* cabecera (de una cama), *f*
headed *a* con cabeza . . .; que tiene la cabeza . . .; de cabeza . . .; (of an article) intitulado. **large h.,** cabezudo
header *n* caída de cabeza, *f;* salto de cabeza, *m*
headgear *n* tocado, *m;* sombrero, gorro, *m*
head-hunting *n* la caza de cabezas, *f*
heading *n naut* el poner la proa en dirección (a); el guiar en dirección (a); (of a book, etc.) título, encabezamiento, *m;* (soccer) golpe de cabeza, *m.* **to come under the h. of,** estar incluido entre; clasificarse bajo
headland *n* cabo, promontorio, *m*
headlight *n naut* faro, *m;* (rw, naut) farol, *m.* **to dip the headlights,** bajar los faros. **to switch on the headlights,** encender los faros (or los faroles)
headline *n* (of a newspaper) titular, *m;* (to a chapter) título de la columna, *m*
headlong *a* precipitado; despeñado. *adv* de cabeza; precipitadamente. **to fall h.,** caer de cabeza
headman *n* cacique, cabecilla, *m;* (foreman) capataz, contramaestre, *m*
headmaster *n* director de colegio, rector, *m*
headmistress *n* directora de colegio, rectora, *f*
head-on collision *n* choque frontal, *m*
head nurse enfermero-jefe, *m*
headphones *n pl* auriculares, *m pl*
headquarters *n mil* cuartel general, *m;* oficina central, *f;* jefatura, *f;* centro, *m*
headrest *n* respaldo, *m;* apoyo para la cabeza, *m*
headstone *n* piedra mortuoria, *f*
headstrong *a* impetuoso, terco, testarudo
headway *n* marcha, *f;* (of ship) progreso, avance, *m.* **to make h.,** avanzar; *fig* hacer progresos; *fig* prosperar
headwind *n* viento en contra, *m*
heady *a* apasionado, violento; impetuoso, precipitado; (obstinate) terco, *fig* (of alcohol) encabezado; *fig* embriagador

heal *vt* curar, sanar; (flesh) cicatrizar. *vi* curar, sanar; cicatrizarse; (superficially) sobresanar
healable *a* curable
healer *n* sanador (-ra), curador (-ra); curandero, *m*
healing *a* curador, sanador; médico. *n* curación, *f;* cura, *f,* remedio, *m*
health *n* salud, *f;* higiene, sanidad, *f.* **Here's to your very good h.!** ¡Salud y pesetas! **He is in good h.,** Disfruta de buena salud. **to drink a person's h.,** beber a la salud de. **to enjoy good h.,** gozar de buena salud. **to look full of h.,** vender salud. **h.-giving,** saludable. **h. inspection,** visita de sanidad, *f.* **h. officer,** inspector de sanidad, *m.* **h. resort,** balneario, *m*
healthiness *n* buena salud, *f;* sanidad, salubridad, *f*
healthy *a* sano; con buena salud; (healthful) saludable. **to be h.,** tener buena salud
heap *n* montón, *m;* rima, pila, *f,* acervo, *m;* (of people) muchedumbre, *f,* tropel, *m. vt* amontonar; apilar; colmar. **in heaps,** a montones. **We have heaps of time,** Nos sobra tiempo, Tenemos tiempo de sobra. **to h. together,** juntar, mezclar. **to h. up, upon,** colmar; amontonar; *agr* hacinar; *fig* acumular
hear *vt* oír; (listen) escuchar; (attend) asistir a; (give audience) dar audiencia (a); (a lawsuit) ver (un pleito); (speak) hablar; (be aware of, feel) sentir. *vi* oír; tener noticias; (learn) enterarse de; (allow) permitir. **H.! H.!** ¡Muy bien! ¡Bravo! **I have heard it said that . . .** He oído decir que . . . **Let me h. from you!** ¡Mándame noticias tuyas! **They were never heard of again,** No se volvió a saber de ellos, No se supo más de ellos. **to h. about,** oír de; (know) saber de, tener noticias de; (receive) recibir información sobre. **to h. from,** tener noticias de; recibir carta de. **to h. of,** enterarse de, saber; recibir información sobre; (allow) permitir
hearer *n* oyente, *mf*
hearing *n* (sense of) oído, *m;* alcance del oído, *m;* presencia, *f;* audición, *f; law* vista (de una causa) *f.* **It was said in my h.,** Fue dicho en mi presencia. **out of h.,** fuera del alcance del oído. **within h.,** al alcance del oído. **have a h. problem,** ser parcialmente sordo
hearing aid acústica, aparato auditivo, aparato acústico, audífono, *m*
hearsay *n* fama, *f,* rumor, *m.* **by h.,** de oídas
hearse *n* coche fúnebre, *m*
heart *n* corazón, *m;* (feelings) entrañas, *f pl;* (of the earth, etc.) seno, corazón, *m;* (of lettuce, etc.) cogollo, repollo, *m;* (suit in cards) copas, *f; bot* médula, *f;* (soul) alma, *f;* (courage) valor, *m;* ánimo, *m.* **at h.,** en el fondo, esencialmente. **by h.,** de memoria. **from the h.,** con toda sinceridad, de todo corazón. **He is a man after my own h.,** Es un hombre de los que me gustan. **I have no h. to do it,** No tengo valor de hacerlo. **in the h. of the country,** en medio del campo. **to break one's h.,** partirse el corazón. **to have one's h. in one's mouth,** tener el alma en un hilo, estar muerto de miedo. **to have no h.,** *fig* no tener entrañas. **to lose h.,** desanimarse, descorazonarse. **to set one's h. on,** poner el corazón en. **to take h.,** cobrar ánimo; *inf* hacer de tripas corazón. **to take to h.,** tomar a pechos. **to wear one's h. on one's sleeve,** tener el corazón en la mano. **with all my h.,** con toda el alma. **h.-ache,** angustia, pena, *f;* **h.-beat,** latido del corazón, *m.* **h.-breaker,** (woman) coqueta, *f;* (man) ladrón de corazones, *m.* **h. disease,** enfermedad del corazón, enfermedad cardíaca, *f.* **h. failure,** colapso cardíaco, *m.* **h.-rending,** desgarrador, angustioso. **h.-searching,** examen de conciencia, *m.* **h.-shaped,** acorazonado, en forma de corazón. **h.-strings,** fibras del corazón, *f pl.* **h.-to-h. talk,** conversación íntima, *f.* **h.-whole,** libre de afectos
heartbreaking *a* desgarrador, angustioso, doloroso, lastimoso
heartbroken *a* acongojado, afligido, transido de dolor
heartburn *n* acidez del estómago, acedia, pirosis, rescoldera, *f*
heartburning *n* rencor, *m,* animosidad, envidia, *f*

hearted *a* de corazón . . . que tiene el corazón . . . **kind-h.,** de buen corazón, bondadoso

hearten *vt* alentar, animar

heartfelt *a* hondo; de todo corazón, sincero; más expresivo

hearth *n* hogar, *m*; chimenea, *f*; *fig* hogar, *m*

heartily *adv* cordialmente; sinceramente; enérgicamente; con entusiasmo; (of eating) con buen apetito; (very) muy, completamente. **I am h. sick of it all,** *inf* Estoy harto hasta los dientes

heartiness *n* cordialidad, *f*; sinceridad, *f*; energía, *f*, vigor, *m*; vehemencia, *f*; entusiasmo, *m*; (of appetite) buen diente, buen apetito, *m*

heartless *a* sin corazón, sin piedad, despiadado, inhumano, cruel

heartlessness *n* falta de corazón, inhumanidad, crueldad, *f*

hearty *a* cordial; sincero; enérgico; vigoroso; robusto; (frank) campechano; (of appetite) voraz; bueno; (big) grande

heat *n* calor, *m*; (in animals) celo, *m*; (of an action) calor, *m*; *fig* vehemencia, fogosidad, *f*; *fig* fuego, *m*; (passion) ardor, *m*, pasión, *f*; (of a race) carrera eliminatoria, *f*. *vt* calentar; (excite) conmover, acalorar, excitar; (annoy) irritar. *vi* calentarse. **dead h.,** empate, *m*. **in h.,** en celo. **in the h. of the moment,** en el calor del momento. **to become heated,** *fig* acalorarse, exaltarse. **white h.,** candencia, incandescencia, *f*. **h. lightning,** fucilazo, *m*. **h. spot,** pápula, *f*; terminación sensible, *f*. **h. stroke,** insolación, *f*. **h. wave,** onda de calor, *f*

heated *a* calentado; caliente; excitado; apasionado

heatedly *adv* con vehemencia, con pasión

heater *n* calentador, *m*; calorífero, *m*; (stove) estufa, *f*; (for plates) calientaplatos, *m*. **water-h.,** calentador de agua, *m*

heath *n* brezal, *m*; yermo, páramo, *m*; *bot* brezo, *m*

heathen *n* pagano (-na); idólatra, *mf*; ateo (-ea), descreído (-da). *a* pagano; ateo; bárbaro

heathenism *n* paganismo, *m*; idolatría, *f*; ateísmo, *m*

heather *n* brezo, *m*

heating *n* calefacción, *f*, *a* calentador; (of drinks) fortificante. **central h.,** calefacción central, *f*

heave *vt* alzar, levantar; *naut* izar; (the anchor, etc.) virar; (throw) arrojar, lanzar; elevar; (extract) extraer; (emit) dar, exhalar. *vi* subir y bajar; palpitar; agitarse. *n* tirón, *m*; (of the sea) vaivén, *m*. **to h. in sight,** aparecer, surgir. **to h. out sail,** *naut* desenvergar. **to h. the lead,** *naut* escandallar. **to h. to,** *naut* estarse a la capa

heaven *n* cielo, *m*; firmamento, *m*; paraíso, *m*. **Heavens!** ¡Cielos! ¡Por Dios! **Thank H.!** ¡Gracias a Dios! **h.-born,** celeste. **h.-sent,** *fig* providencial

heavenliness *n* carácter celestial, *m*; delicia, *f*

heavenly *a* celeste, celestial; divino; *fig* delicioso. **h. body,** astro, *m*

heavily *adv* pesadamente; torpemente; penosamente; (slowly) lentamente; severamente; excesivamente; (of sighing) hondamente; (sadly) tristemente; (of rain, etc.) reciamente, fuertemente; (of wind) con violencia. **He fell h.,** Cayó de plomo. **to lie h. upon,** pesar mucho sobre. **to rain h.,** llover mucho, diluviar

heaviness *n* peso, *m*; (lethargy) torpor, letargo, *m*; sueño, *m*, languidez, *f*; (clumsiness) torpeza, *f*; (severity) severidad, *f*; importancia, responsabilidad, *f*; dificultad, *f*; (gravity) gravedad, *f*; tristeza, melancolía, *f*; (boredom) sosería, insulsez, *f*; (of style) monotonía, ponderosidad, *f*

heaving *n* levantamiento, *m*; (of the anchor, etc.) virada, *f*; (of the sea) vaivén, *m*; (of the breast) palpitación, *f*

heavy *a* pesado; torpe; sin gracia; (slow) lento; (thick) grueso; (strong) fuerte; (hard) duro; grave; difícil; oneroso; responsable, importante; (oppresive) opresivo; penoso; grande; (sad) triste, melancólico; (of the sky) anublado; (of food) indigesto; (tedious)

aburrido, soso; (pompous) pomposo; (of roads) malo; (of scents) fuerte, penetrante; (of sleep, weather) pesado; (weary) rendido; (charged with) cargado de; (of a meal) grande, abundante; (violent) violento; (of a cold, etc.) malo; (drowsy) soñoliento; (torpid) tórpido; (of rain, snow, hail) fuerte, recio; (of firing) intenso; (of sighs) profundo; (of soil) recio, de mucha miga; (*phys chem*) pesado. **to be h.,** pesar mucho. **How h. are you?** ¿Cuánto pesa Vd.? **h.-armed,** pesado; armado hasta los dientes. **h.-eyed,** con ojeras. **h. guns,** artillería pesada, *f*. **h.-handed,** de manos torpes; *fig* tiránico, opresivo. **h.-hearted,** triste, apesadumbrado. **h. industry,** la gran industria, la industria pesada, *f*. **h.-laden,** muy cargado. **h. losses,** *mil* pérdidas cuantiosas, *f pl*. **h.weight,** *sport* peso pesado, *m*

Hebraic *a* hebraico, hebreo, judaico

Hebraism *n* judaísmo, hebraísmo, *m*

Hebraist *n* hebraísta, *m*

Hebrew *n* hebreo (-ea), judío (-ía): (language) hebreo, *m*

Hebrides, the las Hébridas

hecatomb *n* hecatombe, *f*

heckle *vt fig* interrumpir, importunar con preguntas

heckler *n* perturbador (-ra)

heckling *n* interrupción, *f*

hectare *n* hectárea, *f*

hectic *a* (consumptive) hético; (feverish) febril; *fig inf* agitado

hectogram *n* hectogramo, *m*

hectoliter *n* hectolitro, *m*

hector *vt* intimidar, amenazar

hectoring *a* imperioso; amenazador

hectowatt *n elec* hectovatio, *m*

hedge *n* seto, *m*; barrera, *f*. *vt* cercar con un seto; rodear. *vi fig* titubear, vacilar. **h.-hopping,** *aer* vuelo a ras de tierra, *m*. **h.-sparrow,** acentor de bosque, *m*

hedgehog *n* erizo, *m*. **h. position,** *mil* puesto fuerte, *m*

hedonism *n* hedonismo, *m*

hedonist *n* hedonista, *mf*

heed *n* atención, *f*, cuidado, *m*. *vt* atender; observar, considerar; escuchar. **to hacer caso**

heedful *a* atento; cuidadoso

heedless *a* desatento; descuidado, negligente; distraído

heedlessly *adv* sin hacer caso; negligentemente; distraídamente

heedlessness *n* desatención, distracción, *f*; descuido, *m*; negligencia, *f*; inconsideración, *f*

heel *n anat* talón, calcañar, *m*; (of shoe) tacón, *m*; (of a violin, etc., bow) talón, *m*; (remains) restos, *m pl*. *vt* poner tacón a; poner talón a; *naut* hacer zozobrar. *vi naut* zozobrar. **rubber h.,** tacón de goma, *m*. **She let him cool his heels for half an hour,** le dio un plantón de media hora. **to follow on a person's heels,** pisarle (a uno) los talones. **to be down at h.,** (of shoes) estar gastados los tacones; estar desaseado. **to take to one's heels,** apretar a correr, poner pies en polvorosa. **to turn on one's h.,** dar media vuelta. **h.-bone,** zancajo, *m*. **h.-piece,** talón, *m*

heeltap *n* tapa de tacón, *f*; escurridura, *f*

heft *vt* sopesar, tomar al peso

hegemony *n* hegemonía, *f*

heifer *n* ternera, vaquilla, *f*

heigh *interj* (calling attention) ¡oye! ¡ioiga! **h.-ho!** ¡ay!

height *n* altura, *f*; elevación, *f*; altitud, *f*; (stature) estatura, *f*; (high ground) cerro, *m*, colina, *f*; (sublimity) sublimidad, excelencia, *f*; colmo, *m*; (zenith) auge, *m*, cumbre, *f*

heighten *vt* hacer más alto; (enhance) realzar; (exaggerate) exagerar; (perfect) perfeccionar; (intensify) intensificar

heightening *n* elevación, *f*; (enhancement) realce, *m*; (exaggeration) exageración, *f*; (perfection) perfección, *f*; (intensification) intensificación, *f*

heinous *a* atroz, nefando, horrible.

heinousness *n* atrocidad, enormidad, *f*

heir *n* heredero, *m*, *Lat. Am.* asignatario *m*. **h. apparent,**

heredero aparente, *m*. **h.-at-law,** heredero forzoso, *m*. **h. presumptive,** presunto heredero, *m*

heiress *n* heredera, *Lat. Am.* asignataria *f*

heirloom *n* reliquia de familia, *f*; *fig* herencia, *f*

helicopter *n* helicóptero, *m*

helium *n chem* helio, *m*

helix *n geom* hélice, *m*; (*arch geom*) espira, *f*

hell *n* infierno, *m*. **h.-fire,** fuego del infierno, *m*, llamas del infierno, *f pl*

Hellenic *a* helénico

Hellenism *n* helenismo, *m*

Hellenist *n* helenista, *mf*

Hellenize *vt* helenizar

hellish *a* infernal; *inf* horrible, detestable

hello *interj* ¡hola!; (on telephoning someone) ¡oiga! ¡aló!; (answering telephone) *Spain* ¡diga!, ¡aló!, *Colombia* ¡a ver!, *Mexico* ¡bueno!

helm *n* caña del timón, *f*; timón, gobernalle, *m*. **to obey the h.,** obedecer el timón. **to take the h.,** gobernar el timón; ponerse a pilotar

helmet *n* casco, *m*; (in olden days) yelmo, capacete, *m*; (sun) casco colonial, *m*

helminthic *a* helmíntico, vermífugo

helmsman *n* timonero, *m*

help *n* ayuda, *f*; auxilio, socorro, *m*; (protection) favor, *m*, protección, *f*; (remedy) remedio, *m*; (cooperation) cooperación, *f*, concurso, *m*; (domestic) criada, *f*. **A little h. is worth a lot of sympathy,** Más vale un toma que dos te daré. **There's no h. for it,** No hay más remedio. **to call for h.,** pedir socorro a gritos. **without h.,** a solas, sin la ayuda de nadie

help *vt* ayudar; socorrer, auxiliar; (favor) favorecer; (mitigate) aliviar; (contribute to) contribuir a, facilitar; (avoid) evitar. *vi* ayudar. **He cannot h. worrying,** No puede menos de preocuparse. **God h. you!** ¡Dios te ampare! **So h. me God!** ¡Así Dios me salve! **to h. one another,** ayudarse mutuamente, ayudarse los unos a los otros. **to h. oneself,** (to food) servirse. **to h. down, off,** ayudar a bajar; ayudar a apearse. **to h. in,** ayudar a entrar. **to h. along, forward, on,** avanzar, fomentar, promover; contribuir a. **Shall I h. you on with the dress?** ¿Quieres que te ayude a ponerte el vestido? **to h. out,** ayudar a salir; (from a vehicle) ayudar a bajar; (of a difficulty, etc.) sacar; suplir la falta de; ayudar. **to h. over,** ayudar a cruzar; (a difficulty) ayudar a salir (de un apuro); ayudar a vencer (un obstáculo, etc.); (a period) ayudar a pasar. **to h. to,** contribuir a, ayudar en; (food) servir. **to h. up,** ayudar a subir; ayudar a levantarse, levantar

helper *n* auxiliador (-ra); asistente (-ta); (protector) favorecedor (-ra); bienhechor (-ra), *Argentina also* ladero *m*; (colleague) colega, *m*; (co-worker) colaborador (-ra). **He thanked all his helpers,** Dio las gracias a todos los que le habían ayudado

helpful *a* útil, provechoso; (obliging) servicial, atento, *Lat. Am.* acomedido; (favorable) favorable; (healthy) saludable

helpfulness *n* utilidad, *f*; bondad, *f*

helping *n* ayuda, *f*; (of food) porción, ración, *f*, plato, *m*. **Won't you have a second h.?** ¿No quiere usted servirse más (or otra vez)? ¿No quiere usted repetir? **to lend a h. hand (to),** prestar ayuda (a)

helpless *a* desamparado, abandonado; (through infirmity) imposibilitado; impotente, sin fuerzas (para); (shiftless) incompetente, inútil

helplessness *n* desamparo, *m*; invalidez, debilidad, *f*; impotencia, *f*; incompetencia, *f*

helter-skelter *adv* atropelladamente; en desorden. *n* barahunda, *f*

hem *n sew* dobladillo, filete, *m*, bastilla, *f*; (edge) orilla, *f*. *interj* ¡ejem! *vt* hacer dobladillo en, dobladillar. *vi* (cough) fingir toser. **false hem,** *sew* dobladillo falso, *m*. **running hem,** *sew* jareta, *f*. **to hem and haw,** tartamudear; vacilar. **to hem in,** cercar, sitiar

hemisphere *n* hemisferio, *m*

hemispherical *a* hemisférico, semiesférico

hemlock *n bot* cicuta, *f*

hemoglobin *n chem* hemoglobina, *f*

hemophilia *n med* hemofilia, *f*

hemorrhage *n* hemorragia, *f*, flujo de sangre, *m*

hemorrhoids *n pl med* hemorroides, *f*

hemp *n* cáñamo, *m*. **h. cloth,** lienzo, *m*. **h.-seed,** cañamón, *m*

hemstitch *n* vainica, *f*. *vt* hacer vainica en

hen *n* gallina, *f*; (female bird) hembra, *f*. **the hen pheasant,** la hembra del faisán. **hen bird,** pájara, *f*. **hen-coop** or **house,** gallinero, *m*. **hen party,** *inf* reunión de mujeres, *f*. **hen-roost,** nidal, ponedero, *m*

hence *adv* (of place) de aquí; (of time) de ahora, de aquí a; (therefore) por eso, por lo tanto, por consiguiente. *interj* ¡fuera! ¡fuera de aquí! **I shall come to see you a month h.,** Vendré a verte en un mes (or al cabo de un mes). **ten years h.,** de aquí a diez años. **h. the fact that . . . ,** de aquí que. . . . **H. it happens that . . . ,** Por eso sucede que . . .

henceforth *adv* desde aquí en adelante, de hoy en adelante

henchman *n* escudero, *m*; satélite, secuaz, *m*

henna *n* alheña, *f*

henpecked *a* gobernado por su mujer, que se deja mandar por su mujer

her *pers pron direct object* la; (with prepositions) ella. *pers. pron indirect object* le, a ella. *poss a* su, *mf*; sus, *mf pl*, de ella. **I saw her on Wednesday,** La vi el miércoles. **The message is for her,** El recado es para ella. **It is her book,** Es su libro, Es el libro de ella

herald *n* heraldo, *m*; presagio, anuncio, *m*. *vt* proclamar; anunciar, presagiar

heraldic *a* heráldico

heraldry *n* heráldica, *f*

herb *n* hierba, *f*

herbaceous *a* herbáceo

herbage *n* herbaje, *m*; pasto, *m*

herbal *a* herbario. *n* herbolaria, *f*

herbalist *n* herbario, *m*, simplista, *mf*

herbarium *n* herbario, *m*

herbivorous *a* herbívoro

herby *a* herbáceo

Herculean *a* hercúleo

herd *n* manada, *f*; (of cattle) hato, *m*; (race) raza, *f*; (*fig* contemptuous) populacho, *m*, masa, *f*. *vt* reunir en manadas; reunir en hatos; (sheep) reunir en rebaños; guiar las manadas, etc. *vi* ir en manadas, hatos o rebaños; asociarse, reunirse. **h.-instinct,** instinto gregario, *m*; instinto de la masas, *m*

herdsman *n* ganadero, pastor, manadero, *m*; (head herdsman) rabadán, *m*

here *adv* aquí; (at roll-call) ¡presente!; acá; an este punto; ahora. *n* presente, *m*. **And h. he looked at me,** Y a este punto me miró. **Come h.!** ¡Ven acá! **in h.,** aquí dentro. **h. below,** aquí abajo, en la tierra. **h. and there,** aquí y allá. **h., there and everywhere,** en todas partes. **H. I am,** Heme aquí. **h. is . . . ,** he aquí. **. . . H. they are,** Aquí los tienes, Aquí están. **Here's to you!** (on drinking) ¡Salud y pesetas! ¡A tu salud!

hereabouts *adv* por aquí cerca

hereafter *adv* en lo futuro; desde ahora; en adelante. *n* futuro, *m*. **the H.,** la otra vida

hereat *adv* en esto

hereby *adv* por esto, por las presentes

hereditarily *adv* hereditariamente, por herencia

hereditary *a* hereditario

heredity *n* herencia, *f*

herein *adv* en esto; aquí dentro; incluso

hereinafter *adv* después, más abajo, más adelante, en adelante, en lo sucesivo

hereinbefore *adv* en la anterior, en lo arriba citado, en lo antes mencianado, en lo precedente

hereof *adv* de esto

heresy *n* herejía, *f*

heretic *n* hereje, *mf*

heretical *a* herético

hereunder *adv* abajo

hereupon *adv* en esto, en seguida

herewith *adv* junto con esto, con esto; ahora, en esta ocasión

heritage *n* herencia, *f*

hermaphrodite *a* and *n* hermafrodita, *mf*

hermetic *a* hermético

hermit *n* ermitaño, *m*. **h. crab,** paguro, cangrejo ermitaño, *m*

hernia *n* hernia, *f*

hero *n* héroe, *m*. **h.-worship,** culto a los héroes, *m*

heroic *a* heroico, épico

heroin *n chem* heroína, *f*

heroine *n* heroína, *f*

heroism *n* heroísmo, *m*

heron *n* garza, *f*

herpes *n pl* herpes, *mf pl*

herring *n* arenque, *m*

hers *poss pron 3rd sing* (el) suyo, *m*; (la) suya, *f*; (los) suyos, *m pl*; (las) suyas, *f pl*; de ella. This book is h., Este libro es suyo, Este libro es de ella. This book is h., not mine, Este libro es el suyo no el mío. a sister of h., una de sus hermanas, una hermana suya

herself *pron* sí misma, sí; ella misma; (with reflexive verb) se. **She has done it by h.,** Lo ha hecho por sí misma. **She h. told me so,** Ella misma me lo dijo. **She is by h.,** Está a solas, Está sola

hesitancy. See **hesitation**

hesitant *a* indeciso, vacilante, irresoluto. **to be h.,** mostrarse irresoluto

hesitate *vi* vacilar, dudar; titubear. **I do not h. to say . . . ,** No vacilo en decir . . . **He hesitated over his reply,** Tardaba en dar su respuesta

hesitatingly *adv* irresolutamente; titubeando

hesitation *n* vacilación, hesitación, *f*; irresolución, indecisión, *f*; (reluctance) aversión, repugnancia, *f*; titubeo, *m*

heterodox *a* heterodoxo

heterodoxy *n* heterodoxia, *f*

heterogeneity *n* heterogeneidad, *f*

heterogeneous *a* heterogéneo

hew *vt* cortar, tajar; (trees) talar; (a career, etc.) hacerse

hewer *n* partidor, talador, *m*

hexagon *n* hexágono, *m*

hey *interj* ¡he! ¡oye!

heyday *n* apogeo, colmo, *m*; buenos tiempos, *m pl*; reinado, *m*; pleno vigor, *m*

hi *interj* ¡oye! ¡hola!

hiatus *n* hiato, *m*; laguna, *f*, vacío, *m*

hibernate *vi* invernar

hibernation *n* invernada, *f*

hibiscus *n bot* hibisco, *m*

hiccough *n* hipo, *m*. *vi* hipar. *vt* decir con hipo

hidden *a* escondido, secreto, oculto

hide *n* piel, *f*; pellejo, cuero, *m*

hide *vt* esconder, ocultar; (cover) cubrir, tapar; (dissemble) disimular; (meaning) obscurecer. *vi* esconderse; ocultarse, *Mexico* atejanarse; refugiarse. **to h. from each other,** esconderse el uno del otro. **h.-and-seek,** escondite, descanse, dormirlas, *m*

hidebound *a fig* muy conservador, reaccionario, de ideas muy tradicionales

hideous *a* horrible, repulsivo, horroroso; repugnante, odioso

hideously *adv* horriblemente. **to be h. ugly,** (of people) ser más feo que Picio

hideousness *n* fealdad, horribilidad, *f*; repugnancia, *f*

hiding *n* ocultación, *f*; encubrimiento, *m*; refugio, *m*; *inf* paliza, tunda, *f*. **h.-place,** escondite, escondrijo, *m*

hie *vi* apresurarse, ir a prisa

hierarch *n* jerarca, *m*

hierarchical *a* jerárquico

hierarchy *n* jerarquía, *f*

hieroglyph *n* jeroglífico, *m*

higgledy-piggledy *adv* revueltamente, en confusión; en montón, en desorden

high *a* alto; elevado; (with altar, Mass, street, festival) mayor; grande; eminente; aristocrático; (of shooting) fijante; (of quality) superior; excelente; (haughty) orgulloso; (solemn) solemne; (good) bueno; noble; supremo; sumo; (of price) subido; *mus* agudo; (of the sea) tempestuoso, borrascoso; (of wind and explosives) violento, fuerte; (of polish) brillante; (with speed) grande; (with tension, frequency) alto; (with number, etc.) importante, grande; (with colors) subido; (of food) pasado; (angry) enojado, airado; (of cheek bones) saliente, prominente; (well-seasoned) picante; (flattering) lisonjero. *adv* alto; hacia arriba; arriba; (deeply) profundamente; fuertemente; con violencia; (of price) a un precio elevado; (luxuriously) lujosamente; *mus* agudo. **a room 12 ft. h.,** un cuarto de doce pies de altura. **I knew her when she was so h.,** La conocí tamaña. **It is h. time he came,** Ya es hora de que viniese. **on h.,** en alto, arriba; en los cielos. **h. altar,** altar mayor, *m*. **h. and dry,** en la playa, varado; *fig* en seco. **h. and low,** de arriba abajo; por todas partes. **h.-born,** aristocrático, de alta alcurnia. **h.-bred,** (of people) de buena familia; (of animals) de buena raza. **h.-class,** de buena clase; de alta calidad. **h. collar,** alzacuello, *m*. **h. colored,** de colores vivos; *fig* exagerado. **h. command,** (*mil, nav*) alto mando, *m*. **h. court,** tribunal supremo, *m*. **h. day,** día festivo, *m*. **h. explosive,** explosivo violento, *m*. **h.-flown,** hinchado, retumbante, altisonante. **h. frequency,** alta frecuencia, *f*. **h.-handed,** arbitrario, dominador, despótico. **h.-heeled,** *a* de tacón alto. **h. jump,** salto de altura, *m*. **h. land,** tierras altas, *f pl*; eminencia, *f*. **h. life** *Lat. Am.* jáilaif *m*. **h. light,** *art* realce, *m*; acontecimiento de más interés, *m*; momento culminante, *m*. **h. mass,** misa mayor, *f*. **h.-minded,** de nobles pensamientos; arrogante. **h.-necked,** con cuello alto. **h.-pitched,** de tono alto, agudo. **h.-powered,** de alta potencia. **h.-powered car,** coche de muchos caballos, *m*. **h. precision,** suma precisión, *f*. **h. pressure,** *n* alta presión, *f*; *fig* urgencia, *f*; *n* de alta presión; *fig* urgente. **h.-priced,** caro. **h. priest,** sumo pontífice, sumo sacerdote, alto sacerdote, *m*. **h. relief,** alto relieve, *m*. **h. road,** carretera mayor, *f*. **h. school,** instituto de segunda enseñanza, instituto, colegio, liceo, *m*; colegio, liceo, instituto, *m*, escuela secundaria, secundaria, *f*. **h. sea,** marejada, *f*. **h. seas,** alta mar, *f*. **h.-seasoned,** picante. **h. society,** alta sociedad, *f*. **h.-sounding,** altisonante, bombástico. **h.-speed,** de alta velocidad. **h.-spirited,** brioso; alegre. **h.-strung,** nervioso, excitable, sensitivo. **h. tension,** alta tensión, *f*. **h. tide,** marea alta, *f*. **h.-toned,** *mus* agudo; *inf* de alto copete; aristocrático. **h. treason,** alta traición, *f*. **h. water,** marea alta, pleamar, *f*. **h.-water mark,** límite de la marea, *m*; *fig* colmo, *m*; apogeo, *m*

High Andes, the el Altiplano *m*

highball *m Spain* qüisquisoda *f*, *Lat. Am.* jáibol *m*

highbrow *a* and *n* intelectual, *mf*

high-ceilinged *a* alto de techo

higher *a comp* of **high,** más alto; más elevado; superior. **on a h. plane,** en un nivel más alto. **h. education,** enseñanza superior, *f*. **h. mathematics,** la alta matemática, *f*. **h. criticism,** la alta crítica. **h. up,** más arriba. **h. up the river,** río arriba

highest *a superl* of **high,** el más alto; la más alta; los más altos; las más altas; sumo, supremo; excelente. **h. common factor,** *math* máximo común divisor, *m*. **h. references,** (of cook, gardener, etc.) informes inmejorables, *m pl*; *com* referencias excelentes, *f pl*

highland *n* altiplanicie, *f*; montañas, *f pl*, distrito montañoso, *m*. *a* montañoso

highlight *vtr* dar relieve a, destacar

highly *adv* altamente; mucho; muy; extremadamente; grandemente; bien; favorablemente; con lisonja, lisonjeramente. **h. seasoned,** picante. **h. strung,** nervioso, excitable

highness *n* altura, *f*; elevación, *f*; excelencia, *f*; nobleza, *f*; (title) Alteza, *f*. **His Royal H., Her Royal Highness,** Su Alteza Real

high-ranking *a* de alta jerarquía, de alto rango

highway *n* camino real, *m*, carretera, *f*. **h. code,** código de la vía pública (or de la circulación), *m*. **h. robbery,** salteamiento de caminos, atraco, *m*

highwayman *n* salteador de caminos, *m*

highways and byways caminos y veredas

hike *vi* ir de excursión. *n* marcha con equipo, *f*

hiker *n* excursionista, *mf*

hiking *n* excursionismo, *m*; marcha con equipo, *f*

hilarious *a* alegre

hilarity *n* hilaridad, *f*

hill *n* colina, *f*, cerro, otero, *m*; monte, *m*, montaña, *f*; (pile) montón, *m*. **h.-side,** falda de montaña, ladera de una colina, *f*. **h.-top,** cumbre de una colina, *f*

hilliness *n* montuosidad, *f*, lo montañoso

hillman *n* montañés, *m*

hillock *n* altozano, montículo, collado, *m*

hilly *a* montañoso

hilt *n* puño, *m*, empuñadura, *f*

him *pers pron 3rd sing direct object* le, lo; (with prep.) él; *indirect object* le, a él; (with a direct obj. in 3rd person) se. **I gave him the magazine,** Le di la revista. **I gave it to him,** Se lo di a él. **This is for him,** Esto es para él

Himalayas, the los Himalayas, *m pl*

Himalayan *a* himalayo

himself *pron* sí, sí mismo; él mismo; (reflexive) se. **He did it by h.,** Lo hizo por sí mismo. For more examples see **herself**

hind *n* corza, cierva, *f*. *a* trasero, posterior. **h.-quarters,** cuarto trasero, *m*; (of a horse) ancas, *f pl*

hinder *a* trasero, posterior

hinder *vt* impedir, estorbar; embarazar, dificultar; interrumpir. *vi* ser un obstáculo; formar un obstáculo

hinderer *n* estorbador (-ra); interruptor (-ra)

hindmost *a* posterior, postrero, último

hindrance *n* obstáculo, estorbo, impedimento, *m*; perjuicio, *m*; interrupción, *f*

Hindu *a* hindú, *mf*

Hinduism *n* indoísmo, *m*

Hindustani *a* indostanés. *n* (language) indostani, *m*

hinge *n* gozne, pernio, *m*, bisagra, *f*; articulación, *f*; *fig* eje, *m*. *vi* moverse (or abrirse) sobre goznes; *fig* depender (de). *vt* engoznar

hinged *a* con goznes

hint *n* indirecta, insinuación, sugestión, *f*; (advice) consejo, *m*. *vt* dar a entender, decir con medias palabras, insinuar, sugerir. *vi* insinuar. **to take the h.,** darse por aludido

hinterland *n* interior (de un país), *m*

hip *n anat* cadera, *f*; *bot* fruto del rosal silvestre, *m*. **h.-bath,** baño de asiento, *m*. **h.-bone,** hueso ilíaco, *m*. **h.-joint,** articulación de la cadera, *f*. **h.-pocket,** faltriquera, *f*

hipped *a* de caderas

hippodrome *n* hipódromo, *m*

hippopotamus *n* hipopótamo, *m*

hire *n* alquiler, arriendo, *m*; salario, *m*. *vt* alquilar, arrendar; tomar en arriendo; (person) contratar; tomar a su servicio. **to h. out,** alquilar. **for** or **on h.,** de alquiler. **h.-purchase,** compra a plazos, *f*

hireling *n* mercenario, *m*

hirer *n* alquilador (-ra), arrendador (-ra)

hirsute *a* hirsuto. **non-h.** *bot* lampiño

his *poss pron 3rd sing* (el) suyo, *m*; (la) suya, *f*; (los) suyos, *m pl*; (las) suyas, *f pl*; de él. *poss a* su, *mf*; sus, *mf pl*; de él. **his handkerchiefs,** sus pañuelos. **his mother,** su madre, la madre de él. **a sister of his,** una de sus hermanas, una hermana suya. See **hers** for more examples.

Hispanism *n* hispanismo, *m*

Hispanist *n* hispanista, *mf*

hispanize *vt* españolizar

Hispano-American *a* hispano-americano

hiss *n* silbido, *m*; (sputter) chisporroteo, *m*. *vi* silbar

hissing *n* silbido, *m*; chisporroteo, *m*. *a* silbante

hist *interj* ¡chist!

histologist *n* histólogo, *m*

histology *n* histología, *f*

historian *n* historiador (-ra)

historic *a* histórico

historical *a* histórico. **h. truth,** verdad histórica, *f*

historically *adv* históricamente

historiographer *n* historiógrafo, *m*

historiography *n* historiografía, *f*

history *n* historia, *f*. **Biblical h.,** historia sagrada, *f*. **natural h.,** historia natural, *f*

histrionic *a* histriónico

hit *n* golpe, *m*; *aer* impacto, *m*; (success) éxito, *m*; (piece of luck) buena suerte, *f*; (satire) sátira, *f*. *vt* golpear; (buffet) abofetear, pegar; (find) dar con, tropezar con; (attain) acertar; (guess) adivinar; (attract) atraer; (deal) lanzar, dar; (wound) herir, hacer daño (a). **The sun hits me right in the eyes,** El sol me da en la cabeza. **direct hit,** *aer* impacto de lleno, *m*. **lucky hit,** acierto, *m*. **to hit a straight left,** (boxing) lanzar un directo con la izquierda. **to hit the mark,** dar en el blanco; *fig* dar en el clavo. **hit or miss,** acierto o error. **to hit against,** dar contra, estrellar contra. **to hit back,** defenderse; devolver golpe por golpe. **to hit off,** imitar; (a likeness) coger. **to hit out,** abofetear; *fig* atacar; golpear (la pelota) fuera. **to hit upon,** dar con; tropezar con; encontrar por casualidad; (remember) acordarse de

hitch *n* (jerk) sacudida, *f*; nudo fácil de soltar, *m*; *fig* obstáculo, *m*; *fig* dificultad, *f*; (lift, ride) *Mexico* aventón *m* **give s.b. a hitch,** levantar a fulano. *vt* sacudir; (a chair, etc.) arrastrar, empujar; amarrar, enganchar; atar. *vi* (along a seat, etc.) correrse (en); (get entangled) enredarse, cogerse; (rub) rascarse. **without a h.,** sin dificultad alguna, viento en popa; (smoothly) a pedir de boca. **to h. up,** sacudir, dar una sacudida (a)

hitchhike *vi* ir a dedo (Argentina), pedir aventón (Mexico), pedir botella (Cuba), hacer autostop, ir por autostop (Spain)

hither *adv* acá, hacia acá; *a* citerior, más cercano. **h. and thither,** acá y aculla allá

hitherto *adv* hasta ahora, hasta el presente

Hitlerian *a* hitleriano, nacista

Hitlerism *n* hitlerismo, nacismo, *m*

hive *n* (for bees) colmena, *f*; (swarm) enjambre, *m*; *fig* centro, *m*. *vt* (bees) enjambrar. **h. of industry,** centro de industria

hoard *n* acumulación, *f*; provisión, *f*; tesoro, *m*. *vt* acumular, amasar, amontonar; guardar

hoarder *n* acaparador (-ra)

hoarding *n* amontonamiento, *m*; acaparamiento, *m*; (fence) empalizada, cerca, *f*; palizada de tablas, *f*

hoarfrost *n* escarcha, helada blanca, *f*

hoariness *n* (of the hair) canicie, *f*; blancura, *f*; (antiquity) vejez, vetustez, *f*

hoarse *a* ronco; discordante. **to be h.,** tener la voz ronca. **to grow h.,** enronquecerse

hoarsely *adv* roncamente

hoarseness *n* ronquera, *f*; *inf* carraspera, *f*

hoary *a* (of the hair) canoso; blanco; (old) vetusto, antiguo, viejo

hoax *n* estafa, *f*, engaño, *m*; broma pesada, *f*; burla, *f*. *vt* estafar, engañar; burlar

hoaxer *n* burlador (-ra); estafador (-ra)

hob *n* repisa interior del hogar, *f*

hobble *n* (gait) cojera, *f*; traba, maniota, *f*. *vi* cojear. *vt* manear. **h. skirt,** falda muy estrecha, *f*

hobby *n* pasatiempo, *m*, recreación, *f*; manía, afición, *f*. **h.-horse,** caballo de cartón, *m*; *fig* caballo de batalla, *m*

hobgoblin *n* trasgo, duende, *m*

hobnail *n* clavo de herradura, clavo de botas, *m*

hobnailed *a* (of boots) con clavos

hobnob *vi* codearse, tratar con familiaridad

hock *n anat* pernil, *m*; (wine) vino del Rin, *m*

hockey *n* chueca, *m*. **h. ball,** bola, pelota de chueca, *f*. **h. stick,** bastón de chueca, *m*

hocus-pocus *n* juego de pasa pasa, *m*; engaño, *m*, treta, *f*

hod *n* cuezo, *m*

hodgepodge See **hotchpotch**

hoe *n* azadón, *m*, *Chile, Peru* lampa *f*. *vt* azadonar; sachar

hoeing *n* cavadura con azadón, *f*; sachadura, *f*

hog *n* cerdo, puerco, *Peru* cuchí *m*. **to go the whole hog,** ir al extremo. **hogskin,** piel de cerdo, *f*

hoggish *a* porcuno; (greedy) comilón, tragón; (selfish) egoísta

hoist *n* levantamiento, *m*; (lift) montacargas, *m*; (winch) cabria, *f*; (crane) grúa, *f*. *vt* levantar, alzar; (flags) enarbolar; suspender; *naut* izar

hoity-toity *a* picajoso, quisquilloso; presuntuoso

hold *n* asimiento, agarro, *m*, presa, *f*; asidero, *m*; *fig* autoridad, *f*, poder, *m*; *fig* comprensión, *f*; (of a ship) cala, bodega, *f*. **to loose one's h.,** aflojar su presa. **to lose one's h.,** perder su presa. **to seize h. of,** asirse de, echar mano de. **h.-all,** funda, *f*. **h.-up,** (robbery) atraco, robo a mano armada, *m*; (in traffic) atasco (or obstáculo) en el tráfico, *m*; (in work) parada, cesación (de trabajo), *f*

hold *vt* tener; asir, agarrar, coger; retener; (embrace) abrazar; (a post) ocupar; (a meeting, etc.) celebrar; (bear weight of) aguantar, soportar; (own) poseer; *mil* ocupar, defender; (contain) contener; (have in store) reservar; tener capacidad para; (retain) retener; (believe) creer, sostener; (consider) opinar, tener para (mí, etc.); juzgar; (restrain) detener; contener; (of attention, etc.) mantener; (maneuvers) hacer; (observe) guardar. *vi* resistir, aguantar; (be valid) ser válido; regir; (apply) aplicarse; (last) continuar, seguir. *interj* ¡tente! ¡para! **The room won't h. more,** En este cuarto no caben más. **They h. him in great respect,** Le tienen mucho respeto. **The theory does not h. water,** La teoría es falsa, La teoría no es lógica. **to h. one's own,** defenderse, mantenerse en sus trece. **to h. one's breath,** contener la respiración. **to h. one's tongue,** callarse. **to h. sway,** mandar; reinar. **to h. tightly,** agarrar fuertemente; (clasp) estrechar. **H. the line!** (telephone) ¡Aguarde un momento! **to h. back,** *vt* tener; contener; retener; esconder; abstenerse de entregar. *vi* quedarse atrás; vacilar, dudar; tardar en. **to h. by,** seguir; basarse en, apoyarse en. **to h. down,** sujetar; (oppress) oprimir. **to h. fast,** *vt* sujetar fuertemente. *vi* mantenerse firme; *fig* estar agarrado (a). **to h. forth,** *vt* ofrecer; expresar. *vi* hacer un discurso, perorar. **to h. in,** *vt* contener; retener. *vi* contenerse. **to h. off,** *vt* apartar, alejar. *vi* apartarse, alejarse, mantenerse alejado. **to h. on,** seguir, persistir en; aguantar. **to h. out,** *vt* alargar, extender; ofrecer. *vi* aguantar; durar, resistir. **to h. over,** tener suspendido sobre; (postpone) aplazar; *fig* amenazar con. **to h. to,** agarrarse a; atenerse a. **to h. together,** *vt* unir; juntar. *vi* mantenerse juntos. **to h. up,** *vt* (display) mostrar, enseñar; levantar; sostener, soportar; (rob) atracar, saltear; (delay) atrasar; (stop) interrumpir, parar. *vi* mantenerse en pie; (of weather) seguir bueno. **The train has been held up by fog,** El tren viene con retraso a causa de la niebla

holder *n* tenedor *m*, (*f*, la) que tiene; poseedor (-ra); *com* tenedor (-ra); inquilino (-na); propietario (-ia); (support) soporte, *m*; mango, *m*; asa, *f*; (in compounds) porta . . .

holding *n* tención, *f*; posesión, *f*; propiedad, *f*; (leasing) arrendamiento, *m*; (celebration) solemnización, *f*; (of a meeting) el celebrar, el tener; *pl* **holdings,** *com* valores habidos, *m pl*

holding company *n* compañía de cartera, *f*

hole *n* hoyo, *m*, *Lat. Am. also* foramen *m*; boquete, *m*; agujero, *m*; cavidad, *f*; (hollow) depresión, *f*, hueco, *m*; orificio, *m*; (tear) roto, desgarro, *m*; (eyelet) punto, *m*; (in cheese) ojo, *m*; (in stocking) rotura, *f*, punto, *m*; (lair) madriguera, *f*; (nest) nido, *m*; (golf) hoyo, *m*; (fix)

aprieto, *m*. *vt* aguijerear; excavar; (bore) taladrar; *sport* meter la pelota (en). **to h. out,** (golf) meter la pelota en el hoyo. **h.-and-corner,** *a inf* bajo mano, secreto

hole-puncher *n* agujereadora, *f*

holiday *n* día feriado, *m*; día de fiesta, día festivo, *m*; vacación, *f*. *a* festivo, alegre; de vacación; de vacaciones; de excursión; (summer) veraniego. **day's h.,** día de asueto, *m*. **to take a h.,** tomar una vacación; hacer fiesta. **h. camp,** colonia veraniega, *f*. **h.-maker,** excursionista, turista, *mf*; (in the summer) veraneante, *mf* **holidays with pay,** vacaciones retribuidas, *f pl*

holiness *n* santidad, *f*

Holland Holanda, *f*

holland *n* lienzo crudo. *a* holandés. **H. gin,** ginebra holandesa, *f*

hollow *a* hueco; cóncavo; (empty) vacío; (of eyes, etc.) hundido; (of sound) sordo; (of a cough) cavernoso; (echoing) retumbante; (*fig* unreal) vacío, falso; insincero. *adv* vacío; *inf* completamente. *n* hueco, *m*; concavidad, *f*; (hole) hoyo, *m*; cavidad, *f*; (valley) hondonada, *f*, barranco, *m*; (groove) ranura, *f*; (depression) depresión, *f*; (in the back) curvadura, *f*. *vt* excavar, ahuecar; vaciar. **h.-cheeked,** con las mejillas hundidas. **h.-eyed,** con los ojos hundidos, de ojos hundidos

hollowness *n* concavidad, *f*; (falseness) falsedad, *f*; insinceridad, *f*

holly *n* acebo, agrifolio, *m*

holocaust *n* holocausto, *m*

holograph *n* hológrafo, *m*

holster *n* pistolera, *f*

holy *a* santo; sagrado; (blessed) bendito. **most h.,** *a* santísimo. **to make h.,** santificar. **H. Father,** Padre Santo, el Papa, *m*. **H. Ghost,** Espíritu Santo, *m*. **H. Office,** Santo Oficio, *m*, Inquisición, *f*. **H. Orders,** órdenes sagradas, *f pl*. **h. places,** santos lugares, *m pl*. **H. Scripture,** Sagrada Escritura, *f*. **H. See,** Cátedra de San Pedro, *f*. **h. water,** agua bendita, *f*. **H. Souls,** las Ánimas Benditas. **h. water stoup,** acetre, *m*. **H. Week,** Semana Santa, *f*

Holy Land, la Tierra Santa, *f*

homage *n* homenaje, *m*; culto, *m*; reverencia, *f*. **to pay h.,** rendir homenaje

home *n* casa, *f*; hogar, *m*; domicilio, *m*, residencia, *f*; (institution) asilo, *m*; (haven) refugio, *m*; (habitation) morada, *f*; (country of origin) país de origen, *m*; (native land) patria, *f*; (environment) ambiente natural, *m*; *sport* meta, *f*. *a* casero, doméstico; nativo; nacional, del país; indígena. *adv* a casa, hacia casa; (in one's country) en su patria; (returned) de vuelta; (of the feelings) al corazón, al alma; (to the limit) al límite. **at h.,** en casa; *fig* en su elemento; (of games) en campo propio; de recibo. **at-h. day,** día de recibo, *m*. **He shot the bolt h.,** Echó el cerrojo. **one's long h.,** su última morada. **to be at h.,** estar en casa; estar de recibo. **to be away from h.,** estar fuera de casa; estar ausente. **to bring h.,** traer (or llevar) a casa; hacer ver; convencer; llegar al alma; (a crime) probar (contra). **to go h.,** volver a casa; volver a la patria; (be effective) hacer su efecto; (move) herir en lo más vivo. **to make oneself at h.,** ponerse a sus anchas, sentirse como en casa. **Please make yourself at home!** ¡Ha tomado posesión de su casa! **to strike h.,** dar en el blanco; herir; (hit) golpear; herir en lo más vivo; hacerse sentir. **h. affairs,** asuntos domésticos, *m pl*, (Ministry of) Gobernación, *f*. **h.-bred,** criado en el país. **h.-brewed,** fermentado en el país; fermentado en casa. **h.-coming,** regreso al hogar, *m*. **h. counties,** condados alrededor de Londres, *m pl*. **H. Defense,** defensa nacional, *f*. **h. farm,** residencia del propietario de una finca, *f*. **h. for the aged,** asilo de ancianos, *m*. **h. front,** frente doméstico, *m*. **H. Guard,** milicia nacional, *f*. **h. life,** vida de familia, *f*. **h.-made,** casero, de fabricación casera, hecho en casa. **H. Office,** Ministerio de Gobernación, *m*. **H. Rule,** autonomía, *f*. **H. Secretary,** Ministro de Gobernación, *m*. **h. stretch,** último trecho (de una

carrera), *m.* **h. truth,** verdad, *inf* fresca, *f.* **to tell someone a few h. truths,** contarle cuatro verdades
homeless *a* sin casa; sin hogar. **the h.,** los sin techo
homeliness *n* comodidad, *f;* sencillez, *f;* (ugliness) fealdad, *f*
homely *a* doméstico; familiar; (unpretentious) sencillo; llano; (ugly) feo; desabrido
homeopath *n* homeópata, *mf*
homeopathic *a* homeópata
homeopathy *n* homeopatía, *f*
Homeric *a* homérico
homesick *a* nostálgico. **to be h.,** tener morriña
homesickness *n* nostalgia, añoranza, morriña, *f*
homespun *a* tejido en casa; hecho en casa; basto, grueso
homestead *n* hacienda, *f;* casa solariega, *f;* casa, *f*
homeward *adv* hacia casa, en dirección al hogar; de vuelta; hacia la patria. **h.-bound,** en dirección a casa; (of ships) con rumbo al puerto de origen; (of other traffic) de vuelta
homicidal *a* homicida
homicide *n* (act) homicidio, *m;* (person) homicida, *mf*
homily *n ecc* homilía, *f;* sermón, *m*
homing pigeon *n* palomo (-ma) mensajero (-ra)
homogeneity *n* homogeneidad, *f*
homogeneous *a* homogéneo
homologous *a* homólogo
homonym *n* homónimo, *m*
homonymous *a* homónimo
homosexual *a* and *n* homosexual, *mf*
Honduran *a* and *n* hondureño (-ña)
hone *n* piedra de afilar, *f.* *vt* afilar, vaciar
honest *a* honrado; decente, honesto; (chaste) casto; (loyal) sincero, leal; (frank) franco; imparcial. **an h. man,** un hombre de buena fe, un hombre honrado, un hombre decente
honesty *n* honradez, *f;* honestidad, *f;* (chastity) castidad, *f;* sinceridad, *f;* rectitud, imparcialidad, *f*
honey *n* miel, *f.* **h.-bee,** abeja obrera, *f.* **h.-colored,** melado. **h.-pot,** jarro de miel, *m.* **h.-tongued,** melifluo; de pico de oro
honeycomb *n* panal, *m*
honeycombed *a* apanalado
honeydew *n* mielada, *f; fig* ambrosia, *f*
honeyed *a* de miel; *fig* meloso, adulador
honeymoon *n* luna de miel, *f;* viaje de novios, viaje nupcial, *m.* *vi* hacer un viaje nupcial
honeysuckle *n* madreselva, *f*
honor *n* honor, *m;* honra, *f;* honradez, rectitud, integridad, *f; pl* **honors,** honores, *m pl;* condecoraciones, *f pl;* (last h.) honras, pompas fúnebres, *f pl.* *vt* honrar; (God) glorificar; (decorate) condecorar, laurear; (respect) respetar; reverenciar; *com* aceptar; (a toast) beber. **On my h.,** A fe mía. **point of h.,** punto de honor, pundonor, *m.* **word of h.,** palabra de honor, *f.* **Your H.,** (to a judge) Excelentísimo Señor Juez
honorable *a* honorable; glorioso; digno; ilustre; (sensitive of honor) pundonoroso
honorable mention *n* accésit, *m*
honorableness *n* honradez, *f*
honorably *adv* honorablemente; dignamente
honorarium *n* honorario, *m*
honorary *a* honorario, honorífico. **h. member,** socio (-ia) honorario (-ia). **h. mention,** mención honorífica, *f*
hood *n* capucha, caperuza, *f;* (folding, of vehicles) capota, cubierta, cubierta del motor *f;* (of a carriage) caparazón, fuelle, *m;* (of a car) capó, *m,* (university) muceta, *f;* (of a fireplace) campana (de hogar), *f;* (cowl of chimney) sombrerete (de chimenea), *m.* *vt* cubrir con capucha; cubrir; (the eyes) ocultar, cubrir, velar
hooded *a* con capucha
hoodwink *vt* vendar (los ojos); *fig* engañar, embaucar, burlar
hoof *n* casco, *m;* (cloven) pezuña, *f*
hoofed *a* ungulado

hoof it ir a golpe de calcetín
hook *n* gancho, garfio, *m;* (boat-) bichero, *m;* (fish-) anzuelo, *m;* (on a dress) corchete, *m;* (hanger) colgadero, *m;* (claw) garra, *f.* *vt* enganchar; (a dress) abrochar; (fish) pescar, coger; (nab) atrapar, pescar. **by h. or by crook,** a tuertas o a derechas. **left h.,** (boxing) izquierdo, *m.* **right h.,** (boxing) derecho, *m.* **to catch oneself on a h.,** engancharse. **h. and eye,** los corchetes. **h.-nosed,** con nariz de gancho, con nariz aguileña. **h.-up,** *rad* circuito, *m;* transmisión en circuito, *f*
hooked *a* con ganchos; corvo, ganchoso
hooking *n* enganche, *m;* (of a dress) abrochamiento, *m;* (of fish and *inf*) pesca, *f*
hookworm *n* anquilostoma, *m*
hooligan *n* rufián, *m*
hoop *n* aro, arco, *m;* (of a skirt) miriñaque, *m;* (croquet) argolla, *f;* (toy) aro, *m;* círculo, *m.* *vt* poner aros a; *fig* rodear
hoot *n* (of owls) ululación, *f,* grito, *m;* (whistle) silbido, *m;* ruido, clamor, *m.* *vi* (of owls) ulular, gritar; silbar; *aut* avisar con la bocina. **to h. off the stage,** hacer abandonar la escena. **to h. down,** silbar
hooting *n* See **hoot**
hop *n* salto, brinco, *m; bot* lúpulo, *m; bot* flores de oblón, *f pl;* (dance) baile, *m.* *vi* saltar con un pie; andar dando brincos; saltar; (limp) cojear; recoger lúpulo; (of plant) dar lúpulo. *vt* saltar. **hop-garden,** huerto de lúpulo, *m.* **hop-kiln,** horno para secar lúpulo, *m.* **hop-picker,** recolector (-ra) de lúpulo. **hop-picking,** recolección de lúpulos, *f*
hope *n* esperanza, *f;* (faith) confianza, *f;* (expectation) anticipación, expectación, *f;* (probability) probabilidad, *f;* (illusion) ilusión, *f;* sueño, *m.* *vi* esperar. **to live in h. that,** vivir con la esperanza de que. **to lose h.,** desesperarse. **to h. against h.,** esperar sin motivo, esperar lo imposible. **to h. for,** desear. **to h. in,** confiar en
hopeful *a* lleno de esperanzas, confiado; optimista; *(fig)* risueño. *o inf* la esperanza de la casa. **to look h.,** *(fig)* prometer bien
hopefully *adv* con esperanza
hopefulness *n* optimismo, *m; fig* aspecto prometedor, *m*
hopeless *a* desesperado, sin esperanza; irremediable; (of situations) imposible; (of disease) incurable. **to be h.,** (lose hope) desesperarse; (have no remedy) ser irremediable; (of disease) no tener cura. **to make h.,** hacer perder la esperanza, desesperar; dejar sin remedio; (a situation) hacer imposible; (an illness) hacer imposible de curar
hopelessly *adv* sin esperanza; sin remedio; imposiblemente; incurablemente
hopelessness *n* desesperación, *f;* (of an illness) imposibilidad de curar, *f;* lo irremediable; imposibilidad, *f*
hopping mad *Lat. Am.* hecho un ají
hopscotch *n* infernáculo, *m,* rayuela, *f*
horal, horary *a* horario
horde *n* horda, *f*
horizon *n* horizonte, *m*
horizontal *a* horizontal. **h. suspension,** (gymnastics) plancha, *f*
horizontality *n* horizontalidad, *f*
horizontally *adv* horizontalmente
horn *n* (of bull, etc.) cuerno, *m;* (antler) asta, *f;* (of an insect) antena, *f;* (of a snail) tentáculo, *m; mus* cuerno, *m;* trompa, *f;* (of motor and phonograph) bocina, *f, Mexico* kláxon *m;* (of moon) cuerno (de la luna), *m.* **article made of h.,** objeto de cuerno, *m.* **on the horns of a dilemma,** entre la espada y la pared. **h. of plenty,** cuerno de abundancia, *m;* cornucopia, *f.* **h.-rimmed spectacles,** anteojos de concha, *m pl.* **h. thrust,** cornada, *f*
horned *a* cornudo; (antlered) enastado
hornet *n* avispón, abejón, *m*
horny *a* córneo; calloso; duro. **h.-handed,** con manos callosas

horoscope *n* horóscopo, *m*
horrible *a* horrible, repugnante, espantoso; (of price) enorme; *inf* horrible
horribleness *n* horribilidad, *f*, horror, *m*, lo espantoso
horribly *adv* horriblemente
horrid *a* horroroso; desagradable
horridness *n* horror, *m*; lo desagradable
horrific *a* horrífico, horrendo
horrify *vt* horrorizar; escandalizar
horrifying *a* horroroso, horripilante
horror *n* horror, *m*. **h.-stricken,** horrorizado
hors d'œuvres *n pl* entremeses, *m pl*
horse *n* caballo, *m*, *Lat. Am.* cuaco *m*; (cavalry) caballería, *f*; (frame) caballete, *m*; (gymnastics and as punishment) potro, *m*. *a* caballar, caballuno. *vt* montar a caballo. **pack of horses,** caballada, *f*. **to ride a h.,** cabalgar, montar a caballo. **H. Artillery,** artillería montada, *f*. **h. blanket,** manta para caballos, *f*; sudadero *m*, *Lat. Am.* mandil *m*. **h.-block,** montador, *m*. **h.-box,** vagón para caballos, *m*. **h.-breaker,** domador de caballos, *m*. **h.-cab,** simón, *f*. **h.-chestnut,** castaña pilonga, *f*. **h.-chestnut flower,** candela, *f*. **h.-collar,** collera, *f*; collerón *m*. **h.-dealer,** chalán, *m*. **h.-doctor,** veterinario, *m*. **h.-flesh,** carne de caballo, *f*. **h.-fly,** tábano, *m*. **H. Guards,** guardias montadas, *f pl*. **h.-latitudes,** calmas de Cáncer, *f pl*. **h.-laugh,** carcajada, *f*. **h.-master,** maestro de equitación, *m*. **h. meat,** carne de caballo, *f*. **h. pistol,** pistola de arzón, *f*. **h.-play,** payasada, *f*. **h.-power,** caballo de vapor, *m*; potencia, *f*. **a twelve-h.p. car,** un coche de doce caballos. **h.-race,** carrera de caballos, *f*. **h.-radish,** rábano picante, raíz amarga, *m*. **h.-sense,** sentido común, *m*, gramática parda, *f*. **h. show,** exposición de caballos, feria equina *f*; concurso de caballos, *m*. **h.-trainer,** entrenador de caballos, *m*. **h. tram,** tranvía de sangre, *m*. **h. trappings,** monturas, *f pl*. **That's a horse of a different color** Es harina de otro costal, *Argentina, Peru* Esas son otras cuarenta
horseback *n* lomo de caballo, *m*. **on h.,** a caballo. **to ride on h.,** ir a caballo
horseman *n* jinete, cabalgador, *m*
horsemanship *n* equitación, *f*, manejo del caballo, *m*
horseshoe *n* herradura, *f*. **h. arch,** arco de herradura, arco morisco, *m*
horsewoman *n* amazona, *f*
horticultural *a* horticultural. **h. show,** exposición de flores, *f*
horticulturalist *n* horticultor (-ra)
horticulture *n* horticultura, *f*
hosanna *n* hosanna, *m*
hose *n* (tube) manga, *f*; (breeches) calzón, *m*; (stockings) medias, *f pl*; (socks) calcetines, *m pl*. **h. man,** manguero, *m*. **h.-pipe,** manga de riego, manguera, *f*
hosier *n* calcetero (-ra)
hosiery *n* calcetería, *f*. **h. trade,** calcetería *f*
hospice *n* hospicio, *m*; asilo, refugio, *m*
hospitable *a* hospitalario
hospitableness *n* hospitalidad, *f*
hospital *n* hospital, *m*; (school) colegio, *m*. **h. nurse,** enfermera, *f*. **h. ship,** buque hospital, *m*
hospital bed cama hospitalaria, *f*
hospitality *n* hospitalidad, *f*
host *n* huésped, convidador, (of radio or tv program) presentador, *m*; (at an inn) patrón, mesonero, *m*; (army) ejército, *m*; (crowd) multitud, muchedumbre, *f*; *ecc* hostia, *f*; *pl* **hosts,** huestes, *f pl*. **h.-plant,** planta huésped, *f*
hostage *n* rehén, *m*; *fig* prenda, *f*
host country *n* (of an organization) país-sede, *m*
hostel *n* hostería, *f*; club, *m*; residencia de estudiantes, *f*
hostelry *n* hospedería, *f*; parador, mesón, *m*
hostess *n* ama de la casa, *f*; la que recibe a los invitados; la que convida; (of an inn) patrona, mesonera, *f*
hostile *a* enemigo; hostil, contrario (a); (of circumstances, etc.) desfavorable
hostility *n* enemistad, *f*, antagonismo, *m*, mala volun-

tad, *f*; hostilidad, guerra, *f*. **suspension of hostilities,** suspensión de hostilidades, *f*
hot *a* caliente; (of a day, etc.) caluroso; (piquant) picante; ardiente; vehemente, impetuoso; violento; impaciente; colérico; entusiasta; lleno de deseo; *art* intenso; (great) grande, mucho; (vigorous) enérgico. **You are getting very hot now,** *inf* (in a game, etc.) Te estás quemando. **It is hot,** Está caliente; (of weather) Hace calor. **to grow hot,** calentarse; *fig* acalorarse; (of weather) empezar a hacer calor. **to make hot,** calentar; dar calor (a); *inf* dar vergüenza. **hot-blooded,** de sangre caliente; apasionado; colérico. **hot-foot,** aprisa, apresuradamente. **hot-headed,** impetuoso. **hot-plate,** *elec* calientaplatos, *m*. **hot springs,** termas, *f pl*. **hot-tempered,** colérico, irascible. **hot water,** agua caliente, *f*. **hot-water bottle,** bolsa de goma, *f*. **hot-water pipes,** las cañerías del agua caliente
hotbed *n* semillero, vivero, *m*; *fig* semillero, foco, *m*
hotchpotch *n* potaje, *m*; *fig* mezcolanza, *f*, fárrago, *m*
hotel *n* hotel, *m*. **h.-keeper,** hotelero (-ra)
hothead *n* exaltado (-da), fanático (-ca)
hothouse *n* invernáculo, *m*, estufa, *f*. **h. plant,** *fig* planta de estufa, *f*
hotly *adv* calurosamente; con vehemencia; coléricamente
hough *n* *zool* pernil, *m*; (in man) corva, *f*
hound *n* perro de caza, sabueso de artois, *m*; perro, *m*; *inf* canalla, *m*. *vt* cazar con perros; *fig* perseguir; *fig* incitar. **master of hounds,** montero, *m*. **pack of hounds,** jauría, *f*
hour *n* hora, *f*; momento, *m*; ocasión, oportunidad, *f pl*. **hours,** horas, *f pl*. **after hours,** fuera de horas. **at the eleventh h.,** en el último minuto. **by the h.,** por horas; horas enteras. **small hours,** altas horas de la noche, *inf* las tantas, *f pl*. **to keep late hours,** acostarse tarde. **to strike the h.,** dar la hora. **h.-glass,** reloj de arena, *m*. **h.-hand,** horario, *m*. **h. of death,** hora suprema, hora de la muerte, *f*
hourly *a* cada hora; por hora; continuo. *adv* a cada hora; de un momento a otro
house *n* casa, *f*; (home) hogar, *m*; (lineage) familia, *f*, abolengo, *m*; (threat.) sala, *f*, teatro, *m*; *com* casa comercial, *f*; (takings) entrada, *f*; (audience) público, *m*; (of Lords, Commons) cámara, *f*; (college) colegio, *m*; (parliament) parlamento, *m*; (building) edificio, *m*. *a* de casa; de la casa; doméstico. *vt* dar vivienda (a); alojar, recibir (or tener) en casa de uno; (store) poner, guardar. **The cottage will not h. them all,** No habrá bastante lugar para todos ellos en la cabaña, No cabrán todos en la cabaña. **country-h.,** finca, *f*; casa de campo, *f*. **full h.,** casa llena, *f*; *theat* lleno, *m*. **to bring down the h.,** *theat* hacer venirse el teatro abajo. **to keep h.,** llevar la casa; ser ama de casa. **to keep open h.,** tener mesa puesta, ser hospitalario. **to set up h.,** poner casa. **h. of cards,** castillo de naipes, *m*. **H. of Commons,** Cámara de los Comunes, *f*. **H. of Lords,** Cámara de los Lores, *f*. **h.-agent,** agente de casas, *m*. **h.-boat,** barco-habitación, *m*, casa flotante, *f*. **h.-dog,** perro de guardia, *m*; perro de casa, *m*. **h.-fly,** mosca doméstica, *f*. **h. furnisher,** mueblista, *mf*. **h. painter,** pintor de brocha gorda, *m*. **h. party,** reunión en una casa de campo, *f*. **h.-physician,** médico (-ca) interno (-na). **h. porter,** portero, *m*. **h. property,** propiedad inmueble, *f*. **h.-room,** capacidad de una casa, *f*. **h. slipper,** zapatilla, *f*, pantuflo, *m*. **h.-surgeon,** cirujano interno, *m*. **h.-to-h.,** de casa en casa. **h.-warming,** reunión para colgar la cremallera, *f*
housebreaker *n* ladrón de casas, *m*
housebreaking *n* robo de una casa, *m*
houseful *n* casa, *f*
house furnishings *n pl* artefactos para el hogar, accesorios caseros, aparatos electrodomésticos, *m pl*
household *n* casa, *f*; familia, *f*; hogar, *m*. *a* de la casa; doméstico; del hogar. **to be a h. word,** andar en lenguas, *m*. **h. accounts,** cuentas de la casa, *f pl*. **h. duties,**

labores de la casa, *f pl.* **h. gods,** penates, *m pl.* **h. goods,** ajuar, mobiliario, *m.* **h. management,** gobierno de la casa, *m*

householder *n* padre de familia, *m;* dueño (-ña) (or inquilino (-na)) de una casa

house of ill repute *n* burdel, *m,* casa de citas, casa de zorras, casa pública, *f;* lupanar, *m*

housekeeper *n* ama de llaves, *f;* mujer de su casa, *f*

housekeeping *n* gobierno de la casa, *m;* economía doméstica, *f. a* doméstico. **to set up h.,** poner casa

housemaid *n* camarera, sirvienta, *f.* **housemaid's knee,** rodilla de fregona, *f*

housemaker *n* ama de casa, *f*

housetops *n* tejado, *m;* (flat roof) azotea, *f.* **to shout from the h.,** pregonar a los cuatro vientos

housewife *n* madre de familia, mujer de su casa, *f;* (sewing-bag) neceser de costura, *m*

housewifely *a* propio de una mujer de su casa; doméstico; (of a woman) hacendosa

housing *n* provisión de vivienda, *f;* (storage) almacenaje, *m;* alojamiento, *m; inf* casa, vivienda, *f.* **h. scheme,** urbanización, *f.* **h. shortage,** crisis de vivienda, *f,* déficit habitacional, *m*

hovel *n* casucha, *f*

hover *vi* revolotear; (of hawks, etc.) cernerse; estar suspendido; rondar; seguir de cerca, estar al lado (de); *fig* vacilar, dudar

hovering *n* revoloteo, *m;* (of birds of prey) calada, *f; fig* vacilación, *f. a* revolante, que revolotea; que se cierne (sobre); (menacing) que amenaza, inminente

how *adv* cómo; (by what means, in what manner) de qué modo; (at what price) a qué precio; qué; cuánto. *n* el cómo. **to know how,** saber. **For how long?** ¿Por cuánto tiempo? **How are you?** ¿Cómo está Vd.? *inf* ¿Qué tal? **How do you do!** ¡Mucho gusto (en conocerlo/conocerla/conocerlos/conocerlas)! **How old are you?** ¿Qué edad tiene Vd.? **How beautiful!** ¡Qué hermoso! **How big!** ¡Cuán grande! **How early?** ¿Cuán temprano?; ¿Cuánto a más tardar? **How far?** ¿A qué distancia? ¿Hasta qué punto? ¿Hasta dónde? **How fast?** ¿A qué velocidad? **How few!** ¡Qué pocos! **How little!** ¡Qué pequeño!; ¡Qué poco! **How long?** ¿Cuánto tiempo? **How many?** ¿Cuántos? *m pl;* ¿Cuántas? *f pl.* **How much is it?** ¿Cuánto vale? **How much cloth do you want?** ¿Cuánta tela quieres? **How often?** ¿Cuán a menudo? ¿Cuántas veces? **How would you like to go for a walk?** ¿Te gustaría pasearte? **How are you going to Lisbon?** ¿En qué vas a Lisboa?

however *adv* como quiera (que) (followed by subjunctive); por más que (followed by subjunctive); por . . . que (followed by subjunctive). *conjunc* (nevertheless) sin embargo, no obstante. **h. good it is,** por bueno que sea. **h. he does it,** como quiera que lo haga. **h. it may be,** sea como sea. **h. much,** por mucho que

howl *n* aullido, *m;* (groan) gemido, *m;* (cry) grito, *m;* (roar) rugido, bramido, *m;* lamento, *m. vi* aullar; gemir; gritar; rugir, bramar. *vt* chillar. **Each time he opened his mouth he was howled down,** Cada vez que abrió la boca se armó una bronca

howler *n* aullador (-ra). *zool* mono (-na) chillón (-ona); (blunder) coladura, plancha, *f.* **h. monkey** *Lat. Am.* araguato *m*

howling *a* aullante; gemidor; (crying) que llora; bramante, rugiente. *n* los aullidos; (groaning) el gemir, los gemidos; (crying) los gritos; (weeping) el lloro; (roaring) los bramidos, el rugir; los lamentos

hub *n* (of a wheel) cubo (de rueda) *m; fig* centro, *m.* **hub cap,** tapa de cubo, *f*

hubbub *n* algarada, barahúnda, *f*

huckster *n* revendedor (-ra). *vi* revender; (haggle) regatear

huddle *n* (heap) montón, *m;* colección, *f;* (group) corrillo, grupo, *m;* (mixture) mezcla, *f. vt* arrebujar, amontonar; acurrucar, arrebujar; (throw on) echarse. *vi* amontonarse; apiñarse; acurrucarse, arrebujarse

hue *n* color, *m;* matiz, tono, *m;* (of opinion) matiz, *m;* (clamor) clamor, *m,* gritería, *f.* **hue and cry,** alarma, *f*

huff *n* acceso de cólera, *m*

huffily *adv* malhumoradamente; petulantemente

huffiness *n* mal humor, *m;* petulancia, *f;* arrogancia, *f*

hug *n* abrazo, *m. vt* abrazar, apretujar; *fig* acariciar; *naut* navegar muy cerca de. **to hug oneself,** *fig* congratularse

huge *a* enorme, inmenso; gigante; vasto

hugely *adv* inmensamente, enormemente

hugeness *n* inmensidad, enormidad, *f;* vastedad, *f*

Huguenot *a* and *n* hugonote (-ta)

hulk *n* barco viejo, *m;* pontón, *m*

hulking *a* pesado, desgarbado

hull *n naut* casco (de un buque), *m;* (shell) cáscara, *f;* (pod) vaina, *f, vt* mondar

hullabaloo *n* alboroto, tumulto, *m;* vocerío, *m*

hullo *interj* See **hallo**

hum *n* zumbido, *m;* ruido confuso, *m. vi* (sing) canturrear; zumbar; (confused sound) zurrir; (hesitate) vacilar. *vt* (a tune) tararear

human *a* humano. **the h. touch,** el don de gentes. **h. being,** ser humano, hombre, *m*

humane *a* humanitario, humano

humanely *adv* humanitariamente

humaneness *n* humanidad, *f*

humanism *n* humanismo, *m*

humanist *n* humanista, *mf*

humanistic *a* humanista

humanitarian *a* humanitario

humanitarianism *n* humanitarismo, *m*

humanity *n* humanidad, *f;* raza humana, *f.* **the humanities,** las humanidades

humanize *vt* humanizar; (milk) maternizar. *vi* humanizarse

humanly *adv* humanamente

humble *a* humilde; modesto; (cringing) servil; sumiso; pobre. *vt* humillar; mortificar. **to h. oneself,** humillarse

humbleness *n* humildad, *f;* modestia, *f;* (abjectness) servilismo, *m;* sumisión, *f;* pobreza, *f;* (of birth, etc.) obscuridad, *f*

humbling *n* humillación, *f;* mortificación, *f*

humbly *adv* humildemente; modestamente; servilmente

humbug *n* (fraud) embuste, engaño, *m;* (nonsense) disparate, *m,* tontería, *f;* mentira, *f;* (person) farsante, charlatán, *m;* (sweetmeat) caramelo de menta, *m. vt* engañar, embaucar; burlarse de

humdrum *a* monótono; aburrido

humeral *a* humeral. *n ecc* velo humeral, *m*

humerus *n anat* húmero, *m*

humid *a* húmedo

humidity *n* humedad, *f*

humiliate *vt* humillar, mortificar. **to h. oneself,** humillarse

humiliating *a* humillante; degradante

humiliation *n* humillación, mortificación, *f;* degradación, *f*

humility *n* humildad, *f;* modestia, *f*

humming *n* zumbido, *m;* (of a tune) tarareo, *m. a* zumbador. **h.-bird,** pájaro mosca, colibrí, *m.* **h.-top,** trompa, *f*

humoresque *n mus* capricho musical, *m*

humorist *n* humorista, *mf*

humorous *a* humorístico; cómico, risible

humorously *adv* humorísticamente; cómicamente

humorousness *n* humorismo, *m;* lo cómico

humor *n* humor, *m;* humorismo, *m;* (temperament) disposición, *f,* carácter, *m;* (whim) capricho, *m. vt* seguir el humor (a), complacer; satisfacer, consentir en; (a lock, etc.) manejar. **in a good (bad) h.,** de buen (mal) humor. **I am not in the h. to . . .** No estoy de humor para . . . **sense of h.,** sentido de humor, *m*

humored *a* (in compounds) de humor . . . **good-h.,** de buen humor. **ill-h.,** malhumorado, de mal humor

humorless *a* sin sentido humorístico, sin sentido de humor

hump *n* joroba, giba, *f;* (hillock) montecillo, *m; inf* depresión, *f*

humpback *n* giba, joroba, *f;* (person) jorobado (-da), giboso (-sa)

humpbacked *a* jorobado, giboso, corcovado

humph *interj* ¡qué va!; ¡patrañas!

humus *n* humus, mantillo, *m*

hunch *n:* **I have a hunch that . . .** *Mexico* Me late que . . .

hunchback *n* joroba, giba, *f;* (person) jorobado (-da), corcovado (-da), giboso (-sa)

hunchbacked *a* jorobado, giboso, corcovado

hundred *n* ciento, *m;* centenar, *m,* centena, *f. a* ciento; (before nouns and adjectives, excluding numerals, with the exception of mil and millón) cien. **a h. thousand,** cien mil. **one h. and one,** ciento uno. **by the h.,** a centenares. **hundreds of people,** centenares de personas, *m pl.* **h.-millionth,** *a* and *n* cienmillonésimo *m.* **h.-thousandth,** *a* and *n* cienmilésimo *m.*

hundredfold *adv* cien veces. *n* céntuplo, *m*

hundredth *a* centésimo, céntimo. *n* centésimo, *m,* centésima parte, *f*

Hungary Hungría, *f*

Hungarian *a* and *n* húngaro (-ra); (language) húngaro, *m*

hunger *n* hambre, *f;* apetito, *m;* (craving) deseo, *m,* ansia, *f. vi* estar hambriento, tener hambre. **to h. for,** desear, ansiar. **h.-strike,** huelga de hambre, *f*

hungrily *adv* hambrientamente, con hambre; ansiosamente

hungry *a* hambriento; (of land) pobre; (anxious) deseoso. **to be h.,** tener hambre. **to make h.,** dar hambre

hunk *n* rebanada, *f,* pedazo, *m*

hunt *n* caza, cacería, montería, *f;* grupo de cazadores, *m;* (search) busca, *f;* (pursuit) persecución, *f. vt* cazar; cazar a caballo; (search) buscar; rebuscar, explorar; (pursue) perseguir. **to h. down,** perseguir. **to h. for,** buscar. **to h. out,** buscar; descubrir, desenterrar

hunter *n* cazador, *m;* caballo de caza, *m;* (watch) saboneta, *f*

hunting *n* caza, *f;* caza a caballo, *f;* persecución, *f. a* cazador, de caza. **to go h.,** ir a cazar. **h.-box,** pabellón de caza, *m.* **h.-cap,** gorra de montar, *f.* **h.-crop,** látigo para cazar, *m.* **h.-ground,** coto de caza, terreno de caza, *m.* **h.-horn,** cuerno de caza, *m,* corneta de monte, *f.* **h. party,** partido de caza, *m,* cacería, *f*

huntsman *n* cazador, montero, *m*

huntsmanship *n* montería, arte de cazar, *f*

hurdle *n* valla, *f;* zarzo, *m.* **h.-race,** carrera de obstáculos, *f;* carrera de vallas, *f*

hurdy-gurdy *n* organillo, *m*

hurl *vt* lanzar, tirar, arrojar, echar. **to h. oneself,** lanzarse. **to h. oneself against,** arrojarse a (or contra). **to h. oneself upon,** abalanzarse sobre

hurly-burly *n* alboroto, tumulto, *m*

hurrah *interj* ¡hurra! ¡viva! *n* vítor, *m.* **H. for . . . !** ¡Viva . . . !, ¡Vivan . . . ! **to shout h.,** vitorear

hurricane *n* huracán, *m.* **h.-lamp,** lámpara sorda, *f*

hurried *a* apresurado, precipitado; hecho a prisa; superficial

hurriedly *adv* apresuradamente, precipitadamente, con prisa; superficialmente; (of writing) a vuela pluma

hurry *n* prisa, *f;* precipitación, *f;* urgencia, *f;* confusión, *f;* alboroto, *m.* **in a h.,** aprisa. **in a great h.,** aprisa y corriendo. **to be in a h.,** llevar prisa, estar de prisa. **There is no h.,** No corre prisa, No hay prisa

hurry *vt* apresurar, dar prisa, *Lat. Am.* apurar (a); llevar aprisa; hacer andar aprisa; enviar apresuradamente; precipitar; acelerar. *vi* darse prisa; apresurarse. **to h. after,** correr detrás de, seguir apresuradamente. **to h. away,** *vi* marcharse aprisa, marcharse corriendo; huir; salir precipitadamente. *vt* hacer marcharse aprisa; llevar con prisa. **to h. back,** *vi* volver aprisa, apresurarse

a volver. *vt* hacer volver aprisa. **to h. in,** *vi* entrar aprisa, entrar corriendo. *vt* hacer entrar aprisa. **to h. off,** See **to h. away. to h. on,** *vi* apresurarse. *vt* apresurar, precipitar. **to h. out,** salir rápidamente. **to h. over,** hacer rápidamente; concluir aprisa; despachar rápidamente; (travel over) atravesar aprisa; pasar rápidamente por. **to h. toward,** llevar rápidamente hacia; arrastrar hacia; impeler hacia. **to h. up,** *vi* darse prisa. *vt* apresurar, precipitar, *Lat. Am.* apurar; estimular

hurt *n* herida, *f;* (harm) daño, mal, *m;* perjuicio, *m. vt* (wound) herir; (cause pain) doler; hacer daño (a); hacer mal (a); (damage) perjudicar, estropear, *Lat. Am.* afectar; (offend) ofender; (the feelings) mortificar, lastimar, herir. *vi* doler; hacer mal; perjudicarse, estropearse. **I haven't h. myself,** No me he hecho daño. **Does it still h. you?** ¿Te duele todavía? **to h. deeply,** *fig* herir en el alma. **to h. a person's feelings,** herirle (a uno) el amor propio, lastimar, ofender

hurtful *a* nocivo, dañino; injurioso, pernicioso

hurtfulness *n* nocividad, *f;* perniciosidad, *f*

hurtle *vt* lanzar. *vi* lanzarse; volar; caer

husband *n* esposo, marido, *m. vt* economizar, ahorrar. **h. and wife,** los esposos, los cónyuges

husbandry *n* labor de los campos, agricultura, *f;* (thrift) frugalidad, parsimonia, *f*

hush *n* silencio, *m,* tranquilidad, *f. interj* ¡chitón! ¡calla! ¡silencio! *vt* silenciar, hacer callar, imponer silencio (a); (a baby) adormecer; *fig* sosegar, calmar. *vi* callarse, enmudecer. **to h. up,** mantener secreto, ocultar. **h.-h.,** secreto. **h. money,** so-borno, chantaje, *m*

hushaby *interj* ¡duerme!

husk *n* (of grain) cascabillo, *m;* zurrón, *m;* cáscara, *f;* (of chestnut) erizo, *m; vt Lat. Am.* deshojar (corn)

huskily *adv* roncamente

huskiness *n* ronquera, *f; inf* robustez, *f*

husky *a* (of voice) ronco; (Eskimo) esquimal; *inf* robusto, fuerte. *n* perro esquimal, *m*

hussy *n* pícara, bribona, *f*

hustle *vt* empujar, codear; *fig* precipitar; *inf* acelerar. *vi* codearse; andarse de prisa

hut *n* choza, cabaña, barraca, *f, Mexico* jacal, *elsewhere in Lat. Am.* bohío *m*

hutch *n* (chest) arca, *f,* cofre, *m;* (cage) jaula, *f;* (for rabbits) conejera, *f;* (for rats) ratonera, *f; inf* choza, *f*

hutment *n* campamento de chozas, *m*

hyacinth *n* jacinto, *m*

hybrid *a* híbrido; mestizo, mixto. *n* híbrido, *m*

hybridism *n* hibridismo, *m*

hybridization *n* hibridación, *f*

hybridize *vt* cruzar. *vi* producir (or generar) híbridos

hydrangea *n* bot hortensia, *f*

hydrant *n* boca de riego, *f*

hydrate *n chem* hidrato, *m. vt* hidratar

hydraulic *a* hidráulico. **h. engineering,** hidrotecnia, *f*

hydraulics *n* hidráulica, *f*

hydrocarbon *n chem* hidrocarburo, *m*

hydrochloric *a* clorhídrico. **h. acid,** ácido clorhídrico, *m*

hydrogen *n* hidrógeno, *m.* **h. peroxide,** agua oxigenada, *f*

hydrogenation *n* hidrogenación, *f*

hydrogenize *vt* hidrogenizar

hydrolysis *n* hidrólisis, *f*

hydromel *n* aguamiel, *f,* hidromel, *m*

hydropathic *a* hidropático. **h. establishment,** balneario, *m*

hydrophobia *n* hidrofobia, rabia, *f*

hydrophobic *a* hidrofóbico, rabioso

hydroplane *n* hidroplano, *m*

hydrotherapic *a* hidroterápico

hydrotherapy *n* hidroterapia, *f*

hyena *n* hiena, *f*

hygiene *n* higiene, *f.* **personal h.,** higiene privada, *f*

hygienic *a* higiénico

hymen *n anat* himen, *m*; himeneo, *m*
hymeneal *a* nupcial
hymn *n* himno, *m*. **h.-book,** himnario, *m*
hyperbole *n* hipérbole, *f*
hyperbolical *a* hiperbólico
hypercorrection *n* seudocultismo, supercultismo, *m*, ultracorrección, *f*
hypercritic *n* hipercrítico, *m*
hypercritical *a* hipercrítico, criticón
hypersensitive *a* vidrioso, quisquilloso
hypertrophy *n* hipertrofia, *f. vi* hipertrofiarse
hyphen *n* guión, *m*
hypnosis *n* hipnosis, *f*
hypnotic *a* hipnótico. *n* (person) hipnótico (-ca); (drug) hipnótico, narcótico, *m*
hypnotism *n* hipnotismo, *m*
hypnotist *n* hipnotizador (-ra)
hypnotization *n* hipnotización, *f*
hypnotize *vt* hipnotizar

hypo *n* (sodium hyposulphite) hiposulfito sólido, *m*
hypochondria *n* hipocondria, *f*
hypochondriac *n* hipocondríaco (-ca)
hypochondriacal *a* hipocondríaco
hypocrisy *n* hipocresía, *f*; mojigatería, gazmoñería, *f*
hypocrite *n* hipócrita, *mf*; mojigato (-ta). **to be a h.,** ser hipócrita
hypocritical *a* hipócrita; mojigato, gazmoño
hypocritically *adv* hipócritamente, con hipocresía
hypodermic *a* hipodérmico. **h. syringe,** jeringa de inyecciones, *f*
hypotenuse *n geom* hipotenusa, *f*
hypothesis *n* hipótesis, *f*
hypothetical *a* hipotético
hysterectomy *n surg* histerectomía, *f*
hysteria *n med* histerismo, *m*; histeria, *f*, ataque de nervios, *m*
hysterical *a* histérico. **to become h.,** tener un ataque de nervios. **hysterics,** *n pl* ataque de nervios, *m*

I

i *n* (letter) i. *1st pers pron* yo. **It is I,** Soy yo. Normally omitted, the verb alone being used except when **yo** is needed for emphasis, e.g. **Hablo a María,** I speak to Mary, *but* **Yo toco el violín, pero Juan toca el piano,** *I* play the violin, but *John* plays the piano
Iago Yago, *m*
Iberian Peninsula, the la Peninsula Ibérica
Iberian *a* ibero, ibérico. *n* ibero (-ra)
ibex *n zool* íbice, *m*
ice *n* hielo, *m*; (ice cream) helado, *m*. *vt* helar; cubrir de hielo; congelar, cuajar; (a cake, etc.) garapiñar, escarchar, alcorzar. **to ice up,** (*aer, aut*) helarse. **to be as cold as ice,** *inf* estar hecho un hielo. **His words cut no ice,** Sus palabras ni pinchan ni cortan. **ice-age,** edad del hielo, *f*. **ice-ax,** piolet, *m*. **ice-box,** nevera, *f*. **ice-cream,** helado, mantecado, *m*. **ice-cream cone,** cucurucho de helado, *m*. **ice-cream freezer,** heladora, *f*. **ice-cream vendor,** mantequero (-ra). **ice-field,** campo de hielo, *m*. **ice-floe,** témpano de hielo flotante, *m*. **ice hockey,** hockey sobre patines, *m*. **ice-pack,** bolsa para hielo, *f*. **ice-skates,** patines de cuchilla, *m pl*. **ice water,** agua helada, *f*
iceberg *n* iceberg, témpano de hielo, banco de hielo, *m*
icebound *a* aprisionado por el hielo; atascado en el hielo; (of roads, etc.) helado
iced *a* helado; congelado, cuajado; (cakes) garapiñado, escarchado; (of drinks) con hielo. **i. drink,** sorbete, *m*
Iceland Islandia, *f*
Icelander *n* islandés (-esa)
icelandic *a* islandés, islándico. *n* (language) islandés, *m*
icicle *n* carámbano, canelón, cerrión, *m*
icily *adv* fríamente, *fig* frígidamente, con indiferencia, con frialdad
iciness *n* frialdad, frigidez, *f*; *fig* indiferencia, frigidez, *f*
icing *n* helada, *f*, hielo, *m*; (on a cake, etc.) alcorza, capa de azúcar, *f*
icon *n* icono, *m*
iconoclast *n* iconoclasta, *mf*
iconoclastic *a* iconoclasta
iconography *n* iconografía, *f*
iconology *n* iconología, *f*
icy *a* helado; glacial, frío; *med* álgido; *fig* indiferente, desabrido; *poet* frígido, gélido
idea *n* idea, *f*, concepto, *m*; (opinion) juicio, *m*, opinión, *f*; (notion) impresión, noción, *f*; (plan) proyecto, plan, designio, *m*. **to form an i. of,** hacerse una idea de, formar un concepto de. **to have an i. of,** tener una idea de; tener nociones de. **An i. struck me,** Se me ocurrió una idea. **full of ideas,** preñado (or lleno) de ideas. **I had no i. that . . .** No tenía la menor idea de que . . . No sabía que . . . **What an i.!** ¡Qué idea!
ideal *a* ideal; excelente, perfecto; (utopian) utópico;

(imaginary) imaginario, irreal, ficticio. *n* ideal, *m*; modelo, prototipo, *m*
idealism *n* idealismo, *m*
idealist *n* idealista, *mf*
idealistic *a* idealista
idealization *n* idealización, *f*
idealize *vt* idealizar
ideally *adv* idealmente
ideation *n phil* ideación, *f*
idem *adv* ídem
identical *a* idéntico, mismo, igual; muy parecido, semejante
identically *adv* idénticamente
identifiable *a* identificable
identification *n* identificación, *f*. **i. number,** placa de identidad, *f*
identify *vt* identificar. **to i. oneself with,** identificarse con
identity *n* identidad, *f*. **i. card,** cédula personal, *f*; carnet de identidad, *m*. **i. disc,** disco de identidad, *m*
ideogram, ideograph *n* ideograma, *m*
ideography *n* ideografía, *f*
ideological *a* ideológico
ideologist *n* ideólogo (-ga)
ideology *n* ideología, *f*
Ides *n pl* idus, *m pl*
idiocy *n* idiotez, imbecilidad, *f*; (foolishness) necedad, tontería, sandez, *f*
idiom *n* idiotismo, *m*; modismo, *m*, locución, *f*; (language) habla, *f*; lenguaje, *m*
idiomatic *a* idiomático
idiopathy *n med* idiopatía, *f*
idiosyncrasy *n* idiosincrasia, *f*
idiosyncratic *a* idiosincrásico
idiot *n* idiota, imbécil, *mf*; (fool) necio (-ia), tonto (-ta), mentecato (-ta)
idiotic *a* idiota, imbécil; (foolish) necio, tonto, sandío
idle *a* desocupado; indolente, ocioso; (unemployed) cesante, sin empleo; (lazy) perezoso, holgazán; (of machines) parado, inactivo; (useless) vano, inútil, sin efecto; (false) falso, mentiroso, infundado; (stupid) fútil, frívolo. *vi* holgar, estar ocioso; holgazanear, haraganear, gandulear. **to i. away,** malgastar, perder. **to i. away the time,** pasar el rato, matar el tiempo. **i. efforts,** vanos esfuerzos, *m pl*. **i. fancies,** ilusiones, fantasías, *f pl*, sueños, *m pl*, ratos desocupados, *f pl*, ratos perdidos, *m pl*. **i. question,** pregunta ociosa, *f*. **i. tale,** cuento de viejas, *m*. **i. threat,** reto vacuo, *m*
idleness *n* ociosidad, indolencia, inacción, *f*; pereza, holgazanería, gandulería, *f*; (uselessness) inutilidad, futilidad, *f*

idler *n* ocioso (-sa); haragán (-ana); perezoso (-sa), holgazán (-ana), gandul (-la), *Lat. Am.* aplanacalles *mf*
idly *adv* ociosamente, perezosamente; (uselessly) vanamente
idol *n* ídolo, *m.* **a popular i.,** el ídolo de las masas, *m*
idolater *n* idólatra, *mf*; (admirer) amante, *mf* esclavo (-va), admirador (-ra)
idolatrous *a* idólatra, idolátrico
idolatrously *adv* idolatradamente, con idolatría
idolatry *n* idolatría, *f*; (devotion) adoración, pasión, *f*
idolization *n* idolatría, *f*
idolize *vt* idolatrar, adorar
idyll *n* idilio, *m*
idyllic *a* idílico
if *conjunc* si; (even if) aunque, aun cuando; (whenever) cuando, en caso de que; (whether) si. **as if,** como si (foll. by subjunc.). **If he comes, we shall tell him,** Si viene se lo diremos. **If he had not killed the tiger, she would be dead,** Si él no hubiera matado al tigre, ella estaría muerta. **If ever there was one,** Si alguna vez lo hubiera. **if necessary,** si fuese necesario. **if not,** si no, si no es que (e.g., **Poet and philosopher are twins, if not one and the same,** Poeta y filósofo son hermanos gemelos, si no es que la misma cosa). **If only!** ¡Ojalá que! (foll. by subjunc.)
igloo *n* iglú, *m*
igneous *a* ígneo
ignite *vt* encender, pegar fuego (a), incendiar. *vi* prender fuego, incendiarse; arder
ignition *n* ignición, *f*; *aut* encendido, *m.* **i. coil,** *aut* carrete de inducción del encendido, *m.* **i. key,** *aut* llave del contacto, *f*
ignoble *a* innoble, vil, indigno
ignobly *adv* bajamente, vilmente
ignominious *a* ignominioso
ignominiously *adv* ignominiosamente
ignominy *n* ignominia, deshonra, afrenta, *f*
ignoramus *n* ignorante, *mf*
ignorance *n* ignorancia, *f*; (unawareness) desconocimiento, *m.* **to plead i.,** pretender ignorancia
ignorant *a* ignorante; inculto. **He is an i. fellow,** Es un ignorante. **to be i. of,** no saber, ignorar. **to be very i.,** ser muy ignorante, *inf* ser muy burro
ignorantly *adv* ignorantemente, por ignorancia; neciamente
ignore *vt* no hacer caso de, desatender; (omit) pasar por alto de; *law* rechazar; (pretend not to recognize) hacer semblante de no reconocer; (not recognize) no reconocer
iguana *n zool* iguana, *f*
ileac *a anat* ilíaco
ileum *n anat* íleon, *m*
Iliad *n* Ilíada, *f*
ilium *n anat* ilion, *m*
ill *n* mal, *m. a* (sick) enfermo, malo; (bad) malo; (unfortunate) desdichado, funesto. *adv* mal. **to be ill,** estar malo. **to be taken ill,** caer enfermo. **ill-advised,** mal aconsejado; desacertado, imprudente. **ill-advisedly,** imprudentemente. **ill at ease,** incómodo. **ill-bred,** mal criado, mal educado, mal nacido. **ill-breeding,** mala crianza, mala educación, *f.* **ill-disposed,** malintencionado. **ill fame,** mala fama, *f.* **ill-fated,** malhadado, malaventurado, aciago, fatal. **ill-favored,** mal parecido, feúcho. **ill-feeling,** hostilidad, *f*, rencor, *m.* **ill-gotten,** maladquirido. **ill-humor,** mal humor, *m.* **ill-humored,** de mal humor, malhumorado. **ill-luck,** desdicha, mala suerte, malaventura, *f*; infortunio, *m.* **ill-mannered,** mal educado. **ill-natured,** malévolo, perverso. **ill-naturedly,** malignamente. **ill-omened,** nefasto. **ill-spent,** malgastado, perdido. **ill-spoken,** mal hablado. **ill-suited,** malavenido. **ill-timed,** inoportuno, intempestivo. **ill-treat,** maltratar, malparar, tratar mal. **ill-treated,** que ha sido tratado mal; maltrecho. **ill-treatment,** maltratamiento, *m*, crueldad, *f.* **ill-turn,** mala jugada, *f.* **to do an ill-turn,** hacer un flaco servicio. **ill will,** mala

voluntad, *f*; rencor, *m*, ojeriza, *f.* **to bear a person ill will,** guardarle rencor
illegal *a* ilegal; indebido, ilícito
illegality *n* ilegalidad, *f*
illegally *adv* ilegalmente
illegibility *n* ilegibilidad, *f*
illegible *a* ilegible, indescifrable
illegibly *adv* de un modo ilegible
illegitimacy *n* ilegitimidad, *f*; falsedad, *f*
illegitimate *a* ilegítimo, bastardo; falso; ilícito, desautorizado
illegitimately *adv* ilegítimamente
illiberal *a* iliberal; intolerante, estrecho de miras; (mean) avaro, tacaño, ruin
illiberality *n* iliberalidad, *f*; intolerancia, *f*; (avarice) tacañería, avaricia, ruindad, *f*
illiberally *adv* avariciosamente, ruinmente
illicit *a* ilícito, indebido, ilegal
illicitly *adv* ilícitamente, ilegalmente
illicitness *n* ilicitud, ilegalidad, *f*
illimitable *a* ilimitado, sin límites, infinito
illiteracy *n* analfabetismo, *m*
illiterate *a* and *n* analfabeto (-ta), iliterato (-ta)
illness *n* enfermedad, dolencia, *f*, mal, *m*
illogical *a* ilógico; absurdo, irracional
illogicality *n* falta de lógica, *f*; absurdo, *m*, irracionalidad, *f*
illuminant *a* iluminador, alumbrador
illuminate *vt* iluminar, alumbrar; *art* iluminar; (explain) aclarar, ilustrar
illuminated *a* iluminado, encendido; *art* iluminado. **i. sign,** letrero luminoso, *m*
illuminati *n pl* secta de los alumbrados, *f*
illuminating *a* iluminador; (explanatory) aclaratorio. *n art* iluminación, *f*
illumination *n* iluminación, *f*, alumbrado, *m*; (for decoration) luminaria, *f*; *art* iluminación, *f*; *fig* inspiración, *f*
illuminator *n art* iluminador (-ra)
illumine *vt* encender, alumbrar; *fig* inspirar
illusion *n* ilusión, *f*, engaño, *m*; (dream) esperanza, ilusión, *f*, ensueño, *m.* **to harbor illusions,** tener ilusiones
illusive *a* ilusivo, engañoso, falso
illusively *adv* falsamente, aparentemente
illusoriness *n* ilusión, falsedad, *f*, engaño, *m*
illusory *a* ilusorio, deceptivo, falso, irreal
illustrate *vt* ilustrar, aclarar, explicar, elucidar; *art* ilustrar; (prove) probar, demostrar
illustration *n* ejemplo, *m*; ilustración, *f*; *art* grabado, *m*; estampa, *f*; (explanation) elucidación, aclaración, *f*
illustrative *a* ilustrativo, ilustrador, explicativo, aclaratorio
illustrator *n* ilustrador (-ra), grabador (-ra)
illustrious *a* ilustre, famoso, renombrado, distinguido
illustriously *adv* ilustremente, noblemente
illustriousness *n* eminencia, *f*, renombre, *m*, grandeza, *f*
image *n* (optics) imagen, *f*; efigie, imagen, *f*; (religious) imagen, estatua, *f*; *art* figura, *f*; (metaphor) metáfora, expresión, *f*; (of a person) retrato, *m.* **to be the i. of,** ser el retrato de. **sharp i.,** imagen nítida, *f.* **i. breaker,** iconoclasta, *mf.* **i. vendor,** vendedor (-ra) de imágenes
imagery *n art* imaginería, *f*; (style) metáforas, *f pl*
imaginable *a* imaginable
imaginary *a* imaginario; fantástico, de ensueño
imagination *n* imaginación, *f*; imaginativa, fantasía, inventiva, *f*, ingenio, *m*
imaginative *a* imaginativo; fantástico
imagine *vt* imaginar, concebir; idear, proyectar, inventar; figurarse, suponer. **Just i.!** ¡Imagínese usted!
imam *n* imán, *m*
imbecile *a* imbécil; (foolish) necio, estúpido, tonto. *n* imbécil, *mf*; (fool) necio (-ia), tonto (-ta), estúpido (-da)
imbecility *n* imbecilidad, *f*; (folly) necedad, sandez, *f*

imbibe vt embeber, absorber; (drink) sorber, chupar; empaparse de

imbibing n imbibición, absorción, f

imbricate a (zool, bot) imbricado

imbroglio n embrollo, lío, m

imbue vt imbuir, calar, empapar; teñir. **to i. with,** infundir de

imitable a imitable

imitate vt imitar; copiar, reproducir; (counterfeit) contrahacer

imitation n imitación, f; copia, f; remedo, traslado, m. a imitado; falso, artificial

imitative a imitativo; imitador

imitativeness n facultad imitativa (or de imitacion), f

imitator n imitador (-ra); contrahacedor (-ra), falsificador (-ra)

immaculate a inmaculado, puro; (of dress) elegante. **I. Conception,** la Purísima Concepción

immaculately adv inmaculadamente; elegantemente

immaculateness n pureza, f; (of dress) elegancia, f

immanence n inmanencia, inherencia, f

immanent a inmanente; inherente

immaterial a inmaterial, incorpóreo; sin importancia. **It is i. to me,** Me es indiferente, No me importa, Me da lo mismo, Me da igual

immateriality n inmaterialidad, f

immature a inmaturo; precoz; (of fruit) verde

immaturity n falta de madurez, f; precocidad, f

immeasurability n inmensurabilidad, inmensidad, f

immeasurable a inmensurable, inmenso, imponderable

immeasurably adv inmensamente, enormemente

immediate a (of place) inmediato, cercano, contiguo; (of time) próximo, inmediato, directo; (of action) inmediato, perentorio; (on letters) urgente. **to take i. action,** tomar acción inmediata

immediately adv (of place) próximamente, contiguamente; (of time) luego, seguidamente, en el acto, ahora mismo, enseguida; directamente; (as soon as) así que

immemorial a inmemorial, inmemorable

immemorially adv desde tiempo inmemorial

immense a inmenso, enorme; vasto, extenso; infinito

immensely adv inmensamente, enormemente

immensity n inmensidad, f; extensión, vastedad, f

immerse vt sumergir, hundir en, zambullir; bautizar por sumersión. fig **to be immersed in,** estar absorto en

immersion n sumersion, f, hundimiento, m; ast inmersión, f

immigrant a and n inmigrante, mf

immigrate vi inmigrar

immigration n inmigración, f

imminence n inminencia, f

imminent a inminente

immobile a inmóvil, inmoble; impasible, imperturbable

immobility n inmovilidad, f; impasibilidad, imperturbabilidad, f

immobilization n inmovilización, f

immobilize vt inmovilizar

immoderate a inmoderado, excesivo, indebido

immoderately adv inmoderadamente, excesivamente

immoderateness n inmoderación, f, exceso, m

immodest a inmodesto; indecente, deshonesto; (pert) atrevido, descarado

immodestly adv impúdicamente, inmodestamente

immodesty n inmodestia, impudicia, f; deshonestidad, licencia, f; (forwardness) descaro, atrevimiento, m

immolate vt inmolar, sacrificar

immolation n inmolación, f, sacrificio, m

immolator n inmolador (-ra)

immoral a inmoral; licencioso, vicioso; incontinente

immorality n inmoralidad, f

immortal a inmortal; perenne, eterno, imperecedero. n inmortal, mf

immortality n inmortalidad, f; fama inmortal, f

immortalize vt inmortalizar, perpetuar

immortally adv inmortalmente, eternamente, para siempre

immovability n inamovilidad, inmovilidad, f; (of purpose) inflexibilidad, tenacidad, constancia, f

immovable a inmoble, fijo, inmóvil; (of purpose) inconmovible, inalterable, constante. n pl. **immovables** law bienes inmuebles, m pl. ecc **i. feast,** fiesta fija, f

immovably adv inmóvilmente, fijamente

immune a inmune, libre; med inmune. **i. from,** exento de; libre de

immunity n inmunidad, libertad, f; exención, f; med inmunidad, f

immunization n med inmunización, f

immunize vt inmunizar

immure vt emparedar, recluir, encerrar

immutability n inmutabilidad, inalterabilidad, f

immutable a inmutable, inalterable, constante

immutably adv inmutablemente

imp n trasgo, diablillo, duende, m; (child) picaruelo (-la)

impact n impacto, m, impacción, f; choque, m, colisión, f

impair vt perjudicar, echar a perder, deteriorar, empeorar, desmejorar. **to be impaired,** deteriorarse, perjudicarse

impairment n deterioración, perjuicio, empeoramiento, m

impale vt (punishment) empalar; (with a sword) atravesar, espetar

impalement n (punishment) empalamiento, m; atravesamiento, m, transfixión, f

impalpability n impalpabilidad, intangibilidad, f

impalpable a impalpable, intangible; incorpóreo

impart vt comunicar, dar parte (de); conferir

impartial a imparcial, ecuánime

impartiality n imparcialidad, ecuanimidad, entereza, f, desinterés, m

impartially adv imparcialmente, con desinterés

impassability n impracticabilidad, f

impassable a intransitable, impracticable; (of water) invadeable

impasse n callejón sin salida, m

impassibility n impasibilidad, imperturbabilidad, indiferencia, f

impassible a impasible, insensible; indiferente, imperturbable

impassion vt apasionar, conmover

impassioned a apasionado, vehemente, ardiente

impassive a impasible, insensible; indiferente, imperturbable; apático

impassively adv indiferentemente

impassivity n impasibilidad, f; indiferencia, f; apatía, f

impatience n impaciencia, f

impatient a impaciente; intolerante. **to make i.,** impacientar. **to grow i.,** impacientarse, perder la paciencia. **to grow i. at,** impacientarse ante. **to grow i. to,** impacientarse a or por. **to grow i. under,** impacientarse bajo

impatiently adv con impaciencia, impacientemente

impeach vt law denunciar, delatar, acusar, hacer juicio político (Argentina); censurar, criticar, tachar

impeachable a law delatable, denunciable, acusable; censurable

impeacher n acusador (-ra), denunciador (-ra), delator (-ra)

impeachment n law acusación, denuncia, f; reproche, m, queja, f

impeccability n (perfection) impecabilidad, perfección, f; elegancia, f

impeccable a impecable, intachable, perfecto; elegante

impeccably adv perfectamente; elegantemente

impecuniosity n indigencia, probreza, f

impecunious a indigente, pobre

impede vt impedir, obstruir, estorbar; fig dificultar, embarazar

impediment n obstáculo, estorbo, m; fig dificultad, f; law impedimento, m. **to have an i. in one's speech,** tener una dificultad en el hablar

impel vt impulsar, impeler; fig estimular, obligar, mover, constreñir. **I felt impelled (to),** Me sentí obligado (a)

impend vi ser inminente, amenazar

impending a inminente, pendiente

impenetrability n impenetrabilidad, f; fig enigma, secreto, misterio, m

impenetrable a impenetrable; intransitable; denso, espeso; fig enigmático, insondable, secreto

impenetrably adv impenetrablemente, densamente

impenitence n impenitencia, f

impenitent a impenitente, incorregible

impenitently adv sin penitencia

imperative a imperioso, perentorio; gram imperativo; (necessary) esencial, urgente. n mandato, m, orden, f; gram imperativo, m. **in the i.,** en el imperativo

imperatively adv imperativamente

imperativeness n perentoriedad, f; urgencia, importancia, f

imperceptible a imperceptible, insensible

imperceptibly adv imperceptiblemente

imperceptive a insensible

imperfect a imperfecto; incompleto, defectuoso. a and n gram imperfecto m

imperfection n imperfección, f; defecto, desperfecto, m; falta, tacha, f

imperfectly adv imperfectamente

imperial a imperial, imperatorio. n (beard) pera, f. **i. preference,** preferencia dentro del Imperio, f

imperialism n imperialismo, m

imperialist n imperialista, mf

imperialistic a imperialista

imperil vt arriesgar, poner en peligro, aventurar

imperious a imperioso, altivo, arrogante; (pressing) urgente, apremiante

imperiously adv imperiosamente, con arrogancia

imperiousness n autoridad, arrogancia, altivez, f; necesidad, urgencia, f, apremio, m

imperishability n (immortality) inmortalidad, perennidad, f

imperishable a imperecedero, inmarchitable, perenne, eterno

impermanence n inestabilidad, interinidad, f; brevedad, fugacidad, f

impermanent a interino, no permanente

impermeability n impermeabilidad, f

impermeable a impermeable

impersonal a impersonal, objetivo; gram impersonal

impersonality n objetividad, f

impersonally adv impersonalmente

impersonate vt personificar, simbolizar; theat representar

impersonation n personificación, simbolización, f; theat representación, f

impertinence n impertinencia, majadería, insolencia, f; inoportunidad, f; despropósito, m

impertinent a impertinente, insolente; (unseasonable) intempestivo, inoportuno; (irrelevant) fuera de propósito

impertinently adv con insolencia, impertinentemente

imperturbability n imperturbabilidad, serenidad, impasibilidad, f; impavidez, f

imperturbable a imperturbable, impasible, sereno; impávido

imperturbably adv con serenidad, imperturbablemente

impervious a impermeable, impenetrable; fig insensible. **He is i. to arguments,** No hace caso de argumentos

imperviousness n impermeabilidad, impenetrabilidad, f; fig insensibilidad, f

impetigo n med impétigo, m

impetuosity n impetuosidad, temeridad, irreflexión, f

impetuous a impetuoso, temerario, irreflexivo; violento, vehemente

impetuously adv impetuosamente; con vehemencia

impetus n mech ímpetu, m, impulsión, f; fig incentivo, estímulo, impulso, m

impiety n impiedad, irreligión, irreligiosidad, f

impinge (upon) vi chocar con, tropezar con

impious a impío, irreligioso, sacrílego; (wicked) malvado, perverso, malo

impish a travieso, revoltoso, enredador

implacability n implacabilidad, f

implacable a implacable, inexorable, inflexible, riguroso

implacably adv implacablemente

implant vt fig implantar, inculcar, instilar

implantation n fig implantación, instilación, inculcación, f

implement n instrumento, utensilio, m, herramienta, f; (of war) elemento, m. vt cumplir, hacer efectivo; llevar a cabo

implicate vt enredar, envolver; (imply) implicar, contener, llevar en sí; (in a crime) comprometer. **to be implicated in a crime,** estar implicado en un crimen.

implication n implicación, inferencia, repercusión, sugestión, f; (in a crime) complicidad, f

implicit a implícito, virtual, tácito; (absolute) ciego, absoluto, implícito. **with i. faith,** con fe ciega

implicitness n carácter implícito, m, lo implícito

implied a tácito, implícito

implore vt implorar, suplicar

imploring a suplicante, implorante

imploringly adv con encarecimiento, a súplica, de un modo suplicante

imply vt implicar, indicar, presuponer; (mean) querer decir, significar; (hint) insinuar, sugerir

impolicy n indiscreción, imprudencia, impolítica, f

impolite a descortés, mal educado

impolitely adv con descortesía

impoliteness n descortesía, falta de urbanidad, f

impolitic a impolítico

imponderability n imponderabilidad, f

imponderable a imponderable

import vt com importar; (mean) significar, querer decir. a com importado, de importación. n com importación, f; (meaning) significado, sentido, m; (value) importe, valor, m; (contents) contenido, tenor, m; importancia, f. **i. duty,** derechos de importación derechos de entrada, m pl, gravamen a la importación, m. **i. licence,** permiso de importación, m. **i. trade,** negocios de importación, m pl

importable a importable, que se puede importar

importance n importancia, f; valor, alcance, m, magnitud, f; consideración, eminencia, f. **to be fully conscious of one's i.,** tener plena conciencia de su importancia

important a importante; distinguido; presuntuoso, vanidoso. **to be i.,** importar, ser importante. **i. person,** personaje, m, persona importante, f

importantly adv importantemente, con importancia

importation n importación, f; com introducción (or importación) de géneros extranjeros, f

importer n importador (-ra)

importunate a (of a demand) insistente, importuno; (of persons) impertinente, pesado

importunately adv importunadamente

importune vt importunar, asediar, perseguir

importuning n persecución, importunación, f

importunity n importunidad, insistencia, impertinencia, f

impose vt (on, upon) imponer, infligir, cargar; print imponer. vi (on, upon) (deceive) engañar, embaucar

imposing a imponente, impresionante; (of persons) majestuoso, importante

imposition n imposición, f; (burden) impuesto, tributo,

m, carga, *f*; (*print, etc.*) imposición, *f*; (trick) fraude, engaño, *m*, decepción, *f*
impossibility *n* imposibilidad, *f*
impossible *a* imposible. **Nothing is i.,** No hay nada imposible, *inf* De menos nos hizo Dios. **to do the i.,** hacer lo imposible
impostor *n* impostor (-ra), bribón (-ona), embustero (-ra)
imposture *n* impostura, *f*, engaño, fraude, *m*
impotence *n* impotencia, *f*
impotent *a* impotente
impound *vt* acorralar; (water) embalsar; (goods) confiscar
impoverish *vt* empobrecer, depauperar, arruinar; (health) debilitar; (land) agotar
impoverished *a* indigente, necesitado; (of land) agotado
impoverishment *n* empobrecimiento, *m*, ruina, *f*; (of land) agotamiento, *m*
impracticability *n* impracticabilidad, imposibilidad, *f*
impracticable *a* impracticable, no factible, imposible
imprecation *n* imprecación, maldición, *f*
imprecatory *a* imprecatorio, maldiciente
impregnable *a* inexpugnable, inconquistable
impregnate *vt* impregnar, empapar; *biol* fecundar. **to become impregnated,** impregnarse
impregnation *n* impregnación, *f*; *biol* fecundación, fertilización, *f*; *fig* inculcación, *f*
impresario *n* empresario, *m*
imprescriptible *a* imprescriptible, inalienable
impress *vt* imprimir; (on the mind) impresionar; inculcar, imbuir; (with respect) imponer; *mil* reclutar; (of goods) confiscar. *n* impresión, marca, señal, huella, *f*
impression *n* impresión, *f*; marca, señal, huella, *f*; *print* impresión, *f*; efecto, *m*; idea, noción, *f*. **He has the i. that they do not like him,** Sospecha que no les es simpático. **to be under the i.,** tener la impresión
impressionability *n* susceptibilidad, sensibilidad, *f*
impressionable *a* susceptible, impresionable, sensitivo
impressionism *n* impresionismo, *m*
impressionist *n* impresionista, *mf*
impressionistic *a* impresionista
impressive *a* impresionante; emocionante; imponente; majestuoso; enfático
impressively *adv* solemnemente, de modo impresionante; enfáticamente
impressiveness *n* efecto impresionante, *m*, *Lat. Am.* imponencia *f*; grandiosidad, pompa, *f*; majestuosidad, *f*; fuerza, *f*
imprint *n* impresión, señal, marca, huella, *f*; *print* pie de imprenta, *m*. *vt* imprimir; (on the mind) grabar, fijar
imprison *vt* encerrar, encarcelar, aprisionar
imprisonment *n* encarcelación, prisión, *f*, encierro, *m*
improbability *n* improbabilidad, *f*; inverosimilitud, *f*
improbable *a* improbable; inverosímil
improbity *n* improbidad, *f*
impromptu *a* indeliberado, impremeditado, espontáneo. *adv* de improviso, in promptu. *n* improvisación, *f*
improper *a* impropio, inadecuado; incorrecto; indebido; indecente, indecoroso. **i. fraction,** *math* quebrado impropio, *m*
improperly *adv* impropiamente, incorrectamente; indecorosamente
impropriety *n* inconveniencia, *f*; incorrección, *f*; (style) impropiedad, *f*; falta de decoro, *f*
improvable *a* mejorable, perfectible
improve *vt* mejorar; perfeccionar; (beautify) embellecer, hermosear; (land) bonificar; *lit* corregir, enmendar; (cultivate) cultivar; (increase) aumentar; (an opportunity) aprovechar; (strengthen) fortificar; (business) sacar provecho de, explotar. *vi* mejorar; perfeccionarse; (progress) hacer progresos, progresar, adelantarse; *com* subir; (become beautiful) hacerse hermoso, embellecerse; (increase) aumentarse. **to i. upon,** mejorar, perfeccionar; pulir

improvement *n* mejora, *f*; perfeccionamiento, *m*; aumento, *m*; adelantamiento, progreso, *m*; (in health) mejoría, *f*; embellecimiento, *m*; cultivación, *f*; (of land) abono, *m*
improver *n* aprendiz (-za)
improvidence *n* imprevisión, *f*; improvidencia, *f*
improvident *a* impróvido, desprevenido
improvidently *adv* impróvidamente
improvisation *n* improvisación, *f*
improvise *vt* improvisar
improviser *n* improvisador (-ra)
imprudence *n* imprudencia, *f*; desacierto, *m*, indiscreción, *f*
imprudent *a* imprudente; desacertado, indiscreto, mal avisado, irreflexivo
imprudently *adv* imprudentemente; sin pensar
impudence *n* impudencia, *f*, descaro, *m*, insolencia, desvergüenza, *f*, atrevimiento, *m*
impudent *a* impudente, descarado, insolente, desvergonzado, atrevido, *Peru* lisurero
impudently *adv* descaradamente, con insolencia
impugn *vt* impugnar, contradecir, atacar
impugnable *a* impugnable, atacable
impugnment *n* impugnación, *f*
impulse *n* ímpetu, *m*, impulsión, *f*; impulso, estímulo, *m*; incitación, instigación, *f*; motivo, *m*; (fit) arranque, arrebato, acceso, *m*
impulsion *n* ímpetu, *m*, impulsión, *f*; empuje, *m*, arranque, *m*
impulsive *a* impelente; irreflexivo, impulsivo
impulsively *adv* por impulso
impulsiveness *n* irreflexión, *f*; carácter impulsivo, *m*
impunity *n* impunidad, *f*. **with i.,** impunemente
impure *a* impuro; adulterado, mezclado; (indecent) deshonesto, indecente; (dirty) turbio, sucio
impurity *n* impureza, *f*; adulteración, mezcla, *f*; deshonestidad, liviandad, *f*; suciedad, turbiedad, *f*
imputable *a* imputable, atribuible
imputation *n* imputación, atribución, *f*; (in a bad sense) acusación, *f*, reproche, *m*
impute *vt* imputar, achacar, atribuir; acusar, reprochar
imputer *n* imputador (-ra); recriminador (-ra), acusador (-ra)
in *prep* en; a; (of duration) durante, mientras; (with) con; (through) por; dentro de; (under) bajo; (following a superlative) de; (of specified time) dentro de, de aquí a; (with afternoon, etc.) por; (out of) sobre. **course in medieval Catalan literature,** curso de literatura catalana medioeval. **dressed in black,** vestido de negro. **in London,** en Londres. **in the morning,** por la mañana; (in the course of) durante la mañana. **in time,** a tiempo; dentro de algún tiempo. **in a week,** dentro de una semana. **in the best way,** del mejor modo. **in writing,** por escrito. **in anger,** con enojo. **in one's hand,** en la mano. **in addition to,** además de, a más de. **in case,** por si acaso, en caso de que. **in order to,** a fin de, para (foll. by infin.). **in order that,** para que (foll. by subjunc.). **in so far as,** en cuanto. **in spite of,** a pesar de. **in the distance,** a lo lejos, en lontananza. **in the meantime,** entre tanto. **in the middle of,** en el medio de; a la mitad de. **in the style of,** al modo de; a la manera de, a la (francesa, etc.)
in *adv* adentro, dentro; (at home) en casa; (of sun) escondido; (of fire) alumbrado; (in power) en el poder; (of harvest) cosechado; (of boats) entrado (with haber); (of trains) llegado (with haber). **to be in,** estar dentro; haber llegado; estar en casa. **to be in for,** estar expuesto a, correr el riesgo de. **to be in with a person,** ser muy amigo de, estar muy metido con. **Come in!** ¡Adelante! ¡Pase usted! **ins and outs,** sinuosidades, *f pl*; (of river) meandros, *m pl*; (of an affair) pormenores, detalles, *m pl*. **in less time than you can say Jack Robinson,** en menos de Jesús, en un credo, en menos que canta un gallo, en menos que se persigna un cura loco. **in the middle of nowhere,**

donde Cristo dio las tres voces, (Western Hemisphere) donde el diablo perdió el poncho.

in *a* interno. **in-law** (of relations) político. **in-patient,** enfermo (-ma) de hospital

inability *n* incapacidad, inhabilidad, ineptitud, incompetencia, *f*; impotencia, *f*

inaccessibility *n* inaccesibilidad, *f*

inaccessible *a* inaccesible

inaccuracy *n* inexactitud, incorrección, *f*

inaccurate *a* inexacto, incorrecto

inaccurately *adv* inexactamente, erróneamente

inaction *n* inacción, *f*

inactive *a* inactivo, pasivo; (of things) inerte; (lazy) perezoso, indolente; (machinery) parado; (motionless) inmóvil; (at leisure) desocupado, sin empleo

inactivity *n* inactividad, pasividad, *f*; (of things) inercia, *f*; pereza, indolencia, *f*; (of machinery) paro, *m*; inmovilidad, *f*; (leisure) desocupación, *f*

inadaptable *a* inadaptable, no adaptable

inadequacy *n* insuficiencia, escasez, *f*; imperfección, *f*, defecto, *m*

inadequate *a* inadecuado, insuficiente, escaso; imperfecto, defectuoso

inadequately *adv* inadecuadamente

inadmissible *a* inadmisible, no admisible

inadvertence *n* inadvertencia, *f*; equivocación, *f*, descuido, *m*

inadvertent *a* inadvertido, accidental, casual; negligente

inadvertently *adv* inadvertidamente, sin querer

inalienability *n* inalienabilidad, *f*

inalienable *a* inajenable, inalienable

inalterability *n* inalterabilidad, *f*

inalterable *a* inalterable

inalterably *adv* inalterablemente, sin alteración

inane *a* lelo, fatuo, vacío, necio

inanimate *a* (of matter) inanimado; sin vida, exánime, muerto

inanition *n* inanición, *f*

inanity *n* vacuidad, fatuidad, necedad, *f*

inappeasable *a* implacable, riguroso

inapplicability *n* no aplicabilidad, *f*

inapplicable *a* inaplicable

inapposite *a* fuera de propósito, no pertinente, inoportuno

inappreciable *a* inapreciable, imperceptible

inappreciation *n* falta de apreciación, *f*

inappreciative *a* desagradecido, ingrato. **i. of,** insensible a, indiferente a

inapproachable *a* inaccesible, huraño, adusto

inappropriate *a* impropio, inconveniente, inadecuado, incongruente; inoportuno

inappropriately *adv* impropiamente; inoportunamente

inappropriateness *n* impropiedad, inconveniencia, incongruencia, *f*; inoportunidad, *f*

inapt *a* inepto, inhábil; impropio

inaptitude *n* ineptitud, inhabilidad, *f*; impropiedad, *f*

inarticulate *a* (of speech) inarticulado; (reticent) inexpresivo, reservado; indistinto; *anat* inarticulado

inarticulately *adv* indistintamente, de un modo inarticulado

inarticulateness *n* tartamudez, *f*; inexpresión, reserva, *f*; silencio, *m*

inartistic *a* antiartístico, antiestético

inartistically *adv* sin gusto (estético)

inasmuch (as) *adv* puesto que, visto que, dado que

inattention *n* desatención, inaplicación, abstracción, *f*; falta de solicitud, *f*

inattentive *a* desatento, distraído; poco solícito, no atento

inattentively *adv* sin atención, distraídamente

inaudibility *n* imposibilidad de oír, *f*

inaudible *a* inaudible, no audible, ininteligible

inaudibly *adv* indistintamente, de modo inaudible

inaugurate *vt* inaugurar; (open) estrenar, abrir, dedicar; (install) investir, instalar; (initiate) originar, iniciar, dar lugar (a)

inauguration *n* inauguración, *f*; (opening) estreno, *m*, apertura, *f*; (investiture) instalación, investidura, *f*

inauspicious *a* poco propicio, desfavorable; ominoso, triste, infeliz

inauspiciously *adv* en condiciones desfavorables, desfavorablemente; infelizmente, bajo malos auspicios

inauspiciousness *n* condiciones desfavorables, *f pl*; infelicidad, *f*; malos auspicios, *m pl*

inborn *a* innato, instintivo, inherente

inbred *a* innato, inherente, instintivo

Inca *a* incaico, de los incas, *Lat. Am. also* incásico. *n* inca, *m*

incalculability *n* imposibilidad de calcular, *f*; (of persons) volubilidad, veleidad, *f*; infinidad, immensidad, *f*

incalculable *a* incalculable, innumerable; (of persons) voluble, veleidoso, caprichoso; infinito, inmenso

incalculably *adv* enormemente, infinitamente; caprichosamente

incandescence *n* incandescencia, candencia, *f*

incandescent *a* incandescente, candente. **i. light,** luz incandescente, *f*. **to make i.,** encandecer

incantation *n* hechizo, *m*, encantación, *f*, ensalmo, *m*

incapability *n* incapacidad, *f*; inhabilidad, ineptitud, incompetencia, *f*

incapable *a* incapaz; inhábil, incompetente; (physically) imposibilitado

incapacitate *vt* imposibilitar, incapacitar, inutilizar; (disqualify) inhabilitar, incapacitar

incapacitation *n* inhabilitación, *f*

incapacity *n* incapacidad, inhabilidad, *f*

incarcerate *vt* encarcelar

incarceration *n* encarcelación, prisión, *f*

incarnate *a* encarnado. *vt* encarnar

incarnation *n* encarnación, *f*

incautious *a* incauto, imprudente

incautiously *adv* incautamente

incautiousness *n* imprudencia, negligencia, falta de cautela, *f*

incendiary *a* incendiario. **i. bomb,** incendiaria, *f*

incense *n* incienso, *m*; (fig adulación, *f*. *vt* incensar; (annoy) irritar, exasperar, enojar. **i. burner,** incensario, *m*

incentive *n* incentivo, estímulo, motivo, *m*. *a* estimulador, incitativo

inception *n* comienzo, principio, *m*; inauguración, *f*

incertitude *n* incertidumbre, *f*

incessant *a* incesante, continuo, constante

incessantly *adv* incesantemente, sin cesar

incest *n* incesto, *m*

incestuous *a* incestuoso

inch *n* pulgada, *f*. **every i. a man,** hombre hecho y derecho. **Not an i.!** ¡Ni pizca! **within an i. of,** a dos dedos de. **i. by i.,** palmo a palmo, paso a paso. **i. tape,** cinta métrica, *f*

inchoate *a* rudimentario; imperfecto, incompleto

incidence *n* incidencia, *f*

incident *a* propio, característico, incidental. *n* incidente, acontecimiento, *m*, ocurrencia, *f*

incident of navigation *n* accidente de navegación, *m*

incidental *a* incidente, incidental; accidental, accesorio, no esencial. **i. expense,** gasto imprevisto, *m*

incidentally *adv* (secondarily) incidentalmente; (by the way) de propósito

incinerate *vt* incinerar

incineration *n* incineración, cremación, *f*

incinerator *n* incinerador, *m*

incipient *a* incipiente, naciente, rudimentario

incision *n* incisión, *f*; corte, tajo, *m*; *med* abscisión, *f*

incisive *a* (of mind) agudo, penetrante; (of words) mordaz, incisivo, punzante

incisively *adv* en pocas palabras; mordazmente, incisivamente

incisiveness *n* (of mind) agudeza, penetración, *f*; (of words) mordacidad, *f*, sarcasmo, *m*

incisor *n* diente incisivo, *m*

incite *vt* incitar, estimular, animar; provocar, tentar. **to i. to,** mover a, incitar a

incitement *n* incitación, instigación, *f*; estímulo, *m*; tentación, *f*; aliciente, *m*

incivility *n* incivilidad, descortesía, *f*

inclemency *n* inclemencia, *f*, rigor, *m*

inclement *a* inclemente, riguroso, borrascoso

inclination *n* inclinación, *f*; (slope) declive, *m*, pendiente, cuesta, *f*; (tendency) propensión, tendencia, *f*; (liking) afición, *f*; amor, *m*; (bow) reverencia, *f*; *geom* inclinación, *f*

incline *vt* inclinar, torcer; doblar; (cause) inclinar (a), hacer. *vi* inclinarse, torcerse; (tend) tender, propender, inclinarse; (colors) tirar (a). *n* declive, *m*, pendiente, cuesta, inclinación, *f*. **I am inclined to believe it,** Me inclino a creerlo. **I am inclined to do it,** Estoy por hacerlo, Creo que lo haré

inclined *a* torcido, inclinado, doblado; *fig* propenso, adicto. **i. plane,** plano inclinado, *m*

include *vt* incluir, contener, encerrar; comprender, abrazar

including *present part* incluso, inclusive. **not i.,** no comprendido

inclusion *n* inclusión, *f*

inclusive *a* inclusivo. **January 2 to January 12 i.,** del 2 al 12 de enero, ambos inclusivos. **not i. of,** sin contar, exclusivo de. **i. of,** que incluye. **i. terms,** todo incluido, todos los gastos incluidos

incognito *a* and *adv* and *n* incógnito, *m*.

incoherence *n* incoherencia, inconsecuencia, *f*

incoherent *a* incoherente, inconexo, inconsecuente. **an i. piece of writing,** un escrito sin pies ni cabeza

incoherently *adv* con incoherencia

incombustibility *n* incombustibilidad, *f*

incombustible *a* incombustible

income *n* renta, *f*, ingreso, *m*; *com* rédito, *m*. **i.-tax,** impuesto de utilidades, *m*. **i.-tax commissioners,** inspectores de impuestos de utilidades, *m pl*. **i.-tax return,** declaración de utilidades, *f*

incoming *a* entrante; nuevo. *n* entrada, llegada, *f*. *n pl* **incomings,** ingresos, *m pl*

incommensurability *n* inconmensurabilidad, *f*

incommensurable *a* inconmensurable, no conmensurable

incommensurate *a* desproporcionado, desmedido

incommode *vt* incomodar, molestar, fastidiar

incommodious *a* estrecho; incómodo, inconveniente

incommodiousness *n* estrechez, *f*; incomodidad, *f*

incommunicable *a* incommunicable, indecible, inexplicable

incommunicative *a* insociable, intratable, adusto, huraño

incomparable *a* incomparable; sin par, sin igual, excelente

incomparableness *n* excelencia, perfección, *f*

incomparably *adv* incomparablemente, con mucho

incompatibility *n* incompatibilidad, *f*

incompatible *a* incompatible

incompetence *n* incompetencia, ineptitud, inhabilidad, *f*; *law* incapacidad, *f*

incompetent *a* incompetente, incapaz, inepto, inhábil; *law* incapaz

incompetently *adv* inhábilmente

incomplete *a* incompleto; imperfecto, defectuoso; (unfinished) sin terminar, inacabado, inconcluso. **incomplete sentence,** frase que queda colgando, *f*

incompletely *adv* incompletamente; imperfectamente

incompleteness *n* estado incompleto, *m*; imperfección, *f*; inconclusión, *f*

incomprehensibility *n* incomprensibilidad, *f*

incomprehensible *a* incomprensible

incomprehension *n* incomprensión, falta de comprensión, *f*

inconceivable *a* inconcebible, inimaginable

inconclusive *a* inconcluyente, cuestionable, dudoso, no convincente

inconclusiveness *n* carácter inconcluso, *m*, falta de conclusiones, *f*

incongruity *n* incongruencia, desproporción, disonancia, *f*

incongruous *a* incongruente, incongruo; chocante, desproporcionado, disonante

incongruously *adv* incongruentemente, incongruamente

inconsequence *n* inconsecuencia, *f*

inconsequent, inconsequential *a* inconsecuente, ilógico; inconsistente

inconsiderable *a* insignificante

inconsiderate *a* desconsiderado, irreflexivo, irrespetuoso

inconsiderately *adv* sin consideración, desconsideradamente

inconsiderateness *n* desconsideración, falta de respeto, *f*

inconsistency *n* inconsistencia, inconsecuencia, incompatibilidad, contradicción, anomalía, *f*

inconsistent *a* inconsistente, inconsiguiente, incompatible, contradictorio, anómalo

inconsistently *adv* contradictoriamente

inconsolable *a* inconsolable, desconsolado. **to be i.,** estar inconsolable, (*inf* of a woman) estar hecha una Magdalena

inconsolably *adv* desconsoladamente

inconspicuous *a* que no llama la atención; insignificante, humilde, modesto

inconspicuously *adv* humildemente, modestamente

inconspicuousness *n* modestia, humildad, *f*

inconstancy *n* inconstancia, movilidad, *f*; mudanza, veleidad, *f*

inconstant *a* inconstante, mudable, variable; veleidoso, volátil, voluble

incontestable *a* incontestable, evidente, indisputable

incontinence *n* incontinencia, *f*

incontinent *a* incontinente

incontrollable *a* ingobernable, indomable

incontrovertible *a* incontrovertible, incontrastable

inconvenience *n* incomodidad, inconveniencia, *f*; (of time) inoportunidad, *f*. *vt* incomodar, causar inconvenientes (a)

inconvenient *a* incómodo, inconveniente, molesto, embarazoso; (of time) inoportuno. **at an i. time,** a deshora

inconveniently *adv* incómodamente; (of time) inoportunamente

incorporate *vt* incorporar, agregar; comprender, incluir, encerrar. *vi* asociarse, incorporarse. *a* incorpóreo, inmaterial; incorporado, asociado

incorporation *n* incorporación, agregación, *f*; asociación, *f*

incorporeal *a* incorpóreo, inmaterial

incorporeity *n* incorporeidad, inmaterialidad, *f*

incorrect *a* incorrecto; inexacto, erróneo, falso

incorrectness *n* incorrección, *f*

incorrigibility *n* incorregibilidad, *f*

incorrigible *a* incorregible, empecatado

incorrigibly *adv* incorregiblemente, obstinadamente

incorrupt *a* incorrupto; recto, honrado

incorruptibility *n* incorruptibilidad, *f*; honradez, probidad, *f*

incorruptible *a* incorrupto; honrado, incorruptible

incorruption *n* incorrupción, *f*

increase *vt* aumentar, acrecentar; (in numbers) multiplicar; (extend) ampliar, extender; (of price) encarecer, aumentar. *vi* aumentar, crecer; multiplicarse; extenderse; encarecerse, aumentar. *n* aumento, crecimiento, *m*; multiplicación, *f*; (in price) encarecimiento, *m*, alza, *f*; (of water) crecida, *f*; (of moon) creciente, *f*. **It is on the i.,** Va en aumento. **to i. and multiply,** crecer y multiplicar

increasingly *adv* más y más; en creciente, en aumento

incredibility *n* incredibilidad, *f*
incredible *a* increíble; fabuloso, extraordinario. **It seems i.,** Es increíble, *inf* Parece mentira
incredibly *adv* increíblemente
incredulity *n* incredulidad, *f,* escepticismo, *m*
incredulous *a* incrédulo, escéptico
incredulously *adv* con incredulidad, escépticamente
increment *n* aumento, incremento, *m;* adición, añadidura, *f; math* incremento, *m.* **unearned i.,** plusvalía, mayor valía, *f*
incriminate *vt* incriminar
incriminating *a* incriminante, acriminador
incrust *vt* incrustar, encostrar
incrustation *n* incrustación, *f;* (scab) costra, *f*
incubate *vt* empollar; *med* incubar
incubation *n* empolladura, incubación, *f; med* incubación, *f*
incubator *n* incubadora, *f*
incubus *n* íncubo, *m;* (burden) carga, *f*
inculcate *vt* inculcar, implantar, instilar
inculcation *n* inculcación, implantación, instilación, *f*
incumbency *n* posesión, duración de, posesión, duración (de cualquier puesto), *f*
incumbent *a* obligatorio. *n ecc* beneficiado, *m.* **to be i. on,** incumbir a, ser de su obligación
incur *vi* incurrir (en), incidir (en). **to i. an obligation,** contraer una obligación
incurability *n* incurabilidad, *f*
incurable *a* incurable, insanable; *fig* sin solución, irremediable. *n* incurable, *mf*
incurably *adv* incurablemente, irremediablemente
incurious *a* indiferente, sin interés; incurioso, negligente, descuidado
incursion *n* incursión, invasión, irrupción, *f,* acometimiento, *m*
indebted *a* empeñado, adeudado; (obliged) reconocido
indebtedness *n* deuda, *f;* (gratitude) obligación, *f;* agradecimiento, *m*
indecency *n* indecencia, *f*
indecent *a* indecente; obsceno, deshonesto
indecently *adv* torpemente, indecentemente
indecision *n* incertidumbre, vacilación, irresolución, *f*
indecisive *a* indeciso, irresoluto, vacilante
indeclinable *a* indeclinable
indecorous *a* indecoroso, indecente, indigno
indecorum *n* indecoro, *m,* indecencia, *f;* incorrección, *f*
indeed *adv* en efecto, de veras, a la verdad, realmente, por cierto, claro está. *interr* ¿de veras? ¿es posible? **I shall be very glad i.,** Estaré contento de veras. **It is i. an excellent book,** Es en efecto un libro excelente. **There are differences i. between this house and the other,** Hay diferencias, claro está, entre esta casa y la otra
indefatigability *n* resistencia, *f,* aguante, *m,* tenacidad, *f*
indefatigable *a* incansable, infatigable, resistente
indefatigably *adv* infatigablemente
indefensible *a* indefendible, insostenible
indefinable *a* indefinible
indefinite *a* indefinido, incierto; (delicate) sutil, delicado; *gram* indefinido; (vague) vago. *gram* **i. article,** artículo indefinido, *m*
indefinitely *adv* indefinidamente
indefiniteness *n* lo indefinido, el carácter indefinido, *m;* vaguedad, *f*
indelibility *n* resistencia, *f,* lo indeleble; *fig* duración, tenacidad, *f*
indelible *a* indeleble, imborrable; *fig* inolvidable
indelibly *adv* indeleblemente
indelicacy *n* falta de buen gusto, grosería, *f;* (tactlessness) indiscreción, falta de tacto, *f*
indelicate *a* grosero, descortés; indecoroso, inmodesto; (tactless) inoportuno, indiscreto
indemnification *n* indemnización, compensación, *f*
indemnify *vt* indemnizar, compensar
indemnity *n* indemnización, reparación, *f*

indent *vt* endentar, mellar; *print* sangrar
indentation *n* impresión, depresión, *f;* corte, *m,* mella, *f;* línea quebrada, *f,* zigzag, *m*
indenture *n* escritura, *f,* instrumento, *m. vt* escriturar
independence *n* independencia, libertad, *f;* (autonomy) autonomía, *f.* **I. Day,** Fiesta de la Independencia, *f.* **i. movement,** movimiento en favor de la independencia, *m*
independent *a* independiente; libre; (autonomous) autónomo; **i. of,** libre de; aparte de. **a person of i. means,** una persona acomodada
independently *adv* independientemente
indescribability *n* imposibilidad de describir, *f,* lo indescriptible
indescribable *a* indescriptible; indefinible, indecible, inexplicable; incalificable
indestructibility *n* indestructibilidad, *f*
indestructible *a* indestructible
indeterminable *a* indeterminable
indeterminate *a* indeterminado, indefinido, vago; *math* indeterminado
indetermination *n* irresolución, indecisión, duda, vacilación, *f*
index *n* (forefinger) dedo índice, *m;* (of book) tabla de materias, *f,* índice, *m;* (on instruments) manecilla, aguja, *f; math* índice, *m;* (sign) señal, indicación, *f. vt* poner índice (a); poner en el índice. **i. card,** ficha, *f.* **I. expurgatorius,** Índice expurgatorio, *m*
India *n* la India, *f.* **I. paper,** papel de China, *m.* **i.-rubber,** *bot* caucho, *m;* (eraser) goma de borrar, *f.* **i.-rubber tree,** yacio, *m*
Indian *a* and *n* indio (-ia). **I. chief,** cacique, *m.* **I. club,** maza, *f.* **I. corn,** maíz, *m.* **I. ink,** tinta china, *f.* **I. summer,** veranillo, veranillo de San Martín, *m*
Indian Ocean, the el Océano Índico, *m*
indicate *vt* indicar, señalar; (show) denotar, mostrar, anunciar
indication *n* indicación, *f;* señal, *f,* indicio, síntoma, *m;* prueba, *f*
indicative *a* indicador, indicativo, demostrativo; *gram* indicativo. *n gram* indicativo, *m.* **to be i. of,** indicar, señalar
indicator *n* indicador, señalador, *m*
indict *vt* acusar; *law* demandar, enjuiciar
indictable *a* procesable, denunciable, enjuiciable
indictment *n* acusación, *f; law* procesamiento, *m*
indifference *n* indiferencia, apatía, *f,* desinterés, desapego, *m;* imparcialidad, neutralidad, *f;* (coldness) frialdad, tibieza, *f*
indifferent *a* indiferente, apático; imparcial, neutral; frío; (ordinary) regular, ordinario, ni bien ni mal
indifferently *adv* con indiferencia; imparcialmente; friamente
indigence *n* indigencia, necesidad, penuria, *f*
indigenous *a* indígena, nativo, natural
indigent *a* indigente, necesitado, menesteroso
indigestible *a* indigesto
indigestion *n* indigestión, *f, Mexico* insulto *m; fig* empacho, ahíto, *m*
indignant *a* indignado. **to make i.,** indignar
indignantly *adv* con indignación
indignation *n* indignación, cólera, *f*
indignity *n* indignidad, *f;* ultraje, *m*
indigo *n* añil, índigo, *m*
indirect *a* indirecto; oblicuo; tortuoso; *gram* **i. case,** caso oblicuo, *m*
indirectness *n* (of route) rodeo, *m,* desviación, *f;* oblicuidad, *f;* (falsity) tortuosidad, *f*
indiscernible *a* imperceptible
indiscipline *n* indisciplina, falta de disciplina, *f*
indiscreet *a* indiscreto, imprudente, impolítico
indiscretion *n* indiscreción, imprudencia, *f;* (slip) desliz, *m*
indiscriminate *a* general, universal; indistinto, promiscuo
indiscriminately *adv* promiscuamente

indiscrimination *n* universalidad, indistinción, *f*

indispensability *n* indispensabilidad, precisión, necesidad, *f*

indispensable *a* imprescindible, indispensable, insustituible

indispensably *adv* forzosamente, indispensablemente

indispose *vt* indisponer. **to be indisposed,** estar indispuesto, indisponerse

indisposed *a* indispuesto, enfermo, destemplado; (reluctant) maldispuesto

indisposition *n* indisposición, enfermedad, *f*

indisputability *n* verdad manifiesta, certeza, evidencia, *f*

indisputable *a* innegable, incontestable; irrefutable, evidente

indisputably *adv* indisputablemente

indissolubility *n* indisolubilidad, *f*

indissoluble *a* indisoluble

indistinct *a* indistinto; indeterminado, confuso, vago

indistinctly *adv* indistintamente; confusamente, vagamente

indistinctness *n* incertidumbre, vaguedad, indistinción, indeterminación, *f*

indistinguishable *a* indistinguible

individual *a* (single) solo, único; individual, individuo, particular, propio; personal. *n* individuo, *m*, particular, *mf*

individualism *n* individualismo, *m*

individualist *n* individualist, *mf*

individualistic *a* individualista

individuality *n* individualidad, personalidad, *f*; carácter, *m*, naturaleza, *f*

individualize *vt* particularizar, individuar

individually *adv* individualmente, particularmente

indivisibility *n* indivisibilidad, *f*

indivisible *a* incompartible, impartible, indivisible

indivisibly *adv* indivisiblemente

Indo (in compounds) indo. **I.-Chinese,** *a* and *n* indochino (-na). **I.-European,** indoeuropeo. **I.-Germanic,** indogermánico

indocile *a* indócil, desobediente, rebelde

indocility *n* indocilidad, desobediencia, falta de docilidad, *f*

indolence *n* indolencia, pereza, desidia, *f*

indolent *a* indolente, perezoso, holgazán; *med* indoloro

indolently *adv* perezosamente

indomitable *a* indomable, indómito

indoor *a* de casa; de puertas adentro, interno. **i. swimming pool,** piscina bajo techo, *f.* **i. tennis,** tenis en pistas cubiertas, tenis bajo techo, *m*

indoors *adv* en casa; adentro, bajo techo

indorsee *n* endosatario (-ia)

indubitable *a* indudable

indubitably *adv* indudablemente, sin duda

induce *vt* inducir, mover; instigar, incitar; producir, ocasionar; *elec* inducir. **Nothing would i. me to do it,** Nada me induciría a hacerlo

inducement *n* incitamiento, *m*; estímulo, *m*; aliciente, atractivo, *m*; tentación, *f*

induct *vt* instalar; introducir, iniciar

induction *n* instalación, *f*; iniciación, introducción, *f*; *phys* inducción, *f.* **i. coil,** carrete de inducción, *m*

inductive *a* (of reasoning) inductivo; *phys* inductor

indulge *vt* (children) consentir, mimar; (a desire) satisfacer, dar rienda suelta a; (with a gift) agasajar (con), dar gusto (con). **to i. in,** *vt* consentir en. *vi* entregarse a, permitirse, gustar de

indulgence *n* (of children) mimo, cariño excesivo, *m*; (of a desire) propensión (a), afición (a), *f*; (toward others) tolerancia, transigencia, *f*; *ecc* indulgencia, *f*

indulgent *a* indulgente; tolerante, transigente

indult *n ecc* indulto, *m*

industrial *a* industrial. **i. alcohol,** alcohol desnaturalizado, *m.* **i. school,** escuela de artes y oficios, *f, com* **i. shares,** valores industriales, *m pl*

industrialism *n* industrialismo, *m*

industrialist *n* industrial, *m*

industrialization *n* industrialización, *f*

industrialize *vt* industrializar

industrious *a* industrioso, aplicado, diligente

industriously *adv* industriosamente, diligentemente

industriousness *n* industria, laboriosidad, *f*

industry *n* diligencia, aplicación, *f*; (work) trabajo, *m*, labor, *f*; *com* industria, *f*

inebriate *a* borracho, ebrio. *n* borracho (-cha). *vt* embriagar, emborrachar

inebriation *n* embriaguez, borrachera, *f*

inedible *a* incomible, no comestible

inedited *a* inédito

ineffable *a* indecible, inefable

ineffaceable *a* imborrable, indeleble

ineffective *a* ineficaz; vano, fútil. **to be i.,** (of persons) no pinchar ni cortar. **to prove i.,** quedar sin efecto; no tener influencia

ineffectiveness *n* ineficacia, *f*; futilidad, *f*

inefficiency *n* ineficacia, incompetencia, ineptitud, *f*

inefficient *a* ineficaz, incapaz

inefficiently *adv* ineficazmente

inelastic *a* inelástico

inelegance *n* inelegancia, fealdad, vulgaridad, *f*

inelegant *a* inelegante, ordinario, de mal gusto

inelegantly *adv* sin elegancia

ineligibility *n* inelegibilidad, *f*

ineligible *a* inelegible

inept *a* inepto, inoportuno; absurdo, ridículo; (of persons) incompetente, ineficaz

ineptitude *n* ineptitud, *f*; necedad, *f*; (of persons) incapacidad, incompetencia, *f*

ineptly *adv* ineptamente, neciamente

inequality *n* desigualdad, desemejanza, disparidad, *f*; (of surface) escabrosidad, aspereza, *f*; *fig* injusticia, *f*; (of opportunity) diferencia, *f*

inequitable *a* desigual, injusto

inequity *n* injusticia, desigualdad, *f*

ineradicable *a* indeleble, imborrable

ineradicably *adv* indeleblemente

inert *a* inerte, inactivo, pasivo; ocioso, flojo, perezoso

inertia *n* inercia, inacción, *f*; abulia, pereza, *f*; *phys* inercia, *f*

inertly *adv* indolentemente, sin mover, pasivamente

inescapable *a* ineludible, inevitable

inessential *a* no esencial

inestimable *a* inestimable

inevitability *n* fatalidad, necesidad, *f*; lo inevitable

inevitable *a* inevitable, necesario, fatal, forzoso, ineludible

inevitably *adv* inevitablemente, necesariamente, forzosamente

inexact *a* inexacto, incorrecto

inexactitude *n* inexactitud, *f*

inexcusable *a* imperdonable, inexcusable, irremisible

inexcusableness *n* enormidad, *f*; lo inexcusable

inexcusably *adv* inexcusablemente

inexhaustible *a* inagotable, inexhausto

inexorability *n* inflexibilidad, inexorabilidad, *f*

inexorable *a* inexorable, inflexible, duro

inexorably *adv* inexorablemente, implacablemente

inexpediency *n* inoportunidad, inconveniencia, imprudencia, *f*

inexpedient *a* inoportuno; inconveniente; impolítico, imprudente. **to deem i.,** creer inoportuno

inexpensive *a* poco costoso, barato

inexpensiveness *n* baratura, *f*, bajo precio, *m*

inexperience *n* inexperiencia, falta de experiencia, *f*

inexperienced *a* inexperto, novato

inexpert *a* inexperto, imperito

inexpertly *adv* sin habilidad

inexpertness *n* impericia, torpeza, *f*

inexpiable *a* inexpiable

inexplicable *a* inexplicable

inexplicit *a* no explícito

inexplosive *a* inexplosible

inexpressible *a* inexplicable, indecible, inefable

inexpressive *a* inexpresivo; (of persons) reservado, callado, poco expresivo, retraído

inexpressiveness *n* falta de expresión, *f*; (of persons) reserva, *f*, silencio, retraimiento, *m*

inexpugnable *a* inexpugnable

inextinguishable *a* inapagable, inextinguible

inextricable *a* inextricable, intrincado, enmarañado

inextricably *adv* intrincadamente

infallibility *n* infalibilidad, *f*

infallible *a* infalible

infamous *a* infame, torpe, vil, ignominioso; odioso, repugnante

infamously *adv* infamemente

infamy *n* infamia, torpeza, vileza, ignominia, *f*; deshonra, *f*

infancy *n* infancia, niñez, *f*; *law* minoridad, *f*

infant *n* criatura, *f*; crío (-ía), niño (-ña); *law* menor, *mf* **i. school,** escuela de párvulos, *f*

infanticidal *a* infanticida

infanticide *n* (act) infanticidio, *m*; (person) infanticida, *mf*

infantile *a* infantil. **i. paralysis,** parálisis infantil, *f*

infantry *n mil* infantería, *f*

infantryman *n mil* infante, peón, *m*

infatuate *vt* infatuar, embobar

infatuation *n* infatuación, *f*, encaprichamiento, *m*

infect *vt* infectar, contagiar; *fig* pegar, influir; (*fig* in a bad sense) corromper, pervertir, inficionar. **to become infected,** infectarse

infected *a* infecto

infection *n* infección, *f*, contagio, *m*; *fig* influencia, *f*; (*fig* in a bad sense) corrupción, perversión, *f*

infectious *a* infeccioso, contagioso; (*fig* in a bad sense) corruptor; *fig* contagioso

infectiousness *n* contagiosidad, *f*

infelicitous *a* poco apropiado, desacertado

infelicity *n* infelicidad, desdicha, *f*, infortunio, *m*; desacierto, *m*, inoportunidad, *f*

infer *vt* inferir, concluir, educir, deducir, implicar

inferable *a* deducible, demostrable

inference *n* inferencia, deducción, conclusión, *f*

inferential *a* ilativo, deductivo

inferior *a* inferior; (in rank) subordinado, subalterno; (of position) secundario. *n* inferior, *mf* subordinado (-da). **to be not i.,** no ser inferior, *inf* no quedarse en zaga

inferiority *n* inferioridad, *f*. **i. complex,** complejo de inferioridad, *m*

infernal *a* infernal; *poet* inferno, tartáreo

infernally *adv* infernalmente

inferno *n* infierno, *m*

infertile *a* inértil, infecundo, estéril

infertility *n* infertilidad, infecundidad, esterilidad, *f*

infest *vt* infestar. **to be infested with,** plagarse de

infestation *n* infestación, *f*

infidel *n* infiel, gentil, *mf* pagano (-na); (atheist) descreído (-da), ateo (-ea). *a* pagano; infiel, descreído, ateo

infidelity *n* infidelidad, alevosía, perfidia, *f*

infiltrate *vt* infiltrar. *vi* infiltrarse

infiltration *n* infiltración, *f*

infinite *a* infinito, ilimitado; inmenso, enorme; (of number) innumerable, infinito. *n* infinito, *m*

infinitely *adv* infinitamente

infinitesimal *a* infinitesimal. **i. calculus,** cálculo infinitesimal, *m*

infinitive *a* and *n gram* infinitivo, *m*.

infinitude, infinity *n* infinidad, infinitud, *f*; (extent) inmensidad, *f*; (of number) sinfín, *m*; *math* infinito, *m*

infirm *a* achacoso, enfermizo, enclenque; (shaky) inestable, inseguro; (of purpose) irresoluto, vacilante

infirmary *n* enfermería, *f*, hospital, *m*

infirmity *n* achaque, *m*, enfermedad, dolencia, *f*; (fault) flaqueza, falta, *f*

inflame *vt* encender; (excite) acalorar, irritar, provocar; *med* inflamar. *vi* encenderse, arder; acalorarse, irritarse; *med* inflamarse

inflammability *n* inflamabilidad, *f*

inflammable *a* inflamable

inflammation *n* inflamación, *f*

inflammatory *a* inflamador; *med* inflamatorio

inflate *vt* inflar, hinchar; (with pride) engreír, ensoberbecer

inflation *n* inflación, hinchazón, *f*; *com* inflación, *f*

inflationism *n* inflacionismo, *m*

inflator *n mech* bomba para inflar, *f*

inflect *vt* torcer; (voice) modular; *gram* conjugar, declinar

inflection *n* dobladura, *f*; (of voice) tono, acento, *m*, modulación, *f*; *gram* conjugación, declinación, *f*

inflexibility *n* inflexibilidad, dureza, rigidez, *f*

inflexible *a* inflexible, rígido; *fig* inexorable, inalterable

inflexibly *adv* inflexiblemente

inflict *vt* infligir, imponer

infliction *n* imposición, *f*; castigo, *m*

inflorescence *n bot* inflorescencia, *f*

inflow *n* afluencia, *f*, flujo, *m*

influence *n* influencia, *f*, influjo, *m*; ascendiente, *m*; (importance) influencia, importancia, *f*. *vt* influir, afectar; persuadir, inducir. **to have i. over,** (a person) tener ascendiente sobre. *law* **undue i.,** influencia indebida, *f*

influential *a* influyente; (of person) prestigioso, importante

influenza *n med* gripe, *f*, trancazo, *m*

influx *n* influjo, *m*; (of rivers) desembocadura, afluencia, *f*

inform *vt* (fill) infundir, llenar; (tell) informar, enterar, advertir; instruir; (with about) poner al corriente de, participar. *vi* (with against) delatar (a), denunciar. **to i. oneself,** informarse, enterarse. **to be informed about,** estar al corriente de

informal *a* irregular; sin ceremonia, de confianza; (meeting) no oficial, extraoficial

informality *n* irregularidad, *f*; falta de ceremonia, sencillez, *f*; intimidad, *f*

informally *adv* sin ceremonia

informant *n* informante, *mf*; informador (-ra)

information *n* información, instrucción, *f*; noticia, *f*, aviso, *m*; *law* denuncia, delación, *f*. **piece of i.,** información, *f*. **i. bureau,** oficina de información, *f*

informative *a* informativo

informer *n* delator (-ra), denunciador (-ra)

infrared *a phys* infrarrojo, ultrarrojo

infraction *n* contravención, infracción, transgresión, *f*

infrequency *n* infrecuencia, rareza, irregularidad, *f*

infrequent *a* infrecuente, raro, irregular

infrequently *adv* rara vez, infrecuentemente

infringe *vt* infringir, violar, contravenir, quebrantar

infringement *n* contravención, violación, infracción, *f*

infringer *n* infractor (-ra), contraventor (-ra), violador (-ra), transgresor (-ra)

infuriate *vt* enfurecer, enloquecer, enojar. **to be infuriated,** estar furioso

infuse *vt* vaciar, infiltrar; *fig* infundir, inculcar, instilar

infusible *a* infundible

infusion *n* infusión, *f*; *fig* instilación, inculcación, *f*

ingathering *n* cosecha, recolección, *f*

ingenious *a* ingenioso; mañoso, hábil

ingeniously *adv* ingeniosamente, hábilmente

ingenuity *n* ingeniosidad, inventiva, listeza, habilidad, *f*

ingenuous *a* ingenuo, franco, sincero, cándido, sencillo, inocente

ingenuousness *n* ingenuidad, franqueza, sinceridad, *f*; candor, *m*

ingest *vt* ingerir

ingestion *n* ingestión, *f*

inglorious *a* vergonzoso, ignominioso, deshonroso; desconocido, obscuro

ingloriously *adv* vergonzosamente, ignominiosamente; obscuramente

ingloriousness *n* deshonra, ignominia, *f*; obscuridad, *f*
ingoing *a* entrante, que entra. *n* ingreso, *m*, entrada, *f*; *com* **i. and outgoing,** entradas y salidas, *f pl*
ingot *n* pepita, *f*, lingote, *m*; (of any metal) barra, *f*
ingrained *a* innato, natural
ingratiate *vt* (oneself with) congraciarse con, captarse la buena voluntad de, insinuarse en el favor de
ingratiating *a* obsequioso
ingratitude *n* ingratitud, *f*, desagradecimiento, *m*
ingredient *n* ingrediente, *m*
ingress *n* ingreso, *m*; derecho de entrada, *m*
ingrowing *a* que crece hacia adentro. **i. nail,** uñero, *m*
inhabit *vt* habitar, ocupar, vivir en, residir en
inhabitable *a* habitable, vividero
inhabitant *n* habitante, residente, *m*; vecino (-na)
inhabited *a* habitado, poblado
inhalation *n* inspiración, *f*; *med* inhalación, *f*
inhale *vt* aspirar; *med* inhalar
inharmonious *a* *mus* disonante, inarmónico; desavenido, discorde, desconforme. **to be i.,** disonar; (of people) llevarse mal
inhere *vi* ser inherente; pertenecer (a), residir (en)
inherence *n* inherencia, *f*
inherent *a* inherente; innato, intrínseco, natural
inherently *adv* intrínsecamente
inherit *vt* heredar
inheritance *n* herencia, *f*; patrimonio, abolengo, *m*
inheritor *n* heredero, *m*
inhibit *vt* inhibir, impedir; *ecc* prohibir. **be inhibited, became inhibited,** cohibirse
inhibition *n* inhibición, *f*
inhibitory *a* inhibitorio
inhospitable *a* inhospitalario
inhospitably *adv* desabridamente
inhuman *a* inhumano; cruel, bárbaro
inhumanity *n* inhumanidad, crueldad, *f*
inhumanly *adv* inhumanamente, cruelmente
inhume *vt* inhumar, sepultar
inimical *a* enemigo, hostil, opuesto, contrario
inimically *adv* hostilmente
inimitable *a* inimitable
inimitably *adv* inimitablemente
iniquitous *a* inicuo, malvado, perverso, nefando; *inf* diabólico
iniquity *n* iniquidad, maldad, injusticia, *f*
initial *a* inicial. *n* inicial, letra inicial, *f*. *vt* firmar con las iniciales
initially *adv* al principio, en primer lugar
initiate *a* iniciado. *vt* iniciar, poner en pie, empezar, entablar; (a person) admitir
initiation *n* principio, *m*; (of a person) iniciación, admisión, *f*
initiative *n* iniciativa, *f*. **to take the i.,** tomar la iniciativa
initiator *n* iniciador (-ra)
inject *vt* inyectar
injection *n* inyección, *f*. **i. syringe,** jeringa de inyecciones, *f*
injudicious *a* imprudente, indiscreto
injudiciously *adv* imprudentemente
injudiciousness *n* imprudencia, indiscreción, *f*
injunction *n* precepto, mandato, *m*; *law* embargo, *m*
injure *vt* perjudicar, dañar, *Lat. Am.* afectar; menoscabar, deteriorar; (hurt) lastimar, lisiar. **to i. oneself,** hacerse daño
injured *a* (physically) lisiado; (morally) ofendido
injurer *n* perjudicador (-ra)
injurious *a* dañoso, perjudicial, malo; ofensivo, injurioso
injuriously *adv* perjudicialmente
injury *n* perjuicio, daño, *m*; (physical) lesión, *Lat. Am. also* lastimadura *f*; (insult) agravio, insulto, *m*
injustice *n* injusticia, desigualdad, *f*. **You do him an i.,** Le juzgas mal
ink *n* tinta, *f*. *vt* entintar. **copying-ink,** tinta de copiar,

f. **marking-ink,** tinta indeleble, *f.* **printer's ink,** tinta de imprenta, *f.* **ink-stand** or **ink-well,** tintero, *m*
inker *n* print rodillo, *m*
inkling *n* sospecha, noción, *f*
inky *a* manchado de tinta. **i. black,** negro como el betún
inland *n* el interior de un país, *a* interior, mediterráneo; del país, regional. *adv* tierra adentro. **to go i.,** internarse en un país. **I. Revenue,** delegación de contribuciones, *f*. **i. town,** ciudad del interior, *f*
inlay *vt* taracear, ataracear, embutir; incrustar. *n* taracea, *f*, embutido, *m*
inlet *n* entrada, admisión, *f*; *geog* ensenada, *f*. **i. valve,** válvula de admisión, *f*
inmate *n* residente, habitante, *m*; (of hospital) paciente, *mf*; enfermo (-ma); (of prison) prisionero
inmost. See **innermost**
inn *n* posada, fonda, venta, *f*, mesón, *m*. **Inns of Court,** Colegio de Abogados, *m*
innate *a* innato, inherente, instintivo, nativo
innately *adv* naturalmente, instintivamente
innavigable *a* innavegable
inner *a* interior, interno. **i. tube** *aut* cámara de neumatico, cámara de aire, *f*
innermost *a* más adentro; *fig* más íntimo, más hondo
innings *n* (sport) turno, *m*
innkeeper *n* fondista, *mf*; tabernero (-ra), mesonero (-ra), posadero (-ra)
innocence *n* inocencia, *f*; pureza, *f*; (guilelessness) simplicidad, *f*, candor, *m*
innocent *a* inocente, puro; (guiltless) inocente, inculpable; (foolish) simple, tonto, candoroso, inocentón; (harmless) innocuo. *n* inocente, *mf* **Holy Innocents,** Santos Inocentes, *m pl*
innoculator *n* inoculador, *m*
innocuous *a* innocuo, inofensivo
innocuousness *n* inocuidad, *f*
innovate *vt* innovar
innovation *n* innovación, *f*
innovator *n* innovador (-ra)
innuendo *n* indirecta, insinuación, *f*
innumerable *a* innumerable, incalculable. **i. things,** un sinfín de cosas
inobservance *n* inobservancia, *f*, incumplimiento, *m*
inoculate *vt* inocular
inoculation *n* inoculación, *f*
inodorous *a* inodoro
inoffensive *a* inofensivo, innocuo; (of people) pacífico, apacible, manso
inoffensively *adv* inofensivamente
inoffensiveness *n* inocuidad, *f*; (of people) mansedumbre, *f*
inoperable *a* inoperable
inoperative *a* ineficaz, impracticable, inútil
inopportune *a* inoportuno, intempestivo, inconveniente
inopportunely *adv* inoportunamente, a destiempo
inopportuneness *n* inoportunidad, inconveniencia, *f*
inordinate *a* desordenado, excesivo
inordinately *adv* desmedidamente
inorganic *a* inorgánico
inoxidizable *a* inoxidable
input *n* capacidad instalada, *f*, insumo, *m*
inquest *n* law indagación, investigación, *f*
inquietude *n* inquietud, *f*, desasosiego, *m*, agitación, preocupación, *f*
inquire *vt* and *vi* preguntar, averiguar, indagar. **to i. about,** (persons) preguntar por; (things) hacer preguntas sobre. **to i. into,** investigar, examinar, averiguar. **to i. of,** preguntar a. **"I. within,"** «Se dan informaciones»
inquirer *n* indagador (-ra), inquiridor (-ra)
inquiring *a* indagador, inquiridor
inquiringly *adv* interrogativamente
inquiry *n* interrogación, pregunta, *f*; indagación, pes-

quisa, investigación, f; examen, m. **i. office,** oficina de informaciones, f. **on i.,** al preguntar

inquisition n investigación, indagación, f; inquisición, f. **Holy I.,** Santo Oficio, m, Inquisición, f

inquisitive a curioso, inquiridor; preguntador, impertinente, mirón

inquisitively adv con curiosidad, impertinentemente

inquisitiveness n curiosidad, f; impertinencia, f

Inquisitor n ecc inquisidor, m

inquisitorial a inquisitorial, inquisidor

inroad n incursión, f

insalubrious a malsano, insalubre

insane a loco, demente, insano; (senseless) insensato, ridículo. **to become i.,** enloquecer, volverse loco, perder la razón. **to drive i.,** volver a uno el juicio, enloquecer, trastornar. **i. person,** demente, mf, loco (-ca)

insanely adv locamente

insanitary a antihigiénico, malsano

insanity n demencia, locura, f; enloquecimiento, m; (folly) insensatez, ridiculez, f

insatiability n insaciabilidad, f

insatiable a insaciable

insatiably adv insaciablemente

inscribe vt inscribir

inscription n inscripción, f; letrero, m; (of a book) dedicatoria, f; com inscripción, anotación, f, asiento, m

inscrutability n enigma, misterio, m; incomprensibilidad, f

inscrutable a enigmático, insondable, incomprensible, inescrutable

inscrutably adv incomprensiblemente, enigmáticamente

insect n insecto, m. **insects** Lat. Am. bicherío m. **i. powder,** polvos insecticidas, m pl

insecticide a and n insecticida m.

insecure a inseguro, precario

insecurely adv inseguramente

insecurity n inseguridad, f; incertidumbre, inestabilidad, f

inseminate vt fig implantar; med fecundar

insemination n fig implantación, f; med fecundación, f

insensate a (unfeeling) insensible, insensitivo; (stupid) insensato, sin sentido, necio

insensibility n insensibilidad, inconsciencia, f; (stupor) sopor, letargo, m; impasibilidad, indiferencia, f

insensible a insensible, inconsciente; indiferente, impasible, duro de corazón; (scarcely noticeable) imperceptible. **to make i.,** (to sensations) hacer indiferente (a); insensibilizar

insensibly adv insensiblemente, imperceptiblemente

insensitive a insensible, insensitivo; (person) hecho un tronco, hecho un leño

insensitiveness n insensibilidad, f

insentient a insensible

inseparability n inseparabilidad, f

inseparable a inseparable

insert vt insertar, intercalar; (introduce) meter dentro, introducir, encajar; (in a newspaper) publicar

insertion n inserción, intercalación, f; (introduction) introducción, f; metimiento, encaje, m; sew entredós, m; (in a newspaper) publicación, f

inshore a cercano a la orilla. adv cerca de la orilla. **i. fishing,** pesca de arrastre, f

inside a interior, interno. adv adentro, dentro. n interior, m; (contents) contenido, m; (lining) forro, m; (inf stomach) entrañas, f pl. **to turn i. out,** volver al revés. **to walk on the i. of the pavement,** andar a la derecha de la acera. **from the i.,** desde el interior; por dentro. **on the i.,** por dentro, en el interior. **i. information,** información confidencial, f. **i. out,** al revés, de dentro afuera

insidious a insidioso, enganoso, traidor

insidiously adv insidiosamente

insidiousness n insidia, f; engaño, m, traición, f

insight n percepción, perspicacia, intuición, f, atisbo, m

insignia n pl insignias, f pl

insignificance n insignificancia, futilidad, pequeñez, f

insignificant a insignificante; fútil, trivial

insincere a insincero, hipócrita, falso

insincerely adv falsamente, hipócritamente

insincerity n insinceridad, hipocresía, falsedad, falta de sinceridad, doblez, f

insinuate vt insinuar, introducir; (hint) soltar una indirecta, sugerir; (oneself) insinuarse, introducirse con habilidad

insinuation n insinuación, introducción, f; (hint) indirecta, f

insipid a insípido, insulso; (dull) soso

insipidity n insipidez, insulsez, f, desabor, m; (dullness) sosería, f

insist vi insistir; persistir, obstinarse. **to i. on,** insistir en; obstinarse en, hacer hincapié en, aferrarse en (or a)

insistence n insistencia, f; obstinación, pertinacia, f

insistent a insistente; porfiado, obstinaz

insistently adv con insistencia; porfiadamente

insobriety n falta de sobriedad, f; embriaguez, ebriedad, f

insole n (of shoes) plantilla, f

insolence n insolencia, altanería, majadería, frescura, f, atrevimiento, descaro, m

insolent a insolente, arrogante, atrevido, descarado, desmesurado, fresco

insolently adv insolentemente, con descaro

insolubility n insolubilidad, f

insoluble a insoluble

insolvency n in olvencia, f

insolvent a insolvente

insomnia n insomnio, m

insomuch adv (gen. with as or that) de modo (que), así (que), de suerte (que)

inspect vt examinar, investigar, inspeccionar; (officially) registrar, reconocer

inspection n inspección, investigación, f; examen, m; (official) reconocimiento, registro, m

inspector n inspector, m; veedor, interventor, m

inspectorate n inspectorado, m; cargo de inspector, m

inspiration n (of breath) inspiración, aspiración, f; numen, m, inspiración, vena, f. **to find i. in,** inspirarse en.

inspire vt (inhale) aspirar, inspirar; (stimulate) animar, alentar, iluminar; (suggest) sugerir, inspirar; infundir. **to i. enthusiasm,** entusiasmar. **to i. hope,** dar esperanza, esperanzar

inspired a inspirado, intuitivo, iluminado; (of genius) genial

inspirer n inspirador (-ra)

inspiring a alentador, animador; inspirador

inspirit vt alentar, inspirar, estimular, animar

inspiriting a alentador, estimulador

instability n inestabilidad, mutabilidad, inconstancia, f

install vt (all meanings) instalar. **to i. oneself,** instalarse, establecerse

installation n (all meanings) instalación, f

installment n (of a story) entrega, f; com plazo, m, cuota, f. **by installments,** com a plazos. **i. plan,** pago a plazos, pago por cuotas, m

instance n ejemplo, caso, m; (request) solicitación, f, ruego, m; law instancia, f. vt citar como ejemplo, mencionar; demostrar, probar. **for i.,** por ejemplo, verbigracia. **in that i. . . . ,** en el caso . . . **in the first i.,** en primer lugar, primero

instant a inmediato, urgente; com corriente, actual. n instante, momento, m; inf tris, santiamén, m. com **the 2nd i.,** el 2° (segundo) del corriente. **this i.,** (immediately) en seguida

instantaneous a instantáneo. phot **i. exposure,** instantánea, f

instantaneously adv instantáneamente

instantaneousness n instantaneidad, f

instantly adv en seguida, al instante, inmediatamente

instead adv en cambio; (with of) en vez de, en lugar de

instep n empeine, m

instigate vt instigar, incitar, aguijar, animar, provocar; fomentar

instigating a instigador, provocador, fomentador

instigation n instigación, incitación, f; estímulo, m

instigator n instigador (-ra), provocador (-ra), fomentador (-ra)

instil vt instilar; (ideas) inculcar, infundir

instilment n inculcación, implantación, insinuación, f

instinct n instinto, m. **i. with,** imbuido de, lleno de. **by i.,** por instinto, movido por instinto

instinctive a instintivo, espontáneo

instinctively adv por instinto

institute vt instituir, fundar, establecer; (an inquiry) iniciar, empezar. n instituto, m; pl **institutes,** law instituta, f

institution n (creation) fundación, creación, f; institución, f, instituto, m; (beginning) comienzo, m, iniciación, f; (charitable) asilo, m; (custom) uso, m, costumbre, tradición, f

institutional a institucional

instruct vt (teach) instruir, enseñar; (order) mandar, dar orden (a)

instruction n (teaching) instrucción, enseñanza, f; pl **instructions,** (orders) instrucciones, f pl orden, f, mandato, m

instructive a instructivo, instructor, informativo

instructively adv instructivamente

instructiveness n el carácter informativo, lo instructivo

instructor n instructor, preceptor, m

instrument n instrumento, m; (tool) herramienta, f, utensilio, aparato, m; (agent) órgano, agente, medio, m; law instrumento, m, escritura, f. vt mus instrumentar. **percussion i.,** instrumento de percusión, m. **scientific i.,** instrumento científico, m. **stringed i.,** instrumento de cuerda, m. **wind i.,** instrumento de viento, m

instrumental a instrumental; influyente. **to be i. in,** contribuir a

instrumentalist n mus instrumentista, m

instrumentality n mediación, intervención, agencia, f, buenos oficios, m pl

instrumentation n mus instrumentación, f; mediación, f

insubordinate a insubordinado, rebelde, desobediente, refractario

insubordination n insubordinación, rebeldía, desobediencia, f

insubstantial a irreal; insubstancial

insubstantiality n irrealidad, f; insubstancialidad, f

insufferable. See **intolerable**

insufficiency n insuficiencia, falta, carestía, f

insufficient a insuficiente, falto. **"I. Postage,"** «Falta de franqueo»

insufficiently adv insuficientemente

insular a isleño, insular; (narrow-minded) intolerante, iliberal

insularity n carácter isleño, m; (narrow-mindedness) iliberalidad, intolerancia, f

insulate vt aislar

insulating a aislador. **i. tape,** elec cinta aisladora, f

insulation n aislamiento, m

insulator n elec aislador, m

insulin n med insulina, f

insult n insulto, agravio, ultraje, m, afrenta, ofensa, f. vt insultar, ofender, afrentar. **He was insulted,** Fue insultado; Se mostró ofendido

insulter n insultador (-ra)

insulting a insultante, injurioso, ofensivo. **He was very i. to them,** Les insultó, Les trató con menosprecio

insultingly adv con insolencia, ofensivamente

insuperability n dificultades insuperables, f pl, imposibilidad, f, lo insuperable

insuperable a insuperable, invencible

insuperably adv invenciblemente

insupportable a insoportable, inaguantable, intolerable, insufrible

insupportably adv insufriblemente, insoportablemente

insurable a asegurable

insurance n aseguramiento, m; com seguro, m; aseguración, f. **accident i.,** seguro contra accidentes, m. **fire-i.,** seguro contra incendio, m. **life i.,** seguro sobre la vida, m. **maritime i.,** seguro marítimo, m. **National I. Act,** Ley del Seguro Nacional Obligatorio, f. **i. broker,** corredor de seguros, m. **i. company,** compañía de seguros, f. **i. policy,** póliza de seguros, f. **i. premium,** prima de seguros, f

insure vt com asegurar. **to i. oneself,** asegurarse. **the insured,** (person) el asegurado

insurer n asegurador (-ra)

insurgent a insurgente, rebelde; (of sea) invasor. n rebelde, mf insurrecto (-ta)

insurmountable a insalvable, insuperable, invencible, intransitable

insurrection n insurrección, sublevación, f, levantamiento, m

insurrectionary a rebelde, amotinado, insurgente

insusceptible a no susceptible, indiferente, insensible

intact a intacto, íntegro, indemne

intake n (of a stocking) menguado, m; mech aspiración, f; válvula de admisión, f; aer admisión, toma, f; orificio de entrada, m

intangibility n intangibilidad, f

intangible a intangible; incomprensible

integer n math número entero, m

integral a íntegro, intrínseco, inherente; math entero. n math integral, f. **i. calculus,** cálculo integral, m

integrate vt integrar, completar; formar en un todo; math integrar

integrity n integridad, honradez, rectitud, entereza, f

intellect n intelecto, entendimiento, m

intellectual a intelectual, mental. n intelectual

intellectualism n intelectualismo, m, intelectualidad, f

intellectually adv intelectualmente, mentalmente

intelligence n inteligencia, comprensión, mente, f; (quickness of mind) agudeza, perspicacia, f; (news) noticia, f, conocimiento, informe, m. **the latest i.,** las últimas noticias. m. **i. quotient,** cociente de inteligencia, m. **I. Service,** Inteligencia, f; policía secreta, f. **i. test,** prueba de inteligencia, f

intelligent a inteligente

intelligentsia n clase intelectual, intelectualidad, f, inf masa cefálica, f

intelligibility n comprensibilidad, inteligibilidad, f

intelligible a inteligible, comprensible

intelligibly adv inteligiblemente

intemperance n intemperancia, inmoderación, f; exceso en la bebida, m

intemperate a intemperante, destemplado, descomedido; inmoderado; bebedor en exceso

intemperately adv inmoderadamente

intend vt intentar, proponerse, pensar; destinar, dedicar; (mean) querer decir. **to be intended,** estar destinado; tener por fin; querer decir

intendant n intendente, m

intended a pensado, deseado. n inf novio (-ia), futuro (-ra), prometido (-da)

intense a intenso, vivo, fuerte; (of emotions) profundo, hondo, vehemente; (of colors) subido, intenso; (great) extremado, sumo, muy grande

intensification n intensificación, f; aumento, m

intensify vt intensar, intensificar; aumentar

intensity n intensidad, fuerza, f; (of emotions) profundidad, vehemencia, violencia, f; (of colors) intensidad, f

intensive a intensivo

intensive-care unit n sala de terapia intensiva, unidad de cuidados intensivos, unidad de vigilancia intensiva, f

intent n intento, propósito, deseo, m. a atento; (absorbed) absorto, interesado; (on doing) resuelto a, decidido a. **to all intents and purposes,** en efecto, en realidad. **to be i. on,** (reading, etc.) estar absorto en, entregarse a. **with i. to defraud,** con el propósito deliberado de defraudar

intention *n* intención, voluntad, *f*, propósito, pensamiento, proyecto, *m*

intentional *a* intencional, deliberado, premeditado

intentionally *adv* a propósito, intencionalmente, de pensado

intentioned *a* intencionado

intently *adv* atentamente

inter *vt* enterrar, sepultar

inter *pref* inter, entre. **i.-allied,** interaliado, de los aliados. **i.-denominational,** intersectario. **i.-university,** interuniversitario. **i.-urban,** interurbano

interaction *n* interacción, acción recíproca, acción mutua, *f*

intercalate *vt* intercalar, interpolar

intercede *vi* interceder, mediar. **to i. for,** hablar por

intercept *vt* interceptar, detener; entrecoger, atajar

interception *n* interceptación, detención, *f*

intercession *n* mediación, intercesión, *f*

intercessor *n* intercesor (-ra), mediador (-ra)

interchange *n* intercambio, *m*; (of goods) comercio, tráfico, *m*. *vt* cambiar, trocar; alternar

interchangeable *a* intercambiable

intercom *n* teléfono interior, *m*

intercommunicate *vi* comunicarse

intercommunication *n* comunicación mutua, *f*; comercio, *m*

intercostal *a anat* intercostal

intercourse *n* (social) trato, *m*, relaciones, *f pl*; *com* comercio, tráfico, *m*; (of ideas) intercambio, *m*; (sexual) coito, trato sexual, *m*

interdependence *n* dependencia mutua, mutualidad, *f*

interdependent *a* mutuo

interdict *n* interdicto, veto, *m*, prohibición, *f*; *ecc* entredicho, *m*. *vt* interdecir, prohibir, privar; *ecc* poner en entredicho

interdiction *n* interdicción, prohibición, *f*

interest *n* interés, *m*; provecho, *m*; *com* premio, rédito, interés, *m*; (in a firm) participación, *f*; (curiosity) interés, *m*; curiosidad, *f*; simpatía, *f*; (influence) influencia, *f*. *n pl* **interests,** (commercial undertakings) empresas, *f pl*, negocios, *m pl*. *vt* interesar. **to be interested in,** interesarse en, (on behalf of) por. **to be in one's own i.,** ser en provecho de uno, ser en su propio interés. **to bear eight per cent. i.,** dar interés del ocho por ciento. **to pay with i.,** pagar con creces. **to put out at i.,** dar a interés. **in the interests of,** en interés de. **compound i.,** interés compuesto, *m*. **simple i.,** interés sencillo, *m*. **vested interests,** intereses creados, *m pl*

interesting *a* interesante, curioso, atractivo

interestingly *adv* amenamente, de modo interesante

interfere *vi* intervenir, meterse, entremeterse, mezclarse; *inf* mangonear, meter las narices; (with) meterse con; (impede) estorbar, impedir

interference *n* intervención, *f*, entrometimiento, *m*; (obstacle) estorbo, obstáculo, *m*; *phys* interferencia, *f*; *rad* parásitos, *m pl*

interfering *a* entremetido, oficioso; *inf* mangoneador

interim *n* ínterin, intermedio, *Lat. Am. also* interregno *m*. *a* interino, intermedio. **in the i.,** entre tanto, en el ínterin. *com* **i. dividend,** dividendo interino, *m*

interior *a* interior, interno; doméstico. *n* interior, *m*

interject *vt* interponer

interjection *n* exclamación, interjección, *f*; interposición, *f*

interlace *vt* entrelazar, entretejer

interleave *vt* interfoliar, interpaginar

interline *vt* entrerrenglonar, interlinear

interlinear *a* interlineal

interlineation *n* interlineación, *f*

interlining *n* entretela, *f*

interlock *vt* (of wheels, etc.). endentar; trabar; cerrar. *vi* endentarse; entrelazarse, unirse; cerrar

interlocutor *n* interlocutor (-ra)

interloper *n* intruso (-sa); *com* intérlope, *m*

interloping *a* intérlope

interlude *n* intervalo, intermedio, *m*; *mus* interludio, *m*; *theat* entremés, *m*

intermarriage *n* casamiento entre parientes próximos, entre razas distintas, o entre grupos étnicos distintos, *m*

intermarry *vi* contraer matrimonio entre parientes próximos, entre personas de razas distintas, o entre grupos étnicos distintos

intermediary *a* and *n* intermediario (-ia)

intermediate *a* intermedio, medio, medianero. *n* sustancia intermedia, *f*. *vi* intervenir, mediar

interment *n* entierro, *m*

intermezzo *n theat* intermedio, *m*; *mus* intermezzo, *m*

interminable *a* interminable, inacabable

interminably *adv* interminablemente, sin fin, sin cesar

intermingle *vt* entremezclar, entreverar. *vi* mezclarse

intermission *n* intermisión, interrupción, pausa, *f*; *theat* entreacto, *m*. **without i.,** sin pausa, sin tregua

intermittence *n* intermitencia, alternación, *f*

intermittent *a* intermitente, discontinuo; (of fever) intermitente

intermittently *adv* a intervalos, a ratos, a pausas

intern *n med* practicante de hospital *m*, interno (-na), interno de hospital, alumno interno, *m*. *vt* confinar, encerrar

internal *a* interno, interior; (of affairs) doméstico, civil; intrínseco; íntimo. **i.-combustion engine,** motor de combustión interna, *m*

internally *adv* interiormente

international *a* internacional. *n sport* un partido internacional. **i. law,** derecho internacional, *m*

internationalism *n* internacionalismo, *m*

internationalist *n* internacionalista, *mf*

internationalization *n* internacionalización, *f*

internationalize *vt* hacer internacional, poner bajo un control internacional

internecine *a* sanguinario, feroz

internee *n* internado (-da)

internment *n* internamiento, *m*. **i. camp,** campo de internamiento, *m*

interoceanic *a* interoceánico

interpolate *vt* interpolar, intercalar, interponer

interpolation *n* interpolación, inserción, añadidura, *f*

interpolator *n* interpolador (-ra)

interpose *vt* interponer; (a remark) interpolar. *vi* interponerse, intervenir; (interfere) entrometerse; interrumpir

interposition *n* interposición, *f*; entrometimiento, *m*

interpret *vt* interpretar; (translate) traducir; (explain) explicar, descifrar. *vi* interpretar

interpretation *n* interpretación, *f*; (translation) traducción, *f*; (explanation) explicación, *f*

interpretative *a* interpretativo, interpretador

interpreter *n* intérprete, *mf*

interregnum *n* interregno, *m*

interrelation *n* relación mutua, *f*

interrogate *vt* interrogar, examinar, preguntar

interrogating *a* interrogante

interrogation *n* interrogación, *f*, examen, *m*; pregunta, *f*. **mark of i.,** punto de interrogación, *m*

interrogative *a* interrogativo. *n* palabra interrogativa, *f*

interrogatively *adv* interrogativamente

interrogator *n* examinador (-ra), interrogador (-ra)

interrogatory *a* interrogativo. *n* interrogatorio, *m*

interrupt *vt* interrumpir

interruptedly *adv* interrumpidamente

interrupter *n* interruptor (-ra); *elec* interruptor, *m*

interruption *n* interrupción, *f*

intersect *vt* cruzar. *vi* cruzarse, intersecarse

intersection *n* intersección, *f*; cruce, *m*, (of streets) bocacalle, *Lat. Am.* cruza *f*

intersperse *vt* diseminar, esparcir; interpolar, entremezclar

interstice *n* intervalo, intermedio, *m*; (chink) intersticio, *m*, hendedura, *f*

intertwine *vt* entretejer, entrelazar. *vi* entrelazarse

interval *n* intervalo, intermedio, *m*, pausa, *f*; *theat* entreacto, *m*, intermisión, *f*; (in schools) recreo, *m*. **at intervals,** a trechos, de vez en cuando. **lucid i.,** intervalo claro, intervalo lúcido, *m*

intervene *vi* intervenir, tomar parte (en), mediar; (occur) sobrevenir, acaecer; *law* interponerse

intervening *a* intermedio; interventor

intervention *n* intervención, mediación, *f*

interventionist *n pol* partidario (-ia) de la intervención

interview *n* entrevista, *f*, interviev, *m*. *vt* entrevistarse con

interviewer *n* interrogador (-ra); (reporter) reportero, periodista, *m*

interweave *vt* entretejer, entrelazar

interweaving *n* entretejimiento, *m*

intestacy *n* ausencia de un testamento, *f*

intestate *a* and *n* intestado (-da)

intestinal *a* intestinal, intestino. **i. worm,** lombriz intestinal, *f*

intestine *n* intestino, *m*. **large i.,** intestino grueso, *m*. **small i.,** intestino delgado, *m*

intimacy *n* intimidad, *f*, familiaridad, *f*; (of nobility and others) privanza, *f*

intimate *a* íntimo; (of relations) entrañable, estrecho; intrínseco, esencial; (of knowledge) profundo, completo, detallado. *n* amigo (-ga) de confianza. *vt* intimar, dar a entender, indicar. **to become i.,** intimarse. **to be on i. terms with,** tratar de tú (a), ser amigo íntimo de

intimately *adv* íntimamente, al fondo

intimation *n* intimación, indicación, *f*; (hint) insinuación, indirecta, *f*

intimidate *vt* intimidar, aterrar, infundir miedo (a), espantar, acobardar, amedrentar

intimidation *n* intimidación, *f*

intimidatory *a* aterrador, amenazador

into *prep* en; a, al, a la; dentro, adentro; (of transforming, forming, etc.) en. **Throw it i. the fire,** Échalo al (or en el) fuego. **She went i. the house,** Entró en la casa. **to look i.,** mirar dentro de; mirar hacia el interior (de); investigar

intolerable *a* intolerable, insufrible, inaguantable, insoportable, inllevable

intolerableness *n* intolerabilidad, *f*

intolerably *adv* intolerablemente, insufriblemente

intolerance *n* intolerancia, intransigencia, *f*

intolerant *a* intolerante, intransigente; *med* intolerante

intonation *n* entonación, *f*

intone *vt* entonar; *ecc* salmodiar

intoxicant *a* embriagador. *n* bebida alcohólica, *f*

intoxicate *vt* emborrachar, embriagar; *med* intoxicar, envenenar; (excite) embriagar, embelesar

intoxicated *a* borracho; (excited) ebrio, embriagado; *med* intoxicado

intoxicating *a* embriagador

intoxication *n* borrachera, embriaguez, *f*; *med* intoxicación, *f*, envenenamiento, *m*; (excitement) entusiasmo, *m*, ebriedad, *f*

intractability *n* insociabilidad, hurañería, *f*

intractable *a* intratable, insociable, huraño

intramural *adv* intramuros

intransigence *n* intransigencia, intolerancia, *f*

intransigent *a* intransigente, intolerante

intransitive *a* intransitivo, neutro

intrauterine *a med* intrauterino

intravenous *a med* intravenoso

intrepid *a* intrépido, osado, audaz

intrepidity *n* intrepidez, osadía, audacia, *f*

intrepidly *adv* intrépidamente, audazmente

intricacy *n* intrincación, complejidad, *f*

intricate *a* intrincado, complejo

intricately *adv* intrincadamente

intrigue *n* intriga, maquinación, *f*, enredo, *m*; (amorous) lío, *m*. *vi* intrigar, enredar; (amorous) tener un lío. *vt* (interest) atraer, interesar; (with) intrigar con. **to be intrigued** *Lat. Am.* intrigarse

intriguer *n* intrigante, *mf*, urdemalas, *m*, enredador (-ra)

intriguing *a* enredador; (attractive) atrayente, interesante, seductor

intrinsic *a* intrínseco, innato, inherente, esencial

intrinsically *adv* intrínsecamente, esencialmente

introduce *vt* introducir; hacer entrar; insertar, injerir; (a person) presentar; poner de moda, introducir; (a bill) presentar; (a person to a thing) llamar la atención sobre. **Permit me to i. my friend,** Permítame que le presente mi amigo

introduction *n* introducción, *f*; (of a book) prefacio, prólogo, *m*, advertencia, *f*; (of a person) presentación, *f*; inserción, *f*

introductory *a* introductor, preliminar, preparatorio

intromission *n* intromisión, *f*

introspection *n* introspección, *f*

introspective *a* introspectivo

introversion *n psy* introversión *f*

introvert *a* and *n psy* introverso (-sa)

intrude *vt* introducir, imponer. *vi* entremeterse, inmiscuirse. **Do I i.?** ¿Estorbo?

intruder *n* intruso (-sa)

intrusion *n* intrusión, *f*; *geol* intromisión, *f*

intrusive *a* intruso

intuition *n* intuición, *f*. **to know by i.,** intuir, saber por intuición

intuitive *a* intuitivo

inundate *vt* inundar, anegar; *fig* abrumar

inundation *n* inundación, anegación, *f*; *fig* diluvio, *m*, abundancia, *f*

inure *vt* endurecer, habituar

inurement *n* habituación, *f*

invade *vt* invadir, irrumpir, asaltar; *med* invadir

invader *n* invasor (-ra), acometedor (-ra), agresor (-ra)

invading *a* invasor, irruptor

invalid *a* inválido, nulo. **to become i.,** caducar

invalid *a* inválido (-da), enfermo (-ma). **to become an i.,** quedarse inválido. **to i. out of the army,** licenciar por invalidez. **i. carriage,** cochecillo de inválido, *m*

invalidate *vt* invalidar, anular

invalidation *n* invalidación, *f*

invalidity *n* invalidez, nulidad, *f*

invaluable *n* inestimable

invariability *n* invariabilidad, invariación, inalterabilidad, inmutabilidad, *f*

invariable *a* invariable, inmutable, inalterable

invariably *adv* invariablemente, inmutablemente

invariant *n math* invariante, *m*

invasion *n* invasión, irrupción, *f*; *med* invasión, *f*

invective *n* invectiva, diatriba, *f*

inveigh (against) *vi* desencadenarse (contra), prorrumpir en invectivas (contra)

inveigle *vt* seducir, engatusar, persuadir

invent *vt* inventar, descubrir, originar; (a falsehood) fingir; (create) idear, componer

invention *n* invención, *f*, invento, descubrimiento, *m*; (imagination) ingeniosidad, inventiva, *f*; (falsehood) ficción, mentira, *f*; (finding) invención, *f*, hallazgo, *m*

inventive *a* inventor, inventivo; ingenioso, despejado

inventiveness *n* inventiva, *f*

inventor *n* inventor (-ra), autor (-ra)

inventory *n* inventario, *m*; descripción, *f*. *vt* inventariar

inverse *a* inverso. **i. proportion,** razón inversa, *f*

inversely *adv* inversamente, a la inversa

inversion *n* inversión, *f*, trastrocamiento, *m*; *gram* hipérbaton, *m*

invert *vt* invertir, trastornar, trastrocar. **inverted commas,** comilla, *f*

invertebrate *a* and *n* invertebrado *m*.

invest *vt com* invertir; *mil* sitiar, cercar; (foll. by with) poner, cubrir con; (of qualities) conferir, otorgar, dar.

vi (with in) poner dinero en, echar caudal en; *inf* comprar

investigable *a* averiguable

investigate *vt* investigar, estudiar; examinar, averiguar; explorar. **to i. closely** *Lat. Am.* interiorizar

investigation *n* investigación, *f*, estudio, *m*; examen, *m*, averiguación, *f*; encuesta, pesquisa, *f*

investigator *n* investigador (-ra); averiguador (-ra)

investigatory *a* investigador

investiture *n* investidura, instalación, *f*

investment *n* (*com* of money) inversión, *f*, empleo, *m*; *mil* cerco, *m*; (investiture) instalación, *f*; *pl* **investments,** *com* acciones, *f pl*, fondos, *m pl*

investor *n* inversionista, *m*; accionista, *mf*, *Lat. Am.* inversor (-ra) *mf*

inveteracy *n* antigüedad, *f*, lo arraigado

inveterate *a* inveterado, antiguo, arraigado, incurable

invidious *a* odioso, repugnante, injusto

invidiousness *n* injusticia, *f*, lo odioso

invigorate *vt* vigorizar, dar fuerza (a), avivar

invigorating *a* fortaleciente, fortificador, vigorizador

invincibility *n* invencibilidad, *f*

invincible *a* invencible, indomable; *fig* insuperable

inviolability *n* inviolabilidad, *f*

inviolable *a* inviolable

inviolate *a* inviolado

invisibility *n* invisibilidad, *f*

invisible *a* invisible. **i. ink,** tinta simpática, *f*. **i. mending,** zurcido invisible, *m*

invitation *n* invitación, *f*; convite, *m*; (card) tarjeta de invitación, *f*

invite *vt* invitar, convidar; (request) pedir, rogar; (of things) incitar, tentar.

inviting *a* atrayente, incitante; (of food) apetitoso; (of looks) provocativo

invocation *n* invocación, *f*

invocatory *a* invocatorio, invocador

invoice *n* *com* factura, *f*. *vt* facturar. **proforma i.,** factura simulada, *f*. **shipping i.,** factura de expedición, *f*. **i. book,** libro de facturas, *m*

invoke *vt* invocar; suplicar, implorar; (*laws*) acogerse (a)

involuntarily *adv* sin querer, involuntariamente

involuntariness *n* involuntariedad, *f*

involuntary *a* involuntario; instintivo, inconsciente

involve *vt* (entangle) enredar, embrollar, enmarañar; (implicate) comprometer; (imply) implicar, ocasionar, suponer, traer consigo

involved *a* complejo, intrincado; (of style) confuso, obscuro

invulnerability *n* invulnerabilidad, *f*

invulnerable *a* invulnerable

inward *a* interior, interno; íntimo, espiritual. *adv* adentro

inwardly *adv* interiormente; para sí, entre sí

inwards *adv* hacia dentro; adentro

iodine *n* yodo, *m*. **i. poisoning,** yodismo, *m*

ion *n* *chem* ion, *m*

Ionian *a* and *n* jónico (-ca)

Ionic *a* jónico. **i. foot** *poet* jónico, *m*

iota *n* (letter) iota, *f*; jota, pizca, *f*, ápice, *m*. **not an i.,** ni pizca

I.O.U. *n* *com* abonaré, *m*

ipecacuanha *n* ipecacuana, *f*

Iranian *a* and *n* iranio (-ia)

irascibility *n* irascibilidad, iracundia, irritabilidad, *f*

irascible *a* irascible, iracundo, irritable

irate *a* airado, colérico, enojado

ire *n* ira, cólera, furia, *f*

Ireland *n* Irlanda, *f*

iridescence *n* iridiscencia, *f*

iridescent *a* iridiscente. **to look i.,** irisar, tornasolarse

iridium *n* *chem* iridio, *m*

iris *n* *anat* iris, *m*; *bot* irídea, *f*

Irish *a* and *n* irlandés (-esa). **the I.,** los irlandeses

Irish Sea Mar de Irlanda, *f*

irksome *a* fastidioso, tedioso, aburrido

irksomeness *n* tedio, fastidio, aburrimiento, *m*

iron *n* hierro, *m*; (for clothes) plancha, *f*; (tool) utensilio, *m*, herramienta, *f*; (golf) hierro, *m*; *pl* **irons,** grillos, *m pl*, cadenas, *f pl*. *a* de hierro, férreo; *fig* duro, severo. *vt* (linen) planchar; (with out) allanar. **to have too many irons in the fire,** tener demasiados asuntos entre manos. **to put in irons,** echar grillos (a). **to strike while the i. is hot,** A hierro caliente batir de repente. **cast-i.,** hierro colado, *m*. **scrap i.,** hierro viejo, *m*. **sheet i.,** hierro en planchas, *m*. **wrought i.,** hierro dulce, *m*. **i. age,** edad de hierro, *f*. **i.-foundry,** fundición de hierro, *f*. **i. lung,** *med* pulmón de hierro, pulmón de acero, *m*. **i.-mold,** mancha de orín, *f*. **i. smelting furnace,** alto horno, *m*. **i. tonic,** *med* reconstituyente ferruginoso, *m*. **i. will,** voluntad de hierro, *f*

ironclad *a* blindado, acorazado. *n* buque de guerra blindado, acorazado, *m*

ironer *n* planchador (-ra)

ironical *a* irónico

ironically *adv* con ironía, irónicamente

ironing *n* planchado, *m*; ropa por planchar, *f*. *a* de planchar. **i. board,** tabla de planchar, *f*

ironist *n* ironista, *mf*

ironmonger *n* ferretero (-ra). **ironmonger's shop,** ferretería, *f*

ironmongery *n* ferretería, quincallería, *f*

iron sulphide sulfuro de hierro, *m*

ironwork *n* herraje, *m*; obra de hierro, *f*

ironworks *n* herrería, *f*

irony *n* ironía, *f*. *a* (like iron) ferrugiento

Iroquois *a* and *n* iroqués (-esa)

irradiate *vt* irradiar; *fig* iluminar, aclarar

irradiation *n* irradiación, *f*; *fig* iluminación, *f*

irrational *a* ilógico, ridículo, irracional

irrationality *n* irracionalidad, *f*

irreclaimable *a* irrecuperable, irredimible; (of land) inservible, improductivo; irreformable

irreconcilable *a* irreconciliable

irreconcilably *adv* irremediablemente

irrecoverable *a* irrecuperable, incobrable

irredeemable *a* irredimible, perdido. **i. government loan,** deuda perpetua, *f*

irredeemably *adv* perdidamente

irreducible *a* irreducible

irrefutability *n* verdad, *f*

irrefutable *a* irrefutable, indisputable, innegable, irrebatible

irregular *a* irregular; anormal; (of shape) disforme; desordenado; *gram* irregular; (of surface) desigual, escabroso

irregularity *n* irregularidad, *f*; anormalidad, *f*; (of shape) desproporción, irregularidad, *f*; (of surface) escabrosidad, desigualdad, *f*; exceso, *m*, demasía, *f*

irrelevance *n* inconexión, *f*; inoportunidad, *f*; futilidad, poca importancia, *f*; (stupidity) desatino, *m*, impertinencia, *f*

irrelevant *a* inaplicable, fuera de propósito; inoportuno; sin importancia, fútil; (stupid) impertinente

irreligion *n* irreligión, impiedad, *f*

irreligious *a* irreligioso, impío

irremediable *a* irremediable, irreparable

irremediably *adv* sin remedio, irremediablemente

irreparable *a* irreparable

irreplaceable *a* irreemplazable

irrepressible *a* incontrolable, indomable

irreproachable *a* irreprochable, intachable

irresistible *a* irresistible

irresistibleness *n* superioridad, *f*

irresolute *a* irresoluto, indeciso, vacilante

irresoluteness *n* irresolución, indecisión, *f*

irrespective *a* (with of) independiente de, aparte de, sin distinción de

irresponsibility *n* irresponsabilidad, *f*

irresponsible *a* irresponsable

irretrievable *a* irrecuperable

irretrievably *adv* irreparablemente, sin remedio
irreverence *n* irreverencia, *f*
irreverent *a* irreverente, irrespetuoso
irrevocability *n* irrevocabilidad, *f*
irrevocable *a* irrevocable; inquebrantable
irrigable *a* regadío
irrigate *vt agr* poner en regadío, regar; *med* irrigar
irrigation *n agr* riego, *m; med* irrigación, *f.* **i. channel,** cacera, acequia, *f,* canal de riego, *m*
irritability *n* irritabilidad, iracundia, *f*
irritable *a* irritable, irascible, iracundo
irritably *adv* con irritación, airadamente
irritant *a* irritante, irritador. *n* irritador, *m; med* medicamento irritante, *m*
irritate *vt* provocar, estimular; irritar, molestar, exasperar; *med* irritar
irritating *a* irritador, irritante
irritatingly *adv* de un modo irritante
irritation *n* irritación, *f,* enojo, *m; physiol* picazón, *f,* picor, *m*
irruption *n* irrupción, invasión, *f*
isinglass *n* cola de pescado, *f*
Islamic *a* islámico
Islamism *n* islamismo, *m*
Islamite *a* and *n* islamita *mf*
island *n* isla, *f, a* isleño
islander *n* isleño (-ña)
islet *n* isleta, *f;* islote, *m*
isobaric *a* isobárico
isolate *vt* aislar, apartar
isolated *a* aislado, apartado, solitario; único, solo
isolation *n* aislamiento, apartamiento, *m,* soledad, *f*
isolationism *n pol* aislacionismo, aislamientismo, *m*
isolationist *a* and *n pol* aislacionista, aislamientista, *mf*
isomerism *n chem* isomería, *f*
isometric *a* isométrico
isosceles *a* isósceles
isotope *n* isotope, isotopo, *m*
Israelite *a* and *n* israelita *mf*
issue *n* salida, *f;* (result) resultado, *m,* consecuencia, *f;* (of a periodical) número, *m; print* edición, tirada, *f;* (offspring) prole, sucesión, *f;* (of notes, bonds) emisión, *f; med* flujo, *m;* cuestión, *f,* problema, *m. vi* salir, fluir, manar; nacer, originarse; resultar, terminarse. *vt* (an order) expedir, emitir, dictar; publicar, dar a luz;

(of notes, bonds) poner en circulación, librar. **at i.,** en disputa, en cuestión. **to join i.,** llevar la contraria, oponer
isthmian *a* ístmico
isthmus *n* istmo, *m*
it *pron* (as subject) él, *m;* ella, *f;* (gen. omitted with all verbs in Sp.); (as object) lo, *m;* la, *f;* (as indirect object) le (se with an object in 3rd pers.); (meaning that thing, that affair) eso, ello. Sometimes omitted in other cases, e.g. **He has thought it necessary to stay at home,** Ha creído necesario de quedarse en casa. **We heard it said that . . .,** Oímos decir que . . . **to make it perfectly clear that . . .,** dejar bien claro que . . . *n* (slang) garbo, aquél, *m;* atractivos, *m pl.* **Is it not so?** ¿No es así? **That is it,** Eso es. **It's me,** Soy yo
Italy Italia, *f*
Italian *a* and *n* italiano (-na) (language) italiano, *m. art* **I. School,** escuela italiana, *f*
italic *a* (of Italy) itálico; *print* itálico, bastardillo. *n* letra bastardilla, bastardilla, letra itálica, *f.* **italics mine,** el subrayado es mío, los subrayados son míos
italicize *vt* imprimir en bastardilla; dar énfasis (a)
itch *n* sarna, *f; fig* picazón, *f;* prurito, capricho, *m. vi* picar; *fig* sentir picazón; (with to) rabiar por, suspirar por.
itching *n* picazón, *f,* picor, *m. a* sarnoso, picante; *med* pruriginoso. **to have an i. palm,** *fig* ser de la virgen del puño
item *n* ítem, artículo, *m; com* partida, *f;* punto, detalle, *m;* (of a program) número, *m;* asunto, *m. adv* ítem
iterative *a* iterativo
Ithaca Ítaca, *f*
itinerant *a* nómada, errante
itinerary *n* itinerario, *m,* ruta, *f*
its *poss a* su (with pl. obj.) sus. **a book and its pages,** un libro y sus páginas.
itself *pron* él mismo; ella misma, *f;* (with prep.) sí; (with reflex. verb) se; (with noun) el mismo, la misma; (meaning alone) solo. **in i.,** en sí
ivied *a* cubierto de hiedra
ivory *n* marfil, *m. a* ebúrneo, de marfil, marfileño. **vegetable i.,** marfil vegetal, *m.* **i. carving,** talla de marfil, *f*
ivory tower *n* torre de marfil, *f*
ivory-tower *a* de torre de marfil
ivy *n* hiedra, *f*

J

j *n* (letter) jota, *f*
jab *vt* (with a hypodermic needle, etc.) pinchar; introducir (en); clavar (con); (scrape) hurgar; (place) poner. *n* pinchazo, *m;* golpe, *m.* **He jabbed his pistol in my ribs,** Me puso la pistola en las costillas
jabber *vt* and *vi* chapurrear; (of monkeys) chillar
jabbering *n* chapurreo, *m;* (of monkeys) chillidos, *m pl*
Jack *n* Juan, *m;* (man) hombre, *m;* (sailor) marinero, *m;* (in cards) sota, *f;* (for raising weights) gato, *m;* (of a spit) torno, *m;* (of some animals) macho, *m;* (bowls) boliche, *m. vt* (with up) solevantar con gatos. **Union J.,** pabellón británico, *m.* **j.-boot,** bota de montar, *f.* **J.-in-office,** mandarín, funcionario impertinente, *m.* **J.-in-the-box,** faca, *f.* **j.-knife,** navaja, *f.* **J. of all trades,** hombre de muchos oficios, *m.* **jack of all trades, master of none,** aprendiz de todo, oficial de nada. **j.-rabbit,** liebre americana, *f.* **J.-tar,** marinero, *m*
jackal *n* chacal, adive, *m*
jackanapes *n* impertinente, *m;* mequetrefe, *m*
jackass *n* asno, *m;* (fool) tonto, asno, *m.* **laughing j.,** martín pescador, *m*
jacket *n* chaqueta, *f;* americana, *f;* (for boilers, etc.) camisa, *f;* (of a book) forro, *m,* sobrecubierta, *f.* **strait j.,** camisa de fuerza, *f*
jacks *n* (game) matatenas, *f pl,* cantillos, *m pl*

jade *n min* jade, *m;* (horse) rocín, *m;* (woman) mala pécora, *f;* (saucy wench) mozuela, picaruela, *f*
jaded *a* fatigado, agotado, rendido; (of the palate) saciado
jagged *a* dentado
jaguar *n* jaguar, *m*
jai alai *in Mexico* frontón, *m*
jail cárcel, prisión, *f;* encierro, *m. vt* encarcelar. *a* carcelario, carcelero.
jailbird malhechor; presidiario, *m*
jailer *n* carcelero (-ra)
jalopy carcacho, *m,* (Mexico), cafetera rusa, *f,* (Spain)
jalousie *n* celosía, *f*
jam *vt* (ram) apretar; apiñar; estrujar; (a machine) atascar; (radio) causar interferencia (a); (preserve) hacer confitura de. *vi* atascarse. *n* (of people) agolpamiento, *m;* (traffic) atasco, *m;* (preserve) confitura, mermelada, compota, *f.* **He jammed his hat on,** Se encasquetó el sombrero. **She suddenly jammed down on the brakes,** Frenó de repente. **jam-dish,** compotera, *f.* **jam-jar,** pote para confitura, *m*
Jamaican *a* jamaicano, *n* jamaicano (-na)
jamboree *n* campamento, *m*
jamming *n rad* interferencias, *f pl*
jangle *vi* cencerrear; chocar; rechinar. *n* cencerreo, *m;* choque, *m;* rechinamiento, *m*

janissary *n* jenízaro, *m*

janitor *n* portero, *m*; (in a university, etc.) bedel, *m*

January *n* enero, *m*

Japan el Japón, *m*

japan *n* charol, *m. vt* charolar

Japanese *a* japonés. *n* japonés (-esa); (language) japonés, *m*

jar *n* chirrido, *m*; choque, *m*; sacudida, *f*; vibración, *f*; trepidación, *f*; (quarrel) riña, *f*; (receptacle) jarra, *f*; (for tobacco, honey, cosmetics, etc.) pote, *m*; (Leyden) botella (de Leyden), *f. vi* chirriar; vibrar, trepidar; chocar; (of sounds) ser discorde; (of colors) chillar. *vt* sacudir; hacer vibrar. **It jarred on my nerves,** Me atacaba los nervios. **It gave me a nasty jar,** *fig* Me hizo una impresión desagradable. **on the jar,** entreabierto

jardiniere *n* jardinera, *f*

jargon *n* jerga, jerigonza, *f*; monserga, *f*; (technical) lenguaje especial, *m*

jarring *a* discorde, disonante; en conflicto, opuesto; (to the nerves) que ataca a los nervios

jasmine *n* jazmín, *m.* **yellow j.,** jazmín amarillo, *m*

jasper *n min* jaspe, *m*

jaundice *n* ictericia, *f*

jaundiced *a* envidioso; desengañado, desilusionado

jaunt *n* excursión, *f*, *vi* ir de excursión

jauntily *adv* airosamente, con garbo

jauntiness *n* garbo, *m*, gentileza, ligereza, *f*

jaunty *a* garboso, airoso

Javanese *a* javanés. *n* javanés (-esa)

javelin *n* jabalina, *f.* **j. throwing,** lanzamiento de la jabalina, *m*

jaw *n* quijada, *f*; maxilar, *m*; *pl* **jaws,** boca, *f*; (of death, etc.) garras, *f pl*; *mech* quijada, *f*; (narrow entrance) boca, abertura, *f.* **jaw-bone,** mandíbula, *f*; *anat* hueso maxilar, *m*

jay *n* arrendajo, *m*

jazz *n* jazz, *m. vi* bailar el jazz. **j. band,** orquesta de jazz, *f*

jealous *a* celoso; envidioso. **to be j. of,** tener celos de. **to make j.,** dar celos (a)

jealously *adv* celosamente

jealousy *n* celos, *m pl*

jeans *n* vaqueros, *m pl*

jeep *n mil* yip, *m*

jeer *n* burla, mofa, *f*; insulto, *m*, *vi* burlarse; (with at) mofarse de

jeerer *n* mofador (-ra)

jeering *a* mofador. *n* burlas, *f pl*; insultos, *m pl*

jeeringly *adv* burlonamente

jellied *a* en gelatina

jelly *n* jalea, *f*; gelatina, *f. vi* solidificarse. **j.-bag,** manga, *f.* **j.-fish,** aguamala, aguaviva, malagna, medusa, *f*

jeopardize *vt* arriesgar, poner en juego; comprometer

jeopardy *n* peligro, *m*

jeremiad *n* jeremiada, *f*

jerk *n* sacudida, *f. vt* sacudir, dar una sacudida (a); lanzar bruscamente; (pull) tirar de; (push) empujar. *vi* moverse a sacudidas. **I jerked myself free,** Me libré de una sacudida

jerkily *adv* con sacudidas; espasmódicamente; nerviosamente

jerkin *n* justillo, *m*

jerky *a* espasmódico; nervioso (also of style)

jerry-built *a* mal construido, de pacotilla

jersey *n* jersey, *m. a* de jersey; de Jersey. **football j.,** camiseta de fútbol, *f*, jersey de fútbol. *m.* **J. cow,** vaca jerseysa, *f*

Jerusalem Jerusalén, *m*

jest *n* broma, chanza, *f*; (joke) chiste, *m*; (laughingstock) hazmerreír, *m. vi* bromear; burlarse (de). **in j.,** en broma, de guasa

jester *n* burlón (-ona); (practical joker, etc.) bromista, *mf*; (at a royal court) bufón, *m*

jesting *a* en bromas, *f pl*; chistes, *m pl*; burlas, *f pl. a* de broma; burlón

jestingly *adv* en broma

Jesuit *n* Jesuita, *m*

Jesuitical *a* jesuítico

jet *n min* azabache, *m*; (stream) chorro, *m*; (pipe) surtidero, *m*; (burner) mechero, *m*, *vi* chorrear. **jet-black,** negro como el azabache, de azabache. **jet-propelled engine,** motor de retroacción, *m.* **jet-propelled plane,** aeroplano de reacción, *m*

jetsam *n* echazón, *f*; *fig* víctima, *f*

jettison *n* echazón, *f. vt* echar (mercancías) al mar; *fig* librarse de, abandonar

jetty *n* dique, malecón, *m*; (landing pier) embarcadero, muelle, *m*

Jew *n* judío, *m.* **Jew's harp,** birimbao, *m*

jewel *n* joya, alhaja, *f*; (of a watch) rubí, *m*; *fig* alhaja, *f. vt* enjoyar, adornar con piedras preciosas. **j.-box, -case,** joyero, *m*

jeweled *a* adornado con piedras preciosas, enjoyado; (of a watch) montado sobre rubíes

jeweler *n* joyero (-ra). **jeweler's shop,** joyería, *f*

jewelry *n* joyas, *f pl*; artículos de joyería, *m pl*

Jewess *n* judía, *f*

Jewish *a* judío

Jewry *n* judería, *f*

jib *n naut* foque, *m. vi* (of a horse) plantarse; (refuse) rehusar. **to jib at,** vacilar en; mostrarse desinclinado. **jib-boom,** *naut* botalón de foque, *m*

jiffy *n* instante, credo, *m.* **in a j.,** en un decir Jesús, en un credo, en un santiamén

jig *n* (dance) jiga, *f. vi* bailar una jiga; bailar, agitarse, sacudirse. *vt* agitar, sacudir; (sieve) cribar

jigger *n naut* cangreja de mesana, *f*; aparejo de mano, *m*; jigger, *m*

jigsaw puzzle *n* rompecabezas, *m*

jilt *vt* dar calabazas (a)

jingle *n* tintineo, *m*; ruido, *m*; verso, *m*; estribillo, *m. vi* tintinar; sonar; rimar

jingoism *n* jingoísmo, *m*

jitters, to have the no tenerlas todas consigo, no saber dónde meterse

job *n* tarea, *f*; trabajo, *m*; empleo, *m*; (affair) asunto, *m*; (thing) cosa, *f*; (unscrupulous transaction) intriga, *f.* **It is a good (bad) job that . . . ,** Es una buena (mala) cosa que . . . **He has done a good job,** Ha hecho un buen trabajo. **He has lost his job,** Ha perdido su empleo, Le han declarado cesante. **odd-job man,** factótum, *m.* **job-lot,** colección miscelánea, *f*; *com* saldo de mercancías, *m*

jobber *n* (workman) destajista, *m*; (in stocks) agiotista, *m*; *com* corredor, *m*

jobless *a* sin trabajo

jockey *n* jockey, *m. vt* engañar; (with into) persuadir, hacer; (with out of) quitar, robar. **j. cap,** gorra de jockey, *f.* **J. Club,** jockey-club, *m*

jocose *a* jocoso, gracioso, guasón

jocosity *n* jocosidad, *f*

jocular *a* gracioso, alegre; chistoso, zumbón

jocularity *n* alegría, jocosidad, *f*

jocularly *adv* en broma; alegremente

jocund *a* alegre, jovial; jocundo

jocundity *n* alegría, *f*; jocundidad, *f*

jog *vt* empujar; (the memory) refrescar. *vi* ir despacio; andar a trote corto. *n* empujón, *m.* **He jogged me with his elbow,** Me dio con el codo. **jog-trot,** trote corto, *m*

joie de vivre *n* goce de vivir, arregosto de vivir, *m*

join *vt* juntar; unir; añadir; (railway lines) empalmar; juntarse con; (meet) encontrarse (con); reunirse (con); (a club, etc.) hacerse miembro de; (share) acompañar; (regiments, ships) volver (a). *vi* juntarse; unirse; asociarse. *n* unión, *f*; (railway) empalme, *m*; (roads) bifurcación, *f.* **At what time will you j. me?** ¿A qué hora me vendrás a buscar? **He has joined his ship,** Ha vuelto a su buque. **Will you j. me in a drink?** ¿Me quieres acompañar en una bebida? **to j. battle,** librar batalla. **to j. forces,** combinar; *inf* juntar meriendas. **to**

j. in, tomar parte en, participar en. **to j. together,** vt unir, juntar. vi juntarse; asociarse. **to j. up,** alistarse

joiner n carpintero, ensamblador, m,

joinery n ensambladuría, f; carpintería, f

joining n juntura, conjunción, f; (carp etc.) ensambladura, f; fig unión, f

joint n juntura, junta, f; anat coyuntura, articulación, f; (knuckle) nudillo, m; (of meat) cuarto, m; (hinge) bisagra, f; bot nudo, m, a unido; combinado; colectivo; mixto; mutuo; (in compounds) co. vt juntar; (meat) descuartizar. **out of j.,** dislocado; (of the times) fuera de compás. **j. account,** cuenta corriente mutua, f. **j.-heir,** coheredero, m. **j. stock company,** compañía por acciones, sociedad anónima, f

jointed a articulado; (foldable) plegadizo

jointly adv juntamente, en común, colectivamente

joist n sopanda, viga, f

joke n chiste, m; burla, broma, f. vi bromear, chancearse. vt burlarse (de). **Can he take a j.?** ¿Sabe aguantar una broma? **practical j.,** broma pesada, f. **to play a j.,** gastar una broma, hacer una burla

joker n bromista, Argentina also fomista, mf: (in cards) comodín, m

joking n chistes, m pl, bromas, f pl. a chistoso; cómico

jokingly adv en broma, de guasa

jollification n regocijo, m; festividades, fiestas, f pl

jollity n alegría, f, regocijo, m

jolly a alegre, jovial; (tipsy) achispado; (amusing) divertido; (nice) agradable. adv muy. **He is a j. good fellow,** Es un hombre estupendo. **I am j. glad,** Estoy contentísimo, Me alegro mucho

jolt n sacudida, f. vt sacudir. vi (of a vehicle) traquetear

jolting n sacudidas, f pl, sacudimiento, m; (of a vehicle) traqueteo, m

jonquil n bot junquillo, m

Jordan Jordania, f

joss n ídolo chino, m. **j.-stick,** pebete, m

jostle vt empujar, empellar. vi dar empujones, codear

jot n jota, pizca, f. vi (down) apuntar. **not a jot,** ni jota, ni pizca. **to be not worth a jot,** no valer un comino

jotter n taco para notas, m; (exercise book) cuaderno, m

jotting n apunte, m; observación, f

journal n (diary) diario, m; (ship's) diario de navegación, m; (newspaper) periódico, m; (review) revista, f

journalese n lenguaje periodístico, m

journalism n periodismo, Lat. Am. also diarismo, m

journalist n periodista, mf

journalistic a periodístico

journey n viaje, m; expedición, f; trayecto, m; camino, m. vi viajar. **j. by sea,** viaje por mar. **Pleasant j.!** ¡Buen viaje! ¡Feliz viaje! **outward j.,** viaje de ida, m. **return j.,** viaje de regreso, m

Jove n Júpiter, m. **By J.!** ¡Pardiez! ¡Caramba!

jovial a jovial

joviality n jovialidad, f

jowl n (cheek) carrillo, m; (of cattle, etc.) papada, f; (jaw) quijada, f

joy n alegría, f; felicidad, f; deleite, placer, m, vi alegrarse. **I wish you joy,** Te deseo la felicidad. **joy-ride,** excursión en coche, f; vuelo en avión, m. **joy-stick,** (of an airplane) palanca de gobierno, f

joyful a alegre

joyfulness n alegría, f

joyless a sin alegría, triste

joylessness n falta de alegría, tristeza, f

joyous. See **joyful**

jubilant a jubiloso; triunfante

jubilantly adv con júbilo, alegremente; triunfalmente

jubilation n júbilo, m, alegría, f; ruido triunfal, m

jubilee n jubileo, m

jubilee volume n libro de homenaje, libro jubilar, m

Judaic a judaico

Judaism n judaísmo, m

Judas n (traitor and hole) judas, m

Judezmo el judesmo, m

judge n juez, m; (connoisseur) conocedor (-ra) (de);

(umpire) arbitrio, m. vt juzgar; considerar, tener por. vi servir como juez; juzgar. **judging by,** a juzgar por. **to be a good j. of,** ser buen juez de. **to j. for oneself,** formar su propia opinión

judgment, judgement n law fallo, m; sentencia, f; juicio, m; (understanding) entendimiento, discernimiento, m; (opinion) opinión, f, parecer, m. **In my j. . . . ,** Según mi parecer, . . . Según creo yo . . . **Last J.,** Juicio Final, m. **to pass j. on,** law pronunciar sentencia (en o sobre); dictaminar sobre; juzgar. **to sit in j. on,** ser juez de; juzgar. **j.-day,** Día del Juicio, m. **j.-seat,** tribunal, m

judicature n judicatura, f; (court) juzgado, m

judicial a judicial; legal; (of the mind) juicioso. **j. inquiry,** investigación judicial, f. **j. separation,** separación legal, f

judiciary a judicial. n judicatura, f

judicious a juicioso, prudente

judiciously adv prudentemente, juiciosamente

judiciousness n juicio, m, prudencia, sensatez, f

judo n yudo, m

judoka n yudoca, mf

jug n jarro, m; cántaro, m; pote, m; (jail) Argentina, Chile capacha f. vt cul estofar. vi (of nightingale) trinar, cantar. **jugged hare,** n liebre en estofado, f

juggle vi hacer juegos malabares. **to j. out of,** (money, etc.) quitar con engaño, estafar. **to j. with,** fig (facts, etc.) tergiversar, falsificar; (person) engañar

juggler n malabarista, mf: (deceiver) estafador (-ra)

jugglery n prestidigitación, f; juegos malabares, m pl; (imposture) engaño, m, estafa, f; trampas, f pl

jugular a anat yugular. **j. vein,** yugular, m

juice n jugo, m; fig zumo, m. **digestive j.,** jugo digestivo, m

juiciness n jugosidad, f; suculencia, f

juicy a jugoso; suculento

jujube n pastilla, f

jukebox n tocadiscos, vitrola, sinfonola, f

July n julio, m

jumble vt mezclar, confundir. n mezcla confusa, colección miscelánea, confusión, f. **j. sale,** tómbola, f

jump n salto, m; (in prices, etc.) aumento, m. **at one j.,** de un salto. **high j.,** salto de altura, m. **long j.,** salto de longitud, m. **to be on the j.,** inf estar nervioso, tener los nervios en punta

jump vi saltar; dar un salto; brincar; (of tea-cups, etc.) bailar; (throb) pulsar. vt saltar; hacer saltar; (a child) brincar; (omit) pasar por alto de, omitir. **The train jumped the rails,** El tren se descarriló. **to j. out of bed,** saltar de la cama. **to j. to the conclusion that . . . ,** darse prisa a concluir que . . . **to j. about,** dar saltos, brincar; revolverse, moverse de un lado para otro. **to j. at,** saltar sobre; precipitarse sobre; abalanzarse hacia; (an offer) apresurarse a aceptar; (seize) coger con entusiasmo. **to j. down,** bajar de un salto. **to j. over,** saltar; saltar por encima de. **to j. up,** saltar; (on to a horse, etc.) montar rápidamente; levantarse apresuradamente. **to j. with,** (agree) convenir en, estar conforme con

jumper n saltador (-ra); (sailor's) blusa, f; jersey, suéter m, Lat. Am. chompa, f

jumping n salto, m pl. a saltador. **j.-off place,** base avanzada, f; fig trampolín, m. **j.-pole,** pértiga, f

jumpiness n nerviosidad, f

jumpy a nervioso, agitado

junction n unión, f; (of roads) bifurcación, f; (railway) empalme, m; (connection) conexión, f

juncture n coyuntura, f; momento, m; crisis, f, momento crítico, m; (joint) junta, f

June n junio, m

jungle n selva, f. **j.-fever,** fiebre de los grandes bosques, f

junior a joven; hijo; más joven; menos antiguo; subordinado, segundo. n joven, mf **Carmen is my j. by three years,** Carmen es tres años más joven que yo.

James Thomson, Jr., James Thomson, hijo. **the j. school,** los pequeños. **j. partner,** socio menor, *m*

juniper *n bot* enebro, *m*

junk *n* trastos viejos, *m pl;* (nonsense) patrañas, *f pl; naut* junco, *m;* (salt meat) tasajo, *m.* **j.-shop,** tienda de trastos viejos, *f*

junk bond bono-basura, *m*

junketing *n* festividades, *f pl*

juridical *a* jurídico

jurisconsult *n* jurisconsulto, *m*

jurisdiction *n* jurisdicción, *f;* competencia, *f*

jurisprudence *n* jurisprudencia, *f*

jurist *n* jurista, legista, *mf*

juror *n* (miembro del) jurado, *m*

jury *n* jurado, *m.* **to be on the j.,** formar parte del jurado. **j.-box,** tribuna del jurado, *f*

juryman *n* miembro del jurado, *m*

just *a* justo; justiciero; exacto; fiel. **Peter the J.,** Pedro el justiciero

just *adv* justamente, exactamente; precisamente; (scarcely) apenas; (almost) casi; (entirely) completamente; (simply) meramente, solamente, tan sólo; (newly) recién (followed by past part.), recientemente. **He only j. missed being run over,** Por poco le atropellan. **It is j. near,** Está muy cerca. **It is j. the same to me,** Me es completamente igual. **J. as he was leaving,** Cuando estaba a punto de marcharse, En el momento de marcharse. **Just as you arrive in Spain, you must . . .** Nada más llegar a España, tienes que

. . . **That's j. it!** ¡Eso es! ¡Exactamente! **to have j.,** acabar de. **They have j. dined,** Acaban de cenar. **J. as you wish,** Como Vd. quiera. **j. at that moment,** precisamente en aquel momento. **j. by,** muy cerca; al lado. **j. now,** ahora mismo; hace poco; pronto, dentro de poco. **j. yet,** todavía. **They will not come j. yet,** No vendrán todavía. **Just looking** (browser to shopkeeper) Estoy viendo, Estamos viendo

justice *n* justicia, *f;* (judge) juez, *m;* (magistrate) juez municipal, *m.* **to bring to j.,** llevar ante el juez (a). **to do j. to,** (a person) hacer justicia (a); (a meal) hacer honor (a). **to do oneself j.,** quedar bien

justifiable *a* justificable

justifiably *adv* con justicia, justificadamente

justification *n* justificación, *f*

justify *vt* justificar, vindicar; (excuse) disculpar; *print* justificar. **to be justified (in),** tener derecho (a), tener motivo (para), tener razón (en)

justly *adv* justamente; con justicia; con derecho; con razón; exactamente; debidamente

justness *n* justicia, *f;* exactitud, *f*

jut (out) *vi* salir, proyectar; sobresalir

jute *n* yute, *m*

juvenile *a* juvenil; de la juventud; para la juventud; joven; de niños; para niños. *n* joven, *mf.* **j. court,** tribunal de menores, *m.* **j. lead,** *theat* galance, galán joven, *m.* **j. offender,** delincuente infantil, *m*

juxtapose *vt* yuxtaponer

juxtaposition *n* yuxtaposición, *f*

K

k *n* (letter) ka, *f*

kaiser *n* káiser, emperador, *m.* **the K.** el emperador alemán, *m*

kaleidoscope *n* calidoscopio, *m*

kaleidoscopic *a* calidoscópico

kangaroo *n* canguro, *m*

kaolin *n* caolín, *m*

kapok *n* miraguano, *m*

keel *n* quilla, *f. vt* carenar. **to k. over,** volcar; caer; *naut* zozobrar

keelson *n* sobrequilla, *f*

keen *a* (of edges) afilado; agudo; penetrante; vivo; sutil; ardiente; celoso, entusiasta; mordaz; (desirous) ansioso; (of appetite) grande, bueno. **He is a k. tennis player,** Es tenista entusiasta. **Joan has a very k. ear,** Juana tiene un oído muy agudo. **I'm not very k. on apples,** No me gustan mucho las manzanas

keenly *adv* agudamente; vivamente; (of feeling) hondamente; (of looking) atentamente

keenness *n* (of a blade) afiladura, *f;* agudeza, *f;* viveza, *f;* sutileza, *f;* perspicacia, *f;* (enthusiasm) entusiasmo, *m,* afición, *f;* (desire) ansia, *f*

keep *vt* guardar; tener; que darse con; retener; conservar; mantener; (a shop, hotel, etc.) dirigir, tener; (a school) ser director de; (a promise, etc.) cumplir; (the law, etc.) observar, guardar; (celebrate) solemnizar; (a secret) guardar; (books, accounts, a house, in step) llevar; (sheep, etc., one's bed) guardar; (a city, etc.) defender; (domestic animals, cars, etc.) tener; (lodge) alojar; (detain) detener; (reserve) reservar; (cause) hacer. **They had kept this room for me,** Me habían reservado este cuarto. **Dorothy has kept the blue dress,** Dorotea se ha quedado con el vestido azul. **The government could not k. order,** El gobierno no sabía mantener el orden. **I did not know how to k. their attention,** No sabía retener su atención. **Carmen kept quiet,** Carmen guardó silencio, Carmen se calló. **Can you k. a secret?** ¿Sabes guardar un secreto? **to k. an appointment,** acudir a una cita. **to k. in repair,** conservar en buen estado. **to k. someone from doing something,** evitar que uno haga algo. **to k. someone waiting,** hacer que espere uno. **to k.**

something from someone, ocultar algo de uno. **We were kept at it night and day,** Nos hacían trabajar día y noche. **I always k. it by me,** Lo tengo siempre a mi lado (or conmigo). **to k. away,** alejar; mantener a distancia; no dejar venir. **to k. back,** (a crowd, etc.) detener; cortar el paso (a); no dejar avanzar; (retain) guardar, retener; reservar; (tears, words) reprimir, contener; (evidence, etc.) callar, suprimir. **to k. down,** no dejar subir (a); sujetar; (a nation, etc.) oprimir, subyugar; (emotions) dominar; (prices, expenses) mantener bajo; (check) moderar, reprimir. **to k. in,** (feelings) contener; reprimir; (the house) hacer quedarse en casa, no dejar salir; (imprison) encerrar; (school) hacer quedar en la escuela (a). **to k. off,** alejar; tener a distancia (a); cerrar el paso (a), no dejar avanzar; no andar sobre; no tocar; (a subject) no tratar de, no discutir, no tocar. **K. your hands off!** ¡No toques! **to k. on,** guardar; retener; (eyes) fijar en, poner en. **to k. out,** no dejar entrar; excluir. **It is difficult to k. him out of trouble,** Es difícil de evitar que se meta en líos. **to k.** *to,* seguir; limitarse a; adherirse a; **K. to the Left,** «Tome su izquierda», **K. to the right,** «Tome su derecha»; (a path, etc.) seguir por; (one's bed) guardar; (fulfil) cumplir; (oblige) hacer, obligar. **to k. under,** subyugar, oprimir; dominar; controlar. **to k. up,** mantener; (appearances) guardar; conservar; persistir en; (prices) sostener; (in good repair) conservar en buen estado; (go on doing) continuar. **He kept me up late last night,** Anoche me entretuvo hasta muy tarde; Ayer me hizo trasnochar; Anoche me hizo velar. **to k. one's end up,** volver por sí, hacerse fuerte. **to k. up one's spirits,** no desanimarse

keep *vi* quedar; (be) estar; (continue) seguir, continuar; mantenerse; (at home, etc.) quedarse, permanecer; (be accustomed) acostumbrar, soler; (persist) persistir; (of food) conservarse fresco. **How is he keeping?** ¿Cómo está? **to k. in with someone,** cultivar a alguien. **to k. up with the times,** mantenerse al corriente. **to k. at,** seguir; persistir; perseverar; (pester) importunar. **John keeps at it,** Juan trabaja sin descansar. **to k. away,** mantenerse apartado; mantenerse a distancia; no acudir. **to k. back,** hacerse a un lado, apartarse, alejarse. **to k. down,** quedarse tumbado; seguir acurrucado; no levantarse; esconderse. **to k. from,** (doing something) guardarse de. **to k. off,** mantenerse a distancia. **If the storm keeps off,** Si no estalla una tempestad. **If the rain keeps off,** Si no empieza a llover, Si no hay lluvia. **to k. on,** continuar; seguir. **to k. straight on,** seguir derecho. **I'm tired, but I still k. on,** Estoy cansado, pero sigo trabajando. **to k. out,** quedarse fuera. **to k. out of,** (quarrels, trouble, etc.) no meterse en, evitar. **to k. out of sight,** no dejarse ver, no mostrarse, mantenerse oculto. **to k. together,** quedarse juntos; reunirse

keep *n* (of a castle) mazmorra, *f;* (maintenance) subsistencia, *f;* comida, *f.* **for keeps,** para siempre jamás

keeper *n* guarda, *mf;* (in a park, zoo, of a lunatic) guardián, *m;* (of a museum, etc.) director, *m;* (of animals) criador (-ra); (gamekeeper) guardabosque, *m;* (of a boardinghouse, shop, etc.) dueño (-ña); (of accounts, books) tenedor, *m.* **Am I my brother's k.?** ¿Soy yo responsable por mi hermano?

keeping *n* guarda, *f;* conservación, *f;* protección, *f;* (of a rule) observación, *f;* (of an anniversary, etc.) celebración, *f;* (of a person) mantenimiento, *m.* **in k. with,** en armonía con; de acuerdo con. **out of k. with,** en desacuerdo con. **to be in safe k.,** estar en buenas manos; estar en un lugar seguro. **k. back,** retención, *f*

keepsake *n* recuerdo, *m*

keg *n* barrilete, *m*

ken *n* alcance de la vista, *m;* vista, *f;* comprensión, *f*

Kennedy Round, the la serie Kénnedy, *f*

kennel *n* (of a dog) perrera, *f;* (of hounds) jauría, *f;* (dwelling) cuchitril, *m;* (gutter) arroyo, *m.* **k. man,** perrero, *m*

kepi *n* quepis, *m*

Kepler Keplero

kerb, kerbstone See **curb**

kerchief *n* pañuelo, *m;* pañoleta, *f.* **brightly-colored k.,** pañuelo de hierbas, *m*

kernel *n* almendra, semilla, *f; fig* meollo, *m,* esencia, *f*

kerosene *n* petróleo de lámpara, *m;* kerosén, *m*

ketchup *n* salsa de tomate y setas, *f*

kettle *n* caldero, *m, Mexico* marmita, *f.* **pretty k. of fish,** olla de grillos, *f.* **k.-drum,** timbal, *m.* **k.-drum player,** timbalero, *m*

key *n* llave, *f; (fig arch, mus)* clave, *f;* (tone) tono, *m;* (of a piano, typewriter, etc.) tecla, *f; mech* chaveta, *f;* (of a wind instrument) pistón, *m;* (winged fruit) sámara, *f; elec* conmutador, *m.* **major (minor) key,** tono mayor (menor), *m.* **latch-key,** llave de la puerta, *f;* (Yale) llavín, *m.* **master key,** llave maestra, *f;* **skeleton key,** ganzúa, *f.* **He is all keyed up,** Tiene los nervios en punta. **key industry,** industria clave, *f.* **key man,** hombre indispensable, *m.* **key point,** punto estratégico, *m.* **key-ring,** llavero, *m.* **key signature,** *mus* clave, *f.* **key word,** palabra clave, *f*

keyboard *n* teclado, *m*

keyhole *n* ojo de la cerradura, *m.* **through the k.,** por el ojo de la cerradura

keynote *n mus* tónica, *f; fig* piedra clave, idea fundamental, *f*

keystone *n* piedra clave, *f*

khaki *n* caqui, *m*

kick *vt* dar un puntapié (a); golpear; (a goal) chutar. *vi* (of horses, etc.) dar coces, cocear; (of guns) recular. **to k. one's heels,** hacer tiempo. **to kick the bucket,** palmarla, *Lat. Am.* arrancarse. **to k. up a row,** hacer un ruido de mil diablos; (quarrel) armar camorra. **to k. about,** dar patadas (a). **to k. away,** quitar con el pie; lanzar con el pie. **to k. off,** quitar con el pie; lanzar; sacudirse. **k.-off,** *n* golpe de salida, puntapié inicial, saque, *m.* **to k. out,** echar a puntapiés

kick *n* puntapié, *m;* golpe, *m;* coz, *f;* (of guns) culatazo, *m.* **free k.,** golpe franco, *m*

kicking *n* coces, *f pl;* acoceamiento, *m;* pataleo, *m;* golpeamiento, *f*

kid *n* cabrito, *m,* chivo (-va); carne de cabrito, *f;*

(leather) cabritilla, *f; inf* crío, *m.* **kid gloves,** guantes de cabritilla, *m pl*

kidnap *vt* secuestrar

kidnapper *n* secuestrador (-ra); ladrón (-ona) de niños

kidnapping *n* secuestro, *m*

kidney *n* riñón, *m; fig* especie, índole, *f.* **k.-bean,** (plant) judía, *f;* (fruit) habichuela, judía, *f,* fréjol, *Mexico* calamaco, *m*

Kidron Cedrón, *m*

kill *vt* matar; destruir; suprimir. **to k. off,** exterminar. **to k. time,** entretener el tiempo, pasarse las horas muertas. **to k. two birds with one stone,** matar dos pájaros de un tiro. **k.-joy,** aguafiestas, *mf*

killer *n* matador (-ra); (murderer) asesino, *mf*

killing *n* matanza, *f;* (murder) asesinato, *m. a* matador; destructivo; (comic) cómico; ridículo; absurdo; (ravishing) irresistible

kiln *n* horno de cerámica, horno, *m*

kilo *n* kilo, *m*

kilocycle *n elec* kilociclo, *m*

kilogram *n* kilogramo, *m*

kiloliter *n* kilolitro, *m*

kilometer *n* kilómetro, *m*

kilometric *a* kilométrico

kilowatt *n elec* kilovatio, *m*

kin *n* parientes, *m pl;* familia, *f;* clase, especie, *f.* **the next of kin,** los parientes próximos, la familia

kind *n* género, *m,* clase, *f;* especie, *f; inf* tipo, *m.* **He is a queer k. of person,** Es un tipo muy raro. **What k. of cloth is it?** ¿Qué clase de tela es? **Nothing of the k!** ¡Nada de eso! **payment in k.,** pago en especie, *m*

kind *a* bondadoso, bueno; cariñoso, tierno; amable; favorable, propicio. **Will you be so k. as to . . .** Tenga Vd. la bondad de . . . **With k. regards,** Con un saludo afectuoso. **You have been very k. to her,** Vd. ha sido muy bueno para ella. **k.-hearted,** bondadoso. **k.-heartedness,** bondad, benevolencia, *f*

kindergarten *n* jardín de la infancia, kindergarten, *m*

kindle *vt* encender; hacer arder; *fig* avivar. *vi* prender; empezar a arder; encenderse; *fig* inflamarse

kindliness *n* bondad, *f*

kindling *n* encendimiento (del fuego), *m;* (wood) leña menuda, *Lat. Am.* charamusca, *f*

kindly *a* bondadoso; bueno; benévolo; propicio, favorable; (of climate) benigno. *adv* con bondad, bondadosamente; fácilmente. **K. sit down,** Haga el favor de sentarse

kindness *n* bondad, *f;* benevolencia, *f;* amabilidad, *f;* cariño, *m;* favor, *m,* atención, *f*

kindred *n* parentesco, *m;* parientes, *m pl;* familia, *f;* afinidad, *f, a* emparentado; hermano

king *n* (ruler, important person, chess, cards) rey, *m;* (in draughts) dama, *f.* **king's evil,** escrófula, *f.* **k.-bolt,** perno real, *m.* **k.-craft,** arte de reinar, *m,* or *f.* **k.-cup,** *bot* botón de oro, *m.* **K.-of-Arms,** rey de armas, *m.* **k.-post,** pendolón, *m*

kingdom *n* reino, *m.* **animal k.,** reino animal, *m*

kingfisher *n* martín pescador, alción, *m*

kink *n* nudo, *m;* pliegue, *m;* (curl) rizo, *m; fig* peculiaridad, *f*

kinsfolk *n* parientes, *m pl,* familia, *f*

kinship *n* parentesco, *m;* afinidad, *f*

kinsman *n* pariente, deudo, *m*

kinswoman *n* parienta, *f*

kiosk *n* quiosco, *m*

kipper *n* arenque ahumado, *m. vt* ahumar

kiss *n* beso, *m;* (in billiards) pelo, *m. vt* besar; dar un beso (a); (of billiard balls) tocar. **to k. each other,** besarse. **k.-curl,** rizo de la sien, *m,* sortijilla, *f*

kit *n* (tub) cubo, *m;* (for tools, etc.) cajita, caja, *f;* (soldier's) equipo, *m.* **kit-bag,** mochila, *f*

kitchen *n* cocina, *f.* **k.-boy,** pinche (de cocina), *m.* **k.-garden,** huerta, *f.* **k.-maid,** fregona, *f.* **k.-range,** cocina económica, *f.* **k.-sink,** fregadero, *Chile, Mexico, also* lavaplatos, *m.* **k.-stove,** horno de cocina, *m.* **k. utensils,** batería de cocina, *f*

kitchenette *n* cocinilla, *f*

kite *n orn* milano, *m*; cometa, pájara, *f*. **to fly a k.,** hacer volar una cometa. **box-k.,** cometa celular, *f*

kith and kin *n pl* parientes y amigos, *m pl*

kitten *n* gatito (-ta). *vi* (of a cat) parir

kittenish *a* de gatito; juguetón

kitty *n* michito, *m*; (in card games) platillo, *m*

kleptomania *n* cleptomanía, *f*

kleptomaniac *a* cleptómano. *n* cleptómano (-na)

knack *n* destreza, *f*; talento, *m*; (trick) truco, *m*

knapsack *n* mochila, *f*; mil alforja, *f*

knave *n* bellaco, truhán, tunante, *m*; (at cards) sota, *f*

knavery *n* bellaquería, truhanería, *f*

knavish *a* de bribón; taimado, truhanesco

knead *vt* amasar; (massage) sobar; *fig* formar

kneading *n* amasijo, *m*; (massaging) soba, *f*. **k.-trough,** amasadera artesa *f*

knee *n* rodilla, *f*; *fig* ángulo, codillo, *m*. **on bended k.,** de hinojos. **on one's knees,** de rodillas, arrodillado. **to go down on one's knees,** arrodillarse, ponerse de rodillas. **k.-breeches,** calzón corto, *m*; calzón ceñido, *m*; (Elizabethan) gregüescos, *m pl*. **k.-cap,** rótula, *f*. **k.-deep,** hasta las rodillas. **k.-joint,** articulación de la rodilla, *f*; *mech* junta de codillo, *f*. **k.-pad,** rodillera, *f*

kneel (down) *vi* arrodillarse, hincarse de rodillas, ponerse de rodillas

kneeling *a* arrodillado, de rodillas

knell *n* toque de difuntos, tañido fúnebre, *m*; toque de campanas, *m*; *fig* muerte, *f*. *vi* tocar a muerto. *vt* fig anunciar, presagiar

knickerbockers *n pl* bragas, *f pl*; calzón corto, *m*; (women's) pantalones, *m pl*

knickknack *n* chuchería, *f*

knife *n* cuchillo, *m*. **to have one's k. in someone,** tener enemiga (a), querer mal (a). **war to the k.,** guerra a muerte, *f*. **k.-edge,** filo de cuchillo, *m*; fiel de soporte, *m*. **k. grinder,** amolador, *m*. **k.-handle,** mango de cuchillo, *m*. **k. thrust,** cuchillada, *f*

knife, fork, and spoon cuchara, tenedor, y cuchillo

knight *n* caballero, *m*; (chess) caballo, *m*. *vt* armar caballero, calzar la espuela; (in modern usage) dar el título de caballero. **untried k.,** caballero novel, *m*. **k. commander,** comendador, *m*. **k.-errant,** caballero andante, *m*. **k.-errantry,** caballería andante, *f*. **Knight of Labor,** Caballero del Trabajo *m*. **k. of the rueful countenance,** el caballero de la triste figura

knighthood *n* caballería, *f*; (in modern usage) título de caballero, *m*

knightly *a* caballeresco; de caballero; de caballería

knit *vt* and *vi* hacer calceta, hacer media; juntar, ligar; unir. **Isabel is knitting me a jumper,** Isabel me hace un jersey de punto de media. **to k. one's brows,** fruncir el ceño

knitted *a* de punto. **k. goods,** géneros de punto, *m pl*

knitter *n* calcetero (-ra); (machine) máquina de hacer calceta, *f*

knitting *n* acción de hacer calceta, *f*; trabajo de punto, *m*, labor de calceta, *f*; unión, *f*. **k.-machine,** máquina de hacer calceta, *f*. **k.-needle,** aguja de media, aguja de hacer calceta, *f*

knob *n* protuberancia, *f*; (of a door, etc.) perilla, borlita, *f*; (ornamental) bellota, *f*; (of sugar) terrón, *m*; (of a stick) puño, *m*

knock *n* golpe, *m*; choque, *m*; (with a knocker) aldabada, *f*

knock *vt* golpear; chocar (contra). *vi* llamar a la puerta; (of an engine) picar. **to k. one's head against,** chocar con la cabeza contra, dar con la cabeza contra. **to k. about,** *vt* pegar; aporrear. *vi* viajar; vagar, rodar; ca-

llejear. **to k. against,** golpear contra; chocar contra. **to k. down,** derribar; (of vehicles) atropellar, *Mexico* antellevar; (houses, etc.) demoler; (an argument, etc.) destruir; (a tender, etc.) rebajar; (of an auctioneer) rematar al mejor postor. **to k. in,** (nails, etc.) clavar. **to k. into one another,** toparse. **to k. off,** hacer caer; sacudir; quitar; (from price) descontar; (from speed, etc.) reducir; (finish) terminar pronto; (runs in cricket) hacer. **to k. out,** (remove) quitar; (boxing) dejar fuera de combate, noquear; (fig stun) atontar; (an idea, etc.) bosquejar. **to k. over,** volcar. **to k. up,** hacer saltar; (call) llamar; (runs at cricket) hacer; (tire) agotar, rendir; (building) construir toscamente. **to k. up against,** chocar contra; tropezar con. **k.-kneed,** *a* patiabierto. **k.-out,** "knock-out," *m*

knocker *n* (on a door) aldaba, *f*. **k.-up,** despertador, *m*

knocking *n* golpes, *m pl*, golpeo, *m*; (with a knocker) aldabeo, *m*. **k. over,** vuelco, *m*; (by a vehicle) atropello, *m*

knoll *n* altillo, otero, *m*

knot *n* nudo, *m*; (bow) lazo, *m*; (of hair) moño, *m*; *naut* nudo, *m*, milla náutica, *f*; (of people) corrillo, grupo, *m*; (on timber) nudo, *m*. *vt* anudar. *vi* hacer nudos; enmarañarse. **to tie a k.,** hacer un nudo

knotted *a* nudoso

knotty *a* nudoso; *fig* intrincado, difícil, complicado. **a k. problem,** problema espinoso

know *vt* conocer; saber; (understand) comprender; (recognize) reconocer. **I k. her very well by sight,** La conozco muy bien de vista. **John knows Latin,** Juan sabe latín. **How can I k.?** ¿Cómo lo voy a saber yo? **I knew you at once,** Te reconocí en seguida. **They always k. best,** Siempre tienen razón. **Did you k. about Philip?** ¿Has oído lo de Felipe? **to be in the k.,** estar bien informado, estar de buena tinta. **to get to k.,** (a person) llegar a conocer, trabar amistad con. **to make known,** dar a conocer; manifestar. **Who knows?** ¿Quién sabe? **to k. by heart,** saber de coro. **to k. how,** (to do something) saber. **to k. oneself,** conocerse a sí mismo. **k.-it-all,** sabelotodo, *mf*, marisabidilla, *f*

knowing *a* inteligente; malicioso; (of animals) sabio. **There is no k.,** No hay modo de saberlo. **worth k.,** digno de saberse

knowingly *adv* a sabiendas, de intento; conscientemente; (cleverly) hábilmente; (with look, etc.) de un aire malicioso

knowledge *n* conocimiento, *m*. **To the best of my k. the book does not exist,** El libro no existe que yo sepa. **He has a thorough k. of . . .,** Conoce a fondo . . . **lack of k.,** ignorancia, *f*. **He did it without my k.,** Lo hizo sin que lo supiera yo. **It is a matter of common k. that . . .** Es notorio que . . .

knowledgeable *a* sabedor

known *a* conocido

knuckle *n* (of a finger) nudillo, *m*, articulación del dedo, *f*; (of meat) jarrete, *m*. **He knuckled down to his work,** Se puso a trabajar con ahínco. **to k. under,** someterse. **k.-duster,** rompecabezas, *m*

kopeck *n* copec, *f*

Koran *n* Corán, Alcorán, *m*

Korea Corea, *f*

kosher *a* cosher; (slang) genuino

kowtow *vi* saludar humildemente; *fig* bajar la cerviz

Kremlin *n* Kremlín, *m*

kudos *n* prestigio, *m*, gloria, *f*

Kurdish *a* curdo

kyrie eleison *n* kirieleisón, *m*

L

l *n* (letter) ele, *f*

la *n mus* la, *m*

label *n* etiqueta, (on a garment), rótula, *m*, (on a can), *f*; (on a museum specimen, etc.) letrero, *m*; *fig* calificación, *f. vt* poner etiqueta en; marcar, rotular; *fig* calificar, designar, clasificar

labial *a* labial. *n* letra labial, *f*

labor *n* trabajo, *m*; labor, *f*; fatiga, pena, *f*; clase obrera, *f*; (manual workers) mano de obra, *f*; (effort) esfuerzo, *m*; (of childbirth) dolores de parto, *m pl. vi* trabajar; (strive) esforzarse, afanarse; (struggle) forcejar, luchar; (try) procurar, tratar de; avanzar con dificultad; (in childbirth) estar de parto. *vt* elaborar; pulir, perfeccionar. **to l. under,** sufrir; tener que luchar contra. **hard l.,** trabajo arduo, *m; law* trabajos forzosos, *m pl,* presidio, *m.* **Ministry of L.,** Ministerio de Trabajo, *m.* **to be in l.,** estar de parto. **to l. in vain,** trabajar en balde, arar en el mar. **to l. under a delusion,** estar en el error, estar equivocado. **L. Exchange,** Bolsa de Trabajo, *f.* **l. leader,** dirigente sindical, *m.* **L. party,** partido laborista, partido obrero, *m.* **l. question,** cuestión obrera, *f*; (domestic) problema del servicio, *m.* **l.-saving,** *a* que ahorra trabajo. **l. union,** sindicato, *m*

laboratory *n* laboratorio, *m*

labored *a* (of style) premioso, artificial; forzado; (of breathing) fatigoso; (slow) torpe, lento

laborer *n* obrero, *m*; (on the land) labrador, labriego, *m*; (on the roads, etc.) peón, *m*; (by the day) jornalero, *m*

laborious *a* laborioso; arduo, difícil, penoso

laboriously *adv* laboriosamente; con dificultad, penosamente

laboriousness *n* laboriosidad, *f*; dificultad, *f*

Labrador dog *n* perro de Labrador, *m*

labyrinth *n* laberinto, *m*

labyrinthine *a* laberíntico; intrincado

lace *n* (of shoes, corsets, etc.) cordón, *m*; (tape) cinta, *f*; encaje, *m*; (narrow, for trimming) puntilla, *f*; (of gold or silver) galón, *m. vt* and *vi* (shoes, etc.) atarse los cordones; (trim) guarnecer con encajes, etc.; *fig* ornar; (a drink) echar (coñac, etc.) en. **blond l.,** blonda, *f.* **gold l.,** galón de oro, *m.* **point l.,** encaje de aguja, *m.* **l. curtain,** cortina de encaje, *f*; (of net) visillo, *m.* **l. maker** or **seller,** encajero (-ra), *mf.* **l. making,** obra de encaje, *f.* **l.-pillow,** almohadilla para encajes, *f.* **l. shoes,** zapatos con cordones, *m pl*

lacerate *vt* lacerar

laceration *n* laceración, *f*

lachrymal *a* lagrimal, lacrimal

lachrymose *a* lacrimoso

lack *n* falta, *f.* **l. of evidence,** falta de pruebas, *f*; carestía, escasez, *f*; (absence) ausencia, *f*; (need) necesidad, *f. vt* carecer de; no tener; necesitar. *vi* hacer falta; necesitarse. **to l. confidence in oneself,** no tener confianza en sí mismo, carecer de confianza en sí mismo. **l.-luster,** (of eyes) apagado, mortecino. **l. of evidence,** falta de pruebas, *f*

lackadaisical *a* lánguido; indiferente; (dreamy) ensimismado, distraído

lackey *n* lacayo, *m*

laconic *a* lacónico

lacquer *n* laca, *f, vt* dar laca (a), barnizar con laca. **gold l.,** sisa dorada, *f.* **l. work,** laca, *f*

lacquering *n* barnizado de laca, *m*; laca, capa de barniz de laca, *f*

lactate *n* lactato, *m, vi* lactar

lactation *n* lactancia, *f*

lacteal *a* lácteo

lactic *a* láctico

lactose *n* lactosa, *f*

lacuna *n* laguna, *f*

lacy *a* de encaje; parecido a encaje; *fig* transparente, etéreo

lad *n* muchacho, joven, mozalbete, *m*; zagal, *m*; (stable, etc.) mozo, *m.* **He's some l.!** ¡Qué tío que es! **l. of the village,** chulo, *m*

ladder *n* escalera de mano, *f*; *naut* escala, *f*; (in a stocking, etc.) carrera, *f.* **companion l.,** escala de toldilla, *f.* **to l. one's stocking,** escurrirse un punto de las medias

Ladies and gentlemen *n. pl* Señoras y señores, Señoras y caballeros. **ladies' man,** hombre de salón, Perico entre ellas, mujeriego, *m*

lading *n* flete, *m*, carga, *f*

ladle *n* cucharón, cazo, *m. vt* servir con cucharón; (a boat) achicar; *inf* distribuir, repartir

lady *n* dama, *f*; señora, *f*; (English title) milady, *f*; (woman) mujer, *f.* **to be a l.,** ser una señora. **leading l.,** *theat* dama primera, *f.* **Our L.,** Nuestra Señora. **young l.,** señorita, *f*; *inf* novia, *f.* **lady's maid,** doncella, *f.* **l. of the house,** señora de la casa, *f.* **l. bug,** *ent* catalina mariquita, vaca de San Antonio, *f.* **L. Chapel,** capilla de la Virgen, *f.* **L. Day,** día de la Anunciación (de Nuestra Señora), *m.* **l.-help,** asistenta, *f.* **l.-in-waiting,** dama de servicio, *f.* **l.-killer,** ladrón de corazones, castigador, tenorio, *m.* **l.-love,** querida, amada, *f.* **l. mayoress,** alcaldesa, *f*

ladylike *a* de dama; elegante; distinguido; bien educado; delicado; (of men) afeminado

ladyship *n* señoría, *f.* **Your L.,** Su Señoría

lag *vt* recubrir; aislar. *vi* retrasarse; quedarse atrás; ir (or andar) despacio; rezagarse; *naut* roncear. *n* retraso, *m*; *mech* retardación de movimiento, *f*

laggard *n* holgazán (-ana), haragán (-ana)

lagoon *n* laguna, *f*

laid *past part* of verb **to lay. l. up,** (ill) enfermo; *naut* inactivo; (of cars, etc.) fuera de circulación

lair *n* cubil, *m*; guarida, madriguera, *f*

laity *n* legos, *m pl*

lake *n* lago, *m*; (pigment) laca, *f. small l.,** laguna, *f.* **l. dwelling,** vivienda palustre, *f*

lama *n* lama, *m*

lamb *n* cordero (-ra). *vi* parir corderos. **lamb's wool,** lana de cordero. *f*

lambent *a* ondulante, vacilante; centelleante

lamblike *a* manso como un cordero; inocente

lambskin *n* corderina, piel de cordero, *f*

lame *a* estropeado, lisiado; (in the feet) cojo; (of meter) que cojea, malo; (of arguments) poco convincente; frívolo, flojo. *vt* lisiar; hacer cojo. **l. excuse,** pretexto frívolo. **to be l.,** (in the feet) (permanently) ser cojo; (temporarily) estar cojo

lamely *adv* cojeando, con cojera; *fig* sin convicción; mal

lameness *n* cojera, *f*; falta de convicción, *f*

lament *n* lamento, *m*; queja, lamentación, *f. vi* lamentarse; quejarse. *vt* lamentar, deplorar, llorar

lamentable *a* lamentable, deplorable; lastimero

lamentation *n* lamentación, *f*, lamento, *m.* **Book of Lamentations,** Libro de los lamentos, *m*

lamenting *n* lamentación, *f*

lamina *n* lámina, *f*

laminate *a* laminado, laminar. *vt* laminar

lamp *n* lámpara, *f*; (on vehicles, trains, ships and in the street) farol, *m*; luz, *f*; (oil) candil, *m*, lámpara de aceite, *f.* **safety-l.,** lámpara de seguridad, lámpara de los mineros, *f.* **street l.,** farol (de las calles), *m.* **l.-black,** negro de humo, *m.* **l.-chimney,** tubo de una lámpara, *m.* **l. factory** or **shop,** lamparería, *f.* **l.-holder,** portalámpara, *f.* **l.-lighter,** farolero, lamparero, *m.* **l.-post,** farola, *f.* **l.-shade,** pantalla (de lámpara,) *f.* **l. stand,** pie de lámpara, *m*

lamplight *n* luz de la lámpara, *f*; luz artificial, *f.* **in the l.,** a la luz de la lámpara; en luz artificial

lampoon *n* pasquinada, *f*, pasquín, *m, vt* pasquinar, satirizar

lampooner *n* escritor (-ra) de pasquinadas, libelista, *m*

lamprey *n* lamprea, *f*

lance *n* lanza, *f*; (soldier) lancero, *m. vt* alancear; *med* lancinar. **l. in rest,** lanza en ristre, *f.* **l. thrust,** lanzada, *f.* **l.-corporal,** soldado de primera clase, *m*

lancer *n mil* lancero, *m*; *pl* lancers, (dance and music) lanceros, *m pl*

lancet *n* apostemero, *m*, lanceta, *f.* **l. arch,** arco puntiagudo, *m*

land *n* tierra, *f*; terreno, *m*; (country) país, *m*; (region) región, *f*; territorio, *m*; (estate) bienes raíces, *m pl,* tierras, fincas, *f pl. vt* desembarcar; echar en tierra; (*fig place*) poner; *inf* dejar plantado (con); (obtain) obtener; (a fish) sacar del agua; (a blow) dar (un golpe); (leave) dejar. *vi* desembarcar; saltar en tierra; (of a plane) aterrizar; (arrive) llegar; (fall) caer. **to l. on water** *Lat. Am.* acuatizar. **cultivated l.,** tierras cultivadas, *f pl.* **dry l.,** (not sea) tierra firme, *f.* **native l.,** patria, *f;* suelo natal, *m.* **on l.,** en tierra. **to see how the l. lies,** *fig* tantear el terreno. **l. of milk and honey,** jauja, *f,* paraíso, *m.* **l. of promise,** tierra de promisión, *f.* **l. agent,** procurador de fincas, *m.* **l. breeze,** brisa de tierra, *f.* **l. forces,** fuerzas terrestres, *f pl.* **l. law,** leyes agrarias, *f pl.* **l.-locked,** cercado de tierra, mediterráneo **l.-lubber,** marinero de agua dulce, *m.* **l. mine,** mina terrestre, *f.* **l. surveying,** agrimensura, *f.* **l. surveyor,** agrimensor, *m.* **l. tax,** contribución territorial, *f*

landau *n* landó, *m*
landed *a* hacendado. **l. gentry,** hacendados, terratenientes, *m pl.* **l. property,** bienes raíces, *m pl*
landfall *n* derrumbamiento de tierras, *m*
landing *n* desembarque, desembarco, *m;* (landing place) desembarcadero, *m;* *aer* aterrizaje, *m;* (of steps) descanso, rellano, *m,* mesa, mesilla, *f.* **forced l.,** aterrizaje forzoso, *m.* **l. certificate,** *com* tornaguía, *f.* **l. craft,** barcaza de desembarco, *f.* **l. field,** campo de aterrizaje, *m,* pista de vuelo, *f.* **l.-net,** salabardo, *m.* **l. party,** trozo de abordaje, *m.* **l. signal,** *aer* señal de aterrizaje, *f.* **l.-stage,** desembarcadero, *m;* (jetty) atracadero, *m*
landlady *n* patrona, huéspeda, *f*
landlord *n* (of houses, land) propietario, *m;* hotelero, patrón, *m*
landmark *n* (of a hill or mountain) punto destacado, *m;* lugar conocido, *m;* característica, *f; fig* monumento, *m*
landmass *n* unidad territorial, *f*
landowner *n* hacendado, terrateniente, *m*
landscape *n* paisaje, *m;* perspectiva, *f.* **l. gardener,** arquitecto de jardines, *m.* **l. painter,** paisajista, *mf*
landslide *n* desprendimiento de tierras, *m; fig* cambio brusco de la opinión pública, *m*
landward *adv* hacia tierra
lane *n* vereda, senda, *f;* (of traffic) carril, *m,* *Argentina, Spain,* línea, *f*
language *n* lenguaje, *m;* lengua, *f,* idioma, *m.* **modern l.,** lengua viva, *f.* **strong l.,** palabras mayores, *f pl*
languid *a* lánguido
languidness *n* languidez, *f*
languish *vi* languidecer
languishing *a* lánguido; amoroso, sentimental
languishingly *adv* lánguidamente; amorosamente
languor *n* languidez, *f*
languorous *a* lánguido
languorously *adv* con langor
lank *a* flaco, descarnado, alto y delgado; (of hair) lacio
lankiness *n* flacura, *f*
lanky *a* larguirucho, descarnado, *Lat. Am.* largucho
lanoline *n* lanolina, *f*
lantern *n* linterna, *f;* (*naut* and of a lighthouse) farol, *m; arch* linterna, *f;* (small) farolillo, *m.* **dark l.,** linterna sorda, *f.* **magic l.,** linterna mágica, *f.* **l.-jawed,** carilargo. **l. maker,** farolero, *m.* **l. slide,** diapositiva, *f*
lap *n* regazo, *m;* falda, *f;* (knees) rodillas, *f pl;* (lick) lamedura, *f;* (of water) murmurio, susurro, *m;* (in a race) vuelta, *f;* (stage) etapa, *f.* *vt* (wrap) envolver; (cover) cubrir; (fold) plegar; (lick) lamer; (swallow) tragar. *vi* (overlap) traslaparse; estar replegada; (lick) lamer; (of water) murmurar, susurrar, besar. **l.-dog,** perro de faldas, perro faldero, *m*
lapel *n* solapa, *f*
lapidary *a* lapidario
lapidate *vt* lapidar
lapis lazuli *n* lapislázuli, *m*
Laplander *n* lapón (-ona)
lapping *n* (licking) lamedura, *f;* (of water) murmurio, susurro, chapaleteo, *m*

lapse *n* lapso, *m;* (fault) desliz, *m,* falta, *f;* (of time) transcurso, intervalo, *m;* (fall) caída, *f;* (*law* termination) caducidad, *f.* **lapse (into),** *vi* caer (en), recaer (en), reincidir (en); volver a, caer de nuevo (en); (*law* cease) caducar; (*law* pass to) pasar (a); dejar de existir, desaparecer. **after the l. of three days,** después de tres días, al cabo de tres días. **with the l. of years,** en el transcurso de los años
larceny *n* latrocinio, *m*
lard *n* manteca, *f;* lardo, *m.* *vt cul* lardear, mechar; *fig* sembrar (con), adornar (con)
larder *n* despensa, *f*
large *a* grande; grueso; amplio; vasto, extenso; (wide) ancho; considerable; (in number) numeroso; (main, chief) principal; liberal; magnánimo. **at l.,** en libertad, suelto. **on the l. side,** algo grande. **l.-headed,** cabezudo. **l.-hearted,** que tiene un gran corazón, magnánimo. **l. mouth,** boca grande, boca rasgada, *f.* **l.-nosed,** narigudo. **l. scale,** en gran escala. **l.-sized,** de gran tamaño. **l.-toothed,** dentudo, que tiene dientes grandes. **l. type,** letras grandes, *f pl*
largely *adv* grandemente; en gran manera; en so mayor parte, considerablemente; muy; ampliamente; liberalmente; extensamente
largeness *n* gran tamaño, *m;* (of persons) gran talle, *m;* amplitud, *f;* vastedad, extensión, *f;* (width) anchura, *f;* liberalidad, *f;* (generosity) magnanimidad, *f;* grandeza de ánimo, *f*
larger *a comp* más grande, etc. See **large. to grow l.,** crecer, aumentarse. **to make l.,** hacer más grande; aumentar
largesse *n* liberalidad, *f*
largo *n* and *adv mus* largo, *m*
lariat *n* lazo, *m*
lark *n* alondra, *f;* (spree) juerga, *f;* (joke) risa, *f.* **to rise with the l.,** levantarse con las gallinas
larva *n* larva, *f*
laryngeal *a* laríngeo
laryngitis *n* laringitis, *f*
larynx *n* laringe, *f*
lascivious *a* lascivo, lujurioso
lasciviousness *n* lujuria, lascivia, *f*
lash *n* (thong) tralla, *f;* (whip) látigo, *m;* (blow) latigazo, *m;* azote, *m;* (of the eye) pestaña, *f.* *vt* dar latigazos (a); azotar; (of waves) romper contra; (of hail, rain) azotar; (excite) provocar; (the tail) agitar (la cola); (scold) fustigar; (spur) sujetar, atar; *naut* trincar. **to l. out,** (of horses, etc.) dar coces; (in words) prorrumpir (en)
lashing *n* (whipping) azotamiento, *m;* (tying) ligadura, atadura, *f;* amarradura, *f*
lass *n* muchacha, chica, mozuela, *f;* zagala, *f;* niña, *f*
lassitude *n* lasitud, *f*
lasso *n* lazo, *m,* mangana, *Argentina* armada, *f,* *vt* lazar, manganear, *Lat. Am.* lacear
last *vi* durar; subsistir, conservarse; continuar
last *a* último; (with month, week, etc.) pasado; (supreme) extremo, (el) mayor. *adv* al fin; finalmente; por último; después de todos; por última vez; la última vez. *n* el, *m,* (*f,* la) último (-ma); los últimos, *m pl,* (*f pl,* las últimas); (end) fin, *m;* (for shoes) horma, *f.* **at l.,** en fin; por fin, a la postre. **at the l. moment,** a última hora. **I have not been there these l. five years,** Hace cinco años que no voy allá. **John spoke l.,** Juan habló el último. **She came at l.,** Por fin llegó. **to the l.,** hasta el fin. **l. but one,** penúltimo (-ma). **l. hope,** última esperanza, *f;* último recurso, *m.* **l. kick,** *inf* último suspiro, *m.* **l. night,** anoche. **l. week,** la semana pasada
lasting *a* permanente, perdurable; duradero; constante; (of colours) sólido
lastly *adv* en conclusión, por fin, finalmente, por último
latch *n* pestillo, *m,* *vt* cerrar con pestillo. **l.-key,** llave de la puerta, *f;* (Yale) llavín, *m*
late *a* tarde; tardío; (advanced) avanzado; (last) último; reciente; (dead) difunto; (former) antiguo, ex . . . ; (new) nuevo. *adv* tarde. **Better l. than never,** Más vale tarde que nunca. **Helen arrived l.,** Elena llegó

tarde. **The train arrived five minutes l.,** El tren llegó con cinco minutos de retraso. **He keeps l. hours,** Se acuesta muy tarde, Se acuesta a las altas horas de la noche (*inf* a las tantas). **of l.,** últimamente. **to grow l.,** hacerse tarde. **l.-eighteenth-century poetry,** la poesía de fines del siglo diez y ocho; llorado, malogrado (e.g. **the l. Mrs. Smith,** la llorada Sra. Smith, la malograda Sra. Smith);
lateen *a* latino. **l. sail,** vela latina, *f*
lately *adv* recientemente; últimamente, hace poco
latency *n* estado latente, *m*
lateness *n* lo tarde; lo avanzado; retraso, *m*. **the l. of the hour,** la hora avanzada
latent *a* latente
later *a* más tarde; posterior; más reciente. *adv* más tarde; (afterwards) luego, después; posteriormente. **sooner or l.,** tarde o temprano. **l. on,** más tarde
lateral *a* lateral, ladero
late registration *n* matrícula tardía, *f*
latest *a* and *adv sup* último; más reciente, etc. See **late. at the l.,** a lo más tarde, a más tardar. **l. fashion,** última moda, *f*. **l. news,** últimas noticias, *f pl;* novedad, *f*
latex *n* (*bot chem*) látex, *m*
lath *n* listón, *m*. **to be as thin as a l.,** no tener más que el pellejo, estar en los huesos
lathe *n* torno, *m*
lather *n* espuma de jabón, *f,* jabonaduras, *f pl;* (of sweat) espuma, *f. vt* enjabonar; *inf* zurrar. *vi* hacer espuma
lathering *n* jabonadura, *f; inf* tunda, zurra, *f*
Latin *n* latín, *m, a* latino. **Low L.,** bajo latín, *m*. **L.-American,** *a* latinoamericano. *n* latinoamericano (-na)
Latinism *n* latinismo, *m*
Latinist *n* latinista, *mf*
latitude *n* latitud, *f;* libertad, *f*
latitudinal *a* latitudinal
latrine *n* letrina, *f*
latter *a* más reciente; último, posterior; moderno. **the l., éste,** *m;* **ésta,** *f;* esto, *neut;* **éstos,** *m pl;* **éstas,** *f pl.* **the l. half,** la segunda mitad. **toward the l. end of the year,** hacia fines del año. **L.-Day Saint,** santo de los últimos días *m,* santa de los últimos días, *f*
latterly *adv* recientemente, últimamente; en los últimos tiempos; hacia el fin
lattice *n* rejilla, *f;* celosía, reja, *f. vt* poner celosía (a); entrelazar. **l.-work,** enrejado, *m*
latticed *a* (of windows, etc.) con reja
Latvia *n* Latvia, Letonia, *f*
Latvian *a* latvio. *n* latvio (-ia)
laud *n* alabanza, *f; pl.* **lauds,** *ecc* laudes, *f pl. vt* alabar, elogiar
laudability *n* mérito, *m,* lo meritorio
laudable *a* loable, meritorio
laudably *adv* laudablemente
laudatory *a* laudatorio
laugh *n* risa, *f;* carcajada, *f. vi* reír; (smile) sonreír; reírse. **loud l.,** risa estrepitosa, *f.* **to l. in a person's face,** reírsele a uno en las barbas. **to l. loudly,** reírse a carcajadas. **to l. to oneself,** reírse interiormente. **to l. to scorn,** poner en ridículo. **to l. at,** reírse de; burlarse de; ridiculizar
laughable *a* risible, irrisible, ridículo, absurdo
laughing *a* risueño, alegre; (absurd) risible, *n* risa, *f.* **to burst out l.,** reírse a carcajadas. **l.-gas,** gas hilarante, *m.* **l.-stock,** hazmerreír, *m*
laughingly *adv* riendo
laughter *n* risa, *f;* (in a report) risas, *f pl.* **burst of l.,** carcajada, *f.* **to burst into l.,** soltar el trapo, reírse a carcajadas, desternillarse de risa
launch *n* botadura (de un buque), *f;* lancha, *f;* bote, *m;* canoa, *f. vt* (throw) lanzar; (a blow) asestar; (a vessel) botar, echar al agua; (begin) iniciar, dar principio a; (make) hacer. **to l. into,** arrojarse en; entregarse a. **motor l.,** canoa automóvil, *f.* **steam l.,** bote de vapor, *m*

launching *n* botadura (de un buque), *f;* (throwing) lanzamiento, *m;* (beginning) iniciación, *f;* inauguración, *f;* (of a loan, etc.) emisión, *f.* **l. site,** rampa, *f*
launder *vt* lavar y planchar (ropa)
laundress *n* lavandera, *f*
laundromat *n* lavandería automática, *f*
laundry *n* lavadero, *m,* lavandería, *f;* (washing) colada, *f; inf* ropa lavada or ropa para lavar, *f.* **l.-man,** lavandero, *m*
laureate *a* laureado. *n* poeta laureado, *m*
laurel *n* laurel, cerezo, *m, a* láureo. **to crown with l.,** laurear. **l. wreath,** lauréola, *f*
Lausanne *n* Lausana, Losana, *f*
lava *n* lava, *f*
lavabo *n* lavabo, *m; ecc* lavatorio, *m*
lavatory *n* lavabo, *m;* retrete, excusado, *m*
lavender *n* espliego, *m,* lavanda, *f.* **l.-water,** agua de lavanda, *f*
lavish *a* pródigo; profuso, abundante; (spender) *Mexico* disparador. *vt* prodigar
lavishly *adv* pródigamente; en profusión
lavishness *n* prodigalidad, *f;* profusión, abundancia, *f*
law *n* ley, *f;* derecho, *m;* jurisprudencia, *f;* código de leyes, *m. according to law,* según derecho. **canon law,** derecho civil, *m.* **constitutional law,** derecho político, *m.* **criminal law,** derecho penal, *m.* **in law,** por derecho, de acuerdo con la ley; desde el punto de vista legal. **international law,** derecho internacional, *m.* **maritime law,** código marítimo, *m.* **sumptuary law,** ley suntuaria, *f.* **to be the law,** ser la ley. **to go to law,** pleitear (sobre). **to sue at law,** pedir en juicio, poner pleito. **to take the law into one's own hands,** tomar la ley por su propia mano. **law-abiding,** observante de la ley; amigo del orden. **law-breaker,** transgresor (-ra). **law court,** tribunal de justicia, *m;* palacio de justicia, *m.* **law of nature,** ley natural, *f.* **law report,** revista de tribunales, *f.* **law school,** escuela de derecho, *f.* **law student,** estudiante de derecho, *mf*
lawful *a* legítimo; legal; lícito; válido
lawfully *adv* legalmente; legítimamente, lícitamente
lawfulness *n* legalidad, *f;* legitimidad, *f*
lawgiver *n* legislador (-ra)
lawless *a* ilegal; desordenado; ingobernable, rebelde
lawlessness *n* ilegalidad, *f;* desorden, *m;* rebeldía, *f*
lawn *n* césped, prado, *m;* (cloth) estopilla, *f.* **l.-mower,** cortacésped *m,* tundidora de césped, *f,* máquina segadora del césped, *f.* **l.-tennis,** tenis (en pista de hierba), *m*
lawsuit *n* pleito, litigio, *m,* causa, acción, *f*
lawyer *n* abogado (-da). **lawyer's office** or **practice,** bufete, *m*
lax *a* laxo; indisciplinado; vago; descuidado
laxative *n* laxante, *m,* purga, *f, a* laxativo
laxity *n* laxitud, *f;* descuido, *m;* indiferencia, *f*
lay *a* laico, seglar, lego; profano. *n* poema, *m,* trova, *f;* romance, *m;* (song) canción, *f.* **the lay of the land,** la configuración del terreno. **lay brother,** confeso, monigote, *m.* **lay figure,** maniquí, *m.* **lay sister,** (hermana) lega, *f*
lay *vt* and *vi* poner; colocar; dejar; (strike) tumbar; (demolish) derribar; (the dust) matar; (pipes, etc.) instalar; (hands on) asentar (la mano en); (deposit) depositar; (beat down corn, etc.) encamar, abatir; (eggs, keel) poner; (the table) cubrir, poner; (stretch) extender(se); (bury) depositar en el sepulcro; (a bet) hacer; (wager) apostar; (an accusation) acusar; (the wind, etc.) sosegar, amainar; (a ghost) exorcizar; (impute) atribuir, imputar; (impose) imponer; (prepare) prepara; (make) hacer; (open) abrir; (blame, etc.) echar; (claim) reclamar; (reveal) revelar. **Don't lay the blame on me!** ¡No me eches la culpa! **We laid our plans,** Hicimos nuestros planes; Hicimos nuestros preparativos. **to lay siege to,** asediar. **to lay the colors on too thick,** *fig* recargar las tintas. **to lay the foundations,** abrir los cimientos; *fig* crear, establecer; fundar. **to lay about one,** dar garrotazos de ciego. **to lay aside,** poner a un lado; arrinconar; (save) ahorrar;

(cast away) desechar; abandonar; (reserve) reservar; (a person) apartar de sí; (incapacitate) incapacitar. **lay something at somebody's feet,** embutir algo en el guante de fulano. **to lay before,** mostrar; presentar; poner a la vista; revelar. **to lay by,** See **to lay aside. to lay down,** acostar; depositar; (a burden) posar; (arms) rendir; (one's life); entregar; (give up) renunciar (a); (sketchout) trazar, dibujar; (plan) proyectar; (keep) guardar; (as a principle) establecer, sentar; (the law) dictar. **to lay oneself down,** echarse, tumbarse. **to lay in,** (a stock) proveerse de, hacer provisión de; (hoard) ahorrar; (buy) compara. **to lay off,** *naut* virar de bordo; *inf* quitarse de encima. **to lay on,** *vt* colocar sobre; (thrash) pegar; (blows) descargar; (paint, etc.) dar; (water, etc.) instalar; (impose) imponer; (exaggerate) exagerar. *vi* atacar. **to lay open,** abrir; descubrir; revelar; manifestar; exponer. **to lay oneself open to attack,** exponerse a ser atacado. **to lay out,** poner; arreglar; (the dead) amortajar; (one's money) invertir; (at interest) poner a rédito; (plan) planear; (knock down) derribar. **to lay oneself out to,** esforzarse a; tomarse la molestia de. **to lay over,** cubrir; sobreponer; extender sobre. **to lay to,** *vi naut* estar a la capa. **to lay up,** guardar, acumular, atesorar; poner a un lado; (a ship) desarmar; (a car) poner fuera de circulación; (a person) obligar a guardar cama, incapacitar

layabout = lazybones

layer *n* capa, *f*; *geol* estrato, *m*; *min* manto, *m*; (bird) gallina (pata, etc.) ponedera, *f*; (one who bets) apostador (-ra); *agr* acodo, *m*. *vt* (of plants) acodar

layette *n* canastilla, *f*

laying *n* colocación, *f*; puesta, *f*; (of an egg) postura, *f*. **l. down,** depósito, *m*; conservación, *f*; (explanation) exposición, *f*. **l. on of hands,** imposición de manos, *f*. **l. out,** tendedura, *f*; (of money) empleo, *m*; inversión, *f*; (arrangement) arreglo, *m*

layman *n* seglar, *mf*; profano (-na)

layout *n* plan, *m*; diagramación, disposición, *f*; distribución, *f*; esquema, *m*

laze *vi* holgazanear, gandulear, no hacer nada; encontrarse a sus anchas

lazily *adv* perezosamente; indolentemente; lentamente

laziness *n* pereza, holgazanería, *f*; indolencia, *f*; lentitud, *f*

lazy *a* perezoso, holgazán; indolente. **l.bones,** gandul (-la), *Lat. Am.* aplanacalles *mf*

lead *n* (metal) plomo, *m*; (in a pencil) mina, *f*; (plummet) sonda, *f*; *print* interlínea, *f*; *pl* **leads,** (roofs) tejados, *m pl*. *vt* emplomar; guarnecer con plomo; *print* interlinear. **black-l.,** grafito, *m*. **deep-sea l.,** *naut* escandallo, *m*. **white l.,** albayalde, *m*. **to heave the l.,** echar el escandallo, sondar. **l.-colored,** de color de plomo, plomizo. **l. mine,** mina de plomo, *f*. **l. poisoning,** saturnismo, *m*

lead *n* delantera, *f*; primer lugar, *m*; dirección, *f*, mando, *m*; (suggestion) indicación, *f*; (influence) influencia, *f*; (dog's) trailla, *f*; *theat* protagonista, *mf*; *theat* papel principal, *m*; (at cards) mano, *f*

lead *vt* and *vi* (conduct) conducir, llevar; guiar; (induce) mover, persuadir, inducir; inclinar; (cause) hacer, causar; (captain) capitanear, encabezar; dirigir; (channel) encauzar; (with life) llevar; (give) dar; (head) ir a la cabeza de; *mil* mandar; (at cards) salir; (at games) jugar en primer lugar; tomar la delantera; tomar la iniciativa. **to take the l.,** ir delante; ir a la cabeza, tomar la delantera; tomar la iniciativa. **to l. one to think,** hacer pensar. **to l. the way,** mostrar el camino; ir adelante. **to l. along,** llevar (por la mano, etc.), conducir; conducir por; guiar. **to l. astray,** descarriar; desviar (de), seducir (de). **to l. away,** conducir (a otra parte); llevarse (a). **to l. back,** conducir de nuevo; hacer volver. **This path leads back to the village,** Por esta senda se vuelve al pueblo. **to l. in, into,** conducir a (o ante); introducir en, hacer entrar en; invitar a entrar en; (of rooms) comunicarse con;

(sin, etc.) inducir a. **to l. off,** *vi* ir adelante; (begin) empezar; (of rooms) comunicarse con. *vt* hacer marcharse, llevarse (a). **to l. on,** *vt* conducir; guiar; hacer pensar en; (make talk) dar cuerda (a). *vi* ir a la cabeza; tomar la delantera. **to l. out,** conducir afuera; (to dance) sacar. **to l. to,** conducir a; desembocar en, salir a; (cause) dar lugar a, causar; (make) hacer; (incline) inclinar. **This street leads to the square,** Por esta calle se va a la plaza, Esta calle conduce a la plaza. **to l. up to,** conducir a; (in conversation, etc.) preparar el terreno para; preparar; tener lugar antes de, ocurrir antes de

leaden *a* hecho de plomo, plúmbeo; (of skies, etc.) plomizo, de color de plomo, aplomado. **l.-footed,** pesado; lento

leader *n* conductor (-ra); guía, *mf*; jefe (-fa); general, *m*; director (-ra); (in a journal) artículo de fondo, *m*; (of an orchestra) primer violín, *m*. **follow-the-l.,** (game) juego de seguir la fila, *m*

leadership *n* dirección, *f*; jefatura, *f*; *mil* mando, *m*

lead-in *a rad* de entrada. *n rad* conductor de entrada, *m*

leading *n* (leadwork) emplomadura, *f*

leading *n* (guidance) dirección, *f*. *a* principal; primero; importante; eminente. **l. article,** artículo de fondo, *m*; editorial, *m*. **l. card,** primer naipe, *m*. **l. counsel,** abogado (-da) principal. **l. lady,** *theat* dama primera, primera actriz, *f*; (cinema) estrella (de la pantalla), *f*. **l. man,** *theat* primer galán, *m*. **l. question,** pregunta que sugiere la respuesta, *f*; cuestión importante, *f*. **l. strings,** andadores, *m pl*; *fig* tutelaje, *m*

leaf *n* (*bot* and of a page, door, window, table, screen, etc.) hoja, *f*; (petal) pétalo, *m*, *vi* echar hojas. **gold l.,** pan de oro, *m*. **to turn over a new l.,** volver la hoja, hacer libro nuevo, hacer vida nueva. **to turn over the leaves of a book,** hojear (un libro). **l.-bud,** yema, *f*. **l.-mold,** abono verde, *m*. **l. tobacco,** tabaco en hoja, *m*

leafiness *n* frondosidad, *f*

leafless *a* sin hojas

leaflet *n* hojuela, *f*; (pamphlet) folleto, *m*

leafy *a* frondoso

league *n* (measure) legua, *f*; liga, federación, sociedad, *f*; (football) liga, *f*. *vt* aliar; asociar. *vi* aliarse; asociarse, confederarse. **to be in l.,** *inf* estar de manga. **L. of Nations,** Sociedad de las Naciones, *f*

leak *n* (hole) agujero, *m*, grieta, *f*; *naut* vía de agua, *f*; (of gas, liquids, etc.) escape, *m*; (in a roof, etc.) gotera, *f*; *elec* resistencia de escape, *f*. *vi naut* hacer agua; (gas, liquids, etc.) escaparse, salirse; (drip) gotear. **to l. out,** (of news, etc.) trascender, saberse. **to spring a l.,** aparecer una vía de agua, hacer agua

leakage *n* (of gas, liquids) escape, *m*, fuga, *f*; derrame, *m*; pérdida, *f*; (of information) revelación, *f*

leaky *a naut* que hace agua; agujereado; poroso; que tiene goteras

lean *a* magro, seco, enjuto, delgado; (of meat) magro; *fig* pobre, estéril. *n* carne magra, *f*, magro, *m*. **to grow l.,** enflaquecer

lean *vi* inclinarse; apoyarse (en). *vt* apoyar (en); dejar arrimado (en). **to l. out of the window,** asomarse a la ventana. **to l. against,** apoyarse en, recostarse en (o contra). **to l. back,** echarse hacia atrás; recostarse. **to l. over,** inclinarse a. **to l. upon,** apoyarse en; descansar sobre

leaning *n* inclinación, tendencia, *f*; predilección, afición, *f*

leanness *n* magrura, flaqueza, *f*; (of meat) magrez, *f*; *fig* pobreza, *f*

leap *n* salto, *m*; brinco, *m*; (caper) zapateta, *f*; *fig* salto, *m*. *vi* saltar, dar un salto; brincar. *vt* saltar; hacer saltar. **at one l.,** en un salto. **by leaps and bounds,** en saltos. **My heart leaped,** Mi corazón dio un salto. **to l. to the conclusion that . . . ,** saltar a la conclusión de que . . . **to l. to the eye,** saltar a la vista. **l. frog,** salto de la muerte, *m*, pídola *f*. **l. year,** año bisiesto, *m*, salta cabrillas, *f pl*

leaping *a* saltador. *n* saltos, *m pl*

learn *vt* and *vi* aprender; instruirse; enterarse de. **to l. by heart,** aprender de memoria. **to l. from a reliable source,** saber de buena tinta. **to l. from experience,** aprender por experiencia

learned *a* sabio, docto; erudito; (of professions) liberal; versado (en), entendido (en). **a l. society,** una sociedad erudita

learner *n* aprendedor (-ra)

learning *n* saber, *m;* conocimientos, *m pl;* erudición, *f;* estudio, *m;* (literature) literatura, *f*

lease *n* arrendamiento, arriendo, *m;* contrato de arrendamiento, *m. vt* dar en arriendo, arrendar. **on l.,** en arriendo. **to take a new l. on life,** recobrar su vigor.

Lend L. Act, ley de préstamo y arriendo, *f*

leaseholder *n* concesionario, *m;* arrendatario (-ia)

leash *n* (of a dog) traílla, *f*

least *a sup* **little,** mínimo; el (la, etc.) menor; más pequeño. *adv* menos. *n* lo menos. **at l.,** siquiera; por lo menos, al menos. **at the very l.,** a lo menos. **not in the l.,** de ninguna manera, nada. **to say the l. of,** sin exagerar, para no decir más

leather *n* cuero, *m;* piel, *f,* a de cuero; de piel. **patent l.,** charol, *m.* **Spanish l.,** cordobán, *m.* **tanned l.,** curtido, *m.* **l. apron,** mandil, *m.* **l. bag,** saco de cuero, *m.* **l. bottle,** bota, *f.* **l. breeches,** pantalón de montar, *m.* **l. jerkin,** coleto, *m.* **l. shield,** adarga, *f.* **l. strap,** correa, *f.* **l. trade,** comercio en cueros, *m*

leatherette *n* cartón cuero, *m*

leathery *a* de cuero; (of the skin) curtido por la intemperie; (tough) correoso

leave *n* (permission) permiso, *m;* (mil etc.) licencia, *f;* (farewell) despedida, *f. vt* and *vi* dejar; abandonar; salir (de), quitar, marcharse (de), *Lat. Am.* egresar (de . . .); (as surety) empeñar; (by will) legar, mandar; (an employment) darse de baja (de), dejar; (give into the keeping of) entregar; (bid farewell) despedirse (de). **By your l.,** Con permiso de Vd. (Vds.). Con la venia de Vd. (Vds.) **on l.,** de permiso. **l.-taking,** despedidas, *f pl.* **to be left,** quedar. **to be left over,** quedar; sobrar. **Two from four leaves two,** De cuatro a dos van dos. **to take French l.,** despedirse a la inglesa. **to take l. of,** despedirse de. **to take one's l.,** marcharse; despedirse. **to l. a deep impression,** *fig* impresionar mucho; quedar grabado (en). **to l. undone,** dejar de hacer, no hacer; dejar sin terminar. **to l. about,** *vt* dejar por todas partes. *vi* (of time) marcharse a eso de . . . **to l. ajar,** entreabrir, (when opening), entrecerrar (when closing), entornar. **to l. alone,** dejar a solas; dejar en paz; no molestar, no meterse con. **to l. aside,** omitir; prescindir de; olvidar. **to l. behind,** dejar atrás; olvidar. **l. much to be desired,** tener mucho que desear. **to l. off,** *vt* dejar de; abandonar; (garments) no ponerse, quitarse. *vi* terminar. **to l. out,** dejar fuera; dejar a un lado, descontar; omitir; pasar por; (be silent about) callar; suprimir. **to l. to,** dejar para; dejar hacer

leaven *n* levadura, *f,* fermento, *m, vt* fermentar; (*fig* permeate) penetrar (en), infiltrar en, imbuir; (a speech) salpimentar (con)

leaving *n* salida, partida, marcha, *f, Lat. Am.* egreso, *m; pl* **leavings,** sobras, *f pl;* desechos, *m pl*

lecherous *a* lascivo, lujurioso

lechery *n* lascivia, lujuria, *f*

lectern *n* atril, *m;* (in a church) facistol, *m*

lecture *n* conferencia, *f;* (in a university) lección, clase, *f;* discurso, *m;* (*inf* scolding) sermoneo, *m. vi* dar una conferencia; (in a university) dar clase. *vt* (*inf* scold) predicar, sermonear. **l. room,** sala de conferencias, *f;* (in a university) sala de clase, aula, *f*

lecturer *n* conferenciante, *Lat. Am.* conferencista, *mf;* (in a university) auxiliar, *m;* (professor) catedrático (-ca), profesor (-ra)

lectureship *n* auxiliaría, *f*

ledge *n* borde, *m;* capa, *f;* (of a window) alféizar, *m;* (shelf) anaquel, *m*

ledger *n* libro mayor, *m*

leech *n* sanguijuela, *f*

leek *n* puerro, *m*

leer *vi* mirar de soslayo; guiñar el ojo; mirar con los ojos llenos de deseo. *n* mirada de soslayo, *f;* mirada de lascivia, *f*

lees *n pl* heces, *f pl;* sedimento, *m*

leeward *n* sotavento, *m.* **on the l. side,** a sotavento

leeway *n naut* deriva, *f; fig* amplitud, margen de holgura, márgenes de maniobra, *f pl*

left *past part* dejado, etc. See **leave.** *a* izquierdo. *adv* a la izquierda; hacia la izquierda. *n* izquierda, *f.* **on the l.,** a la izquierda. **the L.,** *pol* las izquierdas. **the Left Bank (of Paris)** la Ribera izquierda, la Orilla izquierda **L. face!** ¡Izquierda! **l.-hand,** mano izquierda, *f;* izquierda, *f.* **l.-hand drive,** conducción a la izquierda, *f.* **l.-handed,** zurdo. **l. luggage office,** consigna, *f.* **l.-overs,** sobras, *f pl,* desperdicios, *m pl*

leg *n* pierna, *f;* (of animals, birds, furniture) pata, *f;* (of a triangle) cateto, *m;* (of a pair of compasses, trousers, lamb, veal) pierna, *f;* (of boots, stockings) caña, *f;* (of pork) pernil, *m;* (support) pie, *m;* (stage) etapa, *f;* (of journey) **to be on one's last legs,** estar en las últimas; estar acabándose; estar sin recursos. **to pull a person's leg,** tomar el pelo (a). **leg-pull,** tomadura de pelo, *f.* **leg-of-mutton sleeve,** manga de pernil, *f*

legacy *n* legado, *m,* manda; *f;* herencia, *f*

legal *a* legal; de derecho; jurídico; (lawful, permissible) legítimo, lícito; (of a lawyer) de abogado. **l. expenses,** litisexpensas, *f pl.* **l. inquiry,** investigación jurídica, *f*

legalistics *n. Lat. Am.* abogaderas, abogaderías, *f pl*

legality *n* legalidad, *f*

legalization *n* legalización, *f*

legalize *vt* legalizar; autorizar, legitimar

legally *adv* según la ley; según derecho; legalmente

legal tender *n* moneda de curso liberatorio, *f*

legate *n* legado, *m.* **papal l.,** legado papal, *m*

legatee *n* legatario (-ia), *Lat. Am.* asignatario (-ia)

legation *n* legación, *f*

legend *n* leyenda, *f*

legendary *a* legendario

legerdemain *n* juegos de manos, *m pl*

legged *a* con piernas; de piernas . . . ; de patas . . . a **three-l. stool,** un taburete de tres patas. **long l.,** zancudo

leggings *n pl* polainas, *f pl*

legibility *n* legibilidad, *f*

legible *a* legible

legion *n* legión, *f.* **L. of Honor,** Legión de Honor, *f*

legionary *a* legionario. *n* legionario, *m*

legislate *vt* legislar

legislation *n* legislación, *f*

legislative *a* legislativo, legislador

legislator *n* legislador (-ra)

legislature *n* legislatura, *f*

legitimacy *n* legitimidad, *f;* justicia, *f*

legitimate *a* legítimo; justo

legitimation *n* legitimación, *f*

leisure *n* ocio, *m,* desocupación, *f;* tiempo libre, *m.* **at one's l.,** con sosiego, despacio. **You can do it at your l.,** Puedes hacerlo cuando tengas tiempo. **to be at l.,** estar desocupado, no tener nada que hacer. **l. moments,** ratos perdidos, momentos de ocio, *m pl*

leisured *a* desocupado, libre; sin ocupación; (wealthy) acomodado

leisurely *a* pausado, lento, deliberado; tardo

lemon *n* limón, *m;* (tree) limonero, *m, a* limonado, de color de limón; hecho o sazonado con limón. **l. drop,** pastilla de limón, *f.* **l.-grove,** limonar, *m.* **l.-squash,** limonada natural, *f.* **l.-squeezer,** exprime limones, *m,* exprimidera, *f*

lemonade *n* limonada, *f.* **l. powder,** limonada seca, *f*

lemur *n* lemur, *m*

lend *vt* prestar. **to l. an ear to,** prestar atención a. **It does not l. itself to . . . ,** No se presta a . . . **to l. a hand,** echar una mano, dar una mano

lender *n* el, *m,* (*f,* la) que presta; prestador (-ra); (of money) prestamista, *mf; com* mutuante, *mf*

lending *n* prestación, *f*, préstamo, *m*. **l.-library,** biblioteca circulante, *f*

length *n* largo, *m*; longitud, *f*; (of fabric) corte, *m*; (of a ship) eslora, *f*; (in racing) largo, *m*; distancia, *f*; (in time) duración, *f*; alcance, *m*. **at l.,** por fin, finalmente; (in full) extensamente, largamente. **by a l.,** por un largo. **full-l.,** de cuerpo entero. **three feet in l.,** tres pies de largo. **to go the l. of . . . ,** llegar al extremo de . . .

lengthen *vt* alargar; prolongar; extender. *vi* alargarse; prolongarse; extenderse; (of days) crecer

lengthening *n* alargamiento, *m*; prolongación, *f*; crecimiento, *m*

lengthily *adv* largamente

lengthiness *n* largueza, *f*; prolijidad, *f*

lengthy *a* largo; demasiado largo, larguísimo; (of speech) prolijo; verboso

lenience, leniency *n* lenidad, *f*; indulgencia, *f*

lenient *a* indulgente; poco severo

leniently *adv* con indulgencia

Leningrad Leningrado, *m*

lenitive *a* lenitivo. *n* lenitivo, *m*

lens *n* lente, *m*; (of the eye) cristalino, *m*

Lent *n* Cuaresma, *f*

Lenten *a* de Cuaresma, cuaresmal

lentil *n* lenteja, *f*

lentitude *n* lentitud, *f*

Leo *n* León, *m*

leonine *a* leonino

leopard *n* leopardo, *m*

leper *n* leproso (-sa). **l. colony,** colonia de leprosos, *f*

leprosy *n* lepra, *f*

leprous *a* leproso

lesbian *a* and *n* lesbiana

lesion *n* lesión, *f*

less *a* menor; más pequeño; menos; inferior. *adv* menos; sin. **l. than,** menos de (que). **more or l.,** poco más o menos. **no l.,** nada menos. **none the l.,** sin embargo. **to grow l.,** disminuir. **l. and l.,** cada vez menos

lessee *n* arrendatario (-ia); inquilino (-na)

lessen *vi* disminuir; reducirse. *vt* disminuir; reducir; (lower) rebajar; (disparage) menospreciar

lessening *n* disminución, *f*; reducción, *f*

lesser *a comp* menor; más pequeño. See **little**

lesson *n* lección, *f*. **to give a l.,** dar lección, dar clase; *fig* dar una lección (a). **to hear a l.,** tomar la lección

lessor *n* arrendador (-ra)

lest *conjunc* para que no; por miedo de (que), no sea que. **I did not do it l. they should not like it,** No lo hice por miedo de que no les gustase

let *vt* dejar, permitir; (lease) arrendar. *vi* alquilarse, ser alquilado. **Let** as an expression of the imperative is rendered in Spanish by the subjunctive or the imperative, e.g. **Let them go!** ¡Que se vayan! ¡Déjalos marchar! **He let them go,** Les dejó marchar. **to let fall,** dejar caer. **to let go,** dejar marchar; soltar; poner en libertad (a). **to let loose,** dar suelta a; *fig* desencadenar. **to let one know,** hacer saber, comunicar. **to let the cat out of the bag,** tirar de la manta. **to let th chance slip,** perder la ocasión. **to let alone,** (a thing) no tocar; (a person) dejar en paz, dejar tranquilo; (an affair) no meterse (en or con); (omit) no mencionar, omitir toda mención de. **to let down,** bajar; (by a rope) descolgar; (hair, etc.) dejar caer; (a dress, etc.) alargar; *naut* calar; (disappoint) dejar plantado. **to let in,** dejar entrar; hacer entrar; invitar a entrar; recibir; (insert) insertar. **to let into,** (initiate) iniciar en, admitir en; (a secret) revelar. Other meanings, see **to let in. to let off,** dejar salir; dejar en libertad; exonerar; perdonar; (a gun) descargar; (fireworks, etc.) hacer estallar. **to let out,** dejar salir; poner en libertad; (from a house) acompañar a la puerta; abrir la puerta; *sew* ensanchar; (hire) alquilar; (the fire, etc.) dejar extinguirse. **to let up,** dejar subir; (decrease) disminuir; (end) terminar

let *n* estorbo, impedimento, obstáculo, *m*. **without let or hindrance,** sin estorbo ni obstáculo

lethal *a* letal. **l. weapon,** instrumento de muerte, *m*

lethargic *a* aletargado; letárgico

lethargy *n* letargo, *m*; *med* letargia, *f*

letter *n* (of the alphabet) letra, *f*; (epistle) carta, *f*; *print* carácter, *m*; (lessor) arrendador (-ra); *pl* **letters,** letras, *f pl*; (correspondence) correo, *m*; correspondencia, *f*. *vt* inscribir; imprimir. **capital l.,** letra mayúscula, *f*. **first letters,** *fig* primeras letras, *f pl*. **registered l.,** carta certificada, *f*, certificado, *m*. **small l.,** letra minúscula, *f*. **the l. of the law,** la ley escrita. **to be l.-perfect,** saber de memoria. **to the l.,** *fig* a la letra. **letters patent,** patente, *f*; título de privilegio, *m*. **l.-balance,** pesacartas, *m*. **l.-book,** *com* libro copiador, *m*. **l.-box,** buzón de correos, *m*. **l.-card,** tarjeta postal del gobierno, *f*. **l. of credit,** carta de crédito, *f*. **l. of introduction,** carta de presentación, *f*. **l.-writer,** escritor (-ra) de cartas

lettered *a* culto, instruido; (printed) impreso

lettering *n* inscripción, *f*; letrero, rótulo, *m*

letterpress *n* imprenta, *f*; (not illustrations) texto, *m*

letting *n* (hiring) arrendamiento, *m*

lettuce *n* lechuga, *f*. **l. plant,** lechuguino, *m*. **l. seller,** lechuguero (-ra)

Leuven Lovaina, *f*

Levant, the el Levante, *m*

Levantine *a* and *n* levantino (-na)

levee *n* besamanos, *m*, recepción, *f*

level *n* nivel, *m*; ras, *m*, flor, *f*; llano, *m*; (plain) llanura, *f*; (instrument) nivel, *m*, *a* llano; igual; al nivel (de); uniforme; imparcial. *adv* a nivel; igualmente. *vt* nivelar; igualar; allanar; (a blow) asestar; (a gun) apuntar; (raze) arrasar, derribar; adaptar; hacer uniforme. **on the l.,** a nivel; *fig* de buena fe. **spirit l.,** nivel de burbuja, *m*. **to make l. again,** rellanar. **l. country,** campaña, llanura, *f*. **l. with the ground,** a ras de la tierra. **l. with the water,** a flor de agua. **l. crossing,** paso a nivel, *m*. **l.-headed,** sensato, cuerdo. **l. stretch,** rellano, *m*; llanura, *f*

leveler *n* nivelador (-ra)

leveling *a* nivelador; de nivelación; igualador. *n* nivelación, *f*; allanamiento, *m*; (to the ground) arrasamiento, *m*; igualación, *f*

levelness *n* nivel, *m*; planicie, *f*; igualdad, *f*

lever *n* palanca, *f*; (handle) manivela, *f*; escape de reloj, *m*; (excuse) pretexto, *m*; (means) modo, *m*. *vt* sopalancar. **control l.,** *aer* palanca de mando, *f*. **hand-l.,** palanca de mano, *f*

leverage *n* sistema de palancas, *m*; acción de palanca, *f*; *fig* influencia, fuerza, *f*, poder, *m*

Leviathan *n* leviatán, *m*

levitation *n* levitación, *f*

Levite *n* levita, *m*

Levitical *a* levítico

Leviticus *n* Levítico, *m*

levity *n* levedad, frivolidad, ligereza, *f*

levy *n* exacción (de tributos), *f*; impuesto, *m*; (of a fine) imposición, *f*; *mil* leva, *f*. *vt* (taxes) exigir; (a fine) imponer; (troops) reclutar, enganchar

levying *n* (of a tax) exacción (de tributos), *f*; (of a fine) imposición, *f*; (of troops) leva, *f*

lewd *a* lascivo, lujurioso, impúdico

lewdness *n* lascivia, lujuria, impudicia, *f*

lexicographer *n* lexicógrafo, *m*

lexicography *n* lexicografía, *f*

lexicon *n* léxico, *m*

liability *n* responsabilidad, obligación, *f*; tendencia, *f*; riesgo, *m*; *pl* **liabilities,** obligaciones, *f pl*; *com* pasivo, *m*

liable *a* responsable; propenso (a); expuesto (a); sujeto (a)

liaison *n* lío, *m*; coordinación, *f*. **l. officer,** oficial de coordinación, *m*

liar *n* mentiroso (-sa)

libation *n* libación, *f*

libel *n* libelo, *m*; difamación, *f*, *vt* difamar, calumniar

libeler *n* libelista, *mf* difamador (-ra)

libelous *a* difamatorio

liberal *a* liberal; generoso; abundante. *n* liberal, *mf* **l. profession,** carrera liberal, *f*. **l.-minded,** tolerante. **l.-mindedness,** tolerancia, *f*

liberalism *n* liberalismo, *m*

liberality *n* liberalidad, *f*; generosidad, *f*

liberalize *vt* liberalizar

liberate *vt* (a prisoner) poner en libertad; librar (de); (a gas, etc.) dejar escapar

liberation *n* liberación, *f*; (of a captive) redención, *f*; (of a slave) manumisión, *f*

liberator *n* libertador (-ra)

libertinage *n* libertinaje, *m*

libertine *n* libertino, *m*

libertinism *n* libertinaje, *m*

liberty *n* libertad, *f*; (familiarity) familiaridad, *f*; (right) privilegio, *m*, prerrogativa, *f*; (leave) permiso, *m*. **at l.,** en libertad; desocupado, libre. **I have taken the l. of giving them your name,** Me he tomado la libertad de darles su nombre. **to set at l.,** poner en libertad (a). **to take liberties with,** tratar con familiaridad; (a text) tergiversar. **l. of speech,** libertad de palabra, libertad de expresión, *f*. **l. of thought,** libertad de pensamiento, *f*

libidinous *a* libidinoso

Libra *n* Libra, *f*

librarian *n* bibliotecario (-ia)

librarianship *n* carrera *f*, or empleo *m*, de bibliotecario

library *n* biblioteca, *f*; (book shop) librería, *f*. **l. catalog,** catálogo de la biblioteca, *m*

librettist *n* libretista, *mf*

libretto *n* libreto, *m*

Libya Libia, *f*

Libyan *a* and *n* libio (-ia)

license *n* licencia, *f*, permiso, *m*; autorización, *f*; (driving) carnet de chófer, permiso de conducción, *m*; (of a car) permiso de circulación, *m*; (for a wireless, etc.) licencia, *f*; (marriage) licencia de casamiento, *f*; (excess) libertinaje, desenfreno, *m*. **import l.,** permiso de importación, *m*. **poetic l.,** licencia poética, *f*. **l. number,** (of a car) número de matriculación, *m*. *vt* licenciar; autorizar; (a car) sacar la licencia del automóvil

licensee *n* concesionario (-ia)

licentiate *n* licenciado (-da)

licentious *a* licencioso, disoluto

licentiousness *n* libertinaje, *m*, disipación, *f*

lichen *n* liquen, *m*

licit *a* lícito

lick *vt* lamer; (of waves) besar; (of flames) bailar; (thrash) azotar; (defeat) vencer. **to l. one's lips,** relamerse los labios, chuparse los dedos. **to l. the dust,** morder el polvo

licking *n* lamedura, *f*; (beating) paliza, tunda, *f*; (defeat) derrota, *f*

lid *n* cobertera, *f*; tapa, *f*; (of the eye) párpado, *m*

lie *n* mentira, *f*; invención, falsedad, *f*; mentís, *m*, *vi* mentir. **to give the lie to,** desmentir, dar el mentís. **to lie barefacedly,** mentir por la mitad de la barba. **white lie,** mentira oficiosa, *f*

lie *vi* estar tumbado, estar echado; estar recostado; descansar, reposar; (in the grave) yacer; (be) estar; (be situated) hallarse, estar situado; (stretch) extenderse; (sleep) dormir; (depend) depender; (consist) consistir, estribar; (as an obligation) incumbir. **Here lies . . . ,** Aquí descansa . . . , Aquí yace . . . **It does not lie in my power,** No depende de mí. **to let lie,** dejar; dejar en paz. **to lie at anchor,** estar anclado. **to lie fallow,** estar en barbecho; *fig* descansar. **to lie about,** estar esparcido por todas partes; estar en desorden. **to lie along,** estar tendido a lo largo de; *naut* dar a la banda. **to lie back,** recostarse; apoyarse (en). **to lie by,** estar acostado al lado de; (of things, places) estar cerca (de); descansar. **to lie down,** tenderse, tumbarse, echarse, acostarse; reposar. **Lie down!** (to a dog) ¡Échate! **to lie down under,** tenderse bajo; (an insult) tragar, sufrir. **to lie in,** consistir en; depender de; (of childbirth) estar de parto. **to lie open,** estar abierto; estar ex-

puesto (a); estar al descubierto, estar a la vista. **to lie over,** (be postponed) quedar aplazado. **to lie to,** *naut* estarse a la capa, ponerse en facha. **to lie under,** estar bajo, hallarse bajo; estar bajo el peso de; (be exposed to) estar expuesto a. **to lie with,** dormir con; (concern) tocar (a); corresponder (a)

lie *n* configuración, *f*; disposición, *f*; posición, *f*. **the lie of the land,** la configuración del terreno

lieu *n* lugar, *m*. **in l. of,** en lugar de, en vez de

lieutenant *n* teniente, lugarteniente, *m*; (naval) alférez, *m*. **first l.,** (in the army) primer teniente, teniente, *m*; (in the navy) alférez de navío, *m*. **naval l.,** teniente de navío, *m*. **second l.,** (in the army) segundo teniente, *m*; (in the navy) alférez de fragata, *m*. **l.-colonel,** teniente coronel

life *n* vida, *f*; (being) ser, *m*; (society) mundo, *m*, sociedad, *f*; (vitality) vitalidad, *f*, vigor, *m*, *a* de vida; (of annuities, etc.) vitalicio; (life-saving) de salvamento. **for l.,** de por vida. **from l.,** del natural. **high l.,** gran mundo, *m*, alta sociedad, *f*. **low l.,** vida del hampa, vida de los barrios bajos, *f*. **to the l.,** al vivo. **to lay down one's l.,** entregar la vida. **to take one's l. in one's hands,** jugarse la vida. **l. annuity,** fondo vitalicio, *m*. **l.-belt,** (cinturón) salvavidas, *m*. **l.-blood,** sangre vital, *f*; *fig* nervio, *m*; vigor, *m*. **l.-boat,** (on a ship) bote salvavidas, *m*; (on the coast) lancha de salvamento, *f*. **l.-boat station,** estación de salvamento, *f*. **l.-giving,** vivificante, que da vida; tonificante. **l.-guard,** (soldier) guardia militar, *f*; Guardia de Corps, *f*, (at beach or swimming pool) guardavidas, *mf*. **l.-insurance,** seguro sobre la vida, *m*. **l.-interest,** usufructo, *m*. **l.-jacket,** chaleco salvavidas, *m*. **l.-like,** natural. **l.-line,** cable de salvamento, *m*. **l.-saving,** *a* de salvamento; curativo. **l.-saving apparatus,** aparato salvavidas, *m*. **l.-sized,** de tamaño natural

life cycle *n* ciclo vital, *m*

life imprisonment *n* reclusión perpetua, *f*

life jacket *n* chaleco salvavidas, *f*

lifeless *a* sin vida, muerto; inanimado; *fig* desanimado

lifelessness *n* falta de animación; inercia

lifelong *a* de toda la vida

lifetime *n* vida, *f*

lift *n* esfuerzo para levantar, *m*; acción de levantar, *f*; alza, *f*; (blow) golpe, *m*; (help) ayuda, *f*; (hitch, ride) *Mexico* aventón, *m*, (elevator) ascensor, *m*; (for goods) montacargas, *m*; *pl* **lifts,** *naut* balancines, *m pl*. **to give a l. to,** (help) ayudar; (hitchhiker etc.) dar un aventón.

lift *vt* levantar; alzar, elevar; (pick up) coger; (one's hat) quitarse; (steal) hurtar; exaltar. *vi* (of mist) disiparse; desaparecer. **to l. the elbow,** empinar el codo. **to l. down,** quitar (de); (a person) bajar en brazos. **to l. up,** alzar; erguir, levantar; levantar en brazos

lifting *n* acción de levantar, *f*; levantamiento, alzamiento, *m*

ligament *n* ligamento, *m*

ligature *n* (*surg mus*) ligadura, *f*

light *a* (not dark) claro, con mucha luz, bañado de luz; (of colors) claro; (not heavy, and of sleep, food, troops, movements) ligero; (of reading) de entretenimiento; (irresponsible) frívolo; (easy) fácil; (slight) leve; (of hair) rubio; (happy) alegre; (fickle) inconstante, liviano; (of complexion) blanco. *adv* ligero. **to be l.,** no pesar mucho; estar de día. **to grow l.,** (dawn) clarear; iluminarse. **to make l. of,** no tomar en serio; no preocuparse de; (suffering) sufrir sin quejarse. **l.-colored,** (de color) claro. **l.-fingeredness,** sutileza de manos, *f*. **l.-footed,** ligero de pies. **l.-haired,** de pelo rubio. **l.-headed,** casquivano, ligero de cascos; delirante. **l.-headedness,** ligereza de cascos, frivolidad, *f*; delirio, *m*. **l.-hearted,** alegre (de corazón). **l.-heartedness,** alegría, *f*. **l. horse,** *mil* caballería ligera, *f*. **l. troops,** tropas ligeras, *f pl*. **l.-weight,** *n* (*boxing*) peso ligero, *m*, *a* de peso ligero

light *n* luz, *f*; (day) día, *m*; (match) cerilla, *f*; (of a cigarette, etc.) fuego, *m*; (of a window) cristal, vidrio, *m*; (point of view) punto de vista, *m*; (in a picture) toque de luz, *m; pl* **lights,** (offal) bofes, *m pl.* **against the l.,** al trasluz. **by the l. of,** a la luz de; según. **half-l.,** media luz, *f.* **high light(s),** *art* claros, *m pl; fig* momento culminante, *m;* acontecimiento de más interés, *m.* **to come to l.,** descubrirse. **to put a l. to the fire,** encender el fuego. **l.-year,** año de luz, *m*

light *vt* (a lamp, fire, etc.) encender; iluminar. *vi* encenderse; iluminarse; *fig* animarse; brillar. **to l. upon,** encontrar por casualidad; tropezar con

lighten *vt* (illuminate) iluminar; (of weight) aligerar; (cheer) alegrar; (mitigate) aliviar. *vi* (grow light) clarear; (of lightning) relampaguear; (become less heavy) disminuir de peso, aligerarse; volverse más alegre

lightening *n* aligeramiento, *m;* (easing) alivio, *m;* luz, *f*

lighter *n* (boat) lancha, barcaza, gabarra, *f;* (device) encendedor, *m.* **pocket l.,** encendedor de bolsillo, *m.* **l. man,** gabarrero, *m*

light-fingered *a* ligero de manos

lighthouse *n* faro, *m.* **l.-keeper,** guardafaro, *m*

lighting *n* iluminación, *f;* alumbrado, *m.* **flood l.,** iluminación intensiva, *f.* **l.-up time,** hora de encender los faros, *f*

lightly *adv* ligeramente; fácilmente; (slightly) levemente; ágilmente; sin seriedad. **l. wounded,** levemente herido

lightness *n* ligereza, *f;* poco peso, *m;* agilidad, *f;* (brightness) claridad, *f;* (inconstancy) liviandad, inconstancia, *f;* frivolidad, *f*

lightning *n* relámpago, rayo, *m.* **as quick as l.,** como un relámpago. **to be struck by l.,** ser herido por un relámpago. **l.-rod,** pararrayos, *m*

lightship *n* buque faro, *m*

ligneous *a* leñoso

lignite *n* lignito, *m*

likable *a* simpático

like *a* semejante; parecido; igual, mismo; (characteristic) típico, característico; (likely) probable; (equivalent) equivalente. *adv* como; igual (que); del mismo modo (que). *n* semejante, igual, *mf;* tal cosa, *f;* cosas semejantes, *f pl.* **Don't speak to me l. that,** No me hables así. **He was l. a fury,** Estaba hecho una furia. **They are very l. each other,** Se parecen mucho. **to be l.,** parecerse (a), semejar. **to look l.,** parecer ser (que); tener el aspecto de; (of persons) parecerse (a). **to return l. for l.,** pagar en la misma moneda

like *vt* gustar, agradar; estar aficionado (a), gustar de; (wish) querer. **As you l.,** Como te parezca bien, Como quieras. **If you l.,** Si quieres. **James likes painting,** Jaime está aficionado a la pintura. **Judith does not l. the north of England,** A Judith no le gusta el norte de Inglaterra. **I don't l. to do it,** No me gusta hacerlo. **I should l. him to go to Madrid,** Me gustaría que fuese a Madrid

likelihood *n* posibilidad, *f;* probabilidad, *f*

likely *a* probable; verosímil, creíble, plausible; posible; (suitable) satisfactorio, apropiado; (handsome) bien parecido. *adv* probablemente. **They are not l. to come,** No es probable que vengan

liken *vt* comparar

likeness *n* parecido, *m,* semejanza, *f;* (portrait) retrato, *m*

likewise *adv* igualmente, asimismo, también. *conjunc* además

liking *n* (for persons) simpatía, *f,* cariño, *m;* (for things) gusto, *m,* afición, *f;* (appreciation) aprecio, *m.* **I have a l. for old cities,** Me gustan (or me atraen) las viejas ciudades. **to take a l. to,** (things) aficionarse a; (persons) prendarse de, tomar cariño (a)

lilac *n* lila, *f.* **l. color,** color de lila, *m*

Lilliputian *a* liliputiense. *n* liliputiense, *mf*

lilt *n* canción, *f;* ritmo, *m;* armonía, *f*

lily *n* lirio, *m,* azucena, *f;* (of France) flor de lis, *f.* **l. of the valley,** lirio de los valles, muguete, *m.* **l.-white,** blanco como la azucena

limb *n anat* miembro, *m;* (of a tree) rama, *f*

limbless *a* mutilado

limbo *n* limbo, *m*

lime *n chem* cal, *f;* (for catching birds) liga, hisca, *f;* (linden tree) tilo, *m;* (tree like a lemon) limero, *m;* (fruit) lima, *f. vt* (whiten) encalar; *agr* abonar con cal. **slaked l.,** cal muerta, *f.* **l.-flower,** flor del tilo, tila, *f;* flor del limero, *f.* **l.-juice,** jugo de lima, *m.* **l.-kiln,** calera, *f.* **l.-pit,** pozo de cal, *m.* **l. tree** *Lat. Am.* limo, *m*

limelight *n* luz de calcio, *f; fig* centro de atención, *m;* publicidad, *f.* **to be in the l.,** ser el centro de atención, estar a la vista (de público)

limestone *n* piedra caliza, *f.* **l. deposit,** calar, *m*

limit *n* límite, *m;* confín, *m;* linde, *m,* or *f;* limitación, *f,* *vt* limitar; fijar; (restrict) restringir. **This is the l.!** ¡Este es el colmo! ¡No faltaba más!

limitation *n* limitación, *f;* restricción, *f*

limitative *a* restrictivo, limitativo

limited *a* limitado; restringido; escaso; (of persons) de cortos alcances; *com* anónima. **l. company,** sociedad anónima, *f*

limited monarchy *n* monarquía moderada, *f*

limiting adjective *n* adjetivo determinativo, *m*

limitless *a* sin límites, ilimitado, inmenso

limousine *n* limousina, *f,* coche cerrado, *m*

limp *a* flojo; débil; fláccido; lánguido. *n* cojera, *f. vi* cojear. **to l. off,** marcharse cojeando. **to l. up,** acercarse cojeando; subir cojeando

limpid *a* límpido, cristalino, puro

limpidity *n* limpidez, *f*

limping *a* cojo

limply *adv* flojamente; débilmente; lánguidamente

limpness *n* flojedad, *f;* debilidad, *f;* languidez, *f*

linchpin *n* pezonera, *f*

linden *n* tilo, *m*

line *vt* (furrow) surcar; (troops, etc.) poner en fila; alinear; (clothes, nests, etc.) forrar; (building) revestir; (one's pocket) llenar. *vi* estar en línea, alinearse

line *n* (most meanings) línea, *f;* (cord) cuerda, *f; naut* cordel, *m;* (fishing) sedal, *m;* (railway) vía, *f;* (wrinkle) surco, *m;* arruga, *f;* (row) hilera, ringlera, fila, *f;* (of verse) verso, *m; print* renglón, *m;* (of business) ramo, *m;* profesión, *f;* (interest) especialidad, *f.* **bowling or serving l.,** línea de saque, *f;* **hard lines,** mala suerte, *f;* apuro, *m,* situación difícil, *f.* **in a l.,** en fila; en cola. **in direct l.,** (of descent) en línea recta. **It is not in my l.,** No es una especialidad mía; No es uno de mis intereses. **on the lines of,** conforme a; parecido a. **to cross the l.,** (equator) pasar la línea; (railway) cruzar la vía. **to drop a l.,** escribir unas líneas, poner unas líneas. **to read between the lines,** leer entre líneas. **l.-drawing,** dibujo de líneas, *m.* **l. of battle,** línea de batalla, *f*

lineage *n* linaje, *m,* familia, raza, *f*

lineal *a* lineal

lineament *n* lineamento, *m;* (of the face) facciones, *f pl*

linear *a* lineal. **l. equation,** ecuación de primer grado, *f*

lined *a* rayado, con líneas; (of the face) surcado, arrugado; (of gloves, etc.) forrado. **lined paper,** papel rayado, *m*

linen *n* lino, *m; inf* ropa blanca, *f; a* de lino. **clean l.,** ropa limpia, *f.* **dirty l.,** ropa sucia, *f;* ropa para lavar, *f.* **table-l.,** mantelería, *f.* **l. cupboard,** armario para ropa blanca, *m.* **l. draper,** lencero (-ra). **l.-draper's shop,** lencería, *f.* **l. room,** lencería, *f.* **l. tape,** trenzadera, *f.* **l. thread,** hilo de lino, *m*

liner *n* (ship) transatlántico, *m;* buque de vapor, *m; aer* avión de pasaje, *m*

linesman *n* soldado de línea, *m; sport* juez de línea, *m*

ling *n bot* brezo, *m; icht* especie de abadejo, *f*

linger *vi* (remain) quedarse; tardar en marcharse; ir lentamente; hacer algo despacio

lingerie *n* ropa blanca, *f*

lingering *a* lento; largo, prolongado; melancólico, triste

lingeringly *adv* lentamente; largamente; melancólicamente

linguist *n* lingüista, *mf*

linguistic *a* lingüístico

linguistics *n* lingüística, *f*

liniment *n* linimento, *m*

lining *n* (of a garment, etc.) forro, *m*; (building) revestimiento, *m*

link *n* (in a chain) eslabón, *m*; (of beads) sarta, *f*; *fig* enlace, *m*, cadena, *f*; conexión, *f*; *mech* corredera, *f*; (torch) hacha de viento, *f*. *vt* enlazar, unir; *fig* encadenar. **missing l.,** *fig* estabón perdido, *m*. **to l. arms,** cogerse del brazo

linking *n* encadenamiento, *m*; *fig* conexión, *f*

links *n pl* campo de golf, *m*

linoleum *n* linóleo, *m*

linotype *n* linotipia, *f*

linseed *n* linaza, *f*. **l. cake,** bagazo, *m*. **l.-oil,** aceite de linaza, *m*

lint *n med* hilas, *f pl*; (fluff) borra, *f*

lintel *n* dintel, *m*; (threshold) umbral, *m*

lion *n* león, *m*; *fig* celebridad, *f*. **l. cage** or **den,** leonera, *f*. **l.-hearted,** valeroso. **l.-hunter,** cazador (-ra) de leones. **l.-keeper,** leonero (-ra). **lion's mane,** melena, *f*. **l.-tamer,** domador (-ra) de leones

lioness *n* leona, *f*

lionize *vt* dar bombo (a), hacer la rueda (a), tratar como una celebridad (a)

lion's share *n* parte del león, tajada del león, *f*

lip *n* labio, *m*; (of a vessel) pico, *m*; (of a crater) borde, *m*; *fig* boca, *f*. **to open one's lips,** abrir la boca. **to smack one's lips,** chuparse los dedos. **lip reading,** lectura labial, *f*. **lip-service,** amor fingido, *m*; promesas hipócritas, *f pl*. **lip stick,** lápiz para los labios, *m*

lipped *a* (in compounds) con labios . . . , que tiene labios; (of vessels in compounds) con . . . picos

liquefaction *n* licuefacción, *f*

liquefiable *a* liquidable

liquefy *vt* liquidar. *vi* liquidarse

liqueur *n* licor, *m*. **l.-glass,** copita de licor, *f*. **l.-set,** licorera, *f*

liquid *n* líquido, *m*, *a* líquido; límpido. **l. air,** aire líquido, *m*. **l. measure,** medida para líquidos, *f*

liquidate *vt* liquidar; saldar (cuentas); *mil* soldar

liquidation *n* liquidación, *f*

liquidness *n* liquidez, *f*; fluidez, *f*

liquor *n* licor, *m*. **l. shop,** aguardentería, *f*. **l. traffic,** negocio de vinos y licores, *m*; contrabando, *m*

liquorice *n* regaliz, *m*

lira *n* lira, *f*

Lisbon Lisboa, *f*

lisp *n* ceceo, *m*; balbuceo, *m*, *vi* cecear; balbucir

lisping *a* ceceoso; balbuciente. *n* ceceo, *m*; (of a child, etc.) balbuceo, *m*

lissom *a* flexible; ágil

list *n* lista, *f*; catálogo, *m*; matrícula, *f*; *naut* recalcada, *f*; inclinación, *f*; (tournament) liza, *f*. *vt* hacer una lista de; catalogar; matricular, inscribir. *vi naut* recalcar; inclinarse a un lado. **to enter the lists,** entrar en liza. **l. of wines,** lista de vinos, *f*

listen *vi* escuchar; (attend) attender. **Don't you want to l. to the music?** ¿No quieres escuchar la música? **to l. in,** (to the radio) escuchar la radio; (eavesdrop) escuchar a hurtadillas

listener *n* oyente, *mf*; (to radio) radiooyente, *mf*

listless *a* lánguido, apático, indiferente

listlessly *adv* lánguidamente, indiferentemente

listlessness *n* apatía, languidez, indiferencia, inercia, *f*

litany *n* letanía, *f*

liter *n* litro, *m*

literal *a* literal. **l.-minded,** sin imaginación

literalness *n* literalidad, *f*

literary *a* literario

literary executor *n* depositario de la obra literaria, *m*

literate *a* and *n* literato (-ta)

literature *n* literatura, *f*

lithe *a* flexible; sinuoso y delgado; ágil

litheness *n* flexibilidad, *f*; sinuosidad, *f*; delgadez, *f*; agilidad, *f*

lithograph *n* litografía, *f*, *vt* litografiar

lithographer *n* litógrafo, *m*

lithographic *a* litográfico

lithography *n* litografía, *f*

Lithuania Lituania, *f*

Lithuanian *a* lituano, *n* lituano (-na); (language) lituano, *m*

litigant *n* litigante, *mf*

litigate *vi* and *vt* litigar, pleitear

litigation *n* litigación, *f*

litigious *a* litigioso

litmus *n* tornasol, *m*. **l. paper,** papel de tornasol, *m*

litter *n* litera, *f*; (stretcher) camilla, *f*; (bed) lecho, *m*; cama de paja, *f*; (brood) camada, *f*; (rubbish) cosas en desorden, *f pl*; (papers) papeletas, *f pl*; (untidiness) desarreglo, desorden, *m*, confusión, *f*, *vt* poner en desorden

little *a* pequeño; poco; (scanty) escaso; insignificante; bajo, mezquino. *adv* poco. **a l.,** un poco (de); un tanto. **in l.,** en pequeño. **not a l.,** no poco; bastante. **l. by l.,** poco a poco. **l. or no,** poco o nada. **however l.,** por pequeño que. **as l. as possible,** lo menos posible. **to make l. of,** no dar importancia a; sacar poco en claro de, no comprender bien; no hacer caso de; (persons) acoger mal. **l. by l.,** poco a poco. **l. finger,** dedo meñique, *m*. **l. one,** pequeñuela, *f*, pequeñito, *m*

littleness *n* pequeñez, *f*; poquedad, *f*; mezquindad, *f*; trivialidad, *f*

littoral *a* and *n* litoral, *m*

liturgical *a* litúrgico. **l. calendar,** calendario litúrgico, *m*

liturgical vestment *n* paramento litúrgico, *m*

liturgy *n* liturgia, *f*

live *a* vivo, viviente; (alight) encendido; (of a wire, etc.) cargado de electricidad. **l. cartridge,** cartucho con bala, *m*. **l. coal,** ascua, *f*. **l.-stock,** ganadería, *f*. **l. wire,** conductor eléctrico, *m*; *fig* fuerza viva, *f*

live *vi* vivir; residir, habitar; (of ships) mantenerse a flote; salvarse; subsistir. *vt* (one's life) llevar, pasar. **Long l.!** ¡Viva! **to have enough to l. on,** tener de que vivir. **to l. together,** convivir. **to l. again,** volver a vivir. **to l. at,** vivir en, habitar. **to l. down,** sobrevivir a; (a fault) lograr borrar. **to l. on,** vivir de. **to l. up to,** vivir con arreglo a, vivir en conformidad con; estar al nivel de, merecer. **to l. up to one's income,** vivir al día, gastarse toda la renta

live broadcast *n* emisión en directo, *f*

livelihood *n* vida, subsistencia, *f*. **to make a l.,** ganarse la vida

liveliness *n* vivacidad, vida, *f*; animación, *f*; alegría, *f*

livelong *a* entero, todo; eterno. **all the l. day,** todo el santo día

lively *a* vivo; vivaracho; brioso, enérgico; alegre; bullicioso; animado; (fresh) fresco; (of colours) brilliante; intenso

liver *n* vividor (-ra), el, *m*, (*f*, la) que vive; habitante, *m*; *anat* hígado, *m*. **l. cancer,** cáncer del hígado, *m*. **l. complaint,** mal de hígado, *m*. **l. extract,** extracto de hígado, *m*

livery *n* librea, *f*; uniforme, *m*; *poet* vestiduras, *f pl*. **l. stables,** pensión de caballos, *f*; cochería de alquiler, *f*

livid *a* lívido; cárdeno, amoratado

lividness *n* lividez, *f*

living *a* viviente; vivo, vital. *n* vida, *f*; modo de vivir, *m*; beneficio eclesiástico, *m*. **the l.,** los vivos. **to make one's l.,** ganarse la vida. **l. memory,** memoria de personas vivientes, memoria de los que aún viven, *f*. **l.-room,** sala de estar, *f*. **l. soul,** ser viviente; *inf* bicho viviente, *m*. **l. wage,** jornal básico, *m*

lizard *n* lagarto (-ta). **giant l.,** dragón, *m*. **wall l.,** lagartija, *f*. **l. hole,** lagartera, *f*

llama *n* llama, *f*

load *n* carga, *f*; peso, *m*; (cart) carretada, *f*; *elec* carga, *f*; (quantity) cantidad, *f*. *vt* cargar (con); (with honors) llenar (de); (*fig* weigh down) agobiar (con); (a stick with lead) emplomar; (*elec* and of dice) cargar; (wine) mezclar vino con un narcótico. **to be loaded with**

fruit, estar cargado de fruta. **to l. oneself with,** cargarse de. **to l. the dice,** cargar los dados. **to l. again,** recargar

loader *n* cargador, *m*

loading *n* carga, *f.* **l. depot,** cargadero, *m*

loaf *n* pan, *m;* (French) barra de pan, *f. vi* golfear, vagabundear, gandulear. **l. sugar,** azúcar de pilón, *m*

loafer *n* vago (-ga); azotacalles, *mf;* gandul (-la); golfo (-fa)

loafing *n* gandulería, *f,* vagabundeo, *m*

loam *n* marga, *f*

loamy *a* margoso

loan *n* empréstito, *m;* (lending) prestación, *f;* préstamo, *m. vt* prestar. **l. fund,** caja de empréstitos, *f.* **l. company office,** casa de préstamos, *f*

loath *a* desinclinado, poco dispuesto

loathe *vt* abominar, detestar, odiar, aborrecer; repugnar

loather *n* el, *m,* (*f,* la) que odia; aborrecedor (-ra)

loathing *n* aborrecimiento, odio, *m;* repugnancia, aversión, *f*

loathsome *a* odioso, aborrecible; asqueroso; repugnante

loathsomeness *n* carácter repugnante, *m;* asquerosidad, *f*

lobby *n* pasillo, *m;* antecámara, *f;* (in a hotel, house) vestíbulo, recibidor, *m;* (waiting-room) sala de espera, *f;* (in Parliament) sala de los pasos perdidos, *f. vt* and *vi* cabildear

lobe *n bot* lobo, *m;* (*anat arch*) lóbulo, *m*

lobster *n* langosta, *f;* bogavante, *m.* **l.-pot,** cambín, *m,* nasa, *f*

local *a* local; de la localidad. **l. anesthetic,** anestésico local, *m.* **l. color,** color local, *m*

locale *n* local, *m*

locality *n* localidad, *f;* situación, *f*

localization *n* localización, *f*

localize *vt* localizar

locate *vt* situar; colocar; localizar. **to be located,** situarse; hallarse

location *n* colocación, *f;* emplazamiento, *m;* localidad, *f;* situación, posición, *f*

loch *n* lago, *m*

lock *n* cerradura (of a door, including a vehicle) *f;* (of a gun) cerrojo, *m;* (in wrestling) llave, *f;* (on rivers, canals) presa, *f;* (at a dock) esclusa, *f;* (of hair) mechón, *m,* guedeja, *f;* (ringlet) bucle, *m; pl* **locks,** (hair) cabellos, *m pl,* pelo, *m.* **spring l.,** cerradura de golpe, *f.* **to put a l. on,** poner cerradura a. **under l. and key,** bajo cuatro llaves. **l.-jaw,** trismo, *m.* **l. keeper,** esclusero (-ra) *mf.* **l.-out strike,** huelga patronal, *f*

lock *vt* cerrar con llave; *fig* encerrar; (embrace) abrazar estrechamente; (of wheels, etc.) trabar; (twine) entrelazar. *vi* cerrarse con llave. **to l. in,** cerrar con llave; encerrar. **to l. out,** cerrar la puerta (a); dejar en la calle (a). **to l. up,** encerrar; (imprison) encarcelar

locker *n* (drawer) cajón, *m;* (cupboard) armario, *m; naut* cajonada, *f*

locket *n* guardapelo, *m;* medallón, *m*

locksmith *n* cerrajero, *m.* **locksmith's trade,** cerrajería, *f*

locomotion *n* locomoción, *f*

locomotive *a* locomotor. *n* locomotora, *f*

locum tenens *n* interino (-na)

locust *n* langosta migratoria, *f*

locution *n* locución, *f*

lode *n* filón, *m*

lodestar *n* estrella polar, *f; fig* norte, *m*

lodge *n* casita, garita, *f;* casa de guarda, *f;* (freemason's) logia, *f;* (porter's) portería, *f, vi* hospedarse, alojarse, vivir, parar; penetrar; entrar (en); fijarse (en). *vt* hospedar, alojar; albergar; (a blow) asestar; (a complaint) hacer, dar; (money, etc.) depositar. **to l. an accusation against,** querellarse contra, quejarse de. **l.-keeper,** conserje, *m*

lodger *n* huésped (-eda), *Lat. Am.* alojado (-da)

lodging *n* hospedaje, alojamiento, *m;* (inn) posada, *f;* residencia, *f;* casa, *f.* **l.-house,** casa de huéspedes, *f*

loft *n* desván, sotabanco, *m;* pajar, *m*

loftily *adv* en alto; (proudly) con arrogancia, con altanería

loftiness *n* altura, *f;* sublimidad, *f;* nobleza, *f;* dignidad, *f;* (haughtiness) altanería, soberbia, *f*

lofty *a* alto; sublime; noble; eminente; (haughty) altanero, soberbio

log *n* madero, tronco, *m;* palo, *m;* leño, *m; naut,* diario de a bardo *m,* barquilla, *f.* **to lie like a log,** estar hecho un tronco. **log-book,** *naut* cuaderno de bitácora, *m.* **log-cabin,** cabañas de troncos, *m.* **log-wood,** palo campeche, *m*

logarithm *n* logaritmo, *m*

logarithmic *a* logarítmico

logic *n* lógica, *f*

logical *a* lógico

logician *n* lógico (-ca)

loin *n* ijar, *m;* (of meat) falda, *f; pl* **loins,** lomos, riñones *m pl.* **to gird up one's loins,** *fig* arremangarse los faldones. **l.-cloth,** taparrabo, *m*

loiter *vi* vagabundear, vagar, errar; haraganear; rezagarse

loiterer *n* haragán (-ana); vago (-ga); rezagado (-da)

loll *vi* recostarse (en), apoyarse (en). *vt* (the tongue) sacar

Lombardy-Venetia Lombardo-Véneto, *m*

London Londres, *m*

Londoner *n* londinense, *mf*

lone. See **lonely**

loneliness *n* soledad, *f;* aislamiento, *m*

lonely *a* solitario; solo; aislado, remoto; desierto

lonesome *a* solo, solitario

long *a* largo; prolongado; de largo; (extensive) extenso; (big) grande; (much) mucho. **a l. time,** mucho tiempo. **It is five feet l.,** Tiene cinco pies de largo. **l.-armed,** que tiene los brazos largos. **l.-boat,** falúa, *f.* **l. clothes,** (infant's) mantillas, *f pl.* **l.-distance call,** conferencia telefónica, *f.* **l.-distance race,** carrera de fondo, *f.* **l.-eared,** de orejas largas. **l.-faced,** de cara larga, carilargo. **l.-forgotten,** olvidado hace mucho tiempo. **l.-haired,** que tiene el pelo largo. **l.-headed,** dolicocéfalo; *fig* astuto, sagaz. **l.-legged,** zanquilargo, zancudo. **l.-lived,** que vive hasta una edad avanzada; longevo; duradero. **l.-lost,** perdido hace mucho tiempo. **l.-sighted,** présbita; previsor; sagaz. **l.-standing,** viejo, de muchos años. **l.-suffering,** sufrido, paciente. **l.-tailed,** de cola larga. **l.-waisted,** de talle largo. **l.-winded,** prolijo

long *adv* mucho tiempo; mucho; durante mucho tiempo. **as l. as,** mientras (que). **before l.,** dentro de poco. **the l. and the short of it,** en resumidas cuentas. **How l. has she been here?** ¿Cuánto tiempo hace que está aquí? **not l. before,** poco tiempo antes. **l. ago,** tiempo ha, muchos años ha

long *vi* anhelar, suspirar (por), desear con vehemencia

longanimity *n* longanimidad, *f*

longer *a comp* más largo. *adv comp* más tiempo. **How much l. must we wait?** ¿Cuánto tiempo más hemos de esperar? **He can no l. walk as he used,** Ya no puede andar como antes

longevity *n* longevidad, *f*

longing *a* anheloso, ansioso; de envidia. *n* anhelo, *m,* ansia, *f;* deseo vehemente, *m;* envidia, *f*

longingly *adv* con ansia; impacientemente; con envidia

longish *a* algo largo

longitude *n* longitud, *f*

longitudinal *a* longitudinal

long take *n cinema* toma larga, *f*

loofah *n* esponja vegetal, *f*

look *n* mirada, *f;* (glance) vistazo, *m,* ojeada, *f;* (air) semblante, aire, porte, *m;* (appearance) aspecto, *m;* apariencia, *f.* **good looks,** buen parecer, *m;* guapeza, *f.* **the new l.,** la nueva línea, la nueva silueta, la nueva moda. **to be on the l.-out,** andar a la mira

look *vi* and *vt* mirar; considerar, contemplar; (appear, seem) parecer; tener aire (de); tener aspecto (de); hacer el efecto (de); (show oneself) mostrarse; (of buildings, etc.) caer (a), dar (a); mirar (a).; (seem to be) revelar (e.g., **You don't l. thirty,** No revelas treinta años) **to l. alike,** parecerse. **to l. hopeful,** *fig* prometer bien. **to l. out of the corner of the eye,** mirar de reojo. **to l. (a person) up and down,** mirar de hito en hito. **to l. about one,** mirar a su alrededor; observar. **to l. after,** tener la mirada puesta en, mirar; (care for) cuidar; (watch) vigilar; mirar por. **to l. at,** mirar; considerar; examinar. **He looked at his watch,** Miró su reloj. **He looked at her,** La miró. **to l. away,** desviar los ojos, apartar la mirada. **to l. back,** mirar hacia atrás, volver la cabeza; (in thought) pensar en el pasado. **to l. down,** bajar los ojos; mirar el suelo; mirar hacia abajo. **to l. down upon,** dominar, mirar a; (scorn) despreciar; mirar de arriba para abajo. **to l. for,** buscar; buscar con los ojos; (await) aguardar; (expect) esperar. **to l. forward,** mirar hacia el porvenir; pensar en el futuro; esperar con ilusión. **to l. in,** entrar por un instante, hacer una visita corta. **to l. into,** mirar dentro de; mirar hacia el interior de; estudiar, investigar, *Lat. Am. also* interiorizar. **to l. on,** *vt* mirar; considerar; (of buildings, etc.) dar a. *vi* ser espectador. **to l. on to,** dar a, mirar a. **to l. out,** *vi* (be careful) tener cuidado; (look through) mirar por; asomarse a. *vt* (search) buscar; (find) hallar; (choose) escoger, elegir. **L. out!** ¡Atención! ¡Ojo!, *Mexico* ¡abusado! **to l. out for,** buscar; (await) aguardar, esperar; (be careful) tener cuidado con. **to l. out of,** mirar por; asomarse a. **to l. over,** mirar bien; (persons) mirar de hito en hito; examinar; visitar; (a house) inspeccionar; (a book) hojear; mirar superficialmente. **to l. round,** *vt* (a place) visitar. *vi* volver la cabeza, volverse; mirar hacia atrás. **to l. round for,** buscar con los ojos; buscar por todas partes. **to l. through,** mirar por; mirar a través de; examinar; (search) registrar; (understand) registrar. **to l. to,** (be careful of) tener cuidado de; (attend to) atender a; (care for) cuidar de; (count on) contar con; (resort to) acudir a; (await) esperar. **to l. toward,** mirar hacia, mirar en la dirección de; caer a. **to l. up,** *vi* mirar hacia arriba; (aspire) aspirar; (improve) mejorar. *vt* visitar, ir (or venir) a ver; (turn up) buscar; averiguar. **to l. upon,** mirar. Other meanings see **to l. on.** **They l. upon her as their daughter,** La miran como a una hija suya. **to l. up to,** *fig* respetar.

looking *a* (in compounds) de . . . aspecto, de . . . apariencia. **dirty-l.,** de aspecto sucio. **l.-glass,** espejo, *m*

lookout vigilancia, observación, *f*; (view) vista, *f*, panorama, *m*; (viewpoint) miradero, *m*; *mil* atalaya, *m*; *naut* gaviero, *m*; (*fig* prospect) perspectiva, *f*

loom *n* telar, *m*, *vi* asomar, aparecer

loop *n* (turn) vuelta, *f*; (in rivers, etc.) recodo, *m*, curva, *f*; (fold) pliegue, *m*; bucle, *m*; (fastening) fiador, *m*, presilla, *f*; *aer* rizo, *m*; (knot) nudo corredizo, *m*. **to l. the l.,** *aer* hacer el rizo, hacer rizos. **l.-line,** empalme de ferrocarril, *m*

loophole *n* saetera, aspillera, *f*; *fig* escapatoria, *f*; pretexto, *m*, excusa, *f*

loose *a* suelto; (free) libre; (slack) flojo; (of garments) holgado; (untied) desatado; (unfastened) desprendido; movible; (unchained) desencadenado; en libertad; (of the bowels) suelto (de vientre); (pendulous) colgante; (of a nail, tooth, etc.) inseguro; poco firme; que se mueve; (of knots, etc.) flojo; (of the mind, etc.) incoherente, ilógico; poco exacto; (of style, etc.) vago, impreciso; (of conduct) disoluto, vicioso; (careless) negligente, descuidado. *vt* (untie) desatar; desprender; soltar; aflojar; (of a priest) absolver; *fig* desencadenar. **to break l.,** desprenderse; soltarse; libertarse; escapar; *fig* desencadenarse. **to let l.,** desatar; aflojar; poner en libertad; soltar; *fig* desencadenar; (interject) lanzar. **to turn l.,** poner en libertad; dar salida (a); echar de casa; poner en la calle. **to work l.,** desprenderse; aflojarse;

desvencijarse. **l.-box,** caballeriza, *f*. **l. change,** suelto, *m*. **l.-leaf notebook,** libreta de hojas sueltas, *f*

loosely *adv* flojamente; sueltamente; (vaguely) vagamente; incorrectamente; incoherentemente; (carelessly) negligentemente; (viciously) disolutamente

loosen *vt* (untie) desatar; aflojar; soltar; desasir; (the tongue) desatar; *fig* hacer menos riguroso, ablandar

looseness *n* flojedad, *f*; (of clothing) holgura, *f*; soltura, *f*; relajación, *f*; (of the bowels) diarrea, *f*; (viciousness) licencia, *f*, libertinaje, *m*; (vagueness) vaguedad, *f*; incoherencia, *f*

loosening *n* desprendimiento, *m*; desasimiento, *m*; aflojamiento, *m*

loot *n* botín, *m*, *vt* saquear

looter *n* saqueador (-ra)

looting *n* saqueo, pillaje, *m*, *a* saqueador

lop *vt* mochar; podar; destroncar; cortar de un golpe. *a* (of ears) gacho. **to lop off the ends,** cercenar. **to lop off the top,** desmochar. **lop-sided,** desproporcionado; desequilibrado

lopping *n* desmoche, *m*; poda, *f*

loquacious *a* locuaz, gárrulo

loquacity *n* locuacidad, garrulidad, *f*

lord *n* señor, *m*; (husband) esposo, *m*; (English title) lord, *m*, (*pl* lores); (Christ) Señor, *m*. **feudal l.,** señor de horca y cuchillo, *m*. **my l.,** milord. **my lords,** milores. **Our L.,** Nuestro Señor. **the Lord's Prayer,** el Padrenuestro. **to l. it over,** mandar como señor, mandar a la baqueta. **L. Chamberlain,** camarero mayor, *m*. **L. Chancellor,** gran canciller, *m*. **L. Chief Justice,** presidente del tribunal supremo, *m*. **L.-Lieutenant,** virrey, *m*. **L. Mayor,** alcalde, *m*. **L. Privy Seal,** guardasellos del rey, *m*

lordliness *n* suntuosidad, *f*; liberalidad, munificencia, *f*; dignidad, *f*; (haughtiness) altivez, arrogancia, *f*

lordly *a* señorial, señoril; altivo, arrogante

lordship *n* señoría, *f*; señorío, poder, *m*. **his l.,** su señoría

lore *n* saber, *m*; erudición, *f*; tradiciones, *f pl*

lorgnette *n* impertinentes, *m pl*

lose *vt* perder; hacer perder, quitar; (forget) olvidar. *vi* perder; (of clocks) atrasar. **to be lost in thought,** estar ensimismado, estar absorto. **to l. oneself (in)** perderse (en); abstraerse (en); entregarse (a). **to l. one's footing,** resbalar. **to l. one's way,** extraviarse, perder el camino. **to l. one's self-control,** perder el tino. **to l. one's head,** perder la cabeza. **to l. ground,** perder terreno. **to l. one's voice,** perder la voz. **to l. patience,** perder la paciencia, perder los estribos

loser *n* perdedor (-ra)

losing *a* perdedor. *n* pérdida, *f*

loss *n* pérdida, *f*. **at a l.,** *com* con pérdida; perplejo, dudoso. **heavy losses,** *mil* pérdidas cuantiosas, *f pl*. **loss of blood** *Lat. Am.* desangre *m*. **We are at a l. for words . . . ,** No tenemos palabras para . . .

lot *n* suerte, *f*; fortuna, *f*; lote, *m*; parte, porción, cuota, *f*; (for building) solar, *m*. **a lot of people,** muchas personas. **Our lot would have been very different,** Nuestra suerte hubiera sido muy distinta, Otro gallo nos cantara. **to draw lots,** echar suertes, sortear. **to take the lot,** *inf* alzarse con el santo y la limosna

lotion *n* loción, *f*

lottery *n* lotería, *f*. **l. ticket,** billete de la lotería, *m*

lotus *n* loto, *m*. **l.-eating,** lotofagía, *f*; *fig* indolencia, pereza, *f*

loud *a* fuerte; (noisy) ruidoso, estrepitoso; alto; (gaudy) chillón, llamativo, cursi, *Lat. Am. also* figuroso. *adv* ruidosamente. **l.-speaker,** *rad* altavoz, *Mexico* magnavoz. *m*

loudly *adv* en alta voz; fuertemente; ruidosamente, con estrépito

loudness *n* (noise) ruido, *m*; sonoridad, *f*; (force) fuerza, *f*; (of colors, etc.) mal gusto, *m*, vulgaridad, *f*

lounge *n* sala de estar, *f*; salón, *m*, *vi* reclinarse, ponerse a sus anchas; apoyarse (en); gandulear; vagar. **l. chair,**

poltrona, *f*. **l.-lizard,** *inf* pollo pera, *m*. **l.-suit,** traje americano, *m*
lounger *n* holgazán (-ana); golfo (-fa), azotacalles, *mf*
louse *n* piojo, *m*
lousy *a* piojoso
lout *n* patán, zamacuco, *m*
loutish *a* rústico
lovable *a* amable; simpático
lovableness *n* amabilidad, *f*
love *n* amor, *m*; (friendship) amistad, *f*; (enthusiasm, liking) afición, *f*; (in tennis) cero, *m*, *vt* querer, amar; gustar mucho; tener afición (a). *vi* estar enamorado. **I should l. to dine with you,** Me gustaría mucho cenar con Vds. **to be in l. with,** estar enamorado de. **to fall in l. with,** enamorarse de. **They l. each other,** Se quieren. **to make l. to,** hacer el amor (a), galantear. **l. affair,** amorío, lance de amor, *m*. **l.-bird,** periquito, *m*. **l.-letter,** carta amatoria, carta de amor, *f*. **l.-making,** galanteo, *m*. **l.-philtre,** filtro, *m*. **l.-song,** canción de amor, *f*. **l.-story,** historia de amor, *f*. **l.-token,** prenda de amor, *f*
loveless *a* sin amor
loveliness *n* hermosura, belleza, *f*; encanto, *m*; amabilidad, *f*
lovely *a* hermoso, bello; delicioso; amable; *inf* estupendo
lover *n* amante, *mf*; aficionado (-da)
lovesick *a* enfermo de amor, enamorado
loving *a* amoroso; cariñoso; (friendly) amistoso; de amor
low *a* bajo; de poca altura; (of dresses, etc.) escotado; (of musical notes) grave; (soft) suave; (feeble) débil; (depressed) deprimido, triste, abatido; (plain) sencillo; (of a fever) lento; (of a bow) profundo; pequeño; inferior; humilde; (ill) enfermo; (vile) vil, ruin; obsceno, escabroso. *adv* bajo; cerca de la tierra; en voz baja; (cheaply) barato, a bajo precio. **in a low voice,** en voz baja, paso. **to lay low,** (kill) tumbar; (knock down) derribar; incapacitar. **to lie low,** descansar; estar muerto; esconderse, agacharse; callar. **to run low,** escasear. **low-born,** de humilde cuna. **low-brow,** nada intelectual. **low comedy,** farsa, *f*. **low flying,** *n* bajo vuelo, *m*, a que vuela bajo; terrero, rastrero; que vuela a ras de tierra. **low frequency,** baja frecuencia, *f*. **low Latin,** bajo latín, *m*. **Low Mass,** misa rezada, *f*. **low neck,** escote, *m*. **low-necked,** escotado. **low-pitched,** grave. **low-spirited,** deprimido. **Low Sunday,** domingo de Cuasimodo, *m*. **low tension,** baja tensión, *f*. **low trick,** mala pasada, *f*. **low water,** marea baja, bajamar, *f*; (of rivers) estiaje, *m*
low *vi* berrear, mugir. *n* berrido, mugido, *m*
low-ceiling *a* bajo de techo.
lower *vt* bajar; descolgar; disminuir; (price) rebajar; (a boat, sails) arriar. *vi* (of persons) fruncir el ceño, mostrarse malhumorado; (of the sky) encapotarse, cargarse; (menace) amenazar. **to l. a boat,** arriar un bote. **to l. oneself,** (by a rope, etc.) descolgarse. **to l. the flag,** abatir la bandera
lower *a comp* más bajo; menos alto; bajo; inferior. **l. classes,** clase obrera, *f*, clases bajas, *f pl*. **l. down,** más abajo. **L. House,** Cámara de los Comunes, *f*; cámara baja, *f*. **l. jaw,** mandíbula inferior, *f*. **l. storey,** piso bajo, *m*; piso de abajo, *m*
Lower California Baja California, *f*
lowering *n* abajamiento, *m*; descenso, *m*; (of prices) baja, *f*; (of a boat) arriada, *f*; (of the flag) abatimiento, *m*, *a* (of persons) ceñudo; (of the sky) anublado, encapotado; (threatening) amenazador
lowest *a sup* el (la, etc.) más bajo; el (la, etc.) más profundo; ínfimo
lowing *n* berrido, mugido, *m*
lowland *n* tierra baja, *f*. **the Lowlands,** las tierras bajas de Escocia
lowliness *n* humildad, *f*; modestia, *f*
lowly *a* humilde
lowness *n* poca altura, *f*; situación poco elevada, *f*; pe-

queñez, *f*; (of musical notes) gravedad, *f*; (softness) suavidad, *f*; (feebleness) debilidad, *f*; (sadness) tristeza, *f*, abatimiento, *m*; (of price) baratura, *f*; inferioridad, *f*; humildad, *f*; (vileness) bajeza, *f*; obscenidad, *f*
loyal *a* leal, fiel
loyalist *n* realista, *mf*; defensor (-ra) del gobierno legítimo
loyalty *n* lealtad, fidelidad, *f*
loyalty oath *n* (approximate equivalent) certificado de adhesión, *m*
lozenge *n* pastilla, *f*
lubricant *a* and *n* lubricante *m*
lubricate *vt* lubricar, engrasar
lubricating oil *n* aceite lubricante, *m*
lubrication *n* lubricación, *f*, engrasado, *m*
lubricator *n* lubricador, *m*; engrasador, *m*
Lucerne Lucerna, *f*
lucid *a* lúcido; claro
lucidity *n* lucidez, *f*; claridad, *f*
lucidly *adv* claramente
luck *n* destino, azar, *m*; (good) buenaventura, suerte, *f*. **to bring bad l.,** traer mala suerte. **to try one's l.,** probar fortuna
luckily *adv* por fortuna, afortunadamente, felizmente
luckless *a* desdichado
lucky *a* afortunado; dichoso, venturoso, *Lat. Am. also* lechudo; feliz. **to be l.,** tener buena suerte
lucrative *a* lucrativo
lucre *n* lucro, *m*
lucubration *n* lucubración, *f*
ludicrous *a* absurdo, risible, ridículo
ludicrousness *n* ridiculez, *f*
lug *n* tirón, *m*; (ear and projection) oreja, *f*, *vt* tirar (de); arrastrar. **to lug about,** arrastrar (por); llevar con dificultad. **to lug in,** arrastrar adentro; introducir; hacer entrar. **to lug out,** arrastrar afuera; hacer salir
luggage *n* equipaje, *m*. **excess l.,** exceso de equipaje, *m*. **piece of l.,** bulto, *m*. **to register one's l.,** facturar el equipaje. **l. carrier,** (on buses, etc.) baca, *f*; (on a car) portaequipajes, *m*. **l. porter,** mozo de equipajes, *m*. **l. rack,** (on a car) portaequipajes, *m*; (in a train) rejilla para el equipaje, *f*. **l. receipt,** talón de equipaje, *m*. **l. room,** consigna, *f*. **l. van,** furgón de equipajes, *m*
lugubrious *a* lúgubre
lukewarm *a* tibio, templado; *fig* indiferente, frío
lukewarmness *n* tibieza, *f*; *fig* indiferencia, frialdad, *f*
lull *n* momento de calma, *m*; tregua, *f*; silencio, *m*, *vt* (a child) arrullar, adormecer; (soothe) sosegar, calmar; disminuir, mitigar
lullaby *n* canción de cuna, *f*
lumbago *n* lumbago, *m*
lumbar *a* lumbar
lumber *n* (wood) maderas de sierra, *f pl*; (rubbish) trastos viejos, *m pl*. *vt* amontonar trastos viejos; obstruir. *vi* andar pesadamente; avanzar ruidosamente, avanzar con ruido sordo. **l.-jack,** maderero, ganchero, *m*. **l.-room,** leonera, *f*. **l.-yard,** maderería, *f*, depósito de maderas, *m*
lumbering *a* pesado
luminary *n* lumbrera, *f*
luminosity *n* luminosidad, *f*
luminous *a* luminoso
lump *n* masa, *f*; bulto, *m*; pedazo, *m*; (of sugar) terrón *m*; (swelling) hinchazón, *f*; protuberancia, *f*. *vt* amontonar. **to l. together,** mezclar; incluir. **in the l.,** en la masa; en grueso. **Let him l. it!** ¡Que se rasque! **l. in one's throat,** nudo en la garganta, *m*. **l. of sugar,** terrón de azúcar, *m*. **l. sum,** cantidad gruesa, *f*
lumpishness *n* hobachonería, *f*
lunacy *n* locura, *f*
lunar *a* lunar
lunatic *n* loco (-ca); demente, *mf a* de locos; loco. **l. asylum,** manicomio, *m*
lunch, luncheon *n* almuerzo, *m*, *Mexico* fajina, *f*;

(snack) merienda, *f. vi* almorzar. **l. basket** or **pail,** fiambrera, *f*

lunch counter, luncheonette *Mexico* almuercería, *elsewhere in Lat. Am.* lonchería, *f*

lunette *n* (*arch mil*) luneta, *f*

lung *n* pulmón, *m*

lunge *n* (fencing) estocada, *f*; embestida, *f, vi* dar una estocada; abalanzarse sobre

lurch *n* sacudida, *f*; *naut* guiñada, *f*; tambaleo, *m*; movimiento brusco, *m. vi naut* guiñar; tambalearse; andar haciendo eses. **to leave in the l.,** dejar plantado

lure *n* añagaza, *f*; reclamo, *m*; aliciente, atractivo, *m*; seducción, *f. vt* atraer, tentar

lurid *a* misterioso, fantástico; cárdeno; ominoso; funesto, triste; (orange) anaranjado; (vicissitudinous) accidentado

lurk *vi* acechar, espiar; esconderse

lurking *a* (in ambush) en acecho; (of fear, etc.) vago

luscious *a* delicioso; suculento; meloso; atractivo, apetitoso; sensual

lusciousness *n* suculencia, *f*; melosidad, *f*; atractivo, *m*; sensualidad, *f*

lush *a* jugoso; fresco y lozano; maduro

lust *n* lujuria, lascivia, *f*; codicia, *f*; deseo, *m*. **l. for revenge,** deseo de venganza, *m*

lustful *a* lujurioso, lúbrico, lascivo

luster *n* lustre, brillo, *m*; brillantez, *f*

lusterless *a* sin brillo; mate, deslustrado; (of eyes) apagado

lustrous *a* lustroso

lusty *a* vigoroso, fuerte, lozano

lute *n* laúd, *m*, vihuela, *f*. **l.-player,** vihuelista, *mf*

Lutheran *a* luterano. *n* luterano (-na)

Lutheranism *n* luteranismo, *m*

luxation *n* luxación, *f*

luxuriance *n* lozanía, *f*; exuberancia, superabundancia, *f*

luxuriant *a* lozano; fértil; exuberante

luxuriate *vi* crecer con exuberancia; complacerse (en); disfrutar (de), gozar (de)

luxurious *a* lujoso

luxuriously *adv* lujosamente, con lujo

luxury *n* lujo, *m*. **l. goods,** artículos de lujo, *m pl*

lyceum *n* liceo, *m*

lye *n* lejía, *f*

lying *a* (recumbent) recostado; (untrue) mentiroso, falso. *n* mentiras, *f pl*. **l.-in,** parto, *m*

lymph *n* linfa, *f*; vacuna, *f*

lymphatic *a* linfático; flemático

lynch *vt* linchar

lynching *n* linchamiento, *m*

lynx *n* lince, *m*. **l.-eyed,** de ojos de lince

lyre *n* lira, *f*. **l.-bird,** pájaro lira, *m*

lyric *n* poesía lírica, *f*; poema lírico, *m*; letra (de una canción,) *f*

lyrical *a* lírico

lyricism *n* lirismo, *m*

M

m *n* (letter) eme, *f*

ma'am *n* señora, *f*

macabre *a* macabro

macadam *n* macadán, *m, a* de macadán

macadamize *vt* macadanizar

macaroni *n* macarrones, *m pl*

macaronic *a* macarrónico

macaroon *n* macarrón de almendras, *m*

macaw *n* macagua, *f*, guacamayo, *m*

mace *n* maza, *f*; *cul* macis, *f*. **m.-bearer,** macero, *m*

Macedonian *a* macedón, macedonio. *n* macedonio (-ia)

macerate *vt* macerar. *vi* macerarse

machete *n Mexico* alfanje, *elsewhere* machete, *m*

Machiavellian *a* maquiavélico

Machiavellism *n* maquiavelismo, *m*

machination *n* maquinación, *f*

machine *n* máquina, *f*; mecanismo, *m*; aparato, *m*; instrumento, *m*; organización, *f, vt* trabajar a máquina; *sew* coser a máquina. **m.-gun,** *n* ametralladora, *f. vt* ametrallar. **m.-gun carrier,** portametralladoras, *m*. **m.-gunner,** ametrallador, *m*. **m.-made,** hecho a máquina. **m.-oil,** aceite de motores, *m*. **m.-shop,** taller de maquinaria, *m, Lat. Am.* maestranza, *f*. **m.-tool,** máquina herramienta, *f*

machinery *n* maquinaria, *f*; mecanismo, *m*; organización, *f*; sistema, *m*

machinist *n* maquinista, *mf*; *sew* costurera a máquina, *f*

mackerel *n* caballa, *f*. **m. sky,** cielo aborregado, *m*

mackintosh *n* impermeable, *m*

macrocosm *n* macrocosmo, *m*

mad *a* loco; fuera de sí; (of a dog, etc.) rabioso; furioso. **as mad as a hatter,** loco como una cabra. **to drive mad,** volver loco (a). **to go mad,** volverse loco, enloquecer, perder el seso. **mad with joy (pain),** loco de alegría (dolor). **mad dog,** perro rabioso, *m*

madam *n* señora, *f*; (French form) madama, *f*. **Yes, m.,** Sí señora

madcap *n* locuelo (-la), *f*, botarate, *m*; tarambana, *mf*

madden *vt* enloquecer; enfurecer, exasperar

maddening *a* exasperante, irritador

madder *n bot* rubia, *f*

made *past part* and *a* hecho; formado. **self-m. man,** un

hombre hecho y derecho. **m.-to-measure,** hecho a la medida. **m.-up,** compuesto; (of clothes) confeccionado, ya hecho; (of the face) pintado; (fictitious) inventado, ficticio; artificial

Madeira *n* vino de Madera, *m, a* de Madera

madhouse *n* casa de locos, *f*, manicomio, *m*

madly *adv* locamente; furiosamente

madman *n* loco, *m*

madness *n* locura, *f*; (of a dog, etc.) rabia, *f*; furia, *f*

Madonna *n* Madona, *f*

madrigal *n* madrigal, *m*

Madrilenian *a* madrileño, matritense. *n* madrileño (-ña)

madwoman *n* loca, *f*

Maecenas *n* mecenas, *m*

maelstrom *n* remolino, vórtice, *m*

magazine *n* (store) almacén, *m*; (for explosives) polvorín, *m*, santabárbara, *f*; (periodical) revista, *f*. **m. rifle,** rifle de repetición, *m*

Magdalen *n* magdalena, *f*

magenta *n* color magenta, *m*

maggot *n* gusano, *m*, cresa, *f*; *fig* manía, *f*, capricho, *m*

maggoty *a* gusanoso

Magi, the *n pl* los reyes magos

magic *n* magia, *f*; mágica, *f*; *fig* encanto, *m, a* mágico. **as if by m.,** por ensalmo. **m. lantern,** linterna mágica, *f*

magically *adv* por encanto

magician *n* mago, mágico, brujo, *m*; (conjurer) jugador de manos, *m*

magisterial *a* magistral

magistracy *n* magistratura, *f*

magistrate *n* magistrado, *m*; juez municipal, *m*

Magna Charta *n* Carta Magna, *f*

magnanimity *n* magnanimidad, generosidad, *f*

magnanimous *a* magnánimo, generoso

magnanimously *adv* magnánimamente

magnate *n* magnate, *m*

magnesia *n* magnesia, *f*

magnesium *n* magnesio, *m*. **m. light,** luz de magnesio, *f*

magnet *n* imán, *m*

magnetic *a* magnético; *fig* atractivo. **m. field,** campo magnético, *m*. **m. needle,** brújula, *f*

magnetics *n* la ciencia del magnetismo, *f*

magnetism *n* magnetismo, *m*

magnetization *n* imanación, magnetización, *f*

magnetize *vt* magnetizar, imanar; (hypnotize) magnetizar; *fig* atraer

magnification *n* (by a lens, etc.) aumento, *m*; exageración, *f*

magnificence *n* magnificencia, *f*

magnificent *a* magnífico

magnify *vt* (by lens) aumentar; exagerar; (praise) magnificar

magnifying *a* de aumento, vidrio de aumento. **m. glass,** lente de aumento, *m*

magniloquence *n* grandilocuencia, *f*

magniloquent *a* grandílocuo

magnitude *n* magnitud, *f*

magnolia *n* magnolia, *f*

magnum *n* botella de dos litros, *f*

magpie *n* marica, picaza, *f*

maharaja *n* maharajá, *m*

mahogany *n* caoba, *f*, *a* de caoba

Mahomedan. See **Mohammedan**

maid *n* doncella, muchacha, *f*; virgen, *f*; soltera, *f*; (servant) criada, *f*; (daily) asistenta, *f*. **old m.,** solterona, *f*. **m.-of-all-work,** criada para todo, *f*. **m.-of-honor,** dama de honor, *f*

maiden *n* doncella, joven, soltera, *f*; virgen, *f*; zagala, *f*. *a* de soltera; soltera *f*; virginal; (of speeches, voyages, etc.) primero. **m. lady,** dama soltera, *f*. **m.-name,** apellido de soltera, *m*. **m. speech,** primer discurso, *m*

maidenhood *n* doncellez, virginidad, *f*

maidenly *a* virginal; modesto, modoso; tímido

maidservant *n* criada, sirvienta, *f*

mail *n* mala, *f*; (bag) valija, *f*; correo, *m*; correspondencia, *f*; (armour) cota de malla, *f*. *vt* mandar por correo; armar con cota de malla. **coat of m.,** cota de malla, *f*. **royal m.,** malla real, *f*. **m.-bag,** valija de correo, *f*; portacartas, *m*. **m.-boat,** buque correo, *m*. **m.-cart,** ambulancia de correos, *f*. **m.-clad,** vestido de cota de malla; armado. **m.-coach,** coche correo, *m*, diligencia, *f*. **m.-order,** pedido postal, *m*. **m.-order business,** negocio de ventas por correo, *m*. **m.-plane,** avión postal, *m*. **m. service,** servicio de correos, *m*. **m. steamer,** vapor correo, *m*. **m. train,** tren correo, *m*. **m. van,** (on a train) furgón postal, *m*

mailed *a* de malla; armado. **m. fist,** *fig* puño de hierro, *m*

maim *vt* mancar; mutilar, tullir; estropear

maimed *a* manco; tullido, mutilado

main *a* mayor; principal; más importante, esencial; maestro. *n* (mainland) continente, *m*; (sea) océano, *m*; (pipe) cañería maestra, *f*. **by m. force,** por fuerza mayor. **in the m.,** en general, generalmente; en su mayoría. **m. beam,** viga maestra, *f*. **m. body,** (of a building) ala principal, *f*; (of a church) cuerpo (de iglesia), *m*; (of an army) cuerpo (del ejército), *m*; mayor parte, mayoría, *f*. **m. line,** línea principal, *f*. **m. mast,** palo mayor, *m*. **m. thing,** cosa principal, *f*, lo más importante. **m. wall,** pared maestra, *f*

mainland *n* continente, *m*; tierra firme, *f*

mainly *adv* principalmente; en su mayoría; generalmente

mainsail *n* vela mayor, *f*

mainspring *n* (of a watch) muelle real, *m*; motivo principal, *m*; origen, *m*

mainstay *n* estay mayor, *m*; *fig* sostén principal, *m*

maintain *vt* mantener; sostener; tener; guardar; afirmar

maintainable *a* sostenible; defendible

maintenance *n* mantenimiento, *m*; manutención, *f*, sustento, *m*; conservación, *f*, subsistencia, *f*

maize *n* maíz, *m*. **m. field,** maizal, *m*

majestic *a* majestuoso

majesty *n* majestad, *f*; majestuosidad, *f*. **His** or **Her M.,** Su Majestad

majolica *n* mayólica, *f*

major *a* mayor; principal. *n* mayor de edad, *m*; *mil* comandante. **anthropology major,** alumno con la especialidad en antropología *m*. **m.-domo,** mayordomo, *m*. **m.-general,** general de división, *m*. **m. road,** carretera, *f*; ruta de prioridad, *f*. **m. scale,** escala mayor, *f*

Majorca Mallorca, *f*

majority *n* mayoría, *f*; mayor número, *m*; generalidad, *f*. **to have attained one's m.,** ser mayor de edad

make *vt* hacer; crear; formar; (manufacture) fabricar, confeccionar; construir; (produce) producir; causar; (prepare) preparar; (a bed, a fire, a remark, poetry, friends, enemies, war, a curtsey) hacer; (earn, win) ganar; (a speech) pronunciar; (compel) obligar (a), forzar (a); inclinar (a); (arrive at) alcanzar, llegar (a); (calculate) calcular; (arrange) arreglar; deducir; (be) ser; (equal) ser igual a; (think) creer; (appoint as) constituir (en), hacer; (behave) portarse (como). *vi* (begin) ir (a), empezar (a); (make as though) hacer (como si); (of the tide) crecer; contribuir (a); tender (a). **He made as if to go,** Hizo como si marchara. **to m. as though . . . ,** aparentar, fingir. **It made me ill,** Me hizo sentir mal. **They have made it up,** Han hecho las paces. **They m. a great deal of money,** Hacen (or ganan) mucho dinero. **You cannot m. me believe it,** No puedes hacerme creerlo. **He is making himself ridiculous,** Se está poniendo en ridículo. **to m. ready,** preparar. **to m. the tea,** hacer el té; preparar el té. **Two and two m. four,** Dos y dos son cuatro. **to m. oneself known,** darse a conocer. **to m. one of . . . ,** ser uno de . . . **to m. after,** seguir; correr detrás de. **to m. again,** hacer de nuevo, rehacer. **to m. angry** *Mexico.* amuinar. **to m. away with,** quitar; suprimir; destruir; (kill) matar; (squander) derrochar; (steal) llevarse; hurtar. **to m. away with oneself,** quitarse la vida, suicidarse. **to m. for,** encaminarse a, dirigirse a; (attack) abalanzarse sobre, atacar; (tend to) contribuir a, tender a. **to m. off,** marcharse corriendo, largarse; huir, escaparse. **to m. out,** (discern) distinguir; (prove) probar, justificar; (draw up) redactar; (fill in a form) completar, llenar; (a check, etc.) extender; (an account) hacer; (get on, succeed or otherwise) ir (with bien or mal); (convey) dar la impresión de que; sugerir. **I cannot m. it out,** No lo puedo comprender. **How did you m. out** (get on)? ¿Cómo te fue? **to m. over,** hacer de nuevo, rehacer; (transfer) ceder, traspasar. **to m. up,** hacer; acabar; concluir; (clothes) confeccionar; fabricar; (the face) pintarse, maquillarse; (the fire) echar carbón, etc. a; *print* compaginar; (invent) inventar; (lies) fabricar; (compose) formar; (package) empaquetar; reparar; indemnizar; compensar; (an account) ajustar; preparar; arreglar; (conciliate) conciliar; enumerar; *theat* caracterizarse. **to m. up for,** reemplazar; compensar; (lost time, etc.) recobrar. **to m. up to,** compensar; indemnizar; (flatter) adular, halagar; procurar congraciarse con, procurar obtener el favor de; (court) galantear (con). **m. an impression (on),** dejar(le a fulano) una impresión

make *n* forma, *f*; hechura, *f*; estructura, *f*; confección, *f*; manufactura, *f*; producto, *m*; (trade name) marca, *f*; (character) carácter, temperamento, *m*. **m.-believe,** *n* artificio, pretexto, *m*, *a* fingido, *vi* fingir. **land of m.-believe,** reino de los sueños, *m*. **m.-up,** (for the face, etc.) maquillaje, *m*; *theat* caracterización, *f*; *print* imposición, *f*; (whole) conjunto, *m*; (character) carácter, modo de ser, *m*

maker *n* creador, *m*; autor (-ra); artífice, *mf*; (manufacturer) fabricante, *m*; constructor, *m*; (of clothes, etc.) confeccionador (-ra); (worker) obrero (-ra)

makeshift *n* expediente, *m*, *a* provisional

makeweight *n* añadidura (de peso), *f*, contrapeso, *m*; *fig* suplente, *m*

making *n* creación, *f*; hechura, *f*; (manufacture) fabricación, *f*; construcción, *f*; (of clothes, etc.) confección, *f*; formación, *f*; preparación, *f*; estructura, *f*; composición, *f*; *pl* **makings**, (profits) ganancias, *f pl*; (elements) elementos, *m pl*; germen, *m*; rasgos esenciales, *m pl*, características, *f*. *pl* **m.-up,** (of clothes) confección, *f*; *print* ajuste, *m*; (of the face) maquillaje, *m*; (invention) invención, *f*; fabricación, *f*

maladjustment *n* mal ajuste, *m*; inadaptación, *f*

maladministration *n* desgobierno, *m*, mala administración, *f*; (of funds) malversación, *f*

maladroit *a* torpe

maladroitness *n* torpeza, *f*

malady *n* enfermedad, *f*; mal, *m*

Malaga *n* vino de Málaga, *m*

malaria *n* paludismo, *m*

malarial *a* palúdico. **m. fever,** fiebre palúdica, *f*

Malaya Malasia, *f*, Archipiélago Malayo, *m*

Malayan *a* malayo. *n* malayo (-ya)

malcontent *n* malcontento (-ta). *a* descontento

Maldives Maldivas, *f pl*

male *a* macho; masculino. *n* macho, *m*; varón, *m*. **m. child,** niño, *m*; niño varón, *m*; (son) hijo varón, *m*. **m. flower,** flor masculina, *f*. **m. issue,** sucesión masculina, *f*. **m. nurse,** enfermero, *m*. **m. sex,** sexo masculino, *m*

malediction *n* maldición, *f*

malefactor *n* malhechor (-ra)

malefic *a* maléfico

malevolence *n* malevolencia, *f*

malevolent *a* malévolo, maligno

malformation *n* formación anormal, deformidad, deformación congénita, *f*

malice *n* malicia, *f*; *law* alevosía, *f*. **to bear m.,** guardar rencor

malicious *a* malicioso; maligno, rencoroso

maliciousness *n* malicia, mala intención, *f*

malign *vt* calumniar, difamar. *a* maligno; malévolo

malignancy *n* malignidad, *f*; malevolencia, *f*

malignant *a* maligno; malévolo; *med* maligno

malinger *vi* fingirse enfermo

malingerer *n* enfermo (-ma) fingido (-da)

malingering *n* enfermedad fingida, *f*

mallard *n* pato (-ta), silvestre

malleability *n* maleabilidad, *f*

malleable *a* maleable

mallet *n* mazo, *m*; (in croquet) pala, *f*, mazo, *m*; (in polo) maza (de polo), *f*

mallow *n* malva, *f*

malmsey *n* (wine) malvasía, *f*

malnutrition *n* desnutrición, alimentación deficiente, *f*

malodorous *a* de mal olor, hediondo, fétido

malpractice *n* (wrongdoing) maleficencia, *f*; (by a doctor) tratamiento equivocado, perjudicial o ilegal, *m*; (malversation) malversación, *f*; inmoralidad, *f*

malt *n* malta, *m*. *vt* preparar el malta. **m.-house,** fábrica de malta, *f*. **m. vinegar,** vinagre de malta, *m*

malted milk *n* leche malteada, *f*

malt shop *n* café-nevería, *m*

Maltese *a* maltés (-esa). **M. cat,** gato maltés, *m*. **M. cross,** cruz de Malta, *f*. **M. dog,** perro maltés, *m*

Malthusian *a* maltusiano

Malthusianism *n* maltusianismo, *m*

maltose *n* maltosa, *f*

maltreat *vt* maltratar

maltreatment *n* maltrato, *m*,

mamma *n anat* mama, *f*; (mother) mamá, *f*

mammal *n* mamífero, *m*

mammalian *a* mamífero

mammary *a* mamario. **m. gland,** mama, teta, *f*

mammon *n* becerro de oro, *m*

mammoth *n* mamut, *m*, *a* gigantesco, enorme

man *n* hombre, *m*; varón, *m*; persona, *f*; (servant) criado, *m*; (workman) obrero, *m*; (soldier) soldado, *m*; (sailor) marinero, *m*; (humanity) raza humana, *f*; (husband) marido, *m*; (chess) peón, *m*; (checkers) dama, *f*; (a ship) buque, *m*. **no man,** nadie; ningún hombre. **young man,** joven, *m*. **to a man,** como un solo hombre. **to come to man's estate,** llegar a la edad viril. **Man overboard!** ¡Hombre al agua! **man and wife,** marido y mujer, *m*, cónyuges, esposos, *m pl*. **man about town,** hombre de mundo, señorito, *m*. **man-at-arms,** hombre de armas, *m*. **man-eater,** caníbal, *mf*; tigre, *m*. **man-eating,** *a* antropófago. **man hater,** misántropo, *m*; mujer que odia a los hombres, *f*. **man-hole,** pozo, *m*. **man-hunter,** caníbal, *mf*; (woman) castigadora, *f*. **man in charge,** encargado, *m*. **man in the moon,** mujer de la luna, *f*. **man in the street,** hombre de la calle, hombre medio, *m*. **man of letters,** hombre de letras, literato, *m*; **man of straw,** bausán, *m*; (figure-head) testaferro, *m*. **man of the world,** hombre del mundo, *m*. **man of war,** buque de guerra, *m*. **man-power,** mano de obra, *f*, brazos, *m pl*, (e.g. lack of manpower, falta de brazos, *f*). **man servant,** criado, *m*

man *vt* armar; *mil* poner guarnición (a); ocupar; *naut* tripular; dirigir; *fig* fortificar

manacle *n* manilla, *f*; *pl* **manacles**, esposas, *f pl*; grillos, *m pl*. *vt* poner esposas (a)

manage *vt* manejar; (animals) domar; dirigir; gobernar; administrar; (arrange) agenciar, arreglar; (work) explotar; (do) hacer; (eat) comer. *vi* arreglárselas (para); (get along) ir tirando; (know how) saber hacer; (succeed in) lograr; (do) hacer

manageability *n* lo manejable; flexibilidad, *f*; (of animals, persons) docilidad, mansedumbre, *f*

manageable *a* manejable; flexible; (of persons, animals) dócil

management *n* manejo, *m*; dirección, *f*; gobierno, *m*; administración, *f*; arreglo, *m*; (working) explotación, *f*; *com* gerencia, *f*; *theat* empresa, *f*; conducta, *f*; (economy) economía, *f*; (skill) habilidad, *f*; prudencia, *f*. **the m.,** la dirección, el cuerpo de directores. **domestic m.,** economía doméstica, *f*

manager *n* director, *m*; administrador, *m*; jefe, *m*; *theat* empresario, *m*; *com* gerente, *m*; regente, *m*. **She is not much of a m.,** No es muy mujer de su casa. **manager's office,** dirección, *f*

manageress *n* directora, *f*; administradora, *f*; jefa, *f*

managerial *a* directivo; administrativo. **m. board,** junta directiva, *f*

managership *n* puesto de director, *m*; jefatura, *f*

managing *a* directivo; (officious) mandón, dominante; (niggardly) tacaño

manatee *n* manatí, *m*

mandarin *n* mandarín, *m*; (language) mandarina, *f*. **m. orange,** mandarina, *f*

mandate *n* mandato, *m*. **mandated territory,** territorios bajo mandato, *m pl*

mandatory *a* obligatorio

mandible *n* mandíbula, *f*

mandolin *n* bandolín, *m*, bandurria, *f*

mandrake *n* mandrágora, *f*

mandrill *n* mandril, *m*

mane *n* melena, *f*; (of a horse) crines, *f pl*

maned *a* (in compounds) con melena . . . ; con crines . . .

maneuver *n* maniobra, *f*. *vi* maniobrar, hacer maniobras. *vt* hacer maniobrar; manipular

maneuvering *n* maniobras, *f pl*; maquinaciones, intrigas, *f pl*

manfully *adv* valientemente; vigorosamente

manganate *n* manganato, *m*

manganese *n* manganeso, *m*

mange *n* sarna, *f*; (in sheep) roña, *f*

manger *n* pesebre, *m*

manginess *n* estado sarnoso, *m*

mangle *n* (for clothes) exprimidor de la ropa, *m*. *vt* pasar por el exprimidor; (mutilate) mutilar, lacerar, magullar; (a text) mutilar

mangling *n* (mutilation) mutilación, laceración, *f*

mango *n* mango, *m*

mangy *a* sarnoso

manhandle *vt* maltratar

manhood *n* virilidad, *f*; edad viril, *f*; masculinidad, *f*; los hombres; (manliness) hombradía, *f*, valor, *m*

mania *n* manía, *f*; obsesión, *f*; capricho, *m*, chifladura, *f*, *Lat. Am.* barreno, *m*

maniac *n* maníaco (-ca). *a* maníaco, maniático

manicure *n* manicura, *f*. *vt* arreglar las uñas. **m.-set,** estuche de manicura, *m*

manicurist *n* manicuro (-ra)

manifest *n naut* manifiesto, *m*. *vt* mostrar; hacer patente, probar; manifestarse. *vi* publicar un manifiesto; (of spirits) manifestarse. *a* manifiesto, evidente, claro, patente. **to make m.,** poner de manifiesto

manifestation *n* manifestación, *f*

manifestly *adv* evidentemente, manifiestamente

manifesto *n* manifiesto, *m*

manifold *a* múltiple; numeroso; diverso, vario

manikin *n* enano, *m*; muñeco, *m*; *art* maniquí, *m*

Manila *n* Manila, *f*; cigarro filipino, *m*. **M. hemp,** cáñamo de Manila, *m*

maniple *n* manípulo, *m*

manipulate *vt* manipular

manipulation *n* manipulación, *f*

manipulative *a* manipulador

mankind *n* humanidad, raza humana, *f*, género humano, *m*

manlike *a* de hombre, masculino; varonil; (of a woman) hombruno

manliness *n* masculinidad, hombradía, *f*; virilidad, *f*; valor, *m*; (of a woman) aire hombruno, *m*

manly *a* masculino, de hombre; varonil, viril; valiente; fuerte. **to be very m.,** ser muy hombre, ser todo un hombre

manna *n* maná, *m*

mannequin *n* manequín, modelo, *f*. **m. parade,** exposición de modelos, *f*

manner *n* manera, *f*, modo, *m*; aire, porte, *m*; conducta, *f*; (style) estilo, *m*; (sort) clase, *f*; *gram* modo, *m*; *pl* **manners,** modales, *m pl*, crianza, educación, *f*; (customs) costumbres, *f pl*. **after the m. of,** en (or según) el estilo de. **in a m. of speaking,** en cierto modo, para decirlo así. **in this m.,** de este modo. **to have bad (good) manners,** tener malos (buenos) modales, ser mal (bien) criado. **the novel of manners,** la novela de costumbres

mannered *a* amanerado; (in compounds) . . . educado, de . . . modales; de costumbres . . . **well-m.,** *f*; bien educado, de buenos modales

mannerism *n* amaneramiento, *m*; afectación, *f*; *theat* latiguillo, *m*. **to acquire mannerisms,** amanerarse

mannerliness *n* cortesía, buena educación, urbanidad, *f*

mannerly *a* cortés, bien educado, atento

mannish *a* (of a woman) hombruno; de hombre, masculino

manor *n* feudo, *m*; finca, hacienda, *f*; casa solariega, *f*; señorío, *m*

manorial *a* señorial

mansion *n* mansión, *f*; casa solariega, *f*; hotel, *m*. **m.-house,** casa solariega, *f*; residencia del alcalde de Londres, *f*

manslaughter *n* homicidio, *m*; *law* homicidio sin premeditación, *m*

mantelpiece *n* repisa de chimenea, *f*

mantilla *n* mantilla, *f*

mantle *n* capa, *f*, manto, *m*; *fig* cobertura, *f*; (gas) camiseta, *f*, manguito, *mf*; *zool* manto, *m*. *vt* cubrir; envolver; ocultar. *vi* extenderse; (of blushes) inundar, subirse (a las mejillas)

Mantuan *a* mantuano

manual *a* manual. *n* manual, *m*; *mus* teclado de órgano, *m*. **m. work,** trabajo manual, *m*

manufactory *n* fábrica, *f*, taller, *m*

manufacture *n* fabricación, *f*; manufactura, *f*. *vt* manufacturar, fabricar

manufacturer *n* fabricante, industrial, *m*. **manufacturer's price,** precio de fábrica, *m*

manufacturing *a* manufacturero, fabril. *n* fabricación, *f*

manure *n* estiércol, abono, *m*. *vt* estercolar, abonar. **m. heap,** estercolero, *m*

manuring *n* estercoladura, *f*

manuscript *n* manuscrito, *m*, *a* manuscrito

many *a* muchos (-as); numeroso; diversos (-as); varios (-as). *n* muchos (-as); la mayoría; las masas; muchedumbre, multitud, *f*. **a great m.,** muchísimos, *m pl*, muchísimas, *f pl*; un gran número. **as m. as . . . ,** tantos como . . . **How m. are there?** ¿Cuántos hay? ¿Cuántas hay? **m. a time,** muchas veces. **three too m.,** tres de más. **for m. long years,** por largos años. **m.-colored,** multicolor. **m.-headed,** con muchas cabezas. **m.-sided,** multilátero; polifacético; complicado

Maori *n* maorí, *m*, (*pl* maoríes)

map *n* mapa, *m*; plano, *m*; (chart) carta, *f*. *vt* hacer un mapa (or plano) de. **to map out,** *surv* apear; trazar; (plan) proyectar. **m. ordnance map,** mapa del estado mayor, *m*. **map of the world,** mapamundi, mapa del mundo, *m*. **map-making,** cartografía, *f*

maple *n* (tree) arce, *m*; (wood) madera de arce, *f*. **m.-syrup,** jarabe de arce, *m*

mapping *n* cartografía, *f*

maquiladora *n* maquiladora, *f*

mar *vt* estropear; desfigurar; (happiness) destruir, aguar; frustrar

maraca *n Lat. Am.* alfandoque, *m*

maraschino *n* marrasquino, *m*. **m. cherry,** cerezas en marrasquino, *f pl*

maraud *vi* merodear

marauder *n* merodeador, *m*

marauding *a* merodeador, *n* merodeo, *m*

marble *n* mármol, *m*; (for playing with) canica, *f*, *a* de marmol, marmóreo; *fig* insensible; (of paper, etc.) jaspeado. *vt* jaspear. **m. cutter,** marmolista, *m*. **m. works,** marmolería, *f*

marbled *a* jaspeado

March *n* marzo, *m*. **as mad as a M. hare,** loco como una cabra, loco de atar

march *n* marcha, *f*; (step) paso, *m*; *fig* marcha, *f*, progreso, *m*. **forced m.,** marcha forzada, *f*. **quick m.,** paso doble, *m*. **to steal a m. on,** tomar la delantera (a), ganar por la mano (a). **to strike up a m.,** batir la marcha. **m.-past,** desfile, *m*

march *vi* marchar; (of properties) lindar (con). *vt* hacer marchar, poner en marcha (a). **to m. back,** *vi* regresar (or volver) a pie. *vt* hacer volver a pie. **to m. in,** entrar (a pie) en. **to m. off,** marcharse. **to m. on,** seguir marchando; seguir adelante; avanzar. **to m. past,** desfilar ante

marching *n* marcha, *f*. *a* en marcha; de marcha. **to receive one's m. orders,** recibir la orden de marchar; *inf* ser despedido. **m. order,** orden de marcha, *m*. **m. song,** canción de marcha, *f*

mardi gras *n* martes de carnaval, *m*

mare *n* yegua, *f*

margarine *n* margarina, *f*

margin *n* borde, lado, *m*, orilla, *f*; (of a page) margen, *mf*; reserva, *f*; sobrante, *m*. **in the m.,** al margen

marginal *a* marginal. **m. note,** acotación, nota marginal, *f*

marigold *n* caléndula, maravilla, *f*

marihuana *n* marijuana, *f*. *Lat. Am.* cáñamo *m*

marine *a* marino, de mar; marítimo; naval. *n* (fleet) marina, *f*; (soldier) soldado de marina, *m*. **Tell that to the marines!** ¡Cuéntaselo a tu tía! **mercantile m.,** marina mercante, *f*. **m. forces,** infantería de marina, *f*. **m. insurance,** seguro marítimo, *m*

mariner *n* marinero, marino, *m*. **mariner's compass,** aguja de marear, brújula, *f*

marionette *n* marioneta, *f*, títere, *m*

marital *a* marital

maritime *a* marítimo

mark *n* marca, *f*; señal, *f*; mancha, *f*; impresión, *f*; (target) blanco, *m*; (standard) norma, *f*; (level) nivel, *m*; (distinction) importancia, distinción, *f*; (in examinations) nota, *f*; calificación, *f*; (signature) cruz, *f*; (coin) marco, *m*. *vt* marcar; señalar; (price) poner precio (a); (notice) observar, darse cuenta (de); (characterize) caracterizar. **trade-m.,** marca de fábrica, *f*. **to be beside the m.,** no dar en el blanco; errar el tiro; *fig* no tener nada que ver con; equivocarse. **to hit the m.,** dar en el blanco; *fig* dar en el clavo. **to make one's m.,** firmar con una cruz; distinguirse. **to m. time,** marcar el paso; *fig* hacer tiempo. **to m. down,** (a person) señalar; escoger; (in price) rebajar. **to m. out,** marcar; trazar; definir; (erase) borrar; (a person) escoger; destinar **m. somebody absent,** ponerle a fulano su ausencia. **m. somebody present,** ponerle a fulano su asistencia.

Mark *n* Marcos. **the Gospel according to St. M.,** el Evangelio de San Marcos

marked *a* marcado; señalado; notable; acentuado; particular, especial. **He speaks with a m. Galician accent,** Habla con marcado acento gallego

markedly *adv* marcadamente; notablemente; especialmente, particularmente

marker *n* (billiards) marcador, *m*; (football, etc.) tanteador, *m*

market *n* mercado, *m*; tráfico, *m*; venta, *f*; (price) precio, *m*; (shop) bazar, emporio, *m*. *vt* and *vi* comprar en un mercado; vender en un mercado. **black m.,** mercado negro, estraperlo, *m*. **open m.,** mercado al aire libre, *m*; *fig* mercado libre, *m*. **m. day,** día de mercado, *m*. **m. garden,** huerto, *m*, huerta, *f*. **m. gardener,** hortelano, *m*. **m.-place,** plaza de mercado, *f*; *fig* mercado, *m*. **m. price,** precio corriente, *m*. **m. stall,** tabanco, puesto de mercado, *m*. **m.-woman,** verdulera, *f*

marketable *a* comerciable, vendible; corriente

marketing *n* venta, *f*; compra en un mercado, *f*; mercado, *m*. **to go m.,** ir al mercado

marking *n* marca, *f*; (spot on animals, etc.) pinta, *f*. **m.-ink,** tinta de marcar, *f*. **m.-iron,** ferrete, hierro de marcar, *m*

marksman *n* tirador (-ra)

marksmanship *n* puntería, *f*

marl *n* marga, *f*

marmalade *n* mermelada de naranjas amargas, *f*

marmoset *n* tití, *m*

marmot *n zool* marmota, *f*

maroon *n* (color) marrón, *m*; (slave) cimarrón (-ona); (firework) petardo, *m*. *a* de marrón. *vt* abandonar, dejar

marquee *n* marquesina, *f*

marqueterie *n* marquetería, *f*

marquis *n* marqués, *m*

marriage *n* matrimonio, *m*; unión, *f*; (wedding) boda, *f*, casamiento, *m*. **by m.,** (of relationship) político. **She is an aunt by m.,** tía política. **m. articles,** capitulaciones (matrimoniales), *f pl*. **m. contract,** contrato matrimonial, *m*. **m. license,** licencia de casamiento, *f*. **m. portion,** dote, *mf*. **m. rate,** nupcialidad, *f*. **m. register,** acta matrimonial, *f*. **m. song,** epitalamio, *m*

marriageable *a* casadero

married *past part* and *a* casado; matrimonial, conyugal. **newly-m. couple,** los recién casados. **to get m. to,** casarse con. **m. couple,** matrimonio, *m*, cónyuges, *m pl*. **m. life,** vida conyugal, *f*

married name *n* nombre de casada, *f*

marrow *n* tuétano, *m*, médula, *f*; *fig* meollo, *m*. **to the m. of one's bones,** hasta los tuétanos.

marrowbone *n* hueso medular, *m*. **on one's marrow-bones,** de rodillas

marry *vt* casarse con, contraer matrimonio con; casar; (of a priest) unir en matrimonio; *fig* juntar, unir. *vi* casarse. **to m. again,** volver a casarse

Marseillaise *n* marsellesa, *f*

Marseilles Marsella, *f*

marsh *n* marjal, pantano, *Central America* chagüe, *m*. **m.-mallow,** *bot* malvavisco, *m*. **m. marigold,** calta, *f*

marshal *n* mariscal, *m*, *vt* poner en orden, arreglar; dirigir. **field-m.,** capitán general de ejército, *m*

marshaling *n* ordenación, *f*; dirección, *f*. **m.-yard,** (railway) apartadero ferroviario, *m*

marshy *a* pantanoso

mart *n poet* plaza de mercado, *f*; mercado, emporio, *m*; (auction rooms) martillo, *m*

marten *n* marta, *f*

martial *a* militar; marcial, belicoso. **m. array,** orden de batalla, *m*. **m. law,** derecho militar, *m*; estado de guerra, *m*. **m. spirit,** marcialidad, *f*, espíritu belicoso, *m*

martially *adv* militarmente; marcialmente

Martian *n* marciano

martinet *n mil* ordenancista, *m*; rigorista, *mf*

Martinique Martinica, *f*

Martinmas *n* día de San Martín, *m*

martyr *n* mártir, *mf vt* martirizar

martyrdom *n* martirio, *m*

martyrize *vt* martirizar

marvel *n* maravilla, *f*. **to m. at,** maravillarse de, admirarse de

marvelous *a* maravilloso

marvelousness *n* maravilla, *f*, carácter maravilloso, *m*, lo maravilloso

Marxism *n* marxismo, *m*

Marxist *a* and *n* marxista, *mf*

marzipan *n* mazapán, *m*

mascot *n* mascota, *f*

masculine *a* masculino; varonil, macho; de hombre; (of a woman) hombruno. *n* masculino, *m*

masculinity *n* masculinidad, *f*

mash *n* mezcla, *f*; amasijo, *m*; pasta, *f*, puré, *m*. *vt* mezclar; amasar. **mashed potatoes,** puré de patatas (de papas), *m*

mask *n* máscara, *f*; antifaz, *m*; (death) mascarilla, *f*; (person) máscara, *mf*. *vt* enmascarar; *fig* encubrir, disimular. *vi* ponerse una máscara; disfrazarse. **masked ball,** *m* baile de máscaras, *m*

masker *n* máscara, *mf*

masochism *n* masoquismo, *m*

mason *n* albañil, *m*; (freemason) francmasón, masón, *m*

masonic *a* masónico. **m. lodge,** logia de francmasones, *f*

masonry *n* (trade) albañilería, *f*; mampostería, *f*

masque *n* mascarada, *f*

masquerade *n* mascarada, *f*

masquerader *n* máscara, *mf*

mass *n* misa, *f*. **to hear m.,** oír misa. **to say m.,** celebrar misa. **high m.,** misa mayor, *f*. **low m.,** misa rezada, *f*. **m. book,** libro de misa, *m*

mass *n* masa, *f*; (shape) bulto, *m*; (heap) montón, *m*; (great number) muchedumbre, *f*; (cloud of steam, etc.) nube, *f*. *vt* amasar; *mil* concentrar. *vi* congregarse en masa. **in a m.,** en masa; en conjunto. **the m. (of) . . . ,** la mayoría (de) . . . **the masses,** las masas, el vulgo, el pueblo. **m. formation,** columna cerrada, *f*. **m.-meeting,** mitin, mitin popular, *m*. **m.-production,** fabricación en serie, *f*

massacre *n* matanza, carnicería, *f*, *vt* hacer una carnicería (de)

massage *n* masaje, *m*; (friction) fricción, *f*. *vt* dar un masaje (a)

masseur, masseuse *n* masajista, *mf*

massive *a* macizo; sólido

massively *adv* macizamente; sólidamente

massiveness *n* macicez, *f*; solidez, *f*

mast *n naut* palo, árbol, *m*; (for wireless) mástil, *m*; poste, *m*; (beech) hayuco, *m*; (oak) bellota, *f*. *vt naut* arbolar. **at half-m.,** a media asta. **m.-head,** calcés, tope, *m*

masted *a* arbolado; (in compounds) de . . . palos

449

master *n* (of the house, etc.) señor, amo, *m*; maestro, *m*; *naut* patrón, *m*; (owner) dueño, *m*; (teacher) profesor, maestro, *m*; (young master and as address) señorito, *m*; director, *m*; jefe, *m*; (expert) perito, *m*; (of a military order) maestre, *m*, *a* maestro; superior. *vt* dominar; ser maestro en; dominar, conocer a fondo. **This picture is by an old m.,** Este cuadro es de un gran maestro antiguo. **to be m. of oneself,** ser dueño de sí. **to be one's own m.,** ser dueño de sí mismo; trabajar por su propia cuenta; ser independiente; estar libre. **m. builder,** maestro de obras, *m*. **m. hand,** mano maestra, *f*. **M. of Arts,** maestro (-tra) en artes. **M. of Ceremonies,** maestro de ceremonias, *m*. **M. of Foxhounds,** cazador mayor, *m*. **M. of the Horse,** caballerizo mayor del rey, *m*. **M. of the Rolls,** archivero mayor, *m*. **m.-key,** llave maestra, *f*. **m. mind,** águila, *f*, ingenio, *m*. **m. stroke,** golpe maestro, *m*
masterful *a* imperioso, dominante; autoritario, arbitrario
masterfulness *n* imperiosidad, *f*; arbitrariedad, *f*
masterless *a* sin amo
masterliness *n* maestría, *f*; excelencia, *f*; perfección, *f*
masterly *a* maestro; excelente; perfecto. **m. performance,** obra maestra, *f*; *theat* representación perfecta, *f*; ejecución excelente, *f*
masterpiece *n* obra maestra, *f*
master plan *n* plan regulador, *m*
masterstroke *n* golpe magistral, golpe de maestro, *m*
mastery *n* dominio, *m*; autoridad, *f*; poder, *m*; ventaja, *f*; superioridad, maestría, *f*; conocimiento profundo, *m*. **to gain the m. of,** hacerse el señor de; llegar a dominar
mastic *n* masilla, almáciga, *f*
masticate *vt* masticar, mascar
mastication *n* masticación, *f*
mastiff *n* mastín, alano, *m*
mastodon *n* mastodonte, *m*
mastoid *a* mastoides. *n* apófisis mastoides, *f*
masturbate *vi* masturbarse
masturbation *n* masturbación, *f*
mat *n* esterilla, *f*; alfombrilla, *f*; (on the table) tapete individual, *m*. *vt* (tangle) enmarañar, desgreñar. *vi* enmarañarse
match *n sport* partido, *m*; (wrestling, boxing) lucha, *f*; (fencing) asalto, *m*; (race) carrera, *f*; (contest) concurso, *m*; (equal) igual, *mf*; (pair) pareja, *f*; compañero (-ra); (marriage) boda, *f*, casamiento, *m*; (for lighting) cerilla, *f*, fósforo, *Mexico* cerillo, *m*; (for guns) mecha, *f*. *vt* competir con; (equal) igualar; ser igual (a); hacer juego con; emparejar, aparear; armonizar. *vi* ser igual; hacer juego; armonizarse. **good m.,** *inf* buen partido, *m*. **as thin as a m.,** más delgado que una cerilla. **to meet one's m.,** dar con la horma de su zapato. **to play a m.,** jugar un partido. **m.-box,** cajita de cerillas, fosforera, *f*. **m.-seller,** fosforero (-ra)
matchless *a* incomparable, sin igual, sin par
matchwood *n* madera para cerillas, *f*
mate *n* compañero, camarada, *m*; (spouse) compañero (-ra); pareja, *f*; (on merchant ships) piloto, *m*; (assistant) ayudante, *m*; (at chess) mate, *m*. *vt* (marry) casar, desposar; (animals, birds) aparear, acoplar; (chess) dar jaque mate (a). *vi* casarse; aparearse, acoplarse
maté *n* maté, té del Paraguay, *m*
materfamilias *n* madre de familia, *f*
material *a* material; importante, esencial; considerable; sensible, notable; grave. *n* material, *m*; materia, *f*; (fabric) tela, *f*; tejido, *m*. **raw materials,** materias primas, *f pl*. **writing materials,** utensilios de escritorio, *m pl*; papel de escribir, *m*
materialism *n* materialismo, *m*
materialist *n* materialista, *mf*
materialistic *a* materialista
materiality *n* materialidad, *f*; importancia, *f*
materialization *n* materialización, *f*
materialize *vt* materializar

maternal *a* materno, maternal. **m. grandparents,** abuelos maternos, *m pl*
maternity *n* maternidad, *f*. **m. center,** centro de maternidad, *m*. **m. hospital,** casa de maternidad, *f*
mathematical *a* matemático
mathematician *n* matemático, *m*
mathematics *n pl*; matemáticas, *f pl*. **applied m.,** matemáticas prácticas, *f pl*. **higher m.,** matemáticas superiores, *f pl*. **pure m.,** matemáticas teóricas, *f pl*
matinee *n* función de tarde, *f*
mating *n* (of animals) apareamiento, acoplamiento, *m*; unión, *f*; casamiento, *m*
matins *n pl ecc* maitines, *m pl*
matriarch *n* matriarca, *f*
matriarchal *a* matriarcal
matriarchy *n* matriarcado, *m*
matricide *n* (crime) matricidio, *m*; (person) matricida, *mf*
matriculate *vt* matricular. *vi* matricularse
matriculation *n* matriculación, *f*
matrimonial *a* matrimonial, de matrimonio; marital. **m. agency,** agencia de matrimonios, *f*
matrimony *n* matrimonio, *m*
matrix *n* matriz, *f*
matron *n* matrona, mujer casada, madre de familia, *f*; (of a hospital) matrona, *f*; (of a school) ama de llaves, *f*; directora, *f*. **m. of honor,** (at a wedding) madrina, *f*
matronly *a* de matrona, matronal; respetable; serio
matt *a* mate
matted *a* enmarañado, enredado
matter *n* materia, *f*; substancia, *f*; caso, *m*; cuestión, *f*; asunto, *m*; causa, *f*; (distance) distancia, *f*; (amount) cantidad, *f*; (duration) espacio de tiempo, *m*; (importance) importancia, *f*; *med* pus, *m*; *pl* **matters,** asuntos, *m pl*, etc.; situación, *f*. **as if nothing were the m.,** como si no hubiese pasado nada. **for that m.,** en cuanto a eso. **grey m.,** substancia gris, *f*. **in the m. of,** en el caso de. **It is a m. of taste,** Es cuestión de gusto. **printed m.,** impresos, *m pl*. **What is the m.?** ¿Qué pasa? ¿Qué hay? **What is the m. with him?** ¿Qué tiene? ¿Qué le pasa? **m.-of-course,** cosa natural, *f*. **m.-of-fact,** práctico; sin imaginación; positivista. **m. of fact,** *n* hecho positivo, *m*, realidad, *f*. **As a m. of fact . . . ,** En realidad . . . ; El caso es que . . . **m. of form,** cuestión de fórmula, *f*; pura formalidad, *f*
matter *vi* importar; (discharge) supurar. **What does it m.?** ¿Qué importa? **It doesn't m.,** Es igual, No importa, Da lo mismo
Matterhorn, the el Matterhorn, *m*
matting *n* estera, *f*
mattress *n* colchón, *m*. **spring-m.,** colchón de muelles, *m*. **m.-maker,** colchonero, *m*
mature *a* maduro; *com* vencido. *vt* madurar. *vi* madurarse; *com* vencer
maturity *n* madurez, *f*; edad madura, *f*; (*com* of a bill) vencimiento, *m*
matutinal *a* matutino
maudlin *a* sensiblero; lacrimoso; (tipsy) calamocano
maul *vt* maltratar; herir
maundy *n* lavatorio, *m*. **M. Thursday,** Jueves Santo, *m*
Mauritius Mauricio, *m*, Isla de Francia, *f*
mausoleum *n* mausoleo, *m*
mauve *n* color purpúreo delicado, color de malva, *m*, *a* de color de malva
maw *n* (of a ruminant) cuajar, *m*; (of a bird) buche, *m*; *fig* abismo, *m*
mawkish *a* insípido, insulso; sensiblero; asqueroso
mawkishness *n* insipidez, insulsez, *f*; sensiblería, *f*; asquerosidad, *f*
maxilla *n* hueso maxilar, maxilar, *m*
maxillary *a* maxilar
maxim *n* máxima, *f*
maximum *a* máximo. *n* máximo, *m*
may *v aux* poder; ser posible; (expressing wish, hope) ojalá que . . . , Dios quiera que . . . , or the present subjunctive may be used, e.g. **May you live many**

years! ¡qué! Viva Vd. muchos años! (to denote uncertainty, the future tense of the verb is often used, e.g. **You may perhaps remember the date,** Vd. quizás se acordará de la fecha. **Who may he be?** ¿Quién será?) **May God grant it!** ¡(que) Dios lo quiera! **It may be that . . . ,** Puede ser que . . . , Es posible que . . . , Quizás . . . **He may come on Saturday,** Es posible que venga el sábado; Puede venir el sábado. **May I come in?** ¿Puedo entrar? ¿Se puede entrar? **May I come and see you?** ¿Me das permiso para hacerte una visita? ¿Me dejas venir a verte? **May I go then?** ¿Puedo irme pues? ¿Tengo permiso para marcharme entonces?

May n mayo, m; fig abril, m; bot espina blanca, f. **May Day,** primero de mayo, m. **mayflower,** flor del cuclillo, f. **mayfly,** cachipolla, f. **May queen,** maya, f

maybe adv quizás, tal vez

mayonnaise n mayonesa, f. **m. sauce,** salsa mayonesa, f

mayor n alcalde, Argentina intendente, m

mayoral a de alcalde

mayoralty n Argentina intendencia, f

mayoress n alcaldesa, f

maypole n mayo, m. **m. dance,** danza de cintas, f

maze n laberinto, m; fig perplejidad, f. vt dejar perplejo, aturdir

mazurka n mazurca, f

me pron me; (after a preposition only) mí. **They sent it for me,** Lo mandaron para mí. **Dear me!** ¡Ay de mí!

meadow n prado, m, pradera, f. **m.-sweet,** reina de los prados, f

meager a magro, enjuto, flaco; (scanty) exiguo, escaso, insuficiente; pobre; fig árido

meagerness n exigüidad, escasez, f; pobreza, f; fig aridez, f

meal n comida, f; (flour) harina, f. **to have a good m.,** comer bien. **test m.,** med comida de prueba, f. **m.-time,** hora de comida, f

mealy a harinoso; (of the complexion) pastoso

mean a (middle) medianero; (average) mediano; (humble) humilde; pobre; inferior; bajo, vil, ruin; (avaricious) tacaño, mezquino, Argentina agalludo, Chile, Peru coñete, **m.-spirited,** vil, de alma ruin

mean n medio, m; medianía, f; pl **means,** medio, m; expediente, m; medios, m pl; (financial) recursos, m pl; modo, m, manera, f. **by all means,** por todos los medios; (certainly) ¡ya lo creo! ¡no faltaba más! ¡naturalmente! **by means of,** mediante, por medio de; con la ayuda de. **by no means,** de ningún modo; nada. **by some means,** de algún modo, de alguna manera

mean vt destinar (para); pretender, proponerse; intentar, pensar; querer decir, significar; importar; (wish) querer; (concern, speak about) tratarse (de). vi tener el propósito, tener la intención. **I did not m. to do it,** Lo hice sin querer. **What does this word m.?** ¿Qué significa esta palabra? **What do you m. by that?** ¿Qué quieres decir con eso? **This portrait is meant to be Joan,** Este retrato quiere ser Juana. **What do they m. to do?** ¿Qué piensan (or se proponen) hacer? **Do you really m. it?** ¿Lo dices en serio? **Charles always means well,** Carlos siempre tiene buenas intenciones

meander n meandro, serpenteo, m; camino tortuoso, m, vi serpentear; errar, vagar; (in talk) divagar

meandering n meandros, m pl, serpenteo, m; (in talk) divagaciones, f pl, a serpentino, tortuoso

meaning n intención, voluntad, f; significación, f, significado, m; (of words) acepción, f; (sense) sentido, m; (thought) pensamiento, m. a significante. **double m.,** doble intención, f. **He gave me a m. look,** Me miró con intención. **What is the m. of it?** ¿Qué significa? ¿Qué quiere decir?

meaningful a significante

meaningless a sin sentido; insensato; insignificante

meaningly adv significativamente; con intención

meanness n pobreza, f; inferioridad, f; mediocridad, f;

bajeza, ruindad, f; (stinginess) mezquindad, tacañería, Lat. Am. also lechería, f

meantime, meanwhile n ínterin, m, adv entre tanto, mientras tanto, a todo esto. **in the m.,** mientras tanto, en el ínterin

measles n sarampión, m. **German m.,** rubéola, f

measurable a mensurable

measure n medida, f; capacidad, f; (for measuring) regla, f; número, m; proporción, f; (limit) límite, m; (fig step) medida, f; (metre) metro, m; mus compás, m; (degree) grado, m; manera, f; (parliamentary) proyecto (de ley), m. vt medir; proporcionar, distribuir; (water) aforar; (land) apear; (height of persons) tallar; (for clothes) tomar las medidas (a); (judge) juzgar; (test) probar; (poet traverse) recorrer. **a suit made to m.,** un traje hecho a medida. **in great m.,** en gran manera, en alto grado. **in some m.,** hasta cierto punto. **to m. one's length,** caer tendido. **to take a person's m.,** fig tomar las medidas (a). **to m. up to,** fig estar al nivel de, ser igual a

measured a mesurado, moderado; uniforme; limitado. **to walk with m. tread,** andar a pasos contados

measurement n medición, f; medida, f; dimensión, f

meat n carne, f; (food) alimento, m; (meal) comida, f; fig substancia, f. **to sit at m.,** estar a la mesa. **cold meats,** fiambres, m pl. **m.-ball,** albóndiga, f. **m.-chopper,** picador, m. **m.-dish,** fuente, f. **m.-eater,** comedor (-ra) de carne. **m. extract,** carne concentrada, f. **m.-market,** carnicería, f. **m.-pie,** pastel de carne, m. **m.-safe,** fresquera, f

meaty a carnoso; fig substancial

Mecca la Meca, f

mechanic n mecánico, m

mechanical a mecánico; maquinal

mechanically adv mecánicamente; maquinalmente

mechanical pencil n lapicero, m

mechanics n mecánica, f

mechanism n mecanismo, m; (philosophy) mecanicismo, m

mechanize vt convertir en máquina; (gen. mil) mecanizar; motorizar

medal n medalla, f

medallion n medallón, m

medallist n grabador de medallas, m; el, m, (f, la) que recibe una medalla

meddle vi tocar; meterse (con or en); entremeterse, inmiscuirse; intrigar

meddler n entremetido (-da); intrigante, mf

meddlesome a entremetido; oficioso; impertinente; enredador, intrigante. **to be very m.,** meterse en todo

meddlesomeness n entremetimiento, m; oficiosidad, f; impertinencia, f; intrigas, f pl

media, the los medios informativos, m pl

median a del medio

mediate vi intervenir, mediar, arbitrar; abogar (por). a medio; interpuesto

mediation n mediación, intervención, f; intercesión, f; interposición, f

mediator n mediador (-ra); arbitrador, m; intercesor (-ra)

mediatory a de mediador; intercesor

medical a médico; de medicina; de médico. n inf estudiante de medicina, m. **Army M. Service,** Servicio de Sanidad Militar, m. **m. books,** libros de medicina, m pl. **m. examination,** examen médico, m, exploración médica, f. **m. jurisprudence,** medicina legal, f. **m. knowledge,** conocimientos médicos, m pl. **m. practitioner,** médico (-ca). **m. school,** escuela de medicina, f

medicament n medicamento, m

medicate vt medicar; medicinar

medicated a medicado

medication n medicación, f

medicinal a medicinal

medicine n medicina, f; medicamento, m; (charm) ensalmo, hechizo, m. **patent m.,** específico farmacéutico, *m.* **m. ball,** balón medical, *m.* **m. chest,** botiquín, *m.* **m. man,** hechizador, *m*

medico- *prefix* médico-. **m.-legal,** médicolegal

medieval *a* medieval

medievalism *n* afición a la edad media, *f;* espíritu medieval, *m*

mediocre *a* mediocre

mediocrity *n* mediocridad, *f;* medianía, *f*

meditate *vt* idear, proyectar, meditar. *vi* meditar, reflexionar; pensar, intentar

meditation *n* meditación, *f*

meditative *a* meditabundo, contemplativo; de meditación

meditatively *adv* reflexivamente

Mediterranean *a* mediterráneo. *n* Mar Mediterráneo, *m*

medium *n* medio, *m;* (cooking) término medio, a medio cocer, a medio asar, *m;* (environment) medio ambiente, *m;* (agency) intermediario, *m;* (spiritualism) médium, *m; art* medio, *m,* a mediano; regular; mediocre. **through the m. of,** por medio de. **m.-sized,** de tamaño regular

medlar *n* (fruit) níspola, *f;* (tree) níspero, *m*

medley *n* mezcla, *f;* miscelánea, *f,* a mezclado, mixto

medulla *n* medula, *f*

meek *a* dulce; manso; humilde; modesto; pacífico

meekly *adv* mansamente; humildemente; modestamente

meekness *n* mansedumbre, *f;* humildad, *f;* modestia, *f*

meet *vt* encontrar; encontrarse con; tropezar con; (by arrangement) reunirse con; (make the acquaintance of) conocer (a); (satisfy) satisfacer; cumplir (con); (a bill) pagar, saldar; (refute) refutar; (fight) batirse (con); (confront) hacer frente (a). *vi* juntarse; encontrarse; reunirse; verse; (of rivers) confluir. *n* montería, *f, a* conveniente. **I shall m. you at the station,** Te esperaré en la estación. **Until we m. again!** ¡Hasta la vista! **to go to m.,** ir al encuentro de. **to m. half-way,** encontrar a la mitad del camino; partir la diferencia con; hacer concesiones (a). **to m. the eye,** saltar a la vista. **to m. with,** encontrar; experimentar; sufrir

meeting *n* encuentro, *m;* reunión, *f;* (interview) entrevista, *f;* (of rivers, etc.) confluencia, *f;* (public, etc.) mitin, *m;* (council) concilio, *m;* concurso, *m;* (race) concurso de carreras de caballos, *m.* **creditors' m.,** concurso de acreedores, *m.* **m.-house,** templo de los Cuáqueros, *m.* **m.-place,** lugar de reunión, *m;* lugar de cita, *m;* centro, *m.* **to adjourn the m.,** levantar la sesión. **to call a m.,** convocar una sesión. **to open the m.,** abrir la sesión

megalomania *n* megalomanía, monomanía de grandezas, *f*

megalomaniac *n* megalómano (-na)

megaphone *n* megáfono, portavoz, *m*

Meknès Mequínez, *f*

melancholia *n* melancolía, *f*

melancholy *a* melancólico. *n* melancolía, *f*

mellifluence *n* melifluidad, *f*

mellifluous *a* melifluo; dulce

mellow *a* maduro; dulce; (of wine) rancio; blando; suave; (of sound) melodioso; (slang) alegre; (tipsy) entre dos luces. *vt* madurar; ablandar; suavizar. *vi* madurarse

mellowing *n* maduración, *f*

mellowness *n* madurez, *f;* dulzura, *f;* (of wine) ranciedad, *f;* blandura, *f;* suavidad, *f;* melodia, *f*

melodic *a* melódico

melodious *a* melodioso

melodiously *adv* melodiosamente

melodiousness *n* melodía, *f*

melodrama *n* melodrama, *m*

melodramatic *a* melodramático

melody *n* melodía, *f*

melon *n* melón, *m;* sandía, *f.* **m. bed,** sandiar, *m.* **m.-shaped,** amelonado

melt *vi* derretirse; deshacerse; disolverse; evaporarse;

desaparecer; (of money, etc.) hacerse sal y agua; (relent) enternecerse, ablandarse. *vt* fundir; (snow, etc.) derretir; (*fig* soften) ablandar. **He melted away,** *inf* Se escurrió. **to m. into tears,** deshacerse en lágrimas. **to m. down,** fundir

melting *a* fundente; (forgiving) indulgente; (tender) de ternura; lánguido; dulce. *n* fusión, *f;* derretimiento, *m.* **m. point,** punto de fusión, *m.* **m. pot,** *met* crisol, *m; fig* caldera de razas, *f, m*

member *n* miembro, *m;* (of a club, etc.) socio (-ia). **M. of Parliament,** diputado a Cortes, *m*

membership *n* calidad de miembro, socio(-ia); número de miembros (*or* socios), *m,* composición, integración, *f*

membrane *n* membrana, *f*

membranous *a* membranoso

memento *n* recuerdo, *m*

memoir *n* memoria, *f*

memorable *a* memorable

memorably *adv* memorablemente

memorandum *n* memorándum, *m*

memorial *a* conmemorativo. *n* monumento conmemorativo, *m;* memorial, *m*

memorize *vt* aprender de memoria

memory *n* memoria, *f;* recuerdo, *m.* **from m.,** de memoria. **If my m. does not deceive me,** Si mal no me acuerdo. **in m. of,** en conmemoración de; en recuerdo de

memory span *n* retentiva memorística, *f*

menace *n* amenaza, *f, vt* amenazar

menacing *a* amenazador

menacingly *adv* con amenazas

menagerie *n* colección de fieras, *f;* casa de fieras, *f*

mend *vt* remendar; componer; reparar; (darn) zurcir; (rectify) remediar; reformar; enmendar; (a fire) echar carbón (or leña, etc.) a; (one's pace) avivar. *vi* (in health and of the weather) mejorar. *n* remiendo, *m;* (darn) zurcido, *m.* **to be on the m.,** ir mejorando. **to m. one's ways,** reformarse, enmendarse

mendacious *a* mendaz

mendacity *n* mendacidad, *f*

Mendelism *n* mendelismo, *m*

mender *n* componedor (-ra); (darner) zurcidor (-ra); reparador (-ra); (cobbler and tailor) remendón, *m*

mendicancy *n* mendicidad, *f*

mendicant *a* mendicante. *n* mendicante, *mf.* **m. friar,** fraile mendicante, *m*

mending *n* compostura, *f;* reparación, *f;* (darning) zurcidura, *f;* ropa por zurcir, *f*

menial *a* doméstico; servil; bajo, ruin. *n* criado (-da); lacayo, *m*

meningeal *a* meningeo

meningitis *n* meningitis, *f*

menopause *n* menopausia, *f*

menses *n* menstruación, *f*

menstrual *a* menstrual

menstruate *vi* menstruar

menstruation *n* menstruación, *f,*

mental *a* mental; intelectual. **m. derangement,** enajenación mental, *f.* **m. hospital,** manicomio, *m*

mentality *n* mentalidad, *f*

mentally *adv* mentalmente. **m. deficient,** anormal

menthol *n* mentol, *m*

mention *n* mención, *f;* alusión, *f. vt* hacer mención (de), mencionar, mentar, hablar (de); aludir (a); (quote) citar; (in dispatches) nombrar. **Don't m. it!** (keep silent) ¡No digas nada!; (you're welcome) ¡No hay de que!

mentor *n* mentor, *m*

menu *n* menú, *m;* lista de platos, *f*

meow *vi* maullar. *n* maullido, *m*

Mephistophelean *a* mefistofélico

mercantile *a* mercantil; mercante. **m. law,** derecho mercantil, *m.* **m. marine,** marina mercante, *f*

mercantilism *n* mercantilismo, *m*

mercenariness *n* lo mercenario

mercenary *a* mercenario. *n* (soldier) mercenario, *m*

mercer *n* mercero, *m*
mercerize *vt* mercerizar
mercery *n* mercería, *f*
merchandise *n* mercancía, *f*
merchant *n* traficante (en), *mf*, negociante (en), *m*; comerciante, *Lat. Am.* marchante (-ta), *mf* mercader, *m. a* mercante. **The M. of Venice,** El Mercader de Venecia. **m. navy, service,** marina mercante, *f.* **m. ship,** buque mercante, *m*
merchantman *n* buque mercante, *m*
merciful *a* misericordioso, piadoso; compasivo; clemente; indulgente
mercifully *adv* misericordiosamente; compasivamente; con indulgencia
mercifulness *n* misericordia, *f*; compasión, *f*; indulgencia, *f*
merciless *a* despiadado, inhumano
mercilessly *adv* sin piedad
mercilessness *n* inhumanidad, *f*; falta de compasión, *f*
mercurial *a* mercurial; (changeable) volátil; (lively) vivo
mercury *n* mercurio, *m*; (*ast* and *myth*) Mercurio, *m*. **Mercury's wand,** caduceo, *m*
mercy *n* misericordia, *f*; compasión, *f*; clemencia, *f*; indulgencia, *f*; merced, *f.* **at the m. of,** a la merced de, a la intemperie. **to be at the m. of,** estar a la merced de
mere *a* mero; simple; no más que, solo. *n* lago, *m*
merely *adv* meramente, solamente; simplemente, sencillamente
meretricious *a* (archaic) meretricio; (flashy) de oropel; llamativo, charro
meretriciousness *n* mal gusto, *m*
merge *vt* fundir; *com* fusionar; mezclar. *vi* fundirse; *com* fusionarse; mezclarse
merger *n* combinación, *f*; *com* fusión, *f*
meridian *n* (*geog ast*) meridiano, *m*; (noon) mediodía, *m*; (peak) apogeo, *m*
meringue *n* merengue, *m*, *Lat. Am.* espumilla, *f*
merino *a* de merino; merino. *n* (fabric and sheep) merino, *m*
merit *n* mérito, *m*, *vt* merecer, ser digno de
meritorious *a* meritorio
meritoriously *adv* merecidamente
meritoriousness *n* mérito, *m*
merlon *n* merlón, *m*, almena, *f*
mermaid *n* sirena, *f*
merrily *adv* alegremente
merriment *n* alegría, *f*; júbilo, *m*; regocijo, *m*; diversión, *f*; juego, *m*
merriness *n* alegría, *f*; regocijo, *m*; *inf* ebriedad, *f*
merry *a* alegre; jovial; feliz; regocijado, divertido; (tipsy) calamocano. **to make m.,** divertirse. **to make m. over,** reírse de. **M. Christmas!** ¡Felices Navidades! **m.-andrew,** bufón, *m.* **m.-go-round,** caballitos, *m pl*, tiovivo, *m*, *Lat. Am.* calesita, *f.* **m.-making,** festividades, fiestas, *f pl*
meseta *n* meseta, *f*
mesh *n* malla, *f*; *mech* engranaje, *m*; (network) red, *f*; (snare) lazo, *m*. *vt* coger con red; *mech* endentar
mesmerism *n* mesmerismo, *m*
mesmerize *vt* hipnotizar
mess *n* (of food) plato de comida, *m*; porción, ración, *f*; rancho, *m*; (mixture) mezcla, *f*; (disorder) desorden, *m*; suciedad, *f*; (failure) fracaso, *m*. *vt* (dirty) ensuciar; desordenar; (mismanage) echar a perder. **to be in a m.,** *inf* estar aviado. **to get in a m.,** *inf* hacerse un lío. **to make a m. of,** ensuciar; desordenar; (spoil) echarlo todo a rodar
message *n* mensaje, *m*; recado, *m*; (telegraphic) parte, *m*. **I have to take a m.,** Tengo que hacer un recado
messenger *n* mensajero (-ra); (of telegrams) repartidor, *m*; heraldo, *m*; anuncio, *m*
Messiah *n* Mesías, *m*
Messianic *a* mesiánico
messrs. *n pl* (abbreviation) sres. (from señores), *m pl*
metabolism *n* metabolismo, *m*

metabolize *va* metabolizar
metal *n* metal, *m*; vidrio en fusión, *m*; (road) grava, *f*; her metal, *m*; (mettle) temple, temperamento, *m*; brío, fuego, *m*; *pl* metals, (of a railway) rieles, *m pl*. **m. engraver,** grabador en metal, *m.* **m. polish,** limpiametales, *m.* **m. shavings,** cizallas, *f pl.* **m. work,** metalistería, *f.* **m. worker,** metalario, *m*
metallic *a* metálico
metalloid *n* metaloide, *m*
metallurgic *a* metalúrgico
metallurgist *n* metalúrgico, *m*
metallurgy *n* metalurgia, *f*
metamorphosis *n* metamorfosis, *f*
metaphor *n* metáfora, *f*
metaphorical *a* metafórico
metaphysical *a* metafísico
metaphysician *n* metafísico, *m*
metaphysics *n* metafísica, *f*
metathesis *n* metátesis, *f*
mete (out) *vt* repartir, distribuir
metempsychosis *n* metempsicosis, *f*
meteor *n* meteoro, *m*
meteoric *a* meteórico
meteorite *n* meteorito, *m*
meteorological *a* meteorológico
meteorologist *n* meteorologista, *mf*
meteorology *n* meteorología, *f*
meter *n* (for gas, etc.) contador, *m*; (verse and measure) metro, *m*
methane *n* metano, *m*
method *n* método, *m*; técnica, *f*; táctica, *f*
methodical *a* metódico; ordenado, sistemático
Methodism *n* metodismo, *m*
Methodist *n* metodista, *mf*
methyl *n* metilo, *m.* **m. alcohol,** alcohol metílico, *m*
methylated spirit *n* alcohol desnaturalizado, *m*
meticulous *a* meticuloso; minucioso
meticulously *adv* con meticulosidad
meticulousness *n* meticulosidad, *f*; minuciosidad, *f*
metric *a* métrico. **m. system,** sistema métrico, *m*
metrics *n* métrica, *f*
metronome *n* metrónomo, *m*
metropolis *n* metrópoli, *f*; capital, *f*
metropolitan *a* metropolitano; de la capital. *n ecc* metropolitano, *m*
mettle *n* temple, temperamento, *m*; fuego, brío, *m*; valor, *m*. **You have put him on his m.,** Le has picado en el amor propio
mew *n* (gull) gaviota, *f*; (of a cat) maullido, *m*; (of sea-birds) alarido, *m*. *vi* (of a cat) maullar; (of sea-birds) dar alaridos. **to mew up,** encerrar
mews *n* establos, *m pl*, caballeriza, *f*
Mexican *a* mejicano. *n* mejicano (-na)
Mexico Méjico, *m*
mezzanine *n* entresuelo, *m*
mezzosoprano *n* mezzo-soprano
mi *n mus* mi, *m*
miaow *n* miau, *m*, *vi* maullar
miasma *n* miasma, *m*
miasmatic *a* miasmático
mica *n* mica, *f*
microbe *n* microbio, *m*
microbial *a* microbiano
microbiologist *n* microbiólogo, *m*
microbiology *n* microbiología, *f*
microcosm *n* microcosmo, *m*
microphone *n* micrófono, *m*
microscope *n* microscopio, *m*
microscopic *a* microscópico
microwave *n* microonda, *f*
mid *a* medio. *prep* entre; en medio de; a mediados de. **from mid May to August,** desde mediados de mayo hasta agosto. **a mid-fourteenth century castle,** un castillo de mediados del siglo catorce. **in mid air,** en medio del aire. **in mid channel,** en medio del canal. **in mid winter,** en medio del invierno

midday *n* mediodía, *m, a* del mediodía, meridional. **at m.,** a mediodía

midden *n* muladar, *m*

middle *a* medio; en medio de; del centro; intermedio; (average) mediano. *n* medio, *m*; mitad, *f*; centro, *m*; (waist) cintura, *f.* **in the m. of,** en medio de. **in the m. of nowhere,** donde Cristo dio las tres voces. **toward the m. of the month,** a mediados del mes. **m. age,** edad madura, *f.* **m.-aged,** de edad madura, de cierta edad. **M. Ages,** edad media, *f.* **m. class,** clase media, burguesía, *f, a* de la clase media, burgués. **m. distance,** término medio, *m.* **m. ear,** oído medio, *m.* **m. finger,** dedo de en medio (or del corazón), *m.* **m. way,** *fig* término medio, *m.* **m. weight,** peso medio, *m*

Middle East, the el Oriente Medio, el Levante, *m*

middleman *n* agente de negocios, *m*; (retailer) revendedor, *m*; intermediario, *m*

middling *a* mediano; mediocre; regular, así, así

midge *n* mosquito, *m*, mosca de agua, *f*

midget *n* enano (-na). **m. submarine,** submarino de bolsillo, *m*

midnight *n* medianoche, *f. a* de medianoche; nocturno. **at m.,** a medianoche. **to burn the m. oil,** quemarse las cejas. **m. mass,** misa del gallo, *f*

midriff *n* diafragma, *m*

midship *a* maestro. *n* medio del buque, *m.* **m. beam,** bao maestro, *m.* **m. gangway,** crujía, *f*

midshipman *n* guardiamarina, *m*

midst *n* medio, *m*; seno, *m*, *prep* entre. **in the m. of,** en medio de. **There is a traitor in our m.,** Hay un traidor entre nosotros (or en nuestra compañía)

midstream, *n* **in m.** *m.* en medio de la corriente

midsummer *n* pleno verano, *m*; solsticio estival, *m*; fiesta de San Juan, *f.* **A M. Night's Dream,** El Sueño de la Noche de San Juan

midway *a* and *adv* situado a medio camino; a medio camino, a la mitad del camino; entre. *n* mitad del camino, *f*; medio, *m.* **m. between . . . ,** equidistante de . . . , entre

midwife *n* comadrona, partera, *f*

midwifery *n* obstetricia, *f*

midwinter *n* medio del invierno, *m*

mien *n* aire, *m*; porte, semblante, *m*

might *vi* poder. **It m. or m. not be true,** Podría o no podría ser verdad. **How happy Mary m. have been!** ¡Qué feliz pudo haber sido María! **I thought that you m. have seen him in the theater,** Creí que pudieras haberle visto en el teatro. **That I m. . . . !** ¡Que yo pudiese . . . ! **This m. have been avoided if . . .** Esto podía haberse evitado si . . .

might *n* fuerza, *f*; poder, *m.* **with m. and main,** con todas sus fuerzas

mightily *adv* fuertemente; poderosamente; *inf* muchísimo, sumamente

mightiness *n* fuerza, *f*; poder, *m*; grandeza, *f*

mighty *a* fuerte, vigoroso; poderoso; grande; *inf* enorme; (proud) arrogante. *adv inf* enormemente, muy

migraine *n* migraña, jaqueca, *f*

migrant *a* migratorio, de paso. *n* ave migratoria, ave de paso, *f*

migrate *vi* emigrar

migration *n* migración, *f*

migratory *a* migratorio, de paso; (of people) nómada, pasajero

migratory worker *n* trabajador golondrino, *m*

Milanese *a* milanés. *n* milanés (-esa)

milch *a f,* (of cows) lechera

mild *a* apacible, pacífico; manso; dulce; suave; (of the weather) blando; *med* benigno; (light) leve; (of drinks) ligero; (weak) débil

mildew *n* mildiu, añublo, *m*; moho, *m. vt* anublar; enmohecer. *vi* anublarse; enmohecerse

mildly *adv* suavemente; dulcemente; con indulgencia

mildness *n* apacibilidad, *f*; mansedumbre, *f*; suavidad, *f*;

(of weather) blandura, *f*; dulzura, *f*; indulgencia, *f*; (weakness) debilidad, *f*

mile *n* milla, *f*

mileage *n* distancia en millas, *f*; kilometraje, *m*

milestone *n* hito, *m*, piedra miliaria, *f*; mojón kilométrico, *m*

milfoil *n* milenrama, *f*

militancy *n* carácter militante, *m*; belicosidad, *f*

militant *a* militante, combatiente; belicoso; agresivo. *n* combatiente, *mf*

militarily *adv* militarmente

militariness *n* lo militar, el carácter militar

militarism *n* militarismo, *m*

militarist *n* militarista, *mf*

militaristic *a* militarista

militarization *n* militarización, *f*

militarize *vt* militarizar

military *a* militar; de guerra. **the m.,** los militares. **m. academy,** colegio militar, *m.* **m. camp,** campo militar, *m.* **m. law,** código militar, *m.* **m. man,** militar, *m.* **m. police,** policía militar, *f.* **m. service,** servicio militar, *m*

militate (against) *vi* militar contra

militia *n* milicia, *f*

militiaman *n* miliciano, *m*

milk *n* leche, *f. a* de leche; lácteo. *vt* ordeñar. *vi* dar leche. **to have m. and water in one's veins,** tener sangre de horchata. **condensed m.,** leche condensada, leche en lata, *f.* **m.-can,** lechera, *f.* **m.-cart,** carro de leche, *m.* **m. chocolate,** chocolate con leche, *m.* **m. of magnesia,** leche de magnesia, *f.* **m.-pail,** ordeñadero, *m.* **m.-tooth,** diente de leche, *m.* **m.-white,** blanco como la leche

milkiness *n* lactescencia, *f*; carácter lechoso, *m*; (whiteness) blancura, *f*

milking *n* ordeño, *m.* **m.-machine,** máquina ordeñadora, *f.* **m.-stool,** taburete, banquillo, *m*

milkmaid *n* lechera, *f*

milkman *n* lechero, *m*

milksop *n* marica, *m*

milky *a* lechero; de leche; lechoso, como leche; *ast* lácteo. **the Milky Way** la Vía láctea, *f*

mill *n* molino, *m*; (for coffee, etc.) molinillo, *m*; (factory) fábrica, *f*; taller, *m*; (textile) hilandería, *f*; fábrica de tejidos, *f*; (fight) riña a puñetazos, *f*; pugilato, *m. vt* (grind) moler; (coins) acordonar; (cloth) abatanar; (chocolate) batir. **cotton m.,** hilandería de algodón, *f.* **hand-m.,** molinillo, *m.* **paper-m.,** fábrica de papel, *f.* **saw-m.,** serrería, *f.* **spinning m.,** hilandería, *f.* **water m.,** molino de agua, *m.* **m.-course,** saetín, canal de molino, *m.* **m-dam,** esclusa de molino, *f.* **m.-hand,** obrero (-ra). **m.-pond,** cubo, *m.* **m.-race,** caz, *m.* **m.-wheel,** rueda de molino, *f*

millennial *a* milenario

millennium *n* milenario, *m*

miller *n* molinero, *m.* **miller's wife,** molinera

millet *n* mijo, *m*

milligram *n* miligramo, *m*

milliliter *n* mililitro, *m*

millimeter *n* milímetro, *m*

milliner *n* sombrerero (-ra), modista, *mf* **milliner's shop,** sombrerería, tienda de modista, *f*

millinery *n* sombreros, *m pl*; modas, *f pl*; tienda de modista, *f*

milling *n* molienda, *f*; acuñación, *f*; (edge of coin) cordoncillo, *m.* **m. machine,** fresadora, *f*

million *n* millón, *m.* **the m.,** las masas

millionaire *a* millonario. *n* millonario, *m*

millionairess *n* millonaria, *f*

millionth *a* millonésimo

millstone *n* piedra de moler, muela, *f*

mime *n* (Greek farce and actor) mimo, *m*; (mimicry) mímica, *f*; pantomima, *f. vi* hacer en pantomima

mimetic *a* mímico, imitativo

mimic *a* mímico; (pretended) fingido. *n* imitador (-ra). *vt* imitar, contrahacer; *biol* imitar, adaptarse a

mimicry *n* mímica, imitación, *f*; *biol* mimetismo, *m*

minaret *n* minarete, *m*; (of a mosque) alminar, *m*

minatory *a* amenazador

mince *vt* desmenuzar; (meat) picar; (words) medir (las palabras). *vi* andar con pasos menuditos; andar o moverse con afectación; hacer remilgos. **m.-meat,** carne picada, *f;* (sweet) conserva de fruta y especias, *f*

mincing *a* afectado. *n* acción de picar carne, *f.* **m. machine,** máquina de picar carne, *f*

mincingly *adv* con afectación; con pasos menuditos

mind *n* inteligencia, *f;* espíritu ánimo, *m;* imaginación, *f;* alma, *f;* (memory) memoria, *f,* recuerdo, *m;* (understanding) entendimiento, *m;* (genius) ingenio, *m;* (cast of mind) mentalidad, *f;* (opinion) opinión, *f;* (liking) gusto, *m;* (thoughts) pensamiento, *m;* (intention) propósito, *m,* intención, *f;* (tendency) propensión, inclinación, *f.* **I have a good m. to go away,** Por poco me marcho; Tengo ganas de marcharme. **I have changed my m.,** He cambiado de opinión. **out of m.,** olvidado. **I shall give him a piece of my m.,** Le diré cuatro verdades. **It had quite gone out of my m.,** Lo había olvidado completamente. **I can see it in my mind's eye,** Está presente a mi imaginación. **I shall bear it in m.,** Lo tendré en cuenta. **I thought in my own m. that . . . ,** Pensé por mis adentros que . . . **We are both of the same m.,** Ambos somos de la misma opinión. **to be out of one's m.,** estar fuera de juicio. **to call to m.,** acordarse de. **to have something on one's m.,** estar preocupado. **to make up one's m. (to),** resolverse (a), decidirse (a), determinar; animarse (a). **m.-reader,** adivinador (-ra) del pensamiento

mind *vt* (remember) recordar, no olvidar; (heed) atender a; hacer caso de; tener cuidado de; (fear) tener miedo de; (obey) obedecer; preocuparse de; (object to) molestar; importar; (care for) cuidar. *vi* tener cuidado; molestar; (feel) sentir; (fear) tener miedo; (be the same thing) ser igual. **Do you m. being quiet a moment?** ¿Quieres hacer el favor de callarte un momento? **Do you m. if I smoke?** ¿Le molesta si fumo? **They don't m.,** No les importa, Les da igual. **Never m.!** ¡No se moleste!; ¡No se preocupe!; ¡No importa! ¡Vaya! **M. what you are doing!** ¡Cuidado con lo que haces! **M. your own business!** ¡No te metas donde no te llaman!

minded *a* dispuesto, inclinado; de . . . pensamientos; de . . . disposición

mindful *a* atento (a), cuidadoso (de); que se acuerda (de)

mine *a poss* mío, *m,* (mía, *f;* míos, *m pl;* mías, *f pl*); el mío, *m,* (la mía, *f;* lo mío, *neut;* los míos, *m pl;* las mías, *f pl*); mi (*pl* mis). **a friend of m.,** un amigo mío; uno de mis amigos

mine *n* mina, *f. vt* minar; extraer; sembrar minas en, colocar minas en. *vi* minar; hacer una mina; dedicarse a la minería. **drifting m.,** mina a la deriva, *f.* **land m.,** mina terrestre, *f.* **magnetic m.,** mina magnética, *f.* **to lay mines,** colocar (or sembrar) minas. **m.-sweeper,** dragaminas, buque barreminas, *m*

minefield *n* campo de minas, *m*; barrera de minas, *f*

minelayer *n* barca plantaminas, *f,* barco siembraminas, lanzaminas, *m*

miner *n* minero, *m*; *mil* zapador minador, *m*

mineral *n* mineral, *m, a* mineral. **m. baths,** baños, *m pl.* **m. water,** agua mineral, *f;* gaseosa, *f*

mineralogical *a* mineralógico

mineralogist *n* mineralogista, *m*

mineralogy *n* mineralogía, *f*

mingle *vt* mezclar; confundir. *vi* mezclarse; confundirse

mingling *n* mezcla, *f*

miniature *n* miniatura, *f. a* en miniatura. **m. edition,** edición diamante, *f*

miniature golf *n* minigolf, *m*

miniaturist *n* miniaturista, *mf*

minibus *n* micro, microbús, *Mexico* combi, *m*

minimize *vt* aminorar, reducir al mínimo; mitigar; (underrate) tener en menos, despreciar

minimum *n* mínimo, *m, a* mínimo

mining *n* minería, *f, a* minero; de mina; de minas; de minero. **m. engineer,** ingeniero de minas, *m*

minion *n* favorito (-ta); satélite, *m*; *print* miñona, *f*

minister *n* ministro, *m*. *vi* servir; suministrar, proveer de; (contribute) contribuir (a). **m. of health,** ministro de sanidad, *m.* **m. of war,** ministro de la guerra, *m*

ministration *n ecc* ministerio, *m*; servicio, *m*; agencia, *f*

ministry *n* ministerio, *m.* **m. of food,** Ministerio de Abastecimientos, *m*

mink *n* visón, *m*

minnow *n* pez pequeño de agua dulce, *m*

minor *a* menor. *n* menor de edad, *m*; (logic) menor, *f; mus* tono menor, *m; ecc* menor, *m.* **to be a m.,** ser menor de edad. **m. key,** tono menor, *m.* **m. orders,** *ecc* órdenes menores, *f pl.* **m. scale,** escala menor, *f*

Minorca Menorca, *f*

minority *n* minoría, *f;* (of age) minoridad, *f.* **in the m.,** en la minoría

minster *n* catedral, *f;* monasterio, *m*

minstrel *n* trovador, juglar, *m;* músico, *m;* cantante, *m*

minstrelsy *n* música, *f;* canto, *m;* arte del trovador, *m,* or *f;* gaya ciencia, *f*

mint *n bot* menta, hierbabuena, *f;* casa de moneda, casa de la moneda, ceca, *f; fig* mina, *f;* (source) origen, *m. vt* (money) acuñar; *fig* inventar, *a* (postage stamp) en estado nuevo

minter *n* acuñador, *m; fig* inventor (-ra)

minting *n* (of coins) acuñación, *f; fig* invención, *f*

minuet *n* minué, *m*

minus *a* menos; negativo; desprovisto de; sin. *n* signo menos, *m;* cantidad negativa, *f*

minute *a* menudo, diminuto; insignificante; minucioso

minute *n* minuto, *m;* momento, *m;* instante, *m;* (note) minuta, *f; pl* **minutes,** actas, *f pl.* **in a m.,** en un instante. **m.-book,** libro de actas, minutario, *m.* **m.-hand,** minutero, *m*

minutely *adv* minuciosamente; en detalle; exactamente

minuteness *n* suma pequeñez, *f;* minuciosidad, *f*

minx *n* picaruela, *f;* coqueta, *f*

miracle *n* milagro, *m.* **m.-monger,** milagrero (-ra). **m. play,** milagro, *m*

miraculous *a* milagroso

miraculously *adv* milagrosamente, por milagro

miraculousness *n* carácter milagroso, *m,* lo milagroso

mirage *n* espejismo, *m*

mire *n* fango, lodo, *m;* (miry place) lodazal, *m*

mirror *n* espejo, *m. vt* reflejar. **to look in the m.,** mirarse al espejo. **full-length m.,** espejo de cuerpo entero, *m.* **small m.,** espejuelo, *m*

mirth *n* alegría, *f,* júbilo, *m;* risa, *f;* hilaridad, *f*

mirthful *a* alegre

mirthless *a* sin alegría, triste

miry *a* lodoso, fangoso, cenagoso

misadventure *n* desgracia, *f;* accidente, *m*

misanthrope *n* misántropo, *m*

misanthropic *a* misantrópico

misanthropy *n* misantropía, *f*

misapplication *n* mala aplicación, *f;* mal uso, *m;* abuso, *m*

misapply *vt* aplicar mal; hacer mal uso de; abusar de

misapprehend *vt* comprender mal; equivocarse sobre

misapprehension *n* concepto erróneo, *m;* equivocación, *f,* error, *m*

misappropriate *vt* malversar

misappropriation *n* malversación, *f*

misbehave *vi* portarse mal; (of a child) ser malo

misbehavior *n* mala conducta, *f*

miscalculate *vt* calcular mal; engañarse (sobre)

miscalculation *n* mal cálculo, error, *m;* desacierto, *m*

miscall *vt* mal nombrar; llamar equivocadamente; (abuse) insultar

miscarriage *n med* aborto, *m;* (failure) malogro, fracaso, *m;* (of goods) extravío, *m*

miscarriage of justice *n* yerro en la administración de la justicia, *m*

miscarry *vi med* abortar, malparir; (fail) malograrse, frustrarse; (of goods) extraviarse

miscellaneous *a* misceláneo; vario, diverso

miscellany *n* miscelánea, *f*

mischance *n* mala suerte, *f*; infortunio, *m*, desgracia, *f*; accidente, *m*

mischief *n* daño, *m*; mal, *m*; (wilfulness) travesura, *f*; (person) diablillo, *m*. **m.-maker,** enredador (-ra), chismoso (-sa); alborotador, *m*; malicioso (-sa). **m.-making,** *a* enredador; chismoso; malicioso; alborotador

mischievous *a* dañino, perjudicial, malo; malicioso; chismoso; (wilful) travieso; juguetón; (of glances, etc.) malicioso

mischievously *adv* maliciosamente; con (or por) travesura

mischievousness *n* mal, *m*; malicia, *f*; maleficencia, *f*; travesura, *f*

misconceive *vt* formar un concepto erróneo de; concebir mal, juzgar mal

misconception *n* concepto erróneo, *m*, idea falsa, *f*; error, *m*, equivocación, *f*; engaño, *m*

misconduct *n* mala conducta, *f*. **to m. oneself,** portarse mal

misconstruction *n* mala interpretación, *f*; falsa interpretación, *f*; tergiversación, *f*; mala traducción, *f*

misconstrue *vt* interpretar mal; entender mal; tergiversar; traducir mal

miscount *vt* contar mal, equivocarse en la cuenta de; calcular mal. *n* error, *m*; yerro de cuenta, *m*

miscreant *n* malandrín, *m*; bribón, *m*, *a* vil, malandrín

misdeed *n* delito, malhecho, crimen, *m*

misdemeanor *n* mala conducta, *f*; *law* delito, *m*; ofensa, *f*, malhecho, *m*

misdirect *vt* informar mal (acerca del camino); (a letter) dirigir mal, poner unas señas incorrectas en

miser *n* avaro (-ra)

miserable *a* infeliz, desgraciado; miserable; despreciable; sin valor

miserably *adv* miserablemente

miserliness *n* avaricia, tacañería, *f*

miserly *a* avaro, tacaño

misery *n* miseria, *f*; sufrimiento, *m*; dolor, tormento, *m*

misfire *vi* no dar fuego; (of a motor-car, etc.) hacer falsas explosiones, errar el encendido

misfit *n* traje que no cae bien, *m*; zapato que no va bien, *m*; (person) inadaptado, *m*

misfortune *n* infortunio, *m*, mala suerte, adversidad, *f*; desdicha, desgracia, *f*; mal, *m*

misgive *vt* hacer temer; llenar de duda; hacer recelar; hacer presentir

misgiving *n* temor, *m*; duda, *f*; recelo, *m*; presentimiento, *m*

misgovern *vt* gobernar mal; administrar mal; dirigir mal

misgovernment *n* desgobierno, *m*; mala administración, *f*

misguided *a* mal dirigido; extraviado; engañado; (blind) ciego

misguidedly *adv* equivocadamente

mishap *n* desgracia, *f*; contratiempo, accidente, *m*. **to have a m.,** sufrir una desgracia; tener un accidente

misinform *vt* informar mal; dar informes erróneos (a)

misinformation *n* noticia falsa, *f*; información errónea, *f*

misinterpret *vt* interpretar mal; entender mal; torcer; tergiversar; traducir mal

misinterpretation *n* mala interpretación, *f*; interpretación falsa, *f*; tergiversación, *f*; mala traducción, *f*

misjudge *vt* juzgar mal; equivocarse (en or sobre); tener una idea falsa de

misjudgment *n* juicio errado, *m*; idea falsa, *f*; juicio injusto, *m*

mislay *vt* extraviar, perder

mislead *vt* extraviar; llevar a conclusiones erróneas, despistar; engañar

misleading *a* de falsas apariencias; erróneo, falso; engañoso

mismanage *vt* administrar mal; dirigir mal; echar a perder

mismanagement *n* mala administración, *f*; desgobierno, *m*

misname *vt* mal nombrar; llamar equivocadamente

misnomer *n* nombre equivocado, *m*; nombre inapropiado, *m*

misogynist *n* misógino, *m*

misogyny *n* misoginia, *f*

misplace *vt* colocar mal; poner fuera de lugar

misplaced *a* mal puesto; inoportuno; equivocado

misprint *n* error de imprenta, *m*, errata, *f*, *vt* imprimir con erratas

mispronounce *vt* pronunciar mal

mispronunciation *n* mala pronunciación, *f*

misquotation *n* cita errónea, *f*

misquote *vt* citar mal, citar erróneamente

misrepresent *vt* desfigurar; tergiversar; falsificar

misrepresentation *n* desfiguración, *f*; tergiversación, *f*; falsificación, *f*

misrule *vt* gobernar mal. *n* mal gobierno, desgobierno, *m*; confusión, *f*

miss *n* señorita, *f*

miss *vt* (one's aim) errar (el tiro, etc.); no acertar (a); (let fall) dejar caer; (lose a train, the post, etc., one's footing, an opportunity, etc.) perder; (fall short of) dejar de; no ver; no notar; pasar por alto de; omitir; echar de menos; notar la falta de; no encontrar. *vi* errar; (fail) salir mal, fracasar. **I m. you,** Te echo de menos. **to be missing,** faltar; estar ausente; haberse marchado; haber desaparecido. **to m. one's mark,** errar el blanco. **to m. out,** omitir, pasar por alto de. **She doesn't miss a beat,** (fig.) No se le escapa nada

missal *n* misal, *m*

misshapen *a* deforme

missile *n* arma arrojadiza, *f*; proyectil, *m*

missing *a* que falta; perdido; ausente; *mil* desaparecido

mission *n* misión, *f*

missionary *n* misionero, *m*

missionize *vi* misionar

missis *n* señora, *f*; *inf* mujer, *f*

Mississippi el Misisipí, *m*

missive *n* misiva, *f*

Missouri el Misuri, *m*

misspend *vt* malgastar; desperdiciar; perder

mist *n* bruma, neblina, *f*; vapor, *m*; (drizzle) llovizna, *f*; *fig* nube, *f*. *vt* anublar, empañar. *vi* lloviznar

mistakable *a* confundible

mistake *vt* comprender mal; equivocarse sobre; errar; (with for) confundir con, equivocarse con. *n* equivocación, *f*; error, *m*; inadvertencia, *f*; (in an exercise, etc.) falta, *f*. **And no m.!** *inf* Sin duda alguna. **by m.,** por equivocación; (involuntarily) sin querer. **If I am not mistaken,** Si no me engaño, Si no estoy equivocado. **to make a m.,** equivocarse

mistaken *a* (of persons and things) equivocado; (of things) erróneo; incorrecto

mistakenly *adv* equivocadamente; injustamente, falsamente

mister *n* señor, *m*

mistily *adv* a través de la neblina; obscuramente; indistintamente, vagamente

mistimed *a* intempestivo; inoportuno

mistiness *n* neblina, bruma, *f*; vaporosidad, *f*; obscuridad, *f*

mistletoe *n* muérdago, *m*

mistranslate *vt* traducir mal; interpretar mal

mistranslation *n* mala traducción, *f*; traducción inexacta, *f*

mistress *n* señora, *f*; maestra, *f*; (fiancée) prometida, *f*; (beloved) amada, dulce dueña, *f*; (concubine) amiga, querida, *f.* **M. (Mrs.) Gómez,** Sra Gómez. **m. of the robes,** camarera mayor, *f*

mistrust *vt* desconfiar de, no tener confianza en; dudar de. *n* desconfianza, *f;* recelo, *m,* suspicacia, *f;* aprensión, *f*

mistrustful *a* desconfiado; receloso, suspicaz. **to be m. of,** recelarse de

misty *a* brumoso, nebuloso; vaporoso; (of the eyes) anublado; (of windows, etc.) empañado

misunderstand *vt* comprender mal; tomar en sentido erróneo; interpretar mal

misunderstanding *n* concepto erróneo, error, *m;* equivocación, *f;* (disagreement) desavenencia, *f*

misuse *vt* emplear mal; abusar de; (funds) malversar; (ill-treat) tratar mal. *n* abuso, *m;* (of funds) malversación, *f*

mite *n* (coin) ardite, *m;* (trifle) pizca, *f;* óbolo, *m;* *ent* ácaro, *m*

miter *n* mitra, *f;* *carp* inglete, *m,* *vt* *carp* cortar ingletes en

mitigate *vt* (pain) aliviar; mitigar; suavizar

mitigation *n* (of pain) alivio, *m;* mitigación, *f*

mitten *n* mitón, *m*

mix *vt* mezclar; (salad) aderezar; (concrete, etc.) amasar; combinar, unir; (sociably) alternar (con) (confuse) confundir. *vi* mezclarse; frecuentar la compañía (de); frecuentar; (get on well) llevarse bien

mixed *a* mezclado; vario, surtido; mixto; (confused) confuso. **m. doubles,** parejas mixtas, *f pl.* **m. up,** (in disorder) revuelto; confuso. **m. up with,** implicado en; asociado con

mixer *n* mezclador, *m;* (person) mezclador (-ra); *inf* persona sociable, *f.* **electric m.,** mezclador eléctrico, *m*

mixture *n* mezcla, *f;* (medicine) poción, medicina, *f*

mizzen *n* mesana, *f.* **m.-mast,** palo de mesana, *m.* **m.-sail,** vela de mesana, *f.* **m.-topsail,** sobremesana, *f*

mnemonics *n* mnemotecnia, *f*

Moabite *n* moabita, *mf*

moan *vt* lamentar; llorar. *vi* gemir; quejarse, lamentarse. *n* gemido, *m;* lamento, *m;* quejido, *m*

moaning *n* gemidos, *m pl*

moat *n* foso, *m*

mob *n* (crowd) muchedumbre, multitud, *f;* (rabble) populacho, *m,* gentuza, *f. vt* atropellar; atacar. **mob-cap,** cofia, *f*

mobile *a* móvil; ambulante; (fickle) voluble. **m. canteen,** cantina ambulante, *f*

mobility *n* movilidad, *f*

mobilization *n* movilización, *f*

mobilize *vt* movilizar. *vi* movilizarse

moccasin *n* mocasín, *m*

mocha *n* café de Moca, *m*

mock *vt* ridiculizar; burlarse (de), mofarse (de); (cause to fail) frustrar; (mimic) imitar; (delude) engañar. *vi* mofarse, burlarse, reírse. *a* cómico, burlesco; falso; fingido; imitado. **to make a m. of,** poner en ridículo; hacer absurdo; burlarse de. **m.-heroic,** heroicocómico. **m.-orange,** *bot* jeringuilla, *f.* **m.-turtle soup,** sopa hecha con cabeza de ternera a imitación de tortuga, *f*

mocker *n* mofador (-ra); el, *m,* (*f,* la) que se burla de

mockery *n* mofa, burla, *f;* ridículo, *m;* ilusión, apariencia, *f.* **to make a m. of,** mofarse de; hacer ridículo

mocking *a* burlón. **m. bird,** pájaro burlón, *m*

mockingly *adv* burlonamente

modality *n* modalidad, *f*

mode *n* modo, *m;* manera, *f;* (fashion) moda, *f;* uso, *m,* costumbre, *f*

model *n* modelo, *m;* (artist's) modelo vivo, *m, a* modelo; en miniatura. *vt* modelar; moldear; formar; hacer; planear. **m. display,** (hats, etc.) exposición de modelos, *f.* **m. railway,** ferrocarril en miniatura, *m*

modeler *n* modelador (-ra); diseñador, *m*

modeling *n* modelado, *m;* modelo, *m.* **m. wax,** cera para moldear, *f*

moderate *a* moderado; (of prices, etc.) módico; (fair, medium) regular, mediano; razonable; mediocre. *n*

moderado, *m. vt* moderar; modificar; calmar. *vi* moderarse; calmarse

moderately *adv* moderadamente; módicamente; medianamente; bastante; razonablemente; mediocremente

moderation *n* moderación, *f.* **in m.,** en moderación

moderator *n* moderador, *m;* (Church of Scotland) presidente, *m;* *univ* examinador, *m;* *univ* inspector de exámenes, *m.* **m. lamp,** lámpara de regulador, *f*

modern *a* moderno. *n* modernista, *mf.* **in the m. way,** a la moderna. **m. language,** lengua viva, *f*

modernism *n* modernismo, *m*

modernist *n* modernista, *mf*

modernistic *a* modernista

modernity *n* modernidad, *f*

modernization *n* modernización, *f*

modernize *vt* modernizar

modernness *n* modernidad, *f*

modest *a* modesto; (of a woman) púdico

modesty *n* modestia, *f;* (of a woman) pudor, *m*

modicum *n* porción pequeña, *f;* poco, *m*

modifiable *a* modificable

modification *n* modificación, *f*

modify *vt* modificar. **It has been much modified,** Se ha modificado mucho; Se han hecho muchas modificaciones

modifying *a* modificante, modificador

modish *a* de moda en boga; elegante

modishness *n* elegancia, *f*

modiste *n* modista, *mf*

modulate *vt* and *vi* modular

modulation *n* modulación, *f*

modus vivendi *n* modo de conveniencia, *m*

Mogul *n* mogol. *n* mogol (-la). **the Great M.,** el Gran Mogol

Mohammedan *a* mahometano, agareno

Mohammedanism *n* mahometismo, *m*

Mohican *n* mohican, *m*

moiety *n* mitad, *f*

moiré *n* muaré, *m*

moist *a* húmedo

moisten *vt* humedecer, mojar

moisture *n* humedad, *f*

molar *n* muela, *f, a* molar

molasses *n* melaza, *f*

mold *n* (fungus) moho, *m;* (humus) mantillo, *m;* (ironmould) mancha de orín, *f;* (matrix) molde, *m,* matriz, *f;* *cul* cubilete, *m;* *naut* gálibo, *m;* (for jelly, etc.) molde, *m;* *arch* moldura, *f;* (temperament) temple, *m,* disposición, *f. vt* moldear; (cast) vaciar; *carp* moldurar; *naut* galibar; *fig* amoldar, formar; *agr* cubrir con mantillo. **to m. oneself on,** modelarse sobre. **m.-board,** (of a plough) orejera, *f*

Moldavian *a* moldavo. *n* moldavo (-va)

molder *n* moldeador, *m;* *fig* amolador (-ra); creador (-ra). *vi* desmoronarse, convertirse en polvo; *fig* decaer, desmoronarse; vegetar

moldiness *n* moho, *m*

molding *n* amoldamiento, *m;* vaciado, *m;* *arch* moldura, *f;* *fig* formación,

moldy *a* mohoso, enmohecido; *fig* anticuado

mole *n* (animal) topo, *m;* (spot) lunar, *m;* (breakwater) dique, malecón, *m;* muelle, *m*

molecular *a* molecular

molecule *n* molécula, *f*

molehill *n* topera, *f*

moleskin *n* piel de topo, *f*

molest *vt* molestar; perseguir, importunar; faltar al respeto (a)

molestation *n* importunidad, persecución, *f;* molestia, incomodidad, *f*

mollification *n* apaciguamiento, *m;* mitigación, *f*

mollify *vt* apaciguar, calmar; mitigar

mollusk *n* molusco, *m*

mollycoddle *n* alfeñique, mírame y no me toques, *m;* niño (-ña), mimado (-da)

Moloch *n* Moloc, *m*
molt *vi* mudar, *n* muda, *f*
molten *a* fundido; derretido
Moluccas, the las Malucas, *f pl*
moment *n* momento, *m*; instante *m*; (importance) importancia, *f*. **at this m.,** en este momento. **Do it this m.!** ¡Hazlo al instante (or en seguida)!
momentarily *adv* momentáneamente; cada momento
momentariness *n* momentaneidad, *f*
momentary *a* momentáneo
momentous *a* de suma importancia; crítico; grave
momentousness *n* importancia, *f*; gravedad, *f*
momentum *n* momento, *m*, velocidad adquirida *f*; *fig* ímpetu, *m*. **to gather m.,** cobrar velocidad, acelerar
monarch *n* monarca, *m*
monarchic *a* monárquico
monarchism *n* monarquismo, *m*
monarchist *n* monárquico (-ca)
monarchy *n* monarquía, *f*
monastery *n* monasterio, *m*
monastic *a* monástico. **m. life,** vida de clausura, *f*
monasticism *n* vida monástica, *f*
Monday *n* lunes, *m*
monetary *a* monetario
monetization *n* monetización, *f*
money *n* dinero, *m*; (coin) moneda, *f*; sistema monetario, *m*. **paper m.,** papel moneda, *m*. **ready m.,** dinero contante, *m*. **to make m.,** ganar (or hacer) dinero; enriquecerse. **M. talks,** Poderoso caballero es Don Dinero. **m.-bag,** talega, *f*; (person) ricacho (-cha). **m.-bags,** riqueza, *f*. **m.-box,** alcancía, hucha, *f*. **m.-changer,** cambista, *mf* **m.-lender,** prestamista, *mf* **m.-making,** *n* el hacer dinero; prosperidad, ganancia, *f*. *a* lucrativo, *Lat. Am.* libranza de correos, libranza postal, *f*. **m.-order,** giro postal, *m* (postal)
moneyed *a* adinerado; acomodado
mongoose *n* mangosta, *f*
mongrel *a* mestizo, atravesado. *n* perro mestizo, *m*; (in contempt) mestizo. *m*
monitor *n* monitor, *m*
monitory *a* monitorio. *n ecc* monitorio, *m*
monk *n* monje, *m*. **to become a m.,** hacerse monje, tomar el hábito. **monk's-hood,** acónito, *m*
monkey *n* mono (-na); (imp) diablillo, *m*; (of a pile-driver) pilón de martinete, *m*; (in glass-making) crisol, *m*. **to m. with,** meterse con; entremeterse. **m. nut,** cacahuete, *m*. **m.-puzzle,** (tree) araucaria, *f*. **m. tricks,** monadas, travesuras, diabluras, *f pl*. **m.-wrench,** llave inglesa, *f*
monkish *a* monacal, de monje; monástico
monochromatic *a* monocromo
monochrome *n* monocromo, *m*
monocle *n* monóculo, *m*
monogamist *n* monógamo (-ma)
monogamous *a* monógamo
monogamy *n* monogamia, *f*
monogram *n* monograma, *m*
monograph *n* monografía, *f*, opúsculo, *m*
monolith *n* monolito, *m*
monolithic *a* monolítico
monologue *n* monólogo, *m*
monomania *n* monomanía, *f*
monomaniac *n* monomaníaco (-ca)
monomial *n* monomio, *m*, *a* de un solo término
monoplane *n* monoplano, *m*
monopolist *n* monopolista, *mf*; acaparador (-ra)
monopolization *n* monopolio, *m*
monopolize *vt* monopolizar
monopoly *n* monopolio, *m*
monotheism *n* monoteísmo, *m*
monotheist *n* monoteísta, *mf*
monotone *n* monotonía, *f*
monotonous *a* monótono
monotony *n* monotonía, *f*
monoxide *n* monóxido, *m*
Monroe doctrine *n* monroísmo, *m*

monseigneur *n* monseñor, *m*
monsoon *n* monzón, *mf*
monster *n* monstruo, *m*
monstrance *n* custodia, *f*
monstrosity *n* monstruosidad, *f*
monstrous *a* monstruoso; horrible, atroz; enorme
montage *n* montaje, *m*
month *n* mes, *m*. **He arrived a m. ago,** Llegó hace un mes. **a m. later** *Lat. Am.* al mes
monthly *a* mensual. *adv* mensualmente, cada mes. *n* revista (or publicación) mensual, *f*; *pl* **monthlies,** menstruación, regla, *f*. **m. salary** or **payment,** mensualidad, *f*
monument *n* monumento, *m*
monumental *a* monumental
moo *vi* (of cattle) mugir. *n* mugido, *m*
mood *n* humor, *m*; espíritu, *m*; *gram* modo, *m*
moodily *adv* taciturnamente; tristemente, pensativamente
moodiness *n* mal humor, *m*, taciturnidad, *f*; melancolía, tristeza, *f*
moody *a* taciturno, de mal humor; triste, melancólico, pensativo
mooing *n* (of cattle) mugido, *m*
moon *n* luna, *f*; satélite, *m*; mes lunar, *m*; luz de la luna, *f*. **full m.,** plenilunio, *m*; luna llena, *f*. **new m.,** novilunio, *m*, luna nueva, *f*
moonbeam *n* rayo de luna, *m*
moonless *a* sin luna
moonlight *n* luz de la luna, *f*. **in the m.,** a la luz de la luna. **to do a m. flit,** *inf* mudarse por el aire
moonlighting *n* el pluriempleo, *m*
moonlit *a* iluminado por la luna. **moonlit night,** noche de luna, *f*
moonshine *n* claridad de la luna, *f*; *fig* música celestial, ilusión, *f*
moonstone *n* adularia, *f*
moonstruck *a* lunático
Moor *n* moro (-ra)
moor *n* páramo, brezal, *m*; (marsh) pantano, *m*; (for game) coto, *m*. *vt* amarrar, aferrar; afirmar con anclas o cables. **m.-hen,** polla de agua, *f*
mooring *n* amarre, *m*. **m.-mast,** *aer* poste de amarre, *m*
moorings *n pl* amarradero, *m*
Moorish *a* moro; árabe. **M. architecture,** arquitectura árabe, *f*. **M. girl,** mora, *f*
moorland *n* páramo, brezal, *m*
moose *n* anta, *f*
moot *n* junta, *f*; ayuntamiento, *m*. *a* discutible. *vt* (bring up) suscitar; (discuss) discutir, debatir
mop *n* (implement) trapeador, *m*, *Ecuador*, escoba con fleco, *f*, *elsewhere in Lat. Am.* lampazo, *m*; (of hair) mata (de pelo), *f*. *vt* trapear *Ecuador*; (dry) enjugar, secar. **to mop up,** *inf* limpiar; *mil* acabar con (el enemigo)
mope *vi* replace by tristear. **to m. about,** vagar tristemente
moquette *n* moqueta, *f*
moral *a* moral; (chaste) casto, virtuoso; honrado. *n* (maxim) moraleja, *f*; *pl* **morals,** moralidad, *f*; ética, *f*; moral, *f*; (conduct) costumbres, *f pl*. **m. philosophy,** filosofía moral, *f*. **m. support,** apoyo moral, *m*. **m. tale,** apólogo, *m*
morale *n* moral, *f*
moralist *n* moralista, *m*
morality *n* moralidad, *f*; virtud, *f*; castidad, *f*. **m. play,** moralidad, *f*, drama alegórico, *m*
moralization *n* moralización, *f*
moralize *vt* and *vi* moralizar
moralizer *n* moralizador (-ra)
moralizing *a* moralizador
morally *adv* moralmente
morals. See **moral**
morass *n* marisma, ciénaga, *f*
moratorium *n* moratoria, *f*
Moravian *a* moravo. *n* moravo (-va)
morbid *a* mórbido, mórboso; (of the mind, etc.) insano

morbidezza *n* (*art* and *lit*) morbidez, *f*

morbidity *n* morbidez, *f*

mordacity *n* mordacidad, *f*

mordant *a* mordaz; (of acid) mordiente. *n* mordiente, *m*

more *a* and *adv* más. **The m. he earns, the less he saves,** Cuanto más gana, menos ahorra. **the m. the better,** cuanto más, tanto mejor. **without m. ado,** sin más ni más; sin decir nada. **Would you like some m.?** ¿Quiere Vd. más? (of food) ¿Quiere Vd. repetir? **no m.,** no más; (never) nunca más; (finished) se acabó. **once m.,** otra vez, una vez más. **m. and m.,** cada vez más, más y más. **m. or less,** más o menos; (about) poco más o menos

moreover *adv* además, también; por otra parte

morganatic *a* morganático

morgue *n* depósito de cadáveres, *m*

moribund *a* moribundo

Mormon *a* mormónico. *n* mormón (-ona)

Mormonism *n* mormonismo, *m*

morning *n* mañana, *f*, *a* matutino, de la mañana. **Good m.!** ¡Buenos días! **the next m.,** la mañana siguiente. **very early in the m.,** muy de mañana. **m. coat,** chaqué, *m*. **m. dew,** rocío de la mañana, *m*. **m. paper,** periódico de la mañana, *m*. **m. star,** lucero del alba, *m*. **m. suit,** chaqué, *m*

Moroccan *a* marroquí, marrueco. *n* marrueco (-ca), marroquí, *mf*

Morocco Marruecos, *m*

morocco *n* (leather) marroquí, tafilete, *m*

morose *a* sombrío, taciturno, malhumorado

morosely *adv* taciturnamente

moroseness *n* taciturnidad, *f*; mal humor, *m*

morphia, morphine *n* morfina, *f*. **m. addict,** morfinómano (-na)

morrow *n* mañana, *f*; día siguiente, *m*

Morse code *n* la clave telegráfica de Morse, *f*, el alfabeto de Morse, *m*

morsel *n* pedazo, *m*; (mouthful) bocado, *m*

mortal *a* mortal. *n* mortal, *mf*. **m. sin,** pecado mortal, pecado capital, *m*

mortality *n* mortalidad, *f*

mortally wounded *adv* herido de muerte

mortar *n* (for building) argamasa, *f*; (for mixing and *mil*) mortero, *m*. **m. and pestle,** mortero y majador, *m*. **m.-board,** (in building) cuezo, *m*; (academic cap) birrete, *m*

mortgage *n* hipoteca, *f*. *vt* hipotecar. *a* hipotecario. **to pay off a m.,** redimir una hipoteca

mortgageable *a* hipotecable

mortgaged debt *n* deuda garantizada con una hipoteca, *f*

mortgagee *n* acreedor (-ra) hipotecario (-ia)

mortgagor *n* deudor (-ra) hipotecario (-ia)

mortification *n* mortificación, *f*; humillación, *f*; *med* gangrena, *f*

mortify *vt* mortificar; humillar. *vi med* gangrenarse

mortifying *a* humillante

mortise *n* muesca, *f*. *vt* hacer muescas (en); ensamblar

mortuary *a* mortuorio. *n* depósito de cadáveres, *m*

Mosaic *a* mosaico

mosaic *n* mosaico, *m*

Moscow Moscú, *m*

mosque *n* mezquita, *f*

mosquito *n* mosquito, *m*. **m. net,** mosquitero, *m*

moss *n* musgo, *m*; moho, *m*; (swamp) marjal, *m*

mossgrown *a* musgoso, cubierto de musgo; *fig* anticuado

mossiness *n* estado musgoso, *m*

mossy *a* musgoso

most *a* el (la, los, etc.) más; la mayor parte de; la mayoría de; (el, etc.) mayor. *adv* más; el (la, etc.) más; (extremely) sumamente; (very) muy; (before adjectives sometimes expressed by superlative, e.g. **m. reverend,** reverendísimo, **m. holy,** santísimo, etc.). *n* (highest price) el mayor precio; la mayor parte; el mayor número; lo más. **m. of all,** sobre todo. **m. peo-**

ple, la mayoría de la gente. **at the m.,** a lo más, a lo sumo. **for the m. part,** en su mayor parte; casi todos; generalmente, casi siempre. **to make the m. of,** sacar el mayor partido posible de; aprovechar bien; exagerar

mostly *adv* principalmente; en su mayoría; en su mayor parte; casi siempre; en general, generalmente

mote *n* átomo, *m*; mota, *f*. **to see the m. in our neighbor's eye and not the beam in our own,** ver la paja en el ojo del vecino y no la viga en el nuestro

moth *n* mariposa nocturna, *f*; polilla, *f*. **m.ball,** bola de naftalina, *f*. **m.-eaten,** apolillado

mother *n* madre, *f*; madre de familia, *f*; (of alcoholic beverages) madre, *f*. *vt* cuidar como una madre (a); servir de madre (a); (animals) ahijar. **M. Church,** madre iglesia, *f*; iglesia metropolitana, *f*. **m. land,** (madre) patria, *f*. **m.-of-pearl,** *n* madreperla, *f*, nácar, *m*. *a* nacarado, nacáreo. **M. Superior,** (madre) superiora, *f*. **m. tongue,** lengua materna, *f*

motherhood *n* maternidad, *f*

motherless *a* huérfano de madre, sin madre

motherlike *a* de madre, como una madre

motherliness *n* cariño maternal, *m*

motherly *a* maternal

motif *n* motivo, *m*; tema, *m*; *sew* adorno, *m*

motion *n* movimiento, *m*; *mech* marcha, operación, *f*; mecanismo, *m*; (sign) seña, señal, *f*; (gesture) ademán, gesto, *m*; (carriage) aire, porte, *m*; (of the bowels) movimiento del vientre, *m*, deyección, *f*; (will) voluntad, *f*, deseo, *m*; (proposal in an assembly or debate) proposición, moción, *f*; *law* pedimento, *m*. *vt* hacer una señal (a). *vi* hacer señas. **to set in m.,** poner en marcha. **m. picture,** fotografía cinematográfica, película, *f*. **m.-picture theater,** cine, *m*

motionless *a* inmóvil

motivate *vt* motivar

motive *n* motivo, *m*. *a* motor; motivo. **with no m.,** sin motivo. **m. power,** fuerza motriz, *f*

motley *a* abigarrado, multicolor; (mixed) diverso, vario. *n* traje de colores, *m*, botarga, *f*

motor *n* motor, *m*; automóvil, *m*, *a* motor; movido por motor; con motor; (traveling) de viaje. *vi* ir en automóvil. *vt* llevar en automóvil (a). **m.boat,** lancha automóvil, *f*. **m.bus,** autobús, ómnibus, *m*. **m.car,** automóvil, *m*. **m.-coach,** autobús, *m*. **m.cycle,** motocicleta, *f*. **m.cyclist,** motociclista, *mf* **m.-launch,** canoa automóvil, *f*. **m.oil,** aceite para motores, *m*. **m.-road,** autopista, *f*. **m.-rug,** manta de viaje, *f*. **m.-scooter,** bicicleta con motor, *f*. **m.-spirit,** bencina, *f*

motoring *n* automovilismo, *m*

motorist *n* automovilista, motorista, *mf*

mottled *a* abigarrado; (of marble, etc.) jaspeado, esquizado; manchado (con), con manchas (de); pintado (con)

motto *n* *her* divisa, *f*; mote, *m*; (in a book, etc.) lema, *m*

mound *n* montón, *m*; (knoll) altozano, *m*; (for defence) baluarte, *m*; (for burial) túmulo, *m*

mount *n* (hill, and in palmistry) monte, *m*; (for riding) caballería, *f*; montadura, *f*; (for a picture) borde, *m*. *vt* subir; (machines, etc.) montar; (jewels) engastar; (a picture) poner un borde a; (a play) poner en escena; poner a caballo; proveer de caballo. *vi* montar; subir; (increase) aumentar. **to m. a horse,** subir a caballo, montar. **to m. guard,** mil montar la guardia. **to m. the throne,** subir al trono

mountain *n* montaña, *f*; (mound) montón, *m*. *a* de montaña(s); montano; alpino; alpestre. **to make a m. out of a molehill,** convertir un grano de arena en una montaña. hacer de una pulga un camello, hacer de una pulga un elefante. **m.-chain,** cadena de montañas, *f*. **m. climber** *Lat. Am.* andinista, *mf*. **m. climbing** *Lat. Am.* andinismo, *m*. **m. dweller,** montañés (-esa). **m. railway,** ferrocarril de cremallera, *m*. **m.-side,** falda de una montaña, *f*

mountaineer *n* (inhabitant) montañés (-esa); (climber) alpinista, *mf*. *vi* hacer alpinismo

mountaineering *n* alpinismo, *m*

mountainous *a* montañoso; (huge) enorme

mountebank *n* saltabanco, *m*; charlatán, *m*

mounting *n* (ascent) subida, *f*; ascensión, *f*; (of machinery, etc.) armadura, *f*; montadura, *f*; (of a precious stone) engaste, *m*. **m.-block,** subidero, *m*

mourn *vi* afligirse, lamentarse; (wear mourning) estar de luto. *vt* llorar; lamentar; llevar luto por

mourner *n* lamentador (-ra); (paid) plañidera, *f*; el, *m*, (*f*, la) que acompaña al féretro

mournful *a* triste, acongojado; funesto, lúgubre; fúnebre; lamentable

mournfully *adv* tristemente

mournfulness *n* tristeza, *f*; melancolía, aflicción, *f*, pesar, *m*

mourning *n* aflicción, *f*; lamentación, *f*; luto, *m*. **deep m.,** luto riguroso, *m*. **half m.,** medio luto, *m*. **to be in m.,** estar de luto. **to be in m. for,** llevar luto por. **to come out of m.,** dejar el luto. **m.-band,** (on the hat) tira de gasa, *f*; (on the arm) brazal de luto, *m*. **m.-coach,** coche fúnebre, *m*

mouse *n* ratón (-na); *naut* barrilete, *m*. *vi* cazar ratones. **m.-coloured,** de color de rata. **m.-hole, m.-trap,** ratonera, *f*

mouser *n* gato ratonero, *m*

mousing *n* caza de ratones, *f*

moustache *n* bigote, mostacho, *m*

mousy *a* ratonesco, ratonil

mouth *n* (*anat* human being, of a bottle, cave) boca, *f*; entrada, *f*; (of a river) desembocadura, *f*; (of a channel) embocadero, *m*; (of a wind-instrument) boquilla, *f*. *vt* pronunciar con afectación; (chew) mascar. *vi* clamar a gritos, vociferar. **down in the m.,** *inf* con las orejas caídas. **It makes my m. water,** Se me hace la boca agua. **large m.,** boca rasgada, *f*. **m.-gag,** abrebocas, *m*. **m.-organ,** armónica, *f*. **m.-wash,** antiséptico bucal, *m* (Argentina), enjuague, *m*

mouthed *a* que tiene boca . . . ; de boca . . . **open-m.,** boquiabierto

mouthful *n* bocado, *m*; (of smoke, air) bocanada, *f*

mouthpiece *n* (of wind-instruments, tobacco-pipe, waterpipe) boquilla, *f*; (of a wineskin) brocal, *m*; (spokesman) portavoz, *m*; intérprete, *mf*

movable *a* movible; (of goods) mobiliario. **m. feast,** fiesta movible, *f*

movable type *n* tipos sueltos, *m pl*

movables *n pl* bienes muebles, efectos, *m pl*

move *n* movimiento, *m*; (of household effects) mudanza, *f*; (motion) marcha, *f*; (in a game) jugada, *f*; (*fig* step) paso, *m*; (device) maniobra, *f*. **Whose m. is it?** ¿A quién le toca jugar? **to be on the m.,** estar en movimiento; estar de viaje. **to be always on the m.,** *inf* parecer una lanzadera

move *vt* mover; poner en marcha; (furniture) trasladar; cambiar de lugar; (stir) remover; (shake) agitar, hacer temblar; (transport) transportar; (a piece in chess, etc.) jugar; (pull) arrancar; (impel) impulsar; (incline) inclinar, disponer; (affect emotionally) conmover, emocionar, enternecer; impresionar. *vi* moverse; ponerse en marcha; (walk) andar; ir; avanzar; (a step forward, etc.) dar; (move house) trasladarse; (act) entrar en acción; (in games) hacer una jugada; (progress) progresar; (shake) agitarse, temblar; removerse; (propose in an assembly) hacer una proposición; (in a court of law) hacer un pedimento; (grow) crecer. **to m. about,** pasearse; ir y venir; (of traffic) circular; (remove) trasladarse; (stir, tremble) agitarse. **to m. along,** caminar por; avanzar por. **to m. aside,** *vt* apartar; poner a un lado; (curtains) descorrer. *vi* ponerse a un lado; quitarse de en medio. **to m. away,** *vt* alejar. *vi* alejarse; marcharse; trasladarse; mudar de casa. **to m. back,** retroceder, volver hacia atrás. **to m. down,** bajar, descender. **to m. forward,** adelantarse; avanzar; progresar. **to m. in,** entrar (en); tomar posesión de una casa. **to m. off,** *vt* quitar. *vi* marcharse; ponerse en marcha; alejarse, apartarse. **to m. on,** avanzar; po-

nerse en marcha; circular; (of time) pasar, correr. **to m. out,** *vt* sacar, quitar. *vi* salir; (from a house) mudarse, abandonar (una casa, etc.). **to m. round,** dar vueltas, girar; (turn round) volverse. **to m. to,** (make) hacer, animar (a); causar. **to m. up,** *vt* montar, subir. *vi* montar; avanzar

movement *n* movimiento, *m*; *mech* mecanismo, *m*; (Stock Exchange) actividad, *f*. **encircling m.,** *mil* movimiento envolvente, *m*

mover *n* motor, *m*; móvil, *m*; promotor (-ra); (of a motion, proposer) autor (-ra) de una moción

movie *n inf* cine, *m*. **m. camera,** máquina de impresionar, *f*. **m. star,** estrella de la pantalla, *f*

moving *a* móvil; motor; (affecting) emocionante, conmovedor; impresionante; patético. *n* movimiento, *m*; traslado, *m*; cambio de domicilio, *m*. **m. picture,** fotografía cinematográfica, *f*. **m. staircase,** escalera móvil, *f*

movingly *adv* con emoción; patéticamente

mow *vt* segar. *vi* (grimace) hacer muecas

mowing *n* siega, *f*. **m.-machine,** segadora, *f*

Mr. See **mister**

Mrs. See **mistress**

much *a* mucho. *adv* mucho; (by far) con mucho; (with past part.) muy; (pretty nearly) casi, más o menos. **m. of a size,** más o menos del mismo tamaño. **I was m. angered,** Estuve muy enfadado. **as m. as,** tanto como. **as m. more,** otro tanto. **How m. is it?** ¿Cuánto es? ¿Cuánto cuesta? **however m. . . . ,** por mucho que . . . **not m.,** no mucho. **not to think m. of,** tener en poco (a). **so m. so that,** tanto que. **too m.,** demasiado. **to make m. of,** dar grande importancia a; (a person) apreciar, querer; agasajar; (a child) mimar, acariciar

mucilage *n* mucílago, *m*

muck *n* (dung) estiércol, *m*; (filth) porquería, inmundicia, *f*; suciedad, *f*; (rubbish, of a literary work, etc.) porquería, *n*. **to m. up,** ensuciar; (spoil) estropear por completo

mucky *a* muy sucio; puerco; asqueroso, repugnante

mucosity *n* mucosidad, *f*

mucous *a* mucoso. **m. membrane,** mucosa, *f*

mucus *n* mucosidad, *f*; (from the nose) moco, *m*

mud *n* lodo, barro, fango, *m*. **to stick in the mud,** (of a ship, etc.) embarrancarse. **mudbath,** baño de barro, *m*. **mud wall,** tapia, *f*

muddiness *n* estado fangoso, *m*; (of liquids) turbiedad, *f*; suciedad, *f*

muddle *vt* (bewilder) dejar perplejo, aturdir; (intoxicate) emborrachar; (stupefy) entontecer; (spoil) estropear; embarullar, dejar en desorden; hacer un lío de. *n* desorden, *m*; confusión, *f*; lío, embrollo, *m*. **in a m.,** en desorden; en confusión. **to make a m.,** armar un lío. **to m. away,** derrochar sin ton ni son

muddled *a* desordenado; confuso; estúpido; torpe; (drunk) borracho

muddy *a* fangoso, lodoso, barroso; cubierto de lodo; (of liquids, etc.) turbio; (of the complexion) cetrino. *vt* enlodar, cubrir de lodo; ensuciar; (liquids) enturbiar

mudguard *n* guardabarro, *m*

muezzin *n* almuecín, almuédano, *m*

muff *n* manguito, *m*; (for a car radiator) cubierta para radiador, *f*; (*inf* at games, etc.) maleta, *m*. *vt* dejar escapar (una pelota); (an opportunity) perder

muffin *n* mollete, *m*

muffle *vt* embozar, arrebozar; envolver; encubrir, ocultar, tapar; (stifle sound of) apagar; (oars, bells) envolver con tela para no hacer ruido; *fig* ahogar. **to m. oneself up,** embozarse

muffled *a* (of sound) sordo; confuso; apagado. **m. drum,** tambor enlutado, *m*

muffler *n* bufanda, tapaboca, *f*; (furnace) mufla, *f*; (of a car radiator) cubierta para radiador, *f*; (silencer) silencioso, *m*

mufti *n* mufti, *m*

mug *n* vaso, *m*; (tankard) pichel, tarro, *m*; (face) jeta, *f*; (dupe) primo, *m*; (at games, etc.) maleta, *m*

mulatto *a* mulato. *n* mulato (-ta). **m.-like,** amulatado
mulberry *n* (fruit) mora, *f*; (bush) morera, *f*. **m. plantation,** moreral, *m*
mule *n* mulo (-la); (slipper) mula, chinela, *f*; (spinning-jenny) huso mecánico, *m*
mulish *a* mular; terco como una mula
mulishness *n* terquedad de mula, *f*
mullet *n* (red) salmonete, *m*, trilla, *f*; (grey) mújol, *m*
multicolored *a* multicolor
multifarious *a* numeroso, mucho; diverso, vario
multiform *a* multiforme
multilateral *a* multilátero
multimillionaire *a* archimillonario, multimillonario, *n* multimillonario, *m*
multiple *a* múltiple, múltiplo. *n* múltiplo, *m*
multiple-choice question *n* pregunta optativa, *f*
multiplicand *n* multiplicando, *m*
multiplication *n* multiplicación, *f*. **m. table,** tabla de multiplicación, *f*
multiplicity *n* multiplicidad, *f*
multiplier *n math* multiplicador, *m*; máquina de multiplicar, *f*
multiply *vt* multiplicar. *vi* multiplicarse
multitude *n* multitud, *f*. **the m.,** las masas
multitudinous *a* muy numeroso
mumble *vi* and *vt* musitar, hablar entre dientes; refunfuñar; (chew) mascullar
mummer *n* momero (-ra); máscara, *mf*
mummery *n* momería, *f*; mascarada, *f*
mummification *n* momificación, *f*
mummify *vt* momificar. *vi* momificarse
mummy *n* momia, *f*; carne de momia, *f*; (*inf* mother) mama, *f*. **m. case,** sarcófago, *m*
mumps *n pl* parotiditis, papera, *f*
munch *vt* masticar, mascullar, mascar
mundane *a* mundano
municipal *a* municipal. **m. charter,** fuero municipal, *m*. **m. government,** gobierno municipal, *m*
municipality *n* municipio, *m*
munificence *n* munificencia, *f*
munificent *a* munífico, generoso
munition *n* munición, *f*. *vt* municionar. **m. dump,** depósito de municiones, *m*. **m. factory,** fábrica de municiones, *f*. **m. worker,** obrero (-ra) de una fábrica de municiones
mural *a* mural. *n* pintura mural, *f*
murder *n* asesinato, *m*. *vt* asesinar; dar muerte (a), matar; (a work, etc.) degollar. **He was murdered,** Fue asesinado. **willful m.,** homicidio premeditado, *m*
murderer *n* asesino, *m*
murderess *n* asesina, *f*
murderous *a* homicida; cruel, sanguinario; fatal; imposible, intolerable
murderously *adv* con intento de asesinar; (with look) con ojos asesinos; cruelmente
murkiness *n* obscuridad, lobreguez, *f*, tinieblas, *f pl*
murky *a* lóbrego, negro, obscuro; (of one's past, etc.) negro, accidentado
murmur *n* murmullo, *m*; rumor, *m*; susurro, *m*; (grumble) murmurio, *m*. *vi* murmurar, susurrar; (complain) murmurar, quejarse. *vt* murmurar, decir en voz baja
murmuring *n* murmurio, *m*, *a* que murmura, susurrante
muscatel *a* moscatel. *n* moscatel, *m*. **m. grape,** uva moscatel, *f*
muscle *n* músculo, *m*
Muscovite *a* moscovita. *n* moscovita, *mf*
muscular *a* muscular, musculoso; (brawny) membrudo, fornido. **m. pains,** (in the legs, etc.) agujetas, *f pl*
muscularity *n* fuerza muscular, *f*
musculature *n* musculatura, *f*
Muse *n* musa, *f*
muse *n* meditación, *f*. *vi* meditar, reflexionar, rumiar;

mirar las musarañas, estar distraído. **to m. on,** meditar en (or sobre)
museum *n* museo, *m*
museum of arms *n* museo de armas, *m*, aploteca, *f*
mushroom *n* seta, *f*. *a* de setas; de forma de seta; (upstart) advenedizo; (ephemeral) efímero, de un día. **m.-bed,** setal, *m*. **m.-spawn,** esporas de setas, *f pl*
music *n* música, *f*; armonía, *f*; melodía, *f*. *a* de música. **to set to m.,** poner en música. **m.-hall,** teatro de variedades, *m*; salón de conciertos, *m*. **m. master,** profesor de música, *m*. **m. publisher,** editor de obras musicales, *m*. **m. stand,** atril, *m*; tablado para una orquesta, *m*. **m. stool,** taburete de piano, *m*
musical *a* musical; de música; armonioso, melodioso. **She is very m.,** Es muy aficionada a la música; Tiene mucho talento para la música. **m.-box,** caja de música, *f*. **m. comedy,** zarzuela, *f*. **m. instrument,** instrumento de música, *m*
musical chairs *n* escobas, *f pl*, el juego de sillas, *m sg*
musically *adv* musicalmente; melodiosamente
musician *n* músico (-ca)
musing *n* meditación, *f*; ensueños, *m pl*, *a* pensativo, meditabundo
musingly *adv* reflexivamente
musk *n* (substance) almizcle, *m*; perfume de almizcle, *m*. *a* de almizcle; almizclero; (of scents) almizcleño. **m.-deer,** almizclero, *m*. **m.-rat,** rata almizclera, *f*
musket *n* mosquete, *m*
musketeer *n* mosquetero, *m*
Muslim *a* musulmán, mahometano. *n* musulmán (-ana)
muslin *n* muselina, *f*, *a* de muselina
mussel *n* mejillón, *m*. **m.-bed,** criadero de mejillones, *m*
must *vi* haber de; tener que; deber; (expressing probability) deber de, ser. **This question m. be settled without delay,** Esta cuestión debe ser resuelta sin demora. **You m. do it at once,** Tienes que hacerlo en seguida. **I m. have seen him in the street sometime,** Debo haberle visto en la calle alguna vez. **One m. eat to live,** Se ha de comer para vivir. **Well, go if you m.,** Bueno, vete si no hay más remedio. **It m. be a difficult decision for him,** Debe ser una decisión difícil para él. **It m. have been about twelve o'clock when . . . ,** Serían las doce cuando . . .
must *n* mosto, zumo de la uva, *m*; (mould) moho, *m*
mustang *n* potro mesteño, *m*
mustard *n* mostaza, *f*. **m. gas,** iperita, *f*. **m. plaster,** sinapismo, *m*. **m. pot,** mostacera, *f*. **m. spoon,** cucharita para la mostaza, *f*
muster *n* lista, *f*, rol, *m*; revista, *f*; reunión, *f*, *vt* pasar lista (de); pasar revista (a); reunir. *vi* juntarse, reunirse. **to m. out,** (from the army) dar de baja (a). **to m. up sufficient courage,** cobrar ánimos suficientes. **to pass m.,** pasar revista; ser aceptado. **m.-roll,** *mil* muestra, *f*; *naut* rol de la tripulación, *m*
mustiness *n* moho, *m*; ranciedad, *f*; (of a room, etc.) olor de humedad, *m*
musty *a* mohoso; rancio; que huele a humedad. **to go m.,** enmohecerse
mutability *n* mutabilidad, *f*; inconstancia, inestabilidad, *f*
mutable *a* mudable; inconstante, inestable
mutation *n* mutación, *f*
mute *a* mudo; silencioso. *n* mudo (-da); *mus* sordina, *f*; (phonetics) letra muda, *f*. **deaf m.,** sordomudo (-da)
muted *a* (of sounds) sordo, apagado
mutely *adv* mudamente; en silencio
muteness *n* mudez, *f*; silencio, *m*
mutilate *vt* mutilar; estropear
mutilation *n* mutilación, *f*
mutineer *n* amotinador, rebelde, *m*
mutinous *a* amotinado; rebelde, sedicioso; turbulento
mutiny *n* motín, *m*; sublevación, insurrección, *f*, *vi* amotinarse, sublevarse
mutt *n* chucho, *m*

mutter *vt* and *vi* murmurar, musitar; mascullar, decir (or hablar) entre dientes; gruñir, refunfuñar; (of thunder, etc.) tronar, retumbar. *n* murmurio, *m*; rumor, *m*; retumbo, *m*

mutton *n* carnero, *m*, *a* de carnero. **m.-chop,** chuleta, *f*

mutual *a* mutuo, recíproco; común. **by m. consent,** de común acuerdo. **m. aid society,** sociedad de socorros mutuos, *f*. **m. insurance company,** sociedad de seguros mutuos, *f*

mutual fund *n* fondo de inversiones rentables, *m*

mutualism *n* mutualismo, *m*

mutuality *n* mutualidad, *f*

mutually *adv* mutuamente, recíprocamente

muzzle *n* (snout) hocico, *m*; (for a dog) bozal, *m*; (of a gun) boca, *f*. *vt* abozalar, poner un bozal (a); (*fig* gag) amordazar, imponer silencio (a)

muzzling *n* acción de abozalar, *f*; (*fig* gagging) amordazamiento, *m*

my *a poss* mi, *mf*; mis, *mf pl* **my relatives,** mis parientes. **My goodness!** ¡Dios mío!

myelitis *n* mielitis, *f*

myopia *n* miopía, *f*

myopic *a* miope

myriad *n* miríada, *f*

myrmidon *n* rufián, *m*; asesino, *m*; secuaz, *m*

myrrh *n* mirra, *f*

myrtle *n* mirto, arrayán, *m*

myself *pron* yo mismo; (as a reflexive with a preposition) mí; (with a reflexive verb) me. **I m. sent it,** yo mismo (-ma) lo mandé

mysterious *a* misterioso

mysteriousness *n* misterio, *m*, lo misterioso

mystery *n* misterio, *m*. **m. play,** (religious) misterio, drama litúrgico, *m*; (thriller) comedia de detectives, *f*. **m. story,** novela policíaca, *f*; novela de aventuras, *f*

mystic *a* místico

mysticism *n* misticismo, *m*

mystification *n* mistificación, *f*

mystify *vt* mistificar

myth *n* mito, *m*

mythical *a* mítico

mythologist *n* mitólogo, *m*

mythology *n* mitología, *f*

N

n *n* (letter) ene, *f*

nab *vt inf* atrapar, apresar, agazapar

nabob *n* nabab, *m*; ricacho, *m*

nacre *n* nácar, *m*, madreperla, *f*

nadir *n* nadir, *m*

nag *n* jaca, *f*; (wretched hack) rocín, jamelgo, penco, *m*. *vt* zaherir, echar en cara, regañar; (of one's conscience) remorder; *Lat. Am.* majaderear (pester) *vi* criticar, regañar

nagging *n* zaherimiento, *m*. *a* zaheridor, criticón; (pain) continuo, incesante, constante

naiad *n myth* náyade, *f*

nail *vt* clavar, enclavar; (for ornament) clavetear, tachonar, adornar con clavos. *n* uña, *f*; (mech) clavo, *m*; (animal's) garra, *f*. **to n. down,** sujetar (or cerrar) con clavos. **to n. to (on to),** clavar en. **to n. together,** fijar con clavos. *inf* **on the n.,** en el acto, en seguida. *inf* **to hit the n. on the head,** dar en el clavo. **brass-headed n.,** tachón, *m*. **French n.,** punta de París, *f*. **headless n.,** puntilla, *f*. **hob-n.,** clavo de herradura, *m*. **hook n.,** gancho, *m*. **round-headed n.,** bellota, *f*. **n.-brush,** cepillo para las (or de) uñas, *m*. **n.-file,** lima para las uñas, *f*. **n. head,** cabeza de un clavo, *f*. **n.-puller,** sacaclavos, arrancaclavos, botador, *m*. **n.-scissors,** tijeras para las uñas, *f pl*. **n. trade,** ferretería, *f*. **n. varnish,** barniz para las uñas, *m*

nailed *a* adornado con clavos, claveteado

nailer *n* fabricante de clavos, chapucero, *m*

nailing *n* enclavación, *f*

naive *a* ingenuo, candoroso, espontáneo

naively *adv* ingenuamente, espontáneamente

naiveté *n* ingenuidad, naturalidad, franqueza, *f*; candor, *m*

naked *a* desnudo, nudo, *Peru* calato, *elsewhere in Lat. Am.* encuerado; desabrigado, indefenso, desamparado; (birds) implume; calvo; (truth) simple, sencillo, puro; evidente, patente. **stark n.,** en cueros vivos, tal como le parió su madre. **with the n. sword,** con la espada desnuda. **n. eye,** simple vista, *f*. **n. light,** llama descubierta, *f*

nakedly *adv* nudamente; desabrigadamente; abiertamente, claramente

nakedness *n* desnudez, *f*; *fig* desabrigo, *m*, aridez, *f*; *fig* claridad, *f*. **the truth in all its n.,** la verdad desnuda

namby-pamby *a* soso, insípido, ñoño

name *n* nombre, *m*; título, *m*; fama, opinión, *f*; renombre, crédito, *m*; autoridad, *f*; apodo, mal nombre, *m*. *vt* nombrar, llamar, imponer el nombre de, apellidar; mencionar, señalar; (appoint) designar, elegir; (ships)

bautizar. **by n.,** por nombre. **Christian n.,** nombre de pila, *m*. **in his n.,** en nombre de él, en nombre suyo; de parte de él. **in n. only,** nada más que en nombre. **to be named,** llamarse. **to call** (a person) **names,** poner como un trapo (a). **to go under the n. of,** vivir bajo el nombre de. **to have a good n.,** tener buena fama. **What is her n.?** ¿Cómo se llama? **n. day,** santo, *m*. **n. plate,** (machinery) placa de fábrica, *f*; (streets) rótulo, *m*; (professional) placa profesional, *f*

nameless *a* anónimo; desconocido; (inexpressible) vago, indecible

namely *adv* a saber, es decir

namesake *n* tocayo (-ya)

naming *n* bautizo, *m*; nombramiento, *m*; designación, *f*

nannygoat *n* cabra, *f*

nap *n* (cloth) pelusa, *f*, pelo, tamo, *m*; (plants) vello, *m*, pelusilla, *f*; (sleep) siesta, *f*, sueño, *m*; (cards) napolitana, *f*. **to take a nap,** *vi* dormitar, echar un sueño, echar una siesta. **to take an afternoon nap,** dormir la siesta. **to be caught napping,** estar desprevenido

nape *n* nuca, *f*, cogote, *m*; (animal's) testuz, *m*,

naphtha *n chem* nafta, *f*. **wood n.,** alcohol metílico, *m*

naphthalene *n chem* naftalina, *f*

napkin *n* (table) servilleta, *f*; (babies') pañal, *m*. **n.-ring,** servilletero, *m*

Naples Nápoles, *m*

Napoleonic *a* napoleónico

narcissism *n* narcisismo, *m*

narcissus *n* narciso, *m*

narcosis *n med* narcosis, *f*

narcotic *a med* narcótico, calmante, soporífero. *n med* narcótico, *m*, opiata, *f*

nard *n bot* nardo, *m*, tuberosa, *f*

narrate *vt* narrar, contar; referir, relatar

narration *n* narración, narrativa; relación, descripción, *f*, relato, *m*

narrative *a* narrador, narrativo, narratorio. *n* narrativa, *f*; descripción, *f*

narrator *n* narrador (-ra), relator (-ra), descriptor (-ra)

narrow *vt* estrechar, angostar; reducir, limitar. *vi* reducirse, hacerse más estrecho; (eyes) entornarse; (knitting) menguar. *a* estrecho, angosto; limitado, restringido, reducido, corto; (avaricious) ruin, avaro, mezquino; (ideas) intolerante, intransigente. **"Narrow Road,"** «Camino Estrecho». *n pl* **narrows,** *naut* estrecho, *m*; desfiladero, paso estrecho, *m*. **to have a n. escape,** escapar en una tabla. **n.-brimmed** (hats), de ala estrecha. **n. circumstances,** estrechez, escasez de medios, *f.* **n.-gauge railway,** ferrocarril de vía estrecha (or de vía angosta), *m.* **n. life,** vida de horizontes estrechos, *f.* **n. majority,** escasa mayoría, *f.* **n.-minded,** cerrado al mundo, intolerante, intransigente. **n.-mindedness,** intolerancia, intransigencia, estrechez de miras, *f*

narrowing *n* estrechez, *f,* estrechamiento, *m;* reducción, limitación, *f;* (in knitting) menguado, *m*

narrowly *adv* estrechamente; por poco, con dificultad; atentamente, cuidadosamente. **I n. escaped being run over,** Por poco me atropellan

narrowness *n* estrechez, angostura, *f;* (of means) pobreza, miseria, *f;* (of ideas) intolerancia, intransigencia, *f*

nasal *a* nasal, gangoso. *n* letra nasal, *f*

nasally *adv* nasalmente. **to speak n.,** hablar por las narices, ganguear

nascent *a* naciente

nastily *adv* suciamente; ofensivamente, de un modo insultante; maliciosamente, con malignidad

nastiness *n* suciedad, inmundicia, porquería, *f;* (indecency) obscenidad, indecencia, *f;* (rudeness) insolencia, impertinencia, grosería, *f;* (difficulty) dificultad, *f,* lo malo

nasturtium *n* mastuerzo, *m,* capuchina, *f*

nasty *a* nauseabundo, repugnante; asqueroso, inmundo, sucio; (obscene) indecente, obsceno; desagradable, malo; (malicious) rencoroso, malicioso; violento; malévolo, amenazador; peligroso; difícil. *fig* **to be in a n. mess,** tener el agua al cuello. **to turn n.,** *inf* ponerse desagradable

nation *n* nación, *f,* estado, país, *m;* (people) pueblo, *m*

national *a* nacional; público; patriótico. *n* nacional, *mf.* **n. anthem,** himno nacional, *m.* **n. debt,** deuda pública, *f.* **n. schools,** escuelas públicas, *f pl.* **n. socialism,** nacionalsocialismo, *m.* **n. socialist,** *a* and *n* nacionalsocialista *mf.* **n. syndicalism,** *pol* nacionalsindicalismo, *m.* **n. syndicalist,** *a* and *n pol* nacionalsindicalista, *mf*

nationalism *n* nacionalismo, patriotismo, *m*

nationalist *a* and *n* nacionalista, *mf*

nationality *n* nacionalidad, *f;* nación, *f*

nationalization *n* nacionalización, *f*

nationalize *vt* nacionalizar, *Lat. Am. also* estatizar

National Labor Relations Board *n* Junta Nacional de Relaciones Laborales

nationally *adv* nacionalmente, como nación; del punto de vista nacional

native *a* (of a place) nativo, natal, oriundo; indígena; nacional, típico, del país; (vocabulary) patrimonial (as opposed to borrowed vocabulary); (of genius) natural, innato, instintivo; *min* nativo; (language) vernáculo. *n* nacional, *mf;* natural, *mf;* ciudadano (-na) indígena, aborigen (gen. pl.), *mf;* producto nacional, *m.* **He is a n. of Madrid,** Nació en Madrid, Es natural de Madrid, Es madrileño. **Native American commune** (in Peru) ayllu, *m.* **native informant,** sujeto, *m.* **n. land,** patria, tierra. **n. of the capital** *Lat. Am.* capitalino, *n.* of Río de Janeiro carioca, *mf.* **n. place,** lugar natal, *m.* **n. region,** patria chica, *f.* **n. soil,** terruño, *m.* **n. tongue,** lengua materna, *f*

Native American *movement Lat. Am.* indigenismo, *m*

nativity *n* navidad, natividad, *f;* (manger) nacimiento, *m*

natty *a inf* chulo, majo; coquetón

natural *a* natural; (wild) virgen, salvaje; nativo; (of products) crudo; normal; (usual) acostumbrado, corriente, natural; (of likeness) fiel, verdadero; (illegitimate) ilegítimo, bastardo; (of qualities) innato, instintivo; físico; característico, propio; (of people) inafectado, sencillo, genuino; *mus* natural. *n mus* becuadro, *m; mus* nota natural, *f;* imbécil, *mf* **n. features,** geografía física, *f.* **n. history,** historia natural, *f.* **n. philosophy,** filosofía natural, *f.* **n. science,** ciencias naturales, *f pl.* **n. selection,** selección natural, *f.* **n. state,** estado virgen, *m*

natural child *n* hijo ilegítimo, *m*

naturalism *n* naturalismo, *m*

naturalist *n* (*lit* and *science*) naturalista, *mf*

naturalistic *a* naturalista

naturalization *n* naturalización, *f;* aclimatación, *f.* **n. papers,** carta de naturaleza, *f*

naturalize *vt* naturalizar; aclimatar. **to become naturalized,** naturalizarse

naturally *adv* naturalmente, por naturaleza; normalmente; sin afectación; instintivamente, por instinto; (without art) al natural. **n. curly hair** *Guatemala* colocho, *m*

naturalness *n* naturalidad, *f;* sencillez, desenvoltura, *f;* desembarazo, *m*

nature *n* naturaleza, *f;* (of people) carácter, fondo, temperamento, genio, natural, modo de ser, *m;* (kind) género, *m,* especie, *f;* (essence) condición, esencia, cualidad, *f, art* **from n.,** del natural. **good n.,** bondad natural, afabilidad, *f.* **ill n.,** mala índole, *f.* **nature cure,** naturismo, *m.* **n. curist,** naturista, *mf.* **n. study,** historia natural, *f.* **n. worship,** panteísmo, culto de la naturaleza, *m*

natured *a* de carácter, de índole, con un modo de ser, de condición

naught *n* nada, *f;* cero, *m.* *a* inútil, sin valor. **all for n.,** todo en balde. **to come to n.,** malograrse. **to set at n.,** tener en menos; despreciar

naughtily *adv* traviesamente; con picardía, con malicia

naughtiness *n* travesura, picardía, mala conducta, *f;* malicia, *f*

naughty *a* travieso, pícaro, revoltoso, malo; salado, escabroso, verde (stories, etc.). **to be n.,** (children) ser malo

nausea *n* náusea, *f,* bascas, *f pl,* mareo, *m; fig* asco, *m;* repugnancia, *f*

nauseate *vt* dar náuseas; *fig* repugnar, dar asco

nauseating *a* repugnante, horrible; asqueroso

nauseous *a* nauseabundo, asqueroso; *fig* repugnante

nauseousness *n* náusea, asquerosidad, *f; fig* repugnancia, *f,* asco, *m*

nautical *a* náutico, marítimo. **n. day, twenty-four hours,** singladura, *f*

naval *a* naval; de marina, marítimo. **n. base,** base naval, *f.* **n. engagement,** batalla naval, *f.* **n. hospital,** hospital de marina, *m.* **n. law,** código naval, *m.* **n. officer,** oficial de marina, *m.* **n. power,** poder marítimo, *m.* **n. reservist,** marinero de reserva, *m.* **n. yard,** arsenal, *m*

Navarre Navarra, *f*

nave *n arch* nave, *f;* (of wheels) cubo, *m*

navel *n* ombligo, *m.* **n. string,** cordón umbilical, *m*

navigability *n* navegación, practicabilidad de navegar, *f*

navigable *a* navegable, practicable

navigate *vt* navegar, marear, dirigir (unbuque); *fig* conducir, guiar. *vi* navegar

navigation *n* navegación, *f;* (science of) náutica, marina, *f.* **n. company,** empresa naviera, *f.* **n. laws,** derecho marítimo, *m.* **n. lights,** luces de navegación, *f pl*

navigator *n* navegador, navegante, *m;* piloto, *m*

navvy *n* peón, bracero, jornalero, *m; mech* máquina, excavadora, *f.* **road n.,** peón caminero, *m.* **to work like a n.,** estar hecho un azacán, sudar la gota gorda

navy *n* marina, *f;* armada, *f;* (color) azul marino, *m.* **n. board,** consejo de la armada, *m.* **n. department** ministerio de marina, *m.* **n. estimates,** presupuesto de marina, *m.* **n. list,** escalafón de marina, *m*

nay *adv* no; al contrario, más bien, mejor dicho. *n* negativa, *f,* voto contrario, *m*

Nazarene *a* and *n* nazareno (-na)

Nazareth Nazaret, *m*

Nazi *a* and *n* nacionalsocialista, naci, *mf*

Nazism *n* nacismo, *m*

n.d. (no date) *s.f.* (sin fecha)

Neapolitan *a* and *n* neapolitano (-na)

near *vi* acercarse, aproximarse. *a* cercano, inmediato, contiguo; (of time) inminente, próximo; (relationship) cercano, consanguíneo; (of friends) íntimo, entrañable; (mean) tacaño, avariento

near *prep* cerca de, junto a; hacia, en la dirección de; (of time) cerca de, casi. *adv* cerca, *Central America, Chile, Mexico* lueguito; (time) cerca, próximamente. **to be n. to,** estar cerca de. **to bring n.,** acercar, aproximar. **It was a n. thing,** Escapamos por un pelo. **n. at hand,** a la mano; (time) cerca, inminente. **n.-by,** *a* cercano, inmediato, *Central America, Chile, Mexico* lueguito. *adv* cerca. **n. side,** (of vehicles) lado de la acera, *m.* **n.-sighted,** corto de vista, miope. **n.-sightedness,** miopía, cortedad de vista, *f*

nearest *a comp* and *sup* más cercano, más cerca; más corto. **the n. way,** el camino más corto, el camino directo

nearly *adv* casi; cerca de, aproximadamente; estrechamente; íntimamente. **It touches me n.,** Me toca de cerca, Es de sumo interés para mí. **They n. killed me,** Por poco me matan. **to be n.,** (of age) frisar en, rayar en

nearness *n* (of place) cercanía, proximidad, contigüidad, *Argentina* adyacencia, *f*; (of time) inminencia, proximidad, *f*; (relationship) consanguinidad, *f*; (avarice) avaricia, tacañería, *f*; (dearness) intimidad, amistad estrecha, *f*

neat *a zool* vacuno; elegante, sencillo, de buen gusto; (of the body) bien hecho, airoso, esbelto; (clean) limpio, aseado; (of handwriting) legible, bien proporcionado; pulido, esmerado, acabado; hábil, astuto, diestro; (of liquor, spirits) puro, solo. **to make a n. job of,** hacer (algo) bien

neatly *adv* sencillamente, con elegancia, con primor; con aseo, limpiamente; bien (proporcionado); diestramente, hábilmente

neatness *n* aseo, *m,* limpieza, *f*; elegancia, sencillez, *f*; buen gusto, *m*; destreza, habilidad, *f*; (aptness) pertinencia, *f*

nebula *n ast* nebulosa, *f*

nebulosity *n* nebulosidad, *f*; *ast* nebulosa, *f*; vaguedad, imprecisión, *f*

nebulous *a* nebuloso; vago, impreciso, confuso

necessarily *adv* necesariamente; inevitablemente, sin duda

necessary *a* necesario, inevitable; imprescindible, preciso, indispensable, esencial; obligatorio, debido, forzoso. *n* requisito esencial, *m.* **if n.,** en caso de necesidad; si fuera necesario. **to be n.,** hacer falta; necesitarse

necessitate *vt* necesitar, exigir, requerir, obligar

necessitous *a* pobre, indigente, miserable, necesitado

necessity *n* necesidad, *f*; menester, *m,* (e.g., **an indispensable n.,** un menester imprescindible); consecuencia, *f,* resultado, efecto, *m*; inevitabilidad, fatalidad, *f*; (poverty) indigencia, pobreza, *f.* **Fire and clothing are necessities,** El fuego y el vestir son cosas necesarias. **from n.,** por necesidad. **in case of n.,** si fuese necesario, en caso de necesidad. **of n.,** de necesidad, sin remedio. **physical necessities,** menesteres físicos, *m pl.* **prime n.,** artículo de primera necesidad, *m.* **to be under the n. of,** tener que, tener la necesidad de

Necessity is the mother of invention La necesidad es una gran inventora, La necesidad aguza el ingenio

neck *n* cuello, *m,* garganta, *f*; (of bottles) gollete, cuello, *m*; (of animals) pescuezo, *m*; *geog* istmo, *m,* lengua de tierra, *f*; (of musical instruments) clavijero, mástil, *m*; *sew* escote, *m.* **low-necked,** (of dresses) escotado. **She fell on his n.,** Se colgó de su cuello. **He won by a n.,** Ganó por un cuello; *fig* Ganó por un tris. **to break anyone's n.,** romperle el pescuezo a uno. **to wring the n. of,** torcer el pescuezo (a). **n. and n.,** parejos. **n. or nothing,** todo o nada, perdiz o no comerla. **n. stock,** alzacuello, *m*

neckband *n* tirilla de camisa, *f*

necklace *n* collar, *m*

necklet *n* collar, *m*; (of fur) cuello, *m*

necktie *n* corbata, *f*

necrological *a* necrológico

necrology *n* necrología, *f*

necropolis *n* necrópolis, *f*

nectar *n* néctar, *m*

nectarine *n bot* variedad de melocotón, *f*

need *vt* necesitar, haber menester, requerir, exigir. *vi* ser necesario, hacer falta, carecer; haber (de). **N. I obey?** ¿He de obedecer? **You need to write carefully,** Hay que escribir con cuidado. **The work n. not be done for tomorrow,** No es preciso hacer el trabajo para mañana

need *n* necesidad, *f*; cosa necesaria, *f*; falta; (poverty) indigencia, pobreza, *f*; urgencia, *f*; (shortage) escasez, carestía, *f.* **in case of n.,** en caso de necesidad, en caso de urgencia. **I have n. of two more books,** Me hacen falta dos libros más

needful *a* necesario, preciso; indispensable, esencial. **the n.,** lo necesario

needfulness *n* necesidad, falta, *f*

neediness *n* pobreza, penuria, miseria, estrechez, *f*

needle *n sew* aguja, *f*; (of compass) brújula, aguja imanada, *f*; (monument) obelisco, *m*; (of scales) field, *m,* lengüeta, *f*; (of phonograph) púa, *f*, (of measuring instruments) índice, *m*; *med* aguja de inyecciones, *f. inf* **to be as sharp as a n.,** no tener pelo de tonto. **pack n.,** aguja espartera, *f.* **n.-case,** alfiletero, agujero, *m.* **n. maker,** fabricante de agujas, *m.* **n.-shaped,** en forma de aguja, acicular. *vt Lat. Am.* engorrar

needle and thread hilo y aguja

needless *a* innecesario, superfluo. **n. to say,** claro está que . . ., huelga decir que . . .

needlessly *adv* innecesariamente, inútilmente; en vano, de balde

needlessness *n* superfluidad, *f,* lo innecesario

needlewoman *n* (professional) cosedora, *f*; costurera, *f.* **She is a good n.,** Cose bien (or es una buena cosedora)

needlework *n* labor de aguja, labor blanca, costura, *f*; bordado, *m.* **to do n.,** hacer costura

needs *adv* necesariamente, sin remedio *n pl* necesidades, *f pl.* **if n. must,** si hace falta. **N. must when the devil drives,** A la fuerza ahorcan

needy *a* necesitado, menesteroso, corto de medios, pobre, apurado

ne'er-do-well *n* calavera, perdido, *m.* **to be a n.,** ser de mala madera

nefarious *a* nefario, vil, nefando

nefariously *adv* vilmente, nefariamente

negation *n* negación, *f*

negative *vt* negar, denegar; votar en contra (de), oponerse (a); (prevent) impedir, imposibilitar. *a* negativo. *n* negativa, negación, *f*; repulsa, denegación, *f*; *phot* negativo, *m,* prueba negativa, *f*; *elec* electricidad negativa, *f.* **to reply in the n.,** dar una respuesta negativa

negativeness *n* el carácter negativo, *m*

neglect *vt* descuidar, desatender; abandonar, dejar; (ignore) despreciar, no hacer caso (de); omitir, olvidar. *n* descuido, *m,* desatención, *f*; inobservancia, *f*; abandono, olvido, *m*; desdén, *m,* frialdad, *f.* **to fall into n.,** caer en desuso. **to n. one's obligations,** descuidar sus obligaciones

neglectful *a* negligente, descuidado, omiso

negligee *n* salto de cama, quimono, *m,* bata, *f*

negligence *n* negligencia, *f,* descuido, *m*; flojedad, pereza, *f*; (of dress) desaliño, *m*

negligent *a* negligente, descuidado; remiso, flojo, perezoso

negligently *adv* negligentemente; con indiferencia

negligible *a* insignificante, escaso, insuficiente; sin importancia, desdeñable

negotiable *a* negociable; (of a road) practicable, transitable

negotiate *vt* gestionar, agenciar, tratar; (a bend) tomar;

(an obstacle) salvar, franquear; *vi* negociar. **to n. a bill of exchange,** descontar una letra de cambio. **to n. for a contract,** tratar un contrato

negotiation *n* negociación, *f; com* gestión, transacción, *f;* (of a bend) toma, *f;* (of an obstacle) salto, *m*

negotiator *n* negociador (-ra)

neigh *vi* relinchar. *n* relincho, relinchido, *m*

neighbor *n* vecino (-na); (biblical) prójimo (-ma)

neighborhood *n* vecindad, *f,* vecindario, *m;* cercanía, *f,* afueras, *f pl,* alrededores, *m pl;* a de barrio (e.g. **neighborhood moviehouse,** cine del barrio)

neighboring *a* vecino; cercano, inmediato, adyacente

neighborliness *n* buena vecindad, *f*

neighborly *a* amistoso, sociable, bondadoso. **to be n.,** ser de buena vecindad.

neither *a* ningún; ninguno de los dos, e.g. **N. explanation is right,** Ninguna de las dos explicaciones es correcta. *conjunc* ni, tampoco, e.g. **N. Mary nor John,** Ni María ni Juan. **N. will he give it to her,** Tampoco se lo dará. *pron* ni uno ni otro, ninguno, e.g. **N. of them heard it,** Ni uno ni otro lo oyó.

nemesis *n* némesis, *f;* justicia, *f*

nenuphar *n bot* nenúfar, *m*

neo- *prefix* neo. **neo-Catholic,** *a* and *n* neo-católico (-ca). **neo-Platonic,** neoplatónico. **neo-Platonism,** neoplatonismo, *m*

neolithic *a* neolítico

neologism *n* neologismo, *m*

neon *n chem* neón, *m*

neon sign anuncio luminoso, *m*

neophyte *n* neófito (-ta); aspirante, *mf*

nephew *n* sobrino, *m*

nephritis *n med* nefritis, *f*

nepotism *n* nepotismo, *m*

nerve *n* (*anat bot*) nervio, *m;* valor, ánimo, *m;* vitalidad, *f; inf* descaro, *m,* desvergüenza, frescura, *f. vt* animar, alentar, envalentonar; esforzar; dar fuerza (a). *vi* animarse, esforzarse (a). **My nerves are all on edge,** Se me crispan los nervios. **n.-cell,** neurona, *f.* **to lose one's n.,** perder la cabeza; perder los nervios. **to strain every n.,** hacer un esfuerzo supremo. **n. center,** centro nervioso, *m.* **n.-racking,** espantoso, horripilante. **n. strain,** tensión nerviosa, *f*

nerveless *a* sin nervio; enervado

nerviness *n* nervosidad, *f*

nervous *a* nervioso, asustadizo, tímido; agitado, excitado; (of style) vigoroso. **n. breakdown,** crisis nerviosa, *f.* **n. system,** sistema nervioso, *m*

nervously *adv* nerviosamente; tímidamente

nervousness *n* nervosidad, timidez, *f;* agitación, *f;* (of style) vigor, *m;* energía, *f*

nervy *a* nervioso

nest *vi* anidar, hacerse un nido. *n* (bird's) nido, *m;* (animal's) madriguera, *f;* (of drawers) juego, *m,* serie, *f;* (of thieves) cueva, guarida, *f; inf* casita, *f,* hogar, *m.* **to feather one's n.,** hacer su agosto. **n.-egg,** *fig* nidal, *m.* **n. of eggs,** nidada de huevos, *f*

nestle *vt* apoyar. *vi* apiñarse; hacerse un ovillo. **to n. up to a person,** apretarse contra

nestling *n* pichón, pollo, *m;* pajarito, *m*

net *vt* coger con redes; obtener, coger; cubrir con redes. *vi* hacer redes. *n* red, *f;* (mesh) malla, *f;* (fabric) tul, *m.* **net making,** manufactura de redes, *f*

net *a com* líquido, neto, limpio; (of fabric) de tul. **net amount,** importe líquido, importe neto, *m.* **net balance,** saldo líquido, *m.* **net cost,** precio neto, *m.* **net profit,** beneficio neto (or líquido), *m*

nether *a* inferior, bajero, más bajo. **n. regions,** infierno, *m*

Netherland *a* neerlandés, holandés

Netherlander *n* neerlandés (-esa), holandés (-esa)

Netherlands, the los Países Bajos *m pl*

nethermost *a* lo más bajo, ínfimo, más hondo

netting *n* red, (obra de) malla, *f; naut* jareta, *f;* manufactura de redes, *f;* pesca con redes, *f.* **wire-n.,** tela metálica, malla de alambre, *f*

nettle *vt* picar; *fig* irritar, picar, fastidiar, disgustar. *n* ortiga, *f.* **n.-rash,** urticaria, *f*

network *n* red, malla, randa, *f;* (of communications) sistema, *m,* red, *f*

neuralgia *n* neuralgia, *f*

neuralgic *a* neurálgico

neurasthenia *n* neurastenia, *f*

neurasthenic *a* and *n* neurasténico (-ca)

neuritis *n* neuritis, *f*

neurologist *n* neurólogo, *m*

neurology *n* neurología, *f*

neuropath *n* neurópata, *m*

neuropathic *a* neuropático

neurosis *n* neurosis, *f*

neurosurgeon *n* neurocirujano, *m*

neurotic *a* and *n* neurótico (-ca)

neuter *a* neutro; (of verbs) intransitivo; (*zool bot*) sin sexo

neutral *a* neutral; (*chem mech*) neutro; (of colors) indeciso, indeterminado; (of persons) imparcial, indiferente. *n* neutral, *mf mech* **to go into n.,** pasar a marcha neutra

neutrality *n* neutralidad, *f;* indiferencia, *f;* imparcialidad, *f*

neutralization *n* neutralización, *f*

neutralize *vt* neutralizar

never *adv* nunca, jamás; de ningún modo, no; ni aun, ni siquiera. **Better late than n.,** Más vale tarde que nunca. **Never look a gift horse in the mouth,** A caballo regalado no se le mira el diente. **Were the hour n. so late,** Por más tarde que fuese la hora. **n. again,** nunca jamás. **n. a one,** ni siquiera uno. **n. a whit,** ni pizca. **N. mind!** ¡No importa! ¡No te preocupes! ¡No hagas caso! **n.-ceasing,** continuo, incesante. **n.-ending,** inacabable, eterno, sin fin. **n.-failing,** infalible. **n.-to-be-forgotten,** inolvidable

nevermore *adv* nunca jamás

nevertheless *adv* sin embargo, no obstante, con todo

new *a* nuevo; novel, fresco; distinto, diferente; moderno; (inexperienced) novato, no habituado; reciente. *adv* (in compounds) recién. **as good as new,** como nuevo. **brand-new,** flamante, nuevecito. **newborn,** recién nacido. **new-comer,** recién llegado (-da). **new-fashioned,** de última moda. **new-found,** recién hallado. **new-laid egg,** huevo fresco, *m.* **new moon,** luna nueva, *f,* novilunio, *m.* **new rich,** ricacho (-cha); indio, *m.* **new student,** alumno de nuevo ingreso. **New Testament,** Nuevo Testamento, *m.* **New World,** Nuevo Mundo, *m.* **New York (er),** *a* and *n* neoyorquino (-na). **New Zealand(er),** *a* and *n* neozelandés (-esa)

newel *n* (of stair) alma, *f,* árbol, nabo, *m.* **n.-post,** pilarote (de escalera), *m*

newest *a sup* novísimo; más reciente

Newfoundland Terranova, *f.* **N. dog,** perro de Terranova, *m*

newish *a* bastante nuevo

newly *adv* nuevamente; hace poco, recientemente. The abb. form **recién** is used only with past part, e.g. **the n. painted door,** la puerta recién pintada. **the n.-weds,** los desposados, los recién casados

newness *n* novedad, *f;* inexperiencia, falta de práctica, *f;* innovación, *f*

New Orleans Nueva Orleans, *f*

news *n pl* noticias, *f pl;* nueva, *f;* reporte, aviso, *m;* novedad, *f.* **No n. is good n.,** Falta de noticias, buena señal. **piece of n.,** noticia, *f.* **What's the n.?** ¿Qué hay de nuevo? **n. agency,** agencia de noticias, agencia periodística, *f.* **n.-agent,** agente de la prensa, *m;* vendedor (-ra) de periódicos. **n. bulletin,** *rad* boletín de noticias, *m. inf* **n.-hound,** gacetillero (-ra). **n. item,** noticia de actualidad, *f.* **n.-print,** papel para periódicos, *m.* **n.-room,** gabinete de lectura, *m.* **n. reel,** película noticiaria, revista cinematográfica, *f,* noticiario cinematográfico, noticiero *m,* actualidades, *f pl.*

n.-stand, puesto de periódicos, quiosco de periódicos, *m*. **n. theater,** cine de actualidades, *m*

newsboy *n Lat. Am.* canillito, *m*

newscast *n* noticiario, *m*

newsgirl *n Lat. Am.* canillita, *f*

newsletter circular noticiera, relación de sucesos, *f*

newspaper *n* periódico, diario, noticiero, *m*. **n. clipping, n. cutting,** recorte de periódico, *m*. **n. paragraph,** suelto, *m*. **n. reporter,** reportero (-ra); periodista, *mf* **n. reporting,** reporterismo, *m*. **n. serial,** folletín, *m*, novela por entregas, *f*. **n. vendor,** vendedor (-ra) de periódicos, *m*

news report *n* reportaje, *m*

newsy *a inf* lleno de noticias, noticioso

newt *n* tritón, *m*

Newtonian *a* neutoniano

New York Nueva York, *f*

New Zealand Nueva Zelandia, *f*

next *a* (of place) siguiente, vecino, contiguo; (of time) próximo, siguiente. **on the n. page,** en la página siguiente. **the n. day,** el día siguiente. **the n.-door house,** la casa vecina. **the n. life,** la otra vida. **n. month (yesar),** el mes (año) próximo (or que viene). **n. time,** otra vez, la próxima vez

next *adv* (of time) luego, en seguida; (of place) inmediatamente después. **I come n.,** Ahora me toca a mí. **It is n. to a certainty that . . . ,** Es casi seguro que . . . **the n. best,** el segundo. **the n. of kin,** los pariente más cercarro, *m*, parientes más cercanos, *m pl*. **to wear n. to the skin,** llevar sobre la piel. **n. to,** al lado de, junto a; primero después de; casi. **n. to nothing,** casi nada, muy poco. **What n.?** ¿Qué más?; ¿Y ahora qué?

nib *n* punto, tajo (de una pluma), *m*

nibble *vt* mordiscar, mordisquear, roer; (horses) rozar; (fish) picar; *fig* considerar, tantear; *vi* picar. *n* mordisco, *m*; roedura, *f*

Nicaraguan *a and n* nicaragüeño (-ña)

Nice Niza, *f*

nice *a* escrupuloso, minucioso, exacto; (of persons) simpático, afable, amable; fino; (of things) agradable, bonito; bueno; sutil, delicado; (*inf iron*) bonito. **a n. point,** un punto delicado. **a n. view,** una vista agradable (or bonita). **n.-looking,** guapo. **n. people,** gente fina, *f*; gente simpática, *f*

nicely *adv* muy bien; con elegancia; primorosamente; con amabilidad, gentilmente; agradablemente

Nicene *a* niceno

niceness *n* exactitud, minuciosidad, *f*; (of persons) bondad, amabilidad, *f*; amenidad, hermosura, *f*; lo bonito; sutileza, *f*; refinamiento, *m*

nicety *n* exactitud, *f*; sutileza, *f*, refinamiento, *m*. **niceties,** *n pl* detalles, *m pl*. **to a n.,** con la mayor precisión; a la perfección

niche *n* nicho, templete, *m*; (vaulted) hornacina, *f*, *fig* **to find a n. for oneself,** encontrarse una buena posición; situarse

nick *vt* cortar en muescas, mellar, tarjar. *n* mella, muesca, *f*. **in the n. of time,** en el momento oportuno, a tiempo

nickel *n* níquel, *m*; *com* moneda de níquel, *f*. **n.-plated,** niquelado

nickname *vt* apodar, motejar, apellidar. *n* apodo, sobrenombre, mote, mal nombre, *m*

nicotine *n* nicotina, *f*

nicotinism *n* nicotismo, *m*

nictitating membrane *n anat* membrana nictitante, *f*

niece *n* sobrina, *f*

niggardliness *n* tacañería, avaricia, parsimonia, mezquindad, *f*

niggardly *a* tacaño, avaricioso, mezquino, ruin, miserable

niggling *a* nimio, meticuloso; escrupuloso, minucioso

nigh. See **near**

night *n* noche, *f*; *fig* oscuridad, *f*, tinieblas, *f pl*. **all n.,** toda la noche, la noche entera. **all n. service,** servicio nocturno permanente, *m*. **at** or **by n.,** de noche. **every**

n., todas las noches, cada noche. **Good n.!** ¡Buenas noches! **last n.,** ayer por la noche, anoche, la noche pasada. **restless n.,** noche mala, noche toledana, *f*. **the n. before last,** anteayer por la noche, *m*. **to-n.,** esta noche. **tomorrow n.,** mañana por la noche. **to be n.,** ser de noche. **to spend the n.,** pernoctar, pasar la noche. **n.-bird,** pájaro nocturno, *m*; *inf* trasnochador (-ra). **n.-blindness,** nictalopia, *f*. **n.-cap,** gorro de dormir, *m*. **n. clothes,** traje de dormir, *m*. **n. club,** cabaré *m*. **n. dew,** relente, sereno, *m*. **n. flying,** vuelo nocturno, *m*. **n.-jar,** *orn* chotacabras, *m*. **n.-light,** mariposa, lamparilla, *f*. **n. mail,** último correo, *m*; tren correo de la noche, *m*. **n. school,** escuela nocturna, *f*. **n. shift,** turno de noche, *m*. **n. table** *Mexico* buró, *m*. **n. watch,** ronda de noche, *f*; *naut* sonochada, *f*. **n. watchman,** (in the street) sereno, *m*; (of a building) vigilante nocturno, *m*

nightfall *n* anochecer, crepúsculo, atardecer, *m*

nightgown *n* camisa de noche, *f*

nightingale *n* ruiseñor, *m*

nightly *a* de noche; nocturno, nocturnal. *adv* todas las noches, cada noche

nightmare *n* pesadilla, *f*

nightmarish *a* de pesadilla, horrible

nightshade *n bot* hierba mora, *f*, solano, *m*

nihilism *n* nihilismo, *m*

nihilist *n* nihilista, *mf*

Nile, the el Nilo, *m*

nimble *a* ágil, activo, *México* alacre; vivo, listo. **n.-fingered,** ligero de dedos. **n.-witted,** despierto, vivo

nimbleness *n* agilidad, actividad, *México* alacridad, *f*; viveza, habilidad, *f*

nimbly *adv* ágilmente, ligeramente

nimbus *n* nimbo, *m*, aureola, *f*

nincompoop *n* papirote, *m*, papanatas, *mf* tonto (-ta)

nine *a and n* nueve, *m*. **He is n.,** Tiene nueve años. **the N.,** las nueve Musas. **n. o'clock,** las nueve. **to be dressed up to the nines,** estar hecho un brazo de mar

ninefold *a and adv* nueve veces

ninepins *n* juego de bolos, *m*

nineteen *a and n* diez y nueve, diecinueve *m*

nineteenth *a* décimonono. *n* (of month) el diez y nueve; (of monarchs) diez y nueve. **the n. century,** el siglo diez y nueve

ninetieth *a* nonagésimo, noventa

ninety *a and n* noventa *m*. **n.-one,** noventa y uno. **n.-two,** noventa y dos. **the n.-first chapter,** el capítulo noventa y uno

ninny *n* parapoco, chancleta, *mf*; mentecato (-ta)

ninth *a* noveno, nono. *n* nueve, *m*; (of the month) el nueve (of sovereigns) nono. **one n.,** un noveno

ninthly *adv* en noveno (or nono) lugar

nip *vt* pellizcar, pinchar; mordiscar, morder; (wither) marchitar; (freeze) helar; (run) correr. *vi* pinchar; picar (el viento). *n* pellizco, pinchazo, *m*; mordisco, *m*; (of spirits) trago, *m*; copita, *f*; (in the air) viento frío, hielo, *m*. **to nip in,** colarse dentro, deslizarse en. **to nip off,** pirarse, mudarse. *fig* **to nip in the bud,** cortar en flor

nippers *n pl* alicates, *m pl*; tenacillas, pinzas, *f pl*

nipping *n* pinchadura, *f*; mordedura, *f*. *a* punzante; helado, glacial, mordiente. **n. off,** (of a point) despuntadura, *f*

nipple *n* pezón, *m*; pezón artificial, *m*

nit *n ent* liendre, *f*

nitrate *n chem* nitrato, *m*

nitre *n* salitre, *m*

nitric *a* nítrico

nitrite *n chem* nitrito, *m*

nitro- *prefix chem* nitro. **n.-cellulose,** algodón pólvora, *m*. **n.-glycerine,** nitroglicerina, *f*

nitrogen *n chem* nitrógeno, *m*

no *a* ningún, ninguno, ninguna, e.g. **by no means,** de ningún modo. **No** is often not translated in Sp., e.g. **I have no time,** No tengo tiempo. *adv* no. *n* voto negativo, no, *m*. **to be of no account,** no tener importancia; no significar nada. **to be no good for,** no servir para. **to be of no use,** ser inútil. **to have no connection with,** no tener nada que ver con. **for no reason,** sin motivo alguno. **"No Admittance,"** «Entrada Prohibida.» **no, indeed,** Cierto que no. **no-man's land,** tierra de nadie, *f.* **no more,** no más. **No more of this!** ¡No hablemos más de eso! **no one,** nadie, ninguno. **no sooner,** no bien, tan pronto (como). **no such thing,** no tal. **"No Thoroughfare,"** «Prohibido el Paso.» **whether or not,** sea o no sea

Noah's Ark *n* arca de Noé, *f*

nobility *n* nobleza, *f;* (of rank) aristocracia, nobleza, *f;* (of conduct) caballerosidad, hidalguía, generosidad, bondad, *f;* (grandeur) grandeza, sublimidad, *f.* **the higher n.,** los nobles de primera clase

noble *a* noble; (in rank) aristocrático, noble, linajudo; (of conduct) caballeroso, generoso; (of buildings) sublime, magnífico. *n* noble, *m,* aristócrata, *mf* **to make n.,** ennoblecer. **n.-mindedness,** generosidad, grandeza de alma, *f.* **n. title,** título de nobleza, título del reino, *m*

noblewoman *n* dama noble, mujer noble, aristócrata, *f*

nobly *adv* noblemente, generosamente. **n. born,** noble de nacimiento

nobody *n* nadie, ninguno. **There was n. there,** No había nadie allí. *inf* **a n.,** un (una) cualquiera, una persona insignificante. **n. else,** nadie más, ningún otro

nocturnal *a* nocturno, nocherniego, nocturnal

nocturne *n mus* nocturno, *m*

nod *vt* inclinar la cabeza; hacer una señal (or señas) con la cabeza; *vi* dar cabezadas; cabecear; (of trees) mecerse, inclinarse; inclinar la cabeza. *n* señal (or seña) con la cabeza, *f;* inclinación de la cabeza, *f;* cabeceo, *m,* cabezada, *Lat. Am.* cabeceada, *f.* **A nod is as good as a wink,** A buen entendedor pocas palabras. **He nodded to me as he passed,** Me saludó con la cabeza al pasar. **He signed to me with a nod,** Me hizo una señal con la cabeza

nodding *a* que cabecea; *bot* colgante, inclinado; temblante. *n* cabeceo, *m;* saludo con la cabeza, *m*

noddle *n* mollera, *f*

node *n* (*bot med*) nudo, *m*

nodule *n* nódulo, *m;* nudillo, *m*

noise *n* ruido, son, *m;* tumulto, clamor, estruendo, alboroto, *Central America* embullo, *m.* **to make a n.,** hacer ruido. **to n. abroad,** divulgar, publicar

noiseless *a* silencioso, callado; sin ruido

noiselessness *n* silencio, *m,* falta de ruido, *f*

noisily *adv* ruidosamente

noisiness *n* ruido, estrépito, tumulto, clamor, *m;* (of voices) gritería, *f*

noisome *a* ofensivo; fétido, apestoso

noisy *a* ruidoso; estruendoso; estrepitoso, clamoroso

nomad *a* nómada, errante; (of flocks) trashumante. *n* nómada, *mf*

nomadism *n* nomadismo, *m*

nomenclature *n* nomenclatura, *f*

nominal *a* nominal; titular; insignificante, de poca importancia. **the n. head,** el director en nombre

nominalism *n* nominalismo, *m*

nominally *adv* nominalmente, en nombre

nominate *vt* nombrar, designar, elegir; fijar, señalar

nominating *a* nominador

nomination *n* nombramiento, *m,* nominación, *f;* señalamiento, *m*

nominator *n* nominador (-ra)

nominee *n* nómino propuesto, *m*

non *adv* non; des-; in-; falta de. **non-acceptance,** rechazo, *m.* **non-acquaintance,** ignorancia, *f.* **non-admission,** no admisión, *f;* denegación, *f,* rechazo, *m.* **non-aggression,** no agresión, *f.* **non-alcoholic,** no alcohólico. **non-appearance,** ausencia, *f; law* no comparecencia, contumacia, *f.* **non-arrival,** ausencia, *f;* falta de recibo, *f.* **non-attendance,** falta de asistencia, ausencia, *f.* **non-carbonated,** sin gas. **non-combatant,** no combatiente. **non-commissioned officer,**

oficial subalterno, *m.* **non-committal,** evasivo, equívoco, ambiguo. **non-compliance,** falta de obediencia, *f.* **non-concurrence,** falta de acuerdo, *f.* **non-conducting,** no conductivo. **non-conductor,** mal conductor, *m; elec* aislador, *m.* **non-contagious,** no contagioso. **non-cooperation,** *pol* resistencia pasiva, *f;* no cooperación, *f.* **non-delivery,** falta de entrega, *f.* **non-essential,** no esencial, prescindible. **non-execution,** no cumplimiento, *m.* **non-existence,** no existencia, *f.* **non-existent,** inexistente, no existente. **non-intervention,** no intervención, *f.* **non-manufacturing,** no industrial. **non-member,** visitante, *mf* **non-observance,** incumplimiento, *m;* violación, *f.* **non-payment,** falta de pago, *f.* **non-performance,** falta de ejecución, *f.* **non-poisonous,** no venenoso, innocuo. **non-resistance,** falta de resistencia, *f;* obediencia pasiva, *f.* **non-skid,** antideslizante, antirresbaladizo. **non-smoking,** que no fuma; (of a railway compartment, etc.) para no fumadores. **non-stop,** continuo, incesante; directo, sin parar; *aer* sin escalas

nonagenarian *a* and *n* nonagenario (-ia)

non-aligned *a* no abanderado

non-alignment *n* no abanderamiento *m*

nonce word *n* palabra ocasional, *f*

nonchalance *n* aplomo, *m,* indiferencia, frialdad, calma, *f*

nonchalant *a* indiferente, frío, impasible

nonchalantly *adv* con indiferencia

nonconformist *a* and *n* disidente *mf; a* inconforme, *n,* inconformista, *mf*

nonconformity *n* disidencia, *f*

nondescript *a* indeterminado, indefinido, indeciso, mediocre

none *pron* nadie, ninguno; nada. *a* and *n* ninguno (-na). *adv* no; de ningún modo, de ninguna manera. **I have n.,** No lo tengo, No tengo ninguno. **We have n. of your things,** No tenemos ninguna de tus cosas. **I was n. the worse,** No me hallaba peor. **N. can read his account with pleasure,** Nadie puede leer su narración con gusto. **n. the less,** no menos; sin embargo

nonentity *n* persona sin importancia, medianía, *f,* cero, *m*

nones *n pl ecc* nona, *f;* (Roman Calendar) nonas, *f pl,*

nonplussed *a* cortado, perplejo, confuso

non-profit *a* sin fines de lucro, sin fines lucrativos

non-self-governing *a* no autónomo

nonsense *n* disparate, despropósito, desatino, *m,* absurdidad, *f; inf* galimatías, *m;* pamplina, patraña, *f.* **to talk n.,** hablar sin ton ni son. **N.!** ¡A otro perro con este hueso! ¡Patrañas!

nonsensical *a* absurdo, ridículo, disparatado

noodle *n cul* tallarín, *m; inf* mentecato (-ta), bobo (-ba)

nook *n* escondrijo, lugar retirado, rincón, *m*

noon *n* mediodía, *m; fig* punto culminante, apogeo, *m,* *a* de mediodía, meridional. **at n.,** a mediodía

noose *vt* coger con lazos. *n* lazo corredizo, dogal, *m*

nopal *n bot* nopal, *m*

No Parking «Se Prohibe Estacionar,» «Se Prohibe Estacionarse»

nor *conjunc* ni, no, tampoco. **He removed neither his coat nor his hat,** No se quitó ni el gabán ni el sombrero. **Nor was this the first time,** Y no fue ésta la primera vez. **Nor I,** Ni yo tampoco

Nordic *a* and *n* nórdico (-ca)

norm *n* modelo, *m,* norma, regla, pauta, *f;* (of size) marca, *f;* (*bot zool*) tipo, *m*

normal *a* normal; común, natural, corriente, regular; *math* perpendicular, normal. *n* condición normal, *f,* estado normal, *m; math* normal, *f.* **to become n.,** normalizarse, hacerse normal. **to make n.,** normalizar. **n. school,** escuela normal, *f*

normality *n* normalidad, *f*

normalization *n* normalización, *f*

normalize *vt* normalizar

normally *adv* normalmente

Norman *a* and *n* normando (-da)

Normandy Normandía, *f*

Norse *n* noruego (language), *m*, *a* escandinavo

Norseman *n* normando, viking (*pl* -os), hombre del norte, *m*

north *n* norte, *m*. *a* del norte, septentrional. **n. by west,** norte, cuarta noroeste. **n. of the city,** al norte de la ciudad. **N.-American,** *a* and *n* norte-americano (-na). **n.-east,** *a* and *n* nordeste *m*. **n.-easter,** viento del nordeste, *m*. **n.-easterly,** del nordeste (winds). **n.-eastern,** del nordeste (places). **n.-eastward,** hacia el nordeste. **n.-n.-east,** nornordeste, *m*. **n.-n.-west,** nornorueste, *m*. **n.-polar,** ártico. **N. Star,** estrella del norte, estrella polar, *f*. **n.-west,** noroeste, *m*. **n.-wester,** viento del noroeste, *m*. **n.-westerly,** del noroeste (winds). **n.-westerly gale,** temporal del noroeste, *m*. **n.-western,** del noroeste; situado al noroeste. **n.-westwards,** hacia el noroeste. **n. wind,** el viento del norte, el cierzo

North America, Norteamérica, América del Norte, *f*

northern *a* del norte, septentrional, norteño; (of races) nórdico. **N. Cross,** crucero, *m*. **n. lights,** aurora boreal, *f*

northerner *n* hombre del norte, *m*, habitante del norte, *mf*

northernmost *a sup* al extremo norte, más septentrional

northwards *adv* hacia el norte

Norway Noruega, *f*

Norwegian *a* and *n* noruego (-ga); (language) noruego, *m*

nose *n* nariz, *f*; (of animals) hocico, *m*; (sense of smell) olfato, *m*; (of ships) proa, *f*; (of jug) pico, *m*, boca, *f*; (projecting piece) cuerno, *m*, nariz, *f*; (of airplane) cabeza, *f*, *vt* acariciar con la nariz; avanzar lentamente. *vi* husmear, olfatear. **to n. into,** *inf* meter las narices, poner fazga. **to n. out,** descubrir, averiguar. **to bleed at the n.,** echar sangre por las narices. **to blow one's n.,** sonar (or limpiarse) las narices. **to keep one's n. to the grindstone,** estar sobre el yunque, batir el cobre. *fig* **to lead by the n.,** tener a uno agarrado por las narices. **to pay through the n.,** costar un ojo de la cara. **to speak through the n.,** ganguear. **to turn up one's n.,** *fig* hacer gestos (a), volver la cara. **flat n.,** nariz chata, *f*. **snub n.,** nariz respingona, *f*. **well-shaped n.,** nariz perfilada, *f*. **under one's n.,** bajo las narices de uno. **n.-bag,** cebadera, mochila, *f*; morral, *m*. **n.-bleeding,** *med* epistaxis, *f*; hemorragia de las narices, *f*. **n.-dive,** *aer* descenso de cabeza, picado, *m*. *vi* picar. **n.-piece,** (of microscope) ocular, *m*. **n.-ring,** (of a bull, etc.) narigón, *m*

-nosed *a* de nariz . . . , con la nariz . . .

nosegay *n* ramillete, *m*

nosey Parker *n inf* mequetrefe, *m*; cócora, *Lat. Am.* averigüetas, *Argentina* hurguete, *mf*

No Smoking «Prohibido Fumar», Se Prohibe Fumar

nostalgia *n* nostalgia, añoranza, *f*

nostalgic *a* nostálgico

nostril *n* ventana de la nariz, *f*, *n pl* **nostrils,** narices, *fpl*

nostrum *n* panacea, *f*, curalotodo, *m*; medicina patentada, *f*

not *adv* no; sin; ni, ni siquiera. **Is it not true? We think not,** ¿No es verdad? No lo creemos. **You have seen Mary, have you not?** Vd. ha visto a María, ¿verdad? **not caring whether he came or not,** sin preocuparse de que viniese o no. **not that he will come,** no es decir que venga. **not at all,** de ningún modo; (courtesy) ¡de nada! **not even,** ni siquiera. **not guilty,** no culpable. **not one,** ni uno. **not so much as,** no tanto como; ni siquiera. **It is not so much that, as it is** . . . No es tanto eso, cuanto que . . . **not to say,** por no decir

notability *n* notabilidad, *f*; (person) notable, *mf* persona de importancia, *f*

notable *a* notable, señalado, memorable; digno de atención. *n* persona eminente, *f*, notable, *mf*

notably *adv* notablemente, señaladamente

notary *n* notario, escribano, *m*

notation *n* notación, *f*

notch *vt* cortar muescas (en); mellar, ranurar, entallar. *n* muesca, mella, ranura, entalladura, *f*

note *vt* notar, observar; anotar, apuntar; advertir, hacerse cuenta de. *n mus* nota, *f*; son, acento, *m*; (letter) recado, billete, *m*; anotación, glosa, *f*; apuntación, *f*, apunte, *m*, nota, *f*; (importance) importancia, distinción, *f*; *com* vale, abonaré, *m*; (sign) marca, señal, *f*. **to n. down,** anotar. **worthy of note,** digno de atención. **n.-book,** libro de apuntes, cuaderno, *m*, libreta, *f*. **n.-case,** cartera, *f*, *com* **n. of hand,** pagaré, *m*. **n.-paper,** papel de escribir, *m*. **n.-taker,** apuntador (-ra)

noted *a* célebre, famoso, ilustre, eminente, insigne

noteworthy *a* digno de nota, notable, digno de atención

nothing *n* nada, *f*; la nada; cero, *m*. *adv* en nada. **to come to n.,** anonadarse, fracasar. **to do n.,** no hacer nada. **to do n. but,** no hacer más que. **to have n. to do with,** no tener nada que ver con; *inf* no tener arte ni parte en. **There is n. else to do,** No hay nada más que hacer; No hay más remedio. **There is n. to fear,** No hay de que tener miedo. **We could make n. of the book,** No llegamos a comprender el libro. **for n.,** de balde, en vano; gratis. **next to n.,** casi nada. **n. else or more,** nada más. **n. like,** ni con mucho. **n. much,** poca cosa. **n. new,** nada nuevo. **n. similar,** nada semejante. **n. to speak of,** poca cosa

nothingness *n* nada, *f*

notice *vt* observar, reparar en, darse cuenta (de), marcar, caer en la cuenta (de), fijarse (en). *n* observación, atención, *f*; aviso, *m*, notificación, *f*; anuncio, *m*; (term) plazo, *m*; (review) crítica, *f*. **at short n.,** a corto aviso. **until further n.,** hasta nuevo aviso (or orden). **to attract n.,** atraer la atención. **I hadn't noticed,** No me había fijado. **to be beneath one's n.,** no merecer su atención. **to be under n.,** estar dimitido. **to bring to the n. of,** dar noticia de. **to escape n.,** pasar desapercibido. **to give n.,** hacer saber, informar; (of employer) despedir (a); (of employee) dimitir, dar la dimisión. **to take n. of,** notar, darse cuenta de; hacer caso, atender (a). **n. board,** letrero, tablero de anuncios, *m*. **n. to quit,** desahúcio, *m*

noticeable *a* perceptible, evidente; digno de observación, notable

noticeably *adv* perceptiblemente; notablemente

notifiable *a* declarable, notificable

notification *n* notificación, intimación, advertencia, *f*, aviso, *m*

notify *vt* notificar, comunicar, avisar, intimar, hacer saber

notion *n* noción, idea, *f*, concepto, *m*; (view) opinión, *f*, parecer, *m*; (novelty) novedad, *f*; artículo de fantasía, *m*. **I have a n. that . . . ,** Tengo la idea de que . . . , Sospecho que . . . **I haven't a n.,** No tengo idea

No Tipping «No Se Admiten Propinas»

notoriety *n* notoriedad, publicidad, *f*; escándalo, *m*; persona notoria, *f*

notorious *a* notorio, famoso, conocido; escandaloso, sensacional

notoriously *adv* notoriamente

notwithstanding *prep* a pesar de. *adv* sin embargo, no obstante. *conjunc* aunque, bien que, por más que

nougat *n* turrón, *m*

nought *n math* cero, *m*; nada, *f*

noun *n* substantivo, nombre, *m*

nourish *vt* sustentar, alimentar, nutrir; *fig* fomentar, favorecer

nourishing *a* nutritivo, alimenticio, nutricio

nourishment *n* nutrición, *f*; sustento, *m*; alimento, *m*; *fig* fomento, pasto, *m*

Nova Scotia Nueva Escocia, *f*

novel *a* nuevo, original, inacostumbrado. *n* novela, *f.* **n. of roguery,** novela picaresca, *f*

novelette *n* novela corta, *f*

novelist *n* novelista, *mf*

novelty *n* novedad, *f*; innovación, *f*; cambio, *m*

November *n* noviembre, *m*

novice *n ecc* novicio (-ia); comenzante, principiante, *mf*, aspirante, *m, Lat. Am.* advenedizo (-za)

novocain *n med* novocaína, *f*

now *adv* ahora, actualmente, al presente, a la fecha; en seguida, ahora, inmediatamente; poco ha, hace poco; pues bien. *interj* ¡A ver! ¡Vamos! *conjunc* pero, mas. *n* presente, *m*, actualidad, *f*. **before now,** antes, en otras ocasiones, ya, previamente. **just now,** ahora mismo, hace poco. **now . . . now,** ya . . . ya; sucesivamente, en turno. **now and then,** de vez en cuando, de tarde en tarde. **now that,** ya que, ahora que, dado que. **until now,** hasta el presente, hasta aquí, hasta ahora

nowadays *adv* hoy en día, actualmente, en nuestros días

nowhere *adv* en ninguna parte. **in the middle of n.,** donde Cristo dio las tres voces. **n. else,** en ninguna otra parte. *inf* **n. near,** ni con mucho; muy lejos (de)

nowise *adv* de ningún modo, en modo alguno, de ninguna manera

noxious *a* dañoso, nocivo; pestífero

noxiousness *n* nocividad, *f*

nozzle *n* (of a hose-pipe) boquilla, *f*; *mech* gollete, *m*; tubo de salida, *m*, tobera, *f*; inyector, *m*

n.p. (no place) s.l. (sin lugar)

nuance *n* matiz, *m*, gradación, sombra, *f*

nubile *a* núbil

nuclear *a* nuclear

nucleus *n* núcleo, *m*; centro, foco, *m*

nude *a* desnudo, nudo, *Peru* calato, *elsewhere in Lat. Am.* encuerado

nudge *vt* dar un codazo (a). *n* codazo, *m*

nudism *n* nudismo, *m*

nudist *n* nudista, *mf*

nudity *n* desnudez, *f*

nugget *n min* pepita, *f*

nuisance *n* molestia, incomodidad, *f*, fastidio, *m*; *inf* tostón, *m*, lata, *Lat. Am.* fregada, *Colombia* vaina, *f*. **to make a n. of oneself,** meterse donde no le llaman, ser un pelmazo. **What a n.!** ¡Qué lata! ¡Qué fastidio!, *Colombia* ¡Qué vaina!

null *a* nulo, inválido, sin fuerza legal. **n. and void,** nulo, írrito

nullification *n* anulación, invalidación, *f*

nullity *n* nulidad, *f*

numb *vt* entumecer, entorpecer. *a* entumecido; torpe, dormido; paralizado; *fig* insensible, pasmado. **n. with cold,** entumecido de frío

number *vt* numerar, contar; poner número (a); (pages of a book) foliar; ascender a. *n* número, *m*; (figure) cifra, *f*; (crowd) multitud, muchedumbre, *f*; cantidad, *f*; (of a periodical) ejemplar, *m*; *gram* número, *m*; *pl* versos, *m pl*. **Numbers,** (Bible) Números, *m pl*; **to be numbered among,** figurar entre. **among the n. of,** entre la muchedumbre de. **a n. of,** varios, muchos, una cantidad de. **in great n.,** en gran número; en su mayoría. **6 Peace Street,** Calle de la Paz n⁰ (número) 6. **one of their n.,** uno entre ellos. **n. board,** (racing)

indicador, *m*. **n. plate,** *aut* chapa de identidad, placa de número, *f*

numbering *n* numeración, *f*

numberless *a* innumerable, sin número, sin fin, infinito

numbness *n* entumecimiento, entorpecimiento, *m*; *fig* insensibilidad, *f*

numeral *a* numeral. *n* número, *m*, cifra, *f*; *gram* nombre o adjetivo numeral, *m*

numerator *n* numerador

numerical *a* numérico

numerous *a* numeroso; nutrido, grande; muchos (-as)

numerousness *n* numerosidad, multitud, muchedumbre, *f*

numismatic *a* numismático. *n pl* **numismatics,** numismática, *f*

numismatist *n* numismático, *m*

numskull *n* zote, topo, *m*

nun *n* monja, religiosa, *f*. **to become a nun,** profesar, tomar el hábito, meterse monja

nuncio *n* nuncio, *m*. **acting n.,** pronuncio, *m*

nunnery *n* convento de monjas, *m*

nuptial *a* nupcial. *n pl* **nuptials,** nupcias, *f pl*, enlace, *m*. **n. mass,** *ecc* misa de velaciones, *f*. **n. song,** epitalamio, *m*

nurse *vt* criar; dar de mamar (a), amamantar; (the sick) cuidar, asistir; (fondle) acariciar, mecer; *fig* fomentar, promover. *vi* trabajar como enfermera. *n* (of the sick) enfermera, *f*; (wet) nodriza, ama de leche, *Lat. Am.* criandera, *f*; (children's) niñera, *f*; *fig* fomentador, *m*. **male n.,** enfermero, *m*

nursery *n agr* plantel, vivero semillero, criadero, *m*; (children's room) cuarto de los niños, *m*; *fig* sementera, *f*; semillero, *m*. **n. governess,** aya, *f*. **n. rhyme,** canción infantil, *f*

nurseryman *n* horticultor, *m*; jardinero, *m*

nursing *n* lactancia, crianza, *f*; (of the sick) asistencia, *f*, cuido, *m*. **n. home,** clínica, *f*. **n. mother,** madre lactante, *f*

nurture *vt* alimentar; criar, educar. *n* nutrición, alimentación, *f*; crianza, educación, *f*

nut *vi* coger nueces. *n bot* nuez, *f*; *mech* tuerca, hembra de tornillo, *f, inf* **to be a tough nut to crack,** ser un tío de cuidado. **to crack nuts,** cascar nueces. **to go nutting,** coger nueces. **cashew nut,** anacardo, *m*. **loose nut,** *mech* tuerca aflojada, *f*. **nut-brown,** castaño. **nut tree,** nogal, *m*

nutcrackers *n pl* cascanueces, quebrantanueces, *m*

nutmeg *n* nuez moscada, nuez de especia, *f*

nutria *n zool* nutria, *f*

nutriment *n* nutrimento, alimento, *m*

nutrition *n* nutrición, alimentación, *f*

nutritious, nutritive *a* nutritivo, alimenticio, alible

nutshell *n* cáscara de nuez, *f*. **to put in a n.,** decir en resumidas cuentas, decir en forma apastillada

nutty *a* de nuez

nuzzle *vt* acariciar con la nariz

nylon *n* nilón, nylon, *m*. **n. stockings,** medias de cristal (or de nilón), *f pl*

nymph *n* ninfa, *f*; *ent* crisálida, *f*. **n.-like,** como una ninfa; de ninfa

nymphomania *n* ninfomanía, *f*, furor uterino, *m*

O

o *n* (letter) o, *f, interj* ¡o! **O that . . . !** ¡Ojalá que!

oaf *n* zoquete, zamacuco, *m*

oafish *a* lerdo, bobo

oafishness *n* torpeza, estupidez, *f*

oak *n* (tree and wood) roble, *m, a* de roble. **carved oak,** roble tallado, *m*. **holm-oak,** encina, *f*. **oak-apple,** agalla, *f*. **oak grove,** robledo, *m*

oakum *n* estopa, *f*

oar *n* remo, *m*. **to lie on the oars,** cesar de remar. **to pull at the oars,** bogar, remar. **to put in one's oar,** *inf* meter baza. **to ship the oars,** armar los remos. **to unship the oars,** desarmar los remos. **oar-stroke,** palada, *f*

oarsman *n* remero, bogador, *m*

oarsmanship *n* arte de remar, *m*, or *f*

OAS (Organization of American States) OEA (Organización de los Estados Americanos)

oasis *n* oasis, *m*

oast *n* horno para secar el lúpulo, *m*

oat *n bot* avena, *f*. **wild oat,** avena silvestre, *f*. **to sow one's wild oats,** correrla, andarse a la flor del berro. **oat field,** avenal, *m*

oath *n* juramento, *m*; (curse) blasfemia, *f*, reniego, *m*. **on o.,** bajo juramento. **to break an o.,** violar el juramento. **to put on o.,** tomar juramento, hacer prestar juramento. **to take an o.,** prestar (or hacer) juramento. **to take the o. of allegiance,** jurar la bandera

oatmeal *n* harina de avena, *f*

obduracy *n* obduración, obstinación, terquedad, *f*

obdurate *a* obstinado, terco, porfiado. **He is o. to our requests,** Es sordo a nuestros ruegos

obedience *n* obediencia, sumisión, docilidad, *f*. **blind o.,** obediencia ciega, *f*. **in o. to,** conforme a, de acuerdo con

obedient *a* obediente, sumiso, dócil. **to be o. to,** ser obediente (a), obedecer (a)

obediently *adv* obedientemente, dócilmente. **Yours o.,** Su atento servidor (su att. s.)

obeisance *n* reverencia, cortesía, *f*, saludo, *m*; (homage) homenaje, *m*

obelisk *n* obelisco, *m*

obese *a* obeso, corpulento, grueso, gordo

obesity *n* obesidad, gordura, corpulencia, *f*

obey *vt* and *vi* obedecer. *vt* (carry out) cumplir, observar. **to be obeyed,** ser obedecido

obfuscate *vt* ofuscar, cegar

obfuscation *n* ofuscamiento, *m*, confusión, *f*

obituary *a* mortuorio, necrológico. *n* obituario, *m*, necrología, *f*. **o. column,** (in newspaper) sección necrológica, *f*. **o. notice,** esquela de defunción, *f*

object *n* objeto, artículo, *m*, cosa, *f*; (purpose) propósito, intento, *m*; (aim) fin, término, *m*; *gram* complemento, *m*; *inf* individuo, *m*. *vt* objetar, poner reparos (a). *vi* oponerse, poner objeciones. **I o. to that remark,** Protesto contra esa observación. **If you don't o.,** Si Vd. no tiene inconveniente. **o. finder,** objetivo, *m*. **o. lesson,** lección de cosas, *f*; lección práctica, *f*

objection *n* objeción, protesta, *f*, reparo, *m*; (obstacle) dificultad, *f*, inconveniente, *m*. **to have no o.,** no tener inconveniente. **to raise an o.,** hacer constar una protesta, poner una objeción

objectionable *a* censurable, reprensible; desagradable, molesto

objective *a* objetivo; *gram* acusativo. *n* objeto, propósito, *m*; destinación, *f*; *mil* objetivo, *m*, *gram* **o. case,** caso acusativo, *m*,

objectivism *n phil* objetivismo, *m*

objectivity *n* objetividad, *f*

objector *n* objetante, *mf*, impugnador (-ra). **conscientious o.,** (dissident) el, *m*, (*f*, la) que protesta contra; (pacifist) pacifista, *mf*

oblation *n* oblación, ofrenda, *f*

obligation *n* obligación, *f*; deber, *m*, precisión, *f*; compromiso, *m*. **of o.,** de deber; de precepto. **to be under an o.,** estar bajo una obligación; deber un favor. **to place under an o.,** poner bajo una obligación

obligatory *a* obligatorio, forzoso

oblige *vt* (insist on) obligar, hacer, forzar; (gratify) hacer un favor (a), complacer. **He obliged me with a match,** Me hizo el favor de una cerilla. **They are much obliged to you,** Le están muy reconocidos. **Much obliged!** ¡Se agradece!

obliging *a* atento, condescendiente, complaciente, servicial, *Lat. Am.* acomedido

obligingly *adv* cortésmente

obligingness *n* cortesía, amabilidad, bondad, *f*

oblique *a* oblicuo, sesgado; (indirect) indirecto, evasivo; *gram* oblicuo

obliquely *adv* oblicuamente, al sesgo, sesgadamente; indirectamente. **to place o.,** poner al sesgo

obliquity *n* oblicuidad, *f*, sesgo, *m*; (of conduct, etc.) tortuosidad, *f*

obliterate *vt* borrar; destruir, aniquilar. **to be obliterated,** borrarse; quedar destruido

obliteration *n* testación, *f*; destrucción, *f*. **o. raid,** bombardeo de saturación, *m*

oblivion *n* olvido, *m*. **to cast into o.,** echar al olvido

oblivious *a* olvidadizo, descuidado

oblong *a* oblongo, cuadrilongo, rectangular. *n* rectángulo, cuadrilongo, *m*

obloquy *n* infamia, maledicencia, deshonra, *f*

obnoxious *a* odioso, ofensivo, aborrecible

obnoxiously *adv* odiosamente

obnoxiousness *n* odiosidad, *f*

oboe *n mus* oboe, *m*. **o. player,** oboe, *m*

obol *n* óbolo, *m*

obscene *a* indecente, obsceno, escabroso

obscenely *adv* obscenamente, escabrosamente

obscenity *n* indecencia, obscenidad, *f*

obscurantism *n* obscurantismo, *m*

obscurantist *a* and *n* obscurantista *mf*

obscure *a* (indistinct) obscuro, indistinto; (dark) lóbrego, tenebroso; (remote) retirado, apartado; (puzzling) confuso; (unknown) desconocido; humilde; (difficult to understand) abstruso, obscuro; (vague) vago. *vt* obscurecer; (hide) esconder; (eclipse) eclipsar. **to o. the issue,** hacer perder de vista el problema

obscurely *adv* obscuramente; humildemente, retiradamente; confusamente; vagamente

obscurity *n* (darkness) obscuridad, lobreguez, *f*; (difficulty of meaning) ambigüedad, confusión, vaguedad, *f*; humildad, *f*

obsequies *n pl* exequias, *f pl*, ritos fúnebres, *m pl*

obsequious *a* servil, empalagoso, zalamero

obsequiously *adv* servilmente

obsequiousness *n* servilismo, *m*, sumisión, *f*

observable *a* observable, perceptible, visible; notable

observably *adv* notablemente

observance *n* observancia, *f*, cumplimiento, *m*; práctica, costumbre, *f*; (religious) rito, *m*

observant *a* observador; obediente, atento. **o. of,** observador de; atento a

observation *n* observación, *f*, examen, escrutinio, *m*; (experience) experiencia, *f*; (remark) advertencia, *f*, comento, *m*. **to escape o.,** no ser advertido. **o. car.,** vagón-mirador, *m*, **o. post,** puesto de observación, *m*

observatory *n* observatorio, *m*

observe *vt* (laws) cumplir; (holy days, etc.) guardar; (notice) observar, mirar, notar, ver, reparar en; (remark) decir, advertir; (examine) vigilar, atisbar, examinar; *ast* observar. *vi* ser observador. **to o. silence,** guardar silencio

observer *n* observador (-ra)

obsess *vt* obsesionar, obcecar

obsessed *a* obseso

obsession *n* obsesión, obcecación, idea fija, manía, *f*

obsidian *n min* obsidiana, *f*

obsolescent *a* que se hace antiguo, que cae en desuso

obsolete *a* obsoleto, anticuado; *biol* rudimentario, atrofiado

obstacle *n* obstáculo, impedimento, *m*; dificultad, *f*, inconveniente, *m*. **to put obstacles in the way of,** *fig* dificultar, hacer difícil. **o. race,** carrera de obstáculos, *f*

obstetric *a* obstétrico

obstetrician *n* obstétrico (-ea), médico (-ca) partero (-ra)

obstetrics *n* obstetricia, tocología, *f*

obstinacy *n* obstinación, terquedad, tenacidad, porfía, *f*, tesón, *m*; persistencia, *f*

obstinate *a* terco, porfiado, obstinado, tenaz; refractario; persistente, pertinaz. **to be o.,** ser terco; porfiar. **to be o. about,** obstinarse en.

obstinately *adv* tercamente

obstreperous *a* turbulento, ruidoso

obstruct *vt* obstruir: impedir; cerrar; (thwart) estorbar; (hinder) dificultar, embarazar; (the traffic) obstruir, atascar. *vi* estorbar. **to become obstructed,** obstruirse, cerrarse

obstruction *n* obstrucción, *f*; estorbo, obstáculo, *m*. **to cause a street o.,** obstruir el tráfico

obstructionism *n* obstruccionismo, *m*

obstructionist *n* obstruccionista, *mf*

obstructive *a* estorbador, obstructor

obtain *vt* obtener, conseguir, lograr; recibir; (by threats) arrancar. *vi* estar en boga, estar en vigor, predominar. **to o. on false pretences,** conseguir por engaño

obtainable *a* asequible, alcanzable. **easily o.,** fácil a obtener

obtainer *n* conseguidor (-ra), adquisidor (-ra)

obtainment *n* obtención, *f*, logro, *m*

obtrude *vt* imponer

obtrusion *n* imposición, *f*; importunidad, *f*

obtrusive *a* importuno; entremetido; pretencioso

obtrusiveness *n* importunidad, *f*; entremetimiento, *m*

obtuse *a* (blunt) obtuso, romo; (stupid) estúpido, torpe, lerdo. **o. angle,** obtusángulo, *m*

obtuseness *n* (bluntness) embotamiento, *m*; (stupidity) estupidez, torpeza, *f*

obverse *a* del anverso. *n* anverso, *m*

obviate *vt* obviar, evitar

obvious *a* evidente, manifiesto, patente, obvio, aparente, transparente; poco sutil

obviously *adv* evidentemente, patentemente

obviousness *n* evidencia, transparencia, *f*

occasion *n* ocasión, *f*; oportunidad, *f*, momento oportuno, tiempo propicio, *m*; (reason) motivo, origen, *m*, causa, razón, *f*; (need) necesidad, *f*. *vt* ocasionar, causar, producir. **as o. demands,** cuando las circunstancias lo exigen, en caso necesario. **for the o.,** para la ocasión. **on one o.,** una vez. **on the o. of,** en la ocasión de. **on that o.,** en tal ocasión, en aquella ocasión. **He has given me no o. to say so,** No me ha dado motivos de decirlo. **There is no o. for it,** No hay necesidad para ello. **to have o. to,** haber de, tener que, necesitar. **to lose no o.,** no perder ripio (or oportunidad). **to rise to the o.,** estar al nivel de las circunstancias. **to take this o.,** aprovechar esta oportunidad

occasional *a* (occurring at times) de vez en cuando, intermitente; poco frecuente, infrecuente; (of verse) de ocasión. **o. table,** mesilla, *f*

occasionally *adv* de vez en cuando

occiput *n anat* occipucio, *m*

occlude *vt* obstruir, cerrar; *med* ocluir; *chem* absorber

occlusion *n* cerramiento, *m*; *med* oclusión, *f*; *chem* absorción de gases, *f*

occlusive *a* oclusivo

occult *a* oculto, escondido, misterioso; mágico. **o. sciences,** creencias ocultas, *f pl*

occultation *n ast* ocultación, *f*, eclipse, *m*

occultism *n* ocultismo, *m*

occultist *n* ocultista, *mf*

occupancy *n* ocupación, posesión, *f*; (tenancy) tenencia, *f*

occupant *n* habitante, *mf*; ocupante, *mf*; (tenant) inquilino (-na)

occupation *n* ocupación *f*; (tenure) inquilinato, *m*, tenencia, *f*; (work) trabajo, quehacer, *m*, labor, *f*; (employment) empleo, oficio, *m*; profesión, *f*

occupational *a* de oficio. **o. disease,** enfermedad profesional, *f*

occupier *n* ocupante, *mf*, inquilino (-na)

occupy *vt* ocupar; (live in) vivir en, habitar; (time) emplear, pasar; (take over) apoderarse de, ocupar. **to o. oneself in** or **with,** ocuparse en, ocuparse con. **to be occupied in** or **with,** estar ocupado con, ocuparse en

occur *vi* (happen) suceder, tener lugar, acaecer; (exist) encontrarse, existir; (of ideas) ocurrirse, venirse. **to o. to one's mind,** venírsele a las mientes. **to o. again,** volver a suceder, ocurrir de nuevo. **An idea occurred to her,** Se le ocurrió una idea

occurrence *n* ocurrencia, *f*; incidente, suceso, acontecimiento, *m*. **to be of frequent o.,** ocurrir con frecuencia, acontecer a menudo

ocean *n* océano, *m*; *fig* mar, abundancia, *f*. **o.-going vessel,** buque de alta mar, *m*

Oceania el Mundo Novísmo, *m*

oceanic *a* oceánico

oceanography *n* oceanografía, *f*

ocelot *n zool* ocelote, *m*

ocher *n* ocre, *m*

octagon *n* octágono, *m*

octagonal *a* octagonal

octave *n* (*ecc* metrics, *mus*) octava, *f*

octavo *n* (*print*) libro, etc. en octavo (8°), *m*. **in o.,** en octavo. **large o.,** octavo mayor, *m*. **small o.,** octavo menor, *m*

octet *n mus* octeto, *m*

October *n* octubre, *m*, 2 October 1996, el segundo (2°) de octubre de mil novecientos noventa y seis

octogenarian *a* and *n* octogenario (-ia)

octopus *n* pulpo, *m*

ocular *a* ocular, visual. *n* ocular, *m*

oculist *n* oculista, *mf*

odd *a* (of numbers) impar; (of volumes, etc.) suelto; (strange) raro, curioso, extraño, extravagante; (casual) casual, accidental; (extra) (extra) y pico, y tantos, sobrante; (of gloves, etc.) sin pareja. **at odd moments,** en momentos de ocio. **at odd times,** de vez en cuando. **thirty odd,** treinta y pico. **odd number,** número impare, *m*. **odd or even,** pares o impares. **odd trick,** (at cards) una baza más

oddity *n* excentricidad, rareza, extravagancia, *f*; (person) ente singular, *m*; (curio) objeto curioso, *m*, antigüedad, *f*

oddly *adv* singularmente

oddment *n* bagatela, baratija, *f*

oddness *n* singularidad, rareza, extravagancia, *f*

odds *n pl* diferencia, desigualdad, *f*; (superiority) ventaja, superioridad, *f*; (quarrel) disputa, riña, *f*. **The o. are that . . . ,** Lo más probable es que . . . **to fight against dreadful o.,** luchar contra fuerzas muy superiores. **o. and ends,** (remains) sobras y picos, *f pl*; (trifles) ñaques, *m pl*, chucherías, *f pl*

Odessa Odesa, *f*

odious *a* odioso, detestable, aborrecible, repugnante

odiousness *n* odiosidad, *f*

odium *n* odio, *m*

odor *n* olor, *m*, (fragrance) perfume, aroma, *m*, fragancia, *f*; *fig* sospecha, *f*. **in bad o.,** *fig* en disfavor. **o. of sanctity,** olor de santidad, *m*

odoriferous *a* odorífero; (perfumed) oloroso, perfumado

odorless *a* inodoro

odorous *a* fragante, oloroso

odyssey *n* odisea, *f*

of *prep* de. of has many idiomatic translations which are given as far as possible under the heading of the word concerned. It is also not translated. **I robbed him of his reward,** Le robé su recompensa. **I was thinking of you,** Pensaba en tí. **It was very good of you to . . . ,** Vd. ha tenido mucha bondad de . . . **Your naming of the child Mary,** El que Vd. haya dado el nombre de María al niño. **29th of Sept., 1936,** el 29 de septiembre de 1936. **Of course!** ¡Claro está! ¡Ya lo creo! ¡Naturalmente! **of late,** últimamente. **of the** (before *m, sing*) del; (before *f, sing*) de la; (before *m pl*) de los; (before *f pl*) de las. **to dream of,** soñar con. **to smell of,** oler a tener olor de. **to taste of, etc.,** saber a, tener gusto de.

off *prep* de; fuera de; cerca de; desde; *naut* a la altura de. **from off,** de. **Take your gloves off the table!** ¡Quítate los guantes de la mesa! **The wheel was off the car,** La rueda se había desprendido del coche. **to be off duty,** no estar de servicio; *mil* no estar de guardia. **to lunch off cold meat,** almorzar de carne fría. **off one's head,** chiflado

off *a* (contrasted with near) de la derecha, derecho; (unlikely) improbable, remoto. *adv* (with intransitive verbs of motion) se (e.g. **He has gone off,** Se ha marchado); (contrasted with on) de (e.g. **He has fallen off the horse,** Ha caído del caballo); (of place at a distance) lejos, a distancia de; (of time) generally a verb is used (e.g. **The wedding is three months off,** Faltan tres meses para la boda); (completely) enteramente. **Off** is often not translated in Sp. (e.g. **to put off,** aplazar, **to cut off,** cortar). **day off,** día libre, día de asueto, *m.* **How far off is the house from here? The house is five miles off.** ¿Cuántas millas está la casa de aquí? La casa está a cinco millas de aquí. **His hat is off,** Está sin sombrero, Se ha quitado el sombrero. **The cover is off,** La cubierta está quitada. **The party is off,** Se ha anulado la reunión. **6% off,** un descuento de seis por ciento. *interj* **Off with you!** ¡Márchate! ¡Fuera! **off and on,** de vez en cuando, espasmódicamente. **off color,** (ill) malucho; (of jokes) verde. **off season,** estación muerta, *f.* **off-shore,** a vista de tierra. **off-stage,** entre bastidores

offal *n* (butchers') menudencias, *f pl,* asadura, *f,* menudos, despojos, *m pl;* desperdicio, *m*

offend *vt* ofender; agraviar, insultar; herir; desagradar, disgustar; *vi* ofender, pecar. **to be offended,** resentirse, insultarse. **This offends my sense of justice,** Esto ofende mi sentimiento de justicia. **to o. against,** pecar contra; violar

offender *n* delincuente, *mf;* agraviador (-ra), pecador (-ra), transgresor (-ra). **old o.,** *law* criminal inveterado, *m*

offense *n* ofensa, transgresión, violación, *f;* pecado, *m; law* delito, crimen, *m;* (insult) agravio, *m,* afrenta, *f.* **the first o.,** el primer delito, *m.* **fresh o.,** nuevo delito, *m.* **political o.,** crimen político, *m. law* cuasidelito, *m.* **to commit an o. against,** ofender contra. **to take o.,** resentirse, darse por ofendido

offensive *a* ofensivo, desagradable, repugnante; (insulting) injurioso, agraviador, agresivo. *n mil* ofensiva, *f.* **to take the o.,** tomar la ofensiva

offensiveness *n* lo desagradable; (insult) ofensa, *f;* lo injurioso

offer *n* oferta, *f;* ofrecimiento, *m;* (of help) promesa, *f;* proposición, *f; com* oferta, *f. vt* ofrecer; prometer; (opportunities, etc.) deparar, brindar; tributar. *vi* ofrecerse, ocurrir, surgir. **to o. up,** ofrecer; inmolar, sacrificar. **He did not offer to go,** No hizo ademán de marcharse. **to o. resistance,** oponer resistencia. **o. of marriage,** oferta de matrimonio, *f*

offerer *n* ofrecedor (-ra)

offering *n* ofrecimiento, *m; ecc* ofrenda, oblación, *f,* sacrificio, *m;* regalo, don, *m,* dádiva, *f*

offhand *a* sin preparación, de repente; (casual) casual, despreocupado; (discourteous) brusco, descortés

offhandedly *adv* sin preparación, espontáneamente; negligentemente; bruscamente

office *n* oficina, *m;* (post) cargo, puesto, destino, *m;* (state department) ministerio, *m;* (of a Cabinet minister) cartera, *f;* (room) oficina, *f;* despacho, escritorio, *m;* (of a newspaper) redacción, *f;* (lawyer's) bufete, *m;* departamento, *m; ecc* oficio, *m pl.* **offices,** negocio, *m;* oficinas, *f pl;* (prayers) rezos, *m pl; ecc* oficio, *m pl.* **domestic offices,** dependencias, *f pl.* **good offices,** *fig* buenos oficios, *m pl.* **head o.,** casa central, oficina principal, *f.* **private o.,** despacho particular, *m.* **to be in o.,** estar en el poder. **o.-bearer,** miembro de la junta, *m;* funcionario, *m.* **o.-boy,** mozo de oficina, *m.* **o. employee,** oficinista, *mf.* **o. hours,** horas de oficina, *f pl;* (professions) horas de consulta, *f pl.* **o.-seeker,** aspirante, *m;* pretendiente, *m.* **o. work,** trabajo de oficina, *m*

officer *n* oficial, funcionario, *m;* (police) agente de policía, *m;* (of the Church) dignatario, *m;* (*mil nav aer*) oficial, *m.* *vt* mandar. **commissioned o.,** oficial, *m.* **non-commissioned o.,** oficial subalterno, *m.* **to be well officered,** tener buena oficialidad. **Officers' Training Corps,** Escuela de Oficiales, *f*

office worker *n* oficinista, *mf*

official *a* oficial; autorizado; ceremonioso, grave. *n* funcionario, *m;* oficial público, *m.* **high o.,** funcionario importante. *m.* **o. mourning,** duelo oficial, *m.* **o. receiver,** fiscal de quiebras, *m*

officialdom *n* funcionarismo, *m;* círculos oficiales, *m pl*

officiant *n* oficiante, *m*

officiate *vi* celebrar; oficiar, funcionar

officiating *a* oficiante; celebrante. **o. priest,** sacerdote oficiante, celebrante, *m*

officious *a* oficioso, entremetido

officiousness *n* oficiosidad, *f*

offing *n naut* mar afuera, *m.* **in the o.,** cerca

off season fuera de temporada

offset *n* compensación, *f, vt* compensar, neutralizar

offshoot *n* renuevo, vástago, *m*

offside *a* (of a car) del lado derecho (or izquierda); *sport* fuera de juego

offspring *n* vástago, *m;* descendiente, *mf;* prole, *f;* hijos, *m pl*

often *adv* a menudo, mucho, con frecuencia, frecuentemente, muchas veces. **as o. as,** tan a menudo como, siempre que. **as o. as not,** no pocas veces. **How o.?** ¿Cuántas veces? **It is not o. that . . . ,** No ocurre con frecuencia que . . . **so o.,** tantas veces, con frecuencia. **Do you go there o.?** ¿Va Vd. allí con frecuencia (or frecuentemente)? **Not o.,** Voy rara vez allá

ogival *a arch* ojival

ogive *n arch* ojiva, *f*

ogle *vt* and *vi* comer(se) con los ojos (a), ojear, guiñar el ojo (a). *n* ojeada, *f,* guiño, *m*

ogling *n* guiño, *m,* ojeada, *f*

ogre *n* ogro, *m*

oh! *interj* ¡o! **O no!** ¡Ca! ¡Claro que no!

ohm *n elec* ohmio, *m*

oil *n* aceite, *m;* petróleo, *m;* óleo, *m. vt* aceitar, engrasar, *Argentina* enaceitar; olear, ungir, untar; (bribe) sobornar, untar la mano; *fig* suavizar. *a* aceitero; petrolero. **to pour oil on troubled waters,** echar aceite sobre aguas turbulentas. **to strike oil,** encontrar un pozo de petróleo; *fig* encontrar un filón. **crude oil,** petróleo bruto, *m.* **heavy oil,** aceite pesado, *m.* **thin oil,** aceite ligero, *m. art* **in oils,** al óleo. **oil-bearing,** petrolífero. **oil-box,** engrasador, *m.* **oil-burner,** quemador de petróleo, *m.* **oil-can,** aceitera, *f.* **oil-colors,** pinturas al óleo, *f pl.* **oil field,** yacimiento petrolífero, campo de petróleo, *m.* **oil-filter,** separador de aceite, *m.* **oil-gauge,** nivel de aceite, *m.* **oil lamp,** velón, candil, quinqué, *m.* **oil of turpentine,** aceite de trementina, aguarrás, *m.* esencia de trementina, *f.* **oil-painting,** pintura al óleo, *f.* **oil pipeline,** oleoducto, *m.* **oil shop,** aceitería, *f.* **oil-silk,** encerado, *m.* **oil stove,** estufa de petróleo, *f.* **oil tanker,** *naut* petrolero, *m.* **oil-well,** pozo de petróleo, *m*

oilcake *n* bagazo, *m*

oilcloth *n* hule, *m;* linóleo, *m*

oiler *n* (can) aceitera, *f; naut* petrolero, *m;* lubricador, *m*

oiliness *n* oleaginosidad, untuosidad, *f*

oiling *n* engrasado, *m*

oilskin *n* encerado, *m*

oil seed *n* semilla oleaginosa, *f*

oily *a* aceitoso, grasiento

ointment *n* ungüento, *m,* pomada, *f*

old *a* viejo; antiguo; anciano; (of wines, etc.) añejo; (worn out) usado, gastado; (inveterate) arraigado, inveterado. **How old are you?** ¿Cuántos años tiene usted? **to be sixteen years old,** tener dieciséis años. **He is old enough to know his own mind,** Tiene bastante edad para saber lo que quiere. **to grow old,** envejecer. **to remain an old maid,** quedar soltera, *inf* quedarse para vestir imágenes. **of old,** antiguamente. **prematurely old,** revejido averiado. **old age,** vejez, senectud, *f.* **old bachelor,** solterón, *m.* **old clothes,** ropa vieja (or usada), ropa de segunda mano, *f.* **old-clothes dealer,** ropavejero (-ra). **old-clothes shop,** ropavejería, *f.* **old-established,** viejo. **old-fash-**

ioned, pasado de moda, viejo; (of people) chapado a la antigua. **old lady,** anciana, dama vieja, *f.* **old-looking,** de aspecto viejo, avejentado. **old maid,** solterona, *f.* **old-maidish,** remilgado. **old man,** viejo, *m; theat* barba, *m.* **old salt,** lobo de mar, *m.* **Old Testament,** Antiguo Testamento, *m.* **old wives' tale,** cuento de viejas, *m.* **old woman,** vieja, *f.* **Old World,** Viejo Mundo, mundo antiguo, *m*

old-age home *n* asilo de ancianos, *m*

olden *a* antiguo. **o. days,** días pasados, *m pl*

older *a comp* más viejo, mayor. **The older the madder,** A la vejez viruelas

old hat *n* viejo conocido

oldish *a* bastante viejo, de cierta edad

oldness *n* antigüedad, ancianidad, edad, *f*

oleaginous *a* oleaginoso

oleander *n bot* adelfa, *f,* baladre, *m*

olfactory *a* olfatorio, olfativo

oligarchic *a* oligárquico

oligarchy *n* oligarquía, *f*

olive *n* (tree) olivo, *m;* (fruit) aceituna, oliva, *f, a* aceitunado, *Lat. Am.* aceituno. **wild o. tree,** acebuche, *m.* **o.-complexioned,** con tez aceitunada. **o. green,** verde oliva, *m.* **o. grove,** olivar, *m.* **o. oil,** aceite de oliva, *m*

olympiad *n* olimpíada, *f*

olympian *a* olímpico

olympic *a* olímpico. **o. games,** juegos olímpicos, *m pl*

olympus *n* olimpo, *m*

omasum *n zool* librillo, libro, *m*

omber *n* tresillo, hombre, *m*

omega *n* omega, *f*

omelet *n* tortilla, *f.* **sweet o.,** tortilla dulce, *f*

omen *n* pronóstico, presagio, agüero, *m, vt* agorar, anunciar

ominous *a* ominoso, azaroso, siniestro, amenazante

ominously *adv* ominosamente, con amenazas

omission *n* omisión, *f;* olvido, descuido, *m;* supresión, *f*

omit *vt* omitir; olvidar, descuidar; (suppress) suprimir, excluir, callar, dejar a un lado

omitting *pres part* salvo, excepto

omnibus *n* ómnibus, autobús, *m.* **o. conductor,** cobrador de autobús, *m.* **o. driver,** conductor de autobús, *m.* **o. route,** trayecto de autobús, *m.* **o. service,** servicio de autobuses, *m.* **o. volume,** volumen de obras coleccionadas, *m*

omnipotence *n* omnipotencia, *f*

omnipotent *a* omnipotente, todopoderoso

omnipresence *n* omnipresencia, ubicuidad, *f*

omnipresent *a* ubicuo

omniscience *n* omnisciencia, *f*

omniscient *a* omniscio, omnisciente

omnivorous *a* omnívoro

on *prep* (upon) sobre, en, encima de; (concerning) de, acerca de, sobre; (against) contra; (after) después de; (according to) según; (with gerund) en; (with infin.) al; (at) a; (connected with, employed in) de; (by means of) por, mediante; (near to) cerca de, sobre; (into) en. Untranslated before days of week, dates of month or time of day (e.g. **on Monday,** el lunes. **on Friday afternoons,** los viernes por la tarde). **She has a bracelet on her wrist,** Tiene una pulsera en la muñeca. **He will retire on a good income,** Se jubilará con una buena renta. **on my uncle's death,** después de la muerte (or a la muerte) de mi tío, al morir. **On seeing them, he stopped,** Al verles se paró. **on leave,** con licencia, en uso de licencia. **on the next page,** en la página siguiente. **on this occasion,** en esta ocasión. **on the other hand,** en cambio. **on second thoughts,** luego de pensarlo bien. **on the way,** en camino. **on one side,** a un lado. **on the left,** a la izquierda. **on time,** a tiempo. **on my honor,** bajo palabra de honor. **on pain of death,** so pena de muerte, bajo pena de muerte. **on an average,** por término medio. **on his part,** por su parte. **on and after,** desde, a partir de. **on credit,** de fiado. **on fire,** ardiendo, en

llamas. **on foot,** a pie. **on purpose,** a propósito; con intención. **on,** *adv* puesto (e.g. **She has her gloves on,** Tiene los guantes puestos); (forward) adelante, hacia adelante; (continue, with a verb) seguir, continuar (e.g. **He went on talking,** Siguió hablando). Often **on** is included in Sp. verb (e.g. **The new play is on,** Se ha estrenado la nueva comedia. **The fight is on,** Ya ha empezado la lucha. **On!** *interj* ¡Adelante! **and so on,** y así sucesivamente. **to have on,** llevar puesto. **on and off,** de vez en cuando. **on and on,** sin cesar

onanism *n* onanismo, *m*

once *adv* una vez; (formerly) en otro tiempo, antiguamente; *conjunc* si (e.g. **O. you give him the opportunity,** Si le das la oportunidad). **all at o.,** todo junto, a un mismo tiempo; simultáneamente; (suddenly) súbitamente, de repente. **at o.,** en seguida, inmediatamente, *Lat. Am. also* lueguito. **for o.,** por una vez. **more than o.,** más de una vez. **not o.,** ni siquiera una vez. **o. before,** una vez antes. **o. and for all,** una vez para siempre; por última vez. **o. in a while,** de vez en cuando. **o. more,** otra vez. **o. or twice,** una vez o dos, algunas veces. **o. too often,** una vez demasiado. **O. upon a time,** En tiempos pasados, En tiempos de Maricastaña; (as beginning of a story) Érase una vez, Había una vez, Hubo una vez

once in a blue moon a cada muerte de un obispo

one *a* un, uno, una; (first) primero; (single) único, solo; (indifferent) igual, indiferente; (some, certain) algún, cierto, un (e.g. **one day,** cierto día). *n* uno; (hour) la una; (of age) un año. Often not translated in Sp. (e.g. **I shall take the blue one,** Tomaré el azul). *pron* se; uno. **one's,** su, de uno (e.g. **one's work,** el trabajo de uno). **I for one do not think so,** Yo por uno no lo creo. **It is all one,** Es igual, No hace diferencia alguna. **only one,** un solo. **that one,** ése, *m,* ésa, *f,* eso, *neut.* **this one,** éste, *m,* ésta, *f,* esto, *neut.* **those ones,** ésos, etc. **the one,** el (que), *m,* la (que), *f.* **with one accord,** unánimemente. **one and all,** todos. **one another,** se, uno a otro, mutuamente. **one by one,** uno a uno. **one day,** un día; un día de éstos, algún día. **one-eyed,** tuerto. **one-handed,** manco. **one-sided,** parcial. **one-way street,** *Spain* calle de dirección única, *Argentina* calle de una sola mano, *Mexico* calle de un sentido, calle de una corrida, *f.* **one-way traffic,** tráfico en una sola dirección, *m*

oneiric *a* onírico

oneness *n* unidad, *f*

onerous *a* oneroso, pesado, molesto, gravoso

onerousness *n* pesadez, molestia, dificultad, inconveniencia, *f*

one-seater *n* avión de una plaza, *m*

oneself *pron* se, uno mismo (una misma); (after prep.) sí mismo, sí. **It must be done by o.,** Uno mismo ha de hacerlo

onion *n* cebolla, *f.* **string of onions,** ristra de cebollas, *f.* **young o.,** babosa, *f.* **o. bed,** cebollar, *m.* **o. seed,** cebollino, *m.* **o. seller,** cebollero (-ra)

on-line *a computers* lineal

onlooker *n* espectado (-ra), observador (-ra); testigo, *mf*

only *a* único, solo. *adv* únicamente, sólo; no . . . más (que), tan sólo; con la excepción de, salvo. *conjunc* pero, salvo (que), si no fuera (que). **I shall o. give you three,** No te daré más de tres. **The o. thing one can do,** Lo único que se puede hacer. **I o. wished to see her,** Quería verla nada más. **if o.,** ¡ojalá (que)! **not o. . . . , no sólo . . . o.-begotten,** *a* unigénito. **o. child,** hijo (-ja) único (-ca)

onrush *n* asalto, ataque, acometimiento, *m,* acometida, embestida, *f;* (of water, etc.) acceso, *m;* torrente, *m,* corriente, *f*

onset *n* ataque, *m,* acometida, *f;* (beginning) principio, *m.* **at the first o.,** al primer ímpetu

onslaught *n* asalto, ataque, *m*

onus *n* responsabilidad, *f.* **o. of proof,** obligación de probar, *f*

onward *a* progresivo. *adv* adelante, hacia adelante; (as a command) ¡Adelante!

onyx *n* ónice, *m*

ooze *n* légamo, limo, fango, *m*, lama, *f. vi* exudar, rezumarse; manar; *vt* sudar. **to o. satisfaction,** caérsele (a uno) la baba. **to o. away,** (of money, etc.) desaparecer, volar. **to o. out,** (news) divulgarse

oozing *a* fangoso, legamoso, lamoso

opacity *n* opacidad, *f*

opal *n* ópalo, *m*

opalescence *n* opalescencia, *f*

opalescent *a* opalescente, iridiscente

opaline *a* opalino

opaque *a* opaco

opaqueness *n* opacidad, *f*

op. cit. (opere citato) obra cit. (obra citada)

open *vt* abrir; (a package) desempaquetar, desenvolver; (remove lid) destapar; *Lat. Am.* desenlatar (canned food); (unfold) desplegar; (inaugurate) inaugurar; iniciar, empezar; establecer; (an abscess) cortar; (with arms, heart, eyes) abrir; (with mind, thought) descubrir, revelar; (make accessible) franquear, hacer accesible; (tear) romper; *vi* abrirse; empezar, comenzar; (of a view, etc.) aparecer, extenderse; inaugurarse; (of a career, etc.) prepararse. **to o. fire against,** abrir el fuego contra. **to o. into,** comunicar con, salir a. **to o. into each other,** (of rooms) comunicarse. **to o. on,** mirar a, dar a, caer a. **to o. out,** *vt* abrir; desplegar; revelar. *vi* extenderse; revelarse. **to o. the eyes of,** *fig* desengañar, desilusionar. **to o. up,** abrir; explorar, hacer accesible; revelar; *fig inf* desabrocharse. **to o. with** or **by,** empezar con

open *a* abierto; descubierto; expuesto; (unfenced) descercado; (not private) público; libre; (unfolded) desplegado, extendido; (persuasible) receptivo; no resuelto, pendiente; (frank) franco, candoroso; (with sea) alto; (liberal) generoso, hospitalario; sin prejuicios; *com* abierto, pendiente; sin defensa; (of weather) despejado; (of a letter) sin sellar; (without a lid) destapado; (well-known) manifiesto, bien conocido. *n* aire libre, *m.* **in the o.,** al descubierto. **in the o. air,** aire libre, al raso, a cielo abierto. **to break o.,** forzar. **to cut o.,** abrir de un tajo, cortar. **to leave o.,** dejar abierto. **wide o.,** muy abierto; (of doors) de par en par. **o. boat,** barco descubierto, *m.* **o. car,** coche abierto, *m.* **o. carriage,** carruaje descubierto, *m.* **o. cast,** *min* roza abierta, *f.* **o.-eyed,** con los ojos abiertos. **o.-handed,** generoso, dadivoso, *Lat. Am. also* maniabierto. **o.-hat,** clac, *m.* **o.-house,** teatro de la ópera, *m.* **o. question,** cuestión por decidir, cuestión discutible, *f.* **o. secret,** secreto a voces, *m.* **o. sea,** alta mar, *f.* **o. town,** ciudad abierta, *f.* **o. tramcar,** jardinera, *f.* **o. truck,** vagoneta, *f.* **o.-work,** *sew* calado, enrejado, *m*

opener *n* abridor, *m*

opening *n* abertura, brecha, *f;* orificio, *m;* inauguración, apertura, *f;* principio, *m;* (chance) oportunidad, *f;* (employment) puesto, *m.* **o. price,** *com* (on Exchange) precio de apertura, *m,* primer curso *m*

openly *adv* abiertamente, francamente; públicamente

openness *n* situación expuesta, *f;* espaciosidad, *f;* franqueza, *f;* candor, *m;* imparcialidad, *f*

opera *n* ópera, *f.* **comic o.,** zarzuela, *f.* **o.-cloak,** abrigo de noche, *m.* **o.-glasses,** gemelos de teatro, *m pl.* **o.-hat,** clac, *m.* **o.-house,** teatro de la ópera, *m.* **o. singer,** cantante de ópera, operista, *mf*

operate *vi* funcionar, trabajar; obrar; (with on, upon) producir efecto sobre; influir; *surg* operar; (on Exchange) especular, jugar a la bolsa; *vt* hacer funcionar, manejar; mover, impulsar; dirigir

operatic *a* de ópera, operístico

operating *a* (of surgeons) operante; de operación. **o. table,** mesa de operaciones, *f.* **o. theater,** anfiteatro, *m;* sala de operaciones, *f*

operation *n* funcionamiento, *m,* acción, *f; surg* intervención quirúrgica, operación, *f;* (mil naut) maniobra,

f; manipulación, *f.* **to come into o.,** ponerse en práctica; hacerse efectivo. **to continue in o.,** (laws) seguir en vigor. **to perform an o.,** *surg* operar, praticar una intervención quirúrgica; hacer una maniobra. **to put into o.,** poner en práctica

operative *a* operativo, activo. *n* operario (-ia), obrero (-ra). **to become o.,** tener efecto

operator *n* operario (-ia); (telephone) telefonista, *mf;* (machines, engines) maquinista, *mf; surg* operador, *m*

operetta *n* opereta, *f*

ophthalmologist *n* oftalmólogo, *m*

ophthalmology *n* oftalmología, *f*

opiate *n* opiata, *f,* narcótico, *m, a* opiado

opine *vi* and *vt* opinar, creer

opinion *n* opinión, *f,* parecer, juicio, *m;* concepto, *m,* idea, *f.* **in my o.,** según mi parecer. **to be of the o. that,** ser de la opinión que, opinar que. **to be of the same o.,** estar de acuerdo, concurrir. **public o.,** opinión (or voz) pública, *f*

opinionated *a* terco, obstinado

opium *n* opio, *m.* **o. addict,** opiónamo (-ma). **o. den,** fumadero de opio, *m.* **o. eater,** mascador de opio, opiófago, *m.* **o. smoker,** fumador (-ra) de opio

Oporto Oporto, Porto, *m*

opponent *n* antagonista, *mf,* enemigo (-ga); contrario (-ia), adversario (-ia), competidor (-ra)

opportune *a* oportuno, tempestivo, conveniente, a propósito. **to be o.,** venir al caso. **o. moment,** momento oportuno, *m;* hora propicia, *f*

opportunely *adv* oportunamente. **to come o.,** venir a pelo

opportuneness *n* oportunidad, tempestividad, conveniencia, *f*

opportunism *n* oportunismo, *m*

opportunist *n* oportunista, *Lat. Am. also* maromero (-ra), *mf*

opportunity *n* oportunidad, ocasión, posibilidad, *f.* **to give an o. for,** dar margen para. **to open new opportunities,** abrir nuevos horizontes. **to take the o.,** tomar la oportunidad

opposable *a* oponible

oppose *vt* (counterbalance) oponer, contrarrestar; combatir; hacer frente (a), contrariar, pugnar contra, oponerse (a)

opposed (to) *a* opuesto a, enemigo de, contra

opposing *a* opuesto; enemigo, contrario

opposite *a* (facing) de cara a, frente a, del otro lado de; opuesto; (antagonistic) contrario, antagónico; otro, diferente. *n* contraria, *f,* lo opuesto; antagonista, *mf;* adversario (-ia). **the o. sex,** el otro sexo. **o. leaves,** *bot* hojas opuestas, *f pl.* **o. to,** frente a; distinto de

opposition *n* oposición, *f;* (obstacle) estorbo, impedimento, *m,* dificultad, *f;* resistencia, hostilidad, *f;* (ast pol) oposición, *f;* (difference) contraste, *m,* diferencia, *f. a* de la oposición. **in o.,** en oposición; *pol* en la oposición. **to be in o.,** estar en oposición; *pol* ser de la oposición, estar en la oposición

oppress *vt* oprimir, tiranizar, sojuzgar, apremiar; (of moral causes) abrumar, agobiar, desanimar; (of heat, etc.) ahogar

oppression *n* opresión, tiranía, crueldad, *f;* (moral) agobio, sufrimiento, *m,* ansia, *f;* (difficulty in breathing) sofocación, *f,* ahogo, *m*

oppressive *a* opresivo, tiránico, cruel; (taxes, etc.) gravoso; (of heat) sofocante, asfixiante; agobiador, abrumador

oppressor *n* opresor (-ra), sojuzgador (-ra), tirano (-na)

opprobrious *a* oprobioso, vituperioso; infame

opprobrium *n* oprobio, *m,* ignominia, *f*

opt *vi* optar, escoger, elegir

optic, optical *a* óptico. **o. illusion,** ilusión óptica, *f;* engaño a la vista, trampantojo, *m.* **o. nerve,** nervio óptico, *m*

optician *n* óptico, *m*

optics *n* óptica, *f*

optimism *n* optimismo, *m*

optimist *n* optimista, *mf*
optimistic *a* optimista
optimum *n* lo óptimo; (used as adjective) óptimo
option *n* opción, *f*, (all meanings)
optional *a* discrecional, facultativo
opulence *n* opulencia, riqueza, magnificencia, *f*; (abundance) abundancia, copia, *f*
opulent *a* opulento, rico, acaudalado; abundante
opus *n* obra, composición, *f*
opuscule *n* opúsculo, *m*
or *conjunc* o; (before a word beginning with o or ho) u; (negative) ni. *n her* oro, *m*. **an hour or so,** una hora más o menos, alrededor de una hora. **either . . . or,** o . . . o. **or else, or bien. whether . . . or,** que . . . que, siquiera . . . siquiera, ya . . . ya. **without . . . or,** sin . . . ni
oracle *n* oráculo, *m*
oracular *a* profético, vatídico; ambiguo, misterioso, sibilino; dogmático, magistral
oral *a* verbal, hablado; *anat* oral, bucal
oral cavity *n* cavidad bucal, *f*
orange *n* (tree) naranjo, *m*; (fruit) naranja, *f*; **bitter o.,** naranja amarga, *f*. **blood o.,** naranja dulce, *f*. **tangerine o.,** naranja mandarina, *f*. **o. blossom,** azahar, *m*. **o. color,** color de naranja, *m*. **o.-colored,** de color de naranja, anaranjado. **o.-flower water,** agua de azahar, *f*. **o. grove,** naranjal, *m*. **o. grower** (or **seller**), naranjero (-ra). *m*. **o. peel,** piel de naranja, *f*. **o.-stick,** (for nails) limpiauñas, *m*
orangeade *n* naranjada, *f*; (mineral water) gaseosa, *f*
orangery *n* naranjal, *m*
orangoutan *n zool* orangután, *m*
oration *n* oración, declamación, *f*, discurso, *m*
orator *n* orador (-ra), declamador (-ra)
oratorical *a* oratorio, declamatorio, retórico
oratorio *n mus* oratorio, *m*
oratory *n* oratoria, elocuencia, *f*; *ecc* oratorio, *m*, capilla, *f*
orb *n* orbe, *m*; esfera, *f*, globo, *m*; astro, *m*; *poet* ojo, *m*
orbit *n ast* órbita, *f*; *anat* órbita, cuenca del ojo, *f*
orbital *a anat* orbital
orchard *n* huerto, vergel, *m*; (especially of apples) pomar, *m*
orchestra *n* orquesta, *f*. **with full o.,** con gran orquesta. *theat* **o. seat, o. stall,** butaca de piatea, *f*
orchestral *a* orquestal, instrumental
orchestrate *vt* orquestar, instrumentar
orchestration *n* orquestación, instrumentación, *f*
orchid *n* orquídea, *f*
orchitis *n med* orquitis, *f*
ordain *vt* mandar, disponer, decretar; *ecc* ordenar. **to be ordained as,** *ecc* ordenarse de
ordeal *n hist* ordalías, *f pl*; prueba severa, *f*
order *n* (most meanings) orden, *m*; (command) precepto, mandamiento, decreto, *m*; orden, *f*; (rule) regla, *f*; (for money) libranza postal, *f*; (for goods) pedido, encargo, *m*; (arrangement) método, arreglo, *m*, clasificación, *f*; (condition) estado, *m*; *arch* estilo, *m*; (*zool bot*) orden, *m*; (sort) clase, especie, *f*; (rank) clase social, *f*; *ecc* orden, *f*; (badge) condecoración, insignia, *f*; (association) sociedad, asociación, compañía, *f*; (to view a house, etc.) permiso, *m*; (series) serie, *f*. **His liver is out of o.,** No está bién del hígado. **in good o.,** en buen estado; arreglado. **in o.,** (alphabetical, etc.) en orden; arreglado; (parliamentary) en regla. **in o. that,** para que, a fin de que. **in o. to, a fin de, para. out of o.,** estropeado, descompuesto; (on a notice) No funciona; (parliamentary) fuera del orden del dia. **till further o.,** hasta nueva orden. **o.,** *com* por encargo especial. **to give an o.,** dar una orden; *com* poner un pedido. **to go out of o.,** descomponerse. **to keep in o.,** mantener en orden. **to put in o.,** poner en orden, ordenar. **to take holy orders,** tomar órdenes sagradas. **O.!** ¡Orden! **O. in Council,** orden real, *f*. **o. of knighthood,** orden de caballería, *f*. **o. of the day,** orden del día, *f*. **o. paper,** orden del día, *f*; reglamento, *m*
order *vt* disponer; arreglar; (command) mandar, orde-

nar; (request) rogar, pedir; (direct) dirigir, gobernar; *com* encargar, cometer; (a meal, a taxi) encargar. **I ordered them to do it,** Les mandé hacerlo. **to o. about,** mandar. **to o. back,** hacer volver, mandar que vuelva. **to o. down,** hacer bajar, pedir (a uno) que baje. **to o. in,** mandar entrar. **to o. off,** despedir, decir (a uno) que se vaya. **to o. out,** mandar salir; (the troops) hacer salir la tropa; echar. **to o. up,** mandar subir, hacer subir
orderliness *n* orden, aseo, método, *m*; limpieza, *f*; buena conducta, formalidad, *f*; buena administración, *f*
orderly *a* bien arreglado, metódico; aseado, en orden; (of behaviour) formal, bien disciplinado. *n mil* ordenanza, *m*; ayudante de hospital *m*
ordinal *a* and *n* ordinal *m*
ordinance *n* ordenanza, *f*, reglamento, *m*; *arch* ordenación, *f*; *ecc* rito, *m*
ordinarily *adv* de ordinario, ordinariamente, comúnmente
ordinary *a* (usual) corriente, común, usual, ordinario, normal; (average) mediano, mediocre; (somewhat vulgar) ordinario, vulgar. *n ecc* ordinario, *m*. **out of the o.,** excepcional; poco común. **o. seaman,** marinero, *m*. **o. share,** *com* acción ordinaria, *f*
ordination *n ecc* ordenación, *f*
ordnance *n* artillería, *f*, cañones, *m pl*; pertrechos de guerra, *m pl*. **o. survey map,** mapa del estado mayor, *m*. **o. survey number,** acotación, *f*
ore *n min* mena, *f*, quijo, *Lat. Am.* llampo, *m*
organ *n* (all meanings) órgano, *m*. **barrel-o.,** organillo, órgano de manubrio, *m*. **o.-blower,** entonador (-ra). **o.-grinder,** organillero (-ra). **o.-loft,** tribuna del órgano, *f*. **o.-pipe,** cañón de órgano, *m*. **o.-stop,** registro de órgano, *m*
organdie *n* organdí, *m*
organic *a* orgánico. **o. chemistry,** química orgánica, *f*
organism *n* organismo, *m*
organist *n* organista, *mf*
organization *n* organización, *f*; grupo, *m*, asociación, sociedad, *f*; organismo, *m*
organize *vt* organizar; arreglar. *vi* organizarse; asociarse, constituirse
organizer *n* organizador (-ra)
organizing *a* organizador
orgasm *n med* orgasmo, *m*
orgiastic *a* orgiástico
orgy *n* orgía, *f*
oriel *n arch* mirador, *m*
orient *a poet* naciente, oriental. *n* Oriente, Este, *m*. **pearl of fine o.,** perla de hermoso oriente, *f*
oriental *a* and *n* oriental, *mf*
orientalism *n* orientalismo, *m*
orientalist *n* orientalista, *mf*
orientate *vt* orientar; dirigir, guiar. *vi* mirar (or caer) hacia el este; orientarse
orientation *n* orientación, *f*
orifice *n* orificio, *m*; abertura, boca, *f*
origin *n* origen, génesis, *m*; raíz, causa, *f*; principio, comienzo, *m*; (extraction) descendencia, procedencia, familia, *f*; nacimiento, *m*
original *a* original; primitivo, primero; ingenioso. *n* original, *m*; prototipo, modelo, *m*. **o. sin,** pecado original, *m*
originality *n* originalidad, *f*
originally *adv* originalmente; al principio; antiguamente
originate *vt* (produce) ocasionar, producir, suscitar, iniciar, engendrar; (create) inventar, crear. *vi* originarse, surgir, nacer. **to o. in,** tener su origen en, surgir de, emanar de, venir de
origination *n* origen, principio, génesis, *m*
originator *n* iniciador (-ra), fundador (-ra); autor (-ra), creador (-ra)
oriole *n orn* oropéndola, *f*
Orion *n ast* Orión, *m*

Orkneys, the las Orcades, *f pl*

ornament *n* adorno, *m*; decoración, *f*; *fig* ornamento, *m*; (trinket) chuchería, *f*, *n pl*. **ornaments,** *ecc* ornamentos, *m pl*. *vt* ornar, adornar, decorar, embellecer

ornamental *a* ornamental, decorativo

ornamentation *n* ornamentación, decoración, *f*

ornate *a* vistoso, ornado en demasía, barroco

ornateness *n* elegancia, vistosidad, magnificencia, *f*

ornithological *a* ornitológico

ornithologist *n* ornitólogo, *m*

ornithology *n* ornitología, *f*

orphan *a* and *n* huérfano (-na)

orphanage *n* orfanato, hospicio, *m*

orphanhood *n* orfandad, *f*

Orphean *a* órfico

orthodox *a* ortodoxo

orthodoxy *n* ortodoxia, *f*

orthographic *a* ortográfico

orthography *n* ortografía, *f*

orthopedic *a* ortopédico

orthopedics *n* ortopedia, *f*

orthopedist *n* ortopedista, *mf* ortopédico (-ca)

oscillate *vi* oscilar, fluctuar; (hesitate) dudar, vacilar. *vt* hacer oscilar

oscillation *n* oscilación, fluctuación, vibración, *f*; *elec* oscilación, *f*

oscillator *n* oscilador, *m*

oscillatory *a* oscilante

osculation *n* ósculo, *m*

osier *n bot* mimbre, *m*, or *f*. **o. bed,** mimbrera, *f*

osmic *a chem* ósmico

osmosis *n* (*phys chem*) ósmosis, *f*

osprey *n orn* quebrantahuesos, *m*

osseous *a* óseo

ossification *n* osificación, *f*

ossify *vt* osificar; *vi* osificarse

ossuary *n* osario, *m*

osteitis *n med* osteítis, *f*

Ostend Ostende, *m*

ostensible *a* ostensible; aparente, engañoso, ilusorio

ostensibly *adv* en apariencia, ostensiblemente

ostentation *n* ostentación, *f*; aparato, fausto, boato, alarde, *m*, soberbia, *f*

ostentatious *a* ostentoso; aparatoso, fastuoso, rumboso

ostentatiously *adv* con ostentación

osteology *n* osteología, *f*

osteomyelitis *n med* osteomielitis, *f*

osteopath *n* osteópata, *m*

osteopathy *n* osteopatía, *f*

osteoplasty *n surg* osteoplastia, *f*

ostler *n* mozo de cuadras, establero, *m*

ostracism *n* ostracismo, *m*

ostracize *vt* desterrar; excluir del trato, echar de la sociedad

ostrich *n* avestruz, *m*. **o. farm,** criadero de avestruces, *m*

otalgia *n med* otalgia, *f*, dolor de oídos, *m*

other *a* otro. *pron* el otro, *m*; la otra, *f*; lo otro, *neut adv* (with than) de otra manera que, de otro modo que; otra cosa que. **this hand, not the o.,** esta mano, no la otra. **every o. day,** un día sí y otro no, cada dos días. **no o.,** ningún otro, *m*; otra ninguna, *f*. **someone or o.,** alguien. **the others,** los (las) demás, *m, f pl*; los otros, *m pl*; las otras, *f pl*. **o. people,** otros, *m pl*, los demás

otherwise *adv* de otra manera, de otro modo, otramente; (in other respects) por lo demás, por otra parte; (if not) si no

otitis *n med* otitis, *f*

otologist *n* otólogo, *m*

otology *n* otología, *f*

otter *n zool* nutria, *f*. **o. hound,** perro para cazar la nutria

ottoman *a* otomano, turco. *n* otomana, *f*

ouch! *interj* ¡ax!, ¡huy!

ought *v aux* deber, tener la obligación (de); ser conveniente, convenir; ser necesario (que), tener que. **I o.**

to have done it yesterday, Debía haberlo hecho ayer. **She o. not to come,** No debe (debiera, debería) venir. **He o. to see them tomorrow,** (should) Conviene que les vea mañana; Tiene la obligación de verles mañana; (must) Es necesario que les vea mañana, Tiene que verles mañana

ounce *n* (animal and weight) onza, *f*. **He hasn't an o. of common sense,** No tiene pizca de sentido común

our *a* nuestro

ours *pron* nuestro, *m*; nuestra, *f*; nuestros, *m pl*; nuestras, *f pl*; de nosotros, *m pl*; de nosotras, *f pl*; el nuestro, *m*; la nuestra, *f*; lo nuestro, *neut*; los nuestros, *m pl*; las nuestras, *f pl*. **This book is ours,** Este libro es nuestro (or el nuestro)

ourselves *pron pl* nosotros mismos, *m pl*; nosotras mismas, *f pl*

oust *vt* despedir, desahuciar, expulsar, echar

out *adv* afuera; hacia fuera; (gone out) fuera, salido, ausente; (invested) puesto; (published) publicado, salido; (discovered) conocido, descubierto; (on strike) en huelga; (mistaken) en error, equivocado; (of journeys) de ida, (on ships) de navegación (e.g. **on the second day out,** al segundo día de navegación); (of fire, etc.) extinguido; (at sea) en el mar; (of girls in society) puesta de largo, que ha entrado en sociedad; (of fashion) fuera de moda; (of office) fuera del poder; (in holes) roto, agujereado, andrajoso; (exhausted) agotado; (expired) vencido; (of a watch) llevar . . . minutos (horas) de atraso or de adelanto; (unfriendly) reñido; (way out) salida, *f*; (sport) fuera de juego; (of flowers) abierto; (of chickens) empollado. **a scene out of one of Shakespeare's plays,** una escena de una de las comedias de Shakespeare. **I am out $6,** He perdido seis dólares. **I am out of tea,** Se me ha acabado el té. **to drink out of a glass,** beber de un vaso. **to read out of a book,** leer en un libro. **to speak out,** hablar claro. **Murder will out,** El asesinato se descubrirá.

out-and-out, completo; (with rogue, etc.) redomado.

out of, fuera de; (beyond) más allá de; (through, by) por; (with) con; (without) sin; (from among) entre; (in) en; (with a negative sense) no. **out of breath,** jadeante, sin aliento. **out of character,** impropio. **out of commission,** fuera de servicio. **out of danger,** fuera de peligro. **out of date,** anticuado. **out of hand,** en seguida; indisciplinado. **out of money,** sin dinero. **out of necessity,** por necesidad. **out of one's mind,** loco, demente. **out of order.** See **out of print.** **out of reach,** fuera de alcance, inasequible. **out of season,** fuera de temporada. **out of sight,** fuera del alcance de la vista; invisible. **Out of sight, out of mind,** Ojos que no ven, corazón que no siente. **out of sorts,** indispuesto. **out of temper,** de mal genio. **out of the question,** imposible. **out of the way,** *adv* (of work) terminado, hecho; (remote) fuera del camino; (put aside) arrinconado; donde no estorbe.

out-of-the-way, *a* remoto, aislado; (unusual) extraordinario, singular. **out of this world,** lo máximo, lo último. **out of touch with,** alejado de; sin relaciones con; sin simpatía con. **out of work,** sin empleo, sin trabajo, en paro forzoso. **out-patient,** enfermo (-ma) de un dispensario. **Out!** *interj* ¡Fuera! ¡Fuera de aquí! ¡Márchate! **Out with it!** ¡Hable Vd.! sin rodeos! ¡Hablen claro!

outbalance *vt* exceder, sobrepujar

outbid *vt* pujar, mejorar

outbidding *n* puja, mejora, *f*

outbreak *n* (of war) declaración, *f*; comienzo, *m*; (of disease) epidemia, *f*; (of crimes, etc.) serie, *f*

outbuilding *n* dependencia, *f*, edificio accesorio, anexo, *m*

outburst *n* acceso, arranque, *m*, explosión, *f*

outcast *n* paria, *mf*; desterrado (-da), proscripto (-ta)

outclass *vt* aventajar, ser superior (a), exceder

outcome *n* consecuencia, *f*, resultado, *m*

outcry *n* clamor, grito, *m*; protesta, *f*

outdistance *vt* dejar atrás

outdo *vt* eclipsar, aventajar, sobrepujar

outdoor *a* externo; (of activities) al aire libre; fuera de casa

outdoors *adv* fuera de casa; al aire libre

outer *a* externo, exterior

outer space espacio extraatmosférico, espacio extraterreste, espacio exterior, espacio sideral, espacio sidéreo, espacio ultraterrestre, *m*

outermost *a sup* (el, etc.) más externo, más exterior; extremo, de más allá

outfit *n* equipo, *m*; (of clothes) traje, *m*; (of furniture or trousseau) ajuar, *m*; (gear) pertrechos, avíos, *m pl. vt* aviar equipar

outfitter *n* proveedor (-ra), abastecedor (-ra)

outflank *vt mil* flanquear; ser más listo (que)

outgoing *a* saliente, que sale; cesante. **outgoings,** *n pl* gastos, *m pl*

outgrow *vt* hacerse demasiado grande para; crecer más que; (ideas) perder; (illness) curarse de, curarse con la edad; pasar de la edad de, ser ya viejo para. **to o. one's clothes,** quedársele a uno a chica la ropa. **to o. one's strength,** estar demasiado crecido para su edad

outgrowth *n* excrecencia, *f*; resultado, fruto, *m*, consecuencia, *f*

outhouse *n* edificio accesorio, *m*

outing *n* excursión, vuelta, *f*, paseo, *m*

outlandish *a* extraño, singular, raro; absurdo, ridículo

outlast *vt* durar más que; (outlive) sobrevivir a

outlaw *n* bandido, proscrito, *m*, *vt* proscribir

outlay *n* gasto, desembolso, *m*

outlet *n* salida, *f*; orificio de salida, *m*; (of drains, etc.) desagüe, *m*; (of streets, rivers) desembocadura, *f*; *fig* escape, *m*, válvula de seguridad, *f*

outline *n* perfil, contorno, *m*; (drawing) esbozo, bosquejo, *m*; idea general, *f*; plan general, *m*, *vt* esbozar, bosquejar. **in o.,** en esbozo; en perfil. **to be outlined** (against), dibujarse (contra), destacarse (contra)

outlive *vt* sobrevivir (a); (live down) hacer olvidar

outlook *n* (view) perspectiva, vista, *f*; (opinion) actitud, *f*, punto de vista, *m*; aspecto, *m*, apariencia, *f*; (for trade, etc.) perspectiva, *f*, posibilidades, *f pl*. **o. tower,** atalaya, *f*

outlying *a* remoto, lejano, distante

outmaneuver *vt* superar en estrategia

outmatch *vt* aventajar, superar

outmoded *a* anticuado, pasado de moda

outnumber *vt* ser más numerosos que, exceder en número

out-of-court settlement *n* arreglo pacífico, *m*

out-of-town *a* de las provincias

outpost *n mil* avanzada, *f*, puesto avanzado, *m*

outpouring *n* derramamiento, *m*; efusión, *f*

output *n* producción, *f*. **o. capacity,** capacidad de producción, *f*

outrage *n* barbaridad infamia, atrocidad, *f*; rapto, *m*, violación, *f*. *vt* ultrajar; violar; violentar

outrageous *a* atroz, terrible; desaforado, monstruoso; injurioso; ridículo

outrageousness *n* lo atroz; violencia, furia, *f*; escándalo, *m*; enormidad, *f*; lo excesivo; lo horrible

outré *a* cursi, extravagante

outride *vt* cabalgar más a prisa que

outright *adv* (frankly) de plano (e.g. **to reject outright,** rechazar de plano), francamente, sin reserva; (immediately) en seguida, immediatamente. *a* categórico; completo; franco

outrival *vt* vencer, superar

outrun *vt* correr más que

outset *n* principio, comienzo, *m*

outshine *vt* brillar más que, eclipsar en brillantez; superar, eclipsar

outside *adv* afuera, fuera. *prep* fuera de, al otro lado de, al exterior de; (besides) aparte de, fuera de. *a* externo, exterior; (of labor, etc.) desde fuera; máximo; ajeno. *n* exterior, *m*; superficie, *f*; aspecto, *m*, apariencia, *f*. **at the o.,** a lo sumo, cuando más. **from the o.,** de (or

desde) fuera. **on the o.,** (externally) por fuera. **o. the door,** a la puerta

outsider *n* forastero (-ra); desconocido (-da), *Argentina, Chile also* cuico (-ca); caballo desconocido, *m*; persona poco deseable, *f*

outsize *n* artículo de talla mayor que las corrientes, *m*

outskirts *n pl* alrededores, *m pl*, afueras, immediaciones, cercanías, *f pl*

outspoken *a* franco. **to be o.,** decir lo que se piensa, no tener pelos en la lengua

outspokenness *n* franqueza, *f*,

outspread *a* extendido; (of wings) desplegadas

outstanding *a* excelente; sobresaliente, conspicuo; *com* pendiente, sin pagar. **to be o.,** *com* estar pendiente; *fig* sobresalir. **o. account,** *com* cuenta pendiente, *f*

outstay *vt* quedarse más tiempo que. **to o. one's welcome,** pegársele la silla

outstretched *a* extendido

outstrip *vt* dejar atrás, pasar; aventajar, superar

outvote *vt* reunir más votos que; rechazar por votación

outward *a* exterior, externo; aparente, visible. *adv* exteriormente; hacia fuera; superficialmente. **o. bound,** con rumbo a . . . **o. voyage,** el viaje de ida

outwardly *adv* exteriormente; hacia fuera; en apariencia

outwear *vt* durar más que; gastar

outweigh *vt* exceder, valer más que

outwit *vt* ser más listo que; vencer

outworn *a* anticuado, ya viejo

oval *n* óvalo, *m*, *a* oval, ovalado, aovado

ovarian *a* (*bot zool*) ovárico

ovary *n* ovario, *m*

ovation *n* ovación, recepción entusiasta, *f*

oven *n* horno, *m*. **o. peel,** pala de horno, *f*. **o. rake,** hurgón, *m*

over *prep* (above, upon, over) sobre, encima de; (on the other side) al otro lado de; (across) allende, a través de; (more than) más de; (beyond) más allá de; (of rank) superior a; (during) durante; (in addition) además de; (through) por. *n* (cricket) serie de saques, *f*, *adv* encima; en; por encima; al otro lado; de un lado a otro; enfrente; al lado contrario; de un extremo a otro; (finished) terminado; (ruined) arruinado, perdido; (more) más; (excessively) demasiado, excesivamente; (covered) cubierto (de); (extra) en exceso; (completely) enteramente; (from head to foot) de pies a cabeza, de hito en hito; (of time) pasado. **over** is also used as a prefix. Indicating excess, it is generally translated by demasiado or excesivamente. In other meanings, it is either not translated or its meaning forms part of the verb, being translated as re-, super-, trans-, ultra. Very often a less literal translation is more successful than the employment of the above prefixes. **all o.,** (everywhere) en todas partes; (finished) todo acabado; (covered) cubierto (de); (up and down) de pies a cabeza. **all the world o.,** en todo el mundo. **embroidered all o.,** todo bordado. **He is o. in Germany,** Está en Alemania. **He trembled all o.,** Estaba todo tembloroso. **that which is o.,** el exceso, lo que queda. **to read o.,** leer, repasar. **o. again,** de nuevo. **o. and above,** por encima de, fuera de, en exceso de. **o. and o.,** repetidamente, muchas veces. **o. my signature,** bajo mi firma. **o. six months since . . . ,** más de seis meses desde que . . .

overabundance *n* sobreabundancia, *f*

overabundant *a* sobreabundante

overact *vt* exagerar (un papel)

overall *n* bata, *f*; guardapolvo, *m*; *a* deconjunto (e.g., **overall assessment,** evaluación de conjunto) *pl* **overalls,** mono, *m*

overanxious *a* demasiado ansioso; demasiado inquieto. **to be o.-a.,** preocuparse demasiado

overarch *vt* abovedar

overawe *vt* intimidar, acobardar

overbalance *vt* hacer perder el equilibrio. hacer caer; preponderar. *vi* perder el equilibrio, caer

overbalancing *n* pérdida del equilibrio, caída, *f*; preponderancia, *f*

overbearing *a* dominante, autoritario, imperioso

overboard *adv* al agua, al mar.

overburden *vt* sobrecargar, agobiar

overcast *a* anublado, cerrado, encapotado. *vt sew* sobrehilar. **to become o.**, anublarse

overcharge *n* recargo, *m*; (price) recargo de precio, precio excesivo, *m*. *vt* recargar, cobrar un precio excesivo; *elec* sobrecargar. *vi* cobrar demasiado

overcloud *vt* anublar; *fig* entristecer

overcoat *n* abrigo, sobretodo, gabán, *m*

overcome *vt* vencer, rendir, subyugar; (difficulties) triunfar de, allanar, dominar. *vi* saber vencer. *a* (by sleep, etc.) rendido; (at a loss) turbado, confundido; (by kindness) agradecidísimo

overconfidence *n* confianza excesiva, *f*

overcooked *a* recocido, demasiado cocido

overcrowd *vt* atestar, llenar de bote en bote; (over-populate) sobrepoblar

overcrowding *n* sobrepoblación, *f*

overdo *vt* exagerar; ir demasiado lejos, hacer demasiado; *cul* recocer; (overtire) fatigarse demasiado

overdose *n* dosis excesiva, *f*

overdraft *n com* giro en descubierto, *m*

overdraw *vt* and *vi com* girar en descubierto

over-dressed *a* que viste demasiado; cursi

overdue *a* atrasado; *com* vencido y no pagado

overeat *vi* comer demasiado, atracarse, *Lat. Am.* jambarse

overestimate *vt* estimar en valor excesivo; exagerar, sobreestimar. *n* presupuesto excesivo, *m*; estimación excesiva, *f*

overexcite *vt* sobreexcitar

overexposure *n phot* exceso de exposición, *m*

overfatigue *vt* fatigar demasiado. *n* cansancio excesivo, *m*

overfeeding *n* sobrealimentación, *f*

overflow *vt* inundar, derramarse por; *fig* cubrir, llenar; desbordarse. *vi* (with) rebosar de. *n* inundación, *f*, desbordamiento, derrame, *m*; *fig* residuo, resto, exceso, *m*; (plumbing) sumidero, vertedero, *m*, descarga, *f*. **The river overflowed its banks,** El río se desbordó, El río salió de cauce

overflowing *a* rebosante; superabundante; (its banks) *Lat. Am.* desbocado. **filled to o.,** lleno hasta los bordes. **o. with health,** rebosante de salud, vendiendo salud

overgrown *a* (gawky) talludo; (plants) exuberante, vicioso; frondoso, cubierto de verdura

overhang *vt* caer a, mirar a; colgar; *fig* amenazar. *vi* colgar, sobresalir; *fig* amenazar

overhanging *a* saledizo, sobresaliente; colgante, pendiente

overhaul *vt* examinar, investigar; componer, hacer una inspección general de; (of boats overtaking) alcanzar. *n* examen, *m*, investigación, *f*; *med* exploración general, *f*

overhead *adv* arriba, en lo alto, encima de la cabeza. *a* aéreo, elevado; general, fijo. **o. cable,** cable eléctrico, *m*. **o. expenses,** gastos generales, *m pl*. **o. railway,** ferrocarril aéreo (or elevado), *m*

overhear *vt* (accidentally) oír por casualidad, oír sin querer; (on purpose) alcanzar a oír, lograr oír

overheat *vt* acalorar, hacer demasiado caliente, recalentar. *vi* (in argument) acalorarse; hacerse demasiado caliente

overheating *n* recalentamiento, *m*

overindulge *vt* mimar demasiado; dedicarse a algo con exceso; tomar algo con exceso. *vi* darse demasiada buena vida

overjoyed *a* contentísimo, lleno de alegría, encantado

overland *adv* por tierra. *a* terrestre, trascontinental

overlap *vi* traslaparse; coincidir. *n* traslapo, *m*

overlay *vt* cubrir, dar una capa; (with silver) platear; (with gold) dorar. *n* capa, *f*; cubierta, *f*

overleaf *adv* a la vuelta

overload *vt* sobrecargar, recargar. *n* sobrecarga, *f*

overlook *vt* (face) dar a, mirar a, dominar; (supervise) vigilar, examinar, inspeccionar; (not notice) no notar, pasar por alto, no hacer, caso de, no fijarse en; (neglect) desdeñar; (ignore) no darse cuenta de, ignorar; (excuse) perdonar, tolerar, hacer la vista gorda

overlord *n* señor de horca y cuchillo, señor, jefe, *m*

overmuch *adv* demasiado, en exceso

overnight *adv* la noche pasada, durante la noche; toda la noche. *a* de la víspera, nocturno. **to stay o. with,** pasar la noche con

overpass *n* pasaje elevado, viaducto, *m*

overpay *vt* pagar demasiado

overpayment *n* pago excesivo, *m*

overpopulate *vt* sobrepoblar, become overpopulated recargarse de habitantes (with people), recargarse de animales (with animals)

overpower *vt* vencer, subyugar; (of scents, etc.) trastornar; rendir, dominar

overpowering *a* irresistible

overpraise *vt* encarecer, alabar mucho

overproduce *vt* and *vi* sobreproducir

overproduction *n* sobreproducción, *f*

overrate *vt* exagerar el valor de; (of property) sobrevalorar

overreach *vt* sobrealcanzar. **to o. oneself,** sobrepasarse, ir demasiado lejos

override *vt* (trample) pasar por encima (de); *fig* rechazar, poner a un lado; (bully) dominar; (a horse) fatigar, reventar

overripe *a* demasiado maduro

overrule *vt law* denegar, no admitir; vencer

overrun *vt* (flood) inundar; (ravage) invadir; (infest) plagar, infestar; desbordarse, derramarse

oversea *a* ultramarino, de ultramar. *adv* en ultramar, allende los mares

oversee *vt* vigilar, inspeccionar

overseer *n* capataz, mayoral, sobrestante, contramaestre, *m*; inspector (-ra), veedor (-ra)

oversell *vt* and *vi* vender en exceso

oversensitive *a* demasiado sensitivo; vidrioso; susceptible

oversew *vt* sobrecoser

overshadow *vt* sombrear; *fig* eclipsar, obscurecer; (sadden) entristecer

overshoe *n* chanclo, *m*; (for snow) galocha, *f*

overshoot *vt* tirar más allá del blanco; *fig* exceder, rebasar el límite conveniente, **overshoot the target** (fig.) ir más allá del blanco, ir más allá de lo razonable. **to o. oneself,** exagerar; propasarse, descomedirse

oversight *n* inadvertencia, omisión, equivocación, *f*; descuido, *m*

oversimplify *vt* simplificar en exceso

oversleep *vi* dormir demasiado; *inf* pegársele a uno las sábanas, levantarse demasiado tarde

overspend *vt* and *vi* gastar demasiado

overspread *vt* desparramar, salpicar, esparcir, sembrar; cubrir

overstate *vt* exagerar, encarecer, ponderar

overstatement *n* exageración, ponderación, *f*

overstep *vt* exceder, pasar, violar; rebasar, pasar más allá (de)

overstrain *vt* fatigar demasiado, agotar. *n* fatiga, *f*. **to o. oneself,** esforzarse demasiado, cansarse demasiado

overstrung *a* nervioso, excitable; (piano) de cuerdas cruzadas

oversubscribe *vt* subscribir en exceso

overt *a* abierto, público; manifiesto, evidente

overtake *vt* alcanzar, pasar, dejar atrás; adelantarse (a); (surprise) coger, sorprender; (overwhelm) vencer, dominar

overtax *vt* oprimir de tributos; agobiar, cansar demasiado

overthrow *vt* volcar, echar por tierra, derribar; *fig* vencer, destruir, destronar. *n* vuelco, derribo, *m*; *fig* destrucción, ruina, *f*

overtime *adv* fuera de las horas estipuladas. *n* horas extraordinarias de trabajo, *f pl.* **to work o.,** trabajar horas extraordinarias

overtone *n mus* armónico, *m*

overtop *vt* dominar, sobresalir, elevarse encima de

overture *n mus* obertura, *f*

overturn *vt* volcar, derribar, echar a rodar, echar abajo; (upset) revolver, desordenar. *vi* volcar, venirse abajo, allanarse; estar revuelto

overturning *n* vuelco, salto de campana, *m*

overweening *a* arrogante, insolente, altivo

overweight *n* sobrepeso, exceso en el peso, *m.* **to be o.,** pesar más de lo debido

overwhelm *vt* (conquer) vencer, aplastar, derrotar; (of waves, etc.) sumergir, hundir, inundar, engolfar; (in argument) confundir, dejar confuso, avergonzar; (of grief, etc.) vencer, postrar, dominar; (of work) inundar

overwhelming *a* irresistible, invencible, abrumador, apabullante

overwind *vt* (a watch) dar demasiada cuerda a; romper la cuerda de

overwork *vt* hacer trabajar demasiado (or con exceso); esclavizar. *vi* trabajar demasiado. *n* exceso de trabajo, demasiado trabajo, *m*

overwrought *a* (overworked) agotado por el trabajo, rendido, muy cansado; nerviosísimo, sobreexcitado, exaltado, muy agitado

ovine *a* ovejuno

ovoid *a* ovoide

ovulation *n med* ovulación, *f*

owe *vt* deber, tener deudas (de); deber, estar agradecido (por), estar obligado (a). *vi* estar en deuda, estar endeudado, tener deudas. **He owes his tailor $30,** Le debe treinta dólares a su sastre. **I owe him thanks for his help,** Le estoy agradecido por su ayuda (or Le debo las gracias por . . .). **He owes his success to good fortune,** Su éxito se debe a la suerte

owing *a* sin pagar. **o. to,** debido a, a causa de, por. **We had to stay in o. to the rain,** Tuvimos que quedarnos en casa a causa de la lluvia. **What is o. to you now?** ¿Cuánto se le debe ahora?

owl *n* búho, mochuelo, *Peru* carancho, *m.* **barn** or **screech owl,** lechuza, *f.* **brown owl,** autillo, *m*

owlish *a* parecido a un búho, de búho

own *a* propio. *n* (dearest) bien, *m. vt* poseer, tener, ser dueño de; (recognize) reconocer; (admit) confesar. *vi* confesar. **my (thy, his, our, your) own,** mi (tu, su, nuestro, vuestro) propio, *m,* (*f,* propia); mis (tus, sus, nuestros, vuestros) propios, *m pl,* (*f pl,* propias); (when not placed before a noun) el mío (tuyo, suyo, nuestro, vuestro), la mía (tuya, etc.), los míos (tuyos, etc.), las mías (tuyas, etc.); (relations) los suyos. **in his own house,** en su propia casa. **my (thy, his, etc.) own self,** yo (tú, él) mismo, *m,* (*f,* misma, *m pl,* mismos, *f pl,* mismas). **a room of one's own,** un cuarto para sí (or para uno mismo). **to be on one's own,** ser independiente; estar a solas. **to hold one's own,** mantenerse en sus trece. **to own up,** confesar

owner *n* dueño (-ña), propietario (-ia), posesor (-ra)

ownerless *a* sin dueño, sin amo

ownership *n* posesión, *f,* dominio, *m;* propiedad, *f*

ox *n* buey (*pl* bueyes), *m.* **oxeye daisy,** margarita, *f.* **oxstall,** boyera, *f*

oxidation *n chem* oxidación, *f*

oxide *n chem* óxido, *m*

oxidization *n* oxidación, *f*

oxidize *vt chem* oxidar; *vi* oxidarse

oxygen *n* oxígeno, *m.* **o. mask,** máscara de oxígeno, *f.* **o. tent,** tienda de oxígeno, *f*

oxygenate *vt chem* oxigenar

oxygenation *n chem* oxigenación, *f*

oyez, oyez! *interj* ¡oíd!

oyster *n* ostra, *f.* **o. bed,** pescadero (or criadero) de ostras, *m.* **o. culture,** ostricultura, *f*

ozone *n* ozono, *m*

P

p *n* (letter) pe, *f.* **to mind one's p's and q's,** poner los puntos sobre las íes; ir con pies de plomo

pabulum *n* pábulo, *m;* sustento, *m*

pace *n* paso, *m;* (gait) andar, *m,* marcha, *f;* (of a horse) andadura, *f;* (speed) velocidad, *f. vi* pasear(se), andar; (of a horse) amblar. *vt* recorrer, andar por; marcar el paso para; (with out) medir a pasos. **at a good p.,** a un buen paso. **to keep p. with,** ajustarse al paso de, ir al mismo paso que; andar al paso de; (events) mantenerse al corriente de. **to p. up and down,** pasearse, dar vueltas. **p.-maker,** el que marca el paso

paced *a* de andar . . . ; (of a horse) de andadura . . . ; de paso . . .

pachyderm *n* paquidermo, *m*

Pacific, the el (Océano) Pacífico, *m*

pacific *a geog* pacífico; sosegado, tranquilo, pacífico. **He is of a p. disposition,** Es amigo de la paz

pacification *n* pacificación, *f*

pacificatory *a* pacificador

pacifier *n* pacificador (-ra)

pacifism *n* pacifismo, *m*

pacifist *a* pacifista. *n* pacifista, *mf*

pacify *vt* pacificar; calmar, tranquilizar; aplacar, conciliar

pack *n* (bundle) fardo, lío, *m;* paquete, *m;* (load) carga, *f;* (of hounds) jauría, *f;* (herd) hato, *m;* (of seals) manada, *f;* (of cards) baraja (de naipes), *f;* (of rogues) cuadrilla, *f;* (of lies, etc.) colección, *f;* masa, *f;* (of ice) témpanos flotantes, *m pl;* (Rugby football) delanteros, *m pl;* (for the face) compresa, *f.* **p.-horse,** caballo de carga, *m.* **p.-needle,** aguja espartera, *f.* **p.-saddle,** albarda, *f.* **p.-thread,** bramante, *m*

pack *vt* embalar; empaquetar; envasar; encajonar; (a suit-case, etc.) hacer; (cram) apretar; (crowd) atestar, llenar; (a pipe joint, etc.) empaquetar; (an animal) cargar. *vi* llenar; (one's luggage) hacer el equipaje, hacer el baúl, arreglar el equipaje. **packed like sardines,** como sardinas en banasta. **The train was packed,** El tren estaba lleno de bote en bote. **to p. off,** (a person) despachar; poner de partitas en la calle. **to p. up,** hacer el equipaje; empaquetar; embalar; *inf* liar el hato

package *n* paquete, *m;* bulto, *m;* (bundle) fardo, *m*

packer *n* embalador, *m;* envasador (-ra)

packet *n* paquete, *m;* (of cigarettes, etc.) cajetilla, *f;* (boat) paquebote, *m.* **to make one's p.,** *inf* hacer su pacotilla

packing *n* embalaje, *m;* envoltura, *f;* envase, *m;* (on a pipe, etc.) guarnición, *f.* **I must do my p.,** Tengo que hacer las maletas. **p.-case,** caja de embalaje, *f.* **p.-needle,** aguja espartera, *f*

pact *n* pacto, convenio, *m.* **to make a p.,** pactar

pad *n* almohadilla, *f,* cojinete, *m;* (on a bed, chair) colchoneta, *f;* (on a wound) cabezal, *m;* (for polishing) muñeca, *f;* (hockey) defensa, *f;* (cricket) espinillera, *f;* (writing) bloque, *m;* (of a calendar) taco, *m;* (blotting) secafirmas, *m;* (of a quadruped's foot) pulpejo, *m;* (of fox, hare) pata, *f;* (leaf) hoja grande, *f, vt* almohadillar; acolchar; rellenar, forrar; (out, a book, etc.) meter paja en. **inking-pad,** almohadilla de entintar, *f.* **padded cell,** celda acolchonada, *f.* **shoulder-pad,** (in a garment) hombrera, *f*

padding *n* relleno, *m,* almohadilla, *f;* (material) borra, *f,* algodón, *m; fig* paja, *f,* ripio, *m,*

paddle *n* (oar) canalete, zagual, *m;* paleta, *f;* (flipper) aleta, *f, vt* and *vi* remar con canalete; (dabble) chapotear. **double p.,** remo doble, *m.* **p.-steamer,** vapor de ruedas, vapor de paleta, *m*. **p.-wheel,** rueda de paletas, *f*

paddler *n* remero (-ra); el, *m*, (*f*, la) que chapotea

paddling *n* chapoteo, chapaleo, *m*

paddock *n* prado, *m*, dehesa, *f*; parque, *m*; (near a racecourse) en silla dero, picadero, *m*; (toad) sapo, *m*

padlock *n* candado, *m*, *vt* cerrar con candado, acerrojar

Paduan *a* and *n* paduano (-na)

paean *n* himno de alegría, *m*

pagan *a* and *n* pagano (-na)

paganism *n* paganismo, *m*

page *n* (boy) paje, *m*; (squire) escudero, *m*; (of a book, etc.) página, *f*; *fig* hoja, *f*. *vt* compaginar; (a person) vocear. **on p. nine,** en la página nueve. **to turn the p.,** *fig* volver la hoja

pageant *n* espectáculo, *m*; (procession) desfile, *m*; representación teatral, *f*; fiesta, *f*; *fig* pompa, *f*, aparato, *m*

pageantry *n* pompa, *f*, aparato, *m*, magnificencia, *f*

paginate *vt* paginar

pagination *n* paginación, *f*

pagoda *n* pagoda, *f*

paid *a* pagado; (on a parcel) porte pagado. **p. mourner,** plañidera, *f*. **p.-up share,** acción liberada, *f*

pail *n* cubo, pozal, *m*, cubeta, *f*

pailful *n* cubo (de agua, etc.), *m*

pain *n* dolor, *m*; sufrimiento, *m*; (mental) tormento, *m*, angustia, *f*; *law* pena, *f*; *pl* **pains,** (effort) trabajo, esfuerzo, *m*. *vt* doler; atormentar, afligir. **dull p.,** dolor sordo, *m*. **I have a p. in my head,** Me duele la cabeza. **on p. of death,** so pena de muerte. **to be in great p.,** sufrir mucho. **to take pains,** tomarse trabajo, esforzarse, esmerarse

pained *a* dolorido; afligido; de angustia

painful *a* doloroso; angustioso; fatigoso; (troublesome) molesto; (embarrassing) embarazoso; difícil; (laborious) arduo

painfully *adv* dolorosamente; penosamente; fatigosamente; con angustia; laboriosamente

painfulness *n* dolor, *m*; angustia, aflicción, *f*; tormento, *m*; dificultad, *f*

painless *a* sin dolor, indoloro

painlessly *adv* sin dolor; sin sufrir

painlessness *n* falta de dolor, *f*

painstaking *a* concienzudo; diligente, industrioso; cuidadoso. *n* trabajo, *m*; diligencia, industria, *f*; cuidado, *m*

paint *n* pintura, *f*; (for preserving metal) pavón, *m*; (rouge) colorete, *m*. *vt* pintar. *vi* pintar; pintarse. **The door is painted blue,** La puerta está pintada de azul. **p.-box,** caja de pinturas, *f*. **p.-brush,** pincel, *m*; (for house painting) brocha, *f*

painter *n* pintor (-ra); (house) pintor de brocha gorda, pintor de casas, *m*; (of a boat) boza, *f*. **sign-p.,** pintor de muestras, *m*

painting *n* pintura, *f*; (picture) cuadro, *m*, pintura, *f*

pair *n* par, *m*; (of people) pareja, *f*; (of oxen) yunta, *f*. *vt* parear, emparejar; (persons) unir, casar; (animals) aparear. *vi* parearse; casarse; aparearse. **a carriage and p.,** un landó con dos caballos. **a p. of steps,** una escalera de mano. **a p. of pants a p. of trousers,** unos pantalones. **in pairs,** de dos en dos; por parejas. **to p. off,** *vi* formar pareja; *inf* casarse

pal *n* camarada, compinche, *mf*; amigote, *m*

palace *n* palacio, *m*

paladin *n* paladín, *m*

paleographer *n* paleógrafo, *m*

paleography *n* paleografía, *f*

paleolithic *a* paleolítico

paleology *n* paleología, *f*

paleontology *n* paleontología, *f*

palatable *a* sabroso, apetitoso; *fig* agradable, aceptable

palatableness *n* buen sabor, gusto agradable, *m*; *fig* lo agradable

palatably *adv* agradablemente

palatal *a* paladial. *n* letra paladial, *f*

palatalize *vt* palatizar

palate *n* paladar, *m*. **hard p.,** paladar, *m*. **soft p.,** velo del paladar, *m*

palatial *a* (of a palace) palaciego; (sumptuous) magnífico, suntuoso

pale *n* (stake) estaca, *f*; límite, *m*; *her* palo, *m*, *a* pálido; (wan) descolorido, *Lat. Am. also* lívido; (of colours) claro, desmayado; (of light) tenue, mortecino; (lustreless) sin brillo, muerto. *vi* palidecer, perder el color; *fig* eclipsarse

palely *adv* pálidamente; vagamente, indistintamente

paleness *n* palidez, *f*; (wanness) descoloramiento, *m*, amarillez, *f*; (of light) tenuidad, *f*

palette *n* paleta, *f*. **p.-knife,** espátula, *f*

palimpsest *n* palimpsesto, *m*

palindrome *n* capicúa *f*, (of numbers), palíndromo *m*

paling *n* palizada, estacada, valla, *f*

palisade *n* palenque, *m*, tranquera, palizada, *f*; *mil* estacada, *f*

palish *a* algo pálido; paliducho

pall *n* (on a coffin) paño mortuorio, *m*; (*fig* covering) manto, *m*, capa, *f*; *ecc* palio, *m*; (over a chalice) palia, *f*. *vi* perder el sabor, hacerse insípido; saciarse (de); aburrirse (de), cansarse (de). **The music of Bach never palls on me,** No me canso nunca de la música de Bach

palladium *n min* paladio, *m*; (safeguard) paladión, *m*

pallet *n* jergón, *m*; camilla, *f*; *mech* fiador de rueda, *m*; torno de alfarero, *m*

palliate *vt* (pain) paliar, aliviar; mitigar; (excuse) disculpar, excusar

palliation *n* paliación, *f*; mitigación, *f*; disculpa, *f*

palliative *a* paliativo; (extenuating) atenuante. *n* paliativo, *m*

pallid *a* pálido, *Lat. Am. also* lívido

pallidness *n* palidez, *f*

pallor *n* palidez, *f*

palm *n* (of the hand, and *fig.*, victory) palma, *f*; (measurement) ancho de la mano, *m*; (tree) palmera, *f*. *vt* (a card, etc.) empalmar; (with off) defraudar (con); dar gato por liebre (a). **to bear away the p.,** llevar la palma. **p. branch,** palma, *f*. **p. grove,** palmar, *m*. **p.-oil,** aceite de palma, *m*; (bribe) soborno, *m*. **P. Sunday,** Domingo de Ramos, *m*. **p. tree,** palmera, *Lat. Am.* chonta, *f*

palmate *a* palmeado

palmer *n* peregrino, *m*; (caterpillar) oruga velluda, *f*

palming *n* (in conjuring, etc.) empalme, *m*

palmist *n* quiromántico (-ca)

palmistry *n* quiromancía, *f*

palmy *a* palmar; (flourishing) floreciente; (happy) dichoso, feliz; (prosperous) próspero; triunfante

Palmyra Palmira, *f*

palp *n* palpo, *m*

palpability *n* palpabilidad, *f*

palpable *a* palpable

palpate *vt* palpar

palpation *n* palpación, *f*

palpitate *vi* palpitar

palpitating *a* palpitante

palpitation *n* palpitación, *f*

palsied *a* paralítico

palsy *n* parálisis, *f*, *vt* paralizar

paltriness *n* mezquindad, pequeñez, *f*

paltry *a* mezquino, insignificante, pobre

paludism *n med* paludismo, *m*

pampas *n* pampa, *f*

pamper *vt* mimar, consentir demasiado; criar con mimos, regalar; alimentar demasiado bien

pampered *a* mimado, consentido; demasiado bien alimentado

pamphlet *n* folleto, *m*

pamphleteer *n* folletinista, *mf*

pan *n* (vessel) cazuela, *f*; cacerola, *f*; (brain) cráneo, *m*; (of a balance) platillo, *m*; (of a firelock) cazoleta, *f*, *cinem* toma panorámica *f*, *prefix* pan-. **to pan off,** separar el oro en una gamella. **to pan out,** dar oro; *fig* suceder. **Pan-Americanism,** panamericanismo, *m*

Pan *n* Pan, *m.* **pipes of Pan,** flauta de Pan, *f*
panacea *n* panacea, *f*
panache *n* penacho, *m*
panada *n cul* panetela, *f*
Panama el Panamá, *m*
Panama *a* panameño. (-ña). **P. hat,** sombrero de jipijapa, panamá *m*
pancake *n* fruta de sartén, hojuela, *f.* **p. landing,** *aer* aterrizaje brusco, *m.* **P. Tuesday,** martes de Carnaval, *m*
panchromatic *a* pancromático
pancreas *n* páncreas, *m*
pancreatic *a* pancreático
panda *n zool* panda, *mf*
pandemic *a* pandémico
pandemonium *n* pandemonio
pander *n* alcahuete, *m,* *vi* alcahuetear. **to p. to,** prestarse a; favorecer, ayudar
pandore *n mus* bandola, *f*
pane *n* hoja de vidrio, hoja de cristal, *f;* cuadro, *m*
panegyric *a* panegírico. *n* panegírico, *m*
panel *n* panel, entrepaño, *m; art* tabla, *f;* (in a dress) paño, *m;* (list) lista, *f,* registro, *m;* (jury) jurado, *m;* lista de jurados, *f, vt* labrar a entrepaños; artesonar. **p. doctor,** médico (-ca) de seguros
paneled *a* entrepañado; (of ceilings) artesonado. **p. ceiling,** artesonado, *m*
paneling *n* entrepaños, *m pl;* artesonado, *m*
panful *n* cazolada, *f*
pang *n* punzada (de dolor), *f,* dolor agudo, *m;* dolor, *m;* (anguish of mind) angustia, *f,* tormento, *m;* (of conscience) remordimiento, *m*
panic *n* pánico, *m;* pavor, espanto, *m;* terror súbito, *m,* a pánico. *vi* espantarse. **p.-monger,** alarmista, *mf* **p.-stricken,** aterrorizado, despavorido
panicky *a inf* lleno de pánico; nervioso
pannier *n* (basket) alforja, *f;* cesto, *m;* (bustle) caderillas, *f pl*
panoply *n* panoplia, *f*
panorama *n* panorama, *m*
panoramic *a* panorámico
pansy *n* pensamiento, *m,* trinitaria, *f*
pant *vi* jadear; (of dogs) hipar; resollar; (of the heart) palpitar. *n* jadeo, *m;* palpitación, *f.* **to p. after,** suspirar por
pantaloon *n* (trouser) pantalón, *m;* (Pantaloon) Pantalón, *m*
pantechnicon *n* almacén de muebles, *m;* (van) carro de mudanzas, *m*
pantheism *n* panteísmo, *m*
pantheist *n* panteísta, *mf*
pantheistic *a* panteísta
pantheon *n* panteón, *m*
panther *n* pantera, *f*
panties *n pl* pantalones, *m pl*
panting *a* jadeante, sin aliento. *n* jadeo, *m;* resuello, *m,* respiración difícil, *f;* palpitación, *f*
pantomime *n* pantomima, *f;* revista, *f.* **in p.,** en pantomima; por gestos
pantry *n* despensa, *f*
pants *n pl* calzoncillos, *m pl;* (trousers) pantalones, *m pl.* **p. buttoned down the sides** *Mexico* calzoneras, *f pl*
panzer division *n* división motorizada, *f*
pap *n* (nipple) pezón, *m;* (soft food) papilla, *f*
papa *n* papá, *m*
papacy *n* papado, pontificado, *m*
papal *a* papal, pontificio. **p. bull,** bula pontificia, *f.* **p. nuncio,** nuncio del Papa, nuncio apostólico, *m.* **p. see,** sede apostólica, *f*
papaya *n Cuba* fruta bomba, *f*
paper *n* papel, *m;* hoja de papel, *f;* documento, *m;* (lecture) comunicación, *f;* (newspaper) periódico, *m;* (journal) revista, *f;* (exam.) examen escrito, trabajo, *m;* ejercicio, *m; pl* **papers,** (credentials) documentación, *f,* credenciales, *f pl; com* valores negociables, *m pl;* (packet) paquete, *m,* *a* de papel; para papeles; parecido

al papel. *vt* (a room) empapelar; (a parcel) envolver. **daily p.,** diario, *m.* **in p. covers,** (of books) en rústica. **slip of p.,** papeleta. *f.* **to send in one's papers,** entregar su dimisión. **p. bag,** saco de papel, *m.* **p.-chase,** rally-paper, *m.* **p. clip,** prendedero de oficina, **sujetapapeles,** *Central America* ataché, *elsewhere in Lat. Am.* broche, *m.* **p.-cutting machine,** guillotina, *f.* **p. folder,** plegadera, *f.* **p.-hanger,** empapelador, *m.* **p.-hanging,** empapelado, *m.* **p.-knife,** cortapapel, *m.* **p.-maker,** fabricante de papel, *m.* **p.-making,** manufactura de papel, *f.* **p.-mill,** fábrica de papel, *f.* **p.-money,** papel moneda, *m.* **p.-pulp,** pasta, *f.* **p.-streamer,** serpentina, *f.* **p.-weight,** pisapapeles, *m*
papering *n* (of a room) empapelado, *m*
papery *a* semejante al papel
papier-mâché *n* cartón piedra, *m*
papillary *a* papilar
paprika *n* pimienta húngara, *f*
papyrus *n* papiro, *m*
par *n* par, *f.* **at par,** *com* a la par. **above (below) par,** *com* por encima (*or* debajo) de la par. **He is a little below par,** No está muy bien de salud. **to be on par with,** ser el equivalente de; ser igual a. **par excellence,** por excelencia
parable *n* parábola, *f*
parabola *n geom* parábola, *f*
parachute *n* paracaídas, *m; bot* vilano, *m.* **to p. down,** lanzarse en paracaídas. **p. troops,** cuerpo de paracaidistas, *m*
parachutist *n* paracaidista, *mf*
parade *n* alarde, *m; mil* parada, revista, *f;* (procession) desfile, *m,* procesión, *f;* (promenade) paseo, *m. vt* (display) hacer alarde de, hacer gala de, ostentar; (troops) formar en parada; pasar revista (a); (patrol) recorrer. *vi mil* tomar parte en una parada; desfilar. **to p. up and down,** pasearse. **p.-ground,** campo de instrucción, *m;* plaza de armas, *f*
paradigm *n* paradigma, *m*
paradise *n* paraíso, edén, *m; fig* jauja, *f.* **bird of p.,** ave del paraíso, *f*
paradisiac *a* paradisíaco
paradox *n* paradoja, *f*
paradoxical *a* paradójico
paradoxicality *n* lo paradójico
paraffin *n* parafina, *f, vt* parafinar. **p.-oil,** parafina líquida, *f*
paragon *n* modelo perfecto, dechado, *m*
paragraph *n* párrafo, *m;* (in a newspaper) suelto, *m, vt* dividir en párrafos; escribir un suelto sobre. **new p.,** párrafo aparte, *m*
Paraguay el Paraguay, *m*
Paraguayan *a and n* paraguayo (-ya)
parakeet *n orn* perico, *m*
parallel *a* paralelo; igual; semejante, análogo. *n* línea paralela, *f;* paralelo, *m; mil* paralela, *f; geog* paralelo, *m; print* pleca, *f. vt* poner en paralelo; cotejar, comparar; igualar. **to run p. to,** ser paralelo a; ser conforme a. **p. bars,** paralelas, *f pl*
parallelism *n* paralelismo, *m*
parallelogram *n* paralelogramo, *m*
paralyse *vt* paralizar
paralysis *n* parálisis, *f*
paralytic *a and n* paralítico (-ca)
paramount *a* supremo, sumo
paramour *n* amante, querido, *m;* querida, amiga, *f*
paranoia *n* paranoia, *f*
paranoiac *n* paranoico, *m*
parapet *n* (*arch* and *mil*) parapeto, *m*
paraphernalia *n law* bienes parafernales, *m, p;* (finery) atavíos, adornos, *m pl;* equipo, *m;* arreos, *m pl;* insignias, *f pl*
paraphrase *n* paráfrasis, *f, vt* parafrasear
parasite *n* parásito, *m; inf* zángano, *m,* gorrista, *mf, Mexico* arrimado, *m*
parasitic *a* parásito, parasitario; *med* parasítico
parasitology *n* parasitología, *f*

parasol *n* parasol, quitasol, *m*
parathyroid *a* paratiroides. *n* paratiroides, *f pl*
paratroops *n pl* paracaidistas, *m pl*
paratyphoid *n* paratifoidea, *f*
parboil *vt* sancochar
parcel *n* paquete, *m*; fardo, *m*; (of land) parcela, *f*. **to p. out,** repartir, distribuir; dividir. **to p. up,** envolver, empaquetar. **p. post,** servicio de paquetes, *m*
parceling *n* empaque, *m*; (out) reparto, *m*, distribución, *f*; división, *f*
parch *vt* secar; abrasar, quemar; (roast) tostar. *vi* secarse; quemarse, abrasarse
parched *a* seco, sediento. **p. with thirst,** muerto de sed
parchedness *n* sequedad, aridez, *f*
parchment *n* pergamino, *m*; (of a drum) parche, *m*. **p.-like,** apergaminado
pardon *n* perdón, *m*; *ecc* indulgencia, *f*. *vt* perdonar; indultar, amnistiar. **a general p.,** una amnistia. **I beg your p.!** ¡Vd. dispense!; ¡Perdone Vd.! **to beg p.,** pedir perdón; disculparse. **P.?** ¿Cómo?
pardonable *a* perdonable, disculpable, excusable
pardonableness *n* disculpabilidad, *f*
pardonably *adv* disculpablemente, excusablemente
pardoner *n* vendedor de indulgencias, *m*; perdonador (-ra)
pardoning *n* perdón, *m*; remisión, *f*
pare *vt* (one's nails) cortar; (fruit) mondar; (potatoes, etc.) pelar; (remove) quitar; (reduce) reducir
parent *n* padre, *m*; madre, *f*; (ancestor) antepasado, *m*; (origin) origen, *m*, fuente, *f*; (cause) causa, *f*; (author) autor, *m*; autora, *f*; *pl* **parents,** padres, *m pl*. *a* madre, materno; principal
parentage *n* parentela, *f*; linaje, *m*, familia, alcurnia, *f*; procedencia, *f*, nacimiento, origen, *m*
parental *a* paternal; maternal, de madre
parentally *adv* como un padre; como una madre
parenthesis *n* paréntesis, *m*
parenthetical *a* entre paréntesis; de paréntesis
parenthood *n* paternidad, *f*; maternidad, *f*
pariah *n* paria, *mf*
parietal *a* parietal
paring *n* (act) raedura, *f*; peladura, mondadura, *f*; (shred) brizna, *f*; (refuse) desecho, desperdicio, *m*. **p.-knife,** trinchete, *m*
Paris París, *m*
parish *n* parroquia, *f*; feligresía, *f*, *a* parroquial. **p. church,** parroquia, *f*. **p. clerk,** sacristán de parroquia, *m*. **p. priest,** párroco, *m*. **p. register,** registro de la parroquia, *m*
parishioner *n* parroquiano (-na); feligrés (-esa)
Parisian *a* parisiense. *n* parisiense, *mf*
parity *n* paridad, *f*
park *n* parque, *m*; jardín, *m*. *vt* (vehicles) estacionar; (dump) depositar. **car p.,** parque de automóviles, *m*. **p.-keeper,** guardián del parque, *m*
parking *n* (of vehicles) estacionamiento, *m*; (dumping) depósito, *m*. **p. lights,** *aut* luces de estacionamiento, *f pl*. **p. place,** parque de estacionamiento, *m*
parking meter *n Mexico* estacionómetro, *m*, *Argentina, Spain* parquímetro, *m*, *elsewhere in Lat. Am.* parcómetro, *m*, *Spain* reloj de estacionamiento, *m*
parlance *n* lenguaje, *m*. **in common p.,** en lenguaje vulgar
parley *n* plática, conversación, *f*; discusión, *f*; *mil* parlamento, *m*. *vi mil* parlamentar; discutir; conversar. *vt* hablar
parliament *n* parlamento, *m*; cortes, *f pl*; cuerpo legislativo, *m*
parliamentarian *a* and *n* parlamentario; (of an academy) censor, *m*
parliamentarianism *n* parlamentarismo, *m*,
parliamentary *a* parlamentario. **p. immunity,** inviolabilidad parlamentaria, *f*
parlor *n* salón, gabinete, *m*; sala de recibo, *f*; (in a con-

vent) locutorio, *m*. **p. games,** diversión de salón, *f*, juego de sociedad, *m*. **p.-maid,** camarera, *f*
parlous *a* crítico, malo. *adv* sumamente, muy
Parmesan *a* parmesano, de Parma. *n* parmesano (-na). **P. cheese,** queso de Parma, *m*
Parnassian *a* del parnaso; parnasiano. *n* parnasiano, *m*
Parnassus *n* Parnaso, *m*
parochial *a* parroquial, parroquiano; *fig* provincial
parochialism *n* provincialismo, *m*
parochially *adv* por parroquias
parodist *n* parodista, *mf*
parody *n* parodia, *f*, *vt* parodiar
parole *n* (of convict) libertad vigilada, *f*
paroxysm *n* paroxismo, *m*; ataque, acceso, *m*
parquet (floor) entarimado *m*; (of theater) platea, *f*
parricide *n* (act) parricidio, *m*; (person) parricida, *mf*
parrot *n* papagayo, loro, *m*, *Lat. Am.* cata, *f*
parry *vt* (a blow, and in fencing) parar; rechazar; evitar. *n* parada, *f*; (in fencing) quite, *m*, parada, *f*
parse *vt* analizar
Parsee *n* parsi, *m*
parsimonious *a* parsimonioso
parsimoniously *adv* con parsimonia
parsimony *n* parsimonia, *f*
parsley *n* perejil, *m*
parsnip *n* chirivía, *f*
parson *n* párroco, cura, *m*; (clergyman) clérigo, *m*
parsonage *n* rectoría, *f*
part *n* parte, *f*; porción, *f*; trozo, *m*; *mech* pieza, *f*; (*gram* and of a literary work) parte, *f*; (of a living organism) miembro, *m*; (duty) deber, *m*, obligación, *f*; *theat* papel, *m*; *mus* voz, *f*; *pl* **parts,** (region) partes, *f pl*, lugar, *m*; (talents) partes, dotes, *f pl*. **foreign parts,** países extranjeros, *m pl*, el extranjero. **For my p. . . . ,** Por lo que a mí toca, Por mi parte. **for the most p.,** en su mayoría. **from all parts,** de todas partes. **in p.,** en parte; parcialmente. **spare p.,** pieza de recambio, *f*. **The funny p. of it is . . . ,** Lo cómico del asunto es . . . **the latter p. of the month,** los últimos días del mes, la segunda quincena del mes. **to form p. of,** formar parte de. **to play a p.,** hacer un papel. **to take a person's p.,** apoyar a alguien, ser partidario de alguien. **to take in good p.,** tomar bien. **to take p. in,** tomar parte en, participar en. **p. of speech,** parte de la oración, *f*. **p.-owner,** copropietario (-ia). **p.-time job,** trabajo de unas cuantas horas, *m*
part *vt* distribuir, repartir; dividir; separar (de); (open) abrir. *vi* partir, marcharse; despedirse; (of roads, etc.) bifurcarse; dividirse; (open) abrirse. **to p. one's hair,** hacerse la raya. **to p. from,** (things) separarse de; (people) despedirse de. **to p. with,** separarse de; deshacerse de; perder; (dismiss) despedir (a)
partake *vt* participar de, compartir; tomar parte en. *vi* tomar algo (de comer, de beber). **to p. of,** comer (beber) de; tener rasgos de
partaker *n* partícipe, *mf*
Parthian *a* parto. *n* parto (-ta). **P. shot,** la flecha del parto
partial *a* parcial; (fond of) aficionado (a). **p. eclipse,** eclipse parcial, *m*
partiality *n* parcialidad, *f*; preferencia, predilección, *f*
partially *adv* en parte, parcialmente; (with bias) con parcialidad
participant *a* participante. *n* partícipe, *mf*
participate *vi* participar (de), compartir; tomar parte (en)
participation *n* participación, *f*
participial *a gram* participial
participle *n gram* participio, *m*. **past p.,** participio pasado (or pretérito o pasivo), *m*. **present p.,** participio activo (or presente), *m*
particle *n* partícula, *f*; *fig* átomo, grano, *m*, pizca, *f*; *gram* partícula, *f*
parti-colored *a* bicolor
particular *a* particular; especial; individual; singular; cierto; exacto; escrupuloso; difícil, exigente. *n* detalle,

pormenor, *m;* circunstancia, *f;* caso particular, *m; pl* **particulars,** informes, detalles, *m pl.* **further particulars,** más detalles. **in p.,** en particular; sobre todo. **He is very p. about . . . ,** Es muy exigente en cuanto a . . . ; Le es muy importante . . . , Le importa mucho . . .

particularize *vt* particularizar, detallar; especificar

particularly *adv* en particular; particularmente; sobre todo

parting *n* despedida, *f;* partida, *f;* separación, *f;* (of the hair) raya, crencha, *f;* (cross roads) bifurcación, *f.* a de despedida. **at p.,** al despedirse. **to reach the p. of the ways,** *fig* llegar al punto decisivo

partisan *n* partidario (-ia); (fighter) guerrillero, *m,* a partidario; de guerrilleros

partisanship *n* partidarismo, *m*

partition *n* partición, *f;* división, *f;* (wall) pared, *f,* tabique, *m.* **the p. of Ireland,** la división de Irlanda. *vt* **to p. off** *Lat. Am.* entabicar

partly *adv* en parte

partner *n* asociado (-da); *com* socio (-ia); (dancing) pareja, *f;* (in games, and companion) compañero (-ra); (spouse) consorte, *mf;* (in crime) codelincuente, *mf* **sleeping p.,** socio comanditario, *m.* **working p.,** socio industrial, *m*

partnership *n* asociación, *f; com* sociedad, compañía, *f.* **deed of p.,** artículos de sociedad, *m pl.* **to take into p.,** tomar como socio (a). **to form a p.,** asociarse

partridge *n orn* perdiz, *f.* **young p.,** perdigón, *m*

parturient *a f,* parturienta. *n* parturienta, *f*

parturition *n* parto, *m*

party *n* partido, *m;* grupo, *m;* (of pleasure, etc.) partida, *f;* reunión, fiesta, *f; mil* pelotón, destacamento, *m; law* parte, *f;* (person) interesado (-da); (accessory) cómplice, *mf.* **rescue p.,** pelotón de salvamento, *m.* **to be a p. to,** prestarse a; ser cómplice en. **to give a p.,** dar una fiesta, dar una reunión. **p.-spirit,** espíritu del partido, *m.* **p.-wall,** pared medianera, *f*

parvenu *n* advenedizo (-za)

parvis *n arch* atrio, *m*

Paschal *a* pascual

pass *n* (in an exam.) aprobación, *f;* (crisis) crisis, situación crítica, *f;* estado, *m;* (with the hands) pase, *m;* (permit) permiso, *m; mil* licencia, *f;* (safe-conduct) salvoconducto, *m;* (in football, etc.) pase, *m;* (membership card) carnet, *m;* (defile) desfiladero, paso, puerto, *m; naut* rebasadero, *m;* (fencing) estocada, *f.* **free p.,** billete de favor, *m.* **p.-book,** libreta de banco, *f.* **p. certificate,** (in exams.) aprobado, *m.* **p.-key,** llave maestra, *f*

pass *vi* pasar; (of time) correr, pasar, transcurrir; (happen) occurrir, tomar lugar; (end) cesar, desaparecer; (die) morir. *vt* pasar; hacer pasar; (the butter, etc.) dar, alargar; (in football, hockey) pasar; (excel) aventajar, exceder; (a Bill, an examination) aprobar; (sentence) fallar, pronunciar; (a remark) hacer; (transfer) traspasar; (tolerate) sufrir, tolerar; evacuar. **He passed in psychology,** Aprobó sicología. **to allow to p.,** ceder el paso (a). **to bring to p.,** ocasionar. **to come to p.,** suceder. **to let p.,** (put up with) dejar pasar; no hacer caso de; (forgive) perdonar. **to p. a vote of confidence,** votar una proposición de confianza. **to p. the buck,** *inf* echarle a uno el muerto. **pass the hat, pass the plate,** pasar la gorra. **to p. along,** pasar por; pasar. **to p. away,** pasar; desaparecer; (die) morir, fallecer; (of time) transcurrir. **to p. by,** pasar por, pasar delante de, pasar al lado de; (omit) pasar por alto de, omitir; (ignore) pasar sin hacer caso de. **to p. for,** pasar por. **to p. in,** entrar. **to p. in and out,** entrar y salir. **to p. off,** *vi* pasar; cesar, acabarse; desaparecer; evaporarse, disiparse; (of events) tener lugar. *vt* (oneself) darse por; dar por, hacer pasar por. **to p. a cat off as hare,** dar gato por liebre. **to p. on,** *vi* pasar; seguir su camino, continuar su marcha. *vt* pasar algo de uno a otro. **to p. out,** salir. **to p. over,** pasar por encima de; pasar; cruzar, atravesar; (transfer) traspasar; (disregard) pasar

por alto de, dejar a un lado; omitir. **to p. over in silence,** pasar en silencio (por). **to p. round,** circular. **to p. through,** cruzar, atravesar, pasar por; (pierce) traspasar; *fig* experimentar

passable *a* transitable, pasadero; (fairly good) regular, mediano; tolerable

passably *adv* medianamente, pasaderamente, tolerablemente

passage *n* pasaje, *m;* paso, tránsito, *m;* (voyage) viaje, *m,* travesía, *f;* (corridor) pasillo, *m;* (entrance) entrada, *f;* (way) camino, *m;* (alley) callejón, *m;* (in a mine) galería, *f;* (of time) transcurso, *m;* (of birds) pasa, *f;* (in a book, and *mus*) pasaje, *m;* (occurrence) episodio, incidente, *m;* (of a Bill) aprobación, *f.* **p. money,** pasaje, *m.* **p. of arms,** lucha, *f,* combate, *m;* disputa, *f*

passementerie *n* pasamanería, *f*

passenger *n* viajero (-ra); (on foot) peatón, *m.* **by p. train,** en gran velocidad

passerby *n* transeúnte, paseante, *mf*

passing *a* pasajero; fugitivo; momentáneo. *adv* sumamente, extremadamente. *n* pasada, *f;* paso, *m;* (death) muerte, *f;* (disappearance) desaparición, *f;* (of a law) aprobación, *f.* **in p.,** de paso. **p.-bell,** toque de difuntos, *m*

passing grade *n* calificación mínima aprobatoria, *f*

passion *n* pasión, *f;* (Christ's) Pasión, *f;* (anger) cólera, *f.* **to fly into a p.,** montar en cólera. **p.-flower,** pasionaria, granadilla, *f.* **P. play,** drama de la Pasión, *m.* **P. Sunday,** Domingo de Pasión, *m.* **P. Week,** Semana Santa, *f*

passionate *a* apasionado; (quick-tempered) irascible, colérico; (fervid) vehemente, intenso, ardiente

passionately *adv* con pasión, apasionadamente; (irascibly) coléricamente; (fervidly) con vehemencia, ardientemente

passionless *a* sin pasión, frío; impasible; imparcial

passive *a* pasivo. *n gram* pasiva, *f.* **p. resistance,** resistencia pasiva, *f*

passiveness, passivity *n* pasividad, *f*

Passover *n* Pascua de los judíos, *f*

passport *n* pasaporte, *m*

password *n* contraseña, *f*

past *a* pasado; último; (expert) consumado; (former) antiguo, ex-. *n* pasado, *m;* historia, *f,* antecedentes, *m pl,* prep después de; (in front of) delante de; (next to) al lado de; (beyond) más allá de; (without) sin; fuera de; (of age) más de; (no longer able to) incapaz de. *adv* más allá. (The translation of **past** as an adverb is often either omitted, or included in the verb, e.g. **The years flew by.,** Los años transcurrieron. **for centuries p.,** durante siglos.) **I am p. caring,** Nada me importa ya. **It is a quarter p. ten,** Son las diez y cuarto. **It is p. four o'clock,** Son las siete pasadas, Son después de las cuatro. **what's p. is p.,** lo pasado, pasado. **p. doubt,** fuera de duda. **p. endurance,** insoportable. **p. help,** sin remedio, irremediable. **p. hope,** sin esperanza. **p.-master,** maestro, consumado, experto, *m.* **p. participle,** participio pasado, *m.* **p. president,** ex-presidente, *m.* **p. tense,** (tiempo) pasado, *m*

paste *n* pasta, *f;* (gloy) engrudo, *m.* *vt* (affix) pegar; (glue) engomar, engrudar

pasteboard *n* cartón, *m,* cartulina, *f,* a de cartón, de cartulina

pastel *n art* pastel, *m.* **p. drawing,** pintura al pastel, *f*

pastelist *n* pastelista, *mf*

pasteurization *n* pasteurización, *f*

pasteurize *vt* pasteurizar

pastille *n* pastilla, *f*

pastime *n* pasatiempo, entretenimiento, *m,* diversión, recreación, *f*

pastor *n* pastor, *m*

pastoral *a* pastoril; *ecc* pastoral. *n ecc* pastoral, *f;* (poet *mus*) pastorela, *f*

pastorate *n* pastoría, *f*

pastry *n* (dough) pasta, *f;* pastel, *m,* torta, *f;* pastelería, *f.* **p.-cook,** repostero, *m,* pastelero (-ra)

pasturage *n* (grass, etc.) pasto, *m*; pasturaje, *m*; pastoreo, *m*

pasture *n* (grass, etc.) pasto, herbaje, *m*; pasturaje, *m*; (field) prado, *m*, pradera, dehesa, *f. vi* pacer; pastar. *vt* apacentar, pastar, *Argentina* costear

pasty *a* pastoso; (pale) pálido. *n* empanada, *f*

pat *n* toque, *m*; caricia, *f*; (for butter) molde (de mantequilla), *m. vt* tocar; acariciar, pasar la mano (sobre). *adv* a propósito; oportunamente; fácilmente. **pat of butter,** pedacito de mantequilla, *m*. **pat on the back,** golpe en la espalda, *m*; *fig* elogio, *m*

Patagonian *a* and *n* patagón (-ona)

patch *n* (mend) remiendo, *m*; (piece) pedazo, *m*; (plaster and *aut.*, etc.) parche, *m*; (beauty spot) lunar postizo, *m*; (of ground) parcela, *f*; (of flowers, etc.) masa, *f*; (stain, and *fig*) mancha, *f. vt* (mend) remendar; poner remiendo (a); pegar; (roughly) chafallar; (the face) ponerse lunares postizos. **p. of blue sky,** pedazo de cielo azul. **patch of green grass,** mancha de hierba verde. **to be not a p. on,** no ser de la misma clase que; (of persons) no llegarle a los zancajos de. **to p. up a quarrel,** hacer las paces

patchwork *n* labor de retazos, obra de retacitos, *f*; *fig* mezcla, mezcolanza, *f*. **p. quilt,** centón, *m*

patchy *a* desigual; manchado

patella *n anat* rótula, *f*

patency *n* evidencia, claridad, *f*

patent *a* evidente, patente; patentado. *n* patente, *f. vt* patentar. **p. of nobility,** carta de hidalguía, ejecutoria, *f*. "**P. Applied For,**" «Patente Solicitada.» **Patent Pending** marca en trámite. **p. leather,** *n* charol, *m. a* de charol. **p. medicine,** específico farmacéutico, *m*

patentee *n* el, *m*, (*f*, la) que obtiene una patente; inventor (-ra)

patently *adv* evidentemente, claramente

paterfamilias *n* padre de familia, *m*

paternal *a* paterno, paternal

paternally *adv* paternalmente

paternity *n* paternidad, *f*

path *n* senda, vereda, *f*, sendero, *m*; camino, *m*; (track) pista, *f*; (traject) trayectoria, *f*. **the beaten p.,** el camino trillado

pathetic *a* patético

pathless *a* sin senda

pathogenic *a med* patógeno

pathological *a* patológico

pathologist *n* patólogo, *m*

pathology *n* patología, *f*

pathos *n* lo patético

patience *n* paciencia, *f*. **He tries my p. very much,** Me cuesta mucho no impacientarme con él. **to lose p.,** perder la paciencia; (grow angry) perder los estribos. **to play p.,** hacer solitarios

patient *a* paciente. *n* paciente, *mf*; (ill person) enfermo (-ma); (of a physician) cliente, *mf*

patiently *adv* con paciencia, pacientemente

patina *n* pátina, *f*

patriarch *n* patriarca, *m*

patriarchal *a* patriarcal

patriarchy *n* patriarcado, *m*

patrician *a* and *n* patricio (-ia)

patrimonial *a* patrimonial

patrimony *n* patrimonio, *m*

patriot *n* patriota, *mf*

patriotic *a* patriótico

patriotism *n* patriotismo, *m*

patrol *n* patrulla, *f*; ronda, *f, vi* and *vt* patrullar; rondar; recorrer. **p. boat,** lancha escampavía, *f*. **p. flight,** vuelo de patrulla, *m*

patron *n* (of a freed slave) patrono, *m*; (of the arts, etc.) mecenas, protector, *m*; (customer) parroquiano (-na), cliente, *mf*. **p. saint,** santo (-ta) patrón (-ona)

patronage *n* (protection) patrocinio, *m*; protección, *f*; *ecc* patronato, *m*; (regular custom) clientela, *f*; (of manner) superioridad, *f*

patroness *n* patrona, *f*; protectora, *f*; (of a charity, etc.) patrocinadora, *f*; (of a regiment, etc.) madrina, *f*

patronize *vt* patrocinar; proteger, favorecer; (a shop) ser parroquiano de; (treat arrogantly) tratar con superioridad

patronizing *a* (with air, behavior, etc.) de superioridad, de altivez

patten *n* zueco, chanclo, *m*

patter *n* (jargon) jerga, *f*; charla, *f*; (of rain) azotes, *m pl*; (of feet) son, *m*; golpecitos, *m pl. vt* (repeat) decir mecánicamente. *vi* (chatter) charlar; (of rain) azotar, bailar; correr ligeramente

pattern *n* modelo, *m*; (*sew* and dressmaking) patrón, *m*; (in founding) molde, *m*; (templet) escantillón, *m*; (of cloth, etc.) muestra, *f*; (design) dibujo, diseño, *m*; (example) ejemplar, *m. vt* diseñar; estampar. **p. book,** libro de muestras, *m*

patty *n* empanada, *f*, pastelillo, *m*

paucity *n* poquedad, *f*; corto número, *m*; insuficiencia, escasez, *f*

paunch *n* panza, barriga, *f*

pauper *n* pobre, *mf*

pauperism *n* pauperismo, *m*

pauperization *n* empobrecimiento, *m*

pauperize *vt* empobrecer, reducir a la miseria

pause *n* pausa, *f*; intervalo, *m*; silencio, *m*; interrupción, *f*; *mus* pausa, *f. vi* pausar, hacer una pausa; detenerse, interrumpirse; vacilar. **to give p. to,** hacer vacilar (a)

pave *vt* empedrar, enlosar. **to p. the way for,** facilitar el paso de, preparar el terreno para, abrir el camino de

pavement *n* pavimento, *m*, *Mexico* escarpa, *f*; (sidewalk) acera, *f*. **p.-artist,** pintor callejero, *m*

pavilion *n* pabellón, *m*; (for a band, etc.) quiosco, *m*; (tent) tienda de campaña, *f*

paving *n* pavimentación, *f*; empedrado, *m*; see **pavement. p.-stone,** losa, *f*

paw *n* pata, *f*; (with claws) garra, *f*; *inf* manaza, *f. vt* tocar con la pata; (scratch) arañar; (handle) manosear. *vi* (of a horse) piafar

pawing *n* (of a horse) el piafar; (handling) manoseo, *m*

pawn *n* (chess) peón (de ajedrez), *m*; empeño, *m*; *fig* prenda, *f. vt* empeñar, pignorar; dar en prenda. **p.-ticket,** papeleta de empeño, *f*

pawnbroker *n* prestamista, *mf*

pawnshop *n* casa de préstamos, casa de empeño, *f*, monte de piedad, *m*

pay *n* paga, *f*; (*mil nav*) soldada, *f*; salario, *m*; (of a workman) jornal, *m*; (reward) recompensa, compensación, *f*; (profit) beneficio, provecho, *m*. **pay-day,** día de paga, *m*. **pay-office,** pagaduría, *f*. **pay list, pay-sheet,** nómina, *Mexico* lista de raya, *f*

pay *vt* pagar; (a debt) satisfacer; (spend) gastar; (recompense) remunerar, recompensar; (hand over) entregar; (yield) producir; (a visit) hacer; (attention) prestar; (homage) rendir; (one's respects) presentar. *vi* pagar; producir ganancia; sacar provecho; ser una ventaja, ser provechoso. **It would not pay him to do it,** No le saldría a cuenta hacerlo. **This job doesn't pay,** Este trabajo no da dinero. **to pay a compliment (to),** cumplimentar, decir alabanzas (a), echar una flor (a). **to pay attention,** prestar atención; hacer caso. **to pay cash,** pagar al contado. **to pay in advance,** pagar adelantado, *Lat. Am.* aprontar. **to pay in full,** saldar. **to pay off old scores,** ajustar cuentas viejas. **to pay one's addresses to,** hacer la corte (a), pretender en matrimonio (a). **to pay the penalty,** sufrir el castigo, hacer penitencia. **to pay with interest,** *fig* pagar con creces. **to pay again,** volver a pagar, pagar de nuevo. **to pay back,** devolver, restituir; (money only) reembolsar; *fig* pagar en la misma moneda, vengarse (de). **to pay down,** pagar al contado. **to pay for,** pagar, costear; satisfacer. **to pay in,** ingresar. **to pay off,** (persons) despedir; (a debt) saldar; (a mortgage) cancelar, redimir. **to pay out,** (persons) vengarse de; (money) pagar; (ropes, etc.) arriar. **to pay up,** pagar; pagar por completo; (shares, etc.) redimir

payable *a* pagadero; a pagar; que puede ser pagado

payee *n* tenedor, *m*

payer *n* pagador (-ra)

paying *n*. See **payment**

paymaster *n* pagador, *m*; tesorero, *m*. **P.-General,** ordenador general de pagos, *m*

payment *n* pago, *m*, paga, *f*, *Lat. Am. also* entero, *m*; remuneración, *f*; *fig* recompensa, satisfacción, *f*; *fig* premio, *m*. **in p. of,** en pago de. **on p. of,** mediante el pago de. **p. in advance,** pago adelantado, anticipo, *m*

pea *n* guisante, *m*, *Lat. Am.* alverjana, arveja, *f*. **dry or split pea,** guisante seco, *m*. **sweet pea,** guisante de olor, *m*. **pea-flour,** harina de guisantes, *f*. **pea-green,** verde claro, *m*. **pea-jacket,** chaquetón de piloto, *m*. **pea-shooter,** cerbatana, *f*

peace *n* paz, *f*; tranquilidad, quietud, *f*, sosiego, *m*; *law* orden público, *m*. **P.!** ¡Silencio! **to hold one's p.,** callarse, guardar silencio. **to make p.,** hacer las paces. **P. be upon this house!** ¡Paz sea en esta casa! **p.-footing,** pie de paz, *m*. **p.-loving,** pacífico. **p.-offering,** sacrificio propiciatorio, *m*; satisfacción, oferta de paz, *f*

peaceable *a* pacífico; apacible; tranquilo, sosegado

peaceableness *n* paz, *f*; apacibilidad, *f*; tranquilidad, quietud, *f*, sosiego, *m*

peaceably *adv* pacíficamente; tranquilamente

peaceful *a* pacífico; tranquilo; silencioso. **to come with p. intentions,** venir de paz

peacefully *adv* en paz; pacíficamente; tranquilamente

peacefulness *n* paz, *f*; tranquilidad, calma, quietud, *f*; silencio, *m*; carácter pacífico, *m*

peacemaker *n* pacificador (-ra); conciliador (-ra)

peach *n* (fruit) melocotón, *m*; (tree) melocotonero, melocotón, *m*; (girl) breva, *f*. **p.-colour,** color de melocotón, *m*

peacock *n* pavo real, pavón, *m*. *vi* pavonearse; darse humos. **The p. spread its tail,** El pavo real hizo la rueda

peahen *n* pava real, *f*

peak *n* punta, *f*; (of a cap) visera, *f*; (of a mountain) peñasco, *m*, cumbre, cima, *f*; (mountain itself) pico, *m*; (*naut* of a hull) pico, *m*; *fig* auge, apogeo, *m*; punto más alto, *m*. *vi* consumirse, enflaquecer. **p. hours,** horas de mayor tráfico, *f pl*

peaked *a* en punta; puntiagudo; picudo; (of a cap) con visera; (wan) ojeroso; (thin) delgaducho, macilento, consumido

peal *n* toque (or repique) de campanas, *m*; campanillazo, *m*; carillón, *m*; (noise) estruendo, ruido, *m*; (of thunder) trueno, *m*; (of an organ) sonido, *m*. *vi* repicar; sonar. *vt* tañer, echar a vuelo (las campanas); (of a bell that one presses) hacer sonar, tocar. **a p. of laughter,** una carcajada

peanut *n* cacahuete, *m*. **p. butter,** mantequilla de cacahuete, *f*

pear *n* pera, *f*. **p.-shaped,** piriforme, de figura de pera. **p. tree,** peral, *m*

pearl *n* perla, *f*; (mother-of-pearl) nácar, *m*, *a* de perla; perlero. *vt* (dew) rociar, aljofarar. *vi* pescar perlas; formar perlas. **seed p.,** aljófar, *m*. **p.-ash,** carbonato potásico, *m*. **p.-barley,** cebada perlada, *f*. **p.-button,** botón de nácar, *m*. **p.-fisher,** pescador de perlas, *m*. **p.-fishery,** pescaduría de perlas, *f*. **p.-grey,** gris de perla, *m*

pearly *a* perlino; de perla; nacarado; (dewy) aljofarado

peasant *n* campesino (-na), labrador (-ra). *a* campesino

peasant movement *Mexico* agrarismo, *m*

peasantry *n* campesinos, *m pl*, gente del campo, *f*

peat *n* turba, *f*. **p.-bog,** turbera, *f*

pebble *n* guijarro, *m*, pedrezuela, guija, *f*; (gravel) guijo, *m*; cristal de roca, *m*; lente de cristal de roca, *m*

pebbled, pebbly *a* guijarroso, enguijarrado

peccadillo *n* pecadillo, *m*

peck *n* (of a bird) picotazo, *m*, picada, *f*; (kiss) besito, *m*; (large amount) montón, *m*; multitud, *f*. *vt* (of a bird) picotear; sacar (or coger) con el pico; (kiss) besar rápidamente. *vi* (with at) picotear; picar

pectoral *a* pectoral

peculiar *a* particular, peculiar, individual; propio, característico; (marked) especial; (unusual) extraño, raro, extraordinario

peculiarity *n* peculiaridad, particularidad, *f*; singularidad, *f*; (eccentricity) excentricidad, rareza, *f*

peculiarly *adv* particularmente, peculiarmente; especialmente; extrañamente

pecuniarily *adv* pecuniariamente

pecuniary *a* pecuniario

pedagogic *a* pedagógico

pedagogy *n* pedagogía, *f*

pedal *a* *zool* del pie. *n* pedal, *m*. *vi* pedalear

pedant *n* pedante, *mf*

pedantic *a* pedante

pedantically *adv* con pedantería, pedantescamente

pedantry *n* pedantería, *f*

peddle *vi* ser buhonero. *vt* revender

peddling *n* buhonería, *f*. *a* trivial, insignificante; mezquino

pedestal *n* pedestal, *m*; *fig* fundamento, *m*, base, *f*. **to put on a p.,** *fig* poner sobre un pedestal

pedestrian *n* peatón, peón, *m*, a pedestre; *fig* patoso. **p. traffic,** circulación de los peatones, *f*

pedestrian crosswalk, cruce peatonal *Argentina,* cruce de peatones, *m*

pediatrician *n* pediatra, *mf*

pedigree *n* genealogía, *f*; raza, *f*; (of words) etimología, *f*. *a* (of animals) de raza, de casta. **p. dog,** perro de casta, *m*

pediment *n* *arch* frontón, *m*

pedlar *n* buhonero (-ra), *Lat. Am.* marchante (-ta), *mf*

pedometer *n* pedómetro, cuentapasos, *m*

peel *n* (baker's) pala, *f*; (of fruit, etc.) piel, *f*, hollejo, *m*. *vt* pelar, mondar; (bark) descortezar; *Lat. Am.* deshojar (fruit). *vi* descascararse, descboncharse; (of the bark of a tree) descortezarse

peeling *n* (of fruit, etc.) peladura, monda, *f*; (of bark) descortezadura, *f*; (of paint, etc.) desconchadura, *f*

peep *vi* (of birds) piar; (of mice) chillar; (peer) atisbar, mirar a hurtadillas; (appear) asomar; mostrarse; (of the dawn) despuntar. *n* (of birds) pío, *m*; (of mice) chillido, *m*; (glimpse) vista, *f*; (glance) ojeada, mirada furtiva, *f*; **at the p. of day,** al despuntar el día. **p.-hole,** mirilla, *f*, atisbadero, *m*; escucha, *f*. **p.-show,** óptica, *f*

peeper (eye) avizón *m*

peer *n* par, *m*; igual, *mf*. *vi* atisbar; escudriñar; *fig* asomar, aparecer

peerage *n* nobleza, aristocracia, *f*; dignidad de par, *f*

peeress *n* paresa, *f*

peerless *a* sin par, incomparable, sin igual

peevish *a* displicente, malhumorado; picajoso, vidrioso, enojadizo

peevishness *n* displicencia, *f*, mal humor, *m*; impaciencia, *f*

peg *n* clavija, *f*; (of a tent) estaca, *f*; (of a barrel) estaquilla, *f*; (of a violin, etc.) clavija, *f*; (for coats, etc.) colgador, *m*; (of whisky, etc.) trago, *m*; *fig* pretexto, *m*. *vt* clavar, enclavijar, empernar. **to take down a peg,** bajar los humos (a). **to peg away,** batirse el cobre. **to peg down,** fijar con clavijas; (a tent) sujetar con estacas; (prices) fijar

peignoir *n* peinador, salto de cama, *m*, bata, *f*

pekinese *n* perro (-rra) pequinés (-esa)

pelican *n* pelícano, *m*

pellagra *n* med pelagra, *f*

pellet *n* bolita, *f*; (pill) píldora, *f*; (shot) perdigón, *m*

pellmell *adv* a trochemoche; atropelladamente

pellucid *a* diáfano

Peloponesian *a* and *n* peloponense, *mf*

pelota *n* pelota vasca, *f*. **p. player,** pelotari, *m*

pelt *n* pellejo, *m*; cuero, *m*; (fur) piel, *f*; (blow) golpe, *m*. *vt* llover (piedras, etc.) sobre, arrojar . . . sobre; (questions) disparar; (throw) tirar. *vi* (of rrain) azotar, diluviar

pelvic *a* pélvico, pelviano

pelvis *n* pelvis, *f*
pen *n* (for sheep, etc.) aprisco, *m*; corral, *m*; (paddock) parque, *m*; (for hens) pollera, *f*; (for writing and *fig.*, author, etc.) pluma, *f*. *vt* (shut up) acorralar; encerrar; (write) escribir (con pluma). **pen-and-ink drawing,** dibujo a la pluma, *m*. **pen-holder,** portaplumas, *m*. **pen-name,** seudónimo, *m*. **pen-wiper,** limpiaplumas, *m*
penal *a* penal. **p. code,** código penal, *m*. **p. colony,** colonia penal, *f*. **p. servitude,** trabajos forzados (or forzosos), *m pl*. **p. servitude for life,** cadena perpetua, *f*
penalization *n* castigo, *m*
penalize *vt* penar, imponer pena (a); castigar
penalty *n law* penalidad, *f*; castigo, *m*; (fine) multa, *f*; (risk) riesgo, *m*; *sport* sanción, *m*. **the p. of,** la desventaja de. **under p. of,** so pena de. **p. kick,** (football) penalty, *m*
penance *n* penitencia, *f*. **to do p.,** hacer penitencia
penchant *n* tendencia, *f*; inclinación, *f*
pencil *n* lápiz, *m*; (automatic) lapicero, *m*. *vt* escribir (or dibujar or marcar) con lápiz. **p.-case,** estuche para lápices, *m*. **p.-holder,** lapicero, *m*. **p.-sharpener,** cortalápices, afilalápices, *m*
pendant *n* (jewel) pendiente, *m*; *arch* culo de lámpara, *m*; (*naut* rope) amantillo, *m*; (flag) gallardete, *m*
pending *a* pendiente. *prep* durante. **to be p.,** pender; amenazar
pendulous *a* péndulo; colgante; oscilante
pendulum *n* péndola, *f*, péndulo, *m*
penetrability *n* penetrabilidad, *f*
penetrable *a* penetrable
penetrate *vt* and *vi* penetrar
penetrating *a* penetrante
penetration *n* penetración, *f*
penguin *n* pingüino, pájaro bobo, *m*
penicillin *n* penicilina, *f*
peninsula *n* península, *f*
peninsular *a* peninsular. **P. War,** Guerra de la Independencia, *f*
penis *n* pene, *m*
penitence *n* penitencia, *f*
penitent *a* penitente. *n* penitente, *mf*
penitential *a* penitencial
penitentiary *n ecc* penitenciaria, *f*; casa de corrección, *f*; penitenciaria, *f*, presidio, *m*; cárcel modelo, *f*, *a* penitenciario
penknife *n* cortaplumas, *m*
penmanship *n* caligrafía, *f*
pennant *n naut* gallardete, *m*; banderola, *f*; (ensign) insignia, bandera, *f*
penniless *a* sin un penique, sin blanca; indigente, pobre de solemnidad, *Peru* calato. **to leave p.,** dejar en la miseria; *inf* dejar sin camisa
pennilessness *n* falta de dinero, extrema pobreza, *f*
penning *n* escritura, *f*; (drawing up) redacción, *f*; (of bulls, etc.) acorralamiento, *m*
pennon *n* pendón, *m*, banderola, *f*; (ensign) bandera, insignia, *f*
Pennsylvanian *a* and *n* pensilvano (-na)
penny *n* de un centavo, penique, *m*; perra gorda, *f*. *a* de un penique. **p.-a-liner,** gacetillero, *m*. **p. dreadful,** folletín, *m*, novela por entregas, *f*. **p.-in-the-slot machine,** tragaperras, *m*
pennyworth *n* penique, valor de un penique, *m*
pension *n* pensión, *f*; *mil* retiro, *m*; (grant) beca, *f*; (boardinghouse) pensión de familia, *f*. *vt* pensionar, dar una pensión (a); (with off) jubilar. **old age p.,** pensión para la vejez, *f*. **retirement p.,** pensión vitalicia, *f*
pensioner *n* pensionista, *mf*; (*mil* and *nav*) inválido, *m*
pensive *a* pensativo, meditabundo; cabizbajo, triste
pensively *adv* pensativamente; tristemente
pensiveness *n* reflexión, *f*, meditación profunda, *f*; tristeza, melancolía, *f*
pentagon *n* pentágono, *m*
Pentateuch *n* pentateuco, *m*

Pentecost *n* Pentecostés, *m*, Pascua, *f*
pentecostal *a* de Pentecostés, pascual
penthouse *n* cobertizo, tinglado, *m*, tejavana, *f*
pent-up *a* encerrado; enjaulado; (of emotion) reprimido
penultimate *a* penúltimo. *n* penúltimo, *m*
penurious *a* pobre; escaso; (stingy) tacaño, avaro
penury *n* penuria, *f*
peony *n* peonía, *f*, saltaojos, *m*, rosa albardera, rosa montés, *f*
people *n* pueblo, *m*; nación, *f*; gente, *f*; personas, *f pl*; (used disparagingly, mob) populacho, vulgo, *m*; (inhabitants) habitantes, *m pl*; (subjects) súbditos, *m pl*; (relations) parientes, *m pl*; familia, *f*. *vt* poblar. **little p.,** (children) gente menuda, *f*. **respectable p.,** gente de bien, *f*. **the p. of Burgos,** los habitantes de Burgos. **P. say,** Se dice, La gente dice. **Very few p. think as you do,** Hay muy pocas personas que opinan como Vd. **How are your p.** (family)? ¿Cómo están los de tu casa? ¿Cómo está tu familia? **"People Working"** «Trabajadores»
peopling *n* población, *f*; colonización, *f*
pep *n inf* energía, *f*, ánimo, *m*. **p. talk,** discurso estimulante, *m*. **p. up,** animar
Pepin the Short Pipino el Breve
peplum *n* peplo, *m*
pepper *n* pimienta, *f*; (plant) pimentero, pimiento, *m*, *vt* sazonar con pimienta; (pelt) acribillar; (with questions) disparar; (a literary work with quotations, etc.) salpimentar. **black p.,** pimienta negra, *f*. **red p.,** pimiento, *m*; (cayenne) pimentón, *m*. **p.-castor,** pimentero, *m*
peppercorn *n* grano de pimienta, *m*
peppermint *n* menta, *f*. **p. drop,** pastilla de menta, *f*
peppery *a* picante; (irascible) colérico, irascible
pepsin *n chem* pepsina, *f*
peptic *a* péptico
per *prep* por. **ninety miles per hour,** noventa millas por hora. **ten pesetas per dozen,** diez pesetas la docena. **$60 per annum,** sesenta dólares al año. **per cent.,** por ciento
perambulate *vt* recorrer
perambulator *n* cochecito para niños, *m*
percale *n* percal, *m*
percaline *n* percalina, *f*
perceive *vt* percibir, comprender, darse cuenta de; percibir, discernir
percentage *n* tanto por ciento, *m*; porcentaje, *m*
perceptible *a* perceptible, visible; sensible
perceptibly *adv* visiblemente; sensiblemente
perception *n* percepción, *f*; sensibilidad, *f*
perceptive *a* perceptivo
perch *n icht* perca, *f*; (for birds) percha, *f*; (measure) pértiga, *f*. *vi* posarse (en or sobre). *vt* posar (en or sobre)
percolate *vi* filtrar; *fig* penetrar. *vt* filtrar, colar
percolation *n* filtración, *f*
percolator *n* filtro, *m*. **coffee p.,** colador de café, *m*
percussion *n* percusión, *f*; choque, *m*. **p. cap,** fulminante, *m*. **p. instrument,** instrumento de percusión, *m*
perdition *n* perdición, *f*; ruina, *f*
peregrination *n* peregrinación, *f*
peremptorily *adv* perentoriamente
peremptoriness *n* perentoriedad, *f*
peremptory *a* perentorio; (of manner, etc.) imperioso, autoritario
perennial *a bot* vivaz; perenne; eterno, perpetuo. *n* planta vivaz, *f*
perennially *adv* perennemente
perfect *a* perfecto; (of a work) acabado; completo. *n gram* (tiempo) perfecto, *m*. *vt* perfeccionar; (oneself) perfeccionarse. **to have a p. knowledge of . . . ,** conocer a fondo . . . **They are p. strangers to me,** Me son completamente desconocidos
perfectible *a* perfectible
perfecting *n* perfeccionamiento, *m*; terminación, *f*

perfection *n* perfección, *f*; excelencia, *f*. **to p.,** a la perfección, a las mil maravillas

perfectionist *n* perfeccionista, *mf*

perfidious *a* pérfido

perfidy *n* perfidia, *f*

perforate *vt* perforar, agujerear

perforating *a* perforador

perforation *n* perforación, *f*; agujero, *m*

perforce *adv* a la fuerza, forzosamente

perform *vt* hacer; poner por obra, llevar a cabo; desempeñar, cumplir; ejercer; (a piece of music, etc.) ejecutar; realizar; (a play) representar, dar; (a part in a play) desempeñar (el papel de . . .); (Divine Service) oficiar. *vi theat* trabajar, representar un papel; (a musical instrument) tocar; (sing) cantar; (of animals) hacer trucos

performable *a* hacedero, practicable, ejecutable; *theat* que puede representarse; *mus* tocable

performance *n* ejecución, realización, *f*; desempeño, ejercicio, *m*; cumplimiento, *m*; acción, *f*; hazaña, *f*; (work) obra, *f*; *theat* función, representación, *f*; (*theat* acting of a part) interpretación, *f*; *mus* ejecución, *f*; *mech* potencia, *f*. **first p.,** *theat* estreno, *m*

performer *n mus* ejecutante, *mf*, músico, *m*; *theat* actor (-triz), representante, *mf*; artista, *mf*

performing *a* (of animals) sabio. **p. dog,** perro sabio, *m*

perfume *n* perfume, *m*; fragancia, *f*; aroma, *m*. *vt* perfumar; embalsamar, aromatizar, llenar con fragancia. **p. burner,** perfumador, *m*

perfumer *n* perfumista, *mf*

perfumery *n* perfumería, *f*

perfuming *n* acción de perfumar, *f*, *a* que perfuma

perfunctorily *adv* perfunctoriamente, sin cuidado; superficialmente

perfunctoriness *n* descuido, *m*, negligencia, *f*; superficialidad, *f*

perfunctory *a* perfunctorio, negligente; superficial; ligero, de cumplido

pergola *n* emparrado, cenador, *m*

perhaps *adv* quizá, quizás(s), tal vez

peril *n* peligro, *m*; riesgo, *m*. *vt* poner en peligro; arriesgar. **at one's p.,** a su riesgo. **in p.,** en peligro

perilous *a* peligroso, arriesgado

perimeter *n* perímetro, *m*

perineum *n anat* perineo, *m*

period *n* período, *m*; época, *f*; edad, *f*, tiempo, *m*; duración, *f*; término, plazo, *m*; *gram* período, *m*; (full stop) punto final, *m*; *med* menstruación, regla, *f*. **p. furniture,** muebles de época, *m pl*

periodic *a* periódico

periodical *a* periódico. *n* publicación periódica, revista, *f*

periodicity *n* periodicidad, *f*

peripatetic *a* peripatético

peripheral *a* periférico

periphery *n* periferia, *f*

periphrastic *a* perifrástico

periscope *n* periscopio, *m*

perish *vi* perecer; marchitarse; desaparecer, acabar. **to be perished with cold,** estar muerto de frío

perishable *a* perecedero, frágil

peritoneum *n* peritoneo, *m*

peritonitis *n* peritonitis, *f*

periwig *n* peluca, *f*

periwinkle *n zool* caracol marino, *m*; *bot* vincapervinca, *f*

perjure *vt* perjurar. **to p. oneself,** perjurarse

perjurer *n* perjuro (-ra); perjurador (-ra)

perjury *n* perjurio, *m*. **to commit p.,** jurar en falso, perjurar

perk (up) *vi* levantar la cabeza; recobrar sus bríos, alzar la cabeza; sacar la cabeza

perkiness *n* desenvoltura, gallardía, *f*, despejo, *m*

perky *a* desenvuelto, gallardo; coquetón; atrevido; (gay) alegre

permanence *n* permanencia, *f*; estabilidad, *f*

permanent *a* permanente; estable; (of posts, etc.) fijo. **p. wave,** ondulación permanente, *f*. **p. way,** *rw* vía, *f*

permanganate *n* permanganato, *m*

permeability *n* permeabilidad, *f*

permeable *a* permeable

permeate *vt* penetrar; impregnar; *fig* infiltrar (en)

permeation *n* penetración, *f*; impregnación, *f*; *fig* infiltración, *f*

permissible *a* permisible, admisible; lícito

permission *n* permiso, *m*, licencia, *f*

permissive *a* permisivo, tolerado; (optional) facultativo

permit *vt* permitir; dar permiso (a), dejar; tolerar, sufrir; admitir. *n* permiso, *m*; licencia, *f*; pase, *m*. **Will you p. me to smoke?** ¿Me permites fumar?

permutation *n* permutación, *f*

permute *vt* permutar

pernicious *a* pernicioso. **p. anemia,** anemia perniciosa, *f*

perniciousness *n* perniciosidad, *f*

pernickety *a* tiquismiquis

peroration *n* peroración, *f*

peroxide *n* peróxido, *m*

perpendicular *a* perpendicular. *n* perpendicular, *f*

perpendicularity *n* perpendicularidad, *f*

perpendicularly *adv* perpendicularmente

perpetrate *vt law* perpetrar; cometer

perpetration *n law* perpetración, *f*; comisión, *f*

perpetrator *n* el, *m*, (*f*, la) que comete; *law* autor (-ra); perpetrador (-ra)

perpetual *a* perpetuo, perdurable, eterno; incesante, constante; (life-long) perpetuo

perpetually *adv* perpetuamente; sin cesar; continuamente; constantemente

perpetuate *vt* perpetuar, eternizar; inmortalizar

perpetuation *n* perpetuación, *f*

perpetuity *n* perpetuidad, *f*. **in p.,** para siempre

perplex *vt* dejar perplejo, aturdir, confundir; embrollar

perplexed *a* perplejo, irresoluto; confuso; (of questions, etc.) complicado, intrincado

perplexedly *adv* perplejamente

perplexing *a* difícil; complicado; confuso

perplexity *n* perplejidad, *f*; confusión, *f*

perquisites *n pl* emolumentos, *m pl*; gajes, percances, *m pl*; (tips) propinas, *f pl*

persecute *vt* perseguir; importunar, molestar

persecution *n* persecución, *f*

persecutor *n* perseguidor (-ra)

perseverance *n* perseverancia, *f*

persevere *vi* perseverar

persevering *a* perseverante

perseveringly *adv* con perseverancia, perseverantemente

Persia (la) Persia, *f*

Persian *a* persa; de Persia; pérsico. *n* persa, *mf*; (language) persa, *m*. **P. blinds,** persianas, *f pl*. **P. cat,** gato (-ta) de Angora

persiennes *n pl* persianas, *f pl*

persist *vi* persistir; persistir (en), empeñarse (en), obstinarse (en)

persistence *n* persistencia, *f*

persistent *a* persistente

persistently *adv* con persistencia, persistentemente

person *n* persona, *f*. **first p.,** *gram* primera persona, *f*. **in p.,** en persona. **no p.,** nadie

personable *a* bien parecido

personage *n* personaje, *m*

personal *a* personal; íntimo; particular; en persona; (movable) mueble. **He is to make a p. appearance,** Va a estar presente en persona. **p. column,** (in a newspaper) columna de los suspiros, *f*. **p. equation,** ecuación personal, *f*. **p. estate,** (goods) bienes muebles, *m pl*

personality *n* personalidad, *f*; (insult) personalismo, *m*. **dual p.,** conciencia doble, *f*

personate *vt* (in a play) hacer el papel de; (impersonate) hacerse pasar por

personification *n* personificación, *f*

personify *vt* personificar

personnel *n* personal, *m*

perspective *n* perspectiva, *f*, *a* en perspectiva

perspicacious *a* perspicaz, clarividente, sagaz

perspicacity *n* perspicacia, clarividencia, sagacidad, *f*

perspicuity *n* perspicuidad, claridad, lucidez, *f*

perspicuous *a* perspicuo, claro

perspiration *n* sudor, *m*

perspire *vi* sudar, transpirar

persuadable *a* persuasible

persuade *vt* persuadir; inducir (a), instar (a), mover (a), inclinar (a)

persuasion *n* persuasión, *f*; persuasiva, *f*; opinión, *f*; creencia, *f*; religión, *f*; secta, *f*

persuasive *a* persuasivo. *n* persuasión, *f*; aliciente, atractivo, *m*

persuasively *adv* de un modo persuasivo, persuasivamente

persuasiveness *n* persuasiva, *f*

pert *a* petulante; respondón, desparpajado

pertain *vi* pertenecer (a); tocar (a), incumbir (a), convenir (a); estar relacionado (con)

pertinacious *a* pertinaz

pertinaciously *adv* con pertinacia

pertinacity *n* pertinacia, *f*

pertinence *n* pertinencia, *f*

pertinent *a* pertinente, atinado

pertinently *adv* atinadamente

pertly *adv* con petulancia; con descaro

pertness *n* petulancia, *f*; desparpajo, descaro, *m*

perturb *vt* perturbar, agitar, turbar, inquietar

perturbation *n* perturbación, agitación, inquietud, *f*; confusión, *f*; desorden, *m*

perturbed *a* perturbado, agitado, ansioso, intranquilo

perturbing *a* perturbador, inquietador

Peru el Perú

peruke *n* peluca, *f*

perusal *n* lectura, *f*; examen, *m*

peruse *vt* leer con cuidado, estudiar, examinar

Peruvian *a* and *n* peruano (-na)

pervade *vt* penetrar; llenar, saturar; difundirse por; reinar en

pervasion *n* penetración, *f*

pervasive *a* penetrante

perverse *a* (wicked) perverso, depravado; obstinado; travieso; intratable

perversion *n* perversión, *f*

perversity *n* (wickedness) perversidad, *f*; obstinacia, *f*; travesura, *f*

perversive *a* perversivo

pervert *vt* pervertir; (words, etc.) torcer, tergiversar

pervious *a* penetrable; permeable

pessimism *n* pesimismo, *m*

pessimist *n* pesimista, *mf*

pessimistic *a* pesimista

pessimistically *adv* con pesimismo

pest *n* insecto nocivo, *m*; animal dañino, *m*; parásito, *m*; (pestilence) peste, *f*; *fig* plaga, *f*; (person) mosca, *f*

pester *vt* importunar, molestar, incomodar, *Lat. Am.* acatorrar, cargosear, majaderear. **to p. constantly,** *inf* no dejar a sol ni a sombra

pestering *n* importunaciones, *f pl*; *a* = **annoying**

pestilence *n* pestilencia, peste, *f*; plaga, *f*

pestilential *a* pestilente, pestífero; pernicioso

pestle *n* mano de mortero, *f*, *vt* pistar, machacar, majar

pet *n* animal doméstico, *m*; niño (-ña) mimado (-da); favorito (-ta); (dear) querido (-da); (peevishness) despecho, malhumor, *m*. *vt* acariciar; (spoil) mimar. **to be a great pet,** ser un gran favorito

petal *n* pétalo, *m*, hoja, *f*

Peter *n* Pedro, *m*. **blue P.,** bandera de salida, *f*. **Peter's pence,** los diezmos de San Pedro

peter (out) *vi* desaparecer; agotarse

petition *n* petición, *f*; súplica, *f*; instancia, solicitud, *f*; memorial, *m*. *vt* suplicar; pedir, demandar; dirigir un memorial (a). **to file a p.,** elevar una instancia

petitioner *n* peticionario (-ia)

pet peeve *Lat. Am.* barreno, *m*

Petrarchan *a* petrarquista

petrifaction *n* petrificación, *f*

petrify *vt* petrificar; *inf* dejar seco. **to become petrified,** petrificarse

petrol *n* bencina, gasolina, *f*. *a* de gasolina, de bencina. **to run out of p.,** tener una pana de bencina. **p. gauge,** indicador del nivel de gasolina, *m*. **p. pump,** surtidor de gasolina, *m*. **p. station,** puesto de bencina, *m*, estación de servicio, *f*. **p. tank,** depósito de bencina, *m*

petroleum *n* petróleo, *m*. *a* petrolero; de petróleo. **p. works,** refinería de petróleo, *f*

petrology *n* petrografía, *f*

petrous *a* pétreo

petticoat *n* enagua, *f*; *pl* **petticoats,** (slang) faldas, *f pl*. *a* de faldas, de mujeres; de mujer

pettifogger *n* (lawyer) picapleitos, *m*, rábula, *mf*; (quibbler) sofista, *mf*

pettifogging *a* charlatán, mezquino, trivial

pettiness *n* trivialidad, insignificancia, *f*; pequeñez, *f*; mezquindad, *f*; ruindad, bajeza, *f*

petty *a* trivial, sin importancia, insignificante; inferior; pequeño; mezquino; ruin; bajo. **p. cash,** gastos menores de caja, *m pl*. **p. expense,** gasto menudo, *m*. **p. officer,** suboficial, *m*. **p. thief,** ratero (-ra)

petulance *n* mal humor, *m*, displicencia, irritabilidad, *f*

petulant *a* malhumorado, displicente, enojadizo, irritable

petulantly *adv* displicentemente, con mal humor

petunia *n* petunia, *f*

pew *n* banco (de iglesia), *m*. **p.-opener,** sacristán, *m*

pewter *n* peltre, *m*, *a* de peltre

phalange *n* falange, *f*

phalanx *n* falange, *f*

phallic *a* fálico

phallus *n* falo, *m*

phantasmagoria *n* fantasmagoría, *f*

phantasmagoric *a* fantasmagórico

phantom *n* fantasma, espectro, *m*; sombra, ficción, *f*; visión, *f*

Pharisaical *a* farisaico

Pharisee *n* fariseo, *m*

pharmaceutical *a* farmacéutico; *n* producto farmacéutico, *m*

pharmacist *n* farmacéutico, *m*

pharmacological *a* farmacológico

pharmacologist *n* farmacólogo, *m*

pharmacology *n* farmacología, *f*

pharmacopeia *n* farmacopea, *f*

pharmacy *n* farmacia, *f*

pharyngeal *a* faríngeo

pharyngitis *n* faringitis, *f*

pharynx *n* faringe, *f*

phase *n* fase, *f*; aspecto, *m*; *ast* fase, *f*

pheasant *n* faisán, *m*. **hen p.,** faisana, *f*. **p. shooting,** caza de faisanes, *f*

phenic *a* fénico

phenol *n* fenol, *m*

phenomenal *a* fenomenal

phenomenon *n* fenómeno, *m*

phial *n* redoma, *f*

philander *vi* galantear

philanderer *n* Tenorio, galanteador, *m*

philandering *n* galanteo, *m*

philanthropic *a* filantrópico

philanthropist *n* filántropo, *m*

philanthropy *n* filantropía, *f*

philatelic *a* filatélico

philatelist *n* filatelista, *mf*

philately *n* filatelia, *f*

philharmonic *a* filarmónico

philippic *n* filípica, *f*
Philippine *a* and *n* filipino (-na)
Philippines, the las (Islas) Filipinas, *f pl*
Philistine *a* and *n* filisteo (-ea)
philological *a* filológico
philologist *n* filólogo, *m*
philology *n* filología, *f*
philosopher *n* filósofo, *m*. **philosopher's stone,** piedra filosofal, *f*
philosophic(al) *a* filosófico
philosophize *vi* filosofar
philosophy *n* filosofía, *f*. **moral p.,** filosofía moral, *f*. **natural p.,** filosofía natural, *f*
philter *n* filtro, *m*
phlebitis *n* flebitis, *f*
phlebotomist *n* sangrador, flebotomiano, *m*
phlebotomy *n* flebotomía, *f*
phlegm *n* flema, *f*, *Lat. Am.* desgarro, *m*
phlegmatic *a* flemático
phlox *n* flox, *m*
Phoenician *a* and *n* fenicio (-ia)
phoenix *n* fénix, *f*
phoenitic *a* fonético
phoneticist *n* fonetista, *mf*
phonetics *n* fonética, *f*
phonograph *n* fonógrafo, *m*
phonological *a* fonológico
phonology *n* fonología, *f*
phony *a* falso; espurio. **p. war,** guerra tonta, guerra falsa, *f*
phosphate *n* fosfato, *m*
phosphoresce *vi* fosforecer, ser fosforescente
phosphorescence *n* fosforescencia, *f*
phosphorescent *a* fosforescente
phosphoric *a* fosfórico
phosphorus *n* fósforo, *m*
photo *n* foto, *f*
photochemistry *n* fotoquímica, *f*
photogenic *a* fotogénico
photograph *n* fotografía, *f*. *vt* fotografiar, retratar. **to have one's p. taken,** hacerse retratar
photographer *n* fotógrafo, *m*
photographic *a* fotográfico
photography *n* fotografía, *f*
photogravure *n* fotograbado, *m*
photostat *n* fotostato, *m*
photosynthesis *n* fotosíntesis, *f*
phrase *n* frase, *f*; *mus* frase musical, *f*. *vt* expresar, frasear; redactar. **p.-book,** libro de frases, *m*
phraseology *n* fraseología, *f*
phrasing *n* (drawing up) redacción, *f*; (style) estilo, *m*; *mus* frases, *f pl*
phrenetic *a* frenético
Phrygian *a* and *n* frigio (-ia)
Phrygian cap *n* gorro frigio, *m*
phthisis *n* tisis, *f*
phylactery *n* filactria, *f*
phylloxera *n* filoxera, *f*
physical *a* físico. **p. fitness,** buen estado físico, *m*. **p. geography,** geografía física, *f*. **p. jerks,** ejercicios físicos, *m pl*. **p. sciences,** ciencias físicas, *f pl*. **p. training,** educación física, *f*
physician *n* médico (-ca)
physicist *n* físico, *m*
physics *n* física, *f*
physiognomist *n* fisonomista, *mf*
physiognomy *n* fisonomía, *f*
physiological *a* fisiológico
physiologist *n* fisiólogo, *m*
physiology *n* fisiología, *f*
physiotherapy *n* fisioterapia, *f*
physique *n* físico, *m*
pianist *n* pianista, *mf*
piano, pianoforte *n* piano, *m*. **baby grand p.,** piano de media cola, *m*. **grand p.,** piano de cola, *m*. **upright p.,** piano vertical, *m*. **p. maker,** fabricante de pianos,

m. **p. stool,** taburete de piano, *m*. **p. tuner,** afinador de pianos, *m*
pianola *n* piano mecánico, *m*
picaresque *a* picaresco
piccolo *n* flautín, *m*
pick *n* (tool) pico, zapapico, *m*; (mattock) piqueta, *f*; (choice) selección, *f*; derecho de elección, *m*; (best) lo mejor, lo más escogido; (*fig* cream) flor, nata, *f*. **tooth-p.,** mondadientes, *m*. **p.-a-back,** sobre los hombros, a cuestas. **p.-ax,** zapapico, *m*, alcotana, *f*. **p.-me-up,** tónico, *m*; trago, *m*
pick *vt* (with a pick-ax, make a hole) picar; (pluck, pick up) coger; (remove) sacar; (clean) limpiar; (one's teeth) mondarse (los dientes); (one's nose) hurgarse (las narices); (a bone) roer; (a lock) abrir con ganzúa; (a pocket) bolsear, robar del bolsillo; (peck) picotear; (choose) escoger; (a quarrel) buscar. *vi* (steal) hurtar, robar; (nibble) picar. **I have a bone to p. with you,** Tengo que ajustar unas cuentas contigo. **Take your p.!** ¡Escoja! **to p. and choose,** mostrarse difícil. **to p. to pieces,** *fig* criticar severamente. **to p. one's way through,** abrirse camino entre; andar con precaución por; andar a tientas por. **to p. off,** coger; arrancar; quitar; (shoot) disparar; fusilar. **to p. out,** entresacar; escoger; (recognize) reconocer; (understand) llegar a comprender; (a tune) tocar de oídas; (a song) cantar de oídas; (of colours) contrastar, resaltar. **to p. up,** *vt* (ground, etc.) romper con pico; coger; tomar; recoger; (raise) levantar, alzar; (information, etc.) cobrar, adquirir; (a living) ganar; (make friends with) trabar amistad con; (recover) recobrar; (find) encontrar, hallar; (buy) comprar; (learn) aprender; (a wireless message) interceptar; (a radio station) oír, tener. *vi* recobrar la salud; reponerse; mejorar. *n mech* recobro, *m*
picket *n* estaca, *f*; (*mil* and during strikes) piquete, *m*. *vt* cercar con estacas; poner piquetes ante (or alrededor de); poner de guardia; estacionar
picking *n* (gathering) recolección, *f*; (choosing) selección, *f*; (pilfering) robo, *m*; *pl* **pickings,** desperdicios, *m pl*; (perquisites) gajes, *m pl*; ganancias, *f pl*
pickle *n* (solution) escabeche, *m*; (vegetable, etc.) encurtido, *m*; (plight) apuro, *m*; (child) diablillo, *m*. *vt* encurtir, escabechar
picklock *n* (thief and instrument) ganzúa, *f*
pickpocket *n* carterista, *mf* ratero (-ra)
picnic *n* partida de campo, jira, *f*, picnic, *m*. *vi* llevar la merienda al campo, hacer un picnic
picnicker *n* excursionista, *mf*
pictorial *a* pictórico; ilustrado. *n* revista ilustrada, *f*
pictorially *adv* pictóricamente; en grabados; por imágenes
picture *n* cuadro, *m*; (of a person) retrato, *m*; imagen, *f*; (illustration) grabado, *m*, lámina, *f*; fotografía, *f*; (outlook) perspectiva, *f*; idea, *f*. *vt* pintar; describir; imaginar. **to go to the pictures,** ir al cine. **motion p.,** película, *f*. **talking p.,** película sonora, *f*. **p. book,** libro con láminas, *m*. **p. frame,** marco, *m*. **p. gallery,** museo de pinturas, *m*; galería de pinturas, *f*. **p. hat,** pamela, *f*. **p. palace,** cine, *m*. **p. postcard,** tarjeta postal, *f*. **p. restorer,** restaurador de cuadros, *m*. **p. writing,** pictografía, *f*
picturesque *a* pintoresco
picturesqueness *n* carácter pintoresco, *m*, lo pintoresco; pintoresquismo, *m*
pie *n* (savoury) empanada, *f*; (sweet) pastel, *m*, torta, *f*; (of meat) pastelón, *m*; *print* pastel, *m*. **apple pie,** torta de manzanas, *f*. **to eat humble pie,** bajar las orejas. **to have a finger in the pie,** meter baza
piebald *a* pío; tordo
piece *n* pedazo, *m*; trozo, *m*; parte, porción, *f*; (literary, artistic work, coin, of fabric, at chess, etc. and slang) pieza, *f*; (of luggage) bulto, *m*; (of paper) hoja, *f*; (of ground) parcela, *f*; (of money) moneda, *f*, *vt* remendar; unir, juntar. **a p. of advice,** un consejo. **a p. of bread,** un pedazo de pan; una rebanada de pan. **a p. of folly,** un acto de locura. **a p. of furniture,** un mueble. **a p.**

of insolence, una insolencia. **a p. of news,** una noticia. **a p. of paper,** un papel, una hoja de papel, una cuartilla. **a p. of poetry,** una poesía. **Peter has a five-shilling p.,** Pedro tiene una moneda de cinco chelines. **to break in pieces,** *vt* hacer pedazos, romper. *vi* hacerse pedazos, romperse. **to come or fall to pieces,** deshacerse; (of machines) desarmarse. **to cut in pieces,** cortar en pedazos; (an army) destrozar. **to give a p. of one's mind (to),** decir cuatro verdades (a), decir cuántas son cinco (a). **to go to pieces,** (of persons) hacerse pedazos. **to take to pieces,** (a machine) desmontar; deshacer. **to tear or pull to pieces,** hacer pedazos, despedazar; desgarrar. **p. goods,** géneros en piezas, *m pl*. **p.-work,** trabajo a destajo, *m*. **to do p.-work,** trabajar a destajo. **p.-worker,** destajista, *mf*

piecemeal *adv* en pedazos; a remiendos; en detalle; poco a poco

piecrust *n* pasta, *f*

pied *a* bicolor; abigarrado, de varios colores

pier *n* (jetty) dique, *m*; embarcadero, *m*; malecón, *m*; (of a bridge) pila, *f*; (pillar) columna, *f*; (between windows, etc.) entrepaño, *m*. **p.-glass,** espejo de cuerpo entero, *m*. **p. head,** punta del dique, *f*. **p. table,** consola, *f*

pierce *vt* penetrar; (of sorrow, etc.) traspasar, herir; (bore) agujerear, taladrar. *vi* penetrar

pierced ear *n* oreja perforada, *f*

piercing *a* penetrante; (of the wind, etc.) cortante; (of the voice, etc.) agudo. *n* penetración, *f*

piercingly *adv* de un modo penetrante, agudamente

pietism *n* pietismo, *m*

pietist *n* pietista, *mf*

pietistic *a* pietista

piety *n* piedad, devoción, *f*

piezometer *n* piezómetro, *m*

piffle *n* patrañas, tonterías, *f pl*

pig *n* puerco, cerdo, *Lat. Am.* chancho, *m*; *inf* cochino, *m*; (metal) lingote, *m*. **to buy a p. in a poke,** cerrar un trato a ciegas. **p.-eyed,** de ojos de cerdo. **p.-iron,** arrabio; hierro colado en barras, lingote de fundición, *m*

pigeon *n* paloma, *f*, palomo, *m*; *inf* primo, *m*. *vt* embaucar, engañar. **carrier p.,** paloma mensajera, *f*. **clay p.,** pichón de barro, platillo de arcilla, *m*. **male p.,** pichón, *m*. **pouter p.,** paloma buchona, *f*. **young p.,** palomino, *m*. **p. fancier,** palomero, *m*. **p.-hole,** casilla, *f*. *vt* encasillar. **set of p.-holes,** encasillado, *m*. **p.-shooting,** tiro de pichón, *m*. **p.-toed,** patituerto

piggy bank *n* alcancía, *f*

pigheaded *a* terco, testarudo, *Lat. Am.* empecinado

pigheadedness *n* terquedad, testarudez, *f*

piglet *n* cerdito, *m*

pigment *n* pigmento, *m*

pigmentation *n* pigmentación, *f*

pigskin *n* piel de cerdo, *f*

pigsty *n* pocilga, *f*

pigtail *n* coleta, *f*

pike *n* *mil* pica, *f*, chuzo, *m*; (peak) pico, *m*

pilaster *n* pilastra, *f*

pile *n* estaca, *f*; poste, *m*; (engineering) pilote, *m*; (heap) pila, *f*, montón, *m*; (pyre) pira, *f*; (building) edificio grande, *m*; *elec* pila, *f*; (hair) pelo, *m*; (nap) pelusa, *f*; *pl* piles, *med* almorranas, *f pl*. *vt* clavar pilotes en; apoyar con pilotes; (heap) amontonar; (load) cargar. **to make one's p.,** *inf* hacer su pacotilla. **to p. arms,** poner los fusiles en pabellón. **to p. on,** (coal, etc.) echar; (increase) aumentar. **to p. it on,** exagerar, intensificar; (a table) cargar. **to p. up,** *vi* amontonarse; acumularse; *vt* *Lat. Am.* empilonar; (of a ship) encallar. **p.-driver,** machina, *f*; martinete, *m*. **p. dwelling,** vivienda palustre, sostenida por pilares, *f*

pilfer *vt* sisar, sonsacar, hurtar, ratear, *Mexico* chalequear

pilferer *n* sisador (-ra), ratero (-ra)

pilfering *n* sisa, ratería, *f*

pilgrim *n* peregrino (-na). **pilgrim's staff,** bordón, *m*

pilgrimage *n* peregrinación, *f*; romería, *f*. **to make a p.,** hacer una peregrinación, peregrinar; ir en romería

piling *n* amontonamiento, *m*; (of buildings) pilotaje, *m*

pill *n* píldora, *f*. **to gild the p.,** *fig* dorar la píldora. **p.-box,** caja de píldoras, *f*; casamata, *f*, *mil* nido de ametralladoras, *m*

pillage *vt* pillar, saquear. *n* saqueo, *m*

pillager *n* saqueador (-ra)

pillaging *n* pillaje, *m*, *a* pillador, saqueador

pillar *n* pilar, *m*, columna, *f*; (person) sostén, soporte, *m*. **from p. to post,** de Ceca en Meca. **p. of salt,** estatua de sal, *f*. **the Pillars of Hercules,** las Columnas de Hércules, *f*. **to be a p. of strength,** *inf* ser una roca. **p.-box,** buzón, *m*

pillared *a* con columnas, sostenido por columnas; en columnas

pillion *n* (on a horse, etc.) grupera, *f*; (on a motor-cycle) grupa, *f*. **to ride p.,** ir a la grupa

pillory *n* picota, argolla, *f*. *vt* empicotar; *fig* poner en ridículo; censurar duramente

pillow *n* almohada, *f*; (for lace-making) cojín, *m*; (of a machine) cojinete, *m*. *vt* apoyar; reposar; servir como almohada. **to take counsel of one's p.,** consultar con la almohada. **p.-case,** funda de almohada, *f*

pilot *n* piloto, *m*; *naut* práctico, piloto (de puerto), *m*. *vt* guiar, conducir; (*naut aer*) pilotar, pilotear. **p. boat,** vaporcito del práctico, *m*. **p. jacket,** chaquetón de piloto, *m*. **p. officer,** oficial de aviación, *m*

pilotage *n* pilotaje, *m*; *naut* practicaje, *m*

pilotless *a* sin piloto

pimento *n* pimiento, *m*

pimp *n* rufián, alcahuete, *m*, *vi* alcahuetear

pimple *n* grano, *m*

pimply *a* con granos

pin *n* alfiler, *m*; prendedor, *m*; clavija, *f*; clavo, *m*, chaveta, *f*; (bolt) perno, *m*. *vt* prender con alfileres; (with a peg) enclavijar; fijar; sujetar. **to pin up,** sujetar con alfileres; (the hair) sujetar con horquillas. **I don't care a pin,** No me importa un bledo. **to be on pins,** estar en ascuas. **to suffer from pins and needles,** tener aguijones. **pin-head,** cabeza de alfiler, *f*. **pin-money,** alfileres, *m pl*. **pin-oak,** *bot* pincarrasco, *m*, carrasca, *f*. **pin point,** punta de alfiler, *f*. **pin-prick,** alfilerazo, *m*

pinafore *n* delantal de niño, *m*

pince-nez *n* quevedos, *m pl*

pincers *n pl* pinzas, tenazas, *f pl*, alicates, *m pl*; (of crustaceans) pinzas, *f pl*. **p. movement,** movimiento de pinzas, *m*

pinch *vt* pellizcar; (crush) estrujar; aplastar; apretar; (of the cold) helar; (steal) hurtar, birlar; (arrest) coger, prender. *n* pellizco, torniscón, *m*; pulgarada, *f*; (of snuff) polvo, *m*; (distress) miseria, *f*; (pain) dolor, *m*, angustia, *f*. **at a p.,** en caso de apuro. **to know where the shoe pinches,** saber dónde le aprieta el zapato

pinched *a* (by the cold) helado; (wan) marchito, descolorido

pincushion *n* acerico, *m*

Pindaric *a* pindárico

pine *n* *bot* pino, *m*. *vi* languidecer, marchitarse, consumirse. **to p. for,** anhelar, suspirar por, perecer por. **pitch-p.,** pino de tea, *m*. **p.-apple,** piña de las Indias, *f*, ananás, *m*. **p. cone,** piña, *f*. **p. kernel,** piñón, *m*. **p. needle,** pinocha, *f*. **p. wood,** pinar, *m*, pineda, *f*

pineal *a* en figura de piña; *anat* pineal

ping *n* silbido de una bala, *m*; zumbido, *m*. **p. pong,** tenis de mesa, pingpong, *m*

pinion *n* (wing) ala, *f*; (small feather) piñón, *m*; (in carving) alón, *m*; (wheel) piñón, *m*. *vt* atar las alas de; cortar un piñón de; (a person) atar; (the arms of) trincar, asegurar

pink *n* *bot* clavel, *m*; color de rosa, *m*; (perfection) modelo, *m*; colmo, *m*; (hunting) color rojo, *m*; levitín rojo de caza, *m*. *a* de color de rosa, rosado. *vt* *sew* picar; (pierce) penecrar, atravesar. *vi* (of an engine) picar

pinking *n* *sew* picadura, *f*

pinkish *a* rosáceo
pinnacle *n naut* pinaza, *f*
pinnacle *n* pináculo, *m*
pinpoint *vt* precisar
pint *n* (measure) pinta, *f*
pintle *n* (pin) perno, *m*
pioneer *n* pionero, explorador, *m*; introductor, *m*. **to be a p. in . . . ,** ser el primero en (or a) . . . **pioneering role,** papel de iniciador (e.g. **She played a pioneering role,** jugó un papel de iniciadora)
pious *a* pío, devoto, piadoso
piously *adv* piadosamente, devotamente
pip *n* (of fruit) pepita, *f*; (on cards, dice) punto, *m*; (disease) moquillo, *m*; (of an army, etc., officer) insignia, *f*
pipe *n* (for tobacco) pipa (de fumar) *Argentina* cachimba, *f*; *mus* caramillo, *m*; (boatswain's) pito, *m*; (of a bird) trino, *m*; (voice) voz aguda, *f*; tubo, *m*; (for water, etc.) cañería, *f*; (of a hose) manga, *f*; (of an organ) cañón, *m*; (of wine) pipa, *f*; *pl* **pipes,** *mus* gaita, *f*. *vi* tocar el caramillo (or la gaita); empezar a cantar; silbar; (of birds) trinar. *vt* (a tune) tocar; (sing) cantar; (whistle) llamar con pito; conducir con cañerías; instalar cañerías en. **He smokes a p., Fuma una pipa. I smoked a p.** (of tobacco) **before I went to bed,** Fumé una pipa antes de acostarme. **Put that in your p. and smoke it!** ¡Chúpate eso! **p. clay,** blanquizal, *m*. **p. cleaner,** limpiapipas, *m*. **p. layer,** cañero, fontanero, *m*. **p. laying,** instalación de cañerías, *f*. **p.-line,** cañería, *f*; (oil) oleoducto, *m*. **p. tobacco,** tabaco de pipa, *m*
pipeful *n* pipa, *f*
piper *n* (bagpiper) gaitero, *m*; flautista, *mf*
pipette *n chem* pipeta, *f*
piping *n* sonido del caramillo, *m*; música de la flauta, etc., *f*; (of birds) trinos, *m pl*; voz aguda, *f*; (for water, etc.) cañería, tubería, *f*; *sew* cordoncillo, *m*. **p.-hot,** hirviente
pipkin *n* ollita de barro, *f*
pippin *n* (apple) camuesa, *f*
piquancy *n* picante, *f*
piquant *a* picante
pique *n* (resentment, and score in game) pique, *m*. **to p. oneself upon,** preciarse de, jactarse de. **to be piqued,** estar enojado; *inf* amoscarse
piquet *n* juego de los cientos, *m*
piracy *n* piratería, *f*
pirate *n* pirata, *mf*. *vi* piratear. *vt* publicar una edición furtiva de. **p. edition,** edición furtiva, *f*
piratical *a* pirata, pirático; de pirata, de piratas
pirouette *n* pirueta, *f*
Pisces *n pl* peces, *m pl*
pisciculture *n* piscicultura, *f*
Pisgah Fasga, *f*
pistachio *n* pistacho, *m*
pistil *n bot* pistilo, *m*
pistol *n* pistola, *f*. **p. belt,** charpa, *f*, cinto de pistolas, *m*. **p. case,** pistolera, *f*. **p. shot,** pistoletazo, *m*
piston *n mech* émbolo, pistón, *m*; *mus* pistón, *m*, llave, *f*. **p. ring,** anillo de émbolo, segmento de émbolo, *m*. **p. rod,** biela, *f*. **p. stroke,** carrera del émbolo, *f*
pit *n* hoyo, *m*; foso, *m*; (in a garage) foso de reparación, *m*; *theat* platea, *f*; (trap) trampa, *f*; (scar) hoyo, *m*; precipicio, *m*; (hell) infierno, *m*. *vt* (with smallpox) marcar con viruelas; (against) competir con. **pithead,** boca de mina, *f*. **pit of the stomach,** boca del estómago, *f*. **pit stall,** butaca de platea, *f*
pitch *n chem* pez, brea, *f*, alquitrán, *m*; (place) puesto, *m*; (throwing) lanzamiento, *m*; (distance thrown) alcance, *m*; (for cricket) cancha, *f*; (bowling) saque, *m*; (slope) pendiente, inclinación, *f*; (height) elevación, *f*; *mus* tono, *m*; (*fig* degree) grado, extremo, *m*; (*naut aer*) cabeceo, *m*; (of threads of a screw, etc.) paso, *m*. *vt* (camp) asentar; (a tent, etc.) colocar, poner; (throw) lanzar, arrojar, tirar; (cricket, etc.) lanzar; (fix in) clavar; *mus* graduar el tono de; (tell) narrar. *vi* (fall) caer; *naut* cabecear, zozobrar; *aer* cabecear. **to paint with**

p., embrear. **to p. into,** (attack) acometer, atacar; (scold) desatarse contra; (food) engullir. **p.-black,** negro como la pez; oscuro como boca de lobo. **p.-pine,** pino de tea, *m*. **p.-pipe,** diapasón vocal, *m*
pitched battle *n* batalla campal, *f*
pitcher *n* jarro, cántaro, *m*; (in baseball) lanzador de pelota, *m*
pitcherful *n* jarro (de), *m*
pitchfork *n* horquilla, *f*, aventador, *m*. *vt* levantar con horquilla; *fig* lanzar
pitching *n* (pavement) adoquinado, *m*; (of a ship) socollada, *f*; cabeceo, *m*
piteous *a* lastimero; triste; plañidero; compasivo, tierno
piteousness *n* estado lastimero, *m*; tristeza, *f*; compasión, ternura, *f*
pitfall *n* trampa, *f*; *fig* añagaza, *f*, lazo, peligro, *m*
pith *n bot* médula, *f*; médula espinal, *f*; *fig* meollo, *m*; fuerza, *f*, vigor, *m*; substancia, *f*; quinta esencia, *f*; importancia, *f*
pithiness *n* jugosidad, *f*; fuerza, *f*, vigor, *m*
pithy *a* meduloso; *fig* jugoso; enérgico, vigoroso
pitiable *a* lastimoso, digno de compasión; (paltry) despreciable
pitiful *a* piadoso, compasivo; conmovedor, doloroso, lastimero; (contemptible) miserable
pitifully *adv* lastimosamente
pitiless *a* sin piedad, despiadado
pitilessness *n* crueldad, inhumanidad, *f*
pitman *n* minero, *m*; aserrador de foso, *m*
pittance *n* pitanza, *f*; pequeña porción, *f*; ración de hambre, *f*
pitted *a* picoso
pituitary *a* pituitario
pity *n* piedad, compasión, *f*; lástima, *f*. *vt* compadecerse de, tener lástima (a); compadecer. **It is a p. that . . . ,** Es lástima que . . . **Have p.!** ¡Ten piedad! **to take p. on,** tener lástima (de). **to move to p.,** dar lástima (a), enternecer
pityingly *adv* con lástima
pivot *n* pivote, *m*; eje, *m*; *fig* punto de partida, *m*, *vi* girar sobre un pivote o eje
pivotal *a fig* cardinal, principal, fundamental
pixy *n* duende, *m*. **p. hood,** caperuza, *f*
pizzicato *a* pichigato
placability *n* placabilidad, *f*
placable *a* aplacable, placable
placard *n* cartel, *m*. *vt* fijar carteles (en); publicar por carteles
placate *vt* aplacar, ablandar, apaciguar
placatory *a* placativo
place *n* lugar, *m*; sitio, *m*; (position) puesto, *m*; (seat) asiento, *m*; (laid at table) cubierto, *m*; (square) plaza, *f*; (house) residencia, *f*; (in the country) casa de campo, finca, *f*; (in a book) pasaje, *m*; (in an examination) calificación, *f*; (rank) posición, *f*, rango, *m*; situación, *f*; (employment) empleo, *m*, colocación, *f*. *vt* poner; colocar; (in employment) dar empleo (a); (appoint) nombrar; (an order) dar; (money) invertir; (remember) recordar, traer a la memoria; (size up) fijar; (confidence) poner. **in p.,** en su lugar; apropiado. **in p. of,** en vez de, en lugar de. **in the first p.,** en primer lugar, primero. **in the next p.,** luego, después. **out of p.,** fuera de lugar; inoportuno. **It is not my p. to . . . ,** No me toca a mí de . . . **to give p. to,** conceder el paso (a); ceder (a). **to take p.,** verificarse, tener lugar, ocurrir. **p. of business,** establecimiento, local de negocios, *m*. **p. of worship,** edificio de culto, *m*
placenta *n* placenta, *f*
placid *a* plácido, apacible; calmoso; sereno, sosegado; dulce
placidity *n* placidez, *f*; serenidad, tranquilidad, *f*, sosiego, *m*
placidly *adv* plácidamente
placing *n* colocación, *f*; posición, *f*; localización, *f*
placket *n* abertura (en una falda), *f*
plagiarism *n* plagio, *m*

plagiarist *n* plagiario (-ia)

plagiarize *vt* plagiar, hurtar

plague *n* plaga, *f*; peste, pestilencia, *f.* *vt* importunar, atormentar; plagar

plaice *n* (nearest equivalent) platija, *f*

plaid *n* manta escocesa, *f*; género de cuadros, *m*, *a* a cuadros

plain *a* claro; evidente; (simple) sencillo; llano; sin adorno; (flat) liso, igual; (candid) franco; (with truth, etc.) desnudo; mero; puro, sin mezcla; (of words) redondo; (ugly) feo. *adv* claramente; llanamente; sencillamente; francamente. *n* llanura, *f*, llano, *m*. **the p. truth,** la pura verdad. **p. clothes,** traje de paisano, *m*. **p. clothes man,** detective, *m*. **p. cooking,** cocina sencilla, cocina casera, *f.* **p. dealing,** buena fe, sinceridad, *f.* **p. dweller,** llanero (-ra). **p. living,** vida sencilla, *f.* **p. people,** gente sencilla, *f.* **p. sailing,** *fig* camino fácil, *m.* **p. sewing,** costura, *f.* **p.-song,** canto llano, *m.* **p. speaking,** franqueza, *f.* **p.-spoken,** franco. **in p. English,** sin rodeos, en cristiano (e.g. **Speak in p. English!** Habla sin rodeos! Habla en cristiano!)

plainly *adv* claramente; sencillamente; llanamente; francamente; rotundamente

plainness *n* claridad, *f*; sencillez, *f*; llaneza, *f*; franqueza, *f*; (ugliness) fealdad, *f*

plainsman *n* hombre de las llanuras, *m*

plaint *n* queja, *f*, lamento, *m*; *law* demanda, querella, *f*

plaintiff *n* demandante, *mf*, actor, *m*, parte actora, actora, *f*

plaintive *a* quejumbroso, dolorido; patético

plaintively *adv* quejumbrosamente

plaintiveness *n* melancolía, tristeza, *f*; voz quejumbrosa, *f*

plait *n* trenza, *f. vt* trenzar; tejer. **in plaits,** (of hair) en trenzas

plan *n* plan, *m*; (map) plano, *m*; proyecto, *m. vt* planear; proyectar; proponerse. **the Marshall P.,** el Plan Marshall. **to make a p. of,** trazar un plano de. **to make plans,** hacer planes

planchette *n* mesa giratoria, *f*

plane *n* (tree) plátano, *m*; (tool) cepillo, *m*; *geom* plano, *m*; (level) nivel, *m*; *aer* avión, *m*, plano. *vt* *carp* acepillar, alisar. *vi* *aer* planear

planet *n* planeta, *m*

planetarium *n* planetario, *m*

planetary *a* planetario

planing *n* acepilladura, alisadura, *f*,

plank *n* tabla, *f*; *fig* fundamento, principio, *m*; *pl* **planks,** tablazón, *f. vt* entablar, enmaderar

planking *n* entablado, *m*, tablazón, *f*

plankton *n* plancton, *m*

planned *a* proyectado, planeado; dirigido. **p. economy,** economía dirigida, *f*

planner *n* proyectista, *mf*; autor (-ra) de un plan

planning *n* proyecto, *m*; concepción, *f*

plant *n* *bot* planta, *f*; instalación, *f*, material, *m. vt* plantar; (place) colocar; fijar; (a blow) asestar; (people) establecer; (instil) inculcar, imbuir (con); (conceal) esconder. **p. pot,** florero, *m.* **p. stand,** jardinera, *f*

plantain *n* *bot* llantén, *m*

plantation *n* plantación, *f*; plantío, *m*; *fig* colonia, *f*; introducción, *f*, establecimiento, *m*

planter *n* plantador, cultivador, *m*

planting *n* plantación, *f*; *fig* colonia, *f*; introducción, *f.* **p. out,** trasplante, *m*

plantlike *a* como una planta; de planta

plaque *n* placa, *f*; medalla, *f*

plash *n* (puddle) charco, *m*; (sound) chapaleteo, *m. vt* and *vi* chapotear, chapalear

plasma *n* plasma, *m*

plaster *n* (for walls, etc.) argamasa, *f*; yeso, *m*; *med* parche, emplasto, *m. vt* (walls, etc.) enlucir, enyesar; poner emplastos (a or en); (daub) embadurnar manchar; (cover) cubrir. **p. cast,** vaciado, yeso, *m.* **p. of Paris,** escayola, *f*

plasterer *n* yesero, *m*

plastering *n* revoque, enyesado, guarnecido, *m.* **p. trowel,** fratás, *m*

plastic *a* plástico. *n* plástica, *f*; *pl* **plastics,** materias plásticas, *f pl.* **p. surgery,** cirugía plástica, cirugía estética, *f*

plasticine *n* plasticina, *f*

plasticity *n* plasticidad, *f*

plate *n* plancha, chapa, *f*; (engraving and *phot.*, of a doctor, etc.) placa, *f*; (illustration) lámina, *f*; (cutlery, etc.) vajilla, *f*; (for eating) plato, *m*; (for money) platillo, *m*; electrotipo, *m*; (dental) dentadura postiza, *f. vt* (with armor) blindar; (with metal) planchear; (silver) platear; (electro-plate) niquelar. **silver p.,** vajilla de plata, plata, *f.* **p.-armor,** armadura, *f*; (of a ship) blindaje, *m.* **p.-draining rack,** escurreplatos, *m.* **p.-glass,** vidrio plano, *m.* **p.-rack,** escurridero para platos, *m.* **p. warmer,** calientaplatos, *m*

plateau *n* meseta, altiplanicie, *f*, *Lat. Am.* altiplano, *m*

plateful *n* plato (de), *m*

plater *n* plateador, *m*; platero, *m*

plateresque *a* *arch* plateresco

platform *n* plataforma, *f*; (railway) andén, *m.* **p. ticket,** billete de andén, *m*

plating *n* niquelado, *m*; electrogalvanización, *f*; (with armor) blindaje, *m*

platinum *n* platino, *m.* **p. blonde,** rubia platino, *f*

platitude *n* perogrullada, *f*, lugar común, *m*; trivialidad, vulgaridad, *f*

platitudinous *a* lleno de perogrulladas; trivial

platonic *a* platónico

Platonism *n* platonismo, *m*

Platonist *n* platonista, *mf*

platoon *n* *mil* pelotón, *m*

platter *n* fuente, *f*, trinchero, *m*; plato, *m*

plaudit *n* aplauso, *m*, aclamación, *f*; (praise) elogio, *m*, alabanza, *f*

plausibility *n* plausibilidad, *f*

plausible *a* plausible

plausibly *adv* plausiblemente

play *vi* jugar; (frolic) juguetear, retozar; recrearse, divertirse; *mech* moverse; (on a musical instrument) tocar; (wave) ondear, flotar; *theat* representar; (behave) conducirse. *vt* jugar; (of a searchlight, etc.) enfocar; (direct) dirigir; (a fish) agotar; (a joke, etc.) hacer; (a piece in a game) mover; (a musical instrument or music) tocar; (a string instrument) tañer; (a character in a play) hacer el papel de; (a drama, etc.) representar, poner en escena. **to p. a joke,** gastar una broma, hacer una burla. **to p. fair,** jugar limpio. **to p. false,** jugar sucio, engañar. **to p. the fool,** hacerse el tonto, hacerse el payaso. **to p. at,** jugar a; (pretend) fingir; hacer sin entusiasmo. **to p. off,** confrontar, contraponer. **to p. on.** See **to p. upon. to p. on the . . . ,** (of musical instruments) tocar. **to p. to,** (a person) tocar para. **to p. upon,** tocar; (a person's fears, etc.) explotar. **to p. up to,** (a person) adular, hacer la rueda (a). **to p. with,** jugar con; burlarse de; (an idea) acariciar play, *n* juego, *m*; diversión, *f*, recreo, *m*; (reflection) reflejo, *m*; movimiento libre, *m*; (to the imagination, etc.) rienda suelta, *f*; *mech* holgura, *f*; *lit* pieza dramática, comedia, *f*; (performance) función, representación, *f*; (theater) teatro, *m.* **fair p.,** juego limpio, *m.* **foul p.,** juego sucio, *m*; traición, perfidia, *f.* **to bring into p.,** poner en juego. **to come into p.,** entrar en juego. **to give p. to,** dar rienda a. **p. on words,** juego de palabras, *m.* **p.-pen,** cuadro enrejado, *m*

playact *vi* hacer la comedia

playbill *n* cartel, *m*; programa, *m*

played-out *a* agotado; viejo

player *n* jugador (-ra); *theat* actor (-triz), representante, *mf*; *mus* músico (-ca), tocador (-ra)

playfellow *n* camarada, *mf*; compañero (-ra) de juego, compañero de juegos

playful *a* juguetón; travieso; alegre

playfully *adv* en juego, de broma; alegremente

playfulness *n* carácter juguetón, *m*; travesuras, *f pl*; alegría, *f*

playgoer *n* persona que frecuenta los teatros, *f*; espectador de comedias, *m*

playground *n* patio de recreo, *m*

playing *n* juego, *m*. **p.-cards,** naipes, *m pl*, cartas, *f pl*. **p.-field,** campo de deportes, *m*

playlet *n* comedia corta, *f*

playmate. See **playfellow**

plaything *n* juguete, *m*

playtime *n* recreación, *f*; (in schools) hora de recreo, *f*, recreo, *m*

playwright *n* dramaturgo, *m*, autor (-ra) de comedias

plea *n law* informe, *m*; declaración, *f*; *law* acción, *f*, proceso, *m*; (excuse) pretexto, *m*, excusa, *f*; (entreaty) súplica, *f*. **under p. of,** bajo pretexto de, con excusa de

plead *vi law* pleitear; *law* declarar; suplicar; (of counsel, etc.) abogar (por); interceder (por). *vt* defender en juicio; aducir, alegar; pretender. **to p. guilty,** confesarse culpable. **to p. not guilty,** negar la acusación. **to p. ignorance,** pretender ignorancia

pleading *n* súplicas, *f pl*; *law* defensa, *f*; *pl* **pleadings,** alegatos, *m pl*, *a* implorante

pleasant *a* agradable; placentero; ameno; encantador; dulce; alegre; (of persons) simpático, amable; bueno; divertido

pleasantly *adv* agradablemente; de un modo muy amable; alegremente

pleasantness *n* agrado, *m*; placer, *m*; amabilidad, *f*; alegría, *f*

pleasantry *n* jocosidad, *f*; broma, chanza, *f*

please *vi* dar placer, gustar, dar gusto, agradar; parecer bien, querer, servirse; tener a bien, placer. *vt* deleitar, agradar, gustar; halagar; contentar, satisfacer. **I will do what I p.,** Haré lo que me parezca bien. **If you p.,** Si te parece bien; Con tu permiso. **She is very easy to p.,** Es muy fácil de darle placer. **When you p.,** Cuando Vd. quiera, Cuando a Vd. le venga bien Cuando Vd. guste. **"Please Do Not Disturb,"** «No Molesten.» **P. sit down!** ¡Haga el favor de sentarse! ¡Sírvase de sentarse! **P. God!** ¡Plegue a Dios!

pleased *a* contento (de o con); encantado (de); alegre (de); satisfecho (de o con). **I am p. with my new house,** Estoy contento con mi nueva casa. **I'm p. to meet you,** Mucho gusto (en conocerle), Mucho gusto (en conocerla). **to be p.,** estar contento; complacerse en

pleasing *a* agradable, grato; placentero; halagüeño

pleasurable *a* agradable; divertido, entretenido

pleasure *n* placer, *m*; gusto, *m*; satisfacción, *f*; (will) voluntad, *f*; recreo, *m*; diversión, distracción, *f*. **to give p. (to),** dar placer (a); deleitar, agradar; complacer. **to take p. in,** gustar de, disfrutar de; complacerse en. **I shall do it with great p.,** Lo haré con mucho gusto, Lo haré con mucho placer. **p.-boat,** barco de recreo, *m*. **p.-ground,** parque de atracciones, *m*. **p.-seeking,** amigo de placeres, frívolo. **p. trip,** viaje de recreo, *m*; excursión, *f*

pleasure craft *n* barco de recreo, *m*, (one vessel); barcas de recreo (collectively), *m pl*

pleat *n* pliegue, *m*, *vt* plegar, hacer pliegues en

pleating *n* plegado, *m*

plebeian *a* plebeyo. *n* plebeyo (-ya)

plebiscite *n* plebiscito, *m*. **to take a p.,** hacer un plebiscito

plectrum *n* plectro, *m*

pledge *n* prenda, *f*; empeño, *m*; garantía, *f*; (hostage) rehén, *m*; (toast) brindis, *m*. *vt* empeñar, dar en prenda; garantizar; brindar por; prometer. **to p. oneself,** comprometerse. **to p. support for,** prometer apoyo para

Pleiades *n pl* pléyades, *f pl*

plenary *a* pleno; plenario. **p. indulgence,** indulgencia plenaria, *f*. **p. session,** sesión plenaria, *f*

plenipotentiary *a* plenipotenciario. *n* plenipotenciario, *m*

plenitude *n* plenitud, *f*

plenteous, plentiful *a* copioso, abundante. **to be p.,** abundar

plentifully *adv* en abundancia

plenty *n* abundancia, *f*; en abundancia; de sobra; mucho. *adv inf* bastante. **There is p. of food,** Hay comida en abundancia. **We have p. of time,** Tenemos tiempo de sobra

pleonasm *n* pleonasmo, *m*

plethora *n* plétora, *f*

pleurisy *n* pleuresía, *f*

plexus *n* plexo, *m*

pliability *n* flexibilidad, *f*; docilidad, *f*

pliable, pliant *a* flexible; dócil

pliers *n pl* pinzas, *f pl*, alicates, *m pl*, tenazas, *f pl*

plight *vt* (one's word) empeñar, dar; prometer en matrimonio. *n* (fix) aprieto, apuro, *m*. **to p. one's troth,** dar palabra de matrimonio

plinth *n arch* plinto, *m*

Pliny the Elder Plinio el Antiguo, Plinio el Mayor

Pliny the Younger Plinio el Menor

plod *vi* andar despacio, caminar con trabajo; *fig* trabajar con ahínco

plodder *n* trabajador lento y concienzudo, *m*; (student) empollón (-ona)

plot *n* (of land) parcela, *f*; terreno, solar, *m*; (plan) proyecto, *m*; estratagema, *m*; (literary) intriga, trama, *f*; (story) argumento, *m*; (conspiracy) conjuración, *f*, complot, *m*. *vt* trazar (un plano, etc.); urdir, tramar. *vi* conspirar, intrigar

plotter *n* conspirador (-ra conjurado (-da)

plotting *n* trazado (de un plano, una gráfica), *m*; (conspiracy) conspiración, *f*; maquinaciones, *f pl*; (hatching) trama, *f*

plover *n* ave fría, *f*, chorlito, *m*

plow *n* arado, *m*; *ast* el Carro, la Osa Mayor; (in an examination) escabechina, *f*. *vt* and *vi* arar; *fig* surcar; (in examinations) escabechar, dar calabazas (a), suspender. **plow the sands,** arar en el mar. **p. handle,** esteva, *f*. **to p. up,** roturar

plowman *n* arador, surcador, *m*; (peasant) labrador, *m*

plowshare *n* reja de arado, *f*

pluck *vt* (pick) coger; (a bird) desplumar; *mus* puntear; (in an examination) calabacear escabechar. *vi* tirar (de). *n* (tug) tirón, *m*; (of an animal) asadura, *f*; (courage) coraje, *m*. **to p. up courage,** tomar coraje, sacar ánimos. **to p. off,** quitar. **to p. out,** arrancar; quitar

pluckily *adv* valientemente

pluckiness *n* coraje, valor, *m*

plucky *a* valiente, esforzado, resuelto, animoso

plug *n* tapón, tarugo, *m*; (in building) nudillo, *m*; (of a switchboard) clave, *f*; *elec* enchufe, *m*; (of a w.c.) tirador, *m*; (of a bath, etc.) tapón, *m*; (of tobacco) rollo, *m*. *vt* atarugar, taponar, obturar; (in building) rellenar. *vi* (with away) batirse el cobre, sudar la gota gorda. **to p. in,** enchufar

plum *n* (tree) ciruelo, *m*; (fruit) ciruela, *f*; (raisin) pasa, *f*; (inf prize) breva, golosina, *f*. **p. cake,** pastel de fruta, *m*

plumage *n* plumaje, *m*

plumb *n* plomada, *f*; (sounding-lead) escandallo, *m*. *a* perpendículo; recto; completo. *adv* a plomo, verticalmente; exactamente. *vt* aplomar; *naut* sondar; (fig pierce) penetrar; (understand) comprender. *vi* trabajar como plomero. **p.-line,** plomada, *f*

plumbago *n* plombagina, *f*

plumber *n* plomero, fontanero, *m*; instalador de cañerías, *m*

plumbic *a chem* plúmbico

plumbing *n* plomería, fontanería, *f*; instalación de cañerías, *f*

plumbless *a poet* insondable

plume *n* pluma, *f*; penacho, *m*. *vt* adornar con plumas; desplumar; **to p. itself,** (of a bird) limpiarse las plumas. **to p. oneself on,** echárselas de, hacer alarde de; jactarse de

plumed *a* plumado; con plumas; empenachado

plumelet *n* agujas, *f pl*

plummet *n* plomada, *f*; (weight) plomo, *m*; (sounding-lead) sonda, *f*

plump *a* gordito, llenito; rollizo; hinchado. *adv* de golpe; claramente. *vt* (swell) hinchar, rellenar; (make fall) hacer (or dejar) caer. *vi* (swell) hincharse; engordar; (fall) caer a plomo; dejarse caer. **to p. for,** escoger, dar apoyo (a); votar por. **p.-cheeked,** mofletudo

plumpness *n* gordura, *f*; lo rollizo

plumy *a* como una pluma; plumado

plunder *vt* saquear; pillar; despojar. *n* saqueo, pillaje, *m*; (booty) botín, despojo, *m*

plunderer *n* saqueador (-ra); ladrón (-ona)

plundering *n* saqueo, *m*; despojo, *m. a* saqueador

plunge *vt* chapuzar; sumergir; hundir; meter. *vi* sumergirse; (into water) zambullirse; (rush) precipitarse, lanzarse; *naut* zozobrar; (of a horse) encabritarse; (gamble) jugarse el todo. *n* sumersión, *f*; zambullida, *f*; chapuz, *m*; (rush) salto, *m*; (*fig* step) paso, *m*

plunger *n mech* émbolo, *m*

plunging *n* (of a ship) zozobra, *f*; (of a horse) cabriolas, *f pl*; saltos, *m pl*, For other meanings, see **plunge**

plural *a* plural. *n* plural, *m*. **in the p.,** en el plural. **to make p.,** poner en plural

plurality *n* pluralidad, *f*

pluralize *vt* pluralizar

plus *prep* and *a* más; (*math elec*) positivo. *n* signo más, *m*; *math* cantidad positiva, *f*. **p. fours,** pantalones de golf, *m pl*

plush *n* felpa, *f*; velludo, *m*

plushy *a* felpudo; de felpa

Pluto *n* Plutón, *m*; (pipe-line) oleoducto, *m*

plutocracy *n* plutocracia, *f*

plutocrat *n* plutócrata, *mf*

plutocratic *a* plutocrático

pluviometer *n* pluviómetro, *m*

ply *n* cabo, *m. vt* emplear, usar; manejar; ejercer; ofrecer, servir (con); importunar (con). *vi* hacer el trayecto; hacer el servicio; ir y venir; hacer viajes. **to ply for hire,** tomar viajeros; ofrecerse para ser alquilado

plywood *n* madera contrachapada, *f*

pneumatic *a* neumático. *n* (tire) neumático, *m*. **p. drill,** barreno neumático, *m*

pneumococcus *n* neumococo, *m*

pneumonia *n* pulmonía, *f*. **double p.,** pulmonía doble, *f*

poach *vi* cazar (or pescar) en vedado. *vt* robar caza de un vedado; *fig* invadir; (*fig* steal) hurtar; (eggs) escalfar. **to p. upon another's preserves,** meterse en los asuntos de otro

poacher *n* cazador furtivo, *m*

poaching *n* caza (or pesca) furtiva, *f*

pock *n* pústula, *f*. **p.-mark,** hoyo, *m*. **p.-marked,** picado de viruelas

pocket *n* bolsillo, *m*; bolsillo del reloj, *m*; faltriquera, *f*; *min* bolsa, *f*, depósito, *m*; *fig* bolsa, *f*; (in billiards) tronera, *f. vt* meter (or poner) en el bolsillo; (an insult) tragarse; (in billiards) entronerar; (a profit) ganar; apropiarse. **air-p.,** bolsa de aire, *f*. **to be out of p.,** haber perdido, tener una pérdida. **to have a person in one's p.,** calzarse a una persona. **to p. one's pride,** olvidarse de su orgullo. **p. battleship,** acorazado de bolsillo, *m*. **p.-book,** cartera, *f*. **p. dictionary,** diccionario de bolsillo, *m*. **p.-flap,** portezuela, *f*. **p.-handkerchief,** pañuelo (de bolsillo), *m*. **p.-knife,** cortaplumas, *m*. **p.-lighter,** encendedor de bolsillo, *m*. **p.-money,** alfileres, *m pl*, dinero del bolsillo, *m*. **p. picking,** ratería de carteriza, *f*

pocketful *n* bolsillo lleno (de), *m*; lo que cabe en un bolsillo

pocket of resistance *n* foco de resistencia, *m*

pod *n bot* vaina, *f*; (of a silkworm) capullo, *m. vt* desvainar; mondar. *vi* hincharse, llenarse

podgy *a* gordo, grueso

poem *n* poema, *m*; *pl* **poems,** poesías, *f pl*, versos, *m pl*

poet *n* poeta, *m*. **p. laureate,** poeta laureado, *m*

poetaster *n* poetastro, *m*

poetess *n* poetisa, *f*

poetic *a* poético. **p. licence,** licencia poética, *f*

poeticize *vt* poetizar; hacer un poema (de)

poetics *n* poética, *f*

poetry *n* poesía, *f*; versos, poemas, *m pl*

pogrom *n* pogrom, *m*

poignancy *n* (of emotions) profundidad, violencia, *f*, lo patético, *m*; (of a retort, etc.) mordacidad, acerbidad, *f*

poignant *a* (moving) conmovedor, hondo, agudo; patético; (mordant) mordaz, agudo

poignantly *adv* de un modo conmovedor, patéticamente; mordazmente

poinsettia *n* flor de nochebuena, *f*

point *n* (usual meanings and *ast., math.*, in cards, in a speech, etc.) punto, *m*; característica, *f*; cualidad, *f*; (purpose) motivo, fin, *m*; (question) cuestión, *f*; asunto, *m*; (wit) agudeza, *f*; (significance) significación, *f*; (detail) detalle, *m*; (in rationing) cupón, *m*; (sharp end) punta, *f*; (of a shawl, etc.) pico, *m*; (of land) promontorio, cabo, *m*; (engraving) buril, *m*; (railway) aguja, *f*; (of horses) cabo, *m*. **Mary has many good points,** María tiene muchas cualidades buenas. **There is no p. in being angry,** No hay para que enfadarse. **in p.,** en cuestión; a propósito. **in p. of fact,** en efecto, en verdad. **on the p. of,** a punto de. **to be to the p.,** venir al caso; ser apropiado. **to carry one's p.,** salir con la suya. **to come to the p.,** ir al grano, ir al caso, ir al mollo del asunto. **to make a p. of,** insistir en; tener por principio. **to win on points,** (boxing) ganar por puntos. **p. at issue,** cuestión bajo consideración, *f*, punto en cuestión, *m*. **p.-blank,** a boca de jarro. **p.-duty,** regulación de tráfico, *f*. **p. lace,** encaje de aguja, *m*. **p. of honor,** punto de honor, *m*; cuestión de honor, *f*. **p. or order,** cuestión de orden, *f*. **p. of view,** punto de vista, *m*. **What's your p.?** ¿A dónde quieres llegar con esto?

point *vt* sacar punta (a), afilar; (a moral, etc.) inculcar; (in building) rejuntar; *gram* puntuar; (of dogs) mostrar la caza. **He pointed his gun at them,** Les apuntó con su fusil. **The hands of the clock pointed to seven o'clock,** Las agujas del reloj marcaban las siete. **to p. with the finger,** señalar con el dedo. **to p. at,** señalar, indicar; (with a gun) apuntar; dirigir. **to p. out,** señalar, indicar; enseñar, mostrar; advertir

pointed *a* (sharpened) afilado; (in shape) puntiagudo; picudo; *arch* ojival; *fig* mordaz; satírico; (of a remark, etc.) directo; personal; aparente, evidente

pointedly *adv* explícitamente, categóricamente; mordazmente; directamente; satíricamente

pointedness *n* forma puntiaguda, *f*; (incisiveness) mordacidad, aspereza, *f*; claridad, *f*

pointer *n* (of a clock, weighing-machine, etc.) aguja, *f*; (of a balance) fiel, *m*; (wand) puntero, *m*; *fig* índice, *m*; (dog) perro de muestra, *m*

pointillisme *n art* puntillismo, *m*

pointing *n* (in building) rejuntado, *m*; (of a gun) puntería, *f*

pointless *a* sin motivo, innecesario; fútil; sin importancia

pointlessly *adv* sin motivo, sin necesidad; fútilmente

pointsman *n* (railway) guardagujas, *m*; (policeman) guardia del tráfico, *m*

poise *vt* balancear; pesar. *vi* balancearse; posar, estar suspendido. *n* equilibrio, *m*; (of mind) serenidad de ánimo, sangre fría, *f*; aplomo, *m*; (bearing) porte, aire, *m*

poison *n* veneno, *m*; *fig* ponzoña, *f*, veneno, *m. vt* envenenar; intoxicar; *fig* emponzoñar. **p. gas,** gas asfixiante, *m*

poisoner *n* envenenador (-ra); *fig* corruptor (-ra)

poisoning *n* envenenamiento, *m*; intoxicación, *f*

poisonous *a* venenoso; tóxico; *fig* ponzoñoso, pernicioso. **p. snake,** serpiente venenosa

poisonousness *n* venenosidad, *f*; toxicidad, *f*; *fig* veneno, *m*, ponzoña, *f*

poke *vt* (thrust) clavar; (make) hacer; (the fire) atizar; hurgar; (push) empujar; (put away) arrinconar. *vi* andar a tientas; meterse. **Don't p. your nose into other people's business!** ¡No te metas donde no te llaman! **They poked his eyes out,** Le saltaron los ojos. **to p. fun at,** burlarse de, mofarse de. **to p. the fire,** atizar la lumbre (or el fuego). **to p. about for,** buscar a tientas. **p.-bonnet,** capelina, *f*

poker *n* (game) póker, *m*; (for the fire) hurgón, atizador, *m*. **p. work,** pirograbado, *m*

poky *a* estrecho, ahogado, pequeño; miserable

Poland Polonia, *f*

polar *a* polar. **p. bear,** oso (-sa) blanco (-ca). **p. lights,** aurora boreal, *f*

polarimeter *n* polarímetro, *m*

polarity *n* polaridad, *f*

polarization *n* polarización, *f*

polarize *vt* polarizar

pole *n* palo largo, *m*; poste, *m*; (of a tent) mástil, *m*; (of a cart) pértiga, *f*; *sport* pértiga, garrocha, *f*; (measurement) percha, *f*; (*ast geog biol math elec*) polo, *m*. *vt* (a punt) impeler con pértiga. **from p. to p.,** de polo a polo. **greasy p.,** cucaña, *f*. **under bare poles,** *naut* a palo seco. **p.-ax,** hachuela de mano, *f*; hacha de marinero, *f*; (butcher's) mazo, *m*. **p. jumping,** salto de pértiga, salto a la garrocha, *m*. **p.-star,** estrella polar, *f*

Pole *n* polaco (-ca)

polemic *n* polémica, *f*

polemical *a* polémico

police *n* policía, *f*. *vt* mantener servicio de policía en; mantener el orden público en; administrar, regular. **mounted p.,** policía montada, *f*. **p. constable,** (agente de) policía, guardia urbano, *m*. **p. court,** tribunal de la policía, *m*. **p. dog,** perro de policía, *m*. **p. force,** cuerpo de policía, *m*, policía, *f*. **p. magistrate,** juez municipal, *m*. **p. station,** comisaría de policía, *f*. **p. trap,** puesto oculto de la policía del tráfico, *m*. **p. woman,** policía, *f*

policeman *n* policía, guardia, *Lat. Am.* cívico, *m*

policy *n* política, *f*; táctica, *f*; sistema, *m*; norma de conducta, *f*; ideas, *fpl*, principios, *mpl*; prudencia, *f*; (insurance) póliza, *f*. **fixed premium p.,** póliza a prima fija, *f*. **p.-holder,** asegurado (-da), tenedor (de una póliza), *m*

poliomyelitis *n* poliomielitis, *f*

polish *vt* (metals and wood) pulir; (furniture and shoes) dar brillo (a); (lit works) pulir, limar; (persons) descortezar, civilizar. *n* (shine) brillo, *m*; (furniture) cera para los muebles, *f*; (metal, silver) líquido para limpiar metales, *m*; (for shoes) betún para zapatos, *m*; (varnish) barniz, *m*; (of lit. works) pulidez, elegancia, *f*; (of persons) urbanidad, cultura, *f*. **to p. off,** terminar a prisa; (a person) acabar con; (food) engullir

Polish *a* polaco, polonés. *n* (language) polaco, *m*

polished *a* (of verses, etc.) pulido, elegante; (of person) culto, distinguido; (of manners) fino, cortés

polisher *n* (machine) pulidor, *m*; lustrador, *m*. **floor-p.,** lustrador de piso, *m*. **French p.,** barnizador, *m*

polite *a* cortés, bien educado; atento; elegante

politely *adv* cortésmente; atentamente

politeness *n* cortesía, *f*. **for p. sake,** por cortesía

politic *a* político

political *a* político. **p. agent,** agente político, *m*. **p. economist,** hacendista, *mf* **p. economy,** economía política, *f*

politically *adv* políticamente

politician *n* político (-ca)

politics *n* política, *f*. **to dabble in p.,** meterse en política

polity *n* forma de gobierno, constitución política, *f*

polka *n* polca, *f*

polka-dot *a* con puntos

poll *n* (head of person) cabeza, *f*; (voters' register) lista electoral, *f*; (voting) votación, *f*; (polling booth) colegio electoral, *m*; (counting of votes) escrutinio, *m*. *vt* (trees) desmochar; (vote) votar, dar su voto (a); (obtain votes) obtener, recibir; (count votes) escrutar. **p.-tax,** capitación, *f*

pollard *vt* desmochar. *n* (tree) árbol desmochado, *m*

pollen *n* polen, *m*

pollinate *vt* fecundar con polen

pollination *n* polinización, *f*

polling *n* votación, *f*. **p. booth,** colegio electoral, *m*

pollute *vt* contaminar; ensuciar; profanar; (corrupt morally) corromper

polluter *n* profanador (-ra), corruptor (-ra)

pollution *n* contaminación, *f*; profanación, *f*; corrupción, *f*

polo *n* polo, *m*. **p. mallet,** maza de polo, *f*. **p. player,** jugador de polo, *m*, polista, *mf*

polonaise *n* polonesa, *f*

poltroon *n* cobarde, *m*

polychrome *a* policromo

polygamist *n* polígamo (-ma)

polygamous *a* polígamo

polygamy *n* poligamia, *f*

polygenesis *n* poligenismo, *m*

polyglot *n* poligloto (-ta). **p. Bible,** poliglota, *f*

polygon *n* polígono, *m*

Polynesia Polinesia, *f*

polyp *n* pólipo, *m*

polyphonic *a* polifónico

polyphony *n* polifonía, *f*

polytechnic *n* politécnico

polytheism *n* politeísmo, *m*

polytheistic *a* politeísta

pomade *n* pomada, *f*

pomegranate *n* granada, *f*

Pomeranian *a* pomerano. **P. dog,** perro pomerano, *m*

pommel *n* pomo, *m*, *vt* aporrear

pomp *n* pompa, magnificencia, *f*, fausto, aparato, *m*; ostentación, *f*

Pompeii Pompeya, *f*

pompom *n* pompón, *m*

pomposity *n* pomposidad, presunción, *f*; (of language) ampulosidad, *f*

pompous *a* pomposo, ostentoso; (of style) ampuloso, hinchado; importante. **to be p.,** (of persons) darse tono

pond *n* charca, *f*, estanque, *m*

ponder *vt* ponderar, estudiar, considerar. *vi* meditar (sobre), reflexionar (sobre)

ponderable *a* ponderable

ponderous *a* pesado; macizo; abultado; grave; (dull) pesado, aburrido

ponderously *adv* pesadamente; gravemente

ponderousness *n* pesadez, *f*; gravedad, importancia, *f*

poniard *n* puñal, *m*, *vt* apuñalar

pontiff *n* pontífice, *m*

pontifical *a* pontificio

pontificate *n* pontificado, *m*

pontoneer *n* pontonero, *m*

pontoon *n* pontón, *m*. **p. bridge,** puente de pontones, *m*

pony *n* jaca, *f*

poodle *n* perro (-rra) de aguas, perro de lanas, perro lanudo

pooh-pooh *vt* despreciar, desdeñar. **Pooh!** ¡Bah!

pool *n* (in a river) rebalsa, *f*; charca, *f*, estanque, *m*; (of blood, etc.) charco, *m*; (swimming) *Spain* piscina, *Lat. Am.* alberca, *f*; (in cards) baceta, *f*; *com* asociación, *f*; *fig* fuente, *f*; *pl* **pools,** (football) apuestas benéficas de fútbol, *fpl*. *vt* (resources, etc.) combinar; juntar

poop *n* popa, *f*. **p. lantern,** fanal, *m*

poor *a* pobre; malo; (insignificant or unfortunate) infeliz, desgraciado. **the p.,** los pobres. **to be in p. health,** estar mal de salud. **to be p. stuff,** ser de pacotilla. **to be poorer than a church mouse,** ser más pobre que las ratas. **to have a p. opinion of,** tener en poco (a). **P. me!** ¡Ay de mí! ¡Pecador de mí! **p.-box,**

cepillo, *m.* **p.-law,** ley de asistencia pública, *f.* **p.-spir-
ited,** apocado
poorhouse *n* asilo, *m*
poorly *adv* pobremente; mal. *a* indispuesto, malo
poorness *n* pobreza, *f;* mala calidad, *f;* (lack) carestía, *f;*
(of soil) infertilidad, *f;* (of character) mezquindad, *f*
pop *n* (of a cork) taponazo, *m;* (of a gun) detonación, *f;*
(drink) gaseosa, *f, adv* ¡pum! *vi* (of a cork) saltar; (of
guns) detonar. *vt* (corks) hacer saltar; (a gun, a question, etc.) disparar. **popgun,** escopeta de aire comprimido, *f.* **to pop down,** bajar a presuradamente. **to
pop in,** (visit) dejarse caer; entrar rápidamente. **to
pop off,** marcharse a prisa; (die) estirar la pata, *Lat.
Am.* arrancarse. **to pop up,** subir corriendo; aparecer
de pronto
popcorn *nsg* palomitas (de maíz), rosetas (de maíz) *fpl*
(Spain), cabritos *mpl* (Chile), alborotos *mpl* (Argentina,
Central America, Peru), cabritas *fpl* (elsewhere)
pope *n* Papa, *m*
poplar *n* (black) chopo, álamo, *m;* (white) álamo
blanco, *m.* **p. grove,** alameda, *f*
poplin *n* popelina, *f*
poppy *n* amapola, adormidera, *f*
populace *n* pueblo, *m;* (scornful) populacho, *m*
popular *a* popular; en boga, de moda; cómun. **He is a
p. hero,** Es un héroe popular
popularity *n* popularidad, *f*
popularization *n* vulgarización, *f*
popularize *vt* popularizar, vulgarizar
popularly *adv* popularmente
populate *vt* poblar
population *n* población, *f*
populous *a* populoso; muy poblado
porcelain *n* porcelana, *f*
porch *n* pórtico, *m;* (of a house) portal, *m*
porcine *a* porcino, porcuno
porcupine *n* puerco espín, *m*
pore *n* poro, *m.* **to pore over,** estar absorto en; examinar
cuidadosamente
pork *n* carne de cerdo, *f.* **salt p.,** tocino, *m.* **p. butcher,**
tocinero, *m.* **p. pie,** pastel de carne de cerdo, *m*
pornographic *a* pornográfico
pornography *n* pornografía, *f*
porosity *n* porosidad, *f*
porous *a* poroso
porphyry *n* pórfido, *m*
porpoise *n* marsopa, *f,* puerco marino, *m*
porridge *n* gachas, *f pl, m*
port *n* puerto, *m;* (in a ship) porta, *f;* (larboard) babor,
m; (wine) vino de Oporto, *m;* (mien) porte, *m,* presencia, *f. vt* (the helm) poner a babor; *mil* llevar un fusil
terciado. **to put into p.,** tomar puerto. **to stop at a p.,**
hacer escala en un puerto. **p. dues,** derechos de
puerto, *m pl*
portable *a* portátil; móvil. **p. typewriter,** máquina de
escribir portátil (or de viaje), *f.* **p. wireless,** radio portátil, *f*
portal *n* portal, *m*
portcullis *n* rastrillo, *m*
portend *vt* presagiar, anunciar
portent *n* augurio, presagio, *m;* portento, *m*
portentous *a* ominoso; portentoso; importante
porter *n* (messenger) mozo de cordel, *m;* (of a university, hotel) portero, *m;* (of a block of flats) conserje, *m;*
(railway) mozo de estación, *Argentina* changador, *m;*
(drink) cerveza negra, *f.* **porter's lodge,** portería, *f;*
conserjería, *f*
porterage *n* porte, *m*
portfolio *n* carpeta, *f;* (*pol* of a minister) cartera, *f;* (*pol*
ministry) ministerio, *m*
porthole *n* tronera, *f*
portico *n* pórtico, *m*
portion *n* porción, *f;* parte, *f;* (marriage) dote, *mf;*
(piece) pedazo, *m;* (in a restaurant) ración, *f;* (in life)
fortuna, *f. vt* dividir; repartir; (dower) dotar
portliness *n* corpulencia, *f*

portly *a* corpulento, grueso
portmanteau *n* maleta, *f*
portmanteau word *n* palabra de acarreo, *f*
portrait *n* retrato, *m.* **p. painter,** pintor (-ra) de retratos
portraiture *n* retratos, *m pl;* descripción, pintura, *f*
portray *vt* retratar; pintar, representar; (in words) describir, pintar
portrayal *n* pintura, *f;* retrato, *m;* (in words) descripción, *f*
portrayer *n* retratista, *mf,* pintor (-ra)
portress *n* portera, *f;* (in a convent) tornera, *f*
Portuguese *a* portugués. *n* portugués (-esa); (language) portugués, *m*
pose *vt* colocar; (a problem, etc.) plantear; (a question)
hacer; *vi* colocarse; (with as) echárselas de, dárselas de,
fingir ser; hacerse pasar por. *n* actitud, postura, *f;* (affected) pose, *f;* (deception) engaño, *m*
poser *n* problema difícil, *m;* (in an examination) pega, *f;*
pregunta embarazosa, *f*
position *n* posición, *f;* situación, *f;* actitud, postura, *f;*
condición, *f,* estado, *m;* (post) puesto, empleo, *m.* **He is
not in a p.,** No está en condiciones de . . . , No
está para . . . **to place in p.,** poner en posición, colocar
positive *a* positivo; absoluto; (convinced) convencido,
seguro; (downright) categórico; *inf* completo. *n* realidad, *f; phot* (prueba) positiva, *f*
positively *adv* positivamente; categóricamente
positiveness *n* certitud, seguridad, *f;* terquedad, obstinacia, *f*
positivism *n* positivismo, *m*
posse *n* pelotón, *m;* multitud, muchedumbre, *f*
possess *vt* poseer; gozar (de); (of ideas, etc.) dominar.
to p. oneself of, apoderarse de, apropiarse. **What
possessed you to do it?** ¿Qué te hizo hacerlo?
possession *n* posesión, *f.* **to take p. of,** tomar posesión
de; hacerse dueño de, apoderarse de; (a house, etc.)
entrar en, ocupar
possessive *a* posesivo. *n* posesivo, *m*
possessor *n* poseedor (-ra); dueño (-ña); propietario
(-ia)
possibility *n* posibilidad, *f*
possible *a* posible. **as soon as p.,** cuanto antes, lo más
pronto posible. **to make p.,** hacer posible, posibilitar
possibly *adv* posiblemente; (perhaps) quizás. **I shall
come as soon as I p. can,** Vendré lo más pronto
posible
post *n* (pole) poste, *m;* (of a sentry, etc.) puesto, *m;* (employment) empleo, *m;* (mail) correo, *m; mil* toque, *m. vt*
(a notice) fijar; anunciar; (to an appointment) destinar; (letters, etc.) echar al correo; *com* pasar al libro
mayor; (inform) tener al corriente. *vi* viajar en posta.
"P. no bills!" "Se prohíbe fijar carteles." **registered
p.,** correo certificado, *m.* **p. card,** postal, *f.* **p.-chaise,**
silla de posta, *f.* **p.-date,** posfecha, *f.* **p.-free,** franco de
porte. **p.-haste,** con gran celeridad. **p.-horse,** caballo
de posta, *m.* **p.-impressionism,** post-impresionismo,
m. **p.-mortem,** *n* autopsia, *f.* **p.-natal,** post-natal.
p.-nuptial, postnupcial. **p. office,** correo, *m,* correos,
m pl; (on a train) ambulancia de correos, *f.* **p. office
box,** *Spain* apartado de correos, *m, Lat. Am.* casilla, *f.* **p.
office savings bank,** caja postal de ahorros, *f.*
p.-paid, porte pagado; franco. **p.-war,** *n* postguerra, *f.*
a de la postguerra
postage *n* porte de correos, franqueo, *m.* **p. stamp,**
sello postal, *m, Mexico* timbre, m, *elsewhere in Lat. Am.*
estampilla, *f*
postage meter *n* franqueadora, *f*
postal *a* postal. **p. money order** *Spain* giro postal, *m,
Lat. Am.* libranza de correos, libranza postal, *f.* **p.
order,** orden postal de pago, *f.* **p. packet,** paquete
postal, *m.*
poster *n* cartel, *m. vt* fijar carteles (a or en); anunciar
por carteles. **bill-p.,** fijador de carteles, *m*
poste restante *n* lista de correos, *f*
posterior *a* posterior. *n* trasero, *m,* asentaderas, *f pl*

posteriority *n* posterioridad, *f*
posterity *n* posteridad, *f*
postgraduate *n* estudiante graduado que hace estudios avanzados, *m. a* avanzado; para estudiantes graduados
posthumous *a* póstumo
posthumously *adv* después de la muerte
postman *n* cartero, *m*
postmark *n* matasellos, *m*, *vt* poner matasellos (a)
postmaster *n* administrador de correos, *m*
postmistress *n* administradora de correos, *f*
postpone *vt* aplazar, diferir; retrasar; (subordinate) postergar
postponement *n* aplazamiento, *m*; tardanza, *f*
postscript *n* posdata, *f, Mexico* aumento, *m*
postulate *n* postulado, *m*, *vt* postular
posture *n* postura, actitud, *f*; (of affairs) estado, *m*, situación, *f. vi* tomar una postura
posy *n* (nosegay) ramillete de flores, *m*; flor, *f*; (motto) mote, *m*
pot *n* pote, *m*; tarro, *m*; (flower-) tiesto, *m*; (for cooking) olla marmita, *f*; jarro, *m. vt* plantar en tiestos; conservar en potes. **pot-bellied,** panzudo. **pot-boiler,** obra literaria escrita con el sólo propósito de ganar dinero, *f.* **pot-herb,** hierba que se emplea para sazonar, hortaliza, *f.* **pot-hole,** bache, **pot-luck,** comida ordinaria, *f.* **pot-shot,** tiro fácil, *m*; tiro al azar, *m*
potage *n* potaje, *m*
potash *n* potasa, *f.* **caustic p.,** potasa cáustica, *f*
potassium *n* potasio, *m*
potato *n* patata, *f. sweet* **p.,** batata, *f.* **p. beetle,** coleóptero de la patata, *m.* **p. omelet,** tortilla a la española, *f.* **p. patch,** patatal, *m.* **p. peeler,** pela-patatas, *m*
potency *n* potencia, *f*; fuerza, eficacia, *f*
potent *a* potente, fuerte; eficaz
potentate *n* potentado, *m*
potential *a* potencial; virtual; (*phys gram*) potencial, *n* poder, *m*; *gram* modo potencial, *m*; *phys* energía potencial, *f*; *elec* tensión potencial, *f*
potentiality *n* potencialidad, *f*
pothook *n* garabato de cocina, *m*; palote, *m*; (scrawl) garabato, *m*
potion *n* poción, *f*,
potpourri *n* popurrí, *m*
potter *n* alfarero, *m. vi* gandulear. *vt* perder. **potter's clay,** barro de alfarero, *m.* **potter's wheel,** tabanque, *m.* **potter's workshop,** alfar, *m*
pottery *n* alfarería, *f*; (china) loza, porcelana, *f*
pouch *n* bolsa, *f*; *zool* bolsa marsupial, *f*; (for tobacco) tabaquera, *f*; (for cartridges) cartuchera, *f. vt* embolsar. *vi* bolsear
poulterer *n* pollero (-ra)
poultice *n* apósito, emplasto, *m*, *vt* poner emplastos (a or en)
poultry *n* volatería, *f.* **p. dealer,** gallinero (-ra) vendedor (-ra) de volatería. **p. manure** *Mexico* cuitla, *f.* **p. yard,** gallinero, *m*
poultry farming *n* avicultura, *f*
pounce *n* (swoop) calada, *f. vi* (swoop) calarse; saltar (sobre); agarrar, hacer presa (en); *fig* atacar; descubrir, hacer patente
pound *n* (weight and currency) libra, *f*; (for cattle) corral de concejo, *m*; (thump) golpe, *m. vt* (break up) machacar, pistar; (beat) batir; (thump) golpear, aporrear. **p. sterling,** libra esterlina, *f.* **p. troy,** libra medicinal, *f*
pounding *n* machacamiento, *m*; batimiento, *m*
pour *vt* vaciar, verter; derramar. *vi* correr; (of rain) diluviar, llover a cántaros; (fill) llenar; (of crowds, words, etc.) derramarse. **to p. out the tea,** servir el té. **The crowd poured in,** La multitud entró en tropel
pouring *a* (of rain) torrencial
pout *vi* torcer el gesto; hacer pucheritos
poverty *n* pobreza, *f.* **p.-stricken,** menesteroso, indigente, necesitado
powder *n* polvo, *m*; (face) polvos de arroz, *m pl*; (gun) pólvora, *f. vt* polvorear; (crush) reducir a polvo, pul-

verizar. *vi* ponerse polvos. **p.-flash,** fogonazo, *m.* **p.-flask,** polvorín, *m.* **p.-magazine,** santabárbara, *f.* **p.-mill,** fábrica de pólvora, *f.* **p.-puff,** polvera, borla de empolvarse, *f*
powdered *a* en polvo
powdery *a* polvoriento; friable
power *n* poder, *m*; facultad, capacidad, *f*; vigor, *m*, fuerza, *f*; (*pol* and *math*) potencia, *f*; *mech* fuerza, *f*; influencia, *f.* **as far as lies within my p.,** en cuanto me sea posible. **It does not lie within my p.,** No está dentro de mis posibilidades, No está en mi poder. **the Great Powers,** las grandes potencias. **the powers that be,** los que mandan. **to be in p.,** estar en el poder. **p.-house, p.-station,** central eléctrica, *f.* **p. of attorney,** poderes, *m pl*, procuración, *f.* **to grant p. of attorney (to),** dar poderes (a)
powerful *a* poderoso; fuerte; eficaz; potente; (of arguments, etc.) convincente
powerfully *adv* poderosamente; fuertemente
powerless *a* impotente
power steering *n* dirección asistida *f* (Spain), servo dirección *f*
powwow *n* conferencia, *f*; conversación, *f*
pox *n* sífilis, *f*; (smallpox) viruelas, *f pl*; (chicken-pox) viruelas falsas, *f pl*
practicability *n* factibilidad, *f*
practicable *a* practicable, factible, posible; viable, transitable
practical *a* (doable) factible; práctico; virtual. **p. joke,** burla de consecuencias
practically *adv* prácticamente; en práctica; virtualmente; (in fact) en efecto. **p. nothing,** casi nada
practicalness *n* carácter práctico, *m*
practice *n* (custom) costumbre, *f*; práctica, *f*; ejercicio, *m*; (of a doctor, etc.) clientela, *f*; profesión, *f*; (religious) rito, *m*, ceremonias, *f pl*; (experience) experiencia, *f.* **It is not his p. to . . . ,** No es su costumbre de . . . **to be out of p.,** estar desentrenado. **to put into p.,** poner en práctica. **P. makes perfect,** El ejercicio hace maestro. *vt* tener la costumbre de; practicar; (a profession) ejercer; (a game) entrenarse en; (work at) estudiar; (a musical instrument) tocar; (accustom) acostumbrar. **to p. what one preaches,** predicar con el ejemplo
practiced *a* experimentado; experto
practitioner *n* médico (-ca). **general p.,** médico (-ca) general
pragmatic *a* pragmatista; (historical) pragmático; práctico
pragmatism *n* pragmatismo, *m*
pragmatist *n* pragmatista, *mf*
Prague Praga, *f*
prairie *n* pradera, sabana, pampa, *f*, *a* de la pradera, etc.
praise *vt* alabar; ensalzar, glorificar; elogiar. *n* alabanza, *f*; elogio, *m*; glorificación, *f*, ensalzamiento, *m.* **to p. to the skies,** poner en los cuernos de la luna poner por las nubes, poner sobre las estrellas hacerse lenguas de
praiseworthiness *n* mérito, *m*
praiseworthy *a* digno de alabanza, laudable
prance *vi* (of a horse) caracolear, encabritarse, cabriolar; saltar; andar airosamente. *n* corveta, cabriola, *f*; salto, *m*
prank *n* travesura, diablura, *f.* **to play pranks,** hacer diabluras
prate, prattle *vi* charlar, chacharear; (lisp) balbucir; (of brooks, etc.) murmurar, susurrar.-*vt* divulgar. *n* charla, cháchara, *f*; (lisping) balbuceo, *m*
prattler *n* parlanchín (-ina); (gossip) chismoso (-sa); (child) niño (-ña)
prattling *n* charla, *f*; (lisping) balbuceo, *m*; (of brooks, etc.) murmullo, susurro, ruido armonioso, *m. a* charlatán, gárrulo; balbuciente; (of brooks, etc.) parlero
prawn *n* camarón, *m*
pray *vt* and *vi* suplicar; implorar; rezar, orar. **P. be seated,** Haga el favor de sentarse
prayer *n* rezo, *m*, plegaria, oración, *f*; súplica, *f*; *law* petición, *f.* **p. book,** libro de devociones, devocionario, *m.*

p.-meeting, reunión para rezar, *f.* **p.-rug,** alfombra de rezo, *f*

praying *n* rezo, *m*; suplicación, *f*

pre- *prefix* de antes de (e.g. **pre-World-War-1 publications,** publicaciones de antes de la Primera Guerra Mundial)

preach *vt* and *vi* predicar

preacher *n* predicador (-ra). **to turn p.,** meterse a predicar

preaching *n* predicación, *f, a* predicador

preamble *n* preámbulo, *m*

prearrange *vt* preparar de antemano, predisponer

precarious *a* precario; inseguro; incierto, arriesgado

precariousness *n* condición precaria, *f*; inseguridad, *f*; incertidumbre, *f*

precaution *n* precaución, *f.* **to take precautions,** tomar precauciones

precautionary *a* de precaución; preventivo

precede *vt* preceder (a), anteceder (a); tomar precedencia (a), exceder en importancia (a). *vi* ir delante; tener la precedencia

precedence *n* precedencia, *f*; prioridad, *f*; superioridad, *f.* **to take p. over,** tomar precedencia (a), preceder (a)

precedent *n* precedente, *m, a* precedente. **without p.,** sin precedente

preceding *a* anterior, precedente

precept *n* precepto, *m*

preceptor *n* preceptor, *m*

precinct *n* (police station) *Argentina* comisaría de sección, *Mexico* delegación, *f*

precincts *n pl* recinto, *m*; ámbito, *m*; distrito, barrio, *m*

preciosity *n* afectación, *f*

precious *a* precioso; de gran valor; hermoso; amado; muy querido; (with rogue, etc.) redomado; completo. **p. little,** muy poco. **p. nearly,** casi, por poco . . . **p. stone,** piedra preciosa, *f*

preciousness *n* preciosidad, *f*; gran valor, *m*

precipice *n* precipicio, *m*

precipitancy *n* precipitación, *f*

precipitant *a* precipitado

precipitate *vt* precipitar, despeñar, arrojar; acelerar; *chem* precipitar. *vi* precipitarse. *n* precipitado, *m. a* precipitado, súbito. **to p. oneself,** tirarse, lanzarse

precipitately *adv* precipitadamente

precipitation *n chem* precipitación, *f*; *chem* precipitado, *m*; (rain, etc.) precipitación pluvial, *f*

precipitous *a* precipitoso, escarpado, acantilado

precipitously *adv* en precipicio

precise *a* preciso; exacto; justo; puntual; escrupuloso; formal; claro; pedante, afectado; ceremonioso

precisely *adv* precisamente; exactamente; puntualmente; escrupulosamente; claramente; con afectación; ceremoniosamente. **at six o'clock p.,** a las seis en punto

precision *n* precisión, *f*; exactitud, *f*; puntualidad, *f*; escrupulosidad, *f*; claridad, *f*; afectación, *f*; ceremonia, *f*

preclude *vt* excluir; impedir, hacer imposible

preclusion *n* exclusión, *f*; imposibilidad, *f*

precocious *a* precoz

precocity *n* precocidad, *f*

preconceived *a* preconcebido

preconception *n* idea preconcebida, *f*; (prejudice) prejuicio, *m*

preconcerted *a* concertado de antemano

precursor *n* precursor (-ra)

precursory *a* precursor

predatory *a* rapaz; de rapiña; voraz

predecease *vt* morir antes (de or que); *law* premorir. *n law* premuerto, *m*

predecessor *n* predecesor (-ra); (ancestor) antepasado, *m*

predestination *n* predestinación, *f*

predestine *vt* predestinar

predetermination *n* predeterminación, *f*

predetermine *vt* predeterminar

predicament *n* (logic) predicamento, *m*; situación, *f*; (fix) apuro, *m*; *pl* **predicaments,** categorías, *f pl*

predicate *vt* afirmar. *n* (logic, *gram*) predicado, *m*

predict *vt* predecir, pronosticar, profetizar

prediction *n* predicción, *f*; pronóstico, vaticinio, *m*, profecía, *f*

predilection *n* predilección, *f*

predispose *vt* predisponer

predisposition *n* predisposición, *f*

predominance *n* predominio, *m*

predominant *a* predominante

predominate *vi* predominar

preeminence *n* preeminencia, *f*; primacía, superioridad, *f*

preeminent *a* preeminente; superior; extraordinario

preeminently *adv* preeminentemente; extraordinariamente; por excelencia; entre todos

preen *vt* (of birds) limpiarse; (of people) darse humos, jactarse

preexist *vi* preexistir

preexistence *n* preexistencia, *f*

prefabricated *a* prefabricado

preface *n* prólogo, *m*; *ecc* prefacio, *m*; introducción, *f. vt* dar principio (a), empezar. **He prefaced his remarks by . . . ,** Dijo a modo de introducción

prefatory *a* preliminar, introductorio; a manera de prólogo

prefect *n* prefecto, *m*

prefecture *n* prefectura, *f*

prefer *vt* preferir, gustar más (a); (promote) ascender, elevar; (a charge, etc.) presentar. **to p. a charge against,** pedir en juicio (a). **I p. oranges to apples,** Me gustan más las naranjas que las manzanas, Prefiero las naranjas a las manzanas

preferability *n* preferencia, ventaja, *f*

preferable *a* preferible

preferably *adv* preferiblemente, con preferencia

preference *n* preferencia, *f*; privilegio, *m.* **p. share,** acción privilegiada, acción preferente, *f*

preferential *a* preferente

preferment *n* promoción, *f*, ascenso, *m*; puesto eminente, *m*

preferred *a* preferente; favorito, predilecto. **p. share,** acción preferente, *f*

prefix *vt* anteponer, prefijar; (to a word) poner prefijo (a). *n* prefijo, *m*

pregnancy *n* embarazo, *m*, preñez, *f*

pregnant *a* embarazada, encinta, preñada, *f*; *fig* fértil; *fig* preñado

prehensile *a* prensil

prehistoric *a* prehistórico

prehistory *n* prehistoria, *f*

prejudge *vt* prejuzgar

prejudice *n* prejuicio, *m*; *law* perjuicio, *m. vt* influir, predisponer; (damage) perjudicar. **without p.,** sin perjuicio

prejudiced *a* parcial; con prejuicios

prejudicial *a* perjudicial

prelacy *n* prelacía, *f*; episcopado, *m*

prelate *n* prelado, *m*

preliminarily *adv* preliminarmente

preliminary *a* preliminar. *n* preliminar, *m*

prelude (to) *n* preludio (de) *m*; presagio (de) *m*, *vt* and *vi* preludiar

premature *a* prematuro

prematurely *adv* prematuramente

prematureness *n* lo prematuro

premeditate *vt* premeditar

premeditatedly *adv* premeditadamente, con premeditación

premeditation *n* premeditación, *f*

premier *a* primero, principal. *n* primer minístro, *m*; (in Spain) presidente del Consejo de Ministros, *m*

premiere *n* estreno, *m*

premiership *n* puesto de primer ministro, *m*; *in Spain* presidencia del Consejo de Ministros, *f*

premise *n* (logic) premisa, *f*; *pl* **premises,** local, *m*;

recinto, *m*; establecimiento, *m*; propiedad, *f*; tierras, *f pl*. **on the premises,** en el local; en el establecimiento

premium *n* (prize) premio, *m*, recompensa, *f*; *com* prima, *f*; precio, *m*. **at a p.,** a premio; a una prima; (of shares) sobre la par; *fig* en boga, muy solicitado, en gran demanda

premonition *n* presentimiento, presagio, *m*

premonitory *a* premonitorio

prenatal *a* prenatal, antenatal

preoccupation *n* preocupación, *f*

preoccupied *a* preocupado; abstraído, absorto

preoccupy *vt* preocupar

prepaid *a* porte pagado, franco de porte

preparation *n* preparación, *f*; preparativo, *m*, disposición, *f*; (patent food) preparado, *m*. **I have made all my preparations,** He hecho todos mis preparativos. **The book is in p.,** El libro está en preparación

preparative *a* preparativo. *n* preparativo, *m*

preparatory *a* preparatorio, preparativo; preliminar. **p. school,** escuela preparatoria, *f*, *m*. **p. to,** como preparación para; antes de

prepare *vt* preparar; aparejar, aviar; equipar; (cloth) aprestar. *vi* prepararse; hacer preparativos

preparedness *n* estado de preparación, *m*; preparación, *f*, apercibimiento, *m*

prepay *vt* pagar adelantado, *Lat. Am.* aprontar; (a letter, etc.) franquear

prepayment *n* pago adelantado, *m*; (of a letter, etc.) franqueo, *m*

preponderance *n* preponderancia, *f*

preponderant *a* preponderante, predominante

preponderantly *adv* predominantemente; en su mayoría

preponderate *vi* preponderar; prevalecer (sobre), predominar (sobre)

preposition *n* preposición, *f*

prepossess *vt* predisponer; causar buena impresión (a)

prepossessing *a* atractivo

preposterous *a* ridículo, absurdo

preposterously *adv* absurdamente

preposterousness *n* ridiculez, *f*

Prep School *n* preparatoria, *f*

prepuce *n* prepucio, *m*

Pre-Raphaelite *a* and *n* prerrafaelista, *mf*

prerequisite *n* requisito necesario, esencial, *m*, *a* previamente necesario, esencial

prerogative *n* prerrogativa, *f*

presage *n* presagio, *m*; anuncio, *m*. *vt* presagiar; anunciar

Presbyterian *a* and *n* presbiteriano (-na)

prescience *n* presciencia, previsión, *f*

prescient *a* presciente

prescind *vt* prescindir (de); separar (de). *vi* separarse

prescribe *vt* and *vi* prescribir; *med* recetar; dar leyes; *law* prescribir

prescription *n* prescripción, *f*; *med* receta, *f*

presence *n* presencia, *f*; (ghost) aparición, *f*. **in the p. of,** en presencia de, delante; a vista de. **p. of mind,** presencia de ánimo, serenidad de ánimo, *f*

present *a* presente; actual; (with month) corriente; *gram* presente. **at p.,** al presente, actualmente. **at the p. day,** a la fecha, en la actualidad, hoy día. **P. company excepted!** ¡Mejorando lo presente! **the present writer,** el que suscribe, el que esto escribe, el que estas líneas traza. **to be p. at,** presenciar, ser testigo de; asistir a, acudir a; hallarse en. **p.-day,** de hoy, actual. **p. tense,** *gram* tiempo presente, *m*

present *n* (time) presente, *m*; actualidad, *f*; *gram* tiempo presente, *m*; (gift) regalo, *m*, dádiva, *f*. **By these presents . . . ,** *law* Por estas presentes . . . **to make a p. of,** regalar. **Jane made me a p. of a watch,** Juana me regaló un reloj

present *vt* presentar; ofrecer; manifestar; (a gift) regalar, dar; (*ecc mil*) presentar. **New problems presented themselves,** Nuevos problemas surgieron. **to p. arms,** presentar las armas. **He presented himself**

---

in the office, Se presentó en la oficina. **He presented his friend Mr. Moreno to me,** Me presentó a su amigo el Sr. Moreno

presentable *a* presentable

presentation *n* presentación, *f*; homenaje, *m*; (exhibition) exposición, *f*. **on p.,** *com* a presentación

presentiment *n* presentimiento, *m*, corazonada, *f*. **I had a p. that . . . ,** Tuve el presentimiento de que . . . , Tuve una corazonada que . . . **to have a p. about,** presentir

presently *adv* pronto; en seguida; dentro de poco

preservation *n* conservación, *f*; (from harm) preservación, *f*

preservative *a* preservativo. *n* preservativo, *m*

preserve *vt* preservar (de); guardar; proteger; conservar; *cul* hacer conservas de; (in syrup) almibarar. *n cul* conserva, *f*; (of fruit) compota, confitura, *f*; (covert) coto, *m*. **preserved fruit,** dulce de almíbar, *m*. **p. dish,** compotera, *f*

preserver *n* conservador (-ra); (saviour) salvador (-ra); (benefactor) bienhechor (-ra)

preserving *n* (from harm) preservación, *f*; conservación, *f*. **p. pan,** cazuela para conservas, *f*

preside *vi* (over) presidir; dirigir, gobernar. **He presided at the meeting,** Presidió la reunión

presidency *n* presidencia, *f*

president *n* presidente, *m*; (of a college) rector, *m*. **lady p.,** presidenta, *f*

presidential *a* presidencial

presidentship *n* presidencia, *f*

press *vt* prensar; (juice out of) exprimir; (clothes) planchar; (a bell, a hand, and of a shoe, etc.) apretar, *Mexico* apachurrar; (embrace) dar un abrazo (a); (a stamp, a kiss, etc.) imprimir; (an enemy) hostigar, acosar; (in a game) apretar; (crowd upon) oprimir; (emphasize) insistir en; (urge) instar, instigar; (compel) obligar; apremiar; (oppress) abrumar, agobiar; (paper) satinar; (an advantage) aprovecharse de. **Lola pressed his hand,** Lola le apretó la mano. **Time presses,** El tiempo es breve. **I did not p. the point,** No insistí. **to p. against,** pegar(se) contra. **to p. down,** comprimir; *fig* agobiar. **to p. for,** exigir, reclamar. **to p. forward, on,** avanzar; seguir el camino, continuar la marcha; (hurry) apretar el paso

press *n* (pressure) apretón, *m*; (push) golpe, *m*; (throng) muchedumbre, *f*; (of business, etc.) urgencia, *f*; (apparatus) prensa, *f*; (printing press and publishing firm) imprenta, *f*; (cupboard) armario, *m*. **Associated P.,** Prensa Asociada, *f*. **freedom of the p.,** libertad de la prensa, *f*. **in p., in the p.,** en prensa. **in the p. of battle,** en lo más reñido de la batalla. **to go to p.,** entrar en prensa. **p.-agent,** agente de publicidad, *m*. **p.-box,** tribuna de la prensa, *f*. **p. clipping, p.-cutting,** recorte de prensa, *m*. **p.-gallery,** tribuna de la prensa, *f*. **p.-gang,** ronda de enganche, *f*. **p.-mark,** número de catálogo, *m*. **p. proof,** prueba de imprenta, *f*. **p.-room,** taller de imprenta, *m*. **p.-stud,** botón automático, *m*. **p. conference,** rueda de prensa, entrevista de prensa, conferencia de pensa, *f*

pressing *a* urgente, apremiante; importuno. *n* prensado, *m*, prensadura, *f*; expresión, *f*; (of a garment) planchado, *m*

pressingly *adv* urgentemente, con urgencia; importunamente

pressman *n* tirador, *m*; (journalist) periodista, *m*

pressure *n* presión, *f*; (of the hand) apretón, *m*; apremio, *m*; opresión, *f*; (weight) peso, *m*; (force) fuerza, *f*; urgencia, *f*. **p.-cooker,** cazuela de presión, olla de presión, *f*, presto, *m*. **p.-gauge,** manómetro, *m*

prestidigitation *n* prestidigitación, *f*, juegos de manos, *m pl*

prestige *n* prestigio, *m*

prestigious *a* prestigiado

presumable *a* presumible

presume *vt* presumir; suponer, sospechar; (attempt) pretender. *vi* presumir; tomarse libertades; abusar (de)

presumption *n* presunción, *f;* suposición, *f;* (effrontery) atrevimiento, *m;* insolencia, *f*

presumptive *a* presuntivo; (with heir, etc.) presunto

presumptuous *a* presumido, insolente, presuntuoso; atrevido

presumptuously *adv* presuntuosamente

presumptuousness *n* presunción, presuntuosidad, *f;* atrevimiento, *m*

presuppose *vt* presuponer

presupposition *n* presuposición, *f*

pretence *n* (claim) pretensión, *f;* afectación, *f;* (simulation) fingimiento, *m;* pretexto, *m.* **false pretences,** apariencias fingidas, *f pl;* engaño, *m,* estafa, *f.* **to make a p. of,** fingir. **under p. of,** bajo pretexto de

pretend *vt* dar como pretexto de; aparentar, fingir, simular, hacer el papel (de). *vi* pretender (a); tener pretensiones (de); ser pretendiente (a); fingir

pretended *a* supuesto, fingido; falso

pretender *n* pretendiente, *m;* hipócrita, *mf*

pretension *n* pretensión, *f;* afectación, simulación, *f*

pretentious *a* pretencioso; (of persons) presumido

pretentiousness *f pl,* lo pretencioso

preterite *n* (tiempo) pretérito, *m, a* pretérito, pasado

pretext *n* pretexto, *m.* *vt* pretextar. **under p. of,** bajo pretexto de, so color de

prettily *adv* lindamente; con gracia; agradablemente

prettiness *n* lo bonito; elegancia, *f;* gracia, *f*

pretty *a* bonito; (of women, children) guapo, mono; (of men) lindo; elegante; excelente; *iron* bueno. *adv* bastante; medianamente; (very) muy; (almost) casi. **p. good,** bastante bueno. **p.-p.,** de muñeca; mono. *n* chuchería, *f,* guapos, *m pl.* **p. ways,** monerías, *f pl*

prevail *vi* prevalecer, predominar; ser la costumbre. **to p. against or over,** triunfar de, vencer (a). **to p. on, upon,** inducir, convencer, persuadir. **to be prevailed upon to,** dejarse persuadir a

prevailing *a* prevaleciente; dominante; predominante, reinante; general; común; (fashionable) en boga

prevalence *n* predominio, *m;* existencia, *f;* (habit) costumbre, *f;* (fashion) boga, *f*

prevalent *a* prevaleciente; predominante; general; común; corriente; (fashionable) en boga

prevaricate *vi* tergiversar; *law* prevaricar

prevarication *n* tergiversación, *f,* equívoco, *m*

prevaricator *n* tergiversador (-ra)

prevent *vt* evitar; (hinder) impedir (a)

preventable *a* evitable

prevention *n* prevención, *f;* (preventive) estorbo, obstáculo, *m*

preventive *a* preventivo. *n* preservativo, *m*

preview *n* vista de antemano, *f;* (of a film) avances, *m pl* (Cuba, Mexico), colas, *f pl* (Argentina), cortos *m pl* (Venezuela), sinopsis, *f* (Uruguay), tráiler, *m* (Spain)

previous *a* previo, anterior. **p. to,** antes de

previously *adv* anteriormente, antes, previamente

previousness *n* anterioridad, *f;* inoportunidad, *f*

prevision *n* previsión, *f*

prewar *a* de antes de la guerra

prey *n* presa, *f; fig* víctima, *f;* (booty) botín, *m.* *vi* (of animals) devorar; (plunder) robar, pillar; (of sorrow, etc.) hacer presa (de); agobiar, consumir; (sponge on) vivir a costa de. **to fall a p. to,** ser víctima de

price *n* precio, *m;* valor, *m;* costa, *f.* *vt* evaluar, tasar; poner precio a; preguntar el precio de; fijar el precio de. **at any p.,** a cualquier precio; (whatever the cost) cueste lo que cueste. **at a reduced p.,** a precio reducido. **fixed p.,** precio fijo, *m.* **p. ceiling,** precio máximo, precio tope, *m.* **p. control,** control de precios, *m.* **price list,** lista de precios, *f;* tarifa, *f;* (of shares, etc.) boletín de cotización, *m.* **Prices are subject to change without notice,** Los precios están sujetos a variación sin previo aviso.

priceless *a* inapreciable; (amusing) divertidísimo. **These jewels are p.,** Estas joyas no tienen precio

prick *n* pinchazo, *m;* picadura, *f;* punzada, *f;* (prickle) espina, *f;* (with a goad) aguijonazo, *m;* (with a pin) al-

filerazo, *m;* (with a spur) espolada, *f;* (of conscience) remordimiento, escrúpulo, *m.* *vt* pinchar, punzar; picar; (with remorse) atormentar, causar remordimiento (a); (urge on) incitar. **to p. the ears,** aguzar las orejas

pricking *n* picadura, *f;* punzada, *f.* **prickings of conscience,** remordimientos, *m pl*

prickle *n* espina, *f;* (irritation) escozor, *m*

prickly *a* espinoso; erizado. **p. heat,** salpullido causado por exceso de calor, *m.* **p. pear,** higo chumbo, *m,* chumbera, *f*

pride *n* orgullo, *m;* arrogancia, *f;* (splendour) pompa, *f,* fausto, aparato, *m;* belleza, *f;* vigor, *m;* (of lions) manada, *f.* **to take p. in,** estar orgulloso de. **to p. oneself,** sentirse orgulloso, ufanarse. **to p. oneself upon,** jactarse de, preciarse de

prie-dieu *n* reclinatorio, *m*

prier *n* espía, *mf;* curioso (-sa)

priest *n* sacerdote, *m;* cura, *m.* **high-p.,** sumo sacerdote, *m.* **p.-ridden,** dominado por el clero

priestess *n* sacerdotisa, *f*

priesthood *n* sacerdocio, *m*

priestly *a* sacerdotal

prig *n* fatuo (-ua), mojigato (-ta)

priggish *a* fatuo, gazmoño

priggishness *n* gazmoñería, fatuidad, *f*

prim *a* almidonado, etiquetero; peripuesto; afectado

primacy *n* primacía, *f*

prima donna *n* cantatriz, *f*

primarily *adv* en primer lugar principalmente

primary *a* primario; primitivo; principal. **p. education,** enseñanza primaria, *f.* **p. color,** color primario, *m.* **p. school,** escuela primaria, *f.* **p. election,** elección interna (dentro de un partido), *f*

primate *n* primado, *m*

prime *a* primero; principal; excelente; de primera calidad; de primera clase. *n* (spring) primavera, *f;* (of life, etc.) flor, *f,* vigor, *m;* (best) nata, crema, *f; ecc* prima, *f;* (number) número primo, *m.* *vt* preparar, aprestar; (fire-arms) cebar. **p. the pump,** cebar la bomba; (with paint, etc.) imprimar; (instruct) dar instrucciones (a), informar. **in his p.,** en la flor de su edad. **of p. quality,** de primera calidad. **P. Minister,** Primer Ministro, *m.* **p. necessity,** artículo de primera necesidad, *m*

primer *n* cartilla, *f,* abecedario, *m;* libro de lectura, *m;* (prayer book) devocionario, *m*

primeval *a* primevo, primitivo

priming *n* preparación, *f;* (of fire-arms) cebo, *m;* (of paint, etc.) imprimación, *f;* instrucción, *f*

primitive *a* primitivo; anticuado. *n* primitivo, *m*

primitiveness *n* lo primitivo; carácter primitivo, *m*

primly *adv* afectadamente, con afectación; gravemente

primness *n* afectación, *f;* gravedad, *f*

primogeniture *n* primogenitura, *f*

primordial *a* primordial

primrose *n* primavera, *f;* color amarillo pálido, *m*

prince *n* príncipe, *m.* **P. Consort,** príncipe consorte, *m.* **P. of Wales,** (Britain) príncipe heredero, *m;* (Spanish equivalent) Príncipe de Asturias, *m.* **p. regent,** príncipe regente, *m.* **P. Charming,** el Príncipe Azul, *m*

princeliness *n* magnificencia, *f;* nobleza, *f*

princely *a* principesco; magnífico; noble

princess *n* princesa, *f*

principal *a* principal; fundamental; mayor. *n* principal, jefe, *m;* (of a university) rector, *m;* (of a school) director (-ra); *law* causante, *m; com* capital, *m*

principality *n* principado, *m*

principally *adv* principalmente

principle *n* principio, *m.* **in p.,** en principio

principled *a* de principios . . .

print *n* (mark) impresión, marca, *f;* (type) letra de molde, *f,* tipo, *m;* (of books) imprenta, *f;* (fabric) estampado, *m;* (picture) grabado, *m;* (photograph) positiva impresa, *f;* (mold) molde, *m.* *vt* marcar; imprimir; (on the mind) grabar; *print* tirar, hacer una tirada (de); (in photography) tirar una prueba (de); (publish) sacar a luz, publicar; (fabrics) estampar. **in p.,** impreso; publicado; **He likes to see his name in print,** Le gusta ver su nombre en letras de molde; (available) existente. **to be out of p.,** estar agotado. **p. dress,** vestido estampado, *m*

printed *a* impreso. **p. fabric,** estampado, *m.* **p. matter,** impresos, *m pl*

printer *n* impresor, *m;* tipógrafo, *m.* **printer's devil,** aprendiz de impresor, *m.* **printer's ink,** tinta de imprenta, tinta tipográfica, *f.* **printer's mark,** pie de imprenta, *m*

printing *n* imprenta, *f;* impresión, *f;* (of fabrics) estampación, *f;* (art of) tipografía, *f.* **p. house,** imprenta, *f.* **p. machine,** máquina de imprimir, *f.* **p. press,** prensa tipográfica, *f.* **p. types,** caracteres de imprenta, *m pl*

prior *n* prior, *m, a* anterior, previo. **p. to,** anterior a, antes de

prioress *n* priora, *f*

priority *n* prioridad, *f*

prism *n* prisma, *m;* espectro solar, *m*

prismatic *a* prismático

prison *n* prisión, cárcel, *f.* **p.-breaking,** huida de la prisión, *f.* **p. camp,** campo de prisioneros, *m.* **p. van,** coche celular, *m.* **p. yard,** patio de la prisión, *m*

prisoner *n* prisionero (-ra), preso (-sa). **to take p.,** prender, hacer prisionero (a)

pristine *a* pristino, original

privacy *n* soledad, *f,* aislamiento, retiro, *m;* intimidad, *f;* secreto, *m*

private *a* particular; privado; secreto; confidencial; reservado; íntimo; personal; doméstico; (of hearings, etc.) a puertas cerradas, secreto; (own) propio. *n* (soldier) soldado raso, *m.* **in p.,** en secreto; confidencialmente, de persona a persona. **They wish to be p.,** Quieren estar a solas. **p. company,** sociedad en comandita, *f.* **p. hotel,** pensión, *f.* **p. house,** casa particular, *f.* **p. individual,** particular, *mf.* **p. interview,** entrevista privada, *f.* **p. life,** vida privada, *f.* **p. office,** despacho particular, *m.* **p. secretary,** secretario (-ia) particular. **p. viewing,** (of a film) función privada, *f;* **(of an exhibition)** día de inauguración, *m*

privateer *n* corsario, *m*

privately *adv* privadamente; en secreto; personalmente; confidencialmente; (of hearings) a puertas cerradas

privation *n* privación, *f;* carencia, escasez, *f*

privet *n* alheña, *f*

privilege *n* privilegio, *m;* derecho, *m;* inmunidad, *f. vt* privilegiar

privileged *a* privilegiado; confidencial

privy *a* privado; cómplice; enterado; personal, particular. *n* (latrine) retrete, *m.* **p. council,** consejo privado, *m*

prize *n* premio, *m;* recompensa, *f,* galardón, *m;* (capture) presa, *f. a* que ha ganado un premio; premiado; (huge) enorme; (complete) de primer orden. *vt* estimar, apreciar. **to p. open,** abrir con una palanca. **to carry off the p.,** ganar el premio. **cash p.,** premio en metálico, *m.* **first p.,** primer premio, *m;* (in a lottery) premio gordo, *m.* **p. court,** tribunal de presas, *m.* **p. fight,** partido de boxeo, *m.* **p. fighter,** boxeador, *m.* **p. giving,** distribución de premios, *f.* **p. money,** premio en metálico, *m;* (boxing) bolsa, *f*

pro *prep* pro. **pro forma invoice,** factura simulada, *f*

probability *n* probabilidad, *f*

probable *a* probable

probably *adv* probablemente

probate *n* verificación de un testamento, *f*

probation *n* probación, *f; law* libertad vigilada, *f*

probationary *a* de probación; de prueba

probationer *n* novicio, *m;* estudiante de enfermera, *f;* candidato, *m;* aspirante, *m*

probe *n surg* sonda, cala, tienta, *f. vt surg* tentar; escudriñar

probing *n* sondeo, *m*

probity *n* probidad, integridad, *f*

problem *n* problema, *m;* cuestión, *f.* **p. play,** drama de tesis, *m*

problematic *a* problemático

problem child *n* niño problemático, *m* (male), niña problemática, *f* (female)

proboscis *n* (of an elephant) trompa, *f;* (of an insect) trompetilla, *f*

Probus Probo, *m*

procedure *n* procedimiento, *m*

proceed *vi* seguir el camino, continuar la marcha; avanzar, seguir adelante; ir; proceder; ponerse (a); empezar (a); (say) proseguir; (come to) llegar a, ir a; (of a play, etc.) desarrollarse. **Before we p. any further . . .** Antes de ir más lejos . . . **to p. to blows,** llegar a las manos. **to p. against,** proceder contra, procesar. **to p. from,** venir de. **to p. with,** proseguir; poner por obra; usar

proceeding *n* modo de obrar, *m;* conducta, *f;* procedimiento, *m;* transacción, *f; pl* **proceedings,** (measures) medidas, *f pl,* actos, *m pl;* (of a learned society or a conference) actas, *f pl.* **to take proceedings against,** *law* procesar

proceeds *n pl* producto, *m;* ganancias, *f pl;* beneficios, *m pl.* **net p.,** producto neto, *m*

process *n* proceso, *m;* (method) procedimiento, *m;* (course) curso, *m;* marcha, *f;* (*law zool*) proceso, *m. vt* beneficiar (ore), trasformar, elaborar. **in p. of,** en curso de. **in the p. of time,** con el tiempo marchando el tiempo

processing industry *n* industria de trasformación, industria de elaboración, *f*

procession *n* desfile, *m;* cortejo, *m;* (religious) procesión, *f.* **funeral p.,** cortejo fúnebre, *m.* **to walk in p.,** desfilar

processional *a* procesional

proclaim *vt* proclamar; publicar, pregonar; anunciar; (reveal) revelar; (outlaw) denunciar

proclamation *n* proclamación, *f;* proclama, *f,* anuncio, *m;* declaración, *f*

proclivity *n* proclividad, propensión, *f*

procrastinate *vi* tardar (en decidirse), aplazar su decisión; vacilar; perder el tiempo

procrastination *n* dilación, tardanza, *f;* vacilación, *f;* pereza, *f*

procrastinator *n* perezoso (-sa)

procreate *vt* procrear

procreation *n* procreación, *f*

procreator *n* procreador (-ra)

proctor *n* procurador, *m; univ* censor, *m*

procurable *a* procurable; asequible

procure *vt* obtener, conseguir, lograr

procurement *n* obtención, *f,* logro, *m*

procurer *n* alcahuete, *m*

procuress *n* alcahueta, celestina, trotaconventos, *f*

prod *n* (with a bayonet, etc.) punzada, *f; fig* pinchazo, *m. vt* punzar; (in the ribs, etc.) clavar; *fig* pinchar

prodigal *a* and *n* pródigo (-ga)

prodigality *n* prodigalidad, *f*

prodigally *adv* pródigamente

prodigious *a* prodigioso

prodigiousness *n* prodigiosidad, *f;* enormidad, *f*

prodigy *n* prodigio, *m;* portento, *m.* **child p.,** niño prodigio

produce *vt* producir; dar frutos; (show) mostrar, presentar; (take out) sacar; (occasion) causar, traer consigo, ocasionar; (shares, etc.) rendir; *geom* prolongar; (a play) poner en escena. *n* producto, *m;* víveres, comestibles, *m pl*

producer *n* productor (-ra); *theat* director de escena, *m*

product *n* producto, *m;* (result) fruto, resultado, *m,* consecuencia, *f; math* producto, *m*

production *n* producción, *f;* producto, *m; geom* prolongación, *f;* (of a play) dirección escénica, *f;* (performance) producción, *f.* **p. cost,** coste de producción, *m*

productive *a* productivo

productivity *n* productividad, *f*

profanation *n* profanación, *f*
profane *a* profano; sacrílego, blasfemo. *vt* profanar
profaner *n* profanador (-ra)
profanity *n* profanidad, *f*; blasfemia, *f*
profess *vt* (assert) afirmar, manifestar; declarar; (a faith, a profession, teach) profesar; (feign) fingir; (pretend) tener pretensiones de. *vi* (as a monk or nun) tomar estado, entrar en religión. **He professed himself surprised,** Se declaró sorprendido
professed *a* declarado; *ecc* profeso; ostensible, fingido
profession *n* profesión, *f*; carrera, *f*; declaración, *f*. **p. of faith,** profesión de fe, *f*. **the learned professions,** las carreras liberales
professional *a* profesional; de la profesión; de profesión; de carrera. **p. diplomat,** diplomático (-ca) de carrera. **p. etiquette,** etiqueta profesional, *f*. **p. man,** hombre profesional, *m*; hombre de carrera liberal, *m*
professor *n* catedrático (-ca), profesor (-ra)
professorate *n* profesorado, *m*
professorial *a* de catedrático; de profesor
professorship *n* cátedra, *f*
proffer *vt* proponer; ofrecer. *n* oferta, *f*
proficiency *n* pericia, habilidad, *f*
proficient *a* proficiente, experto, adepto, perito
profile *n* perfil, *m*. *vt* perfilar. **in p.,** de perfil
profit *n* provecho, *m*; utilidad, *f*; ventaja, *f*; *com* ganancia, *f*, *vt* aprovechar. *vi* ganar; *com* sacar ganancia. **to p. by,** aprovechar. **gross p.,** ganancia total, *f*. **p. and loss,** ganancias y pérdidas, *f pl*. **p. sharing,** participación en las ganancias, participación de utilidades, *f*
profitable *a* provechoso, útil, ventajoso; lucrativo. **p. use,** aprovechamiento, *m*
profitably *adv* con provecho, provechosamente; lucrativamente
profiteer *n* estraperlista, *mf*
profit incentive *n* acicate del lucro, *m*
profitless *a* sin provecho, infructuoso, inútil
profligacy *n* libertinaje, *m*
profligate *a* licencioso, disoluto. *n* libertino, *m*
profound *a* profundo
profundity *n* profundidad, *f*
profuse *a* profuso; pródigo; lujoso
profusely *adv* profusamente; pródigamente; lujosamente
profusion *n* profusión, abundancia, *f*; prodigalidad, *f*; exceso, *m*
progenitor *n* progenitor, *m*; (ancestor) antepasado, *m*
progeny *n* prole, *f*
prognosis *n* prognosis, *f*; presagio, *m*; *med* pronóstico, *m*
prognosticate *vt* pronosticar, presagiar
prognostication *n* pronosticación, *f*; pronóstico, presagio, augurio, *m*
program *n* programa, *m*
progress *n* progreso, *m*; avance, *m*; (betterment) mejora, *f*; (of events) marcha, *f*. *vi* avanzar, marchar; (improve) progresar, adelantar; mejorar. **to make p.,** adelantarse; hacer progresos
progression *n* progresión, *f*
progressive *a* progresivo; avanzado; *pol* progresista. *n pol* progresista, *mf*
progressiveness *n* carácter progresivo, *m*
prohibit *vt* prohibir; defender; (prevent) impedir, privar. **His health prohibited him from doing it,** Su salud le impidió hacerlo
prohibition *n* prohibición, *f*; interdicción, *f*; (of alcohol) prohibicionismo, *m*
prohibitionist *n* prohibicionista, *mf*
prohibitive *a* prohibitivo, prohibitorio
project *vt* (all meanings) proyectar. *vi* sobresalir; destacarse. *n* proyectil, plan, *m*
projectile *n* proyectil, *m*, *a* arrojadizo
projecting *a* saliente; (of teeth) saltón
projection *n* (hurling) lanzamiento, *m*; prominencia, protuberancia, *f*; (other meanings) proyección, *f*
projector *n* proyectista, *mf*; proyector, *m*

proletarian *a* proletario
proletariate *n* proletariado, *m*
prolific *a* prolífico; fecundo, fértil
prolix *a* prolijo
prolixity *n* prolijidad, *f*
prolog *n* prólogo, *m*, *vt* prologar
prolong *vt* prolongar
prolongation *n* prolongación, *f*
promenade *n* paseo, *m*; bulevar, *m*; avenida, *f*. *vi* pasearse. *vt* recorrer, andar por, pasearse por. **p. deck,** cubierta de paseo, *f*
Promethean *a* de Prometeo
prominence *n* prominencia, *f*; protuberancia, *f*; eminencia, *f*; importancia, *f*
prominent *a* prominente, saliente; (of eyes, teeth) saltón; (distinguished) eminente, distinguido. **They placed the vase in a p. position,** Pusieron el florero muy a la vista. **to play a p. part,** desempeñar un papel importante. **p. eyes, ojos** saltones, *m pl*
promiscuous *a* promiscuo
promiscuousness *n* promiscuidad, *f*
promise *n* promesa, *f*; (hope) esperanza, *f*; (word) palabra, *f*; (future) porvenir, *m*. *vt* and *vi* prometer. **a young man of p.,** un joven de porvenir. **to break one's p.,** faltar a su palabra; no cumplir una promesa. **to keep one's p.,** guardar su palabra; cumplir su promesa. **to p. and do nothing,** apuntar y no dar. **under p. of,** bajo palabra de. **p. of marriage,** palabra de matrimonio, *f*
promised *a* prometido. **P. Land,** Tierra de promisión, *f*
promising *a* que promete bien, que promete mucho; prometedor; (of the future, etc.) halagüeño; (of persons) que llegará
promissory *a* promisorio. **p. note,** pagaré, abonaré, *m*
promontory *n* promontorio, *m*
promote *vt* fomentar, promover; provocar; (aid) favorecer, proteger; avanzar; estimular; (to a post) ascender; (an act bill) promover; *com* negociar
promoter *n* promotor (-ra); instigador (-ra); (*theat* etc.) empresario, *m*
promotion *n* (encouragement) fomento, *m*; (furtherance) adelanto, *m*; protección, *f*, favorecimiento, *m*; (in employment, etc.) promoción, *f*, ascenso, *m*; (of a company, etc.) creación, *f*
prompt *a* pronto; diligente; presuroso; puntual; rápido; *com* inmediato. *vt* impulsar, incitar, mover; dictar; insinuar; *theat* apuntar; (remind) recordar. **He came at five o'clock p.,** Vino a las cinco en punto. **p. book,** libro del traspunte, *m*. **p. box,** concha (del apuntador), *f*
prompter *n* *theat* apuntador, (in the wings) traspunte, *m*
prompting *n* sugestión, *f*; instigación, *f*; *pl* **promptings,** impulso, *m*; (of the heart, etc.) dictados, *m pl*
promptitude *n* prontitud, presteza, *f*; prisa, expedición, *f*; puntualidad, *f*
promptly *adv* inmediatamente, en seguida; con prontitud, con celeridad; puntualmente
promptness *n* See **promptitude**
promulgate *vt* promulgar; divulgar, diseminar
promulgation *n* promulgación, *f*; divulgación, diseminación, *f*
prone *a* postrado; inclinado, propenso
proneness *n* postración, *f*; inclinación, tendencia, propensión, *f*
prong *n* (pitchfork) horquilla, *f*; (of a fork) diente, *m*, púa, *f*
pronged *a* dentado, con púas
pronoun *n* pronombre, *m*
pronounce *vt* pronunciar; declarar; articular
pronounced *a* marcado; perceptible; bien definido
pronouncement *n* pronunciamiento, *m*
pronunciation *n* pronunciación, *f*; articulación, *f*
proof *n* prueba, *f*; demostración, *f*; ensayo, *m*; *law* testimonio, *m*; (*phot print*) prueba, *f*; *math* comprobación, *f*, *a* hecho a prueba (de); impenetrable (a); *fig* insensible

(a). *vt* (raincoats, etc.) impermeabilizar. **in p. whereof,** en fe de lo cual. **p. against bombs,** a prueba de bombas. **p. reading,** corrección de pruebas, *f*

prop *n* apoyo, puntal, estribadero, *m*; (for a tree) horca, *f*, rodrigón, *m*; *naut* escora, *f*; *fig* báculo, *m*, columna, *f*, apoyo, *m*. *vt* apoyar; apuntalar; (a tree) ahorquillar; (a building) acodalar; *naut* escorar; *fig* sostener. **He propped himself against the wall,** Se apoyó en el muro, Se arrimó al muro

propaganda *n* propaganda, *f*

propagandist *n* propagandista, *mf*

propagate *vt* propagar. *vi* propagarse

propagation *n* propagación, *f*

propagator *n* propagador (-ra)

propel *vt* propulsar, empujar, mover

propeller *n* propulsor, *m*; *mech* hélice, *f*

propelling, *f*. **p. pencil,** lapicero, *m*

propensity *n* propensión, tendencia, inclinación, *f*

proper *a* propio; apropiado; correcto; decente; (prim) afectado; serio, formal; (exact) justo, exacto; (suitable (for)) bueno (para), apto (para); (true) verdadero; (characteristic) peculiar; *her* natural; (with rascal, etc.) redomado; (handsome) guapo. **If you think it p.,** Si te parece bien. **p. noun,** nombre propio, *m*

properly *adv* decentemente; correctamente; propiamente; bien. **to do (a thing) p.,** hacer algo bien. **p. speaking,** propiamente dicho, hablando con propiedad

propertied *a* propietario, hacendado; (rich) pudiente, adinerado

property *n* propiedad, *f*; (belongings) bienes, *m pl*; posesiones, *f pl*; (estate) hacienda, *f*; (quality) cualidad, *f*; *pl* **properties,** *theat* accesorios, *m pl*. **personal p.,** bienes muebles, *m pl*; cosas personales, *f pl*. **real p.,** bienes raíces, *m pl*. **p. man,** *theat* encargado de los accesorios, *m*. **p. owner,** propietario (-ia). **p. tax,** contribución sobre la propiedad, *f*

prophecy *n* profecía, *f*; predicción, *f*

prophesier *n* See **prophet**

prophesy *vt* profetizar; presagiar, predecir. *vi* hacer profecías

prophet *n* profeta, *m*

prophetess *n* profetisa, *f*

prophetic *a* profético

prophylactic *a* and *n* profiláctico, *m*

propinquity *n* propincuidad, proximidad, *f*; (relationship) parentesco, *m*

propitiate *vt* propiciar; apaciguar, conciliar

propitiation *n* propiciación, *f*

propitiator *n* propiciador (-ra)

propitiatory *a* propiciador

propitious *a* propicio, favorable

propitiousness *n* lo propicio

proportion *n* proporción, *f*; parte, *f*; porción, *f*; *pl* **proportions,** proporciones, *f pl*; dimensiones, *f pl*. *vt* proporcionar; repartir, distribuir. **in p.,** en proporción; conforme (a), según; *com* a prorrata. **in p. as,** a medida que. **out of p.,** desproporcionado. **He has lost all sense of p.,** Ha perdido su equilibrio (mental)

proportional *a* proporcional; en proporción (a); proporcionado (a). **p. representation,** representación proporcional, *f*

proportionally *adv* proporcionalmente, en proporción

proportionate *a* proporcionado; proporcional. *vt* proporcionar

proportionately *adv* See **proportionally**

proposal *n* proposición, *f*; oferta, *f*; (plan) propósito, proyecto, *m*. **p. of marriage,** oferta de matrimonio, *f*

propose *vt* proponer; ofrecer; (a toast) dar, brindar. *vi* pretender, intentar, tener la intención de; pensar; (marriage) declararse

proposer *n* proponente, *m*; (of a motion) autor (-ra) de una proposición

proposition *n* proposición, *f*; (plan) proyecto, propósito, *m*

propound *vt* proponer; plantear, presentar

proprietary *a* propietario; de propiedad

proprietor *n* propietario, *m*; dueño, *m*

proprietorship *n* propiedad, pertenencia, *f*

proprietress *n* propietaria, *f*; dueña, *f*

propriety *n* decoro, *m*; conveniencia, *f*; corrección, *f*

propulsion *n* propulsión, *f*

propulsive *a* propulsor

prorogation *n* prorrogación, *f*

prorogue *vt* prorrogar, suspender (la sesión de una asamblea legislativa)

pros and cons el pro y el contra

prosaic *a* prosaico

proscenium *n* proscenio, *m*

proscribe *vt* proscribir

proscription *n* proscripción, *f*

prose *n* prosa, *f*. **p. writer,** prosista, *mf*

prosecute *vt* proseguir, llevar adelante; (*law* a person) procesar; (*law* a claim) pedir en juicio

prosecution *n* prosecución, *f*; cumplimiento, *m*; *law* acusación, *f*; (*law* party) parte actora, *f*. **in the p. of his duty,** en el cumplimiento de su deber

prosecutor *n* demandante, actor, *m*. **public p.,** fiscal, *m*

proselyte *n* prosélito, *m*

proselytism *n* proselitismo, *m*

prose writer *n* prosador, *m*

prosody *n* prosodia, *f*

prospect *n* perspectiva, *f*; esperanza, *f*; probabilidad, *f*; (in mining) indicio de filón, *m*; criadero (de oro, etc.), *m*. *vi* explorar; (of a mine) prometer (bien), dar buenas esperanzas. *vt* explorar, inspeccionar; examinar. **He is a man with good prospects,** Es un hombre de porvenir

prospecting *n* la prospección, *f*

prospective *a* en expectativa, futuro; previsor

prospector *n* explorador, operador, *m*

prospectus *n* prospecto, programa, *m*

prosper *vi* prosperar. *vt* favorecer, prosperar

prosperity *n* prosperidad, *f*

prosperous *a* próspero; favorable

prostate *n* próstata, *f*

prostitute *n* prostituta, *f*, *vt* prostituir

prostitution *n* prostitución, *f*

prostrate *a* tendido; postrado; abatido. *vt* derribar; arruinar; (by grief, etc.) postrar; (oneself) postrarse

prostration *n* postración, *f*; abatimiento, *m*. **nervous p.,** neurastenia, *f*

prosy *a* aburrido, árido; pedestre, prosaico; verboso, prolijo

protagonist *n* protagonista, *mf*

protean *a* proteico

protect *vt* proteger

protection *n* protección, *f*; defensa, *f*; garantía, *f*; abrigo, *m*; refugio, *m*; (passport) salvoconducto, *m*; *pol* proteccionismo, *m*

protectionism *n* proteccionismo, *m*

protectionist *n* proteccionista, *mf*

protective *a* protector; *pol* proteccionista

protector *n* protector, *m*

protectorate *n* protectorado, *m*

protectress *n* protectriz, *f*

protein *n* proteína, *f*

protest *vt* protestar; *law* hacer el protesto de una letra de cambio. *vi* declarar; insistir (en); hacer una protesta. *n* protesta, *f*; *law* protesto, *m*. **under p.,** bajo protesta. **to p. against,** protestar contra

Protestant *a* and *n* protestante, *mf*

Protestantism *n* protestantismo, *m*

protestation *n* protestación, *f*

protester *n* el, *m*, (*f*, la) que protesta

protest literature *n* literatura de denuncia, *f*

protocol *n* protocolo, *m*, *vt* protocolizar

protoplasm *n* protoplasma, *m*

prototype *n* prototipo, *m*

protract *vt* prolongar; dilatar

protracted *a* prolongado; largo

protraction *n* prolongación, *f*

protractor *n* (*geom* and *surv*) transportador, *m*. **p. muscle,** músculo extensor, *m*

protrude *vt* sacar fuera. *vi* salir fuera; sobresalir

protuberance *n* protuberancia, *f*

protuberant *a* protuberante, prominente

proud *a* orgulloso; arrogante; noble; glorioso; magnífico; *Mexico* alzado. **to be p.,** enorgullecerse. **to make p.,** enorgullecer; hacer orgulloso. **to be p. of,** ser orgulloso de, pagarse de, gloriarse en. **p. flesh,** carnosidad, *f*, bezo, *m*

proudly *adv* con orgullo, orgullosamente

provable *a* demostrable

prove *vt* probar; demostrar; (experience) experimentar, sufrir; poner a prueba; (a will) verificar; (show) mostrar; confirmar. *vi* resultar, salir (bien or mal)

provenance *n* origen, *m*

Provençal *a* provenzal. *n* provenzal, *mf*; (language) provenzal, *m*

Provence Provenza, *f*

provender *n* forraje, *m*; *inf* provisiones, *f pl*

proverb *n* refrán, *m*; proverbio, *m*. **collection of proverbs,** refranero, *m*. **Book of Proverbs,** Proverbios, *m pl*

proverbial *a* proverbial

proverbially *adv* proverbialmente

provide *vt* proporcionar, dar; proveer, surtir, suplir; (stipulate) estipular; preparar (por); tomar precauciones (contra); sufragar los gastos (de); proporcionar medios de vida (a); señalar una pensión (a). **to p. oneself with,** proveerse de

provided (that) *conjunc* si; a condición de que, siempre que, con tal que

providence *n* providencia, *f*

provident *a* próvido, previsor, prudente; económico

providential *a* providencial

providentially *adv* providencialmente

providently *adv* próvidamente, prudentemente

provider *n* proveedor (-ra)

province *n* provincia, *f*; esfera, *f*; función, incumbencia, *f*

provincial *a* provincial, de provincia; provinciano. *n* provinciano (-na); *ecc* provincial, *m*

provincialism *n* provincialismo, *m*

provision *n* provisión, *f*; (stipulation) estipulación, *f*; *pl* **provisions,** provisiones, *f pl*; víveres, comestibles, *m pl*. *vt* abastecer, aprovisionar. **to make p. for,** hacer provisión para, proveer de. **to make p. for one's family,** asegurar el porvenir de su familia. **p. merchant,** vendedor (-ra) de comestibles

provisional *a* provisional, interino

provisioning *n* aprovisionamiento, abastecimiento, *m*

proviso *n* condición, estipulación, disposición, *f*

provisory *a* provisional; condicional

provocation *n* provocación, *f*

provocative *a* provocativo, provocador

provocatively *adv* de un modo provocativo

provoke *vt* provocar; suscitar; incitar, excitar; (irritate) sacar de madre (a), indignar

provoker *n* provocador (-ra); instigador (-ra)

provoking *a* provocativo; (irritating) enojoso, irritante

provost *n* preboste, *m*; (of a college) director, *m*; (in Scotland) alcalde, *m*. **p.-marshal,** capitán preboste, *m*

prow *n* proa, *f*

prowess *n* valor, *m*, destreza, *f*; proeza, *f*

prowl *vi* and *vt* rondar; cazar al acecho

prowler *n* rondador (-ra); ladrón (-ona)

proximity *n* proximidad, *Argentina* adyacencia, *f*

proximo *adv* en (or del) mes próximo

proxy *n* poder, *m*; delegación, *f*; apoderado, *m*; delegado (-da); substituto (-ta). **to be married by p.,** casarse por poderes

prude *n* mojigata, beata, *f*

prudence *n* prudencia, *f*

prudent *a* prudente

prudently *adv* con prudencia

prudery *n* mojigatería, beatería, damería, gazmoñería, *f*

prudish *a* mojigato, gazmoño, remilgado

prune *n* ciruela pasa, *f*; color de ciruela, *m*, *vt* podar; (cut) cortar; reducir

pruning *n* poda, *f*; reducción, *f*. **p. knife,** podadera, *f*

prurient *a* lascivo, lujurioso, salaz

Prussia Prusia, *f*

Prussian *a* and *n* prusiano (-na). **P. blue,** azul de Prusia, *m*

prussic acid *n* acido prúsico, *m*

pry *vi* escudriñar; acechar, espiar, fisgonear; (meddle) entremeterse, meterse donde no le llaman. *vt* See **prize**

prying *n* fisgoneo, *m*; curiosidad, *f*, *a* fisgón, curioso

psalm *n* salmo, *m*. **to sing psalms,** salmodiar

psalmist *n* salmista, *m*

psaltery *n* salterio, *m*

pseudo- *a* seudo. **p.-learned,** erudito a la violeta

pseudonym *n* seudónimo, *m*

psychiatrist *n* siquiatra, *m*

psychiatry *n* siquiatría, *f*

psychic *a* síquico

psychoanalysis *n* sicoanálisis, *mf*

psychoanalyst *n* sicoanalista, *mf*

psychoanalyze *vt* sicoanalizar

psychological *a* sicológico

psychologist *n* sicólogo (-ga)

psychology *n* sicología, *f*

psychopathic *a* sicopático

psychosis *n* sicosis, *f*

psychotherapy *n* sicoterapia, *f*

ptomaine poisoning *n* intoxicación por tomaínas, *f*

puberty *n* pubertad, *f*

pubescent *a* púber

pubic *a* púbico

pubis *n* pubis, *m*

public *a* and *n* público *m*. **in p.,** en público. **p. assistance,** asistencia pública, *f*. **p. funds,** hacienda pública, *f*. **p. health,** higiene pública, *f*. **p.-house,** taberna, *f*. **p. opinion,** opinión pública, *f*. *inf* el qué dirán. **p.-spirited,** patriótico. **p. thoroughfare,** vía pública, *f*. **p. works,** obras públicas, *f pl*

publican *n* tabernero, *m*

publication *n* publicación, *f*

publicist *n* publicista, *mf*

publicity *n* publicidad, *f*

publicity agent *n* publicista, *mf*

publish *vt* publicar, divulgar, difundir; (a book, etc.) dar a luz, dar a la prensa, publicar; (of a publisher) editar. **to p. abroad,** pregonar a los cuatro vientos. **to p. banns of marriage,** correr las amonestaciones

publisher *n* publicador (-ra); (of books) editor (-ra)

publishing *n* publicación, *f*. **p. house,** casa editorial, *f*. **the p. world,** el mundo de la edición, *m*

puck *n* trasgo, *m*; diablillo, picaruelo, *m*

pucker *vt* (one's brow, etc.) fruncir; (crease) arrugar. *vi* arrugarse. *n* frunce, *m*; arruga, *f*; (fold) bolsa, *f*

puckering *n* fruncido, *m*; arrugas, *f pl*

puckish *a* travieso

pudding *n* pudín, budín, *m*. **black p.,** morcilla, *f*

puddle *n* charco, *m*

puerile *a* pueril

puerperal *a* puerperal. **p. fever,** fiebre puerperal, *f*

Puerto Rican *a* and *n* puertorriqueño (-ña), *a* boricua, *n* borinqueño (-ña)

puff *vt* and *vi* (blow) soplar; (at a pipe, etc.) chupar; (smoke) lanzar bocanadas de humo; (make pant) hacer jadear; (advertise) dar bombo (a); (distend) hinchar; (make conceited) envanecerse; (of a train, etc.) bufar; resoplar. *n* soplo, *m*; (of smoke, etc.) bocanada, *f*; (of an engine, etc.) resoplido, bufido, *m*; (for powder) borla (para polvos), *f*; (pastry) bollo, *m*; (advertisement) bombo, *m*. **to be puffed up,** *fig* hincharse, inflarse. **p. of wind,** ráfaga de aire, *f*. **p.-ball,** bejín, *m*.

p.-pastry, hojaldre, *m,* or *f.* **p.-sleeve,** manga de bullón, *f*

puffiness *n* hinchazón, *f*

puffy *a* (of the wind) a ráfagas; (panting) jadeante; (swollen) hinchado

pug *n* (dog) doguino, *m.* **p.-nosed,** de nariz respingona

pugilism *n* boxeo, pugilato, *m*

pugilist *n* pugilista, *mf,* boxeador, *m*

pugnacious *a* pugnaz, belicoso

pugnacity *n* pugnacidad, belicosidad, *f*

pull *n* tirón, *m;* sacudida, *f;* golpe, *m;* (row) paseo en barco, *m;* (with the oars) golpe (de remos), *m;* (at a bell) tirón, *m;* (bell-rope) tirador, *m;* (at a bottle) trago, *m;* (strain) fuerza, *f;* atracción, *f;* (struggle) lucha, *f;* (advantage) ventaja, *f;* (influence) influencia, *f, Central America, Mexico* arranque *m.* **to give a p.,** tirar (de), dar un tirón (a). **to have plenty of p.,** *inf* tener buenas aldabas

pull *vt* tirar (de); (drag) arrastrar; (extract) sacar; (a boat) remar; (gather) coger; *print* imprimir. **He pulled the trigger (of his gun),** Apretó el gatillo. **He was sitting by the fire pulling at his pipe,** Estaba sentado cerca del fuego fumando su pipa. **to p. a hat well down on the head,** calarse el sombrero. **to p. a person's leg,** tomar el pelo (a). **to p. oneself together,** componer el semblante, serenarse; recobrar el aplomo; (tidy oneself) arreglarse. **to p. apart,** *vt* separar; romper en dos. *vi* separarse; romperse en dos. **to p. away,** *vt* arrancar; quitar. *vi* tirar con esfuerzo. **to p. back,** tirar hacia atrás; hacer retroceder (a); retener. **to p. down,** hacer bajar, obligar a bajar; (objects) bajar; (buildings) derribar, demoler; (humble) humillar; degradar; (weaken) debilitar. **to p. in,** tirar hacia dentro; hacer entrar; (a horse) enfrenar; (expenditure) reducir. **to p. off,** arrancar; (clothes) quitarse; (a deal) cerrar (un trato), concluir con éxito; (win) ganar. **to p. on,** *vt* (gloves, etc.) meterse, ponerse. *vi* seguir remando. **to p. open,** abrir; abrir rápidamente. **to p. out,** hacer salir; obligar a salir; (teeth, daggers, etc.) sacar; (hair) arrancar. **to p. round, through,** *vt* ayudar a reponerse (a); sacar de un aprieto. *vi* restablecerse; reponerse, cobrar la salud, sanar. **to p. together,** obrar de acuerdo; (get on) llevarse (bien or mal). **He pulled himself together very quickly,** Se repuso muy pronto. **to p. up,** *vt* montar, subir; (a horse) sofrenar; (stop) parar; (by the root) desarraigar, extirpar; (interrupt) interrumpir; (scold) reñir. *vi* parar(se); (restrain oneself) reprimirse, contenerse

pullet *n* polla, *f*

pulley *n* polea, *f; naut* garrucha, *f.* **p. wheel,** roldana, *f*

pulling *n* tracción, *f;* tirada, *f;* arranque, *m*

pullover *n* jersey, *m, Lat. Am.* chompa, *f*

pulmonary *a* pulmonar

pulp *n* pulpa, *f;* (of fruit) carne, *f;* (paper) pasta, *f;* (of teeth) bulbo dentario, *m. vt* reducir a pulpa; deshacer (el papel). **to beat to a p.,** *inf* poner como un pulpo

pulpit *n* púlpito, *m*

pulpy *a* pulposo; *bot* carnoso

pulsate *vi* pulsar, latir

pulsation *n* pulsación, *f,* latido, *m*

pulsatory *a* pulsante, pulsativo, latiente

pulse *n* pulso, *m;* pulsación, *f,* latido, *m;* vibración, *f;* (vegetable) legumbre, *f, vi* pulsar, latir; vibrar. **to take a person's p.,** tomar el pulso (a)

pulverization *n* pulverización, *f*

pulverize *vt* pulverizar

puma *n* puma, *f, Lat. Am.* león, *m*

pumice *n* piedra pómez, *f*

pummel *vt* aporrear

pump *n mech* bomba, *f;* (for water, etc.) aguatocha, *f; naut* pompa, *f;* (slipper) escarpín, *m, vt* bombear, extraer por medio de una bomba; (for information) sondear, sonsacar. **hand-p.,** bomba de mano, *f.* **to work a p.,** darle a la bomba

pumpkin *n* calabaza, *f, Central America* ayote, *m, Chile* zapallo, *m;* (plant) calabacera, *f*

pun *n* retruécano, *m*

punch *n* (drink) ponche, *m;* (blow) puñetazo, golpe, *m; mech* punzón, *m;* (for tickets, etc.) taladro, *m; inf* fuerza, *f. vt* (perforate) taladrar, punzar; estampar; (hit) dar un puñetazo (a). **p.-ball,** pelota de boxeo, *f.* **p.-bowl,** ponchera, *f*

Punchinello *n* Polichinela, *m.* **Punch and Judy show,** títeres, *m pl*

punctilious *a* formal, puntual, puntilloso

punctiliousness *n* formalidad, puntualidad, *f*

punctual *a* puntual

punctually *adv* puntualmente

punctuate *vt* puntuar

punctuation *n* puntuación, *f*

puncture *n* pinchazo, *m;* perforación, *f; surg* punción, *f. vt* pinchar; perforar; punzar. **We have a p. in the right tire,** Tenemos un pinchazo en el neumático derecho

pungency *n* picante, *m;* acerbidad, mordacidad, *f*

pungent *a* picante; acerbo, mordaz

Punic *a* púnico, cartaginés

punish *vt* castigar; maltratar

punishable *a* punible

punishment *n* castigo, *m;* pena, *f;* maltrato, *m*

punitive *a* punitivo

punt *n* batea, *f. vt* impeler una batea con una pértiga; ir en batea; (a ball) golpear, dar un puntapié (a). *a* excel. **puny** *a* débil, encanijado; insignificante; pequeño

pup *n* cachorro (-rra). *vi* parir la perra

pupa *n* crisálida, *f*

pupil *n* alumno (-na), discípulo (-la); (of the eye) pupila, niña (del ojo), *f; law* pupilo (-la). *a* escolar. **day p.,** alumno (-na) externo (-na). **p. teacher,** maestro (-tra) alumno (-na)

puppet *n* títere, *m,* marioneta, *f;* muñeca, *f;* (person) maniquí, *m.* **p. show,** función de títeres, *f.* **p. showman,** titiritero, titerero, *m*

puppy *n* perrito (-ta), cachorro (-rra)

purblind *a* ciego; (short-sighted and *fig*) miope

purchasable *a* comprable, que puede comprarse; *fig* sobornable

purchase *vt* comprar; adquirir; *fig* lograr, conseguir. *n* compra, *f;* adquisición, *f; mech* apalancamiento, *m;* fuerza, *f;* (lever) palanca, *f,* aparejo, *m; fig* influencia, *f.* **p. tax,** impuesto de lujo, *m*

purchaser *n* comprador (-ra)

purchasing *n* See **purchase. p. power,** poder de adquisición, *m*

pure *a* puro. **p.-bred,** de raza

purgation *n* purgación, *f*

purgative *a* purgativo. *n* purga, *f*

purgatorial *a* del purgatorio; (expiatory) purgatorio

purgatory *n* purgatorio, *m*

purge *n* purgación, *f;* (laxative) purga, *f; pol* depuración, *f;* purificación, *f. vt* purgar; *pol* depurar; purificar; expurgar

purging *n* purgación, *f; pol* depuración, *f; fig* purificación, *f*

purification *n* purificación, *f*

purificatory *a* purificador, purificatorio, que purifica

purifier *n* purificador (-ra)

purify *vt* purificar; (metals) acrisolar; refinar; depurar; (purge) purgar

purist *n* purista, *mf*

puritan *a* and *n* puritano (-na)

Puritanism *n* puritanismo, *m*

purity *n* pureza, *f*

purl *vi* (of a stream, etc.) murmurar, susurrar. *n* (of a stream, etc.) susurro, murmullo, *m*

purlieu *n* límite, *m; pl* **purlieus,** alrededores, *m pl,* inmediaciones, *f pl;* (slums) barrios bajos, *m pl*

purling *a* murmurante, que susurra, parlero. *n* murmullo, susurro, *m*

purloin *vt* hurtar, robar

purple *n* púrpura, *f*, *a* purpúreo. *vt* purpurar, teñir de púrpura. *vi* purpurear

purplish *a* purpurino, algo purpúreo

purport *vt* dar a entender, querer decir; significar; indicar; parecer; tener el objeto de; pretender. *n* importe, *m*; sentido, significado, *m*; objeto, *m*

purpose *n* objeto, *m*; propósito, fin, *m*; intención, *f*; proyecto, *m*; designio, *m*; determinación, voluntad, *f*; efecto, *m*; ventaja, utilidad, *f*, *vi and vt* proponerse; pensar, tener el propósito (de), intentar. **It will serve my p.,** Servirá para lo que yo quiero. **for the p. of . . .,** con el propósito de . . . , con el fin de . . . for purposes of . . . para efectos de . . . **on p.,** de propósito, expresamente, *Central America* adifés. **to no p.,** inútilmente; en vano

purposeful *a* resuelto; de substancia

purposeless *a* irresoluto, vacilante, vago; sin objeto; inútil

purposely *adv* expresamente, de intento

purr *vi* ronronear. *n* ronroneo, *m*

purse *n* bolsa, *f*; monedero, portamonedas, *m*. **to p. one's lips,** apretar los labios

purser *n naut* contador, sobrecargo, *Argentina* comisario, *m*. **purser's office,** contaduría, *f*

pursuance *n* cumplimiento, desempeño, *m*, prosecución, *f*. **in p. of,** en cumplimiento de; en consecuencia de

pursuant *a and adv* según; conforme (a), de acuerdo (con); en consecuencia (de)

pursue *vt* perseguir; seguir; (search) buscar; (hunt) cazar; (a submarine, etc.) dar caza (a); (continue) proseguir, continuar; (an occupation) dedicarse (a), ejercer

pursuer *n* perseguidor (-ra)

pursuit *n* perseguimiento, *m*; (search) busca, *f*; (hunt) caza, *f*; (performance) prosecución, *f*, desempeño, *m*; (employment) ocupación, *f*. **in p. of,** en busca de. **p. plane,** avión de caza, *m*

purulence *n* purulencia, *f*

purulent *a* purulento

purvey *vt* proveer, surtir, suministrar; abastecer; procurar

purveyance *n* suministro, abastecimiento, *m*; provisión, *f*

purveyor *n* suministrador (-ra), proveedor (-ra), bastecedor (-ra)

pus *n* pus, *m*

push *n* empujón, *m*; empellón, *m*; impulso, *m*; (of a person) empuje, *m*, energía, *f*; (attack) ataque, *m*; ofensiva, *f*; (effort) esfuerzo, *m*; crisis, *f*, momento crítico, *m*. **at a push,** *inf* en caso de necesidad; en un aprieto, si llegara el caso. **to give the p. to,** *inf* despedir (a). **p.-bicycle,** bicicleta, *f*. **p.-button,** botón, *m*; botón de llamada, *m*. **p.-cart,** carretilla de mano, *f*; (child's) cochecito de niño, *m*

push *vt* empujar; (jostle) empellar, dar empellones (a); (a finger in one's eye, etc.) clavar; (a button) apretar; (*fig* a person) proteger, ayudar; dar publicidad (a); (a claim, etc.) insistir en; (compel) obligar. *vi* empujar; dar empujones, empellar. **I am pushed for time,** Me falta tiempo. **He is pushed for money,** Está apurado por dinero. **I have pushed my finger in my eye,** Me he clavado el dedo en el ojo. **to p. against,** empujar contra; lanzarse contra; empellar, dar empellones (a). **to p. aside, away,** apartar con la mano; rechazar, alejar. **to p. back,** (hair, etc.) echar hacia atrás; (people) hacer retroceder; rechazar. **to p. by,** pasar. **to p. down,** hacer bajar; hacer caer; (demolish) derribar. **to p. forward,** *vt* empujar hacia delante, hacer avanzar; (a plan, etc.) llevar adelante. *vi* adelantarse a empujones; avanzar; seguir el camino. **to p. oneself forward,** *fig* abrirse camino; entremeterse; darse importancia. **to p. in,** *vt* empujar; hacer entrar; clavar, hincar. *vi* entrar a la fuerza; entremeterse. **to p. off,** *vt* apartar con la mano (a); *inf* quitar de encima (a). *vi naut* desatracar; *inf* ponerse en camino. **to p. open,**

empujar, abrir. **to p. out,** *vt* empujar hacia fuera; hacer salir; echar. *vi naut* zarpar. **to p. through,** *vt* (business, etc.) despachar rápidamente; (a crowd) abrirse camino por. *vi* aparecer, mostrarse. **to p. to,** cerrar. **to p. up,** empujar; hacer subir; (windows, etc.) levantar. **be pushing up the daises,** mirar los árboles de raíz

pushing *a* enérgico, emprendedor; ambicioso; agresivo. **by p. and shoving,** a empellones, a empujones

pusillanimity *n* pusilanimidad, *f*

pusillanimous *a* pusilánime

puss *n* micho (-cha). **P.! P.!** ¡Miz, Miz!

pustule *n* pústula, *f*

put *vt* poner; colocar; (pour out) echar; aplicar; emplear; (estimate) calcular; presentar; (ask) preguntar; (say) decir; (express) expresar; (a question) hacer; (a problem) plantear; (the weight) lanzar; (rank) estimar. **As the Spanish put it,** Como dicen los españoles. **If I may put it so,** Si puedo expresarlo así, Por así decirlo. **hard put to it,** En dificultades, apurado. **How will you put it to her?** ¿Cómo se lo vas a explicar a ella? **to put ashore,** echar en tierra (a). **to put a child to bed,** acostar a un niño. **to put in order,** arreglar; ordenar, *Lat. Am.* acotejar. **to put out of joint,** dislocar. **to put out of order,** estropear. **to put to death,** matar; (judicially) ajusticiar. **to put about,** *vt* (a rumor) diseminar, divulgar; (worry) preocupar. *vi naut* virar, cambiar de rumbo **to put a roof on =roof** *vt*. **to put aside,** poner a un lado; descartar; (omit) omitir, pasar por alto de; (fears, etc.) desechar. **to put away,** quitar; guardar; poner en salvo; arrinconar; (thoughts) desechar, ahuyentar; (save) ahorrar; (banish) despedir, alejar; (a wife) repudiar, divorciar; (food) tragar. **to put back,** *vt* echar hacia atrás; hacer retroceder; (replace) devolver, restituir; (the clock) retrasar; (retard) retardar, atrasar. *vi* volver; *naut* volver a puerto. **to put down,** depositar; poner en el suelo; (the blinds) bajar; (an umbrella) cerrar; (a rebellion) sofocar; (gambling, etc.) suprimir; (humble) abatir, humillar; degradar; (silence) hacer callar; (reduce) reducir, disminuir; (write) apuntar, anotar; (a name) inscribir; (to an account) poner a la cuenta de; (estimate) juzgar, creer; (impute) atribuir. **The book is so interesting that it's hard to put down,** El libro es tan interesante que es difícil dejarlo. **to put forth,** (leaves, flowers, sun's rays) echar; (a book) publicar, dar a luz; (a hand) alargar; (an arm) extender; (show) manifestar, mostrar; (strength, etc.) desplegar; (use) emplear. **to put forward,** avanzar; (a clock) adelantar; (a suggestion, etc.) hacer; (propose) proponer; (a case) presentar. **to put oneself forward,** ponerse en evidencia. **to put in,** poner dentro; (a hand, etc.) introducir; (liquids) echar en; (a government) poner en el poder; (an employment) nombrar, colocar; (insert) insertar; (a claim) presentar; (say) decir. **I shall put in two hours' work before bedtime,** Trabajaré por dos horas antes de acostarme. **He put in a good word for you,** Habló en tu favor. **to put in writing,** poner por escrito. **to put in for,** (an employment) solicitar (un empleo); (as a candidate) presentarse como candidato para. **to put into,** meter dentro (de); (words) expresar; (port) arribar, hacer escala en (un puerto). **to put off,** desechar; (garments) quitarse, despojarse (de); (postpone) diferir, aplazar; (evade) evadir, entretener; quitarse de encima (a), desembarazarse (de); (confuse) desconcertar; (discourage) desanimar; quitar el apetito (a). **to put on,** poner sobre; (clothes) ponerse; (pretend) fingir, afectar; poner; (a play) poner en escena; (the hands of a clock) adelantar; (weight) engordar, poner carnes; (add) añadir; (sport score) hacer; (bet) apostar; (the light) encender; (assume) tomar; (the brake) frenar; (abuse) abusar de, engañar. **He put the kettle on the fire,** Puso la tetera en el fuego. **to put on airs and graces,** darse humos. **to put on probation,** dar el azul a, poner a prueba a. **to put on more trains,** poner más trenes. **put one's foot down,** ponerle a

fulano el alto. **to put out,** *vt* (eject) echar, expulsar; hacer salir; poner en la calle; (a tenant) desahuciar; (one's hand) alargar; (one's arm) extender; (one's tongue) sacar; (eyes) saltar; (fire, light) apagar, extinguir; (leaves, etc.) echar; (horns) sacar; (head) asomar, sacar; (use) emplear; (give) entregar, dar; (at interest) dar a interés; (finish) terminar; (dislocate) dislocar; (worry) desconcertar; turbar; poner los nervios en punta (a); (anger) enojar; (inconvenience) incomodar; (a book) publicar; (a boat) echar al mar. *vi* (of a ship) hacerse a la vela, zarpar. **to put out to grass,** mandar a pacer. **We put out to sea,** Nos hicimos a la mar. **to put the cart before the horse,** poner la carreta por delante de los bueyes. **to put through,** (perform) desempeñar; concluir, terminar; (thrust) meter; (subject to) someter a; (exercise) ejercitar; (on the telephone) poner en comunicación (con). **to put together,** juntar; (a machine, etc.) montar, armar. **to put two and two together,** atar cabos. **to put up,** *vt* (sails, a flag) izar; (raise a window) levantar, cerrar; (open a window, or an umbrella) abrir; (one's hands, etc.) poner en alto; (one's fists) alzar; (a prayer) ofrecer, hacer; (as a candidate) nombrar; (for sale) poner (a la venta); (the price) aumentar; (a prescription) preparar; (food) conservar; (pack) empaquetar; (a sword) envainar; (lodge) alojar; (a petition) presentar; (build) construir; *mech* montar; (*inf* plan) arreglar. *vi* alojarse. **to put upon,** abusar (de); oprimir; (accuse) imputar, acusar (de). **to put up to,** incitar (a), instigar (a); dar informaciones sobre; poner al corriente (de). **to put up with,** tolerar, soportar, aguantar; resignarse a; contentarse con, conformarse con
putative *a* supuesto; (of relationship) putativo
putrefaction *n* putrefacción, *f*
putrefy *vt* pudrir. *vt* pudrirse, descomponerse

putrid *a* pútrido; *inf* apestoso
putt *vt* and *vi* patear.
putting *n* acción de poner, *f*; colocación, *f*. **p. forward of the clock,** adelanto de la hora, *m*. **p. off,** tardanza, dilación, *f*. **p. the weight,** lanzamiento del peso, *m*. **p. up,** (for office) candidatura, *f*. **p. green,** pista de golf en miniatura, *f*
putty *n* masilla, *f*, *vt* enmasillar, rellenar con masilla
puzzle *vt* dejar perplejo; desconcertar; confundir; embrollar. *n* problema, *m*; dificultad, *f*; enigma, *m*; (perplexity) perplejidad, *f*; (game) rompecabezas, *m*. **to p. out,** procurar resolver; encontrar la solución de. **to p. over,** pensar en, meditar sobre. **I am puzzled by . . . ,** Me trae (or tiene) perplejo . . . . **to be puzzled** *Lat. Am.* intrigarse
pygmy *a* and *n* pigmeo (-ea)
pyjamas *n* pijama, *m*
pylon *n* pilón, *m*; poste, *m*; (at an airport) poste de señales, *m*
pylorus *n* píloro, *m*
pyorrhœa *n* piorrea, *f*
pyramid *n* pirámide, *f*
pyramidal *a* piramidal
pyre *n* pira, *f*
Pyrenean *a* pirineo, pirenaico
Pyrenees, the los Pirineos, *m pl*
pyromancy *n* piromancia, *f*
pyrotechnic *a* pirotécnico
pyrotechnics *n* pirotecnia, *f*
pyrotechnist *n* pirotécnico, *m*
Pyrrhic *a* pírrico
Pythagorean *a* and *n* pitagórico (-ca)
Pythian *a* pitio
python *n* pitón, *m*
pythoness *n* pitonisa, *f*

Q

q *n* (letter) cu, *f*
quack *vi* (of a duck) graznar. *n* (of a duck) graznido, *m*; (charlatan) charlatán, farsante, *m*; curandero, *m*. **q. doctor,** matasanos, medicastro, curandero, *m*. **q. medicine,** curanderismo, *m*
quackery *n* charlatanería, *f*, charlatanismo, *m*
quadrangle *n* cuadrángulo, *m*; (courtyard) patio, *m*
quadrangular *a* cuadrangular
quadratic *a* cuadrático. **q. equation,** cuadrática, ecuación de segundo grado, *f*
quadrature *n* (*math ast*) cuadratura, *f*
quadrennial *a* cuadrienal
quadrilateral *a* and *n* cuadrilátero *m*
quadrille *n* cuadrilla, *f*; (card game) cuatrillo, *m*
quadruped *a* and *n* cuadrúpedo *m*
quadruple *a* cuádruple. *vt* cuadruplicar. *n* cuádruplo, *m*
quadruplet *n* serie de cuatro cosas, *f*; bicicleta de cuatro asientos, *f*; uno (una) de cuatro niños (-as) gemelos (-as)
quadruplication *n* cuadruplicación, *f*
quaff *vt* beber a grandes tragos, vaciar de un trago
quagmire *n* tremedal, pantano, *m*; *fig* cenagal, *m*
quail *n* codorniz, *f*; (U.S.A.) parpayuela, *f*. *vi* cejar, retroceder; temblar, acobardarse
quaint *a* pintoresco; curioso, raro; (eccentric) excéntrico, extravagante
quaintly *adv* de un modo pintoresco; curiosamente; con extravagancia
quaintness *n* lo pintoresco; rareza, singularidad, *f*; (eccentricity) extravagancia, *f*
quake *vi* estremecerse, vibrar; temblar. *n* estremecimiento, *m*; (of the earth) terremoto, *m*. **to q. with fear,** temblar de miedo
Quaker *n* cuáquero (-ra)
quaking *a* temblón; tembloroso. *n* temblor, *m*; estremecimiento, *m*. **q. ash,** álamo temblón, *m*

qualifiable *a* calificable
qualification *n* calificación, *f*; requisito, *m*; capacidad, aptitud, *f*; (reservation) reservación, salvedad, *f*
qualified *a* apto, competente; (of professions) con título universitario; habilitado; limitado
qualify *vt* habilitar; calificar; modificar; suavizar; *vi* habilitarse; prepararse; llenar los requisitos
qualifying *a gram* calificativo
qualitative *a* cualitativo
quality *n* cualidad, *f*; calidad, *f*; propiedad, *f*. **This cloth is of good q.,** Esta tela es de buena calidad. **the q.,** la alta sociedad, la aristocracia
qualm *n* náusea, *f*; mareo, desmayo, *m*; (of conscience) escrúpulo, remordimiento, *m*
quandary *n* incertidumbre, perplejidad, *f*; dilema, apuro, *m*. **to be in a q.,** estar perplejo
quantitative *a* cuantitativo
quantity *n* cantidad, *f*; gran cantidad, *f*. **unknown q.,** incógnita, *f*
quantum *n* cantidad, *f*; tanto, *m*. **q. theory,** teoría de la quanta, *f*
quarantine *n* cuarentena, *f*, *vt* someter a cuarentena
quarrel *vi* pelear, disputar; (scold) reñir; (find fault) criticar. *n* pelea, disputa, *Argentina* arenga, *f*; (glazier's) diamante de vidriero, *m*. **to pick a q. with,** armar pleito con, reñir con, *Chile, Peru* cruzar. **to q. with,** reñir con, romper con; quejarse de
quarreller *n* reñidor (-ra)
quarrelling *n* disputas, altercaciones, *f pl*
quarrelsome *a* pendenciero, peleador, belicoso
quarrelsomeness *n* belicosidad, pugnacidad, *f*
quarry *n* cantera, *f*; *fig* mina, *f*; (prey) presa, *f*; víctima, *f*. *vt* explotar una cantera; examinar
quarrying *n* explotación de canteras, *f*; cantería, *f*
quarryman *n* cantero, *m*
quart *n* cuarto de galón, *m*

quartan *a* cuartanal. *n* (fever) cuartana, *f*
quarter *n* (fourth part) cuarta parte, *f*, cuarto, *m*; (of a year) trimestre, *m*; (of an hour, the moon, a ton, an animal, etc.) cuarto, *m*; (of the compass) cuarta, *f*; *naut* cuartelada, *f*; (of a town) barrio, *m*; (mercy) cuartel, *m*; *her* cuartel, *m*; dirección, *f*; origen, *m*, fuente, *f*; *pl* **quarters,** vivienda, *f*; alojamiento, *m*; (barracks) cuartel, *m*. *vt* cuartear; (a body) descuartizar, hacer cuartos (a); (troops) alojar; (in barracks) acuartelar; *her* cuartelar. **a q. of an hour,** un cuarto de hora. **at close quarters,** de cerca. **hind quarters,** cuartos traseros, *m pl*. It **is a q. to four,** Son las cuatro menos cuarto. **It is a q. past four,** Son las cuatro y cuarto. **q.-day,** primer día de un trimestre, *m*. **q.-deck,** alcázar, *m*; cuerpo de oficiales de un buque, *m*. **q.-mile,** cuarto de milla, *m*. **q.-plate,** cuarto de placa, *m*. **q.-sessions,** sesión trimestral de los juzgados municipales, *f*. **q.-staff,** barra, *f*. **q.-tone,** cuarto de tono, *m*
quartering *n* (punishment) descuartizamiento, *m*; *her* cantón, *m*
quarterly *a* trimestral, trimestre. *n* publicación trimestral, *f*, *adv* trimestralmente
quartermaster *n mil* cabo furriel, *m*; *nav* maestre de víveres, cabo de mar, *m*. **q.-general,** intendente de ejército, *m*
quartet *n* cuarteto, *m*
quarto *n* papel en cuarto, *m*; libro en cuarto, *m*. **in q.,** en cuarto
quartz *n* cuarzo, *m*
quash *vt law* anular, derogar; *inf* sofocar, reprimir
quasi *a* and *adv* cuasi
quasimodo *n* cuasimodo, *m*
quatrain *n* cuarteta, *f*
quaver *vi* vibrar; temblar; (trill) trinar, hacer quiebros. *vt* decir con voz temblorosa. *n* vibración, *f*; trémolo, *m*; (trill) trino, *m*; (musical note) corchea, *f*
quaveringly *adv* con voz temblorosa
quavery *a* trémulo, tembloroso
quay *n* muelle, *m*
queasiness *n* náusea, *f*; escrupulosidad, *f*
queasy *a* propenso a la náusea; nauseabundo; delicado, escrupuloso
queen *n* reina, *f*; (in a Spanish pack of cards) caballo, *m*; (in a French or English pack and in chess) reina, *f*. **to q. it,** conducirse como una reina; mandar. **q. bee,** maestra, abeja reina, *f*. **q. cell,** maestril, *m*. **q. mother,** reina madre, *f*. **q. regent,** reina regente, *f*
queenliness *n* majestad de reina, *f*
queenly *a* de reina; regio
queer *a* raro; extraño, singular; ridículo; (shady) sospechoso; (ill) malucho, algo enfermo; (mad) chiflado
queerly *adv* extrañamente; ridiculamente
queerness *n* rareza, extrañeza, singularidad, *f*; ridiculez, *f*
quell *vt* subyugar; reprimir; apaciguar, calmar
quench *vt* apagar; calmar; satisfacer. **to q. one's thirst,** apagar la sed
quenching *n* apagamiento, *m*; satisfacción, *f*
querulous *a* quejumbroso
querulousness *n* hábito de quejarse, *m*; quejumbre, *f*
query *n* pregunta, *f*; duda, *f*; punto de interrogación, *m*. *vt* preguntar; dudar (de); poner en duda. *vi* hacer una pregunta; expresar una duda
quest *n* busca, *f*; (adventure) demanda, *f*. **in q. of,** en busca de
question *n* pregunta, *f*; problema, *m*; asunto, *m*; cuestión, *f*; (discussion) debate, *m*, discusión, *f*. *vt* and *vi* interrogar; examinar; poner en duda, dudar de; preguntarse; hacer preguntas. **beyond q.,** fuera de duda. **to ask a q.,** hacer una pregunta. **without q.,** sin duda. **It is out of the q.,** Es completamente imposible. **It is a q. of whether . . . ,** Se trata de si . . . **q.-mark,** punto interrogante, *m*
questionable *a* cuestionable, discutible, dudoso; equívoco, sospechoso

questionableness *n* lo discutible; carácter dudoso, *m*; carácter sospechoso, *m*
questioner *n* preguntador (-ra); interrogador (-ra)
questioning *n* preguntas, *f pl*; interrogatorio, *m*
questioningly *adv* interrogativamente
questionnaire *n* cuestionario, *m*
quetzal *n* (money and *orn*) quetzal, *m*
queue *n* coleta, *f*; cola, *f*, *vi* formar cola; hacer cola
quibble *n* equívoco, subterfugio, *m*; sutileza, *f*; (pun) retruécano, *m*. *vi* hacer uso de subterfugios; sutilizar
quibbler *n* sofista, *mf*
quibbling *n* sofistería, *f*, sofismas, *m pl*, sutilezas, *f pl*
quick *a* vivo; agudo; penetrante; sagaz; rápido, veloz; (ready) pronto; ágil, activo; (light) ligero. *adv* rápidamente; (soon) pronto. *n* carne viva, *f*; *fig* lo vivo. **Be q.!** ¡Date prisa! **He was very q.,** Lo hizo muy aprisa; Volvió (or Fue, according to sense) rápidamente. **the q. and the dead,** los vivos y los muertos. **to cut to the q.,** herir en lo más vivo. **q. march,** paso doble, *m*. **q.-sighted,** de vista aguda; perspicaz. **q. step,** paso rápido, *m*. **q.-tempered,** de genio vivo, colérico. **q. time,** compás rápido, *m*; *mil* paso doble, *m*. **q.-witted,** de ingenio agudo
quicken *vt* vivificar; animar; acelerar; excitar, avivar. *vi* vivificarse; despertarse; renovarse; acelerarse; (stir) moverse. **to q. one's step,** acelerar el paso
quicklime *n* cal viva, *f*
quickly *adv* rápidamente; (soon) pronto; (immediately) en seguida; (promptly) con presteza; vivamente
quickness *n* viveza, *f*; (of wit, etc.) agudeza, *f*; rapidez, velocidad, *f*; (promptness) prontitud, *f*; agilidad, *f*; (lightness) ligereza, *f*; (understanding) penetración, sagacidad, *f*
quicksand *n* arena movediza, *f*; *fig* cenagal, *m*
quicksilver *n* azogue, mercurio, *m*, *vt* azogar
quiescence *n* reposo, *m*; quietud, tranquilidad, *f*; inactividad, *f*; pasividad, *f*
quiescent *a* quieto; inactivo; pasivo
quiet *a* tranquilo; quieto; silencioso; quedo; monótono; inactivo; (informal) sin ceremonia; (simple) sencillo; (of the mind) sereno; (of colours, etc.) suave. *n* tranquilidad, quietud, *f*; silencio, *m*; paz, *f*; (of mind) serenidad, *f*. *vt* tranquilizar, sosegar; calmar. **to be q.,** callarse; no hacer ruido. **Be q.!** ¡Estate quieto! ¡A callar!
quietism *n* quietismo, *m*
quietist *n* quietista, *mf*
quietistic *a* quietista
quietly *adv* tranquilamente; en silencio; sin ruido; en calma; (simply) sencillamente; dulcemente
quietness *n* tranquilidad, quietud, *f*; calma, *f*; paz, *f*; silencio, *m*
quietus *n* (quittance) quitanza, *f*, finiquito, *m*; golpe de gracia, *m*; muerte, *f*
quill *n* pluma de ave, *f*; (of a feather) cañón, *m*; (pen) pluma, *f*; (of a porcupine) púa, *f*. **q.-driver,** cagatintas, *mf*
quilt *n* colcha, *f*, edredón, *m*. *vt* acolchar. **q. maker,** colchero, *m*
quilting *n* acolchamiento, *m*; colchadura, *f*
quince *n* (tree and fruit) membrillo, *m*. **q. cheese,** carne de membrillo, *f*. **q. jelly,** jalea de membrillo, *f*
quincentenary *n* quinto centenario, *m*
quinine *n* quinina, *f*
quinsy *n* angina, *f*
quintessence *n* quinta esencia, *f*
quintessential *a* quintaesenciado
quintet *n* quinteto, *m*
quintuple *a* quíntuplo
quintuplet *n* quintupleto, *m*; uno (una) de cinco niños (-as) gemelos (-as)
quip *n* agudeza, salida, *f*; (hint) indirecta, *f*; donaire, *m*, chanza, burla, *f*
quire *n* (of paper) mano (de papel), *f*
quirk *n* (quip) agudeza, salida, *f*; (quibble) sutileza, evasiva, *f*, (gesture) gesto, *m*

quit *vt* abandonar; dejar; renunciar (a). *vi* marcharse, *inf* tomar las de Villadiego, poner pies en polvorosa; (slang) dejar de, cesar de. **notice to q.,** aviso de desahúcio, *m*

quite *adv* completamente, enteramente; totalmente; del todo; (very) muy; (fairly) bastante. **It is not q. the thing to do,** Esto es algo que no se hace. **Q. so!** ¡Claro!; ¡Eso es! Se comprende. **It is not q. so good as we hoped,** No es tan bueno como esperábamos. **Peter is q. grown-up,** Pedro está hecho un hombre (*or* es todo un hombre)

quits *adv* quito, descargado. **be q.,** estar en paz

quittance *n* quitanza, *f*; recibo, *m*; recompensa, *f*

quitter *n* desertor (-ra); cobarde, *mf*

quiver *vi* temblar; vibrar; estremecerse; palpitar; (of light) titilar. *n* (for arrows) aljaba, *f*, carcaj, *m*. See also **quivering**

quivering *a* tremulante; vibrante; palpitante. *n* temblor, *m*; estremecimiento, *m*

quixotic *a* quijotesco

quixotism *n* quijotismo, *m*

quiz *n* examen parcial, *m*. *vt* tomar el pelo (a); burlarse (de); (stare) mirar de hito en hito (a)

quizzical *a* burlón; cómico; estrafalario

quizzically *adv* burlonamente; cómicamente

quoin *n* piedra angular, *f*; ángulo, *m*; (wedge) cuña, *f*. *vt* meter cuñas (a)

quoit *n* tejo, *m*; *pl* **quoits,** juego de tejos, *m*

quondam *a* antiguo

quorum *n* quórum, *m*. **to form a q.,** hacer un quórum

quota *n* cuota, *f*

quotable *a* citable; (Stock Exchange) cotizable

quota system *n* tablas diferenciales, *f pl*

quotation *n* citación, *f*; cita, *f*; *com* cotización, *f*. **q. mark,** comilla, *f*

quote *vt* citar; *com* cotizar. *n inf* comilla, *f*

quoth *vt* q. **I,** dije yo. **q. he,** dijo él

quotient *n* cociente, *m*. **intelligence q.,** cociente intelectual, *m*

R

r *n* (letter) erre, *f*

rabbet *n* ranura, *f*, rebajo, *m*. *vt* ensamblar a rebajo. **r.-joint,** junta a rebajo, *f*

rabbi *n* rabí, rabino, *m*. **grand r.,** gran rabino, *m*

rabbinical *a* rabínico

rabbinism *n* rabinismo, *m*

rabbit *n* conejo (-ja). *a* conejuno, de conejo. *vi* cazar conejos. **young r.,** gazapo, *m*. **r.-hutch,** jaula para conejos, *f*. **r.-warren,** conejera, *f*

rabble *n* populacho, vulgo, *m*, plebe, *f*

Rabelaisian *a* rabelasiano

rabid *a* rabioso; fanático; furioso, violento

rabies *n* rabia, hidrofobia, *f*

raccoon *n* mapache, *m*

race *n* carrera, *f*; (current) corriente, *f*; (prize) premio, *m*; (breed) raza, *f*; casta, estirpe, *f*; (family) linaje, *m*, familia, *f*; (scornful) ralea, *f*; (struggle) lucha, *f*. *vi* tomar parte en una carrera; correr de prisa; asistir a concursos de carreras de caballos; (of a machine) dispararse. *vt* (racer) correr; competir en una carrera (con); desafiar a una carrera. **flat r.,** carrera llana, *f*. **mill-r.,** caz, *m*. **to run a r.,** tomar parte en una carrera; *fig* hacer una carrera. **r.-card,** programa de carreras de caballos, *m*. **r. hatred,** odio de razas, *m*. **r.-meeting,** concurso de carreras de caballos, *m*. **r. suicide,** suicidio de la raza, *m*. **r.-track,** pista, *f*

racecourse hipódromo, *m*; estadio, *m*

racehorse *n* caballo de carreras, *m*

racer *n* (horse) caballo de carreras, *m*; (person) carrerista, *mf*; (car) coche de carreras, *m*; (boat) yate de carreras, *m*; (bicycle) bicicleta de carreras, *f*

rachitic *a* raquítico

racial *a* racial, de raza

racialism *n* rivalidad de razas, *f*

raciness *n* sabor, *m*; savia, *f*, picante, *m*

racing *n sport a pl; mech* disparo, *m*, *a* de carreras; hípico. **r. calendar,** calendario de concursos de carreras de caballos, *m*. **r. car,** coche de carreras, *m*. **r. cycle,** bicicleta de carreras, *f*

rack *n* (for hay) percha (del pesebre), *f*; (in a railway compartment) rejilla, *f*; (for billiard cues) taquera, *f*; (for clothes) percha, *f*; (for torture) potro, *m*; *mech* cremallera, *f*. *vt* poner en el potro, torturar; atormentar. **to be on the r.,** estar en el potro **to r. one's brains,** devanarse los sesos, quebrarse la cabeza. **r. and ruin,** ruina total, *f*. **r. railway,** ferrocarril de cremallera, *m*, *m*

racket *n sport* raqueta, *f*; (din) barahúnda, *f*; ruido, estrépito, *m*; confusión, *f*; (bustle) bullicio, *m*, agitación, *f*; (swindle) estafa, *f*; (binge) parranda, *f*. **to play rackets,** jugar a la raqueta

racking *n* tortura, *f*; (of wine) trasiego, *m*, *a* torturante; (of a pain or cough) persistente

racoon *n* mapache, *m*

racquet *n* See **racket**

racy *a* picante; sabroso

radar *n* radar, *m*

raddled *a* pintado de almagre; mal pintado

radial *a* radial

radiance *n* resplandor, brillo, *m*, luminosidad, *f*

radiant *a* radiante; brillante, luminoso. *n geom* línea radial, *f*. **r. heat,** calor radiante, *m*

radiantly *adv* con resplandor; brillantemente; con alegría

radiate *vi* radiar. *vt* irradiar

radiation *n* irradiación, *f*; *geom* radiación, *f*

radiator *n* (for central heating and of a car) radiador, *m*; (stove) calorífero, *m*

radical *a* radical. *n* (*math chem*) radical, *m*; *pol* radical, *mf*

radicalism *n* radicalismo, *m*

radio *n* radio, *f*; radiocomunicación, *f*. **r. amateur, r. enthusiast,** radioaficionado (-da). **r. announcer,** locutor (-ra). **r. broadcast,** radioemisión, radiodifusión, *f*. **r. listener,** radiooyente, *mf* **r. receiver,** (technical) radiorreceptor, *m*; (usual word) aparato de radio, *m*. **r. transmitter,** radiotransmisor, *m*

radioactive *a* radiactivo

radioactive fallout *n* caída radiactiva, llovizna radiactiva, precipitación radiactiva, *f*

radioactivity *n* radiactividad, *f*

radiofrequency *n* radiofrecuencia, *f*

radiolocation *n* radiolocación, *f*

radiologist *n* radiólogo, *m*

radiology *n* radiología, *f*

radiometer *n* radiómetro, *m*

radiometry *n* radiometría, *f*

radioscopy *n* radioscopia, *f*

radiotherapeutics, radiotherapy *n* radioterapia, *f*

radish *n* rábano, *m*. **horse-r.,** rábano picante, *m*

radium *n* radio, *m*

radius *n* (*geom anat*) radio, *m*; (of a wheel) rayo, *m*; (scope) alcance, *m*

raffia *n* rafia, *f*

raffish *a* disoluto, libertino

raffle *n* rifa, *f*, sorteo, *m*; lotería, *f*. *vt* rifar, sortear

raffling *n* sorteo, *m*, rifa, *f*

raft *n* balsa, *f*; (timber) armadía, *f*. *vt* transportar en balsa; cruzar en balsa

rafter *n* (of a roof) viga, traviesa, *f*; (raftsman) balsero, *m*

raftered *a* con vigas

rag *n* jirón, guiñapo, *m*; (for cleaning) paño, trapo, *m*;

(for papermaking) estraza, *f;* (of smoke, etc.) penacho, *m;* (newspaper) papelucho, *m; pl* **rags,** harapos, *m pl; inf* viejos hábitos, *m pl. vt* (tease) tomar el pelo (a); burlarse de; hacer una broma pesada (a). **r.-and-boneman, ragpicker,** andrajero, trapero (Mexico), pepinador, *m.* **r. doll,** muñeca de trapo, *f*

ragamuffin *n* galopín, *m*

rage *n* (anger) cólera, rabia, ira, *f;* (of the elements) furia, violencia, *f;* (ardour) entusiasmo, ardor, *m;* (fashion) boga, moda, *f;* (craze) manía, *f;* (of the poet) furor, *m. vi* (be angry) rabiar, estar furioso; (of the sea) encresparse, alborotarse, enfurecerse; (of wind, fire, animals) bramar, rugir; (of pain) rabiar; (be prevalent) prevalecer, desencadenarse. **to r. against,** protestar furiosamente contra; culpar amargamente (de). **to be all the r.,** *inf* ser la última moda. **to fly into a r.,** montar en cólera. **to put into a r.,** hacer rabiar

ragged *a* harapiento, andrajoso; roto; (uneven) desigual, (rugged) peñascoso, áspero, escabroso; (serrated) serrado; dentellado; (of a coastline) accidentado; (unfinished) inacabado, sin terminar; (of style) descuidado, sin pulir

raggedness *n* harapos, *m pl;* estado andrajoso, *m;* aspereza, escabrosidad, *f;* lo serrado; lo accidentado; (of style) falta de elegancia, tosquedad, *f*

raging *a* furioso, rabioso; violento; (roaring) bramante; (of the sea) bravío; intenso. *n* furia, *f;* violencia, *f;* intensidad, *f*

raglan *n* raglán, *m.* **r. sleeve,** manga raglán, *f*

ragout *n* estofado, *m*

ragpicker *n* trapero (-ra)

ragtime *n* música sincopada, *f*

raid *n* incursión, correría, *f;* asalto, ataque, *m;* (by the police) razzia, *f;* (by aircraft) bombardeo, *m, vt* invadir; atacar, asaltar; apoderarse de; hacer una razzia en; (by aircraft) bombear, bombardear; (pillage) pillar, saquear. **obliteration r.,** bombardeo de saturación, *m*

raider *n* corsario, *m;* atacador, asaltador, *m;* (aircraft) avión enemigo, *m*

rail *n* barra, *f;* antepecho, *m;* (of a staircase) barandilla, *f,* pasamano, *m;* (track) riel, *m;* (railway) ferrocarril, *m;* (of a ship) barandilla, *f;* (of a chair) travesaño, *m pl.* **rails,** (fence) cerca, barrera, palizada, *f. vt* cercar con una palizada, poner cerca a; mandar por ferrocarril. **by r.,** por ferrocarril. **to run off the rails,** descarrilar. **to r. at,** protestar contra; prorrumpir en invectivas contra, injuriar de palabra (a)

railing *n* barandilla, *f;* antepecho, *m,* enrejado, *m;* (grille) reja, *f;* (jeers) burlas, *f pl;* insultos, *m pl,* injurias, *f pl;* quejas, *f pl*

raillery *n* jocosidad, tomadura de pelo, *f;* sátiras, *f pl*

railway *n* ferrocarril, *m;* vía férrea, *f,* camino de hierro, *m, a* de ferrocarril, ferroviario. **elevated r.,** ferrocarril aéreo, *m.* **narrow gauge r.,** ferrocarril de vía estrecha, *m.* **r. buffet,** fonda, *f,* (or restaurante, *m*) de estación. **r. carriage,** departamento de tren, *m.* **r. company,** compañía de ferrocarriles, *f.* **r. crossing,** paso a nivel, *m.* **r. engine,** locomotora, *f.* **r. guard,** jefe del tren, *m.* **r. guide,** guía de ferrocarriles, *f.* **r. line,** vía férrea, *f.* **r. marshalling yard,** apartadero ferroviario, *m.* **r. passenger,** viajero (-ra) en un tren. **r. platform,** andén, *m.* **r. porter,** mozo de estación, *m.* **r. siding,** vía muerta, *f.* **r. signal,** disco de señales, *m.* **r. station,** estación (de ferrocarril), *f.* **r. system,** sistema ferroviario, *m.* **r. ticket,** billete de tren, *m*

railwayman *n* ferroviario, empleado de los ferrocarriles, *m*

raiment *n* ropa, *f; poet* hábitos, *m pl*

rain *n* lluvia, *f. vi* and *vt* llover. **a r. of arrows,** una lluvia de flechas. **fine r.,** llovizna, *f.* **to r. cats and dogs,** llover a cántaros. **to r. hard,** diluviar. **r. cloud,** nubarrón, *m.* **r.-gauge,** pluviómetro, *m*

rainbow *n* arco iris, arco de San Martín, *m*

raincoat *n* abrigo impermeable, *m*

raindrop *n* gota de lluvia, *f*

rainfall *n* cantidad llovida, *f;* (shower) aguacero, *m*

rainless *a* sin lluvia, seco

rainstorm *n* chaparrón, *m,* tempestad de lluvia, *f*

rainwater *n* lluvia, *f;* agua lluvia, *f*

rainy *a* lluvioso. **r. day,** día de lluvia, *m; fig* tiempo de escasez, *m*

raise *vt* levantar; alzar; (the hat) quitar; solevantar; (dough) fermentar; (erect) erigir, edificar; (dust) levantar; elevar; (promote) ascender; (increase) aumentar; hacer subir; (spirits, memories) evocar; (the dead) resucitar; (cause) causar; dar lugar (a); hacer concebir; (a question, a point) hacer; plantear; (breed or educate) criar; (a crop) cultivar; (an army) alistar; (gather together) juntar; (a subscription) hacer; (money, etc.) obtener, hallar; (a siege, etc.) levantar, alzar; (a laugh, a protest, etc.) suscitar, provocar; (utter) poner, dar; (a fund) abrir. **to r. oneself,** incorporarse. **He succeeded in raising himself,** Logró alzarse; Logró mejorar su posición. **He raised their hopes unduly,** Les hizo concebir esperanzas desmesuradas. **to r. an objection (to),** poner objeción (a). **to r. an outcry,** armar un alboroto. **to r. a point,** hacer una observación; plantear una cuestión. **to r. a siege,** levantar un sitio. **to r. Cain,** armar lo de Dios es Cristo. **to r. one's voice,** alzar la voz

raised *a* (in relief) en relieve; (embossed) de realce

raiser *n* (breeder) criador (-ra); (cultivator) cultivador (-ra); (educator) educador (-ra); autor (-ra); fundador (-ra); (of objections, etc.) suscitador (-ra)

raisin *n* pasa, *f*

raising *n* levantamiento, *m;* alzamiento, *m;* (of a building, monument) erección, *f;* elevación, *f;* (increase) aumento, *m;* provocación, *f;* fundación, *f;* (breeding or education) crianza, *f;* (of spirits) evocación, *f;* (of the dead) resucitación, *f;* producción, *f;* (of crops) cultivo, *m*

rake *n agr* rastrillo, *m,* rastra, *f;* (for the fire) hurgón, *m;* (croupier's) raqueta, *f;* (of a mast, funnel) inclinación, *f;* (person) tenorio, calavera, *m. vt agr* rastrillar; (a fire, etc.) hurgar; (sweep) barrer; recoger; (ransack) buscar (en); (with fire) enfilar, tirar a lo largo de; (scan) escudriñar. *vi* trabajar con el rastrillo; (slope) inclinarse. **r. off,** tajada, *f.* **to r. together,** juntar con el rastrillo; amontonar; ahorrar. **to r. up,** (revive) resucitar, desenterrar

raking *n* rastrillaje, *m;* (the fire, etc.) hurgonada, *f*

rakish *a* (of a ship) de palos muy inclinados, (dissolute) disoluto, libertino; (dashing) elegante

rakishly *adv* disolutamente; elegantemente

rakishness *n* (licentiousness) libertinaje, *m,* disipación, disolución, *f;* (elegance) elegancia, *f*

rally *vt* reunir; *mil* rehacer; (faculties) concentrar; (tease) tomar el pelo (a). *vi* reunirse; *mil* rehacerse; (revive) mejorar, recobrar las fuerzas; (of markets, etc.) mejorar *n* reunión, *f*

rallying *n* reunión, *f;* (of faculties, etc.) concentración, *f;* (recovery) mejora, *f.* **r. point,** punto de reunión, *m*

ram *n zool* carnero, morueco, *m; ast* Aries, Carnero, *m;* (mil etc.) ariete, *m;* (tool) pisón, *m; nav* espolón, *m, vt* golpear con ariete o espolón; (of a gun) atacar; apisonar; meter a la fuerza; hacer tragar a la fuerza; (squeeze) apretar; (crowd) atestar

Ramadan *n* ramadán, *m*

ramble *vi* vagar, vagabundear; hacer una excursión. *vt* errar por

rambler *n* excursionista, *mf;* paseante, *mf; bot* rosa trepante, *f*

rambling *a* (of houses) encantado; laberíntico; (straggly) disperso; (of thought, etc.) incoherente, inconexo. *n* vagabundeo, *m;* excursiones, *f pl;* paseo, *m;* (digression) digresiones, *f pl;* (delirium) desvaríos, *m pl*

ramification *n* ramificación, *f*

ramify *vi* ramificarse, tener ramificaciones. *vt* ramificar; dividir en ramales

rammer *n* pisón de empedrador, *m;* baqueta (de fusil), *f;* (of a ship) espolón, *m*

ramp *n* rampa, *f;* (swindle) estafa, *f;* (storm, commotion) tormenta, *f*

rampage *vi* alborotarse; bramar

rampant *a* salvaje; *her* rampante; (of persons) impaciente, furioso; (of plants, growth) lozano, exuberante; desenfrenado; (rife) prevaleciente, predominante

rampart *n* muralla, *f;* terraplén, *m; fig* baluarte, *m. vt* abaluartar, abastionar

ramrod *n* baqueta, *f*

ramshackle *a* destartalado, ruinoso; desvencijado; (badly made) mal hecho

ranch *n* rancho, *m*, hacienda (de ganado), *Lat. Am.* estancia, *f*

rancher *n* ranchero (-ra), *Lat. Am.* estanciero (-ra) *mf*

rancid *a* rancio

rancorous *a* rencoroso

rancor *n* rencor, encono, *m*

random *n* azar, *m, a* fortuito, al azar; sin orden ni concierto. **at r.,** a la ventura, al azar; sin pensar; (of shooting) sin apuntar. **to talk at r.,** hablar a trochemoche

range *n* línea, hilera, *f;* (of mountains) cadena, *f;* serie, *f;* clase, *f;* variedad, *f;* (of goods) surtido, *m;* (of a gun, voice, vision, etc.) alcance, *m;* (area) extensión, área, *f;* esfera de actividad, *f;* (scope) alcance, *m;* (of voice, musical instrument) compás, *m;* (of colors) gama, *f;* (for shooting) campo de tiro, *m;* (for cooking) cocina económica, *f.* **at close r.,** de cerca. **out of r.,** fuera de alcance. **within r.,** al alcance. **r.-finder,** (of guns, cameras) telémetro, *m.* **r. of mountains,** cadena de montañas, *f;* sierra, *f*

range *vt poet* arreglar; alinear; ordenar; clasificar; (a gun, etc.) apuntar; (place oneself) ponerse; sumarse (a); (roam) recorrer; (scan) escudriñar. *vi* extenderse; (roam) vagar; (of plants) crecer (en); variar, fluctuar; oscilar, vacilar; (of guns, etc.) alcanzar; (of the mind) pasar (por); (include) incluir

ranger *n* (wanderer) vagabundo, *m;* (keeper) guardabosque, *m; mil* batidor, *m*

ranging *n* arreglo, *m;* alineación, *f;* ordenación, *f;* clasificación, *f;* (roving) vida errante, *f*

rank *n* línea, *f;* fila, *f;* grado, *m;* clase, *f;* rango, *m;* categoría, *f;* posición, *f;* calidad, *f;* distinción, *f. vt* ordenar; clasificar; (estimate) estimar; poner (entre). *vi* ocupar un puesto; tener un grado, rango, etc.; estar al nivel (de); ser igual (a); contarse (entre). *a* (luxuriant) lozano, exuberante; fértil; (thick) espeso; (rancid) rancio; (complete) consumado; completo; (foul-smelling) fétido; *fig* repugnante, aborrecible; (very) muy. **of the first r.,** de primera calidad; de primera clase; de distinción. **the r. and file,** los soldados, la tropa; las masas, hombres de filas, *m pl,* mujeres de fila, *f pl,* la mayoría; los socios ordinarios (de un club, etc.). **to break ranks,** *mil* romper filas. **to rise from the ranks,** ascender de las filas. **to r. high,** ocupar alta posición; ser de los mejores (de). **to r. with,** estar al nivel de; (be numbered among) contarse entre, figurar entre

rankle *vi fig* irritar, molestar; envenenarse la vida, hacerse odioso

rankly *adv* ranciamente; lozanamente; con exuberancia; abundantemente; groseramente

rankness *n* rancidez, *f;* olor rancio, *m;* fertilidad, lozanía, *f;* exuberancia, *f,* vigor, *m;* enormidad, *f*

ransack *vt* (search) registrar; (pillage) saquear; *fig* buscar en

ransacking *n* (searching) registro, *m;* (sacking) saqueo, *m*

ransom *n* rescate, *m,* redención, *f;* liberación, *f. vt* rescatar, redimir

ransomer *n* rescatador (-ra)

ransoming *n* redención, *f;* liberación, *f*

rant *vi* declamar a gritos, vociferar; despotricar (contra); desvariar; hablar por hablar, hablar sin ton ni son. *n* declamación, vociferación, *f;* desvarío, *m*

ranter *n* declamador (-ra); agitador populachero, *m;* predicador chillón, *m*

rap *n* golpecito, *m;* toque, *m;* (with the knocker) aldabada, *f;* (worthless trifle) ardite, maravedí, *m. vt and vi* golpear; tocar. **He doesn't care a rap,** No le importa un ardite. **to rap at the door,** tocar a la puerta. **to rap with the knuckles,** golpear con los nudillos. **to rap out an oath,** proferir una blasfemia

rapacious *a* rapaz

rapacity *n* rapacidad, *f*

rape *n* (carrying off) rapto, *m.* **the Rape of the Sabine Women,** el Rapto de las Sabinas, *m; law* estupro, *m;* violación, *f; bot* nabo silvestre, *m. vt* (carry off) raptar, robar; violar, forzar

rapid *a* rápido. *n* rápido, *m.* **r. combustion,** combustión activa, *f*

rapidity *n* rapidez, *f*

rapidly *adv* rápidamente, con rapidez

rapids *npl Argentina* correntada, *f sg*

rapier *n* estoque, *m;* espadin, *m*

rapine *n* rapiña, *f*

rapping *n* golpecitos, *m pl;* golpeo, *m;* toques, *m pl;* (of the knocker) aldabeo, *m*

rapscallion *n* bribón, *m*

rapt *past part* and *a* arrebatado; absorto; extático, extasiado

rapture *n* arrebato, *m;* éxtasis, *m;* transporte, *m;* embriaguez, *f;* entusiasmo, *m*

rapturous *a* embelesado; extático; entusiasta

rapturously *adv* extáticamente; con entusiasmo

rare *a* raro; extraordinario; exótico; infrecuente

raree show *n* barracón de los fenómenos, barracón de las atracciones, *m*

rarefaction *n* rarefacción, *f*

rarefy *vt* rarefacer. *vi* rarefacerse

rareness *n* rareza, *f;* singularidad, *f;* infrecuencia, *f*

rarity *n* raridad, *f;* (uncommonness and rare object) rareza, *f*

rascal *n* sinvergüenza, *m;* truhán, bribón, pícaro, *m;* (affectionately) picaruelo, *m*

rascality *n* bellaquería, truhanería, *f*

rascally *a* redomado; vil, ruin, canallesco

rash *a* temerario, precipitado; imprudente. *n* erupción, *f,* salpullido, *m*

rasher *n* magra, *f;* (of bacon) torrezno, *m*

rashly *adv* temerariamente, precipitadamente; imprudentemente, con imprudencia

rashness *n* temeridad, precipitación, *f;* imprudencia, *f*

rasp *n* escofina, *f,* rallo, *m;* sonido áspero, *m. vt* raspar, escofinar; (get on one's nerves) poner los nervios en punta (a)

raspberry *n* frambuesa, *f.* **r.-cane,** frambueso, *m.* **r. jam,** mermelada de frambuesa, *f*

rasping *a* (of the voice) áspero, estridente

rat *n* rata, *f;* desertor, *m;* (black leg) esquirol, *m. vi* cazar ratas; ser desertor; ser esquirol. **rat-catcher,** cazador de ratas, *m.* **rat poison,** matarratas, *m,* raticida, *f.* **rattrap,** ratonera, *f*

ratable *a* sujeto a contribución; imponible; valuable

ratafia *n* ratafía, *f*

rataplan *n* rataplán, *m*

ratchet *n mech* trinquete, *m;* (of a watch) disparador, *m.* **r.-drill,** carraca, *f.* **r.-wheel,** rueda dentada con trinquete, *f*

rate *n* velocidad, *f;* razón, proporción, *f;* (of exchange) tipo, *m;* tanto, *m;* precio, *m;* clase, *f;* modo, *m,* manera, *f; naut* clasificación, *f;* (tax) contribución, *f,* impuesto, *m; pl* **rates,** (of a house) inquilinato, *m. vt* tasar; estimar; fijar el precio (a); *naut* clasificar; imponer una contribución (de); (scold) reñir. **at a great r.,** rápidamente, velozmente. **at a r. of,** a razón de; a una velocidad de. **at any r.,** de todos modos; por lo menos; sea como fuere. **at this r.,** de este modo; a este paso; a esa cuenta; en esta proporción; (with seguir) así. **first-r.,** de primera clase. **rates and taxes,** contribuciones e impuestos, *f pl.* **r. of climb,** *aer* velocidad ascensional, *f.* **r. of exchange,** tipo de cambio, *m.* **r.-payer,** contribuyente, *mf*

rather *adv* más bien; antes; (more willingly) de mejor gana; (somewhat) algo, un poco; (perhaps) quizás; mejor dicho; (fairly) bastante; (very) muy; mucho; al contrario. **R.!** ¡Ya lo creo! **or r.,** o más bien. **anything r. than . . . ,** todo menos . . . He had r., Preferiría. **r. than,** antes que, en vez de

ratification *n* ratificación, *f*; (of a bill) aprobación, *f*

ratifier *n* ratificador (-ra)

ratify *vt* ratificar

ratifying *n* ratificación, *f*, *a* ratificatorio

rating *n* tasación, *f*; valuación, *f*; clasificación, *f*; impuesto, *m*, contribución, *f*; repartición de impuestos, *f*; (of a ship's company) graduación, *f*; (scolding) reprensión, *f*

ratio *n* razón, *f*; proporción, *f*. **in direct r.,** en razón directa

ratiocinate *vi* raciocinar

ratiocination *n* raciocinación, *f*

ration *n* ración, *f*. *vt* racionar. **r.-book,** cartilla de racionamiento, *f*

rational *a* racional; razonable, juicioso. *n* ser racional, *m*

rationalism *n* racionalismo, *m*

rationalist *n* racionalista, *mf*

rationalistic *a* racionalista

rationality *n* racionalidad, *f*; justicia, *f*

rationalization *n* racionalización, *f*; justificación, *f*

rationalize *vt* hacer racional; concebir racionalmente; *math* quitar los radicales (a); justificar

rationing *n* racionamiento, *m*

rattan *n* rota, *f*, bejuco, *m*; junquillo, *m*

ratteen *n* ratina, *f*

ratter *n* perro ratonero, *m*; gato que caza ratas, *m*

ratting *n* caza de ratas, *f*; deserción, *f*

rattle *vi* hacer ruido; rechinar, crujir; (of loose windows, etc.) zangolotearse; (knock) golpear; tocar; (patter) bailar; sonar; (of the dying) dar un estertor. *vt* (shake) sacudir; hacer vibrar; (jolt) traquetear; (do rapidly) acabar rápidamente; (confuse) aturdir, hacer perder la cabeza (a); desconcertar. **to r. along,** deslizarse (or correr) rápidamente. **to r. off,** (repeat) decir rápidamente; terminar apresuradamente. **to r. on about,** charlar mucho de, hablar sin cesar sobre

rattle *n* rechinamiento, crujido, *m*; zangoloteo, *m*; ruido, *m*; son (de la lluvia, etc.), *m*; (in the throat) estertor, *m*; ʃof a rattlesnake) cascabel, *m*; (child's) sonajero, *m*; matraca, *f*; carraca, *f*; (chatter) charla, *f*. **r.-headed,** de cabeza de chorlito, casquivano

rattlesnake *n* serpiente de cascabel, *f*, crótalo, *m*

rattling *n* See **rattle**

raucous *a* ronco, estridente

raucousness *n* ronquedad, *f*, estridor, *m*

ravage *vt* devastar; (pillage) saquear; destruir; (spoil) estropear. *n* devastación, *f*; destrucción, *f*; estrago, *m*

ravager *n* devastador (-ra); saqueador (-ra)

rave *vi* desvariar, delirar; (of the elements) bramar, rugir. **to r. about,** hablar con entusiasmo de; delirar por. **to r. against,** vociferar contra, despotricarse contra

ravel *vt* deshilar, destejer; *fig* enredar. **to r. out,** deshilarse; *fig* desenredarse, desenmarañarse

raven *n* cuervo, *m*, *a* negro como el azabache

ravening *a* rapaz, salvaje

Ravenna Rávena, *f*

ravenous *a* voraz

ravenously *adv* vorazmente

ravenousness *n* voracidad, *f*

ravine *n* cañada, *f*, barranco, cañón, *m*

raving *n* delirio, *m*, desvaríos, *m pl*. *a* delirante; violento; bravío

ravioli *n* ravioles, *m pl*

ravish *vt* (carry off) arrebatar, raptar; extasiar, encantar; (rape) violar, forzar

ravisher *n* raptador, *m*; violador, *m*

ravishing *n* violación, *f*, *a* encantador

ravishment *n* violación, *f*; arrobamiento, *m*; transporte, éxtasis, *m*

raw *a* (of meat, etc.), silk, leather, weather) crudo; bruto; (inexpert) bisoño; (of flesh) vivo; *com* en bruto. **raw-boned,** huesudo. **raw hand,** novato (-ta). **raw material,** primera materia, *f*. **raw materials,** materias primas, *f pl*. **raw score,** puntuación bruta, *f*. **raw silk,** seda cruda, seda en rama, *f*. **raw sugar,** azúcar bruto, *m*

rawhide *a* de cuero crudo

rawness *n* crudeza, *f*; inexperiencia, *f*; (of weather) humedad, *f*

ray *n* rayo, *m*; (line) raya, *f*; (radius) radio, *m*; (fish) raya, *f*. **cathode rays,** rayos catódicos, *m pl*

rayon *n* rayón, *m*

raze *vt* arrasar, asolar; demoler; (erase) borrar, tachar

razor *n* navaja, *f*. **electric r.,** máquina de afeitar eléctrica, *f*. **safety r.,** máquina de afeitar, *f*. **slash with a r.,** navajada, *f*. **r. blade,** hoja de afeitar, *f*. **r. case,** navajero, *m*. **r. strop,** suavizador, *m*

re *n mus* re, *m*; *prep law* causa, *f*; *com* concerniente a

re *prefix* (attached to verb) re-; (after the verb) de nuevo; (followed by infin.) volver a . . . **to re-count,** volver a contar, contar de nuevo, recontar

reabsorb *vt* resorber

reabsorption *n* reabsorción, resorción, *f*

reach *vt* (stretch out) alargar; extender; alcanzar; llegar hasta; (arrive at) llegar a; (achieve) lograr, obtener. *vi* extenderse; alcanzar; penetrar. *n* alcance, *m*; extensión, *f*; poder, *m*; capacidad, *f*; (of a river) tabla, *f*. **as far as the eye could r.,** hasta donde alcanzaba la vista. **He reached home very soon,** Llegó muy pronto a casa. **out of r.,** fuera de alcance. **to r. a deadlock,** llegar a un punto muerto. **within r.,** al alcance. **within easy r.,** de fácil acceso; a corta distancia. **to r. after,** procurar alcanzar; hacer esfuerzos para obtener. **to r. back,** (of time) remontarse. **to r. down,** bajar. **r.-me-downs,** ropa hecha, *f*

react *vi* reaccionar. *vt* hacer de nuevo; *theat* volver a representar

reaction *n* reacción, *f*

reactionary *a* and *n* reaccionario (-ia)

reactive *a* reactivo

read *vt* leer; (a riddle, etc.) adivinar; descifrar; interpretar; (study) estudiar; (the Burial Service, etc.) decir; (correct) corregir; (of thermometers, etc.) marcar. *vi* leer; estudiar; (be written) estar escrito, decir. **The play acts better than it reads,** La comedia es mejor representada que leída. **to r. aloud,** leer en voz alta. **to r. between the lines,** leer entre líneas. **to r. proofs,** corregir pruebas. **to r. to oneself,** leer para sí. **to r. about,** leer; (learn) enterarse de. **to r. again,** volver a leer, leer otra vez. **to r. on,** continuar leyendo. **to r. out,** leer en alta voz. **to r. over,** leer; leerlo todo. **to r. over and over again,** leer muchas veces, leer y releer.

read *past part* leído, etc. **well-r.,** releído; instruido, culto

readability *n* legibilidad, *f*; interés, *m*, amenidad, *f*

readable *a* legible; interesante

readdress *vt* dirigir de nuevo (una carta, etc.); poner la nueva dirección (en una carta, etc.)

reader *n* lector (-ra); *ecc* lector, *m*; (proof) corrector de pruebas, *m*; (citation collector for a dictionary) cedulista, *mf*; (university) profesor (-ra) auxiliar a cátedra; (book) libro de lectura, *m*. **to be a great r.,** leer mucho. **the Spanish r.** (reader of Spanish books) el lector de español

readily *adv* fácilmente; en seguida, inmediatamente; de buena gana, con placer

readiness *n* prontitud, expedición, *f*; buena voluntad, *f*; (of speech, etc.) facilidad, *f*. **in r.,** preparado. **r. of wit,** viveza de ingenio, *f*

reading *n* lectura, *Lat. Am. also* leída, *f*; (erudition) conocimientos, *m pl*; (recital) declamación, *f*; (lecture) conferencia, *f*; (study) estudio, *m*; interpretación, *f*; (of a thermometer, etc.) registro, *m*; (of a will) apertura, *f*. **at one reading** *Lat. Am.* de una leída. **r.-book,** libro de lectura, *m.* **r.-desk,** atril, *m.* **r.-glass,** lente para leer, *m,* carlita, *f.* **r.-lamp,** lámpara de sobremesa, *f.* **r.-matter,** material de lectura, *m.* **r.-room,** gabinete de lectura, *m,* sala de lectura, *f*

readjourn *vt* (a meeting) suspender (la sesión) de nuevo

readjust *vt* reajustar, reacomdar; *vi* reacomodarse

readjustment *n* reajuste, *m,* reacomodación, *f*

readmission *n* readmisión, *f*

ready *a* listo, preparado; dispuesto; pronto; (on the point of) a punto de; (easy) fácil; (near at hand) a la mano; (with money) contante; (with wit, etc.) vivo; (available) disponible; (nimble) ágil, ligero. **I am r. to do it,** Estoy dispuesto a hacerlo. **in r. cash,** en dinero contante. **to get r.,** prepararse; (dress) vestirse. **to make r.,** *vt* preparar; aprestar; *print* imponer. *vi* prepararse, disponerse. **r.-made,** hecho; confeccionado. **r.-made clothing,** ropa hecha, *f.* **r. money,** dinero contante, *m.* **r.-witted,** de ingenio vivo

reaffirm *vt* afirmar de nuevo; reiterar, volver a repetir

reaffirmation *n* reiteración, *f*

reafforestation *n* nuevas plantaciones, *f pl*

reagent *n* reactivo, *m*

real *a* real; verdadero; efectivo; (with silk, etc.) puro; sincero. **r. estate, r. property,** bienes raíces, *m pl*

realism *n* realismo, *m*

realist *n* realista, *mf*

realistic *a* realista

reality *n* realidad, *f;* verdad, *f*

realizable *a* realizable; factible

realization *n* realización, *f;* comprensión, *f*

realize *vt* (understand) darse cuenta de, hacerse cargo de; realizar; (make real) dar vida (a); (accomplish) llevar a cabo; *com* realizar; (gain) adquirir

really *adv* realmente; en verdad; en realidad; en efecto; (frankly) francamente. **R.?** ¿De veras?

realm *n* reino, *m,* dominios, *m pl; fig* esfera, *f*

realty *n* bienes raíces, *m pl*

ream *n* resma, *f*

reanimate *vt* reanimar

reap *vt* segar; *fig* cosechar, recoger

reaper *n* segador (-ra); (machine) segadora mecánica, *f*

reaping *n* siega, *f; fig* cosecha, *f.* **r.-machine,** segadora mecánica, *f*

reappear *vi* reaparecer

reappearance *n* reaparición, *f*

reapplication *n* nueva aplicación, *f;* (of paint, etc.) otra capa, *f;* (for a post, etc.) neuva solicitud, *f*

reapply *vt* aplicar de nuevo; (paint, etc.) dar otra capa (de); (for a post, etc.) mandar una nueva solicitud

reappoint *vt* designar de nuevo

rear *vt* (lift) alzar, levantar; (breed, educate) criar; (build) erigir, construir. *vi* (of horses) encabritarse, corcovear

rear *n* cola, *f;* parte de atrás, *f;* parte posterior, *f;* última fila, *f;* (background) fondo, *m; inf* trasera, *f; mil* retaguardia, *f. a* de atrás; trasero; último; posterior; de última fila; *mil* de retaguardia. **in the r.,** por detrás; a la cola; a retaguardia. **to bring up the r.,** cerrar la marcha. **r.-admiral,** contra almirante, *m.* **r.-axle,** eje trasero, *m.* **r.-guard,** retaguardia, *f.* **r. lamp,** faro trasero, *m.* **r. rank,** última fila, *f.* **r. view,** vista por detrás, *f;* vista posterior, *f*

rearing *n* (breeding) cría, *f;* (education) crianza, *f*

rearm *vt* rearmar. *vi* rearmarse

rearmament *n* rearmamento, *m*

rearrange *vt* volver a arreglar; arreglar de otra manera; (a literary work) refundir, adaptar

rearrangement *n* nuevo arroglo, *m;* (of a literary work) refundición, adaptación, *f*

reascend *vi* and *vt* subir de nuevo, subir otra vez; montar de nuevo (sobre)

reason *n* razón, *f.* **I have plenty of r. to . . .** No me faltarían motivos para . . . *vi* and *vt* razonar. **to r. out of,** disuadir de. **by r. of,** a causa de, con motivo de; en virtud de. **for this r.,** por esto, por esta razón. **out of**

all r., fuera de razón. **to stand to r.,** ser lógico, estar puesto en razón. **with r.,** con razón. **r. of state,** razón de estado, *f*

reasonable *a* razonable; racional

reasonableness *n* lo razonable; moderación, *f;* justicia, *f;* racionalidad, *f*

reasonably *adv* razonablemente; con razón; bastante

reasoning *n* razonamiento, *m*

reassemble *vt* reunir otra vez. *vi* juntarse de nuevo

reassert *vt* afirmar de nuevo, reiterar

reassertion *n* reiteración, *f*

reassess *vt* tasar de nuevo; repartir de nuevo; (a work of art) hacer una nueva apreciación (de)

reassessment *n* nueva tasación, *f;* nuevo repartimiento, *m;* (of a work of art) nueva estimación, *f*

reassume *vt* reasumir

reassumption *n* reasunción, *f*

reassurance *n* afirmación repetida, *f;* confianza restablecida, *f*

reassure *vt* asegurar de nuevo; tranquilizar, confortar

reassuring *a* tranquilizador, consolador

rebate *n* rebaja, *f,* descuento, *m;* reducción, *f. vt* rebajar, descontar; reducir. **to r. pro rata,** ratear

rebec *n mus* rabel, *m*

rebel *n* rebelde, *mf,* insurrecto (-ta). *vi* rebelarse, sublevarse. **r. leader,** cabecilla, *m*

rebellion *n* rebelión, *f*

rebellious *a* rebelde; revoltoso; refractario

rebelliousness *n* rebeldía, *f*

rebind *vt* atar de nuevo; (a book) reencuadernar

rebirth *n* renacimiento, *m*

rebore *vt* (an engine) descarbonizar

reboring *n* (of an engine) descarburación, *f*

reborn, to be *vi* renacer; ser reincarnado

rebound *a* (of books) reencuadernado. *vi* rebotar; repercutir; (revive) reavivarse. *n* rebote, resalto, *m;* reacción, *f,* rechazo, *m*

rebuff *n* repulsa, *f,* desaire, *m;* contrariedad, *f. vt* rechazar; contrariar

rebuild *vt* reedificar

rebuilding *n* reedificación, *f*

rebuke *n* reconvención, represión, censura, *f,* reproche, *m, vt* reprender, censurar, reprochar

rebukingly *adv* en tono de censura; con represión, con reprobación

rebut *vt* refutar

rebuttal *n* refutación, *f*

recalcitrance *n* terquedad, obstinacia, *f;* rebeldía, *f*

recalcitrant *a* reacio, recalcitrante

recall *vt* llamar; hacer volver; (dismiss) destituir; (ambassador, etc.) retirar; (remind or remember) recordar; (revoke) revocar. *n* llamada, *f; mil* toque de llamada, *m;* (of ambassadors, etc.) retirada, *f;* (dismissal) destitución, *f.* **beyond r.,** irrevocable; (forgotten) olvidado

recant *vt* retractar, retirar. *vi* desdecirse (de), retractarse

recantation *n* recantación, *f*

recapitulate *vt* recapitular, resumir

recapitulation *n* recapitulación, *f*

recapture *vt* volver a prender, hacer prisionero nuevamente; (a place) volver a tomar; (a ship) represar

recast *vt* (metals, a literary work) refundir; (alter) cambiar; (reckon) volver a calcular

recasting *n* (metals, a literary work) refundición, *f*

recede *vi* retroceder; alejarse (de), separarse (de); desviarse (de); retirarse; desaparecer; (diminish) disminuir; (of prices) bajar

receding *a* que retrocede, etc.

receipt *n* recibo, *m;* (for money) recibí, *m;* (recipe) receta, *f; pl* **receipts,** ingresos, *m pl. vt* firmar (or extender) recibo. **on r. of,** al recibir. **to acknowledge the r. of,** acusar recibo de. **r. book,** libro talonario, *m*

receive *vt* and *vi* recibir; admitir, aceptar; acoger; (money) percibir, cobrar; (lodge) hospedar, alojar; (contain) contener. **to r. one's degree** *Lat. Am.* diplomarse. **to be well received,** tener buena acogida

receiver *n* recibidor (-ra); (of stolen goods) receptador

(-ra); (in bankruptcies) síndico, *m*; (for other legal business) receptor, *m*; (of a telephone) auricular, *m*; *elec* receptor, *m*; *rad* radiorreceptor, *m*. **to hang up (the r.),** colgar (el auricular)

receivership *n* sindicatura, *f*; receptoría, *f*

receiving *n* recibimiento, *m*; (of money, etc.) cobranza, *f*, percibo, *m*; (of stolen goods) encubrimiento, *m*. *a* que recibe; recipiente; de recepción. **r. set,** aparato de radio, *m*

recency *n* lo reciente; novedad, *f*

recent *a* reciente; nuevo. **in r. years,** en estos últimos años

recently *adv* recientemente; (before past participles) recién. **until r.,** hasta hace poco. **r. painted,** recién pintado

receptacle *n* receptáculo, recipiente, *m*; *bot* receptáculo, *m*

reception *n* recepción, *f*; recibo, *m*; (welcome) acogida, *f*; (of evidence) recepción, *f*. **r. room,** pieza de recibo, *f*, gabinete, *m*

receptive *a* receptivo; susceptible

receptiveness *n* sensibilidad, susceptibilidad, *f*

recess *n* (holiday) vacaciones, *f pl*; (during school hours) hora de recreo, *f*; (*fig* heart) seno, *m*, entrañas, *f pl*; (of the soul, heart) hondón, *m*; (in a coastline, etc.) depresión, *f*; (in a wall) nicho, *m*; (alcove) alcoba, *f*. **parliamentary r.,** interregno parlamentario, *m*

recessional *n* himno que se canta mientras se retiran los eclesiásticos y el coro, *m*

recharge *vt* (a gun, etc.) recargar; acusar de nuevo

recipe *n* receta, *f*

recipient *n* recibidor (-ra); el, *m*, (*f*, la) que recibe. *a* recipiente; receptivo

reciprocal *a* recíproco

reciprocate *vt* reciprocar; *mech* producir movimiento de vaivén. *vi mech* oscilar, tener movimiento alternativo; corresponder; ser recíproco

reciprocation *n* reciprocación, *f*; reciprocidad, correspondencia, *f*

reciprocity *n* reciprocidad, *f*

recital *n* narración, relación, *f*; enumeración, *f*; recitación, *f*; *mus* recital, *m*

recitation *n* recitación, *f*

recitative *n* recitado, *m*

recite *vt* recitar, repetir; narrar; declamar. *vi* decir una recitación

reciter *n* recitador (-ra); declamador (-ra)

reckless *a* temerario, audaz; precipitado; descuidado (de); indiferente (a); excesivo; imprudente

recklessly *adv* temerariamente; descuidadamente; imprudentemente

recklessness *n* temeridad, audacia, *f*; descuido, *m*; imprudencia, *f*; indiferencia, *f*

reckon *vt* calcular, computar; contar; enumerar; (believe) considerar, juzgar; (attribute) atribuir; (think) creer (que). **to r. up,** echar cuentas, calcular. **to r. with,** contar con; tomar en serio

reckoner *n* calculador (-ra). **ready r.,** tablas matemáticas, *f pl*

reckoning *n* cálculo, *m*, calculación, *f*; cuenta, *f*; *fig* retribución, *f*, castigo, *m*; *naut* estima, *f*. **the day of r.,** el día de ajuste de cuentas; el día del juicio final. **to be out in one's r.,** equivocarse en el cálculo; engañarse en el juicio

reclaim *vt* (land) entarquinar; (reform) reformar; (tame) domesticar; (claim) reclamar; (restore) restaurar

reclamation *n* (of land) entarquinamiento, *m*; cultivo, *m*; (reform) reformación, *f*; (restoration) restauración, *f*; (claiming) reclamación, *f*

recline *vt* apoyar; recostar; reclinar; descansar, reposar. *vi* recostarse, reclinarse; estar tumbado; apoyarse; descansar

reclining *n* reclinación, *f*. *a* inclinado; acostado; (of statues) yacente

recluse *a* solitario, *n* recluso (-sa); solitario (-ia); ermitaño, *m*, anacoreta, *mf*

recognition *n* reconocimiento, *m*

recognizable *a* que puede reconocerse; identificable

recognizance *n* reconocimiento, *m*; *law* obligación, *f*

recognize *vt* reconocer; confesar

recoil *n* reculada, *f*; (of a gun) culatazo, *m*; (refusal) rechazo, *m*; (result) repercusión, *f*; (repugnance) aversión, repugnancia, *f*. *vi* recular; retroceder; repercutir; sentir repugnancia

recoin *vt* acuñar de nuevo

recollect *vt* acordarse de, recordar. **to r. oneself,** reponerse, recobrarse

recollection *n* recuerdo, *m*, memoria, *f*

recommence *vt* and *vi* empezar de nuevo

recommend *vt* recomendar; aconsejar; encargar

recommendable *a* recomendable

recommendation *n* recomendación, *f*

recommendatory *a* recomendatorio

recommender *n* el, *m*, (*f*, la) que recomienda

recompense *n* recompensa, *f*, *vt* recompensar

recomposition *n* recomposición, *f*

reconcilability *n* posibilidad de reconciliación, *f*; compatibilidad, *f*

reconcilable *a* reconciliable; compatible; conciliable

reconcile *vt* reconciliar; (quarrels) componer, ajustar; (opposing theories, etc.) conciliar. **to r. oneself (to),** aceptar; acostumbrarse (a); resignarse (a)

reconciler *n* reconciliador (-ra)

reconciliation *n* reconciliación, *f*; (of theories, etc.) conciliación, *f*

reconciliatory *a* reconciliador

recondite *a* recóndito

recondition *vt* reconeficiar

reconnaissance *n* reconocimiento, *m*; exploración, *f*. **r. flight,** vuelo de reconocimiento, *m*. **r. plane,** avión de reconocimiento, *m*

reconnoiter *n mil* reconocer; explorar. *vi mil* practicar un reconocimiento; correr la campaña

reconnoitering *n* reconocimiento, *m*, *a* de reconocimiento

reconquer *vt* reconquistar

reconquest *n* reconquista, *f*

reconsecrate *vt* consagrar de nuevo

reconsider *vt* considerar de nuevo, volver a considerar; volver a discutir

reconsideration *n* nueva consideración, *f*; nueva discusión, *f*

reconstitute *vt* reconstituir

reconstitution *n* reconstitución, *f*

reconstruct *vt* reconstruir

reconstruction *n* reconstrucción, *f*

reconversion *n* reconversión, *f*

recopy *vt* copiar de nuevo

record *vt* apuntar; inscribir; (recount) contar, escribir; recordar; registrar; (of thermometers, etc.) marcar, registrar; hacer un disco de gramófono de; (radio, cinema) impresionar. *n* relación, *f*; crónica, *f*; historia, *f*; (soldier's) hoja de servicios, *f*; (past) antecedentes, *m pl*; documento, *m*; inscripción, *f*; (entry) partida, *f*; testimonio, *m*; (memory) recuerdo, *m*; registro, *m*; (gramophone) disco de gramófono, *m*; *sport* record, *m*, plusmarca, *f*; *pl* **records,** *m pl*; (notes) notas, *f pl*; (facts) datos, *m pl*; anales, *m pl*. **keeper of the records,** archivero, *m*. **off the r.,** confidencialmente. **on r.,** escrito; registrado; inscrito en los anales de la historia. **to break a r.,** supremar precedentes. **r.-holder,** plusmarquista, *mf*

recorder *n* registrador, *m*; archivero, *m*; *law* juez, *m*; (historian) historiador, *m*; *mus* caramillo, *m*; *mech* contador, indicador, *m*; (scientific) aparato registrador, *m*

recording *a* registrador. **r. apparatus,** (cinema, radio, gramophone) máquina de impresionar, *f*; (scientific) aparato registrador, *m*. **r. van,** carro de sonido, *m*

recount *vt* contar de nuevo; (tell) referir, narrar, contar

recoup *vt* compensar, indemnizar; recobrar; desquitarse de

recourse *n* recurso, *m*. **to have r. to,** recurrir, *a*

recover *vt* (regain) recobrar; *fig* reconquistar; (retrieve) rescatar; *law* reivindicar. *vi* reponerse; (in health) recobrar la salud, sanar, curarse; *law* ganar un pleito. **to r. consciousness,** volver en sí

recoverable *a* recuperable

recovery *n* (regaining) recobro, *m*, recuperación, *f*; (of money) cobranza, *f*; (retrieval) rescate, *m*; *fig* reconquista, *f*; (from illness) mejoría, convalecencia, *f*; restablecimiento, *m*; *law* reivindicación, *f*

recreant *a* traidor, falso, desleal. *n* apóstata, *mf* traidor (-ra)

recreate *vt* recrear

recreation *n* recreación, *f*; (break in schools) recreo, *m*. **r. hall,** sala de recreo, *f*

recreative *a* recreativo

recriminate *vi* recriminar

recrimination *n* recriminación, reconvención, *f*

recriminator *n* recriminador (-ra)

recriminatory *a* recriminador

recross *vt* volver a cruzar, cruzar de nuevo

recrudesce *vi* recrudecer

recrudescence *n* recrudescencia, *f*

recrudescent *a* recrudescente

recruit *n* recluta, *m*. *vt* reclutar; (restore) reponer

recruiting *n* reclutamiento, *m*. **r. office,** caja de reclutamiento, *f*

rectal *a* rectal

rectangle *n* rectángulo, *m*

rectangular *a* rectangular

rectifiable *a* rectificable

rectification *n* rectificación, *f*

rectifier *n* rectificador, *m*

rectify *vt* rectificar

rectilinear *a* rectilíneo

rectitude *n* rectitud, *f*

rector *n* (of a university or school) rector, *m*; (priest) párroco, *m*

rectorship *n* rectorado, *m*

rectory *n* rectoral, rectoría, *f*

rectum *n* recto, *m*

recumbent *a* recostado, reclinado; (of a statue) yacente

recuperable *a* recuperable

recuperate *vt* recuperar, recobrar. *vi* restablecerse, reponerse; recuperarse

recuperation *n* recuperación, *f*

recuperative *a* recuperativo

recur *vi* presentarse a la imaginación; volver (sobre); presentarse de nuevo, aparecer otra vez; repetirse; reproducirse

recurrence *n* reaparición, *f*; repetición, *f*

recurrent *a* periódico; *med* recurrente

red *a* rojo; (of wine) tinto. *n* color rojo, *m*; (in billiards) mingo, *m*, bola roja, *f*; *pol* rojo, *m*. **to catch red-handed,** coger con el hurto en las manos; coger con las manos en la masa, coger en el acto. **to grow red,** enrojecerse, ponerse rojo; volverse rojo. **red-berried,** con bayas rojas. **red cabbage,** lombarda, *f*. **red cedar,** cedro dulce, *m*. **red corpuscle,** glóbulo rojo, *m*. **Red Cross,** Cruz Roja, *f*. **red currant,** grosella, *f*. **red currant bush,** grosellero, *m*. **red-eyed,** con los ojos inyectados. **red fir,** pino silvestre, *m*. **red flush,** (in the sky) arrebol, *m*. **red-gold,** bermejo; (of hair, etc.) rojo. **red-haired,** pelirrojo, de pelo rojo. **red-handed,** con las manos ensangrentadas; *fig* en el acto. **red-head** (person) pelirrojo (-ja). **red-heat,** incandescencia, *f*. **red-hot,** candente. *m*. **red-lead,** minio, *m*. **red-letter,** de fiesta; extraordinario. **red-letter day,** día de fiesta, *m*; día extraordinario, *m*. **red mullet,** salmonete, *m*, trilla, *f*. **red ocher,** almagre, *m*. **red pepper,** pimiento, *m*; (cayenne) pimentón, *Lat. Am.* ají, *m*, **Red Sea,** mar Rojo, mar Bermejo, *m*. **red tape,** balduque, *m*; formulismo, *m*; burocracia, *f*. **red wine,** vino tinto, *m*

redbreast *n* petirrojo, *m*

redden *vt* rojear, enrojecer; pintar de rojo. *vi* enrojecerse, ponerse rojo; volverse rojo

reddish *a* rojizo

redeem *vt* (a mortgage, bonds, etc.) amortizar; (from pawn) desempeñar; (a promise, etc.) cumplir; libertar; redimir; compensar; (a fault) expiar; (reform) reformar; (rescue) rescatar

redeemable *a* redimible; amortizable

redeemer *n* rescatador (-ra); salvador (-ra); *theol* Redentor, *m*

redeeming *a* redentor; compensatorio. **r. feature,** compensación, *f*; rasgo bueno, *m*. **There is no r. feature in his work,** No hay nada bueno en su obra

redemption *n* (of a mortgage, etc.) amortización, *f*; (from pawn) desempeño, *m*; (of a promise, etc.) cumplimiento, *m*; (ransom, etc.) rescate, *m*; *theol* redención, *f*; compensación, *f*; (of a fault) expiación, *f*; reformación, *f*

redemptive *a* redentor

redescend *vi* bajar de nuevo

rediscovery *n* nuevo descubrimiento, *m*

redistribute *vt* distribuir de nuevo, volver a distribuir

redistribution *n* nueva distribución, *f*

redness *n* rojez, *f*, color rojo, *m*

redolent *a* fragante, oloroso; *fig* evocador (de)

redouble *vt* redoblar. *vi* redoblarse

redoubling *n* redoblamiento, *m*

redoubt *n* reducto, *m*

redoubtable *a* formidable, terrible; valiente

redound *vi* redundar (en)

redress *vt* rectificar; reparar; remediar; hacer justicia (a); corregir

reduce *vt* reducir; disminuir; (in price) rebajar; abreviar; (exhaust, weaken) agotar; (impoverish) empobrecer; (degrade) degradar. **to r. to the ranks,** *mil* volver a las filas; degradar. **to be in reduced circumstances,** estar en la indigencia

reducible *a* reducible

reduction *n* reducción, *f*; (in price) rebaja, *f*

redundance *n* redundancia, *f*

redundant *a* redundante; superfluo, excesivo

reduplicate *vt* reduplicar

reduplication *n* reduplicación, *f*

reecho *vt* repetir; devolver el son de, hacer reverberar. *vi* repercutirse, reverberar

reed *n bot* caña, *f*; (arrow) saeta, *f*; (pipe) caramillo, *m*; (in wind-instruments) lengüeta, *f*; *arch* junquillo, *m*; (in a loom) peine, *m*; (pastoral poetry) poesía bucólica, *f*. *vt* (thatch) bardar con cañas

reedit *vt* reeditar, volver a editar

reedy *a* juncoso, lleno de cañas; (of the voice) silbante

reef *n* arrecife, escollo, encalladero, *m*; *min* filón, *m*; *naut* rizo, *m*. *vt naut* arrizar. **to take in reefs,** *naut* hacer el rizo. **r.-knot,** nudo de marino, *m*

reek *n* humo, *m*; olor, *m*. *vi* humear; oler (de); *fig* recordar, hacer pensar (en)

reeky *a* humoso

reel *n* carrete, *m*; devanadera, *f*; (of a fishing rod) carrete, carretel, *m*; (cinema) cinta, *f*; (dance) baile escocés, *m*. *vt* devanar. *vi* tambalear, titubear; (of ships, etc.) cabecear; temblar; oscilar. **to r. about drunkenly,** (of persons) andar haciendo eses, arrimarse a las paredes. **to r. off,** recitar; enumerar; decir rápidamente

reelect *vt* reelegir

reelection *n* reelección, *f*

reeligible *a* reelegible

reeling *n* tambaleo, *m*; andar vacilante, *m*; (of a ship, etc.) cabeceo, *m*; oscilación, *f*

reembarcation *n* reembarque, *m*

reembark *vt* reembarcar. *vi* reembarcarse

reemerge *vi* reaparecer

reemergence *n* reaparición, *f*

reenact *vt* revalidar (una ley); decretar de nuevo

reenactment *n* revalidación (de una ley), *f*; nuevo decreto, *m*

reengage *vt* contratar de nuevo

reengagement *n* nuevo contrato, *m*

reenlist *vt* and *vi* alistar(se) de nuevo
reenlistment *n* reenganche, *m*
reenter *vt* volver a entrar (en); reingresar (en)
reentry *n* segunda entrada, *f*, reingreso, *m*
reequip *vt* equipar de nuevo
reestablish *vt* restablecer; restaurar
reestablishment *n* restablecimiento, *m*; restauración, *f*
reeve *vt naut* laborear, guarnir
reexamination *n* reexaminación, *f*; nuevo examen, *m*; *law* nuevo interrogatorio, *m*
reexamine *vt* reexaminar; *law* interrogar de nuevo
reexport *vt* reexportar
reexportation *n* reexportación, *f*
refashion *vt* volver a hacer; formar de nuevo
refection *n* refección, *f*
refectory *n* refectorio, *m*
refer *vt* atribuir (a); (send) enviar, remitir; (assign) referir (a), relacionar (con). *vi* referirse (a); aludir (a); hablar (de)
referee *n* árbitro, *m*; *law* juez arbitrador, *m*; (reference) garante, *mf* fiador (-ra). *vi* servir de árbitro
reference *n* referencia, *f*; consulta, *f*; mención, *f*; alusión, *f*; (relation) relación, *f*; *pl* **references,** *com* referencias, *f pl*. **for r.,** para consulta. **in r. to,** con referencia a, respecto a, en cuanto a. **terms of r.,** puntos de consulta, *m pl*. **work of r.,** libro de consulta, *m*
reference book *n* libro de consulta, *m*
referendum *n* referéndum, *m*
refill *vt* rellenar; rehenchir; (pen) llenar de nuevo con tinta. *n* (for a pencil) mina de recambio, *f*
refine *vt* refinar; (metals) acrisolar; (fats) clarificar; *fig* perfeccionar, pulir, refinar
refined *a* refinado; fino; culto; cortés; elegante; delicado; (subtle) sutil; (affected) afectado
refinement *n* refinamiento, *m*; finura, *f*; cultura, *f*; cortesía, *f*; elegancia, *f*; delicadeza, *f*; (subtlety) sutileza, *f*; (affectation) afectación, *f*
refiner *n* refinador, *m*
refinery *n* refinería, *f*
refining *n* refinación, *f*; *fig* refinamiento, *m*
refit *vt* reparar; *naut* embonar
refitting *n* reparación, *f*; *naut* embonada, *f*
reflect *vt* reflejar; reflexionar. *vi* reflejar; reflexionar (sobre), pensar (en), meditar (sobre). **This offer reflects credit on him,** Esta oferta le hace honor. **to r. on, upon,** reflexionar sobre; (disparage) desacreditar; (affect unfavorably) perjudicar
reflecting *a* reflector
reflection *n phys* reflexión, *f*; reflejo, *m*; consideración, *f*, pensamiento, *m*; (aspersion) censura, *f*, reproche, *m*. **upon mature r.,** después de pensarlo bien
reflective *a phys* reflector; reflexivo, pensativo, meditabundo
reflectively *adv* reflexivamente
reflector *n* reflector, *m*; (shade) pantalla, *f*
reflex *a* reflejo. *n* reflejo, *m*; acción refleja, *f*. **r. action,** acción refleja, *f*
refloat *vt* (a ship) poner otra vex a flote, desvarar
reflux *n* reflujo, *m*
reform *n* reforma, *f*. *a* de reforma; reformista. *vt* reformar; formar de nuevo. *vi* reformarse
reformation *n* reformación, *f*; **Reformation,** Reforma, *f*
reformatory *a* reformatorio, reformador. *n* reformatorio, *m*, casa de corrección, *f*
reformer *n* reformador (-ra), reformista, *mf*
refract *vt* refractar
refraction *n* refracción, *f*
refractive *a* refringente
refractoriness *n* terquedad, obstinacia, *f*; rebeldia, indocilidad, *f*
refractory *a* (of substances) refractario; recalcitrante, intratable, rebelde
refrain *n* estribillo, estrambote, *m*
refrain *vi* abstenerse (de), evitar
refresh *vt* refrescar

refreshing *a* refrescante; atractivo; estimulante; interesante
refreshment *n* (solace) solaz, reposo, *m*; recreación, *f*, deleite, *m*; (food and (or) drink) refresco, *m*. **r.-room,** (at a station) fonda, *f*. **r. stand** *Mexico* fresquería, *f*
refrigerate *vt* refrigerar; enfriar; refrescar
refrigeration *n* refrigeración, *f*; enfriamiento, *m*. **r. chamber,** cámara frigorífica, *f*
refrigerative *a* refrigerante, frigorífico
refrigerator *n* refrigerador, *m*, nevera, *f*
refringent *a* refringente
refuel *vt* (a furnace) cargar con carbón, etc.; (of a ship) tomar carbón; (of an airplane, motor vehicle) tomar bencina
refuge *n* refugio, *m*; asilo, *m*; (resort) recurso, *m*; subterfugio, *m*; (traffic island) refugio para peatones, *m*. **to take r.,** refugiarse; resguardarse (de)
refugee *a* refugiado. *n* refugiado (-da)
refulgence *n* refulgencia, *f*
refulgent *a* refulgente
refund *vt* reembolsar; devolver
refunding *n* reembolso, *m*; devolución, *f*
refurbish *vt* restaurar; renovar; (a literary work) refundir
refurnish *vt* amueblar de nuevo
refusal *n* negativa, *f*; (rejection) rechazo, *m*; (option) opción, *f*; preferencia, *f*
refuse *vt* negar; (reject) rechazar. *vi* negarse (a), rehusar; (of a horse) resistirse a saltar
refuse *n* desecho, *m*; desperdicios, *m pl*; residuo, *m*; basura, *f*. *a* de desecho. **r. dump,** muladar, *m*
refutable *a* refutable
refutation *n* refutación, *f*
refute *vt* refutar
regain *vt* recobrar, recuperar; cobrar; ganar de nuevo; *fig* reconquistar. **to r. one's breath,** cobrar aliento. **to r. consciousness,** volver en sí
regal *a* regio, real
regale *vt* regalar, agasajar; recrear, deleitar
regalia *n* regalía, *f*; insignias reales, *f pl*; distintivos, *m pl*, insignias, *f pl*
regally *adv* regiamente
regard *vt* mirar; observar; considerar; (respect) respetar; (concern) importar, concernir; relacionarse con. *n* mirada, *f*; atención, *f*; (esteem) aprecio, *m*, estimación, *f*; respeto, *m*; veneración, *f*; (relation) referencia, *f*; *pl* **regards,** recuerdos, saludos, *m pl*. **He has little r. for their feelings,** Le importan poco sus susceptibilidades. **With kindest regards,** Con mis saludos más afectuosos. **as regards, with r. to,** con referencia a, respecto a, en cuanto a
regardful *a* atento (a), cuidadoso (de); que se preocupa (de)
regarding *prep* tocante a, en cuanto a, respecto de
regardless *a* negligente (de); indiferente (a), insensible (a); que no se interesa (en); que no se inquieta (por); sin preocuparse (de)
regatta *n* regata, *f*
regency *n* regencia, *f*
regeneracy *n* regeneración, *f*
regenerate *vt* regenerar. *a* regenerado
regeneration *n* regeneración, *f*
regenerative *a* regenerador
regenerator *n* regenerador (-ra)
regent *n* regente, *mf*
régime *n* régimen, *m*
regimen *n* (*gram med*) régimen, *m*,
regiment *n* regimiento, *m*. *vt* regimentar. **r. of the line,** tropa de línea, *f*
regimental *a* de (un) regimiento, perteneciente a un regimiento
regimentation *n* regimentación, *f*
region *n* región, *f*
regional *a* regional
regionalism *n* regionalismo, *m*
regionalist *n* regionalista, *mf*

regionalistic *a* regionalista

register *n* (record and *mech mus print*) registro, *m*; (of ships, etc.) matrícula, *f*; lista, *f. vt* registrar; matricular; (a ship) abanderar; inscribir; (one's child in a school) anotar (Argentina), inscribir; (of thermometers, etc.) marcar; (letters) certificar; (luggage) facturar; (in one's mind) grabar; (emotion) mostrar, manifestar. *vi* (at a hotel, etc.) registrarse; *print* estar en registro. **cash r.,** caja registradora, *f.* **r. of births, marriages and deaths,** registro civil, *m*

registered letter *n* carta certificada, *f*

registrar *n* registrador, *m*; archivero, *m*; secretario, *m*; (of a school) jefe de inscripciones, secretario general (the latter has many more duties). **r. of births, marriages and deaths,** secretario del registro civil, *m*. **registrar's office,** oficina del registro civil, *f*

registration *n* registro, *m*; inscripción, *f*; (of a vehicle, etc.) matrícula, *f*; *naut* abanderamiento, *m*; (of a letter, etc.) certificación, *f.* **r. number,** número de matrícula, *m*

registry *n* registro, *m*; inscripción, *f*; matrícula, *f.* **r. office,** oficina del registro civil, *f*; (for servants) agencia doméstica, *f*

regression *n* regresión, *f*, retroceso, *m*

regret *vt* sentir; lamentar, pesar; arrepentirse (de); (miss) echar de menos (a). *n* sentimiento, pesar, *m*; (remorse) remordimiento, *m*. **I r. very much that . . . ,** Me pesa mucho que . . . , Siento mucho que . . . **to send one's regrets,** mandar sus excusas

regretful *a* lleno de pesar; arrepentido; lamentable, deplorable. **He was most r. that . . . ,** Lamentaba mucho que . . .

regretfully *adv* con pesar

regrettable *a* lamentable, deplorable; doloroso; (with loss, etc.) sensible

regrettably *adv* lamentablemente; sensiblemente

regroup *vt* arreglar de nuevo; formar de nuevo; reorganizar

regular *a* regular; normal; (ordinary) corriente, común; (in order) en regla; (*gram bot ecc mil geom*) regular. *n ecc* regular, *m*; (soldier) soldado de línea, *m*; (officer) militar de carrera, *m*; (client) parroquiano habitual, *m*

regularity *n* regularidad,

regularization *n* regularización, *f*

regularize *vt* regularizar

regularly *adv* regularmente

regulate *vt* regular; ajustar, arreglar; (direct) dirigir; reglamentar

regulation *n* regulación, *f*; arreglo, *m*; (rule) reglamento, *m*, *a* de reglamento; normal

regulative *a* regulador

regulator *n mech* regulador, *m*

regurgitate *vt* and *vi* regurgitar

regurgitation *n* regurgitación, *f*

rehabilitate *vt* rehabilitar

rehabilitation *n* rehabilitación, *f*

rehash *vt* (a literary work, etc.) refundir

rehearing *n* nueva audición, *f*, (of a case) revisión, *f*

rehearsal *n theat* ensayo, *m*; recitación, *f*; relación, narración, *f.* **dress r.,** ensayo general, *m*

rehearse *vt theat* ensayar; recitar; (narrate) narrar; enumerar

reheat *vt* recalentar

reign *n* reinado, *m. vi* reinar; predominar

reigning *a* reinante; predominante

reimburse *vt* reembolsar

reimbursement *n* reembolso, *m*

reimport *vt* importar de nuevo, reimportar, *n* reimporte, *m*

reimportation *n* reimportación, *f*

reimpose *vt* reimponer

reimposition *n* reimposición, *f*

reimprison *vt* encarcelar de nuevo, reencarcelar

reimprisonment *n* reencarcelamiento, *m*

rein *n* rienda, *f. vt* llevar las riendas (de); (hold back) refrenar. **to give r. to,** *fig* dar rienda suelta (a)

reincarnation *n* reencarnación, *f*

reincorporate *vt* reincorporar

reincorporation *n* reincorporación, *f*

reindeer *n* reno, *m*

reinforce *vt* reforzar; (concrete) armar; fortalecer. **reinforced concrete,** *n* hormigón armado, *m*

reinforcement *n* reforzamiento, *m*; (*mil nav fig*) refuerzo, *m*

reins. *n* See **rein**

reinsert *vt* volver a insertar

reinstall *vt* reinstalar; rehabilitar

reinstalment *n* reinstalación, *f*; rehabilitación, *f*; restablecimiento, *m*

reinstate *vt* reponer, restablecer; reinstalar; rehabilitar

reinstatement *n* restablecimiento, *m*; rehabilitación, *f*

reinsurance *n* reaseguro, *m*

reinsure *vt* reasegurar

reintegrate *vt* reintegrar

reintegration *n* reintegración, *f*

reinter *vt* enterrar de nuevo

reinvest *vt* reinvertir

reinvestment *n* reinversión, *f*

reinvigorate *vt* reanimar, dar nuevo vigor (a)

reinvite *vt* invitar de nuevo (a)

reissue *n* nueva emisión, *f*; (of a book, etc.) nueva edición, reimpresión, *f. vt* hacer una nueva emisión (de); reeditar, publicar de nuevo

reiterate *vt* reiterar, repetir

reiteration *n* reiteración, *f*

reiterative *a* reiterativo

reject *vt* rechazar, rehusar; repudiar; repulsar; desechar

rejection *n* rechazamiento, *m*; repudiación, refutación, *f*; repulsa, *f*

rejoice *vt* alegrar, regocijar. *vi* alegrarse (de), regocijarse (de), gloriarse (en)

rejoicing *n* regocijo, júbilo, *m*, alegría, *f*; algazara, *f*, fiestas, *f pl*

rejoin *vt* and *vi* juntar de nuevo; volver a; reunirse con; (reply) contestar, replicar

rejoinder *n* contestación, respuesta, *f*

rejuvenate *vt* rejuvenecer

rejuvenation *n* rejuvenecimiento, *m*

rekindle *vt* encender de nuevo; despertar, reavivar. *vi* encenderse de nuevo; reavivarse

relapse *n* reincidencia, recaída, *f*; *med* recidiva, *f. vi* reincidir (en); *med* recaer

relapsed *a* relapso

relate *vt* (recount) relatar, narrar; relacionar; unir; (of kinship) emparentar. *vi* ajustarse (a); referirse (a). **The first fact is not related to the second,** El primer hecho no tiene nada que ver con el segundo

related *a* relacionado; (by kinship) emparentado. **John is well-r.,** Juan es de buena familia; Juan es de familia influyente; Juan tiene buenas relaciones

relater *n* narrador (-ra)

relation *n* (narrative) relación, narración, *f*; conexión, *f*; relación, *f*; (kinship) parentesco, *m*; (person) pariente (-ta). **in r. to,** con relación a, en cuanto a

relationship *n* parentesco, *m*; conexión, relación, *Lat. Am.* atingencia, *f*

relative *a* relativo. *n* pariente (-ta); *pl* **relatives,** parientes, *m pl*, parentela, *f*

relativism *n* relativismo, *m*

relativity *n* relatividad, *f*

relax *vt* relajar; aflojar; soltar; (make less severe) ablandar; (decrease) mitigar. *vi* relajarse; aflojar; (rest) descansar

relaxation *n* relajación, *f*; aflojamiento, *m*; ablandamiento, *m*; mitigación, *f*; (rest) descanso, reposo, *m*; (pastime) pasatiempo, *m*; (amusement) diversión, *f*

relaxing *a* relajante; (of climate) enervante

relay *n* (position of horses) parada, *f*; (shift) tanda, *f*; relevo, *m*; *elec* relais, *m*; *rad* redifusión, *f. vt* enviar por posta; *elec* reemitir; *rad* retransmitir; (lay again) colocar de nuevo. **r. race,** carrera de equipo, carrera de relevos, *f*

release *vt* soltar; (hurl) lanzar; (set free) poner en libertad (a); librar (de); absolver; (surrender) renunciar (a); dar al público, poner en circulación; (lease again) realquilar. *n* soltura, *f*; lanzamiento, *m*; liberación, *f*; (from pain) alivio, *m*; remisión, *f*; exoneración, *f*; publicación, *f*; (of films) representación, *f*; *law* soltura, *f*

relegate *vt* relegar

relegation *n* relegación, *f*

relent *vi* ablandarse, enternecerse; ceder

relenting *n* enternecimiento, desenojo, *m*

relentless *a* implacable, inexorable; despiadado

relentlessly *adv* inexorablemente; sin piedad

relentlessness *n* inexorabilidad, *f*; falta de piedad, *f*

relet *vt* realquilar

relevance *n* conexión, *f*; pertinencia, *f*; aplicabilidad, *f*

relevant *a* relativo; pertinente, a propósito, oportuno; aplicable

reliability *n* seguridad, *f*; formalidad, *f*; confianza, *f*; exactitud, *f*; veracidad, *f*

reliable *a* seguro; formal; digno de crédito, de confianza, solvente digno de confianza; exacto; veraz

reliably *adv* seguramente; de una manera digna de confianza; exactamente

reliance *n* confianza, *f*. **to place r. on,** tener confianza en

reliant *a* confiado

relic *n* vestigio, rastro, *m*; *ecc* reliquia, *f*

relict *n* viuda, *f*

relief *n* (alleviation) alivio, *m*; desahogo, *m*; (help) socorro, *m*, ayuda, *f*; beneficencia, *f*; *mil* relevo, *m*; (pleasure) placer, *m*, satisfacción, *f*; (consolation) consuelo, *m*; *law* remisión, *f*; *art* relieve, *m*. **high r.,** alto relieve, *m*. **low r.,** bajo relieve, *m*. **r. map,** mapa en relieve, *m*. **r. train,** tren de socorro, *m*

relieve *vt* aliviar; aligerar, suavizar; mitigar; (one's feelings, etc.) desahogar; (*mil* and to take the place of) relevar; (free) librar; (dismiss) destituir; (remove) quitar; (rob) robar; (help) socorrer, remediar; (redeem) redimir; (ornament) adornar; (from a wrong) hacer justicia (a)

relieving *n* alivio, *m*; aligeramiento, *m*; mitigación, *f*; (of the feelings) desahogo, *m*; *mil* relevo, *m*; (help) socorro, *m*. **r. arch,** sobrearco, *m*

relight *vt* volver a encender. *vi* encenderse de nuevo

religion *n* religión, *f*

religiosity *n* religiosidad, *f*

religious *a* religioso; en religión; piadoso, crevente; devoto. *n* religioso (-sa). **r. orders,** órdenes religiosas, *f pl*. **r. toleration,** libertad de cultos, *f*

religiousness *n* religiosidad, *f*

relinquish *vt* abandonar; (one's grip) soltar; renunciar; desistir (de), dejar (de); (a post) dimitir (de)

relinquishment *n* abandono, *m*; renuncia, *f*; dejamiento, *m*; (of a post) dimisión, *f*

reliquary *n* relicario, *f*

relish *n* gusto, *m*; sabor, *m*; (touch, smack) dejo, *m*; condimento, *m*; apetito, *m*, gana, *f*. *vt* gustar de; comer con apetito; saborear, paladear; *fig* seducir, atraer, gustar. *vi* tener gusto (de). **I do not much r. the idea,** No me seduce la idea

relishing *n* saboreo, *m*; (enjoyment) goce, *m*, fruición, *f*; consideración, *f*

relive *vt* vivir de nuevo, volver a vivir

reload *vt* recargar

reluctance *n* repugnancia, desgana, *f*. **with r.,** a regañadientes, de mala gana

reluctant *a* poco dispuesto (a), que tiene repugnancia a (hacer algo), sin gana; (forced) forzado; artificial; (hesitating) vacilante

reluctantly *adv* de mala gana, con repugnancia, a disgusto

rely on *vi* contar con, confiar en, depender de

remain *vi* quedar; permanecer; (be left over) sobrar; continuar. **I r. yours faithfully . . . ,** (in a letter) Queda de Vd. su att. s.s. . . . **It remains to be written,** Queda por escribir

remainder *n* resto, *m*; restos, *m pl*, sobras, *f pl*; residuo,

m. **The r. of the people went away,** Los demás se marcharon

remaining *pres. part* and *a* que queda; sobrante. **r. to be paid** *Lat. Am.* impago

remains *n pl* restos, *m pl*; sobras, *f pl*, desperdicios, *m pl*; ruinas, *f pl*

remake *vt* rehacer; reformar

remand *vt* *law* reencarcelar. *n* *law* reencarcelamiento, *m*

remark *n* observación, *f*; nota, *f*; comentario, *m*. *vt* and *vi* observar; notar. **to r. on,** comentar, hacer una observación sobre

remarkable *a* notable, singular, extraordinario

remarkably *adv* singularmente

remarriage *n* segundas nupcias, *f pl*, segundo casamiento, *m*

remarry *vt* volver a casar (a). *vi* casarse en segundas nupcias; volver a casarse

remediable *a* remediable

remedial *a* remediador; curativo, terapéutico

remedy *n* remedio, *m*; recurso, *m*, *vt* remediar; curar

remember *vt* recordar; tener presente; acordarse de. *vi* acordarse; no olvidarse. **R. me to your mother,** Dale recuerdos míos a tu madre. **If I r. rightly . . . ,** Si bien me acuerdo . . . **And r. that I shall do no more!** ¡Y no olvides que no haré más!

remembrance *n* recuerdo, *m*; memoria, *f*; *pl* **remembrances,** recuerdos, *m pl*

remind *vt* recordar

reminder *n* recuerdo, *m*; (warning) advertencia, *f*. **a gentle r.,** una indirecta, una insinuación

reminisce *vi* *inf* recordar viejas historias

reminiscence *n* reminiscencia, *f*, recuerdo, *m*

reminiscent *a* evocador, que recuerda; de reminiscencia; que piensa en el pasado. **to be r. of,** recordar; *inf* oler a

reminiscently *adv* evocadoramente, como si recordara

remiss *a* negligente, descuidado

remission *n* remisión, *f*

remissly *adv* negligentemente

remissness *n* negligencia, *f*, descuido, *m*

remit *vt* remitir; *com* remesar, enviar. *vi* (pay) pagar

remittance *n* remesa, *f*, envío, *m*

remitter *n* remitente, *mf*

remnant *n* resto, *m*; (of fabric) retal, retazo, *m*; (relic) vestigio, *m*, reliquia, *f*. **r. sale,** saldo, *m*

remodel *vt* rehacer; reformar; modelar de nuevo; (a play, etc.) refundir

remodeling *n* reformación, *f*; (of a play, etc.) refundición, *f*

remonstrance *n* protesta, *f*; reconvención, *f*

remonstrate *vi* protestar, objetar. **to r. with,** reprochar, reconvenir

remorse *n* remordimiento, *m*

remorseful *a* lleno de remordimientos; penitente, arrepentido

remorsefully *adv* con remordimiento

remorseless *a* sin conciencia, sin remordimientos; despiadado, inflexible

remorselessness *n* inexorabilidad, crueldad, dureza, *f*

remote *a* distante, lejano; remoto; aislado; ajeno; (slight) leve, vago. **r. control,** mando a distancia, *m*

remotely *adv* remotamente

remoteness *n* distancia, *f*; aislamiento, *m*; alejamiento, *m*; (vagueness) vaguedad, *f*

remount *vt* subir de nuevo, montar de nuevo; *mil* remontar. *vi* (go back to) remontar (a), derivarse (de). *n* *mil* remonta, *f*

removable *a* que puede quitarse; (of collars, etc.) de quita y pon; transportable; (of officials, etc.) amovible

removal *n* acción de quitar o levantar, *f*; sacamiento, *m*; separación, *f*; eliminación, *f*; alejamiento, *m*; traslado, *m*; (from office, etc.) deposición, *f*; supresión, *f*; asesinato, *m*. **r. van,** carro de mudanzas, *m*

remove *vt* quitar; retirar; levantar; sacar; apartar; separar; eliminar; trasladar; (from office) destituir; suprimir; asesinar. *vi* trasladarse. *n* grado, *m*; distancia, *f*; (departure) partida, *f*. **to r. oneself,** quitarse de en medio. **to r. one's hat,** descubrirse. **first cousin once removed,** hijo de primo carnal, primo hermano del padre, primo hermano de la madre, *m*

remunerate *vt* remunerar

remuneration *n* remuneración, *f*

remunerative *a* remunerador

renaissance *n* renacimiento, *m*, *a* renacentista

Renaissance man *n* hombre del Renacimiento, *m*

Renaissance woman *n* mujer del Renacimiento, *f*

renal *a* renal

rename *vt* poner otro nombre (a)

renascent *a* renaciente, que renace

rend *vt* desgarrar, rasgar; *fig* lacerar; (split) hender; *fig* dividir. **to r. from,** arrancar (a). **to r. the air,** (with cries, etc.) llenar el aire

render *vt* (return) devolver; dar; rendir; (make) hacer; (help, service) prestar; interpretar; (translate) traducir; (fat) derretir y clarificar

rendering *n* versión, *f*; interpretación, *f*

rendezvous *n* cita, *f*; lugar de cita, *m*; reunión, *f*. *vi* reunirse

rending *n* desgarro, *m*; hendimiento, *m*

renegade *a* renegado. *n* renegado (-da)

renew *vt* renovar; (resume) reanudar; (a lease, etc.) prorrogar

renewable *a* renovable

renewal *n* renovación, *f*; (resumption) reanudación, *f*; (of a lease, etc.) prorrogación, *f*

renewed *a* renovado; nuevo

rennet *n* cuajo, *m*

renounce *vt* renunciar; (a throne) abdicar; renegar (de), repudiar; abandonar. *vi law* desistir; (cards) renunciar

renouncement *n* renuncia, *f*; (of a throne) abdicación, *f*; repudiación, *f*

renovate *vt* renovar; limpiar; restaurar

renovation *n* renovación, *f*; limpiadura, *f*; restauración, *f*

renovator *n* renovador (-ra)

renown *n* renombre, *m*, fama, *f*

renowned *a* renombrado, famoso

rent *n* (tear) rasgadura, *f*; desgarro, *m*; abertura, *f*; raja hendedura, *f*; (discord) división, *f*; (hire) alquiler, *m*; arrendamiento, *m*. *vt* arrendar, alquilar. **r.-free,** sin pagar alquiler

rentable *a* alquilable, arrendable

rental. See **rent**

renter *n* arrendador (-ra)

rentier *n* rentista, *mf*

renting *n* alquiler, arrendamiento, *m*

renumber *vt* numerar de nuevo

renunciation *n* renunciación, renuncia, *f*

reoccupy *vt* volver a ocupar, ocupar otra vez

reopen *vt* abrir de nuevo, volver a abrir. *vi* abrirse nuevamente, abrirse otra vez

reopening *n* reapertura, *f*

reorder *vt* ordenar de nuevo, *com* volver a pedir. *n com* nuevo pedido, *m*

reorganization *n* reorganización, *f*

reorganize *vt* reorganizar

reorganizing *a* reorganizador

repack *vt* reembalar; reenvasar; volver a hacer (una maleta)

repaint *vt* pintar de nuevo

repainting *n* nueva pintura, *f*

repair *vt* arreglar (e.g. a machine) componer, remendar; reparar; restaurar; rehacer. *vi* (with to) dirigirse a, ir a; acudir a. *n* arreglo *m*, reparación, *f*; compostura, *f*; restauración, *f*. **to keep in r.,** conservar en buen estado

repairable *a* que se puede componer

repairer *n* componedor (-ra); restaurador (-ra)

repairing *a* reparador

reparable *a* reparable; remediable

reparation *n* reparación, *f*

repartee *n* respuestas, agudezas, *f pl*; *inf* dimes y diretes, *m pl*

repast *n* comida, *f*; (light) colación, *f*

repatriate *vt* repatriar

repatriation *n* repatriación, *f*

repay *vt* reembolsar; recompensar, pagar; pagar en la misma moneda. *vi* pagar. **It well repays a visit,** Vale la pena de visitarse

repayable *a* reembolsable

repayment *n* reembolso, *m*; pago, retorno, *m*

repeal *n* abrogación, revocación, *f*, *vt* abrogar, rescindir, revocar

repeat *vt* repetir; reiterar; (renew) renovar; duplicar. *n* repetición, *f*

repeated *a* reiterado; redoblado

repeatedly *adv* reiteradamente, repetidamente

repeater *n* repetidor (-ra); reloj de repetición, *m*; arma de repetición, *f*

repel *vt* repeler; ahuyentar; (spurn) rechazar; *phys* resistir; repugnar

repellent *a* repulsivo

repent *vt* arrepentirse de. *vi* arrepentirse

repentance *n* arrepentimiento, *m*, penitencia, *f*

repentant *a* arrepentido, penitente, contrito

repentantly *adv* arrepentidamente, con contrición

repeople *vt* repoblar

repeopling *n* repoblación, *f*

repercuss *vt* repercutir (en)

repercussion *n* repercusión, *f*

repercussive *a* repercusivo

repertory *n* repertorio, *m*

repetition *n* repetición, *f*; recitación, *f*

repetitive *a* iterativo

repine *vi* afligirse (de); quejarse (de); padecer nostalgia

repining *n* pesares, *m pl*; quejas, *f pl*, descontento, *m*; nostalgia, *f*

replace *vt* (put back) reponer, colocar de nuevo; restituir, devolver; (renew) renovar; (in a post, etc.) reemplazar, substituir

replaceable *a* restituible; renovable; reemplazable

replacement *n* reposición, *f*; restitución, devolución, *f*; renovación, *f*; reemplazo, *m*

replant *vt* replantar

replanting *n* replantación, *f*

replenish *vt* rellenar

replenishment *n* relleno, *m*

replete *a* repleto

repletion *n* repleción, *f*

replica *n* réplica, *f*

reply *n* respuesta, contestación, *f*, *vi* responder, contestar. **Awaiting your r.,** En espera de sus noticias. **in his r.,** en su respuesta

repolish *vt* repulir

repopulate *vt* repoblar

repopulation *n* repoblación, *f*

report *n* (rumor) voz, *f*, rumor, *m*; (reputation) fama, *f*; (news) noticia, *f*; (journalistic) reportaje, *m*; (*mil nav* and from school) parte, *f*; (weather) boletín, *m*; (proceedings) actas, *f pl*; (statement) informe, *m*; relación, *f*; (of a gun, etc.) detonación, *f*; explosión, *f*. *vt* dar cuenta de, relatar; informar; (measure) registrar; (*mil nav*) dar parte de; comunicar; (journalistic) hacer un reportaje de; (transcribe) transcribir; (accuse) denunciar; quejarse de. *vi* presentar informe; ser reportero; (present oneself) presentarse, comparecer. **It is reported that . . . ,** Se informa que . . .

report card *n* boletín de calificaciones, *m*

reporter *n* reportero (-ra); *law* relator, *m*

reporting *n* reporterismo, *m*

repose *n* reposo, *m*; quietud, *f*; tranquilidad, serenidad, *f*. *vt* reposar, descansar; reclinar; (place) poner. *vi* reposar; tener confianza (en); basarse (en)

repository *n* repositorio, depósito, *m*; almacén, *m*; (furniture) guardamuebles, *m*; (person) depositario (-ia)

repoussé (work) *n* repujado, *m*. **to work in r.,** repujar

reprehend *vt* reprender, reprobar
reprehensible *a* reprensible
reprehension *n* reprensión, *f*
represent *vt* representar; significar
representation *n* representación, *f*
representational *a art* realista
representative *a* que representa; representativo. *n* representante, *mf*
repress *vt* reprimir
repression *n* represión, *f*
repressive *a* represivo
reprieve *vt law* aplazar la ejecución (de); *fig* dar una tregua (a)
reprimand *n* reprimenda, *f, vt* reprender
reprint *n* reimpresión, tirada aparte, separata, *f, vt* reimprimir
reprinting *n* reimpresión, *f*
reprisal *n* represalia, *f.* **to take reprisals,** tomar represalias
reproach *n* reproche, *m*; censura, *f*; (shame) vergüenza, *f. vt* reprochar; censurar, echar en cara, afear
reproachful *a* severo; lleno de reproches; de censura; (shameful) vergonzoso
reproachfully *adv* con reprobación, con reprensión, severamente
reproachfulness *n* severidad, *f.* **the r. of my gaze,** mi mirada llena de reproches
reprobate *n* réprobo (-ba)
reproduce *vt* reproducir. *vi* reproducirse
reproducible *a* reproductible
reproduction *n* reproducción, *f*
reproductive *a* reproductor; de reproducción
reproof *n* reconvención, *f*
reprove *vt* censurar, culpar; reprender
reprovingly. See **rebukingly**
reptile *a* and *n* reptil, *m*
republic *n* república, *f.* **the r. of letters,** la república de las letras
republican *a* and *n* republicano (-na)
republicanism *n* republicanismo, *m*
republish *vt* publicar de nuevo; volver a editar
repudiate *vt* repudiar; negar, rechazar
repudiation *n* repudiación, *f*
repugnance *n* repugnacia, *f*
repugnant *a* repugnante; contrario; opuesto. **to be r. to,** repugnar (a)
repulse *vt* repulsar, repeler; rebatir, refutar; (refuse) rechazar, *n* repulsa, *f*; refutación, *f*; rechazo, *m*
repulsion *n phys* repulsión, *f*; repugnancia, aversión, *f*
repulsive *a* repulsivo, repugnante, repelente
repulsiveness *n* carácter repulsivo, *m*; aspecto repugnante, *m*
reputable *a* honrado, respetable, formal
reputation *n* reputación, *f*; fama, *f*, renombre, *m.* **to have the r. of,** ser reputado como, pasar por
reputed *a* supuesto; putativo
reputedly *adv* según la opinión común, según dice la gente
request *n* ruego, *m*, petición, *f*; instancia, *f*; solicitud, *f*; *com* demanda, *f. vt* pedir, rogar; suplicar; solicitar. **in r.,** en boga; solicitado; en demanda, **on r.,** a solicitud. **r. stop,** (for buses) parada discrecional, *f*
requiem *n* réquiem, *m.* **r. mass,** misa de difuntos, *f*
require *vt* exigir, requerir; necesitar; (wish) desear; invitar. *vi* ser necesario
required *a* necesario; obligatorio
requirement *n* deseo, *m*; requisito, *m*; formalidad, *f*; estipulación, *f*; necesidad, *f*
requisite *n* requisito, *m. a* necesario, requisito, preciso. **to be r.,** ser necesario, ser menester hacer falta
requisition *vt mil* requisar
requisitioning *n* requisa, *f*
requital *n* recompensa, *f*; compensación, satisfacción, *f*
requite *vt* pagar, recompensar; (affection) corresponder a
reread *vt* releer

reredos *n* retablo, *m*
resale *n* reventa, *f*
rescind *vt* rescindir
rescission *n* rescisión, *f*
rescue *vt* salvar; librar; *mil* rescatar. *n* socorro, *m*; salvamento, *m*; *mil* rescate, *m.* **to go to the r. of,** ir al socorro de. **r. party,** expedición de salvamento, *f*; *mil* expedición de rescate, *f*
rescuer *n* salvador (-ra)
reseal *vt* resellar
research *n* investigación, *f, vt* investigar
researcher *n* investigador (-ra)
reseda *n bot* reseda, *f*
resell *vt* revender
resemblance *n* parecido, *m*, semejanza, *f.* **The two sisters bear a strong r. to each other,** Las dos hermanas se parecen mucho
resemble *vt* parecerse (a). **Mary doesn't r. her mother,** María no se parece a su madre
resent *vt* resentirse de; ofenderse por, indignarse por; tomar a mal
resentful *a* resentido; ofendido, indignado, agraviado; vengativo
resentfully *adv* con resentimiento; con indignación
resentment *n* resentimiento, *m*
reservation *n* reservación, *f*; reserva, *f*; territorio reservado, *m*; santuario, *m.* **mental r.,** reserva mental, *f*
reserve *n* reserva, *f. vt* reservar. *a* de reserva. **without r.,** sin reserva
reserved *a* reservado; callado, taciturno. **r. compartment,** reservado, *m.* **r. list,** (*mil nav*) sección de reserva, *f*
reservedly *adv* con reserva
reservist *n* reservista, *mf*
reservoir *n* depósito, *m*; cisterna, *f*, aljibe, tanque, *m*
reset *vt* montar de nuevo
resettle *vt* repoblar; rehabilitar; (a dispute) llegar a un nuevo acuerdo sobre
resettlement *n* repoblación, *f*; rehabilitación, *f*; (of a dispute) nuevo acuerdo, *m*
reshape *vt* reformar
reship *vt* reembarcar
reshipment *n* reembarque, *m*
reshuffle *vt* volver a barajar; *fig* cambiar
reside *vi* residir, habitar; vivir
residence *n* residencia, *f*; permanencia, estada, *f*; domicilio, *m*
resident *a* residente; (of a servant) que duerme en casa; interno. *n* residente, *mf*; (diplomacy) residente, *m.* **r. of the capital** *Lat. Am.* capitalino (-na) *mf.* **r. of Rio de Janeiro** carioca, *mf*
residential *a* residencial
residue *n* resto, *m*; (*law, chem*) residuo, *m*
residuum *n* residuo, *m.*
resign *vt* renunciar (a); ceder; resignar. *vi* dimitir. **to r. oneself,** resignarse
resignation *n* resignación, *f*; (from a post) dimisión, *f.* **to send in one's r.,** dimitir
resigned *a* resignado
resignedly *adv* con resignación
resilience *n* elasticidad, *f*
resilient *a* elástico
resin *n* resina, *f, Central America, Mexico* copal, *m*; (solid, for violin bows, etc.) colofonia, *f*
resinous *a* resinoso
resist *vt* and *vi* (bear) aguantar; (impede) impedir; (repel, ward off) resistir; rechazar; hacer frente (a); oponerse (a); negarse (a)
resistance *n* resistencia, *f*; aguante, *m*, tenacidad, *f*; oposición, *f*; repugnancia, *f.* **passive r.,** resistencia pasiva, *f.* **r. coil,** *elec* resistencia, *f.* **r. movement,** movimiento de resistencia, *m*
resistant *a* resistente
resister *n* el, *m*, (*f*, la) que resiste
resole *vt* remontar
resolute *a* resuelto, decidido

resolutely *adv* resueltamente

resolution *n* resolución, *f*; (proposal placed before a legislative body, etc.) proposición, *f*; propósito, *m*

resolve *vt* resolver; desarrollar, deshacer (an abbreviation, acronym, or initialism). *vi* resolverse. *n* propósito, *m*; (of character) resolución, firmeza, *f*

resonance *n* resonancia, *f*; sonoridad, *f*

resonant *a* resonante; reverberante, sonoro

resort *n* recurso, *m*; punto de reunión. *m*; (frequentation) frecuentación, *f*; (gathering) concurrencia, *f*; reunión, *f*. *vi* acudir (a), acogerse (a); hacer uso (de); pasar (a); (frequent) frecuentar, concurrir. **health r.,** balneario, *m*. **holiday r.,** playa de verano, *f*; pueblo de veraneo, *m*. **in the last r.,** en último recurso

resound *vi* resonar, retumbar, retronar; *fig* tener fama, ser celebrado. *vt* hacer reverberar; *fig* celebrar

resounding *a* retumbante, resonante

resource *n* recurso, *m*; (of character) inventiva, *f*; *pl* **resources**; recursos, fondos, *m pl*

resourceful *a* ingenioso

resourcefulness *n* ingeniosidad, *f*

respect *n* respeto, *m*; consideración, *f*; (reference, regard) respecto, *m*; *pl* **respects**, (greetings) saludos, *m pl*; homenaje, *m*. *vt* respetar; honrar; (concern, regard) concernir, tocar (a). **in other respects,** por lo demás. **in r. of,** tocante a, respecto a. **in some respects,** desde algunos puntos de vista. **out of r. for,** por consideración a

respectability *n* respetabilidad, *f*

respectable *a* respetable; pasable; considerable

respectably *adv* respetablemente

respected *a* and *part* respetado; apreciado, estimado; digno de respeto, honrado

respectful *a* respetuoso

respectfully *adv* respetuosamente

respectfulness *n* aire respetuoso, *m*; conducta respetuosa, *f*

respecting *prep* con respecto a, en cuanto a, tocante a; a propósito de

respective *a* respectivo; relativo

respectively *adv* respectivamente

respiration *n* respiración, *f*

respirator *n* respirador, *m*

respiratory *a* respiratorio

respire *vt* and *vi* respirar; exhalar; descansar

respite *n* tregua, pausa, *f*; respiro, *m*; *law* espera, *f*. *vt* dar tregua (a); (postpone) aplazar; (relieve) aliviar

resplendence *n* resplandor, *m*, refulgencia, *f*, esplendor, fulgor, *m*

resplendent *a* resplandeciente, refulgente, relumbrante. **He was r. in a new uniform,** Lucía (or Ostentaba) un nuevo uniforme. **to be r.,** ser resplandeciente; relumbrar, refulgir

resplendently *adv* esplendorosamente

respond *vi* responder; contestar; (obey) obedecer; reaccionar

respondent *n* (in a suit) demandado (-da)

response *n* respuesta, *f*; *ecc* responso, *m*

responsibility *n* responsabilidad, *f*

responsible *a* responsable

responsive *a* simpático; sensible, sensitivo

responsiveness *n* simpatía, *f*; sensibilidad, *f*

rest *n* descanso, *m*; reposo, *m*; (the grave) última morada, *f*; tranquilidad, paz, *f*; inacción, *f*; (prop) soporte, apoyo, *m*; base, *f*; (for a lance) ristre, *m*; (for a rifle) apoyo, *m*; *mus* silencio, *m*, pausa, *f*; (in verse) cesura, *f*. **t. in r.,** en ristre. **the r.,** el resto; los demás, los otros. **to set at r.,** calmar, tranquilizar; (remove) quitar. **r.-cure,** cura de reposo, *f*. **r.-house,** hospedería, *f*; refugio, *m*. **r.-room, lounge,** sala de descanso, *f*; (toilet) excusado, retrete, *m*; (in theaters) saloncillo, *m*

rest *vi* reposar, descansar; (lie down) acostarse, echarse; (stop) cesar, parar; estar en paz; apoyarse (en); descansar (sobre); posar; depender (de); (remain) quedar. *vt* descansar; dar un descanso (a); (lean) apoyar; basar (en). **It rests with them,** Depende de ellos. **These**

valuable documents now rest in the Library of Congress, Estos valiosos documentos han parado en la Biblioteca del Congreso. **May he r. in peace!** ¡Que en paz descanse! **to r. assured,** estar seguro. **to r. on one's oars,** cesar de remar; descansar

restate *vt* repetir, afirmar de nuevo

restatement *n* repetición, *f*

restaurant *n* restaurante, restorán, *m*. **r.-car,** coche-comedor, *m*

restful *a* descansado; tranquilo, sosegado

resting *n* reposo, *m*. **last r.-place,** última morada, *f*. **r.-place,** descansadero, *m*; refugio, *m*

restitution *n* restitución, *f*

restive *a* (of a horse) repropio, ingobernable; inquieto, agitado; impaciente

restiveness *n* inquietud, agitación, *f*; impaciencia, *f*

restless *a* agitado; inquieto, intranquilo; turbulento; sin reposo; (wakeful) desvelado; (ceaseless) incesante. **r. night,** noche desvelada, noche intranquila, *inf* noche toledana, *f*

restlessly *adv* agitadamente; con inquietud; turbulentamente; incesantemente

restlessness *n* agitación, *f*; inquietud, intranquilidad, *f*; turbulencia, *f*; falta de reposo, *f*; (wakefulness) desvelo, *m*; movimiento incesante, *m*

restock *vt* (with goods) surtir de nuevo; proveer de nuevo; restablecer; repoblar

restoration *n* restauración, *f*; renovación, *f*; restablecimiento, *m*; (returning) restitución, *f*

restorative *a* and *n* restaurativo *m*

restore *vt* restaurar; restituir; devolver; restablecer; reponer; (repair) reformar, reparar; reconstruir; (to former rank, etc.) rehabilitar. **He restored the book to its place,** Devolvió el libro a su sitio

restorer *n* restaurador (-ra)

restrain *vt* refrenar; reprimir; (restrict) limitar, restringir; (prevent) impedir; desviar; (detain) recluir. **to r. oneself,** contenerse

restrained *a* moderado, mesurado; sobrio; (of emotion) contenido

restraining *a* restrictivo; moderador, calmante

restraint *n* freno, *m*; restricción, *f*; limitación, *f*; prohibición, *f*; compulsión, *f*; (reserve) reserva, *f*; moderación, *f*

restrict *vt* restringir; limitar

restriction *n* restricción, *f*; limitación, *f*

restrictive *a* restrictivo

result *n* resultado, *m*; consecuencia, resulta, *f*; solución, *f*. *vi* resultar. **as the r. of,** de resultas de

resultant *a* resultante; consecuente. *n* resultado, *m*; *mech* resultante, *f*

resume *vt* reasumir; (continue) reanudar, continuar; (summarize) resumir

résumé *n* resumen, *m*, recapitulación, *f*

resummon *vt* convocar de nuevo (a); citar de nuevo (a)

resumption *n* (renewal) reanudación, *f*; reasunción, *f*

resurgence *n* resurgimiento, *m*

resurrect *vt* *inf* desenterrar; resucitar

resurrection *n* resurrección, *f*

resuscitate *vt* and *vi* resucitar

resuscitation *n* resurrección, *f*; renovación, *f*; renacimiento, *m*

retail *n* venta al por menor, reventa, *f*. *adv* al por menor. *vt* (goods) vender al por menor, revender; (tell) contar; repetir. **r. trade,** comercio al por menor, *m*

retailer *n* vendedor (-ra) al por menor; (of a story) narrador (-ra); el, *m*, (*f*, la) que cuenta algo

retain *vt* retener; guardar; conservar; (a barrister) ajustar; (hire) contratar

retainer *n* (dependent) criado, dependiente, *m*; partidario, adherente, *m*; (fee) honorario, *m*; *pl* **retainers,** séquito, *m*; adherentes, *m pl*, gente, *f*

retaining wall *n* muro de contención, *m*

retake *vt* volver a tomar; reconquistar

retaking *n* reconquista, *f*

retaliate *vt* vengarse de, desquitarse de. *vi* vengarse, tomar represalias

retaliation *n* represalias, *f pl*; desquite, *m*, satisfacción, *f*. **law of r.,** talión, *m*,

retaliatory *a* de represalias; de desquite

retard *vt* retardar

retch *vi* tener náuseas, procurar vomitar

retching *n* náusea, basca, *f*

retell *vt* repetir, volver a contar

retention *n* retención, *f*; conservación, *f*

retentive *a* retentivo

retentiveness *n* poder de retención, *m*; (memory) retentiva, *f*

reticence *n* reticencia, reserva, *f*

reticent *a* reservado, inexpresivo, taciturno

retina *n* retina, *f*

retinue *n* séquito, acompañamiento, *m*, comitiva, *f*

retire *vi* retirarse; (to bed) recogerse, acostarse; (from a post) jubilarse. *vt* retirar; jubilar. **to r. from a post,** *mil* rendir el puesto

retired *a* retirado; (remote) apartado, aislado; (hidden) escondido; (former) antiguo; (from employment, etc.) jubilado; (of an officer) retirado. **to place on the r. list,** jubilar; (*mil nav*) dar el retiro (a)

retirement *n* retirada, *f*; (solitude) apartamiento, aislamiento, *m*; retiro, *m*; (superannuation) jubilación, *f*

retiring *a* que se retira; (from a post) dimitente; (with pension, etc.) de jubilación; (reserved) reservado; modesto

retort *vi* replicar. *vt* retorcer; devolver (una acusación, etc.). *n* réplica, *f*; contestación, *f*; *chem* retorta, *f*

retouch *vt* retocar

retrace *vt* volver a trazar; volver a andar (un camino); (one's steps) volver sobre sus pasos, volver atrás; (in memory) rememorar, recordar; buscar el origen (de); (recount) narrar, contar

retract *vt* retractar, retirar; (draw back) retraer. *vi* retractarse

retraction *n* retracción, *f*

retranslate *vt* hacer una nueva traducción (de)

retransmission *n* retransmisión, *f*

retread *vt* pisar de nuevo; (tires) recauchetear

retreat *n* retirada, *f*; (*mil* signal) retreta, *f*; (refuge and *ecc*) retiro, *m*. *vi* retirarse; retroceder; refugiarse

retreat house *n* casa de ejercicios, *f*

retreating *a* que se retira; que retrocede; *mil* que se bate en retirada

retrench *vt* reducir; disminuir; *vi* economizar, hacer economías

retrenchment *n* disminución, reducción, *f*; economías, *f pl*

retrial *n* (of a person) nuevo proceso, *m*; (of a case) revisión, *f*

retribution *n* retribución, *f*; justo castigo, *m*, pena merecida, *f*

retrievable *a* recuperable, que puede recobrarse; reparable

retrieval *n* recuperación, *f*; reparación, *f*; (of game) cobra, *f*; (of one's character) rehabilitación, *f*

retrieve *vt* (game, of dogs) cobrar; (regain) recobrar, recuperar; restaurar; reparar; restablecer; (one's character) rehabilitar. *vi* cobrar la caza

retriever *n* (dog) perdiguero (-ra)

retroactive *a* retroactivo

retrocede *vi* retroceder

retrograde *a* retrógrado

retrogression *n* retrogradación, regresión, *f*; *med* retroceso, *m*

retrogressive *a* retrógrado

retrospect *n* mirada retrospectiva, *f*, examen del pasado, *m*. **in r.,** retrospectivamente

retrospection *n* retrospección, *f*

retrospective *a* retrospectivo

retrospectively *adv* retrospectivamente

retry *vt* (a case) rever; (a person) procesar de nuevo

return *vi* regresar, *Lat. Am.* devolverse; volver; reapa-

recer; presentarse de nuevo; *law* revertir; (answer) contestar, responder. *vt* (give back or put back) devolver; (a ball) restar; (a kindness, visit) pagar; restituir; (reciprocate) corresponder (a); recompensar; contestar (a); dar; rendir; (yield) producir; (a verdict) fallar, pronunciar; (report) dar parte de; anunciar; (exchange) cambiar; (elect) elegir. *n* regreso, *m*; vuelta, *f*; (giving or putting back) devolución, *f*; pago, *m*; restitución, *f*; correspondencia, *f*; recompensa, *f*; (reply) respuesta, *f*; (reappearance) reaparición, *f*; reinstalación, *f*; repetición, *f*; (gain) ganancia, *f*, provecho, *m*; rendimiento, *m*; (exchange) cambio, *m*; (report) parte oficial, *f*; informe, *m*; lista, *f*; (election) elección, *f*; *pl* **returns,** tablas estadísticas, *f pl*; (of an election) resultados, *m pl*. **Many happy returns!** ¡Feliz cumpleaños! **by return mail,** a vuelta de correo. **on my (his, etc.) r.,** a la vuelta, cuando vuelva. **to r. like for like,** pagar en la misma moneda. **r. journey, r. trip,** viaje de vuelta, *m*. **r. match,** partido de vuelta, *m*. **r. ticket,** billete de ida y vuelta, *m*; billete de vuelta, *m*

returnable *a* restituible; susceptible a ser devuelto; (on approval) a prueba; *law* devolutivo

returning *a* que vuelve. *n* See **return**

"Return to Sender" «Al remitente»

reunion *n* reunión, *f*

reunite *vt* reunir. *vi* reunirse

revaccinate *vt* revacunar

revaccination *n* revacunación, *f*

reveal *vt* revelar; descubrir

revealer *n* revelador (-ra)

revealing *a* revelador. *n* revelación, *f*; descubrimiento, *m*

reveille *n* *mil* diana, *f*

revel *vi* divertirse; regocijarse (en); gozarse (en); entregarse (a); (carouse) ir de parranda; emborracharse. *n* algazara, jarana, *f*; *pl* **revels,** fiestas, festividades, *f pl*

revelation *n* revelación, *f*; descubrimiento, *m*; (in the Bible) Apocalipsis, *m*

reveler *n* convidado alegre, *m*; (at night) trasnochador (-ra); (drunk) borracho (-cha); (masked) máscara, *mf*

revelry *n* festividades, *f pl*, regocijo, *m*; orgías, *f pl*, *Central America* embullo, *m*

revenge *n* venganza, *f*. *vt* vengarse de; desquitarse de

revengeful *a* vengativo

revengefully *adv* vengativamente

revengefulness *n* deseo de venganza, *m*; carácter vengativo, *m*

revenger *n* vengador (-ra)

revenue *n* rentas públicas, *f pl*; (treasury) fisco, *m*; *com* rédito, *m*, ingresos, *m pl*; beneficio, *m*. **Inland R.,** delegación de contribuciones, *f*. **r. officer,** agente fiscal, *m*

reverberate *vt* and *vi* (of sound) retumbar, resonar; (of light, etc.) reverberar

reverberation *n* (reflection) reverberación, *f*; (of sound) retumbo, eco, *m*

revere *vt* reverenciar, venerar, honrar

reverence *n* reverencia, *f*, *vt* reverenciar

reverend *a* reverendo

reverent *a* reverente

reverie *n* ensueño, *m*

reversal *n* inversión, *f*; (of a verdict) revocación, *f*

reverse *vt* invertir; (a steam engine) dar contra vapor (a); (a vehicle) poner en marcha atrás; (arms) llevar a la funerala; (a judgment, etc.) revocar, derogar. *vi* (dancing) dar vueltas al revés. *n* lo contrario, lo opuesto; (back) dorso, revés, *m*; (change) cambio, *m*; (check) revés, *m*, vicisitud, *f*; (loss) pérdida, *f*; (defeat) derrota, *f*; *mech* marcha atrás, *f*, *a* inverso; contrario, opuesto. **quite the r.,** todo el contrario. **r. turn,** (of an engine) cambio de dirección, *m*; (in dancing) vuelta al revés, *f*

reversible *a* reversible

reversion *n* reversión, *f*; *biol* atavismo, *m*; (of offices) futura, *f*; (of property) reversión, *f*

revert *vi law* revertir; volver (a)

review *n* examen, análisis, *m*; juicio crítico, *m*; (journal and *mil*) revista, *f*; (criticism) revista, reseña, *f*; *law* revisión, *f*. *vt* examinar, analizar; (*mil* etc.) pasar revista (a); revisar; repasar; (a book, etc.) reseñar; *law* revisar. *vi* escribir revistas

review article *n* artículo de reseña, *m*

reviewer *n* revistero (-ra), crítico, *m*

revile *vt* injuriar, maldecir, difamar

reviler *n* maldiciente, *m*, insultador (-ra)

reviling *n* insultos, *m pl*, injurias, *f pl*

revisal *n* revisión, *f*

revise *vt* revisar; repasar; corregir; (change) cambiar

reviser *n* revisor, *m*; corrector de pruebas, *m*

revision *n* revisión, *f*; repaso, *m*; corrección de pruebas, *f*

revisit *vt* volver a visitar, visitar de nuevo

revival *n* resurgimiento, *m*; renovación, *f*; (awakening) despertamiento, *m*; restablecimiento, *m*; resurrección, *f*; (of learning) renacimiento, *m*; *theat* reposición, *f*; (religious) despertar religioso, *m*

revive *vi* reponerse; restablecerse; resucitar; renovarse; renacer; cobrar fuerzas; (recover consciousness) volver en sí. *vt* hacer revivir; resucitar; restablecer; renovar; restaurar; despertar; (fire, colours) avivar

reviver *n* resucitador (-ra)

revivification *n* revivificación, *f*

revivify *vt* revivificar

revocable *a* revocable

revocation *n* revocación, *f*

revoke *vt* revocar, anular, derogar; (wills) quebrantar. *vi* revocar, anular; (at cards) renunciar. *n* (cards) renuncio, *m*

revolt *n* rebelión, *f*, *vi* rebelarse, sublevarse. *vt* repugnar, indignar, dar asco (a)

revolting *a* repugnante, asqueroso; (rebellious) rebelde

revolution *n* revolución, *f*; (turn) vuelta, *f*, giro, *m*

revolutionary *a* and *n* revolucionario (-ia)

revolutionize *vt* revolucionar

revolve *vi* dar vueltas, girar; suceder periódicamente. *vt* hacer girar; (ponder) revolver, discurrir

revolver *n* revólver, *m*

revolving *a* giratorio; que vuelve; periódico. **r. chair,** silla giratoria, *f*. **r. door,** puerta giratoria, *f*. **r. stage,** escenario giratorio, *m*

revue *n theat* revista, *f*

revulsion *n* revulsión, *f*

revulsive *a med* revulsivo

rev up *vt* (an engine) calentar

reward *n* recompensa, *f*; retribución, *f*. *vt* recompensar; satisfacer, premiar

rewarding *a* premiador; que recompensa. *n* recompensación, *f*. **a rewarding experience,** una experiencia compensadora, *f*

rewrite *vt* escribir de nuevo; volver a escribir; redactar otra vez

rhapsody *n* rapsodia, *f*

rheostat *n* reóstato, *m*

rhetoric *n* retórica, *f*

rhetorical *a* retórico; declamatorio

rhetorician *n* retórico (-ca)

rheumatic *a* reumático. **r. fever,** reumatismo poliarticular agudo, *m*

rheumatism *n* reumatismo, reuma, *m*

rheumy *a* catarroso; (of the eyes) legañoso

Rhine, the el Rin, *m*

rhinestone *n* circón, *m*

rhinoceros *n* rinoceronte, *m*

Rhodes Rodas, *f*

rhododendron *n* rododendro, *m*

rhubarb *n* ruibarbo, *m*

rhyme *n* rima, *f*; verso, *m*. *vi* and *vt* rimar. **without r. or reason,** sin ton ni son; a tontas y a locas

rhymer *n* rimador (-ra)

rhyming *a* rimador

rhythm *n* ritmo, *m*

rhythmic *a* rítmico

rib *n* (*anat, bot, aer, naut, arch*) costilla, *f*; (of an umbrella or fan) varilla, *f*; (in cloth) cordoncillo, *m*, lista, *f*

ribald *a* escabroso, ribaldo, indecente

ribaldry *n* ribaldería, escabrosidad, indecencia, *f*

ribbed *a* con costillas; (of cloth) listado, con listas

ribbon *n* cinta, *f*; tira, *f*; (tatter) jirón, *m*. **to tear to ribbons,** hacer jirones

rice *n* arroz, *m*. *a* de arroz; con arroz. **r. field,** arrozal, *m*. **r.-paper,** papel de paja de arroz, *m*. **r.-pudding,** arroz con leche, *m*

rich *a* rico; opulento; (happy) dichoso; (of land, etc.) fértil; abundante; (of objects) magnífico, suntuoso, hermoso; precioso; (of food) exquisito; suculento; (highly seasoned) muy sazonado; (creamy) con mucha nata; (of colours) brillante, vivo. **new r.,** ricacho (-cha). **newly-r.,** advenedizo. **to grow r.,** enriquecerse, *Lat. Am. also* fondearse

riches *n* riqueza, *f*

richly *adv* ricamente; abundantemente; magníficamente; bien

richness *n* riqueza, *f*; opulencia, *f*; (of land, etc.) fertilidad, *f*; abundancia, *f*; (of objects) magnificencia, suntuosidad, hermosura, *f*; preciosidad, *f*; (of food) gusto exquisito, *m*; suculencia, *f*; (piquancy) gusto picante, *m*; (of colours) viveza, *f*

rickets *n* raquitismo, *m*

rickety *a med* raquítico; destartalado, desvencijado; (unsteady) tambaleante; cojo

rickshaw *n* riksha, *m*

ricochet *n* rebote, *m*, *vi* rebotar

rid *vt* librar (de). **to get rid of,** librarse de; quitarse de encima (a); perder, quitarse; (dismiss) despedir. **to rid oneself of,** librarse de, deshacerse de

riddance *n* libramiento, *m*

riddle *n* acertijo, *m*; enigma, problema, *m*; misterio, *m*; (sieve) tamiz de alambre, *m*; *vt* (guess) adivinar; (sift) cribar; (with holes) acribillar

ride *vi* (a horse) montar a caballo, cabalgar; pasear a caballo; (a mule, a bicycle) montar en, pasear en; (a vehicle, train) ir en; (a carriage, car) andar en, pasear en; (float) flotar; (on the wind) dejarse llevar por el viento; ser llevado por el viento; (go) ir; (come) venir; (a distance) hacer . . . a caballo, en coche, etc.; *naut* estar al ancla; *mech* tener juego. *vt* (a horse, mule, bicycle) montar; ir montado sobre; manejar; (a race) hacer; (float) flotar en; (cleave, the sea, etc.) surcar. *n* paseo (a caballo, en bicicleta, en coche, etc.), *m*; viaje (en un autobús, de tren, etc.), *m*; (bridle path) camino de herradura, *m*; cabalgata, *f*, desfile a caballo, *m*; (hitch, lift) *Mexico* aventón, *m*. **a r. on horseback,** un paseo a caballo. **They gave me a r. in their car,** (e.g. to see the sights) Me llevaron a paseo en su auto, (a lift to a certain place) Me dieron un aventón. **ride at anchor,** estar fondeado. **to r. a bicycle,** montar en bicicleta. **to r. rough-shod over,** mandar a la baqueta (a), mandar a puntapiés (a). **to r. sidesaddle,** cabalgar a mujeriegas. **to r. at,** embestir con. **to r. away,** marcharse, alejarse; marcharse a caballo, etc. **to r. back,** volver; volver a caballo, en bicicleta, etc. **to r. behind,** seguir a caballo; ir inmediatamente detrás (de); (on the back seat) ocupar el asiento de atrás; (on the same animal) cabalgar en la grupa. **to r. down,** atropellar; (trample) pisotear, pasar por encima de. **to r. on,** seguir su camino. **to r. out,** salir a paseo en caballo, etc.; irse a paseo en coche, etc.; (a storm) hacer frente a, luchar con. **to r. over,** pasar por encima de; recorrer. **to r. up,** *vi* llegar, acercarse; (of a tie, etc.) subir. *vt* montar

rider *n* cabalgador (-ra); jinete, *m*; persona que va en coche, etc., *f*; (on a bicycle) ciclista, *mf*; (on a motorcycle) motociclista, *mf*; (horsebreaker) domador de caballos, *m*; (clause) añadidura, *f*; corolario, *m*

ridge *n* cumbre, cima, *f*; (of mountains) cordillera, sierra, *f*; (of a roof, of a nose) caballete, *m*; *agr* lomo, caballón, *m*; (wrinkle) arruga, *f*; (on coins) cordoncillo, *m*. *vt* surcar; formar lomos (en); (wrinkle) arrugar

ridicule *n* ridículo, *m, vt* poner en ridículo, ridiculizar, burlarse (de), mofarse (de)

ridiculous *a* ridículo, absurdo

riding *a* cabalgante; que va a caballo; montado (a, en, sobre); *naut* al ancla; (in compounds) de equitación; de montar. *n* equitación, *f*; paseo a caballo; en bicicleta, etc., *m*; acción de ir a caballo, etc., *f*; (district) comarca, *f*. **r.-boots,** botas de montar, *f pl*. **r.-habit,** traje de montar, *m*; (woman's) amazona, *f*. **r.-master,** profesor de equitación, *m*. **r.-saddle,** silla de montar, *f*. **r.-school,** escuela de equitación, *f*

rife *a* común; corriente; frecuente; prevalente; abundante; general. **r. with,** abundante en; lleno de

riffraff *n* desperdicios, *m pl*; (rabble) gentuza, canalla, *f*

rifle *n* rifle, fusil rayado, *m. vt* robar; (a suitcase, etc.) desvalijar; (a gun) rayar. **r.-case,** *Mexico* carcaj, *m*. **r.-range,** campo de tiro, *m*. **r.-sling,** portafusil, *m*. **r.-shot,** fusilazo, *m*

rifleman *n* fusilero, *m*

rifler *n* saqueador (-ra)

rifling *n* (robbing) saqueo, robo, *m*; (of a suitcase, etc.) desvalijamiento, *m*

rift *n* hendedura, abertura, *f*; grieta, *f*

rig *n naut* aparejo, *m*; *inf* atavío, *m. vt* (a ship) aparejar; equipar; (elections) falsificar. **to rig out,** proveer de; equipar con; ataviar. **to rig up,** arreglar; armar, construir

rigging *n* (of a ship) aparejo, *m*

right *a* recto; correcto; conveniente, debido; apropiado; exacto; (opposite of left hand) derecho; (straight) directo; en línea recta; razonable; (true) verdadero, genuino, legítimo; (just) justo; (prudent) prudente; (in health) sano. **All r.!** ¡Está bien! **I feel all r.,** Me siento perfectamente bien, Estoy bien. **He is the r. man for the job,** Él es el hombre que hace falta para el puesto. **It is the r. word,** Es la palabra apropiada. **on the r.,** a la derecha. **to be r.,** (of persons) tener razón. **to make r.,** poner en orden; arreglar. **r.-angle,** ángulo recto, *m*. **r.-angled,** rectangular. **r.-angled triangle,** triángulo rectángulo, *m*. **the R. Bank (of Paris),** la Orilla derecha, la Ribera derecha, *f*. **r. hand,** *n* (mano) derecha, diestra, *f*; derecha, *f*; (person) brazo derecho, *m. a* de la mano derecha; de la derecha; a la derecha. **r.-handed,** derecho; diestro, hábil. **r. mind,** entero juicio, *m*. **r.-minded,** juicioso, prudente; honrado. **r.-of-way,** derecho a la vía, *m*

right *adv* directamente; inmediatamente; derechamente; correctamente; debidamente; exactamente; bien; (quite, thoroughly) completamente; honradamente; (very) muy. **r. on,** adelante; en frente. **R. about face!** ¡Media vuelta a la derecha! **r. at the bottom,** al fondo; al final; el último (de la clase, etc.). **r. at the end of his speech,** al fin de su discurso. **r. away,** **r. now** en seguida, inmediatamente, *Mexico* ahorita, *elsewhere in Lat. Am.* lueguito

right *n* razón, *f*; verdad, *f*; justicia, *f*; (good) bien, *m*; derecho, *m*; (not left side) derecha, *f*; (of political parties) derechas, *f pl*. **r. and wrong,** el bien y el mal. "All rights reserved," «Derechos reservados.» **by rights,** por derecho. **It is on the r.,** Está a la derecha. **to exercise one's r.,** usar de su derecho. **r. of association,** derecho de asociación, *m*. **r. of way,** derecho de paso, *m*. **to be in the r.,** tener razón; estar en su derecho

right *vt* enderezar; rectificar; corregir; poner en orden; *naut* enderezar; hacer justicia (a). **to r. wrongs,** deshacer agravios

righteous *a* recto, virtuoso, justo; justificado

righteously *adv* virtuosamente; justamente

righteousness *n* rectitud, integridad, virtud, *f*; justicia, *f*

rightful *a* justo; legítimo; verdadero

rightfully *adv* justamente; legitimamente; verdaderamente

rightfulness *n* justicia, *f*; legitimidad, *f*; verdad, *f*

rightly *adv* justamente; debidamente; correctamente; bien. **r. or wrongly,** mal que bien

rightness *n* rectitud, *f*; derechura, *f*; justicia, *f*; exactitud, *f*

rigid *a* rígido; inflexible; severo, riguroso

rigidity *n* rigidez, *f*; inflexibilidad, *f*; severidad, *f*

rigmarole *n* monserga, *f*, galimatías, *m*, jerigonza, *f*

rigor *n* rigor, *m*

rigorous *a* riguroso

rigor *n* rigor, *m*

rile *vt inf* irritar, sacar de tino (a)

rim *n* borde, *m*; orilla, *f*; (of a wheel) llanta, *f*, aro, *m*

rime *n* escarcha, *f*, *vt* cubrir con escarcha. See also **rhyme**

rind *n* (of fruit) cáscara, corteza, *f*; (of cheese) costra, *f*; (of bacon) piel, *f*

ring *n* círculo, *m*; (round the eyes) ojera, *f*; (for curtains, etc.) anilla, *f*; (for the finger) anillo, *m*, sortija, *f*; (for children's games, etc.) corro, *m*; (for the ears) arete, *m*; (of smoke and for the nose) anillo, *m*; (for hitching, etc.) argolla, *f*; (for boxing) cuadrilátero, *m*; (on a racecourse) picadero, *m*; (at a circus, bull-fight) ruedo, redondel, *m*; *fig* arena, *f*; (group) camarilla, *f*, grupo, *m*; (metallic sound) sonido metálico, *m*; resonancia, *f*; (tinkle) tintín, *m*; (of a bell) repique, tañido, son (de la campana), *m*; (of bells) juego de campanas, *m*; (of laughter, etc.) ruido, *m*; (of truth, etc.) apariencia, *f*. **r.-bolt,** *naut* cáncamo, *m*. **r. finger,** dedo anular, *m*. **r.-master,** director de circo, *m*

ring *vt* (surround) cercar, rodear; (a bull, etc.) poner un anillo (a); (sound) hacer sonar; sonar; (a door bell, etc.) tocar, apretar; (bells) echar a vuelo; (announce by pealing the bells) anunciar, proclamar; sonar, tañer. *vi* (of bells) sonar; (re-echo) resonar; (of the ears) zumbar; (tinkle) tintinar. **to r. the bell,** tocar la campana; tocar el timbre. **to r. off,** colgar el teléfono. **to r. up,** llamar por teléfono, telefonear

ringing *n* acción de tocar las campanas o el timbre, *f*; toque, *m*; repique, *m*; campanilleo, *f*; (in the ears) zumbido, *m. a* resonante, sonoro. **r. signal,** señal de llamada, *f*. **the r. of the bells,** el son de las campanas

ringleader *n* cabecilla, *m*

ringlet *n* rizo, bucle, *m*

ringworm *n* tiña, *f*

rink *n* pista, *f*. **skating-r.,** sala de patinar, *f*; pista de patinar, *f*

rinse *n* enjuague, *m*; enjuagadura, *f*; (of clothes) aclarado, *m. vt* enjuagar; (clothes) aclarar; lavar

rinsing *n* See **rinse**; *pl* **rinsings,** lavazas, *f pl, a* aclarar

Rio de Janeiro *n* Río de Janeiro, *f*; *a* carioca, *formal* fluminense, *mf*

riot *n* motín, *m*; tumulto, *m*; desorden, *m*; exceso, *m*; orgía, *f*; disipación, *f. vi* amotinarse; alborotarse; entregarse a la disipación (or al placer); (enjoy) gozar, disfrutar. **to run r.,** hacer excesos; perder el freno; desmandarse; *fig* extenderse por todas partes; crecer en abundancia, cubrir todo

rioter *n* amotinador (-ra); alborotador (-ra)

riotous *a* sedicioso; bullicioso; disoluto; desordenado; desenfrenado

riotousness *n* sedición, *f*; disolución, *f*; excesos, *m pl*, desenfreno, *m*; desorden, *m*

rip *vt* rasgar; (unsew) descoser; (wood, etc.) partir; (make) hacer. *vi* rasgarse. *n* rasgón, *f*; rasgadura, *f*; desgarro, *m*; (libertine) calavera, *m*. **to rip off,** arrancar; quitar. **to rip open,** abrir; (an animal) abrir en canal

riparian *a* and *n* ribereño (-ña)

ripe *a* maduro; preparado; perfecto, acabado

ripen *vt* and *vi* madurar

ripeness *n* madurez, *f*

ripening *n* maduración, *f*

ripping *n* rasgadura, *f*; (unstitching) deshiladura, *f. a inf* estupendo

ripple *n* rizo, *m*; onda, *f*; (of sound) murmullo, *m. vt* rizar. *vi* rizarse; murmurar

rippling *n* rizado, *m*; murmullo, *m*

rise *vi* ascender; subir; levantarse; ponerse de pie; (of a meeting) suspenderse; (from the dead) resucitar; (grow) crecer; (swell) hincharse; (of sun, moon) salir; (of sound, gradient, price, stock exchange quotations) subir; (of river source) nacer; (in revolt) sublevarse, rebelarse; (to the mind) presentarse, surgir; (appear) aparecer; (of buildings, etc.) elevarse, alzarse; (in the world) mejorar de posición; (originate) originarse (en), proceder (de); (of mercury) alzarse; (of fish) picar. **He has risen in my estimation,** Ha ganado en mi estimación. **She rose early,** Se levantó temprano. **The color rose in her cheeks,** Se le subieron los colores a la cara. **to r. to the occasion,** estar al nivel de las circunstancias. **to r. to one's feet,** ponerse de pie. **to r. to the bait,** morder el anzuelo. **to r. again,** levantarse de nuevo; resucitar; renovarse, suscitarse otra vez. **to r. above,** alzarse por encima de; mostrarse superior a

rise *n* ascensión, *f*; subida, *f*; levantamiento, *m*; (in price, temperature) alza, *f*; (increase) aumento, *m*; (of the sun, moon) salida, *f*; (of a river) nacimiento, *m*; (origin) origen, *m*; (growth, development) desarrollo, crecimiento, *m*; (promotion) ascenso, *m*; (slope) cuesta, *f*; pendiente, *f*; (high ground) eminencia, altura, *f*. **to give r. to,** dar lugar a, causar. **r. and fall,** subida y baja, *f*; (of the voice) ritmo, *m*; (of music) cadencia, *f*; (of institutions) grandeza y decadencia, *f*. **r. to power,** subida al poder, *f*

riser *n* el, *m*, (*f*, la) que se levanta; (of a step) contrahuella, *f*. **early r.,** madrugador (-ra). **late r.,** el, *m*, (*f*, la) que se levanta tarde

risibility *n* risibilidad, *f*

risible *a* risible

rising *n* subida, *f*; (of the source of rivers) nacimiento, *m*; (overflowing of rivers) crecimiento, *m*; (of sun, moon) salida, *f*; (from the dead) resurrección, *f*; (rebellion) sublevación, insurrección, *f*; (of the tide) crecida, *f*; (of bread) levadura, *f*; (of an assembly) suspensión, *f*; (of a theater curtain) subida, *f*; (literary) renacimiento, *m*, *a* creciente; naciente; saliente; (promising) de porvenir; (young) joven. **the r. generation,** los jóvenes, la generación joven. **He is r. forty,** Raya en los cuarenta. **He likes early r.,** Le gusta madrugar. **On the r. of the curtain . . . ,** Al levantarse el telón . . . **the r. of the moon,** la salida de la luna, *f*. **the r. tide,** la marea creciente

risk *n* riesgo, *m*; peligro, *m. vt* arriesgar; atreverse (a), osar. **at the r. of,** al riesgo de. **to take a r.,** tomar un riesgo; correr peligro. **to r. everything on the outcome,** jugar el todo por el todo

risk capital *n* capital-riesgo, *m*

riskiness *n* peligro, *m*

risky *a* arriesgado, peligroso

rissole *n* risol, *m*, (*pl* risoles)

rite *n* rito, *m*

rite of passage *n* rito de tránsito, *m*

ritual *a* ritual. *n* rito, *m*, ceremonia, *f*

ritualist *n* ritualista, *mf*

ritualistic *a* ritualista

rival *n* rival, *mf a* competidor; rival. *vt* rivalizar con, competir con

rivalry *n* rivalidad, *f*

river *n* río, *m. a* del río; fluvial. **r.-basin,** cuenca de un río, *f*. **r.-bed,** lecho, cauce (de un río), *m*. **r. civilization,** civilización fluvial, *f*. **r.-god,** dios de los ríos, *m*. **r.-mouth,** ría, *f*. **r. port,** puerto fluvial, *m*

riverside *n* ribera, orilla de un río, *f. a* de la(s) orilla(s) de un río; situado a la orilla de un río; ribereño

rivet *n* remache, roblón, *m. vt* remachar; clavar; *fig* fijar, concentrar; *fig* cautivar, absorber

Riviera, the la Riviera, *f*

riveter *n* remachador, *m*

riveting *n* remachado, remache, *m*; *fig* fijación, concentración, *f*; *fig* absorción, *f*. **r. machine,** remachadora, *f*

rivulet *n* riachuelo, arroyo, *m*

road *n* camino, *m*; carretera, *f*; ruta, *f*; *pl* **roads,** *naut* rada, *f*. **high r.,** camino real, *m*. **main r.,** carretera, *f*. **secondary r.,** carretera de segunda clase, *f*. **on the r. to . . . ,** en el camino de . . . **to get out of the r.,** *inf* quitarse de en medio. **to go by r.,** ir por carretera. **"R. up!"** «Carretera en reparaciones.» **r.-book,** guía de carreteras, *f*. **r. house,** albergue de carretera, *m*. **r. maker,** constructor de caminos, *m*; (navvy) peón caminero, *m*. **r. making,** construcción de caminos, *f*. **r. map,** mapa de carreteras, *m*. **r. sign,** señal de carretera, señal de tránsito, señal vial, *f*, poste indicador, *m*. **The r. to hell is paved with good intentions,** El camino del infierno está empedrado de buenas intenciones. **"R. Repairs,"** «Camino en Reparación»

roadmender *n* peón caminero, *m*

roadside *n* borde del camino, *m*, *a* al lado del camino

roadstead *n* rada, *f*

roadster *n* automóvil de turismo, *m*; bicicleta de carreras, *f*; caballo de aguante, *m*; buque fondeado en rada, *m*

roadway *n* calzada, carretera, *f*

roam *vi* vagar, vagabundear, andar errante. *vt* errar por

roamer *n* vagabundo (-da), hombre errante, *m*

roaming *n* vagabundeo, *m*; excursiones, *f pl*, paseos, *m pl*; *a* errante, vagabundo; nómada

roan *a* roano, sabino. *n* caballo roano, *m*

roar *vi* rugir; (of a bull, of the wind, of a person in anger) bramar; dar voces; (of the fire) crepitar; (of cannon) retumbar; (of thunder) estallar. *vt* gritar. *n* rugido, bramido, *m*; (shout) grito, *m*; (of the fire) crepitación, *f*; (of cannon, thunder) estallido, *m*; (noise) ruido, *m*. **to r. with laughter,** reírse a carcajadas

roaring *n* (of horses) asma de los caballos, *f*, For other meanings, see under **roar.** *a* rugiente, bramante; *inf* magnífico. **to do a r. trade,** hacer un buen negocio

roast *n* asado, *m*, carne asada, *f. a* asado; tostado. *v asar*; (coffee and to warm one's feet, etc.) tostar; (metals) calcinar; (scold) desollar vivo (a). *vi* asarse; tostarse. **r. beef,** rosbif, *m*

roaster *n* asador, *m*; (for coffee or peanuts) tostador, *m*; (for chestnuts, etc.) tambor, *m*

roasting *n* asación, *f*; (of coffee) tostado, *m*; (of metals) calcinación, *f*. **r. spit,** asador, *m*

rob *vt* robar; quitar, privar (de). **They have robbed her of her pocketbook,** Le han robado la cartera

robber *n* ladrón (-ona); (footpad) salteador de caminos, *m*; (brigand) bandido, *m*

robbery *n* robo, *m*. **It's daylight r.!** ¡Es un desuello! **to commit a r.,** cometer un robo. **r. with violence,** robo armado, *m*

robe *n* traje talar, *m*; (of a monk, nun) hábito, *m*; (of a priest, etc.) sotana, *f*; *poet* manto, *m*; (infant's) mantillas, *f pl*; *pl* **robes,** traje de ceremonia, *m. vt* vestir; cubrir, revestir (de). *vi* vestirse. **bath r.,** albornoz, *m*

robin *n* petirrojo, *m*

roble *n* rublo, *m*

robot *n* hombre mecánico, *m*; *aer* piloto mecánico, *m*. **traffic r.,** torre del tráfico, *f*, aparato automático, *m*. **r. plane,** avión sin piloto, *m*

robust *a* robusto; fuerte, vigoroso. **to make r.,** robustecer

robustness *n* robustez, *f*; vigor, *m*, fuerza, *f*

rock *n* roca, *f*; (in the sea) abrojo, escollo, *m*; peña, *f*, peñasco, *m*. **as firm as a r.,** como una roca. **to be on the rocks,** *inf* estar a la cuarta pregunta. **r. bottom,** *n* fondo, *m. a* mínimo, más bajo. **r. crystal,** cuarzo, *m*. **r.-garden,** jardincito rocoso, jardín alpestre, *m*. **r.-plant,** planta alpestre, *f*. **r.-rose,** heliantemo, *m*. **r.-salt,** sal gema, *f*

rock *vt* mecer; (shake) hacer temblar, sacudir; (to sleep) arrullar. *vi* mecerse; balancearse; tambalearse; agitarse; temblar

rocker *n* (of a chair, cradle) balancín, *m*; (chair) mecedora, *f*

rockery *n* jardincito rocoso, *m*

rocket *n* cohete, volador, *m*. *vi* lanzarse. **r.-launching aircraft,** caza lanzacohetes, *f*

rockiness *n* abundancia de rocas, *f*; fragosidad, escabrosidad, *f*

rocking *n* balanceo, *m*; (staggering) tambaleo, *m*; oscilación, *f*; (of an infant) arrullo, *m*. **r.-chair,** mecedora, *f*. **r.-horse,** caballo balancín, caballo mecedor, *m*

rocky *a* rocoso; de roca; roqueño; (rough) fragoso, escabroso; (rugged) peñascoso, escarpado. **the R. Mountains,** las Montañas Rocosas, *f pl*

rococo *n* rococó, *m*

rod *n* vara, *f*; bastón de mando, *m*; (for fishing) caña, *f*; (measure) pértiga, *f*; (surveying) jalón, *m*; palo, *m*; (for punishment) vergajo, *m*; *mech* vástago, *m*. **connecting rod,** biela, *f*. **to fish with rod and line,** pescar con caña

rodent *n* and *n* roedor, *m*

roe *n* (deer) corzo (-za); (of fish) hueva, *f*. **soft roes,** lechas, *f pl*

rogue *n* bribón (-ona), pícaro (-ra), pillo (-lla), *Argentina* farabute, *mf*; *law* vago, *m*; (affectionate) picaruelo (-la)

roguery *n* truhanería, picardía, *f*; (knaves) pícaros, *m pl*; (mischief) travesuras, *f pl*. **novel of r.,** novela picaresca, *f*

roguish *a* picaresco, bellaco; (mischievous) travieso, juguetón; malicioso

roguishly *adv* como un pícaro; con malicia

roguishness *n* picardía, bribonería, bellaquería, *f*; (mischievousness) travesuras, *f pl*; malicia, *f*

role *n* papel, *m*

roll *n* rollo, *m*; (list) rol, *m*, lista, *f*; (of bread) panecillo, *Mexico* bolillo, *m*; (of a drum) redoble, *m*; (of thunder) tronido, *m*; (of cloth) pieza, *f*; (of tobacco) rollo, *m*; (of meat, etc.) pastel, *m*; (of a ship) balanceo, *m*; *pl* **rolls,** (records) archivos, *m pl*. **He has a nautical r.,** Tiene un andar de marinero. **to call the r.,** pasar lista. **r. film,** película fotográfica, *f*. **r. of honour,** lista de honor, *f*. **r.-on corset,** faja elástica, *f*, corsé de goma, *m*. **r.-top desk,** buró de cierre enrollable, *m*

roll *vi* rodar; dar vueltas; (wallow) revolcarse; (of a ship) balancearse, bambolearse; (in money, etc.) nadar; (flow) correr, fluir; (*fig* of time) pasar tranquilamente; (of vehicle) rodar; pasar rodando; (of country) ondular; (of the sea) ondear; (of drums) redoblar; (of thunder) retumbar. *vt* hacer rodar; arrollar; (a cigarette) liar; (metals) laminar; (move) mover; (the eyes) guiñar (los ojos); (the ground) apisonar; (pastry) aplanar; (of an organ) sonar; (a drum) redoblar. **Mary rolled her eyes heavenwards,** María puso los ojos en blanco. **to r. away,** alejarse; desaparecer; (of time) pasar. **to r. back,** volver, retirarse; desaparecer. **to r. by,** pasar rodando; desaparecer. **to r. down,** bajar rodando, rodar por. **to r. in,** llegar en gran cantidad (or en gran número). **to r. off,** caer de. **to r. on,** seguir su marcha; fluir sin cesar; seguir su curso; (of time) avanzar. **to r. out,** (metal) laminar; (pastry) aplanar; (bring out) sacar; desenrollar. **to r. over,** *vt* volcar; tumbar; dar la vuelta (a). *vi* dar la vuelta; volverse al otro lado. **to r. up,** arrollar; envolver; (of hedgehogs, etc.) enroscarse, hacerse un ovillo

roll-call vote *n* votación nominal, *f*

roller *n* rodillo, *m*; cilindro, *m*; (wheel, castor) rueda, *f*; (for flattening the ground) apisonadora, *f*; *print* rodillo, *m*; (wave) ola grande, *f*. **r.-bandage,** venda, *f*. **r. canary,** canario de raza flauta, *m*. **r.-skate,** patín de ruedas, *m*. **r.-skating,** patinaje de ruedas, *m*. **r.-towel,** toalla continua, *f*

rollicking *a* alegre, jovial; juguetón

rolling *a* rodante; (of landscape) ondulante, quebrado. *n* rodadura, *f*; (wallowing) revuelco, *m*; (of metals) laminación, *f*; (of a ship) balanceo, *m*; (rolling up) enrollamiento, *m*. **r.-pin,** rollo, rodillo de pastelero, *m*. **r.-stock,** material móvil ferroviario, *m*

Roman *a* romano, de los romanos; (of noses and *print*) romano. *n* romano (-na). **in R. fashion,** a la romana. **R. Catholic,** *a* católico; católico apostólico romano. *n*

el católico (-ca). **R. Catholicism,** catolicismo, *m*. **R. figures,** números romanos, *m pl*. **R. nose,** nariz romana, *f*. **R. road,** vía romana, *f*. **R. type,** *print* tipo romano, *m*

Romance *a* (of languages) romance. *n* (language) romance, *m*

romance *n* novela de caballería, *f*; romance, *m*; aventura, *f*; cuento, *m*, novela, *f*; romanticismo, *m*; *mus* romanza, *f*. *vi* inventar ficciones; exagerar

romancer *n* romancerista, *mf*; mentiroso (-sa), embustero (-ra)

Romanesque *a* románico; romanesco

romantic *a* and *n* romántico (-ca)

romantically *adv* románticamente; de un modo romántico

romanticism *n* romanticismo, *m*

romanticist *n* romántico (-ca)

Rome Roma, *f*

romp *vi* juguetear, brincar, retozar, loquear; correr rápidamente. *n* locuelo (-la), saltaparedes, *mf*; (game) retozo, *m*. **The horse romped home easily,** El caballo ganó la carrera fácilmente

rompers *n* mono, *m*

romping *n* juegos, *m pl*, travesuras, *f pl*

rondo *n* rondó, *m*

rood *n* cruz, *f*; crucifijo, *m*; cuarto de acre, *m*. **By the r.!** ¡Por mi santiguada!

roof *n* tejado, techado, *m*; (of a motor-car, bus) tejadillo, *m*; (of coaches, etc.) imperial, *f*; cubierta, *f*; (of the mouth) paladar, *m*; (bower) enramada, *f*; (of heaven) bóveda (del cielo), *f*. *vt* techar, tejar, *Lat. Am.* entechar; (shelter) abrigar. **r.-garden,** azotea, *f*. **r.-gutter,** canalera, *f*

roofer *n* techador, *m*; constructor de tejados, *m*

rook *n* chova, *f*, grajo, *m*; (chess) torre, *f*. *vt* engañar, estafar; (overcharge) desollar vivo (a)

rookery *n* manada de grajos, *f*; colonia de grajos, aves marinas or focas, *f*

room *n* (in a house) habitación, *f*, cuarto, *m*; sala, *f*; cámara, *f*; (behind a shop) trastienda, *f*; (space) sitio, espacio, *m*; lugar, *m*; (opportunity) oportunidad, *f*; (cause) motivo, *m*, causa, *f*. *vi* alojarse. **bath-r.,** cuarto de baño, *m*. **dining-r.,** comedor, *m*. **drawing-r.,** salón, *m*. **There is no r. for us in this car,** No cabemos en este coche. **There is still r. for improvement,** Se puede mejorar todavía. **There isn't r. for anything else,** No cabe más. **to be r.,** caber, haber sitio. **to make r.,** hacer sitio

roomed *a* (in compounds) de . . . habitaciones; de . . . salas

roominess *n* espaciosidad, amplitud, amplitud de habitación, *f*; (of garments) holgura, *f*

rooming house *n* casa de huéspedes, *f*

roommate *n* compañero de cuarto, compañero de pieza, *m*

roomy *a* espacioso, amplio; (of garments) holgado

roost *n* percha de gallinero, *f*, *Lat. Am.* dormidero, *m*. *vi* dormir en una percha; recogerse. **to rule the r.,** ser el amo del cotarro

rooster *n* gallo, *m*,

root *n* raíz, *f*; *gram* radical, *m*; *mus* base, *f*; origen, *m*; explicación, *f*. *vt* arraigar; *fig* fijar, clavar. *vi* echar raíces; *fig* arraigarse; (of pigs, etc.) hozar, escarbar; revolver. **to r. out,** arrancar de raíz; *fig* desarraigar; (destroy) extirpar. **cubed r.,** raíz cúbica, *f*. **from the r.,** (entirely) de raíz. **square r.,** raíz cuadrada, *f*. **to cut close to the r.,** cortar a raíz

rooted *a* (in compounds) de raíces . . . ; arraigado

rope *n* soga, cuerda, *f*; (hawser) maroma, *f*; *naut* cabo, *m*; (tight-rope) cable, *m*, cuerda de volatinero, *f*; (string) ristra, sarta, *f*; hilo, *m*; *pl* **ropes,** (boxing) cuerdas del cuadrilátero, *f pl*. *vt* encordelar, atar con cuerdas. **to r. in,** encerrar; (a person) enganchar, coger. **a r. of pearls,** una sarta de perlas. **to give a person plenty of r.,** dar mucha latitud (a). **to know the ropes,** conocer todos los trucos. **r.-ladder,** escala de

cuerda, *f.* **r.-maker,** cordelero (-ra), soguero, *m.*
r.-making, cordelería, soguería, *f.* **r.-trick,** truco de la
cuerda, *m.* **r.-walk,** cordelería, *f.* **r.-yarn,** *naut* filás-
tica, *f*

rosary *n* rosario, *m.* **to say the r.,** rezar el rosario

rose *n* rosa, *f;* color de rosa, *m;* (rosette) roseta, *f; arch*
rosetón, *m;* (of watering-can) pomo, *m,* roseta, *f. a de*
rosa, rosado. **to see the world through r.-colored**
spectacles, ver las cosas en color de rosa. **to turn to**
r., volverse color de rosa, rosear. **r.-bay,** *bot* rododafne,
adelfa, *f.* **r.-bush,** rosal, *m.* **r.-color,** color de rosa, rosa,
m. **r.-colored,** de color de rosa, rosado. **r.-garden,**
rosalera, rosaleda, *f.* **r. grower,** cultivador (-ra) de
rosas. **r. hip,** escaramujo, *m.* **r. leaf,** hoja de rosa, *f;*
pétalo de rosa, *m.* **r.-like,** como una rosa, de rosa.
r.-red, de color de rosa; como una rosa. **climbing**
r.-tree, rosal trepador, *m.* **dwarf r.-tree,** rosal bajo, *m.*
standard r.-tree, rosal de tallo, *m.* **r.-water,** agua de
rosas, *f.* **r.-window,** rosetón, *m,* rosa, *f.* **r.-wood,** palo
de rosa, *m*

rosé *a* (of wines) rosado

rosebud *n* capullo de rosa, *m*

rosemary *n* romero, *m*

rosin *n* (solid, for violin-bows, etc.) colofonia, *f;* resina,
f. vt dar con colofonia; dar con resina

rosiness *n* color de rosa, *m*

roster *n* lista, *f;* registro, *m,* matrícula, *f*

rostrum *n* tribuna, *f; zool* pico, *m;* (of a ship) espolón, *m*

rosy *a* róseo, rosado; sonrosado; *fig* de color de rosa,
halagüeño; optimista. **r.-cheeked,** con (de) mejillas
sonrosadas

rot *n* putrefacción, podredumbre, *f;* (in trees) caries, *f;*
(in sheep) comalía, *f;* (slang) patrañas, *f pl,* disparates,
m pl, vi pudrirse; descomponerse; *fig* echarse a perder;
(slang) decir disparates. *vt* pudrir; *fig* corromper;
(slang) tomar el pelo (a)

rota *n* lista, *f;* orden del día, *m*

rotary *a* rotativo. **r. printing press,** rotativa, *f*

rotary telephone *n* teléfono de discado, *m*

rotate *vi* girar, dar vueltas; alternarse. *vt* hacer girar

rotating *a* rotativo; giratorio

rotation *n* rotación, *f;* turno, *m.* **in r.,** por turnos. **r. of**
crops, rotación de cultivos, *f*

rotatory *a* rotatorio

rote, to learn by *vt* aprender de memoria, aprender por
repetición, aprender de cotorra

rotogravure *n* rotograbado, *m*

rotten *a* putrefacto; podrido; (of bones, teeth) cariado;
dañado, echado a perder; *fig* corrompido; (slang)
pésimo. **to smell r.,** oler a podredumbre; apestar

rottenness *n* putrefacción, podredumbre, *f; fig* corrupción, *f*

rotter *n* (slang) perdido, *m*

rotting *n* pudrición, *f, a* que se pudre

rotund *a* rotundo

rotunda *n* rotonda, *f*

rotundity *n* redondez, *f;* rotundidad, *f*

roué *n* calavera, libertino, *m*

rouge *n* colorete, *m, vt* and *vi* pintar de rojo, poner(se)
colorete

rough *a* áspero; duro; (of country) fragoso, escabroso;
(uneven) desigual; (stormy) borrascoso, tempestuoso;
(of the sea) encrespado, bravo; (of movement) violento; (bristling) erizado, *fig* de (movement) violento; (bristling) erizado; (of the hair) despeinado; (unpolished) tosco; basto; (unskilled, clumsy) torpe; (of
sounds, tastes) áspero; (of persons) rudo, inculto; (severe) severo; (of behavior) brutal; (of manners)
brusco; (rude) grosero; (approximate) aproximado.
adv duramente, mal. *n* estado tosco, *m;* (person)
matón, *m.* **in the r.,** en bruto; (roughed out) bosquejado. **to grow r.,** (of the sea) encresparse, embravecerse. **to take the r. with the smooth,** *fig*
aceptar la realidad; tomar lo bueno con lo malo. **to r.**
it, luchar contra las dificultades, pasar apuros; llevar
una vida sencilla; vivir mal. **to r. out,** bosquejar. **r.**
and ready, improvisado; provisional. **r. and tumble,**

n camorra, pendencia, *f.* **r.-cast,** *vt* dar una primera
capa de mezcla gruesa (a); bosquejar. **r. diamond,** diamante bruto (or en bruto), *m.* **r.-draft,** borrador, *m;*
bosquejo, *m.* **r.-haired,** (of a dog) de pelo crespo.
r.-hewn, modelado toscamente; desbastado; *fig* cerril,
tosco. **r.-house,** jarana, *f.* **r.-rider,** domador (de caballos), *m.* **r. sketch,** bosquejo, esbozo, *m.* **r.-spoken,**
malhablado

roughen *vt* poner áspero. *vi* ponerse áspero

roughly *adv* rudamente, toscamente; duramente; brutalmente; bruscamente; (of tastes, sounds) ásperamente; (approximately) aproximadamente, más o
menos

roughness *n* aspereza, *f;* dureza, *f;* tosquedad, *f;* rudeza,
f; (of the sea, wind) braveza, *f;* violencia, *f;* (of manner)
brusquedad, *f;* brutalidad, *f;* (vulgarity) grosería, *f.* **the**
r. of the way, la aspereza del camino

roulette *n* ruleta, *f*

round *a* redondo; (plump) rollizo; rotundo, categórico;
sonoro. **a r. sum,** una cantidad redonda; un número
redondo. **to walk at a r. pace,** andar a un buen paso.
r. dance, baile en ruedo, *m.* **r.-faced,** carilleno, de cara
redonda. **r.-house,** cuerpo de guardia, *m; naut* tum-
badillo, *m.* **r.-shouldered,** cargado de espaldas. **r.**
table, mesa redonda, *f;* (of King Arthur) Tabla
Redonda, *f.* **r. trip,** viaje redondo, viaje de ida y vuelta,
m. **r.-up,** rodeo de ganado, *m;* arresto, *m*

round *n* círculo, *m;* esfera, *f;* redondez, *f;* (slice) rodaja,
f; (of a ladder) peldaño, *m;* (patrol and *mil*) ronda, *f;*
circuito, *m;* vuelta, *f,* giro, *m;* serie, *f;* rutina, *f;* (of ammunition) andanada, descarga, *f;* (of cartridge) cartucho con bala, *m;* (of applause, etc.) salva, *f;* (of golf)
partido, *m;* (in a fight) asalto, *m; sport* vuelta, *f;* (of
drinks) ronda, *f;* (doctor's) visitas, *f pl*

round *vt* redondear; (*fig* complete) acabar, perfeccionar;
(go round, e.g. a corner) dar vuleta (a), doblar, trasponer; rodear, cercar; (of a ship) doblar. *vi* redondearse. **to r. off,** redondear; terminar; coronar. **to r.**
up, (cattle) rodear. **to r. upon,** volverse contra

round *adv* alrededor, en derredor; por todos lados; a la
redonda, en torno; en circunferencia; en conjunto (**r.** is
not translated in Spanish, e.g. **I shall come r. to your**
house, Vendré a tu casa). *prep* alrededor de. **all the**
year r., todo el año, el año entero. **r. about,** a la
redonda de, al derredor de; (nearly) cerca de; (of time
by the clock) a eso de. **The road is closed and we**
shall have to go r., El camino está cerrado y ten-
dremos que dar una vuelta. **to come r.,** volver; dejarse
persuadir; recobrar su buen humor. **to go r.,** (spin) dar
vueltas; (of the wind) cambiar. **There is enough to go**
r., Hay bastante para todos

roundabout *a* indirecto; desviado; vago. *n* tiovivo, *m;*
(traffic) redondel, *m.* **He spoke in a r. way,** Hablaba
con circunloquios. **We went there by a r. way,**
Fuimos dando un rodeo

roundly *adv* en redondo; rotundamente, claramente

roundness *n* redondez, *f;* rotundidad, *f*

rouse *vt* despertar; animar; excitar; suscitar, provocar.
to r. oneself, despertarse; animarse (a hacer algo)

rousing *a* que despierta; (moving) emocionante; (enthusiastic) entusiasta; grande, bueno

rout *n* (rabble) chusma, *f;* (party) sarao, *m;* (defeat) derrota, *f;* (meeting) reunión, *f. vt* derrotar, poner en
fuga; vencer

route *n* ruta, *f;* camino, *m;* itinerario, *m.* **r. march,** marcha de maniobras, *f*

routine *n* rutina, *f, a* rutinario, de rutina

rove *vi* vagar, errar

rover *n* vagabundo (-da); pirata, *m*

roving *a* vagabundo, errante; ambulante

row *n* (line) hilera, fila, hila, *f;* (in a theater, etc.) fila, *f;*
(string) ristra, *f;* (in a boat) paseo en bote, *m;* (commotion) alboroto, *m;* (noise) ruido, *m;* (shindy) gresca,
camorra, *f;* (scolding) regaño, *m, vi* (a boat) remar,
bogar. *vt* conducir remando; (scold) regañar. **to be a**

row, (shindy) haber la de San Quintín. **to start a row,** (shindy) armar camorra.
rowboat *n* bote de remos, *m*
rowdiness *n* alboroto, *m*
rowdy *a* alborotador. *n* trafalmejas, *mf* rufián, *m*. **rowdy party** *Lat. Am.* fandango, *m*
rower *n* remero (-ra), bogador (-ra)
rowing *a* que rema; de remos. *n* deporte del remo, *m*; paseo en bote, *m*. **r.-boat,** bote de remos, *m*. **r.-club,** club náutico, *m*. **r.-seat,** bancada, *f*. **r.-stroke,** bogada, *f*
royal *a* real; regio. *n naut* sobrejuanete, *m*. **r. academy,** real academia, *f*. **r. eagle,** águila real, *f*. **R. Highness,** Alteza Real, *f*. **r. letters patent,** cédula real, *f*. **R. Mail,** mala real, *f*. **R. Standard,** estandarte real, *m*
royalist *a* and *n* realista, *mf*
royally *adv* realmente; regiamente
royalty *n* realeza, *f*; miembro de la familia real, *m*; tanto por ciento de los ingresos, *m*; derechos de autor, *m pl*
R.R. (abbrev. of *railroad*) F.R. (abbrev. of *ferrocarril*)
rub *vt* frotar, estregar; fregar; rozar; friccionar; (make sore) raspar. **to rub one's hands together,** frotarse las manos. **to rub the wrong way,** frotar a contrapelo. **to rub against,** rozar. **to rub along,** *inf* ir tirando. **to rub down,** (a horse) bruzar; limpiar; (dry) secar; (wear down) desgastar. **to rub in,** dar fricciones con; frotar con; (an idea, etc.) machacar. **to rub off,** *vt* quitar (frotando); borrar. *vi* borrarse; separarse (de). **to rub out,** *vt* borrar. *vi* borrarse. **to rub up,** (polish) limpiar; *fig* refrescar
rub *n* frotación, *f*; roce, *m*; fricción, *f*; *fig* obstáculo, *m*; dificultad, *f*. **to give a rub,** frotar, etc. **rub-a-dub,** rataplán, *m*
rubber *a* de caucho, de goma. *n* caucho, *m*, goma, *f*; (for erasing) goma de borrar, *f*; (masseur) masajista, *mf*; (at whist, etc.) partida, *f*; *pl* **rubbers,** zapatos de goma, chanclos, *m pl*. **synthetic r.,** caucho artificial, *m*. **r. band,** goma, banda de goma, *f*. **r. belt,** *mech* correa de transmisión de caucho, *f*. **r.-plant, tree,** cauchera, *f*, *Central America, Mexico* hule, *m*. **r. plantation,** cauchal, *m*. **r.-plantation worker** cauchero (-a) *mf*. **r. planter,** cauchero, *m*. **r. stamp,** estampilla, *f*
rubbing *n* frotación, *f*; fricción, *f*; roce, *m*; (of floors, dishes, etc.) fregado, *m*
rubbish *n* basura, *f*; desperdicios, *m pl*, desecho, *m*; (of goods) pacotilla, *f*; (nonsense) pamplinas, patrañas, *f pl*, disparates, *m pl*. **r. cart,** carro del basurero, *m*
rubbishy *a* sin valor, malo; (of goods) de pacotilla, de calidad inferior
rubble *n* escombros, *m pl*; cascote, *m*; piedra bruta, *f*
rubicund *a* rubicundo
rubric *n* rúbrica, *f*
ruby *n* rubí, *m*. *a* de rubíes; de rubí. **r. lips,** labios de rubí, *m pl*
rucksack *n* mochila, *f*
rudder *n* timón, gobernalle, *m*
ruddiness *n* rubicundez, *f*; rojez, *f*; frescura, *f*
ruddy *a* rubicundo; rojo; frescote; (of animals) barcino
rude *a* tosco; vigoroso; grosero, descortés
rudely *adv* toscamente; groseramente
rudeness *n* rudeza, *f*; tosquedad, *f*; grosería, incivilidad, descortesía, *f*
rudiment *n* rudimento, *m*
rudimentary *a* rudimentario
rue *vt* lamentar, llorar. *n bot* ruda, *f*
rueful *a* triste, melancólico; lamentable
ruefulness *n* tristeza, *f*
ruff *n* golilla, lechuguilla, *f*; (of a bird) collarín de plumas, *m*; (of an animal) collarín de pelo, *m*
ruffian *n* rufián, *m*
ruffle *n sew* volante fruncido, *m*; (of a bird) collarín de plumas, *m*; (of an animal) collarín de pelo, *m*; (ripple) rizo, *m*; (annoyance) irritación, *f*. *vt* (ripple) rizar; (pleat) fruncir; (feathers) erizar; (hair) despeinar; agitar; (annoy) irritar, incomodar

ruffling *n* (rippling) rizado, *m*; (pleating) fruncido, *m*; (of the temper) irritación, *f*
rug *n* (floor) alfombra, *f*; manta de viaje, *f*. **rug strap,** portamantas, *m*
rugged *a* áspero, escabroso; escarpado, abrupto; (wrinkled) arrugado; tosco; (harsh) duro, severo; inculto; rudo; mal acabado; vigoroso
ruggedness *n* aspereza, escabrosidad, *f*; lo escarpado; dureza, severidad, *f*; rudeza, *f*; vigor, *m*
ruin *n* ruina, *f*. *vt* arruinar; echar a perder, estropear por completo; (a woman) perder
ruination *n* ruina, perdición, *f*
ruined *a* arruinado; en ruinas
ruinous *a* ruinoso; en ruinas
rule *n* regla, *f*; gobierno, *m*; autoridad, *f*, mando, *m*; administración, *f*; (reign) reinado, *m*; (of a court, etc.) orden, *f*; (for measuring) regla, *f*; *print* regleta, *f*; *pl* **rules,** reglas, *f pl*; reglamento, *m*. *vt* gobernar; regentar, regir; (control) dominar; (of a chairman, etc.) disponer, decidir; (guide) guiar; (lines) reglar. *vi* gobernar; (of a monarch) reinar; (of prices) mantenerse; estar en boga, prevalecer. **as a r.,** por regla general, en general. **slide-r.,** regla de cálculo, *f*. **to make it a r.,** tener por regla; tener por costumbre; tener por máxima. **to r. out,** excluir; *law* no admitir. **to r. over,** (of a king, etc.) reinar sobre. **r. of the road,** reglamento del tráfico, *m*. **r. of thumb,** regla empírica, *f*; rutina, *f*
ruler *n* gobernador (-ra); soberano (-na); (master) amo (ama); (for ruling lines) regla, *f*
ruling *a* regente; dominante; (current) vigente. *n* gobierno, *m*; *law* decisión, *f*, fallo, *m*; (with lines) rayado, *m*. **r. pen,** tiralíneas, *m*
rum *n* ron, *m*
Rumanian *a* rumano. *n* rumano (-na); (language) rumano, *m*
rumble *vi* retumbar, tronar; (of vehicles) rugir; crujir. *n* retumbo, trueno, *m*; rugido, *m*; ruido sordo, *m*; rumor, *m*; crujido, *m*
rumbling *a* que retumba, etc. *n* ruido sordo, *m*; retumbo, *m*; crujido, *m*; (in the bowels) rugido, *m*
ruminant *a* and *n* rumiante, *mf*
ruminate *vi* and *vt* rumiar
rumination *n* rumia, *f*; meditación, reflexión, *f*
rummage *vt* revolver, desordenar, trastornar; explorar. **to r. out,** desenterrar
rumor *n* rumor, *m*, fama, *f*. **It is rumored that . . . ,** Hay rumores de que . . . , La voz corre que . . . , Se dice que . . .
rump *n* (of an animal) nalgas, ancas, *f pl*; cuarto trasero, *m*; (of man) rabadilla, *f*; (scornful) culo, *m*, posaderas, *f pl*. **r.-steak,** solomillo, *m*
rumple *vt* arrugar; desordenar
run *vi* correr; acudir; (flee) huir; (rush) precipitarse, lanzarse; (in a race) tomar parte en una carrera; competir; (pass over) deslizarse (por); (of machines) andar, marchar; (of traffic) circular; (leave, of trains, ships, etc.) salir; (ply between) hacer el trayecto entre . . . y . . . ; (flow) fluir, correr; (into the sea, of rivers) desembocar (en); (spurt) chorrear, manar; (drip) gotear; (leak) dejar fugar (el agua, etc.); (of colors) correrse; caer; (of tears) correr; derramarse; (of eyes) llorar; (melt) derretirse; (of a sore) supurar; (travel or go) ir; moverse; (work) trabajar; funcionar; (of editions of a book) agotarse; (of a play) representarse; (cross) cruzar; (elapse) correr; transcurrir, pasar; (become) hacerse; (of wording) decir; (be current) correr; (for parliament, etc.) hacerse candidato; (navigate) navegar; (spread) extenderse; (be) estar, ser; (of thoughts) pasar; (last) durar; (tend) tender (a). *vt* (a race, a horse) correr; (drive) conducir; (a business, etc.) administrar; dirigir; (govern) gobernar, regir; (hunt) cazar; perseguir; (water, etc.) hacer correr; (pierce) clavar; introducir; (push) empujar; (one's hand, eye, etc.) pasar; (risks, etc.) correr; (possess) tener; establecer un servicio de (autobuses, etc.); (smuggle) hacer contrabando de. **The ship ran aground,** El barco encalló. **to run dry,** se-

carse; agotarse. **to run in the family,** estar en la familia. **to run into debt,** endeudarse, contraer deudas. **to run to seed,** granar; agotarse. **Steamers run daily between Barcelona and Mallorca,** Hay servicio diario de vapores entre Barcelona y Mallorca. **A stab of pain ran up his leg,** Sintió un dolor agudo en la pierna. **Feeling was running high,** Los ánimos estaban excitados. **My arrangements ran smoothly,** Mis planes marchaban bien. **Funds are running low,** El dinero escasea. **The tune runs in my head,** Tengo la canción metida en la cabeza. **The message runs like this,** El mensaje reza así, El mensaje dice así. **He ran his fingers through his hair,** Se mesaba los cabellos. **to run about,** andar de un lado a otro, correr por todas partes; (gad) corretear. **to run across,** cruzar corriendo; (meet) topar con, tropezar con. **to run after,** correr detrás (de); perseguir; buscar. **to run against,** (collide with) dar contra; (meet) tropezar con. **to run at,** abalanzarse hacia, precipitarse sobre; atacar. **to run away,** huir, escaparse; (slip away) escurrirse; (of a horse) dispararse, desbocarse. **to run away with,** huir con, fugarse con; (carry off) arrebatar; (steal) llevarse; (imagine) imaginarse, figurarse; (of temper, etc.) dominar, poseer. **to run back,** volver corriendo; llegar corriendo; retroceder rápidamente, correr hacia atrás. **to run backwards,** correr hacia atrás; **to run backwards and forwards,** ir y venir. **to run behind,** correr detrás (de); quedarse atrás; (be late) estar atrasado. **to run down,** *vi* bajar corriendo; descender, bajar; (of a clock) parar; (of a battery) gastarse; (of liquids) correr; fluir; (drop by drop) destilar. *vt* (capture) coger; alcanzar; (a person by a vehicle) atropellar; (a ship) echar a pique; (disparage) hablar mal de. **run-down,** (in health) agotado; (of a clock) parado. **to run for,** buscar corriendo; correr para coger (el autobús, etc.); (president, etc.) ser candidato para. **to run in,** *vi* entrar corriendo. *vt* arrestar; hacer prisionero; *print* encerrar. **to run into,** tropezar con; chocar con; (plunge into) meterse de cabeza en; (of sums of money, etc.) ascender a; (of streets, rivers, etc.) desembocar en. **to run off,** *vi* escaparse corriendo; marcharse corriendo. *vt* deslizarse por; (drain) vaciar; *print* imprimir; (print) componer. **to run off with,** huir con. **to run on,** correr delante; continuar; (of the mind) pensar en, entregarse a; hablar sin cesar; *print* recorrer. **to run out,** *vi* salir corriendo; (of liquids) derramarse; salir; (end) acabarse; agotarse; (project) sobresalir. *vt* (cricket) coger al lanzador fuera de la línea de saque. **to run out of,** no tener más de, haber terminado. **to run over,** *vi* rebosar; derramarse. *vt* (of a vehicle) atropellar, pasar por encima de, *Mexico* atellevar; (peruse) repasar; revisar. **run pell-mell,** salir pitando, salir volando, salvarse por pies. **to run through,** correr por; pasar por; recorrer; (go directly) ir directamente (a); (pierce) traspasar, pasar de parte a parte; (squander) derrochar, malbaratar; (read) hojear, leer por encima de. **to run up,** *vt* (hoist) izar; hacer de prisa; construir rápidamente; (incur) incurrir. *vi* subir corriendo; (of plants) trepar (por); (shrink) encogerse; (of expenses) aumentar. **to run up to time,** llegar a su hora. **to run up against,** tropezar con; (opposition, etc.) encontrar.

run *n* carrera, corrida, *f*; (excursion) visita, excursión, *f*; (cricket) carrera, *f*; (walk) paseo, *m*; (by train or sea) viaje, *m*; (by bus, train) trayecto, *m*; (sea crossing) travesía, *f*; (distance run) recorrido, *m*; (of events, etc.) curso, *m*; marcha, *f*; (of markets, etc.) tendencia, *f*; (rhythm) ritmo, *m*; dirección, *f*; distancia, *f*; *mus* serie de notas, *f*; serie, *f*; duración, *f*; *theat* serie de representaciones, *f*; (freedom to use) libre uso, *m*; (majority) mayoría, *f*; (on a bank) asedio, *m*; (on a book, etc.) demanda, *f*; (for sheep, etc.) terreno de pasto, *m*; (for fowls) gallinero, *m* (in a stocking) *Lat. Am.* acarraladura, *f*, *m*. **a run of bad luck,** una temporada de mala suerte. **at a run,** corriendo. **in the long run,** a la larga, al fin y al cabo. **on the run,** en fuga; ocupado.

Prices came down with a run, Los precios bajaron de golpe. **take-off run,** *aer* recorrido de despegue, *m*

runaway *a* fugitivo; (of a horse) desbocado

rung *n* (of a ladder) peldaño, *m*; (of a chair) travesaño, *m*; (lath) listón, *m*

runner *n* corredor (-ra); (carrier of sedan chair, etc.) silletero, *mf*; (smuggler) contrabandista, *m*; (courier) estafeta, *f*; (messenger) mensajero, *m*; (ring) anillo movible, pasador corredizo, *m*; rueda móvil, *f*; (of a sledge) patín, *m*; *bot* tallo rastrero, *m*. **r.-up,** el segundo

running *a* corredor; (of water, bank accounts) corriente; (of a knot) corredizo; (of a sore) supurante; (continuous) continuo; (consecutive) consecutivo. *n* carrera, *f*; marcha, *f*; funcionamiento, *m*; administración, *f*; gobierno, *m*; dirección, *f*; (flowing) derrame, *m*; (of trains, buses, etc.) servicio, *m*; (smuggling) contrabando, *m*; (of a sore) supuración, *f*. **six times r.,** seis veces consecutivas. **The car is in r. order,** El auto está en buen estado. **r. away,** fuga, *f*. **r.-board,** (of a car, etc.) estribo, *m*; (of a locomotive) plataforma, *f*. **r. costs,** gastos de mantenimiento, *m pl*; (railway) gastos de tracción, *m pl*. **r. fight,** acción de retirada, *f*. **r.-knot,** lazo corredizo, *m*. **r. title,** *print* título de la columna, *m*

run-off match *n* desempate, *m*

runway *n* (for launching a ship) grada, *f*; (of an airfield) pista de aterrizaje, *f*

rupee *n* rupia, *f*

rupestrian *a* rupestre

rupture *n* rompimiento, *m*, rotura, *f*; ruptura, *f*; *med* hernia, *f*

ruptured *a med* herniado, quebrado

rupturing *n* ruptura, *f*

rural *a* rural, campestre, del campo; agrario

ruse *n* artimaña, treta, ardid, *f*

rush *n bot* junco, *m*; acometida, *f*; ataque, *m*; (of water) torrente, *m*; (bustle) bullicio, *m*; (speed) prisa, *f*; precipitación, *f*; acceso, *m*; (crowd) tropel, *m*, masa, *f*; (struggle) lucha, *f*; furia, *f*. *vi* precipitarse, lanzarse; agolparse. *vt* llevar rápidamente (a); despachar rápidamente; precipitar; (attack) asaltar, atacar; (capture) tomar, capturar; hacer de prisa; (a bill) hacer aprobar de prisa. **to r. upon,** abalanzarse hacia; embestir. **in a r.,** en tropel, en masa; de prisa. **to r. to a conclusion,** precipitarse a una conclusión. **r.-bottomed,** con asiento de enea. **r. hour,** hora de mayor circulación, *f*, hora de aglomeración, hora-pico (Argentina), hora brava (Argentina, informal). **r. order,** pedido urgente, *m*

rushy *a* juncoso

russet *a* rojizo; rojo. **r. apple,** manzana asperiega, *f*

Russia Rusia, *f*

Russian *a* ruso. *n* ruso (-sa); (language) ruso, *m*. **R. leather,** piel de Rusia, *f*

rust *n* herrumbre, *f*, orín, *m*; moho, *m*; (disease) añublo, tizón, *m*. *vt* aherrumbrar; enmohecer. *vi* aherrumbrarse; enmohecerse

rustic *a* rústico; campesino, aldeano; (scornful) palurdo, grosero. *n* aldeano, *m*; (scornful) patán, *m*

rusticate *vi* rusticar, vivir en el campo. *vt* enviar al campo

rustication *n* rusticación, *f*

rusticity *n* rusticidad, *f*

rustiness *n* herrumbre, *f*; enmohecimiento, *m*; color rojizo, *m*; *fig* falta de práctica, *f*

rustle *n* susurro, *m*; murmurio, *m*; (of silk, a dress, etc.) frufrú, *m*; (of paper, etc.) crujido, *m*. *vi* susurrar; murmurar; crujir. *vt* (a paper) hacer crujir

rustless *a* inoxidable

rustling *n see* **rustle**

rusty *a* herrumbroso; enmohecido, mohoso; (red) rojizo, (worn out) usado, viejo; (out of practice) descostumbrado; (forgotten) empolvorado, oxidado (e.g. **My Portuguese is rusty,** Mi portugués está empolvorado)

rut *n* rodera, *f*, bache, surco, *m*; *fig* sendero trillado, *m*; *fig* rutina, *f*; (sexual appetite) celo, *m*, *vi* estar en celo

ruthless *a* inhumano, insensible, despiadado; inexorable, inflexible

ruthlessly *adv* inhumanamente; inflexiblemente, inexorablemente

ruthlessness *n* inhumanidad, *f*; inflexibilidad, inexorabilidad, *f*

rye *n* centeno, *m*. **rye field,** centenar, *m*

S

s *n* (letter) ese, *f*

sabbatarian *a* sabatario

Sabbath *n* (Jewish) sábado, *m*; (Christian) domingo, *m*

sabbatical *a* sabático

sable *n* (animal and fur) marta, *f*; *her* sable, *m*. *a her* sable; *poet* negro

sabotage *n* sabotaje, *m*, *vt* cometer un acto de sabotaje en

saboteur *n* saboteador, *m*

sabre *n* sable, *m*; (soldier) jinete, *m*. *vt* dar sablazos (a), acuchillar. **s. cut, thrust,** sablazo, *m*

sac *n biol* saco, *m*

saccharin *n* sacarina, *f*

sachet *n* sachet, *m*; bolsa, *f*. **handkerchief s.,** bolsa para pañuelos, *f*

sack *n* (bag) saco, *m*; *mil* saqueo, saqueamiento, saco, *m*. *vt* meter en sacos; (dismiss) dar pasaporte (a), despedir; *mil* saquear. **to get the s.,** recibir el pasaporte. **to give the s.,** dar el pasaporte (a), poner de patitas en la calle (a). **s. coat,** saco, *m*

sackcloth *n* harpillera, *f*. **to repent in s. and ashes,** ponerse cenizas en la cabeza

sacking *n* harpillera, *f*; *mil* saqueo, *m*

sacrament *n* sacramento, *m*; Eucaristía, *f*. **the Blessed S.,** el Santísimo Sacramento. **to receive the Holy S.,** comulgar. **to receive the last sacraments,** recibir los sacramentos, recibir la Extremaunción

sacramental *a* sacramental

sacramentalist *n* sacramentario (-ia)

sacred *a* sagrado; sacro, santo; consagrado. **Nothing is s. to them,** No hay nada sagrado para ellos, No respetan nada. **the S. Heart of Jesus,** el Sagrado Corazón (de Jesús). **S. to the memory of . . .** Consagrado a la memoria de . . . **s. music,** música sagrada, *f*

sacredness *n* carácter sagrado, *m*; santidad, *f*; inviolabilidad, *f*

sacrifice *n* sacrificio, *m*. *vt* and *vi* sacrificar. **s. of the mass,** sacrificio del altar, *m*

sacrificial *a* sacrificador; del sacrificio

sacrilege *n* sacrilegio, *m*

sacrilegious *a* sacrílego

sacristan *n* sacristán, *m*

sacristy *n* sacristía, *f*

sacrosanct *a* sacrosanto

sacrum *n anat* sacro, *m*

sad *a* triste; melancólico; (of a mistake) deplorable, funesto; *inf* redomado; (pensive) pensativo. **How s.!** ¡Qué lástima! ¡Qué triste! **It made me s.,** Me entristeció

sadden *vt* entristecer, acongojar, afligir

saddle *n* (riding) silla de montar, *Lat. Am.* albarda, *f*; (of a bicycle, etc.) sillín, *m*; *mech* silla, *f*; *anat* espalda, *f*. *vt* ensillar. **to s. with the responsibility of,** echar la responsabilidad de (a). **s. of mutton,** lomo de carnero, *m*. **s.-bag,** alforja, *Lat. Am.* buchaca, *f*. **s.-cloth,** mantilla de silla, *f*. **s.-tree,** arzón, *m*

saddler *n* sillero, guarnicionero, *m*

Sadducee *n* saduceo (-ea)

sadism *n* sadismo, *m*

sadist *n* sadista, *mf*

sadistic *a* sadístico

sadly *adv* tristemente; (very) muy

sadness *n* tristeza, melancolía, *f*

safe *a* al abrigo (de); seguro; salvo; (certain) cierto; prudente; digno de confianza. *n* caja de caudales, *f*; (for food) alacena, *f*. **I stood beneath a tree s. from the** rain, Estaba de pie bajo un árbol, al abrigo de la lluvia. **to put something in a s. place,** poner algo en salvo; poner algo en un lugar seguro. **s. and sound,** sano y salvo. **s.-conduct,** salvoconducto, *m*. **s.-keeping,** lugar seguro, *m*; (of a person) buenas manos, *f pl*

safeguard *n* protección, garantía, *f*; precaución, *f*. *vt* proteger, guardar; tomar precauciones (contra)

safely *adv* seguramente; sin accidente, sin novedad, sano y salvo; sin peligro. **You may s. tell him,** Puedes decírselo con toda seguridad. **to put** (something) **away s.,** poner (algo) en un lugar seguro

safety *n* seguridad, *f*. *a* de seguridad; (of locks) de golpe. **a place of s.,** un lugar seguro. **in s.,** en salvo, en seguro; con seguridad. **to believe in s. first,** poner la seguridad en primer lugar. **to play for s.,** jugar seguro. **with complete s.,** con toda seguridad. **s.-belt,** (cinto) salvavidas, *m*. **s.-catch,** fiador, *m*. **s.-curtain,** telón de seguridad, telón contra incendios, *m*. **s.-fuse,** espoleta de seguridad, *f*. **s.-glass,** vidrio inastillable, *m*. **s.-island,** refugio para peatones, *m*. **s.-lamp,** lámpara de seguridad, *f*. **s.-latch,** pestillo de golpe, *m*. **s.-lock,** (of fire-arms) seguro, *m*; (of doors, etc.) cerradura de seguridad, *f*. **s.-pin,** imperdible, *m*. **s.-razor,** máquina de afeitar, *f*. **s.-valve,** válvula de seguridad, *f*

saffron *n* azafrán, *m*, *a* azafranado, de color de azafrán.

sag *vi* doblegarse, ceder; inclinarse; *naut* caer a sotavento; (of prices) bajar; (of spirits, etc.) flaquear

saga *n* saga, *f*; epopeya, *f*

sagacious *a* sagaz, perspicaz; (of animals) sabio

sagacity *n* sagacidad, perspicacia, *f*; (of animals) sagacidad, *f*

sage *n* sabio, *m*; *bot* salvia, *f*. *a* sabio; sagaz; cuerdo

Sagittarius *n* Sagitario, *m*

Sahara, the el Sáhara, *m*

said *a* antedicho; tal dicho. **No sooner s. than done,** Dicho y hecho. **the s. Mr. Martínez,** el tal Sr. Martínez

sail *n* (of a ship) vela, *f*; (sailing-ship) velero, *m*; (of a windmill) aspa, *f*; *mech* ala, *f*; (trip) paseo en barco, *m*. *vi* navegar; ir en barco; dar un paseo en barco; (leave) salir en barco; zarpar; (of swans, etc.) deslizarse; (of clouds, etc.) flotar. *vt* (a ship) gobernar; (the sea) navegar por. **She sailed into the room,** Entró majestuosamente en la sala. **The ship sailed at eight knots,** El buque navegaba a ocho nudos. **to go for a s.,** dar un paseo en barco. **to s. round the world,** dar la vuelta al mundo. **to s. the seas,** navegar por los mares. **to set s.,** darse a la vela, zarpar. **to take in the sails,** amainar. **s.-maker,** velero, *m*. **to s. into,** entrar en barco; (of a boat) ir río arriba

sailcloth *n* lona, *f*

sailing *n* navegación, *f*; (departure) salida, *f*. **It's all plain s.,** Todo va viento en popa. **s.-boat,** bote de vela, *m*. **s.-ship,** buque de vela, velero, *m*

sailor *n* marinero, *m*. **John is a bad s.,** Juan se marea fácilmente. **to be a good s.,** no marearse. **s.-blouse,** marinera, *f*. **s.-suit,** traje de marinero, *m*

saint *n* santo (-ta); (before masculine names of Sts., excluding Sts. Dominic and Thomas) San; *inf* ángel, *m*. **All Saints' Day,** el día de Todos los Santos. **saint's day,** fiesta de un santo (or de una santa), *f*; (of a person) santo, *m*. **St. Bernard dog,** perro de San Bernardo, *m*. **St. John the Baptist,** San Juan Bautista. **St. Martin's summer,** el veranillo de San Martín. **St. Vitus's dance,** el baile de San Vito

sainthood *n* santidad, *f*

saintliness *n* santidad, *f*

saintly *a* de santo; de santa; santo; *inf* angelical

Saint Petersburg San Petersburgo, *m*

sake *n* amor, *m*; causa, *f*. **for God's s.,** por el amor de Dios. **for the s. of,** para; por amor de. **to talk for talking's s.,** hablar por hablar

salable *a* vendible

salaciousness *n* salacidad, *f*

salad *n* ensalada, *f*; (lettuce) lechuga, *f*. **fruit s.,** macedonia de frutas, *f*. **s.-bowl,** ensaladera, *f*. **s.-dressing,** aderezo, aliño, *m*, salsa para ensalada, *f*. **s.-oil,** aceite para ensaladas, *m*

salamander *n* salamandra, *f*

salaried *a* a sueldo; (of posts) retribuido

salary *n* sueldo, salario, *m*

sale *n* venta, *f*; (auction) almoneda, subasta pública, *f*. **(clearance) s.,** liquidación, *f*, saldo, *m*, *Mexico* barata, *f*. **to be on s.,** estar de venta. **"Piano for s.,"** «Se vende un piano.» **s. price,** precio de venta, *m*; precio de saldo, *m*

sales contract *n* contrato de compraventa, *m*

salesman *n* dependiente de tienda, *m*; (traveller) viajante, *m*

salesmanship *n* arte de vender, *mf*

salesroom *n* salón de ventas, *m*

saleswoman *n* dependiente de tienda, vendedera, *f*

salient *a* saliente; *fig* prominente, conspicuo, notable, *n* saliente, *m*. **s. angle,** ángulo saliente, *m*

saline *a* salino. *n* (marsh) saladar, *m*; *med* salino, *m*

saliva *n* saliva, *f*

salivary *a* salival

salivate *vi* salivar

salivation *n* salivación, *f*

sallow *a* cetrino, oliváceo, lívido

sallowness *n* amarillez, lividez, *f*; palidez, *f*

sally *n* (*mil* etc.) salida, *f*; (quip) ocurrencia, salida, *f*. *vi* hacer una salida, salir. **s. forth,** ponerse en camino

salmon *n* salmón, *m*; color de salmón, *m*. **s.-net,** salmonera, *f*. **s. trout,** trucha asalmonada, *f*

salon *n* salón, *m*

Salonika Salónica, *f*

saloon *n* sala, *f*; (of a steamer) cámara, *f*, salón, *m*; (on train, for sleeping) departamento de coche cama, *m*; (on train, for dining) coche comedor, *m*; *aut* coche cerrado, *m*. **billiard s.,** salón de billares, *m*. **dancing s.,** salón de baile, *m*. **hair-dresser's s.,** salón de peluquero, *m*. **s. bar,** bar, *m*

salsify *n bot* salsifí, *m*

salt *n* sal, *f*; (spice) sabor, *m*; (wit) sal, agudeza, *f*. *a* salobre, salino; salado; (of land) salitroso. *vt* (season) poner sal en; (cure) salar. **kitchen s.,** sal de cocina, *f*. **old s.,** *inf* lobo de mar, *m*. **rock s.,** sal gema, *f*. **sea s.,** sal marina, *f*. **to be not worth one's s.,** no merecer el pan que se come. **to take with a pinch of s.,** tomar con su grano de sal. **s.-cellar,** salero, *m*. **s. lagoon,** albufera, *f*. **s. lake,** lago salado, *m*. **s. marsh,** saladar, *m*. **s. meat,** carne salada, cecina, *f*. **s. merchant,** salinero, *m*. **s.-mine,** mina de sal, *f*. **s.-spoon,** cucharita de sal, *f*. **s. water,** agua salada, *f*; agua de mar, *f*. **s.-water fish,** pez de mar, *m*. **s.-works,** salinas, *f pl*

saltiness *n* sabor de sal, *m*; salobridad, *f*

salting *n* saladura, *f*; (salt marsh) saladar, *m*

saltless *a* sin sal, soso, insípido; *fig* soso

saltpeter *n* salitre, *m*. **s. bed,** salitral, *m*. **s. works,** salitrería, *f*

salty *a* salado; salobre

salubrious *a* salubre, saludable, sano

salubriousness *n* salubridad, *f*

salutary *a* saludable, beneficioso

salutation *n* salutación, *f*, saludo, *m*

salute *vt* and *vi* saludar. *n* saludo, *m*; (of guns) salva, *f*. **to fire a s.,** hacer salvas, saludar con . . . salvas. **The soldier saluted them,** El soldado les saludó. **to take the s.,** tomar el saludo. **saluting base,** puesto de mando, *m*

Salvadoran, Salvadorian *a* and *n* salvadoreño (-ña)

salvage *n* salvamento, *m*, *vt* salvar

salvation *n* salvación, *f*. **to work out one's own s.,** salvar el alma. **the S. Army,** el Ejército de la Salvación, *m*

salve *n* pomada, *f*; *fig* bálsamo, *m*. *vt* curar; (overcome) vencer; (soothe) tranquilizar; *naut* salvar. **to s. one's conscience,** tranquilizar la conciencia

salver *n* salva, bandeja, *f*

salvo *n* (of guns or applause) salva, *f*; (reservation) salvedad, reservación, *f*. **s. of applause,** salva de aplausos, *f*

Samaritan *a* and *n* samaritano (-na)

same *a* mismo; igual; parecido; idéntico. *adv* lo mismo; del mismo modo. **all the s.,** sin embargo; con todo, a pesar de eso. **at the s. time,** al mismo tiempo; a la vez. **just the s.,** igual; (nevertheless) sin embargo. **He bowed deeply and I did the s.,** Él hizo una profunda reverencia y yo hice lo mismo. **They do not look at things the s. as we do,** No ven las cosas del mismo modo que nosotros. **If it is the s. to her,** Si le da igual. **It's all the s.,** Es igual, Lo mismo da, Es todo uno. **Ávila, capital of the province of the s. name,** Ávila, capital de la provincia de su nombre

"Same-Day Service" «En el día» (Argentina)

sameness *n* identidad, *f*; semejanza, *f*, parecido, *m*; monotonía, *f*

samovar *n* samovar, *m*

sampan *n* (boat) champán, *m*

sample *n* muestra, *f*; prueba, *f*; ejemplo, *m*. *vt* sacar una muestra de; (try) probar. **s. book,** muestrario, *m*

sampler *n* probador, *m*; (of wines) catador, *m*; *sew* dechado, *m*

sanatorium *n* sanatorio, *m*

sanctification *n* santificación, *f*; consagración, *f*

sanctify *vt* santificar; consagrar

sanctimonious *a* santurrón, mojigato, beato

sanctimoniousness *n* beatería, mojigatería, santurronería, *f*

sanction *n* sanción, *f*. *vt* sancionar; autorizar. **to apply sanctions,** *pol* aplicar sanciones

sanctity *n* santidad, *f*; lo sagrado; inviolabilidad, *f*. **odor of s.,** olor de santidad, *f*

sanctuary *n* santuario, *m*; (historical) sagrado, sagrado asilo, *m*; refugio, asilo, *m*. **to take s.,** acogerse a sagrado; refugiarse

sand *n* arena, *f*; (for drying writing) arenilla, *f*; granos de arena, *m pl*; *pl* **sands,** playa, *f*; (of life) horas de la vida, *f pl*. *vt* arenar. **to plough the s.,** arar en el mar. **s.-bag,** *n* saco de arena, *m*. *vt* (a building) proteger con sacos de arena; (a person) golpear con un saco de arena. **s.-bank,** banco de arena, *m*, barra, *f*. **to run on a s.-bank,** encallar. **s.-colored,** de color de arena. **s.-dune,** médano, *m*. **s.-paper,** *n* papel de lija, *m*. *vt* pulir con papel de lija, lijar. **s.-pit,** arenal, *m*. **s. shoes,** alpargatas, *f pl*

sandal *n* sandalia, *f*, *Central America* caite, *m*; (rope-soled) alpargata, *f*. **s.-wood,** sándalo, *m*

sandiness *n* naturaleza arenosa, *f*; (of hair) color bermejo, *m*

sandstone *n* arenisca, *f*

sandstorm *n* tempestad de arena, *f*; simún, *m*

sandwich *n* emparedado, bocadillo, *m*. *vt* insertar. **I found myself sandwiched between two fat men,** Me encontré aplastado entre dos hombres gordos. **s.-man,** hombre sándwich, *m*

sandy *a* arenoso; sabuloso; (of hair) rojo, rufo, bermejo. **a s. beach,** una playa arenosa

sane *a* de juicio sano; razonable, prudente; sesudo. **He is a very s. person,** Es un hombre con mucho sentido común. **to be s.,** estar en su juicio; (of a policy, etc.) ser prudente, ser razonable

sangfroid *n* sangre fría, *f*; aplomo, *m*

sanguinary *a* sanguinario

sanguine *a* (of complexion) rubicundo; sanguíneo; optimista, confiado. *n* (drawing) sanguina, *f*. **to be s.**

about the future, ser optimista acerca del porvenir, tener confianza en el porvenir

sanhedrin *n* sanedrín, *m*

sanitary *a* sanitario; higiénico, **s. inspector,** inspector de sanidad, *m.* **s. napkin, s. towel,** servilleta higiénica, toalla sanitaria, *mf,* paño higiénico, *m*

sanitation *n* higiene, *f;* sanidad pública, *f;* (apparatus) instalación sanitaria, *f*

sanity *n* juicio sano, *m;* prudencia, *f;* (common sense) sentido común, *m,* sensatez, *f*

Santa Claus *n* (Spanish equivalent) los Reyes Magos, *m pl*

São Paulo San Pablo, *m*

sap *n* (*bot* and *fig*) savia, *f; mil* zapa, *f. vt* (undermine) debilitar, agotar; *mil* zapar

sapidity *n* sapidez, *f*

sapling *n* arbolillo, *m*

sapper *n mil* zapador, *m*

Sapphic *a* sáfico. **S. verse,** verso sáfico, *m*

sapphire *n* zafiro, *m. a* de zafiros; cerúleo, de zafiro

Saracen *a* and *n* sarraceno (-na)

Saragossa Zaragoza, *f*

sarcasm *n* sarcasmo, *m*

sarcastic *a* sarcástico

sarcastically *adv* con sarcasmo, sarcásticamente

sarcophagus *n* sarcófago, *m*

sardine *n* sardina, *f.* **packed like sardines,** como sardinas en banasta. **s.-net,** sardinal, *m*

Sardinia Cerdeña, *f*

Sardinian *a* and *n* sardo (-da)

sardonic *a* sardónico

sarsaparilla *n* zarzaparrilla, *f*

sash *n* (with uniform) faja, *f;* (belt) cinto, cinturón, *m;* (of a window) cerco, *m.* **s. window,** ventana de guillotina, *f*

Satan *n* Satanás, *m*

satanic *a* satánico

satchel *n* saquito de mano, *m,* bolsa, *f;* (school) vademécum, *m;* cartapacio, *m,* cartera, *f*

sate *vt* saciar, hartar; satisfacer

sateen *n* satén, *m*

satellite *n* satélite, *m*

satiable *a* saciable

satiate *vt* saciar, hartar; satisfacer. *a* harto; repleto

satiety *n* saciedad, *f*

satin *n* raso, *m. a* de raso; (glossy) lustroso, terso. *vt* (paper) satinar

satiny *a* arrasado; lustroso, brillante

satire *n* sátira, *f*

satiric *a* satírico

satirist *n* escritor (-ra) satírico (-ca)

satirize *vt* satirizar

satisfaction *n* satisfacción, *f;* (contentment) contento, *m,* satisfacción, *f;* (for sin) expiación, *f;* (of a debt) pago, *m;* desquite, *m;* recompensa, *f.* **to demand s.,** pedir satisfacción. **to give** (someone) **s.,** dar contento (a), alegrar

satisfactorily *adv* satisfactoriamente

satisfactoriness *n* carácter satisfactorio, *m,* lo satisfactorio

satisfactory *a* satisfactorio; (for sin) expiatorio

satisfy *vt* satisfacer; (convince) convencer; (allay) tranquilizar, apaciguar. **I am satisfied with him,** Estoy satisfecho (Estoy contento) con él. **The explanation did not s. me,** La explicación no me convenció. **to s. oneself that . . . ,** asegurarse de que . . . **to s. one's thirst,** apagar la sed

satisfying *a* que satisface; satisfactorio; (of food) nutritivo

satrap *n* sátrapa, *m*

saturate *vt* saturar (de), empapar (de); *chem* saturar; *fig* imbuir; *fig* empapar. **to s. oneself in,** (a subject) emparparse en

saturation *n* saturación, *f.* **s. point,** (*chem* etc.) punto de saturación, *m*

Saturday *n* sábado, *m*

Saturn *n* Saturno, *m*

saturnine *a* saturnino, taciturno

satyr *n* sátiro, *m*

sauce *n* salsa, *f;* (thick fruit) compota, *f; inf* insolencia, *f.* **s.-boat,** salsera, *f*

saucepan *n* cazuela, cacerola, *f.* **double s.,** baño de María, *m*

saucer *n* platillo, *m.* **s. flying s.,** platillo volante, *m.* **s.-eyed,** con ojos redondos

sauciness *n* impertinencia, insolencia, *f*

saucy *a* respondón, descarado; (cheerful) alegre; (of hats, etc.) coquetón, majo

sauerkraut *n* chucruta, *f*

saunter *vi* pasearse, vagar, *n* paseo, *m,* vuelta, *f*

sausage *n* chorizo, *m;* salchicha, *f.* **s.-balloon,** globo cautivo, *m.* **s.-curl,** bucle, *m.* **s.-machine,** choricera, *f.* **s.-maker,** choricero (-ra)

savage *a* salvaje; feroz; (cruel) inhumano, cruel; (furious) furioso. *n* salvaje, *mf*

savagely *adv* bárbaramente; ferozmente; furiosamente

savagery *n* salvajismo, *m;* ferocidad, *f;* brutalidad, crueldad, *f*

savannah *n* sabana, *f.* **s. dweller,** sabanero (-ra)

save *vt* salvar; (keep) guardar; conservar; reservar; (money, one's clothes, etc.) ahorrar; (time) ganar; (avoid) evitar. *vi* salvar; hacer economías; ahorrar. **He saved my life,** Me salvó la vida. **They have saved a room for me,** Me han reservado una habitación. **to s. appearances,** guardar las apariencias. **to s. oneself trouble,** ahorrarse molestias. **to s. the situation,** estar al nivel de las circunstancias

save *prep* salvo, excepto, menos. *conjunc* sino, a menos que; con la excepción de. **all s. one,** todos menos uno. **all the conspirators s. he,** todos los conspiradores con la excepción de él

saving *a* frugal, económico; (stingy) tacaño, avaricioso; (clause) condicional. *n* salvación, *f;* (of money, time, etc.) ahorro, *m,* economía, *f; pl* **savings,** ahorros, *m pl. prep* salvo, excepto, fuera de. *conjunc* con excepción de que, fuera de que. **s. grace,** único mérito, *m.* **savings bank,** caja de ahorros, *f.* **savings fund,** montepío, *m*

savior *n* salvador (-ra). **the S.,** el Salvador, el Redentor

savor *n* sabor, gusto, *m;* (aftertaste) dejo, *m;* (zest) salsa, *f. vi* saber (a), tener sabor (de); *fig* oler (a). *vt* saborear; paladear; (flavor) sazonar

savoriness *n* buen sabor, *m;* (of a district) respetabilidad, *f*

savory *a* sabroso, apetitoso; (not sweet) no dulce; (of places) respetable; (of reputation, etc.) bueno. *n* entremés salado, *m.* **s. omelette,** tortilla, *f*

Savoy Saboya, *f*

saw *n* (maxim) sentencia, *f;* (proverb) refrán, decir, *m;* (tool) sierra, *f. vt* aserrar, *Lat. Am.* aserruchar; (the air) cortar. *vi* usar una sierra. **two-handled saw,** tronzador, *m.* **saw-fish,** pez sierra, *m.* **saw-mill,** molino de aserrar, *m.* **saw-pit,** aserradero, *m*

sawdust *n* aserrín, *m*

sawinghorse *n* caballete de aserrar, *m*

sawyer *n* aserrador, *m*

Saxon *a* and *n* sajón (-ona)

Saxony Sajonia, *f*

saxophone *n* saxófono, saxofón *m*

say *vt* decir; recitar. *vi* decir. **Let us say that the house is worth \$100,000,** Pongamos por ejemplo que la casa vale cien mil dólares. **He has no say in the matter,** No entra ni sale en el asunto. **I have said my say,** He dicho lo que quería. **They say,** Se dice, Dicen, La gente dice. **You don't say!** ¡Calle! ¿De veras? ¡Imposible! **that is to say . . . ,** es decir . . . ; esto es . . . , a saber . . . **to say one's prayers,** rezar, decir sus oraciones. **to say again,** volver a decir; decir otra vez, repetir. **to say over and over again,** repetir muchas veces, decir repetidamente. **What do you say to that?** ¿Qué dices a esto?

saying *n* decir, *m;* (proverb) refrán, *m;* (maxim) sentencia, *f.* **As the s. is,** Como suele decirse; Según el

refrán. **It goes without s.,** Huelga decir. **It's only a s.,**
Es un decir, nada más

scab n (of a wound) costra, f; (disease) escabro, m;
(blackleg) esquirol, m

scabbard n vaina (de espada), f

scabby a costroso; (diseased) roñoso, sarnoso

scabies n sarna, f. **s. mite,** arador de la sarna, m

scaffold n (in building) andamio, m; (for execution)
cadalso, patíbulo, m. **to go to the s.,** ir al patíbulo;
acabar en el patíbulo

scaffolding n andamiada, f; (building, scaffold) andamio, m

scald vt escaldar; quemar; (instruments) esterilizar. n
quemadura, escaldadura, f. **to s. oneself,** escaldarse.
scalding hot, hirviendo

scale n (of a balance) platillo, m; zool escama, f; bot brác-
tea, f; bot hojuela, f; (flake) laminita, f; (mus, math) escala, f; (of charges, etc.) tarifa, f; (of salaries) escalafón,
m; (of a thermometer) escala, f. vt escalar; (fish) escamar. **major s.,** escala mayor, f. **minor s.,** escala
menor, f. **on a grand s.,** en gran escala. **on a small s.,**
en pequeña escala. **pair of scales,** balanza, f; (for
heavy weights) báscula, f. **social s.,** escala social, f. **The
Scales,** ast Libra, f. **to draw to s.,** dibujar a escala. **to
turn the scales,** pesar; fig inclinar la balanza. **to s.
down,** (art and of charges) reducir

scaling n (of fish) escamadura, f; (of buildings) desconchadura, f; (ascent) escalamiento, m

scallop n (icht and badge) venera, f; concha, f; sew onda,
f, festón, m. vt cul guisar en conchas; sew ondear, festonear

scalp n anat pericráneo, m; cuero cabelludo, m; fig
trofeo, m. vt escalpar. **s.-hunter,** cazador de cabelle-
ras, m

scalpel n escalpelo, m

scaly a escamoso, conchado; (of boilers) incrustado

scamp n bribón, granuja, m, vt (work) frangollar

scamper vi retozar, brincar; correr. n carrerita, f. **to s.
off,** salvarse por los pies, huir; marcharse corriendo

scan vt (verse) medir, escandir; (examine) escudriñar,
examinar; (glance at) dar un vistazo (a)

scandal n escándalo, m; maledicencia, f; (slander) calumnia, f. **to talk s.,** murmurar

scandalize vt escandalizar

scandalous a escandaloso; infame; calumnioso

scandalously adv escandalosamente

scandalousness n carácter escandaloso, m

Scandinavia Escandinavia, f

Scandinavian a escandinavo. n escandinavo (-va);

scant a escaso; insuficiente

scantily adv insuficientemente

scantiness n escasez, f; insuficiencia, f

scanty a insuficiente; escaso; (of hair) ralo; (of crops,
etc.) pobre

scapegoat n víctima propiciatoria, f; cabeza de turco, f.
to be a s. for, pagar el pato por

scapegrace n bribón, m

scapula n anat escápula, f

scapulary n ecc escapulario, m

scar n cicatriz, f; fig señal, f. vt marcar con una cicatriz.
to s. over, cicatrizarse

scarab n escarabajo, m; escarabajo sagrado, m

scarce a escaso; insuficiente; raro. adv poet apenas. **to
make oneself s.,** largarse, pirarse, escabullirse; ausentarse, esconderse

scarcely adv apenas; no bien; casi; (with difficulty) a
duras penas, con dificultad. **It is s. likely he said
that,** No es muy probable que lo hubiese dicho. **There
were s. twenty people in the building,** Había
apenas veinte personas en el edificio. **S. anyone likes
his pictures,** Sus cuadros no le gustan a casi nadie

scarcity n escasez, insuficiencia, f; (famine) carestía, f;
(rarity) rareza, f

scare vt asustar, espantar, llenar de miedo (a), Lat. Am.
also julepear; intimidar. n susto, pánico, m; alarma, f.
What a s. I got! ¡Qué susto me he llevado! **to s. away,**
ahuyentar. **to be scared** Lat. Am. julepearse

scarecrow n espantapájaros, m; inf estantigua, f,
mamarracho, espantajo, m

scaremonger n alarmista, mf

scarf n bufanda, f; (tie) corbata, f; mil faja, f

scarlatina n med escarlatina, f

scarlet n escarlata, f. a de color escarlata. **to turn s.,** (of
persons) enrojecerse. **s. fever,** escarlatina, f. **s. hat,** ecc
capelo (cardenalicio), m. **s. runner,** bot judía verde, f

scatheless a ileso, sano y salvo

scathing a mordaz, cáustico

scatter vt esparcir, sembrar con; (benefits, etc.) derramar; (put to flight) derrotar; dispersar; disipar; (fig
frustrar; (squander) derrochar, desparramar. vi dispersarse. **The crowd scattered,** La muchedumbre se dis-
persó. **s.-brained,** de cabeza de chorlito, atolondrado

scattered a disperso; esparcido

scattered showers n lluvias aisladas, f pl

scattering n dispersión, f; (defeat) derrota, f; esparcimiento, m; (small number) número pequeño, m

scavenge vt (streets) recoger la basura de, barrer

scavenger n (of the streets) barrendero, m; (dustman)
basurero, m; zool animal que se alimenta de carne
muerta, m; (insecto que se alimenta de estiércol, m. vt
See **scavenge**

scenario n escenario, m

scene n escena, f; teatro, lugar, m; espectáculo, m; (theat
décor) decoración, f; (of a play) escena, f; (view) vista,
perspectiva, f; (fig of hounds) viento, m; (of game,
etc.) rastro, viento, m; (fig of person) nariz, f; (trail)
pista, f. **to lose the s.,** perder la pista. **to s. danger,**
oler el peligro. **to throw off the s.,** despistar. **s.-bot-
tle,** frasco de perfume, m. **s.-spray,** pulverizador, m

scenery n theat decorado, m; (landscape) paisaje, m

scenic a dramático; escénico; pintoresco. **s. railway,**
montaña rusa, f

scenography n escenografía, f

scent vt perfumar; (smell) oler; (out) husmear, olfatear;
(suspect) sospechar. n perfume, m; fragancia, f, aroma,
m; (smell) olor, m; (of hounds) viento, m; (of game,
etc.) rastro, viento, m; (fig of person) nariz, f; (trail)
pista, f. **to lose the s.,** perder la pista. **to s. danger,**
oler el peligro. **to throw off the s.,** despistar. **s.-bot-
tle,** frasco de perfume, m. **s.-spray,** pulverizador, m

scented a perfumado; (of roses, etc.) de olor, oloroso;
(in compounds) de . . . olfato. **s. sweet pea,** guisante
de olor, m

scentless a sin olor; inodoro

scepter n cetro, m

sceptic n escéptico (-ca)

sceptical a escéptico

scepticism n escepticismo, m

schedule n lista, m; programa, m; (of taxes) clase, f; (of
trains, etc.) horario, m. vt poner en una lista; inventariar

scheme n plan, m; proyecto, m; diagrama, esquema, m;
(summary) resumen, m; (of colors, etc.) combinación,
f; (plot) intriga, maquinación, f. vt proyectar. vi planear, formar planes; (intrigue) intrigar, conspirar.
color s., combinación de colores, f

schemer n (plotter) intrigante, mf

scheming a intrigante; astuto. n planes, proyectos, m pl;
intrigas, maquinaciones, f pl

schism n cisma, mf

schismatic a cismático. n cismático (-ca)

scholar n (at school) colegial (-la); (disciple) alumno
(-na); (student) estudiante, mf; (learned person)
erudito (-ta), hombre de letras, m; (scholarship holder)
becario, m. **to be a poor s.,** fig ser analfabeto

scholarly a de sabio, de hombre de letras; erudito

scholarship n erudición, f; saber, m; (exhibition) beca,
f. **s. holder,** becario, m

scholastic a escolar, escolástico; pedante; (medieval)
escolástico, m. **the s. profession,** el magisterio

school *n* escuela, *f;* colegio, *m;* academia, *f; univ* departamento, *m;* (faculty) facultad, *f;* (of fish) banco, *m. vt* enseñar, instruir; formar; disciplinar. **in s.,** en clase. **day s.,** escuela, *f,* colegio, *m.* **the Florentine s.,** (of painting) la escuela florentina. **the lower s.,** los alumnos del preparatorio. **private s.,** colegio particular, *m.* **s.-bag,** vademécum, *m.* **s.-book,** libro escolar, *m.* **s.-days,** los días de escuela; los años de colegio. **in his s.-days,** cuando él iba a la escuela. **s.-fees,** gastos de la enseñanza, *m pl,* cuota escolar, *f.*

schoolboy *n* muchacho de escuela, colegial, *m*

school district *n* sector escolar, *m*

schoolfellow *n* compañero de colegio, condiscípulo, *m*

schoolgirl *n* colegiala, *f*

schooling *n* educación, enseñanza, *f*

schoolmaster *n* maestro de escuela, professor, *Mexico* escuelante, *m*

schoolmistress *n* maestra de escuela, profesora, *f*

school of hard knocks *n* universidad sin tejados, *f*

schoolroom *n* aula, sala de clase, salón de clase, *m*

sciatic *a* ciático

sciatica *n* ciática, *f*

science *n* ciencia, *f*

scientific *a* científico; exacto, sistemático

scientist *n* hombre de ciencia, *m,* científico (-ca)

scimitar *n* cimitarra, *f*

scintilla *n fig* átomo, vestigio, *m*

scintillate *vi* centellear, lucir, chispear; (of persons) brillar

scion *n* (sucker) acodo, *m;* (shoot) vástago, renuevo, *m;* (human) descendiente, *mf.* **s. of a noble race,** vástago de una raza noble, *m*

scissors *n pl* tijeras, *f pl, Argentina* cortante, *msg.* **s.-sharpener,** amolador, *m*

sclerosis *n med* esclerosis, *f*

sclerotic *n anat* esclerótica, *f*

scoff *n* burla, mofa, *f. vi* burlarse. **to s. at,** burlarse de, mofarse of

scoffer *n* mofador (-ra) (at religion, etc.) incrédulo (-la)

scoffing *a* burlón. *n* mofas, burlas, *f pl*

scold *n* virago, *f, vt* reñir, reprender

scolding *n* represión, increpación, *f*

sconce *n* cubo de candelero, *m;* candelabro de pared, *m;* cornucopia, *f*

scone *n* bollo, *m*

scoop *n* pala de mano, *f;* cuchara de draga, *f;* (boat) achicador, *m;* (financial) golpe, *m;* (journalistic) éxito periodístico, *m. vt* sacar con pala (de); sacar con cuchara (de); (shares, etc.) comprar, obtener. **to s. out,** vaciar; excavar; (bail) achicar

scooter *n* (child's) patinete, patín del diablo, *m;* monopatín, *m*

scope *n* alcance, *m;* esfera de acción, *f;* lugar, *m.* **to give full s. to,** dar rienda suelta a. **to have full s.,** tener plena oportunidad; tener todas las facilidades. **within the s. of,** dentro del alcance de

scorbutic *a med* escorbútico

scorch *vt* chamuscar; (the skin) tostar; (of the sun) abrasar, quemar; (wither) agostar. **to s. along,** ir como un relámpago. **scorching,** *a* abrasador, ardiente; *fig* mordaz

score *n* (scratch) rasguño, *m;* señal, *f;* (crossing out) raya, *f;* (reckoning) cuenta, *f,* escote, *m;* (notch) muesca, *f; sport* tanteo, *m,* puntuación, *Lat. Am.* anotación, *f;* (point) punto, tanto, *m;* (twenty) veintena, *f;* (reason) motivo, *m,* causa, *f;* respecto, *m; mus* partitura, *f. vt* marcar; rayar; (erase) tachar, borrar; (cricket runs, etc.) hacer; (goals) marcar; (points) ganar; (reckon) apuntar. **s. a triumph,** apuntarse un triunfo; *mus* instrumentar; (for orchestra) orquestar. *vi* (be fortunate) llevar la ventaja. **to pay off old scores,** ajustar cuentas viejas. **to s. off someone,** ganar un punto (a), triunfar de. **upon that s.,** a ese respecto; por esa causa. **Upon what s.?** ¿Con qué motivo? **s.-board,** marcador, *m*

scorer *n* (of a goal, etc.) tanteador, *m;* (keeper of score) marcador, *m*

scoria *n* escoria, *f*

scorn *n* desprecio, desdén, *m. vt* despreciar, desdeñar; reírse de. **to s. to do,** no dignarse hacer

scornful *a* desdeñoso, despreciativo

scornfully *adv* desdeñosamente, con desprecio

Scorpion *n* Escorpión, *m*

scorpion *n* escorpión, alacrán, *m; ast* Escorpión, *m*

Scot *n* escocés, *m*

scotch *vt* (kill) matar; (thwart) frustrar; (a wheel) calzar

Scotland Escocia, *f*

Scotswoman *n* escocesa, *f*

Scottish *a* escocés

scoundrel *n* canalla, sinvergüenza, *mf*

scour *vt* (traverse) recorrer, batir; (pans, etc.) fregar, estregar; (free from) limpiar (de); (of water) arrastrar

scourge *vt* azotar, flagelar; castigar, mortificar. *n* disciplinas, *f pl; fig* verdugo, *m,* plaga, *f*

scout *n* mil batidor, explorador, *m. vi mil* explorar, reconocer. *vt* (flout) rechazar a mano airada, rechazar con desdén. **boy s.,** muchacho explorador, *m*

scowl *vi* fruncir el ceño. *n* ceño, *m.* **to s. at,** mirar con ceño

scowling *a* amenazador

scragginess *n* magrez, flaqueza, *f*

scraggy *a* flaco, magro, descarnado

scramble *vi* trepar. *vt* (throw) arrojar; (eggs) revolver. **scrambled eggs,** huevos revueltos, *m pl.* **to s. for,** andar a la rebatiña por; (for coins, etc.) luchar para. **to s. up,** escalar; subir a gatas

scrap *n* pedazo, *m;* fragmento, *m;* pizca, brizna, *f;* (shindy) suiza, camorra, *f;* (boxing) combate de boxeo, *m; pl* **scraps,** desperdicios, *m pl;* (food) restos de la comida, *m pl. vt* desechar; (expunge) borrar; *vi* (fight) armar camorra. **a few scraps of news,** algunas noticias. **Do you mind not coming? Not a s.,** ¿Te importa no venir? Ni pizca. **s.-book,** álbum de recortes, *m;* **s.-heap,** depósito de basura, *m; fig* olvido, *m.* **s. iron,** chatarra, *f,* hierro viejo, *m*

scrape *vt* raspar, rascar, raer; (one's shoes) restregar; (a musical instrument) rascar. *n* rasguño, *m;* ruido de raspar, *m;* (predicament) lío, apuro, *m;* dificultad, *f.* **to s. acquaintance with,** trabar amistad con. **to s. along,** *inf* ir tirando. **to s. away,** rascar; quitar. **to s. through,** (an examination) aprobar justo. **to s. together,** amontonar poco a poco

scrappy *a* escaso; fragmentario; (incoherent) descosido. **a s. meal,** una comida escasa

scratch *vt* arañar; (the earth) escarbar; (rub) rascar; (a hole) hacer; (sketch) dibujar, trazar; (a horse) retirar de una carrera. *vi* arañar; rascar; escarbar; (of a pen) rasguear; (back out) retirarse. *n* arañazo, *m;* (of a pen) rasgueo, *m;* (in a race) línea de salida, *f;* (in games) cero, *m.* *a* improvisado. **The dog scratched at the door,** El perro arañó la puerta. **to come up to s.,** estar al nivel de las circunstancias. **to s. one's head,** rascarse la cabeza. **to s. a person's eyes out,** sacar los ojos con las uñas (a). **to s. the surface of,** (a subject) tratar superficialmente. **to s. out,** tachar

scrawl *vi* hacer garabatos. *vt* garabatear, garrapatear. *n* garabato, *m*

scream *vt* and *vi* chillar. *n* chillido, *m.* **It was a perfect s.** Era para morirse de risa. **to s. with laughter,** reírse a carcajadas, morirse de risa

screaming *n* chillidos, *m pl. a* chillador; (piercing) penetrante, agudo; (funny) divertidísimo

screech *vi* chillar; (of owls, etc.) ulular; graznar. *n* chillido, *m,* ululación, *f;* graznido, *m.* **s.-owl,** úlula, *f*

screed *n* arenga, *f;* cita larga, *f*

screen *n* biombo, *m;* (wire) tela metálica, *f;* (nonfolding) mampara, *f;* (eco) cancel, *m;* (cinema, television) pantalla, *f;* (of trees, etc., and *mil*) cortina, *f;* (*fig* protection) abrigo, *m. vt* proteger; (shelter) abrigar; (hide) esconder, ocultar; (a light) proteger con pantalla; (a film) proyectar; (sieve) cribar, cerner; (examine) investigar.

to s. from view, ocultar la vista (de), esconder. **s. star,** estrella de la pantalla, *f*

screw *n* tornillo, *m*; (propeller) hélice, *f*; vuelta de tornillo, *f*; presión, *f*; (miser) tacaño, *m*; (salary) salario, *m*. *vt* atornillar; torcer; apretar, oprimir. **He has a s. loose,** Le falta un tornillo. **to s. down,** sujetar con tornillos. **to s. up,** cerrar con tornillos. **to s. up one's courage,** tomar coraje. **to s. up one's eyes,** desojarse, entornar los ojos. **s.-driver,** destornillador, *Mexico* desarmador, *m*

scribble *vt* escribir de prisa, *vi* garabatear, garrapatear; escribir, ser autor. *n* garabato, garrapato, *m*; mala letra, letra ilegible, *f*; (note) billete, *m*

scribbler *n* el, *m*, (*f*, la) que tiene mala letra; (author) autor (-ra) malo (-la)

scribbling *n* garabateo, *m*. **s.-block,** bloque de papel, *m*

scribe *n* escribiente, copista, *mf*; (Jewish history) escriba, *m*

scrimmage *n* reyerta, pelea, camorra, *f*; (Rugby) mêlée, *f*

script *n* letra cursiva, *f*; *print* plumilla, *f*; manuscrito, *m*; *law* escritura, *f*; examen escrito, *m*; (film) escenario, *m*

scriptural *a* bíblico

Scripture *n* Sagrada Escritura, *f*. **Scriptures,** Escrituras, *f pl*; (of non-Christian religions) los libros sagrados

scrofula *n* escrófula, *f*

scrofulous *a* escrofuloso

scroll *n* (of paper, etc.) rollo, *m*; pergamino, *m*; (flourish) rúbrica, *f*; (of an Ionic capital) voluta, *f*. **s. of fame,** lista de la fama, *f*

scrotum *n anat* escroto, *m*

scrounge *vi* sablear. *vt* dar un sablazo (a); hurtar

scrounger *n* sablista, *mf*, *Mexico* lapa, *f*

scrub *vt* fregar; limpiar; restregar. *n* fregado, *m*; limpieza, *f*; fricción, *f*; (brushwood) matorral, breñal, *m*, maleza, *f*

scrubbing *n* fregado, *m*. **s.-brush,** cepillo para el suelo, *m*

scrubby *a* (of plants) anémico; (of persons) insignificante, pobre; (of land) cubierto de maleza

scruff *n* nuca, *f*, pescuezo, *m*

scruple *n* escrúpulo, *m*. *vi* tener escrúpulos. **to have no scruples,** no tener escrúpulos

scrupulous *a* escrupuloso; exacto, meticuloso

scrupulously *adv* escrupulosamente; meticulosamente

scrupulousness *n* escrupulosidad, *f*; meticulosidad, *f*

scrutinize *vt* escudriñar, examinar, *Lat. Am. also* interiorizar; (votes) escrutar

scrutinizer *n* escudriñador (-ra); (of votes) escrutador (-ra)

scrutinizing *a* escrutador

scrutiny *n* escrutinio, *m*

scud *vi* correr; deslizarse; flotar. **to s. before the wind,** ir viento en popa

scuffle *vi* pelear, forcejear, andar a la rebatiña. *n* refriega, pelea, sarracina, arrebatiña, *f*

scull *n* remo, *m*. *vi* remar

scullery *n* fregadero, *m*. **s. maid,** fregona, *f*

sculptor *n* escultor, *m*, escultora, *f*

sculptural *a* escultural, escultórico

sculpture *n* escultura, *f*, *vt* esculpir

scum *n* espuma, *f*; (dregs) heces, *f pl*. *vt* espumar. **s. of the earth,** las heces de la sociedad

scupper *n naut* clava, *f*. *vt* abrir las clavas (de); (frustrate) frustrar, destruir

scurrility *n* grosería, indecencia, *f*

scurrilous *a* grosero, indecente

scurry *vi* echar a correr. *n* fuga precipitada, *f*; (of rain) chaparrón, *m*; (of snow) remolino, *m*. **to s. off,** escabullirse. **to s. through,** hacer de prisa, terminar rápidamente

scurvy *a* tiñoso, vil, ruin. *n* escorbuto, *Mexico* berbén, *m*. **a s. trick,** una mala pasada

scuttle *n* (trap-door) escotillón, *m*; *naut* escotilla, *f*; (for coal) carbonera, *f*; (flight) huida precipitada, *f*. *vt* (a

boat) echar a pique, *vi* (run away) escabullirse, apretar a correr

scythe *n* dalle, *m*, guadaña, *f*, *vt* dallar, segar

sea *n* mar, *m*, or *f*; ola, *f*; multitud, *f*. **Black Sea,** Mar Negro. **Mediteranean Sea,** (Mar) Mediterráneo, *m*. **at sea,** en el mar; perplejo. **beyond the seas,** allende los mares. **by sea,** por mar. **by the sea,** a la orilla del mar. **high seas,** alta mar, *f*. **the seven seas,** todos los mares del mundo. **to go to sea,** hacerse marinero. **to put to sea,** hacerse a la mar, hacerse a la vela. **sea-anemone,** anémone de mar. *f*. **sea-bathing,** baños de mar, *m pl*. **sea-breeze,** brisa de mar, *f*. **sea captain,** capitán de mar, *m*. **sea chart,** carta de marear, *f*. **sea-coast,** litoral, *m*, costa marítima, *f*. **sea-cow,** manatí, *m*. **sea dog,** lobo de mar, *m*. **sea-foam,** espuma de mar, *f*. **sea-girt,** rodeado por el mar. **sea-going,** de altura; navegante. **sea-going craft,** embarcación de alta mar, *f*. **sea-green,** verdemar, *m*. **sea-gull,** gaviota, *f*. **sea-horse,** caballo marino, *m*. **sea-legs,** piernas de marino, *f pl*. **sea-level,** nivel del mar, *m*. **sea-lion,** león marino, *m*. **sea-mist,** bruma, *f*. **sea-nymph,** nereida, *f*. **sea-power,** potencia naval, *f*. **sea-serpent,** serpiente de mar, *f*. **sea-sick,** mareado. **to be sea-sick,** marearse. **sea-sickness,** mal de mar, *m*. **sea-trip,** viaje por mar, *m*. **sea-urchin,** erizo de mar, *f*. **sea-wall,** dique de mar, *m*

seafarer *n* (traveller) viajero (-ra) por mar; (sailor) marinero, *m*

seafaring *a* marinero, marino. *n* viajes por mar, *m pl*; vida del marinero, *f*

seal *n zool* foca *f*, lobo marino, *m*; piel de foca, *f*; sello, *m*; (stamp) estampillo, timbre, *m*; *vt* sellar; (stamp) estampar; (letters, etc.) cerrar; *vi* cazar focas. **His fate is sealed,** Su suerte está determinada. **His lips were sealed,** Sus labios estaban cerrados. **under my hand and s.,** firmado y sellado por mí. **s.-ring,** sortija de sello, *f*

sealing wax *n* lacre, *m*

sealskin *n* piel de foca, *f*

seam *n sew* costura, *f*; *naut* costura de los tablones, *f*; *anat* sutura, *f*; *surg* cicatriz, *f*; (wrinkle) arruga, *f*, surco, *m*; *geol* capa, *f*, yacimiento, *m*; *min* vena, *f*, filón, *m*. *vt* coser; juntar; (a face) surcar, arrugar

seaman *n* marinero, *m*; hombre de mar, *m*; navegante, *m*. **able-bodied s.,** marinero práctico, *m*

seamanlike *a* de marinero, marino; de buen marinero

seamanship *n* marinería, *f*; náutica, *f*

seamstress *n* costurera, *f*

seamy *a* con costuras. **the s. side of life,** el lado peor de la vida

seance *n* sesión, junta, *f*; sesión de espiritistas, *f*

seaplane *n* hidroavión, hidroplano, *m*

seaport *n* puerto de mar, *m*

sear *a* marchito. *vt* agostar, secar; (a wound) cauterizar; marchitar, ajar; (a conscience) endurecer

search *vt* registrar; (a wound) explorar; examinar; escudriñar; investigar. *vi* buscar. *n* busca, *f*; (of luggage, etc.) reconocimiento, *m*. **in s. of,** en busca de. **to s. after, for,** buscar; ir al encuentro de. **to s. out,** ir en busca de; preguntar por. **right of s.,** (international law) derecho de visita, *m*. **s.-party,** pelotón de salvamento, *m*. **s.-warrant,** auto de reconocimiento, auto de registro domiciliario, orden de allanamiento, orden de cateo, *m*

searching *a* escrutador; penetrante; minucioso. **a s. look,** una mirada penetrante. **a s. wind,** un viento penetrante. **a s. question,** una pregunta perspicaz

searchlight *n* reflector, proyector, *m*

seashore *n* playa, *f*; orilla del mar, *f*

seaside *n* orilla del mar, *f*; playa, *f*. **to go to the s.,** ir al mar, ir a la playa

season *n* estación, *f*; sazón, *f*; temporada, *f*; tiempo, *m*. *vt* (food) sazonar; (wood, wine) madurar; (accustom) acostumbrar, aclimatar; (with wit, etc.) salpimentar; (temper) templar, moderar. *vi* madurarse. **at that s.,** a la sazón. **close s.,** veda, *f.* **in s.,** en sazón; a su tiempo. **out of s.,** fuera de sazón; fuera de tiempo, inoportuno. **the dead s.,** la estación muerta. **the autumn s.,** el otoño; (for social functions, etc.) la temporada de otoño. **s.-ticket,** billete de abono, *m*

seasonable *a* de estación; tempestivo, oportuno

seasonably *adv* en sazón; oportunamente

seasonal *a* estacional; de temporada

seasonal worker *n* trabajador por temporada, *m*

seasoned *a* (of food) sazonado; (of wood, etc.) maduro. **highly-s.,** (of a dish) picante, con muchas especies

seasoning *n cul* condimento, *m*; madurez, *f*; aclimatación, *f*; *fig* salsa, sal, *f*

seat *n* asiento, *m*; (bench) banco, *m*; (chair) silla, *f*; (in a cinema, etc.) localidad, *f*; (*theat* etc., ticket) entrada, *f*; (of a person) trasero, *m*, asentaderas, *f pl*; (of trousers) fondillos, *m pl*; (of government, etc.) sede, capital, *f*; (of war, etc.) teatro, *m*; (place) sitio, lugar, *m*; (house) casa solar, *f. vt* sentar; poner en una silla (a); encontrar sitio; (of buildings) tener . . . asientos; (a chair) poner asiento (a). **The hall seats a thousand,** La sala tiene mil asientos, Hay mil asientos en la sala. **Please be seated!** ¡Haga el favor de sentarse! **to be seated,** estar sentado; sentarse. **to have a good s.,** (on a horse) caer bien a caballo. **to hold a s. in parliament,** ser diputado a Cortes. **to keep one's s.,** permanecer sentado. **to take a s.,** tomar asiento, sentarse. **s.-back,** respaldo, *m*; **s. belt,** cinturón de seguridad, *m*

seater *n* de . . . asientos. **four-s.,** automóvil de cuatro asientos, *m*

seaweed *n* alga marina, *f*; (edible) *Lat. Am.* cochayuyo, *m*

seaworthy *a* (of a ship) en buen estado; marinero

sebaceous *a* sebáceo

secede *vi* retirarse (de); separarse (de)

secessionist *n* secesionista, *mf*; *pol* separatista, *mf. a* secesionista; *pol* separatista

secluded *a* apartado, retirado; solitario

seclusion *n* reclusión, *f*; apartamiento, retiro, *m*; soledad, *f*

second *a* segundo; otro; igual. *adv* en segundo lugar; después. *n* segundo, *m*; (in a duel) padrino, *m*; (helper) ayudante, *m*; (boxing) segundo, *m*; (railway compartment) departamento de segunda (clase), *m*; *mus* segunda, *f*; (of time) segundo, *m*; (moment) instante, momento, *m. vt* secundar; (a motion) apoyar; *mil* ayudar. **the s. of May,** el dos de mayo. **James the S.,** Jaime el segundo. **on s. thoughts,** después de pensarlo bien. **every s. day,** cada dos días. **They live on the s. floor,** Viven en el primer piso (since the ground floor is not counted separately in Spanish speaking areas, the American second floor = the Spanish primer piso). **the s. largest,** el más grande menos uno. **to be s. to none,** no ser inferior a ninguno; (of persons) no ser inferior a nadie; no ceder a nadie. **to come off s.,** llegar el segundo; ser vencido. **seconds hand,** (of watch) segundero, *m*. **s.-in-command,** segundo, *m*; subjefe, *m*. **s.-best,** segundo. **My s.-best hat,** Mi sombrero número dos. **to come off s.-best,** salir mal parado; ser vencido. **s. class,** segunda clase, *f*. **s.-class,** de segunda clase; de calidad inferior; mediocre. **s. cousin,** primo (-ma) segundo (-a). **s. gear,** segunda velocidad, *f*. **s.-hand,** a usado; de ocasión; no nuevo. *adv* de segunda mano. **s.-hand car,** un coche de segunda mano. **s.-hand clothing,** ropa usada, *f*. **s.-hand shop** *Lat. Am.* cambalache, *m*. **s. lieutenant,** *mil* subteniente, segundo teniente, *m*; *nav* alférez de fragata, *m*. **s.-rate,** *a* inferior, mediocre. **s. sight,** doble vista, *f*

secondary *a* secundario; subordinado; accesorio; poco importante. **s. school** colegio, liceo. **s. education,** enseñanza secundaria, *f*

seconder *n* ayudante, *m*; el, *m*, (*f,* la) que apoya una proposición

secondly *adv* en segundo lugar

secrecy *n* secreto, *m*; reserva, *f*, silencio, *m*. **in the s. of one's own heart,** en lo más íntimo de su corazón

secret *a* secreto; clandestino; (of persons) reservado, taciturno; (secluded) remoto, apartado; oculto; misterioso. *n* secreto, *m*; (key) clave, *f*. **a s. code,** un código secreto. **in s.,** en secreto, secretamente. **open s.,** secreto a voces. **to keep a s.,** guardar un secreto. **to keep s.,** tener secreto, ocultar. **s. drawer,** secreto, *m*. **S. Service,** servicio de espionaje, *m*

secretaire *n* secreter, escritorio, *m*

secretarial *a* de secretario. **s. college,** academia comercial, *f*

secretariat *n* secretaría, *f*

secretary *n* secretario (-ia). **private s.,** secretario (-ia) particular. **S. of State,** ministro, *m*; Ministro de Estado, *m*

secrete *vt* esconder, ocultar; *med* secretar

secretion *n* escondimiento, *m*; *med* secreción, *f*

secretive *a* reservado, callado

secretly *adv* en secreto, secretamente; ocultamente, a escondidas

sect *n* secta, *f*

sectarian *a* and *n* sectario (-ia)

section *n* sección, *f*; porción, *f*; subdivisión, *f*; (of a law) artículo, *m. vt* seccionar. **conic s.,** sección cónica, *f*

sectional *a* en secciones. **s. bookcase,** biblioteca desmontable, *f*

sector *n* sector, *m*

secular *a* (very old) secular; (lay) seglar; laico; profano. **s. music,** música profana, *f*. **s. school,** escuela laica, *f*

secularization *n* secularización, *f*

secularize *vt* secularizar

secure *a* seguro; (certain) asegurado; (safe) en seguridad; sano y salvo; (firm) firme; fijo; (confident (in)) confiado (en). *vt* asegurar; (insure) garantizar; (lock) cerrar; (confine) prender; (acquire) adquirir, obtener; lograr, conseguir

securely *adv* seguramente; en seguridad, sin peligro; con confianza; (firmly) firmemente

security *n* seguridad, *f*; protección, defensa, *f*; garantía, *f*; (faith) confianza, *f*; *com* fianza, *f*; (person) fiador, *m*; *pl* **securities,** valores, títulos, *m pl*. **government securities,** papel del Estado, *m*. **to give s.,** *com* dar fianza. **to stand s. for,** *com* salir fiador de

sedan-chair *n* silla de manos, *f*

sedate *a* tranquilo, sosegado; formal, serio, grave

sedately *adv* sosegadamente; seriamente

sedateness *n* sosiego, *m*, tranquilidad, *f*; formalidad, compostura, *f*

sedative *a* and *n* sedativo, calmante *m*

sedentary *a* sedentario

sediment *n* sedimento, *m*, *Lat. Am.* concho, *m*

sedimentation *n* sedimentación, *f*

sedition *n* sedición, *f*

seditious *a* sedicioso

seduce *vt* seducir

seducer *n* seductor, *m*

seduction *n* seducción, *f*

seductive *a* seductivo, atractivo; persuasivo

sedulous *a* asiduo, diligente

see *n* sede, *f*. **The Holy S.,** la Santa Sede, *f*

see *vt* and *vi* ver; mirar; (understand) comprender; (visit) visitar; (attend to) atender a; ocuparse de. **He sees the matter quite differently,** Él mira el asunto de un modo completamente distinto, Su punto de vista sobre el asunto es completamente distinto. **You are not fit to be seen,** No eres nada presentable. **See you next Tuesday!** ¡Hasta el miércoles que viene! **I see!** ¡Ya! ¡Ahora comprendo! **Let's see!** ¡Vamos a ver! **Shall I see you home?** ¿Quieres que te acompañe a casa? **to go and see,** ir a ver. **to see red,** echar chispas. **to see the sights,** visitar los monumentos. **to see life,** ver mundo. **to see service,** servir (en el ejército, etc.). **to see about,** atender a; pensar en; ocuparse de. **to see after,** cuidar de; atender (a); ocuparse de. **to see again,** volver a ver. **to see into,** investigar, examinar.

to see off, (at the station, etc.) ir a despedir; acompañar. **to see out,** (a person) acompañar a la puerta; (a play, etc.) quedarse hasta el fin (de); no dejar el puesto. **to see over,** inspeccionar. **to see through,** (a house, etc.) inspeccionar; (a person) calarle las intenciones; (a mystery) penetrar; (a person through trouble) ayudar. **to see it through,** llevarlo al cabo; quedarse hasta el fin. **to see to,** atender a; ocuparse de; encargarse de. **to see to everything,** encargarse de todo

seed *n* semilla, *f*; simiente, *f*; (of fruit) pepita, *f*, grano, *m*; *fig* germen, *m*; (offspring) prole, descendencia, *f*. *vi* granar. *vt* sembrar. **s.-bed,** almáciga, *f*, semillero, *m*. **s.-pearl,** aljófar, *m*. **s.-plot,** sementera; *f*; *fig* semillero, *m*. **s.-time,** tiempo de sembrar, *m*

seedling *n* planta de semilla, *f*

seedsman *n* tratante en semillas, *m*

seedy *a* granado; (of clothes) raído, roto; (of persons) andrajoso, desharrapado; infeliz, desgraciado; (ill) indispuesto, malucho

seeing *n* vista, *f*; visión, *f*. **It is worth s.,** Vale la pena de verse. **s. that . . . ,** visto que, dado que, como que. **S. is believing,** Ver es creer

seek *vt* buscar; solicitar, pretender; (demand) pedir; (investigate) investigar; (to do something) procurar, tratar de. **They are much sought after,** Son muy populares, Están en demanda. **to s. after,** buscar; perseguir. **to s. for,** buscar

seeker *n* el, *m*, (*f*, la) que busca; investigador (-ra)

seem *vi* parecer. **He seemed honest,** Parecía honrado. **It seemed to me,** Me pareció a mí. **It seems that they were both at home last night,** Parece ser que ambos estaban en casa anoche

seeming *a* aparente; supuesto

seemingly *adv* aparentemente; en apariencia

seemliness *n* decoro, *m*

seemly *a* decoroso, decente

seep *vi* filtrar; rezumarse

seer *n* profeta, *m*

seesaw *n* columpio, *m*; vaivén, *m*. *vi* columpiarse; balancearse, oscilar. *a* de vaivén, oscilante

seethe *vi* hervir; *fig* bullir

segment *n* segmento, *m*

segregate *vt* segregar. *vi* segregarse. *a* segregado

segregation *n* segregación, *f*

Seine, the el Sena, *m*

seismic *a* sísmico

seismograph *n* sismógrafo, *m*

seismological *a* sismológico

seismology *n* sismología, *f*

seize *vt law* embargar; apoderarse de; asir; (a person) prender; coger; (a meaning) comprender; (an occasion, etc.) aprovecharse de; (of emotions) dominar; (of illnesses) atacar. *vi mech* atascarse. **He was seized by fear,** Le dominó el miedo. **to s. the opportunity,** aprovecharse de la oportunidad. **to s. upon a pretext,** valerse de un pretexto

seizure *n* asimiento, *m*; (of property) embargo, secuestro, *m*; (of a person) captura, *f*; arresto, *m*; *med* ataque, *m*

seldom *adv* rara vez, raramente; pocas veces

select *a* escogido, selecto; exclusivista. *vt* escoger

selection *n* selección, *f*. **selections from Cervantes,** trozos escogidos de Cervantes, *m pl*. **to make a s. from,** escoger entre. **s. committee,** comité de selección, *m*

selective *a* selectivo

self *n* mismo (-a), propio (-a); sí mismo (-a), se; personalidad, *f*; ser, *m*. **all by one's s.,** sin ayuda de nadie; solo; *inf* solito. **my other s.,** mi otro yo. **my better s.,** mi mejor parte. **the s.,** el yo. **s.-abasement,** humillación de sí mismo, *f*. **s.-acting,** automático. **s.-apparent,** evidente, patente. **s.-appointed,** nombrado por uno mismo. **s.-assertion,** presunción, *f*. **s.-assertive,** presumido. **s.-assurance,** confianza en sí mismo, *f*; aplomo, *m*; (impertinence) cara dura, frescura, *f*. **s.-centered,** egocéntrico. **s.-colored,** del mismo

color; de su color natural. **s.-command,** dominio de sí mismo, *m*; sangre fría, ecuanimidad, *f*. **s.-complacent,** satisfecho de sí mismo. **s.-conceit,** vanidad, arrogancia, petulancia, *f*. **s.-confidence,** confianza en sí mismo, *f*; aplomo, *m*. **s.-confident,** seguro de sí mismo, lleno de confianza en sí mismo. **s.-conscious,** turbado, confuso, apocado. **s.-consciousness,** turbación, confusión, *f*, apocamiento, azoramiento, *m*. **s.-contained,** (of a person) reservado, poco comunicativo; dueño de sí mismo; (of things) completo; (of flats, etc.) independiente; con entrada independiente. **s.-contradictory,** contradictorio. **s.-control,** dominio de sí mismo, *m*; ecuanimidad, serenidad, sangre fría, *f*. **s.-controlled,** dueño de sí mismo; ecuánime, sereno. **s.-deception,** engaño de sí mismo, *m*; ilusiones, *f pl*. **s.-defense,** defensa propia, *f*. **s.-denial,** abnegación, *f*; renunciación, *f*; frugalidad, *f*. **s.-destruction,** suicidio, *m*. **s.-determination,** libre albedrío, *m*; (of peoples) autonomía, *f*; independencia, *f*. **s.-educating,** autodidacto. **s.-esteem,** respeto para uno mismo, *m*; amor propio, *m*. **s.-evident,** aparente, que salta a la vista. **s.-explanatory,** que se explica a sí mismo; evidente. **s.-generating,** autógeno. **s.-government,** (of a person) dominio de sí mismo, *m*; (of a state) autonomía, *f*. **s.-importance,** presunción, petulancia, *f*. **s.-important,** pagado de sí mismo. **to be s.-important,** darse importancia, darse tono. **s.-indulgence,** indulgencia con sí mismo, *f*; (of food, drink, etc.) excesos, *m pl*, falta de moderación, *f*. **s.-indulgent,** indulgente con sí mismo; dado a los placeres, sibarita. **s.-interest,** propio interés, *m*. **s.-knowledge,** conocimiento de sí mismo, *m*. **s.-love,** egolatría, *f*. **s.-made man,** hombre que ha llegado a su posición actual por sus propios esfuerzos, *m*. **self-medication,** automedicación, *f*. **s.-opinionated,** terco, obstinaz. **s.-portrait,** autorretrato, *m*. **s.-possessed,** dueño de sí mismo; reservado; de sangre fría. **s.-possession,** aplomo, *m*, sangre fría, serenidad, *f*. **s.-preservation,** protección de sí mismo, *f*. **s.-reliance,** independencia, *f*; confianza en sí mismo, *f*. **s.-reliant,** independiente; confiado en sí mismo. **s.-reproach,** remordimiento, *m*. **s.-respect,** respeto de sí mismo, *m*; amor propio, *m*, dignidad, *f*. **s.-respecting,** que se respeta; que tiene amor propio **s.-restraint,** dominio de sí mismo, *m*; moderación, *f*. **s.-righteous,** farisaico. **s.-sacrifice,** abnegación, *f*. **s.-sacrificing,** abnegado. **s.-same,** mismo, idéntico. **s.-satisfaction,** satisfacción de sí mismo, *f*; vanidad, *f*; (of desires, etc.) satisfacción, indulgencia, *f*. **s.-satisfied,** satisfecho de sí mismo, pagado de sí mismo. **s.-seeking,** a egoísta, interesado. *n* egoísmo, *m*. **s.-starter,** *mech* arranque automático, *m*. **s.-styled,** autodenominado, autotitulado, llamado por sí mismo. **s.-sufficiency,** suficiencia, *f*; presunción, *f*. **s.-sufficient,** que basta a sí mismo; contento de sí mismo. **s.-supporting,** que vive de su propio trabajo; (of an institution, business) independiente. **s.-taught,** autodidacto. **s.-willed,** voluntarioso

selfish *a* egoísta, interesado

selfishly *adv* interesadamente; por egoísmo

selfishness *n* egoísmo, *m*

sell *vt* vender. *vi* vender; venderse. **They sold him to his enemies,** Le vendieron a sus enemigos. **House to s.,** «Se vende una casa.» **to s. at a loss,** malvender, vender con pérdida. **to s. for cash,** vender al contado. **to s. retail,** vender al por menor. **to s. wholesale,** vender al por mayor. **to s. one's life dearly,** vender cara la vida. **They sold the chair for $10,** Vendieron la silla por diez dólares. **to s. off,** (goods) liquidar, saldar. **to s. out,** vender; agotar. **The best edition is sold out,** La mejor edición está agotada. **All the nylons have been sold out,** Se han vendido todas las medias de nilón (de cristal). **to s. up,** vender

seller *n* vendedor (-ra); comerciante (en), *m*

selling *n* venta, *f*. **s. off,** liquidación, *f*. **s. price,** precio de venta, *m*

selvage *n* (in cloth) orillo, *m*

semantics *n* semántica, *f*

semaphore *n* semáforo, *m*, *vt* and *vi* hacer señales semafóricas (a)

semaphoric *a* semafórico

semblance *n* apariencia, *f*. **to put on a s. of woe,** aparentar ser triste

semen *n* semen, *m*, esperma, *f*

semester *n* semestre, *m*

semi *prefix* semi; medio. **s.-conscious,** medio consciente. **s.-detached house,** casa doble, *f*

semicircle *n* semicírculo, *m*

semicircular *a* semicircular

semicolon *n* punto y coma, *m*

semidetached *a* (house) apartado

semiformal *a* de media ceremonia

seminarist *n* seminarista, *mf*

seminary *n* seminario, *m*; (for girls) colegio interno, *m*

Semite *n* semita, *mf*

Semitic *a* semítico, semita

Semitism *n* semitismo, *m*

semolina *n* sémola, *f*

senate *n* senado, *m*

senator *n* senador, *m*

senatorial *a* senatorio

send *vt* enviar, mandar; *com* remitir; (a ball) lanzar; (grant) conceder; permitir; (inflict) afligir (con). **I sent Jane for it,** Envié a Juana a buscarlo. **He sent us word that he could not come,** Nos mandó un recado diciéndonos que no podía venir. **to s. mad,** hacer enloquecer. **to s. packing,** mandar a paseo. **to s. again,** volver a mandar. **to s. away,** *vt* enviar; (dismiss) destituir; despedir; (scare off) ahuyentar, *vi* enviar a otra parte. **to s. back,** (goods) devolver; (persons) volver. **to s. down,** hacer bajar; (rain, etc.) mandar, derramar; (a student) suspender, expulsar. **to s. in,** mandar; (persons) hacer entrar, introducir; (food) servir; (a bill) presentar; (one's name) dar. **Please s. him in!** ¡Sírvase de invitarle a entrar! **to s. in one's resignation,** mandar su dimisión. **to s. off,** enviar, mandar; (goods) despachar; (persons) destituir; (scare) ahuyentar. **s.-off,** *n* despedida, *f*. **a good s.-off,** una despedida afectuosa. **to s. on,** (a letter) hacer seguir; (instructions) transmitir. **to s. out,** hacer salir; mandar; (emit) despedir, dar; (new shoots, etc.) echar. **to s. round,** (the hat, etc.) hacer circular. **to s. up,** enviar arriba; mandar subir, hacer subir; mandar, enviar; (a ball) lanzar

sender *n* remitente, *mf*; *elec* transmisor, *m*

sending *n* envío, *m*

Senegal Senegal, *m*

Senegalese *a* and *n* senegalés (-esa)

senile *a* senil

senility *n* senilidad, *f*

senior *a* mayor, de mayor edad; más antiguo. **Martinez s.,** Martínez padre. **Charles is Mary's s. by five years,** Carlos es cinco años mayor que María. **s. member,** decano, *m*

seniority *n* ancianidad, *f*; antigüedad, *f*

senna *n bot* sena, *f*

sensation *n* sensación, *f*; sentimiento, *m*; impresión, *f*. **to create a s.,** causar una sensación

sensational *a* sensacional

sensationalism *n phil* sensualismo, *m*; efectismo, *m*

sensationalist *n phil* sensualista, *mf*; efectista, *mf*

sense *n* sentido, *m*. *vt* sentir. **in a s.,** hasta cierto punto; desde un punto de vista. **in the full s. of the word,** en toda la extensión de la palabra. **common s.,** sentido común, *m*. **He has no s. of smell,** No tiene olfato. **the five senses,** los cinco sentidos. **to be out of one's senses,** estar fuera de sí, estar trastornado. **You must be out of your senses!** ¡Debes de haber perdido el juicio! ¡Estás loco! **to come to one's senses,** (after unconsciousness) volver en sí; (after folly) recobrar el sentido común. **to talk s.,** hablar con sentido común, hablar razonablemente. **s. organ,** órgano de los sentidos, *m*. **have a good s. of direction,** saber orientarse, tener buena orientación. **have no s. of smell,** ser incapaz de percibir olores. **have no s. of taste,** ser incapaz de distinguir gustos

senseless *a* (unconscious) sin sentido, insensible; desmayado; (silly) necio, estúpido. **to knock s.,** derribar, tumbar

senselessness *n* falta de sentido común, *f*; locura, absurdidad, *f*

sensibility *n* sensibilidad, *f*

sensible *a* sensible; (conscious) consciente (de); sesudo. **to be s. of,** estar consciente de; estar persuadido de

sensibly *adv* sensiblemente; sesudamente, cuerdamente

sensitive *a* sensitivo; susceptible (a); impresionable. **s. plant,** sensitiva, *f*

sensitivity *n* sensibilidad, *f*; susceptibilidad, *f*; delicadeza, *f*

sensitize *vt phot* sensibilizar

sensory *a* sensorio

sensual *a* sensual; voluptuoso

sensualism *n* sensualismo, *m*

sensualist *n* sensualista, *mf*

sensuality *n* sensualidad, *f*

sensually *adv* sensualmente

sensuous *a* sensorio

sensuousness *n* sensualidad, *f*

sentence *n law* sentencia, *f*; (penalty) pena, *f*; *gram* frase, *f*; (maxim) máxima, sentencia, *f*. *vt* sentenciar, condenar. **to pass s.,** pronunciar sentencia, fallar. **under s. of,** bajo pena de

sententious *a* sentencioso

sentient *a* sensible

sentiment *n* sentimiento, *m*; (sentimentality) sentimentalismo, *m*; opinión, *f*

sentimental *a* sentimental; (mawkish) sensiblero

sentimentalist *n* romántico (-ca), persona sentimental, *f*

sentimentality *n* sentimentalismo, *m*, sensiblería, *f*

sentimentalize *vt* idealizar

sentimentally *adv* sentimentalmente

sentinel *n* centinela, *mf*

sentry *n* centinela, *m*. **to be on s. duty,** estar de guardia. **s.-box,** garita de centinela, *f*

separable *a* separable

separate *a* separado; distinto; independiente. *vt* separar; dividir. *vi* separarse; (of husband and wife) separarse de bienes y de cuerpos

separately *adv* separadamente; aparte

separation *n* separación, *f*; *law* separación de bienes y de cuerpos, *f*

separatism *n* separatismo, *m*

separatist *a* and *n* separatista *mf*

Sephardic *a* Sefardí

sepia *n* (color and fish) sepia, *f*

September *n* setiembre, septiembre, *m*

septic *a* séptico

septicemia *n* septicemia, *f*

septuagenarian *n* setentón (-ona); septuagenario (-ia)

septum *n* septo, tabique, *m*

sepulcher *n* sepulcro, *m*

sepulchral *a* sepulcral

sequel *n* (of a story, etc.) continuación, *f*; consecuencia, *f*; resultado, *m*

sequence *n* sucesión, *f*; serie, *f*; orden, *mf*; (at cards) serie, *f*; *gram* correspondencia, *f*; (*ecc* and cinema) secuencia, *f*. **s. of tenses,** correspondencia de los tiempos, *f*

sequestered *a* aislado, remoto

sequestrate *vt* secuestrar

sequestration *n* secuestro, *m*,

sequin *n* lentejuela, *f*

seraglio *n* serrallo, *m*

seraph *n* serafín, *m*

seraphic *a* seráfico

seraphim *n* serafín, *m*

Serbia Servia, *f*

Serbian *a* servio. *n* servio (-ia); (language) servio, *m*
serenade *n* serenata, *f, vt* dar una serenata (a)
serene *a* sereno. **His S. Highness,** Su Alteza Serenísima
serenity *n* serenidad, *f;* tranquilidad, *f*
serf *n* siervo (-va)
serfdom *n* servidumbre, *f*
serge *n* estameña, *f;* (silk) sarga, *f*
sergeant *n mil* sargento, *m;* (police) sargento de policía, *m*. **s.-at-arms,** macero, *m*. **s.-major,** sargento instructor, *m*
serial *a* en serie; (of a story) por entregas. *n* novela por entregas, *f*. **s. number,** número de serie, *m*
sericulture *n* sericultura, *f*
series *n* serie, *f;* cadena, *f; math* serie, progresión, *f*. **in s.,** en serie
serious *a* serio; sincero; verdadero; (of illness, etc.) grave; importante. **He was s.** (not laughing) **when he said it,** Lo dijo en serio. **He is very s. about it,** Lo toma muy en serio. **to grow s.,** (of persons) ponerse serio; (of events) hacerse grave
seriously *adv* seriamente; en serio; gravemente. **to take** (something) **s.,** tomar (algo) en serio. **to take oneself s.,** tomarse muy en serio
seriousness *n* seriedad, *f;* gravedad, *f*. **in all s.,** en serio, seriamente
sermon *n* sermón, *m*
sermonize *vt* and *vi* sermonear
serpent *n* serpiente, *f; mus* serpentón, *m*
serpentine *a* serpentino; (of character) tortuoso. *n min* serpentina, *f*
serrated *a* serrado; dentellado
serried *a* apretado, apiñado
serum *n* suero, *m*
servant *n* servidor (-ra); (domestic) criado (-da); (employee) empleado (-da); (slave and *fig*) siervo (-va); *pl* **servants,** (domestic) servidumbre, *f,* servicio, *m*. **I remain your obedient s.,** Quedo de Vd. atento y seguro servidor (att. y s.s.). **civil s.,** empleado del estado, *m*. **general s.,** criada para todo, *f*. **man s.,** criado, *m*. **the s. problem,** el problema del servicio. **Your s., sir,** Servidor de Vd., señor. **s.-girl,** criada, *f*
serve *vt* servir (a); ser útil (a); satisfacer; (in a shop) despachar; (an apprenticeship, etc.) hacer; (a prison sentence) cumplir; (treat) tratar; (of stallion) cubrir; (a warrant, etc.) ejecutar; (a notice) entregar; (a ball) servir; (on a jury, etc.) formar parte de; *naut* aforrar. **I re**servir; (mil, nav) hacer el servicio. *n sport* saque, *m*. **It serves you right!** ¡Lo tienes merecido! **to s. at table,** servir a la mesa. **to s. as,** servir de. **to s. out,** distribuir; servir. **Serves 8,** (recipe) Da 8 porciones
server *n ecc* acólito, *m; sport* saque, *m;* (tray) bandeja, *f;* (for fish, etc.) pala, *f*
service *n* servicio, *m; ecc* oficio, *m;* servicio de mesa, *m;* (of a writ) entrega, *f; sport* saque, *m*. **coffee s.,** juego de café, *m*. **diplomatic s.,** cuerpo diplomático, *m*. **At your s.,** Para servir a Vd., A su disposición. **on active s.,** en acto de servicio; en el campo de batalla. **to go into s.,** (of servants) ir a servir. **to render s.,** prestar servicios. **s. tree,** serbal, *m*
serviceable *a* (of persons) servicial; (of things) servible, utilizable; útil; (lasting) duradero
service road *n* vía de servicio, *f*
serviette *n* servilleta, *f*. **s. ring,** servilletero, *m*
servile *a* servil, *Lat. Am. also* incondicional
servility *n* servilismo *m*
serving *a* sirviente; al servicio (de). **s. maid,** criada, *f*. **s. table,** trinchero, *m*
servitude *n* servidumbre, esclavitud, *f*. **penal s.,** cadena perpetua, *f*
session *n* sesión, *f;* junta, *f*. **petty sessions,** tribunal de primera instancia, *m*
set *vt* poner; colocar; fijar; (seeds, etc.) plantar; (bones) reducir, componer; (gems) engastar, montar; (a clock) regular; (sails) desplegar; (the teeth of a saw) trabar, triscar; (congeal) hacer coagular; (a trap) armar; (a

snare) tender; (a razor) afilar; (make ready) preparar; (type) componer; (cause) hacer; *mus* poner en música; *mus* adaptar; (order) mandar; (prescribe) dar, asignar; (estimate) estimar, evaluar; (an example, etc.) dar; (establish) establecer, crear. *vi* (of the sun, etc.) ponerse; (solidify) coagularse; solidificarse; (of tides) fluir; (of the wind) soplar; (of dogs) hacer punta. **The joke set him laughing,** El chiste le hizo reír. **set an example,** dar ejemplo, dar el ejemplo. **set a precedent,** sentar precedente. **to set a person's mind at rest,** tranquilizar, sosegar. **to set a trap,** armar lazo. **to set at ease,** poner a sus anchas (a), hacer cómodo (a). **to set at naught,** despreciar. **to set eyes on,** poner los ojos en. **to set fire to,** pegar fuego a, incendiar. **to set free,** poner en libertad, librar (de). **to set in motion,** poner en marcha. **to set one's teeth,** apretar los dientes. **to set people talking,** dar que hablar a la gente. **to set the fashion,** fijar la moda; poner de moda. **to set the alarm at seven o'clock,** poner el despertador a las siete. **to set the table,** poner la mesa. **to set to work,** ponerse a trabajar. **to set about,** *vi* (begin) ponerse (a); empezar; (undertake) emprender. *vt* (a rumour, etc.) divulgar. **They set about each other,** Empezaron a golpearse, Vinieron a las manos. **to set against,** indisponer (con), enemistar (con); hacer el enemigo (de), ser hostil (a); (balance) oponer, balancear. **to set oneself against,** oponerse a; atacar, luchar contra. **to set aside,** poner a un lado; apartar; (discard) desechar; (omit) omitir, pasar por alto de; dejar aparte, excluir; (keep) reservar; (money, etc.) ahorrar; (reject) rechazar; (quash) anular. **to set back,** retrasar; hacer retroceder. **set-back,** *n* revés, *m;* contrariedad, *f*. **to set before,** poner ante; (facts) exponer; (introduce) presentar. **to set down,** poner en tierra; depositar; (of a bus, etc.) dejar; (in writing) poner por escrito; anotar, apuntar; narrar, contar; (attribute) atribuir; (fix) fijar, formular; (believe to be) creer. **Passengers are set down at . . . ,** Los viajeros pueden apearse en . . . **to set forth,** *vt* (one's opinions, etc.) exponer; publicar; (display) exhibir, mostrar; (make) hacer. *vi* ponerse en camino. **to set going,** poner en marcha; echar a andar. **to set in,** empezar; (of the tide) fluir. **A reaction has set in,** Se ha hecho sentir una reacción. **to set off,** *vt* (explode) hacer estallar; (cause) hacer; (heighten) realzar; hacer resaltar; (counterbalance) contraponer. *vi* partir; ponerse en camino. **set-off,** *n* contraste, *m,* contraposición, *f*. **to set off against,** contraponer. **to set on,** *vt* (a dog) azuzar; (incite) instigar, incitar. *vi* atacar. **to set out,** *vt* (state) exponer, manifestar; (embellish) realzar; (display) arreglar, disponer. *vi* ponerse en camino, partir. **to set over,** (rule) tener autoridad sobre, gobernar. **to set to,** (begin to) ponerse a, empezar a; (work) ponerse a trabajar. **set-to,** *n* lucha, *f;* (boxing) asalto, *m;* (quarrel) pelea, riña, *f*. **to set up,** *vt* (a monument, etc.) erigir, levantar; (fix) fijar; (apparatus, machinery) montar; (exalt) exaltar; (found) establecer, *Lat. Am. also* instaurar; crear; (propound) exponer; (a howl, etc.) dar; (equip with) proveer de; instalar; (make strong) robustecer; fortificar; (type) componer; (raise) alzar. *vi* establecerse; dárselas de. **He sets himself up as a painter,** Se las da de pintor. **to set** (a person) **up as a model,** poner como modelo (a). **to set up house,** poner casa. **to set up a business,** establecer un comercio. **set-up,** *n* establecimiento, *m;* arreglo, *m*. **to set upon,** atacar
set *n* (of sun, etc.) puesta, *f,* ocaso, *m;* (of the head, etc.) porte, *m;* (of a garment) corte, *m;* (of the tide, etc.) dirección, *f;* (slant) inclinación, *f;* (*fig* drift) tendencia, *f,* movimiento, *m;* (of the teeth of a saw) triscamiento, *m;* (of men, houses, etc.) grupo, *m;* (of tools, golf clubs, china, etc.) juego, *m;* (gang) pandilla, camarilla, *f;* clase, *f;* (*dance*) tanda, *f;* (tennis) partido, *f; theat* decoración, *f; rad* aparato de radio, *m,* radio, *f*. **coffee set,** juego de café, *m*. **all-mains set,** radio de corriente eléctrica, *f*. **battery set,** radio de batería, *f*. **portable**

set

set, radio portátil, *f.* **the smart set,** el mundo elegante. **to have a shampoo and set,** hacerse lavar y marcar (el pelo). **to make a set,** hacer juego. **to make a dead set at,** hacer un ataque vigoroso (a), atacar resueltamente; procurar insinuarse en el favor de. **set of teeth,** dentadura, *f*
set *a* fijo; inmóvil; (of a smile) forzado; (of a task) asignado; (of times) señalado, fijo; (prescribed) prescrito, establecido; (firm) firme; (resolved) resuelto; (well-known) consabido; (obstinate) terco, nada adaptable. **well set-up,** apuesto, bien plantado. **He is set on doing it,** Se empeña en hacerlo. **to be dead set against,** estar completamente opuesto a. **set phrase,** frase hecha, *f.* **set-square,** cartabón, *m*
setter *n* (perro) séter, perdiguero, *m.* **s.-on,** instigador (-ra)
setting *n* (of the sun, etc.) puesta, *f;* (of mortar, etc.) fraguado, *m;* (of a jelly) solidificación, *f;* (of jewels) engaste, *m,* montadura, *f;* (of bones) aliño, *m;* (of teeth of saw) traba, *f;* (of razor) afiladura, *f;* (of a trap) armadura, *f;* (of a machine, etc.) ajuste, *m;* (frame) marco, *m; mus* arreglo, *m; theat* decorado, *m;* (emplacement) lecho, *m.* **the s. sun,** el sol poniente. **s. free,** liberación, *f.* **s. off,** partida, salida, *f.* **s. out,** ida, marcha, *f;* principio, *m.* **s.-up,** creación, institución, *f,* establecimiento, *m;* (of a machine) montaje, *m; print* composición, *f*
settle *vt* colocar; asegurar; afirmar; (a country) colonizar; (live in) establecer (en); (populate) poblar; (in a profession, etc.) dar; (install) instalar; (the imagination, etc.) sosegar, calmar; (resolve) resolver; (arrange) disponer, arreglar; (differences) componer, concertar; (an opponent, etc.) confundir; (a bill) saldar, pagar; (a claim) satisfacer; (clarify) depositar, clarificar; (end) poner fin (a). *vi* establecerse; (of weather) serenarse; (to work, etc.) empezar a, ponerse a; aplicarse a; (decide) decidirse; (alight) posarse; (of foundations, etc.) asentarse; (of a ship) zozobrar; (of sediment) depositarse; (of liquid) clarificarse. **to s. accounts with,** *fig* ajustar cuentas con. **to s. down,** establecerse, arraigarse; adaptarse (a); (become calm) sosegarse, calmarse; sentar el juicio; (of foundations) asentarse; (of a ship) zozobrar; (of sediment) depositarse. **to s. in,** *vt* instalar. *vi* instalarse. **to s. on,** (choose) escoger; (decide on) decidirse (a). **to s. a pension on,** señalar pensión (a). **to s. up,** *vt* (one's affairs) poner en orden; (bill) pagar, saldar. *vi* llegar a un acuerdo; pagar cuentas
settled *a* fijo; permanente; invariable; (of countries) colonizado; (of weather) sereno
settlement *n* (of a country) colonización, *f;* (of a dispute) arreglo, ajuste, *m;* (of a question) solución, *f;* decisión, *f;* (of a bill) saldo, pago, *m,* liquidación, *f;* (of an obligation) satisfacción, *f;* (colony) colonia, *f;* (creation) creación, institución, *f;* establecimiento, arraigo, *m.* **deed of s.,** escritura de donación, *f.* **marriage s.,** contrato matrimonial, *m;* **s. out of court,** arreglo pacífico, *m*
settler *n* colono, *m;* colonizador (-ra)
seven *a* and *n* siete *m.* **It is s. o'clock,** Son las siete. **the s. deadly sins,** los siete pecados capitales
seventeen *a* diecisiete, diez y siete. *n* diecisiete, *m.* **She is just s.,** Acaba de cumplir los diez y siete años
seventeenth *a* décimoséptimo; (of monarchs and of the month) diez y siete. *n* décimoséptimo, *m.* **Louis the S.,** Luis diez y siete. **the s. of June,** el diez y siete de junio
seventh *a* séptimo; (of the month) siete. *n* séptimo, *m;* séptima parte, *f; mus* séptima, *f.* **Edward the S.,** Eduardo séptimo. **the s. of August,** el siete de agosto
seventieth *a* septuagésimo, setentavo. *n* setentavo, *m*
seventy *a* and *n* setenta, *m*
sever *vt* separar; romper; dividir
several *a* distinto, diferente; respectivo; varios, *m pl,* (*f pl,* varias); algunos, *m pl,* (*f pl,* algunas)

shake

severally *adv* separadamente; individualmente; independientemente
severance *n* separación, *f;* (of friendship, etc.) ruptura, *f*
severe *a* severo; riguroso; fuerte; duro; (of style) austero; (of pain) agudo; (of illness) grave
severely *adv* severamente; intensamente; gravemente
severity *n* severidad, *f;* intensidad, *f;* (of weather) inclemencia, *f;* (of illness) gravedad, *f*
sew *vt* and *vi* coser, *Lat. Am.* costurar, costurear. **to sew on,** coser, pegar
sewage *n* aguas residuales, *f pl.* **s. system,** alcantarillado, *m*
sewer *n* alcantarilla, cloaca, *f,* albañal, *m*
sewing *n* costura, *f.* **s. bag,** costurero, *m.* **s. cotton,** hilo de coser, *m.* **s.-machine,** máquina de coser, *f.* **s. silk,** torzal, *m*
sex *n* sexo, *m.* **the fair sex,** el bello sexo. **the weaker sex,** el sexo débil. **sex appeal,** atractivo, *m*
sexagenarian *n* sexagenario (-ia)
sexless *a* neutro; frígido
sexologist *n* sexólogo (-ga)
sexology *n* sexología, *f*
sextant *n* sextante, *m*
sexton *n* sacristán, *m;* sepulturero, *m;* (bell-ringer) campanero, *m*
sexual *a* sexual
sexuality *n* sexualidad, *f*
Sforza Esforcia, *f*
sh! *interj* ¡Chitón! ¡Chis!
shabbily *adv* (of dressing) pobremente; (of treatment) mezquinamente
shabbiness *n* pobreza, *f;* estado andrajoso, *m;* (of behavior) mezquindad, ruindad, *f*
shabby *a* (of persons) desharrapado, andrajoso, *Lat. Am.* maltraído; (of garments) raído, roto; (of a neighborhood, etc.) pobre; (mean) ruin, mezquino
shack *n* choza, *f, Mexico* jacal, *elsewhere in Lat. Am.* bohío *m*
shackle *n* traba, *f; pl* **shackles,** grillos, *m pl,* esposas, *f pl; fig* cadenas, *f pl.* *vt* poner esposas (a), encadenar; (a horse) apear; *fig* atar; (impede) estorbar
shad *n* sábalo, *m*
shade *n* sombra, *f;* (in a picture) toque de obscuro, *m;* (for the eyes) visera, *f;* (of a lamp) pantalla, *f;* (ghost) espectro, fantasma, *m;* (of color) matiz, *m;* (tinge) dejo, *m.* *vt* sombrear, dar sombra (a); (the face, etc.) proteger, resguardar; (a drawing) esfumar. **in the s.,** a la sombra. **80° in the s.,** ochenta grados a la sombra. **to put (a person) in the s.,** eclipsar
shadiness *n* sombra, *f*
shading *n* sombra, *f; art* degradación, *f*
shadow *n* sombra, *f;* obscuridad, *f;* (in a picture) toque de obscuro, *m.* *vt* sombrear; obscurecer; (a person) seguir **to cast a s.,** proyectar una sombra. **to s. forth,** indicar; simbolizar. **s. show,** sombras chinescas, *f pl*
shadowy *a* umbroso; vago, indistinto, indefinido
shady *a* sombreado, umbrío; sombrío; (of persons, etc.) sospechoso. **It was s. in the wood,** Hacía sombra en el bosque
shaft *n* fuste, *m;* (arrow) flecha, saeta, *f,* dardo, *m;* (of a golf club, etc.) mango, *m;* (of a cart) vara, *f; mech* árbol, eje, *m;* (of a column and a feather) cañón, *m;* (of light) rayo, *m;* (of a mine) pozo, tiro, *m;* (air-shaft) conducto de aire, ventilador, *m.* **cam-s.,** árbol de levas, *m.* **driving s.,** árbol motor, *m*
shaggy *a* peludo; lanudo
shagreen *n* chagrén, *f*
shah *n* sha, *m*
shake *vt* sacudir; agitar; hacer temblar; (weaken) debilitar, hacer flaquear. *vi* estremecerse; temblar; (trill) trinar. **He managed to s. himself free,** Consiguió librarse por una sacudida. **to s. hands,** darse la mano, estrecharse la mano. **to s. one's finger at,** señalar con el dedo (a). **to s. one's fist at,** amenazar con el puño (a). **to s. one's head,** mover la cabeza; negar con la

540

cabeza. **to s. one's sides,** (with laughter) reírse a carcajadas. **to s. with fear,** temblar de miedo. **to s. down,** sacudir, hacer caer. **s.-down,** *n* cama improvisada, *f*. **to s. off,** sacudirse; librarse (de), perder; quitar de encima (a). **to s. out,** (unfurl) desplegar; sacudir. **to s. up,** agitar; sacudir, remover

shake *n* sacudida, *f*; (of the head) movimiento (de la cabeza), *m*; (of the hand) apretón (de manos), *m*; temblor, *m*; *mus* trino, gorjeo, *m*. **in two shakes,** *inf* en un periquete. **to give a person a good s.,** sacudir violentamente (a)

Shakespearean *a* shakespeariano

shakiness *n* inestabilidad, *f*; poca firmeza, *f*; temblor, *m*; lo dudoso. **the s. of his voice,** su voz trémula

shaking *n* sacudimiento, *m*; temblor, *m*; (of windows, etc.) zangoloteo, *m*

shaky *a* inestable; poco firme; (of hands, etc.) tembloroso; (of the voice) trémulo; (of gait) vacilante; dudoso

shale *n* esquisto, *m*

shall *v aux* (expressing simple future) **I s. arrive tomorrow,** Llegaré mañana. **S. we go to the sea next week?** ¿Iremos al mar la semana próxima?; (expressing obligation, compulsion) **You s. not go out,** No has de salir, No quiero que salgas. **He s. see her immediately,** Tiene que verla en seguida; (as a polite formula) **S. I go?** ¿Quiere Vd. que vaya? **S. we buy the soap?** ¿Quiere Vd. que compremos el jabón? ¿Compraremos el jabón?

shallot *n bot* chalote, *m*, ascalonia, *f*

shallow *a* poco profundo; (of a receptacle) llano; (of persons) superficial, frívolo; (of knowledge, etc.) superficial, ligero, somero. *n* bajío, *m*

shallowness *n* poca profundidad, *f*; superficialidad, *f*

sham *vt* fingir, simular. *n* farsa, *f*; imitación, *f*; engaño, *m*; (person) farsante, *m*. *a* falso; espurio. **to s. illness,** fingirse enfermo. **to s. dead,** hacer la mortecina. **You're just a s.,** Eres un farsante

sham battle *n mil* simulacro de combate, simulacro guerrero, *m*

shamble *vi* andar arrastrándose. *n* andar pesado, *m*; *pl* **shambles,** matadero, *m*; *fig* carnicería, *f*

shambling *a* pesado, lento

shame *n* vergüenza, *f*; ignominia, *f*; deshonra, *f*. *vt* avergonzar; deshonrar. **For s.!** ¡Qué vergüenza! **What a s.!** ¡Qué lástima! **to put to s.,** avergonzar

shamefaced *a* (bashful) vergonzoso, tímido; (ashamed) avergonzado

shamefacedly *adv* vergonzosamente, tímidamente; con vergüenza

shameful *a* vergonzoso, escandaloso; indecente

shamefully *adv* escandalosamente

shameless *a* desvergonzado; impúdico, indecente

shamelessly *adv* desvergonzadamente

shamelessness *n* desvergüenza, poca vergüenza, *f*; impudicia, deshonestidad, *f*

shampoo *n* champú, *m*. *vt* dar un champú (a); dar un masaje (a). **dry s.,** champú seco, *m*

shank *n* zanca, *f*; *mech* pierna, *f*; (handle) mango, *m*; (of a button) rabo, *m*, cola, *f*. **go on Shank's mare, ride on Shank's mare,** caminar en coche de San Francisco, ir en boricua de Villadiego

shanty *n* choza, *f*

shanty town *n* barriada (Peru), callampa, población, población, callampa (Chile), *f*, rancho (Venezuela), *m*, villa-miseria (Argentina), *f*

shape *n* forma, *f*; bulto, *m*; fantasma, *m*; (of a garment) corte, *m*; (of a person) talle, *m*; *cul* molde, *m*; (of a hat) forma, *f*. *vt* formar; (a garment) cortar; (ideas) dar forma (a); adaptar; (stone, etc.) labrar; (one's life) dominar. *vi* (of events) desarrollarse. **to go out of s.,** perder la forma. **to take s.,** tomar forma. **to s. one's course,** dirigirse (hacia, a); *naut* dar el rumbo. **to s. well,** prometer bien

shaped *a* de forma de . . . , que tiene figura de . . . **pear-s.,** piriforme

shapeless *a* informe; disforme

shapelessness *n* informidad, *f*; deformidad, *f*

shapeliness *n* belleza de forma, *f*; simetría, *f*

shapely *a* bien formado; simétrico

share *n* porción, *f*; parte, *f*; cuota, *f*; contribución, *f*; (part ownership) interés, *m*; (in a company) acción, *f*. *vt* distribuir; compartir; dividir; tomar parte en. *vi* participar (de); tomar parte (en). **to fall to one's s.,** tocar, corresponder. **to go shares with,** dividir con, compartir con. **to take a s. in the conversation,** tomar parte en la conversación. **paid-up s.,** *com* acción liberada, *f*. **to s. out,** repartir, distribui

sharecropper *Lat. Am.* agregado (-da), *mf*

shareholder *n* accionista, *mf*

sharer *n* partícipe, *mf*

shark *n icht* tiburón, *m*; *inf* caimán, *m*

sharp *a* (of edges) afilado, cortante, *Lat. Am. also* filoso, filudo; (of points) punzante, puntiagudo; (of features, etc.) anguloso; (of bends, etc.) brusco; (of outlines, etc.) definido, distinto; (of pain, sound) agudo; (marked) marcado; (intense) intenso; (of winds, glance, etc.) penetrante; (of hearing) fino; (of appetite) bueno; (of showers) fuerte; (quick) rápido; (clever, etc.) vivo, listo; perspicaz; (of children) despierto, precoz; (unscrupulous) astuto, sin escrúpulos; (of criticism, remarks) mordaz; (of rebukes, sentences, etc.) severo; (of winters, etc.) riguroso; (of fighting) encarnizado; (of taste) picante; (sour) ácido; *mus* sostenido. *adv* en punto; puntualmente. *n mus* sostenido, *m*. **at five o'clock s.,** a las cinco en punto. **Look s.!** ¡Date prisa! **s.-edged,** afilado. **s.-eyed,** con ojos de lince; de mirada penetrante. **s.-featured,** de facciones angulosas. **s.-nosed,** de nariz puntiaguda. **s.-pointed,** puntiagudo. **s. practice,** procedimientos poco honrados, *m pl*. **s.-tongued,** de lengua áspera. **s. turn,** curva brusca, curva cerrada, *f*. **s.-witted,** de inteligencia viva, listo

sharpen *vt* (knives) afilar, amolar; (pencils, etc.) sacar punta (a); (wits, etc.) despabilar; (appetite) abrir. **This walk has sharpened my appetite,** Este paseo me ha abierto el apetito. **to s. one's claws,** afilarse las uñas

sharper *n inf* caballero de industria, timador, *m*; (at cards) fullero, *m*

sharply *adv* claramente; bruscamente; severamente; ásperamente

sharpness *n* (of cold, etc.) intensidad, *f*; severidad, *f*; (cleverness) agudeza, perspicacia, *f*; (of a child) precocidad, *f*; (sarcasm, etc.) mordacidad, *f*; aspereza, *f*; brusquedad, *f*

sharpshooter *n* franco tirador, *m*

sharpsighted *a* de vista penetrante, listo, perspicaz

shatter *vt* romper, quebrantar; hacer añicos; *fig* destrozar. **You have shattered my illusions,** Has destrozado todas mis ilusiones

shave *vt* afeitar, rasurar; (wood, etc.) acepillar. *vi* afeitarse; (of razors) afeitar. *n* afeitada, *f*. **to have a s.,** hacerse afeitar. **to have a close s.,** *inf* escapar por un pelo

shaving *n* afeitada, *f*; (of wood, etc.) viruta, acepilladura, *f*. **s.-bowl,** bacía, *f*. **s.-brush,** brocha de afeitar, *f*. **s.-glass,** espejo de afeitar, *m*. **s.-soap,** jabón de afeitar, *m*. **s.-stick,** barra de jabón de afeitar, *f*

shawl *n* chal, mantón, rebozo, *m*

she *pers pron* ella; la; (female) hembra, *f*; (translated by fem. ending in the case of animals, etc., e.g. **she bear,** osa, **she cat,** gata) **It is her,** Es ella. **she who is dancing,** la que baila

sheaf *n* (of corn, etc.) gavilla, garba, *f*; (of arrows) haz, *m*; (of papers, etc.) paquete, atado, *m*. **to bind in sheaves,** agavillar

shear *vt* (sheep) esquilar, trasquilar; tonsurar; cortar; (cloth) tundir

shearer *n* (of sheep) esquilador, *m*

shearing *n* (of sheep) esquileo, *m*, tonsura, *f*; (of cloth) tunda, *f*. **s. machine,** esquiladora, *f*. **s. season,** esquileo, *m*

shears *n pl* tijeras grandes, *f pl*, cizalla, *f*

sheath n vaina, f. **s.-knife,** cuchillo de monte, m
sheathe vt envainar; naut aforrar
shed vt derramar; (skin, etc.) mudar; perder; (remove) quitarse, desprenderse de; (get rid of) deshacerse de. n cobertizo, sotechado, m; cabaña, f. **to s. light on,** echar luz sobre, iluminar
sheen n lustre, m; brillo, m
sheep n oveja, f; carnero, m; ganado lanar, m. **He is the black s. of the family,** Es el garbanzo negro de la familia. **to cast sheep's eyes at,** lanzar miradas de carnero degollado. **s. breeder,** ganadero, m. **s.-dip,** desinfectante para ganado, m. **s.-dog,** perro de pastor, m. **s.-like,** ovejuno, de oveja. **s.-shearing,** esquileo, m
sheepfold n aprisco, redil, m
sheepish a tímido, vergonzoso; estúpido
sheepishly adv tímidamente
sheepishness n timidez, cortedad, f; estupidez, f
sheepskin n piel de carnero, f. **s. jacket,** zamarra, f
sheer a puro; completo, absoluto; (steep) escarpado, acantilado; a pico; (of fabrics) transparente; ligero, fino. adv completamente; de un golpe; (perpendicularly) a pico. **to s. off,** desviarse; largarse, marcharse
sheet n (bed) sábana, f; (shroud) mortaja, f; (of paper) hoja, f; cuartilla, f; (pamphlet) folleto, m; (news) periódico, m, hoja, f; (of metal, etc.) lámina, plancha, f; (of water, etc.) extensión, f; naut escota, f. vt poner sábanas en; envolver en sábanas; (a corpse) amortajar. **to be as white as a s.,** estar pálido como un muerto. **s. bend,** (knot) nudo de tejedor, m. **s. glass,** vidrio en lámina, m. **s. iron,** hierro en planchas, m
sheik n jeque, m
shekel n (coin) siclo, m; pl **shekels,** dinero, m
shelf n estante, anaquel, m; (reef) banco de arena, bajío, m; (of rock) escalón, m. **to be on the s.,** inf quedarse para tía, quedarse para vestir imágenes
shell n (of small shellfish) concha, f; (of tortoise) coraza, f; (of insects, lobsters, etc.) caparazón, m; (of a nut) cáscara, f; (of an egg) cascarón, m; (of peas, beans) vaina, f; (com and mus) concha, f; (of a building) casco, m; (outside) exterior, m; (empty form) apariencia, f; mil granada, f. vt pelar; (nuts) descascarar; (beans, etc.) desvainar; mil bombardear. **to be under s.-fire,** sufrir un bombardeo. **s. shock,** neurosis de guerra, f
shellfish n crustáceo, m; (as food) marisco, m
shelling n mil bombardeo, m
shelter n abrigo, amparo, m; refugio, m; asilo, m. vt dar asilo (a); abrigar; (defend) amparar, proteger; (hide) esconder. vi refugiarse; resguardarse; esconderse
sheltered a abrigado
sheltering a protector
shelve vt (books) poner en un estante; (persons) destituir; (questions, etc.) aplazar, arrinconar; proveer de estantes, vi (slope) inclinarse, formar declive; (of sea bed) formar escalones
shelving a inclinado; (of ocean bed) acantilado
shepherd n pastor, m. vt guardar; guiar, conducir. **s. boy,** zagal, m. **shepherd's pouch,** zurrón, m
shepherdess n pastora, f
sherbet n sorbete, m
sheriff n (in U.K.) sheriff, m; (U.S.A.) jefe de la policía, m
sherry n (vino de) jerez, m. **dry s.,** jerez seco, m
shield n escudo, m; (round) rodela, f; her escudo de armas, m; fig defensa, f, amparo, m. vt proteger, amparar. **to s. a person,** proteger a una persona. **to s. one's eyes from the sun,** proteger los ojos del sol. **s.-bearer,** escudero, m
shift vt mover; trasladar; quitar, librarse de; cambiar. vi moverse; (of the wind) girar; cambiar. n cambio, m; (expedient) recurso, expediente, m; (dodge) artificio, m, trampa, f; (of workmen) tanda, f; turno, m. **to make s.,** arreglárselas (para hacer algo); procurar (hacer algo); (manage) ir tirando. **to s. for oneself,** componérselas, arreglárselas. **to s. the scenes,** theat cambiar de decoración. **to s. the helm,** naut cambiar el timón. **to work in shifts,** trabajar por turnos

shiftiness n falta de honradez, informalidad, f; astucia, f
shifting a (of light, etc.) cambiante; (of sand, etc.) movedizo; (of wind) mudable; (of moods) voluble. **s. sand,** arena movediza, f
shiftless a perezoso; sin energía, ineficaz
shiftlessness n pereza, f; falta de energía, f
shifty a (tricky) tramposo, astuto; (dishonest) informal, falso; (of gaze) furtivo. **s.-eyed,** a de mirada furtiva
Shiite a and n chiita
shilling n chelín, m. **nine shillings in the £,** nueve chelines por libra. **to cut off with a s.,** desheredar
shilly shally n irresolución, vacilación, f, vi estar irresoluto, titubear, no saber qué hacer
shimmer vi rielar; relucir. n luz trémula, f; resplandor, m; viso, m
shin n espinilla, f; (of beef) corvejón, m. **to s. up,** trepar
shindy n suiza, reyerta, tasquera, f. **to kick up a s.,** armar camorra
shine vi brillar; resplandecer, relucir, relumbrar. vt (shoes) dar lustre (a). n brillo, m; lustre, m; (shoeshine) Mexico bola, f. **in rain or s.,** en buen o mal tiempo. **to s. with happiness,** radiar felicidad. **to take the s. out of,** eclipsar
shingle n (pebbles) guijarros, m pl; cascajo, m; carp barda, f; (hair) pelo a la garçonne, m; pl **shingles,** med zona, f, herpe zóster, m. vt (the hair) cortar a la garçonne
shining a resplandeciente, brillante, reluciente; radiante. **s. with happiness,** radiante de felicidad. **s. example,** ejemplo notable, m
shintoism n sintoísmo, m
shiny a brillante; lustroso, terso; (of trousers, etc.) reluciente; (of paper) glaseado
ship n buque, barco, m; (sailing) velero, m. vt embarcar; (oars) armar. vi embarcar; (as a member of crew) embarcarse. **on board s.,** a bordo. **to s. a sea,** embarcar agua. **to take s.,** embarcar. **to s. off,** mandar. **ship's boat,** lancha, f. **ship's boy,** grumete, m. **ship's carpenter,** carpintero de ribera, m. **ship's company,** tripulación, f. **s.-breaker,** desguazador, m. **s.-canal,** canal de navegación, m. **s.-load,** cargamento, m
shipbuilder n constructor de buques, arquitecto naval, m
shipbuilding n construcción naval, f
shipment n embarque, m; despacho por mar, m; (consignment) remesa, f
shipowner n naviero, m
shipper n naviero, m; importador, m; exportador, m
shipping n embarque, m; buques, barcos, m pl; (of a country) marina, f. **s. agent,** consignatario de buques, m. **s. company,** compañía de navegación, f. **s. offices,** oficinas de una compañía de navegación, f pl
shipshape a en buen orden; bien arreglado
shipwreck n naufragio, m, vt hacer naufragar, echar a pique
shipwrecked person n náufrago (-ga). **to be shipwrecked,** naufragar
shipyard n astillero, varadero, m
shire n condado, m
shirk vt eludir, esquivar; desentenderse de. vi faltar al deber
shirker n gandul (-la); persona que no cumple con su deber, f
shirr vt fruncir
shirt n camisa, f. **dress s.,** camisa de pechera dura, f. **hair-s.,** cilicio, m. **in one's shirt-sleeves,** en mangas de camisa. **s.-blouse,** blusa sencilla, f. **s.-collar,** cuello de camisa, m. **s. factory** or **shop,** camisería, f. **shirt-front,** pechera, f. **s.-maker,** camisero (-ra)
shirting n tela para camisas, f
shiver vi temblar, tiritar; dar diente con diente; (of a boat) zozobrar. vt (break) hacer añicos, romper; (sails) sacudir. n temblor, estremecimiento, m; escalofrío, m; (of glass, etc.) fragmento, m, astilla, f. **You give me the shivers,** Me das escalofríos

shivery *a* tembloroso; friolero. **I feel s.,** Tengo escalofríos

shoal *n* (of fish) banco, *m*; gran cantidad, *f*; (of people) multitud, muchedumbre, *f*; (water) bajo fondo, *m*; (sand-bank) banco, bajío, *m*, a poco profundo. **I know shoals of people in Valencia,** Conozco a muchísima gente de Valencia

shock *n* choque, *m*; *elec* conmoción, *f*; *med* shock, *m*; (*med* stroke) conmoción cerebral, *f*; (fright) sobresalto, susto, *m*. *vt* sacudir, dar una sacudida (a); chocar; escandalizar, horrorizar. *vi* chocar. **electric s.,** conmoción eléctrica, *f*. **She is easily shocked,** Ella se escandaliza fácilmente. **s. of hair,** mata de pelo, *f*. **s. absorber,** *mech* amortiguador, *m*; *aut* amortiguador (de los muelles), *m*. **s. troops,** tropas de asalto, *f pl*, elementos de choque, *m pl*

shocking *a* escandaloso; repugnante, horrible; espantoso. **How s.!** ¡Qué horror! **s. bad,** malísimo

shockingly *adv* horriblemente

shod *a* calzado; (of horses) herrado

shoddy *n* pacotilla, *f*. *a* de pacotilla; espurio, falso

shoe *n* zapato, *m*; (horse) herradura, *f*; (*naut mech*) zapata, *f*. *vt* (horses) herrar. **I should not like to be in his shoes,** No me gustaría estar en su pellejo. **That is quite another pair of shoes,** Eso es harina de otro costal. **to cast a s.,** (of horses) desherrarse, perder una herradura. **to put on one's shoes,** ponerse los zapatos, calzarse. **to remove one's shoes,** quitarse los zapatos, descalzarse. **wooden shoes,** zuecos, *m pl*. **s.-buckle,** hebilla de zapato, *f*. **s.-lace,** cordón de zapato, *m*. **s.-leather,** cuero para zapatos, *m*; calzado, *m*. **s.-scraper,** limpiabarros, *m*, estregadera, *f*. **s.-shop,** zapatería, *f*

shoeblack *n* betún, *m*; (person) limpiabotas, *m*

shoehorn *n* calzador, *m*

shoemaker *n* zapatero (-ra)

shoemaking *n* fabricación de calzado, zapatería, *f*

shoeshine *n Mexico* bola, *f*

shoo! *interj* ¡fuera!; ¡zape! *vt* ahuyentar

shoot *vt* (throw) lanzar; precipitar; (empty) vaciar; (a rapid) salvar; (rays, etc.) echar; (an arrow, a gun, etc.) disparar; (a person, etc.) pegar un tiro a (a); *sport* tirar; *mil* fusilar, pasar por las armas, *Lat. Am.* afusilar; (a film) hacer, impresionar. *vi* lanzarse, precipitarse; (of pain) latir; (sprout) brotar; disparar; tirar; (at football) tirar a gol, chutar. **to s. a glance at,** lanzar una mirada (a). **I was shot in the foot,** Una bala me hirió en el pie. **to s. the sun,** *naut* tomar el sol. **to s. ahead,** tomar la delantera. **to s. at,** tirar a, *Lat. Am.* abalear. **to s. at** *Central America, Mexico* balacear. **to s. by,** pasar como una bala. **to s. down,** *aer* derribar; matar de un tiro. **to s. up,** (of children) espigarse; (of prices) subir mucho; (of cliffs, etc.) elevarse

shoot *n* partida de caza, *f*; tiro, *m*; *bot* renuevo, retoño, *m*

shooting *n* tiro, *m*; caza con escopeta, *f*; (of guns) tiroteo, *m* (of an arrow) disparo, *m*; (of a film) rodaje, *m*. **to go s.,** ir a cazar con escopeta. **s.-box,** pabellón de caza, *m*. **s. butts,** tiradero, *m*. **s. dog,** perro de caza, *m*. **s.-gallery,** tiro al blanco, *m*. **s. match,** concurso de tiro, *m*. **s. pain,** punzada de dolor, *f*. **s. party,** partida de caza, *f*. **s. practice,** ejercicios de tiro, *m pl*. **s.-range,** campo de tiro, *m*. **s. star,** estrella fugaz, *f*

shop *n* tienda, *f*; (workshop) taller, *m*. *vi* ir de compras, ir de tiendas; comprar. **to talk s.,** hablar de negocios. **s.-assistant,** dependiente (-ta). **s.-soiled,** deslucido. **s.-steward,** representante de los obreros de una fábrica o taller, *m*. **s. window,** escaparate, *Mexico* aparador, *m*

shopkeeper *n* tendero (-ra), *Chile* despachero (-ra)

shoplifter *n* ladrón (-ona) de tiendas, ratero (-ra) de las tiendas

shoplifting *n* ratería en las tiendas, *f*

shopper *n* comprador (-ra)

shopping *n* compra, *f*; compras, *f pl*. **to go s.,** ir de com-

pras. **s. basket,** cesta para compras, *f*. **s. center,** centro comercial, *m*

shopwalker *n* jefe de recepción, *m*

shore *n* orilla, ríbera, *f*; costa, *f*; (sands) playa, *f*. **off s.,** en alta mar. **on s.,** en tierra. **to come on s.,** desembarcar. **to s. up,** apuntalar, acodalar; *fig* apoyar

short *a* corto; (of persons) bajo; breve; (of temper) vivo; insuficiente; distante (de); (brusque) seco; (of money) alcanzado. *adv* súbitamente; brevemente. *n* (vowel) vocal breve, *m*; *pl* **shorts,** calzones cortos, *m pl*. **for s.,** para mayor brevedad. **for a s. time,** por poco tiempo. **in a s. time,** dentro de poco. **in s.,** en breve, en resumen, en pocas palabras. **on s. notice,** con poco tiempo de aviso. **s. of,** con la excepción de, menos. **to be s.,** faltar, ser escaso. **to be s. with someone,** tratar con sequedad (a). **to fall s. of expectations,** no cumplir las esperanzas. **to go s. of,** pasarse sin. **to grow s.,** escasear. **s.-circuit,** corto circuito, *m*. **s. cut,** atajo, *Lat. Am.* desecho, *m*. **s.-haired,** pelicorto. **s.-handed,** falto de mano de obra. **s.-lived,** de vida corta; efímero, fugaz. **to be short-lived,** tener vida corta. **s.-sighted,** corto de vista. **s.-sightedness,** miopía, cortedad de vista, *f*. **s. story,** cuento, *m*. **s.-tempered,** irascible, irritable, de genio vivo. **s.-waisted,** corto de talle. **s.-winded,** corto de resuello; asmático

shortage *n* falta, escasez, *f*; carestía, *f*. **water s.,** carestía de agua, *f*

shortcoming *n* defecto, *m*; imperfección, *f*

shorten *vt* acortar; reducir, disminuir; abreviar. *vi* acortarse

shorthand *n* taquigrafía, estenografía, *f*. *a* taquigráfico, estenográfico

shortly *adv* dentro de poco, pronto; brevemente, en resumen, en pocas palabras; (curtly) bruscamente, secamente

shortness *n* cortedad, *f*; brevedad, *f*; (of a person) pequeñez, *f*; (lack) falta, *f*; (of memory, sight) cortedad, *f*; brusqueness) sequedad, brusquedad, *f*. **s. of breath,** falta de aliento, respiración difícil, *f*

shot *n* perdigón, *m*; *inf* perdigones, *m pl*; bala, *f*; (firing) tiro, *m*; (person) tirador (-ra); (stroke, etc.) golpe, *m*, tirada, *f*; (cinema) fotograma, *m*, a (of silk) tornasolado. **at one s.,** de un tiro. **like a s.,** *fig* como una bala. **to exchange shots,** tirotearse. **to fire a s.,** disparar un tiro. **to have a s. at,** probar suerte. **s.-gun,** escopeta, *f*. **s. silk,** seda tornasolada, *f*

should *v aux* (expressing future) **I s. like to go to the sea,** Me gustaría ir al mar; (expressing conditional) **I s. like to see them if I could,** Me gustaría verlos si pudiera; (expressing obligation) **You s. go at once,** Debes ir en seguida; (expressing probability) **They s. arrive tomorrow,** Seguramente llegarán mañana; (expressing doubt) **If the moment s. be opportune,** Si el momento fuera oportuno. **I s. just think so!** ¡Ya lo creo! ¡No lo dudo!

shoulder *n* hombro, *m*; (of mutton) espalda, *f*; (of a hill) falda, *f*. *vt* echar al hombro, echar sobre sí; (a responsibility) cargar con, hacerse responsable para; (jostle) dar codazos (a). **s. to s.,** hombro a hombro. **S. arms!** ¡Armas al hombro! **s.-blade,** omoplato, *m*. **s.-knot,** charretera, *f*. **s.-pad,** hombrera, *f*. **s.-strap,** *mil* dragona, *f*; (of a dress, etc.) tirante, *m*; (of a water carrier, etc.) correón, *m*

shouldered *a* de hombros . . . , de espaldas . . . **round-s.,** cargado de espaldas

shout *vi* gritar, hablar a gritos. *vt* gritar. *n* grito, *m*. **shouts of applause,** aclamaciones, *f pl*, aclamaciones, *m pl*. **to s. from the housetops,** pregonar a los cuatro vientos. **to s. with laughter,** reírse a carcajadas. **to s. down,** silbar. **to s. out,** gritar

shouting *n* gritos, *m pl*, vocerío, clamor, *m*; (applause) aclamaciones, *f pl*

shove *vt* empujar; poner. *n* empujón, *m*. **to s. along,** empujar. **to s. aside,** empujar a un lado; apartar a codazos. **to s. away,** rechazar. **to s. back,** hacer retroceder. **to s. forward,** hacer avanzar, empujar hacia adelante. **to s. off,** (a boat) echar afuera. **to s. out,** empujar hacia fuera

shovel *n* pala, *f. vt* traspalar. **s. hat,** sombrero de teja, *m*

show *vt* mostrar; hacer ver; (disclose) descubrir; revelar; (exhibit) exhibir; (indicate) indicar; (prove) demostrar, probar; (conduct) conducir, llevar, guiar; (explain) explicar; (oneself) presentarse. *vi* mostrarse; verse; parecer. **to s. cause,** mostrar causa. **to s. fight,** ofrecer resistencia. **s. signs of,** dar señales de. **to s. itself,** declararse, asomarse, surgir. **to s. to the door,** acompañar a la puerta. **to s. in,** (a person) hacer entrar, introducir (en). **to s. off,** *vt* exhibir; realzar; (new clothes, etc.) lucir. *vi* darse importancia; pavonearse. **to s. out,** (a person) acompañar a la puerta; (in anger) poner de patitas en la calle. **to s. through,** *vi* trasparentarse. *vt* conducir por. **to s. up,** *vt* invitar a subir; (a fraud, etc.) descubrir; (a swindler) desenmascarar; (defects) revelar. *vi* (stand out) destacarse; (be present) asomarse, asistir

show *n* (exhibition) exposición, *f*; espectáculo, *m*; (sign) indicio, *m*, señal, *f*; (ostentation) pompa, *f*, aparato, *m*, ostentación, *f*; (appearance) apariencia, *f*; (affair) negocio, *m*. **to give the s. away,** echar los títeres a rodar. **to make a s. of,** hacer gala de. **s.-case,** escaparate, *m*, vitrina, *f*. **s. of hands,** votación por manos levantadas, *f*. **s.-room,** salón de muestras, *m*

showdown *n* cartas boca arriba, *m*

shower *n* chaparrón, chubasco, *m*; (of spray, etc.) chorro, *m*; (of stones, arrows, etc.) lluvia, *f*; (of honors) cosecha, *f*; (bridal) despedida de soltera, despedida de soltería, *f. vt* derramar; rociar; mojar; llover. *vi* chaparrear, llover. **shower (bath)** ducha, *f, Argentina* baño de China, *f*

shower cap *n* gorro de ducha, *m*

showery *a* lluvioso

showily *adv* aparatosamente, con ostentación

showiness *n* ostentación, *f*; esplendor, *m*, magnificencia, *f*

showman *n* director de un espectáculo de feria, *m*; titiritero, *m*; pregonero, *m*

showy *a* vistoso; ostentoso, *Lat. Am. also* figuroso

shrapnel *n* granada, *m*, granada de metralla, *f*

shred *n* fragmento, *m*; (of cloth) jirón, *m*; brizna, *f*; *fig* pizca, *f. vt* desmenuzar. **to tear in shreds,** hacer pedazos

shrew *n zool* musaraña, *f*; (woman) fiera, *f*

shrewd *a* sagaz, perspicaz; prudente; (of the wind) penetrante; (pain) punzante. **to have a s. idea of,** tener una buena idea de. **a s. diplomat,** un fino diplomático

shrewdly *adv* sagazmente, con perspicacia; prudentemente

shrewdness *n* sagacidad, perspicacia, *f*; prudencia, *f*

shrewish *a* regañón

shrewishness *n* mal genio, *m*

shriek *vi* chillar, gritar. *vt* decir a voces, gritar. *n* chillido, *m*; grito agudo, *m*. **shrieks of laughter,** carcajadas, *f pl*

shrieking *n* gritos, chillidos, *m pl*

shrift to give short, enviar normala (a), enviar a paseo (a)

shrill *a* estridente, agudo

shrillness *n* estridencia, *f*

shrimp *n* camarón, *m*, gamba, *f*, *vi* pescar camarones

shrine *n* relicario, *m*; sepulcro de santo, *m*; templete, *m*, capilla, *f*; santuario, *m*

shrink *vi* encogerse; contraerse; disminuir, reducirse. *vt* encoger; reducir, disminuir; desaparecer; disiparse. **I shrank from doing it,** Me repugnaba hacerlo. **to s. away from,** retroceder ante; recular ante; huir de. **to s. back,** recular (ante)

shrinkage *n* encogimiento, *m*; contracción, *f*; reducción, disminución, *f*

shrinking *a* tímido

shrive *vt* confesar

shrivel *vi* avellanarse; (of persons, through old age)

acartonarse, apergaminarse; (wither) marchitarse; arrugarse. *vt* arrugar; secar, marchitar

shroud *n* sudario, *m*, mortaja, *f*; *naut* obenque, *m*. **to wrap in a s.,** amortajar

Shrove Tuesday *n* martes de carnaval, *m*

shrub *n* arbusto, *m*; matajo, *m*

shrubbery *n* arbustos, *m pl*, maleza, *f*; bosquecillo, *m*

shrug *vi* encogerse de hombros. *n* encogimiento de hombros, *m*

shrunken *a* contraído; acartonado, apergaminado; seco, marchito. **shrunken head,** cabeza reducida, *f*

shudder *vi* estremecerse; vibrar. *n* estremecimiento, *m*; escalofrío, *m*; (of an engine, etc.) vibración, *f*

shuffle *vt* (the feet) arrastrar; (scrape) restregar; (cards) barajar; (papers) mezclar. *vi* arrastrar los pies, arrastrarse; (cards) barajar; *fig* tergiversar. *n* (of the cards) barajadura, *f*; *fig* evasiva, *f*; embuste, *m*. **to s. along,** andar arrastrando los pies

shuffling *n* el arrastrar, *m*, (e.g. **the shuffling of chairs,** el arrastrar de sillas)

shun *vt* evitar, rehuir, esquivar

shunt *vt rw* apartar; *elec* shuntar. *vi rw* hacer maniobras

shunting *n* (of trains) maniobras, *f pl*

shut *vt* and *vi* cerrar. **to s. again,** volver a cerrar. **to s. down,** *vt* cerrar; (a machine) parar. *vi* (of factories, etc.) cerrar. **to s. in,** encerrar; (surround) cercar, rodear. **to s. off,** (water, etc.) cortar; (isolate) aislar (de). **to s. out,** excluir; obstruir, impedir; negar la entrada (a). **to s. up,** *vt* cerrar; encerrar; *inf* hacer callar (a); *vi inf* callarse, cerrar la boca. **to s. oneself up,** encerrarse

shutter *n* (window) contraventana, *f*, postigo, *m*; (of a camera) obturador, *m*; (of a fireplace) campana (de hogar), *f. vt* poner contraventanas (a); cerrar los postigos de

shuttle *n* (weaver's, and sewing-machine) lanzadera, *f*, (airplane service) puente aéreo, *m*. **s.-cock,** volante, *m*, gallito, *m*

shy *a* (of animals) tímido, salvaje; (of persons) huraño, tímido; vergonzoso. *vi* (of a horse) respingar; (of persons) asustarse (de). *vt* (a ball, etc.) lanzar. *n* (of a horse) respingo, *m*; (of a ball) lanzamiento, *m*; (try) prueba, tentativa, *f*. **to fight shy of,** procurar evitar. **to have a shy at,** probar

shyly *adv* tímidamente; con vergüenza, vergonzosamente

shyness *n* timidez, *f*; huranía, *f*; vergüenza, *f*

Siamese *a* siamés. *n* siamés (-esa); (language) siamés, *m*. **S. cat,** gato siamés, *m*

sic *vt* atacar; abijar, azuzar (a dog); *adv* así (in academic prose)

Sicilian *a* and *n* siciliano (-na)

Sicily Sicilia, *f*

sick *a* enfermo; mareado. **the s.,** los enfermos. **to be s.,** vomitar; estar enfermo. **to be s. of,** estar harto de. **to feel s.,** sentirse mareado. **to be on the s.-list,** estar enfermo. **s.-bed,** lecho de dolor, *m*. **s.-headache,** jaqueca, con náuseas, *f*. **s.-leave,** *mil* permiso por enfermedad, *m*. **s.-nurse,** enfermera, *f*

sicken *vt* caer enfermo, enfermar; (feel sick) marearse; (recoil from) repugnar; (weary of) cansarse (de), aburrirse (de); *vt* marear; dar asco (a), repugnar; cansar, aburrir. **It sickens me,** Me da asco. **He is sickening for measles,** Muestra síntomas de sarampión

sickening *a* nauseabundo; repugnante; (tedious) fastidioso

sickle *n* hoz, segadera, *f*

sickliness *n* falta de salud, *f*; náusea, *f*; (paleness) palidez, *f*

sickly *a* enfermizo, achacoso, malucho, *Lat. Am.* farruto, *Central America, Mexico* fifiriche; (of places, etc.) malsano; (pale) pálido; débil; (of a smell) nauseabundo; (mawkish) empalagoso

sickness *n* enfermedad, *f*; mal, *m*; náusea, *f*, mareo, *m*

side *n* lado, *m*; (hand) mano, *f*; (of a river, etc.) orilla, *f*, margen, *m*; (of a person) costado, *m*; (of an animal) ijada, *f*; (of a hill) falda, pendiente, ladera, *f*; (of a ship) banda, *f*, costado, *m*; (aspect) aspecto, *m*; punto de vista, *m*; (party) partido, grupo, *m*; (team) equipo, *m*; (of descent) lado, *m*. *a* lateral, de lado; oblicuo. **on all sides,** por todas partes. **on both sides,** por ambos lados. **s. by s.,** lado a lado. **the other s. of the picture,** el revés de la medalla. **to change sides,** cambiar de partido. **to pick sides,** escoger el equipo. **to put on s.,** darse tono, alzar el gallo. **to split one's sides,** desternillarse de risa, reírse a carcajadas. **to s. with,** declararse por, ponerse al lado de, tomar el partido de. **wrong s. out,** al revés. **s.-car,** sidecar, asiento lateral, *m*. **s.-chain,** *chem* cadena lateral, *f*. **s.-dish,** entremés, *m*. **s. door,** puerta lateral, *f*. **s.-face,** *a* de perfil. *n* perfil, *m*. **s.-glance,** mirada de soslayo, *f*. **s.-issue,** cuestión secundaria, *f*. **s.-line,** negocio accesorio, *m*; ocupación secundaria, *f*; *rw* vía secundaria, *f*. **s.-saddle,** silla de señora, silla de montar de lado, *f*. **s.-show,** (at a fair) barraca, *f*, puesto de feria, *m*; exhibición secundaria, *f*; función secundaria, *f*. **s.-table,** trinchero, *m*. **s.-track,** *n rw* apartadero, *m*. *vt* desviar (de), apartar (de). **s.-view,** perfil, *m*. **s.-walk,** acera, *f Mexico* banqueta *f*, *elsewhere in Lat. Am.* andén *m*, vereda *f*. **s.-whiskers,** patillas, *f pl*

sidelight *n* luz lateral, *f*; (on a ship) ojo de buey, *m*; *fig* información incidental, *f*

sidelong *adv* de lado, lateralmente; (of glances) de soslayo. *a* oblicuo

side road *n* camino lateral, *m*

sideways *adv* oblicuamente, de lado; (edgeways) de soslayo. *a* de soslayo

siding *n rw* apartadero, *m*

sidle *vi* andar (or ir) de lado. **to s. up to,** acercarse servilmente a; arrimarse (a)

siege *n* asedio, sitio, cerco, *m*. **to lay s. to,** poner cerco (a), sitiar, asediar cercar. **to raise a s.,** levantar un sitio

sienna *n* tierra de siena natural, *f*. **burnt s.,** tierra de siena tostada, *f*

sieve *n* cedazo, tamiz, *m*, criba, *f*, *Lat. Am.* arnero, *m*, *vt* tamizar, cerner, cribar

sift *vt* (sieve) cerner, cribar; (sugar, etc.) salpicar (con); (a question) escudriñar, examinar minuciosamente

sifting *n* cribado, *m*; (of a question) investigación minuciosa, *f*; *pl* **siftings,** cerniduras, *f pl*

sigh *vi* suspirar; (of the wind) susurrar. *n* suspiro, *m*; (of the wind) susurro, *m*. **to s. for,** suspirar por; lamentar

sighing *n* suspiros, *m pl*; (of the wind) susurro, *m*

sight *n* vista, *f*; visión, *f*; espectáculo, *m*; (fright) estantigua, *f*. *vt* ver, divisar; (aim) apuntar. **front s.,** (of guns) alza, *f*. **short s.,** (of eyes) vista corta, *f*. **at first s.,** a primera vista. **in s.,** a la vista. **in s. of,** a vista de. **out of s.,** que no está a la vista; perdido de vista. **Out of s., out of mind,** Ojos que no ven, corazón que no siente. **to be lost to s.,** perderse de vista. **to lose s. of,** perder de vista (a). **to catch a s. of,** vislumbrar. **to come in s.,** aparecer, asomarse. **to know by s.,** conocer de vista (a). **s.-reading,** lectura a primera vista, *f*

sightly *a* hermoso; deleitable

sightseeing *n* turismo, *m*. **to go s.,** visitar los monumentos, ver los puntos de interés

sightseer *n* curioso (-sa); turista, *mf*

sign *n* señal, *f*; seña, *f*; indicio, *m*; (of the zodiac and *mus*) signo, *m*; marca, *f*; *ecc* símbolo, *m*; (of a shop, etc.) muestra, *f*, rótulo, *m*; (symptom) síntoma, *m*. *vt* firmar; indicar; *ecc* persignar. **as a s. of,** en señal de. **to converse by signs,** hablar por señas. **to make the s. of the cross over,** santiguar. **to show signs (of),** dar señas (de); indicar. **s.-painter,** pintor de muestras, *m*

signal *n* señal, *f*. *vt* señalar; hacer señas (a). *vi* hacer señales. *a* insigne, notable. **fog-s.,** señal de niebla, *f*. **landing s.,** *aer* señal de aterrizaje, *f*. **to give the s. for,** dar la señal para. **s.-box,** garita de señales, *f*. **s. code,** *naut* código de señales, *m*

signalize *vt* señalar, distinguir

signaler *n* señalador, *m*

signalman *n rw* guardavía, *m*

signatory *a and n* signatario (-ia)

signature *n* firma, *f*; (*mus* and *print*) signatura, *f*

signboard *n* letrero, *m*, muestra, *f*

signet *n* sello, *m*. **s.-ring,** anillo de sello, *m*

significance *n* significación, *f*, significado, *m*; importancia, *f*

significant *a* significativo, significante; expresivo; importante

significantly *adv* significativamente; expresivamente

signify *vt* significar; querer decir; importar. *vi* significar, tener importancia; importar

signpost *n* indicador de dirección, *m*

silage *n* forraje conservado en silo, *m*

silence *n* silencio, *m*, *interj* ¡silencio! *vt* hacer callar, imponer silencio (a); silenciar. **to keep s.,** guardar silencio, callarse. **to pass over in s.,** pasar en silencio (por), pasar por alto de. **S. gives consent,** Quien calla otorga

silencer *n* (of fire-arms) silencioso, *m*; *aut* silenciador, silencioso, *m*

silent *a* silencioso. **to become s.,** enmudecer; callar. **to remain s.,** callarse, guardar silencio; permanecer silencioso. **s. partner,** *n* socio (-ia) comanditario (-ia)

silent film, silent movie *n* película muda, *f*

silently *adv* silenciosamente, en silencio

silhouette *n* silueta, *f*. *vt* representar en silueta; destacar. **in s.,** en silueta. **to be silhouetted against the sky,** destacarse contra el sielo

silica *n* sílice, *f*

silk *n* seda, *f*, *a* de seda. **artificial s.,** seda artificial, *f*. **floss s.,** seda ocal, *f*. **sewing s.,** seda de coser, *f*. **twist s.,** seda cordelada, *f*. **as smooth as s.,** como una seda. **s. growing,** sericultura, *f*. **s. hat,** sombrero de copa, *m*. **s. merchandise,** sedería, *f*. **s. stocking,** media de seda, *f*

silken *a* de seda; sedoso

silkiness *n* carácter sedoso, *m*; suavidad, *f*

silk-screen process *n* imprenta por tamiz, imprenta serigráfica, imprenta tamigráfica, impresión con estarcido de seda, *f*, proceso tamigráfico, *m*, serigrafía, tamigrafía, *f*

silkworm *n* gusano de seda, *m*

silky *a* sedoso; (of wine) suave

sill *n* (of a window) alféizar, antepecho, *m*; (of a door) umbral, *m*

silliness *n* tontería, estupidez, *f*

silly *a* tonto, estúpido; imbécil, *Central America also* azurrumbado. *n* tonto (-ta). **You are a s. ass,** Eres un imbécil

silo *n* silo, *m*

silt *n* aluvión, *m*, sedimentación, *f*. **to s. up,** *vt* cegar (or obstruir) con aluvión. *vi* cegarse con aluvión

silver *n* plata, *f*. *a* de plata; argénteo; (of the voice, etc.) argentino. *vt* platear; (mirrors) azogar; (hair) blanquear. **s. birch,** abedul, *m*. **s. fox,** zorro plateado, *m*. **s.-gry,** gris perla, *m*. **s.-haired,** de pelo entrecano. **s.-paper,** papel de estaño, *m*. **s.-plate,** *n* vajilla de plata, *f*. *vt* platear. **s.-tongued,** de pico de oro; de voz argentina. **s. wedding,** bodas de plata, *f pl*

silversmith *n* platero, *m*. **silversmith's shop,** platería, *f*

silvery *a* plateado, argentado; (of sounds) argentino

simian *a* símico

similar *a* parecido (a), semejante (a); similar; *geom* semejante. **to be s. to,** asemejarse (a), parecerse (a)

similarity *n* parecido, *m*, semejanza, similitud, *f*

similarly *adv* de un modo parecido, asimismo

simile *n* símil, *m*

simmer *vi* hervir a fuego lento; *fig* estar a punto de estallar. **to s. down,** *fig* moderarse poco a poco. **to s. over,** *fig* estallar

simper *vi* sonreírse bobamente

simpering *n* sonrisilla tonta, *f*

simperingly *adv* con sonrisa necia

simple *a* sencillo; simple; ingenuo, inocente; crédulo; (humble) humilde; (mere) mero. **s.-hearted,** ino-

cente, cándido, sin malicia. **s.-minded,** ingenuo; crédulo. **s.-mindedness,** ingenuidad, *f*; credulidad, *f*
simpleton *n* primo (-ma); papanatas, *m*, tonto (-ta)
simplicity *n* sencillez, *f*; simplicidad, candidez, *f*
simplifiable *a* simplificable
simplification *n* simplificación, *f*
simplify *vt* simplificar
simply *adv* sencillamente; simplemente, meramente; absolutamente
simulacrum *n* simulacro, *m*
simulate *vt* fingir, aparentar, simular
simulation *n* simulación, *f*, fingimiento, *m*
simultaneous *a* simultáneo
simultaneously *adv* simultáneamente; al mismo tiempo (que)
simultaneousness *n* simultaneidad, *f*
sin *n* pecado, *m*, *vi* pecar; faltar (a)
since *adv* desde entonces, desde (que). *prep* desde. *conjunc* desde que; ya que, puesto que. **a long time s.,** hace mucho. **not long s.,** hace poco. **How long is it s.
. . . ?** ¿Cuánto tiempo hace que . . . ? **s. then,** desde entonces
sincere *a* sincero
sincerely *adv* sinceramente. **Yours s.,** Su afectísimo . . .
sincerity *n* sinceridad, *f*
sine *n* math seno, *m*
sinecure *n* canonjía, sinecura, *f*, empleo de aviador (Mexican slang), *m*
sinew *n* tendón, *m*; *pl* **sinews,** nervio, *m*, fuerza, *f*
sinewy *a* (stringy) fibroso; musculoso, nervudo
sinful *a* (of persons) pecador; (of thoughts, acts) pecaminoso
sinfulness *n* pecado, *m*; culpabilidad, perversidad, maldad, *f*
sing *vi* cantar; (of the ears) zumbar; (of wind, water) murmurar, susurrar; (of a cat) ronronear. *vt* cantar. **to s. a child to sleep,** dormir a un niño cantando. **to s. another song,** *inf* bajar el tono. **to s. small,** hacerse el chiquito. **to s. the praises of,** hacer las alabanzas de. **to s. out,** vocear, gritar. **s.-song,** *n* cantaría, *f*; concierto improvisado, *m*. *a* monótono
Singapore Singapur, *m*
singe *vt* chamuscar; (a fowl) aperdigar; (hair) quemar las puntas de los cabellos
singer *n* cantor (-ra); (professional) cantante, *mf*; (bird) ave cantora, *f*
singing *n* canto, *m*; (of the ears) zumbido, *m*. *a* cantante. **s.-bird,** ave cantora, *f*. **s.-master,** maestro de cantar, *m*
single *a* único; sencillo; solo; simple; (individual) particular; individual; (unmarried) soltero. *n* (tennis) juego sencillo, individual, *m*. **in s. file,** de reata. **to s. out,** escoger; singularizar. **s. bed,** cama de monja, *f*. **s. bedroom,** habitación individual, habitación con una sola cama, *f*. **s.-breasted,** (of coats) recto. **s. combat,** combate singular, *m*. **s. entry,** *com* partida simple, *f*. **s.-handed,** de una mano; para una sola persona; sin ayuda, solo, en solitario. **s.-minded,** sin doblez, sincero de una sola idea. **s. ticket,** billete sencillo, *m*
singleness *n* celibato, *m*, soltería, *f*. **with s. of purpose,** con un solo objeto
single room *Mexico* cuarto sencillo, *m*
singlet *n* camiseta, *f*
singly *adv* separadamente, uno a uno; a solas, solo; sin ayuda
singular *a* and *n* singular, *m*
singularity *n* singularidad, *f*
singularly *adv* singularmente
sinister *a* siniestro
sink *vi* ir al fondo; bajar; hundirse; (of ships) irse a pique, naufragar; sumergirse; disminuir; caer (en); penetrar; (of persons, fires) morir; (of the sun, etc.) ponerse. *vt* (a ship) echar a pique; sumergir; hundir; dejar caer; bajar; (wells) cavar; reducir, disminuir; (invest) invertir; (one's identity, etc.) tener secreto; (differ-

ences) olvidar; (engrave) grabar. **My heart sank,** Se me cayeron las alas del corazón. **He sank to his knees,** Cayó de rodillas. **He is sinking fast,** Está en las últimas. **Their words began to s. in,** Sus palabras empezaban a tener efecto (or hacer mella). **I found her sunk in thought,** La encontré ensimismada. **to s. one's voice,** bajar la voz. **to s. down on a chair,** dejarse caer en una silla. **to s. into misery,** caer en la miseria. **to s. under,** (a responsibility, etc.) estar agobiado bajo
sink *n* (kitchen) fregadero, *Chile, Mexico also* lavaplatos, *m*; sumidero, *m*, sentina, *f*. **s. of iniquity,** sentina, *f*
sinker *n* (engraver) grabador (-ra); (of a fishing line) plomada, *f*
sinking *n* hundimiento, *m*; (of the sun) puesta, *f*; (of wells) cavadura, *f*; sumergimiento, *m*. **the s. of a boat,** el hundimiento de un buque. **with s. heart,** con la muerte en el alma. **s. fund,** fondo de amortización, *m*
sinless *a* sin pecado, inocente, puro
sinner *n* pecador (-ra)
sinuous *a* sinuoso, tortuoso; flexible, ágil
sinus *n* (anat etc.) seno, *m*
sip *vt* sorber; (wine) saborear, paladear. *n* sorbo, *m*
siphon *n* sifón, *m*, *vt* sacar con sifón
sir *n* señor, *m*; (British title) sir. **Dear s.,** Muy Señor mío
sire *n* (to a monarch) Señor, *m*; (father) padre, *m*; (stallion) semental, *m*. *vt* procrear, engendrar
siren *n* sirena, *f*. **s. suit,** mono, *m*
sirloin *n* solomillo, *Mexico* diezmillo, *m*
sirocco *n* siroco, *m*
sister *n* hermana, *f*; (before nun's christian name) Sor; (hospital) hermana del hospital, *f*; enfermera, *f*. **s. language,** lengua hermana, *f*. **s. ship,** buque gemelo, *m*. **s.-in-law,** cuñada, hermana política, *f*. **S. of Mercy,** Hermana de la Caridad, *f*
sisterhood *n* hermandad, *f*; comunidad de monjas, *f*
sisterly *a* de hermana
sit *vi* sentarse; estar sentado; (of birds) posarse; (of hens) empollar; (in Parliament, etc.) ser diputado; (of a committee, etc.) celebrar sesión; (on a committee, etc.) formar parte de; (function) funcionar; (of garments, food, and *fig*) sentar. **to sit a horse,** mantenerse a caballo; montar a caballo. **to sit oneself,** sentarse, tomar asiento. **to sit by,** (a person) sentarse (or estar sentado) al lado de. **to sit for** (a portrait) servir de modelo para; hacerse retratar. **to sit tight,** no moverse. **to sit down,** sentarse; (besiege) sitiar. **to sit on,** sentarse (en or sobre); (eggs) empollar; (a committee, etc.) formar parte de; (investigate) investigar; (snub) dejar aplastado (a). **to sit out,** quedarse hasta el fin (de). **to sit out a dance,** conversar un baile. **to sit up,** incorporarse en la cama; tenerse derecho; (at night) velar; (of dogs, etc.) pedir. **to sit up and take notice,** abrir los ojos. **to sit up in bed,** incorporarse en la cama. **to sit up late,** estar de pie hasta muy tarde
sit-down strike *n* huelga de brazos caídos, huelga de sentados, *f*
site *n* sitio, local, *m*; (for building) solar, *m*
sitting *n* asentada, *f*; (of Parliament, etc.) sesión, *f*; (for a portrait) estadia, *f*; (of eggs) nidada, *f*. **at a s.,** de una asentada. **s.-room,** sala de estar, *f*
situated *a* situado. **How is he s.?** ¿Cómo está situado? ¿Cuál es su situación?
situation *n* situación, *f*; (job) empleo, *m*
six *a* and *n* seis, *m*. **It is six o'clock,** Son las seis. **Everything is at sixes and sevens,** Todo está en desorden. **six-foot,** de seis pies. **six hundred,** seiscientos (-as)
sixfold *a* séxtuplo
sixteen *a* and *n* diez y seis, dieciséis, *m*. **John is s.,** Juan tiene dieciséis años
sixteenth *a* décimosexto; (of the month) (el) diez y seis; (of monarch) diez y seis. *n* dieciseisavo, *m*
sixth *a* sexto; (of the month) (el) seis; (of monarchs) sexto. *n* seisavo, *m*; sexta parte, *f*; *mus* sexta, *f*. **Henry the S.,** Enrique sexto. **May the s.,** el seis de mayo

sixtieth *a* sexagésimo. *n* sesentavo, *m*; sexagésima parte, *f*

sixty *a* and *n* sesenta *m*. **John has turned s.,** Juan ha pasado los sesenta

sizable *a* bastante grande

size *n* tamaño, *m*; dimensión, *f*; (height) altura, *f*; (measurement) medida, *f*; talle, *m*; (in gloves, etc.) número, *m*; (glue) cola, *f*. *vt* clasificar por tamaños; (glaze, etc.) encolar. **to s. up,** tomar las medidas (a).

sizzle *vi* chisporrotear, chirriar. *n* chisporroteo, chirrido, *m*

skate *n* patín, *m*; *icht* raya, *f*, *vi* patinar

skater *n* patinador (-ra)

skating *n* patinaje, *m*. **s. rink,** sala de patinar, *f*; pista de hielo, pista de patinar, *f*, patinadero, *m*

skein *n* madeja, *f*

skeleton *n* esqueleto, *m*; (of a building) armadura, *f*; (of a literary work) esquema, *m*. **s. key,** ganzúa, *f*

sketch *n* croquis, apunte, *m*; (for a literary work) esbozo, esquema, *m*; (article) cuadro, artículo, *m*; (description, *f*; *theat* entremés, sainete, *m*. *vt* dibujar; esbozar, bosquejar; trazar; describir. **s.-book,** álbum de croquis, *m*

sketchily *adv* incompletamente

sketching *n* arte de dibujar, *mf*. **He likes s.,** Le gusta dibujar

sketchy *a* bosquejado; incompleto; escaso

skewer *n* broqueta, *f*, *vt* espetar

ski *n* esquí, *m*, *vi* esquiar

skid *n* (of a vehicle) patinazo, *m*, *vi* patinar

skidding *n* patinaje, *m*

skier *n* esquiador (-ra), *mf*

skiff *n* esquife, *m*

skiing *n* patinaje sobre la nieve, *m*, el esquiar. **to go s.,** ir a esquiar

skill *n* habilidad, *f*

skilled *a* hábil; experto

skilled worker *n* obrero calificado, *m*

skillful *a* hábil

skim *vt* espumar; (milk) desnatar, *Lat. Am.* descremar; (touch lightly) deslizarse sobre, rozar; (a book) hojear

skimp *vt* escatimar; escasear; (work) frangollar. *vi* ser parsimonioso

skimpy *a* escaso

skin *n* tez, *f*, cutis, *m*; piel, *f*; (of fruit) pellejo, *m*, piel, *f*; (for wine) odre, pellejo, *m*; (on milk) espuma, *f*. *vt* despellejar; pelar, mondar; (graze) hacerse daño (a); *inf* desollar. **next to one's s.,** sobre la piel. **to s. over,** cicatrizarse. **to have a thin s.,** *fig* ser muy susceptible. **to save one's s.,** salvar el pellejo. **s.-deep,** superficial. **s.-tight,** escurrido, muy ajustado

skinflint *n* avaro (-ra)

skinny *a* flaco, descarnado, magro

skip *vi* retozar, brincar, saltar; saltar a la comba; (bolt) largarse, escaparse. *vt* saltar; (a book) hojear; (omit) omitir; pasar por alto de. *n* brinco, pequeño salto, *m*

skipper *n* *naut* patrón, *m*; (*inf* and *sport*) capitán, *m*

skirmish *vi* escaramuzar. *n* escaramuza, *f*

skirt *n* falda, *f*; (edge) margen, borde, *m*, orilla, *f*; (of a jacket, etc.) faldón, *m*. *vt* ladear; (hug) rodear, ceñir

skit *n* sátira, *f*; parodia, *f*

skittish *a* (of a horse) retozón; (of persons) frívolo; caprichoso

skittle *n* bolo, *m*; *pl* **skittles,** juego de bolos, *m*. **s. alley,** pista de bolos, bolera, *f*

skulk *vi* estar en acecho; esconderse; rondar

skull *n* cráneo, *m*; calavera, *f*. **s.-cap,** gorro, casquete, *m*; (for ecclesiastics) solideo, *m*

skunk *n* *zool* mofeta, *f*, chingue, mapurite, yaguré, zorrillo, zorrino, zorro hediondo, *m*

sky *n* cielo, *m*. **to praise to the skies,** poner en los cuernos de la luna. **s.-blue,** *n* azul celeste, *m*. *a* de color azul celeste, cerúleo. **s.-high,** hasta las nubes, hasta el cielo. **s.-line,** horizonte, *m*. **s.-scraper,** rascacielos, *m*. **s.-sign,** anuncio luminoso, *m*

skylight *n* claraboya, *f*, tragaluz, *m*

slab *n* bloque, *m*; losa, *f*, *Lat. Am. also* laja; plancha, *f*

slack *a* lento; flojo; (lazy) perezoso; negligente, descuidado; *com* encalmado; débil. *vi* ser perezoso. **the s. season,** la estación muerta. **to be s. in one's work,** ser negligente en el trabajo. **to s. off,** disminuir sus esfuerzos; dejar de trabajar

slacken *vt* and *vi* aflojar; disminuir, reducir. **The wind slackened,** El viento amainaba, El viento aflojaba. **to s. one's efforts,** disminuir sus esfuerzos. **to s. speed,** disminuir la velocidad

slackening *n* aflojamiento, *m*; disminución, *f*

slacker *n* gandul (-la)

slackness *n* flojedad, *f*; pereza, falta de energía, *f*; negligencia, *f*; *com* desanimación, *f*

slacks *n* *pl* pantalones, *m* *pl*

slake *vt* (one's thirst and lime) apagar; satisfacer

slam *vt* cerrar de golpe; golpear. *n* (of a door) portazo, *m*; golpe, *m*; (cards) capote, *m*. **He went out and slammed the door,** Salió dando un portazo

slander *n* calumnia, *f*, *vt* calumniar

slanderer *n* calumniador (-ra)

slanderous *a* calumnioso

slang *n* argot, *m*, jerga, *f*, *vt* poner como un trapo (a), llenar de insultos

slant *vi* estar al sesgo; inclinarse; ser oblicuo. *vt* inclinar. *n* inclinación, *f*; oblicuidad, *f*. **on the s.,** inclinado; oblicuo

slanting *a* al sesgo, inclinado; oblicuo

slap *vt* pegar con la mano. *n* bofetada, *f*; palmada, *Lat. Am.* cachetada, *f*. **to s. on the back,** golpear en la espalda. **s.-dash,** (of persons) irresponsable, descuidado; (of work) chapucero, sin cuidado

slash *vt* (gash, also sleeves, etc.) acuchillar; cortar; (with a whip) dar latigazos (a). *n* cuchillada, *f*; corte, *m*; latigazo, *m*

slashing *a* mordaz, severo

slat *n* tablilla, *f*, *vi* (of sails) dar zapatazos, zapatear

slate *n* pizarra, *f*, esquisto, *m*; (for roofs and for writing) pizarra, *f*, *vt* (a roof) empizarrar; (censure) criticar severamente, censurar. **s.-colored,** apizarrado. **s. pencil,** pizarrín, *m*. **s. quarry,** pizarrería, *f*, pizarral, *m*

slater *n* pizarrero, *m*

slating *n* empizarrado, *m*; (criticism) crítica severa, censura, *f*; (scolding) peluca, *f*

slattern *n* pazpuerca, *f*

slatternly *a* desgarbado, desaliñado

slaughter *n* matanza, *f*; carnicería, *f*. *vt* (animals) sacrificar, matar; matar, hacer una carnicería de. **s.-house,** matadero, *m*

slaughterer *n* jifero, carnicero, *m*

Slav *a* and *n* eslavo (-va)

slave *n* esclavo (-va). *vi* trabajar como un negro. **white s. traffic,** trata de blancas, *f*. **s.-bangle,** esclava, *f*. **s.-driver,** capataz de esclavos, negrero, *m*; *fig* negrero, sayón de esclavos, *m*. **s.-trade,** trata de esclavos, *f*

slaver *n* negrero, *m*

slaver *vi* babear. *n* baba, *f*

slavering *a* baboso

slavery *n* esclavitud, *f*; trabajo muy arduo, *m*

slavish *a* de esclavo; servil

slavishly *adv* como esclava; servilmente

Slavonic *a* eslavo. *n* (language) eslavo, *m*, lengua eslava, *f*

slay *vt* matar; asesinar

slayer *n* matador (-ra); asesino, *mf*

slaying *n* matanza, *f*; asesinato, *m*

sledge *n* trineo, *m*. *vi* ir en trineo. *vt* transportar por trineo. **s.-hammer,** acotillo, *m*

sleek *a* liso, lustroso; (of general appearance) pulcro, bien aseado, elegante; (of manner) obsequioso

sleekness *n* lustre, *m*, lisura, *f*; (of an animal) gordura, *f*; elegancia, *f*

sleep *n* sueño, *m*, *vi* dormir; reposar, descansar. *vt* dormir. **a deep s.,** un sueño pesado. **He walks in his s.,** Es un sonámbulo. **to court s.,** conciliar el sueño. **to go to s.,** dormirse; entumecerse. **My foot has gone to s.,**

Se me ha dormido (*or* Se me ha entumecido) el pie. **to send a person to s.,** adormecer. **to s. like a top,** dormir como un lirón. **to s. oneself sober,** dormir la mona. **to s. in,** dormir tarde; dormir en casa. **to s. off,** (a cold, etc.) curarse . . . durmiendo; (drunkenness) dormirla. **to s. on,** *vt* (consider) dormir sobre, consultar con la almohada. *vi* seguir durmiendo. **to s. out,** dormir fuera de casa; dormir al aire libre

sleeper *n* durmiente, *mf; rw* traviesa, *f;* (on a train) coche cama, *m.* **to be a bad s.,** dormir mal. **to be a good s.,** dormir bien.

sleepily *adv* soñolientamente

sleepiness *n* somnolencia, *f;* letargo, *m*

sleeping *a* durmiente. *n* el dormir. **between s. and waking,** entre duerme y vela. **s.-bag,** saco-cama, *m.* **s.-car,** coche camas, *m.* **s.-draught,** narcótico, *m.* **s. partner,** *n* socio (-ia) comanditario (-ia). **s. sickness,** enfermedad del sueño, *f*

sleepless *a* (of persons) insomne, desvelado; (unremitting) incansable; (of the sea, etc.) en perpetuo movimiento. **to spend a s. night,** pasar una noche en vela, pasar una noche toledana, pasar una noche sin dormir

sleeplessness *n* insomnio, *m*

sleepwalker *n* sonámbulo (-la)

sleepwalking *n* sonambulismo, *m*

sleepy *a* soñoliento; letárgico. **to be s.,** tener sueño. **s.-head,** lirón, *m,* marmota, *f*

sleet *n* aguanieve, cellisca, nevisca, *f, vi* caer aguanieve, cellisquear, neviscar

sleeve *n* manga, *f;* (of a hose pipe, etc.) manguera, *f; mech* manguito, *m.* **to have something up one's s.,** traer algo en la manga

sleeved *a* con mangas . . . ; de . . . manga(s)

sleeveless *a* sin manga. **s. shirt** *Lat. Am.* cusma, *f*

sleigh *n* trineo, *m, vi* ir en trineo

sleight of hand *n* prestidigitación, *f;* juego de manos, *m*

slender *a* delgado; esbelto; tenue; escaso; pequeño; ligero. **Their means are very s.,** Sus recursos son muy escasos. **It is a very s. hope,** Es una esperanza muy remota

slenderness *n* delgadez, *f;* esbeltez, *f;* tenuidad, *f;* escasez, *f*

sleuth *n* (dog) sabueso, *m; inf* detective, *m*

slice *n* lonja, tajada, *f;* (of fruit) raja, *f;* (of bread, etc.) rebanada, *f;* (share) parte, porción, *f;* (for fish, etc.) pala, *f. vt* cortar en tajadas, etc.; rajar; cortar

slick *a* hábil, diestro

slide *vi* deslizarse, resbalar; (over a question) pasar por alto de; (into a habit, etc.) caer (en). *n* resbalón, *m;* pista de hielo, *f;* (chute) tobogán, *m;* (of a microscope) portaobjetos, *m;* (lantern) diapositiva, *f;* (for the hair) pasador, *m;* (of rock, etc.) desprendimiento, *m; mech* guía, *f.* **to let things s.,** dejar rodar la bola. **s.-rule,** regla de cálculo, *f*

sliding *a* resbaladizo; corredizo; movible. **s.-door,** puerta corrediza, puerta de corradera, *f.* **s.-roof,** techo corredizo, *m.* **s.-scale,** escala graduada, *f.* **s.-seat,** asiento movible, *m;* (in a rowing-boat) bancada corrediza, *f*

slight *a* delgado; débil, frágil; ligero; (small) pequeño; escaso; (trivial) insignificante, poco importante. *vt* desairar, despreciar, *Mexico* descolar. *n* desaire, desprecio, *m;* falta de respeto, *f*

slighting *a* despreciativo, de desprecio

slightingly *adv* con desprecio

slightly *adv* ligeramente; poco. **I only know her s.,** La conozco muy poco. **s. built,** de talle delgado

slightness *n* (slimness) delgadez, *f;* ligereza, *f;* (triviality) poca importancia, insignificancia, *f*

slim *a* delgado; escaso. *vi* adelgazarse. **He has very s. chances of success,** Tiene muy pocas posibilidades de conseguir el éxito

slime *n* légamo, limo, lodo, cieno, *m;* (of a snail) limazo, *m; fig* cieno, *m*

sliminess *n* limosidad, *f;* viscosidad, *f*

slimness *n* delgadez, *f;* escasez, *f*

slimy *a* limoso, legamoso; pecinoso, viscoso; (of persons) rastrero, servil

sling *vt* arrojar, lanzar; tirar con honda; (a sword, etc.) suspender; (lift) embragar; (a limb) poner en cabestrillo. *n* (for missiles) honda, *f; naut* balso, *m;* (for a limb) cabestrillo, *m,* charpa, *f*

slink *vi* (away, off) escurrirse, escabullirse

slip *vi* resbalar, deslizar; (stumble) resbalar, tropezar; (fall) caer; (out of place) salirse; (become untied) desatarse; (steal away) escabullirse; (glide) deslizarse; (of years) correr, pasar; (skid) patinar. *vt* deslizar; (garments, shoes) ponerse; (dogs, cables) soltar; (an arm round, etc.) pasar; *rw* desacoplar; (escape) escaparse de; (free oneself of) librarse de. *n* resbalón, *m;* (skid) patinazo, *m;* (stumble) tropezón, traspié, *m;* (oversight) inadvertencia, *f;* (mistake) falta, equivocación, *f;* (moral lapse) desliz, *m;* (petticoat) combinación, *f;* (cover) funda, *f; bot* vástago, *m; print* galerada, *f;* (of paper) papeleta, *f; pl* **slips,** *naut* anguilas, *f pl.* **It slipped my memory,** Se me fue de la memoria. **There's many a s. 'twixt the cup and the lip,** Del dicho al hecho hay muy gran trecho, De la mano a la boca desaparece la sopa. **to give** (someone) **the slip,** escaparse de. **You ought not to let the opportunity s.,** No debes perder la oportunidad. **to let s. a secret,** revelar un secreto. **to let s. an exclamation,** soltar (dar) una exclamación. **to s. into,** colarse en, deslizarse en. **to s. into,** colarse en, deslizarse en. **to s. into one's clothes,** vestirse rápidamente. **to s. on,** (a garment) ponerse. **to s. out,** salir a hurtadillas; escaparse; (of information) divulgarse. **s. of a boy,** mozalbete, joven imberbe, *m.* **s. of the tongue,** error de lengua, *m.* **s.-knot,** nudo corredizo, *m*

slipcover *n* cubierta, cubierta para muebles, funda, funda para muebles, *f*

slipper *n* babucha, chinela, *f,* pantuflo, *m;* (heelless) chancleta, *f;* (dancing) zapatilla de baile, *f.* **s.-shaped,** achinelado

slippered *a* en zapatillas

slippery *a* resbaladizo; poco firme, inestable; (of persons) informal, sin escrúpulos

slipshod *a* descuidado, negligente; poco correcto

slit *vt* cortar; hender, rajar; (the throat) degollar. *n* cortadura, *f;* resquicio, *m.* **to s. open,** abrir un tajo

slither *vi* resbalar; deslizarse

sliver *n* raja, *f;* (of wood) astilla, *f;* (of cloth) tira, *f*

slobber *vi* babear; (blubber) gimotear, *n* baba, *f*

sloe *n* (fruit) endrina, *f;* (tree) endrino, *m.* **s.-colored,** endrino. **s.-eyed,** con ojos de mora

slog *vt* golpear duramente. **to s. away,** batirse el cobre, trabajar como un negro

slogan *n* grito de batalla, *m;* reclamo, *m;* frase hecha, *f;* mote, *m*

slop *n* charco, *m; pl* **slops,** agua sucia, *f;* alimentos líquidos, *m pl. vi* derramarse, verterse. *vt* verter, derramar

slope *n* inclinación, *f;* pendiente, *f;* (of a mountain, etc.) falda, ladera, cuesta, *f;* vertiente, *mf. vi* inclinarse; estar en declive; bajar (hacia). **to s. down,** declinar

sloping *a* inclinado; en declive; (of shoulders) caídos, *m pl*

sloppy *a* casi líquido; (muddy) lodoso, lleno de barro; (of work) chapucero; (of persons) baboso, sobón. **s. sentiment,** sensiblería, *f*

slot *n* ranura, muesca, *f.* **s.-machine,** máquina expendedora, *f,* expendedor, *m;* (in amusement arcades, etc.) tragaperras, *m*

sloth *n* pereza, indolencia, *f; zool* perezoso, *m*

slothful *a* perezoso, indolente

slouch *n* inclinación del cuerpo, *f. vi* andar cabizbajo, andar arrastrando los pies. **to s. about,** vagar, golfear. **s.-hat,** sombrero gacho, *m*

slough *n* (bog) cenagal, pantano, *m,* marisma, *f;* (of a snake) camisa, *f. vt* (a skin) mudar; (prejudices, etc.) desechar

Slovak *n* eslovaco (-ca)

Slovakian *a* eslovaco

sloven *n* puerco, *m*; (at work) chapucero, *m*

Slovene *a* and *n* esloveno (-na)

slovenliness *n* desaseo, desaliño, *m*; (carelessness) descuido, *m*, negligencia, *f*; (of work) chapucería, *f*

slovenly *a* desgarbado, desaseado, *Central America* descacharrado, *Lat. Am.* distraído; (careless) descuidado, negligente; (of work) chapucero

slow *a* despacio; lento, *Lat. Am.* demorón; (stupid) torpe; tardo; (of clocks) atrasado; (boring) aburrido; (inactive) flojo. *adv* despacio, lentamente. **I was not s. to . . .** , No tardé en . . . , *Lat. Am.* No dilaté en . . . **The clock is ten minutes s.,** El reloj lleva diez minutos de atraso. **to s. down,** aflojar el paso; ir más despacio. **s.-motion,** velocidad reducida, *f.* **s. train,** tren ómnibus, *m*. **s.-witted,** lerdo tardo

"Slow Down" «Moderar Su Velocidad»

slow learner *n* alumno de lento aprendizaje, *m*

slowly *adv* despacio, lentamente; poco a poco

slowness *n* lentitud, *f*; (delay) tardanza, *f*; (stupidity) torpeza, estupidez, *f*

slug *n* babosa, *f*

sluggard *n* gandul (-la), perezoso (-a)

sluggish *a* perezoso; (of the market) flojo; (of temperament, etc.) calmoso, flemático; (slow) lento

sluggishness *n* pereza, *f*; (of the market) flojedad, *f*; (slowness) lentitud, *f*

sluice *n* esclusa, *f*; canal, *m*, acequia, *f*. **to s. down,** lavar; echar agua sobre; (a person) dar una ducha (a), dar un baño (a). **s.-gate,** compuerta de esclusa, *f*; tajaderas, *f pl*, tablacho, *m*

slum *nsg* (inner-city slum) barrio bajo (understood everywhere), arrabales *mpl* (Argentina, Uruguay), banda de miseria *fsg* (Argentina), barracas *fpl* (Mexico), barriada *fsg* (Peru), callampa *fsg* (Chile), cantegriles *mpl* (Spain, Uruguay), chabolas *fpl* (Spain), clandestinos *mpl* (Colombia), morenales *mpl* (Honduras), orillas *fpl* (Mexico), población *fsg* (Chile), pueblo joven *msg* (Peru), ranchos *mpl* (Venezuela), tugurios *mpl* (Colombia), villa-miseria *fsg* (Argentina), rancherío *msg*, ribera *fpl*, villorio *msg* (elsewhere in Lat. Am.); (in Brazil) favelas *fpl*; (slum on the outskirts of an urban area) suburbio *msg*

slumber *vi* dormir; (go to sleep) dormirse, caer dormido; (be latent) estar latente. *n* sueño, *m*

slump *n com* baja repentina, *f*; *fig* baja, racha mala, *f. vi com* bajar repentinamente. **the s.,** la crisis económica. **to s. into an armchair,** dejarse caer en un sillón

slur *vt* (words) comerse sílabas o letras (de); (in writing) unir (las palabras); (*mus* of notes) ligar. **to cast a s. on,** difamar, manchar. **to s. over,** pasar por alto de, omitir, suprimir

slush *n* lodo, *m*; agua nieve, *f*; (sentimentality) ñoñería, *f*

sly *a* astuto, taimado, socarrón, *Lat. Am.* macuco; disimulado; (arch) malicioso. **on the sly,** a hurtadillas.

sly person *Mexico* fistol, *m*

slyness *n* astucia, socarronería, *f*; disimulo, *m*; malicia, *f*

smack *n* (taste) sabor, gusto, *m*; (tinge) dejo, *m*; (blow) golpe, *m*; (with the hand) bofetada, palmada, *f*; (with a whip) latigazo, *m*; (crack of whip) restallido, chasquido, *m*; (kiss) beso sonado, *m*; (boat) lancha de pescar, *f. vi* (taste of) tener gusto de, saber a; (be tinged with) oler a. *vt* (a person) dar una bofetada; (slap) pegar con la mano. **to s. one's lips over,** chuparse los dedos

small *a* pequeño; menudo; menor; poco; (petty) mezquino, vulgar. *n* parte estrecha, *f.* **a s. number,** un pequeño número. **to make a person look s.,** humillar. **to make oneself s.,** hacerse chiquito. **s.-arms,** armas portátiles, *f pl.* **s. change,** suelto, *m*. **s. craft,** embarcaciones menores, *f pl.* **s. farm** *Lat. Am.* chacra, *Central America* labor, *f.* **s. fry,** pececillos, *m pl*; (children) gente menuda, *f*; gente sin importancia, *f.* **s. hours,** altas horas de la noche, *f pl.* **s.-minded,** adocenado, de cortos alcances. **s.-talk,** trivialidades, *f pl*, charla frívola, *f*

smallholding *n Lat. Am.* chacra, *f*

smallish *a* bastante pequeño; más bien pequeño que grande

smallpox *n* viruelas, *f pl*

smart *vi* picar; dolerse (de). *n* escozor, *m*; dolor, *m*. *a* severo; vivo; rápido; pronto; (competent) hábil; (clever) listo; (unscrupulous) cuco, astuto; (of personal appearance) majo; elegante, distinguido, *Lat. Am. also* fachoso; (neat) aseado; (fashionable, etc.) de moda; de buen tono. **to s. for,** ser castigado por. **to s. under,** sufrir

smarten *vt* embellecer. *vi* (up) ponerse elegante; mejorar. **I must go and s. myself up a little,** Tengo que arreglarme un poco

smartness *n* viveza, *f*; prontitud, rapidez, *f*; (cleverness) despejo, *m*, habilidad, *f*; (wittiness) agudeza, *f*; (astuteness) cuquería, astucia, *f*; (of dress, etc.) elegancia, *f*; buen tono, *m*

smash *vt* romper, quebrar; (a ball, etc.) golpear; (annihilate) destruir; (an opponent) aplastar. *vi* romperse, quebrarse; hacerse pedazos; (collide) chocar (con, contra); estallarse (contra); (financially) hacer bancarrota. *n* rotura, *f*; quebrantamiento, *m*; estruendo, *m*; (financial) quiebra, ruina, *f*; (car, etc.) accidente, *m*; desastre, *m*, catástrofe, *f.* **to s. to atoms,** hacer trizas. **to s. up,** hacer pedazos. **s. and grab raid,** atraco a mano armada, *m*

smash hit *n* éxito arrollador, éxito rotundo, *m*

smattering *n* conocimiento superficial, *m*, tintura, *f*, barniz, *m*

smear *n* mancha, *f*; *biol* frotis, *m*. *vt* embadurnar (de); manchar (con), ensuciar (con); (oneself) untarse; (blur) borrar

smell *n* (sense of) olfato, *m*; (odor) olor, *m*. *vt* oler. *vi* oler; tener olor; (disagreeably) oler mal, tener mal olor; (stink) apestar. **How good it smells!** ¡Qué bien huele! **to s. of,** oler a. **to s. out,** husmear

smelling *n* olfateo, *m*. **s.-bottle,** frasco de sales, *m*. **s.-salts,** sales (inglesas), *f pl*

smelt *vt* fundir. *n* (fish) eperlano, *m*

smelter *n* fundidor, *m*

smelting *n* fundición, *f.* **s. furnace,** horno de fundición, *m*

smile *vi* sonreír; reírse. *vt* expresar con una sonrisa. *n* sonrisa, *f.* **Mary smiled her thanks,** María dio las gracias con una sonrisa. **smile at adversity,** ponerse buena cara a mal tiempo. **to s. at threats,** reírse de las amenazas

smiling *a* sonriente, risueño

smilingly *adv* sonriendo, con una sonrisa, con cara risueña

smirch *vt* manchar. *n* mancha, *f*

smirk *vi* sonreír con afectación; hacer visajes. *n* sonrisa afectada, *f*

smirking *a* afectado; sonriente

smite *vt* golpear; (kill) matar; (punish) castigar; (pain) doler; (of bright light, sounds, etc.) herir; (cause remorse) remorder. **My conscience smites me,** Tengo remordimientos de conciencia. **to be smitten by,** *inf* estar prendado de. **I was smitten by a desire to smoke,** Me entraron deseos de fumar

smith *n* herrero, *m*. **smith's hammer,** destajador, *m*

smithereens *n pl* añicos, *m pl*

smithy *n* herrería, *f*

smock *n* blusa, *f*; (child's) delantal, *m*

smoke *n* humo, *m*. *vi* humear, echar humo; (tobacco) fumar. *vt* ahumar; ennegrecer; (tobacco) fumar. **smoked glasses,** gafas ahumadas, *f pl.* **s. helmet,** casco respiratorio, *m*. **s.-screen,** cortina de humo, *f.* **s. signal,** ahumada, *f.* **s.-stack,** chimenea, *f*

smokeless *a* sin humo

smoker *n* fumador (-ra)

smoking *a* humeante. *n* el fumar. **"S. Prohibited,"** «Se prohíbe fumar.» **non-s. compartment,** *rw* departamento de no fumadores, *m*. **s.-carriage,** *rw* departamento para fumadores, *m*. **s.-room,** fumadero, *m*

smoky *a* humeante; lleno de humo; (black) ahumado

smooth *a* liso; igual; (of the skin, etc.) suave; (of water) calmo, tranquilo; (flattering, etc.) lisonjero; obsequioso; afable. *vt* allanar; (hair, etc.) alisar; (paths, etc.) igualar. **to s. down,** (a person) tranquilizar, calmar. **to s. over,** (faults) exculpar. **to s. the way for,** allanar el camino para. **s.-faced,** barbilampiño, lampiño, bien afeitado, todo afeitado; *fig* obsequioso, untuoso. **s.-haired,** de pelo liso. **s.-spoken,** de palabras lisonjeras; obsequioso

smoothly *adv* lisamente; (of speech) afablemente; con lisonjeras. **Everything was going s.,** Todo iba viento en popa

smoothness *n* igualdad, *f*; lisura, *f*; (of skin, etc.) suavidad, *f*; (of water) calma, tranquilidad, *f*; (of manner, etc.) afabilidad, *f*

smother *vt* ahogar, sofocar; (a fire) apagar; (cover) envolver, cubrir

smoulder *vi* arder sin llama, arder lentamente; (of passions, etc.) arder; estar latente

smouldering *a* que arde lentamente; *fig* latente

smudge *vt* manchar, ensuciar; (blur) borrar. *n* mancha, *f*

smug *a* satisfecho de sí mismo, pagado de sí mismo; farisaico

smuggle *vt* pasar de contrabando. *vi* hacer contrabando

smuggler *n* contrabandista, *mf*

smuggling *n* contrabando, *m*

smugly *adv* con presunción, de un aire satisfecho

smugness *n* satisfacción de sí mismo, *f*; fariseísmo, *m*

smut *n* copo de hollín, *m*; mancha, *f*; (disease) tizón, *m*

smutty *a* tiznado; ahumado; *inf* verde

snack *n* tentempié, piscolabis, bocado, *Lat. Am.* botana, *f*. **to take a s.,** tomar un piscolabis

snack bar *n* merendero, *m*, *Lat. Am.* lonchería, *f*

snaffle *n* filete, *m*. *vt* (a horse) refrenar. **s.-bridle,** bridón, *m*

snag *n* (of a tree) tocón, *m*; (of a tooth) raigón, *m*; (problem) busilis, *m*; obstáculo inesperado, *m*

snail *n* caracol, *m*. **at a snail's pace,** a paso de tortuga

snake *n* serpiente, *f*. **s.-charmer,** encantador de serpientes, *m*

snakelike *a* de serpiente; serpentino

snap *vt* morder; (break) romper; (one's fingers) castañetear; (a whip) chasquear; (down a lid, etc.) cerrar de golpe; (beaks, etc.) cerrar ruidosamente; *phot* sacar una instantánea de. *vi* partirse; quebrarse; hablar bruscamente. *n* (bite) mordedura, *f*; golpe seco, *m*; chasquido, *m*; rotura, *f*; (clasp) cierre, *m*; (of weather) temporada, *f*; (spirit) vigor, brío, *m*; *phot* instantánea, *f*. **to s. at,** procurar morder; (an invitation, etc.) aceptar gustoso. **to s. one's fingers at,** *fig* burlarse de. **to s. up,** coger, agarrar; (a person) cortar la palabra (a), interrumpir. **s.-fastener,** botón de presión, *m*

snapdragon *n* dragón, *m*, becerra, boca de dragón, *f*

snappily *adv* irritablemente

snappishness *n* irritabilidad, *f*

snappy *a* irritable; vigoroso

snapshot *n* instantánea, foto, *f*

snare *n* cepo, lazo, *m*, trampa, *f*; *fig* red, *f*. *vt* coger en el lazo; *fig* enredar

snarl *vi* (of dogs) regañar; (cats, etc.) gruñir. *n* regañamiento, *m*; gruñido, *m*

snarling *n* regañamiento, *m*; gruñidos, *m pl*, *a* gruñidor

snatch *vt* asir; agarrar; (enjoy) disfrutar; (an opportunity) tomar, aprovecharse de. *n* asimiento, agarro, *m*; (of time) rato, *m*; instante, *m*; (of song) fragmento, *m*. **to make a s. at,** procurar agarrar; alargar la mano hacia. **to s. a hurried meal,** comer aprisa. **to s. away,** arrebatar, quitar; (carry off) robar. **to s. up,** coger rápidamente; coger en brazos

sneak *vi* deslizarse (en), colarse (en); (lurk) rondar; (inform) acusar. *n* mandilón, *m*; (accuser) acusón (-ona). **to s. off,** escabullirse, irse a hurtadillas. **s.-thief,** *n* garduño (-ña)

sneaker *n* (shoe) zapatilla de tenis, *f*

sneaking *a* furtivo, ruin, mezquino; secreto

sneer *vi* sonreír irónicamente; burlarse, mofarse. *n* sonrisa sardónica, sonrisa de desprecio, *f*; burla, mofa, *f*. **to s. at,** mofarse de, burlarse de; hablar con desprecio de

sneering *a* mofador, burlón

sneeringly *adv* con una sonrisa sardónica; burlonamente

sneeze *vi* estornudar. *n* estornudo, *m*. **It's not to be sneezed at,** No es moco de pavo

sniff *vi* respirar fuertemente; resollar. *vt* oler, olfatear; aspirar. **to s. at,** oler. **to s. out,** *inf* husmear

snigger *vi* reírse por lo bajo, reírse disimuladamente. *n* risa disimulada, *f*

snip *vt* cortar con tijeras; cortar, quitar. *n* tijeretada, *f*; (of cloth, etc.) recorte, pedacito, *m*

sniper *n* *mil* paco, *m*

snippet *n* pedacito, fragmento, *m*; (of prose, etc.) trocito, *m*; (of news) noticia, *f*

snivel *vi* lloriquear, gimotear

sniveling *n* lloriqueo, gimoteo, *m. a* llorón; mocoso

snob *n* esnob, *mf*

snobbery *n* snobismo, *m*

snobbish *a* esnob

snood *n* (for the hair) redecilla, *f*; (turkey's) moco (de pavo), *m*; (fishing) cendal, *m*

snoop *vi* espiar; entremeterse

snooper *n* *Lat. Am.* averigüetas, *mf*

snooze *vi* dormitar, echar un sueño. *n* sueñecito, *m*; (afternoon) siesta, *f*

snore *vi* roncar. *n* ronquido, *m*

snoring *n* ronquidos, *m pl*

snort *vi* bufar; resoplar. *n* bufido, *m*; resoplido, *m*

snout *n* hocico, *m*; (of a pig) jeta, *f*

snow *n* nieve, *f*. *vi* nevar. *vt* nevar; *fig* inundar. **to s. under** (with), inundar con. **to be snowed up,** estar aprisionado por la nieve. **s.-blindness,** deslumbramiento causado por la nieve, *m*. **s.-boot,** bota para la nieve, *f*. **s.-bound,** aprisionado por la nieve; bloqueado por la nieve. **s.-capped,** coronado de nieve. **s.-clad,** cubierto de nieve. **s.-drift,** acumulación de nieve, *f*. **s.-field,** ventisquero, *m*. **s.-goggles,** gafas ahumadas, *f pl*. **s.-line,** límite de las nieves perpetuas, *m*. **s.-man,** figura de nieve, *f*. **s.-plough,** quitanieve, *m*. **s.-shoe,** raqueta de nieve, *f*. **s.-white,** blanco como la nieve

snowball *n* bola de nieves, *f*; *bot* bola de nieve, *f*

snowdrop *n* campanilla de invierno, violeta de febrero, *f*

snowfall *n* nevada, *f*

snowflake *n* copo de nieve, *m*

snowstorm *n* ventisca, *f*

snowy *a* nevoso; de nieve

snub *vt* repulsar; desairar, tratar con desdén, *Mexico* descolar. *n* repulsa, *f*, desaire, *m*; (nose) nariz respingona, *f*. **s.-nosed,** de nariz respingona

snuff *vt* (breathe) oler, olfatear; inhalar; (a candle) atizar, despabilar. *n* (of a candle) moco, *m*, despabiladura, *f*; (tobacco) rapé, *m*. **to take s.,** tomar rapé. **to s. out,** extinguir. **s.-box,** caja de rapé, tabaquera, *f*

snuffers *n pl* tenacillas, despabiladeras, *f pl*

snuffle *vi* hacer ruido con la nariz; respirar fuerte; (in speaking) ganguear

snuffling *a* mocoso; (of the voice) gangoso

snug *a* caliente; cómodo; (hidden) escondido, **to have a s. income,** tener el riñón bien cubierto, ser acomodado

snuggle *vi* hacerse un ovillo; acomodarse; ponerse cómodo. **to s. up to,** arrimarse a, apretarse contra

snugly *adv* cómodamente

snugness *n* comodidad, *f*

so *adv* así; de este modo, de esta manera; por lo tanto; tanto; (before adjs. and advs. but not before **más, mejor, menos, peor,** where **tanto** is used) tan; (in the same way) del mismo modo, de igual modo; (therefore) de modo que, de manera que; (also) también; (approximately) más o menos, aproximadamente. **Is that so?** ¿De veras? **if so . . . ,** si así es

. . . **He has not yet done so,** no lo ha hecho todavía. **I told you so!** ¡Ya te lo dije yo! **So be it!** ¡Así sea! **so far,** hasta aquí; hasta ahora. **so forth,** etcétera. **So long!** ¡Nos vemos! **so much,** tanto. **So much the worse for them,** Tanto peor para ellos. **so to speak** . . . , por decirlo así. **so as to,** a fin de, para. **so long as,** con tal que, a condición de que. **so on,** etcétera. **so soon as,** tan pronto como. **so that,** de suerte que, de modo que, para que; con que. **so-and-so,** *n* fulano (-na); mengano (-na). **so-called.** así llamado, supuesto. **so-so,** así-así, regular

soak *vt* remojar; empapar; (skins) abrevar. *vi* estar en remojo. *n* remojo, *m*; (rain) diluvio, *m*; (booze) borrachera, *f*. **to s. into,** filtrar en; penetrar. **to s. through,** penetrar; filtrar **so-called,** así llamado, supuesto. **so-so,** así, regular

soaked *a* remojado. **He is s. to the skin,** Está calado hasta los huesos

soaking *n* remojo, *m*; empapamiento, *m*,

soap *n* jabón, *m*. *vt* jabonar; (flatter) enjabonar. **a tablet of s.,** una pastilla de jabón. **soft s.,** jabón blando, *m*. **toilet s.,** jabón de tocador, jaboncillo, *m*. **s.-bubble,** burbuja de jabón, *f*. **s. dish,** jabonera, *f*. **s. factory,** jabonería, *f*. **s.-flakes,** copos de jabón, *m pl*

soapbark tree *n* quillay, palo de jabón, *m*

soap box *n lit* caja de jabón, *f*; *fig* tribuna callejera, *f*

soap opera *n* radionovela (on radio), telenovela (on television), *f*; serial lacrimógeno (derogatory), *m*

soapsuds *n pl* jabonaduras, *f pl*

soapy *a* cubierto de jabón; jabonoso

soar *vi* remontarse; *fig* elevarse; (of prices, etc.) subir de golpe

soaring *n* remonte, vuelo, *m*; *fig* aspiración, *f*; (of prices, etc.) subida repentina, *f*

sob *vi* sollozar. *n* sollozo, *m*. **to sob one's heart out,** llorar a lágrima viva. **to sob out,** decir sollozando, decir entre sollozos

s.o.b. *n* (son of a bitch) hache de pe (hijo de puta)

sobbing *n* sollozos, *m pl*, *a* sollozante

sober *a* sobrio; moderado; (of colors) obscuro. **s.-minded,** serio; reflexivo

sobriety *n* sobriedad, *f*; moderación, *f*; seriedad, *f*; calma, tranquilidad, *f*

sobriquet *n* apodo, *m*

soccer *n* fútbol (Asociación), *m*

sociability *n* sociabilidad, *f*

sociable *a* sociable; amistoso

sociably *adv* sociablemente; amistosamente

social *a* social; sociable. *n* reunión, velada, *f*. **s.-democrat,** *a and n* socialdemócrata, *mf*. **s. event,** acontecimiento social, *m*. **s. insurance,** previsión social, *f*. **s. services,** servicios sociales, *m pl*. **s. work,** asistencia social, *f*

socialism *n* socialismo, *m*

socialist *a* socialista, laborista. *n* socialista, *mf*

socialization *n* socialización, *f*

socialize *vt* socializar

socially *adv* socialmente

society *n* sociedad, *f*; (fashionable) mundo elegante, *m*, alta sociedad, *f*; compañía, *f*. **to go into s.,** (of girls) ponerse de largo; entrar en el mundo elegante. **s. hostess,** dama de sociedad, *f*. **society for the prevention of cruelty to animals,** sociedad protectora de animales, *f*. **s. news,** noticias de sociedad, *f pl*

sociological *a* sociológico

sociologist *n* sociólogo (-ga)

sociology *n* sociología, *f*

sock *n* calcetín, *m*; (for a shoe) plantilla, *f*

socket *n mech* encaje, cubo, ojo, *m*; (of a lamp, and *elec*) enchufe, *m*; (of the eye) órbita, cuenca, *f*; (of a tooth) alvéolo, *m*; (of a joint) fosa, *f*. **His eyes stared out of their sockets,** Sus ojos estaban fuera de su órbita

Socratic *a* socrático

sod *n* césped, *m*; (cut) tepe, *m*

soda *n* sosa, *f*. **caustic s.,** sosa cáustica, *f*. **s.-ash,** car-

bonato sódico, *m*. **s.-fountain,** aparato de aguas gaseosas, *m*. **s.-water,** sifón, *m*

sodden *a* saturado, empapado

sodium *n* sodio, *m*.

Sodomite *n* sodomita, *mf*

sodomy *n* sodomía, *f*

sofa *n* sofá, *m*

soft *a* blando; suave; muelle; (flabby) flojo; (of disposition, etc.) dulce; (effeminate) muelle, afeminado; (lenient) indulgente; (easy) fácil; (silly) tonto. **to have a s. spot for,** (a person) tener una debilidad para. **s. coal,** carbón bituminoso, *m*. **s. drink,** bebida no alcohólica, *f*. **s. felt hat,** sombrero flexible, *m*. **s. fruit,** fruta blanda, *f*. **s.-boiled,** (of eggs) pasado por agua; (of persons) inocente, ingenuo. **s.-hearted,** de buen corazón; compasivo, bondadoso. **s.-heartedness,** buen corazón, *m*, bondad, *f*. **s.-spoken,** de voz suave; que habla con dulzura, meloso. **s. water,** agua blanda, *f*

soften *vt* ablandar, reblandecer) (weaken) debilitar; (mitigate) mitigar, suavizar; (the heart, etc.) enternecer. *vi* reblandecerse; enternecerse

softening *n* reblandecimiento, *m*; (relenting) enternecimiento, *m*

softly *adv* suavemente; dulcemente, tiernamente; sin ruido, silenciosamente

softness *n* blandura, *f*; suavidad, *f*; (sweetness, etc.) dulzura, *f*; (of character) debilidad de carácter, *f*; (silliness) necedad, estupidez, *f*

soggy *a* empapado de agua; saturado

soil *n* tierra, *f*; (country) país, *m*, tierra, *f*. *vt* ensuciar; *fig* manchar. **my native s.,** mi tierra, mi patria

soiled *a* sucio. **s. linen,** ropa sucia, *f*

soiree *n* velada, *f*

sojourn *vi* morar, residir, permanecer. *n* residencia, permanencia, *f*

sojourner *n* morador (-ra), residente, *mf*

sol *n mus* sol, *m*. **sol-fa,** *n* solfa, *f*, solfeo, *m*. *vt* solfear

solace *n* consuelo, solaz, *m*. *vt* consolar; solazar

solar *a* solar. **s. plexus,** *anat* plexo solar, *m*. **s. system,** sistema solar, *m*

solder *n* soldadura, *f*, *vt* soldar

soldering *n* soldadura, *f*

soldier *n* soldado, *m*; militar, *m*. **He wants to be a s.,** Quiere ser militar

soldierly *a* militar; marcial

soldiery *n* soldadesca, *f*

sole *n* (of a foot) planta, *f*; (of a shoe) suela, *f*; (of a plough) cepa, *f*; *icht* lenguado, *m*, suela, *f*. *vt* (shoes) solar, poner suela (a). *a* solo, único; exclusivo. **s. right,** exclusiva, *f*, derecho exclusivo, *m*

solecism *n* solecismo, *m*

solely *adv* sólo; únicamente, puramente; meramente

solemn *a* solemne; grave; serio; (sacred) sagrado. **Why do you look so s.?** ¿Por qué estás tan serio?

solemnity *n* solemnidad, *f*

solemnization *n* solemnización, celebración, *f*

solemnize *vt* solemnizar

solemnly *adv* solemnemente; gravemente

solicit *vt* solicitar; implorar, rogar encarecidamente

solicitation *n* solicitación, *f*

solicitor *n* abogado (-da)

solicitous *a* ansioso (de), deseoso (de); solícito, atento; (worried) preocupado

solicitude *n* solicitud, *f*, cuidado, *m*; (anxiety) preocupación, *f*

solid *a* sólido; macizo; (of persons) serio, formal; (unanimous) unánime. *n* sólido, *m*. **a s. meal,** una comida fuerte. **He slept for ten s. hours,** Durmió por diez horas seguidas. **solid-colored material,** tela lisa, *f*. **s. food,** alimentos sólidos, *m pl*. **s. geometry,** geometría del espacio, *f*. **s. gold,** oro de ley, *m*. **s. tire,** llanta de goma maciza, *f*

solidarity *n* solidaridad, *f*

solidification *n* solidificación, *f*

solidify *vt* solidificar. *vi* solidificarse; congelarse

solidity n solidez, f; unanimidad, f
solidly adv sólidamente
soliloquize vi soliloquiar, hablar a solas
soliloquy n soliloquio, m
solitaire n (diamond and game) solitario, m
solitary a solitario; solo, aislado, único. **He was in s. confinement for three months,** Estuvo incomunicado durante tres meses. **There is not a s. one,** No hay ni uno
solitude n soledad, f
solo n (performance and cards) solo, m. **to sing a s.,** cantar un solo. **It was his first s. flight,** Era su primer vuelo a solas
soloist n solista, mf
solstice n solsticio, m. **summer s.,** solsticio vernal, m. **winter s.,** solsticio hiemal, m
solubility n solubilidad, f
soluble a soluble
solution n solución, f
solvable a que se puede resolver, soluble
solve vt resolver, hallar la solución de
solvency n solvencia, f
solvent a com solvente; (chem and fig) disolvente. n disolvente, m
somatic a somático
somber a sombrío
somberly adv sombríamente
somberness n lo sombrío; sobriedad, f; melancolía, f
some a alguno (-a), algunos (-as); (before a masculine sing. noun) algún; unos (-as); un poco de, algo de; (as a partitive, often not translated, e.g. **Give me s. wine,** Dame vino); (approximately) aproximadamente, unos (-as). pron algunos (-as), unos (-as); algo, un poco. **I should like s. strawberries,** Me gustaría comer unas fresas. **s. day,** algún día. **S. say yes, others no,** Algunos dicen que sí, otros que no. **There are s. sixty people in the garden,** Hay unas sesenta personas en el jardín
somebody, someone n alguien, mf. **s. else,** otro (-a), otra persona, f. **S. or other said that the book is worth reading,** No sé quién dijo que el libro vale la pena de leerse. **to be s.,** inf ser un personaje
somehow adv de un modo u otro, de alguna manera. **S. I don't like them,** No sé por qué, pero no me gustan
somersault n salto mortal, m, vi dar un salto mortal
something n algo, m, alguna cosa, f. adv algún tanto. **Would you like s. else?** ¿Quiere Vd. otra cosa? **He left s. like fifty thousand pounds,** Dejó algo así como cincuenta mil libras. **He has s. to live for,** Tiene para que vivir
sometime adv algún día, alguna vez; en algún tiempo. a ex-. **Come and see me s. soon,** Ven a verme algún día de estos. **He will have to go abroad s. or another,** Tarde o temprano, tiene que ir al extranjero. **s. last month,** durante el mes pasado
sometimes adv algunas veces, a veces. **s. happy, s. sad,** algunas veces feliz y otras triste, ora feliz ora triste
somewhat adv algo; algún tanto, un tanto; un poco. **I am s. busy,** Estoy algo ocupado. **He is s. of a lady-killer,** Tiene sus puntos de castigador, Tiene algo de castigador
somewhere adv en alguna parte. **s. about,** por ahí. **s. else,** en otra parte
somnambulism n somnambulismo, m
somnambulist n somnámbulo (-la)
somnolence n somnolencia, f
somnolent a soñoliento; soporífero
son n hijo, m. **son-in-law,** yerno, hijo político, m
sonata n sonata, f
song n canto, m; canción, f; (poem) poema, verso, m. **It's nothing to make a s. about,** No es para tanto. **to break into s.,** ponerse a cantar. **to be not worth an old s.,** no valer un pito. **the S. of Songs,** Cantar de los Cantares, m. **s.-bird,** ave canora, f. **s.-book,** libro de canciones, m. **s.-writer,** compositor (-ra) de canciones
sonic adj sónico. **sonic boom,** estampido sónico, m

sonnet n soneto, m
sonorous a sonoro
sonorousness n sonoridad, f
soon adv pronto; dentro de poco, luego. **as s. as,** así que, en cuanto, luego que, no bien . . . **as s. as possible,** lo antes posible, lo más pronto posible, con la mayor antelación posible, cuanto antes. **s. after,** poco después (de). **See you s.!** ¡Hasta pronto! **sooner or later,** tarde o temprano. **the sooner the better,** cuanto antes mejor. **No sooner had he left the house, when . . .** Apenas hubo dejado la casa, cuando . . . **Emily would sooner go to London,** Emilia preferiría ir a Londres (A Emilia le gustaría más ir a Londres)
soot n hollín, m, vt cubrir de hollín
soothe vt tranquilizar, calmar; (pain) aliviar, mitigar
soothing a calmante, tranquilizador, sosegador; (of powders, etc.) calmante
soothingly adv con dulzura; suavemente; como un consuelo
soothsayer n adivino (-na), adivinador (-ra)
soothsaying n adivinanza, f
sooty a cubierto de hollín; negro como el hollín
sop n sopa, f; (bribe) soborno, m
sophism n sofisma, m
sophist n hist sofista, m; (quibbler) sofista, mf
sophistic a phil sofista; (of persons, arguments) sofístico
sophisticated a nada ingenuo; mundano; (cultured) culto
sophistication n falta de simplicidad, f; mundanería, f; cultura, f
sophistry n sofistería, f
Sophoclean a sofocleo
soporific a soporífico
sopping a muy mojado. **s. wet,** hecho una sopa
soprano n (voice and part) soprano, m; (singer) soprano, tiple, mf
sorcerer n encantador, mago, brujo, m
sorceress n hechicera, bruja, f
sorcery n sortilegio, m, hechicería, brujería, f; encanto, m
sordid a sórdido; (of motives, etc.) ruin, vil
sordidness n sordidez, f; (of motives, etc.) vileza, bajeza, f
sordine n mus sordina, f
sore a doloroso, malo; (sad) triste; (annoyed) enojado; (with need, etc.) extremo. n llaga, Lat. Am. also lacra, f; (on horses, etc., caused by girths) matadura, f; fig herida, f; recuerdo doloroso, m. **to open an old s.,** fig renovar la herida. **running s.,** úlcera, f. **s. throat,** dolor de garganta, m
sorely adv grandemente; muy; urgentemente. **He was s. tempted,** Tuvo grandes tentaciones
soreness n dolor, m; (resentment) amargura, f, resentimiento, m; (ill-feeling) rencor, m
sorrel a alazán. n (horse) alazán, m; bot acedera, f
sorrow n pesar, m, aflicción, pesadumbre, f; tristeza, f. vi afligirse; entristecerse. **To my great s.,** Con gran pesar mío. **s.-stricken,** afligido, agobiado de pena
sorrowful a afligido, angustiado; triste
sorrowfully adv con pena, tristemente
sorrowing a afligido. n aflicción, f; lamentación, f
sort n especie, f; clase, f; tipo, m. vt separar (de); clasificar. **a s. of hat,** una especie de sombrero. **all sorts of,** toda clase de. **He is a good s.,** Es buen chico. **He is a queer s.,** Es un tipo raro. **in some s.,** hasta cierto punto. **I am out of sorts,** Estoy destemplado. **Nothing of the s.!** ¡Nada de eso!
sorter n oficial de correos, m; clasificador (-ra)
sorting n clasificación, f
sotto voce adv a sovoz, en voz baja
soul n alma, f; espíritu, m; (departed) ánima, f; (being) ser, m; (life) vida, f; (heart) corazón, m. **All Souls' Day,** Día de los Difuntos, m. **He is a good s.!** ¡Es un bendito! **She is a simple s.,** Ella es una alma de Dios. **without seeing a living s.,** sin ver un bicho viviente. **Upon my s.!** ¡Por mi vida! **s. in purgatory,** alma en pena, f. **s.-stirring,** emocionante

soulful *a* sentimental, emocional; espiritual; romántico
soulless *a* sin alma; mecánico
sound, *n* sonido, *m*; son, *m*; ruido, *m*; (strait) estrecho, *m*. *vi* sonar; hacer ruido; resonar; (seem) parecer. *vt* sonar; (the horn, the alarm, musical instrument) tocar; (express) expresar; proclamar; (praise) celebrar; *naut* hondear; *med* tentar; (the chest) auscultar; (try to discover) tentar, sondar; (experience) experimentar. **to the s. of,** al son de. **s.-box,** (of a gramophone) diafragma, *m*. **s.-detector,** fonolocalización de aviones, *f*. **s.-film,** película sonora, *f*. **s.-proof,** (of radio studios, etc.) aislado de todo sonido. **s.-track,** guía sonora, banda sonora, *f*. **s.-wave,** onda sonora, *f*
sound *a* sano; (of a person) perspicaz; (reasonable) lógico, razonable; (of a policy, etc.) prudente; (of an argument, etc.) válido; (of an investment) seguro; (solvent) solvente; (good) bueno; (deep) profundo. *adv* profundamente, bien
sounding *n naut* sondeo, *m*; *pl* **soundings,** sondas, *f pl*. *a* sonoro. **to take soundings,** sondar, echar la plomada. **s.-board,** tabla de armonía, *f*
soundless *a* sin ruido, silencioso
soundly *adv* sanamente; juiciosamente, prudentemente; bien; (deeply) profundamente
soundness *n* (of a person) perspicacia, *f*; (of a policy, etc.) prudencia, *f*; (of an argument, etc.) validez, fuerza, *f*; (financial) solvencia, *f*
soup *n* sopa, *f*. **clear s.,** consommé, *m*. **thick s.,** puré, *m*. **to be in the s.,** *inf* estar aviado. **s.-ladle,** cucharón, *m*. **s.-plate,** plato sopero, *m*. **s.-tureen,** sopera, *f*
sour *a* ácido, agrio; (of milk) agrio; (of persons, etc.) agrio, desabrido. *vt* agriar. **to go s.,** volverse agrio. **S. grapes!** ¡Están verdes!
source *n* (of a river, etc.) nacimiento, *m*; fuente, *f*; (of infection) foco, *m*. **to know from a good s.,** saber de buena tinta
sourly *adv* agriamente
sourness *n* acidez, agrura, *f*; acrimonia, *f*
south *n* sur, *m*; mediodía, *m*. *a* del sur. *adv* hacia el sur. **S. African,** *a* and *n* sudafricano (-na). **S. American,** *a* and *n* sudamericano (-na). **s.-east,** *n* sudeste, *m*. *a* del sudeste. *adv* hacia el sudeste. **s.-easterly,** *a* del sudeste; al sudeste. *adv* hacia el sudeste. **s.-eastern,** *a* del sudeste. **s.-s.-east,** *n* sudsudeste, *m*. **s.-s.-west,** sudsudoeste, *m*. **s.-west,** *n* sudoeste, *m*. *a* del sudoeste. *adv* hacia el sudoeste. **s.-west wind,** viento sudoeste, ábrego, *m*. **s.-westerly,** *a* del sudoeste. *adv* hacia el sudoeste. **s.-western,** *a* del sudoeste
South Africa República Sudafricana, *f*
South America América del Sur, *f*
southerly *a* del sur; hacia el sur. **The house has a s. aspect,** La casa está orientada al sur
southern *a* del sur; del mediodía; meridional. **S. Cross,** Cruz, *f*, Crucero, *m*. **s. express,** sudexpreso, *m*
southerner *n* habitante del sur, *m*
South Sea Mar del Sur, Mar del Pacífico, *m*
southward *a* del sur; al sur. *adv* hacia el sur
souvenir *n* recuerdo, *m*
sovereign *a* soberano. *n* soberano (-na); (coin) soberano, *m*
sovereignty *n* soberanía, *f*
soviet *n* soviet, *m*; a soviético
Soviet Union, the la Unión Soviética, *f*
sow *n* cerda, puerca, marrana, *f*; (of a wild boar) jabalina, *f*; (of iron) galápago, *m*
sow *vt* sembrar; esparcir; diseminar
sower *n* sembrador (-ra)
sowing *n* sembradura, siembra, *f*. **s. machine,** sembradera, *f*. **s. time,** tiempo de la siembra, *m*
soya bean *n* soja, *f*
spa *n* balneario, *m*; (spring) manantial mineral, *m*, caldas, *f pl*
space *n* espacio, *m*; (of time) temporada, *f*; intervalo, *m*; (print, mus) espacio, *m*. *vt* espaciar. **blank s.,** blanco, *m*. **s.-bar,** tecla de espacios, *f*, espaciador, *m*

spacious *a* espacioso; amplio
spaciousness *n* espaciosidad, *f*; amplitud, *f*
spade *n* pala, azada, *f*; (cards) espada, *f*. **to call a s. a s.,** llamar al pan pan y al vino vino, llamar a las cosas por su nombre. **s.-work,** trabajo preparatorio, *m*, labor de pala, *f*
spaghetti *n* fideos, macarrones, *m pl*
Spain España, *f*
span *vt* medir a palmos; rodear; medir; (cross) atravesar, cruzar. *n* palmo, *m*; espacio, *m*, duración, *f*; (of a bridge) vano, *m*; (of wing, *aer, zool*) envergadura, *f*; (distance) distancia, *f*. **single-s. bridge,** puente de vano único. **the brief s. of human life,** la corta duración de la vida humana
spangle *n* lentejuela, *f*; (tinsel) oropel, *m*. *vt* adornar con lentejuelas; sembrar (de), esparcir (de). **spangled with stars,** sembrado de estrellas
Spaniard *n* español (-la). **a young S.,** un joven español
spaniel *n* perro de aguas, perro sabueso español *m*; (cocker) sabueso, *m*
Spanish *a* español. *n* (language) español, castellano, *m*. **a S. girl,** una muchacha española. **in S. fashion,** a la española. **S. American,** *a* and *n* hispanoamericano (-na). **S. broom,** retama de olor, *f*. **S. fly,** cantárida, *f*
Spanish America Hispanoamérica, *f*
spank *vt* pegar con la mano, azotar. *n* azotazo, *m*. **to s. along,** correr rápidamente; (of a horse) galopar
spanking *n* azotamiento, vapuleo, *m*
spanner *n* llave inglesa, llave de tuercas, *f*
spar *n naut* mastel, *m*; *min* espato, *m*; (boxing) boxeo, *m*; (quarrel) disputa, *f*. *vi* boxear; (argue) disputar
spare *a* (meager) frugal, escaso; (of persons) enjuto, flaco; (available) disponible; (extra) de repuesto. *n* recambio, *m*. **s. part,** pieza de recambio, pieza de repuesto, *f*. **s. room,** cuarto de amigos, *m*. **s. time,** ratos de ocio, *m pl*, tiempo disponible, *m*. **s. tire** *Mexico* llanta de refación, *f*. **s. wheel,** rueda de repuesto, *f*
spare *vt* (expense, etc.) escatimar; ahorrar; (do without) pasarse sin; (give) dar; (a life, etc.) perdonar; (avoid) evitar; dispensar de; (grant) hacer gracia de; (time) dedicar. **I cannot s. her,** No puedo estar sin ella. **They have no money to s.,** No tienen dinero de sobra. **to be sparing of,** ser avaro de
sparingly *adv* frugalmente; escasamente. **to eat s.,** comer con frugalidad
spark *n* chispa, *f*; (gallant) pisaverde, *m*. *vi* chispear, echar chispas
sparking *a* chispeante. *n* emisión de chispas, *f*. **s.-plug,** bujía de encendido, *f*
sparkle *vi* centellear, rutilar, destellar; *fig* brillar; (of wines) ser espumoso. *n* centelleo, destello, *m*; *fig* brillo, *m*
sparkling *a* rutilante, centelleante, reluciente; *fig* brillante, chispeante; (of wines) espumante
sparring match *n* combate de boxeo amistoso, *m*
sparrow *n* gorrión, *m*. **s.-hawk,** gavilán, esparaván, *m*
sparse *a* claro, ralo; esparcido
sparsely *adv* escasamente
Sparta Esparta, *f*
Spartan *a* and *n* espartano (-na)
spasm *n* espasmo, *m*; ataque, *m*; acceso, *m*
spasmodic *a* espasmódico; intermitente
spasmodically *adv* espasmódicamente
spat *n* (gaiter) polaina de tela, *f*
spate *n* crecida, *f*; *fig* torrente, *m*. **in s.,** crecido
spatter *vt* salpicar; (*fig* smirch) manchar. *vi* rociar. *n* salpicadura, *f*; rociada, *f*
spatula *n* espátula, *f*
spawn *vt* and *vi* desovar; engendrar. *n* huevas, *f pl*, freza, *f*; (offspring) producto, *m*
speak *vi* hablar; pronunciar un discurso; (sound) sonar. *vt* decir; (French, etc.) hablar. **She never spoke to him again,** Nunca volvió a dirigirle la palabra. **roughly speaking,** aproximadamente, más o menos. **Speaking for myself,** En cuanto a mí, Por mi parte. **without speaking,** sin decir nada, sin hablar. **to s.**

for, (a person) hablar por. **to s. for itself,** hablar por sí mismo, ser evidente. **to s. one's mind,** decir lo que se piensa. **to s. of,** hablar de. **to s. out,** hablar claro; hablar alto. **to s. up for,** (a person) hablar en favor de (alguien)

speaker *n* el, *m,* (*f,* la) que habla; (public) orador (-ra). **the S.,** el Presidente de la Cámara de los Comunes

speaking *a* hablante; para hablar; elocuente, expresivo. *n* habla, *f,* discurso, *m.* **They are not on s. terms,** No se hablan. **within s. distance,** al habla. **s.-trumpet,** portavoz, *m.* **s.-tube,** tubo acústico, *m*

spear *n* lanza, *f;* (javelin) venablo, *m;* (harpoon) arpón, *m.* *vt* herir con lanza, alancear; (fish) arponear. **s.-head,** punta de la lanza, *f.* **s.-thrust,** lanzada, *f*

special *a* especial; particular; extraordinario. *n* (train) tren extraordinario, *m.* **s. correspondent,** corresponsal extraordinario, *m.* **s. friend,** amigo (-ga) del alma, amigo íntimo

specialist *n* especialista, *mf*

speciality *n* particularidad, *f;* especialidad, *f*

specialization *n* especialización, *f*

specialize *vt* especializar. *vi* especializarse

specially *adv* especialmente; particularmente; sobre todo

species *n* especie, *f;* raza, *f*

specific *a* específico; explícito. *n* específico, *m.* **s. gravity,** peso específico, *m,* densidad, *f*

specifically *adv* específicamente; explícitamente

specification *n* especificación, *f*

specify *vt* especificar

specimen *n* espécimen, *m;* ejemplo, *m; inf* tipo, *m*

specious *a* especioso. **s. arguments** *Lat. Am.* abogaderas, abogaderías,*f pl*

speciousness *n* plausibilidad, *f;* apariencia engañosa, *f*

speck *n* pequeña mancha, *f;* punto, *m;* átomo, *m;* (on fruit) maca, *f*

speckle *vt* motear, manchar

speckled *a* abigarrado; con manchas . . .

spectacle *n* espectáculo, *m;* escena, *f; pl* **spectacles,** gafas, *f pl,* anteojos, *m pl.* **s.-case,** cajita para las gafas, *f*

spectacled *a* con gafas, que lleva gafas

spectacular *a* espectacular

spectator *n* espectador (-ra)

spectral *a* espectral

specter *n* espectro, fantasma, *m*

spectrum *n phys* espectro, *m*

speculate *vi* especular (sobre, acerca de); *com* especular (en)

speculation *n* especulación, *f*

speculative *a* especulativo

speculator *n* especulador (-ra)

speech *n* habla, *f;* palabra, *f;* (idiom) lenguaje, *m;* (language) idioma, *m; gram* oración, *f;* (address) discurso, *m;* disertación, *f.* **part of s.,** parte de la oración, *f.* **to make a s.,** pronunciar un discurso. **s.maker,** orador (-ra)

speechless *a* mudo; sin habla; desconcertado, turbado

speed *n* prisa, rapidez, *f;* velocidad, *f. vt* dar la bienvenida (a); conceder éxito (a); (accelerate) acelerar. *vi* darse prisa; correr a toda prisa; (of arrows) volar. **at full s.,** a toda prisa; a toda velocidad; a todo correr. **maximum s.,** velocidad máxima, *f.* **with all s.,** a toda prisa. **s. of impact,** velocidad del choque, *f.* **s.-boat,** lancha de carrera, *f.* **s.-limit,** velocidad máxima, *f,* límite de velocidad, *m*

speedily *adv* aprisa, rápidamente; prontamente

speediness *n* rapidez, prisa, celeridad, *f;* prontitud, *f*

speeding *n* exceso de velocidad, *m.* **s. up,** aceleración, *f*

speedometer *n* cuentakilómetros, *m*

speedway *n* autódromo, *m,* pista de ceniza, *f*

speedy *a* rápido; pronto

spell *n* ensalmo, hechizo, *m;* encanto, *m;* (bout) turno, *m;* (interval) rato, *m;* temporada, *f. vt* (a word) deletrear; (a word in writing) escribir; (mean) significar; (be) ser. **a s. of good weather,** una temporada de

buen tiempo. **by spells,** a ratos. **to learn to s.,** aprender la ortografía. **s.-bound,** encantado, fascinado; asombrado

spelling *n* deletreo, *m;* ortografía, *f.* **s.-book,** silabario, *m; s.* **mistake,** falta de ortografía, *f*

spelling bee *n* certamen de deletreo, *m*

spend *vt* gastar; (time, etc.) pasar; perder; consumir, agotar. *vi* gastar, hacer gastos. **to s. lavishly** *Mexico* disparar. **to s. oneself,** agotarse

spendthrift *n* derrochador (-ra), manirroto (-ta). *a* despilfarrado, pródigo

spent *a* agotado, rendido. **The night is far s.,** La noche está avanzada. **s. bullet,** bala fría, *f*

sperm *n biol* esperma, *f; fig* sabor, *m;* (trace) dejo, *m. vt* especiar. **s. cupboard,** especiero, *m*

spermaceti *n* esperma de ballena, *f*

sphere *n* esfera, *f.* **s. of influence,** zona de influencia, *f*

spherical *a* esférico

sphinx *n* esfinge, *f.* **s.-like,** de esfinge

spice *n* especia, *f; fig* sabor, *m;* (trace) dejo, *m. vt* especiar. **s. cupboard,** especiero, *m*

spick and span *a* limpio como una patena; (brand-new) flamante; (of persons) muy compuesto

spicy *a* especiado; aromático; *fig* picante

spider *n* araña, *f.* **spider's web,** telaraña, *f*

spidery *a* de araña; lleno de arañas. **s. writing,** letra de patas de araña, *f*

spigot *n* espiche, *m*

spike *n* punta (de hierro, etc.), *f;* escarpia, *f;* (for boots) clavo, *m; bot* espiga, *f. vt* clavetear; (a cannon) clavar

spill *vt* derramar. *n* (fall) caída, *f*

spilling *n* derramamiento, derrame, *m*

spin *vt* hilar; (a cocoon) tejer; (a top) bailar; (a ball) tornear; (a coin) lanzar. *vi* hilar; girar, bailar. *n* vuelta, *f;* paseo, *m.* **to send spinning downstairs,** hacer rodar por la escalera (a). **to s. a yarn,** contar un cuento. **to s. out,** prolongar

spinach *n* espinaca, *f*

spinal *a* espinal. **s. anaesthesia,** raquianestesia, *f.* **s. column,** columna vertebral, *f*

spindle *n* huso, *m; mech* eje, *m.* **s.-shaped,** ahusado

spine *n anat* espinazo, *m,* columna vertebral, *f; bot* espina, *f;* (of a porcupine, etc.) púa, *f*

spineless *a zool* invertebrado; *fig* débil

spinet *n* espineta, *f*

spinner *n* hilandero (-ra); máquina de hilar, *f*

spinney *n* arboleda, *f;* bosquecillo, *m*

spinning *n* hilado, *m;* hilandería, *f.* **s.-machine,** máquina de hilar, *f.* **s.-top,** trompo, *m,* peonza, *f.* **s.-wheel,** rueca, *f*

spinster *n* soltera, *f.* **confirmed s.,** solterona, *f*

spiny *a* con púas; espinoso

spiral *a* espiral; en espiral. *n* espiral, *f*

spirally *adv* en espiral

spire *n* (of a church) aguja, *f;* espira, *f*

spirit *n* espíritu, *m;* alma, *f;* (ghost) aparecido, fantasma, *m;* (outstanding person) ingenio, *m,* inteligencia, *f;* (disposition) ánimo, *m;* (courage) valor, espíritu, *m;* (for a lamp, etc.) alcohol, *m.* **the Holy S.,** El Espíritu Santo. **to be in high spirits,** no caber de contento, saltar de alegría. **to be in low spirits,** estar desalentado, estar deprimido. **to be full of spirits,** ser bullicioso, tener mucha energía. **to keep up one's spirits,** sostener el valor. **to s. away,** quitar secretamente, hacer desaparecer; (kidnap) secuestrar. **s.-level,** nivel de burbuja, *m.* **s.-stove,** cocinilla, *f*

spirited *a* animado, vigoroso; fogoso, animoso, brioso

spiritless *a* sin espíritu, apático; flojo, débil; (depressed) abatido, desalentado; (cowardly) sin valor, cobarde

spiritual *a* espiritual

spiritualism *n* espiritismo, *m; phil* espiritualismo, *m*

spiritualist *n* espiritista, *mf; phil* espiritualista, *mf*

spiritualistic *a* espiritista; *phil* espiritualista. **s. séance,** sesión espiritista, *f*

spirituality *n* espiritualidad, *f*

spiritually *adv* espiritualmente

spirituous *a* espiritoso

spirt *vi, vt, n*. See **spurt**

spit *n* (for roasting) espetón, asador, *m*; (sand-bank) banco de arena, *m*; (of land) lengua de tierra, *f*; (spittle) saliva, *f*. **the spit of, the spit and image of, the spitting image of,** la imagen viva de, la segunda edición de, *f*. *vt* (skewer) espetar; (saliva, etc.) escupir; (curses, etc.) vomitar. *vi* escupir, expectorar; (of a cat) fufear, decir fu; (sputter) chisporrotear; (rain) lloviznar

spite *n* malevolencia, mala voluntad, hostilidad, *f*; rencor, *m*, ojeriza, *f*. *vt* contrariar, hacer daño (a). **He has a s. against them,** Les tiene rencor. **in s. of,** a pesar de; a despecho de

spiteful *a* rencoroso, malévolo

spitefully *adv* malévolamente; con rencor; por maldad; por despecho

spitefulness *n* malevolencia, *f*; rencor, *m*

spitfire *n* cascarrabias, *mf*, furia, *f*

spittle *n* saliva, *f*

splash *vt* salpicar (de); manchar (con). *vi* derramarse, esparcirse, chapotear, chapalear. *n* chapoteo, *m*; (of rain, etc.) chapaleteo, *m*; (stain or patch) mancha, *f*. **John was splashing about in the sea,** Juan chapoteaba en el mar. **to make a s.,** *fig* causar una sensación. **s.-board,** alero, *m*

spleen *n anat* bazo, *m*; esplín, *m*

splendid *a* espléndido; magnífico; glorioso; excelente

splendidly *adv* espléndidamente; magníficamente; excelentemente

splendor *n* resplandor, *m*; magnificencia, *f*; (of exploits, etc.) esplendor, brillo, *m*

splice *vt* (ropes, timbers) empalmar; (marry) unir, casar. *n* empalme, *m*

splint *n surg* férula, *f*. **to put in a s.,** entablar

splinter *vt* astillar, hacer astillas. *vi* hacerse astillas

splintery *a* astilloso

split *vi* henderse; resquebrajarse; (of seams) nacerse; abrirse; dividirse. *vt* hender; partir; dividir; abrir; (the atom) escindir. *n* hendedura, *f*; grieta, *f*; división, *f*; (in fabric) rasgón, *m*; (quarrel) ruptura, *f*. **to s. hairs,** andar en quisquillas, pararse en pelillos, sutilizar. **I have a splitting headache,** Tengo un dolor de cabeza que me trae loco. **to s. one's sides,** reírse a carcajadas, desternillarse de risa. **You have spoilt my fun,** Me has aguado la fiesta. **s.-sport,** aguafiestas, *mf*

spoilt *a* (of a child, etc.) mimado, consentido, malacostumbrado

spoke *n* (of a wheel) rayo, *m*; (of a ladder) travesaño, peldaño, *m*; *naut* cabilla (de la rueda del timón), *f*

spoken *a* hablado. **well-s.,** bien hablado; cortés

spokesman *n* portavoz, *m*. **to be s.,** llevar la palabra

spoliation *n* expoliación, *f*; despojo, *m*

sponge *n* esponja, *f*; (cadger) gorrón (-ona); (cake) bizcocho, *m*. *vt* limpiar con esponja. **to s.,** *inf* vivir de gorra. **s.-holder,** esponjera, *f*

sponger *n* gorrón (-ona), vividor, *m*, sablista, *mf*

sponginess *n* esponjosidad, *f*

sponging *n* esponjadura, *f*; *inf* sablazo, *m*

spongy *a* esponjoso

sponsor *n* garante, *mf*; valedor (-ra), patron (-na); (godfather) padrino, *m*; (godmother) madrina, *f*, (radio and TV) auspiciador, patrocinador, *m*

spontaneity *n* espontaneidad, *f*

spontaneous *a* espontáneo. **s. combustion,** combustión espontánea, *f*

spontaneously *adv* espontáneamente

spook *n* fantasma, espectro, *m*

spool *n* (for thread) bobina, *f*, carrete, *m*; (in a sewing machine) canilla, *f*; (of a fishing rod) carrete, *m*

spoon *n* cuchara, *f*. *vt* sacar con cuchara. *vi* (slang) besuquearse. **to s.-feed,** dar de comer con cuchara (a); tratar como un niño (a)

spoonful *n* cucharada, *f*

spoor *n* pista, huella de animal, *f*; rastro, *m*

sporadic *a* esporádico

spore *n bot* espora, *f*; *zool* germen, *m*

sport *n* deporte, sport, *m*; deportismo, *m*; (jest) broma, *f*; (game) juego, *m*; (plaything) juguete, *m*; (pastime) pasatiempo, *m*. *vi* jugar; recrearse, divertirse. *vt* llevar; ostentar, lucir. **He is a s.,** Es un buen chico. **to make s. of,** burlarse de. **sports car,** coche de deporte, *m*. **sports ground,** campo de recreo, *m*. **sports jacket,** chaqueta de deporte, americana, *f*. **sports shirt,** camisa corta, *f*

sporting *a* deportista; caballeroso. **I think there is a s. chance,** Me parece que hay una posibilidad de éxito

sporting goods *n* artículos de deporte, efectos de deportes, *m pl*

sportive *a* juguetón; bromista

sportsman *n* deportista, *m*; aficionado al sport, *m*; *fig* caballero, señor, *m*; buen chico, *m*

sportsmanlike *a* de deportista; caballeroso

sportsmanship *n* deportividad, *f*

spot *n* mancha, *f*; pinta, *f*; (on the face, etc.) peca, *f*; grano, *m*; (place) sitio, *m*; lugar, *m*; (of liquor) trago, *m*; (of food) bocado, *m*; (of rain) gota, *f*. *vt* manchar; motear; (recognize) reconocer; (understand) darse cuenta de, comprender. **a tender s.,** *fig* debilidad, *f*. **on the s.,** en el acto. **s. ball,** (billiards) pinta, *f*. **s. cash,** dinero contante, *m*

spotless *a* saltando de limpio; sin mancha; inmaculado; puro; virgen

spotlight *n* luz del proyector, *f*; proyector, *m*

spotted *a* (stained) manchado; (of animals, etc.) con manchas; (of garments, etc.) con pintas

spotty *a* lleno de manchas; moteado; (pimply) con granos

spouse *n* esposo, *m*; esposa, *f*

spout *vi* chorrear; *inf* hablar incesantemente. *vt* arrojar; vomitar; *inf* declamar, recitar. *n* (of a jug, etc.) pico, *m*; (for water, etc.) tubo, *m*, cañería, *f*; canalón, *m*; (gust) ráfaga, nube, *f*. **down s.,** tubo de bajada, *m*

spouting *n* chorreo, *m*; *inf* declamación, *f*

sprachgefühl *n* sentido del idioma, *m*

sprain *vt* dislocar, torcer. *n* dislocación, *f*, esguince, *m*. **Victoria has sprained her foot,** Victoria se ha torcido el pie

sprat *n* sardineta, *f*

sprawl *vi* recostarse (en); extenderse; (of plants) trepar. **He went sprawling,** Cayó cuan largo era

spray *n* (branch) ramo, *m*; (of water, etc.) rocío, *m*; (of the sea) espuma, *f*; (mechanical device) pulverizador, *m*. *vt* pulverizar; rociar; regar; (the throat) jeringar

spread *vt* tender; cubrir (de); poner; (stretch out) extender; (open out) desplegar; (of disease, etc.) propagar; diseminar; divulgar, difundir. *vi* extenderse; propagarse; difundirse; divulgarse; (become general) generalizarse. *n* extensión, *f*; expansión, *f*; propagación, *f*; divulgación, *f*; (aer and of birds) envergadura, *f*. **Carmen s. her hands to the fire,** Carmen extendió las manos al fuego. **The peacock s. its tail,** El pavo real hizo la rueda. **The dove s. its wings,** La paloma desplegó sus alas. **to s. out,** vt extender; desplegar; (scatter) esparcir, vi extenderse. **spread like wildfire,** correr como pólvora en reguero, propagarse como un reguero de pólvora, ser un reguero de pólvora

spreading *n* (of a disease) propagación, *f*; (of knowledge, etc.) divulgación, *f*; expansión, *f*; extensión, *f*

spree *n* juerga, parranda, *f*; excursión, *f*. **to go on the s.,** ir de juerga, ir de picos pardos

sprig *n* ramita, *f*; (of heather, etc.) espiga, *f*; (scion) vástago, *m*

sprightliness *n* vivacidad, *f*, despejo, *m*; energía, *f*

sprightly *a* vivaracho, despierto; enérgico

spring *vi* saltar, brincar; (become) hacerse; (seek) buscar; (of plants, water) brotar; (of tears) arrasar, llenar; (from) originarse (en), ser causado (por); inspirarse (en). *vt* (a mine) volar; (a trap) soltar. **to s. a surprise,** dar una sorpresa. **to s. a surprise on a person,** coger a la imprevista (a). **to s. at a person,** precipitarse sobre. **to s. to one's feet,** ponerse de pie de un salto. **to s. back,** saltar hacia atrás; recular; volver a su sitio. **to s. open,** abrirse súbitamente. **to s. up,** (of plants) brotar, crecer; (of difficulties, etc.) surgir, asomarse

spring *n* (jump) salto, brinco, *m*; (of water) fuente, *f*, manantial, *m*; (season) primavera, *f*; (of a watch, etc.) resorte, *m*; (of a mattress, etc.) muelle, *m*. *a* primaveral. *vi* saltar, brincar. **at one s.,** en un salto. **to give a s.,** dar un salto. **s.-board,** trampolín, *m*. **s.-mattress,** colchón de muelles, *m*. **s.-tide,** marea viva, *f*

springiness *n* elasticidad, *f*

springlike *a* primaveral

springtime *n* primavera, *f*

sprinkle *vt* esparcir; salpicar; rociar

sprinkling *n* salpicadura, *f*; rociadura, *f*; pequeño número, *m*. **a s. of snow,** una nevada ligera

sprint *vi* esprintar. *n* sprint, *m*

sprite *n* trasgo, *m*; hada, *f*

sprout *vi* brotar, despuntar, retoñar, tallecer; germinar. *vt* salir. *n* brote, retoño, pimpollo, *m*; germen, *m*. **Brussels sprouts,** coles de Bruselas, *f pl*

spruce *a* peripuesto, muy aseado, pulido; elegante, *n bot* pícea, *f*. **to s. oneself up,** arreglarse, ponerse elegante

spruceness *n* aseo, buen parecer, *m*, elegancia, *f*

spry *a* activo, ágil

spur *n* espuela, *f*; aguijada, *f*; (of a bird) espólon, *m*; *bot* espuela, *f*; (of a mountain range) espolón, estribo, *m*; *fig* estímulo, *m*. *vt* espolear, picar con la espuela; calzarse las espuelas; *fig* estimular, incitar, *Lat. Am.* espuelar. **on the s. of the moment,** bajo el impulso del momento

spurious *a* espurio; falso

spurn *vt* rechazar; tratar con desprecio; menospreciar

spurt *vi* (gush) chorrear, borbotar; brotar, surgir; (in racing, etc.) hacer un esfuerzo supremo. *vt* hacer chorrear; lanzar. *n* (jet) chorro, *m*; esfuerzo supremo, *m*

sputter *vi* chisporrotear; crepitar; (of a pen) escupir; (of a person) balbucir

sputtering *n* chisporroteo, *m*; crepitación, *f*; (of a person) balbuceo, *m*

sputum *n* esputo, *m*

spy *vt* observar, discernir. *vi* espiar, ser espía. *n* espía, *mf*. **to spy out the land,** explorar el terreno. **to spy upon, espiar;** seguir los pasos (a). **spy-glass,** catalejo, *m*

spying *n* espionaje, *m*

squabble *n* disputa, *f*; riña, *f*. *vi* pelearse; disputar

squabbling *n* riñas, querellas, *f pl*; disputas, *f pl*

squad *n* escuadra, *f*; pelotón, *m*

squadron *n mil* escuadrón, *m*; *nav* escuadra, *f*; *aer* escuadrilla, *f*; (of persons) pelotón, *m*. **s.-leader,** comandante, *m*

squalid *a* escuálido; (of quarrels, etc.) sórdido, mezquino

squall *vi* berrear; chillar. *n* berrido, *m*; chillido, *m*; (storm) chubasco, turbión, *m*; (storm) chubasco, turbión, *m*; *fig* tormenta, tempestad, *f*

squalor *n* escualidez, *f*; sordidez, mezquindad, *f*

squander *vt* derrochar, tirar, desperdiciar; (time, etc.) malgastar

squanderer *n* derrochador (-ra)

squandering *n* derroche, desperdicio, dispendio, *m*; (of time, etc.) pérdida, *f*, desperdicio, *m*

square *n math* cuadrado, *m*; rectángulo, *m*; (of a chessboard) escaque, *m*; (of a draughtboard and of graph paper) casilla, *f*; (in a town) plaza, *f*; (of troops) cuadro,

m, a cuadrado; justo; igual; (honest) honrado, formal; (unambiguous) redondo, categórico; *math* cuadrado. **She wore a silk s. on her head,** Llevaba un pañuelo de seda en la cabeza. **five s. feet,** cinco pies cuadrados. **nine feet s.,** nueve pies en cuadro. **on the s.,** honradamente. **a s. dance,** contradanza, *f*. **a s. meal,** una buena comida. **s. dealing,** trato limpio, *m*. **The account is s.,** La cuenta está justa. **to get s. with,** desquitarse (de), vengarse de. **s. measure,** medida de superficie, *f*. **s. root,** raíz cuadrada, *f*. **s.-shouldered,** de hombros cuadrados

square *vt* cuadrar; *carp* escuadrar; (arrange) arreglar; (bribe) sobornar; (reconcile) acomodar; *math* cuadrar. *vi* conformarse (con), cuadrar (con). **to s. the circle,** cuadrar el círculo. **to s. one's shoulders,** enderezarse. **to s. accounts with,** saldar cuentas con. **to s. up to,** (a person) avanzar belicosamente hacia

squarely *adv* en cuadro; directamente; sin ambigüedades, rotundamente; (honestly) de buena fe, honradamente

squareness *n* cuadratura, *f*; (honesty) honradez, buena fe, *f*

squash *vt* aplastar. *vi* aplastarse; apretarse. *n* aplastamiento, *m*; (of fruit, etc.) pulpa, *f*; (of people) agolpamiento, *m*; muchedumbre, *f*; (drink) refresco (de limón, etc.), *m*, (sport) frontón con raqueta, *m*

squashy *a* blando y húmedo

squat *vi* acuclillarse, agacharse, agazaparse ponerse en cuclillas; estar en cuclillas; (on land, etc.) apropiarse sin derecho. *a* rechoncho

squatter *n* intruso (-sa); colono usurpador, *m*

squatter town *n.* See **shanty town**

squawk *vi* graznar; lanzar gritos agudos. *n* graznido, *m*; grito agudo, *m*

squeak *vi* (of carts, etc.) chirriar, rechinar; (of shoes) crujir; (of persons, mice, etc.) chillar; (slang) cantar. *n* chirrido, crujido, *m*; chillido, *m*. **to have a narrow s.,** escapar por un pelo

squeaking *n* chirrido, rechinamiento, *m*; crujido, *m*; (of humans, mice, etc.) chillidos, *m pl*

squeal *vi* lanzar gritos agudos, chillar; (complain) quejarse; (slang) cantar. *n* grito agudo, chillido, *m*

squealing *n* gritos agudos, chillidos, *m pl*

squeamish *a* que se marea fácilmente; mareado; (nauseated) asqueado; delicado; remilgado

squeamishness *n* tendencia a marearse, *f*; delicadeza, *f*; remilgos, *m pl*

squeeze *vt* apretar; estrujar; (fruit) exprimir; (extort) arrancar; (money from) sangrar. *n* (of the hand, etc.) apretón, *m*; estrujón, *m*; (of fruit juice) algunas gotas (de). **It was a tight s. in the car,** Íbamos muy apretados en el coche. **He was in a tight s.,** Se encontraba en un aprieto. **to s. one's way through the crowd,** abrirse camino a codazos por la muchedumbre. **to s. in,** *vt* hacer sitio para. *vi* introducirse con dificultad (en)

squelch *vi* gorgotear, chapotear. *vt* aplastar

squib *n* (firework) rapapiés, buscapiés, *m*; (lampoon) pasquinada, *f*

squid *n* calamar, *m*

squint *n* estrabismo, *m*; mirada furtiva, *f*; *inf* vistazo, *m*, mirada, *f*. *vi* ser bizco; bizcar. **to s. at,** mirar de soslayo. **s.-eyed,** bizco. **to be s.-eyed,** mirar contra el gobierno

squire *n* escudero, *m*; hacendado, *m*. *vt* escoltar, acompañar

squirm *vi* retorcerse; (with embarrassment) no saber dónde meterse. *n* retorcimiento, *m*. **to s. along the ground,** arrastrarse por el suelo

squirrel *n* ardilla, *f*

squirt *vt* (liquids) lanzar. *vi* chorrear, salir a chorros. *n* chorro, *m*; (syringe) jeringa, *f*

stab *vt* apuñalar, dar de puñaladas (a); herir. *n* puñalada, *f*; herida, *f*; (of pain, and *fig*) pinchzo, *m*. **a s. in the back,** una puñalada por la espalda

stability *n* estabilidad, *f*; solidez, firmeza, *f*

stabilize *vt* estabilizar

stable *a* estable; fijo, firme. *n* cuadra, caballeriza, *f*; (for cows, etc.) establo, *m*. *vt* poner en la cuadra; alojar. **s.-boy,** mozo de cuadra, *m*

stack *n* (of hay) niara, *f*, almiar, *m*; (heap) montón, *m*; (of rifles) pabellón, *m*; (of a chimney) cañón, *m*. *vt agr* hacinar; amontonar; *mil* poner (las armas) en pabellón

stacked *a* (woman) abultada de pechera

stadium *n* estadio, *m*

staff *n* vara, *f*; (bishop's, and *fig*) báculo, *m*; (pilgrim's) bordón, *m*; (pole) palo, *m*; (flagstaff) asta, *f*; (of an office, etc.) personal, *m*; (editorial) redacción, *f*; (corps) cuerpo, *m*; *mil* plana mayor, *f*, estado mayor, *m*; *mus* pentagrama, *m*. *vt* proveer de personal. **general s.,** estado mayor general, *m*. **s. officer,** *mil* oficial de estado mayor, *m*

stag *n* ciervo, *m*. **s.-beetle,** ciervo volante, *m*. **s.-hunting,** caza del ciervo, *f*

stage *n* (for workmen) andamio, *m*; (of a microscope) portaobjetos, *m*; *theat* escena, *f*, tablas, *f pl*; teatro, *m*; (of development, etc.) etapa, *f*; fase, *f*. *vt theat* escenificar, poner en escena; *theat* representar; (a demonstration, etc.) arreglar. **by easy stages,** poco a poco; (of a journey) a pequeñas etapas. **to come on the s.,** salir a la escena. **to go on the s.,** hacerse actor (actriz), dedicarse al teatro. **s. carpenter,** tramoyista, *m*. **s.-coach,** diligencia, *f*. **s.-craft,** arte de escribir para el teatro, *f*; arte escénica, *f*. **s.-direction,** acotación, *f*. **s.-door,** entrada de los artistas, *f*. **s.-effect,** efecto escénico, *m*. **s.-fright,** miedo al público, *m*. **s.-hand,** tramoyista, sacasillas, metesillas y sacamuertos, *m*. **s. manager,** director de escena, *m*. **s.-whisper,** aparte, *m*

stager, old *n* veterano, *m*

stagger *vi* tambalear; andar haciendo eses; (hesitate) titubear, vacilar. *vt* desconcertar. *n* titubeo, tambaleo, *m*; *aer* decalaje, *m*. **staggered working hours,** horas de trabajo escalonadas, *f pl*

staggering *a* tambaleante; (surprising) asombroso, sorprendente; (dreadful) espantoso. **a s. blow,** un golpe que derriba

staging *n* (scaffolding) andamio, *m*; *theat* producción, *f*; representación, *f*; decorado, *m*

stagnancy *n* (of water) estancación, *f*; (inactivity) estagnación, *f*; paralización, *f*

stagnant *a* estancado; paralizado. **to be s.,** estar estancado. **s. water,** agua estancada, *f*

stagnate *vi* estancarse; estar estancado; (of persons) vegetar

stagnation *n* (of water) estancación, *f*; estagnación, *f*; parálisis, *f*

staid *a* serio, formal, juicioso

staidness *n* seriedad, formalidad, *f*

stain *vt* manchar; (dye) teñir. *n* mancha, *f*; colorante, *m*. **without a s.,** *fig* sin mancha. **stained glass,** vidrio de color, *m*. **s.-remover,** quitamanchas, *m*

stainless *a* sin mancha; inmaculado, puro

stair *n* escalón, peldaño, *m*; escalera, *f*; *pl* **stairs,** escalera, *f*. **a flight of stairs,** una escalera; un tramo de escaleras. **below stairs,** abajo. **s.-carpet,** alfombra de escalera, *f*. **s.-rod,** varilla para alfombra de escalera, *f*

staircase *n* escalera, *f*. **spiral s.,** escalera de caracol, *f*

stake *n* estaca, *f*; (for plants) rodrigón, *m*; (gaming) envite, *m*, apuesta, *f*; (in an undertaking) interés, *m*; *pl* **stakes,** (prize) premio, *m*; (race) carrera, *f*. *vt* estacar; (plants) rodrigar; (bet) jugar. **at s.,** en juego; en peligro. **to be burnt at the s.,** morir en la hoguera. **to s. one's all,** jugarse el todo por el todo. **to s. a claim,** hacer una reclamación. **to s. out,** jalonar

stalactite *n* estalactita, *f*

stalagmite *n* estalagmita, *f*

stale *a* no fresco; (of bread, etc.) duro, seco; (of air) viciado; viejo; pasado de moda; (tired) cansado

stalemate *n* (chess, checkers) tablas, *f pl*; *fig* punto muerto, *m*. **to reach a s.,** llegar a un punto muerto

staleness *n* rancidez, *f*; (of bread, etc.) dureza, *f*; (of news, etc.) falta de novedad, *f*

stalk *n bot* tallo, *m*; *bot* pedúnculo, *m*; (of a glass) pie, *m*. *vi* andar majestuosamente; *fig* rondar. *vt* (game) cazar al acecho; (a person) seguir los pasos (a)

stalking horse *n* boezuelo, *m*; *fig* pretexto, *m*

stall *n* (in a stable) puesto (individual), *m*; (stable) establo, *m*; (choir) silla de coro, *f*; (in a fair, etc.) barraca, *f*, puesto, *m*; *theat* butaca, *f*; (finger-stall) dedal, *m*. *vt* (an engine) cortar accidentalmente. *vi aut* pararse de pronto; *aer* perder velocidad; (of a cart, etc.) atascarse. **pit s.,** *theat* butaca de platea, *f*

stalling *n aut* parada accidental, *f*; *aer* pérdida de velocidad, *f*. **Stop s.!** ¡Déjate de rodeos!

stallion *n* semental, *m*

stalwart *a* robusto, fornido; leal; valiente

stalwartness *n* robustez, *f*; lealtad, *f*; valor, *m*

stamina *n* resistencia, *f*

stammer *vi* tartamudear; (hesitate in speaking) titubear, balbucir. *n* tartamudez, *f*; titubeo, balbuceo, *m*

stammerer *n* tartamudo (-da)

stammering *a* tartamudo; balbuciente. *n* tartamudeo, *m*; balbuceo, *m*

stamp *vt* estampar; imprimir; (documents) timbrar; pegar el sello de correo (a); (characterize) sellar; (*fig* engrave) grabar; (coins) acuñar; (press) apisonar; (with the foot) golpear con los pies, patear; (in dancing) zapatear. *n* (with the foot) patada, *f*, golpe con los pies, *m*; (mark, etc.) marca, *f*; (rubber, etc.) estampilla, *f*; matasellos, *m*; cuño, *m*; (for documents) póliza, *f*; timbre, *m*; (for letters) sello, *m*; *Mexico* timbre, *m*, *elsewhere in Lat. Am.* estampilla, *f*, (machine) punzón, *m*; mano de mortero, *f*; (*fig* sign) sello, *m*; (kind) temple, *m*, clase, *f*. **The events of that day are stamped on my memory,** Los acontecimientos de aquel día están grabados en mi memoria. **to s. out,** (a fire, etc.) extinguir, apagar; (resistance, etc.) vencer; destruir. **postage-s.,** sello de correos, *m*. **s.-album,** álbum de sellos, *m*. **s.-machine,** expendedor automático de sellos de correo, *m*

stampede *n* fuga precipitada, *f*; pánico, *m*. *vi* huir precipitadamente; (of animals) salir de estampía; huir en desorden. *vt* hacer perder la cabeza (a), sembrar el pánico entre

stamping *n* selladura, *f*; (of documents) timbrado, *m*; (of fabrics, etc.) estampado, *m*; (with the feet) pataleo, *m*; (in dancing) zapateo, *m*

stance *n* posición de los pies, *f*; postura, *f*

stanch *vt* restañar

stand *vi* estar de pie; ponerse de pie, incorporarse; estar; hallarse; sostenerse; ser; ponerse; (halt) parar; (remain) permanecer, quedar. *vt* (endure) resistir; tolerar; sufrir; (entertain) convidar. **S.!** ¡Alto! **as things s.,** tal como están las cosas. **I cannot s. any more,** No puedo más. **I cannot s. him,** No le puedo ver. **Nothing stands between them and ruin,** No hay nada entre ellos y la ruina. **I stood him a drink,** Le convidé a un trago. **How do we s.?** ¿Cómo estamos? **It stands to reason that . . . ,** Es lógico que . . . **Edward stands six feet,** Eduardo tiene seis pies de altura. **to s. accused of,** ser acusado de. **to s. godfather (or godmother) to,** sacar de pila (a). **to s. in need (of),** necesitar, tener necesidad (de). **to s. on end,** (of hair) ponerse de punta, despeluzarse. **to s. one in good stead,** ser útil, ser ventajoso. **to s. one's ground,** no ceder, tenerse fuerte. **to s. to attention,** cuadrarse, permanecer en posición de firmes. **to s. well with,** tener buenas relaciones con, ser estimado de. **to s. aside,** tenerse a un lado; apartarse; (in favor of someone) retirarse. **to s. back,** quedarse atrás; recular, retroceder. **to s. by,** estar de pie cerca de; estar al lado de; estar presente (sin intervenir); ser espectador; estar preparado; (one's friends) ayudar, proteger; (a promise, etc.) atenerse (a); ser fiel (a); (of a ship) mantenerse listo. **s.-by,** *n* recurso, *m*. **to s. for,** representar; simbolizar; (mean) significar; (Parliament, etc.) presentarse como candidato; (put up with) tolerar, sufrir. **to s. in,** colaborar. **to s. in with,** estar de acuerdo con, ser partidario de; compartir. **to s. off,** mantenerse a distancia. **to s. out,** (in relief, and *fig.* of persons) destacarse; (be firm) resistir, mantenerse firme; *naut* gobernar más afuera. **S. out of the way!** ¡Quítate del medio! **to s. over,** (be postponed) quedar aplazado. **to s. up,** estar de pie; ponerse de pie, incorporarse; tenerse derecho. **to s. up against,** resistir; oponerse a. **to s. up for,** defender; volverpor. **to s. up to,** hacer cara a

stand *n* puesto, *m*; posición, actitud, *f*; (for taxis, etc.) punto, *m*; (in a market, etc.) puesto, *m*; *sport* tribuna, *f*; (for a band) quiosco, *m*; (of a dish, etc.) pie, *m*; *mech* sostén, *m*; (opposition) resistencia, oposición, *f*. **to make a s. against,** oponerse resueltamente (a); ofrecer resistencia (a). **to take one's s.,** fundarse (en), apoyarse (en). **to take up one's s. by the fire,** ponerse cerca del fuego

standard *n* (flag) estandarte, *m*, bandera, *f*; (for gold, weights, etc.) marco, *m*; norma, *f*; convención, regla, *f*; (of a lamp) pie, *m*; (pole) poste, *m*; columna, *f*; (level) nivel, *m. a* corriente; normal; típico; clásico. **It is a s. type,** Es un tipo corriente. **gold s.,** patrón de oro, *m.* **s. author,** autor clásico, *m.* **s. formula,** fórmula clásica, *f.* **s. of living,** nivel de vida, *m.* **s.-bearer,** abanderado, *m.* **s.-lamp,** lámpara vertical, *f*

standardization *n* (of armaments, etc.) unificación de tipos, *f*; (of dyestuffs, medicinals, etc.) control, *m*, estandardización, *f*

standardize *vt* hacer uniforme; controlar

standing *a* de pie, derecho; permanente, fijo; constante. *n* posición, *f*; reputación, *f*; importancia, *f*; antigüedad, *f.* **It is a quarrel of long s.,** Es una riña antigua. **s. committee,** comisión permanente, *f.* **s. room,** sitio para estar de pie, *m.* **s. water,** agua estancada, *f.* **standoffish,** frío, etiquetero; altanero. **standoffishness,** frialdad, *f*; altanería, *f.* **standpoint,** punto de vista, *m*

standstill *n* parada, *f*; pausa, *f.* **at a s.,** parado; (of industry) paralizado

stanza *n* estrofa, estancia, *f*

staple *n* (fastener) grapa, *f*; (of wool, etc.) hebra, fibra, *f*; producto principal (de un país), *m*; (raw material) materia prima, *f*; *a* principal; más importante; corriente

stapler, (device) cosepapeles, engrapador, *m*, atrochadora (Argentina), *f*

star *n* (all meanings) estrella, *f*; (asterisk) asterisco, *m. vt* estrellar, sembrar de estrellas; marcar con asterisco. *vi* (*theat* cinema) presentarse como estrella, ser estrella. **stars and stripes,** las barras y las estrellas. **to be born under a lucky s.,** tener estrella. **to see stars,** ver estrellas. **s.-gazing,** observación de las estrellas, *f*; ensimismamiento, *m.* **s.-spangled,** estrellado, tachonado de estrellas, sembrado de estrellas. **s.-turn,** gran atracción, *f*

starboard *n naut* estribor, *m*

starch *n* almidón, *m*, las harinas, *f pl, vt* almidonar

starchy *a* almidonado; (of food) feculento; *fig* tieso, entonado, etiquetero

stare *vi* mirar fijamente; abrir mucho los ojos. *n* mirada fija, *f.* **stony s.,** mirada dura, *f.* **to s. at,** (a person) clavar la mirada en; mirar de hito en hito (a). **The explanation stares one in the face,** La explicación salta a la vista (or está evidente). **to s. into space,** mirar las telarañas. **to s. out of countenance,** avergonzar con la mirada

starfish *n* estrella de mar, *f*

staring *a* (of colors) chillón, llamativo, encendido. **s. eyes,** ojos saltones, *m pl*; ojos espantados, *m pl*

stark *a* rígido; *poet* poderoso; absoluto. **s. staring mad,** loco de atar. **s.-naked,** en cueros vivos, en pelota

starless *a* sin estrellas

starlight *n* luz de las estrellas, *f, a* estrellado

starry *a* estrellado, sembrado de estrellas

start *vi* estremecerse, asustarse; saltar; (set out) salir; ponerse en camino; (of a train, a race) arrancar; ponerse en marcha; *aer* despegar; (begin) empezar; (of

timbers) combarse. *vt* empezar; (a car, etc.) poner en marcha; (a race) dar la señal de partida; (a hare, etc.) levantar; (cause) provocar, causar; (a discussion, etc.) abrir; iniciar. *n* (fright) susto, *m*; (setting out) partida, salida, *f*; (beginning) principio, comienzo, *m*; (starting-point of a race) arrancadero, *m*; *aer* despegue, *m*; (advantage) ventaja, *f.* **at the s.,** al principio. **for a s.,** para empezar. **from s. to finish,** desde el principio hasta el fin. **She started to cry,** Se puso a llorar. **He has started his journey to Canada,** Ha empezado su viaje al Canadá. **I started up the engine,** Puse el motor en marcha. **to get a s.,** asustarse; tomar la delantera. **to give** (a person) **a s.,** asustar, dar un susto (a); dar la ventaja (a). **to give** (a person) **a s. in life,** ayudar a alguien a situarse en la vida. **to make a fresh s. (in life),** hacer vida nueva, empezar la vida de nuevo. **to s. after,** lanzarse en busca de; salir tras. **to s. back,** retroceder; emprender el viaje de regreso; marcharse. **to s. off,** salir, partir; ponerse en camino. **to s. up,** *vi* incorporarse bruscamente, ponerse de pie de un salto; (appear) surgir, aparecer. *vt* (an engine) poner en marcha

starter *n* iniciador (-ra); (for a race) starter, juez de salida, *m*; (competitor in a race) corredor, *m*; (of a car, etc.) arranque, *m*

starting *n* (setting out) salida, partida, *f*; (beginning) principio, *m*; (fear) estremecimiento, *m*; susto, *m.* **s.-gear,** palanca de arranque, *f.* **s.-handle,** manivela de arranque, *f.* **s.-point,** punto de partida, *m; fig* arrancadero, punto de arranque, *m.* **s.-post,** puesto de salida, *m*

startle *vt* asustar, sobresaltar, alarmar. **The news startled him out of his indifference,** Las noticias le hicieron salir de su indiferencia

startling *a* alarmante; (of dress, etc.) exagerado; (of colors) chillón

starvation *n* hambre, *f; med* inanición, *f.* **s. diet,** régimen de hambre, *m.* **s. wage,** ración de hambre, *f*

starve *vi* morir de hambre; pasar hambre, no tener bastante que comer; no comer. *vt* matar de hambre; privar de alimentos (a). **I am simply starving,** Tengo una hambre canina, Me muero de hambre. **to s. with cold,** *vi* morir de frío. *vt* matar de frío

starved *a* muerto de hambre, hambriento. **s. of affection,** hambriento de cariño

starving *a* que muere de hambre, hambriento

state *n* estado, *m*; condición, *f*; (anxiety) agitación, ansiedad, *f*; (social) rango, *m*; (pomp) magnificencia, pompa, *f*; (government, etc.) Estado, *m*; nación, *f. a* de Estado; de gala, de ceremonia. **the married s.,** el estado matrimonial. **s. of war,** estado de guerra. **in s.,** con gran pompa. **to lie in s.,** (of a body) estar expuesto. **s. apartments,** habitaciones de gala, *f pl.* **s. banquet,** comida de gala, *f.* **s. coach,** coche de gala, *m.* **s. control,** control por el Estado, *m.* **S. Department,** Ministerio de Estado, *m.* **s. education,** instrucción pública, *f.* **State of the Union message,** Mensaje al Congreso, *m.* **s. papers,** documentos de Estado, *m pl*

state *vt* decir (que), afirmar (que); (one's case, etc.) exponer; explicar; *math* proponer

statecraft *n* arte de gobernar, *m*

stated *a* arreglado, indicado; fijo. **the s. date,** la fecha indicada. **at s. intervals,** a intervalos fijos

statehood *n* estadidad, *f*

stateliness *n* dignidad, *f*; majestad, *f*

stately *a* majestuoso; imponente; noble; digno

statement *n* afirmación, declaración, *f*; resumen, *m*; exposición, *f; law* deposición, *f; com* estado de cuenta, *m.* **to make a s.,** hacer una declaración

stateroom *n* sala de recepción, *f*; (on a ship) camarote, *m*

statesman *n* hombre de estado, *m*

statesmanlike *a* de hombre de estado

statesmanship *n* arte de gobernar, *m*

static *a* estático

statics *n* estática, *f*

station *n* (place) puesto, sitio, *m*; (*rw* and *ecc*) estación,

stationary — step

stationary *f;* (social) posición social, *f; naut* apostadero, *m; surv* punto de marca, *m. vt* estacionar, colocar, poner. **to s. oneself,** colocarse. **Stations of the Cross,** Estaciones, *f pl.* **s.-master,** jefe de la estación, *m*

stationary *a* estacionario; inmóvil; *ast* estacional

stationer *n* papelero (-ra). **stationer's shop,** papelería, *f*

stationery *n* papelería, *f,* efectos de escritorio, *m pl;* papel de escribir, *m*

station wagon *n* pisicorre, coche camioneta, coche rural, *m*

statistical *a* estadístico

statistician *n* estadista, *m*

statistics *n* estadística, *f*

statuary *a* estatuario. *n* estatuaria, *f;* estatuas, *f pl;* (sculptor) estatuario, *m*

statue *n* estatua, *f;* imagen, *f*

statuesque *a* escultural

statuette *n* figurilla, *f*

stature *n* estatura, *f;* (moral, etc.) valor, *m*

status *n* (*law* etc.) estado, *m;* posición, *f;* rango, *m.* **What is his s. as a physicist?** ¿Cómo se le considera entre los físicos? **social s.,** posición social, *f;* rango social, *m*

statute *n* ley, *f;* acto legislativo, *m;* estatuto, *m;* regla, *f.* **s. book,** código legal, *m*

statutory *a* establecido; reglamentario; estatutario

staunch *a* leal, fiel; firme, constante. *vt* restañar

staunchness *n* lealtad, fidelidad, *f;* firmeza, *f*

stave *n* (of a barrel, etc.) duela, *f;* (of a ladder) peldaño, *m;* (stanza) estrofa, *f; mus* pentagrama, *m.* **to s. in,** abrir boquete en; romper a golpes; quebrar. **to s. off,** apartar, alejar; (delay) aplazar, diferir; (avoid) evitar; (thirst, etc.) dominar

stay *vt* detener; (a judgment, etc.) suspender. *vi* permanecer; quedarse; detenerse; (of weather, etc.) durar; (lodge) hospedarse, vivir. **to come to s.,** venir a ser permanente. **to s. a person's hand,** detenerle a fulano el brazo. **to s. at home,** quedarse en casa. **s.-at-home,** *a* casero. *n* persona casera, *f.* **to s. the course,** terminar la carrera. **S.! Say no more!** ¡Calle! ¡No diga más! **to s. away,** ausentarse. **to s. up,** no acostarse; velar. **to s. with,** quedarse con; alojarse con; quedarse en casa de, vivir con

stay *n* estancia, permanencia, *f;* residencia, *f;* (restraint) freno, *m; law* suspensión, *f;* (endurance) aguante, *m,* resistencia, *f; naut* estay, *m;* (prop) puntal, *m; fig* apoyo, soporte, *m; pl* **stays,** corsé, *m*

stead *n* lugar, *m.* **in the s. of,** en el lugar de, como substituto de. **It has stood me in good s.,** Me ha sido muy útil

steadfast *a* fijo; constante; firme; tenaz. **s. gaze,** mirada fija, *f*

steadfastly *adv* fijamente; con constancia; firmemente; tenazmente

steadfastness *n* fijeza, *f;* constancia, *f;* firmeza, *f;* tenacidad, *f*

steadily *adv* firmemente; (without stopping) sin parar; continuamente; (assiduously) diligentemente; (uniformly) uniformemente. **Prices have gone up s.,** Los precios no han dejado de subir. **He looked at it s.,** Lo miraba sin pestañear (or fijamente)

steadiness *n* estabilidad, *f;* firmeza, *f;* constancia, *f;* (of persons) seriedad, formalidad, *f;* (of workers) diligencia, asiduidad, *f*

steady *a* firme; seguro; fijo; constante; uniforme; continuo; estacionario; (of persons) serio, formal, juicioso; (of workers) diligente, asiduo. *vt* afirmar; (persons) hacer más serio (a); (nerves, etc.) calmar, fortificar. **a s. job,** un empleo seguro. **S.!** ¡Calma!; *naut* ¡Seguro! **He steadied himself against the table,** Se apoyó en la mesa

steak *n* tajada, *f;* biftec, *Argentina* bife, *m*

steal *vt* robar, hurtar; tomar. *vi* robar, ser ladrón; (glide) deslizarse; (overwhelm) dominar, ganar insensiblemente (a). **to s. a kiss,** robar un beso. **to s. a look**

at, mirar de soslayo (or de lado). **to s. away,** escurrirse, escabullirse; marcharse a hurtadillas. **to s. in,** deslizarse en, colarse en

stealthily *adv* a hurtadillas; a escondidas, furtivamente

stealthiness *n* carácter furtivo, *m*

stealthy *a* furtivo; cauteloso

steam *n* vapor, *m. a* de vapor. *vi* echar vapor. *vt cul* cocer al vapor; (clothes) mojar; (windows, etc.) empañar. **to have the s. up,** estar bajo presión. **The windows are steamed,** Los cristales están empañados. **s.-boiler,** caldera de vapor, *f.* **s.-engine,** máquina de vapor, *f.* **s.-hammer,** maza de fragua, *f.* **s.-heat,** calefacción por vapor, *f.* **s.-roller,** *lit* apisonadora, *fig* fuerza arrolladora, *f*

steamboat *n* vapor, *m*

steamer *n cul* marmita al vacío, *f; naut* buque de vapor, *m*

steamship *n* buque de vapor, piróscafo, *m*

steamy *a* lleno de vapor

steed *n* corcel, *m*

steel *n* (metal, and *poet* sword) acero, *m;* (for sharpening) afilón, *m. a* de acero; acerado. *vt* acerar; *fig* endurecer. **to be made of s.,** *fig* ser de bronce. **He cannot s. himself to do it,** No puede persuadirse a hacerlo. **to s. one's heart,** hacerse duro de corazón. **cold s.,** arma blanca, *f.* **stainless s.,** acero inoxidable, *m.* **s.-engraving,** grabado en acero, *m*

steel mill *n* fábrica de acero, *f*

steep *a* acantilado, escarpado; precipitoso; (of stairs, etc.) empinado; (of price) exorbitante. *vt* (soak) remojar, empapar; *fig* absorber; (in a subject) empapar (en). *n* remojo, *m.* **It's a bit s.!** *inf* ¡Es un poco demasiado!

steeping *n* remojo, *m,* maceración, *f*

steeple *n* campanario, *m,* torre, *f;* aguja, *f*

steeplechase *n* steeplechase, *m,* carrera de obstáculos, *f*

steepness *n* carácter escarpado, *m,* lo precipitoso

steer *vt naut* gobernar (a car, etc.) conducir; *fig* guiar, conducir. *vi naut* timonear; *naut* navegar; *aut* conducir. *n zool* novillo, *m.* **to s. clear of,** evitar. **to s. one's way through the crowd,** abrirse paso entre la muchedumbre

steerage *n* gobierno, *m;* (stern) popa, *f;* (quarters) entrepuente, *m.* **to go s.,** viajar en tercera clase

steering *n naut* gobierno, *m;* (tiller, etc.) gobernalle, timón, *m;* (of a vehicle) conducción, *f.* **s.-column,** barra de dirección, *f.* **s.-wheel,** *aut* volante de dirección, *m; naut* rueda del timón, *f*

stellar *a* estelar

stem *n* (of a tree) tronco, *m;* (of a plant) tallo, *m;* (of a glass, etc.) pie, *m;* (*mus* of a note) rabo, *m;* (of a pipe) tubo, *m;* (of a word) radical, *m. vt* (check) contener; (the tide) ir contra; (the current) vencer; (dam) estancar. **from s. to stern,** de proa a popa

stench *n* tufo, hedor, *m,* hediondez, *f,* Lat. Am. *also* fortaleza, *f*

stencil *n* patrón para estarcir, *m;* estarcido, *m. vt* estarcir

stenographer *n* estenógrafo (-fa), taquígrafo (-fa)

stenography *n* estenografía, taquigrafía, *f*

stentorian *a* estentóreo

step *n* paso, *m;* (footprint) huella, *f;* (measure) medida, *f;* (of a stair, etc.) escalón, peldaño, *m,* grada, *f;* (of a ladder) peldaño, *m;* (of vehicles) estribo, *m;* (grade) escalón, *m; mus* intervalo, *m.* **at every s.,** a cada paso. **flight of steps,** escalera, *f;* (before a building, etc.) escalinata, *f.* **in steps,** en escalones. **to bend one's steps towards,** dirigirse hacia. **to keep in s.,** llevar el paso. **to take a s.,** dar un paso. **to take steps,** tomar medidas. **s. by s.,** paso a paso; poco a poco. **s.-dance,** baile típico, *m.* **s.-ladder,** escalera de tijera, *f*

step *vi* dar un paso; pisar; andar. **Please s. in!** Sírvase de entrar. **Will you s. this way, please?** ¡Haga el favor de venir por aquí! **to s. aside,** ponerse a un lado; desviarse; *fig* retirarse (en favor de). **to s. in,** entrar; intervenir (en); (meddle) entrometerse. **He stepped**

into the train, Subió al tren. **to s. on,** pisar. **to s. on board,** *naut* ir a bordo. **to s. out,** salir; (from a vehicle) bajar; (a dance) bailar. **He stepped out a moment ago,** Salió hace un instante

stepbrother *n* hermanastro, medio hermano, *m*

stepchild *n* hijastro (-ra)

stepdaughter *n* hijastra, *f*

stepfather *n* padrastro, *m*

stepmother *n* madrastra, *f*

steppingstone *n* pasadera, *f*; *fig* escabel, escalón, *m*

stepsister *n* hermanastra, media hermana, *f*

stepson *n* hijastro, *m*

stereotype *n* estereotipia, *f*, clisé, *m*, *vt* (*print* and *fig*) estereotipar

sterile *a* estéril; árido

sterility *n* esterilidad, *f*; aridez, *f*

sterilization *n* esterilización, *f*

sterilize *vt* esterilizar

sterilizer *n* esterilizador, *m*

sterling *a* esterlina *f*; *fig* genuino. **pound s.,** libra esterlina, *f*

stern *a* severo, austero; duro. *n naut* popa, *f*

sternly *adv* con severidad, severamente, duramente

sternness *n* severidad, *f*; dureza, *f*

sternum *n anat* esternón, *m*

stethoscope *n* estetoscopio, *m*

stevedore *n* estibador, *m*

stew *vt* guisar a la cazuela, estofar; (mutton, etc.) hervir; (fruit) cocer. *n* estofado, *m*; *inf* agitación, *f*. **to be in a s.,** *inf* sudar la gota gorda. **stewed fruit,** compota de frutas, *f*. **s.-pot,** cazuela, olla, *f*, puchero, *m*

steward *n* administrador, *m*; mayordomo, *m*; (provision) despensero, *m*; *naut* camarero, *m*

stewardess *n naut* camarera, *f*

stick *vt* clavar (en); hundir (en); (put) poner; sacar; (stamps, etc.) pegar; fijar; (endure) resistir; tolerar. *vi* clavarse, hundirse; estar clavado; pegarse; (remain) quedar; (in the mud, etc.) atascarse, embarrancarse; (on a reef) encallarse; (in the throat, etc.) atravesarse; (stop) detenerse. **It sticks in my throat,** *inf* No lo puedo tragar. **Friends always s. together,** Los amigos no se abandonan. **The nickname stuck to him,** El apodo se le quedó. **to s. at,** persistir en; desistir (ante); pararse (ante); tener escrúpulos sobre. **to s. at nothing,** no tener escrúpulos. **He stuck at his work,** Siguió trabajando. **to s. down,** pegar. **to s. one's nose into other people's business** *Mexico* entrucharse. **to s. out,** *vi* proyectar; sobresalir. *vt* (one's chest) inflar; (one's tongue) sacar. **His ears s. out,** Tiene las orejas salientes. **to s. to,** (one's job) no dejar; (one's plans) adherirse (a); (one's principles) ser fiel (a); (one's friends) no abandonar; (one's word, etc.) cumplir; atenerse a. **to s. up,** *vi* (of hair) erizarse, ponerse de punta; salirse. *vt* clavar; (a notice) fijar. **to s. up for,** (a person) defender

stick *n* estaca, *f*; (for the fire) leña, *f*; (walking-s.) bastón, *m*; (of office) vara, *f*; (of sealing-wax, etc.) barra, *f*; palo, *m*; (baton) batuta, *f*; (of celery) tallo, *m*. **in a cleft s.,** entre la espada y la pared. **to give** (a person) **the s.,** dar palo (a)

stickiness *n* viscosidad, *f*

stickingplaster *n* esparadrapo, *m*

stick-in-the-mud *n* chapado a la antigua, *m*

stickler *n* rigorista, *mf*. **to be a s. for etiquette,** ser etiquetero

sticky *a* pegajoso, viscoso; *fig* difícil

stiff *a* rígido; inflexible; tieso; (of paste, etc.) espeso; (of manner) distante; (of a bow, etc.) frío; (of a person) almidonado, etiquetero; severo; (of examinations, etc.) difícil; (strong) fuerte; (of price, etc.) alto, exorbitante; (of a shirt front, etc.) duro. **s. with cold,** aterido de frío. **s. neck,** torticolis, *m*. **s.-necked,** terco, obstinaz

stiffen *vt* reforzar; atiesar; (paste, etc.) hacer más espeso; (*fig* strengthen) robustecer; (make more obstinate) hacer más tenaz. *vi* atiesarse; endurecerse;

(straighten oneself) enderezarse; (of manner) volverse menos cordial; (become firmer) robustecerse; (become more obstinate) hacerse más tenaz. **The breeze stiffened,** Refrescó el viento

stiffly *adv* tiesamente; rígidamente; obstinadamente

stiffness *n* rigidez, *f*; tiesura, *f*; dureza, *f*; (of manner) frialdad, *f*; (obstinacy) terquedad, obstinación, *f*; (of an examination, etc.) dificultad, *f*

stifle *vt* ahogar, sofocar; apagar; suprimir

stifling *a* sofocante, bochornoso

stigma *n* estigma, *m*

stigmatize *vt* estigmatizar

stile *n* (nearest equivalent) portilla con escalones, *f*

still *a* tranquilo; inmóvil; quedo; silencioso; (of wine) no espumoso. *n* silencio, *m*. **in the s. of the night,** en el silencio de la noche. **Keep s.!** ¡Estate quieto! **to keep s.,** quedarse inmóvil, no moverse. **s.-birth,** nacimiento de un niño muerto, *m*. **s.-born,** nacido muerto. **s. life,** *art* bodegón, *m*, naturaleza muerta, *f*

still *vt* hacer callar, acallar; calmar, tranquilizar; apaciguar; (pain) aliviar

still *adv* todavía, aún; (nevertheless) sin embargo, no obstante; (always) siempre. **I think she s. visits them every week,** Me parece que sigue visitándoles cada semana. **s. and all,** con todo y eso. **s. more,** aún más. **s. to be paid** *Lat. Am.* impago

still *n* alambique, *m*. **salt water s.,** adrazo, *m*

stillness *n* quietud, tranquilidad, *f*; silencio, *m*. **in the s. of the night,** en el silencio de la noche

stilt *n* zanco, *m*

stilted *a* ampuloso, campanudo, hinchado

stimulant *a* and *n* estimulante, *m*

stimulate *vt* estimular; incitar (a), excitar (a)

stimulating *a* estimulante; (encouraging) alentador; (inspiring) sugestivo, inspirador

stimulation *n* excitación, *f*; (stimulus) estímulo, *m*

stimulus *n* estímulo, *m*; *med* estimulante, *m*; (incentive) impulso, incentivo, *m*; acicate, aguijón, *m*

sting *vt* picar, pinchar; (of snakes, etc.) morder; (of hot dishes) resquemar; (of hail, etc.) azotar; (pain) atormentar; (provoke) provocar (a), incitar (a). *n* (*zool* organ) aguijón, *m*; *bot* púa, *f*; (of a scorpion) uña, *f*; (of a serpent) colmillo, *m*; (pain and wound) pinchazo, *m*; (serpent's) mordedura, *f*; (stimulus) acicate, estímulo, *m*; (torment) tormento, dolor, *m*

stingily *adv* avaramente, tacañamente

stinginess *n* tacañería, avaricia, *f*

stinging *a* picante; *fig* mordaz; (of blows) que duele

stingy *a* tacaño, avaro, mezquino, *Argentina* agalludo, *Chile, Peru* coñete

stink *vi* apestar, heder, oler mal. *n* tufo, *m*, hediondez, *Lat. Am. also* fortaleza, *f*

stinking *a* apestoso, hediondo, fétido, mal oliente

stint *vt* escatimar; limitar. *n* límite, *m*, restricción, *f*. **without s.,** sin límite; sin restricción

stipend *n* estipendio, salario, *m*

stipple *vt art* puntear. *n* punteado, *m*

stipulate *vi* estipular, poner como condición. *vt* estipular, especificar. **They stipulated for a five-day week,** Pusieron como condición (*or* Estipularon) que trabajasen cinco días por semana

stipulation *n* estipulación, *f*; condición, *f*

stir *vt* agitar; revolver; (the fire) atizar; (move) mover; (emotionally) conmover, impresionar; (the imagination) estimular. *vi* moverse. *n* movimiento, *m*; conmoción, *f*; (bustle) bullicio, *m*; sensación, *f*. **to make a s.,** causar una sensación. **to s. one's coffee,** revolver el café. **to s. up discontent,** fomentar el descontento

stirring *a* conmovedor, emocionante, impresionante; (of times, etc.) turbulento, agitado

stirrup *n* estribo, *m*. **s.-cup,** última copa, *f*. **s.-pump,** bomba de mano (para líquidos), *f*

stitch *n* (action) puntada, *f*; (result) punto, *m*; *surg* punto de sutura, *m*; (pain) punzada, *f*, pinchazo, *m*. *vt* coser; *surg* suturar

stoat *n* armiño, *m*; (weasel) comadreja, *f*

stock n (of a tree) tronco, m; (of a rifle) culata, f; (handle) mango, m; (of a horse's tail) nabo, m; (stem for grafting etc.) injerto, m; (race) raza, f; (lineage) linaje, m, estirpe, f; (supply) provisión, f; reserva, f; (of merchandise) surtido, m; cul caldo, m; (collar) alzacuello, m; bot alhelí, m; (government) papel del estado, m, valores públicos, m pl; (financial) valores, m pl, (of a company) capital, m; pl **stocks,** hist cepo, m; (of goods) existencias, f pl, stock, m, a corriente; del repertorio. **in s. en existencia. lives.,** ganado m. **rolling-s.,** rw materia móvil ferroviario, m. **s. phrase** frase hecha, f. **s. size,** talla corriente, f. **to lay in a s. of,** hacer provisión de, almacenar, **to stand s.-still,** quedarse completamente inmóvil. **to take s. of,** hacer inventario. **to take s. of,** inventariar; examinar, considerar. **s.-breeder,** ganadero, m. **s.-broker,** corredor de bolsa, bolsista, m. **s. exchange,** bolsa, f. **s.-in-hand,** com existencias, f pl. **s.-in-trade** (com etc.) capital, m. **s.-raising,** cría de ganados, ganadería, f. **s.-taking,** com inventario, m

stock vt proveer (de), abastecer (de); (of shops) tener existencia de

stockade n estacada, empalizada, f, vt empalizar

stocking n media, f. **nylon stockings,** medias de cristal (or de nilón), f pl

stocky a rechoncho, doblado, achaparrado

stodgy a (of food) indigesto; (of style, etc.) pesado, amazacotado

stoic a and n estoico (-ca)

stoical a estoico

stoke vt (a furnace, etc.) cargar, alimentar; (a fire) echar carbón, etc., en. **s.-hole,** cuarto de fogoneros, m; naut cámara de calderas, f

stoker n fogonero, m; (mechanical) cargador, m

stole n (ecc and of fur, etc.) estola, f

stolid a impasible, imperturbable

stolidly adv imperturbablemente

stomach n estómago, vientre, m; apetito, estómago, m; (courage) corazón, valor, m. vt digerir; (tolerate) tragar, sufrir. **s.ache,** dolor de estómago, m

stone n piedra, f; (gem) piedra preciosa, f; (of cherries, etc.) hueso, m; (of grapes, etc.) pepita, f; med cálculo, m. a de piedra. vt apedrear; (a wall, etc.) revestir de piedra; (fruit) deshuesar. **to pave with stones,** empedrar. **to leave no s. unturned,** no dejar piedra sin remover. **within a stone's throw,** a corta distancia, a un paso. **S. Age,** edad de piedra, f. **s.-breaker,** cantero, picapedrero, m. **s.-cold,** muy frío, completamente frío **s.-deaf,** a completamente sordo. **s.-fruit,** fruta de hueso, f. **s.-mason,** mazonero, albañil, m; picapedrero, m. **s.-quarry,** pedrera, cantera, f

stonily adv fríamente; fijamente, sin pestañear

stoniness n lo pedregoso; (of hearts, etc.) dureza, f; (of stares, etc.) fijeza, inmovilidad, f

stoning n apedreamiento, m, lapidación, f

stony a pedregoso; (of hearts, etc.) duro, insensible, empedernido; (of a stare, etc.) fijo, duro

stool n banquillo, taburete, m; (feces) excremento, m

stoop vi inclinarse, doblarse; encorvarse; ser cargado de espaldas; andar encorvado; (demean oneself) rebajarse (a). vt inclinar, doblar. n inclinación, f; cargazón de espaldas, f

stooping a inclinado, doblado; (of shoulders) cargado

stop vt (a hole) obstruir, atascar; (a leak) cegar, tapar; (a tooth) empastar; (stanch) restañar; (the traffic, etc.) parar; detener; (prevent) evitar; (discontinue) cesar (de), dejarse de; (cut off) cortar; (end) poner fin (a), acabar con; (payment) suspender. vi parar; detenerse; cesar; terminar; (stay) quedarse, permanecer. **I stopped myself from saying what I thought,** Me abstuve de decir lo que pensaba, Me mordí la lengua. **They stopped the food-supply,** Cortaron los suministros. **to s. beating about the bush,** dejarse de historias. **to s. one's ears,** fig taparse los oídos. **to s. payments,** suspender pagos

stop n parada, f; pausa, f; interrupción, f; cesación, f; (of

an organ) registro, m. **"Stop,"** (road sign) «Alto.» **full s.,** gram punto, m. **tram s.,** parada de tranvía, f. **to come to a full s.,** pararse de golpe; cesar súbitamente. **to put a s. to,** poner fin a, poner coto a, acabar con. f pl. **s.-watch,** cronógrafo, m

stopgap n (person) tapagujeros, m; substituto, m

stoppage n parada, f; cesación, f; suspensión, f; interrupción, f; pausa, f; (obstruction) impedimento, m; obstrucción, f. **s. of work,** suspensión de trabajo, f

stopper n tapón, m; obturador, m, vt cerrar con tapón, taponar

stopping n parada, f; cesación, f; suspensión, f; (of a tooth) empaste, m. **without s.,** sin parar. **without s. to draw breath,** de un aliento. **s.-place,** paradero, m; (of buses, etc.) parada, f. **s. train,** tren ómnibus, m. **s. up,** obturación, f

storage n almacenamiento, m; (charge) almacenaje, m; (place) depósito, m. **cold s.,** cámara frigorífica, f. **s. battery,** acumulador, m

store n provisión, f; abundancia, f; reserva, f; (of knowledge, etc.) tesoro, m; (for furniture, etc.) depósito, almacén, m; pl **stores,** (shop) almacenes, m pl; (food) provisiones, f pl; (mil etc.) pertrechos, m pl. vt proveer; guardar, acumular; tener en reserva; (furniture, etc.) almacenar; (hold) caber en, tomar. **in s.,** en reserva; en depósito, en almacén. **to set s. by,** estimar en mucho; dar importancia a. **to set little s. by,** estimar en poco; conceder poca importancia a. **s.-room,** despensa, f

storehouse n almacén, m; fig mina, f, tesoro, m

storekeeper = shopkeeper

storied a de . . . pisos. **two-s.,** de dos pisos

stork n cigüeña, f

storm n tempestad, tormenta, f, temporal, m; fig tempestad, f; mil asalto, m. vt mil tomar por asalto, asaltar. vi (of persons) bramar de cólera. **to take by s.,** tomar por asalto; fig cautivar, conquistar. **s. cloud,** nubarrón, m. **s.-signal,** señal de temporal, f. **s.-tossed,** a sacudido por la tempestad. **s. troops,** tropas de asalto, f pl. **s. window,** contravidriera, f

stormily adv tempestuosamente; con tormenta

storming n (mil etc.) asalto, m; violencia, f. **s.-party,** pelotón de asalto, m

stormy a tempestuoso; de tormenta; (of life, etc.) borrascoso; (of meetings, etc.) tempestuoso

story n historia, f; cuento, m; anécdota, f; (funny) chiste, m; (plot) argumento, enredo, m; (fib) mentira, f; (floor) piso m. **It's always the same old s.,** Es siempre la misma canción (or historia). **That is quite another s.,** Eso es harina de otro costal, Argentina, Peru esas son otras cuarenta. **short s.,** cuento, m. **s. book,** libro de cuentos, m. **s. teller,** cuentista, mf; (fibber) mentiroso (-sa)

stout a fuerte; (brave) intrépido, indómito; (fat) gordo, grueso; (firm) sólido, firme; (decided) resuelto; vigoroso. n (drink) cerveza negra, f. **s.-hearted,** valiente, intrépido

stove n estufa, f; (open, for cooking) cocina económica, f; (gas, etc., for cooking) cocina, f, fogón, m. **s. dealer:** **s. maker** Argentina fumista, mf; **s. pipe,** tubo de la chimenea, m

stow vt meter, poner; colocar; (hide) esconder; (cargo) estibar, arrimar

stowaway n polizón, llovido, m, vi embarcarse secretamente

straddle vi (nav etc.) graduar el tiro. vt montar a horcajadas en. **s.-legged,** patiabierto

strafe vt bombardear concentradamente; castigar; reñir

straggle vi rezagarse; vagar en desorden; dispersarse; estar esparcido; extenderse

straggler n rezagado (-da)

straight a derecho; recto; (of hair) lacio; directo; (tidy) en orden; (frank) franco; (honest) honrado. adv derecho; en línea recta; directamente. **Keep s. on!** ¡Siga Vd. derecho! **to go s. to the point,** dejarse de rodeos, ir al grano. **to look s. in the eyes,** mirar derecho en los ojos. **s. away,** inmediatamente, en seguida. **s. out,** sin rodeos

straighten *vt* enderezar; poner derecho; poner en orden; arreglar. *vi* ponerse derecho; enderezarse. **to s. one's face,** componer el semblante. **to s. the line,** *mil* rectificar el frente. **to s. out,** poner en orden; *fig* desenredar. **to s. oneself up,** erguirse

straightforward *a* honrado, sincero; franco; (simple) sencillo. **s. answer,** respuesta directa, *f*

straightforwardly *adv* honradamente; francamente

straightforwardness *n* honradez, integridad, *f*; franqueza, *f*; (simplicity) sencillez, *f*

straightness *n* derechura, rectitud, *f*; (of persons) honradez, probidad, *f*

straightway *adv* al instante, inmediatamente

strain *vt* estirar; forzar; esforzar; (one's eyes) quebrarse; (one's ears) aguzar (el oído); (a muscle, etc.) torcer; (a friendship) pedir demasiado (a), exigir demasiado (de); (a person's patience, etc.) abusar (de); (words) tergiversar; (embrace) abrazar estrechamente (a); (filter) filtrar; *cul* colar. *vi* hacer un gran esfuerzo, esforzarse (para). *n* tirantez, *f*; tensión, *f*; (effort) esfuerzo, *m*; (sprain) torcedura, *f*; (nervous) tensión nerviosa, *f*; *mech* esfuerzo, *m*; (breed) raza, *f*; *biol* cepa, *f*; (tendency) tendencia, *f*; (heredity) herencia, *f*; rasgo, *m*, vena, *f*; (style) estilo, *m*; *mus* melodía, *f*; (of mirth, etc.) son, ruido, *m*; (poetry) poesía, *f*. **to s. a point,** hacer una excepción. **to s. after effect,** buscar demasiado el efecto

strained *a* tenso; (of muscles, etc.) torcido; (of smiles, etc.) forzado. **s. relations,** *pol* estado de tirantez, *m*

strainer *n* filtro, *m*; coladero, *m*

strait *n geog* estrecho, *m*. **to be in great straits,** estar en un apuro. **s. laced,** *fig* de manga estrecha

straiten *vt* estrechar; limitar, **in straitened circumstances,** en la necesidad

Strait of Magellan Estrecho de Magallanes, *m*

Straits Settlements Establecimientos del Estrecho, *m pl*

strand *n* (shore) playa, *f*; (of a river) ribera, orilla, *f*; (of rope) cabo, ramal, *m*; (of thread, etc.) hebra, *f*; (of hair) trenza, *f*. *vt* and *vi* (a ship) encallar, varar. **to be stranded,** hallarse abandonado; (by missing a train, etc.) quedarse colgado. **to leave stranded,** abandonar, dejar plantado (a)

strange *a* (unknown) desconocido; nuevo; (exotic, etc.) extraño, singular; extraordinario; raro; exótico. **I felt very s. in a s. country,** Me sentía muy solo en un país desconocido. **He is a very s. person,** Es una persona muy rara

strangely *adv* extrañamente, singularmente; de un modo raro

strangeness *n* novedad, *f*; singularidad, *f*; rareza, *f*

stranger *n* desconocido (-da); (from a foreign country) extranjero (-ra); (from another region, etc.) forastero (-ra).

strangle *vt* estrangular; (a sob, etc.) ahogar

stranglehold *n* collar de fuerza, *m*. **to have a s. (on),** tener asido por la garganta; paralizar

strap *n* correa, *f*; tirante de botas, *m*, *vt* atar con correas

strapping *a* rozagante, robusto

Strasburg Estrasburgo, *m*

stratagem *n* estratagema, *f*, ardid, *m*

strategic *a* estratégico

strategist *n* estratego, *m*

strategy *n* estrategia, *f*

stratification *n* estratificación, *f*

stratosphere *n* estratosfera, *f*

stratum *n geol* estrato, *m*, capa, *f*; (social, etc.) estrato, *m*

straw *n* paja, *f*. **I don't care a s.,** No se me da un bledo. **to be not worth a s.,** no valer un ardite. **to be the last s.,** ser el colmo. **to drink through a s.,** sorber con una paja. **s. hat,** sombrero de paja, *m*. **s.-colored,** pajizo

strawberry *n* (plant and fruit, especially small or wild)

fresa, *f*; (large cultivated) fresón, *m*. **s. bed,** fresal, *m*. **s. ice,** helado de fresa, *m*

stray *vi* errar, vagar; perderse; (from a path, etc., also *fig*) descarriarse. *n* animal perdido, *m*; niño (-ña) sin hogar. *a* descarriado, perdido; errante; (sporadic) esporádico

stray bullet *n* bala perdida, *f*

streak *n* raya, *f*; (in wood and stone) vena, *f*; (of light) rayo, *m*; (of humor, etc.) rasgo, *m*. *vt* rayar. **like a s. of lightning,** como un relámpago

streaky *a* rayado; (of bacon) entreverado

stream *n* arroyo, riachuelo, *m*; río, *m*; (current) corriente, *f*; (of words, etc.) torrente, *m*. *vi* correr, fluir; manar, brotar; (float) flotar, ondear. *vt* (blood, etc.) manar, echar. **The tears streamed down Jean's cheeks,** Las lágrimas corrían por las mejillas de Juana. **s.-lined,** fuselado

stream-of-consciousness *n* escritura automática, *f*, fluir de la conciencia, *m*, flujo de la subconciencia, *m*; monólogo interior, *m*

streamer *n* gallardete, *m*, serpentina, *f*; (on a hat, etc.) cinta colgante, *f*, siguemepollo, *m*

street *n* calle, *f*. **the man in the s.,** el hombre medio. **at s. level,** a ras de suelo. **s. arab,** golfo, *m*. **s. cries,** gritos de vendedores ambulantes, *m pl*. **s. entertainer,** saltabanco, *m*. **s. brawl, s. fight,** algarada callejera, *f*. **s. fighting,** luchas en las calles, *f pl*. **s. musician,** músico ambulante, *m*. **s.-sweeper,** barrendero, *m*. **s.-walker,** buscona, prostituta, *f*

strength *n* fuerza, *f*; (of colors, etc.) intensidad, *f*; (of character) firmeza (de carácter), *f*; (of will) resolución, decisión, *f*; *mil* complemento, *m*. **The enemy is in s.,** El enemigo está presente en gran número. **by sheer s.,** a viva fuerza. **on the s. of,** confiando en, en razón de

strengthen *vt* fortificar; consolidar; reforzar. *vi* fortificarse; consolidarse; reforzarse

strengthening *a* fortificante; tonificante. *n* refuerzo, *m*; fortificación, *f*; consolidación, *f*

strenuous *a* activo, enérgico; vigoroso; (arduous) arduo

strenuously *adv* enérgicamente, vigorosamente

strenuousness *n* energía, *f*; vigor, *m*; (arduousness) arduidad, *f*

streptococcus *n med* estreptococo, *m*

streptomycine *n med* estreptomicina, *f*

stress *n* tensión, *f*; impulso, *m*; importancia, *f*, énfasis, *m*; *gram* acento (tónico), *m*; acentuación, *f*; *mech* esfuerzo, *m*. *vt* acentuar; poner énfasis en, insistir en. **under s. of circumstance,** impulsado por las circunstancias. **times of s.,** tiempos turbulentos, *m pl*. **to lay great s. on,** insistir mucho en; dar gran importancia a

stretch *vt* (make bigger) ensanchar; (pull) estirar; (one's hand, etc.) alargar, extender; (knock down) tumbar. *vi* ensancharse; dar de sí; ceder; extenderse. **to s. oneself,** estirarse, desperezarse. **to s. as far as,** llegar hasta, extenderse hasta. **to s. a point,** hacer una concesión. **to s. one's legs,** estirar las piernas

stretch *n* estirón, *m*; tensión, *f*; (of country, etc.) extensión, *f*; (scope) alcance, *m*. **by a s. of the imagination,** con un esfuerzo de imaginación. **He can sleep for hours at a s.,** Puede dormir durante horas enteras

stretcher *n* (for gloves) ensanchador, *m*; dilatador, *m*; (for canvas) bastidor, *m*; (for wounded, etc.) camilla, *f*. **s.-bearer,** camillero, *m*

strew *vt* esparcir; derramar

stricken *a* (wounded) herido; (ill) enfermo; (with grief) afligido, agobiado de dolor. **s. in years,** entrado en años

strict *a* exacto; estricto; escrupuloso; severo

strictly *adv* exactamente; estrictamente; severamente, con severidad. **s. speaking,** en rigor, en realidad

strictness *n* exactitud, *f*; escrupulosidad, *f*; rigor, *m*; severidad, *f*

stricture *n fig* crítica severa, censura, *f*. **to pass strictures on,** criticar severamente

stride *vi* andar a pasos largos, dar zancadas; cruzar a grandes trancos. *vt* cruzar de un tranco; poner una pierna en cada lado de. *n* zancada, *f*, paso largo, tranco, *m*. **to s. up and down,** dar zancadas

strident *a* estridente; (of colors) chillón

strife *n* lucha, *f*, conflicto, *m*

strike *vt* golpear; pegar, dar una bofetada (a); (wound) herir; (a coin) acuñar; (a light) encender; (of a snake) morder; (a blow) asestar, dar; (of ships, a rock, etc.) chocar contra; estrellarse contra; (flags) bajar, arriar; (a tent) desmontar; (camp) levantar; (come upon) llegar a; (discover) encontrar por casualidad, tropezar con; hallar, descubrir; (seem) parecer; (impress) impresionar; (of ideas) ocurrirse; (an attitude) tomar, adoptar; (of a clock) dar; (a balance) hacer; (a bargain) cerrar, llegar a; (level) nivelar; (cuttings) enraciar. *vi* golpear; (of a clock) dar la hora; (of a ship) encallar; (go) ir; (penetrate) penetrar; (of a cutting) arraigar; (sound) sonar. **He struck the table with his fist,** Golpeó la mesa con el puño. **I was very much struck by the city's beauty,** La belleza de la ciudad me impresionó mucho. **The news struck fear into their hearts,** La noticia les llenó el corazón de miedo. **The clock struck three,** El reloj dio las tres. **The hour has struck,** *fig* Ha llegado la hora. **How did the house s. you?** ¿Qué te pareció la casa? **to s. a bargain,** cerrar un trato. **to s. a blow,** asestar un golpe. **to s. across country,** ir a campo traviesa. **to s. an attitude,** tomar una actitud. **to s. home,** dar en el blanco; herir; herir en lo más vivo; hacerse sentir. **to s. at,** asestar un golpe (a); acometer, embestir; atacar. **to s. down,** derribar; (of illness) acometer. **to s. off,** (a head, etc.) cortar; (a name) borrar, tachar; (print) imprimir. **to s. out,** *vi* asestar un golpe (a); (of a swimmer) nadar; echarse, lanzarse. *vt* (a word, etc.) borrar, rayar; (begin) iniciar. **to s. through,** (cross out) rayar, tachar; (of the sun's rays, etc.) penetrar. **to s. up,** *vt* tocar; empezar a cantar; (a friendship) trabar. *vi* empezar a tocar. **to s. up a march,** *mil* batir la marcha

strike *n* huelga, *f*. *vi* declararse en huelga. **go-slow s.,** tortuguismo, *m*. **lock-out s.,** huelga patronal, *f*. **sit-down s.,** huelga de brazos caídos, *f*. **to go on s.,** declararse en huelga. **s.-breaker,** esquirol, *m*. **s.-pay,** subsidio de huelga, *m*

striker *n* huelguista, *mf*

striking *a* notable, sorprendente; (impressive) impresionante; que llama la atención; llamativo

string *n* bramante, *m*; cuerda, *f*; (ribbon) cinta, *f*; (of beads, etc.) sarta, *f*; (of onions) ristra, *f*; (of horses, etc.) reata, *f*; hilera, *f*; (of a bridge) cable, *m*; (of oaths, lies) sarta, serie, *f*; (of beans) fibra, *f*. *vt* encordar; (beads, etc.) ensartar; (beans) quitar las fibras (de). **He is all strung up,** Se le crispan los nervios. **the strings,** los instrumentos de cuerda. **a s. of pearls,** un collar de perlas. **for strings,** *mus* para arco. **to pull strings,** *fig* manejar los hilos. **to s. up,** (an instrument) templar; (a person) pender, ahorcar. **s. bean,** judía verde, *f*, *Central America, Mexico* ejote, *m*

stringed *a* (of musical instruments) de cuerda. **s. instrument,** instrumento de cuerda, *m*

stringent *a* estricto, severo

stringy *a* fibroso; filamentoso; correoso; arrugado

strip *vt* desnudar; despojar (de), quitar; robar; (a cow) ordeñar hasta agotar la leche. *vi* desnudarse. *n* (tatter) jirón, *m*; tira, lista, *f*; (of wood) listón, *m*; (of earth) pedazo, *m*; (*geog* of land) zona, *f*. **to s. off,** *vt* quitar; (bark from a tree) descortezar; (one's clothes) despojarse de. *vi* desprenderse, separarse. **to s. the leaves from,** **to s. the petals from** *Lat. Am.* deshojar

stripe *n* raya, lista, *f*; (*mil* etc.) galón, *m*; (lash) azote, *m*. *vt* rayar. **the stripes of the tiger,** las rayas del tigre

striped *a* listado, a rayas; con rayas. **s. trousers,** pantalón de corte, *m*

stripling *n* joven imberbe, pollo, mancebo, *m*

strive *vi* esforzarse (a); pugnar (por, para); trabajar (por); (fight against) luchar contra, pelear con. **He was**

striving to understand, Pugnaba por (or Se esforzaba a) comprender

stroke *n* (blow) golpe, *m*; (of the oars) golpe del remo, *m*, remada, *f*; (at billards) tacada, *f*; (in golf) tirada, *f*; (in swimming) braza, *f*; (of a clock) campanada, *f*; (of a pen) rasgo de la pluma, *m*; (of a brush) pincelada, *f*; *mech* golpe de émbolo, *m*; (caress) caricia con la mano, *f*. *vt* acariciar con la mano. **on the s. of six,** al acabar de dar las seis. **to have a s.,** tener un ataque de apoplejía. **s. of genius,** rasgo de ingenio, *m*. **s. of good luck,** racha de buena suerte, *f*

stroll *vi* pasearse, vagar. *n* vuelta, *f*, paseo, *m*. **to go for a s.,** dar una vuelta

stroller *n* paseante, *mf*

strolling *a* errante; ambulante. **s. player,** *n* cómico (-ca) ambulante

strong *a* fuerte; vigoroso; robusto; *Argentina* alentado; enérgico; firme; poderoso; (of colours) intenso, vivo; (of tea, coffee) cargado; *gram* fuerte. **The government took s. measures,** El gobierno tomó medidas enérgicas. **They gave very s. reasons,** Alegaron unas razones muy poderosas. **Grammar is not his s. point,** La gramática no es su punto fuerte. **The enemy is s. in numbers,** El enemigo es numéricamente fuerte. **The society is four thousand s.,** La sociedad tiene cuatro mil miembros. **s. box,** caja de caudales, *f*. **s. man,** hombre fuerte, *m*; (in a circus) hércules, *m*. **s.-minded,** de espíritu fuerte; independiente. **s. room,** cámara acorazada, *f*

stronghold *n* fortaleza, *f*; refugio, *m*

strongly *adv* vigorosamente; fuertemente; firmemente

strop *n* (razor) suavizador, *m*, *vt* suavizar

structural *a* estructural

structure *n* estructura, *f*; edificio, *m*; construcción, *f*

struggle *vi* luchar; pelear; disputarse, *Lat. Am.* abrocharse (con . . .); *n* lucha, *f*; combate, *m*; conflicto, *m*. **to s. to one's feet,** luchar por levantarse. **without a s.,** sin luchar

struggling *a* pobre, indigente, que lucha para vivir

strum *vt* (a stringed instrument) rascar; tocar mal

strut *vi* pavonearse. *vt* (prop) apuntalar. *n* pavonada, *f*; (prop) puntal, *m*. **to s. out,** salir de un paso majestuoso

stub *n* (of a tree) tocón, *m*; (of a pencil, candle, etc.) cabo, *m*; pedazo, fragmento, *m*; (of a cigarette or cigar) colilla, *f*. **s.-book,** talonario, *m*

stubborn *a* inquebrantable, tenaz; persistente; (pig-headed) terco, testarudo, *Lat. Am.* empecinado

stubbornness *n* tenacidad, *f*; terquedad, testarudez, *f*

stucco *n* estuco, *m*, *vt* estucar

stuck past part. of **stick. be stuck** (for an answer) = **be stumped**

stuck-up *a* = haughty

stud *n* (of horses) caballeriza, *f*; (nail) tachón, *m*; (for collars) pasador para camisas, *m*. *vt* tachonar; sembrar. **dress s.,** botón de la pechera, *m*. **s.-farm,** potrero, *m*

student *n* estudiante, *mf*. *a* estudiantil. **students** (as a body) *Lat. Am.* estudiantado, *msg*.

student body *n* *Lat. Am.* estudiantado, *m*

studied *a* estudiado; calculado; (of style) cerebral, reflexivo; (intentional) deliberado

studio *n* estudio, *m*. **broadcasting s.,** estudio de emisión, *m*

studious *a* estudioso, aplicado; (deliberate) intencional, deliberate; (eager) solícito, ansioso

studiously *adv* estudiosamente; con intención, deliberadamente; solícitamente

study *n* estudio, *m*; solicitud, *f*, cuidado, *m*; investigación, *f*; (room) gabinete, cuarto de trabajo, *m*. *vt* ocuparse de, cuidar de, atender a; considerar; estudiar; examinar; (the stars) observar; (try) procurar. *vi* estudiar. **in a brown s.,** en Babia. **to make a s. of,** hacer un estudio de, estudiar. **to s. for an examination,** prepararse para un examen

stuff *n* substancia, materia, *f*; (fabric) tela, *f*, paño, *m*; (rubbish) cachivaches, *m pl*, cosas, *f pl*. *a* de estofa. *vt* henchir; llenar; *cul* rellenar; (with food) ahitar (de);

(cram) atestar, apretar; (furniture) rehenchir; (an animal, bird) disecar; (put) meter, poner. **S. and nonsense!** ¡Patrañas! **to be poor s.**, ser de pacotilla; no valer para nada

stuffed animal *n* animal disecado, *m*

stuffiness *n* mala ventilación, *f*; falta de aire, *f*; calor, *m*

stuffing *n* (of furniture) rehenchimiento, *m*; *cul* relleno, *m*

stuffy *a* mal ventilado, poco aireado, ahogado

stumble *vi* tropezar; dar un traspié; (in speaking) tartamudear. *n* tropezón, *m*; traspié, *m*. **to s. through a speech,** pronunciar un discurso a tropezones. **to s. against,** tropezar contra. **to s. upon, across,** tropezar con; encontrar por casualidad

stumblingblock *n* tropiezo, impedimento, *m*

stump *n* (of a tree) tocón, *m*; (of an arm, leg) muñón, *m*; (of a pencil, candle) cabo, *m*; (of a tooth) raigón, *m*; (of a cigar) colilla, *f*; (cricket) poste, montante, *m*; *art* esfumino, *m*; (leg) pata, *f*. *vt* (disconcert) desconcertar; *art* esfumar; recorrer. **to s. up,** *inf* pagar. **be stumped** (for an answer) *Mexico* atrojarse

stun *vt* dejar sin sentido (a); aturdir de un golpe (a); (astound) pasmar

stunning *a* aturdidor; que pasma; *inf* estupendo

stunt *vt* impedir el crecimiento de; encanijar. *n* (advertising) anuncio de reclamo, *m*; recurso (para conseguir algo), *m*; proeza, *f*

stunted *a* (of trees, etc.) enano; (of children) encanijado; (of intelligence) inmaduro

stupefy *vt* atontar, embrutecer; causar estupor (a), asombrar

stupendous *a* asombroso; enorme

stupid *a* (with sleep, etc.) atontado; (silly) estúpido, tonto, *Lat. Am.* baboso, *Central America* azurumbado. *n* tonto (-ta)

stupidity *n* estupidez, *f*; tontería, *f*

stupor *n* estupor, *m*

sturdiness *n* robustez, *f*, vigor, *m*; firmeza, tenacidad, *f*

sturdy *a* robusto, vigoroso, fuerte; firme, tenaz

sturgeon *n* *icht* esturión, *m*

stutter *vi* tartamudear. *vt* balbucir. *n* tartamudeo, *m*

stutterer *n* tartamudo (-da)

stuttering *a* tartamudo; balbuciente. *n* tartamudeo, *m*

sty *n* (pig) pocilga, *f*; *med* orzuelo, *m*

Stygian *a* estigio

style *n* (for etching) buril, *m*; (lit, art, arch, etc.) estilo, *m*; (fashion) moda, *f*; (model) modelo, *m*; (behavior, etc.) tono, *m*; elegancia, *f*; (kind) especie, clase, *f*; (designation) tratamiento, *m*; *vt* llamar, nombrar. **the latest styles from Madrid,** los últimos modelos de Madrid. **He has a very individual s.,** Su estilo es muy personal. **They live in great s.,** Viven en gran lujo

stylet *n* estilete, *m*

stylish *a* elegante

stylishness *n* elegancia, *f*

stylist *n* estilista, *mf*

stylize *vt* estilizar

suasion *n* persuasión, *f*

suasive *a* suasorio, persuasivo

suave *a* afable, cortés, urbano; (of wine) suave

suavity *n* afabilidad, urbanidad, *f*

subaltern *n* *mil* subalterno, *m*, *a* subalterno, subordinado

subcommittee *n* subcomisión, *f*

subconscious *a* subconsciente. **the s.,** la subconsciencia

subconsciously *adv* subconscientemente

subcutaneous *a* subcutáneo

subdivide *vt* subdividir. *vi* subdividirse

subdivision *n* subdivisión, *f*

subdominant *n* *mus* subdominante, *f*

subdue *vt* subyugar, sojuzgar, vencer; (one's passions) dominar; (colors, voices) suavizar; (lessen) mitigar; apagar

subdued *a* (of colors) apagado; (of persons) sumiso;

(depressed) deprimido, melancólico. **in a s. voice,** en voz baja

subheading *n* subtítulo, *m*

subhuman *a* subhumano

subject *a* sujeto; sometido (a); expuesto (a). *n* (of a country) súbdito (-ta); sujeto, *m*; (of study) asignatura, materia, *f*; (theme) tema, *m*; (gram, phil) sujeto, *m*. *vt* subyugar; someter. **It can only be done s. to his consent,** Podrá hacerse únicamente si él lo consiente. **He is a British s.,** Es súbdito británico. **to change the s.,** cambiar de conversación. **to s. to criticism,** criticar (a). **s.-matter,** materia, *f*; (of a letter) contenido, *m*

subjection *n* sujeción, *f*; sometimiento, *m*. **He was in a state of complete s.,** Estaba completamente sumiso. **to bring into s.,** subyugar

subjective *a* subjetivo

subjectiveness *n* subjetividad, *f*

subjectivism *n* subjetivismo, *m*

subjoin *vt* añadir, adjuntar

subjugate *vt* subyugar, someter

subjugation *n* subyugación, *f*

subjunctive *a* and *n* subjuntivo *m*

sublet *vt* subarrendar. *n* subarriendo, *m*

sublimate *vt* sublimar. *n* sublimado, *m*

sublimation *n* sublimación, *f*

sublime *a* sublime; absoluto, completo; extremo. **the s.,** lo sublime

sublimely *adv* sublimemente; completamente

submachine gun *n* pistola ametralladora, metralleta, *f*, subfusil ametrallador, *m*

submarine *a* submarino. *n* submarino, *m*. **midget s.,** submarino enano, submarino de bolsillo, *m*. **s. chaser,** cazasubmarino, *m*

submerge *vt* sumergir; inundar. *vi* sumergirse. **The submarine submerged,** El submarino se sumergió

submergence *n* sumergimiento, *m*, sumersión, *f*; hundimiento, *m*

submersible *a* sumergible

submersion *n* sumersión, *f*; hundimiento, *m*

submission *n* sometimiento, *m*; sumisión, resignación, *f*; docilidad, *f*

submissive *a* sumiso, dócil, manso

submissively *adv* sumisamente, con docilidad

submissiveness *n* sumisión, docilidad, *f*

submit *vt* someter (a); doblarse ante; (a scheme, etc.) someter; presentar; (urge) proponer. *vi* someterse; resignarse; (surrender) rendirse, entregarse. **to s. to arbitration,** someter a arbitraje

subnormal *a* anormal

subordinate *a* subordinado; subalterno, inferior; secundario. *n* subordinado (-da). *vt* subordinar

subordination *n* subordinación, *f*

suborn *vt* sobornar, cohechar

subpena *n* citación, *f*, *vt* citar

subplot *n* intriga secundaria, trama secundaria, *f*

subscribe *vt* and *vi* subscribir; (to a periodical, etc.) abonarse (a)

subscriber *n* subscriptor (-ra); abonado (-da)

subscription *n* subscripción, *f*; (to a periodical, series of concerts, etc.) abono, *m*; (to a club) cuota, *f*

subsection *n* subsección, *f*

subsequent *a* subsiguiente, subsecuente; posterior. **s. to,** después de, posterior a. **s. upon,** de resultas de

subsequently *adv* más tarde; subsiguientemente; posteriormente

subservience *n* servilidad, *f*; utilidad, *f*

subservient *a* servil; subordinado; útil

subside *vi* (of water) bajar; (of ground) hundirse; (of foundations) asentarse; disminuir; calmarse; (be quiet) callarse. **to s. into a chair,** dejarse caer en un sillón

subsidence *n* hundimiento, *m*; desplome, derrumbamiento, *m*; (of floods) bajada, *f*; (of anger, etc.) apaciguamiento, *m*

subsidiary *a* subsidiario

subsidize *vt* subvencionar

subsidy *n* subvención, *f*, subsidio, *m*; prima, *f*

subsist *vi* subsistir
subsistence *n* subsistencia, *f*
subsoil *n* subsuelo, *m*
substance *n* substancia, *f*
substantial *a* substancial; sólido; importante
substantially *adv* substancialmente; sólidamente
substantiate *vt* establecer, verificar; justificar
substantiation *n* comprobación, verificación, *f*; justificación, *f*
substantive *a* real, independiente; *gram* substantivo. *n gram* substantivo, *m*
substitute *n* substituto (-ta); (material) substituto, *m. vt* substituir, reemplazar. **to be a s. for,** hacer las veces de
substitution *n* substitución, *f*, reemplazo, *m*
substratum *n* substrato, *m*
subterfuge *n* subterfugio, *m*; evasiva, *f*
subterranean *a* subterráneo
subtitle *n* subtítulo, *m*; (on films) guión, *m*
subtle *a* sutil; delicado; penetrante; (crafty) astuto
subtlety *n* sutileza, *f*; delicadeza, *f*; (craftiness) astucia, *f*
subtly *adv* sutilmente; con delicadeza
subtract *vt* restar, substraer
subtraction *n* resta, substracción, *f*
suburb *n* suburbio, *m*; *pl* **suburbs,** las afueras, *f pl* los arrabales, *m pl*
suburban *a* suburbano
subvention *n* subvención, *f*
subversion *n* subversión, *f*
subversive *a* subversivo
subvert *vt* subvertir
subway *n* (passageway) pasaje subterráneo, *m*; (underground railway) metro (Spain, Puerto Rico), subte (Argentina), *m*
succeed *vt* seguir (a); suceder (a); heredar. *vi* seguir (a); suceder (a); (be successful) tener éxito. **I did not s. in doing it,** No logré hacerlo. **to s. to the throne,** subir al trono
succeeding *a* subsiguiente; futuro; consecutivo; sucesivo
success *n* éxito, *m*; triunfo, *m.* **to be a s.,** tener éxito. **The film was a great s.,** La película tuvo mucho éxito.
successful *a* que tiene éxito; afortunado, venturoso; próspero, *Lat. Am.* exitoso
successfully *adv* con éxito; prósperamente
succession *n* sucesión, *f*; (series) serie, *f*; (inheritance) herencia, *f*; (descendants) descendencia, *f.* **in s.,** sucesivamente
successive *a* sucesivo
successor *n* sucesor (-ra)
succinct *a* sucinto, conciso
succinctly *adv* sucintamente, brevemente, en pocas palabras
succor *vt* socorrer, auxiliar. *n* socorro, *m*, ayuda, *f*
succulence *n* suculencia, *f*
succulent *a* suculento
succumb *vi* sucumbir; someterse, ceder
such *a* tal; parecido, semejante; así; tanto; (before an adjective, adverb) tan. *n* el, *m*, (*f*, la) que, los, *m pl*, (*f pl*, las) que; tal. **s. men,** tales hombres. **I have never seen s. magnificence,** Nunca no he visto tanta magnificencia. **s. an important man,** un hombre tan importante. **s. pictures as these,** cuadros como estos. **S. is life!** ¡Así es la vida! **science as s.,** la ciencia como tal. **s.-and-s.,** tal y tal
suchlike *a* parecido, semejante; de esta clase
suck *vt* chupar; (the breast) mamar; sorber; (of a vacuum cleaner, etc.) aspirar. *n* chupada, *f*; succión, *f.* **to s. down,** tragar. **to s. up,** aspirar; absorber
sucker *n zool* ventosa, *f*; *bot* acodo, mugrón, *m*; (greenhorn) primo, *m*; (pig) lechón, *m*
suckingpig *n* lechón, cochinillo, *m*
suckle *vt* amamantar, dar el pecho (a)
suction *n* succión, *f*; aspiración, *f.* **s.-pump,** bomba aspirante, *f*
Sudan, the el Sudán, *m*

Sudanese *a* and *n* sudanés (-esa)
sudden *a* súbito; (unexpected) inesperado, impensado; (of bends) brusco. **all of a s.,** de repente; súbitamente
suddenly *adv* súbitamente; de pronto, de repente
suddenness *n* carácter repentino, *m*; (of a bend, etc.) brusquedad, *f*
suds *n pl* jabonaduras, *f pl*; espuma, *f*
sue *vt law* proceder contra, pedir en juicio; *law* demandar; (beg) suplicar. **to sue for peace,** pedir la paz
suede *n* ante, *m.* **s. glove,** guante de ante, *m*
suet *n* sebo, *m*
Suez Canal, the el Canal de Suez, *m*
suffer *vt* sufrir, padecer; pasar, experimentar; (tolerate) tolerar, sufrir; (allow) permitir. *vi* sufrir. **She suffers from her environment,** es la víctima de su medio ambiente
sufferance *n* tolerancia, *f.* **on s.,** por tolerancia
sufferer *n* enfermo (-ma); víctima, *f*
suffering *n* sufrimiento, padecimiento, *m*; dolor, *m. a* sufriente
suffice *vi* ser suficiente, bastar. *vt* satisfacer
sufficiency *n* suficiencia, *f*; (of money) subsistencia, *f*
sufficient *a* suficiente, bastante. **to be s.,** bastar, ser suficiente
sufficiently *adv* suficientemente, bastante
suffix *n gram* sufijo, *m*
suffocate *vt* ahogar, sofocar, asfixiar. *vi* sofocarse, asfixiarse
suffocating *a* sofocante, asfixiante
suffocation *n* sofocación, asfixia, *f*; ahogo, *m*
suffrage *n* sufragio, *m*; voto, *m.* **universal s.,** sufragio universal, *m*
suffragette *n* sufragista, *f*
suffuse *vt* bañar, inundar, cubrir
sugar *n* azúcar, *m. vt* azucarar. **brown s.,** azúcar moreno, *m.* **loaf s.,** azúcar de pilón, *m.* **white s.,** azúcar blanco, *m.* **to s. the pill,** dorar la píldora. **s.-almond,** peladilla, *f.* **s.-basin,** azucarera, *f.* **s.-beet,** remolacha, *f.* **s.-candy,** azúcar candi, *m.* **s.-cane,** caña de azúcar, *f.* **s.-cane syrup,** miel de caña, *f.* **s.-paste,** alfeñique, *m*, alcorza, *f.* **s.-refinery,** fábrica de azúcar, *f.* **s.-tongs,** tenacillas para azúcar, *f pl*
sugary *a* azucarado; *fig* meloso, almibarado
suggest *vt* implicar; indicar, dar a entender; sugerir; (advise) aconsejar; (hint) insinuar; (evoke) evocar. **I suggested they should go to London,** Les aconsejé que fueran a Londres. **An idea suggested itself to him,** Se le ocurrió una idea
suggestion *n* sugestión, *f*; insinuación, *f*
suggestive *a* sugestivo; estimulante
suicidal *a* suicida. **s. tendency,** tendencia suicida, tendencia al suicidio, *f*
suicide *n* (act) suicidio, *m*; (person) suicida, *mf.* **to commit s.,** darse la muerte, quitarse la vida suicidarse
suit *n* (request) petición, súplica, *f*; oferta de matrimonio, *f*; *law* pleito, *m*; (of clothes) traje, *Colombia, Venezuela* flus, *m*; (cards) palo, *m*; (of cards held) serie, *f*, *vt* convenir; sentar; ir bien (a); venir bien (a); (adapt) adaptar. **S. yourself!** ¡Haz lo que quieras! **The arrangement suits me very well,** El arreglo me viene muy bien. **The climate doesn't s. me,** El clima no me sienta bien. **The color does not s. you,** El color no te va bien. **to follow s.,** seguir el ejemplo (de); (cards) jugar el mismo palo. **s.-case,** maleta, *f*
suitability *n* conveniencia, *f*; aptitud, *f*
suitable *a* conveniente; apropiado; apto; a propósito. **Not s. for children,** No apto para menores. **to make s. for,** adaptar a las necesidades de
suitably *adv* convenientemente; apropiadamente
suite *n* (of retainers, etc.) séquito, acompañamiento, *m*; (of furniture, etc.) juego, *m*; *mus* suite, *f.* **private s.,** habitaciones particulares, *f pl.* **s. of rooms,** apartamiento, *m*
suitor *n law* demandante, *m*; pretendiente, *m*
sulk *vi* ponerse malhumorado, ser mohíno
sulkiness *n* mohína, *f*, mal humor, *m*

sulky *a* mohíno, malhumorado

sullen *a* taciturno, hosco; malhumorado, sombrío; (of a landscape, etc.) triste, sombrío

sullenly *adv* taciturnamente, hoscamente

sullenness *n* taciturnidad, hosquedad, *f*, mal humor, *m*

sully *vt* desdorar, empañar; manchar

sulphur *n* azufre, *m*

sulphuric *a* sulfúrico

sulphurous *a* sulfuroso

sultan *n* sultán, *m*

sultriness *n* bochorno, calor sofocante, *m*

sultry *a* bochornoso, sofocante

sum *n* suma, *f*; total, *m*; cantidad, *f*; (in arithmetic) problema (de aritmética), *m*. *vt* sumar, calcular. **in sum,** en suma; en resumen. **to sum up,** recapitular; resumir; (a person) tomar las medidas (a)

summarily *adv* someramente; *law* sumariamente

summarize *vt* resumir brevemente; compendiar

summary *a* somero; *law* sumario. *n* resumen, sumario, compendio, *m*. **summary records,** actas resumidas, *f pl*

summer *n* verano, estío, *m*. **to spend the s.,** veranear. **s.-house,** cenador, *m*. **s.-time,** verano, *m*; hora de verano, *f*. **s. wheat,** trigo tremesino, *m*

summing-up *n* recapitulación, *f*

summit *n* cima, cumbre, *f*; *fig* apogeo, *m*

summitry *n* diplomacia en la cumbre, *f*

summon *vt* llamar, hacer venir; mandar, requerir; *law* citar. **to s. up one's courage,** cobrar ánimos

summons *n* llamamiento, *m*; *mil* intimación, *f*; *law* citación, *f*. *vt law* citar

sump *n* (of a motor-car) pozo colector, *m*; *min* sumidero, *m*

sumptuous *a* suntuoso, lujoso, magnífico

sumptuousness *n* suntuosidad, magnificencia, *f*

sun *n* sol, *m*. **The sun was shining,** Hacía sol, El sol brillaba. **to bask in the sun,** tomar el sol. **sun-bathing,** baños de sol, *m pl*. **sun-blind,** toldo para el sol, *m*. **sun-bonnet,** capelina, *f*. **sun-glasses,** gafas ahumadas, *f pl*. **sun-helmet,** casco colonial, *m*. **sun-spot,** *ast* mancha del sol, *f*; (freckle) peca, *f*. **sun-worship,** adoración del sol, *f*

sunbeam *n* rayo de sol, *m*

sunburn *n* quemadura del sol, *f*; bronceado, *m*

sunburnt *a* quemado por el sol; bronceado, tostado por el sol

sundae *n* helado de frutas, *m*

Sunday *n* domingo, *m*. **in his S. best,** en su traje dominguero, endomingado. **S. school,** escuela dominical, *f*

Sunday's child *n* niño nacido de pies, niño nacido un domingo, niño mimado de la fortuna

sunder *vt* dividir en dos, hender; separar

sundial *n* reloj de sol, reloj solar, *m*

sundown *n* puesta del sol, *f*

sundry *a* varios (-as). *n pl* **sundries,** artículos diversos, *m pl*; *com* varios, *m pl*. **all and s.,** todo el mundo, todos y cada uno

sunflower *n* girasol, tornasol, *m*, trompeta de amor, *f*

sunken *a* (of eyes, etc.) hundido

sun letter *n* letra solar, *f*

sunless *a* sin sol

sunlight *n* luz del sol, *f*, rayos del sol, *m pl*. **artificial s.,** sol artificial, *m*. **in the s.,** al sol

sunny *a* de sol; bañado de sol; asoleado; expuesto al sol; (face) risueño; (of disposition, etc.) alegre. **to be s.,** hacer sol

sunrise *n* salida del sol, *f*. **from s. to sunset,** de sol a sol

sunset *n* puesta del sol, *f*. **at s.,** a la caída (or puesta) del sol

sunshade *n* parasol, quitasol, *m*, sombrilla, *f*

sunshine *n* luz del sol, *f*. **in the s.,** al sol

sunstroke *n* insolación, *f*

sup *vt* sorber. *vi* cenar. *n* sorbo, *m*

super *n* (actor) comparsa, *mf*; (film) superproducción, *f*; (of a beehive) alza, *f*

superabundance *n* superabundancia, sobreabundancia, *f*

superabundant *a* superabundante, sobreabundante. **to be s.,** sobreabundar

superannuate *vt* (retire) jubilar

superannuated *a* (retired) jubilado; (out-of-date) anticuado

superannuation *n* (retirement and pension) jubilación, *f*

superb *a* magnífico, espléndido

superbly *adv* magníficamente

supercargo *n naut* sobrecargo, *m*

supercharger *n* (aut, aer) compresor, *m*

supercilious *a* altanero, altivo, orgulloso; desdeñoso

superciliousness *n* altanería, altivez, *f*, orgullo, *m*; desdén, *m*

superficial *a* superficial

superficiality *n* superficialidad, *f*

superficially *adv* superficialmente

superfine *a* superfino

superfluity *n* superfluidad, *f*

superfluous *a* superfluo. **to be s.,** sobrar

superfortress *n aer* superfortaleza volante, *f*

superhuman *a* sobrehumano

superimpose *vt* sobreponer

superintend *vt* superentender, dirigir

superintendent *n* superintendente, *mf*; director (-ra); (school) inspector; (police) subjefe de la policía, *m*

superior *a* superior; (in number) mayor; (smug) desdeñoso. *n* superior (-ra). **Mother S.,** (madre) superiora, *f*. **s. to,** superior a; encima de

superiority *n* superioridad, *f*

superlative *a* extremo, supremo; *gram* superlativo. *n gram* superlativo, *m*

superlatively *adv* en sumo grado, superlativamente

superman *n* superhombre, *m*

supernatural *a* sobrenatural

supernumerary *a and n* supernumerario (-ia)

superposition *n* superposición, *f*

superscribe *vt* sobrescribir; poner el sobrescrito (a)

superscription *n* (on letters, documents) sobrescrito, *m*; leyenda, *f*

supersede *vt* reemplazar; suplantar

supersensible *a* suprasensible

superstition *n* superstición, *f*

superstitious *a* supersticioso

supertax *n* impuesto suplementario, *m*

supervene *vi* sobrevenir

supervise *vt* superentender, vigilar; dirigir

supervision *n* superintendencia, *f*; dirección, *f*

supervisor *n* superintendente, *mf*; inspector (-ra); director (-ra)

supine *a* supino; indolente, negligente. *n gram* supino, *m*

supper *n* cena, *f*. **the Last S.,** la Última Cena. **to have s.,** cenar. **s.-time,** hora de cenar, *f*

supplant *vt* suplantar; usurpar; reemplazar

supplanter *n* suplantador (-ra)

supple *a* flexible; dócil, manso; (fawning) adulador, servil, lisonjero

supplement *n* suplemento, *m*; (of a book) apéndice, *m*

supplementary *a* suplementario; adicional

suppleness *n* flexibilidad, *f*; docilidad, *f*; servilidad, *f*

suppliant *a and n* suplicante, *mf*

supplicate *vt and vi* suplicar

supplication *n* suplicación, *f*; súplica, *f*

supply *vt* proveer (de); suministrar; proporcionar, dar; (a deficiency) suplir; (a post) llenar; (a post temporarily) reemplazar. *n* suministro, surtimiento, *m*; provisión, *f*; (of electricity, etc.) suministro, *m*; *com* oferta, *f*; (person) substituto (-ta); *pl* **supplies,** *com* existencias, *f pl*; *mil* pertrechos, *m pl*; víveres, *m pl*, provisiones, *f pl*. **s. and demand,** oferta y demanda, *f*

support *vt* apoyar, sostener; mantener; (endure) soportar; (a cause) apoyar, defender; (corroborate) confirmar, vindicar. *n* apoyo, *m*; sostén, *m*; soporte, *m*. **to**

speak in s. of, defender, abogar por. **to s. oneself,** ganarse la vida, mantenerse

supporter *n* apoyo, *m*; defensor (-ra); partidario (-ia)

suppose *vt* suponer; imaginar(se); creer. **always supposing,** dado que, en el caso de que. **Supposing he had gone out?** ¿Y si hubiera salido? **I don't s. they will go to Spain,** No creo que vayan a España. **He is supposed to be clever,** Tiene fama de listo

supposed *a* supuesto; que se llama a sí mismo

supposition *n* suposición, hipótesis, *f*

suppress *vt* reprimir; (yawns, etc.) ahogar; contener; (heresies, rebellions, books, etc.) suprimir; (dissemble) disimular, esconder; (a heckler, etc.) hacer callar

suppressed *a* reprimido; contenido; disimulado

suppression *n* represión, *f*; supresión, *f*; disimulación, *f*

suppurate *vi* supurar

suppuration *n* supuración, *f*

supremacy *n* supremacía, *f*

supreme *a* supremo; sumo. **with s. indifference,** con suma indiferencia. **s. court,** tribunal supremo, *m*

surcharge *n* sobrecarga, *f*

sure *a* seguro; cierto. *adv* seguramente. **Be s. to . . . !** ¡Ten cuidado de . . . ! ¡No dejes de . . . ! **to be s.,** seguramente, sin duda; ¡claro!; (fancy!) ¡no me digas!; ¡qué sorpresa! **I am not so s. of that,** No diría yo tanto. **Come on Thursday for s.,** Venga el jueves sin falta. **It is s. to rain tomorrow,** Seguramente va a llover mañana. **to make s. of,** asegurarse de. **to be (or feel) s.,** estar seguro. **s.-footed,** de pie firme, seguro

surely *adv* seguramente; sin duda, ciertamente; por supuesto

sureness *n* seguridad, *f*; certeza, *f*

surety *n* garantía, fianza, *f*; (person) garante, *mf*. **to go s. for,** ser fiador (de), salir garante (por)

surf *n* resaca, *f*; rompiente, *m*; oleaje, *m*. **s.-board,** aquaplano, *m*. **s.-riding,** patinaje sobre las olas, *m*

surface *n* superficie, *f*; exterior, *m*. *a* superficial. *vi* (of a submarine) salir a la superficie. **on the s.,** en apariencia

surface mail *n* correo por vía ordinaria, servicio ordinario, servicio per vía de superficie, *m*

surfeit *n* exceso, *m*, superabundancia, *f*; saciedad, *f*. *vt* hartar; saciar

surge *vi* (of waves) embravecerse, hincharse; (of crowds) agitarse, bullir; (of emotions) despertarse. *n* (of sea, crowd, blood) oleada, *f*; (of anger) ola, *f*. **The blood surged into his face,** La sangre se le subió a las mejillas

surgeon *n* cirujano, *m*; (nav, mil) médico, *m*

surgery *n* cirugía, *f*; (doctor's) consultorio, *m*; (dispensary) dispensario, *m*

surgical *a* quirúrgico

surliness *n* mal genio, *m*, taciturnidad, *f*; brusquedad, *f*

surly *a* taciturno, huraño, malhumorado; brusco

surmise *n* conjetura, suposición, *f*. *vt* conjeturar, adivinar; imaginar, suponer. *vi* hacer conjeturas

surmount *vt* superar, vencer; coronar

surname *n* apellido, *m*, *vt* denominar, nombrar

surpass *vt* superar, exceder; aventajarse (a); eclipsar

surpassing *a* sin par, incomparable

surplus *n* exceso, sobrante, *m*; (com of accounts) superávit, *m*. **sale of s. stock,** liquidación de saldos, *f*

surplusage *n* material de desecho, *m*

surprise *n* sorpresa, *f*; asombro, *m*. *vt* sorprender; asombrar. **to s.** (someone) **in the act,** coger en el acto. **to take** (a person) **by s.,** sorprender (a). **He was surprised into admitting it,** Cogido a la imprevista, lo confesó

surprising *a* sorprendente

surrealism *n* surrealismo, *m*

surrealist *a* and *n* surrealista, *mf*

surrender *vt* rendir, entregar; (goods) ceder, renunciar (a). *vi* rendirse, entregarse; abandonarse. *n* rendición, capitulación, *f*; entrega, *f*; (of goods) cesión, *f*; (of an insurance policy) rescate, *m*. **to s. oneself to remorse,** abandonarse (or entregarse) al remor-

dimiento. **to s. unconditionally,** entregarse a discreción

surreptitious *a* subrepticio

surreptitiously *adv* subrepticiamente, a hurtadillas

surround *vt* rodear; cercar; *mil* asediar, sitiar. *n* borde, *m*. **Peter was surrounded by his friends,** Pedro estaba rodeado por sus amigos

surrounding *a* (que está) alrededor de; vecino. **the s. country,** los alrededores

surroundings *n pl* cercanías, *f pl*, alrededores, *m pl*; (environment) medio, *m*; (medio) ambiente, *m*

surtax *n* impuesto suplementario, *m*

surveillance *n* vigilancia, *f*

survey *vt* contemplar, mirar; (events, etc.) pasar en revista; estudiar; (land, etc.) agrimensurar; (of facts, etc.) inspeccionar. *n* vista general, *f*; inspección, *f*; (of facts, etc.) examen, *m*; estudio, *m*; (of land, etc.) apeo, *m*; (of literature, etc.) bosquejo, breve panorama, *m*

surveying *n* agrimensura, *f*

surveyor *n* agrimensor, *m*; (superintendent) inspector, *m*; superintendente, *m*

survival *n* supervivencia, *f*. **s. of the fittest,** supervivencia de los más aptos, *f*

survive *vt* sobrevivir a. *vi* sobrevivir; (of customs) subsistir, durar

survivor *n* sobreviviente, *mf*

susceptibility *n* susceptibilidad, *f*; tendencia, *f*; *pl* **susceptibilities,** sensibilidad, *f*

susceptible *a* susceptible; impresionable; sensible; (to love) enamoradizo. **He is s. to bronchitis,** Es susceptible a la bronquitis

suspect *a* and *n* sospechoso (-sa). *vt* sospechar; dudar; imaginar, suponer. *vi* tener sospechas

suspend *vt* suspender. **suspended animation,** muerte aparente, *f*

suspender *n* liga, *f*; *pl* **suspenders,** (braces) tirantes del pantalón, *m pl*. **s.-belt,** faja, *f*

suspense *n* incertidumbre, *f*. **to keep** (a person) **in s.,** dejar en la incertidumbre (a)

suspension *n* suspensión, *f*. **s.-bridge,** puente colgante, *m*. **s. of payments,** suspensión de pagos, *f*

suspicion *n* sospecha, *f*; (touch) dejo, *m*; cantidad muy pequeña, *f*. **to be above s.,** estar por encima de toda sospecha. **to be under s.,** estar bajo sospecha. **I had no suspicions . . . ,** No sospechaba . . .

suspicious *a* (by nature) suspicaz; sospechoso. **to make s.,** hacer sospechar

suspiciously *adv* suspicazmente, desconfiadamente; de un modo sospechoso. **It seems s. like . . . ,** Tiene toda la apariencia de . . .

suspiciousness *n* carácter sospechoso, *m*, lo sospechoso; suspicacia, *f*

sustain *vt* sostener; mantener; sustentar; apoyar; corroborar, confirmar; (a note) prolongar. **to s. injuries,** recibir heridas

sustenance *n* mantenimiento, *m*; sustento, *m*, alimentos, *m pl*

suture *n* sutura, *f*

svarabhakti *adj* esvarabático

svelte *a* esbelto, gentil

swab *vt naut* lampacear; limpiar con lampazo; *surg* taponar. *n* lampazo, *m*; *surg* torunda, *f*, tampón, *m*

swaddle *vt* envolver; (infants) fajar

swaddling clothes *n pl* pañales, *m pl*. **to be still in s. clothes,** *fig* estar en mantillas, estar en pañales

swagger *vi* fanfarronear, pavonearse; darse importancia. *n* pavoneo, *m*; aire importante, *m*; (coat) tonto, *m*. *a* majo; de última moda

swaggering *a* fanfarrón, jactancioso; importante

Swahili suaili; *n* suaili, *m*

swain *n* zagal, *m*; enamorado, *m*; pretendiente, amante, *m*

swallow *vt* tragar, engullir. *n* trago, *m*; sorbo, *m*; *orn* golondrina, *f*. **to s. an insult (a story),** tragar un insulto (una historia). **to s. one's words,** retractarse. **to**

s. one's pride, bajar la cerviz, humillarse. **to s. up,** tragar; absorber. **s.-tailed coat,** frac, *m*

swamp *n* pantano, *m*, marisma, *f, Argentina* fachinal, *f, Central America* chagüe, *m. vt* sumergir; (a boat) echar a pique, hundir; (inundate) inundar

swampy *a* pantanoso

swan *n* cisne, *m*. **swan's down,** plumón de cisne, *m*. **s.-song,** canto del cisne, *m*

swank *n* pretensiones, *f pl, vi* darse humos

sward *n* césped, *m*, hierba, *f*

swarm *n* enjambre, *m*; (of people) muchedumbre, multitud, *f*; tropel, *m. vi* (of bees) enjambrar; (of other insects) pulular; (of carriages) (of people) hormiguear, bullir, pulular. *vt* (climb) trepar. **to s. with,** estar infestado de

swarthiness *n* tez morena, *f*; color moreno, *m*

swarthy *a* moreno

swashbuckler *n* perdonavidas, matasiete, *m*

swashbuckling *a* matamoros, valentón, fanfarrón

swastika *n* esvástica, cruz gamada, *f*

swathe *vt* envolver; fajar; (with bandages) vendar

swathing *n* envoltura, *f*; (bandages) vendas, *f pl*

sway *vi* balancearse; oscilar; (stagger, of persons) bambolearse; (totter, of things) tambalearse; (of carriages) cabecear; (gracefully, in walking) cimbrarse. *vt* balancear, mecer; oscilar; hacer tambalear; (influence) influir, inclinar; (govern) regir, gobernar. *n* balanceo, *m*; oscilación, *f*; vaivén, *m*; tambaleo, *m*; (influence) ascendiente, dominio, *m*, influencia, *f*; (rule) imperio, poder, *m*. **to hold s. over,** gobernar, regir

swear *vt* jurar; (*law* etc.) declarar bajo juramento. *vi* jurar; (curse) echar pestes, blasfemar. **to s. at,** maldecir. **to s. by,** jurar por; poner fe implícita en. **to be sworn in,** prestar juramento. **to s. in,** tomar juramento (a). **to s. to,** atestiguar

sweat *n* sudor, *m*, *inf* trabajo arduo, *m. vi* sudar. *vt* sudar; hacer sudar; (workers) explotar. **by the s. of one's brow,** con el sudor de la frente, con el sudor del rostro. **s.-gland,** glándula sudorípara, *f*

sweated *a* (of persons) explotado; (of labor) mal retribuido

sweater *n* suéter, jersey, *m*

sweating *n* transpiración, *f*; (of workers) explotación, *f*

sweaty *a* sudoroso

Swede *n* sueco (-ca); (vegetable) naba, *f*

Sweden Suecia, *f*

sweep *vi* extenderse (por); (cleave) surcar; pasar rápidamente (por); invadir; dominar; andar majestuosamente; (with a brush) barrer. *vt* barrer; pasar (por); (the strings of a musical instrument) rasguear; (the sea) navegar por; (mines) barrer; (the horizon, etc.) examinar; (a chimney) deshollinar; (with a brush) barrer; (remove) arrebatar; quitar; llevarse; (abolish) suprimir. **to s. along,** *vt* (of the current, crowds, etc.) arrastrar. *vi* pasar majestuosamente; correr rápidamente (por). **to s. aside,** apartar con la mano; abandonar; (a protest) desoír, no hacer caso de. **to s. away,** barrer; (remove) llevarse; destruir; suprimir. **to s. down,** *vt* barrer; (carry) arrastrar. *vi* (of cliffs, etc.) bajar; (of an enemy) abalanzarse (sobre); lanzarse (por). **to s. off,** barrer; (a person) llevarse sin perder tiempo; arrebatar con violencia (a). **to be swept off one's feet,** ser arrastrado (por); perder el balance; (of emotion) ser dominado por. **to s. on,** seguir su avance inexorable; seguir su marcha. **to s. up,** recoger, barrer

sweep *n* barredura, *f*; (of a chimney) deshollinador, *m*; (of the tide) curso, *m*; (of a scythe, etc.) golpe, *m*; (range) alcance, *m*; (fold) pliegue, *m*; (curve) curva, *f*; (of water, etc.) extensión, *f*; (of wings) envergadura, *f*. **with a s. of the arm,** con un gesto del brazo. **to make a clean s. of,** hacer tabla rasa de

sweeping *a* completo; comprensivo; demasiado general; radical. **a s. judgment,** un juicio demasiado general. **s. change,** cambio radicale, *m pl*. **s. brush,** escoba, *f*

sweepings *n pl* barreduras, *f pl*; residuos, *m pl*; (of society) heces, *f pl*

sweepstake *n* lotería, *f*

sweet *a* dulce; (of scents) oloroso, fragante; (of sounds) melodioso, dulce; (charming) encantador; amable; (pretty) bonito. *n* bombón, *m*; golosina, *f*; (at a meal) (plato) dulce, *m*; dulzura, *f*; (beloved) amor, *m*, querido (-da). **How s. it smells!** ¡Qué buen olor tiene! **the sweets of life,** las dulzuras de la vida. **s.-pea,** guisante de olor, *m*, haba de las Indias, *f*. **s.-potato,** batata, *f, Lat. Am.* boniato, camote, *m*. **s.-scented,** perfumado, fragante. **s.-tempered,** amable, de carácter dulce. **s.-toothed,** goloso. **s.-william,** *bot* clavel de la China, clavel de ramillete, clavel de San Isidro, ramillete de Constantinopla, *m*, minutisa, *f*

sweetbread *n* lechecillas, *f pl*

sweeten *vt* azucarar; endulzar. **Cervantes sweetens one's bitter moments,** Cervantes endulza los momentos ásperos

sweetheart *n* amante, *mf*, amado (-da); (as address) querido (-da)

sweetish *a* algo dulce

sweetly *adv* dulcemente; (of scents) olorosamente; (of sounds) melodiosamente; (of behaviour, etc.) amablemente

sweetness *n* dulzura, *f*; (of scents) buen olor, *m*, fragancia, *f*; (of sounds) melodía, dulzura, *f*; (of character) bondad, amabilidad, *f*

sweet potato *n* batata, *f*, boniato, buniato, camote, *m*

sweet sixteen *n* (age) los dieciséis abriles, *m pl*; (party) quinceañera (at age fifteen) *f*

sweet turnip *Central America* jícama, *f*

swell *vi* hincharse; (of the sea) entumecerse; crecer; aumentarse. *vt* hinchar; aumentar. *n* (of the sea) oleada, *f*, oleaje, *m*; (of the ground) ondulación, *f*; (of sound) crescendo, *m*; (increase) aumento, *m*; (dandy) pisaverde, elegante, *m*; (important person) pájaro gordo, *m*; (at games, etc.) espada, *m*. *a* estupendo; elegantísimo; de primera, excelente. **to suffer from swelled head,** tener humos, darse importancia. **This foot is swollen,** Este pie está hinchado (or tumefacto). **The refugees have swelled the population,** Los refugiados han aumentado la población. **eyes swollen with tears,** ojos arrasados de lágrimas. **to s. with pride,** hincharse de orgullo

swelling *n* hinchazón, *f*; *med* tumefacción, *f*; (bruise, etc.) chichón, *m*

swelter *vi* abrasarse; arder. *n* bochorno, calor sofocante, *m*

swerve *vi* desviarse; apartarse (de); torcerse. *n* desvío, *m*

swift *a* rápido, veloz; pronto. *adv* velozmente, rápidamente. *n orn* vencejo, *m*. **s.-flowing,** (of rivers, etc.) de corriente rápida. **s.-footed,** de pies ligeros

swiftly *adv* rápidamente, velozmente

swiftness *n* rapidez, velocidad, *f*; prontitud, *f*

swim *vi* nadar; flotar; (glide) deslizarse; (fill) inundarse. *vt* (a horse) hacer nadar; pasar a nado; nadar. *n* natación, *f*. **eyes swimming with tears,** ojos inundados de lágrimas. **He enjoys a s.,** Le gusta nadar. **My head swims,** Se me va la cabeza. **Everything swam before my eyes,** Todo parecía bailar ante mis ojos. **to be in the s.,** formar parte (de), ser (de); (be up to date) estar al corriente. **to s. the Channel,** atravesar el canal de la Mancha a nado. **to s. with the tide,** Nada mal corriente

swimmer *n* nadador (-ra). **He is a bad s.,** Nada mal

swimming *n* natación, *f*; (of the head) vértigo, *m*. **s.-bath,** piscina, *f*. **s.-costume,** traje de baño, *m*. **s.-pool,** piscina, *Lat. Am.* alberca, *f*

swindle *vt* engañar, estafar; defraudar (de). *n* estafa, *f*, timo, *m*; engaño, *m*; impostura, *f, Lat. Am.* cambullón, *Argentina* forro, *m*

swindler *n* estafador (-ra), trampeador (-ra); engañador (-ra)

swine *n* cerdo, puerco, *m*; (person) cochino (-na). **a herd of s.,** una manada de cerdos

swineherd *n* porquero, *m*

swing *vi* balancearse; oscilar; (hang) colgar, pender; columpiarse; girar; dar la vuelta; (of a boat) bornear. *vt* balancear; (hang) colgar; (rock) mecer; (in a swing, etc.) columpiar; hacer oscilar; (raise) subir. *n* oscilación, *f*; vaivén, *m*; balanceo, *m*; (rhythm) ritmo, *m*; (seat, etc.) columpio, *m*; (reach) alcance, *m*. **The door swung open,** La puerta se abrió silenciosamente. **He swung the car round,** Dio la vuelta al auto. **He swung himself into the saddle,** Montó de un salto. **to be in full s.,** estar a toda marcha. **to go with a s.,** tener mucho éxito. **s.-boat,** columpio, *m*. **s.-bridge,** puente giratorio, *m*. **s.-door,** puerta giratoria, *f*

swinging *a* oscilante; pendiente; rítmico. *n* balanceo, *m*; oscilación, *f*; vaivén, *m*; ritmo, *m*. **s. stride,** andar rítmico, *m*

swinish *a* porcuno, de cerdo; cochino, sucio

swipe *vt* golpear duro; aplastar; (steal) *Mexico* chalequear. *n* golpe fuerte, *m*

swirl *vi* arremolinarse. *n* remolino, *m*

swish *vt* (of an animal's tail) agitar, mover, menear; (of a cane) blandir; (thrash) azotar. *vi* silbar; (of water) susurrar; (of a dress, etc.) crujir. *n* silbo, *m*; (of water) susurro, murmullo, *m*; (of a dress, etc.) crujido, *m*

Swiss *a* and *n* suizo (-za)

switch *n* vara, *f*; (riding) látigo, *m*; (of hair) trenza, *f*; *elec* interruptor, *m*; *rw* aguja, *f*; (*rw* siding) desviadero, *m*. *vt* azotar; (a train) desviar; *elec* interrumpir; (transfer) trasladar; (of an animal, its tail) remover, mover rápidamente. **to s. off,** (*elec* and telephone) cortar; (*rad* and *aut*) desconectar. **to s. on,** conectar; (a light) poner (la luz); (a radio) encender

switchboard *n* cuadro de distribución, *m*

Switzerland Suiza, *f*

swivel *n* torniquete, *m*; anillo móvil, *m*; pivote, *m*. *vi* girar sobre un eje; dar una vuelta. **s.-chair,** silla giratoria, *f*. **s.-door,** puerta giratoria, *f*

swoon *vi* desvanecerse, desmayarse. *n* desmayo, desvanecimiento, *m*

swoop *vi* calarse, abatirse; (of robbers, etc.) abalanzarse (sobre). *n* calada, *f*. **at one fell s.,** de un solo golpe

sword *n* espada, *f*; sable, *m*. **to measure swords with,** cruzar espadas con. **to put to the s.,** pasar a cuchillo (a). **s.-arm,** brazo derecho, *m*. **s.-belt,** talabarte, *m*. **s.-cut,** sablazo, *m*. **s.-dance,** danza de espadas, *f*. **s.-fish,** pez espada, pez sierra, espadarte, *m*, jifia, *f*. **s.-play,** esgrima, *f*; manejo de la espada, *m*. **s.-stick,** bastón de estoque, *m*. **s.-thrust,** golpe de espada, *m*; estocada, *f*

swordsman *n* espadachín, *m*; esgrimidor, *m*

swordsmanship *n* manejo de la espada, *m*; esgrima, *f*

sybarite *a* and *n* sibarita, *mf*

sybaritic *a* sibarítico, sibarita

sycamore *n* sicomoro, *m*; falso plátano, *m*

sycophancy *n* servilismo, *m*

sycophant *n* sicofanta, *m*

syllabic *a* silábico

syllable *n* sílaba, *f*

syllabus *n* programa, *m*; compendio, *m*

syllogism *n* silogismo, *m*

sylph *n* sílfide, *f*, silfo, *m*; (woman) sílfide, *f*; (hummingbird) colibrí, *m*. **s.-like,** de sílfide; como una sílfide

sylvan *a* selvático, silvestre; rústico

symbiosis *n* simbiosis, *f*

symbol *n* símbolo, emblema, *m*; *math* símbolo, *m*; (of rank, etc.) insignia, *f*

symbolical *a* simbólico

symbolism *n* simbolismo, *m*

symbolist *n* simbolista, *mf*

symbolize *vt* simbolizar

symmetrical *a* simétrico

symmetry *n* simetría, *f*

sympathetic *a* simpático; compasivo; (of the public, etc.) bien dispuesto. *n anat* gran simpático, *m*. **s. words,** palabras de simpatía, *f pl*. **s. ink,** tinta simpática, *f*

sympathetically *adv* simpáticamente; con compasión

sympathize *vi* simpatizar (con); (understand) comprender; (condole) compadecerse (de), condolerse (de); dar el pésame

sympathizer *n* partidario (-ia)

sympathy *n* simpatía, *f*; compasión, *f*. **Paul is in s. with their aims,** Pablo está de acuerdo con sus objetos. **Please accept my s.,** (on a bereavement) Le acompaño a Vd. en su sentimiento

symphonic *a* sinfónico

symphony *n* sinfonía, *f*

symposium *n* colección de artículos, *f*

symptom *n* síntoma, *m*; señal, *f*, indicio, *m*. **to show symptoms of,** dar indicios de

symptomatic *a* sintomático

synagogue *n* sinagoga, *f*

synchronization *n* sincronización, *f*

synchronize *vi* coincidir, tener lugar simultáneamente; sincronizarse. *vt* sincronizar

synchronous *a* sincrónico

syncopate *vt* (*gram mus*) sincopar

syncopation *n mus* síncopa, *f*

syncope *n* (*med gram*) síncope, *m*

syndical *a* sindical

syndicalism *n* sindicalismo, *m*

syndicalist *n* sindicalista, *mf*

syndicate *n* sindicato, *m*, *vt* sindicar

syndication *n* sindicación, *f*

synod *n ecc* sínodo, *m*

synonym *n* sinónimo, *m*

synonymous *a* sinónimo

synopsis *n* sinopsis, *f*

synoptic *a* sinóptico

syntax *n* sintaxis, *f*

synthesis *n* síntesis, *f*

synthetic *a* sintético

synthetize *vt* sintetizar

syphilis *n* sífilis, *f*

syphilitic *a* and *n* sifilítico (-ca)

Syracuse Siracusa, *f*

syren *n*. See **siren**

Syria Siria, *f*

Syrian *a* and *n* siríaco (-ca), sirio (-ia)

syringe *n* jeringa, *f*, *vt* jeringar

syrup *n* jarabe, *m*; (for bottling fruit, etc.) almíbar, *m*

syrup cake *Argentina* chancaca, *f*

syrupy *a* siroposo

system *n* sistema, *m*; régimen, *m*; método, *m*; (body) organismo, *m*. **He has no s. in his work,** No tiene método en su trabajo. **the nervous s.,** el sistema nervioso. **the feudal s.,** el feudalismo, el sistema feudal

systematic *a* sistemático, metódico

systematically *adv* sistemáticamente, metódicamente

systematization *n* sistematización, *f*

systematize *vt* sistematizar

systole *n med* sístole, *f*

T

t *n* (letter) te, *f. a* en T, en forma de T. **T bandage,** vendaje en T, *m*. **T square,** regla T, *f*
tab *n* oreja, *f*
tabby *n* gato romano, *m*; (female) gata, *f*; *inf* vieja chismosa, *f*
tabernacle *n* tabernáculo, *m*; templo, *m*; *arch* templete, *m*; *ecc* custodia, *f*
tabes *n med* tabes, *f*
table *n* mesa, *f*; (food) comida, mesa, *f*; (of the law, weights, measures, contents, etc.) tabla, *f*; (of land) meseta, *f*; (of prices) lista, tarifa, *f. vt* (parliament) poner sobre la mesa; enumerar, apuntar, hacer una lista de. **to clear the t.,** alzar (or levantar) la mesa. **to lay the t.,** cubrir (or poner) la mesa. **to have a t.-d'hôte meal,** tomar el menú. **to rise from t.,** levantarse de la mesa. **to sit down to t.,** ponerse a la mesa. **The tables are turned,** Se volvió la tortilla. **side t.,** aparador, trinchero, *m*. **small t.,** mesilla, *f*. **t. of contents,** tabla de materias, *f*, índice, índice de materias, índice general, *m*. **t.-centrepiece,** centro de mesa, *m*. **t.-cloth,** mantel, *m*. **t.-companion,** comensal, *mf* **t.-knife,** cuchillo de mesa, *m*. **t.-lamp,** quinqué, *m*; lámpara de mesa, *f*. **t.-land,** meseta, *f*. **t.-leg,** pata de una mesa, *f*. **t.-linen,** mantelería, *f*. **t.-napkin,** servilleta, *f*. **t.-runner,** camino de mesa, *m*. **t.-spoon,** cuchara para los legumbres, *f*. **t.-talk,** conversación de sobremesa, *f*. **t.-turning,** mesas que dan vueltas, *f pl*. **t.-ware,** artículos para la mesa, *m pl*
table d'hôte *n Spain* el menú, *m*, *Mexico* comida corrida *f*
tableau *n* cuadro, *m*. **tableaux vivants,** cuadros vivos, *m pl*
tablespoonful *n* cucharada, *f*
tablet *n* tabla, *f*; (with inscription) tarjeta, losa, lápida, *f*; *med* comprimido, *m*, tableta, *f*; (of soap, chocolate) pastilla, *f*. **writing t.,** taco de papel, *m*
tabloid *n* comprimido, *m*, pastilla, *f*
taboo *n* tabú, *m. a* prohibido, tabú. *vt* declarar tabú, prohibir
tabor *n mus* tamboril, tamborín, *m*. **t. player,** tamborilero, *m*
tabouret *n* (stool) taburete, *m*; (for embroidery) tambor de bordar, *m*; *mus* tamborilete, *m*
tabulate *vt* resumir en tablas; hacer una lista de, catalogar
tabulation *n* distribución en tablas, *f*
tacit *a* tácito
taciturn *a* taciturno, sombrío, reservado, de pocas palabras
tack *n* (nail) tachuela, puntilla, *f*; *sew* hilván, embaste, *m*; *naut* amura, *f*; *naut* puño de amura, *m*; *naut* bordada, *f*; *fig* cambio de política, *m. vt* clavar con tachuelas; *sew* hilvanar, embastar; *fig* añadir. *vi naut* virar; *fig* cambiar de política, adoptar un nuevo plan de acción. **t. puller,** sacabrocas, *m*
tackle *n* aparejo, *m*; maniobra, *f*; *naut* cuadernal, *m*, jarcia, *f*; (gear) aparejos, avíos, *m pl*; (football) carga, *f*. *vt* agarrar, asir; *fig* atacar, abordar; (football) cargar; (undertake) emprender; (a problem) luchar con. **t.-block,** polea, *f*
tacky *a* pegajoso, viscoso
tact *n* tacto, *m*, discreción, diplomacia, delicadeza, *f*
tactful *a* lleno de tacto, diplomático, discreto
tactfully *adv* discretamente, diplomáticamente
tactical *a* táctico
tactically *adv* según la táctica; del punto de vista táctico
tactician *n* táctico, *m*
tactics *n pl* táctica, *f*
tactile *a* táctil; tangible
tactless *a* que no tiene tacto, sin tacto alguno, indiscreto

tactlessly *adv* impolíticamente, indiscretamente
tactlessness *n* falta de tacto, *f*
tadpole *n* renacuajo, *m*
taffeta *n* tafetán, *m*
tag *n* herrete, *m*; (label) marbete, *m*, etiqueta, *f*; (of tail) punta del rabo, *f*; (of boot) tirador de bota, *m*; (game) marro, *m*; (rag) arrapiezo, *m*; (quotation) cita bien conocida, *f*; (of song, poem) refrán, *m*. **to play t.,** jugar al marro
Tagus *n* el Tajo, *m*
tail *n* cola, *f*, rabo, *m*; (plait) trenza, *f*; (wisp of hair) mechón, *m*; (of a comet) cola, cabellera, *f*; (of a note in music) rabito, *m*; (of a coat) faldón, *m*; (of a kite) cola, *f*; (of the eye), rabo, *m*; (retinue) séquito, *m*, banda, *f*; (of an aeroplane) cola, *f*; (end) fin, *m*; (of coin) cruz, *f*; (line) fila, cola, *f. vt* seguir de cerca, pisarle (a uno) los talones. **to t. after,** seguir de cerca. **to t. away,** disminuir; desaparecer, perderse de vista. **to t. on,** unir, juntar. **to turn t.,** volver la espalda, poner los pies en polvorosa. **with the t. between the legs,** con el rabo entre piernas. **t.-board,** (of a cart) escalera, *f*. **t.-coat,** frac, *m*. **t.-end,** extremo, *m*; fin, *m*; lo último. **t.-feather,** pena, *f*. **t.-fin,** aleta caudal, *f*; *aer* timón de dirección, *m*. **t.-light,** farol trasero, *m*, *Mexico* calavera, *f*. **t.-piece,** (of a violin, etc.) cola, *f*; *print* marmoset, culo de lámpara, *m*. **t. spin** *aer* barrena de cola, *f*. **t. wind,** viento de cola, *m*
tailed *a* de rabo. **big-t.,** rabudo, de cola grande. **long-t.,** rabilargo. **short-t.,** rabicorto
tailless *a* rabón, sin rabo
tailor *n* sastre, *m*. **t.-made,** *n* traje sastre, *m*, *a* de hechura de sastre. **tailor's shop,** sastrería, *f*
tailoress *n* sastra, *f*
tailoring *n* sastrería, *f*; (work) corte, *m*
taint *n* corrupción, *f*; infección, *f*; (blemish) mancha, *f*; (tinge) dejo, *m. vt* corromper, pervertir; inficionar; (meat) corromper. *vi* corromperse, inficionarse; (meat) corromperse
take *vt* tomar; (receive) aceptar; (remove) quitar; (pick up) coger; (grab) asir, agarrar; *math* restar; (carry) llevar; (a person) traer, llevar; (guide) conducir, guiar; (win) ganar; (earn) cobrar, percibir; obtener; (make prisoner) hacer prisionero, prender; (a town, etc.) tomar, rendir, conquistar; (appropriate) apoderarse de, apropiarse; (steal) robar, hurtar; (ensnare) coger, cazar con trampas; (fish) pescar, coger; (a trick, in cards) hacer (una baza); (an illness) contraer, coger; (by surprise) sorprender, coger desprevenido (a); (attract) atraer; (drink) beber; (a meal) tomar; (select) escoger; (hire) alquilar; (suppose) suponer; (a journal) estar abonado a; (use) emplear, usar; (impers., require) necesitarse, hacer falta; (purchase) comprar; (assume) adoptar, asumir; (a leap) dar (un salto); (a walk) dar (un paseo); (a look) echar (un vistazo); (measures) tomar (medidas); (the chair) presidir; (understand) comprender; (a photograph) sacar (una fotografía); (believe) creer; (consider) considerar; (a note) apuntar; (jump over) saltar; (time) tomar, emplear. **I t. size three in shoes,** Calzo el número tres. **to t. to be,** (believe) suponer; (mistake) creer quivocadamente. **to t. (a thing) badly,** tomarlo (or llevarlo) a mal. **The book took me two hours to read,** Necesité dos horas para leer el libro, Leí el libro en dos horas. **And this, I t. it, is Mary?** ¿Y supongo que ésta será María? **to be taken with,** ser entusiasta de; (of persons) estar prendado de. **to t. aback,** desconcertar, coger desprevenido (a). **to t. again,** volver a tomar; llevar otra vez; (a photograph) retratar otra vez. **to t. along,** llevar; traer. **to t. a long time,** tardar, *Lat. Am.* dilatar. **to t. away,** quitar; llevarse. **to t. back,** devolver; (retract) retractar; (receive) recibir (algo) devuelto. **to t. down,**

bajar; (a building) derribar; (machinery) desmontar; (hair) deshacerse (el cabello); (swallow) tragar; (in writing) apuntar; (humble) quitar los humos (a), humillar. **to t. for,** creer, imaginar; (a walk, etc.) llevar a; (mistake) creer erróneamente; tomar por. **Whom do you t. me for?** ¿Por quién me tomas? **to. t. for granted (assume),** dar por descontado, dar por lecho, dar por sentado, dar por supuesto; (underestimate) no hacer caso de, tratar con indiferencia. **t. the lion's share (of),** llevarse la parte del león (de), llevarse la tajada del león (de). **t. shape,** cobrar perfiles más nítidos, estructurarse con más nitidez, ir adquiriendo consistencia, tomar forma. **t. the law into one's own hands,** tomar la justicia por la mano. **to t. from,** privar, quitar de; (subtract) restar; substraer de. **to t. in,** (believe) tragar, creer; (sail) acortar las velas; (deceive) engañar; (lead in) hacer entrar; (accept) recibir, aceptar. **to t. off,** quitar; (surgically) amputar; (one's hat, etc.) quitarse (el sombrero); (eyes) sacar; (take away) llevarse; (mimic) imitar; (ridicule) ridiculizar; (unstick) despegar; (discount) descontar. **to t. on,** emprender; aceptar; (at sports) jugar. **to t. on oneself,** encargarse de, tomar por su cuenta, asumir. **to t. out,** sacar; extraer; (remove) quitar; (outside) llevar fuera; (for a walk) llevar a paseo; (obtain) obtener, sacar; (tire) agotar, rendir. **to t. over,** tomar posesión de; asumir; (show) mostrar, conducir por. **t. the bull by the horns,** ir al toro por los cuernos. **take seriously,** tomar en serio. **to t. up,** subir; (pick up) recoger; tomar; (a challenge, etc.) aceptar; (a dress, etc.) acortar; (absorb) absorber; (of space) ocupar; (of time) ocupar, hacer perder; (buy) comprar; (adopt) dedicarse a; (arrest) arrestar, prender; (criticize) censurar, criticar; (begin) empezar; (resume) continuar

take *vi* tomar; (be successful) tener éxito; (of vaccination, etc.) prender; (a good (bad) photograph) salir bien (mal). **to t. after,** salir a, parecerse a; (of conduct) seguir el ejemplo de; **to t. off,** salir; *aer* despegar. **to t. on,** *inf* lamentarse. **to t. to,** dar: gustar; darse a; (of persons) tomar cariño a; (grow accustomed) acostumbrarse a. **to t. up with,** hacerse amigo de

take *n* toma, *f*; cogida, *f*; *print* tomada, *f*; *theat* taquilla, *f*. **t.-in,** engaño, *m*. **t.-off,** *aer* (recorrido de) despegue, *m*; caricatura, *f*; sátira, *f*

taking *n* toma, *f*; secuestro, *m*, *n pl* **takings,** ingresos, *m pl*; *theat* taquilla, entrada, *f. a* atractivo, encantador; simpático; (of disease) contagioso

talc *n min* talco, *m*

talcum powder *n* talco, polvo de talco, *m*

tale *n* (recital) narración, historia, *f*; relato, *m*; cuento, *m*; leyenda, historia, fábula, *f*; (number) cuenta, *f*, número, *m*; (gossip) chisme, *m*. **old wives' t.,** cuento de viejas, *m*. **to tell a t.,** contar una historia. **to tell tales,** contar cuentos; revelar secretos, chismear

talebearer *n* correveidile, *mf*; chismoso (-sa), soplón (-ona)

talebearing *n* el chismear, *m*

talent *n* (coin) talento, *m*; (ability) ingenio, *m*; habilidad, *f.* **the best t. in Spain,** la flor de la cultura española

talented *a* talentoso, ingenioso

talisman *n* talismán, *m*

talit taled, *m*

talk *vi* and *vt* hablar, decir. **to t. business,** hablar de negocios. **to t. for talking's sake,** hablar por hablar. **to t. French,** hablar francés. **to t. nonsense,** decir disparates. **to t. too much,** hablar demasiado; *inf* hablar por los codos, irse (a uno) la lengua. **to t. about,** hablar de; conversar sobre. **to t. at,** decir algo a alguien para que lo entienda otro. **Are you talking at me?** ¿Lo dices por mí? **to t. away,** seguir hablando; disipar. **to t. into,** persuadir, inducir (a). **to t. of,** hablar de; charlar sobre. **to t. on,** hablar acerca de (or sobre); (continue) seguir hablando. **to t. out of,** disuadir de. **to t. out of turn,** meterse donde no le llaman, meter la pata. **to t. over,** hablar de; discutir, considerar. **to t.**

round, persuadir. **to t. to,** (address) hablar a; (consult) hablar con; (scold) reprender. **to t. to each other,** hablarse. **to t. up,** hablar claro

talk *n* conversación, *f*; (informal lecture) charla, *f*; (empty words) palabras, *f pl*; (notoriety) escándalo, *m*; rumor, *m*. **There is t. of . . . ,** Se dice que . . . ; Se habla de que. **to give a t.,** dar una charla. **to indulge in small t.,** hablar de cosas sin importancia, hablar de naderías

talkative *a* locuaz, gárrulo, hablador, decidor. **to be very t.,** ser muy locuaz; *inf* tener mucha lengua

talkativeness *n* locuacidad, garrulidad, *f*

talker *n* hablador (-ra), conversador (-ra); (lecturer) orador (-ra); (in a derogatory sense) fanfarrón (-ona), charlatán (-ana). **to be a good t.,** hablar bien, ser buen conversacionista

talking *a* que habla, hablante; (of birds, dolls, etc.) parlero. **to give a good t. to,** dar una paliza (a). **t.-film,** película sonora, *f*. **t.-machine,** fonógrafo, *m*

tall *a* alto; (of stories) exagerado. **five feet tall,** de cinco pies de altura

tallboy *n* cómoda alta, *f*

tallness *n* altura, *f*; estatura, talla, *f*; (of stories) lo exagerado

tallow *n* sebo, *m*. **t. candle,** vela de sebo, *f*. **t. chandler,** velero (-ra). **t.-faced,** con cara de color de cera

tallowy *a* seboso

tall tale *Peru* bacho, *m*

tally *n* tarja, tara, *f*; cuenta, *f. vt* llevar la cuenta (de). *vi* estar conforme, cuadrar

Talmud *n* Talmud, *m*

Talmudic *a* talmúdico

tamable *a* domable, domesticable

tambour *n mus* tambor, *m*; (for embroidery) tambor (or bastidor) para bordar, *m*

tambourine *n* pandereta, *f*

tame *a* domesticado, manso; (spiritless) sumiso; (dull) aburrido, soso. *vt* domar, domesticar; (curb) reprimir, gobernar, domar, suavizar. **to grow t.,** domesticarse

tamer *n* domador (-ra)

taming *n* domadura, *f*. **The T. of the Shrew,** La Fierecilla Domada

tamp *vt* apisonar; (in blasting) atacar (un barreno)

tamper *vi* (with) descomponer, estropear; (meddle with) meterse con; (witnesses) sobornar; (documents) falsificar

tampon *n surg* tampón, tapón, *m*, *vt* taponar

tan *vt* curtir, adobar; (of sun) tostar, quemar; (slang) zurrar. *vi* tostarse por el sol. *n* color café claro, *m*; bronceado, cutis tostado, *m*. *a* de color café claro

tandem *n* tándem, *m*

tang *n* (of sword, etc.) espiga, *f*; (flavor) fuerte sabor, *m*; (sound) retintín, *m*

tangent *a* and *n* tangente *f*. **to fly off at a t.,** *fig* salir por la tangente

tangerine *a* and *n* tangerino (-na). **t. orange,** naranja mandarina, *f*

tangible *a* tangible; *fig* real

Tangier Tánger, *m*

tangle *n* embrollo, enredo, nudo, *m*; (of streets) laberinto, *m*; *fig* confusión, *f. vt* embrollar, enmarañar; (entangle) enredar; *fig* poner en confusión, complicar. *vi* enmarañarse

tank *n* tanque, depósito (de agua, etc.), *m*; cisterna, *f*; (as a reservoir) aljibe, estanque, *m*; *mil* tanque, carro de asalto, *m*. **t. up** (get drunk) *Argentina* acatarrarse

tankard *n* pichel, bock, *m*

tanker *n* petrolero, *m*

tanned *a* bronceado, quemado por el sol, dorado por el sol

tanner *n* curtidor, *m*; (slang) medio chelín, *m*. **tanner's scraper,** descarnador, *m*. **tanner's vat,** noque, *m*

tannery *n* curtiduría, *f*

tannic *a chem* tánico. **t. acid,** ácido tánico, *m*

tannin *n chem* tanino, *m*

tanning *n* curtido, adobamiento, *m*

tantalize vt tentar, atormentar, provocar

tantalizing a tentador, atormentador; provocativo

tantamount a equivalente, igual. **to be t. to,** ser equivalente a

tantrum n pataleta, rabieta, f, berrinche, m

taoism n taoísmo, m

taoist n taoísta, mf

tap n (blow) pequeño golpe, toque ligero, m; palmadita, f; (for drawing water, etc.) grifo, m, llave, f; (of a barrel) canilla, f; (brew of liquor) clase de vino, f; (tap-room) bar con mostrador, m; (tool) macho de terraja, m; (piece of leather on shoe) tapa, f; pl **taps,** mil toque de apagar las luces, m. vt (strike) golpear ligeramente, dar una palmadita a; (pierce) horadar; (a barrel) decentar; surg hacer una puntura en; (trees) sangrar; elec derivar (una corriente); (of water, current) tomar; (information) descubrir; (telephone) escuchar las conversaciones telefónicas. vi golpear ligeramente. **to tap at the door,** llamar suavemente a la puerta. **on tap,** en tonel. **screw-tap,** terraja, f. **tap-dance,** claqué, m. **tap-root,** raíz pivotante, f

tape n (linen) cinta de hilo, f; (cotton) cinta de algodón, f; (telegraph machine) cinta de papel, f; (surveying) cinta para medir, f. **adhesive t.,** cinta adhesiva, f. **red t.,** balduque, m; fig burocracia, f; formulismo, m. **t.-machine,** telégrafo de cotizaciones, bancarias, m. **t.-measure,** cinta métrica, f

taper n bujía, cerilla, f; ecc cirio, m. vi ahusarse, rematar en punta. vt afilar

tapering a cónico, piramidal; (of fingers) afilado

tapestried a cubierto de tapices, tapizado

tapestry n tapiz, m. **t. weaver,** tapicero, m

tapeworm n tenia, lombriz solitaria, f

tapioca n tapioca, f

tapir n zool danta, f

tapis, to be on the estar sobre el tapete

tar n alquitrán, m, brea, f. vt embrear, alquitranar. **to tar and feather,** emplumar. **coal t.,** alquitrán mineral, m

tarantella n tarantela, f

tarantula n tarántula, f

tardily adv tardíamente; lentamente

tardiness n tardanza, lentitud, f

tardy a (late) tardío; (slow) lento; (reluctant) desinclinado

tare n bot yero, m; (in the Bible) cizaña, f; com tara, f; (of a vehicle) peso en vacío, m

target n blanco (de tiro), m; (shield) rodela, tarja, f. **t. practice,** tiro al blanco, m

tariff n tarifa, f. **to put a t. on,** tarifar

tarlatan n tarlatana, f

tarmac n alquitranado, m

tarn n lago de montaña, m

tarnish n deslustre, m. vt deslustrar, empañar; fig obscurecer, manchar. vi deslustrarse

tarpaulin n alquitranado, encerado, m

tarred a alquitranado, embreado

tarring n embreadura, f

tarry vi tardar, detenerse

tart a ácido, acerbo, agridulce; fig áspero. n tarta, f; pastelillo de fruta, m

tartan n naut tartana, f; (plaid) tartán, m

tartar n chem tártaro, m; (in teeth) sarro, tártaro, m; **cream of t.,** (cremor) tártaro, m. **t. emetic,** tártaro emético, m. **Tartar,** a and n tártaro (-ra)

Tartary Tartaria, f

tartly adv ásperamente, agriamente

tartness n acidez, f; fig aspereza, f

task n tarea, labor, f; empresa, f; misión, f. **to take to t.,** regañar, censurar. **t.-force,** (naval or military) contingente, m

taskmaster n el que señala una tarea; amo, m

tassel n borla, f; (of corn) panoja, espiga, f

taste n gusto, m; (flavor) sabor, m; (specimen) ejemplo, m, idea, f; (small quantity) un poco, muy poco; (liking) afición, inclinación, f; (of drink) sorbo, trago, m; (tinge)

dejo, m. vt (appraise) probar; gustar, percibir el gusto de; (experience) experimentar, conocer. vi tener gusto, tener sabor. **a matter of t.,** cuestión de gusto. **Each to his own t.,** Entre gustos no hay disputa. **He had not tasted a bite,** No había probado bocado. **in bad (good) t.,** de mal (buen) gusto; de mal (buen) tono. **to have a t. for,** ser aficionado a, gustar de. **to t.,** cul a gusto, a sabor. **to t. of,** tener gusto de, saber a

tasted a (in compounds) de sabor . . .

tasteful a de buen gusto

tastefully adv con buen gusto

tastefulness n buen gusto, m

tasteless a insípido, soso, insulso; de mal gusto

tastelessness n insipidez, insulsez, f; mal gusto, m

taster n catador, m; (vessel) catavino, m

tasting n saboreo, m, gustación, f, a (in compounds) de sabor . . .

tasty a apetitoso, sabroso

tatter n andrajo, harapo, m; jirón, m. **to tear in tatters,** hacer jirones

tattered a andrajoso, haraposo

tatting n frivolité, m

tattoo n tatuaje, m; mil retreta, f; (display) parada militar, f. vt tatuar

tattooing n tatuaje, m; tamboreo, m

taunt n mofa, f, insulto, escarnio, m. vt insultar, atormentar. **to t. with,** echar en cara

taunting a insultante, burlón, insolente

tauntingly adv burlonamente, insolentemente

Taurus n tauro, toro, m

taut a tieso, tirante, tenso; en regla; naut **to make t.,** tesar

tauten vt tesar; poner tieso

tautness n tensión, f

tautological a tautológico

tautology n tautología, f

tavern n taberna, f; (inn) mesón, m, posada, f. **t.-keeper,** tabernero, m

tawdrily adv llamativamente, de un modo cursi

tawdriness n charrería, f

tawdry a chillón, charro, cursi

tawny a leonado

tax n contribución, gabela, imposición, f; fig carga, f; vt imponer contribuciones (a); law tasar; fig cargar, abrumar. **to tax with,** tachar (de), acusar (de). **direct (indirect) tax,** contribución directa (indirecta), f. **tax-collector,** recaudador de contribuciones, m. **tax-free,** libre de impuestos. **tax-rate,** tarifa de impuestos, f, cupo, m. **tax-register,** lista de contribuyentes, f

taxable a imponible, sujeto a impuestos

taxation n imposición de contribuciones (or impuestos), f

tax evasion n evasión tributaria, f

taxi n taxi, Mexico libre, m. vi ir en un taxi; aer correr por tierra. **t. driver,** chófer de un taxi, taxista, m. **t. rank, taxi stand,** parada de taxis, f

taxidermist n taxidermista, mf

taxidermy n taxidermia, f

taximeter n taxímetro, m

taxpayer n contribuyente, mf

taxpaying a tributario, que paga contribuciones

tax reform n reforma impositiva, reforma tributaria, f

tea n (liquid) té, m; (meal) merienda, f. **to have tea,** tomar el té, merendar. **tea-caddy,** bote para té, m. **tea-chest,** caja para té, f. **tea-cosy,** cubretetera, m. **tea-cup,** taza para té, f. **tea-dance,** té baile, m. **tea-kettle** or **tea-pot,** tetera, f. **tea-leaf,** hoja de té, f. **tea-party,** reunión para tomar el té, f. **tea-room,** salón de té, m. **tea-rose,** rosa de té, f. **tea-set,** juego de té, m. **tea-strainer,** colador de té, m. **tea-time,** hora de té, f. **tea-urn,** samowar, m, tetera para hacer té, f. **tea-wagon,** carrito para el té, m

teach vt (a person) enseñar, instruir; (a subject) enseñar; (to lecture on) ser profesor de; (a lesson) dar una lección de. vi (be a teacher) dedicarse a la enseñanza. **to teach at . . . ,** desempeñar una cátedra en . . . **to t.**

a person Spanish, enseñar el castellano a alguien. **to t. how to,** enseñar a (followed by infin.)

teachability *n* docilidad, *f*

teachable *a* educable; dócil

teacher *n* preceptor, *m;* profesor, maestro, *m.* **woman t.,** profesora, maestra, *f*

teaching *n* enseñanza, *f;* (belief) doctrina, *f, a* docente. **t. profession,** magisterio, *m*

teaching method *n* método didáctico, *f*

teak *n bot* teca, *f;* (wood) madera de teca, *f*

team *n* (of horses) tiro, *m;* (of oxen, mules) par, *m,* pareja, yunta, *f; sport* partido, equipo, *m;* compañía, *f,* grupo, *m. vt* enganchar, uncir. **t.-work,** cooperación, *f*

teamster *n* gañán, *m*

tear *vt* rasgar; romper; lacerar; (in pieces) hacer pedazos, despedazar; (scratch) arañar; *fig* atormentar. **to t. asunder,** romper; desmembrar. **to t. away,** arrancar, quitar violentamente. **to t. down,** derribar, echar abajo. **to t. off,** arrancar; desgajar. **to t. oneself away,** arrancarse, desgarrarse. **to t. one's hair,** arrancarse los pelos, mesarse. **to t. open,** abrir apresuradamente. **to t. up,** hacer pedazos; (uproot) arrancar, desarraigar.

tear *vi* rasgarse; romper; correr precipitadamente. **to t. along,** correr rápidamente (por). **to t. away,** marcharse corriendo. **to t. down,** bajar corriendo. **to t. into,** entrar corriendo en. **to t. off,** irse precipitadamente, marcharse corriendo. **to t. up,** subir corriendo; llegar corriendo; atravesar rápidamente

tear *n* lágrima, *f;* (drop) gota, *f.* **with tears in one's eyes,** con lágrimas en los ojos. **to shed tears,** llorar, lagrimear. **to wipe away one's tears,** secarse las lágrimas. **t.-drop,** lágrima, *f.* **t.-duct,** conductor lacrimal, *m.* **t.-gas,** gas lacrimante, *m.* **t.-stained,** mojado de lágrimas

tear *n* (rent) rasgón, *m*

tearful *a* lloroso, lacrimoso

tearfully *adv* con lágrimas en los ojos

tearing *n* rasgadura, *f,* desgarro, *m*

tearjerker *n* drama lacrimón, *m*

tease *vt* (card) cardar; (annoy) fastidiar, irritar, molestar; (chaff) tomar el pelo (a), embromar; (pester) importunar. *n* bromista, *mf*

teasel *n bot* cardencha, *f, vt* cardar

teaser *n* (problem) rompecabezas, *m;* (person) bromista, *mf*

teaspoon *n* cucharita, *f*

teaspoonful *n* cucharadita, *f*

teat *n* pezón, *m;* (of animals) teta, *f*

technical *a* técnico. **t. offence,** *law* cuasidelito, *m.* **t. school,** escuela industrial, *f*

technicality *n* carácter técnico, *m;* tecnicismo, *m;* detalle técnico, *m*

technician *n* técnico, *m*

technicolor *n* tecnicolor, *m*

technique *n* técnica, *f;* ejecución, *f;* mecanismo, *m*

technological *a* tecnológico

technologist *n* tecnólogo, *m*

technology *n* tecnología, *f*

teddy bear *n* osito de trapo, *m*

tedious *a* aburrido, tedioso, pesado

tediously *adv* aburridamente

tediousness *n* aburrimiento, *m,* pesadez, *f*

tedium *n* tedio, *m,* monotonía, *f*

tee *n sport* meta, *f;* (golf) tee, *m;* (letter) te, *f;* cosa en forma de t., *f. vt* (golf) colocar la pelota en el tee

teem *vi* rebosar (de), abundar (en); pulular, hormiguear, estar lleno (de); (with rain) diluviar

teeming *a* prolífico, fecundo. **t. with,** abundante en, lleno de

teens *n pl* números y años desde trece hasta diez y nueve; edad de trece a diez y nueve años de edad. **to be still in one's t.,** no haber cumplido aún los veinte

teeter *vi* balancearse, columpiarse

teethe *vi* endentecer, echar los dientes

teething *n* dentición, *f.* **t.-ring,** chupador, *m*

teetotal *a* abstemio

teetotalism *n* abstinencia completa de bebidas alcohólicas, *f*

teetotaller *n* abstemio (-ia)

teetotum *n* perinola, *f*

telecast *vt* telefundir

telecommunication *n* telecomunicación, *f*

telegram *n* telegrama, *m*

telegraph *n* telégrafo, *m. vi* telegrafiar; *fig* hacer señas. *vt* telegrafiar, enviar por telégrafo. **t. line,** línea telegráfica, *f.* **t. office,** central de telégrafos, *f.* **t. pole,** poste telegráfico, *m.* **t. wire,** hilo telegráfico, *m*

telegraphic *a* telegráfico

telegraphist *n* telegrafista, *mf*

telegraphy *n* telegrafía, *f.* **wireless t.,** telegrafía sin hilos, *f*

telemetry *n* telemetría, *f*

teleology *n* teleología, *f*

telepathic *a* telepático

telepathy *n* telepatía, *f*

telephone *n* teléfono, *m. vi* telefonear. *vt* telefonear, llamar por teléfono. **to be on the t.,** (speaking) estar communicando; (of subscribers) tener teléfono. **dial t.,** teléfono automático, *m.* **t. call,** comunicación telefónica, *f;* conversación telefónica, *f.* **t. call box,** teléfono público, *m.* **t. directory,** guía de teléfonos, *f.* **t. exchange,** central telefónica, *f.* **t. number,** número de teléfono, *m.* **t. operator,** telefonista, *mf* **t. receiver,** receptor telefónico, *m.* **t. wire,** hilo telefónico, *m*

telephonic *a* telefónico

telephonist *n* telefonista, *mf*

telephony *n* telefonía, *f.* **wireless t.,** telefonía sin hilos, *f*

teleprinter *n* teletipo, *m*

telescope *n* telescopio, catalejo, *m. vt* enchufar. *vi* enchufarse, meterse una cosa dentro de otra

telescopic *a* telescópico; de enchufe

televise *vt* trasmitir por televisión

television *n* televisión, *f.* **on television,** por televisión. **I saw her on television,** La vi por televisión

television series *n* serie televisiva, *f*

tell *vt* contar, narrar; decir; revelar; expresar; (the time, of clocks) marcar; (inform) comunicar, informar; (show) indicar, manifestar; (explain) explicar; distinguir; (order) mandar; (compute) contar. *vi* decir; (have effect) producir efecto. **We cannot t.,** No sabemos. **Who can t.?** ¿Quién sabe? **T. that to the marines!;** Cuéntaselo a tu tía! **to t. its own tale,** hacer ver por sí mismo lo que hay. **to t. again,** volver a decir; contar otra vez. **to t. off,** regañar, reñir; (on a mission) despachar, mandar. **to t. on,** delatar. **to t. upon,** afectar

teller *n* narrador (-ra); (of votes) escrutador (-ra) de votos; (payer) pagador; (bank) cajero (-ra), *m*

telling *a* notable, significante. *n* narración, *f*

telltale *n* chismoso (-sa), soplón (-ona); (informer) acusón (-ona); *fig* indicio, *m,* señal, *f, a* revelador

temerity *n* temeridad, *f*

temper *n* (of metals) temple, *m;* (nature) naturaleza, *f,* carácter, *m;* espíritu, *m;* (mood) humor, *m;* (anger) mal genio, *m. vt* (of metals) templar; moderar, mitigar; mezclar. *vi* templarse. **bad (good) t.,** mal (buen) humor. **to keep one's t.,** no enojarse, no impacientarse. **to lose one's t.,** enojarse, perder la paciencia

tempera *n art* templa, *f.* **in t.,** al temple, *m*

temperament *n* temperamento, *m;* modo de ser, natural, *m,* naturaleza, índole, *f; mus* temple, *m*

temperamental *a* natural, innato; caprichoso

temperamentally *adv* por naturaleza

temperance *n* moderación, templanza, *f;* sobriedad, abstinencia, *f*

temperate *a* moderado; sobrio; (of regions) templado. **t. zone,** zona templada, *f*

temperately *adv* sobriamente

temperateness *n* moderación, sobriedad, mesura, *f;* (of regions) templanza, *f*

temperature *n* temperatura, *f.* **to have a t.,** tener fiebre

tempered *a* de humor . . . , de genio . . . **to be good (bad) t.,** ser de buen (mal) humor
tempering *n* temperación, *f*
tempest *n* tempestad, borrasca, *f,* temporal, *m; fig* tormenta, *f*
tempest in a teapot borrasca en un vaso de agua, *m*
tempestuous *a* tempestuoso, borrascoso; *fig* impetuoso, violento
tempestuousness *n* lo tempestuoso; *fig* impetuosidad, violencia, *f*
temple *n* templo, *m; anat* sien, *f*
tempo *n mus* tiempo, *m*
temporal *a* temporal; (transient) transitorio, fugaz; *anat* temporal. *n anat* hueso temporal, *m*
temporality *n* temporalidad, *f*
temporarily *adv* provisionalmente
temporariness *n* interinidad, *f*
temporary *a* provisional, interino
temporize *vi* ganar tiempo; contemporizar
temporizing *n* contemporización, *f, a* contemporizador
tempt *vt* tentar; atraer, seducir
temptation *n* tentación, *f;* aliciente, atractivo, *m*
tempter *n* tentador (-ra)
tempting *a* tentador, atrayente; seductor
ten *a* diez; (of the clock) las diez, *f pl;* (of age) diez años, *m pl, n* diez, *m;* (a round number) decena, *f;* **ten-millionth,** *a* and *n* diezmillonésimo *m.* **ten months old,** diezmesino. **ten syllable,** decasílabo. **ten thousand,** *a* and *n* diez mil *m.* **There are ten thousand soldiers,** Hay diez mil soldados. **ten-thousandth,** *a* and *n* diezmilésimo *m*
tenable *a* sostenible, defendible
tenacious *a* tenaz; (stubborn) porfiado, obstinaz, terco; (sticky) adhesivo. **to be t. of life,** estar muy apegado a la vida
tenaciously *adv* tenazmente; porfiadamente
tenacity *n* tenacidad, *f;* porfía, *f;* tesón, *m*
tenancy *n* inquilinato, *m;* tenencia, *f*
tenant *n* arrendatario (-ia), inquilino (-na); habitante, *m;* morador (-ra). **t. farmer** *Chile* inquilino (-na), *mf*
tench *n icht* tenca, *f*
tend *vt* cuidar, atender; guardar; vigilar. *vi* tender; inclinarse (a), propender (a)
tendency *n* tendencia, inclinación, propensión, *f;* proclividad, *f*
tendentious *a* tendencioso
tender *n* guardián, *m; com* oferta, propuesta, *f; naut* falúa, *f;* (of a railway engine) ténder, *m.* **legal t.,** moneda corriente, *f*
tender *a* tierno; delicado; (of conscience) escrupuloso; (of a subject) espinoso; compasivo, afectuoso, sensible; muelle, blando. **t.-hearted,** compasivo, tierno de corazón
tender *vt* ofrecer; dar; presentar. *vi* hacer una oferta. **to t. condolences,** dar el pésame. **to t. one's resignation,** presentar la dimisión. **to t. thanks,** dar las gracias
tenderly *adv* tiernamente
tenderness *n* ternura, *f;* sensibilidad, *f;* delicadeza, *f;* dulzura, *f;* indulgencia, *f;* compasividad, benevolencia, *f;* escrupulosidad, *f;* mimo, cariño, *m*
tendon *n anat* tendón, *m.* **t. of Achilles,** tendón de Aquiles, *m*
tenement *n* casa de vecindad, *f;* vivienda, *f, Lat. Am.* conventillo, *m; poet* morada, *f*
Teneriffe Tenerife, *f*
tenet *n* principio, dogma, *m,* doctrina, *f*
tenfold *a* décuplo. *adv* diez veces
tennis *n* tenis, *m.* **to play t.,** jugar al tenis. **t. ball,** pelota de tenis, *f.* **t. court,** campo de tenis, *m,* cancha de tenis, pista de tenis, *f.* **tennis club,** club de tenis, *m.* **t. racket,** raqueta de tenis, *f;* **tennis shoe,** zapatilla de tenis, *f*
tenon *n carp* espiga, *f, vt* espigar
tenor *n* curso, *m;* tenor, contenido, *m; mus* tenor, *m; mus* alto, *m;* (mus. instrument) viola, *f. a mus* de tenor

tense *n gram* tiempo, *m. a* tirante, estirado, tieso; tenso
tenseness *n* tirantez, *f;* tensión, *f*
tensile *a* tensor; extensible
tension *n* tensión, *f; elec* voltaje, *m,* tensión, *f;* (of sewing-machine) tensáhilo, *m.* **state of t.,** (diplomatic) estado de tirantez, *m*
tent *n* tienda (de campaña), *Lat. Am.* carpa, *f;* (bell) pabellón, *m; surg* tienda, *f.* **oxygen t.,** tienda oxígena, *f.* **to pitch tents,** armar las tiendas de campaña; acamparse. **to strike tents,** plegar tiendas. **t. fly,** toldo de tienda, *m.* **t. maker,** tendero, *m.* **t. peg,** clave que sujeta las cuerdas de una tienda, *f.* **t. pole,** mástil (or montante) de tienda, *m*
tentacle *n* tentáculo, *m*
tentative *a* tentativo, interino, provisional, de prueba, *n* tentativa, *f,* ensayo, *m*
tentatively *adv* por vía de ensayo, experimentalmente
tenth *a* décimo; (of monarchs) diez; (of the month) (el) diez. *n* décimo, *m;* (part) décima parte, *f; mus* decena, *f*
tenthly *adv* en décimo lugar
tenuity *n* tenuidad, *f;* sutilidad, *f;* delgadez, *f*
tenuous *a* tenue; sutil; delgado; fino
tenure *n* tenencia, posesión, *f;* (duration) duración, *f;* (of office) administración, *f*
tepid *a* tibio
tepidity *n* tibieza, *f*
tercentenary *n* tercer centenario, *m*
tercet *n* terceto, *m*
term *n* (limit) límite, fin, *m;* (period) plazo, tiempo, período, *m;* (schools, universities) trimestre, *m; (math, law, logic)* término, *m;* (word) expresión, palabra, *f pl.* **terms,** (conditions) condiciones, *f pl;* (charges) precios, *m pl,* tarifa, *f;* (words) términos, *m pl,* palabras, *f pl. vt* llamar, calificar. **for a t. of years,** por un plazo de años. **in plain terms,** en palabras claras. **on equal terms,** en condiciones iguales. **to be on bad (good) terms with,** estar en (or tener) malas (buenas) relaciones con. **to come to terms,** llegar a un acuerdo; hacer las paces. **What are your terms?** ¿Cuáles son sus condiciones? (price) ¿Cuáles son sus precios? **terms of sale,** condiciones de venta, *f pl*
termagant *n* arpía, fiera, *f*
terminable *a* terminable
terminal *a* terminal, final; (of schools, universities) trimestre. *n* término, *m; elec* borne, *m;* (schools, universities) examen de fin de trimestre, *m;* (railway) estación terminal, *f;* (arch and figure) término, *m; arch* remate, *m*
terminate *vt* limitar; terminar, concluir, poner fin (a). *vi* terminarse, concluirse (por); cesar
termination *n* terminación, conclusión, *f;* fin, *m; gram* terminación, *f;* cabo, remate, *m*
terminology *n* nomenclatura, terminología, *f*
terminus *n* (railway) estación terminal, *f;* (arch and figure) término, *m; arch* remate, *m; myth* Término
termite *n ent* termita, *f*
term paper *n* trabajo de examen, *m*
terms of trade *n* relación de los precios de intercambio, *f*
terrace *n* terraza, *f, vt* terraplenar
terraced *a* en terrazas; con terrazas
terracotta *n* terracota, *f*
terrain *n* terreno, campo, *m,* región, *f*
terrapin *n* tortuga de agua dulce, *f*
terrestrial *a* terrestre, terrenal
terrible *a* terrible, pavoroso, espantoso; *inf* tremendo
terribleness *n* terribilidad, *f,* lo horrible
terrier *n* terrier, *m; inf* soldado del ejército territorial, *m*
terrific *a* espantoso, terrible; *inf* atroz, tremendo
terrify *vt* aterrorizar, espantar, horrorizar, *Lat. Am. also* julepear. **to be terrified** *Lat. Am.* julepearse
terrifying *a* aterrador, espantoso
territorial *a* territorial. *n* soldado del ejército territorial, *m*
territoriality *n* territorialidad, *f*
territory *n* región, comarca, *f;* (state) territorio, *m;* ju-

risdicción, *f.* **mandated territory,** territorio bajo mandato, *m pl*

terror *n* terror, pavor, espanto, *m.* **the Reign of T.,** el Reinado del Terror, *m.* **t.-stricken,** espantado, muerto de miedo

terrorism *n* terrorismo, *m*

terrorist *n* terrorista, *m*

terrorization *n* aterramiento, *m*

terrorize *vt* aterrorizar

terse *a* conciso, sucinto; seco, brusco

tersely *adv* concisamente; secamente

terseness *n* concisión, *f*; brusquedad, *f*

tertiary *a* tercero; *geol* terciario. *n ecc* terciario, *m*

tessera *n* tesela, *f*

test *n* (proof) prueba, *f*; examen, *m*; investigación, *f*; (standard) criterio, *m*, piedra de toque, *f*; *chem* análisis, *m*; (trial) ensayo, *m*; *zool* concha, *f*. *vt chem* ensayar; probar, poner a prueba; examinar; (eyes) graduar (la vista). **to put to the t.,** poner a prueba. **to stand the t.,** soportar la prueba. **t. match,** partido internacional de cricket, *m.* **t. meal,** *med* comida de prueba, *f*. **t. pilot,** *aer* piloto de pruebas, *m.* **t. tube,** tubo de ensayo, *m*

testament *n* testamento, *m.* **the New T.,** el Nuevo Testamento, *m.* **the Old T.,** el Antiguo Testamento, *m*

testamentary *a* testamentario

testate *a* testado

testator *n* testador, *m*, **(testatrix,** testadora, *f*)

testicle *n* testículo, *m*

testification *n* testificación, *f*

testify *vt* and *vi* declarar, atestar; *law* atestiguar, testificar, dar fe

testily *adv* malhumoradamente

testimonial *n* recomendación, *f*; certificado, *m*; (tribute) homenaje, *m*

testimony *n* testimonio, *m*, declaración, *f*; (proof) prueba, *f*. **in t. whereof,** en fe de lo cual. **to bear t.,** atestar

testiness *n* mal humor, *m*, irritación, *f*

testing grounds *n* campo de experimentación, campo de pruebas, *m*

testy *a* enojadizo, irritable, irascible, quisquilloso

tetanus *n* tétano, *m*

tether *n* traba, atadura, maniota, *f*. *vt* atar con una correa. **to be at the end of one's t.,** acabarse la resistencia; acabarse la paciencia

Teutonic *a* teutónico

text *n* texto, *m*; (subject) tema, *m*; (motto) lema, *m*; (of a musical composition) letra, *f*. **t.-book,** libro de texto, *m*

textile *a* textil, de tejer. *n* textil, *m*, materia textil, *f*; tejido, *m*

textual *a* textual

texture *n* (material and *biol*) tejido, *m*; textura, *f*

Thailand Tailandia, *f*

thalamus *n* (*anat, bot*) tálamo, *m*

Thames, the *n* el Támesis, *m.* **to set the T. on fire,** descubrir la pólvora

than *conjunc* que; (between **more, less,** or **fewer** and a number) de; (in comparisons of inequality) que, but que becomes *a* del (de la, de los, de las) que if the point of comparison is a noun in the principal clause, which has to be supplied mentally to fill up the ellipsis; (*b*) de lo que if there is no noun to act as a point of comparison, e.g. **He was older than I thought,** Era más viejo de lo que yo pensaba. **They have less than they deserve,** Tienen menos de lo que merecen. **They lose more money than (the money) they earn,** Pierden más dinero del que ganan. **He will meet with more opposition than he thought,** Va a encontrar más oposición de la que pensaba. **I have more books than you,** Tengo más libros que tú. **She has fewer than nine and more than five,** Ella tiene menos de nueve y más de cinco

thank *vt* agradecer, dar las gracias (a). **to t. for,** agradecer. **I will t. you to be more polite,** Le agradecería que fuese más cortés. **He has himself to t. for it,** Él

mismo tiene la culpa de ello. **No, t. you,** No, muchas gracias. **T. goodness!** ¡Gracias a Dios!

thank *n* (now in pl. only, **thanks**) gracias, *f pl.* **a vote of thanks,** un voto de gracias. **Many thanks!** ¡Muchas gracias! **to return thanks,** dar las gracias. **thanks to,** merced a, debido a. **thanks to you,** gracias a tí. **t.-offering,** ofrecimiento en acción de gracias, *m*

thankful *a* agradecido. **I am t. to see,** Me alegro de ver; Me es grato ver

thankfully *adv* con gratitud, agradecido

thankfulness *n* agradecimiento, *m*; gratitud, *f*

thankless *a* ingrato; desagradecido; desagradable

thanksgiving *n* acción de gracias, *f*. **t. service,** servicio de acción de gracias, *m.* **Thanksgiving (Day),** *n* día de acción de dar gracias, día de gracias, *m*

that *dem a* ese, *m*; esa, *f*; aquel, *m*; aquella, *f, dem. pron* ése, *m*; ésa, *f*; eso, *neut*; aquél, *m*; aquélla, *f*; aquello, *neut*; (standing for a noun) el, *m*; la, *f*; lo, *neut* **All t. there is,** Todo lo que hay. **His temperament is t. of his mother,** Su temperamento es el de su madre. **We have not come to t. yet,** Todavía no hemos llegado a ese punto. **T. is what I want to know,** Eso es lo que quiero saber. **with t.,** con eso; (thereupon) en eso. **Go t. way,** Vaya Vd. por allí; Tome Vd. aquel camino. **T. is to say . . . ,** Es decir . . . **What do you mean by t.?** ¿Qué quieres decir con eso? **The novel is not as bad as all t.,** La novela no es tan mala como tú piensas (*or* como dicen, etc.)

that *pron. rel* que; el cual, *m*; la cual, *f*; lo cual, *neut*; (of persons) a quien, *mf*; a quienes, *mf pl*; (with from) de quien, *mf*; de quienes, *mf pl*; (of place) donde. **The letter t. I sent you,** la carta que te mandé. **The box t. John put them in,** la caja en la cual los puso Juan. **The last time t. I saw her,** La última vez que la vi

that *conjunc* que; (of purpose) para que; afin de que; (before infin.) para; (because) porque. **O t. he would come!** ¡Ojalá que viniese! **so t.,** para que; (before infin.) para; (as a result) de manera que; de modo que. **It is better t. he should not come,** Es mejor que no venga. **now t.,** ahora que

thatch *n* barda, *f*, *vt* bardar

thaw *n* deshielo, *m.* *vt* deshelar; derretir. *vi* deshelarse; derretirse

the *def art.* el, *m*; la, *f*; lo, *neut*; los, *m pl*; las, *f pl*; (before feminine sing. noun beginning with stressed a or ha) el; (untranslated between the name and number of a monarch, pope, ruler, e.g. **Charles the Tenth,** Carlos diez). *adv* (before a comparative) cuanto, tanto más. **at the** *or* **to the,** al, *m*, (also before feminine sing. noun beginning with a or ha); a la, *f*; a lo, *neut*; a los, *m pl*; a las, *f pl.* **from the** *or* **of the,** del, *m*, (also before feminine sing. noun beginning with stressed a or ha); de la, *f*; de lo, *neut*; de los, *m pl*; de las, *f pl.* **the one,** see **one. The sooner the better,** Cuanto antes mejor. **The room will be all the warmer,** El cuarto estará tanto más caliente

theater *n* teatro, *m*; (lecture) anfiteatro, *m*; (drama) teatro, *m*, obra dramática, *f*; (scene) teatro, *m*, escena, *f*. **t. attendant,** acomodador (-ra)

theater-in-the-round *n* teatro circular, teatro en círculo, *m*

theatin *a* and *n ecc* teatino *m*

theatrical *a* teatral. *n pl* **theatricals,** funciones teatrales, *f pl.* **amateur theatricals,** función de aficionados, *f.* **t. company,** compañía de teatro, *f.* **t. costumier,** mascarero (-ra), alquilador (-ra) de disfraces. **t. manager,** empresario de teatro, *m*

theatricality *n* teatralidad, *f*

theban *a* and *n* tebeo (-ea), tebano (-na)

Thebes Tebas, *f*

thee *pers pron* te; (after prep.) tí. **with t.,** contigo

theft *n* robo, hurto, *m*

their *poss a* su, *mf sing*; sus, *pl*; de ellos, *m pl*; de ellas, *f pl.* **They have t. books,** Tienen sus libros. **I have t. books,** Tengo los libros de ellos

theirs *poss pron* (el) suyo, *m*; (la) suya, *f*; (los) suyos, *m* *pl*; (las) suyas, *f pl*; de ellos, *m pl*; de ellas, *f pl*. **These hats are t.,** Estos sombreros son los suyos

them *pers pron* ellos, *m pl*; ellas, *f pl*; (as object of a verb) los, *m pl*; las, *f pl*; (to them) les

thematic *a* temático

theme *n* tema, asunto, *m*; tesis, *f*; *mus* tema, motivo, *m*

themselves *pers pron pl* ellos mismos, *m pl*; ellas mismas, *f pl*, *reflexive pron* sí; sí mismos; (with a reflexive verb) se. **They t. told me about it,** Ellos mismos me lo dijeron. **They left it for t.,** Lo dejaron para sí (mismos)

then *adv* (of future time) entonces; (of past time) a la sazón, en aquella época, entonces; (next, afterwards) luego, después, en seguida; (in that case) en este caso, entonces; (therefore) por consiguiente. *a* de entonces. *n* entonces, *m*. *conjunc* (moreover) además; pues. **And what t.?** ¿Y qué pasó después?; ¿Y qué pasará ahora?; ¿Y qué más? **by t.,** por entonces. **now and t.,** de vez en cuando. **now . . . t.,** ya . . . ya, ora . . . ora. **since t.,** desde aquel tiempo; desde entonces; desde aquella ocasión. **until t.,** hasta entonces; hasta aquella época. **well t.,** bien, pues. **t. and there,** en el acto, en seguida; allí mismo

thence *adv* desde allí, de allí; (therefore) por eso, por esa razón, por consiguiente

thenceforth *adv* de allí en adelante, desde entonces

theocracy *n* teocracia, *f*

theocratic *a* teocrático

theologian *n* teólogo, *m*

theological *a* teológico, teologal

theologize *vi* teologizar

theology *n* teología, *f*

theorem *n* teorema, *m*

theoretical *a* teórico

theoretically *adv* teóricamente, en teoría

theorist *n* teórico, *m*

theorize *vi* teorizar

theory *n* teoría, *f*

theosophical *a* teosófico

theosophist *n* teósofo, *m*

theosophy *n* teosofía, *f*

therapeutic *a* terapéutico. *n* **therapeutics,** terapéutica, *f*

therapeutist *n* terapeuta, *mf*

therapy *suffix* terapia, *f*

there *adv* allí; ahí, allá; (at that point) en eso; (used pronominally as subject of verb) haber, e.g. **T. was once a king,** Hubo una vez un rey; **What is t. to do here?** ¿Qué hay que hacer aquí? *interj* ¡vaya!; (I told you so) ¡ya ves! ¡ya te lo dije yo!; (in surprise) ¡toma! **about t.,** cerca de allí. **down t.,** allí abajo. **in t.,** allí dentro. **out t.,** allí fuera. **over t.,** ahí; allá a lo lejos. **up t.,** allí arriba. **T. came a time when . . . ,** Llegó la hora cuando . . . **T. it is!** ¡Allí está! **t. is** or **t. are,** hay. **t. was** or **t. were,** había, hubo. **t. may be,** puede haber, quizás habrá. **t. must be,** tiene que haber. **t. will be,** habrá. **T., t.!** (to a child, etc.) ¡Vamos!

thereabouts *adv* (near to a place) cerca de allí, por ahí, allí cerca; (approximately) approximadamente, cerca de

thereafter *adv* después, después de eso

thereby *adv* (near to that place) por allí cerca; (by that means) con lo cual, de este modo

therefore *adv* por lo tanto, por eso, así, por consiguiente; por esta razón

therein *adv* (inside) allí dentro; (in this, that particular) en estre, en eso, en ese particular

thereinafter *adv* posteriormente, más adelante

thereupon *adv* (in consequence) por consiguiente, por lo tanto; (at that point) luego, en eso; (immediately afterwards) inmediatamente después, en seguida

thermal *a* termal. **t. springs,** aguas termales, termas, *f pl*

thermodynamics *n* termodinámica, *f*

thermoelectric *a* termoeléctrico

thermometer *n* termómetro, *m*

Thermopylae Termópilas, *f*

thermos flask *n* termos, *m*

thermostat *n* termostato, *m*

thermostatic *a* termostático

thesaurus *n* tesoro, tesauro, *m*

these *dem pron pl* of **this,** éstos, *m pl*; éstas, *f pl, dem a* estos, *m pl*; estas, *f pl*. **Are not t. your flowers?** ¿No son éstas tus flores? **T. pictures have been sold,** Estos cuadros han se han vendito

thesis *n* tesis, *f*

Thespian *a* dramático

Thessaly Tesalia, *f*

they *pers pron pl* ellos, *m pl*; ellas, *f pl*; (people) se (followed by sing. verb). **T. say,** Dicen, Se dice

thick *a* espeso; (big) grueso, (wall) grueso, (string, cord) gordo; (vapors) denso; (muddy) turbio; (dense, close) tupido apretado; (numerous) numeroso, repetido, continuo; (full of) lleno (de); (of voice) velado, indistinto; (obtuse) estúpido, lerdo; (friendly) íntimo. *adv* densamente; continuamente, sin cesar. **three feet t.,** de tres pies de espesor. **That's a bit t.!** ¡Eso es un poco demasiado! **to be as t. as thieves,** estar unidos como los dedos de la mano. **t.-lipped,** con labios gruesos, bezudo. **t.-headed,** estúpido, lerdo. **t.-skinned,** de piel gruesa; *zool* paquidermo; *fig* sin vergüenza, insensible. **t. stroke,** (of letters) grueso, *m*

thick *n* espesor, *m*; parte gruesa, *f*; lo más denso; (of a fight) lo más reñido; centro, *m*. **in the t. of,** en el centro (de), en medio de

thicken *vt* espesar; (increase) aumentar, multiplicar; *cul* espesar. *vi* espesarse; condensar; aumentar, multiplicarse; (of a mystery, etc.) complicarse; hacerse más denso; *cul* espesarse

thickening *n* hinchamiento, *m*; gordura, *f*; (cul and of paints) espesante, *m*

thicket *n* matorral, soto, *m*, maleza, *f*; (grove) boscaje, *m*

thickly *adv* densamente; espesamente; continuamente, sin cesar; (of speech) indistintamente

thickness *n* espesor, *m*; grueso, *m*; densidad, *f*; (of liquids) consistencia, *f*; (layer) capa, *f*; (of speech) dificultad (en el hablar), *f*

thickset *a* doblado

thief *n* ladrón (-ona); (in a candle) moco de vela, *m*. **Stop t.!** ¡Ladrones! **thieves' den,** *fig* cueva de ladrones, *f*

thieve *vi* hurtar, robar. *vt* robar

thievish *a* ladrón

thigh *n* muslo, *m*. **t.-bone,** fémur, *m*

thimble *n* dedal, *m*

thimbleful *n* lo que cabe en un dedal; *fig* dedada, *f*

thin *a* delgado; (lean) flaco; (small) pequeño; delicado; fino; (of air, light) tenue, sutil; (clothes) ligero; (sparse) escaso; transparente; (watery) aguado; (of wine) bautizado; (not close) claro; (of arguments) flojo. *vt* adelgazar; aclarar; *agr* limpiar; reducir. *vi* adelgazarse; afilarse; reducirse. **somewhat t.,** (of persons) delgaducho, algo flaco. **to grow t.,** enflaquecer; afilarse. **to make t.,** hacer adelgazar volver flaco. **t.-clad,** ligero de ropa; mal vestido. **t.-faced,** de cara delgada. **t.-lipped,** de labios apretados. **t.-skinned,** de piel fina; *fig* sensitivo, sensible

thine. See **theirs.** *poss pron* (el) tuyo, *m*; (la) tuya, *f*; (los) tuyos, *m pl*; (las) tuyas, *f pl*; tu, *mf*; tus, *mf pl*; de tí. **The fault is t.,** La culpa es tuya, La culpa es de tí

thing *n* cosa, *f*; objeto, artículo, *m*; (affair) asunto, *m*; (contemptuous) sujeto, tipo, *m*; (creature) ser, *m*, criatura, *f*; *pl* **things,** (belongings) efectos, trastos, *m pl*; (luggage) equipaje, *m*; (clothes) trapitos, *m pl*; (circumstances) circunstancias, condiciones, *f pl*. **above all things,** ante todo, sobre todo. **a very pretty little t.,** (child) una pequeña muy mona. **as things are,** tal como están las cosas. **for one t.,** en primer lugar. **Her behavior is not quite the t.,** La conducta de ella no está bien vista. **It is a bad t. that . . . ,** Lo malo es que . . . **It is a good t. that . . . ,** Menos mal que . . . ; Lo bueno es que . . . **No such t.!** ¡No hay tal!; ¡Nada de eso! **Poor t.!** ¡Pobrecito!; (woman) ¡Pobre mujer!; (man) ¡Pobre hombre! **to be just the t.,** venir al pelo. **with one t. and another,** entre unas cosas y otras. **I like things Spanish,** Me gusta lo español

think *vt* and *vi* pensar; (believe) creer; (deem) considerar, juzgar; imaginar; (suspect) sospechar; (opine) ser de opinión (que). **And to t. that . . . !** ¡Y pensar que . . . ! **As you t. fit,** Como usted quiera, Como a usted le parezca bien. **He thought as much,** Se lo figuraba. **He little thought that . . . !** ¡Cuán lejos estaba de pensar que . . . ! **He thinks nothing of . . . ,** No le importa . . . ; Desprecia, Tiene una opinión bastante mala de. **I don't t. so,** No lo creo. **I should just t. not!** ¡Claro que no! ¡Eso sí que no! **I should just t. so!** ¡Claro! ¡Ya lo creo! **It makes me t. of . . . ,** Me hace pensar en . . . **One might t.,** Podría creerse . . . **to t. better of something,** cambiar de opinión, considerar mejor. **to t. highly (badly) of,** tener buen (mal) concepto sobre. **to t. over carefully,** pensarlo bien, considerar detenidamente; *inf* consultar con la almohada. **to t. proper,** creer conveniente. **to t. to oneself,** pensar para sí (or entre sí). **to t. too much of oneself,** pensar demasiado en sí; tener demasiada buena opinión de sí mismo; tener humos. **What do you t. about it?** ¿Qué te parece? **to t. about,** (of persons) pensar en; (of things) pensar de (or sobre); meditar, considerar, reflexionar sobre. **to t. for,** pensar por. **to t. of,** pensar en; pensar de (or sobre). **What do you t. of this?** ¿Qué te parece esto? **to t. out,** idear, proyectar, hacer planes para; (a problem) resolver. **to t. over,** pensar; reflexionar sobre, meditar sobre. **I shall t. it over,** Lo pensaré.

thinker *n* pensador, *m*

thinking *n* pensamiento, *m*, reflexión, meditación, *f*; juicio, *m*; opinión, *f*, parecer, *m*. *a* pensador; inteligente; racional; serio. **To my way of t.,** Según pienso yo, A mi parecer. **way of t.,** modo de pensar, *m*

thinly *adv* delgadamente; esparcidamente; (lightly) ligeramente; poco numeroso

thinness *n* delgadez, *f*; (leanness) flaqueza, *f*; sutileza, tenuidad, *f*; (lack) escasez, *f*; pequeño número, *m*; poca consistencia, *f*

third *a* tercero (tercer before *m, sing* noun); (of monarchs) tercero; (of the month) (el) tres. *n* tercio, *m*, tercera parte, *f*; *mus* tercera, *f*. **T. time lucky!** ¡A la tercera va la vencida! **t. class,** *n* tercera clase, *f*. *a* de tercera clase. **t. party,** tercera persona, *f*. **t.-party insurance,** seguro contra tercera persona, *m*. **t. person,** tercero (-ra); *gram* tercera persona, *f*. **t.-rate,** de tercera clase

thirdly *adv* en tercer lugar

thirst *n* sed, *f*; *fig* deseo, *m*, ansia, *f*; entusiasmo, *m*. **to satisfy one's t.,** apagar (or matar) la sed

thirsty *a* sediento. **to be t.,** tener sed. **to make t.,** dar sed.

thirteen *a* and *n* trece *m*. **t. hundred,** *a* and *n* mil trescientos *m*

thirteenth *a* décimotercio; (of monarchs) trece; (of month) (el) trece, *m*. *n* décimotercio, trezavo, *m*

thirtieth *a* trigésimo; (of month) (el) treinta, *m*. *n* treintavo, *m*

thirty *a* and *n* treinta, *m*. **t.-first,** treinta y uno

this *dem a* este, *m*; esta, *f*, *dem pron* éste, *m*; ésta, *f*; esto, *neut* **by t. time,** a esta hora, ya. **like t.,** de este modo, así. **T. is Wednesday,** Hoy es miércoles. **What is all t.?** ¿Qué es todo esto?

thistle *n* cardo, *m*. **t.-down,** papo de cardo, vilano de cardo, *m*

thither *adv* allá, hacia allá; a ese fin. *a* más remoto

thong *n* correa, tira, *f*

thoracic *a* torácico

thorax *n* tórax, *m*

thorn *n* espina, *f*; (tree) espino, *m*; *fig* abrojo, *m*, espina, *f*. **to be a t. in the flesh of,** ser una espina en el costado de. **t. brake,** espinar, *m*

thornless *a* sin espinas

thorny *a* espinoso; *fig* difícil, arduo

thorough *a* completo; perfecto; (conscientious) concienzudo; (careful) cuidadoso. **t.-bred,** (of animals) de pura raza, de casta; (of persons) bien nacido. **t.-paced,** cabal, consumado

thoroughfare *n* vía pública, *f*. **"No t.,"** «Prohibido el paso», Calle cerrada

thoroughly *adv* completamente; (of knowing a subject) a fondo; concienzudamente

thoroughness *n* perfección, *f*; minuciosidad, *f*

those *dem a pl* of **that,** esos, *m pl*; esas, *f pl*; aquellos, *m pl*; aquellas, *f pl*, *dem pron* ésos, *m pl*; ésas, *f pl*; aquéllos, *m pl*; aquéllas, *f pl*; (standing for a noun) los, *m pl*; las, *f pl*. **t. who,** quienes, *mf pl*; los que, *m pl*; las que, *f pl*. **t. that** or **which,** los que, *m pl*; las que, *f pl*. **Your eyes are t. of your mother,** Tus ojos son los de tu madre

thou *pers pron* tú

though *conjunc* (followed by subjunc. when doubt is implied or uncertain future time) aunque, bien que; (nevertheless) sin embargo, no obstante; (in spite of) a pesar de que; (but) pero. **as t.,** como si (followed by subjunc.). **even t.,** aunque (followed by subjunc.)

thought *n* pensamiento, *m*; meditación, reflexión, *f*. **some thoughts on . . .** algunas reflexiones sobre . . . ; opinión, *f*; consideración, *f*; idea, *f*, propósito, *m*; (care) cuidado, *m*, solicitud, *f*; *inf* pizca, *f*. **on second thought,** después de pensarlo bien. **The t. struck him,** Se le ocurrió la idea. **to collect one's thoughts,** orientarse; informarse (de). **t.-reading,** adivinación del pensamiento, *f*. **t.-transference,** telepatía, transmisión del pensamiento, *f*

thoughtful *a* pensativo, meditabundo; serio; especulativo; (provident) previsor; (kind) atento, solícito; cuidadoso; (anxious) inquieto, intranquilo

thoughtfully *adv* pensativamente; seriamente; (providently) con previsión; (kindly) atentamente, solícitamente

thoughtfulness *n* natural reflexivo, *m*, seriedad, *f*; (kindness) solicitud, atención, *f*; (forethought) previsión, *f*

thoughtless *a* irreflexivo; (careless) descuidado, negligente; (unkind) inconsiderado; (silly) necio, estúpido

thoughtlessly *adv* sin pensar, irreflexivamente; negligentemente

thoughtlessness *n* irreflexión, *f*; descuido, *m*, negligencia, *f*; (unkindness) inconsideración, *f*; (silliness) neciedad, *f*

thousand *a* mil. *n* mil, *m*; millar, *m* one *a* mil, *m*. **one t. three hundred,** *a* mil trescientos, *m pl*; mil trescientas, *f pl*. *n* mil trescientos, *m pl*. **two (three) t.,** dos (tres) mil. **by thousands,** por millares; por miles. **t.-fold,** mil veces más

thousandth *a* and *n* milésimo *m*

Thrace Tracia, *f*

thrall *n* esclavo (-va); esclavitud, *f*

thrash *vt* azotar, apalear *Mexico* festejar, *Lat. Am.* humear; *agr* trillar, desgranar; *inf* triunfar sobre, derrotar. *vi, agr* trillar el grano; arrojarse, agitarse. *fig* **to t. out,** ventilar

thrashing *n* apaleamiento, *m*, paliza, *f*, *Lat. Am. also* azotera, *f*; *agr* See **threshing**

thread *n* hilo, *m*; (fibre) hebra, fibra, *f*, filamento, *m*; (of a screw) filete, *m*; *fig* hilo, *m*, *a* de hilo. *vt* (a needle) enhebrar; (beads) ensartar; (make one's way) colarse a través de, atravesar; pasar por. **to hang by a t.,** pender de un hilo. **to lose the t. of,** *fig* perder el hilo de

threadbare *a* raído; muy usado; *fig* trivial, viejo

threadlike *a* como un hilo, filiforme

threadworm *n m*, lombriz intestinal, *f*

threat *n* amenaza, *f*

threaten *vt* and *vi* amenazar. **to t. with,** amenazar con

threatening *a* amenazador. *n* amenazas, *f pl*

threateningly *adv* con amenazas

three *a* and *n* tres *m*; (of the clock) las tres, *f pl*; (of one's age) tres años, *m pl*. **t.-color process,** tricromía, *f*.

t.-colored, tricolor. **t.-cornered,** triangular; (of hats) rincones de. **t. traffic,** tráfico directo, *m.* **t. train,** tren de tres picos, tricornio. **t.-cornered hat,** sombrero de directo, *m*
tres picos, tricornio. *m.* **t. decker,** *naut* navío de tres **throughout** *prep* por todo; durante todo. *adv* com-
puentes, *m;* novela larga, *f.* **t. deep,** en tres hileras. **t.** pletamente; (from beginning to end) desde el principio
hundred, *a* and *n* trescientos *m.* **t.-hundredth,** *a* and hasta el fin; (everywhere) en todas partes
n tricentésimo *m.* **t.-legged,** de tres patas. **t.-legged** **throw** *vt* arrojar, lanzar, echar; (fire) disparar; (pottery)
stool, banqueta, *f.* **t.-per-cents,** accion al tres por plasmar; (knock down) derribar; (slough) mudar (la
ciento (3%), *f.* **t.-phase,** *elec* trifásico. **t.-ply,** (of yarn) piel); (cast off) despojarse de; (a rider) desmontar; (a
triple; (of wood) de tres capas. **t.-quarter,** de tres cuar- glance) echar, dirigir (una mirada, etc.); (silk) torcer;
tos. **t. quarters of an hour,** tres cuartos de hora, *m pl.* (dice) echar; (light) dirigir, enfocar. **to t. oneself at**
t.-sided, trilátero. **t. speed gear box,** cambio de mar- **the head of,** echarse a la cabeza de. **to t. open,** abrir
cha de tres velocidades, *m.* **t.-stringed,** *mus* de tres de par en par; abrir. **to t. overboard,** *naut* echar al
cuerdos. **t. thousand,** *a* tres mil, *mf pl; n* tres mar; desechar; (desert) abandonar. **to t. about,** espar-
mil, *m* cir, desparramar; derrochar. **to t. aside,** echar a un
threefold *a* triple lado, desechar; abandonar, dejar. **to t. away,** tirar;
Three Musketeers, the los Tres Mosqueteros desechar, *Lat. Am.* botar; (spend) malgastar, derrochar;
threescore *a* and *n* sesenta, *m pl* (waste) sacrificar; (of opportunities) malograr, perder.
threesome *n* partido de tres, *m* **to t. back,** devolver; echar hacia atrás. **to t. down,**
thresh *vt* trillar, desgranar. *vi* trillar el grano. **to t. out,** derribar, dar en el suelo con; echar abajo; (arms) ren-
ventilar dir. **to t. down the glove,** arrojar el guante. **to t. one-**
threshing *n* trilla, *f.* **t. floor,** era, *f.* **t. machine,** tri- **self down,** tumbarse, echarse; (descend) echarse
lladora, *f* abajo. **to t. oneself down from,** arrojarse de. **to t. in,**
threshold *n* umbral, *Lat. Am. also* dintel, *m; psy* limen, echar dentro; (give extra) añadir; (the clutch) embra-
m; fig comienzo, principio, *m;* (entrance) entrada, *f.* **to** gar; insertar; (a remark) hacer (una observación). **to t.**
cross the t., atravesar (or pisar) los umbrales **off,** despojarse de; quitarse; (refuse) rechazar; sacu-
thrice *adv* tres veces dirse; (get rid of) despedir; (renounce) renunciar; (ex-
thrift *n* frugalidad, parsimonia, *f* hale) emitir, despedir; (verses) improvisar. **to t. on,**
thriftless *a* malgastador, manirroto echar sobre; (garments) ponerse. **to t. oneself upon,**
thrifty *a* frugal, económico lanzarse sobre. **to t. out,** expeler; hacer salir; plantar
thrill *n* estremecimiento, *m;* emoción, *f. vt* conmover, en la calle; (utter) proferir, soltar; (one's chest) inflar;
emocionar; penetrar. *vi* estremecerse, emocionarse (discard) tirar, desechar, *Lat. Am.* botar; **to t. over,**
thriller *n* libro, *m,* (or comedia, *f)* sensacional; (detec- (desert) abandonar, dejar. **to t. up,** (build) levantar;
tive novel) novela policíaca, *f* lanzar en el aire; (a post, etc.) renunciar (a), abando-
thrilling *a* sensacional, espeluznante; (moving) emo- nar; vomitar, *Central America, Mexico* deponer
cionante, conmovedor **throw** *n* echada, *f;* tiro, *m;* (at dice) lance, *m;* jugada, *f;*
thrive *vi* prosperar, medrar; enriquecerse, tener éxito; (wrestling) derribo, *m.* **within a stone's t.,** a tiro de
(grow) desarrollarse, robustecerse; florecer; (of plants) piedra. **t.-back,** retroceso, *m; biol* atavismo, *m*
acertar **thrower** *n* tirador (-ra), lanzador (-ra)
thriving *a* próspero; floreciente; robusto, vigoroso **throwing** *n* lanzamiento, *m,* lanzada, *f.* **t. the ham-**
throat *n* garganta, *f;* orificio, *m;* (narrow entry) paso, *m.* **mer,** lanzamiento del martillo, *m*
sore t., dolor de garganta, *m.* **to cut one's t.,** cortarse **thrum** *vt* and *vi* tocar mal; (of keyed instruments) tela garganta. **to take by the t.,** asir (or agarrar) por la clear; (of stringed instruments) rascar las cuerdas (de)
garganta **thrust** *n* empujón, *m;* (with a sword) estocada, *f;* (fenc-
throat cancer *n* cáncer de la garganta, *m* ing) golpe, *m;* (with a lance) bote, *m;* ataque, *m;* asalto,
throaty *a* indistinto, ronco *m. vt* empujar; (put) meter; (insert) introducir; (pierce)
throb *n* latido, *m;* pulsación, *f;* vibración, *f; fig* es- atravesar; (out, through, of the head, etc.) asomar. *vi*
tremecimiento, *m. vi* palpitar, latir; vibrar acometer, atacar, embestir; meterse, introducirse; (in-
throbbing *n* pulsación, *f;* vibración, *f. a* palpitante; vi- trude) entrometerse; (fencing) dar un golpe. **to t.**
brante. **t. pain,** dolor pungente, *m* **aside,** empujar a un lado; (proposals) rechazar. **to t.**
throe *n* dolor, *m,* agonía, angustia, *f.* **in the throes of,** **back,** hacer retroceder, empujar hacia atrás; (words)
en medio de; luchando con; en las garras de. **throes of** tragarse; (thoughts) apartar, rechazar. **to t. down,**
childbirth, dolores de parto, *m pl.* **throes of death,** empujar hacia abajo; hacer bajar; *fig* reprimir. **to t. for-**
agonía de la muerte, *f* **ward,** empujar hacia delante; hacer seguir. **to t. one-**
thrombosis *n med* trombosis, *f* **self forward,** adelantarse; *fig* ponerse delante de los
throne *n* trono, *m;* (royal power) corona, *f,* poder real, otros, darse importancia. **to t. in,** introducir; (stick)
m. vt elevar al trono. **speech from the t.,** el discurso hincar; (insert) intercalar. **to t. on,** hacer seguir; em-
de la corona, *m* pujar sobre; (garments) ponerse rápidamente. **to t.**
throng *n* muchedumbre, multitud, *f. vi* apiñarse **oneself in,** introducirse; entrometerse. **to t. out,**
remolinarse, acudir. *vt* atestar, llenar de bote en bote echar fuera; hacer salir, echar; expulsar; (the tongue)
throttle *n mech* regulador, *m; aut* estrangulador, *m; inf* sacar (la lengua); (the head, etc.) asomar. **to t.**
garganta, *f. vt* estrangular; *fig* ahogar, suprimir. **to** **through,** atravesar; (pierce) traspasar. **to t. one's**
open (close) the t., abrir (cerrar) el estrangulador **way through,** abrirse paso por. **to t. upon,** imponer,
throttling *n* estrangulación, *f* hacer aceptar
through *prep* por; al través de; de un lado a otro de; por **thud** *n* sonido sordo, *m;* golpe sordo, *m*
medio de; (between) entre; por causa de; gracias a. *adv* **thug** *n* asesino, criminal, *m*
al través; de un lado a otro; (whole) entero, todo; **thumb** *n* pulgar, *m. vt* hojear; ensuciar con los dedos.
(from beginning to end) desde el principio hasta el fin; **under the t. of,** *fig* en el poder de. **t. index,** índice
(to the end) hasta el fin. *a* (of passages, etc.) que va pulgar, *m.* **t.-mark,** huella del dedo, *f.* **t.-screw,** tor-
desde . . . hasta . . . ; (of trains) directo. **to look t. the** nillo de orejas, *m,* **t.-stall,** dedil, *m.* **t.-tack,** chinche, *m*
window, mirar por la ventana, asomarse a la ventana. **thump** *n* golpe, porrazo, *m. vt* and *vi* golpear, aporrear;
to be wet t., estar calado hasta los huesos; estar muy (the ground, of rabbits) zapatear
mojado. **to carry t.,** llevar a cabo. **to fall t.,** caer por; **thunder** *n* trueno, *m;* (of hooves, etc.) estampido, *m;*
(fail) fracasar. **to sleep the whole night t.,** dormir estruendo, *m. vi* tronar; retumbar; *fig* fulminar. *vt* gritar
durante toda la noche, dormir la noche entera. **t. and** en una voz de trueno, rugir. **to t. along,** avanzar como
t., completamente. **through the length and** el trueno; galopar ruidosamente. **t.-clap,** trueno, *m.*
breadth of, a lo largo y a lo ancho de, hasta los últimos **t.-cloud,** nube de tormenta, *f,* nubarrón, *m.* **t.-storm,**

tronada, f. **t. struck,** muerto, estupefacto. **to be thun-derstruck,** quedarse frío

thunderbolt n rayo, m

thunderer n fulminador, m. **the Thunderer,** Júpiter tonante, Júpiter tronante, m; el «Times» londinense, m

Thuringia Turingia, f

Thursday n jueves, m. **Holy T.,** Jueves Santo, m

thus adv así; de este modo; en estos términos; hasta este punto. **t. far,** hasta ahora; hasta este punto; hasta aquí. **Thus it is that . . . ,** Así es que . . .

thwack n golpe, m; vt golpear

thwart vt frustrar, impedir

thy poss a tu, mf; tus, m pl, and f pl

thyme n bot tomillo, m

thymus n anat timo, m

thyroid a tiroideo. **t. gland,** tiroides, f

thyself poss pron tu mismo, m; tu misma, f; (with prep.) tí mismo, m; tí misma, f; (in a reflexive verb) te

tiara n tiara, f

Tiberias Tiberíades, f

Tibetan a and n tibetano (-na); (language) tibetano, m

tibia n anat tibia, f

tic n (twitch) tic nervioso, m

tick n ent ácaro, m; (sound) tictac, m; (cover) funda de colchón, f; inf fiado, crédito, m; (mark) marca, f vi hacer tictac. vt poner una marca contra. **on t.,** inf al fiado. **to t. off,** poner una marca contra; inf reñir. **to t. over,** aut andar, marchar

ticket n billete, Lat. Am. boleto, m; (for an entertainment) entrada, localidad, f; (label) etiqueta, f; (pawn) papeleta de empeño, f; (for luggage) talón, m; (pol U.S.A.) candidatura, f, vt marcar. **to take one's t.,** sacar el billete (or for entertainment) la entrada, f). **excursion t.,** billete de excursión, m. **return t.,** billete de ida y vuelta, m. **season t.,** billete de abono, m. **single t.,** billete sencillo, m. **t. agency,** (for travel) agencia de viajes, f; (for entertainments) agencia de teatros, f. **t. collector or inspector,** revisor, m. **t. holder,** tenedor de billete, m; abonado (-da). **t. office,** (railway) despacho de billetes, m; taquilla, Lat. Am. boletería, f. **t.-of-leave,** libertad condicional, f. **t. punch,** sacabocados, m; (on tramcars) clasificador de billetes, m

ticking n (sound) tictac, m; (cloth) cotí, m

tickle vt hacer cosquillas (a), cosquillear; irritar; (gratify) halagar; (amuse) divertir. vi tener cosquillas; hacer cosquillas; ser irritante

ticklish a cosquilloso; (of persons) difícil, vidrioso; (of affairs) espinoso, delicado

tidal a de marea. **t. wave,** marejada, f; fig ola popular, f

tidbit n See titbit

tiddlywinks n juego de la pulga, m

tide n marea, f; (season) tiempo, m, estación, f; (trend) corriente, f; (progress) curso, m; marcha, f. vi (with over) vencer, superar; aguardar la ocasión. **to go against the t.,** ir contra la corriente. **to go with the t.,** seguir la corriente. **high t.,** marea alta, f. **low t.,** marea baja, f; bajamar, m. **neap t.,** marea muerta, f. **t. mark,** lengua del agua, f

tidily adv aseadamente; en orden, metódicamente

tidiness n aseo, m; buen orden, m

tidings n pl noticias, nuevas, f pl

tidy a aseado; metódico; en orden; pulcro; inf considerable. vt poner en orden, asear; limpiar; (oneself) arreglarse

tie n lazo, m, atadura, f; (knot) nudo, m; (for the neck) corbata, f; sport empate, m; mus ligado, m; arch tirante, m; (spiritual bond) lazo, m; (burden) carga, responsabilidad, f, **tie clasp,** pisa corbata, mf. **tie-pin,** alfiler de corbata, Mexico fistol, m. **tie seller,** corbatero (-ra)

tie vt atar; (bind) ligar; (lace) lacear; (a knot) hacer; (with a knot) anudar; (unite) unir; (fig bind) constreñir, obligar; (limit) limitar, restringir; (occupy) ocupar, entretener; (hamper) estorbar, impedir. vi atarse; sport empatar. **to tie one's tie,** hacer la corbata. **to tie down,** atar a; limitar; obligar. **They tied him down**

to a chair, Le ataron a una silla. **to tie together,** enlazar, ligar; unir. **to tie up,** liar, atar; (wrap) envolver; recoger; naut amarrar, atracar; (restrict) limitar, restringir; (invest) invertir

tie-breaker n desempate, m

tier n fila, hilera, f. **in tiers,** en gradas; (of a dress) en volantes

tiff n disgusto, m

tiger n tigre, m. **t.-cat,** gato (-ta) atigrado (-da). **t.-lily,** tigridia, f

tigerish a atigrado, de tigre; salvaje, feroz

tight a apretado; (not leaky) hermético, impermeable; (taut) tieso, tirante; (narrow) estrecho; (trim) compacto; (of clothes) muy ajustado; (shut) bien cerrado; naut estanco; (risky) peligroso, difícil; (miserly) tacaño, Argentina agalludo; (of money, goods) escaso; (tipsy) borracho, Mexico abombado. **become t., get t.** (get tipsy) Mexico abombarse. **to be t.-fisted,** ser como un puño. **to hold t.,** agarrar fuerte. **t. corner,** fig aprieto, lance apretado, m. **t.-rope,** cuerda de volatinero, cuerda floja, Lat. Am. maroma, f. **t.-rope walker,** alambrista, equilibrista, mf; volatinero (-ra), bailarín de la cuerda floja, m, Lat. Am. maromero (-ra), mf. **t.-rope walker's pole,** balancín, m

tighten vt estrechar, apretar, Lat. Am. atesar; (stretch) estirar; (of saddle girths) cinchar. vi estrecharse; estirarse. **t. up** Lat. Am. atesar

tightly adv estrechamente

tightness n estrechez, f; tirantez, tensión, f; (feeling of constriction) opresión, f; (drunkenness) emborrachamiento, m

tights n pl mallas, f pl

tile n teja, f; (for flooring) baldosa, losa, f; (ornamental) azulejo, m; (hat) chistera, f. vt tejar; embaldosar. **t. floor,** enlosado, embaldosado, m. **t. manufacturer,** tejero, m. **t. works** or **yard,** tejar, m, (Colombia) galpón m

tiler n solador, m; tejero, m

till n (for money) cajón, m. vt agr cultivar, labrar. prep hasta. conjunc hasta que

tillable a laborable

tiller n agr labrador, m; bot mugrón, renuevo, vástago, m; naut caña del timón, f

tilling n agr cultivo, laboreo, m

tilt n inclinación, f; ladeo, m; (fight) torneo, m, justa, f. vt inclinar; ladear; (a drinking vessel) empinar. vi inclinarse; ladearse; (fight) justar. **to t. against,** fig arremeter contra, atacar. **at full t.,** a todo correr. **t. hammer,** martinete de báscula, m. **t.-yard,** palestra, f

tilting n incinación, f; (fighting) justas, f pl. a inclinado

timber n madera de construcción, f; (trees) árboles de monte, m pl; bosque, m; (beam) viga, f; naut cuaderna, f. vt enmaderar. **t. line,** límite del bosque maderable, m. **t. merchant,** maderero, m. **t. wolf,** lobo gris, m. **t. work,** maderaje, m. **t. yard,** maderería, f, corral de madera, m

timbered a enmaderado; (with trees) arbolado

timbre n mus timbre, m

timbrel n mus tamborete, tamboril, m

time n (in general) tiempo, m; (epoch) época, edad, f; tiempos, m pl; (of the year) estación, f; (by the clock) hora, f; (lifetime) vida, f; (particular moment of time) momento, m; (occasion) sazón, ocasión, f; (day) día, m; (time allowed) plazo, m; (in repetition) vez, f; mus compás, m; mil paso, m. vt ajustar al tiempo; hacer con oportunidad; (regulate) regular; calcular el tiempo que se emplea en hacer una cosa; (a blow) calcular. **all the t.,** todo el tiempo; continuamente, sin cesar. **a long t.,** mucho tiempo. **a long t. ago,** mucho tiempo ha, hace mucho tiempo. **at a t.,** a la vez, al mismo tiempo; (of period) en una época. **at any t.,** a cualquier hora; en cualquier momento; (when you like) cuando gustes. **at no t.,** jamás, nunca. **at some t.,** alguna vez; en alguna época. **at some t. or another,** un día u otro; en una u otra ocasión; en alguna época. **at that t.,** en aquella época; en la sazón; en aquel instante. **at the**

one t., de una vez. **at the present t.,** en la actualidad, al presente. **at the proper t.,** a su debido tiempo; a la hora señalada; a la hora conveniente. **at the same t.,** al mismo tiempo. **at the same t. as,** mientras, a medida que; al mismo instante que, **at times,** a veces, en ocasiones. **behind the times,** fig atrasado de noticias; pasado de moda. **behind t.,** atrasado. **by that t.,** para entonces. **every t.,** cada vez; siempre. **for some t.,** durante algún tiempo. **for some t. past,** de algún tiempo a esta parte. **for the t. being,** de momento, por ahora, por lo pronto. **from this t.,** desde hoy; desde esta fecha. **from this t. forward,** de hoy en adelante. **from t. to t.,** de vez en cuando, de cuando en cuando, de tarde en tarde. **in a month's t.,** en un mes. **in a short t.,** en breve, dentro de poco. **in good t.,** puntualmente; temprano. **in my t.,** en mis días, en mis tiempos. **in olden times,** antiguamente, en otros tiempos. **in the course of t.,** andando el tiempo, en el transcurso de los años. **in the t. of,** en la época de. **in t.,** (promptly) a tiempo; con el tiempo. **in t. to come,** en el porvenir. **It is t. to . . . ,** Es hora de . . . **many times,** frecuentemente, muchas veces. **Once upon a t.,** Érase una vez, Una vez había, Érase que érase. Érase que se era. **Since t. out of mind,** Desde tiempo inmemorial. **the last (next) t.,** la última (próxima) vez. **this t. of year,** esta estación del año. **T. hangs heavy on his hands,** El tiempo se le hace interminable. **T. flies,** El tiempo vuela. **T. will tell!** ¡El tiempo lo dirá! ¡Veremos lo que veremos! **What t. is it?** ¿Qué hora es? **The t. is . . . ,** La hora es . . . **within a given t.,** dentro de un plazo dado. **to be out of t.,** estar fuera de compás. **to gain t.,** ganar tiempo. **to have a good t.,** pasarlo bien, divertirse. **to have a bad t.,** pasarlo mal; *inf* tener un mal cuarto de hora. **to have no t. to,** no tener tiempo para + noun or pronoun, no tener tiempo de + infinitive. **to keep t.,** guardar el compás. **to kill t.,** engañar (or entretener) el tiempo. **to mark t.,** marcar el paso; *fig* hacer tiempo. **to pass the t.,** pasar el rato; pasar el tiempo. **to pass the t. of day,** saludar. **to serve one's t.,** (to a trade) servir el aprendizaje; (in prison) cumplir su condena; *mil* hacer el servicio militar. **to take t. to,** tomar tiempo para. **to take t. by the forelock,** asir la ocasión por la melena. **to waste t.,** perder el tiempo. **t. exposure,** pose, *f.* **t. fuse,** espoleta de tiempo, espoleta graduada, *f.* **t.-honored,** tradicional, consagrado por el tiempo. **t.-keeper,** capataz, *m;* reloj, *m.* **t.-saving,** que ahorra el tiempo. **t.-server,** lameculos, *mf* **t.-signal,** señales horarias, *f pl.* **t.-table,** horario, *m;* itinerario, programa, *m;* (railway) guía de ferrocarriles, *f.* **t. to come,** porvenir, *m,* lo venidero

timed *a* calculado; **(ill-)** intempestivo; **(well-)** oportuno

timeless *a* eterno

timeliness *n* tempestividad, oportunidad, *f*

timely *a* oportuno

timepiece *n* reloj, *m*

time zone *n* huso esférico, huso horario, *m*

timid *a* tímido, asustadizo, medroso; **(shy)** vergonzoso

timidity *n* timidez, *f;* vergüenza, *f*

timing *n* medida del tiempo, *f; mech* regulación, *f;* (timetable) horario, *m*

timorous *a* timorato, apocado, asustadizo

timorousness *n* encogimiento, *m,* timidez, *f*

tin *n* (metal) estaño, *m;* (container) lata, *f;* (sheet) hojalata, *f;* (money) plata, *f. vt* estañar; (place in tins) envasar en lata; cubrir con hojalata, hoja de aluminio, *f.* **tin-foil,** papel de estaño, *m.* **tin hat,** casco de acero, *m.* **tin opener,** abrelatas, abridor de latas, *m.* **tin-plate,** hojalata, *f.* **tin soldier,** soldado de plomo, *m.* **tin ware,** hojalatería, *f*

tincture *n* tintura, *f,* tinte, *m; med* tintura, *f;* (trace) dejo, *m;* (veneer) capa, *f. vt* teñir, tinturar

tinder *n* yesca, *f.* **t. box,** yescas, lumbres, *f pl*

tinge *n* tinte, matiz, *m; fig* dejo, toque, *m. vt* matizar, tinturar; *fig* tocar

tingle *n* picazón, comezón, *f;* (thrill) estremecimiento,

m. vi picar; (of ears) zumbar; (thrill) estremecerse (de); vibrar

tingling *n* picazón, *f;* (of the ears) zumbido, *m;* (thrill) estremecimiento, *m*

tinker *n* calderero remendón, *m. vt* remendar. *vi* chafallar. **to t. with,** jugar con

tinkle *n* tilín, retintín, *m;* campanilleo, *m;* cencerreo, *m. vi* tintinar. *vt* hacer tintinar

tinkling *n* retintín, tintineo, *m;* campanilleo, *m*

tinned *a* (of food) en lata, en conserva

tinsel *n* oropel, *m;* (cloth) lama de oro o plata, *f,* brocadillo, *m; fig* oropel, *m. a* de oropel; de brocadillo; *fig* charro. *vt* adornar con oropel

tinsmith *n* hojalatero, estañador, *m*

tint *n* tinta, *f,* color, *m;* matiz, *m;* tinte, *m. vt* colorar, teñir; matizar

tinting *n* tintura, *f,* teñido, *m*

tiny *a* diminuto, minúsculo, menudo, chiquito

tip *n* punta, *f;* cabo, *m,* extremidad, *f;* (of an umbrella, etc.) regatón, *m;* (of a lance) borne, *m;* (of a cigarette) boquilla, *f;* (of a shoe) puntera, *f;* (of a finger) yema, *f;* (for rubbish) depósito de basura, *m;* (gratuity) propina, *f;* (information) informe oportuno, *m;* (tap) golpecito, *m.* **to have on the tip of one's tongue,** tener en la punta de la lengua. **tip-cart,** volquete, *m.* **tip-up seat,** asiento plegable, *m*

tip *vt* inclinar; volcar, voltear; (drinking vessel) empinar; poner regatón, etc. (a); *poet* tocar, golpear ligeramente; (reward) dar propina (a). *vi* inclinarse; (topple) tambalearse; (reward) dar propina. **to tip the wink,** guiñar el ojo (a). **to tip off,** (liquids) echar; hacer caer; (inform) decir en secreto; informar oportunamente. **to tip over,** *vt* volcar; hacer caer. *vi* volcarse; caer; (of a boat) zozobrar. **to tip up,** *vt* (a seat) levantar; (money) proporcionar (el dinero); (upset) volcar; hacer perder el equilibrio. *vi* (of a seat) levantarse; (lose the balance) perder el equilibrio

tipple *n* bebida, *f. vt* beber, sorber. *vi* empinar el codo

tippler *n* borracho (-cha)

tipsily *adv* como borracho

tipsy *a* achispado, algo borracho, *Lat. Am.* mamado. **to be t.,** estar entre dos luces, estar entre dos velas

tiptoe (on) *adv* de puntillas; *fig* excitado, ansioso. **to stand on t.,** ponerse de puntillas, empinarse

tirade *n* diatriba, *f*

tire *n* (of a cart, etc.) llanta, *f; aut* neumático, *Lat. Am.* caucho, *m;* (of a perambulator, etc.) rueda de goma, *f.* **balloon t.,** neumático balón, *m.* **pneumatic t.,** neumático, *m.* **slack t.,** neumático desinflado, *m.* **solid t.,** neumático macizo, *m.* **spare t.,** neumático de recambio (or de repuesto), *m.* **t. burst,** estallido de un neumático, *m.* **t. valve,** válvula de cámara (del neumático), *f*

tire *vt* cansar, fatigar; (bore) aburrir. *vi* cansarse, fatigarse; aburrirse. **to be tired of,** estar cansado de. **to grow tired,** empezar a cansarse. **to t. out,** rendir de cansancio

tired *a* cansado, fatigado. **to be sick and t. of,** estar hasta la coronilla (de), (of persons) con. **t. of,** cansado de; disgustado de

tiredness *n* cansancio, *m,* fatiga, *f;* aburrimiento, *m*

tireless *a* infatigable, incansable

tiresome *a* fastidioso, molesto, pesado; (dull) aburrido

tiresomeness *n* pesadez, *f,* fastidio, *m;* tedio, aburrimiento, *m*

tiring *a* fatigoso

tissue *n* (cloth) tisú, *m,* lama, *f;* (paper) pañuelito *m; biol* tejido, *m;* (series) serie, sarta, *f.* **t. paper,** papel de seda, *m*

tit *n orn* paro, *m.* **tit for tat,** tal para cual

Titan *n* titán, *m*

titanic *a* titánico

titbit *n* golosina, *f*

tithe *n* décima, *f;* fracción, pequeña parte, *f, vt* diezmar. **t. gatherer,** diezmero (-ra)

titillate *vt* titilar, estimular

titivate *vi* arreglarse

title *n* título, *m*; (right) derecho, *m*; documento, *m*. **to give a t. to,** intitular; ennoblecer. **t. deed,** títulos de propiedad, *m*. **t. page,** portada, *f*. **t. role,** papel principal, *m*

titter *vi* reírse disimuladamente. *n* risa disimulada, *f*

tittle *n* adarme, tilde, ápice, *m*

titular *a* titular; nominal

to *prep* a; (as far as) hasta; (in the direction of) en dirección a, hacia; (with indirect object) a; (until) hasta; (compared with) en comparación con, comparado con; (against) contra; (according to) según; (as) como; (in) en; (so that, in order to, for the purpose of) para; (indicating possession) a, de; (of time by the clock) menos; (by) por; (before verbs of motion or which imply motion) a (sometimes para); (before some other verbs) de; en; (before verbs of beginning, inviting, exhorting, obliging) a; (indicating indirect object) a; (before a subjunctive or infinitive indicating future action or obligation) que. **To** is often not translated. With most Spanish infinitives no separate translation is necessary, e.g. leer, decir, to read, to speak. Some verbs are always followed by a preposition (e.g. **to begin to speak,** empezar a hablar, etc.). *adv* (shut) cerrado. **to come to,** volver en sí. **to lie to,** *naut* ponerse a la capa. **to and from,** de un lado a otro. **face to face,** cara a cara. **He has been a good friend to them,** Ha sido un buen amigo para ellos. **That is new to me,** Eso es nuevo para mí. **He went to London,** Se fue a Londres. **to go to France (Canada),** ir a Francia (al Canadá). **the road to Madrid,** la carretera de Madrid. **She kept the secret to herself,** Guardó el secreto para sí. **to go to the dentist,** ir al dentista. **We give it to them,** Se lo damos a ellos. **It belongs to me,** Pertenece a mí. **What does it matter to you?** ¿Qué te importa a tí? **I wish to see him,** Quiero verle. **They did it to help us,** Lo hicieron para ayudarnos. **I have to go to see her,** Tengo que ir a verla. **to this day,** hasta hoy, hasta el presente. **It is a quarter to six,** Son las seis menos cuarto. **to the house of . . ., to . . .'s** a casa de. *Lat. Am. also* donde (e.g. **My wife went to her friend's house** Mi mujer fue a casa de su amiga, Mi mujer fue donde su amiga). **to the last shilling,** hasta el último chelín. **the next to me,** el que me sigue. **closed to the public,** cerrado para el público

toad *n* sapo, *m*

toady *n* lameculos, *mf* adulador (-ra). *vt* lamer el culo (a), adular

toast *n cul* tostada, *f*; (drink) brindis, *m*. *vt* tostar; brindar, beber a la salud de. *vi* brindar. **buttered t.,** mantecada, *f*. **t.-rack,** portatostadas, *m*

toaster *n* (device) tostador, *m*; (person) brindador, *m*

toasting *n* tostadura, *f*, tueste, *m*, *a* de tostar. **t.-fork,** tostadera, *f*

tobacco *n* tabaco, *m*. *a* tabacalero. **black** or **cut t.,** picadura, *f*. **leaf t.,** tabaco de hoja, *m*. **mild t.,** tabaco flojo, *m*. **pipe t.,** tabaco de pipa, *m*. **plug t.,** tabaco para mascar, *m*. **strong t.,** tabaco fuerte, *m*. **Turkish t.,** tabaco turco, *m*. **Virginian t.,** tabaco rubio, *m*. **t.-pipe,** pipa (de pipa), *f*. **t.-pipe cleaner,** escobillón para limpiar pipas, *m*. **t. plantation,** tabacal, *m*. **t. planter,** tabacalero (-ra). **t. poisoning,** tabaquismo, *m*. **t.-pouch** or **jar,** tabaquera, *f*

tobacconist *n* tabaquero (-ra). **tobacconist's shop,** tabaquería, *Lat. Am.* cigarrería, *f*, expendio, *m*

toboggan *n* tobogán, *m*. *vi* ir en tobogán. **t. run,** pista de tobogán, *f*

tocsin *n* rebato, *m*

today *adv* hoy; ahora, actualmente, al presente, hoy día. *n* el día de hoy. **from t.,** desde hoy. **from t. forward,** de hoy en adelante

toddle *vi* hacer pinos, empezar a andar; (stroll) dar una vuelta; (leave) marcharse

toddy *n* ponche, *m*

toe *n* dedo del pie, *m*; (cloven) pezuña, *f*; uña, *f*; (of furniture) base, *f*, pie, *m*; (of stockings, shoes) punta, *f*. **He**

stepped on my toe, Me pisó el dedo del pie. **big toe,** dedo pulgar del pie, dedo gordo del pie, *m*. **little toe,** dedo pequeño del pie, *m*. **to toe the line,** ponerse en la raya; *fig* cumplir con su deber. **toe-cap,** puntera, *f*. **toe-dancing,** baile de puntillas, *m*. **toe-nail,** uña del dedo del pie, *f*

toffee *n* caramelo, *m*

toga *n* toga, *f*

together *adv* junto; (uninterruptedly) sin interrupción; (in concert) simultáneamente, a la vez, al mismo tiempo; (consecutively) seguido. **t. with,** junto con; en compañía de; (simultaneously) a la vez que

toil *n* labor, *f*, trabajo, *m pl*. **toils,** lazos, *m pl*; *fig* redes, *f pl*. *vi* trabajar, afanarse. **to t. along,** caminar penosamente (por); adelantar con dificultad. **to t. up,** subir penosamente

toiler *n* trabajador (-ra)

toilet *n* tocado, *m*; atavío, *m*; vestido, *m*; (w.c.) retrete, excusado, *m*; (for ladies) tocador, *m*. **to make one's t.,** arreglarse. **t. case,** neceser, *m*. **t.-paper,** papel higiénico, *m*. **t.-powder,** polvos de arroz, *m pl*. **t. roll,** rollo de papel higiénico, *m*. **t.-set,** juego de tocador, *m*. **t. soap,** jabón de olor, jabón de tocador, *m*

toiling *n* trabajo duro, *m*, *a* laborioso, trabajador

token *n* señal, muestra, *f*; prueba, *f*; (presage) síntoma, indicio, *m*; (remembrance) recuerdo, *m*. **as a t. of,** en señal de; como recuerdo de

Tokyo Tokio, *m*

tolerable *a* tolerable, soportable, llevadero; (fairly good) mediano, mediocre, regular

tolerably *adv* bastante

tolerance *n* tolerancia, *f*; paciencia, indulgencia, *f*

tolerant *a* tolerante; indulgente

tolerate *vt* tolerar, sufrir, soportar; permitir

toleration *n* tolerancia, *f*; indulgencia, paciencia, *f*. **religious t.,** libertad de cultos, *f*

toll *n* (of a bell) tañido, doble, *m*; (for passage) peaje, portazgo, *m*; (for grinding) derecho de molienda, *m*. *vt* and *vi* doblar, tañer. **to t. the hour,** dar la hora. **t. call,** conferencia telefónica interurbana, llamada a larga distancia, *f*. **t. gate,** barrera de peaje, *f*. **t. house,** oficina de portazgos, *f*

toll booth *n* caseta de pago, *f*

tolling *n* tañido, clamor (de las campanas), *m*

Tom *n* Tomás, *m*; (cat) gato, *m*. **Tom, Dick and Harry,** Fulano, Zutano y Mengano

tomahawk *n* hacha de guerra de los indios, *f*

tomato *n* tomate, jitomate (Mexico) *m*. **t. plant,** tomatera, *f*. **t. sauce,** salsa de tomate, *f*

tomb *n* tumba, *f*, sepulcro, *m*

tombac *n* tombac, *m*, tumbaga, *f*

tomboy *n* muchachote, torbellino, *m*

tombstone *n* piedra mortuoria, *f*, monumento funerario, *m*

tome *n* tomo, volumen, *m*

tomfoolery *n* necedad, tontería, *f*; payasada, *f*

tommy gun *n* pistola automática

tomorrow *adv* mañana, *f*. **a fortnight t.,** mañana en quince. **the day after t.,** pasado mañana. **t. afternoon (morning),** mañana por la tarde (mañana). **T. is Friday,** Mañana es viernes

ton *n* tonelada, *f*

tonality *n* tonalidad, *f*

tone *n* tono, *m*; (mus, med, art) tono, *m*; (of the voice) acento, *m*, entonación, *f*; (of musical instruments) sonido, *m*; (shade) matiz, *m*. *vt* entonar; *phot* virar. **to t. down,** *vt* (art, mus) amortiguar; *fig* suavizar, modificar. *vi* (art, mus) amortiguarse; *fig* suavizarse, modificarse. **to t. in with,** (of colors) *vt* armonizar con. *vi* armonizarse, corresponder en tono o matiz. **to t. up,** *vt* subir de color, intensificar el color de; *med* entonar, robustecer. **t. poem,** poema sinfónico, *m*

tonelessly *adv* sin tono; apáticamente

tongs *n pl* tenazas, *f pl*; tenacillas, *f pl*. **curling t.,** tenacillas para el pelo, *f pl*. **sugar t.,** tenacillas para azúcar, *f pl*

tongue *n anat* lengua, *f;* (language) idioma, *m*, lengua, *f;* (speech) modo de hablar, *m*, habla, *f; mus* lengüeta, *f;* (of buckle) diente, *m;* (of shoe) oreja, *f;* (of land) lengua, *f;* (of a bell) badajo, *m;* (flame) lengua, *f.* **My t. ran away with me,** *inf* Se me fue la mula. **to give t.,** ladrar. **to hold one's t.,** cerrar el pico, tener la boca. **t. of fire,** lengua de fuego, *f.* **t. tied,** con impedimento en el habla; turbado, confuso; mudo. **t.-twister,** trabalenguas, *m*

-tongued *a* de voz . . .

tonic *a* tónico. *n med* tónico, reconstituyente, *m; mus* tónica, *f*

tonight *adv* and *n* esta noche

tonnage *n* tonelaje, porte, *m;* (duty) derecho de tonelaje, *m*

tonner *n naut* de . . . toneladas

tonsil *n* amígdala, *f*

tonsillitis *n* amigdalitis, *f*

tonsure *n ecc* tonsura, *f,* *vt* tonsurar

tonsured *a* tonsurado

too *adv* demasiado; (very) muy; también; además. **too hard,** demasiado difícil, demasiado rígido; (of persons) demasiado duro. **too much,** demasiado. **too often,** con demasiada frecuencia

tool *n* herramienta, *f;* utensilio, *m;* instrumento, *m;* (person) criatura, *f. vt* labrar con herramienta; (a book) estampar en seco. **t.-bag,** capacho, *m.* **t. box,** caja de herramientas, *f*

tooling *n* (of books) estampación en seco, *f*

toot *n* sonido de bocina, *m, vi* sonar una bocina

tooth *n* diente, *m;* muela, *f;* (of comb) púa, *f;* (taste) gusto, paladar, *m;* (cog) diente de rueda, *m;* (of saw) diente, *m. vt* dentar; mellar. *vi mech* engranar. **armed to the teeth,** armado hasta los dientes. **double t.,** muela, *f.* **false teeth,** dentadura postiza, *f.* **set of teeth,** dentadura, *f.* **to cut one's teeth,** echar los dientes. **to have a sweet t.,** ser muy goloso. **to show one's teeth,** enseñar los dientes. **t.-brush,** cepillo para los dientes, *m.* **t. drawing,** extracción de un diente, *f.* **t.-paste,** pasta dentífrica, *f*

toothache *n* dolor de muelas, *m*

toothed *a* con dientes; dentado

toothless *a* desdentado, sin dientes; (of combs) sin púas

toothpick *n* mondadientes, *m*

top *n* (summit) cima, cumbre, *f;* (of a tree) copa, *f;* (of the head) coronilla, *f;* (of a page) cabeza, *f;* (crest) copete, *m,* cresta, *f;* (surface) superficie, *f;* (of a wall) coronamiento, *m;* (tip) punta, *f;* (point) ápice, *m;* (of a tram, bus) imperial, baca, *f;* (of a wave) cresta, *f;* (acme) auge, *m;* (of a class) primero (de la clase), *m;* (highest rank) último grado, *m;* (of a plant) hojas, *f pl;* (of a piano) cima, *f; naut* cofa, *f;* (head of a bed, etc.) cabeza, *f;* (lid) tapadera, *f;* (toy) trompo, peón, *m;* (humming) trompa, *f, a* más alto; máximo; (chief) principal, primero. *vt* (cover) cubrir de; (cut off) desmochar; (come level with) llegar a la cima de; (rise above) elevarse por encima (de), coronar, dominar; (be superior to) exceder, aventajar; (golf) topear. **at the top,** a la cabeza; a la cumbre. **from top to bottom,** de arriba abajo. **on top of,** encima de; (besides) en adición a, además de. **to be top-dog,** ser un gallito. **to sleep like a top,** dormir como un lirón. **top boots,** botas de campaña, *f pl.* **top-dog,** vencedor, *m;* poderoso, *m.* **top-hat,** sombrero de copa, *m.* **top-heavy,** más pesado por arriba que por abajo

topaz *n* topacio, jacinto occidental, *m*

topcoat *n* sobretodo, gabán, *m*

top floor *n* piso alto, *m*

topic *n* asunto, tema, *m*

topical *a* tópico; actual

topknot *n* cresta, *f,* penacho, *m;* (of birds) moño, *m;* copete, *m*

topmast *n* mastelero, *m*

topmost *a* más alto; más importante

topographer *n* topógrafo, *m*

topographical *a* topográfico

topography *n* topografía, *f*

topple *vi* tambalearse, estar al punto de caer. **to t. down,** volcarse; derribarse; caer. **to t. over,** *vi* venirse abajo; perder el equilibrio. *vt* derribar, hacer caer

topsail *n* gavia, *f*

topsyturvy *a* desordenado. *adv* en desorden, patas arriba, de arriba abajo

toque *n* toca, *f*

torch *n* antorcha, hacha, tea, *f.* **electric t.,** lamparilla eléctrica, *f.* **t.-bearer,** hachero, *m*

torchlight *n* luz de antorcha, *f.* **by t.,** a la luz de las antorchas

torment *n* tormento, *m,* angustia, *f;* (torture) tortura, *f;* suplicio, *m;* mortificación, *f;* disgusto, *m. vt* atormentar, martirizar; (torture) torturar; molestar

tormentor *n* atormentador (-ra)

tornado *n* tornado, *m*

torpedo *n* torpedo, *m; icht* pez torpedo, *m. vt* torpedear. **self-propelling t.,** torpedo automóvil, *m.* **t.-boat,** torpedero, *m.* **t.-boat destroyer,** cazatorpedero, contratorpedero, *m.* **t. netting,** red contra torpedos, *f.* **t. station,** base de torpederos, *f.* **t. tube,** tubo lanzatorpedos, *m*

torpedoing *n* torpedeamiento, torpedeo, *m*

torpid *a* aletargado, entorpecido; (of the mind) torpe, tardo, apático

torpidity, torpor *n* letargo, *m;* apatía, *f*

torrent *n* torrente, *m*

torrential *a* torrencial

torrid *a* tórrido. **t. zone,** zona tórrida, *f*

torsion *n* torsión, *f*

torso *n* torso, *m*

tort *n law* tuerto, *m*

tortoise *n* tortuga, *f.* **t.-shell,** carey, *m. a* de carey

tortuous *a* tortuoso

tortuousness *n* tortuosidad, *f*

torture *n* tortura, *f,* tormento, *m;* angustia, *f. vt* torturar, dar tormento (a); martirizar

torturer *n* atormentador (-ra)

torturing *a* torturador, atormentador; angustioso

toss *n* sacudimiento, *m,* sacudida, *f;* (of the head) movimiento (de cabeza), *m;* (bull fighting) cogida, *f;* (from a horse) caída de caballo, *f. vt* echar, lanzar; agitar, sacudir; (of bulls) acornear. *vi* agitarse; (of plumes, etc.) ondear; (in a boat) balancearse a la merced de las olas; jugar a cara o cruz. **to t. a coin** *Mexico* echar un volado. **to t. in a blanket,** mantear, dar una manta (a). **to t. aside,** echar a un lado; abandonar. **to t. off,** beber de un trago. **to t. up,** jugar a cara o cruz

tot *n* (child) nene (-na), crío (-ía); (of drink) vaso pequeño, *m.* **to tot up,** sumar

total *a* total; absoluto, completo, entero. *n* total, *m,* suma, *f. vt* sumar. *vi* ascender (a). **t. employment,** ocupación total, *f.* **t. war,** guerra total, *f*

totalitarian *a* totalitario

totality *n* totalidad, *f*

totally *adv* totalmente, completamente

totem *n* tótem, *m*

totemism *n* totemismo, *m*

totter *vi* (of persons) bambolearse; tambalear, estar al punto de caer; *fig* aproximarse a su fin

tottering *a* vacilante; tambaleante. *n* bamboleo, *m;* tambaleo, *m*

toucan *n orn* tucán, *m*

touch *vt* tocar; (brush against) rozar; (reach) alcanzar; (musical instruments) tocar; (move) emocionar, enternecer; (spur on) aguijar; (food) tomar; (affect) influir, afectar; (arouse) despertar, estimular; (equal) compararse con, igualar; (consider) tratar ligeramente (de); (money) dar un sablazo (a). *vi* tocarse; imponer las manos para curar. **I have not touched a bite,** No he probado un bocado. **This touches me nearly,** Esto me toca de cerca. **to t. at,** hacer escala en, tocar en (un puerto). **to t. down on water** *Lat. Am.* acuatizar. **to t. off,** descargar. **to t. up,** retocar; corregir. **to t. upon,**

(a subject) tratar superficialmente de, tratar ligeramente de; hablar de; considerar

touch *n* (sense of) tacto, *m*; (contact) toque, contacto, *m*; (brushing) roce, *m*; (tap) golpe ligero, *m*; palmadita, *f*; (of an illness) ataque ligero, *m*; *mus* dedeo, *m*; (little) dejo, *m*; (test) prueba, *f*, toque, *m*; *art* toque, *m*, pincelada, *f*. **by the t.,** a tiento. **in t. with,** en relaciones con; en comunicación con; al corriente de. **to give the finishing t.,** dar la última pincelada; dar el último toque. **t.-line,** (football) línea de toque, línea lateral, *f*. **t.-me-not,** *inf* erizo, *m*. **t.-stone,** piedra de toque, *f*

touched *a* emocionado, conmovido

touchiness *n* susceptibilidad, *f*, *Argentina* acometividad, *f*

touching *a* patético, conmovedor. *prep* tocante a, acerca de. *n* tocamiento, *m*

touchy *a* susceptible, quisquilloso, vidrioso

tough *a* (hard) duro; vigoroso, fuerte, robusto; resistente; (of character) tenaz, firme; (of a job) difícil; espinoso. *n* chulo, *m*

toughen *vt* endurecer. *vi* endurecerse

toughness *n* dureza, *f*; vigor, *m*, fuerza, *f*; resistencia, *f*; tenacidad, firmeza, *f*; dificultad, *f*

toupee *n* tupé, *m*

tour *n* viaje, *m*, excursión, *f*. *vi* viajar. *vt* viajar por. **circular t.,** viaje redondo, *m*. **on t.,** *theat* en tour, de gira

touring *a* de turismo. *n* turismo, *m*; viaje, *m*. **t. car,** coche de turismo, *m*

tourist *n* turista, *mf*; viajero (-ra). **t. agency,** agencia de turismo, *f*, patronato de turismo, *m*. **t. ticket,** billete kilométrico, *m*

tournament *n* torneo, *m*, justa, *f*; (of games) concurso, *m*

tourniquet *n* torniquete, *m*

tousle *vt* despeinar; desordenar el pelo

tout *n* buhonero, *m*. **to t. for,** pescar, solicitar

tow *n* remolque, *m*; (rope) estopa, *f*. *vt* (*naut, aut*) remolcar. **on tow,** a remolque. **tow-path,** camino de sirga, *m*. **tow rope,** cable de remolque, *m*

towage *n* remolque, *m*; (fee) derechos de remolque, *m pl*

towards *prep* hacia, en dirección a; (of time) sobre, cerca de; (concerning) tocante a; (with persons) para, con

towel *n* toalla, *f*. *Lat. Am. also* limpiamanos, *m*. **roller t.,** toalla continua, *f*. **t. rail,** toallero, *m*

toweling *n* tela para toallas, *f*

tower *n* torre, *f*; (fortress) fortaleza, *f*; (belfry) campanario, *m*; (large) torreón, *m*. *vi* elevarse. **to t. above,** destacarse sobre, sobresalir; *fig* sobrepujar, superar

towered *a* torreado; de las . . . torres. **high t.,** de las altas torres

towering *a* elevado; dominante; orgulloso; *fig* violento, terrible

town *n* población, *f*, pueblo, *m*; ciudad, *f*. **t. clerk,** secretario de ayuntamiento, *m*. **t. council,** concejo municipal, *m*. **t. councilor,** concejero municipal, *m*. **t. crier,** pregonero, *m*. **t. hall,** (casa de) ayuntamiento, casa consistorial, *f*. **t. house,** casa de ciudad, *f*. **t. planning,** urbanismo, *m*; reforma urbana, *f*. **t. wall,** muralla, *f*

"Town Ahead" «Poblado Próximo»

townsman *n* ciudadano, *m*

town worthy *n* persona principal de la ciudad, *f*

toxic *a* tóxico

toxicological *a* toxicológico

toxicologist *n* toxicólogo, *m*

toxicology *n* toxicología, *f*

toxin *n* toxina, *f*

toy *n* juguete, *m*. *vi* (with) jugar con; acariciar. **toy maker,** fabricante de juguetes, *m*

toyshop *n* juguetería, tienda de juguetes, *f*

trace huella, pista, *f*, rastro, *m*; vestigio, *m*; indicio, *m*, evidencia, *f*; (of a harness) tirante, *m*; (touch) dejo, *m*; (of fear, etc.) sombra, *f*. *vt* trazar; (through transparent paper) calcar; seguir la pista (de); (write) escribir; (discern) distinguir; investigar; descubrir; determinar; (walk) atravesar, recorrer. **to t. back,** (of ancestry, etc.) hacer remontar (a)

traceable *a* que se puede trazar; atribuible

tracer *n* trazador (-ra). **t. bullet,** bala luminosa, *f*

tracery *n* tracería, *f*

trachea *n anat* tráquea, *f*

trachoma *n med* tracoma, *f*

tracing *n* calco, *m*; trazo, *m*; seguimiento, *m*. **t.-paper,** papel de calcar, *m*

track *n* huella, *f*, rastro, *m*; (for racing, etc.) pista, *f*; (of wheels) rodada, *f*; (railway) vía, *f*; (of a boat) estela, *f*; (path) senda, vereda, *f*; (sign) señal, evidencia, *f*; (course) ruta, *f*. *vt* rastrear, seguir la pista (de); *naut* sirgar. **to t. down,** seguir y capturar. **double t.,** vía doble, *f*. **off the t.,** extraviado; (of a train) descarrilado; *fig* por los cerros de Úbeda. **side t.,** desviadero, *m*. **to keep t. of,** *inf* no perder de vista (a); seguir las fortunas de

trackless *a* sin camino; sin huella; (of trams, etc.) sin rieles; (untrodden) no pisado

tract *n* tracto, *m*; región, *f*; *anat* vía, *f*; (written) tratado, *m*

tractability *n* docilidad, *f*

tractable *a* dócil

traction *n* tracción, *f*. **t.-engine,** máquina de arrastre (or de tracción), *f*

tractor *n* máquina de arrastre, *f*; tractor, *m*

trade *n* comercio, *m*; tráfico, *m*; negocio, *m*; industria, *f*; (calling) oficio, *m*, profesión, *f*; (dealers) comerciantes, *mf pl*. *vi* comerciar, traficar. *vt* cambiar. **to t. on,** explotar, aprovecharse de. **by t.,** de oficio, por profesión. **t.-mark,** marca de fábrica, *f*. **t.-name,** razón social, *f*. **t. price,** precio para el comerciante, *m*. **t. union,** sindicato, *m*. **T. Union Congress,** Congreso de Sindicatos, *m*. **t. unionism,** sistema de sindicatos obreros, *m*. **t.-winds,** vientos alisios, *m pl*

trader *n* comerciante, traficante, *mf*; mercader, *m*; (boat) buque mercante, *m*

tradesman *n* tendero, *m*. **tradesmen's entrance,** puerta de servicio, *f*

trading *n* comercio, tráfico, *m*. *a* mercantil, comerciante, mercante. **t. ship,** buque mercante, *m*. **t. station,** factoría, *f*

tradition *n* tradición, *f*

traditional *a* tradicional; del lugar

traditionalism *n* tradicionalismo, *m*

traditionalist *n* tradicionalista, *mf*

traditionally *adv* según la tradición, tradicionalmente

traduce *vt* calumniar, denigrar, vituperar

traducer *n* calumniador (-ra)

traffic *n* comercio, negocio, *m*; tráfico, *m*; (in transit) transporte, *m*; (in movement) circulación, *f*. *vi* comerciar, traficar, negociar. **to cause a block in the t.,** interrumpir la circulación. **t. block,** obstrucción del tráfico, *f*, atasco en la circulación, *m*. **t. indicator,** (on a car) indicador de dirección, *m*. **t. island,** refugio para peatones, salvavidas, *m*. **t. light,** disco, *m*, luz (de tráfico) *f*, semáforo, *m*. **t. roundabout,** redondel, *m*

trafficker *n* traficante, *mf*

tragedian *n* trágico, *m*

tragedy *n* tragedia, *f*

tragic *a* trágico

tragicomedy *n* tragicomedia, *f*

tragicomic *a* tragicómico

trail *n* rastro, *m*, pista, huella, *f*; (path) sendero, *m*; (of a comet) cola, cabellera, *f*. *vt* rastrear, seguir el rastro de; (drag) arrastrar; (the anchor) garrar. *vi* arrastrar; (of plants) trepar. **on t. of,** en busca de; siguiendo el rastro de; **put somebody on the t. of . . .** darle a fulano la pista de . . .

trailer *n* cazador (-ra); perseguidor (-ra); *aut* remolque, *m*; (cinema) anuncio de próximas atracciones, *m*; *bot* talle rastrero, *m*

train *n* (railway) tren, *m*; (of a dress) cola, *f*; (retinue) séquito, *m*; (procession) desfile, *m*, comitiva, *f*; (series) serie, sucesión, f; (of gunpowder) reguero de pólvora, m. **down t.,** tren descendente, m. **excursion t.,** tren de excursionistas, m. **express t.,** exprés, tren expreso, m. **fast t.,** rápido, m. **goods t.,** tren de mercancías, m. **mail t.,** tren correo, m. **next t.,** próximo tren, m. **passenger t.,** tren de pasajeros, m. **stopping t.,** tren ómnibus, m. **through t.,** tren directo, m. **up t.,** tren ascendente, m. **t.-bearer,** paje que lleva la cola, m; dama de honor, f; (of a cardinal, etc.) caudatario, m. **t.-ferry,** buque transbordador, m. **t.-oil,** aceite de ballena, m. **t. service,** servicio de trenes, m

train vt educar; adiestrar; enseñar; *sport* entrenar; (firearms) apuntar; (plants) guiar; (accustom) habituar, acostumbrar; (a horse for racing) entrenar; (circus) amaestrar. vi educarse; adiestrarse; *sport* entrenarse

trainer n (of men and racehorses) entrenador, m; (of performing animals) domador, m

training n educación, f; enseñanza, instrucción, f; *sport* entrenamiento, m. **t.-college,** escuela normal, f. **t.-ship,** buque escuela, m

trait n rasgo, m, característica, f

traitor n traidor, m

traitress n traidora, f

trajectory n trayectoria, f

tram n tranvía, m. a tranviario. **t. conductor,** cobrador de tranvía, m. **t. depot,** cochera de tranvías, f. **t. stop,** parada de tranvía, f

trammel n (of a horse) traba, f; *fig* obstáculo, estorbo, m. vt travar; *fig* estorbar, impedir

tramp n (person) vagabundo (-da); vago (-ga); (walk) caminata, f, paseo largo, m; ruido de pasos, m; *naut* vapor volandero, m. vi ir a pie; patear; vagabundear. vt vagar por

trample n pisoteo, m; (of feet) ruido de pasos, m. vt pisotear, pisar, hollar. vi pisar fuerte. **to t. on,** *fig* atropellar humillar

trance n rapto, arrobamiento, m; *med* catalepsia, f

tranquil a tranquilo, apacible; sereno, sosegado

tranquilizer n calmante, m

tranquility n tranquilidad, paz, quietud, f; serenidad, f; sosiego, m; calma, f

tranquilize vt tranquilizar, sosegar, calmar

tranquilizing a sosegador, tranquilizador

trans *prefix* trans-. **t.-Pyrenean,** a transpirenaico. **to t.-ship,** trasbordar. **t.-shipment,** trasbordo, m. **t.-Siberian,** trasiberiano

transact vt despachar, hacer. vi despachar un negocio

transaction n desempeño, m; negocio, m; transacción, operación, f; *pl* **transactions** (of a society) actas, f *pl*

transatlantic a transatlántico. **t. liner,** transatlántico, m

transcend vt exceder, superar, rebasar. vi trascender

transcendence n superioridad, f; trascendencia, f

transcendental a trascendental

transcontinental a transcontinental

transcribe vt trascribir, copiar; *mus* trascribir, adaptar

transcriber n copiador (-ra); *mus* adaptador (-ra)

transcript n traslado, trasunto, m; (student's) certificado de estudios, certificado de materias aprobadas, m, constancia de estudios, copia del expediente académico, hoja de estudios, f

transcription n trascripción, copia, f, trasunto, m; *mus* trascripción, adaptación, f, arreglo, m

transept n *arch* transepto, crucero, m

transfer n traslado, m; trasferencia, f, traspaso, m; *law* cesión, enajenación, f; (picture) calcomanía, f. vt trasladar; trasferir; pasar; *law* enajenar, ceder; estampar; calcografiar. vi trasbordarse. **deed of t.,** escritura de cesión, f. **t.-paper,** papel de calcar, f

transferable a trasferible

transferee n cesionario (-ia)

transference n traslado, m; transferencia, f; *law* cesión, enajenación, f

transferor n cesionista, *mf*

transfiguration n trasfiguración, f

transfigure vt trasfigurar, trasformar

transfix vt traspasar; *fig* paralizar

transfixion n trasfixión, f

transform vt trasformar; convertir, cambiar. **It is completely transformed,** Está completamente trasformado

transformation n trasformación, f; conversión, f, cambio, m

transformative a trasformador

transformer n *elec* trasformador, m

transfuse vt trasfundir

transfusion n trasfusión, f. **blood t.,** trasfusión de sangre, f

transgress vt exceder, sobrepasar; (violate) contravenir, violar, pecar contra. vi pecar

transgression n contravención, trasgresión, f; pecado, m

transgressor n trasgresor (-ra), pecador (-ra)

transient a transitorio, fugaz, pasajero; perecedero

transiently adv pasajeramente

transit n tránsito, paso, m; trasporte, m; *ast* tránsito, m. **in t.,** de tránsito

transition n transición, f; cambio, m; tránsito, paso, m

transitional a de transición, transitorio

transitive a *gram* transitivo, activo. **t. verb,** verbo transitivo, verbo activo, m

transitively adv transitivamente

transitorily adv transitoriamente; provisionalmente

transitoriness n brevedad, f, lo fugaz

transitory a transitorio, fugaz, pasajero, breve

translatable a traducible

translate vt traducir; interpretar; (transfer) trasladar

translation n traducción, f; versión, f; traslado, m

translator n traductor (-ra)

translucence n traslucidez, f

translucent a traslúcido, trasparente

transmigrate vi trasmigrar

transmigration n trasmigración, f

transmissibility n trasmisibilidad, f

transmissible a trasmisible

transmission n trasmisión, f

transmit vt trasmitir; remitir, dar

transmitter n trasmisor (-ra); *rad* radiotrasmisor, m; *elec* trasmisor, m

transmutable a trasmutable

transmutation n trasmutación, f

transmute vt trasmutar

transoceanic a transoceánico

transom n *carp* travesaño, m; *naut* yugo de popa, m

transpacific a traspacífico

transparency n trasparencia; diafanidad, f; (picture) trasparente, m

transparent a trasparente; diáfano; (of style) claro, limpio

transpiration n traspiración, f

transpire vi traspirar; rezumarse; hacerse público; *inf* acontecer. vt exhalar

transplant vt trasplantar

transplantation n trasplante, m, trasplantación, f,

transport n trasporte, m; *naut* navío de trasporte, m; *aer* avión de trasporte, m; (fit) acceso, paroxismo, m. vt trasportar; (convicts) deportar; *fig* (joy) colmar; (rage) llenar

transportable a trasportable

transportation n trasporte, m; (convicts) deportación, f

transporter n trasportador (-ra)

transpose vt trasponer; *mus* trasportar

transposition n trasposición, f

transversal a and n trasversal, m

transverse a trasverso, trasversal

transversely adv trasversalmente

trap n trampa, f, cepo, m; (net) lazo, m, red, f; (for mice, rats) ratonera, f; *mech* sifón de depósito, m; pequeño carruaje de dos ruedas, m; (door) puerta caediza, f; *theat* escotillón, m; *pl* **traps,** trastos, m *pl*; equipaje, m. vt coger con trampa; hacer caer en el lazo; *fig* tender el lazo. *vi* armar una trampa; armar lazo. **to fall into a t.,** *fig* caer en la trampa. **to pack one's traps,** liar el hato

trapeze *n* trapecio (de gimnasia), *m*

trapper *n* cazador de animales de piel, *m*

trappings *n pl* arneses, jaeces, *m pl*; arreos, aderezos, *m pl*, galas, *f pl*

trash *n* paja, hojarasca, *f*; (of sugar, etc.) bagazo, *m*; trastos viejos, *m pl*; cachivaches, *m pl*; (literary) paja, *f*

trashy *a* de ningún valor, inútil, despreciable

traumatic *a med* traumático

traumatism *n med* traumatismo, *m*

travail *n* dolores de parto, *m pl*. *vi* estar de parto; trabajar

travel *n* el viajar, viajes, *m pl*. *vi* viajar; ver mundo; (of traffic) circular, pasar, ir. *vt* viajar por; recorrer; (with number of miles) hacer. **to t. over,** viajar por; recorrer. **t. worn,** fatigado por el viaje

travel agent *n* agente de viajes, *mf*

traveled *a* que ha viajado, que ha visto muchas partes

traveler *n* viajero (-ra); pasajero (-ra). **commercial t.,** viajante, *mf* **traveler's check,** cheque de viajeros, *m*. **traveler's joy,** *bot* clemátide, *f*

traveling *n* viajes, *m pl. a* viajero; para (or de) viajar; (itinerant) ambulante. **t. crane,** grúa móvil, *f*. **t. expenses,** gastos de viaje, *m pl*. **t. requisites,** objetos de viaje, *m pl*. **t. rug,** manta, *f*. **t. show,** circo ambulante, *m*

traversable *a* atravesable, transitable, practicable

traverse *n carp* travesaño, *m*; *law* negación, *f*; (*mil arch*) través, *m*; (crossing) travesía, *f*, *a* transversal. *adv* transversalmente. *vt* atravesar, cruzar; *law* negar

travesty *n* parodia, *f*, *vt* parodiar

trawl *vt* rastrear. *vi* pescar a la rastra. **t.-net,** red de arrastre, *f*

trawler *n* barco barredero, *m*; pescador a la rastra, *m*

trawling *n* pesca a la rastra, *f*

tray *n* bandeja, *f*; (of a balance) platillo, *m*; (in a wardrobe, etc.) cajón, *m*; (trough) artesa, *f*

treacherous *a* traidor, falso, pérfido, fementido; (of memory) infiel; engañoso; (of ice, etc.) peligroso

treacherously *adv* traidoramente, a traición

treachery *n* perfidia, traición, falsedad, *f*

treacle *n* melado, *m*

tread *n* pisada, *f*; paso, *m*; (of a stair) peldaño, *m*; (of tire) pastilla, *f*; (walk) andar, porte, *m*, *vi* pisar; (trample) pisotear; hollar; (oppress) oprimir. *vt* hollar; (a path) abrir; recorrer; caminar por; bailar. **to t. the grapes,** pisar las uvas. **to t. the stage,** pisar las tablas. **to t. under foot,** hollar; pisotear. **to t. on,** pisar. **to t. on one's heels,** pisarle los talones a uno; seguir de cerca. **to t. out,** (a measure) bailar

treading *n* pisoteo, *m*

treadle *n* pedal, *m*; (of a loom) cárcola, *f*

treadmill *n* molino de rueda de escalones, *m*; *fig* rueda, *f*

treason *n* traición, *f*. **high t.,** alta traición, lesa majestad, *f*

treasonable *a* desleal, traidor

treasonably *adv* traidoramente

treasure *n* tesoro, *m*; riqueza, *f*, caudal, *m*; *fig* perla, *f*. *vt* atesorar; acumular (or guardar) riquezas; (a memory) guardar. **t. trove,** tesoro hallado, *m*

treasurer *n* tesorero (-ra)

treasury *n* tesorería, *f*; (government department) Ministerio de Hacienda, *m*; (anthology) tesoro, *m*. **t. bench,** banco del Gobierno, *m*

treat *n* (pleasure) gusto, placer, *m*; (present) obsequio, *m*; (entertainment) fiesta, *f*. *vt* tratar; *med* tratar, curar; (regale) obsequiar. *vi* (stand host) convidar; (of) tratar de, versar sobre; (with) negociar con

treatise *n* tesis, monografía, disertación, *f*, tratado, *m*

treatment *n* tratamiento, *m*; (of persons) conducta hacia, *f*, modo de obrar con, *m*; *med* tratamiento, *m*; (*lit, art*) procedimiento, *m*, técnica, *f*

treaty *n* tratado, pacto, *m*; (bargain) contrato, *m*

treble *n mus* tiple, *m*; voz de tiple, *f*. *a* triple; *mus* so-

breagudo. *vt* triplicar; *vi* triplicarse. **t. clef,** clave de sol, *f*

trebling *n* triplicación, *f*

tree *n* árbol, *m*; (for shoes) horma, *f*; (of a saddle) arzón, *m*. **breadfruit t.,** árbol del pan, *m*. **Judas t.,** árbol de amor, *m*. **t. of knowledge,** árbol de la ciencia, *m*. **t.-covered,** arbolado. **t.-frog,** rana de San Antonio, *f*

treeless *a* sin árboles

trefoil *n* trébol, trifolio, *m*

trek *n* caminar, andar

trellis *n* enrejado, *m*; (for plants) espaldera, *f*. *vt* cercar con un enrejado; construir espalderas

tremble *vi* temblar; estremecerse; trepidar; vibrar; (sway) oscilar; (of flags) ondear; agitarse; ser tembloroso. **His fate trembled in the balance,** Su suerte estaba en la balanza. **to t. all over,** temblar de pies a cabeza

trembling *n* temblor, *m*; estremecimiento, *m*; trepidación, *f*; vibración, *f*; (fear) agitación, ansiedad, *f*; temor, *m*. *a* tembloroso; trémulo

tremendous *a* terrible, espantoso; formidable; grande; importante; *inf* tremendo; enorme

tremendously *adv* terriblemente; *inf* enormemente

tremor *n* temblor, movimiento sísmico, *m*; (thrill) estremecimiento, *m*; vibración, *f*

tremulous *a* trémulo, tembloroso; vacilante; tímido

tremulously *adv* trémulamente; tímidamente

tremulousness *n* lo tembloroso; vacilación, *f*; timidez, *f*

trench *n* zanja, *f*, foso, *m*; (for irrigation) acequia, *f*; *mil* trinchera, *f*. *vt* hacer zanjas (en); acequiar; *mil* atrincherar. **t.-fever,** tifus exantemático, *m*. **t.-foot,** pie de trinchera, *m*. **t.-mortar,** mortero de trinchera, *m*

trenchant *a* mordaz

trencher *n* trinchero, *m*

trend *n* curso, rumbo, *m*; *fig* tendencia, *f*; dirección, *f*. *vi* *fig* tender

trepan *vt surg* trepanar

trepanning *n surg* trepanación, *f*

trepidation *n* trepidación, *f*

trespass *n* violación de propiedad, *f*; ofensa, *f*; pecado, *m*; (in the Lord's Prayer) deuda, *f*. *vi* (on land) entrar sin derecho, violar la propiedad; (upon) entrar sin permiso en; (with patience, etc.) abusar de; (against) pecar contra, infringir

trespasser *n* violador (-ra) de la ley de propiedad. **"Trespassers will be prosecuted,"** «Entrada prohibida,» «Prohibido el paso»

tress *n* (plait) trenza, *f*; rizo, bucle, *m*; *pl* **tresses,** cabellera, *f*

trestle *n* caballete, *m*; armazón, *m*. **trestle-table,** mesa de caballete, *f*

triad *n* terna, *f*; *mus* acorde, *m*

trial *n* prueba, *f*, ensayo, *m*; examen, *m*; (experiment) tentativa, *f*, experimento, *m*; (misfortune) desgracia, pena, *f*; (nuisance) molestia, *f*; *law* vista de una causa, *f*. **on t.,** a prueba; *law* en proceso. **to bring to t.,** procesar. **to stand one's t.,** ser procesado. **t. run,** marcha de ensayo, *f*. **t. trip,** *naut* viaje de ensayo, *m*

trial and error *n* tanteos, *m*. **by trial and error,** por tanteos.

triangle *n* triángulo, *m*. **acute-angled t.,** triángulo acutángulo, *m*. **obtuse-angled t.,** triángulo obtusángulo, *m*. **right-angled t.,** triángulo rectángulo, *m*. **the eternal t.,** el eterno triángulo

triangular *a* triangular, triángulo

triangulation *n* (in surveying) triangulación, *f*

tribal *a* tribal

tribe *n* tribu, *f*

tribesman *n* miembro de una tribu, *m*

tribulation *n* tribulación, *f*; pena, aflicción, desgracia, *f*

tribunal *n* (seat) tribunal, *m*; (court) juzgado, *m*; (confessional) confesionario, *m*

tribunary *a* tribúnico

tribunate *n* tribunado, *m*

tribune *n* (person) tribuno, *m*; tribuna, *f*

tributary *a* and *n* tributario *m*
tribute *n* tributo, *m*; contribución, imposición, *f*
trice *n* tris, soplo, *m*. **in a t.,** en un periquete, en un avemaría, en dos trancos
tricentennial *a* de trescientos años; *n* tercer centenario, tricentenario, *m*
trick *n* (swindle) estafa, *f*, engaño, *m*; (ruse) truco, *m*, estratagema, ardid, *f*; (mischief) travesura, *f*; burla, *f*; (illusion) ilusión, *f*; (habit) costumbre, *f*; (affectation) afectación, *f*; (jugglery) juego de manos, *m*; (knack) talento, *m*; (at cards) baza, *f*. *vt* engañar, estafar; (with out) adornar, ataviar; (with into) inducir fraudulentamente. *vi* trampear. **dirty t.,** *inf* mala pasada, perrada, *f*. **His memory plays him tricks,** La memoria le engaña. **to play a t. on,** gastar una broma (a). **to play tricks,** hacer travesuras. **t. riding,** acrobacia ecuestre, *f*
trickery *n* maullería, superchería, *f*; fraude, engaño, *m*
trickle *n* chorrito, hilo (de agua, etc.) *m*. *vi* gotear. **to t. down,** deslizar por, correr por, escurrir por
trickling *n* goteo, *m*; (sound) murmullo, *m*
trickster *n* embustero (-ra), trampeador (-ra). **to be a t.,** ser buena maula
tricky *a* informal, maullero; (of things) difícil; complicado; (clever) ingenioso; (person) = **crafty**
tricolor *a* tricolor
tricycle *n* triciclo, *m*
tried *a* probado
triennial *a* trienal
trifle *n* (object) baratija, fruslería, *f*; pequeñez, tontería, bagatela, *f*; *cul*, *f*; (small amount) pequeña cantidad, *f*, muy poco (de); (adverbially) algo. *vi* entretenerse, jugar. *vt* (away) malgastar. **to t. with,** jugar con
trifler *n* persona frívola, *f*; (with affections) seductor (-ra)
trifling *a* insignificante, sin importancia, trivial
trigger *n* (of a fire-arm) gatillo, *m*; *mech* tirador, *m*
trigonometric *a* trigonométrico
trigonometry *n* trigonometría, *f*
trilingual *a* trilingüe
trill *n* trino, *m*, *vi* trinar
trillion *n* trillón, *m*
trilogy *n* trilogía, *f*
trim *a* aseado; bien arreglado; bien ajustado; elegante; bonito; (of sail) orientado. **She has a t. waist,** Tiene un talle juncal. *n* orden, *m*; buen estado, *m*; buena condición, *f*; (toilet) atavío, *m*. *vt* arreglar; (tidy) asear; pulir; (ornament) ornar, adornar; (adapt) ajustar, adaptar; *sew* guarnecer; (lamps) despabilar; (a fire) atizar; (hair, moustache) atusar, recortar; (trees) mondar, atusar; *carp* alisar; (sails) templar, orientar; (distribute weight in a boat) equilibrar; (of quill pens) tajar. *vi* (waver) nadar entre dos aguas. **to t. oneself up,** arreglarse
trimly *adv* aseadamente; lindamente
trimmer *n* guarnecedor (-ra); contemporizador (-ra)
trimming *n* arreglo, *m*; guarnición, *f*; (on a dress) pasamanería, *f*; adorno, *m*; *agr* poda, *f*; adaptación, *f*, ajuste, *m*; *pl* **trimmings,** accesorios, *m pl*
trimness *n* aseo, buen orden, *m*; buen estado, *m*; elegancia, lindeza, *f*; (slimness) esbeltez, *f*
Trinidad and Tobago Trinidad, *f*, y Tobago, *m*
Trinidadian *n* and *a* trinitario
Trinity *n* Trinidad, *f*
trinket *n* joya, alhaja, *f*; dije, *m*, chuchería, baratija, *f*
trinomial *a math* de tres términos. *n math* trinomio, *m*
trio *n* trío, *m*
trip *n* excursión, *f*; viaje, *m*; (slip) traspié, tropiezo, *m*; (in wrestling) zancadilla, *f*; (mistake) desliz, *m*. *vi* (stumble) tropezar, caer; (move nimbly) andar airosamente, ir (or correr) ligeramente; (frolic) bailar, saltar; (wrestling, games) echar la zancadilla; (err) equivocarse; cometer un desliz. *vt* (up) hacer caer; echar la zancadilla (a); coger en una falta; hacer desdecirse; coger en un desliz; *naut* levantar (el ancla)
tripartite *a* tripartito

tripartition *n* tripartición, *f*
tripe *n* callos, *m pl*
triple *a* triple. *vt* triplicar. *vi* triplicarse
triplet *n poet* terceto, *m*; *mus* tresillo, *m*; cada uno (una) de tres hermanos (hermanas) gemelos (-as)
triplicate *a* triplicado. *vt* triplicar
triplication *n* triplicación, *f*
tripod *n* trípode, *m*
Tripoli Trípoli, *m*
tripper *n* turista, excursionista, *mf*
tripping *a* ligero, ágil
trippingly *adv* ligeramente
triptych *n* tríptico, *m*
trite *a* vulgar, trivial
triteness *n* trivialidad, vulgaridad, *f*
triumph *n* triunfo, *m*. *vi* triunfar; (over) triunfar de, vencer
triumphal *a* triunfal. **t. arch,** arco de triunfo, *m*
triumphant *a* triunfante, victorioso
triumvirate *n* triunvirato, *m*
trivet *n* trébedes, *f pl*, trípode, *m*
trivial *a* trivial, frívolo; insignificante, sin importancia
triviality *n* trivialidad, frivolidad, *f*; insignificancia, *f*
trochlea *n anat* tróclea, *f*
trodden *a* trillado, batido
troglodyte *a* and *n* troglodita, *mf*
Trojan *a* and *n* troyano (-na). **the T. War,** la guerra de Troya, *f*
trolley *n elec* trole, *m*; (for children) carretón, *m*. **t.-bus,** trolebús, *m*. **t. car** tranvía, *m*. **t.-pole,** trole, *m*
trollop *n* tarasca, ramera, *f*
trombone *n* trombón, *m*. **t. player,** trombón, *m*
troop *n* banda, muchedumbre, *f*; *theat* compañía, *f*; (of cavalry) escuadrón, *m*; *pl* **troops,** *mil* tropas, *f pl*; ejército, *m*. *vi* ir en tropel, congregarse; (with away) marcharse en tropel, retirarse; (with out) salir en masa. **fresh troops,** tropas frescas, *f pl*. **storm troops,** tropas de asalto, *f pl*. **t.-ship,** transporte de guerra, *m*
trooper *n* soldado de caballería, *m*
trope *n* tropo, *m*
trophy *n* trofeo, *m*
tropic *a* and *n* trópico, *m*
tropical *a* tropical; (figurative) figurativo
tropism *n* tropismo, *m*
trot *n* trote, *m*. *vi* trotar. *vt* hacer trotar. **to t. out,** *inf* sacar a relucir
troth *n* fe, *f*; palabra, *f*. **to plight one's t.,** dar palabra de matrimonio, desposarse
trotting *a* trotón. *n* trote, *m*
troubadour *n* trovador, *m*, *a* trovadoresco
trouble *n* (grief) aflicción, angustia, *f*; (difficulty) dificultad, *f*; (effort) esfuerzo, *m*; pena, desgracia, *f*; (annoyance) disgusto, sinsabor, *m*; (unrest) confusión, *f*, disturbio, *m*; (illness) enfermedad, *f*; mal, *m*; (disagreement) desavenencia, *f*. **The t. is . . . ,** Lo malo es; La dificultad está en que . . . **to be in t.,** estar afligido; estar en un apuro, estar entre la espada y la pared. **to be not worth the t.,** no valer la pena. **to stir up t.,** revolver el ajo; armar un lío. **to take the t. to,** tomarse la molestia de.
trouble *vt* turbar; agitar; afligir, inquietar; (badger) importunar; (annoy) molestar; (cost an effort) costar trabajo (e.g., **Learning Spanish did not t. him much,** No le costó mucho trabajo aprender el castellano). *vi* preocuparse; darse la molestia; inquietarse
troubled *a* agitado; inquieto; preocupado; (of life) accidentado, borrascoso. **to fish in t. waters,** pescar en agua turbia, pescar en río revuelto
troublemaker *n Lat. Am.* buscapleitos, *mf*
troublesome *a* dificultoso; molesto; inconveniente; importuno; fastidioso
trough *n* gamella, *f*; (for kneading bread) artesa, *f*; (of the waves) seno, *m*; (meteorological) mínimo, *m*. **drinking t.,** abrevadero, *m*. **stone t.,** pila, *f*
trounce *vt* zurrar, apalear; *fig* fustigar
troupe *n* compañía, *f*

trousers *n pl* pantalones, *m pl*. **plus four t.**, pantalones de golf, *m pl*. **striped t.**, pantalón de corte, *m*. **t. pocket,** bolsillo del pantalón, *m*. **t. press,** prensa para pantalones, *f*

trousseau *n* ajuar de novia, *m*

trout *n* trucha, *f*

trowel *n agr* almocafre, *m*; (mason's) paleta, *f*, palustre, *m*

troy weight *n* peso de joyería, *m*

truant *n* novillero, *m*; haragán (-ana). *a* haragán, perezoso. **to play t.**, (from school) hacer novillos; ausentarse

truce *n* tregua, *f*; suspensión, cesación, *f*

truck *n* (lorry) camión, *m*; carretilla de mano, *f*; (railway) vagón de carga, *m*; (intercourse) relaciones, *f pl*; (trash) cachivaches, *m pl*, cosas sin valor, *f pl*

truckage *n* camionaje, *m*; acarreo, *m*

truckle *vi* humillarse, no levantar los ojos. **t. bed,** carriola, *f*

truculence *n* truculencia, agresividad, *f*

truculent *a* truculento, agresivo

trudge *vi* caminar a pie; andar con dificultad, caminar lentamente, andar trabajosamente, *n* caminata, *f*

true *a* verdadero; real; leal, sincero; fiel; exacto; honesto; genuino; auténtico; alineado, a plomo. **That is t. of . . .** Es propio de . . . *adv* realmente; exactamente. **t.-bred,** de casta legítima. **t.-hearted,** leal, fiel, sincero

truffle *n* trufa, *f*. **to stuff with truffles,** trufar

truism *n* perogrullada, *f*

truly *adv* lealmente; realmente, verdaderamente; en efecto, por cierto; sinceramente, de buena fe. **Yours t.,** su seguro servidor (su s.s.)

trump *n* (cards) triunfo, *m*; son de la trompeta, *m*; *inf* gran persona, joya, *f*. *vt* ganar con el triunfo. **to t. up,** inventar. **t.-card,** naipe de triunfo, *m*

trumpery *a* de pacotilla; ineficaz. *n* oropel, *m*

trumpet *n* trompeta, *f*. *vt* trompetear; *fig* pregonar. *vi* (of elephant) barritar. **ear.-t.,** trompetilla (acústica), *f*. **speaking t.,** portavoz, *m*. **t. blast,** trompetazo, *m*. **t. shaped,** en trompeta

trumpeter *n* trompetero, trompeta, *m*

trumpeting *n* trompeteo, *m*; (of elephant) barrito, *m*

truncate *a* truncado. *vt* truncar

truncheon *n* porra (de goma), *f*; bastón de mando, *m*. **blow with a t.,** porrazo, *m*

trunk *n* (*anat bot*) tronco, *m*; (elephant's) trompa, *f*; (railway) línea principal, *f*; baúl, *m*; cofre, *m*; (of a car) *Lat. Am.* baúl *m*; *pl* **trunks,** (Elizabethan, etc.) trusas, *f pl*; calzoncillos cortos, *m pl*. **wardrobe t.,** baúl mundo, *m*. **t.-call,** conferencia telefónica, *f*. **t.-line,** tronco, *m*. **t.-road,** carretera de primera clase, carretera mayor, *f*

truss *n med* braguero, *m*; (of straw, etc.) haz, *m*; (of blossom) racimo, *m*; (framework) armazón, *f*. *vt* atar; cul espetar; (a building) apuntalar

trust *n* fe, confianza, *f*; deber, *m*; *law* fideicomiso, *m*; (credit) crédito, *m*; esperanza, expectación, *f*; *com* trust, *m*. *vt* tener confianza en; confiar en; esperar; creer; *com* dar crédito (a). *vi* confiar; *com* dar crédito. **in t.,** en confianza; en administración, en depósito. **on t.,** al fiado

trustee *n* guardián, *m*; *law* fideicomisario, depositario, consignatario, *m*

trustful *a* confiado

trusting *a Lat. Am.* creído

trustingly *adv* confiadamente

trust release *n* extinción de fideicomiso, *f*

trustworthiness *n* honradez, probidad, integridad, *f*; (of statements) exactitud, *f*

trustworthy *a* digno de confianza, honrado; fidedigno, seguro; exacto

trusty *a* leal, fiel; firme, seguro

truth *n* verdad, *f*; realidad, *f*; exactitud, *f*. **the plain t.,** la pura verdad. **to tell the t.,** decir la verdad

truthful *a* veraz; exacto, verdadero

truthfulness *n* veracidad, *f*; exactitud, *f*

try *vt* and *vi* procurar, tratar de; (test) probar, ensayar;

(a case, *law*) ver (el pleito); (strain) poner a prueba; (tire) cansar, fatigar; (annoy) molestar, exasperar; (afflict) hacer sufrir, afligir; (attempt) intentar; (judge) juzgar; (the weight of) tomar a pulso; (assay) refinar. *n* tentativa, *f*; (football) tiro, *m*. **Try as he would . . . ,** Por más que hizo . . . **to try hard to,** hacer un gran esfuerzo para. **to try one's luck,** probar fortuna. **to try on,** (clothes) probarse (un vestido, etc.). **to try out,** poner a prueba, probar. **to try to,** tratar de, procurar

trying *a* molesto; fatigoso; irritante; (painful) angustioso, penoso

tryst *n* cita, *f*; lugar de cita, *m*. *vt* citar. *vi* citarse

tsar *n* zar, *m*

tsarina *n* zarina, *f*

tsetse fly *n* mosca tsetsé, *f*

tub *n* cuba, *f*, artesón, *m*; cubeta, *f*. *vi* bañarse. **tub thumper,** *inf* gerundio, *m*

tuba *n mus* tuba, *f*

tube *n* tubo, *m*; (railway) metro, ferrocarril subterráneo, *m*; tubo, *m*; *anat* trompa, *f*. **Eustachian t.,** *anat* trompa de Eustaquio, *f*. **Fallopian t.,** trompa de Falopio, *f*. **inner t.,** *aut* cámara de aire, *f*. **speaking t.,** tubo acústico, *m*. **test t.,** tubo de ensayo, *m*

tuber *n* tubérculo, *m*. **kind of tuber resembling a sweet potato** *Central America* malanga, *f*

tubercular *a* tuberculoso

tuberculosis *n* tuberculosis, *f*

tuberose *n* nardo, *m*, tuberosa, *f*

tubing *n* tubería, *f*

tuck *n sew* alforzar, *f*; pliegue, *m*. *vt* recoger; *sew* alforzar. *vi* hacer alforzas. **to t. in,** (in bed) arropar; *inf* tragar. **to t. under,** poner debajo; doblar. **to t. up,** (in bed) arropar; (skirt) sofaldar; (sleeves) arremangar

tucker *n* camisolín, *m*

Tuesday *n* martes, *m*. **Shrove T.,** martes de carnaval, *m*

tuft *n* (bunch) manojo, *m*; (on the head) copete, moño, *m*, cresta, *f*; (tassel) borla, *f*; mechón, *m*

tufted *a Lat. Am.* copetudo

tug *n* tirón, *m*; sacudida, *f*; (boat) remolcador, *m*. *vt* tirar de; halar; sacudir. *vi* tirar con fuerza. **to give a tug,** dar una sacudida. **tug of war,** *lit* lucha de la cuerda, *f*; *fig* estira y afloja, *msg*

tuition *n* (teaching) instrucción, enseñanza, *f*; lecciones, *f pl*; (fee) cuota, *f*

tulip *n* tulipán, *m*. **t. wood,** palo de rosa, *m*

tulle *n* tul, *m*

tumble *n* caída, *f*; (somersault) tumbo, *m*; voltereta, *f*. *vi* caer; (acrobats) voltear, dar saltos. *vt* hacer caer; desarreglar. **to t. down,** venirse abajo; caer por. **t. down,** ruinoso, destartalado. **to t. off,** caer de. **to t. out,** *vt* hacer salir; arrojar. *vi* salir apresuradamente. **to t. over,** *vt* tropezar con. *vi* volcarse. **to t. to,** *inf* caer en la cuenta

tumbler *n* (acrobat) volteador (-ra); vaso para beber, *m*

tumefaction *n* tumefacción, *f*

tumor *n* tumor, *m*

tumult *n* alboroto, tumulto, *m*; conmoción, agitación, *f*; confusión, *f*

tumultuous *a* tumultuoso, alborotado; ruidoso; confuso; turbulento, violento

tumulus *n* túmulo, *m*

tun *n* tonel, *m*, cuba, *f*, *vt* entonelar, embarrilar

tune *n* melodía, *f*; son, *m*; armonía, *f*; *fig* tono, *m*; *inf* suma, *f*. *vt mus* afinar, templar; *rad* sintonizar; (up, an engine) ajustar (un motor). *vi* (in) sintonizar el receptor; (up, *mus*) templar (afinar) los instrumentos. **in t.,** *mus* afinado, templado; *fig* armonioso; (agreement) de acuerdo, conforme. **out of t.,** *mus* desafinado, destemplado. **to be out of t.,** desentonar; discordar; *fig* no armonizar, no estar en armonía. **to go out of t.,** desafinar. **to put out of t.,** destemplar. **to change one's t.,** *inf* bajar el tono

tuneful *a* melodioso

tunefully *adv* melodiosamente, armoniosamente

tunefulness *n* melodía, *f*

tuneless *a* disonante, discordante
tuner *n* afinador, templador, *m*; *rad* sintonizador, *m*
tungsten *n* tungsteno, *m*
tunic *n* túnica, *Lat. Am. also* cusma, *f*
tuning *n* afinación, *f*; *rad* sintonización, *f*. **t. fork,** diapasón normal, *m*. **t. key,** templador, *m*
Tunis Túnez, *m*
Tunisian *a* and *n* tunecino (-na)
tunnel *n* túnel, *m*. *vt* hacer (or construir) un túnel por. *vi* hacer un túnel
tunneling *n* construcción de túneles, *f*; horadación, *f*
tunny *n* atún, *m*. **striped t.,** bonito, *m*. **t. fishery,** almadraba, *f*
turban *n* turbante, *m*
turbid *a* turbio; *fig* confuso, **to make t.,** enturbiar
turbine *n* turbina, *f*
turbulence *n* turbulencia, *f*; desorden, *m*; agitación, *f*
turbulent *a* turbulento; alborotado; (stormy) borrascoso; agitado
tureen *n* sopera, *f*
turf *n* césped, *m*; (fuel) turba, *f*; (racing) carreras de caballos, *f pl*
turgid *a* turgente, hinchado; (of style) pomposo
turgidity *n* turgencia, *f*; pomposidad, *f*
Turk *n* turco (-ca). **Turk's head,** (duster) deshollinador, *m*; *naut* cabeza de turco, *f*
Turkey Turquía, *f*
turkey *n* (cock) pavo, *m*; (hen) pava, *f*; **t. red,** rojo turco, *m*
Turkish *a* turco. *n* (language) turco, idioma turco, *m*. **T. bath,** baño turco, *m*. **T. slipper,** babucha, *f*. **T. towel,** toalla rusa, *f*
turmeric *n* cúrcuma, *f*. **t. paper,** papel de cúrcuma, *m*
turmoil *n* alboroto, tumulto, desorden, *m*
turn *n* turno, *m*; (twist) torcimiento, *m*; (bend) recodo, *m*, vuelta, *f*; (in a river) meandro, *m*; (in a road) viraje, *m*; (revolution) vuelta, revolución, *f*; (direction) dirección, *f*; (in spiral stair) espira, *f*; *theat* número, *m*; (change) cambio, *m*; vicisitud, *f*; (appearance) aspecto, *m*; (service) servicio, *m*; (nature) índole, naturaleza, *f*; (of phrase) giro, *m*, expresión, *f*; (walk) vuelta, *f*, paseo, *m*; (talent) talento, *m*. **a sharp t.,** (in a road) un viraje rápido. **at every t.,** a cada instante; en todas partes. **bad t.,** flaco servicio, *m*. **by turns,** por turnos. **good t.,** servicio, favor, *m*. **in its t.,** a su vez. **in t.,** sucesivamente. **Now it's my t.,** Ahora me toca a mí. **The affair has taken a new t.,** El asunto ha cambiado de aspecto. **turn of the century,** vuelta del siglo, *f*; **turn of the millenium,** vuelta del milenio, *f*. **to a t.,** *cul* a la perfección. **to have a t. for,** tener talento para. **to take turns at,** alternar en. **t.-table,** (railway) plataforma, *f*; (of a gramophone) disco giratorio, *m*. **t. up,** barahúnda, conmoción, *f*; (of trousers) dobladillo (del pantalón), *m*
turn *vt* (on a lathe) tornear; (revolve) dar vueltas a, girar; (a key, door handle, etc.) torcer; (the leaves of a book) hojear; (the brain) trastornar; (a screw) enroscar; (the stomach) revolver (el estómago), marear; (go round) doblar, dar la vuelta a; (change) cambiar, mudar; (translate) traducir, verter; (dissuade) disuadir; (deflect) desviar; (apply) adaptar; (direct, move) volver; (concentrate) dirigir; concentrar; (turn over) volver del revés al derecho; (upside-down) volver lo de arriba abajo; (make) hacer, volver; (make sour) volver agrio; (transform) transformar convertir; *mil* envolver. **He has turned thirty,** Ha cumplido los treinta. **He said it without turning a hair,** Lo dijo sin pestañear. **He turned his head,** Volvió la cabeza. **They have turned the corner,** Han doblado la esquina; *fig* Han pasado la crisis. **"Please t. over,"** «A la vuelta (de la página).» **to t. a deaf ear to,** no dar oídos a, no hacer caso de. **to t. one's hand to,** aplicarse a. **to t. to account,** sacar ventaja (de). **to t. adrift,** dejar a la merced de las olas; echar de casa, poner en la calle; abandonar. **to t. against,** causar aversión, hacer hostil. **to t. aside,** desviar. **to t. away,** despedir; rechazar;

(the head, etc.) volver; desviar. **to t. back,** hacer volver; enviar de nuevo; (raise) alzar; (fold) doblar; (the clock) retrasar. **to t. down,** doblar; (gas) bajar; (a glass, etc.) poner boca abajo; (reject) rechazar; (a suitor) dar calabazas (a). **to t. from,** alejar de, desviar de. **to t. in,** doblar hacia dentro; entregar. **to t. in one's toes,** ser patizambo. **to t. inside out,** volver al revés. **to t. into,** (enter) entrar en; (change) cambiar en, transformar en; convertir en; (translate) traducir a. **to t. off,** (dismiss) despedir; (from) desviarse de, dejar; (light) apagar; (water) cortar; *mech* cerrar; (disconnect) desconectar; (avoid) evitar; (refuse) rechazar. **to t. off the tap,** (water, gas) cerrar la llave (del agua, del gas). **to t. on,** (light) encender; (water, gas, etc.) abrir la llave (del agua, del gas); (steam) dar (vapor); (electric current) establecer (la corriente eléctrica); (eyes) fijar. **to t. out,** (expel) expeler, echar; (dismiss) despedir; (animals) echar al campo; (produce) producir; (dress) vestir; (equip) equipar, guarnecer; (a light) apagar. **to t. over,** (the page) volver (la hoja); (transfer) ceder, traspasar; revolver; (upset) volcar; considerar, pensar. **to t. round,** dar vuelta (a); girar; (empty) descargar. **to t. up,** levantar; apuntar; hacia arriba; (the earth) labrar, cavar; (a glass) poner boca arriba; (one's sleeves, skirt) arremangar; (fold) doblar. **to t. up one's nose at,** mirar con desprecio. **to t. upon,** atacar, volverse contra, acometer; depender de, estribar en. **to t. upside down,** volver lo de arriba abajo; revolver; revolcar
turn *vi* (in a lathe) tornear; (revolve) girar, dar vueltas; (depend) depender (de); torcer; volverse; dar la vuelta; girar sobre los talones; dirigirse (a, hacia); (move) mudar de posición; (deviate) desviarse (de); (be changed) convertirse (en); (become) hacerse, venir a ser; (begin) meterse (a); (take to) dedicarse a; (seek help) acudir; (change behavior) enmendarse, corregirse; (the stomach) revolver (el estómago); (go sour) agriarse, avinagrarse; (rebel) sublevarse. **He turned to the left,** Dio la vuelta a la izquierda; Torció hacia la izquierda. **My head turns,** (with giddiness) Se me va la cabeza. **to t. about,** voltearse, dar la vuelta. **to t. against,** coger aversión (a), disgustarse con; volverse hostil (a). **to t. aside,** desviarse; dejar el camino. **to t. away,** volver la cabeza; apartarse; alejarse. **to t. back,** volver atrás; volver de nuevo; retroceder; volver sobre sus pasos. **to t. down,** doblarse; reducirse. **to t. from,** alejarse de; apartarse de, huir de. **to t. in,** doblar hacia dentro; (retire) acostarse. **to t. into,** transformarse en; convertirse en. **to t. off,** (depart from) desviarse (de); (fork) torcer, bifurcarse. **to t. out,** estar vuelto hacia fuera; (leave home) salir de casa; (rise) levantarse (de la cama); (arrive) llegar, presentarse; (attend) asistir, acudir; (result) resultar. **to t. over,** mudar (or cambiar) de posición, revolverse; (upset) voltearse, volcarse. **to t. round,** girar; volverse; cambiar de frente; cambiar de dirección, dar la vuelta; (*aut, aer*) virar; (change views) cambiar de opinión; (change sides) cambiar de partido. **to t. round and round,** dar vueltas, girar. **to t. to,** (apply to) acudir a; (begin) ponerse a; (become) convertirse en; (face) dirigirse hacia; (address) dirigirse a. **to t. up,** (crop up) surgir, aparecer; (arrive) llegar; (happen) acontecer; (be found again) volver a hallarse, reaparecer; (cards) venir; (of hats) levantar el ala; (of hair, etc.) doblarse. **His nose turns up,** Tiene la nariz respingona
turncoat *n* desertor (-ra), renegado (-da). **to become a t.,** volver la casaca
turned-up *a* (of hats) con el ala levantada; (of noses) respingona
turner *n* (craftsman) tornero, torneador, *m*
turnery *n* tornería, *f*
turning *n* (bend) vuelta, *f*; (turnery) tornería, *f*; (of milk, etc.) agrura, *f*; *pl* **turnings,** *sew* ensanche, *m*. **t.-point,** punto decisivo, *m*, crisis, *f*. **t. yellow** *Lat. Am.* amarilloso
turnip *n* nabo, *m*. **t. field,** nabar, *m*

turnover *n com* ventas, *f pl*; *cul* pastelillo, *m*
turnpike *n* barrera de portazgo, *f*
turnstile *n* torniquete, *m*
turpentine *n* aguarrás, *m*, trementina, *f*
turpitude *n* infamia, maldad, *f*
turquoise *n* turquesa, *f*
turret *n* torrecilla, almenilla, *f*; *naut* torre blindada, *f*
turreted *a* con torres, guarnecido de torres; en forma de torre
turtle *n* (dove) tórtolo (-la); (sea) tortuga de mar, *f*. **to turn t.,** voltearse patas arriba; *naut* zozobrar. **t. soup,** sopa de tortuga, *f*
Tuscan *a* and *n* toscano (-na)
Tuscany Toscana, *f*
tusk *n* colmillo, *m*
tussle *n* lucha, *f*; agarrada, *f*. *vi* luchar, pelear; tener una agarrada
tutelage *n* tutela, *f*
tutelar *a* tutelar
tutor *n* (private) ayo, *m*; profesor (-ra); (Roman law) tutor, *m*; (supervisor of studies) preceptor. *vt* enseñar, instruir. *vi* ser profesor, dar clases
tutorial *n* (university) seminario, *m*; (private) clase particular, *f*
tutoring *n* enseñanza, instrucción, *f*
TWA la TWA, *f*, (pronounced as if written *túa*)
twaddle *n* disparates, *m pl*, tonterías, patrañas, *f pl*
twain *a* and *n* dos, *m*
twang *n* punteado de una cuerda, *m*; (of a guitar) zumbido, *m*; (in speech) gangueo, *m*. *vt* puntear; (las cuerdas de un instrumento) rasguear. **to speak with a t.,** hablar con una voz gangosa
tweak *n* pellizco, *m*; sacudida, *f*, tirón, *m*. *vt* pellizcar; sacudir, tirar
tweed *n* mezcla, *f*, cheviot, *m*
tweezers *n pl* pinzas, tenacillas, *f pl*
twelfth *a* duodécimo; (of the month) (el) doce; (of monarchs) doce. *n* duodécimo, *m*; (part) dozavo, *m*, duodécima parte, *f*. **T.-night,** Día de Reyes, *m*, Epifanía, *f*
twelve *a* and *n* doce *m*; (of age) doce años, *m pl*. **o'- clock,** las doce; (mid-day) mediodía, *m*; (midnight) media noche, *f*, las doce de la noche. **t.-syllabled,** dodecasílabo
twentieth *a* vigésimo; (of the month) (el) veinte; (of monarchs) veinte, *n* vigésimo, *m*; (part) vientavo, *m*, vigésima parte, *f*
twenty *a* veinte; (of age) veinte años, *m pl*, *n* veinte, *m*; (score) veintena, *f*. **t.-first,** vigésimo primero; (of date) (el) veintiuno, *m*, (In modern Spanish the ordinals above *décimo* "tenth" are generally replaced by the cardinals, e.g. **the twenty-ninth chapter,** el capítulo veintinueve.)
twice *adv* dos veces. **t. as many** or **as much,** el doble
twiddle *vt* jugar con; hacer girar. *vi* girar; vibrar. *n* vuelta, *f*. **to t. one's thumbs,** dar vuelta a los pulgares, estar mano sobre mano
twig *n* ramita, pequeña rama, *f*
twilight *n* crepúsculo, *m*; media luz, *f*. *a* crepuscular. **in the t.,** en el crepúsculo; en la media luz. **t. sleep,** parto sin dolor, *m*
twin *a* gemelo, mellizo; doble. *n* gemelo (-la), mellizo (-za); (of objects) pareja, *f*, par, *m*. **t.-engined,** bimotor. **t. screw,** (*naut aer*) de dos hélices
twine *n* bramante, cordel, *m*; guita, *f*. *vt* enroscar; (weave) tejer; (encircle) ceñir; (round, about) abrazar. *vi* (of plants) trepar; entrelazarse; (wind) serpentear
twinge *n* punzada, *f*, dolor agudo, *m*; *fig* remordimiento, tormento, *m*. *vi* causar un dolor agudo
twining *a* *bot* trepante, voluble. **t. plant,** planta enredadera (or trepante), *f*
twinkle *vi* centellear, chispear, titilar; (of eyes) brillar; (of feet) moverse rápidamente, bailar. *n* (in the eye) chispa, *f*
twinkling *n* centelleo, *m*; titilación, *f*; (of the eye) brillo, *m*; (glimpse) vislumbre, *m*; *fig* instante, momento, *m*. *a*

titilante, centelleador. **in a t.,** en un dos por tres. **in the t. of an eye,** en un abrir y cerrar de ojos
twin-tailed comet *n* ceratias, *m*
twirl *n* rotación, vuelta, *f*; pirueta, *f*. *vi* hacer girar; voltear; torcer; (a stick, etc.) dar vueltas (a). *vi* girar, dar vueltas; dar piruetas
twirp *n* *inf* renacuajo, *m*
twist *n* (skein) mecha, *f*; trenza, *f*; (yarn) torzal, *m*; (of tobacco) rollo, *m*; (of bread) rosca de pan, *f*; (act of twisting) torcimiento, *m*, torsión, *f*; (in a road, etc.) recodo, *m*, curva, vuelta, *f*; (pull) sacudida, *f*; (contortion) regate, esguince, *m*; (in a winding stair) espira, *f*; (in ball games) efecto, *m*; (in a person's nature) peculiaridad, *f*; falta de franqueza, *f*; (to words) interpretación, *f*. *vi* torcer; enroscar; (plait) trenzar; (wring) estrujar; (weave) tejer; (encircle) ceñir; (a stick, etc.) dar vueltas a; (of hands) crispar; (distort) interpretar mal, torcer. *vi* torcerse; enroscarse; (wind) serpentear; dar vueltas; (coil) ensortijarse; (writhe) undular, retorcerse; (of a stair) dar vueltas
twisted *a* torcido, *Mexico* chueco; (of persons) contrahecho
twisting *n* torcimiento, *m*; torcedura, *f*; serpenteo, *m*; (interlacing) entrelazamiento, *m*. *a* sinuoso, serpenteado
twitch *n* sacudida, *f*, tirón, *m*; (nervous) contracción nerviosa, *f*. *vt* tirar bruscamente, quitar rápidamente; agarrar; (ears, etc.) mover; (hands) crispar, retorcer. *vi* crisparse; (of ears, nose) moverse
twitching *n* sacudida, *f*; (contraction) crispamiento, *m*, contracción nerviosa, *f*; (pain) punzada, *f*; (of conscience) remordimiento, *m*
twitter *n* piada, *f*, gorjeo, *m*. *vi* piar, gorjear
two *a* and *n* dos, *m*; (of the clock) (las) dos, *f pl*; (of age) dos años, *m pl*. *a* de dos. **in two,** en dos partes. **in two's,** de dos en dos, uno o dos; algunos, *m pl*; algunas, *f pl*. **two against two,** dos a dos. **two by two,** de dos en dos, a pares. **Two can live as cheaply as one,** Donde come uno comen dos. **to put two and two together,** atar cabos. **two-edged,** de dos filos. **two-faced,** de dos caras; *fig* de dos haces. **to be two-faced,** hacer a dos caras; *fig* de dos cabezas; bicéfalo. **two hundred,** *a* and *n* doscientos, *m*. **two hundredth,** *a* ducentésimo. *n* ducentésima parte, *f*; doscientos, *m*. **two-legged,** bípedo. **two-ply,** de dos hilos. **two-seater,** *a* de dos asientos. **two-speed gear box,** cambio de marcha de dos velocidades, *m*. **two-step,** paso doble, *m*. **two of a kind,** (well-matched) tal para cual. **two-way switch,** *elec* interruptor de dos direcciones, *m*
twofold *a* doble. *adv* doblemente, dos veces
twosome *n* partido de dos, *m*
two swords' theory *n* teoría de los dos gladios, *f*
tying *n* ligadura, *f*; atadura, *f*
tympanum *n* (*anat*, *arch*) tímpano, *m*
type *n* tipo, *m*; *print* carácter, *m*, letra de imprenta, *f*, tipo, *m*. *vt* and *vi* escribir a máquina. **t. case,** caja de imprenta, *f*. **t. founder,** fundidor de letras de imprenta, *m*. **t. foundry,** fundición de tipos, *f*. **t.-setter,** cajista, *mf* **t.-setting,** composición tipográfica, *f*
typewrite *vt* and *vi* escribir a máquina
typewriter *n* máquina de escribir, *f*
typewriting *n* mecanografía, *f*, *a* mecanográfico
typewritten *a* escrito a máquina
typhoid *n* tifoidea, fiebre tifoidea, *f*
typhoon *n* tifón, *m*
typhus *n* tifus, tabardillo pintado, *m*
typical *a* típico, característico; simbólico. **t. Mexican dish** (of food) antojito, *m*
typify *vt* simbolizar, representar; ser ejemplo de
typist *n* mecanografista, *mf*; mecanógrafo (-fa)
typographic *a* tipográfico
typography *n* tipografía, *f*
typographer *n* tipógrafo, *m*
tyrannical *a* tiránico, despótico

tyrannization *n* tiranización, *f*
tyrannize *vi* tiranizar
tyranny *n* tiranía, *f*, despotismo, *m*
tyrant *n* déspota, *m*, tirano (-na)

Tyre Tiro, *m*
tyro *n* novicio (-cia), tirón (-ona), advenedizo (-za), *mf*
Tyrol, the el Tirol
Tyrolese *a* and *n* tirolés (-esa)

U

U *n* (letter) u, *f.* **U-boat,** submarino, *m.* **u-shaped,** en forma de U
ubiquitous *a* ubicuo, omnipresente
ubiquity *n* ubicuidad, omnipresencia, *f*
udder *n* ubre, teta, mama, *f*
ugh *interj* ¡uf!
ugliness *n* fealdad, *f*; (moral) perversidad, *f*; (of a situation) peligro, *m*, lo difícil
ugly *a* feo, *Lat. Am. also* feroz; (morally) repugnante, asqueroso, perverso; (of a situation) peligroso, difícil; (of a wound) grave, profundo; (of a look) amenazador; *inf* desagradable; (of weather) borrascoso. **to make u.,** afear, hacer feo
Ukraine Ucrania, *f*
Ukrainian *a* and *n* ucranio (-ia)
ukulele *n* mus ucelele, *m*
ulcer *n* úlcera, *f, Lat. Am. also* lacra
ulcerate *vt* ulcerar. *vi* ulcerarse
ulceration *n* ulceración, *f*
ulcerous *a* ulceroso
ulterior *a* (of place) ulterior; (of time) posterior, ulterior; (of motives) interesado, oculto; **ulterior motive,** segunda intención, *f*
ultimate *a* último; fundamental, esencial
ultimately *adv* por fin, al final; esencialmente
ultimatum *n* ultimátum, *m*
ultimo *adv* del mes anterior
ultra *a* exagerado, extremo. *prefix* ultra-. **u-red,** ultra-rrojo. **u.-violet,** ultravioleta
ultramarine *a* ultramarino. *n* azul de ultramar, *m*
ultramontane *a* ultramontano
ululation *n* ululación, *f*, ululato, *m*
umbilical *a* umbilical
umbilicus *n* ombligo, *m*
umbra *n ast* cono de sombra, *m*
umbrage *n poet* sombra, *f*; resentimiento, enfado, *m*. **to take u.,** ofenderse, resentirse
umbrella *n* paraguas, *m*. **u. maker,** paragüero (-ra). **u. shop,** paragüería, *f.* **u. stand,** paragüero, *m*
umpire *n sport* árbitro, *m*; *law* juez arbitrador, tercero en discordia, *m*. *vt* arbitrar
un- *prefix* Used before adjectives, adverbs, abstract nouns, verbs and translated in Spanish by **in-, des-, nada, no, poco, sin,** as well as in other ways
unabashed *a* desvergonzado, descarado, insolente; (calm) sereno, sosegado
unabashedly *adv* sin rubor
unabated *a* no disminuido; cabal, entero
unabbreviated *a* íntegro, sin abreviar
unable *a* incapaz, impotente; (physical defect) imposibilitado. **to be u. to,** no poder, serle a uno imposible. **to be u. to control,** no poder controlar
unabridged *a.* See **unabbreviated**
unaccented *a* sin acento
unacceptability *n* lo inaceptable
unacceptable *a* inaceptable
unaccepted *a* rechazado, no aceptado
unaccommodating *a* poco complaciente, nada servicial
unaccompanied *a* solo, sin compañía; *mus* sin acompañamiento
unaccomplished *a* incompleto, sin terminar, inacabado; (not clever) sin talento
unaccountability *n* lo inexplicable; falta de responsabilidad, irresponsabilidad, *f*
unaccountable *a* inexplicable; irresponsable
unaccountably *adv* inexplicablemente, extrañamente

unaccredited *a* no acreditado, extraoficial
unaccustomed *a* no habituado; (unusual) desacostumbrado, insólito, inusitado
unacknowledged *a* no reconocido; (of letter) sin contestación, por contestar; no correspondido, sin devolver; (of crimes, etc.) inconfeso, no declarado
unacquainted *a* que no conoce; que desconoce, que ignora; no habituado. **to be u. with,** no conocer; ignorar; no estar acostumbrado a
unadaptable *a* inadaptable (also of persons)
unadorned *a* sin adorno sencillo, que no tiene adornos
unadulterated *a* sin mezcla, no adulterado, natural; genuino, verdadero; puro
unadventurous *a* nada aventurero, que no busca aventuras, tímido; tranquilo, sin incidente
unadvisability *n* imprudencia, *f*; inoportunidad, *f*
unadvisable *a* imprudente; inoportuno, no conveniente
unadvisedly *adv* imprudentemente
unesthetic *a* antiestético
unaffected *a* natural, llano, sin melindres; impasible; genuino, sincero. **u. by,** no afectado por
unaffectedly *adv* sin afectación
unaffectedness *n* naturalidad, sencillez, *f*; sinceridad, franqueza, *f*
unaffiliated *a* no afiliado
unafraid *a* sin temor
unaided *a* sin ayuda, solo a solas
unaired *a* sin ventilar, no ventilado; húmedo, sin airear
unalloyed *a* sin mezcla, puro
unalterability *n* lo inalterable; constancia, *f*
unalterable *a* inalterable; invariable, constante
unambiguous *a* no ambiguo, nada dudoso, claro
unambitious *a* sin ambición; modesto
unamusing *a* nada divertido
unanimity *n* unanimidad, *f*
unanimous *a* unánime
unanimously *adv* unánimemente, por unanimidad. **carried u.,** adoptado por unanimidad
unanswerability *n* imposibilidad de negar, *f*; lo irrefutable
unanswerable *a* incontestable, incontrovertible, incontrastable, irrefutable
unanswered *a* no contestado, sin contestar; (unrequited) no correspondido
unapparent *a* no aparente
unappealable *a* inapelable
unappeasable *a* implacable
unappeased *a* no satisfecho; implacable
unappetizing *a* no apetitoso; (unattractive) repugnante, feo
unappreciated *a* desestimado, no apreciado, tenido en poco; (misunderstood) mal comprendido
unapproachable *a* inaccesible
unapproachableness *n* inaccesibilidad, *f*
unappropriated *a* no concedido; libre
unapproved *a* sin aprobar, no aprobado
unarm *vt* desarmar. *vi* desarmarse, quitarse las armas
unarmed *a* desarmado; indefenso; (zool, bot) inerme
unarranged *a* no arreglado, sin clasificar; (accidental) fortuito, casual
unartistic *a* no artístico
unascertainable *a* no verificable
unashamed *a* sin vergüenza; tranquilo, sereno; insolente, descarado
unasked *a* sin pedir; no solicitado; espontáneo; (uninvited) no convidado

unassailable *a* inexpugnable; irrefutable; incontestable

unassisted *a*. See **unaided**

unassuming *a* modesto, sin pretensiones

unattached *a* suelto; *law* no embargado; *mil* de reemplazo; independiente

unattainable *a* inasequible, irrealizable

unattainableness *n* imposibilidad de alcanzar (or realizar), *f*; inaccesibilidad

unattended *a* solo, sin acompañamiento; (of ill person) sin tratamiento; (of entertainment, etc.) no concurrido

unattested *a* sin atestación

unattractive *a* poco atrayente, desagradable, antipático, feo

unattractiveness *n* fealdad, falta de hermosura, *f*; lo desagradable

unauthentic *a* no auténtico, sin autenticidad; apócrifo

unauthorized *a* no autorizado

unavailable *a* inaprovechable

unavailing *a* inútil, vano

unavenged *a* no vengado, sin castigo

unavoidable *a* inevitable, preciso, necesario. **to be u.,** no poder evitarse, no tener remedio

unavoidableness *n* inevitabilidad, necesidad, *f*

unavoidably *adv* irremediablemente

unaware *a* ignorante; inconsciente. **to be u. of,** ignorar, desconocer; no darse cuenta de

unawareness *n* ignorancia, *f*, desconocimiento, *m*; inconsciencia, *f*

unawares *adv* (by mistake) sin querer, inadvertidamente; (unprepared) de sobresalto, de improviso, inopinadamente. **He caught me u.,** Me cogió desprevenido

unbalance *vt* desequilibrar, hacer perder el equilibrio; *fig* trastornar

unbalanced *a* desequilibrado; *fig* trastornado; *com* no balanceado

unbaptized *a* no bautizado, sin bautizar

unbar *vt* desatrancar; *fig* abrir

unbearable *a* intolerable, insufrible, inaguantable, insufrible, insoportable

unbearably *adv* insoportablemente

unbeatable *a* inmejorable

unbeaten *a* (of paths) no frecuentado, no pisado; (of armies) no derrotado, no batido; invicto

unbecoming *a* impropio, inapropiado, inconveniente; indecoroso, indigno; indecente; (of clothes) que no va bien, que sienta mal

unbelief *n* incredulidad, *f*

unbelievable *a* increíble

unbelievably *adv* increíblemente

unbeliever *n* incrédulo (-la), descreído (-da)

unbeloved *a* no amado

unbend *vt* desencorvar, enderezar; entretenerse, descansar; (*naut* of sails) desenvergar; (*naut* of cables) desamarrar. *vi* enderezarse; mostrarse afable

unbending *a* inflexible, rígido, tieso; *fig* inexorable, inflexible, duro, terco; (amiable) afable, jovial

unbiased *a* imparcial, ecuánime

unbidden *a* espontáneo; (uninvited) no convidado, no invitado

unbind *vt* desligar, desatar; (bandages) desvendar; (books) desencuadernar

unbleached *a* crudo, sin blanquear

unblemished *a* no manchado; (pure) sin mancha, inmaculado, puro

unblessed *a* no bendecido, no consagrado; (accursed) maldito; (unhappy) desdichado

unblushing *a* desvergonzado, insolente

unbolt *vt* descerrojar, desempernar

unborn *a* sin nacer, no nacido todavía; venidero

unbosom *vt* confesar, declarar. **to u. oneself,** abrir su pecho a (or con)

unbought *a* no comprado; gratuito, libre; (not bribed) no sobornado

unbound *a* suelto, libre; (of books) en rama, no encuadernado

unbounded *a* ilimitado, infinito; inmenso

unbowed *a* erguido; no encorvado; (undefeated) invicto

unbreakable *a* irrompible, inquebrantable

unbridled *a* desenfrenado, violento; licencioso

unbroken *a* no quebrantado, intacto, entero; continuo, incesante; no interrumpido; (of soil) virgen; (of a horse) indomado; inviolado; (of the spirit) indómito; (of a record) no batido

unbrotherly *a* poco fraternal, indigno de hermanos

unbuckle *vt* deshebillar

unburden *vt* descargar; aliviar. **to u. oneself,** (express one's feelings) desahogarse

unburied *a* insepulto

unburnt *a* no quemado; incombusto

unbusinesslike *a* informal; poco comercial, descuidado

unbutton *vt* desabrochar, desabotonar

uncalled *a* no llamado, no invitado. **u.-for,** impertinente; innecesario

uncannily *adv* misteriosamente

uncanniness *n* lo misterioso

uncanny *a* misterioso, horroroso, pavoroso

uncared-for *a* abandonado, desatendido, desamparado

uncarpeted *a* sin alfombra

uncaught *a* no prendido, libre

unceasing *a* continuo, incesante, sin cesar, constante

unceasingly *adv* incesantemente, sin cesar

uncensored *a* no censurado

unceremonious *a* sin ceremonia, familiar; descortés, brusco

unceremoniousness *n* falta de ceremonia, familiaridad, *f*; incivilidad, descortesía, *f*

uncertain *a* incierto, dudoso; inseguro; precario; (hesitant) indeciso, vacilante, irresoluto

uncertainly *adv* inciertamente

uncertainty *n* incertidumbre, duda, *f*; inseguridad, *f*; irresolución, *f*

uncertificated *a* sin certificado (of teachers, etc.) sin título

uncertified *a* sin garantía; no garantizado; (of lunatics) sin certificar

unchain *vt* desencadenar

unchallenged *a* incontestable

unchangeable *a* invariable, inalterable, inmutable

unchangeableness *n* invariabilidad, inalterabilidad, *f*

unchanging *a* inmutable, invariable

uncharitable *a* nada caritativo, duro; intolerante, intransigente

uncharitableness *n* falta de caridad, *f*; intolerancia, intransigencia

uncharitably *adv* sin caridad; con intolerancia

unchaste *a* incasto, incontinente; deshonesto, impuro, lascivo

unchecked *a* desenfrenado; (unproved) no comprobado; *com* no confrontado

unchivalrous *a* nada galante, nada caballeroso

unchristened *a* no bautizado, sin bautizar

unchristian *a* (heathen) pagano; poco cristiano, indigno de un cristiano, nada caritativo

uncircumcised *a* incircunciso

uncircumscribed *a* incircunscripto

uncivil *a* descortés, incivil

uncivilizable *a* reacio a la civilización

uncivilized *a* no civilizado, bárbaro, salvaje, inculto

uncivilly *adv* descortésmente

unclad *a* sin vestir; desnudo

unclasp *vt* (jewelery) desengarzar; desabrochar; (of hands) soltar, separar

unclassifiable *a* inclasificable

unclassified *a* sin clasificar

uncle *n* tío, *m*; (pawnbroker) prestamista, *m*

unclean *a* sucio, puerco, inmundo; deseaseado; impuro, obsceno; (ritually) poluto

uncleanliness *n* suciedad, porquería, *f*; deseaseo, *m*; falta de limpieza, *f*

uncleanly *a* sucio, puerco; desaseado
uncleanness *n* suciedad, *f*; impureza, obscenidad, inmoralidad, *f*
unclench *vt* (of hands) abrir
Uncle Tom's Cabin La Cabaña del Tío Tom
unclouded *a* sin nubes, despejado, claro
uncoil *vt* desarrollar. *vi* desovillarse; (of snakes) desanillarse
uncollected *a* disperso; no cobrado; (in confusion) confuso, desordenado
uncolored *a* incoloro; *fig* imparcial, objetivo, sencillo
uncombed *a* despeinado, sin peinar
uncomfortable *a* incómodo; (anxious) intranquilo, inquieto, desasosegado, preocupado; (awkward) molesto, difícil, desagradable. **to be u.,** (people) estar incómodo; (anxious) estar preocupado; (of things) ser incómodo
uncomfortableness *n* incomodidad, *f*; malestar, *m*; intranquilidad, preocupación, *f*; dificultad, *f*; lo desagradable
uncomfortably *adv* incómodamente; intranquilamente; desagradablemente
uncomforted *a* desconsolado, sin consuelo
uncommercial *a* no comercial
uncommon *a* poco común, extraordinario, singular, raro, extraño; infrecuente; insólito
uncommonly *adv* extraordinariamente, muy; infrecuentemente, raramente
uncommonness *n* infrecuencia, rareza, *f*; singularidad, *f*
uncommunicative *a* reservado, poco expresivo
uncommunicativeness *n* reserva, *f*
uncomplaining *a* resignado, que no se queja
uncomplainingly *adv* con resignación
uncompliant *a* sordo, inflexible
uncomplicated *a* sencillo, sin complicaciones
uncomplimentary *a* descortés, poco halagüeño, ofensivo
uncompromising *a* inflexible, estricto, intolerante; irreconciliable
unconcealed *a* no oculto; abierto
unconcern *n* indiferencia, frialdad, *f*, desapego, *m*; (lack of interest) apatía, despreocupación, *f*; (nonchalance) desenfado, *m*, frescura, *f*
unconcerned *a* indiferente, frío, despegado, apático, despreocupado; desenfadado, fresco
unconcernedly *adv* con indiferencia; sin preocuparse; con desenfado
unconditional *a* incondicional, absoluto. **u. surrender,** rendición incondicional, *f*
unconditionally *adv* incondicionalmente; *mil* a discreción
unconfessed *a* inconfeso
unconfined *a* suelto, libre; ilimitado; sin estorbo
unconfirmed *a* no confirmado; (report) sin confirmar
uncongenial *a* incompatible, antipático; desagradable, repugnante
uncongeniality *n* incompatibilidad, antipatía, *f*; repugnancia, *f*; lo desagradable
unconnected *a* inconexo; *mech* desconectado; (relationship) sin parentesco; (confused) incoherente
unconquerable *a* invencible, indomable, inconquistable
unconquered *a* no vencido
unconscientious *a* poco concienzudo
unconscionable *a* excesivo, desmedido; sin conciencia
unconscious *a* inconsciente; (senseless) insensible, sin sentido; espontáneo; (unaware) ignorante. **to be u. of,** ignorar; perder la consciencia de. **to become u.,** perder el sentido
unconsciously *adv* inconscientemente, involuntariamente
unconsciousness *n* inconsciencia, *f*; (hypnosis, swoon) insensibilidad, *f*; (unawareness) ignorancia, falta de conocimiento, *f*
unconsecrated *a* no consagrado

unconsidered *a* indeliberado; sin importancia, trivial
unconstitutional *a* anticonstitucional, inconstitucional
unconstitutionally *adv* inconstitucionalmente
unconstrained *a* libre; voluntario; sin freno
uncontaminated *a* incontaminado; puro, sin mancha, impoluto
uncontested *a* sin oposición
uncontradicted *a* sin contradicción; incontestable
uncontrollable *a* irrefrenable, incontrolable, inmanejable; (temper) ingobernable; indomable
uncontrolled *a* libre, no controlado; desenfrenado, desgobernado
unconventional *n* poco convencional; bohemio, excéntrico, extravagante; original
unconventionality *a* excentricidad, extravagancia, independencia de ideas, *f*; (of a design) originalidad, *f*
unconversant *a* poco familiar, poco versado (en)
unconverted *a* no convertido; sin transformar
unconvinced *a* no convencido
unconvincing *a* no convincente, poco convincente, que no me (nos, etc.) convence; frívolo
uncooked *a* crudo, no cocido, sin cocer
uncork *vt* destapar, descorchar, quitar el corcho
uncorrected *a* sin corregir, no corregido
uncorroborated *a* no confirmado, sin confirmar
uncorrupted *a* incorrupto; puro, no pervertido; (unbribed) no sobornado, honrado
uncorruptible *a* incorruptible
uncountable *a* innumerable
uncounted *a* no contado, sin cuenta
uncouple *vt* soltar; desenganchar, desconectar
uncouth *a* grosero, chabacano, tosco, patán
uncouthness *n* grosería, tosquedad, patanería, *f*
uncover *vt* descubrir; (remove lid of) destapar; (remove coverings of) desabrigar, desarropar; (leave unprotected) desamparar; (disclose) revelar, dejar al descubierto. *vi* descubrirse, quitar el sombrero
uncovered *a* descubierto; desnudo; sin cubierta
uncreated *a* increado
uncritical *a* sin sentido crítico, poco juicioso
uncross *vt* (of legs) descruzar
uncrossed *a* (of check) sin cruzar
uncrowned *a* antes de ser coronado; sin corona
unction *n* unción, *f*; untadura, *f*, untamiento, *m*; (unguent) ungüento, *m*; (zeal) fervor, *m*; (flattery) insinceridad, hipocresía, *f*; (relish) gusto, entusiasmo, *m*. **extreme u.,** extremaunción, *f*
unctuous *a* untuoso, craso; insincero, zalamero
uncultivable *a* incultivable
uncultivated *a* inculto, yermo; (barbarous) salvaje, bárbaro; (uncultured) inculto, tosco; no cultivado
uncultured *a* inculto, iletrado
uncurbed *a* sin freno; *fig* desenfrenado
uncurl *vt* desrizar *vi* desrizarse; desovillarse
uncurtained *a* sin cortinas; con las cortinas recogidas
uncut *a* sin cortar, no cortado; (of gems) sin labrar
undamaged *a* indemne, sin daño
undated *a* sin fecha
undaunted *a* intrépido, atrevido
undeceive *vt* desengañar, desilusionar
undecided *a* (of question) pendiente, indeciso; dudoso; vacilante, irresoluto
undecipherable *a* indescifrable; ilegible
undeclared *a* no declarado
undefended *a* indefenso
undeferable *a* inaplazable
undefiled *a* impoluto, incontaminado; puro
undefinable *a* indefinible; inefable, vago
undefined *a* indefinido; indeterminado
undelivered *a* no recibido; (speech) no pronunciado; (not sent) no enviado
undemonstrative *a* poco expresivo, reservado
undeniable *a* incontestable, innegable, indudable; excelente; inequívoco, evidente
undeniably *adv* indudablemente

undenominational *a* sin denominación

undependable *a* indigno de confianza

under *prep* debajo de; bajo; (in) en; (less than) menos de, menos que; (at the orders of) a las órdenes de, al mando de; (in less time than) en menos de; (under the weight of) bajo el peso de; (at the foot of) al abrigo de; (for less than) por menos de; (at the time of) en la época de, en tiempos de; (according to) según, conforme a, en virtud de (e.g. **under the law,** en virtud de la ley); (of monarchs) bajo (or durante) el reinado de; (of rank) inferior a; (in virtue of) en virtud de; (of age) menor de; (with penalty, pretext, etc.) so; en; a (see below for examples); (*agr* of fields) plantado de, sembrado de. **u. arms,** bajo las armas. **u. contract,** bajo contrato. **u. cover,** al abrigo, bajo cubierto. **u. cover of,** bajo pretexto de, so color de. **u. fire,** bajo fuego. **u. oath,** bajo juramento. **u. pain of,** so pena de. **u. sail,** a la vela. **u. separate cover,** bajo cubierta separada, en sobre apartado, por separado. **u. steam,** al vapor. **u. way,** en camino; en marcha; en preparación. **to be u. an obligation,** deber favores; (to) tener obligacion de; estar obligado a

under *a* inferior; (of rank) subalterno, subordinado; bajo, bajero. *adv* debajo; abajo; más abajo; menos; (for less) para menos; (ill) mal; (insufficient) insuficiente. **to bring u.,** someter. **to keep u.,** dominar, subyugar

underact *vt* hacer un papel sin fogosidad

underarm *n* sobaco, *m*. *a* sobacal; (of bowling) de debajo del brazo. **to serve u.,** sacar por debajo

underbid *vt* ofrecer menos que

underbred *a* mal criado, mal educado

undercharge *vt* cobrar menos de lo debido

underclothes *n* ropa interior, *f*, paños menores, *m pl*

undercurrent *n* corriente submarina, *f*; *fig* tendencia oculta, *f*

undercut *n* (of meat) filete, *m*

underdeveloped *a* de desarrollo atrasado; *phot* no revelado lo suficiente

underdog *n* víctima, *f*; débil, paciente, *m*. **underdogs,** los de abajo, *m pl*

underdone *a* (of meat) crudo, medio asado

underdress *vt* and *vi* vestir(se) sin bastante elegancia

underestimate *vt* tasar en menos; desestimar, menospreciar

underfeed *vt* alimentar insuficientemente

underfoot *adv* debajo de los pies, en el suelo

undergo *vt* sufrir, padecer, pasar por. **undergo surgery,** someterse a la cirugía

undergraduate *n* estudiante no graduado, *m*

underground *a* subterráneo; *fig* oculto, secreto. *adv* bajo tierra, debajo de la tierra; *fig* en secreto, ocultamente. *n* sótano, *m*; metro, ferrocarril subterráneo, *m*

undergrown *a* enclenque

undergrowth *n* maleza, *f*

underhand *adv fig* bajo mano, ocultamente, a escondidas. *a fig* secreto, oculto

underlie *vt* estar debajo de; servir de base a, caracterizar

underline *vt* subrayar

underling *n* subordinado (-da)

underlying *a* fundamental, básico, esencial

undermentioned *a* abajo citado

undermine *vt* socavar, excavar; minar, destruir poco a poco

undermining *n* socava, excavación, *f*; destrucción, *f*, *a* minador

underneath *adv* debajo. *prep* bajo, debajo de

undernourished *a* mal alimentado

undernourishment *n* desnutrición, *f*

underpaid *a* insuficientemente retribuido, mal pagado

underpass *n* pasaje por debajo, *m*

underpay *vt* pagar mal, remunerar (or retribuir) deficientemente

underpayment *n* retribución mezquina, *f*, pago insuficiente, *m*

underpin *vt* apuntalar, socalzar

underpopulated *a* con baja densidad de población

underprivileged *a* menesteroso, pobre, necesitado

underrate *vt* tasar en menos; tener en poco, desestimar, menospreciar

underripe *a* verde

undersecretary *n* subsecretario (-ia)

undersell *vt* vender a un precio más bajo que

undershirt *n Spain* camiseta, *Lat. Am.* franela, *f*

underside *n* revés, envés, *m*

undersigned *a* infrascrito, suscrito. **the u.,** el abajo firmado, el infrascrito

undersized *a* muy pequeño, enclenque, enano

underskirt *n* enagua, *f*; refajo, *m*

underslung *a aut* con bajo centro de gravedad

understand *vt* comprender, entender; (know) saber; (be acquainted with) conocer; (hear) oír, tener entendido; (mean) sobrentender. *vi* comprender, entender; oír, tener entendido. **to u. each other,** comprenderse. **It being understood that . . .,** Bien entendido que . . .

understandable *a* comprensible; inteligible. **It is very u. why he does not wish to come,** Se comprende muy bien por qué no quiere venir

understanding *n* (intelligence) entendimiento, *m*, inteligencia, *f*; (agreement) acuerdo, *m*; (knowledge) conocimiento, *m*; (wisdom) comprensión, sabiduría, *f*. *a* inteligente; sabio; (sympathetic) comprensivo, simpático. **to come to an u.,** ponerse de acuerdo

understandingly *adv* con inteligencia; con conocimiento (de); con simpatía

understate *vt* decir menos que, rebajar, describir sin énfasis

understatement *n* moderación, *f*

understudy *n* sobresaliente, *mf*. *vt* sustituir

undertake *vt* comprometerse a, encargarse de; emprender, abarcar, acometer

undertaker *n* empresario, director de pompas fúnebres, *m*

undertaking *n* empresa, tarea, *f*; garantía, promesa, *f*; (funerals) funeraria, *f*

undertone *n* voz baja, *f*; *art* color tenue (or apagado), *m*. **in an u.,** en voz baja

undervalue *vt* tasar en menos; tener en poco, despreciar

underwater *a* subacuático, submarino. **underwater flipper,** aleta de bucear

underweight *a* de bajo peso, que pesa menos de lo debido, flaco

underworld *n* (hell) infierno, averno, *m*; (slums) hampa, *f*, fondos bajos de la sociedad, *m pl*; heces de la sociedad, *f pl*. **u. slang** *Peru* cantuja *f*

underwrite *vt com* asegurar contra riesgos; reasegurar; obligarse a comprar todas las acciones de una compañía no subscritas por el público, mediante un pago convenido

underwriter *n* asegurador, *m*; reasegurador, *m*

underwriting *n* aseguro, *m*; reaseguro, *m*

undeserved *a* inmerecido, no merecido

undeserving *a* indigno, desmerecedor; que no merece

undesirable *a* no deseable; nocivo, pernicioso; (unsuitable) inconveniente

undesired *a* no deseado; no solicitado, no buscado

undesirous *a* no deseoso

undestroyed *a* sin destruir, no destruido, intacto

undetected *a* no descubierto

undeveloped *a* no desarrollado; rudimentario; inmaturo; (of a country) no explotado, virgen; *phot* no revelado; (of land) sin cultivar

undeviating *a* directo; constante, persistente

undigested *a* no digerido, indigesto

undignified *a* sin dignidad; poco serio; indecoroso

undiluted *a* sin diluir, puro

undiminished *a* no disminuido, sin disminuir, cabal, íntegro

undimmed *a* no obscurecido, brillante

undiplomatic *a* impolítico, indiscreto

undirected *a* sin dirección; (of letters) sin señas

undiscernible *a* imperceptible, invisible

undiscerning *a* sin percepción, obtuso, sin discernimiento

undisciplined *a* indisciplinado

undisclosed *a* no revelado, secreto

undiscouraged *a* animoso, sin flaquear, sin desaliento

undiscovered *a* no descubierto, ignoto

undiscriminating *a* sin distinción; sin sentido crítico

undisguised *a* sin disfraz; abierto, claro

undismayed *a* intrépido, impávido; sin desaliento

undisposed *a* desinclinado; (of property) no enajenado, no invertido

undisputed *a* incontestable, indisputable

undistinguishable *a* indistinguible

undistinguished *a* (of writers) poco conocido; indistinto; sin distinción

undisturbed *a* sin tocar; tranquilo, sereno, impasible

undivided *a* indiviso, íntegro; junto; completo, entero

undo *vt* anular; reparar; desatar, deshacer; desasir; abrir

undoing *n* anulación, *f*; (reparation) reparación, *f*; (opening) abrir, *m*; ruina, *f*

undomesticated *a* salvaje, no domesticado; poco casero

undone *a* and *part* sin hacer; deshecho; arruinado, perdido. **I am undone!** ¡Estoy perdido! **to come u.,** desatarse. **to leave u.,** dejar sin hacer

undoubted *a* indubable, evidente, incontestable

undoubtedly *adv* sin duda

undramatic *a* no dramático

undreamed *a* no soñado. **u. of,** inopinado, no imaginado

undress *vt* desnudar, desvestir, *Peru* calatear. *vi* desnudarse. *n* traje de casa, *m*; paños menores, *m pl*; *mil* traje de cuartel, *m*

undressed *a* desnudo; en paños menores; (of wounds) sin curar; *com* en rama, en bruto

undrinkable *a* impotable

undue *a* excesivo, indebido; injusto; impropio; (of a bill of exchange) por vencer

undulant *a* ondulante. **u. fever,** fiebre mediterránea, fiebre de Malta, *f*

undulate *vi* ondular, ondear

undulating *a* ondulante

undulation *n* ondulación, undulación, *f*, ondeo, *m*; fluctuación, *f*

undulatory *a* ondulatorio, undoso

unduly *adv* excesivamente, demasiado, indebidamente; injustamente

undutiful *a* desobediente, irrespetuoso

undutifulness *n* desobediencia, falta de respeto, *f*

undying *a* inmortal, imperecedero; eterno

unearned *a* no ganado; inmerecido

unearth *vt* desenterrar; *fig* descubrir, sacar a luz

unearthing *n* desenterramiento, *m*; *fig* descubrimiento, *m*, revelación, *f*

unearthly *a* sobrenatural; misterioso, aterrador, espantoso, *Lat. Am. also* extraterrenal

uneasily *adv* con dificultad; incómodamente; inquietamente

uneasiness *n* malestar, *m*; (discomfort) incomodidad, *f*; (anxiety) inquietud, intranquilidad, *f*, desasosiego, *m*

uneasy *a* incómodo; inseguro; inquieto, intranquilo, desasosegado; aturdido, turbado. **to become u.,** inquietarse

uneatable *a* incomible

uneaten *a* no comido

uneconomical *a* poco económico, costoso, caro

unedifying *a* poco edificante

unedited *a* inédito

uneducated *a* ignorante; ineducado, inculto, indocto

unembarrassed *a* sereno, tranquilo, imperturbable; (financially) sin deudas, acomodado

unemotional *a* frío, impasible

unemployable *a* sin uso, inservible; (of persons) inútil para el trabajo

unemployed *a* sin empleo; (out of work) sin trabajo, parado; desocupado, ocioso; inactivo. *n* paro obrero, *m*. **the u.,** los sin trabajo, los cesantes, los desocupados

unemployment *n* paro forzoso, *m*. **u. benefit,** subvención contra el paro obrero, *f*. **u. insurance,** seguro contra el paro obrero, *m*,

unencumbered *a* libre, independiente; (of estates) libre de gravamen; (untaxable) saneado

unending *a* perpetuo, eterno, sin fin; inacabable, constante, continuo, incesante

unendurable *a* insoportable, insufrible, intolerable

unenlightened *a* ignorante

unenterprising *a* poco emprendedor, tímido

unenthusiastic *a* sin entusiasmo, tibio

unenviable *a* no envidiable

unequal *a* desigual; inferior; (out of proportion) desproporcionado; injusto; insuficiente; incapaz; (of ground) escabroso. **to be u. to the task,** ser incapaz de la tarea; no tener fuerzas para la tarea

unequalled *a* sin igual, incomparable, sin par, único

unequally *adv* desigualmente

unequivocal *a* inequívoco; redondo, claro, franco

unerring *a* infalible; seguro

unerringly *adv* infaliblemente; sin equivocarse

unessential *a* no esencial

uneven *a* desigual; (of roads) escabroso, quebrado; (of numbers) impar; irregular

unevenly *adv* desigualmente

unevenness *n* desigualdad, *f*; desnivel, *m*, irregularidad, *f*. **the unevenness of the terrain,** lo desigual del terreno, lo accidentado del terreno, *m*

uneventful *a* sin incidentes, sin acontecimientos notables; tranquilo

unexaggerated *a* nada exagerado

unexamined *a* no examinado, sin examinar

unexampled *a* sin igual, sin par

unexceptionable *a* intachable, irreprensible; correcto; impecable, perfecto

unexhausted *a* no agotado; inexhausto

unexpected *a* inesperado, imprevisto, inopinado, impensado; repentino, súbito

unexpectedly *adv* inesperadamente; de repente

unexpectedness *n* lo inesperado

unexpired *a* (of bill of exchange) no vencido; (of lease) no caducado

unexplored *a* inexplorado

unexpressed *a* no expresado; tácito, sobrentendido

unexpurgated *a* sin expurgar, completo

unfading *a* inmarcesible, inmarchitable; eterno, inmortal

unfailing *a* inagotable; inexhausto; seguro; indefectible

unfailingly *adv* siempre, constantemente; sin faltar

unfair *a* injusto; vil, bajo, soez; de mala fe, engañoso; (of play) sucio

unfairly *adv* injustamente; de mala fe

unfairness *n* injusticia, *f*; mala fe, *f*

unfaithful *a* infiel; desleal; inexacto, incorrecto. **to be u. to,** ser infiel a; faltar a

unfaithfulness *n* infidelidad, *f*; deslealtad, *f*; inexactitud, *f*

unfaltering *a* sin vacilar; resuelto, firme

unfamiliar *a* poco familiar; desconocido. **to be u. with,** ser ignorante de

unfashionable *a* pasado de moda, fuera de moda; poco elegante

unfashionableness *n* falta de elegancia, *f*

unfashionably *adv* contra la tendencia de la moda; sin elegancia

unfasten *vt* desatar; desabrochar, desenganchar; abrir; aflojar; soltar

unfathomable *a* insondable; impenetrable, inescrutable

unfavorable *a* desfavorable, adverso, contrario

unfavorably *adv* desfavorablemente

unfeathered *a* implume, sin plumas

unfeeling *a* insensible, impasible, frío; duro, cruel

unfeigned *a* sincero, natural, verdadero

unfenced *a* descercado, sin tapia; abierto

unfermented *a* no fermentado;

unfetter *vt* desencadenar, destrabar; poner en libertad, librar

unfilial *a* poco filial, desobediente

unfinished *a* incompleto, inacabado; sin acabar; imperfecto

unfit *a* incapaz; incompetente, inepto; (unsuitable) impropio; (useless) inservible, inadecuado; (unworthy) indigno; (ill) enfermo, malo. *vt* inhabilitar, incapacitar. **u. for human consumption,** impropio para el consumo humano

unfitness *n* incapacidad, *f*; incompetencia, ineptitud, *f*; impropiedad, *f*; falta de mérito, *f*; falta de salud, *f*

unfix *vt* desprender, despegar, descomponer; soltar. **to come unfixed,** desprenderse

unflagging *a* incansable, infatigable; persistente, constante

unflattering *a* poco halagüeño

unflinching *a* inconmovible, resuelto, firme

unfold *vt* desplegar, desdoblar; tender; abrir; (plans) revelar, descubrir; contar, manifestar. *vi* abrirse

unfolding *a* que se abre. *n* despliegue, *m*; revelación, *f*; narración, *f*

unforced *a* libre; espontáneo; fácil; natural

unforeseen *a* imprevisto, inesperado

unforgettable *a* inolvidable

unforgivable *a* inexcusable, imperdonable

unforgiving *a* implacable, que no perdona, inexorable

unforgotten *a* no olvidado

unformed *a* informe; rudimentario; inmaturo; (inexperienced) inexperto, sin experiencia

unfortunate *a* desdichado, infortunado, desgraciado, desventurado. *n* desdichado (-da); pobre, *mf*; (prostitute) perdida, *f*

unfortunately *adv* por desdicha, desgraciadamente

unfounded *a* infundado, inmotivado, sin fundamento, injustificado

unframed *a* sin marco

unfrequented *a* poco frecuentado, solitario, retirado, aislado

unfriendliness *n* hostilidad, falta de amistad, frialdad, *f*; huraña, insociabilidad, *f*

unfriendly *a* hostil, enemigo; (of things, events) perjudicial; huraño, insociable

unfrock *vt* degradar, exclaustrar

unfruitful *a* estéril, infecundo; infructuoso, improductivo, vano

unfulfilled *a* incumplido, sin cumplir; malogrado

unfurl *vt* desplegar; *naut* izar (las velas)

unfurnished *a* desamueblado, sin muebles; desprovisto (de), sin

ungainliness *n* falta de gracia, torpeza, *f*, desgarbo, *m*

ungainly *a* desgarbado

ungallant *a* poco caballeroso, nada galante

ungenerous *a* poco generoso; avaro, tacaño, mezquino; injusto

ungentlemanly *a* poco caballeroso, indigno de un caballero

unglazed *a* sin vidriar; (paper) sin satinar; deslustrado

ungloved *a* sin guante(s)

unglue *vt* desencolar, despegar

ungodliness *n* impiedad, *f*

ungodly *a* impío, irreligioso

ungovernable *a* ingobernable, indomable; irrefrenable

ungraceful *a* desagraciado, desgarbado, sin gracia

ungracious *a* desagradable, poco cortés, desdeñoso

ungraciousness *n* descortesía, aspereza, inurbanidad, *f*

ungrammatical *a* antigramatical, incorrecto

ungrateful *a* ingrato, desagradecido; desagradable, odioso

ungratefulness *n* ingratitud, *f*; lo desagradable

ungrounded *a* infundado; sin motivo

ungrudging *a* no avaro, liberal; generoso, magnánimo

ungrudgingly *adv* de buena gana

unguarded *a* indefenso, sin protección; descuidado; indiscreto, imprudente; sin reflexión

unguided *a* sin guía

unhallowed *a* impío, profano

unhampered *a* desembarazado, libre

unhappily *adv* desafortunadamente, por desgracia

unhappiness *n* infelicidad, desgracia, desdicha, tristeza, *f*

unhappy *a* infeliz, desgraciado, desdichado, triste; (illfated) aciago, funesto, malhadado; (remark) inoportuno, inapropiado

unharmed *a* ileso, sano y salvo; (of things) indemne, sin daño

unharness *vt* desaparejar; desenganchar; desarmar

unhealthiness *n* falta de salud, *f*; (of place) insalubridad, *f*

unhealthy *a* enfermizo; malsano, insalubre

unheard *a* no oído; sin ser escuchado; desconocido. **u.-of,** inaudito, no imaginado

unheeding *a* distraído; desatento, sin prestar atención (a); descuidado

unhelpful *a* poco servicial; inútil

unhesitating *a* resuelto, decidido; pronto, inmediato

unhesitatingly *adv* sin vacilar

unhinge *vt* desgoznar, desquiciar; (of the mind) trastornar

unhitch *vt* desenganchar; descolgar

unholy *a* impío, sacrílego

unhonored *a* sin que se reconociese sus méritos; despreciado; (check) protestado

unhook *vt* desenganchar; desabrochar; descolgar

unhoped-for *a* inesperado

unhurt *a* ileso, incólume, sano y salvo; (of things) sin daño

unicellular *a* unicelular

unicolored *a* unicolor

unicorn *n* unicornio, *m*

unidentified *a* no reconocido, no identificado

unification *n* unificación, *f*

uniform *a* uniforme; igual, constante, invariable; homogéneo. *n* uniforme, *m*. **in full u.,** de gran uniforme. **to make u.,** uniformar, igualar, hacer uniforme

uniformity *n* uniformidad, igualdad, *f*

uniformly *adv* uniformemente

unify *vt* unificar; unir

unilateral *a* unilateral

unimaginable *a* inimaginable, no imaginable

unimaginative *a* sin imaginación

unimpaired *a* no disminuido; sin alteración; intacto, entero; sin menoscabo

unimpeachable *a* irreprochable, intachable

unimportance *n* no importancia, insignificancia, trivialidad, *f*

unimportant *a* sin importancia, nada importante, insignificante, trivial, *Lat. Am. also* intrascendente

unimpressive *a* poco impresionante; nada conmovedor; (of persons) insignificante

uninflammable *a* no inflamable, incombustible

uninfluenced *a* no afectado (por), libre (de)

uninformed *a* ignorante

uninhabitable *a* inhabitable

uninhabited *a* deshabitado, inhabitado, vacío, desierto

uninjured *a* ileso; sin daño

uninspired *a* sin inspiración; pedestre, mediocre

uninstructive *a* nada instructivo

uninsured *a* no asegurado

unintelligent *a* nada inteligente, corto de alcances, tonto

unintelligibility *n* incomprensibilidad, *f*, lo ininteligible

unintelligible *a* ininteligible, incomprensible

unintentional *a* involuntario, inadvertido

unintentionally *adv* sin querer, involuntariamente

uninterested *a* no interesado, despreocupado

uninteresting *a* sin interés, poco interesante, soso

uninterrupted *a* ininterrum pido, sin interrupción; continuo, incesante

uninvited *a* no invitado, no convidado, sin invitación; (unlooked-for) no buscado

uninviting *a* poco atrayente; inhospitalario

union *n* unión, *f*; *mech* manguito de unión, *m*; conexión, *f*; (poverty) asociación, *f*; (of trade) gremio de oficios, *m*; sindicato (obrero), *m*; (workhouse) asilo, *m*; (U.S.A.) Estados Unidos de América, *m pl*

unionism *n* unionismo, *m*

unionist *n pol* unionista, *mf*

unique *a* único, sin igual, sin par

uniqueness *n* unicidad, *f*; lo singular

unisexual *a* unisexual

unison *n* unisonancia, *f*. **in u.,** al unísono

unit *n* unidad, *f*. **u. bookcase,** librería en secciones, *f*

Unitarian *a* and *n* unitario (-ia)

Unitarianism *n* unitarismo, *m*

unite *vt* unir, juntar; combinar, incorporar; (of countries) unificar; (of energies, etc.) reunir. *vi* unirse, juntarse; reunirse, concertarse; convenirse

united *a* unido; junto. **the U. Nations,** las Naciones Unidas, *f pl*

unitedly *adv* unidamente; armoniosamente, de acuerdo

United States of America los Estados Unidos de Norteamérica, *m pl*

unity *n* unidad, *f*; *math* la unidad; unión, *f*; conformidad, armonía, *f*. **the three unities,** las tres unidades

universal *a* universal; general; común. **to make u.,** universalizar, generalizar. **u. joint,** junta universal, *f*; *aut* cardán, *m*

universalize *vt* universalizar

universe *n* universo, *m*; creación, *f*, mundo, *m*

university *n* universidad, *f*. *a* universitario. **u. degree,** grado universitario, *m*

unjust *a* injusto

unjustifiable *a* injustificable, indisculpable, inexcusable

unjustifiably *adv* injustificadamente, inexcusablemente

unjustly *adv* injustamente, sin razón

unkempt *a* despeinado; desaseado, sucio

unkind *a* nada bondadoso, nada amable; poco complaciente; duro, cruel; desfavorable, nada propicio

unkindly *adv* sin bondad; con dureza, cruelmente

unkindness *n* falta de bondad, *f*; severidad, crueldad, dureza, *f*, rigor, *m*; acto de crueldad, *m*

unknowable *a* impenetrable, incomprehensible, insondable

unknowingly *adv* sin querer, involuntariamente; sin saberlo; insensiblemente

unknown *a* ignoto, desconocido; *math* incógnito. *n* lo desconocido, misterio, *m*; *math* incógnita, *f*; (person) desconocido (-da), forastero (-ra). *math* **u. quantity,** incógnita, *f*

unlabeled *a* sin etiqueta

unlace *vt* desenlazar; desatar

unladylike *a* indigno (or impropio) de una dama; vulgar, ordinario, cursi

unlamented *a* no llorado, no lamentado

unlatch *vt* alzar el pestillo de, abrir

unlawful *a* ilegal, ilícito

unlawfulness *n* ilegalidad, *f*

unlearn *vt* olvidar, desaprender

unleash *vt* soltar

unleavened *a* ázimo, sin levadura

unless *conjunc* a no ser que, a menos que, como no, si no (all followed by subjunc.); salvo, excepto, con excepción de

unlicensed *a* no autorizado, sin licencia

unlike *a* disímil, desemejante; distinto, diferente. *prep* a distinción de, a diferencia de, al contrario de. **They are quite u.,** No se parecen nada

unlikeliness *n* improbabilidad, *f*

unlikely *a* improbable, inverosímil; arriesgado

unlikeness *n* desemejanza, diferencia, *f*

unlimited *a* ilimitado, infinito, inmenso; sin restricción; excesivo, exagerado. **unlimited telephone,** teléfono no medido (Argentina)

unlined *a* no forrado, sin forro; sin rayas; (of face) sin arrugas

unlit *a* no iluminado, oscuro, sin luz

unload *vt* descargar; aligerar; *naut* hondear; (of shares) deshacerse de. *vi* descargar

unloading *n* descarga, *f*, descargue, *m*

unlock *vt* desencerrar, abrir; *fig* revelar, descubrir

unlooked-for *a* inopinado, inesperado

unloose *vt* desatar; soltar; poner en libertad

unlovable *a* indigno del querer; antipático, poco amable; repugnante

unloveliness *n* falta de hermosura, fealdad, *f*

unlovely *a* nada hermoso, feo; desagradable

unluckily *adv* desafortunadamente, por desgracia

unluckiness *n* mala suerte, *f*; (unsuitability) inoportunidad, *f*; lo nefasto, lo malo

unlucky *a* de mala suerte; desdichado, desgraciado, infeliz; (ill-omened) funesto, nefasto, fatal; inoportuno, inconveniente

unmanageable *a* indomable, indócil; ingobernable, inmanejable; (unwieldy) difícil de manejar, pesado

unmannerliness *n* mala crianza, descortesía, *f*

unmannerly *a* mal educado, descortés

unmarketable *a* invendible

unmarriageable *a* incasable

unmarried *a* soltero, célibe

unmask *vt* desenmascarar; *fig* quitar la careta (a). *vi* quitarse la máscara; *fig* quitarse la careta, descubrirse

unmeaning *a* sin sentido, vacío, sin significación

unmelodious *a* sin melodía, discorde

unmendable *a* incomponible

unmentionable *a* que no se puede mencionar; indigno de mencionarse

unmerciful *a* sin piedad, sin compasión; cruel, despiadado, duro

unmerited *a* inmerecido, desmerecido

unmethodical *a* poco metódico

unmindful *a* olvidadizo; desatento; negligente. **u. of,** sin pensar en, olvidando

unmistakable *a* inequívoco; manifiesto, evidente, indudable

unmistakably *adv* indudablemente

unmitigated *a* no mitigado; completo, absoluto; (of rogue) redomado

unmixed *a* sin mezcla; puro, sencillo; (free) limpio

unmoor *vt* desamarrar

unmoral *a* amoral, no moral; sin fin didáctico

unmounted *a* desmontado

unmoved *a* fijo; (unemotional) impasible, frío; (determined) firme, inmutable, inexorable

unmuffle *vt* desembozar, descubrir

unmusical *a* sin afición a la música; sin oído (para la música); inarmónico

unnamable *a* que no se puede nombrar, innominable

unnatural *a* desnaturalizado; (of vices, etc.) contra natural; innatural; (of style) rebuscado; artificial; inhumano, cruel

unnaturalness *n* lo monstruoso; lo innatural; artificialidad, *f*; inhumanidad, *f*

unnavigable *a* innavegable, no navegable

unnecessarily *adv* inútilmente, innecesariamente, sin necesidad

unnecessariness *n* inutilidad, *f*; superfluidad, *f*; lo innecesario

unnecessary *a* innecesario, superfluo, inútil

unneighborly *a* de mala vecindad, impropio de vecinos, poco servicial

unnerve *vt* acobardar quitar el valor, desanimar

unnoticed *a* inadvertido, no observado

unobjectionable *a* *Lat. Am.* inobjetable

unobliging *a* nada servicial

unobservable *a* inobservable
unobservant *a* inobservante
unobserved *a* sin ser notado, desapercibido
unobtainable *a* inalcanzable, inasequible
unobstructed *a* no obstruido; sin obstáculos; libre
unobtrusive *a* discreto, modesto
unobtrusiveness *n* discreción, modestia, *f*
unoccupied *a* (at leisure) desocupado, ocioso, sin ocupación; vacío, vacante, libre; (untenanted) deshabitado
unofficial *a* no oficial
unopened *a* sin abrir, cerrado; (of exhibitions, etc.) no inaugurado
unopposed *a* sin oposición
unorganized *a* inorganizado; *biol* inorgánico
unoriginal *a* poco original
unorthodox *a* heterodoxo
unostentatious *a* sencillo, modesto, sin ostentación
unostentatiousness *n* sencillez, modestia, falta de ostentación, *f*
unpack *vt* desempaquetar; (trunks) vaciar; (bales) desembalar. *vi* desempaquetar; deshacer las maletas
unpacking *n* desembalaje, *m*
unpaid *a* sin pagar, no pagado, *Lat. Am. also* impago
unpalatable *a* de mal sabor; desagradable
unparalleled *a* sin paralelo, sin par, sin igual
unpardonable *a* imperdonable, inexcusable, irremisible
unparliamentary *a* poco parlamentario
unpatriotic *a* antipatriótico
unpaved *a* sin empedrar
unperceived *a* inadvertido, sin ser notado
unperturbed *a* impasible, sin alterarse, sereno
unpleasant *a* desagradable, desapacible; ofensivo; (troublesome) enfadoso, molesto
unpleasantly *adv* desagradablemente
unpleasantness *n* lo desagradable; disgusto, sinsabor, *m*; (disagreement) disputa, riña, *f*
unpleasing *a* nada placentero; desagradable, sin atractivos
unplug *vt* desenchufar
unpolished *a* sin pulir, tosco, mate; *fig* inculto, cerril. **u. diamond,** diamante en bruto, *m*
unpolluted *a* impoluto, incontaminado; puro, sin pervertir
unpopular *a* impopular
unpopularity *n* impopularidad, *f*
unpractical *a* impracticable, imposible; (of persons) sin sentido práctico
unpracticed *a* no practicado; inexperto, inhábil
unpraiseworthy *a* inmeritorio
unprecedented *a* sin precedente, inaudito
unprejudiced *a* sin prejuicios, imparcial
unpremeditated *a* sin premeditación, indeliberado, impremeditado
unprepared *a* sin preparación, no preparado; desprevenido; desapercibido (unready)
unpreparedness *n* falta de preparación, imprevisión, *f*, desapercibimiento, *m*
unprepossessing *a* poco atrayente, antipático
unpresentable *a* impresentable
unpretentious *a* sin pretensiones, modesto
unpriced *a* sin precio
unprincipled *a* sin consciencia, sin escrúpulos
unprinted *a* sin imprimir, no impreso
unprocurable *a* inalcanzable, inasequible
unproductive *a* improductivo; infructuoso, estéril
unproductiveness *n* infructuosidad, *f*; esterilidad, *f*
unprofessional *a* sin profesión; contrario a la ética profesional
unprofitable *a* improductivo, infructuoso; sin provecho; inútil; nada lucrativo
unprogressive *a* reaccionario
unpromising *a* poco halagüeño
unpronounceable *a* impronunciable

unpropitious *a* desfavorable, nada propicio, nada halagüeño
unprosperous *a* impróspero
unprotected *a* sin protección; (of persons) indefenso, desválido
unproved *a* no probado, sin demostrar
unprovided *a* desapercibido, desprovisto. **u. for,** sin provisión (para); sin medios de vida, desamparado
unprovoked *a* no provocado, sin provocación; sin motivo
unpublished *a* inédito, no publicado, sin publicar
unpunctual *a* no puntual, retrasado
unpunctuality *n* falta de puntualidad, *f*, retraso, *m*
unpunctually *adv* sin puntualidad, tarde, con retraso
unpunishable *a* no punible
unpunished *a* impune, sin castigo
unpurchasable *a* que no puede comprarse
unqualified *a* incapaz, incompetente; (with professions) sin título; (downright) incondicional, absoluto
unquenchable *a* inextinguible, inapagable; insaciable
unquestionable *a* indiscutible, indudable, indubitable
unquestionably *adv* indudablemente
unquiet *a* inquieto, intranquilo; agitado
unravel *vt* deshilar; destejer; (a mystery, etc.) desentrañar, desembrollar, descifrar
unraveling *n* deshiladura, *f*; aclaración, *f*
unreadable *a* ilegible
unreadiness *n* falta de preparación, *f*, desapercibimiento, *m*; lentitud, *f*
unready *a* desapercibido, desprevenido; lento
unreal *a* irreal; falso, imaginario, ilusorio; ficticio; artificial; insincero, hipócrita; ideal; incorpóreo
unreality *n* irrealidad, *f*; falsedad, *f*; artificialidad, *f*; lo quimérico
unreasonable *a* irrazonable, irracional; disparatado, extravagante; (with price, etc.) exorbitante, excesivo
unreasonableness *n* irracionalidad, *f*; exorbitancia, *f*
unreasonably *adv* irracionalmente
unreasoning *a* irracional; sin motivo, sin causa
unreceipted *a* sin recibo
unrecognizable *a* que no puede reconocerse; imposible de reconocer
unrecognized *a* no reconocido
unreconciled *a* no resignado, no reconciliado
unrectified *a* no corregido, sin rectificar
unredeemed *a* no redimido; no mitigado; (of pledges) sin desempeñar
unrefined *a* no refinado, impuro; inculto, grosero
unreformed *a* no reformado
unrefuted *a* no refutado
unregenerate *a* no regenerado
unregretted *a* no llorado, sin lamentar
unrehearsed *a* sin preparación; *theat* sin ensayar; (extempore) improvisado
unrelated *a* inconexo; (of persons) sin parentesco
unrelenting *a* implacable, inflexible, inexorable
unreliability *n* incertidumbre, *f*; el no poder confiar en, informalidad, inestabilidad, *f*
unreliable *a* incierto, dudoso, indigno de confianza; (of persons) informal
unrelieved *a* no aliviado; absoluto, complete, total
unremitting *a* incansable
unremunerative *a* sin remuneración, no remunerado
unrepealed *a* vigente
unrepentant *a* impenitente
unrepresentative *a* poco representativo
unrepresented *a* sin representación
unrequited *a* no correspondido
unreserved *a* no reservado; expresivo, comunicativo, expansivo, franco
unreservedly *adv* sin reserva; con toda franqueza
unresisting *a* sin oponer resistencia
unresolved *a* sin resolverse, vacilante; incierto, dudoso, inseguro sin solución
unresponsive *a* flemático; insensible, sordo
unresponsiveness *n* flema, *f*; insensibilidad, *f*

unrest *n* desasosiego, *m*, agitación, inquietud, *f*
unrestful *a* agitado, inquieto, intranquilo
unrestrained *a* desenfrenado; ilimitado, sin límites; sin reserva
unrestricted *a* sin restricción; ilimitado
unrevealed *a* no revelado, por descubrir, no descubierto
unrewarded *a* sin premio, no recompensado
unrighteous *a* injusto, malo, perverso
unrighteousness *n* injusticia, *f*; maldad, perversidad, *f*
unripe *a* verde, inmaturo
unripeness *n* falta de madurez, *f*
unrivaled *a* sin igual, sin par
unroll *vt* desarrollar. *vi* desarrollarse; (unfold) desplegarse (a la vista)
unromantic *a* poco (or nada) romántico
unruffled *a* sereno, plácido, ecuánime; no arrugado; (of hair) liso
unruliness *n* turbulencia, indisciplina, *f*; insubordinación, rebeldía, *f*
unruly *a* ingobernable, revoltoso; refractario, rebelde; (of hair) indomable
unsaddle *vt* desensillar; derribar (del caballo, etc.)
unsafe *a* inseguro; peligroso; arriesgado; (to eat) nocivo
unsafeness *n* inseguridad, *f*; peligro, riesgo, *m*
unsaid *a* sin decir, no dicho
unsalable *a* invendible
unsalaried *a* no asalariado
unsalted *a* soso, sin sal
unsanitary *a* antihigiénico
unsatisfactoriness *n* lo insatisfactorio
unsatisfactory *a* poco (or nada) satisfactorio; no aceptable
unsatisfied *a* no satisfecho; descontento; no convencido; (hungry) no harto; *com* no saldado
unsatisfying *a* que no satisface
unsavoriness *n* insipidez, *f*, mal sabor, *m*; lo desagradable; sordidez, suciedad, *f*
unsavory *a* insípido, de mal sabor; desagradable; sórdido, sucio
unscalable *a* inascendible, virgen
unscathed *a* sin daño, ileso
unscented *a* sin perfume, sin olor, no fragante
unscholarly *a* nada erudito; indigno de un erudito
unscientific *a* no científico
unscrew *vt* destornillar, *Lat. Am.* desenroscar. *vi* destornillarse
unscrewing *n* destornillamiento, *m*
unscrupulous *a* sin escrúpulos, poco escrupuloso, desaprensivo
unscrupulousness *n* falta de escrúpulos, desaprensión, *f*
unseal *vt* desellar, romper (or quitar) el sello (de)
unseasonable *a* intempestivo, fuera de sazón; inoportuno, inconveniente. **at an u. hour,** a una hora inconveniente, a deshora
unseasonableness *n* lo intempestivo, inoportunidad, *f*
unseasonably *adv* intempestivamente; a deshora; inoportunamente
unseasoned *a cul* sin sazonar, soso; (wood) verde; no maduro, sin madurar
unseat *vt* (from horse) tirar, echar al suelo; *pol* desituir
unseaworthy *a* innavegable
unseemliness *n* falta de decoro, *f*; indecencia, *f*
unseemly *a* indecoroso, indigno; indecente; impropio
unseen *a* no visto, invisible; inadvertido; secreto, oculto. *n* versión al libro abierto, *f*. **the u.,** lo invisible
unselfish *a* desinteresado, abnegado, nada egoísta; generoso
unselfishness *n* abnegación, *f*; desinterés, *m*; generosidad, *f*
unsentimental *a* no sentimental
unserviceable *a* inservible, inútil, que no sirve para nada, sin utilidad
unsettle *vt* desarreglar; desorganizar; hacer inseguro; agitar, perturbar

unsettled *a* inconstante, variable; *com* pendiente, sin pagar; incierto; sin resolver; (of estates) sin solucionar
unshackle *vt* desencadenar
unshakable *a* inconmovible, firme
unshapely *a* desproporcionado
unshaven *a* sin afeitar
unsheathe *vt* desenvainar, sacar
unsheltered *a* desabrigado, desamparado; no protegido, sin protección; (of places) sin abrigo, expuesto; (from) sin defensa contra
unship *vt* desembarcar; (the oars) desarmar
unshod *a* descalzo; (of a horse) sin herraduras
unshorn *a* sin esquilar; intonso
unshrinkable *a* que no se encoge
unshrinking *a* intrépido; resoluto, sin vacilar
unsightly *a* feo, horrible, repugnante, antiestético
unsinkable *a* insumergible
unskilled *a* inexperto, inhábil, imperito, torpe
unsmokable *a* (of tobacco) infumable
unsociability *n* insociabilidad, huraña, esquivez, *f*
unsociable *a* insociable, huraño, esquivo, arisco
unsocial *a* insocial, antisocial
unsold *a* no vendido, sin vender
unsolder *vt* desoldar, desestañar
unsoldierly *a* indigno de un soldado; poco marcial
unsophisticated *a* ingenuo, inocente, cándido
unsought *a* no solicitado; no buscado
unsound *a* enfermo; defectuoso; (rotten) podrido; (fallacious) erróneo, poco convincente; (of persons) informal, indigno de confianza; (of religious views) heterodoxo. **of u. mind,** insano
unsoundness *n* lo defectuoso; mal estado, *m*; falsedad, *f*; informalidad, *f*; heterodoxia, *f*
unsparing *a* severo, implacable; generoso, pródigo
unspeakable *a* indecible, inefable; que no puede mencionarse, horrible
unspecified *a* no especificado
unspoilt *a* intacto; ileso, indemne; no corrompido; no estropeado; (of children) no mimado
unspoken *a* no pronunciado
unsportsmanlike *a* indigno de un cazador; indigno de un deportista; nada caballeroso. **to play in an u. way,** jugar sucio
unstable *a* inestable; variable; inconstante; vacilante, irresoluto
unstained *a* no manchado; no teñido; inmaculado, sin mancha
unstamped *a* sin sello; no sellado
unstatesmanlike *a* impropio (or indigno) de un hombre de estado
unsteadiness *n* inestabilidad, falta de firmeza, *f*; inconstancia, *f*
unsteady *a* inestable, inseguro; inconstante
unstick *vt* desapegar
unstitch *vt* desapuntar
unstressed *a* sin énfasis; (of syllables) sin acento
unstudied *a* no estudiado; natural, espontáneo
unsubstantial *a* insubstancial; ligero; irreal, imaginario; incorpóreo; aparente
unsuccessful *a* sin éxito; infructuoso. **to be u.,** no tener éxito
unsuccessfully *adv* en vano, sin éxito
unsuitability *n* impropiedad, *f*; inconveniencia, incongruencia, *f*; incapacidad, *f*; inoportunidad, *f*
unsuitable *a* inapropiado; inconveniente; impropio; inservible; incapaz; inoportuno
unsung *a* no cantado; no celebrado en verso
unsupported *a* sin apoyo; sin defensa; no favorecido
unsurmountable *a* insuperable, infranqueable
unsurpassable *a* inmejorable, insuperable
unsurpassed *a* sin par
unsuspecting *a* no suspicaz, confiado, no receloso
unswerving *a* directo; sin vacilar, constante
unsymmetrical *a* asimétrico
unsympathetic *a* indiferente, incompasivo; antipático
unsystematic *a* sin sistema, asistemático, no metódico

untalented *a* sin talento

untamed *a* indomado, cerril, bravío, no domesticado; desenfrenado, violento. **u. horse** *Lat. Am.* bellaco, *m*

unteach *vt* desenseñar

untenable *a* insostenible

untenanted *a* desalquilado, deshabitado; vacío, desierto

unthankful *a* ingrato, desagradecido

unthinkable *a* inconcebible; imposible

unthinking *a* sin reflexión; desatento; indiscreto

unthinkingly *adv* sin pensar

unthread *vt* deshebrar

untidily *adv* en desorden, sin aseo

untidiness *n* desorden, *m*; desaseo, desaliño, *m*; falta de pulcritud, *f*

untidy *a* desarreglado; desaseado; abandonado; en desorden, sin concierto

untie *vt* desatar, desanudar; (knots) deshacer

until *prep* hasta. *conjunc* hasta que. (The subjunc. is required in clauses referring to future time, e.g. **No venga usted hasta que le avise yo,** Don't come until I tell you. In clauses referring to past or present time the indicative is generally used, e.g. **No la reconocí hasta que se volvió,** I didn't recognize her until she turned round)

untilled *a* sin cultivar

untimeliness *n* inoportunidad, *f*; lo prematuro

untimely *a* inoportuno, intempestivo; prematuro

untiring *a* incansable, infatigable

unto *prep* hacia

untold *a* no revelado; no narrado; sin decir, no dicho; incalculable

untouchable *a* que no puede tocarse, intangible; (of castes) intocable

untouched *a* sin tocar; intacto, incólume

untrained *a* indisciplinado; inexperto; no adiestrado

untranslatable *a* intraducible

untraveled *a* no frecuentado; (of persons) provinciano

untried *a* no experimentado. **u. knight,** caballero novel, *m*

untrodden *a* no hollado, no frecuentado; inexplorado, virgen

untroubled *a* tranquilo, sosegado

untrue *a* mentiroso, falso, engañoso; ficticio, imaginario; traidor, desleal; infiel

untrustworthiness *n* incertidumbre, inseguridad, *f*; (of persons) informalidad, *f*

untrustworthy *a* indigno de confianza; incierto, dudoso; desleal

untruth *n* mentira, falsedad, *f*; ficción, *f*

untruthful *a* mentiroso; falso

untruthfulness *n* falsedad, *f*

untwist *vt* destorcer

unused *a* no empleado; desacostumbrado; inusitado; (postage stamp) sin sellar

unusual *a* fuera de lo común, desacostumbrado; extraño, raro, peregrino, extraordinario

unusually *adv* excepcionalmente; infrecuentemente

unusualness *n* lo insólito; rareza, *f*

unutterable *a* indecible, inexpresable

unvarnished *a* sin barnizar; *fig* sencillo

unvarying *a* invariable, constante, uniforme

unveil *vt* quitar el velo; (memorial) descubrir; *fig* revelar. *vi* quitarse el velo; revelarse, quitarse la careta

unventilated *a* sin ventilación; sin aire, ahogado; (of topics) no discutido

unverifiable *a* que no puede verificarse

unverified *a* sin verificar

unvisited *a* no visitado; no frecuentado

unvoiced *a* no expresado

unwanted *a* no deseado; superfluo, de más

unwarlike *a* nada marcial, pacífico

unwarranted *a* sin garantía; inexcusable, injustificable

unwary *a* incauto, imprudente

unwashed *a* sin lavar; sucio

unwatched *a* no vigilado

unwavering *a* resuelto, firme; inexorable; (gaze) fijo

unwaveringly *adv* sin vacilar; inexorablemente

unwearied *a* incansable; infatigable

unwelcome *a* mal acogido; inoportuno; desagradable

unwell *a* indispuesto

unwholesome *a* malsano, nocivo, insalubre

unwholesomeness *n* insalubridad, *f*

unwieldiness *n* pesadez, dificultad de manejarse, *f*

unwieldy *a* pesado, abultado, difícil de manejar

unwilling *a* desinclinado, reluctante

unwillingly *adv* de mala gana

unwillingness *n* falta de inclinación, repugnancia, *f*

unwind *vt* desenvolver; (thread) desdevanar, desovillar. *vi* desarrollarse; desdevanarse

unwise *a* imprudente, indiscreto, incauto; (lacking wisdom) tonto

unwisely *adv* imprudentemente, indiscretamente

unwitting *a* inconsciente

unwittingly *adv* sin darse cuenta

unwomanly *a* poco femenino

unwonted *a* insólito, inusitado

unworkable *a* impráctico

unworkmanlike *a* chapucero, charanguero

unworldly *a* poco, mundano, espiritual

unworn *a* sin llevar, nuevo

unworthiness *n* indignidad, *f*

unworthy *a* indigno

unwounded *a* no herido, sin herida, ileso

unwrap *vt* desenvolver, desempapelar

unwritten *a* no escrito. **u. law,** ley consuetudinaria, *f*

unyielding *a* duro, firme; (of persons) inflexible, terco, resuelto, obstinado

unyoke *vt* desuncir, quitar el yugo

up *adv* (high) arriba, en alto; (higher) hacia arriba; (out of bed) levantado; (standing) de pie; (finished) concluido, terminado; (of time) llegado; (excited) agitado; (rebellious) sublevado; (of sun, etc.) salido; (come or gone up) subido; (of universities) en residencia; (for discussion) bajo consideración; (abreast of) al lado, al nivel; (incapable) incapaz, incompetente; (ill) enfermo, indispuesto. **"Up,"** (on elevators) **"Para subir."** (For various idiomatic uses of **up** after verbs, see verbs themselves.) *a* (in a few expressions only) ascendente. *prep* en lo alto de; hacia arriba de; a largo de; (with country) en el interior de; (with current) contra. **to be up in arms,** sublevarse, rebelarse. **to be very hard up,** ser muy pobre, estar a la cuarta pregunta. **to drink up,** beberlo todo. **to go or come up,** subir. **to lay up,** acumular. **to speak up,** hablar en voz alta. **He has something up his sleeve,** Tiene algo en la manga. **It is all up,** Todo se acabó, Mi gozo en el pozo. **It is not up to much,** Vale muy poco; No es muy fuerte. **It is up to you,** Tú dirás, Tú harás lo que te parezca. **What is he up to?** ¿Qué está tramando? **What's up?** ¿Qué pasa? ¿Qué hay? **up and down,** *adv* bajando y subiendo, de arriba abajo; de un lado a otro; por todas partes. **up-and-down,** *a* fluctuante; (of roads) ondulante; (of life) accidentado, borrascoso. **ups and downs,** vicisitudes, *f pl*, altibajos, *m pl*. **up-grade,** subida, *f*. **up in,** versado en, perito en. **well up in,** fuerte en. **up North,** al norte; en el norte; hacia el norte. **up there,** allí arriba, allí en lo alto. **up to,** hasta; (aware) al corriente de, informado de. **up to date,** *adv* hasta la fecha. **up-to-date,** *a* de última moda; al día. **up to now,** hasta ahora. **up train,** tren ascendente. **Up with . . . !** ¡Arriba! **Up you go!** (to children) ¡Upa!

upbraid *vt* reprender, echar en cara

upbringing *n* crianza, educación, *f*

upcountry *n* tierra adentro, *f*; lo interior (de un país). *a* de tierra adentro, del interior. *adv* tierra adentro, hacia el interior

update *vt* actualizar, poner al día

upheaval *n* solevantamiento, *m*; trastorno, *m*

uphill *a* ascendente; penoso, fatigoso, difícil. *adv* cuesta arriba, pecho arriba

uphold *vt* sostener, apoyar; (help) ayudar, consolar;

(protect) defender; (countenance) aprobar; *law* confirmar

upholder *n* sostenedor (-ra), defensor (-ra)

upholster *vt* entapizar, tapizar

upholsterer *n* tapicero, *m*

upholstery *n* tapicería, *f*; (of car) almohadillado, *m*

upkeep *n* mantenimiento, *m*, conservación, *f*

upland *n* tierra alta, *f*, *a* alto, elevado

uplift *vt* elevar. *n* elevación, *f*; *inf* fervor, *m*

upon *prep*. See **on**

upper *a comp* superior; alto; de arriba. *n* (of shoe) pala, *f*, *sport* **u.-cut**, golpe de abajo arriba, upper-cut, *m*. **U. Egypt,** Alto Egipto, *m*. **u. hand,** dominio, *m*; superioridad, ventaja, *f*. **u. house,** cámara alta, *f*; senado, *m*. **u. ten,** los diez primeros

upper classes *a* clases altas, capas altas, *f pl*

uppermost *a* más alto, más elevado; predominante, principal; más fuerte. *adv* en primer lugar; en lo más alto. **to be u.,** predominar

upright *a* recto, derecho; vertical; (honorable) honrado, digno, recto. *n* (stanchion) mástil, soporte, palo derecho, montante, *m*. *adv* en pie; derecho

uprightly *adv* rectamente, honradamente

uprightness *n* rectitud, honradez, probidad, *f*

uprising *n* insurrección, sublevación, *f*

uproar *n* alboroto, tumulto, estrépito, *m*, conmoción, *f*

uproarious *a* tumultuoso, estrepitoso

uproot *vt* desarraigar, *Lat. Am.* destroncar; *fig* arrancar; (destroy) extirpar

uprooting *n* desarraigo, *m*; arranque, *m*; extirpación, *f*

upset *vt* volcar; (overthrow) derribar, echar abajo; (frustrate) contrariar; desarreglar; (distress) trastornar, turbar; (of food) hacer mal. *vi* volcarse. *n* vuelco, *m*; trastorno, *m*. **u. price,** tipo de subasta, *m*

upsetting *a* turbante, inquietante

upshot *n* resultado, *m*; consecuencia, *f*

upside *n* lado superior, *m*; parte superior, *f*; (of trains) andén ascendente, *m*. **u. down,** al revés, de arriba abajo; en desorden

upstairs *adv* arriba, en el piso de arriba; (with go or come) al piso de arriba

upstanding *a* gallardo, guapo. **an u. young man (woman),** un buen mozo (una buena moza)

upstart *n* arribista, *mf*; advenedizo (-za), insolente, *mf*; presuntuoso (-sa)

upstream *a* and *adv* contra la corriente, agua arriba, río arriba

upturned *a* (of noses) respingada

upward *a* ascendente, hacia arriba

upwards *adv* hacia arriba; en adelante. **u. of,** más de

Urals, the los Urales, *m pl*

uranium *n min* uranio, *m*

Uranus *n ast* Urano, *m*

urban *a* urbano, ciudadano

urban renewal *n* renovación urbana, renovación urbanística, *f*

urbane *a* cortés, urbano, fino

urbanity *n* urbanidad, cortesía, finura, *f*

urbanization *n* urbanización, *f*

urbanize *vt* urbanizar

urchin *n* galopín, granuja, pilluelo, *m*

ureter *n anat* uréter, *m*

urethra *n anat* uretra, *f*

urge *vt* empujar, impeler; incitar, estimular, azuzar, animar; pedir con urgencia, recomendar con ahínco, instar, insistir (en). *n* instinto, impulso, *m*; deseo, *m*; ambición, *f*

urgency *n* urgencia, *f*; importancia, perentoriedad, *f*

urgent *a* urgente; importante, apremiante, perentorio. **to be u.,** urgir

urgently *adv* urgentemente

uric *a* úrico

urinal *n* orinal, urinario, *m*

urinalysis *n* análisis de orina, urinálisis, *m*

urinary *a* urinario

urinary tract *n* conducto urinario, *m*, vías urinarias, *f pl*

urinate *vi* orinar

urine *n* orín, *m*

urn *n* urna, *f*; (for coffee) cafetera, *f*; (for tea) tetera, *f*

Ursa *n ast* osa, *f*. **U. Major,** osa mayor, *f*. **U. Minor,** osa menor, *f*

urticaria *n med* urticaria, *f*

Uruguayan *a* and *n* uruguayo (-ya)

us *pron* nos; (with prep.) nosotros. **He came toward us,** Vino hacia nosotros

usable *a* aprovechable, servible

usage *n* (handling) tratamiento, *m*; uso, *m*, costumbre, *f*

use *n* uso, *m*; manejo, empleo, *m*; (custom) costumbre, *f*; (need) necesidad, *f*; (usefulness) aprovechamiento, *m*; *law* usufructo, *m*. **directions for use,** direcciones para el uso, *f pl*, **for the use of . . .,** para uso de . . . **in use,** en uso. **out of use,** anticuado; fuera de moda. **to be of no use,** no servir; ser inútil. **to have no use for,** no tener necesidad de; *inf* tener en poco. **to make use of,** servirse de, aprovechar; *law* ejercer. **to put to use,** poner en uso, poner en servicio

use *vt* usar; (employ) emplear; (utilize) servirse de, utilizar; (handle) manejar; hacer uso de; (consume) gastar, consumir; (treat) tratar; practicar. **to use up,** agotar, acabar con; consumir. *vi impers* acostumbrar, soler (e.g. **It used to happen that . . . ,** Solía ocurrir que . . .). **(Used to** and the verb which follows are often translated simply by the imperfect tense of the following verb, e.g. **I used to see her every day,** La veía todos los días. Use of the verbs **acostumbrar** or **soler** to translate used to adds emphasis to the statement)

used *a* and *past part* acostumbrado, habituado; empleado; (clothes) usado; (postage stamp) sellado. **to become u. to,** acostumbrarse a

useful *a* útil; provechoso; servicial

usefully *adv* útilmente; con provecho

usefulness *n* utilidad, *f*; valor, *m*

useless *a* inútil; vano, infructuoso. **to render u.,** inutilizar

uselessness *n* inutilidad, *f*

user *n* el, *m*, (f, la) que usa, comprador (-ra)

usher *n* ujier, *m*; (in a theater) acomodador (-ra). *vt* introducir, anunciar; acomodar

usual *a* usual, acostumbrado, habitual; normal, común. **as u.,** como siempre. **in the u. form,** *com* al usado; como de costumbre. **with their usual courtesy,** con la cortesía que les es característica

usually *adv* por lo general, ordinariamente. **We u. go out on Sundays,** Acostumbramos salir los domingos

usurer *n* usurero (-ra)

usurious *a* usurario

usurp *vt* usurpar; asumir, arrogarse

usurpation *n* usurpación, *f*; arrogación, *f*

usurper *n* usurpador (-ra)

usurping *a* usurpador

usury *n* usura, *f*. **to practice u.,** usurear, dar (or tomar) a usura

utensil *n* utensilio, instrumento, *m*; herramienta, *f*. **kitchen utensils,** batería de cocina, *f*

uterine *a med* uterino

uterus *n* útero, *m*

utilitarian *a* utilitario

utilitarianism *n* utilitarismo, *m*

utility *n* utilidad, *f*; ventaja, *f*; beneficio, provecho, *m*. **u. goods,** artículos fabricados bajo la autorizacion del gobierno, *m pl*

utilizable *a* utilizable, aprovechable

utilization *n* empleo, aprovechamiento, *m*

utilize *vt* utilizar, servirse de; aprovechar

utmost *a* (outermost) extremo; (farthest) más remoto, más distante; (greatest) mayor, más grande. *n* lo más; todo lo posible. **to do one's u.,** hacer todo lo posible, hacer todo lo que uno pueda

utopian *a* utópico

utter *a* completo, total; terminate, absoluto; sumo, extremo. **He is an u. fool,** Es un tonto de capirote
utter *vt* pronunciar, proferir, decir, hablar; (a sigh, cry, etc.) dar; (express) manifestar, expresar, explicar; (coin) poner en circulación; (a libel) publicar; (disclose) revelar, descubrir

utterance *n* expresión, manifestación, *f*; pronunciación, *f*; (style) lenguaje, *m*
utterly *adv* enteramente, completamente
uttermost *a*. See **utmost**
uvula *n anat* úvula, *f*
uxorious *a* uxorio

V

v *n* (letter) ve, *f*; pieza en forma de V, *f*
vacancy *n* vacío, *m*; vacancia, *f*; (mental) vacuidad, *f*; (of offices, posts) vacante, *f*; (leisure) desocupación, ociosidad, *f*; (gap, blank) vacío, *m*, laguna, *f*
vacant *a* vacío; despoblado, deshabitado; (free) libre; (of offices, etc.) vacante; (leisured) ocioso; (absentminded) distraído; (vague) vago; (foolish) estúpido, estólido
vacantly *adv* distraídamente; estúpidamente
vacate *vt* dejar vacío; (a post) dejar; (a throne) renunciar a; dejar vacante; *mil* evacuar; *law* anular, rescindir
vacation *n* (of offices) vacante, *f*; (holiday) vacaciones, *f pl, f.* **the long v.,** las vacaciones de verano. **to be on a v.,** estar de vacaciones
vaccinate *vt* vacunar
vaccination *n* vacunación, *f*
vaccine *n* vacuna, *f*
vacillate *vi* (sway) oscilar; (hesitate) vacilar, titubear, dudar
vacillating *a* vacilante
vacillation *n* vacilación, *f*
vacuity *n* vacuidad, *f*
vacuous *a* desocupado, ocioso; estúpido, vacío
vacuum *n* vacío, *m*. **v. brake,** freno al vacío, *m*. **v. cleaner,** aspirador de polvo, *m*. **v. flask,** termos, *m*. **v. pump,** bomba neumática, *f*. **vacuum-shelf dryer,** secador al vacío, *m*
vade mecum *n* vademécum, *m*
vagabond *n* vagabundo (-da); vago, *m*; (beggar) mendigo (-ga). *a* vagabundo, errante
vagabondage *n* vagabundeo, *m*, vagancia, *f*
vagary *n* (whim) capricho, antojo, *m*, extravagancia, *f*; (of the mind) divagación, *f*
vagina *n* vagina, *f*
vaginal *a* vaginal
vagrancy *n* vagancia, *f*
vagrant *n* vago, *m*, *a* vagabundo, errante
vague *a* vago; indistinto; equívoco, ambiguo; (uncertain) incierto
vaguely *adv* vagamente
vagueness *n* vaguedad, *f*
vain *a* vano; (fruitless) infructuoso; (useless) inútil; (unsubstantial) fútil, insubstancial; fantástico; (empty) vacío; (worthless) despreciable; (conceited) vanidoso, presumido. **in v.,** en vano, en balde, inútilmente. **v. about,** orgulloso de
vainglorious *a* vanaglorioso
vaingloriousness *n* vanagloria, *f*
vainly *adv* vanamente; inútilmente; (conceitedly) vanidosamente, con vanidad
valance *n* cenefa, *f*
vale *n* (valley) valle, *m*. *interj* ¡adiós! *n* (good-bye) vale, *m*
valediction *n* despedida, *f*; vale, *m*
valedictory *a* de despedida
Valencian *a* and *n* valenciano (-na)
valency *n chem* valencia, *f*
valet *n* criado, *m*. **v. de chambre,** ayuda de cámara, *m*
valetudinarian *a* valetudinario
Valhalla *n* el Valhala, *m*
valiant *a* valiente, esforzado, animoso, bravo
valiantly *adv* valientemente
valid *a* válido, valedero; (of laws in force) vigente
validate *vt* validar
validation *n* validación, *f*
validity *n* validez, *f*

validly *adv* válidamente
valise *n* valija, *f*, saco de viaje, *m*
Valkyrie *n* Valquiria, *f*
valley *n* valle, *m*
valor *n* valor, *m*, valentía, *f*
valorous *a* valoroso, esforzudo, intrépido
valse *n* vals, *m*
valuable *a* valioso; costoso; precioso; estimable; excelente. *n pl* **valuables,** objetos de valor, *m pl*
valuableness *n* valor, *m*
valuation *n* valuación, tasación, *f*; estimación, *f*
valuator *n* tasador, *m*
value *n* valor, *m*; precio, *m*; estimación, *f*; importancia, *f*; (*gram mus*) valor, *m*; *pl* **values,** valores morales, principios, *m pl*. *vt* tasar, valorar; estimar; apreciar; tener en mucho; hacer caso de; considerar. **to be of v.,** ser de valor
valued *a* apreciado, estimado; precioso
valueless *a* sin valor; insignificante
valuer *n* tasador, *m*
valve *n* (*elec, mech, anat*) válvula, *f*; (*bot, zool*) valva, *f*
valved *a* con válvulas; (in compounds) de . . . válvulas
valvular *a* valvular
vamp *n* (of a shoe) pala (de zapato), *f*; (patch) remiendo, *m*; *mus* acompañamiento improvisado, *m*; *inf* aventurera, *f*. *vt* (of shoes) poner palas (a); (patch) remendar; *mus* improvisar un acompañamiento; (of a woman) fascinar, engatusar
vampire *n* vampiro, *m*
van *n* (*mil, nav, fig*) vanguardia, *f*; camión, *m*; (for delivery) camión de reparto, *m*; (for furniture) conductora de muebles, *f*; (removal) carro de mudanzas, *m*; (mail) camión postal, *m*; (for bathing) caseta de baño, *f*; (for guard on trains) furgón de equipajes, *m*; (railroad car) vagón, *m*
vandal *n* and *n* vándalo (-la); bárbaro (-ra)
vandalism *n* vandalismo, *m*
Vandyke *n* cuadro de Vandyke, *m*. **V. beard,** perilla, *f*. **V. collar,** cuello de encaje, *m*
vane *n* (weathercock) veleta, *f*; (of a windmill) aspa, *f*; (of a propeller) paleta, *f*; (of a feather) barba, *f*; (of a surveying instrument) pínula, *f*
vanguard *n* vanguardia, *f*. **in the v.,** a vanguardia; *fig* en la vanguardia
vanilla *n* vainilla, *f*
vanish *vi* desaparecer; desvanecerse; disiparse
vanishing *n* desaparición, *f*; disipación, *f*. **v. cream,** crema desvanecedora, *f*. **v. point,** punto de la vista, *m*
vanity *n* vanidad, *f*. **v. case,** polvera de bolsillo, *f*
vanquish *vt* vencer, derrotar
vanquisher *n* vencedor (-ra)
vantage *n* ventaja (also in tennis), *f*. **v.-ground,** posición ventajosa, *f*, sitial de privilegio, *m*
vapid *a* insípido, insulso; (of speeches, etc.) soso, aburrido, insípido
vapidity *n* insipidez, sosería, *f*
vapor *n* vapor, *m*; *pl* **vapors,** (hysteria) vapores, *m pl*. *vi* (boast) jactarse, baladronear; decir disparates. **v. bath,** baño de vapor, *m*
vaporizable *a* vaporizable
vaporization *n* vaporización, *f*
vaporize *vt* vaporizar. *vi* vaporizarse
vaporizer *n* vaporizador, *m*
vaporous *a* vaporoso
variability *n* variabilidad, *f*

variable *a* variable. *n math* variable, *f*
variably *adv* variablemente
variance *n* variación, *f*, cambio, *m*; desacuerdo, *m*, disensión, *f*; diferencia, contradicción, *f*. **at v.**, en desacuerdo, reñidos; hostil (a), opuesto (a); (of things) distinto (de), en contradicción (con)
variant *n* variante, *f*
variation *n* variación, *f*; cambio, *m*; variedad, *f*; diferencia, *f*; (*mus* magnetism) variación, *f*
varicose *a* varicoso
varied success éxito vario, *m*
variegate *vt* abigarrar, matizar, salpicar
variegated *a* abigarrado; variado; mezclado
variegation *n* abigarramiento, *m*; diversidad de colores, *f*
variety *n* variedad, *f*; diversidad, *f*; (choice) surtido, *m*. **v. show,** función de variedades, *f*
various *a* vario, diverso; diferente
variously *adv* diversamente
varix *n* várice, *f*
varnish *n* barniz, *m*. *vt* barnizar; (pottery) vidriar; (conceal) disimular. **copal v.,** barniz copal, *m*. **japan v., charol japonés,** *m*. **lacquer v.,** laca, *f*. **v. remover,** (for nails) quitaesmalte, *m*
varnishing *n* barnizado, *m*; (of pottery) vidriado, *m*
vary *vt* variar; cambiar; diversificar; modificar. *vi* variar; cambiar; (be different) ser distinto (de); (deviate) desviarse (de); (disagree) estar en desacuerdo, distar, estar en contradicción. **to v. directly (indirectly),** *math* variar en razón directa (inversa)
varying *a* variante, cambiante, diverso
vascular *a* vascular
vase *n* vaso, jarrón, *m*; urna, *f*
vaseline *n* vaselina, *f*
vassal *n* vasallo (-lla); esclavo (-va), siervo (-va). *a* tributario
vast *a* vasto, extenso; enorme; grande. *n* vastedad, inmensidad, *f*
vastly *adv* enormemente; muy; con mucho
vastness *n* vastedad, extensión, *f*; inmensidad, *f*; enormidad, *f*, gran tamaño, *m*; grandeza, *f*
vat *n* cuba, tina, *f*; alberca, *f*, estanque, *m*. **dyeing vat,** cuba de tintorero, *f*. **tanning vat,** noque, *m*. **wine vat,** lagar, *m*
Vatican *a* and *n* Vaticano, *m*
vaticinate *vt* and *vi* vaticinar, profetizar
vaticination *n* vaticinio, *m*, predicción, *f*
vaudeville *n* vodevil, *m*, zarzuela cómica, *f*
vault *n arch* bóveda, *f*; caverna, *f*; (for wine) bodega, cueva, *f*; (in a bank) cámara acorazada, *f*; (in a church) cripta, *f*; sepultura, *f*; (of the sky) bóveda celeste, *f*; (leap) salto, *m*; voltereta, *f*. *vi* (jump) saltar; (with a pole) saltar con pértiga; saltar por encima de; voltear. *vt arch* abovedar; saltar
vaulted *a* abovedado
vaulter *n* saltador (-ra)
vaulting *n* construcción de bóvedas, *f*; bóvedas, *f pl*; edificio abovedado, *m*; (jumping) salto, *m*. **v.-horse,** potro de madera, *m*
vaunt *vi* jactarse (de), hacer gala (de); triunfar (sobre). *vt* ostentar, sacar a relucir; (praise) alabar. *n* jactancia, *f*
veal *n* ternera, *f*. **v.-cutlet,** chuleta de ternera, *f*
vector *n* vector, *m*
Veda *n* Veda, *m*
veer *vi* (of the wind) girar; (of a ship) virar; *fig* cambiar (de opinión, etc.). *vt* virar
vegetable *n* vegetal, *m*; legumbre, *f*; *pl* **vegetables,** (green and generally cooked) verduras, *f pl*; (raw green) hortalizas, *f pl*. **v. dish,** fuente de legumbres, *f*. **v. garden,** huerto de legumbres, *m*; **v. ivory,** marfil vegetal, *m*. **v. kingdom,** reino vegetal, *m*. **v. soup,** sopa de hortelano, *f*
vegetal *a* vegetal
vegetarian *a* and *n* vegetariano (-na)
vegetarianism *n* vegetarianismo, *m*

vegetate *vi* vegetar
vegetation *n* vegetación, *f*
vehemence *n* vehemencia, *f*; violencia, *f*; impetuosidad, *f*; pasión, *f*, ardor, *m*
vehement *a* vehemente; violento; impetuoso; apasionado
vehemently *adv* con vehemencia; violentamente; con impetuosidad; apasionadamente
vehicle *n* vehículo, *m*; (means) medio, *m*; instrumento, *m*
vehicular *a* vehicular, de los vehículos; de los coches. **v. traffic,** circulación de los coches, *f*; los vehículos
veil *n* velo, *m*; (curtain) cortina, *f*; (disguise) disfraz, *m*; (excuse) pretexto, *m*; (appearance) apariencia, *f*. *vt* velar; cubrir con un velo; (hide) tapar, encubrir; (dissemble) disimular; (disguise) disfrazar. **to take the v.,** tomar el velo, profesar
vein *n* (*anat, bot*) vena, *f*; (*geol, min*) veta, *f*, filón, *m*; (in wood) fibra, hebra, *f*; (*fig* streak) rasgo, *m*; (inspiration) vena, *f*; (mood) humor, *m*
veined, veiny *a* venoso; de venas; veteado
velar *a* velar
vellum *n* vitela, *f*
velocity *n* velocidad, *f*; rapidez, *f*
velodrome *n* velódromo, *m*
velours *n* terciopelo, *m*
velvet *n* terciopelo, *m*, *a* hecho de terciopelo; aterciopelado
velveteen *n* pana, *f*, velludillo, *m*
velvety *a* aterciopelado
venal *a* venal
venality *n* venalidad, *f*
vend *vt* vender
vendor *n* vendedor (-ra)
veneer *vt* chapear, taracear; (conceal) disimular, disfrazar. *n* taraceado, chapeado, *m*; (plate) chapa, hoja para chapear, *f*; (*fig* gloss) barniz, *m*, apariencia, *f*
venerability *n* venerabilidad, respetabilidad, *f*
venerable *a* venerable
venerate *vt* venerar, reverenciar
veneration *n* veneración, *f*
venerator *n* venerador (-ra)
venereal *a* venéreo. **v. disease,** enfermedad venérea, *f*
Venetian *a* and *n* veneciano (-na). **v. blinds,** persianas, celosías, *f pl*
Venezuelan *a* and *n* venezolano (-na)
vengeance *n* venganza, *f*
vengeful *a* vengativo
venial *a* venial
veniality *n* venialidad, *f*
Venice Venecia, *f*
venison *n* venado, *m*
venom *n* veneno, *m*
venomous *a* venenoso; maligno, malicioso
venomously *adv* con malignidad, maliciosamente
venomousness *n* venenosidad, *f*; malignidad, *f*
venous *a* venoso
vent *n* abertura, *f*; salida, *f*; (air-hole) respiradero, *m*; (in pipes) ventosa, *f*; (in fire-arms) oído, *m*; *anat* ano, *m*; (*fig* outlet) desahogo, *m*; expresión, *f*. *vt* dejar escapar; (pierce) agujerear; (discharge) emitir, vomitar; (relieve) desahogar; expresar, dar expresión (a), dar rienda suelta (a)
venter *n law* vientre, *m*
ventilate *vt* ventilar; discutir
ventilation *n* ventilación, *f*
ventilator *n* ventilador, *m*
ventricle *n* ventrículo, *m*
ventriloquism *n* ventriloquia, *f*
ventriloquist *n* ventrílocuo (-ua)
venture *n* ventura, *f*; riesgo, *m*; aventura, *f*; especulación, *f*. *vt* arriesgar, aventurar; (stake) jugar; (state) expresar. *vi* aventurarse; (dare) atreverse, osar; permitirse. **at a v.,** a la ventura. **to v. on,** arriesgarse a; probar ventura con; lanzarse a; (a remark) permitirse. **to v. out,** atreverse a salir

venturesome *a* atrevido, audaz; (dangerous) arriesgado, peligroso

venturesomeness *n* atrevimiento, *m,* temeridad, *f;* (risk) riesgo, peligro, *m*

Venus *n* (planet) Venus, *m;* (woman) venus, *f*

veracious *a* veraz, verídico; verdadero

veracity *n* veracidad, *f;* verdad, *f*

veranda *n* veranda, *f*

verb *n* verbo, *m.* **auxiliary v.,** verbo auxiliar, *m.* **intransitive v.,** verbo intransitivo (neutro), *m.* **reflexive v.,** verbo reflexivo, *m.* **transitive v.,** verbo transitivo, *m*

verbal *a* verbal

verbally *adv* de palabra, verbalmente

verbatim *a* textual. *adv* textualmente, palabra por palabra

verbiage *n* verbosidad, palabrería, *f*

verbose *a* verboso, prolijo

verbosity *n* verbosidad, *f*

verdancy *n* verdura, *f,* verdor, *m*

verdant *a* verde

verdict *n law* veredicto, fallo, *m,* sentencia, *f;* opinión, *f;* juicio, *m.* **to bring in a v.,** fallar sentencia.

verdigris *n* cardenillo, verdin, *m*

verdure *n* verdura, *f,* verdor, *m; fig* lozanía, *f*

verge *n* (wand) vara, *f;* (edge) margen, borde, *m;* (of a lake, etc.) orilla, *f;* (horizon) horizonte, *m; fig* víspera, *f,* punto, *m.* **on the v. of,** al margen de, a la orilla de. **to be on the v. of,** *fig* estar a punto de; estar en vísperas de

verger *n* macero, *m;* (in a church) pertiguero, *m*

verifiable *a* verificable

verification *n* verificación, *f*

verifier *n* verificador (-ra)

verify *vt* verificar, confirmar; probar

verily *adv* de veras, en verdad

verisimilitude *n* verosimilitud, *f*

veritable *a* verdadero

veritably *adv* verdaderamente

verity *n* verdad, *f*

vermicelli *n* fideos, *m pl*

vermilion *n* bermellón, *m*

vermin *n* bichos dañinos, *m pl;* (insects) parásitos, *m pl*

vermouth *n* vermut, *m*

vernacular *a* vernáculo; nativo; vulgar. *n* lengua popular, *f;* lenguaje vulgar, *m*

versatile *a zool* versátil; inconstante, voluble; (clever) de muchos talentos; de muchos intereses; adaptable; completo, cabal

versatility *n* (cleverness) muchos talentos, *m pl;* adaptabilidad, *f*

verse *n* verso, *m;* (stanza) estrofa, *f;* (in the Bible) versículo, *m;* (poetry) poesía, *f,* versos, *m pl.* **to make verses,** escribir versos

versed *a* versado, experimentado

versicle *n* versículo, *m*

versification *n* versificación, *f*

versifier *n* versificador (-ra)

versify *vt* and *vi* versificar

version *n* versión, *f;* traducción, *f;* interpretación, *f*

versus *prep* contra

vertebra *n* vértebra, *f*

vertebral *a* vertebral

vertebrate *n* vertebrado, *m*

vertex *n* (*geom, anat*) vértice, *m; ast* cenit, *m;* cumbre, *f*

vertical *a* vertical

verticality *n* verticalidad, *f*

vertiginous *a* vertiginoso

vertigo *n* vértigo, *m*

verve *n* brío, *m,* fogosidad, *f*

very *a* mismo; (mere) mero; (true) verdadero; (with adjective and comparative) más grande; *inf* mismísimo; (complete) perfecto, completo. **The v. thought of it made him laugh,** Sólo con pensarlo se rió (*or* La mera idea le hizo reír). **this v. minute,** este mismísimo instante. **the v. day,** el mismo día

very *adv* muy; mucho; demasiado; (exactly) exactamente; completamente; absolutamente. **He is v. worried,** Está muy preocupado. **He is not v. well,** (i.e. rather ill) Está bastante bien. **This cloth is the v. best,** Esta tela es la mejor que hay. **I like it v. much,** Me gusta muchísimo. **He is v. much pleased,** Está muy contento. **so v. little,** tan poco; tan pequeño. **v. well,** muy bien

vesicle *n* vesícula, *f*

vesper *n* estrella vespertina, *f,* héspero, *m; pl* **vespers,** *ecc* vísperas, *f pl*

vessel *n* vasija, *f,* recipiente, *m;* (boat) barco, buque, *m;* (anat, bot) vaso, *m*

vest *n* camiseta, *f;* (waistcoat) chaleco, *m. vt* vestir; (with authority, etc.) revestir de; (property, etc.) hacer entrega de, ceder. *vi* tener validez; (dress) vestirse. **vested interests,** intereses creados, *m pl.* **v.-pocket,** bolsillo del chaleco, *m.* **v.-pocket camera,** cámara de bolsillo, *f*

vestal *a* vestal; virgen, casto. *n* vestal, *f;* virgen, *f*

vestibule *n* vestíbulo, *m;* (anteroom) antecámara, *f;* (of a theatre box) antepalco, *m; anat* vestíbulo, *m*

vestige *n* vestigio, rastro, *m;* sombra, *f; biol* rudimento, *m*

vestment *n* hábito, *m; ecc* vestidura, *f*

vestry *n* vestuario, *m,* sacristía, *f*

vesture *n* traje, hábito, *m,* vestidura, *f*

Vesuvius Vesubio, *m*

veteran *a* veterano; de los veteranos; aguerrido; anciano; experimentado. *n* veterano (-na)

veterinary *a* veterinario. **v. science,** veterinaria, *f.* **v. surgeon,** veterinario, *m*

veto *n* veto, *m;* prohibición, *f. vt* poner el veto; prohibir

vex *vt* contrariar, irritar; enojar; (make impatient) impacientar; fastidiar; (afflict) afligir, acongojar; (worry) inquietar

vexation *n* contrariedad, irritación, *f;* enojo, enfado, *m;* (impatience) impaciencia, *f;* fastidio, *m;* aflicción, *f;* inquietud, *f;* disgusto, *m*

vexatious *a* irritante; enojoso; enfadoso; fastidioso, molesto

vexatiousness *n* fastidio, *m,* molestia, *f;* incomodidad, *f;* contrariedad, *f*

vexed *a* discutido; contencioso; (thorny) espinoso, difícil

vexing *a* irritante; molesto; enfadoso

via *n* vía, *f, prep* por, por la vía de

viability *n* viabilidad, *f*

viable *a* viable

viaduct *n* viaducto, *m*

vial *n* frasco, *m,* ampolleta, *f*

vibrant *a* vibrante

vibrate *vi* vibrar; (of machines) trepidar; oscilar. *vt* hacer vibrar, vibrar

vibration *n* vibración, *f;* trepidación, *f;* oscilación, *f, Lat. Am.* cimbrón, *m*

vibrator *n elec* vibrador, *m; rad* oscilador, *m*

vicar *n* vicario, *m;* (of a parish) cura, *m.* **v.-general,** vicario general, *m*

vicarious *a* vicario; sufrido por otro; experimentado por otro

vicariously *adv* por delegación; por substitución. **I know it only vicariously,** Lo conozco sólo por referencia

vice *n* vicio, *m;* defecto, *m;* (in a horse) vicio, resabio, *m;* (tool) tornillo de banco, *m, prefix* vice. **v.-admiral,** vicealmirante, *m.* **v.-chairman,** vice-presidente (-ta). **v.-chancellor,** vicecanciller, *m.* **v.-consul,** vice-cónsul, *m.* **v.-consulate,** vice-consulado, *m.* **v.-president,** vicepresidente (-ta)

viceroy *n* virrey, *m*

viceversa *adv* viceversa

vicinity *n* vecindad, *f;* (nearness) cercanía, proximidad, *f.* **to be in the v. of,** estar en la vecindad de

vicious *a* vicioso. **v. circle,** círculo vicioso, *m*

viciousness *n* viciosidad, *f;* (in a horse) resabios, *m pl*

vicissitude *n* vicisitud, *f*
vicissitudinous *a* accidentado, vicisitudinario
victim *n* víctima, *f*
victimization *n* sacrificio, *m*; tormento, *m*
victimize *vt* hacer víctima (de); sacrificar; ser víctima (de), sufrir; (cheat) estafar, engañar
victor *n* víctor, vencedor, *m*
victoria *n* victoria, *f*
Victorian *a* victoriano
victorious *a* victorioso, triunfante. **to be v.**, triunfar, salir victorioso
victoriously *adv* victoriosamente, triunfalmente
victory *n* victoria, *f*
victress *n* vencedora, *f*
victual *n* vitualla, vianda, *f*; *pl* **victuals,** víveres, *m pl*, provisiones, *f pl. vt* avituallar; abastecer. *vi* tomar provisiones
victualler *n* abastecedor (-ra), proveedor (-ra)
victualling *n* abastecimiento, *m*
vide *Latin imperative* véase, véanse
videlicet *adv* a saber
video, *n* vídeo, *m*
videotape *n* videograbación, videocinta, *f*
vie *vi* (with) competir con; rivalizar con; (with a person for) disputar; luchar con
Vienna Viena, *f*
Viennese *a* and *n* vienés (-esa)
view *n* vista, *f*; perspectiva, *f*, panorama, *m*; (landscape) paisaje, *m*; escena, *f*; inspección, *f*; (judgment) opinión, *f*, parecer, *m*; consideración, *f*; (appearance) apariencia, *f*; aspecto, *m*; (purpose) propósito, *m*, intención, *f*; (sight) alcance de la vista, *m*; (show) exposición, *f*; *vt* examinar; inspeccionar; (look at) mirar; (see) ver, contemplar; considerar. **in v. of,** en vista de. **in my v.,** en mi opinión, segun creo yo. **on v.,** a la vista. **to keep in v.,** no perder de vista; *fig* no olvidar, tener presente. **to take a different v.,** pensar de un modo distinto. **to v. a house,** inspeccionar una casa. **with a v. to,** con el propósito de. **v.-finder,** enfocador, *m*. **v.-point,** punto de vista, *m*
viewer *n* espectador (-ra); examinador (-ra)
viewing *n* inspección, *f*, examen, *m*
vigil *n* vela, vigilia, *f*; *ecc* vigilia, *f*
vigilance *n* vigilancia, *f*, desvelo, *m*
vigilant *a* vigilante, desvelado
vigilantly *adv* vigilantemente
vignette *n* viñeta, *f*
vigorous *a* vigoroso, enérgico, fuerte; *Argentina* alentado
vigorously *adv* con vigor
vigor *n* vigor, *m*, fuerza, *f*
Viking *n* vikingo, *m*
vile *a* vil; bajo; despreciable; infame; *inf* horrible
vilely *adv* vilmente; *inf* mal, horriblemente
vileness *n* vileza, *f*; bajeza, *f*; infamia, *f*
vilification *n* vilipendio, *m*, difamación, *f*
vilifier *n* difamador (-ra)
vilify *vt* vilipendiar, difamar
villa *n* villa, torre, casa de campo, *f*; hotel, *m*
village *n* aldea, *f*, pueblo, *m*. **v. shop** *Lat. Am.* esquina, *f*
villager *n* aldeano (-na)
villain *n* *hist* villano, *m*; malvado, *m*
villainous *a* malvado; infame; vil
villainously *adv* vilmente   >
villainy *n* vileza, infamia, maldad, *f*
vindicate *vt* vindicar, justificar; defender
vindication *n* vindicación, justificación, *f*; defensa, *f*
vindicative *a* vindicativo, vindicador, justificativo
vindicator *n* vindicador (-ra)
vindictive *a* vengativo; rencoroso
vindictively *adv* vengativamente; rencorosamente
vindictiveness *n* deseo de venganza, *m*; rencor, *m*
vine *n* vid, parra, *f*; (twining plant) enredadera, *f*. **v.-arbor,** emparrado, *m*. **v.-branch,** sarmiento, *m*. **v.-clad,** cubierto de parras. **v.-grower,** vinicultor, *m*.

v.-growing, vinicultura, *f*. **v.-leaf,** hoja de parra, *f*. **v.-pest,** filoxera, *f*. **v.-stock,** cepa, *f*
vinegar *n* vinagre, *m*. **v.-cruet,** vinagrera, *f*. **v.-sauce,** vinagreta, *f*
vinegary *a* vinagroso
vineyard *n* viña, *f*, viñedo, *m*. **v.-keeper,** viñador, *m*
vinification *n* vinificación, *f*
vinosity *n* vinosidad, *f*
vinous *a* vinoso
vintage *n* vendimia, *f*; (of wine) cosecha (de vino), *f*
vintner *n* vinatero, *m*
viola *n* (*mus, bot*) viola, *f*. **v. player,** viola, *mf*
violate *vt* (desecrate) profanar; (infringe) contravenir, infringir; (break) romper; (ravish) violar
violation *n* profanación, *f*; (infringement) contravención, *f*; (rape) violación, *f*
violator *n* violador (-ra); (ravisher) violador, *m*
violence *n* violencia, *f*
violent *a* violento
violently *adv* con violencia
violet *n* violeta, *f*. *a* violado, **v. color,** violeta, color violado, *m*
violin *n* violín, *m*
violinist *n* violinista, *mf*
violoncellist *n* violoncelista, *mf*
violoncello *n* violoncelo, *m*
viper *n* víbora, *f*
viperish *a* viperino
virago *n* virago, *f*,
Virgilian *a* virgiliano
virgin *n* virgen, *f*; (sign of the zodiac) Virgo, *m. a* virginal; (untouched) virgen. **the V.,** la Virgen. **v. soil,** tierra virgen, *f*
virginal *a* virginal
virginity *n* virginidad, *f*
Virgo *n* Virgo, *m*
virile *a* viril
virility *n* virilidad, *f*
virtual *a* virtual
virtue *n* virtud, *f*
virtuosity *n* virtuosidad, *f*
virtuoso *n* virtuoso (-sa)
virtuous *a* virtuoso
virulence *n* virulencia, *f*
virulent *a* virulento
virulently *adv* con virulencia
virus *n* virus, *m*
visa *n* visado, *m*
visage *n* cara, *f*, rostro, *m*; semblante, aspecto, *m*
viscera *n* víscera, *f*
visceral *a* visceral
viscid *a* viscoso
viscosity *n* viscosidad, *f*
viscount *n* vizconde, *m*
viscountess *n* vizcondesa, *f*
viscous *a* viscoso
visé *n* visado, *m*, *vt* visar
visibility *n* visibilidad, *f*. **poor v.,** mala visibilidad, *f*
visible *a* visible; aparente, evidente
visibly *adv* visiblemente; a ojos vistas
Visigoth *n* visigodo (-da)
Visigothic *a* visigodo, visigótico
vision *n* visión, *f*; (eyesight) vista, *f*. **field of v.,** campo visual, *m*
visionary *a* and *n* visionario (-ia)
visit *n* visita, *f*; (inspection) inspección, *f*; (doctor's) visita de médico, *f*. *vt* visitar; hacer una visita (a); ir a ver; inspeccionar; (frequent) frecuentar; (Biblical) visitar. **to be visited by an epidemic,** sufrir una epidemia. **to go visiting,** ir de visita. **to pay a v.,** hacer una visita
visitation *n* visita, *f*; *ecc* visitación, *f*; (inspection) inspección, *f*; (punishment) castigo, *m*
visiting *a* de visita. **v. card,** tarjeta de visita, *f*. **v. card case,** tarjetero, *m*. **visiting hours,** horas de visita, *f pl*
visitor *n* visita, *f*; (official) visitador, *m*

visor *n* visera, *f*
vista *n* vista, perspectiva, *f*
visual *a* visual. **the v. arts,** las artes visuales
visualize *vt* and *vi* imaginarse, ver mentalmente
vital *a* vital; esencial; trascendental
vitalism *n* vitalismo, *m*
vitality *n* vitalidad, *f*
vitalize *vt* vitalizar, vivificar; reanimar
vitals *n pl* partes vitales, *f pl*; *fig* entrañas, *f pl*
vitamin *n* vitamina, *f*
vitiate *vt* viciar; corromper, contaminar
viticultural *a* vitícola
viticulture *n* viticultura, *f*
vitreous *a* vítreo, vidrioso
vitrification *n* vitrificación, *f*
vitrify *vt* vitrificar. *vi* vitrificarse
vitriol *n* vitriolo, ácido sulfúrico, *m*
vitriolic *a* vitriólico
Vitruvius Vitrubio, *m*
vituperable *a* vituperable
vituperate *vt* vituperar
vituperation *n* vituperio, *m*
vituperative *a* vituperador
vivacious *a* animado, vivaracho
vivaciously *adv* animadamente
vivacity *n* vivacidad, animación, *f*
viva voce *a* oral. *n* examen oral, *m*
vivid *a* vivo; brillante; intenso; (of descriptions, etc.) gráfico
vividly *adv* vivamente; brillantemente
vividness *n* vivacidad, *f*; intensidad, *f*; (strength) fuerza, *f*
vivification *n* vivificación, *f*
vivify *vt* vivificar, avivar
vivifying *a* vivificante
vivisection *n* vivisección, *f*
vixen *n* raposa, zorra, *f*; (woman) arpía, *f*
viz *adv* a saber
vizier *n* visir, *m*. **grand v.,** gran visir, *m*
vocabulary *n* vocabulario, *m*
vocal *a* vocal. **v. cords,** cuerdas vocales, *f pl*
vocalist *n* cantante, *mf*, voz, *f*
vocalization *n* vocalización, *f*
vocalize *vt* vocalizar
vocation *n* vocación, *f*; oficio, *m*; empleo, *m*; profesión, *f*
vocational *a* profesional; práctico. **vocational guidance,** guía vocacional, orientación profesional, *f*. **v. training,** instrucción práctica, *f*; enseñanza de oficio, *f*
vociferate *vt* gritar. *vi* vociferar, vocear
vociferation *n* vociferación, *f*
vociferous *a* (noisy) ruidoso; vocinglero, clamoroso
vociferously *adv* ruidosamente; a gritos
vodka *n* vodca, *m*
vogue *n* moda, *f*. **in v.,** en boga, de moda
voice *n* voz, *f*. *vt* expresar, interpretar, hacerse eco de; hablar. **in a loud v.,** en voz alta. **in a low v.,** en voz baja
voiced *a* (in compounds) de voz . . . ; hablado
void *a* (empty) vacío; (vacant) vacante; deshabitado; (lacking in) privado (de), desprovisto (de); (without) sin; *law* inválido, nulo; sin valor. *n* vacío, *m*. *vt* evacuar; *law* anular; invalidar
voile *n* espumilla, *f*
volatile *a* volátil; (light) ligero; (changeable) voluble, inconstante
volatility *n* volatilidad, *f*; ligereza, *f*; volubilidad, *f*
volatilization *n* volatilización, *f*
volatilize *vt* volatilizar. *vi* volatilizarse
volcanic *a* volcánico
volcano *n* volcán, *m*. **extinct v.,** volcán extinto, *m*
volition *n* volición, *f*; voluntad, *f*
volley *n* (of stones, etc.) lluvia, *f*; (of fire-arms) descarga, *f*; (of cannon, naval guns) andanada, *f*; *sport* voleo, *m*; (of words, etc.) torrente, *m*; (of applause etc.)

as a salute) salva, *f*. *vt sport* volear; (abuse, etc.) dirigir. *vi* lanzar una descarga, hacer una descarga
volt *n elec* voltío, *m*; (of a horse and in fencing) vuelta, *f*. **v.-ampere,** voltamperio, *m*
voltage *n* voltaje, *m*. **v. control,** mando del voltaje, *m*
voltaic *a* voltaico
Voltairian *a* volteriano
voltmeter *n* voltímetro, *m*
volubility *n* garrulidad, locuacidad, *f*
voluble *a* gárrulo, locuaz
volume *n* (book) tomo, *m*; (amount, size, space) volumen, *m*; (of water) caudal (de río), *m*; (mass) masa, *f*; (of smoke) humareda, *f*, nubes de humo, *f pl*
volumed *a* (in compounds) en . . . volúmenes, de . . . tomos
volumetric *a* volumétrico
voluminous *a* voluminoso
voluminousness *n* lo voluminoso
voluntarily *adv* voluntariamente
voluntariness *n* carácter voluntario, *m*
voluntary *a* voluntario; espontáneo; libre; (charitable) benéfico; (intentional) intencional, deliberado. *n* solo de órgano, *m*
volunteer *n mil* voluntario (-ia). *a* de voluntarios. *vt* ofrecer; contribuir; expresar. *vi* ofrecerse para hacer algo; *mil* alistarse, ofrecerse a servir como voluntario
volunteering *n* voluntariado, *m*
voluptuary *n* voluptuoso (-sa); sibarita, *mf*
voluptuous *a* voluptuoso
voluptuously *adv* voluptuosamente
voluptuousness *n* voluptuosidad, *f*; sensualidad, *f*
volute *n arch* voluta, *f*
vomit *vt* and *vi* vomitar; arrojar, devolver, *Central America, Mexico* deponer. *n* vómito, *m*
vomiting *n* vómito, *m*
voodoo *n* vudú, *m*
voracious *a* voraz
voracity *n* voracidad, *f*
vortex *n* torbellino, *m*, vorágine, *f*; *fig* vórtice, *m*
votaress, votary *n* devoto (-ta), adorante, *mf*; partidario (-ia)
vote *n* voto, *m*; (voting) votación, *f*; (suffrage) sufragio, *m*; (election) elección, *f*. *vt* votar; asignar; nombrar; elegir; (consider) tener por. *vi* votar, dar el voto. **casting v.,** voto de calidad, *m*. **to put to the v.,** poner a votación. **to v. down,** desechar, rechazar. **v. of confidence,** voto de confianza, *m*. **v. of thanks,** voto de gracias, *m*
voter *n* votante, *mf*, votador (-ra); elector (-ra)
voting *n* votación, *f*; elección, *f*. *a* de votar; electoral. **v. paper,** papeleta de votación, *f*
votive *a* votivo. **v. offering,** exvoto, *m*
vouch *vt* atestiguar, afirmar; garantizar; responder (de)
voucher *n* (guarantor) fiador (-ra); (guarantee) garantía, *f*; (receipt) recibo, *m*; (proof) prueba, *f*; documento justificativo, *m*; vale, bono, *m*
vouchsafe *vt* conceder, otorgar
vouchsafement *n* concesión, *f*, otorgamiento, *m*
vow *n* voto, *m*; promesa solemne, *f*. *vt* hacer voto (de), hacer promesa solemne (de); jurar. **to take a vow,** hacer un voto
vowel *n* vocal, *f*
voyage *n* viaje (por mar), *m*; travesía, *f*. *vi* viajar por mar. **Good v.!** ¡Buen viaje!, Feliz viaje!
voyager *n* viajero (-ra)
vulcanite *n* ebonita, *f*
vulcanization *n* vulcanización, *f*
vulcanize *vt* vulcanizar
vulgar *a* vulgar; (ill-bred) ordinario, cursi; (in bad taste) de mal gusto; trivial; adocenado; (coarse) grosero. *n* vulgo, populacho, *m*. **v. fraction,** fracción común, *f*
vulgarism *n* vulgarismo, *m*; vulgaridad, *f*
vulgarity *n* vulgaridad, *f*; grosería, *f*; mal tono, *m*, cursilería, *f*
vulgarize *vt* vulgarizar; popularizar
vulgarly *adv* vulgarmente; comúnmente; groseramente

Vulgate *n* Vulgata, *f*
vulnerability *n* vulnerabilidad, *f*
vulnerable *a* vulnerable

vulpine *a* vulpino; astuto
vulture *n* buitre, *Argentina* carancho, *m*
vulva *n* vulva, *f*

W

w *n* ve doble, *f*
wabble *vi.* See **wobble**
wad *n* (of straw, etc.) atado, *m*; (of notes, etc.) rollo, *m*; (in a gun) taco, *m*. *vt sew* acolchar; (furniture) emborrar; (guns) atacar; (stuff) rellenar
wadding *n* borra, *f*; (lining) entretela, *f*; (for guns) taco, *m*; (stuffing) relleno, *m*
waddle *n* anadeo, *m*, *vi* anadear
waddling *a* patojo, que anadea
wade *vi* and *vt* andar (en el agua, etc.); vadear; (paddle) chapotear. **to w. in,** entrar en (el agua, etc.); *fig* meterse en. **to w. through,** (a book) leer con dificultad; estudiar detenidamente; ir por
wader *n* el, *m*, (*f*, la) que vadea; (bird) ave zancuda, *f*; *pl* **waders,** botas de vadear, *f pl*
wafer *n* (host) hostia, *f*; (for sealing) oblea, *f*; (for ices) barquillo, *m*
waffle *n cul* fruta de sartén, *f*
waft *vt* llevar por el aire o encima del agua; hacer flotar; (stir) mecer; (of the wind) traer. *n* (fragrance) ráfaga de olor, *f*
wag *n* (of the tail) coleada, *f*; movimiento, *m*; meneo, *m*; (jester) bromista, *mf*. *vt* mover ligeramente; agitar; (of the tail) menear (la cola), colear. *vi* menearse; moverse; oscilar; (of the world) ir. **And thus the world wags,** Y así va el mundo
wage, wages *n* salario, *m*; *fig* premio, galardón, *m*. **minimum wage,** salario mínimo, *m*. **wages clerk,** pagador (-ra). **wage-earner,** asalariado (-da); (worker) trabajador (-ra)
wage *vt* emprender; sostener; hacer. **to w. war,** hacer guerra
wager *n* (bet) apuesta, *f*; (test) prueba, *f*, *vt* (bet) apostar; (pledge) empeñar. **to lay a w.,** hacer una apuesta
wages *n pl.* See **wage**
waggish *a* zumbón, jocoso; cómico
waggishness *n* jocosidad, *f*
waggle *vt* menear; mover; agitar; oscilar. *vi* menearse; moverse; agitarse; oscilar. *n* meneo, movimiento, *m*; oscilación, *f*
wagon *n* carro, *m*; carreta, *f*; (railway) vagón, *m*. **w.-lit,** coche cama, *m*. **w.-load,** carretada, *f*; vagón, *m*
wagoner *n* carretero, *m*
Wagnerian *a* wagneriano
waif *n* niño (-ña) sin hogar; animal perdido o abandonado, *m*; objeto extraviado, *m*; objeto sin dueño, *m*. **waifs and strays,** niños abandonados, *m pl*
wail *n* lamento, gemido, *m*; (complaint) queja, *f*. *vi* lamentarse, gemir; quejarse (de). *vt* lamentar, deplorar
wailer *n* lamentador (-ra)
wailing *n* lamentaciones, *f pl*, gemidos, *m pl*, *a* lamentador, gemidor
wainscot *n* entablado de madera, *m*. *vt* enmaderar; poner friso de madera (a)
waist *n* cintura, *f*; (blouse) blusa, *f*; (belt) cinturón, *m*; (bodice) corpiño, *m*; (narrowest portion) cuello, *m*; garganta, *f*; *naut* combés, *m*. **w.-band,** pretina, *f*. **w.-deep,** hasta la cintura. **w.-line,** cintura, *f*. **w. measurement,** medida de la cintura, *f*. **w.-coat,** chaleco, *m*. **w. strap,** trincha, *f*
wait *vi* and *vt* esperar, aguardar; (serve) servir. **to keep waiting,** hacer esperar. **to w. at table,** servir a la mesa. **to w. on oneself,** servirse a sí mismo; cuidarse a sí mismo; hacer las cosas por sí solo. **to w. one's time,** aguardar la ocasión. **to w. for,** (until) esperar hasta que; (of persons) esperar (a), aguardar (a); (in ambush) acechar. **to w. upon,** (serve) servir a; (visit)

visitar; presentar sus respetos (a); (*fig* accompany) acompañar; (follow) seguir a
wait *n* espera, *f*; (pause) pausa, *f*, intervalo, *m*; (ambush) asechanza, *f*; *pl* **waits,** coro de nochebuena, *m*. **to lie in w. for,** estar en acecho para
waiter *n* camarero, mozo, *m*; (tray) bandeja, *f*
waiting *n* espera, *f*. *a* que espera; de espera; de servicio. **lady-in-w.,** dama de servicio, *f*. **w.-maid,** camarera, doncella, *f*. **w.-room,** (of a bus station, etc.) sala de espera, *f*; (of an office) antesala, *f*
waitress *n* camarera, *f*
waive *vt* renunciar (a); desistir (de)
wake *vi* estar despierto; despertarse; (watch) velar. *vt* despertar; (a corpse) velar (a). *n* vela, *f*; vigilia, *f*; (of a corpse) velatorio, *m*; (holiday) fiesta, *f*; (of a ship) estela, *f*. **in the w. of,** *naut* en la estela de; después de; seguido por
wakeful *a* vigilante; (awake) despierto. **to be w.,** pasar la noche en vela
wakefulness *n* vigilancia, *f*; (sleeplessness) insomnia, *f*
waken *vi* despertarse. *vt* despertar; (call) llamar
waking *a* despierto; de vela. *n* despertar, *m*; (watching) vela, *f*
wale *n* (weal) verdugo, *m*, huella de azote, *f*, *vt* azotar
Wales (País de) Gales, *m*
walk *n* (pace) paso, *m*; (modo de) andar, *m*; (journey on foot) paseo, *m*, vuelta, *f*; (long) caminata, *f*; (promenade) paseo, *m*, avenida, *f*; (path) senda, *f*; (rank) clase social, *f*; esfera, *f*; profesión, *f*; ocupación, *f*. **quick w.,** paseo rápido, *m*; (pace) andar rápido, *m*. **to go for a w.,** ir de paseo. **to take a w.,** dar un paseo (or una vuelta), pasear. **to take for a w.,** llevar a paseo, sacar a paseo. **w.-out,** (strike) huelga, *f*. **w.-over,** triunfo, *m*, (or victoria, *f*) fácil. **w. past,** desfile, *m*
walk *vi* andar; caminar; ir a pie; (take a walk) pasear, dar un paseo; (of ghosts) aparecer; (behave) conducirse. *vt* hacer andar; (take for a walk) sacar a paseo; andar de una parte a otra (de), recorrer; (a specified distance) hacer a pie, andar; (a horse) llevar al paso. **to w. abroad,** dar un paseo; salir. **to w. arm in arm,** ir de bracero. **to w. past,** pasar; (in procession) desfilar. **to w. quickly,** andar de prisa. **to w. slowly,** andar despacio, andar lentamente. **to w. the hospitals,** estudiar en los hospitales. **to w. the streets,** recorrer las calles; vagar por las calles. **to w. about,** pasearse; ir y venir. **to w. after,** seguir (a), ir detrás de. **to w. along,** andar por; recorrer. **to w. away,** marcharse, irse. **to w. away with,** (win) ganar, llevarse; (steal) quitar, tomar, alzarse con. **to w. back,** volver; volver a pie, regresar a pie. **to w. down,** bajar; bajar a pie; andar por. **to w. in,** entrar en; entrar a pie en; (walk about) pasearse en. **to w. on,** seguir andando; (step on) pisar. **to w. out,** salir. **to w. over,** andar por; llevar la victoria (a); triunfar fácilmente sobre. **to w. round,** dar la vuelta a. **to w. round and round,** dar vueltas. **to w. up,** subir andando; subir. **to w. up and down,** dar vueltas, ir y venir
walker *n* (pedestrian) peatón, *m*; andador (-ra); (promenader) paseante, *mf*
walking *n* el andar; (excursion on foot) paseo, *m*. *a* andante; de andar; a pie; ambulante. **at a w. pace,** a un paso de andadura. **w. encyclopedia,** enciclopedia ambulante, *f*. **w. match,** marcha atlética, *f*. **w.-stick,** bastón, *m*. **w. tour,** excursión a pie, *f*
Walkyrie *n* valquiria, *f*
wall *n* muro, *m*; (rampart) muralla, *f*; (*fig* and of an organ, cavity, etc.) pared, *f*. **partition w.,** tabique, *m*.

Walls have ears, Las paredes oyen. **w. lizard,** lagartija, *f.* **w. map,** mapa mural, *m.* **w.-painting,** pintura mural, *f.* **w.-paper,** papel pintado, *m.* **w. socket,** *elec* enchufe, *m*

wall *vt* cercar con un muro; amurallar. **to w. in,** murar. **to w. up,** tapiar, tabicar

wallet *n* cartera, *f;* bolsa de cuero, *f*

wallflower *n* alhelí, *m*

Walloon *a* and *n* valón (-ona)

wallop *n* golpe, *m,* *vt* tundir, zurrar

wallow *vi* revolcarse; encenagarse; (in riches, etc.) nadar (en). *n* revuelco, *m*

walnut *n* (tree and wood) nogal, *m;* (nut) nuez de nogal, *f*

walrus *n* morsa, *f*

waltz *n* vals, *m,* *vi* valsar

wan *a* ojeroso, descolorido; (of the sky, etc.) pálido, sin color

wand *n* vara, *f;* (conductor's) batuta, *f.* **magic w.,** varita mágica, *f*

wander *vi* errar, vagar; (deviate) extraviarse; (from the subject) desviarse del asunto; divagar; (be delirious) delirar. *vt* vagar por, errar por, recorrer

wanderer *n* vagabundo (-da); hombre, *m,* (*f,* mujer) errante; (traveler) viajero (-ra)

wandering *a* errante; vagabundo; nómada; (traveling) viajero; (delirious) delirante; (of thoughts, the mind) distraído; (of cells, kidneys, etc.) flotante. *n* vagancia, *f;* viaje, *m;* (delirium) delirio, *m;* (digression) divagación, *f;* (of a river, etc.) meandro, *m.* **the w. Jew,** el judío errante

wane *vi* (of the moon, etc.) menguar; (decrease) disminuir; (*fig* decay) decaer. *n* (of the moon) menguante de la luna, *f;* mengua, *f;* disminución, *f;* decadencia, *f*

waning *a* menguante

wanly *adv* pálidamente; *fig* tristemente

wanness *n* palidez, *f;* *fig* tristeza, *f*

want *vt* (lack) carecer de, faltar; (need) necesitar, haber menester de; (require or wish) querer, desear; (demand) exigir; (ought) deber; (do without) pasarse sin. *vi* hacer falta; carecer (de); (be poor) estar necesitado. **I don't w. to,** No quiero, No me da la gana. **to be wanted,** hacer falta; (called) ser llamado. **You are wanted on the telephone,** Te llaman por teléfono

wanted se necesita; (advertisement) demanda, *f.* **Estelle wants me to write a letter,** Estrella quiere que escriba una carta. **What do you w. me to do?** ¿Qué quiere Vd. que haga?; ¿En qué puedo servirle? **What does Paul w.?** ¿Qué quiere Pablo?; (require) ¿Qué necesita Pablo? **He wants (needs) a holiday,** Le hacen falta unas vacaciones, Necesita unas vacaciones

want *n* (lack) falta, *f;* escasez, carestía, *f;* (need) necesidad, *f;* (poverty) pobreza, indigencia, *f;* (absence) ausencia, *f;* (wish) deseo, *m;* exigencia, *f.* **in w. of,** por falta de; en la ausencia de. **to be in w.,** estar en la necesidad, ser indigente

wanting *a* deficiente (en); falto (de); (scarce) escaso; ausente; (in intelligence) menguado. *prep* (less) menos; (without) sin. **to be w.,** faltar. **to be w. in,** carecer de

wanton *a* (playful) juguetón; (wilful) travieso; (loose) suelto, libre; (unrestrained) desenfrenado; extravagante; excesivo; (caprichoso; (dishevelled) en desorden; (reckless) indiscreto; (of vegetation) lozano; (purposeless) inútil; imperdonable; frívolo; (unchaste) disoluto; lascivo. *n* mujer disoluta, *f;* ramera, *f;* (child) niño (-ña) juguetón (-ona)

wantonly *adv* innecesariamente; sin motivo; excesivamente; lascivamente

war *n* guerra, *f. a* de guerra; guerrero. *vi* guerrear. **at war with,** en guerra con. **cold war,** guerra tonta, *f.* **on a war footing,** en pie de guerra. **We are at war,** Estamos en guerra. **to be on the war-path,** *fig inf* buscar pendencia, tratar de armarla. **to declare war on,** declarar la guerra (a). **to make war on,** hacer la guerra (a). **war to the death,** guerra a muerte, *f.* **war**

correspondent, corresponsal en el teatro de guerra, *m.* **war-cry,** alarido de guerra, grito de combate, grito de guerra *m.* **war-dance,** danza guerrera, *f.* **war horse,** caballo de batalla, *m.* **war loan,** empréstito de guerra, *m.* **war-lord,** adalid, caudillo, jefe militar, *m.* **war material,** pertrechos de guerra, *m pl;* municiones, *f pl.* **war memorial,** monumento a los caídos, *m.* **war minister,** Ministro de la Guerra, *m.* **war neurosis,** neurosis de guerra, *f.* **War Office,** Ministerio de la Guerra, *m.* **war plane,** avión de guerra, *m.* **war-ship,** barco (or buque) de guerra, *m.* **war-wearied,** agotado por la guerra

warble *vt* and *vi* trinar; gorjear; murmurar. *n* trino, *m;* gorjeo, *m;* murmurio, *m*

ward *n* protección, *f;* (of a minor) pupilo (-la); (of locks, keys) guarda, *f;* (of a city) barrio, distrito, *m;* (of a hospital, etc.) sala, *f;* (of a prison) celda, *f;* (fencing) guardia, *f.* **w.-room,** cuarto de los oficiales, *m.* **w. sister,** hermana de una sala de hospital, *f*

ward *vt* proteger, defender. **to w. off,** desviar; evitar

warden *n* guardián, *m;* director (-ra); (of a prison) alcaide, *m;* (of a church) mayordomo de la iglesia, *m;* (of a port) capitán, *m*

warder *n* (gaoler) guardián, *m;* alabardero, guardia, *m*

Wardour-Street English *n* inglés arcaizante de magüerista, *m*

wardress *n* guardiana, *f*

wardrobe *n* guardarropa, ropero, *m;* (clothes) ropa, *f; theat* vestuario, *m.* **w. trunk,** baúl mundo, *m*

ware *n* mercadería, *f;* (pottery) loza, *f; pl* **wares,** mercancías, *f pl*

war effort *n* esfuerzo bélico, esfuerzo de guerra, esfuerzo guerrero, *m*

warehouse *n* almacén, *m, vt* almacenar

warehouseman *n* almacenero, *m*

warfare *n* guerra, *f;* lucha, *f;* arte militar, *m,* or *f.* **chemical w.,** guerra química, *f*

war head *n* (of torpedo) cabeza de combate, punto de combate, *f;* (of missile) detonante, *m*

war heroe *n* héroe de guerra, *m*

war heroine *n* heroína de guerra, *f*

warily *adv* con cautela, cautelosamente; prudentemente

wariness *n* cautela *f;* prudencia, *f*

warlike *a* belicoso, guerrero; militar, de guerra; marcial. **war-spirit,** espíritu belicoso, *m,* marcialidad, *f*

warm *a* caliente; (lukewarm) tibio; (hot) caluroso; (affectionate) cordial, cariñoso, afectuoso; (angry) acalorado; (enthusiastic) entusiasta, ardiente; (art) cálido; (of coats, etc.) de abrigo; (fresh) fresco, reciente; *inf* adinerado. *vt* calentar; *fig* encender; entusiasmar. *vi* calentarse; *fig* entusiasmarse (con). **to have a w. at the fire,** calentarse al lado del fuego. **to be w.,** (of things) estar caliente; (of coats, etc.) ser de abrigo; (of the weather) hacer calor; (of people) tener calor. **to grow w.,** calentarse; (grow angry) excitarse, agitarse; (of a discussion) hacerse acalorado. **to keep w.,** conservar caliente; calentar. **to keep oneself w.,** estar caliente, no enfriarse. **to w. up,** calentar. **w.-blooded,** de sangre caliente; ardiente. **w.-hearted,** de buen corazón; generoso; afectuoso, cordial. **w.-heartedness,** buen corazón, *m;* generosidad, *f;* cordialidad, *f*

warming *n* calentamiento, *m;* calefacción, *f. a* calentador; para calentar. **w.-pan,** calentador, *m*

warmly *adv* (affectionately) cordialmente, afectuosamente; con entusiasmo; (angrily) acaloradamente. **to be w. wrapped up,** estar bien abrigado

warmonger *n* atizador de guerra, belicista, fautor de guerra, fomentador de guerra, propagador (-ra) de guerra

warmth *n* calor, *m*

warn *vt* advertir; prevenir; amonestar; (inform) avisar

warning *n* advertencia, *f;* aviso, *m;* amonestación, *f;* (lesson) lección, *f;* escarmiento, *m;* alarma, *f. a* amonestador; de alarma. **to give w.,** prevenir, advertir; (dismiss) despedir. **to take w.,** escarmentar

warningly *adv* indicando el peligro; con alarma; con amenaza

warp *vt* torcer; combar; *naut* espiar; (the mind) pervertir. *vi* torcerse; combarse, bornearse; *naut* espiarse. *n* (in a fabric) urdimbre, *f*; (in wood) comba, *f*, torcimiento, *m*; *naut* espía, *f*. **w. and woof,** trama y urdimbre, *f*

warping *n* (of wood) combadura, *f*; (weaving) urdidura, *f*; *naut* espía, *f*; (of the mind) perversión, *f*. **w. frame,** urdidera, *f*

warrant *n* autoridad, *f*; justificación, *f*; autorización, *f*; garantía, *f*; decreto de prisión, *m*; orden, *f*; *com* orden de pago, *f*; *mil* nombramiento, *m*; motivo, *m*, razón, *f*. *vt* justificar; autorizar; garantizar, responder por; asegurar. **pay w.,** boletín de pago, *m*

warrantable *a* justificable

warrantor *n* garante, *mf*

warranty *n* autorización, *f*; justificación, *f*; *law* garantía, *f*

warren *n* (for hunting) vedado, *m*; (rabbit) conejera, *f*; vivar, *m*, madriguera, *f*

warrior *n* guerrero, *m*; soldado, *m*

Warsaw Varsovia, *f*

wart *n* verruga, *f*

wary *a* cauto, cauteloso; prudente

wash *vt* lavar; (dishes) fregar; (lave) bañar; (clean) limpiar; (furrow) surcar; (wet) regar, humedecer; (with paint) dar una capa de color o de metal. *vi* lavarse; lavar ropa. **Two of the crew were washed overboard,** El mar arrastró a dos de los tripulantes. **Will this material w.?** ¿Se puede lavar esta tela? ¿Es lavable esta tela? **to w. ashore,** echar a la playa. **w. away,** (remove by washing) quitar lavando; derrubiar; (water or waves) arrastrar, llevarse. **to w. one's hands,** lavarse las manos. **to look washed out,** estar ojeroso. **to w. down,** lavar; limpiar; (remove) llevarse; (accompany with drink) regar. **to w. off,** *vt* quitar lavando; hacer desaparecer; borrar; (of waves, etc.) llevarse; (of color) desteñir. *vi* borrarse; desteñirse. **to w. up,** lavar los platos, fregar la vajilla; (cast up) desechar. **w. one's dirty laundry in public,** sacar los más sucios trapillos a la colada

wash *n* lavadura, *f*, lavado, *m*; baño, *m*; (clothes) ropa para lavar, ropa sucia, *f*; colada, *f*; (of the waves) chapoteo, *m*; (lotion) loción, *f*; (coating) capa, *f*; (silt) aluvión, *m*. **w.-basin,** palangana, *f*; lavabo, *m*. **w.-board,** tabla de lavar, *f*. **w.-house,** lavadero, *m*. **w.-leather,** gamuza, badana, *f*. **w.-out,** fracaso, *m*. **w.-stand,** aguamanil, lavabo, *m*. **w.-tub,** cuba de lavar, *f*

washable *a* lavable

washer *n* lavador (-ra); (washerwoman) lavandera, *f*; (machine) lavadora, *f*; *mech* arandela, *f*

washerwoman *n* lavandera, *f*

washing *n* lavamiento, *m*; ropa sucia, ropa para lavar, *f*; ropa limpia, *f*; ropa, *f*; (bleaching) blanqueadura, *f*; (toilet) abluciones, *f pl*; *ecc* lavatorio, *m*; *pl* **washings,** lavazas, *f pl*. **There is a lot of w. to be done,** Hay mucha ropa que lavar. **w.-board,** tabla de lavar, *f*. **w.-day,** día de colada, *f*. **w.-machine,** lavadora, máquina de lavar, *f*. **w.-soda,** carbonato sódico, *m*. **w.-up,** lavado de los platos, *m*. **w.-up machine,** fregador mecánico de platos, *m*

wasp *n* avispa, *f*, *Lat. Am. also* jicote, *m*. **wasp's nest,** avispero, *m*. **w.-waisted,** (of clothes) ceñido, muy ajustado

waspish *a* enojadizo, irascible; malicioso; mordaz

waste *vt* desperdiciar, derrochar, malgastar; (time) perder; consumir; corroer; (devastate) asolar, devastar; echar a perder; malograr; disipar; agotar. *vi* gastarse; consumirse; perderse. **to w. time,** perder el tiempo. **to w. away,** (of persons) demacrarse, consumirse

waste *n* (wilderness) yermo, desierto, *m*; (vastness) inmensidad, vastedad, *f*; (loss) pérdida, *f*; (squandering) despilfarro, derroche, *m*; diminución, *f*; (refuse) desechos, *m pl*; (of cotton, etc.) borra, *f*; disipación, *f*. *a* (of land) sin cultivar; yermo; inútil; desechado, de dese-

cho; superfluo. **to lay w.,** devastar. **w. land,** yermo, *m*; tierras sin cultivar, *f pl*. **w. paper,** papel usado, papel de desecho, *m*. **w.-paper basket,** cesto para papeles, *m*. **w.-pipe,** desaguadero, tubo de desagüe, *m*

wasteful *a* pródigo, derrochador, manirroto; antieconómico; ruinoso; inútil

wastefully *adv* pródigamente; antieconómicamente; inútilmente

wastefulness *n* prodigalidad, *f*, despilfarro, *m*; pérdida, *f*; gasto inútil, *m*; falta de economía, *f*

waster *n* gastador (-ra); disipador (-ra); (loafer) golfo, *m*

watch *vi* velar; mirar. *vt* mirar; observar; guardar; (await) esperar; (spy upon) espiar, acechar. **to w. for,** buscar aguardar. **to w. over,** vigilar, guardar; (care for) cuidar; proteger. **watch out!** *Mexico* ¡abusado!

watch *n* (at night) vela, *f*; (wakefulness) desvelo, *m*; observación, vigilancia, *f*; (mil naut) guardia, *f*; (sentinel) centinela, *m*; (watchman) sereno, vigilante, *m*; (guard) ronda, *f*; (timepiece) reloj de bolsillo, *m*. **to be on the w.,** estar al acecho, estar al alerta, estar a la mira. **to keep w.,** vigilar. **dog w.,** media guardia, *f*. **pocket w.,** reloj de bolsillo, *m*. **wrist w.,** reloj de pulsera, *m*. **w.-case,** caja de reloj, relojera, *f*. **w.-chain,** cadena de reloj, leontina, *f*. **w.-dog,** perro guardián, *m*. **w.-glass,** cristal de reloj, *m*. **w.-making,** relojería, *f*. **w.-night,** noche vieja, *f*. **w.-spring,** muelle de reloj, *m*, espiral, *f*

watcher *n* observador (-ra); espectador (-ra); (at a sick bed) el, *m*, (*f*, la) que vela a un enfermo

watchful *a* vigilante, alerto; observador; atento, cuidadoso

watchfully *adv* vigilantemente; atentamente

watchfulness *n* vigilancia, *f*; cuidado, *m*; desvelo, *m*

watching *n* observación, *f*; (vigil) vela, *f*

watchmaker *n* relojero (-ra). **watchmaker's shop,** relojería, *f*

watchman *n* vigilante, sereno, *m*; guardián, *m*

watchword *n* (password) consigna, contraseña, *f*; (motto) lema, *m*

water *n* agua, *f*; (tide) marea, *f*; (of precious stones) aguas, *f pl*; (urine) orina, *f*; (quality) calidad, clase, *f*. *a* de agua; por agua; acuático; hidráulico. **fresh w.,** (not salt) agua dulce, *f*; agua fresca, *f*. **hard w.,** agua cruda, *f*. **high w.,** marea alta, *f*. **low w.,** marea baja, *f*. **of the first w.,** de primera clase. **running w.,** agua corriente, *f*. **soft w.,** agua blanda, *f*. **to make w.,** *naut* hacer agua; orinar. **to take the waters,** tomar las aguas. **under w.,** *adv* debajo del agua. *a* acuático. **w.-bird,** ave acuática, *f*. **w. blister,** ampolla, *f*. **w.-boatman,** chinche de agua, *f*. **w.-borne,** flotante. **w.-bottle,** cantimplora, *f*. **w.-brash,** acedia, *f*. **w.-butt,** barril, *m*, pipa, *f*. **w.-carrier,** aguador (-ra). **w.-cart,** carro de regar, *m*. **w.-closet,** retrete, excusado, *m*. **w.-color,** acuarela, *f*. **w.-color painting,** pintura a la acuarela, *f*. **w.-colorist,** acuarelista, *mf* **w.-cooled,** enfriado por agua. **w.-cooler,** cantimplora, *f*. **w.-finder,** zahorí, *m*. **w. front,** (wharf) muelle, *m*; puerto, *m*; litoral, *m*. **w.-gauge,** indicador de nivel de agua, *m*, vara de aforar, *f*. **w.-glass,** vidrio soluble, silicato de sosa, *m*. **w. heater,** calentador de agua, *m*. **w.-ice,** helado, *m*. **w.-level,** nivel de las aguas, *m*. **w.-lily,** nenúfar, *m*, azucena de agua, *f*. **w.-line,** lengua de agua, *f*; (of a ship) línea de flotación, *f*. **w.-logged,** anegado en agua. **w.-main,** cañería maestra de agua, *f*. **w. man,** barquero, *m*. **w.-melon,** sandía, *f*. **w. mill,** aceña, *f*. **w.-nymph,** náyade, *f*. **w.-pipe,** cañería del agua, *f*. **w. pitcher,** jarro, *m*. **w. plant,** planta acuática, *f*. **w.-polo,** polo acuático, *m*. **w.-power,** fuerza hidráulica, *f*. **w.-rate,** cupo del consumo de agua, *m*. **w. snake,** culebra de agua, *f*. **w. softener,** generador de agua dulce, *m*; purificador de agua, *m*. **w. spaniel,** perro (-rra) de aguas. **w. sprite,** ondina, *f*. **w.-supply,** abastecimiento de agua, *m*; traída de aguas, *f*. **w. tank,** depósito para agua, *m*. **w. tower,** arca de agua, *f*. **w. wave,** ondulado al agua, *m*. **w.-way,** canal, río, *m*, o vía *f*, navegable. **w.-wheel,** rueda hidráulica, *f*, azud, *m*; (for irrigation) aceña, *f*. **w. wings,** nadaderas, *f pl*

water *vt* (irrigate, sprinkle) regar; (moisten) mojar; (cattle, etc.) abrevar; (wine, etc.) aguar; diluir con agua; (bathe) bañar. *vi* (of animals) beber agua; (of engines, etc.) tomar agua; (of the eyes, mouth) hacerse agua. **My mouth waters,** Se me hace agua la boca
watercourse *n* corriente de agua, *f*; cauce, *m*; lecho de un río, *m*
watercress *n* berro, mastuerzo, *m*
watered *a* regado, abundante en agua; (of silk) tornasolado
watered-down *fig* pasado por agua
waterfall *n* salto de agua, *m*, cascada, catarata, *f*
wateriness *n* humedad, *f*; acuosidad, *f*
watering *n* riego, *m*; irrigación, *f*; (of eyes) lagrimeo, *m*; (of cattle, etc.) el abrevar (a); *naut* aguada, *f*. **w.-can,** regadera, *f*. **w.-cart,** carro de regar, *m*. **w.-place,** (for animals) aguadero, *m*; (for cattle) abrevadero, *m*; (spa) balneario, *m*; (by the sea) playa de veraneo, *f*
watermark *n* (in paper) filigrana, *f*; nivel del agua, *m*. *vt* filigranar
waterproof *a* impermeable; a prueba de agua. *n* impermeable, *m*. *vt* hacer impermeable, impermeabilizar
water-repellent *a* repelente al agua
watershed *n* vertiente, *f*; línea divisoria de las aguas, *f*; (river-basin) cuenca, *f*
waterspout *n* bomba marina, manga, trompa, *f*
watertight *a* impermeable, estanco; a prueba de agua; (of arguments, etc.) irrefutable
watertightness *n* impermeabilidad, *f*
waterworks *n* establecimiento para la distribución de las aguas, *m*; obras hidráulicas, *f pl*
watery *a* (wet) húmedo; acuoso; (of the sky) de lluvia; (of eyes) lagrimoso, lloroso; (sodden) mojado; (of soup, etc.) claro; insípido
watt *n* vatio, *m*. **w. hour,** vatio hora, *m*. **w.-meter,** vatímetro, *m*
wattage *n* vatiaje, *m*
wattle *n* zarzo, *m*; (of turkey) barba, *f*; (of fish) barbilla, *f*
wave *vi* ondear; ondular; flotar; hacer señales. *vt* (brandish) blandir; agitar; (the hair) ondular; ondear; hacer señales (de). **They waved goodby to him,** Le hicieron adiós con la mano; Le hicieron señas de despedida; Se despidieron de él agitando el pañuelo
wave *n* (of the sea) ola, *f*; *phys* onda, *f*; (in hair or a surface) ondulación, *f*; (movement) movimiento, *m*; (of anger, etc.) ráfaga, *f*. **long w.,** onda larga, *f*. **medium w.,** onda media, *f*. **short w.,** onda corta, *f*. **sound w.,** onda sonora, *f*. **to have one's hair waved,** hacerse ondular el pelo. **w. band,** franja undosa, escala de longitudes de onda, *f*. **w. crest,** cresta de la ola, cabrilla, *f*. **w.-length,** longitud de onda, *f*
wavelet *n* pequeña ola, olita, *f*; (ripple) rizo (del agua), *m*
wave of immigration una inmigración, *f*
waver *vi* ondear; oscilar; (hesitate) vacilar, titubear; (totter) tambalearse; (weaken) flaquear
waverer *n* irresoluto (-ta), vacilante, *m*
wavering *n* vacilación, irresolución, *f*. *a* oscilante; vacilante, irresoluto; flotante
waving *n* ondulación, *f*; oscilación, *f*; agitación, *f*; movimiento, *m*. *a* ondulante; oscilante; que se balancea
wavy *a* ondulado; flotante
wax *n* cera, *f*; (cobblers') cerote, *m*; (in the ear) cerilla, *f*. *a* de cera. *vt* encerar. *vi* crecer; hacerse; ponerse. **to wax enthusiastic,** entusiasmarse. **waxed paper,** papel encerado, *m*. **wax chandler,** cerero, *m*. **wax doll,** muñeca de cera, *f*. **wax modeling,** modelado en cera, *m*, ceroplástica, *f*. **wax taper,** blandón, *m*
waxen *a* de cera; como la cera; de color de cera
waxing *n* enceramiento, *m*; (of the moon) crecimiento, *m*; aumento, *m*
wax museum *n* museo de cera, *m*
waxwork *n* figura de cera, *f*
waxy *a*. See **waxen**
way *n* camino, *m*; senda, *f*; paso, *m*; ruta, *f*; (railway,

etc.) vía, *f*; dirección, *f*; rumbo, *m*; distancia, *f*; (journey) viaje, *m*; (sea crossing) travesía, *f*; avance, progreso, *m*; (*naut* etc.) marcha, *f*; método, *m*; modo, *m*; (means) medio, *m*; manera, *f*; (habit) costumbre, *f*; (behavior) conducta, *f*, modo de obrar, *m*; (line of business, etc.) ramo, *m*; (state) estado, *m*, condición, *f*; (course) curso, *m*; (respect) punto de vista, *m*; (particular kind) género, *m*; (scale) escala, *f*. **a long way off,** a gran distancia, a lo lejos. **a short way off,** a poca distancia, no muy lejos. **by way of,** pasando por; por vía de; como; por medio de; a modo de. **by the way,** de paso; durante el viaje; durante la travesía; a propósito; entre paréntesis. **in a small way,** en pequeña escala. **in a way,** hasta cierto punto; desde cierto punto de vista. **in many ways,** de muchos modos; por muchas cosas. **in no way,** de ningún modo; nada. **in the way,** en el medio. **in the way of,** en cuanto a, tocante a; en materia de. **I went out of my way to,** Dejé el camino para; Me di la molestia de. **Is this the way to . . . ?** ¿Es este el camino a . . . ? **Make way!** ¡Calle! **Milky Way,** vía láctea, *f*. **on the way,** en camino; al paso; durante el viaje. **out of the way,** puesto a un lado; arrinconado; apartado, alejado; (imprisoned) en prisión; fuera del camino; remoto; (unusual) original. **over the way,** en frente; al otro lado (de la calle, etc.). **right of w.,** derecho de paso, *m*. **The ship left on its way to . . . ,** El barco zarpó con rumbo a . . . **the Way of the Cross,** vía crucis, *f*. **This way!** ¡Por aquí!; De este modo, Así. **this way and that,** en todas direcciones, por todos lados. **"This way to . . . ,"** «Dirección a . . .» **A . . . under way,** en camino; en marcha; en preparación. **to bar the way,** cerrar el paso. **to be in the way,** estorbar. **to be out of the way of doing,** haber perdido la costumbre de hacer (algo). **to clear the way,** abrir paso, abrir calle; *fig* preparar el terreno. **to force one's way through,** abrirse paso por. **to find a way,** encontrar un camino; *fig* encontrar medios. **to find one's way,** hallar el camino; orientarse. **to get into the way of,** contraer la costumbre de. **to get under way,** *naut* zarpar, hacerse a la vela; ponerse en marcha. **to give way,** ceder; (break) romper. **to go a long way,** ir lejos; contribuir mucho (a). **to have one's own way,** salir con la suya. **to keep out of the way,** *vt* and *vi* esconder(se); mantener(se) alejado; mantener(se) apartado. **to lose one's way,** perder el camino; desorientarse; *fig* extraviarse. **to make one's way,** abrirse paso. **to make one's way down,** bajar. **to make one's way round,** dar la vuelta a. **to make one's way up,** subir. **to make way,** hacer lugar; hacer sitio; dar paso (a). **to pay one's way,** ganarse la vida; pagar lo que se debe. **to prepare the way for,** preparar el terreno para. **to put out of the way,** poner a un lado; apartar; (kill) matar; (imprison) poner en la cárcel; hacer cautivo (a). **to see one's way,** poder ver el camino; poder orientarse; ver el modo de hacer algo; ver cómo se puede hacer algo. **ways and means,** medios y arbitrios, *m pl*. **way back,** camino de regreso, *m*; vuelta, *f*. **way down,** bajada, *f*. **way in,** entrada, *f*. **way out,** salida, *f*. **way round,** camino alrededor, *m*; solución, *f*; modo de evitar . . . , *m*. **way through,** paso, *m*. **way up,** subida, *f*
wayfarer *n* transeúnte, *mf*; viajero (-ra)
wayfaring *a* que va de viaje; errante, ambulante
waylay *vt* asechar, salir al paso (de)
wayside *n* borde del camino, *m*. *a* (of flowers) silvestre; (by the side of the road) en la carretera
wayward *a* caprichoso; desobediente; voluntarioso; travieso; rebelde
waywardness *n* desobediencia, indocilidad, *f*; voluntariedad, *f*; travesura, *f*; rebeldía, *f*
we *pron* nosotros, *m pl*; nosotras, *f pl*, (Usually omitted except for emphasis or for clarity.) **We are in the garden,** Estamos en el jardín. **We have come, but they are not here,** Nosotros hemos venido pero ellos no están aquí
weak *a* débil; flojo; frágil; delicado; (insecure) inseguro;

(of arguments) poco convincente; (of prices, markets, etc.) flojo, en baja; (sickly) *Lat. Am.* farruto, *Central America, Mexico* fifiriche. **w.-eyed,** de vista floja. **w.-kneed,** débil de rodillas; *fig* sin voluntad. **w.-minded,** sin carácter; pusilánime; **w. spot,** debilidad, *f;* flaco, *m;* lado débil, *m;* desventaja, *f*
weaken *vt* debilitar; (diminish) disminuir. *vi* debilitarse; flaquear, desfallecer; (give way) ceder
weakening *n* debilitación, *f. a* debilitante; enervante
weaker *a comp* más débil. **the w. sex,** el sexo débil
weakling *n* ser delicado, *m,* persona débil, *f;* cobarde, *m; inf* alfeñique, *m*
weakly *a* enfermizo, delicado, enclenque. *adv* débilmente
weakness *n* debilidad, *f;* imperfección, *f*
weal *n* bienestar, *m;* prosperidad, *f;* (blow) verdugo, *m*
wealth *n* riqueza, *f;* abundancia, *f;* bienes, *m pl*
wealthy *a* rico, adinerado, acaudalado; abundante (en)
wean *vt* destetar, ablactar; separar (de); privar (de); enajenar el afecto de; (of ideas) desaferrar (de)
weaning *n* ablactación, *f,* destete, *m*
weapon *n* arma, *f; pl* **weapons,** (*zool, bot*) medios de defensa, *m pl.* **steel w.,** arma blanca, *f*
wear *n* uso, *m;* gasto, *m;* deterioro, *m;* (fashion) moda, boga, *f.* **for hard w.,** para todo uso. **for one's own w.,** para su propio uso. **for evening w.,** para llevar de noche. **for summer w.,** para llevar en verano. **w. and tear,** uso y desgaste, *m;* deterioro natural, *m*
wear *vt* llevar; llevar puesto; traer; usar; (have) tener; (exhibit) mostrar; (be clad in) vestir; (waste) gastar; deteriorar; (make) hacer; (exhaust) agotar, cansar, consumir. *vi* (last) durar; (of persons) conservar(se); (of time) correr; avanzar. **She wears well,** Está bien conservada. **to w. one's heart on one's sleeve,** tener el corazón en la mano. **to w. the trousers,** *fig inf* llevar los pantalones. **to w. well,** durar mucho. **to w. away,** *vt* gastar, roer; (rub out) borrar; consumir. *vi* (of time) pasar lentamente, transcurrir despacio. **to w. down,** gastar; consumir; reducir; agotar las fuerzas de; destruir; (tire) fatigar. **to w. off,** *vt* destruir; borrar. *vi* quitarse; borrarse; *fig* desaparecer, pasar. **to w. on,** (of time) transcurrir, correr, pasar. **to w. out,** *vt* usar; romper con el uso; consumir, acabar con; (exhaust) agotar; (tire) rendir. *vi* usarse; romperse con el uso; consumirse
wearable *a* que se puede llevar
wearer *n* el, *m,* (*f,* la) que lleva alguna cosa
weariness *n* cansancio, *m,* fatiga, lasitud, *f;* aburrimiento, *m;* aversión, repugnancia, *f*
wearing *n* uso, *m;* desgaste, *m. a* (tiring) agotador; cansado. **w. apparel,** ropa, *f*
wearisome *a* cansado; laborioso; aburrido, tedioso, pesado
wearisomeness *n* cansancio, *m;* aburrimiento, tedio, hastío, *m*
weary *a* cansado, fatigado; aburrido; hastiado; impaciente; tedioso, enfadoso. *vt* cansar, fatigar; aburrir; hastiar; molestar. *vi* cansarse, fatigarse; aburrirse. **to w. for,** anhelar, suspirar por; (miss) echar de menos (a). **to w. of,** aburrirse de; (things) impacientarse de; (people) impacientarse con
weasel *n* comadreja, *f*
weather *n* tiempo, *m;* intemperie, *f;* (storm) tempestad, *f. a naut* del lado del viento; de barlovento. *vt* (of rain, etc.) desgastar; curtir; secar al aire; *naut* pasar a barlovento; (bear) aguantar, capear; (survive) sobrevivir a; luchar con. *vi* curtirse a la intemperie. **Andrew is a little under the w.,** Andrés está algo destemplado; (with drink) Andrés tiene una mona; (depressed) Andrés está melancólico. **to be bad (good) w.,** hacer mal (buen) tiempo. **What is the w. like?** ¿Qué tiempo hace? ¿Cómo está el tiempo? **w.-beaten,** curtido por la intemperie. **w. chart,** carta meteorológica, *f.* **w. conditions,** condiciones meteorológicas, *f pl.* **w. forecast,** pronóstico del tiempo, *m.* **w.-hardened,** endurecido a la intemperie. **w. prophet,** meteorologista,

mf **w. report,** boletín meteorológico, *m.* **w.-worn,** gastado por la intemperie; curtido por la intemperie
weathercock *n* veleta, *f*
weathering *n* desintegración por la acción atmosférica, *f*
weather-resistant *a* resistente a la intemperie
weave *vt* tejer; trenzar; entrelazar; *fig* tejer. *vi* tejer. *n* tejido, *m;* textura, *f*
weaver *n* tejedor (-ra)
weaving *n* tejido, *m;* tejeduría, *f.* **w. machine,** telar, *m*
web *n* tejido, *m;* tela, *f;* (network) red, *f;* (spider's) telaraña, *f;* (of a feather) barba, *f;* (of birds, etc.) membrana interdigital, *f;* (of intrigue) red, *f;* (snarl) lazo, *m,* trampa, *f.* **web-foot,** pie palmado, *m.* **web-footed,** palmípedo.
webbed *a* (of feet) unido por una membrana
wed *vt* casarse con; (join in marriage, cause to marry) casar; *fig* unir. *vi* estar casado; casarse
wedded *a* casado; matrimonial, conyugal; *fig* unido (a); aficionado (a), entusiasta (de), devoto (de); aferrado (a). **to be w. to one's own opinion,** estar aferrado a su propia opinión
wedding *n* boda, *f,* casamiento, *m;* (with golden, etc.) bodas, *f pl;* (union) enlace, *m, a* de boda, nupcial, matrimonial, conyugal; de novios, de la novia. **golden w.,** bodas de oro, *f pl.* **silver w.,** bodas de plata, *f pl.* **w. bouquet,** ramo de la novia, *m.* **w.-breakfast,** banquete de bodas, *m.* **w.-cake,** torta de la boda, *f,* pan de la boda, *m.* **w.-day,** día de la boda, *m.* **w.-march,** marcha nupcial, *f.* **w.-present,** regalo de boda, regalo de la boda, *m.* **w.-ring,** anillo de la boda, *m, Lat. Am.* argolla, *f.* **w. trip,** viaje de novios, *m*
wedge *n* cuña, *f;* (under a wheel) calza, alzaprima, *f; mil* cuña, mella, *f;* (of cheese) pedazo, *m. vt* acuñar, meter cuñas; (a wheel) calzar; (fix) sujetar. **to be the thin end of the w.,** ser el principio, ser el primer paso. **to drive a w.,** *mil* hacer mella, practicar una cuña. **to w. oneself in,** introducirse con dificultad (en). **w.-shaped,** cuneiforme
wedlock *n* matrimonio, *m*
Wednesday *n* miércoles, *m*
wee *a* pequeñito, chiquito. **a wee bit,** un poquito
weed *n* mala hierba, *f;* tabaco, *m;* (cigar) cigarro, *m;* (person) madeja, *f;* (*fig* evil) cizaña, *f. vt* carpir, desherbar, sachar, sallar, escardar. *Lat. Am.* desmalezar; *fig* extirpar, arrancar. **w.-grown,** cubierto de malas hierbas. **to w. out,** extirpar; quitar
weeder *n* (person) escardador (-ra); (implement) sacho, *m*
weedy *a* lleno de malas hierbas; *fig* raquítico
week *n* semana, *f.* **in a w.,** de hoy en ocho (días); en una semana; después de una semana. **once a w.,** una vez por semana. **a w. ago,** hace una semana. **a w. later** *Lat. Am.* a la semana. **Michael will come a w. from today,** Miguel llegará hoy en ocho. **w. in, w. out,** semana tras semana. **w.-day,** día de trabajo, día laborable, día de la semana que no sea el domingo. **on weekdays,** entre semana, *m.* **w.-end,** fin de semana, *m.* **w.-end case,** saco de noche, *m*
weekly *a* semanal, semanario; de cada semana. *adv* semanalmente, cada semana. *n* semanario, *m,* revista semanal, *f*
weep *vt and vi* llorar. **to w. for,** (a person) llorar (a); (on account of) llorar por; (with happiness, etc.) llorar de. **They wept for joy,** Lloraron de alegría
weeping *n* lloro, llanto, *m,* lágrimas, *f pl. a* lloroso, que llora; (of trees) llorón. **w.-willow,** sauce llorón, *m*
weevil *n* gorgojo, *m*
weigh *vt* pesar; (consider) considerar, ponderar, tomar en cuenta; comparar; (the anchor) levar. *vi* pesar; ser de importancia. **to w. anchor,** zarpar, levar el ancla, hacerse a la vela. **to w. down,** pesar sobre; sobrecargar; hacer inclinarse bajo; *fig* agobiar. **to be weighed down,** hundirse por su propio peso; *fig* estar agobiado. **to w. out,** pesar. **to w. with,** influir (en). **w.-bridge,** báscula, *f*

weighing *n* pesada, *f*; (weight) peso, *m*; (of the anchor) leva, *f*; (consideration) ponderación, consideración, *f*.

w.-machine, báscula, *f*

weight *n* peso, *m*; (heaviness) pesantez, *f*; cargo, *m*; (of a clock and as part of a system) pesa, *f*; *fig* peso, *m*, importancia, *f. vt* cargar; (a stick) emplomar; aumentar el peso (de); poner un peso (a). **gross w.,** peso bruto, *m*. **heavy w.,** peso pesado, *m*. **light w.,** peso ligero, *m*. **middle w.,** peso medio, *m*. **net w.,** peso neto, *m*. **to lose w.,** adelgazar. **loss of w.,** (of a person) adelgazamiento, *m*. **to put on w.,** cobrar carnes, hacerse más gordo. **to put the w.,** *sport* lanzar el peso. **to throw one's w.** about, *inf* darse importancia. **to try the w. of,** sopesar. **weights and measures,** pesas y medidas, *f pl.* **weightlifting,** halterofilia, *f*

weighty *a* pesado; (influential) influyente; importante, de peso; grave

weir *n* presa, esclusa, *f*; (for fish) cañal, *m*

weird *a* misterioso, sobrenatural; fantástico; mágico; (queer) raro, extraño. **the W. Sisters,** las Parcas

weirdly *adv* misteriosamente; fantásticamente; (queerly) de un modo raro, extrañamente

weirdness *n* misterio, *m*; cualidad fantástica, *f*; lo sobrenatural; (queerness) rareza, *f*

welcome *a* bienvenido; (pleasant) grato, agradable. *n* bienvenida, *f*; buena acogida, *f*; (reception) acogida, *f. vt* dar la bienvenida (a); acoger con alegría, acoger con entusiasmo; agasajar, festejar; (receive) acoger, recibir; recibir con gusto. **W.!** ¡Bienvenido! **to bid w.,** dar la bienvenida (a). **You are w.,** Estás bienvenido. **You are w. to it,** Está a su disposición

welcoming *a* acogedor, cordial, amistoso

weld *vt* soldar; combinar; unificar

welder *n* soldador, *m*

welding *n* soldadura, *f*; unión, fusión, *f*

welfare *n* bienestar, bien, *m*; (health) salud, *f*; prosperidad, *f*; intereses, *m pl*. **w. state,** estado benefactor, estado de beneficencia, estado socializante, *m*. **w. work,** trabajo social, *m*

well *a* bien; bien de salud; bueno; conveniente; (advantageous) provechoso; favorable; (happy) feliz; (healed) curado; (recovered) repuesto. **I am very w.,** Estoy muy bien. **to get w.,** ponerse bien. **to make w.,** curar. **w. enough,** bastante bien

well *adv* bien; (very) muy; favorablemente; convenientemente; (easily) sin dificultad. **as w.,** también. **as w. as,** tan bien como; además de. **That's all very w. but . . . ,** Todo eso está muy bien pero . . . **to be w. up in,** estar versado en. **to get on w. with,** llevarse bien con. **Very w.!** ¡Está bien!; Muy bien. **w. and good,** bien está. **w. now,** ahora bien. **w. then,** conque; pues bien. **w.-advised,** bien aconsejado; prudente. **w.-aimed,** certero. **w.-appointed,** bien provisto; (furnished) bien amueblado. **w.-attended,** concurrido. **w.-balanced,** bien equilibrado. **w.-behaved,** bien educado; (of animals) manso. **w.-being,** bienestar, *m*; felicidad, *f*. **w.-born,** bien nacido, de buena familia. **w.-bred,** bien criado, bien educado; (of animals) de pura raza. **w.-chosen,** bien escogido. **w.-defined,** bien definido. **w.-deserved,** bien merecido. **w.-disposed,** bien dispuesto; favorable; bien intencionado. **w.-doing,** *n* el obrar bien; obras de caridad, *f pl, a* bondadoso, caritativo. **w.-done,** *a* bien hecho. *interj* ¡bravo! **w.-educated,** instruido, culto. **w.-favored,** guapo, de buen parecer. **w.-founded,** bien fundado. **w.-groomed,** elegante. **w.-grounded,** bien fundado; bien instruido. **w.-informed,** instruido; culto, ilustrado. **w.-intentioned,** bien intencionado. **w.-known,** bien conocido, notorio, *Lat. Am.* de notado. **w.-meaning,** bien intencionado. **w.-modulated,** armonioso. **w.-off,** acomodado, adinerado; feliz. **w.-read,** culto, instruido. **w.-shaped,** bien hecho; bien formado. **w.-shaped nose,** nariz perfilada, *f*. **w.-spent,** bien empleado. **w.-spoken,** bien hablado; bien dicho. **w.-stocked,** bien provisto. **w.-suited,** apropiado. **w.-timed,** oportuno. **w.-to-do,** acomo-

dado, rico. **w.-wisher,** amigo (-ga). **w.-worn,** raído; (of paths) trillado

well *n* pozo, *m*; (of a stair) caja, *f*; cañón de escalera, *m*; (fountain) fuente, *f*, manantial, *m*; (of a fishing boat) vivar, *m*; (of a ship) sentina, *f*. **w.-sinker,** pocero, *m*

well *vi* chorrear, manar, brotar, fluir

Welsh *a* galés, de Gales. *n* (language) galés, *m*. **the W.,** los galeses

Welshman *n* galés, *m*

Welshwoman *n* galesa, *f*

welt *n* (of shoe) vira, *f*, cerquillo, *m*; (in knitting) ribete, *m*; (weal) verdugo, *m*

Weltanschauung *n* cosmovisión, postura de vida, *f*

welter *vi* revolcarse; bañarse (en), nadar (en). *n* confusión, *f*, tumulto, *m*; mezcla, *f*. **w.-weight,** peso welter, *m*

wench *n* mozuela, muchacha, *f*

wend *vt* dirigir, encaminar. *vi* ir. **to w. one's way,** dirigir sus pasos, seguir su camino

west *n* oeste, *m*; poniente, *m*; occidente, *m. a* del oeste; occidental. *adv* hacia el oeste, a poniente; al occidente. **W. Indian,** de las Antillas, de las Indias Occidentales. **w.-north-w.,** oesnorueste, *m*. **w.-south-w.,** oessudueste, *m*. **w. wind,** viento del oeste, poniente, *m*

westerly *a* del oeste; hacia el oeste; occidental

western *a* occidental; del oeste. *n* (novel) novela caballista, *f*; (film) película del oeste, *f*

Western Hemispheric americano

westernized *a* influido por el occidente

westernmost *a* más al oeste

West Indies Indias Occidentales, *f pl*

westward *a* que está al oeste. *adv* hacia el oeste; hacia el occidente

wet *a* mojado; húmedo; (rainy) lluvioso. *vt* mojar; humedecer. *n* (rain) lluvia, *f*. **"Mind the wet paint!"** «¡Cuidado, recién pintado!» **to be wet,** estar mojado; (of the weather) llover. **to get wet,** mojarse. **wet blanket,** *fig* aguafiestas, *mf* **wet through,** (of persons) calado, hecho una sopa. **wet-nurse,** nodriza, *Lat. Am.* criandera, *f*

wetting *n* mojada, *f*; humectación, *f*; (soaking) remojo, *m*

whack *n* golpe, *m*; (try) tentativa, *f*; (portion) porción, parte, *f. vt* golpear, aporrear, pegar

whale *n* ballena, *f*. **sperm w.,** cachalote, *m*. **w.-oil,** aceite de ballena, *m*

whalebone *n* barbas de ballena, *f pl*, ballena, *f*

whaler *n* (man) ballenero, pescador de ballenas, *m*; (boat) buque ballenero, *m*

whaling *a* ballenero. *n* pesca de ballenas, *f*. **w.-gun,** cañón arponero, *m*

wharf *n* muelle, embarcadero, descargadero, *m, vt* amarrar al muelle

what *a pron* (interrogative and exclamatory) qué; cómo; (relative) que; el que, *m*; la que, *f*; lo que, *neut*; los que, *m pl*; las que, *f pl*; (which, interrogative) cuál, *mf*; cuáles, *mf pl*; (how many) cuantos, *m pl*; cuantas, *f pl*; (interrogative and exclamatory) cuántos, *m pl*; cuántas, *f pl*; (how much, interrogative and exclamatory) cuánto, *m*; cuánta, *f*. **And w. not,** Y qué sé yo qué más. **Make w. changes you will,** Haz los cambios que quieras. **W. confidence he had . . . ,** La confianza que tenía . . . **W. is this called?** ¿Cómo se llama esto? **W. did they go there for?** ¿Por qué fueron? **W. do you take me for?** ¿Por quién me tomas? **That was not w. he said,** No fue eso lo que dijo. **to know what's w.,** saber cuántas son cinco. **You have heard the latest news, w.?** Has oído las últimas noticias, ¿verdad? **W. a pity!** ¡Qué lástima! **W., do you really believe it?** ¿Lo crees de veras? **W. else?** ¿Qué más? **W. for?** ¿Para qué? **what's-his-name,** fulano (-na) de tal, *m*. **W. ho!** ¡Hola! **W. if . . . ?** ¿Qué será si . . . ? **W. is the matter?** ¿Qué pasa? ¿Qué hay? **w. though . . . ,** aun cuando . . . ; ¿Qué importa qué? **w. with one thing, w. with another,** entre una cosa y otra. **What's more, . . .** Es más, . . .

whatever *a pron* cuanto; todo lo que; cualquier cosa que; cualquier. **W. sacrifice is necessary,** Cualquier sacrificio que sea necesario. **W. I have is yours,** Todo lo que tenga es vuestro. **W. happens,** Venga lo que venga. **It is of no use w.,** No sirve absolutamente para nada

wheal *n.* See **weal**

wheat *n* trigo, *m. a* de trigo. **summer w.,** trigo tremesino, *m.* **whole w.,** *a* de trigo entero. **w.-ear,** espiga de trigo, *f.* **w.-field,** trigal, *m.* **w.-sheaf,** gavilla de trigo, *f*

wheedle *vt* lagotear, engatusar, *Lat. Am. also* engaratusar; (flatter) halagar; (with out) sacar con mimos

wheedling *a* zalamero, mimoso; marrullero. *n* lagotería, *f*, mimos, *m pl;* (flattery) halagos, *m pl;* marrullería, *f*

wheel *n* rueda, *f;* (bicycle) bicicleta, *f;* (for steering a ship) timón, *m;* rueda del timón, *f;* (for steering a car) volante, *m;* (for spinning) rueca, *f;* (potter's) rueda de alfarero, *f;* (of birds) vuelo, *m;* (turn) vuelta, *f; mil* conversión, *f.* **Catherine w.,** (firework) rueda de Santa Catalina, *f.* **back w.,** rueda trasera, *f.* **front w.,** rueda delantera, *f.* **to break on the w.,** enrodar. **to go on wheels,** ir en ruedas; *fig* ir viento en popa. **to take the w.,** (in a ship) tomar el timón; tomar el volante. **w. of fortune,** rueda de la fortuna, *f.* **w.-chair,** silla de ruedas, *f.* **w.-house,** timonera, *f.* **w.-mark,** rodada, *f*

wheel *vt* hacer rodar; (push) empujar; (drive) conducir; transportar; llevar; pasear; (turn) hacer girar. *vi* girar; dar vueltas; ir en bicicleta. **to w. about,** cambiar de frente; volverse; cambiar de rumbo

wheelbarrow *n* carretilla, *f*

wheeled *a* de . . . ruedas; con ruedas. **w. chair,** silla de ruedas, *f*

wheeler-dealer *n Lat. Am.* ardilla, *f*

wheeling *n* rodaje, *m; mil* conversión, *f;* (of birds) vuelos, *m pl,* vueltas, *f pl.* **free-w.,** rueda libre, *f*

wheelwright *n* carpintero de carretas, ruedero, *m*

wheeze *vi* ser asmático, jadear, respirar fatigosamente, resollar

wheezing *n* resuello, jadeo, *m;* respiración fatigada, *f*

whelp *n* cachorro (-rra). *vi and vt* parir

when *adv* cuando (interrogative, ¿cuándo?); (as soon as) tan pronto como, en cuanto; (meaning 'and then') y luego, y entonces; (although) aunque. **I will see you w. I return,** Te veré cuando vuelva. **W. he came to see me he was already ill,** Cuando vino a verme estaba enfermo ya. **We returned a week ago, since w. I have not been out,** Volvimos hace ocho días y desde entonces no he salido. **Since w.?** ¿Desde cuándo?

whence *adv* de donde (interrogative, de dónde); a donde (interrogative a dónde); por donde, de que; por lo que. **W. does he come?** ¿De dónde viene? **W. comes it that?** ¿Cómo es que . . . ?

whenever *adv* cuando quiera que, siempre que; cada vez que, todas las veces que; cuando

where *adv pron* donde (interrogative, dónde); en donde; en que (interrogative, en qué); (to where with verbs of motion) a donde (interrogative, a dónde); (from where with verbs of motion) de donde (interrogative, de dónde). **W. are you going to?** ¿A dónde va Vd.? **This is w. we get out,** (of a bus, etc.) Nos apeamos aquí

whereabouts *adv* (interrogative) dónde; (relative) donde. *n* paradero, *m*

whereas *conjunc* (inasmuch as) visto que, ya que; (although) mientras (que)

whereat *adv* por lo cual; a lo cual

whereby *adv* cómo; por qué; por el cual, con el cual

wherefore *adv* (why) por qué; por lo cual. *n* porqué, *m*

wherein *adv* en donde (interrogative, en dónde); en que (interrogative, en qué)

whereinto *adv* en donde; dentro del cual; en lo cual

whereof *adv* de que; (whose) cuyo

whereon *adv* sobre que; en qué

whereto *adv* adonde; a lo que

whereupon *adv* dónde; sobre lo cual, con lo cual; en consecuencia de lo cual

wherever *adv* dondequiera (que), en cualquier sitio; adondequiera (que). **Sit w. you like,** Siéntate donde te parezca bien

wherewith *adv* con que (interrogative, con qué)

wherewithal *n* lo necesario; dinero necesario, *m*

whet *vt* (knives, etc.) afilar, amolar, aguzar; (curiosity, etc.) excitar, estimular

whether *conjunc* si; que; sea que, ya que. **W. he will or no,** Que quiera, que no quiera. **w. or not,** si o no

whetstone *n* afiladera, amoladera, piedra de amolar, *f*

whetting *n* aguzadura, amoladura, *f;* (of curiosity, etc.) estimulación, excitación, *f*

whey *n* suero (de la leche), *m*

which *a* and *pron* cuál, *mf;* cuáles, *mf pl;* que (interrogative, qué); el cual, *m;* la cual, *f;* lo cual, *neut;* los cuales, *m pl;* las cuales, *f pl;* el que, *m;* la que, *f;* lo que, *neut;* los que, *m pl;* las que, *f pl;* (who) quien. **all of w.,** todo lo cual, etc. **in w.,** en donde, en el que; donde. **the w.,** el cual, la cual, etc. **W. would you like?** ¿Cuál quieres? **The documents w. I have seen,** Los documentos que he visto. **W. way have we to go?** ¿Por dónde hemos de ir?

whichever *a* and *pron* cualquiera (que), *mf;* cualesquiera, *mf pl;* el que, en; la que, *f;* (of persons only) quienquiera (que), *mf;* quienesquiera (que), *mf pl* **Give me w. you like,** Dame el que quieras. **I shall take w. of you would like to come,** Me llevaré a cualquiera de Vds. que guste de venir

whiff *n* (of air) soplo, *m;* vaho, *m;* fragancia, *f*

while *n* rato, *m;* momento, *m;* tiempo, *m.* **after a w.,** al cabo de algún tiempo, después de algún tiempo. **a little w. ago,** hace poco. **all this w.,** en todo este tiempo. **at whiles,** a ratos, de vez en cuando. **between whiles,** de cuando en cuando; entre tanto. **It is worth your w. to do it,** Vale la pena de hacerse. **Mary smiled the w.,** María mientras tanto se sonreía. **once in a w.,** de vez en cuando; en ocasiones

while *conjunc* mientras (que); al (followed by an infinitive); al mismo tiempo que; a medida que; (although) aunque; si bien. **w. I was walking down the street,** mientras andaba por la calle, al andar yo por la calle. *vt* **to w. (away),** pasar, entretener. **to w. away the time,** pasar el rato

whim *n* capricho, antojo, *m;* manía, *f;* extravagancia, *f;* fantasía, *f*

whimper *n* quejido, sollozo, gemido, *m, vi* lloriquear, quejarse, sollozar, gemir

whimpering *n* lloriqueo, llanto, *m, a* de lloriquea

whimsical *a* antojadizo, caprichoso; fantástico

whimsicality *n* capricho, *m,* extravagancia, *f;* fantasía, *f*

whimsically *adv* caprichosamente; fantásticamente

whine *vi* gimotear, lloriquear; quejarse

whining *n* gimoteo, lloriqueo, *m;* quejumbres, *f pl. a* que lloriquea; quejumbroso

whinny *n* relincho, hin, *m, vi* relinchar

whip *vt* azotar; pegar; *cul* batir; *sew* sobrecoser; (ropes, etc.) ligar; (defeat) vencer. *vi* moverse rápidamente. **to w. down,** (of rain) bajar volando, bajar corriendo. *vt* arrebatar (de). **to w. in,** entrar precipitadamente (en), penetrar apresuradamente (en). **to w. off,** cazar a latigazos, despachar a golpes; (remove) quitar rápidamente; (persons) llevar corriendo, llevar aprisa. **to w. open,** abrir rápidamente. **to w. out,** *vt* (draw) sacar rápidamente; (utter) saltar diciendo (que); proferir. *vi* escabullirse, escaparse, salir apresuradamente. **to w. round,** volverse de repente. **to w. up,** (horses, etc.) avivar con el látigo; (snatch) coger de repente agarrar; (gather) reunir. *vi* (mount) subir corriendo

whip *n* azote, zurriago, *Lat. Am.* chicote, *m;* (riding) látigo, *m.* **blow with a w.,** latigazo, *m.* **to have the w.-hand,** mandar, tener la sartén por el mango; tener la ventaja. **w.-cord,** tralla del látigo, *f*

whippet *n* especie de perro (-rra) lebrero (-ra)

whipping *n* paliza, *f,* vapuleo, azotamiento, *m.* **w. post,** picota, *f.* **w. top,** trompo, *m,* peonza, *f*

whirl *n* vuelta, *f,* giro, *m;* rotación, *f; fig* torbellino, *m. vi* girar; dar vueltas; (dance) bailar, danzar. *vt* hacer girar; dar vueltas (a); (carry) llevar rápidamente. **to w. along,** volar (por), pasar aprisa (por); dejar atrás los vientos, correr velozmente. **to w. past,** pasar volando (por); pasar como una exhalación. **to w. through,** atravesar rápidamente, cruzar volando

whirligig *n* perinola, *f;* (merry-go-round) tiovivo, *m*

whirlpool *n* vórtice, remolino, *m; fig* vorágine, *f*

whirlwind *n* torbellino, *m,* manga de viento, *f*

whirr *n* zumbido, *m;* (of wings) ruido (de las alas), *m. vi* girar; zumbar

whirring *n* zumbido, *m;* ruido, *m. a* que gira; que zumba

whisk *n* cepillo, *m; cul* batidor, *m;* (movement) movimiento rápido, *m. vt cul* batir; (wag) menear, mover rápidamente; (with off, away) quitar rápidamente; sacudir; arrebatar; (take away a person) llevarse (a). *vi* moverse rápidamente; andar rápidamente

whiskers *n pl* mostacho, *m,* patillas, barbas, *f pl;* (of a feline) bigotes, *m pl*

whiskered *a* bigotudo

whisky *n* güisqui, *m*

whisper *n* cuchicheo, *m;* (rumour) voz, *f;* (of leaves, etc.) susurro, murmullo, *m. vi and vt* cuchichear, hablar al oído; (of leaves, etc.) susurrar; (of rumors) murmurar. **in a w.,** al oído, en un susurro

whisperer *n* cuchicheador (-ra); (gossip) murmurador (-ra)

whispering *n* cuchicheo, *m;* susurro, *m;* (gossip) murmurio, *m.* **w. gallery,** galería de los murmullos, *f. inf* sala de los secretos, *f*

whistle *n* (sound) silbido, silbo, *m;* (instrument) pito, silbato, *m; inf* gaznate, *m. vi and vt* silbar. **blast on the w.,** pitido, *m.* **to w. for,** llamar silbando; *inf* esperar sentado, buscar en vano

whistler *n* silbador (-ra)

whistling *n* silbido, *m, a* silbador

whit *n* pizca, *f,* bledo, *m.* **not a w.,** ni pizca

Whit, Whitsun *a* de Pentecostés. **W. Monday,** lunes de Pentecostés, *m*

white *a* blanco; pálido; puro. *n* color blanco, blanco, *m;* (pigment) pintura blanca, *f;* (whiteness) blancura, *f;* (of egg) clara (del huevo), *f;* (person) blanco, *m.* **Elizabeth went w.,** Isabel se puso pálida. **the w.,** (billiards) la blanca. **the w. of the eye,** lo blanco del ojo. **w. ant,** hormiga blanca, termita, *f.* **w. cabbage,** repollo, *m.* **w. caps,** (of waves) cabrillas, *f pl;* (of mountains) picos blancos, *m pl.* **w. clover,** trébol blanco, *m.* **w. corpuscle,** glóbulo blanco, *m.* **w. currant,** grosella blanca, *f.* **w. elephant,** elefante (-ta) blanco (-ca). **w. ensign,** pabellón blanco, *m.* **w.-faced,** de cara pálida. **w. fish,** pescado blanco, *m.* **w. flag,** bandera blanca, *f.* **w.-haired,** de pelo blanco. **w. heat,** calor blanco, *m,* candencia, *f;* ardor, *m.* **w. horses,** cabrillas, palomas, *f pl.* **w.-hot,** incandescente. **W. House, the,** la Casa Blanca, *f.* **w. lead,** albayalde, *m.* **w. lie,** mentira inocente, mentira oficiosa, mentira piadosa, la mentirilla, *f.* **w. man,** blanco, hombre de raza blanca, *m.* **the white man's burden,** la misión sagrada de la civilización blanca, *f.* **w. meat,** carne blanca, pechuga, *f.* **w. paper,** libro blanco, *m.* **w. sauce,** salsa blanca, *f.* **w. slave,** víctima de la trata de blancas, *f.* **w. slavery,** trata de blancas, *f.* **w. sugar,** azúcar blanco, azúcar de flor, *m.* **w. woman,** mujer de raza blanca, *f*

whiten *vt* blanquear. *vi* blanquearse

whiteness *n* blancura, *f;* palidez, *f;* pureza, *f; poet* nieve, *f*

whitening *n* blanqueo, *m;* blanco de España, *m;* blanco para los zapatos, *m*

whitewash *vt* blanquear, jalbegar, encalar; *(fig* of faults) disculpar, justificar

whitewashing *n* blanqueo, *m,* encaladura, *f*

whither *adv* (interrogative) adónde; (with a clause) adonde

whithersoever *adv* adondequiera

whiting *n* blanco de España, *m;* blanco para los zapatos, *m;* (fish) pescadilla, *f,* merlango, *m*

whitish *a* blanquecino

whitlow *n* panadizo, *m*

Whitsunday *n* domingo de Pentecostés, *m*

Whitsuntide *n* pascua de Pentecostés, *f*

whittle *n* navaja, *f. vt* cercenar, cortar; (sharpen) afilar, sacar punta (a); tallar; *fig* reducir. **to w. away, down,** *fig* reducir a nada

whizz *n* silbido, zumbido, *m, vi* silbar, zumbar

whizzing *n* silbido, *m, a* que zumba

who *pron* (interrogative) quién, *mf;* quiénes, *mf pl;* (relative) quien, *mf;* quienes, *mf pl;* que; (in elliptical constructions the person that, etc.) el que, *m;* la que, *f;* los que, *m pl;* las que, *f pl*

whoa *interj* ¡so!

whoever *pron* quienquiera (que); cualquiera (que); quien. **Give it to w. you like,** Dáselo a quien te parezca bien

whole *a* (healthy) sano; (uninjured) ileso, entero; todo. *n* todo, *m;* total, *m;* totalidad, *f;* conjunto, *m.* **on the w.,** por regla general, en general; en conjunto. **the w. week,** la semana entera, toda la semana. **w.-hearted,** sincero, genuino; entusiasta. **w.-heartedly,** de todo corazón. **w.-heartedness,** sinceridad, *f;* entusiasmo, *m.* **w. length,** de cuerpo entero. **w. number,** número entero, *m*

wholemeal *n* harina de trigo entero, *f, a* de trigo entero

wholeness *n* totalidad, *f;* integridad, *f;* todo, *m*

wholesale *a com* al por mayor; en grueso; *fig* general; en masa. *n* venta al por mayor, *f.* **w. price,** precio al por mayor, *m.* **w. trade,** comercio al por mayor, *m*

wholesaler *n* comerciante al por mayor, *mf* mercader de grueso, *m*

wholesome *a* sano; saludable; (edifying) edificante

wholesomeness *n* sanidad, *f;* lo sano; lo saludable

wholly *adv* completamente, enteramente, totalmente; integralmente; del todo

whom *pron* quien; a quien, *mf;* a quienes, *mf pl;* (interrogative) quién, *mf;* a quiénes, *mf pl;* al que, *m;* a la que, *f;* a los que, *m pl;* a las que, *f pl.* **from w.,** de quien, *f;* (interrogative) de quién. **the man w. you saw,** el hombre a quien viste

whoop *n* alarido, grito, *m;* estertor de la tos ferina, *m. vi* dar gritos, chillar; (whooping-cough) toser

whooping cough *n* tos ferina, coqueluche, *f*

whore *n* puta, ramera, *f, Lat. Am.* araña, *f*

whorl *n* (of a shell) espira, *f; bot* verticilo, *m;* (of a spindle) tortera, *f*

whorled *a bot* verticilado; (of shells) en espira

whose *pron* cuyo, *m;* cuya, *f;* cuyos, *m pl;* cuyas, *f pl;* de quien, *mf;* de quienes, *mf pl;* (interrogative) de quién, de quiénes; **W. daughter is she?** ¿De quién es ella la hija? **This is the writer w. name I always forget,** Este es el autor cuyo nombre siempre olvido

whosoever *pron.* See **whoever**

why *adv* (*interrogative*) por qué; (on account of which) por el cual, *m;* por la cual, *f;* por lo cual, *neut;* por los cuales, *m pl;* por las cuales, *f pl;* (how) cómo. *n* ni porqué, *m, interj* ¡qué!; ¡cómo!; ¡toma!; sí. **not to know the why or wherefore,** no saber ni el porqué ni el cómo, no saber ni el qué ni el por qué. **Why! I have just come,** ¡Si no hago más de llegar! **Why not?** ¿Por qué no? ¡Cómo no!

wick *n* mecha, torcida, *f*

wicked *a* malo; malvado, perverso; pecaminoso; malicioso; (mischievous) travieso

wickedly *adv* mal; perversamente; maliciosamente

wickedness *n* maldad, *f;* perversidad, *f;* pecado, *m;* (mischievousness) travesura, *f*

wicker *n* mimbre, *m, a* de mimbre

wicket *n* postigo, portillo, *m;* (half-door) media puerta, *f;* (at cricket) meta, *f.* **w.-keeper,** guardameta, *m*

wide *a* ancho; (in measurements) de ancho; vasto; extenso; grande; amplio; (loose) holgado; (distant) lejos; liberal; general, comprensivo. *adv* lejos; completamente. **far and w.,** por todas partes. **to be too w.,** ser muy ancho; estar muy ancho; (of garments) venir muy ancho. **two feet w.,** dos pies de ancho. **w.-awake,** muy despierto; despabilado; vigilante. **w.-eyed,** con los ojos muy abiertos; asombrado. **w.-open,** abierto de par en par

widely *adv* extensamente; generalmente; (very) muy

widen *vt* ensanchar; extender. *vi* ensancharse; extenderse

widening *n* ensanche, *m*; extensión, *f*

widespread *a* universal, generalizado; extenso; esparcido. **to become w.,** generalizarse

widow *n* viuda, *f*. *vt* dejar viuda; dejar viudo; *fig* privar. **to be a grass w.,** estar viuda. **to become a w.,** enviudar, perder al esposo. **widow's pension,** viudedad, *f*. **widow's weeds,** luto de viuda, *m*

widowed *a* viudo

widower *n* viudo, *m*. **to become a w.,** perder a la esposa, enviudar

widowerhood, widowhood *n* viudez, *f*

width *n* anchura, *f*; (of cloth) ancho, *m*; (of mind) liberalismo, *m*. **double w.,** (cloth) doble ancho, *m*

wield *vt* (a scepter) empuñar; (power, etc.) ejercer; (a pen, sword) manejar

wife *n* esposa, mujer, *f*; mujer, *f*; comadre, *f*. **husband and w.,** los cónyuges, los esposos. **old wives' tale,** cuento de viejas, *m*. **The Merry Wives of Windsor,** Las alegres comadres de Windsor. **to take to w.,** contraer matrimonio con, tomar como esposa (a)

wifely *a* de esposa, de mujer casada; de mujer de su casa; conyugal

wig *n* peluca, *f*; (hair) cabellera, *f*. **top wig,** peluquín, *m*. **wigmaker,** peluquero, *m*

wigged *a* con peluca, de peluca

wigging *n* (scolding) peluca, *f*

wigwam *n* tienda de indios, *f*

wild *a* (of animals, men, land) salvaje; (barren) desierto, yermo; (mountainous) riscoso, montañoso; (of plants, birds) silvestre; montés; (disarranged) en desorden, desarreglado; (complete) absoluto, completo; (dissipated) disipado; vicioso; (foolish) alocado; (of the sea) bravío; (of weather, etc.) borrascoso; (mad with delight, etc.) loco; (frantic, mad) frenético, loco; (with 'talk,' etc.) extravagante; insensato, desatinado; (shy) arisco; (incoherent) inconexo, incoherente; (frightened) alarmado, espantado; (wilful) travieso, indomable. *n* tierra virgen, *f*; desierto, *m*; soledad, *f*. **It made me w.,** (angry) Me hizo rabiar. **to run w.,** volver al estado silvestre; (of persons) llevar una vida de salvajes; volverse loco. **to shoot w.,** errar el tiro. **to spread like w. fire,** propagarse como el fuego. **w. beast,** fiera, *f*. **w. boar,** jabalí, *m*. **w. cat,** gato montés, *Lat. Am.* lince, *m*. **w. duck,** pato silvestre, *m*. **w. goat,** cabra montesa, *f*. **w.-goose chase,** caza infructuosa, *f*; empresa quimérica, *f*. **w. oats,** avenas locas, *f pl*; *fig* indiscreciones de la juventud, *f pl*. **to sow one's w. oats,** andarse a la flor del berro

wilderness *n* desierto, *m*; yermo, páramo, despoblado, *m*; soledad, *f*; (jungle) selva, *f*; (maze) laberinto, *m*; infinidad, *f*

wildly *adv* en un estado salvaje; sin cultivo; (rashly) desatinadamente; sin reflexión, sin pensar; (incoherently) incoherentemente; (stupidly, of looking, etc.) tontamente; (in panic) con ojos espantados, con terror en los ojos, alarmado

wildness *n* salvajez, *f*; estado silvestre, *m*; naturaleza silvestre, *f*; (ferocity) ferocidad, *f*; (of the wind, sea) braveza, *f*; (of the wind) violencia, *f*; (impetuosity) impetuosidad, *f*; (of statements, etc.) extravagancia, *f*; (incoherence) incoherencia, *f*; (disorder) desorden, *m*; (wilfulness, of children) travesuras, *f pl*; (of the expression) gesto espantado, *m*

wile *n* estratagema, *f*, engaño, *m*, ardid, *f*

wilily *adv* astutamente

wiliness *n* astucia, *f*

will *n* voluntad, *f*; albedrío, *m*; (wish) deseo, *m*; (pleasure) discreción, *f*, placer, *m*; (legal document) testamento, *m*. **against my w.,** contra mi voluntad. **at w.,** a voluntad; a gusto; a discreción. **free w.,** libre albedrío, *m*. **of one's own free w.,** por su propia voluntad. **iron w.,** voluntad de hierro, *f*. **last w. and testament,** última disposición, última voluntad, *f*. **to do with a w.,** hacer con toda el alma, hacer con entusiasmo. **to make one's w.,** otorgar (hacer) su testamento. **w.-power,** fuerza de voluntad, *f*

will *vt* querer; disponer, ordenar; (bequeath) legar, dejar en testamento, mandar; (oblige) sugestionar (a una persona) para que haga algo; hipnotizar. *vi aux.* querer; (As a sign of the future it is not translated separately in Spanish) **I w. come tomorrow,** Vendré mañana. **John does not approve, but I w. go,** Juan no lo aprueba pero yo quiero ir. **Do what you w.,** Haga lo que a Vd. le parezca bien, Haga lo que Vd. quiera; Haga lo que haga. **Boys w. be boys,** Los niños son siempre niños. **He w. not (won't) do it,** No lo hará; No quiere hacerlo

willful *a* rebelde, voluntarioso; (of children) travieso; (of crimes, etc.) premeditado

willfully *adv* voluntariosamente; intencionalmente; (of committing crimes) con premeditación

willfulness *n* rebeldía, *f*; (obstinacy) terquedad, obstinación, *f*

William the Silent Guillermo el Taciturno

willing *a* dispuesto, inclinado; (serviceable) servicial; deseoso; espontáneo; complaciente; gustoso; (willingly) de buena gana. **to be w.,** estar dispuesto (a), querer; consentir (en)

willingly *adv* de buena gana, con gusto

willingness *n* buena voluntad, *f*; deseo de servir, *m*; complacencia, *f*; (consent) consentimiento, *m*

will-o'-the-wisp *n* fuego fatuo, *m*

willow *n* sauce, *m*. **weeping w.,** sauce llorón, *m*. **w.-pattern china,** porcelana de estilo chino, *f*. **w. tree,** sauce, *m*

willowy *a* lleno de sauces; (slim) cimbreño, esbelto, alto y delgado

willy nilly *adv* de buen o mal grado, mal que bien

wilt *vi* (of plants) marchitarse, secarse; *fig* languidecer; ajarse. *vt* marchitar; *fig* ajar; hacer languidecer

wily *a* astuto, chuzón

wimple *n* toca, *f*

win *vt* ganar; (reach) alcanzar, lograr; (a victory, etc.) llevarse; conquistar. *vi* ganar; triunfar. *n* triunfo, *m*. **to win back,** volver a ganar; recobrar

wince *vi* retroceder, recular; (flinch) quejarse; (of a horse) respingar. *n* respingo, *m*. **without wincing,** sin quejarse; estoicamente

winch *n* cabria, *f*; (handle) manubrio, *m*

wind *n* viento, *m*; aire, *m*; (flatulence) flatulencia, *f*; (breath) respiración, *f*, aliento, *m*; (idle talk) paja, *f*. **breath of w.,** soplo de viento, *m*. **following w.,** viento en popa, *m*. **high w.,** viento alto, viento fuerte, *m*. **land w.,** viento terrenal, *m*. **It's an ill w. that blows nobody good,** No hay mal que por bien no venga. **There is something in the w.,** Hay algo en el aire, Se trama algo. **to get w. of,** husmear. **to sail before the w.,** navegar de viento en popa. **The w. stiffened,** Refrescó el viento. **You took the w. out of his sails,** Le deshinchaste las velas. **w.-instrument,** instrumento de viento, *m*. **w.-proof,** a prueba del viento. **w.-swept,** expuesto a todos los vientos. **w. storm,** ventarrón, *m*

wind *vi* serpentear; desfilar lentamente; torcerse. *vt* (turn) dar vueltas (a); (a handle) manejar, mover; (a watch) dar cuerda (a); (wool, etc.) devanar, ovillar; (wrap) envolver; (of arms, embrace) rodear (con); (a horn) tocar. **to w. off,** devanar; desenrollar. **to w. round,** (wrap) envolver; (skirt) rodear; (embrace) ceñir con (los brazos); (pass by) pasar por; deslizarse por; (of snakes) enroscarse. **to w. up,** (a watch) dar cuerda (a); (thread) devanar; (conclude) concluir; *com* liquidar; (excite) agitar, emocionar

windbag *n* pandero, *m,* sacamuelas, *mf*

winder *n* (person) devanador (-ra); (machine) devanadera, *f;* (of a clock) llave, *f*

windfall *n* fruta caída del árbol, *f;* (good luck) breva, *f;* ganancia inesperada, lotería, *f*

windiness *n* tiempo ventoso, *m;* situación expuesta a todos los vientos, *f;* (of speech) pomposidad, verbosidad, *f*

winding *a* tortuoso; (e.g., road) sinuoso; serpentino; en espiral. *n* tortuosidad, *f;* meandro, recoveco, *m,* vuelta, curva, *f.* **w. sheet,** mortaja, *f,* sudario, *m.* **w. stair,** escalera de caracol, *f.* **w.-up,** conclusión, *f; com* liquidación, *f*

windlass *n* torno, *m*

windless *a* sin viento

windmill *n* molino de viento, *m*

window *n* ventana, *f;* (of a shop) escaparate, *Mexico* aparador, *m;* (in a train, car, bank, etc.) ventanilla, *f;* (booking office) taquilla, *f;* (of a church) vidriera, *f.* **casement w.,** ventana, *f.* **sash w.,** ventana de guillotina, *f.* **small w.,** ventanilla, *f.* **stained glass w.,** vidriera, *f.* **to lean out of the w.,** asomarse a la ventana. **to look out of the w.,** mirar por la ventana. **w. blind,** (Venetian) persiana, *f;* transparente, *m;* (against the sun) toldo, *m.* **w.-dresser,** decorador (-ra) de escaparates. **w. frame,** marco de ventana, *m.* **w.-pane,** cristal (de ventana), *m.* **w.-shutter,** contraventana, *f.* **w.-sill,** repisa de la ventana, *f,* alféizar, *m*

windpipe *n* tráquea, *f*

windscreen *n* parabrisas, guardabrisa, *m.* **w.-wiper,** limpiaparabrisas, limpiavidrios, *m*

windward *n* barlovento, *m.* *a* de barlovento. *adv* a barlovento

windy *a* ventoso; expuesto al viento; (of style) hinchado, pomposo. **It is w.,** Hace viento

wine *n* vino, *m;* zumo fermentado (de algunas frutas), *m. a* de vino; de vinos; para vino. **in w.,** *cul* en vino; (drunk) ebrio, borracho. **heavy w.,** vino fuerte, *m.* **light w.,** vino ligero, *m.* **local w.,** vino del país, *m.* **matured w.,** vino generoso, *m.* **red w.,** vino tinto, *m.* **thin w.,** vinillo, *m.* **white w.,** vino blanco, *m.* **w.-cellar,** bodega, cueva, *f.* **w.-colored,** de color de vino. **w.-cooler,** cubo para enfriar vinos, *m.* **w. country,** tierra de vino, *f.* **w. decanter,** garrafa para vino, *f.* **w.-grower,** vinicultor (-ra). **w.-growing,** *n* vinicultura, *f. a* vinícola. **w. lees,** zupia, *f.* **w. merchant,** comerciante en vinos, *mf.* vinatero, *m.* **w.-press,** lagar, *m.* **w.-taster,** catavinos, *m.* **w. waiter,** bodeguero, *m*

wineskin *n* bota, *f,* odre, pellejo, *m*

wing *n* (of a bird and *zool, arch, aer, mil, bot*) ala, *f;* (flight) vuelo, *m; theat* bastidor, *m; fig* protección, *f. vt* dar alas (a); llevar sobre las alas; (wound) herir en el ala; herir en el brazo; volar por. *vi* volar. **beating of wings,** batir de alas, aleteo, *m.* **in the wings,** *theat* entre bastidores. **to w. al** vuelo. **to clip a (per son's) wings,** cortar (*or* quebrar) las alas (a). **under his w.,** bajo su protección. **w.-case,** (élitro de un insecto), *m.* **w. chair,** sillón con orejas, *m.* **w.-commander,** teniente coronel de aviación, *m.* **w.-span,** (*zool* and *aer*) envergadura, *f.* **w.-spread,** extensión del ala, *f.* **w.-tip,** punta del ala, *f*

winged *a* alado, con alas; (in compounds) de alas . . .; (swift) alado; (of style) elevado, alado

wink *vi* (blink) pestañear; (as a signal, etc.) guiñar; (of stars, etc.) titilar, rutilar, parpadear, centellear. *vt* guiñar (el ojo). *n* pestañeo, *m;* guiño, *m.* **not to sleep a w.,** no pegar los ojos. **to take forty winks,** echar una siesta. **to w. at,** guiñar el ojo (a); (ignore) hacer la vista gorda

winking *n* (blinking) parpadeo, *m;* (as a signal) guiños, *m pl;* (of stars, etc.) titilación, *f,* pestañeo, *m. a* (of stars, etc.) titilante. **like w.,** en un abrir y cerrar de ojos.

winner *n* ganador (-ra); vencedor (-ra)

winning *a* ganador; vencedor; (attractive) encantador.

n ganancia, *f.* **w. number,** número galardonado, número premiado, número vencedor, *m.* **w.-post,** meta, *f.* **w. side,** *sport* equipo vencedor, *m;* (politics, etc.) partido vencedor, *m*

winnings *n* ganancias, *f pl*

winnow *vt* aventar, abalear; *fig* separar

winnower *n* aventador (-ra)

winnowing *n* abaleo, aventamiento, *m; fig* separación, *f.* **w. fork,** bieldo, *m.* **w. machine,** aventador mecánico, *m*

winsome *a* sandunguero; dulce, encantador

winsomeness *n* sandunga, *f;* encanto, *m,* dulzura, *f*

winter *n* invierno, *m. a* de invierno; hiemal. *vi* pasar el invierno, invernar. *vt* (of cattle, etc.) guardar en invierno. **in w.,** en invierno, durante el invierno. **w. clothes,** ropa de invierno, *f.* **w. palace,** palacio de invierno, *m.* **w. pasture** *Lat. Am.* invernada, *f.* **w. quarters,** invernadero, *m.* **w. season,** invierno, *m;* temporada de invierno, *f.* **w. sleep,** invernada, *f.* **w. solstice,** solsticio hiemal, *m.* **w. sports,** deportes de nieve, *m pl.* **w. wheat,** trigo de invierno, *m*

wintry *a* de invierno; invernal; (of a smile, etc.) glacial

wipe *vt* limpiar; (rub) frotar; (dry) secar; (remove) quitar. *n* limpión, *m;* (blow) golpe de lado, *m.* **to w. one's eyes,** enjugarse las lagrimas. **to w. off, out,** limpiar; (remove) quitar; (erase) borrar; (kill) destruir completamente, exterminar; (a military force) destrozar; (a debt) cancelar

wire *n* alambre, *m;* hilo metálico, *m;* telégrafo (eléctrico), *m; inf* telegrama, *m. vt* atar con alambre; (fence) alambrar; (snare) coger con lazo de alambre; (of electrical equipment, etc.) instalar; (telegraph) telegrafiar. *vi* (telegraph) telegrafiar. **barbed w.,** alambre espinoso, *m;* (person) fuerza viva, *f.* **w.-cutters,** cortaalambres, *m pl.* **w. entanglement,** *mil* alambrada, *f.* **w. fence,** alambrera, *f,* cercado de alambre, *m.* **w. gauze,** tela metálica, *f.* **w. nail,** punta de París, *f.* **w.-netting,** malla de alambre, *f.* **w.-pulling,** influencias secretas, *f pl;* intrigas políticas, *f pl*

wiredraw *vt* estirar (alambre), tirar (el hilo de hierro, plata, etc.); (arguments, etc.) sutilizar

wiredrawer *n* estirador, *m*

wireless *a* sin hilos; (of a message) radiotelegráfico; por radio. *n* telegrafía sin hilos; *f;* radiotelefonía, *f;* (telegram) radiocomunicación, *f;* (broadcasting) radio, *f. vt* radiotelegrafiar. **Let's listen to the w.,** Vamos a escuchar la radio. **portable w.,** radio portátil, *f.* **w. engineer,** ingeniero radio-telegrafista, *m.* **w. enthusiast,** radioaficionado (-da). **w. licence,** permiso de radiorreceptor, *m.* **w. operator,** radiotelegrafista, *mf.* **w. room,** cuarto de telegrafía sin hilos, *m.* **w. set,** aparato de radio, *m.* **w. station,** estación de radiotelegrafía, *f;* (broadcasting) radioemisora, *f.* **w. telegraph,** telégrafo sin hilos, *m.* **w. telegraphy,** telegrafía sin hilos, *f.* **w. telephony,** telefonía sin hilos, *f.* **w. transmission,** radioemisión, *f*

wiretap *n* poner escucha a

wiring *n* instalación de alambres eléctricos, *f*

wiry *a* semejante al alambre; (of persons) nervudo

wisdom *n* sabiduría, *f;* (learning) saber, *m;* (judgment) juicio, *m.* **Book of W.,** Libro de la Sabiduría, *m.* **w.-tooth,** muela del juicio, *f*

wise *a* sabio; juicioso, prudente; (informed) enterado, informado. **a w. man,** un sabio. **in no w.,** de ningún modo. **the W. Men of the East,** los magos. **w. guy,** *inf* toro corrido, *m*

wisely *adv* sabiamente; prudentemente, con prudencia

wish *n* deseo, *m.* **Best wishes for the New Year,** Los mejores deseos para el Año Nuevo. **w.-bone,** espoleta, *f*

wish *vt* querer; desear; ansiar; (with 'good morning', etc.) dar. **I w. he were here!** ¡Ojalá que estuviera aquí! **Theresa wishes us to go,** Teresa quiere que vayamos. **I w. it had happened otherwise,** Quisiera que las cosas hubiesen pasado de otra manera. **I w.**

you would make less noise, Me gustaría que hicieses menos ruido. I only w. one thing, Solamente deseo una cosa. I w. you good luck, Te deseo mucha suerte. I wished him a merry Christmas, Le deseé unas Pascuas muy felices, Le felicité las Pascuas. to w. a prosperous New Year, desear un próspero Año Nuevo. to w. good-by, despedirse (de). to w. good day, dar los buenos días. to w. for, desear

wisher *n* el que, *m*, (*f*, la que) desea, deseador (-ra)

wishful *a* deseoso; ansioso; ávido. w. thinking, ilusiones, *f pl*; optimismo injustificado, optimismo exagerado, *m*

wisp *n* mechón, *m*; jirón, *m*; trozo, pedazo, *m*

wistaria *n* vistaria, *f*

wistful *a* ansioso; triste; patético; (envious) envidioso; (regretful) de pesar; (remorseful) de remordimiento; (thoughtful) pensativo

wistfully *adv* con ansia; tristemente; patéticamente; con envidia; con pesar; con remordimiento; pensativo

wistfulness *n* ansia, *f*; tristeza, *f*; (envy) envidia, *f*; (regret) pesar, *m*; (remorse) remordimiento, *m*; (thoughtfulness) lo pensativo, lo distraído

wit, to wit *v* a saber

wit *n* (reason) juicio, *m*; agudeza, gracia, *f*, rasgo de ingenio, *m*; ingenio, *m*; inteligencia, *f*, talento, *m*; (person) hombre de ingenio, *m*; mujer de ingenio, *f*. my five wits, mis cinco sentidos. to be at one's wits' end, no saber qué hacer. to live by one's wits, ser caballero de industria. to lose one's wits, perder el juicio

witch *n* bruja, *f*. witches' sabbath, aquelarre, *m*. w.-doctor, hechizador, mago, *m*. witch-hazel, carpe, *m*; loción de carpe, *f*

witchcraft *n* brujería, *f*; sortilegio, encantamiento, *m*

witchery *n* brujería, *f*; *fig* encanto, *m*, magia, *f*

with *prep* con; en compañía de; en casa de; (against) contra; (among) entre; en; (by) por; (towards) hacia; para con; (according to) según; (notwithstanding) a pesar de; a; (concerning) con respecto a; en el caso de. Rose is w. Antony, Rosa está con Antonio. He was w. his dog, Estaba acompañado por su perro. He pulled at it w. both hands, Lo tiró con las dos manos. filled w. fear, lleno de miedo. to shiver w. cold, temblarse de frío. the girl w. golden hair, la muchacha del pelo dorado. They killed it w. one blow, Lo mataron de un solo golpe. It rests w. you to decide, Tú tienes que decidirlo; Te toca a tí decidirlo. to begin w., *adv* para empezar; *v* empezar por. w. all speed, a toda prisa. to part w., desprenderse de; (of people) despedirse; separarse de. w. that . . ., (at once) en esto . . . (disease and poverty, etc.) are still with us, están todavía en el mundo

withal *adv* además; al mismo tiempo. *prep* con

withdraw *vt* retirar; (words) retractar; (remove) quitar, privar (de); (a legal action) apartar. *vi* retirarse; retroceder; apartarse; irse

withdrawal *n* retirada, *f*; (retirement) retiro, *m*; apartamiento, *m*

withdrawn *a* (abstracted) ensimismado, meditabundo

wither *vi* marchitarse, secarse, ajarse. *vt* marchitar, secar, ajar; *fig* hacer languidecer, matar; (snub) avergonzar

withered *a* marchito, mustio; muerto; (of persons) acartonado, seco

witheredness *n* marchitez, *f*; sequedad, *f*

withering *a* que marchita; (scorching) abrasador, ardiente; (scornful) despreciativo, desdeñoso; (biting) mordaz, cáustico

withers *n* cruz, *f*

withhold *vt* retener; detener; (restrain) refrenar; apartar; (refuse) negar; abstenerse de; (refuse to reveal) ocultar

withholding *n* detención, *f*; (refusal) negación, *f*

within *adv* dentro, adentro; en el interior; en casa; *fig* en su interior. He stayed w., Se quedó dentro. Is Mrs. González w.? ¿Está en casa de la Sra. González?

within *prep* dentro de; el interior de; en; entre; (within range of) al alcance de; a la distancia de; (near) cerca de; a poco de; (of time) en el espacio de, en; dentro de; (almost) por poco, casi. He was w. an ace of being killed, Por poco le matan. to be w. hearing, estar al alcance de la voz. seen from w., visto desde dentro. twice w. a fortnight, dos veces en quince días. w. himself, por sus adentros, entre sí. w. an inch of, *fig* a dos dedos de. w. a few miles of Edinburgh, a unas millas de Edimburgo. w. a short distance, en una corta distancia; a poca distancia

without *prep* sin; (outside) fuera de; (beyond) más allá de. *adv* exteriormente; por fuera; hacia afuera; fuera. It goes w. saying, No hay que decir. w. more ado, sin más ni más. w. my knowledge, que yo lo supiese. w. regard for, sin miramientos por. w. saying more, sin decir más. without batting an eyelash, sin sobresaltos

withstand *vt* resistir, oponerse (a); soportar

withstanding *n* resistencia, oposición (a), *f*

witless *a* sin seso, tonto, necio

witness *n* (evidence) testimonio, *m*; (person) testigo, *mf*; espectador (-ra). in w. whereof, en fe de lo cual. to bear w., atestiguar, dar testimonio. to bring forward witnesses, hacer testigos. w. my hand, en fe de lo cual, firmo. w.-box, puesto de los testigos, *m*. w. for the defence, testigo de descargo, *mf*. w. for the prosecution, testigo de cargo, *mf*

witness *vt* (show) mostrar, señalar; (see) ser testigo de, ver, presenciar; *law* atestiguar. *vi* dar testimonio; servir de testigo

witticism *n* rasgo de ingenio, donaire, *m*, agudeza, *f*

wittily *adv* ingeniosamente, donairosamente, agudamente

wittiness *n* viveza de ingenio, donosura, *f*

witty *a* salado, gracioso. w. sally, agudeza, *f*

wizard *n* mago, hechicero, *m*

wizardry *n* magia, *f*

wizened *a* seco, arrugado; (of persons) acartonado

wobble *vi* tambalearse, balancearse; (quiver) temblar; oscilar; *mech* galopar; (stagger) titubear; *fig* vacilar

wobbly *a* que se bambolea; inestable; *fig* vacilante

woe *n* dolor, *m*; congoja, aflicción, *f*; mal, desastre, infortunio, *m*. Woe is me! ¡Ay de mí! ¡Desdichado de mí!

woebegone *a* angustiado

woeful *a* triste; doloroso; funesto

woefully *adv* tristemente; dolorosamente

wolf *n* lobo (-ba). a w. in sheep's clothing, un lobo en piel de cordero. to cry w., gritar «el lobo!» to keep the w. from the door, ponerse a cubierto del hambre. w.-cub, lobezno, *m*. w.-hound, perro lobo, *m*. w. pack, manada de lobos, *f*

wolfish *a* lobuno, de lobo

wolfram *n* volframio, *m*

woman *n* mujer, *f*; hembra, *f*; (lady-in-waiting) dama de servicio, *f*. a fine figure of a w., una real hembra. w. doctor, médica, *f*. w.-hater, misógino, *m*. w. of the town, mujer de la vida airada, *f*. w. of the world, mujer de mundo, *f*

womanhood *n* feminidad, *f*; sexo feminino, *m*

womanish *a* afeminado

womankind *n* sexo feminino, las mujeres

womanliness *n* feminidad, *f*; carácter femenino, *m*

womanly *a* femenino, de mujer

womb *n* útero, *m*, matriz, *f*; *fig* seno, *m*

women's dormitory *n* residencia para señoritas, *f*

wonder *n* maravilla, *f*; prodigio, *m*; portento, milagro, *m*; (surprise) sorpresa, *f*; admiración, *f*; asombro, *m*; (problem) enigma, *m*; misterio, *m*. *vi* admirarse, asombrarse, maravillarse; sorprenderse. *vt* (ask oneself) preguntarse; desear saber. I wondered what the answer would be, Me preguntaba qué sería la respuesta. It is no w. that . . ., No es mucho que . . . , No es sorprendente que . . . It is one of the wonders of the world, Es una de las maravillas del mundo. to

work wonders, hacer milagros. **to w. at,** asombrarse de, maravillarse de; sorprenderse de. **w.-working,** milagroso

wonderful *a* maravilloso; magnífico; asombroso; *inf* estupendo

wonderfully *adv* maravillosamente; admirablemente

wondering *a* de asombro, sorprendido; perplejo

wonderingly *adv* con asombro

wonderland *n* mundo fantástico, *m*; reino de las hadas, *m*; país de las maravillas, *m.* **"Alice in W.,"** Alicia en el país de las maravillas

wonderment *n.* See **wonder**

wondrous *a* maravilloso.

wont *n* costumbre, *f. vi* soler. **as he was w.,** Como solía

won't. See **will not**

wonted *a* sólito, acostumbrado

woo *vt* galantear; hacer la corte (a), solicitar amores a; cortejar, *Lat. Am.* afilar. *fig* solicitar; perseguir

wood *n* bosque, *m*; madera, *f*; (for the fire, etc.) leña, *f*; (cask) barril, *m. a* de madera; (of the woods) selvático. **dead w.,** ramas muertas, *f pl*; *fig* paja, *f.* **w. alcohol,** alcohol metílico, *m.* **w.-anemone,** anémona de los bosques, *f.* **w.-block floor,** entarimado, *m.* **w.-borer,** xiló-fago, *m.* **w.-carver,** tallista, *mf* **w.-carving,** talla en madera, *f.* **w.-craft,** conocimiento del campo, *m.* **w.-cut,** grabado en madera, *m.* **w.-cutter,** leñador, *m.* **w.-engraver,** grabador (-ra) en madera. **w.-engraving,** grabado al boj, *m.* **w.-fibre,** fibra de madera, *f.* **w.-louse,** cochinilla, *f.* **w.-nymph,** ninfa de los bosques, *f.* **w.-pigeon,** paloma torcaz, *f.* **w.-pile,** pila de leña, leñera, *f.* **w.-pulp,** pulpa de madera, *f.* **w.-shaving,** acepilladura, *f.* **w.-splinter,** tasquil, *m*; astilla, *f.* **w.-wind,** *mus* madera, *f.* **w.-worm,** carcoma, *f*

wooded *a* provisto de árboles, plantado de árboles, arbolado

wooden *a* de madera; de palo; (of smiles) mecánico; (stiff) indiferente, sin emoción; (clumsy) torpe; (of character) inflexible. **He has a w. leg,** Tiene una pata de palo. **w. beam,** madero, *m*; viga de madera, *f.* **w. bridge,** pontón, *m.* **w. galley,** *print* galerín, *m*

woodland *n* bosques, *m pl. a* de bosque; silvestre

woodpecker *n* pájaro carpintero, picamaderos, *m*

woodshed *n* leñera, *f*

woodwork *n* maderaje, *m*; molduras, *f pl*; carpintería, *f*

woody *a* leñoso; arbolado, con árboles. **w. tissue,** tejido leñoso, *m*

wooer *n* pretendiente, galanteador, *m*

woof *n* trama, *f*

wooing *n* galanteo, *m*

wool *n* lana, *f. a* de lana; lanar. **to go w.-gathering,** estar distraído. **to pull the w. over a person's eyes,** engañar como a un chino. **w.-bearing,** lanar. **w.-carding,** cardadura de lana, *f.* **w.-growing,** cría de ganado lanar, *f.* **w. merchant,** comerciante en lanas, *mf*, lanero, *m.* **w.-pack,** fardo de lana, *m.* **w. trade,** comercio de lana, *m*

woollen *a* de lana; lanar. *n* paño de lana, *m*; género de punta de lana, *m*

woolliness *n* lanosidad, *f*

woolly *a* lanudo, lanoso; de lana; *bot* velloso; (of hair) lanoso, crespo. *n* género de punta de lana, *m*; (sweater) jersey, *m*

word *n* palabra, *f*; *gram* vocablo, *m*; *theol* verbo, *m*; (maxim) sentencia, *f*, dicho, *m*; (message) recado, *m*; (news) aviso, *m*, noticias, *f pl*; (*mil* command) voz de mando, *f*; (order) orden, *f*; (password) contraseña, *f*; (term) término, *m. vt* expresar; formular; (draw up) redactar; escribir. **He was as good as his w.,** Fue hombre de palabra. **I do not know how to w. this letter,** No sé cómo redactar esta carta. **in a w.,** en una palabra; en resumidas cuentas. **by w. of mouth,** de palabra. **I give you my w. for it,** Le doy mi palabra de honor. **in other words,** en otros términos; en efecto. **the W. (of God),** el Verbo (de Dios). **to have a w. with,** hablar con; conversar con; entablar conversa-

ción con. **to leave w.,** dejar recado. **to have words with,** tener palabras con. **to keep one's w.,** cumplir su palabra

word index *n* índice de vocablos, *m*

wordiness *n* palabrería, verbosidad, *f*

wording *n* fraseología, *f*; expresión, *f*; estilo, *m*; (terms) términos, *m pl*; (drawing up) redacción, *f*

wordy *a* verboso, prolijo

work *n* trabajo, *m*; (sewing) labor, *f*; (literary, artistic production and theological) obra, *f*; (behavior) acción, *f*, acto, *m*; (employment) empleo, *m*; (business affairs) negocios, *m pl*; *pl* **works,** obras, fortificaciones, *f, pl*; obras públicas, *f pl*; construcciones, *f pl*; (of a machine) mecanismo, *m*; motor, *m*; (factory) fábrica, *f*, taller, *m.* **w. of art,** obra de arte. **w. accident,** accidente del trabajo, *m.* **w.-bag,** bolsa de costura, *f*, saco de labor, *m.* **w.-box,** (on legs) costurero, *m*; (small) neceser de costura, *m.* **w.-people,** obreros (-as). **w.-room,** taller, *m*; (study) estudio, *m*; (for sewing) cuarto de costura, *m.* **w.-table,** banco de taller, *m*; (for writing) mesa de escribir, *f*

work *vi* trabajar, *Central America also* laborar; *sew* hacer labor de aguja, coser; (embroider) bordar; *mech* funcionar, marchar; (succeed) tener éxito; ser eficaz; (be busy) estar ocupado; (be employed) tener empleo; (of the face) demudarse, torcerse; (ferment) fermentar; (operate) obrar *vt* trabajar; operar, hacer funcionar; mover; (control) manejar; (a mine) explotar; (embroider) bordar; (wood) tallar; (a problem) resolver; calcular; (iron, etc.) labrar; (the soil) cultivar; (a ship) maniobrar; (do) hacer; (bring about) efectuar; traer consigo; producir; (agitate oneself) agitarse, emocionarse, conmoverse. **to w. in repoussé,** repujar. **to w. loose,** desprenderse. **to w. one's passage,** trabajar por el pasaje. **to w. overtime,** trabajar horas extraordinarias. **to w. two ways,** ser espada de dos filos. **to w. at,** trabajar en; ocuparse en; dedicarse a; elaborar. **to w. in,** *vt* introducir; insinuar. *vi* combinarse. **to w. into,** penetrar en. **to w. off,** usar, emplear; (get rid of) deshacerse de, librarse de. **to w. on, upon,** influir en; obrar sobre; estar ocupado en. **to w. out,** *vt* calcular; resolver; (a mine, topic, etc.) agotar; (develop) elaborar, desarrollar; trazar; planear; (find) encontrar. *vi* llegar (a); resultar; venir a ser. **to w. up,** crear; (promote) fomentar; producir; (excite) agitar, excitar; (fashion) dar forma (a), labrar; (finish) terminar

workable *a* laborable; factible, practicable; (of a mine) explotable

workableness *n* practicabilidad, *f*

workaday *a* de todos los días; prosaico

workbench banco de mecánico, *f*, banco de taller, banco de trabajo, *m*, mesa de trabajo, *f*

workday *n* día de trabajo, día laborable, *m*

worker *n* trabajador (-ra); (manual) obrero (-ra); (of a machine) operario (-ia). **w.-ant,** hormiga obrera, *f.* **w.-bee,** abeja obrera, *f*

workhouse *n* asilo, *m*

working *a* de trabajo; (of capital) de explotación; trabajador, que trabaja; obrero. *n* trabajo, *m*; (of a machine, organism, institution) funcionamiento, *m*; explotación, *f*; (of a mine) laboreo, *m*; (of a ship) maniobra, *f*; (of metal, stone, wood) labra, *f*; operación, *f*; (result) efecto, resultado, *m*; (calculation) cálculo, *m.* **"Not w.,"** «No funciona.» **to be in w. order,** funcionar bien. **w.-class,** clase obrera, *f*; pueblo, *m.* **w.-clothes,** ropa de trabajo, *f.* **w.-day,** día de trabajo, *m.* **w.-hours,** horas de trabajo, horas hábiles, *f pl.* **w. hypothesis,** postulado, *m.* **w.-man,** obrero, *m*; trabajador, *m.* **w.-out,** elaboración, *f*; ensayo, *m.* **w.-plan,** plan de trabajo, *m.* **w.-woman,** obrera, *f*; trabajadora, *f*

workless *a* sin trabajo

workman *n* obrero, *m*; (agricultural) labrador, *m*

workmanlike *a* bien hecho, bien acabado; (clever) hábil

workmanship *n* trabajo, *m*; manufactura, *f*; hechura, *f*; (cleverness) habilidad, *f*

workshop *n* taller, *m*

world *n* mundo, *m*. **For all the w. as if . . . ,** Exactamente como si . . . **to see the w.,** ver mundo. **to treat the w. as one's oyster,** ponerse el mundo por montera. **w. without end,** por los siglos de los siglos. **w.-power,** potencia mundial, gran potencia, *f*. **w.-wide,** mundial, universal

world almanac *n* compendio mundial, *m*

worldliness *n* mundanería, *f*, conocimiento del mundo, *m*; frivolidad, vanidad mundana, *f*; egoísmo, *m*; prudencia, *f*

worldly *a* de este mundo; mundano; humano; profano; frívolo. **to be w.-wise,** tener mucho mundo

worm *n* gusano, *m*; lombriz, *f*; *chem* serpentín, *m*; (of a screw) tornillo sinfín, *m*; (person) gusano, *m*; *fig* gusano roedor, remordimiento, *m*. **intestinal w.,** lombriz intestinal, *f*, gusano de la conciencia. **w.-eaten,** carcomido. **w.-hole,** picadura de gusano, lombriguera, *f*. **w.-powder,** polvos antihelmínticos, *m pl*. **w.-shaped,** vermiforme. **having worms, suffering from worms** *Lat. Am.* lombriciento

worm *vt* (a dog) dar un vermífugo (a). *vi* arrastrarse como un gusano. **to w. one's way into,** deslizarse en; *fig* insinuarse en, introducirse en. **to w. out,** (secrets, information) sonsacar

wormwood *n* ajenjo, *m*

wormy *a* gusanoso, lleno de gusanos

worn *a* (of garments) raído; estropeado; gastado; (of paths) trillado; (of the face) arrugado, cansado. **w. out,** acabado; muy usado; (tired) rendido; (exhausted) agotado

worrier *n* inquietador (-ra); receloso (-sa); aprensivo (-va)

worry *n* preocupación, inquietud, ansiedad, *f*; problema, cuidado, *m*. *vt* (prey) zamarrear; preocupar, inquietar; molestar; importunar. *vi* estar preocupado, estar intranquilo, inquietarse. **Don't worry,** Pierda cuidado, No pase cuidado

worrying *a* inquietante, perturbador; molesto

worse *a comp* peor; inferior. *adv* peor; menos. *n* lo peor. **so much the w.,** tanto peor. **to be w. off,** estar peor; estar en peores circunstancias; ser menos feliz. **to be the w. for wear,** ser muy usado; estar ajado; ser ya viejo. **to grow w.,** empeorarse; (of an ill person) ponerse peor. **w. and w.,** de mal en peor, peor que peor. **w. than ever,** peor que nunca

worsen *vt* agravar, hacer peor; exasperar. *vi* agravarse, empeorarse; exasperarse

worsening *n* agravación, *f*, empeoramiento, *m*; exasperación, *f*

worship *n* culto, *m*; adoración, *f*; veneración, *f*. *vt* adorar; reverenciar. *vi* adorar; rezar; dar culto (a). **place of w.,** edificio de culto, *m*. **Your W.,** vuestra merced

worshipful *a* venerable, respetable

worshipper *n* adorador (-ra); *pl* **worshippers,** (in a church, etc.) fieles, *m pl*, congregación, *f*

worshipping *n* adoración, *f*, culto, *m*

worst *a* el (la, etc.) peor; más malo. *adv* el (la, etc.) peor. *n* el (la, etc.) peor; lo peor. *vt* vencer, derrotar; triunfar sobre **If the w. comes to the w.,** En el peor de los casos. **The w. of it is that . . . ,** Lo peor es que . . . **to have the w. of it,** salir perdiendo, llevar la peor parte

worsted *n* estambre, *m*, *a* de estambre

worth *n* valor, *m*; precio, *m*; mérito, *m*, *a* (que) vale; de precio de; cuyo valor es de; equivalente a; (que) merece; digno de. **He bought six hundred pesetas w. of sweets,** Compró seiscientas pesetas de dulces. **He sang for all he was w.,** Cantó con toda su alma. **It is w. seeing,** Es digno de verse, Vale la pena de verse. **to be w.,** valer. **to be w. while,** valer la pena, merecer la pena

worthily *adv* dignamente

worthiness *n* mérito, valor, *m*

worthless *a* sin valor; sin mérito; inútil; malo; (of persons) vil, despreciable, indigno

worthlessness *n* falta de valor, *f*; falta de mérito, *f*; inutilidad, *f*; (of persons) bajeza, vileza, *f*

worthy *a* digno de respeto, benemérito, respetable; digno, merecedor; meritorio. *n* varón ilustre, hombre célebre, *m*; héroe, *m*; (*inf iron*) tío, *m*. **to be w. of,** ser digno de, merecer

would *preterite* and *subjunctive* of **will.** (indicating a conditional tense) **They w. come if . . . ,** Vendrían si . . . ; (indicating an imperfect tense) **Often he w. sing,** Muchas veces cantaba, **Now and then a blackbird w. whistle,** De vez en cuando silbó un mirlo; (expressing wish, desire) **What w. they?** ¿Qué quieren? **The place where I w. be,** El lugar donde quisiera estar. **W. I were at home!** ¡Ojalá que estuviese en casa! **I thought that I w. tell you,** Se me ocurrió la idea de decírselo. **It w. seem that . . . ,** Parece ser que . . . , **Según parece . . . ;** Se diría que . . . **He said that he w. never have done it,** Dijo que no lo hubiera hecho nunca. **They w. have been killed if he had not rescued them,** Habrían sido matados si él no los hubiese salvado. **He w. go,** Se empeñó en ir. **He w. not do it,** Rehusó hacerlo, Se resistió a hacerlo; No quiso hacerlo. **This w. probably be the house,** Sin duda esta sería la casa. **W. you be good enough to . . . ,** Tenga Vd. la bondad de . . . , Haga el favor de . . .

would-be *a* supuesto; llamado; aspirante (a); en esperanza de (followed by infin.); (frustrated) frustrado, malogrado

wound *n* herida, lesión, *Lat. Am. also,* lastimadura, *f*. *vt* herir; (the feelings) lastimar, lacerar. **deep w.,** herida penetrante, *f*. **the wounded,** los heridos.

wounding *n* herida, *f*, *a fig* lastimador

wraith *n* fantasma, espectro, *m*, sombra, *f*

wrangle *vi* discutir; altercar, disputar acaloradamente; reñir; (bargain) regatear. *n* argumento, *m*; disputa, *f*, altercado, *m*; riña, *f*

wrangler *n* disputador (-ra); (Cambridge University) laureado en matemáticas, *m*

wrangling *n* disputas, *f pl*, altercación, *f*; (bargaining) regateo, *m*

wrap *vt* envolver; arrollar; cubrir; abrigar; (conceal) ocultar. *n* envoltorio, *m*; abrigo, *m*; *pl* **wraps,** abrigos y mantas de viaje, *m pl*. **W. yourself up well!** ¡Abrígate bien! **to be wrapped up in,** estar envuelto en; *fig* estar entregado a, estar absorto en; (a person) estar embelesado con

wrapper *n* envoltura, *f*; embalaje, *m*; (of a newspaper) faja, *f*; (of a book) sobrecubierta, *f*; (dressing-gown) bata, *f*, salto de cama, *m*

wrapping *n* envoltura, cubierta, *f*. **w.-paper,** papel de envolver, *m*

wrath *n* ira, *f*

wrathful *a* airado

wreak *vt* ejecutar; (anger, etc.) descargar. **to w. one's vengeance,** vengarse

wreath *n* guirnalda, *f*; corona, *f*; trenza, *f*. **funeral w.,** corona funeraria, *f*

wreathe *vt* trenzar; (entwine) entrelazar (de); (garland) coronar (de), enguirnaldar (con); (encircle) ceñir, rodear; (a face in smiles) iluminar

wreck *n* naufragio, *m*; buque naufragado, *m*; destrucción, *f*; *fig* ruina, *f*; (remains) restos, *m pl*; (person) sombra, *f*. *vt* hacer naufragar; destruir; *fig* arruinar; hacer fracasar. **I am a complete w.,** *inf* Estoy hecho una ruina. **to be wrecked,** irse a pique, naufragar; *fig* arruinarse; frustrarse

wreckage *n* naufragio, *m*; restos de naufragio, *m pl*; ruinas, *f pl*; (of a car, plane, etc.) restos, *m pl*; accidente, *m*

wrecked *a* naufragado

wrecker *n* destructor (-ra); (of ships) raquero, *m*

wrench *n* (jerk) arranque, *m*; (pull) tirón, *m*; (sprain) torcedura, *f*; (tool) llave, *f*; (pain) dolor, *m*. *vt* arrancar;

forzar; torcer, dislocar. **He has wrenched his arm,** Se ha torcido el brazo

wrest vt arrebatar, arrancar

wrestle vi luchar. n lucha grecorromana, f; fig lucha, f. **to w. with,** fig luchar con; luchar contra, Lat. Am. abrocharse (con . . .)

wrestler n luchador, m

wrestling n lucha grecorromana, f. **all-in-w.,** lucha libre, f. **w.-match,** lucha, f

wretch n infeliz, mf; (ruffian) infame, m; (playful) picaruelo (-la). **a poor w.,** un pobre diablo

wretched a (unhappy) infeliz, desdichado; miserable; pobre; (ill) enfermo; horrible; malo; mezquino; despreciable; lamentable

wretchedly adv tristemente; pobremente; muy mal; ruinmente

wretchedness n infelicidad, desdicha, f; miseria, pobreza, f; escualidez, f; ruindad, f

wriggle vi agitarse, moverse; menearse; serpear, culebrear; retorcerse. n See under **wriggling**. **to w. into,** insinuarse en, deslizarse dentro (de). **to w. out,** escaparse. **to w. out of a difficulty,** extricarse de una dificultad

wriggling n meneo, m; retorcimiento, m; serpenteo, culebreo, m

wring vt torcer; estrujar; exprimir; arrancar; (force) forzar. **to w. one's hands,** restregarse las manos. **to w. the neck of,** torcer el pescuezo (a). **to w. out,** exprimir; estrujar

wringer n torcedor (-ra); (for clothes) exprimidor de ropa, m

wringing n torsión, f. **w.-machine,** exprimidor de ropa, m

wrinkle n arruga, f; pliegue, m; inf noción, f. vt arrugar. vi arrugarse. **to w. one's brow,** (frown) fruncir el ceño; (in perplexity) arrugar la frente

wrinkling n arrugamiento, m

wrinkly a arrugado

wrist n muñeca, f. **w.-band,** tira del puño de la camisa, f. **w. bandage,** pulsera, f

wristlet n pulsera, f; manguito elástico, m. **w. watch,** reloj de pulsera, m

writ n escritura, f; law decreto judicial, mandamiento, m; orden, f; título ejecutorio, m; hábeas corpus, m. **Holy W.,** la Sagrada Escritura. **to issue a w.,** dar orden. **to serve a w.,** notificar una orden. **w. of privilege,** auto de excarcelación, m

write vt and vi escribir; fig mostrar. **He writes a good hand,** Tiene buena letra. **I shall w. to them for a list,** Les escribiré pidiendo una lista. **to w. back,** contestar por escrito; contestar a una carta. **to w. down,** poner por escrito; anotar, apuntar; describir. **to w. for,** escribir para; escribir para pedir algo; escribir algo en vez de otra persona. **to w. off,** escribir; escribir rápidamente; cancelar. **to w. on,** seguir escribiendo; escribir sobre. **to w. out,** copiar; redactar. **to w. over again,** escribir de nuevo, escribir otra vez, volver a escribir. **to w. up,** redactar; com poner al día; (praise) escribir alabando

writer n escritor (-ra); autor (-ra). **the present w.,** el que, m, (f, la que) esto escribe. **writer's cramp,** calambre del escribiente, m

writhe vi retorcerse

writhing n retorsión, f

writing n escritura, f; (work) escrito, m; inscripción, f; documento, m; (style) estilo, m; (hand) letra, f; el arte de escribir; trabajo literario, m. **in one's own w.,** de su propia letra. **in w.,** por escrito. **w.-case,** escribanía, f. **w.-desk,** escritorio, m. **w.-pad,** taco de papel, m. **w.-paper,** papel de escribir, m. **w.-table,** mesa de escribir, f

written a escrito

wrong a injusto; mal; equivocado, erróneo; inexacto; falso; incorrecto; desacertado; inoportuno. **It is the w. one,** No es el que hacía falta; No es el que quería. **to be in the w. place,** estar mal situado; estar mal colocado. **to be w.,** estar mal; no tener razón; (mistaken) estar equivocado; (of deeds or things) estar mal hecho; (be unjust) ser injusto; (of clocks) andar mal. **to do w.,** hacer mal; obrar mal. **to get out of bed on the w. side,** levantarse del izquierdo. **to go w.,** (of persons) descarriarse; (of affairs) ir mal; salir mal; frustrarse; (of apparatus) estropearse, no funcionar. **We have taken the w. road,** Nos hemos equivocado de camino. **You were very w. to . . . ,** Has hecho muy mal en . . . **w.-headed,** terco, obstinado; disparatado. **w.-headedness,** terquedad, obstinación, f. **w. number,** (telephone) número errado, m. **w. side,** revés, m; lado malo, m. **w. side out,** al envés; al revés

wrong adv mal; injustamente; sin razón; incorrectamente; equivocadamente; (inside out) al revés. **to get it w.,** (a sum) calcular mal; (misunderstand) comprender mal

wrong n mal, m; injusticia, f; perjuicio, m; ofensa, f; agravio, m; culpa, f; error, m. **to be in the w.,** no tener razon; haber hecho mal. **to put one in the w.,** echar la culpa (a), hacer responsable (de)

wrong vt hacer mal (a); perjudicar; ser injusto con; ofender

wrongdoer n malhechor (-ra); pecador (-ra); perverso (-sa)

wrongdoing n maldad, maleficencia, f; pecado, m; injusticia, f

wrongful a injusto; perjudicial; falso

wrongfully adv injustamente; falsamente

wrongly adv injustamente; erróneamente, equivocadamente; perversamente; mal

wrongness n mal, m; injusticia, f; falsedad, f; inexactitud, f, error, m

wrought a forjado; labrado; (hammered) batido; trabajado. **w. iron,** hierro dulce, hierro forjado, m. **w. up,** muy excitado, muy agitado, muy nervioso

wry a torcido; tuerto; triste; pesimista; desilusionado; irónico. **wry face,** mueca f, de desengaño, de ironía, de disgusto, etc. **make a wry face,** torcer el gesto, Mexico engestarse. **wry neck,** orn torcecuello, m

wryly adv tristemente; irónicamente

Wuthering Heights Cumbres borrascosas

wye n (letter) ye, i griega, f; horquilla, cosa en forma de Y, f

X

x n equis, f

x-ray vt tomar una radiografía (de). **x-ray,** rayo x, m pl. **x-ray examination,** examen con rayos x, m. **x-ray photograph,** radiografía, f

xylophone n xilófono, m

Y

y *n* (letter) i griega, ye, *f*
yacht *n* yate, *m*. **y. club,** club marítimo, *m*. **y. race,**
  regata de yates, *f*
yachting *n* navegación en yate, *f*, paseo en yate, *m*
yachtsman *n* deportista náutico, balandrista, balandrismo, *m*
yam *n* batata, *f*, *Lat. Am.* boniato, camote, *m*
yank *n* tirón, *m*, sacudida, *f*. *vt* dar un tirón (a); sacar de
  un tirón
Yankee *a* and *n* yanqui, *mf*
yap *vi* ladrar. *n* ladrido, *m*
yapper *n* (yapping dog) gozque, gozquejo, *m*
yapping *n* ladridos, *m pl*, a que ladra
yard *n* (measure) yarda, *f*; *naut* verga, *f*; corral, *m*;
  (courtyard) patio, *m*. *vt* acorralar. **goods y.,** estación de
  mercancías, *f*. **y.-arm,** penol (de la verga), *m*. **y.-stick,**
  vara de medir de una yarda, *f*
yarn *n* hilaza, *f*; hilo, *m*; (story) historia, *f*, cuento, *m*. **to
  spin a y.,** contar una historia
yaw *vi naut* guiñar; *aer* serpentear. *n naut* guiñada, *f*; *aer*
  serpenteo, *m*
yawn *vi* bostezar; quedarse con la boca abierta; (of
  chasms, etc.) abrirse. *n* bostezo, *m*. **to stifle a y.,** ahogar un bostezo
yawning *a* abierto. *n* bostezos, *m pl*
yea *adv* en verdad, ciertamente; y aun . . . no sólo . . .
  sino. *n* si, *m*
year *n* año, *m*; *pl* **years,** años, *m pl*, edad, *f*. **We are
  getting on in years,** Nos vamos haciendo viejos. **He
  is five years old,** Tiene cinco años. **all the y. round,**
  todo el año, el año entero. **by the y.,** al año. **every
  other y.,** cada dos años, un año sí y otro no. **in after
  years,** en años posteriores. **last y.,** el año pasado. **next
  y.,** el año próximo. el año que viene. **y. after y.,** año
  tras año. **New Y.,** Año Nuevo, *m*. **to see the New Y.
  in,** ver empezar el Año Nuevo. **New Year's Day,** día
  de Año Nuevo, *m*. **(A) Happy New Y.!** ¡Feliz Año
  Nuevo! **y.-book,** anuario, *m*. **a y. later** *Lat. Am.* al año
yearling calf *n* becerra *f*
yearly *a* anual. *adv* anualmente, cada año; una vez
  al año
yearn *vi* anhelar, suspirar (por); desear vivamente
yearning *n* sed, ansia, *f*; anhelo, deseo vehemente, *m*. *a*
  ansioso; anhelante; (tender) tierno
yeast *n* levadura, *f*
yell *vi* and *vt* chillar; gritar. *n* chillido, *m*; grito, *m*
yelling *n* chillidos, *m pl*; gritos, *m pl*, gritería, *f*
yellow *a* amarillo; (of hair) rubio; (cowardly) cobarde;
  (newspaper) amarillista, sensacionalista. **to turn y.,** *vi*
  ponerse amarillo; amarillear. *vt* volver amarillo. **y.
  fever,** fiebre amarilla, *f*. **y.-hammer,** *orn* emberizo, *m*
yellowing *n* amarilleo, *m*
yellowish *a* amarillento, *Lat. Am.* amarilloso
yellowness *n* amarillez, *f*
yellow pages *n* páginas amarillas, páginas doradas, *f pl*
yelp *vi* gañir. *n* gañido, *m*
yelping *n* gañidos, *m pl*
yen *n* (currency) yen, *m*; (desire) deseo vivo, *m*
yeoman *n* pequeño propietario rural, *m*; soldado de caballería, *m*. **Y. of the Guard,** alabardero de la Casa
  Real, *m*
yes *adv* sí. **Yes?** ¿De verdad? ¿Y qué pasó después? ¿Y
  entonces? **to say yes,** decir que sí; dar el sí. **yes-man,**
  amenista, sacristán de amén, *m*
yesterday *adv* ayer. *n* ayer, *m*. **the day before y.,** anteayer
yet *adv* aún, todavía. **as yet,** hasta ahora; todavía. **He
  has not come yet,** No ha venido todavía. **yet again,**
  otra vez
yet *conjunc* sin embargo, no obstante, con todo; pero.

The book is well written and yet I do not like it,
  El libro está bien escrito, y sin embargo no me gusta
yew *n* tejo, *m*; madera de tejo, *f*
Yiddish *n* yídis, yídish, yídico, *m*; *a* yídico
yield *vt* producir; dar; (grant) otorgar; (afford) ofrecer;
  (surrender) ceder. *vi* producir; (submit) rendirse,
  someterse; (of disease) responder; (give way) flaquear,
  doblegarse; dar de sí; (consent) consentir (en); (to circumstances, etc.) ceder (a), sucumbir (a). *n* producción, *f*, producto, *m*; *com* rédito, *m*; (crop) cosecha, *f*. **to
  y. to temptation,** ceder a la tentación. **to y. up,** entregar; devolver
yielding *a* flexible; (soft) blando; dócil, sumiso; fácil;
  condescendiente
yogurt *n* yogur, *m*
yoke *n* yugo, *m*; (of oxen) yunta, *f*; (for pails) balancín,
  m; (of a garment) canesú, *m*; *fig* férula, *f*, yugo, *m*. *vt*
  uncir, acoplar. **to throw off the y.,** sacudir el yugo
yokel *n* patán, rústico, *m*
yolk *n* (of an egg) yema, *f*
yonder *a* aquel, *m*; aquella, *f*; aquellos, *m pl*; aquellas, *f
  pl*. *adv* allí; allí a lo lejos
yore *n* **in days of y.,** antaño; en otro tiempo
you *pers pron nominative* (polite form) usted (Vd.), *mf*;
  ustedes (Vds.), *mf pl*; (familiar form) *sing* tu, *mf*; (plural) vosotros, *m pl*; vosotras, *f pl*; (one) uno, *m*; una, *f*;
  se (followed by 3rd pers. sing. of verb). *pers pron accusative* (polite form) le, *m*; la, *f*; les, *m pl*; las, *f pl*; a usted, a
  ustedes; (informal form) te, *mf*, os, *mf pl*; (after most
  prepositions) ti, *mf*; vosotros, *m pl*; vosotras, *f pl*. **Are
  you there?** (telephone) ¡Oiga! **I gave the parcel to
  you,** Te (os) di el paquete; Di el paquete a usted (a
  ustedes). **I shall wait for you in the garden,** Te (os)
  esperaré en el jardín; Esperaré a Vds. (a Vd.) en el jardín. **This present is for you,** Este regalo es para tí
  (para vosotros, para Vd. (Vds.)). **Away with you!**
  ¡Vete! ¡Marchaos! **Between you and me,** Entre tú y
  yo. **you can't eat your cake and have it too,** no hay
  rosa sin espinas. **You never can tell,** No se sabe
  nunca, Uno no sabe nunca
young *a* joven; nuevo, reciente; inexperto; poco avanzado. *n* cría, *f*, hijuelos, *m pl*. **y. blood,** *inf* pollo pera,
  m. **y. girl,** jovencita, *f*. **y. man** joven, *m*. **y. people,**
  jóvenes, *m pl*. **in his y. days,** en su juventud. **The
  night is y.,** La noche está poca avanzada. **to grow y.
  again,** rejuvenecer. **with y.,** (of animals) preñada *f*
younger *a* más joven; menor. **Peter is his y. brother,**
  Pedro es su hermano menor. **to look y.,** parecer más
  joven
youngish *a* bastante joven
youngster *n* jovencito, chico, muchacho, *m*; niño, *m*
your *a poss* (polite form) su (*pl* sus), de usted (Vd.), (*pl*
  de ustedes (Vds.)); (familiar form) tu (*pl* vuestro). **I
  have y. papers,** Tengo tus (vuestros) papeles; Tengo
  los papeles de Vd. (*or* de Vds.). **How is y. mother?**
  ¿Cómo está su (tu) madre? **It is y. turn,** Te toca a ti, Le
  toca a Vd.
yours *pron poss* (polite form) (el) suyo, *m*; (la) suya, *f*;
  (los) suyos, *m pl*; (las) suyas, *f pl*; el, *m*; la, *f*; lo, *neut*; los,
  m pl; las, *f pl*; de usted (Vd.), *mf sing* or de ustedes
  (Vds.), *mf pl*; (familiar form) (el) tuyo, *m*; (la) tuya, *f*;
  (los) tuyos, *m pl*; (las) tuyas, *f pl*; (el) vuestro, *m*; (la)
  vuestra, *f*; (los) vuestros, *m pl*; (las) vuestras, *f pl*. **This
  is a picture of y.,** (addressing one person), Este es uno
  de los cuadros de usted (Vd.), Este es uno de tus cuadros. **This hat is mine,** el. **It is y.,** Este sombrero es
  el mío, no es el tuyo. **The horse is y.,** El caballo es tuyo
  (de Vd.). **Y. affectionately,** Un abrazo de tu amigo
  . . . **Y. faithfully,** Queda de Vd. su att. (atentísimo) s.s.
  (seguro servidor). **Y. sincerely,** Queda de Vd. su aff.
  (afectuoso)

yourself *pron pers* (familiar form *sing*) tú mismo, *m*; tú misma, *f*; (after a preposition) tí, *mf*; (polite form) usted (Vd.) mismo, *m*; usted misma, *f*; *pl* **yourselves,** (familiar form) vosotros mismos, *m pl*; vosotras mismas, *f pl*; (polite form) ustedes (Vds.) mismos, *m pl*; ustedes mismas, *f pl*. **This is for y.,** Esto es para ti; Esto es para Vd.

youth *n* juventud, *f*; (man) joven, chico, mozalbete, *m*; (collectively) jóvenes, *m pl*, juventud, *f*

youthful *a* joven, juvenil; de la juventud
yowl *n* gañido, aullido, *m*. *vi* gañir, aullar
Yucatan *a* yucateco
yucca *n bot* yuca, *f*
Yugoslav *n* yugoeslavo (-va). *a* yugoeslavo
Yugoslavia Yugoeslavia, *f*
Yukon, the el Yukón, *m*
Yule *n* Navidad, *f*. **y.-log,** leño de Navidad, *m*. **y-tide,** Navidades, *f pl*

Z

z *n* (letter) zeda, zeta, *f*
zeal *n* celo, entusiasmo, *m*; ardor, fervor, *m*
zealot *n* fanático (-ca)
zealous *a* celoso, entusiasta
zealously *adv* con entusiasmo
zebra *n* cebra, *f*
zenith *n* cenit, *m*; *fig* apogeo, punto culminante, *m*
zephyr *n* céfiro, *m*, brisa, *f*
zero *n* cero, *m*. **below z.,** bajo cero. **z. hour,** hora cero, *f*
zest *n* sabor, gusto, *m*; entusiasmo, *m*. **to eat with z.,** comer con buen apetito. **to enter on with z.,** emprender con entusiasmo
zigzag *n* zigzag, *m*. *a* and *adv* en zigzag. *vi* zigzaguear, hacer zigzags, serpentear; (of persons) andar haciendo eses
Zimbabwe Zimbabue
zinc *n* cinc, *m*. **z. oxide,** óxido de cinc, *m*
Zion *n* Sión, *m*

Zionism *n* sionismo, *m*
Zionist *n* and *a* sionista
zip *n* (of a bullet) silbido, *m*; *inf* energía, *f*. **zip fastener,** cierre de cremallera, *m*
zip code *n* código postal, *m*
zipper *n* cremallera, *f*, cierre relámpago, cierre, cerrador, *m*
zircon *n* circón, *m*
zither *n* cítara, *f*
zodiac *n* zodiaco, *m*
zone *n* zona, *f*; faja, *f*
zoo *n* jardín zoológico, *m*
zoological *a* zoológico. **Z. garden,** jardín zoológico, *m*
zoologist *n* zoólogo, *m*
zoology *n* zoología, *f*
zoom *n* zumbido, *m*. *vi* zumbar; *aer* empinarse
Zulu *a* and *n* zulú *mf*
Zuyder Zee, the el Zuyderzée, *m*

Numbers/Números

Cardinal/Cardinales

one	1	uno, una
two	2	dos
three	3	tres
four	4	cuatro
five	5	cinco
six	6	seis
seven	7	siete
eight	8	ocho
nine	9	nueve
ten	10	diez
eleven	11	once
twelve	12	doce
thirteen	13	trece
fourteen	14	catorce
fifteen	15	quince
sixteen	16	dieciséis
seventeen	17	diecisiete
eighteen	18	dieciocho
nineteen	19	diecinueve
twenty	20	veinte
twenty-one	21	veintiuno
twenty-two	22	veintidós
thirty	30	treinta
thirty-one	31	treinta y uno
thirty-two	32	treinta y dos
forty	40	cuarenta
fifty	50	cincuenta
sixty	60	sesenta
seventy	70	setenta
eighty	80	ochenta
ninety	90	noventa

one hundred	100	cien
one hundred one	101	ciento uno
one hundred two	102	ciento dos
two hundred	200	doscientos, -as
three hundred	300	trescientos, -as
four hundred	400	cuatrocientos, -as
five hundred	500	quinientos, -as
six hundred	600	seiscientos, -as
seven hundred	700	setecientos, -as
eight hundred	800	ochocientos, -as
nine hundred	900	novecientos, -as
one thousand	1,000	mil
two thousand	2,000	dos mil
one hundred thousand	100,000	cien mil
one million	1,000,000	un millón
two million	2,000,000	dos millones

Ordinal/Ordinales*

first	1st /	1°	primero
second	2nd /	2°	segundo
third	3rd /	3°	tercero
fourth	4th /	4°	cuarto
fifth	5th /	5°	quinto
sixth	6th /	6°	sexto
seventh	7th /	7°	séptimo
eighth	8th /	8°	octavo
ninth	9th /	9°	noveno
tenth	10th /	10°	décimo

*Spanish ordinal numbers are used as adjectives: el primer hombre, los primeros hombres, la primera mujer, las primeras mujeres, etc.

Weights and Measures/Pesos y Medidas

1 centímetro	=	.3937 inches	1 kilolitro	=	264.18 gallons
1 metro	=	39.37 inches	1 inch	=	2.54 centímetros
1 kilómetro	=	.621 mile	1 foot	=	.305 metros
1 centigramo	=	.1543 grain	1 mile	=	1.61 kilómetros
1 gramo	=	15.432 grains	1 grain	=	.065 gramos
1 kilogramo	=	2.2046 pounds	1 pound	=	.455 kilogramos
1 tonelada	=	2.204 pounds	1 ton	=	.907 toneladas
1 centilitro	=	.338 ounces	1 ounce	=	2.96 centilitros
1 litro	=	1.0567 quart (liquid);	1 quart	=	1.13 litros
		.908 quart (dry)	1 gallon	=	4.52 litros

Signs/Señales

Caution	Precaución	**No smoking**	Prohibido fumar
Danger	Peligro	**No admittance**	Entrada prohibida
Exit	Salida	**One way**	Dirección única
Entrance	Entrada	**No entry**	Dirección prohibida
Stop	Alto	**Women**	Señoras or Mujeres or Damas
Closed	Cerrado	**Men**	Señores or Hombres or Caballeros
Open	Abierto	**Ladies' Room**	Cuarto de Damas
Slow	Despacio	**Men's Room**	Servicio

Days of the Week/Días de la Semana

Sunday	domingo	Thursday	jueves
Monday	lunes	Friday	viernes
Tuesday	martes	Saturday	sábado
Wednesday	miércoles		

Months/Meses

January	enero	October	octubre
February	febrero	November	noviembre
March	marzo	December	diciembre
April	abril		
May	mayo		
June	junio		
July	julio		
August	agosto		
September	septiembre		

Useful Phrases/Locuciones Útiles

Good day or Good morning! ¡Buenos días!
Good afternoon! ¡Buenas tardes!
Good night or Good evening! ¡Buenas noches!
Hello! ¡Hola!
Welcome! ¡Bienvenido!
See you later! ¡Hasta luego!
Goodbye! ¡Adiós!
How are you? ¿Cómo está usted?
I am fine, thank you. Estoy bien, gracias.
I am pleased to meet you. Mucho gusto en conocerle.
May I introduce . . . Quisiera presentar . . .
Thank you very much. Muchas gracias.
You're welcome. De nada *or* No hay de qué.
Please. Por favor.
Excuse me. Con permiso.
Good luck! ¡Buena suerte!
To your health! ¡Salud!

Please help me. Ayúdeme, por favor.
I don't know. No sé.
I don't understand. No entiendo.
Do you understand? ¿Entiende usted?
I don't speak Spanish. No hablo español.
Do you speak English? ¿Habla usted inglés?
How do you say . . . in Spanish? ¿Cómo se dice . . . en español?
What do you call this? ¿Cómo se llama esto?
Speak slowly, please. Hable despacio, por favor.
Please repeat. Repita, por favor.
I don't like it. No me gusta.
I am lost. Ando perdido *or* Me he extraviado.

What is your name? ¿Cómo se llama usted?
My name is . . . Me llamo . . .
I am an American. Soy norteamericano.
Where are you from? ¿De dónde es usted?
I'm from . . . Soy de . . .

How is the weather? ¿Qué tiempo hace?
It's cold (hot) today. Hace frío (calor) hoy.
What time is it? ¿Qué hora es?

How much is it? ¿Cuánto es?
It is too much. Es mucho.
What do you wish? ¿Qué desea usted?
I want to buy . . . Quiero comprar . . .
May I see something better? ¿Podría ver algo mejor?
May I see something cheaper? ¿Podría ver algo menos caro?
It is not exactly what I want. No es precisamente lo que quiero.

I am hungry. Tengo hambre.
I am thirsty. Tengo sed.
Where is there a restaurant? ¿Dónde hay restaurante?
I have a reservation. Tengo reservación.
I would like . . . Quisiera . . . ; Me gustaría . . .
Please give me . . . Me da . . .
Please bring me . . . Me trae . . .
May I see the menu? ¿Se puede ver el menú?
The bill, please. La cuenta, por favor.
Is service included in the bill? ¿El servicio está incluido en la cuenta?
Where is there a hotel? ¿Dónde hay hotel?
Where is the post office? ¿Dónde está el correo?
Is there any mail for me? ¿Tengo correo?
Where can I mail this letter? ¿Dónde se puede echar esta carta?

Take me to . . . Lléveme a . . .
I believe I am ill. Creo que estoy enfermo.
Please call a doctor. Por favor, llame al médico.

Please call the police. Por favor, llame a la policía.

I want to send a telegram. Quiero poner telegrama.

As soon as possible. Cuanto antes.

Round trip. Ida y vuelta.

Please help me with my luggage. Por favor, ayúdeme con el equipaje.

Where can I get a taxi? ¿Dónde hay taxi?

What is the fare to . . . ¿Cuánto es el pasaje hasta . . . ?

Please take me to this address. Por favor, lléveme a esta dirección.

Where can I change my money? ¿Dónde se puede cambiar dinero?

Where is the nearest bank? ¿Dónde está el banco más cercano?

Can you accept my check? ¿Aceptará cheque?

Do you accept traveler's checks? ¿Aceptan cheques de viaje?

What is the postage? ¿Cuánto es el franqueo?

Where is the nearest drugstore? ¿Dónde está la farmacia más cercana?

Where is the men's (women's) room? ¿Dónde está el servicio de caballeros (de señoras)?

Please let me off at . . . Por favor, déjeme bajar en . . .

Right away! ¡Pronto!

Help! ¡Socorro!

Who is it? ¿Quién es?

Just a minute! ¡Un momento no más!

Come in! ¡Pase usted!

Pardon me. Dispense usted.

Stop! ¡Pare!

Look out! ¡Cuidado!

Hurry! ¡De prisa! *or* ¡Dése prisa!

Go on! ¡Siga!

To (on, at) the right. A la derecha.

To (on, at) the left. A la izquierda.

Straight ahead. Adelante.